the essential
study bible

CONTEMPORARY ENGLISH VERSION

Notes prepared by Eric Yost and adapted from
The Learning Bible Contemporary English Version

G.P. PUTNAM'S SONS
AMERICAN BIBLE SOCIETY

the essential study bible

*everything you need
for a deeper understanding
of the bible*

CONTEMPORARY ENGLISH VERSION

G. P. Putnam's Sons
Publishers Since 1838
Published by the Penguin Group

Penguin Group (USA) Inc., 375 Hudson Street, New York, New York 10014, USA • Penguin Group (Canada), 90 Eglinton Avenue East, Suite 700, Toronto, Ontario M4P 2Y3, Canada (a division of Pearson Penguin Canada Inc.) • Penguin Books Ltd, 80 Strand, London WC2R 0RL, England • Penguin Ireland, 25 St Stephen's Green, Dublin 2, Ireland (a division of Penguin Books Ltd) • Penguin Group (Australia), 250 Camberwell Road, Camberwell, Victoria 3124, Australia • (a division of Pearson Australia Group Pty Ltd) • Penguin Books India Pvt Ltd, 11 Community Centre, Panchsheel Park, New Delhi–110 017, India • Penguin Group (NZ), Cnr Airborne and Rosedale Roads, Albany, Auckland 1310, New Zealand (a division of Pearson New Zealand Ltd) • Penguin Books (South Africa) (Pty) Ltd, 24 Sturdee Avenue, Rosebank, Johannesburg 2196, South Africa

Penguin Books Ltd, Registered Offices: 80 Strand, London WC2R 0RL, England

ISBN 978-0-399-15388-4

Printed in the United States of America
1 3 5 7 9 10 8 6 4 2

Book design by Claire Vaccaro

foreword

to the Contemporary English Version

Languages are spoken before they are written. And far more communication is done through the spoken word than through the written word. In fact, more people *hear* the Bible read than read it for themselves. Traditional translations of the Bible count on the *reader's* ability to understand a *written* text. But the *Contemporary English Version* differs from most other English Bibles in that it takes into consideration the needs of the *hearer,* as well as those of the reader, who may not be familiar with traditional biblical language.

The *Contemporary English Version* has been described as a "user-friendly" and a "mission-driven" translation that can be *read aloud* without stumbling, *heard* without misunderstanding, and *listened to* with enjoyment and appreciation, because the language is contemporary and the style is lucid and lyrical.

preface

A Word about the Contemporary English Version

Translation it is that opens the window, to let in the light; that breaks the shell, that we may eat the kernel; that puts aside the curtain, that we may look into the most holy place; that removes the cover of the well, that we may come by the water. ("The Translators to the Reader," King James Version, 1611).

The most important document in the history of the English language is the *King James Version* of the Bible. To measure its spiritual impact on the English speaking world would be more impossible than counting the grains of sand along the ocean shores. Historically, many Bible translators have attempted in some measure to *retain the form* of the *King James Version*. But the translators of the *Contemporary English Version* of the Bible have diligently sought to *capture the spirit* of the *King James Version* by following certain principles set forth by its translators in the document "The Translators to the Reader," which was printed in the earliest editions.

This is the Word of God, which we translate

Accuracy, beauty, clarity, and dignity—all of these can and must be achieved in the translation of the Bible. After all, as the translators of the King James Version stated, "This is the Word of God, which we translate."

Every attempt has been made to produce a text that is faithful to the *meaning* of the original. In order to assure the *accuracy* of the *Contemporary English Version*, the Old Testament was translated directly from the Hebrew and Aramaic texts published by the United Bible Societies (*Biblia Hebraica*

Stuttgartensia, fourth edition corrected). And the New Testament was translated directly from the Greek text published by the United Bible Societies (third edition corrected and compared with the fourth revised edition).

The drafts in their earliest stages were sent for review and comment to a number of biblical scholars, theologians, and educators representing a wide variety of church traditions. In addition, drafts were sent for review and comment to all English-speaking Bible Societies and to more than forty United Bible Societies translation consultants around the world. Final approval of the text was given by the American Bible Society Board of Trustees on the recommendation of its Translations Subcommittee.

We desire that Scripture . . . may be understood

That the Scripture may be understood even by ordinary people was a primary goal of the translators of the *King James Version*. And they raised the question, "What can be more available thereto than to deliver God's book unto God's people in a tongue which they understand?" Martin Luther also did his translation for the common people, and he established the following guidelines:

We do not have to inquire of the literal Latin, how we are to speak German . . . Rather we must inquire about this of the mother in the home, the children on the street, the common man in the marketplace. *We must be guided by their language, the way they speak, and do our translating accordingly.*

Today more people hear the Bible read aloud than read it for themselves! And statistics released by the National Center for Education indicate that "almost half of U.S. adults have very limited reading and writing skills." If this is the case, a contemporary translation must be a text that an inexperienced reader can *read aloud* without stumbling, that someone unfamiliar with traditional biblical terminology can *hear without misunderstanding*, and that everyone can *listen to with enjoyment* because the style is lucid and lyrical.

In order to attain these goals of clarity, beauty, and dignity, the translators of the *Contemporary English Version* carefully studied every word, phrase, clause, and paragraph of the original. Then, with equal care, they struggled to discover the best way to translate the text, so that it would be suitable both for *private* and *public* reading, and for *memorizing*. The result is an English text that is enjoyable and easily understood by the vast majority of English speakers, regardless of their religious or educational background.

In the *hearing* of a translation, even the inclusion of a simple word like "and" can make a significant difference. Matthew 2.9 of the *Contemporary English Version* reads as follows: "The wise men listened to what the king said and then left. *And* the star they had seen in the east went on ahead of them until it stopped over the place where the child was."

"And" at the beginning of the second sentence assists both the person who reads the text aloud and those who must depend upon hearing it read. Like all other punctuation marks, the period after "left" is silent, and so the text without "And" could possibly be *heard* as, "The wise men listened to what the king said and then left the star they had seen in the east." However, as the text now stands, the oral reader must pause briefly for a breath before "And," which will signal the hearer that a new sentence has begun.

As another example, try reading the following two sentences aloud: "You yourselves admit, then, that you agree with what your ancestors did" and "for it was better with me then than now." both suffer from potential tongue twisters ("admit, then, that" and "then than"). But the first is doubly difficult because it consists of a lengthy series of unaccented syllables that do not allow the reader to take a breath. In the *Contemporary English Version* every attempt has been made to avoid these and other kinds of constructions that could possibly prove problematic for oral reading.

According to the rules of English grammar, the pronoun *he* must refer back to *God* in the following sentence: "The other, however, rebuked him saying, 'Don't you fear *God*? You received the same sentence *he* did.'" But the reference is actually to Jesus, who is mentioned earlier in the passage. Traditional translations assume that the reader can study the printed text and finally figure out the meaning, but the *Contemporary English Version* is concerned equally with the reader and the hearer. And in many situations, the *hearer* may have only *one* chance to understand what is read aloud.

In poetry, the *appearance of the text on the page* is important, since in oral reading there is a tendency to stress the last word on a line and to pause momentarily before going to the next line, especially if the second line is indented. Compare the three following examples, where the lines of the same text have been broken improperly (left column) and properly (right column):

He brought me out into a broad
    place.
With the loyal you show yourself
    loyal.
The Lord my God lights up
    my darkness.

He brought me out
    into a broad place.
With the loyal
    you show yourself loyal.
The Lord my God
    lights up my darkness.

No fault is to be found with the translation itself. Yet there is a significant difference in the *appearance* of the text on the page, because the lines on the right have been *measured,* in order to prevent unfortunate runovers. In this form, the text not only looks better on the page, but it is easier to read and memorize, and it avoids such disastrous combinations as "He brought me out into a broad" or "With the loyal you show yourself" or "The Lord my God lights up." Moreover, both formats require exactly the same amount of lines.

The first translation in the history of the English Bible to develop a text with measured poetry lines is the *Contemporary English Version,* in which the translators have consciously created a text that will not suffer from unfortunate line breaks when published in double columns. *Accuracy* is the main concern of translators, but it must be realized that in the translation of biblical poetry, what the reader *sees* is what will be *said,* and what others will *hear.* This means that lines improperly broken can easily lead to a misunderstanding of the text, especially for those who must depend upon *hearing* the Scriptures read.

Hebrew poetry has its own systems of sound, rhyme, and rhythm, as well as a *form* that involves much repetition. It is impossible in English to retain the sounds, rhymes, and rhythms of the Hebrew text, but traditional translations have attempted to reproduce the frequent repetition, in which a second line will repeat or expand, either negatively or positively, the thoughts of the previous line. However, this repetition is often ineffective for those English speakers who are unaccustomed to the poetic style of the biblical authors. And so, the translators of the *Contemporary English Version* have followed the example of Martin Luther in the translation of poetry:

Whoever would speak German *must not use Hebrew style.* Rather he must see to it—once he understands the Hebrew author—that he concentrates on the sense of the text, asking himself, "Pray tell, what do the Germans say in such a situation?" Once he has the German words to serve his purpose, let him drop the Hebrew words and *express the meaning freely* in the best German he knows.

The qualities that many critics value most in modern poetry are effortless *economy* and *exactness* of language. It is hoped that readers will discover similar features in the poetry of the *Contemporary English Version,* which strives for beauty and dignity, as much as for accuracy and clarity. In this translation, the poetry often requires fewer lines than do traditional translations, but the *integrity, intent,* and *impact* of the original are consistently maintained. Note, for example, the rendering of Job 38.14,15:

> Early dawn outlines the hills
> like stitches on clothing
>   or sketches on clay.
> But its light is too much
> for those who are evil,
>   and their power is broken.

Whenever the contents of two or more verses have been joined together and rearranged in the poetic sections of the *Contemporary English Version,* this is signaled by an asterisk (*) before the first verse number in the series.

In everyday speech, "gender generic" or "inclusive" language is used, because it sounds most natural to people today. This means that where the biblical languages require masculine nouns or pronouns when both men and women are intended, this intention must be reflected in translation, though the English *form* may be very different from that of the original. The Greek text of Matthew 16.24 is literally, "If anyone wants to follow me, *he* must deny *himself* and take up *his* cross and follow me." The *Contemporary English Version* shifts to a form which is still accurate, and at the same time more effective in English: "If any of *you* want to be my followers, *you* must forget about *yourself*. *You* must take up *your* cross and follow me."

Since its publication, diverse groups of people around the world have read and enjoyed the *Contemporary English Version*. To better meet the needs of these global audiences, the *Contemporary English Version* has undergone a revision that addressed issues raised in reviews and feedback from readers. This revision has led to an edition that replaces many of the American idioms used in the first edition with others that communicate more meaningfully to all the English-speaking audiences around the world.

Variety of translations is profitable

The translators of the *King James Version* said, ". . . variety of translations is profitable for the finding out of the sense of the Scriptures" and "We affirm and avow that the very meanest translation of the Bible in English, set forth by men of our profession . . . contains the Word of God, nay is the Word of God." They even stated, "No cause therefore why the Word translated should be denied to be the Word, or forbidden to be current, notwithstanding that some imperfections and blemishes may be noted in the setting forth of it."

Each English translation is, in its own right, the Word of God, yet each translation serves to meet the needs of a different audience. In this regard, the *Contemporary English Version* should be considered a *companion*— the *mission* arm—of traditional translations, because it takes seriously the words of the apostle Paul that "faith comes by hearing."

It has pleased God in his divine providence

Translating the Bible may be compared to living the life of faith. God has not given us all the answers for our pilgrim journey, but we have been provided with all that we need to know in order to be saved. As the translators of the *King James Version* observed:

> . . . it has pleased God in His divine providence here and there to scatter those words and sentences of that difficulty and doubtfulness, not in doctrinal points that concern salvation (for in such it has been vouched that the Scriptures are plain), but in matters of less moment, that fearfulness would better beseem us than confidence . . .
>
> For as it is a fault of incredulity, to doubt of those things that are evident; so to determine of such things that the Spirit of God has left (even in the mind of the judicious) questionable, can be no less than presumption.

Bible translators do not have the privilege and luxury of working from the original manuscripts of either the Old or New Testament. Indeed, there are numerous difficult passages where decisions must be made concerning what word or words actually belong in the text, and what these words may, in fact, mean. At such places, the best a translator can do is to give what seems to be one possible meaning for the difficult text and to indicate this by a note, which was also what the King James translators did: ". . . so diversity of signification and sense in the margin, where the text is not clear, must needs be good; yea, is necessary, as we are persuaded." Fortunately, these "words and sentences of that difficulty and doubtfulness" do not in any way leave unclear the central message of the Bible or any of its major doctrines.

Editorial specialists, translators, clergy, and lay readers provided invaluable feedback and suggestions on the first edition of the *Contemporary English Version*. The input over the years since the first edition appeared has prompted the translators to revisit a small number of places where rewording was thought necessary to emend matters that might cause confusion or were deemed inaccuracies. This revised edition also addressed matters of stylistic consistency, smoother language for reading and hearing, and words or phrases that were perceived as dated or less used in general readership.

Having and using as great helps as were needful

The translators of the *Contemporary English Version* have not created new or novel interpretations of the text. Rather, it was their goal to express mainstream interpretations of the text in current, everyday English. To do so required *listening* carefully to each word of the biblical text, to the way in which English is spoken today, to the remarks of their reviewers, and especially to the Spirit of God. Once again the comments of the translators of the *King James Version* are appropriate.

> Neither did we think much to consult the translators or commentators . . . but neither did we disdain to revise that which we had done, and to bring to the anvil that which we had hammered; but having and using as great helps as were needful, and fearing no reproach for slowness, nor coveting praise for expedition, we have at length, through the good hand of the Lord upon us, brought forth the work to that pass that you see.

The translators of the *Contemporary English Version* are indebted to all translators and biblical scholars who have gone before them and have made it possible to understand something of the languages, cultures, and history of biblical times. And, together with the apostle Paul, they confess: *We don't have the right to claim that we have done anything on our own. God gives us what it takes to do all that we do.* (2 Corinthians 3.5)

Offer praise to God our Savior because of our Lord Jesus Christ! (Jude 24,25)

how to use the essential study bible

The *Essential Study Bible* is a great way to discover God's Word. Whether you began reading the Bible as a child or whether you are taking on this challenge for the first time, *The Essential Study Bible* will help you get the most out of the time you set aside for this important educational and spiritual experience.

GETTING YOU POINTED IN THE RIGHT DIRECTION

When church groups are surveyed and asked why they don't read the Bible on their own more often, the most frequent replies are "I don't know where to begin" and "I began at the beginning with GENESIS, but couldn't get through LEVITICUS." The Bible is a difficult book to read and even a modern translation can be hard to understand, because the events and customs it describes happened a long time ago. *The Essential Study Bible* narrows down the vast amount of information that's out there to bring you—in clear, simple language—the most essential historical, geographical, cultural, and religious facts and concepts you need to have a good understanding of the Bible. Because the Bible is a collection of many books, it doesn't matter which book of the Bible you read first. Some people like to begin with GENESIS. Others want to learn about Jesus right away, and they select one of the Gospels. Wherever you begin, *The Essential Study Bible* has a number of tools to help you find your footing and head you in the right direction on the path of discovery.

INTRODUCTIONS AND OUTLINES

A special Introduction begins each book of the Bible. The Introductions give information about who may have written the book and when it may have been written. It also introduces the book's important themes and provides you with clues to understanding its structure, including an outline of the book's contents. In addition, *The Essential Study Bible* has Introductions to the Old and New Testaments. These introductions will give you a quick overview of the books contained in each section and can help you decide which ones you'll want to read first.

GETTING YOU THE INFORMATION YOU NEED

The Essential Study Bible is designed so that you'll have everything you need to understand what's going on in the Bible.

The Essential Study Bible features:

The Contemporary English Version Translation

The translators of the *Contemporary English Version (CEV)* did many things to make the Bible easy to read and understand. They took special care to make sure that figures of speech and customs—which ancient people would have understood, but which modern people cannot—have been phrased in ways that are clear and to the point. For more about the *CEV* translation, see the Preface called "The Contemporary English Version" on pg vii.

Notes

The Essential Study Bible provides three categories of notes, which appear in the outside columns on each page, near their Scripture references. Each of these categories is marked with its own symbol:

● Information on ancient history and cultures, geography, plants, animals, tools, materials, and objects—the important background information you need to go deeper into your Bible study!

■ Clear and simple explanations of the religious and social ideas and concepts used in the Bible.

⊙ Web References—so you can continue your Bible study online. Web References help you connect to over one hundred mini-articles on important Bible topics, provided by The American Bible Society's Bible Resource Center. The links to these articles can be found at www.essential studybible.com.

Find Your Way Fast by Chapter and Verse

With The Essential Study Bible, you're never lost without a guide. The CEV conventions (shown below) help you locate the exact Scripture passage you want. They're easy to learn, easy to remember, and useful for a lifetime.

HOW TO LOOK UP A SCRIPTURE REFERENCE
Like many books, the Bible is divided into units (called "books" of the Bible). Each book is divided into chapters. However, unlike most books, chapters are divided into much smaller units called "verses" (usually consisting of a sentence or two). Both chapters and verses are numbered.

BOOK TITLE ABBREVIATION 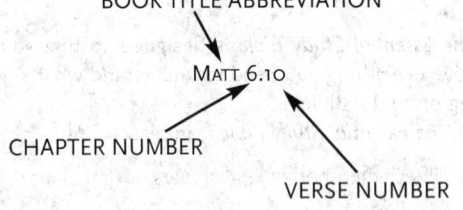MATT 6.10 CHAPTER NUMBER VERSE NUMBER	MATT 6.10-14 INDICATES VERSES 10 THROUGH 14 WITHIN CHAPTER 6 MATT 6.10—7.21 INDICATES ALL VERSES FROM CHAPTER 6, VERSE 10 THROUGH CHAPTER 7, VERSE 21

The more often you look up Scripture references, the easier it becomes. Soon you will be familiar with the Bible book abbreviations used and this system of notation. In the meantime, the "Alphabetical Listing with Abbreviations" located immediately after the "Contents" page will help you become familiar with abbreviations you don't recognize.

Parallel Text References

Sometimes the smaller headings that divide the Bible text are followed by "parallel text references" in parentheses. Here is an example, found in the sixteenth chapter of the book of Matthew:

> ### Who Is Jesus?
> (Mark 8.27-30; Luke 9.18-21)

A parallel text is a Scripture passage that is very similar to the one that follows on the page. These appear frequently in the Gospels, but they appear in other books as well.

Feature Articles

Some important topics call for more information than can be given in a simple margin note or mini-article. *The Essential Study Bible* also includes special feature articles that give you a longer explanation of important topics. These are contained in the back of the book. A complete list of these articles is given on the contents page.

Footnotes

The *CEV* Bible was translated into English from ancient Greek and Hebrew manuscripts. These manuscripts are very old and were copied out by hand, so they do not always agree with one another word for word. When these differences occur, the translators had to decide which manuscript to use in the translation. The *CEV* translators often listed other possible renderings in footnotes to the Bible verses. The footnotes also identify when the original language text is unclear and explain other decisions the translators had to make. Together, the footnotes and the notes in the margin of *The Essential Study Bible* will give the information you need for a solid understanding of the Bible.

Charts

The Essential Study Bible contains a section of special charts in the back of the book. These charts summarize detailed information and display it in a way that is easy for you to look up. You'll be directed to these charts as necessary by special callouts, which follow certain marginal notes in **bold.** Also, at the back of *The Essential Study Bible*, pgs 1863–1866, is a Bible Timeline that provides an easy-to-follow overview of the history of the ancient world from the earliest times through the time of the apostles.

Maps

The events described in the Bible occurred over more than a thousand years and in places as far apart as Egypt, Palestine, Greece, and Rome. To help you keep track of the way the "Bible Lands" changed from one era to the next, *The Essential Study Bible* provides 16 full-color, topographical maps keyed to specific periods of history. Located at the back of this volume, these maps provide a good overview of the ancient Near East and include most of the place names you will encounter when reading the Bible. You'll be directed to these maps as necessary by special callouts, which follow certain marginal notes in **bold**.

HELPING YOU CONNECT WITH THE BIBLE'S MESSAGE

Most people who read the Bible are looking for more than information about ancient people and customs. They believe (or hope) it contains truth, comfort, and spiritual insight. They look to the Bible for guidance in their daily lives. *The Essential Study Bible* has a number of features that will help you understand and appreciate the enduring importance of God's Word.

Questions about Each Book of the Bible

Reflection Questions are provided at the end of each Scripture book. These questions are intended to help you review the content and meaning of each book, and consider how each book of the Bible relates to your life today. You can answer these questions silently to yourself, keep a devotional journal of your responses, or use the questions as a discussion guide for group Bible study.

Memory Verses

Many people find comfort and strength from memorizing Scripture verses. A number of important and inspirational verses have been highlighted at the bottom of *The Essential Study Bible* pages. These are by no means the *only* verses worth memorizing, but they do represent the kinds of messages that you'll discover each time you read the Bible.

Bible Reading Plans

At the back of *The Essential Study Bible* are two Bible reading plans. Select the one that best matches your needs and fits into your schedule. Most people who make a practice of reading the Bible say they benefit most from reading the Bible on a daily basis—regardless of how much or how little time they set aside to do this. The Reading Plans in *The Essential Study Bible* are:

1. *Read Through the Bible in a Year*
   Many people have always wanted to read the Bible all the way through. This plan provides a scheme that allows you to read some Old Testament and some New Testament every day. Be prepared to spend about a half hour every day in order to complete your reading on schedule.

2. *Moment with Scripture*
   Many people feel pulled in a hundred different directions and complain about too many demands on their time. Reading the Bible is a wonderful way to "get one's bearings" before facing all these challenges. This plan only requires five minutes a day. The passages selected are especially geared to people who are caught up in the "rush of life."

It's never too soon to begin discovering God's Word for yourself . . . or to re-discover it, if you set the Bible aside because you found it difficult to understand. *The Essential Study Bible* gives you the help you need to make Bible reading a consistent part of your life. Start reading it today!

Your teachings are wonderful,
and I respect them all.
Understanding your word
brings light to the minds
of ordinary people.
I honestly want to know
everything you teach.
Psalm 119.129-131

contents

Charts and Tables

How to Use This Book

Bible Maps

Alphabetical Listing with Abbreviations

Old Testament

Book	Short	Long	Book	Short	Long
Amos	Am	Amos	Judges	Jg	Judg
1 Chronicles	1 Ch	1 Chr	1 Kings	1 K	1 Kgs
2 Chronicles	2 Ch	2 Chr	2 Kings	2 K	2 Kgs
Daniel	Dn	Dan	Lamentations	Lm	Lam
Deuteronomy	Dt	Deut	Leviticus	Lv	Lev
Ecclesiastes	Ec	Eccl	Malachi	Ml	Mal
Esther	Es	Esth	Micah	Mic	Mic
Exodus	Ex	Exod	Nahum	Nh	Nah
Ezekiel	Ez	Ezek	Nehemiah	Ne	Neh
Ezra	Ezra	Ezra	Numbers	Nu	Num
Genesis	Gn	Gen	Obadiah	Ob	Obad
Habakkuk	Hb	Hab	Proverbs	Pr	Prov
Haggai	Hg	Hag	Psalms	Ps	Ps
Hosea	Ho	Hos	Ruth	Ru	Ruth
Isaiah	Is	Isa	1 Samuel	1 S	1 Sam
Jeremiah	Jr	Jer	2 Samuel	2 S	2 Sam
Job	Job	Job	Song of Songs	Sgs	Song
Joel	Jl	Joel	Zechariah	Zec	Zech
Jonah	Jon	Jonah	Zephaniah	Zep	Zeph
Joshua	Js	Josh			

New Testament

Book	Short	Long	Book	Short	Long
Acts	Ac	Acts	Mark	Mk	Mark
Colossians	Co	Col	Matthew	Mt	Matt
1 Corinthians	1 C	1 Cor	1 Peter	1 P	1 Pet
2 Corinthians	2 C	2 Cor	2 Peter	2 P	2 Pet
Ephesians	Eph	Eph	Philemon	Phm	Phlm
Galatians	Ga	Gal	Philippians	Phil	Phil
Hebrews	He	Heb	Revelation	Rev	Rev
James	Jas	Jas	Romans	Ro	Rom
John	Jn	John	1 Thessalonians	1 Th	1 Thes
1 John	1 Jn	1 John	2 Thessalonians	2 Th	2 Thes
2 John	2 Jn	2 John	1 Timothy	1 Ti	1 Tim
3 John	3 Jn	3 John	2 Timothy	2 Ti	2 Tim
Jude	Jd	Jude	Titus	Titus	Titus
Luke	Lk	Luke			

the old testament

The "Old Testament" is the name Christians have given to the Jewish Scriptures and the first part of the Christian Bible. When the earliest Christians quoted from "Scripture," they quoted from the Jewish Scriptures. It was not until after the New Testament books were written in the first and second centuries A.D. that Christians started referring to the Jewish Scriptures as the "Old Testament."

Composed over a period of at least one thousand years, the Old Testament is actually many different books of various kinds written by many different writers. Some parts of the Old Testament date back to around 1200 B.C. Originally, they were stories that were told from generation to generation. They were eventually written down and gathered together into longer collections (like the stories about Abraham in Gen 12–24). The books of the Old Testament were written in Hebrew, the language of the people of Israel, though a few of the later books (or parts of books) were written in Aramaic, a closely related language.

The Old Testament is a record of Israel's experience of what God is like and what the people who worship God should be like (Lev 20.7,8). It proclaims the LORD God as the creator of the world (Gen 1; Ps 104), and describes God as one who promises to bless. God's "blessings" are described in the agreements (covenants) God made with the people of Israel. Much of the Old Testament tells the story of how God's chosen people struggled to keep their part of this agreement with God, and how God continually offered guidance and forgiveness when they disobeyed.

Both Jews and Christians view the Old Testament as a sacred book that has meaning and authority for their lives. All Christian groups agree that the Old Testament deals in a special way with the relationship between God and God's people, while it also provides a background for understanding the message of the New Testament. The four major sections of the Old Testament are the Pentateuch, the Historical Books, the Books of Wisdom and Poetry, and the Prophetic Books.

THE PENTATEUCH

The "Pentateuch" is a term used to describe the first five books of the Old Testament (Genesis—Deuteronomy). The great narratives of the Pentateuch begin with stories about how God created the world and its people (Gen 1–5). This is followed by the story of Noah and the great flood, and a story explaining why there are different human languages (Gen 6–11). These stories are sometimes described as "pre-history." In Genesis 12 the history of God's people begins: God chooses Abraham and his wife Sarah to leave their home and go to a new land (Canaan). God promises Abraham that his descendants will become a great nation and eventually make the land of Canaan their home (Gen 12.1-3; 17.1-8). GENESIS also describes how the promises of God begin to be fulfilled through the descendants of Abraham and Sarah, including Isaac, Jacob, and their families.

As EXODUS begins, these promises are in question because Abraham and Sarah's descendants are living as slaves in Egypt. But God hears the people begging for help and chooses Moses to lead the people out of Egypt (Exod 3.4-12). This great event, known as the "exodus," is told about in exciting detail in EXODUS. Israel's time of slavery in Egypt became a lesson for future generations. Because God cared about the people of Israel and responded to them when they were suffering and oppressed, they were to treat others, especially the poor and powerless, with fairness and justice (Exod 23.6-9; Lev 25.35-38; Deut 5.6,12-15).

The second major event in EXODUS is the agreement (covenant) that the LORD makes with Moses and the people of Israel at Mount Sinai. In this agreement, God gives the laws and instructions that would guide how the people were to live and worship. At Sinai, God made it clear what the people of Israel must do in order to show that they were God's "holy" people. These laws and instructions are found in Exodus 20–40; LEVITICUS; selected portions of NUMBERS; and in Moses' sermons in DEUTERONOMY. The remainder of NUMBERS tells about the years of wandering through the desert. The narratives in this book focus on the way the LORD God continued to care for the people even in the terrible years they spent in the desert.

The Pentateuch ends with the people of Israel camped across the Jordan River from Canaan, ready to enter the land God had promised them. The final words of DEUTERONOMY describe the death of Moses and the choice of Joshua as the next leader of Israel. Because the main human figure of the Pentateuch is Moses, these books have traditionally been called the "Books of Moses."

HISTORICAL BOOKS

Christians call the Old Testament books that follow the Pentateuch—beginning with JOSHUA and ending with ESTHER—the Historical Books. These books describe Israel's history as a people in the land of Canaan. Although these books are called "historical," they are different from history books of today. The descriptions of events in these books are more often concerned with an important religious teaching about God and God's relationship with Israel than they are about the historical facts of the events themselves.

These books can be thought of as telling one long story that took place from around 1250 B.C. to 150 B.C. Within this story are five key events.

Israel's settlement in the land of Canaan. JOSHUA and JUDGES describe how the people of Israel entered Canaan and settled in various regions and cities. Sometimes this settlement was peaceful, but at other times it was more difficult. These two books also describe how the Israelites lived throughout Canaan as separate tribes, each with its own leader (called a judge).

Israel's Monarchy. The second key event describes the change from this tribal system of government to a monarchy ruled by a king. The books of 1 and 2 SAMUEL tell how Saul was chosen to be the first king of Israel and describe the events that led to David becoming the second king of Israel. An important part of this event was David's choosing of Jerusalem to be the capital of Israel.

The Divided Kingdom. David's son Solomon became king after David died. Solomon built the first temple in Jerusalem and increased the influence and wealth of Israel. But his policy of forcing the Israelites to work on his building projects for little pay, together with his sin of allowing the worship of foreign idols, led to a revolt shortly after his death. The result was a divided kingdom. The books of 1 and 2 KINGS and 1 and 2 CHRONICLES describe the reigns of the kings who ruled the northern and southern kingdoms from about 931 B.C. to 586 B.C.

Defeat and exile of these two kingdoms. Though warned by prophets like Amos and Hosea, the northern kingdom (Israel) continued to worship idols and to disobey God's Law. This led to their defeat by the Assyrians in 722 B.C. The southern kingdom (Judah) was ruled by kings descended from

David, but it, too, did not listen to the warnings of prophets like Isaiah, Jeremiah, and Ezekiel. When the people and some of their leaders were unfaithful to the LORD, the LORD allowed the Babylonians to defeat them in 586 B.C. and force many of Judah's leading citizens to live as exiles in Babylonia.

The return from exile. In 539 B.C., King Cyrus of Persia defeated Babylonia and allowed the Jewish people to return home and reclaim their land. EZRA and NEHEMIAH describe how the people were able to return to Judah, rebuild the walls and temple of Jerusalem, and rededicate themselves to being God's people.

BOOKS OF WISDOM AND POETRY

The Books of Wisdom and Poetry—JOB through SONG OF SONGS—make up the section of the Christian Bible that follows the Pentateuch and the Historical Books. The Books of Wisdom and Poetry include excellent examples of Hebrew poetry. While some of these books fall into the category of "wisdom" writings (like JOB, ECCLESIASTES, and PROVERBS), the others are collections of love poems (SONG OF SONGS) or worship prayers and songs (PSALMS).

Books of Wisdom. The Wisdom writings explore important questions about life and give advice for practical living, especially in community with others. But these writings make it clear that true wisdom is a gift that "comes from the LORD," who gives helpful advice to everyone who obeys God's Law (Prov 2.6,7; 6.23).

The story of JOB focuses on the question, "Why do innocent people suffer?" Job is a faithful man who must struggle with the loss of his family, his home, and his wealth. In his sadness and despair he cries out for answers, and God responds. ECCLESIASTES focuses on the question of finding meaning in life. The writer asks why human beings must work and wonders about the real source of happiness. PROVERBS celebrates human wisdom and the wisdom that comes from God's Law as the way to a

happy and prosperous life. Some of these sayings are said to come from King Solomon (Prov 1.1; 10.1), but others are words of people from other nations (Prov 30.1; 31.1). The collection called PROVERBS likely includes wisdom sayings from as many as five centuries later.

Books of Poetry. Although many of the books in the Old Testament include sections of poetry, two books in this section are written entirely in poetic form. SONG OF SONGS is a beautiful example of Hebrew poetry. It was originally written as a love poem to describe the joy and extreme happiness of two people in love. But it has also been understood in some Jewish traditions as a description of God's love for Israel, and in some Christian traditions as a description of Christ's love for the Church.

PSALMS is named after the Greek word *psalmos*, which means "song." The songs and prayers found in this book were used by the Hebrew people to express their relationship with God. They cover a whole range of human emotions from joy to anger, and from hope to despair. Many of the psalms were written for use in group worship, while others were likely written as private prayers but also were used in worship. Psalms includes songs of praise to God the Creator; songs of sorrow and anger; prayers of confession; prayers of thanksgiving; hymns to celebrate the crowning of kings; and prayers celebrating God's Law and Wisdom.

PROPHETIC BOOKS

The books beginning with ISAIAH and ending with MALACHI belong to a section of the Christian Bible called the Prophetic Books. These books record God's messages to the people of Israel and Judah in the form of speeches or sermons, visions, and life experiences of prophets who preached between about 750 and 450 B.C. Some of the messages are of judgment and warning, while others focus on forgiveness and renewal. The Prophetic Books in the Christian Bible are often divided into two categories: the "Major Prophets" and the "Book of the Twelve." The

"Twelve" are sometimes referred to as the "Minor Prophets" because their speeches and sermons are much shorter than those of the "Major Prophets."

The Role of the Prophet. In the Bible, a "prophet" is a person called to speak for God and deliver God's messages to people. Prophets did not simply predict the future, but rather observed what was going on around them and delivered God's messages for those situations. The prophets usually introduced their speeches with the words "The LORD says." These words show that the prophets did not speak their own messages, but considered themselves messengers of God who had the authority to speak for God to the people.

The Message of the Prophet. Because some prophets spoke as early as 760 B.C. and others as late as 445 B.C., their messages are sometimes very different in emphasis. For example, Amos, Micah, and Zephaniah preached about the need for the people to change how they acted toward God and each

other, so that they could avoid being punished like the foreign nations around them. Others, like Jeremiah and Ezekiel, warned the people about the coming defeat of Jerusalem and the exile of its people to Babylonia and promised a future time when God's people will be delivered and return to Jerusalem. Still others, like Haggai, Zechariah, and Malachi preached to people who had returned from exile and were working to rebuild the temple in Jerusalem and begin the worship of God again. The messages of ISAIAH seem to address all these periods of Israel's history and span the events leading up to and following the return from exile in Babylonia.

Some of the Prophetic Books reflect historical settings much later than when the prophets themselves actually lived. Their messages seem to have been adapted and edited by people who faced different social and religious situations. This shows that the messages of the Prophetic Books address issues of permanent importance: proper worship of God, justice and equality, and caring for oppressed and mistreated people.

genesis

How did the world begin? Who were God's chosen people?
Find the answer to these questions and more in GENESIS.

WHAT MAKES GENESIS SPECIAL?

The word *genesis* comes from a Greek word meaning "beginning." And this is a book about beginnings—the beginning of the world, the beginning of the human race, and the beginning of the people of Israel. GENESIS includes a number of family lists (genealogies) to explain how the Israelite people are related to each other and to other peoples and nations.

GENESIS is also a book of faith, which means that it is mainly concerned with who God is and how God has been involved in the lives of people from the time of creation. It records how God created the world and how the people of Israel became God's people. The book also tells how the first human beings broke the perfect relationship they had with God in the Garden of Eden. GENESIS shows that God did not give up on human beings, but instead chose Abram and Sarai (later called Abraham and Sarah) to leave their home and go to Canaan, a land God promised to give to Abram and his descendants. God also promised Abram that his descendants would be a great people who would bring God's blessings to all the other nations of the world (12.1-3).

WHAT'S THE STORY BEHIND THE SCENE?

According to tradition, Moses is considered the author and collector of the first five books of the Bible, including GENESIS. The Bible (1 Kgs 6.1) and other ancient documents indicate that Moses lived sometime between 1400 and 1250 B.C. In the past two centuries, however, Bible scholars have suggested

that GENESIS reached its final form much later than the time of Moses, perhaps as late as the time of Israel's exile in Babylon (587–538 B.C.). No matter who wrote the book, its main message is clear: The God of Abraham, Sarah, and their descendants (the people of Israel) is the creator of the world and acts in history to save all people.

HOW IS GENESIS CONSTRUCTED?

GENESIS can be divided into two main parts: Chapters 1—11 cover the creation of the world and the earliest human families, as well as the Great Flood and the creation of different languages. Chapters 12—50 tell the story of the ancestors of the people of Israel, beginning with Abraham and Sarah, and ending with their grandson Jacob's family living in Egypt. A broad outline of the book follows these two main sections.

The beginning of human history (1.1—11.25)
    God creates the universe and all living things
    (1.1—2.25)
    Sin in Eden (3.1—4.16)
    The first generations of human beings
    (4.17—5.32)
    Noah and his descendants (6.1—11.25)
The beginning of God's people, Israel
    (11.26—50.26)
    Abraham, Sarah, and Isaac (11.26—23.20)
    Isaac and his family (24.1—28.9)
    Jacob and Esau and their families (28.10—36.43)
    The story of Jacob's son, Joseph (37.1—50.26)

Genesis describes many beginnings. The book opens with poetic accounts of how God created the earth and human beings. Later on, Genesis tells of another kind of beginning—the beginning of God's special people, the Israelites. The story of creation tells how human beings rebelled against God and were forced to leave their earthly paradise. When human wickedness caused God to destroy the world in a great flood, God saved the faithful man Noah and his family so that they could begin life again. However, it is with the stories of Abraham, his son Isaac, and his grandson Jacob, that the focus of Genesis changes. Beginning with Abraham's story, Genesis tells how God formed a people who would later be known as Israel. God called Abraham and instructed him to leave his homeland in the east and journey to a new land, promising him many descendants. Later, it seemed that God's promise would not come true when a great famine threatened the family of Jacob (Israel) and forced them to leave the land God had promised to their ancestor Abraham and move to Egypt. But Genesis shows how God continued to supply all their needs. Joseph, one of Abraham's great-grandchildren, who had been sold into slavery in Egypt by his brothers, had come to power under Egypt's king. Because of his high status he was able to help his brothers and their families during their time of need.

Outline

The Story of Creation

1 In the beginning God
created the heavens
and the earth.[a]
²The earth was barren,
with no form of life;[b]
it was under a roaring ocean
covered with darkness.
But the Spirit of God[c]
was moving over the water.

THE FIRST DAY

³God said, "I command light to shine!"
And light started shining. ⁴God looked at
the light and saw that it was good. He separated light from darkness ⁵and named the
light "Day" and the darkness "Night."
Evening came, then morning—that was
the first day.[d]

THE SECOND DAY

⁶God said, "I command a dome to separate the water above it from the water below it." ⁷And that's what happened. God
made the dome ⁸and named it "Sky."
Evening came, then morning—that was
the second day.

THE THIRD DAY

⁹God said, "I command the water under
the sky to come together in one place, so
there will be dry ground." And that's what
happened. ¹⁰God named the dry ground
"Land," and he named the water "Ocean."
God looked at what he had done and saw
that it was good.
¹¹God said, "I command the earth to
produce all kinds of plants, including fruit
trees and grain." And that's what happened. ¹²The earth produced all kinds of
vegetation. God looked at what he had

■ 1.1 *God created the heavens and the earth:* GENESIS describes God as the creator of everything that exists. In the opening verses of this book of beginnings, "the heavens and the earth" stands for the universe and all its galaxies, stars, and planets. The earth is described as a formless, watery mass. Ancient peoples viewed the earth as a flat disc stretched over the oceans (Ps 136.6). The sky also was believed to be a great ocean that was kept from flooding the earth by a solid bowl or dome called "Sky" (1.8). Before the earth was created, these two watery masses were mixed together, but on the second day God separated them, just as he separated the light from the darkness on the first day (1.3-5). The writer of PSALMS, like the author of GENESIS, says one of the ways God creates is with words (Ps 33.6; 148.5). For example, God gave a command for light to shine, and it happened (1.3.). And then, God commanded the lights (the sun and moon and stars) that separate day from night to appear (1.14-19). Ancient people feared the darkness and welcomed each new day as a reminder of God's victory over the dark chaos at creation.

■ 1.1 *God:* The Hebrew name translated as "God" here and throughout 1.1—2.3 is *Elohim*. It is a plural form of *El*, and can refer to "gods," but here it means the one true God who creates.

● 1.5 *Evening came . . . the first day:* The Jewish day began at sundown, so a full day was measured from evening to evening.

---

[a]**1.1** *the heavens and the earth:* "The heavens and the earth" stood for the universe. [b]**1.1,2** *In . . . life:* Or "When God began to create the heavens and the earth, the earth was barren with no form of life." [c]**1.2** *the Spirit of God:* Or "a mighty wind." [d]**1.5** *the first day:* A day was measured from evening to evening.

1.26 *Now we will make humans . . . like us:* The plural (we, us) may refer to God and the heavenly beings that make up God's heavenly court (11.7; Isa 6.8; 1 Kgs 22.19). The Hebrew word for "human" here is *adam,* which is also the name of the first human created (3.20). Humans alone are "like" God, which means they have a special relationship with God and represent God on earth by ruling over the other creatures. Also, the word *adam* comes from the same Hebrew word as "soil" (*adaman*). People are true "earth"-lings.

2.3 *God blessed the seventh day and . . . rested:* The Hebrew verb translated as "rested" is the basis for the word *sabbath,* which means "rest." God's rest is one reason given for the Sabbath Commandment in the Law of Moses.

2.4 LORD *God:* In 1.1—2.4, the Hebrew name translated as "God" is *Elohim.* In a second description of creation beginning with 2.4, the name used for God combines the Hebrew words *Yahweh* and *Elohim.* In CEV these are translated as "LORD God." While *Elohim* is a general name for God, *Yahweh* is a more particular name. It is the name God told Moses to use when telling the Hebrew people who it was who had sent Moses to speak to them (Exod 3.14,15).

LORD (YHWH)

done, and it was good. ¹³Evening came, then morning—that was the third day.

THE FOURTH DAY

¹⁴God said, "I command lights to appear in the sky and to separate day from night and to show the time for seasons, special days, and years. ¹⁵I command them to shine on the earth." And that's what happened. ¹⁶God made two powerful lights, the brighter one to rule the day and the other[e] to rule the night. He also made the stars. ¹⁷Then God put these lights in the sky to shine on the earth, ¹⁸to rule day and night, and to separate light from darkness. God looked at what he had done, and it was good. ¹⁹Evening came, then morning—that was the fourth day.

THE FIFTH DAY

²⁰God said, "I command the ocean to be full of living creatures, and I command birds to fly above the earth." ²¹So God made the giant sea monsters and all the living creatures that swim in the ocean. He also made every kind of bird. God looked at what he had done, and it was good. ²²Then he gave the living creatures his blessing—he told the ocean creatures to increase and live everywhere in the ocean and the birds to increase everywhere on earth. ²³Evening came, then morning—that was the fifth day.

THE SIXTH DAY

²⁴God said, "I command the earth to give life to all kinds of tame animals, wild animals, and reptiles." And that's what happened. ²⁵God made every one of them. Then he looked at what he had done, and it was good.

²⁶God said, "Now we will make humans, and they will be like us. We will let them rule the fish, the birds, and all other living creatures."

²⁷So God created humans to be like himself; he made men and women. ²⁸God gave them his blessing and said:

Have a lot of children! Fill the earth with people and bring it under your control. Rule over the fish in the ocean, the birds in the sky, and every animal on the earth.

²⁹I have provided all kinds of fruit and grain for you to eat. ³⁰And I have given the green plants as food for everything else that breathes, including animals, both wild and tame, and birds. And so it was.

³¹God looked at what he had done. All of it was very good! Evening came, then morning—that was the sixth day.

2 So the heavens and the earth and everything else were created.

THE SEVENTH DAY

²By the seventh day God had finished his work, and so he rested. ³God blessed the seventh day and made it special, because on that day he rested from his work.

⁴That's how God created the heavens and the earth.

The Garden of Eden

When the LORD God made the heavens and the earth, ⁵no grass or plants were growing anywhere. God had not yet sent any rain, and there was no one to work the land. ⁶But streams[f] came up from the ground and watered the earth.

⁷The LORD God took some soil from the ground and made a man.[g] God breathed

---

[e]**1.16** *the brighter . . . the other:* The sun and the moon. But they are not called by their names, because in Old Testament times some people worshiped the sun and the moon as though they were gods.
[f]**2.6** *streams:* Or "mist." [g]**2.7** *man:* In Hebrew "man" comes from the same word as "ground."

God looked at what he had done. All of it was very good! GEN 1.31

life into the man, and the man started breathing. ⁸The LORD made a garden in a place called Eden, which was in the east, and he put the man there.

⁹The LORD God filled the garden with all kinds of beautiful trees and fruit trees. Two other trees were in the middle of the garden. One of these gave life—the other gave the wisdom to know the difference between right and wrong.

¹⁰From Eden a river flowed out to water the garden, then it divided into four rivers. ¹¹The first one is the Pishon River that flows through the land of Havilah, ¹²where pure gold, rare perfumes, and precious stones are found. ¹³The second is the Gihon River that winds through Ethiopia.^h ¹⁴The Tigris River that flows east of Assyria is the third, and the fourth is the Euphrates River.

¹⁵The LORD God put the man in the Garden of Eden to take care of it and to look after it. ¹⁶But the LORD told him, "You may eat fruit from any tree in the garden, ¹⁷except the one that has the power to let you know the difference between right and wrong. If you eat any fruit from that tree, you will die before the day is over!"

¹⁸The LORD God said, "It isn't good for the man to live alone. I will make a suitable partner for him." ¹⁹⁻²⁰So the LORD took some soil and made animals and birds. He brought them to the man to see what names he would give each of them. Then the man named the tame animals and the birds and the wild animals. That's how they got their names.

None of these was the right kind of partner for the man. ²¹So the LORD God made him fall into a deep sleep, and he took out one of the man's ribs. Then after closing the man's side, ²²the LORD made a woman out of the rib.

The LORD God brought her to the man, ²³and the man exclaimed,

"Here is someone like me!
She is part of my body,
   my own flesh and bones.
She came from me, a man.
So I will name her Woman!"ⁱ

²⁴That's why a man will leave his own father and mother. He marries a woman, and the two of them become like one person. ²⁵Although the man and his wife were both naked, they were not ashamed.

The First Sin

3 The snake was sneakier than any of the other wild animals that the LORD God had made. One day it came to the woman and asked, "Did God tell you not to eat fruit from any tree in the garden?"

²The woman answered, "God said we could eat fruit from any tree in the garden, ³except the one in the middle. He told us not to eat fruit from that tree or even to touch it. If we do, we will die."

⁴"No, you won't!" the snake replied. ⁵"God understands what will happen on the day you eat fruit from that tree. You will see what you have done, and you will know the difference between right and wrong, just as God does."

⁶The woman stared at the fruit. It looked beautiful and tasty. She wanted the wisdom that it would give her, and she ate some of the fruit. Her husband was there

^h**2.13** *Ethiopia:* The Hebrew text has "Cush," which was a region south of Egypt that included parts of the present countries of Ethiopia and Sudan.   ⁱ**2.23** *a man . . . Woman:* In Hebrew the words "man" and "woman" are similar.

2.10-14 *Eden . . . Euphrates River:* In Hebrew, *Eden* means "pleasure" or "delight." The location of the Garden of Eden is described here as being somewhere in Mesopotamia. **(See Map 1 on pg 1879.)**

2.15 *take care of it:* As part of the "rule" over creation that God gave humans (1.26-29), the man is expected to take care of the Garden of Eden.

2.18-23 *suitable partner . . . Woman:* The animals and birds were not the right kind of partner for man, so woman was created. The woman is made from the man's rib, and not from the earth like the animals (2.19-20). Man and woman come from the same flesh (2.23) and together represent the human race.

3.1 *snake:* In the Old Testament, the snake came to represent the evil in the world that is able to tempt human beings to disobey God. In both the Old and New Testaments, an image of a snake is sometimes used to describe evil persons or nations or instruments of punishment (Ps 58.1-5; Deut 32.33; Isa 14.29; Jer 8.16,17; Matt 3.7; 23.33; Luke 3.7). In REVELATION Satan is described as a snake (Rev 12.9,13-15; 20.2). That is why the snake in the Garden of Eden is sometimes referred to as Satan, even though GENESIS does not say this and also does not clearly say where evil came from.

CR   Satan

3.16-18 *suffer terribly . . . ground will produce thorns*: As punishment for disobeying God, the woman will have pain during childbirth and the man will have to work hard to grow food, since the ground will naturally produce weeds, thorns, and thistles. After a lifetime of work, human beings will die and turn back into the soil God made them from.

3.21 *God made clothes*: Even though Adam and Eve disobeyed, God continued to take care of them.

3.22 *tree*: To be near this tree meant being in the presence of God. But to be sent away from this tree (3.23) shows how Adam and Eve's relationship with God was broken, and living forever with God was now impossible. The New Testament tells how God gives people new life, which includes one day being able to eat from the tree of life (Rev 22.14).

3.24 *God put winged creatures*: These winged creatures have traditionally been called *cherubim* (the plural of the Hebrew word *cherub*). They guarded sacred areas (Exod 25.18-22; 1 Kgs 8.6,7) and are often pictured as looking like the Sphinx of Egypt, having a human head and lion's body (Ezek 41.18-20) or like the human-headed bulls and lions that guarded ancient Mesopotamian temples.

with her, so she gave some to him, and he ate it too. **7**At once they saw what they had done, and they realized they were naked. Then they sewed fig leaves together to cover themselves.

8Late in the afternoon, when the breeze began to blow, the man and woman heard the Lord God walking in the garden. So they hid behind some trees.

Sin Brings a Curse

9The Lord God called out to the man and asked, "Where are you?"

10The man answered, "I was naked, and when I heard you walking through the garden, I was frightened and hid!"

11"How did you know you were naked?" God asked. "Did you eat any fruit from that tree in the middle of the garden?"

12"It was the woman you put here with me," the man said. "She gave me some of the fruit, and I ate it."

13The Lord God then asked the woman, "What have you done?"

"The snake tricked me," she answered, "and I ate some of that fruit."

14So the Lord God said to the snake:
"Because of what you have done,
you will be the only animal
   to suffer this curse—
For as long as you live,
you will crawl on your stomach
   and eat dirt.
15You and this woman
   will hate each other;
your descendants and hers
   will always be enemies.
One of hers will strike you
   on the head,
and you will strike him
   on the heel."

16Then the Lord God said to the woman,
"You will suffer terribly
   when you give birth.
But you will still desire
   your husband,
   and he will rule over you."

17The Lord said to the man,
"You listened to your wife
and ate the fruit
   I told you not to eat.
And so, the ground
will be under a curse
   because of what you did.
As long as you live,
you will have to struggle
   to grow enough food.
18Your food will be plants,
but the ground will produce
   thorns and thistles.
19You will sweat all your life
   to earn a living;
you were made out of soil,
and you will once again
   turn into soil."

20The man Adam^j named his wife Eve^k because she would become the mother of all who live.

21Then the Lord God made clothes out of animal skins for the man and his wife.

22The Lord said, "They now know the difference between right and wrong, just as we do. But they must not be allowed to eat fruit from the tree that lets them live forever." **23**So the Lord God sent them out of the Garden of Eden, where they would have to work the ground from which the man had been made. **24**Then God put

^j**3.20** *The man Adam*: In Hebrew "man" and "Adam" are the same.   ^k**3.20** *Eve*: In Hebrew "Eve" sounds like "living."

winged creatures at the entrance to the garden and a flaming, flashing sword to guard the way to the life-giving tree.

Cain Murders Abel

4 Adam[l] and Eve had a son. Then Eve said, "I'll name him Cain because I got[m] him with the help of the Lord." [2]Later she had another son and named him Abel.

Abel became a sheep farmer, but Cain farmed the land. [3]One day, Cain gave part of his harvest to the Lord, [4]and Abel also gave an offering to the Lord. He killed the first-born lamb from one of his sheep and gave the Lord the best parts of it. The Lord was pleased with Abel and his offering, [5]but not with Cain and his offering. This made Cain so angry that he could not hide his feelings.

[6]The Lord said to Cain:

What's wrong with you? Why do you look so angry? [7]If you had done the right thing, you would be smiling.[n] But you did the wrong thing, and now sin is waiting to attack you like a lion. Sin wants to destroy you, but don't let it!

[8]Cain said to his brother Abel, "Let's go for a walk."[o] And when they were out in a field, Cain attacked and killed him.

[9]Afterwards the Lord asked Cain, "Where is Abel?"

"How should I know?" he answered. "Am I supposed to look after my brother?"

[10]Then the Lord said:

Why have you done this terrible thing? You killed your own brother,

and his blood flowed onto the ground. Now his blood is calling out for me to punish you. [11]And so, I'll put you under a curse. Because you killed Abel and made his blood run out on the ground, you will never be able to farm it again. [12]When you try to farm the land, it won't produce anything for you. From now on, you'll be without a home, and you'll spend the rest of your life wandering from place to place.

[13]"This punishment is too hard!" Cain said. [14]"You're making me leave my home and live far from you.[P] I will have to wander about without a home, and just anyone could kill me."

[15]"No!"[q] the Lord answered. "Anyone who kills you will be punished seven times worse than I am punishing you." So the Lord put a mark on Cain to warn everyone not to kill him. [16]But Cain had to go far from the Lord and live in the Land of Wandering,[r] which is east of Eden.

More and More People

[17]Later, Cain and his wife had a son named Enoch. At the time Cain was building a town, and so he named it Enoch after his son. [18]Then Enoch had a son named Irad, who had a son named Mehujael, who had a son named Methushael, who had a son named Lamech. [19]Lamech married Adah, then Zillah. [20-21]Lamech and Adah had two sons, Jabal and Jubal. Their son Jabal was the first to live in tents and raise sheep and goats. Jubal was the first to play harps and flutes.

[l]**4.1** *Adam:* See the note at 3.20. [m]**4.1** *Cain . . . got:* In Hebrew "Cain" sounds like "got." [n]**4.7** *you would be smiling:* Or "I would have accepted your offering." [o]**4.8** *Cain said to his brother Abel, "Let's . . . walk."* Most ancient translations; Hebrew "Cain spoke to his brother Abel." [P]**4.14** *live . . . you:* It was generally believed that the Lord was with his people only in their own land. [q]**4.15** *No:* Three ancient translations; Hebrew "Very well!" [r]**4.16** *Wandering:* The Hebrew text has "Nod," which means "wandering."

4.3,4 *Cain . . . Abel:* Abel's sacrifice of a first-born lamb was proper and pleasing to God (Exod 13.2,12,15; Lev 27.26; Heb 11.4). Although grain offerings were usually considered good, Cain may not have offered God the "first," or best, part of his harvest. **(See the chart Sacrifices and Offerings on pg 1828.)**

Sin

4.10,11 *blood . . . curse:* Blood was believed to be the life-source of animals and human beings (Lev 17.11,14). Cain was cursed, just as the ground was earlier put under a curse (3.17).

Blood

4.14 *live far from you:* Ancient peoples often believed that their gods lived or looked after particular places. This thinking is reflected in Cain's concern. Later, the Hebrew people would discover that their God was not limited to a particular place.

4.15 *mark:* Just what kind of mark is not clear. The mark was a sign of God's protection and mercy.

4.17,18 *Cain . . . Lamech:* Counting Adam, the number of the first generations is seven, a number that symbolizes perfection. **(See the chart Numbers in the Bible on pg 1844.)**

Cain answered the Lord, "Am I supposed to look after my brother?" Gen 4.9

4.23 *two wives:* It was not unusual in ancient times for a man to have more than one wife (16.1-3; 29.16-30).

5.1-4 *God created men and women . . . Adam . . . Seth:* The same phrase that describes how the first man (Adam) was created to be like God is now used to describe how Adam's son, Seth, was made like Adam.

5.3-32 *Adam . . . Noah:* The number of generations from Adam to Noah is ten and equal about 8,400 years. Whether these years are meant to be taken as an exact number or as symbolic numbers has been debated, especially when compared to archaeological discoveries. For example, Enoch's years are 365 (5.23,24), the same number of days in a year, meaning he had a full life.

In Hebrew the name Noah sounds like "comfort," which emphasizes Noah's part in how God delivered the human race from the flood and promised never to destroy humankind this way again (9.11-17). **(See the chart Numbers in the Bible on pg 1844.)**

Genealogies in the Bible

6.1-4 *supernatural beings . . . Nephilim:* The supernatural beings probably refer to angels or other heavenly beings in God's heavenly court. The children born to the women who married these heavenly beings were called Nephilim, which means "fallen ones." Most likely they are similar to the giant beings mentioned in Num 13.31-33 and Deut 2.10,11; 9.2.

[22]Lamech and Zillah had a son named Tubal Cain who made tools out of bronze and iron. They also had a daughter, whose name was Naamah.

[23]One day, Lamech said to his two wives, "A young man wounded me, and I killed him. [24]Anyone who tries to get even with me will be punished ten times more than anyone who tries to get even with Cain."

[25]Adam and his wife had another son. They named him Seth, because they said, "God has given[s] us a son to take the place of Abel, who was killed by his brother Cain." [26]Later, Seth had a son and named him Enosh.

About this time people started worshiping the LORD.[t]

Descendants of Adam

5 [1-2]God created men and women to be like himself. He gave them his blessing and called them human beings. The following is a list of the descendants of Adam, the first man:

[3-4]When Adam was 130, he had a son who was just like him, and he named him Seth. Adam had more children [5]and died at the age of 930.

[6]When Seth was 105, he had a son named Enosh. [7]Seth had more children [8]and died at the age of 912.

[9]When Enosh was 90, he had a son named Kenan. [10]Enosh had more children [11]and died at the age of 905.

[12]When Kenan was 70, he had a son named Mahalalel. [13]Kenan had more children [14]and died at the age of 910.

[15]When Mahalalel was 65, he had a son

named Jared. [16]Mahalalel had more children [17]and died at the age of 895.

[18]When Jared was 162, he had a son named Enoch. [19]Jared had more children [20]and died at the age of 962.

[21]When Enoch was 65, he had a son named Methuselah, [22]and during the next 300 years he had more children. Enoch truly loved God, [23-24]and God took him away at the age of 365.

[25]When Methuselah was 187, he had a son named Lamech. [26]Methuselah had more children [27]and died at the age of 969.

[28]When Lamech was one 182, he had a son. [29]Lamech said, "I'll name him Noah because he will give us comfort,[u] as we struggle hard to make a living on this land that the LORD has put under a curse." [30]Lamech had more children [31]and died at the age of 777.

[32]After Noah was 500 years old, he had three sons and named them Shem, Ham, and Japheth.

The LORD Will Send a Flood

6 [1-2]More and more people were born, until finally they spread all over the earth. Some of their daughters were so beautiful that supernatural beings[v] came down and married the ones they wanted. [3]Then the LORD said, "I won't let my life-giving breath remain in anyone forever.[w] No one will live for more than 120 years."[x]

[4]The children of the supernatural beings who had married these women became famous heroes and warriors. They were called Nephilim and lived on the earth at that time and even later.

[s]4.25 *Seth . . . given:* In Hebrew "Seth" sounds like "given." [t]4.26 *worshiping the LORD:* Or "worshiping in the name of the LORD." [u]5.29 *Noah . . . comfort:* In Hebrew "Noah" sounds like "comfort." [v]6.1,2 *supernatural beings:* Or "angels." [w]6.3 *I won't . . . forever:* One possible meaning for the difficult Hebrew text. [x]6.3 *No one . . . years:* Or "In fact, they will all be destroyed in about 100 years" (that is, at the time of the flood).

God created men and women to be like himself. He gave them his blessing and called them human beings.
GEN 5.1-2

[5]The LORD saw how bad the people on earth were and that everything they thought and planned was evil. [6]He was sorry that he had made them, [7]and he said, "I'm going to destroy every person on earth! I'll even wipe out animals, birds, and reptiles. I'm sorry I ever made them."

[8]But the LORD was pleased with Noah, [9]and this is the story about him. Noah was the only person who lived right and obeyed God. [10]He had three sons: Shem, Ham, and Japheth.

[11-12]God knew that everyone was terribly cruel and violent. [13]So he told Noah:

Cruelty and violence have spread everywhere. Now I'm going to destroy the whole earth and all its people. [14]Get some good lumber and build a boat. Put rooms in it and cover it with tar inside and out. [15]Make it 450 feet long, 75 feet wide, and 45 feet high. [16]Build a roof[y] on the boat and leave a space of about 18 inches between the roof and the sides.[z] Make the boat three stories high and put a door on one side.

[17]I'm going to send a flood that will destroy everything that breathes! Nothing will be left alive. [18]But I solemnly promise that you, your wife, your sons, and your daughters-in-law will be kept safe in the boat.[a]

[19-20]Take into the boat with you a male and a female of every kind of animal and bird, as well as a male and a female of every reptile. I don't want them to be destroyed. [21]Store up enough food both for yourself and for them. [22]Noah did everything God told him to do.

The Flood

7 The LORD told Noah:
Take your whole family with you into the boat, because you are the only one on this earth who pleases me. [2]Take seven pairs of every kind of animal that can be used for sacrifice[b] and one pair of all others. [3]Also take seven pairs of every kind of bird with you. Do this so there will always be animals and birds on the earth. [4]Seven days from now I will send rain that will last for 40 days and nights, and I will destroy all other living creatures I have made.

[5-7]Noah was 600 years old when he went into the boat to escape the flood, and he did everything the LORD had told him to do. His wife, his sons, and his daughters-in-law all went inside with him. [8-9]He obeyed God and took a male and a female of each kind of animal and bird into the boat with him. [10]Seven days later a flood began to cover the earth.

[11-12]The water under the earth started gushing out everywhere, the sky opened like windows, and rain poured down for 40 days and nights. All this began on the seventeenth day of the second month of the year. [13]On that day Noah and his wife went into the boat with their three sons, Shem, Ham, and Japheth, and their wives. [14]They took along every kind of animal, tame and wild, including the birds. [15]Noah took a male and a female of every living creature with him, [16]just as God had told him to do. And when they were all in the boat, the LORD closed the door.

[17-18]For 40 days the rain poured down without stopping. And the water became

[y]6.16 roof: Or "window." [z]6.16 leave . . . sides: One possible meaning for the difficult Hebrew text.
[a]6.18 boat: One possible meaning for the difficult Hebrew text of verse 18. [b]7.2 animal . . . for sacrifice: Hebrew "clean animals." Animals that could be used for sacrifice were called "clean," and animals that could not be used were called "unclean."

6.14 *good lumber . . . build a boat:* The type of wood Noah used is uncertain. The Hebrew word used for boat here is often translated as "ark." This same Hebrew word also is used for the floating basket that was used to save the baby Moses (Exod 2.3-5). The boat is about the length of one and a half modern American football fields.

7.2 *seven pairs . . . used for sacrifice:* Compare this verse to 6.19,20. The number seven is a sacred number. Animals that could be sacrificed according to the Law of Moses were called "clean" animals, and animals that could not be sacrificed were called "unclean." Extra "clean" animals would have been needed for the sacrifices to please the LORD that Noah would later make (8.20) and for food (9.3). **(See the article People of the Law: The Religion of Israel on pg 1794.)**

Purity (Clean and Unclean)

7.4 *40 days and nights:* In the Bible, this length of time is often associated with a time of preparation. **(See the chart Numbers in the Bible on pg 1844.)**

7.11-12 *water under the earth . . . sky opened like windows:* The water did not simply fall as rain, but also came out of the ground like geysers gushing from underground oceans. This flood is described as the reversal of what God did to overcome the watery chaos at the time of creation, when he separated the dry land (earth) from the water below and above the earth (1.7).

An Ancient Flood Story

7.22-23 *destroyed everything that breathed:* Except for the people and animals on the boat, the gift of breath, which God gave at creation (1.30; 2.7), was taken away.

8.1 *God made a wind blow:* Compare the order of events in chapters 8 and 9 to the order of events in chapter 1. This new beginning after the flood is like the beginning of creation: 8.1 (1.2); 8.2 (1.6,7); 8.5 (1.20); 8.17 (1.24); 9.1,2 (1.28).

8.4 *Ararat mountains:* Probably refers to the area northwest of ancient Mesopotamia known as Urartu (modern-day northeast Turkey or Armenia). **(See Map 1 on pg 1879.)**

8.6-8 *send out a raven . . . a dove:* A raven is a black bird that can survive in difficult circumstances. They were considered "unclean" birds because according to the Law of Moses they were not acceptable for eating or as sacrifices for sin (see Deut 14.14).

Doves are "clean" birds, similar to pigeons. They could be easily trained to carry messages. According to the Law of Moses they were acceptable sacrifices for sin for poor people who couldn't afford to sacrifice a larger animal.

8.21 *sinful things . . . evil thoughts:* The flood didn't destroy sin, which causes evil thoughts in human beings from the time they are young. But God promises not to destroy all living things because of sin.

deeper and deeper, until the boat started floating high above the ground. [19-20]Finally, the mighty flood was so deep that even the highest mountain peaks were almost 25 feet below the surface of the water. [21]Not a bird, animal, reptile, or human was left alive anywhere on earth. [22-23]The LORD destroyed everything that breathed. Nothing was left alive except Noah and the others in the boat. [24]A hundred fifty days later, the water started going down.

The Water Goes Down

8 God did not forget about Noah and the animals with him in the boat. So God made a wind blow, and the water started going down. [2]God stopped up the places where the water had been gushing out from under the earth. He also closed up the sky, and the rain stopped. [3]For 150 days the water slowly went down. [4]Then on the seventeenth day of the seventh month of the year, the boat came to rest somewhere in the Ararat mountains. [5]The water kept going down, and the mountain tops could be seen on the first day of the tenth month.

[6-7]Forty days later Noah opened a window to send out a raven, but it kept flying around until the water had dried up. [8]Noah wanted to find out if the water had gone down, so he sent out a dove. [9]Deep water was still everywhere, and when the dove could not find a place to land, it flew back to the boat. Then Noah held out his hand and helped it back in. [10]Seven days later Noah sent the dove out again. [11]It returned in the evening, holding in its beak a green leaf from an olive tree. Noah knew the water was finally going down. [12]He waited seven more days

before sending the dove out again, and this time it did not return.

[13]Noah was now 601 years old. And by the first day of that year, almost all the water had gone away. Noah made an opening in the roof of the boat[c] and saw that the ground was getting dry. [14]By the twenty-seventh day of the second month, the earth was completely dry.

[15]God said to Noah, [16]"You, your wife, your sons, and your daughters-in-law may now leave the boat. [17]Let out the birds, animals, and reptiles, so they can mate and live all over the earth." [18]After Noah and his family had left the boat, [19]the living creatures left in groups of their own kind.

The LORD's Promise for the Earth

[20]Noah built an altar where he could offer sacrifices to the LORD. Then he offered on the altar one of each kind of animal and bird that could be used for a sacrifice.[d] [21]The smell of the burning offering pleased the LORD, and he said:

Never again will I punish the earth for the sinful things its people do. All of them have evil thoughts from the time they are young, but I will never destroy everything that breathes, as I did this time.
[22]As long as the earth remains,
there will be planting
and harvest,
cold and heat;
winter and summer,
day and night.

God's Promise to Noah

9 God said to Noah and his sons:
I am giving you my blessing.

[c]**8.13** *made . . . boat:* One possible meaning for the difficult Hebrew text. [d]**8.20** *animal . . . sacrifice:* See the note at 7.2.

Have a lot of children and grand-children, so people will live every-where on this earth. [2]All animals, birds, reptiles, and fish will be afraid of you. I have placed them under your control, [3]and I have given them to you for food. From now on, you may eat them, as well as the green plants that you have always eaten. [4]But life is in the blood, and you must not eat any meat that still has blood in it. [5-6]I cre-ated humans to be like me, and I will punish any animal or person that takes a human life. If an animal kills someone, that animal must die. And if a person takes the life of another, that person must be put to death.

[7]I want you and your descendants to have many children, so people will live everywhere on earth.

[8]Again, God said to Noah and his sons: [9]I am going to make a solemn prom-ise to you and to everyone who will live after you. [10]This includes the birds and the animals that came out of the boat. [11]I promise every living creature that the earth and those living on it will never again be destroyed by a flood. [12-13]The rainbow that I have put in the sky will be my sign to you and to every living creature on earth. It will remind you that I will keep this prom-ise forever. [14]When I send clouds over the earth, and a rainbow appears in the sky, [15]I will remember my promise to you and to all other living creatures. Never again will I let floodwaters de-stroy all life. [16]When I see the rainbow in the sky, I will always remember the promise that I have made to every liv-ing creature. [17]The rainbow will be the sign of that solemn promise.

[e]9.27 *more and more:* In Hebrew "Japheth" sounds like "more and more."

Noah and His Family

[18]Noah and his sons, Shem, Ham, and Japheth, left the boat. Ham later had a son named Canaan. [19]All people on earth are descendants of Noah's three sons.

[20]Noah farmed the land and was the first to plant a vineyard. [21]One day he got drunk and was lying naked in his tent. [22]Ham entered the tent and saw him naked, then went back outside and told his brothers. [23]Shem and Japheth put a robe over their shoulders and walked backwards into the tent. Without looking at their fa-ther, they placed it over his body.

[24]When Noah sobered up and learned what his youngest son had done, [25]he said,

"I now put a curse on Canaan!
He will be the lowest slave
    of his brothers.
[26]I ask the LORD my God
    to bless Shem
and make Canaan his slave.
[27]I pray God will give Japheth
    more and more[e] land
and let him take over
    the territory of Shem.
May Canaan be his slave."

[28]Noah lived 350 years after the flood [29]and died at the age of 950.

The Descendants of Noah

10 After the flood Shem, Ham, and Japheth had many descendants.

The Descendants of Japheth

[2-5]Japheth's descendants had their own languages, tribes, and land. They were Gomer, Magog, Madai, Javan, Tubal, Meshech, and Tiras.

9.3,4 *you may eat them . . . must not eat . . . blood:* Meat is here added to the food God provided at the time of creation (1.29). But because blood was thought to carry life, it was not to be eaten (Lev 17.10-14; Deut 12.23,24).

Blood

9.9 *solemn promise:* The Hebrew word for this phrase is sometimes translated as "covenant," which means an agreement between two or more persons (or groups). Most ancient cov-enants stated what both parties would do to keep the terms of the agreement. But here, God alone is making an un-conditional promise not to destroy the earth by a flood (9.11,15). The rainbow will be a sign of this promise. Noah's part of the agreement is not stated.

Agreements (Covenants)

Wine

9.22-27 *Ham . . . Canaan:* Canaan is the son of Ham, Noah's youngest son. Because Noah curses Canaan, some have suggested that it was actu-ally Canaan who saw Noah naked and told his uncles. Later, the Israelites, who were descendants of Shem, did enter and take over the land of the Canaanites, the descendants of Canaan. The curse could imply that the Canaan-ites became Israel's slaves because of their evil sexual actions. For example, Canaanite worship included having sex with temple prostitutes who served the Canaanite fertility goddess.

God said to Noah, "I promise every living creature that the earth and those living on it will never again be destroyed by a flood." GEN 9.11

10.6-20 *Ham's descendants:* These tribes and nations were mainly located in northeastern Africa and Canaan, but certain ancestors such as the warrior Nimrod ruled city-states in Babylonia, another name for southern Mesopotamia, and Nineveh in Assyria, which was in the northern part of the Tigris and Euphrates River valleys.

The land of Cush has been identified with the region south of Egypt that included parts of the present countries of Ethiopia and Sudan. (See Map 1 on pg 1879 and the article The Ancient World: Peoples, Powers, and Politics on pg 1780.)

10.21-31 *Shem's descendants:* These descendants were "Shemites," later modified to Semites. The people known as Israel descended from the Hebrew people (children of Eber), one group of ancient Semitic peoples. Elam was an early name for Assyria, and Aram was an early name for Syria.

Sheba was probably located in southwest Arabia. The queen of Sheba made a famous visit to King Solomon of Israel (1 Kgs 10.1-13). Ophir, in southern Arabia or in Africa, was an important source of gold for Solomon (1 Kgs 9.28; 10.11).

11.2-4 *Babylonia . . . tower:* A number of tall temples (called ziggurats) were built in ancient Mesopotamia to honor the gods. They usually had a square base with sloping stepped sides leading up to an altar area at the top. These towers were meant to be stairways to heaven.

Gomer was the ancestor of Ashkenaz, Riphath, and Togarmah.

Javan was the ancestor of Elishah, Tarshish, Kittim, and Dodanim,[f] who settled along the coast.

The Descendants of Ham

[6-20]Ham's descendants had their own languages, tribes, and land. They were Ethiopia,[g] Egypt, Put, and Canaan.

Cush[h] was the ancestor of Seba, Havilah, Sabtah, Raamah, and Sabteca.

Raamah was the ancestor of Sheba and Dedan.

Cush was also the ancestor of Nimrod, a mighty warrior whose strength came from the LORD. This is why people say: "You hunt like Nimrod with the strength of the LORD!" Nimrod first ruled in Babylon, Erech, and Accad, all of[i] which were in Babylonia.[j] From there Nimrod went to Assyria and built the great city of Nineveh. He also built Rehoboth-Ir and Calah, as well as Resen, which is between Nineveh and Calah.

Egypt was the ancestor of Ludim, Anamim, Lehabim, Naphtuhim, Pathrusim, Casluhim, and Caphtorim, the ancestor of the Philistines.[k]

Canaan's sons were Sidon and Heth. Canaan was also the ancestor of the Jebusites, the Amorites, the Girgashites, the Hivites, the Arkites, the Sinites, the Arvadites, the Zemarites, and the Hamathites.

Later the Canaanites spread from the territory of Sidon and settled as far away as Gaza in the direction of Gerar. They also went as far as Lasha in the direction of Sodom, Gomorrah, Admah, and Zeboiim.

The Descendants of Shem

[21-31]Shem's descendants had their own languages, tribes, and land. He was the older brother of Japheth and the ancestor of the tribes of Eber.

Shem was the ancestor of Elam, Asshur, Arpachshad, Lud, and Aram.

Aram was the ancestor of Uz, Hul, Gether, and Mash.

Arpachshad was the father of Shelah and the grandfather of Eber, whose first son was named Peleg,[l] because it was during his time that tribes divided up the earth. Eber's second son was Joktan.

Joktan was the ancestor of Almodad, Sheleph, Hazarmaveth, Jerah, Hadoram, Uzal, Diklah, Obal, Abimael, Sheba, Ophir, Havilah, and Jobab. Their land reached from Mesha in the direction of Sephar, the hill country in the east.

[32]This completes the list of Noah's descendants. After the flood their descendants became nations and spread all over the world.

The Tower of Babel

11 At first everyone spoke the same language, [2]but after some of them moved from the east[m] and settled in Babylonia,[n] [3-4]they said:

Let's build a city with a tower that reaches to the sky! We'll use hard

[f]10.2-5 *Dodanim:* Most Hebrew manuscripts; some Hebrew manuscripts and one ancient translation have "Rodanim." [g]10.6-20 *Ethiopia:* See the note at 2.13. [h]10.6-20 *Cush:* See the note at 2.13. [i]10.6-20 *and Accad, all of:* Or "Accad, and Calneh." [j]10.6-20 *Babylonia:* The Hebrew text has "Shinar," another name for Babylonia. [k]10.6-20 *Casluhim, and Caphtorim, the ancestor of the Philistines:* Hebrew "Caphtorim, and Casluhim, the ancestor of the Philistines." The Philistines were from Caphtor (see Jeremiah 47.4; Amos 9.7), better known as Crete. [l]10.21-31 *Peleg:* In Hebrew "Peleg" means "divided." [m]11.2 *from the east:* Or "to the east." [n]11.2 *Babylonia:* See the note at 10.6-20.

bricks and tar instead of stone and mortar. We'll become famous, and we won't be scattered all over the world. [5]But when the LORD came down to look at the city and the tower, [6]he said:

These people are working together because they all speak the same language. This is just the beginning. Soon they will be able to do anything they want. [7]Let's go down and confuse them! We'll make them speak different languages, and they won't be able to understand each other.

[8-9]So the people had to stop building the city, because the LORD confused their language and scattered them all over the earth. That's how the city of Babel[o] got its name.

The Descendants of Shem

[10-11]Two years after the flood, when Shem was 100, he had a son named Arpachshad. He had more children and died at the age of 600. This is a list of his descendants:

[12]When Arpachshad was 35, he had a son named Shelah. [13]Arpachshad had more children and died at the age of 438. [14]When Shelah was 30, he had a son named Eber. [15]Shelah had more children and died at the age of 433. [16]When Eber was 34, he had a son named Peleg. [17]Eber had more children and died at the age of 464. [18]When Peleg was 30, he had a son named Reu. [19]Peleg had more children and died at the age of 239. [20]When Reu was 32 he had a son named Serug. [21]Reu had more children and died at the age of 239.

[22]When Serug was 30, he had a son named Nahor. [23]Serug had more children and died at the age of 230. [24]When Nahor was 29, he had a son named Terah. [25]Nahor had more children and died at the age of 148.

The Descendants of Terah

[26-28]After Terah was 70 years old, he had three sons: Abram, Nahor, and Haran, who became the father of Lot. Terah's sons were born in the city of Ur in Chaldea,[P] and Haran died there before the death of his father. The following is the story of Terah's descendants. [29-30]Abram married Sarai, but she was not able to have children. And Nahor married Milcah, who was the daughter of Haran and the sister of Iscah. [31]Terah decided to move from Ur to the land of Canaan. He took along Abram and Sarai and his grandson Lot, the son of Haran. But when they came to the city of Haran,[q] they settled there instead. [32]Terah lived to be 205 years old and died in Haran.

The LORD Chooses Abram

12 The LORD said to Abram:
Leave your country, your family, and your relatives and go to the land that I will show you. [2]I will bless you and make your descendants into a great nation. You will become famous and be a blessing to others. [3]I will bless those who bless you, but I will put a curse on anyone who puts a curse on you. Everyone on earth will be blessed because of you.[r]

● 11.10-25 *Shem . . . Terah:* The list of Shem's descendants in these verses continues the genealogy in 5.3-32, that began with Adam and ended with Noah. The list here (11.10-25) traces the genealogy to Terah, the father of Abram (Abraham). Another version of Shem's genealogy is found in 10.21-31.

● 11.26-32 *Terah . . . Haran:* These verses list the immediate family of Abram, whose descendants became the people of Israel. Haran is the name of one of Terah's sons, as well as the name of a place (11.31).

● 11.26-31 *Ur in Chaldea . . . Haran:* Chaldea was a region at the northern end of the Persian Gulf. Ur was on the main trade routes from Mesopotamia to the Mediterranean Sea. Terah wanted to go to Canaan, which was west of Chaldea, but traveling directly west meant traveling through the dangerous Arabian Desert. The safer route to Canaan was northwest along the Euphrates River Valley to Haran and then turning southwest toward Canaan. **(See Map 1 on pg 1879 and the article Trade and Travel on pg 1806.)**

● 12.1-3 *Abram:* The name Abram means "exalted father." His name later is changed to Abraham (17.4,5).

◌ Abraham

---

[o]**11.8,9** *Babel:* In Hebrew "Babel" sounds like "confused."   [P]**11.26-28** *Ur in Chaldea:* Chaldea was a region at the head of the Persian Gulf. Ur was on the main trade routes from Mesopotamia to the Mediterranean Sea.   [q]**11.31** *Haran:* About 550 miles northwest of Ur.   [r]**12.3** *Everyone . . . you:* Or "Everyone on earth will ask me to bless them as I have blessed you."

12.4-5 *Canaan:* Canaan included lands that today make up the states of Israel, Lebanon, and southern Syria. The Canaanites were descendants of Noah's son, Ham (10.6-20). **(See Map 1 on pg 1879.)**

12.9 *Southern Desert:* The Southern Desert is also known as the Negev, the area south and west of the Dead Sea, which formed a land bridge between Canaan, the Sinai Peninsula, and Egypt. **(See Map 3 on pg 1881.)**

Egypt

12.19 *I've married her:* The king of Egypt took Sarai into his palace, where she was expected to be part of the community of women who were the king's wives (a harem). By letting the king think that Sarai was his sister, Abram put the LORD's promise (12.1-3) at risk. **(See the article The Ancient World: Peoples, Powers, and Politics on pg 1780.)**

King of Egypt (Pharaoh)

13.10-12 *Sodom and Gomorrah . . . Zoar . . . Jordan Valley:* The Jordan Valley stretched from Lake Galilee in the north to Zoar, which was at the southern end of the present Dead Sea. The location of Sodom and Gomorrah is not certain, but they may have been in the Siddim Valley (14.1-4), the area that is now covered by the southern part of the Dead Sea. Settling near Sodom was risky, since the people there were seen as being evil (13.13; 19.1-29). **(See Map 3 on pg 1881.)**

4-5 Abram was 75 years old when the LORD told him to leave the city of Haran. He obeyed and left with his wife Sarai, his nephew Lot, and all the possessions and slaves they had acquired while in Haran.

When they came to the land of Canaan, **6**Abram went as far as the sacred tree of Moreh in a place called Shechem. The Canaanites were still living in the land at that time, **7**but the LORD appeared to Abram and promised, "I will give this land to your family forever." Abram then built an altar there for the LORD.

8Abram traveled to the hill country east of Bethel and camped between Bethel and Ai, where he built another altar and worshiped the LORD. **9**Later, Abram started out toward the Southern Desert.

Abram in Egypt

10-11 The crops failed, and there was no food anywhere in Canaan. So Abram and his wife Sarai went to live in Egypt for a while. But just before they got there, Abram said, "Sarai, you are really beautiful! **12**When the Egyptians see you, they will murder me because I am your husband. But they won't kill you. **13**Please save my life by saying you are my sister."

14As soon as Abram and Sarai arrived in Egypt, the Egyptians noticed how beautiful she was. **15**The king's[s] officials told him about her, and she was taken to his house. **16**The king was good to Abram because of Sarai, and Abram was given sheep, cattle, donkeys, slaves, and camels.

17Because of Sarai, the LORD struck the king and everyone in his palace with terrible diseases. **18**Finally, the king sent for Abram and said to him, "What have you done to me? Why didn't you tell me Sarai

was your wife? **19**Why did you make me believe she was your sister? Now I've married her. Take her and go! She's your wife."

20So the king told his men to let Abram and Sarai take their possessions and leave.

Abram and Lot Separate

13 Abram and Sarai took everything they owned and went to the Southern Desert. Lot went with them.

2Abram was very rich. He owned many cattle, sheep, and goats, and had a lot of silver and gold. **3**Abram moved from place to place in the Southern Desert. And finally, he went north and set up his tents between Bethel and Ai, **4**where he had earlier camped and built an altar. There he worshiped the LORD.

5Lot, who was traveling with him, also had sheep, goats, and cattle, as well as his own family and slaves. **6-7**At this time the Canaanites and the Perizzites were still living in the same area, and so there wasn't enough pastureland left for Abram and Lot with all of their animals. Besides this, the men who took care of Abram's animals and the ones who took care of Lot's animals started quarreling.

8Abram said to Lot, "We are close relatives. We shouldn't argue, and our men shouldn't be fighting one another. **9**There is plenty of land for you to choose from. Let's separate. If you go north, I'll go south; if you go south, I'll go north."

10This happened before the LORD had destroyed the cities of Sodom and Gomorrah. And when Lot looked around, he saw there was plenty of water in the Jordan Valley. All the way to Zoar the valley was as green as the garden of the LORD or the land of Egypt. **11**So Lot chose the whole Jordan

---

[s]12.15 *The king's:* The Hebrew text has "Pharaoh's," a Hebrew word sometimes used for the king of Egypt.

Valley for himself, and as he started out toward the east, he and Abram separated. [12]Abram stayed in the land of Canaan. But Lot settled near the cities of the valley and put up his tents not far from Sodom, [13]where the people were evil and sinned terribly against the LORD.

Abram Moves to Hebron

[14]After Abram and Lot had gone their separate ways, the LORD said to Abram:

Look around to the north, south, east, and west. [15]I will give you and your family all the land you can see. It will be theirs forever! [16]I will give you more descendants than there are specks of dust on the earth, and someday it will be easier to count those specks of dust than to count your descendants. [17]Now walk back and forth across the land, because I am going to give it to you.

[18]Abram took down his tents and went to live near the sacred trees of Mamre at Hebron, where he built an altar in honor of the LORD.

Abram Rescues Lot

14 About this time, King Amraphel of Babylonia,[t] King Arioch of Ellasar, King Chedorlaomer of Elam, and King Tidal of Goiim [2]attacked King Bera of Sodom, King Birsha of Gomorrah, King Shinab of Admah, King Shemeber of Zeboiim, and the king of Bela, a city also known as Zoar. [3-4]King Chedorlaomer and his allies had ruled these last five kings for twelve years, but in the thirteenth year the kings rebelled and joined forces in Sid-

dim Valley, which is now covered by the southern part of the Dead Sea.

[5]A year later King Chedorlaomer and his allies attacked and defeated the Rephaites in Ashteroth-Karnaim, the Zuzites in Ham, and the Emites in Shaveh-Kiriathaim. [6]They also defeated the Horites in the hill country of Edom,[u] as far as El-Paran, near the desert.

[7]They went back to the city of Enmishpat, better known as Kadesh. Then they captured all the land that belonged to the Amalekites, and they defeated the Amorites who were living in Hazazon-Tamar.

[8-9]At Siddim Valley, the armies of the kings of Sodom, Gomorrah, Admah, Zeboiim, and Bela fought the armies of King Chedorlaomer of Elam, King Tidal of Goiim, King Amraphel of Babylonia, and King Arioch of Ellasar. The valley [10]was full of tar pits, and when the troops from Sodom and Gomorrah started running away, some of them fell into the pits. Others escaped to the hill country. [11]Their enemies took everything of value from Sodom and Gomorrah, including their food supplies. [12]They also captured Abram's nephew Lot, who lived in Sodom. They took him and his possessions and then left.

[13]At this time Abram the Hebrew was living near the oaks that belonged to Mamre the Amorite. Mamre and his brothers Eshcol and Aner were Abram's friends. Someone who had escaped from the battle told Abram [14]that his nephew Lot had been taken away. Three hundred and eighteen of Abram's servants were fighting men, so he took them and followed the enemy as far north as the city of Dan.

[15]That night, Abram divided up his

[t]**14.1** *Babylonia:* See the note at 10.6-20.   [u]**14.6** *Edom:* The Hebrew text has "Seir," another name for Edom.

13.18 *sacred trees of Mamre at Hebron:* Mamre, a town named after one of Abram's Amorite friends (14.13), was near Hebron, located about 20 miles south of Jerusalem. It is where Sarah would later die (23.1). **(See Map 1 on pg 1879.)**

14.1-4 *King Amraphel . . . Dead Sea:* The kings named in 14.1 were from the lands to the east of Canaan. The kings named in 14.2 were leaders of cities in southern Canaan. They battled in the Siddim Valley, located 1,300 feet below sea level. **(See Map 1 on pg 1879.)**

14.5-7 *Ashteroth-Karnaim . . . Hazazon-Tamar:* The places and the peoples who were attacked by the eastern king, Chedorlaomer, lived in the lands east and southwest of the Jordan River and Dead Sea. Edom was south of the Dead Sea. Kadesh was located in the Southern Desert (see 12.4-9) and was later known as Kadesh-Barnea (Num 32.8). The constant warfare in the area where Lot had chosen to live threatened his family and flocks.

14.13 *Abram the Hebrew . . . Mamre the Amorite:* Abram is the first person in the Bible to be called a "Hebrew." Ancient sources other than the Bible speak of a people known as *Habiru* or *Apiru*, which may be related to the name Hebrew. These people were described as poor immigrants or foreigners who wandered from place to place but did not own land or property in a specific place.

14.18 *King Melchizedek of Salem . . . priest of God Most High:* Melchizedek means "king of justice," and "Salem" means "peace" (see Heb 7.2). Salem probably is a shortened form of Jerusalem. In ancient countries, a leader or king often performed the religious duties of a priest. "God Most High" was the name of the highest Canaanite god in Jerusalem. Abram identifies God Most High with "the LORD" (14.22; see also Num 24.16; Ps 46.4) and gives Melchizedek a tenth of all he owns. A tenth was considered a king's share (1 Sam 8.15,17). Melchizedek is also mentioned in Ps 110.4.

15.2 *Eliezer of Damascus:* Abram probably recruited Eliezer to be one of his servants as he traveled south from Haran to Canaan. Eliezer may be the "most trusted servant" named in 24.2. A law found in writings from ancient Babylonia said that a slave could be adopted if a couple had no children. In such a case, the servant would inherit his master/father's wealth and property.

15.8-10 *Abram asked . . . Abram obeyed:* These verses describe an ancient ceremony showing that an agreement is being made. Animals were cut in two, and the persons making the agreement walked between these parts (Jer 34.17-19).

Agreements (Covenants)

troops, attacked from all sides, and won a great victory. But some of the enemy escaped to the town of Hobah north of Damascus, **16**and Abram went after them. He brought back his nephew Lot, together with Lot's possessions and the women and everyone else who had been captured.

Abram Is Blessed by Melchizedek

17Abram returned after he had defeated King Chedorlaomer and the other kings. Then the king of Sodom went to meet Abram in Shaveh Valley, which is also known as King's Valley.

18King Melchizedek of Salem was a priest of God Most High. He brought out some bread and wine **19**and said to Abram:

"I bless you in the name
of God Most High,
Creator of heaven and earth.
20All praise belongs
to God Most High
for helping you defeat
your enemies."

Then Abram gave Melchizedek a tenth of everything.

21The king of Sodom said to Abram, "All I want are my people. You can keep everything else."

22Abram answered:

The LORD God Most High made the heavens and the earth. And I have promised him **23**that I won't keep anything of yours, not even a sandal strap or a piece of thread. Then you can never say that you are the one who made me rich. **24**Let my share be the food that my men have eaten. But Aner, Eshcol, and Mamre went with

me, so give them their share of what we brought back.

The LORD's Promise to Abram

15 Later the LORD spoke to Abram in a vision, "Abram, don't be afraid! I will protect you and reward you greatly."

2But Abram answered, "LORD All-Powerful, you have given me everything I could ask for, except children. And when I die, Eliezer of Damascus will get all I own.**ᵛ** **3**You have not given me any children, and this servant of mine will inherit everything."

4The LORD replied, "No, he won't! You will have a son of your own, and everything you have will be his." **5**Then the LORD took Abram outside and said, "Look at the sky and see if you can count the stars. That's how many descendants you will have." **6**Abram believed the LORD, so the LORD was pleased with him and accepted him.

The LORD Makes Another Promise to Abram

7The LORD said to Abram, "I brought you here from Ur in Chaldea, and I gave you this land."

8Abram asked, "LORD God, how can I know the land will be mine?"

9Then the LORD told him, "Bring me a three-year-old cow, a three-year-old female goat, a three-year-old ram, a dove, and a young pigeon."

10Abram obeyed the LORD. Then he cut**ʷ** the animals in half and laid the two halves of each animal opposite each other on the

---

ᵛ15.2 *And . . . own:* One possible meaning for the difficult Hebrew text. **ʷ15.10** *cut:* In Hebrew "cut" sounds something like "agreement." What follows shows that the LORD is making an agreement with Abram.

---

ground. But he did not cut the doves and pigeons in half. **11**And when birds came down to eat the animals, Abram chased them away.

12As the sun was setting, Abram fell into a deep sleep, and everything became dark and frightening. **13-15**Then the LORD said:

Abram, you will live to an old age and die in peace.

But I solemnly promise that your descendants will live as foreigners in a land that doesn't belong to them. They will be forced into slavery and abused for 400 years. But I will terribly punish the nation that enslaves them, and they will leave with many possessions.

16Four generations later,[x] your descendants will return here and take this land, because only then will the people who live here[y] be so sinful that they deserve to be punished.

17Sometime after sunset, when it was very dark, a smoking cooking pot[z] and a flaming fire passed between the two halves of each animal. **18**At that time the LORD made an agreement with Abram and told him:

I will give your descendants the land east of the Shihor River[a] on the border of Egypt as far as the Euphrates River. **19**They will possess the land of the Kenites, the Kenizzites, the Kadmonites, **20**the Hittites, the Perizzites, the Rephaites, **21**the Amorites, the Canaanites, the Girgashites, and the Jebusites.

Hagar and Ishmael

16 Abram's wife Sarai had not been able to have any children. But she owned a young Egyptian slave woman named Hagar, **2**and Sarai said to Abram, "The LORD has not given me any children. Sleep with my slave, and if she has a child, it will be mine."[b] Abram agreed, **3**and Sarai gave him Hagar to be his wife. This happened after Abram had lived in the land of Canaan for ten years. **4**Later, when Hagar knew she was going to have a baby, she became proud and treated Sarai hatefully.

5Then Sarai said to Abram, "It's all your fault![c] I gave you my slave woman, but she has been hateful to me ever since she found out she was pregnant. You have done me wrong, and you will have to answer to the LORD for this."

6Abram said, "All right! She's your slave—do whatever you want with her." Then Sarai began treating Hagar so harshly that she finally ran away.

7Hagar stopped to rest at a spring in the desert on the road to Shur. While she was there, the angel of the LORD came to her **8**and asked, "Hagar, where have you come from, and where are you going?"

She answered, "I'm running away from Sarai, my owner."

9The angel said, "Go back to Sarai and be her slave. **10-11**I will give you a son, who will be called Ishmael,[d] because I have heard your cry for help. And someday I

● 15.13-16 *promise:* God's promise to Abram included the news that his descendants would live as slaves in Egypt (see Exod 1.1-14; 12.40,41; Acts 7.6,7) for 400 years.

● 15.18 *Shihor River . . . Euphrates:* The Shihor was a brook in the wilderness area between Egypt and Canaan, and the Euphrates River was in Mesopotamia. Only during the reign of King David did the people of Israel control this much land. **(See Map 1 on pg 1879.)**

● 16.3 *Sarai gave . . . Hagar to be his wife:* When ten years had passed (compare 15.4 and 16.3), and Sarai still was not pregnant, she told Abram to take her slave Hagar as a wife. Ancient Assyrian marriage laws dating to the time before Abram allowed a man to sleep with his wife's slave if his wife could not get pregnant and have children. The children of the slave would belong to the husband's wife. Abram was 85 years old when he slept with Hagar (see 12.4; 16.15,16).

● 16.10-12 *Ishmael . . . wild donkey:* God's promise to Hagar is repeated in 17.20 and fulfilled in 25.13-16. Ishmael's descendants would be wandering herders living free in the Southern Desert like wild donkeys (see Job 24.5; Hos 8.9).

[x]**15.16** *Four generations later:* This may refer to the "400" of verses 13-15. [y]**15.16** *people who live here:* The Hebrew text has "Amorites," a name sometimes used of the people who lived in Palestine before the Israelites. [z]**15.17** *smoking cooking pot:* One possible meaning for the difficult Hebrew text. The smoke and fire represent the presence of the LORD. [a]**15.18** *Shihor River:* See Joshua 13.2-7. [b]**16.2** *Sleep . . . mine:* It was the custom for a wife who could not have children to let her husband sleep with one of her slave women. The children of the slave would belong to the wife. [c]**16.5** *It's . . . fault:* Or "I hope you'll be punished for what you did to me!" [d]**16.10,11** *Ishmael:* In Hebrew "Ishmael" sounds like "God hears."

16.14 *Kadesh and Bered:* Probably located in the southwest part of the area called the Southern Desert. (See Map 3 on pg 1881.)

17.2 *solemn promise:* Earlier promises of God to Abram (12.2,3; 13.14-16; 15.4,5) did not include any requirements, except that Abram go to Canaan. In this agreement (17.1-22) God tells Abraham to practice circumcision as a way to keep his part of the agreement (17.9-14).

Agreements (Covenants)

17.10-11 *circumcise:* "Circumcision" was the ceremony of cutting off the foreskin of a male's penis. This was a common rite among many people in the ancient Near East, though the reasons why are not clear. God commanded circumcision as a physical sign that Abraham's descendants were God's chosen people (17.12-14). Circumcision was a requirement in the Law of Moses (34.21-23; Lev 12.3).

Circumcision

17.15 *Sarah:* Both "Sarai" and "Sarah" mean "princess." This name emphasizes that Sarah would be the mother of Israel's rulers (17.16).

17.20 *father of twelve princes:* See 25.13-16, which describes the fulfillment of this promise about Ishmael.

will give you so many descendants that no one will be able to count them all. ¹²But your son will live far from his relatives; he will be like a wild donkey, fighting everyone, and everyone fighting him."

¹³Hagar thought, "Have I really seen God and lived to tell about it?"ᵉ So from then on she called him, "The God Who Sees Me."ᶠ ¹⁴That's why people call the well between Kadesh and Bered, "The Well of the Living One Who Sees Me."ᵍ

¹⁵⁻¹⁶Abram was 86 years old when Hagar gave birth to their son, and he named him Ishmael.

God's Promise to Abraham

17 When Abram was 99 years old, the LORD appeared to him again and said, "I am God All-Powerful. If you obey me and always do right, ²I will keep my solemn promise to you and give you more descendants than can be counted." ³Abram bowed with his face to the ground, and God said:

⁴⁻⁵I promise that you will be the father of many nations. So now I'm changing your name from Abram to Abraham.ʰ ⁶I will give you a lot of descendants, and they will become great nations. Some of them will even be kings.

⁷I will always keep the promise I have made to you and your descendants, because I am your God and their God. ⁸I will give you and them the land in which you are now a foreigner. I will give the whole land of Canaan to your family forever, and I will be their God.

⁹Abraham, you and all future members of your family must promise to obey me. ¹⁰⁻¹¹As the sign that you are keeping this promise, you must circumcise every man and boy in your family. ¹²⁻¹³From now on, your family must circumcise every baby boy when he is eight days old. You must even circumcise any man or boy you have as a slave, both those born in your homes and those you buy from foreigners. This will be a sign that my promise to you will last forever. ¹⁴Any man who isn't circumcised hasn't kept his part of the promise and cannot be one of my people.

¹⁵Abraham, from now on your wife's name will be Sarah instead of Sarai. ¹⁶I will bless her, and you will have a son by her. She will become the mother of nations, and some of her descendants will even be kings.

¹⁷Abraham bowed with his face to the ground and thought, "I am almost 100 years old. How can I become a father? And Sarah is 90. How can she have a child?" So he started laughing. ¹⁸Then he asked God, "Why not let Ishmaelⁱ inherit what you have promised me?"

¹⁹But God answered:

No! You and Sarah will have a son. His name will be Isaac,ʲ and I will make an everlasting promise to him and his descendants.

²⁰However, I have heard what you asked me to do for Ishmael, and so I will also bless him with many descendants. He will be the father of twelve princes, and I will make his family a great nation. ²¹But your son Isaac will

ᵉ16.13 *Have . . . it:* One possible meaning for the difficult Hebrew text.   ᶠ16.13 *The God Who Sees Me:* Or "The God I Have Seen."   ᵍ16.14 *The Well . . . Me:* Or "Beer-Lahai-Roi" (see 25.11).   ʰ17.4,5 *Abraham:* In Hebrew "Abraham" sounds like "father of many nations."   ⁱ17.18 *Ishmael:* Ishmael was the son of Sarah's slave Hagar (see 16.1-16).   ʲ17.19 *Isaac:* In Hebrew "Isaac" sounds like "laugh."

God said to Abram, "I promise that you will be the father of many nations . . . I will give the whole land of Canaan to your family forever, and I will be their God." GEN 17.4-8

be born about this time next year, and the promise I am making to you and your family will be for him and his descendants forever.

²²God finished speaking to Abraham and then left.

²³⁻²⁷On that same day Abraham obeyed God by circumcising Ishmael. Abraham was also circumcised, and so were all the other men and boys in his household, including his servants and slaves. He was 99 years old at the time, and his son Ishmael was 13.

The LORD Promises Abraham a Son

18 One hot summer afternoon while Abraham was sitting by the entrance to his tent near the sacred trees of Mamre, the LORD appeared to him. ²Abraham looked up and saw three men standing nearby. He quickly ran to meet them, bowed with his face to the ground, ³and said, "Please come to my home where I can serve you. ⁴I'll have some water brought, so you can wash your feet, then you can rest under a tree. ⁵Let me get you some food to give you strength before you leave. I would be honored to serve you."

"Thank you very much," they answered. "We accept your offer."

⁶Abraham went quickly to his tent and said to Sarah, "Hurry! Get a large sack of flour and make some bread." ⁷After saying this, he rushed off to his herd of cattle and picked out one of the best calves, which his servant quickly prepared. ⁸He then served his guests some yogurt and milk together with the meat.

While they were eating, he stood near them under the tree, ⁹and they asked, "Where's your wife Sarah?"

"She is right there in the tent," Abraham answered.

¹⁰One of the guests was the LORD, and he said, "I'll come back about this time next year, and when I do, Sarah will already have a son."

Sarah was behind Abraham, listening at the entrance to the tent. ¹¹Abraham and Sarah were very old, and Sarah was well past the age for having children. ¹²So she laughed and said to herself, "Now that I am worn out and my husband is old, will I really know such happiness?"ᵏ

¹³The LORD asked Abraham, "Why did Sarah laugh? Does she doubt that she can have a child in her old age? ¹⁴I am the LORD! There is nothing too difficult for me. I'll come back next year at the time I promised, and Sarah will already have a son."

¹⁵Sarah was so frightened that she lied and said, "I didn't laugh."

"Yes, you did!" he answered.

Abraham Prays for Sodom

¹⁶When the three men got ready to leave, they looked down toward Sodom, and Abraham walked part of the way with them.

¹⁷The LORD said to himself, "I should tell Abraham what I am going to do, ¹⁸since his family will become a great and powerful nation that will be a blessing to all the other nations on earth.ˡ ¹⁹I have chosen him to teach his family to obey me forever and to do what is right and fair. If they do, I will give Abraham many descendants, just as I promised."

²⁰The LORD said, "Abraham, I have heard

ᵏ**18.12** *know such happiness:* Either the joy of making love or the joy of having children.
ˡ**18.18** *that will be . . . on earth:* Or "and all other nations on earth will ask me to bless them as I have blessed his family."

● **18.16** *three men:* It appears that these "men" were two angels and the LORD. Abraham greeted them with respect and invited them to his home. He prepared a meal, brought water for them to wash their feet (18.4), and stood nearby like a servant (18.8) as they ate. These are common examples of hospitality in the ancient Near East.

◷ Angels

18.23 *those who are good:* The word "good" here is sometimes translated as "righteous," which means being right with God, or living according to God's Law. The ancient Israelites believed that the evil done by one or a few can spoil a whole community (Deut 21.1-9). Here Abraham argues the opposite: that a few good people could help save a whole community that was mostly evil.

19.8 *I have two daughters . . . They are guests in my home:* According to the ancient customs of hospitality, Lot was expected to make his two guests as comfortable and safe as possible. But by offering the men of Sodom his own daughters so that his guests would be protected, Lot actually put them, his daughters, and himself in greater danger. As it turned out, it was his guests (the angels) who ended up protecting Lot.

19.9 *You're a foreigner:* Lot had moved to the area around Sodom after parting with Abraham (13.8-12). Compare the hostility of the people of Sodom toward Lot with the Egyptian's reaction to Moses (Exod 2.14; Acts 7.27).

that the people of Sodom and Gomorrah are doing all kinds of evil things. [21]Now I am going down to see for myself if those people really are that bad. If they aren't, I would like to know."

[22]The men turned and started toward Sodom. But the LORD stayed with Abraham. [23]And Abraham asked him, "LORD, when you destroy the evil people, are you also going to destroy those who are good? [24]Wouldn't you spare the city if there are only 50 good people in it? [25]You surely wouldn't let them be killed when you destroy the evil ones. You are the judge of all the earth, and you do what is right."

[26]The LORD replied, "If I find 50 good people in Sodom, I will save the city to keep them from being killed."

[27]Abraham answered, "I am nothing more than the dust of the earth. Please forgive me, LORD, for daring to speak to you like this. [28]But suppose there are only 45 good people in Sodom. Would you still wipe out the whole city?"

"If I find 45 good people," the LORD replied, "I won't destroy the city."

[29]"Suppose there are just 40 good people?" Abraham asked.

"Even for them," the LORD replied, "I won't destroy the city."

[30]Abraham said, "Please don't be angry, LORD, if I ask you what you will do if there are only 30 good people in the city."

"If I find 30," the LORD replied, "I still won't destroy it."

[31]Then Abraham said, "I don't have any right to ask you, LORD, but what would you do if you find only 20?"

"Because of them, I won't destroy the city," was the LORD's answer.

[32]Finally, Abraham said, "Please don't get angry, LORD, if I speak just once more. Suppose you find only 10 good people there."

"For the sake of 10 good people," the LORD told him, "I still won't destroy the city."

[33]After speaking with Abraham, the LORD left, and Abraham went back home.

The Evil City of Sodom

19 That evening, while Lot was sitting near the city gate,[m] the two angels[n] arrived in Sodom. When Lot saw them, he got up, bowed down low, [2]and said, "Gentlemen, I am your servant. Please come to my home. You can wash your feet, spend the night, and be on your way in the morning."

They told him, "No, we'll spend the night in the city square." [3]But Lot kept insisting, until they finally agreed and went home with him. He quickly baked some bread,[o] cooked a meal, and they ate.

[4]Before Lot and his guests could go to bed, every man in Sodom, young and old, came and stood outside his house [5]and started shouting, "Where are your visitors? Send them out, so we can have sex with them!"

[6]Lot went outside and shut the door behind him. [7]Then he said, "Friends, please don't do such a terrible thing! [8]I have two daughters who have never had sex. I'll bring them out, and you can do what you want with them. But don't harm these men. They are guests in my home."

[9]"Don't get in our way," the crowd answered. "You're a foreigner. What right do you have to order us around? We'll do worse things to you than we're going to do to them."

[m]**19.1** *near the city gate:* In a large area where the people would gather for community business and for meeting with friends.   [n]**19.1** *two angels:* The two men of 18.22.   [o]**19.3** *bread:* The Hebrew text has "bread without yeast," which could be made quickly when guests came without warning.

The crowd kept arguing with Lot. Finally, they rushed toward the door to break it down. ¹⁰But the two angels in the house reached out and pulled Lot safely inside. ¹¹Then they struck blind everyone in the crowd, and none of them could even find the door.

¹²⁻¹³The two angels said to Lot, "The LORD has heard many terrible things about the people of Sodom, and he has sent us here to destroy the city. Take your family and leave. Take every relative you have in the city, as well as the men your daughters are going to marry."

¹⁴Lot went to the men who were engaged to his daughters and said, "Hurry up and get out of here! The LORD is going to destroy this city." But they thought he was joking, and they laughed at him.

¹⁵Early the next morning the two angels tried to make Lot hurry and leave. They said, "Take your wife and your two daughters and get away from here as fast as you can! If you don't, every one of you will be killed when the LORD destroys the city." ¹⁶At first, Lot just stood there. But the LORD wanted to save him. So the angels took Lot, his wife, and his two daughters by the hand and led them out of the city. ¹⁷When they were outside, one of the angels said, "Run for your lives! Don't even look back. And don't stop in the valley. Run to the hills, where you'll be safe."

¹⁸⁻¹⁹Lot answered, "You have done us a great favor, sir. You have saved our lives, but please don't make us go to the hills. That's too far away. The city will be destroyed before we can get there, and we will be killed when it happens. ²⁰There's a town near here. It's only a small place, but my family and I will be safe, if you let us go there."

²¹"All right, go there," he answered. "I

won't destroy that town. ²²Hurry! Run! I can't do anything until you are safely there."

The town was later called Zoar^P because Lot had said it was small.

Sodom and Gomorrah Are Destroyed

²³The sun was coming up as Lot reached the town of Zoar, ²⁴and the LORD sent burning sulfur down like rain on Sodom and Gomorrah. ²⁵He destroyed those cities and everyone who lived in them, as well as their land and the trees and grass that grew there.

²⁶On the way, Lot's wife looked back and was turned into a block of salt.

²⁷That same morning Abraham got up and went to the place where he had stood and spoken with the LORD. ²⁸He looked down toward Sodom and Gomorrah and saw smoke rising from all over the land— it was like a flaming furnace.

²⁹When God destroyed the cities of the valley where Lot lived, he remembered his promise to Abraham and saved Lot from the terrible destruction.

Moab and Ammon

³⁰Lot was afraid to stay on in Zoar. So he took his two daughters and moved to a cave in the hill country. ³¹One day his older daughter said to her sister, "Our father is old, and there are no men anywhere for us to marry. ³²Let's get our father drunk! Then we can sleep with him and have children." ³³That night they got their father drunk, and the older daughter got in bed with him, but he was too drunk even to know she was there.

³⁴The next day the older daughter said to her sister, "I slept with my father last

P**19.22** *Zoar:* In Hebrew "Zoar" sounds like "small."

19.17-23 *Run to the hills . . . Zoar:* This probably refers to the hills of Moab to the east (19.30,37). But first Lot and his family went to the small town of Zoar, a few miles south of the Dead Sea. **(See Map 1 on pg 1879.)**

19.26 *Lot's wife . . . block of salt:* Salt formations can be seen near the southern end of the Dead Sea.

19.30-38 *his two daughters . . . ancestor of the Ammonites:* By telling how Lot's daughters deceived him into being the father of their children, these verses explain the shameful origin of two of Israel's closest neighbors. The daughters perhaps felt they had no other chance of having children.

night. We'll get him drunk again tonight,
so you can sleep with him, and we can each
have a child." 35 That night they got their
father drunk, and this time the younger
sister slept with him. But once again he was
too drunk even to know she was there.
36 That's how Lot's two daughters had
children. 37 The older daughter named her
son Moab,[q] and he is the ancestor of the
Moabites. 38 The younger daughter named
her son Benammi,[r] and he is the ancestor
of the Ammonites.

Abraham and Sarah at Gerar

20 Abraham moved to the Southern
Desert, where he settled between
Kadesh and Shur. Later he went to Gerar,
and while there 2 he told everyone that his
wife Sarah was his sister. So King Abimelech of Gerar had Sarah brought to him.
3 But God came to Abimelech in a dream
and said, "You have taken a married woman
into your home, and for this you will die!"
4-5 Abimelech said to the Lord, "Don't
kill me! I haven't slept with Sarah. Didn't
they say they were brother and sister? I am
completely innocent."
6 Then God continued:

I know you are innocent. That's why
I kept you from sleeping with Sarah
and doing anything wrong. 7 Her husband is a prophet. Let her go back to
him, and his prayers will save you from
death. But if you don't return her, you
and all your people will die.

8 Early the next morning Abimelech sent
for his officials, and when he told them
what had happened, they were frightened.
9 Abimelech then called in Abraham and
said:

Look what you've done to us! What
have I ever done to you? Why did you
make me and my nation guilty of such
a terrible sin? 10 What were you thinking when you did this?

11 Abraham answered:

I did it because I didn't think any of
you respected God, and I was sure that
someone would kill me to get my wife.
12 Besides, she is my half sister. We have
the same father, but different mothers.
13 When God made us leave my father's home and start wandering, I
told her, "If you really love me, then
tell everyone that I am your brother."

14 After Abimelech had given Abraham
some sheep, cattle, and slaves, he sent
Sarah back 15 and told Abraham he could
settle anywhere in his country. 16 Then he
said to Sarah, "I have given your brother
1,000 pieces of silver as proof to everyone
that you have done nothing wrong."[s]
17-18 Meanwhile, God had kept Abimelech's wife and slaves from having children. But Abraham prayed, and God let
them start having children again.

Sarah Has a Son

21 The LORD was good to Sarah and
kept his promise. 2 Although Abraham was very old, Sarah had a son exactly
at the time God had said. 3 Abraham
named his son Isaac, 4 and when the boy
was eight days old, Abraham circumcised
him, just as God had commanded.
5 Abraham was 100 years old when Isaac
was born, 6 and Sarah said, "God has made
me laugh.[t] And now everyone will laugh
with me. 7 Who would have dared to tell
Abraham that someday I would have a

[q] **19.37** *Moab*: In Hebrew "Moab" sounds like "from (my) father." [r] **19.38** *Benammi*: In Hebrew "Benammi" means "son of my relative." [s] **20.16** *as proof . . . wrong*: One possible meaning for the difficult Hebrew text. [t] **21.6** *God has made me laugh*: In Hebrew "Isaac" sounds like "laugh."

● 19.37,38 *Moabites . . . Ammonites:* Moab was located to the east of the Dead Sea. Ammon was a land east of the Jordan River valley. The Moabites and Ammonites would later become enemies of Abraham's descendants, Israel (Judg 10.11-18; 1 Sam 14.47,48; 2 Kgs 3.21-27; 2 Chr 20.11). **(See Map 3 on pg 1881.)**

● 20.1 *Gerar:* Gerar was located at the southern end of Philistine territory, about halfway between Gaza near the Mediterranean coast and Beersheba. **(See Map 3 on pg 1881.)**

● 20.4-5 *Abimelech:* Possibly the father or grandfather of the later king with the same name (26.1). In Hebrew the name means "my father is king."

● 20.7 *Her husband is a prophet:* This refers to Abraham, whose role as a prophet was to pray to God (18.22-33) and to make sure his family obeyed God by following the rite of circumcision (17.7-14). Abraham was the first man to be called prophet in the Bible. **(See the article Prophets and Prophecy on pg 1791.)**

● 20.12 *half sister:* Marriage with a half sister apparently was permitted in ancient times (2 Sam 13.13). Later the Law of Moses would forbid this kind of marriage (Lev 18.9,11; 20.17).

● 20.16 *pieces of silver:* These were not coins, but pieces of silver that likely weighed about a shekel each. The shekel was the common unit of weight in the ancient Near East.

child? But in his old age, I have given him a son."

⁸The time came when Sarah no longer had to nurse Isaac,ᵘ and on that day Abraham gave a big feast.

Hagar and Ishmael Are Sent Away

⁹⁻¹⁰One day, Sarah noticed Hagar's son Ishmaelᵛ playing,ʷ and she said to Abraham, "Get rid of that Egyptian slave woman and her son! I don't want him to inherit anything. It should all go to my son."ˣ

¹¹Abraham was worried about Ishmael. ¹²But God said, "Abraham, don't worry about your slave woman and the boy. Just do what Sarah tells you. Isaac will inherit your family name, ¹³but the son of the slave woman is also your son, and I will make his descendants into a great nation."

¹⁴Early the next morning Abraham gave Hagar an animal skin full of water and some bread. Then he put the boy on her shoulder and sent them away.

They wandered around in the desert near Beersheba, ¹⁵and after they had run out of water, Hagar put her son under a bush. ¹⁶Then she sat down a long way off, because she could not bear to watch him die. And she cried bitterly.

¹⁷When God heard the boy crying, the angel of God called out to Hagar from heaven and said, "Hagar, why are you worried? Don't be afraid. I have heard your son crying. ¹⁸Help him up and hold his hand, because I will make him the father of a great nation." ¹⁹Then God let her see a well. So she went to the well and filled the skin with water, then gave some to her son.

²⁰⁻²¹God blessed Ishmael, and as the boy grew older, he became an expert at hunting with his bow and arrows. He lived in the Paran Desert, and his mother chose an Egyptian woman for him to marry.

A Peace Treaty

²²About this time Abimelech and his army commander Phicol said to Abraham, "God blesses everything you do! ²³Now I want you to promise in the name of God that you will always be loyal to me and my descendants, just as I have always been loyal to you in this land where you have lived as a foreigner." ²⁴And so, Abraham promised he would.

²⁵One day, Abraham told Abimelech, "Some of your servants have taken over one of my wells."

²⁶"This is the first I've heard about it," Abimelech replied. "Why haven't you said something before? I don't have any idea who did it." ²⁷Abraham gave Abimelech some sheep and cattle, then the two men made a peace treaty.

²⁸Abraham separated seven female lambs from his flock of sheep, ²⁹and Abimelech asked, "Why have you done this?"

³⁰Abraham replied, "I want you to accept these seven lambs as proof that I dug this well." ³¹So they called the place Beersheba,ʸ because they made a treaty there.

³²When the treaty was completed,

21.20-21 *God blessed Ishmael:* Compare to 16.6-12. Even though Sarah did not want Ishmael to inherit anything, God did bless Ishmael and promised to make his descendants a great nation (25.12-18).

21.20-21 *Paran Desert:* This desert was located on the Sinai Peninsula, between Canaan and Egypt. **(See Map 2 on pg 1880.)**

21.31 *Beersheba:* Though this name means "Well of Good Fortune" or "Peace Treaty Well," it has also been called the "Well of Seven," since Abraham chose seven female lambs to seal his treaty with Abimelech.

ᵘ**21.8** *no longer had to nurse Isaac:* In ancient Israel mothers nursed their children until they were about three years old. Then there was a family celebration. ᵛ**21.9,10** *Ishmael:* The son of Abraham and Hagar, who was Sarah's slave woman (see 16.1-16). ʷ**21.9,10** *playing:* Hebrew; one ancient translation "playing with her son Isaac." ˣ**21.9,10** *Get rid . . . son:* When Abraham accepted Ishmael as his son, it gave Ishmael the right to inherit part of what Abraham owned. But slaves who were given their freedom lost the right to inherit such property. ʸ**21.31** *Beersheba:* Meaning "Well of Good Fortune" or "Peace Treaty Well."

21.32 *Philistines:* This group of people came from Caphtor (Jer 47.4; Amos 9.7), which may be Crete or the islands of the Aegean Sea. They were not part of the peoples that were related to Abraham's descendants. The land of the Philistines refers to the plains area along the Mediterranean Sea coast from Joppa to south of Gaza. **(See Map 3 on pg 1881.)**

22.7-8 *lamb for the sacrifice:* In ancient times, offering burned sacrifices was a way to worship God, and to maintain, restore, or celebrate the relationship between the giver and God. In this story, Abraham is prepared to offer his son, the child of God's promise. The death of Isaac would be a direct threat to the agreement God had made with Abraham and Sarah (15.5). **(See the chart Sacrifices and Offerings on pg 1828.)**

22.13 *a ram caught by its horns:* Rams are male sheep. Besides eating the meat they provided, people in Palestine used the skins of rams for making tents and the curved horns of rams for making trumpets (called "shofars") and containers for holding oil. Their long broad tails contained fat which was burned as an offering to the LORD (see Lev 3.9; 7.3; 8.25).

22.20-24 *Nahor . . . Maacah:* Nahor (11.26-28) had twelve sons by two different wives. These sons became the ancestors of twelve Aramean tribes, just as Abraham's grandson Jacob would become the ancestor of the twelve tribes of Israel (49.28). The list introduces Bethuel, whose daughter Rebekah later marries Isaac (chapter 24).

Abimelech and his army commander Phicol went back to the land of the Philistines. ³³Abraham planted a tamarisk tree[z] in Beersheba and worshiped the eternal LORD God. ³⁴Then Abraham lived a long time as a foreigner in the land of the Philistines.

The LORD Tells Abraham To Offer Isaac as a Sacrifice

22 Some years later God decided to test Abraham, so he spoke to him. Abraham answered, "Here I am, LORD."

²The LORD said, "Go get Isaac, your only son, the one you dearly love! Take him to the land of Moriah, and I will show you a mountain where you must sacrifice him to me on the fires of an altar." ³So Abraham got up early the next morning and chopped wood for the fire. He put a saddle on his donkey and set out with Isaac and two servants for the place where God had told him to go.

⁴Three days later Abraham looked off in the distance and saw the place. ⁵He told his servants, "Stay here with the donkey, while my son and I go over there to worship. We will come back."

⁶Abraham put the wood on Isaac's shoulder, but he carried the hot coals and the knife. As the two of them walked along, ⁷⁻⁸Isaac said, "Father, we have the coals and the wood, but where is the lamb for the sacrifice?"

"My son," Abraham answered, "God will provide the lamb."

The two of them walked on, and ⁹when they reached the place that God had told him about, Abraham built an altar and placed the wood on it. Next, he tied up his son and put him on the wood. ¹⁰He then

took the knife and got ready to kill his son. ¹¹But the LORD's angel shouted from heaven, "Abraham! Abraham!"

"Here I am!" he answered.

¹²"Don't hurt the boy or harm him in any way!" the angel said. "Now I know that you truly obey God, because you were willing to offer him your only son."

¹³Abraham looked up and saw a ram caught by its horns in the bushes. So he took the ram and sacrificed it instead of his son. ¹⁴Abraham named that place "The LORD Will Provide." And even now people say, "On the mountain of the LORD it will be provided."[a]

¹⁵The LORD's angel called out from heaven a second time:

¹⁶You were willing to offer your only son to the LORD, and so he makes you this solemn promise, ¹⁷"I will bless you and give you such a large family, that someday your descendants will be more numerous than the stars in the sky or the grains of sand along the seashore. They will defeat their enemies and take over the cities where their enemies live. ¹⁸You have obeyed me, and so you and your descendants will be a blessing to all nations on earth."

¹⁹Abraham and Isaac went back to the servants who had come with him, and they returned to Abraham's home in Beersheba.

The Children of Nahor

²⁰⁻²³Abraham's brother Nahor had married Milcah, and Abraham was later told that they had eight sons. Uz was their firstborn; Buz was next, and then there was

[z]21.33 *tamarisk tree:* A tall shade tree that has deep roots and needs little water. [a]22.14 *The LORD Will Provide . . . it will be provided:* Or "The LORD Will Be Seen . . . the LORD will be seen" or "It (a ram) Will Be Seen . . . it (a ram) will be seen."

"Now I know that you truly obey God, because you were willing to offer him your only son." GEN 22.12

Kemuel the father of Aram; their other five sons were: Chesed, Hazo, Pildash, Jidlaph, and Bethuel the father of Rebekah. [24]Nahor also had another wife.[b] Her name was Reumah, and she had four sons: Tebah, Gaham, Tahash, and Maacah.

Sarah's Death and Burial

23 [1-2]When Sarah was 127 years old, she died in Kiriath-Arba, better known as Hebron, in the land of Canaan. After Abraham had mourned for her, [3]he went to the Hittites and said, [4]"I live as a foreigner in your land, and I don't own any property where I can bury my wife. Please let me buy a piece of land."

[5-6]"Sir," they answered, "you are an important man. Choose the best place to bury your wife. None of us would refuse you a resting place for your dead."

[7]Abraham bowed down [8]and replied, "If you are willing to let me bury my wife here, please ask Zohar's son Ephron [9]to sell me Machpelah Cave at the end of his field. I'll pay what it's worth, and all of you can be witnesses."

[10]Ephron was sitting there near the city gate, when Abraham made this request, and he answered, [11]"Sir, the whole field, including the cave, is yours. With my own people as witnesses, I freely give it to you as a burial place for your dead."

[12]Once again, Abraham bowed down [13]and said to Ephron, "In front of these witnesses, I offer you the full price, so I can bury my wife. Please accept my offer."

[14-15]"But sir," the man replied, "the property is worth only 400 pieces of silver. Why should we haggle over such a small amount? Take the land. It's yours."

[16-18]Abraham accepted Ephron's offer and paid him the 400 pieces of silver in front of everyone at the city gate. That's how Abraham came to own Ephron's property east of Mamre[c] which included the field with all of its trees, as well as Machpelah Cave at the end of the field. [19]So Abraham buried his wife Sarah in Machpelah Cave that was in the field [20]he had bought from the Hittites.

A Wife for Isaac

24 Abraham was now a very old man. The LORD had made him rich, and he was successful in everything he did. [2]One day, Abraham called in his most trusted servant and said to him, "Solemnly promise me [3]in the name of the LORD, who rules heaven and earth, that you won't choose a wife for my son Isaac from the people here in the land of Canaan. [4]Instead, go back to the land where I was born and find a wife for him from among my relatives."

[5]But the servant asked, "What if the young woman I choose refuses to leave home and come here with me? Should I send Isaac there to look for a wife?"

[6]"No!" Abraham answered. "Don't ever do that, no matter what. [7]The LORD who rules heaven brought me here from the land where I was born and promised that he would give this land to my descendants forever. When you go back there, the LORD will send his angel ahead of you to help you find a wife for my son. [8]If the woman refuses to come along, you don't have to keep this promise. But don't ever take my son back there." [9]So the servant gave Abraham his word that he would do everything he had been told to do.

[10]Soon after that, the servant loaded ten

---

[b]22.24 *another wife:* This translates a Hebrew word for a woman who was legally bound to a man, but without the full privileges of a wife.   [c]23.16-18 *Mamre:* A place just north of Hebron.

24.10 *camels . . . gifts:* Camels are stubborn animals, but they are very valuable as pack animals, because they can easily carry up to 350 pounds of goods long distances with little water and food. The gifts included gold items (24.22) and clothing (24.53), and may have included food. (See the article Trade and Travel on pg 1806.)

24.11 *late afternoon:* The women took water from the well at this time of day, because it was beginning to get cool.

24.29-30 *Laban:* Laban is Rebekah's brother. His daughters, Leah and Rachel, later would marry Isaac's son Jacob (29-31).

24.31-33 *Come home . . . brought in food:* Compare Laban's hospitality to that of Abraham.

In the ancient Near East, the customs of hospitality required that the owner of a house take care of and protect any stranger he invited to stay in his house. Travelers who were not taken into someone's home would have no status or protection in the community. Once a host agreed to take in strangers he was expected to treat his guests as if they were family members, to serve them the best meals, and to give them places of honor. Any host who did not meet these expectations brought shame to himself, his family, and the community. In addition, any disrespect shown to the guest by the community was considered an offense against the host. See also 18.1-15 and 19.1-11.

of Abraham's camels with valuable gifts. Then he set out for the city in northern Syria,[d] where Abraham's brother Nahor lived.

[11]When he got there, he let the camels rest near the well outside the city. It was late afternoon, the time when the women came out for water. [12]The servant prayed:

You, Lord, are the God my master Abraham worships. Please keep your promise to him and let me find a wife for Isaac today. [13]The young women of the city will soon come to this well for water, [14]and I'll ask one of them for a drink. If she gives me a drink and then offers to get some water for my camels, I'll know she is the one you have chosen and that you have kept your promise to my master.

[15-16]While he was still praying, a beautiful unmarried young woman came by with a water jar on her shoulder. She was Rebekah, the daughter of Bethuel, the son of Abraham's brother Nahor and his wife Milcah. Rebekah walked past Abraham's servant, then went over to the well, and filled her water jar. When she started back, [17]Abraham's servant ran to her and said, "Please let me have a drink of water."

[18]"I'll be glad to," she answered. Then she quickly took the jar from her shoulder and held it while he drank. [19-20]After he had finished, she said, "Now I'll give your camels all the water they want." She quickly poured out water for them, and she kept going back for more, until his camels had drunk all they wanted. [21]Abraham's servant did not say a word, but he watched everything Rebekah did, because

he wanted to know for certain if this was the woman the Lord had chosen.

[22]The servant had brought along an expensive gold ring and two large gold bracelets. When Rebekah had finished bringing the water, he gave her the ring for her nose[e] and the bracelets for her arms. [23]Then he said, "Please tell me who your father is. Does he have room in his house for me and my men to spend the night?"

[24]She answered, "My father is Bethuel, the son of Nahor and Milcah. [25]We have a place where you and your men can stay, and we also have enough straw and feed for your camels."

[26]Then the servant bowed his head and prayed, [27]"I thank you, Lord God of my master Abraham! You have led me to his relatives and kept your promise to him."

[28]Rebekah ran straight home and told her family everything. [29-30]Her brother Laban heard her tell what the servant had said, and he saw the ring and the bracelets she was wearing. So Laban ran out to Abraham's servant, who was standing by his camels at the well. [31]Then Laban said, "The Lord has brought you safely here. Come home with me. There's no need for you to keep on standing outside. I have a room ready for you in our house, and there's also a place for your camels."

[32]Abraham's servant went home with Laban, where Laban's servants unloaded his camels and gave them straw and feed. Then they brought water into the house, so Abraham's servant and his men could wash their feet. [33]After that, they brought in food. But the servant said, "Before I eat, I must tell you why I have come."

"Go ahead and tell us," Laban answered.

[d]24.10 *northern Syria:* The Hebrew text has "Aram-Naharaim," probably referring to the land around the city of Haran (see also 25.20; 28.2,6; 31.18,20; 33.18; 35.23-26; 46.8-15, where CEV translates "Paddan-Aram" as "northern Syria"; and 48.7, where CEV translates "Paddan" as "northern Syria").
[e]24.22 *ring for her nose:* Nose-rings were popular jewelry items, as were earrings.

34The servant explained:

I am Abraham's servant. **35**The LORD has been good to my master and has made him very rich. He has given him many sheep, goats, cattle, camels, and donkeys, as well as a lot of silver and gold, and many slaves. **36**Sarah, my master's wife, didn't have any children until she was very old. Then she had a son, and my master has given him everything. **37**I solemnly promised my master that I would do what he said. And he told me, "Don't choose a wife for my son from the women in this land of Canaan. **38**Instead, go back to the land where I was born and find a wife for my son from among my relatives."

39I asked my master, "What if the young woman refuses to come with me?"

40My master answered, "I have always obeyed the LORD, and he will send his angel to help you find my son a wife from among my own relatives. **41**But if they refuse to let her come back with you, then you are freed from your promise."

42When I came to the well today, I silently prayed, "You, LORD, are the God my master Abraham worships, so please lead me to a wife for his son **43**while I am here at the well. When a young woman comes out to get water, I'll ask her to give me a drink. **44**If she gives me a drink and offers to get some water for my camels, I'll know she is the one you have chosen."

45Even before I had finished praying, Rebekah came by with a water jar on her shoulder. When she had filled the jar, I asked her for a drink. **46**She quickly lowered the jar from her shoulder and said, "Have a drink. Then I'll get water for your camels." So I drank, and after that she got some water for my camels. **47**I asked her who her father was, and she answered, "My father is Bethuel the son of Nahor and Milcah." At once I put the ring in her nose and the bracelets on her arms. **48**Then I bowed my head and gave thanks to the God my master Abraham worships. The LORD had led me straight to my master's relatives, and I had found a wife for his son.

49Now please tell me if you are willing to do the right thing for my master. Will you treat him fairly, or do I have to look for another young woman?

50Laban and Bethuel answered, "The LORD has done this. We have no choice in the matter. **51**Take Rebekah with you; she can marry your master's son, just as the LORD has said." **52**Abraham's servant bowed down and thanked the LORD. **53**Then he gave clothing, as well as silver and gold jewelry, to Rebekah. He also gave expensive gifts to her brother and her mother.

54Abraham's servant and the men with him ate and drank, then spent the night there. The next morning they got up, and the servant told Rebekah's mother and brother, "I would like to go back to my master now."

55"Let Rebekah stay with us for a week or ten days," they answered. "Then she may go."

56But he said, "Don't make me stay any longer. The LORD has already helped me find a wife for my master's son. Now let us return."

57They answered, "Let's ask Rebekah what she wants to do." **58**They called her and asked, "Are you willing to leave with this man at once?"

"Yes," she answered.

59So they agreed to let Rebekah and an

24.40 *his angel:* In the Bible, angels act both as messengers and servants of God.

Angels

24.50 *the LORD has done this:* The story of finding a wife for Isaac often mentions that the LORD is guiding events (24.21,26,27,48,56)

"I bowed my head and gave thanks to the God my master Abraham worships. The LORD had led me straight to my master's relatives." GEN 24.48

25.1-4 *Keturah . . . Eldaah:* Abraham would have been close to 140 years old by this time, if his marriage to Keturah happened after Sarah died. The descendants of Abraham and Keturah were the first ancestors of certain Arabic tribes, including the Midianites who were desert wanderers. Moses' father-in-law Jethro was a Midianite priest (Exod 2.15-22).

25.5-6 *left everything to Isaac:* Ancient laws allowed for a man to give a greater share of his property to his oldest son. The Law of Moses later said that at least a double share of a father's property should be given to the first-born son when the father died (Deut 21.15-17). Technically, Hagar's son Ishmael was Abraham's first-born. Abraham gave Ishmael and his other sons gifts, but reserved the bulk of his property for Isaac, the son of God's promise (18.1-15).

Birthright

25.13-16 *Ishmael had twelve sons:* Many of the names in this list are of Arab origin. Arab tradition names Ishmael as their ancestor. Ishmael's sons were the ancestors of twelve tribes (as predicted in 17.20), just as Israel was later organized into twelve tribes (49.1-28; Josh 13.14—19.51).

old family servant woman[f] leave immediately with Abraham's servant and his men. [60]They gave Rebekah their blessing and said, "We pray that God will give you many children and grandchildren and that he will help them defeat their enemies." [61]Afterwards, Rebekah and the young women who were to travel with her prepared to leave. Then they got on camels and left with Abraham's servant and his men.

[62]At that time Isaac was living in the southern part of Canaan near a place called "The Well of the Living One Who Sees Me."[g] [63-65]One evening he was walking out in the fields, when suddenly he saw a group of people approaching on camels. So he started toward them. Rebekah saw him coming; she got down from her camel, and asked, "Who is that man?"

"He is my master Isaac," the servant answered. Then Rebekah covered her face with her veil.[h]

[66]The servant told Isaac everything that had happened.

[67]Isaac took Rebekah into the tent[i] where his mother had lived before she died, and Rebekah became his wife. He loved her and was comforted over the loss of his mother.

Abraham Marries Keturah

25 Abraham married Keturah, [2]and they had six sons: Zimran, Jokshan, Medan, Midian, Ishbak, and Shuah. [3]Later, Jokshan became the father of Sheba and Dedan, and when Dedan grew up, he had three sons: Asshurim, Letushim, and Leummim. [4]Midian also had five sons: Ephah, Epher, Hanoch, Abida, and Eldaah.

[5-6]While Abraham was still alive, he gave gifts to the sons of Hagar and Keturah. He also sent their sons to live in the east far from his son Isaac, and when Abraham died, he left everything to Isaac.

The Death of Abraham

[7-8]Abraham died at the ripe old age of 175. [9-10]His sons Isaac and Ishmael buried him east of Hebron[j] in Machpelah Cave that was part of the field Abraham had bought from Ephron son of Zohar the Hittite. Abraham was buried there beside his wife Sarah. [11]God blessed Isaac after this, and Isaac moved to a place called "The Well of the Living One Who Sees Me."[k]

Ishmael's Descendants

[12]Ishmael was the son of Abraham and Hagar, the slave woman of Sarah. [13]Ishmael had twelve sons, in this order: Nebaioth, Kedar, Adbeel, Mibsam, [14]Mishma, Dumah, Massa, [15]Hadad, Tema, Jetur, Naphish, and Kedemah. [16]Each of Ishmael's sons was a tribal chief, and a village was named after each of them.

[17-18]Ishmael had settled in the land east of his brothers, and his sons[l] settled everywhere from Havilah to Shur, east of Egypt on the way to Asshur.[m] Ishmael was 137 when he died.

[f]**24.59** *old family servant woman:* Probably Deborah, who had taken care of Rebekah from the time she was born (see 35.8). [g]**24.62** *Who Sees Me:* Or "I Have Seen." [h]**24.63-65** *covered . . . veil:* Since the veiling of a bride was part of the wedding ceremony, this probably means that she was willing to become the wife of Isaac. [i]**24.67** *took . . . tent:* This shows that Rebekah is now the wife of Isaac and the successor of Sarah as the leading woman in the tribe. [j]**25.9,10** *Hebron:* See the note at 23.16-18. [k]**25.11** *The Well . . . Sees Me:* Or "Beer-Lahai-Roi." (see 16.14). [l]**25.17,18** *sons:* Or "descendants." [m]**25.17,18** *Havilah to Shur . . . Asshur:* The exact location of these places is not known.

The Birth of Esau and Jacob

[19]Isaac was the son of Abraham, [20]and he was 40 years old when he married Rebekah, the daughter of Bethuel. She was also the sister of Laban, the Aramean from northern Syria.[n]

Almost 20 years later, [21]Rebekah still had no children. So Isaac asked the LORD to let her have a child, and the LORD answered his prayer.

[22]Before Rebekah gave birth, she knew she was going to have twins, because she could feel them inside her, fighting each other. She thought, "Why is this happening to me?" Finally, she asked the LORD why her twins were fighting, [23]and he told her:

"Your two sons will become
    two separate nations.[o]
The younger of the two
    will be stronger,
and the older son
    will be his servant."

[24]When Rebekah gave birth, [25]the first baby was covered with red hair, so he was named Esau.[p] [26]The second baby grabbed on to his brother's heel, so they named him Jacob.[q] Isaac was 60 years old when they were born.

Esau Sells His Rights as the First-Born Son

[27]As Jacob and Esau grew older, Esau liked the outdoors and became a good hunter, while Jacob lived the quiet life of a shepherd.[r] [28]Esau would take the meat of wild animals to his father Isaac, so Isaac loved him more, but Jacob was his mother's favorite son.

[29]One day, when Jacob was cooking some stew, Esau came home hungry [30]and said, "I'm starving to death! Here and now give me some of that red stew!" That's how Esau got the name "Edom."[s]

[31]Jacob replied, "Sell me your rights as the first-born son."[t]

[32]"I'm about to die," Esau answered. "What good will those rights do me?"

[33]But Jacob said, "Promise me your birthrights, here and now!" And that's what Esau did. [34]Jacob then gave Esau some bread and some of the bean stew, and when Esau had finished eating and drinking, he just got up and left, showing how little he thought of his rights as the first-born.

Isaac and Abimelech

26 Once during Abraham's lifetime, the fields had not produced enough grain, and now the same thing happened. So Isaac went to King Abimelech of the Philistines in the land of Gerar, [2]because the LORD had appeared to Isaac and said:

Isaac, stay away from Egypt! I will show you where I want you to go. [3]You will live there as a foreigner, but I will be with you and bless you. I will keep my promise to your father Abraham by giving this land to you and your descendants.

[4]I will give you as many descendants as there are stars in the sky, and I will give your descendants all of this land. They will be a blessing to every nation

25.23 *older son will be his servant:* According to ancient customs, younger sons ranked below the oldest son. Here, the Lord is telling Rebekah that the expected order will be reversed. God's actions overrule human laws and customs. See also Rom 9.11,12.

25.30 *Edom:* The land of Edom, or Seir, was south and southeast of the Dead Sea. The Edomites descended from Esau (36.1-43). The descendants of Jacob (the Israelites) often battled with the Edomites (Num 20.14-21; Obad 9,10). **(See Map 2 on pg 1880.)**

25.31 *rights as the first-born son:* In addition to a double-share of the property, the older son inherited leadership of the family.

Birthright

26.5 *Abraham did everything I told him to do:* Even though God gave the Law to Moses many years after Abraham died (Exod 19,20), Abraham's faithful obedience in the past (17.9-14, 23-27; 22.9-18) was to be an example of how the people should be loyal to God's commands.

26.15-22 *stopped up the wells . . . named "Lots of Room":* Apparently the Philistines threw dirt into the wells that Isaac used (26.17). But Isaac cleaned them out and called them by the names his father had given them which meant that he claimed ownership of the wells. Disputes over wells and water rights were common in the ancient Near East (26.18-20) and continue to be today, because the land is dry most of the year (see also 13.6-11; 21.25; 36.7). The Hebrew names for the wells mentioned are *Esek* ("Quarrel"), *Sitnah* ("Jealous"), and *Rehoboth* ("Lots of Room").

26.30 *big feast:* Important agreements were often celebrated with a feast (31.54; Exod 24.11).

on earth,[u] [5]because Abraham did everything I told him to do.

[6]Isaac moved to Gerar [7]with his beautiful wife Rebekah. He was afraid that someone might kill him to get her, and so he told everyone that Rebekah was his sister. [8]After Isaac had been there a long time, King Abimelech looked out a window and saw Isaac hugging and kissing Rebekah. [9]Abimelech called him in and said, "Rebekah must be your wife! Why did you say she is your sister?"

"Because I thought someone would kill me," Isaac answered.

[10]"Don't you know what you've done?" Abimelech exclaimed. "If someone had slept with her, you would have made our whole nation guilty!" [11]Then Abimelech warned his people that anyone who even touched Isaac or Rebekah would be put to death.

[12]Isaac planted grain and had a good harvest that same year. The LORD blessed him, [13]and Isaac was so successful that he became very rich. [14]In fact, the Philistines were jealous of the large number of sheep, goats, and slaves that Isaac owned, [15]and they stopped up the wells that Abraham's servants had dug before his death. [16]Finally, Abimelech said, "Isaac, I want you to leave our country. You have become too powerful to stay here."

[17]Isaac left and settled in Gerar Valley, [18]where he cleaned out those wells that the Philistines had stopped up. Isaac also gave each of the wells the same name[v] that Abraham had given to them. [19]While his servants were digging in the valley, they found a spring-fed well. [20]But the shepherds of Gerar Valley quarreled with Isaac's shepherds and claimed the water belonged

to them. So this well was named "Quarrel," because they had quarreled with Isaac. [21]Isaac's servants dug another well, and the shepherds also quarreled about it. So that well was named "Jealous." [22]Finally, they dug one more well. There was no quarreling this time, and the well was named "Lots of Room," because the LORD had given them room and would make them very successful.

[23]Isaac went on to Beersheba, [24]where the LORD appeared to him that night and told him, "Don't be afraid! I am the God who was worshiped by your father Abraham, my servant. I will be with you and bless you, and because of Abraham I will give you many descendants." [25]Isaac built an altar there and worshiped the LORD. Then he set up camp, and his servants started digging a well.

[26]Meanwhile, Abimelech had left Gerar and was taking his advisor Ahuzzath and his army commander Phicol to see Isaac. [27]When they arrived, Isaac asked, "Why are you here? Didn't you send me away because you hated me?"

[28]They answered, "We now know for certain that the LORD is with you, and we have decided there needs to be a peace treaty between you and us. So let's make a solemn agreement [29]not to harm each other. Remember, we have never hurt you, and when we sent you away, we let you go in peace. The LORD has truly blessed you."

[30]Isaac gave a big feast for them, and everyone ate and drank. [31]Early the next morning Isaac and the others made a solemn agreement, then he let them go in peace.

[32]Later that same day Isaac's servants came and said, "We've struck water!" [33]So

[u]**26.4** *They . . . on earth:* Or "All nations on earth will ask me to bless them."   [v]**26.18** *gave . . . same name:* By doing this Isaac claimed ownership of the wells.

Isaac named the well Shibah,^{w} and the town is still called Beersheba.^{x}

Esau's Foreign Wives

^{34}When Esau was 40 years old, he married Judith the daughter of Beeri the Hittite and Basemath the daughter of Elon the Hittite. ^{35}But these two women brought a lot of grief to Esau's parents Isaac and Rebekah.

Isaac Blesses Jacob

27 Isaac was old and almost blind, when he called in his first-born son Esau, who asked him, "Father, what can I do for you?"

^{2}Isaac replied, "I am old and might die at any time. ^{3}So go hunting with your bow and arrows and kill a wild animal. ^{4}Cook some of that tasty food that I love so much and bring it to me. I want to eat it once more and give you my blessing before I die."

^{5}Rebekah had been listening, and as soon as Esau left to go hunting, ^{6}she said to Jacob, "I heard your father tell Esau ^{7}to kill a wild animal and cook some tasty food for him before he dies. Your father said this because he wants to bless your brother with the Lord as his witness. ^{8}Now, my son, listen carefully to what I want you to do. ^{9}Go and kill two of your best young goats and bring them to me. I'll cook the tasty food that your father loves so much. ^{10}Then you can take it to him, so he can eat it and give you his blessing before he dies."

^{11}"My brother Esau is a hairy man," Jacob reminded her. "And I am not. ^{12}If my father touches me and realizes I am trying to trick him, he will put a curse on me instead of giving me a blessing."

^{13}Rebekah insisted, "Let his curse fall on me! Just do what I say and bring me the meat." ^{14}So Jacob brought the meat to his mother, and she cooked the tasty food that his father liked. ^{15}Then she took Esau's best clothes and put them on Jacob. ^{16}She also covered the smooth part of his hands and neck with goatskins ^{17}and gave him some bread and the tasty food she had cooked.

^{18}Jacob went to his father and said, "Father, here I am."

"Which one of my sons are you?" his father asked.

^{19}Jacob replied, "I am Esau, your firstborn, and I have done what you told me. Please sit up and eat the meat I have brought. Then you can give me your blessing."

^{20}Isaac asked, "My son, how did you find an animal so quickly?"

"The Lord your God was kind to me," Jacob answered.

^{21}"My son," Isaac said, "come closer, where I can touch you and find out if you really are Esau." ^{22}Jacob went closer. His father touched him and said, "You sound like Jacob, but your hands feel hairy like Esau's." ^{23}And so Isaac blessed Jacob, thinking he was Esau.

^{24}Isaac asked, "Are you really my son Esau?"

"Yes, I am," Jacob answered.

^{25}So Isaac told him, "Serve me the wild meat, and I can give you my blessing."

Jacob gave him some meat, and he ate it. He also gave him some wine, and he drank it. ^{26}Then Isaac said, "Son, come over here

● 26.34 *Esau . . . Hittite:* Esau was Isaac and Rebekah's oldest son and the twin of Jacob (25.19-33). Esau also married Ishmael's daughter Mahalath (28.9). Compare this list with 36.2-3. Why the names are different is not clear. Perhaps Esau married more than three different women.

■ 27.4 *give you my blessing:* Spoken promises and deathbed blessings were important in the lives of ancient peoples (48.8-20; 49.1-28; Deut 33; Josh 23). What was said by the person giving these blessings was considered as valid as any written law. In fact, such blessings were considered so powerful, they could not be taken back (27.33).

^{w}26.33 *Shibah:* In Hebrew "Shibah" sounds something like "good luck" and "promise."
^{x}26.33 *Beersheba:* Meaning "Well of Good Fortune" or "Peace Treaty Well."

27.29 *rule over your brothers:* Isaac's blessing fulfilled what God had told Rebekah (25.23). See also 12.3; Num 24.9.

27.33 *blessing:* Esau also wanted a blessing, but Isaac could not undo the blessing he had already given Jacob which gave Jacob the right to rule over Esau (27.29). The blessing was to be the birthright of the first-born, but Esau had earlier sold his birthright to Jacob (25.27-33).

27.39,40 *Your home . . . you will break loose:* Edom was a mostly dry, hilly area, not fertile and green like the Jordan Valley in Canaan (36.6-8). Living by the sword is a reference to Edom's disputes with Israel (Amos 1.11,12; Joel 3.19; Obad 1-21; Ezek 25.12-14). But the people of Israel did recognize the Edomites as their "relatives" (Deut 23.7,8). King Jehoshaphat of Judah controlled Edom at a time when Edom had no king (1 Kgs 22.47). When Jehoram was king of Judah, the Edomites broke free (2 Kgs 8.20-22).

and kiss me." **27**While Jacob was kissing him, Isaac caught the smell of his clothes and said:

"The smell of my son
is like a field
the LORD has blessed.
28God will bless you, my son,
with dew from heaven
and with fertile fields,
rich with grain and grapes.
29Nations will be your servants
and bow down to you.
You will rule over your brothers,
and they will kneel
at your feet.
Anyone who curses you
will be cursed;
anyone who blesses you
will be blessed."

30Right after Isaac had given Jacob his blessing and Jacob had gone, Esau came back from hunting. **31**He cooked the tasty food, brought it to his father, and said, "Father, please sit up and eat the meat I have brought you, so you can give me your blessing."

32"Who are you?" Isaac asked.

"I am Esau, your first-born son."

33Isaac started trembling and said, "Then who brought me some wild meat right before you came in? I ate it and gave him a blessing that cannot be taken back."

34Esau cried out in great distress, "Father, give me a blessing too!"

35Isaac answered, "Your brother tricked me and stole your blessing."

36Esau replied, "My brother deserves the name Jacob,[y] because he has already cheated me twice. The first time he cheated me out of my rights as the first-born son, and now he has cheated me out of

my blessing." Then Esau asked his father, "Don't you have any blessing left for me?"

37"My son," Isaac answered, "I have made Jacob the ruler over you and your brothers, and all of you will be his servants. I have also promised him all the grain and grapes that he needs. There's nothing left that I can do for you."

38"Father," Esau asked, "don't you have more than one blessing? You can surely give me a blessing too!" Then Esau started crying again.

39So his father said:

"Your home will be far
from that fertile land,
where dew comes down
from the heavens.
40You will live by the power
of your sword
and be your brother's slave.
But when you decide to be free,
you will break loose."

41Esau hated his brother Jacob because he had stolen the blessing that was supposed to be his. So he said to himself, "Just as soon as my father dies, I'll kill Jacob."

42When Rebekah found out what Esau planned to do, she sent for Jacob and told him, "Son, your brother Esau is just waiting for a chance to kill you. **43**Now listen carefully and do what I say. Go to the home of my brother Laban in Haran **44**and stay with him for a while. When Esau stops being angry **45**and forgets what you have done to him, I'll send for you to come home. Why should I lose both of my sons on the same day?"[z]

46Rebekah later told Isaac, "Those Hittite wives of Esau are making my life miserable! If Jacob marries a Hittite woman, I'd be better off dead."

[y]27.36 *Jacob:* In Hebrew "Jacob" sounds like "cheat." [z]27.45 *lose . . . day:* Esau would be hunted down as a murderer if he killed Jacob, and so Rebekah would lose both of her sons.

"*Jacob . . . has already cheated me . . . out of my rights as the first-born son, and now he has cheated me out of my blessing.*" GEN 27.36

Isaac's Instructions to Jacob

28 Isaac called in Jacob, then gave him
a blessing, and said:
Don't marry any of those Canaanite
women. 2Go at once to your mother's
father Bethuel in northern Syria[a] and
choose a wife from one of the daughters of Laban, your mother's brother.
3I pray that God All-Powerful will bless
you with many descendants and let you
become a great nation. 4May he bless
you with the land he promised Abraham, so that you will take over this
land where we now live as foreigners.
5Isaac then sent Jacob to stay with
Rebekah's brother Laban, the son of
Bethuel the Aramean.

Esau Marries the Daughter of Ishmael

6Esau found out that his father Isaac had
blessed Jacob and had warned him not to
marry any of the Canaanite women. He
also learned that Jacob had been sent to
find a wife in northern Syria[b] 7and that he
had obeyed his father and mother. 8Esau
already had several wives, but he now realized how much his father hated the
Canaanite women. 9So he married Ishmael's daughter Mahalath, who was the
sister of Nebaioth[c] and the granddaughter
of Abraham.

Jacob's Dream at Bethel

10Jacob left the town of Beersheba and
started out for Haran. 11At sunset he
stopped for the night and went to sleep,
resting his head on a large rock. 12In a
dream he saw a ladder that reached from
earth to heaven, and God's angels were going up and down on it.
13The LORD was standing beside the ladder[d] and said:
I am the LORD God who was worshiped by Abraham and Isaac. I will
give to you and your family the land
on which you are now sleeping.
14Your descendants will spread over
the earth in all directions and will become as numerous as the specks of
dust. Your family will be a blessing to
all people.[e] 15Wherever you go, I will
watch over you, then later I will bring
you back to this land. I won't leave
you—I will do all I have promised.
16Jacob woke up suddenly and thought,
"The LORD is in this place, and I didn't even
know it." 17Then Jacob became frightened
and said, "What a frightening place! It must
be the house of God and the gateway to
heaven."
18When Jacob got up early the next
morning, he took the rock that he had
used for a pillow and stood it up as a place
of worship. Then he poured olive oil on the
rock to dedicate it to God, 19and he named
the place Bethel.[f] Before that it had been
named Luz.
20Jacob solemnly promised God, "If you
go with me and watch over me as I travel,
and if you give me food and clothes 21and
bring me safely home again, you will be my
God. 22This rock will be your house, and I
will give back to you a tenth of everything
you give me."

[a]28.2 *northern Syria*: See the note at 24.10. [b]28.6 *northern Syria*: See the note at 24.10.
[c]28.9 *Nebaioth*: Ishmael's oldest son (see 25.13). [d]28.13 *the ladder*: Or "Jacob" or "the stairway."
[e]28.14 *Your family . . . people*: Or "All people will ask me to bless them as I have blessed your family."
[f]28.19 *Bethel*: In Hebrew "Bethel" means "House of God."

28.1,2 *Canaanite women . . . Bethuel in northern Syria . . . Laban:* Isaac wanted the family line to continue and not be mixed with the Canaanites, who worshiped a number of gods but not the God he and Abraham worshiped.

28.12 *ladder:* This ladder was more like the kind of stairway that went up the side of a Mesopotamian temple. In Jacob's dream, the LORD stands above the ladder (28.13).

28.15 *Wherever you go . . . I won't leave you:* The gods of certain peoples, such as the ancient Mesopotamians, were connected to particular places, and they only gave protection within that area. But the LORD God of Abraham and Isaac promised to be with Jacob no matter where he went.

28.18 *place of worship . . . olive oil:* In ancient times stones were often used at places set apart to honor a god (Josh 24.26). Olive oil was poured on objects like these marker stones to dedicate them to God. This was called "anointing" (Gen 35.14; Exod 30.25-31; 1 Sam 10.1).

Angels

28.22 *a tenth:* Jacob's promise to give one tenth may refer to his offering part of his flock of sheep or goats as a sacrifice to God. Some years later, Jacob did have his own flocks (31.1-18, 38-42). Giving a tenth (tithe) of one's crops or animal herds later became a requirement for all the people of Israel according to the Law of Moses (Num 18.21-24).

29.14 *like one of my own family:* This phrase translates Hebrew words which literally mean "my flesh and blood" or "my bone and flesh."

29.18 *seven years:* Seven was considered a perfect or complete number in ancient times. **(See the chart Numbers in the Bible on pg 1844.)**

29.23-30 *married her . . . Laban also gave Zilpah . . . Bilhah:* In ancient Palestine marriages were important family events even though couples did not exchange vows as in modern weddings. Instead, a couple was considered married if they slept together. Laban brought Leah to Jacob's tent at night, and Leah was probably wearing a veil over her face. The festivities celebrating the couple's union often lasted as long as a week (29.27; see also Judg 14.12,17). Giving a servant was a wedding custom taken from old Babylonian wedding contracts (see also 29.28-30).

Jacob Arrives at Laban's Home

29 As Jacob continued on his way to the east, ²he looked out in a field and saw a well where shepherds took their sheep for water. Three flocks of sheep were lying around the well, which was covered with a large rock. ³Shepherds would roll the rock away when all their sheep had gathered there. Then after the sheep had been watered, the shepherds would roll the rock back over the mouth of the well.

⁴Jacob asked the shepherds, "Where are you from?"

"We're from Haran," they answered.

⁵Then he asked, "Do you know Nahor's grandson Laban?"

"Yes we do," they replied.

⁶"How is he?" Jacob asked.

"He's fine," they answered. "And here comes his daughter Rachel with the sheep."

⁷Jacob told them, "Look, the sun is still high up in the sky, and it's too early to bring in the rest of the flocks. Water your sheep and take them back to the pasture."

⁸But they replied, "We can't do that until they all get here, and the rock has been rolled away from the well."

⁹While Jacob was still talking with the men, his cousin Rachel came up with her father's sheep. ¹⁰When Jacob saw her and his uncle's sheep, he rolled the rock away and watered the sheep. ¹¹He then kissed Rachel and started crying because he was so happy. ¹²He told her that he was the son of her aunt Rebekah, and she ran and told her father about him.

¹³As soon as Laban heard the news, he ran out to meet Jacob. He hugged and kissed him and brought him to his home, where Jacob told him everything that had

happened. ¹⁴Laban said, "You are my nephew, and you are like one of my own family."

Jacob Marries Leah and Rachel

After Jacob had been there for a month, ¹⁵Laban said to him, "You shouldn't have to work without pay, just because you are a relative of mine. What do you want me to give you?"

¹⁶⁻¹⁷Laban had two daughters. Leah was older than Rachel, but her eyes didn't sparkle,ᵍ while Rachel was beautiful and had a good figure. ¹⁸Since Jacob was in love with Rachel, he answered, "If you will let me marry Rachel, I'll work seven years for you."

¹⁹Laban replied, "It's better for me to let you marry Rachel than for someone else to have her. So stay and work for me." ²⁰Jacob worked seven years for Laban, but the time seemed like only a few days, because he loved Rachel so much.

²¹Jacob said to Laban, "The time is up, and I want to marry Rachel now!" ²²So Laban gave a big feast and invited all their neighbors. ²³But that evening he brought Leah to Jacob, who married her and spent the night with her. ²⁴Laban also gave Zilpah to Leah as her servant woman.

²⁵The next morning Jacob found out that he had married Leah, and he asked Laban, "Why did you do this to me? Didn't I work to get Rachel? Why did you trick me?"

²⁶Laban replied, "In our country the older daughter must get married first. ²⁷After you spend this weekʰ with Leah, you may also marry Rachel. But you will have to work for me another seven years."

²⁸⁻³⁰At the end of the week of celebration, Laban let Jacob marry Rachel, and he

ᵍ29.16,17 *but her eyes didn't sparkle:* Or "and her eyes sparkled." ʰ29.27 *this week:* The wedding feast lasted for seven days (see Judges 14.12,17).

gave her his servant woman Bilhah. Jacob loved Rachel more than he did Leah, but he had to work another seven years for Laban.

[31]The LORD knew that Jacob loved Rachel more than he did Leah, and so he gave children to Leah, but not to Rachel. [32]Leah gave birth to a son and named him Reuben.[i] Then she said, "The LORD has taken away my sorrow. Now my husband will love me more than he does Rachel." [33]She had a second son and named him Simeon,[j] because she said, "The LORD has heard that my husband doesn't love me." [34]When Leah's third son was born, she said, "Now my husband will hold me close." So this son was named Levi.[k] [35]She had one more son and named him Judah,[l] because she said, "I'll praise the LORD!"

Problems between Rachel and Leah

30 Rachel was very jealous of Leah for having children, and she said to Jacob, "I'll die if you don't give me some children!"

[2]But Jacob became upset with Rachel and answered, "Don't blame me! I'm not God."

[3]"Here, take my servant Bilhah," Rachel told him. "Have children by her, and I'll let them be born on my knees to show that they are mine."

[4]Then Rachel let Jacob marry Bilhah, [5]and they had a son. [6]Rachel named him Dan,[m] because she said, "God has answered my prayers. He judged in my favor

and has given me a son." [7]When Bilhah and Jacob had a second son, [8]Rachel said, "I've struggled hard with my sister, and I've won!" So she named the boy Naphtali.[n]

[9]When Leah realized she could not have any more children, she let Jacob marry her servant Zilpah, [10]and they had a son. [11]"I'm really lucky," Leah said, and she named the boy Gad.[o] [12]When they had another son, [13]Leah exclaimed, "I'm happy now, and all the women will say how happy I am." So she named him Asher.[p]

Love Flowers

[14]During the time of the wheat harvest, Reuben found some love flowers[q] and took them to his mother Leah. Rachel asked Leah for some of them, [15]but Leah said, "It's bad enough that you stole my husband! Now you want my son's love flowers too."

"All right," Rachel answered. "Let me have the flowers, and you can sleep with Jacob tonight."

[16]That evening when Jacob came in from the fields, Leah told him, "You're sleeping with me tonight. I hired you with my son's love flowers."

They slept together that night, [17]and God answered Leah's prayers by giving her a fifth son. [18]Leah shouted, "God has rewarded me for letting Jacob marry my servant," and she named the boy Issachar.[r] [19]When Leah had another son, [20]she exclaimed, "God has given me a wonderful gift, and my husband will praise me for giving him six sons." So she named the boy

29.32-35 *Leah gave birth to . . . Levi . . . Judah:* Levi was the ancestor of Aaron, whose descendants were Israel's priests. Judah was the ancestor of Israel's King David.

30.3 *born on my knees:* Rachel may have wanted to be present at the birth, but most likely this phrase was meant as a symbol of adoption (see 48.10-12).

30.18-21 *Dinah:* No explanation is given for the meaning of Dinah's name. For more about Dinah, see 34.1-24.

---

[i]**29.32** *Reuben:* In Hebrew "Reuben" means, "Look, a son!" [j]**29.33** *Simeon:* In Hebrew "Simeon" sounds like "someone who hears." [k]**29.34** *hold me close . . . Levi:* In Hebrew "Levi" sounds like "hold (someone) close." [l]**29.35** *Judah:* In Hebrew "Judah" sounds like "praise." [m]**30.6** *Dan:* In Hebrew "Dan" means "judge." [n]**30.8** *Naphtali:* In Hebrew "Naphtali" means "struggle" or "contest." [o]**30.11** *Gad:* In Hebrew "Gad" means "lucky." [p]**30.13** *Asher:* In Hebrew "Asher" means "happy." [q]**30.14** *love flowers:* Also called "mandrakes," a flowering plant that was thought to give sexual powers. [r]**30.18** *Issachar:* In Hebrew "Issachar" sounds like "reward."

● 30.22-24 *Joseph:* For more about Joseph, see chapters 37; 39–50 and the chart Jacob's Children and Their Mothers on pg 1824.

■ 30.27-28 *I'm sure:* The Hebrew text here refers to knowledge received by some form of divination, which means trying to discover the wishes of the gods by a number of means, including magic, fortunetelling, reading fluids in a cup (44.5), communicating with the dead (1 Sam 28.3-25), inspecting the liver and other organs of dead animals, reading dreams (41.1-32), and casting lots (drawing objects out of a container). Later the Law of Moses would ban most of these things in Israel (Lev 19.26; Deut 18.10-14).

Zebulun.^{s} ^{21}Later, Leah had a daughter and named her Dinah.

$^{22-23}$Finally, God remembered Rachel— he answered her prayer by giving her a son. "God has taken away my disgrace," she said. ^{24}"I'll name the boy Joseph,^{t} and I'll pray that the LORD will give me another son."

Jacob and Laban

^{25}After Joseph was born, Jacob said to Laban, "Release me from our agreement^u and let me return to my own country. ^{26}You know how hard I've worked for you, so let me take my wives and children and leave."

$^{27-28}$But Laban told him, "If you really are my friend, stay on, and I'll pay whatever you ask. I'm sure^v the LORD has blessed me because of you."

^{29}Jacob answered:

You've seen how hard I've worked for you, and you know how your flocks and herds have grown under my care. ^{30}You didn't have much before I came, but the LORD has blessed everything I have ever done for you. Now it's time for me to start looking out for my own family.

^{31}"How much do you want me to pay you?" Laban asked.

Then Jacob told him:

I don't want you to pay me anything. Just do one thing, and I'll take care of your sheep and goats. ^{32}Let me go through your flocks and herds and

take the sheep and goats that are either spotted or speckled^w and the black lambs. That's all you need to give me. ^{33}In the future you can easily find out if I've been honest. Just look and see if my animals are either spotted or speckled, or if the lambs are black. If they aren't, they've been stolen from you.

^{34}"I agree to that," was Laban's response. ^{35}Before the end of the day, Laban had separated his spotted and speckled animals and the black lambs from the others and had put his sons in charge of them. ^{36}Then Laban made Jacob keep the rest of the sheep and goats at a distance of three days' journey.

^{37}Jacob cut branches from some poplar trees and from some almond and evergreen trees. He peeled off part of the bark and made the branches look spotted and speckled. ^{38}Then he put the branches where the sheep and goats would see them^x while they were drinking from the water trough. The goats mated there ^{39}in front of the branches, and their young were spotted and speckled.

^{40}Some of the sheep that Jacob was keeping for Laban were already spotted. And when the others were ready to mate, he made sure that they faced in the direction of the spotted and black ones. In this way, Jacob built up a flock of sheep for himself and did not put them with the other sheep.

^{41}When the stronger sheep were mating near the drinking place, Jacob made sure that the spotted branches were there.

---

^{s}**30.20** *Zebulun:* In Hebrew "Zebulun" sounds like "give" and "praise." ^{t}**30.24** *Joseph:* In Hebrew "Joseph" sounds like "take away" and "add." ^{u}**30.25** *Release . . . agreement:* Jacob had agreed to work seven years for each of Laban's two daughters (see 29.18). ^{v}**30.27,28** *I'm sure:* The Hebrew says he found this out by some kind of magic, such as fortunetelling. ^{w}**30.32** *spotted or speckled:* In ancient times sheep were usually white, and goats were usually black or dark brown; only a few sheep would have black spots, and only a few goats would have white spots. ^{x}**30.38** *would see them:* It was believed by some that what sheep and goats saw at the time of breeding would determine the color of their young.

⁴²But he would not put out the branches when the weaker animals were mating. So Jacob got all of the healthy animals, and Laban got what was left. ⁴³Jacob soon became rich and successful. He owned many sheep, goats, camels, and donkeys, as well as a lot of slaves.

Jacob Runs from Laban

31 Jacob heard that Laban's sons were complaining, "Jacob is now a rich man, and he got everything he owns from our father." ²Jacob also noticed that Laban was not as friendly as he had been before. ³One day the LORD said, "Jacob, go back to your relatives in the land of your ancestors, and I will be with you."

⁴Jacob sent for Rachel and Leah to meet him in the pasture where he kept his sheep, ⁵and he told them:

Your father isn't as friendly with me as he used to be, but the God my ancestors worshiped has been on my side. ⁶You know that I have worked hard for your father ⁷and that he keeps cheating me by changing my wages time after time. But God has protected me. ⁸When your father said the speckled sheep would be my wages, all of them were speckled. And when he said the spotted ones would be mine, all of them were spotted. ⁹That's how God has taken sheep and goats from your father and given them to me.

¹⁰Once, when the flocks were mating, I dreamed that all the rams were either spotted or speckled. ¹¹Then God's angel called me by name. I answered, ¹²and he said, "Notice that all the rams are either spotted or speckled. I know everything Laban is doing to you, ¹³and I am the God you worshiped at Bethel,ʸ when you poured olive oil on a rock and made a promise to me. Leave here at once and return to the land where you were born."

¹⁴Rachel and Leah said to Jacob:

There's nothing left for us to inherit from our father. ¹⁵He treats us like foreigners and has even cheated us out of the bride priceᶻ that should have been ours. ¹⁶So do whatever God tells you to do. Even the property God took from our father and gave to you really belongs to us and our children.

¹⁷Then Jacob, his wives, and his children got on camels and left ¹⁸northern Syriaᵃ for the home of his father Isaac in Canaan. Jacob took along all his flocks, herds, and other property.

¹⁹Before Rachel left, she stole the household idolsᵇ while Laban was out shearing his sheep. ²⁰Jacob tricked Laban the Arameanᶜ by not saying that he intended to leave. ²¹When Jacob crossed the Euphrates River and headed for the hill country of Gilead, he took with him everything he owned.

Laban Catches Up with Jacob

²²Three days later Laban found out that Jacob had gone. ²³So he took some of his relatives along and chased after Jacob for seven days, before catching up with him in

31.3 *land of your ancestors:* This means Canaan (see 31.17,18).

31.4 *Jacob sent for Rachel and Leah:* According to legal customs, Rachel and Leah belonged to their father's house and were considered part of his property (see Ruth 4.5,10), so Jacob asked their opinion about what to do.

31.9 *God has . . . given them to me:* Jacob gives credit to God for helping him gain large flocks, rather than his own idea to use speckled sticks (30.37-42). This is a common theme in these stories of Israel's ancestors: God is at work in the common events of people's lives and in their actions.

Canaanite Gods and Goddesses

31.21 *hill country of Gilead:* Gilead was the area east of the Jordan River between Lake Galilee and the Dead Sea. It had high pasture lands and fertile lowlands where grain was grown. **(See Maps 1 and 6 on pgs 1879 and 1884.)**

ʸ**31.13** *you . . . Bethel:* Or "who appeared to you at Bethel." ᶻ**31.15** *bride price:* Usually the husband-to-be paid a bride price to the father of the bride. But Jacob didn't pay Laban a bride price for either Rachel or Leah. Instead he was tricked into working 14 years to get the bride he loved. So there was no money for either of Laban's daughters. ᵃ**31.18** *northern Syria:* See the note at 24.10. ᵇ**31.19** *household idols:* These were thought to protect the household from danger. It is also possible that the person who had them would inherit the family property. ᶜ**31.20** *the Aramean:* Meaning someone from northern Syria (see the note at 24.10).

31.27 *tambourines and harps:* A tambourine is a circular frame with metal disks attached that jingle when the frame is shaken or hit. The harp here was probably a lyre, a stringed musical instrument that could be held by hand.

31.35 *my period:* In ancient times, anything a woman sat on while having her period was considered ritually unclean (Lev 15.19-23).

the hill country of Gilead. **24**But God appeared to Laban in a dream that night and warned, "Don't say a word to Jacob. Don't make a threat or a promise."

25Jacob had set up camp in the hill country of Gilead, when Laban and his relatives came and set up camp in another part of the hill country. Laban went to Jacob **26**and said:

Look what you've done! You've tricked me and run off with my daughters like a kidnapper. **27**Why did you sneak away without telling me? I would have given you a going-away party with singing and with music on tambourines and harps. **28**You didn't even give me a chance to kiss my own grandchildren and daughters goodbye. That was really foolish. **29**I could easily hurt you, but the God your father worshiped has warned me not to make any threats or promises.

30I can understand why you were eager to return to your father, but why did you have to steal my idols?

31Jacob answered, "I left secretly because I was afraid you would take your daughters from me by force. **32**If you find that any one of us has taken your idols, I'll have that person killed. Let your relatives be witnesses. Show me what belongs to you, and you can take it back." Jacob did not realize that Rachel had stolen the household idols.

33Laban searched the tents of Jacob, Leah, and the two servant women,**d** but did not find the idols. Then he went to Rachel's tent. **34**She had already hidden them in the cushion she used as a saddle and was sitting on it. Laban searched everywhere and did not find them. **35**Rachel said, "Father, please don't be angry with me for not getting up; I'm having my period." Laban kept on searching, but still did not find the idols.

36Jacob became very angry and said to Laban:

What have I done wrong? Have I committed some crime? Is that why you hunted me down? **37**After searching through everything I have, did you find anything of yours? If so, put it here, where your relatives and mine can see it. Then we can decide what to do.

38In all the 20 years that I've worked for you, not one of your sheep or goats has had a miscarriage, and I've never eaten even one of your rams. **39**If a wild animal killed one of your sheep or goats, I paid for it myself. In fact, you demanded the full price, whether the animal was killed during the day or at night.**e 40**I sweated every day, and I couldn't sleep at night because of the cold.

41I had to work 14 of these 20 long years to earn your two daughters and another 6 years to buy your sheep and goats. During that time you kept changing my wages. **42**If the fearsome God**f** worshiped by Abraham and my father Isaac had not been on my side, you would have sent me away without a thing. But God saw my hard work, and he knew the trouble I was in, so he helped me. Then last night he told you how wrong you were.

---

d31.33 *two servant women:* Bilhah and Zilpah (see 30.4,9). **e**31.39 *you demanded . . . night:* A shepherd was not responsible for sheep and goats killed by wild animals, if the shepherd could supply proof of how they were killed. **f**31.42 *fearsome God:* One possible meaning for the difficult Hebrew text.

Jacob and Laban Make an Agreement

43Laban said to Jacob, "Leah and Rachel are my daughters, and their children belong to me. All these sheep you are taking are really mine too. In fact, everything you have belongs to me. But there is nothing I can do to keep my daughters and their children. **44**So I am ready to make an agreement with you, and we will pile up some large rocks here to remind us of the agreement."

45After Jacob had set up a large rock, **46**he told his men to get some more rocks and pile them up next to it. Then Jacob and Laban ate a meal together beside the rocks. **47**Laban named the pile of rocks Jegar Sahadutha.**g** But Jacob named it Galeed.**h** **48**Laban said to Jacob, "This pile of rocks will remind us of our agreement." That's why the place was named Galeed. **49**Laban also said, "This pile of rocks means that the LORD will watch us both while we are apart from each other." So the place was also named Mizpah.**i**

50Then Laban said:

If you mistreat my daughters or marry other women, I may not know about it, but remember, God is watching us! **51-52**Both this pile of rocks and this large rock have been set up between us as a reminder. I must never go past them to attack you, and you must never come past them to attack me. **53**My father Nahor, your grandfather Abraham, and their ancestors all worshiped the same God, and he will make sure that we each keep the agreement.

Then Jacob made a promise in the name of the fearsome God**j** his father Isaac had worshiped. **54**Jacob killed an animal and offered it as a sacrifice there on the mountain, and he invited his men to eat with him. After the meal they spent the night on the mountain. **55**Early the next morning, Laban kissed his daughters and his grandchildren goodbye, then he left to go back home.

Jacob Gets Ready To Meet Esau

32 As Jacob was on his way back home, some of God's angels came and met him. **2**When Jacob saw them, he said, "This is God's camp." So he named the place Mahanaim.**k**

3Jacob sent messengers on ahead to Esau, who lived in the land of Seir, also known as Edom. **4**Jacob told them to say to Esau, "Master, I am your servant! I have lived with Laban all this time, **5**and now I own cattle, donkeys, and sheep, as well as many slaves. Master, I am sending these messengers in the hope that you will be kind to me."

6When the messengers returned, they told Jacob, "We went to your brother Esau, and now he is heading this way with 400 men."

7Jacob was so frightened that he divided his people, sheep, cattle, and camels into two groups. **8**He thought, "If Esau attacks one group, perhaps the other can escape." **9**Then Jacob prayed:

You, LORD, are the God who was worshiped by my grandfather Abraham and by my father Isaac. You told me to return home to my family, and you promised to be with me and make me successful. **10**I don't deserve all the

31.47-49 *pile of rocks:* Making a pile of rocks was a way to leave evidence of an agreement between people, or between people and God (28.18-22; Josh 4.4-7).

32.1 *God's angels:* In Hebrew the word for "angel" means "messenger." In the Bible, angels act both as messengers and servants of God.

Angels

32.2 *Mahanaim:* Mahanaim was close to where the Jabbok River flows into the Jordan. It was important later in the history of Israel (2 Sam 2.8,9; 17.24-29; 1 Kgs 4.14).

32.4 *Master, I am your servant:* Jacob shows his humility toward Esau.

---

g31.47 *Jegar Sahadutha:* In Aramaic "Jegar Sahadutha" means "a pile of rocks to remind us."
h31.47 *Galeed:* In Hebrew "Galeed" means "a pile of rocks to remind us." **i**31.49 *Mizpah:* In Hebrew "Mizpah" sounds like "a place from which to watch." **j**31.53 *fearsome God:* See the note at 31.42.
k32.2 *Mahanaim:* In Hebrew "Mahanaim" means "two camps."

32.22-23 *Jabbok River:* This small river flows west into the Jordan River about 20 miles north of the Dead Sea. (See Map 3 on pg 1881.)

32.24 *man:* This means God or an angel of God (32.30).

32.28 *Israel:* Abraham's descendants eventually were known as the people of Israel and Israelites. In the Bible, Israel is the nation made up of the twelve tribes descended from Jacob.

⟨R⟩   Israel

32.30 *Peniel:* In Hebrew "Peniel" means "face of God." Seeing God's face was believed to bring death (Exod 33.20), but Jacob survived.

32.32 *muscle on his hip:* This rule about not eating the hip tendon is not found anywhere else in the Bible, but it is found in later writings of Judaism.

good things you have done for me, your servant. When I first crossed the Jordan, I had only my walking stick, but now I have two large groups of people and animals. [11]Please rescue me from my brother. I am afraid he will come and attack not only me, but my wives and children as well. [12]But you have promised that I would be a success and that someday it will be as hard to count my descendants as it is to count the grains of sand along the seashore.

[13]After Jacob had spent the night there, he chose some animals as gifts for Esau: [14-15]200 female goats and 20 males, 200 female sheep and 20 males, 30 female camels with their young, 40 cows and 10 bulls, and 20 female donkeys and 10 males.

[16]Jacob put servants in charge of each herd and told them, "Go ahead of me and keep a space between each herd." [17]Then he said to the servant in charge of the first herd, "When Esau meets you, he will ask whose servant you are. He will want to know where you are going and who owns those animals in front of you. [18]So tell him, 'They belong to your servant Jacob, who is coming this way. He is sending them as a gift to his master Esau.'"

[19]Jacob also told the men in charge of the second and third herds and those who followed to say the same thing when they met Esau. [20]And Jacob told them to be sure to say that he was right behind them. Jacob hoped the gifts would make Esau friendly, so Esau would be glad to see him when they met. [21]Jacob's men took the gifts on ahead of him, but he spent the night in camp.

Jacob's Name Is Changed to Israel

[22-23]Jacob got up in the middle of the night and took his wives, his eleven children, and everything he owned across to the other side of the Jabbok River for safety. [24]Afterwards, Jacob went back and spent the rest of the night alone.

A man came and fought with Jacob until just before daybreak. [25]When the man saw that he could not win, he struck Jacob on the hip and threw it out of joint. [26]They kept on wrestling until the man said, "Let go of me! It's almost daylight."

"You can't go until you bless me," Jacob replied.

[27]Then the man asked, "What is your name?"

"Jacob," he answered.

[28]The man said, "From now on, your name will no longer be Jacob. You will be called Israel,[1] because you have wrestled with God and with men, and you have won."

[29]Jacob said, "Now tell me your name."

"Don't you know who I am?" he asked. And he blessed Jacob.

[30]Jacob said, "I have seen God face to face, and I am still alive." So he named the place Peniel.[m] [31]The sun was coming up as Jacob was leaving Peniel. He was limping because he had been struck on the hip, [32]and the muscle on his hip joint had been injured. That's why even today the people of Israel don't eat the hip muscle of any animal.

[1]**32.28** *Israel:* In Hebrew one meaning of "Israel" is "a man who wrestles with God."   [m]**32.30** *Peniel:* In Hebrew "Peniel" means "face of God."

"Your name will no longer be Jacob. You will be called Israel, because you have wrestled with God and with men, and you have won." GEN 32.28

Jacob Meets Esau

33 Later that day Jacob met Esau coming with his 400 men. So Jacob told his children to walk with their mothers. [2]The two servant women, Zilpah and Bilhah, together with their children went first, followed by Leah and her children, then by Rachel and Joseph. [3]Jacob himself walked in front of them all, bowing to the ground seven times as he came near his brother.

[4]But Esau ran toward Jacob and hugged and kissed him. Then the two brothers started crying.

[5]When Esau noticed the women and children he asked, "Whose children are these?"

Jacob answered, "These are the children the LORD has been kind enough to give to me, your servant."

[6]Then the two servant women and their children came and bowed down to Esau. [7]Next, Leah and her children came and bowed down; finally, Joseph and Rachel also came and bowed down.

[8]Esau asked Jacob, "Why did you send those herds I met along the road?"

"Master," Jacob answered, "I sent them so you would be friendly to me."

[9]"But, brother, I already have plenty," Esau replied. "Keep them for yourself."

[10]"No!" Jacob said. "Please accept them as a sign of your friendship for me. When you welcomed me and I saw your face, it was like seeing the face of God. [11]Please accepts these as gifts I brought to you. God has been good to me, and I have everything I need." Jacob kept insisting until Esau agreed.

[12]"Let's get ready to travel," Esau said. "I'll go along with you."

[13]But Jacob answered, "Master, you know traveling is hard on children, and I have to look after the sheep and goats that are nursing their young. If my animals travel too much in one day, they will all die. [14]Why don't you go on ahead and let me travel along slowly with the children, the herds, and the flocks. We can meet again in the country of Edom."

[15]Esau replied, "Let me leave some of my men with you."

"You don't have to do that," Jacob answered. "I am happy, simply knowing that you are friendly to me."

[16]So Esau left for Edom. [17]But Jacob went to Succoth,[n] where he built a house for himself and set up shelters for his animals. That's why the place is called Succoth.

Jacob Arrives at Shechem

[18]After leaving northern Syria,[o] Jacob arrived safely at Shechem in Canaan and set up camp outside the city. [19]The land where he camped was owned by the descendants of Hamor, the father of Shechem. So Jacob paid them 100 pieces of silver[p] for the property, [20]then he set up his tents and built an altar there to honor the God of Israel.

Dinah Is Raped

34 Dinah, the daughter of Jacob and Leah, went to visit some of the women who lived nearby. [2]She was seen by Hamor's son Shechem, the leader of the Hivites, and he grabbed her and raped her. [3]But Shechem was attracted to Dinah, so he told her how much he loved her.

[n]**33.17** *Succoth:* In Hebrew "Succoth" means "shelters." [o]**33.18** *northern Syria:* See the note at 24.10. [p]**33.19** *pieces of silver:* Or "lambs" or "cattle."

● 33.2 *Rachel and Joseph:* Jacob had his favorite wife (Rachel) and her son (Joseph) walk at the rear, where it was safer.

● 33.3 *bowing . . . seven times:* This ancient act of showing honor and humility toward another is also described in writings found at Tell el-Amarna in Egypt and dating to the fourteenth century B.C.

■ 33.11 *these as gifts:* In Hebrew, the word for "gifts" can also mean "blessing." This may be Jacob's attempt to return at least a part of the "blessing" he stole from his brother (27.1-40).

● 33.13 *travel too much:* Jacob's family and flocks had traveled over 300 miles by foot in a short time since leaving Haran (31.21-23). **(See Map 1 on pg 1879.)**

● 33.16 *Succoth:* Succoth is thought to have been a few miles west of Mahanaim, just north of where the Jabbok River flows into the Jordan. **(See Map 3 on pg 1881.)**

● 33.19—34.2 *Hamor, the father of Shechem . . . Dinah . . . Hivites:* The Bible also refers to Hamor as the founder of the town of Shechem (Josh 24.32; Judg 9.28). He apparently named his son after the town. For Dinah, see also 30.21 and 46.8-15. The Hivites may also be the people known as the Horites, who may have settled in the area around Mount Seir but were later pushed out by the descendants of Esau, the Edomites.

34.7 *Nothing is more disgraceful:* In ancient Israel rape was not seen just as an act of violence against the victim, it was also seen as something that insulted and brought shame to the entire tribe and nation. Compare this story to the rape and murder of the Levite's wife in Judg 19.

34.14 *circumcised:* If Hamor's son and other Hivite men were circumcised, they could be part of the people of Israel. In addition to the possibility of gaining the wife he desired, Shechem saw a chance to gain part of the property of Jacob's family (34.22,23).

34.25 *Simeon and Levi:* Dinah's full brothers, whose mother was Leah (29.33,34; 30.21). Later, Simeon and Levi's own descendants were to be scattered because of the violent revenge they took on the men of Shechem (49.5-7). Their action caused Jacob to leave the area around Shechem and move on to Bethel (34.30; 35.1)

[4]Shechem even asked his father to arrange for him to marry her.

[5]Meanwhile, Jacob heard what had happened. But his sons were out in the fields with the cattle, so he did not do anything at the time. [6]Hamor arrived at Jacob's home [7]just as Jacob's sons were coming in from work. When they learned that their sister had been raped, they became furiously angry, because nothing is more disgraceful than rape, and it must not be tolerated.

[8]Hamor said to Jacob and his sons:

My son Shechem really loves Dinah. Please let him marry her. [9]Why don't you start letting your families marry into our families and ours marry into yours? [10]You can share this land with us. Move freely about until you find the property you want; then buy it and settle down here.

[11]Shechem added, "Do this favor for me, and I'll give whatever you want. [12]Ask anything, no matter how expensive. I'll do anything, just let me marry Dinah."

[13]Jacob's sons wanted to get even with Shechem and his father because of what had happened to their sister. [14]So they tricked them by saying:

You're not circumcised![q] It would be a disgrace for us to let you marry Dinah now. [15]But we will let you marry her, if you and the other men in your tribe agree to be circumcised. [16]Then your families can marry into ours, and ours can marry into yours, and we can live together like one nation. [17]But if you don't agree to be circumcised, we'll take Dinah and leave this place.

[18]Hamor and Shechem liked what was said. [19]Shechem was the most respected person in his family, and he was so in love with Dinah that he hurried off to get everything done. [20]The two men met with the other leaders of their city and told them:

[21]These people really are friendly. Why not let them move freely about until they find the property they want? There's enough land here for them and for us. Then our families can marry into theirs, and theirs can marry into ours.

[22]We have to do only one thing before they will agree to stay here and become one nation with us. Our men will have to be circumcised just like theirs. [23]Just think! We'll get their property, as well as their flocks and herds. All we have to do is to agree, and they will live here with us.

[24]Every grown man followed this advice and got circumcised.

Dinah's Brothers Take Revenge

[25]Three days later the men who had been circumcised were still weak from pain. So Simeon and Levi,[r] two of Dinah's brothers, attacked with their swords and killed every man in the town, [26]including Hamor and Shechem. Then they took Dinah and left. [27]Jacob's other sons came and took everything they wanted. All this was done because of the horrible thing that had happened to their sister. [28]They took sheep, goats, donkeys, and everything else that was in the town or the countryside. [29]After taking everything of value from the houses, they dragged away the wives and children of their victims.

[30]Jacob said to Simeon and Levi, "Look

[q]34.14 *You're not circumcised:* Israelite boys were circumcised when they were eight days old, and no uncircumcised man could be part of the people of Israel.   [r]34.25 *Simeon and Levi:* Dinah's full brothers.

what you've done! Now I'm in real trouble with the Canaanites and Perizzites who live around here. There aren't many of us, and if they attack, they'll kill everyone in my household."

31They answered, "Was it right to let our own sister be treated that way?"

Jacob Returns to Bethel

35 God told Jacob, "Return to Bethel, where I appeared to you when you were running from your brother Esau. Make your home there and build an altar for me."

2Jacob said to his family and to everyone else who was traveling with him:

Get rid of your foreign gods! Then make yourselves acceptable to worship God and put on clean clothes. **3**Afterwards, we'll go to Bethel. I will build an altar there for God, who answered my prayers when I was in trouble and who has always been at my side.

4So everyone gave Jacob their idols and their earrings,^{s} and he buried them under the oak tree near Shechem.

5While Jacob and his family were traveling through Canaan, God terrified the people in the towns so much that no one dared bother them. **6**Finally, they reached Bethel, also known as Luz. **7**Jacob built an altar there and called it "God of Bethel," because that was the place where God had appeared to him when he was running from Esau. **8**While they were there, Rebekah's personal servant Deborah^t died. They buried her under an oak tree and called it "Weeping Oak."

God Blesses Jacob at Bethel

9-11 After Jacob came back to the land of Canaan, God appeared to him again. This time he gave Jacob a new name and blessed him by saying:

I am God All-Powerful, and from now on your name will be Israel^u instead of Jacob. You will have many children. Your descendants will become nations, and some of the men in your family will even be kings. **12**I will give you the land that I promised Abraham and Isaac, and it will belong to your family forever.

13After God had gone, **14**Jacob set up a large rock, so that he would remember what had happened there. Then he poured wine and olive oil on the rock to show that it was dedicated to God, **15**and he named the place Bethel.^{v}

Benjamin Is Born

16Jacob and his family had left Bethel and were still a long way from Ephrath, when the time came for Rachel's baby to be born. **17**She was having a rough time, but the woman who was helping her said, "Don't worry! It's a boy." **18**Rachel was at the point of death, and right before dying, she said, "I'll name him Benoni."^{w} But Jacob called him Benjamin.^{x}

19Rachel was buried beside the road to Ephrath, which is also called Bethlehem. **20**Jacob set up a tombstone over her grave, and it is still there. **21**Jacob, also known as Israel, traveled to the south of Eder Tower, where he set up camp.

22During their time there, Jacob's oldest

35.2-4 *foreign gods . . . idols and their earrings:* The gods were probably the small household gods mentioned in 31.19, but Jacob's family members might have collected small statues of Canaanite gods, such as Baal.

Canaanite Gods and Goddesses

35.2 *make yourselves acceptable . . . clean clothes:* Those who wanted to worship God or come into God's presence needed to become ritually "clean" first (see Exod 19.10-14). Specific instructions for this kind of cleansing were later given in the Law of Moses (Lev 16.1-4; Num 8.5-8).

35.9-11 *God . . . gave Jacob a new name:* This appears to be another version of Jacob's name being changed (32.24-30), of God's promises to him (17.4-8; 28.13-15), and of his dedicating the rock at Bethel (28.18-22).

35.21 *Eder Tower:* This means "tower of the flock," probably referring to a watchtower built to keep watch over flocks of sheep and goats and protect them from robbers and wild animals.

---

^{s}**35.4** *earrings:* These would have had symbols of foreign gods on them. ^{t}**35.8** *Deborah:* See 24.59 and the note there. ^{u}**35.9-11** *Israel:* See the note at 32.28. ^{v}**35.15** *Bethel:* See the note at 28.19. ^{w}**35.18** *Benoni:* In Hebrew "Benoni" means "Son of my Sorrow." ^{x}**35.18** *Benjamin:* In Hebrew "Benjamin" can mean "Son at my Right Side" (the place of power).

Jacob said, "God . . . answered my prayers when I was in trouble and . . . has always been at my side." GEN 35.3

35.23-26 *Jacob had twelve sons:* See 29.28—30.23. This section says that Benjamin was also born in the north, though 35.18 says Benjamin was born to Rachel at Ephrath in the south.

36.4-5, 9-14 *Esau and his three wives had five sons:* Compare the list in 36.4-5 to the list in 36.9-14, which also includes Esau's grandchildren. Esau's descendants were the people of Edom, or Seir.

Timna is called "the other wife," of Eliphaz. This translates a Hebrew word for a woman who was legally bound to a man, but without the full privileges of a wife.

36.15-19 *clans:* Clans are groups of people who claim a common ancestor. The list of clans given here is another way of identifying the descendants of Esau. Compare this list with the previous one (36.9-14) and the list found in 1 Chr 1.35-37.

son Reuben slept with Bilhah, who was one of Jacob's other wives.[y] And Jacob found out about it.

Jacob's Twelve Sons

[23-26]Jacob had twelve sons while living in northern Syria.[z] His first-born Reuben was the son of Leah, who later gave birth to Simeon, Levi, Judah, Issachar, and Zebulun. Leah's servant Zilpah had two sons: Gad and Asher.

Jacob and his wife Rachel had Joseph and Benjamin. Rachel's servant woman Bilhah had two more sons: Dan and Naphtali.

Isaac Dies

[27]Jacob went to his father Isaac at Hebron, also called Mamre or Kiriath-Arba, where Isaac's father Abraham had lived as a foreigner. [28-29]Isaac died at the ripe old age of 180, then his sons Esau and Jacob buried him.

Esau's Family

36 Esau, also known as Edom, had many descendants. [2]He married three Canaanite women: The first was Adah, the daughter of Elon the Hittite; the second was Oholibamah, the daughter of Anah and the granddaughter of Zibeon the Hivite; [3]the third was Basemath, who was Ishmael's daughter and Nebaioth's sister.

[4-5]Esau and his three wives had five sons while in Canaan. Adah's son was Eliphaz; Basemath's son was Reuel; Oholibamah's three sons were Jeush, Jalam, and Korah.

[6]Esau took his children and wives, his relatives and servants, his animals and pos-

sessions he had acquired while in Canaan, and moved far from Jacob. [7]He did this because the land was too crowded and could not support him and his brother with their flocks and herds. [8]That's why Esau made his home in the hill country of Seir.

[9-14]Esau lived in the hill country of Seir and was the ancestor of the Edomites. Esau had three wives: Adah, Basemath, and Oholibamah. Here is a list of his descendants: Esau and Adah had a son named Eliphaz, whose sons were Teman, Omar, Zepho, Gatam, and Kenaz. Timna was the other wife[a] of Esau's son Eliphaz, and she had a son named Amalek.

Esau and Basemath had a son named Reuel, whose sons were Nahath, Zerah, Shammah, and Mizzah.

Esau and Oholibamah had three sons: Jeush, Jalam, and Korah.

Chiefs and Leaders in Edom

[15]Esau and Adah's oldest son was Eliphaz, and the clans that descended from him were Teman, Omar, Zepho, Kenaz, [16]Korah, Gatam, and Amalek. These and Esau's other descendants lived in the land of Edom.

[17]The clans that descended from Esau and Basemath's son Reuel were Nahath, Zerah, Shammah, and Mizzah.

[18]The clans that descended from Esau and Oholibamah the daughter of Anah were Jeush, Jalam, and Korah. [19]All of these clans descended from Esau, who was known as Edom.

[20]Seir was from the Horite tribe that had lived in Edom before the time of Esau. The clans that had descended from him were Lotan, Shobal, Zibeon, Anah, [21]Dishon, Ezer, and Dishan.

[y]**35.22** *other wives:* See the note at 22.24. Bilhah had been Rachel's servant woman (see 29.28-30). [z]**35.23-26** *northern Syria:* See the note at 24.10. [a]**36.9-14** *other wife:* See the note at 22.24.

²²Lotan's sons were Hori and Heman; his sister was Timna.

²³Shobal's sons were Alvan, Manahath, Ebal, Shepho, and Onam.

²⁴Zibeon's sons were Aiah and Anah— the same Anah who found an oasis[b] in the desert while taking the donkeys of his father out to pasture.

²⁵Anah's children were Dishon and Oholibamah.

²⁶Dishon's sons were Hemdan, Eshban, Ithran, and Cheran.

²⁷Ezer's sons were Bilhan, Zaavan, and Akan.

²⁸Dishan's sons were Uz and Aran.

²⁹The clans of the Horites were Lotan, Shobal, Zibeon, Anah, ³⁰Dishon, Ezer, and Dishan, and they lived in the land of Seir.

³¹⁻³⁹Before there were kings in Israel, the following kings ruled Edom one after another:

Bela son of Beor from Dinhabah;

Jobab son of Zerah from Bozrah;

Husham from the land of Teman;

Hadad son of Bedad from Avith
   (Bedad had defeated the Midianites
   in Moab);

Samlah from Masrekah;

Shaul from the city of Rehoboth on
   the Euphrates River;

Baal Hanan son of Achbor;

Hadar from the city of Pau (his wife
   Mehetabel was the daughter of
   Matred and the granddaughter of
   Mezahab).

⁴⁰The clans that descended from Esau took their names from their families and the places where they lived. They are Timna, Alvah, Jetheth, ⁴¹Oholibamah, Elah, Pinon, ⁴²Kenaz, Teman, Mibzar, ⁴³Magdiel, and Iram. These clans descended from Esau, who was known as Edom, the father of the Edomites. They took their names from the places where they settled.

Joseph and His Brothers

37 ¹Jacob lived in the land of Canaan, where his father Isaac had lived, ²and this is the story of his family.

When Jacob's son Joseph was 17 years old, he took care of the sheep with his brothers, the sons of Bilhah and Zilpah.[c] But he was always telling his father all sorts of bad things about his brothers.

³Jacob loved Joseph more than he did any of his other sons, because Joseph was born when Jacob was very old. Jacob had even given Joseph a fancy coat[d] ⁴which showed that Joseph was his favorite son, and so Joseph's brothers hated him and would not be friendly to him.

⁵One day, Joseph told his brothers what he had dreamed, and they hated him even more. ⁶Joseph said, "Let me tell you about my dream. ⁷We were out in the field, tying up bundles of wheat. Suddenly my bundle stood up, and your bundles gathered around and bowed down to it."

⁸His brothers asked, "Do you really think you are going to be king and rule over us?" Now they hated Joseph more than ever because of what he had said about his dream.

⁹Joseph later had another dream, and he told his brothers, "Listen to what else I dreamed. The sun, the moon, and eleven stars bowed down to me."

¹⁰When he told his father about this dream, his father became angry and said, "What's that supposed to mean? Are your mother and I and your brothers all going

36.31-39 *Before there were kings in Israel:* The land of Edom was ruled by kings long before Israel was (Num 20.14).

37.3 *fancy coat:* The coat probably was a long robe with sleeves, normally worn by wealthy men, and not the more common sleeveless coat (like a long open vest) worn for everyday work (2 Sam 13.18).

37.9 *eleven stars:* Often in the ancient world the positions of the sun, the moon, and the stars were studied for signs of God's purpose (1.14-18), but their appearance in Joseph's dream had a specific meaning that his father and brothers seemed to understand.

37.10 *your mother:* Joseph's mother was Rachel, whose death was told in 35.18-20. It is unclear why Jacob is referring to her here.

[b]36.24 *an oasis:* One possible meaning for the difficult Hebrew text.   [c]37.2 *Bilhah and Zilpah:* See 30.1-13.   [d]37.3 *fancy coat:* Or "a coat of many colors" or "a coat with long sleeves."

Joseph said, "Let me tell you about my dream . . . The sun, the moon, and eleven stars bowed down to me." GEN 37.6-9

37.17 *Dothan*: The ancient city of Dothan was about 13 miles north of Shechem. **(See Map 3 on pg 1881.)**

37.25 *Ishmaelites . . . Gilead . . . Egypt*: The Ishmaelites were descendants of Ishmael, the son of Abraham and the Egyptian slave woman Hagar (16.1-16; 25.12-18). The Ishmaelites were generally known as desert wanderers and caravan traders.

Egypt

37.25 *all kinds of spices*: According to the Hebrew, these included a special balm or ointment, made from trees in Gilead, known for its healing power (Jer 8.22; 46.11) and myrrh, a dark-red gum with a strong smell and a bitter taste that comes from a bush or tree grown in Arabia and Africa. Myrrh was often crushed into powder and used to make expensive perfumes and ointments.

37.34 *tore his clothes and wore sackcloth*: These are two ways ancient people showed their sadness when mourning (see also 37.29).

to come and bow down to you?" [11]Joseph's brothers were jealous of him, but his father kept wondering about the dream.

Joseph Is Sold and Taken to Egypt

[12]One day when Joseph's brothers had taken the sheep to a pasture near Shechem, [13]his father Jacob said to him, "I want you to go to your brothers. They are with the sheep near Shechem."

"Yes, sir," Joseph answered.

[14]His father said, "Go and find out how your brothers and the sheep are doing. Then come back and let me know." So he sent him from Hebron Valley.

Joseph was near Shechem [15]and wandering through the fields, when a man asked, "What are you looking for?"

[16]Joseph answered, "I'm looking for my brothers who are watching the sheep. Can you tell me where they are?"

[17]"They're not here anymore," the man replied. "I overheard them say they were going to Dothan."

Joseph left and found his brothers in Dothan. [18]But before he got there, they saw him coming and made plans to kill him. [19]They said to one another, "Look, here comes the hero of those dreams! [20]Let's kill him and throw him into a pit and say that some wild animal ate him. Then we'll see what happens to those dreams."

[21]Reuben heard this and tried to protect Joseph from them. "Let's not kill him," he said. [22]"Don't murder him or even harm him. Just throw him into a well out here in the desert." Reuben planned to rescue Joseph later and take him back to his father.

[23]When Joseph came to his brothers, they pulled off his fancy coat[e] [24]and threw him into a dry well.

[25]As Joseph's brothers sat down to eat, they looked up and saw a caravan of Ishmaelites coming from Gilead. Their camels were loaded with all kinds of spices that they were taking to Egypt. [26]So Judah said, "What will we gain if we kill our brother and hide his body? [27]Let's sell him to the Ishmaelites and not harm him. After all, he is our brother." And the others agreed.

[28]When the Midianite merchants came by, Joseph's brothers took him out of the well, and for 20 pieces of silver they sold him to the Ishmaelites[f] who took him to Egypt.

[29]When Reuben returned to the well and did not find Joseph there, he tore his clothes in sorrow. [30]Then he went back to his brothers and said, "The boy is gone! What am I going to do?"

[31]Joseph's brothers killed a goat and dipped Joseph's fancy coat in its blood. [32]After this, they took the coat to their father and said, "We found this! Look at it carefully and see if it belongs to your son."

[33]Jacob knew it was Joseph's coat and said, "It's my son's coat! Joseph has been torn to pieces and eaten by some wild animal."

[34]Jacob mourned for Joseph a long time, and to show his sorrow he tore his clothes and wore sackcloth.[g] [35]All of Jacob's children came to comfort him, but he refused to be comforted. "No," he said, "I will go to my grave, mourning for my son." So Jacob kept on grieving.

[e]37.23 *fancy coat*: Or "a coat of many colors" or "a coat with long sleeves."   [f]37.28 *Midianite . . . Ishmaelites*: According to 25.1,2,12 both the Midianites and the Ishmaelites were descendants of Abraham, and in Judges 8.22-24 the two names are used of the same people. It is possible that in this passage "Ishmaelite" has the meaning "nomadic traders," while "Midianite" refers to their ethnic origin.   [g]37.34 *sackcloth*: A rough dark-colored cloth made from goat or camel hair and used to make grain sacks. It was worn in times of trouble or sorrow.

³⁶Meanwhile, the Midianites had sold Joseph in Egypt to a man named Potiphar, who was the king's[h] official in charge of the palace guard.

Judah and Tamar

38 About that time Judah left his brothers in the hill country and went to live near his friend Hirah in the town of Adullam. ²While there he met the daughter of Shua, a Canaanite man. Judah married her, ³and they had three sons. He named the first one Er; ⁴she named the next one Onan. ⁵The third one was born when Judah was in Chezib, and she named him Shelah.

⁶Later, Judah chose Tamar as a wife for Er, his oldest son. ⁷But Er was very evil, and the LORD took his life. ⁸So Judah told Onan, "It's your duty to marry Tamar and have a child for your brother."[i]

⁹Onan knew the child would not be his,[j] and when he had sex with Tamar, he made sure that she would not get pregnant. ¹⁰The LORD wasn't pleased with Onan and took his life too.

¹¹Judah did not want the same thing to happen to his son Shelah, and he told Tamar, "Go home to your father and live there as a widow until my son Shelah is grown." So Tamar went to live with her father.

¹²Some years later Judah's wife died, and he mourned for her. He then went with his friend Hirah to the town of Timnah, where his sheep were being sheared. ¹³Tamar found out that her father-in-law Judah was going to Timnah to shear his sheep. ¹⁴She also realized that Shelah was now a grown man, but she had not been allowed to marry him. So she decided to dress in something other than her widow's clothes and to cover her face with a veil. After this, she sat outside the town of Enaim on the road to Timnah.

¹⁵When Judah came along, he did not recognize her because of the veil. He thought she was a prostitute ¹⁶and asked her to sleep with him. She asked, "What will you give me if I do?"

¹⁷"One of my young goats," he answered.

"What will you give me to keep until you send the goat?" she asked.

¹⁸"What do you want?" he asked in return.

"The ring on that cord around your neck," was her reply. "I also want the special walking stick[k] you have with you." He gave them to her, they slept together, and she became pregnant.

¹⁹After returning home, Tamar took off the veil and dressed in her widow's clothes again.

²⁰Judah asked his friend Hirah take a goat to the woman, so he could get back the ring and walking stick, but she wasn't there. ²¹Hirah asked the people of Enaim, "Where is the prostitute who sat along the road outside your town?"

"There's never been one here," they answered.

²²Hirah went back and told Judah, "I couldn't find the woman, and the people

[h]**37.36** *the king's:* See the note at 12.15. [i]**38.8** *It's your duty . . . child . . . brother:* If a man died without having children, his brother was to marry the dead man's wife and have a child, who was to be considered the child of the dead brother (see Deuteronomy 25.5,6). [j]**38.9** *the child . . . not be his:* When Judah died, Onan would get his dead brother's share of the inheritance, but if his dead brother had a son, the inheritance would go to him instead. [k]**38.18** *ring . . . walking stick:* The ring was shaped like a cylinder and could be rolled over soft clay as a way of sealing special documents. The walking stick was probably a symbol of power and the sign of leadership in the tribe, though it may have been a shepherd's rod.

38.27-30 *twins ... Perez ... Zerah*: Perez was an ancestor of King David (Ruth 4.18-22) and was named along with Zerah as two clans of the tribe of Judah (Num 26.19-22). Compare this story to the story of the birth of the twins, Jacob and Esau (25.24-26).

39.5 *bless*: The promise to Abraham that his descendants would be a blessing to other nations was being fulfilled in Joseph (12.2,3; 30.27-30).

39.9 *sin against God*: Wanting another person's wife or husband was prohibited in the Law of Moses (Exod 20.17).

Sin

Ten Commandments

of Enaim said no prostitute had ever been there."

23"If you couldn't find her, we'll just let her keep the things I gave her," Judah answered. "And we'd better forget about the goat, or else we'll look like fools."

24About three months later someone told Judah, "Your daughter-in-law Tamar has behaved like a prostitute, and now she's pregnant!"

"Drag her out of town and burn her to death!" Judah shouted.

25As Tamar was being dragged off, she sent someone to tell her father-in-law, "The man who gave me this ring, this cord, and this walking stick is the one who got me pregnant."

26"Those are mine!" Judah admitted. "She's a better person than I am, because I broke my promise to let her marry my son Shelah." After this, Judah never slept with her again.

27-28Tamar later gave birth to twins. But before either of them was born, one of them stuck a hand out of her womb. The woman who was helping tied a red thread around the baby's hand and explained, "This one came out first."

29At once his hand went back in, and the other child was born first. The woman then said, "What an opening you've made for yourself!" So they named the baby Perez.[l]

30When the brother with the red thread was born, they named him Zerah.[m]

Joseph and Potiphar's Wife

39 The Ishmaelites took Joseph to Egypt and sold him to Potiphar, the king's[n] official in charge of the palace

guard. 2-3So Joseph lived in the home of Potiphar, his Egyptian owner.

Soon Potiphar realized that the LORD was helping Joseph to be successful in whatever he did. 4Potiphar liked Joseph and made him his personal assistant, putting him in charge of his house and all of his property. 5Because of Joseph, the LORD began to bless Potiphar's family and fields. 6Potiphar left everything up to Joseph, and with Joseph there, the only decision he had to make was what he wanted to eat.

Joseph was well-built and handsome, 7and Potiphar's wife soon noticed him. She asked him to make love to her, 8but he refused and said, "My master isn't worried about anything in his house, because he has placed me in charge of everything he owns. 9No one in my master's house is more important than I am. The only thing he hasn't given me is you, and that's because you are his wife. I won't sin against God by doing such a terrible thing as this." 10She kept begging Joseph day after day, but he refused to do what she wanted or even to go near her.

11One day, Joseph went to Potiphar's house to do his work, and none of the other servants were there. 12Potiphar's wife grabbed hold of his coat and said, "Make love to me!" Joseph ran out of the house, leaving his coat there in her hands.

13When this happened, 14she called in her servants and said, "Look! This Hebrew has come just to make fools of us. He tried to rape me, but I screamed for help. 15And when he heard me scream, he ran out of the house, leaving his coat with me."

16Potiphar's wife kept Joseph's coat until her husband came home. 17Then she said,

[l]38.29 *Perez*: In Hebrew "Perez" sounds like "opening." [m]38.30 *Zerah*: In Hebrew "Zerah" means "bright," probably referring to the red thread. [n]39.1 *the king's*: See the note at 12.15.

"That Hebrew slave of yours tried to rape me! [18]But when I screamed for help, he left his coat and ran out of the house."

[19]Potiphar became very angry [20]and threw Joseph in the same prison where the king's prisoners were kept.

While Joseph was in prison, [21]the LORD helped him and was good to him. He even made the jailer like Joseph so much that [22]he put him in charge of the other prisoners and of everything that was done in the jail. [23]The jailer did not worry about anything, because the LORD was with Joseph and made him successful in all that he did.

Joseph Tells the Meaning of the Prisoners' Dreams

40 [1-3]While Joseph was in prison, both the king's[o] personal servant[p] and his chief cook made the king angry. So he had them thrown into the same prison with Joseph. [4]They spent a long time in prison, and the official in charge of the palace guard,[q] made Joseph their servant.

[5]One night each of the two men had a dream, but their dreams had different meanings. [6]The next morning, when Joseph went to see the men, he could tell they were upset, [7]and he asked, "Why are you so worried today?"

[8]"We each had a dream last night," they answered, "and there is no one to tell us what they mean."

Joseph replied, "Doesn't God know the meaning of dreams? Now tell me what you dreamed."

[9]The king's personal servant told Joseph, "In my dream I saw a vine [10]with three branches. As soon as it budded, it blossomed, and its grapes became ripe. [11]I held the king's cup and squeezed the grapes into it, then I gave the cup to the king."

[12]Joseph said:

This is the meaning of your dream. The three branches stand for three days, [13]and in three days the king will pardon you. He will make you his personal servant again, and you will serve him his wine, just as you used to do. [14]But when these good things happen, please don't forget to tell the king about me, so I can get out of this place. [15]I was kidnapped from the land of the Hebrews, and here in Egypt I haven't done anything to deserve being thrown in jail.

[16]When the chief cook saw that Joseph had given a good meaning to the dream, he told Joseph, "I also had a dream. In it I was carrying three breadbaskets stacked on top of my head. [17]The top basket was full of all kinds of baked things for the king, but birds were eating them."

[18]Joseph said:

This is the meaning of your dream. The three baskets are three days, [19]and in three days the king will cut off your head. He will hang your body on a pole, and birds will come and peck at it.

[20]Three days later, while the king was celebrating his birthday with a dinner for his officials, he sent for his personal servant and the chief cook. [21]He put the personal servant back in his old job [22]and had the cook put to death.

Everything happened just as Joseph had said it would, [23]but the king's personal servant completely forgot about Joseph.

■ 39.21 *the LORD helped him:* The usual punishment for rape, the crime Joseph was being accused of, was the death penalty. Imprisonment, with the hope of eventual release, was a much lighter sentence. As in other stories in GENESIS, God is being given credit for the hero's good fortune.

● 40.1-3 *king's personal servant:* The Hebrew translated here as "personal servant" actually refers to a king's chief "cup bearer," an important and trusted official in the royal court. Cup bearers personally served wine to the king and were sometimes asked to taste the wine before the king drank any of it, to make sure it wasn't poisoned.

● 40.5 *dreams had different meanings:* In the ancient world dreams were thought to have specific meanings and could predict the future if they were correctly interpreted. God sometimes spoke to people in dreams (20.3; 28.10-15; Matt 1.20-23).

● 40.15 *jail:* The Hebrew word translated "jail" in this verse is the same word translated as "pit" in (37.20,28) and "dry well" (37.24) earlier in the Joseph story. Through this clever word play Joseph's being in jail is compared to his being in the pit back in Canaan.

[o]**40.1-3** *the king's:* See the note at 12.15.   [p]**40.1-3** *personal servant:* The Hebrew text has "cup bearer," an important and trusted official in the royal court, who personally served wine to the king. [q]**40.4** *the palace guard:* Possibly Potiphar (see 39.1).

● 41.1 *Nile River:* The Nile River, the world's second longest river, floods its banks each year leaving fresh muddy soil behind that is good for growing crops. This annual flooding of the Nile was so important to maintaining the fertility of the land that the Nile itself came to be considered one of Egypt's gods. Cattle often stood in the waters of the Nile up to their necks (41.3) to stay out of the sun and keep away insects. **(See Map 2 on pg 1880.)**

⊂R King of Egypt (Pharaoh)

⊂R Egypt

● 41.6 *a wind from the desert:* A hot wind that blew from the desert area west of the Nile valley and dried up crops. This was known in the area as a "sirocco" wind.

■ 41.16 *God can give a good meaning:* The episode about the king's dreams is meant to show that Joseph's God is more powerful than the Egyptian magic and wisdom. For other examples of how the Lord God's power is superior to that of a foreign king's court magicians, see Exod 7.8-12; 8.16-19; 9.11; Dan 5.8,15-28.

● 41.27 *seven years... won't be enough grain:* Long periods of drought and grain shortages were not common in Egypt because the Nile River overflowed nearly every year, providing water for crops.

Joseph Interprets the King's Dreams

41 Two years later the king[r] of Egypt dreamed he was standing beside the Nile River. [2]Suddenly, seven fat, healthy cows came up from the river and started eating grass along the bank. [3]Then seven ugly, skinny cows came up out of the river and [4]ate the fat, healthy cows. When this happened, the king woke up.

[5]The king went back to sleep and had another dream. This time seven full heads of grain were growing on a single stalk. [6]Later, seven other heads of grain appeared, but they were thin and scorched by a wind from the desert. [7]The thin heads of grain swallowed the seven full heads. Again the king woke up, and it had only been a dream.

[8]The next morning the king was upset. So he called in his magicians and wise men and told them what he had dreamed. None of them could tell him what the dreams meant.

[9]The king's personal servant said:

Now I remember what I was supposed to do. [10]When you were angry with me and your chief cook, you threw us both in jail in the house of the captain of the guard. [11]One night we both had dreams, and each dream had a different meaning. [12]A young Hebrew, who was a servant of the captain of the guard, was there with us at the time. When we told him our dreams, he explained what each of them meant, [13]and everything happened just as he said it would. I got my job back, and the cook was put to death.

[14]The king sent for Joseph, who was quickly brought out of jail. He shaved, changed his clothes, and went to the king.

[r]**41.1** *the king:* See the note at 12.15.

[15]The king said to him, "I had a dream, yet no one can explain what it means. I am told that you can interpret dreams."

[16]"Your Majesty," Joseph answered, "I can't do it myself, but God can give a good meaning to your dreams."

[17]The king told Joseph:

I dreamed I was standing on the bank of the Nile River. [18]I saw seven fat, healthy cows come up out of the river, and they began feeding on the grass. [19]Next, seven skinny, bony cows came up out of the river. I have never seen such terrible looking cows anywhere in Egypt. [20]The skinny cows ate the fat ones. [21]But you couldn't tell it, because these skinny cows were just as skinny as they were before. At once, I woke up.

[22]I also dreamed that I saw seven heads of grain growing on one stalk. The heads were full and ripe. [23]Then seven other heads of grain came up. They were thin and scorched by a wind from the desert. [24]These heads of grain swallowed the full ones. I told my dreams to the magicians, but none of them could tell me the meaning of the dreams.

[25]Joseph replied:

Your Majesty, both of your dreams mean the same thing, and in them God has shown what he is going to do. [26]The seven good cows stand for seven years, and so do the seven good heads of grain. [27]The seven skinny, ugly cows that came up later also stand for seven years, as do the seven bad heads of grain that were scorched by the desert wind. The dreams mean there will be seven years when there won't be enough grain.

[28]It is just as I said—God has shown

what he intends to do. ²⁹For seven years Egypt will have more than enough grain, ³⁰but that will be followed by seven years when there won't be enough. The good years of plenty will be forgotten, and everywhere in Egypt people will be starving. ³¹The famine will be so bad that no one will remember that once there had been plenty. ³²God has given you two dreams to let you know that he has definitely decided to do this and that he will do it soon.

³³Your Majesty, you should find someone who is wise and will know what to do, so that you can put him in charge of all Egypt. ³⁴Then appoint some other officials to collect one fifth of every crop harvested in Egypt during the seven years when there is plenty. ³⁵Give them the power to collect the grain during those good years and to store it in your cities. ³⁶It can be stored until it is needed during the seven years when there won't be enough grain in Egypt. This will keep the country from being destroyed because of the lack of food.

Joseph Is Made Governor over Egypt

³⁷The king[s] and his officials liked this plan. ³⁸So the king said to them, "Who could possibly handle this better than Joseph? After all, the Spirit of God is with him."

³⁹The king told Joseph, "God is the one who has shown you these things. No one else is as wise as you are or knows as much

as you do. ⁴⁰I'm putting you in charge of my palace, and everybody will have to obey you. No one will be over you except me. ⁴¹You are now governor of all Egypt!"

⁴²Then the king took off his royal ring and put it on Joseph's finger. He gave him fine clothes to wear and placed a gold chain around his neck. ⁴³He also let him ride in the chariot next to his own, and people shouted, "Make way for Joseph!" So Joseph was governor of Egypt.

⁴⁴The king told Joseph, "Although I'm king, no one in Egypt is to do anything without your permission." ⁴⁵He gave Joseph the Egyptian name Zaphenath Paneah. And he let him marry Asenath, the daughter of Potiphera, a priest in the city of Heliopolis.[t] Joseph traveled all over[u] Egypt.

⁴⁶Joseph was 30 when the king made him governor, and he went everywhere for the king. ⁴⁷For seven years there were big harvests of grain. ⁴⁸Joseph collected and stored up the extra grain in the cities of Egypt near the fields where it was harvested. ⁴⁹In fact, there was so much grain that they stopped keeping record, because it was like counting the grains of sand along the beach.

⁵⁰Joseph and his wife had two sons before the famine began. ⁵¹Their first son was named Manasseh, which means, "God has let me forget all my troubles and my family back home." ⁵²His second son was named Ephraim, which means "God has made me a success[v] in the land where I suffered."[w]

⁵³Egypt's seven years of plenty came to an end, ⁵⁴and the seven years of famine began, just as Joseph had said. There was not enough food in other countries, but all over Egypt there was plenty. ⁵⁵When the

41.38 *Spirit of God:* The king of Egypt recognizes that Joseph's ability as a manager is from God.

41.41-43 *governor . . . chariot:* The symbols of royal authority given to Joseph were a ring with the king's symbol (see Esth 3.10), a special robe (see Esth 6.11), and a golden neck chain (see Dan 5.7,29). Riding in a royal chariot was a sign of great power. **(See the article Trade and Travel on pg 1806.)**

41.45 *Egyptian name . . . Asenath:* The ceremony of making Joseph an Egyptian official ended with him receiving an Egyptian name that may mean "God speaks, he lives." Though the king used Joseph to serve his political purposes, he did not realize that Joseph's promotion was part of God's greater plan (45.5-8; 50.19,20).

The name of Joseph's new wife, "Asenath," may mean "belonging to Neith" (an Egyptian goddess). Her father Potiphera's name may mean "given by Ra" (the sun god).

41.45 *Heliopolis:* This name in Greek means "city of the sun" and was located about six miles northeast of modern Cairo.

[s]**41.37** *The king:* See the note at 12.15.   [t]**41.45** *Heliopolis:* The Hebrew text has "On," which is better known by its Greek name "Heliopolis."   [u]**41.45** *traveled all over:* Or "extended his authority over all."   [v]**41.52** *God has made me a success:* Or "God has given me children."   [w]**41.52** *Ephraim . . . suffered:* In Hebrew "Ephraim" actually means either "fertile land" or "pastureland."

41.57 *from all over the world:* This probably refers to all the nearby lands in the Middle East.

42.3,4 *Ten of Joseph's brothers . . . Benjamin:* Joseph's brothers may have thought he was dead because so much time had passed since they sold him to a caravan, or, they may have preferred to tell Joseph the same story they had told their father as a way of keeping the Egyptian official (Joseph) from learning how they had mistreated their own brother. The youngest brother was Benjamin (42.4), who was born to Rachel, making him Joseph's only full brother. See also 29.31-30.23; 35.16-18.

42.7-8 *They did not recognize Joseph:* Joseph was a teenager when the brothers had sold him as a slave nearly 20 years earlier. He would have changed, and they would not have expected to see him as a powerful ruler in Egypt.

42.15 *swear by the life of the king:* Because the king (pharaoh) was considered to be like a god, this was a very powerful oath.

42.18 *I respect God:* Joseph's brothers might have been surprised to hear an Egyptian official declare his respect for God.

42.23 *interpreter:* Joseph spoke Egyptian, but Hebrew was his first language. Speaking Hebrew, however, might have given away his identity to his brothers.

famine finally struck Egypt, the people asked the king for food, but he said, "Go to Joseph and do what he tells you to do."

56The famine became bad everywhere in Egypt, so Joseph opened the storehouses and sold the grain to the Egyptians. 57People from all over the world came to Egypt to buy grain, because the famine was so severe in their countries.

Joseph's Brothers Go to Egypt To Buy Grain

42 When Jacob found out there was grain in Egypt, he said to his sons, "Why are you just sitting here, staring at one another? 2I have heard there is grain in Egypt. Go down and buy some, so we won't starve to death."

3Ten of Joseph's brothers went to Egypt to buy grain. 4But Jacob did not send Joseph's younger brother Benjamin with them; he was afraid that something might happen to him. 5So Jacob's sons joined others from Canaan who were going to Egypt because of the terrible famine.

6Since Joseph was governor of Egypt and in charge of selling grain, his brothers came to him and bowed with their faces to the ground. 7-8They did not recognize Joseph, but at once he knew who they were, though he pretended not to know. Instead, he spoke harshly and asked, "Where do you come from?"

"From the land of Canaan," they answered. "We've come here to buy grain."

9Joseph remembered what he had dreamed about them and said, "You're spies! You've come here to find out where our country is weak."

10"No sir," they replied. "We're your servants, and we have only come to buy grain. 11We're honest men, and we come from the same family—we're not spies."

12"That isn't so!" Joseph insisted. "You've come here to find out where our country is weak."

13But they explained, "Sir, we come from a family of twelve brothers. The youngest is still with our father in Canaan, and one of our brothers is dead."

14Joseph replied:

It's like I said. You're spies, 15and I'm going to find out the truth. I swear by the life of the king that you won't leave this place until your youngest brother comes here. 16Choose one of you to go after your brother, while the rest of you stay in jail. That will show whether you are telling the truth. But if you are lying, I swear by the life of the king that you are spies!

17Joseph kept them all under guard for three days, 18before saying to them:

Since I respect God, I'll give you a chance to save your lives. 19If you are honest men, one of you must stay here in jail, and the rest of you can take the grain back to your starving families. 20But you must bring your youngest brother to me. Then I'll know that you are telling the truth, and you won't be put to death.

Joseph's brothers agreed 21and said to one another, "We're being punished because of Joseph. We saw the trouble he was in, but we refused to help him when he begged us. That's why these terrible things are happening."

22Reuben spoke up, "Didn't I tell you not to harm the boy? But you wouldn't listen, and now we have to pay the price for killing him."

23They did not know that Joseph could understand them, since he was speaking through an interpreter. 24Joseph turned away from them and cried, but soon he turned back and spoke to them again. Then he had Simeon tied up and taken away while they watched.

Joseph's Brothers Return to Canaan

25Joseph gave orders for his brothers' grain sacks to be filled with grain and for their money[x] to be put in their sacks. He also gave orders for them to be given food for their journey home. After this was done, 26they each loaded the grain on their donkeys and left.

27When they stopped for the night, one of them opened his sack to get some grain for his donkey, and at once he saw his moneybag. 28"Here's my money!" he told his brothers. "Right here in my sack."

They were trembling with fear as they stared at one another and asked themselves, "What has God done to us?"[y]

29When they returned to the land of Canaan, they told their father Jacob everything that had happened to them:

30The governor of Egypt was rude and treated us like spies. 31But we told him, "We're honest men, not spies. 32We come from a family of twelve brothers. The youngest is still with our father in Canaan, and the other is dead."

33Then the governor of Egypt told us, "I'll find out if you really are honest. Leave one of your brothers here with me, while you take the grain to your starving families. 34But bring your youngest brother to me, so I can be certain that you are honest men and not spies. After that, I'll let your other brother go free, and you can stay here and trade."

35When the brothers started emptying their sacks of grain, they found their mon-eybags in them. They were frightened, and so was their father Jacob, 36who said, "You have already taken my sons Joseph and Simeon from me. And now you want to take away Benjamin! Everything is against me."

37Reuben spoke up, "Father, if I don't bring Benjamin back, you can kill both of my sons. Trust me with him, and I'll bring him back."

38But Jacob said, "I won't let my son Benjamin go down to Egypt with the rest of you. His brother is already dead, and he is the only son I have left.[z] I am an old man, and if anything happens to him on the way, I'll die from sorrow, and all of you will be to blame."

Joseph's Brothers Return to Egypt with Benjamin

43 The famine in Canaan got worse, 2until finally, Jacob's family had eaten all the grain they had bought in Egypt. So Jacob said to his sons, "Go back and buy some more grain."

3-5Judah replied, "The governor strictly warned us that we would not be allowed to see him unless we brought our youngest brother with us. If you let us take Benjamin along, we will go and buy grain. But we won't go without him!"

6Jacob asked, "Why did you cause me so much trouble by telling the governor you had another brother?"

7They answered, "He asked a lot of questions about us and our family. He wanted to know if you were still alive and if we had any more brothers. All we could do was answer his questions. How could we know

42.28 *What has God done to us:* The brothers believed God was directing what was happening to them, but they did not understand why.

42.37 *both of my sons:* As the oldest son, Reuben felt responsible for Benjamin's safety, as he had earlier for Joseph (37.17-22).

43.3-5 *Judah:* At this point in the story, Judah begins to speak for his brothers (see also 44.14-34; 46.28). The tribe of Judah eventually would become the most important among the tribes of Israel (49.8-10). David, Israel's most famous king, would be from the tribe of Judah (1 Chr 2.1-17). Compare Judah's offer in 43.9 with Reuben's offer (42.37).

---

[x]**42.25** *money:* Probably in the form of small pieces of silver and/or other precious or semi-precious metals; there were no coins or paper money at this time. [y]**42.28** *What has God…us:* They thought God had put the money in their bags, so they would be caught and punished. [z]**42.38** *only son I have left:* Jacob had only two sons by Rachel, his favorite wife.

43.11 *a gift . . . honey, spices, pistachio nuts, and almonds:* Bringing gifts to someone who had superior power or position was an ancient custom.

43.14 *God All-Powerful:* The meaning of the Hebrew for this title, *El Shaddai,* is uncertain. One possible meaning is "God, the One of the Mountains" (see also 35.9-11; Exod 6.2,3). *El* was one of the most common names for god among the Canaanites, who believed that El was not the only god, but the one who ruled over all the other gods. In the Jewish Scriptures this name frequently refers to the God of Israel.

Names of God

43.23 *God . . . must have put the money there:* See 42.28. The servant's words repeat the main theme of the Joseph story: God is at work directing events for the good of his chosen people.

43.32 *Egyptians sat at yet another table:* They probably sat apart from the Hebrews because of religious or ritual purity rules (see also Exod 8.26).

he would tell us to bring along our brother?"

[8] Then Judah said to his father, "Let Benjamin go with me, and we will leave at once, so that none of us will starve to death. [9] I promise to bring him back safely, and if I don't, you can blame me as long as I live. [10] If we had not wasted all this time, we could already have been there and back twice."

[11] Their father said:

If Benjamin must go with you, take the governor a gift of some of the best things from our own country, such as perfume, honey, spices, pistachio nuts, and almonds.[a] [12] Also take along twice the amount of money for the grain, because there must have been some mistake when the money was put back in your sacks. [13] Take Benjamin with you and leave at once.

[14] When you go in to see the governor, I pray that God All-Powerful will be good to you and that the governor will let your other brother and Benjamin come back home with you. But if I must lose my children, I suppose I must.

[15] The brothers took the gifts, twice the amount of money, and Benjamin. Then they hurried off to Egypt. When they stood in front of Joseph, [16] he saw Benjamin and told the servant in charge of his house, "Take these men to my house. Slaughter an animal and cook it, so they can eat with me at noon."

[17] The servant did as he was told and took the brothers to Joseph's house. [18] But on the way they got worried and started thinking, "We are being taken there because of the money that was put back in our sacks last time. He will arrest us, make us his slaves, and take our donkeys."

[19] So when they arrived at Joseph's house, they said to the servant in charge, [20] "Sir, we came to Egypt once before to buy grain. [21] But when we stopped for the night, we each found in our grain sacks the exact amount we had paid. We have brought that money back, [22] together with enough money to buy more grain. We don't know who put the money in our sacks."

[23] "It's all right," the servant replied. "Don't worry. The God you and your father worship must have put the money there, because I received your payment in full." Then he brought Simeon out to them.

[24] The servant took them into Joseph's house and gave them water to wash their feet. He also tended their donkeys. [25] The brothers got their gifts ready to give to Joseph at noon, since they had heard they were going to eat there.

[26] When Joseph came home, they gave him the gifts they had brought, and they bowed down to him. [27] After Joseph had asked how they were, he said, "What about your elderly father? Is he still alive?"

[28] They answered, "Your servant our father is still alive and well." And again they bowed down to Joseph.

[29] When Joseph looked around and saw his brother Benjamin, he said, "This must be your youngest brother, the one you told me about. God bless you, my son."

[30] Then, because of his love for Benjamin, he rushed off to his room and cried. [31] After washing his face and returning, he was able to control himself and said, "Serve the meal!"

[32] Joseph was served at a table by himself, and his brothers were served at another. The Egyptians sat at yet another table, because Egyptians felt it was disgusting to eat with Hebrews. [33] To the surprise of Joseph's

[a] 43.11 *honey, spices, pistachio nuts, and almonds:* Some of these foods were still available in Canaan, but the main food was bread, and there was no grain to make bread.

When Joseph . . . saw his brother Benjamin, he said, "This must be your youngest brother, the one you told me about. God bless you, my son." GEN 43.29

brothers, they were seated in front of him according to their ages, from the oldest to the youngest. **34**They were served food from Joseph's table, and Benjamin was given five times as much as each of the others. So Joseph's brothers ate and drank with him and had a good time.

The Missing Cup

44 **1-2**Later, Joseph told the servant in charge of his house, "Fill the men's grain sacks with as much as they can hold and put their money in the sacks. Also put my silver cup in the sack of the youngest brother." The servant did as he was told.

3Early the next morning, the men were sent on their way with their donkeys. **4**But they had not gone far from the city when Joseph told the servant, "Go after those men! When you catch them, say, 'My master has been good to you. So why have you stolen his silver cup? **5**Not only does he drink from his cup, but he also uses it to learn about the future. You have done a terrible thing.'"

6When the servant caught up with them, he said exactly what Joseph had told him to say. **7**But they replied, "Sir, why do you say such things? We would never do anything like that! **8**We even returned the money we found in our grain sacks when we got back to Canaan. So why would we want to steal any silver or gold from your master's house? **9**If you find that one of us has the cup, then kill him, and the rest of us will become your slaves."

10"Good!" the man replied, "I'll do what you have said. But only the one who has the cup will become my slave. The rest of you can go free."

11Each of the brothers quickly put his sack on the ground and opened it.

12Joseph's servant started searching the sacks, beginning with the one that belonged to the oldest brother. When he came to Benjamin's sack, he found the cup. **13**This upset the brothers so much that they began tearing their clothes in sorrow. Then they loaded their donkeys and returned to the city.

14When Judah and his brothers got there, Joseph was still at home. So they bowed down to Joseph, **15**who asked them, "What have you done? Didn't you know I could find out?"

16"Sir, what can we say?" Judah replied. "How can we say we are innocent, when God has shown we are guilty? And now all of us are your slaves, especially the one who had the cup."

17Joseph told them, "I would never punish all of you. Only the one who was caught with the cup will become my slave. The rest of you are free to go home to your father."

Judah Pleads for Benjamin

18Judah went over to Joseph and said:

Sir, you have as much power as the king**b** himself, and I am only your slave. Please don't get angry if I speak. **19**You asked us if our father was still alive and if we had any more brothers. **20**So we told you, "Our father is a very old man. In fact, he was already old when Benjamin was born. Benjamin's brother is dead. Now Benjamin is the only one of the two brothers who is still alive, and our father loves him very much."

21You ordered us to bring him here, so you could see him for yourself. **22**We told you that our father would die if Benjamin left him. **23**But you warned us that we could never see you

b44.18 *the king*: See the note at 12.15.

43.33,34 *were seated . . . oldest to the youngest . . . five times as much:* Joseph is both following the usual custom for treating guests and breaking the custom at the same time. He arranged the brothers at their table so that the oldest would have the place of honor, but he gave special treatment to the youngest, Benjamin, by giving him the largest portions.

Birthright

44.1-5 *money . . . silver cup . . . to learn about the future:* The servant claims that Joseph's cup is important, because Joseph uses it to practice divination, or telling future events by reading objects that are put into liquid in his cup.

44.20 *one of the two brothers:* This refers to Benjamin and Joseph. Judah believes Joseph is dead.

44.27 *favorite wife . . . two sons:* This means Rachel, Joseph, and Benjamin.

45.5 *God is the one who sent me:* God's promise to Abraham (12.1-3), the main theme of the Joseph story, is repeated again. See also 50.19,20; Acts 7.9,10.

45.8 *highest official:* Sometimes translated as "father of Pharaoh," meaning the prime minister or vizier.

45.10 *Goshen:* This area of grazing land was in the eastern part of the Nile River delta of northern Egypt. Because Joseph's family would "live near me" in Goshen, it is assumed that the palace of the Egyptian king was in or near this region at this time.

again, unless our youngest brother came with us. **24**So we returned to our father and reported what you had said.

25Later our father sent us back here to buy more grain. **26**But we told him, "We can't go back to Egypt without our youngest brother. We will never be let in to see the governor, unless he is with us."

27Sir, our father then reminded us that his favorite wife had given birth to two sons. **28**One of them was already missing and had not been seen for a long time. My father thinks the boy was torn to pieces by some wild animal, **29**and he said, "I am an old man. If you take Benjamin from me, and something happens to him, I will die of a broken heart."

30That's why Benjamin must be with us when I go back to my father. He loves him so much **31**that he will die if Benjamin doesn't come back with me. **32**I promised my father that I would bring him safely home. If I don't, I told my father he could blame me the rest of my life.

33Sir, I am your slave. Please let me stay here in place of Benjamin and let him return home with his brothers. **34**How can I face my father if Benjamin isn't with me? I couldn't bear to see my father in such sorrow.

Joseph Tells His Brothers Who He Is

45 Since Joseph could no longer control his feelings in front of his servants, he sent them out of the room. When he was alone with his brothers, he told them, "I am Joseph." **2**Then he cried so loudly that the Egyptians heard him and told about it in the king's[c] palace.

3Joseph asked his brothers if his father was still alive, but they were too frightened to answer. **4**Joseph told them to come closer to him, and when they did, he said:

Yes, I am your brother Joseph, the one you sold into Egypt. **5**Don't worry or blame yourselves for what you did. God is the one who sent me ahead of you to save lives.

6There has already been a famine for two years, and for five more years no one will plow fields or harvest grain. **7**But God sent me on ahead of you to keep your families alive and to save you in this wonderful way. **8**After all, you weren't really the ones who sent me here—it was God. He made me the highest official in the king's court and placed me over all Egypt.

9Now hurry back and tell my father that his son Joseph says, "God has made me ruler of Egypt. Come here as quickly as you can. **10**You will live near me in the region of Goshen with your children and grandchildren, as well as with your sheep, goats, cattle, and everything else you own. **11**I will take care of you there during the next five years of famine. But if you don't come, you and your family and your animals will starve to death."

12All of you, including my brother Benjamin, can tell by what I have said that I really am Joseph. **13**Tell my father about my great power here in Egypt and about everything you have seen. Hurry and bring him here.

14Joseph and Benjamin hugged each other and started crying. **15**Joseph was still crying as he kissed each of his other broth-

[c]**45.2** *the king:* See the note at 12.15.

Joseph told his brothers, "Yes, I am your brother Joseph . . . Don't worry or blame yourselves for what you did. God is the one who sent me ahead of you to save lives." GEN 45.4,5

ers. After this, they started talking with Joseph.

¹⁶When it was told in the palace that Joseph's brothers had come, the king and his officials were happy. ¹⁷So the king said to Joseph:

Tell your brothers to load their donkeys and return to Canaan. ¹⁸Tell them to bring their father and their families here. I will give them the best land in Egypt, and they can eat and enjoy everything that grows there. ¹⁹Also tell your brothers to take some wagons from Egypt for their wives and children to ride in. And be sure they bring their father. ²⁰They can leave their possessions behind, because they will be given the best of everything in Egypt.

²¹Jacob's sons agreed to do what the king had said. And Joseph gave them wagons and food for their trip home, just as the king had ordered. ²²Joseph gave some new clothes to each of his brothers, but to Benjamin he gave five new outfits and 300 pieces of silver. ²³To his father he sent ten donkeys loaded with the best things in Egypt, and ten other donkeys loaded with grain and bread and other food for the return trip. ²⁴Then he sent his brothers off and told them, "Don't argue on the way home!"

²⁵Joseph's brothers left Egypt, and when they arrived in Canaan, ²⁶they told their father that Joseph was still alive and was the ruler of Egypt. But their father was so surprised that he could not believe them. ²⁷Then they told him everything Joseph had said. When he saw the wagons Joseph had sent, he felt much better ²⁸and said, "Now I can believe you! My son Joseph must really be alive, and I will get to see him before I die."

Jacob and His Family Go to Egypt

46 Jacob packed up everything he owned and left for Egypt. On the way he stopped near the town of Beersheba and offered sacrifices to the God his father Isaac had worshiped. ²That night, God spoke to him in a dream and said, "Jacob! Jacob!"

"Here I am," Jacob answered.

³God said, "I am God, the same God your father worshiped. Don't be afraid to go to Egypt. I will give you so many descendants that one day they will become a nation. ⁴I will go with you to Egypt, and later I will bring your descendants back here. Your son Joseph will be at your side when you die."

⁵⁻⁷Jacob and his family set out from Beersheba and headed for Egypt. His sons put him in the wagon that the king^d had sent for him, and they put their small children and their wives in the other wagons. Jacob's whole family went to Egypt, including his sons, his grandsons, his daughters, and his granddaughters. They took along their animals and everything else they owned.

⁸⁻¹⁵When Jacob went to Egypt, his children who were born in northern Syria^e also went along with their families.

Jacob and his wife Leah had a total of 33 children, grandchildren, and great-grandchildren, but two of their grandchildren had died in Canaan.

Their oldest son Reuben took his sons Hanoch, Pallu, Hezron, and Carmi.

Their son Simeon took his sons Jemuel, Jamin, Ohad, Jachin, Zohar, and Shaul, whose mother was a Canaanite.

Their son Levi took his sons Gershon, Kohath, and Merari.

^d**46.5-7** *the king:* See the note at 12.15.   ^e**46.8-15** *northern Syria:* See the note at 24.10.

46.19-22 *Asenath . . . two sons, Manasseh and Ephraim:* See 41.45, 50-52.

46.27 *total of 70:* This number, given in the ancient Hebrew text, includes Jacob and Joseph and the two sons born to Joseph and Asenath, who were already living in Egypt. Seventy was considered an ideal and complete number. Acts 7.14 lists the number of Jacob's descendants in Egypt as 75, following the ancient Greek translation of the Hebrew Scriptures (see also Exod 1.1-5).

46.34 *shepherds . . . Egyptians did not like:* Egyptians thought that the wandering sheep herders from the east were inferior and did not like to mix with them. Joseph wanted to tell the king that his brothers were shepherds, so the king would give them their own area (Goshen), apart from Egypt's main population farther up river.

ᑫᔆ   Nomads (Wandering Herders)

Their son Judah took his sons Shelah, Perez, and Zerah. Judah's sons Er and Onan had died in Canaan. Judah's son Perez took his sons Hezron and Hamul.

Their son Issachar took his sons Tola, Puvah, Jashub,[f] and Shimron.

Their son Zebulun took his sons Sered, Elon, and Jahleel.

Their daughter Dinah also went.

[16-18]Jacob and Zilpah, the servant woman Laban had given his daughter Leah, had a total of 16 children, grandchildren, and great-grandchildren.

Their son Gad took his sons Ziphion, Haggi, Shuni, Ezbon, Eri, Arodi, and Areli.

Their son Asher took his sons Imnah, Ishvah, Ishvi, and Beriah, who took his sons, Heber and Malchiel.

Serah, the daughter of Asher, also went.

[19-22]Jacob and Rachel had 14 children and grandchildren.

Their son Joseph was already in Egypt, where he had married Asenath, daughter of Potiphera, the priest of Heliopolis.[g] Joseph and Asenath had two sons, Manasseh and Ephraim.

Jacob and Rachel's son Benjamin took his sons Bela, Becher, Ashbel, Gera, Naaman, Ehi, Rosh, Muppim, Huppim, and Ard.

[23-25]Jacob and Bilhah, the servant woman Laban had given his daughter Rachel, had seven children and grandchildren.

Their son Dan took his son Hushim.

Their son Naphtali took his sons Jahzeel, Guni, Jezer, and Shillem.

[26]Sixty-six members of Jacob's family went to Egypt with him, not counting his daughters-in-law. [27]Jacob's two grandsons who were born there made it a total of 70 members of Jacob's family in Egypt.

[28]Jacob had sent his son Judah ahead of him to ask Joseph to meet them in Goshen. [29]So Joseph got in his chariot and went to meet his father. When they met, Joseph hugged his father around the neck and cried for a long time. [30]Jacob said to Joseph, "Now that I have seen you and know you are still alive, I am ready to die."

[31]Then Joseph said to his brothers and to everyone who had come with them:

I must go and tell the king[h] that you have arrived from Canaan. [32]I will tell him that you are shepherds and that you have brought your sheep, goats, cattle, and everything else you own. [33]The king will call you in and ask what you do for a living. [34]When he does, be sure to say, "We are shepherds. Our families have always raised sheep." If you tell him this, he will let you settle in the region of Goshen.

Joseph wanted them to say this to the king, because the Egyptians did not like to be around anyone who raised sheep.

47 [1-2]Joseph took five of his brothers to the king and told him, "My father and my brothers have come from Canaan. They have brought their sheep, goats, cattle, and everything else they own to the region of Goshen."

Then he introduced his brothers to the king, [3]who asked them, "What do you do for a living?"

"Sir, we are shepherds," was their answer. "Our families have always raised sheep. [4]But in our country all the pastures are dried up, and our sheep have no grass to eat. So we, your servants, have come here. Please let us live in the region of Goshen."

[f]46.8-15 *Jashub:* The Samaritan Hebrew Text and one ancient translation; the Standard Hebrew Text "Iob." [g]46.19-22 *Heliopolis:* See the note at 41.45. [h]46.31 *the king:* See the note at 12.15.

⁵The king said to Joseph, "It's good that your father and brothers have arrived. ⁶I will let them live anywhere they choose in the land of Egypt, but I suggest that they settle in Goshen, the best part of our land. I would also like for your finest shepherds to watch after my own sheep and goats."

⁷Then Joseph brought his father Jacob and introduced him to the king. Jacob gave the king his blessing, ⁸and the king asked him, "How old are you?"

⁹Jacob answered, "I have lived only 130 years, and I have had to move from place to place. My parents and my grandparents also had to move from place to place. But they lived much longer, and their life was not as hard as mine." ¹⁰Then Jacob gave the king his blessing once again and left. ¹¹Joseph obeyed the king's orders and gave his father and brothers some of the best land in Egypt near the city of Rameses. ¹²Joseph also provided food for their families.

A Famine in Egypt

¹³The famine was bad everywhere in Egypt and Canaan, and the people were suffering terribly. ¹⁴So Joseph sold them the grain that had been stored up, and he put the money[i] in the king's treasury. ¹⁵But when everyone had run out of money, the Egyptians came to Joseph and demanded, "Give us more grain! If you don't, we'll soon be dead, because our money's all gone."

¹⁶"If you don't have any money," Joseph answered, "give me your animals, and I'll let you have some grain." ¹⁷From then on, they brought him their horses and donkeys and their sheep and goats in exchange for grain.

Within a year Joseph had collected every animal in Egypt. ¹⁸Then the people came to him and said:

Sir, there's no way we can hide the truth from you. We are broke, and we don't have any more animals. We have nothing left except ourselves and our land. ¹⁹Don't let us starve and our land be ruined. If you'll give us grain to eat and seed to plant, we'll sell ourselves and our land to the king.[j] We'll become his slaves.

²⁰The famine became so severe that Joseph finally bought every piece of land in Egypt for the king ²¹and made everyone the king's slaves,[k] ²²except the priests. The king gave the priests a regular food allowance, so they did not have to sell their land. ²³Then Joseph said to the people, "You and your land now belong to the king. I'm giving you seed to plant, ²⁴but one fifth of your crops must go to the king. You can keep the rest as seed or as food for your families."

²⁵"Sir, you have saved our lives!" they answered. "We are glad to be slaves of the king." ²⁶Then Joseph made a law that one fifth of the harvest would always belong to the king. Only the priests did not lose their land.

Jacob Becomes an Old Man

²⁷The people of Israel made their home in the land of Goshen, where they became prosperous and had large families. ²⁸Jacob himself lived there for 17 years, before dying at the age of 147. ²⁹When Jacob knew he did not have long to live, he called in

---

● 47.7-10 *gave the king his blessing:* This probably refers to a greeting that included Jacob's blessing of well-being and long life. However, since Jacob refers to his grandparents (Abraham and Sarah), he may have used a form of the blessing found in 12.2,3.

⋯ King of Egypt (Pharaoh)

● 47.11 *near the city of Rameses:* The city of Rameses was located in Goshen in the northeast part of the Nile River delta. It was probably named for the Egyptian king, Rameses II (about 1279–1212 B.C.), who ruled for many years after the time of Joseph. The name of the city was probably added to 47.11 by a later editor to help readers clearly identify where Jacob's family settled. (See Map 2 on pg 1880.)

● 47.22 *priests:* At times in ancient Egypt the priests had enough power and influence to remove one king and replace him with another, or to change a form of worship. This may be why the king of Egypt did not take the land belonging to the priests.

● 47.24 *one fifth:* A fifth of the crops were taken during the seven years of plenty (41.34), but now all land belonged to the king as well.

---

[i]47.14 *money:* See the note at 42.25. [j]47.19 *the king:* See the note at 12.15. [k]47.21 *made . . . slaves:* One ancient translation and the Samaritan Hebrew Text; the Standard Hebrew Text "made everyone move to the cities."

48.5,6 *I accept them as my own . . . inheritance:* By adopting Joseph's sons as his own, Jacob gave them the same status as his own oldest sons, Reuben and Simeon. Jacob named Ephraim first, even though Manasseh was older, which meant Ephraim received Jacob's main blessing. Actually, because of his earlier sin (35.22), Reuben would lose his birthright to Joseph and Joseph's sons (49.3,4; 1 Chr 5.1,2). This scene explains why in later passages, the Joseph tribe is divided into two tribes, Manasseh and Ephraim, each receiving land like other tribes of Israel.

Birthright

48.13 *left . . . right:* The right side was the place of greater authority or power. Joseph placed Manasseh there because he was the oldest. This is why Joseph was upset when Jacob crossed his hands and gave the blessing of the first-born to Ephraim (48.17-19).

Joseph and said, "If you really love me, you must make a solemn promise not to bury me in Egypt. [30]Instead, bury me in the place where my ancestors are buried."

"I will do what you have asked," Joseph answered.

[31]"Will you give me your word?" Jacob asked.

"Yes, I will," Joseph promised. After this, Jacob bowed down and prayed at the head of his bed.

Jacob Blesses Joseph's Two Sons

48 Joseph was told that his father Jacob had become very sick. So Joseph went to see him and took along his two sons, Manasseh and Ephraim. [2]When Joseph arrived, someone told Jacob, "Your son Joseph has come to see you." Jacob sat up in bed, but it took almost all his strength.

[3]Jacob told Joseph:

God All-Powerful appeared to me at Luz in the land of Canaan, where he gave me his blessing [4]and promised, "I will give you a large family with many descendants that will grow into a nation. And I am giving you this land that will belong to you and your family forever."

[5]Then Jacob went on to say:

Joseph, your two sons Ephraim and Manasseh were born in Egypt, but I accept them as my own, just as Reuben and Simeon are mine. [6]Any children you have later will be considered yours, but their inheritance will come from Ephraim and Manasseh. [7]Unfortunately, your mother Rachel died in Canaan after we had left northern Syr-

ia[l] and before we reached Bethlehem.[m] And I had to bury her along the way.

[8-10]Jacob was very old and almost blind. He did not recognize the two boys, and so he asked Joseph, "Who are these boys?"

Joseph answered, "They are my sons. God has given them to me here in Egypt."

"Bring them to me," Jacob said. "I want to give them my blessing." Joseph brought the boys to him, and he hugged and kissed them.

[11]Jacob turned to Joseph and told him, "For many years I thought you were dead and that I would never see you again. But now God has even let me live to see your children." [12]Then Joseph made his sons move away from Jacob's knees,[n] and Joseph bowed down in front of him with his face to the ground.

[13]After Joseph got up, he brought his two sons over to Jacob again. He led his younger son Ephraim to the left side of Jacob and his older son Manasseh to the right. [14]But before Jacob gave them his blessing, he crossed his arms, putting his right hand on the head of Ephraim and his left hand on the head of Manasseh. [15]Then he gave Joseph his blessing and said:

My grandfather Abraham and my father Isaac worshiped the LORD God. He has been with me all my life, [16]and his angel has kept me safe. Now I pray that he will bless these boys and that my name and the names of Abraham and Isaac will live on because of them. I ask God to give them many children and many descendants as well.

[17]Joseph did not like it when he saw his father place his right hand on the head of the younger son. So he tried to move his father's right hand from Ephraim's head

[l]**48.7** *northern Syria:* See the note at 24.10.   [m]**48.7** *Bethlehem:* The Hebrew text has "Ephrath, that is, Bethlehem."   [n]**48.12** *move . . . Jacob's knees:* The two boys were placed either on or between Jacob's knees, as a sign that he had accepted them as his sons.

and place it on Manasseh. ¹⁸Joseph said, "Father, you have made a mistake. This is the older boy. Put your right hand on him."

¹⁹But his father said, "Son, I know what I am doing. It's true that Manasseh's family will someday become a great nation. But Ephraim will be even greater than Manasseh, because his descendants will become many great nations."

²⁰Jacob told him that in the future the people of Israel would ask God's blessings on one another by saying, "I pray for God to bless you as much as he blessed Ephraim and Manasseh." Jacob put Ephraim's name first to show that he would be greater than Manasseh. ²¹After that, Jacob said, "Joseph, you can see that I won't live much longer. But God will be with you and will lead you back to the land he promised our family long ago. ²²Meanwhile, I'm giving you the hillside^o I captured from the Amorites."

Jacob Blesses His Sons

49 ^{*1}Jacob called his sons together and said:

My sons, I am Jacob,
  your father Israel.
²Come, gather around,
  as I tell your future.

³Reuben, you are my oldest,
  born at the peak of my powers;
    you were an honored leader.
⁴Uncontrollable as a flood,
  you slept with my wife
    and disgraced my bed.
And so you no longer deserve
  the place of honor.

⁵Simeon and Levi,
  you are brothers,
    each a gruesome sword.
⁶I never want to take part
  in your plans or deeds.
You slaughtered people
  in your anger,
and you crippled cattle
  for no reason.
⁷Now I place a curse on you
because of
  your fierce anger.
Your descendants
will be scattered
  among the tribes of Israel.

⁸Judah, you will be praised
  by your brothers;
they will bow down to you,
  as you defeat your enemies.
⁹My son, you are a lion
  ready to eat your victim!
You are terribly fierce;
  no one will bother you.
¹⁰You will have power and rule
  until nations obey you^P
  and come bringing gifts.
¹¹You will tie your donkey
  to a choice grapevine
and wash your clothes
  in wine from those grapes.
¹²Your eyes are darker than wine,
  your teeth whiter than milk.

¹³Zebulun, you will settle
  along the seashore
and provide safe harbors
  as far north as Sidon.

¹⁴Issachar, you are a strong donkey
  resting in the meadows.^q

48.19 *But Ephraim . . . greater than Manasseh:* Later in Israel's history the tribe of Ephraim would become very powerful, and during the time when Israel was divided into two kingdoms, the whole northern kingdom was sometimes called Ephraim.

49.3 *Reuben:* He was Jacob's oldest son (29.32).

49.5-7 *Simeon and Levi:* Verse 6 refers to the revenge these two brothers took against the men at Shechem because of the rape of Dinah, their sister (34.25-29). When the tribes of Israel later settled in Canaan, the tribe of Simeon was eventually absorbed into the tribe of Judah. The Levi tribe became Israel's priests. The number of Jacob's sons was twelve and stood for the twelve tribes of Israel. But since the Levi tribe could not own land (Deut 10.9), the land that would have gone to Joseph's tribe was divided between his two sons, Manasseh and Ephraim, making the total of land-owning tribes twelve.

Israel's Priests

Israel

49.8-12 *Judah:* Judah was the fourth son born to Jacob and Leah (29.35), but his older brothers (Reuben, Simeon, and Levi) had done things that made them lose their rights of leadership (see 35.22; 34.25-29). Judah would become the leading tribe in the south. King David belonged to the Judah tribe.

49.16-21 *Dan . . . Gad . . . Asher . . . Naphtali*: The reference to Dan as a snake may be to its sneak attack on Laish (Judg 18.1-2,27-29) The tribe of Gad settled east of the Jordan River, where they were open to attack by the Moabites (see Josh 13.24-28; 2 Kgs 3.4,5). The tribe of Asher settled on fertile farmland (Josh 19.24-31), which meant they would always have plenty of food. The Naphtali tribe settled in the hill country north of Lake Galilee (Josh 19.32-39) and may have been known for being independent and free, like deer that roam the woods.

49.22-26 *Joseph*: The Joseph tribe was divided according to his two sons, Ephraim and Manasseh. The "fruitful vine" probably refers to Ephraim, whose name in Hebrew sounds like the word for "fruitful." As vines tend to grow over whatever surrounds them, the Joseph tribes tended to try to expand the boundaries of their land (Josh 17.14-18). The Joseph tribes were large (49.25) and were blessed by much wealth.

49.24 *Shepherd . . . rock*: Shepherds lead and protect their flocks, just as God leads and protects his people (Ps 23.1; Isa 40.11). The ideal leader of Israel would be like a good shepherd (Ezek 34.23; John 10.14-16). "Rock" is often used to describe God, who is Israel's defense (Deut 32.15; Ps 18.2).

49.27 *Benjamin*: Some of the descendants of Benjamin were fierce and brutal warriors (Judg 3.12-30; 19.1-21.24).

¹⁵You found them so pleasant
   that you worked too hard
   and became a slave.

¹⁶Dan,ʳ you are the tribe
   that will bring justice
   to Israel.
¹⁷You are a snake that bites
   the heel of a horse,
   making its rider fall.

¹⁸Our Lord, I am waiting
   for you to save us.

¹⁹Gad,ˢ you will be attacked,
   then attack your attackers.

²⁰Asher, you will eat food
   fancy enough for a king.

²¹Naphtali, you are a wild deer
   with lovely fawns.ᵗ

²²Joseph, you are a fruitful vine
   growing near a stream
   and climbing a wall.ᵘ
²³Enemies attacked with arrows,
   refusing to show mercy.
²⁴But you stood your ground,
   swiftly shooting back
   with the help of Jacob's God,
   the All-Powerful One—
his name is the Shepherd,
   Israel's mighty rock.ᵛ
²⁵Your help came from the God
   your father worshiped,
   from God All-Powerful.
God will bless you with rain
   and streams from the earth;

he will bless you
   with many descendants.
²⁶My son, the blessings I give
   are better than the promise
   of ancient mountains
   or eternal hills.ʷ
Joseph, I pray these blessings
   will come to you,
because you are the leader
   of your brothers.

²⁷Benjamin, you are a fierce wolf,
   destroying your enemies
   morning and evening.

²⁸These are the twelve tribes of Israel, and this is how Jacob gave each of them their proper blessings.

Jacob's Death

²⁹⁻³¹Jacob told his sons:

Soon I will die, and I want you to bury me in Machpelah Cave. Abraham bought this cave as a burial place from Ephron the Hittite, and it is near the town of Mamre in Canaan. Abraham and Sarah are buried there, and so are Isaac and Rebekah. I buried Leah there too. ³²Both the cave and the land that goes with it were bought from the Hittites.

³³When Jacob had finished giving these instructions to his sons, he lay down on his

50 bed and died. ¹Joseph started crying, then leaned over to hug and kiss his father.

²Joseph gave orders for Jacob's body to be embalmed, ³and it took the usual 40 days.

ʳ**49.16** *Dan*: In Hebrew "Dan" means "justice" or "judgment."   ˢ**49.19** *Gad*: In Hebrew "Gad" sounds like "attack."   ᵗ**49.21** *with lovely fawns*: Or "speaking lovely words."   ᵘ**49.22** *wall*: One possible meaning for the difficult Hebrew text.   ᵛ**49.24** *mighty rock*: The Hebrew text has "rock," which is sometimes used in poetry to compare the Lord to a mountain where his people can run for protection from their enemies.   ʷ**49.26** *eternal hills*: One possible meaning for the difficult Hebrew text.

The Egyptians mourned 70 days for Jacob. ⁴When the time of mourning was over, Joseph said to the Egyptian leaders, "If you consider me your friend, please speak to the king^x for me. ⁵Just before my father died, he made me promise to bury him in his burial cave in Canaan. If the king will give me permission to go, I will come back here."

⁶The king answered, "Go to Canaan and keep your promise to your father."

⁷⁻⁹When Joseph left Goshen with his brothers, his relatives, and his father's relatives to bury Jacob, many of the king's highest officials and even his military chariots and cavalry went along. The Israelites left behind only their children, their cattle, and their sheep and goats.

¹⁰After crossing the Jordan River, Joseph stopped at Atad's threshing place, where they all mourned and wept seven days for Jacob. ¹¹The Canaanites saw this and said, "The Egyptians are in great sorrow." Then they named the place "Egypt in Sorrow."^y

¹²So Jacob's sons did just as their father had instructed. ¹³They took him to Mamre in Canaan and buried him in Machpelah Cave, the burial place Abraham had bought from Ephron the Hittite.

¹⁴After the funeral, Joseph, his brothers, and everyone else returned to Egypt.

Joseph's Promise to His Brothers

¹⁵After Jacob died, Joseph's brothers said to each other, "What if Joseph still hates us and wants to get even with us for all the cruel things we did to him?"

¹⁶So they sent this message to Joseph:

Before our father died, ¹⁷he told us, "You did some cruel and terrible things to Joseph, but you must ask him to forgive you."

Now we ask you to please forgive the terrible things we did. After all, we serve the same God that your father worshiped.

When Joseph heard this, he started crying.

¹⁸Right then, Joseph's brothers came and bowed down to the ground in front of him and said, "We are your slaves."

¹⁹But Joseph told them, "Don't be afraid! I have no right to change what God has decided. ²⁰You tried to harm me, but God made it turn out for the best, so that he could save all these people, as he is now doing. ²¹Don't be afraid! I will take care of you and your children." After Joseph said this, his brothers felt much better.

Joseph's Death

²²Joseph lived in Egypt with his brothers until he died at the age of 110. ²³Joseph lived long enough to see Ephraim's children and grandchildren. He also lived to see the children of Manasseh's son Machir, and he welcomed them into his family. ²⁴Before Joseph died, he told his brothers, "I won't live much longer. But God will take care of you and lead you out of Egypt to the land he promised Abraham, Isaac, and Jacob. ²⁵Now promise me that you will take my body with you when God leads you to that land."

²⁶So Joseph died in Egypt at the age of 110; his body was embalmed and put in a coffin.

50.2-4 *embalmed . . . mourning:* Embalming was an ancient Egyptian custom that was done by removing internal organs and using linen and spices to fill the body cavities. In Egypt the bodies of important kings were also wrapped in long linen bandages, becoming mummies. The process of embalming took 40 days, and the time of mourning for Jacob lasted 70 days, or about the same amount of time the Egyptian people mourned the death of one of their kings.

Burial

50.10 *Jordan River . . . Atad's threshing place:* The Jordan River begins in the streams near Mount Hermon, which come together and run south into Lake Galilee. The river then flows south from Lake Galilee to the Dead Sea. It formed a natural boundary between Canaan and its neighbors to the east. Atad's threshing place was likely a flat area located in a high open place exposed to the wind. During threshing, grain stalks were crushed on the floor, and then thrown into the air. The heavier grain fell to the floor, but the light chaff was blown away in the wind. (See Map 3 on pg 1881.)

50.20 *God made it turn out for the best:* Here is one final statement of this key theme in the Joseph stories: God is at work in human events and can make good things happen even when a person's intentions are evil. With Joseph, the people of Israel have begun to fulfill God's promise that they would be a blessing to others (12.1-3).

---

^x**50.4** *the king:* See the note at 12.15.   ^y**50.11** *Egypt in Sorrow:* Or "Abel-Mizraim."

Reflection Questions About Genesis 1.1—50.26

1. Why do you think the first three chapters of GENESIS were written? What beliefs or perspectives are being passed on?

2. How does the Bible's description of creation fit with modern theories about how the world began? Do you see any conflicts between the two? Why or why not?

3. From the story in chapter 3, how would you explain what "sin" is? What effects of human sin do you see in the world today?

4. Why did God send a flood to destroy the earth and its people (6.4-7,11-13)? Why was Noah chosen to build the boat? What promise did God make to Noah after the flood waters went down (8.21; 9.9-11)? What do you make of the existence of a flood story in the writings of a number of ancient peoples?

5. Why did the people try to build the tower at Babel (11.1-4)? How did God respond to the tower building? Why? If God created human beings "to be like himself" (1.27), what was wrong with building a tower that got the people "closer" to God in the heavens?

6. What are the three main promises God made to Abraham and his descendants (12.1-3; 15.5-7;

17.1-8)? What were Abraham and his descendants expected to do in order to hold up their part of the agreement with God (17.9-14)?

7. What promise did Jacob receive at Bethel while he was dreaming (28.10-15; see also 35.9-15)? What did Jacob promise God in return (28.20-22)? Jacob's name was changed to what? Where did this happen (32.22-30; 35.9-11)? Why is this important for the history of God's people, the descendants of Abraham?

8. Who was Joseph and what were his dreams (37.19)? How did Joseph's brothers react to his dreams? Why? What did they do to Joseph (37.10-34)? What is the overall message of the story of Joseph in the Bible?

9. Compare Genesis 50.20 to Romans 8.28. How does God bring good results out of bad situations? What examples can you think of?

10. Complete these statements.
    - My favorite part of GENESIS is . . . because . . .
    - One new thing I learned from reading GENESIS is . . .
    - After reading GENESIS, one question I still have is . . .

exodus

Who was Moses, and how was he involved in two of the most important events in the history of the people of Israel?

WHAT MAKES EXODUS SPECIAL?

The word "exodus" comes from a Greek word meaning "exit" or "the way out." Those who wrote the Greek version of the Old Testament (the Septuagint) named the book EXODUS to emphasize how God chose Moses to lead the Hebrew people out of slavery in Egypt. The Hebrew title of the book means "These are the names," a phrase that appears in Genesis 46.8 and lists the names of some of Israel's ancestors. This title emphasizes how EXODUS continues the story of God's people, begun in GENESIS.

EXODUS describes two key events in the history of the people of Israel. The first event is the exodus from Egypt. The second key event in the book occurs at Mount Sinai, where God gives Moses and the people the Ten Commandments and the laws that are to guide how they will worship and live together as God's people. The agreement God made with the people at Sinai was built on the promises God had first made to Abraham (Exod 33.1-3; see also Gen 12.1-3; 17.1-8). But in order to receive God's promised blessings the people had to be loyal to God alone and follow God's commands (Exod 23.20-33).

WHAT'S THE STORY BEHIND THE SCENE?

According to 1 Kings 6.1, the exodus from Egypt occurred 480 years before the fourth year of King Solomon's reign. Solomon ruled from about 970 to 931 B.C. That would mean that the exodus occurred around 1446 B.C. However, 480 may be a symbolic number for twelve generations. The small amount of historical evidence that exists (the name Rameses in Exod 1.11) seems to point to Sety I and Rameses II as the Egyptian kings at the time of Israel's slavery and escape from Egypt. This would date the exodus shortly after 1300 B.C.

HOW IS EXODUS CONSTRUCTED?

The following outline divides the book into three major sections, based primarily on the location of events.

Moses leads the people out of Egypt (1.1—13.16)
    Troubled times for Israel and Moses (1.1—2.25)
    God chooses Moses (3.1—4.31)
    The God of Israel versus Egypt's king (5.1—11.10)
    Passover and exodus (12.1—13.16)
Moses leads the people in the desert (13.17—18.27)
    Escape through the sea (13.17—15.21)
    God provides water and food (15.22—17.7)
    Victory in battle and the appointment of judges (17.8—18.27)
Moses and the people of Israel at Mount Sinai (19.1—40.38)
    God gives Moses the Law (19.1—24.18)
    God gives instructions for worship (25.1—31.18)
    The people rebel, but God remains faithful (32.1—33.23)
    God's instructions are carried out (34.1—40.38)

Exodus continues the story of God's people begun in Genesis. Jacob's family has settled in Egypt, where they have eventually prospered. Fearing the growing number of Hebrews in his kingdom, a new Egyptian king forces them into slave labor. Moses, the Israelite leader chosen by God, confronts the Egyptian king and demands freedom for the Hebrew people. God helps Moses win freedom for the people and lead them safely out of Egypt. On their way back to the land God promised to Abraham, God appears to Moses on Mount Sinai and gives him the Law, instructions that the people are to live by. An entire generation of Israelites do not accept the Law, but God remains faithful to them nonetheless, protecting them as they journey through the desert and preparing the way for the fulfillment of his promise in future generations. Although Exodus is full of human drama, God stands above the characters and guides their story to his purpose. In this book, we see the power and mercy of God, who acts as rescuer, teacher, and protector.

Outline

The People of Israel Suffer

1 [1-5]When Jacob went to Egypt, his son Joseph was already there. So Jacob took his eleven other sons and their families. They were: Reuben, Simeon, Levi, Judah, Issachar, Zebulun, Benjamin, Dan, Naphtali, Gad, and Asher. Altogether, Jacob had 70 children, grandchildren, and great-grandchildren[a] who went with him.

[6]After Joseph, his brothers, and everyone else in that generation had died, [7]the people of Israel became so numerous that the whole region of Goshen was full of them.

[8]Many years later a new king came to power. He did not know what Joseph had done for Egypt, [9]and he told the Egyptians:

There are too many of those Israelites in our country, and they are becoming more powerful than we are. [10]If we don't outsmart them, their families will keep growing larger. And if our country goes to war, they could easily fight on the side of our enemies and escape from Egypt.

[11]The Egyptians put slave bosses in charge of the people of Israel and tried to wear them down with hard work. Those bosses forced them to build the cities of Pithom and Rameses,[b] where the king[c] could store his supplies. [12]But even though the Israelites were mistreated, their families grew larger, and they took over more land. Because of this, the Egyptians feared them worse than before [13]and made them work so hard [14]that their lives were miserable. The Egyptians were cruel to the people of Israel and forced them to make bricks and to mix mortar and to work in the fields.

[15]Finally, the king called in Shiphrah and Puah, the two women who helped the

---

[a]**1.1-5** *70 children . . . great-grandchildren*: See Genesis 46.8-27.   [b]**1.11** *Pithom and Rameses*: This is the only mention of Pithom in the Bible; its exact location is unknown, though it was probably in the northern Delta of Egypt. Rameses is the famous Delta city that was the home of Rameses II; its exact location is also unknown.   [c]**1.11** *the king*: The Hebrew text has "Pharaoh," a Hebrew word sometimes used for the title of the king of Egypt.

1.1-5 *Jacob . . . great-grandchildren*: Jacob was the grandson of Abraham and son of Isaac (Gen 25.19-26). Jacob's son Joseph had been sold by his jealous brothers to slave traders and ended up in Egypt (Gen 37.12-36), where he eventually became an important Egyptian official (Gen 41.37-56). When a severe food shortage (famine) hit Canaan, Jacob's sons went to Egypt to ask for food and were reunited with Joseph. Shortly after, Jacob and his sons and their families moved to Egypt (Gen 46.8-27). They were given their own land in the area of Egypt known as Goshen (Gen 47.27), where they settled. The tribes of Israel were named for Jacob's sons.

1.7 *Goshen*: This area of pastureland was in the eastern part of the Nile River delta on the Mediterranean coast. The palace of the Egyptian king was in or near this region at this time. As the Hebrews filled the land, God's promise of many descendants was coming true (Gen 17.1,2; 22.17; Acts 7.17). (See Map 2 on pg 1880.)

King of Egypt (Pharaoh)

Egypt

1.14 *bricks . . . mortar*: Handmade mud bricks were made of a mixture of river-mud or clay plus a bit of straw to help them hold together better. Mortar was made of clay and sand or chalky lime or gypsum rock mixed with water. It was used to hold the bricks in place or to cover the bricks like plaster.

1.16 *kill him:* In ancient Hebrew cultures the family line was passed on through the males, so killing the male babies was thought to be the way to wipe out that culture.

1.22 *everyone in the nation:* Since the Egyptian people participated in trying to get rid of Hebrew male babies, they suffered the consequences of God's judgment.

Disasters (Plagues)

Moses

Hebrew[d] mothers when they gave birth. [16]He told them, "If a Hebrew woman gives birth to a girl, let the child live. If the baby is a boy, kill him!"

[17]But the two women were faithful to God and did not kill the boys, even though the king had told them to. [18]The king called them in again and asked, "Why are you letting those baby boys live?"

[19]They answered, "Hebrew women have their babies much quicker than Egyptian women. By the time we arrive, their babies are already born." [20-21]God was good to the two women because they truly respected him, and he blessed them with children of their own.

The Hebrews kept increasing [22]until finally, the king gave a command to everyone in the nation, "As soon as a Hebrew boy is born, throw him into the Nile River! But you can let the girls live."

Moses Is Born

2 A man from the Levi tribe married a woman from the same tribe, [2]and she later had a baby boy. He was a beautiful child, and she kept him inside for three months. [3]But when she could no longer keep him hidden, she made a basket out of reeds and covered it with tar. She put him in the basket and placed it in the tall grass along the edge of the Nile River. [4]The baby's older sister[e] stood off at a distance to see what would happen to him.

[5]About that time one of the king's[f] daughters came down to take a bath in the river, while her servant women walked along the river bank. She saw the basket in the tall grass and sent one of them to pull it out of the water. [6]When the king's daughter opened the basket, she saw the baby crying and felt sorry for him. She said, "This must be one of the Hebrew babies."

[7]At once the baby's older sister came up and asked, "Do you want me to get a Hebrew woman to take care of the baby for you?"

[8]"Yes," the king's daughter answered.

So the girl brought the baby's mother, [9]and the king's daughter told her, "Take care of this child, and I will pay you."

The baby's mother carried him home and took care of him. [10]And when he was old enough, she took him to the king's daughter, who adopted him. She named him Moses[g] because she said, "I pulled him out of the water."

Moses Escapes from Egypt

[11]After Moses had grown up, he went out to where his own people were hard at work, and he saw an Egyptian beating one of them. [12]Moses looked around to see if anyone was watching, then he killed the Egyptian and hid his body in the sand.

[13]When Moses went out the next day, he saw two Hebrews fighting. So he went to the man who had started the fight and asked, "Why are you beating up one of your own people?"

[14]The man answered, "Who put you in charge of us and made you our judge? Are you planning to kill me, just like you killed that Egyptian?"

This frightened Moses because he was sure that people must have found out what had happened. [15]When the king[h] heard what Moses had done, he wanted to kill him. But Moses escaped and went to the land of Midian.

[d]**1.15** *Hebrew:* An earlier term for "Israelite." [e]**2.4** *older sister:* Miriam, the sister of Moses and Aaron. [f]**2.5** *the king's:* See the note at 1.11. [g]**2.10** *Moses:* In Hebrew "Moses" sounds like "pull out." [h]**2.15** *the king:* See the note at 1.11.

One day, when Moses was sitting by a well, [16]the seven daughters of Jethro, the priest of Midian,[i] came up to water their father's sheep and goats. [17]Some shepherds tried to chase them away, but Moses came to their rescue and watered their animals. [18]When Jethro's daughters returned home, their father asked, "Why have you come back so early today?"

[19]They answered, "An Egyptian rescued us from the shepherds, and he even watered our sheep and goats."

[20]"Where is he?" Jethro asked. "Why did you leave him out there? Invite him to eat with us."

[21]Moses agreed to stay on with Jethro, who later let his daughter Zipporah marry Moses. [22]And when she had a son, Moses said, "I will name him Gershom,[j] since I am a foreigner in this country."

[23]After the death of the king of Egypt, the Israelites still complained because they were forced to be slaves. They cried out for help, [24]and God heard their loud cries. He did not forget the promise he had made to Abraham, Isaac, and Jacob, [25]and because he knew what was happening to his people, he felt sorry for them.

God Speaks to Moses

3 One day, Moses was taking care of the sheep and goats of his father-in-law Jethro, the priest of Midian, and Moses decided to lead them across the desert to Sinai,[k] the holy mountain. [2]There an angel of the LORD appeared to him from a burning bush. Moses saw that the bush was on fire, but it was not burning up. [3]"This is strange!" he said to himself. "I'll go over and see why the bush isn't burning up."

[4]When the LORD saw Moses coming near, he called him by name from the bush, and Moses answered, "Here I am."

[5]God replied, "Don't come any closer. Take off your sandals—the ground where you are standing is holy. [6]I am the God who was worshiped by your ancestors Abraham, Isaac, and Jacob."

Moses was afraid to look at God, and so he hid his face.

[7]The LORD said:

I have seen how my people are suffering as slaves in Egypt, and I have heard them beg for my help because of the way they are being mistreated. I feel sorry for them, [8]and I have come down to rescue them from the Egyptians.

I will bring my people out of Egypt into a country where there is a lot of good land, rich with milk and honey. I will give them the land where the Canaanites, Hittites, Amorites, Perizzites, Hivites, and Jebusites now live. [9]My people have begged for my help, and I have seen how cruel the Egyptians are to them. [10]Now go to the king! I am sending you to lead my people out of his country.

[11]But Moses said, "Who am I to go to the king and lead your people out of Egypt?"

[12]God replied, "I will be with you. And you will know that I am the one who sent you, when you worship me on this mountain after you have led my people out of Egypt."[l]

[13]Moses answered, "I will tell the people

2.19 *Egyptian:* Moses was actually a Hebrew, but he was wearing Egyptian clothing and had his hair cut in an Egyptian style, having been adopted by the Egyptian royal family.

2.23 *death of the king:* The new king (possibly Rameses II) treated the Israelite people as cruelly as the previous king had.

King of Egypt (Pharaoh)

2.24 *promise:* God's help was based on promises made to the Israelites' ancestors: Abraham (Gen 15.13-18; 17.1-9), Isaac (Gen 17.19; 26.24), and Jacob (Gen 35.9-12).

3.2 *burning bush:* Fire and smoke often signal the presence of God in the Bible (Gen 15.17,18; Exod 13.21,22; 19.16-19; Judg 13.20). The Hebrew word for bush (*seneh*) sounds like Sinai.

3.4 *LORD:* In the CEV, "LORD" is usually the translation for the Hebrew word *Yahweh*.

LORD (YHWH)

3.5 *Take off your sandals . . . holy:* Removing sandals may have been an ancient custom connected with holy places, though it was not required in the Law of Moses. What made the place holy was the special presence of God.

[i]2.16 *Jethro, the priest of Midian:* Hebrew "the priest of Midian." But see 3.1; 4.18; 18.1-4 where his name is given. In the Hebrew of verse 18 he is spoken of as "Reuel," which may have been the name of the tribe to which Jethro belonged. [j]2.22 *Gershom:* In Hebrew "Gershom" sounds like "foreigner." [k]3.1 *Sinai:* The Hebrew text has "Horeb," another name for Sinai. [l]3.12 *I will be with you . . . out of Egypt:* Or "I will be with you. This bush is a sign that I am the one sending you, and it is a promise that you will worship me on this mountain after you have led my people out of Egypt."

3.16 *leaders of Israel:* The Hebrew word here refers to "those with beards," meaning the older and experienced men who were the heads of each clan or tribe.

3.18 *offer a sacrifice:* Offering sacrifices to gods and goddesses was a common worship practice in the ancient world (Gen 22.13,14). These sacrifices were a way to maintain, restore, or celebrate the relationship between the giver and God. Before the Law of Moses commanded sacrifices to be done by Israel's priests, sacrifices were offered by the head of each family. **(See the chart Sacrifices and Offerings on pg 1828.)**

4.2-4 *walking stick . . . snake:* The king of Egypt often wore a head piece that included a metal cobra, or snake which symbolized the king's majesty and power. Turning the walking stick to a snake and back again may have been meant to show that the LORD was more powerful than Egypt's king, who was considered a god by the Egyptians.

   Egypt

of Israel that the God their ancestors worshiped has sent me to them. But what should I say, if they ask me your name?"

14-15 God said to Moses:

I am the eternal God. So tell them that the LORD,[m] whose name is "I Am," has sent you. This is my name forever, and it is the name that people must use from now on.

16Call together the leaders of Israel and tell them that the God who was worshiped by Abraham, Isaac, and Jacob has appeared to you. Tell them I have seen how terribly they are being treated in Egypt, **17**and I promise to lead them out of their troubles. I will give them a land rich with milk and honey, where the Canaanites, Hittites, Amorites, Perizzites, Hivites, and Jebusites now live.

18The leaders of Israel will listen to you. Then you must take them to the king of Egypt and say, "The LORD God of the Hebrews has appeared to us. Let us walk three days into the desert, where we can offer a sacrifice to him." **19**But I know that the king of Egypt won't let you go unless something forces him to. **20**So I will use my mighty power to perform all kinds of miracles and strike down the Egyptians. Then the king will send you away.

21After I punish the Egyptians, they will be so afraid of you that they will give you anything you want. You are my people, and I will let you take many things with you when you leave the land of Egypt. **22**Every Israelite woman will go to her Egyptian neighbors or to any Egyptian woman living with them and ask them for gold and silver jewelry and for their finest clothes. The Egyptians will give them to you, and you will put these fine things on your sons and daughters. Carry all this away when you leave Egypt.

The LORD Gives Great Power to Moses

4 Moses asked the LORD, "Suppose everyone refuses to listen to my message, and no one believes that you really appeared to me?"

2The LORD answered, "What's that in your hand?"

"A walking stick," Moses replied.

3"Throw it down!" the LORD commanded. So Moses threw the stick on the ground. It immediately turned into a snake, and Moses jumped back.

4"Pick it up by the tail!" the LORD told him. And when Moses did this, the snake turned back into a walking stick.

5"Do this," the LORD said, "and the Israelites will believe that you have seen me, the God who was worshiped by their ancestors Abraham, Isaac, and Jacob."

6Next, the LORD commanded Moses, "Put your hand inside your shirt." Moses obeyed, and when he took it out, his hand had turned white as snow—like someone with leprosy.[n]

7"Put your hand back inside your shirt," the LORD told him. Moses did so, and when he took it out again, it was as healthy as the rest of his body.

8-9 Then the LORD said, "If no one be-

[m]3.14,15 *LORD:* The Hebrew text has "Yahweh," which is usually translated "LORD" in the CEV. Since it seems related to the word translated "I am," it may mean "I am the one who is" or "I will be what I will be" or "I am the one who brings into being."   [n]4.6 *leprosy:* The word translated "leprosy" was used for many different kinds of skin diseases.

lieves either of these miracles, take some water from the Nile River and pour it on the ground. The water will immediately turn into blood."

[10]Moses replied, "I have never been a good speaker. I wasn't one before you spoke to me, and I'm not one now. I am slow at speaking, and I can never think of what to say."

[11]But the LORD answered, "Who makes people able to speak or makes them deaf or unable to speak? Who gives them sight or makes them blind? Don't you know that I am the one who does these things? [12]Now go! When you speak, I will be with you and give you the words to say."

[13]Moses begged, "LORD, please send someone else to do it."

[14]The LORD became angry with Moses and said:

What about your brother Aaron, the Levite? I know he is a good speaker. He is already on his way here to visit you, and he will be happy to see you again. [15-16]Aaron will speak to the people for you, and you will be like me, telling Aaron what to say. I will be with both of you as you speak, and I will tell each of you what to do. [17]Now take this walking stick and use it to perform miracles.

Moses Returns to Egypt

[18]Moses went to his father-in-law Jethro and asked, "Please let me return to Egypt to see if any of my people are still alive."

"All right," Jethro replied. "I hope all goes well."

[19]But even before this, the LORD had told Moses, "Leave the land of Midian and re-turn to Egypt. Everyone who wanted to kill you is now dead." [20]So Moses put his wife and sons on donkeys and headed for Egypt, holding the walking stick that had the power of God.

[21]On the way the LORD said to Moses:

When you get to Egypt, go to the king and work the miracles I have shown you. But I will make him so stubborn that he will refuse to let my people go. [22]Then tell him that I have said, "Israel is my first-born son, [23]and I commanded you to release him, so he could worship me. But you refused, and now I will kill your first-born son."

Zipporah's Son Is Circumcised

[24]One night while Moses was in camp, the LORD was about to kill him. [25]But Zip-porah[o] circumcised her son with a flint knife. She touched his[p] legs with the skin she had cut off and said, "My dear son, this blood will protect you."[q] [26]So the LORD did not harm Moses. Then Zipporah said, "Yes, my dear, you are safe because of this cir-cumcision."[r]

Aaron Is Sent To Meet Moses

[27]The LORD sent Aaron to meet Moses in the desert. So Aaron met Moses at Mount Sinai[s] and greeted him with a kiss. [28]Moses told Aaron what God had sent him to say; he also told him about the miracles God had given him the power to perform.

[29]Later they brought together the lead-ers of Israel, [30]and Aaron told them what the LORD had sent Moses to say. Then Moses worked the miracles for the people,

[o]4.25 Zipporah: The wife of Moses (see 2.16-21).   [p]4.25 his: Either Moses or the boy.   [q]4.25 My dear son . . . you: Or "My dear husband, you are a man of blood" (meaning Moses).   [r]4.26 you are . . . circumcision: Or "you are a man of blood."   [s]4.27 Mount Sinai: Hebrew "the mountain of God."

● 4.14 Aaron, the Levite: Both Moses and Aaron were from the Israelite tribe of Levi. Later, Aaron and his descen-dants were assigned the task of being priests. Aaron was the first high priest of Israel (27.21—28.3).

● 4.22 Israel is my first-born son: Jacob, the grandson of Abraham, was renamed "Israel" (Gen 32.28). Jacob's (Israel's) sons became the original an-cestors of the tribes of Israel. Ancient laws allowed for a father to give a greater share of his property to his oldest son. As God's "first-born," the people of Israel had the special privileges and inheritance reserved for the first-born (Deut 21.15-17).

◌⃟ Birthright

● 4.24,25 circumcised . . . blood will protect you: "Circumcision" was the cer-emony of cutting off the foreskin of a male's penis. According to God's agree-ment with Abraham, Hebrew fathers were responsible for making sure the males in their families were circum-cised. This was to show that Abraham's descendants were God's chosen people (17.9-14; 34.21-23; see also Lev 12.3). Perhaps Moses had not yet circumcised his own son, and this made God angry. So, Zipporah, Moses' wife, came to the res-cue by circumcising their son instead. She used a knife made of a hard sharp-ened rock. As a daughter of a priest (2.16) she was likely familiar with reli-gious rituals. She put some of the blood which flowed from the cut on Moses' or the boy's leg, which probably was meant to symbolize the genitals. Blood was believed to have saving or protective power (see 12.21-23).

Blood

Circumcision

5.3 LORD *God of the Hebrews . . . sacrifices:* "Hebrews" is another name for Israelites, the descendants of Abraham, Isaac, and Jacob. Ancient sources other than the Bible speak of a people known as *Habiru* or *Apiru*, which may be related to the name Hebrew. These people were described as poor immigrants or foreigners who wandered from place to place but did not own land or property in a specific place.

5.7,8 *straw . . . same number of bricks:* In ancient times, bricks were often made by adding straw to a mud or clay mixture. Collecting enough straw to make large numbers of bricks would have taken a lot of time. Though this job was added to the Hebrew slaves' brick making, the number of bricks they had to make did not change. They had to work longer and harder to complete their assigned tasks.

31and everyone believed. They bowed down and worshiped the LORD because they knew that he had seen their suffering and was going to help them.

Moses and Aaron Go to the King of Egypt

5 Moses and Aaron went to the king[t] of Egypt and told him, "The LORD God says, 'Let my people go into the desert, so they can honor me with a celebration there.'"

2"Who is this LORD and why should I obey him?" the king replied. "I refuse to let you and your people go!"

3They answered, "The LORD God of the Hebrews, has appeared to us. Please let us walk three days into the desert where we can offer sacrifices to him. If you don't, he may strike us down with terrible troubles or with war."

4-5The king said, "Moses and Aaron, why are you keeping these people from working? Look how many you are keeping from doing their work. Now everyone get back to work!"

6That same day the king gave orders to his Egyptian slave bosses and to the Israelite men directly in charge of the Israelite slaves. He told them:

7"Don't give the slaves any more straw[u] to put in their bricks. Force them to find their own straw wherever they can, 8but they must make the same number of bricks as before. They are lazy, or else they would not beg me to let them go and sacrifice to their God. 9Make them work so hard that they won't have time to listen to these lies.

10The slave bosses and the men in charge of the slaves went out and told them, "The king says he will not give you any more straw. 11Go and find your own straw wherever you can, but you must still make as many bricks as before."

12The slaves went all over Egypt, looking for straw. 13But the slave bosses were hard on them and kept saying, "Each day you have to make as many bricks as you did when you were given straw." 14The bosses beat the men in charge of the slaves and said, "Why didn't you force the slaves to make as many bricks yesterday and today as they did before?"

15Finally, the men in charge of the slaves went to the king and said, "Why are you treating us like this? 16No one brings us any straw, but we are still ordered to make the same number of bricks. We are beaten with whips, and your own people are to blame."

17The king replied, "You are lazy— nothing but lazy! That's why you keep asking me to let you go and sacrifice to your LORD. 18Get back to work! You won't be given straw, but you must still make the same number of bricks."

19The men knew they were in deep trouble when they were ordered to make the same number of bricks each day. 20After they left the king, they went to see Moses and Aaron, who had been waiting for them. 21Then the men said, "We hope the LORD will punish both of you for making the king and his officials hate us. Now they even have an excuse to kill us."

The LORD's Promise to Moses

22Moses left them and prayed, "Our LORD, why have you brought so much

[t]5.1 *the king:* See the note at 1.11.   [u]5.7 *straw:* The straw made the mud bricks stronger and kept them from shrinking, cracking, or losing their shape.

They bowed down and worshiped the LORD *because they knew that he had seen their suffering and was going to help them.* EXOD 4.31

trouble on your people? Is that why you sent me here? ²³Ever since you told me to speak to the king,ᵛ he has caused nothing but trouble for these people. And you haven't done a thing to help."

6 The LORD God told Moses:
Soon you will see what I will do to the king. Because of my mighty power, he will let my people go, and he will even chase them out of his country.

²My name is the LORD.ʷ ³But when I appeared to Abraham, Isaac, and Jacob, I came as God All-Powerful and did not use my name. ⁴I made an agreement and promised them the land of Canaan, where they were living as foreigners. ⁵Now I have seen how the people of Israel are suffering because of the Egyptians, and I will keep my promise.

⁶Here is my message for Israel: "I am the LORD! And with my mighty power I will punish the Egyptians and free you from slavery. ⁷I will accept you as my people, and I will be your God. Then you will know that I was the one who rescued you from the Egyptians. ⁸I will bring you into the land that I solemnly promised to Abraham, Isaac, and Jacob, and it will be yours. I am the LORD!"

⁹When Moses told this to the Israelites, they were too discouraged and mistreated to believe him.

¹⁰Then the LORD told Moses ¹¹to demand that the king of Egypt let the Israelites leave. ¹²But Moses replied, "I'm not a powerful speaker. If the Israelites won't listen to me, why should the king of Egypt?" ¹³But the LORD sent Aaron and

Moses with a message for the Israelites and for the king. He also ordered Aaron and Moses to free the people from Egypt.

Family Record of Aaron and Moses

¹⁴The following men were the heads of their ancestral clans:

The sons of Reuben, Jacob'sˣ oldest son, were Hanoch, Pallu, Hezron, and Carmi.

¹⁵The sons of Simeon were Jemuel, Jamin, Ohad, Jachin, Zohar, and Shaul, the son of a Canaanite woman.

¹⁶Levi lived to be 137; his sons were Gershon, Kohath, and Merari.

¹⁷Gershon's sons were Libni and Shimei.

¹⁸Kohath lived to be 133; his sons were Amram, Izhar, Hebron, and Uzziel.

¹⁹Merari's sons were Mahli and Mushi. All of the above were from the Levi tribe.

²⁰Amram lived to be 137. He married his father's sister Jochebed, and they had two sons, Aaron and Moses.

²¹Izhar's sons were Korah, Nepheg, and Zichri.

²²Uzziel's sons were Mishael, Elzaphan, and Sithri.

²³Aaron married Elisheba. She was the daughter of Amminadab and the sister of Nahshon; they had four sons, Nadab, Abihu, Eleazar, and Ithamar.

²⁴Korah's sons were Assir, Elkanah, and Abiasaph.

²⁵Aaron's son Eleazar married one of Putiel's daughters, and their son was Phinehas. This ends the list of those

6.3 *God All-Powerful:* In Hebrew "God All-Powerful" is *El Shaddai,* which means "God, the One of the Mountains" (Gen 35.9-11). *El* was one of the most common names for god among the Canaanites. The Canaanites did not believe that El was the only god, but they believed that he ruled over all the other gods. In the Jewish Scriptures/Old Testament this name frequently refers to the God of Israel.

6.14-25 *ancestral clans . . . sons of Reuben . . . Simeon . . . Levi tribe:* Ancestral clans are groups of extended families who are descended from a common male ancestor. Tribes are made up of all the clans who are descended from a single male ancestor (for Israelites, one of Jacob's sons). Only the three oldest of Jacob's twelve sons are mentioned in this list (genealogy), since the story is mainly concerned with describing the family history of Moses and Aaron. They were from the Levi tribe and so were part of the family that became Israel's priests.

Genealogies in the Bible

Israel

ᵛ**5.23** *the king:* See the note at 1.11. ʷ**6.2** *My name is the* LORD: See the note at 3.14,15. ˣ**6.14** *Jacob:* The Hebrew text has "Israel," Jacob's name after God renamed him.

"I am the LORD*! And with my mighty power I will punish the Egyptians and free you from slavery. I will accept you as my people, and I will be your God."* EXOD 6.6,7

7.1 *prophet:* A prophet is someone who speaks God's message. The message the prophet speaks is called a "prophecy." While the prophets of the Bible sometimes told what would happen in the future, they mainly observed what was happening around them and then delivered God's message for that situation. (See the article Prophets and Prophecy on pg 1791.)

7.3-4 *I will make the king so stubborn:* Throughout the story, the king acts in a stubborn way on his own (7.13,14,22; 8.15,19,32; 9.7), or the LORD acts to make the king even more stubborn (9.12; 10.1,20,27; 11.10; 14.8). The king's stubbornness leads to many disasters that reveal the power of Israel's God (9.16).

7.7 *80 years old:* Compare to 2.11, where Moses is said to be "grown up," meaning he was probably between 20 and 40 years old when he ran away from Egypt. He spent at least 40 years in Midian before returning to Egypt.

7.12 *swallowed:* When Aaron's walking stick swallowed the snakes thrown down by the magicians, it showed the LORD's power over the Egyptian gods. (See the article Miracles, Magic, and Medicine on pg 1820.)

7.19 *hold his stick over the water:* For Aaron to do this he needed to stretch out his arm. The outstretched arm is often a symbol of God's power or protection in the Bible (15.12,16; Deut 5.15; Isa 14.27; 40.10).

who were the heads of clans in the Levi tribe. **26**The LORD had commanded Aaron and Moses to lead every family and tribe of Israel out of Egypt, **27**and so they told the king of Egypt to set the people of Israel free.

The LORD Commands Moses and Aaron To Speak to the King

28When the LORD spoke to Moses in the land of Egypt, **29**he said, "I am the LORD. Tell the king^y of Egypt everything I say to you." **30**But Moses answered, "You know I am a very poor speaker, and the king will never listen to me."

7 The LORD said:
I am going to let your brother Aaron speak for you. He will tell your message to the king, just as a prophet speaks my message to the people. **2**Tell Aaron everything I say to you, and he will order the king to let my people leave his country. **3-4**But I will make the king so stubborn that he won't listen to you. He won't listen even when I do many terrible things to him and his nation. Then I will bring a final punishment on Egypt, and the king will let Israel's families and tribes go. **5**When this happens, the Egyptians will know that I am the LORD.

6Moses and Aaron obeyed the LORD **7**and spoke to the king. At the time, Moses was 80 years old, and Aaron was 83.

A Stick Turns into a Snake

8-9 The LORD said, "Moses, when the king^y asks you and Aaron to perform a miracle, command Aaron to throw his walking stick down in front of the king, and it will turn into a snake."

10Moses and Aaron went to the king and his officials and did exactly as the LORD had commanded—Aaron threw the stick down, and it turned into a snake. **11**Then the king called in the wise men and the magicians, who used their secret powers to do the same thing— **12**they threw down sticks that turned into snakes. But Aaron's snake swallowed theirs. **13**The king behaved just as the LORD had said and stubbornly refused to listen.

The Nile River Turns into Blood

14The LORD said to Moses:
The Egyptian king^y stubbornly refuses to change his mind and let the people go. **15**Tomorrow morning take the stick that turned into a snake, then wait beside the Nile River for the king. **16**Tell him, "The LORD God of the Hebrews sent me to order you to release his people, so they can worship him in the desert. But until now, you have paid no attention.

17"The LORD is going to do something to show you that he really is the LORD. I will strike the Nile with this stick, and the water will turn into blood. **18**The fish will die, the river will stink, and none of you Egyptians will be able to drink the water."

19Moses, then command Aaron to hold his stick over the water. And when he does, every drop of water in Egypt will turn into blood, including rivers, canals, ponds, and even the water in buckets and jars.

20Moses and Aaron obeyed the LORD. Aaron held out his stick, then struck the

^y 6.29; 7.8,9,14 *the king:* See the note at 1.11.

Nile, as the king and his officials watched. The river turned into blood, [21]the fish died, and the water smelled so bad that none of the Egyptians could drink it. Blood was everywhere in Egypt.

[22]But the Egyptian magicians used their secret powers to do the same thing. The king did just as the LORD had said—he stubbornly refused to listen. [23]Then he went back to his palace and never gave it a second thought. [24]The Egyptians had to dig holes along the banks of the Nile for drinking water, because water from the river was unfit to drink.

Frogs

[25]Seven days after the LORD had struck the Nile, [1]he said to Moses:

8 Go to the palace and tell the king[z] of Egypt that I order him to let my people go, so they can worship me. [2]If he refuses, I will cover his entire country with frogs. [3]Warn the king that the Nile will be full of frogs, and from there they will spread into the royal palace, including the king's bedroom and even his bed. Frogs will enter the homes of his officials and will find their way into ovens and into the bowls of bread dough. [4]Frogs will be crawling on everyone—the king, his officials, and every citizen of Egypt.

[5]Moses, now command Aaron to hold his stick over the water. Then frogs will come from all rivers, canals, and ponds in Egypt, and they will cover the land.

[6]Aaron obeyed, and suddenly frogs were everywhere in Egypt. [7]But the magicians used their secret powers to do the same thing.

[8]The king sent for Moses and Aaron and told them, "If you ask the LORD to take these frogs away from me and my people, I will let your people go and offer sacrifices to him."

[9]"All right," Moses answered. "You choose the time when I am to pray for the frogs to stop bothering you, your officials, and your people, and for them to leave your houses and be found only in the river."

[10]"Do it tomorrow!" the king replied.

"As you wish," Moses agreed. "Then everyone will discover that there is no god like the LORD, [11]and frogs will no longer be found anywhere, except in the Nile."

[12]After Moses and Aaron left the palace, Moses begged the LORD to do something about the frogs he had sent as punishment for the king. [13]The LORD listened to Moses, and the frogs died everywhere—in houses, yards, and fields. [14]The dead frogs were placed in piles, and the whole country began to stink. [15]But when the king saw that things were now better, he again did just as the LORD had said he would and stubbornly refused to listen to Moses and Aaron.

Gnats

[16]The LORD said to Moses, "Command Aaron to strike the ground with his walking stick, and everywhere in Egypt the dust will turn into gnats." [17]They obeyed, and when Aaron struck the ground with the stick, gnats started swarming on people and animals. In fact, every speck of dust in Egypt turned into a gnat. [18]When the magicians tried to use their secret powers to do this,[a] they failed, and gnats stayed on people and animals.

[z]8.1 *the king*: See the note at 1.11.   [a]8.18 *to do this*: Or "to get rid of the gnats."

7.19-24 *water in buckets and jars . . . dig holes*: Any water that came from streams, ponds, and irrigation canals fed by the river turned to blood, even water collected in buckets or jars. The Bible doesn't explain where the Egyptian magicians found fresh water to turn to blood. But the devastating effect of what Moses and Aaron had done by God's power was so great that the Egyptians had to dig wells to find underground water that didn't come from the river.

7.25 *Seven days*: The number "seven" symbolized completeness. (See the chart Numbers in the Bible on pg 1844.)

8.2 *frogs*: Frogs thrive in marshes and along rivers. They were known to be a nuisance in areas near the Nile River. A huge swarm of frogs was a disaster the people of Egypt would have been very familiar with, though the one described here was clearly bigger than usual.

8.5,6 *hold his stick over the water . . . Aaron obeyed*: Aaron not only speaks for Moses but also does the action that causes God's miracle to happen.

● 8.22-23 *Goshen:* The Egyptians made the Hebrew people live apart from the general Egyptian population, because Hebrew customs and habits were different from those of the Egyptians (Gen 43.32).

● 8.26 *would disgust the Egyptians:* Apparently, the Hebrews' religious practices, which included animal sacrifices, were considered disgusting by the Egyptians. Moses demanded that the Hebrew people go far away into the desert to offer sacrifices to God, so the Egyptians wouldn't be angered or disgusted by watching the sacrifices.

● 9.3 *terrible disease:* The exact disease is not known, but swarms of flies can carry disease-causing bacteria such as anthrax, which is deadly to animals that live in herds and flocks. The Egyptians worshiped certain animal-headed gods, such as Apis (bull), Mnevis (cow), and Khnum (ram). This disaster symbolized God's power over the Egyptian animal gods.

● 9.8 *ashes from a stove:* The stove was probably built out of bricks that had been hand-made by the Hebrew people. The type of sores or boils that affected the people may have been caused by the same kind of bacteria that caused the animals to get sick and die. In humans, this kind of bacteria can cause sores that burn and turn black, the color of soot or ashes.

¹⁹The magicians told the king,[b] "God has done this."

But, as the Lord had said, the king was too stubborn to listen.

Flies

²⁰The Lord said to Moses:

Early tomorrow morning, while the king[b] is on his way to the river, go and say to him, "The Lord commands you to let his people go, so they can worship him. ²¹If you don't, he will send swarms of flies to attack you, your officials, and every citizen of your country. Your houses will be full of flies, and the ground will crawl with them. ²²⁻²³"The Lord's people in Goshen won't be bothered by flies, but your people in the rest of the country will be tormented by them. That's how you will know that the Lord is here in Egypt. This miracle will happen tomorrow."

²⁴The Lord kept his promise—the palace and the homes of the royal officials swarmed with flies, and the rest of the country was infested with them as well. ²⁵Then the king sent for Moses and Aaron and told them, "Go ahead and sacrifice to your God, but stay here in Egypt."

²⁶"That's impossible!" Moses replied. "Any sacrifices we offer to the Lord our God would disgust the Egyptians, and they would stone us to death. ²⁷No indeed! The Lord has ordered us to walk three days into the desert before offering sacrifices to him, and that's what we have to do."

²⁸Then the king told him, "I'll let you go into the desert to offer sacrifices, if you don't go very far. But in the meantime, pray for me."

²⁹"Your Majesty," Moses replied, "I'll

[b]8.19,20; 9.1 *the king:* See the note at 1.11.

pray for you as soon as I leave, and by tomorrow the flies will stop bothering you, your officials, and the citizens of your country. Only make sure that you're telling the truth this time and that you really intend to let our people offer sacrifices to the Lord."

³⁰After leaving the palace, Moses prayed, ³¹and the Lord answered his prayer. Not a fly was left to pester the king, his officials, or anyone else in Egypt. ³²But the king turned stubborn again and would not let the people go.

Dead Animals

9 The Lord sent Moses with this message for the king[b] of Egypt:

The Lord God of the Hebrews commands you to let his people go, so they can worship him. ²If you keep refusing, ³he will bring a terrible disease on your horses and donkeys, your camels and cattle, and your sheep and goats. ⁴But the Lord will protect the animals that belong to the people of Israel, and none of theirs will die. ⁵Tomorrow is the day the Lord has set to do this.

⁶It happened the next day—all of the animals belonging to the Egyptians died, but the Israelites did not lose even one. ⁷When the king found out, he was still too stubborn to let the people go.

Sores

⁸The Lord said to Moses and Aaron:

Take a few handfuls of ashes from a stove and you, Moses, throw them into the air. Be sure the king is watching. ⁹The ashes will blow across the land of Egypt, causing sores to break out on people and animals.

[10]So they took a few handfuls of ashes and went to the king.[c] Moses threw them into the air, and sores immediately broke out on the Egyptians and their animals. [11]The magicians were suffering so much from the sores, that they could not even come to Moses. [12]Everything happened just as the Lord had told Moses—he made the king too stubborn to listen to Moses and Aaron.

Hailstones

[13]The Lord told Moses to get up early the next morning and say to the king:[c]

The Lord God of the Hebrews commands you to let his people go, so they can worship him! [14]If you don't, he will send his worst plagues to strike you, your officials, and everyone else in your country. Then you will find out that no one can oppose the Lord. [15]In fact, he could already have sent a terrible disease and wiped you from the face of the earth. [16]But he has kept you alive, just to show you his power and to bring honor to himself everywhere in the world.

[17]You are still determined not to let the Lord's people go. [18]All right. At this time tomorrow, he will bring on Egypt the worst hailstorm in its history. [19]You had better give orders for every person and every animal in Egypt to take shelter. If they don't, they will die.

[20]Some of the king's officials were frightened by what the Lord had said, and they hurried off to make sure their slaves and animals were safe. [21]But others paid no attention to his threats and left their slaves and animals out in the open.

[22]Then the Lord told Moses, "Stretch your arm toward the sky, so that hailstones will fall on people, animals, and crops in the land of Egypt." [23-24]Moses pointed his walking stick toward the sky, and hailstones started falling everywhere. Thunder roared, and lightning flashed back and forth, striking the ground. This was the worst storm in the history of Egypt. [25]People, animals, and crops were pounded by the hailstones, and bark was stripped from trees. [26]Only Goshen, where the Israelites lived, was safe from the storm.

[27]The king sent for Moses and Aaron and told them, "Now I have really sinned! My people and I are guilty, and the Lord is right. [28]We can't stand any more of this thunder and hail. Please ask the Lord to make it stop. Your people can go—you don't have to stay in Egypt any longer."

[29]Moses answered, "As soon as I leave the city, I will lift my arms in prayer. When the thunder and hail stop, you will know that the earth belongs to the Lord. [30]But I am certain that neither you nor your officials really fear the Lord God."

[31]Meanwhile, the flax and barley crops had been destroyed by the storm because they were ready to ripen. [32]But the wheat crops[d] ripen later, and they were not damaged.

[33]After Moses left the royal palace and the city, he lifted his arms in prayer to the Lord, and the thunder, hail, and drenching rain stopped. [34]When the king realized that the storm was over, he disobeyed once more. He and his officials were so stubborn [35]that he refused to let the Israelites go. This was exactly what the Lord had said would happen.

[c]9.10,13 *the king:* See the note at 1.11.   [d]9.32 *wheat crops:* The Hebrew text mentions two kinds of wheat.

■ 9.11 *magicians:* As the disasters continue, the power of the magicians decreases.

■ 9.16 *to show you his power:* The disasters God sent upon Egypt revealed God's power (Rom 9.17).

⊗ Disasters (Plagues)

● 9.18 *tomorrow:* Moses' announcement allows time for people who believed the threat to get their animals into shelter (9.20,21).

■ 9.22 *Stretch your arm toward the sky:* This was a common posture for prayer (see 9.29).

■ 9.27 *I have really sinned:* Sin is turning away from God and disobeying God's Law. The Egyptian king admits he is guilty of resisting God.

⊗ Sin

■ 9.30 *fear the Lord God:* The Hebrew word translated as "fear" also means "to respect" or "to honor." The Hebrew name translated as "God" here is *Elohim,* another name Israel used for the one true God.

⊗ Names of God

10.4 *locusts:* Locusts can cause severe food shortages called famines. In the spring, hungry young locusts often migrated west toward Egypt, blown by prevailing east winds (10.13). Locusts are described in the Bible as a symbol of God's judgment (see Joel 1.4-7; Amos 7.1-3; Mal 3.9-11).

Locusts

10.13 *east wind:* During the months of March and April, the most common winds in Egypt come from the dry areas to the east. (See Map 2 on pg 1880.)

10.17 *Forgive me:* To "forgive" means to remove any penalty or judgment that one deserves because of sinful actions. God's forgiveness not only removes this penalty but wipes out the guilt associated with the sin.

Sin

Locusts

10 The LORD said to Moses:
Go back to the king.[e] I have made him and his officials stubborn, so that I could work these miracles. [2]I did this because I want you to tell your children and your grandchildren about my miracles and about my harsh treatment of the Egyptians. Then all of you will know that I am the LORD.

[3]Moses and Aaron went to the king and told him that the LORD God of the Hebrews had said:

How long will you stubbornly refuse to obey? Release my people so they can worship me. [4]Do this by tomorrow, or I will cover your country with so many locusts[f] [5]that you won't be able to see the ground. Most of your crops were ruined by the hailstones, but these locusts will destroy what little is left, including the trees. [6]Your palace, the homes of your officials, and all the other houses in Egypt will overflow with more locusts than have ever been seen in this country.

After Moses left the palace, [7]the king's officials asked, "Your Majesty, how much longer is this man going to be a troublemaker? Why don't you let the people leave, so they can worship the LORD their God? Don't you know that Egypt is a disaster?"

[8]The king had Moses and Aaron brought back, and he said, "All right, you may go and worship the LORD your God. But first tell me who will be going."

[9]"Everyone, young and old," Moses answered. "We will even take our sheep, goats, and cattle, because we want to hold a celebration in honor of the LORD."

[10]The king replied, "The LORD had better watch over you on the day I let you leave with your families! You're up to no good. [11]Do you want to worship the LORD? All right, take only the men and go." Then Moses and Aaron were chased out of the palace.

[12]The LORD told Moses, "Stretch your arm toward Egypt. Swarms of locusts will come and eat everything left by the hail."

[13]Moses held out his walking stick, and the LORD sent an east wind that blew across Egypt the rest of the day and all that night. By morning, locusts [14]were swarming everywhere. Never before had there been so many locusts in Egypt, and never again will there be so many. [15]The ground was black with locusts, and they ate everything left on the trees and in the fields. Nothing green remained in Egypt—not a tree or a plant.

[16]At once the king sent for Moses and Aaron. He told them, "I have sinned against the LORD your God and against you. [17]Forgive me one more time and ask the LORD to stop these insects from killing every living plant."

[18]Moses left the palace and prayed. [19]Then the LORD sent a strong west wind[g] that swept the locusts into the Red Sea.[h] Not one locust was left anywhere in Egypt, [20]but the LORD made the king so stubborn that he still refused to let the Israelites go.

Darkness

[21]The LORD said to Moses, "Stretch your arm toward the sky, and everything will be

[e]**10.1** *the king:* See the note at 1.11. [f]**10.4** *locusts:* A type of grasshopper that comes in swarms and causes great damage to crops. [g]**10.19** *west wind:* The Hebrew text has "wind from the sea," referring to the Mediterranean Sea (see verse 13). [h]**10.19** *Red Sea:* Hebrew *yam suph,* here referring to the Gulf of Suez, since the term is extended to include the northwestern arm of the Red Sea (see also the note at 13.18).

covered with darkness thick enough to touch." [22]Moses stretched his arm toward the sky, and Egypt was covered with darkness for three days. [23]During that time, the Egyptians could not see each other or leave their homes, but there was light where the Israelites lived.

[24]The king[i] sent for Moses and told him, "Go worship the LORD! And take your families with you. Just leave your sheep, goats, and cattle."

[25]"No!" Moses replied. "You must let us offer sacrifices to the LORD our God, [26]and we won't know which animals we will need until we get there. That's why we can't leave even one of them here."

[27]This time the LORD made the king so stubborn [28]that he said to Moses, "Get out and stay out! If you ever come back, you're dead!"

[29]"Have it your way," Moses answered. "You won't see me again."

Moses Warns the Egyptians That the LORD Will Kill Their First-Born Sons

11 The LORD said to Moses:

I am going to punish the king[i] of Egypt and his people one more time. Then the king will gladly let you leave his land. In fact, he will even chase you out. [2]Now go and tell my people to ask their Egyptian neighbors for gold and silver jewelry.

[3]So the LORD made the Egyptians greatly respect the Israelites, and everyone, including the king's officials, considered Moses an important leader.

[4]Moses went to the king and said:

I have come to let you know what the LORD is going to do. About mid-night he will go through the land of Egypt, [5]and wherever he goes, the first-born son in every family will die. Your own son will die, and so will the son of the lowest slave woman. Even the first-born males of your cattle will die. [6]Everywhere in Egypt there will be loud crying. Nothing like this has ever happened before or will ever happen again.

[7]But there won't be any need for the Israelites to cry. Things will be so quiet that not even a dog will be heard barking. Then you Egyptians will know that the LORD is good to the Israelites, even while he punishes you. [8]Your leaders will come and bow down, begging me to take my people and leave your country. Then we will leave.

Moses was very angry; he turned and left the king.

[9]What the LORD had earlier said to Moses came true. He had said, "The king of Egypt won't listen. Then I will perform even more miracles." [10]So the king of Egypt saw Moses and Aaron work miracles, but the LORD made him stubbornly refuse to let the Israelites leave his country.

The Passover

12 Some time later the LORD said to Moses and Aaron:

[2]This month[j] is to be the first month of the year for you. [3]Tell the people of Israel that on the tenth day of this month the head of each family must choose a lamb or a young goat for his family to eat. [4-5]If any family is too small to eat the whole animal, they must share it with their next-door neighbors. Choose either a sheep or a

[i]10.24; 11.1 *The king*: See the note at 1.11.   [j]12.2 *This month*: Abib (also called Nisan), the first month of the Hebrew calendar, from about mid-March to mid-April.

10.22 *darkness:* The darkness could have been caused by the kind of blinding sandstorm that blows across Egypt from the desert in the early spring. See also Ps 105.28; Rev 16.10.

11.5 *lowest slave woman:* The "slave woman" here refers to a non-Hebrew slave woman whose task was grinding grain into flour by hand.

12.2 *first month of the year:* See the chart Pilgrimage Festivals on pg 1799.

12.4-5 *nothing wrong with it:* These animals had to be healthy and have no defects (see Lev 1.3,10).

12.7 *blood...put on the... door:* To protect themselves from God's final punishment of the Egyptians (11.4-6; 12.29,30).

12.8 *bitter herbs and thin bread:* The herbs probably were endive or chicory. Their bitter taste would remind the people of their bitter years as slaves in Egypt. Yeast is a tiny yellowish fungus that causes the dough to rise. Bread that has no yeast is flat and is called "thin bread." Thin bread was served at Passover as a reminder of how quickly the people had to leave Egypt. There wasn't even time to let the bread dough rise.

12.11 *Passover Festival:* The "Passover" is related to the Hebrew word translated as "pass over" in 12.13,27. This festival was celebrated as a remembrance of how God saved the people from the final disaster and helped them escape from slavery in Egypt.

Passover and the Festival of Thin Bread

12.24-25 *country promised to you:* This refers to Canaan. About 40 years passed from the time the Israelite people left Egypt until they finally entered the promised land of Canaan (Num 14.31-35).

goat, but it must be a one-year-old male that has nothing wrong with it. And it must be large enough for everyone to have some of the meat. [6]Each family must take care of its animal until the evening of the fourteenth day of the month, when the animals are to be killed. [7]Some of the blood must be put on the two doorposts and above the door of each house where the animals are to be eaten. [8]That night the animals are to be roasted and eaten, together with bitter herbs and thin bread made without yeast. [9]Don't eat the meat raw or boiled. The entire animal, including its head, legs, and insides, must be roasted. [10]Eat what you want that night, and the next morning burn whatever is left. [11]When you eat the meal, be dressed and ready to travel. Have your sandals on, carry your walking stick in your hand, and eat quickly. This is the Passover Festival in honor of me, your LORD.

[12]That same night I will pass through Egypt and kill the first-born son in every family and the first-born male of all animals. I am the LORD, and I will punish the gods of Egypt. [13]The blood on the houses will show me where you live, and when I see the blood, I will pass over you. Then you won't be bothered by the terrible disasters I will bring on Egypt.

[14]Remember this day and celebrate it each year as a festival in my honor. [15]For seven days you must eat bread made without yeast. And on the first of these seven days, you must remove all yeast from your homes. If you eat anything made with yeast during this festival, you will no longer be part of Israel. [16]Meet together for worship on the first and seventh days of the festi-

val. The only work you are allowed to do on either of these two days is that of preparing the bread.

[17]Celebrate this Festival of Thin Bread as a way of remembering the day that I brought your families and tribes out of Egypt. And do this each year. [18]Begin on the evening of the fourteenth day of the first month by eating bread made without yeast. Then continue this celebration until the evening of the twenty-first day. [19]During these seven days no yeast is allowed in anyone's home, whether they are native Israelites or not. If you are caught eating anything made with yeast, you will no longer be part of Israel. [20]Stay away from yeast, no matter where you live. No one is allowed to eat anything made with yeast!

[21]Moses called the leaders of Israel together and said:

Each family is to pick out a sheep and kill it for Passover. [22]Make a brush from a few small branches of a hyssop plant and dip the brush in the bowl that has the blood of the animal in it. Then brush some of the blood above the door and on the posts at each side of the door of your house. After this, everyone is to stay inside until morning.

[23]During that night the LORD will go through the country of Egypt and kill the first-born son in every Egyptian family. He will see where you have put the blood, and he will not come into your house. His angel that brings death will pass over and not kill your first-born sons.

[24-25]After you have entered the country promised to you by the LORD, you and your children must continue to celebrate Passover each year. [26]Your children will ask you, "What are we

celebrating?" ²⁷And you will answer, "The Passover animal is killed to honor the LORD. We do these things because on that night long ago the LORD passed over the homes of our people in Egypt. He killed the first-born sons of the Egyptians, but he spared our children from death."

After Moses finished speaking, the people of Israel knelt down and worshiped the LORD. ²⁸Then they left and did what Moses and Aaron had told them to do.

Death for the First-Born Sons

²⁹At midnight the LORD killed the first-born son of every Egyptian family, from the son of the king^k to the son of every prisoner in jail. He also killed the first-born male of every animal that belonged to the Egyptians.

³⁰That night the king, his officials, and everyone else in Egypt got up and started crying bitterly. In every Egyptian home, someone was dead.

The People of Israel Escape from Egypt

³¹During the night the king^k sent for Moses and Aaron and told them, "Get your people out of my country and leave us alone! Go and worship the LORD, as you have asked. ³²Take your sheep, goats, and cattle, and get out. But ask your God to be kind to me."

³³The Egyptians did everything they could to get the Israelites to leave their country as quickly as possible. They said, "Please hurry and leave. If you don't, we will all be dead." ³⁴So the Israelites quickly made some bread dough and put it in pans. But they did not mix any yeast in

^k**12.29,31** *the king*: See the note at 1.11.

the dough to make it rise. They wrapped cloth around the pans and carried them on their shoulders.

³⁵The Israelites had already done what Moses had told them to do. They had gone to their Egyptian neighbors and asked for gold and silver and for clothes. ³⁶The LORD had made the Egyptians friendly toward the people of Israel, and they gave them whatever they asked for. In this way they carried away the wealth of the Egyptians when they left Egypt.

³⁷The Israelites walked from the city of Rameses to the city of Succoth. There were about 600,000 of them, not counting women and children. ³⁸Many other people went with them as well, and there were also a lot of sheep, goats, and cattle. ³⁹They left Egypt in such a hurry that they did not have time to prepare any food except the bread dough made without yeast. So they baked it and made thin bread.

⁴⁰⁻⁴¹The LORD's people left Egypt exactly 430 years after they had arrived. ⁴²On that night the LORD kept watch for them, and on this same night each year Israel will always keep watch in honor of the LORD.

Instructions for Passover

⁴³The LORD gave Moses and Aaron the following instructions for celebrating Passover:

Only Israelites may eat the Passover meal.

⁴⁴Your slaves may eat the meal if they have been circumcised, ⁴⁵but no foreigners who work for you are allowed to have any.

⁴⁶The entire meal must be eaten inside, and no one may leave the house during the celebration.

No bones of the Passover lamb may

12.37 *Succoth*: In Hebrew "Succoth" means "booths." Its location is not certain, though it may have been near the area of Pithom.

12.44,45 *slaves . . . circumcised . . . foreigners*: Two groups of non-Israelites are mentioned in these verses. Even though the Israelites were slaves in Egypt, they apparently also had some slaves that they had bought from slave traders, such as the Midianites or Ishmaelites (Gen 37.28,36). Foreigners who lived and worked among the Israelite people were not circumcised and so could not eat the Passover meal.

13.9 *sign on your hand . . . forehead:* Identifying seals, rings, or ornaments were worn on the hands or head (see also 13.16; Deut 6.8; 11.18; Prov 3.3). This passage may have led to the later practice of writing Scripture texts on small pieces of parchment and putting them in small leather boxes called phylacteries. These were then strapped to the head and left arm before morning prayers (Deut 6.4-9; Matt 23.5).

Purity (Clean and Unclean)

be broken. ⁴⁷And all Israelites must take part in the meal. ⁴⁸If anyone who isn't an Israelite wants to celebrate Passover with you, every man and boy in that family must first be circumcised. Then they may join in the meal, just like native Israelites. No uncircumcised man or boy may eat the Passover meal! ⁴⁹This law applies both to native Israelites and to those foreigners who live among you. ⁵⁰The Israelites obeyed everything the LORD had commanded Moses and Aaron to tell them. ⁵¹And on that same day the LORD brought Israel's families and tribes out of Egypt.

Dedication of the First-Born

13 The LORD said to Moses, ²"Dedicate to me the first-born son of every family and the first-born males of your flocks and herds. These belong to me."

The Festival of Thin Bread

³⁻⁴Moses said to the people:

Remember this day in the month of Abib.¹ It is the day when the LORD's mighty power rescued you from Egypt, where you were slaves. Do not eat anything made with yeast. ⁵The LORD promised your ancestors that he would bring you into the land of the Canaanites, Hittites, Amorites, Hivites, and Jebusites. It is a land rich with milk and honey.

Each year during the month of Abib, celebrate these events in the following way: ⁶For seven days you are to eat bread made without yeast, and on the seventh day you are to celebrate a festival in honor of the LORD. ⁷During those seven days, you must not eat anything made with yeast or even have yeast anywhere near your homes. ⁸Then on the seventh day you must explain to your children that you do this because the LORD brought you out of Egypt.

⁹This celebration will be like wearing a sign on your hand or on your forehead, because then you will pass on to others the teaching of the LORD, whose mighty power brought you out of Egypt. ¹⁰Celebrate this festival each year at the same time.

¹¹The LORD will give you the land of the Canaanites, just as he promised you and your ancestors. ¹²From then on, you must give him every first-born son from your families and every first-born male from your animals, because these belong to him. ¹³You can spare the life of a first-born donkey^m by sacrificing a lamb; if you don't, you must break the donkey's neck. You must spare every first-born son.

¹⁴In the future your children will ask what this ceremony means. Explain it to them by saying, "The LORD used his mighty power to rescue us from slavery in Egypt. ¹⁵The king^n stubbornly refused to set us free, so the LORD killed the first-born male of every animal and the first-born son of every Egyptian family. This is why we sacrifice to the LORD every first-born

---

¹13.3,4 *Abib*: Or Nisan, the first month of the Hebrew calendar, from about mid-March to mid-April. ^{m}13.13 *donkey*: This was the only "unclean" animal that had to be spared; the first-born of all "clean" animals (sheep, goats, cattle) had to be sacrificed. Donkeys were important because they were the basic means of transportation. ^{n}13.15 *The king*: See the note at 1.11.

Moses said to the people: "Pass on to others the teaching of the LORD, whose mighty power brought you out of Egypt."
EXOD 13.9

male of every animal and save every first-born son."

¹⁶This ceremony will serve the same purpose as a sign on your hand or on your forehead to tell how the LORD's mighty power rescued us from Egypt.

The LORD Leads His People

¹⁷After the king^o had finally let the people go, the LORD did not lead them through Philistine territory,^P though that was the shortest way. God had said, "If they are attacked, they may decide to return to Egypt." ¹⁸So he led them around through the desert and toward the Red Sea.^q

The Israelites left Egypt, prepared for battle.

¹⁹Moses had them take the bones of Joseph, whose dying words had been, "God will come to your rescue, and when he does, be sure to take my bones with you."

²⁰The people of Israel left Succoth and camped at Etham at the border of Egypt near the desert. ²¹⁻²²During the day the LORD went ahead of his people in a thick cloud, and during the night he went ahead of them in a flaming fire. That way the LORD could lead them at all times, whether day or night.

The Israelites Cross the Red Sea

14 At Etham the LORD said to Moses:
²Tell the people of Israel to turn back

and camp across from Pi-Hahiroth near Baal-Zephon, between Migdol and the Red Sea.^r ³The king^s will think you were afraid to cross the desert and that you are wandering around, trying to find another way to leave the country. ⁴I will make the king stubborn again, and he will try to catch you. Then I will destroy him and his army. People everywhere will praise me for my victory, and the Egyptians will know that I really am the LORD.

The Israelites obeyed the LORD and camped where he told them.

⁵When the king of Egypt heard that the Israelites had finally left, he and his officials changed their minds and said, "Look what we have done! We let them get away, and they will no longer be our slaves."

⁶The king got his war chariot and army ready. ⁷He commanded his officers in charge of his 600 best chariots and all his other chariots to start after the Israelites. ⁸The LORD made the king so stubborn that he went after them, while the Israelites proudly^t went on their way. ⁹But the king's horses and chariots and soldiers caught up with them while they were camping by the Red Sea near Pi-Hahiroth and Baal-Zephon.

¹⁰When the Israelites saw the king coming with his army, they were frightened and begged the LORD for help. ¹¹They also complained to Moses, "Wasn't there enough room in Egypt to bury us? Is that why you brought us out here to die in the

---

^o**13.17** *the king*: See the note at 1.11.   ^P**13.17** *Philistine territory*: The shortest land route from the Nile Delta to Canaan; it was the southern section of the major road that led to Megiddo and then on to Mesopotamia by way of Asia Minor.   ^q**13.18** *Red Sea*: Hebrew *yam suph*, "Sea of Reeds," one of the marshes or fresh water lakes, near the eastern part of the Nile Delta. This identification is based on Exodus 13.17—14.9, which lists the towns on the route of the Israelites before crossing the sea. In the Greek translation of the Scriptures made about 200 B.C., the "Sea of Reeds" was named "Red Sea."   ^r**14.2** *Red Sea*: Hebrew *hayyam*, "the Sea," understood as *yam suph*, "Sea of Reeds" (see also the note at 13.18).   ^s**14.3** *The king*: See the note at 1.11.   ^t**14.8** *proudly*: Or "victoriously."

● **13.17,18** *Philistine territory... desert... Red Sea*: The Philistine territory was the narrow strip of land along the sea, bordering on the southwest part of Canaan. The Israelites could easily be attacked on this main road, so God led them southeast toward Succoth, Etham (13.20), and the Red Sea. **(See Map 2 on pg 1880.)**

● **14.2** *Pi-Hahiroth... Baal-Zephon... Migdol... Red Sea*: Pi-Hahiroth may have been an Egyptian temple site east of Baal-Zephon (Num 33.7). Baal was the Canaanite god, whose home was believed to be "Zaphon," or Mount Casius on the coast of northern Syria. Baal-Zephon may refer to an ancient temple site near one of the lakes in northern Sinai, either Menzaleh or Sarbonis. In Hebrew *Migdol* means "Tower," and may refer to a fort built along the northern Sinai coast, east of the lake area mentioned above. All of the locations mentioned seem to point to a water crossing in northern Sinai and not at the location today known as the Red Sea. **(See Map 2 on pg 1880.)**

● **14.6** *war chariot and army*: A war chariot had a single axle and two wheels, and was usually drawn by one or two horses. Two or three soldiers could ride in a chariot. The speed and mobility of chariots made it easy for chariot drivers to gain on fleeing enemy armies or to quickly change positions and attack their enemies from behind.

14.14 *The Lord will fight for you:* Israel's God is often described in the Jewish Scriptures/Old Testament as a warrior who fights for them (Exod 14.25; 15.3; Deut 1.30; Josh 10.14; 2 Sam 5.22-24; Ps 24.8).

Holy War (The Lord's Battles)

14.17 *chariots and cavalry:* Cavalry refers to warriors who ride on horseback. Because of their usefulness in warfare, horses were owned almost exclusively by kings, and the power of kings in the ancient world was often measured by the number of horses and chariots they had at their command.

14.19 *God's angel:* Likely refers to the cloud and pillar of fire that led the Israelites (see 13.21,22). In Hebrew the word for "angel" means "messenger." In 14.24, the Lord himself is said to be in the fiery cloud.

Angels

14.31 *servant Moses:* The Hebrew word for "servant" here refers to one who serves as a high official in the court of the Lord (Num 12.8; Deut 34.5). This title was used to describe other important Israelite leaders such as, the military leader Joshua (Josh 24.29), and Israel's greatest king, David (2 Sam 3.18).

15.1-21 *this song in praise:* Many scholars think that portions of the songs in this chapter, especially "Miriam's Song" (15.21), are some of the oldest writings in the entire Bible.

desert? Why did you bring us out of Egypt anyway? [12]While we were there, didn't we tell you to leave us alone? We'd rather be slaves in Egypt than die in this desert!"

[13]But Moses answered, "Don't be afraid! Be brave, and you will see the Lord save you today. These Egyptians will never bother you again. [14]The Lord will fight for you, and you won't have to do a thing."

[15]The Lord said to Moses, "Why do you keep calling out to me for help? Tell the Israelites to move forward. [16]Then hold your walking stick over the sea. The water will open up and make a road where they can walk through on dry ground. [17]I will make the Egyptians so stubborn that they will go after you. Then I will be praised because of what happens to the king and his chariots and cavalry. [18]The Egyptians will know for sure that I am the Lord."

[19]All this time God's angel had gone ahead of Israel's army, but now he moved behind them. A large cloud had also gone ahead of them, [20]but now it moved between the Egyptians and the Israelites. The cloud gave light to the Israelites, but made it dark for the Egyptians, and during the night they could not come any closer.

[21]Moses stretched his arm over the sea, and the Lord sent a strong east wind that blew all night until there was dry land where the water had been. The sea opened up, [22]and the Israelites walked through on dry land with a wall of water on each side.

[23]The Egyptian chariots and cavalry went after them. [24]But before daylight the Lord looked down at the Egyptian army from the fiery cloud and made them panic. [25]Their chariot wheels got stuck,[u] and it was hard for them to move. So the Egyptians said to one another, "Let's leave these

people alone! The Lord is on their side and is fighting against us."

[26]The Lord told Moses, "Stretch your arm toward the sea—the water will cover the Egyptians and their cavalry and chariots." [27]Moses stretched out his arm, and at daybreak the water rushed toward the Egyptians. They tried to run away, but the Lord drowned them in the sea. [28]The water came and covered the chariots, the cavalry, and the whole Egyptian army that had followed the Israelites into the sea. Not one of them was left alive. [29]But the sea had made a wall of water on each side of the Israelites, so they walked through on dry land.

[30]On that day, when the Israelites saw the bodies of the Egyptians washed up on the shore, they knew that the Lord had saved them. [31]Because of the mighty power he had used against the Egyptians, the Israelites worshiped him and trusted him and his servant Moses.

The Song of Moses

15 Moses and the Israelites sang this song in praise of the Lord:

I sing praises to the Lord
  for his great victory!
He has thrown the horses
  and their riders
    into the sea.
[2]The Lord is my strength,
  the reason for my song,
    because he has saved me.
I praise and honor the Lord—
  he is my God and the God
    of my ancestors.
[3]The Lord is his name,

[u]**14.25** *stuck:* The Samaritan Hebrew text and two ancient translations; Hebrew "came off."

and he is a warrior!
4He threw the chariots and army
of Egypt's king[v]
into the Red Sea,[w]
and he drowned the best
of the king's officers.
5They sank to the bottom
just like stones.

6With the tremendous force
of your right arm, our LORD,
you crushed your enemies.
7What a great victory was yours,
when you defeated everyone
who opposed you.
Your fiery anger wiped them out,
as though they were straw.
8You were so furious
that the sea piled up
like a wall,
and the ocean depths
curdled like cheese.

9Your enemies boasted
that they would
pursue and capture us,
divide up our possessions,
treat us as they wished,
then take out their swords
and kill us right there.
10But when you got furious,
they sank like lead,
swallowed by ocean waves.

11Our LORD, no other gods
compare with you—
Majestic and holy!
Fearsome and glorious!
Miracle worker!
12When you signaled
with your right hand,

your enemies were swallowed
deep into the earth.

13The people you rescued
were led by your powerful love
to your holy place.
14Nations learned of this
and trembled—
Philistines shook with horror.
15The leaders of Edom and of Moab
were terrified.
Everyone in Canaan fainted,
16   struck down by fear.
Our LORD, your powerful arm
kept them still as a rock
until the people you rescued
to be your very own
had marched by.

17You will let your people settle
on your own mountain,
where you chose to live
and to be worshiped.
18Our LORD, you will rule forever!

The Song of Miriam

19The LORD covered the royal Egyptian cavalry and chariots with the sea, after the Israelites had walked safely through on dry ground. 20Miriam the sister of Aaron was a prophet. So she took her tambourine and led the other women out to play their tambourines and to dance. 21Then she sang to them:

"Sing praises to the LORD
for his great victory!
He has thrown the horses
and their riders into the sea."

[v]15.4 *Egypt's king*: See the note at 1.11.   [w]15.4 *Red Sea*: See the note at 13.18.

15.6 *right arm*: In ancient times, the "right side" was thought to be the side of power.

15.13 *holy place*: This translates a Hebrew word that often refers to the place where shepherds live, or a field of green grass as in Psalm 23.2. Sometimes this word is used to describe the promised land of Canaan (13.5).

15.14,15 *Philistines . . . Edom . . . Moab*: The Philistine rulers were quite powerful and often battled with Israel in the days of the judges and later during the time of Israel's kings. The land of Edom, or Seir, was south and southeast of the Dead Sea. The Edomites descended from Esau (Gen 36.1-43). The descendants of Jacob (the Israelites) sometimes fought with the Edomites (Num 20.14-21; Obad 9,10). Moab was located to the east of the Dead Sea. The Moabites and Ammonites would later become enemies of Israel (Judg 10.11-18; 1 Sam 14.47,48; 2 Kgs 3.21-27; 2 Chr 20.10,11).

15.17 *your own mountain . . . worshiped*: This mountain probably refers to Mount Zion in Jerusalem. King Solomon built the first temple in which to worship the LORD on Mount Zion about 350 years after Moses led the Israelite people out of Egypt.

Zion

15.20 *Miriam . . . prophet*: Miriam is most likely the "older sister" who helped rescue the baby Moses by finding a Hebrew woman (Moses' own mother) to take care of him for the king's daughter who had found him in the Nile and adopted him (2.1-10).

15.22 *Shur Desert:* The Shur Desert was located east of Goshen in the northwestern part of the Sinai Peninsula. Moses probably found water at an oasis known as Marah (15.23), which today is often identified with a bitter spring at Hawwarah, located on the eastern shore of the Gulf of Suez. (See Map 2 on pg 1880.)

15.27—16.1 *Elim . . . Sinai Desert . . . Mount Sinai:* Elim means "large trees," and is often identified with the brook known as Gharandel, south of Hawwarah. The Sinai Desert stretches across the Sinai Peninsula between the Gulf of Suez and the Gulf of Aqaba.

16.8 *meat:* Refers to the meat of quails (see 16.13), small brown or sandy-colored birds that usually migrated to the region of Palestine in large flocks during March or April.

Bitter Water at Marah

[22]After the Israelites left the Red Sea,[x] Moses led them through the Shur Desert for three days, before finding water. [23]They did find water at Marah, but it was bitter, which is how that place got its name.[y] [24]The people complained and said, "Moses, what are we going to drink?"

[25]Moses asked the LORD for help, and the LORD told him to throw a certain piece of wood into the water. Moses did so, and the water became fit to drink.

At Marah the LORD tested his people and also gave them some laws and teachings. [26]Then he said, "I am the LORD your God, and I cure your diseases. If you obey me by doing right and by following my laws and teachings, I won't punish you with the diseases I sent on the Egyptians."

[27]Later the Israelites came to Elim, where there were twelve springs and 70 palm trees. So they camped there.

The LORD Sends Food from Heaven

16 On the fifteenth day of the second month after the Israelites had escaped from Egypt, they left Elim and started through the western edge of the Sinai Desert[z] in the direction of Mount Sinai. [2]There in the desert they started complaining to Moses and Aaron, [3]"We wish the LORD had killed us in Egypt. When we lived there, we could at least sit down and eat all the bread and meat we wanted. But you have brought us out here into this desert, where we are going to starve."

[4]The LORD said to Moses, "I will send bread[a] down from heaven like rain. Tell the people to go out each day and gather only enough for that day. That's how I will see if they obey me. [5]But on the sixth day of each week they must gather and cook twice as much."

[6]Moses and Aaron told the people, "This evening you will know that the LORD was the one who rescued you from Egypt. [7]And in the morning you will see his glorious power, because he has heard your complaints against him. Why should you grumble to us? Who are we?"

[8]Then Moses continued, "You will know it is the LORD when he gives you meat each evening and more than enough bread each morning. He is really the one you are complaining about, not us—we are nobodies—but the LORD has heard your complaints."

[9]Moses turned to Aaron and said, "Bring the people together, because the LORD has heard their complaints."

[10]Aaron was speaking to them, when everyone looked out toward the desert and saw the bright glory of the LORD in a cloud. [11]The LORD said to Moses, [12]"I have heard my people complain. Now tell them that each evening they will have meat and each morning they will have more than enough bread. Then they will know that I am the LORD their God."

[13]That evening a lot of quails came and landed everywhere in the camp, and the next morning dew covered the ground. [14]After the dew had gone, the desert was covered with thin flakes that looked like frost. [15]The people had never seen anything like this, and they started asking each other, "What is it?"[b]

Moses answered, "This is the bread that the LORD has given you to eat. [16]And he or-

[x]15.22 *Red Sea:* See the note at 13.18.   [y]15.23 *Marah . . . name:* In Hebrew "Marah" means "bitter."   [z]16.1 *the western edge of the Sinai Desert:* Hebrew "the Sin Desert."   [a]16.4 *bread:* This was something like a thin wafer, and it was called "manna," which in Hebrew means, "What is it?"   [b]16.15 *What is it:* See the note at 16.4.

The LORD said to Moses, "I will send bread down from heaven like rain." EXOD 16.4

ders you to gather about two quarts[c] for each person in your family—that should be more than enough."

[17]They did as they were told. Some gathered more and some gathered less. [18]Everyone had exactly what they needed, just the right amount.

[19]Moses told them not to keep any overnight. [20]Some of them disobeyed, but the next morning what they kept was stinking and full of worms, and Moses was angry.

[21]Each morning everyone gathered as much as they needed, and in the heat of the day the rest melted. [22]However, on the sixth day of the week, everyone gathered enough to have four quarts, instead of two. When the leaders reported this to Moses, [23]he told them that the LORD had said, "Tomorrow is the Sabbath, a sacred day of rest in honor of me. So gather all you want to bake or boil, and make sure you save enough for tomorrow."

[24]The people obeyed, and the next morning the food smelled fine and had no worms. [25]"You may eat the food," Moses said. "Today is the Sabbath in honor of the LORD, and there won't be any of this food on the ground today. [26]You will find it there for the first six days of the week, but not on the Sabbath."

[27]A few of the Israelites did go out to look for some, but there was none. [28]Then the LORD said, "Moses, how long will you people keep disobeying my laws and teachings? [29]Remember that I was the one who gave you the Sabbath. That's why on the sixth day I provide enough bread for two days. Everyone is to stay home and rest on the Sabbath." [30]And so they rested on the Sabbath.

[31]The Israelites called the bread manna.[d] It was white like coriander seed and delicious as wafers made with honey. [32]Moses told the people that the LORD had said, "Store up two quarts of this manna, because I want future generations to see the food I gave you during the time you were in the desert after I rescued you from Egypt."

[33]Then Moses told Aaron, "Put some manna in a jar and store it in the place of worship for future generations to see."

[34]Aaron followed the LORD's instructions and put the manna in front of the sacred chest for safekeeping. [35-36]The Israelites ate manna for 40 years, before they came to the border of Canaan that was a settled land.[e]

The LORD Gives Water from a Rock

17 The Israelites left the desert and moved from one place to another each time the LORD ordered them to. Once they camped at Rephidim,[f] but there was no water for them to drink.

[2]The people started complaining to Moses, "Give us some water!"

Moses replied, "Why are you complaining to me and trying to put the LORD to the test?"

[3]But the people were thirsty and kept on complaining, "Moses, did you bring us out of Egypt just to let us and our families and our animals die of thirst?"

[4]Then Moses prayed to the LORD, "What am I going to do with these people? They are about to stone me to death!"

[5]The LORD answered, "Take some of the leaders with you and go ahead of the rest of the people. Also take along the walking

16.23 *Sabbath:* The Sabbath was the seventh day of the week, and commemorated the day that God rested after finishing the work of creation (Gen 2.2,3). Sabbath means "rest" or to "stop working" and resting on the Sabbath became an important way for Jewish people to honor God (20.8-11; Deut 5.12-15). Picking up bread (manna), quails, or grain on the Sabbath would have been considered work, so it was forbidden. **(See the chart Pilgrimage Festivals on pg 1799.)**

16.33 *jar . . . in the place of worship:* Moses commands Aaron to do this, since he would later become the first high priest of Israel (28.1). The high priest was the only person who could place something near the sacred chest. This jar was said to be made of gold. The "place of worship" likely refers to the sacred tent (25–27), though the directions on how to make it had not yet been given to Moses.

16.34 *sacred chest:* The directions for building the sacred chest are given in Exodus 25.10-19.

The Sacred Chest

17.4 *stone me:* Piling or dropping stones on someone was one of the most common forms of capital punishment in Israelite society (Lev 24.23).

---

[c]**16.16** *two quarts:* The Hebrew measure is an omer. In the CEV "omer" is usually translated "two quarts." [d]**16.31** *manna:* See the note at 16.4. [e]**16.35,36** *land:* The Hebrew text adds, "An omer is one tenth of an ephah." See the note at 16.16. [f]**17.1** *Rephidim:* The last stopping place for the Israelites between the Red Sea and Mount Sinai; the exact location is not known.

17.7 *Massah . . . Meribah:* Compare this verse to Numbers 20.7-13 and Deuteronomy 6.16; 9.22. This location must have been near the base of Mount Sinai.

17.8-10 *Amalekites . . . Joshua . . . Hur:* The Amalekites were descendants of Amalek, grandson of Esau (Gen 36.15, 16). They were a nomadic people living mostly in the area south and east of the Dead Sea. In later times, the Amalekites raided the Israelites living in Canaan (Judg 6.1-35; 1 Sam 30.1-20). See also 1 Chr 4.41-43.

Joshua, whose name means "the LORD saves," was appointed to lead Israel after the death of Moses (Deut 1.38; 31.14; 34.9).

Not much is known about Hur, but this leader from the tribe of Judah must have been important to be standing on the hilltop with Moses and Aaron. Along with Aaron, Hur would later be responsible for resolving any arguments among the Israelites while Moses went up Mount Sinai to receive the Law from the LORD (24.14).

18.2-4 *Eliezer:* In Hebrew "Eliezer" means "God has helped me," a reference to how Moses was saved from the king of Egypt (1.22—2.15). See also Acts 7.29.

18.12 *offered sacrifices:* A portion of the food prepared for sacrifice was used in a meal of celebration. Meals were also a common way to complete an agreement (Gen 26.30; 31.54; Exod 24.11).

stick with which you struck the Nile River. [6]When you get to the rock at Mount Sinai,[g] I will be there with you. Strike the rock with the stick, and water will pour out for the people to drink." Moses did this while the leaders watched.

[7]The people had complained and tested the LORD by asking, "Is the LORD really with us?" So Moses named that place Massah, which means "testing" and Meribah, which means "complaining."

Israel Defeats the Amalekites

[8]When the Israelites were at Rephidim, they were attacked by the Amalekites. [9]So Moses told Joshua, "Have some men ready to attack the Amalekites tomorrow. I will stand on a hilltop, holding this walking stick that has the power of God."

[10]Joshua led the attack as Moses had commanded, while Moses, Aaron, and Hur stood on the hilltop. [11]The Israelites outfought the Amalekites as long as Moses held up his arms, but they started losing whenever he lowered them. [12]After a while, his arms were so tired that Aaron and Hur got a rock for him to sit on. Then they stood beside him and supported his arms in the same position until sunset. [13]That's how Joshua defeated the Amalekites.

[14]Afterwards, the LORD said to Moses, "Write an account of this victory and read it to Joshua. I want the Amalekites to be forgotten forever."

[15]Moses built an altar and named it "The LORD Gives Me Victory." [16]Then Moses explained, "This is because I depended on the LORD.[h] But in future generations, the LORD will fight the Amalekites again and again."

Jethro Visits Moses

18 Jethro was the priest of Midian and the father-in-law of Moses. He heard what the LORD God had done for Moses and his people, after rescuing them from Egypt.

[2-4]In the meantime, Moses had sent his wife Zipporah and her two sons to stay with Jethro, and he had welcomed them. Moses was still a foreigner in Midian when his first son was born, and so Moses said, "I'll name him Gershom."[i]

When his second son was born, Moses said, "I'll name him Eliezer,[j] because the God my father worshiped has saved me from the king of Egypt."[k]

[5-6]While Israel was camped in the desert near Mount Sinai,[l] Jethro sent Moses this message: "I am coming to visit you, and I am bringing your wife and two sons."

[7]When they arrived, Moses went out and bowed down in front of Jethro, then kissed him. After they had greeted each other, they went into the tent, [8]where Moses told him everything the LORD had done to protect Israel against the Egyptians and their king. He also told him how the LORD had helped them in all of their troubles.

[9]Jethro was so pleased to hear this good news about what the LORD had done, [10]that he shouted, "Praise the LORD! He rescued you and the Israelites from the Egyptians and their king. [11]Now I know that the LORD is the greatest God, because he has rescued Israel from their arrogant enemies." [12]Jethro offered sacrifices to God. Then Aaron and Israel's leaders came to eat with Jethro there at the place of worship.

[g]17.6 *Sinai:* The Hebrew text has "Horeb," another name for Sinai. [h]17.16 *This . . . LORD:* One possible meaning for the difficult Hebrew text. [i]18.2-4 *Gershom:* See the note at 2.22. [j]18.2-4 *Eliezer:* In Hebrew "Eliezer" means "God has helped me." [k]18.2-4 *saved . . . Egypt:* See 2.1-15. [l]18.5,6 *Mount Sinai:* Hebrew "the mountain of God."

Jethro shouted, "*Praise the LORD! He rescued you and the Israelites from the Egyptians and their king. Now I know that the LORD is the greatest God.*" EXOD 18.10,11

Judges Are Appointed
(Deuteronomy 1.9-18)

[13]The next morning Moses sat down at the place where he decided legal cases for the people, and everyone crowded around him until evening. [14]Jethro saw how much Moses had to do for the people, and he asked, "Why are you the only judge? Why do you let these people crowd around you from morning till evening?"

[15]Moses answered, "Because they come here to find out what God wants them to do. [16]They bring their complaints to me, and I make decisions on the basis of God's laws."

[17]Jethro replied:

That isn't the best way to do it. [18]You and the people who come to you will soon be worn out. The job is too much for one person; you can't do it alone. [19]God will help you if you follow my advice. You should be the one to speak to God for the people, [20]and you should teach them God's laws and show them what they must do to live right.

[21]You will need to appoint some competent leaders who respect God and are trustworthy and honest. Then put them over groups of 10, 50, 100, and 1,000. [22]These judges can handle the ordinary cases and bring the more difficult ones to you. Having them to share the load will make your work easier. [23]This is the way God wants it done. You won't be under nearly as much stress, and everyone else will return home feeling satisfied.

[24]Moses followed Jethro's advice. [25]He chose some competent leaders from every tribe in Israel and put them over groups of 10, 50, 100, and 1,000. [26]They served as judges, deciding the easy cases themselves, but bringing the more difficult ones to Moses.

[27]After Moses and his father-in-law Jethro had said goodbye to each other, Jethro returned home.

At Mount Sinai

19 [1-2]The Israelites left Rephidim[m] and arrived at the desert near Mount Sinai, where they set up camp at the foot of the mountain. This was two months after they had left Egypt.

[3]Moses went up the mountain to meet with the Lord God, who told him to say to the people:

[4]You saw what I did in Egypt, and you know how I brought you here to me, just as a mighty eagle carries its young. [5]Now if you will faithfully obey me, you will be my very own people. The whole world is mine, [6]but you will be my holy nation and serve me as priests.

Moses, that is what you must tell the Israelites.

[7]After Moses went back, he reported to the leaders what the Lord had said, [8]and they all promised, "We will do everything the Lord has commanded." So Moses told the Lord about this.

[9]The Lord said to Moses, "I will come to you in a thick cloud and let the people hear me speak to you. Then they will always trust you." Again Moses reported to the Lord what the people had said.

[10]Once more the Lord spoke to Moses:

Go back and tell the people that today and tomorrow they must get themselves ready to meet me. They

[m]**19.1,2** *Rephidim:* See the note at 17.1.

18.13-20 *legal cases . . . God's laws . . . live right:* This refers to disputes between Israelites that had to be settled by a judge. In the desert, the people turned to Moses as judge, but he couldn't do all the work of settling disputes by himself. Moses used God's laws. Though the laws had yet to be given in written form (chapter 20), the basis for some of the laws that governed the Israelites' life together were based, in part, on laws that existed in some other cultures of the day.

Law

19.3 *Lord God:* The Hebrew name translated as "God" here is *Elohim.* It is a plural form of *El,* and can refer to "gods," but here it is used with Lord (Yahweh) to refer to Israel's one true God.

Names of God

19.6 *priests:* Though the descendants of Aaron, the members of the Levi tribe, were officially appointed as Israel's priests (28.1; Num 18.20-32), all the people were God's holy people, which means that they had been chosen and set apart to serve God.

Israel's Priests

19.10 *get themselves ready . . . wash their clothes:* This refers to a ritual known as "consecration," which included washing clothes and the body to remove any trace of contact with something that had made them ritually unclean (19.14,15; Deut 23.10,11).

19.12 *touch any part of the mountain:* God's holiness has a physical aspect. There is danger in coming into contact with God's holiness. See also Heb 12.18-20.

19.15 *not to have sex:* Sex was not considered sinful, but was believed to make one ritually unclean for a day (Lev 15.18; Deut 23.10,11; 1 Sam 21.4,5).

20.1-3 *I am the LORD your God:* The Ten Commandments (20.2–17) are based on an ancient form of treaty between a ruler and his people. In such a treaty, the ruler identifies himself and refers to acts done on behalf of his people (20.2). Then the ruler gives the laws that the people are to live by in order to keep their part of the treaty. The ruler promises to protect and help the people, who promise in return to be loyal and obedient to the ruler alone.

Ten Commandments

Agreements (Covenants)

20.5 *idols:* Refers to objects made of wood, stone, or metal, commonly worshiped by many ancient peoples. No lifeless image could stand for Israel's God, who was a "living" God (Isa 44.9-20). See also Exod 34.17; Lev 19.3,4; 26.1; Deut 4.15-20; 27.15.

must wash their clothes [11] and be ready by the day after tomorrow, when I will come down to Mount Sinai, where all of them can see me. [12] Warn the people that they are forbidden to touch any part of the mountain. Anyone who does will be put to death, [13] either with stones or arrows, and no one must touch the body of the person being put to death in this way. Even an animal that touches this mountain must be put to death. You may go up the mountain only after a signal is given on the trumpet. [14] After Moses went down the mountain, he gave orders for the people to wash their clothes and make themselves acceptable to worship God. [15] He told them to be ready in three days and not to have sex in the meantime.

The LORD Comes to Mount Sinai

[16] On the morning of the third day there was thunder and lightning. A thick cloud covered the mountain, a loud trumpet blast was heard, and everyone in camp trembled with fear. [17] Moses led them out of the camp to meet God, and they stood at the foot of the mountain. [18] Mount Sinai was covered with smoke because the LORD had come down in a flaming fire. Smoke poured out of the mountain just like a furnace, and the whole mountain shook. [19] The trumpet blew louder and louder. Moses spoke, and God answered him with thunder.

[20] The LORD came down to the top of Mount Sinai and told Moses to meet him there. [21] Then he said, "Moses, go and warn the people not to cross the boundary that

you set at the foot of the mountain. They must not cross it to come and look at me, because if they do, many of them will die. [22] Only the priests may come near me, and they must obey strict rules before I let them. If they don't, they will be punished."

[23] Moses replied, "The people cannot come up the mountain. You warned us to stay away because it is holy."

[24] Then the LORD told Moses, "Go down and bring Aaron back here with you. But the priests and people must not try to push their way through, or I will rush at them like a flood!"

[25] After Moses had gone back down, he told the people what the LORD had said.

The Ten Commandments
(Deuteronomy 5.1-21)

20 God said to the people of Israel: [2] I am the LORD your God, the one who brought you out of Egypt where you were slaves.

[3] Do not worship any god except me. [4] Do not make idols that look like anything in the sky or on earth or in the ocean under the earth. [5] Don't bow down and worship idols. I am the LORD your God, and I demand all your love. If you reject me, I will punish your families for three or four generations. [6] But if you love me and obey my laws, I will be kind to your families for thousands of generations.

[7] Do not misuse my name.[n] I am the LORD your God, and I will punish anyone who misuses my name.

[8] Remember that the Sabbath Day belongs to me. [9] You have six days when you can do your work, [10] but the

[n]**20.7** *misuse my name:* Probably includes breaking promises, telling lies after swearing to tell the truth, using the LORD's name as a curse word or a magic formula, and trying to control the LORD by using his name.

God said to the people of Israel: "I am the LORD your God, the one who brought you out of Egypt where you were slaves. Do not worship any god except me." EXOD 20.1-3

seventh day of each week belongs to me, your God. No one is to work on that day—not you, your children, your slaves, your animals, or the foreigners who live in your towns. ¹¹In six days I made the sky, the earth, the oceans, and everything in them, but on the seventh day I rested. That's why I made the Sabbath a special day that belongs to me.

¹²Respect your father and your mother, and you will live a long time in the land I am giving you.

¹³Do not murder.

¹⁴Be faithful in marriage.

¹⁵Do not steal.

¹⁶Do not tell lies about others.

¹⁷Do not desire to possess anything that belongs to another person—not a house, a wife, a husband, a slave, an ox, a donkey, or anything else.

The People Are Afraid
(Deuteronomy 5.23-33)

¹⁸The people trembled with fear when they heard the thunder and the trumpet and saw the lightning and the smoke coming from the mountain. They stood a long way off ¹⁹and said to Moses, "If you speak to us, we will listen. But don't let God speak to us, or we will die!"

²⁰"Don't be afraid!" Moses replied. "God has come only to test you, so that by obeying him you won't sin." ²¹But when Moses went near the thick cloud where God was, the people stayed a long way off.

Idols and Altars

²²The LORD told Moses to say to the people of Israel:

With your own eyes you saw me speak to you from heaven. ²³So you must never make idols of silver or gold to worship in place of me.^o

²⁴Build an altar out of earth, and offer on it your sacrifices^p of sheep, goats, and cattle. Wherever I choose to be worshiped, I will come down to bless you. ²⁵If you ever build an altar for me out of stones, do not use any tools to chisel the stones, because that would make the altar unfit for use in worship. ²⁶And don't build an altar that requires steps; you might expose yourself when you climb up.

Hebrew Slaves
(Deuteronomy 15.12-18)

21 The LORD gave Moses the following laws for his people:
²If you buy a Hebrew slave, he must remain your slave for six years. But in the seventh year you must set him free, without cost to him. ³If he was single at the time you bought him, he alone must be set free. But if he was married at the time, both he and his wife must be given their freedom. ⁴If you give him a wife, and they have children, only the man himself must be set free; his wife and children remain the property of his owner.

⁵But suppose the slave loves his wife and children and his owner so much that he won't leave them. ⁶Then he must stand beside either the door or the doorpost at the

^o**20.23** *in place of me:* Or "together with me."   ^p**20.24** *sacrifices:* The Hebrew text mentions two types of sacrifices: Sacrifices to please the LORD (traditionally called "whole burnt offerings") and sacrifices to ask the LORD's blessing (traditionally called "peace offerings").

20.12 *Respect:* Children were expected to care for parents (Ps 91.15) and to show them the greatest respect (Lev 19.3,4; 20.9; Deut 27.14-26). Note that this command comes with a promise.

20.13 *murder:* Some modern translations substitute "kill," but this commandment does not forbid all forms of killing. Rather, it refers to taking a life without just cause.

20.20 *test . . . sin:* The visible presence of God in the thunder and smoke (19.16-19) tested the people's courage. But their fear was not to keep them from living up to their promises to trust the LORD God and to obey the LORD's commands.

20.26 *expose yourself:* Priests were to wear full-length clothes and special underwear (28.42). Unlike some of their ancient neighbors, the religion of Israel did not include sexual practices. This set the Israelites apart from other peoples and their religions. Requiring priests to remain fully covered in the presence of God may have been a way to make sure no such sexual practices entered Israel's religious rituals.

21.2 *slave:* The Israelites were not to keep other Hebrews as slaves longer than six years, unless the slave asked to continue serving his master. The slave's ear was pierced as a sign of his or her life-long commitment (21.6). See also Lev 25.39-46; Jer 34.8-20.

21.7,8 *young woman . . . bought back*: The rights of female slaves were protected. If she did not please her owner, the owner was obligated to sell her back to her family or to another Israelite who wished to marry her. A woman who became the wife of her owner's son was to be treated as part of the family.

21.13,14 *run for safety . . . holding on to my altar*: The "places" were towns set aside as places of refuge (Num 35.9-34; Deut 4.41-43; 19.1-13; Josh 20.1-9). The LORD's altar was like the cities of refuge. A person who caused accidental death could hold on to the horns of an altar and be protected from the death penalty, until proven guilty (1 Kgs 1.50-53; 2.28-34).

Safe Towns

place of worship,q while his owner punches a small hole through one of his ears with a sharp metal rod. This makes him a slave for life.

7A young woman who was sold by her father doesn't gain her freedom in the same way that a man does. **8**If she doesn't please the man who bought her to be his wife, he must let her be bought back.r He cannot sell her to foreigners; this would break the contract he made with her. **9**If he selects her as a wife for his son, he must treat her as his own daughter.

10If the man later marries another woman, he must continue to provide food and clothing for the one he bought and to treat her as a wife. **11**If he fails to do any of these things, she must be given her freedom without paying for it.

Murder and Other Violent Crimes

The LORD said:
12Death is the punishment for murder. **13**But if you did not intend to kill someone, and I, the LORD, let it happen anyway, you may run for safety to a place that I have set aside. **14**If you plan in advance to murder someone, there's no escape, not even by holding on to my altar.s You will be dragged off and killed.

15Death is the punishment for attacking your father or mother.

16Death is the punishment for kidnapping. If you sell the person you kidnapped, or if you are caught with that person, the penalty is death.

17Death is the punishment for cursing your father or mother.

18Suppose two of you are arguing, and you hit the other with either a rock or your fist, without causing a fatal injury. If the victim has to stay in bed, **19**and later has to use a stick when walking outside, you must pay for the loss of time and do what you can to help until the injury is completely healed. That's your only responsibility.

20Death is the punishment for beating to death any of your slaves. **21**However, if the slave lives a few days after the beating, you are not to be punished. After all, you have already lost the services of that slave who was your property.

22Suppose a pregnant woman suffers a miscarriaget as the result of an injury caused by someone who is fighting. If she isn't badly hurt, the one who injured her must pay whatever fine her husband demands and the judges approve. **23**But if she is seriously injured, the payment will be life for life, **24**eye for eye, tooth for tooth, hand for hand, foot for foot, **25**burn for burn, cut for cut, and bruise for bruise.

26If you hit one of your slaves and cause the loss of an eye, the slave must be set free. **27**The same law applies if you knock out a slave's tooth—the slave goes free.

28A bull that kills someone with its horns must be killed and its meat destroyed, but the owner of the bull isn't responsible for the death.

29Suppose you own a bull that has been in the habit of attacking people, but you have refused to keep it fenced in. If that bull kills someone, both you and the bull must be put to death by stoning. **30**However, you may save your own life by paying whatever fine is demanded. **31**This same

q21.6 *at the place of worship*: The Hebrew text has "in the presence of God," which probably refers to the place where God was worshiped. r21.8 *bought back*: Either by her family or by another Israelite who wanted to marry her. s21.14 *altar*: As a rule, anyone who ran to the altar was safe from the death penalty, until proven guilty. t21.22 *suffers a miscarriage*: Or "gives birth before her time."

law applies if the bull gores someone's son or daughter. ³²If the bull kills a slave, you must pay the slave owner 30 pieces of silver for the loss of the slave, and the bull must be killed by stoning.

³³Suppose someone's ox or donkey is killed by falling into an open pit that you dug or left uncovered on your property. ³⁴You must pay for the dead animal, and it becomes yours.

³⁵If your bull kills someone else's, yours must be sold. Then the money from your bull and the meat from the dead bull must be divided equally between you and the other owner.

³⁶If you refuse to fence in a bull that is known to attack others, you must replace any animal it kills, but the dead animal will belong to you.

Property Laws

The Lord said:

22 If you steal an ox and slaughter or sell it, you must replace it with five oxen; if you steal a sheep and slaughter it or sell it, you must replace it with four sheep. ²⁻⁴But if you cannot afford to replace the animals, you must be sold as a slave to pay for what you have stolen. If you steal an ox, donkey, or sheep, and are caught with it still alive, you must pay the owner double.

If you happen to kill a burglar who breaks into your home after dark, you are not guilty. But if you kill someone who breaks in during the day, you are guilty of murder.

⁵If you allow any of your animals to stray from your property and graze^u in someone else's field or vineyard, you must repay the damage from the best part of your own harvest of grapes and grain.

⁶If you carelessly let a fire spread from your property to someone else's, you must pay the owner for any crops or fields destroyed by the fire.

⁷Suppose a neighbor asks you to keep some silver or other valuables, and they are stolen from your house. If the thief is caught, the thief must repay double. ⁸But if the thief isn't caught, some judges^v will decide if you are the guilty one.

⁹Suppose two people claim to own the same ox or donkey or sheep or piece of clothing. Then the judges^w must decide the case, and the guilty person will pay the owner double.

¹⁰Suppose a neighbor who is going to be away asks you to keep a donkey or an ox or a sheep or some other animal, and it dies or gets injured or is stolen while no one is looking. ¹¹If you swear with me as your witness that you did not harm the animal, you do not have to replace it. Your word is enough. ¹²But if the animal was stolen while in your care, you must replace it. ¹³If the animal was attacked and killed by a wild animal, and you can show the remains of the dead animal to its owner, you do not have to replace it.

¹⁴Suppose you borrow an animal from a neighbor, and it gets injured or dies while the neighbor isn't around. Then you must replace it. ¹⁵But if something happens to the animal while the owner is present, you do not have to replace it. If you had leased the animal, the money you paid the owner will cover any harm done to it.

Laws for Everyday Life

The Lord said:

¹⁶Suppose a young woman has never had sex and isn't engaged. If a man talks

^u**22.5** *graze:* Or "eat everything." ^v**22.8** *some judges:* Or "I." ^w**22.9** *the judges:* Or "I."

22.1-4 *ox . . . sheep . . . donkey:* Good animals were highly valued by their owners and were a sign of wealth. Their loss threatened their owners' livelihood. In the ancient Babylonian law code of Hammurabi, a thief who could not repay what he or she had stolen would be put to death instead of being sold as a slave. **(See the article Trade and Travel on pg 1806.)**

22.2-4 *after dark . . . during the day:* Killing someone in defense of one's home during the night was allowed. During daylight, however, a person could identify a robber and later seek repayment. But killing the thief without giving the thief a chance to repay was considered murder.

22.5 *vineyard:* This is a place where grapes are grown on vines. Grape-growing and wine making would be an important part of Israel's economy once they settled in Canaan, the land God promised to them. See Num 13.23,24.

Wine

22.16,17 *bride price:* This payment showed that the bride now belonged to her husband's family and no longer to her father's. If the bride had already had sex, the bride price was meant to make up for the dishonor to the father whether or not he agreed to let his daughter marry the man she had slept with.

22.18 *witchcraft:* Witchcraft was forbidden by the Law of Moses (Lev 19.26), since relying on spirits or powers other than God showed a lack of faith in the one true God. See also Deut 18.10,11.

22.21 *foreigners:* The Israelites were to remember their experience as slaves in Egypt in order to act with fairness and justice toward non-Israelites and those in their society who could not easily take care of their own needs, such as widows and orphans. See also Exod 23.9; Lev 19.33,34; Deut 24.17,18.

Foreigners (Aliens)

23.6 *justice in court:* God's concern for justice toward all people, especially the poor, is clear in the Law of Moses and in the writings of Israel's prophets (Amos 5.21-24; Hos 6.6; Isa 1.10-17).

Justice

23.11,12 *seventh year . . . seventh day:* Every seventh year the people were to let the land rest, just as they were to rest every seventh day. This rest also provided for the poor who didn't own their own land.

her into having sex, he must pay the bride price[x] and marry her. [17]But if her father refuses to let her marry the man, the bride price must still be paid.

[18]Death is the punishment for witchcraft.

[19]Death is the punishment for having sex with an animal.

[20]Death is the punishment for offering sacrifices to any god except me.

[21]Do not mistreat or abuse foreigners who live among you. Remember, you were foreigners in Egypt.

[22]Do not mistreat widows or orphans. [23]If you do, they will beg for my help, and I will come to their rescue. [24]In fact, I will get so angry that I will kill your men and make widows of their wives and orphans of their children.

[25]Don't charge interest when you lend money to any of my people who are in need. [26]Before sunset you must return any coat taken as security for a loan, [27]because that is the only cover the poor have when they sleep at night. I am a merciful God, and when they call out to me, I will come to help them.

[28]Don't speak evil of me[y] or of the ruler of your people.

[29]Don't fail to give me the offerings of grain and wine that belong to me.[z]

Dedicate to me your first-born sons [30]and the first-born of your cattle and sheep. Let the animals stay with their mothers for seven days, then on the eighth day give them to me, your God.

[31]You are my chosen people, so don't eat the meat of any of your livestock that was killed by a wild animal. Instead, feed the meat to dogs.

Equal Justice for All

The LORD said:

23 Don't spread harmful rumors or help a criminal by giving false evidence.

[2]Always tell the truth in court, even if everyone else is[a] dishonest and stands in the way of justice. [3]And don't favor the poor, simply because they are poor.

[4]If you find an ox or a donkey that has wandered off, take it back where it belongs, even if the owner is your enemy.

[5]If a donkey is overloaded and falls down, you must do what you can to help, even if it belongs to someone who doesn't like you.[b]

[6]Make sure that the poor are given equal justice in court. [7]Don't bring false charges against anyone or sentence an innocent person to death. I won't forgive you if you do.

[8]Don't accept bribes. Judges are blinded and justice is twisted by bribes.

[9]Don't mistreat foreigners. You were foreigners in Egypt, and you know what it is like.

Laws for the Sabbath

The LORD said:

[10]Plant and harvest your crops for six years, [11]but let the land rest during the seventh year. The poor are to eat what they want from your fields, vineyards, and olive trees during that year, and when they have all they want from your fields, leave the rest for wild animals.

[12]Work the first six days of the week, but rest and relax on the seventh day. This law

[x]**22.16** *bride price:* It was the custom for a man to pay his wife's family a bride price before the actual wedding ceremony took place. [y]**22.28** *me:* Or "your judges." [z]**22.29** *Don't fail . . . me:* One possible meaning for the difficult Hebrew text. [a]**23.2** *everyone else is:* Or "the authorities are." [b]**23.5** *you:* One possible meaning for the difficult Hebrew text of verse 5.

The LORD said, "Do not mistreat or abuse foreigners who live among you. Remember, you were foreigners in Egypt."
EXOD 22.21

is not only for you, but for your oxen, donkeys, and slaves, as well as for any foreigners among you.

¹³Make certain that you obey everything I have said. Don't pray to other gods or even mention their names.

Three Annual Festivals

(Exodus 34.18-26; Deuteronomy 16.1-17)

The LORD said:

¹⁴Celebrate three festivals each year in my honor.

¹⁵Celebrate the Festival of Thin Bread by eating bread made without yeast, just as I have commanded.ᶜ Do this at the proper time during the month of Abib,ᵈ because it is the month when you left Egypt. And make certain that everyone brings the proper offerings.

¹⁶Celebrate the Harvest Festivalᵉ each spring when you start harvesting your wheat, and celebrate the Festival of Sheltersᶠ each autumn when you pick your fruit.

¹⁷Your men must come to these three festivals each year to worship me.

¹⁸Do not offer bread made with yeast when you sacrifice an animal to me. And make sure that the fat of the animal is burned that same day.

¹⁹Each year bring the best part of your first harvest to the place of worship.

Don't boil a young goat in its mother's milk.

A Promise and a Warning

The LORD said:

²⁰I am sending an angel to protect you and to lead you into the land I have ready for you. ²¹Carefully obey everything the angel says, because I am giving him complete authority, and he won't tolerate rebellion. ²²If you faithfully obey him, I will be a fierce enemy of your enemies. ²³My angel will lead you into the land of the Amorites, Hittites, Perizzites, Canaanites, Hivites, and Jebusites, and I will wipe them out. ²⁴Don't worship their gods or follow their customs. Instead, destroy their idols and shatter their stone images.

²⁵Worship only me, the LORD your God! I will bless you with plenty of food and water and keep you strong. ²⁶Your women will give birth to healthy children, and everyone will live a long life.

²⁷I will terrify those nations and make your enemies so confused that they will run from you. ²⁸I will make the Hivites, Canaanites, and Hittites panic as you approach. ²⁹But I won't do all this in the first year, because the land would become poor, and wild animals would be everywhere. ³⁰Instead, I will force out your enemies little by little and give your nation time to grow strong enough to take over the land.

³¹I will see that your borders reach from the Red Seaᵍ to the Euphrates River and from the Mediterranean Sea to the desert. I will let you defeat the people who live there, and you will force them out of the land. ³²But you must not make any agreements with them or with their gods.

ᶜ**23.15** *as I have commanded*: See 12.14-20.   ᵈ**23.15** *Abib*: See the note at 12.2.   ᵉ**23.16** *Harvest Festival*: Traditionally called the "Festival of Weeks" and known in New Testament times as "Pentecost." ᶠ**23.16** *Festival of Shelters*: The Hebrew text has "Festival of Ingathering" (so also in 34.22), which was the final harvesting of crops and fruits before the autumn rains began. But the usual name was "Festival of Shelters." ᵍ**23.31** *Red Sea*: Hebrew *yam suph*, here referring to the Gulf of Aqaba, since the term is extended to include the northeastern arm of the Red Sea (see also the note at 13.18).

23.14-17 *three festivals . . . Your men must come:* Although the Israelites would come to celebrate a number of festivals, the three festivals described here would continue to have special importance for the Jewish people. **(See the chart Pilgrimage Festivals on pg 1799.)**

Passover and the Festival of Thin Bread

23.23 *Amorites . . . Jebusites:* These peoples worshiped a number of different gods and made statues or special poles (34.13) honoring them. Israel was to worship God alone (20.3-6).

23.31 *Euphrates River:* The Euphrates River formed the western boundary of Mesopotamia. The desert here probably refers to the Southern Desert to the southeast of Canaan. Only during the time of King Solomon did Israel control the amount of land mentioned in this verse (1 Kgs 4.21). **(See Maps 2, 4, and 7 on pgs 1880, 1882, and 1885.)**

24.1-4 *Nadab and Abihu... 70... twelve tribes:* Nadab and Abihu were Aaron's oldest sons (6.23). Eleazar, not Nadab, would become high priest after Aaron because Nadab and Abihu were killed for disobeying the Lord (Lev 10.1,2; Num 3.4; 20.25-28). Seventy was considered a complete or full number. The leaders probably represented each of Israel's twelve tribes (see also 19.7).

Blood

24.11 *saw God:* Moses had been warned not to let the people come close enough to see God, because this could cause death (19.20-22). Only those selected to represent the people (Moses and the priests) could come into the presence of God. Here, Israel's leaders are allowed to see God up close. See also Ezek 44.3.

24.17-18 *40 days and nights:* The number 40 is an important number in the Bible. It stands for a long time or for a generation. **(See the chart Numbers in the Bible on pg 1844.)**

Fire

25.4-6 *blue, purple, and red wool... olive oil:* The colors of wool requested were considered royal colors because these shades of dyes were expensive to make.

Oil extracted from olives had many uses in the ancient world. It was used for cooking and food preparation, as fuel for lamps, and as an important ingredient in perfumes and medicinal ointments. As indicated here, it was also used for ceremonial purposes (ordaining priests and dedicating sacred objects).

33Don't let them stay in your land. They will trap you into sinning against me and worshiping their gods.

The People Agree To Obey God

24 The Lord said to Moses, "Come up to me on this mountain. Bring along Aaron, as well as his two sons Nadab and Abihu, and 70 of Israel's leaders. They must worship me at a distance, 2but you are to come near. Don't let anyone else come up."

3Moses gave the Lord's instructions to the people, and they all promised, "We will do everything the Lord has commanded!" 4Then Moses wrote down what the Lord had said.

The next morning Moses got up early. He built an altar at the foot of the mountain and set up a large stone for each of the twelve tribes of Israel. 5He also sent some young men to burn offerings and to sacrifice bulls as special offerings[h] to the Lord. 6Moses put half of the blood from the animals into bowls and sprinkled the rest on the altar. 7Then he read aloud the Lord's commands and promises, and the people shouted, "We will obey the Lord and do everything he has commanded!"

8Moses took the blood from the bowls and sprinkled it on the people. Next, he told them, "With this blood the Lord makes his agreement with you."

9Moses and Aaron, together with Nadab and Abihu and the 70 leaders, went up the mountain 10and saw the God of Israel. Under his feet was something that looked like a pavement made out of sapphire,[i] and it was as bright as the sky.

11Even though these leaders of Israel saw

God, he did not punish them. So they ate and drank.

Moses on Mount Sinai

12The Lord said to Moses, "Come up on the mountain and stay here for a while. I will give you the two flat stones on which I have written the laws that my people must obey." 13Moses and Joshua his assistant got ready, then Moses started up the mountain to meet with God.

14Moses had told the leaders, "Wait here until we come back. Aaron and Hur will be with you, and they can settle any arguments while we are away."

15When Moses went up on Mount Sinai, a cloud covered it, 16and the bright glory of the Lord came down and stayed there. The cloud covered the mountain for six days, and on the seventh day the Lord told Moses to come into the cloud. 17-18Moses did so and stayed there 40 days and nights. To the people, the Lord's glory looked like a blazing fire on top of the mountain.

The Sacred Tent
(Exodus 35.4-9)

25 The Lord said to Moses: 2Tell everyone in Israel who wants to give gifts that they must bring them to you. 3Here is a list of what you are to collect: Gold, silver, and bronze; 4blue, purple, and red wool; fine linen; goat hair; 5tanned ram skins; fine leather; acacia wood; 6olive oil for the lamp; sweet-smelling spices to mix with the incense and with the oil for dedicating the tent and ordaining the priests; 7and onyx[j] stones and other gems for the sacred vest and the

[h]24.5 *special offerings:* Often translated "peace offerings," which were to make peace between God and his people, who ate certain parts of the sacrificed animal. [i]24.10 *sapphire:* A precious stone, blue in color. [j]25.7 *onyx:* A precious stone with bands of different colors.

breastpiece. **8**I also want them to build a special place where I can live among my people. **9**Make it and its furnishings exactly like the pattern I will show you.

The Sacred Chest
(Exodus 37.1-9)

The LORD said to Moses:

10Tell the people to build a chest of acacia wood 45 inches long, 27 inches wide, and 27 inches high. **11**Cover it inside and out with pure gold and put a gold edging around the lid. **12**Make four gold rings and attach one of them to each of the four legs of the chest. **13**Make two poles of acacia wood. Cover them with gold **14**and put them through the rings, so the chest can be carried by the poles. **15**Don't ever remove the poles from the rings. **16**When I give you the Ten Commandments written on two flat stones, put them inside the chest.

17Make the lid of the chest out of pure gold. **18-19**Then hammer out two winged creatures of pure gold and fasten them to the lid at the ends of the chest. **20**The creatures must face each other with their wings spread over the chest. **21**Inside it place the two flat stones with the Ten Commandments on them and put the gold lid on top of the chest. **22**I will meet you there**k** between the two creatures and tell you what my people must do and what they must not do.

The Table for the Sacred Bread
(Exodus 37.10-16)

The LORD said:

23Make a table of acacia wood 36 inches long, 18 inches wide, and 27 inches high.

24-25 Cover it with pure gold and put a gold edging around it with a border 3 inches wide.**l** **26**Make four gold rings and attach one to each of the legs **27-28**near the edging. The poles for carrying the table are to be placed through these rings and are to be made of acacia wood covered with gold. **29-30**The table is to be kept in the holy place, and the sacred loaves of bread must always be on it. All bowls, plates, jars, and cups for wine offerings are to be made of pure gold and set on this table.

The Lampstand
(Exodus 37.17-24)

The LORD said:

31Make a lampstand of pure gold. The whole lampstand, including its decorative flowers, must be made from a single piece of hammered gold **32**with three branches on each of its two sides. **33**There are to be three decorative almond blossoms on each branch **34**and four on the stem. **35**There must also be a blossom where each pair of branches comes out from the stem. **36**The lampstand, including its branches and decorative flowers, must be made from a single piece of hammered pure gold. **37**The lamp on the top and those at the end of each of its six branches must be made so as to shine toward the front of the lampstand. **38**The tongs and trays for taking care of the lamps are to be made of pure gold. **39**The lampstand and its equipment will require 75 pounds of pure gold, **40**and they must be made according to the pattern I showed you on the mountain.

k25.22 *I will meet you there:* It was believed that God had his earthly throne on the lid of the sacred chest. **l**25.24,25 *a gold edging . . . wide:* Or "a gold edging around it 3 inches wide."

26.1-8 *sacred tent...linen... winged creatures...goat hair:* This sacred tent was the place where the people were to meet God (29.42,43), who lived among the people (Exod 25.8). The sacred tent is traditionally called the "tabernacle," which means "dwelling place." It became the place of worship, where the people brought gifts and priests offered sacrifices to God. The tent's curtains were made of fine red, blue, or purple linen and were decorated with winged creatures like those that were on the lid of the sacred chest. The tent itself was made of coarse goat hair woven in eleven sections, ram skins dyed red, and fine leather.

The Sacred Tent

26.15-30 *framework of acacia wood:* The tent was supported by a framework of acacia wood slats or frames placed on heavy silver stands and connected with five crossbars.

26.31-34 *curtain...holy place... most holy place:* Inside the tent, a linen curtain was hung to separate the holy place, which contained the table for the sacred bread, the lampstand, the altar of incense (30.1-6), and the lamp (27.20, 21), from the most holy place, where it was believed that God had his earthly throne on the lid of the sacred chest.

26.36 *entrance:* The entrance was made of fine linen, embroidered with wool, not woven like the curtain separating the holy spaces inside the tent (see 26.31-34).

Curtains and Coverings for the Sacred Tent

(Exodus 36.8-19)

The LORD said to Moses:

26 The top of the sacred tent must be made from ten pieces of the finest linen, woven with blue, purple, and red wool and embroidered with figures of winged creatures. **2**Make each piece 14 yards long and 2 yards wide **3**and sew them together into two panels with five sections each. **4-6**Put 50 loops of blue cloth along one of the wider sides of each panel, then fasten the two panels at the loops with 50 gold hooks.

7-8 As the material for protecting the tent, use goat hair to weave eleven sections of cloth 15 yards by 2 yards each. **9**Sew five of the sections together to make one panel. Then sew the other six together to make a second panel, and fold the sixth section double over the front of the tent. **10**Put 50 loops along one of the wider sides of each panel **11**and fasten the two panels at the loops with 50 bronze hooks. **12-13**The panel of goat hair will be a yard longer than the tent itself, so fold half a yard of the material behind the tent and on each side as a protective covering. **14**Make two more coverings—one with tanned ram skins and the other with fine leather.

The Framework for the Sacred Tent

(Exodus 36.20-34)

The LORD said:

15Build a framework of acacia wood for the walls of the sacred tent. **16**Make each frame 15 feet high and 27 inches wide **17**with two wooden pegs near the bottom.

18-21 Place two silver stands under each frame with sockets for the pegs, so the frames can be joined together. Put 20 of these frames along the south side and 20 more along the north. **22**For the back wall along the west side use six frames **23-24**with two more at the southwest and northwest corners. Make certain that these corner frames are joined from top to bottom. **25**Altogether, this back wall will have eight frames with two silver stands under each one.

26-27 Make five crossbars for each of the wooden frames, **28**with the center crossbar running the full length of the wall. **29**Cover the frames and the crossbars with gold and attach gold rings to the frames to run the crossbars through. **30**Then set up the tent in the way I showed you on the mountain.

The Curtain inside the Sacred Tent

(Exodus 36.35-38)

The LORD said:

31-33 Make a curtain to separate the holy place from the most holy place. Use fine linen woven with blue, purple, and red wool, and embroidered with figures of winged creatures. Cover four acacia wood posts with gold and set them each on a silver stand. Then fasten gold hooks to the posts and hang the curtain there.

34Inside the most holy place, put the sacred chest that has the place of mercy on its lid.[m] **35**Outside the most holy place, as you face the curtain, put the table for the sacred bread on the right side and the gold lampstand on the left.

36For the entrance to the tent, use a piece of fine linen woven with blue, purple, and red wool and embroidered with fancy

---

[m]**26.34** *place of mercy on its lid:* It was believed that God had his earthly throne on the lid of the sacred chest, and from this place he showed mercy to his people.

needlework. **37**Cover five acacia wood posts with gold and set them each on a bronze stand. Then put gold hooks on the posts and hang the curtain there.

The Altar for Offering Sacrifices
(Exodus 38.1-7)

The LORD said to Moses:

27 Use acacia wood to build an altar seven and a half feet square and four and a half feet high, **2**and make each of the four top corners stick up like the horn of a bull. Then cover the whole altar with bronze, including the four horns. **3**All the equipment for the altar must also be made of bronze—the pans for the hot ashes, the shovels, the sprinkling bowls, the meat forks, and the fire pans. **4-5**Halfway up the altar build a ledge around it, and cover the bottom half of the altar with a decorative bronze grating. Then attach a bronze ring beneath the ledge at the four corners of the altar. **6-7**Cover two acacia wood poles with bronze and put them through the rings for carrying the altar. **8**Construct the altar in the shape of an open box, just as you were shown on the mountain.

The Courtyard around the Sacred Tent
(Exodus 38.9-20)

The LORD said:

9-15 Surround the sacred tent with a courtyard 150 feet long on the south and north and 75 feet wide on the east and west. Use 20 bronze posts on bronze stands for the south and north and ten for the west. Then hang a curtain of fine linen on the posts along each of these three sides by using silver hooks and rods.

Place three bronze posts on each side of the entrance at the east and hang a curtain seven and a half yards wide on each set of posts. **16**Use four more of these posts for the entrance way, then hang on them an embroidered curtain of fine linen ten yards long and woven with blue, purple, and red wool.

17-18 Make the curtains that surround the courtyard two and a half yards high and hang them from the bronze posts with silver hooks and rods. **19**Make the rest of the equipment for the sacred tent of bronze, including the pegs for the tent and for the curtain surrounding the courtyard.

The Oil for the Lamp in the Holy Place
(Leviticus 24.1-4)

The LORD said to Moses:

20Command the people of Israel to supply you with the purest olive oil. Do this so the lamp will keep burning **21**in front of the curtain that separates the holy place from the most holy place, where the sacred chest is kept. Aaron and his sons are responsible for keeping the lamp burning every night in the sacred tent. The Israelites must always obey this command.

The Clothes for the High Priest
(Exodus 39.1-7)

The LORD said to Moses:

28 Send for your brother Aaron and his sons Nadab, Abihu, Eleazar, and Ithamar. They are the ones I have chosen from Israel to serve as my priests. **2**Make Aaron some beautiful clothes that are worthy of a high priest. **3**Aaron is to be dedicated as my high priest, and his clothes must be made only by persons who possess skills that I have given them. **4**Here are the items that need to be made: a breastpiece, a priestly vest, a robe, an embroidered shirt, a turban, and a sash. These sacred clothes are to be made for your brother Aaron and his

27.9-15 *courtyard:* The courtyard surrounding the sacred tent was about half the size of an American football field. The curtain surrounding the courtyard was about seven and a half feet high (27.17,18), or about half the height of the tent itself. In the courtyard were the bronze altar (27.1-7) and the large bronze bowl used by the priests to wash their hands and feet (30.18-21). The sacred tent took up the western half of the courtyard, and the bronze altar of sacrifice was in the middle of the eastern half. The entrance to the courtyard was on the east end of the courtyard, so the tent opening faced east toward the rising sun.

27.20 *lamp:* The lamp in the holy place was probably a simple oil lamp that had to be filled with enough oil at sunset so it would burn until sunrise, when it was likely put out (see 30.8,9; 1 Sam 3.3). This lamp symbolized God's presence in the sacred tent.

Israel's Priests

28.2 *clothes . . . worthy of a high priest:* The clothes are described in detail in Exodus 28.4-39. Israel's high priest was in charge of the other priests and was the only one who could enter the most holy place in the sacred tent (Lev 16.1-19). Aaron would later be "dedicated" as Israel's first high priest (see 29.5-7).

28.6-8 *priestly vest:* This vest, sometimes referred to as an "ephod," was made of fine linen woven with royal shades of wool. The sash was like a wide belt used to help hold the vest in place. On the shoulder straps two onyx stones were engraved with the names of the twelve tribes of Israel. **(See the article People of the Law: The Religion of Israel on pg 1794.)**

Israel

28.15 *breastpiece:* The breastpiece was like a flat wool and linen pouch that contained an inner pocket, formed by doubling over the material (28.16). In the pouch were kept the small objects used to receive answers from God.

28.31-35 *robe . . . pomegranates . . . bells:* The long robe made of blue wool was worn under the vest. At the bottom of the robe were to be woven shapes in the form of pomegranates. One was not supposed to approach earthly rulers without being formally announced. The sound of the bells was intended to announce to God that the high priest was coming into the holy place. The sound of the bells also let people outside the holy place know that the high priest was still alive and moving about.

sons who will be my priests. [5]Use only gold and fine linen, woven with blue, purple, and red wool, for making these clothes.

The Vest for the High Priest
(Exodus 39.2-7)

The LORD said:

[6-8]Make the entire priestly vest of fine linen skillfully woven with blue, purple, and red wool, and decorate it with gold. It is to have two shoulder straps to support it and a sash that fastens around the waist. [9-12]Put two onyx[n] stones in gold settings, then attach one to each of the shoulder straps. On one of these stones engrave the names of Israel's first six sons in the order of their birth. And do the same with his remaining six sons on the other stone. In this way Aaron will always carry the names of the tribes of Israel when he enters the holy place, and I will never forget my people. [13-14]Attach two gold settings to the shoulder straps and fasten them with two braided chains of pure gold.

The Breastpiece for the High Priest
(Exodus 39.8-21)

The LORD said:

[15]From the same costly material make a breastpiece for the high priest to use in finding out what I want my people to do. [16]It is to be nine inches square and folded double [17]with four rows of three precious stones: In the first row put a carnelian, a

chrysolite, and an emerald; [18]in the second row a turquoise, a sapphire, and a diamond; [19]in the third row a jacinth, an agate, and an amethyst; [20]and in the fourth row a beryl, an onyx, and a jasper.[o] Mount the stones in delicate gold settings [21]and engrave on each of them the name of one of the twelve tribes of Israel.

[22-25]Attach two gold rings to the upper front corners of the breastpiece and fasten them with two braided gold chains to gold settings on the shoulder straps. [26]Attach two other gold rings to the lower inside corners next to the vest [27]and two more near the bottom of the shoulder straps right above the sash. [28]Then take a blue cord and tie the two lower rings on the breastpiece to those on the vest. This will keep the breastpiece in place.

[29]In this way Aaron will have the names of the twelve tribes of Israel written on his heart each time he enters the holy place, and I will never forget my people. [30]He must also wear on his breastpiece the two small objects[p] that he uses to receive answers from me.

The Other High-Priestly Clothes
(Exodus 39.22-26,30,31)

The LORD said:

[31]Under his vest Aaron must wear a robe of blue wool [32]with an opening in the center for his head. Be sure to bind the material around the collar to keep it from wearing out. [33-34]Along the hem of the robe weave pomegranates[q] of blue, purple,

[n]**28.9-12** *onyx:* See the note at 25.7.   [o]**28.20** *jasper:* The stones mentioned in verses 17-20 are of different colors: *carnelian* is deep red or reddish white; *chrysolite* is olive green; *emerald* is green; *turquoise* is blue or blue green; *sapphire* is blue; *diamond* is colorless or white; *jacinth* is reddish orange; *agate* has circles of brown and white; *amethyst* is deep purple; *beryl* is green or bluish green; *onyx* has bands of different colors; and *jasper* is usually green or clear.   [p]**28.30** *two small objects:* The Hebrew text has "urim and thummim," which may have been made of wood, stone, or metal, and were used in some way to receive answers from God.   [q]**28.33,34** *pomegranates:* A bright red fruit that looks like an apple.

and red wool with a gold bell between each of them. ³⁵If Aaron wears these clothes when he enters the holy place as my high priest, the sound of the bells will be heard, and his life will not be in danger.

³⁶On a narrow strip of pure gold engrave the words: "Dedicated to the LORD." ³⁷Fasten it to the front of Aaron's turban with a blue cord, ³⁸so he can wear it on his forehead. This will show that he will take on himself the guilt for any sins the people of Israel commit in offering their gifts to me, and I will forgive them.

³⁹Make Aaron's robe and turban of fine linen and decorate his sash with fancy needlework.

The Clothes for the Other Priests
(Exodus 39.27-29)

⁴⁰Since Aaron's sons are priests, they should also look dignified. So make robes, sashes, and special caps for them. ⁴¹Then dress Aaron and his sons in these clothes, pour olive oil on their heads, and ordain them as my priests.

⁴²Make linen shorts for them that reach from the waist down to the thigh, so they won't expose themselves. ⁴³Whenever they enter the sacred tent or serve at the altar or enter the holy place, they must wear these shorts, or else they will be guilty and die. This same rule applies to any of their descendants who serve as priests.

Instructions for Ordaining Priests
(Leviticus 8.1-36)

The LORD said to Moses:

29 When you ordain Aaron and his sons to serve me as priests, choose a young bull and two rams that have nothing wrong with them. ²Then from your finest flour make three batches of dough without yeast. Shape some of it into larger loaves, some into smaller loaves mixed with olive oil, and the rest into thin wafers brushed with oil. ³Put all of this bread in a basket and bring it when you come to sacrifice the three animals to me.

⁴Bring Aaron and his sons to the entrance of the sacred tent and tell them to wash themselves. ⁵Dress Aaron in the priestly shirt, the robe that goes under the sacred vest, the vest itself, the breastpiece, and the sash. ⁶Put on his turban with its narrow strip of engraved gold ⁷and then ordain him by pouring olive oil on his head.

⁸Next, dress Aaron's sons in their special shirts, ⁹caps, and sashes,ʳ then ordain them, because they and their descendants will always be priests.

¹⁰Lead the bull to the entrance of the sacred tent, where Aaron and his sons will lay their hands on its head. ¹¹Kill the bull near my altar in front of the tent. ¹²Use a finger to smear some of its blood on each of the four corners of the altar and pour out the rest of the blood on the ground next to the altar. ¹³Then take the fat from the animal's insides, as well as the lower part of the liver and the two kidneys with their fat, and send them up as an offering to me in the smoke from the altar. ¹⁴But the meat, the skin, and the food still in the bull's stomach must be burned outside the camp as an offering to ask forgiveness for the sins of the priests.ˢ

¹⁵Bring one of the rams to Aaron and his sons and tell them to lay their hands on its head. ¹⁶Kill the ram and splatter its blood against all four sides of the altar. ¹⁷Cut up

ʳ**29.9** *sashes:* One ancient translation; Hebrew "the sashes of Aaron and his sons." ˢ**29.14** *for the sins of the priests:* When a sacrifice for the forgiveness of sins was made for someone other than priests, the part that was not burned on the altar could be eaten by the priests (see Leviticus 5.13; 6.26).

◼ **28.38** *take on himself the guilt . . . sins:* If an Israelite or one of the priests mistakenly sinned, that is, did not follow proper procedures while offering a sacrifice, his error (sin) would fall on the high priest's head, at least in a symbolic way (see Lev 22.3, for example). So, the gold plate may have been thought to act as a sort of magnet, attracting these improper actions.

◉ Israel's Priests

◼ **29.1** *ordain:* To ordain meant "to choose and to set apart for a special purpose." Olive oil was poured on the head of the person who was being ordained or chosen (28.41; 29.7). This pouring of oil is also known as "anointing."

◉ Messiah (Chosen One)

● **29.4** *wash themselves:* Washing the hands and feet was a requirement before offering sacrifices (30.18-21). If a priest had touched something that was ritually unclean he could make the sacrifice unclean and unfit for God (40.12; Lev 16.3,4; Heb 10.22).

◉ Purity (Clean and Unclean)

● **29.10-12** *bull . . . blood:* A bull was offered as a sin offering (29.14). The choicest parts of the bull were burned on the altar (Lev 3.3-5).

● **29.14** *offering . . . for the sins of the priests:* The contents of the bull's stomach were thought of as containing the sins and were to be burned outside the camp (Heb 13.11-13).

29.20,21 *blood on Aaron's right ear . . . their clothes:* The blood was believed to have purifying power and to keep the priest safe from ritual uncleanness.

◯ Blood

29.35-37 *seven days . . . the altar will become so holy:* The number seven was considered a sacred number signifying completeness. Olive oil was used to dedicate or "anoint" people or things in order to make them holy. To be holy meant "to be set apart," usually for a special purpose, or to be dedicated to God.

29.38-43 *Each day . . . sacrifice:* The priests were to offer daily sacrifices on the bronze altar (27.1-8) in the courtyard outside the entrance to the sacred tent. The sacrifices offered in the morning and at twilight before sunset included a young lamb, two pounds of flour and about one quart of pure olive oil.

the ram, wash its insides and legs, and lay all of its parts on the altar, including the head. [18]Then make sure that the whole animal goes up in smoke with a smell that pleases me.

[19]Bring the other ram to Aaron and his sons and tell them to lay their hands on its head. [20]Kill the ram and place some of its blood on Aaron's right ear lobe, his right thumb, and the big toe of his right foot. Do the same for each of his sons and splatter the rest of the blood against the four sides of the altar. [21]Then take some of the blood from the altar, mix it with the oil used for ordination, and sprinkle it on Aaron and his clothes, and also on his sons and their clothes. This will show that they and their clothes have been dedicated to me.

[22]This ram is part of the ordination service. So remove its right hind leg,[t] its fat tail, the fat on its insides, as well as the lower part of the liver and the two kidneys with their fat. [23]Take one loaf of each kind of bread[u] from the basket, [24]and put this bread, together with the meat, into the hands of Aaron and his sons. Then they will lift it all up[v] to show that it is dedicated to me. [25]After this, put the meat and bread on the altar and send them up in smoke with a smell that pleases me.

[26]You may eat the choice ribs from this second ram, but you must first lift them up[v] to show that this meat is dedicated to me.

[27-28]In the future, when anyone from Israel offers the ribs and a hind leg of a ram either to ordain a priest or to ask for my blessing, the meat belongs to me, but it may be eaten by the priests. This law will never change.

[29-30]After Aaron's death, his priestly clothes are to be handed down to each descendant who succeeds him as high priest, and these clothes must be worn during the seven-day ceremony of ordination.

[31]Boil the meat of the ordination ram in a sacred place, [32]then Aaron and his sons are to eat it together with the three kinds of bread[w] at the entrance to the sacred tent. [33]At their ordination, a ceremony of forgiveness was performed for them with this sacred food, and only they have the right to eat it. [34]If any of the sacred food is left until morning, it must be completely burned.

[35]Repeat this ordination ceremony for Aaron and his sons seven days in a row, just as I have instructed you. [36]Each day you must offer a bull as a sacrifice for sin and as a way of purifying the altar. In addition, you must smear the altar with olive oil to make it completely holy. [37]Do this for seven days, and the altar will become so holy that anyone who touches it will become holy.

Daily Sacrifices
(Leviticus 6.8-13; Numbers 28.1-8)

The LORD said:

[38]Each day you must sacrifice two lambs a year old, [39]one in the morning and one in the evening. [40-41]With each lamb offer two pounds of your finest flour mixed with a quart of pure olive oil, and also pour out a quart of wine as an offering. The smell of this sacrifice on the fires of the altar will be pleasing to me. [42-43]You and your descendants must always offer this sacrifice on the altar at the entrance to the sacred tent.

People of Israel, I will meet and speak with you there, and my shining glory will

---

[t]**29.22** *right hind leg:* This was usually given to the officiating priest (see Leviticus 7.33).   [u]**29.23** *each kind of bread:* See verses 2,3.   [v]**29.24,26** *lift it all up:* Or "wave it all."   [w]**29.32** *three kinds of bread:* See verses 2,3.

make the place holy. [44]Because of who I am, the tent will become sacred, and Aaron and his sons will become worthy to serve as my priests. [45]I will live among you as your God, [46]and you will know that I am the LORD your God, the one who rescued you from Egypt, so that I could live among you.

The Altar for Burning Incense
(Exodus 37.25-28)

The LORD said to Moses:

30 Build an altar of acacia wood where you can burn incense. [2]Make it 18 inches square and 36 inches high, and make each of its four corners stick up like the horn of a bull. [3]Cover it with pure gold and put a gold edging around it. [4]Then below the edging on opposite sides attach two gold rings through which you can put the poles for carrying the altar. [5]These poles are also to be made of acacia wood covered with gold.

[6]Put the altar in front of the inside curtain of the sacred tent. The chest with the place of mercy[x] is kept behind that curtain, and I will talk with you there. [7-8]From now on, when Aaron takes care of the lamps each morning and evening, he must burn sweet-smelling incense to me on the altar. [9]Burn only the proper incense on the altar and never use it for grain sacrifices or animal sacrifices or drink offerings. [10]Once a year Aaron must purify the altar by smearing on its four corners[y] the blood of an animal sacrificed for sin, and this practice must always be followed. The altar is sacred because it is dedicated to me.

The Money for the Sacred Tent

[11]The LORD said to Moses:
[12]Find out how many grown men there

are in Israel and require each of them to pay me to keep him safe from danger while you are counting them. [13-15]Each man over 19, whether rich or poor, must pay me the same amount of money, weighed according to the official standards. [16]This money is to be used for the upkeep of the sacred tent, and because of it, I will never forget my people.

The Large Bronze Bowl
(Exodus 38.8)

[17]The LORD said to Moses:
[18-21]Make a large bronze bowl and a bronze stand for it. Then put them between the altar for sacrifice and the sacred tent, so the priests can wash their hands and feet before entering the tent or offering a sacrifice on the altar. Each priest in every generation must wash himself in this way, or else he will die right there.

The Oil for Dedication and Ordination
(Exodus 37.29)

[22]The LORD said to Moses:
[23-25]Mix a gallon of olive oil with the following costly spices: twelve pounds of myrrh, six pounds of cinnamon, six pounds of cane, and twelve pounds of cassia. Measure these according to the official standards. Then use this sacred mixture [26]for dedicating the tent and chest, [27]the table with its equipment, the lampstand with its equipment, the incense altar with all its utensils, [28]the altar for sacrifices, and the large bowl with its stand. [29]By dedicating them in this way, you will make them so holy that anyone who even touches them will become holy.
[30]When you ordain Aaron and his sons as

[x]**30.6** *place of mercy*: See the note at 26.34.   [y]**30.10** *four corners*: See 27.2; 30.2.

30.1 *altar of acacia wood . . . incense:* Incense was made of frankincense, other gums and spices, and salt, which together produced a sweet smell when burned. The smoke from the burning incense represented the prayers that went up to God (Ps 141.2; Rev 5.8). The altar for burning incense was in the holy place.

30.13-16 *money . . . used for the upkeep of the sacred tent:* A count (census) of the number of Israelite men was taken every so often to determine who had duty as a priest, and to keep track of offerings made to support the sacred tent, and later, the temple in Jerusalem. The amount owed by each Israelite male was half a shekel, which at this time was a piece of gold or silver that weighed about one fifth of an ounce. Coins were not yet in use. See also 38.25,26; Matt 17.24.

30.18-21 *large bronze bowl . . . wash:* The bowl was made from bronze mirrors donated by Israelite women (see 38.8). Bronze was made by melting and mixing together copper and tin.

30.23-31 *olive oil . . . costly spices . . . dedicated to the LORD:* Myrrh, cinnamon and cassia were mixed with olive oil and used to dedicate items in the sacred tent and to ordain priests. To be holy meant "to be set apart," usually for a special purpose, or to be dedicated to God. **(See the chart Spices and Perfumes on pg 1835.)**

30.34-36 *costly spices stacte . . . frankincense . . . sacred chest:* Stacte is a sweet-smelling gum resin similar to myrrh. Onycha comes from mollusk shells, and galbanum is a resin that comes from the milky juice of the root of a carrot-like plant that was plentiful in Persia and Syria. Frankincense comes from a white gummy substance produced by certain trees in the Middle East. It was often pounded into a valuable powder that was burned to make a sweet smell. **(See the chart Spices and Perfumes on pg 1835.)**

The Sacred Chest

31.2 *Bezalel . . . Judah tribe:* In Hebrew *Bezalel* means "In the Shadow (Protection) of God." The Judah tribe would settle in the area west of the Dead Sea after the Israelites settled in Canaan, the land God promised to them. King David and his son Solomon, who built the first temple to the LORD in Jerusalem, were from the Judah tribe.

31.3-5 *Spirit:* This refers to the presence of God, which gives special gifts or abilities.

31.6 *Oholiab . . . tribe of Dan:* His name means "My Tent Is the Father (God)." The members of the Dan tribe eventually settled just to the north of the Judah tribe.

my priests, sprinkle them with some of this oil, ³¹and say to the people of Israel: "This oil must always be used in the ordination service of a priest. It is holy because it is dedicated to the LORD. ³²So treat it as holy! Don't ever use it for everyday purposes or mix any for yourselves. ³³If you do, you will no longer belong to the LORD's people."

The Sweet-Smelling Incense

³⁴⁻³⁵Mix equal amounts of the costly spices stacte, onycha, galbanum, and pure frankincense, then add salt to make the mixture pure and holy. ³⁶Pound some of it into powder and sprinkle it in front of the sacred chest, where I meet with you. Be sure to treat this incense as something very holy. ³⁷It is truly holy because it is dedicated to me, so don't ever make any for yourselves. ³⁸If you ever make any of it to use as perfume, you will no longer belong to my people.

The LORD Chooses Bezalel and Oholiab
(Exodus 35.30—36.1)

31 The LORD said to Moses: ²I have chosen Bezalel[z] from the Judah tribe to make the sacred tent and its furnishings. ³⁻⁵Not only have I filled him with my Spirit, but I have given him wisdom and made him a skilled craftsman who can create objects of art with gold, silver, bronze, precious stones, and wood. ⁶I have appointed Oholiab[a] from the tribe of Dan to work with him, and I have also given skills to those who will help them make everything exactly as I have commanded you: ⁷⁻¹¹the sacred tent with its furnishings, the sacred chest with its place

of mercy, the table with all that is on it, the lamp with its equipment, the incense altar, the altar for sacrifices with its equipment, the bronze bowl with its stand, the beautiful priestly clothes for Aaron and his sons, the oil for dedication and ordination services, and the sweet-smelling incense for the holy place.

Laws for the Sabbath

¹²⁻¹³Moses told the Israelites that the LORD had said:

The Sabbath belongs to me. Now I command you and your descendants to always obey the laws of the Sabbath. By doing this, you will know that I have chosen you as my own. ¹⁴⁻¹⁵Keep the Sabbath holy. You have six days to do your work, but the Sabbath is mine, and it must remain a day of rest. If you work on the Sabbath, you will no longer be part of my people, and you will be put to death.

¹⁶Every generation of Israelites must respect the Sabbath. ¹⁷This day will always serve as a reminder, both to me and to the Israelites, that I made the heavens and the earth in six days, then on the seventh day I rested and relaxed. ¹⁸When God had finished speaking to Moses on Mount Sinai, he gave him the two flat stones on which he had written all his laws with his own hand.

The People Make an Idol To Worship
(Deuteronomy 9.6-29)

32 After the people saw that Moses had been on the mountain for a long time, they went to Aaron and said,

[z]**31.2** *Bezalel:* Hebrew "Bezalel, son of Uri and grandson of Hur."   [a]**31.6** *Oholiab:* Hebrew "Oholiab son of Ahisamach."

"Every generation of Israelites must respect the Sabbath. This day will always serve as a reminder . . . that I made the heavens and the earth in six days, then on the seventh day I rested." EXOD 31.16,17

"Make us an image of a god who will lead and protect us. Moses brought us out of Egypt, but nobody knows what has happened to him."

²Aaron told them, "Bring me the gold earrings that your wives and sons and daughters are wearing." ³Everybody took off their earrings and brought them to Aaron, ⁴then he melted them and made an idol in the shape of a young bull.

All the people said to one another, "This is the god who brought us out of Egypt!"

⁵When Aaron saw what was happening, he built an altar in front of the idol and said, "Tomorrow we will celebrate in honor of the LORD." ⁶The people got up early the next morning and killed some animals to be used for sacrifices and others to be eaten. Then everyone ate and drank so much that they began to carry on like wild people.

⁷The LORD said to Moses:

Hurry back down! Those people you led out of Egypt are acting like fools. ⁸They have already stopped obeying me and have made themselves an idol in the shape of a young bull. They have bowed down to it, offered sacrifices, and said that it is the god who brought them out of Egypt. ⁹Moses, I have seen how stubborn these people are, ¹⁰and I'm angry enough to destroy them, so don't try to stop me. But I will make your descendants into a great nation.

¹¹Moses tried to get the LORD God to change his mind:

Our LORD, you used your mighty power to bring these people out of Egypt. Now don't become angry and destroy them. ¹²If you do, the Egyptians will say that you brought your people out here into the mountains just to get rid of them. Please don't be angry with your people. Don't destroy them!

¹³Remember the solemn promise you made to Abraham, Isaac, and Jacob. You promised that someday they would have as many descendants as there are stars in the sky and that you would give them land.

¹⁴So even though the LORD had threatened to destroy the people, he changed his mind and let them live.

¹⁵⁻¹⁶Moses went back down the mountain with the two flat stones on which God had written all of his laws with his own hand, using both sides of the stones.

¹⁷When Joshua heard the noisy shouts of the people, he said to Moses, "A battle must be going on down in the camp."

¹⁸But Moses replied, "It doesn't sound like they are shouting because they have won or lost a battle. It sounds more like a wild party!"

¹⁹As Moses got closer to the camp, he saw the idol, and he also saw the people dancing around. This made him so angry that he threw down the stones and broke them to pieces at the foot of the mountain. ²⁰He melted the idol the people had made, and he ground it into powder. He scattered it in their water and made them drink it. ²¹Moses asked Aaron, "What did these people do to harm you? Why did you make them sin in this terrible way?"

²²Aaron answered:

Don't be angry with me. You know as well as I do that they are determined to do evil. ²³They even told me, "That man Moses led us out of Egypt, but now we don't know what has happened to him. Make us a god to lead us." ²⁴Then I asked them to bring me their gold earrings. They took them off and gave them to me. I threw the gold into a fire, and out came this bull.

²⁵Moses knew that the people were out of control and that it was Aaron's fault. And now they had made fools of

---

● **32.1** *image of a god:* A statue or idol (32.4), which was forbidden in the laws Moses received from the LORD on Mount Sinai (20.3-5).

● **32.4** *young bull:* The statue may have looked like the Egyptian bull-god Apis or one of the gods worshiped by the Canaanites. Many centuries later, King Jeroboam of Israel (northern kingdom) used similar words to describe the golden calves he set up as objects of worship in the towns of Bethel and Dan (1 Kgs 12.26-30). See also Acts 7.41.

■ **32.11** *LORD . . . change his mind:* Moses' prayers had an effect on the LORD's actions toward the Hebrew people. The people broke their earlier promise to worship only God, and so they deserved punishment. Moses pleaded with God not to destroy the people he had chosen. See also Num 14.13-19.

● **32.18** *shouting . . . wild party:* Victory over an enemy was celebrated by a special kind of high-pitched shouting. Sometimes a sort of yodel-like singing was done at weddings and funerals. What Moses heard was not a victory shout but wild, unorganized singing and yelling.

● **32.19** *idol . . . threw down the stones:* The people broke their promise (agreement) to worship only the LORD, so Moses broke the stones.

⊗ Agreements (Covenants)

⊗ Sin

32.26 *men of the Levi tribe:* Not all the Levites joined Moses, since Exodus 32.29 and Deuteronomy 33.9 suggest that some were later killed. At first, all the descendants of Levi may have been considered Israel's priests. Eventually, only those members of the tribe of Levi who could prove they were descendants of Aaron were considered Israel's true priests (Num 18.20-32; Neh 11.10-18). "Levites" then came to mean those members of the tribe of Levi who were not descended from Aaron. Their job was to take care of the tent of meeting and to assist the priests.

Israel's Priests

32.35 *terrible disease:* The people may have become ill from drinking the water that had gold powder in it (32.20), but this is not certain. The retelling of this event in DEUTERONOMY does not include this detail (see Deut 9.6-29).

33.4-5 *fancy jewelry . . . mourning:* Removing jewelry during times of mourning was a way of showing sorrow (Ezek 26.16).

33.7 *"meeting tent":* This is not the sacred tent of meeting (27.21), which was to stand in the center of the Israelite camp. This tent, which was probably used before the sacred tent was built, was a place to go and hear a special message from the LORD.

themselves in front of their enemies. ²⁶So Moses stood at the gate of the camp and shouted, "Everyone who is on the LORD's side come over here!"

Then the men of the Levi tribe gathered around Moses, ²⁷and he said to them, "The LORD God of Israel commands you to strap on your swords and go through the camp, killing your relatives, your friends, and your neighbors."

²⁸The men of the Levi tribe followed his orders, and that day they killed about 3,000 men. ²⁹Moses said to them, "You obeyed the LORD and did what was right, and so you will serve as his priests for the people of Israel. It was hard for you to kill your own sons and brothers, but the LORD has blessed you and made you his priests today."

³⁰The next day Moses told the people, "This is a terrible thing you have done. But I will go back to the LORD to see if I can do something to keep this sin from being held against you."

³¹Moses returned to the LORD and said, "The people have committed a terrible sin. They have made a gold idol to be their god. ³²But I beg you to forgive them. If you don't, please wipe my name out of your book."[b]

³³The LORD replied, "I will wipe out of my book the name of everyone who has sinned against me. ³⁴Now take my people to the place I told you about, and my angel will lead you. But when the time comes, I will punish them for this sin."

³⁵So the LORD punished the people of Israel with a terrible disease for talking Aaron into making the gold idol.

The LORD Tells Israel To Leave Mount Sinai

33 The LORD said to Moses:
You led the people of Israel out of Egypt. Now get ready to lead them to the land I promised their ancestors Abraham, Isaac, and Jacob. ²⁻³It is a land rich with milk and honey, and I will send an angel to force out those people who live there—the Canaanites, the Amorites, the Hittites, the Perizzites, the Hivites, and the Jebusites. But I will not go with my people. They are so rebellious that I would destroy them before they get there.

⁴⁻⁵Even before the LORD said these harsh things, he had told Moses, "These people really are rebellious, and I would kill them at once, if I went with them. But tell them to take off their fancy jewelry, then I'll decide what to do with them." So the people started mourning, ⁶and after leaving Mount Sinai,[c] they stopped wearing fancy jewelry.

The LORD Is with His People

⁷Moses used to set up a tent far from camp. He called it the "meeting tent," and whoever needed some message from the LORD would go there. ⁸Each time Moses went out to this tent, everyone would stand at the entrance to their own tents and watch him enter. ⁹⁻¹¹Then they would bow down because a thick cloud would come down in front of the tent, and the LORD would speak to Moses face to face, just like a friend. Afterwards, Moses would return to camp, but his young assistant Joshua[d] would stay at the tent.

[b]**32.32** *your book:* The people of Israel believed that the LORD kept a record of the names of his people, and anyone whose name was removed from that book no longer belonged to the LORD. [c]**33.6** *Mount Sinai:* The Hebrew text has "Mount Horeb," another name for Sinai. [d]**33.9-11** *Joshua:* Hebrew "Joshua son of Nun."

The LORD Promises To Be with His People

[12]Moses said to the LORD, "I know that you have told me to lead these people to the land you promised them. But you have not said who will go along to help me. You have said that you are my friend and that you are pleased with me. [13]If this is true, let me know what your plans are, then I can obey and continue to please you. And don't forget that you have chosen this nation to be your own."

[14]The LORD said, "I will go with you and give you peace."

[15]Then Moses replied, "If you aren't going with us, please don't make us leave this place. [16]But if you do go with us, everyone will know that you are pleased with your people and with me. That way, we will be different from the rest of the people on earth."

[17]So the LORD told him, "I will do what you have asked, because I am your friend and I am pleased with you."

[18]Then Moses said, "I pray that you will let me see you in all of your glory."

[19]The LORD answered:

All right. I am the LORD, and I show mercy and kindness to anyone I choose. I will let you see my glory and hear my holy name, [20]but I won't let you see my face, because anyone who sees my face will die. [21]There is a rock not far from me. Stand beside it, [22]and before I pass by in all of my shining glory, I will put you in a large crack in the rock. I will cover your eyes with my hand until I have passed by. [23]Then I will take my hand away, and you will see my back. You will not see my face.

[e]34.5 *the* LORD: See the note at 3.14,15.

The Second Set of Commandments

(Deuteronomy 10.1-5)

34 One day the LORD said to Moses, "Cut two flat stones like the first ones I made, and I will write on them the same commandments that were on the two you broke. [2]Be ready tomorrow morning to come up Mount Sinai and meet me at the top. [3]No one is to come with you or to be on the mountain at all. Don't even let the sheep and cattle graze at the foot of the mountain." [4]So Moses cut two flat stones like the first ones, and early the next morning he carried them to the top of Mount Sinai, just as the LORD had commanded.

[5]The LORD God came down in a cloud and stood beside Moses there on the mountain. God spoke his holy name, "the LORD."[e] [6]Then he passed in front of Moses and called out, "I am the LORD God. I am merciful and very patient with my people. I show great love, and I can be trusted. [7]I keep my promises to my people forever, but I also punish anyone who sins. When people sin, I punish them and their children, and also their grandchildren and great-grandchildren."

[8]Moses quickly bowed down to the ground and worshiped the LORD. [9]He prayed, "LORD, if you really are pleased with me, I pray that you will go with us. It is true that these people are sinful and rebellious, but forgive our sin and let us be your people."

A Promise and Its Demands

(Exodus 23.14-19; Deuteronomy 7.1-5; 16.1-17)

[10]The LORD said:

I promise to perform miracles for you that have never been seen anywhere

---

LORD (YHWH)

34.6,7 *I am merciful . . . great-grandchildren:* These verses use formula-style language to describe several characteristics of God's nature. First, they speak of God's love and faithfulness (see also Neh 9.17; Ps 86.15; 103.8; 145.8; Jonah 4.2). But they also say God hates sin and punishes those who are unfaithful or disobedient. Here, God's anger is described as being so great that even the descendants of the rebellious person are punished (see also 20.5; Num 14.18; Nah 1.3). Later in Israelite history, the prophets Jeremiah and Ezekiel speak of a time when people will be responsible for their own sins and no child will be punished for the sins of the parent (see Jer 31.29,30; Ezek 18.1-32).

The LORD told Moses, *"I am the* LORD, *and I show mercy and kindness to anyone I choose. I will let you see my glory and hear my holy name."* EXOD 33.19

Gods and Goddesses

34.15,16 *sacrificial meals... marry their women:* To eat food that had been sacrificed to a foreign god would mean being disloyal to the LORD God of Israel (1 Cor 8; 10.18-21). The sacrificial meals of the Moabites and Canaanites sometimes included ritual prostitution (Num 25.1,2; Judg 2.17; 8.33; Hos 9.10). Marriage between Hebrew men and foreign women was also a temptation to follow other gods. At various times in Israel's history, such intermarriage was viewed as a severe problem (see, for example, Ezra 9.1-4).

34.29-35 *face was shining ... veil:* Moses' face reflected God's glory (Exod 29.42,43; 33.18). The people may have been afraid that Moses had become a god. The veil acted to hide Moses' shining face, either because some were afraid of it or because he did not want the people to see the glory of God fade from his face.

on earth. Neighboring nations will stand in fear and know that I was the one who did these marvelous things. [11]I will force out the Amorites, the Canaanites, the Hittites, the Perizzites, the Hivites, and the Jebusites, but you must do what I command you today. [12]Don't make treaties with any of those people. If you do, it will be like falling into a trap. [13]Instead, you must destroy their altars and tear down the sacred poles[f] they use in the worship of the goddess Asherah. [14]I demand your complete loyalty—you must not worship any other god! [15]Don't make treaties with the people there, or you will soon find yourselves worshiping their gods and taking part in their sacrificial meals. [16]Your men will even marry their women and be influenced to worship their gods.

[17]Don't make metal images of gods.

[18]Don't fail to observe the Festival of Thin Bread in the month of Abib.[g] Obey me and eat bread without yeast for seven days during Abib, because that is the month you left Egypt.

[19]The first-born males of your families and of your flocks and herds belong to me. [20]You can save the life of a first-born donkey[h] by sacrificing a lamb; if you don't, you must break the donkey's neck. You must save every first-born son.

Bring an offering every time you come to worship.

[21]Work for six days and rest on the seventh day, even during the seasons for plowing and harvesting. [22]Celebrate the Harvest Festival[i] each spring when you start harvesting your wheat, and celebrate the Festival of Shelters[j] each autumn when you pick your fruit.

[23]Your men must come to worship me three times a year, because I am the LORD God of Israel. [24]As you advance, I will force the nations out of your land and enlarge your borders. Then no one will try to take your property when you come to worship me these three times each year.

[25]When you sacrifice an animal on the altar, don't offer bread made with yeast. And don't save any part of the Passover meal for the next day.

[26]I am the LORD your God, and you must bring the first part of your harvest to the place of worship.

Don't boil a young goat in its mother's milk.

[27]The LORD told Moses to put these laws in writing, as part of his agreement with Israel. [28]Moses stayed on the mountain with the LORD for 40 days and nights, without eating or drinking. And he wrote down the Ten Commandments, the most important part of God's agreement with his people.

Moses Comes Down from Mount Sinai

[29]Moses came down from Mount Sinai, carrying the Ten Commandments. His face was shining brightly because the LORD had been speaking to him. But Moses did not know at first that his face was shining. [30]When Aaron and the others looked at Moses, they saw this, and they were afraid to go near him. [31]Moses called out for

[f]**34.13** *sacred poles:* Or "trees," used as symbols of Asherah, the goddess of fertility.   [g]**34.18** *Abib:* See the note at 12.2.   [h]**34.20** *donkey:* See the note at 13.13.   [i]**34.22** *Harvest Festival:* See the note at 23.16.
[j]**34.22** *Festival of Shelters:* See the note at 23.16.

Aaron and the leaders to come to him, and he spoke with them. ³²Then the rest of the people of Israel gathered around Moses, and he gave them the laws that the Lord had given him on Mount Sinai.

³³The face of Moses kept shining, and after he had spoken with the people, he covered his face with a veil. ³⁴Moses would always remove the veil when he went into the sacred tent to speak with the Lord. And when he came out, he would tell the people everything the Lord had told him to say. ³⁵They could see that his face was still shining. So after he had spoken with them, he would put the veil back on and leave it on until the next time he went to speak with the Lord.

Laws for the Sabbath

35 Moses called together the people of Israel and told them that the Lord had said:

²You have six days in which to do your work. But the seventh day must be dedicated to me, your Lord, as a day of rest. Whoever works on the Sabbath will be put to death. ³Don't even build a cooking fire at home on the Sabbath.

Offerings for the Sacred Tent
(Exodus 25.1-9; 35.10-19)

⁴Moses told the people of Israel that the Lord had said:

⁵I will welcome an offering from anyone who wants to give something. You may bring gold, silver, or bronze; ⁶blue, purple, or red wool; fine linen; goat hair; ⁷tanned ram skin or fine leather; acacia wood; ⁸olive oil for the lamp; sweet-smelling spices for the oil of dedication and for the incense; or

⁹onyx[k] stones or other gems for the sacred vest and breastpiece.

¹⁰If you have any skills, you should use them to help make what I have commanded: ¹¹the sacred tent with its covering and hooks, its framework and crossbars, and its post and stands; ¹²the sacred chest with its carrying poles, its place of mercy, and the curtain in front of it; ¹³the table with its carrying poles and all that goes on it, including the sacred bread; ¹⁴the lamp with its equipment and oil; ¹⁵the incense altar with its carrying poles and sweet-smelling incense; the ordination oil; the curtain for the entrance to the sacred tent; ¹⁶the altar for sacrifices with its bronze grating, its carrying poles, and its equipment; the large bronze bowl with its stand; ¹⁷the curtains with the posts and stands that go around the courtyard and the curtain at the entrance; ¹⁸the pegs and ropes for the tent and the courtyard; ¹⁹and the finely woven priestly clothes for Aaron and his sons.

Gifts for the Lord

²⁰Moses finished speaking, and everyone left. ²¹Then those who wanted to bring gifts to the Lord, brought them to be used for the sacred tent, the worship services, and the priestly clothes. ²²Men and women came willingly and gave all kinds of gold jewelry such as pins, earrings, rings, and necklaces. ²³Everyone brought their blue, purple, and red wool, their fine linen, and their cloth made of goat hair, as well as their ram skins dyed red and their fine leather. ²⁴Anyone who had silver or bronze or acacia wood brought it as a gift to the Lord.

²⁵The women who were good at weaving cloth brought the blue, purple, and red

[k]35.9 *onyx:* See the note at 25.7.

35.5-9 *offering . . . breastpiece:* Many of the items mentioned in these verses were described as being used to create parts of the sacred tent and its furnishings.

35.10 *skills . . . help make what I have commanded:* In addition to bringing physical gifts (35.5-9), the people were encouraged to share their skill and energy to make the sacred tent and the many objects that were to be used in worship.

Holy Spirit

35.34 Oholiab from the tribe of Dan: Like Bezalel, Oholiab was chosen by the LORD to do the important work of creating everything that was needed for the sacred tent. But it is the LORD who prepared them for this work and who gave them the skills to carry it out according to the instructions the LORD gave to Moses, including the ability to teach others.

wool and the fine linen they had made. **26**And the women who knew how to make cloth from goat hair were glad to do so.

27The leaders brought different kinds of jewels to be sewn on the special clothes and the breastpiece for the high priest. **28**They also brought sweet-smelling spices to be mixed with the incense and olive oil that were for the lamps and for ordaining the priests. **29**Moses had told the people what the LORD wanted them to do, and many of them decided to bring their gifts.

Bezalel and Oholiab
(Exodus 31.1-11)

30Moses said to the people of Israel:

The LORD has chosen Bezalel[l] of the Judah tribe. **31-33**Not only has the LORD filled him with his Spirit, but he has given him wisdom and made him a skilled craftsman who can create objects of art with gold, silver, bronze, precious stones, and wood. **34**The LORD is urging him and Oholiab[m] from the tribe of Dan to teach others. **35**And he has given them all kinds of artistic skills, including the ability to design and embroider with blue, purple, and red wool and to weave fine linen.

36 The LORD has given to Bezalel, Oholiab, and others the skills needed for building a place of worship, and they will follow the LORD's instructions.

2Then Moses brought together these workers who were eager to work, **3**and he gave them the gifts that the people of Israel had donated for building the place of worship. In fact, so much was being given each morning, **4**that finally everyone stopped working **5**and said, "Moses, there is already more than we need for what the LORD has

assigned us to do." **6**So Moses sent word for the people to stop giving, and they did. **7**But there was already more than enough to do what needed to be done.

The Curtains and Coverings for the Sacred Tent
(Exodus 26.1-14)

8-9 The skilled workers got together to make the sacred tent and its linen curtains that were woven with blue, purple, and red wool and embroidered with figures of winged creatures. Each of the ten panels was 14 yards long and 2 yards wide, **10**and they were sewn together to make two curtains with five panels each. **11-13**Then 50 loops of blue cloth were put along one of the wider sides of each curtain, and the two curtains were fastened together at the loops with 50 gold hooks.

14-15 As the material for protecting the tent, goat hair was used to weave eleven sections 15 yards by 2 yards each. **16**These eleven sections were joined to make two panels, one with five and the other with six sections. **17**Fifty loops were put along one of the wider sides of each panel, **18**and the two panels were fastened at the loops with 50 bronze hooks. **19**Two other coverings were made—one with fine leather and the other with ram skins dyed red.

The Framework for the Sacred Tent
(Exodus 26.15-30)

20Acacia wood was used to build the framework for the walls of the sacred tent. **21**Each frame was 15 feet high and 27 inches wide **22-26**with two wooden pegs near the bottom. Then two silver stands were placed under each frame with sockets for

[l]**35.30** *Bezalel:* See the note at 31.2.   [m]**35.34** *Oholiab:* Hebrew "Oholiab son of Ahisamach."

the pegs, so they could be joined together. Twenty of these frames were used along the south side and 20 more along the north. [27]Six frames were used for the back wall along the west side [28-29]with two more at the southwest and northwest corners. These corner frames were joined from top to bottom. [30]Altogether, along the back wall there were eight frames with two silver stands under each of them.

[31-33]Five crossbars were made for each of the wooden frames, with the center crossbar running the full length of the wall. [34]The frames and crossbars were covered with gold, and gold rings were attached to the frames to run the crossbars through.

The Inside Curtain for the Sacred Tent
(Exodus 26.31-37)

[35]They made the inside curtain[n] of fine linen woven with blue, purple, and red wool, and embroidered with figures of winged creatures. [36]They also made four acacia wood posts and covered them with gold. Then gold rings were fastened to the posts, which were set on silver stands. [37]For the entrance to the tent, they used a curtain of fine linen woven with blue, purple, and red wool and embroidered with fancy needlework. [38]They made five posts, covered them completely with gold, and set each of them on a gold-covered bronze stand. Finally, they attached hooks for the curtain.

The Sacred Chest
(Exodus 25.10-22)

37 Bezalel built a chest of acacia wood 45 inches long, 27 inches wide, and 27 inches high. [2]He covered it inside and out with pure gold and put a gold edging around the top. [3]He made four gold rings and attached one of them to each of the four legs of the chest. [4]Then he made two poles of acacia wood, covered them with gold, [5]and put them through the rings, so the chest could be carried by the poles.

[6]The entire lid of the chest, which was made of pure gold, was the place of mercy.[o] [7-9]On each of the two ends of the chest he made a winged creature of hammered gold. They faced each other, and their wings covered the place of mercy.

The Table for the Sacred Bread
(Exodus 25.23-30)

[10]Bezalel built a table of acacia wood 36 inches long, 18 inches wide, and 27 inches high. [11-12]He covered it with pure gold and put a gold edging around it with a border 3 inches wide.[P] [13]He made four gold rings and attached one to each of the legs [14]near the edging. The poles for carrying the table were placed through these rings [15]and were made of acacia wood covered with gold. [16]Everything that was to be set on the table was made of pure gold— the bowls, plates, jars, and cups for wine offerings.

The Lampstand
(Exodus 25.31-40)

[17]Bezalel made a lampstand of pure gold. The whole lampstand, including its decorative flowers, was made from a single piece of hammered gold, [18]with three branches on each of its two sides. [19]There were three decorative almond blossoms on each branch [20]and four on the stem.

36.35 *inside curtain:* The curtain inside the sacred tent that separated the holy place from the most holy place.

The Sacred Chest

37.1 *acacia wood:* Acacia wood comes from a kind of evergreen tree. Its beautiful wood is harder and darker in color than oak.

37.6 *lid of the chest:* The lid of the chest has also been called a "mercy seat," where God sat and judged the people with overwhelming kindness (mercy) and told them what they must do (25.22).

37.21 *blossom:* The lampstand was decorated with golden leaves or blossoms patterned after the almond tree, one of the first trees to bloom each spring in Canaan.

38.1 *altar:* The main altar used for offering sacrifices was made of acacia wood covered with bronze. The altar was to have a decorative bronze edge all the way around the top with corners that resembled bulls' horns.

The Sacred Tent

²¹There was also a blossom where each pair of branches came out from the stem. ²²The lampstand, including its branches and decorative flowers, was made from a single piece of hammered pure gold. ²³⁻²⁴The lamp and its equipment, including the tongs and trays, were made of about 75 pounds of pure gold.

The Altar for Burning Incense
(Exodus 30.1-5)

²⁵For burning incense, Bezalel made an altar of acacia wood. It was 18 inches square and 36 inches high with each of its four corners sticking up like the horn of a bull. ²⁶He covered it with pure gold and put a gold edging around it. ²⁷Then below the edging on opposite sides he attached two gold rings through which he put the poles for carrying the altar. ²⁸These poles were also made of acacia wood and covered with gold.

The Oil for Dedication and the Incense
(Exodus 30.22-38)

²⁹Bezalel mixed the sacred oil for dedication and the pure spices for the sweet-smelling incense.

The Altar for Offering Sacrifices
(Exodus 27.1-8)

38 Bezalel built an altar of acacia wood for offering sacrifices. It was seven and a half feet square and four and a half feet high ²with each of its four corners sticking up like the horn of a bull, and it was completely covered with bronze. ³The equipment for the altar was also made of bronze—the pans for the hot ashes, the shovels, the bowls, the meat forks, and the fire pans. ⁴About halfway up the altar he built a ledge around it and covered the bottom half of the altar with a decorative bronze grating. ⁵Then he attached a bronze ring beneath the ledge at the four corners to put the poles through. ⁶He covered two acacia wood poles with bronze and ⁷put them through the rings for carrying the altar, which was shaped like an open box.

The Large Bronze Bowl
(Exodus 30.18-21)

⁸Bezalel made a large bowl and a stand out of bronze from the mirrors of the women who helped at the entrance to the sacred tent.

The Courtyard around the Sacred Tent
(Exodus 27.9-19)

⁹⁻¹⁷Around the sacred tent Bezalel built a courtyard 150 feet long on the south and north and 75 feet wide on the east and west. He used twenty bronze posts on bronze stands for the south and north and ten for the west. Then he hung a curtain of fine linen on the posts along each of these three sides by using silver hooks and rods. He placed three bronze posts on each side of the entrance at the east and hung a curtain seven and a half yards wide on each set of posts.
¹⁸⁻¹⁹For the entrance to the courtyard, Bezalel made a curtain ten yards long, which he hung on four bronze posts that were set on bronze stands. This curtain was two and a half yards high, the same height as the one for the rest of the courtyard, and was made of fine linen embroidered and woven with blue, purple, and red wool. He hung the curtain on the four posts, using

silver hooks and rods. **20**The pegs for the tent and for the curtain around the tent were made of bronze.

The Sacred Tent

21-23 Bezalel had worked closely with Oholiab,[q] who was an expert at designing and engraving, and at embroidering blue, purple, and red wool. The two of them completed the work that the LORD had commanded to be done.

Moses put Aaron's son Ithamar in charge of the Levites who kept record of the metals used for the sacred tent. **24**According to the official weights, the amount of gold given was 2,209 pounds, **25**and the silver that was collected when the people were counted[r] came to 7,550 pounds. **26**Everyone who was counted paid the required amount, and there was a total of 603,550 men who were 20 years old or older.

27Seventy-five pounds of the silver were used to make each of the 100 stands for the sacred tent and the curtain. **28**The remaining 50 pounds of silver were used for the hooks and rods and for covering the tops of the posts.

29Five thousand three hundred pounds of bronze were given. **30**And it was used to make the stands for the entrance to the tent, the altar and its grating, the equipment for the altar, **31**the stands for the posts that surrounded the courtyard, including those at the entrance to the courtyard, and the pegs for the tent and the courtyard.

Making the Priestly Clothes

(Exodus 28.1-14)

39 Beautiful priestly clothes were made of blue, purple, and red wool for Aaron to wear when he performed his duties in the holy place. This was done exactly as the LORD had commanded Moses.

2-3 The entire priestly vest was made of fine linen, woven with blue, purple, and red wool. Thin sheets of gold were hammered out and cut into threads that were skillfully woven into the vest. **4-5**It had two shoulder straps to support it and a sash that fastened around the waist. **6**Onyx[s] stones were placed in gold settings, and each one was engraved with the name of one of Israel's sons. **7**Then these were attached to the shoulder straps of the vest, so the LORD would never forget his people. Everything was done exactly as the LORD had commanded Moses.

The Breastpiece

(Exodus 28.15-30)

8The breastpiece was made with the same materials and designs as the priestly vest. **9**It was nine inches square and folded double **10**with four rows of three precious stones: A carnelian, a chrysolite, and an emerald were in the first row; **11**a turquoise, a sapphire, and a diamond were in the second row; **12**a jacinth, an agate, and an amethyst were in the third row; **13**and a beryl, an onyx, and a jasper[t] were in the fourth row. They were mounted in a delicate gold setting, **14**and on each of them was engraved the name of one of the twelve tribes of Israel.

[q]**38.21-23** *Bezalel . . . Oholiab*: Hebrew "Bezalel son of Uri and grandson of Hur of the Judah tribe had worked closely with Oholiab son of Ahisamach from the tribe of Dan." [r]**38.25** *counted*: See 30.11-16; Numbers 1. [s]**39.6** *Onyx*: See the note at 25.7. [t]**39.13** *jasper*: For the stones mentioned in verses 10-13, see the note at 28.20.

● 38.21-23 *Ithamar:* Later, Ithamar was put in charge of the work done by the men from two Levite clans, the Gershonites and Merarites (Num 4.21-33).

● 38.24-26 *official weights . . . required amount:* The weights of gold, silver, and bronze mentioned in these verses are given in pounds, but are based on the Hebrew weights known as shekels and talents. A talent was equal to about 75 pounds. So, for example, the amount of gold in 38.24 (2,209 pounds) was equal to nearly 29 1/2 talents. The amount of silver given was over 100 talents (7,550 pounds). A shekel was about 2/5 of an ounce. So, each pound (16 ounces) would equal about 40 shekels. That would make a total of nearly 302,000 shekels of silver, or about a half a shekel for each of the 603,550 men mentioned in verse 26.

It is interesting to note that the total number of men mentioned here seems to be based on the census taken in NUMBERS (1.20-46). See also Matt 17.24.

39.42-43 *blessing*: Moses blessed them for their gifts and for the work they did in creating the sacred tent and its furnishings.

40.2 *first day of the year*: Abib (also called Nisan) is the first month of the Hebrew calendar, from mid-March to mid-April. **(See the chart Pilgrimage Festivals on pg 1799.)**

15-18Two gold rings were attached to the upper front corners of the breastpiece and fastened with two braided gold chains to gold settings on the shoulder straps. 19Two other gold rings were attached to the lower inside corners next to the vest, 20and two more near the bottom of the shoulder straps right above the sash. 21To keep the breastpiece in place, a blue cord was used to tie the two lower rings on the breastpiece to those on the vest. These things were done exactly as the LORD had commanded Moses.

The Clothes for the Priests

(Exodus 28.31-43)

22The priestly robe was made of blue wool 23with an opening in the center for the head. The material around the collar was bound so as to keep it from wearing out. 24-26Along the hem of the robe were woven pomegranatesᵘ of blue, purple, and red wool with a bell of pure gold between each of them. This robe was to be worn by Aaron when he performed his duties.

27-29Everything that Aaron and his sons wore was made of fine linen woven with blue, purple, and red wool, including their robes and turbans, their fancy caps and underwear, and even their sashes that were embroidered with needlework.

30The words "Dedicated to the LORD" were engraved on a narrow strip of pure gold, 31which was fastened to Aaron's turban. These things were done exactly as the LORD had commanded Moses.

The Work Is Completed

(Exodus 35.10-19)

32So the people of Israel finished making everything the LORD had told Moses to make. 33Then they brought it all to Moses: the sacred tent and its equipment, including the hooks, the framework and crossbars, and its posts and stands; 34the covering of tanned ram skins and fine leather; the inside curtain; 35the sacred chest with its carrying poles and the place of mercy; 36the table with all that goes on it, including the sacred bread; 37the lampstand of pure gold, together with its equipment and oil; 38the gold-covered incense altar; the ordination oil and the sweet-smelling incense; the curtain for the entrance to the tent; 39the bronze altar for sacrifices with its bronze grating, its carrying poles, and its equipment; the large bronze bowl with its stand; 40the curtain with its posts and cords, and its pegs and stands that go around the courtyard; everything needed for the sacred tent; 41and the finely woven priestly clothes for Aaron and his sons.

42-43When Moses saw that the people had done everything exactly as the LORD had commanded, he gave them his blessing.

The LORD's Tent Is Set Up

40 The LORD said to Moses: 2Set up my tent on the first day of the yearᵛ 3and put the chest with the Ten Commandments behind the inside curtain.ʷ 4Bring in the table and set on it those things that are made for it. Also bring in the lampstand and attach the lamps to it. 5Then place the gold altar of incense in front of the sacred chest and hang a curtain at the entrance to the tent. 6Set the altar for burning sacrifices in front of the entrance to my tent. 7Put the large

ᵘ39.24-26 *pomegranates*: See the note at 28.33,34.   ᵛ40.2 *first day of the year*: See the note at 12.2.
ʷ40.3 *inside curtain*: Separating the holy place from the most holy place.

When Moses saw that the people had done everything exactly as the LORD had commanded, he gave them his blessing.
EXOD 39.42-43

bronze bowl between the tent and the altar and fill the bowl with water. [8]Surround the tent and the altar with the wall of curtains and hang the curtain that was made for the entrance.

[9]Use the sacred olive oil to dedicate to me the tent and everything in it. [10]Do the same thing with the altar for offering sacrifices and its equipment [11]and with the bowl and its stand. [12]Bring Aaron and his sons to the entrance of the tent and tell them to wash themselves. [13]Dress Aaron in the priestly clothes, then use the sacred olive oil to ordain him and dedicate him to me as my priest. [14]Put the priestly robes on Aaron's sons [15]and ordain them in the same way, so they and their descendants will always be my priests.

[16]Moses followed the Lord's instructions. [17]And on the first day of the first month[x] of the second year, the sacred tent was set up. [18]The posts, stands, and framework were put in place, [19]then the two layers of coverings were hung over them. [20]The stones with the Ten Commandments written on them were stored in the sacred chest, the place of mercy[y] was put on top of it, and the carrying poles were attached. [21]The chest was brought into the tent and set behind the curtain in the most holy place. These things were done exactly as the Lord had commanded Moses.

[22]The table for the sacred bread was put along the north wall of the holy place, [23]after which the bread was set on the table. [24]The lampstand was put along the south wall, [25]then the lamps were attached to it there in the presence of the Lord. [26]The gold incense altar was set up in front of the curtain, [27]and sweet-smelling incense was burned on it. These things were done exactly as the Lord had commanded Moses.

[28]The curtain was hung at the entrance to the sacred tent. [29]Then the altar for offering sacrifices was put in front of the tent, and animal sacrifices and gifts of grain were offered there. [30]The large bronze bowl was placed between the altar and the entrance to the tent. It was filled with water, [31]then Moses and Aaron, together with Aaron's sons, washed their hands and feet. [32]In fact, they washed each time before entering the tent or offering sacrifices at the altar. These things were done exactly as the Lord had commanded Moses.

[33]Finally, Moses had the curtains hung around the courtyard and at the entrance.

The Glory of the Lord

[34]Suddenly the sacred tent was covered by a thick cloud and filled with the glory of the Lord. [35]And so, Moses could not enter the tent. [36]Whenever the cloud moved from the tent, the people would break camp and follow; [37]then they would set up camp and stay there, until it moved again. [38]No matter where the people traveled, the Lord was with them. Each day his cloud was over the tent, and each night a fire could be seen in the cloud.

● 40.17 *first day . . . second year:* The sacred tent was set up exactly one year after the Israelite people began their exodus out of Egypt and celebrated the first Passover (12.2-41).

[x]**40.17** *first month*: See the note at 12.2. [y]**40.20** *place of mercy*: See the note at 26.34.

No matter where the people traveled, the Lord was with them. Each day his cloud was over the tent, and each night a fire could be seen in the cloud. Exod 40.38

Reflection Questions About Exodus 1.1—40.38

1. In the time between Joseph's death (Gen 50.22) and Moses' birth (Exod 2.1,2), what had happened to the Hebrew people living in Egypt? How was God's promise to Abraham and his descendants being threatened (Gen 17.1-9; Exod 1.15-22)?

2. Describe how the LORD chose Moses to lead the people of Israel out of slavery in Egypt. What was Moses worried about? How did the LORD deal with his worries (3.1—4.23)?

3. What was the purpose of the many disasters (plagues) that God sent upon Egypt (9.16)? What kinds of disasters (plagues) would be especially horrible in our day?

4. Retrace the journey of the Israelites from the time they left Egypt until they reached Mount Sinai (13.17—18.27). Name three key events that took place during that journey.

5. Why did Moses appoint judges to help him settle disputes among the Israelites?

6. Describe the scene at Mount Sinai when the LORD God came to give the laws and instructions to Moses and the Israelite people (19.16-25).

7. How does 20.2 serve as a bridge between the events of the exodus and the giving of the laws and instructions? Which of the commandments in 20.2-17 relate to the people's relationship with God? Which relate to their relationship with one another?

8. What was the sacred chest, and where was it to be kept? What was to be kept in it? What was important about the lid of the sacred chest (25.10-22)?

9. In the agreement between God and the Israelites at Sinai, what did God promise? What did God demand in return (34.10-26)?

10. Complete this sentence: "After reading EXODUS, I wonder . . ."

leviticus

Blood sacrifices, grain offerings, and special holy days—read LEVITICUS *to find out how these were an important part of the ongoing relationship between the people of Israel and the* LORD.

WHAT MAKES LEVITICUS SPECIAL?

The name of this book in the Hebrew Scriptures is taken from the first word of the book, which is translated in English as "The LORD spoke." "Leviticus" is the name given to this book in the Greek version of the Old Testament (the Septuagint). It is related to "Levites," the descendants of Levi who had special assigned duties in Israel's priesthood. But this book mentions the Levites only once (25.32-34), and most of the duties described in the book were to be done by the priests from Aaron's family, who actually performed the sacrifices. The Levites did the basic work of preparing sacrifices, cleaning the holy place, and carrying the sacred objects used in Israel's worship service from place to place.

WHAT'S THE STORY BEHIND THE SCENE?

LEVITICUS is the third book in the Pentateuch, as the first five books of the Old Testament are called by Christians. It follows EXODUS, which describes the laws God gave at Mount Sinai and provides instructions for building the sacred tent of meeting and all the holy objects that were to be used in worship. As it exists today, the book probably combines material from the time of Moses with teachings about God's Law that reflect the settled life of Israel in Canaan many years after Moses' death. By then, the people were no longer worshiping in the movable sacred tent that they had used for so many years in the Sinai desert and in Canaan, but were worshiping the LORD in the glorious temple built by Solomon in Jerusalem around 950 B.C. Even so, much of the religious practices described in LEVITICUS continued to be carried out by priests in the temple.

HOW IS LEVITICUS CONSTRUCTED?

The following outline divides the book into two main sections with a number of important divisions.

Israel: Community sacrifice and purity (1.1—16.34)
    Five kinds of sacrifices (1.1—7.38)
    The ordination and work of Israel's priests (8.1—10.20)
    Cleaning out impurity (11.1—16.34)
Israel: God's holy people (17.1—27.34)
    Laws for all God's people (17.1—20.27)
    Laws for the priests and religious festivals (21.1—25.55)
    Keeping promises: The blessings of obedience (26.1—27.34)

Leviticus contains many of the laws for worship and sacrifice that God gave the Israelites. The book also describes the Great Day of Forgiveness (Yom Kippur) and other important religious festivals. Leviticus also gives instruction about religious purity (identifying those things which are clean and those which are unclean), as well as laws that describe the way the people are to treat one another and the kindness they are to show to the poor. In this way, Leviticus emphasizes the responsibilities and duties of God's people—how they should act if they are to be worthy of having God live among them. At the same time, the book makes clear that God's rules are intended to unite the people and help them to live better lives.

Outline

1

1-3 The LORD spoke to Moses from the sacred tent and gave him instructions for the community of Israel to follow when they offered sacrifices.

Sacrifices To Please the LORD

The LORD said:

Sacrifices to please me[a] must be completely burned on the bronze altar.[b]

Bulls or rams or goats[c] are the animals to be used for these sacrifices. If the animal is a bull, it must not have anything wrong with it. Lead it to the entrance of the sacred tent, and I will let you know if it is[d] acceptable to me. **4**Lay your hand on its head, and I will accept the animal as a sacrifice for taking away your sins.

5After the bull is killed in my presence, some priests from Aaron's family will offer its blood to me by splattering it against the four sides of the altar.

6Skin the bull and cut it up, **7**while the priests pile wood on the altar fire to make it start blazing. **8-9**Wash the bull's insides and hind legs, so the priests can lay them on the altar with the head, the fat, and the rest of the animal. A priest will then send all of it up in smoke with a smell that pleases me.

10If you sacrifice a ram or a goat, it must not have anything wrong with it. **11**Lead the animal to the north side of the altar, where it is to be killed in my presence. Then some of the priests will splatter its blood against the four sides of the altar.

12-13 Cut up the animal and wash its insides and hind legs. A priest will put these parts on the altar with the head, the fat,

---

[a]**1.1-3** *Sacrifices to please me:* These sacrifices have traditionally been called "whole burnt offerings" because the whole animal was burned on the altar. A main purpose of such sacrifices was to please the LORD with the smell of the sacrifice, and so in the CEV they are often called "sacrifices to please the LORD." [b]**1.1-3** *bronze altar:* This altar for offering sacrifices was in front of the entrance to the sacred tent; it was made of acacia wood covered with bronze. A smaller altar for offering incense was inside the tent; it was made of acacia wood covered with gold. [c]**1.1-3** *goats:* Hebrew "male goats." [d]**1.1-3** *if it is:* Or "if you are."

■ 1.1-3 *LORD:* In the CEV, "LORD" is usually the translation for the Hebrew name for God, *Yahweh.*

⊂⊃ LORD (YHWH)

■ 1.4 *Lay your hand on:* This was done to show that the sins of the one who brought the animal to be sacrificed were transferred to the animal, and that God would accept the sacrifice and forgive these sins.

■ 1.4 *taking away your sins:* Sin is turning away from God and disobeying God's laws. Israel's priests offered animal sacrifices as a substitute for the sins of the people. See also 4.1—6.7, 24-30.

⊂⊃ Sin

● 1.5 *blood:* Because blood represented life (Gen 4.10,11), it was sacred and not to be eaten (7.26,27; 17.10-14; 19.26; Deut 12.23,24; 15.23). It also had power to protect (Exod 4.25; 12.7,13) and was a sign of the bond between God and the people. Blood splattered or smeared on the altar or on the people had cleansing power and showed that something or someone was dedicated to God (Exod 29.10-21).

⊂⊃ Blood

2.3 rest of this sacrifice: Unlike the whole burnt offerings (1.1-3), which had to be completely burned up, a portion of these grain offerings was to be saved and eaten by the priests in the sacred courtyard of the sacred tent (6.16,17). Israel's priests came from the Levite tribe, which did not receive tribal land when the people of Israel entered Canaan. So, Israel's priests and their families were to be supported by the people from the tribes that did receive land. This meant that Levites could keep portions of the offerings brought by the Israelite people (Num 18.21-24).

2.4,5 bread . . . for this sacrifice: Four different kinds of bread could be used for sacrifices: oven-baked loaves or wafers (2.4), bread made over the fire in a shallow pan (2.5,6) or fried in a covered pan (2.7). No recipe was to include yeast.

2.12 first part: This includes the first harvested grains and the foods made from the first grains harvested. The "first part" was given to honor God and to remember that the people's blessings came from God (23.9-12; Num 18.11,12,26-30; Deut 26.1-15).

2.13 Salt: Salt was used to preserve food in ancient times, so it was sprinkled on sacrifices as a symbol of the lasting agreement between God and God's people.

and the rest of the animal. Then he will send all of it up in smoke with a smell that pleases me.

[14]If you offer a bird for this kind of sacrifice, it must be a dove or a pigeon. [15]A priest will take the bird to the bronze altar, where he will wring its neck and put its head on the fire. Then he will drain out its blood on one side of the altar, [16]remove the bird's craw with what is in it,[e] and throw them on the ash heap at the east side of the altar.[f] [17]Finally, he will take the bird by its wings, tear it partially open,[g] and send it up in smoke with a smell that pleases me.

Sacrifices To Give Thanks to the LORD

The LORD said:

2 When you offer sacrifices to give thanks to me,[h] you must use only your finest flour. Put it in a dish, sprinkle olive oil and incense on the flour, [2]and take it to the priests from Aaron's family. One of them will scoop up the incense together with a handful of the flour and oil. Then, to show that the whole offering belongs to me, the priest will lay this part on the bronze altar and send it up in smoke with a smell that pleases me. [3]The rest of this sacrifice is for the priests; it is very holy because it was offered to me.

[4]If you bake bread in an oven for this sacrifice, use only your finest flour, but without any yeast. You may make the flour into a loaf mixed with olive oil, or you may make it into thin wafers and brush them with oil.

[5]If you cook bread in a shallow pan for this sacrifice, use only your finest flour. Mix it with olive oil, but do not use any yeast. [6]Then break the bread into small pieces and sprinkle them with oil. [7]If you cook your bread in a pan with a lid on it, you must also use the finest flour mixed with oil.

[8]You may prepare sacrifices to give thanks in any of these three ways. Bring your sacrifice to a priest, and he will take it to the bronze altar. [9]Then, to show that the whole offering belongs to me, the priest will lay part of it on the altar and send it up in smoke with a smell that pleases me. [10]The rest of this sacrifice is for the priests; it is very holy because it was offered to me.

[11]Yeast and honey must never be burned on the altar, so don't ever mix either of these in a grain sacrifice. [12]You may offer either of them separately,[i] when you present the first part of your harvest to me, but they must never be burned on the altar.

[13]Salt is offered when you make an agreement with me, so sprinkle salt on these sacrifices.

[14]Freshly cut grain, either roasted or coarsely ground,[j] must be used when you offer the first part of your grain harvest. [15]You must mix in some olive oil and put incense on top, because this is a grain sacrifice. [16]A priest will sprinkle all of the incense and some of the grain and oil on the altar and send them up in smoke to show that the whole offering belongs to me.

---

[e]**1.16** *with what is in it:* One possible meaning for the difficult Hebrew text.   [f]**1.16** *ash heap at the east side of the altar:* Ashes were piled here, then once a day they were taken to the ash heap outside the camp (see 4.11,12; 6.10,11).   [g]**1.17** *tear it partially open:* Or "tear it open without pulling off the wings."   [h]**2.1** *sacrifices to give thanks to me:* These sacrifices have traditionally been called "grain offerings." A main purpose of such sacrifices was to thank the LORD with a gift of grain, and so in the CEV they are sometimes called "sacrifices to give thanks to the LORD."   [i]**2.12** *You . . . separately:* One possible meaning for the difficult Hebrew text.   [j]**2.14** *either . . . ground:* Or "roasted and coarsely ground."

Sacrifices To Ask the LORD's Blessing

The LORD said:

3 When you offer sacrifices to ask my blessing,[k] you may offer either a bull or a cow, but there must be nothing wrong with the animal. [2]Lead it to the entrance of the sacred tent, lay your hand on its head, and have it killed there. A priest from Aaron's family will splatter its blood against the four sides of the altar.

[3]Offer all of the fat on the animal's insides, [4]as well as the lower part of the liver and the two kidneys with their fat. [5]Some of the priests will lay these pieces on the altar and send them up in smoke with a smell that pleases me, together with the sacrifice that is offered to please me.[l]

[6]Instead of a bull or a cow, you may offer any sheep or goat that has nothing wrong with it. [7]If you offer a sheep, you must present it to me at the entrance to the sacred tent. [8]Lay your hand on its head and have it killed there. A priest will then splatter its blood against the four sides of the altar. [9]Offer the fat on the tail, the tailbone, and the insides, [10]as well as the lower part of the liver and the two kidneys with their fat. [11]One of the priests will lay these pieces on the altar and send them up in smoke as a food offering for me.

[12]If you offer a goat, you must also present it to me [13]at the entrance to the sacred tent. Lay your hand on its head and have it killed there. A priest will then splatter its blood against the four sides of the altar. [14]Offer all of the fat on the animal's insides, [15]as well as the lower part of the liver and the two kidneys with their fat. [16]One of the priests will put these pieces on the altar and send them up in smoke as a food offering with a smell that pleases me.

All fat belongs to me. [17]So you and your descendants must never eat any fat or any blood, not even in the privacy of your own homes.[m] This law will never change.

Sacrifices for Sin
(Leviticus 6.24-30)

4 The LORD told Moses [2]to say to the community of Israel:

Offer a sacrifice to ask forgiveness when you sin by accidentally doing something I have told you not to do.

When the High Priest Sins

The LORD said:

[3]When the high priest sins, he makes everyone else guilty too. And so, he must sacrifice a young bull that has nothing wrong with it. [4]The priest will lead the bull to the entrance of the sacred tent, lay his hand on its head, and kill it there. [5]He will take a bowl of the blood inside the tent, [6]dip a finger in the blood, and sprinkle some of it seven times toward the sacred chest behind the curtain. [7]Then, in my presence, he will smear some of the blood on each of the four corners of the incense altar, before pouring out the rest at the foot of the bronze altar[n] near the entrance to the tent.

[8-10]The priest will remove the fat from the bull, just as he does when he sacrifices a

---

• 3.3-5 *fat . . . sacrifice that is offered to please me:* This refers to the layer of fat right below the skin and around the animal's internal organs. Fat belonged to the LORD (3.16).

• 4.1 *Moses:* God chose Moses to lead Israel out of slavery in Egypt (Exod 3–15), and to receive God's laws, including the laws concerning sacrifices (Exod 19–40; Lev 1–3).

∝   Moses

■ 4.2 *sacrifice to ask forgiveness:* Sometimes referred to as "sin offerings," but they are actually done in order to clean or purify one who unintentionally sinned or accidentally did something that was against God's law. Different objects of sacrifice were used for different individuals and for the whole people.

• 4.3 *high priest sins:* Israel's high priest was in charge of the other priests and was the only one who could enter the most holy place in the sacred tent. Aaron was ordained as Israel's first high priest (Exod 29.5-7), so later high priests were regarded as descendants of Aaron. The best animals, rather than injured animals, were to be offered to God. Bulls were an especially valuable sacrifice, see 4.4-12.

■ 4.5-7 *blood . . . seven times . . . bronze altar:* The sprinkling of blood purified the altar. This was done seven times, because seven was a sacred number symbolizing perfection or completeness.

---

[k]3.1 *sacrifices to ask my blessing:* These sacrifices have traditionally been called "peace offerings" or "offerings of well-being." A main purpose was to ask for the LORD's blessing, and so in the CEV they are sometimes called "sacrifices to ask the LORD's blessing." [l]3.5 *sacrifice . . . to please me:* See the note at 1.1-3. [m]3.17 *not even . . . homes:* Or "no matter where you live." [n]4.7 *incense altar . . . bronze altar:* See the note at 1.1-3.

4.13 *whole nation is still guilty:* The idea that all the people of the nation are guilty because of the actions of a few was an important understanding for ancient Israel. A bull was also used as a sacrifice for the sins of the whole nation.

4.26 *sacrifice is offered to ask my blessing:* The offering to ask forgiveness followed a pattern similar to the offering to ask God's blessing.

4.27-32 *ordinary people . . . female goat . . . lamb:* People who were not priests or leaders were to bring a female goat or a lamb as a sacrifice for the forgiveness of sins.

4.32 *lamb . . . nothing wrong with it:* Meaning it could have no blemish or deformity (22.21-24).

bull to ask my blessing.o This includes the fat on the insides, as well as the lower part of the liver and the two kidneys with their fat. He will then send it all up in smoke.

11-12The skin and flesh of the bull, together with its legs, insides, and the food still in its stomach, are to be taken outside the camp and burned on a wood fire near the ash heap.P

When the Whole Nation Sins

The LORD said:

13When the nation of Israel disobeys me without meaning to, the whole nation is still guilty. 14Once you realize what has happened, you must sacrifice a young bull to ask my forgiveness. Lead the bull to the entrance of the sacred tent, 15where your tribal leaders will lay their hands on its head, before having it killed in my presence.

16The priest will take a bowl of the animal's blood inside the sacred tent, 17dip a finger in the blood, and sprinkle some of it seven times toward the sacred chest behind the curtain. 18Then, in my presence, he must smear some of the blood on each of the four corners of the incense altar, before pouring out the rest at the foot of the bronze altarq near the entrance to the tent. 19-21After this, the priest will remove the fat from the bull and send it up in smoke on the altar. Finally, he will burn its remains outside the camp, just as he did with the other bull. By this sacrifice the sin of the whole nation will be forgiven.

When a Tribal Leader Sins

The LORD God said:

22Any tribal leader who disobeys me without knowing it is still guilty. 23As soon

as the leader realizes what has happened, he must sacrifice a goatr that has nothing wrong with it. 24This is a sacrifice for sin. So he will lay his hand on the animal's head, before having it killed in my presence at the north side of the bronze altar. 25The priest will dip a finger in the blood, smear some of it on each of the four corners of the altar, and pour out the rest at the foot of the altar. 26Then he must send all of the fat up in smoke, just as he does when a sacrifice is offered to ask my blessing.s By this sacrifice the leader's sin will be forgiven.

When Ordinary People Sin

The LORD said:

27When any of you ordinary people disobey me without meaning to, you are still guilty. 28As soon as you realize what you have done, you must sacrifice a female goat that has nothing wrong with it. 29Lead the goat to the north side of the bronze altar and lay your hand on its head, before having it killed. 30Then a priest will dip a finger in the blood; he will smear some of it on each of the four corners of the altar and pour out the rest at the foot of the altar. 31After this, the priest will remove all of the fat, just as he does when an animal is sacrificed to ask my blessing.s The priest will then send the fat up in smoke with a smell that pleases me. This animal is sacrificed so that I will forgive you ordinary people when you sin.

32If you offer a lamb instead of a goat as a sacrifice for sin, it must be a female that has nothing wrong with it. 33Lead the lamb to the altar and lay your hand on its head, before having it killed. 34The priest will dip a finger in the blood, smear some of it on

o4.8-10 *to ask my blessing:* See the note at 3.1.   P4.11,12 *ash heap:* See the note at 1.16.   q4.18 *incense altar . . . bronze altar:* See the note at 1.1-3.   r4.23 *goat:* See the note at 1.1-3.   s4.26,31 *sacrifice . . . blessing:* See the note at 3.1.

each of the four corners of the altar, and pour out the rest at the foot of the altar. ³⁵After this, all of the fat must be removed, just as when an animal is sacrificed to ask my blessing. Then the priest will send it up in smoke to me, together with a food offering, and your sin will be forgiven.

The Lord said:

5 If you refuse to testify in court about something you saw or know has happened, you have sinned and can be punished.

²You are guilty and unfit to worship me, if you accidentally touch the dead body of any kind of unclean animal.

³You are guilty if you find out that you have accidentally touched anything unclean that comes from a human body.

⁴You are guilty the moment you realize that you have made a hasty promise to do something good or bad.

⁵As soon as you discover that you have committed any of these sins, you must confess what you have done. ⁶Then you must bring a female sheep or goat to me as the price for your sin. A priest will sacrifice the animal, and you will be forgiven.

⁷If you are poor and cannot afford to bring an animal, you may bring two doves or two pigeons. One of these will be a sacrifice to ask my forgiveness, and the other will be a sacrifice to please me. ⁸Give both birds to the priest, who will offer one as a sacrifice to ask my forgiveness. He will wring its neck without tearing off its head, ⁹splatter some of its blood on one side of the bronze altar, and drain out the rest at the foot of the altar. ¹⁰Then he will follow the proper rules for offering the other bird as a sacrifice to please me.

You will be forgiven when the priest offers these sacrifices as the price for your sin. ¹¹If you are so poor that you cannot afford doves or pigeons, you may bring two pounds of your finest flour. This is a sacrifice to ask my forgiveness, so don't sprinkle olive oil or sweet-smelling incense on it. ¹²Give the flour to a priest, who will scoop up a handful and send it up in smoke together with the other offerings. This is a reminder that all of the flour belongs to me. ¹³By offering this sacrifice, the priest pays the price for any of these sins you may have committed. The priest gets to keep the rest of the flour, just as he does with grain sacrifices.

Sacrifices To Make Things Right
(Leviticus 7.1-10)

¹⁴⁻¹⁵The Lord told Moses what the people must do to make things right when they find out they have cheated the Lord without meaning to:

If this happens, you must either sacrifice a ram that has nothing wrong with it or else pay the price of a ram with the official money used by the priests. ¹⁶In addition, you must pay what you owe plus a fine of 20 percent. Then the priest will offer the ram as a sacrifice to make things right, and you will be forgiven.

¹⁷⁻¹⁹If you break any of my commands without meaning to, you are still guilty, and you can be punished. When you realize what you have done, you must either bring to the priest a ram that has nothing wrong with it or else pay him for one. The priest will then offer it as a sacrifice to make things right, and you will be forgiven.

Other Sins
That Need Sacrifices or Payments
(Numbers 5.5-10)

6 ¹⁻³The Lord told Moses what the people must do when they commit other sins against the Lord:

You have sinned if you rob or cheat

6.8-9 *daily sacrifices*: In ancient Israel a new day was said to begin at sunset, so the priests placed the animal for the daily sacrifice to please the LORD on the bronze altar in the evening and let it burn throughout the night.

6.13 *altar fire . . . must never go out*: The very first sacrifices offered by Aaron on the altar were burned up by a fire sent from the LORD (9.24). The altar fire was to be kept burning so that all later sacrifices could be consumed by fire that had its beginning with the LORD's miraculous fire.

6.20 *ordained*: People who were ordained were chosen and set apart for a special purpose, or dedicated to the LORD. Olive oil was poured on their head as a sign that they had been chosen (Exod 28.41; 29.7). This pouring of oil is also known as "anointing." The full description of the ordination of Israel's priests is given in Exodus 29.1-37 and Leviticus 8.1-36.

6.20 *regular morning and evening sacrifices*: Ordination offerings included a one-pound grain offering at the regular time of the morning and evening sacrifices. This bread offering was to be completely burned up and not eaten.

someone, if you keep back money or valuables left in your care, or if you find something and claim not to have it.

⁴When this happens, you must return what doesn't belong to you ⁵and pay the owner a fine of 20 percent. ⁶⁻⁷In addition, you must either bring to the priest a ram that has nothing wrong with it or else pay him for one. The priest will then offer it as a sacrifice to make things right, and you will be forgiven for what you did wrong.

Daily Sacrifices
(Exodus 29.38-43; Numbers 28.1-8)

⁸⁻⁹The LORD told Moses to tell Aaron and his sons how to offer the daily sacrifices that are sent up in smoke to please the LORD:ᵗ

You must put the animal for the sacrifice on the altar in the evening and let it stay there all night. But make sure the fire keeps burning. ¹⁰The next morning you will dress in your priestly clothes, including your linen underwear. Then clean away the ashes left by the sacrifices and pile them beside the altar. ¹¹Change into your everyday clothes, take the ashes outside the camp, and pile them in the special place.ᵘ

¹²The fire must never go out, so put wood on it each morning. After this, you are to lay an animal on the altar next to the fat that you sacrifice to ask my blessing.ᵛ Then send it all up in smoke to me.

¹³The altar fire must always be kept burning—it must never go out.

Sacrifices To Give Thanks to the LORD

The LORD said:

¹⁴When someone offers a sacrifice to give thanks to me,ʷ the priests from Aaron's family must bring it to the front of the bronze altar, ¹⁵where one of them will scoop up a handful of the flour and oil, together with all the incense on it. Then, to show that the whole offering belongs to me, he will lay all of this on the altar and send it up in smoke with a smell that pleases me. ¹⁶⁻¹⁷The rest of it is to be baked without yeast and eaten by the priests in the sacred courtyard of the sacred tent. This bread is very holy, just like the sacrifices for sin or the sacrifices for making things right, and I have given this part to the priests from what is offered to me on the altar.

¹⁸Only the men in Aaron's family are allowed to eat this bread, and they must go through a ceremony to be made holy before touching it.ˣ This law will never change.

When Priests Are Ordained

¹⁹The LORD spoke to Moses ²⁰and told him what sacrifices the priests must offer on the morning and evening of the day they are ordained:

It is the same as the regular morning and evening sacrifices—a pound of flour ²¹mixed with olive oil and cooked in a shallow pan. The bread must then be crumbled into small piecesʸ and sent up in smoke with a smell that pleases me. ²²⁻²³Each of

ᵗ6.8,9 *to please the* LORD: See the note at 1.1-3.   ᵘ6.11 *ashes . . . in the special place*: See the note at 1.16.   ᵛ6.12 *sacrifice to ask my blessing*: See the note at 3.1.   ʷ6.14 *a sacrifice to give thanks to me*: See the note at 2.1.   ˣ6.18 *and they . . . touching it*: One possible meaning for the difficult Hebrew text.   ʸ6.21 *crumbled . . . pieces*: One possible meaning for the difficult Hebrew text.

Aaron's descendants who is ordained as a priest must perform this ceremony and make sure that the bread is completely burned on the altar. None of it may be eaten!

Sacrifices for Sin

(Leviticus 4.1,2)

[24]The Lord told Moses [25]how the priests from Aaron's family were to offer the sacrifice for sin:

This sacrifice is very sacred, and the animal must be killed in my presence at the north side of the bronze altar. [26]The priest who offers this sacrifice must eat it in the sacred courtyard of the sacred tent, [27]and anyone or anything that touches the meat will be holy.[z] If any of the animal's blood is splattered on the clothes of the priest, they must be washed in a holy place. [28]If the meat was cooked in a clay pot, the pot must be destroyed,[a] but if it was cooked in a bronze pot, the pot must be scrubbed and rinsed with water.

[29]This sacrifice is very holy, and only the priests may have any part of it. [30]None of the meat may be eaten from the sacrifices for sin that require blood to be brought into the sacred tent.[b] These sacrifices must be completely burned.

Sacrifices To Make Things Right

(Leviticus 5.14-19)

The Lord said:

7 The sacrifice to make things right is very sacred. [2]The animal must be killed in the same place where the sacrifice to please me[c] is killed, and the animal's blood must be splattered against the four sides of the bronze altar. [3]Offer all of the animal's fat, including the fat on its tail and on its insides, [4]as well as the lower part of the liver and the two kidneys with their fat. [5]One of the priests will lay these pieces on the altar and send them up in smoke to me. [6]This sacrifice for making things right is very holy. Only the priests may eat it, and they must eat it in a holy place.[d]

[7]The ceremony for this sacrifice and the one for sin are the same, and the meat may be eaten only by the priest who performs this ceremony of forgiveness.

[8]In fact, the priest who offers a sacrifice to please me[e] may keep the skin of the animal, [9]just as he may eat the bread from a sacrifice to give thanks to me.[f] [10]All other grain sacrifices—with or without olive oil in them—are to be divided equally among the priests of Aaron's family.

Sacrifices To Ask the Lord's Blessing

The Lord said:

[11]Here are the instructions for offering a sacrifice to ask my blessing:[g] [12]If you offer it to give thanks, you must offer some bread together with it. Use the finest flour to make three kinds of bread without yeast—two in the form of loaves mixed with olive oil and one in the form of thin wafers brushed with oil. [13]You must also make some bread with yeast. [14]Give me one loaf or wafer from each of these four kinds of bread, after which they will belong to the priest who splattered the blood against the bronze altar.

[15]When you offer an animal to ask a

■ 6.25,26 *sacrifice for sin . . . eat it in the sacred courtyard:* Some of the sacrifices to ask forgiveness were "holy" and were to be eaten by the priest who offered the sacrifice (6.26,29). But sacrifices for sin that required blood to be brought into the sacred tent (4.1-21) were not to be eaten but burned completely on the bronze altar (6.30).

■ 6.27,28 *anyone or anything that touches . . . clay pot:* The sacrificial meat and juices were holy but absorbed the sin or impurity the sacrifice was meant to get rid of. Persons or objects that came into contact with this sacrifice could become polluted by the impurities that the sacrifice had absorbed. The priests had to clean the blood and juices of the sacrifice from their clothes, and clay pots that held the sacrifice had to be destroyed, since clay absorbed the juices and could not be fully cleansed.

■ 7.1 *sacrifice to make things right:* The animal to be sacrificed was killed near the entrance of the sacred tent. This sacrifice was very holy and was to be eaten by the priests in the "holy place," the courtyard of the sacred tent (6.16,17).

● 7.11 *sacrifice to ask my blessing:* Rules for three different kinds of "peace" or "well-being" sacrifice are given. This first is a thank offering using four different kinds of bread.

[z]**6.27** *that touches . . . holy:* One possible meaning for the difficult Hebrew text. [a]**6.28** *clay pot . . . destroyed:* Juice from the meat cannot be completely cleaned from a clay pot. [b]**6.30** *that require blood . . . tent:* See 4.1-21. [c]**7.2** *sacrifice to please me:* See the note at 1.1-3. [d]**7.6** *holy place:* The courtyard of the sacred tent (see 6.16,17). [e]**7.8** *sacrifice to please me:* See the note at 1.1-3. [f]**7.9** *sacrifice to give thanks to me:* See the note at 2.1. [g]**7.11** *sacrifice to ask my blessing:* See the note at 3.1.

7.29-30 *sacrifice to ask my blessing:* The choice ribs were to be kept and eaten by the priest who offered the sacrifice. These ribs were to be waved above the priest's head to show that they were being dedicated to the LORD.

7.38 *desert at Mount Sinai:* God gave the Ten Commandments and the rest of the laws to Moses and the people at Mount Sinai, which was probably located somewhere on the dry Sinai Peninsula.

8.6 *wash themselves:* To make themselves ritually clean, not just to remove dirt.

8.7-9 *priestly shirt . . . sacred vest . . . breastpiece . . . turban:* The shirt was a special embroidered shirt (Exod 28.4,5), and the vest, traditionally referred to as an "ephod," was made of fine linen and colorful wool (Exod 28.6-14). The sash was like a wide belt used to help hold the vest in place. The belt that held the two parts of the vest in place had twelve onyx stones, each engraved with the name of one of the twelve tribes of Israel, who were named after the sons of Jacob (Gen 29.31—30.24; 35.23-26).

The sacred breastpiece was like a flat wool and linen pouch that contained an inner pocket, formed by doubling over the material (Exod 28.16). In the pouch were kept the small objects (also known as the Urim and Thummim) used to receive answers from God. The turban was a kind of headdress that included cloth rolled at its base that was thick enough to support a gold strip.

blessing from me or to thank me, the meat belongs to you, but it must be eaten the same day. [16]It is different with the sacrifices you offer when you make me a promise or voluntarily give me something. The meat from those sacrifices may be kept and eaten the next day, [17-18]but any that is left over must be destroyed. If you eat any of it after the second day, your sacrifice will be useless and unacceptable, and you will be both disgusting and guilty.

[19]Don't eat any of the meat that has touched something unclean. Instead, burn it. The rest of the meat may be eaten by anyone who is clean and acceptable to me. [20-21]But don't eat any of this meat if you have become unclean by touching something unclean from a human or an animal or from any other creature. If you do, you will no longer belong to the community of Israel.

[22]The LORD told Moses [23]to say to the people:

Don't eat the fat of cattle, sheep, or goats. [24]If one of your animals dies or is killed by some wild animal, you may do anything with its fat except eat it. [25]If you eat the fat of an animal that can be used as a sacrifice to me, you will no longer belong to the community of Israel. [26]And no matter where you live, you must not eat the blood of any bird or animal, [27]or you will no longer belong to the community of Israel.

[28]The LORD also told Moses [29-30]to say to the people of Israel:

If you want to offer a sacrifice to ask my blessing, you must bring the part to be burned and lay it on the bronze altar. But you must first lift up[h] the choice ribs with their fat to show that the offering is dedicated to me. [31]A priest from Aaron's family

[h]7.29,30 *lift up:* Or "wave."

will then send the fat up in smoke, but the ribs belong to the priests. [32-33]The upper joint of the right hind leg is for the priest who offers the blood and the fat of the animal. [34]I have decided that the people of Israel must always give the choice ribs and the upper joint of the right hind leg to Aaron's descendants [35]who have been ordained as priests to serve me. [36]This law will never change. I am the LORD!

[37]These are the ceremonies for sacrifices to please the LORD, to give him thanks, and to ask for his blessing or his forgiveness, as well as the ceremonies for those sacrifices that demand a payment and for the sacrifices that are offered when priests are ordained. [38]While Moses and the people of Israel were in the desert at Mount Sinai, the LORD commanded them to start offering these sacrifices.

The Ceremony for Ordaining Priests
(Exodus 29.1-37)

8 The LORD said to Moses:
[2]Send for Aaron and his sons, as well as their priestly clothes, the oil for ordination, the bull for the sin offering, the two rams, and a basket of bread made without yeast. [3]Then bring the whole community of Israel together at the entrance to the sacred tent.

[4]Moses obeyed the LORD, and when everyone had come together, [5]he said, "We are here to follow the LORD's instructions."

[6]After Moses told Aaron and his sons to step forward, he told them to wash themselves. [7]He put the priestly shirt and robe on Aaron and wrapped the sash around his waist. Then he put the sacred vest on

Aaron and fastened it with the finely woven belt. **8**Next, he put on Aaron the sacred breastpiece that was used in finding out what the Lord wanted his people to do. **9**He placed the turban on Aaron's head, and on the front of the turban was the narrow strip of thin gold as a sign of his dedication to the Lord.

10Moses then dedicated the sacred tent and everything in it to the Lord by sprinkling them with some of the oil for ordination. **11**He sprinkled the bronze altar seven times, and he sprinkled its equipment, as well as the large bronze bowl and its base. **12**He also poured some of the oil on Aaron's head to dedicate him to the Lord. **13**Next, Moses dressed Aaron's sons in their shirts, then tied sashes around them and put special caps on them, just as the Lord had commanded.

14Moses led out the bull that was to be sacrificed for sin, and Aaron and his sons laid their hands on its head. **15**After it was killed, Moses dipped a finger in the blood and smeared some of it on each of the four corners of the bronze altar, before pouring out the rest at the foot of the altar. This purified the altar and made it a fit place for offering the sacrifice for sin. **16**Moses then took the fat on the bull's insides, as well as the lower part of the liver and the two kidneys with their fat, and sent them up in smoke on the altar fire. **17**Finally, he took the skin and the flesh of the bull, together with the food still in its stomach, and burned them outside the camp, just as the Lord had commanded.

18Moses led out the ram for the sacrifice to please the Lord.[i] After Aaron and his sons had laid their hands on its head, **19**Moses killed the ram and splattered its blood against the four sides of the altar. **20-21**Moses had the animal cut up, and he washed its insides and hind legs. Then he laid the head, the fat, and the rest of the ram on the altar and sent them up in smoke with a smell that pleased the Lord. All this was done just as the Lord had commanded.

22Moses led out the ram for the ceremony of ordination. Aaron and his sons laid their hands on its head, **23**and it was killed. Moses smeared some of its blood on Aaron's right earlobe, some on his right thumb, and some on the big toe of his right foot. **24**Moses did the same thing for Aaron's sons, before splattering the rest of the blood against the four sides of the altar. **25**He took the animal's fat tail, the fat on its insides, and the lower part of the liver and the two kidneys with their fat, and the right hind leg. **26**Then he took from a basket some of each of the three kinds of bread[j] that had been made without yeast and had been dedicated to the Lord.

27Moses placed the bread on top of the meat and gave it all to Aaron and his sons, who lifted it up[k] to show that it was dedicated to the Lord. **28**After this, Moses placed it on the fires of the altar and sent it up in smoke with a smell that pleased the Lord. This was part of the ordination ceremony. **29**Moses lifted up[k] the choice ribs of the ram to show that they were dedicated to the Lord. This was the part that the Lord had said Moses could have.

30Finally, Moses sprinkled the priestly clothes of Aaron and his sons with some of the oil for ordination and with some of the blood from the altar. So Aaron and his sons, together with their priestly clothes, were dedicated to the Lord.

31Moses said to Aaron and his sons:

■   8.18 *sacrifice to please the Lord*: In the ceremony of ordination, the sin offering was followed by a sacrifice to please the Lord and a sacrifice to thank the Lord (8.26).

■   8.23 *smeared . . . its blood on Aaron's right earlobe . . . thumb . . . big toe*: The practice of smearing blood on persons or statues of gods was common in the ancient Near East. The words spoken during these rituals showed that the smearing was intended to protect the person or object from evil forces. See also Exod 4.24,25.

---

[i]**8.18** *sacrifice to please the Lord*: See the note at 1.1-3.   [j]**8.26** *three kinds of bread*: Made from the finest wheat flour; olive oil was mixed into part of the dough, and some of it was made into thin wafers brushed with oil (see Exodus 29.2,3).   [k]**8.27,29** *lifted it up*: See the note at 7.29,30.

9.1 *Eight days later:* That is, after the seven-day ordination ceremony was over. The priests began their official duties by offering sacrifices for the people.

9.8 *sacrifice for his sins:* "His" refers to the high priest. Aaron is making this sacrifice for his own sins. Later, high priests who were to be descendants of Aaron would be required to make similar sacrifices. (See the chart Sacrifices and Offerings on pg 1828.)

The LORD told me that you must boil this meat at the entrance to the sacred tent and eat it there with the bread. [32]Burn what is left over [33]and stay near the entrance to the sacred tent until the ordination ceremony ends seven days from now. [34]We have obeyed the LORD in everything that has been done today, so that your sins may be forgiven.[l] [35]The LORD has told me that you must stay near the entrance to the tent for seven days and nights, or else you will die.

[36]Aaron and his sons obeyed everything that the LORD had told Moses they must do.

The First Sacrifices Offered by Aaron and His Sons

9 Eight days later Moses called together Aaron, his sons, and Israel's leaders. [2]Then he said to Aaron:

Find a young bull and a ram that have nothing wrong with them. Offer the bull to the LORD as a sacrifice for sin and the ram as a sacrifice to please him.[m]

[3]Tell the people of Israel that they must offer sacrifices as well. They must offer a goat[n] as a sacrifice for sin, and a bull and a ram as a sacrifice to please the LORD. The bull and the ram must be a year old and have nothing wrong with them. [4]Then the people must offer a bull and a ram as a sacrifice to ask the LORD's blessing[o] and also a grain sacrifice[p] mixed with oil. Do this, because the LORD will appear to you today.

[5]After the animals and the grain had been brought to the front of the sacred tent, and the people were standing there in the presence of the LORD, [6]Moses said:

The LORD has ordered you to do this, so that he may appear to you in all of his glory. [7]Aaron, step up to the altar and offer the sacrifice to please the LORD, then offer the sacrifices for the forgiveness of your sins and for the sins of the people, just as the LORD has commanded.

[8]Aaron stepped up to the altar and killed the bull that was to be the sacrifice for his sins. [9]His sons brought him the blood. He dipped a finger in it, smeared some on the four corners of the bronze altar, and poured out the rest at its foot. [10]But he sent up in smoke the fat, the kidneys, and the lower part of the liver, just as the LORD had commanded Moses. [11]Then Aaron burned the skin and the flesh outside the camp.

[12]After Aaron had killed the ram that was sacrificed to please the LORD, Aaron's sons brought him the blood, and he splattered it against all four sides of the altar. [13]They brought him each piece of the animal, including the head, and he burned them all on the altar. [14]He washed the insides and the hind legs and also sent them up in smoke.

[15]Next, Aaron sacrificed the goat for the sins of the people, as he had done with the sacrifice for his own sins. [16]And so, he burned this sacrifice on the altar in the proper way. [17]He also presented the grain sacrifice and burned a handful of the flour on the altar as part of the morning sacrifice.

[18]Finally, he killed the bull and the ram as a sacrifice to ask the LORD's blessing on the people. Aaron's sons brought him the

[l]8.34 *forgiven:* One possible meaning for the difficult Hebrew text of verse 34. [m]9.2 *sacrifice to please him:* See the note at 1.1-3. [n]9.3 *goat:* See the note at 1.1-3. [o]9.4 *to ask the LORD's blessing:* See the note at 3.1. [p]9.4 *grain sacrifice:* To give thanks to the LORD (see the note at 2.1).

blood, and he splattered it against the four sides of the altar. [19]His sons placed all the fat, as well as the kidneys and the lower part of the liver [20]on top of the choice ribs. [21]Then Aaron burned the fat on the altar and lifted up[q] the ribs and the right hind leg to show that these were dedicated to the LORD. This was done just as the LORD had instructed Moses.

[22]Aaron held out his hand and gave the people his blessing, before coming down from the bronze altar where he had offered the sacrifices. [23]He and Moses went into the sacred tent, and when they came out, they gave the people their blessing. Then the LORD appeared to the people in all of his glory. [24]The LORD sent fiery flames that burned up everything on the altar, and when everyone saw this, they shouted and fell to their knees to worship the LORD.

Nadab and Abihu

10 Nadab and Abihu were two of Aaron's sons, but they disobeyed the LORD by burning incense to him on a fire pan, when they were not supposed to.[r] [2]Suddenly the LORD sent fiery flames and burned them to death. [3]Then Moses told Aaron that this was exactly what the LORD had meant when he said:

"I demand respect
    from my priests,
and I will be praised
    by everyone!"

Aaron was speechless.

[4]Moses sent for Mishael and Elzaphan, the two sons of Aaron's uncle Uzziel. Then he told them, "Take these two dead relatives of yours outside the camp far from the entrance to the sacred tent." [5]So they dragged the dead men away by their clothes.

[6]Then Moses told Aaron and his other two sons, Eleazar and Ithamar:

Don't show your sorrow by messing up your hair and tearing your priestly clothes, or the LORD will get angry. He will kill the three of you and punish everyone else. It's all right for your relatives, the people of Israel, to mourn for those he destroyed by fire. [7]But you are the LORD's chosen priests, and you must not leave the sacred tent, or you will die.

Aaron and his two sons obeyed Moses. [8]The LORD said to Aaron:

[9]When you or your sons enter the sacred tent, you must never drink beer or wine. If you do, you will die right there! This law will never change. [10]You must learn the difference between what is holy and what isn't holy and between the clean and the unclean. [11]You must also teach the people of Israel everything that I commanded Moses to say to them.

[12]Moses told Aaron and his two sons, Eleazar and Ithamar:

The grain sacrifice that was offered to give thanks to the LORD[s] is very holy. So make bread without yeast from the part that wasn't sent up in smoke and eat it beside the altar. [13]The LORD has said that this belongs to you and your sons, and that it must be eaten in a holy place. [14-15]But the choice ribs and the hind leg that were lifted up[t] may be eaten by your entire family, as long as you do so in an acceptable place.[u] These parts are yours from the sacrifices that

9.23,24 *LORD appeared . . . fiery flames:* Flames, fire, and smoke often signal God's presence in the Bible (Gen 15.17,18; Exod 3.1-6; 13.21,22; 19.16-19; Judg 13.20; Rev 1.12-16). The fire may have come from the most holy place in the sacred tent (Exod 25.22).

Fire

10.4,5 *Mishael and Elzaphan . . . dragged the dead men away:* These men were Aaron's cousins (Exod 6.22). They dragged Nadab and Abihu by their clothes so as not to have any contact with the corpses, which would have made them unclean.

10.6 *messing . . . hair and tearing . . . clothes:* Like wearing sackcloth and rubbing ashes on the body and face, these acts were done to show extreme sadness (Gen 37.29; Lev 13.45; Jonah 3.4-9). Aaron and his other sons were not to leave the camp (10.7) and join the other mourners. That would have made them ritually unclean and unfit to perform priestly duties.

10.9 *beer or wine:* The priests could not drink alcoholic beverages while on duty, because drinking too much might impair a priest's judgment, causing him to make mistakes when trying to follow the correct procedures for making a sacrifice.

10.14-15 *acceptable place . . . sacrifices . . . to ask the LORD's blessing:* The "acceptable place" mentioned here is the courtyard of the sacred tent (6.24-26).

[q]9.21 *lifted up:* See the note at 7.29,30.   [r]10.1 *when they . . . to:* One possible meaning for the difficult Hebrew text.   [s]10.12 *grain sacrifice . . . to give thanks to the LORD:* See the note at 2.1.   [t]10.14,15 *lifted up:* See the note at 7.29,30.   [u]10.14,15 *acceptable place:* See 6.24-30.

10.19 *what has happened to me:* Aaron may be referring to the death of his older sons or to something that happened to him to make him ritually unclean.

11.4-8 *animals . . . unclean:* See Deut 14.4-21. Animals that "chew the cud" are cattle, sheep, and goats. Pigs, which do not "chew the cud," eat a wide variety of things, including carrion. This may be one reason they were considered unclean.

Purity (Clean and Unclean)

11.9-12 *anything that lives in water:* Fish with scales were clean, but other water creatures like eels were considered unclean.

11.24-28 *animals:* These animals include pigs, cats, dogs, and other animals that walk on their paws.

11.32,33 *something made of wood . . . clay pot:* Unclean things could also transfer their impurity to other objects. Most things could be washed to remove the impurity, but clay pots had to be destroyed, since the porous clay soaked up the impurity. If they weren't destroyed, anything that was put in the pot would become unclean, as would anyone who ate something from an unclean pot. See also 6.28.

11.36 *spring or a cistern:* Water sources that came out of the ground were not made unclean by the body of a dead animal.

the people offer to ask the LORD's blessing.[v] This is what the LORD has commanded, and it will never change.

[16]When Moses asked around and learned that the ram for the sin sacrifice had already been burned on the altar, he became angry with Eleazar and Ithamar and said, [17]"Why didn't you eat the meat from this sacrifice in an acceptable place? It is very holy, and the LORD has given you this sacrifice to remove Israel's sin and guilt. [18]Whenever an animal's blood isn't brought into the sacred tent, I commanded you to eat its meat in an acceptable place, but you burned it instead."

[19]Their father Aaron replied, "Today two of my sons offered the sacrifice for sin and the sacrifice to please the LORD, and look what has happened to me! Would the LORD have approved if I had eaten the sacrifice for sin?"

[20]Moses was satisfied with Aaron's reply.

Clean and Unclean Animals
(Deuteronomy 14.3-21)

11 The LORD told Moses and Aaron [2]to say to the community of Israel:

You may eat [3]any animal that has divided hoofs and chews the cud.[w] [4-8]But you must not eat animals such as camels, rock badgers, and rabbits that chew the cud but don't have divided hoofs. And you must not eat pigs—they have divided hoofs, but don't chew the cud. All of these animals are unclean,[x] and you are forbidden even to touch their dead bodies.

[9-12]You may eat anything that lives in water and has fins and scales. But it would be disgusting for you to eat anything else that lives in water, and you must not even touch their dead bodies.

[13-19]Eagles, vultures, buzzards, crows, ostriches, hawks, sea gulls, owls, pelicans, storks, herons, hoopoes,[y] and bats are also disgusting, and you are forbidden to eat any of them.

[20-23]The only winged insects you may eat are locusts, grasshoppers, and crickets. All other winged insects that crawl are too disgusting for you to eat.

[24-28]Don't even touch the dead bodies of animals that have divided hoofs but don't chew the cud. And don't touch the dead bodies of animals that have paws. If you do, you must wash your clothes, but you are still unclean until evening.

[29-30]Moles, rats, mice, and all kinds of lizards are unclean. [31]Anyone who touches their dead bodies or anything touched by their dead bodies becomes unclean until evening. [32]If something made of wood, cloth, or leather touches one of their dead bodies, it must be washed, but it is still unclean until evening. [33]If any of these animals is found dead in a clay pot, the pot must be broken to pieces, and everything in it becomes unclean. [34]If you pour water from this pot on any food, that food becomes unclean, and anything drinkable in the pot becomes unclean.

[35]If the dead body of one of these animals touches anything else, including ovens and stoves, that thing becomes unclean and must be destroyed. [36]A spring or a cistern where one of these dead animals is

[v]10.14,15 *to ask the LORD's blessing:* See the note at 3.1.   [w]11.3 *chews the cud:* Some animals that eat grass and leaves have more than one stomach and chew their food a second time after it has been partly digested in the first stomach. This partly digested food is called the "cud."   [x]11.4-8 *unclean:* In the Old Testament "clean" and "unclean" refer to whatever makes a person, animal, or object acceptable or unacceptable to God. For example, a person became unclean by eating certain foods, touching certain objects, and having certain kinds of diseases or bodily discharges.
[y]11.13-19 *Eagles . . . hoopoes:* Some of the birds in this list are difficult to identify.

found is still clean, but anyone who touches the animal becomes unclean. **37**If the dead body of one of these animals is found lying on seeds that have been set aside for planting, the seeds remain clean. **38**But seeds that are soaking in water become unclean, if the dead animal is found in the water.

39If an animal that may be eaten happens to die, and you touch it, you become unclean until evening. **40**If you eat any of its meat or carry its body away, you must wash your clothes, but you are still unclean until evening.

41-42 Don't eat any of those disgusting little creatures that crawl or walk close to the ground. **43**If you eat any of them, you will become just as disgusting and unclean as they are. **44**I am the Lord your God, and you must dedicate yourselves to me and be holy, just as I am holy. Don't become disgusting by eating any of these unclean creatures. **45**I brought you out of Egypt so that I could be your God. Now you must become holy, because I am holy!

46-47I have given these laws so that you will know what animals, birds, and fish are clean and may be eaten, and which ones are unclean and may not be eaten.

What Women Must Do after Giving Birth

12 The Lord told Moses **2**to say to the community of Israel:

If a woman gives birth to a son, she is unclean for seven days, just as she is during her monthly period. **3**Her son must be circumcised on the eighth day, **4**but her loss of blood keeps her from being completely clean for another 33 days. During this time she must not touch anything holy or go to

the place of worship. **5**Any woman who gives birth to a daughter is unclean for two weeks, just as she is during her period. And she won't be completely clean for another 66 days.

6When the mother has completed her time of cleansing, she must come to the front of the sacred tent and bring to the priest a year-old lamb as a sacrifice to please me**z** and a dove or a pigeon as a sacrifice for sin. **7**After the priest offers the sacrifices to me, the mother will become completely clean from her loss of blood, whether her child is a boy or a girl. **8**If she cannot afford a lamb, she can offer two doves or two pigeons, one as a sacrifice to please me and the other as a sacrifice for sin.

Skin Diseases

13 The Lord told Moses and Aaron to say to the people:

2If sores or boils or a skin rash should break out and start spreading on your body, you must be brought to Aaron or to one of the other priests. **3**If the priest discovers that the hair in the infected area has turned white and that the infection seems more than skin deep, he will say, "This is leprosy**a**—you are unclean."

4But if the infected area is white and only skin deep, and if the hair in it hasn't turned white, the priest will order you to stay away from everyone else for seven days. **5**If the disease hasn't spread by that time, he will order you to stay away from everyone else for another seven days. **6**Then if the disease hasn't become any worse or spread, the priest will say, "You are clean. It is only a sore. After you wash your clothes, you may go home."

7However, if the disease comes back, you

z12.6 *sacrifice to please me:* See the note at 1.1-3.   **a13.3** *leprosy:* The word translated "leprosy" was used for many different kinds of skin diseases.

I am the Lord your God, and you must dedicate yourselves to me and be holy, just as I am holy. Lev 11.44

13.8 *spreading:* Non-spreading scabs were not considered unclean.

13.18-19 *sore that . . . swells:* This probably refers to boils or other skin swelling due to infections.

13.25 *burn has turned into leprosy:* Burns don't turn to leprosy, but burns that become infected were considered leprous and unclean.

13.29 *sore on your head or chin:* Persons with diseases or sores on the head that were only skin deep and didn't spread would be declared clean after seven days and after their clothes were washed (13.33). Normal baldness didn't make one unclean, but sores that broke out on the bald spot could be called unclean.

must return to the priest. [8]If it is discovered that the disease has started spreading, he will say, "This is leprosy—you are unclean."

[9]Any of you with a skin disease must be brought to a priest. [10]If he discovers that the sore spot is white with pus and that the hair around it has also turned white, [11]he will say, "This is leprosy. You are unclean and must stay away from everyone else." [12-13]But if the disease has run its course and only the scars remain, he will say, "You are clean." [14-15]If the sores come back and turn white again, he will say, "This is leprosy—you are unclean."

[16-17]However, if the sores heal and only white spots remain, the priest will say, "You are now clean."

[18-19]If you have a sore that either swells or turns reddish-white after it has healed, then you must show it to a priest. [20]If he discovers that the hair in the infected area has turned white and that the infection seems more than skin deep, he will say, "This is leprosy—you are unclean." [21]But if the white area is only on the surface of the skin and hasn't become any worse, and if the hair in it hasn't turned white, he will tell you to stay away from everyone else for seven days.

[22]If the sore begins spreading during this time, the priest will say, "You are unclean because you have a disease." [23]But if it doesn't spread, and only a scar remains, he will say, "You are now clean."

[24]If you have a burn that gets infected and turns red or reddish-white, [25]a priest must examine it. Then if he discovers that the hair in the infected area has turned white and that the infection seems more than skin deep, he will say, "The burn has turned into leprosy, and you are unclean." [26]But if the priest finds that the hair in the infected area hasn't turned white and that the sore is only skin deep and it is healing,

he will tell you to stay away from everyone else for seven days. [27]On the seventh day the priest will examine you again, and if the infection is spreading, he will say, "This is leprosy—you are unclean." [28]However, if the infection hasn't spread and has begun to heal, and if only a scar remains, he will say, "Only a scar remains from the burn, and you are clean."

[29]If you have a sore on your head or chin, [30]it must be examined by a priest. If the infection seems more than skin deep, and the hair in it has thinned out and lost its color, he will say, "This is leprosy—you are unclean." [31]On the other hand, if he discovers that the itchy spot is only skin deep, but that the hair still isn't healthy, he will order you to stay away from everyone else for seven days. [32]By that time, if the itch hasn't spread, if the hair seems healthy, and if the itch is only skin deep, [33]you must shave off the hair around the infection, but not those on it. Then the priest will tell you to stay away from everyone else for another seven days. [34]By that time, if the itch hasn't spread and seems no more than skin deep, he will say, "You are clean; now you must wash your clothes."

[35-36]Later, if the itch starts spreading, even though the hair is still healthy, the priest will say, "You are unclean." [37]But if he thinks you are completely well, he will say, "You are clean."

[38]If white spots break out on your skin, [39]but the priest discovers that it is only a rash, he will say, "You are clean."

[40-41]If you become bald on any part of your head, you are still clean. [42-43]But if a priest discovers that a reddish-white sore has broken out on the bald spot and looks like leprosy, he will say, [44]"This is leprosy—you are unclean."

[45]If you ever have leprosy, you must tear your clothes, leave your hair uncombed, cover the lower part of your face, and go

around shouting, "I'm unclean! I'm unclean!" **46**As long as you have the disease, you are unclean and must live alone outside the camp.

47-50 If a greenish or reddish spot[b] appears anywhere on any of your clothing or on anything made of leather, you must let the priest examine the clothing or the leather. He will put it aside for seven days, **51**and if the mildew has spread in that time, he will say, "This is unclean **52**because the mildew has spread." Then he will burn the clothing or the piece of leather.

53If the priest discovers that the mildew hasn't spread, **54**he will tell you to wash the clothing or leather and put it aside for another seven days, **55**after which he will examine it again. If the spot hasn't spread, but is still greenish or reddish, the clothing or leather is unclean and must be burned. **56**But if the spot has faded after being washed, he will tear away the spot. **57**Later, if the spot reappears elsewhere on the clothing or the leather, you must burn it. **58**Even if the spot completely disappears after being washed, it must be washed again before it is clean.

59These are the rules for deciding if clothing is clean or unclean after a spot appears on it.

The Ceremony for People Healed of Leprosy

14 The LORD told Moses to say to the people:

2-3 After you think you are healed of leprosy,[c] you must ask for a priest to come outside the camp and examine you. And if you are well, **4**he will order someone to bring out two live birds that are acceptable for sacrifice, together with a stick of cedar wood, a piece of red yarn, and a branch from a hyssop plant. **5**The priest will order someone to kill one of the birds over a clay pot of spring water. **6**Then he will dip the other bird, the cedar, the red yarn, and the hyssop in the blood of the dead bird. **7**Next, he will sprinkle you seven times with the blood and say, "You are now clean." Finally, he will release the bird and let it fly away.

8After this you must wash your clothes, shave your entire body, and take a bath before you are completely clean. You may move back into camp, but you must not enter your tent for seven days. **9**Then you must once again shave your head, face, and eyebrows, as well as the hair on the rest of your body. Finally, wash your clothes and take a bath, and you will be completely clean.

10On the eighth day you must bring to the priest two rams and a year-old female lamb that have nothing wrong with them; also bring a half pint of olive oil and six pounds of your finest flour mixed with oil. **11**Then the priest will present you and your offerings to me at the entrance to my sacred tent. **12**There he will offer one of the rams, together with the pint of oil, as a sacrifice to make things right.[d] He will also lift them up[e] to show that they are dedicated to me. **13**This sacrifice is very holy. It belongs to the priest and must be killed in the same place where animals are killed as sacrifices for sins and as sacrifices to please me.[f]

14The priest will smear some of the blood from this sacrifice on your right ear lobe, some on your right thumb, and some on the big toe of your right foot. **15**He will

13.47-52 *spot . . . mildew:* Those who wore clothes with mildew would be considered ritually impure (unclean). If mildew spread on leather or a garment, the garment was to be destroyed.

14.2-3 *leprosy:* A person who had recovered from leprosy needed to show himself to the priest so that the priest could confirm that the leper was healed. If so, the healed leper could make the prescribed sacrifice and rejoin the Israelite community. Jesus was aware of this practice and insisted that the lepers he healed show themselves to a priest.

14.6 *dip:* Dipping the objects in blood may have been thought to transfer the person's uncleanness to the blood, which had the power to purify. The live bird then flew away carrying the impurity with it.

14.8 *wash . . . shave:* After washing and shaving twice, washing his clothes and staying out of his tent for seven days, a person was considered clean and could once again be part of his family and the whole people of God.

14.12 *sacrifice to make things right:* Part of this sacrifice was to be lifted up or waved to show that it was dedicated to the LORD. This sacrifice was done in case the unclean person had touched a sacred object or entered a holy space while unclean, and the sacrifice was to be made at the entrance to the sacred tent.

---

[b]**13.47-50** *spot:* The Hebrew word translated "spot" and "mildew" in verses 47-59 is the same one translated "leprosy" earlier in the chapter.   [c]**14.2,3** *leprosy:* See the note at 13.3.   [d]**14.12** *sacrifice to make things right:* See 7.1-10.   [e]**14.12** *lift them up:* See the note at 7.29,30.   [f]**14.13** *sacrifices to please me:* See the note at 1.1-3.

14.21 *If you are poor:* The Law includes a number of instructions on how the Israelites were to treat the poor.

14.34 *Canaan:* Canaan was the land God promised to give Abraham and his descendants (Gen 17.7,8; Exod 3.8). **(See Map 3 on pg 1881.)**

Palestine

14.36 *Empty the house:* People or objects removed from the house before the inspection were considered clean.

14.40-41 *unclean place outside the town:* This probably refers to a dumping area for garbage and other unclean items.

14.45-47 *house torn down . . . wash your clothes:* If mildew reappeared, the whole building was to be destroyed and taken away from the camp or town. Anyone who entered a diseased house was considered unclean and had to wash to purify himself or herself.

then pour some of the olive oil into the palm of his left hand, [16]dip a finger of his right hand into the oil, and sprinkle some of it seven times toward the sacred tent. [17]Next, the priest will smear some of the oil on your right ear lobe, some on your right thumb, and some on the big toe of your right foot, [18-20]and he will pour the rest of the oil from his palm on your head. Then he will offer the other two animals—one as a sacrifice for sin and the other as a sacrifice to please me, together with a grain sacrifice. After this you will be completely clean.

[21]If you are poor and cannot afford to offer this much, you may offer a ram as a sacrifice to make things right, together with a half pint of olive oil and two pounds of flour mixed with oil as a grain sacrifice. The priest will then lift these up[g] to dedicate them to me. [22]Depending on what you can afford, you must also offer either two doves or two pigeons, one as a sacrifice for sin and the other as a sacrifice to please me. [23]The priest will offer these to me in front of the sacred tent on the eighth day.

[24-25]The priest will kill this ram for the sacrifice to make things right, and he will lift it up[g] with the olive oil in dedication to me. Then he will smear some of the blood on your right ear lobe, some on your right thumb, and some on the big toe of your right foot.

[26]The priest will pour some of the olive oil into the palm of his left hand, [27]then dip a finger of his right hand in the oil and sprinkle some of it seven times toward the sacred tent. [28]He will smear some of the oil on your right ear lobe, some on your right thumb, and some on the big toe of your right foot, just as he did with the blood of the sacrifice to make things right. [29-31]And

he will pour the rest of the oil from his palm on your head.

Then, depending on what you can afford, he will offer either the doves or the pigeons together with the grain sacrifice. One of the birds is the sacrifice for sin, and the other is the sacrifice to please me. After this you will be completely clean.

[32]These are the things you must do if you have leprosy and cannot afford the usual sacrifices to make you clean.

When There Is Mildew in a House

[33]The LORD told Moses and Aaron to say to the people:

[34]After I have given you the land of Canaan as your permanent possession, here is what you must do, if I ever put mildew[h] on the walls of any of your homes. [35]First, you must say to a priest, "I think there is mildew on the wall of my house."

[36]The priest will reply, "Empty the house before I inspect it, or else everything in it will be unclean."

[37]If the priest discovers greenish or reddish spots that go deeper than the surface of the walls, [38]he will have the house closed for seven days. [39]Then he will return and check to see if the mildew has spread. [40-41]If so, he will order someone to scrape the plaster from the walls, remove the stones covered with mildew, then haul everything off and dump it in an unclean place outside the town. [42]Afterwards the wall must be repaired with new stones and fresh plaster.

[43]If the mildew appears a second time, [44]the priest will come and say, "This house is unclean. It's covered with mildew that can't be removed." [45]Then he will have the house torn down and every bit of wood,

[g]14.21,24,25 *lift these up:* See the note at 7.29,30. [h]14.34 *mildew:* The Hebrew word translated "mildew" is the same one translated "leprosy" and "spot" in chapter 13.

stone, and plaster hauled off to an unclean place outside the town. **46**Meanwhile, if any of you entered the house while it was closed, you will be unclean until evening. **47**And if you either slept or ate in the house, you must wash your clothes.

48On the other hand, if the priest discovers that mildew hasn't reappeared after the house was newly plastered, he will say, "This house is clean—the mildew has gone." **49**Then, to show that the house is now clean, he will get two birds, a stick of cedar wood, a piece of red yarn, and a branch from a hyssop plant and bring them to the house. **50**He will kill one of the birds over a clay pot of spring water **51-52**and let its blood drain into the pot. Then he will dip the cedar, the hyssop, the yarn, and the other bird into the mixture of blood and water. Next, he will sprinkle the house seven times with the mixture, then the house will be completely clean. **53**Finally, he will release the bird and let it fly away, ending the ceremony for purifying the house.

54-57 These are the things you must do if you discover that you are unclean because of an itch or a sore, or that your clothing or house is unclean because of mildew.

Sexual Uncleanness

15 The LORD told Moses and Aaron **2**to say to the community of Israel:

Any man with an infected penis is unclean, **3**whether it is stopped up or keeps dripping. **4**Anything that he rests on or sits on is also unclean, **5-7**and if you touch either these or him, you must wash your clothes and take a bath, but you still remain unclean until evening.

8If you are spit on by the man, you must wash your clothes and take a bath, but you

still remain unclean until evening. **9-10**Any saddle or seat on which the man sits is unclean. And if you touch or carry either of these, you must wash your clothes and take a bath, but you still remain unclean until evening. **11**If the man touches you without first washing his hands, you must wash your clothes and take a bath, but you still remain unclean until evening. **12**Any clay pot that he touches must be destroyed, and any wooden bowl that he touches must be washed.

13Seven days after the man gets well, he will be considered clean, if he washes his clothes and takes a bath in spring water. **14**On the eighth day he must bring either two doves or two pigeons to the front of my sacred tent and give them to a priest. **15**The priest will offer one of the birds as a sacrifice for sin and the other as a sacrifice to please me,[i] then I will consider the man completely clean.

16Any man who has a flow of semen must take a bath, but he still remains unclean until evening. **17**If the semen touches anything made of cloth or leather, these must be washed, but they still remain unclean until evening. **18**After having sex, both the man and the woman must take a bath, but they still remain unclean until evening.

19When a woman has her monthly period, she remains unclean for seven days, and if you touch her, you must take a bath, but you remain unclean until evening. **20-23**Anything that she rests on or sits on is also unclean, and if you touch either of these, you must wash your clothes and take a bath, but you still remain unclean until evening. **24**Any man who has sex with her during this time becomes unclean for seven days, and anything he rests on is also unclean.

[i]**15.15** *sacrifice to please me*: See the note at 1.1-3.

15.28-30 *Seven days after . . . sacrifice:* Seven days after her monthly period stopped, a woman was to bring a sacrifice to ask forgiveness (a "sin offering") and a sacrifice to please the LORD. Then she would be considered clean again. That meant that a woman had to spend a significant part of each month at home and not go near the place of worship.

☙ The Sacred Chest

16.7,8 *goats . . . demon Azazel:* On the Great Day of Forgiveness two goats were to be offered for the people's sins (compare this to 4.13-15, which says a bull is to be offered for the nation's sin). One goat was killed and sacrificed, and the other was sent away to Azazel, an evil demon that was believed to live in the desert. (See the chart Pilgrimage Festivals on pg 1799.)

16.12 *fire pan . . . bronze altar . . . incense:* The fire pan was made of bronze and was used at the bronze altar of sacrifice (Exod 27.3).

16.13 *place of mercy:* The smoke from the burning incense was to cover God's presence on the place of mercy and protect the high priest who came into God's presence.

16.14 *sprinkle some of the blood:* The blood sprinkled seven times in front of the sacred chest was from the bull (16.11). Then Aaron sprinkled blood from the goat inside the most holy place, in order to take away the sins of the people.

[25]Any woman who has a flow of blood outside her regular monthly period is unclean until it stops, just as she is during her monthly period. [26]Anything that she rests on or sits on during this time is also unclean, just as it would be during her period. [27]If you touch either of these, you must wash your clothes and take a bath, but you still remain unclean until evening.

[28]Seven days after the woman gets well, she will be considered clean. [29]On the eighth day, she must bring either two doves or two pigeons to the front of my sacred tent and give them to a priest. [30]He will offer one of the birds as a sacrifice for sin and the other as a sacrifice to please me; then I will consider the woman completely clean.

[31]When any of you are unclean, you must stay away from the rest of the community of Israel. Otherwise, my sacred tent will become unclean, and the whole nation will die.

[32-33]These are the things you men must do if you become unclean because of an infected penis or if you have a flow of semen. And these are the things you women must do when you become unclean either because of your monthly period or an unusual flow of blood. This is also what you men must do if you have sex with a woman who is unclean.

The Great Day of Forgiveness

16 [1-2]Two of Aaron's sons had already lost their lives for disobeying the LORD,[j] so the LORD told Moses to say to Aaron:

I, the LORD, appear in a cloud over the place of mercy on the sacred chest, which is behind the inside curtain[k] of the sacred tent. And I warn you not to go there except at the proper time. Otherwise, you will die!

[3]Before entering this most holy place, you must offer a bull as a sacrifice for your sins[l] and a ram as a sacrifice to please me.[m] [4]You will take a bath and put on the sacred linen clothes, including the underwear, the robe, the sash, and the turban. [5]Then the community of Israel will bring you a ram and two goats, both of them males. The goats are to be used as sacrifices for sin, and the ram is to be used as a sacrifice to please me.

[6]Aaron, you must offer the bull as a sacrifice of forgiveness for your own sins and for the sins of your family. [7]Then you will lead the two goats into my presence at the front of the sacred tent, [8]where I will show you[n] which goat will be sacrificed to me and which one will be sent into the desert to the demon Azazel.[o] [9]After you offer the first goat as a sacrifice for sin, [10]the other one must be presented to me alive, before you send it into the desert to take away the sins of the people.

[11]You must offer the bull as a sacrifice to ask forgiveness for your own sins and for the sins of your family. [12]Then you will take a fire pan of live coals from the bronze altar, together with two handfuls of finely ground incense, into the most holy place. [13]There you will present them to me by placing the incense on the coals, so that the place of mercy will be covered with a cloud of smoke. Do this, or you will die right there! [14]Next, use a finger to sprinkle

---

[j]16.1,2 *lost . . . disobeying the LORD*: See 10.1,2.   [k]16.1,2 *inside curtain*: That separated the holy place from the most holy place.   [l]16.3 *for your sins*: See 4.3-12.   [m]16.3 *sacrifice to please me*: See the note at 1.1-3.   [n]16.8 *I will show you*: The Hebrew text has "you must cast lots to find out." Pieces of wood or stone (called "lots") were used to find out what God wanted his people to do.   [o]16.8 *Azazel*: It was believed that a demon named Azazel lived in the desert.

some of the blood on the place of mercy, which is on the lid of the sacred chest; then sprinkle blood seven times in front of the chest.

¹⁵Aaron, you must next sacrifice the goat for the sins of the people, and you must sprinkle its blood inside the most holy place, just as you did with the blood of the bull. ¹⁶By doing this, you will take away the sins that make both the most holy place and the people of Israel unclean. Do the same for the sacred tent, which is here among the people. ¹⁷Only you are allowed in the sacred tent from the time you enter until the time you come out. ¹⁸After leaving the tent, you will purify the bronze altar by smearing each of its four corners with some of the blood from the bull and from the goat. ¹⁹Use a finger to sprinkle the altar seven times with the blood, and it will be completely clean from the sins of the people.

²⁰After you have purified the most holy place, the sacred tent, and the bronze altar, you must bring the live goat to the front of the tent. ²¹There you will lay your hands on its head, while confessing every sin the people have committed, and you will appoint someone to lead the goat into the desert, so that it can take away their sins. ²²Finally, this goat that carries the heavy burden of Israel's sins must be released deep in the desert.

²³⁻²⁴Aaron, after this you must go inside the sacred tent, take a bath, put on your regular priestly clothes, and leave there the clothes you put on before entering the most holy place. Then you will come out and offer sacrifices to please me and sacrifices for your sins and for the sins of the people. ²⁵The fat from these sacrifices for

sin must be sent up in smoke on the bronze altar.

²⁶The one who led the goat into the desert and sent it off to the demon Azazel must take a bath and wash his clothes before coming back into camp. ²⁷The remains of the bull and the goat whose blood was taken into the most holy place must be taken outside the camp and burned. ²⁸And whoever does this must take a bath and change clothes before coming back into camp.

The LORD told Moses to say to the people:
²⁹On the tenth day of the seventh month^P of each year, you must go without eating to show sorrow for your sins, and no one, including foreigners who live among you, is allowed to work. ³⁰This is the day on which the sacrifice for the forgiveness of your sins will be made in my presence, ³¹and from now on, it must be celebrated each year. Go without eating and make this a day of complete rest just like the Sabbath. ³²The high priest must offer the sacrifices for cleansing from sin, while wearing the sacred linen clothes. ³³He will offer these sacrifices for the most holy place, the sacred tent, the bronze altar, all the priests, and for the whole community. ³⁴You must celebrate this day each year— it is the Great Day of Forgiveness^q for all the sins of the people of Israel.

Moses did exactly as the LORD had commanded.

Where To Offer Sacrifices

17 The LORD told Moses ²to tell Aaron, his sons, and everyone else in Israel: ³⁻⁴Whenever you kill any of your cattle,

---

^{P}16.29 *seventh month*: Tishri (also called Ethanim), the seventh month of the Hebrew calendar, from about mid-September to mid-October. ^{q}16.34 *Great Day of Forgiveness*: Traditionally known as the Day of Atonement.

■   16.21 *confessing every sin the people:* The confession of sins along with the laying of hands transferred the sins of the people to the goat. The goat that was sent into the desert has traditionally been called the "scapegoat."

●   16.23-24 *regular priestly clothes:* The clothes the high priest had worn in the most holy place were left behind, because they had been in the presence of God.

●   16.26 *one who led the goat . . . take a bath and wash his clothes:* The person who led the goat out of the camp carrying the people's sins and those who removed the remains of the bull and goat from the camp had to wash and change clothes, since they had come into contact with holy things. See also Heb 13.11.

●   16.29-31 *go without eating . . . like the Sabbath:* To go without eating is also called fasting. People fasted during times of mourning. Here, fasting is done to show sorrow for sins on the Great Day of Forgiveness. The Sabbath was the weekly day of rest that began at sunset on Friday and ended with a blessing (benediction) at sunset on Saturday. Observing the Sabbath, which means to "rest" or to "stop working" was a rule for all Jewish people (Exod 20.8-11; Deut 5.12-15). **(See the chart Pilgrimage Festivals on pg 1799.)**

Moses told the people: "You must celebrate this day each year—it is the Great Day of Forgiveness for all the sins of the people of Israel." LEV 16.34

17.11 *Life is in the blood:* Blood drained from an animal killed while hunting was to be covered with dirt, so it could not be used in an improper ceremony, such as idol worship involving blood.

18.5 *I am the LORD:* What set the people of Israel apart from their neighbors was that God had chosen them and given them laws that they were to follow with loyalty and obedience.

18.6 *sex with . . . relatives:* Just as the people's faith in the LORD was to set them apart from their neighbors, so was their lifestyle. Following strict rules about sexual behavior was one way to set themselves apart.

Purity (Clean and Unclean)

18.21 *god Molech:* This name is related to the Hebrew name for "king" (*melech*) but it is changed slightly, so that it sounds like the word for "shame." People sacrificed their children to this Ammonite god by burning them in the Hinnom Valley near Jerusalem (20.1-5; Deut 12.31; 2 Kgs 16.3; 17.17; 23.10; Jer 7.30,31; 19.4-5; Ezek 16.20,21; 20.31).

sheep, or goats as sacrifices to me, you must do it at the entrance to the sacred tent. If you don't, you will be guilty of pouring out blood, and you will no longer belong to the community of Israel. **5**And so, when you sacrifice an animal to ask my blessing,[r] it must not be done out in a field, **6**but in front of the sacred tent. Then a priest can splatter its blood against the bronze altar and send its fat up in smoke with a smell that pleases me. **7**Don't ever turn from me again and offer sacrifices to goat-demons. This law will never change.

8Remember! No one in Israel, including foreigners, is to offer a sacrifice anywhere **9**except at the entrance to the sacred tent. If you do, you will no longer belong to my people.

Do Not Eat Blood

The LORD said:

10I will turn against any of my people who eat blood. This also includes any foreigners living among you. **11**Life is in the blood, and I have given you the blood of animals to sacrifice in place of your own. **12**That's also why I have forbidden you to eat blood. **13**Even if you should hunt and kill a bird or an animal, you must drain out the blood and cover it with soil.

14The life of every living creature is in its blood. That's why I have forbidden you to eat blood and why I have warned you that anyone who does will no longer belong to my people.

15If you happen to find a dead animal and eat it, you must take a bath and wash your clothes, but you are still unclean until evening. **16**If you don't take a bath, you will suffer for what you did wrong.

Forbidden Sex

18 The LORD told Moses **2**to tell the people of Israel:

I am the LORD your God! **3**So don't follow the customs of Egypt where you used to live or those of Canaan where I am bringing you. **4**I am the LORD your God, and you must obey my teachings. **5**Obey them and you will live. I am the LORD.

6Don't have sex with any of your close relatives, **7**especially your own mother. This would disgrace your father. **8**And don't disgrace him by having sex with any of his other wives. **9**Don't have sex with your sister or stepsister, whether you grew up together or not. **10**Don't disgrace yourself by having sex with your granddaughter **11**or half sister **12-13**or a sister of your father or mother. **14**Don't disgrace your uncle by having sex with his wife. **15**Don't have sex with your daughter-in-law **16**or sister-in-law. **17**And don't have sex with the daughter or granddaughter of any woman that you have earlier had sex with. You will be having sex with her closest relatives, and that will make you unclean. **18**As long as your wife is alive, don't cause trouble for her by taking one of her sisters as a second wife.

19When a woman is having her monthly period, she is unclean, so don't have sex with her.

20Don't have sex with another man's wife—that would make you unclean.

21Don't sacrifice your children on the altar fires to the god Molech. I am the LORD your God, and that would disgrace me.

22It is disgusting for a man to have sex with another man.

23Anyone who has sex with an animal is unclean.

[r]**17.5** *sacrifice . . . to ask my blessing:* See the note at 3.1.

²⁴Don't make yourselves unclean by any of these disgusting practices of those nations that I am forcing out of the land for you. They made themselves ²⁵and the land so unclean, that I punished the land because of their sins, and I made it vomit them up. ²⁶⁻²⁷Now don't do these sickening things that make the land filthy. Instead, obey my laws and teachings. ²⁸Then the land won't become sick of you and vomit you up, just as it did them. ²⁹⁻³⁰If any of you do these vulgar, disgusting things, you will be unclean and no longer belong to my people. I am the LORD your God, and I forbid you to follow their sickening way of life.

Moral and Religious Laws

19 The LORD told Moses ²to say to the community of Israel:

I am the LORD your God. I am holy, and you must be holy too! ³⁻⁴Respect your father and your mother, honor the Sabbath, and don't make idols or images. I am the LORD your God.

⁵When you offer a sacrifice to ask my blessing,ˢ be sure to follow my instructions. ⁶You may eat the meat either on the day of the sacrifice or on the next day, but you must burn anything left over on the third day. ⁷If you eat any of it on the third day, the sacrifice will be disgusting to me, and I will reject it. ⁸In fact, you will be punished for not respecting what I say is holy, and you will no longer belong to the community of Israel.

⁹When you harvest your grain, always leave some of it standing along the edges of your fields and don't pick up what falls on the ground. ¹⁰Don't strip your grapevines clean or gather the grapes that fall off the vines. Leave them for the poor and for those foreigners who live among you. I am the LORD your God.

¹¹Do not steal or tell lies or cheat others. ¹²Do not misuse my name by making promises you don't intend to keep. I am the LORD your God.

¹³Do not steal anything or cheat anyone, and don't fail to pay your workers at the end of each day.ᵗ

¹⁴I am the LORD your God, and I command you not to make fun of the deaf or to cause a blind person to stumble.

¹⁵Be fair, no matter who is on trial— don't favor either the poor or the rich.

¹⁶Don't be a gossip, but never hesitate to speak up in court, especially if your testimony can save someone's life.ᵘ

¹⁷Don't hold grudges. On the other hand, it's wrong not to correct someone who needs correcting. ¹⁸Don't be angry or try to take revenge. I am the LORD, and I command you to love others as much as you love yourself.

¹⁹Breed your livestock animals only with animals of the same kind, and don't plant two kinds of seed in the same field or wear clothes made of different kinds of material.

²⁰If a man has sex with a slave woman who is promised in marriage to someone else, he must pay a fine, but they are not to be put to death. After all, she was still a slave at the time.ᵛ ²¹⁻²²The man must bring a ram to the entrance of the sacred tent and give it to a priest, who will then offer it as a sacrifice to me, so the man's sins will be forgiven.

ˢ**19.5** *sacrifice . . . to ask my blessing:* See the note at 3.1.   ᵗ**19.13** *to pay . . . end of each day:* Day laborers needed their wages to buy food for their evening meal, which was the main meal of the day.
ᵘ**19.16** *but never . . . someone's life:* One possible meaning for the difficult Hebrew text.
ᵛ**19.20** *time:* One possible meaning for the difficult Hebrew text of verse 20.

■ 18.24 *disgusting practices of those nations:* Though Israel had not yet entered Canaan, this verse refers to the people they would force out when they took over that land. Disgusting practices probably refers to idol worship.

❧ Canaanite Gods and Goddesses

■ 18.25 *I punished the land:* Immoral living pollutes the land itself (makes it unclean). This is part of the basis for the idea of a "holy land," which remains clean (acceptable to God) if all people who live there, including foreigners (17.8,10), obey God's laws.

■ 19.9 *leave some:* Being a holy people did not simply mean Israelites shall avoid doing things that would make them unclean. It also meant they should look out for the needs of others, especially the poor, who were allowed to pick up leftover grain after the harvest (23.22). See also 23.22; Deut 24.19-22; Ruth 2.1-3.

■ 19.19 *same kind . . . two kinds:* This may be based on the belief that in creation God separated everything according to their own species (Gen 1). Keeping things separate was seen as following the natural order of God's created world. See Deut 22.9-11.

19.24 *fruit must be set apart:* Meaning dedicated or presented as holy to the LORD.

19.26 *practice any kind of witchcraft:* Witchcraft included casting spells, fortunetelling, and trying to talk to the spirits of the dead (19.31; Deut 18.10,11). Witchcraft was forbidden by the Law of Moses.

19.29 *temple prostitutes:* This may refer to the practice of women serving as prostitutes at the temple of a foreign god such as the fertility god Baal. But such activities disgraced the land.

20.2 *Death by stoning:* Dropping or placing heavy stones on someone was one of the most common forms of execution in Israelite society.

²³After you enter the land, you will plant fruit trees, but you are not to eat any fruit from them for the first three years. ²⁴In the fourth year the fruit must be set apart, as an expression of thanks ²⁵to me, the LORD God. Do this, and in the fifth year, those trees will produce an abundant harvest of fruit for you to eat.

²⁶Don't eat the blood of any animal.

Don't practice any kind of witchcraft.

²⁷⁻²⁸I forbid you to shave any part of your head or beard or to cut and tattoo yourself as a way of worshiping the dead.

²⁹Don't let your daughters serve as temple prostitutes—this would bring disgrace both to them and the land.

³⁰I command you to respect the Sabbath and the place where I am worshiped.

³¹Don't make yourselves disgusting to me by going to people who claim they can talk to the dead.

³²I command you to show respect for older people and to obey me with fear and trembling.

³³Don't mistreat any foreigners who live in your land. ³⁴Instead, treat them as well as you treat your own people and love them as much as you love yourself. Remember, you were once foreigners in the land of Egypt. I am the LORD your God.

³⁵⁻³⁶Use honest scales and don't cheat when you weigh or measure anything.

I am the LORD your God. I rescued you from Egypt, ³⁷and I command you to obey my laws.

Penalties for Disobeying God's Laws

20 The LORD told Moses ²to say to the community of Israel:

Death by stoning is the penalty for any citizens or foreigners in the country who sacrifice their children to the god Molech. ³They have disgraced both the place where I am worshiped and my holy name, and so I will turn against them and no longer let them belong to my people. ⁴Some of you may let them get away with human sacrifice, ⁵but not me. If any of you worship Molech, I will turn against you and your entire family, and I will no longer let you belong to my people.

⁶I will be your enemy if you go to someone who claims to speak with the dead, and I will destroy you from among my people. ⁷Dedicate yourselves to me and be holy because I am the LORD your God. ⁸I have chosen you as my people, and I expect you to obey my laws.

⁹If you curse your father or mother, you will be put to death, and it will be your own fault.

¹⁰If any of you men have sex with another man's wife, both you and the woman will be put to death.

¹¹Having sex with one of your father's wives disgraces him. So both you and the woman will be put to death, just as you deserve. ¹²It isn't natural to have sex with your daughter-in-law, and both of you will be put to death, just as you deserve. ¹³It's disgusting for men to have sex with one another, and those who do will be put to death, just as they deserve. ¹⁴It isn't natural for a man to marry both a woman and her daughter, and so all three of them will be burned to death. ¹⁵⁻¹⁶If any of you have sex with an animal, both you and the animal will be put to death, just as you deserve.

¹⁷If you marry one of your sisters, you will be punished, and the two of you will be disgraced by being openly forced out of the community. ¹⁸If you have sex with a woman during her monthly period, both you and the woman will be cut off from the people of Israel. ¹⁹The sisters of your father and mother are your own relatives, and you will be punished for having sex

with any of them. ²⁰If you have sex with your uncle's wife, neither you nor she will ever have any children. ²¹And if you marry your sister-in-law, neither of you will ever have any children.^w

²²Obey my laws and teachings. Or else the land I am giving you will become sick of you and throw you out. ²³The nations I am chasing out did these disgusting things, and I hated them for it, so don't follow their example. ²⁴I am the LORD your God, and I have promised you their land that is rich with milk and honey. I have chosen you to be different from other people. ²⁵That's why you must make a difference between animals and birds that I have said are clean and unclean^x—this will keep you from becoming disgusting to me. ²⁶I am the LORD, the holy God. You have been chosen to be my people, and so you must be holy too.

²⁷If you claim to receive messages from the dead, you will be put to death by stoning, just as you deserve.

Instructions for Priests

21 The LORD gave Moses these instructions for Aaron's sons, the priests:

Touching a dead body will make you unclean. So don't go near a dead relative, ²except your mother, father, son, daughter, brother, ³or an unmarried sister, who has no husband to take care of her. ⁴Don't make yourself unclean by attending the funeral of someone related to you by marriage.^y ⁵Don't shave any part of your head or trim your beard or cut yourself to show that you are mourning. ⁶I am the LORD your God, and I have chosen you alone to offer sacrifices of food to me on the altar. That's why you must keep yourselves holy. ⁷Don't marry a divorced woman or a woman who has served as a temple prostitute. You are holy, ⁸because I am holy. And so, you must be treated with proper respect, since you offer food sacrifices to me, the God of holiness.

⁹If any of you priests has a daughter who disgraces you by serving as a temple prostitute, she must be burned to death.

¹⁰If you are the high priest, you must not mess up your hair or tear your clothes in order to mourn for the dead. ¹¹Don't make yourself unclean by going near a dead body, not even that of your own father or mother. ¹²If you leave the sacred place to attend a funeral, both you and the sacred place become unclean, because you are the high priest.

¹³If you are the high priest, you must marry only a virgin ¹⁴from your own tribe. Don't marry a divorced woman or any other woman who has already had sex, including a temple prostitute. ¹⁵In this way, your descendants will be qualified to serve me. Remember—I am the LORD, and I have chosen you.

¹⁶The LORD told Moses ¹⁷⁻¹⁸to say to Aaron:

No descendant of yours can ever serve as my priest if he is blind or lame, if his face is disfigured, if one leg is shorter than the other, ¹⁹if either a foot or a hand is paralyzed, ²⁰if he is a hunchback or a dwarf, if an eye or his skin is diseased, or if his testicles have been damaged. ²¹These men may not serve as my priests and burn sacrifices to me. ²²They may eat the food offerings presented to me, ²³but they may not enter

● *21.1 the priests:* The regulations in chapter 21 were given to keep the priests from becoming ritually impure, making them unfit to do their work on behalf of the people.

● *21.13 marry only a virgin:* Since the office of high priest was passed on within a family, a young man would know he was next in line to be high priest even while his father was still the acting high priest (6.22,23). The young man was to marry a Levite woman, but one from a different clan.

● *21.17-20 blind . . . damaged:* Just as animals given for sacrifice could not have any defects, so those who handled the sacrifices or entered the holy place of the sacred tent were to be without defects. By modern standards, this seems harsh, but this rule was based on the Israelite understanding of holiness, which meant that all things chosen and dedicated to God were to represent the perfection of God's creation. Although men with such defects could not serve at the altar, they were not abandoned by the community. They could eat the food the priests ate and likely helped the priests with certain tasks, such as getting rid of the ashes from the daily sacrifice.

^w**20.21** *And . . . children:* According to Deuteronomy 25.5,6 a man was supposed to marry his brother's widow if his brother had died without having children. Otherwise, such marriages were forbidden (see also Matthew 22.23-33; Mark 12.18-27; Luke 20.27-40). ^x**20.25** *clean and unclean:* See the note at 11.4-8. ^y**21.4** *marriage:* One possible meaning for the difficult Hebrew text of verse 4.

22.8 *killed by a wild animal . . . natural death:* The rule for ordinary people was not as strict (17.15). The priests were to rely on the food that came from portions of the sacrifices they offered. To eat food from other sources showed a lack of faith. This rule was more than a diet restriction; it had to do with the priests trusting in God to provide for their needs.

22.10,11 *servants . . . slave:* Paid laborers could not eat any of the sacred food, that is, portions of the sacrificial meat, bread, and grains. But slaves who lived in the households of the priestly families could eat the sacred food. Even though the Israelites had themselves been slaves in Egypt, they apparently also had some slaves that they had bought from slave traders, such as the Midianites or Ishmaelites (see Gen 37.28,36). The Hebrew people were not to keep slaves longer than six years, unless the slave asked to continue serving his master. The slave's ear was pierced as a sign of his life-long commitment (Exod 21.6).

22.25 *foreigner:* This means someone who was not born into an Israelite family. Only animals bred and raised by the Israelites could be used for sacrifices.

Foreigners (Aliens)

22.29 *sacrifice to give thanks:* This is not the sacrifice to give thanks described in chapter 2, which involved grain and bread offerings. This offering of thanks can include an animal sacrifice (7.12-16).

the sacred place or serve me at the altar. Remember—I am the Lord, the one who makes a priest holy. ²⁴Moses told all of this to Aaron, his sons, and the people of Israel.

The Offerings Are Holy

22 The Lord told Moses ²to say to Aaron and his sons:

I am the Lord God, and I demand that you honor my holy name by showing proper respect for the offerings brought to me by the people of Israel. ³If any of you are unclean when you accept an offering for me, I will no longer let you serve as a priest. ⁴None of you may take part in the sacred meals while you have a skin disease or an infected penis, or after you have been near a dead body or have had a flow of semen, ⁵or if you have touched an unclean creature of any sort, including an unclean person. ⁶⁻⁷Once you are unclean, you must take a bath, but you still cannot eat any of the sacred food until evening. ⁸I command you not to eat anything that is killed by a wild animal or dies a natural death. This would make you unclean. ⁹Obey me, or you will die on duty for disgracing the place of worship. Remember—I am the Lord, the one who makes a priest holy.

¹⁰Only you priests and your families may eat the food offerings; these are too sacred for any of your servants. ¹¹However, any slave that you own, including those born into your household, may eat this food. ¹²If your daughter marries someone who isn't a priest, she can no longer have any of this food. ¹³But if she returns to your home, either widowed or divorced, and has no children, she may join in the meal. Only members of a priestly family can eat this food, ¹⁴and anyone else who accidentally

does so, must pay for the food plus a fine of 20 percent.

¹⁵I warn you not to treat lightly the offerings that are brought by the people of Israel. ¹⁶Don't let them become guilty of eating this sacred food. Remember—I am the Lord, the one who makes these offerings holy.

Acceptable Sacrifices

¹⁷The Lord told Moses ¹⁸to tell Aaron and his sons and everyone else the rules for offering sacrifices. He said:

The animals that are to be completely burned on the altar ¹⁹⁻²⁰must have nothing wrong with them, or else I won't accept them. Bulls or rams or goatsᶻ are the animals to be used for these sacrifices.

²¹When you offer a sacrifice to ask my blessing,ᵃ there must be nothing wrong with the animal. This is true, whether the sacrifice is part of a promise or something you do voluntarily. ²²Don't offer an animal that is blind or injured or that has an infection or a skin disease. ²³If one of your cattle or lambs has a leg that is longer or shorter than the others, you may offer it voluntarily, but not as part of a promise. ²⁴As long as you live in this land, don't offer an animal with injured testicles. ²⁵And don't bring me animals you bought from a foreigner. I won't accept them, because they are no better than one that has something wrong with it.

²⁶The Lord told Moses to say:

²⁷Newborn cattle, sheep, or goats must remain with their mothers for seven days, but on the eighth day, you may send them up in smoke to me, and I will accept the offering. ²⁸Don't sacrifice a newborn animal and its mother on the same day.

²⁹When you offer a sacrifice to give

ᶻ**22.19,20** *goats:* See the note at 1.1-3.   ᵃ**22.21** *sacrifice to ask my blessing:* See the note at 3.1.

thanks[b] to me, you must do it in a way that is acceptable. [30]Eat all of the meat that same day and don't save any for the next day. I am the LORD your God!

[31]Obey my laws and teachings—I am the LORD. [32-33]I demand respect from the people of Israel, so don't disgrace my holy name. Remember—I am the one who chose you to be priests and rescued all of you from Egypt, so that I would be your LORD.

Religious Festivals

23 The LORD told Moses [2]to say to the community of Israel:

I have chosen certain times for you to come together and worship me.

[3]You have six days when you can do your work, but the seventh day of each week is holy because it belongs to me. No matter where you live, you must rest on the Sabbath and come together for worship. This law will never change.

Passover and the Festival of Thin Bread
(Numbers 28.16-25)

The LORD said:

[4-5]Passover is another time when you must come together to worship me, and it must be celebrated on the evening of the fourteenth day of the first month[c] of each year. [6]The Festival of Thin Bread begins on the fifteenth day of that same month; it lasts seven days, and during this time you must honor me by eating bread made without yeast. [7]On the first day of this festival you must rest from your work and come together for worship. [8]Each day of this festi-

val you must offer sacrifices. Then on the final day you must once again rest from your work and come together for worship.

Offering the First Part of the Harvest

[9]The LORD told Moses [10]to say to the community of Israel:

After you enter the land I am giving you, the first bundle of wheat from each crop must be given to me. So bring it to a priest [11]on the day after the Sabbath. He will lift it up[d] in dedication to me, and I will accept you. [12]You must also offer a sacrifice to please me.[e] So bring the priest a one-year-old lamb that has nothing wrong with it [13]and four pounds of your finest flour mixed with olive oil. Then he will place these on the bronze altar and send them up in smoke with a smell that pleases me. Together with these, you must bring a quart of wine as a drink offering. [14]I am your God, and I forbid you to eat any new grain or anything made from it until you have brought these offerings. This law will never change.

The Harvest Festival
(Numbers 28.26-31)

The LORD said:

[15]Seven weeks after you offer this bundle of grain, each family must bring another offering of new grain. [16]Do this exactly 50 days later, which is the day following the seventh Sabbath. [17]Bring two loaves of bread to be lifted up[f] in dedication to me. Each loaf is to be made with yeast and with four pounds of the finest flour from the first part of your harvest.

[b]**22.29** *sacrifice to give thanks:* See 7.12.   [c]**23.4,5** *first month:* Abib (also called Nisan), the first month of the Hebrew calendar, from about mid-March to mid-April.   [d]**23.11** *lift it up:* See the note at 7.29,30.   [e]**23.12** *sacrifice to please me:* See the note at 1.1-3.   [f]**23.17** *lifted up:* See the note at 7.29,30.

23.4-5 *Passover . . . first month:* The "Passover" is related to the Hebrew verb translated as "pass over" in Exodus 12.1-13,23,27. This festival was celebrated as a remembrance of how God acted to save the Israelite people from slavery in Egypt. See also Deut 16.1,2. The first month of the Hebrew calendar is Abib (also called Nisan), which lasts from about mid-March to mid-April. **(See the chart Pilgrimage Festivals on pg 1799.)**

23.6 *Festival of Thin Bread:* This feast began the day after Passover and lasted seven days (Num 28.16-25). The thin bread that was to be eaten during Passover and the Festival of Thin Bread was a reminder of how quickly the people had to leave Egypt. They did not have time to let the dough for their bread rise.

GR Passover and the Festival of Thin Bread

23.14 *new grain:* The newest (first-cut) grain belonged to God. Requiring this offering reminded the people that God was the source of the peoples' blessings.

23.16 *50 days later:* Fifty days after offering the first grain offering during the Festival of Thin Bread, a new offering was brought to the Harvest Festival, also known as the Feast of Weeks and later as Pentecost (see Acts 2.1; 20.16; 1 Cor 16.8). The people presented grain to God as a sign of thanks and to show confidence that God would continue to meet their needs. See also Exod 23.16; 34.22; Deut 16.9-12.

23.24-25 *seventh month . . . trumpets*: The Festival of Trumpets was observed by trumpet blasts, special sacrifices, and rest from work. Trumpets were also blown on the first day of every month ("new moon," Ps 81.3). These trumpets were probably hammered metal horns made of silver (Num 10.2) that measured about a foot long. Today, this first day of the seventh month is known as *Rosh Hashanah*, meaning "the beginning of the year."

23.27 *Great Day of Forgiveness*: This festival is also known as *Yom Kippur*.

23.34 *Festival of Shelters*: This festival took place at the end of the fall harvest (Exod 23.16; Deut 16.13-17) and lasted for seven days. In addition to giving thanks to God for the fall harvest, the people were to build and live in shelters made of tree branches (23.40-42). The temporary shelters were to be a reminder of how the people lived in the wilderness after leaving Egypt. See also Neh 8 and Ezek 45.25. This festival is traditionally known as Sukkoth or the "Feast of Tabernacles."

[18]At this same time, the entire community of Israel must bring seven lambs that are a year old, a young bull, and two rams. These animals must have nothing wrong with them, and they must be offered as a sacrifice to please me.[g] You must also offer the proper grain and wine sacrifices with each animal.[h] [19]Offer a goat[i] as a sacrifice for sin, and two rams a year old as a sacrifice to ask my blessing.[j] [20]The priest will lift up[k] the rams together with the bread in dedication to me. These offerings are holy and are my gift to the priest. [21]This is a day of celebration and worship, a time of rest from your work. You and your descendants must obey this law.

[22]When you harvest your grain, always leave some of it standing around the edges of your fields and don't pick up what falls on the ground. Leave it for the poor and for those foreigners who live among you. I am the LORD your God!

The Festival of Trumpets
(Numbers 29.1-6)

[23]The LORD told Moses [24-25]to say to the people of Israel:

The first day of the seventh month[l] must be a day of complete rest. Then at the sound of the trumpets, you will come together to worship and to offer sacrifices on the altar.

The Great Day of Forgiveness
(Numbers 29.7-11)

[26]The LORD God said to Moses:

[27]The tenth day of the seventh month[l] is the Great Day of Forgiveness.[m] It is a solemn day of worship; everyone must go without eating to show sorrow for their sins, and sacrifices must be burned. [28]No one is to work on that day—it is the Great Day of Forgiveness, when sacrifices will be offered to me, so that I will forgive your sins. [29]I will destroy anyone who refuses to go without eating. [30-31]None of my people are ever to do any work on that day—not now or in the future. And I will wipe out those who do! [32]This is a time of complete rest just like the Sabbath, and everyone must go without eating from the evening of the ninth to the evening of the tenth.

The Festival of Shelters
(Numbers 29.12-40)

[33]The LORD told Moses [34]to say to the community of Israel:

Beginning on the fifteenth day of the seventh month,[n] and continuing for seven days, everyone must celebrate the Festival of Shelters in honor of me. [35]No one is to do any work on the first day of the festival—it is a time when everyone must come together for worship. [36]For seven days, sacrifices must be offered on the altar. The eighth day is also to be a day of complete rest, as well as a time of offering sacrifices on the altar and of coming together for worship.

[37]I have chosen these festivals as times when my people must come together for worship and when animals, grain, and wine are to be offered on the proper days. [38]These festivals must be celebrated in addition to the Sabbaths and the times when you offer special gifts or sacrifices to keep a promise or as a voluntary offering.

g**23.18** *sacrifice to please me*: See the note at 1.1-3.   h**23.18** *proper grain . . . animal*: See Numbers 15.1-16.   i**23.19** *goat*: See the note at 1.1-3.   j**23.19** *sacrifice to ask my blessing*: See the note at 3.1.   k**23.20** *lift up*: See the note at 7.29,30.   l**23.24,25,27** *seventh month*: See the note at 16.29.   m**23.27** *Great Day of Forgiveness*: See the note at 16.34.   n**23.34** *seventh month*: See the note at 16.29.

[39]Remember to begin the Festival of Shelters on the fifteenth day of the seventh month after you have harvested your crops. Celebrate this festival for seven days in honor of me and don't do any work on the first day or on the day following the festival. [40]Pick the best fruit from your trees[o] and cut leafy branches to use during the time of this joyous celebration in my honor. [41]I command you and all of your descendants to celebrate this festival during the seventh month of each year. [42]For seven days every Israelite must live in a shelter, [43]so future generations will know that I made their ancestors live in shelters when I brought them out of Egypt. I am the Lord your God.

[44]This is how Moses instructed the people of Israel to celebrate the Lord's festivals.

Caring for the Lamps
(Exodus 27.20,21)

24 The Lord told Moses [2]to say to the community of Israel:

You must supply the purest olive oil for the lamps in the sacred tent, so they will keep burning. [3-4]Aaron will set up the gold lampstand in the holy place of the sacred tent. Then he will light the seven lamps that must be kept burning there in my presence, every night from now on. This law will never change.

The Sacred Bread

The Lord said:

[5]Use your finest flour to bake twelve loaves of bread about four pounds each, [6]then take them into the sacred tent and lay them on the gold table in two rows of six loaves. [7]Alongside each row put some pure incense that will be sent up by fire in place of the bread as an offering to me. [8]Aaron must lay fresh loaves on the table each Sabbath, and priests in all generations must continue this practice as part of Israel's agreement with me. [9]This bread will always belong to Aaron and his family; it is very holy because it was offered to me, and it must be eaten in a holy place.[P]

Punishment for Cursing the Lord

[10-11]Shelomith, the daughter of Dibri from the tribe of Dan, had married an Egyptian, and they had a son. One day their son got into a fight with an Israelite man in camp and cursed the name of the Lord. So the young man was dragged off to Moses, [12]who had him guarded while everyone waited for the Lord to tell them what to do.

[13]Finally, the Lord said to Moses:

[14]This man has cursed me! Take him outside the camp and tell the witnesses to lay their hands on his head. Then command the whole community of Israel to stone him to death. [15-16]And warn the others that everyone else who curses me will die in the same way, whether they are Israelites by birth or foreigners living among you.

[17]Death is also the penalty for murder, [18]but the killing of an animal that belongs to someone else requires only that the animal be replaced. [19]Personal injuries to others must be dealt with in keeping with the crime—[20]a broken bone for a broken bone, an eye for an eye, or a tooth for a tooth. [21]It's possible to pay the owner for an animal that has been killed, but death is

---

[o]**23.40** *best fruit from your trees:* One possible meaning for the difficult Hebrew text.   [P]**24.9** *holy place:* The courtyard of the sacred tent (see 6.16,17).

● **23.40-42** *fruit . . . leafy branches . . . shelter:* The kind of fruit is unclear. The shelters were to be made of the branches of leafy trees, such as the olive, myrtle, and palm. See also Neh 8.13-16.

● **24.5,6** *finest flour . . . twelve loaves . . . on the gold table:* Finest flour was made of wheat. Twelve fresh loaves representing the twelve tribes of Israel were to be placed on the holy table every Sabbath (24.8). The loaves were an ongoing offering to God and a reminder of God's blessings. The gold table, also located in the holy place of the sacred tent, probably resembled a modern coffee table with a raised ridge all around its top.

■ **24.10-11** *cursed the name of the Lord:* This phrase can mean a number of things, such as, using God's name to break promises, telling lies after swearing to tell the truth, using the Lord's name as a curse word or a magic formula, and trying to control the Lord by using the name. But the young man here may have said the sacred name of God, which was not to be spoken aloud. See also Exod 3.14,15; Lev 19.12; Deut 5.11.

● **24.14** *witnesses lay their hands . . . stone him:* Speaking God's sacred name aloud affected not only the speaker but all those who heard it as well. The laying on of hands transferred the bad effect (guilt) from the hearers back to the one who spoke the name.

25.4 *seventh year . . . let your fields and vineyards rest:* The year of rest was intended to help the soil regain some of the nutrients lost in the previous growing seasons. The plants and grasses that grew up during the year of rest would be plowed into the soil to make it richer and more fertile.

25.9,10 *seventh month . . . Great Day of Forgiveness . . . fiftieth year:* The last year of seven seven-year cycles was the Year of Celebration, traditionally known as the Jubilee year. During this year property was to be returned to its original owners (25.11,13). This was done so that each Israelite tribe could hold on to the land they were given when they first entered the land of Canaan (Num 34.1-29; Josh 15.1-14). Deuteronomy 15.1-11 adds that during this year debts should be canceled and any crops that grew on their own were to be left for the poor.

25.14-15 *Year of Celebration:* Land bought one year before the Year of Celebration had to be returned to the family that originally owned it. The price would be low, since the land would only have one year to produce crops. The price of the land was really a rental fee paid for the right to grow crops on the land and sell its produce.

25.25 *relative must buy:* If a relative cannot buy the land, it can be sold, but the original owner must buy it back along with a fair rental price when he can afford to.

the penalty for murder. **22**I am the LORD your God, and I demand equal justice both for you Israelites and for those foreigners who live among you. **23**When Moses finished speaking, the people did what the LORD had told Moses, and they stoned to death the man who had cursed the LORD.

The Seventh Year
(Deuteronomy 15.1-11)

25 When Moses was on Mount Sinai, the LORD told him **2**to say to the community of Israel:

After you enter the land that I am giving you, it must be allowed to rest one year out of every seven. **3**You may raise grain and grapes for six years, **4**but the seventh year you must let your fields and vineyards rest in honor of me, your LORD. **5**This is to be a time of complete rest for your fields and vineyards, so don't harvest anything they produce. **6-7**However, you and your slaves and your hired workers, as well as any domestic or wild animals, may eat whatever grows on its own.

The Year of Celebration

The LORD said to his people:
8Once every 49 years **9**on the tenth day of the seventh month,q which is also the Great Day of Forgiveness,r trumpets are to be blown everywhere in the land. **10**This fiftieth years is sacred—it is a time of freedom and of celebration when everyone will receive back their original property, and slaves will return home to their families. **11**This is a year of complete celebration, so don't plant any seed or harvest

what your fields or vineyards produce. **12**In this time of sacred celebration you may eat only what grows on its own.

13During this year, all property must go back to its original owner. **14-15**So when you buy or sell farmland, the price is to be determined by the number of crops it can produce before the next Year of Celebration. Don't try to cheat. **16**If it is a long time before the next Year of Celebration, the price will be higher, because what is really being sold are the crops that the land can produce. **17**I am the LORD your God, so obey me and don't cheat anyone.

18-19 If you obey my laws and teachings, you will live safely in the land and enjoy its abundant crops. **20**Don't ever worry about what you will eat during the seventh year when you are forbidden to plant or harvest. **21**I will see to it that you harvest enough in the sixth year to last for three years. **22**In the eighth year you will live on what you harvested in the sixth year, but in the ninth year you will eat what you plant and harvest in the eighth year.

23No land may be permanently bought or sold. It all belongs to me—it isn't your land, and you only live there for a little while.

24When property is being sold, the original owner must be given the first chance to buy it.

25If any of you Israelites become so poor that you are forced to sell your property, your closest relative must buy it back, **26**if that relative has the money. Later, if you can afford to buy it, **27**you must pay enough to make up for what the present owner will lose on it before the next Year of Celebration, when the property would become yours again. **28**But if you don't have the money to pay the present owner a fair

q25.9 *seventh month:* See the note at 16.29. r25.9 *Great Day of Forgiveness:* See the note at 16.34.
s25.10 *fiftieth year:* The year following seven periods of seven years.

price, you will have to wait until the Year of Celebration, when the property will once again become yours.

²⁹If you sell a house in a walled city, you have only one year in which to buy it back. ³⁰If you don't buy it back before that year is up, it becomes the permanent property of the one who bought it, and it will not be returned to you in the Year of Celebration. ³¹But a house out in a village may be bought back at any time just like a field. And it must be returned to its original owner in the Year of Celebration. ³²If any Levites own houses inside a walled city, they will always have the right to buy them back. ³³And any houses that they do not buy back will be returned to them in the Year of Celebration, because these homes are their permanent property among the people of Israel. ³⁴No pasture-land owned by the Levi tribe can ever be sold; it is their permanent possession.

Help for the Poor

The LORD said:

³⁵If any of your people become poor and unable to support themselves, you must help them, just as you are supposed to help foreigners who live among you. ³⁶-³⁷Don't take advantage of them by charging any kind of interest or selling them food for profit. Instead, honor me by letting them stay where they now live. ³⁸Remember—I am the LORD your God! I rescued you from Egypt and gave you the land of Canaan, so that I would be your God.

³⁹Suppose some of your people become so poor that they have to sell themselves and become your slaves. ⁴⁰Then you must treat them as servants, rather than as slaves. And in the Year of Celebration they are to be set free, ⁴¹so they and their children may return home to their families and property. ⁴²I brought them out of Egypt to be my servants, not to be sold as slaves. ⁴³So obey me, and don't be cruel to the poor.

⁴⁴If you want slaves, buy them from other nations ⁴⁵or from the foreigners who live in your own country, and make them your property. ⁴⁶You can own them, and even leave them to your children when you die, but do not make slaves of your own people or be cruel to them.

⁴⁷Even if some of you Israelites become so much in debt that you must sell yourselves to foreigners in your country, ⁴⁸you still have the right to be set free by a relative, such as a brother ⁴⁹or uncle or cousin, or some other family member. In fact, if you ever get enough money, you may buy your own freedom ⁵⁰by paying your owner for the number of years you would still be a slave before the next Year of Celebration. ⁵¹-⁵²The longer the time until then, the more you will have to pay. ⁵³And even while you are the slaves of foreigners in your own country, your people must make sure that you are not mistreated. ⁵⁴If you cannot gain your freedom in any of these ways, both you and your children will still be set free in the Year of Celebration. ⁵⁵People of Israel, I am the LORD your God, and I brought you out of Egypt to be my own servants.

Blessings for Obeying the LORD

The LORD said:

26 I am the LORD your God! So don't make or worship idols or images. ²Respect the Sabbath and honor the place where I am worshiped, because I am the LORD.

³Faithfully obey my laws, ⁴and I will send rain to make your crops grow and your trees produce fruit. ⁵Your harvest of grain and grapes will be so abundant, that you won't know what to do with it all. You will

25.29 *sell a house:* If an owner wanted to buy back his house within a year of selling it, the new owner had to sell it back. But after a year, the new owner owned the house and could decide what to do with it.

25.35 *poor . . . foreigners:* The poor were those who were forced to sell their property or land. A poor Israelite could rely on a relative's help (25.26), become a servant of another Israelite (25.39), or become a slave for a foreigner living in the land of the Israelites (25.47-50). The people of God were to look after the needs of the poor (Exod 22.25; Isa 1.17; Amos 5.10-13).

Foreigners (Aliens)

The Poor

25.39 *your slaves:* This refers to poor Israelites who became paid servants of other Israelites. In the Year of Celebration they returned to their families, who once again would own the land originally given to them.

26.2 *Sabbath . . . place:* The place of worship refers to the sacred tent and courtyard. During King Solomon's reign Israel's "sacred place" became the temple in Jerusalem.

26.3-6 *Faithfully obey . . . will bless your country:* If the people obey God's laws, God will give them many different blessings.

26.18 *seven times:* The number seven symbolized completeness or perfection. Israel's punishment would be total and complete. **(See the chart Numbers in the Bible on pg 1844.)**

26.19 *hold back the rain:* Ancient Hebrews understood the sky to be like a solid bowl set over the earth (Gen 1.6-8), held up by high mountains (Job 26.11). Rain and snow were said to fall when God opened windows or doors in the sky (Ps 78.23). A sky dome made of "iron" would be very solid, hard for rain to penetrate.

26.20 *no harvest:* Just the opposite of the abundant harvest as a blessing for faithfulness (26.4,5,10).

26.30 *destroy your shrines . . . tear down . . . altars:* This probably refers to worship places dedicated to worshiping idols. This describes the situation that would come to pass in Israel some centuries after the time of Moses, when the people of Israel had built shrines to honor Canaanite gods and goddesses (1 Kgs 16.29-33; 22.52, 53; 2 Kgs 14.3,4).

Exile

26.39 *your sins:* Here "sins" refers to Israel's people worshiping idols and treating their neighbors or the poor among them unfairly (Isa 48.1-11; Jer 11.9-13; Mic 2.1-3; Amos 2.4,5; 5.10-15).

eat and be satisfied, and you will live in safety. [6]I will bless your country with peace, and you will rest without fear. I will wipe out the dangerous animals and protect you from enemy attacks. [7]You will chase and destroy your enemies, [8]even if there are only 5 of you and 100 of them, or only 100 of you and 10,000 of them. [9]I will treat you with such kindness that your nation will grow strong, and I will also keep my promises to you. [10]Your barns will overflow with grain each year. [11]I will live among you and never again look on you with disgust. [12]I will walk with you—I will be your God, and you will be my people. [13]I am the LORD your God, and I rescued you from Egypt, so that you would never again be slaves. I have set you free; now walk with your heads held high.

Punishment for Disobeying the LORD

The LORD said:

[14-15]If you disobey me and my laws, and if you break our agreement, [16]I will punish you terribly, and you will be ruined. You will be struck with incurable diseases and with fever that leads to blindness and depression. Your enemies will eat the crops you plant, [17]and I will turn from you and let you be destroyed by your attackers. You will even run at the very rumor of attack. [18]Then, if you still refuse to obey me, I will punish you seven times for each of your sins, [19]until your pride is completely crushed. I will hold back the rain, so the sky above you will be like iron, and the ground beneath your feet will be like copper. [20]All of your hard work will be for nothing—and there will be no harvest of grain or fruit.

[21]If you keep rebelling against me, I'll punish you seven times worse, just as your sins deserve! [22]I'll send wild animals to at-

tack you, and they will gobble up your children and livestock. So few of you will be left that your roads will be deserted.

[23]If you remain my enemies after this, [24]I'll remain your enemy and punish you even worse. [25]War will break out because you broke our agreement, and if you escape to your walled cities, I'll punish you with horrible diseases, and you will be captured by your enemies. [26]You will have such a shortage of bread, that ten women will be able to bake their bread in the same oven. Each of you will get only a few crumbs, and you will go hungry.

[27]Then if you don't stop rebelling, [28]I'll really get furious and punish you terribly for your sins! [29]In fact, you will be so desperate for food that you will eat your own children. [30]I'll destroy your shrines and tear down your incense altars, leaving your dead bodies piled on top of your idols. And you will be disgusting to me. [31]I'll wipe out your towns and your places of worship and will no longer be pleased with the smell of your sacrifices. [32]Your land will become so desolate that even your enemies who settle there will be shocked when they see it. [33]After I destroy your towns and ruin your land with war, I'll scatter you among the nations.

[34-35]While you are prisoners in foreign lands, your own land will enjoy years of rest and refreshment, as it should have done each seventh year when you lived there. [36-37]In the land of your enemies, you will tremble at the rustle of a leaf, as though it were a sword. And you will become so weak that you will stumble and fall over each other, even when no one is chasing you. [38]Many of you will die in foreign lands, [39]and others of you will waste away in sorrow as the result of your sins and the sins of your ancestors.

[40-41]Then suppose you realize that I turned against you and brought you to the

I will walk with you—I will be your God, and you will be my people. LEV 26.12

land of your enemies because both you and your ancestors had stubbornly sinned against me. If you humbly confess what you have done and start living right, [42]I'll keep the promise I made to your ancestors Abraham, Isaac, and Jacob. I will bless your land [43]and let it rest during the time that you are in a foreign country, paying for your rebellion against me and my laws.

[44]No matter what you have done, I am still the LORD your God, and I will never completely reject you or become absolutely disgusted with you there in the land of your enemies. [45]While nations watched, I rescued your ancestors from Egypt so that I would be their God. Yes, I am your LORD, and I will never forget our agreement.

[46]Moses was on Mount Sinai when the LORD gave him these laws and teachings for the people of Israel.

Making Promises to the LORD

27 The LORD told Moses [2]to say to the community of Israel:

If you ever want to free someone who has been promised to me, [3-7]you may do so by paying the following amounts, weighed according to the official standards:

50 pieces of silver for men
    ages 20 to 60,
and 30 pieces for women;
20 pieces of silver
    for young men ages 5 to 20,
and 10 pieces
    for young women;
15 pieces of silver for men
ages 60 and above
    and 10 pieces for women;
5 pieces of silver for boys

ages 1 month to 5 years,
    and 3 pieces for girls.

[8]If you have promised to give someone to me and can't afford to pay the full amount for that person's release, you will be taken to a priest, and he will decide how much you can afford.

[9]If you promise to sacrifice an animal to me, it becomes holy, and there is no way you can set it free. [10]If you try to substitute any other animal, no matter how good, for the one you promised, they will both become holy and must be sacrificed. [11]Donkeys are unfit for sacrifice, so if you promise me a donkey,[t] you must bring it to the priest, [12]and let him determine its value. [13]But if you want to buy it back, you must pay an additional 20 percent.

[14]If you promise a house to me, a priest will set the price, whatever the condition of the house. [15]But if you decide to buy it back, you must pay an additional 20 percent.

[16]If you promise part of your family's land to me, its value must be determined by the amount of seed needed to plant the land, and the rate will be ten pieces of silver for every bushel of seed. [17]If this promise is made in the Year of Celebration,[u] the land will be valued at the full price. [18]But any time after that, the price will be figured according to the number of years before the next Year of Celebration. [19]If you decide to buy back the land, you must pay the price plus an additional 20 percent, [20]but you cannot buy it back once someone else has bought it. [21]When the Year of Celebration comes, the land becomes holy because it belongs to me, and it will be given to the priests.

[22]If you promise me a field that you have

● 26.42 *Abraham, Isaac, and Jacob:* God promised Israel's earliest ancestors land and many descendants. God also promised to bless them, so that they could be a blessing to other nations (Gen 12.1-3). See also Gen 17.7,8; 26.3,4; 28.13,14.

● 27.2 *free someone . . . promised to me:* This refers to people who had been dedicated to serving the LORD by a promise or vow. To free someone from this service meant overriding the vow with a payment of money.

● 27.3-7 *official standards . . . silver:* The standard payments probably were based on how much work an individual would be able to do. A strong mature male would normally be able to do more work that required physical strength.

■ 27.9 *promise . . . holy:* An animal promised as a sacrificial offering became holy, that is, "dedicated to the LORD," and couldn't be set free or exchanged for a different animal. Unclean animals, such as donkeys, that had been promised could be bought back for the priest's price plus an additional 20 percent.

● 27.16-21 *your family's land . . . given to the priests:* Israel's land was divided among the descendants of Israel's twelve tribes. Families within each tribe were probably given their own pieces of land. The sale of lands dedicated to the LORD was complicated. Buying back dedicated family land was charged according to ten pieces of silver for every bushel of seed (27.16).

[t]27.11 *Donkeys . . . donkey:* The Hebrew text has "If you promise me an unclean animal," which probably refers to a donkey (see Exodus 13.13; 34.20).   [u]27.17 *Year of Celebration:* See 25.8-34.

bought, ²³its value will be decided by a priest, according to the number of years before the next Year of Celebration, and the money you pay will be mine. ²⁴However, on the next Year of Celebration, the land will go back to the family of its original owner. ²⁵Every price will be set by the official standards.

Various Offerings

The LORD said:

²⁶All first-born animals of your flocks and herds are already mine, and so you cannot promise any of them to me. ²⁷If you promise me a donkey,^v you may buy it back by adding an additional 20 percent to its value. If you don't buy it back, it can be sold to someone else for whatever a priest has said it is worth.

²⁸Anything that you completely dedicate to me must be completely destroyed.^w It cannot be bought back or sold. Every person, animal, and piece of property that you dedicate completely is only for me. ²⁹In fact, any humans who have been promised to me in this way must be put to death.

³⁰Ten percent of everything you harvest is holy and belongs to me, whether it grows in your fields or on your fruit trees. ³¹If you want to buy back this part of your harvest, you may do so by paying what it is worth plus an additional 20 percent.

³²When you count your flocks and herds, one out of ten of every newborn animal^x is holy and belongs to me, ³³no matter how good or bad it is. If you substitute one animal for another, both of them become holy, and neither can be bought back.

³⁴Moses was on Mount Sinai when the LORD gave him these laws for the people of Israel.

^v**27.27** *donkey:* See the note at verse 11. ^w**27.28** *completely dedicate . . . completely destroyed:* In order to show that something belonged completely to the LORD and could not be used by anyone else, it was destroyed. This law most often applied to towns and people captured in war (see Joshua 6.16,17). ^x**27.32** *one out of ten of every newborn animal:* Or "one out of every ten animals."

Reflection Questions About Leviticus 1.1—27.34

1. The LORD gave Moses instructions for five different types of sacrifices. What was the purpose of each kind of sacrifice? Who was assigned the task of making these sacrifices (chapters 1–5)?

2. How did the laws of sacrifice help define the relationship between God and the Israelite people?

3. Describe some of the reasons the "sacrifices for sin" were to be made (4.1—5.13). For what other reasons did people have to bring an offering or payment to "makes things right" (5.14—6.7)? When you think of "making things right" in society today, what comes to mind?

4. What does it mean to be "holy"? What do the laws of sacrifice and cleanness have to do with being holy? Read Leviticus 11.44,45. How is it possible to live up to that command?

5. Describe what happened on the Great Day of Forgiveness (16.1-34). Who alone could enter the most holy place in the sacred tent on that day? What was the "scapegoat"?

6. Review the laws in chapter 19. Which do you think are most relevant for life today? Why? Which laws do you wish people were more careful about following? Why?

7. Review the religious festivals in chapter 23. What was the purpose of each festival?

8. How were the laws of ancient Israel set up to help those who were poor or those who had become poor (25.35-55)?

9. What blessings were promised to those who faithfully obeyed God's laws? What were the punishments for disobeying (chapter 26)?

10. What words, phrases, or passages are especially helpful to you in understanding the meaning of LEVITICUS? How do you think people should understand the laws given in LEVITICUS today?

numbers

*God was leading the Israelites to the promised land, so
why was their trip bumpy and filled with detours?*

WHAT MAKES NUMBERS SPECIAL?

The title "NUMBERS" comes from the Greek (*Arithmoi*) and later Latin (*Numeri*) names for this book. The title in Hebrew is based on a word that means "in the desert." Both titles reflect what the book is about. Many lists of groups and numbers of people are included (see 1.20; 3.21; 7.12; 26.5; 26.57), but more important is the description of the Israelites' desert journey toward the land God promised them. That land represented true freedom and escape from slavery in Egypt.

NUMBERS describes the Israelite people's journey in the desert wilderness. There they learn how God wishes them to be organized, how the Levites are to help Israel's priests. They also find out who will be chosen to lead them when they enter Canaan. The account of the Israelites' desert journey also shows the rebellious side of the people. They complain that God has brought them out to the wilderness to starve or to die of thirst. They plot to get rid of their leaders, Moses and Aaron. Because of these sins, God does not allow them an easy path to the land of promise. Instead, the older generation who left Egypt (including Moses) must wander for 40 years and eventually die in the desert wilderness. Only those in the younger generation (14.22,23,29,30) would follow the faithful leaders, Joshua and Caleb, into Canaan. The lesson is that those who obey and trust God will receive God's blessings.

WHAT'S THE STORY BEHIND THE SCENE?

NUMBERS is the fourth book of the five-part section of the Old Testament known as the Pentateuch. It continues the story of the wandering Israelite people begun in EXODUS and continued in LEVITICUS. While LEVITICUS describes the Israelite people learning God's laws concerning holiness as they camp at Mount Sinai, NUMBERS depicts the Israelite people on the move. Moses has traditionally been identified as the book's author, and much of the material in the book may date back that far. But it is likely that scribes and editors who lived centuries later put the book in the form we know today.

HOW IS NUMBERS CONSTRUCTED?

NUMBERS is made up of different kinds of material, and there are many ways of looking at its organization. The following outline uses a geographical way of structuring the book.

Israel in camp at Sinai (1.1—10.10)
 The people are counted and organized (1.1—2.34)
 The duties of the priests and Levites (3.1—4.49)
 Instructions for God's holy people (5.1—10.10)
Israel's journey from Sinai to Moab (10.11—22.1)
 From Sinai to the Paran Desert (10.11—12.16)
 Trouble at the Paran Desert Camp at Kadesh (13.1—20.13)
 From Kadesh to Moab (20.14—22.1)
The Moab Camp. Preparing to enter Canaan (22.2—36.13)
 The stories of Balaam and the worship of Baal (22.2—25.18)
 Counting and instructing a new generation (26.1—30.16)
 Getting ready to cross the Jordan River (31.1—36.13)

The Hebrew title for the book of Numbers is "In the Desert." As the book begins, the people of Israel are camped in the Sinai Desert. The Lord commands Moses to count the people, and gives the Israelites rules for their time of traveling and instructions for worship. The people begin their journey to the promised land of Canaan, pass through the land of Kadesh, and try to enter Canaan from the south, but are forced to detour around the country of Edom. Numbers also describes the people's disobedience and tells how they often grumbled against the Lord during their years in the desert. After the Lord chooses Joshua to be the leader of the people after Moses' death, the Israelites defeat the Midianites, and finally come to the mountains overlooking the promised land.

Outline

The People of Israel Are Counted

1 The people of Israel had left Egypt and were living in the Sinai Desert. Then on the first day of the second month[a] of the second year, when Moses was in the sacred tent the LORD said:

2-3 I want you and Aaron to find out how many people are in each of Israel's clans and families. And make a list of all the men 20 years and older who are able to fight in battle. 4-15 The following twelve family leaders, one from each tribe, will help you:

Elizur son of Shedeur
　from Reuben,
Shelumiel son of Zurishaddai
　from Simeon,
Nahshon son of Amminadab
　from Judah,
Nethanel son of Zuar
　from Issachar,
Eliab son of Helon
　from Zebulun,
Elishama son of Ammihud
　from Ephraim,
Gamaliel son of Pedahzur
　from Manasseh,
Abidan son of Gideoni
　from Benjamin,
Ahiezer son of Ammishaddai
　from Dan,
Pagiel son of Ochran
　from Asher,
Eliasaph son of Deuel
　from Gad,
and Ahira son of Enan
　from Naphtali.

16-17 Moses and Aaron, together with these twelve tribal leaders, 18 called together the people that same day. They were counted according to their clans and families. Then Moses and the others listed the names of the men twenty years and older, 19 just as the LORD had commanded.

[a] 1.1 second month: Ziv, the second month of the Hebrew calendar, from about mid-April to mid-May.

1.1 *The people of Israel:* The Israelites are traditionally understood to be the descendants of Abraham's grandson Jacob (also called Israel). Because of these relationships they shared a common identity and believed themselves to be the inheritors of the promise God made to Abraham (Gen 12.1-7) and reaffirmed with Jacob (Gen 28.10-15). This promise includes the gift of the land of Canaan. For the blessings each son received from Jacob, see Gen 48.1—49.28. For the blessings Moses gave to the twelve tribes before they entered Canaan, see Deut 33. **(See the chart Jacob's Children and Their Mothers on pg 1824.)**

Israel

LORD (YHWH)

1.2-3 *Aaron . . . Israel's clans:* The descendants of Aaron, the brother of Moses, were assigned the task of being priests. Aaron was the first high priest of Israel (see Exod 27.21—28.3). Each of Israel's twelve tribes was divided into clans, and each clan included a number of families. Only males 20 years or older were to be counted, because they were the ones expected to fight in battle.

1.4-15 *twelve family leaders . . . from Reuben . . . Naphtali:* These verses list the twelve tribes that would later be given land in Canaan. The tribes were named for the sons of Jacob. Ephraim and Manasseh were the sons of Jacob's son Joseph. Each received a share of land in Canaan (see Gen 48). The tribe of Levi was given special duties but did not receive a share of the land.

1.20-46 *Reuben . . . Naphtali:* Gad is listed third in this list, instead of eleventh as in the previous list (1.4-15). This is probably because the family was supposed to camp on the south side of the sacred tent next to Reuben and Simeon (2.10-15). The total of 603,550 fighting men has been questioned by many Bible scholars as being too large, but an agreement has not been reached on a more accurate number.

1.47 *Levi tribe:* The descendants of Levi, the son of Jacob and Leah (Gen 29.34). The Levite tribe did not receive a share of the land of Canaan (Deut 10.9), but they were given towns and nearby pasturelands (see 35.1-8; Josh 21.1-42). The Levites helped the priests by taking care of the sacred tent and its furnishings and by carrying them from camp to camp.

2.3-8 *Judah . . . Zebulun:* The first tribes mentioned are called by the names of the fourth, fifth, and sixth sons of Jacob and Leah (Gen 29.35; 30.16-20). Judah was given a place of honor among his brothers when Jacob blessed his sons (Gen 49.8-10). Judah's warriors were to lead the other tribes into battle. **(See the chart Israel on the March on pg 1830.)**

2.10-15 *Reuben . . . Gad:* Reuben and Simeon were the first and second sons of Jacob and Leah (Gen 29.31-33). Reuben lost his position as Jacob's first-born son because he slept with Bilhah, one of Jacob's wives. See Gen 35.22; 49.3,4. Gad was Jacob's seventh son and his first son by Leah's maid Zilpah (Gen 30.9,10).

20-46The number of men from each tribe who were at least 20 years old and strong enough to fight in Israel's army was as follows:

46,500 from Reuben,
   the oldest son of Jacob,[b]
59,300 from Simeon,
45,650 from Gad,
74,600 from Judah,
54,400 from Issachar,
57,400 from Zebulun,
40,500 from Ephraim,
32,200 from Manasseh,
35,400 from Benjamin,
62,700 from Dan,
41,500 from Asher,
53,400 from Naphtali.

The total number of men registered by Moses, Aaron, and the twelve leaders was 603,550.

47But those from the Levi tribe were not included 48because the LORD had said to Moses:

49When you count the Israelites, do not include those from the Levi tribe. 50-51Instead, give them the job of caring for the sacred tent, its furnishings, and the objects used for worship. They will camp around the tent, and whenever you move, they will take it down, carry it to the new camp, and set it up again. Anyone else who tries to go near it must be put to death. 52The rest of the Israelites will camp in their own groups and under their own banners. 53But the Levites will camp around the sacred tent to make sure that no one goes near it and makes me furious with the Israelites. 54The people of Israel did everything the LORD had commanded.

[b]1.20-46 *Jacob:* The Hebrew text has "Israel," Jacob's name after God renamed him.

Instructions for Setting Up Israel's Camp

2 The LORD told Moses and Aaron 2how the Israelites should arrange their camp:

Each tribe must set up camp under its own banner and under the flags of its ancestral families. These camps will be arranged around the sacred tent, but not close to it.

3-4Judah and the tribes that march with it must set up camp on the east side of the sacred tent, under their own banner. The 74,600 troops of the tribe of Judah will be arranged by divisions and led by Nahshon son of Amminadab. 5-6On one side of Judah will be the tribe of Issachar, with Nethanel son of Zuar as the leader of its 54,400 troops. 7-8On the other side will be the tribe of Zebulun, with Eliab son of Helon as the leader of its 57,400 troops. 9These 186,400 troops will march into battle first.

10-11Reuben and the tribes that march with it must set up camp on the south side of the sacred tent, under their own banner. The 46,500 troops of the tribe of Reuben will be arranged by divisions and led by Elizur son of Shedeur. 12-13On one side of Reuben will be the tribe of Simeon, with Shelumiel son of Zurishaddai as the leader of its 59,300 troops. 14-15On the other side will be the tribe of Gad, with Eliasaph son of Deuel as the leader of its 45,650 troops. 16These 151,450 troops will march into battle second.

17Marching behind Reuben will be the Levites, arranged in groups, just as they are camped. They will carry the sacred tent and their own banners.

18-19Ephraim and the tribes that march

with it must set up camp on the west side of the sacred tent, under their own banner. The 40,500 troops of the tribe of Ephraim will be arranged by divisions and led by Elishama son of Ammihud. [20-21]On one side of Ephraim will be the tribe of Manasseh, with Gamaliel son of Pedahzur as the leader of its 32,200 troops. [22-23]On the other side will be the tribe of Benjamin, with Abidan son of Gideoni as the leader of its 35,400 troops. [24]These 108,100 troops will march into battle third.

[25-26]Dan and the tribes that march with it must set up camp on the north side of the sacred tent, under their own banner. The 62,700 troops of the tribe of Dan will be arranged by divisions and led by Ahiezer son of Ammishaddai. [27-28]On one side of Dan will be the tribe of Asher, with Pagiel son of Ochran as the leader of its 41,500 troops. [29-30]On the other side will be the tribe of Naphtali with Ahira son of Enan as the leader of its 53,400 troops. [31]These 157,600 troops will march into battle last.

[32]So all the Israelites in the camp were counted according to their ancestral families. The troops were arranged by divisions and totaled 603,550. [33]The only Israelites not included were the Levites, just as the LORD had commanded Moses.

[34]Israel did everything the LORD had told Moses. They arranged their camp according to clans and families, with each tribe under its own banner. And that was the order by which they marched into battle.

The Sons of Aaron

3 When the LORD talked with Moses on Mount Sinai, [2]Aaron's four sons, Nadab, Abihu, Eleazar, and Ithamar, [3]were the ones to be ordained as priests. [4]But the LORD killed Nadab and Abihu in the Sinai Desert when they used fire that was unacceptable[c] in their offering to the LORD.[d] And because Nadab and Abihu had no sons, only Eleazar and Ithamar served as priests with their father Aaron.

The Duties of the Levites

[5]The LORD said to Moses:

[6]Assign the Levi tribe to Aaron the priest. They will be his assistants [7]and will work at the sacred tent for him and for all the Israelites. [8]The Levites will serve the community by being responsible for the furnishings of the tent. [9]They are assigned to help Aaron and his sons, [10]who have been appointed to be priests. Anyone else who tries to perform the duties of a priest must be put to death.

[11-13]Moses, I have chosen these Levites from all Israel, and they will belong to me in a special way. When I killed the first-born sons of the Egyptians, I decided that the first-born sons in every Israelite family and the first-born males of their flocks and herds would be mine.[e] But now I accept these Levites in place of the first-born sons of the Israelites.

The Levites Are Counted

[14]In the Sinai Desert the LORD said to Moses, [15]"Now I want you to count the men and boys in the Levi tribe by families and by clans. Include every one at least a

c3.4 *fire that was unacceptable*: One possible meaning for the difficult Hebrew text.   d3.4 *the LORD killed Nadab and Abihu . . . to the LORD*: See Leviticus 10.1,2.   e3.11-13 *When I killed . . . mine*: See Exodus 13.1,2,11-16.

2.25-30 *Dan . . . Naphtali*: Dan led the northern camp as the first-born son of Jacob and Rachel's maid Bilhah (Gen 30.4-6). Naphtali was Jacob and Bilhah's second son (Gen 30.7,8), and Asher was Jacob's second son with Leah's maid Zilpah (Gen 30.9-13).

2.34 *clans and families*: Clans are groups of extended families who are descended from a common male ancestor. Tribes are made up of all the clans who are descended from a single male ancestor (for the Israelites, one of Jacob's sons).

Genealogies in the Bible

3.2 *Aaron's four sons*: All of Aaron's sons were ordained by Moses at Mount Sinai (Exod 29.1-37; 30.22-33; 40.12-15; Lev 8). Nadab and Abihu died when they did not follow correct procedures for offering a sacrifice.

3.11-13 *first-born*: In ancient societies, the first-born son often held a special place in the family structure. As Israel was preparing to leave Egypt, the LORD told Moses that Israel's first-born sons and the first-born of the flocks were to be dedicated, that is, set apart to honor and serve the LORD (Exod 13.1,2,11-16; see also Lev 27.26). Now, the Levites are to take the place of first-born sons, freeing the families from this obligation.

3.21 *Gershon clans:* These clans were in charge of putting up and taking down the tent covering and curtains, except the curtain in front of the most holy place. **(See the chart Israel on the March on pg 1830.)**

3.27 *Kohath clans:* The Kohathites took care of the sacred objects (see Exod 25.10-40; 30.1-10) in the sacred tent. They were not allowed to touch or look at these sacred objects, so the priests from Aaron's family covered them first (4.4-12). Then the Kohath clan could carry them from place to place.

3.32 *Levite leaders:* Aaron and his sons were the leaders of the Levite clans. They functioned as Israel's priests and made sure the other clans did their assigned work. They camped in the most important location, near the entrance of the sacred tent on the east side.

3.33 *Merari clans:* They were responsible for setting up and taking down the framework that held the tent together (see Exod 26.15-30). They also carried these objects each time the Israelite tribes moved to a new location.

3.40,41 *first-born . . . Levites as substitutes:* By assigning the Levites the special duties connected with religious rites, God frees other Israelite families from the obligation to dedicate their first-born sons to serve the LORD at the sacred tent. The number of Levites (22,000; see 3.39) did not equal the total number of first-born in Israel (22,273; see 3.46), so the extra 273 had to be paid for (see Lev 27.1-7).

month old." [16]So Moses obeyed and counted them.

[17]Levi's three sons, Gershon, Kohath, and Merari, had become the heads of their own clans. [18]Gershon's sons were Libni and Shimei. [19]Kohath's sons were Amram, Izhar, Hebron, and Uzziel. [20]And Merari's sons were Mahli and Mushi. These were the sons and grandsons of Levi, and they had become the leaders of the Levite clans.

[21]The two Gershon clans were the Libnites and Shimeites, [22]and they had 7,500 men and boys at least one month old. [23-24]The Gershonites, under the leadership of Eliasaph son of Lael, were to camp on the west side of the sacred tent. [25]Their duties at the tent included taking care of the tent itself, along with its outer covering, the curtain for the entrance, [26]the curtains hanging inside the courtyard around the tent, as well as the curtain and ropes for the entrance to the courtyard and its altar. The Gershonites were responsible for setting these things up and taking them down.

[27]The four Kohath clans were the Amramites, Izharites, Hebronites, and the Uzzielites, [28]and they had 8,600[f] men and boys at least one month old. [29-30]The Kohathites, under the leadership of Elizaphan son of Uzziel, were to camp on the south side of the sacred tent. [31]Their duties at the tent included taking care of the sacred chest, the table for the sacred bread, the lampstand, the altars, the objects used for worship, and the curtain in front of the most holy place. The Kohathites were responsible for setting these things up and taking them down.

[32]Eleazar son of Aaron was the head of the Levite leaders, and he made sure that the work at the sacred tent was done.

[33]The two Merari clans were the Mah-

lites and the Mushites, [34]and they had 6,200 men and boys at least one month old. [35]The Merarites, under the leadership of Zuriel son of Abihail, were to camp on the north side of the sacred tent. [36-37]Their duties included taking care of the tent frames and the pieces that held the tent up: the bars, the posts, the stands, and its other equipment. They were also in charge of the posts that supported the courtyard, as well as their stands, tent pegs, and ropes. The Merari clans were responsible for setting these things up and taking them down.

[38]Moses, Aaron, and his sons were to camp in front of the sacred tent, on the east side, and to make sure that the Israelites worshiped in the proper way. Anyone else who tried to do the work of Moses and Aaron was to be put to death.

[39]So Moses and Aaron obeyed the LORD and counted the Levites by their clans. The total number of Levites at least one month old was 22,000.

The Levites Are Accepted as Substitutes for the First-Born Sons

[40]The LORD said to Moses, "Make a list and count the first-born sons at least one month old in each of the Israelite families. [41]They belong to me, but I will accept the Levites as substitutes for them, and I will accept the Levites' livestock as substitutes for the Israelites' first-born livestock."

[42]Moses obeyed the LORD and counted the first-born sons; [43]there were 22,273 of them.

[44]Then the LORD said, [45]"The Levites will belong to me and will take the place of the first-born sons; their livestock will take the place of the Israelites' first-born livestock.

[f]**3.28** 8,600: Hebrew; some manuscripts of one ancient translation "8,300."

⁴⁶But since there are more first-born sons than Levites, the extra 273 men and boys must be bought back from me. ⁴⁷For each one, you are to collect five pieces of silver, weighed according to the official standards. ⁴⁸This money must then be given to Aaron and his sons."

⁴⁹Moses collected the silver from the extra 273 first-born men and boys, ⁵⁰and it amounted to 1,365 pieces of silver, weighed according to the official standards. ⁵¹Then he gave it to Aaron and his sons, just as the Lord had commanded.

The Duties of the Kohathite Clans

4 The Lord told Moses and Aaron: ²⁻³Find out how many men between the ages of 30 and 50 are in the four Levite clans of Kohath. Count only those who are able to work at the sacred tent.

⁴The Kohathites will be responsible for carrying the sacred objects used in worship at the sacred tent. ⁵When the Israelites are ready to move their camp, Aaron and his sons will enter the tent and take down the curtain that separates the sacred chest from the rest of the tent. They will cover the chest with this curtain, ⁶and then with a piece of fine leather, and cover it all with a solid blue cloth. After this they will put the carrying poles in place.

⁷Next, Aaron and his sons will use another blue cloth to cover the table for the sacred bread.⁸ On the cloth they will place the dishes, the bowls for incense, the cups, the jugs for wine, as well as the bread itself. ⁸They are to cover all of this with a bright red cloth, and then with a piece of fine leather, before putting the carrying poles in place.

⁹With another blue cloth they will cover the lampstand, along with the lamps, the lamp snuffers, the fire pans, and the jars of oil for the lamps. ¹⁰All of this will then be covered with a piece of fine leather and placed on a carrying frame.

¹¹The gold incense altar[h] is to be covered with a blue cloth, and then with a piece of fine leather, before its carrying poles are put in place.

¹²Next, Aaron and his sons will take blue cloth and wrap all the objects used in worship at the sacred tent. These will need to be covered with a piece of fine leather, then placed on a carrying frame.

¹³They are to remove the ashes from the bronze altar and cover it with a purple cloth. ¹⁴On that cloth will be placed the utensils used at the altar, including the fire pans, the meat forks, the shovels, and the sprinkling bowls. All of this will then be covered with a piece of fine leather, before the carrying poles are put in place.

¹⁵When the camp is ready to be moved, the Kohathites will be responsible for carrying the sacred objects and the furnishings of the sacred tent. But Aaron and his sons must have already covered those things so the Kohathites won't touch them and die.

¹⁶Eleazar son of Aaron the priest will be in charge of the oil for the lamps, the sweet-smelling incense, the grain for the sacrifices, and the olive oil used for dedications and ordinations. Eleazar is responsible

⚫ 4.6 *carrying poles:* The Kohathites carried the sacred objects by putting wood poles covered with gold through gold loops attached to corners or legs of those objects (Exod 25.12-14).

⚫ 4.9 *lampstand:* The lampstand (see Exod 25.31-40) was made of pure gold and had seven branches with small clay saucer-like lamps attached to the end of each branch. The light from the lamps represented the glory of God (Exod 29.43).

⬛ 4.15 *won't touch them and die:* The sacred objects were holy and were not to be touched by anyone except the priests who represented the people before God. Touching a sacred object could be disastrous (see 2 Sam 6.1-7; Exod 19.12,13, 20-24).

⬛ 4.16 *dedications and ordinations:* Objects or people could be dedicated to the Lord, that is, set apart to honor or serve him. To "ordain" also means to set apart to serve God, but it usually refers to people who have been chosen for a specific task, such as a priest or king. Ordination was usually accompanied by pouring oil on the person's head as a sign of being chosen. This pouring of oil is also known as "anointing." See also Exod 29.1-7; Lev 8.12; 1 Sam 10.1; 16.12,13.

---

g4.7 *sacred bread:* This bread was offered to the Lord and was a symbol of his presence in the sacred tent. It was put out on a special table and was replaced with fresh bread each Sabbath (Leviticus 24.5-9).   **h4.11** *gold incense altar:* This altar for offering incense was inside the sacred tent; it was made of acacia wood covered with gold. A large altar for offering sacrifices was in front of the entrance to the tent; it was made of acacia wood covered with bronze (see verse 13).

● 4.34-49 *Levi tribe . . . 8,580:* The first Levite census (3.14-39) counted all Levite males one month and older (22,000), whereas this second census counts males between 30 and 50 years old, those directly responsible for the sacred tent and its objects.

■ 5.3 *clean:* In the Old Testament "clean" and "unclean" refer to whatever makes a person, animal, or object acceptable or unacceptable to God. See also Deut 14.4-21. Bodily discharges included blood (including blood flow from menstruation or childbirth), semen, or pus from sores or infections (see Lev 12; 15; 17.10-14). Touching a dead body or certain dead animals could also make a person ritually unclean (Lev 11.35,39,40; 21.1-12).

Ⅽ੪ Purity (Clean and Unclean)

■ 5.6-8 *sinned . . . sacrifice:* Sin is turning away from God and disobeying God's laws. In this case the LORD is talking about cheating a neighbor in any way (see Lev 6.1-7). To remove the guilt of the sin, the neighbor was to be repaid in full plus 20 percent more. In addition, a sacrifice was to be offered by the priest.

Ⅽ੪ Sin

for seeing that the sacred tent, its furnishings, and the sacred objects are taken care of.

$^{17-20}$The Kohathites must not go near or even look at the sacred objects until Aaron and his sons have covered those objects. If they do, their entire clan will be wiped out. So make sure that Aaron and his sons go into the tent with them and tell them what to carry.

The Duties of the Gershonite Clans

^{21}The LORD said to Moses:

$^{22-23}$Find out how many men between the ages of 30 and 50 are in the two Levite clans of Gershon. Count only those who are able to work at the sacred tent.

^{24}The Gershonites will be responsible ^{25}for carrying the curtains of the sacred tent, its two outer coverings,[i] the curtain for the entrance to the tent, ^{26}the curtains hanging around the courtyard of the tent, and the curtain and ropes for the entrance to the courtyard. The Gershonites are to do whatever needs to be done to take care of these things, ^{27}and they will carry them wherever Aaron and his sons tell them to. ^{28}These are the duties of the Gershonites at the sacred tent, and Ithamar son of Aaron will make sure they do their work.

The Duties of the Merarite Clans

$^{29-30}$The LORD said:

Moses, find out how many men between 30 and 50 are in the two Levite clans of Merari, but count only those who are able to work at the sacred tent.

^{31}The Merarites will be responsible for carrying the frames of the tent and its

other pieces, including the bars, the posts, and the stands, ^{32}as well as the posts that support the courtyard, together with their stands, tent pegs, and ropes. The Merarites are to be told exactly what objects they are to carry, ^{33}and Ithamar son of Aaron will make sure they do their work.

The Levites Are Counted Again

$^{34-49}$Moses, Aaron, and the other Israelite leaders obeyed the LORD and counted the Levi tribe by families and clans, to find out how many men there were between the ages of 30 and 50 who could work at the sacred tent. There were 2,750 Kohathites, 2,630 Gershonites, and 3,200 Merarites, making a total of 8,580. Then they were all assigned their duties.

People Are Sent Outside the Camp

5 The LORD told Moses $^{2-3}$to say to the people of Israel, "Put out of the camp everyone who has leprosy[j] or a bodily discharge or who has touched a dead body. Now that I live among my people, their camp must be kept clean."

^{4}The Israelites obeyed the LORD's instructions.

The Penalty for Committing a Crime
(Leviticus 6.1-7)

^{5}The LORD told Moses ^{6}to say to the community of Israel:

If any of you commit a crime against someone, you have sinned against me. ^{7}You must confess your guilt and pay the victim in full for whatever damage has

[i]**4.25** *two outer coverings:* See Exodus 26.14. [j]**5.2,3** *leprosy:* The word translated "leprosy" was used for many different kinds of skin diseases.

been done, plus a fine of 20 percent. [8]If the victim has no relative who can accept this money, it belongs to me and will be paid to the priest. In addition to that payment, you must take a ram for the priest to sacrifice so your sin will be forgiven.

[9-10]When you make a donation to the sacred tent, that money belongs only to the priest, and each priest will keep what is given to him.

A Suspicious Husband

[11]The LORD told Moses [12-14]to say to the people of Israel:

Suppose a man becomes jealous and suspects that his wife has been unfaithful, but he has no proof. [15]He must take his wife to the priest, together with two pounds of ground barley as an offering to find out if she is guilty. No olive oil or incense is to be put on that offering.

[16]The priest will lead the woman to my altar and make her stand there. [17]He will then pour sacred water into a clay jar and stir in some dust from the floor of the sacred tent. [18-22]Next, he will remove her veil, then hand her the barley offering, and say, "If you have been faithful to your husband, this water won't harm you. But if you have been unfaithful, it will bring down the LORD's curse—you will never be able to give birth to a child, and everyone will curse your name."

Then the woman will answer, "If I am guilty, let it happen just as you say."

[23]The priest will write these curses on special paper and wash them off into the bitter water, [24]so that when the woman drinks this water, the curses will enter her body. [25]He will take the barley offering from her and lift it up[k] in dedication to me, the LORD. Then he will place it on my altar

[k]**5.25** *lift it up*: Or "wave it."

[26]and burn part of it as a sacrifice. After that, the woman must drink the bitter water.

[27]If the woman has been unfaithful, the water will immediately make her unable to have children, and she will be a curse among her people. [28]But if she is innocent, her body will not be harmed, and she will still be able to have children.

[29-30]This is the ceremony that must take place at my altar when a husband suspects that his wife has been unfaithful. The priest must tell the woman to stand in my presence and carefully follow these instructions. [31]If the husband is wrong, he will not be punished; but if his wife is guilty, she will be punished.

Rules for Nazirites

6 The LORD told Moses [2]to say to the people of Israel:

If any of you want to dedicate yourself to me by vowing to become a Nazirite, [3]you must no longer drink any wine or beer or use any kind of vinegar. Don't drink grape juice or eat grapes or raisins— [4]not even the seeds or skins.

[5]The hair of a Nazirite is sacred to me, and as long as you are a Nazirite, you must never cut your hair.

[6]During the time that you are a Nazirite, you must never go close to a dead body, [7-8]not even that of your father, mother, brother, or sister. That would make you unclean. Your hair is the sign that you are dedicated to me, so remain holy.

[9]If someone suddenly dies near you, your hair is no longer sacred, and you must shave it seven days later during the ceremony to make you clean. [10]Then on the next day, bring two doves or two pigeons to the priest at the sacred tent. [11]He will

5.12-14 *no proof*: The Law of Moses said that two witnesses were needed to convict someone of a crime (Deut 17.6; 19.15). If a woman's unfaithfulness had been observed by witnesses, she would have been tried in the normal way and likely punished by death (Lev 20.10). Here, however, the man suspects his wife's guilt but cannot prove it, so the punishment can't be death.

5.17 *clay jar*: A clay jar was used and then broken so that the curses dissolved in the water it held.

5.31 *If the husband is wrong*: The husband had the right to accuse his wife, but there was no comparable law that allowed a woman to accuse her husband of being unfaithful if no witnesses were available (5.12-14).

6.2 *Nazirite*: Nazirites were not priests. They were people who dedicated themselves to being ritually clean and serving God. This dedication meant they did things that set them apart from others. They didn't drink alcohol, and they didn't cut their hair, because even their hair was considered holy. (See the story of Samson in Judg 16.4-31.) See also Judg 13.2-14; Luke 1.15.

6.9-12 *no longer sacred . . . sacrifice*: If a Nazirite did touch a dead body, he or she also had to go through a cleansing ritual that included shaving off the hair and bringing offerings used as a sacrifice for sin and a sacrifice to please God. Even priests who were made unclean by touching a dead body did not have to go through a purification ritual this elaborate.

6.14,15 *nothing wrong . . . without yeast:* The animals to be offered had to be in perfect health (see Lev 22.21-24). Yeast is a fungus used to make dough rise when mixed with water and flour. Bread that has no yeast, or leaven, is flat and is called "thin bread" (unleavened bread). See Lev 2.1-7. **(See the chart Sacrifices and Offerings on pg 1828.)**

6.23 *bless the people:* One function of the priests was to bless the people of Israel (see also Lev 9.22,23; Deut 10.8; 21.4-5; 2 Chr 30.27). The word translated "peace" in 6.26 is from the Hebrew word *shalom,* which means total well-being, not simply an absence of war.

7.3 *carts and twelve oxen:* Probably two-wheeled carts. Oxen were strong animals used for hauling large objects and pulling plows. **(See the article Trade and Travel on pg 1806.)**

offer one of the birds as a sacrifice for sin and the other as a sacrifice to please me.[l] You will then be forgiven for being too near a dead body, and your hair will again become sacred. [12]But the dead body made you unacceptable, so you must make another vow to become a Nazirite and be dedicated once more. Finally, a year-old ram must be offered as the sacrifice to make things right.

[13]When you have completed your promised time of being a Nazirite, go to the sacred tent [14]and offer three animals that have nothing wrong with them: a year-old ram as a sacrifice to please me, a year-old female lamb as a sacrifice for sin, and a full-grown ram as a sacrifice to ask my blessing.[m] [15]Wine offerings and grain sacrifices must also be brought with these animals. Finally, you are to bring a basket of bread made with your finest flour and olive oil, but without yeast. Also bring some thin wafers brushed with oil.

[16]The priest will take these gifts to my altar and offer them, so that I will be pleased and will forgive you. [17]Then he will sacrifice the ram and offer the wine, grain, and bread.

[18]After that, you will stand at the entrance to the sacred tent, shave your head, and put the hair in the fire where the priest has offered the sacrifice to ask my blessing.

[19]Once the meat from the ram's shoulder has been boiled, the priest will take it, along with one loaf of bread and one wafer brushed with oil, and give them to you. [20]You will hand them back to the priest, who will lift them up[n] in dedication to me. Then he can eat the meat from the ram's

shoulder, its choice ribs, and its hind leg, because this is his share of the sacrifice. After this, you will no longer be a Nazirite, and you will be free to drink wine.

[21]These are the requirements for Nazirites. However, if you can afford to offer more, you must do so.

The Blessing for the People

[22]The LORD told Moses, [23]"When Aaron and his sons bless the people of Israel, they must say:

[24]I pray that the LORD
   will bless and protect you,
[25]and that he will show you mercy
   and kindness.
[26]May the LORD be good to you
   and give you peace."

[27]Then the LORD said, "If Aaron and his sons ask me to bless the Israelites, I will give them my blessing."

The Leaders Bring Gifts to the Sacred Tent

7 When Moses had finished setting up the sacred tent, he dedicated it to the LORD, together with its furnishings, the altar, and its equipment. [2]Then the twelve tribal leaders of Israel, the same men who had been in charge of counting the people,[o] came to the tent [3]with gifts for the LORD. They brought six strong carts and twelve oxen—one ox from each leader and a cart from every two.

[4]The LORD said to Moses, [5]"Accept these

[l]**6.11** *sacrifice to please me:* This sacrifice has traditionally been called a "whole burnt offering," because the whole animal was burned on the altar. A main purpose of such a sacrifice was to please the LORD with the smell of the sacrifice, and so in the CEV it is often called "a sacrifice to please the LORD." [m]**6.14** *sacrifice to ask my blessing:* This sacrifice has traditionally been called a "peace offering" or an "offering of well-being." A main purpose of such a sacrifice was to ask the LORD's blessing, and so in the CEV it is often called a "sacrifice to ask the LORD's blessing." [n]**6.20** *lift them up:* See the note at 5.25. [o]**7.2** *the same men . . . the people:* See 1.1-19.

gifts, so the Levites can use them here at the sacred tent for carrying the sacred things."

⁶Then Moses took the carts and oxen and gave them to the Levites, ⁷⁻⁸who were under the leadership of Ithamar son of Aaron. Moses gave two carts and four oxen to the Gershonites for their work, and four carts and eight oxen to the Merarites for their work. ⁹But Moses did not give any to the Kohathites, because they were in charge of the sacred objects that had to be carried on their shoulders.

¹⁰On the day the altar was dedicated, the twelve leaders brought offerings for its dedication. ¹¹The LORD said to Moses, "Each day one leader is to give his offering for the dedication."

¹²⁻⁸³So each leader brought the following gifts:

   a silver bowl that weighed over three pounds and a silver sprinkling bowl weighing almost two pounds, both of them filled with flour and olive oil as grain sacrifices and weighed according to the official standards;

   a small gold dish filled with incense;

   a young bull, a full-grown ram, and a year-old ram as sacrifices to please the LORD;^p

   a goat^q as a sacrifice for sin;

   and two bulls, five full-grown rams, five goats, and five rams a year old as sacrifices to ask the LORD's blessing.^r

The tribal leaders brought their gifts and offerings in the following order:

On the first day
   Nahshon from Judah,
on the second day
   Nethanel from Issachar,
on the third day
   Eliab from Zebulun,

on the fourth day
   Elizur from Reuben,
on the fifth day
   Shelumiel from Simeon,
on the sixth day
   Eliasaph from Gad,
on the seventh day
   Elishama from Ephraim,
on the eighth day
   Gamaliel from Manasseh,
on the ninth day
   Abidan from Benjamin,
on the tenth day
   Ahiezer from Dan,
on the eleventh day
   Pagiel from Asher,
on the twelfth day
   Ahira from Naphtali.

⁸⁴⁻⁸⁸And so when the altar was dedicated to the LORD, these twelve leaders brought the following gifts:

   12 silver bowls and 12 silver sprinkling bowls, weighing a total of about 60 pounds, according to the official standards;

   12 gold dishes filled with incense and weighing about three pounds;

   12 bulls, 12 full-grown rams, and 12 rams a year old as sacrifices to please the LORD, along with the proper grain sacrifices;

   12 goats as sacrifices for sin;

   and 24 bulls, 60 full-grown rams, 60 goats, and 60 rams a year old as sacrifices to ask the LORD's blessing.

⁸⁹Whenever Moses needed to talk with the LORD, he went into the sacred tent, where he heard the LORD's voice coming from between the two winged creatures above the lid of the sacred chest.

7.5 *sacred things:* These included the sacred objects in the sacred tent and the tent itself (see 3.17-37).

7.7-9 *Gershonites . . . Kohathites:* The Gershonites (3.21-26) and Merarites (3.33-37) could use carts to haul the tent curtains and framing, but the Kohathites (3.27-31) had to carry the sacred objects from the sacred tent by hand.

7.12-83 *gifts . . . weighed according to the official standards . . . incense . . . sacrifice:* The gifts included two silver bowls. One was used to catch the blood from a sacrifice so it could be sprinkled on the altar (Lev 16.18,19). Sacrifices to please the LORD have traditionally been called "whole burnt offerings" because the whole animal was burned on the altar. A main purpose of such a sacrifice was to please the LORD with the smell of the sacrifices.

7.89 *lid of the sacred chest:* The lid of the sacred chest has also been called a "mercy seat," where God said he would sit and judge the people with overwhelming kindness, or mercy, and tell them what they must do (Exod 25.22). The winged creatures, also known as "cherubim," probably looked like the Sphinx of Egypt, having a human head and lion's body (Ezek 41.18,19) or like the human-headed bulls and lions that guarded ancient Mesopotamian temples. See also 1 Sam 4.4; 2 Sam 6.2; Ps 80.1.

---

^p**7.12-83** *sacrifices to please the LORD:* See the note at 6.11.   ^q**7.12-83** *goat:* Hebrew "male goat."
^r**7.12-83** *sacrifices to ask the LORD's blessing:* See the note at 6.14.

8.6,7 *Levites must be acceptable . . . wash:* The Levites had to become ritually clean before they could serve at the sacred tent. This was done by sprinkling them with the water that washes away sins (19.9,17-19), which was not the same as the sacred water (5.17). They also had to shave their bodies and wash their clothes.

8.8 *sacrifice:* The proper grain sacrifice was the sacrifice to give thanks (Lev 2). The sacrifice for sin was actually done to clean or purify those who had unintentionally sinned by disobeying God's laws or those who had accidentally done something God told them not to do. Like the high priest, the Levites were to offer a bull (see Lev 4.3).

8.10 *place their hands on them:* Touching (laying hands on) connected the people with those chosen for the special work, just as the laying of hands identified the one making a sacrifice with the object being sacrificed (see Lev 3.2). The sins of the people were transferred to the bull that was sacrificed.

8.12 *Sacrifice . . . for the forgiveness of sin . . . pleased:* One bull was sacrificed as a sin offering and the other as a whole burnt thanks offering to please God.

8.24-25 *Levites . . . between the ages of 25 and 50:* Compare these verses to 4.2,3. The age differences may be a clue that the ages for Levite workers varied among periods of Israel's history.

Aaron Puts the Gold Lamps in Place

8 The LORD said to Moses, [2]"Tell Aaron to put the seven lamps on the lampstand so they shine toward the front."

[3]Aaron obeyed and placed the lamps as he was told. [4]The lampstand was made of hammered gold from its base to the decorative flowers on top, exactly like the pattern the LORD had described to Moses.

Instructions for Ordaining the Levites

[5]The LORD said to Moses:

[6]The Levites must be acceptable to me before they begin working at the sacred tent. So separate them from the rest of the Israelites [7]and sprinkle them with the water that washes away their sins. Then have them shave their entire bodies and wash their clothes.

[8]They are to bring a bull and its proper grain sacrifice of flour mixed with olive oil. And they must bring a second bull as a sacrifice for sin.

[9]Then you, Moses, will call together all the people of Israel and send the Levites to my sacred tent, [10]where the people will place their hands on them. [11]Aaron will present the Levites to me as a gift from the people, so that the Levites will do my work.

[12]After this, the Levites are to place their hands on the heads of the bulls. Sacrifice one of the bulls for the forgiveness of sin, and the other to make sure that I am pleased. Then the Levites will be acceptable to me. [13]They will stand at my altar in front of Aaron and his sons, who will dedicate the Levites to me.

[14]This ceremony will show that the Levites are different from the other Israelites and belong to me in a special way. [15]After they have been made acceptable and have been dedicated, they will be allowed to work at my sacred tent. [16]They are mine and will take the place of the first-born Israelite sons. [17]When I killed the oldest sons of the Egyptians, I decided that the first-born sons in each Israelite family would be mine, as well as every first-born male from their flocks and herds. [18]But now I have chosen these Levites as substitutes for the first-born sons, [19]and I have given them as gifts to Aaron and his sons to serve at the sacred tent. I will hold them responsible for what happens to anyone who gets too close to the sacred tent.[s]

The Levites Are Dedicated to the LORD

[20]Moses, Aaron, and the other Israelites made sure that the Levites did everything the LORD had commanded. [21]The Levites sprinkled themselves with the water of forgiveness and washed their clothes. Then Aaron brought them to the altar and offered sacrifices to forgive their sins and make them acceptable to the LORD. [22]After this, the Levites worked at the sacred tent as assistants to Aaron and his sons, just as the LORD had commanded.

[23]The LORD also told Moses, [24-25]"Levites who are between the ages of 25 and 50 must work at my sacred tent. But once they turn 50, they must retire. [26]They may help the other Levites in their duties, but they must no longer be responsible for any work themselves. Remember this when you assign their duties."

[s]8.19 *I will hold . . . sacred tent:* One possible meaning for the difficult Hebrew text.

Regulations for Celebrating Passover

9 During the first month of Israel's second year in the Sinai Desert,[t] the LORD had told Moses [2]to say to the people, "Celebrate Passover [3]in the evening of the fourteenth day of this month[u] and do it by following all the regulations." [4-5]Moses told the people what the LORD had said, and they celebrated Passover there in the desert in the evening of the fourteenth day of the first month.

[6]Some people in Israel's camp had touched a dead body and had become unfit to worship the LORD, and they could not celebrate Passover. But they asked Moses and Aaron, [7]"Even though we have touched a dead body, why can't we celebrate Passover and offer sacrifices to the LORD at the same time as everyone else?"

[8]Moses said, "Wait here while I go into the sacred tent and find out what the LORD says about this."

[9]The LORD then told Moses [10]to say to the community of Israel:

If any of you or your descendants touch a dead body and become unfit to worship me, or if you are away on a long journey, you may still celebrate Passover. [11]But it must be done in the second month,[v] in the evening of the fourteenth day. Eat the Passover lamb with thin bread and bitter herbs, [12]and don't leave any of it until morning or break any of the animal's bones. Be sure to follow these regulations.

[13]But if any of you are fit to worship me, and yet refuse to celebrate Passover when you are not away on a journey, you will no longer belong to my people. You will be punished because you did not offer sacrifices to me at the proper time.

[14]Anyone, including foreigners who live among you, can celebrate Passover, if they follow all the regulations.

The Cloud over the Sacred Tent

(Exodus 40.34-38)

[15-16]As soon as the sacred tent was set up,[w] a thick cloud appeared and covered it. The cloud was there each day, and during the night, a fire could be seen in it. [17-19]The LORD used this cloud to tell the Israelites when to move their camp and where to set it up again. As long as the cloud covered the tent, the Israelites did not break camp. But when the cloud moved, they followed it, and wherever it stopped, they camped and stayed there, [20-22]whether it was only one night, a few days, a month, or even a year. As long as the cloud remained over the tent, the Israelites stayed where they were. But when the cloud moved, so did the Israelites. [23]They obeyed the LORD's commands and went wherever he directed Moses.

---

[t]**9.1** *first month . . . Sinai Desert:* The book of Numbers begins in the second month of the second year (see 1.1), so 9.1-5 refers to a Passover celebration that had already taken place. [u]**9.3** *this month:* Abib (also called Nisan), the first month of the Hebrew calendar, from about mid-March to mid-April. [v]**9.11** *second month:* See the note at 1.1. [w]**9.15,16** *As soon as the sacred tent was set up:* According to Exodus 40.17, this took place "on the first day of the first month of the second year" of the Israelites' stay in the desert.

■ **9.2-5** *Passover . . . this month:* The name "Passover" is related to the Hebrew verb translated as "pass over" in Exodus 12.13,23,27. This festival was celebrated as a remembrance of how God acted to save the Israelite people from slavery in Egypt. "This month" refers to Abib. **(See the chart Pilgrimage Festivals on pg 1799.)**

❧ Passover and the Festival of Thin Bread

● **9.11** *second month:* Those who were considered ritually unclean at the time of the actual Passover Festival could celebrate a month later after they had become acceptable to God again. See also 2 Chr 30.1-4.

● **9.11** *Passover lamb . . . thin bread:* Lamb was served at the first Passover (Exod 12.3) along with thin bread and bitter herbs (Exod 12.8), which symbolized the Israelites' bitter years of slavery in Egypt.

● **9.14** *foreigners:* Refers to non-Israelites who had settled among the Israelite people. The non-Israelite males could celebrate Passover as long as they were circumcised (see Exod 12.48,49). Foreigners were not punished if they decided not to celebrate the Passover, but Israelites were (9.13).

❧ Foreigners (Aliens)

❧ Circumcision

The Silver Trumpets

10 The LORD told Moses: ²Have someone make two trumpets out of hammered silver. These will be used to call the people together and to give the signal for moving your camp. ³If both trumpets are blown, everyone is to meet with you at the entrance to the sacred tent. ⁴But if just one is blown, only the twelve tribal leaders need to come together.

⁵⁻⁶Give a signal on a trumpet when it is time to break camp. The first blast will be the signal for the tribes camped on the east side, and the second blast will be the signal for those on the south. ⁷But when you want everyone to come together, sound a different signal on the trumpet. ⁸The priests of Aaron's family will be the ones to blow the trumpets, and this law will never change.

⁹Whenever you go into battle against an enemy attacking your land, give a warning signal on the trumpets. Then I, the LORD, will hear it and rescue you. ¹⁰During the celebration of the New Moon Festival and other religious festivals, sound the trumpets while you offer sacrifices. This will be a reminder that I am the LORD your God.

The Israelites Begin Their Journey

¹¹On the twentieth day of the second month[x] of that same year, the cloud over the sacred tent moved on. ¹²So the Israelites broke camp and left the Sinai Desert. And some time later, the cloud stopped in the Paran Desert.[y] ¹³This was the first time the LORD had told Moses to command the people of Israel to move on.

¹⁴Judah and the tribes that camped alongside it marched out first, carrying their banner. Nahshon son of Amminadab was the leader of the Judah tribe, ¹⁵Nethanel son of Zuar was the leader of the Issachar tribe, ¹⁶and Eliab son of Helon was the leader of the Zebulun tribe.

¹⁷The sacred tent had been taken down, and the Gershonites and the Merarites carried it, marching behind the Judah camp.

¹⁸Reuben and the tribes that camped alongside it marched out second, carrying their banner. Elizur son of Shedeur was the leader of the Reuben tribe, ¹⁹Shelumiel son of Zurishaddai was the leader of the Simeon tribe, ²⁰and Eliasaph son of Deuel was the leader of the Gad tribe.

²¹Next were the Kohathites, carrying the objects for the sacred tent, which was to be set up before they arrived at the new camp.

²²Ephraim and the tribes that camped alongside it marched next, carrying their banner. Elishama son of Ammihud was the leader of the Ephraim tribe, ²³Gamaliel son of Pedahzur was the leader of the Manasseh tribe, ²⁴and Abidan son of Gideoni was the leader of the Benjamin tribe.

²⁵Dan and the tribes that camped alongside it were to protect the Israelites against an attack from behind, and so they marched last, carrying their banner. Ahiezer son of Ammishaddai was the leader of the tribe of Dan, ²⁶Pagiel son of Ochran was the leader of the Asher tribe, ²⁷and Ahira son of Enan was the leader of the Naphtali tribe.

²⁸This was the order in which the Israelites marched each time they moved their camp.

²⁹Hobab[z] the Midianite, the father-in-law of Moses, was there. And Moses said to

[x]**10.11** *second month:* See the note at 1.1. [y]**10.12** *the Paran Desert:* Probably a general name for the northernmost part of the Sinai Desert. [z]**10.29** *Hobab:* Hebrew "Hobab son of Reuel."

him, "We're leaving for the place the LORD has promised us. He has said that all will go well for us. So come along, and we will make sure that all goes well for you."

³⁰"No, I won't go," Hobab answered. "I'm returning home to be with my own people."

³¹"Please go with us!" Moses said. "You can be our guide because you know the places to camp in the desert. ³²Besides that, if you go, we will give you a share of the good things the LORD gives us."

³³The people of Israel began their journey from Mount Sinai.ᵃ They traveled three days, and the Levites who carried the sacred chest led the way, so the LORD could show them where to camp. ³⁴And the cloud always stayed with them.

³⁵Each day as the Israelites began their journey, Moses would pray, "Our LORD, defeat your enemies and make them run!" ³⁶And when they stopped to set up camp, he would pray, "Our LORD, stay close to Israel's thousands and thousands of people."

The Israelites Complain

11 One day the Israelites started complaining about their troubles. The LORD heard them and became so angry that he destroyed the outer edges of their camp with fire. ²When the people begged Moses to help, he prayed, and the fire went out. ³They named the place "Burning,"ᵇ because in his anger the LORD had set their camp on fire.

The People Grumble about Being Hungry

⁴One day some foreigners among the Israelites became greedy for food, and even the Israelites themselves began moaning,

"We don't have any meat! ⁵In Egypt we could eat all the fish we wanted, and there were cucumbers, melons, all kinds of onions, and garlic. ⁶But we're starving out here, and the only food we have is this manna."

⁷The manna was like small whitish seeds ⁸⁻⁹and tasted like something baked with sweet olive oil. It appeared at night with the dew. In the morning the people would collect the manna, grind or crush it into flour, then boil it and make it into thin wafers.

¹⁰The Israelites stood around their tents complaining. Moses heard them and was upset that they had made the LORD angry. ¹¹He prayed:

I am your servant, LORD, so why are you doing this to me? What have I done to deserve this? You've made me responsible for all these people, ¹²but they're not my children. You told me to nurse them along and to carry them to the land you promised their ancestors. ¹³They keep whining for meat, but where can I get meat for them? ¹⁴This job is too much for me. How can I take care of all these people by myself? ¹⁵If this is the way you're going to treat me, just kill me now and end my miserable life!

Seventy Leaders Are Chosen To Help Moses

¹⁶The LORD said to Moses:

Choose 70 of Israel's respected leaders and go with them to the sacred tent. ¹⁷While I am talking with you there, I will give them some of your authority, so they can share responsibility for my people. You will no longer have to care for them by yourself.

ᵃ10.33 *Mount Sinai:* Hebrew "the LORD's mountain." ᵇ11.3 *Burning:* Or "Taberah."

■ 11.1 *fire:* Fire is often a sign of God's judgment in the Bible. Here the fire may have been lightning or wild fire caused by lightning.

◌ꝑ Fire

● 11.4 *foreigners:* Food was scarce on the long desert journey, and some of those who had come with the Israelites when they left Egypt missed the food available there. Their complaining caused the Israelites to complain too.

● 11.6 *manna:* God provided this unusual food described as white, sweet wafers every day except on the Sabbath (see Exod 16.1-31). In Hebrew, "manna" means "What is it?" after the reaction of the Israelites upon finding it on the ground for the first time.

● 11.12 *land you promised their ancestors:* Canaan, the land God promised to give Abraham and his descendants (Gen 17.7,8; Exod 3.8).

■ 11.16 *70 . . . leaders:* The number seven symbolized completeness and perfection, as in the seven days of creation. Because it is a multiple of the complete number seven, "70" was also considered an important number. The leaders were probably older men who had led the clans in each tribe. (See the chart Numbers in the Bible on pg 1844.)

11.18 *make themselves acceptable:* The people were to prepare for this gift from God by bathing themselves and washing their clothes to make themselves ritually clean and by abstaining from sex (see Exod 19.10-15).

11.25 *Lord's Spirit . . . prophets:* The Spirit refers to God's power, which gives special gifts or abilities. In ancient Israel, prophets were sometimes described as having ecstatic experiences after the LORD'S Spirit took control of them (see, for example, 1 Sam 10.5,6; 19.20-24). **(See the article Prophets and Prophecy on pg 1791.)**

11.31 *quails:* A small brown or sandy-colored bird that usually migrated to the region of Palestine in large flocks during March or April. The people were only to eat what they needed, to show that they trusted God would continue to provide food for them, but many took baskets full of quails in order to dry the meat for eating later.

12.1-3 *Miriam and Aaron . . . Ethiopia:* Moses' sister and brother (see Exod 4.14; 15.20; Num 26.59). Ethiopia is a region to the south of Egypt. The "woman from Ethiopia" is not identified by name anywhere in the Bible. Some scholars think she may have been a woman Moses married some time after marrying Zipporah the Midianite (Exod 18.2-4). Others have suggested that the word translated as "Ethiopia" (*Cush*) can also refer to a place in northern Arabia and could include areas where Midianites lived. If so, Aaron and Miriam could actually be objecting to Moses' marriage to Zipporah.

[18]As for the Israelites, I have heard them complaining about not having meat and about being better off in Egypt. So tell them to make themselves acceptable to me, because tomorrow they will have meat. [19-20]In fact, they will have meat day after day for a whole month—not just a few days, or even 10 or 20. They turned against me and wanted to go back to Egypt. Now they will eat meat until they get sick of it.

[21]Moses replied, "At least 600,000 grown men are here with me. How can you say there will be enough meat to feed them and their families for a whole month? [22]Even if we butchered all our sheep and cattle, or caught every fish in the sea, we wouldn't have enough to feed them."

[23]The LORD answered, "I can do anything! Watch and you'll see my words come true."

[24]Moses told the people what the LORD had said. Then he chose 70 respected leaders and went with them to the sacred tent. While the leaders stood in a circle around the tent, Moses went inside, [25]and the LORD spoke with him. Then the LORD took some authority[c] from Moses and gave it to the 70 leaders. And when the LORD's Spirit took control of them, they started shouting like prophets. But they did it only this one time.

[26]Eldad and Medad were two leaders who had not gone to the tent. But when the Spirit took control of them, they began shouting like prophets right there in camp. [27]A boy ran to Moses and told him about Eldad and Medad.

[28]Joshua[d] was there helping Moses, as he had done since he was young. And he said to Moses, "Sir, you must stop them!"

[29]But Moses replied, "Are you concerned what this might do to me? I wish the LORD would give his Spirit to all his people so everyone could be a prophet." [30]Then Moses and the 70 leaders went back to camp.

The LORD Sends Quails

[31]Some time later the LORD sent a strong wind that blew quails in from the sea until Israel's camp was completely surrounded with birds, piled up about three feet high for miles in every direction. [32]The people picked up quails for two days—each person filled at least 50 bushels. Then they spread them out to dry. [33]But before the meat could be eaten, the LORD became angry and sent a deadly disease through the camp.

[34]After they had buried the people who had been so greedy for meat, they called the place "Graves for the Greedy."[e]

[35]Israel then broke camp and traveled to Hazeroth.

Miriam and Aaron Are Jealous of Moses

12 [1-3]Although Moses was the most humble person in all the world, Miriam and Aaron started complaining, "Moses had no right to marry that woman from Ethiopia![f] Who does he think he is? The LORD has spoken to us, not just to him."

The LORD heard their complaint [4]and told Moses, Aaron, and Miriam to come to the entrance of the sacred tent. [5]There the LORD appeared in a cloud and told Aaron

[c]**11.25** *some authority:* Or "some of the Spirit's power." [d]**11.28** *Joshua:* Hebrew "Joshua son of Nun." [e]**11.34** *Graves for the Greedy:* Or "Kibroth-Hattaavah." [f]**12.1-3** *Ethiopia:* The Hebrew text has "Cush," which was a region south of Egypt that included parts of the present countries of Ethiopia and Sudan.

The LORD answered, "I can do anything! Watch and you'll see my words come true." NUM 11.23

and Miriam to come closer. **6**Then after commanding them to listen carefully, he said:

"I, the Lord, speak to prophets
in visions and dreams.
7But my servant Moses
is the leader of my people.
8He sees me face to face,
and everything I say to him
is perfectly clear.
You have no right to criticize
my servant Moses."

9The Lord became angry with Aaron and Miriam. And after the Lord left **10**and the cloud disappeared from over the sacred tent, Miriam's skin turned white with leprosy.**g** When Aaron saw what had happened to her, **11**he said to Moses, "Sir, please don't punish us for doing such a foolish thing. **12**Don't let Miriam's flesh rot away like a child born dead!"

13Moses prayed, "Lord God, please heal her."

14But the Lord replied, "Miriam would be disgraced for seven days if her father had punished her by spitting in her face. So make her stay outside the camp for seven days, before coming back."

15The people of Israel did not move their camp until Miriam returned seven days later. **16**Then they left Hazeroth and set up camp in the Paran Desert.

Twelve Men Are Sent into Canaan
(Deuteronomy 1.19-33)

13 The Lord said to Moses, **2**"Choose a leader from each tribe and send them into Canaan to explore the land I am giving you."

3So Moses sent twelve tribal leaders from Israel's camp in the Paran Desert **4-16**with orders to explore the land of Canaan. And here are their names:

Shammua son of Zaccur
from Reuben,
Shaphat son of Hori
from Simeon,
Caleb son of Jephunneh
from Judah,
Igal son of Joseph
from Issachar,
Joshua son of Nun
from Ephraim,**h**
Palti son of Raphu
from Benjamin,
Gaddiel son of Sodi
from Zebulun,
Gaddi son of Susi
from Manasseh,
Ammiel son of Gemalli
from Dan,
Sethur son of Michael
from Asher,
Nahbi son of Vophsi
from Naphtali,
and Geuel son of Machi
from Gad.

17Before Moses sent them into Canaan, he said:

After you go through the Southern Desert of Canaan, continue north into the hill country **18**and find out what those regions are like. Be sure to remember how many people live there, how strong they are, **19-20**and if they live in open towns or walled cities. See if the land is good for growing crops and find out what kinds of trees grow there. It's time for grapes to ripen, so try to bring back some of the fruit that grows there.

g12.10 *leprosy*: See the note at 5.2,3. **h**13.4-16 *Joshua . . . Ephraim*: Hebrew "Hoshea son of Nun from Ephraim; Moses renamed him Joshua."

13.17-22 *Southern Desert of Canaan . . . Hebron:* The twelve men traveled from the Paran Desert north to the Zin Desert (13.21; Josh 15.1-4). The hill country may refer to the hilly area of the southern Desert or to the hills of Southern Canaan itself (see 14.40). The twelve spies were to go as far north as Rehob near Lebo-Hamath. The location of Rehob itself is unknown. Lebo-Hamath, meaning "entrance to Hamath," may refer to the pass near Mount Hermon at the entrance to southern Lebanon (see Judg 18.27-29), or it may refer to the city north of Damascus on the Orontes River, which would correspond to Israel's northern boundary at the time of King David (see 2 Sam 10.6-19). Assuming the more southern location of Israel's northern border, the men would have had to cover the 500-mile round-trip in 40 days (see 13.25).

Zoan was a city located in the eastern part of the Nile Delta in Egypt. Hebron, a city in southern Canaan, was where the spies saw the Anakim peoples.

13.23-24 *pomegranates and figs:* The pomegranate is a bright red fruit about the size of a large apple that has a lot of seeds surrounded by a sweet-tasting pulp. Figs are sweet fruits from bushy trees that grow as high as 30 feet.

13.26 *Kadesh in the Paran Desert:* Kadesh probably refers to an oasis located about 50 miles south of Beer-sheba in the Zin Desert (see 20.1) Also known as Kadesh-Barnea (see 32.8; 34.4).

13.29 *Mediterranean Sea . . . Jordan River:* The Mediterranean Sea formed Canaan's western boundary, and the Jordan River was Canaan's main river running south from the mountains near Mount Hermon to Lake Galilee and then on to the Dead Sea. **(See Map 3 on pg 1881.)**

13.33 *Nephilim:* This is a legendary race of giant people with human mothers and heavenly beings as fathers (see Gen 6.4). Their name means "fallen ones." The reports from Canaan compared the Anakim to these legendary giants. Only Caleb and Joshua (14.5-9) argued that the Israelites, with God on their side, could defeat any enemy.

14.6 *tore their clothes in sorrow:* Tearing one's clothing was a way ancient people showed sorrow or sadness. See also Gen 37.29,34; Judg 11.35.

[21]The twelve men left to explore Canaan from the Zin Desert in the south all the way to the town of Rehob near Lebo-Hamath in the north. [22]As they went through the Southern Desert, they came to the town of Hebron, which was seven years older than the Egyptian town of Zoan. In Hebron, they saw the three Anakim[i] clans of Ahiman, Sheshai, and Talmai. [23-24]When they got to Bunch Valley,[j] they cut off a branch with such a huge bunch of grapes, that it took two men to carry it on a pole. That's why the place was called Bunch Valley. Along with the grapes, they also took back pomegranates[k] and figs.

The Men Report Back to the People

[25]After exploring the land of Canaan for 40 days, [26]the twelve men returned to Kadesh in the Paran Desert and told Moses, Aaron, and the people what they had seen. They showed them the fruit [27]and said:

Look at this fruit! The land we explored is rich with milk and honey. [28]But the people who live there are strong, and their cities are large and walled. We even saw the three Anakim[l] clans. [29]Besides that, the Amalekites live in the Southern Desert; the Hittites, Jebusites, and Amorites are in the hill country; and the Canaanites[m] live along the Mediterranean Sea and the Jordan River.

[30]Caleb calmed down the crowd and said, "Let's go and take the land. I know we can do it!"

[31]But the other men replied, "Those people are much too strong for us." [32]Then

they started spreading rumors and saying, "We won't be able to grow anything in that soil. And the people are like giants. [33]In fact, we saw the Nephilim who are the ancestors of the Anakim. They were so big that we felt as small as grasshoppers."

The Israelites Rebel against Moses

14 After the Israelites heard the report from the twelve men who had explored Canaan, the people cried all night [2]and complained to Moses and Aaron, "We wish we had died in Egypt or somewhere out here in the desert! [3]Is the LORD leading us into Canaan, just to have us killed and our women and children captured? We'd be better off in Egypt." [4]Then they said to one another, "Let's choose our own leader and go back."

[5]Moses and Aaron bowed down to pray in front of the crowd. [6]Joshua and Caleb tore their clothes in sorrow [7]and said:

We saw the land ourselves, and it's very good. [8]If we obey the LORD, he will surely give us that land rich with milk and honey. [9]So don't rebel. We have no reason to be afraid of the people who live there. The LORD is on our side, and they won't stand a chance against us!

[10]The crowd threatened to stone Moses and Aaron to death. But just then, the LORD appeared in a cloud at the sacred tent.

Moses Prays for the People

[11]The LORD said to Moses, "I have done great things for these people, and they still

---

[i]**13.22** *Anakim:* Perhaps a group of very large people (see Deuteronomy 2.10,11,20,21). [j]**13.23,24** *Bunch Valley:* Or "Eshcol Valley." [k]**13.23,24** *pomegranates:* A bright red fruit that looks like an apple. [l]**13.28** *Anakim:* See the note at verse 22. [m]**13.29** *Amalekites . . . Hittites . . . Jebusites . . . Amorites . . . Canaanites:* These people lived in Canaan before the Israelites.

reject me by refusing to believe in my power. [12]So they will no longer be my people. I will destroy them, but I will make you the ancestor of a nation even stronger than theirs."

[13-16]Moses replied:

With your mighty power you rescued my people from Egypt, so please don't destroy us here in the desert. If you do, the Egyptians will hear about it and tell the people of Canaan. Those Canaanites already know that we are your people, and that we see you face to face. And they have heard how you lead us with a thick cloud during the day and flaming fire at night. But if you kill us, they will claim it was because you weren't powerful enough to lead us into Canaan as you promised.

[17]Show us your great power, Lord. You promised [18]that you love to show mercy and kindness. And you said that you are very patient, but that you will punish everyone guilty of doing wrong—not only them but their children and grandchildren as well.

[19]You are merciful, and you treat people better than they deserve. So please forgive these people, just as you have forgiven them ever since they left Egypt.

[20]Then the Lord said to Moses:

In answer to your prayer, I do forgive them. [21]But as surely as I live and my power has no limit, [22-23]I swear that not one of these Israelites will enter the land I promised to give their ancestors. These people have seen my power in Egypt and in the desert, but they will never see Canaan. They have disobeyed and tested me too many times.

[24]But my servant Caleb isn't like the others. So because he has faith in me, I will allow him to cross into Canaan, and his descendants will settle there.

[25]Now listen, Moses! The Amalekites and the Canaanites live in the valleys of Canaan.[n] And tomorrow, you'll need to turn around and head back into the desert toward the Red Sea.[o]

The Israelites Are Punished for Complaining

[26]The Lord told Moses and Aaron [27-28]to give this message to the people of Israel:

You sinful people have complained against me too many times! Now I swear by my own life that I will give you exactly what you wanted.[p] [29]You will die right here in the desert, and your dead bodies will cover the ground. You have insulted me, and none of you men who are over 20 years old [30]will enter the land that I solemnly promised to give you as your own—only Caleb and Joshua[q] will go in.

[31]You were worried that your own children would be captured. But I, the Lord, will let them enter the land you have rejected. [32]You will die here in the desert! [33]Your children will wander around in this desert 40 years, suffering because of your sins, until all of you are dead. [34]I will punish you

[n]**14.25** *The Amalekites and the Canaanites . . . valleys of Canaan:* That is, all possible ways into Canaan were blocked. [o]**14.25** *Red Sea:* Hebrew *yam suph*, here referring to the Gulf of Aqaba, since the term is extended to include the northeastern arm of the Red Sea (see also the note at Exodus 13.18). [p]**14.27,28** *wanted:* See verse 2. [q]**14.30** *Caleb and Joshua:* Hebrew "Caleb son of Jephunneh and Joshua son of Nun."

● 14.22-23 *not one of these Israelites:* These are the older generation of Israelites who escaped from Egypt. They will die in the desert during the 40-year period of wandering because they complained and tested God too often (14.29,34). See also Heb 3.18.

● 14.24 *Caleb:* Caleb was from the tribe of Judah. For his trust in God, he and his descendants were later given choice land in Canaan (see Josh 14.6-14).

● 14.25 *valleys of Canaan . . . Red Sea:* The valley passages leading into Canaan from the south were blocked by the Amalekites and Canaanites so the Israelites had to go southeast toward the Red Sea, which here refers to the Gulf of Aqaba, the northeastern arm of the Red Sea.

■ 14.27-28 *sinful people . . . what you wanted:* Here the sin is lack of trust. God promises to give them what they asked for in 14.2, namely to die in the desert.

■ 14.33 *children will wander . . . 40 years:* Though the older generation will die, God hears Moses' prayer for mercy and will allow their children to enter Canaan, after first suffering hardship in the desert for 40 years. The number 40 is an important number in the Bible. It is used to stand for a long period of time. The flood during the time of Noah (Gen 7.12) lasted 40 days and nights. Jesus was tempted in the wilderness for 40 days (Mark 1.12). **(See the chart Numbers in the Bible on pg 1844.)**

14.44 *sacred chest:* God was present with the Israelites as long as they carried the sacred chest (7.89). When they tried to enter Canaan without it, they were doing so without God's blessing.

14.45 *hill country . . . Hormah:* The hill country here refers to southern Canaan. The exact location of Hormah is uncertain, but it probably was somewhere just south of Beersheba.

15.4-5 *sacrifice a young ram . . . wine:* Offerings for the sacrifices to ask God's blessing (see Lev 3.1) and the sacrifice to give thanks to the LORD (see Lev 6.14-17). Since the offerings include things that must be grown (grain), cultivated (olives), or fermented (wine) some scholars have suggested that these laws reflect the time when the people had begun to settle in the land.

15.6-7 *flour mixed with . . . olive oil:* The flour was probably wheat flour. Olive oil was collected by crushing olives in a bowl and then pouring the olive pulp into a cloth basket. The oil that dripped through the cloth was used in cooking and burned in lamps.

severely every day for the next 40 years—one year for each day that the land was explored. ³⁵You sinful people who ganged up against me will die here in the desert.

³⁶Ten of the men sent to explore the land had brought back bad news and had made the people complain against the LORD. ³⁷So he sent a deadly disease that killed those men, ³⁸but he let Joshua and Caleb live.

The Israelites Fail To Enter Canaan
(Deuteronomy 1.41-45)

³⁹The people of Israel were very sad after Moses gave them the LORD's message. ⁴⁰So they got up early the next morning and got ready to head toward the hill country of Canaan. They said, "We were wrong to complain about the LORD. Let's go into the land that he promised us."

⁴¹But Moses replied, "You're disobeying the LORD! Your plan won't work, ⁴²⁻⁴³so don't even try it. The LORD refuses to help you, because you turned your backs on him. The Amalekites and the Canaanites are your enemies, and they will attack and defeat you."

⁴⁴But the Israelites ignored Moses[r] and marched toward the hill country, even though the sacred chest and Moses did not go with them. ⁴⁵The Amalekites and the Canaanites came down from the hill country, defeated the Israelites, and chased them as far as the town of Hormah.

Laws about Sacrifices

15 The LORD told Moses ²to give the Israelites the following laws about offering sacrifices:

³Bulls or rams or goats[s] are the animals that you may burn on the altar as sacrifices to please me.[t] You may also offer sacrifices voluntarily or because you made a promise, or because they are part of your regular religious ceremonies. The smell of the smoke from these sacrifices is pleasing to me.

⁴⁻⁵If you sacrifice a young ram or goat, you must also offer two pounds of your finest flour mixed with a quart of olive oil as a grain sacrifice. A quart of wine must also be poured on the altar.

⁶⁻⁷And if the animal is a full-grown ram, you must offer four pounds of flour mixed with one and a half quarts of olive oil. One and a half quarts of wine must also be poured on the altar. The smell of this smoke is pleasing to me.

⁸If a bull is offered as a sacrifice to please me or to ask my blessing,[u] ⁹you must offer six pounds of flour mixed with two quarts of olive oil. ¹⁰Two quarts of wine must also be poured on the altar. The smell of this smoke is pleasing to me.

¹¹⁻¹³If you are a native Israelite, you must obey these rules each time you offer a bull, a ram, or a goat as a sacrifice. ¹⁴And the foreigners who live among you must follow these rules. ¹⁵⁻¹⁶This law will never change. I am the LORD, and I consider all people the same, whether they are Israelites or foreigners living among you.

¹⁷⁻¹⁹When you eat food in the land that I am giving you, remember to set aside some of it as an offering to me. ²⁰From the first batch of bread dough that you make after each new grain harvest, make a loaf of bread and offer it to me, just as you offer grain. ²¹All your descendants must follow this law and offer part of the first batch of bread dough.

²²⁻²³The LORD also told Moses to tell the

---

[r]**14.44** *ignored Moses:* One possible meaning for the difficult Hebrew text. [s]**15.3** *goats:* See the note at 7.12-83. [t]**15.3** *sacrifices to please me:* See the note at 6.11. [u]**15.8** *to ask my blessing:* See the note at 6.14.

people what must be done if they ever disobey his laws:

24If all of you disobey one of my laws without knowing it, you must offer a bull as a sacrifice to please me, together with a grain sacrifice, a wine offering, and a goat as a sacrifice for sin. **25**Then the priest will pray and ask me to forgive you. And since you did not mean to do wrong, and you offered sacrifices, **26**the sin of everyone—both Israelites and foreigners among you—will be forgiven.

27But if one of you does wrong without knowing it, you must sacrifice a year-old female goat as a sacrifice for sin. **28**The priest will then ask me to forgive you, and your sin will be forgiven.

29The law will be the same for anyone who does wrong without meaning to, whether an Israelite or a foreigner living among you.

30-31 But if one of you does wrong on purpose, whether Israelite or foreigner, you have sinned against me by disobeying my laws. You will no longer belong to my people.

A Man Put to Death for Gathering Firewood on the Sabbath

32Once, while the Israelites were traveling through the desert, a man was caught gathering firewood on the Sabbath.ᵛ **33**He was taken to Moses, Aaron, and the rest of the community. **34**But no one knew what to do with him, so he was not allowed to leave. **35**Then the LORD said to Moses, "Tell the people to take that man outside the camp and stone him to death!" **36**So he was

killed, just as the LORD had commanded Moses.

The Tassels on the People's Clothes

37The LORD told Moses **38**to say to the people of Israel, "Sew tassels onto the bottom edge of your clothes and tie a blue string to each tassel. **39-40**These will remind you that you must obey my laws and teachings. And when you do, you will be dedicated to me and won't follow your own sinful desires. **41**I am the LORD your God who led you out of Egypt."

Korah, Dathan, and Abiram Lead a Rebellion

16 **1-2**Korah son of Izhar was a Levite from the Kohathite clan. One day he called together Dathan, Abiram, and Onʷ from the Reuben tribe, and the four of them decided to rebel against Moses. So they asked 250 respected Israelite leaders for their support, and together they went to Moses **3**and Aaron and said, "Why do you think you're so much better than everyone else? We're part of the LORD's holy people, and he's with all of us. What makes you think you're the only ones in charge?"

4When Moses heard this, he knelt down to pray.ˣ **5**Then he said to Korah and his followers:

Tomorrow morning the LORD will show us the person he has chosen to be his priest, and that man will faithfully serve him.

6-7 Korah, here is what you and your followers must do: Get some fire pans, fill them with coals and incense, and

---

ᵛ**15.32** *a man . . . Sabbath*: No work was to be done on the Sabbath (see Exodus 31.12-17).
ʷ**16.1,2** *Dathan, Abiram, and On*: Hebrew "Dathan and Abiram the sons of Eliab, and On son of Peleth."   ˣ**16.4** *he knelt down to pray*: Or "he fell to his knees in sorrow."

■ **15.24** *disobey . . . without knowing it*: Breaking God's laws, even without knowing it, still called for offering sacrifices. Unintentional sins, such as touching sacred objects or going near the sacred tent when ritually unclean, affected the whole people of God, and so everyone needed forgiveness.

● **15.32** *Sabbath*: The Sabbath was the weekly day of rest that began at sunset on Friday and ended at sunset on Saturday. **(See the chart Pilgrimage Festivals on pg 1799.)**

● **15.35** *stone him*: Stoning was a common form of capital punishment in Israelite society. It was inflicted for crimes against God, such as working on the Sabbath. Stoning was done outside the camp to keep from disturbing the holiness of the camp. See also Lev 24.14,23.

● **15.38** *tassels*: The tassels would wave about when people walked reminding them to obey God's laws and teachings. Today Jewish prayer shawls still include such tassels. See also Deut 22.12.

16.14 *You keep promising:* Dathan and Abiram's complaint seems to focus on the fact that Moses' promise to lead the people to the rich land of Canaan is taking too long. They claim that they would be better off going back to Egypt where they had rich farmland. They have already begun to forget that they were also slaves in Egypt.

place them near the sacred tent. And the man the LORD chooses will be his priest.ʸ Korah, this time you Levites have gone too far!

8-9 You know that the God of Israel has chosen you Levites from all Israel to serve him by being in charge of the sacred tent and by helping the community to worship in the proper way. What more do you want? **10**The LORD has given you a special responsibility, and now, Korah, you think you should also be his priest. **11**You and your followers have rebelled against the LORD, not against Aaron.

12Then Moses sent for Dathan and Abiram, but they sent back this message: "We won't come! **13**It's bad enough that you took us from our rich farmland in Egypt to let us die here in the desert. Now you also want to boss us around! **14**You keep promising us rich farmlands with fertile fields and vineyards—but where are they? Stop trying to trick these people. No, we won't come to see you."

15Moses was very angry and said to the LORD, "Don't listen to these men! I haven't done anything wrong to them. I haven't taken as much as a donkey."

16Then he said to Korah, "Tomorrow you and your followers must go with Aaron to the LORD's sacred tent. **17**Each of you take along your fire pan with incense in it and offer the incense to the LORD."

18The next day the men placed incense and coals in their fire pans and stood with Moses and Aaron at the entrance to the sacred tent. **19**Meanwhile, Korah had convinced the rest of the Israelites to rebel against their two leaders.

When that happened, the LORD appeared in all his glory **20**and said to Moses and Aaron, **21**"Get away from the rest of the Israelites so I can kill them at once!"

22But the two men bowed down and prayed, "Our God, you gave these people life. Why would you punish everyone here when only one man has sinned?"

23The LORD answered Moses, **24**"Tell the people to stay away from the tents of Korah, Dathan, and Abiram."

25Moses walked over to Dathan and Abiram, and the other leaders of Israel followed. **26**Then Moses warned the people, "Get away from the tents of these sinful men! Don't touch anything that belongs to them or you'll be wiped out." **27**So everyone moved away from those tents, except Korah, Dathan, Abiram, and their families.

28Moses said to the crowd, "The LORD has chosen me and told me to do these things—it wasn't my idea. And here's how you will know: **29**If these men die a natural death, it means the LORD hasn't chosen me. **30**But suppose the LORD does something that has never been done before. For example, what if a huge crack appears in the ground, and these men and their families fall into it and are buried alive, together with everything they own? Then you will know they have turned their backs on the LORD!"

31As soon as Moses said this, the ground under the men opened up **32-33**and swallowed them alive, together with their families and everything they owned. Then the ground closed back up, and they were gone.

34The rest of the Israelites heard their screams, so they ran off, shouting, "We don't want that to happen to us!"

35Suddenly the LORD sent a fire that burned up the 250 men who had offered incense to him.

36Then the LORD said to Moses, **37**"Tell Aaron's son Eleazar to take the fire pans

ʸ**16.6,7** *Get some fire pans . . . his priest:* Only priests could offer incense at the sacred altar; anyone else who tried would be killed. In this case, the man who lived would be the one the LORD had chosen.

from the smoldering fire and scatter the coals. The pans are now sacred, **38**because they were used for offering incense to me. Have them hammered into a thin layer of bronze as a covering for the altar. Those men died because of their sin, and now their fire pans will become a warning for the rest of the community."

39Eleazar collected the pans and had them hammered into a thin layer of bronze as a covering for the altar, **40**just as the LORD had told Moses. The pans were a warning to the Israelites that only Aaron's descendants would be allowed to offer incense to the LORD. Anyone else who tried to would be punished like Korah and his followers.

The Israelites Rebel and Are Punished

41The next day the people of Israel again complained against Moses and Aaron, "The two of you killed some of the LORD's people!"

42As the people crowded around them, Moses and Aaron turned toward the sacred tent, and the LORD appeared in his glory in the cloud covering the tent. **43**So Moses and Aaron walked to the front of the tent, **44**where the LORD said to them, **45**"Stand back! I am going to wipe out these Israelites once and for all."

They immediately bowed down and prayed. **46**Then Moses told Aaron, "Grab your fire pan and fill it with hot coals from the altar. Put incense in it, then quickly take it to where the people are and offer it to the LORD, so they can be forgiven. The LORD is very angry, and people have already started dying!"

47-48 Aaron did exactly what he had been told. He ran over to the crowd of people and stood between the dead bodies and the people who were still alive. He placed the incense on the pan, then offered it to the LORD and asked him to forgive the people's sin. The disease immediately stopped spreading, and no one else died from it. **49**But 14,700 Israelites were dead, not counting those who had died with Korah and his followers.

50Aaron walked back and stood with Moses at the sacred tent.

Aaron's Walking Stick Blooms and Produces Almonds

17 The LORD told Moses: **2-3**Call together the twelve tribes of Israel and tell the leader of each tribe to write his name on the walking stick he carries as a symbol of his authority. Make sure Aaron's name is written on the one from the Levi tribe, then collect all the sticks.

4Place these sticks in the tent right in front of the sacred chest where I appear to you. **5**I will then choose a man to be my priest, and his stick will sprout. After that happens, I won't have to listen to any more complaints about you.

6Moses told the people what the LORD had commanded, and they gave him the walking sticks from the twelve tribal leaders, including Aaron's from the Levi tribe. **7**Moses took them and placed them in the LORD's sacred tent.

8The next day when Moses went into the tent, flowers and almonds were already growing on Aaron's stick. **9**Moses brought the twelve sticks out of the tent and showed them to the people. Each of the leaders found his own and took it.

10But the LORD told Moses, "Put Aaron's stick back! Let it stay near the sacred chest as a warning to anyone who might think of rebelling. If these people don't stop their grumbling about me, I will wipe them out." **11**Moses did what he was told.

■ *16.37-39 pans are now sacred . . . bronze:* Eleazar, Aaron's son, took the fire pans from the fire, probably because the high priest (Aaron) was not allowed to touch anything that was dead (see Lev 21.10,11; also Num 19.1-3). The pans were considered sacred, or holy, because they had been used to offer incense to the LORD. Verse 38 offers an explanation of how the altar of sacrifice became covered in bronze (compare this to Exod 27.1,2; 38.1,2).

■ *16.46 incense . . . offer it . . . so they can be forgiven:* Offering incense was not the usual way for priests to make offerings and sacrifices to forgive the sins of the people (see Lev 4.1— 5.19; 6.24-30), but in this case speed was important because the people had already started dying.

● *16.47-48 disease:* It is unclear what disease started killing the people. In the Bible the LORD sometimes uses disease to punish those who disobey or oppose God (see Exod 9.15; Lev 26.14,15; Num 12.9-15; 14.36,37; 25.1-9; Deut 28.21-27; 2 Sam 24.1-17; Jer 14.11,12).

● *17.2-3 walking stick:* A walking stick symbolized a leader's power and authority (see Exod 7.8-12; 14.15-17).

● *17.8 flowers and almonds:* Almond trees grow wild in Palestine and Syria and reach a height of 14 to 18 feet. They bloom as early as January and produce a pulpy fruit with a hard stone surrounding the almond seed or nut.

18.1 *Levites of the Kohath clan:* The Levites helped the priests (1.47-53), but they could not go near the sacred objects or altar to offer sacrifices.

18.8-9 *will receive part of the sacrifices:* When the Israelites entered the land of Canaan, the Levite tribe could not farm the land because they were needed to take care of the sacred tent. Therefore God tells Aaron that they deserve a part of the people's offerings to support themselves and their families.

■ 18.14 *completely dedicated to me:* Those things completely dedicated to the LORD are called *cherem* in Hebrew. These are things taken away from humans and given to God forever. Sometimes they were even destroyed so they could never be used again (see Josh 6.15-19). See also Lev 27.28; Num 21.1-3; 1 Sam 15.3. But here God tells Aaron that these things can be used by the priests.

18.17 *Splatter their blood on the altar:* Because blood was thought to be the source of life (see Gen 4.10,11), it was to be completely drained when sacrificing an animal (17.10-14; Deut 12.23, 24). Blood splattered or smeared on the altar or on the people had cleansing power and showed that something or someone was dedicated to God (see also Exod 29.10-21).

Blood

¹²The Israelites cried out to Moses, "We're done for ¹³and doomed if we even go near the sacred tent!"

The Duties of the Priests and Levites

18 The LORD said to Aaron:
You, your sons, and the other Levites of the Kohath clan, are responsible for what happens at the sacred tent.[z] And you and your sons will be responsible for what the priests do. ²The Levites are your relatives and are here to help you in your service at the tent. ³You must see that they perform their duties. But if they go near any of the sacred objects or the altar, all of you will die. ⁴No one else is allowed to take care of the sacred tent or do anything connected with it. ⁵Follow these instructions, so I won't become angry and punish the Israelites ever again.

⁶I alone chose the Levites from all the other tribes to belong to me, and I have given them to you as your helpers. ⁷But only you and your sons can serve as priests at the altar and in the most holy place. Your work as priests is a gift from me, and anyone else who tries to do that work must be put to death.

The Priests' Share of Offerings Given to the LORD
(Deuteronomy 18.1-8)

⁸⁻⁹The LORD said to Aaron:
I have put you in charge of the sacred gifts and sacrifices that the Israelites bring to me. And from now on, you, your sons, and your descendants will receive part of the sacrifices for sin, as well as part of the grain sacrifices, and the sacrifices to make things right. Your share of these sacrifices will be the parts not burned on the altar. ¹⁰Since these things are sacred, they must be eaten near the sacred tent, but only men are allowed to eat them.

¹¹You will also receive part of the special gifts and offerings that the Israelites bring to me. Any member of your family who is clean and acceptable for worship can eat these things. ¹²For example, when the Israelites bring me the first batches of oil, wine, and grain, you can have the best parts of those gifts. ¹³And the first part of the crops from their fields and vineyards also belongs to you. The people will offer this to me, then anyone in your family who is clean may have some of it.

¹⁴Everything in Israel that has been completely dedicated to me[a] will now belong to you.

¹⁵The first-born son in every Israelite family, as well as the first-born males of their flocks and herds, belong to me. But every first-born son and first-born donkey[b] must be bought back from me. ¹⁶The price for a first-born son who is at least one month old will be five pieces of silver, weighed according to the official standards. ¹⁷However, all first-born cattle, sheep, and goats belong to me and cannot be bought back. Splatter their blood on the altar and send their fat up in smoke, so I can smell it and be pleased. ¹⁸You are allowed to eat the meat of those animals, just as you can eat the choice ribs and the right hind leg of special sacrifices.

¹⁹From now on, the sacred offerings that the Israelites give to me will belong to you,

[z]18.1 *are responsible . . . sacred tent:* Or "are to make sure that no one gets near the sacred tent."
[a]18.14 *that has been completely dedicated to me:* This translates a Hebrew word that describes property and things that were taken away from humans and given to God forever. Sometimes such things had to be completely destroyed (see Joshua 6.15-19). [b]18.15 *donkey:* The Hebrew text has "unclean animal," which probably refers to a donkey (see Exodus 13.13; 34.20).

your sons, and your daughters. This is my promise to you and your descendants, and it will never change.

²⁰You will not receive any land in Israel as your own. I am the LORD, and I will give you whatever you need.

What the Levites Receive

The LORD said to Aaron:

²¹Ten percent of the Israelites' crops and one out of every ten of their newborn animals belong to me. But I am giving all this to the Levites as their pay for the work they do at the sacred tent. ²²⁻²³They are the only ones allowed to work at the tent, and they must not let anyone else come near it. Those who do come near must be put to death, and the Levites will also be punished. This law will never change.

Since the Levites won't be given any land in Israel as their own, ²⁴they will be given the crops and newborn animals that the Israelites offer to me.

What the Levites Must Give

²⁵The LORD told Moses ²⁶to say to the Levites:

When you receive from the people of Israel ten percent of their crops and newborn animals, you must offer a tenth of that to me. ²⁷Just as the Israelites give me part of their grain and wine, you must set aside part of what you receive ²⁸as an offering to me. That amount must then be given to Aaron, ²⁹so the best of what you receive will be mine.

³⁰After you have dedicated the best parts to me, you can eat the rest, just as the Israelites eat part of their grain and wine after offering them to me.ᶜ ³¹Your share may be eaten anywhere by anyone in your family, because it is your pay for working at the sacred tent. ³²You won't be punished for eating it, as long as you have already offered the best parts to me.

The gifts and sacrifices brought by the people must remain sacred, and if you eat any part of them before they are offered to me, you will be put to death.

The Ceremony To Wash Away Sin

19 ¹⁻²The LORD gave Moses and Aaron the following law:

The people of Israel must bring Moses a reddish-brown cow that has nothing wrong with it and that has never been used for plowing. ³Moses will give it to Eleazar the priest, then it will be led outside the camp and killed while Eleazar watches. ⁴He will dip his finger in the blood and sprinkle it seven times in the direction of the sacred tent. ⁵Then the whole cow, including its skin, meat, blood, and insides must be burned. ⁶A priestᵈ is to throw a stick of cedar wood, a hyssopᵉ branch, and a piece of red yarn into the fire.

⁷After the ceremony, the priest is to take a bath and wash his clothes. Only then can he go back into the camp, but he remains unclean and unfit for worship until evening. ⁸The man who burned the cow must also wash his clothes and take a bath, but he is also unclean until evening.

⁹A man who isn't unclean must collect the ashes of the burnt cow and store them outside the camp in a clean place. The people of Israel can mix these ashes with the water used in the ceremony to wash away sin. ¹⁰The man who collects the ashes

ᶜ**18.30** *just as the Israelites . . . to me:* One possible meaning for the difficult Hebrew text.
ᵈ**19.6** *A priest:* Or "Eleazar." ᵉ**19.6** *hyssop:* A plant with small clusters of blue flowers and sweet-smelling leaves.

18.21 *Ten percent:* This ten percent, also known as a "tithe," was given to the Levites in return for their care of the sacred tent and because they did not receive a share of land. See also Lev 27.30-33; Deut 14.22-29; 2 Chr 31.5,6.

18.26 *a tenth of that to me:* The Levites had to offer a tenth of the gifts given to them (18.21) to the LORD. These gifts went to the priests from Aaron's family.

19.1-2 *reddish-brown cow . . . nothing wrong with it:* The cow was to be burned as a sacrifice and its ashes used in a ceremony to wash away sin (19.9) and to cleanse someone who had touched a dead body (19.11,12). It had to be an animal that had nothing wrong with it (see Lev 4.28; 14.10; 22.19,20) and one that had not done any common work (see Deut 15.19; 21.3). The cow's reddish-brown color probably was meant to connect it with the color of blood, which had the power to purify.

19.3 *Eleazar . . . outside the camp:* The high priest (Aaron) was not allowed to leave the sacred tent area (Lev 21.10-12), so Eleazar (Aaron's son) took the cow outside the camp. Normally sacrifices were made at the altar near the sacred tent.

19.10 *unclean:* Because the cow had been sacrificed to God it was considered holy. Touching holy things could make a person ritually unclean and could even be dangerous (see Exod 19.10-15; Lev 6.24-28; Num 16.26).

19.11 *touch a dead body . . . seven days:* Coming into contact with a dead body made a person ritually unclean (see also Lev 11; 21.1; Num 31.19-24). To become clean again, a person had to go through a ceremonial washing using the ashes of a red cow (19.17-19). "Seven" was a number symbolizing a complete cycle. See also Lev 12.2; 14.8; 15.

19.13 *making my sacred tent unclean:* A person who was unclean had to stay away from both the rest of the community and the sacred tent to avoid making them unclean.

19.21 *whoever touches this water:* Even the person who sprinkled the unclean person with the water (19.17,18) is made unclean. But this uncleanness is temporary, lasting only until sundown.

20.1 *Zin Desert . . . Kadesh:* It is unclear how many years have passed, but it may be near the end of the 40-year period in the desert.

must wash his clothes, but will remain unclean until evening. This law must always be obeyed by the people of Israel and the foreigners living among them.

What Must Be Done after Touching a Dead Body

The LORD said:

[11]If you touch a dead body, you will be unclean for seven days. [12]But if you wash with the water mixed with the cow's ashes on the third day and again on the seventh day, you will be clean and acceptable for worship. You must wash yourself on those days; if you don't, you will remain unclean. [13]Suppose you touch a dead body, but refuse to be made clean by washing with the water mixed with ashes. You will be guilty of making my sacred tent unclean and will no longer belong to the people of Israel.

[14]If someone dies in a tent while you are there, you will be unclean for seven days. And anyone who later enters the tent will also be unclean. [15]Any open jar in the tent is unclean.

[16]If you touch the body of someone who died or was killed, or if you touch a human bone or a grave, you will be unclean for seven days.

[17-18]Before you can be made clean, someone who is clean must take some of the ashes from the burnt cow and stir them into a pot of spring water. That same person must dip a hyssop branch in the water and ashes, then sprinkle it on the tent and everything in it, including everyone who was inside. If you have touched a human bone, a grave, or a dead body, you must be sprinkled with that water. [19]If this is done on the third day and on the seventh day, you will be clean. Then after you take a

bath and wash your clothes, you can worship that evening.

[20]If you are unclean and refuse to be made clean by washing with the water mixed with ashes, you will be guilty of making my sacred tent unclean, and you will no longer belong to the people of Israel. [21]These laws will never change.

The man who sprinkled the water and the ashes on you when you were unclean must also wash his clothes. And whoever touches this water is unclean until evening. [22]When you are unclean, everything you touch becomes unclean, and anyone who touches you will be unclean until evening.

Water from a Rock

20 The people of Israel arrived at the Zin Desert during the first month[f] and set up camp near the town of Kadesh. It was there that Miriam died and was buried.

[2]The Israelites had no water, so they went to Moses and Aaron [3]and complained, "Moses, we'd be better off if we had died along with the others in front of the LORD's sacred tent.[g] [4]You brought us into this desert, and now we and our livestock are going to die! [5]Egypt was better than this horrible place. At least there we had grain and figs and grapevines and pomegranates.[h] But now we don't even have any water."

[6]Moses and Aaron went to the entrance to the sacred tent, where they bowed down. The LORD appeared to them in all of his glory [7-8]and said, "Moses, get your walking stick.[i] Then you and Aaron call the people together and command that rock to give you water. That's how you will

[f]20.1 *first month:* See the note at 9.3.   [g]20.3 *if we had died . . . sacred tent:* See 16.41-49.   [h]20.5 *pomegranates:* See the note at 13.23,24.   [i]20.7,8 *walking stick:* A symbol of his authority.

provide water for the people of Israel and their livestock."

⁹Moses obeyed and took his stick from the sacred tent. ¹⁰After he and Aaron had gathered the people around the rock, he said, "Look, you rebellious people, and you will see water flow from this rock!" ¹¹He raised his stick in the air and struck the rock two times. At once, water gushed from the rock, and the people and their livestock had water to drink.

¹²But the LORD said to Moses and Aaron, "Because you refused to believe in my power, these people did not respect me. And so, you will not be the ones to lead them into the land I have promised."

¹³The Israelites had complained against the LORD, and he had shown them his holy power by giving them water to drink. So they named the place Meribah, which means "Complaining."

Israel Isn't Allowed To Go through Edom

¹⁴Moses sent messengers from Israel's camp near Kadesh with this message for the king of Edom:

We are Israelites, your own relatives, and we're sure you have heard the terrible things that have happened to us. ¹⁵Our ancestors settled in Egypt and lived there a long time. But later the Egyptians were cruel to us, ¹⁶and when we begged our LORD for help, he answered our prayer and brought us out of that land.

Now we are camped at the border of your territory, near the town of Kadesh. ¹⁷Please let us go through your country. We won't go near your fields or vineyards, and we won't drink any water from your wells. We will stay on the main road^j until we leave your territory.

¹⁸But the king of Edom answered, "No, I won't let you go through our country! And if you try, we will attack you."

¹⁹Moses sent back this message: "We promise to stay on the main road, and if any of us or our livestock drink your water, we will pay for it. We just want to pass through."

²⁰But the king insisted, "You can't go through our land!"

Then Edom sent out its strongest troops ²¹to keep Israel from passing through its territory. So the Israelites had to go in another direction.

Aaron Dies

²²After the Israelites had left Kadesh and had gone as far as Mount Hor ²³on the Edomite border, the LORD said, ²⁴"Aaron, this is where you will die. You and Moses disobeyed me at Meribah, and so you will not enter the land I promised the Israelites. ²⁵Moses, go with Aaron and his son Eleazar to the top of the mountain. ²⁶Then take Aaron's priestly robe from him and place it on Eleazar. Aaron will die there."

²⁷Moses obeyed, and everyone watched as he and Aaron and Eleazar walked to the top of Mount Hor. ²⁸Moses then took the priestly robe from Aaron and placed it on Eleazar. Aaron died there.

When Moses and Eleazar came down, ²⁹the people knew that Aaron had died, and they mourned his death for 30 days.

---

^{j}20.17 *the main road*: The Hebrew text has "the King's Highway," which was an important trade route through what is today the country of Jordan. It connected the city of Damascus in Syria with the Gulf of Aqaba in southern Jordan.

■ 20.12 *you refused to believe*: Though not clear in this story, other Bible passages describe the sin of Moses and Aaron as disobedience (20.24; 27.14), lack of respect for God (Deut 32.50,51), or speaking in anger (Ps 106.32,33).

● 20.14 *Edom*: The people of Edom were descendants of Jacob's brother Esau (Gen 25.24-26; 36.1) and usually described as enemies of Israel (24.18; 1 Sam 14.47-48; 2 Sam 8.13-14). Edom was directly south of the Dead Sea between Zin Desert and Moab. **(See Map 2 on pg 1880.)**

● 20.29 *mourned . . . 30 days*: The normal time of mourning was seven days, but the people mourned Aaron's death for 30 days.

21.1 *Arad . . . Atharim:* Arad was located about 50 miles north of Kadesh in the Southern Desert of Canaan. The location of Atharim is unknown.

21.3 *Hormah:* Hormah is many miles northwest of the Edom location mentioned in 20.21 and opposite the direction the Israelites had to travel to "go around Edom" in 21.4. This has led some scholars to suggest that this part of chapter 21 may be out of place.

21.6 *poisonous snakes:* Because the Hebrew word translated as "poisonous snakes" comes from a word for fire, the bite of these creatures probably caused a burning pain.

21.8 *snake out of bronze:* Bronze is made by mixing copper and tin. In some ancient cultures people believed that the power of a dangerous creature could be controlled by creating an image of that creature.

21.10-16 *Oboth . . . Beer:* The Israelites have gone all the way around the south of Edom and now they are in the area to the east of Moab. The Zered River gorge lay between northern Edom and southern Moab. From the Zered they traveled north on the eastern edge of Moab to the Arnon River which flows into the Dead Sea and formed the boundary between Moab and Ammon. The meaning of "Beer" in Hebrew is "well," but its location is uncertain. (See Map 4 on pg 1882.)

21.18 *scepters:* A scepter is a ceremonial staff that was a symbol of a ruler's power.

Israel Defeats the Canaanites at Hormah

21 The Canaanite king of Arad lived in the Southern Desert of Canaan, and when he heard that the Israelites were on their way to the village of Atharim, he attacked and took some of them hostage.
[2]The Israelites prayed, "Our Lord, if you will help us defeat these Canaanites, we will completely destroy their towns and everything in them, to show that they belong to you."[k]
[3]The Lord answered their prayer and helped them wipe out the Canaanite army and completely destroy their towns. That's why one of the towns is named Hormah, which means "Destroyed Place."

Moses Makes a Bronze Snake

[4]The Israelites had to go around the territory of Edom, so when they left Mount Hor, they headed south toward the Red Sea.[l] But along the way, the people became so impatient [5]that they complained against God and said to Moses, "Did you bring us out of Egypt, just to let us die in the desert? There's no water out here, and we can't stand this awful food!"
[6]Then the Lord sent poisonous snakes that bit and killed many of them.
[7]Some of the people went to Moses and admitted, "It was wrong of us to insult you and the Lord. Now please ask him to make these snakes go away."
Moses prayed, [8]and the Lord answered, "Make a snake out of bronze and place it on top of a pole. Anyone who gets bitten can look at the snake and be saved from death."

[9]Moses obeyed the Lord. And all of those who looked at the bronze snake lived, even though they had been bitten by the poisonous snakes.

Israel's Journey to Moab

[10]As the Israelites continued their journey to Canaan, they camped at Oboth, [11]then at Iye-Abarim in the desert east of Moab, [12]and then in the Zered Gorge. [13]After that, they crossed the Arnon River gorge and camped in the Moabite desert bordering Amorite territory. The Arnon was the border between the Moabites and the Amorites. [14]A song in *The Book of the Lord's Battles*[m] mentions the town of Waheb with its creeks in the territory of Suphah. It also mentions the Arnon River, [15]with its valleys that lie alongside the Moabite border and extend to the town of Ar.
[16]From the Arnon, the Israelites went to the well near the town of Beer, where the Lord had said to Moses, "Call the people together, and I will give them water to drink."
[17]That's also the same well the Israelites sang about in this song:
> Let's celebrate!
> The well has given us water.
[18]With their royal scepters,
> our leaders pointed out
> where to dig the well.

The Israelites left the desert and camped near the town of Mattanah, [19]then at Nahaliel, and then at Bamoth. [20]Finally, they reached Moabite territory, where they camped near Mount Pisgah[n] in a valley overlooking the desert north of the Dead Sea.

[k]21.2 *completely destroy . . . belong to you:* The complete destruction of a town and everything in it, including its people and animals, showed that the town belonged to the Lord and could no longer be used by humans. [l]21.4 *Red Sea:* See the note at 14.25. [m]21.14 *The Book of the Lord's Battles:* This may have been a collection of ancient war songs. [n]21.20 *Mount Pisgah:* This probably refers to the highest peak in the Abarim Mountains in Moab.

Israel Defeats King Sihon the Amorite

(Deuteronomy 2.26-37)

21The Israelites sent this message to King Sihon of the Amorites:

22Please let us pass through your territory. We promise to stay away from your fields and vineyards, and we won't drink any water from your wells. As long as we're in your land, we'll stay on the main road.[o]

23But Sihon refused to let Israel travel through his land. Instead, he called together his entire army and marched into the desert to attack Israel near the town of Jahaz. 24Israel defeated them and took over the Amorite territory from the Arnon River gorge in the south to the Jabbok River gorge in the north. Beyond the Jabbok was the territory of the Ammonites, who were much stronger than Israel.

25The Israelites settled in the Amorite towns, including the capital city of Heshbon with its surrounding villages. 26King Sihon had ruled from Heshbon, after defeating the Moabites and taking over their land north of the Arnon River gorge. 27That's why the Amorites had written this poem about Heshbon:

Come and rebuild Heshbon,
King Sihon's capital city!
28His armies marched out
like fiery flames,
burning down the town of Ar
and destroying[p] the hills
along the Arnon River.
29You Moabites are done for!
Your god Chemosh
deserted your people;
they were captured, taken away
by King Sihon the Amorite.
30We completely defeated Moab.
The towns of Heshbon and Dibon,
of Nophah and Medeba
are ruined and gone.[q]

31After the Israelites had settled in the Amorite territory, 32Moses sent some men to explore the town of Jazer. Later, the Israelites captured the villages surrounding it and forced out the Amorites who lived there.

Israel Defeats King Og of Bashan

(Deuteronomy 3.1-11)

33The Israelites headed toward the region of Bashan, where King Og ruled, and he led his entire army to Edrei to meet Israel in battle.

34The LORD said to Moses, "Don't be afraid of Og. I will help you defeat him and his army, just as you did King Sihon who ruled in Heshbon. Og's territory will be yours."

35So the Israelites wiped out Og, his family, and his entire army—there were no survivors. Then Israel took over the land of Bashan.

22 Israel moved from there to the hills of Moab, where they camped across the Jordan River from the town of Jericho.

King Balak of Moab Hires Balaam To Curse Israel

2-3When King Balak[r] of Moab and his people heard how many Israelites there were and what they had done to the Amorites, he and the Moabites were terrified and panicked. 4They said to the Midianite

[o]21.22 *the main road*: See the note at 20.17. [p]21.28 *destroying*: One ancient translation; Hebrew "the rulers of." [q]21.30 *gone*: One possible meaning for the difficult Hebrew text of verse 30.
[r]22.2,3 *Balak*: Hebrew "Balak son of Zippor."

21.21 *King Sihon of the Amorites:* Also called "king of Heshbon" (Deut 2.26; 3.6; Josh 12.5), because Heshbon was where the king ruled (21.25; Deut 1.4; Josh 12.2; 13.10). The Amorites lived in Canaan in the area that would later be claimed by the tribe of Judah (Exod 3.8; 1 Chr 1.14; Deut 1.19-27) and in the hill country east of the Jordan River. They were Israel's enemies until King Solomon defeated them (1 Kgs 9.20,21).

21.24 *Jabbok . . . Ammonites:* The Jabbok River formed the southern boundary of Ammon, a land east of the Jordan River valley and north of Moab. The Ammonites and Moabites had a common ancestor, and both were enemies of Israel. **(See Map 3 on pg 1881.)**

21.29 *Moabites:* Moab was located east of the Dead Sea.

Canaanite Gods and Goddesses

21.33 *Bashan . . . Edrei:* Bashan was a wide area of fertile land on the eastern side of the Jordan River, known for its rich pastures, forests, and herds of cattle (see Ps 22.12; Isa 2.13; Ezek 27.6; Zech 11.2). Edrei was located about 30 miles east of Lake Galilee.

22.1 *hills of Moab . . . Jordan River . . . Jericho:* From these hills the Israelites could see Canaan, the land God promised them. It was west of the Jordan River, the main waterway in the area running south from Lake Galilee to the Dead Sea. Jericho was a very ancient city controlled at this time by the Canaanites. **(See Map 2 on pg 1880.)**

22.5 *Balaam son of Beor:* Balaam had a reputation as a fortuneteller, prophet, and diviner. In the Bible he is remembered in both negative and positive ways. The exact location of Pethor is unclear.

22.8 *LORD's answer:* Divination was the practice of trying to discover information about the future by looking at the inner organs of a sacrificed animal or by reading the pattern of oil droplets in a cup of water. Balaam was not an Israelite and did not follow Israel's LORD (Yahweh), so it is surprising when he tells Balak's officials that he has to listen for the LORD's answer (22.18). (See the articles Prophets and Prophecy and Miracles, Magic, and Medicine on pgs 1791 and 1820.)

22.9 *God:* The Hebrew name translated as "God" in these verses is *Elohim.*

Names of God

22.22-26 *God was angry . . . angel:* The story does not tell exactly why God was angry, since God had already given Balaam permission to go (22.20, 35). In Hebrew the word for "angel" also means "messenger." In the Bible, angels act both as messengers and servants of God.

Angels

leaders, "That huge mob of Israelites will wipe out everything in sight, like a bull eating grass in a field."

So King Balak [5]sent a message to Balaam son of Beor who lived among his relatives in the town of Pethor near the Euphrates River. It said:

I need your help. A large group of people has come here from Egypt and settled near my territory. [6]They are too powerful for us to defeat, so would you come and place a curse on them? Maybe then we can run them off. I know that anyone you bless will be successful, but anyone you curse will fail.

[7]The leaders of Moab and Midian left and took along money to pay Balaam. When they got to his house, they gave him Balak's message.

[8]"Spend the night here," Balaam replied, "and tomorrow I will tell you the LORD's answer." So the officials stayed at his house.

[9]During the night, God asked Balaam, "Who are these people at your house?"

[10]"They are messengers from King Balak of Moab," Balaam answered. "He sent them [11]to ask me to go to Moab and put a curse on the people who have come there from Egypt. They have settled everywhere around him, and he wants to run them off."

[12]But God replied, "Don't go with Balak's messengers. I have blessed those people who have come from Egypt, so don't curse them."

[13]The next morning, Balaam said to Balak's officials, "Go on back home. The LORD says I cannot go with you."

[14]The officials left and told Balak that Balaam refused to come.

[15]Then Balak sent a larger group of officials, who were even more important than the first ones. [16]They went to Balaam and told him that Balak had said, "Balaam, if you come to Moab, [17]I'll pay you very well and do whatever you ask. Just come and place a curse on these people."

[18]Balaam answered, "Even if Balak offered me a palace full of silver or gold, I wouldn't do anything to disobey the LORD my God. [19]You are welcome to spend the night here, just as the others did. I will find out if the LORD has something else to say about this."

[20]That night, God said, "Balaam, I'll let you go to Moab with Balak's messengers, but do only what I say."

[21]So Balaam got up the next morning and saddled his donkey, then left with the Moabite officials.

Balaam and His Donkey Meet an Angel

[22]Balaam was riding his donkey to Moab, and two of his servants were with him. But God was angry that Balaam had gone, so one of the LORD's angels stood in the road to stop him. [23]When Balaam's donkey saw the angel standing there with a sword, it walked off the road and into an open field. Balaam had to beat the donkey to get it back on the road.

[24]Then the angel stood between two vineyards, in a narrow path with a stone wall on each side. [25]When the donkey saw the angel, it walked so close to one of the walls that Balaam's foot scraped against the wall. Balaam beat the donkey again.

[26]The angel moved once more and stood in a spot so narrow that there was no room for the donkey to go around. [27]So it just lay down. Balaam lost his temper, then picked up a stick and whacked the donkey.

[28]When that happened, the LORD told the donkey to speak, and it asked Balaam, "What have I done that made you beat me three times?"

²⁹"You made me look stupid!" Balaam answered. "If I had a sword, I'd kill you here and now!"

³⁰"But you're my owner," answered the donkey, "and you've ridden me many times. Have I ever done anything like this before?"

"No," Balaam admitted.

³¹Just then, the LORD let Balaam see the angel standing in the road, holding a sword, and Balaam bowed down.

³²The angel said, "You had no right to treat your donkey like that! I was the one who blocked your way, because I don't think you should go to Moab.ˢ ³³If your donkey had not seen me and stopped those three times, I would have killed you and let the donkey live."

³⁴Balaam replied, "I was wrong. I didn't know you were trying to stop me. If you don't think I should go, I'll return home at once."

³⁵"It's all right for you to go," the LORD's angel answered. "But you must say only what I tell you." So Balaam went on with Balak's officials.

King Balak Meets Balaam

³⁶When Balak heard that Balaam was coming, he went to meet him at the town of Ir on the Arnon River, which is the northern border of Moab. ³⁷Balak asked, "Why didn't you come when I invited you the first time? Did you think I wasn't going to pay you?"

³⁸"I'm here now," Balaam answered. "But I will say only what God tells me to say."

³⁹They left and went to the town of Kiriath-Huzoth, ⁴⁰where Balak sacrificed cattle and sheep and gave some of the meat to Balaam and the officials who were with him.

⁴¹The next morning, Balak took Balaam to the town of Bamoth-Baal. From there, Balaam could see some of the Israelites.ᵗ

Balaam's First Message

23 Balaam said to Balak, "Build seven altars here, then bring seven bulls and seven rams."

²After Balak had done this, they sacrificed a bull and a ram on each altar. ³Then Balaam said, "Wait here beside your offerings, and I'll go somewhere to be alone. Maybe the LORD will appear to me. If he does, I will tell you everything he says." And he left.

⁴When God appeared to him, Balaam said, "I have built seven altars and have sacrificed a bull and a ram on each one."

⁵The LORD gave Balaam a message, then sent him back to tell Balak. ⁶When Balaam returned, he found Balak and his officials standing beside the offerings.

⁷Balaam said:

"King Balak of Moab brought me
from the hills of Syria
to curse Israel
and announce its doom.
⁸But I can't go against God!
He did not curse
or condemn Israel.

*⁹"From the mountain peaks,
I look down and see Israel,
the obedient people of God.
¹⁰They are living alone in peace.

ˢ**22.32** *I don't think you should go to Moab:* One possible meaning for the difficult Hebrew text.
ᵗ**22.41** *Balaam could see some of the Israelites:* For a curse to work, the people or thing being cursed had to be seen.

23.16 *message:* Messages spoken by prophets are sometimes called "oracles."

23.20 *bless these people:* God's blessing could not be taken away once it was promised (see 22.12), just as a curse could not be taken back once it was spoken (see Gen 27.1-40).

23.21 *Israel's king is the LORD God:* Though the books of the Bible are not necessarily arranged as they were written, this is the first place in the Old Testament that Israel's God is described as a king (see also Ps 8.1,9; 145.1; Isa 41.21-24). It is noteworthy that this affirmation of Israel's God is made by Balaam, a foreigner.

23.23 *magic charms:* As a diviner, Balaam may also have practiced magic, but his words here point out that magic charms could not work against the Israelites because they were protected by God.

23.28 *Mount Peor:* Not mentioned anywhere else in the Bible, it may have been near Beth-Peor.

24.1 *did not use any magic:* Balaam may have examined the inner organs of the sacrificed animals (see 22.40), but there is no evidence that he had relied on magic when he received the first two messages from God.

24.1 *desert:* North of the Dead Sea on the east side of the Jordan River (see 23.28).

And though they are many,
they don't bother
the other nations.

"I hope to obey God
for as long as I live
and to die in such peace."

¹¹Balak said, "What are you doing? I asked you to come and place a curse on my enemies. But you have blessed them instead!" ¹²Balaam answered, "I can say only what the LORD tells me."

Balaam's Second Message

¹³Balak said to Balaam, "Let's go somewhere else. Maybe if you see a smaller part of the Israelites, you will be able to curse them for me." ¹⁴So he took Balaam to a field on top of Mount Pisgah where lookouts were stationed.ᵘ Then he built seven altars there and sacrificed a bull and a ram on each one.

¹⁵"Wait here beside your offerings," Balaam said. "The LORD will appear to me over there."

¹⁶The LORD appeared to Balaam and gave him another message, then he told him to go and tell Balak. ¹⁷Balaam went back and saw him and his officials standing beside the offerings.

Balak asked, "What did the LORD say?" ¹⁸Balaam answered:

"Pay close attention
to my words—
¹⁹God is no mere human!
He doesn't tell lies
or change his mind.
God always keeps his promises.

²⁰"My command from God
was to bless these people,

and there's nothing I can do
to change what he has done.
²¹Israel's king is the LORD God.
He lives there with them
and intends them no harm.
²²With the strength of a wild ox,
God led Israel out of Egypt.
²³No magic charms can work
against them—
just look what God has done
for his people.
²⁴They are like angry lions
ready to attack;
and they won't rest
until their victim
is gobbled up."

²⁵Balak shouted, "If you're not going to curse Israel, then at least don't bless them."

²⁶"I've already told you," Balaam answered. "I will say only what the LORD tells me."

Balaam's Third Message

²⁷Balak said to Balaam, "Come on, let's try another place. Maybe God will let you curse Israel from there." ²⁸So he took Balaam to Mount Peor overlooking the desert north of the Dead Sea.

²⁹Balaam said, "Build seven altars here, then bring me seven bulls and seven rams." ³⁰After Balak had done what Balaam asked, he sacrificed a bull and a ram on each altar.

24 Balaam was sure that the LORD would tell him to bless Israel again. So he did not use any magic to find out what the LORD wanted him to do, as he had the first two times. Instead, he looked out toward the desert ²and saw the tribes of Israel camped below. Just then, God's Spirit took control of him, ³and Balaam said:

ᵘ**23.14** *a field . . . where lookouts were stationed:* Or "Zophim Field on the top of Mount Pisgah."

"I hope to obey God for as long as I live and to die in such peace." NUM 23.10

"I am the son of Beor,
  and my words are true,^{v}
    so listen to my message!
^{4}It comes from the LORD,
  the God All-Powerful.
I bowed down to him
  and saw a vision of Israel.

^{5}"People of Israel,
  your camp is lovely.
^{6}It's like a grove of palm trees^w
  or a garden beside a river.
You are like tall aloe trees
  that the LORD has planted,
or like cedars
  growing near water.
^{7}You and your descendants
  will prosper like an orchard
    beside a stream.
Your king will rule with power
and be a greater king
  than Agag the Amalekite.^{x}
^{8}With the strength of a wild ox,
  God led you out of Egypt.
You will defeat your enemies,
shooting them with arrows^y
  and crushing their bones.
^{9}Like a lion you lie down,
  resting after an attack.
Who would dare disturb you?

"Anyone who blesses you
  will be blessed;
anyone who curses you
  will be cursed."

^{10}When Balak heard this, he was so furious that he pounded his fist against his hand and said, "I called you here to place a curse on my enemies, and you've blessed them three times. ^{11}Leave now and go home! I told you I would pay you well, but since the LORD didn't let you do what I asked, you won't be paid."

^{12}Balaam answered, "I told your messengers ^{13}that even if you offered me a palace full of silver or gold, I would still obey the LORD. And I explained that I would say only what he told me. ^{14}So I'm going back home, but I'm leaving you with a warning about what the Israelites will someday do to your nation."

Balaam's Fourth Message

^{15}Balaam said:

"I am the son of Beor,
  and my words are true,^{z}
    so listen to my message!
^{16}My knowledge comes
  from God Most High,
    the LORD All-Powerful.
I bowed down to him
  and saw a vision of Israel.

^{17}"What I saw in my vision
  hasn't happened yet.
But someday, a king of Israel
  will appear like a star.
He will wipe out you Moabites^a
and destroy^b those tribes
  who live in the desert.^{c}

24.4 *God All-Powerful . . . bowed down:* "Bowed down" may also mean to fall down in a kind of trance, something prophets sometimes did when they received visions from God.

Names of God

24.6 *palm . . . aloe trees:* Probably the date palm, which is common in this region. It can grow taller than 60 feet and live up to 200 years. The aloe tree should not be confused with the aloe plant. It is valued for its bark's sweet-smelling resin.

24.16 *God Most High . . . Lord All-Powerful:* "God Most High" is a translation of the Hebrew *El Elyon*, the Canaanite god in Jerusalem (Gen 14.8-24), here identified with "the LORD."

24.17 *king of Israel . . . Moabites:* King David of Israel defeated the Moabites and Edomites (2 Sam 8.2, 13,14) at least 200 years after Balaam's message.

^{v}**24.3** *my words are true:* One possible meaning for the difficult Hebrew text. ^{w}**24.6** *grove of palm trees:* Or "green valley." ^{x}**24.7** *Agag the Amalekite:* The Amalekites were long-time enemies of the Israelites (see Exodus 17.8-16), and Agag was one of their most powerful kings. ^{y}**24.8** *shooting them with arrows:* One possible meaning for the difficult Hebrew text. ^{z}**24.15** *my words are true:* One possible meaning for the difficult Hebrew text. ^{a}**24.17** *you Moabites:* Or "the territories of Moab." ^{b}**24.17** *destroy:* The Standard Hebrew Text; the Samaritan Hebrew Text "the skulls of." ^{c}**24.17** *those tribes . . . desert:* The Hebrew text has "the descendants of Sheth," which probably refers to the people who lived in the desert areas of Canaan before the Israelites.

24.21,22 *Kenites . . . Assyria:* The Kenites were descendants of Hobab, the father-in-law of Moses (Judg 4.11). Assyria was a very powerful country in biblical times. But there is no known record of the Assyrians ever defeating the Kenites.

24.24 *Cyprus . . . Assyria and Eber:* Cyprus is a translation of the word *Kittim*, which may stand for the island of Cyprus or may refer to a number of peoples who sailed from the west to invade the Middle East (see Jer 2.10; Dan 11.30). Eber may refer to a land to the east of the Euphrates River, such as Babylonia (see Josh 24.3; Isa 7.20). In Genesis 10.21-31 Eber is listed as one of Israel's ancestors.

25.1 *Acacia:* The area of Moab across the Jordan River from Jericho, where the Israelites were camped (see 22.1; 33.49; Josh 2.1; 3.1).

25.2,3 *ceremonies . . . Baal Peor:* After having sex, the Moabite women convinced the Israelite men to join in a sacrifice ceremony to the Moabite gods, which included Baal Peor. Baal was the name of a number of fertility gods worshiped in different parts of the region. Peor refers to the place this particular Baal was worshiped. (See also 31.16; Deut 4.3; Hos 9.10.)

25.8 *deadly disease:* The text does not say what this disease was, but verse 6 seems to show the people's reaction to it.

[18]Israel will conquer Edom
    and capture the land
    of that enemy nation.
[19]The king of Israel will rule
    and destroy the survivors
    of every town there.[d]

[20]"And I saw this vision
    about the Amalekites:[e]
Their nation is now great,
    but it will someday
    disappear forever.[f]

[21]"And this is what I saw
    about the Kenites:[g]
They think they're safe,
    living among the rocks,
[22]but they will be wiped out
    when Assyria conquers them.[h]

[23]"No one can survive
    if God plans destruction.[i]
[24]Ships will come from Cyprus,
    bringing people who will invade
    the lands of Assyria and Eber.
But finally, Cyprus itself
    will be ruined."

[25]After Balaam finished, he started home, and Balak also left.

The Israelites Worship Baal

25 While the Israelites were camped at Acacia, some of the men had sex with Moabite women. [2]These women then invited the men to ceremonies where sacri-fices were offered to their gods. The men ate the meat from the sacrifices and worshiped the Moabite gods.

[3]The LORD was angry with Israel because they had worshiped the god Baal Peor. [4]So he said to Moses, "Take the Israelite leaders who are responsible for this and have them killed in front of my sacred tent where everyone can see. Maybe then I will stop being angry with the Israelites."

[5]Moses told Israel's officials,[j] "Each of you must put to death any of your men who worshiped Baal."

[6]Later, Moses and the people were at the sacred tent, crying, when one of the Israelite men brought a Midianite[k] woman to meet his family. [7]Phinehas, the grandson of Aaron[l] the priest, saw the couple and left the crowd. He found a spear [8]and followed the man into his tent, where he ran the spear through the man and into the woman's stomach. The LORD immediately stopped punishing Israel with a deadly disease, [9]but 24,000 Israelites had already died.

[10]The LORD said to Moses, [11]"In my anger, I would have wiped out the Israelites if Phinehas had not been faithful to me. [12-13]But instead of punishing them, I forgave them. So because of the loyalty that Phinehas showed, I solemnly promise that he and his descendants will always be my priests."

[14]The Israelite man that was killed was Zimri son of Salu, who was one of the leaders of the Simeon tribe. [15]And the Midianite woman killed with him was Cozbi, the

[d]**24.19** *every town there:* Or "Ir in Moab." [e]**24.20** *the Amalekites:* See the note at 24.7. [f]**24.20** *but . . . forever:* One possible meaning for the difficult Hebrew text. [g]**24.21** *the Kenites:* A group of people who lived in the desert south of Israel. [h]**24.22** *them:* One possible meaning for the difficult Hebrew text of verse 22. [i]**24.23** *destruction:* One possible meaning for the difficult Hebrew text of verse 23. [j]**25.5** *officials:* These were special leaders who were probably responsible for an entire tribe or part of a tribe. [k]**25.6** *Midianite:* Used here as a general term for various peoples who lived east of the Jordan River. Some of these people were probably ruled by the Moabite king (see Genesis 36.35). [l]**25.7** *Phinehas . . . Aaron:* Hebrew "Phinehas, son of Eleazar and grandson of Aaron."

daughter of a Midianite clan leader named Zur.

[16]The LORD told Moses, [17-18]"The Midianites are now enemies of Israel, so attack and defeat them! They tricked the people of Israel into worshiping their god at Peor, and they are responsible for the death of Cozbi, the daughter of one of their own leaders."

The Israelites Are Counted a Second Time

26 After the LORD had stopped the deadly disease from killing the Israelites, he said to Moses and Eleazar son of Aaron, [2]"I want you to find out how many Israelites are in each family. Then make a list of every man 20 years and older who is able to serve in Israel's army."

[3]Israel was now camped in the hills of Moab across the Jordan River from the town of Jericho. Moses and Eleazar told them [4]what the LORD had said about counting the men 20 years and older, just as Moses and their ancestors had done when they left Egypt.[m]

[5-7]There were 43,730 men from the tribe of Reuben, the oldest son of Jacob.[n] These men were from the clans of Hanoch, Pallu, Hezron, and Carmi. [8]Pallu was the father of Eliab [9]and the grandfather of Nemuel, Dathan, and Abiram. These are the same Dathan and Abiram who had been chosen by the people, but who followed Korah and rebelled against Moses, Aaron, and the LORD. [10]That's when the LORD made the earth open up and swallow Dathan, Abiram, and Korah. At the same time, fire destroyed 250 men as a warning to the other Israelites.[o] [11]But the Korahite clan wasn't destroyed.

[12-14]There were 22,200 men from the tribe of Simeon; they were from the clans of Nemuel, Jamin, Jachin, Zerah, and Shaul.

[15-18]There were 40,500 men from the tribe of Gad; they were from the clans of Zephon, Haggi, Shuni, Ozni, Eri, Arod, and Areli.

[19-22]There were 76,500 men from the tribe of Judah; they were from the clans of Shelah, Perez, and Zerah, as well as Hezron and Hamul, whose ancestor was Perez. Judah's sons Er and Onan had died in Canaan.[p]

[23-25]There were 64,300 men from the tribe of Issachar; they were from the clans of Tola, Puvah, Jashub, and Shimron.

[26-27]There were 60,500 men from the tribe of Zebulun; they were from the clans of Sered, Elon, and Jahleel.

[28-34]There were 52,700 men from the tribe of Manasseh son of Joseph; they were from the clan of Machir, the clan of Gilead his son, and the clans of his six grandsons: Iezer, Helek, Asriel, Shechem, Shemida, and Hepher. Zelophehad son of Hepher had no sons, but he had five daughters: Mahlah, Noah, Hoglah, Milcah, and Tirzah.[q]

[35-37]There were 32,500 men from the tribe of Ephraim son of Joseph; they were from the clans of Shuthelah, Becher, Tahan, and Eran the son of Shuthelah.

[38-41]There were 45,600 men from the tribe of Benjamin; they were from the clans of Bela, Ashbel, Ahiram, Shephupham, Hupham, as well as from Ard and Naaman, the two sons of Bela.

[m]26.4 *just as . . . Egypt:* One possible meaning for the difficult Hebrew text.   [n]26.5-7 *Jacob:* The Hebrew text has "Israel," Jacob's name after God renamed him.   [o]26.10 *Israelites:* See 16.1-35.
[p]26.19-22 *Judah's sons . . . Canaan:* See Genesis 38.1-10.   [q]26.28-34 *Zelophehad . . . Tirzah:* See also 27.1-11; 36.1-12.

26.1 *Eleazar:* After Aaron died, his son Eleazar became Israel's high priest (20.27,28).

26.2 *list of every man:* Forty years had passed since the first census. This second census counted the Israelite men in the next generation, those who would be allowed to enter the promised land of Canaan.

26.5-18 *Reuben . . . God:* See the chart Israel Counted Twice on pg 1829.

● **26.51** *total number:* Compare this total to the total in 1.46. In the second counting, the clans of each tribe are also listed.

● **26.53** *Divide the land of Canaan among these tribes:* The tribe of Levi was not given a share of the land. The results of the second counting were also used to determine how much land would be given to each tribe. See also Josh 13.8—19.48 for another account of how the land was divided among Israel's tribes. The author of JOSHUA says that Moses gave land east of the Jordan River to Reuben, Gad, and half of the tribe of Manasseh (Josh 13.8; 14.1,2). It was Joshua who later divided the land among those in Canaan, to the west of the Jordan River.

● **27.3** *our father died . . . left no sons:* Zelophehad died along with the others who were punished for rebelling against God (13.1—14.45). In Israel, property was usually passed from father to son. If a man had no son, his daughters would share his land.

42-43 There were 64,400 men from the tribe of Dan; they were all from the clan of Shuham.

44-47 There were 53,400 men from the tribe of Asher; they were from the clans of Imnah, Ishvi, and Beriah, and from the two clans of Heber and Malchiel, the sons of Beriah. Asher's daughter was Serah.

48-50 There were 45,400 men from the tribe of Naphtali; they were from the clans of Jahzeel, Guni, Jezer, and Shillem.

51The total number of Israelite men listed was 601,730.

52The LORD said to Moses, **53**"Divide the land of Canaan among these tribes, according to the number of people in each one, **54**so the larger tribes have more land than the smaller ones. **55-56**I will show you[r] what land to give each tribe, and they will receive as much land as they need, according to the number of people in it."

57The tribe of Levi included the clans of the Gershonites, Kohathites, Merarites, **58**as well as the clans of Libni, Hebron, Mahli, Mushi, and Korah. Kohath the Levite was the father of Amram, **59**the husband of Levi's daughter Jochebed, who was born in Egypt. Amram and Jochebed's three children were Aaron, Moses, and Miriam. **60**Aaron was the father of Nadab, Abihu, Eleazar, and Ithamar. **61**But Nadab and Abihu had died when they offered fire that was unacceptable to the LORD.[s]

62In the tribe of Levi there were 23,000 men and boys at least a month old. They were not listed with the other tribes, because they would not receive any land in Canaan.

63Moses and Eleazar counted the Is-raelites while they were camped in the hills of Moab across the Jordan River from Jericho. **64**None of the people that Moses and Aaron had counted in the Sinai Desert were still alive, **65**except Caleb son of Jephunneh and Joshua son of Nun. The LORD had said that everyone else would die there in the desert.[t]

The Daughters of Zelophehad Are Given Land

27 Zelophehad[u] was from the Manasseh tribe, and he had five daughters, whose names were Mahlah, Noah, Hoglah, Milcah, and Tirzah.

2One day his daughters went to the sacred tent, where they met with Moses, Eleazar, and some other leaders of Israel, as well as a large crowd of Israelites. The young women said:

3You know that our father died in the desert. But it was for something he did wrong, not for joining with Korah in rebelling against the LORD.

Our father left no sons **4**to carry on his family name. But why should his name die out for that reason? Give us some land like the rest of his relatives in our clan, so our father's name can live on.

5Moses asked the LORD what should be done, **6**and the LORD answered:

7Zelophehad's daughters are right. They should each be given part of the land their father would have received.

8Tell the Israelites that when a man dies without a son, his daughter will inherit his land. **9**If he has no daugh-

[r]**26.55,56** *I will show you:* The Hebrew text has "Cast lots to find out." Pieces of wood or stone (called "lots") were used to find out what the LORD wanted his people to do.   [s]**26.61** *Nadab and Abihu . . . the LORD:* See 3.1-4 and Leviticus 10.1,2.   [t]**26.64,65** *None of the people . . . the desert:* See 14.26-30.
[u]**27.1** *Zelophehad:* Hebrew "Zelophehad son of Hepher son of Gilead son of Machir son of Manasseh son of Joseph." Also see 26.28-34; 36.1-12.

ter, his brothers will inherit the land. [10]But if he has no brothers, his father's brothers will inherit the land. [11]And if his father has no brothers, the land must be given to his nearest relative in the clan. This is my law, and the Israelites must obey it.

Joshua Is Appointed Israel's Leader
(Deuteronomy 31.1-8)

[12]The Lord said to Moses, "One day you will go up into the Abarim Mountains, and from there you will see the land I am giving the Israelites. [13]After you have seen it, you will die,[v] just like your brother Aaron, [14]because both of you disobeyed me at Meribah near the town of Kadesh in the Zin Desert. When the Israelites insulted me there, you didn't believe in my holy power."[w]

[15]Moses replied, [16]"You are the Lord God, and you know what is in everyone's heart. So I ask you to appoint a leader for Israel. [17]Your people need someone to lead them into battle, or else they will be like sheep wandering around without a shepherd."

[18]The Lord answered, "Joshua son of Nun can do the job. Place your hands on him to show that he is the one to take your place. [19]Then go with him and tell him to stand in front of Eleazar the priest and the Israelites. Appoint Joshua as their new leader [20]and tell them they must now obey him, just as they obey you. [21]But Joshua must depend on Eleazar to find out from me[x] what I want him to do as he leads Israel into battle."

[22]Moses followed the Lord's instruc-tions and took Joshua to Eleazar and the people, [23]then he placed his hands on Joshua and appointed him Israel's leader.

Regular Daily Sacrifices
(Exodus 29.38-43; Leviticus 6.8-13)

28 The Lord told Moses [2]to say to the people of Israel:

Offer sacrifices to me at the appointed times of worship, so that I will smell the smoke and be pleased.

[3]Each day offer two rams a year old as sacrifices to please me.[y] The animals must have nothing wrong with them; [4]one will be sacrificed in the morning, and the other in the evening. [5]Along with each of them, two pounds of your finest flour mixed with a quart of olive oil must be offered as a grain sacrifice. [6]This sacrifice to please me was first offered at Mount Sinai. [7]Finally, along with each of these two sacrifices, a quart of wine must be poured on the altar as a drink offering. [8]The second ram will be sacrificed that evening, along with the other offer-ings, just like the one sacrificed that morn-ing. The smell of the smoke from these sacrifices will please me.

The Sacrifice on the Sabbath

The Lord said:

[9-10]On the Sabbath, in addition to the regular daily sacrifices,[z] you must sacrifice two rams a year old to please me.[a] These rams must have nothing wrong with them, and they will be sacrificed with a drink offering and four pounds of your finest flour mixed with olive oil.

27.12-14 *Abarim Mountains . . . Meribah . . . Zin Desert:* The Abarim Mountains stretched around the north-ern end of the Dead Sea on the east side of the Jordan River.

27.18 *Joshua . . . Place your hands on him:* Moses placed his hands on Joshua to show that his power would be passed on to Joshua. Laying hands on a person was also a way to show that the person was chosen for a special task.

27.21 *Joshua must depend on Eleazar to find out:* Joshua was Israel's military leader, but he had to get advice from the high priest Eleazar who used pieces of wood or stone called urim or "lots" to find out what the Lord wanted. Exactly how the *urim* was used is not known.

28.26 *Harvest Festival:* This festival, also known as the Feast of Weeks, took place 50 days after the Festival of Thin Bread (Lev 23.15,16). The people presented grain to God as a sign of thanks and to show confidence that God would continue to meet their needs. **(See the chart Pilgrimage Festivals on pg 1799.)**

The Sacrifices on the First Day of the Month

The LORD said:

[11]On the first day of each month, bring to the altar two bulls, one full-grown ram, and seven rams a year old that have nothing wrong with them. Then offer these as sacrifices to please me.[b] [12]Six pounds of your finest flour mixed with olive oil must be offered with each bull as a grain sacrifice. Four pounds of flour mixed with oil must be offered with the ram, [13]and two pounds of flour mixed with oil must be offered with each of the young rams. The smell of the smoke from these sacrifices will please me.

[14-15]Offer one and a half quarts of wine as a drink offering with each bull, one and a half quarts with the ram, and one quart with each of the young rams.

Finally, you must offer a goat[c] as a sacrifice for sin.

These sacrifices are to be offered on the first day of each month, in addition to the regular daily sacrifices.[d]

The Sacrifices during Passover and the Festival of Thin Bread
(Leviticus 23.4-8)

The LORD said:

[16]Celebrate Passover in honor of me on the fourteenth day of the first month[e] of each year. [17]The following day will begin the Festival of Thin Bread, which will last for a week. During this time you must honor me by eating bread made without yeast.

[18]On the first day of this festival, you must rest from your work and come together for worship. [19]Bring to the altar two bulls, one full-grown ram, and seven rams a year old that have nothing wrong with them. And then offer these as sacrifices to please me.[f] [20]Six pounds of your finest flour mixed with olive oil must be offered with each bull as a grain sacrifice. Four pounds of flour mixed with oil must be offered with the ram, [21]and two pounds of flour mixed with oil must be offered with each of the young rams. [22]Also offer a goat[g] as a sacrifice for the sins of the people. [23-24]All of these are to be offered each day of the festival in additional to the regular sacrifices,[h] and the smoke from them will please me. [25]Then on the last day of the festival, you must once again rest from work and come together for worship.

The Sacrifices during the Harvest Festival
(Leviticus 23.15-22)

The LORD said:

[26]On the first day of the Harvest Festival, you must rest from your work, come together for worship, and bring a sacrifice of new grain. [27]Offer two young bulls, one full-grown ram, and seven rams a year old as sacrifices to please me.[i] [28]Six pounds of your finest flour mixed with olive oil must be offered with each bull as a grain sacrifice. Four pounds of flour mixed with oil must be offered with the ram, [29]and two pounds of flour mixed with oil must be offered with each of the young rams. [30]Also offer a goat[j] as a sacrifice for sin. [31]The animals must have nothing wrong with them

---

[b]**28.11** *sacrifices . . . to please me*: See the note at 6.11.   [c]**28.14,15** *goat*: See the note at 7.12-83.
[d]**28.14,15** *regular daily sacrifices*: See 28.1-8.   [e]**28.16** *first month*: See the note at 9.3.   [f]**28.19** *sacrifices to please me*: See the note at 6.11.   [g]**28.22** *goat*: See the note at 7.12-83.   [h]**28.23,24** *regular sacrifices*: See 28.1-8.   [i]**28.27** *sacrifices to please me*: See the note at 6.11.   [j]**28.30** *goat*: See the note at 7.12-83.

and are to be sacrificed along with the regular daily sacrifices.[k]

The Sacrifices at the Festival of Trumpets
(Leviticus 23.23-25)

The LORD said:

29 On the first day of the seventh month,[l] you must rest from your work and come together to celebrate at the sound of the trumpets. [2]Bring to the altar one bull, one full-grown ram, and seven rams a year old that have nothing wrong with them. And then offer these as sacrifices to please me.[m] [3]Six pounds of your finest flour mixed with olive oil must be offered with the bull as a grain sacrifice. Four pounds of flour mixed with oil must be offered with the ram, [4]and two pounds of flour mixed with oil must be offered with each of the young rams. [5]You must also offer a goat[n] as a sacrifice for sin. [6]These sacrifices will be made in addition to the regular daily sacrifices[o] and the sacrifices for the first day of the month.[p] The smoke from these sacrifices will please me.

The Sacrifices on the Great Day of Forgiveness
(Leviticus 23.26-32)

The LORD said:

[7]The tenth day of the seventh month[q] is the Great Day of Forgiveness.[r] On that day you must rest from all work and come together for worship. Show sorrow for your sins by going without food, [8]and bring to the altar one young bull, one full-grown ram, and seven rams a year old that have nothing wrong with them. Then offer these as sacrifices to please me.[s] [9]Six pounds of your finest flour mixed with olive oil must be offered with the bull as a grain sacrifice. Four pounds of flour mixed with oil must be offered with the ram, [10]and two pounds of flour mixed with oil must be offered with each of the young rams. [11]A goat[t] must also be sacrificed for the sins of the people. You will offer these sacrifices in addition to the sacrifice to ask forgiveness and the regular daily sacrifices.[u]

The Sacrifices during the Festival of Shelters
(Leviticus 23.33-44)

The LORD said:

[12]Beginning on the fifteenth day of the seventh month[v] and continuing for seven days, everyone must celebrate the Festival of Shelters in honor of me.

[13]On the first day, you must rest from your work and come together for worship. Bring to the altar 13 bulls, 2 full-grown rams, and 14 rams a year old that have nothing wrong with them. Then offer these as sacrifices to please me.[w] [14]Six pounds of your finest flour mixed with olive oil must be offered with each bull as a grain sacrifice. Four pounds of flour mixed with oil must be offered with each of the rams, [15]and two pounds of flour mixed

● 29.1 *seventh month . . . celebrate:* The seventh month of the Hebrew calendar, Tishri (also known as Ethanim), runs from about mid-September to mid-October. The first day of this month was the start of the Festival of Trumpets, which was observed by horn blasts, special sacrifices, and rest from work. Today, this first day of the seventh month is known as *Rosh Hashanah,* meaning "the beginning of the year." It is not clear why the seventh month marks the beginning of a new year.

● 29.12 *Festival of Shelters:* The Festival of Shelters took place at the end of the fall harvest (Exod 23.16; Deut 16.13-17). The people were to build shelters made of tree branches. They were to live in them for seven days (Lev 23.42) to recall the temporary shelters their ancestors lived in as they wandered in the desert. **(See the chart Pilgrimage Festivals on pg 1799.)**

[k]**28.31** *regular daily sacrifices:* See 28.1-8.   [l]**29.1** *seventh month:* Tishri (also called Ethanim), the seventh month of the Hebrew calendar, from about mid-September to mid-October.   [m]**29.2** *sacrifices to please me:* See the note at 6.11.   [n]**29.5** *goat:* Hebrew "male goat."   [o]**29.6** *regular daily sacrifices:* See 28.1-8.   [p]**29.6** *sacrifices . . . month:* See 28.11-15.   [q]**29.7** *seventh month:* See the note at 29.1.   [r]**29.7** *Great Day of Forgiveness:* Traditionally known as the Day of Atonement.   [s]**29.8** *sacrifices to please me:* See the note at 6.11.   [t]**29.11** *goat:* See the note at 7.12-83.   [u]**29.11** *regular daily sacrifices:* See 28.1-8.   [v]**29.12** *seventh month:* See the note at 29.1.   [w]**29.13** *sacrifices to please me:* See the note at 6.11.

30.2 *a promise to the* LORD: Promises, also known as vows, were taken very seriously. Once a person made a vow, it could not be taken back.

❧   Making Promises (Vows)

● 30.3-16 *young woman . . . Widows . . . married woman:* The laws concerning promises made by women show that men were in charge of ancient Israelite society. Fathers could overrule a vow made by an unmarried daughter living at home, and husbands could overrule promises made by their wives. But the husband had only one day to object to his wife's promise. Widows and divorced women who made vows were expected to keep any promises they made to the LORD.

with oil must be offered with each of the young rams. [16]You must also offer a goat[x] as a sacrifice for sin. These are to be offered in addition to the regular daily sacrifices.[y]

[17-34]For the next six days of the festival, you will sacrifice one less bull than the day before, so that on the seventh day, seven bulls will be sacrificed. The other sacrifices and offerings must remain the same for each of these days.

[35]On the eighth day, you must once again rest from your work and come together for worship. [36]Bring to the altar one bull, one full-grown ram, and seven rams a year old that have nothing wrong with them. Then offer these as sacrifices to please me. [37]You must also offer the proper grain sacrifices and drink offerings of wine with each animal. [38]And offer a goat[z] as the sacrifice to ask forgiveness for the people. These sacrifices are made in addition to the regular daily sacrifices.[a]

[39]You must offer all these sacrifices to me at the appointed times of worship, together with any offerings that are voluntarily given or given because of a promise.

[40]Moses told the people of Israel everything the LORD had told him about the sacrifices.

Making Promises to the LORD

30 The LORD told Moses to say to Israel's tribal leaders:

[2]When one of you men makes a promise to the LORD,[b] you must keep your word.

[3]Suppose a young woman who is still living with her parents makes a promise to the LORD. [4]If her father hears about it and says nothing, she must keep her promise. [5]But if he hears about it and objects, then she no longer has to keep her promise. The LORD will forgive her, because her father did not agree with the promise.

[6-7]Suppose a woman makes a promise to the LORD and then gets married. If her husband later hears about the promise but says nothing, she must do what she said, whether she meant it or not. [8]But if her husband hears about the promise and objects, she no longer has to keep it, and the LORD will forgive her.

[9]Widows and divorced women must keep every promise they make to the LORD.

[10]Suppose a married woman makes a promise to the LORD. [11]If her husband hears about the promise and says nothing, she must do what she said. [12]But if he hears about the promise and does object, she no longer has to keep it. The LORD will forgive her, because her husband would not allow her to keep the promise. [13]Her husband has the final say about any promises she makes to the LORD. [14]If her husband hears about a promise and says nothing about it for a whole day, she must do what she said—since he did not object, the promise must be kept. [15]But if he waits until the next day to stop her from keeping her promise, he is the one who must be punished.

[16]These are the laws that the LORD gave Moses about husbands and wives, and about young daughters who still live at home.

Israel's War against Midian

31 The LORD said to Moses, [2]"Before you die, make sure that the Midianites are punished for what they did to Israel."[c]

[3]Then Moses told the people, "The LORD wants to punish the Midianites. So tell our

[x]**29.16** *goat:* See the note at 7.12-83.   [y]**29.16** *regular daily sacrifices:* See 28.1-8.   [z]**29.38** *goat:* See the note at 7.12-83.   [a]**29.38** *regular daily sacrifices:* See 28.1-8.   [b]**30.2** *a promise to the* LORD: Either the promise of a gift or the promise to do something.   [c]**31.2** *Midianites . . . to Israel:* See 25.1-18.

men to prepare for battle. **4**Each tribe will send 1,000 men to fight."

5Twelve thousand men were picked from the tribes of Israel, and after they were prepared for battle, **6**Moses sent them off to war. Phinehas the son of Eleazar went with them and took along some things from the sacred tent[d] and the trumpets for sounding the battle signal.

7The Israelites fought against the Midianites, just as the LORD had commanded Moses. They killed all the men, **8**including Balaam son of Beor and the five Midianite kings, Evi, Rekem, Zur, Hur, and Reba. **9**The Israelites captured every woman and child, then led away the Midianites' cattle and sheep, and took everything else that belonged to them. **10**They also burned down the Midianite towns and villages.

11Israel's soldiers gathered together everything they had taken from the Midianites, including the captives and the animals. **12-13**Then they returned to their own camp in the hills of Moab across the Jordan River from Jericho, where Moses, Eleazar, and the other Israelite leaders met the troops outside camp.

14Moses became angry with the army commanders **15**and said, "I can't believe you let the women live! **16**They are the ones who followed Balaam's advice and invited our people to worship the god Baal Peor. That's why the LORD punished us by killing so many of our people. **17**You must put to death every boy and all the women who have ever had sex. **18**But do not kill the young women who have never had sex. You may keep them for yourselves."

19Then Moses said to the soldiers, "If you killed anyone or touched a dead body, you are unclean and have to stay outside the camp for seven days. On the third and seventh days, you must go through a ceremony to make yourselves and your captives clean. **20**Then wash your clothes and anything made from animal skin, goat's hair, or wood."

21-23 Eleazar then explained, "If you need to purify something that won't burn, such as gold, silver, bronze, iron, tin, or lead, you must first place it in a hot fire. After you take it out, sprinkle it with the water that purifies. Everything else should only be sprinkled with the water. Do all of this, just as the LORD commanded Moses. **24**Wash your clothes on the seventh day, and after that, you will be clean and may return to the camp."

Everything Taken from the Midianites Is Divided

25The LORD told Moses: **26-27**Make a list of everything taken from the Midianites, including the captives and the animals. Then divide them between the soldiers and the rest of the people. Eleazar the priest and the family leaders will help you.

28-29 From the half that belongs to the soldiers, set aside for the LORD one out of every 500 people or animals and give these to Eleazar.

30From the half that belongs to the people, set aside one out of every 50 and give these to the Levites in charge of the sacred tent.

31Moses and Eleazar followed the LORD's instructions **32-35**and listed everything that had been taken from the Midianites. The list included 675,000 sheep and goats, 72,000 cattle, 61,000 donkeys, and 32,000 young women who had never had sex.

36-47 Each half included 337,500 sheep

---

d**31.6** *Phinehas . . . sacred tent*: Phinehas would serve as the priest during the battle, so he took along the things needed to ask God what he wanted done.

• **31.6** *Phinehas . . . things from the sacred tent*: Eleazar, the high priest, was not allowed to leave the sacred tent area or touch dead bodies, so Phinehas was sent out with the army as Israel's priest. The battle with the Midianites was considered a Holy War because the priest and holy objects were present (see also Deut 20; Josh 6.1-21). It is not clear which sacred objects were taken into battle. It could possibly have been the sacred chest itself.

Holy War (The LORD's Battles)

■ **31.9-18** *Israelites captured . . . do not kill the young women*: Because the war against Midian was a Holy War, the people and property captured were to be dedicated to the LORD. This meant killing the men and destroying the towns. According to Deuteronomy 20.16 and Leviticus 27.28,29 all people and animals dedicated to God and captured in a Holy War were to be destroyed. But Deuteronomy 20.10-15 says women and children were to be kept as slaves. In this case, Moses wanted all the women who were not virgins killed, because some of them had persuaded the Israelites to worship Baal Peor and had had sex with some Israelite men (see 25.1-18). Young women who had not had sex were to be kept as slaves.

Purity (Clean and Unclean)

• **31.28-30** *set aside for the LORD . . . the Levites*: A portion of everything captured in battle, as well as a portion of anything grown, went to the priest and Levites.

32.1 *the regions of Jazer and Gilead:* Jazer's exact location is unknown (21.32), but it probably was in the same general area as Gilead, a high area of fertile grasslands east of the Jordan River (see Gen 31.21,47,48).

32.16,17 *Let us build places . . . prepare to fight:* Moses and the tribes of Reuben and Gad reached a compromise. The Reuben and Gad tribes would fight in Canaan to the west of the Jordan River, but once the other tribes were settled in the land, they could come back and own the land east of the Jordan (32.20-22). **(See Map 3 on pg 1881.)**

and goats, 36,000 cattle, 30,500 donkeys, and 16,000 young women. From the half that belonged to the soldiers, Moses counted out 675 sheep and goats, 72 cattle, 61 donkeys, and 32 women and gave them to Eleazar to be dedicated to the LORD. Then from the half that belonged to the people, Moses set aside one out of every 50 animals and women, as the LORD had said, and gave them to the Levites.

[48]The army commanders went to Moses [49]and said, "Sir, we have counted our troops, and not one soldier is missing. [50]So we want to give the LORD all the gold jewelry we took from the Midianites. It's our gift to him for watching over us and our troops."

[51]Moses and Eleazar accepted the jewelry from the commanders, [52]and its total weight was over 400 pounds. [53]This did not include the things that the soldiers had kept for themselves. [54]So Moses and Eleazar placed the gold in the LORD's sacred tent to remind Israel of what had happened.[e]

Land East of the Jordan River Is Settled

(Deuteronomy 3.12-22)

32 The tribes of Reuben and Gad owned a lot of cattle and sheep, and they saw that the regions of Jazer and Gilead had good pastureland. [2]So they went to Moses, Eleazar, and the other leaders of Israel and said, [3-4]"The LORD has helped us capture the land around the towns of Ataroth, Dibon, Jazer, Nimrah, Heshbon, Elealeh, Sebam, Nebo, and Beon. That's good pastureland, and since we own cattle and sheep, [5]would you let us stay here east of the Jordan River and have this land as our own?"

[6]Moses answered:

You mean you'd stay here while the rest of the Israelites go into battle? [7]If you did that, it would discourage the others from crossing over into the land the LORD promised them. [8]This is exactly what happened when I sent your ancestors from Kadesh-Barnea to explore the land. [9]They went as far as Eshcol Valley, then returned and told the people that we should not enter it. [10]The LORD became very angry. [11]And he said that no one who was 20 years or older when they left Egypt would enter the land he had promised to Abraham, Isaac, and Jacob. Not one of those people believed in the LORD's power, [12]except Caleb and Joshua.[f] They remained faithful to the LORD, [13]but he was so angry with the others that he forced them to wander around in the desert for 40 years. By that time everyone who had sinned against him had died.

[14]Now you people of Reuben and Gad are doing the same thing and making the LORD even angrier. [15]If you reject the LORD, he will once again abandon his people and leave them here in the desert. And you will be to blame!

[16]The men from Reuben and Gad replied:

Let us build places to keep our sheep and goats, and towns for our wives and children, [17]where they can stay and be safe. Then we'll prepare to fight and lead the other tribes into battle. [18]We will stay with them until they have settled in their own tribal lands. [19]The land on this side of the Jordan River will be ours, so we won't expect to receive any on the other side.

[e]**31.54** *to remind . . . happened:* Or "so the LORD would continue to help Israel."   [f]**32.12** *Caleb and Joshua:* See the note at 14.30.

20Moses said:

You promised that you would be ready to fight for the Lord. 21You also agreed to cross the Jordan and stay with the rest of the Israelites, until the Lord forces our enemies out of the land. If you do these things, 22then after the Lord helps Israel capture the land, you can return to your own land. You will no longer have to stay with the others. 23But if you don't keep your promise, you will sin against the Lord and be punished.

24Go ahead and build towns for your wives and children, and places for your sheep and goats. Just be sure to do what you have promised.

25The men from Reuben and Gad answered:

Sir, we will do just what you have said. 26Our wives and children and sheep and cattle will stay here in the towns in Gilead. 27But those of us who are prepared for battle will cross the Jordan and fight for the Lord.

28Then Moses said to Eleazar, Joshua, and the family leaders, 29"Make sure that the tribes of Gad and Reuben prepare for battle and cross the Jordan River with you. If they do, then after the land is in your control, give them the region of Gilead as their tribal land. 30But if they break their promise, they will receive land on the other side of the Jordan, like the rest of the tribes."

31The tribes of Gad and Reuben replied, "We are your servants and will do whatever the Lord has commanded. 32We will cross the Jordan River, ready to fight for the Lord in Canaan. But the land we will inherit as our own will be on this side of the river."

33So Moses gave the tribes of Gad, Reuben, and half of Manassehg the territory and towns that King Sihon the Amorite had ruled, as well as the territory and towns that King Og of Bashan had ruled.h

34The tribe of Gad rebuilt the towns of Dibon, Ataroth, Aroer, 35Atroth-Shophan, Jazer, Jogbehah, 36Beth-Nimrah, and Beth-Haran. They built walls around them and also built places to keep their sheep and goats.

37The tribe of Reuben rebuilt Heshbon, Elealeh, Kiriathaim, 38Sibmah, as well as the towns that used to be known as Nebo and Baal-Meon. They renamed all those places.

39The clan of Machir from the tribe of East Manasseh went to the region of Gilead, captured its towns, and forced out the Amorites. 40So Moses gave the Machirites the region of Gilead, and they settled there.

41Jair from the Manasseh tribe captured villages and renamed them "Villages of Jair."i

42Nobah captured the town of Kenath with its villages and renamed it Nobah.

Israel's Journey from Egypt to Moab

33 As Israel traveled from Egypt under the command of Moses and Aaron, 2Moses kept a list of the places they camped, just as the Lord had instructed. Here is the record of their journey:

3-4Israel left the Egyptian city of Rameses on the fifteenth day of the first month.j This was the day after the Lord had punished Egypt's gods by killing the first-born sons in every Egyptian family. So while the Egyptians were burying the bodies, they

● 32.29 32.34-37 *Gad . . . Reuben:* See Joshua 13.15-28 for another account of the lands given to the Reuben and Gad tribes.

● 32.39-42 *Machir . . . Nobah:* Machir was one of Manasseh's sons (see Josh 13.30-31). East Manasseh was the area east of the Jordan. This tribe also owned land west of the Jordan River after the Israelites took over Canaan (Josh 17.1-13). Jair was probably in the Bashan region (see Josh 13.30-31). Nobah is usually identified with the Nobah mentioned in Judges 8.11, which would place it near Jogbehah in the region west or northwest of modern-day Amman, Jordan.

● 33.3-4 *Rameses . . . first month:* The city of Rameses was probably located in Goshen in the northeast part of the Nile River Delta. See Exod 12.1-3.

---

g32.33 *half of Manasseh*: Or "East Manasseh." h32.33 *ruled*: One possible meaning for the difficult Hebrew text of verse 33. i32.41 *Villages of Jair*: Or "Havvoth-Jair." j33.3,4 *first month*: See the note at 9.3.

33.5-15 *Succoth . . . Sinai Desert:*
Succoth may have been near Pithom,
and Pi-Hahiroth may have been near
Baal-Zephon, an ancient temple site
close to one of the lakes in northern
Sinai. In Hebrew *Migdol* means "Tower,"
and may refer to a fort built along the
northern Sinai coast, Baal-Zephon. Here
the Red Sea refers to the northwestern
arm of the Red Sea known as the Gulf
of Suez. The location of the Etham
Desert is unknown. Elim means "large
trees," and is often said to be near the
brook known as Gharandel. The Sinai
Desert stretches across the Sinai Peninsula between the Gulf of Suez and the
Gulf of Aqaba. Rephidim was the last
stopping place between the Red Sea
and Mount Sinai (see Exod 17.1-7).

Canaanite Gods and Goddesses

watched the Israelites proudly[k] leave their
country.

⁵After the Israelites left Rameses, they
camped at Succoth, ⁶and from there, they
moved their camp to Etham on the edge
of the desert. ⁷Then they turned back
toward Pi-Hahiroth, east of Baal-Zephon,
and camped near Migdol. ⁸They left Pi-
Hahiroth,[l] crossed the Red Sea,[m] then
walked three days into the Etham Desert
and camped at Marah. ⁹Next, they camped
at Elim, where there were 12 springs of
water and 70 palm trees. ¹⁰They left Elim
and camped near the Red Sea,[n] ¹¹then
turned east and camped along the western
edge of the Sinai Desert.[o] ¹²⁻¹⁴From there
they went to Dophkah, Alush, and
Rephidim, where they had no water.[p]
¹⁵They left Rephidim and finally reached
the Sinai Desert.

¹⁶⁻³⁶As Israel traveled from the Sinai
Desert to Kadesh in the Zin Desert, they
camped at Kibroth-Hattaavah, Hazeroth,
Rithmah, Rimmon-Perez, Libnah, Rissah,
Kehelathah, Mount Shepher, Haradah,
Makheloth, Tahath, Terah, Mithkah,
Hashmonah, Moseroth, Bene-Jaakan, Hor-
Haggidgad, Jotbathah, Abronah, Ezion-
Geber, and finally Kadesh. ³⁷When they
left Kadesh, they came to Mount Hor, on
the border of Edom.

³⁸That's where the LORD commanded
Aaron the priest to go to the top of the
mountain. Aaron died there on the first
day of the fifth month,[q] 40 years after the
Israelites left Egypt. ³⁹He was 123 years old
at the time.

⁴⁰It was then that the Canaanite king of
Arad, who lived in the Southern Desert of
Canaan, heard that Israel was headed that
way.

⁴¹⁻⁴⁷The Israelites left Mount Hor and
headed toward Moab. Along the way, they
camped at Zalmonah, Punon, Oboth, Iye-
Abarim in the territory of Moab, Dibon-
Gad, Almon-Diblathaim, at a place near
Mount Nebo in the Abarim Mountains,
⁴⁸and finally in the lowlands of Moab across
the Jordan River from Jericho. ⁴⁹Their
camp stretched from Beth-Jeshimoth to
Acacia.

The LORD's Command
To Conquer Canaan

⁵⁰While Israel was camped in the lowlands of Moab across the Jordan River from
Jericho, the LORD told Moses ⁵¹to give the
people of Israel this message:

When you cross the Jordan River
and enter Canaan, ⁵²you must force
out the people living there. Destroy
their idols and tear down their altars.
⁵³Then settle in the land—I have
given it to you as your own.

⁵⁴I will show you[r] how to divide the
land among the tribes, according to
the number of clans in each one, so
that the larger tribes will have more
land than the smaller ones.

⁵⁵If you don't force out all the people there, they will be like splinters in
your eyes and thorns in your back.
They will always be trouble for you,

---

[k]33.3,4 *proudly:* Or "bravely." [l]33.8 *Pi-Hahiroth:* Two ancient translations and the Samaritan He-
brew Text; the Standard Hebrew Text "a place near Hahiroth." [m]33.8 *Red Sea:* Hebrew *hayyam,* "the
Sea," understood as *yam suph,* "Sea of Reeds" (see also the note at Exodus 13.18). [n]33.10 *Red Sea:*
Hebrew *yam suph,* here referring to the Gulf of Suez, since the term is extended to include the
northwestern arm of the Red Sea (see also the note at Exodus 13.18). [o]33.11 *the western edge of the
Sinai Desert:* Hebrew "the Sin Desert." [p]33.12-14 *Rephidim . . . no water:* See Exodus 17.1-7.
[q]33.38 *fifth month:* Ab, the fifth month of the Hebrew calendar, from about mid-July to mid-August.
[r]33.54 *I will show you:* See the note at 26.55,56.

56and I will treat you as severely as I planned on treating them.

Israel's Borders

34 The LORD told Moses **2**to tell the people of Israel that their land in Canaan would have the following borders:
3The southern border will be the Zin Desert and the northwest part of Edom. This border will begin at the south end of the Dead Sea. **4**It will go west from there, but will turn southward to include Scorpion Pass, the village of Zin, and the town of Kadesh-Barnea. From there, the border will continue to Hazar-Addar and on to Azmon. **5**It will run along the Egyptian Gorge and end at the Mediterranean Sea.
6The western border will be the Mediterranean Sea.
7The northern border will begin at the Mediterranean, then continue eastward to Mount Hor.§ **8**After that, it will run to Lebo-Hamath and across to Zedad, which is the northern edge of your land. **9**From Zedad, the border will continue east to Ziphron and end at Hazar-Enan.
10The eastern border will begin at Hazar-Enan in the north, then run south to Shepham, **11**and on down to Riblah on the east side of Ain. From there, it will go south to the eastern hills of Lake Galilee,† **12**then follow the Jordan River down to the north end of the Dead Sea.
The land within those four borders will belong to you.
13Then Moses told the people, "You will receive the land inside these borders. It will be yours, but the LORD has commanded you to divide it among the nine and a half tribes. **14**The tribes of Reuben, Gad, and East Manasseh have already been given their land **15**across from Jericho, east of the Jordan River."

The Leaders Who Will Divide the Land

16The LORD said to Moses, **17**"Eleazar the priest and Joshua son of Nun will divide the land for the Israelites. **18**One leader from each tribe will help them, **19-28**and here is the list of their names:
Caleb son of Jephunneh from Judah,
Shemuel son of Ammihud from Simeon,
Elidad son of Chislon from Benjamin,
Bukki son of Jogli from Dan,
Hanniel son of Ephod from Manasseh,
Kemuel son of Shiphtan from Ephraim,
Elizaphan son of Parnach from Zebulun,
Paltiel son of Azzan from Issachar,
Ahihud son of Shelomi from Asher,
and Pedahel son of Ammihud from Naphtali."

29These are the men the LORD commanded to help Eleazar and Joshua divide the land for the Israelites.

§**34.7** *Mount Hor:* Not the same as in 33.37. †**34.11** *Lake Galilee:* The Hebrew text has "Lake Chinnereth," an earlier name for Lake Galilee.

34.3-12 *southern border . . . Dead Sea:* The borders described in these verses do not accurately describe Israel's borders at any time in history. Also, the land in Canaan is limited here to lands west of the Jordan River and does not include the lands promised to Reuben, Gad, and East Manasseh (see Num 32). The southern boundary ran from the south end of the Dead Sea southwest through the Zin Desert through the Scorpion Pass (location unknown) to Kadesh-Barnea. Then it turned northwest following the Egyptian Gorge, probably modern Wadi el-Arish (Kadesh-Barnea), ending at the Mediterranean Sea, which formed the western boundary. The northern boundary began at a point on the Mediterranean parallel to Mount Hor (not the Mount Hor where Aaron died) and ran east to Lebo-Hamath. The exact location of Zedad is unknown, but may have been northeast of Damascus. The eastern boundary went south from Hazar-Enan (unknown) to Lake Galilee. From there it followed the Jordan River into the Dead Sea. **(See Map 3 on pg 1881.)**

34.17,18 *Eleazar . . . Joshua . . . One leader from each tribe:* Eleazar was Aaron's son (see 20.26). Other than Caleb, the leaders listed in 34.19-28 are new names who represent the new generation of Israelites who will enter Canaan. Eleazar and Joshua will lead this new generation. The tribes are listed from south to north, except for Manasseh, which is listed before Ephraim because Manasseh was the first-born of Joseph's two sons.

35.6 *Safe Towns:* Also known as "cities of refuge," these were set aside to protect those who accidentally killed someone. At this time in Israel's history, the male relative closest to the victim had the right to avenge the death (35.16-19). A person found guilty of murder at a trial would be taken from the Safe Town and put to death. If found innocent, the person could stay in the Safe Town, protected from the relative's revenge (35.25). "Anyone" in 35.15 is understood as including non-Israelite strangers and those traveling through the land.

Safe Towns

35.28 *until the high priest dies:* The shedding of blood, whether accidental or intentional, was against God's Law (Exod 20.13) and polluted the land (Gen 4.10,11; Num 35.33). Penalties had to be paid and sacrifices offered to make the person and the land clean again (see Exod 21.12-36; Lev 4.1—5.19). The high priest's death was considered sufficient payment for the blood of victims who were killed while he was high priest. See also Deut 17.5-7; 19.15.

The Towns for the Levites

35 While the people of Israel were still camped in the lowlands of Moab across the Jordan River from Jericho, the LORD told Moses ²to say to them:

When you receive your tribal lands, you must give towns and pastures to the Levi tribe. ³That way, the Levites will have towns to live in and pastures for their animals. ⁴-⁵The pasture around each of these towns must be in the shape of a square, with the town itself in the center. The pasture is to measure 3,000 feet on each side, with 1,500 feet of land outside each of the town walls. This will be the Levites' pastureland.

⁶Six of the towns you give them will be Safe Towns where a person who has accidentally killed someone can run for protection. But you will also give the Levites 42 other towns, ⁷so they will have a total of 48 towns with their surrounding pastures.

⁸Since the towns for the Levites must come from Israel's own tribal lands, the larger tribes will give more towns than the smaller ones.

The Safe Towns
(Deuteronomy 19.1-13; Joshua 20.1-9)

⁹The LORD then told Moses ¹⁰to tell the people of Israel:

After you have crossed the Jordan River and are settled in Canaan, ¹¹choose Safe Towns, where a person who has accidentally killed someone can run for protection. ¹²If the victim's relatives think it was murder, they might try to take revenge.ᵘ Anyone accused of murder can run to one

of these Safe Towns for protection and not be killed before a trial is held.

¹³There are to be six of these Safe Towns, ¹⁴three on each side of the Jordan River. ¹⁵They will be places of protection for anyone who lives in Israel and accidentally kills someone.

Laws about Murder and Accidental Killing

The LORD said:

¹⁶-¹⁸Suppose you hit someone with a piece of iron or a large stone or a dangerous wooden tool. If that person dies, then you are a murderer and must be put to death ¹⁹by one of the victim's relatives. He will take revengeᵛ for his relative's death as soon as he finds you.

²⁰-²¹Or suppose you get angry and kill someone by pushing or hitting or by throwing something. You are a murderer and must be put to death by one of the victim's relatives.

²²-²⁴But if you are not angry and accidentally kill someone in any of these ways, the townspeople must hold a trial and decide if you are guilty. ²⁵If they decide that you are innocent, you will be protected from the victim's relative and sent to stay in one of the Safe Towns until the high priest dies. ²⁶But if you ever leave the Safe Town ²⁷and are killed by the victim's relative, he cannot be punished for killing you. ²⁸You must stay inside the town until the high priest dies; only then can you go back home.

²⁹The community of Israel must always obey these laws.

³⁰Death is the penalty for murder. But

ᵘ**35.12** *the victim's relatives . . . revenge:* At this time in Israel's history, the clan would appoint the closest male relative to find and kill a person who had killed a member of their clan.   ᵛ**35.19** *the victim's relatives . . . revenge:* See the note at verse 12.

no one accused of murder can be put to death unless there are at least two witnesses to the crime. **31**You cannot give someone money to escape the death penalty; you must pay with your own life! **32**And if you have been proven innocent of murder and are living in a Safe Town, you cannot pay to go back home; you must stay there until the high priest dies.

33-34I, the LORD, live among you people of Israel, so your land must be kept pure. But when a murder takes place, blood pollutes the land, and it becomes unclean. If that happens, the murderer must be put to death, so the land will be clean again. Keep murder out of Israel!

The Laws about Married Women and Land

36 One day the family leaders from the Gilead clan of the Manasseh tribe went to Moses and the other family leaders of Israel **2**and said, "Sir, the LORD has said that he will show^w what land each tribe will receive as their own. And the LORD has commanded you to give the daughters of our relative Zelophehad^x the land that he would have received. **3**But if they marry men from other tribes of Israel, the land they receive will become part of that tribe's

inheritance and will no longer belong to us. **4**Even when land is returned to its original owner in the Year of Celebration,^y we will not get back Zelophehad's land—it will belong to the tribe into which his daughters married."

5So Moses told the people that the LORD had said:

These men from the Manasseh tribe are right. **6**I will allow Zelophehad's daughters to marry anyone, as long as those men belong to one of the clans of the Manasseh tribe.

7Tribal land must not be given to another tribe—it will remain the property of the tribe that received it. **8-9**In the future, any daughter who inherits land must marry someone from her own tribe. Israel's tribal land is never to be passed from one tribe to another. **10-11**Mahlah, Tirzah, Hoglah, Milcah, and Noah the daughters of Zelophehad obeyed the LORD and married their uncles' sons **12**and remained part of the Manasseh tribe. So their land stayed in their father's clan.

13These are the laws that the LORD gave to Moses and the Israelites while they were camped in the lowlands of Moab across the Jordan River from Jericho.

● 36.1-3 *Gilead . . . no longer belong to us:* Gilead was a grandson of Joseph's son Manasseh. The Gilead clan leaders went to Moses because they were upset about his earlier ruling concerning the daughters of Zelophehad (27.1-11). They were worried that, if the daughters married outside their clan, the land would transfer to the husbands' clans.

● 36.4-9 *Year of Celebration . . . tribal land:* This sacred year for Israel, traditionally called the "Year of Jubilee" occurred every fiftieth year, after seven cycles of seven years each (see Lev 25.8-55). During this year, all property had to go back to its original owner. But here, if a daughter married outside the tribe, the property belonged to her husband's tribe and so could not be returned. To protect the Manasseh tribe from losing the land given to Zelophehad's daughters, Moses made the daughters marry men from one of the Manasseh clans. Then the rule was made to apply to all daughters who inherited land (36.8-9).

---

^w**36.2** *that he will show:* See the note at 26.55,56.   ^x**36.2** *Zelophehad:* See also 26.28-34; 27.1-11.
^y**36.4** *Year of Celebration:* This was a sacred year for Israel, traditionally called the "Year of Jubilee." During this year, all property had to go back to its original owner. But here, the property was not sold; it became part of the other tribe's land when the daughter who owned it married into that tribe. So the property could not be returned even during this year.

Reflection Questions About Numbers 1.1—36.13

1. Who helped Moses and Aaron count the people of Israel? Why were the people counted (chapter 1)?

2. What happened during the celebration of Passover (9.1-14)? What important event was being remembered in this celebration?

3. How did the Israelites know when to break camp in the Sinai Desert? In what order did they march (10.11-28)? Where did the Levite clans (Gershonites, Merarites, and Kohathites) march, and what did they carry?

4. Why was the ceremony to wash away sin important to the people of Israel (chapter 19)? Notice that the phrase "You will be guilty of making my sacred tent unclean and you will no longer belong to the people of Israel" occurs twice (in 19.13 and 20). What does this mean? What is the relationship between "being clean" and belonging to God's people?

5. In chapter 20, what did the people complain about? How did Moses and Aaron respond to the complaint? Why did God decide to punish Aaron and Moses (20.1-13)?

6. Why did King Balak and the Midianite leaders hire the prophet Balaam (22.2—24.25)? Did Balak get what he expected from Balaam? Summarize the key points of Balaam's four messages.

7. Forty years passed between the first census of the Israelite people (chapter 1) and the second census (chapter 26). What had happened to the older generation of Israelites that came out of Egypt?

8. How important was the offering of sacrifices to God to the Israelites in daily life, worship, and special festivals (chapters 28,29)? How important in daily life are offerings, worship, and religious ceremonies today?

9. Describe the Israelites' battle with the Midianites (chapter 31). What happened to the Midianites' lands? Read the note at 31.9-18. What is your reaction to the concept of a "Holy War"?

10. Think of NUMBERS as a family travel album. What pictures from this album stand out in your mind? Are there any pictures you would not want to show other people? Why or why not?

deuteronomy

Was DEUTERONOMY, *the ancient book of Law, discovered in the temple during the reign of King Josiah? If so, it may have been the first book of the Bible to be recognized as Holy Scripture. Listen as Moses speaks powerful words about God's Law to the people of Israel.*

WHAT MAKES DEUTERONOMY SPECIAL?

DEUTERONOMY comes from a Greek word meaning "second law." Those who prepared the Greek version of the Old Testament (the Septuagint) thought the "copy of God's law" in Deuteronomy 17.18 was a "second law." But, DEUTERONOMY is not to be understood as a "second law." Rather, it is a retelling or renewal of the law God gave Moses on Mount Sinai. The Hebrew title of the book, "These are the words (that Moses spoke)," more correctly sums up what DEUTERONOMY is all about. DEUTERONOMY is presented as Moses' last words to the generation of Israelites who are ready to enter the promised land. The "words" are a series of speeches that Moses made to the people of Israel before his death.

DEUTERONOMY is located at an important place in the Old Testament. It is the fifth and concluding book in the section of the Bible known as The Law, or Torah, which means "teaching" (see also the Introduction to the Pentateuch). It continues the story of God's people that began in EXODUS, LEVITICUS, and NUMBERS. The LORD chose the people of Israel, brought them out of slavery in Egypt, and at Sinai gave to them and their leader Moses the laws and commandments that they were to live by. In this way, DEUTERONOMY looks backward, emphasizing what the LORD has already done. But the words of Moses also look forward and are meant to be teaching for future genera-

tions as well. God's agreement with the people of Israel, as presented in DEUTERONOMY, forms the basis of and provides an introduction to the history of Israel found in the books of JOSHUA, JUDGES, 1 and 2 SAMUEL, and 1 and 2 KINGS.

HOW IS DEUTERONOMY CONSTRUCTED?

The following outline divides the book into five major sections, based primarily on the speeches of Moses:

Setting the scene (1.1-5a)
The first speech. Moses reviews the past
  (1.5b—4.43)
    God's faithfulness in the wilderness
    (1.5b—3.29)
    Challenge to hear the word of the LORD (4.1-43)
The second speech. Moses tells what the LORD
  demands (4.44—29.1)
    Love God and obey God's laws (4.44—11.31)
    How to live as God's people (12.1—26.15)
    Renewing the agreement (26.16—29.1)
The third speech. Israel must keep its agreement
  with the LORD (29.2—30.20)
Final speeches and the death of Moses (31.1—34.12)
    A leader for the people and a place for the Law
    (31.1-29)
    The song and the blessing of Moses (31.30—
    33.29)
    Moses dies (34.1-12)

Deuteronomy is the final book in the section of the Bible known as "The Pentateuch" or "Torah" (The Law). Presented as a series of speeches given by Moses, it restates many of the laws and teachings given in Exodus, Leviticus, and Numbers. Deuteronomy reminds God's people of the faithfulness and saving power of God, and stresses the importance of people's gratitude for all the Lord has done. These final speeches of Moses also provide future generations with important lessons on how to live in a way that is faithful to their agreement or covenant with the Lord.

Outline

The Final Speeches of Moses

1 1-5This book contains the speeches that Moses made while Israel was in the land of Moab, camped near the town of Suph in the desert east of the Jordan River. The town of Paran was in one direction from their camp, and the towns of Tophel, Laban, Hazeroth, and Dizahab^a were in the opposite direction.

Earlier, Moses had defeated the Amorite King Sihon of Heshbon. Moses had also defeated King Og of Bashan, who used to live in Ashtaroth for part of the year and in Edrei for the rest of the year.

Although it takes only eleven days to walk from Mount Sinai^b to Kadesh-Barnea by way of the Mount Seir Road, these speeches were not made until 40 years after Israel left Egypt.^c

THE FIRST SPEECH: MOSES REVIEWS THE PAST

The LORD's Command at Mount Sinai

The LORD had given Moses his laws for the people of Israel. And on the first day of the eleventh month,^d Moses began explaining those laws by saying:

^6People of Israel, when we were in our camp at Mount Sinai,^e the LORD our God told us:

You have stayed here long enough. ^7Leave this place and go into the land

---

^a1.1-5 *Suph . . . Paran . . . Tophel, Laban, Hazeroth, and Dizahab*: The exact location of these towns is not known.   ^b1.1-5 *Mount Sinai*: The Hebrew text has "Horeb," another name for Mount Sinai. ^c1.1-5 *Egypt*: The Israelites would soon enter Canaan, but they would have entered the land of Canaan from Kadesh-Barnea 40 years earlier if they had not rebelled against God (see verses 6-40). ^d1.1-5 *eleventh month*: Shebat, the eleventh month of the Hebrew calendar, from about mid-January to mid-February.   ^e1.6 *Mount Sinai*: See the note at 1.1-5.

1.1-5 *Moses . . . Israel:* Moses led the Hebrew people (later, the Israelites) out of slavery in Egypt, received the Law of the LORD at Mount Sinai, and led the people in battle during their time of wandering in the desert wilderness. As DEUTERONOMY begins, Moses is nearing the end of his life, and he knows he will not be able to enter the promised land of Canaan (1.37). When Moses delivers the speeches in DEUTERONOMY, the Israelites are preparing to cross into the promised land. **(See the article The Ancient World: Peoples, Powers, and Politics on pg 1780.)**

Moses

Israel

Egypt

1.1-5 *40 years:* The number "40" is an important number in the Bible. It stands for a long period of time or for a generation. **(See the chart Numbers in the Bible on pg 1844.)**

1.1-5 *LORD . . . his laws:* "LORD" is the translation of the Hebrew *Yahweh*, God's personal name in the Jewish Scriptures. The "laws" here refer to the Law of Moses, which includes the Ten Commandments and other laws that God gave Moses on Mount Sinai (see Exod 20–24).

Agreements (Covenants)

Law

LORD (YHWH)

1.8 *Canaanites . . . your ancestors Abraham, Isaac, and Jacob:* The Canaanites lived in the land God promised to give Abraham and his descendants (Gen 17.7,8). God promised Abraham that his descendants would form a great nation (see Gen 12.1-3; 15.4-6). This promise was repeated to Isaac, Abraham's son (Gen 26.2-4), and again to Jacob, Abraham's grandson (Gen 28.13; 35.9-12).

1.15-17 *official leaders . . . judges . . . foreigner . . . me:* "Official leaders" (1.15) have a variety of civil and military duties. "Judges" (1.16) have the duty of deciding legal cases. Even foreigners, those who were not part of the Israelite people, are to be treated fairly. Only the most difficult cases are to be brought to Moses (1.17).

1.23 *twelve men . . . each tribe:* The twelve men are named in Numbers 13.4-15. Israel was made up of twelve tribes descended from the twelve sons of Jacob. The promised land was eventually divided up among these twelve tribes. The Joseph tribe was divided into two tribes representing his sons, Ephraim and Manasseh. That would make thirteen, but the Bible always counts only twelve. The Levi tribe is often not counted, because it was not given land in Canaan (Num 35.1-8; Deut 10.9; Josh 21.1-42).

that belongs to the Amorites and their neighbors the Canaanites. This land includes the Jordan River valley, the hill country, the western foothills, the Southern Desert, the Mediterranean seacoast, the Lebanon Mountains, and all the territory as far as the Euphrates River. [8]I give you this land, just as I promised your ancestors Abraham, Isaac, and Jacob. Now you must go and take the land.

Leaders Were Appointed

(Exodus 18.13-27)

Moses said:

[9]Right after the LORD commanded us to leave Mount Sinai,[f] I told you:

Israel, being your leader is too big a job for one person. [10]The LORD our God has blessed us, and so now there are as many of us as there are stars in the sky. [11]God has even promised to bless us a thousand times more, and I pray that he will. [12]But I cannot take care of all your problems and settle all your arguments alone. [13]Each tribe must choose some experienced men who are known for their wisdom and understanding, and I will make those men the official leaders of their tribes. [14]You answered, "That's a good idea!" [15]Then I took these men, who were already wise and respected leaders, and I appointed them as your official leaders. Some of them became military officers in charge of groups of 1000, or 100, or 50, or 10, [16]and others became judges. I gave these judges the following instructions:

When you settle legal cases, your decisions must be fair. It doesn't matter if the case is between two Israelites, or

between an Israelite and a foreigner living in your community. [17]And it doesn't matter if one is helpless and the other is powerful. Don't be afraid of anyone! No matter who shows up in your court, God will help you make a fair decision.

If any case is too hard for you, bring the people to me, and I will make the decision.

[18]After I gave these instructions to the judges, I taught you the LORD's commands.

Men Were Sent To Explore the Hill Country

(Numbers 13.1-33)

Moses said to Israel:

[19]The LORD had commanded us to leave Mount Sinai[f] and go to the hill country that belonged to the Amorites, so we started out into the huge desert. You remember how frightening it was, but soon we were at Kadesh-Barnea, [20-21]and I told you, "We have reached the hill country. It belongs to the Amorites now, but the LORD our God is giving it to us. He is the same God our ancestors worshiped, and he has told us to go in and take this land, so don't hesitate and be afraid."

[22]Then all of you came to me and said, "Before we go into the land, let's send some men to explore it. When they come back, they can tell us about the towns we will find and what roads we should take to get there."

[23]It seemed like a good idea, so I chose twelve men, one from each tribe. [24]They explored the hill country as far as Bunch Valley[g] [25]and even brought back some of the fruit. They said, "The LORD our God is giving us good land."

[f]1.6,9,19 *Mount Sinai:* See the note at 1.1-5. [g]1.24 *Bunch Valley:* Or "Eshcol Valley," famous for its large bunches of grapes.

Israel Refused To Obey the LORD
(Numbers 14.1-45)

Moses said to Israel:

26 You did not want to go into the land, and you refused to obey the LORD your God. **27** You stayed in your tents and grumbled, "The LORD must hate us—he brought us out of Egypt, just so he could hand us over to the Amorites and get rid of us. **28** We are afraid, because the men who explored the land told us that the cities are large, with walls that reach to the sky. The people who live there are taller and stronger than we are,[h] and some of them are Anakim.[i] We have nowhere to go."

29 Then I said, "Don't worry! **30** The LORD our God will lead the way. He will fight on our side, just as he did when we saw him do all those things to the Egyptians. **31** And you know that the LORD has taken care of us the whole time we've been in the desert, just as you might carry one of your children."

32 But you still would not trust the LORD, **33** even though he had always been with us in the desert. During the daytime, the LORD was in the cloud, leading us in the right direction and showing us where to camp. And at night, he was there in the fire.[j]

34 You had made the LORD angry, and he said:

35 You people of this generation are evil, and I refuse to let you go into the good land that I promised your ancestors. **36** Caleb son of Jephunneh is the only one of your generation that I will allow to go in. He obeyed me completely, so I will give him and his descendants the land he explored.

37 The LORD was even angry with me because of you people, and he said, "Moses, I won't let you go into the land either. **38** Instead, I will let Joshua[k] your assistant lead Israel to conquer the land. So encourage him."

39 Then the LORD spoke to you again:

People of Israel, you said that your innocent young children would be taken prisoner in the battle for the land. But someday I will let them go into the land, and with my help they will conquer it and live there.

40 Now, turn around and go back into the desert by way of Red Sea[l] Road.

41 Then you told me, "We disobeyed the LORD our God, but now we want to obey him. We will go into the hill country and fight, just as he told us to do." So you picked up your weapons, thinking it would be easy to take over the hill country.

42 But the LORD said, "Moses, warn them not to go into the hill country. I won't help them fight, and their enemies will defeat them."

43 I told you what the LORD had said, but you paid no attention. You disobeyed him and went into the hill country anyway. You thought you were so great! **44** But when the Amorites in the hill country attacked from their towns, you ran from them as you would run from a swarm of bees, The

---

[h] **1.28** *The people . . . we are:* Most Hebrew manuscripts; a few Hebrew manuscripts and one ancient translation "the people who live there are stronger than we are, and there are more of them than there are of us." [i] **1.28** *Anakim:* Perhaps a group of very tall people that lived in or near Palestine before the Israelites. See also 2.10,11,20,21; Numbers 13.33. [j] **1.33** *the cloud . . . the fire:* See Exodus 40.34-38; Numbers 9.15-23. [k] **1.38** *Joshua:* Hebrew "Joshua son of Nun." [l] **1.40** *Red Sea:* Hebrew *yam suph,* here referring to the Gulf of Aqaba, since the term is extended to include the northeastern arm of the Red Sea (see also the note at 11.4).

● **1.26-28** *You did not . . . nowhere to go:* The Israelites refused to take possession of the land the LORD gave them (1.20,21). Their fear was stronger than their memory of God's power and ability to save them. See also 9.23; Heb 3.16.

● **1.30-32** *do all those things to the Egyptians . . . not trust the LORD:* God brought disasters and death upon the Egyptians to force them to release the Israelites from slavery (Exod 7.14—15.21). As the people made their way through the desert, God continued to care for them (Exod 15.22—18.27), but they failed to trust God.

■ **1.33** *the cloud . . . the fire:* Clouds, fire, and smoke often signal the presence of God in the Bible (Gen 5.17,18; Exod 3.1-6; 19.16-19; 24.15-18; Judg 13.20).

⊗ Fire

● **1.35** *this generation:* Meaning the first generation of Israelites who left Egypt but rebelled against the LORD in the wilderness (Num 14.26-30).

● **1.36-38** *Caleb . . . Moses . . . Joshua:* Caleb and Joshua were the only spies who encouraged the people to trust God and enter Canaan (Num 13.25-33; 14.1-10). For his trust in God, Caleb and his descendants are later given some of the best land in Canaan (Josh 14.6-14). Joshua was chosen to lead the people of Israel (31.3). Here, Moses cannot enter the promised land because, as the representative of the people, he shares their guilt (1.37; 4.21).

1.44-46 *Red Sea Road:* The Red Sea Road went through the Arabah desert region south of the Dead Sea to the Gulf of Aqabah. **(See Map 2 on pg 1880.)**

2.3-19 *Turn and go north . . . into Ammon:* Moses reminds the people that the LORD had warned them not to create a conflict with the Edomites (2.4-7), the Moabites (2.9), or the Ammonites (2.18,19).

2.8,9 *Arabah Road . . . Ar:* Here, the Arabah region refers to the area south of the Dead Sea that extends to the Gulf of Aqaba and the Red Sea ports. Archaeologists usually have claimed that Elath was another name for Ezion-Geber, a port city in Edom. **(See Map 2 on pg 1880.)**

2.12 *Horites:* The Hebrew word *hor* means "cave," so the Horites may have been cave-dwelling people in Edom.

2.14 *38 years after:* God made the Israelites wander in the desert for 40 years until the older generation died, as punishment for their rebellion (2.7; Num 14.27-35).

Amorites chased your troops into Seir[m] as far as Hormah, killing them as they went. [45]Then you came back to the place of worship at Kadesh-Barnea and wept, but the LORD would not listen to your prayers.

Israel Spent Years in the Desert

Moses said to Israel:

[46]After we had been in Kadesh for a few months, we obeyed the LORD and headed back into the desert by way of Red Sea[n] Road. [1]We spent many years wandering around outside the hill country of Seir,[o] [2]until the LORD said:

Moses, [3]Israel has wandered in these hills long enough. Turn and go north. [4] And give the people these orders: "Be very careful, because you will soon go through the land that belongs to your relatives, the descendants of Esau.[p] They are afraid of you, [5]but don't start a war with them. I have given them the hill country of Seir, so I won't give any of it to you, not even enough to set a foot on. [6]And as you go through their land, you will have to buy food and water from them."

[7]The LORD has helped us and taken care of us during the past 40 years that we have been in this huge desert. We've had everything we needed, and the LORD has blessed us and made us successful in whatever we have done.

[8]We went past the territory that belonged to our relatives, the descendants of Esau.[q] We followed Arabah Road that starts in the south at Elath and Ezion-Geber, then we turned onto the desert road that leads to Moab.

[9] The LORD told me, "Don't try to start a war with Moab. Leave them alone, because I gave the land of Ar[r] to them,[s] and I will not let you have any of it."

Tribes That Lived near Canaan

[10]Before the LORD gave the Moabites their land, a large and powerful tribe lived there. They were the Emim, and they were as tall as the Anakim. [11]The Moabites called them Emim, though others sometimes used the name Rephaim[t] for both the Anakim and the Emim.

[12]The Horites used to live in Seir, but the Edomites[u] took over that region. They killed many of the Horites and forced the rest of them to leave, just as Israel did to the people in the land that the LORD gave them.

Israel Crossed the Zered Gorge

Moses said to Israel:

[13]When we came to the Zered Gorge along the southern border of Moab, the LORD told us to cross the gorge into Moab, and we did. [14] This was 38 years after we left

[m]**1.44** *Seir:* An area of hills and mountains that was part of the territory of Edom.   [n]**1.46** *Red Sea:* See the notes at 1.40; 11.4.   [o]**2.1** *hill country of Seir:* See the note at 1.44.   [p]**2.4** *your relatives, the descendants of Esau:* Esau was the brother of Jacob, the ancestor of the nation of Israel. Esau's descendants were also known as the nation of Edom.   [q]**2.8** *We went past . . . Esau:* According to Numbers 20.14-21, the king of Edom did not let the Israelites go through his land.   [r]**2.9** *Ar:* One of the main cities of Moab (see Numbers 21.28); sometimes it may have stood for the whole territory of Moab. [s]**2.9** *them:* The Hebrew text has "the descendants of Lot"; the nation of Moab descended from Moab, who was the son of Lot, the nephew of Abraham.   [t]**2.10,11** *Emim . . . Anakim . . . Rephaim:* These may refer to a group or groups of very tall people that lived in or near Palestine before the Israelites (see also Numbers 13.33).   [u]**2.12** *Edomites:* The Hebrew text has "the descendants of Esau," who became the nation of Edom.

Kadesh-Barnea, and by that time all the men who had been in the army at Kadesh-Barnea had died, just as the LORD had said they would. **15-16**The LORD kept getting rid of[v] them until finally none of them were left.

17Then the LORD told me, **18**"Moses, now go past the town of Ar and cross Moab's northern border. **19**into Ammon. But don't start a war with the Ammonites. I gave them[w] their land, and I won't give any of it to Israel."

More Nations That Lived near Canaan

20Before the Ammonites conquered the land that the LORD had given them, some of the Rephaim used to live there, although the Ammonites called them Zamzummim. **21**The Zamzummim were a large and powerful tribe and were as tall as the Anakim.[x] But the LORD helped the Ammonites, and they killed many of the Zamzummim and forced the rest to leave. Then the Ammonites settled there. **22**The LORD helped them as he had helped the Edomites,[y] who killed many of the Horites in Seir and forced the rest to leave before settling there themselves.

23A group called the Avvim used to live in villages as far south as Gaza, but the Philistines[z] killed them and settled on their land.

Israel Crossed the Arnon Gorge

Moses said:

24After we went through Ammon, the LORD told us:

Israel, pack up your possessions, take down your tents, and cross the Arnon River gorge.[a] The territory of the Amorite King Sihon of Heshbon lies on the other side of the river, but I now give you his land. So attack and take it! **25**Today I will start making all other nations afraid of you. They will tremble with fear when anyone mentions you, and they will be terrified when you show up.

The Defeat of King Sihon of Heshbon

(Numbers 21.21-30)

Moses said to Israel:

26After we had crossed the Arnon and had set up camp in the Kedemoth Desert, I sent messengers to King Sihon of Heshbon, telling him that his nation and ours could be at peace. I said:

27Please let Israel go across your country. We will walk straight through, without turning off the road. **28-29**You can even sell us food and water, and we will pay with silver. We need to reach the Jordan River and cross it, because the LORD our God is giving us the land on the west side. The Edomites and Moabites[b] have already let us cross their land. Please let us cross your land as well.

● **2.23** *Avvim . . . Gaza . . . Philistines:* Little is known about the Avvite peoples who lived in Gaza. Gaza was one of the greatest trade centers of biblical Palestine. For a time the area around it was named Philistia for the Philistine peoples who killed the Avvim and settled there. **(See Map 1 on pg 1879.)**

■ **2.24** *I now give you . . . take it!* The idea that the LORD would fight for the Israelite people and help them conquer other peoples and lands is sometimes referred to as "holy war." In a holy war, God commands the battle and fights against the enemy, who must be completely destroyed along with all that they own.

✎ Holy War (The LORD's Battles)

● **2.26-29** *Kedemoth Desert . . . Jordan River:* The Kedemoth Desert was east of the Dead Sea and Jordan River, and south of Heshbon. **(See Map 4 on pg 1882.)**

---

[v]**2.15,16** *getting rid of:* Or "sending diseases on."   [w]**2.19** *them:* The Hebrew text has "descendants of Lot"; the nation of Ammon descended from Benammi, who was the son of Lot, the nephew of Abraham.   [x]**2.21** *Anakim:* See the note at 2.10,11.   [y]**2.22** *Edomites:* See the note at 2.12.
[z]**2.23** *Philistines:* The Hebrew text has "the Caphtorim from Caphtor," probably referring to the Philistines who originally came from Crete.   [a]**2.24** *Arnon River gorge:* The northern boundary of Moab's territory and the southern boundary of Sihon's kingdom.   [b]**2.28,29** *Edomites and Moabites:* Hebrew "descendants of Esau, who live in Seir and Moabites who live in Ar."

2.32-37 *Jahaz . . . Arnon River gorge . . . Gilead . . . Jabbok River:* These places help to trace the movement of the Israelites into Canaan. The location of Jahaz is unknown. Gilead was a high area of fertile grasslands east of the Jordan River (Gen 31.21,47,48). **(See Map 6 on pg 1884.)**

Holy War (The LORD's Battles)

3.3-10 *Argob . . . Edrei:* The Argob region east of the Jordan River formed part of the kingdom of Og. Sidon was a city and seaport on the Mediterranean coast. The beautiful Mount Hermon in Lebanon is over 9,200 feet high. Salecah marked the eastern boundary of Bashan. **(See Maps 4 and 5 on pgs 1882 and 1883.)**

3.11 *coffin:* Large stone coffins have been found in Bashan. Rabbah bordered the Ammonite territory. The size of the coffin supports the idea that the Rephaim were large people.

3.12-17 *Arnon River gorge . . . Mount Pisgah:* The places mentioned describe the area given to the Reuben and Gad tribes. Lake Galilee is a freshwater lake in the hills of northern Palestine. Mount Pisgah is probably one of the mountains north of Mount Nebo. **(See Map 2 on pg 1880.)**

30-31 But Sihon refused to let us go across his country, because the LORD made him stubborn and eager to fight us. The LORD told me, "I am going to help you defeat Sihon and take his land, so attack him!"

32We met Sihon and his army in battle at Jahaz, **33**and the LORD our God helped us defeat them. We killed Sihon, his sons, and everyone else in his army. **34**Then we captured and destroyed every town in Sihon's kingdom, killing everyone, **35**but keeping the livestock and everything else of value. **36**The LORD helped us capture every town from the Arnon River gorge north to the boundary of Gilead, including the town of Aroer on the edge of the gorge and the town in the middle of the gorge. **37**However, we stayed away from all the Ammonite towns, both in the hill country and near the Jabbok River, just as the LORD had commanded.

The Defeat of King Og of Bashan
(Numbers 21.31-35)

Moses said to Israel:

3 When we turned onto the road that leads to Bashan, King Og of Bashan led out his whole army to fight us at Edrei. **2**But the LORD told me, "Moses, don't be afraid of King Og. I am going to help you defeat him and his army and take over his land. Destroy him and his people, just as you did with the Amorite King Sihon of Heshbon."

3-6 The LORD our God helped us destroy Og and his army and conquer his entire kingdom of Bashan, including the Argob region. His kingdom had lots of villages and 60 towns with high walls and gates that locked with bars. We completely destroyed[c] them all, killing everyone, **7**but keeping the livestock and everything else of value.

8Sihon and Og had ruled Amorite kingdoms east of the Jordan River. Their land stretched from the Arnon River gorge in the south to Mount Hermon in the north, and we captured it all. **9**Mount Hermon is called Mount Sirion by the people of Sidon, and it is called Mount Senir by the Amorites. **10**We captured all the towns in the highlands, all of Gilead, and all of Bashan as far as Salecah and Edrei, two of the towns that Og had ruled.

Og's Coffin

11King Og was the last of the Rephaim,[d] and his coffin[e] is in the town of Rabbah in Ammon. It is made of hard black rock[f] and is thirteen and a half feet long and six feet wide.

The Land East of the Jordan River Is Divided
(Numbers 32.1-42)

Moses said to Israel:

12-17I gave some of the land and towns we captured to the tribes of Reuben and Gad. Their share started at the Arnon River gorge in the south, took in the town of Aroer on the edge of the gorge, and went far enough north to include the southern half of the Gilead region. The northern part of their land went as far east as the upper Jabbok River gorge, which formed

[c]**3.3-6** *completely destroyed:* The Hebrew word means that the town was given completely to the LORD, and since it could not be used for normal purposes any more, it had to be destroyed. Every person was killed and sometimes all the animals as well.   [d]**3.11** *Rephaim:* See the note at 2.10,11.   [e]**3.11** *coffin:* Or "bed."   [f]**3.11** *hard black rock:* The Hebrew text has "iron," which probably refers to basalt, a hard black rock.

their border with the Ammonites.[g] I also gave them the eastern side of the Jordan River valley, from Lake Galilee[h] south to the Dead Sea[i] below the slopes of Mount Pisgah.

I gave the northern half of Gilead and all of the Bashan region to half the tribe of Manasseh.[j] Bashan had belonged to King Og, and the Argob region in Bashan used to be called the Land of the Rephaim. Jair from the Manasseh tribe conquered the Argob region as far west as the kingdoms of Geshur and Maacah. The Israelites even started calling Bashan by the name "Villages of Jair,"[k] and that is still its name. I gave the northern half of Gilead to the Machir clan.[l]

18-19 At that time I told the men of Reuben, Gad, and East Manasseh:

The LORD our God told me to give you this land with its towns, and that's what I have done. Now your wives and children can stay here with your large flocks of sheep and goats and your large herds of cattle. But all of you men that can serve in our army must cross the Jordan River and help the other tribes, because they are your relatives. 20 The LORD will let them defeat the enemy nations on the west side of the Jordan and take their land. Afterwards, you can come back here to the land I gave you.

21-22 Then I told Joshua, "You saw how the LORD our God helped us destroy King Sihon and King Og. So don't be afraid! Wherever you go, the LORD will fight on your side and help you destroy your enemies."

God Refused To Let Moses Enter Canaan

Moses said to Israel:

23 At that time I prayed and begged, 24 "Our LORD, it seems that you have just begun to show me your great power. No other god in the sky or on earth is able to do the mighty things that you do. 25 The land west of the Jordan is such good land. Please let me cross the Jordan and see the hills and the Lebanon Mountains."

26 But the LORD was angry with me because of you people,[m] and he refused to listen. "That's enough!" he said. "I don't want to hear any more. 27 Climb to the top of Mount Pisgah and look north, south, east, and west. Take a good look, but you are not going to cross the Jordan River. 28 Joshua will lead Israel across the Jordan to take the land, so help him be strong and brave and tell him what he must do."

29 After this we stayed in the valley at Beth-Peor.

Israel Must Obey God

Moses said:

4 Israel, listen to these laws and teachings! If you obey them, you will live, and you will go in and take the land that the LORD is giving you. He is the God your ancestors worshiped, 2 and now he is your God. I am telling you everything he has

---

■ 3.18-20 *At that time . . . I gave you:* Before the Reuben, Gad, and East Manasseh tribes settled down in eastern Canaan, they were to help the armies of the other nine and one half tribes to conquer western Canaan. See also Josh 1.12-15.

● 3.23 *I prayed and begged:* Moses was not allowed to enter the promised land of Canaan (Num 20.1-13; see also Deut 32.49-52).

● 3.25-29 *land west of the Jordan:* Canaan, the promised land, lay west of the Jordan River. Moses was allowed to see Canaan from the top of Mount Pisgah, one peak in the mountainous region known as Abarim (32.48-52; Num 27.12-14; 33.47). **(See Map 2 on pg 1880.)**

● 3.28 *Joshua:* Joshua was Moses' loyal assistant and was on the mountain when Moses received the Law (Exod 32.17). He was also a military general (Exod 17.8-13) and one of the spies Moses sent into Canaan (Num 13). Joshua and Caleb were the only Israelites of their generation allowed to live long enough to enter Canaan. See also 34.9.

■ 4.1-4 *Israel, listen . . . still alive today:* Moses recalls how God destroyed the Israelites who worshiped the god Baal Peor (Num 25) as a way of reminding the people of this truth: If you obey and honor God, you will live; if you turn away from God, you will die.

4.9-14 *You must be . . . the Jordan River:* Remembering God's saving acts is a frequent theme in DEUTERONOMY (5.15; 7.18; 8.2; 9.27; 11.2-4; 16.1-4; 24.18,22; 32.7). In the incident recalled here (Exod 19), God spoke the words of the Ten Commandments.

4.16-18 *idols . . . shaped like men . . . fish:* Israel's LORD God was a living God, and no image or idol could be made that could represent God. See also Exod 20.4,5; 34.17; Lev 26.1; Deut 5.8,9; 27.10; Isa 44.6-20.

4.19 *sun or moon or stars, don't . . . worship them:* Some ancient religions were based on worshiping stars and constellations, as well as the sun and moon. But Israel was chosen for a special relationship with the one true God, who led them out of slavery in Egypt (Exod 12–14). No other god was to be the object of Israel's worship. See also Exod 20.4; Lev 26.1; Deut 5.8.

4.25-31 *Soon you will . . . with your ancestors:* Moses warns the people not to forget the law and not to worship idols. If they do, the nation will be destroyed, and the few remaining people will be forced to leave the promised land. But if the people turn back to God and worship only God, God will keep the promises made with the people and show them mercy. **(See the article From Joshua to the Exile: The People of Israel in the Promised Land on pg 1783.)**

commanded, so don't add anything or take anything away.

[3]You saw how he killed everyone who worshiped the god Baal Peor.[n] [4]But all of you that were faithful to the LORD your God are still alive today.

[5-8]No other nation has laws that are as fair as the ones the Lord my God told me to give you. If you faithfully obey them when you enter the land, you will show other nations how wise you are. In fact, everyone that hears about your laws will say, "That great nation certainly is wise!" And what makes us greater than other nations? We have a God who is close to us and answers our prayers.

[9]You must be very careful not to forget the things you have seen God do for you. Keep reminding yourselves, and tell your children and grandchildren as well. [10]Do you remember the day you stood in the LORD's presence at Mount Sinai?[o] The LORD said, "Moses, bring the people of Israel here. I want to speak to them so they will obey me as long as they live, and so they will teach their children to obey me too."

[11]Mount Sinai[o] was surrounded by deep dark clouds, and fire went up to the sky. You came to the foot of the mountain, [12]and the LORD spoke to you from the fire. You could hear him and understand what he was saying, but you couldn't see him. [13]The LORD said he was making an agreement with you, and he told you that your part of the agreement is to obey the Ten Commandments. Then the LORD wrote these Commandments on two flat stones.

[14]That's when the LORD commanded me to give you the laws and teachings you must obey in the land that you will conquer west of the Jordan River.

Don't Worship Idols

Moses said to Israel:

[15]When God spoke to you from the fire, he was invisible. So be careful [16]not to commit the sin of worshiping idols. Don't make idols to be worshiped, whether they are shaped like men, women, [17]animals, birds, [18]reptiles, or fish. [19]And when you see the sun or moon or stars, don't be tempted to bow down and worship them. The LORD put them there for all the other nations to worship. [20]But you are the LORD's people, because he rescued you from Egypt, that fiery furnace.

[21]The LORD was angry with me because of what you said,[P] and he told me that he would not let me cross the Jordan River into the good land that he is giving you.[q] [22]So I must stay here and die on this side of the Jordan, but you will cross the river and take the land.

[23]Always remember the agreement that the LORD your God made with you, and don't make an idol in any shape or form. [24]The LORD will be angry if you worship other gods, and he can be like a fire destroying everything in its path.

[25-26]Soon you will cross the Jordan River and settle down in the land. Then in the years to come, you will have children, and they will give you grandchildren. After many years, you might lose your sense of right and wrong and make idols, even though the LORD your God hates them. So I am giving you fair warning today, and I call the earth and the sky as witnesses. If you ever make idols, the LORD will be angry, and you won't have long to live, because the LORD will let you be wiped out. [27]Only a few of you will survive, and the LORD will force you to leave the land and

[n]**4.3** *Baal Peor:* See Numbers 25.1-9. [o]**4.10,11** *Mount Sinai:* See the note at 1.1-5. [P]**4.21** *what you said:* Or "you people." [q]**4.21** *The LORD was angry . . . giving you:* See 1.37; 3.26.

will scatter you among the nations. **28**There you will have to worship gods made of wood and stone, and these are nothing but idols that can't see or hear or eat or smell.

29-30 In all of your troubles, you may finally decide that you want to worship only the LORD. And if you turn back to him and obey him completely, he will again be your God. **31**The LORD your God will have mercy—he won't destroy you or desert you. The LORD will remember his promise, and he will keep the agreement he made with your ancestors.

32-34 When the LORD your God brought you out of Egypt, you saw how he fought for you and showed his great power by performing terrifying miracles. You became his people, and at Mount Sinai you heard him talking to you out of fiery flames. And yet you are still alive! Has anything like this ever happened since the time God created humans? No matter where you go or who you ask, you will get the same answer. No one has ever heard of another god even trying to do such things as the LORD your God has done for you.

35-36 The LORD wants you to know he is the only true God, and he wants you to obey him. That's why he let you see his mighty miracles and his fierce fire on earth, and why you heard his voice from that fire and from the sky.

37The LORD loved your ancestors and decided that you would be his people. So the LORD used his great power to bring you out of Egypt. **38**Now you face other nations more powerful than you are, but the LORD has already started forcing them out of their land and giving it to you.

39So remember that the LORD is the only true God, whether in the sky above or on the earth below. **40**Today I am explaining his laws and teachings. And if you always obey them, you and your descendants will live long and be successful in the land the LORD is giving you.

Safe Towns

41-43 Moses said, "People of Israel, you must set aside the following three towns east of the Jordan River as Safe Towns: Bezer in the desert highlands belonging to the Reuben tribe; Ramoth in Gilead, belonging to the Gad tribe; and Golan in Bashan, belonging to the Manasseh tribe. If you kill a neighbor without meaning to, and if you had not been angry with that person, you can run to one of these towns and find safety."[r]

THE SECOND SPEECH: MOSES TELLS WHAT THE LORD DEMANDS

Israel at Beth-Peor

44-46 The Israelites had come from Egypt and were camped east of the Jordan River near Beth-Peor, when Moses gave these laws and teachings. The land around their camp had once belonged to King Sihon of Heshbon. But Moses and the Israelites defeated him **47**and King Og of Bashan, and took their lands. These two Amorite kings had ruled the territory east of the Jordan River **48**from the town of Aroer on the edge of the Arnon River gorge, north to Mount Hermon.[s] **49**Their land included the eastern side of the Jordan River valley,

4.32-34 *terrifying miracles:* This likely refers to the way God acted to save the people in Egypt.

4.41-43 *Safe Towns:* Also traditionally known as "cities of refuge," these cities were set aside to protect those who accidentally killed someone. At this time in Israel's history, "revenge killing" was an accepted form of execution. A victim's clan could appoint a close male relative to track down and kill a person who had killed a member of their clan. If the person who killed someone was found guilty of intentional murder at a trial, he or she could be taken from the Safe Town and put to death. If found innocent, the person could stay in the Safe Town to be protected from the relative's revenge killing (Num 35.25-27). See also Exod 21.12-14; Num 35.6-18; Deut 19.1-13; Josh 20.2-9.

4.44-49 *Egypt . . . Beth-Peor . . . Mount Pisgah:* These verses are a second introduction to DEUTERONOMY. It took 40 years of wandering for the Israelites to reach this camp at Beth-Peor. After defeating kings and peoples on the east side of the Jordan River, they are getting ready to cross over to the lands west of the river.

---

[r]**4.41-43** *find safety:* From the victim's clan, who might appoint one of their men to track down and put to death the killer (see also 19.1-13). [s]**4.48** *Hermon:* The Hebrew text also includes the name "Sion," probably another form of "Sirion," the name used by the Sidonians.

5.12 *Sabbath:* This day of rest began at sunset on Friday and ended with a blessing (benediction) at sunset on Saturday. The emphasis here is a concern that servants and animals get a day of rest, to remind the people of Israel that they once were slaves in Egypt and that the LORD rescued them from slavery. See also Exod 16.23-30; 23.12; 31.12-15; 34.21; 35.2; and Lev 23.3.

5.16 *Respect:* Children were expected to care for parents and to show them the greatest respect (Lev 19.3,4; 20.9). Note that this command comes with a promise.

5.17 *murder:* Some modern translations substitute "kill." This commandment does not forbid all forms of killing, but rather refers to taking a life without just cause.

5.18 *faithful in marriage:* This commandment forbids sex between a married and an unmarried person or between married persons not married to each other.

5.19 *steal:* Here, stealing also refers to kidnapping and selling someone into slavery (Exod 24.7).

5.20 *tell lies:* This includes spreading rumors and giving false testimony that would help a criminal (Exod 23.1).

5.21 *Do not desire:* This refers both to greedy attitudes (jealousy) and actions. Compare this list to the list in Exodus 20.17. See also Rom 7.7; 13.9.

as far south as the Dead Sea[t] below the slopes of Mount Pisgah.

The Ten Commandments
(Exodus 20.1-17)

5 Moses called together the people of Israel and said:

Today I am telling you the laws and teachings that you must follow, so listen carefully. [2]The LORD our God made an agreement with our nation at Mount Sinai.[u] [3]That agreement wasn't only with[v] our ancestors but with us, who are here today. [4]The LORD himself spoke to you out of the fire, [5]but you were afraid of the fire and refused to go up the mountain. So I spoke with the LORD for you, then I told you that he had said:

[6]I am the LORD your God, the one who brought you out of Egypt where you were slaves.

[7]Do not worship any god except me.

[8]Do not make idols that look like anything in the sky or on earth or in the ocean under the earth. [9]Don't bow down and worship idols. I am the LORD your God, and I demand all your love. If you reject me and worship idols, I will punish your families for three or four generations. [10]But if you love me and obey my laws, I will be kind to your families for thousands of generations.

[11]Do not misuse my name.[w] I am the LORD your God, and I will punish anyone who misuses my name.

[12]Show respect for the Sabbath Day—it belongs to me. [13] You have six days when you can do your work,

[14]but the seventh day of the week belongs to me, your God. No one is to work on that day—not you, your children, your oxen or donkeys or any other animal, not even those foreigners who live in your towns. And don't make your slaves do any work. [15]This special day of rest will remind you that I reached out my mighty arm and rescued you from slavery in Egypt.

[16]Respect your father and mother, and you will live a long and successful life in the land I am giving you.

[17]Do not murder.

[18]Be faithful in marriage.

[19]Do not steal.

[20]Do not tell lies about others.

[21]Do not desire to possess anything that belongs to another person—not a house, a wife, a husband, a slave, an ox, a donkey, or anything else.

[22] When we were gathered at the mountain, the LORD spoke to us in a loud voice from the dark fiery cloud. The LORD gave us these commands, and only these. Then he wrote them on two flat stones and gave them to me.

The People Were Afraid
(Exodus 20.18-21)

Moses said to Israel:

[23]When fire blazed from the mountain, and you heard the voice coming from the darkness, your tribal leaders came to me [24]and said:

Today the LORD our God has shown us how powerful and glorious he is. He spoke to us from the fire, and we learned that people can live, even

---

[t]**4.49** *the Dead Sea:* Hebrew "the Sea of the Arabah."　　[u]**5.2** *Mount Sinai:* See the note at 1.1-5.
[v]**5.3** *wasn't only with:* Hebrew "wasn't with."　　[w]**5.11** *misuse my name:* Probably includes breaking promises, telling lies after swearing to tell the truth, using the LORD's name as a curse word or a magic formula, and trying to control the LORD by using his name.

though God speaks to them. **25**But we don't want to take a chance on being killed by that terrible fire, and if we keep on hearing the LORD's voice, we will die. **26**Has anyone else ever heard the only true God speaking from fire, as we have? And even if they have, would they live to tell about it? **27**Moses, go up close and listen to the LORD. Then come back and tell us, and we will do everything he says. **28**The LORD heard you and said:

Moses, I heard what the people said to you, and I approve. **29**I wish they would always worship me with fear and trembling and be this willing to obey me! Then they and their children would always enjoy a successful life. **30**Now, tell them to return to their tents, **31**but you come back here to me. After I tell you my laws and teachings, you will repeat them to the people, so they can obey these laws in the land I am giving them.

Moses said:

32Israel, you must carefully obey the LORD's commands. **33**Follow them, because they make a path that will lead to a long successful life in the land the LORD your God is giving you.

The Most Important Commandment

Moses said to Israel:

6 The LORD told me to give you these laws and teachings,**x** so you can obey them in the land he is giving you. Soon you will cross the Jordan River and take that land. **2**And if you and your descendants want to live a long time, you must always worship the LORD and obey his laws. **3**Pay attention, Israel! Our ancestors worshiped the LORD, and he promised to give us this land that is rich with milk and honey. Be careful to obey him, and you will become a successful and powerful nation.

4 Listen, Israel! The LORD our God is the only true God!**y** **5**So love the LORD your God with all your heart, soul, and strength. **6**Memorize his laws **7**and tell them to your children over and over again. Talk about them all the time, whether you're at home or walking along the road or going to bed at night, or getting up in the morning. **8**Write down copies and tie them to your wrists and foreheads to help you obey them. **9**Write these laws on the door frames of your homes and on your town gates.

Worship Only the LORD

Moses said to Israel:

10The LORD promised your ancestors Abraham, Isaac, and Jacob that he would give you this land. Now he will take you there and give you large towns, with good buildings that you didn't build, **11**and houses full of good things that you didn't put there. The LORD will give you wells**z** that you didn't have to dig, and vineyards and olive orchards that you didn't have to plant. But when you have eaten so much that you can't eat any more, **12**don't forget it was the LORD who set you free from slavery and brought you out of Egypt. **13**Worship and obey the LORD your God with fear and trembling, and promise that you will be loyal to him.

14Don't have anything to do with gods that are worshiped by the nations around

---

x6.1 *these laws and teachings:* Or "the following commandment with its laws and teachings" (see 6.4,5). **y6.4** *The LORD . . . true God:* Or "Only the LORD is our God." **z6.11** *wells:* Cisterns cut into the rock to collect rainwater.

5.28-31 *Moses . . . I approve . . . my laws:* The LORD approves the people's confidence in Moses and gives to him the laws and teachings that he will pass on to the people. If the people obey, future generations will have success in the new land.

6.4 *Listen, Israel:* Jewish tradition calls these verses the "Shema," because the first Hebrew word of the passage is *shema*, which means "listen" or "hear." This confession of faith in the LORD, the one true God, is to be recited twice a day. The Hebrew word translated as "love" (6.5) can mean a holy respect and awe. To love with one's heart and soul was to love with one's entire being. See also 10.12,13; 11.13-15; 13.3-5; 26.16; 30.2,6,8-10; Mark 12.29,30.

6.6-8 *Memorize . . . tie them to your wrists and foreheads:* The people were to take these words to heart ("memorize") and to show them in public. Some Jewish people put Scripture passages in small leather pouches (phylacteries) and tied them to their wrists and foreheads.

6.10,11 *buildings . . . wells:* Because Canaan was already a settled area, Moses said that the people of Israel will not have to build houses, dig wells, or plant vineyards.

6.16 *Massah:* Where the people tested God's patience with their complaining (Exod 17.1-7; Num 20.2-13).

7.1 *Hittites . . . Jebusites:* The Hittites were a strong force in Canaan from the time of Abraham to around 1300 B.C. (see also Gen 10.6-20). The Girgashites came from Canaan, son of Ham and grandson of Noah (Gen 10.16). The Perizzites may have lived in the open country as opposed to the Canaanites who lived in walled cities. The Hivites may also be the people known as the Horites, and may have settled in the area around Mount Seir. The Jebusites lived in and around Jerusalem until King David took over that city (2 Sam 5.6-9).

7.2 *the LORD will force them out . . . you must destroy:* The Hebrew word ("herem") translated here as "destroy" is a term used in holy war settings. Another practical aspect of total destruction was the removal of temptations that would cause Israel to turn their backs on the LORD.

7.5 *altars . . . sacred stones . . . poles:* The people of Israel were to tear down these sacred objects and destroy these altar stones. Carved wooden poles were set up in honor of Asherah, the Canaanite goddess of fertility.

7.8 *mighty arm . . . rescued you from . . . Egypt:* The LORD's "mighty arm" is an image often used to describe the LORD's protection or power, especially in battle (Exod 15.12,16; Deut 5.15; Isa 40.10).

you. [15]If you worship other gods, the LORD will be furious and wipe you off the face of the earth. The LORD your God is with you, [16]so don't try to make him prove that he can help you, as you did at Massah.[a] [17]Always obey the laws that the LORD has given you [18-19]and live in a way that pleases him. Then you will be able to go in and take this good land from your enemies, just as he promised your ancestors.

[20]Someday your children will ask, "Why did the LORD give us these laws and teachings?"

[21]Then you will answer:

We were slaves of the king of Egypt, but the LORD used his great power and set us free. [22]We saw him perform miracles and make horrible things happen to the king, his officials, and everyone else. [23]The LORD rescued us from Egypt, so he could bring us into this land, as he had promised our ancestors. [24-25]That's why the LORD our God demands that we obey his laws and worship him with fear and trembling. And if we do, he will protect us and help us be successful.

Force the Other Nations Out of the Land
(Exodus 34.11-16)

Moses said:

7 People of Israel, the LORD your God will help you take the land of the Hittites, the Girgashites, the Amorites, the Canaanites, the Perizzites, the Hivites, and the Jebusites. These seven nations have more people and are stronger than Israel, but when you attack them, [2]the LORD will force them out of the land. Then you must destroy them without mercy. Don't make

[a]6.16 *Massah:* See Exodus 17.1-7; Numbers 20.2-13.

any peace treaties with them, [3]and don't let your sons and daughters marry any of them. [4]If you do, those people will lead your descendants to worship other gods and to turn their backs on the LORD. That will make him very angry, and he will quickly destroy Israel.

[5]So when you conquer these nations, tear down the altars where they worship their gods. Break up their sacred stones, cut down the poles that they use in worshiping the goddess Asherah, and throw their idols in the fire.

The LORD's Chosen People

Moses said:

[6]Israel, you are the chosen people of the LORD your God. There are many nations on this earth, but he chose only Israel to be his very own. [7]You were the weakest of all nations, [8]but the LORD chose you because he loves you and because he had made a promise to your ancestors. Then with his mighty arm, he rescued you from the king of Egypt, who had made you his slaves.

[9]You know that the LORD your God is the only true God. So love him and obey his commands, and he will faithfully keep his agreement with you and your descendants for a thousand generations. [10]But if you turn against the LORD, he will quickly destroy you. [11]So be sure to obey his laws and teachings I am giving you today.

The LORD Will Bless You if You Obey
(Deuteronomy 28.1-14; Leviticus 26.3-13)

Moses said to Israel:

[12]If you completely obey these laws, the LORD your God will be loyal and keep the

agreement he made with you, just as he promised our ancestors. [13]The LORD will love you and bless you by giving you many children and plenty of food, wine, and olive oil. Your herds of cattle will have many calves, and your flocks of sheep will have many lambs. [14]God will bless you more than any other nation—your families will grow and your livestock increase. [15]You will no longer suffer with the same horrible diseases that you sometimes had in Egypt. You will be healthy, but the LORD will make your enemies suffer from those diseases.

Destroy the Nations and Their Gods

Moses said to Israel:

[16]When the LORD helps you defeat your enemies, you must destroy them without pity! And don't get trapped into worshiping their gods. [17]You may be thinking, "How can we destroy these nations? They are more powerful than we are." [18]But stop worrying! Just remember what the LORD your God did to Egypt and its king. [19]You saw how the LORD used his tremendous power to work great miracles and bring you out of Egypt. And he will again work miracles for you when you face these enemies you fear so much. [20]Some of them may try to survive by hiding from you, but the LORD will make them panic, and soon they will be dead.[b] [21]So don't be frightened when you meet them in battle. The LORD your God is great and fearsome, and he will fight at your side.

[22]As you attack these nations, the LORD will force them out little by little. He won't let you get rid of them all at once—if he

did, there wouldn't be enough people living in the land to keep down the number of wild animals. [23-24]But when you attack your enemies, the LORD will make them panic, and you will easily destroy them. You will defeat their kings one after another until they are gone, and no one will remember they ever lived.

[25]After you conquer a nation, burn their idols. Don't get trapped into wanting the silver or gold on an idol. Even the metal on an idol is disgusting to the LORD, [26]so destroy it. If you bring it home with you, both you and your house will be destroyed. Stay away from those disgusting idols!

The LORD Takes Care of You

Moses said:

8 Israel, do you want to go into the land the LORD promised your ancestors? Do you want to capture it, live there, and become a powerful nation? Then be sure to obey every command I am giving you.

[2]Don't forget how the LORD your God has led you through the desert for the past 40 years. He wanted to find out if you were truly willing to obey him and depend on him, [3]so he made you go hungry. Then he gave you manna,[c] a kind of food that you and your ancestors had never even heard about. The LORD was teaching you that people need more than food to live—they need every word that the LORD has spoken.

[4]Over the past 40 years, your clothing hasn't worn out, and your feet haven't swollen. [5]So keep in mind that the LORD has been correcting you, just as parents correct their children. [6]Obey the commands the LORD your God has given you and worship him with fear and trembling.

[7]The LORD your God is bringing you into

[b]**7.20** *make them . . . dead:* Or "send hornets to kill them."   [c]**8.3** *manna:* See Exodus 16.1-36.

7.15 *diseases:* This probably refers to the kind of diseases that the Egyptians suffered (Exod 9.8-11; 15.26).

7.26 *disgusting idols:* The Hebrew word, *toebhah,* translated here as "disgusting," is the strongest word used in the Old Testament for something that is totally displeasing to God. It shows how terrible the worship of idols or other gods was considered to be. To worship another god was to reject the LORD.

8.3 *manna:* God provided this unusual food in the wilderness (Exod 16.13-31). In Hebrew, "manna" means "What is it?" At night, insects feeding on tamarisk trees in the southern desert secrete a sticky white substance that Arabs call *man.* It has a sweet taste like the manna that tasted like honey wafers (Exod 16.1-36). Though God gave food to keep their bodies alive, Moses makes the point that the LORD's word (commands, 8.6) is the true source of life.

8.8-9 *copper:* Copper and iron ore are found in the mountains of Lebanon and in regions east of the Sea of Galilee. Ancient copper mines dating back to Israel's King Solomon have also been discovered south of the Dead Sea.

8.10-20 *give praise to the Lord . . . always obey . . . destroy you:* Moses reminds the people to guard against pride when they begin to enjoy the rich blessings waiting for them in Canaan. They should not forget how the Lord has saved them in the past—by freeing them from slavery in Egypt (8.14) and by providing them with water (Num 20.2-13) and manna in the wilderness. They are to remember that what they earned was not their own doing, but was a gift from God (8.17,18). If they forget the Lord or fail to thank the Lord for these blessings, they may be punished.

9.1-6 *Israel, listen . . . Abraham, Isaac, and Jacob:* This passage presents the reasons for the holy war soon to take place when Israel enters Canaan. The Israelites are not stronger, and they are not such "good" people. But the Lord will help the Israelites gain victory because the other nations are evil and because God made a promise to give the land to the descendants of Abraham, Isaac, and Jacob.

a good land with streams that flow from springs in the valleys and hills. **8-9**You can dig for copper in those hills, and the stones are made of iron ore. And you won't go hungry. Wheat and barley fields are everywhere, and so are vineyards and orchards full of fig, pomegranate,^d and olive trees, and there is plenty of honey.

Don't Forget the Lord

Moses said to Israel:

10After you eat and are full, give praise to the Lord your God for the good land he gave you. **11**Make sure that you never forget the Lord or disobey his laws and teachings that I am giving you today. If you always obey them, **12**you will have plenty to eat, and you will build good houses to live in. **13**You will get more and more cattle, sheep, silver, gold, and other possessions.

14But when all this happens, don't be proud! Don't forget that you were once slaves in Egypt and that it was the Lord who set you free. **15**Remember how he led you in that huge and frightening desert where poisonous snakes and scorpions live. There was no water, but the Lord split open a rock, and water poured out so you could drink. **16**He also gave you manna,^e a kind of food your ancestors had never even heard about. The Lord was testing you to make you trust him, so that later on he could be good to you.

17When you become successful, don't say, "I'm rich, and I've earned it all myself." **18**Instead, remember that the Lord your God gives you the strength to make a living. That's how he keeps the promise he made to your ancestors.

19-20 But I'm warning you—if you forget the Lord your God and worship other gods, the Lord will destroy you, just as he destroyed the nations you fought.

Why the Lord Will Help Israel

Moses said:

9 Israel, listen to me! You will soon cross the Jordan River and go into the land to force out the nations that live there. They are more powerful than you are, and the walls around their cities reach to the sky. **2**Some of these nations are descendants of the Anakim.^f You know how tall and strong they are, and you've heard that no one can defeat them in battle. **3**But the Lord your God has promised to go ahead of you, like a raging fire burning everything in its path. So when you attack your enemies, it will be easy for you to destroy them and take their land.

4-6 After the Lord helps you wipe out these nations and conquer their land, don't think he did it because you are such good people. You aren't good—you are stubborn! No, the Lord is going to help you, because the nations that live there are evil, and because he wants to keep the promise he made to your ancestors Abraham, Isaac, and Jacob.

When Israel Made an Idol
(Exodus 32)

Moses said to Israel:

7Don't ever forget how you kept rebelling and making the Lord angry the whole time you were in the desert. You rebelled from the day you left Egypt until the day you arrived here.

8At Mount Sinai^g you made the Lord so angry that he was going to destroy you.

^d**8.8,9** *pomegranate:* A bright red fruit that looks like an apple.   ^e**8.16** *manna:* See the note at 8.3.
^f**9.2** *Anakim:* See the note at 2.10,11.   ^g**9.8** *Mount Sinai:* See the note at 1.1-5.

When you become successful, don't say, "I'm rich, and I've earned it all myself." Instead, remember that the Lord your God gives you the strength to make a living. Deut 8.17,18

9-11 It happened during those 40 days and nights that I was on the mountain, without anything to eat or drink. He had told me to come up there so he could give me the agreement he made with us. And this agreement was actually the same Ten Commandments[h] he had announced to you when he spoke from the fire on the mountain. The LORD had written them on two flat stones with his own hand. But after giving me the two stones, **12**he said:

Moses, hurry down the mountain to those people you led out of Egypt. They have already disobeyed me and committed the terrible sin of making an idol.

13I've been watching the Israelites, and I've seen how stubborn and rebellious they are. **14**So don't try to stop me! I am going to wipe them out, and no one on earth will remember they ever lived. Then I will let your descendants become an even bigger and more powerful nation than Israel.

Moses said:

15Fire was raging on the mountaintop as I went back down, carrying the two stones with the commandments on them. **16**I saw how quickly you had sinned and disobeyed the LORD your God. There you were, worshiping the metal idol you had made in the shape of a calf. **17**So I threw down the two stones and smashed them before your very eyes.

18-20I bowed down at the place of worship and prayed to the LORD, without eating or drinking for 40 days and nights. You had committed a terrible sin by making that idol, and the LORD hated what you had done. He was angry enough to destroy all of you and Aaron as well. So I prayed for you and Aaron as I had done before, and this time the LORD answered my prayers.[i]

21It was a sin for you to make that idol, so I threw it into the fire to melt it down. Then I took the lump of gold, ground it into powder, and threw the powder into the stream flowing down the mountain.

22You also made the LORD angry when you were staying at Taberah,[j] at Massah,[k] and at Kibroth-Hattaavah.[l] **23**Then at Kadesh-Barnea the LORD said, "I am giving you the land, so go ahead and take it!" But since you didn't trust the LORD, you rebelled and disobeyed his command.[m] **24**In fact, you've rebelled against the LORD for as long as he has[n] known you.

25After you had made the idol in the shape of a calf, the LORD said he was going to destroy you. So I lay face down in front of the LORD for 40 days and nights **26**and prayed:

Our LORD, please don't wipe out your people. You used your great power to rescue them from Egypt and to make them your very own. **27**Israel's ancestors Abraham, Isaac, and Jacob obeyed you faithfully. Think about them, and not about Israel's stubbornness, evil, and sin. **28**If you destroy your people, the Egyptians will say, "The LORD promised to give Israel land, but he wasn't powerful enough to keep his promise. In fact, he hated them so much that he took them into the

⬤ **9.22,23** *Taberah . . . Kadesh-Barnea:* The exact location of Taberah is unknown. It means "burning," so the name recalls God's burning anger at the people's complaining (Num 11.3). The first place the Israelites stopped after leaving Mount Sinai was Kibroth-Hattaavah, which means "Graves for the Greedy" (Num 11.18-34). Kadesh-Barnea was the oasis where the Israelites stayed after leaving Mount Sinai. The people also failed to trust and obey the LORD God while they were at Kadesh (Num 13.1—14.38; also Heb 3.16). **(See Map 2 on pg 1880.)**

◼ **9.26-29** *and prayed . . . from Egypt:* Moses argues that God should forgive the people and not destroy them, because God chose them (9.26), because their ancestors were faithful to God's promise to Abraham (9.27), and because nations will say that God is not powerful enough to keep his promise to the people.

---

[h]**9.9-11** *Ten Commandments:* Hebrew "commandments." [i]**9.18-20** *as I had done before . . . prayers:* This may refer to Moses' praying for Israel before he came down from the mountain (see Exodus 32.11-14). [j]**9.22** *Taberah:* See Numbers 11.1-3. [k]**9.22** *Massah:* See the note at 6.16. [l]**9.22** *Kibroth-Hattaavah:* See Numbers 11.31-34. [m]**9.23** *Kadesh-Barnea . . . you rebelled and disobeyed his command:* See Numbers 13; 14. [n]**9.24** *he has:* The Samaritan Hebrew Text and one ancient translation; the Standard Hebrew Text "I have."

10.1-3 *flat stones . . . wooden chest . . . acacia wood:* These flat stones may have been like other ancient "steles" (upright stones) that were carved with words and illustrations. Some nations used these to announce their laws. The wooden chest Moses made to hold the law stones is described here as a plain box made of acacia wood.

The Sacred Chest

Ten Commandments

10.6 *Aaron:* Aaron was the brother of Moses and Miriam. He was of the tribe of Levi and served as Israel's first high priest (Exod 28.1-3; Lev 8.1—9.24; Num 18.1-20). Like Moses, Aaron was not allowed to enter the promised land (Num 20.7-13; 33.38). On the border of Edom, Moses took Aaron up Mount Hor and gave Aaron's high priest's clothing to Aaron's son Eleazar. Aaron died there at the age of 123 (Num 20.23-28).

10.8 *tribe of Levi:* Levi was the son of Jacob and Leah (Gen 29.34). His descendants became the proper family line for Israel's priests (Exod 6.16-25; 32.26-29; Num 3.5-8). Eventually only those members of the tribe of Levi who could prove they were descendants of Aaron were considered Israel's true priests (Num 18.20-32; Neh 11.10-18). Levite men who were not descended from Aaron were assigned to take care of the meeting tent and to assist the priests.

Israel's Priests

desert and killed them." [29]But you, our LORD, chose the people of Israel to be your own, and with your mighty power you rescued them from Egypt.

The Second Set of Commandments
(Exodus 34.1-10)

Moses said to the people:

10 The LORD told me to chisel out two flat stones, just like the ones he had given me earlier. He also commanded me to make a wooden chest, then come up the mountain and meet with him. [2]He told me that he would write on the new stones the same words he had written on the ones I broke, and that I could put these stones in this sacred chest.

[3]So I made a chest out of acacia wood, and I chiseled two flat stones like the ones I broke. Then I carried the stones up the mountain, [4]where the LORD wrote the Ten Commandments on them, just as he had done the first time. The commandments were exactly what he had announced from the fire, when you were gathered at the mountain.

After the LORD returned the stones to me, [5]I took them down the mountainside and put them in the chest, just as he had commanded. And they are still there.

Aaron Died
(Numbers 20.22-29)

Moses said to Israel:

[6]Later we set up camp at the wells belonging to the descendants of Jaakan.[o] Then we moved on and camped at Moserah,

where Aaron died and was buried, and his son Eleazar became the priest. [7]Next, we camped at Gudgodah and then at Jotbathah, where there are flowing streams.

The Levites Were Appointed To Carry the Chest

Moses said to Israel:

[8]After I put the two stones in the sacred chest,[P] the LORD chose the tribe of Levi, not only to carry the chest, but also to serve as his priests at the place of worship and to bless the other tribes in his name. And they still do these things. [9]The LORD promised that he would always provide for the tribe of Levi, and that's why he won't give them any land, when he divides it among the other tribes.

The LORD Answered the Prayers of Moses
(Exodus 34.9,10,27-29)

Moses said to Israel:

[10]When I had taken the second set of stones up the mountain, I spent 40 days and nights there, just as I had done before. Once again, the LORD answered my prayer and did not destroy you. [11]Instead, he told me, "Moses, get ready to lead the people into the land that I promised their ancestors."[q]

What the LORD Wants

Moses said:

[12]People of Israel, what does the LORD your God want from you? The LORD wants you to respect and follow him, to love and

[o]10.6 *the wells . . . Jaakan:* Or "Beeroth Bene-Jaakan." [P]10.8 *After . . . chest:* Or "After Israel reached Jotbathah." [q]10.11 *lead . . . ancestors:* The LORD would later tell Moses that he would not be allowed to enter the land (see 1.37; 3.23-28; Numbers 20.10-12).

serve him with all your heart and soul, [13]and to obey his laws and teachings that I am giving you today. Do this, and all will go well for you.

[14]Everything belongs to the Lord your God, not only the earth and everything on it, but also the sky and the highest heavens. [15]Yet the Lord loved your ancestors and wanted them to belong to him. So he chose them and their descendants rather than any other nation, and today you are still his people.

[16]Remember your agreement with the Lord and stop being so stubborn. [17]The Lord your God is more powerful than all other gods and lords, and his tremendous power is to be feared. His decisions are always fair, and you cannot bribe him to change his mind. [18]The Lord defends the rights of orphans and widows. He cares for foreigners and gives them food and clothing. [19]And you should also care for them, because you were foreigners in Egypt.

[20]Respect the Lord your God, be faithful, and serve only him, making promises in his name. [21]Offer your praises to him, because you have seen him work such terrifying miracles for you.

[22]When your ancestors went to live in Egypt, there were only 70 of them. But the Lord has blessed you, and now there are more of you than there are stars in the sky.

If You Are Loyal to the Lord, He Will Bless You

Moses said to Israel:

11 The Lord is your God, so you must always love him and obey his laws and teachings. [2]Remember, he corrected you and not your children. You are the ones who saw the Lord use his great power [3]when he worked miracles in Egypt, making terrible things happen to the king and all his people. [4]And when the Egyptian army chased you in their chariots, you saw the Lord drown them and their horses in the Red Sea.[r] Egypt still suffers from that defeat!

[5]You saw what the Lord did for you while you were in the desert, right up to the time you arrived here. [6]And you saw how the Lord made the ground open up in the middle of our camp underneath the tents of Dathan and Abiram,[s] who were swallowed up along with their families, their animals, and their tents.

[7]With your own eyes, you saw the Lord's mighty power do all these things.

[8]Soon you will cross the Jordan River, and if you obey the laws and teachings I'm giving you today, you will be strong enough to conquer the land [9]that the Lord promised your ancestors and their descendants. It's rich with milk and honey, and you will live there and enjoy it for a long time. [10]It's better land than you had in Egypt, where you had to struggle just to water your crops.[t] [11]But the hills and valleys in the promised land are watered by rain from heaven,[u] [12]because the Lord your

10.18,19 *orphans and widows . . . foreigners:* Orphans and widows were completely dependent on others in Hebrew society. Foreigners were without the support of their own people and were more likely to be treated unfairly. The Israelites were to treat such people fairly, just as God does (10.17), and just as God treated the Israelites when they were defenseless slaves in Egypt (10.19). See also Exod 22.21-24; Lev 19.33.

Justice

10.22 *70:* See Genesis 46.15-27, which lists the members of Jacob's family who went to Egypt. In the Bible "70" is often meant as a complete number, but is not always to be taken as an exact number. The number of Jacob's descendants fulfilled the Lord's promise to Abraham (Gen 15.5; 22.17). **(See the chart Numbers in the Bible on pg 1844.)**

11.6 *Dathan and Abiram:* Along with Korah, these two men led a rebellion against Moses, but the Lord punished them and their families (Num 16.1-33).

[r]**11.4** *Red Sea:* Hebrew *yam suph,* "Sea of Reeds," one of the marshes or fresh water lakes near the eastern part of the Nile Delta. This identification is based on Exodus 13.7—14.9, which lists towns on the route of the Israelites before crossing the sea. In the Greek translation of the Scriptures made about 200 B.C., the "Sea of Reeds" was named "Red Sea." [s]**11.6** *Dathan and Abiram:* Hebrew "Dathan and Abiram, the sons of Eliab from the Reuben tribe." [t]**11.10** *where . . . crops:* One possible meaning for the difficult Hebrew text. [u]**11.10,11** *to water your crops . . . rain from heaven:* Egypt was flat and had very little rain. All water for crops had to come from the Nile River.

11.18-20 *tie them to your wrists . . . foreheads . . . door frames:* Many Jews today continue the practice of memorizing the Law (Scripture) by placing verses in containers called mezuzahs and attaching them to their door frames.

11.24 *Southern Desert . . . Mediterranean Sea:* The places mentioned formed the approximate south-north and east-west boundaries of Israel's kingdom as it existed under the rule of David (2 Sam 8.1-12) and Solomon (1 Kgs 4.20-25). **(See Maps 3 and 4 on pgs 1881 and 1882.)**

11.29,30 *Mount Gerizim . . . Gilgal:* The ceremony mentioned is explained in Deuteronomy 27.11-26. The sacred trees of Moreh were near Shechem. See Gen 12.6-18; 35.4. Gilgal means "circle" and probably refers to a circle of stones. **(See Map 3 on pg 1881.)**

Canaanite Gods and Goddesses

God keeps his eye on this land and takes care of it all year long.

13 The LORD your God commands you to love him and to serve him with all your heart and soul. If you obey him, **14-15**he will send rain at the right seasons,ᵛ so you will have more than enough food, wine, and olive oil, and there will be plenty of grass for your cattle.

16But watch out! You will be tempted to turn your backs on the LORD. And if you worship other gods, **17**the LORD will become angry and keep the rain from falling. Nothing will grow in your fields, and you will die and disappear from the good land that the LORD is giving you.

18Memorize these laws and think about them. Write down copies and tie them to your wrists and your foreheads to help you obey them. **19**Teach them to your children. Talk about them all the time—whether you're at home or walking along the road or going to bed at night, or getting up in the morning. **20**Write them on the door frames of your homes and on your town gates. **21**Then you and your descendants will live a long time in the land that the LORD promised your ancestors. Your families will live there as long as the sky is above the earth.

22Love the LORD your God faithfully and obey all the laws and teachings I'm giving you today. If you live the way the LORD wants, **23**he will help you take the land. And even though the nations there are more powerful than you, the LORD will force them to leave when you attack. **24**You will capture the land everywhere you go, from the Southern Desert to the Lebanon Mountains, and from the Euphrates River west to the Mediterranean

Sea. **25**No one will be able to stand up to you. The LORD will make everyone terrified of you, just as he promised.

26You have a choice—do you want the LORD to bless you, or do you want him to put a curse on you? **27**Today I am giving you his laws, and if you obey him, he will bless you. **28**But if you disobey him and worship those gods that have never done anything for you, the LORD will put a curse on you.

29After the LORD your God helps you take the land, you must have a ceremony where you announce his blessings from Mount Gerizim and his curses from Mount Ebal. **30**You know that these two mountains are west of the Jordan River in land now controlled by the Canaanites living in the Jordan River valley. The mountains are west of the road near the sacred trees of Moreh on the other side of Gilgal.

31Soon you will cross the Jordan River to conquer the land that the LORD your God is giving you. And when you have settled there, **32**be careful to obey his laws and teachings that I am giving you today.

Only One Place To Worship the LORD

Moses said to Israel:

12 Now I'll tell you the laws and teachings that you have to obey as long as you live. Your ancestors worshiped the LORD, and he is giving you this land. **2**But the nations that live there worship other gods. So after you capture the land, you must completely destroy their places of worship—on mountains and hills or in the shade of large trees. **3**Wherever these nations worship their gods, you must tear

---

ᵛ**11.14,15** *rain . . . seasons:* In Palestine, almost all the rain for the year comes during the months from October through April.

down their altars, break their sacred stones, burn the sacred poles[w] used in worshiping the goddess Asherah, and smash their idols to pieces. Destroy these places of worship so completely that no one will remember they were ever there. **4**Don't worship the LORD your God in the way those nations worship their gods.

5-19 Soon you will cross the Jordan, and the LORD will help you conquer your enemies and let you live in peace, there in the land he has given you. But after you are settled, life will be different. You must not offer sacrifices just anywhere you want to. Instead, the LORD will choose a place somewhere in Israel where you must go to worship him. All of your sacrifices and offerings must be taken there, including sacrifices to please the LORD[x] and any gift you promise or voluntarily give him. That's where you must also take one tenth of your grain, wine, and olive oil,[y] as well as the first-born of your cattle, sheep, and goats.[z] You and your family and servants will eat your gifts and sacrifices[a] and celebrate there at the place of worship, because the LORD your God has made you successful in everything you have done. And since Levites will not have any land of their own, you must ask some of them to come along and celebrate with you.

Sometimes you may want to kill an ani-mal for food and not as a sacrifice. If the LORD has blessed you and given you enough cows or sheep or goats, then you can butcher one of them where you live. You can eat it just like the meat from a deer or gazelle that you kill when you go hunting. And even those people who are unclean and unfit for worship can have some of the meat. But you must not eat the blood of any animal—let the blood drain out on the ground.

20-21 The LORD has promised that later on he will give Israel more land, and some of you may not be able to travel all the way from your homes to the place of worship each time you are hungry for meat.[b] But the LORD will give you cattle, sheep, and goats, and you can butcher any of those animals at home and eat as much as you want. **22**It is the same as eating the meat from a deer or a gazelle that you kill when you go hunting. And in this way, anyone who is unclean and unfit for worship can have some of the meat.[c]

23-24 But don't eat the blood. It is the life of the animal, so let it drain out on the ground before you eat the meat. **25**Do you want the LORD to make you successful? Do you want your children to be successful even after you are gone? Then do what pleases the LORD and don't eat blood.

26-27 All sacrifices and offerings to the

● 12.5-19 *one tenth of your grain . . . olive oil . . . first-born:* The Israelites had to give one tenth of their harvest of these products to the LORD each year (Lev 27.30-33; Deut 14.22-29; 26.12,13). Israel's first-born sons and the first-born of the flocks were to be dedicated to the LORD (Exod 13.2). See also Lev 27.26; Deut 15.19-22.

● 12.5-19 *you can butcher:* Butchering animals for food was permitted at home, as long as the blood was not eaten. Since this meat is not eaten as part of a sacrifice, those eating it do not have to be "clean" (12.20,21).

◌ Purity (Clean and Unclean)

◌ Blood

● 12.20-27 *place of worship . . . the place where he chooses:* The law in Exodus 20.24 allowed the worship of the LORD at several different locations. But Moses' words suggest that in the land of Canaan, one place of worship will be established. This likely refers to King David setting up the sacred tent in Jerusalem (2 Sam 6.16-18) and to King Solomon building Israel's first temple there (1 Kgs 8.1-21).

---

[w]**12.3** *sacred poles:* Or "trees," used as symbols of Asherah, the goddess of fertility.   [x]**12.5-19** *sacrifices to please the LORD:* These sacrifices have traditionally been called "whole burnt offerings" because the whole animal was burned on the altar. A main purpose of such sacrifices was to please the LORD with the smell of the sacrifice, and so in the CEV they are often called "sacrifices to please the LORD."   [y]**12.5-19** *one tenth of your grain, wine, and olive oil:* The Israelites had to give one tenth of their harvest of these products to the LORD each year (see 14.22-29; 26.12,13; Leviticus 27.30-33).   [z]**12.5-19** *the first-born of your cattle, sheep, and goats:* The Israelites had to sacrifice these to the LORD (see 15.19-22).   [a]**12.5-19** *sacrifices:* Some sacrifices were completely burned on the altar; in other sacrifices, part of the animal was burned and part was given to the priests, but most of the meat was eaten by the worshipers as a sacred meal.   [b]**12.20,21** *meat:* Usually eaten only on special occasions, such as during a sacred meal when sacrifices were offered to the LORD.   [c]**12.22** *anyone . . . the meat:* Only those who were properly prepared for worship, or "clean," could eat a sacred meal, but anyone could eat this kind of meat.

12.31 *nations worship their gods . . . burn their sons and daughters:* The practice of making children walk through fire was especially true of the cult of the god Molech (Lev 18.21; 20.2-5; Deut 18.10,11; 2 Kgs 21.4-7; 23.10; Jer 7.31).

13.1-2 *prophet:* A prophet is God's messenger. The message the prophet speaks is called a "prophecy." The prophets of the Bible sometimes foretold what would happen in the future, but they mainly observed what was happening around them and then delivered God's message for that situation. Some Israelites assumed that anyone who performed miracles was a prophet who received that power from God. But any person who tries to lead the people to worship other gods is not a prophet of God and should not be followed. God used such a person as a test of the people's faithfulness. **(See the article Prophets and Prophecy on pg 1791.)**

13.6-10 *stone them:* Stoning someone was one of the most common forms of capital punishment among the Israelites. The accused persons were forced to stand in a small pit, and people would throw large rocks down on them in order to crush and kill them.

13.14 *disgusting thing:* This refers to the worship of an idol.

13.15-17 *kill every one . . . sacrifice to the LORD your God:* A city that worships other gods is to be destroyed, just like cities that are captured in holy war, so it can be purified and dedicated to God.

LORD must be taken to the place where he chooses to be worshiped. If you offer a sacrifice to please the LORD, all of its meat must be burned on the altar. You can eat the meat from certain kinds of sacrifices, but you must always pour out the animal's blood on the altar.

28If you obey these laws, you will be doing what the LORD your God says is right and good. Then he will help you and your descendants be successful.

Worship the LORD in the Right Way

Moses said:

29Israel, as you go into the land and attack the nations that are there, the LORD will get rid of them, and you can have their land.

30But that's when you must be especially careful not to ask, "How did those nations worship their gods? Shouldn't we worship the LORD in the same way?" 31No, you should not! The LORD hates the disgusting way those nations worship their gods, because they even burn their sons and daughters as sacrifices.

32Obey all the laws and teachings I am giving you. Don't add any, and don't take any away.

Don't Worship Other Gods

Moses said to Israel:

13 1-2Someday a prophet[d] may come along who is able to perform miracles or tell what will happen in the future. Then the prophet may say, "Let's start worshiping some new gods—some gods that we know nothing about." 3If the prophet says this, don't listen! The LORD your God will be watching to find out whether or not

you love him with all your heart and soul. 4You must be completely faithful to the LORD. Worship and obey only the LORD and do this with fear and trembling, 5because he rescued you from slavery in Egypt.

If a prophet tells you to disobey the LORD your God and to stop worshiping him, then that prophet is evil and must be put to death.

6-10Someone else may say to you, "Let's worship other gods." That person may be your best friend, your brother or sister, your son or daughter, or your own dear wife or husband. But you must not listen to people who say such things. Instead, you must stone them to death. You must be the first to throw the stones, then others from the community will finish the job. Don't show any pity.

The gods worshiped by other nations have never done anything for you or your ancestors. People who ask you to worship other gods are trying to get you to stop worshiping the LORD, who rescued you from slavery in Egypt. So put to death anyone who asks you to worship another god. 11And when the rest of Israel hears about it, they will be afraid, and no one else will ever do such an evil thing again.

12After the LORD your God gives you towns to live in, you may hear a rumor about one of the towns. 13You may hear that some worthless people have talked everyone there into worshiping other gods, even though these gods had never done anything for them. 14You must carefully find out if the rumor is true. Then if the people of that town have actually done such a disgusting thing in your own country, 15you must take your swords and kill every one of them, and their livestock too. 16-17Gather all the possessions of the people who lived there, and pile them up in

[d]13.1,2 *a prophet:* Hebrew adds "or a dreamer of dreams," another name for a prophet.

If you obey these laws, you will be doing what the LORD your God says is right and good. Then he will help you and your descendants be successful. DEUT 12.28

the marketplace, without keeping any-thing for yourself. Set the pile and the whole town on fire, and don't ever rebuild the town. The whole town will be a sacri-fice to the LORD your God. Then he won't be angry anymore, and he will have mercy on you and make your nation stronger, just as he promised your ancestors. 18That's why you must do what the LORD your God says is right. I am giving you his laws and teachings today, and you must obey them.

Don't Mourn like Other Nations

Moses said:

14 People of Israel, you are the LORD's children, so when you mourn for the dead, you must not cut yourselves or shave your forehead.e 2Out of all the na-tions on this earth, the LORD your God chose you to be his own. You belong to the LORD, so don't behave like those who wor-ship other gods.

Animals That Can Be Eaten
(Leviticus 11.1-47)

3Don't eat any disgusting animals.
4-5You may eat the meat of cattle, sheep, and goats; wild sheep and goats; and gazelles, antelopes, and all kinds of deer. 6It is all right to eat meat from any animals that have divided hoofs and also chew the cud.f
7But don't eat camels, rabbits, and rock badgers. These animals chew the cud but do not have divided hoofs. You must treat

them as unclean. 8And don't eat pork, since pigs have divided hoofs, but they do not chew their cud. Don't even touch a dead pig!
9You can eat any fish that has fins and scales. But there are other creatures that live in the water, 10and if they do not have fins and scales, you must not eat them. Treat them as unclean.
11You can eat any clean bird. 12-18But don't eat the meat of any of the following birds: eagles, vultures, falcons, kites, ravens, ostriches, owls, sea gulls, hawks, pelicans, ospreys, cormorants, storks, herons, and hoopoes.g You must not eat bats. 19Swarm-ing insects are unclean, so don't eat them. 20However, you are allowed to eat certain kinds of winged insects.h
21 You belong to the LORD your God, so if you happen to find a dead animal, don't eat its meat. You may give it to foreigners who live in your town or sell it to foreigners who are visiting your town.
Don't boil a young goat in its mother's milk.

Give the LORD Ten Percent of Your Harvest

Moses said:
22People of Israel, every year you must set aside ten percent of your grain harvest. 23Also set aside ten percent of your wine and olive oil, and the first-born of every cow, sheep, and goat. Take these to the place where the LORD chooses to be wor-shiped, and eat them there. This will teach you to always respect the LORD your God.
24But suppose you can't carry that ten

e14.1 *when you mourn . . . forehead:* Or "you must not worship Baal, cutting yourselves and shaving your forehead." f14.6 *chew the cud:* Some animals that eat grass and leaves have more than one stomach, and they chew their food a second time, after it has been partly digested in the first stomach. This partly digested food is called "cud." g14.12-18 *eagles . . . hoopoes:* Some of the birds in this list are difficult to identify. h14.20 *certain kinds of winged insects:* These were locusts, crickets, and grasshoppers; see Leviticus 11.21,22.

14.1 *when you mourn . . . fore-head:* Shaving the head (Job 1.20; Isa 3.24; 15.2; 22.12; Ezek 7.18; Amos 8.10; Mic 1.16) or cutting the skin (Jer 16.6; 41.5) were done as signs of mourn-ing. But here and in Leviticus 19.27,28; and 21.5 such shaving and cutting is forbidden, probably because it was con-nected with the worship of other gods.

14.2 *the LORD your God chose you:* The Israelites were chosen by God and so were to set themselves apart from those who worshiped other gods. See also Exod 19.5,6; Deut 4.20; 7.6; 26.18; Isa 41.8,9; 1 Pet 2.9; Titus 2.14.

Purity (Clean and Unclean)

14.21 *dead animal:* An animal that had died naturally would contain blood, which could not be eaten.

14.21 *young goat in its mother's milk:* Some religions prepared a sacri-fice by cooking it in milk. The Israelites may have been forbidden to do so to avoid imitating such pagan customs. This law forms the basis for the dietary practice of not mixing meat and dairy foods in later Judaism.

15.1-10 *Every seven years:* Only DEUTERONOMY says that debts should be canceled every seven years. In other books, the land is to be allowed to rest every seven years, and the poor are to eat what grows naturally during that year (Exod 23.10,11; Lev 25.1-5). Plants and grasses that grew during the year of rest would be plowed into the soil to make it more fertile.

15.11 *poor and needy:* Even though the law (15.4-6) was supposed to eliminate poverty in Israel, this verse probably reflects the view that people will not always properly care for the poor and needy who live in the land. See also Matt 26.11; Mark 14.7; John 12.8.

15.12-17 *slaves:* Slavery was extremely common in the ancient Near East. The Israelites also had slaves, including some of their own Israelite people who had to work for someone to repay a debt. The Israelites were not to keep slaves longer than six years, and when the slaves were released, the owners were supposed to provide them with enough so that they could remain independent (15.12-15). If the slave chose to continue serving his master, the slave's ear was pierced as a sign of his life-long commitment (15.16,17; Exod 21.6). Compare this to the rules concerning female slaves (21.7-11). See also Lev 25.39-46; Jer 34.8-20.

⟲ Slaves and Servants in the Time of Jesus

percent of your harvest to the place where the LORD chooses to be worshiped. If you live too far away, or if the LORD gives you a big harvest, [25]then sell this part and take the money there instead. [26]When you and your family arrive, spend the money on food for a big celebration. Buy cattle, sheep, goats, wine, beer, and if there are any other kinds of food that you want, buy those too. [27]And since people of the Levi tribe won't own any land for growing crops, remember to ask the Levites to celebrate with you.

[28]Every third year, instead of using the ten percent of your harvest for a big celebration, bring it into town and put it in a community storehouse. [29]The Levites have no land of their own, so you must give them food from the storehouse. You must also give food to the poor who live in your town, including orphans, widows, and foreigners. If they have enough to eat, then the LORD your God will be pleased and make you successful in everything you do.

Loans
(Leviticus 25.1-7)

Moses said:

15 [1-2]Every seven years you must announce, "The LORD says loans do not need to be paid back." Then if you have loaned money to another Israelite, you can no longer ask for payment.[i] [3]This law applies only to loans you have made to other Israelites. Foreigners will still have to pay back what you have loaned them.

[4-6]No one in Israel should ever be poor. The LORD your God is giving you this land, and he has promised to make you very successful, if you obey his laws and teachings

that I'm giving you today. You will lend money to many nations, but you won't have to borrow. You will rule many nations, but they won't rule you.

[7]After the LORD your God gives land to each of you, there may be poor Israelites in the town where you live. If there are, then don't be mean and selfish with your money. [8]Instead, be kind and lend them what they need. [9]Be careful! Don't say to yourself, "Soon it will be the seventh year, and then I won't be able to get my money back." It would be horrible for you to think that way and to be so selfish that you refuse to help the poor. They are your relatives, and if you don't help them, they may ask the LORD to decide whether you have done wrong. And he will say that you are guilty. [10]You should be happy to give the poor what they need, because then the LORD will make you successful in everything you do.

[11]There will always be some Israelites who are poor and needy. That's why I am commanding you to be generous with them.

Setting Slaves Free
(Exodus 21.1-11)

Moses said to Israel:

[12]If any of you buy Israelites as slaves, you must set them free after six years. [13]And don't just tell them they are free to leave— [14]give them sheep and goats and a good supply of grain and wine. The more the LORD has given you, the more you should give them. [15]I am commanding you to obey the LORD as a reminder that you were slaves in Egypt before he set you free. [16]But one of your slaves may say, "I

[i]15.1,2 *The LORD says . . . no longer ask for payment:* Or "'The LORD says loans do not need to be paid back this year.' Then if you have loaned money to another Israelite, you cannot ask for payment until the next year."

love you and your family, and I would be better off staying with you, so please don't make me leave." **17**Take the slave to the door of your house and push a sharp metal rod through one earlobe and into the door. Such slaves will belong to you for life, whether they are men or women.

18Don't complain when you have to set a slave free. After all, you got six years of service at half the cost of hiring someone to do the work.[j]

First-Born Animals
(Leviticus 27.26,27; Numbers 18.15-18)

Moses said to Israel:

19If the first-born animal of a cow or sheep or goat is a male, it must be given to the LORD. Don't put first-born cattle to work or cut wool from first-born sheep. **20**Instead, each year you must take the first-born of these animals to the place where the LORD your God chooses to be worshiped. You and your family will sacrifice them to the LORD and then eat them as part of a sacred meal.

21But if the animal is lame or blind or has something else wrong with it, you must not sacrifice it to the LORD your God. **22**You can butcher it where you live, and eat it just like the meat of a deer or gazelle that you kill while hunting. Even those people who are unclean and unfit for worship can have some. **23**But you must never eat the blood of an animal—let it drain out on the ground.

Passover
(Exodus 12.1-20; Leviticus 23.4-8)

Moses said:

16 People of Israel, you must celebrate Passover in the month of Abib,[k] because one night in that month years ago, the LORD your God rescued you from Egypt. **2**The Passover sacrifice must be a cow, a sheep, or a goat, and you must offer it at the place where the LORD chooses to be worshiped. **3-4**Eat all of the meat of the Passover sacrifice that same night. But don't serve bread made with yeast at the Passover meal. Serve the same kind of thin bread that you ate when you were slaves suffering in Egypt[l] and when you had to leave Egypt quickly. As long as you live, this thin bread will remind you of the day you left Egypt.

For seven days following Passover,[m] don't make any bread with yeast. In fact, there should be no yeast anywhere in Israel.

5Don't offer the Passover sacrifice in just any town where you happen to live. **6**It must be offered at the place where the LORD chooses to be worshiped. Kill the sacrifice at sunset, the time of day when you left Egypt.[n] **7**Then cook it and eat it there at the place of worship, returning to your tents the next morning.

8Eat thin bread for the next six days. Then on the seventh day, don't do any work. Instead, come together and worship the LORD.

---

[j]**15.18** *six years . . . work*: Or "six years of service, and it cost you no more than if you had hired someone to do the work"; or "six years of service, for what you would have had to pay a worker for two years." [k]**16.1** *in the month of Abib*: Abib (also called Nisan), the first month of the Hebrew calendar, from about mid-March to mid-April. Passover was celebrated on the evening of the fourteenth of Abib (see Exodus 12.6; Leviticus 23.4,5). [l]**16.3,4** *the same kind . . . in Egypt*: One possible meaning for the difficult Hebrew text. [m]**16.3,4** *seven days following Passover*: This period was called the Festival of Thin Bread (see also verse 16). [n]**16.6** *sunset, the time of day when you left Egypt*: Or "sunset on the same date as when you left Egypt."

■ 15.19 *first-born animal*: First-born male animals were not to be kept and sold for profit, but they were to be offered as a sacrifice to God at God's chosen place of worship. If the animal was unfit for sacrifice (15.21), it could be eaten at home like any other meat.

● 16.3-4 *seven days following Passover*: This period was called the Festival of Thin Bread (16.16). The "Passover" celebration is related to the Hebrew word translated as "pass over" in Exodus 12.1-20,23,27. Passover was celebrated as a remembrance of how God saved the people from the final disaster and acted to help them escape from slavery in Egypt. It was to be celebrated on the fourteenth day of the first month starting at twilight. The Festival of Thin Bread was to begin the next day and to last for seven days (Lev 23.4-8; Num 28.16-25; Exod 12.1-20; 13.3-8).

Passover and the Festival of Thin Bread

● 16.8 *thin bread*: This bread was flat, because it was baked without yeast, which is added to bread dough to make it rise. The thin bread was made and eaten as a reminder that the Hebrew people had to leave Egypt so quickly that they didn't have time to let their bread dough rise before baking it.

16.10-11 *Harvest Festival:* The Harvest Festival celebrated grain harvests (Exod 23.16; 34.22). The people thanked God by bringing gifts of grain (Lev 23.15-21; Num 28.26-31).

16.13-15 *Festival of Shelters:* The Festival of Shelters (Exod 23.16) was one of three yearly celebrations that would eventually be celebrated in Jerusalem. During this seven-day celebration, the people were to give thanks to God for the fall harvest and to build and live in shelters made of tree branches (Lev 23.39-43). These shelters were a reminder of the temporary shelters their ancestors lived in after they left Egypt and wandered in the desert. **(See the chart Pilgrimage Festivals on pg 1799.)**

16.18-19 *judges:* It is not clear if this system of selecting judges differed from the system described earlier (Exod 18.13-27; Deut 1.9-17). It is only clear that judges must be fair and honest and not take bribes (Exod 23.6-8; Lev 19.15). Local town councils apparently had the authority to settle arguments and make economic and political decisions for the community. Israel's system of local government and courts was unique, because it was based on God's laws and the command to treat all people equally, whether they were rich or poor, powerful or weak.

The Harvest Festival
(Exodus 34.22; Leviticus 23.15-21)

Moses said to Israel:

9Seven weeks after you start your grain harvest, **10-11**go to the place where the LORD chooses to be worshiped and celebrate the Harvest Festival[o] in honor of the LORD your God. Bring him an offering as large as you can afford, depending on how big a harvest he has given you. Be sure to take along your sons and daughters and all your servants. Also invite the poor, including Levites, foreigners, orphans, and widows. **12**Remember that you used to be slaves in Egypt, so obey these laws.

The Festival of Shelters
(Leviticus 23.33-43; Numbers 29.12-38)

Moses said to Israel:

13-15 After you have finished the grain harvest and the grape harvest,[P] take your sons and daughters and all your servants to the place where the LORD chooses to be worshiped. Celebrate the Festival of Shelters for seven days. Also invite the poor, including Levites, foreigners, orphans, and widows. The LORD will give you big harvests and make you successful in everything you do. You will be completely happy, so celebrate this festival in honor of the LORD your God.

Three Festivals at the Place of Worship
(Exodus 23.14-17)

Moses said:

16Each year there are three festivals when all Israelite men must go to the place where the LORD chooses to be worshiped. These are the Festival of Thin Bread, the Harvest Festival,[q] and the Festival of Shelters. And don't forget to take along a gift for the LORD. **17**The bigger the harvest the LORD gives you, the bigger your gift should be.

Treat Everyone with Justice

Moses said to Israel:

18-19 After you are settled in the towns that you will receive from the LORD your God, the people in each town must appoint judges and other officers. Those of you that become judges must be completely fair when you make legal decisions, even if someone important is involved. Don't take bribes to give unfair decisions. Bribes keep people who are wise from seeing the truth and turn honest people into liars.[r]

20People of Israel, if you want to enjoy a long and successful life, make sure that everyone is treated with justice in the land the LORD is giving you.

Don't Set Up Sacred Poles or Stones

Moses said to Israel:

21When you build the altar for offering sacrifices to the LORD your God, don't set up a sacred pole[s] for the worship of the goddess Asherah. **22**And don't set up a sacred stone! The LORD hates these things.

---

[o]**16.10,11** *Harvest Festival:* Traditionally called the "Festival of Weeks," and known in New Testament times as "Pentecost." [P]**16.13-15** *After you . . . harvest:* Leviticus 23.34 gives the exact date as the fifteenth day of the seventh month of the Hebrew calendar, which would be early in October. [q]**16.16** *Harvest Festival:* See the note at 16.10,11. [r]**16.18,19** *turn . . . liars:* Or "keep innocent people from getting justice." [s]**16.21** *sacred pole:* See the note at 12.3.

Sacrifices That Have Something Wrong with Them

Moses said to Israel:

17 If an ox or a sheep has something wrong with it, don't offer it as a sacrifice to the LORD your God—he will be disgusted!

Put To Death People Who Worship Idols

Moses said to Israel:

2-3 The LORD your God is giving you towns to live in. But later, a man or a woman in your town may start worshiping other gods, or even the sun, moon, or stars.[t] I have warned you not to worship other gods, because whoever worships them is disobeying the LORD and breaking the agreement he made with you. **4**So when you hear that someone in your town is committing this disgusting sin, you must carefully find out if that person really is guilty. **5-7**But you will need two or three witnesses—one witness isn't enough to prove a person guilty.

Get rid of those who are guilty of such evil. Take them outside your town gates and everyone must stone them to death. But the witnesses must be the first to throw stones.

Difficult Cases

Moses said to Israel:

8-12 It may be difficult to find out the truth in some legal cases in your town. You may not be able to decide if someone was killed accidentally or murdered. Or you may not be able to tell whether an injury or some property damage was done by accident or on purpose. If the case is too difficult, take it to the court at the place where the LORD your God chooses to be worshiped.

This court will be made up of one judge and several priests[u] who serve at the LORD's altar. They will explain the law to you and give you their decision about the case. Do exactly what they tell you, or you will be put to death. **13**When other Israelites hear about it, they will be afraid and obey the decisions of the court.

The King

Moses said:

14People of Israel, after you capture the land the LORD your God is giving you, and after you settle on it, you will say, "We want a king, just like the nations around us."

15Go ahead and appoint a king, but make sure that he is an Israelite and that he is the one the LORD has chosen.

16The king should not have many horses, especially those from Egypt. The LORD has said never to go back there again. **17** And the king must not have a lot of wives—they might tempt him to be unfaithful to the LORD.[v] Finally, the king must not try to get huge amounts of silver and gold.

18The official copy of God's laws[w] will be kept by the priests of the Levi tribe. So, as soon as anyone becomes king, he must go to the priests and write out a copy of these

[t]**17.2,3** *sun, moon, or stars:* Some people thought these were gods and worshiped them.
[u]**17.8-12** *several priests:* The Hebrew text has "the priests, the Levites"; priests belonged to the Levi tribe.   [v]**17.17** *a lot of wives . . . unfaithful to the LORD:* A king would often marry the daughter of another king that he was making a treaty with. These foreign women would naturally want to worship their own gods, and would want their husband the king to do so as well.   [w]**17.18** *God's laws:* Or "God's laws for the king."

17.1 *something wrong:* Any animal offered as a sacrifice was to be in perfect and whole condition (Exod 12.4,5; Lev 22.20-25).

17.5-7 *two or three witnesses:* Witnesses who accused someone of a crime punishable by death were supposed to be the first to throw stones if the person they accused was found guilty. This was meant to keep people from falsely accusing someone. Two witnesses were needed (Num 35.30; Deut 19.15), so one person alone could not charge someone falsely. These requirements show God's concern for justice as part of the law.

17.8-13 *It may be difficult . . . decisions of the court:* Cases that are too difficult for the local judges to decide (16.18-20) are to be taken to a court at the place of worship. God chose the place, as well as the judge and the priests who interpret the law, so the decision is to be taken as the LORD's.

17.14 *We want a king:* When the people of Israel first took over Canaan, they did not have a king. Each tribe had leaders, and in times of national danger, God chose a special leader to help the people fight off their enemies (see JUDGES). Eventually, the people begged for a king (1 Sam 8.4-22). Unlike other nations, Israel's king was to be chosen by God and was to rule according to God's laws (17.19,20). The LORD God alone was to be the supreme ruler of Israel, and the king's future was in God's hands.

18.6 *Any Levite . . . go to the place:* The priests and other Levites from the Levi tribe were assigned to work at the temple in Jerusalem for a period of time each year. While serving at the place of worship, they would receive a portion of the food offerings brought by the people.

Israel's Priests

18.10-11 *sacrifice your son or daughter . . . tell fortunes:* Some ancient fortunetellers thought they could learn the future by watching the flight of birds, examining fluid in a cup, looking at the livers of dead animals, observing the movement of the stars and planets, or trying to contact the spirits of the dead. Telling fortunes or practicing witchcraft were forbidden by God's Law (Exod 22.18; Lev 19.26,31; Deut 18.14).

18.15 *prophet . . . like me:* In the Bible, Moses is described as a prophet (Deut 34.10; Acts 3.22; 7.37). He did not receive the kind of visions and dreams God gave to other "prophets," but God spoke directly to Moses (Num 12.6-8).

laws while they watch. [19]Each day the king must read and obey these laws, so that he will learn to worship the LORD with fear and trembling [20]and not think that he's better than everyone else.

If the king completely obeys the LORD's commands, he and his descendants will rule Israel for many years.

Special Privileges for Priests and Levites
(Numbers 18.8-32)

Moses said to Israel:

18 The people of the Levi tribe, including the priests, will not receive any land. Instead, they will receive part of the sacrifices that are offered to the LORD, [2] because he has promised to provide for them in this way.

[3]When you sacrifice a bull or sheep, the priests will be given the shoulder, the jaws, and the stomach.[x] [4]In addition, they will receive the first part of your grain harvest and part of your first batches of wine and olive oil.[y] You must also give them the first wool that is cut from your sheep each year. [5]Give these gifts to the priests, because the LORD has chosen them and their descendants out of all the tribes of Israel to be his special servants at the place of worship.

[6]Any Levite can leave his hometown, and go to the place where the LORD chooses to be worshiped, [7]and then be a special servant of the LORD[z] there, just like all the other Levites. [8]Some Levites may have money from selling family possessions, and others may not. But all Levites serving at the place of worship will receive

the same amount of food from the sacrifices and gifts brought by the people.

Don't Do Disgusting Things

Moses said to Israel:

[9]Soon you will go into the land that the LORD your God is giving you. The nations that live there do things that are disgusting to the LORD, and you must not follow their example. [10-11]Don't sacrifice your son or daughter. And don't try to use any kind of magic or witchcraft to tell fortunes[a] or to cast spells or to talk with spirits of the dead.

[12]The LORD is disgusted with anyone who does these things, and that's why he will help you destroy the nations that are in the land. [13]Never be guilty of doing any of these disgusting things!

A Prophet like Moses

Moses said to Israel:

[14]You will go in and take the land from nations that practice magic and witchcraft. But the LORD your God won't allow you to do those things. [15]Instead, he will choose one of your own people to be a prophet just like me, and you must do what that prophet says. [16]You were asking for a prophet the day you were gathered at Mount Sinai[b] and said to the LORD, "Please don't let us hear your voice or see this terrible fire again—if we do, we will die!"

[17]Then the LORD told me:

Moses, they have said the right thing. [18]So when I want to speak to them, I will choose one of them to be a prophet like you. I will give my mes-

[x]18.3 *stomach:* Certain portions of the stomach were considered a delicacy. [y]18.4 *grain . . . olive oil:* An Israelite was supposed to offer the first part of the harvest as a gift to the LORD (see Leviticus 23.10,11). [z]18.7 *a special servant of the LORD:* Or "one of the LORD's priests." [a]18.10,11 *tell fortunes:* Fortunetellers thought they could learn secrets or learn about the future by watching the flight of birds or looking at the livers of animals or in many other ways. [b]18.16 *Mount Sinai:* See the note at 1.1-5.

sage to that prophet, who will tell the people exactly what I have said. ¹⁹Since the message comes from me, anyone who doesn't obey the message will have to answer to me.

²⁰But if I haven't spoken, and a prophet claims to have a message from me, you must kill that prophet, and you must also kill any prophet who claims to have a message from another god.

Moses said to Israel:

²¹You may be asking yourselves, "How can we tell if a prophet's message really comes from the LORD?" ²²You will know, because if the LORD says something will happen, it will happen. And if it doesn't, you will know that the prophet was falsely claiming to speak for the LORD. Don't be afraid of any prophet whose message doesn't come from the LORD.

Safe Towns

(Numbers 35.9-28; Joshua 20.1-9)

Moses said to Israel:

19 Soon you will go into the land and attack the nations. The LORD your God will destroy them and give you their lands, towns, and homes. Then after you are settled, ²⁻⁴you must choose three of your towns to be Safe Towns. Divide the land into three regions with one Safe Town near the middle of each, so that a Safe Town can be easily reached from anywhere in your land.

Then, if one of you accidentally kills someone, you can run to a Safe Town and find protection from being put to death. But you must not have been angry with the person you killed.

⁵For example, suppose you and a friend go into the forest to cut wood. You are chopping down a tree with an ax, when the ax head slips off the handle, hits your friend, and kills him. You can run to one of the Safe Towns and save your life. ⁶You don't deserve to die, since you did not mean to harm your friend. But he did get killed, and his relatives might be very angry. They might even choose one of the men from their family to track you down and kill you. If it is too far to one of the Safe Towns, the victim's relative might be able to catch you and kill you. ⁷That's why I said there must be three Safe Towns.

⁸⁻⁹Israel, the LORD your God has promised that if you obey his laws and teachings I'm giving you, and if you always love him, then he will give you the land he promised your ancestors. When that happens, you must name three more Safe Towns in the new territory. ¹⁰You will need them, so innocent people won't be killed on your land while they are trying to reach a Safe Town that is too far away. You will be guilty of murder, if innocent people lose their lives because you didn't name enough Safe Towns in the land the LORD your God will give you.

¹¹But what if you really do commit murder? Suppose one of you hates a neighbor. So you wait in a deserted place, kill the neighbor, and run to a Safe Town. ¹²If that happens, the leaders of your town must send messengers to bring you back from the Safe Town. They will hand you over to one of the victim's relatives, who will put you to death.

¹³Israel, for the good of the whole country, you must kill anyone who murders an innocent person. Never show mercy to a murderer!

Property Lines

Moses said to Israel:

¹⁴ In the land the LORD is giving you, there are already stones set up to mark the

18.18-22 *that prophet . . . falsely claiming:* It is unclear who Moses is describing. Since the prophet is to be killed, later Christian interpreters compared this prophet to Christ. Two methods are given for deciding if a prophet speaks for God: (1) Anyone who speaks in the name of another god is not from God; and (2) if what is predicted comes true, the prophet was speaking for God.

19.2-13 *Safe Towns . . . Never show mercy to a murder:* If an innocent person is killed because a Safe Town is too far away, the whole nation is guilty of murder (19.10), and anyone guilty of murder is to die without mercy (19.13).

19.14 *stones:* Stones were used to mark property lines and to establish who owned fields and portions of land. Moving a boundary marker was a crime forbidden in Israel's law (Deut 27.14-26; Prov 22.28).

19.15 *witnesses:* Israel's justice system depended heavily on witnesses. Any witness who was discovered lying was severely punished (19.19-21).

20.1 *The Lord your God . . . help you fight:* In a holy war, the side having the most soldiers, horses, and chariots will not necessarily win the battle, because victory comes from God, and not from human efforts or strength. Israel is reminded how the Lord helped them cross the Red Sea, where the Lord destroyed the Egyptians' chariots and cavalry.

20.2 *priest:* Priests were the religious leaders of the communities. They reminded the army before a battle that the Lord God would fight along with them. Sometimes the priests went into battle with the troops (Josh 6.4-21; 2 Chr 20.14-23).

20.10-15 *a town that is far from your land:* A town that was outside the boundaries of Canaan was allowed to surrender. If it did, the people would become slaves; if not, all the men were to be killed and the women, children, and property were to be divided among the soldiers.

20.16 *towns in the land:* Captured towns in the land of Canaan were to be completely destroyed.

property lines between fields. So don't move those stones.

Witnesses Must Tell the Truth

Moses said to Israel:

¹⁵Before you are convicted of a crime, at least two witnesses must be able to testify that you did it.

¹⁶If you accuse someone of a crime, but seem to be lying, ¹⁷⁻¹⁸then both you and the accused must be taken to the court at the place where the Lord is worshiped. There the priests and judges will find out if you are lying or telling the truth.

If you are lying and the accused is innocent, ¹⁹⁻²¹then you will be punished without mercy. You will receive the same punishment the accused would have received if found guilty, whether it means losing an eye, a tooth, a hand, a foot, or even your life.

Israel, the crime of telling lies in court must be punished. And when people hear what happens to witnesses that lie, everyone else who testifies in court will tell the truth.

Laws for Going to War

Moses said to Israel:

20 If you have to go to war, you may find yourselves facing an enemy army that is bigger than yours and that has horses and chariots. But don't be afraid! The Lord your God rescued you from Egypt, and he will help you fight. ²Before you march into battle, a priest will go to the front of the army ³and say, "Soldiers of Israel, listen to me! Today when you go into battle, don't be afraid of the enemy, and when you see them, don't panic. ⁴The Lord your God will fight alongside you and help you win the battle."

⁵Then the tribal officials will say to the troops:

If any of you have built a new house, but haven't yet moved in, you may go home. It isn't right for you to die in battle and for somebody else to live in your new house.

⁶If any of you have planted a vineyard but haven't had your first grape harvest, you may go home. It isn't right for you to die in battle and for somebody else to enjoy your grapes.

⁷If any of you are engaged to be married, you may go back home and get married. It isn't right for you to die in battle and for somebody else to marry the woman you are engaged to.

⁸Finally, if any of you are afraid, you may go home. We don't want you to discourage the other soldiers.

⁹When the officials are finished giving these orders, they will appoint officers to be in command of the army.

¹⁰⁻¹⁵Before you attack a town that is far from your land, offer peace to the people who live there. If they surrender and open their town gates, they will become your slaves. But if they reject your offer of peace and try to fight, surround their town and attack. Then, after the Lord helps you capture it, kill all the men. Take the women and children as slaves and keep the livestock and everything else of value.

¹⁶Whenever you capture towns in the land the Lord your God is giving you, be sure to kill all the people and animals. ¹⁷He has commanded you to completely wipe out the Hittites, the Amorites, the Canaanites, the Perizzites, the Hivites, and the Jebusites. ¹⁸If you allow them to live, they will persuade you to worship their disgusting gods, and you will be unfaithful to the Lord.

¹⁹When you are attacking a town, don't

chop down its fruit trees, not even if you have had the town surrounded for a long time. Fruit trees aren't your enemies, and they produce food that you can eat, so don't cut them down. **20**You may need wood to make ladders and towers to help you get over the walls and capture the town. But use only trees that you know are not fruit trees.

Unsolved Murder

Moses said to Israel:

21 Suppose the body of a murder victim is found in a field in the land the LORD your God is giving you, and no one knows who the murderer is. **2**The judges and other leaders from the towns around there must find out what town is the closest to where the body was found. **3**The leaders from that town will go to their cattle herds and choose a young cow that has never been put to work.^c **4-5**They and some of the priests will take this cow to a nearby valley where there is a stream, but no crops. Once they reach the valley, the leaders will break the cow's neck.

The priests must be there, because the LORD your God has chosen them to be his special servants at the place of worship. The LORD has chosen them to bless the people in his name and to be judges in all legal cases, whether property or injury is involved.

6The town leaders will wash their hands over the body of the dead cow **7**and say, "We had no part in this murder, and we don't know who did it. **8-9**But since an innocent person was murdered, we beg you, our LORD, to accept this sacrifice and forgive Israel. We are your people, and you

rescued us. Please don't hold this crime against us."

If you obey the LORD and do these things, he will forgive Israel.

Marrying a Woman Taken Prisoner in War

Moses said to Israel:

10From time to time, you men will serve as soldiers and go off to war. The LORD your God will help you defeat your enemies, and you will take many prisoners. **11-13**One of these prisoners may be a beautiful woman, and you may want to marry her. But first you must bring her into your home, and have her shave her head, cut her nails, get rid of her foreign clothes, and start wearing Israelite clothes. She will mourn a month for her father and mother, then you can marry her.

14Later on, if you are not happy with the woman, you can divorce her, and she can go free. But you have slept with her as your wife, so you cannot sell her as a slave or make her into your own slave.

Rights of a First-Born Son

Moses said to Israel:

15-17 Suppose a man has two wives and loves one more than the other. The first son of either wife is the man's first-born son, even if the boy's mother is the wife the man doesn't love. Later, when the man is near death and is dividing up his property, he must give a double share to his first-born son, simply because he was the first to be born.

^c**21.3** *young cow . . . work:* Cows and oxen pulled plows and wagons.

● **21.1-9** *murder . . . don't hold this crime against us:* Murder was against God's Law (Exod 20.13; Deut 5.17), and the spilled blood of a murder victim made the land "unclean" and useless until the murderer was found and executed (Gen 4.10,11; Num 35.33,34). If the murderer was not found, the town nearest to the murder was required to conduct a ceremony of purification to remove that guilt and make the land clean again. After breaking the neck of a young cow, the town leaders were to wash their hands over the dead body as the blood of the cow washed down the stream. This symbolized the washing away of guilt. By performing this ceremony and asking God's forgiveness, the community took responsibility for the crime.

Purity (Clean and Unclean)

● **21.15-17** *two wives . . . first-born son:* Having more than one wife was not unusual, but it often created problems. This law protects the rights of a man's first-born son, even if he is not the son of the most-favored wife. Ancient laws allowed for a man to give a greater share of his property to his oldest son. Because a widow depended on her son for support, this law also protected the less-favored wife.

Birthright

● 21.18 *rebellious son:* Stoning a rebellious son to death was meant to serve as a lesson to others and to protect the family, the primary unit in the Israelite society.

● 21.19 *town gate:* Many cities were built with walls around them for protection. A town wall usually had a central gate, where people could enter the city. The town gate was also used as a gathering place where the town leaders heard and decided disputes.

● 21.22 *hang the dead body on a tree:* This was allowed only on the day of execution. It was done to warn others and to remind them that one person's sins affected and shamed the entire community. Because the hanged body was considered cursed by God, it had to be buried by evening so that the land would not become "unclean."

A Son Who Rebels

Moses said to Israel:

18A father and a mother may have a stubborn and rebellious son who refuses to obey them even after he has been punished. **19**If a son is like that, his parents must drag him to the town gate, where the leaders of the town hold their meetings. **20**The parents will tell the leaders, "This son of ours is stubborn and never obeys. He spends all his time drinking and partying." **21**The men of the town will stone that son to death, because they must get rid of the evil he brought into the community. Everyone in Israel will be afraid when they hear how he was punished.

The Body of a Criminal

Moses said to Israel:

22If a criminal is put to death, and you hang the dead body on a tree, **23**you must not leave it there overnight. Bury it the same day, because the dead body of a criminal hanging on a tree will bring God's curse on the land. The LORD your God is giving this land to you, so don't make it unclean by leaving the bodies of executed criminals on display.

Helping Others

Moses said to Israel:

22 If you see a cow or sheep wandering around lost, take the animal back to its owner. **2**If the owner lives too far away, or if you don't know who the owner is, take the animal home with you and take care of it. The owner will come looking for the animal, and then you can give it back. **3**That's what you should do if you find anything that belongs to someone else. Do whatever you can to help, whether you find a cow or sheep or donkey or some clothing.

4Oxen and donkeys that carry heavy loads can stumble and fall, and be unable to get up by themselves. So as you walk along the road, help anyone who is trying to get an ox or donkey back on its feet.

Don't Pretend To Be the Opposite Sex

Moses said to Israel:

5Women must not pretend to be men, and men must not pretend to be women.**d** The LORD your God is disgusted with people who do that.

Don't Take a Mother Bird

Moses said to Israel:

6-7 As you walk along the road, you might see a bird's nest in a tree or on the ground. If the mother bird is in the nest with either her eggs or her baby birds, you are allowed to take the baby birds or the eggs, but not the mother bird. Let her go free, and the LORD will bless you with a long and successful life.

Put a Wall around Your Flat Roof

8If you build a house, make sure to put a low wall around the edge of the flat roof.**e** Then if someone falls off the roof and is killed, it won't be your fault.

d22.5 *pretend to be men . . . pretend to be women:* Or "wear men's clothing . . . wear women's clothing."
e22.8 *flat roof:* Houses usually had flat roofs. In hot dry weather, it was cooler on the roof than in the house, and so roofs were used for sleeping and living quarters, and for entertaining guests.

Laws against Mixing Different Things

Moses said to Israel:

[9]If you plant a vineyard, don't plant any other fruit tree or crop in it. If you do plant something else there, you must bring to the place of worship everything you harvest from the vineyard.

[10]Don't hitch an ox and a donkey to your plow at the same time.

[11]When you weave cloth for clothing, you can use thread made of flax[f] or wool, but not both together. [12]And when you make a coat, sew a tassel on each of the four corners.

When a Husband Accuses His Wife

Moses said to Israel:

[13]Suppose a man starts hating his wife soon after they are married. [14]He might tell ugly lies about her, and say, "I married this woman, but when we slept together, I found out she wasn't a virgin."

[15]If this happens, the bride's father and mother must go to the town gate to show the town leaders the proof that the woman was a virgin. [16]Her father will say, "I let my daughter marry this man, but he started hating her [17]and accusing her of not being a virgin. But he is wrong, because here is proof that she was a virgin!" Then the bride's parents will show them the bed sheet from the woman's wedding night.

[18]The town leaders will beat the man with a whip [19]because he accused his bride of not being a virgin. He will have to pay her father 100 pieces of silver and will never be allowed to divorce her.

[20]But if the man was right and there is no proof that his bride was a virgin, [21]the men of the town will take the woman to the door of her father's house and stone her to death.

This woman brought evil into your community by sleeping with someone before she got married, and you must get rid of that evil by killing her.

Laws about Illegal Sex

Moses said:

[22]People of Israel, if a man is caught having sex with someone else's wife, you must put them both to death. That way, you will get rid of the evil they have done in Israel.

[23-24]If a man is caught in town having sex with an engaged woman who isn't screaming for help, they both must be put to death. The man is guilty of having sex with a married woman.[g] And the woman is guilty because she didn't call for help, even though she was inside a town and people were nearby. Take them both to the town gate and stone them to death. You must get rid of the evil they brought into your community.

[25]If an engaged woman is raped out in the country, only the man will be put to death. [26]Do not punish the woman at all; she has done nothing wrong, and certainly nothing deserving death. This crime is like murder, [27]because the woman was alone out in the country when the man attacked her. She screamed, but there was no one to help her.

---

[f]**22.11** *flax:* The stalks of flax plants were harvested, soaked in water, and dried, then their fibers were separated and spun into thread, which was woven into linen cloth.   [g]**22.23,24** *engaged woman . . . married woman:* An engaged woman was legally married, but had not yet slept with her husband or started living with him.

● **22.9-11** *If you plant . . . not both together:* The Israelites believed that God separated everything according to its own species at the time of creation (Gen 1). Breeding, planting, and even the making of cloth were to follow the natural order of God's created world. See Lev 19.19.

● **22.13-21** *man . . . by killing her:* A woman's sexual behavior was judged strictly in ancient Israelite society. Women who married were expected to be virgins at the time of the wedding. If it could be proved that a woman was not a virgin, she was killed so that her evil influence could not corrupt the community (22.21). The execution was done outside her father's door as a public show of the shame she had brought upon her family. To discourage false charges a man could be beaten and heavily fined for lying about a woman's virginity. Any fine paid for falsely accusing a woman was paid to her father, not to her (22.19,28,29).

● **22.22** *having sex with someone else's wife:* This law forbidding sex with another man's wife (adultery) was intended to protect a husband's rights over his wife or the woman he was engaged to marry. An engaged woman was legally married even if she had not yet slept with her husband or started living with him. If a man had sex with a married or engaged woman, both were to die. But an engaged woman could avoid death if she was heard screaming for help (22.23,24) or if the act took place where no one could hear her (22.25). In that case, the man was guilty of rape and was to be put to death.

23.1 *a man's private parts:* A man whose private parts have been cut off is called a "eunuch." Eunuchs were common in the ancient world, and they usually served as court officials. Excluding eunuchs from membership in God's community reflects the belief that all things chosen or dedicated to God were to represent the perfection of God's creation.

23.3-7 *Ammonites or Moabites . . . Edomites and Egyptians:* The history recalled here does not fit entirely with other biblical passages. Moab did hire Balaam to curse Israel (Num 22.1-6), but Ammon is not mentioned as being involved. Ammon may be excluded from God's people because both Ammon and Moab were born out of an improper relationship between Lot and his daughters (Gen 19.20-38). The Edomites had refused to let Israel pass through their land, but they will be included because they are relatives. The Egyptians, who had held the Israelites as slaves (Exod 1.1-22), will be included because they helped Joseph and his father Jacob's family (Gen 41.37-57; 46.1—47.26).

23.9 *camp is acceptable:* A camp that was acceptable to God was part of the holy war tradition. Like blood, semen was considered sacred, since it carried the "seed" of life. The natural flow of semen caused a man to be unclean for a day, and so he could not be in camp during that time (Lev 15.16-18). Other bodily discharges were also considered unclean, so toilets had to be placed outside the camp.

[28]Suppose a woman isn't engaged to be married, and a man forces her to have sex with him. If he is caught, [29]they will be forced to get married. He must give her father 50 pieces of silver as a bride-price and[h] can never divorce her.

[30]A man must not marry a woman who was married to his father. This would be a disgrace to his father.

Who Cannot Become One of the LORD's People

Moses said to Israel:

23 If a man's private parts have been crushed or cut off,[i] he cannot fully belong to the LORD's people.

[2]No one born outside of a legal marriage, or any of their descendants for ten generations, can fully belong to the LORD's people.

[3] No Ammonites or Moabites, or any of their descendants for ten generations, can become part of Israel, the LORD's people. [4]This is because when you came out of Egypt, they refused to provide you with food and water. And besides, they hired Balaam[j] to put a curse on you. [5] But the LORD your God loves you, so he refused to listen to Balaam and turned Balaam's curse into a blessing. [6]Don't even think of signing a peace treaty with Moab or Ammon.

[7]But Edomites are your relatives, and you lived as foreigners in the country of Egypt. Now you must be kind to Edomites and Egyptians [8]and let their great-grandchildren become part of Israel, the LORD's people.

Keep the Army Camp Acceptable

Moses said to Israel:

[9]When you men go off to fight your enemies, make sure your camp is acceptable to the LORD.

[10]For example, if something happens at night that makes a man unclean and unfit for worship, he[k] must go outside the camp and stay there [11]until late afternoon. Then he must take a bath, and at sunset he can go back into camp.

[12]Set up a place outside the camp to be used as a toilet area. [13]And make sure that you have a small shovel in your equipment. When you go out to the toilet area, use the shovel to dig a hole. Then, after you relieve yourself, bury the waste in the hole. [14]You must keep your camp clean of filthy and disgusting things. The LORD is always present in your camp, ready to rescue you and give you victory over your enemies. But if he sees something disgusting in your camp, he may turn around and leave.

Runaway Slaves from Other Countries

Moses said:

[15]When runaway slaves from other countries come to Israel and ask for protection, you must not hand them back to their owners. [16]Instead, you must let them choose which one of your towns they want to live in. Don't be cruel to runaway slaves.

[h]22.28,29 *forces her to have sex with him . . . bride-price and:* Or "talks her into sleeping with him. Then if they are caught,[29] he will have to marry her. He must give her father 50 pieces of silver as a bride-price and." [i]23.1 *a man's private parts have been crushed or cut off:* This was sometimes done to show devotion to pagan gods. [j]23.4 *Balaam:* Hebrew "Balaam son of Beor from Pethor." [k]23.10 *if something . . . worship, he:* Or "if a man has a flow of semen at night, he is unclean and unfit for worship, and he."

Temple Prostitutes

Moses said:

[17]People of Israel, don't any of you ever be temple prostitutes.[l] [18]The LORD your God is disgusted with men and women who are prostitutes of any kind, and he will not accept a gift from them, even if it had been promised to him.

Interest on Loans

Moses said:

[19]When you lend money, food, or anything else to another Israelite, you are not allowed to charge interest. [20]You can charge a foreigner interest. But if you charge other Israelites interest, the LORD your God will not let you be successful in the land you are about to take.

Sacred Promises to the LORD

Moses said:

[21]People of Israel, if you make a sacred promise to give a gift to the LORD, then do it as soon as you can. If the LORD has to come looking for the gift you promised, you will be guilty of breaking that promise. [22]On the other hand, if you never make a sacred promise, you can't be guilty of breaking it. [23]You must keep whatever promises you make to the LORD. After all, you are the one who chose to make the promises.

Eating Someone Else's Produce

[24]If you go into a vineyard that belongs to someone else, you are allowed to eat as many grapes as you want while you are there. But don't take any with you when you leave. [25]In the same way, if you are in a grain field that belongs to someone else, you can pick heads of grain and eat the kernels. But don't cut down the stalks of grain and take them with you.

A Law about Divorce

Moses said to Israel:

24 Suppose a woman was divorced by her first husband because he found something disgraceful about her.[m] He wrote out divorce papers, gave them to her, and sent her away. [2]Later she married another man, [3]who then either divorced her in the same way or died. [4]Since she has slept with her second husband, she cannot marry her first husband again. Their marriage would pollute the land that the LORD your God is giving you, and he would be disgusted.

Newlyweds

Moses said to Israel:

[5]If a man and a woman have been married less than one year, he must not be sent off to war or sent away to do forced labor. He must be allowed to stay home for a year and be happy with his wife.

Loans

Moses said to Israel:

[6]When you lend money to people, you are allowed to keep something of theirs as a guarantee that they will pay back the loan. But don't take one or both of their millstones, or else they may starve. They need these stones for grinding grain into flour to make bread.

[l]23.17 *temple prostitutes:* Some Canaanites worshiped by going to their temples and having sex with prostitutes that represented their gods. [m]24.1 *something disgraceful about her:* One possible meaning for the difficult Hebrew text.

Prostitution in the Bible

23.19 *interest:* Coins or paper money were not used by the Israelites at this time, but pieces of gold and silver were used like money to buy and trade. The cost of borrowing gold or silver pieces was called interest, or the amount charged over and above the amount actually borrowed. See also Lev 25.35-38; Deut 15.7-11; Exod 22.25.

23.21 *a sacred promise:* It was a common practice to promise God something in return for having a prayer request granted. Promises, also known as vows, were taken very seriously. Once a person made a vow, it could not be taken back. See also Num 30.1-6; Matt 5.33.

Making Promises (Vows)

24.1-4 *divorced:* In ancient Israel, a husband could easily divorce his wife, though he had to state his grounds for divorce. If the woman married a second man, the husband who divorced her could not marry her again, even if the second husband died. This law probably was intended to discourage men from deciding too quickly to write out divorce papers. Marriage and proper sexual behavior were to be taken seriously. Disobeying the law in these matters could pollute the land. See Matt 5.31; 19.7; Mark 10.4.

24.8 *leprosy:* The word translated "leprosy" was used for many different kinds of skin diseases. The strict rules about being ritually clean or unclean helped to stop the spread of skin diseases. Some skin diseases were contagious, but skin diseases and burns that were not contagious were also treated as if they made a person unclean.

24.15 *Pay them . . . each day:* Much of the hiring was done for seasonal work and on a day-to-day basis. Poor workers probably used most of the money they earned for food. See also Lev 19.13.

24.16 *put to death:* In the ancient world the entire family or community was often held responsible for the actions of one of its members.

Foreigners (Aliens)

24.19-21 *forget to bring in . . . grain . . . olives . . . grapes:* Some grain or fruit was to be left behind in fields, orchards, and vineyards, so the poor could pick it and eat.

Kidnapping

Moses said to Israel:

[7]If you are guilty of kidnapping Israelites and forcing them into slavery, you will be put to death to remove this evil from the community.

Skin Diseases

Moses said to Israel:

[8]I have told the priests[n] what to do if any of you have leprosy,[o] so do exactly what they say. [9]And remember what the LORD your God did to Miriam[p] after you left Egypt.

Loans

Moses said to Israel:

[10]When you lend money to people, you are allowed to keep something of theirs as a guarantee that the money will be paid back. But you must not go into their house to get it. [11]Wait outside, and they will bring out the item you have agreed on.

[12]Suppose someone is so poor that a coat is the only thing that can be offered as a guarantee on a loan. Don't keep the coat overnight. [13]Instead, give it back before sunset, so the owner can keep warm and sleep and ask the LORD to bless you. Then the LORD your God will notice that you have done the right thing.

Poor People's Wages

Moses said:

[14]If you hire poor people to work for you, don't hold back their pay,[q] whether they are Israelites or foreigners who live in your town. [15]Pay them their wages at the end of each day, because they live in poverty and need the money to survive. If you don't pay them on time, they will complain about you to the LORD, and he will punish you.

The Death Penalty

Moses said to Israel:

[16]Parents must not be put to death for crimes committed by their children, and children must not be put to death for crimes committed by their parents. Don't put anyone to death for someone else's crime.

Don't Mistreat the Powerless

Moses said to Israel:

[17]Make sure that orphans and foreigners are treated fairly. And if you lend money to a widow and want to keep something of hers to guarantee that she will pay you back, don't take any of her clothes. [18]You were slaves in Egypt until the LORD your God rescued you. That's why I am giving you these laws.

Leave Some of Your Harvest for the Poor

Moses said to Israel:

[19]If you forget to bring in a stack of harvested grain, don't go back in the field to get it. Leave it for the poor, including foreigners, orphans, and widows, and the LORD will make you successful in everything you do.

[20]When you harvest your olives, don't try to get them all for yourself, but leave

---

[n]**24.8** *the priests:* See the note at 17.8-12. [o]**24.8** *leprosy:* The word "leprosy" was used for many different kinds of skin diseases. [p]**24.9** *what the LORD your God did to Miriam:* See Numbers 12.1-16. [q]**24.14** *don't hold back their pay:* The Dead Sea Scrolls; the Standard Hebrew Text "treat them right."

some for the poor. [21]And when you pick your grapes, go over the vines only once, then let the poor have what is left. [22]You lived in poverty as slaves in Egypt until the LORD your God rescued you. That's why I am giving you these laws.

Whipping as Punishment for a Crime

Moses said to Israel:

25 [1-2]Suppose you and someone else each accuse the other of doing something wrong, and you go to court, where the judges decide you are guilty. If your punishment is to be beaten with a whip,[r] one of the judges will order you to lie down, and you will receive the number of lashes you deserve. [3]Forty lashes is the most that you can be given, because more than that might make other Israelites think you are worthless.

Don't Muzzle an Ox

Moses said to Israel:

[4] Don't muzzle an ox while it is threshing grain.[s]

A Son for a Dead Brother

Moses said to Israel:

[5-6]Suppose two brothers are living on the same property, when one of them dies without having a son to carry on his name. If this happens, his widow must not marry anyone outside the family. Instead, she must marry her late husband's brother, and their first son will be the legal son of the dead man.

[7]But suppose the brother refuses to marry the widow. She must go to a meet-ing of the town leaders at the town gate and say, "My husband died without having a son to carry on his name. And my husband's brother refuses to marry me so I can have a son."

[8]The leaders will call the living brother to the town gate and try to persuade him to marry the widow. But if he doesn't change his mind and marry her, [9]she must go over to him while the town leaders watch. She will pull off one of his sandals and spit in his face, while saying, "That's what happens to a man who won't help provide descendants for his dead brother." [10]From then on, that man's family will be known as "the family of the man whose sandal was pulled off."

When Two Men Fight

Moses said to Israel:

[11]If two men are fighting, and the wife of one man tries to rescue her husband by grabbing the other man's private parts, [12]you must cut off her hand. Don't have any mercy.

Be Honest in Business

Moses said to Israel:

[13-14]Don't try to cheat people by having two sets of weights or measures, one to get more when you are buying, and the other to give less when you are selling. [15]If you weigh and measure things honestly, the LORD your God will let you enjoy a long life in the land he is giving you. [16]But the LORD is disgusted with anyone who cheats or is dishonest.

25.1-2 *go to court:* Beating as a punishment was allowed, but only after a trial and in view of a judge. The limit of 40 blows was later changed to 39 to allow for a miscount (2 Cor 11.24). To "lie down," may mean that the blows were given to the soles of the feet.

25.5 *one of them dies without having a son:* This law assured that a man who died without a son could have his name carried on and his property kept in the family (Gen 38.6-26; Ruth 4.10; also Matt 22.24; Mark 12.19).

25.9 *pull off one of his sandals and spit in his face:* To make a deal legal, one person took off a sandal and gave it to the other (Ruth 4.7,8). To have one's sandal pulled off and to be spit at in the face in public was a great disgrace.

25.13-14 *two sets of weights or measures:* A standard system of weights was to be used when measuring grain in a scale. Sometimes a seller added dust to the grain or used a lighter than legal weight to measure it, so the buyer got less for his money. Or, when buying grain a merchant might use heavier weights to balance the grain, so he could get more grain for his money. These dishonest practices were forbidden (Exod 20.15; Lev 19.35,36; Prov 20.10).

[r]25.1,2 *whip:* Or "rod." [s]25.4 *threshing grain:* Oxen were used at the threshing place to walk on heads of grain, or pull heavy slabs of wood over it, to separate the kernels from the husks.

25.17 *Amalekites:* The Amalekites were descendants of Amalek,
(Gen 36.15,16). They likely were wandering herders who attacked the Israelites
on their way out of Egypt, but God
helped Israel defeat them (Exod 17.8-14;
1 Sam 15.2-9). Even though they were
enemies who lived outside Canaan
(20.10-15) they were to be treated like
those who are to be totally destroyed
(see 20.16).

26.2-11 *first things . . . place:* When
the first part of the harvest is presented
to God at the place of worship, the
people are to remember how God rescued them from Egypt and give thanks
for the gift of a new land. A farmer was to
offer these gifts at the time of harvest. It
is not clear whether this ceremony was a
one-time event or part of the Harvest Festival or Festival of Shelters.

26.3 *priest:* Israel's priests offered
proper sacrifices to God, taught the
people what was ritually clean and unclean, and made arrangements for Israel's yearly religious festivals.

Israel's Priests

26.5 *homeless, an Aramean:* This
refers to Jacob, who wandered from
southern Canaan to Haran and back
(Gen 27–35), later went to Egypt
(Gen 46.3-7), and was married to two
Aramean women (Gen 28.5; 29.16-28).
During Jacob's time in Egypt, his family
grew to great numbers (Exod 1.1-7). The
tribes of Israel were named after Jacob's sons.

Wipe Out Amalek

Moses said:

[17]People of Israel, do you remember
what the Amalekites did to you after you
came out of Egypt? [18]You were tired, and
they followed along behind, attacking
those who could not keep up with the others. This showed that the Amalekites have
no respect for God.

[19]The LORD your God will help you capture the land, and he will give you peace.
But when that day comes, you must wipe
out Amalek so completely that no one will
remember they ever lived.

Give the LORD the First Part of Your Harvest

Moses said to Israel:

26 The LORD is giving you the land,
and soon you will conquer it, settle
down, [2]and plant crops. And when you begin harvesting each of your crops, the very
first things you pick must be put in a basket. Take them to the place where the
LORD your God chooses to be worshiped,
[3]and tell the priest, "Long ago the LORD our
God promised our ancestors that he would
give us this land. And today, I thank him
for keeping his promise and giving me a
share of the land."

[4]The priest will take the basket and set it
in front of the LORD's altar. [5]Then, standing
there in front of the place of worship, you
must pray:

My ancestor was homeless,
an Aramean who went to live
in Egypt.
There were only a few

in his family then,
but they became great
and powerful,
a nation of many people.

[6]The Egyptians were cruel
and had no pity on us.
They mistreated our people
and forced us into slavery.
[7]We called out for help
to you, the LORD God
of our ancestors.
You heard our cries;
you knew we were in trouble
and abused.
[8]Then you terrified the Egyptians
with your mighty miracles
and rescued us from Egypt.
[9]You brought us here
and gave us this land
rich with milk and honey.
[10]Now, LORD, I bring to you
the best of the crops
that you have given me.

After you say these things, place the basket in front of the LORD's altar and bow
down to worship him.

[11]Then you and your family must celebrate by eating a meal at the place of worship to thank the LORD your God for giving
you such a good harvest. And remember to
invite the Levites and the foreigners who
live in your town.

Ten Percent of the Harvest

Moses said to Israel:

[12]Every year you are to give ten percent
of your harvest to the LORD.[t] But every
third year,[u] this ten percent must be given

[t]**26.12** *Every year . . . LORD:* See 14.22-29.   [u]**26.12** *every third year:* Probably the third and sixth years of
the seven-year cycle described in 15.1-11 and Leviticus 25.1-7.

to the poor who live in your town, including Levites, foreigners, orphans, and widows. That way, they will have enough to eat. [13]Then you must pray:

Our Lord and our God, you have said that ten percent of my harvest is sacred. I have obeyed your command and given this to the poor, including the Levites, foreigners, orphans, and widows.

[14]I have not eaten any of this sacred food while I was in mourning; in fact, I never touched it when I was unclean.[v] And none of it has been offered as a sacrifice to the spirits of the dead. I have done everything exactly as you commanded.

[15]Our Lord, look down from your temple in heaven and bless us and our land. You promised our ancestors that you would give us this land rich with milk and honey, and you have kept your promise.

The Lord Is Your God, and You Are His People

Moses said to Israel:

[16]Today the Lord your God has commanded you to obey these laws and teachings with all your heart and soul.

[17]In response, you have agreed that the Lord will be your God, that you will obey all his laws and teachings, and that you will listen when he speaks to you.

[18] Since you have agreed to obey the Lord, he has agreed that you will be his people and that you will belong to him, just as he promised. [19]The Lord created all nations, but he will make you more famous than any of them, and you will receive more praise and honor. You will belong only to the Lord your God, just as he promised.

Build an Altar on Mount Ebal

27 Moses stood together with the leaders and told the people of Israel:

Obey all the laws and teachings that I am giving you today. [2-4]Soon you will enter the land that the Lord your God is giving to you. He is the God your ancestors worshiped, and he has promised that this land is rich with milk and honey.

After you cross the Jordan River, go to Mount Ebal. Set up large slabs of stone, then cover them with white plaster and write on them a copy of these laws.

[5]At this same place, build an altar for offering sacrifices to the Lord your God. But don't use stones that have been cut with iron tools. [6]Look for stones that can be used without being cut. Then offer sacrifices to please the Lord,[w] burning them completely on the altar. [7]Next, offer sacrifices to ask the Lord's blessing,[x] and serve the meat at a sacred meal where you will celebrate in honor of the Lord.

[8]Don't forget to write out a copy of these laws on the stone slabs that you are going to set up. Make sure that the writing is easy to read.

Curses on Those Who Disobey

[9]Moses stood together with the priests[y] and said, "Israel, be quiet and listen to me!

[v]26.14 *in mourning . . . unclean*: Touching a dead body made a person unclean and unfit to worship God. Ten percent of the harvest belonged to God, and was not to be touched by an unclean person. [w]27.6 *sacrifices to please the Lord*: See the note at 12.5-19. [x]27.7 *sacrifices to ask the Lord's blessing*: These sacrifices have traditionally been called "peace offerings" or "offerings of well-being." A main purpose was to ask for the Lord's blessing, and so in the CEV they are sometimes called "sacrifices to ask the Lord's blessing." [y]27.9 *priests*: See the note at 17.8-12.

ଔ   Purity (Clean and Unclean)

■ 26.16-18 *obey these laws . . . you will be his people*: This passage concludes the presentation of the law that began with chapter 12 (compare 12.1 with 26.16). Though 12.1—26.15 strongly emphasizes obeying the Lord, these final verses (26.16-19) also emphasize the people's personal relationship with God. The people are to obey, not simply as a duty, but as a loving response to the care and blessing they have first received from the Lord God.

● 27.2-4 *enter the land . . . cross the Jordan River . . . to Mount Ebal*: While the Israelites are still camped in Moab, east of the Jordan River, Moses gives instructions for a ceremony at Mount Ebal near Shechem. The ceremony presented here calls for announcing both blessings and curses (27.12,13), but only the curses appear in 27.14-26.

● 27.2-5 *slabs of stone . . . altar*: Putting important writings on stones was common in the ancient world. A mixture of clay and lime was added to give the stones a smooth, light surface for the writing. It is not known why the altar stones were not to be cut with iron tools (27.5).

● 27.9 *Today you have become the people of the Lord*: This statement is based on the agreement recorded in 26.16-19. This new agreement does not replace the first agreement made at Mount Sinai, but renews it. It is important that each new generation renew its commitment to obeying and serving the Lord (6.1-9).

27.12-13 *The tribes:* It is not known why some tribes were chosen to pronounce the blessings and others were chosen to agree to the LORD's curses.

27.14-26 *curse:* In Israelite thought, the spoken word was powerful. This was especially true of curses and blessings. Some of the curses were for those who disobeyed various Commandments: idol worship (Exod 20.4,5; Lev 19.3,4); disrespecting parents (Exod 20.12); murder (Deut 5.17). Other curses were for various other laws: moving property lines (see 19.14); causing a blind person to stumble (Lev 19.14); treating the poor unfairly (Lev 19.33,34; Deut 24.17,18); improper sexual relations (Lev 18.8,9,23; Deut 22.22-30); and taking bribes (see 16.18-19).

28.1-13 *obey . . . Israel will be wealthy and powerful:* The blessings in 28.1-14 correspond to the curses given in 28.15-44. A list of blessings and curses was often included in ancient treaties. They were meant to assure that both sides would act according to the terms of the treaty. In DEUTERONOMY, blessings and curses are used in the same way. Israel will receive blessings if they obey the LORD's laws and teachings and do not worship other gods (28.1,2,14; 26.16-19; 27.9,10; 28.1,2,9,13), but curses will follow disobedience (27.14-26; 28.15,45).

28.4 *many children . . . flocks:* Children were considered proof of God's love and blessing, as were good crops and large herds and flocks. A large family was a special blessing (Ps 127.3-5).

Today you have become the people of the LORD your God.[z] [10]So you must obey his laws and teachings that I am giving you."

[11]That same day, Moses gave them the following instructions:

[12-13]After you cross the Jordan River, you will go to Mount Gerizim and Mount Ebal.[a] The tribes of Simeon, Levi, Judah, Issachar, Ephraim, Manasseh,[b] and Benjamin will go up on Mount Gerizim, where they will bless the people of Israel. The tribes of Reuben, Gad, Asher, Zebulun, Dan, and Naphtali will go up on Mount Ebal where they will agree to the curses.

[14-26]The people of the Levi tribe will speak each curse in a loud voice, then the rest of the people[c] will agree to that curse by saying, "Amen!" Here are the curses:

We ask the LORD to put a curse on anyone who makes an idol or worships idols, even secretly. The LORD is disgusted with idols.

We ask the LORD to put a curse on all who do not show respect for their father and mother.

We ask the LORD to put a curse on anyone who moves the rocks that mark property lines.

We ask the LORD to put a curse on anyone who tells blind people to go the wrong way.

We ask the LORD to put a curse on anyone who keeps the poor from getting justice, whether these poor are foreigners, widows, or orphans.

We ask the LORD to put a curse on any man who sleeps with his father's wife; that man has shown no respect for his father's marriage.

We ask the LORD to put a curse on anyone who has sex with an animal.

We ask the LORD to put a curse on any man who sleeps with his sister or his half sister or his mother-in-law.

We ask the LORD to put a curse on anyone who commits murder, even when there are no witnesses to the crime.

We ask the LORD to put a curse on anyone who accepts money to murder an innocent victim.

We ask the LORD to put a curse on anyone who refuses to obey his laws.

And so, to each of these curses, the people will answer, "Amen!"

The LORD Will Bless You if You Obey

Moses said to Israel:

28 [1-2]Today I am giving you the laws and teachings of the LORD your God. Always obey them, and the LORD will make Israel the most famous and important nation on earth, and he will bless you in many ways.

[3]The LORD will make your businesses and your farms successful.

[4]You will have many children. You will harvest large crops, and your herds of cattle and flocks of sheep and goats will produce many young.

[5]You will have plenty of bread[d] to eat.

[6]The LORD will make you successful in your daily work.

[7]The LORD will help you defeat your enemies and make them scatter in all directions.

[8]The LORD your God is giving you the

[z]27.9 *Today you have become the people of the LORD your God:* As a result of the agreement that the LORD had made with them, recorded in 26.16-19.   [a]27.12,13 *Mount Gerizim and Mount Ebal:* These mountains were separated by a valley.   [b]27.12,13 *Ephraim, Manasseh:* The Hebrew text has "Joseph"; the descendants of Joseph formed the two tribes of Ephraim and Manasseh.   [c]27.14-26 *the rest of the people:* Or "all the people who are standing on Mount Ebal."   [d]28.5 *bread:* The main food of the Israelites.

Moses . . . said, "Israel, be quiet and listen to me! Today you have become the people of the LORD your God. So you must obey his laws and teachings that I am giving you." DEUT 27.9,10

land, and he will make sure you are successful in everything you do. Your harvests will be so large that your storehouses will be full.

⁹If you follow and obey the LORD, he will make you his own special people, just as he promised. ¹⁰Then everyone on earth will know that you belong to the LORD, and they will be afraid of you.

¹¹The LORD will give you a lot of children and make sure that your animals give birth to many young. The LORD promised your ancestors that this land would be yours, and he will make it produce large crops for you.

¹²The LORD will open the storehouses of the skies where he keeps the rain, and he will send rain on your land at just the right times. He will make you successful in everything you do. You will have plenty of money to lend to other nations, but you won't need to borrow any yourself.

¹³Obey the laws and teachings that I'm giving you today, and the LORD your God will make Israel a leader among the nations, and not a follower. Israel will be wealthy and powerful, not poor and weak. ¹⁴But you must not reject any of his laws and teachings or worship other gods.

The LORD Will Put Curses on You if You Disobey

(Leviticus 26.14-46)

Moses said:

¹⁵Israel, today I am giving you the laws and teachings of the LORD your God. And if you don't obey them all, he will put many curses on you.

¹⁶Your businesses and farms will fail.

¹⁷You won't have enough bread[e] to eat.

¹⁸You'll have only a few children, your crops will be small, and your herds of cattle

[e]**28.17** *bread:* The main food of the Israelites.

and flocks of sheep and goats won't produce many young.

¹⁹The LORD will make you fail in everything you do.

²⁰No matter what you try to accomplish, the LORD will confuse you, and you will feel his anger. You won't last long, and you may even meet with disaster, all because you rejected the LORD.

²¹⁻²³The LORD will send terrible diseases to attack you, and you will never be well again. You will suffer with burning fever and swelling and pain until you die somewhere in the land that you captured.

The LORD will make the sky overhead seem like a bronze roof that keeps out the rain, and the ground under your feet will become as hard as iron. Your crops will be scorched by the hot east wind or ruined by mildew. ²⁴He will send dust and sandstorms instead of rain, and you will be wiped out.

²⁵The LORD will let you be defeated by your enemies, and you will scatter in all directions. You will be a horrible sight for the other nations to see, ²⁶and no one will disturb the birds and wild animals while they eat your dead bodies.

²⁷The LORD will make you suffer with diseases that will cause oozing sores or crusty itchy patches on your skin or boils like the ones that are common in Egypt. And there will be no cure for you! ²⁸You will become insane and go blind. The LORD will make you so confused, ²⁹that even in bright sunshine you will have to feel your way around like a blind person, who cannot tell day from night. For the rest of your life, people will beat and rob you, and no one will be able to stop them.

³⁰A man will be engaged to a woman, but before they can get married, she will be raped by enemy soldiers. Some of you will

28.12 *storehouses of the skies:* In ancient times, God was said to keep the rain, snow, hail, and wind in storehouses above the sky dome that covered the earth. When God opened a window in the sky, rain or snow would fall through and water the earth. See Gen 1.6-8; 8.2; Job 38.22-30; Ps 135.7; Jer 10.13; 51.16.

28.21-23 *terrible diseases:* The exact diseases are not known. Diseases often were connected to the LORD's punishment (Lev 26.16; 1 Kgs 8.37; Jer 14.12). One of the disasters that God sent upon Egypt was an epidemic of sores on people and animals (Exod 9.9).

28.21-23 *sky . . . a bronze roof . . . ground . . . hard as iron:* This passage gives a picture of drought conditions when crops dry up and animals die of thirst. Dry times also produced severe dust and sand storms that blew over the land from the desert areas to the east and south of Canaan.

28.36 *taken captive . . . worship idols:* This curse is the opposite of the promise of national greatness for Israel (28.7,10,13). This curse did come true in Israel's later history. The Assyrians defeated the northern kingdom of Israel in 722 B.C. and took many of its people into exile (2 Kgs 17.5-23). In 587 or 586 B.C. Babylonia defeated the southern kingdom of Judah and many of its leaders, including the king, were captured and taken to live in exile in Babylonia (2 Kgs 24.8—25.21). The people would have been introduced to the gods worshiped in those countries. It was sometimes thought that only the gods of a country could be worshiped within the borders of that country. (See the article From Joshua to the Exile: The People of Israel in the Promised Land on pg 1783.)

Locusts

28.40 *olive oil . . . hair:* Olive oil was used for cooking, making ointments, and combing the hair.

build houses, but never get to live in them. If you plant a vineyard, you won't be around long enough to enjoy the first harvest. ³¹Your cattle will be killed while you watch, but you won't get to eat any of the meat. Your donkeys and sheep will be stolen from you, and no one will be around to force your enemies to give them back. ³²Your sons and daughters will be dragged off to a foreign country, while you stand there helpless. And even if you watch for them until you go blind, you will never see them again.

³³You will work hard on your farms, but everything you harvest will be eaten by foreigners, who will mistreat you and abuse you for the rest of your life.

³⁴What you see will be so horrible that you will go insane, ³⁵and the LORD will punish you from head to toe with boils that never heal.

³⁶The LORD will let you and your king be taken captive to a country that you and your ancestors have never even heard of, and there you will have to worship idols[f] made of wood and stone. ³⁷People of nearby countries will shudder when they see your terrible troubles, but they will still make fun of you.

³⁸You will plant a lot of seed, but gather a small harvest, because locusts[g] will eat your crops. ³⁹You will plant vineyards and work hard at taking care of them, but you won't gather any grapes, much less get any wine, because the vines themselves will be eaten by worms. ⁴⁰Even if your olive trees grow everywhere in your country, the olives will fall off before they are ready, and there won't be enough olive oil for combing your hair.[h]

⁴¹Even your children will be taken as prisoners of war.

⁴²Locusts[i] will eat your crops and strip your trees of leaves and fruit.

⁴³Foreigners in your towns will become wealthy and powerful, while you become poor and powerless. ⁴⁴You will be so short of money that you will have to borrow from those foreigners. They will be the leaders in the community, and you will be the followers.

More Curses for Disobedience

Moses said:

⁴⁵Israel, if you don't obey the laws and teachings that the LORD your God is giving you, he will send these curses to chase, attack, and destroy you. ⁴⁶Then everyone will look at you and your descendants and realize that the LORD has placed you under a curse.

⁴⁷If the LORD makes you wealthy, but you don't joyfully worship and honor him, ⁴⁸he will send enemies to attack you and make you their slaves. Then you will live in poverty with nothing to eat, drink, or wear, and your owners will work you to death.

⁴⁹Foreigners who speak a strange language will be sent to attack you without warning, just like an eagle swooping down. ⁵⁰They won't show any mercy, and they will have no respect for old people or pity for children. ⁵¹They will take your cattle, sheep, goats, grain, wine, and olive oil, then leave you to starve.

⁵²All over the land that the LORD your God gave you, the enemy army will surround your towns. You may feel safe inside

[f]**28.36** *have to worship idols:* It was sometimes thought that only the gods of a country could be worshiped within the borders of that country.   [g]**28.38** *locusts:* A type of grasshopper that comes in swarms and causes great damage to plant life.   [h]**28.40** *olive oil . . . hair:* Olive oil was used for combing the hair.   [i]**28.42** *Locusts:* See the note at 28.38.

your town walls, but the enemy will tear them down, ⁵³while you wait in horror. Finally, you will get so hungry that you will eat the sons and daughters that the LORD gave you. ⁵⁴⁻⁵⁵Because of hunger, a man who had been gentle and kind will eat his own children and refuse to share the meal with his brother or wife or with his other children. ⁵⁶⁻⁵⁷A woman may have grown up in such luxury that she never had to put a foot on the ground. But times will be so bad that she will secretly eat both her newborn baby and the afterbirth, without sharing any with her husband or her other children.

Disobedience Brings Destruction

Moses said to Israel:

⁵⁸You must obey everything in *The Book of God's Law.* Because if you don't respect the LORD, ⁵⁹he will punish you and your descendants with incurable diseases, ⁶⁰like those you were so afraid of in Egypt. ⁶¹Remember! If the LORD decides to destroy your nation, he can use any disease or disaster, not just the ones written in *The Book of God's Law.*

⁶²There are as many of you now as the stars in the sky, but if you disobey the LORD your God, only a few of you will be left. ⁶³The LORD is happy to make you successful and to help your nation grow while you conquer the land. But if you disobey him, he will be just as happy to pull you up by your roots.

⁶⁴Those of you that survive will be scattered to every nation on earth, and you will have to worship stone and wood idols[j] that never helped you or your ancestors. ⁶⁵You will be restless—always longing for home, but never able to return. ⁶⁶You will

live in constant fear of death. ⁶⁷Each morning you will wake up to such terrible sights that you will say, "I wish it were night!" But at night you will be terrified and say, "I wish it were day!"

⁶⁸I told you never to go back to Egypt. But now the LORD himself will load you on ships and send you back. Then you will even try to sell yourselves as slaves, but no one will be interested.

The Agreement in Moab

29 So Moses finished telling the Israelites what they had to do in order to keep the agreement the LORD was making with them in Moab, which was in addition to the one the LORD had made with them at Mount Sinai.[k]

THE THIRD SPEECH: ISRAEL MUST KEEP ITS AGREEMENT WITH THE LORD

The LORD Is Your God

²⁻³Moses called the nation of Israel together and told them:

When you were in Egypt, you saw the LORD perform great miracles that caused trouble for the king, his officials, and everyone else in the country. ⁴⁻⁶He has even told you, "For 40 years I, the LORD, led you through the desert, but your clothes and your sandals didn't wear out, and I gave you special food.[l] I did these things so you would realize that I am your God."

But the LORD must give you a change of heart before you truly understand what you have seen and heard.

⁷When we first camped here, King Sihon of Heshbon and King Og of Bashan attacked,

[j]**28.64** *have to worship . . . idols*: See the note at 28.36. [k]**29.1** *Mount Sinai*: See the note at 1.1-5.
[l]**29.4-6** *I gave . . . food*: Hebrew "you didn't eat bread or drink any wine or beer."

29.1 *agreement . . . in Moab . . . at Mount Sinai:* The agreement at Moab contains much of what is found in DEUTERONOMY, beginning with Moses' speech at 4.1. This agreement is similar to the first agreement that the LORD made with Moses and the people at Mount Sinai (Exod 19–40). Both agreements include the Ten Commandments, but each has much material that is different from the other.

Agreements (Covenants)

29.2-3 *When you were in Egypt:* This review of God's saving acts is a typical Israelite way to confess faith in God.

29.4-6 *40 years . . . change of heart:* Even God's miracles and saving help did not convince the people to be faithful. This would take a change of heart. See also Jer 31.31-34.

29.16-17 *Egyptians worship disgusting idols:* The ancient Egyptians worshiped many gods, including animal-headed gods such as Apis (bull), Mnevis (cow), and Khnum (ram). The Nile River was worshiped like a god, because its floods made the land fertile. The king of Egypt (pharaoh) was also considered a god.

29.18 *root . . . produces . . . poisonous fruit:* One person worshiping idols could influence the rest of the Israelite people and lead to punishment for all (29.19). See also Heb 12.15.

29.23 *Sodom . . . Zeboiim:* The LORD destroyed Sodom and Gomorrah because of the evil people who lived there (Gen 18.16-28; 19.24,25). Admah and Zeboiim were located near Sodom and Gomorrah (Gen 10.19) and were likely destroyed at the same time (Hos 11.8).

29.25 *they rejected the agreement:* The nations wonder why God's chosen people have been defeated and sent into exile. The answer: Israel worshiped other gods. This act of disobedience caused the LORD to punish them with the curses described in *The Book of God's Law.*

but we defeated them. [8]Then we captured their land and divided it among the tribes of Reuben, Gad, and East Manasseh.

Keep the Agreement

Moses said:

[9]Israel, the LORD has made an agreement with you, and if you keep your part, you will be successful in everything you do. [10-12]Today everyone in our nation is standing here in the LORD's presence, including leaders and officials, parents and children, and even those foreigners who cut wood and carry water for us. We are at this place of worship to promise that we will keep our part of the agreement with the LORD our God.

[13-15]In this agreement, the LORD promised that you would be his people and that he would be your God. He first made this promise to your ancestors Abraham, Isaac, and Jacob, and today the LORD is making this same promise to you. But it isn't just for you; it is also for your descendants.

[16-17]When we lived in Egypt, you saw the Egyptians worship disgusting idols of wood, stone, silver, and gold. Then as we traveled through other nations, you saw those people worship other disgusting idols. [18]So make sure that everyone in your tribe remains faithful to the LORD and never starts worshiping gods of other nations.

If even one of you worships idols, you will be like the root of a plant that produces bitter, poisonous fruit. [19]You may be an Israelite and know all about the LORD's agreement with us, but he won't bless you if you rebel against him. You may think you can get away with it, but you will cause

the rest of Israel to be punished along with you.[m] [20-21]The LORD will be furious, and instead of forgiving you, he will separate you from the other tribes. Then he will destroy you, by piling on you all the curses in *The Book of God's Law,* and you will be forgotten forever.

[22]The LORD will strike your country with diseases and disasters. Your descendants and foreigners from distant countries will see that your land [23] has become a scorching desert of salt and sulfur, where nothing is planted, nothing sprouts, and nothing grows. It will be as lifeless as the land around the cities of Sodom, Gomorrah, Admah, and Zeboiim, after the LORD became angry and destroyed them.[n]

[24]People from other nations will ask, "Why did the LORD destroy this country? Why was he so furious?"

[25]And they will be given this answer:

Our ancestors worshiped the LORD, but after he brought them out of Egypt and made an agreement with them, they rejected the agreement [26]and decided to worship gods that had never helped them. The LORD had forbidden Israel to worship these gods, [27-28]and so he became furious and punished the land with all the curses in *The Book of God's Law.* Then he pulled up Israel by the roots and tossed them into a foreign country, where they still are today.

[29]The LORD our God hasn't explained the present or the future, but he has commanded us to obey the laws he gave to us and our descendants.

[m]**29.19** *you will cause the rest of Israel to be punished along with you:* Hebrew "The mud will be swept away as well as the dust."   [n]**29.23** *Sodom . . . destroyed them:* See Genesis 18.16-28.

The LORD promised that you would be his people and that he would be your God. He first made this promise to your ancestors . . . and today the LORD is making this same promise to you. DEUT 29.13-15

The Lord Will Bring You Back

Moses said to Israel:

30 I have told you everything the Lord your God will do for you, and I've also told you the curses he will put on you if you reject him. He will scatter you in far-away countries, but when you realize that he is punishing you, **2**return to him with all your heart and soul and start obeying the commands I have given to you today. **3-4**Then he will stop punishing you and treat you with kindness. He may have scattered you to the farthest countries on earth, but he will bring you back **5**to the land that had belonged to your ancestors and make you even more successful and powerful than they ever were.

6You and your descendants are stubborn, but the Lord will make you willing to obey him and love him with all your heart and soul, and you will enjoy a long life.

7Then the Lord your God will remove the curses from you and put them on those enemies who hate and attack you.

8You will again obey the laws and teachings of the Lord, **9**and he will bless you with many children, large herds and flocks, and abundant crops. The Lord will be happy to do good things for you, just as he did for your ancestors. **10**But you must decide once and for all to worship him with all your heart and soul and to obey everything in *The Book of God's Law.*

Choose Life, Not Death

Moses said to Israel:

11You know God's laws, and it isn't impossible to obey them. **12**His commands aren't in heaven, so you can't excuse yourselves by saying, "How can we obey the Lord's commands? They are in heaven, and no one can go up to get them, then bring them down and explain them to us." **13**And you can't say, "How can we obey the Lord's commands? They are across the sea, and someone must go across, then bring them back and explain them to us." **14**No, these commands are nearby and you know them by heart. All you have to do is obey!

15Today I am giving you a choice. You can choose life and success or death and disaster. **16-18**I am commanding you to be loyal to the Lord, to live the way he has told you, and to obey his laws and teachings. You are about to cross the Jordan River and take the land that he is giving you. If you obey him, you will live and become successful and powerful.

On the other hand, you might choose to disobey the Lord and reject him. So I'm warning you that if you bow down and worship other gods, you won't have long to live.

19Now I call the sky and the earth to be witnesses that I am offering you this choice. Will you choose for the Lord to make you prosperous and give you a long life? Or will he put you under a curse and kill you? Choose life! **20**Be completely faithful to the Lord your God, love him, and do whatever he tells you. The Lord is the only one who can give life, and he will let you live a long time in the land that he promised to your ancestors Abraham, Isaac, and Jacob.

FINAL SPEECHES AND THE DEATH OF MOSES

Joshua Is Appointed the Leader of Israel

31 Moses again spoke to the whole nation of Israel:

2I am 120 years old, and I am no longer able to be your leader. And besides that, the Lord your God has told me that he won't let me cross the Jordan River. **3-5**But he has

30.1 *everything the Lord your God will do for you . . . curses:* This refers to the blessings promised to Israel if they obey the Lord and worship only him.

30.3-4 *He may have scattered you . . . but:* In this passage, it sounds as if Israel is already in exile. But they are reminded that if they turn back to God and obey God's laws, God will return them to the land and bless them. This promise was made by a number of Israel's prophets many centuries after the time of Moses (see Isa 48.1—49.7; Jer 3.12-19; Ezek 11.15-21; Hos 14.1-9).

30.15 *choose life:* Here, choosing life means obeying the laws and commands God gave the people. Those who obey are promised a life full of blessings.

31.2 *120 years old:* This is three times 40 years. Since the Hebrews considered a generation to be about 40 years, this may simply mean that Moses was a man old enough to have seen his grandchildren become adults.

Be completely faithful to the Lord your God, love him, and do whatever he tells you. The Lord is the only one who can give life. Deut 30.20

31.9 *laws and teachings*: This is the agreement (covenant) the people made with God at Mount Sinai and the explanations and teachings about it (4.1—29.1). In ancient times, copies of agreements between nations were often placed before the gods at the worship centers of the nations involved. Israel was commanded to keep its agreement with God in the sacred chest at God's chosen place of worship.

31.10-11 *Festival of Shelters . . . every seventh year . . . repaid*: Reading the law and teaching it to the people of Israel was one of the main jobs of a priest (33.10; Mal 2.4-9). Every seven years the laws were to be read at one of the required festivals, so that each generation would hear and learn them.

31.19 *the words to a new song*: The words of the song are given in 32.1-43. The song will not be forgotten and will stand as proof that the Israelites know God's laws and have no excuse for breaking them (31.21).

promised that he and Joshua will lead you across the Jordan to attack the nations that live on the other side. The LORD will destroy those nations just as he destroyed Sihon and Og, those two Amorite kings. Just remember—whenever you capture a place, kill everyone who lives there.

6Be brave and strong! Don't be afraid of the nations on the other side of the Jordan. The LORD your God will always be at your side, and he will never abandon you.

7Then Moses called Joshua up in front of the crowd and said:

Joshua, be brave and strong as you lead these people into their land. The LORD made a promise long ago to Israel's ancestors that this land would someday belong to Israel. That time has now come, and you must divide up the land among the people. **8** The LORD will lead you into the land. He will always be with you and help you, so don't ever be afraid of your enemies.

Read These Laws

9Moses wrote down all of these laws and teachings and gave them to the priests and the leaders of Israel. The priests were from the Levi tribe, and they carried the sacred chest that belonged to the LORD. **10-11**Moses told these priests and leaders:

Each year the Israelites must come together to celebrate the Festival of Shelters at the place where the LORD chooses to be worshiped. You must read these laws and teachings to the people at the festival every seventh year, the year when loans do not need to be repaid.º **12-13**Everyone must come—men, women, children, and even the foreigners who live in your towns. And each new generation will

listen and learn to worship the LORD their God with fear and trembling and to do exactly what is said in God's Law.

Israel Will Reject the LORD

14The LORD told Moses, "You will soon die, so bring Joshua to the sacred tent, and I will appoint him the leader of Israel."

Moses and Joshua went to the sacred tent, **15**and the LORD appeared in a thick cloud right over the entrance to the tent. **16**The LORD said:

Moses, you will soon die. But Israel is going into a land where other gods are worshiped, and Israel will reject me and start worshiping these gods. The people will break the agreement I made with them, **17**and I will be so furious that I will abandon them and ignore their prayers. I will send disasters and suffering that will nearly wipe them out. Finally, they will realize that the disasters happened because I abandoned them. **18**They will pray to me, but I will ignore them because they were evil and started worshiping other gods.

19Moses and Joshua, I am going to give you the words to a new song. Write them down and teach the song to the Israelites. If they learn it, they will know what I want them to do, and so they will have no excuse for not obeying me. **20**I am bringing them into the land that I promised their ancestors. It is a land rich with milk and honey, and the Israelites will have more than enough food to eat. But they will get fat and turn their backs on me and start worshiping other gods. The Israelites will reject me and break the agreement that I made with them.

º**31.10,11** *every seventh year . . . repaid*: See 15.1,2 and the note there.

[21]When I punish the Israelites and their descendants with suffering and disasters, I will remind them that they know the words to this song, so they have no excuse for not obeying me.

I will give them the land that I promised, but I know the way they are going to live later on.

[22]Moses at once wrote down the words to the song,[p] and he taught it to the Israelites.

[23] The LORD told Joshua, "Be brave and strong! I will help you lead the people of Israel into the land that I have promised them."

[24]Moses wrote down all these laws and teachings in a book, [25]then he went to the Levites who carried the sacred chest and said:

[26]This is *The Book of God's Law.* Keep it beside the sacred chest that holds the agreement the LORD your God made with Israel. This book is proof that you know what the LORD wants you to do. [27]I know how stubborn and rebellious you and the rest of the Israelites are. You have rebelled against the LORD while I have been alive, and it will only get worse after I am gone. [28]So call together the leaders and officials of the tribes of Israel. I will bring this book and read every word of it to you, and I will call the sky and the earth as witnesses that all of you know what you are supposed to do.

[29]I am going to die soon, and I know that in the future you will stop caring about what is right and what is wrong, and so you will disobey the LORD and stop living the way I told you to live. The LORD will be angry, and terrible things will happen to you.

The Song of Moses

[30]Moses called a meeting of all the people of Israel, so he could teach them the words to the song that the LORD had given him. And here are the words:

32 Earth and Sky,
listen to what I say!
[2]Israel, I will teach you.
My words will be like gentle rain
on tender young plants,
or like dew on the grass.

[3]Join with me in praising
the wonderful name
of the LORD our God.
[4]The LORD is a mighty rock,[q]
and he never does wrong.
God can always be trusted
to bring justice.
[5]But you lie and cheat
and are unfaithful to him.
You have disgraced yourselves
and are no longer worthy
to be his children.[r]
[6]Israel, the LORD is your Father,
the one who created you,
but you repaid him
by being foolish.
[7]Think about past generations.
Ask your parents
or any of your elders.
They will tell you
[8]that God Most High
gave land to every nation.
He assigned a guardian angel
to each of them,[s]

[p]**31.22** *the words to the song*: See 32.1-43. [q]**32.4** *mighty rock*: The Hebrew text has "rock," which is sometimes used in poetry to compare the LORD to a mountain where his people can run for protection from their enemies. [r]**32.5** *and are unfaithful . . . children*: One possible meaning for the difficult Hebrew text. [s]**32.8** *He assigned . . . them*: The Dead Sea Scrolls and one ancient translation; the Standard Hebrew Text "So there were as many nations as Israel (that is, Jacob) had children."

31.21 *know the way they are going to live later on:* This refers to Israel worshiping other gods after they have settled in the promised land.

31.24-26 *Moses wrote . . . in a book . . . beside the sacred chest:* These verses continue the thought begun in 31.9-13. The book (*The Book of God's Law*) is to be used along with the laws (commandments) written on stone slabs and kept inside the sacred chest.

32.8 *Most High . . . guardian angel:* The name "Most High" emphasizes God's control over all of creation (Gen 14.19). Angels are part of God's heavenly court. They are beings who tell God's messages to people or protect those who belong to God.

Names of God

Angels

The LORD is a mighty rock, and he never does wrong. God can always be trusted to bring justice. DEUT 32.4

● **32.13** *helped you capture the land:* Moses' song is written in a way that sounds as if the people have already taken over Canaan and have been living in the land.

● **32.13** *Olive trees . . . honey:* Olive trees often grew on rocky hillsides, and bees sometimes built their hives between rocks.

■ **32.16,17** *disgusting idols . . . useless gods:* The gods of other nations were not like Israel's living LORD God, so they were useless to help.

■ **32.20,21** *You are unfaithful . . . worshiped worthless idols:* Though the LORD saved the people of Israel from slavery in Egypt and helped them take over the land of Canaan, they turned their backs on the LORD by worshiping other gods.

■ **32.22** *breathe out fire . . . world of the dead:* Fire is often connected with the LORD's judgment against those who are evil or disobedient (Gen 19.23-29; Lev 10.1,2; Isa 4.4; Joel 2.1-3; Matt 13.36-42).

In ancient Hebrew thought, the "world of the dead" was a deep underground pit that lay beneath a great underground sea. The Hebrew name for the underground world of the dead was *Sheol,* described in the Bible as a totally silent place where no one knows or feels anything (Job 10.21,22; Ps 88.12; 94.17).

⁹but the LORD himself
    takes care of Israel.ᵗ

¹⁰Israel, the LORD discovered you
    in a barren desert
      filled with howling winds.
    God became your fortress,
    protecting you as though
      you were his own eyes.
¹¹The LORD was like an eagle
    teaching its young to fly,
    always ready to swoop down
    and catch them on its back.
¹²Israel, the LORD led you,
    and without the aid
      of a foreign god,
¹³he helped you
    capture the land.
    Your fields were rich
      with grain.
    Olive trees grew
      in your stony soil,
    and honey was found
      among the rocks.
¹⁴Your flocks and herds
    produced milk and yogurt,
    and you got choice meat
    from your sheep and goats
      that grazed in Bashan.
    Your wheat was the finest,
      and you drank the best wine.

¹⁵Israel,ᵘ you grew fat and rebelled
    against God, your Creator
    you rejected the Mighty Rock,ᵛ
      your only place of safety.
¹⁶You made God jealous and angry

by worshiping disgusting idols
    and foreign gods.
¹⁷You offered sacrifices
    to demons, those useless godsʷ
      that never helped you,
    new gods that your ancestors
      never worshiped.
¹⁸You turned away
    from God, your Creator;
    you forgot the Mighty Rock,ˣ
      the source of your life.
¹⁹You were the LORD's children,
    but you made him angry.
    Then he rejected you ²⁰and said,
    "You are unfaithful
      and can't be trusted.
    So I won't answer your prayers;
    I'll just watch and see
      what happens to you.
²¹You worshiped worthless idols,
    and made me jealous
      and angry!
    Now I will send a cruelʸ
      and worthless nation
    to make you jealous and angry.

²²"My people, I will breathe out fire
    that sends you down
      to the world of the dead.
    It will scorch your farmlands
    and burn deep down
      under the mountains.
²³I'll send disaster after disaster
    to strike you like arrows.
²⁴You'll be struck by starvation
    and deadly diseases,
    by the fangs of wild animals

ᵗ**32.9** *Israel:* The Hebrew text has "Jacob," another name for Israel's ancestor.   ᵘ**32.15** *Israel:* The Standard Hebrew Text has "Jeshurun," a rare name for Israel related to a word meaning "honest." The Samaritan Hebrew Text and one ancient translation also use "Jacob," another name for the ancestor of the nation of Israel.   ᵛ**32.15** *Mighty Rock:* See the note at 32.4.   ʷ**32.16,17** *disgusting idols . . . foreign gods . . . demons . . . those useless gods:* Different ways of referring to gods of other nations.   ˣ**32.18** *Mighty Rock:* See the note at 32.4.   ʸ**32.21** *cruel:* One possible meaning for the difficult Hebrew text.

and poisonous snakes.
25 Young and old alike
 will be killed in the streets
 and terrified at home.

26 "I wanted to scatter you,
 so no one would remember
 that you had ever lived.
27 But I dreaded the sound
 of your enemies saying,
 'We defeated Israel with no help
 from the LORD.'"

28 People of Israel,
 that's what the LORD
 has said to you.
 But you don't have good sense,
 and you never listen
 to advice.
29 If you did, you could see
 where you are headed.
30 How could one enemy soldier
 chase a thousand
 of Israel's troops?
 Or how could two of theirs
 pursue ten thousand of ours?
 It can only happen if the LORD
 stops protecting Israel
 and lets the enemy win.
31 Even our enemies know
 that only our God
 is a Mighty Rock.**z**

32 Our enemies are grapevines
 rooted in the fields
 of Sodom and Gomorrah.**a**
 The grapes they produce
 are full of bitter poison;
33 their wine is more deadly
 than cobra venom.
34 But the LORD has written
 a list of their sins

and locked it in his vault.
35 Soon our enemies will get
 what they deserve**b** —
 suddenly they will slip,
 and total disaster
 will quickly follow.

36 When only a few
 of the LORD's people remain,
 when their strength is gone,
 and some of them are slaves,
 the LORD will feel sorry for them
 and give them justice.

37 But first the LORD will say,
 "You ran for safety to other gods—
 couldn't they help you?
38 You offered them wine
 and your best sacrifices.
 Can't those gods help you now
 or give you protection?
39 Don't you understand?
 I am the only God;
 there are no others.
 I am the one who takes life
 and gives it again.
 I punished you with suffering.
 But now I will heal you,
 and nothing can stop me!

40 "I make this solemn promise:
 Just as I live forever,
41 I will take revenge
 on my hateful enemies.
 I will sharpen my sword
 and let it flash
 like lightning.
42 My arrows will get drunk
 on enemy blood;
 my sword will taste the flesh
 and the blood of the enemy.

■ **32.26,27** *I wanted to scatter you:* It is important that other nations not misunderstand Israel's punishment as a lack of God's authority. If Israel is spared, it will be to prove God's power to others, not because the people deserve it.

● **32.38** *offered them wine . . . best sacrifices:* The first part of Israel's wine, grain, and livestock were to be sacrificed as a gift of thanks to the LORD. But some Israelites offered these things to other gods, especially the Canaanite gods that were believed to be responsible for giving rain and making the land fertile for growing good crops.

---

z32.31 *Mighty Rock:* See the note at 32.4.   **a32.32** *Sodom and Gomorrah:* Two cities that the LORD destroyed because their people were so evil (see Genesis 18.16—19.28).   **b32.35** *our enemies . . . deserve:* The Samaritan Hebrew Text and one ancient translation; the Standard Hebrew Text "I will pay them back."

"Don't you understand? I am the only God; there are no others." DEUT 32.39

32.47 *The Law . . . can give you a long life:* The Law of the LORD refers to the commandments and laws given to Moses and the people, and is included in parts of the first five books of the Old Testament. Those who obey the Law are often described as choosing the path of life and blessing (Ps 1.2,3; Prov 4.10-13).

Law

33.2 *Mount Paran:* Mount Paran appears to be the same as Mount Sinai. If not, its location is not known. The Paran Desert (Num 10.13) is often assumed to be on the Sinai peninsula, south of the Negeb and west of the Arabah. **(See Map 2 on pg 1880.)**

33.6 *Reuben:* Reuben lost his right as first-born son to inherit leadership of the family because he had an affair with one of his father's wives (Gen 35.22; 49.4). The tribe is described here as being very small. It disappeared by the tenth century B.C.

It will kill prisoners,
and cut off the heads
    of their leaders."[c]

[43]Tell the heavens to celebrate
and all gods to bow down
    to the LORD,[d]
because he will take revenge
on those hateful enemies
    who killed his people.
He will forgive the sins of Israel
and purify their land.[e]

[44-45]Moses spoke the words of the song so that all the Israelites could hear, and Joshua[f] helped him. When Moses had finished, [46]he said, "Always remember this song I have taught you today. And let it be a warning that you must teach your children to obey everything written in *The Book of God's Law.* [47]The Law isn't empty words. It can give you a long life in the land that you are going to take."

Moses Will See the Land

[48] Later that day the LORD said to Moses: [49]Go up into the Abarim Mountain range here in Moab across the Jordan River valley from Jericho. And when you reach the top of Mount Nebo, you will be able to see the land of Canaan, which I am giving to Israel. [50]Then you will die and be buried on the mountaintop, just as your brother Aaron died and was buried on Mount Hor. [51]Both of you were unfaithful to me at

Meribah Spring near Kadesh in the Zin Desert.[g] I am God, but there in front of the Israelites, you did not treat me with the honor and respect I deserve. [52]So I will give the land to the people of Israel, but you will only get to see it from a distance.

Moses Blesses the Tribes of Israel

33 Moses was a prophet, and before he died, he blessed the tribes of Israel by saying:

[2]The LORD came from Mount Sinai.
From Edom, he gave light
    to his people,
and his glory was shining
    from Mount Paran.
Thousands of his warriors
were with him, and fire
    was at his right hand.[h]
[3]The LORD loves the tribes
of Israel,[i]
    and he protects his people.
They listen to his words
    and worship at his feet.
*[4]I called a meeting
    of the tribes of Israel[j]
    and gave you God's Law.
[5]Then you and your leaders
    made the LORD your king.

[6]Tribe of Reuben, you will live,
even though your tribe
    will always be small.[k]

[c]32.42 *leaders:* Or "long-haired warriors," who let their hair grow to show that they had made sacred promises to their gods. [d]32.43 *Tell . . . LORD:* The Dead Sea Scrolls and one ancient translation; the Standard Hebrew Text "Let the nations, his people, celebrate." [e]32.43 *because he will . . . land:* One possible meaning for the difficult Hebrew text. [f]32.44,45 *Joshua:* The Hebrew text has "Hoshea," another form of Joshua's name. [g]32.51 *Both of you were unfaithful . . . the Zin Desert:* See Numbers 20.1-13. [h]33.2 *Thousands . . . right hand:* One possible meaning for the difficult Hebrew text. [i]33.3 *the tribes of Israel:* Or "the nations." [j]33.4 *Israel:* The Hebrew text also uses the name "Jeshurun," a rare name for "Israel." [k]33.6 *even though . . . small:* One possible meaning for the difficult Hebrew text.

⁷The LORD will listen to you,
  tribe of Judah, as you beg
    to come safely home.
  You fought your enemies alone;[l]
    now the LORD will help you.

⁸At Massah and Meribah Spring,[m]
  the LORD tested you,
    tribe of Levi.
  You were faithful,[n]
  and so the priesthood[o] belongs
    to the Levi tribe.
⁹Protecting Israel's agreement
    with the LORD
  was more important to you
  than the life of your father
    or mother,
  or brothers or sisters,
    or your own children.[p]

¹⁰You teach God's laws to Israel,[q]
  and at the place of worship
    you offer sacrifices
    and burn incense.
¹¹I pray that the LORD will bless
  everything you do,
  and make you strong enough
    to crush your enemies.

¹²The LORD Most High[r] loves you,
    tribe of Benjamin.
  He will live among your hills
    and protect you.

¹³Descendants of Joseph,
  the LORD will bless you
    with precious water
    from deep wells
      and with dew from the sky.
¹⁴Month by month, your fruit
    will ripen in the sunshine.
¹⁵You will have a rich harvest
    from the slopes
      of the ancient hills.
¹⁶The LORD who appeared
    in the burning bush
  wants to give you the best
    the land can produce,
  and it will be a princely crown
    on Joseph's head.

¹⁷The armies of Ephraim
    and Manasseh
  are majestic and fierce
    like a bull or a wild ox.
  They will run their spears
    through faraway nations.

¹⁸Be happy, Zebulun,
    as your boats set sail;
  be happy, Issachar,
    in your tents.
¹⁹The sea will make you wealthy,
  and from the sandy beach
    you will get treasure.[s]
  So invite the other tribes[t]
  to celebrate with you
    and offer sacrifices to God.

²⁰Tribe of Gad,
  the LORD will bless you
    with more land.
  So shout his praises!

33.7 *Judah:* Judah was Jacob and Leah's fourth son. He was a leader among his brothers and was given a special blessing by Jacob (Gen 49.8-12). Moses speaks of the tribe as having trouble with an enemy. Judah did suffer at the hands of the Philistines in the eleventh century B.C.

33.12 *Benjamin:* Benjamin was Jacob's youngest son. His mother was Rachel. The tribe of Benjamin became known as warriors, living up to the name of "fierce wolf" (Gen 49.27).

33.13-17 *Joseph . . . Ephraim and Manasseh:* Joseph was Jacob and Rachel's first son. Joseph's two sons, Ephraim and Manasseh, were adopted by Jacob. Several important leaders in Israel's history came from this tribe, including Joshua (Josh 1.1-11), Samuel (1 Sam 3.19,20; 7.6,9-13,15-17), and Jeroboam (1 Kgs 11.26-40).

33.18 *Zebulun:* Zebulun was Jacob's tenth son and Leah's sixth and final son. See also Gen 49.13.

33.18 *Issachar:* Issachar was Jacob's ninth son and Leah's fifth. See also Gen 49.14,15.

---

[l]**33.7** *beg . . . alone:* One possible meaning for the difficult Hebrew text.   [m]**33.8** *Massah and Meribah Spring:* See Exodus 17.1-7; Numbers 20.1-13.   [n]**33.8** *the LORD tested you, tribe of Levi. You were faithful:* Or "the LORD tested me. I was faithful" or "the LORD tested Aaron and me. We were faithful."   [o]**33.8** *priesthood:* The Hebrew text has "your thummim and your urim," objects that were used by priests to get answers from God.   [p]**33.9** *Protecting Israel's agreement . . . your own children:* See Exodus 32.25-29.   [q]**33.10** *Israel:* See the note at 32.9.   [r]**33.12** *Most High:* One possible meaning for the difficult Hebrew text.   [s]**33.19** *sandy beach . . . treasure:* Possibly a reference to glass made from sand; glass was rare and very valuable.   [t]**33.19** *other tribes:* Or "nations."

● **33.20** *like a lion:* Gad was Jacob's seventh son. His mother was Zilpah, Leah's maid. When Leah could no longer have children, she saw Gad's birth as a sign of good fortune and so named him Gad, which means "fortune or lucky" (Gen 30.11). Gad was the strongest of the tribes and was known for its fine warriors (1 Chr 12.8).

● **33.22** *Dan:* Dan was Jacob's fifth son. His mother was Rachel's maid, Bilhah, who was also the mother of Naphtali (33.23). See also Gen 49.16,17.

● **33.23** *Naphtali:* Naphtali was Jacob's sixth son. His mother was Bilhah, Rachel's maid. His name means "struggle" or "contest," and reflects the struggles between Rachel and Leah (Gen 30.1-8). See also Gen 49.21.

● **33.24** *Asher:* Asher was Jacob's eighth son. His mother was Leah's maid, Zilpah, who was also the mother of Gad (33.20,21). See also Gen 49.20.

● **34.1-3** *Moab . . . Jericho . . . Zoar:* Moses is following God's command (32.48-52). Mount Nebo was probably one peak of the ridge known as Mount Pisgah. Jericho was a Canaanite city just west of the Jordan River and north of the Dead Sea (Josh 5.13—6.25). Zoar was probably located near the southern shore of the Dead Sea. **(See Maps 3 and 4 on pgs 1881 and 1882.)**

Your tribe is like a lion
ripping up its victim.
[21] Your leaders met together
and chose the best land
for your tribe,
but you obeyed the LORD
and helped the other tribes.[u]

[22] Tribe of Dan,
you are like a lion cub,
startled by a snake.[v]

[23] The LORD is pleased with you,
people of Naphtali.
He will bless you
and give you the land
to the west and the south.[w]

[24] The LORD's greatest blessing
is for you, tribe of Asher.
You will be the favorite
of all the other tribes.
You will be rich with olive oil
[25] and have strong town gates
with bronze and iron bolts.
Your people will be powerful
for as long as they live.

[26] Israel,[x] no other god
is like ours—
the clouds are his chariot
as he rides across the skies
to come and help us.
[27] The eternal God
is our hiding place;
he carries us in his arms.
When God tells you

to destroy your enemies,
he will make them run.
[28] Israel, you will live in safety;
your enemies will be gone.[y]
The dew will fall from the sky,
and you will have plenty
of grain and wine.
[29] The LORD has rescued you
and given you more blessings
than any other nation.
He protects you like a shield
and is your majestic sword.
Your enemies will bow in fear,
and you will trample
on their backs.

The Death of Moses

34 Sometime later, Moses left the lowlands of Moab. He went up Mount Pisgah to the peak of Mount Nebo,[z] which is across the Jordan River from Jericho. The LORD showed him all the land as far north as Gilead and the town of Dan. [2] He let Moses see the territories that would soon belong to the tribes of Naphtali, Ephraim, Manasseh, and Judah, as far west as the Mediterranean Sea. [3] The LORD also showed him the land in the south, from the valley near the town of Jericho, known as The City of Palm Trees, down to the town of Zoar.

[4] The LORD said, "Moses, this is the land I was talking about when I solemnly promised Abraham, Isaac, and Jacob that I would give land to their descendants. I have let you see it, but you will not cross the Jordan and go in."

[u]**33.21** *tribes:* One possible meaning for the difficult Hebrew text of verse 21. The Gad tribe asked for some of the land east of the Jordan River, but promised that their warriors would cross the Jordan and help the other tribes take over the land west of the Jordan (see Numbers 32.1-33; Joshua 4.10-13). [v]**33.22** *startled by a snake:* Or "jumping out from the forest of Bashan." [w]**33.23** *land to the west and the south:* Or "land south as far as Lake Galilee." [x]**33.26** *Israel:* See the note at 33.4. [y]**33.28** *your enemies will be gone:* One possible meaning for the difficult Hebrew text. [z]**34.1** *Mount Pisgah . . . Mount Nebo:* Mount Nebo was probably one peak of the ridge known as Mount Pisgah.

[5]And so, Moses the LORD's servant died there in Moab, just as the LORD had said. [6]The LORD buried him in a valley near the town of Beth-Peor, but even today no one knows exactly where. [7]Moses was 120 years old when he died, yet his eyesight was still good, and his body was strong.

[8]The people of Israel stayed in the lowlands of Moab, where they mourned and grieved 30 days for Moses, as was their custom.

Joshua Becomes the Leader of Israel

[9]Before Moses died, he had placed his hands on Joshua, and the LORD had given Joshua wisdom. The Israelites paid attention to what Joshua said and obeyed the commands that the LORD had given Moses.

Moses Was a Great Prophet

[10]There has never again been a prophet in Israel like Moses. The LORD spoke face to face with him [11]and sent him to perform powerful miracles in the presence of the king of Egypt and his entire nation. [12]No one else has ever had the power to do such great things as Moses did for everyone to see.

34.9 *wisdom:* Here wisdom refers to the ability to understand and carry out God's will.

Wisdom

34.10-12 *a prophet . . . power to do such great things:* Moses was a prophet who understood God's will, interpreted it for the people, and carried it out as God's servant. He was also Israel's leader, priest, and judge.

Moses

Reflection Questions About Deuteronomy 1.1—34.12

1. Why did God cause the Israelites to wander in the desert for 40 years (1.26—2.7)?

2. What events does Moses recall to prove to the people that the LORD is the only true God (4.1-8,29-40)?

3. What must the people of Israel do to take the land God promised to give them (4.1,2)?

4. What, if anything, surprises you about the laws or the culture reflected in this section of DEUTERONOMY (4.44—29.1)?

5. What does the LORD God want from his people (6.4-9; 10.12,13)?

6. Idol worship is described as being like a poison in the community (29.18). Explain what this means. What "idols" are worshiped in modern culture? How does worship of idols "poison" our communities?

7. What was the historical situation that Israel understood to be its punishment for disobedience? What is the reward for changing (30.1-10)?

8. The challenge to choose life or disaster is described clearly in the words of Moses. Why did the Israelites have difficulty choosing life? How can you "choose life" (30.15-20)?

9. Why did God not allow Moses to enter Canaan, the promised land (3.23-28; 32.49-52; Num 20.1-13)?

10. How does your new understanding of DEUTERONOMY affect the way you understand other parts of the Bible?

joshua

God keeps promises. Read Joshua *to see how God helped the people enter into and settle the land he had promised to give their ancestor Abraham.*

WHAT MAKES JOSHUA SPECIAL?

Joshua describes how the tribes of Israel conquered and divided the promised land of Canaan. The title of the book comes from its leading character, Joshua, who was chosen to lead Israel after Moses died. But the real hero is the Lord, who helped the people conquer the land. By doing so, the Lord kept the promise that was part of the agreements made with Israel's ancestors.

Joshua is part of the great story, Deuteronomy through 2 Kings, which tells of Israel's life as God's special people in the promised land. A key theme in this work is that the land is a gift from the Lord, and remaining loyal to the Lord and the Lord's Law are the conditions for keeping the land. Joshua records events that took place around 1250 to 1225 B.C. It reports the swift and sometimes miraculous capture of many cities and towns in Canaan. With Joshua in command, the united tribes of Israel crossed the Jordan River and cut through the center of the land, eventually taking over the lands to the south and to the north.

WHAT'S THE STORY BEHIND THE SCENE?

Archaeologists have discovered evidence that parts of Canaan were attacked in the period between 1300 and 1200 B.C. While some key places were destroyed or captured under Joshua, not all the places where Canaanites lived were taken over by the people of Israel. It was not until the time of King David (around 1000 B.C.) that the tribes of Israel were united in one kingdom and were solidly in place in the land of Canaan. Even then, Canaanite culture and religion continued to influence the people of Israel for many more centuries. According to the biblical authors, it was the worship of Canaanite idols that led, in part, to the fall of the northern kingdom (Israel) in 722 B.C. and to the fall of the southern kingdom (Judah) in 586 B.C.

HOW IS JOSHUA CONSTRUCTED?

The book of Joshua has two main parts. The first half (1–12) is a series of stories about the capture of key cities and towns in Canaan. It includes many stories that explain the origin of a landmark in Israel. The second half (13–22) consists of tribal boundaries and city lists. The twelve tribes each got a share of the land, while the Levites were given special cities scattered throughout Israel. The concluding chapters of the book (23, 24) report Joshua's farewell and death as well as the important gathering at Shechem where the people of Israel promised to obey the Lord God, now that they had settled in the promised land.

The book may be outlined in the following way:

Conquest of western Canaan (1.1—12.24)
    Entering the promised land (1.1—5.12)
    The Lord leads Israel in battle (5.13—12.24)
Division of the promised land (13.1—22.34)
The last days of Joshua (23.1—24.33)
    Joshua's farewell address (23.1-16)
    The ceremony at Shechem and three burials (24.1-33)

This book is named after Joshua, who was chosen by God to lead the Israelites after the death of Moses. The book describes how the Israelites conquered Canaan under Joshua's leadership and divided the land among the twelve tribes of Israel. The book emphasizes that the land promised to their ancestor Abraham, and now to them, is a gift from the Lord. When the Israelites are united in their obedience to the Lord, they are able to conquer the Canaanite cities, even those that are protected by thick walls like Jericho. Even before Canaan is completely under Israel's control, the Lord tells Joshua to divide the land west of the Jordan River among each of the twelve tribes. The book ends with Joshua's farewell speech. In it, the elderly Joshua urges the people to remain faithful to the Lord. Then, at an important meeting at Shechem, Joshua urges the people to renew their agreement to worship only the Lord and no other gods.

Outline

Joshua Becomes
the Leader of Israel

1 Moses, the LORD's servant, was dead. So the LORD spoke to Joshua son of Nun, who had been the assistant of Moses. The LORD said:

²My servant Moses is dead. Now you must lead Israel across the Jordan River into the land I'm giving to all of you. ³Wherever you go, I'll give you that land, as I promised Moses. ⁴It will reach from the Southern Desert to the Lebanon Mountains in the north, and to the northeast as far as the great Euphrates River. It will include the land of the Hittites,[a] and the land from here at the Jordan River to the Mediterranean Sea on the west. ⁵Joshua, I will always be with you and help you as I helped Moses, and no one will ever be able to defeat you.

⁶⁻⁸Long ago I promised the ancestors of Israel that I would give this land to their descendants. So be strong and brave! Be careful to do everything my servant Moses taught you. Never stop reading *The Book of the Law*[b] he gave you. Day and night you must think about what it says. If you obey it completely, you and Israel will be able to take this land.

⁹I've commanded you to be strong and brave. Don't ever be afraid or discouraged! I am the LORD your God, and I will be there to help you wherever you go.

The Eastern Tribes
Promise To Help

¹⁰Joshua ordered the tribal leaders ¹¹to go through the camp and tell everyone:

In a few days we will cross the Jordan River to take the land that the LORD our God is giving us. So prepare as

---

[a]**1.4** *the land . . . Hittites*: This refers to the northern part of Syria, which had been the southernmost part of the Hittite Empire. [b]**1.6-8** *the Law*: Or "Teachings."

● **1.1** *Moses . . . Joshua:* Moses, the great leader who had brought the Hebrews out of Egypt and through the wilderness wanderings of 40 years, was dead. Joshua was chosen to take his place (Deut 34.1-10). Since his youth, Joshua had been Moses' assistant or lieutenant (Exod 24.13; 33.9-11; Num 11.28). Before Moses died, he placed his hands on Joshua to show that he would take Moses' place as the leader of the twelve tribes of Israel (Num 27.12-23; Deut 31.1-8). Here in Joshua 1.2-9 the LORD orders Joshua to lead Israel into Canaan and promises to be with Joshua and the people wherever they go.

○૪ Moses

● **1.2-4** *Jordan River . . . to the Mediterranean Sea:* The land promised to Moses (Exod 3.8) and described here covered more than the land of Canaan. It included the entire area between the Jordan River to the Mediterranean Sea. Its southern boundary was the Southern Desert, also known as the Negev. It stretched north to the Lebanon Mountains and included parts of Syria.

■ **1.6-8** *Long ago I promised . . . If you obey:* The promise of a land the people could call their own was first given to Abraham (Gen 17.7,8). But obeying God's Law became a condition both for taking the land and remaining in the land. "The Book of the Law," here probably refers to the core of what is now DEUTERONOMY (most likely Deut 12–26).

"I've commanded you to be strong and brave. Don't ever be afraid or discouraged! I am the LORD your God, and I will be there to help you wherever you go." JOSH 1.9

1.12 *tribes of Reuben, Gad, and East Manasseh:* A tribe is a large group of people descended from a common ancestor. The twelve tribes are named for the twelve sons of Jacob, who was renamed Israel.

1.13-15 *help them . . . then you can come back:* Even though the land they would settle was already secure, the men of the eastern tribes were ordered to lead the attack on Canaan. After Israel conquered the lands west of the Jordan River, these tribes could return to their territories on the eastern side of the Jordan. (See Map 3 on pg 1881.)

Palestine

2.1 *Rahab:* Possibly an innkeeper, Rahab is identified here as a prostitute. She and her family would later become part of the Hebrew people (6.21-25).

2.2 *king of Jericho:* The "king" was probably the chief ruler of the town. Canaan's cities were not united under one government; each village had its own leader. At the time Israel invaded Canaan (about 1250 B.C.), Jericho was only six acres in area. The king knew Rahab's house would be a likely place to find the spies.

2.3-7 *town gate:* Many towns and cities had walls with heavy gates that were closed at night for protection. The area just inside the town gate was an important meeting place during the day.

much food as you'll need for the march into the land.

[12]Joshua told the men of the tribes of Reuben, Gad, and East Manasseh:[c]

[13-14]The LORD's servant Moses said that the LORD our God has given you land here on the east side of the Jordan River, where you could live in peace. Your wives and children and your animals can stay here in the land Moses gave you. But all of you that can serve in our army must pick up your weapons and lead the men of the other tribes across the Jordan River. They are your relatives, so you must help them [15]conquer the land that the LORD is giving them. The LORD will give peace to them as he has given peace to you, and then you can come back and settle here in the land that Moses promised you. [16]The men answered:

We'll cross the Jordan River and help our relatives. We'll fight anywhere you send us. [17-18]If the LORD our God will help you as he helped Moses, and if you are strong and brave, we will obey you as we obeyed Moses. We'll even put to death anyone who rebels against you or refuses to obey you.

Rahab Helps the Israelite Spies

2 Joshua chose two men as spies and sent them from their camp at Acacia with these instructions: "Go across the river and find out as much as you can about the whole region, especially about the town of Jericho."

The two spies left the Israelite camp at Acacia and went to Jericho, where they decided to spend the night at the house of a prostitute[d] named Rahab.

[2]But someone found out about them and told the king of Jericho, "Some Israelite men came here tonight, and they are spies." [3-7]So the king sent soldiers to Rahab's house to arrest the spies.

Meanwhile, Rahab had taken the men up to the flat roof of her house and had hidden them under some piles of flax plants[e] that she had put there to dry.

The soldiers came to her door and demanded, "Let us have the men who are staying at your house. They are spies."

She answered, "Some men did come to my house, but I didn't know where they had come from. They left about sunset, just before it was time to close the town gate.[f] I don't know where they were going, but if you hurry, maybe you can catch them."

The guards at the town gate let the soldiers leave Jericho, but they closed the gate again as soon as the soldiers went through. Then the soldiers headed toward the Jordan River to look for the spies at the place where people cross the river.

[8]Rahab went back up to her roof. The spies were still awake, so she told them:

[9]I know that the LORD has given Israel this land. Everyone shakes with fear because of you. [10]We heard how the LORD dried up the Red Sea[g] so you

[c]1.12 *East Manasseh:* The half of Manasseh that settled east of the Jordan River. [d]2.1 *prostitute:* Rahab was possibly an innkeeper. [e]2.3-7 *flax plants:* The stalks of flax plants were harvested, soaked in water, and dried, then their fibers were separated and spun into thread, which was woven into linen cloth. [f]2.3-7 *gate:* Many towns and cities had walls with heavy gates that were closed at night for protection. [g]2.10 *Red Sea:* Hebrew *yam suph*, "Sea of Reeds," one of the marshes or fresh water lakes near the eastern part of the Nile Delta. This identification is based on Exodus 13.17—14.9, which lists the towns on the route of the Israelites before crossing the sea. In the Greek translation of the Scriptures made about 200 B.C., the "Sea of Reeds" was named "Red Sea."

could leave Egypt. And we heard how you destroyed Sihon and Og, those two Amorite kings east of the Jordan River. [11]We know that the LORD your God rules heaven and earth, and we've lost our courage and our will to fight.

[12]Please promise me in the LORD's name that you will be as kind to my family as I have been to you. Do something to show [13]that you won't let your people kill my father and mother and my brothers and sisters and their families.

[14]"Rahab," the spies answered, "if you keep quiet about what we're doing, we promise to be kind to you when the LORD gives us this land. We pray that the LORD will kill us if we don't keep our promise!"[h]

[15]Rahab's house was built into the town wall,[i] and one of the windows in her house faced outside the wall. She gave the spies a rope, showed them the window, and said, "Use this rope to let yourselves down to the ground outside the wall. [16]Then hide in the hills. The men who are looking for you won't be able to find you there. They'll give up and come back after a few days, and you can be on your way."

[17-20]The spies said:

You made us promise to let you and your family live. We will keep our promise, but you can't tell anyone why we were here. You must tie this red rope on your window when we attack, and your father and mother, your brothers, and everyone else in your family must be here with you. We'll take the blame if anyone who stays in this house gets hurt. But anyone who leaves your house will be killed, and it won't be our fault.

[21]"I'll do exactly what you said," Rahab promised. Then she sent them on their way and tied the red rope to the window.

[22]The spies hid in the hills for three days while the king's soldiers looked for them along the roads. As soon as the soldiers gave up and returned to Jericho, [23]the two spies went down into the Jordan valley and crossed the river. They reported to Joshua and told him everything that had happened. [24]"We're sure the LORD has given us the whole country," they said. "The people there shake with fear every time they think of us."

Israel Crosses the Jordan River

3 Early the next morning, Joshua and the Israelites packed up and left Acacia. They went to the Jordan River and camped there that night. [2]Two days later[j] their leaders went through the camp, [3-4]shouting, "When you see some of the priests[k] carrying the sacred chest, you'll know it is time to cross to the other side. You've never been there before, and you won't know the way, unless you follow the chest. But don't get too close! Stay about half a mile back."

[5]Joshua told the people, "Make yourselves acceptable[l] to worship the LORD,

---

2.24 *We're sure the LORD has given us the whole country:* The Israelite spies express their confidence and show that they accept what God wants to do for the Israelite people. Their confidence, most likely, was reinforced by Rahab's words. Although she was a Canaanite, she knew the LORD was going to give the land to the Israelites.

3.3-4 *priests carrying the sacred chest:* The sacred chest was considered the place where God was present with the people of Israel. The priests who came from the Levite clan of Kohath had earlier been assigned the task of carrying the sacred chest (Num 4.1-6).

The Sacred Chest

3.5 *Make yourselves acceptable:* The people's crossing of the Jordan River into the promised land of Canaan includes the parts of a religious ceremony—a rite of purification (3.5), a procession (3.6), a sermon (3.9-13), and setting up a memorial (4.9).

---

[h]**2.14** *We pray . . . promise:* Or "If you save our lives, we will save yours!" [i]**2.15** *wall:* In ancient times, cities and larger towns had high walls around them to protect them against attack. Sometimes houses were built against the wall so that the city wall formed one wall of the house. This added strength to the city wall. [j]**3.2** *Two days later:* The Hebrew text has "At the end of three days," two days after they had set up camp. [k]**3.3,4** *the priests:* The Hebrew text has "the priests, the Levites"; priests belonged to the tribe of Levi. [l]**3.5** *Make yourselves acceptable:* People had to do certain things to make themselves acceptable to worship the LORD (see Leviticus 7.20,21; 15.2,33; 22.4-8; Deuteronomy 23.10,11).

3.10 *Canaanites . . . Jebusites:* This was a common list of the peoples living in Palestine at the time of the conquest. The Canaanites were said to be descendants of Noah's son Ham. The Hittites were a dominant force in Canaan from the time of Abraham to around 1300 B.C. The exact identity of the Hivites, Girgashites, and Perizzites is not certain. The Amorites lived in the hill country of Canaan at the time the Israelites invaded. The Jebusites controlled the area around Jerusalem until Israel's King David took over that city.

4.2-3 *set up those rocks:* Two descriptions of the monument stones are given here, perhaps indicating two different sets of stones. One monument was set up at the Gilgal camp (4.1-3, 19,20), while the other was placed in the bed of the Jordan River (4.9).

4.6-7 *Someday your children will ask:* As in Exodus 13.14 and Deuteronomy 6.20, the concern is for future generations to know and remember the ways that the LORD has acted on behalf of the people.

because he is going to do some amazing things for us."

⁶Then Joshua turned to the priests and said, "Take the chest and cross the Jordan River ahead of us." So the priests picked up the chest by its carrying poles and went on ahead.

⁷The LORD told Joshua, "Beginning today I will show the people that you are their leader, and they will know that I am helping you as I helped Moses. ⁸Now, tell the priests who are carrying the chest to go a little way into the river and stand there."

⁹Joshua spoke to the people:

Come here and listen to what the LORD our God said he will do! ¹⁰The Canaanites, the Hittites, the Hivites, the Perizzites, the Girgashites, the Amorites, and the Jebusites control the land on the other side of the river. But the living God will be with you and will force them out of the land when you attack. And now, God is going to prove that he's powerful enough to force them out. ¹¹⁻¹³Just watch the sacred chest that belongs to the LORD, the ruler of the whole earth. As soon as the priests carrying the chest step into the Jordan, the water will stop flowing and pile up as if someone had built a dam across the river.

The LORD has also said that each of the twelve tribes should choose one man to represent it.

¹⁴The Israelites packed up and left camp. The priests carrying the chest walked in front, ¹⁵until they came to the Jordan River. The water in the river had risen over its banks, as it often does in springtime.ᵐ But as soon as the feet of the priests touched the water, ¹⁶⁻¹⁷the river stopped

flowing, and the water started piling up at the town of Adam near Zarethan. No water flowed toward the Dead Sea, and the priests stood in the middle of the dry riverbed near Jericho while everyone else crossed over.

The People Set Up a Monument

4 After Israel had crossed the Jordan, the LORD said to Joshua:

²⁻³Tellⁿ one man from each of the twelve tribes to pick up a large rock from where the priests are standing. Then tell the men to set up those rocks as a monument at the place where you camp tonight.

⁴Joshua chose twelve men; then he called them together ⁵and said:

Go to the middle of the riverbed where the sacred chest is, and pick up a large rock. Carry it on your shoulder to our camp. There are twelve of you, so there will be one rock for each tribe. ⁶⁻⁷Someday your children will ask, "Why are these rocks here?" Then you can tell them how the water stopped flowing when the chest was being carried across the river. These rocks will always remind our people of what happened here today.

⁸The men followed the instructions that the LORD had given Joshua. They picked up twelve rocks, one for each tribe, and carried them to the camp, where they put them down.

⁹Joshua set up a monument next to the place where the priests were standing. This monument was also made of twelve large rocks, and it is still there in the middle of the river.

ᵐ3.15 *springtime:* Or "harvest time"; the grain harvest was in late spring.   ⁿ4.1-3 *Joshua . . . Tell:* Or "Joshua, you and the other leaders must tell."

The People of Israel Set Up Camp at Gilgal

10-13 The army got ready for battle and crossed the Jordan with everyone else. They marched quickly past the sacred chest[o] and into the desert near Jericho. Forty thousand soldiers from the tribes of Reuben, Gad, and East Manasseh[p] led the way, as Moses had ordered.[q]

The priests stayed right where they were until the people had followed the orders that the LORD had given Moses and Joshua. Then they watched as the priests carried the chest the rest of the way across.

14-18"Joshua," the LORD said, "tell the priests to come up from the Jordan and bring the chest with them." So Joshua went over to the priests and told them what the LORD had said. And as soon as the priests carried the chest past the highest place that the floodwaters of the Jordan had reached, the river flooded its banks again.

That's how the LORD showed the Israelites that Joshua was their leader.[r] For the rest of Joshua's life, they respected him as they had respected Moses.

19It was the tenth day of the first month[s] of the year when Israel crossed the Jordan River. They set up camp at Gilgal, which was east of the land controlled by Jericho. **20**The men who had carried the twelve rocks from the Jordan brought them to Joshua, and they made them into a monument. **21**Then Joshua told the people:

Years from now your children will ask you why these rocks are here. **22-23**Tell them, "The LORD our God dried up the Jordan River so we could walk across. He did the same thing here for us that he did for our people at the Red Sea,[t] **24**because he wants everyone on earth to know how powerful he is. And he wants us to worship only him."

5 The Amorite kings west of the Jordan River and the Canaanite kings along the Mediterranean Sea lost their courage and their will to fight, when they heard how the LORD had dried up the Jordan River to let Israel go across.

Israel Gets Ready To Celebrate Passover

2While Israel was camped at Gilgal, the LORD said, "Joshua, make some flint knives[u] and circumcise the rest of the Israelite men and boys."[v]

3Joshua made the knives, then circumcised those men and boys at Haaraloth Hill.[w] **4-7**This had to be done, because none of Israel's baby boys had been circumcised during the 40 years that Israel had wandered through the desert after leaving Egypt.

And why had they wandered for 40 years?

---

[o]**4.10-13** *the sacred chest:* The Hebrew text has "the LORD." The army was marching past the sacred chest, which was a symbol of God's throne on earth (see 1 Samuel 4.4 and Exodus 25.10-22; 37.1-9).
[p]**4.10-13** *Forty thousand soldiers from the tribes of Reuben, Gad, and East Manasseh:* Or "There were forty thousand soldiers altogether, and those from the tribes of Reuben, Gad, and East Manasseh."
[q]**4.10-13** *Moses . . . ordered:* See Numbers 32.16-32; Joshua 1.12-16. [r]**4.14-18** *leader:* See 3.7. [s]**4.19** *first month:* Abib (also called Nisan), the first month of the Hebrew calendar, from about mid-March to mid-April. [t]**4.22,23** *Red Sea:* See the note at 2.10. [u]**5.2** *flint knives:* Flint is a stone that can be chipped until it forms a very sharp edge. [v]**5.2** *circumcise . . . men and boys:* They could not celebrate Passover unless they were circumcised (see Exodus 12.43-49). [w]**5.3** *Haaraloth Hill:* Or "Foreskin Hill."

4.14-18 *the LORD showed the Israelites:* Joshua's role as leader is demonstrated by this crossing, as promised by the LORD in 1.5,17,18; 3.7. When Moses died his leadership was honored, but many stories in EXODUS and NUMBERS show how the Israelites had questioned Moses' leadership.

Moses

4.19 *first month:* The first month of the Hebrew calendar, Abib (also called Nisan), is from mid-March to mid-April. (See the chart Pilgrimage Festivals on pg 1799.)

4.19 *Gilgal:* Located near Jericho, Gilgal was an important worship site before Jerusalem was established as the only proper place for Israelites to make sacrifices.

5.1 *Amorite . . . Canaanite:* These terms are used loosely to describe the groups of people who lived in Palestine. Each Canaanite city had its own king.

5.2 *flint knives . . . circumcise:* Flint is a stone that can be chipped until it forms a very sharp edge. Bronze tools had replaced stone by this time, but the ancient stone tools were required for this circumcision ritual.

Circumcision

"The LORD our God dried up the Jordan River so we could walk across. He did the same thing here for us that he did for our people at the Red Sea." JOSH 4.22-23

5.10 *Passover:* Passover was celebrated as a remembrance of how God acted to save the Israelite people from slavery in Egypt.

Passover and the Festival of Thin Bread

5.11-12 *manna . . . roasted grain . . . thin bread:* These verses mark the end of one era and the beginning of another. Manna was the special food that God provided for the Israelites while they were in the desert. Now that they were beginning a settled life in Canaan, they could grow the grains that would be an important part of their diet. Israelites were supposed to eat bread made without yeast (thin bread) for the week following Passover during the Festival of Thin Bread.

5.15 *Take off your sandals:* This was done to show respect for God, just as Moses had done when he encountered God on Mount Sinai. The account appears to be incomplete, as no instructions are given; perhaps the story is continued in 6.2-5.

6.4 *march slowly around the town:* Jericho was located at the crossroads of several important trade routes in the Jordan River valley. Though it was a center for trade and business, Jericho was small by modern standards, only six acres in size. So, the Israelites are able to march around it slowly seven times in one day. (See the chart Numbers in the Bible on pg 1844.)

It was because right after they left Egypt, the men in the army had disobeyed the LORD. And the LORD had said, "None of you men will ever live to see the land that I promised Israel. It is a land rich with milk and honey, and someday your children will live there, but not before you die here in the desert."

⁸Everyone who had been circumcised needed time to heal, and they stayed in camp.

⁹The LORD told Joshua, "It was a disgrace for my people to be slaves in Egypt, but now I have taken away that disgrace." So the Israelites named the place Gilgal,ˣ and it still has that name.

¹⁰Israel continued to camp at Gilgal in the desert near Jericho, and on the fourteenth day of the same month,ʸ they celebrated Passover.

¹¹⁻¹²The next day, God stopped sending the Israelites mannaᶻ to eat each morning, and they started eating food grown in the land of Canaan. They ate roasted grainᵃ and thin breadᵇ made of the barley they had gathered from nearby fields.

Israel Captures Jericho

¹³One day, Joshua was near Jericho when he saw a man standing some distance in front of him. The man was holding a sword, so Joshua walked up to him and asked, "Are you on our side or on our enemies' side?"

¹⁴"Neither," he answered. "I am here because I am the commander of the LORD's army."

Joshua fell to his knees and bowed down to the ground. "I am your servant," he said. "Tell me what to do."

¹⁵"Take off your sandals," the commander answered. "This is a holy place."

So Joshua took off his sandals.

6 Meanwhile, the people of Jericho had been locking the gates in their town wall because they were afraid of the Israelites. No one could go out or come in.

²⁻³The LORD said to Joshua:

With my help, you and your army will defeat the king of Jericho and his army, and you will capture the town. Here is how to do it: March slowly around Jericho once a day for six days. ⁴Take along the sacred chest and tell seven priests to walk in front of it, carrying trumpets.ᶜ

But on the seventh day, march slowly around the town seven times while the priests blow their trumpets. ⁵Then the priests will blast on their trumpets, and everyone else will shout. The wall will fall down, and your soldiers can go straight in from every side.

⁶Joshua called the priests together and said, "Take the chest and tell seven priests to carry trumpets and march ahead of it."

⁷⁻¹⁰Next, he gave the army their orders: "March slowly around Jericho. A few of you will go ahead of the chest to guard it, but most of you will follow it. Don't shout

ˣ**5.9** *Gilgal:* In Hebrew "Gilgal" sounds like "take away." ʸ**5.10** *the same month:* See the note at 4.19. ᶻ**5.11,12** *manna:* The special food that God provided for the Israelites while they were in the desert for 40 years. It was about the size of a small seed, and it appeared on the ground during the night, except on the Sabbath. It was gathered early in the morning, ground up, and then baked or boiled (see Exodus 16.13-36; Numbers 11.4-9). ᵃ**5.11,12** *roasted grain:* Roasted grain was made by cooking the grain in a dry pan or on a flat rock, or by holding a bunch of grain stalks over a fire. ᵇ**5.11,12** *thin bread:* Bread made without yeast. Israelites were not supposed to eat bread made with yeast for the week following Passover. That week is called the Festival of Thin Bread (see Exodus 12.14-20; 13.3-7). ᶜ**6.4** *trumpets:* These were hollowed-out ram's horns.

Joshua told the army, "Don't shout the battle cry or yell or even talk until the day I tell you to. Then let out a shout!"

the battle cry or yell or even talk until the day I tell you to. Then let out a shout!"

As soon as Joshua finished giving the orders, the army started marching. One group of soldiers led the way, with seven priests marching behind them and blowing trumpets. Then came the priests carrying the chest, followed by the rest of the soldiers. [11]They obeyed Joshua's orders and carried the chest once around the town before returning to camp for the night.

[12-14]Early the next morning, Joshua and everyone else started marching around Jericho in the same order as the day before. One group of soldiers was in front, followed by the seven priests with trumpets and the priests who carried the chest. The rest of the army came next. The seven priests blew their trumpets while everyone marched slowly around Jericho and back to camp. They did this once a day for six days.

[15]On the seventh day, the army got up at daybreak. They marched slowly around Jericho the same as they had done for the past six days, except on this day they went around seven times. [16]Then the priests blew the trumpets, and Joshua yelled:

Get ready to shout! The LORD will let you capture this town. [17]But you must destroy it and everything in it, to show that it now belongs to the LORD.[d] The woman Rahab helped the spies we sent,[e] so protect her and the others who are inside her house. But kill everyone else in the town. [18-19]The silver and gold and everything made of bronze and iron belong to the LORD and must be put in his treasury. Be careful to follow these instructions, because if you see something you want and take it, the LORD will destroy Israel. And it will be all your fault.[f]

[20]The priests blew their trumpets again, and the soldiers shouted as loud as they could. The walls of Jericho fell flat. Then the soldiers rushed up the hill, went straight into the town, and captured it. [21-25]They killed everyone, men and women, young and old, everyone except Rahab and the others in her house. They even killed every cow, sheep, and donkey.

Joshua said to the two men who had been spies, "Rahab kept you safe when I sent you to Jericho. We promised to protect her and her family, and we will keep that promise. Now go into her house and bring them out."

The two men went into Rahab's house and brought her out, along with her father and mother, her brothers, and her other relatives. Rahab and her family had to stay in a place just outside the Israelite army camp.[g] But later they were allowed to live among the Israelites, and her descendants still do.

The Israelites took the silver and gold and the things made of bronze and iron and put them with the rest of the treasure that was kept at the LORD's house.[h] Finally, they set fire to Jericho and everything in it.

[26]After Jericho was destroyed, Joshua warned the people, "Someday a man will rebuild Jericho, but the LORD will put a

● 6.12-15 *marching around Jericho ... On the seventh day:* The effect of this strategy was to make the enemy afraid while giving the troops exercise and keeping their morale high. The way Israel marched around Jericho is more like a religious ritual than a true battle plan. On the seventh day the priests and troops marched around Jericho seven times. Preparation for the battle was perfectly complete.

❧ Holy War (The LORD's Battles)

● 6.18-19 *bronze:* This metal was made by melting and mixing copper and tin. Because it was harder than copper, bronze could be used to make weapons. Because it was shiny when polished, it was also used to make decorative items.

❧ Purity (Clean and Unclean)

❧ The Sacred Tent

[d]**6.17** *destroy . . . now belongs to the LORD:* Destroying a city and everything in it, including its people and animals, showed that it belonged to the LORD and could no longer be used by humans. [e]**6.17** *sent:* See 2.1,21. [f]**6.18,19** *Be careful . . . fault:* One ancient translation; Hebrew "Don't keep any of it for yourself. If you do, the LORD will destroy both you and Israel." [g]**6.21-25** *camp:* Rahab and her family were Canaanites and were considered unclean. If they stayed in the Israelite army camp, the LORD would not help the Israelite army in battle (see Deuteronomy 23.9-14). However, Rahab and her family later became part of Israel. [h]**6.21-25** *the LORD's house:* A name for the place of worship, which at that time was the sacred tent.

what will happen to anyone who re-builds Jericho. This is exactly what hap-pened to Hiel of Bethel many years later (1 Kgs 16.34).

7.2 *town of Ai:* The site was eleven miles north of Jerusalem and two miles east of Bethel. Ai was an unwalled vil-lage at that time. (See Map 3 on pg 1881.)

curse on him, and the man's oldest son will die when he starts to build the town wall. And by the time he finishes the wall and puts gates in it, all his children will be dead."[i]

[27]The LORD helped Joshua in everything he did, and Joshua was famous everywhere in Canaan.

Achan Is Punished for Stealing from the LORD

7 The LORD had said that everything in Jericho belonged to him.[j] But Achan[k] from the Judah tribe took some of the things from Jericho for himself. And so the LORD was angry with the Israelites, because one of them had disobeyed him.[l]

[2]While Israel was still camped near Jeri-cho, Joshua sent some spies with these in-structions: "Go to the town of Ai[m] and find out whatever you can about the re-gion around the town."

The spies left and went to Ai, which is east of Bethel and near Beth-Aven. [3]They went back to Joshua and reported, "You don't need to send the whole army to attack Ai—2,000 or 3,000 troops will be enough. Why bother the whole army for a town that small?"

[4-5]Joshua sent about 3,000 soldiers to at-tack Ai. But the men of Ai fought back and chased the Israelite soldiers away from the town gate and down the hill to the stone quarries.[n] Thirty-six Israelite soldiers were killed, and the Israelite army felt discour-aged.

[6]Joshua and the leaders of Israel tore their clothes and put dirt on their heads to show their sorrow. They lay facedown on the ground in front of the sacred chest un-til sunset. [7]Then Joshua said:

Our LORD, did you bring us across the Jordan River just so the Amorites could destroy us? This wouldn't have happened if we had agreed to stay on the other side of the Jordan. [8]I don't even know what to say to you, since Is-rael's army has turned and run from the enemy. [9]Everyone will think you weren't strong enough to protect your people. Now the Canaanites and everyone else who lives in the land will surround us and wipe us out.

[10]The LORD answered:

Stop lying there on the ground! Get up! [11]I said everything in Jericho be-longed to me and had to be destroyed. But the Israelites have kept some of the things for themselves. They stole from me and hid what they took. Then they lied about it. [12]What they stole was supposed to be destroyed, and now Israel itself must be destroyed. I cannot help you anymore until you do exactly what I have said. That's why Is-rael turns and runs from its enemies instead of standing up to them.

[13]Tell the people of Israel, "Tomor-row you will meet with the LORD your God, so make yourselves acceptable to worship him. The LORD says that you have taken things that should have been destroyed. You won't be able to stand up to your enemies until you get rid of those things.

[14]"Tomorrow morning everyone must gather near the place of worship.

[i]6.26 *by the time . . . dead:* Or "when he puts gates into the town wall, his youngest son will die." [j]7.1 *belonged to him:* See the note at 6.17. [k]7.1 *Achan:* The Hebrew text has "Achan, son of Carmi, grandson of Abdi, and great-grandson of Zerah." [l]7.1 *the LORD was angry . . . disobeyed him:* Even though only one person had disobeyed, it meant that the LORD's instructions to the people of Israel had not been followed, and the whole nation was held responsible. [m]7.2 *of Ai:* Or "called The Ruins." [n]7.4,5 *stone quarries:* Or "Shebarim."

"The LORD says that you have taken things that should have been destroyed. You won't be able to stand up to your enemies until you get rid of those things." JOSH 7.13

You will come forward tribe by tribe, and the LORD will show which tribe is guilty. Next, the clans in that tribe must come forward, and the LORD will show which clan is guilty. The families in that clan must come, and the LORD will point out the guilty family. Finally, the men in that family must come, [15]and the LORD will show who stole what should have been destroyed. That man must be put to death, his body burned, and his possessions thrown into the fire. He has done a terrible thing by breaking the sacred agreement that the LORD made with Israel."

[16]Joshua got up early the next morning and brought each tribe to the place of worship, where the LORD showed that the Judah tribe was guilty. [17]Then Joshua brought the clans of Judah to the LORD, and the LORD showed that the Zerah clan was guilty. One by one he brought the leader of each family in the Zerah clan to the LORD, and the LORD showed that Zabdi's family was guilty. [18]Finally, Joshua brought each man in Zabdi's family to the LORD, and the LORD showed that Achan was the guilty one.

[19]"Achan," Joshua said, "the LORD God of Israel has decided that you are guilty. So tell me what you did, and don't try to hide anything."

[20]"It's true," Achan answered. "I sinned and disobeyed the LORD God of Israel. [21-22]While we were in Jericho, I saw a beautiful Babylonian robe, 200 pieces of silver, and a gold bar that weighed the same as 50 pieces of gold. I wanted them for myself, so I took them. I dug a hole under my tent and hid the silver, the gold, and the robe."

Joshua told some people to run to Achan's tent, where they found the silver, the gold, and the robe. [23]They brought them back and put them in front of the sacred chest, so Joshua and the rest of the Israelites could see them. [24]Then everyone took Achan and the things he had stolen to Trouble Valley.° They also took along his sons and daughters, his cattle, donkeys, and sheep, his tent, and everything else that belonged to him.

[25]Joshua said, "Achan, you caused us a lot of trouble. Now the LORD is paying you back with the same kind of trouble."

The people of Israel then stoned to death Achan and his family. They made a fire and burned the bodies, together with what Achan had stolen, and all his possessions. [26]They covered the remains with a big pile of rocks, which is still there. Then the LORD stopped being angry with Israel.

That's how the place came to be called Trouble Valley.

Israel Destroys the Town of Ai

8 [1-2]The LORD told Joshua:

Don't be afraid, and don't be discouraged by what happened at the town of Ai. Take the army and attack again. But first, order part of the army to set up an ambush on the other side of the town. I will help you defeat the king of Ai and his army, and you will capture the town and the land around it. Destroy Ai and kill its king as you did at Jericho. But you may keep the livestock and everything else you want.

[3-4]Joshua quickly got the army ready to attack Ai. He chose 30,000 of his best soldiers and gave them these orders:

Tonight, while it is dark, march to Ai and take up a position behind the town. Get as close to the town as you can without being seen, and be ready to attack.

° 7.24 *Trouble Valley*: Or "Achor Valley."

8.5-6 *we'll run away:* The plan calls for a force under Joshua to act as decoys, drawing the enemy army out of the city. This force is positioned to the north of Ai, while the ambush force is west of the town.

8.9 *Bethel:* Bethel was located eleven miles north of Jerusalem and two miles west of Ai. It was an important town in Israel's history. **(See Map 3 on pg 1881.)**

8.16-17 *Not one man was left:* The decoy attack works. The northern war party draws the troops out of the city, the western ambush easily captures the city, and the men of Ai are caught between the two forces.

8.28-29 *every building in Ai was burned . . . rocks are still there:* As with Jericho (6.17), nothing is to remain of Canaanite, pagan influences. The people of Israel are to be holy, set apart from that culture. The dead king's body is to be taken down as commanded in Deuteronomy 21.22,23. The Israelites set up memorial stones here as they had previously next to the Jordan River (4.9) and in Trouble Valley (7.26). They could still be seen at the time JOSHUA was written.

⁵⁻⁶The rest of the army will come with me and attack near the gate. When the people of Ai come out to fight, we'll run away and let them chase us. They will think we are running from them just like the first time. But when we've let them chase us far enough away, ⁷you come out of hiding. The LORD our God will help you capture the town. ⁸Then set it on fire, as the LORD has told us to do. Those are your orders, ⁹now go!

The 30,000 soldiers went to a place on the west side of Ai, between Ai and Bethel, where they could hide and wait to attack.

That night, Joshua stayed in camp with the rest of the army. ¹⁰Early the next morning he got his troops ready to move out, and he and the other leaders of Israel led them to Ai. ¹¹They set up camp in full view of the town, across the valley to the north. ¹²Joshua had already sent 5,000 soldiers to the west side of the town to hide and wait to attack. ¹³Now all his troops were in place. Part of the army was in the camp to the north of Ai, and the others were hiding to the west, ready to make a surprise attack. That night, Joshua went into the valley.ᴾ

¹⁴⁻¹⁵The king of Ai saw Joshua's army, so the king and his troops hurried out early the next morning to fight them. Joshua and his army pretended to be beaten, and they let the men of Ai chase them toward the desert. The king and his army were facing the Jordan valley as Joshua had planned.

The king did not realize that some Israelite soldiers were hiding behind the town. ¹⁶⁻¹⁷So he called out every man in Ai to go after Joshua's troops. They all rushed out to chase the Israelite army, and they left the town gates wide open. Not one man was left in Ai or in Bethel.�q

Joshua let the men of Ai chase him and his army farther and farther away from Ai. ¹⁸Finally, the LORD told Joshua, "Point your swordʳ at the town of Ai, because now I am going to help you defeat it!"

As soon as Joshua pointed his sword at the town, ¹⁹the soldiers who had been hiding jumped up and ran into the town. They captured it and set it on fire.

²⁰⁻²¹When Joshua and his troops saw smoke rising from the town, they knew that the other part of their army had captured it. So they turned and attacked.

The men of Ai looked back and saw smoke rising from their town. But they could not escape, because the soldiers they had been chasing had suddenly turned and started fighting. ²²⁻²⁴Meanwhile, the other Israelite soldiers had come from the town and attacked the men of Ai from the rear. The Israelites captured the king of Ai and brought him to Joshua. They also chased the rest of the men of Ai into the desert and killed them.ˢ

The Israelite army went back to Ai and killed everyone there. ²⁵⁻²⁶Joshua kept his sword pointed at the town of Ai until every last one of Ai's 12,000 people was dead. ²⁷But the Israelites took the animals and the other possessions of the people of Ai, because this was what the LORD had told Joshua to do.

²⁸⁻²⁹Joshua made sure every building in Ai was burned to the ground. He told his men to kill the king of Ai and hang his body on a tree. Then at sunset he told the

ᴾ8.13 *valley:* This may refer either to the Jordan River valley or to the valley between the Israelite camp and Ai.   q8.16,17 *Ai or in Bethel:* Hebrew; one ancient translation "Ai."   ʳ8.18 *sword:* Or "spear."   ˢ8.22-24 *Joshua. They also chased . . . them:* Or "Joshua. The men of Ai had chased the Israelites into the desert, but the Israelites killed them there."

Israelites to take down the body,[t] throw it in the gateway of the town, and cover it with a big pile of rocks. Those rocks are still there, and the town itself has never been rebuilt.

Joshua Reads the Blessings and Curses
(Deuteronomy 27.1-26)

30-32 One day, Joshua led the people of Israel to Mount Ebal, where he told some of his men, "Build an altar for offering sacrifices to the LORD. And use stones that have never been cut with iron tools,[u] because that is what Moses taught in *The Book of the Law*."[v]

Joshua offered sacrifices to please the LORD[w] and to ask his blessing.[x] Then with the Israelites still watching, he copied parts of *The Book of the Law*[y] of Moses onto stones.

33-35 Moses had said that everyone in Israel was to go to the valley between Mount Ebal and Mount Gerizim, where they were to be blessed. So everyone went there, including the foreigners, the leaders, officials, and judges. Half of the people stood on one side of the valley, and half on the other side, with the priests from the Levi tribe standing in the middle with the sacred chest. Then in a loud voice, Joshua read the blessings and curses from *The Book of the Law*[y] of Moses.[z]

The People of Gibeon Trick the Leaders of Israel

9 **1-2**The kings west of the Jordan River heard about Joshua's victories, so they got together and decided to attack Joshua and Israel. These kings were from the hill country and from the foothills to the west, as well as from the Mediterranean seacoast as far north as the Lebanon Mountains. Some of them were Hittites, others were Amorites or Canaanites, and still others were Perizzites, Hivites, or Jebusites.

3The people of Gibeon had also heard what Joshua had done to Jericho and Ai. **4**So they decided that some of their men should pretend to be messengers to Israel from a faraway country.[a] The men put worn-out bags on their donkeys and found some old wineskins that had cracked and had been sewn back together. **5**Their sandals were old and patched, and their clothes were worn out. They even took along some dry and crumbly bread. **6**Then they went to the Israelite camp at Gilgal, where they said to Joshua and the men of Israel, "We have come from a country that is far from here. Please make a peace treaty with us."

7-8 The Israelites replied, "But maybe you really live near us. We can't make a peace treaty with you if you live nearby."[b]

The Gibeonites[c] said, "If you make a peace treaty with us, we will be your servants."

[t]**8.28,29** *take down the body*: See Deuteronomy 21.22,23. [u]**8.30-32** *use stones . . . iron tools*: See Exodus 20.25. [v]**8.30-32** *taught . . . Law*: Or "commanded . . . Teachings." [w]**8.30-32** *sacrifices to please the LORD*: These sacrifices have been traditionally called "whole burnt offerings" because the whole animal was burned on the altar. A main purpose of such sacrifices was to please the LORD with the smell of the sacrifice, and so in the CEV they are often called "sacrifices to please the LORD." [x]**8.30-32** *to ask his blessing*: These sacrifices have traditionally been called "peace offerings," or "offerings of well-being." A main purpose was to ask for the LORD's blessing, and so in the CEV they are often called "sacrifices to ask the LORD's blessing." [y]**8.30-32,33-35** *Law*: Or "Teachings." [z]**8.33-35** *the blessings . . . Moses*: Or "all of *The Book of the Law of Moses*, including the blessings and the curses." [a]**9.4** *So . . . country*: One possible meaning for the difficult Hebrew text. [b]**9.7,8** *nearby*: See Deuteronomy 20.10-18. [c]**9.7,8** *Gibeonites*: Hebrew "Hivites."

8.30-32 *Mount Ebal*: Located about 20 miles from Ai in central Canaan. Moses had earlier received instructions about the ceremony that was to take place at Ebal after the people had crossed into Canaan (Deut 11.29, 30; 27.2-8). The ceremony in 8.30-35 is similar to the one in 24.1-28.

8.30-32 *stones . . . iron tools*: Even though bronze tools were in common use, ancient stone tools were required for this ritual (Exod 20.25).

8.33-35 *valley between Mount Ebal and Mount Gerizim . . . the foreigners*: Between Mounts Ebal and Gerizim is a valley and the city of Shechem. By gaining control of the high ground above this important mountain pass, the Israelites could control a large area in central Palestine. The ceremony described here may point to the fact that some of Canaan was taken over by peace treaties and not by warfare.

9.3,4 *people of Gibeon . . . pretend to be messengers*: Gibeon was six miles northwest of Jerusalem. Having heard of Israel's victories, the Gibeonites decided to try and trick the Israelites into signing a peace treaty.

9.6 *make a peace treaty*: People from far away could expect to make peace with the Israelites, while the people of Canaan could not (Exod 23.31-33; 34.11-16; Deut 7.1-4; 20.10-18).

● 9.9,10 *Egypt . . . Og . . . Sihon:* The cunning Gibeonites say that they know about the Israelites' escape from Egypt and how they defeated the Amorite kings, Og and Sihon, but they make no mention of what happened at the nearby cities of Jericho or Ai, even though they are very aware of it (9.3).

● 9.14,15 *tried . . . food . . . swore that Israel would keep this promise:* The Israelites may have tried the Gibeonites' food to see if it really was old or to simply show that they wanted peace. Ancient treaties often included the sharing of gifts or a meal (Gen 21.22-31). The Israelites trusted their own judgment rather than asking the LORD for advice. By swearing (taking an oath), the leaders were committed to the peace treaty (9.19-21).

● 9.16-17 *Gibeon . . . Kiriath-Jearim:* These towns were 20 to 30 miles west of the Israelite camp at Gilgal. Chephirah, Beeroth, and Kiriath-Jearim are towns within a five mile radius of Gibeon (Gibeah). **(See Map 3 on pg 1881.)**

■ 9.19-21 *If we break our promise:* Even though the Gibeonites tricked Israel into making a peace treaty with them, the Gibeonites were not harmed, because once a treaty is made it cannot be broken. In Hebrew thought and practice, the spoken word had great power.

Making Promises (Vows)

"Who are you?" Joshua asked. "Where do you come from?"

They answered:

⁹We are your servants, and we live far from here. We came because the LORD your God is so famous. We heard what the LORD did in Egypt ¹⁰and what he did to those two Amorite kings on the other side of the Jordan: King Og of Bashan, who lived in Ashtaroth, and King Sihon of Heshbon.

¹¹Our leaders and everyone who lives in our country told us to meet with you and tell you that all of us are your servants. They said to ask you to make a peace treaty with our people. They told us to be sure and take along enough food for our journey. ¹²See this dry, crumbly bread of ours? It was hot out of the oven when we packed the food on the day we left our homes. ¹³These cracked wineskins were new when we filled them, and our clothes and sandals are worn out because we have traveled so far.

¹⁴The Israelites tried some of the food,ᵈ but they did not ask the LORD if he wanted them to make a treaty. ¹⁵So Joshua made a peace treaty with the messengers and promised that Israel would not kill their people. Israel's leaders swore that Israel would keep this promise.

¹⁶⁻¹⁷A couple of days later,ᵉ the Israelites found out that these people actually lived in the nearby towns of Gibeon, Chephirah, Beeroth, and Kiriath-Jearim.ᶠ So the Israelites left the place where they had camped

and arrived at the four towns two days later.ᵍ ¹⁸But they did not attack the towns, because the Israelite leaders had sworn in the name of the LORD that they would let these people live.

The Israelites complained about their leaders' decision not to attack, ¹⁹⁻²¹but the leaders reminded them, "We promised these people in the name of the LORD God of Israel that we would let them live, so we must not harm them. If we break our promise, God will punish us. We'll let them live, but we'll make them cut wood and carry water for our people."

²²Joshua told some of his soldiers, "I want to meet with the Gibeonite leaders. Bring them here."

When the Gibeonites came, Joshua said, "You live close to us. Why did you lie by claiming you lived far away? ²³So now you are under a curse, and from now on your people will have to send workers to cut wood and carry water for the place of worship."ʰ

²⁴The Gibeonites answered, "The LORD your God told his servant Moses that you were to kill everyone who lives here and take their land for yourselves. We were afraid you would kill us, and so we tricked you into making a peace treaty. But we agreed to be your servants, ²⁵and you are strong enough to do anything to us that you want. We just ask you to do what seems right."

²⁶Joshua did not let the Israelites kill the Gibeonites, ²⁷but he did tell the Gibeonites that they would have to be servants of the

ᵈ9.14 *tried . . . food:* Probably to see if it really was old or to show that they wanted peace. ᵉ9.16,17 *A couple . . . later:* The Hebrew text has "At the end of three days," meaning two days after the day the treaty was made. ᶠ9.16,17 *Gibeon, Chephirah, Beeroth, and Kiriath-Jearim:* These towns were 20 to 30 miles west of the Israelite camp at Gilgal. ᵍ9.16,17 *A couple of days . . . later:* Or "A couple of days later, the Israelites moved their camp to the area near the towns of Gibeon, Chephirah, Beeroth, and Kiriath-Jearim. When they arrived, they realized that they had made a peace treaty with the people of these nearby towns!" ʰ9.23 *the place of worship:* The Hebrew text has "God's house," which at that time was the sacred tent.

nation of Israel. They would have to cut firewood and bring it for the priests to use for burning sacrifices on the LORD's altar, wherever the LORD decided the altar would be. The Gibeonites would also have to carry water for the priests. And that is still the work of the Gibeonites.

Joshua Commands the Sun To Stand Still

10 King Adonizedek of Jerusalem[i] heard that Joshua had captured and destroyed the town of Ai, and then killed its king as he had done at Jericho. He also learned that the Gibeonites had signed a peace treaty with Israel. [2]This frightened Adonizedek and his people. They knew that Gibeon was a large town, as big as the towns that had kings, and even bigger than the town of Ai had been. And all of the men of Gibeon were warriors. [3]So Adonizedek sent messages to the kings of four other towns: King Hoham of Hebron, King Piram of Jarmuth, King Japhia of Lachish, and King Debir of Eglon. The messages said, [4]"The Gibeonites have signed a peace treaty with Joshua and the Israelites. Come and help me attack Gibeon!"

[5]When these five Amorite kings called their armies together and attacked Gibeon, [6]the Gibeonites sent a message to the Israelite camp at Gilgal: "Joshua, please come and rescue us! The Amorite kings from the hill country have joined together and are attacking us. We are your servants, so don't let us down. Please hurry!"

[7]Joshua and his army, including his best warriors, left Gilgal. [8]"Joshua," the LORD said, "don't be afraid of the Amorites. They will run away when you attack, and I will help you defeat them."

[9]Joshua marched all night from Gilgal to Gibeon and made a surprise attack on the Amorite camp. [10]The LORD made the enemy panic, and the Israelites started killing them right and left. They[j] chased the Amorite troops up the road to Beth-Horon and kept on killing them, until they reached the towns of Azekah and Makkedah.[k] [11]And while these troops were going down through Beth-Horon Pass,[l] the LORD made huge hailstones fall on them all the way to Azekah. More of the enemy soldiers died from the hail than from the Israelite weapons.

[12-13]The LORD was helping the Israelites defeat the Amorites that day. So about noon, Joshua prayed to the LORD loud enough for the Israelites to hear:

> "Our LORD, make the sun stop
> in the sky over Gibeon,
> and the moon stand still
> over Aijalon Valley."[m]
> So the sun and the moon
> stopped and stood still
> until Israel defeated its enemies.

This poem can be found in *The Book of Jashar*.[n] The sun stood still and didn't go down for about a whole day. [14]Never before and never since has the LORD done anything like that for someone who prayed. The LORD was really fighting for Israel.

[15]After the battle, Joshua and the Israelites went back to their camp at Gilgal.

10.1 *Jerusalem:* Jerusalem was not an Israelite city at this time. It was first settled by the Jebusites. The Israelites burned the city, but it was evidently resettled. Eventually David captured it (2 Sam 5.6-10), made it the capital of Israel, and renamed it the City of David.

Jerusalem

10.3 *Adonizedek . . . kings of four other towns:* This alliance is made up of five kings, or chiefs of five cities to the south of Gibeon. This is their first attempt at an offensive action. However, the action is aimed at Gibeon, not Israel. The peace treaty of 9.15, meant that Israel would let Gibeon live; it also meant that Israel would defend the Gibeonites against their enemies. **(See Map 3 on pg 1881.)**

10.5 *Amorite:* The Amorites are described in Genesis 10.6-20 as descendants of Noah's grandson Canaan.

10.12-13 *Book of Jashar:* This book, now lost, may have been a collection of ancient war songs praising national heroes.

10.14 *The LORD was really fighting:* The LORD fulfills the promise made to Joshua (1.5).

Holy War (The LORD's Battles)

---

[i]10.1 *Jerusalem:* Jerusalem was not an Israelite city at this time.   [j]10.10 *They:* Or "The LORD."
[k]10.10 *Makkedah:* A total distance of about 25 miles.   [l]10.11 *Beth-Horon Pass:* A two-mile long, steeply-sloping valley between the towns of Upper Beth-Horon and Lower Beth-Horon.
[m]10.12,13 *Aijalon Valley:* A valley southwest of Beth-Horon Pass.   [n]10.12,13 *Book of Jashar:* This book may have been a collection of ancient war songs.

10.24 *put your feet on their necks:* This custom was done as a gesture of total domination and defeat .

10.28-34 *Makkedah . . . Libnah . . . Lachish . . . Eglon:* Joshua takes the chief towns of the region that guarded the approach to the southern highlands. No details are given.

10.40 *Joshua captured towns everywhere:* This is a summary of the conquest of the south. The Southern Desert, also called the Negev, is a dry region south of Beersheba. Joshua does as the LORD commanded, offering up the enemy as a sacrifice to God.

Joshua Kills the Five Enemy Kings

16While the enemy soldiers were running from the Israelites, the five enemy kings ran away and hid in a cave near Makkedah. **17**Joshua's soldiers told him, "The five kings have been found in a cave near Makkedah."

18Joshua answered, "Roll some big stones over the mouth of the cave and leave a few soldiers to guard it. **19**But you and everyone else must keep going after the enemy troops, because they will be safe if they reach their walled towns. Don't let them get away! The LORD our God is helping us get rid of them." **20**So Joshua and the Israelites almost wiped out the enemy soldiers. Only a few safely reached their walled towns.

21The Israelite army returned to their camp at Makkedah, where Joshua was waiting for them. No one around there dared say anything bad about the Israelites. **22**Joshua told his soldiers, "Now, move the rocks from the entrance to the cave and bring those five kings to me."

23The soldiers opened the entrance to the cave and brought out the kings of Jerusalem, Hebron, Jarmuth, Lachish, and Eglon. **24**After Joshua had called the army together, he forced the five kings to lie down on the ground. Then he called his officers forward and told them, "You fought these kings along with me, so put your feet on their necks." The officers did this, **25**and Joshua continued, "Don't ever be afraid or discouraged. Be brave and strong. This is what the LORD will do to all your enemies."

26Joshua killed the five kings and told his men to hang each body on a tree. Then at sunset **27**he told some of his troops, "Take the bodies down and throw them into the cave where the kings were found. Cover the entrance to the cave with big rocks."

Joshua's troops obeyed his orders, and those rocks are still there.

Joshua Continues the Fighting

28Later that day, Joshua captured Makkedah and killed its king and everyone else in the town, just as he had done at Jericho.

29Joshua and his army left Makkedah and attacked the town of Libnah. **30**The LORD let them capture the town and its king, and they killed the king and everyone else, just as they had done at Jericho.

31Joshua then led his army to Lachish, and they set up camp around the town. They attacked, **32**and the next day the LORD let them capture the town. They killed everyone, as they had done at Libnah. **33**King Horam of Gezer arrived to help Lachish, but Joshua and his troops attacked and destroyed him and his army.

34From Lachish, Joshua took his troops to Eglon, where they set up camp surrounding the town. They attacked, **35**captured it that same day, then killed everyone, as they had done at Lachish.

36Joshua and his army left Eglon and attacked Hebron. **37**They captured the town and the nearby villages, then killed everyone, including the king. They destroyed Hebron in the same way they had destroyed Eglon.

38Joshua and the Israelite army turned and attacked Debir. **39**They captured the town, and its nearby villages. Then they destroyed Debir and killed its king, together with everyone else, just as they had done with Hebron and Libnah.

40Joshua captured towns everywhere in the land: In the central hill country and the foothills to the west, in the Southern Desert and the region that slopes down toward the Dead Sea. Whenever he captured a town, he would kill the king and everyone else, as the LORD God of Israel had commanded. [41]Joshua wiped out towns from Kadesh-Barnea to Gaza, everywhere in the region of Goshen,[o] and as far north as Gibeon. [42-43]The LORD fought on Israel's side, so Joshua and the Israelite army were able to capture these kings and take their land. They fought one battle after another, then they went back to their camp at Gilgal after capturing all that land.

Joshua Captures Towns in the North

11 King Jabin of Hazor heard about Joshua's victories, so he sent messages to many nearby kings and asked them to join him in fighting Israel. He sent these messages to King Jobab of Madon, the kings of Shimron and Achshaph, [2]the kings in the northern hill country and in the Jordan River valley south of Lake Galilee,[p] and the kings in the foothills and in Naphath-Dor to the west. [3]He sent messages to the Canaanite kings in the east and the west, to the Amorite, Hittite, Perizzite, and Jebusite kings in the hill country, and to the Hivite kings in the region of Mizpah, near the foot of Mount Hermon.[q]

[4-5]The kings and their armies went to Merom Pond,[r] where they set up camp, and got ready to fight Israel. It seemed as though there were more soldiers and horses and chariots than there are grains of sand on a beach.

[6]The LORD told Joshua:

Don't let them frighten you! I'll help you defeat them, and by this time tomorrow they will be dead.

When you attack, the first thing you have to do is to cripple their horses. Then after the battle is over,[s] burn their chariots.

[7]Joshua and his army made a surprise attack against the enemy camp at Merom Pond[t] [8-9]and crippled the enemies' horses.[u] Joshua followed the LORD's instructions, and the LORD helped Israel defeat the enemy. The Israelite army even chased enemy soldiers as far as Misrephoth-Maim to the northwest,[v] the city of Sidon to the north, and Mizpeh Valley to the northeast.[w] None of the enemy soldiers escaped alive. The Israelites came back after the battle and burned the enemy's chariots.

[10]Up to this time, the king of Hazor had controlled the kingdoms that had joined together to attack Israel, so Joshua led his army back and captured Hazor. They killed its king [11]and everyone else, then they set the town on fire.

[12-15]Joshua captured all the towns where the enemy kings had ruled. These towns were built on small hills,[x] and Joshua did not set fire to any of these towns, except Hazor. The Israelites kept the animals

[o]**10.41** *Goshen*: A region between the hill country of Judah and the desert further south. Not the same Goshen as in Genesis 47.4-6. [p]**11.2** *Lake Galilee*: The Hebrew text has "Lake Chinnereth," an earlier name. [q]**11.3** *Mizpah, near the foot of Mount Hermon*: Probably the same region as Mizpeh Valley in verses 8,9, but different from the two other places named Mizpeh in 15.37-41; 18.25-28, and also different from the Mizpah mentioned in Genesis 31.49 and Judges 10.17. [r]**11.4,5** *Pond*: Or "Gorge." [s]**11.6** *When . . . over*: Or "After the battle is over, cripple their horses and burn their chariots." [t]**11.7** *Pond*: See the note at 11.4,5. [u]**11.8,9** *and crippled the enemies' horses*: It is also possible that the Israelites crippled the enemies' horses after the battle at the same time they burned the enemies' chariots; see the note at 11.6. [v]**11.8,9** *Misrephoth-Maim . . . northwest*: Or "the town of Misrephoth to the northwest" or "the Misrephoth River." [w]**11.8,9** *northeast*: These three areas were 20 to 35 miles north of Merom. [x]**11.12-15** *small hills*: Towns were often built on top of the ruins of a previous town that had been destroyed. When this happened many times at one place, a hill was formed.

11.1 *King Jabin of Hazor:* This powerful king organized an army of troops from surrounding cities in the far north country of Palestine. Jabin was a noted enemy of Israel. Hazor, nine miles north of Lake Galilee, was noted in Egyptian and Mesopotamian records as a chief Canaanite city.

11.4-5 *soldiers . . . grains of sand:* The terrifying odds against Israel in the north of Palestine were made more threatening by the enemies' horses and chariots. Israel did not have horses or chariots at this time.

11.8-9 *crippled the enemies' horses:* Most likely the Israelites crippled the enemies' horses after the battle at the same time they burned the enemies' chariots. It was not until the time of Solomon (ruled from about 970 to 931 B.C.) that the Israelites used horses for military purposes (1 Kings 10.26-29). Depending on chariots and a cavalry indicates trust in material resources and not in God (Isa 31.1).

11.12-15 *These towns . . . Joshua did not set fire:* The old walled cities of the lowlands were not destroyed. The Israelites had their greatest success in the hills where the Canaanite chariots could not be used.

11.17-18 *Mount Halak . . . Mount Hermon:* This is a summary of Israel's conquests as in 10.40-43, with the addition of northern Palestine. Battles against the kings in the north continued for a "long time."

11.19-20 *why the* LORD *made the people . . . stubborn:* The LORD causes the Canaanites to be stubborn, just as it is God who made the king of Egypt stubborn (Exod 4.21).

11.21 *the Anakim:* This was a group of very large people who lived in Palestine before the Israelites. Sons of Anak, they are described as descendants of the legendary giants called Nephilim (Gen 6.4).

11.22 *Gaza, Gath, and Ashdod:* These cities on the coastal plain, plus Ashkelon and Ekron, made up the five cities of the Philistine alliance.

12.1 *Arnon River . . . Mount Hermon:* The Arnon River flowed into the Dead Sea and formed the boundary between Moab and Ammon. Mount Hermon was located near the southern border of Lebanon.

12.4 *Rephaim:* Like the Anakim, this may have been a group of large people who lived in Palestine before the Israelites.

and everything of value from these towns, but they killed everyone who lived in them, including their kings. That's what the LORD had told his servant Moses to do, that's what Moses had told Joshua to do, and that's exactly what Joshua did.

¹⁶Joshua and his army took control of the northern and southern hill country, the foothills to the west, the Southern Desert, the whole region of Goshen,^y and the Jordan River valley. ¹⁷⁻¹⁸They took control of the land from Mount Halak near the country of Edom in the south to Baal-Gad in Lebanon Valley at the foot of Mount Hermon in the north. Joshua and his army were at war with the kings in this region for a long time, but finally they captured and put to death the last king.

¹⁹⁻²⁰The LORD had told Moses that he wanted the towns in this region destroyed and their people killed without mercy. That's why the LORD made the people in the towns stubborn and determined to fight Israel. The only town that signed a peace treaty with Israel was the Hivite town of Gibeon. The Israelite army captured the rest of the towns in battle.

²¹During this same time, Joshua and his army killed the Anakim^z from the northern and southern hill country. They also destroyed the towns where the Anakim had lived, including Hebron, Debir, and Anab. ²²There were not any Anakim left in the regions where the Israelites lived, although there were still some in Gaza, Gath, and Ashdod.^a

²³That's how Joshua captured the land,

just as the LORD had commanded Moses, and Joshua divided it up among the tribes.

Finally, there was peace in the land.

The Kings Defeated by the Israelites

12 Before Moses died, he and the people of Israel had defeated two kings east of the Jordan River. These kings had ruled the region from the Arnon River gorge in the south to Mount Hermon in the north, including the eastern side of the Jordan River valley.

²The first king that Moses and the Israelites defeated was an Amorite, King Sihon of Heshbon.^b The southern border of his kingdom ran down the middle of the Arnon River gorge, taking in the town of Aroer on the northern edge of the gorge. The Jabbok River separated Sihon's kingdom from the Ammonites on the east. Then the Jabbok turned west and became his northern border, so his kingdom included the southern half of the region of Gilead. ³Sihon also controlled the eastern side of the Jordan River valley from Lake Galilee^c south to Beth-Jeshimoth and the Dead Sea. In addition to these regions, he ruled the town called Slopes of Mount Pisgah^d and the land south of there at the foot of the hill.

⁴Next, Moses and the Israelites defeated King Og of Bashan,^e who lived in the town of Ashtaroth part of each year and in Edrei the rest of the year. Og was one of the last of the Rephaim.^f ⁵His kingdom stretched

^y**11.16** *Goshen:* See the note at 10.41.   ^z**11.21** *Anakim:* Perhaps a group of very large people that lived in Palestine before the Israelites (see Numbers 13.33 and Deuteronomy 2.10,11,20,21).   ^a**11.22** *Gaza, Gath, and Ashdod:* Towns in Philistia.   ^b**12.2** *King Sihon of Heshbon:* See Numbers 21.21-31.   ^c**12.3** *Lake Galilee:* See the note at 11.2.   ^d**12.3** *the town called Slopes of Mount Pisgah:* Or "the slopes of Mount Pisgah."   ^e**12.4** *King Og of Bashan:* See Numbers 21.33-35.   ^f**12.4** *Rephaim:* Perhaps a group of very large people that lived in Palestine before the Israelites (see Deuteronomy 2.10,11,20,21).

north to Mount Hermon, east to the town of Salecah, and included the land of Bashan as far west as the borders of the kingdoms of Geshur and Maacah. He also ruled the northern half of Gilead.

[6] Moses, the LORD's servant, had led the people of Israel in defeating Sihon and Og. Then Moses gave their land to the tribes of Reuben, Gad, and East Manasseh.

[7-8]Later, Joshua and the Israelites defeated many kings west of the Jordan River, from Baal-Gad in Lebanon Valley in the north to Mount Halak near the country of Edom in the south. This region included the hill country and the foothills, the Jordan River valley and its western slopes, and the Southern Desert. Joshua and the Israelites took this land from the Hittites, the Amorites, the Canaanites, the Perizzites, the Hivites, and the Jebusites. Joshua divided up the land among the tribes of Israel.

The Israelites defeated the kings of the following towns west of the Jordan River:
[9-24]Jericho, Ai near Bethel, Jerusalem, Hebron, Jarmuth, Lachish, Eglon, Gezer, Debir, Geder, Hormah, Arad, Libnah, Adullam, Makkedah, Bethel, Tappuah, Hepher, Aphek, Lasharon,[g] Madon, Hazor, Shimron-Meron, Achshaph, Taanach, Megiddo, Kedesh, Jokneam on Mount Carmel, Dor in Naphath-Dor, Goiim in Galilee,[h] and Tirzah.[i]
There were 31 of these kings in all.

The Land Israel Had Not Yet Taken

13 Many years later, the LORD told Joshua:

Now you are very old, but there is still a lot of land that Israel has not yet taken. [2-7]First, there is the Canaanite territory that starts at the Shihor River just east of Egypt and goes north to Ekron. The southern part of this region belongs to the Avvites and the Geshurites,[j] and the land around Gaza, Ashdod, Ashkelon, Gath, and Ekron belongs to the five Philistine rulers.

The other Canaanite territory is in the north. Its northern border starts at the town of Arah, which belongs to the Sidonians. From there, it goes to Aphek,[k] then along the Amorite border[l] to Hamath Pass.[m] The eastern border starts at Hamath Pass and goes south to Baal-Gad at the foot of Mount Hermon, and its southern boundary runs west from there to Misrephoth-Maim.[n] This northern region includes the Lebanon Mountains and the land that belongs to the Gebalites[o] and the Sidonians who live in the hill country from the Lebanon Mountains to Misrephoth-Maim.

With my help, Israel will capture these Canaanite territories and force out the people who live there. But you must divide up the land from the

● 12.7-24 *defeated the kings . . . towns west of the Jordan:* Thirty-one Canaanite towns are listed, including those defeated under Moses and many not previously mentioned in Joshua. Jerusalem was taken from the Jebusites by King David (2 Sam 5.6-10). This most likely is due to the fact that the author drew upon a number of oral and written sources. These lists of towns and kings concludes the Joshua account of the conquest of Canaan.

■ 13.1 *Many years later:* This verse seems to pick up where 11.23 ends. Joshua, now an old man (as in 23.1,2), is commanded to divide western Canaan among the nine and a half tribes.

● 13.2-7 *Shihor River . . . Gaza . . . Misrephoth-Maim:* The areas mentioned represent the ideal borders of Israel. These lands roughly describe the lands captured by King David some 200 years after the time of Joshua. Israel never held all these lands, yet they were regarded as Canaanite lands promised to Israel by God. The border town Aphek mentioned in these verses is not the same Aphek as in 12.9-24. **(See Map 4 on pg 1882.)**

[g]12.9-24 *Aphek, Lasharon:* Or "Aphek in the Sharon Plain."   [h]12.9-24 *Galilee:* One ancient translation; Hebrew "Gilgal."   [i]12.9-24 *Jericho . . . Tirzah:* There are some differences in this list between the Hebrew and several ancient translations.   [j]13.2-7 *Geshurites:* Not the same Geshur as in 12.5 and 13.11. One ancient translation has "Gezerites." Gezer was a town north of Ekron that the Israelites did not capture (see Judges 1.29).   [k]13.2-7 *Aphek:* Not the same Aphek as in 12.9-24. [l]13.2-7 *Amorite border:* What had been the southern border of the old Amorite kingdom of Amurru. [m]13.2-7 *Hamath Pass:* Or "Lebo-Hamath."   [n]13.2-7 *Misrephoth-Maim:* Or "Misrephoth" or "the Misrephoth River."   [o]13.2-7 *Gebalites:* Gebal was another name for Byblos.

Phoenicia

13.14 *the Levi tribe:* Israel's priests came from the Levi tribe. **(See the chart Sacrifices and Offerings on pg 1828.)**

Israel's Priests

13.15 *Reuben tribe:* Reuben and Simeon, Jacob's first and second sons (Gen 29.31-33), lost their normal position of leadership among the tribes because of their evil actions (Gen 49.3-7). The Reuben tribe was given territory to the east of the Dead Sea.

13.17-21 *Heshbon . . . Pisgah:* On the northern border of the Reuben tribe, the city of Heshbon had belonged to King Sihon, who was defeated by Moses (2.10, Sihon and Og). Mount Pisgah probably refers to the highest peak in the Abiram Mountains in Moab. From this spot, the Israelites could likely see the land of Canaan.

13.22 *Balaam:* Balaam was a fortuneteller hired by the Moabite King Balak to curse the Israelites. Balaam was unable to deliver the curse, giving Israel a blessing instead (Num 22.2—24.25). Later, Moses ordered Balaam killed, because he had invited the people to worship the Canaanite god Baal (Num 31.7-16).

13.25 *Gilead region:* The territory given to Gad bordered the Reuben territory on the north. It included the highlands north and south of the Jabbok River. **(See Map 3 on pg 1881.)**

Jordan River to the Mediterranean Sea[P] among the nine tribes and the half of Manasseh that don't have any land yet. Then each tribe will have its own land.

The Land East of the Jordan River

[8]Moses had already given land east of the Jordan River to the tribes of Reuben, Gad, and half of Manasseh. [9]This region stretched north from the town in the middle of the Arnon River valley, and included the town of Aroer on the northern edge of the valley. It covered the flatlands of Medeba north of Dibon, [10]and took in the towns that had belonged to Sihon, the Amorite king of Heshbon. Some of these towns were as far east as the Ammonite border. [11-12]Geshur and Maacah were part of this region, and so was the whole territory that King Og had ruled, that is, Gilead, Mount Hermon, and all of Bashan as far east as Salecah. Og had lived in Ashtaroth part of each year, and he had lived in Edrei the rest of the year. Og had been one of the last of the Rephaim,[q] but Moses had defeated Sihon and Og and their people[r] and had forced them to leave their land. [13]However, the Israelites did not force the people of Geshur and Maacah to leave, and they still live there among the Israelites.

Why Moses Did Not Give Land to the Levi Tribe

[14]Moses did not give any land to the Levi tribe, because the LORD God of Israel had told them, "Instead of land, you will receive the sacrifices offered at my altar."

The Land Moses Gave to the Reuben Tribe

[15]Moses gave land to each of the clans in the Reuben tribe. [16]Their land started in the south at the town in the middle of the Arnon River valley, took in the town of Aroer on the northern edge of the valley, and went as far north as the flatlands around Medeba. [17-21]The Amorite King Sihon had lived in Heshbon and had ruled the towns in the flatlands. Now Heshbon belonged to Reuben, and so did the following towns in the flatlands: Dibon, Bamoth-Baal, Beth-Baal-Meon, Jahaz, Kedemoth, Mephaath, Kiriathaim, Sibmah, Zereth-Shahar on the hill in the valley, Beth-Peor, Slopes of Mount Pisgah, and Beth-Jeshimoth.

Moses defeated Sihon and killed him and the Midianite chiefs who ruled parts of his kingdom for him. Their names were Evi, Rekem, Zur, Hur, and Reba. [22]The Israelites also killed Balaam the son of Beor, who had been a fortuneteller.

[23]This region with its towns and villages was the land for the Reuben tribe, and the Jordan River was its western border.

The Land Moses Gave to the Gad Tribe

[24]Moses also gave land to each of the clans in the Gad tribe. [25]It included the town of Jazer, and in the Gilead region their territory took in the land and towns as far east as the town of Aroer[s] just west of Rabbah.[t] This was about half of the land that had once belonged to the Ammonites. [26]The land given to Gad stretched from Heshbon in the south to Ramath-Mizpeh and Betonim in the north, and even fur-

[P]13.2-7 *from . . . Sea:* One ancient translation; the Hebrew text does not have these words. [q]13.11,12 *Rephaim:* See the note at 12.4. [r]13.11,12 *Sihon . . . people:* Or "the Rephaim." [s]13.25 *Aroer:* Not the same town as the Aroer in verse 16. [t]13.25 *Rabbah:* The capital city of Ammon.

ther north to Mahanaim and Lidebor.[u] [27]Gad also received the eastern half of the Jordan River valley, which had been ruled by King Sihon of Heshbon. This territory stretched as far north as Lake Galilee,[v] and included the towns of Beth-Haram, Beth-Nimrah, Succoth, and Zaphon. [28]These regions with their towns and villages were given to the Gad tribe.

The Land Moses Gave to Half the Manasseh Tribe

[29]Moses gave land east of the Jordan River to half of the clans from the Manasseh tribe. [30-31]Their land started at Mahanaim and took in the region that King Og of Bashan had ruled, including Ashtaroth and Edrei, the two towns where he had lived. The villages where the Jair clan settled were part of Manasseh's land, and so was the northern half of the region of Gilead. The clans of this half of Manasseh had 60 towns in all.

The Manasseh tribe is sometimes called the Machir tribe, after Manasseh's son Machir.

[32]That was how Moses divided up the Moab Plains to the east of Jericho on the other side of the Jordan River, so these two and a half tribes would have land of their own. [33]But Moses did not give any land to the Levi tribe, because the LORD had promised that he would always provide for them.

The Land West of the Jordan River

14 [1-5]Nine and a half tribes still did not have any land, although two and a half tribes had already received land east of the Jordan River. Moses had divided that land among them, and he had also said that the Levi tribe would not receive a large region like the other tribes. Instead, the people of Levi would receive towns and the nearby pastures for their sheep, goats, and cattle. And since the descendants of Joseph had become the two tribes of Ephraim and Manasseh, there were still nine and a half tribes that needed land. The LORD had told Moses that he would show those tribes[w] how to divide up the land of Canaan.

When the priest Eleazar, Joshua, and the leaders of the families and tribes of Israel met to divide up the land of Canaan, the LORD showed them how to do it.

Joshua Gives Hebron to Caleb

[6]One day while the Israelites were still camped at Gilgal, Caleb the son of Jephunneh went to talk with Joshua. Caleb belonged to the Kenaz clan, and many other people from the Judah tribe went with Caleb. He told Joshua:

You know that back in Kadesh-Barnea the LORD talked to his prophet Moses about you and me. [7]I was 40 years old at the time Moses sent me from Kadesh-Barnea into Canaan as a spy. When I came back and told him about the land, everything I said was true. [8]The other spies said things that made our people afraid, but I completely trusted the LORD God. [9]The same day I came back, Moses told me, "Since you were faithful to the LORD God, I promise that the places where

● 13.29-31 *Manasseh . . . Machir:* Manasseh and Ephraim were the sons of Jacob's son Joseph. Each received a share of land in Canaan. Half of the Manasseh tribe settled east of the Jordan, and their land was to the north of Gad. "Machir" seems to stand for western Manasseh.

■ 14.1-5 *Moses had divided that land . . . people of Levi . . . descendants of Joseph:* This division of the land was first reported in Numbers 26.52-56; 34.13. The tribes who fought together would take possession of the land in an orderly fashion, with the largest tribes receiving more than the smallest. The tribes of Reuben, Gad, and East Manasseh had already received their portion under Moses. Joseph's sons Ephraim and Manasseh were blessed by Jacob and counted as his own (Gen 48.5). The Levi tribe was set apart for the service of the LORD and didn't receive a share of land.

● 14.6 *Caleb:* Caleb and Joshua had been sent to spy out the land of Canaan along with ten other spies. Only Caleb and Joshua encouraged the people to enter the land. Because they were faithful, Joshua and Caleb were the only two of that generation allowed to enter into the promised land.

---

[u]13.26 *Lidebor:* This may be another name for Lodebar, a town a few miles east of the Jordan River and about ten miles south of Lake Galilee.   [v]13.27 *Lake Galilee:* See the note at 11.2.   [w]14.1-5 *he would show those tribes:* The Hebrew text has "those tribes must cast lots to find out." Pieces of wood or stone (called "lots") were used to find out what God wanted his people to do.

15.1 *Judah tribe:* Judah was the son of Jacob and Leah (Gen 29.35; 30.16-20). He was given a place of honor among his brothers when Jacob blessed his sons (Gen 49.8-10). Israel's King David was from the tribe of Judah. **(See Map 3 on pg 1881.)**

15.3 *Kadesh-Barnea:* This town in the desert of Paran was southwest of the Dead Sea and 55 miles south of Beersheba. **(See Map 4 on pg 1882.)**

you went as a spy will belong to you and your descendants forever."

[10]Joshua, it was 45 years ago that the LORD told Moses to make that promise, and now I am 85. Even though Israel has moved from place to place in the desert, the LORD has kept me alive all this time as he said he would. [11]I'm just as strong today as I was then, and I can still fight as well in battle.

[12]So I'm asking you for the hill country that the LORD promised me that day. You were there. You heard the other spies talk about that part of the hill country and the large, walled towns where the Anakim[x] live. But maybe the LORD will help me take their land, just as he promised.

[13]Joshua prayed that God would help Caleb, then he gave Hebron to Caleb and his descendants. [14]And Hebron still belongs to Caleb's descendants, because he was faithful to the LORD God of Israel.

[15]Hebron used to be called Arba's Town,[y] because Arba had been one of the greatest[z] of the Anakim.

There was peace in the land.

Judah's Land

15 The clans of the Judah tribe were given land that went south along the border of Edom, and at its farthest point south it even reached the Zin Desert. [2]Judah's southern border started at the south end of the Dead Sea. [3]As it went west from there, it ran south of Scorpion Pass[a]

to Zin, and then came up from the south to Kadesh-Barnea. It continued past Hezron up to Addar, turned toward Karka, [4]and ran along to Azmon. After that, it followed the Egyptian Gorge and ended at the Mediterranean Sea. This was also Israel's southern border.

[5]Judah's eastern border ran the full length of the Dead Sea.

The northern border started at the northern end of the Dead Sea.[b] [6]From there it went west up to Beth-Hoglah, continued north of Beth-Arabah, and went up to the Monument of Bohan,[c] who belonged to the Reuben tribe. [7]From there, it went to Trouble Valley[d] and Debir,[e] then turned north and went to Gilgal,[f] which is on the north side of the valley across from Adummim Pass. It continued on to En-shemesh, Enrogel, [8]and up through Hinnom Valley on the land sloping south from Jerusalem. The city of Jerusalem itself belonged to the Jebusites.

Next, the border went up to the top of the mountain on the west side of Hinnom Valley and at the north end of Rephaim Valley. [9]At the top of the mountain it turned and went to Nephtoah Spring and then to the ruins[g] on Mount Ephron. From there, it went to Baalah, which is now called Kiriath-Jearim.

[10]From Baalah the northern border curved west to Mount Seir and then ran along the northern ridge of Mount Jearim, where Chesalon is located. Then it went down to Beth-Shemesh[h] and over to Timnah. [11]It continued along to the hillside

[x]**14.12** *Anakim:* See the note at 11.21.   [y]**14.15** *Arba's Town:* Or "Kiriath-Arba."   [z]**14.15** *Arba's Town, because . . . greatest:* Hebrew; one ancient translation "Arba's Town. It was one of the main towns."   [a]**15.3** *Scorpion Pass:* Or "Akrabbim Pass."   [b]**15.5** *at . . . Dead Sea:* One possible meaning for the difficult Hebrew text.   [c]**15.6** *Monument of Bohan:* Or "Bohan Rock," possibly a natural rock formation.   [d]**15.7** *Trouble Valley:* Or "Achor Valley."   [e]**15.7** *Debir:* Not the same town as in 10.38,39.   [f]**15.7** *Gilgal:* Not the same "Gilgal" as in 4.19.   [g]**15.9** *ruins:* Hebrew; one ancient translation "towns."   [h]**15.10** *Beth-Shemesh:* Probably the same town as the Ir-Shemesh of 19.41-46. Two other towns were also named Beth-Shemesh (see 19.17-23 and 19.35-39).

north of Ekron, curved around to Shik-keron, and then went to Mount Baalah. After going to Jabneel, the border finally ended at the Mediterranean Sea, [12]which was Judah's western border.

The clans of Judah lived within these borders.

Caleb's Land
(Judges 1.12-15)

[13]Joshua gave Caleb some land among the people of Judah, as God had told him to do. Caleb's share was Hebron, which at that time was known as Arba's Town,[i] because Arba was the famous ancestor of the Anakim.[j]

[14]Caleb attacked Hebron and forced the three Anakim clans of[k] Sheshai, Ahiman, and Talmai to leave. [15]Next, Caleb started a war with the town of Debir, which at that time was called Kiriath-Sepher. [16]He told his men, "The man who captures Kiriath-Sepher can marry my daughter Achsah."

[17]Caleb's nephew Othniel[l] captured Kiriath-Sepher, and Caleb let him marry Achsah. [18]Right after the wedding, Achsah started telling Othniel that he[m] ought to ask her father for a field. She went to see her father, and while she was getting down from[n] her donkey, Caleb asked her, "What's bothering you?"

[19]She answered, "I need your help. The land you gave me is in the Southern Desert, so I really need some spring-fed ponds[o] for a water supply."

Caleb gave her a couple of small ponds, named Higher Pond and Lower Pond.[p]

Towns in Judah's Land

[20]The following is a list of the towns in each region given to the Judah clans:

[21-32]The first region was located in the Southern Desert along the border with Edom, and it had the following 29 towns with their surrounding villages:

Kabzeel, Eder, Jagur, Kinah, Dimonah, Aradah,[q] Kedesh, Hazor of Ithnan,[r] Ziph, Telem, Bealoth, Hazor-Hadattah, Kerioth-Hezron, which is also called Hazor, Amam, Shema, Moladah, Hazar-Gaddah, Heshmon, Beth-Pelet, Hazar-Shual, Beersheba and its surrounding villages,[s] Baalah, Iim, Ezem, Eltolad, Chesil, Hormah, Ziklag, Madmannah, Sansannah, Lebaoth, Shilhim, and Enrimmon.[t]

[33-36]The second region was located in the northern part of the lower foothills, and it had the following 14 towns with their surrounding villages:

Eshtaol, Zorah, Ashnah, Zanoah, En-Gannim, Tappuah, Enam, Jarmuth, Adullam, Socoh, Azekah, Shaaraim, Adithaim, Gederah, and Gederothaim.

[37-41]The third region was located in the southern part of the lower foothills, and it had the following 16 towns with their surrounding villages:

Zenan, Hadashah, Migdalgad, Dilan, Mizpeh, Joktheel, Lachish, Bozkath,

15.12 *Judah's western border:* The cities along the Mediterranean coastal plain were never under Israelite control until King David's time.

15.17 *Othniel:* He later was chosen to be a judge (leader) of Israel for 40 years (Judg 3.7-11).

15.21-32 *The first region:* Judah's first region was a large area in the south with Beersheba as its center. This region was in the lowlands or plains west of Judah's central mountains, with Adullam being the southernmost town and Gederah the northernmost.

15.37-41 *The third region:* Most of the towns named are unknown.

---

[i]15.13 *Arba's Town:* See the note at 14.15.   [j]15.13 *Anakim:* See the note at 11.21.   [k]15.14 *clans of:* Or "warriors."   [l]15.17 *Caleb's nephew Othniel:* Hebrew "Othniel the son of Caleb's brother Kenaz."   [m]15.18 *Achsah . . . Othniel . . . he:* Hebrew; one manuscript of one ancient translation and two ancient translations of the parallel in Judges 1.14 "Othniel . . . Achsah . . . she."   [n]15.18 *getting down from:* One possible meaning for the difficult Hebrew text.   [o]15.19 *spring-fed ponds:* Or "wells."   [p]15.19 *small ponds . . . Pond . . . Pond:* Or "wells . . . Well . . . Well."   [q]15.21-32 *Aradah:* One possible meaning for the difficult Hebrew text.   [r]15.21-32 *Hazor of Ithnan:* One ancient translation; Hebrew "Hazor and Ithnan."   [s]15.21-32 *its . . . villages:* One ancient translation; Hebrew "Biziothiah."   [t]15.21-32 *Enrimmon:* One ancient translation; Hebrew "Ain and Rimmon."

15.42-44 *The fourth region:* This district lies between the second and third; it is centered around Mareshah, 14 miles northwest of Hebron.

15.45-47 *The fifth region:* This region includes the major Philistine cities of Ekron, Ashdod, and Gaza.

15.48-51 *The sixth region:* This region was to the north of the first region. Debir is one of its important towns.

15.52-54 *The seventh region:* This region was in the heart of the southern highlands. Its center is Hebron, perhaps the most important city in Judah at that time. It was at Hebron where, many years later, the people of Judah crowned David king (2 Sam 2.4). Hebron was David's base of operations until he captured Jerusalem, nineteen miles to the north.

15.55-57 *The eighth region:* This region was on the eastern edge of the highlands south of Hebron. Jezreel is not the same town as in 19.17-23; Gibeah is not the same as in 18.25-38.

15.58-59 *The ninth region:* Its center was Beth-Zur, about four miles north of Hebron.

15.58-59 *The tenth region:* The center of this region was six miles south of Jerusalem at Bethlehem, where David was later born (1 Sam 17.12).

15.61-62 *The twelfth region:* En-Gedi is about midway along the western shore of the Dead Sea.

Eglon, Cabbon, Lahmas,[u] Chitlish, Gederoth, Beth-Dagon, Naamah, and Makkedah.

42-44 The fourth region was located in the central part of the lower foothills, and it had the following nine towns with their surrounding villages:

Libnah, Ether, Ashan, Iphtah, Ashnah, Nezib, Keilah, Achzib, and Mareshah.

45-47 The fifth region was located along the Mediterranean seacoast, and it had the following towns with their surrounding settlements and villages:

Ekron and the towns between there and the coast, Ashdod and the larger towns nearby, Gaza, the towns from Gaza to the Egyptian Gorge, and the towns along the coast of the Mediterranean Sea.

48-51 The sixth region was in the southwestern part of the hill country, and it had the following eleven towns with their surrounding villages:

Shamir, Jattir, Socoh, Dannah, Kiriath-Sannah, which is now called Debir, Anab, Eshtemoh,[v] Anim, Goshen, Holon, and Giloh.

52-54 The seventh region was located in the south-central part of Judah's hill country, and it had the following nine towns with their surrounding villages:

Arab, Dumah,[w] Eshan, Janim, Beth-Tappuah, Aphekah, Humtah, Kiriath-Arba, which is now called Hebron, and Zior.

55-57 The eighth region was located in

the southeastern part of the hill country, and it had the following ten towns with their surrounding villages:

Maon, Carmel, Ziph, Juttah, Jezreel,[x] Jokdeam,[y] Zanoah, Kain, Gibeah,[z] and Timnah.

58-59 The ninth region was located in the central part of Judah's hill country, and it had the following six towns with their surrounding villages:

Halhul, Beth-Zur, Gedor, Maarath, Beth-Anoth, and Eltekon.

The tenth region was located in the north-central part of Judah's hill country, and it had the following eleven towns with their surrounding villages:

Tekoa, Ephrath, which is also called Bethlehem, Peor, Etam, Culon, Tatam, Shoresh, Kerem, Gallim, Bether, and Manahath.[a]

60The eleventh region was located in the northern part of Judah's hill country, and it had the following two towns with their surrounding villages:

Rabbah, and Kiriath-Baal, which is also called Kiriath-Jearim.

61-62 The twelfth region was located in the desert along the Dead Sea, and it had the following six towns with their surrounding villages:

Beth-Arabah, Middin, Secacah, Nibshan, Salt Town, and En-Gedi.

The Jebusites

63The Jebusites lived in Jerusalem, and the people of the Judah tribe could not

[u]**15.37-41** *Lahmas:* Most Hebrew manuscripts; many other Hebrew manuscripts and one manuscript of one ancient translation "Lahmam." [v]**15.48-51** *Eshtemoh:* Another spelling for the name Eshtemoa (see 21.9-19). [w]**15.52-54** *Dumah:* Most Hebrew manuscripts; some Hebrew manuscripts and one ancient translation "Rumah." [x]**15.55-57** *Jezreel:* Not the same Jezreel as in 19.17-23. [y]**15.55-57** *Jokdeam:* Hebrew; one ancient translation "Jorkeam." [z]**15.55-57** *Gibeah:* Not the same Gibeah as in 18.25-28. [a]**15.58,59** *The tenth region . . . Manahath:* One ancient translation; the Hebrew text does not have these words.

capture the city and get rid of them. That's why Jebusites still live in Jerusalem along with the people of Judah.[b]

Ephraim's Land

16 [1-4]Ephraim and Manasseh are the two tribes descended from Joseph, and the following is a description of the land they received. The southern border of their land started at the Jordan River east of the spring at Jericho. From there it went west through the desert up to the hill country around Bethel. From Bethel it went to Luz and then[c] to the border of the Archites in Ataroth.[d] It continued west down to the land that belonged to the Japhlet clan, then went on to Lower Beth-Horon, Gezer, and the Mediterranean Sea.

[5]The following is a description of the land that was divided among the clans of the Ephraim tribe. Their southern border started at Ataroth-Addar and went west to Upper Beth-Horon [6-8]and the Mediterranean Sea. Their northern border started on the east at Janoah, curved a little to the north, then came back south to Michmethath and Tappuah, where it followed the Kanah Gorge west to the Mediterranean Sea.

The eastern border started on the north near Janoah and went between Janoah on the southwest and Taanath-Shiloh on the northeast. Then it went south to Ataroth, Naarah, and on as far as the edge of the land that belonged to Jericho. At that point it turned east and went to the Jordan River.

The clans of Ephraim received this region as their tribal land. [9]Ephraim also had some towns and villages that were inside Manasseh's tribal land.

[10]Ephraim could not force the Canaanites out of Gezer, so there are still some Canaanites who live there among the Israelites. But now these Canaanites have to work as slaves for the Israelites.

Manasseh's Land
West of the Jordan River

17 [1-6]Manasseh was Joseph's oldest son, and Machir was Manasseh's oldest son. Machir had a son named Gilead, and some of his descendants had already received the regions of Gilead and Bashan because they were good warriors. The other clans of the Manasseh tribe descended from Gilead's sons Abiezer, Helek, Asriel, Shechem, Hepher, and Shemida. The following is a description of the land they received.

Hepher's son Zelophehad did not have any sons, but he did have five daughters: Mahlah, Noah, Hoglah, Milcah, and Tirzah. One day the clans that were descendants of Zelophehad's five daughters went to the priest Eleazar, Joshua, and the leaders of Israel. The people of these clans said, "The LORD told Moses to give us land just as he gave land to our relatives."[e]

Joshua followed the LORD's instructions and gave land to these five clans, as he had given land to the five clans that had descended from Hepher's brothers.[f] So

16.1-4 *Ephraim and Manasseh:* Ephraim was the larger of the two, and one of the most powerful tribes. With the division of the kingdom in 931 B.C., Ephraim became one of the names for the northern kingdom, which included the ten northernmost tribes. **(See Map 3 on pg 1881.)**

16.1-4 *The southern border:* This boundary ran from Jericho to the Mediterranean Sea. Compared to the description of the Judah boundaries, the details here are sketchy. The Joseph tribes occupy the central hill country north of Jerusalem, with Ephraim in the south and Manasseh in the north.

16.10 *Ephraim could not force . . . Gezer:* Because their horses and chariots helped them hold the plains region of Palestine, some Canaanites remained in Ephraim tribal lands. Their status as "slaves" reflects different conditions from that of the conquest. Over 200 years later, Israel's King Solomon also used the Canaanite population for forced labor (1 Kgs 9.20-22). But intermarriage between Israelites and Canaanites and the worship of Canaanite gods was an ongoing problems for Israel's tribes.

17.1-6 *Manasseh . . . Machir . . . Gilead:* In Numbers 26.28-34, six clans of Manasseh are listed as descendants of Machir's son Gilead. The names of three of his sons are also the names of Canaanite cities (Shechem, Hepher, and Tirzah).

[b]**15.63** *Jebusites . . . Judah:* Israel captured Jerusalem in King David's time, but even then the Jebusites were not forced to leave. [c]**16.1-4** *it . . . then:* Or "which is also called Luz, it went."
[d]**16.1-4** *Ataroth:* This is the same Ataroth as Ataroth-Addar in verse 5, but a different Ataroth from the one in verses 6-8. [e]**17.1-6** *The LORD told Moses . . . relatives:* See Numbers 27.1-11; 36.1-12.
[f]**17.1-6** *the clans that were descendants of Zelophehad's five daughters . . . Hepher's brothers:* Or "Zelophehad's five daughters went to the priest Eleazar, Joshua, and the leaders of Israel. The five sisters said, 'The LORD told Moses to give us land just as he gave land to our relatives.' Joshua followed the LORD's instructions and gave land to these five sisters, as he had given land to Hepher's brothers."

● 17.7 *land of the Manasseh tribe:*
The land described in 17.7-11 is the land
given to the part of the Manasseh tribe
that settled west of the Jordan River.
Combined with the east Manasseh
lands, this tribe held the most territory
of all the tribes. **(See Map 3 on pg
1881.)**

■ 17.14 *the Joseph tribes:* This refers
to Ephraim and Manasseh (14.1-5). The
Ephraim and Manasseh tribes that
lived west of the Jordan act here as one
tribe, as they were treated in 16.1-4.
Their request for more land is based on
two arguments: God has continually
shown mercy to them, and they have
too many people for the land area they
were given. Their dissatisfaction is evidence of quarreling among the tribes.

● 17.15 *hill country . . . forest:* The
rugged hill country that covered a good
portion of the Joseph tribal territories
was difficult to farm. The dissatisfied
Joseph tribes were invited to clear the
forests of the Perizzites (3.10) and the
Rephaim (12.4).

● 18.1 *they met at Shiloh:* For this
religious ceremony the scene has shifted
from Gilgal to Shiloh, an important religious site for Israel in the time before
David. The sacred chest was kept in
Shiloh until it was taken by the Philistines
around 1050 B.C.

☞   The Sacred Tent

Manasseh's land west of the Jordan River
was divided into ten parts.

7The land of the Manasseh tribe went
from its northern border with the Asher
tribe south to Michmethath, which is to
the east of Shechem. The southern border
started there, but curved even farther
south to include the people who lived
around Tappuah Spring.**g** **8**The town of
Tappuah was on Manasseh's border with
Ephraim. Although the land around Tappuah belonged to Manasseh, the town itself belonged to Ephraim.

9-10 Then the border went west to the
Kanah Gorge and ran along the northern
edge of the gorge to the Mediterranean
Sea. The land south of the gorge belonged
to Ephraim. And even though there were a
few towns that belonged to Ephraim north
of the gorge, the land north of the gorge
belonged to Manasseh.

The western border of Manasseh was the
Mediterranean Sea, and the tribe shared a
border with the Asher tribe on the northwest and with the Issachar tribe on the
northeast.

11Manasseh was supposed to have the
following towns with their surrounding
villages inside the borders of Issachar's and
Asher's tribal lands:

> Beth-Shan, Ibleam, Endor, Taanach,
> Megiddo, and Dor, which is also called
> Naphath.**h**

12But the people of Manasseh could not
capture these towns, so the Canaanites
kept on living in them. **13**When the Israelites grew stronger, they made the
Canaanites in these towns work as their
slaves, though they never did force them
to leave.

Joseph's Descendants Ask for More Land

14One day the Joseph tribes**i** came to
Joshua and asked, "Why didn't you give us
more land? The LORD has always been kind
to us, and we have too many people for this
small region."

15Joshua replied, "If there's not enough
room for you in the hill country of
Ephraim, then go into the forest that belonged to the Perizzites and the Rephaim.**j**
Clear out the trees and make more room
for yourselves there."

16"Even if we do that," they answered,
"there still won't be enough land for us in
the hill country. And we can't move down
into Jezreel Valley, because the Canaanites
who live in Beth-Shan and in other parts of
the valley have iron chariots."

17"Your tribes do have a lot of people,"
Joshua admitted. "I'll give you more land.
Your tribes are powerful, **18**so you can have
the rest of the hill country, but it's a forest,
and you'll have to cut down the trees and
clear the land. You can also have Jezreel
Valley. Even though the Canaanites there
are strong and have iron chariots, you can
force them to leave the valley."

Joshua Gives Out the Rest of the Land

18 After Israel had captured the land,
they met at Shiloh and set up the
sacred tent.**k** **2**There were still seven tribes
without any land, **3-7**so Joshua told the
people:

> The Judah tribe has already settled
> in its land in the south, and the Joseph

---

g17.7 *to include . . . Tappuah Spring:* Hebrew; one ancient translation "to Jassiben-Tappuah" or "and
turns toward Tappuah Spring." **h**17.11 *Dor . . . Naphath:* One possible meaning for the difficult
Hebrew text. **i**17.14 *Joseph tribes:* Ephraim and the half of Manasseh that lived west of the Jordan
River. **j**17.15 *Rephaim:* See the note at 12.4. **k**18.1 *sacred tent:* Or "meeting tent."

tribes[l] have settled in their land in the north. The tribes of Gad, Reuben, and East Manasseh already have the land that the Lord's servant Moses gave them east of the Jordan River. And the people of Levi won't receive land like the other tribes. Instead, they will serve the Lord as priests.

But the rest of you haven't done a thing to take over any land. The Lord God who was worshiped by your ancestors has given you the land, and now it's time to go ahead and settle there.

Seven tribes still don't have any land. Each of these tribes should choose three men, and I'll send them to explore the remaining land. They will divide it into seven regions, write a description of each region, and bring these descriptions back to me. I will find out[m] from the Lord our God what region each tribe should get.

[8]Just before the men left camp, Joshua repeated their orders: "Explore the land and write a description of it. Then come back to Shiloh, and I will find out from the Lord how to divide the land."

[9]The men left and went across the land, dividing it into seven regions. They wrote down a description of each region, town by town, and returned to Joshua at the camp at Shiloh. [10]Joshua found out from the Lord how to divide the land, and he told the tribes what the Lord had decided.

Benjamin's Land

[11]Benjamin was the first tribe chosen to receive land. The region for its clans lay between the Judah tribe on the south and the Joseph tribes[n] on the north. [12]Benjamin's northern border started at the Jordan River and went up the ridge north of Jericho, then on west into the hill country as far as the Beth-Aven Desert. [13-14]From there it went to Luz, which is now called Bethel. The border ran along the ridge south of Luz, then went to Ataroth-Orech[o] and on as far as the mountain south of Lower Beth-Horon. At that point it turned south and became the western border. It went as far south as Kiriath-Baal, a town in Judah now called Kiriath-Jearim.

[15]Benjamin's southern border started at the edge of Kiriath-Jearim and went east to the ruins[p] and on to Nephtoah Spring. [16]From there it went to the bottom of the hill at the northern end of Rephaim Valley. The other side of this hill faces Hinnom Valley, which is on the land that slopes south from Jerusalem.[q] The border went down through Hinnom Valley until it reached Enrogel.

[17]At Enrogel the border curved north and went to Enshemesh and on east to Geliloth,[r] which is across the valley from Adummim Pass. Then it went down to the Monument of Bohan,[s] who belonged to the Reuben tribe. [18]The border ran along the hillside north of Beth-Arabah,[t] then down into the Jordan River valley. [19]Inside the valley it went south as far as the northern hillside of Beth-Hoglah. The last

[l]18.3-7 *Joseph tribes:* See the note at 17.14.   [m]18.3-7 *find out:* Hebrew "cast lots to find out" (see the note at 14.1-5).   [n]18.11 *Joseph tribes:* See the note at 17.14.   [o]18.13,14 *Ataroth-Orech:* One ancient translation; Hebrew "Ataroth-Addar."   [p]18.15 *the ruins:* One possible meaning for the difficult Hebrew text.   [q]18.16 *Jerusalem:* Hebrew "the Jebusite town."   [r]18.17 *Geliloth:* Probably another name for Gilgal.   [s]18.17 *Monument of Bohan:* See the note at 15.6.   [t]18.18 *hillside north of Beth-Arabah:* One ancient translation (see also the border description in 15.6); Hebrew "the northern hillside overlooking the Jordan River valley."

19.1-9 *Simeon . . . inside Judah's territory:* Simeon was the second son born to Jacob and Leah (Gen 29.31-33). Simeon and Jacob's first son Reuben lost their normal position of leadership among the tribes because of their evil actions (Gen 49.3-7). The tribal boundaries for Simeon are not given because Simeon became absorbed into the larger tribe of Judah. The towns listed for Simeon are in the southern part of Judah.

19.10-12 *Zebulun:* Zebulun was the sixth son born to Jacob and Leah (Gen 30.16-20). The five tribes listed in 19.10-48 settled in the Galilee region. It is not possible to trace their borders with accuracy. Zebulun's region is roughly the western half of the southern Galilean hills. **(See Map 3 on pg 1881.)**

section of the border went from there to the northern end of the Dead Sea,[u] at the mouth of the Jordan River. [20]The Jordan River itself was Benjamin's eastern border.

These were the borders of Benjamin's tribal land, where the clans of Benjamin lived.

[21-24]One region of Benjamin's tribal land had twelve towns with their surrounding villages. Those towns were Jericho, Beth-Hoglah, Emek-Keziz, Beth-Arabah, Zemaraim, Bethel, Avvim, Parah, Ophrah, Chephar-Ammoni, Ophni, and Geba.

[25-28]In the other region there were the following 14 towns with their surrounding villages: Gibeon, Ramah, Beeroth, Mizpeh, Chephirah, Mozah, Rekem, Irpeel, Taralah, Zelah, Haeleph, Gibeah, Kiriath-Jearim,[v] and Jerusalem, which is also called Jebusite Town.

These regions are the tribal lands of Benjamin.

Simeon's Land

19 Simeon was the second tribe chosen to receive land, and the region for its clans was inside Judah's borders. [2-6]In one region of Simeon's tribal land there were the following 13 towns with their surrounding villages:

Beersheba, Shema,[w] Moladah, Hazar-Shual, Balah, Ezem, Eltolad, Bethul, Hormah, Ziklag, Beth-Marcaboth, Hazar-Susah, Beth-Lebaoth, and Sharuhen.

[7]In another region, Simeon had the following four towns with their surrounding villages:

Enrimmon,[x] Tachan,[y] Ether, and Ashan.

[8]Simeon's land also included all the other towns and villages as far south as Baalath-Beer, which is also called Ramah of the South.

[9]Simeon's tribal land was actually inside Judah's territory. Judah had received too much land for the number of people in its tribe, so part of Judah's land was given to Simeon.

Zebulun's Land

[10-12]Zebulun was the third tribe chosen to receive land. The southern border for its clans started in the west at the edge of the gorge near Jokneam. It went east to the edge of the land that belongs to the town of Dabbesheth, and continued on to Maralah and Sarid. It took in the land that belongs to Chislothtabor, then ended at Daberath.

The eastern border went up to Japhia [13]and continued north to Gath-Hepher, Ethkazin, and Rimmonah,[z] where it curved[a] toward Neah [14]and became the northern border. Then it curved south around Hannathon and went as far west as Iphtahel Valley.

---

[u]**18.19** *northern . . . Dead Sea:* One possible meaning for the difficult Hebrew text.   [v]**18.25-28** *Kiriath-Jearim:* One ancient translation; Hebrew "Kiriath."   [w]**19.2-6** *Shema:* One ancient translation and some manuscripts of another ancient translation (see also the list at 15.21-32); Hebrew and some manuscripts of one ancient translation "Sheba." The list in 1 Chronicles 4.28 does not have either "Shema" or "Sheba."   [x]**19.7** *Enrimmon:* Some Hebrew manuscripts and one ancient translation; most Hebrew manuscripts "Ain, Rimmon."   [y]**19.7** *Tachan:* Some manuscripts of one ancient translation; the Hebrew text does not have this word.   [z]**19.13** *Rimmonah:* Or "Rimmon."   [a]**19.13** *Rimmonah . . . curved:* One possible meaning for the difficult Hebrew text.

[15]Zebulun had twelve towns with their surrounding villages. Some of these were Kattath, Nahalal, Shimron, Jiralah,[b] and Bethlehem.[c]

[16]This is the tribal land, and these are the towns and villages of the Zebulun clans.

Issachar's Land

[17-23]Issachar was the fourth tribe chosen to receive land. The northern border for its clans went from Mount Tabor east to the Jordan River. Their land included the following 16 towns with their surrounding villages:

Jezreel, Chesulloth, Shunem, Haph-araim, Shion, Anaharath, Debirath,[d] Kishion, Ebez, Remeth, En-Gannim, Enhaddah, Beth-Pazzez, Tabor,[e] Sha-hazumah and Beth-Shemesh.[f]

Asher's Land

[24-26]Asher was the fifth tribe chosen to receive land, and the region for its clans included the following towns:

Helkath, Hali, Beten, Achshaph, Al-lammelech, Amad, and Mishal.

Asher's southern border ran from the Mediterranean Sea southeast along the Shihor-Libnath River at the foot of Mount Carmel, [27]then east to Beth-Dagon. On the southeast, Asher shared a border with Zebulun along the Iphtahel Valley. On the eastern side their border ran north to Beth-Emek, went east of Cabul, and then on to Neiel, [28]Abdon,[g] Rehob, Hammon, Kanah, and as far north as the city of Sidon. [29-31]Then it turned west to become the northern border and went to Ramah[h] and the fortress-city of Tyre.[i] Near Tyre it turned toward Hosah and ended at the Mediterranean Sea.

Asher had a total of 22 towns with their surrounding villages, including Mahalab,[j] Achzib, Acco,[k] Aphek, and Rehob.

Naphtali's Land

[32-34]Naphtali was the sixth tribe chosen to receive land. The southern border for its clans started in the west, where the tribal lands of Asher and Zebulun meet near Hukkok. From that point it ran east and southeast along the border with Zebulun as far as Aznoth-Tabor. From there the border went east to Heleph, Adami-Nekeb, Jabneel,[l] then to the town called Oak in Zaanannim,[m] and Lakkum. The southern border ended at the Jordan River, at the edge of the town named Jehudah.[n] Naphtali shared a border with Asher on the west.

[35-39]The Naphtali clans received this region as their tribal land, and it included

---

19.17-23 *Issachar:* Issachar was the fifth son of Jacob and Leah (Gen 30.16-18). In Genesis 49.14,15 Issachar is compared to a donkey that is satisfied to rest and willing to become a slave to others, which may refer to its later service of King Solomon (1 Kgs 4.6; 5.13; 9.21) or to serving its Canaanite neighbors. This tribe's territory forms a rough square.

19.24-26 *Asher:* Asher was Jacob's second son with Leah's servant Zilpah (Gen 30.9-13). The Asher tribe's northern border ran along the edge of the Galilean mountains to the territory of Tyre.

19.31 *Tyre:* Part of Tyre, the Phoenician walled city, was built on an island in the Mediterranean Sea about half a mile from shore. It was never under Israelite control. Years later, its king, Hiram, would be an important ally of Israel.

Phoenicia

19.32-34 *Naphtali:* Naphtali was the second son of Jacob and Rachel's servant Bilhah (Gen 30.4-8). This tribe held land in the Galilean highlands. Its northern border is not given but, like Asher, it bordered Phoenician territory. (See Map 3 on pg 1881.)

---

[b]19.15 *Jiralah:* Some Hebrew manuscripts and two ancient translations; most Hebrew manuscripts "Idalah." [c]19.15 *Bethlehem:* This town is different from the Bethlehem in 15.58,59. [d]19.17-23 *Debirath:* One ancient translation; Hebrew "Rabbith." Debirath is probably the same place as Daberath in verse 12. [e]19.17-23 *Mount Tabor . . . Tabor:* In Hebrew the name "Tabor" is used only once. It was probably intended as the name of a town located at the foot of Mount Tabor and which formed one point on the northern border of Issachar. [f]19.17-23 *Beth-Shemesh:* Not the same Beth-Shemesh as in 15.10 or 19.35-39. [g]19.28 *Abdon:* A few Hebrew manuscripts and one ancient translation; most Hebrew manuscripts "Ebron." [h]19.29-31 *Ramah:* Not the same "Ramah" as in 18.25-28 or 19.35-39. [i]19.29-31 *fortress-city of Tyre:* Tyre was a walled city built on an island about half a mile from shore. [j]19.29-31 *Mahalab:* One possible meaning for the difficult Hebrew text. [k]19.29-31 *Acco:* One ancient translation; Hebrew "Ummah." [l]19.32-34 *Jabneel:* This town is not the same Jabneel as in 15.11. [m]19.32-34 *the town . . . Zaanannim:* Or "the oak tree in the town of Zaanannim." [n]19.32-34 *at . . . Jehudah:* One possible meaning for the difficult Hebrew text.

19 towns with their surrounding villages. The following towns had walls around them:

Ziddim, Zer, Hammath, Rakkath, Chinnereth, Adamah, Ramah,[o] Hazor, Kedesh, Edrei,[p] Enhazor, Iron, Migdalel, Horem, Beth-Anath, and Beth-Shemesh.[q]

Dan's Land

40-46 Dan was the seventh tribe chosen to receive land, and the region for its clans included the following towns:

Zorah, Eshtaol, Ir-Shemesh,[r] Shaalabbin, Aijalon, Ithlah, Elon, Timnah, Ekron, Eltekeh, Gibbethon, Baalath, Jehud, Azor,[s] Beneberak, Gath-Rimmon, Mejarkon, and Rakkon.

Dan's tribal land[t] went almost as far as Joppa. 47-48 Its clans received this land and these towns with their surrounding villages.

Later, when enemies[u] forced them to leave their tribal land, they went to the town of Leshem. They attacked the town, captured it, and killed the people who lived there. Then they settled there themselves and renamed the town Dan after their ancestor.

Joshua's Land

49-51 The Israelites were still gathered in Shiloh in front of the sacred tent,[v] when Eleazar the priest, Joshua, and the family leaders of Israel finished giving out the land to the tribes. The LORD had told the people to give Joshua whatever town he wanted. So Joshua chose Timnath-Serah in the hill country of Ephraim, and the people gave it to him. Joshua went to Timnath-Serah, rebuilt it, and lived there.

The Safe Towns

(Numbers 35.9-15; Deuteronomy 19.1-13)

20 One day the LORD told Joshua:

2 When Moses was still alive, I commanded him to tell the Israelites about the Safe Towns. Now you tell them that it is time to set up these towns. 3-4 If a person accidentally kills someone and the victim's relatives say it was murder, they might try to take revenge.[w] Anyone accused of murder can run to one of the Safe Towns and be safe from the victim's relatives. The one needing protection will stand at the entrance to the town gate and explain to the town leaders what happened. Then the leaders will bring that person in and provide a place to live in their town.

5 One of the victim's relatives might come to the town, looking for revenge. But the town leaders must not simply hand over the person accused of murder. After all, the accused and the victim had been neighbors, not enemies. 6 The citizens of that Safe Town must come together and hold a trial.

[o] **19.35-39** *Ramah*: Not the same "Ramah" as in 18.25-28 or 19.29-31. [p] **19.35-39** *Edrei*: Not the same Edrei as the town in Bashan east of the Jordan River where King Og had lived (see 12.4; 13.11,12,30,31). [q] **19.35-39** *Beth-Shemesh*: Not the same Beth-Shemesh as in 15.10 or 19.17-23. [r] **19.40-46** *Ir-Shemesh*: Possibly the same town as the Beth-Shemesh of 15.10. [s] **19.40-46** *Azor*: Some manuscripts of one ancient translation; the Hebrew text does not have this word. [t] **19.40-46** *Gath-Rimmon, Mejarkon, and Rakkon. Dan's tribal land*: Or "Gath-Rimmon, and Rakkon. Dan's tribal land also included the Yarkon River and." [u] **19.47,48** *enemies*: Probably the Philistines. [v] **19.49-51** *sacred tent*: Or "meeting tent." [w] **20.3,4** *revenge*: At this time in Israel's history, the clan could appoint a close male relative to find and kill a person who had killed a member of their clan.

● 19.40-46 *Dan:* Dan was the first-born son of Jacob and Rachel's servant Bilhah (Gen 30.4-6). No border list is given for this tribe. The towns listed fall in the second and fifth regions of Judah (15.21-32,45-47).

● 19.47-48 *Then they settled there themselves:* Ancient tradition locates Dan in the south along the Mediterranean coastal plain (19.40-46). Sometime before David became king of Israel, the tribe migrated to the north and took territory around the town of Leshem, also called Laish. The "enemies" who forced them to leave were probably the Philistines. For a different account of the migration see Judges 17,18.

● 19.49-51 *Timnath-Serah:* This town was located 17 miles southwest of Shechem and 10 miles northwest of Bethel. Joshua is from the tribe of Ephraim (Num 13.4-16). Timnath-Serah is given to Joshua as a reward for his services, as Hebron was given to Caleb in 14.13. This is the proper last act in the land distribution.

● 20.2-8 *Safe Towns:* All six of these towns appear in chapter 21, where they belong to the Levites. The cities serve both sides of the Jordan River and are spaced to cover the north, south, and center of the land. The presence of the priests also helped ensure the condition of safety in these towns. The reasons for this are given in Deuteronomy 19.10.

Safe Towns

They may decide that the victim was killed accidentally and that the accused is not guilty of murder.

Everyone found not guilty[x] must still live in the Safe Town until the high priest dies. Then they can go back to their own towns and their homes that they had to leave behind.

[7]The Israelites decided that the following three towns west of the Jordan River would be Safe Towns:

Kedesh in Galilee in Naphtali's hill country, Shechem in Ephraim's hill country, and Kiriath-Arba in Judah's hill country. Kiriath-Arba is now called Hebron.

[8]The Israelites had already decided on the following three towns east of the Jordan River:

Bezer in the desert flatlands of Reuben, Ramoth in Gilead, which was a town that belonged to Gad, and Golan in Bashan, which belonged to Manasseh.

[9]These Safe Towns were set up, so that if Israelites or even foreigners who lived in Israel accidentally killed someone, they could run to one of these towns. There they would be safe until a trial could be held, even if one of the victim's relatives came looking for revenge.

Levi's Towns

21 [1-2]While the Israelites were still camped at Shiloh in the land of Canaan, the family leaders of the Levi tribe went to speak to the priest Eleazar, Joshua, and the family leaders of the other Israelite tribes. The leaders of Levi said, "The LORD told Moses that you have to give us towns and provide pastures for our animals."[y]

[3]Since the LORD had said this, the leaders of the other Israelite tribes agreed to give some of the towns and pastures from their tribal lands to Levi. [4]The leaders asked the LORD to show them[z] in what order the clans of Levi would be given towns, and which towns each clan would receive.

The Kohath clans were first. The descendants of Aaron, Israel's first priest,[a] were given 13 towns from the tribes of Judah, Simeon, and Benjamin. [5]The other members of the Kohath clans received 10 towns from the tribes of Ephraim, Dan, and West Manasseh. [6]The clans that were descendants of Gershon were given 13 towns from the tribes of Issachar, Asher, Naphtali, and East Manasseh. [7]The clans that were descendants of Merari[b] received 12 towns from the tribes of Reuben, Gad, and Zebulun.

[8]The LORD had told Moses that he would show the Israelites which towns and pastures to give to the clans of Levi, and he did.

TOWNS FROM JUDAH, SIMEON, BENJAMIN

[9-19]The descendants of Aaron from the Kohath clans of Levi were priests, and they were chosen to receive towns first. They were given 13 towns and the pastureland around them. Nine of these towns were from the tribes of Judah and Simeon and four from Benjamin.

Hebron, Libnah, Jattir, Eshtemoa, Holon, Debir, Ashan,[c] Juttah, and Beth-Shemesh

20.9 *foreigners:* The cities provided protection for foreigners as well. Anyone who lived in the land was to be safeguarded.

Foreigners (Aliens)

21.1-2 *Levi tribe . . . give us towns:* The Levites were given 48 towns (21.41,42) with pasturelands by the other tribes. The Levites did not control these cities, but they served as priests there. This division of the land ensured that the priests were scattered among the tribes. The actual selection of the Levite towns was determined by casting lots.

21.4-7 *Kohath . . . Gershon . . . Merari:* These are the names of the three major clans of the Levi tribe. The Kohath clans are given towns and pastureland in 21.9-26, the Gershon clans in 21.27-33, and the Merari clans in 21.34-40. Although Gershon was Levi's oldest son, the Kohath clan gets the most towns, most likely because Israel's first high priest, Aaron, had been a member of this clan.

21.9-19 *Aaron . . . receive towns first:* The descendants of Aaron from the Kohath clans were given priority because of Aaron's importance as the Israelite's first high priest.

Israel's Priests

[x]**20.6** *not guilty:* If the person was found to be guilty of murder, the citizens of the Safe Town were to let the victim's relatives kill the murderer (see Deuteronomy 19.11-13).   [y]**21.1,2** *The LORD told Moses . . . animals:* See Numbers 35.1-8.   [z]**21.4** *asked the LORD to show them:* Hebrew "cast lots to find out." See the note at 14.1-5.   [a]**21.4** *The descendants . . . priest:* Hebrew text; three ancient translations "The priests, the descendants of Aaron." The male descendants of Aaron would also be priests.   [b]**21.4-7** *Kohath . . . Gershon . . . Merari:* Sons of Levi, the ancestor of the tribe of Levi.   [c]**21.9-19** *Ashan:* One ancient translation and the parallel in 1 Chronicles 6.59; Hebrew "Ain."

21.27-33 *descendants of Gershon*: The Gershon clans were in charge of setting up and taking down the tent's covering and curtains, except the curtain in front of the most holy place (Num 4.21-28). The Gershon towns and pastures were in the tribal territories of East Manasseh, Issachar, Asher, and Naphtali.

21.34-40 *descendants of Merari*: The Merarites were responsible for setting up and taking down the framework that held the sacred tent together (Num 4.29-33). They also carried these objects when the Israelite tribes moved to a new location. The Merari towns and pastures were in the tribal territories of Zebulun, Reuben, and Gad. **(See Map 3 on pg 1881.)**

21.43-45 *The LORD gave . . . The LORD promised*: This summary of the conquest emphasizes the LORD's role in helping Israel capture and settle Canaan. This fulfilled the ancient promises made to Israel (1.6-8). Though Israel had settled in the land, the enemies around them were not yet completely under Israel's control. Battles would continue off and on for many years.

were from Judah and Simeon. Hebron, located in the hill country of Judah, was earlier called Arba's Town.[d] It had been named after Arba, the ancestor of the Anakim.[e] Hebron's pasturelands went along with the town, but its farmlands and the villages around it had been given to Caleb.[f] Hebron was also one of the Safe Towns for people who had accidentally killed someone.

Gibeon, Geba, Anathoth, and Almon were from Benjamin.

TOWNS FROM EPHRAIM, DAN, WEST MANASSEH

20-26 The rest of the Kohath clans of the Levi tribe received ten towns and the pastureland around them. Four of these towns were from the tribe of Ephraim, four from Dan, and two from West Manasseh.

Shechem, Gezer, Kibzaim, and Beth-Horon were from Ephraim. Shechem was located in the hill country, and it was also one of the Safe Towns for people who had accidentally killed someone.

Elteke, Gibbethon, Aijalon, and Gath-Rimmon were from Dan.

Taanach and Jibleam[g] were from West Manasseh.

TOWNS FROM EAST MANASSEH, ISSACHAR, ASHER, NAPHTALI

27-33 The clans of Levi that were descendants of Gershon received 13 towns and the pastureland around them. Two of these towns were from the tribe of East Manasseh, four from Issachar, four from Asher, and three from Naphtali.

Golan in Bashan and Beeshterah were from East Manasseh.

Kishion, Daberath, Jarmuth, and En-Gannim were from Issachar.

Mishal, Abdon, Helkath, and Rehob were from Asher.

Kedesh in Galilee, Hammothdor, and Kartan were from Naphtali. Golan in Bashan and Kedesh in Galilee were also Safe Towns for people who had accidentally killed someone.

TOWNS FROM ZEBULUN, REUBEN, GAD

34-40 The rest of the Levi clans were descendants of Merari, and they received twelve towns with the pastureland around them. Four towns were from the tribe of Zebulun, four from Reuben, and four from Gad.

Jokneam, Kartah, Rimmonah,[h] and Nahalal were from Zebulun.

Bezer, Jazah, Kedemoth, and Mephaath were from Reuben. Bezer was located in the desert flatlands east of the Jordan River across from Jericho.[i]

Ramoth in Gilead, Mahanaim, Heshbon, and Jazer were from Gad.

Bezer and Ramoth in Gilead were Safe Towns[j] for people who had accidentally killed someone.

41-42 The people of the Levi tribe had a total of 48 towns within Israel, and they had pastures around each one of their towns.

Israel Settles in the Land

43The LORD gave the Israelites the land he had promised their ancestors, and they captured it and settled in it. **44**There still were enemies around Israel, but the LORD kept his promise to let his people live in

[d]**21.9-19** *Arba's Town*: See the note at 14.15.   [e]**21.9-19** *Anakim*: See the note at 11.21.   [f]**21.9-19** *Caleb*: See 14.6-14.   [g]**21.20-26** *Jibleam*: One ancient translation and the parallel in 1 Chronicles 6.70; Hebrew "Gath-Rimmon."   [h]**21.34-40** *Rimmonah*: One possible meaning for the difficult Hebrew text. [i]**21.34-40** *Bezer . . . Jericho*: One possible meaning for the difficult Hebrew text.   [j]**21.34-40** *Bezer and Ramoth in Gilead were Safe Towns*: One ancient translation; Hebrew "Ramoth in Gilead was a Safe Town."

peace. And whenever the Israelites did have to go to war, no enemy could defeat them. The LORD always helped Israel win. [45]The LORD promised to do many good things for Israel, and he kept his promise every time.

The Two and a Half Tribes Return Home

22 Joshua held a meeting with the men of the tribes of Reuben, Gad, and East Manasseh, and he told them:

[2-3]You have obeyed every command of the LORD your God and of his servant Moses. And you have done everything I've told you to do. It's taken a long time, but you have stayed and helped your relatives. [4]The LORD promised to give peace to your relatives, and that's what he has done. Now it's time for you to go back to your own homes in the land that Moses gave you east of the Jordan River.

[5]Moses taught you to love the LORD your God, to be faithful to him, and to worship and obey him with your whole heart and with all your strength. So be very careful to do everything Moses commanded.

[6-9]You've become rich from what you've taken from your enemies. You have big herds of cattle, lots of silver, gold, bronze, and iron, and plenty of clothes. Take everything home with you and share with the people of your tribe.

I pray that God will be kind to you. You are now free to go home.

The tribes of Reuben and Gad started back to Gilead, their own land. Moses had given the land of Bashan to the East Manasseh tribe, so they started back along with Reuben and Gad. God had told Moses that these two and a half tribes should conquer Gilead and Bashan, and they had done so.

Joshua had given land west of the Jordan River to the other half of the Manasseh tribe, so they stayed at Shiloh in the land of Canaan with the rest of the Israelites.

[10-11]The tribes of Reuben, Gad, and East Manasseh reached the western side of the Jordan River valley[k] and built a huge altar there beside the river.

When the rest of the Israelites heard what these tribes had done,[l] [12]the Israelite men met at Shiloh to get ready to attack the two and a half tribes. [13]But first they sent a priest, Phinehas the son of Eleazar, to talk with the two and a half tribes. [14]Each of the ten tribes at Shiloh sent the leader of one of its families along with Phinehas.

[15]Phinehas and these leaders went to Gilead and met with the tribes of Reuben, Gad, and East Manasseh. They said:

[16]All of the LORD's people have gathered together and have sent us to find out why you are unfaithful to our God. You have turned your backs on the LORD by building that altar. Why are you rebelling against him? [17]Wasn't our people's sin at Peor[m] terrible enough for you? The LORD punished us by sending a horrible sickness that killed many of us, and we still suffer because of that sin.[n] [18]Now you are turning your backs on the LORD again.

22.6-9 *You've become rich... share with the people:* Reuben, Gad, and East Manasseh have fulfilled their obligations to help; now they can return home. They go back with a share of the things taken from those they had conquered.

22.13 *Phinehas:* The eagerness of Phinehas is first seen in Numbers 25.6-13. He is grandson of Aaron and son of Eleazar, the high priest during the conquest. This is the first time he is mentioned in JOSHUA. Here, Phinehas and ten leaders from each of the western tribes were sent to investigate the rumor and resolve the problem.

22.17 *our people's sin at Peor:* At the time of the wanderings in the desert, the Israelites worshiped the Moabite gods and the Canaanite god Baal at Acacia. Phinehas' fierce, swift action stopped the deadly disease sent by the LORD as a punishment (Num 25).

[k]**22.10,11** *western . . . valley:* Or "the town of Geliloth, which is in the land of Canaan near the Jordan River." [l]**22.10,11** *built a huge altar . . . tribes had done:* According to Deuteronomy 12.5-14, the LORD wanted the Israelites to have only one altar for offering sacrifices. To build another altar would be to disobey the LORD. [m]**22.17** *our people's sin at Peor:* See Numbers 25. [n]**22.17** *we still . . . sin:* Or "There are still people in Israel who want to worship other gods."

"Moses taught you to love the LORD your God, to be faithful to him, and to worship and obey him with your whole heart and with all your strength." JOSH 22.5

22.24-25 *we were worried*: The east Jordan tribes explain their action. They fear that at some future time, the tribes in western Palestine might disown them. So, they set up the altar, not for sacrifices (22.23), but as a sign of their unity with the rest of Israel. They are bound together by faith in one God.

22.27-29 *the LORD's altar . . . sacred tent*: At this time, the sacred tent was portable, and so was the altar used for sacrifices at the sacred tent. The tent was set up at Shiloh, west of the Jordan River. The issue here is that only one place for sacrifices is commanded by Moses in Deuteronomy 12.5-19. The eastern tribes insist they have not built an altar for sacrifices, but as a memorial. These verses provide evidence of conflict and a potential feud between the two and a half tribes who settled east of the Jordan and the tribes who settled west of the Jordan.

If you don't stop rebelling against the LORD at once, he will be angry with the whole nation. [19]If you don't think your land is a fit place to serve God, then move across the Jordan and live with us in the LORD's own land, where his sacred tent is located. But don't rebel against the LORD our God or against us by building another altar besides the LORD's own altar.[o] [20] Don't you remember what happened when Achan was unfaithful[p] and took some of the things that belonged to God? This made God angry with the entire nation. Achan died because he sinned, but he also caused the death of many others.

[21]The tribes of Reuben, Gad, and East Manasseh answered:

[22]The LORD is the greatest God! We ask him to be our witness, because he knows whether or not we were rebellious or unfaithful when we built that altar. If we were unfaithful, then we pray that God won't rescue us today. Let us tell you why we built that altar, [23]and we ask the LORD to punish us if we are lying. We didn't build it so we could turn our backs on the LORD. We didn't even build it so we could offer animal or grain sacrifices to please the LORD or ask his blessing.

[24-25]We built that altar because we were worried. Someday your descendants might tell our descendants, "The LORD made the Jordan River the boundary between us Israelites and you people of Reuben and Gad. The LORD is Israel's God, but you're not part of Israel, so you can't take part in worshiping the LORD."

Your descendants might say that and try to make our descendants stop worshiping and obeying the LORD. [26]That's why we decided to build the altar. It isn't for offering sacrifices, not even sacrifices to please the LORD.[q] [27-29]To build another altar for offering sacrifices would be the same as turning our backs on the LORD and rebelling against him. We could never do that! No, we built the altar to remind us and you and the generations to come that we will worship the LORD. And so we will keep bringing our sacrifices to the LORD's altar, there in front of his sacred tent. Now your descendants will never be able to say to our descendants, "You can't worship the LORD."

But if they do say this, our descendants can answer back, "Look at this altar our ancestors built! It's like the LORD's altar, but it isn't for offering sacrifices. It's here to remind us and you that we belong to the LORD, just as much as you do."

[30-31]Phinehas and the clan leaders were pleased when they heard the tribes of Reuben, Gad, and East Manasseh explain why they had built the altar. Then Phinehas told them, "Today we know that the LORD is helping us. You have not been unfaithful to him, and this means that the LORD will not be angry with us."

[32]Phinehas and the clan leaders left Gilead and went back to Canaan to tell the Israelites about their meeting with the Reuben and Gad tribes. [33]The Israelites were happy and praised God. There was no more talk about going to war and wiping out the tribes of Reuben and Gad.

[34]The people of Reuben and Gad named

---

[o]**22.19** *or against . . . altar*: Or "by building another altar besides the LORD's own altar. That would even make us into rebels along with you." [p]**22.20** *Achan was unfaithful*: See 7.1,26. [q]**22.26** *sacrifices to please the LORD*: See the note at 8.30-32.

the altar "A Reminder to Us All That the LORD Is Our God."r

Joshua's Farewell Speech

23 The LORD let Israel live in peace with its neighbors for a long time, and Joshua lived to a ripe old age. 2One day he called a meeting of the leaders of the tribes of Israel, including the old men, the judges, and the officials. Then he told them:

I am now very old. 3You have seen how the LORD your God fought for you and helped you defeat the nations who lived in this land. 4-5There are still some nations left, but the LORD has promised you their land. So when you attack them, he will make them run away. I have already divided their land among your tribes, as I did with the land of the nations I defeated between the Jordan River and the Mediterranean Sea.

6Be sure that you carefully obey everything written in *The Book of the Law*s of Moses and do exactly what it says.

7Don't have anything to do with the nations that live around you. Don't worship their gods or pray to their idols or make promises in the names of their gods. 8Be as faithful to the LORD as you have always been.

9When you attacked powerful nations, the LORD made them run away, and no one has ever been able to stand up to you. 10Any one of you can defeat a thousand enemy soldiers, because

the LORD God fights for you, just as he promised. 11Be sure to always love the LORD your God. 12-13Don't ever turn your backs on him by marrying people from the nations that are left in the land. Don't even make friends with them. I tell you that if you are friendly with those nations, the LORD won't chase them away when you attack. Instead, they'll be like a trap for your feet, a whip on your back, and thorns in your eyes. And finally, none of you will be left in this good land that the LORD has given you.

14I will soon die, as everyone must. But deep in your hearts you know that the LORD has kept every promise he ever made to you. Not one of them has been broken. 15-16Yes, when the LORD makes a promise, he does what he has promised. But when he makes a threat, he will also do what he has threatened. The LORD is our God. He gave us this wonderful land and made an agreement with us that we would worship only him. But if you worship other gods, it will make the LORD furious. He will start getting rid of you, and soon not one of you will be left in this good land that he has given you.

We Will Worship and Obey the LORD

24 Joshua called the tribes of Israel together for a meeting at Shechem. He asked the leaders, including the old men, the judges, and the officials, to come up and stand near the sacred tent.t 2Then

---

● **23.1,2** *Joshua . . . called a meeting:* The place is not known. This is not the same assembly as in chapter 24. Joshua's speech here is a fitting conclusion to the book, balancing the material in 1.1-9 and drawing together the themes first raised at the beginning of the book.

■ **23.11-13** *love the LORD . . . Don't ever turn:* This teaching, indeed the entire farewell address, closely follows Moses' speech in Deuteronomy 6,7. This is a significant warning which recognizes that intermarriage can cause divided loyalties.

✎ Foreigners (Aliens)

● **23.12-13** *a trap . . . a whip . . . thorns:* Foreign nations are described here as a source of constant trouble as in Judges 2.3. The biggest danger is that the people of Israel will lose the land that they have begun to settle. This view of foreigners contrasts sharply with the message of RUTH and with God's plan for Israel as reported in Isaiah 49.6; 51.4,5; 55.5; 56.6-8.

■ **23.15-16** *made an agreement:* The agreement is based on *The Book of the Law of Moses* and calls for being faithful to the LORD God and not worshiping other gods (Josh 23.6-8).

✎ Agreements (Covenants)

---

r**22.34** *named . . . God:* Or "gave a name to the altar. They explained, 'This altar is here to remind us all that the LORD is our God'"; most Hebrew manuscripts. A few Hebrew manuscripts and one ancient translation "named the altar 'Reminder.' They explained, 'This altar is here to remind us all that the LORD is our God.'" s**23.6** *Law:* See the note at 8.30-32. t**24.1** *near . . . tent:* Or "in front of the sacred chest"; Hebrew "in the presence of God."

"Be as faithful to the LORD as you have always been."
JOSH 23.8

24.5-6 *those horrible things*: This refers to the disasters God sent upon Egypt when Egypt's king would not release the Hebrew people from slavery.

Disasters (Plagues)

24.7 *You lived in the desert*: This summary of the history of God's saving acts follows the biblical record and Deuteronomy 26.5-11, but does not mention the events at Mount Sinai or the wilderness wanderings, which are described in Exodus 15.22—40.38 and Numbers 1–20.

24.14 *Get rid of the idols*: Joshua's speech provided an opportunity for the Israelites who had been living according to the Law of Moses (1.6-8) to rededicate themselves to worshiping the LORD. Others who had been taken into the people of Israel during the time of settlement were also challenged to "choose here and now" whether they would worship the LORD or keep worshiping their other gods. While in Egypt the people had worshiped the sacred bull idol representing the fertility god Apis. The gods of Mesopotamia beyond the Euphrates River included Marduk, the chief god of Babylon, and Bel, who was similar to the Canaanite fertility god Baal.

Joshua told everyone to listen to this message from the LORD, the God of Israel:

Long ago your ancestors lived on the other side of the Euphrates River, and they worshiped other gods. This continued until the time of your ancestor Terah and his two sons, Abraham and Nahor. ³But I brought Abraham across the Euphrates River and led him through the land of Canaan. I blessed him by giving him Isaac, the first in a line of many descendants. ⁴Then I gave Isaac two sons, Jacob and Esau. I gave Esau the hill country of Mount Seir, but your ancestor Jacob and his children went to live in Egypt.

⁵⁻⁶Later I sent Moses and his brother Aaron to help your people, and I made all those horrible things happen to the Egyptians. I brought your ancestors out of Egypt, but the Egyptians got in their chariots and on their horses and chased your ancestors, catching up with them at the Red Sea.ᵘ ⁷Your people cried to me for help, so I put a dark cloud between them and the Egyptians. Then I opened up the sea and let your people walk across on dry ground. But when the Egyptians tried to follow, I commanded the sea to swallow them, and they drowned while you watched.

You lived in the desert for a long time, ⁸then I brought you into the land east of the Jordan River. The Amorites were living there, and they fought you. But with my help, you defeated them, wiped them out, and took their land. ⁹King Balak decided that his nation Moab would go to war against you, so he asked Balaamᵛ to come and put a curse on you. ¹⁰But I

wouldn't listen to Balaam, and I rescued you by making him bless you instead of curse you.

¹¹You crossed the Jordan River and came to Jericho. The rulers of Jericho fought you, and so did the Amorites, the Perizzites, the Canaanites, the Hittites, the Girgashites, the Hivites, and the Jebusites. I helped you defeat them all. ¹²Your enemies ran from you, but not because you had swords and bows and arrows. I made your enemies panic and run away, as I had done with the two Amorite kings east of the Jordan River.

¹³You didn't have to work for this land—I gave it to you. Now you live in towns you didn't build, and you eat grapes and olives from vineyards and trees you didn't plant.

¹⁴Then Joshua told the people:

Worship the LORD, obey him, and always be faithful. Get rid of the idols your ancestors worshiped when they lived on the other side of the Euphrates River and in Egypt. ¹⁵But if you don't want to worship the LORD, then choose here and now! Will you worship the same idols your ancestors did? Or since you're living on land that once belonged to the Amorites, maybe you'll worship their gods. I won't. My family and I are going to worship and obey the LORD!

¹⁶The people answered:

We could never worship other gods or stop worshiping the LORD. ¹⁷The LORD is our God. We were slaves in Egypt as our ancestors had been, but we saw the LORD work miracles to set our people free and to bring us out of Egypt. Even though other nations

ᵘ**24.5,6** *Red Sea*: See the note at 2.10. ᵛ**24.9** *King Balak . . . Balaam*: The Hebrew text has "King Balak the son of Zippor . . . Balaam the son of Beor."

were all around us, the LORD protected us wherever we went. [18]And when we fought the Amorites and the other nations that lived in this land, the LORD made them run away. Yes, we will worship and obey the LORD, because the LORD is our God.

[19]Joshua said:

The LORD is fearsome; he is the one true God, and I don't think you are able to worship and obey him in the ways he demands. You would have to be completely faithful, and if you sin or rebel, he won't let you get away with it. [20]If you turn your backs on the LORD and worship the gods of other nations, the LORD will turn against you. He will make terrible things happen to you and wipe you out, even though he had been good to you before.

[21]But the people shouted, "We won't worship any other gods. We will worship and obey only the LORD!"

[22]Joshua said, "You have heard yourselves say that you will worship and obey the LORD. Isn't that true?"

"Yes, it's true," they answered.

[23]Joshua said, "But you still have some idols, like those the other nations worship. Get rid of your idols! You must decide once and for all that you really want to obey the LORD God of Israel."

[24]The people said, "The LORD is our God, and we will worship and obey only him."

[25]Joshua helped Israel make an agreement with the LORD that day at Shechem. Joshua made laws for Israel [26]and wrote

them down in *The Book of the Law*[w] *of God.* Then he set up a large stone under the oak tree at the place of worship in Shechem [27]and told the people, "Look at this stone. It has heard everything that the LORD has said to us. Our God can call this stone as a witness if we ever reject him."

[28]Joshua sent everyone back to their homes.

Joshua, Joseph, and Eleazar Are Buried

[29]Not long afterwards, the LORD's servant Joshua died at the age of 110. [30]The Israelites buried him in his own land at Timnath-Serah, north of Mount Gaash in the hill country of Ephraim.

[31]As long as Joshua lived, Israel worshiped and obeyed the LORD. There were other leaders old enough to remember everything that the LORD had done for Israel. And for as long as these men lived, Israel continued to worship and obey the LORD.

[32]When the people of Israel left Egypt, they brought the bones of Joseph along with them. They took the bones to the town of Shechem and buried them in the field that Jacob had bought for 100 pieces of silver[x] from Hamor, the founder of Shechem. The town and the field both[y] became part of the land belonging to the descendants of Joseph.

[33]When Eleazar the priest[z] died, he was buried in the hill country of Ephraim on a hill that belonged to his son Phinehas.

24.18 *we will worship and obey the* LORD: Joshua challenges the people and warns them that breaking their agreement with the LORD will lead to terrible things, including their destruction as a nation. The agreement calls for their discipline and devotion. Their enthusiasm will not be enough.

24.33 *Eleazar:* 14.1-5 (Eleazar). The death of these leaders marks the end of an era of faithfulness.

[w]24.26 *Law:* See the note at 8.30-32.   [x]24.32 *pieces of silver:* One possible meaning for the difficult Hebrew word.   [y]24.32 *town . . . both:* One possible meaning for the difficult Hebrew text.
[z]24.33 *Eleazar the priest:* Hebrew "Eleazar the son of Aaron."

Reflection Questions About Joshua 1.1—24.33

1. Who was Joshua? What does the LORD promise him (1.1-9)?

2. How does Rahab show her faith in the LORD (2.1-11)? How is she "rewarded" (2.12-14)?

3. Compare the crossing of the Jordan River (3.1-17) with the crossing of the Red Sea (Exod 14). How are they similar? Different? What purpose was this miracle crossing meant to serve (3.10; 4.6,7,22-23)?

4. In what ways do the events in chapter 5 mark the end of an old era and the beginning of the new?

5. What person or event in Joshua 1–5 do you find most inspiring? Why?

6. What were the "rules" of holy war (chapter 6)? Why were these rules so important at that time in Israel's history?

7. How does the account of the war against the five kings (10.1-15) make it clear that the LORD was fighting for Israel? Who does God "fight for" today?

8. What was the purpose of the Safe Towns (20.1-9)? What does their existence reveal about the relationship of punishment and justice in Israelite society?

9. Re-read Joshua's farewell speech (23.1-16). What were his key points? What were his instructions concerning how the Israelites were to live in relationship to the other people in the land? Would Joshua's advice work in today's world? Why or why not?

10. Name two things you learned from studying JOSHUA.

judges

*Who were the "judges" of Israel, and how did God use
them? Read JUDGES to find out.*

WHAT MAKES JUDGES SPECIAL?

JUDGES is part of the great story, from DEUTERONOMY
through 2 KINGS, which tells of God's special people,
the Israelites, in the promised land of Canaan. In order for the people of Israel to survive as a nation,
they had to obey God's Law and worship the LORD
God only. If they did this, they would remain in the
land of Canaan and receive the LORD's blessings,
but the Israelites did not show a strong and lasting
commitment to the agreement they had made with
the LORD.

The people had to learn that they were to worship only the LORD, and that when they were
unfaithful, the LORD would punish them. However,
even though they often abandoned the LORD, the
LORD did not give up on them.

WHAT'S THE STORY BEHIND THE SCENE?

The period of the judges starts with the death of
Joshua around 1200 B.C. and continues at least until
Samuel, the last of the judges, chooses Saul as the
first king of Israel in about 1030 B.C. Israel at this
time was a loosely bound group of tribes rather than
a single, united country. Canaanite culture and religion remained a heavy influence that tempted the
Israelites to disobey and forget God.

The judges who led Israel during this violent and
unsettled time were not judges in a legal sense, although Deborah and Samuel did sometimes play a
legal role. The CEV uses the word "leaders" for these
heroes who led the people in battle and sometimes
in their faith.

HOW IS JUDGES CONSTRUCTED?

JUDGES mainly consists of a series of independent
stories that focus on the leaders (judges) who came
to rescue Israel's tribes (3.7—16.31). The opening
two chapters set the stage for the stories of the
judges, while the final chapters (17–21) do not mention the judges at all. In the final chapters, the threat
to Israel is not from outside enemies but from those
inside Israel who continued to turn away from the
LORD. The final chapters make it clear that Israel
was suffering from lack of leadership and from a
lack of loyalty to the LORD. These chapters hint that
Israel's problems might begin to be solved, if a king
could be chosen to rule over all the tribes.

The following summary is one way the book can be
outlined:

Israel invades Canaan but turns away from the
   LORD (1.1—3.6)
The stories of Israel's chosen leaders, the judges
   (3.7—16.31)
   Othniel, Ehud, and Shamgar (3.7-31)
   Deborah (4.1—5.31)
   Gideon (6.1—8.35)
   Abimelech, Tola, and Jair (9.1—10.5)
   Jephthah, Ibzan, Elon, and Abdon (10.6—12.15)
   Samson (13.1—16.31)
Israel's troubled times continue (17.1—21.25)
   The tribe of Dan and their place of worship
   (17.1—18.31)
   The crime at Gibeah and civil war against the
   tribe of Benjamin (19.1—21.25)

After Joshua's death (around 1200 B.C.), no single leader came forward to unite the people. God's people faced many challenges—disagreements among the twelve tribes, battles with the native peoples of Canaan, and the threat of foreign religions that would lead people to become unfaithful to the Lord. Judges tells of special leaders, called "judges," who were chosen by the Lord to help Israel's tribes. Though some of these judges were involved in legal matters, they were primarily military leaders who united the people in battles against their enemies. Most of the stories in Judges follow a pattern. The people disobey God's Law, and the Lord sends enemies to punish them. When the people call upon the Lord for help and protection, God sends a judge to help them defeat their enemies. But after the death of the judge, the people once again fall away from the Lord, and the pattern repeats itself. Even though the people make the same mistakes over and over, the Lord repeatedly reaches out to the people and offers them a chance to renew their agreement with him.

Outline

The Tribes of Judah and Simeon Fight the Canaanites

1 After the death of Joshua, the Israelites asked the LORD, "Which of our tribes should attack the Canaanites first?"

²"Judah!" the LORD answered. "I'll help them take the land."

³The people of Judah went to their relatives, the Simeon tribe, and said, "Canaanites live in the land God gave us. Help us fight them, and we will help you."

Troops from Simeon came to help Judah. ⁴⁻⁵Together they attacked an army of 10,000 Canaanites and Perizzites at Bezek, and the LORD helped Judah defeat them. During the battle, Judah's army found out where the king of Bezek[a] was, and they attacked there. ⁶The king tried to escape, but soldiers from Judah caught him. They cut off his thumbs and big toes, ⁷and he said, "I've cut off the thumbs and big toes of 70 kings and made those kings crawl around under my table for scraps of food. Now God is paying me back."

The army of Judah took the king of Bezek along with them to Jerusalem, where he died. ⁸They attacked Jerusalem,[b] captured it, killed everyone who lived there, and then burned it to the ground.

⁹Judah's army fought the Canaanites who lived in the hill country, the Southern Desert, and the foothills to the west. ¹⁰After that, they attacked the Canaanites who lived at Hebron, defeating the three clans called[c] Sheshai, Ahiman, and Talmai. At that time, Hebron was called Kiriath-Arba.

¹¹From Hebron, Judah's army went to attack Debir, which at that time was called Kiriath-Sepher. ¹²Caleb[d] told his troops,

---

[a]**1.4,5** *king of Bezek:* Or "Adoni-Bezek." [b]**1.8** *Jerusalem:* This probably refers to towns and villages belonging to Jerusalem but lying in Judah's territory south of the city wall. Jerusalem itself was just inside Benjamin's territory, but was not captured by Israel at this time (see verse 21; Joshua 15.5-9; 18.15-18). [c]**1.10** *clans called:* Or "warriors." [d]**1.12** *Caleb:* One of the leaders of Judah; see Joshua 14.6-14 and Numbers 13.6,30; 14.6,10,20-24. For verses 12-15, see Joshua 15.13-19.

1.16 *Kenite . . . Amalekites:* The Kenites lived in the northern part of the Sinai Peninsula, an area rich in copper mines. The Amalekites descended from Esau (Gen 36.15,16). They were nomads who lived primarily south and east of the Dead Sea. They were enemies of Israel.

1.16 *Jericho . . . Arad:* Jericho was an important city on the trade routes from the east to Canaan. It was the first city the Israelites captured after crossing into Canaan. Arad was 15 miles south of Hebron.

Holy War (The LORD's Battles)

1.18-19 *Gaza, Ashkelon, Ekron:* Three of the five main Philistine cities are mentioned here. The Philistines controlled the land along the Mediterranean coast and were often at war with Israel. Israel never controlled these cities. (See Map 3 on pg 1881.)

1.18-19 *iron chariots:* The Philistine warriors used wooden chariots with iron armor plates, but the Israelites did not. A battle chariot was pulled by one or more horses and carried one or more soldiers.

1.20 *three Anakim:* The Anakim were a group of very large people that lived in Palestine before the Israelites.

1.22-23 *Ephraim and Manasseh . . . Bethel:* The Ephraim and Manasseh tribes were named for Joseph's two sons (Gen 48.1-19). Ephraim was one of Israel's most powerful tribes. Bethel was a holy place in central Canaan, about 12 miles north of Jerusalem. (See Map 3 on pg 1881.)

"The man who captures Kiriath-Sepher can marry my daughter Achsah."

[13]Caleb's nephew Othniel captured Kiriath-Sepher, so Caleb let him marry Achsah. Othniel was the son of Caleb's younger brother Kenaz.[e] [14]Right after the wedding, Achsah started telling Othniel that he[f] ought to ask her father for a field. She went to see her father, and while she was getting down from[g] her donkey, Caleb asked, "What's bothering you?"

[15]She answered, "I need your help. The land you gave me is in the Southern Desert, so please give me some spring-fed ponds for a water supply."

Caleb gave her a couple of small ponds named Higher Pond and Lower Pond.[h]

[16]The people who belonged to the Kenite clan were the descendants of the father-in-law of Moses. They left Jericho[i] with the people of Judah and settled near Arad in the Southern Desert of Judah not far from the Amalekites.[j]

[17]Judah's army helped Simeon's army attack the Canaanites who lived at Zephath. They completely destroyed[k] the town and renamed it Hormah.[l]

[18-19]The LORD helped the army of Judah capture Gaza, Ashkelon, Ekron, and the land near those towns. They also took the hill country. But the people who lived in the valleys had iron chariots, so Judah was not able to make them leave or to take their land.

[20]The tribe of Judah gave the town of Hebron to Caleb, as Moses had told them to do. Caleb defeated the three Anakim[m] clans[n] and took over the town.

The Benjamin Tribe Does Not Capture Jerusalem

[21]The Jebusites were living in Jerusalem, and the Benjamin tribe did not defeat them or capture the town. That's why Jebusites still live in Jerusalem along with the people of Benjamin.

The Ephraim and Manasseh Tribes Capture Bethel

[22-23]The Ephraim and Manasseh tribes[o] were getting ready to attack Bethel, which at that time was called Luz. And the LORD helped them when they sent spies to find out as much as they could about Bethel. [24]While the spies were watching the town, a man came out, and they told him, "If you show us how our army can get into the town,[p] we will make sure that you aren't harmed." [25]The man showed them, and the two Israelite tribes attacked Bethel, killing everyone except the man and his family. The two tribes made the man and

[e]1.13 *Othniel was the son of . . . Kenaz:* Or "Othniel and Caleb both belonged to the Kenaz clan, but Othniel was younger than Caleb." [f]1.14 *Achsah . . . Othniel . . . he:* Hebrew; two ancient translations "Othniel . . . Achsah . . . she." [g]1.14 *getting down from:* One possible meaning for the difficult Hebrew text. [h]1.15 *spring-fed ponds . . . small ponds . . . Higher Pond and Lower Pond:* Or "wells . . . wells . . . Higher Well and Lower Well." [i]1.16 *Jericho:* The Hebrew text has "Town of Palm Trees," another name for Jericho. [j]1.16 *not far . . . Amalekites:* One possible meaning for the difficult Hebrew text. [k]1.17 *completely destroyed:* The Hebrew word means that the town was given completely to the LORD, and since it could not be used for normal purposes anymore, it had to be destroyed. [l]1.17 *Hormah:* In Hebrew "Hormah" sounds like "completely destroyed." [m]1.20 *Anakim:* Perhaps a group of very tall people that lived in Palestine before the Israelites (see Numbers 13.33 and Deuteronomy 2.10,11,20,21). [n]1.20 *clans:* See the note at 1.10. [o]1.22,23 *The Ephraim and Manasseh tribes:* The Hebrew text has "The Joseph family," which was divided into these two tribes named after Joseph's sons. [p]1.24 *If you . . . town:* Sometimes there were small doors in the town wall that could be opened from the inside even when the main town gates were shut and locked.

his family leave, ²⁶so they went to the land of the Hittites,^q where he built a town. He named the town Luz, and that is still its name.

Israel Does Not Get Rid of All the Canaanites

²⁷⁻²⁸Canaanites lived in the towns of Beth-Shan, Taanach, Dor, Ibleam, Megiddo, and all the villages nearby. The Canaanites were determined to stay, and the Manasseh tribe never did get rid of them. But later on, when the Israelites grew more powerful, they made slaves of the Canaanites.

²⁹ The Ephraim tribe did not get rid of the Canaanites who lived in Gezer, so the Canaanites lived there with Israelites all around them.

³⁰The Zebulun tribe did not get rid of the Canaanites who lived in Kitron and Nahalol, and the Canaanites stayed there with Israelites around them. But the people of Zebulun did force the Canaanites into slave labor.

³¹⁻³²The Asher tribe did not get rid of the Canaanites who lived in Acco, Sidon, Ahlab, Achzib, Helbah, Aphik, and Rehob, and the Asher tribe lived with Canaanites all around them.

³³The Naphtali tribe did not get rid of the Canaanites who lived in Beth-Shemesh and Beth-Anath, but they did force the Canaanites into slave labor. The Naphtali tribe lived with Canaanites around them.

³⁴The Amorites^r were strong enough to keep the tribe of Dan from settling in the valleys, so Dan had to stay in the hill country.

³⁵The Amorites on Mount Heres and in Aijalon and Shaalbim were also determined to stay. Later on, as Ephraim and Manasseh grew more powerful, they forced those Amorites into slave labor.

The Amorite-Edomite Border

³⁶The old Amorite-Edomite border used to go from Sela through Scorpion Pass^s into the hill country.^t

The LORD's Angel Speaks to Israel

2 The LORD's angel went from Gilgal to Bochim^u and gave the Israelites this message from the LORD:

I promised your ancestors that I would give this land to their families, and I brought your people here from Egypt. We made an agreement that I promised never to break, ²and you promised not to make any peace treaties with the other nations that live in the land. Besides that, you agreed to tear down the altars where they sacrifice to their idols. Why haven't you kept your promise?

³And so, I'll stop helping you defeat your enemies. Instead, they will be there to trap^v you into worshiping their idols.

⁴The Israelites started crying loudly, ⁵and they offered sacrifices to the LORD. From then on, they called that place "Crying."^w

---

^q1.26 *land of the Hittites*: The Hittites had an empire centered in what is now Turkey. At one time their empire reached south into Syria, north of Israel.   ^r1.34 *Amorites*: Used in the general sense of nations that lived in Canaan before the Israelites.   ^s1.36 *Scorpion Pass*: Or "Akrabbim Pass."   ^t1.36 *country*: One possible meaning for the difficult Hebrew text of verse 36.   ^u2.1 *Bochim*: In Hebrew "Bochim" means "crying" (see verse 5).   ^v2.3 *trap*: One possible meaning for the difficult Hebrew text.   ^w2.5 *Crying*: Or "Bochim."

● 1.26 *Hittites:* The Hittites had an empire centered in what is now Turkey. At one time their empire reached south into Syria, the area just north of Israel.

● 1.34 *Amorites:* Used here to mean many of the non-Israelite nations that lived in Canaan. The Amorites are described in Genesis 10.6-20 as descendants of Canaan, the son of Ham.

● 1.35 *Later on . . . slave labor:* The native population was not forced into slave labor until the time of David and Solomon.

■ 2.1 *The LORD's angel:* A supernatural being who tells God's messages to people.

∝ Angels

■ 2.2 *kept your promise:* The Israelites broke their promises to God and worshiped other gods (Num 25; Judg 2.11-13).

∝ Agreements (Covenants)

2.11-13 *the idols of Baal and Astarte:* The Canaanites believed that Baal was the most powerful god. Astarte was the Canaanite goddess of fertility. Those who worshiped her believed she could give them many children, abundant crops, and their animals lots of young.

Canaanite Gods and Goddesses

2.16 *special leaders . . . judges:* These special leaders became military leaders of their own tribe or several tribes. After defeating enemies, the judges governed their tribe or tribes until they died. In addition to leading Israelites in battle, these leaders also decided legal cases and sometimes performed religious duties.

2.20—3.6 *broken the agreement . . . test Israel . . . worshiping foreign gods:* Israel broke their agreement with the Lord by worshiping other gods. These verses explain why the Canaanites and other enemies were still present in the promised land. Foreign peoples were left in Canaan as a test to see if the Israelites would hold to the terms of their agreement with the Lord. The second reason why enemies were still present is that each generation must learn how to defend itself against its enemies (3.1-2). The third reason enemies remained is that Israelites had married them (3.4-6). Marrying these people caused divided loyalties, and in Israel's case, it led to the worship of foreign gods.

Israel Stops Worshiping the Lord

6-9 Joshua had been faithful to the Lord. And after Joshua sent the Israelites to take the land they had been promised, they remained faithful to the Lord until Joshua died at the age of 110. He was buried on his land in Timnath-Heres, in the hill country of Ephraim north of Mount Gaash. Even though Joshua was gone, the Israelites were faithful to the Lord during the lifetime of those men who had been leaders with Joshua and who had seen the wonderful things the Lord had done for Israel.

10 After a while the people of Joshua's generation died, and the next generation did not know the Lord or any of the things he had done for Israel. **11-13** The Lord had brought their ancestors out of Egypt, and they had worshiped him. But now the Israelites stopped worshiping the Lord and worshiped the idols of Baal and Astarte, as well as the idols of other gods from nearby nations.

The Lord was so angry **14-15** with the Israelites that he let other nations raid Israel and steal their crops and other possessions. Enemies were everywhere, and the Lord always let them defeat Israel in battle. The Lord had warned Israel he would do this, and now the Israelites were miserable.

The Lord Chooses Leaders for Israel

16 From time to time, the Lord would choose special leaders known as judges.[x] These judges would lead the Israelites into battle and defeat the enemies that made raids on them. **17** In years gone by, the Is-

raelites had been faithful to the Lord, but now they were quick to be unfaithful and to refuse even to listen to these judges. The Israelites disobeyed the Lord, and instead of worshiping him, they worshiped other gods.

18 When enemies made life miserable for the Israelites, the Lord felt sorry for them. He would choose a judge and help that judge rescue Israel from its enemies. The Lord was kind to Israel as long as that judge lived. **19** But afterwards, the Israelites would become even more sinful than their ancestors had been. The Israelites were stubborn—they simply would not stop worshiping other gods or following their teachings.

The Lord Lets Enemies Test Israel

20 The Lord was angry with Israel and said:

The Israelites have broken the agreement I made with their ancestors. They won't obey me, **21** so I'll stop helping them defeat their enemies. Israel still had a lot of enemies when Joshua died, **22** and I'm going to let those enemies stay. I'll use them to test Israel, because then I can find out if Israel will worship and obey me as their ancestors did.

23 That's why the Lord had not let Joshua get rid of those enemy nations all at once.

3 **1-2** And the Lord had another reason for letting these enemies stay. The Israelites needed to learn how to fight in war, just as their ancestors had done. Each new generation would have to learn by fighting **3** the Philistines and their five rulers, as well as the Canaanites, the Sido-

---

[x]**2.16** *special leaders known as judges:* The Hebrew text has "judges." In addition to leading Israelites in battle, these special leaders also decided legal cases and sometimes performed religious duties.

In years gone by, the Israelites had been faithful to the Lord, but now they were quick to be unfaithful. Judg 2.17

nians, and the Hivites that lived in the Lebanon Mountains from Mount Baal-Hermon to Hamath Pass.[y]

[4]Moses had told the Israelites what the LORD had commanded them to do, and now the LORD was using these nations to find out if Israel would obey. [5-6]But they refused. And some of them even married Canaanites, Hittites, Amorites, Perizzites, Hivites, and Jebusites who lived all around them. That's how they started worshiping foreign gods.

Othniel

[7]The Israelites sinned against the LORD by forgetting him and worshiping idols of Baal and Astarte. [8]This made the LORD angry, so he let Israel be defeated by King Cushan Rishathaim of northern Syria,[z] who ruled Israel eight years and made everyone pay taxes. [9]The Israelites begged the LORD for help, and so he chose Othniel to rescue them. Othniel was the son of Caleb's younger brother Kenaz.[a] [10]The Spirit of the LORD took control of Othniel, and he led Israel in a war against Cushan Rishathaim. The LORD let Othniel win, [11]and Israel was at peace until Othniel died about 40 years later.

Ehud

[12]Once more the Israelites started disobeying the LORD. So he let them be defeated by King Eglon of Moab, [13]who had joined forces with the Ammonites and the Amalekites to attack Israel. Eglon and his army captured Jericho.[b] [14]Then he ruled Israel for 18 years and forced the Israelites to pay heavy taxes.

[15-16]The Israelites begged the LORD for help, and the LORD chose Ehud[c] from the Benjamin tribe to rescue them. They put Ehud in charge of taking the taxes to King Eglon, but before Ehud went, he made a double-edged dagger. Ehud was left-handed, so he strapped the dagger to his right thigh, where it was hidden under his robes.

[17-18]Ehud and some other Israelites took the taxes to Eglon, who was a very fat man. As soon as they gave the taxes to Eglon, Ehud said it was time to go home.

[19-20]Ehud went with the other Israelites as far as the statues[d] at Gilgal.[e] Then he turned back and went upstairs to the room[f] where Eglon had his throne. Ehud said, "Your Majesty, I need to talk with you in private."

Eglon replied, "Don't say anything yet!" His officials left the room, and Eglon stood up as Ehud came closer.

"Yes," Ehud said, "I have a message for you from God!" [21]Ehud pulled out the dagger with his left hand and shoved it so far into Eglon's stomach [22-23]that even the handle was buried in his fat. Ehud left the dagger there. Then after closing and locking the doors to the room, he climbed through a window onto the porch[g] [24]and left.

3.8-10 *King Cushan Rishathaim . . . Othniel . . . Spirit of the LORD*: Cushan ruled in northern Syria, also known as the land of the Arameans. Nothing else is known about this king. Othniel is the hero of 1.13 and Joshua 15.17. The "Spirit" is the power of God at work in the world. It is when the Spirit of the LORD takes control of him that Othniel becomes victorious. (See Map 4 on pg 1882.)

Holy Spirit

3.12,13 *Moab . . . Ammonites . . . Amalekites . . . Jericho*: The Moabites and Ammonites were said to be the descendants of Lot's sons. Historically, both nations were enemies of Israel. The Amalekites were nomadic tribes who lived mostly in the area southeast of the Dead Sea. They were early enemies of Israel.

3.14 *heavy taxes*: Taxes were most likely paid in silver pieces or in goods such as olive oil, wine, animal hides, or wool.

[y]3.3 *Hamath Pass*: Or "Lebo-Hamath." [z]3.8 *northern Syria*: The Hebrew text has "Aram-Naharaim," probably referring to the land around the city of Haran (see Genesis 24.10; 25.20; 28.2,6; 31.18,20; 33.18; 35.23-26; 46.8-15; 48.7). [a]3.9 *Othniel was the son of . . . Kenaz*: See the note at 1.13. [b]3.13 *Jericho*: See the note at 1.16. [c]3.15,16 *Ehud*: Hebrew "Ehud the son of Gera." [d]3.19,20 *statues*: Or "stone idols" or "stone monuments." [e]3.19,20 *Gilgal*: About a mile and a half from Jericho, where Eglon probably was (see verse 13). [f]3.19,20 *upstairs . . . room*: Houses usually had flat roofs, and sometimes a room was built on one corner of the roof where it could best catch the breeze and be kept cooler than the rest of the house. [g]3.22,23 *he climbed . . . porch*: One possible meaning for the difficult Hebrew text.

3.27-28 *trumpet:* This was probably a hollowed out ram's horn. Ehud signals the troops and blocks the Moabite forces from retreating across the Jordan River.

4.2 *Jabin of Hazor:* This king organized nearby Canaanite kings to fight against Joshua and the Israelites. (Josh 11.1-11)

4.4,5 *Deborah . . . legal cases:* As a prophet, Deborah would have spoken God's message. She also settled legal cases, as our modern judges do. But she is best remembered for her role in leading two of Israel's tribes (4.6) in battle against the forces of Jabin. The "Palm Tree" in 4.5 is sometimes confused with the oak tree near Bethel where a different Deborah had been buried (Gen 35.8). **(See the article Prophets and Prophecy on pg 1791.)**

4.6,7 *Mount Tabor . . . Kishon River:* Mount Tabor stands alone in the northeast corner of Jezreel Valley, southeast of Lake Galilee. The Kishon River is actually a stream that flows west through the Esdraelon Plain. **(See Map 3 on pg 1881.)**

When the king's officials came back and saw that the doors were locked, they said, "The king is probably inside relieving himself." 25They stood there waiting until they felt foolish, but Eglon still didn't open the doors. Finally, they unlocked the doors and found King Eglon lying dead on the floor. 26But by that time, Ehud had already escaped past the statues.[h]

Ehud went to the town of Seirah 27-28in the hill country of Ephraim and started blowing a trumpet as a signal to call the Israelites together. When they came, he shouted, "Follow me! The Lord will help us defeat the Moabites."

The Israelites followed Ehud down to the Jordan valley, and they captured the places where people cross the river on the way to Moab. They would not let anyone go across, 29and before the fighting was over, they killed about 10,000 Moabite warriors—not one escaped alive.

30Moab was so badly defeated that it was a long time before they were strong enough to attack Israel again. And Israel was at peace for 80 years.

Shamgar

31Shamgar the son of Anath was the next to rescue Israel. In one battle, he used a sharp wooden pole[i] to kill 600 Philistines.

Deborah and Barak

4 After the death of Ehud, the Israelites again started disobeying the Lord. 2So the Lord let the Canaanite King Jabin of Hazor conquer Israel. Sisera, the commander of Jabin's army, lived in Harosheth-Ha-Goiim. 3Jabin's army had 900 iron chariots, and for 20 years he made life miserable for the Israelites, until finally they begged the Lord for help.

4Deborah the wife of Lappidoth was a prophet and a leader[j] of Israel during those days. 5She would sit under Deborah's Palm Tree between Ramah and Bethel in the hill country of Ephraim, where Israelites would come and ask her to settle their legal cases.

6One day, Barak the son of Abinoam was in Kedesh in Naphtali, and Deborah sent word for him to come and talk with her. When he arrived, she said:

I have a message for you from the Lord God of Israel! You are to get together an army of 10,000 men from the Naphtali and Zebulun tribes and lead them to Mount Tabor. 7The Lord will trick Sisera into coming out to fight you at the Kishon River. Sisera will be leading King Jabin's army as usual, and they will have their chariots, but the Lord has promised to help you defeat them.

8"I'm not going unless you go!" Barak told her.

9"All right, I'll go!" she replied. "But I'm warning you that the Lord is going to let a woman defeat Sisera, and no one will honor you for winning the battle."

Deborah and Barak left for Kedesh, 10where Barak called together the troops from Zebulun and Naphtali. Ten thousand soldiers gathered there, and Barak led them out from Kedesh. Deborah went too.

11At this time, Heber of the Kenite clan was living near the village of Oak in Zaanannim,[k] not far from Kedesh. The Kenites were descendants of Hobab, the father-in-law of Moses, but Heber had

---

[h]**3.26** *statues:* See the note at 3.19,20. [i]**3.31** *sharp wooden pole:* The Hebrew text has "cattle prod," a pole with a sharpened tip or metal point at one end. [j]**4.4** *leader:* See 2.16 and the note there. [k]**4.11** *the village . . . Zaanannim:* Or "the oak tree in the town of Zaanannim."

moved and had set up his tents away from the rest of the clan.

¹²When Sisera learned that Barak had led an army to Mount Tabor, ¹³he called his troops together and got all 900 iron chariots ready. Then he led his army away from Harosheth-Ha-Goiim to the Kishon River.

¹⁴Deborah shouted, "Barak, it's time to attack Sisera! Because today the LORD is going to help you defeat him. In fact, the LORD has already gone on ahead to fight for you."

Barak led his 10,000 troops down from Mount Tabor. ¹⁵And during the battle, the LORD confused Sisera, his chariot drivers, and his whole army. Everyone was so afraid of Barak and his army, that even Sisera jumped down from his chariot and tried to escape. ¹⁶Barak's forces went after Sisera's chariots and army as far as Harosheth-Ha-Goiim.

Sisera's entire army was wiped out. ¹⁷Only Sisera escaped. He ran to Heber's camp, because Heber and his family had a peace treaty with the king of Hazor. Sisera went to the tent that belonged to Jael, Heber's wife. ¹⁸She came out to greet him and said, "Come in, sir! Please come on in. Don't be afraid."

After they had gone inside, Sisera lay down, and Jael covered him with a blanket. ¹⁹"Could I have a little water?" he asked. "I'm thirsty."

Jael opened a leather bottle and poured him some milk, then she covered him back up.

²⁰"Stand at the entrance to the tent," Sisera told her. "If someone comes by and asks if anyone is inside, tell them 'No.'"

²¹Sisera was exhausted and soon fell fast asleep. Jael took a hammer and drove a tent-peg through his head into the ground, and he died.

²²Meanwhile, Barak had been following Sisera, and Jael went out to meet him. "The man you're looking for is inside," she said. "Come in and I'll show him to you."

They went inside, and there was Sisera—dead and stretched out with a tent-peg through his skull.

²³That same day God defeated the Canaanite King Jabin while the Israelites looked on, and his army was no longer powerful enough to attack the Israelites. ²⁴Jabin grew weaker while the Israelites kept growing stronger, until at last the Israelites destroyed him.

Deborah and Barak Sing for the LORD

5 After the battle was over that day, Deborah and Barak sang this song:

²We praise you, LORD!
Our soldiers volunteered,
    ready to follow you.
³Listen, kings and rulers,
    while I sing for the LORD,
    the God of Israel.

*⁴Our LORD, God of Israel,
    when you came from Seir,
        where the Edomites live,
⁵ rain poured from the sky,
    the earth trembled,
        and mountains shook.

⁶In the time of Shamgar
        son of Anath,
    and now again in Jael's time,
roads were too dangerous
        for caravans.
Travelers had to take
    the back roads,
⁷and villagers couldn't work
    in their fields.[1]

[1]5.7 *villagers . . . fields*: One possible meaning for the difficult Hebrew text.

4.14 *fight for you*: Deborah declares that the battle is actually the LORD's, and the victory will be God's as well.

◌ Holy War (The LORD's Battles)

● 4.16,17 *Heber's camp . . . Jael*: The camp of Heber the Kenite was at Kedesh (4.11), about 40 miles northeast of the battle site at the foot of Mount Tabor (4.6,7). Sisera thought he would be safe hiding out in Heber's clan, because they had a peace treaty with the king of Hazor. But Heber's wife Jael is more loyal to the Kenites' friends, the Israelites. She kills Sisera, fulfilling Deborah's prediction that a woman would defeat Sisera (4.9).

■ 5.3,4 *LORD . . . God of Israel*: In CEV "LORD" is used for the Hebrew, Yahweh. The LORD is Israel's personal God, who chose them and lives among them.

◌ LORD (YHWH)

● 5.4 *Seir*: This is another name for Edom, southeast of the Dead Sea. The LORD is pictured coming from a desert area, bringing a heavy rain that causes the Kishon River to flood and the enemy chariots to be stuck in the mud (5.21,22). All nature responds as God comes to Israel's aid. (See Map 4 on pg 1882.)

Deborah shouted . . . "The LORD has already gone on ahead to fight for you." JUDG 4.14

5.11-18 *LORD's people marched . . .
Naphtali:* This great procession echoes
Psalm 68.24-27, including the roll call
of Israel's tribes. "Machir" in 5.14 is the
Manasseh tribe (1.22,23). **(See Map 3
on pg 1881.)**

Israel

5.19 *Taanach . . . Megiddo:* These
two cities were in the northern hill
country. The stream probably refers to
one of the streams that flows into the
Kishon River. It was common practice
for the army that won a battle to take
everything of value ("our silver") from
the dead enemy soldiers.

5.20,21 *From their pathways . . .
River:* In ancient times, the stars were
sometimes regarded as supernatural
beings. The poetry here has the heavens above and the waters below fighting on God's side for Israel.

Then Deborah[m] took command,
    protecting Israel as a mother
    protects her children.

[8]The Israelites worshiped
        other gods,
    and the gates of their towns
        were then attacked.[n]
    But they had no shields
        or spears to fight with.
[9]I praise you, LORD,
        and I am grateful
    for those leaders and soldiers
        who volunteered.
[10]Listen, everyone!
    Whether you ride a donkey
        with a padded saddle
        or have to walk.
[11]Even those who carry water[o]
        to the animals will tell you,
    "The LORD has won victories,
        and so has Israel."

    Then the LORD's people marched
        down to the town gates
[12]and said, "Deborah, let's go!
    Let's sing as we march.
        Barak, capture our enemies."

[13]The LORD's people who were left
    joined with their leaders
        and fought at my side.[p]
[14]Troops came from Ephraim,
    where Amalekites once lived.

    Others came from Benjamin;
        officers and leaders came
        from Machir and Zebulun.
[15]The rulers of Issachar
        came along with Deborah,
    and Issachar followed Barak
        into the valley.

    But the tribe of Reuben
        was no help at all![q]
[16]Reuben, why did you stay
        among your sheep pens?[r]
    Was it to listen to shepherds
        whistling for their sheep?
    No one could figure out
        why Reuben wouldn't come.[s]
[17]The people of Gilead stayed
        across the Jordan.
    Why did the tribe of Dan
        remain on their ships
    and the tribe of Asher
    stay along the coast
        near the harbors?

[18]But soldiers of Zebulun
        and Naphtali
    risked their lives
        to attack the enemy.[t]
[19]Canaanite kings fought us
    at Taanach by the stream
        near Megiddo[u]—
    but they couldn't rob us
        of our silver.[v]
[20]From their pathways in the sky

[m]**5.7** *Deborah:* Or "I, Deborah."   [n]**5.8** *The Israelites . . . attacked:* One possible meaning for the
difficult Hebrew text.   [o]**5.11** *Even . . . water:* One possible meaning for the difficult Hebrew text.
[p]**5.13** *side:* One possible meaning for the difficult Hebrew text of verse 13.   [q]**5.15** *But . . . at all:* Or
"But the people of Reuben couldn't make up their minds."   [r]**5.16** *sheep pens:* Or "campfires."
[s]**5.16** *No . . . come:* Or "The people of Reuben couldn't make up their minds."   [t]**5.18** *to attack the
enemy:* One possible meaning for the difficult Hebrew text.   [u]**5.19** *stream near Megiddo:* Probably
refers to one of the streams that flow into the Kishon River.   [v]**5.19** *rob us of our silver:* The army that
won a battle would take everything of value from the dead enemy soldiers.

the stars[w] fought Sisera,
²¹and his soldiers were swept away
    by the ancient Kishon River.

I will march on and be brave.

²²Sisera's horses galloped off,
    their hoofs thundering
        in retreat.

²³The LORD's angel said,
    "Put a curse on Meroz Town!
Its people refused
to help the LORD fight
    his powerful enemies."

²⁴But honor Jael,
    the wife of Heber
        from the Kenite clan.
Give more honor to her
    than to any other woman
        who lives in tents.
Yes, give more honor to her
    than to any other woman.
²⁵Sisera asked for water,
    but Jael gave him milk—
        cream in a fancy cup.
²⁶She reached for a tent-peg
    and held a hammer
        in her right hand.
And with a blow to the head,
    she crushed his skull.
²⁷Sisera sank to his knees
    and fell dead at her feet.

²⁸Sisera's mother looked out
    through her window.
    "Why is he taking so long?"
        she asked.
    "Why haven't we heard

his chariots coming?"
²⁹She and her wisest women
    gave the same answer:
³⁰"Sisera and his troops
    are finding treasures
        to bring back—
a woman, or maybe two,
    for each man,
and beautiful dresses
    for those women to wear."[x]

³¹Our LORD, we pray
that all your enemies
    will die like Sisera.
But let everyone who loves you
shine brightly like the sun
    at dawn.

Midian Steals Everything from Israel

6 There was peace in Israel for about 40 years. ¹Then once again the Israelites started disobeying the LORD, so he let the nation of Midian control Israel for seven years. ²The Midianites were so cruel that many Israelites ran to the mountains and hid in caves.

³Every time the Israelites planted crops, the Midianites invaded Israel together with the Amalekites and other eastern nations. ⁴⁻⁵They rode in on their camels, set up their tents, and then let their livestock eat the crops as far as the town of Gaza. The Midianites stole food, sheep, cattle, and donkeys. Like a swarm of locusts,[y] they could not be counted, and they ruined the land wherever they went.

⁶⁻⁷The Midianites took almost everything

- 5.22 *Sisera's horses:* Israelite armies marched on foot rather than horseback. It was not until the time of Solomon that horses were used by Israel for military purposes (1 Kgs 10.26-29). Depending on chariots and a cavalry indicated trust in material resources and not in God (Ps 20.7; 33.17; Isa 31.1).

- 5.24 *Jael:* Jael is not an Israelite, but God did use her to put an end to the enemy commander Sisera.

- 5.28-30 *Sisera's mother . . . treasures:* Sisera's mother and other Canaanite women wait for their husbands and sons to return from battle. They are worried about how long the battle is taking, but are hopeful that the delay is for good reasons. The reader, on the other hand, knows that all the Canaanite soldiers are dead.

- 6.2,3 *Midianites . . . Amalekites:* The Midianites mainly lived in the eastern part of the Arabian Desert, but they were nomads who lived in tents and moved from place to place looking for good pasturelands and water for their herds. Perhaps food and water shortages led the Midianites and other peoples who lived in the eastern part of the Arabian Desert to move into Israel's tribal lands in Canaan. (See Map 2 on pg 1880.)

-   Nomads (Wandering Herders)

-   Locusts

---

[w]5.20 *stars:* In ancient times, the stars were sometimes regarded as supernatural beings.   [x]5.30 *and beautiful . . . wear:* One possible meaning for the difficult Hebrew text.   [y]6.4,5 *locusts:* Insects like grasshoppers that travel in swarms and cause great damage to crops.

6.11 *threshing grain*: In threshing, stalks of grain were beaten by hand or walked on by oxen in order to separate the kernels from the rest (chaff). Threshing was done outdoors on a hard floor made of packed clay soil or rock. Usually the chaff was thrown in the air so the wind would blow it away while the heavier grain kernels fell back down to the threshing floor. Joash was threshing in a pit, so a cloud of dust and chaff would not attract a Midianite raid (6.4-5).

6.22 *I'm going to die*: It was not until the angel vanished that Gideon realized who his visitor was. Some people believed that if they saw one of the LORD's angels, they would die (13.22).

that belonged to the Israelites, and the Israelites begged the LORD for help. **8-9**Then the LORD sent a prophet to them with this message:

I am the LORD God of Israel, so listen to what I say. You were slaves in Egypt, but I set you free and led you out of Egypt into this land. And when nations here made life miserable for you, I rescued you and helped you get rid of them and take their land. **10**I am your God, and I told you not to worship Amorite gods, even though you are living in the land of the Amorites. But you refused to listen.

The LORD Chooses Gideon

11One day an angel from the LORD went to the town of Ophrah and sat down under the big tree that belonged to Joash, a member of the Abiezer clan. Joash's son Gideon was nearby, threshing grain in a shallow pit, where he could not be seen by the Midianites.

12The angel appeared and spoke to Gideon, "The LORD is helping you, and you are a strong warrior."

13Gideon answered, "Please don't take this wrong, but if the LORD is helping us, then why have all of these awful things happened? We've heard how the LORD performed miracles and rescued our ancestors from Egypt. But those things happened long ago. Now the LORD has abandoned us to the Midianites."

14Then the LORD himself said, "Gideon, you will be strong, because I am giving you the power to rescue Israel from the Midianites."

15Gideon replied, "But how can I rescue Israel? My clan is the weakest one in Manasseh, and everyone else in my family is more important than I am."

16"Gideon," the LORD answered, "you can rescue Israel because I am going to help you! Defeating the Midianites will be as easy as beating up one man."

17Gideon said, "It's hard to believe that I'm actually talking to the LORD. Please do something so I'll know that you really are the LORD. **18**And wait here until I bring you an offering."

"All right, I'll wait," the LORD answered.

19Gideon went home and killed a young goat, then started boiling the meat. Next, he opened a big sack of flour and made it into thin bread.**z** When the meat was done, he put it in a basket and poured the broth into a clay cooking pot. He took the meat, the broth, and the bread and placed them under the big tree.

20God's angel said, "Gideon, put the meat and the bread on this rock, and pour the broth over them." Gideon did as he was told. **21**The angel was holding a walking stick, and he touched the meat and the bread with the end of the stick. Flames jumped from the rock and burned up the meat and the bread.

When Gideon looked, the angel was gone. **22**Gideon realized that he had seen one of the LORD's angels. "Oh!" he moaned. "Now I'm going to die."**a**

23"Calm down!" the LORD told Gideon. "There's nothing to be afraid of. You're not going to die."

24Gideon built an altar for worshiping the LORD and called it "The LORD Calms Our Fears." It still stands there in Ophrah, a town in the territory of the Abiezer clan.

---

z6.19 *thin bread*: Bread made without yeast, since there was no time for the dough to rise.
a6.22 *Now I'm going to die*: The Hebrew text has "I have seen an angel of the LORD face to face." Some people believed that if they saw one of the LORD's angels, they would die (see 13.22).

Gideon Tears Down Baal's Altar

[25] That night the LORD spoke to Gideon again:

Get your father's second-best bull, the one that's seven years old. Use it to pull down the altar where your father worships Baal and cut down the sacred pole[b] next to the altar. [26] Then build an altar for worshiping me on the highest part of the hill where your town is built. Use layers of stones for my altar, not just a pile of rocks. Cut up the wood from the pole, make a fire, kill the bull, and burn it as a sacrifice to me.

[27] Gideon chose ten of his servants to help him, and they did everything God had said. But since Gideon was afraid of his family and the other people in Ophrah, he did it all at night.

[28] When the people of the town got up the next morning, they saw that Baal's altar had been knocked over, and the sacred pole next to it had been cut down. Then they noticed the new altar covered with the remains of the sacrificed bull.

[29] "Who could have done such a thing?" they asked. And they kept on asking, until finally someone told them, "Gideon the son of Joash did it."

[30] The men of the town went to Joash and said, "Your son Gideon knocked over Baal's altar and cut down the sacred pole next to it. Hand him over, so we can kill him!"

[31] The crowd pushed closer and closer, but Joash replied, "Are you trying to take revenge for Baal? Are you trying to rescue Baal? If you are, you will be the ones who are put to death, and it will happen before another day dawns. If Baal really is a god, let him take his own revenge on someone who tears down his altar."

[32] That same day, Joash changed Gideon's name to Jerubbaal, explaining, "He tore down Baal's altar, so let Baal take revenge himself."[c]

Gideon Defeats the Midianites

[33] All the Midianites, Amalekites, and other eastern nations got together and crossed the Jordan River. Then they invaded the land of Israel and set up camp in Jezreel Valley.

[34] The LORD's Spirit took control of Gideon, and Gideon blew a trumpet as a signal for the men in the Abiezer clan to follow him. [35] He also sent messengers to the tribes of Manasseh, Asher, Zebulun, and Naphtali, telling the men of these tribes to come and join his army. Then they set out toward the enemy camp.

[36-37] Gideon prayed to God, "I know that you promised to help me rescue Israel, but I need proof. Tonight I'll spread a sheep skin on the stone floor of that threshing-place over there. If you really will help me rescue Israel, then tomorrow morning let there be dew on the skin, but let the stone floor be dry."

[38] And that's just what happened. Early the next morning, Gideon got up and checked the sheep skin. He squeezed out enough water to fill a bowl. [39] But Gideon prayed to God again. "Don't be angry with me," Gideon said. "Let me try this just one more time, so I'll really be sure you'll help me. Only this time, let the skin be dry and the stone floor be wet."

[40] That night, God made the stone floor wet with dew, but he kept the sheep skin dry.

6.25 *Baal . . . altar . . . sacred pole:* Baal, the Canaanite god of fertility, was being worshiped at this time by Gideon's family and by the other people of the town. A bull was often used as a symbol for Baal. Ancient readers probably would have seen the humor in Gideon using an old, "second-best" bull to pull down the altar of Baal. The sacred pole was a symbol of Asherah, the Canaanite goddess of fertility

Canaanite Gods and Goddesses

6.34 *The LORD's Spirit took control:* This phrase is used frequently in JUDGES to indicate the moment when a person becomes one of God's chosen leaders (a judge).

Holy Spirit

6.36-39 *I need proof . . . prayed to God again:* As in 6.17, Gideon asks for a sign that it is really God leading him (6.36,37). God honors his request, but then Gideon prays to God again. Even persons of faith, such as Gideon, may sometimes have doubts.

---

[b] 6.25 *sacred pole:* Or "sacred tree," used as a symbol of Asherah, the Canaanite goddess of fertility.
[c] 6.32 *Jerubbaal . . . take revenge himself:* In Hebrew, "Jerubbaal" means "Let Baal take revenge."

7.1 *Fear Spring... Moreh Hill:* Fear Spring is at the base of Mount Gilboa in the Jezreel Valley. Moreh Hill is about five miles north of Fear Spring.

7.2 *your army is too big:* God will fight on behalf of Israel. This is God's battle and God's victory. Israel will be so outnumbered that it cannot win by its power alone.

7.5 *those who lap... those who kneel down:* The soldiers who knelt most likely put their faces directly into the water. This would have made it impossible for them to see an enemy approach and suggests that they might not be alert fighters in the battlefield. The soldiers who lapped water from their hands were probably better prepared to grab their weapons at a moment's notice. If so, then God seems to have chosen the more astute warriors. Even so, the emphasis in this passage, as in other parts of JUDGES, is that God is the one who brings victory and he does not need a large army to do so.

7 Early the next morning, Gideon and his army got up and moved their camp to Fear Spring.[d] The Midianite camp was to the north, in the valley at the foot of Moreh Hill.[e]

[2]The LORD said, "Gideon, your army is too big. I can't let you win with this many soldiers. The Israelites would think that they had won the battle all by themselves and that I didn't have anything to do with it. [3]So call your troops together and tell them that anyone who is really afraid can leave Mount Gilead[f] and go home."

Twenty-two thousand men returned home, leaving Gideon with only 10,000 soldiers.

[4]"Gideon," the LORD said, "you still have too many soldiers. Take them down to the spring and I'll test them. I'll tell you which ones can go along with you and which ones must go back home."

[5]When Gideon led his army down to the spring, the LORD told him, "Watch how each man gets a drink of water. Then divide them into two groups—those who lap the water like a dog and those who kneel down to drink."

[6]Three hundred men scooped up water in their hands and lapped it, and the rest knelt to get a drink. [7]The LORD said, "Gideon, your army will be made up of everyone who lapped the water from their hands. Send the others home. I'm going to rescue Israel by helping you and your army of 300 defeat the Midianites."

[8]Then Gideon gave these orders, "You 300 men stay here. The rest of you may go home, but leave your food and trumpets with us."

Gideon's army camp was on top of a hill overlooking the Midianite camp in the valley.

[9]That night, the LORD said to Gideon. "Get up! Attack the Midianite camp. I am going to let you defeat them, [10]but if you're still afraid, you and your servant Purah should sneak down to their camp. [11]When you hear what the Midianites are saying, you'll be brave enough to attack."

Gideon and Purah worked their way to the edge of the enemy camp, where soldiers were on guard duty. [12]The camp was huge. The Midianites, Amalekites, and other eastern nations covered the valley like a swarm of locusts.[g] And it would be easier to count the grains of sand on a beach than to count their camels. [13]Gideon overheard one enemy guard telling another, "I had a dream about a flat[h] loaf of barley bread that came tumbling into our camp. It hit the headquarters tent,[i] and the tent flipped over and fell to the ground."

[14]The other soldier answered, "Your dream must have been about Gideon, the Israelite commander. It means God will let him and his army defeat the Midianite army and everyone else in our camp."

[15]As soon as Gideon heard about the dream and what it meant, he bowed down to praise God. Then he went back to the Israelite camp and shouted, "Let's go! The LORD is going to let us defeat the Midianite army."

[16]Gideon divided his little army into three groups of 100 men, and he gave each soldier a trumpet and a large clay jar with a burning torch inside. [17-18]Gideon said, "When we get to the enemy camp, spread out and surround it. Then wait for me to blow a signal on my trumpet. As soon as

[d]7.1 *Fear Spring:* Or "Harod Spring."   [e]7.1 *Moreh Hill:* About 5 miles north of Fear Spring.
[f]7.3 *Mount Gilead:* Usually "Gilead" refers to an area east of the Jordan River, but in this verse it refers to a place near Jezreel Valley west of the Jordan.   [g]7.12 *locusts:* See the note at 6.4,5.
[h]7.13 *flat:* Or "moldy."   [i]7.13 *the headquarters tent:* Or "a tent."

Gideon shouted, "Let's go! The LORD is going to let us defeat the Midianite army." JUDG 7.15

you hear it, blow your trumpets and shout, 'Fight for the LORD! Fight for Gideon!' "

[19]Gideon and his group reached the edge of the enemy camp a few hours after dark, just after the new guards had come on duty.[j] Gideon and his soldiers blew their trumpets and smashed the clay jars that were hiding the torches. [20]The rest of Gideon's soldiers blew the trumpets they were holding in their right hands. Then they smashed the jars and held the burning torches in their left hands. Everyone shouted, "Fight with your swords for the LORD and for Gideon!"

[21]The enemy soldiers started yelling and tried to run away. Gideon's troops stayed in their positions surrounding the camp [22]and blew their trumpets again. As they did, the LORD made the enemy soldiers pull out their swords and start fighting each other.

The enemy army tried to escape from the camp. They ran to Acacia Tree Town, toward Zeredah,[k] and as far as the edge of the land that belonged to the town of Abel-Meholah near Tabbath.[l]

[23]Gideon sent word for more Israelite soldiers to come from the tribes of Naphtali, Asher, and both halves of Manasseh[m] to help fight the Midianites. [24]He also sent messengers to tell all the men who lived in the hill country of Ephraim, "Come and help us fight the Midianites! Put guards at every spring, stream, and well, as far as Beth-Barah before the Midianites can get to them. And guard the Jordan River."

Troops from Ephraim did exactly what Gideon had asked, [25]and they even helped chase the Midianites on the east side of the Jordan River. These troops captured Raven and Wolf,[n] the two Midianite leaders. They killed Raven at a large rock that has come to be known as Raven Rock, and they killed Wolf near a wine-pit that has come to be called Wolf Wine-Pit.[o]

The men of Ephraim brought the heads of the two Midianite leaders to Gideon. **8** [1]But the men were really upset with Gideon and complained, "When you went to war with Midian, you didn't ask us to help! Why did you treat us like that?"

[2]Gideon answered:

Don't be upset! Even though you came later, you were able to do much more than I did. It's just like the grape harvest: The grapes your tribe doesn't even bother to pick are better than the best grapes my family can grow. [3]Besides, God chose you to capture Raven and Wolf. I didn't do a thing compared to you.

By the time Gideon had finished talking, the men of Ephraim had calmed down and were no longer angry with him.

Gideon Finishes Destroying the Midianite Army

[4]After Gideon and his 300 troops had chased the Midianites across the Jordan River, they were exhausted. [5]The town of

● 7.23 *both halves of Manasseh:* Half of Manasseh lived east of the Jordan River, and the other half lived west of the river. Gideon first asked men from these tribes to join his army shortly after becoming a leader (judge). See 6.35. At this point, Gideon needed more than the little army of 300 to chase away the Midianites. **(See Map 3 on pg 1881.)**

● 8.1 *Why did you treat us like that:* Ephraim was the last tribe that Gideon called to this battle with the Midianites (7.24), and so they felt slighted. This conflict probably reflects the long rivalry between the tribes of Manasseh (Gideon's tribe) and Ephraim that went back to the time when Jacob blessed Joseph's youngest son Ephraim before the older Manasseh. Ephraim was always the more powerful of the two tribes.

● 8.2 *Don't be upset:* In his speech to the Ephraim tribe, Gideon shows great diplomatic skill. He uses the example of the grapes to say that his tribe is nothing next to Ephraim. His humble words have a calming effect.

[j]**7.19** *a few hours after dark, just . . . duty:* The Hebrew text has "at the beginning of the second watch, just . . . duty." The night was divided into three periods called "watches," each about four hours long, and different guards would come on duty at the beginning of each watch. The first watch began at sunset, so the beginning of the second watch would have been shortly after 10:00 P.M. [k]**7.22** *Zeredah:* Some Hebrew manuscripts; most Hebrew manuscripts "Zererah"; these may be different names for the town of Zarethan in the Jordan River valley. [l]**7.22** *Acacia Tree Town . . . Zeredah . . . Abel-Meholah near Tabbath:* These were places east of the Jordan River. [m]**7.23** *both halves of Manasseh:* Half of Manasseh lived east of the Jordan River, and the other half lived on the west. [n]**7.25** *Raven and Wolf:* Or "Oreb and Zeeb." [o]**7.25** *Raven Rock . . . Wolf Wine-Pit:* Or "Oreb Rock . . . Zeeb Wine-Pit."

8.5 *Succoth:* This town was on the east side of the Jordan River in the territory of Gad.

8.7 *make a whip out of thorns:* In the ancient Near East thorns and thistles were plentiful in the dry season. A whip made of thorns would have caused severe injury.

8.8-11 *Penuel . . . Karkor . . . Nomad Road:* Penuel was several miles east of Succoth on the Jabbok River. Karkor was about 100 miles east of the Dead Sea, in the Arabian Desert. The Nomad Road was named for the desert nomads, people who moved from place to place.

Nomads (Wandering Herders)

8.20 *Jether was young:* Gideon wanted to insult the kings by having a young boy kill them. But his son doesn't have the heart to kill them.

8.22,23 *be our king . . . Only the LORD:* The Israelites will later make a similar request for a king in 1 Samuel 8.4,5. As God's special people, the only ruler they were to have was God. To ask for an earthly king showed a lack of faith or even rejection of God (1 Sam 10.19).

Kingship in Israel

Succoth was nearby, so he went there and asked, "Please give my troops some food. They are worn out, but we have to keep chasing Zebah and Zalmunna, the two Midianite kings."

⁶The town leaders of Succoth answered, "Why should we feed your army? We don't know if you really will defeat Zebah and Zalmunna."

⁷"Just wait!" Gideon said. "After the LORD helps me defeat them, I'm coming back here. I'll make a whip out of thorns and rip the flesh from your bones."

⁸After leaving Succoth, Gideon went to Penuel and asked the leaders there for some food. But he got the same answer as he did at Succoth. ⁹"I'll come back safe and sound," Gideon said, "but when I do, I'm going to tear down your tower!"ᴾ

¹⁰Zebah and Zalmunna were in Karkorᵠ with an army of 15,000 troops. They were all that was left of the army of the eastern nations, because 120,000 of their warriors had been killed in the battle.

¹¹Gideon reached the enemy camp by going east along Nomadʳ Road past Nobah and Jogbehah. He made a surprise attack, ¹²and the enemy panicked. Zebah and Zalmunna tried to escape, but Gideon chased and captured them.

¹³After the battle, Gideon set out for home. As he was going through Heres Pass, ¹⁴he caught a young man who lived in Succoth. Gideon asked him who the town officials of Succoth were, and the young man wrote down 77 names.

¹⁵Gideon went to the town officials and said, "Here are Zebah and Zalmunna. Remember how you made fun of me? You said, 'We don't know if you really will defeat those two Midianite kings. So why should we feed your worn-out army?'"

¹⁶Gideon made a whip from thorn plants and used it to beat the town officials. ¹⁷Afterwards he went to Penuel, where he tore down the tower and killed all the town officials.ˢ

¹⁸Then Gideon said, "Zebah and Zalmunna, tell me about the men you killed at Tabor."

"They were a lot like you," the two kings answered. "They were dignified, almost like royalty."

¹⁹"They were my very own brothers!" Gideon said. "I swear by the living LORD that if you had let them live, I would let you live."

²⁰Gideon turned to Jether, his oldest son. "Kill them!" Gideon said.

But Jether was young,ᵗ and he was too afraid to even pull out his sword.

²¹"What's the matter, Gideon?" Zebah and Zalmunna asked. "Do it yourself, if you're not too much of a coward!"

Gideon jumped up and killed them both. Then he took the gold ornaments from the necks of their camels.

The Israelites Ask Gideon To Be Their King

²²After the battle with the Midianites, the Israelites said, "Gideon, you rescued us! Now we want you to be our king. Then after your death, your son and then your grandson will rule."

²³"No," Gideon replied, "I won't be your king, and my son won't be king either.

ᴾ**8.9** *tower:* Towers were often part of a town wall. ᵠ**8.10** *Karkor:* A little over 100 miles east of the Dead Sea. ʳ**8.11** *Nomad:* A person who lives in a tent and moves from place to place. ˢ**8.17** *all . . . officials:* Or "every man in town." ᵗ**8.20** *young:* Gideon wanted to insult the kings by having a young boy kill them.

Only the Lord is your ruler. [24]But I will ask you to do one thing: Give me all the earrings you took from the enemy."

The enemy soldiers had been Ishmaelites,[u] and they wore gold earrings.

[25]The Israelite soldiers replied, "Of course we will give you the earrings." Then they spread out a robe on the ground and tossed the earrings on it. [26]The total weight of this gold was over 40 pounds. In addition, there was the gold from the camels' ornaments and from the beautiful jewelry worn by the Midianite kings. Gideon also took their purple robes.

[27-29]Gideon returned to his home in Ophrah and had the gold made into a statue, which the Israelites soon started worshiping. They were unfaithful to God, and even Gideon and his family were trapped into worshiping the statue.[v]

The Midianites had been defeated so badly that they were no longer strong enough to attack Israel. And so Israel was at peace for the remaining 40 years of Gideon's life.

Gideon Dies

[30]Gideon had many wives and 70 sons. [31]He even had a wife[w] who lived at Shechem.[x] They had a son, and Gideon named him Abimelech.

[32]Gideon lived to be an old man. And when he died, he was buried in the family tomb in his hometown of Ophrah, which belonged to the Abiezer clan.

[33]Soon after Gideon's death, the Israelites turned their backs on God again. They set up idols of Baal and worshiped Baal Berith[y] as their god. [34]The Israelites forgot that the Lord was their God, and that he had rescued them from the enemies who lived around them. [35]Besides all that, the Israelites were unkind to Gideon's family, even though Gideon had done so much for Israel.

Abimelech Tries To Be King

9 Abimelech the son of Gideon[z] went to Shechem. While there, he met with his mother's relatives [2]and told them to say to the leaders of Shechem, "Do you think it would be good to have all 70 of Gideon's sons ruling us? Wouldn't you rather have just one man be king? Abimelech would make a good king, and he's related to us."

[3]Abimelech's uncles talked it over with the leaders of Shechem who agreed, "Yes, it would be better for one of our relatives to be king." [4]Then they gave Abimelech 70 pieces[a] of silver from the temple of their god Baal Berith.[b]

Abimelech used the silver to hire a gang of rough soldiers who would do anything for money. [5]Abimelech and his soldiers went to his father's home in Ophrah and

8.30,31 *many wives . . . . a wife who lived at Shechem:* At this time Israelite men had as many wives as they could support. Some, such as the wife at Shechem, were known as "concubines." These women were legally bound to the man but did not have full privileges of a primary wife. Apparently, Gideon's wife at Shechem lived with her parents, and Gideon visited her from time to time.

8.33 *idols:* Idols were images or statues that represented foreign gods.

Canaanite Gods and Goddesses

9.1 *Abimelech:* His father, Gideon, rejected the offer of kingship (8.23). His mother was a concubine from Shechem (8.31), a city where Baal was worshiped (9.4), and the home of earlier Canaanite kings or chieftains (9.28). Abimelech was influenced by his background and Canaanite relatives to seek to become king of the lands controlled by the Shechemites. It is clear that God was not behind this plan, because the author does not call Abimelech a "judge" or say that the Lord's Spirit took control of him. God is only mentioned at 9.23, 24 and 9.56,57 of this story, and then only as one who punishes Abimelech.

9.4 *70 pieces of silver:* A gold piece usually weighed one shekel, or about two-fifths of an ounce. Seventy pieces would have been about 28 ounces of silver, but "70" is probably meant to symbolize a very large amount. The silver came from a pagan temple honoring Baal.

---

[u]8.24 *Ishmaelites:* According to Genesis 25.1,2,12, both Ishmaelites and Midianites were descendants of Abraham. It is possible that in this passage "Ishmaelites" has the meaning "nomadic traders," while "Midianites" (verses 22,26-29) refers to their ethnic origin. [v]8.27-29 *statue . . . statue:* Or "sacred priestly vest . . . vest." [w]8.31 *wife:* This translates a Hebrew word for a woman who was legally bound to a man, but without the full privileges of a wife. [x]8.31 *who lived at Shechem:* Sometimes marriages were arranged so that the wife lived with her parents, and the husband visited her from time to time. [y]8.33 *Baal Berith:* Or "Baal of the Agreement" or "the Lord of the Agreement." [z]9.1 *Gideon:* The Hebrew text has "Jerubbaal," another name for Gideon (see 6.32). [a]9.4 *70 pieces:* About 28 ounces. [b]9.4 *Baal Berith:* See the note at 8.33.

9.7 *Mount Gerizim:* This mountain was located south of Shechem in territory of Ephraim. **(See Map 3 on pg 1881.)**

9.7 *listen to me:* Jotham tells a story which is a fable. This fable has talking trees and a moral—that the monarchy can bring trouble. Also note that the king is not chosen by God, but is picked as a last resort.

brought out Gideon's other sons to a large rock, where they murdered all 70 of them. Gideon's youngest son Jotham hid from the soldiers, but he was the only one who escaped.

6The leaders of Shechem, including the priests and the military officers,[c] met at the tree next to the sacred rock[d] in Shechem to crown Abimelech king. **7**Jotham heard what they were doing. So he climbed to the top of Mount Gerizim and shouted down to the people who were there at the meeting:

> Leaders of Shechem,
> listen to me,
> and maybe God
> will listen to you.

8Once the trees searched
  for someone to be king;
they asked the olive tree,
  "Will you be our king?"
9But the olive tree replied,
  "My oil brings honor
    to people and gods.
I won't stop making oil,
  just so my branches can wave
    above the other trees."

10Then they asked the fig tree,
  "Will you be our king?"
11But the fig tree replied,
  "I won't stop growing
    my delicious fruit,
  just so my branches can wave
    above the other trees."

12Next they asked the grape vine,
  "Will you be our king?"

13But the grape vine replied,
  "My wine brings cheer
    to people and gods.
I won't stop making wine,
  just so my branches can wave
    above the other trees."

14Finally, they went
  to the thornbush and asked,
  "Will you be our king?"
15The thornbush replied,
  "If you really want me
    to be your king,
  then come into my shade
    and I will protect you.
But if you're deceiving me,
  I'll start a fire
that will spread out and destroy
  the cedars of Lebanon."[e]

After Jotham had finished telling this story, he said:

16-18 My father Gideon risked his life for you when he fought to rescue you from the Midianites. Did you reward Gideon by being kind to his family? No, you did not! You attacked his family and killed all 70 of his sons on that rock.

And was it right to make Abimelech your king? He's merely the son of my father's slave girl.[f] But just because he's your relative, you made him king of Shechem.

19So, you leaders of Shechem, if you treated Gideon and his family the way you should have, then I hope you and Abimelech will make each other very happy. **20**But if it was wrong to treat Gideon and his family the way you did,

[c]**9.6** *including the priests and the military officers:* The Hebrew text has "and the Millo house," another name for the temple of Baal Berith. It probably also served as a military fortress. [d]**9.6** *tree . . . rock:* One ancient translation; Hebrew "propped-up sacred tree." [e]**9.15** *cedars of Lebanon:* The cedars that grew in the Lebanon mountains were some of the largest trees in that part of the world. [f]**9.16-18** *son of . . . slave girl:* See 8.31.

then I pray that Abimelech will destroy you with fire, and I pray that you will do the same to him.

²¹Jotham ran off and went to live in the town of Beer, where he could be safe from his brother Abimelech.

Abimelech Destroys Shechem

²²Abimelech had been a military commander of Israel for three years, ²³⁻²⁴when God decided to punish him and the leaders of Shechem for killing Gideon's 70 sons.

So God turned the leaders of Shechem against Abimelech. ²⁵Then they sent some men to hide on the hilltops and watch for Abimelech and his troops, while they sent others to rob everyone that went by on the road. But Abimelech found out what they were doing.

²⁶One day, Gaal son of Ebed went to live in Shechem. His brothers moved there too, and soon the leaders of Shechem started trusting him.

²⁷The time came for the grape harvest, and the people of Shechem went into their vineyards and picked the grapes. They gathered the grapes and made wine. Then they went into the temple of their god and threw a big party. There was a lot of eating and drinking, and before long they were cursing Abimelech.

²⁸Gaal said:

Hamor was the founder of Shechem, and one of his descendants should be our ruler. But Abimelech's father was Gideon, so Abimelech isn't really one of us. He shouldn't be our king, and we shouldn't have to obey him or Zebul, who rules Shechem for him. ²⁹If I were the ruler of Shechem, I'd get rid of that

Abimelech. I'd tell him, "Get yourself an even bigger army, and we will still defeat you."

³⁰Zebul was angry when he found out what Gaal had said. ³¹And so he sent some messengers to Abimelech. But they had to pretend to be doing something else, or they would not have been allowed to leave Shechem.ᵍ Zebul told the messengers to say:

Gaal the son of Ebed has come to Shechem along with his brothers, and they have persuaded the people to let Gaal rule Shechem instead of you. ³²This is what I think you should do. Lead your army here during the night and hide in the fields. ³³Get up the next morning at sunrise and rush out of your hiding places to attack the town. Gaal and his followers will come out to fight you, but you will easily defeat them.

³⁴So one night, Abimelech led his soldiers to Shechem. He divided them into four groups, and they all hid near the town.

³⁵The next morning, Gaal went out and stood in the opening of the town gate. Abimelech and his soldiers left their hiding places, ³⁶and Gaal saw them. Zebul was standing there with Gaal, and Gaal remarked, "Zebul, that looks like a crowd of people coming down from the mountaintops."

"No," Zebul answered, "it's just the shadows of the mountains. It only looks like people moving."

³⁷"But Zebul, look over there," Gaal said. "There's a crowd coming down from the sacred mountain,ʰ and another group is coming along the road from the tree where people talk with the spirits of the dead."

³⁸Then Zebul replied, "What good is all of

ᵍ9.31 *But . . . Shechem:* One possible meaning for the difficult Hebrew text.   ʰ9.37 *sacred mountain:* The Hebrew text has "the navel of the land," which probably refers to Mount Gerizim as a sacred mountain linking heaven and earth.

9.21 *Beer:* The exact location of this place is unknown, but most likely it was somewhere north of Shechem and south of Lake Galilee. "Beer" means "well" and frequently appears as part of place names throughout Palestine.

9.22 *military commander of Israel:* As a result of his military campaigns, Abimelech ruled Shechem and some other Canaanite and Israelite cities (9.41), but he did not rule over all of Israel. It must be noted, too, that he was made king of Shechem by the elders there, not by the LORD.

9.27 *grape harvest:* This was a festival time. Note that the celebration takes place in Shechem in a temple of one of the Canaanite gods.

9.28 *Hamor:* He was the first Canaanite ruler of Shechem (Gen 33.18, 19; Josh 24.32). Gaal calls on the people of Shechem to remember the old days and the old Canaanite kings (here, chiefs of the city of Shechem). The point of Gaal's speech is that Abimelech is not a Shechemite, and that he should be overthrown. Zebul, Abimelech's deputy, sends this news to Abimelech (9.31).

9.34 *Abimelech led his soldiers:* They were camped at Arumah, about five miles from Shechem (9.41).

9.38 *go out and fight:* Zebul taunts Gaal into battle but then forces him out of town (9.41).

9.46-49 *the temple fortress . . . set them on fire:* Some leaders hid out in the temple of the Canaanite god they served, perhaps thinking their god would protect them from Abimelech's soldiers. Instead, they die by fire, which fulfills Jotham's curse upon them (9.15-20).

9.50 *Thebez:* This town was about twelve miles northeast of Shechem.

9.54-57 *kill me . . . Jotham's curse:* It was considered a disgrace for a man to be killed by a woman. Shechem already has been punished (9.3-6,42-49) for supporting Abimelech as king even though he wasn't worthy. Now, with Abimelech's death, Jotham's curse is fulfilled (9.15,19-21).

10.1,2 *Tola . . . leader:* Of the total of twelve special leaders named in Judges, some are only mentioned briefly, including Tola and Jair in 10.1-5. Tola is from the Issachar tribe (Num 26.23-25). It is unclear which nation was oppressing Israel at this time or how Tola helped Israel.

your bragging now? You were the one who said Abimelech shouldn't be the ruler of Shechem. Out there is the army that you made fun of. So go out and fight them!"

^{39}Gaal and the leaders of Shechem went out and fought Abimelech. ^{40}Soon the people of Shechem turned and ran back into the town. However, Abimelech and his troops were close behind and killed many of them along the way.

^{41}Abimelech stayed at Arumah,[i] and Zebul forced Gaal and his brothers out of Shechem.

^{42}The next morning, the people of Shechem were getting ready to work in their fields as usual, but someone told Abimelech about it. ^{43}Abimelech divided his army into three groups and set up an ambush in the fields near Shechem. When the people came out of the town, he and his army rushed out from their hiding places and attacked. ^{44}Abimelech and the troops with him ran to the town gate and took control of it, while two other groups attacked and killed the people who were in the fields. ^{45}He and his troops fought in Shechem all day, until they had killed everyone in town. Then he and his men tore down the houses and buildings and scattered salt[j] everywhere.

^{46}Earlier that day, the leaders of the temple of El Berith[k] at Shechem had heard about the attack. So they went into the temple fortress, ^{47}but Abimelech found out where they were. ^{48}He led his troops to Mount Zalmon, where he took an ax and chopped off a tree branch. He lifted the branch onto his shoulder and shouted, "Hurry! Cut off a branch just as I did."

^{49}When they all had branches, they followed Abimelech back to Shechem. They piled the branches against the fortress and set them on fire, burning down the fortress and killing about 1,000 men and women.

^{50}After destroying Shechem, Abimelech went to Thebez. He surrounded the town and captured it. ^{51}But there was a tall fortress in the middle of the town, and the town leaders and everyone else went inside. Then they barred the gates and went up to the flat roof.

^{52}Abimelech and his army rushed to the fortress and tried to force their way inside. Abimelech himself was about to set the heavy wooden doors on fire, ^{53}when a woman on the roof dropped a large rock[l] on his head and cracked his skull. ^{54}The soldier who carried his weapons was nearby, and Abimelech told him, "Take out your sword and kill me. I don't want people to say that I was killed by a woman!"

So the soldier ran his sword through Abimelech. ^{55}And when the Israelite soldiers saw that their leader was dead, they went back home.

^{56}That's how God punished Abimelech for killing his brothers and bringing shame on his father's family. ^{57}God also punished the people of Shechem for helping Abimelech.[m] Everything happened just as Jotham's curse said it would.

Tola

10 Tola was the next person to rescue Israel. He belonged to the Issachar tribe, but he lived in Shamir, a town in the hill country of Ephraim. His father was

---

[i]**9.41** *Arumah:* About five miles from Shechem.   [j]**9.45** *scattered salt:* This may have been part of a ceremony to place a curse on the town.   [k]**9.46** *temple of El Berith:* The Hebrew text also calls all or part of this temple the "Fortress of Shechem." El Berith, "the God of the Agreement," was also known as Baal Berith, "the Lord of the Agreement" (see also 8.33; 9.4).   [l]**9.53** *large rock:* One that was used in the grinding of grain.   [m]**9.57** *helping Abimelech:* Hebrew "their evil" (see 9.3,4).

Puah, and his grandfather was Dodo. [2]Tola was a leader[n] of Israel for 23 years, then he died and was buried in Shamir.

Jair

[3]The next leader[n] of Israel was Jair, who lived in Gilead. He was a leader for 22 years. [4]He had 30 sons, and each son had his own mule[o] and was in charge of one town in Gilead. Those 30 towns are still called The Settlements of Jair.[P] [5]When he died, he was buried in the town of Kamon.

Israel Is Unfaithful to God

[6]Before long, the Israelites began disobeying the LORD by worshiping Baal, Astarte, and gods from Syria, Sidon, Moab, Ammon, and Philistia.

[7]The LORD was angry with Israel and decided to let Philistia and Ammon conquer them. [8]So the same year that Jair died, Israel's army was crushed by these two nations. For 18 years, Ammon was cruel to the Israelites who lived in Gilead, the region east of the Jordan River that had once belonged to the Amorites. [9]Then the Ammonites began crossing the Jordan and attacking the tribes of Judah, Benjamin, and Ephraim. Life was miserable for the Israelites. [10]They begged the LORD for help and confessed, "We were unfaithful to you, our LORD. We stopped worshiping you and started worshiping idols of Baal."

[11-12]The LORD answered:

In the past when you came crying to me for help, I rescued you. At one time or another I've rescued you from the Egyptians, the Amorites, the Ammon-

ites, the Philistines, the Sidonians, the Amalekites, and the Maonites.[q] [13-14]But I'm not going to rescue you any more! You've left me and gone off to worship other gods. If you're in such big trouble, go and cry to them for help!

[15]"We have been unfaithful to you," the Israelites admitted. "If we must be punished, do it yourself, but please rescue us from the Ammonites."

[16]Then the Israelites got rid of the idols of the foreign gods, and they began worshiping only the LORD. Finally, there came a time when the LORD could no longer stand to see them suffer.

The Ammonites Invade Gilead

[17]The rulers of Ammon called their soldiers together and led them to Gilead, where they set up camp.

The Israelites gathered at Mizpah[r] and set up camp there. [18]The leaders of Gilead asked each other, "Who can lead an attack on the Ammonites?" Then they agreed, "If we find someone who can lead the attack, we'll make him the ruler of Gilead."

Jephthah

11 [1-5]The leaders of the Gilead clan decided to ask a brave warrior named Jephthah son of Gilead to lead the attack against the Ammonites.

Even though Jephthah belonged to the Gilead clan, he had earlier been forced to leave the region where they had lived. Jephthah was the son of a prostitute, but his half brothers were the sons of his father's wife.

---

[n]10.2,3 *leader*: See 2.16 and the note there. [o]10.4 *each son had his own mule*: A sign that the family was wealthy. [P]10.4 *The Settlements of Jair*: Or "Havvoth-Jair." [q]10.11,12 *Maonites*: Hebrew; one ancient translation "Midianites." [r]10.17 *Mizpah*: In chapters 10–12, Mizpah is the name of a town in Gilead (see 11.29), not the same town as the Mizpah of chapters 20,21.

● 10.3-5 *Gilead . . . Settlements of Jair . . . Kamon:* Gilead was the territory east of the Jordan River in the highlands north and south of the Jabbok River. The "Settlements" were 30 towns, each governed by one of Jair's sons. See also Josh 13.30,31. The exact location of Kamon is unknown. **(See Map 6 on pg 1884.)**

● 10.6 *worshiping Baal . . . gods:* Baal and Astarte were the chief Canaanite gods, while the other nations surrounding Israel's tribes turned to similar gods for protection and blessings.

✎ Canaanite Gods and Goddesses

● 10.7 *Ammon:* The Ammonites, who lived east of the Jordan River, began crossing the Jordan River to attack the tribes west of the southern part of the Jordan. **(See Map 3 on pg 1881.)**

■ 10.10 *They begged . . . and confessed:* The Israelites say that they are sorry for worshiping other gods, but God is not swayed at first (10.13-14). Eventually, the people get rid of the Canaanite idols, so the LORD helps them (10.16).

● 11.1-5 *Gilead clan . . . son of a prostitute:* A clan was a group of families who were related to each other. A group of clans made up a tribe. The Gilead clan was in the Manasseh tribe that lived east of the Jordan River.

As the son of a prostitute, Jephthah was not a likely candidate for leadership. Nevertheless he is a military hero, and a special leader appointed by God (11.29). **(See Map 3 on pg 1881.)**

✎ Prostitution in the Bible

11.10 *the LORD is a witness:* See Gen 31.45-49, where an agreement is made between Jacob and Laban at this same site.

Making Promises (Vows)

11.13,14 *the land really belongs to me . . . Jephthah sent the messengers:* The king of Ammon declares that he deserves to have the land back because it was stolen from him (11.13). Jephthah argues that the Israelites moved into the land after conquering it at the time of Moses (11.14-27). At that time it did not belong to either Ammon or Moab, but to the Amorites (under King Sihon). However, the argument does not convince the king of Ammon (11.28). According to Joshua 13.15-32, two and a half tribes (Reuben, Gad, and East Manasseh) settled east of the Jordan River. This land was promised to them from the time of Moses. **(See Map 3 on pg 1881.)**

One day his half brothers told him, "You don't really belong to our family, so you can't have any of the family property." Then they forced Jephthah to leave home.

Jephthah went to the country of Tob, where he was joined by a number of men who would do anything for money.

So the leaders of Gilead went to Jephthah and said, **6**"Please come back to Gilead! If you lead our army, we will be able to fight off the Ammonites."

7"Didn't you hate me?" Jephthah replied. "Weren't you the ones who forced me to leave my family? You're only coming to me now because you're in trouble."

8"But we do want you to come back," the leaders said. "And if you lead us in battle against the Ammonites, we will make you the ruler of Gilead."

9"All right," Jephthah said. "If I go back with you and the LORD lets me defeat the Ammonites, will you really make me your ruler?"

10"You have our word," the leaders answered. "And the LORD is a witness to what we have said."

11So Jephthah went back to Mizpah[r] with the leaders of Gilead. The people of Gilead gathered at the place of worship and made Jephthah their ruler. Jephthah also made promises to them.

12After the ceremony, Jephthah sent messengers to say to the king of Ammon, "Are you trying to start a war? You have invaded my country, and I want to know why!"

13The king of Ammon replied, "Tell Jephthah that the land really belongs to me, all the way from the Arnon River in the south, to the Jabbok River in the north,

and west to the Jordan River. When the Israelites came out of Egypt, they stole it. Tell Jephthah to return it to me, and there won't be any war."

14Jephthah sent the messengers back to the king of Ammon, **15**and they told him that Jephthah had said:

Israel hasn't taken any territory from Moab or Ammon. **16**When the Israelites came from Egypt, they traveled across the desert to the Red Sea[s] and then to Kadesh. **17** They sent messengers to the king of Edom and said, "Please, let us go through your country." But the king of Edom refused. They also sent messengers to the king of Moab, but he wouldn't let them cross his country either. And so the Israelites stayed at Kadesh.

18A little later, the Israelites set out into the desert, going east of Edom and Moab, and camping on the eastern side of the Arnon River gorge. The Arnon is the eastern border of Moab, and since the Israelites didn't cross it, they didn't even set foot in Moab.

19The Israelites sent messengers to the Amorite King Sihon of Heshbon. "Please," they said, "let our people go through your country to get to our own land."

20Sihon didn't think the Israelites could be trusted, so he called his army together. They set up camp at Jahaz, then they attacked the Israelite camp. **21**But the LORD God helped Israel defeat Sihon and his army. Israel took over all of the Amorite land where Sihon's people had lived, **22**from the Arnon River in the south to the Jab-

[r]**11.11** *Mizpah:* In chapters 10–12, Mizpah is the name of a town in Gilead (see 11.29), not the same town as the Mizpah of chapters 20,21.   [s]**11.16** *Red Sea:* Hebrew *yam suph,* here referring to the Gulf of Aqaba, since the term is extended to include the northeastern arm of the Red Sea (see also the note at Exodus 13.18).

bok River in the north, and from the desert in the east to the Jordan River in the west. ²³The messengers also told the king of Ammon that Jephthah had said:

The LORD God of Israel helped his nation get rid of the Amorites and take their land. Now do you think you're going to take over that same territory? ²⁴If Chemosh your god[t] takes over a country and gives it to you, don't you have a right to it? And if the LORD takes over a country and gives it to us, the land is ours!

²⁵ Are you better than Balak the son of Zippor? He was the king of Moab, but he didn't quarrel with Israel or start a war with us.

²⁶For 300 years, Israelites have been living in Heshbon and Aroer and the nearby villages, and in the towns along the Arnon River gorge. If the land really belonged to you Ammonites, you wouldn't have waited until now to try to get it back.

²⁷I haven't done anything to you, but it's certainly wrong of you to start a war. I pray that the LORD will show whether Israel or Ammon is in the right.

²⁸But the king of Ammon paid no attention to Jephthah's message.

²⁹Then the LORD's Spirit took control of Jephthah, and Jephthah went through Gilead and Manasseh, raising an army. Finally, he arrived at Mizpah in Gilead, where ³⁰he promised the LORD, "If you will let me defeat the Ammonites ³¹and come home safely, I will sacrifice to you whoever comes out to meet me first."

³²From Mizpah, Jephthah attacked the Ammonites, and the LORD helped him defeat them.

³³Jephthah and his army destroyed the 20 towns between Aroer and Minnith, and others as far as Abel-Keramim. After that, the Ammonites could not invade Israel any more.

Jephthah's Daughter

³⁴When Jephthah returned to his home in Mizpah, the first one to meet him was his daughter. She was playing a tambourine and dancing to celebrate his victory, and she was his only child.

³⁵"Oh no!" Jephthah cried. Then he tore his clothes in sorrow and said to his daughter, "I made a sacred promise to the LORD, and I must keep it. Your coming out to meet me has broken my heart."

³⁶"Father," she said, "you made a sacred promise to the LORD, and he let you defeat the Ammonites. Now, you must do what you promised, even if it means I must die. ³⁷But first, please let me spend two months, wandering in the hill country with my friends. We will cry together, because I can never get married and have children."

³⁸"Yes, you may have two months," Jephthah said.

She and some other girls left, and for two months they wandered in the hill country, crying because she could never get married and have children. ³⁹Then she went back to her father. He did what he had promised, and she never got married.

That's why ⁴⁰every year, Israelite girls walk around for four days, weeping for[u] Jephthah's daughter.

11.25 *Balak:* He was a Moabite king at the time the people of Israel were on their way to settle in the promised land of Canaan (Num 22.1-6).

11.26 *Heshbon:* Along the northern border of the Reuben tribe, Heshbon had belonged to King Sihon, who was defeated by Moses. The "300 years" of Israelite settlement may refer to the total number of years the judges mentioned in the book so far had served plus the 18 years that Ammon oppressed the Israelites in Gilead. But it is unlikely that the Israelite people had been settled near Heshbon this long.

11.30,31 *If you will let me . . . I will sacrifice to you:* The tragedy of this bargain with God is that it is not necessary. Jephthah is already possessed by the Spirit (11.29), so his victory is assured. For "whoever," Jephthah may have meant "whatever." Because homes had courtyards for domestic animals, Jephthah most likely expected that the first thing to meet him would have been a sheep or a goat to be offered as a sacrifice.

Making Promises (Vows)

11.40 *every year . . . for four days:* This religious rite was probably performed at some point in Israel's history, but it is not mentioned anywhere else in the Bible.

[t]11.24 *Chemosh your god:* Chemosh was actually the national god of Moab, not Ammon. The land that Ammon was trying to take over had belonged to the Moabites before belonging to the Amorites (see Numbers 21.26). So the Ammonites may have thought that Chemosh controlled it.
[u]11.40 *weeping for:* Or "remembering."

12.1-5 *Ephraim tribe . . . Gilead*: The Ephraim tribe complained that they were not involved in the war against the Ammonites, perhaps because they wanted a share of the money and goods that had been captured. The men of Ephraim then claim that the people of Gilead are living on land that actually belongs to Ephraim (12.4). So Jephthah squashes the Ephraim threat and orders tight security placed on the east bank of the Jordan River, so no one from Ephraim can get into Gilead (the tribal land belonging to Gad).

12.6 *Shibboleth*: This is Hebrew for "ear of corn." The Ephraimites apparently had their own pronunciation for this word, and so their dialect gave them away.

12.8 *Ibzan . . . from Bethlehem*: Ibzan was from the town of Bethlehem in the territory of Zebulun, not Bethlehem in Judah. (See Map 3 on pg 1881.)

12.12 *Aijalon*: This is not the Aijalon in the Manasseh or Ephraim territory (Judg 1.35), but another Aijalon farther north in the Zebulun territory.

12.13-15 *Abdon . . . 40 sons . . . donkey*: Donkeys at this time were commonly used as pack animals and for transportation, though not everyone could afford to keep one. The fact that each son owned a donkey was a sign that the family was wealthy. It was not until the time of King Solomon (around 970 B.C.) that the horse came to be used in Palestine.

The Ephraim Tribe Fights Jephthah's Army

12 The men of the Ephraim tribe got together an army and went across the Jordan River to Zaphon to meet with Jephthah. They said, "Why did you go to war with the Ammonites without asking us to help? Just for that, we're going to burn down your house with you inside!"

²"But I did ask for your help," Jephthah answered. "That was back when the people of Gilead and I were having trouble with the Ammonites, and you wouldn't do a thing to help us. ³So when we realized you weren't coming, we risked our lives and attacked the Ammonites. And the LORD let us defeat them. There's no reason for you to come here today to attack me."

⁴But the men from Ephraim said, "You people of Gilead are nothing more than refugees from Ephraim. You even live on land that belongs to the tribes of Ephraim and Manasseh."ᵛ

So Jephthah called together the army of Gilead, then they attacked and defeated the army from Ephraim. ⁵The army of Gilead also posted guards at all the places where the soldiers from Ephraim could cross the Jordan River to return to their own land.

Whenever one of the men from Ephraim would try to cross the river, the guards would say, "Are you from Ephraim?"

"No," the man would answer, "I'm not from Ephraim."

⁶The guards would then tell them to say "Shibboleth," because they knew that people of Ephraim could say "Sibboleth," but not "Shibboleth."

If the man said "Sibboleth," the guards would grab him and kill him right there. Altogether, 42,000 men from Ephraim were killed in the battle and at the Jordan.

⁷Jephthah was a leaderʷ of Israel for six years, before he died and was buried in his hometown Mizpahˣ in Gilead.

Ibzan

⁸Ibzan, the next leaderʸ of Israel, came from Bethlehem. ⁹He had 30 daughters and 30 sons, and he let them all marry outside his clan.

Ibzan was a leader for seven years, ¹⁰before he died and was buried in Bethlehem.

Elon

¹¹Elon from the Zebulun tribe was the next leaderʸ of Israel. He was a leader for ten years, ¹²before he died and was buried in Aijalon that belonged to the Zebulun tribe.

Abdon

¹³⁻¹⁵Abdon the son of Hillel was the next leaderʸ of Israel. He had 40 sons and 30 grandsons, and each one of them had his own donkey.ᶻ Abdon was a leader for eight years, before he died and was buried in his hometown of Pirathon, which is located in the part of the hill country of Ephraim where Amalekites used to live.

Samson Is Born

13 Once again the Israelites started disobeying the LORD. So he let the Philistines take control of Israel for 40 years.

ᵛ**12.4** *You people of Gilead . . . Ephraim and Manasseh*: One possible meaning for the difficult Hebrew text.   ʷ**12.7** *leader*: See 2.16 and the note there.   ˣ**12.7** *his hometown Mizpah*: One possible meaning for the difficult Hebrew text.   ʸ**12.8,11,13-15** *leader*: See 2.16 and the note there.   ᶻ**12.13-15** *each . . . donkey*: A sign that the family was wealthy.

²Manoah from the tribe of Dan lived in the town of Zorah. His wife was not able to have children, ³⁻⁵but one day an angel from the LORD appeared to her and said:

You have never been able to have any children, but very soon you will be pregnant and have a son. He will belong to God[a] from the day he is born, so his hair must never be cut. And even before he is born, you must not drink any wine or beer or eat any food forbidden by God's laws.

Your son will begin to set Israel free from the Philistines.

⁶She went to Manoah and said, "A prophet who looked like an angel of God came and talked to me. I was so frightened, that I didn't even ask where he was from. He didn't tell me his name, ⁷but he did say that I'm going to have a baby boy. I'm not supposed to drink any wine or beer or eat any food forbidden by God's laws. Our son will belong to God for as long as he lives."

⁸Then Manoah prayed, "Our LORD, please send that prophet again and let him tell us what to do for the son we are going to have."

⁹God answered Manoah's prayer, and the angel went back to Manoah's wife while she was resting in the fields. Manoah wasn't there at the time, ¹⁰so she found him and said, "That same man is here again! He's the one I saw the other day."

¹¹Manoah went with his wife and asked the man, "Are you the one who spoke to my wife?"

"Yes, I am," he answered.

¹²Manoah then asked, "When your promise comes true, what rules must he obey and what will be his work?"

¹³"Your wife must be careful to do everything I told her," the LORD's angel answered. ¹⁴"She must not eat or drink anything made from grapes. She must not drink wine or beer or eat anything forbidden by God's laws. I told her exactly what to do."

¹⁵"Please," Manoah said, "stay here with us for just a little while, and we'll fix a young goat for you to eat." ¹⁶Manoah didn't realize that he was really talking to one of the LORD's angels.

The angel answered, "I can stay for a little while, although I won't eat any of your food. But if you would like to offer the goat as a sacrifice to the LORD, that would be fine."

¹⁷Manoah said, "Tell us your name, so we can honor you after our son is born."

¹⁸"No," the angel replied. "You don't need to know my name. And if you did, you couldn't understand it."

¹⁹So Manoah took a young goat over to a large rock he had chosen for an altar, and he built a fire on the rock. Then he killed the goat, and offered it with some grain as a sacrifice to the LORD. But then an amazing thing happened. ²⁰The fire blazed up toward the sky, and the LORD's angel went up toward heaven in the fire. Manoah and his wife bowed down low when they saw what happened.

²¹Although the angel didn't appear to them again, they realized he was one of the LORD's angels. ²²Manoah said, "We have seen an angel.[b] Now we're going to die."[c]

²³"The LORD isn't going to kill us," Manoah's wife responded. "The LORD accepted our sacrifice and grain offering, and he let us see something amazing. Besides, he told us that we're going to have a son."

²⁴Later, Manoah's wife did give birth to a son, and she named him Samson. As the

---

[a]13.3-5 *belong to God*: The Hebrew text has "be a Nazirite of God." Nazirites were dedicated to God and had to follow special rules to stay that way (see Numbers 6.1,21).   [b]13.22 *angel*: The Hebrew text has "god," which can be used of God or of other supernatural beings.   [c]13.22 *We have seen an angel. Now we're going to die*: Some people believed that if they saw the LORD or one of the LORD's angels, they would die.

13.2 *Zorah*: Located on the border between Judah and Dan 15 miles west of Jerusalem. **(See Map 3 on pg 1881.)**

13.3-5 *belong to God*: This phrase in Hebrew means he will be a Nazirite. Nazirites dedicated themselves to God and had to follow special rules to show their commitment. Their strict lifestyle is outlined in Numbers 6.1-21. Among other things, they were not to cut their hair, drink wine or beer, or have any contact with a dead body. They were also supposed to follow the laws concerning clean and unclean food (Lev 11).

Purity (Clean and Unclean)

13.19 *a sacrifice to the LORD*: Sacrifices were gifts to God that included certain animals, grains, fruits, and sweet-smelling spices. Israelites offered sacrifices to give thanks to God, to ask for God's forgiveness and blessing, and to make payment for a wrong. **(See the chart Sacrifices and Offerings on pg 1828.)**

13.24 *Samson*: This name is related to the Hebrew word for sun. A miracle birth (13.2), concerned parents (13.8), and God's blessing are typical ways for biblical authors to call attention to special individuals.

14.2 *I want . . . Get her for me:* Samson was strong physically, but seemed to be weak in other ways. He was stubborn and had to have his own way, and he was attracted to non-Israelite women. Marriage with foreigners was forbidden throughout much of Israel's history, because such marriages could lead to worshiping foreign gods (3.5-6).

At this time, marriage was not a matter of personal choice. Rather, parents (or the father alone) chose who their children would marry.

14.5 *lion:* This large strong animal was dangerous not only to domestic animals but also to humans. Lions often hide in small hollows in the ground and wait for their prey to pass by. They can kill smaller animals with a blow of the paw and kill larger ones by biting them on the throat.

14.9,10 *he didn't tell them . . . skeleton of a lion . . . party:* Samson didn't tell them because eating anything that had touched a skeleton was against God's laws. Further, as a Nazirite, Samson was not permitted to go close to a dead body. The Hebrew term for "party" here means a social gathering that involves a lot of drinking. Again, as a Nazirite, Samson was not allowed to drink wine, beer, or even grape juice.

14.12 *riddle:* A riddle was a saying with a hidden meaning. Riddles were often used in the ancient world to test a person's intelligence and wisdom. People who could answer difficult riddles were usually considered more worthy of rewards and positions of authority.

boy grew, the LORD blessed him. ²⁵Then, while Samson was staying at Dan's Camp[d] between the towns of Zorah and Eshtaol, the Spirit of the LORD took control of him.

Samson Gets Married

14 One day, Samson went to Timnah, where he saw a Philistine woman. ²When he got back home, he told his parents, "I saw a Philistine woman in Timnah, and I want to marry her. Get her for me!"[e]

³His parents answered, "There are a lot of women in our clan and even more in the rest of Israel. Those Philistines are pagans. Why would you want to marry one of their women?"

"She looks good to me," Samson answered. "Get her for me!"

⁴At that time, the Philistines were in control of Israel, and the LORD wanted to stir up trouble for them. That's why he made Samson desire that woman.

⁵As Samson and his parents reached the vineyards near Timnah, a fierce young lion suddenly roared and attacked Samson. ⁶But the LORD's Spirit took control of Samson, and with his bare hands he tore the lion apart, as though it had been a young goat. His parents didn't know what he had done, and he didn't tell them.

⁷When they got to Timnah, Samson talked to the woman, and he was sure that she was the one for him.

⁸Later,[f] Samson returned to Timnah for the wedding. And when he came near the place where the lion had attacked, he left the road to see what was left of the lion. He was surprised to see that bees were living in

the lion's skeleton, and that they had made some honey. ⁹He scooped up the honey in his hands and ate some of it as he walked along. When he got back to his parents, he gave them some of the honey, and they ate it too. But he didn't tell them he had found the honey in the skeleton of a lion.[g]

¹⁰While Samson's father went to make the final arrangements with the bride and her family, Samson threw a big party,[h] as grooms[i] usually did. ¹¹When the Philistines saw what Samson was like, they told 30 of their young men to stay with him at the party.

¹²Samson told the 30 young men, "This party will last for seven days. Let's make a bet: I'll tell you a riddle, and if you can tell me the answer before the party is over, I'll give each of you a shirt and a full change of clothing. ¹³But if you can't tell me the answer, then each of you will have to give me a shirt and a full change of clothing."

"It's a bet!" the Philistines said. "Tell us the riddle."

¹⁴Samson said:

Once so strong and mighty—
   now so sweet and tasty!

Three days went by, and the Philistine young men had not come up with the right answer. ¹⁵Finally, on the seventh[j] day of the party they went to Samson's bride and said, "You had better trick your husband into telling you the answer to his riddle. Have you invited us here just to rob us? If you don't find out the answer, we will burn you and your family to death."

¹⁶Samson's bride went to him and started crying in his arms. "You must really

[d]**13.25** *Dan's Camp:* Or "Mahaneh-Dan."   [e]**14.2** *Get her for me:* At that time, parents arranged marriages for their children.   [f]**14.8** *Later:* Or "The following year."   [g]**14.9** *But he didn't tell them . . . skeleton of a lion:* To eat anything that had touched a skeleton was against God's laws (see Leviticus 11.27-40).   [h]**14.10** *party:* The Hebrew term means a party that involved a lot of drinking.   [i]**14.10** *grooms:* Or "warriors."   [j]**14.15** *Finally, on the seventh:* Hebrew; three ancient translations "on the fourth."

hate me," she sobbed. "If you loved me at all, you would have told me the answer to your riddle."

"But I haven't even told my parents the answer!" Samson replied. "Why should I tell you?"

[17]For the entire seven days of the party, she had been whining and trying to get the answer from him. But that seventh day she put so much pressure on Samson that he finally gave in and told her the answer. She went straight to the young men and told them.

[18]Before sunset that day, the men of the town went to Samson with this answer:

A lion is the strongest—
honey is the sweetest!

Samson replied,

This answer you have given me
doubtless came
from my bride-to-be.

[19]Then the LORD's Spirit took control of Samson. He went to Ashkelon,[k] where he killed 30 men and took their clothing. Samson then gave it to the 30 young men at Timnah and stormed back home to his own family.

[20]The father of the bride made Samson's wife marry one of the 30 young men that had been at Samson's party.[l]

15 Later, during the wheat harvest, Samson went to visit the young woman he thought was still his wife.[m] He brought along a young goat as a gift and said to her father, "I want to go into my wife's bedroom."

"You can't do that," he replied. [2]"When you left the way you did, I thought you were divorcing[n] her. So I arranged for her to marry one of the young men who were at your party. But my younger daughter is even prettier, and you can have her as your wife."

[3]"This time," Samson answered, "I have a good reason for really hurting some Philistines."

Samson Takes Revenge

[4]Samson went out and caught 300 foxes and tied them together in pairs with oil-soaked rags around their tails. [5]Then Samson took the foxes into the Philistine wheat fields that were ready to be harvested. He set the rags on fire and let the foxes go. The wheat fields went up in flames, and so did the stacks of wheat that had already been cut. Even the Philistine vineyards and olive orchards burned.

[6]Some of the Philistines started asking around, "Who could have done such a thing?"

"It was Samson," someone told them. "He married the daughter of that man in Timnah, but then the man gave Samson's wife to one of the men at the wedding."

The Philistine leaders went to Timnah and burned to death Samson's wife and her father.[o]

[7]When Samson found out what they had done, he went to them and said, "You killed them! And I won't rest until I get even with you." [8]Then Samson started hacking them to pieces with his sword.[P]

Samson left Philistia and went to live in the cave at Etam Rock. [9]But it wasn't long

14.18 *Before sunset that day*: At this time, marriage was official after the seventh day of the wedding festivities. However, Samson leaves the woman's home on sunset of the last day, meaning the marriage rite has not been completed or made official.

14.19 *the LORD's Spirit*: In contrast to other judges, Samson never leads an army, and his feuds are motivated by personal revenge not by a desire to rescue the Israelite tribes from hostile neighbors. When the LORD's Spirit takes control of him, Samson gains superhuman strength (also 14.6; 15.13-14; 16.28-30).

14.19 *Ashkelon*: This was a major Philistine town on the southern Mediterranean coast, about 20 miles from Timnah. Samson robs Ashkelon in order to pay his personal debt to Timnah. (See Map 3 on pg 1881.)

15.4 *foxes*: The Hebrew word is also used for jackals, animals very much like foxes. Jackals stay together in packs during the day and sometimes hide in caves where hunters try to trap and kill them.

15.8,9 *cave at Etam . . . Judah*: Samson belonged to the Dan tribe, but Etam Rock was a few miles southwest of Bethlehem in the territory of the Judah tribe. The people of Judah do not want a confrontation with the Philistines (15.10), and they have no reason to support this wild man from Dan. (See Map 3 on pg 1881.)

15.15 *jawbone of a donkey:* Note that this act occurs at a place called "Jawbone" (15.9). After snapping the ropes tied around him, Samson uses a jawbone as a curved, sickle-like weapon. As a Nazirite, he is to have no contact with corpses or skeletons (14.9). The story, however, would have delighted Israelites who were tired of foreign oppressors.

16.3 *Hebron:* Hebron was in the southern highlands of Judah, about a 40-mile uphill walk from Gaza. This story of Samson's superhuman strength no doubt thrilled early listeners. Many would have wondered what could defeat him. **(See Map 3 on pg 1881.)**

before the Philistines invaded Judah[q] and set up a huge army camp at Jawbone.[r]

[10]The people of Judah asked, "Why have you invaded our land?"

The Philistines answered, "We've come to get Samson. We're going to do the same things to him that he did to our people."

[11]Three thousand men from Judah went to the cave at Etam Rock and said to Samson, "Don't you know that the Philistines rule us, and they will punish us for what you did?"

"I was only getting even with them," Samson replied. "They did the same things to me first."

[12]"We came here to tie you up and turn you over to them," said the men of Judah.

"I won't put up a fight," Samson answered, "but you have to promise not to hurt me yourselves."

[13-14]"We promise," the men said. "We will only tie you up and turn you over to the Philistines. We won't kill you." Then they tied up his hands and arms with two brand-new ropes and led him away from Etam Rock.

When the Philistines saw that Samson was being brought to their camp at Jawbone, they started shouting and ran toward him. But the LORD's Spirit took control of Samson, and Samson broke the ropes, as though they were pieces of burnt cloth. [15]Samson glanced around and spotted the jawbone of a donkey. The jawbone had not yet dried out, so it was still hard and heavy. Samson grabbed it and started hitting Philistines—he killed 1,000 of them! [16]After the fighting was over, he made up

this poem about what he had done to the Philistines:

> I used a donkey's jawbone
> to kill a thousand men;
> I beat them with this jawbone
> over and over again.[s]

[17]Samson tossed the jawbone on the ground and decided to call the place Jawbone Hill.[t] It is still called that today.

[18]Samson was so thirsty that he prayed, "Our LORD, you helped me win a battle against a whole army. Please don't let me die of thirst now. Those heathen Philistines will carry off my dead body."

[19]Samson was tired and weary, but God sent water gushing from a rock.[u] Samson drank some and felt strong again.

Samson named the place Caller Spring,[v] because he had called out to God for help. The spring is still there at Jawbone.

[20]Samson was a leader[w] of Israel for 20 years, but the Philistines were still the rulers of Israel.

Samson Carries Off the Gates of Gaza

16 One day while Samson was in Gaza, he saw a prostitute and went to her house to spend the night. [2]The people who lived in Gaza found out he was there, and they decided to kill him at sunrise. So they went to the city gate and waited all night in the guardrooms on each side of the gate.[x]

[3]But Samson got up in the middle of the night and went to the town gate. He pulled the gate doors and doorposts out of the

[q]15.9 *Judah:* Samson belonged to the Dan tribe, but his hideout in the cave at Etam Rock was in Judah, a few miles southwest of Bethlehem. [r]15.9 *Jawbone:* Or "Lehi" (see verse 17). [s]15.16 *I beat . . . again:* One possible meaning for the difficult Hebrew text. [t]15.17 *Jawbone Hill:* Or "Ramath-Lehi." [u]15.19 *God sent . . . a rock:* One possible meaning for the difficult Hebrew text. [v]15.19 *Caller Spring:* Or "Enhakkore." [w]15.20 *leader:* See 2.16 and the note there. [x]16.2 *guardrooms . . . gate:* The gate was often in a part of the town wall that was thicker and taller than the rest of the wall, and that had rooms where guards stayed when they were on duty.

wall and put them on his shoulders. Then he carried them all the way to the top of the hill that overlooks Hebron,[y] where he set the doors down, still closed and locked.

Delilah Tricks Samson

[4]Some time later, Samson fell in love with a woman named Delilah, who lived in Sorek Valley. [5]The Philistine rulers[z] went to Delilah and said, "Trick Samson into telling you what makes him so strong and what can make him weak. Then we can tie him up so he can't get away. If you find out his secret, we will each give you 1,100 pieces of silver."[a]

[6]The next time Samson was at Delilah's house, she asked, "Samson, what makes you so strong? How can I tie you up so you can't get away? Come on, you can tell me."

[7]Samson answered, "If someone ties me up with seven new bowstrings that have never been dried,[b] it will make me just as weak as anyone else."

[8-9]The Philistine rulers gave seven new bowstrings to Delilah. They also told some of their soldiers to go to Delilah's house and hide in the room where Samson and Delilah were. If the bowstrings made Samson weak, they would be able to capture him.

Delilah tied up Samson with the bowstrings and shouted, "Samson, the Philistines are attacking!"

Samson snapped the bowstrings, as though they were pieces of scorched string. The Philistines had not found out why Samson was so strong.

[10]"You lied and made me look like a fool," Delilah said. "Now tell me. How can I really tie you up?"

[11]Samson answered, "Use some new ropes. If I'm tied up with ropes that have never been used, I'll be just as weak as anyone else."

[12]Delilah got new ropes, and again some Philistines hid in the room. Then she tied up Samson's arms and shouted, "Samson, the Philistines are attacking!"

Samson snapped the ropes as if they were threads.

[13]"You're still lying and making a fool of me," Delilah said. "Tell me how I can tie you up!"

"My hair is in seven braids," Samson replied. "If you weave my braids into the threads on a loom and nail the loom[c] to a wall, then I will be as weak as anyone else."

[14]While Samson was asleep, Delilah wove his braids into the threads on a loom and nailed the loom to a wall.[d] Then she shouted, "Samson, the Philistines are attacking!"

Samson woke up and pulled the loom free from its posts in the ground and from the nails in the wall. Then he pulled his hair free from the woven cloth.

[15]"Samson," Delilah said, "you claim to love me, but you don't mean it! You've made me look like a fool three times now, and you still haven't told me why you are so strong." [16]Delilah started nagging and pestering him day after day, until he couldn't stand it any longer.

[17]Finally, Samson told her the truth. "I have belonged to God[e] ever since I was

[y]16.3 Hebron: About 40 miles from Gaza. [z]16.5 Philistine rulers: There were five rulers, each one controlling part of Philistia. [a]16.5 silver: About 140 pounds of silver altogether. [b]16.7 new bowstrings . . . dried: The string for a bow was often made from sinews or internal organs of animals. These strings were made while the animal tissues were still moist, and they became much stronger, once they were dry. [c]16.13 loom: A large wooden frame on which cloth is woven. [d]16.13,14 If you weave . . . to a wall: Some manuscripts of one ancient translation; Hebrew "Weave my braids into the threads on a loom. She nailed the loom to a wall." [e]16.17 belonged to God: See the note at 13.3-5.

16.23 *their god Dagon:* This Philistine god was father of Baal and god of grain, with temples in Ashdod and Gaza. The temple had a large flat roof where the big party with lots of drinking took place.

Canaanite Gods and Goddesses

16.28 *watching Samson... prayed:* Samson may have been in a courtyard visible from the roof (16.27). In his prayer, Samson claims that his power comes from God.

16.31 *They buried him... and Zorah and Eshtaol:* Several family members were often buried in one tomb, which was often a cave cut into bedrock. Zorah and Eshtaol were listed as part of the Dan tribal territory in Joshua 19.40-46, but in Joshua 15.33-36 they are listed as part of Judah.

Burial

born, so my hair has never been cut. If it were ever cut off, my strength would leave me, and I would be as weak as anyone else."

[18]Delilah realized that he was telling the truth. So she sent someone to tell the Philistine rulers, "Come to my house one more time. Samson has finally told me the truth."

The Philistine rulers went to Delilah's house, and they brought along the silver they had promised her. [19]Delilah had lulled Samson to sleep with his head resting in her lap. She signaled to one of the Philistine men as she began cutting off Samson's seven braids. And by the time she was finished, Samson's strength was gone. Delilah tied him up [20]and shouted, "Samson, the Philistines are attacking!"

Samson woke up and thought, "I'll break loose and escape, just as I always do." He did not realize that the LORD had stopped helping him.

[21]The Philistines grabbed Samson and poked out his eyes. They took him to the prison in Gaza and chained him up. Then they put him to work, turning a millstone to grind grain. [22]But they didn't cut his hair any more, so it started growing back.

[23]The Philistine rulers threw a big party and sacrificed a lot of animals to their god Dagon. The rulers said:

> Samson was our enemy,
>   but our god Dagon
>   helped us capture him!

[24-25]Everyone there was having a good time, and they shouted, "Bring out Samson—he's still good for a few more laughs!"

The rulers had Samson brought from the prison, and when the people saw him, this is how they praised their god:

> Samson ruined our crops
>   and killed our people.
> He was our enemy,
>   but our god helped us
>   capture him.

They made fun of Samson for a while, then they told him to stand near the columns that supported the roof. [26]A young man was leading Samson by the hand, and Samson said to him, "I need to lean against something. Take me over to the columns that hold up the roof."

[27]The Philistine rulers were celebrating in a temple packed with people and with 3,000[f] more on the flat roof. They had all been watching Samson and making fun of him.[g]

[28]Samson prayed, "Please remember me, LORD God. The Philistines poked out my eyes, but make me strong one last time, so I can take revenge for at least one of my eyes!"[h]

[29]Samson was standing between the two middle columns that held up the roof. He felt around and found one column with his right hand, and the other with his left hand. [30]Then he shouted, "Let me die with the Philistines!" He pushed against the columns as hard as he could, and the temple collapsed with the Philistine rulers and everyone else still inside. Samson killed more Philistines when he died than he had killed during his entire life.

[31]His brothers and the rest of his family went to Gaza and took his body back home. They buried him in his father's tomb,[i]

[f]16.27 *3,000:* Hebrew; some manuscripts of one ancient translation "700." [g]16.27 *They . . . him:* Samson may have been in a courtyard visible from the roof. [h]16.28 *one of my eyes:* Or "my eyes." [i]16.31 *buried him in his father's tomb:* Several family members were often buried in one tomb.

Samson prayed, "Please remember me, LORD God . . . make me strong one last time." JUDG 16.28

which was located between Zorah and Esh-taol.

Samson was a leader[j] of Israel for 20 years.

Micah Makes Idols and Hires a Priest

17 Micah[k] belonged to the Ephraim tribe and lived in the hill country. [2]One day he told his mother, "Do you remember those 1,100 pieces of silver[l] that were stolen from you? I was there when you put a curse on whoever stole them. Well, I'm the one who did it."

His mother answered, "I pray that the LORD will bless[m] you, my son."

[3-4]Micah returned the silver to his mother, and she said, "I give this silver to the LORD, so my son can use it to make an idol." Turning to her son, she said, "Micah, now the silver belongs to you."

But Micah handed it back to his mother. She took 200 pieces[n] of the silver and gave them to a silver worker, who made them into an idol.[o] They kept the idol in Micah's house. [5]He had a shrine for worshiping God there at his home, and he had made some idols and a sacred priestly vest. Micah chose one of his own sons to be the priest for his shrine.

[6]This was before kings ruled Israel, so all the Israelites did whatever they thought was right.

[7-8]One day a young Levite came to Micah's house in the hill country of Ephraim. He had been staying with one of the clans of Judah in Bethlehem, but he had left Bethlehem to find a new place to live[p] where he could be a priest.[q]

[9]"Where are you from?" Micah asked.

"I am a Levite from Bethlehem in Judah," the man answered, "and I'm on my way to find a new place to live."

[10]Micah said, "Why don't you stay here with me? You can be my priest and tell me what God wants me to do. Every year I'll give you ten pieces of silver and one complete set of clothes, and I'll provide all your food."

The young man went for a walk, [11-12]then he agreed to stay with Micah and be his priest. He lived in Micah's house, and Micah treated him like one of his own sons. [13]Micah said, "I have a Levite as my own priest. Now I know that the LORD will be kind to me."

18 These things happened before kings ruled Israel.

The Tribe of Dan Takes Micah's Priest and Idols

About this time, the tribe of Dan was looking for a place to live. The other tribes had land, but the people of Dan did not really have any to call their own. [2]The tribe chose five warriors to represent their clans and told them, "Go and find some land where we can live."

The warriors left the area of Zorah and Eshtaol and went into the hill country of Ephraim. One night they stayed at Micah's house, [3]because they heard the young Levite talking, and they knew from his accent that he was from the south. They asked him, "What are you doing here? Who brought you here?"

[j]16.31 *leader:* See 2.16 and the note there. [k]17.1 *Micah:* The Hebrew also uses the longer form "Micaiah." [l]17.2 *1,100 . . . silver:* About 28 pounds. [m]17.2 *curse . . . bless:* A curse could not be taken back, but it could be made powerless by a blessing. [n]17.3,4 *200 pieces:* About five pounds. [o]17.3,4 *idol:* Probably carved from wood and covered with the silver. [p]17.7,8 *place to live:* The people of the Levi tribe did not have a large area of land like the other tribes. [q]17.7,8 *to find . . . priest:* Or "and was on his way to find a new place to live."

● 17.1 *Micah . . . Ephraim tribe:* A number of people in the Bible are called Micah, a name that means "who is like the LORD?" This Micah should not be confused with the prophet who lived at the same time as the prophet Isaiah.

● 17.7-8 *a young Levite:* God chose the men of one Levite family, the descendants of Moses' brother Aaron, to be Israel's priests. The other men from this tribe helped with work in the sacred tent and later in the temple. The Levites were not given territory like the other tribes. Instead, they were to be supported by the rest of the tribes by receiving a portion of the sacrifices given to the LORD.

◯R   Israel's Priests

● 17.7-8 *Bethlehem:* This town six miles south of Jerusalem was where Rachel was buried (Gen 35.19) and where Israel's greatest king, David, was born (1 Sam 17.12).

● 17.10 *You can be my priest:* Micah had already made his son the household priest (17.5). Now he seizes the opportunity to get a genuine Levite for the job. Micah is convinced that he then will have God's favor, or perhaps simply have better luck.

● 18.1 *the tribe of Dan:* Ancient tradition locates the tribe of Dan in the south along the Mediterranean coastal plain (Josh 19.40-48). They were hemmed in by the tribe of Ephraim to the north, the tribes of Benjamin and Judah to the east, and the Philistines to the south. **(See Map 3 on pg 1881.)**

18.7 *Laish . . . Sidon:* Laish was southwest of Mount Hermon in the north, at the headwaters of the Jordan River. Sidon was in Phoenician territory on the Mediterranean coast 20 miles north of Tyre. Laish was defenseless ("had no walls") and had no allies. **(See Map 3 on pg 1881.)**

4The Levite replied, "Micah hired me as his priest." Then he told them how well Micah had treated him.

5"Please talk to God for us," the men said. "Ask God if we will be successful in what we are trying to do."

6"Don't worry," answered the priest. "The LORD is pleased with what you are doing."

7The five men left and went to the town of Laish, whose people were from Sidon,ʳ but Sidon was too far away to protect them. Even though their town had no walls, the people thought they were safe from attack. So they had not asked anyone elseˢ for protection, which meant that the tribe of Dan could easily take over Laish.ᵗ

8The five men went back to Zorah and Eshtaol, where their relatives asked, "Did you find any land?"

9-10"Let's go!" the five men said. "We saw some very good land with enough room for all of us, and it has everything we will ever need. What are you waiting for? Let's attack and take it. You'll find that the people think they're safe, but God is giving the land to us."

11Six hundred men from the tribe of Dan strapped on their weapons and left Zorah and Eshtaol with their families.ᵘ **12**One night they camped near Kiriath-Jearim in the territory of Judah, and that's why the place just west of Kiriath-Jearim is still known as Dan's Camp.ᵛ **13**Then they went into the hill country of Ephraim.

When they came close to Micah's house, **14**the five men who had been spies asked the other warriors, "Did you know that someone in this village has several idols and a sacred priestly vest? What do you think we should do about it?"

15-18 The 600 warriors left the road and went to the house on Micah's property where the young Levite priest lived. They stood at the gate and greeted the priest. Meanwhile, the five men who had been there before went into Micah's house and took the sacred priestly vest and the idols.

"Hey!" the priest shouted. "What do you think you're doing?"

19"Quiet!" the men said. "Keep your mouth shut and listen. Why don't you come with us and be our priest, so you can tell us what God wants us to do? You could stay here and be a priest for one man's family, but wouldn't you rather be the priest for a clan or even a whole tribe of Israel?"

20The priest really liked that idea. So he took the vest and the idols and joined the others **21**from the tribe of Dan. Then they turned and left, after putting their children, their cattle, and the rest of their other possessions in front.

22They had traveled for some time before Micah asked his neighbors to help him get his things back. He and his men caught up with the people of Dan **23**and shouted for them to stop.

They turned to face him and asked, "What's wrong? Why did you bring all these men?"

24Micah answered, "You know what's wrong. You stole the godsʷ I made, and you took my priest. I don't have anything left."

25"We don't want to hear any more about it," the people of Dan said. "And if you make us angry, you'll only get yourself

ʳ**18.7** *whose people . . . Sidon:* One possible meaning for the difficult Hebrew text. ˢ**18.7** *anyone else:* Hebrew; one ancient translation has "the Arameans," who were a short distance to the north. ᵗ**18.7** *which . . . Laish:* One possible meaning for the difficult Hebrew text. ᵘ**18.11** *Eshtaol with their families:* Hebrew "Eshtaol" (see verse 21). ᵛ**18.12** *Dan's Camp:* See the note at 13.25. ʷ**18.24** *gods:* Or "god."

and your family killed." [26]After saying this, they turned and left.

Micah realized there was no way he could win a fight with them, and so he went back home.

The Tribe of Dan Captures Laish

[27-28]The tribe of Dan took Micah's priest and the things Micah had made, and headed for Laish, which was located in a valley controlled by the town of Beth-Rehob. Laish was defenseless, because it had no walls and was too far from Sidon for the Sidonians to help defend it. The leaders of Laish had not even asked nearby towns to help them in case of an attack.

The warriors from Dan made a surprise attack on Laish, killing everyone and burning it down. Then they rebuilt the town and settled there themselves. [29]But they named it Dan, after one of Israel's[x] sons, who was the ancestor of their tribe.

[30-31]Even though the place of worship[y] was in Shiloh, the people of Dan set up the idol Micah had made. They worshiped the idol, and the Levite was their priest. His name was Jonathan, and he was a descendant of Gershom the son of Moses.[z] His descendants served as priests for the tribe of Dan, until the people of Israel were taken away as prisoners by their enemies.

A Woman Is Murdered

19 Before kings ruled Israel, a Levite[a] was living deep in the hill country of the Ephraim tribe. He married[b] a woman from Bethlehem in Judah, [2]but she was unfaithful and went back to live with her family in Bethlehem.

Four months later [3]her husband decided to try and talk her into coming back. So he went to Bethlehem, taking along a servant and two donkeys. He talked with his wife, and she invited him into her family's home. Her father was glad to see him [4]and did not want him to leave. So the man stayed three days, eating and drinking with his father-in-law.

[5]When everyone got up on the fourth day, the Levite started getting ready to go home. But his father-in-law said, "Don't leave until you have a bite to eat. You'll need strength for your journey."

[6]The two men sat down together and ate a big meal. "Come on," the man's father-in-law said. "Stay tonight and have a good time."

[7]The Levite tried to leave, but his father-in-law insisted, and he spent one more night there. [8]The fifth day, the man got up early to leave, but his wife's father said, "You need to keep up your strength! Why don't you leave right after lunch?" So the two of them started eating.

[9]Finally, the Levite got up from the meal, so he and his wife and servant could leave. "Look," his father-in-law said, "it's already late afternoon, and if you leave now, you won't get very far before dark. Stay with us one more night and enjoy yourself. Then you can get up early tomorrow morning and start home."

[10]But the Levite decided not to spend the night there again. He had the saddles put on his two donkeys, then he and his wife

---

[x]18.29 *Israel's*: Israel was another name for Jacob, the father of the twelve ancestors of the tribes of Israel. [y]18.30,31 *place of worship*: The Hebrew text has "house of God," which at this time was probably the sacred tent. [z]18.30,31 *Moses*: Some manuscripts of two ancient translations; the Standard Hebrew Text has "Manasseh," but written in a special way that tells the reader "Moses" had been changed to "Manasseh." [a]19.1 *a Levite*: Someone from the Levi tribe, which had no tribal lands of its own. [b]19.1 *married*: See the note at 8.31.

● 18.30-31 *Dan set up the idol . . . until the people of Israel were taken away*: Dan later became a center for idol worship (1 Kgs 12.28-30). Located 20 miles north of Jerusalem, Shiloh was an important religious site for Israel and many other ancient peoples. Israel kept the sacred chest—containing the flat stones with the Ten Commandments written on them—at Shiloh, until the Philistines stole it around 1050 B.C. (1 Sam 4.3,4). Eventually, Israel's King David defeated the Philistines and got the sacred chest back. The people were "taken away" in 722 B.C. when Assyria conquered the northern kingdom of Israel and forced many of Israel's citizens to live in other lands. **(See the article From Joshua to the Exile: The People of Israel in the Promised Land on pg 1783.)**

CR   The Sacred Chest

CR   Exile

● 19.1 *a Levite . . . Ephraim tribe*: The Levites did not have tribal land, but were scattered throughout all the tribes to serve as priests. The woman from Bethlehem was not a full legal wife, but a "concubine" (8.27-31).

19.15 *spend the night:* People usually considered it a duty to ask travelers to spend the night in their homes, since there were often no other places to stay. This lack of hospitality proved to be the least of their troubles in Gibeah.

19.16 *this man... from... Ephraim:* While the Benjaminites failed to do the proper thing, the old man from Ephraim extends an invitation to the weary travelers.

19.22-24 *Send him out... do whatever else:* According to customs of hospitality, the old man was expected to protect his male guest. Offering the Benjaminite men his daughter and the Levite's wife (concubine) shows how strongly he felt about his duty to keep this custom. It also shows that men often controlled what happened to a woman and that women had few legal rights. Though the Law of Moses did have strong rules against illegal sex, including rape, the story is another example of the lawlessness of the time.

19.29 *he... cut her body into twelve pieces:* The gruesome act of cutting up the dead woman's body and distributing the pieces to Israel's twelve tribes is a dramatic call to action. Her murder is seen as not just a personal tragedy, but an insult to all the people of Israel. Ironically, her dismemberment brings the people together and makes them act as one to avenge this insult.

and servant traveled as far as Jebus, which is now called Jerusalem. [11]It was beginning to get dark, and the man's servant said, "Let's stop and spend the night in this town where the Jebusites live."

[12]"No," the Levite answered. "They aren't Israelites, and I refuse to spend the night there. We'll stop for the night at Gibeah, [13]or maybe we can even reach Ramah[c] before dark."

[14]They walked on and reached Gibeah in the territory of Benjamin just after sunset. [15]They left the road and went into Gibeah. But the Levite couldn't find a house where anyone would let them spend the night, and they sat down in the open area just inside the town gates.

[16]Soon an old man came in through the gates on his way home from working in the fields. Most of the people who lived in Gibeah belonged to the tribe of Benjamin, but this man was originally from the hill country of Ephraim. [17]He noticed that the Levite was just in town to spend the night. "Where are you going?" the old man asked. "Where did you come from?"

[18]"We've come from Bethlehem in Judah," the Levite answered. "We went there on a visit. Now we're going to the place where the LORD is worshiped, and later we will return to our home in the hill country of Ephraim. But no one here will let us spend the night[d] in their home. [19]We brought food for our donkeys and bread and wine for ourselves, so we don't need anything except a place to sleep."

[20]The old man said, "You are welcome to spend the night in my home and to be my guest, but don't stay out here!"

[21]The old man brought them into his house and fed their donkeys. Then he and his guests washed their feet[e] and began eating and drinking. [22]They were having a good time, when some worthless men of that town surrounded the house and started banging on the door and shouting, "A man came to your house tonight. Send him out, so we can have sex with him!"

[23]The old man went outside and said, "My friends, please don't commit such a horrible crime against a man who is a guest in my house. [24]Let me send out my daughter instead. She's a virgin. And I'll even send out the man's wife.[f] You can rape them or do whatever else you want, but please don't do such a horrible thing to this man."

[25]The men refused to listen, so the Levite grabbed his wife and shoved her outside. The men raped her and abused her all night long. Finally, they let her go just before sunrise, [26]and it was almost daybreak when she went back to the house where her husband[g] was staying. She collapsed at the door and lay there until sunrise.

[27]About that time, her husband woke up and got ready to leave. He opened the door and went outside, where he found his wife lying at the door with her hands on the doorstep. [28]"Get up!" he said. "It's time to leave."

But his wife didn't move.[h]

He lifted her body onto his donkey and left. [29]When he got home, he took a butcher knife and cut her body into twelve

[c]19.13 *Gibeah ... Ramah:* It was about three miles from Jerusalem to Gibeah, and another three miles to Ramah.   [d]19.18 *spend the night:* People usually considered it a duty to ask travelers to spend the night in their homes, since there were often no other places to stay.   [e]19.21 *washed their feet:* This was a custom, since people wore open sandals and their feet would be dirty after walking on the dirt roads or working in the fields.   [f]19.24 *wife:* See the note at 8.31.   [g]19.26 *husband:* Or "owner"; the Hebrew word may mean that she was his slave and had no legal rights.   [h]19.28 *move:* Hebrew; one ancient translation "move. She was dead."

pieces. Then he told some messengers, "Take one piece to each tribe of Israel [30]and ask everyone if anything like this has ever happened since Israel left Egypt. Tell them to think about it, talk it over, and tell us what should be done."

Everyone who saw a piece of the body said, "This is horrible! Nothing like this has ever happened since the day Israel left Egypt."[i]

Israel Gets Ready for War

20 [1-3]The Israelites called a meeting of the nation. And since they were God's people, the meeting was held at the place of worship in Mizpah. Men who could serve as soldiers came from everywhere in Israel—from Dan in the north, Beersheba in the south, and Gilead east of the Jordan River. Four hundred thousand of them came to Mizpah, and they each felt the same about what those men from the tribe of Benjamin had done.

News about the meeting at Mizpah reached the tribe of Benjamin.

As soon as the leaders of the tribes of Israel took their places, the Israelites said, "How could such a horrible thing happen?"

[4]The husband of the murdered woman answered:

My wife[j] and I went into the town of Gibeah in Benjamin to spend the night. [5]Later that night, the men of Gibeah surrounded the house. They wanted to kill me, but instead they raped and killed my wife. [6]It was a terrible thing for Israelites to do! So I cut up her body and sent the pieces everywhere in Israel.

[7]You are the people of Israel, and you must decide today what to do about the men of Gibeah.

[8]The whole army was in agreement, and they said, "None of us will go home. [9-10]We'll send one tenth of the men from each tribe to get food for the army. And we'll ask God[k] who should attack Gibeah, because those men[l] deserve to be punished for committing such a horrible crime in Israel."

[11]Everyone agreed that Gibeah had to be punished.

[12]The tribes of Israel sent messengers to every town and village in Benjamin. And wherever the messengers went, they said, "How could those worthless men in Gibeah do such a disgusting thing? [13]We can't allow such a terrible crime to go unpunished in Israel! Hand the men over to us, and we will put them to death."

But the people of Benjamin refused to listen to the other Israelites. [14]Men from towns all over Benjamin's territory went to Gibeah and got ready to fight Israel. [15]The Benjamin tribe had 26,000 soldiers, not counting the 700 who were Gibeah's best warriors. [16]In this army there were 700 left-handed experts who could sling a rock[m] at a target the size of a hair and hit it every time.

● 20.1-3 *Mizpah . . . Dan . . . Beersheba:* People from every tribe gathered in Mizpah in the Benjamin district, a worship site eight miles north of Jerusalem. "From Dan to Beersheba" indicates the whole of Canaan from north to south. **(See Map 3 on pg 1881.)**

● 20.1-3 *tribe of Benjamin:* Benjamin was the youngest son of Jacob, and the smallest of the tribes (1 Sam 9.21). This tribe ignores the summons, supports the town of Gibeah, and prepares for war. The men of Gibeah who raped the Levite's wife should have been judged according to the Law of Moses, but because this was a lawless time, their evil act leads to a civil war.

● 20.9-10 *ask God:* Answers to questions put to the LORD were often determined by a method known as casting lots. Small pieces of wood or stone called "lots" were used to find out what God wanted the people to do. It was similar to flipping a coin or drawing straws, but it was believed that God controlled the outcome.

● 20.16 *sling a rock:* Benjamin's warriors were known as sharpshooters, using slings made from leather straps to hurl rocks with precision (1 Chr 12.2).

[i]19.29,30 *he told some messengers . . . since the day Israel left Egypt:* One ancient translation; Hebrew "he told some messengers, 'Take one piece to each tribe of Israel.' Everyone who saw a piece of the body said, 'This is horrible! Nothing like this has ever happened since Israel left Egypt. Think of it! Let's talk it over and decide what to do.'" [j]20.4 *wife:* See the note at 8.31. [k]20.9,10 *ask God:* The Hebrew text has "use lots to decide"; small pieces of wood or stone called "lots" were used to find out what God wanted his people to do. [l]20.9,10 *those men:* One Hebrew manuscript and one ancient translation; The Standard Hebrew text "the men of Geba." [m]20.16 *sling a rock:* By using a sling made from a leather strap.

20.26-28 *crying and not eating*: After being defeated by the Benjamin tribe, the Israelites mourned their losses by crying out to God and by fasting (going without eating). Mourning was also done by tearing one's clothes and rubbing dirt on one's body. The slaughter of the Israelites was immense.

The Sacred Chest

20.26-28 *Phinehas*: Phinehas is the grandson of Aaron and son of Eleazar, the high priest during the conquest of Canaan.

20.31-41 *a different plan*: The battle plan used here is similar to that used by Joshua in the campaign against the town of Ai (Josh 8).

20.31-41 *set the town on fire*: The smoke signals the destruction of Gibeah and the ambush. Just when the Benjaminites thought all was going well, the rest of Israel defeats them. Over 25,000 men of Benjamin were killed and only 600 survived (20.47).

[17]The other Israelite tribes organized their army and found they had 400,000 experienced soldiers. [18]So they went to the place of worship at Bethel[n] and asked God, "Which tribe should be the first to attack the people of Benjamin?"

"Judah," the LORD answered.

[19]The next morning the Israelite army moved its camp to a place near Gibeah. [20]Then they left their camp and got into position to attack the army of Benjamin.

The War Between Israel and Benjamin

[21]Benjamin's soldiers came out of Gibeah and attacked, and when the day was over, 22,000 Israelite soldiers lay dead on the ground.

[22-24]The people of Israel went to the place of worship and cried until sunset. Then they asked the LORD, "Should we attack the people of Benjamin again, even though they are our relatives?"

"Yes," the LORD replied, "attack them again!"

The Israelite soldiers encouraged each other to be brave and to fight hard. Then the next day they went back to Gibeah and took up the same positions as they had before.

[25]That same day, Benjamin's soldiers came out of Gibeah and attacked, leaving another 18,000 Israelite soldiers dead on the battlefield.

[26-28]The people of Israel went to the place of worship at Bethel,[n] where the sacred chest was being kept. They sat on the ground, crying and not eating for the rest of the day. Then about sunset, they offered sacrifices to please the LORD and to ask his blessing.[o] Phinehas[p] the priest then prayed, "Our LORD, the people of Benjamin are our relatives. Should we stop fighting or attack them again?"

"Attack!" the LORD answered. "Tomorrow I will let you defeat them."

[29]The Israelites surrounded Gibeah, but stayed where they could not be seen. [30]Then the next day, they took the same positions as twice before, [31-41]but this time they had a different plan. They said, "When the men of Benjamin attack, we will run off and let them chase us away from the town and into the country roads."

The soldiers of Benjamin attacked the Israelite army and started pushing it back from the town. They killed about 30 Israelites in the fields and along the road between Gibeah and Bethel. The men of Benjamin were thinking, "We're mowing them down like we did before."

The Israelites were running away, but they headed for Baal-Tamar, where they regrouped. They had set an ambush, and they were sure it would work. Ten thousand of Israel's best soldiers had been hiding west of Gibeah,[q] and as soon as the men of Benjamin chased the Israelites into the countryside, these 10,000 soldiers made a surprise attack on the town gates. They dashed in and captured Gibeah, killing everyone there. Then they set the town on fire, because the smoke would be the signal for the other Israelite soldiers to turn and attack the soldiers of Benjamin.

The fighting had been so heavy around the soldiers of Benjamin, that they did not know the trouble they were in. But then they looked back and saw clouds of smoke rising from the town. They looked in front

[n]20.18,26-28 *place . . . Bethel*: The Hebrew text has "beth-el," which means "house of God." This could refer to the town of Bethel, to the place of worship at Mizpah, or to the sacred tent at Shiloh (see 18.30,31). [o]20.26-28 *sacrifices . . . blessing*: See Leviticus 1–3. [p]20.26-28 *Phinehas*: Hebrew "Phinehas the son of Eleazar the son of Aaron." [q]20.31-41 *west of Gibeah*: Three ancient translations; Hebrew "in a field at Geba."

and saw the soldiers of Israel turning to attack. This terrified them, because they realized that something horrible was happening. And it was horrible—over 25,000[r] soldiers of Benjamin died that day, and those who were left alive knew that the LORD had given Israel the victory.

[42] The men of Benjamin headed down the road toward the desert, trying to escape from the Israelites. But the Israelites stayed right behind them, keeping up their attack. Men even came out of the nearby towns to help kill the men of Benjamin, [43] who were having to fight on all sides. The Israelite soldiers never let up their attack.[s] They chased and killed the warriors of Benjamin as far as a place directly east of Gibeah,[t] [44] until 18,000 of these warriors lay dead.

[45] Some other warriors of Benjamin turned and ran down the road toward Rimmon Rock in the desert. The Israelites killed 5,000 of them on the road, then chased the rest until they had killed[u] 2,000 more. [46] Twenty-five thousand soldiers of Benjamin died that day, all of them experienced warriors. [47] Only 600 of them finally made it into the desert to Rimmon Rock, where they stayed for four months.

[48] The Israelites turned back and went to every town in Benjamin's territory, killing all the people and animals, and setting the towns on fire.

Wives for the Men of Benjamin

21 When the Israelites had met at Mizpah before the war with Benjamin,[v] they had made this sacred promise: "None of us will ever let our daughters marry any man from Benjamin."

[2] After the war with Benjamin, the Israelites went to the place of worship at Bethel and sat there until sunset. They cried loudly and bitterly [3] and prayed, "Our LORD, you are the God of Israel. Why did you let this happen? Now one of our tribes is almost gone."

[4] Early the next morning, the Israelites built an altar and offered sacrifices to please the LORD and to ask his blessing.[w] [5] Then they asked each other, "Did any of the tribes of Israel fail to come to the place of worship? We made a sacred promise that anyone who didn't come to the meeting at Mizpah would be put to death."

[6] The Israelites were sad about what had happened to the Benjamin tribe, and they said, "One of our tribes was almost wiped out. [7] Only a few men of Benjamin weren't killed in the war. We need to get wives for them, so the tribe won't completely disappear. But how can we do that, after promising in the LORD's name that we wouldn't let them marry any of our daughters?"

[8-9] Again the Israelites asked, "Did any of the tribes stay away from the meeting at Mizpah?"

After asking around, they discovered that no one had come from Jabesh in Gilead. [10-11] So they sent 12,000 warriors with these orders: "Attack Jabesh in Gilead and kill everyone, except the women who have never been married."

[12] The warriors attacked Jabesh in Gilead, and returned to their camp at Shiloh in Canaan[x] with 400 young women.

20.45 *Rimmon Rock:* This was located about three miles east of Bethel. **(See Map 3 on pg 1881.)**

20.48 *killing all the people:* The civil war ends with the tribe of Benjamin almost completely wiped out (21.15). The "Holy War" tactics that had guided the Israelites in their defeat of foreign enemies in Canaan were now used against one of their own tribes (Benjamin). Only 600 male survivors were left at Rimmon Rock (20.47).

21.5 *sacred promise . . . put to death:* See the first oath at 21.1. Here we find out that a second oath was made at the meeting of the tribes at Mizpah (20.1-3). This oath to kill anyone who didn't come to the meeting at Mizpah would cause more bloodshed and death, but it also allowed the Israelite tribes to make things up to the men of the Benjamin tribe that had been nearly wiped out.

21.12 *400 young women:* The young unmarried women of Jabesh in Gilead are given as wives to the surviving men of the Benjamin tribe, since all the women of the Benjamin tribe had been killed. Sparing young women's lives and then claiming them as war prizes is also seen in Numbers 31.17,18 and Judges 5.30. But the 400 women mentioned here are not enough for the 600 warriors (20.47).

---

[r]**20.31-41** *over 25,000:* Hebrew "25,100." [s]**20.42,43** *Men even came out . . . their attack:* One possible meaning for the difficult Hebrew text. [t]**20.43** *Gibeah:* Or "Geba." [u]**20.45** *until . . . killed:* Or "as far as Gidom, killing." [v]**21.1** *the Israelites . . . Benjamin:* See 20.1-3. [w]**21.4** *sacrifices . . . blessing:* See the note at 20.26-28. [x]**21.12** *in Canaan:* Jabesh was in Gilead, across the Jordan River from the land of Canaan.

21.22 *you won't be under the curse:* The vow of 21.1 was not technically violated, as the women were kidnapped, and their parents did not actually give them to the Benjaminites.

21.24,25 *Afterwards . . . Israel wasn't ruled by a king:* The book seems to end with the tribes of Israel at peace (21.24). But the writer repeats the phrase (17.6; 18.1; 19.1), which leaves the impression that Israel will continue to have a difficult time until a king rules all the tribes. Until then, every person and every tribe will do what each thinks is right, meaning that civil war, needless violence, and acts of cruelty and injustice will continue.

[13]The Israelites met and sent messengers to the men of Benjamin at Rimmon Rock, telling them that the Israelites were willing to make peace with them. [14]So the men of Benjamin came back from Rimmon Rock, and the Israelites let them marry the young women from Jabesh. But there weren't enough women.

[15]The Israelites were very sad, because the LORD had almost wiped out one of their tribes. [16]Then their leaders said:

All the women of the Benjamin tribe were killed. How can we get wives for the men of Benjamin who are left? [17]If they don't have children, one of the Israelite tribes will die out. [18]But we can't let the men of Benjamin marry any of our daughters. We made a sacred promise not to do that, and if we break our promise, we will be under our own curse.

[19]Then someone suggested, "What about the LORD's Festival that takes place each year in Shiloh? It's held north of Bethel, south of Lebonah, and just east of the road that goes from Bethel to Shechem."

[20]The leaders told the men of Benjamin who still did not have wives:

Go to Shiloh and hide in the vineyards near the festival. [21]Wait there for the young women of Shiloh to come out and perform their dances. Then rush out and grab one of the young women, then take her home as your wife. [22]If the fathers or brothers of these women complain about this, we'll say, "Be kind enough to let those men keep your daughter. After all, we couldn't get enough wives for all the men of Benjamin in the battle at Jabesh. And because you didn't give them permission to marry your daughters, you won't be under the curse we earlier agreed on."[y]

[23]The men of Benjamin went to Shiloh and hid in the vineyards. The young women soon started dancing, and each man grabbed one of them and carried her off. Then the men of Benjamin went back to their own land and rebuilt their towns and started living in them again.

[24]Afterwards, the rest of the Israelites returned to their homes and families.

Israel Was Not Ruled by a King

[25]In those days Israel wasn't ruled by a king, and everyone did what they thought was right.

[y]21.22 *on:* One possible meaning for the difficult Hebrew text of verse 22.

In those days Israel wasn't ruled by a king, and everyone did what they thought was right. JUDG 21.25

Reflection Questions About Judges 1.1—21.25

1. In the first chapter of JUDGES, what is the condition of Israel's tribes in Canaan?

2. What promise did God make to Israel's ancestors about the land of Canaan? What did the Israelites promise to do in return (2.1,2)? Why did the LORD stop helping Israel defeat its enemies (2.3)?

3. What was the main role of Israel's "judges" (2.16-19)? How is this role different from or similar to what you might expect?

4. Why were many of Israel's enemies still in Canaan, even after the Israelites had invaded the land (2.20—3.6)?

5. Who was Deborah? In what ways does she show special leadership (4.1-14)?

6. When Gideon was chosen to be a judge, how did he respond (6.11-24)? How many times did Gideon ask for proof from the LORD (6.17-40)? Why do you think he needed this proof?

7. What were the miraculous events that accompanied Samson's birth (13.2-25)? Does Samson fit the role of a judge? How is he different from other judges in the book? What are your thoughts or questions about God's choice of Samson as a leader?

8. Which, if any, of the events in chapters 19–21 would not be tolerated in our society today? Why? What seems to have been the attitude toward women in the ancient times? What was women's status?

9. What point does the writer of JUDGES seem to be making in 21.25 (also 17.6; 18.1; 19.1)? How does this fit with Gideon's response to the people in 8.22,23?

10. How is the idea of "everyone doing what they think is right" encouraged in our society today? How does this idea fit with honoring God and living a life of faith?

ruth

Trying to survive when the odds are against you can be difficult. Read the story of Ruth and her mother-in-law Naomi to find out how a brave and loyal woman survived under difficult circumstances to become the great-grandmother of King David.

WHAT MAKES RUTH SPECIAL?

RUTH is a beautiful story that teaches many things. The story quietly shows how God is concerned with the life of ordinary people, and works to fulfill his purposes in unexpected ways. By telling the story of a Moabite girl whose care for her mother-in-law brings her to Israel, RUTH shows how God works in the lives of people who are faithful; how helping others and being loyal to family and friends can change lives and bring happiness; and that God's goodness is for everyone, not just for people who are born Jews.

The story of Ruth showed the people it was written for, the people of Israel, how God can use not only the Jews but people of other nations to work out God's plans in the world. Ruth was not from any of the tribes of Israel but from Moab. She left the security of her own family to live in Israel with her mother-in-law Naomi and to take care of this childless widow. The last verses of the story (4.13-22) tell how Ruth and her descendants became ancestors of Israel's greatest king, David.

WHAT'S THE STORY BEHIND THE SCENE?

The story of Ruth tells about events that happened during the time of the judges, which was a period of around 200 years before David became king of Israel in 1000 B.C. Many of the Hebrew terms and customs that are mentioned in the story come from this time, but some of the language and laws at work in the book come from as late as 250 B.C. This may mean that the final version of the story was written down centuries after the time when the events in the story took place.

HOW IS RUTH CONSTRUCTED?

RUTH is like a short story with interesting characters and a plot that leads to a happy conclusion. But, it is a story with an important message about God and God's people. It can be divided in this way:

Ruth decides to leave Moab (1.1-22)
Ruth in Israel (2.1—4.22)

Set in the time of the judges, before Israel was ruled by kings, Ruth is written in a form that resembles an ancient short story. It tells of a family from Bethlehem who, when their crops fail, are forced to move to the country of Moab, east of the Dead Sea. While living there, the family's sons marry Moabite women. After ten years, the father and sons die. Naomi, the widowed mother, learns that the land around Bethlehem is again yielding good harvests and decides to return to her home. She attempts to persuade her daughters-in-law to remain in Moab. Orpah agrees, but Ruth insists on returning with Naomi to Judah. In Bethlehem, Ruth's devotion and loyalty to her mother-in-law attract the attention of Naomi's wealthy relative Boaz. Even though Ruth is a Gentile, Boaz, a Jew, marries her. Their descendants become ancestors of Israel's King David.

Outline

Ruth Is Loyal to Naomi

1 [1-2]Before Israel was ruled by kings, Elimelech from the clan of Ephrath lived in the town of Bethlehem. His wife was named Naomi, and their two sons were Mahlon and Chilion. But when their crops failed in Israel, they moved to the country of Moab.[a] And while they were there, [3]Elimelech died, leaving Naomi with only her two sons.

[4]Later, Naomi's sons married Moabite women. One was named Orpah and the other Ruth. About ten years later, [5]Mahlon and Chilion also died. Now Naomi had no husband or sons.

[6-7]When Naomi heard that the LORD had given his people a good harvest, she and her two daughters-in-law got ready to leave Moab and go to Judah. As they were on their way there, [8]Naomi said to them,

"Don't you want to go back home to your own mothers? You were kind to my husband and sons, and you've always been kind to me. I pray that the LORD will be just as kind to you. [9]May he give each of you another husband and a home of your own."

Naomi kissed them. They cried [10]and said, "We want to go with you and live among your people."

[11]But she replied, "My daughters, why don't you return home? What good will it do you to go with me? Do you think I could have more sons for you to marry?[b] [12]You must go back home, because I am too old to marry again. Even if I got married tonight and later had more sons, [13]would you wait for them to become old enough to marry? No, my daughters! Life is harder for me than it is for you, because the LORD has turned against me."[c]

[a]1.1,2 *Moab:* The people of Moab worshiped idols and were usually enemies of the people of Israel.
[b]1.11 *for you to marry:* When a married man died and left no children, it was the custom for one of his brothers to marry his widow. Any children they had would then be thought of as those of the dead man, so that his family name would live on.   [c]1.13 *Life . . . me:* Or "I'm sorry that the LORD has turned against me and made life so hard for you."

● 1.1-2 *Before Israel was ruled by kings:* After Joshua led the Israelite people into the land of Canaan, the land was divided among Israel's twelve tribes. During this time, God chose leaders known as "judges" to help the people protect their land and to remind them to remain faithful to God. **(See Map 3 on pg 1881.)**

● 1.1-2 *Moab:* Moab was a land east of the Dead Sea. The people of Moab were not part of Israel, but were considered to be descendants of Lot, the nephew of Abraham (Gen 11.31; 19.30-38). The tribes of Israel stayed in Moab (Num 22–24) on their way from Egypt to Canaan, the land God had promised to give them. The people of Moab worshiped idols and were enemies of the people of Israel (Deut 23.3-6).

● 1.4 *Orpah . . . Ruth:* In Hebrew "Orpah" means "neck" or "back of the head." "Ruth" means "friend" or "companion."

1.19 *Bethlehem:* This town, whose name means "house of bread" would come to be known as King David's hometown (1 Sam 20.6; Luke 2.4). It is located in the highlands about six miles south of Jerusalem on the main north-south ridge that runs through Palestine.

1.22 *barley harvest:* Barley and wheat were the two most important grains in the ancient Near East. Barley was the cheaper of the two and was used mainly to feed cattle. But it was also used by poor people for making bread.

2.1-3 *grain left . . . workers:* It was the custom at harvest time to leave some stalks of grain in the field for poor people, widows, orphans, and foreigners to pick up. Naomi and Ruth had little money or food after coming back to Bethlehem from Moab. As widows, it would not have been unusual for them to take advantage of the law allowing them to pick unharvested grain.

2.1-3 *Boaz:* Boaz was a wealthy relative of Elimelech. His name means "strength" or "sharp mind."

2.10 *I come from another country:* Because the people of Moab were sometimes enemies of Israel (Deut 23.3-6), the Jewish people who first heard this story might have been surprised that Boaz was so kind toward Ruth, who was from Moab.

Foreigners (Aliens)

---

¹⁴They cried again. Orpah kissed her mother-in-law goodbye, but Ruth held on to her. ¹⁵Naomi then said to Ruth, "Look, your sister-in-law is going back to her people and to her gods! Why don't you go with her?"

¹⁶Ruth answered,

"Please don't tell me
   to leave you
      and return home!
I will go where you go,
   I will live where you live;
your people will be my people,
   your God will be my God.
¹⁷I will die where you die
   and be buried beside you.
May the LORD punish me
if we are ever separated,
   even by death!"ᵈ

¹⁸When Naomi saw that Ruth had made up her mind to go with her, she stopped urging her to go back.

¹⁹They reached Bethlehem, and the whole town was excited to see them. The women who lived there asked, "Can this really be Naomi?"

²⁰Then she told them, "Don't call me Naomi any longer! Call me Mara,ᵉ because God has made my life bitter. ²¹I had everything when I left, but the LORD has brought me back with nothing. How can you still call me Naomi, when God has turned against me and made my life so hard?"

²²The barley harvest was just beginning when Naomi and Ruth, her Moabite daughter-in-law, arrived in Bethlehem.

Ruth Meets Boaz

2 ¹⁻³ One day, Ruth said to Naomi, "Let me see if I can find someone who will let me pick up the grain left in the fields by the harvest workers."ᶠ

Naomi answered, "Go ahead, my daughter." So immediately Ruth went out to pick up grain in a field. She didn't know it was owned by Boaz, a relative of Naomi's husband Elimelech, as well as a rich and important man.

⁴When Boaz arrived from Bethlehem and went out to his field, he said to the harvest workers, "The LORD bless you!"

They replied, "And may the LORD bless you!"

⁵Then Boaz asked the man in charge of the harvest workers, "Who is that young woman?"

⁶The man answered, "She is the one who came back from Moab with Naomi. ⁷She asked if she could pick up grain left by the harvest workers, and she has been working all morning without a moment's rest."ᵍ

⁸Boaz went over to Ruth and said, "I think it would be best for you not to pick up grain in anyone else's field. Stay here with the women ⁹and follow along behind them, as they gather up what the men have cut. I have warned the men not to bother you, and whenever you are thirsty, you can drink from their water jars."

¹⁰Ruth bowed down to the ground and said, "You know I come from another country. Why are you so good to me?"

¹¹Boaz answered, "I've heard how you've helped your mother-in-law ever since your husband died. You even left your own father and mother to come and live in a for-

---

ᵈ**1.17** *even by death:* Or "by anything but death."   ᵉ**1.20** *Mara:* In Hebrew "Naomi" means "pleasant," and "Mara" means "bitter."   ᶠ**2.1-3** *grain left . . . workers:* It was the custom at harvest time to leave some grain in the field for the poor to pick up (see Leviticus 19.10; 23.22).   ᵍ**2.7** *she has . . . rest:* One possible meaning for the difficult Hebrew text.

Ruth told Naomi, *"I will go where you go, I will live where you live; your people will be my people, your God will be my God."* RUTH 1.16

eign land among people you don't know.
¹²I pray that the LORD God of Israel will reward you for what you have done. And
now that you have come to him for protection, I pray that he will bless you."

¹³Ruth replied, "Sir, it's good of you to
speak kindly to me and make me feel so
welcome. I'm not even one of your servants."

¹⁴At mealtime Boaz said to Ruth, "Come,
eat with us. Have some bread and dip it in
the sauce." At once she sat down with the
workers, and Boaz handed her some roasted
grain. Ruth ate all she wanted and had some
left over.

¹⁵When Ruth left to start picking up
grain, Boaz told his men, "Don't stop her,
even if she picks up grain from where it is
stacked. ¹⁶Be sure to pull out some stalks
of grain from the bundles and leave them
on the ground for her. And don't speak
harshly to her!"

¹⁷Ruth worked in the field until evening.
Then after she had pounded the grain off
the stalks, she had a large basket full of
grain. ¹⁸She took the grain to town and
showed Naomi how much she had picked
up. Ruth also gave her the food left over
from her lunch.

¹⁹Naomi said, "Where did you work today? Whose field was it? God bless the man
who treated you so well!" Then Ruth told
her that she had worked in the field of a
man named Boaz.

²⁰ "The LORD bless Boaz!" Naomi replied.
"He[h] has shown that he is still loyal to the
living and to the dead. Boaz is a close relative, one of those who is supposed to look
after us."

²¹Ruth told her, "Boaz even said I could
stay in the field with his workers until they
had finished harvesting all his grain."

²²Naomi replied, "My daughter, it's good

that you can pick up grain alongside the
women who work in his field. Who knows
what might happen to you in someone
else's field!" ²³And so, Ruth stayed close to
the women, while picking up grain in his
field.

Ruth worked in the fields until the barley and wheat were harvested. And all this
time she lived with Naomi.

Naomi Makes Plans for Ruth

3 One day, Naomi said to Ruth:
It's time I found you a husband,
who will give you a home and take
care of you.

²You have been picking up grain
alongside the women who work for
Boaz, and you know he is a relative of
ours. Tonight he will be threshing the
grain. ³Now take a bath and put on
some perfume, then dress in your best
clothes. Go where he is working, but
don't let him see you until he has
finished eating and drinking. ⁴Watch
where he goes to spend the night, then
when he is asleep, lift the cover and lie
down at his feet.[i] He will tell you what
to do.

⁵Ruth answered, "I'll do whatever you
say." ⁶She went out to the place where
Boaz was working and did what Naomi had
told her.

⁷After Boaz finished eating and drinking
and was feeling happy, he went over and
fell asleep near the pile of grain. Ruth
slipped over quietly. She lifted the cover
and lay down near his feet.

⁸In the middle of the night, Boaz suddenly woke up and was shocked to see a
woman lying at his feet. ⁹"Who are you?"
he asked.

"Sir, I am Ruth," she answered, "and you

2.23 *wheat:* Wheat is a highly valued grain that is usually harvested in
late May or early June, several weeks after the harvesting of barley. People
ground wheat into flour and used it for
making bread and other baked foods.

3.1 *time I found you a husband:* In
ancient Israel, unmarried women and
widows had a difficult time supporting
themselves. Since property was owned
by men who passed it on to their sons,
it was very important for a woman to
have a husband or sons to protect her
and take care of her.

3.4 *lift the cover . . . feet:* By telling
Ruth to lie under the cover next to
Boaz, Naomi was hoping that Boaz
would want to marry Ruth. Although
the Law of Moses required Boaz to take
care of the needs of the widow of his
dead relative, the Law did not require
him to marry Ruth.

3.7 *was feeling happy . . . fell
asleep:* Boaz was likely feeling very relaxed from the food and from the wine
he had been drinking. It was customary
to sleep in the fields during harvest
time in order to protect the newly-cut
grain from robbers.

[h]2.20 *He:* Or "The LORD." [i]3.4 *lift the cover . . . feet:* To ask for protection and possibly for marriage.

3.9 *spread the edge of your cover over me:* If Boaz followed this request, it was a sign that he agreed to marry Ruth.

3.12 *an even closer relative:* Boaz knew that the Law of Moses gave Ruth's closest male relative the first chance to marry her. If that relative refused, then Boaz would be free to marry Ruth. See also 2.20.

3.14 *did not want anyone to know:* Ruth left before daylight, so people would not know she had slept beside Boaz the night before. If people had seen Ruth, they could have said that Boaz had already made a commitment to marry her.

4.6 *property I already own:* Boaz invited Ruth's other close relative to buy the land that had belonged to Naomi's husband Elimelech. If he bought the land, it would mean that he agreed to support Elimelech's whole family and that he agreed to marry Ruth. If he married Ruth, part of his property would have to be passed on to Ruth and any children she would have.

4.7,8 *took off one of his sandals:* This custom was a public sign in ancient Israel that a purchase involving land or property was complete.

are the relative who is supposed to take care of me. So spread the edge of your cover over me."[j]

[10]Boaz replied:

The LORD bless you! This shows how truly loyal you are to your family. You could have looked for a younger man, either rich or poor, but you didn't. [11]Don't worry, I'll do what you have asked. You are respected by everyone in town.

[12]It's true that I am one of the relatives who is supposed to take care of you, but there is someone who is an even closer relative. [13]Stay here until morning, then I will find out if he is willing to look after you. If he isn't, I promise by the living God to do it myself. Now go back to sleep until morning.

[14]Ruth lay down again, but she got up before daylight, because Boaz did not want anyone to know she had been there. [15]Then he told her to spread out her cape. And he filled it with grain and placed it on her shoulder.

When Ruth got back to town, [16]Naomi asked her[k] what had happened, and Ruth told her everything. [17]She also said, "Boaz gave me this grain, because he didn't want me to come back without something for you."

[18]Naomi replied, "Just be patient and don't worry about what will happen. He won't rest until everything is settled today!"

Ruth and Boaz Get Married

4 In the meanwhile, Boaz had gone to the meeting place at the town gate and was sitting there when the other close relative came by. So Boaz invited him to come over and sit down, and he did. [2]Then Boaz got ten of the town leaders and also asked them to sit down. After they had sat down, [3]he said to the man:

Naomi has come back from Moab and is selling the land that belonged to her husband Elimelech. [4]I'm telling you about this, since you are his closest relative and have the right to buy the property. If you want it, you can buy it now. These ten men and the others standing here can be witnesses. But if you don't want the property, let me know, because I am next in line.

The man replied, "I'll buy it!"

[5]"If you do buy it from Naomi," Boaz told him, "you must also marry Ruth. Then if you have a son by her, the property will stay in the family of Ruth's first husband."

[6]The man answered, "If that's the case, I don't want to buy it! That would make problems with the property I already own.[l] You may buy it yourself, because I cannot."

[7] To make a sale legal in those days, one person would take off a sandal and give it to the other. [8]So after the man had agreed to let Boaz buy the property, he took off one of his sandals and handed it to Boaz.

[9]Boaz told the town leaders and everyone else:

All of you are witnesses that today I have bought from Naomi the property that belonged to Elimelech and his two sons, Chilion and Mahlon. [10]You are also witnesses that I have agreed to marry Mahlon's widow Ruth, the Moabite woman. This will keep the

[j]**3.9** So . . . me: To show that he would protect and take care of her.   [k]**3.15,16** When . . . her: Some Hebrew manuscripts and two ancient translations; most Hebrew manuscripts "Boaz went back to town. [16]Naomi asked Ruth."   [l]**4.6** property . . . own: This property would then have to be shared with Ruth and her children as well as with his own family.

property in his family's name, and he will be remembered in this town.

[11]The town leaders and the others standing there said:

We are witnesses to this. And we pray that the LORD will give your wife many children, just as he did Leah and Rachel, the wives of Jacob. May you be a rich man in the tribe of Ephrath and an important man in Bethlehem. [12]May the children you have by this young woman make your family as famous as the family of Perez,[m] the son of Tamar and Judah.

[13]Boaz married Ruth, and the LORD blessed her with a son. [14]After his birth, the women said to Naomi:

Praise the LORD! Today he has given you a grandson to take care of you. We pray that the boy will grow up to be famous everywhere in Israel. [15]He will[n] make you happy and take care of you in your old age, because he is the son of your daughter-in-law. And she loves you more than seven sons of your own would love you.

[16]Naomi loved the boy and took good care of him. [17]The neighborhood women named him Obed, but they called him "Naomi's Boy."

When Obed grew up he had a son named Jesse, who later became the father of King David. [18-22]Here is a list of the ancestors of David: Jesse, Obed, Boaz, Salmon, Nahshon, Amminadab, Ram, Hezron, and Perez.

4.12 *Perez, the son of Tamar and Judah:* Perez was one of the sons of Judah (Gen 38.27-30) and Tamar, a Canaanite woman who had been married to another of Judah's sons. Perez was an ancestor of Boaz and of many others who lived in Bethlehem. See also verses 18-22.

4.14,15 *Praise the LORD . . . love you:* These words, like other blessings in the Bible (Gen 12.1-3; 27.27-29), are a declaration of the many good things God has done and will do in the future.

Blessed (Happy)

4.17 *Obed . . . Jesse . . . King David:* In Hebrew, "Obed" means "worshiper." Obed's grandson was David, Israel's greatest king. David was the son of Jesse, a wealthy sheep farmer.

David

4.17 *Naomi's Boy:* Even though Obed was not technically the son or grandson of Naomi, the women of Bethlehem knew that because of Ruth's son Naomi's family would continue and Naomi's place in the community was once again secure.

4.18-22 *list of the ancestors:* Knowing who your ancestors were was important in ancient Israel.

Genealogies in the Bible

[m]4.12 *Perez:* One of the sons of Judah; he was an ancestor of Boaz and of many others who lived in Bethlehem. [n]4.14,15 *We pray that . . . famous . . .* [15]*He will:* Or "We pray that the LORD will be praised everywhere in Israel. [15]Your grandson will."

Reflection Questions About Ruth 1.1—4.22

1. When Naomi's sons died, Naomi believed that God had turned against her and Ruth (1.1-22). Why did she feel so desperate? Have you ever felt this desperate or have you known anyone who felt bitter like Naomi? If so, what caused these feelings and how did you or your friend get through this difficult period?

2. Naomi's daughters-in-law both loved Naomi but made very different decisions about how to go on with their lives (1.6-18). What did Orpah do? What did Ruth do? Why do you think Ruth wanted to go with Naomi to Judah?

3. What did Ruth do to help Naomi when they got to Bethlehem in Judah (2.1-18)? What seem to have been the risks for women who did this kind of work? How could the fact that Ruth was a foreigner (from Moab) have made the situation even more difficult?

4. In chapter 3 Naomi helps Ruth to find a husband. Why do you think she felt this was an important thing to do?

5. How would you describe the mood at the end of the story? How are Naomi's feelings after the birth of her grandson (4.14-17) different from her feelings at the end of chapter one? How does she show her gratitude? How did Naomi's grandson Obed become a blessing for all the people of Israel?

1 samuel

*Exciting stories of Samuel, Saul, and David fill the pages of
1 SAMUEL. Read how they struggled with themselves, with each
other, and with God, and how they transformed Israel from a
group of tribes governed by judges to a nation ruled by a king.*

WHAT MAKES 1 SAMUEL SPECIAL?

FIRST SAMUEL is the beginning of one long book that
was split in two because it was too long to fit on one
scroll. (2 SAMUEL is the second half.) Together they
tell of the lives of Samuel, Saul, and David—three
people who were chosen by the LORD. But the real
story in these books is how all three, in spite of their
human flaws, helped to make Israel a strong nation.

This book tells how God chose the earliest kings in
ancient Israel. For two centuries the Israelites had
been loosely organized as a group of twelve tribes
ruled by temporary leaders, called judges, chosen by
God in times of need. Samuel, the last of these leaders, had to deal with God because of Israel's request
for a new kind of leader—a king similar to the ones
that ruled other nations. But some people saw the request for a human king as going against Israel's ancient belief in God as king. FIRST SAMUEL presents the
views of both sides: 8.1-22 (against); 9.1—10.16 (for);
10.17-27 (against); 11.1-11 (for); 11.12—12.25 (against).

God reluctantly agreed to let Israel have a king,
but reminded them that they must still keep their
solemn promise to obey the LORD (as described in
Genesis 17.7-9 and Exodus 24). But Saul did not
obey and did not want to be replaced by David, the
new king chosen by God. As David himself would
later learn, even kings must obey the LORD.

WHAT'S THE STORY BEHIND THE SCENE?

The two books of SAMUEL cover just over a century of
Israel's history—1080 to 970 B.C. FIRST SAMUEL
opens with a loosely organized group of twelve
tribes. By the end of 2 SAMUEL, however, David is
the king of a unified and powerful nation. The story
of Israel's religious growth during the same time is
also impressive. FIRST SAMUEL describes how the
Israelites gathered several times a year to worship
and offer sacrifices to the LORD. As 2 SAMUEL
closes, Jerusalem has become the center of worship, and David has built an altar at the place where
his son Solomon would later build a magnificent
temple.

HOW IS 1 SAMUEL CONSTRUCTED?

The book can be divided into three major sections,
one for each of its main characters—Samuel, Saul,
and David:

Originally, 1 and 2 Samuel were one book. Together, they describe Israel's history from about 1080 to 970 B.C., from the birth of the prophet Samuel to the death of King David. These books not only tell about the lives of three of Israel's early national heroes—Samuel, Saul, and David—but they also describe how Israel went from being a loosely-knit group of tribes ruled by judges to being a strong nation ruled by kings. First Samuel begins with the story of Samuel; it tells of his birth, his calling by the Lord, and his career as prophet and military leader. When the people insisted that Samuel appoint a king to rule over them like the ones who ruled the nations around them, the Lord told Samuel to select Saul from the tribe of Benjamin to be Israel's first king. King Saul eventually displeased the Lord and as a result of his disobedience the Lord told Samuel that Saul could no longer be king and directed Samuel to select David, a shepherd youth from the tribe of Judah, to be the next king of Israel. Later, when Saul became David's enemy, Samuel helped David escape from Saul. First Samuel ends with an account of the death of Saul and his sons in battle against the Philistines. Second Samuel will take up the story and tell how David, the one God chose to replace Saul, becomes king of a united and powerful Israelite kingdom.

Outline

Hannah Asks the LORD for a Child

1 Elkanah lived in Ramah,[a] a town in the hill country of Ephraim. His great-great-grandfather was Zuph, so Elkanah was a member of the Zuph clan of the Ephraim tribe. Elkanah's father was Jeroham, his grandfather was Elihu, and his great-grandfather was Tohu.

[2]Elkanah had two wives,[b] Hannah and Peninnah. Although Peninnah had children, Hannah did not have any.

[3]Once a year Elkanah traveled from his hometown to Shiloh, where he worshiped the LORD All-Powerful and offered sacrifices. Eli was the LORD's priest there, and his two sons Hophni and Phinehas served with him as priests.[c]

[4]Whenever Elkanah offered a sacrifice, he gave some of the meat[d] to Peninnah and some to each of her sons and daughters. [5]But he gave Hannah even more, because[e] he loved Hannah very much, even though the LORD had kept her from having children of her own.

[6]Peninnah liked to make Hannah feel miserable about not having any children, [7]especially when the family went to the house of the LORD[f] each year.

One day, Elkanah was there offering a sacrifice, when Hannah began crying and refused to eat. [8]So Elkanah asked, "Hannah, why are you crying? Why won't you eat? Why do you feel so bad? Don't I mean more to you than ten sons?"

[9]When the sacrifice had been offered, and they had eaten the meal, Hannah got

---

[a]1.1 *Ramah*: The Hebrew has "Ramathaim," a longer form of "Ramah" (see verse 19).   [b]1.2 *two wives*: Having more than one wife was allowed in those times.   [c]1.3 *Eli . . . priests*: One ancient translation; Hebrew "Hophni and Phinehas, the two sons of Eli, served the LORD as priests."   [d]1.4 *meat*: For some sacrifices, like this one, only part of the meat was burned. Some was given to the priest, and the rest was eaten by the family and guests of the worshiper (see Leviticus 3.1-17; 7.11-18).   [e]1.5 *even more, because*: One ancient translation; Hebrew "only one; he."   [f]1.7 *house of the LORD*: Another name for the place of worship at Shiloh, which still may have been the sacred tent at this time.

● 1.1 *Ephraim*: Ephraim was the area of Canaan given to the tribe of Ephraim when the people of Israel moved into the land and divided it among the twelve tribes of Israel. Each tribe was descended from one of Jacob's twelve sons. (See Map 3 on pg 1881.)

Israel

● 1.3 *Once a year . . . worshiped . . . sacrifices*: Israelite males were required to go to the central place of worship three times each year. Elkanah probably went during the Festival of Shelters, when the people thanked God for their harvests. (See the chart Sacrifices and Offerings on pg 1828.)

LORD (YHWH)

Names of God

■ 1.5 *even though the LORD. . . . children of her own*: Many Israelites believed that children were gifts that God would give or withhold. Children were also considered a sign of God's blessing. Seeing others celebrate God's blessings, it is natural that Hannah would be upset that she did not have a child.

● 1.7 *house of the LORD*: This may have been a temple that was later destroyed by the Philistines. More likely, it refers to the sacred tent that the LORD told Moses to set up and where the people made sacrifices and worshiped the LORD.

The Sacred Tent

1.11 *promise to give him . . . never be cut:* Hannah's promise is like what God had required of Samson's mother (Judg 13.3-5). Each of their sons would serve God. Leaving the child's hair uncut would show that he would belong to the LORD forever. See also Num 6.1-21.

1.12-13 *drunk:* In those times, people usually prayed aloud. Hannah prayed silently. When Eli saw her lips moving, he thought she had had too much to drink and was mumbling to herself.

up and went to pray. Eli was sitting in his chair near the door to the place of worship. **10**Hannah was heartbroken and was crying as she prayed, **11**"LORD All-Powerful, I am your servant, but I am so miserable! Please let me have a son. I promise to give him to you for as long as he lives, and his hair will never be cut."**g**

12-13 Hannah prayed silently to the LORD for a long time. But her lips were moving, and Eli thought she was drunk. **14**"How long are you going to stay drunk?" he asked. "Sober up!"

15-16"Sir, please don't think I'm no good!" Hannah answered. "I'm not drunk, and I haven't been drinking. But I do feel miserable and terribly upset. I've been praying all this time, telling the LORD about my problems."

17Eli replied, "Go home. Everything will be fine. The God of Israel will answer your prayer."

18"Sir, thank you for being so kind to me," Hannah said. Then she left, and after eating something, she felt much better.

Samuel Is Born

19Elkanah and his family got up early the next morning and worshiped the LORD. Then they went back home to Ramah. Later the LORD blessed Elkanah and Hannah **20**with a son. She named him Samuel because she had asked the LORD for him.**h**

Hannah Gives Samuel to the LORD

21The next time Elkanah and his family went to offer their yearly sacrifice, he took along a gift that he had promised to give to the LORD. **22**But Hannah stayed home, because she had told Elkanah, "Samuel and I won't go until he's old enough for me to stop nursing him. Then I'll give him to the LORD, and he can stay there at Shiloh for the rest of his life."

23"You know what's best," Elkanah said. "Stay here until it's time to stop nursing him. I'm sure the LORD will help you do what you have promised."**i** Hannah did not go to Shiloh until she stopped nursing Samuel.

24-25 When it was the time of year to go to Shiloh again, Hannah and Elkanah**j** took Samuel to the LORD's house. They brought along a three-year-old bull,**k** a 20-pound sack of flour, and a clay jar full of wine. Hannah and Elkanah offered the bull as a sacrifice, then brought the little boy to Eli.

26"Sir," Hannah said, "a few years ago I stood here beside you and asked the LORD **27**to give me a child. Here he is! The LORD gave me just what I asked for. **28**Now I am giving him to the LORD, and he will be the LORD's servant for as long as he lives."

g1.11 *his hair . . . cut:* Never cutting the child's hair would be a sign that he would belong to the LORD (see Numbers 6.1,21, especially verse 5). **h**1.20 *him:* In Hebrew "Samuel" sounds something like "Someone from God" or "The name of God" or "His name is God." **i**1.23 *the LORD . . . promised:* The Dead Sea Scrolls and two ancient translations; the Standard Hebrew Text "the LORD will do what he said." **j**1.24,25 *When it was the time of year to go to Shiloh again, Hannah and Elkanah:* The Dead Sea Scrolls and one ancient translation; the Standard Hebrew Text "she." **k**1.24,25 *a three-year-old bull:* The Dead Sea Scrolls and two ancient translations; the Standard Hebrew Text "three bulls."

Hannah Prays

2 Elkanah[l] worshiped the LORD there at Shiloh, and [1]Hannah prayed:

You make me strong
and happy, LORD.
You rescued me.
Now I can be glad
and laugh at my enemies.

[2]No other god[m] is like you.
And with you we are safer
than on a high mountain.[n]
[3]I can tell those proud people,
"Stop your boasting!
Nothing is hidden from the LORD,
and he judges what we do."

[4]Our LORD, you break
the bows of warriors,
but you give strength
to everyone who stumbles.
[5]People who once
had plenty to eat
must now hire themselves out
for only a piece of bread.
But you give the hungry more
than enough to eat.
A woman did not have a child,
and you gave her seven,
but a woman who had many
was left with none.
[6]You take away life,
and you give life.
You send people down
to the world of the dead
and bring them back again.

[7]Our LORD, you are the one
who makes us rich or poor.

You put some in high positions
and bring disgrace on others.
[8]You lift the poor and homeless
out of the garbage dump
and give them places of honor
in royal palaces.

You set the world on foundations,
and they belong to you.
[9]You protect your loyal people,
but everyone who is evil
will die in darkness.

We cannot win a victory
by our own strength.
[10]Our LORD, those who attack you
will be broken in pieces
when you fight back
with thunder from heaven.
You will judge the whole earth
and give power and strength
to your chosen king.

Samuel Stays with Eli

[11]Elkanah and Hannah went back home to Ramah, but the boy Samuel stayed to help Eli serve the LORD.

Eli's Sons

[12-13]Eli's sons were priests, but they were dishonest and refused to obey the LORD. So, while people were boiling the meat from their sacrifices, these priests would send over a servant with a large, three-pronged fork. [14]The servant would stick the fork into the cooking pot, and whatever meat came out on the fork was taken back to Eli's two sons. That was how they treated

2.1-10 *Hannah prayed . . . your chosen king:* Beginning and ending books with similar expressions was common in Hebrew literature. Several phrases in Hannah's prayer are repeated in David's prayer at the end of these books (2 Sam 22). For example: "rock" (1 Sam 2.2, translated as "high mountain" in the CEV; 2 Sam 22.2,3); "world of the dead" (1 Sam 2.6; 2 Sam 22.6); "thunder" (1 Sam 2.10; 2 Sam 22.14); "chosen king" (1 Sam 2.10; 2 Sam 22.51). Scholars believe that parts of this prayer are taken from older prayers that were used to give thanks after receiving God's help. The prayer celebrates God's power to change human situations from bad to good so that those in need are helped. For example, the hungry are given food, and a woman without a child is given seven children.

2.6 *world of the dead:* The dead were thought to live as shadows far beneath the earth in a place called Sheol.

Hell

---

[l]1.28 *Elkanah:* Or "They" or "Samuel." [m]2.2 *god:* The Hebrew text has "holy one," a term for supernatural beings or gods. [n]2.2 *mountain:* One possible meaning for the difficult Hebrew text of verse 2.

"You make me strong and happy, LORD. You rescued me . . . No other god is like you. And with you we are safer than on a high mountain." 1 SAM 2.1,2

2.18,19 *a special linen garment . . . clothes:* Fine linen was a luxury and a symbol of purity. Priests wore special linen garments nobody else could wear: a long vest with a sash, an embroidered shirt, and other things. Samuel was a small child, but his mother made him clothes just like the ones Eli wore. The Hebrew word translated here as "clothes" means a long, sleeveless vest.

2.28-29 *here where I live:* The sacred chest was promised to be God's home among God's chosen people, the Israelites.

every Israelite who came to offer sacrifices in Shiloh. [15]Sometimes, when people were offering sacrifices, the servant would come over, even before the fat had been cut off and sacrificed to the LORD.[o]

Then the servant would tell them, "The priest doesn't want his meat boiled! Give him some raw meat that he can roast!"

[16]Usually the people answered, "Take what you want. But first, let us sacrifice the fat to the LORD."

"No," the servant would reply. "If you don't give it to me now, I'll take it by force."

[17]Eli's sons did not show any respect for the sacrifices that the people offered. This was a terrible sin, and it made the LORD very angry.

Hannah Visits Samuel

[18]The boy Samuel served the LORD and wore a special linen garment[p] [19]and the clothes[q] his mother made for him. She brought new clothes every year, when she and her husband came to offer sacrifices at Shiloh.

[20]Eli always blessed Elkanah and his wife and said, "Samuel was born in answer to your prayers. Now you have given him to the LORD. I pray that the LORD will bless you with more children to take his place." After Eli had blessed them, Elkanah and Hannah would return home.

[21]The LORD was kind to Hannah, and she had three more sons and two daughters. But Samuel grew up at the LORD's house in Shiloh.

Eli Warns His Sons

[22]Eli was now very old, and he heard what his sons were doing to the people of Israel.[r] [23-24]"Why are you doing these awful things?" he asked them. "I've been hearing nothing but complaints about you from all of the LORD's people. [25]If you harm another person, God can help make things right between the two of you. But if you commit a crime against the LORD, no one can help you!"

But the LORD had already decided to kill them. So he kept them from listening to their father.

A Prophet Speaks to Eli

[26]Each day, as Samuel grew older, the LORD was pleased with him, and so were the people.

[27]One day a prophet came to Eli and gave him this message from the LORD:

When your ancestors were slaves of the king of Egypt, I came and showed them who I am. [28-29]Out of all the tribes of Israel, I chose your family to be my priests. I wanted them to offer sacrifices and burn incense to me and to find out from me what I want my people to do. I commanded everyone to bring their sacrifices here where I live, and I allowed you and your family to keep those that were not offered to me on the altar.

But you honor your sons instead of me! You don't respect[s] the sacrifices

[o]**2.15** *sacrificed to the LORD:* The fat belonged to the LORD and was supposed to be burned as a sacrifice before the rest of the animal was cooked and eaten (see Leviticus 3.3,4,9,10,14,15). [p]**2.18** *a special linen garment:* Either a loin cloth or a jacket or a vest worn only by priests. [q]**2.19** *clothes:* The Hebrew word means a sleeveless coat or robe that was worn by priests. Samuel was a small child, but his mother made him clothes just like those worn by priests. [r]**2.22** *Israel:* The Dead Sea Scrolls and one ancient translation; the Standard Hebrew Text adds "He heard that his sons were even sleeping with the women who worked at the entrance to the sacred tent." [s]**2.28,29** *don't respect:* The Standard Hebrew Text; the Dead Sea Scrolls and one ancient translation "are greedy for."

and offerings that are brought to me, and you've all grown fat from eating the best parts.

³⁰I am the LORD, the God of Israel. I promised to always let your family serve me as priests, but now I tell you that I cannot do this any longer! I honor anyone who honors me, but I put a curse on anyone who hates me. ³¹The time will come when I will kill you and everyone else in your family. Not one of you will live to an old age. ³²Your family[t] will have a lot of trouble. I will be kind to Israel,[u] but everyone in your family will die young. ³³If I let anyone from your family be a priest, his[v] life will be full of sadness and sorrow. But most of the men in your family will die a violent death![w] ³⁴To prove to you that I will do these things, your two sons, Hophni and Phinehas, will die on the same day.

³⁵I have chosen someone else to be my priest, someone who will be faithful and obey me. I will always let his family serve as priests and help my chosen king. ³⁶But if anyone is left from your family, he will come to my priest and beg for money or a little bread. He may even say to my priest, "Please let me be a priest, so I will at least have something to eat."

The LORD Speaks to Samuel

3 ¹⁻²Samuel served the LORD by helping Eli the priest, who was by that time almost blind. In those days, the LORD hardly ever spoke directly to people, and he did not appear to them in dreams very often. But one night, Eli was asleep in his room, ³and Samuel was sleeping on a mat near the sacred chest in the LORD's house. They had not been asleep very long[x] ⁴when the LORD called out Samuel's name.

"Here I am!" Samuel answered. ⁵Then he ran to Eli and said, "Here I am. What do you want?"

"I didn't call you," Eli answered. "Go back to bed."

Samuel went back.

⁶Again the LORD called out Samuel's name. Samuel got up and went to Eli. "Here I am," he said. "What do you want?"

Eli told him, "Son, I didn't call you. Go back to sleep."

⁷The LORD had not spoken to Samuel before, and Samuel did not recognize the voice. ⁸When the LORD called out his name for the third time, Samuel went to Eli again and said, "Here I am. What do you want?"

Eli finally realized that it was the LORD who was speaking to Samuel. ⁹So he said, "Go back and lie down! If someone speaks to you again, answer, 'I'm listening, LORD. What do you want me to do?'"

Once again Samuel went back and lay down.

¹⁰The LORD then stood beside Samuel and called out as he had done before, "Samuel! Samuel!"

"I'm listening," Samuel answered. "What do you want me to do?"

¹¹The LORD said:

Samuel, I am going to do something in Israel that will shock everyone who hears about it! ¹²I will punish Eli and his family, just as I promised. ¹³He

3.3 *mat . . . sacred chest . . . the* LORD's *house:* Samuel's sleeping mat could have been a cloth sack with wool, feathers, or straw inside, or a pad of animal skins. Sleeping mats were usually rolled up each morning and stored along a wall.

The Sacred Chest

---

[t]**2.32** *Your family:* Or "My house of worship." [u]**2.31,32** *Not one . . . to Israel:* The Standard Hebrew Text; the Dead Sea Scrolls and one ancient translation do not have these words. [v]**2.33** *his:* The Dead Sea Scrolls and one ancient translation; the Standard Hebrew Text "your." [w]**2.33** *die a violent death:* The Dead Sea Scrolls and one ancient translation; the Standard Hebrew Text "die." [x]**3.3** *They . . . long:* The Hebrew text has "The lamp of God was still burning." An olive oil lamp would go out after a few hours if the wick was not adjusted.

"I'm listening, LORD. What do you want me to do?"
1 SAM 3.9

3.20 *prophet:* Prophets received messages from God to pass on to other people. Prophets were important Israelite leaders and advisors through much of Israel's history. **(See the article Prophets and Prophecy on pg 1791.)**

4.1 *Philistines:* The Philistines lived in an area along the Mediterranean Sea about 50 miles long and 20 miles wide. They had five main cities in that small area: Ekron, Gath, Ashdod, Ashkelon, and Gaza. Although each city had its own ruler, the rulers worked together to make the Philistines stronger. They were often at war with Israel. **(See Map 3 on pg 1881.)**

4.3 *the LORD's agreement:* The "LORD's agreement" with Israel was written on two flat stones with the Ten Commandments that were kept in the sacred chest.

Ten Commandments

Agreements (Covenants)

4.6 *Hebrews:* In the Jewish Scriptures, the use of the word "Hebrews" (instead of "Israelites" or "the people") usually shows that the person who is speaking is not an Israelite.

4.7 *The gods have come into their camp:* The Philistines worshiped several gods and might have assumed the Israelites did, too. But the Israelites were God's special people, since they had agreed to worship only the LORD.

knew that his sons refused to respect me,[y] and he let them get away with it, even though I said I would punish his family forever. [14]I warned Eli that sacrifices or offerings could never make things right! His family has done too many disgusting things.

[15]The next morning, Samuel got up and opened the doors to the LORD's house. He was afraid to tell Eli what the LORD had said. [16]But Eli told him, "Samuel, my boy, come here!"

"Yes, sir!" Samuel answered.

[17]Eli said, "What did God say to you? Tell me everything. I'll ask God to punish you terribly if you don't tell me every word he said!"

[18]Samuel told Eli everything. Then Eli said, "He is the LORD, and he will do what's right."

The LORD Helps Samuel

[19]As Samuel grew up, the LORD helped him and made everything Samuel said come true. [20]From the town of Dan in the north to the town of Beersheba in the south, everyone in the country knew that Samuel was truly the LORD's prophet. [21]The LORD often appeared to Samuel at Shiloh 4 and told him what to say. [1]Then Samuel would speak to the whole nation of Israel.

The Philistines Capture the Sacred Chest

One day the Israelites went out to fight the Philistines. They set up camp near Ebenezer, and the Philistines camped at Aphek. [2]The Philistines made a fierce attack. They defeated the Israelites and killed about 4,000 of them.

[3]The Israelite army returned to their camp, and the leaders said, "Why did the LORD let us lose to the Philistines today? Let's get the sacred chest where the LORD's agreement with Israel is kept. Then the LORD[z] will help us and rescue us from our enemies."

[4]The army sent some soldiers to bring back the sacred chest from Shiloh, because the LORD All-Powerful has his throne on the winged creatures on top of the chest. As Eli's two sons, Hophni and Phinehas, [5]brought the chest into camp, the army cheered so loudly that the ground shook. [6]The Philistines heard the noise and said, "What are those Hebrews shouting about?"

When the Philistines learned that the sacred chest had been brought into the camp, [7]they were scared to death and said:

The gods have come into their camp. Now we're in real trouble! Nothing like this has ever happened to us before. [8]We're in big trouble! Who can save us from these powerful gods? They're the same gods who made all those horrible things happen to the Egyptians in the desert.

[9]Philistines, be brave and fight hard! If you don't, those Hebrews will rule us, just as we've been ruling them. Fight and don't be afraid.

[10]The Philistines did fight. They killed 30,000 Israelite soldiers, and all the rest ran off to their homes. [11]Hophni and Phinehas were killed, and the sacred chest was captured.

Eli Dies

[12]That same day a soldier from the tribe of Benjamin ran from the battlefront to Shiloh. He had torn his clothes and put dirt on his head to show his sorrow. [13]He

[y]3.13 *refused . . . me:* Or "were insulting everyone."   [z]4.3 *LORD:* Or "chest."

went into town and told the news about the battle, and everyone started crying.

Eli was afraid that something might happen to the sacred chest. So he was sitting on his chair beside the road, just waiting. **14-15**He was 98 years old and blind, but he could hear everyone crying, and he asked, "What's all that noise?"

The soldier hurried over and told Eli, **16**"I escaped from the fighting today and ran here."

"Young man, what happened?" Eli asked.

17"Israel ran away from the Philistines," the soldier answered. "Many of our people were killed, including your two sons, Hophni and Phinehas. But worst of all, the sacred chest was captured."

18Eli was still sitting on a chair beside the wall of the town gate. And when the man said that the Philistines had taken the sacred chest, Eli fell backwards. He was a very heavy old man, and the fall broke his neck and killed him. He had been a leader[a] of Israel for 40 years.

19The wife of Phinehas was about to give birth. And soon after she heard that the sacred chest had been captured and that her husband and his father had died, her baby came. The birth was very hard, **20**and she was dying. But the women taking care of her said, "Don't be afraid—it's a boy!"

She didn't pay any attention to them. **21-22**Instead she kept thinking about losing her husband and her father-in-law. So she said, "My son will be named Ichabod,[b] because the glory of Israel left our country when the sacred chest was captured."

God Causes Trouble for the Philistines

5 The Philistines took the sacred chest from near Ebenezer to the town of Ashdod. **2**They brought it into the temple of their god Dagon and put it next to the statue of Dagon, which they worshiped.

3When the people of Ashdod got up early the next morning, they found the statue lying facedown on the floor in front of the sacred chest. They put the statue back where it belonged. **4**But early the next morning, it had fallen over again and was lying facedown on the floor in front of the chest. The body of the statue was still in one piece, but its head and both hands had broken off and were lying on the stone floor in the doorway. **5**This is why the priests and everyone else step over that part of the doorway when they enter the temple of Dagon in Ashdod.

6The LORD caused a lot of trouble for the people of Ashdod and their neighbors. He made sores break out all over their bodies,[c] and everyone was in a panic.[d] **7**Finally, they said, "The God of Israel did this. He is the one who caused all this trouble for us and our god Dagon. We've got to get rid of this chest."

8The people of Ashdod invited all the Philistine rulers to come to Ashdod, and they asked them, "What can we do with the sacred chest that belongs to the God of Israel?"

"Send it to Gath," the rulers answered. But after they took it there, **9**the LORD made sores break out on everyone in town. The people of Gath were frightened, **10**so they sent the sacred chest to Ekron. But

4.21-22 *Ichabod:* Ichabod means "where is the glory?" or "there is no glory." Phinehas' wife saw the loss of the sacred chest as losing the LORD, because a cloud of glory marked the LORD's presence at the sacred chest.

5.2 *statue of Dagon:* Dagon was a god of rain and fertility and the Philistines' most important god. Dagon was originally worshiped in Mesopotamia but by 2000 B.C. was more widely worshiped throughout the ancient Near East. As the Canaanites began to trade with Mesopotamia they learned about their god Dagon, and adopted him as their own. When the Philistines conquered Canaan, Dagon also became their god.

5.6 *sores . . . bodies:* Probably bubonic plague, a disease spread by fleas carried by rats or mice.

5.8-10 *Gath . . . Ekron:* These were two of the five main Philistine cities. The name "Gath" comes from a word meaning "winepress," something that was very common throughout the region because there were so many vineyards. As a result, many cities were called Gath, but most had a second name to help tell them apart (Gath-Rimmon and Moresheth-Gath, for example). The Philistines' Gath might have been about twelve miles east of Ashdod. (See Map 3 on pg 1881.)

[a]**4.18** *leader:* The Hebrew word means that Eli may have been an army commander, a judge, and a priest. [b]**4.21,22** *Ichabod:* Ichabod means "where is the glory?" or "there is no glory." [c]**5.6** *sores . . . bodies:* Or "He struck them with bubonic plague." [d]**5.6** *panic:* Two ancient translations add "Rats came from their ships, and people were dying right and left."

6.5 *five gold models of the rats:* The Philistines used gold to try to impress God. When they sent the models of the sores and the rats, they were admitting that Israel's God had sent the disease and rats. The Philistines also might have hoped that by sending away the symbols of the disease, they could send away the disease itself.

6.7 *two cows that . . . have never pulled a cart:* Cows have to be trained to pull a cart, and usually cows will not leave a nursing calf. The Philistines believed that if untrained cows left their calves and pulled the cart away, that would be a clear sign that God had caused the disease and was taking the sacred chest back to the Israelites.

6.9 *Beth-Shemesh:* Four cities with this name appear in the Jewish Scriptures. This one was near the Philistine border, about 16 miles southwest of Jerusalem. Archaeologists have excavated Beth-Shemesh three times in the last century and have concluded that people lived here as early as 2000 B.C.

6.13 *wheat:* The wheat harvest usually took place in May and June. Wheat has been grown in this part of the world since at least 8300 B.C. and was a regular part of the ancient Near Eastern diet.

before they could take it through the town gates, the people of Ekron started screaming, "They've brought the sacred chest that belongs to the God of Israel! It will kill us and our families too!"

The Philistines Send Back the Sacred Chest

11The people of Ekron called for another meeting of the Philistine rulers and told them, "Send this chest back where it belongs. Then it won't kill us."

Everyone was in a panic, because God was causing a lot of people to die, **12**and those who had survived were suffering from the sores. They all cried to their gods for help.

6 After the sacred chest had been in Philistia for seven months,[e] **2**the Philistines called in their priests and fortunetellers, and asked, "What should we do with this sacred chest? Tell us how to send it back where it belongs!"

3"Don't send it back without a gift," the priests and fortunetellers answered. "Send along something to Israel's God to make up for taking the chest in the first place. Then you will be healed, and you will find out why the LORD was causing you so much trouble."

4"What should we send?" the Philistines asked.

The priests and fortunetellers answered:

There are five Philistine rulers, and they all have the same disease that you have. **5**So make five gold models of the sores and five gold models of the rats that are wiping out your crops. If you honor the God of Israel with this gift, maybe he will stop causing trouble for you and your gods and your crops.

6Don't be like the Egyptians and their king. They were stubborn, but when Israel's God was finished with them, they had to let Israel go.

7Get a new cart and two cows that have young calves and that have never pulled a cart. Hitch the cows to the cart, but take the calves back to their barn. **8**Then put the chest on the cart. Put the gold rats and sores into a bag and put it on the cart next to the chest. Then send it on its way.

9Watch to see if the chest goes on up the road to the Israelite town of Beth-Shemesh. If it goes back to its own country, you will know that it was the LORD who made us suffer so badly. But if the chest doesn't go back to its own country, then the LORD had nothing to do with the disease that hit us—it was simply bad luck.

10The Philistines followed their advice. They hitched up the two cows to the cart, but they kept their calves in a barn. **11**Then they put the chest on the cart, along with the bag that had the gold rats and sores in it.

12The cows went straight up the road toward Beth-Shemesh, mooing as they went. The Philistine rulers followed them until they got close to Beth-Shemesh.

13The people of Beth-Shemesh were harvesting their wheat[f] in the valley. When they looked up and saw the chest, they were so happy that they stopped working and started celebrating.

14-15 The cows left the road and pulled the cart into a field that belonged to Joshua from Beth-Shemesh, and they stopped beside a huge rock. Some men from the tribe of Levi were there. So they took the chest off the cart and placed it on the rock, and then they did the same thing with the bag

[e]**6.1** *months:* One ancient translation adds "and rats were everywhere" or "and rats ate the crops."
[f]**6.13** *wheat:* The wheat harvest took place in May and June.

of gold rats and sores. A few other people chopped up the cart and made a fire. They killed the cows and burned them as sacrifices to the LORD. After that, they offered more sacrifices.

[16]When the five rulers of the Philistines saw what had happened, they went back to Ekron that same day.

[17]That is how the Philistines sent gifts to the LORD to make up for taking the sacred chest. They sent five gold sores, one each for their towns of Ashdod, Gaza, Ashkelon, Gath, and Ekron. [18]They also sent one gold rat for each walled town and for every village that the five Philistine rulers controlled. The huge stone[g] where the Levites set the chest is still there in Joshua's field as a reminder of what happened.

The Sacred Chest Is Sent to Kiriath-Jearim

[19]Some of the men of Beth-Shemesh looked inside the sacred chest, and the LORD God killed 70[h] of them. This made the people of Beth-Shemesh very sad, [20]and they started saying, "No other God is like the LORD! Who can go near him and stay alive? We'll have to send the chest away from here. But where can we send it?"

[21]They sent messengers to tell the people of Kiriath-Jearim, "The Philistines have sent back the sacred chest. Why don't you take it and keep it there with you?"

7 The people of Kiriath-Jearim got the chest and took it to Abinadab's house, which was on a hill in their town. They chose his son Eleazar to take care of it, [2]and it stayed there for 20 years.

During this time everyone in Israel was very sad and begged the LORD for help.[i]

The People of Israel Turn Back to the LORD

[3]One day, Samuel told all the people of Israel, "If you really want to turn back to the LORD, then prove it. Get rid of your foreign idols, including the ones of the goddess Astarte. Turn to the LORD with all your heart and worship only him. Then he will rescue you from the Philistines."

[4]The people got rid of their idols of Baal and Astarte and began worshiping only the LORD.

[5]Then Samuel said, "Tell everyone in Israel to meet together at Mizpah, and I will pray to the LORD for you."

[6]The Israelites met together at Mizpah with Samuel as their leader. They drew water from the well and poured it out as an offering to the LORD. On that same day they went without eating to show their sorrow, and they confessed they had been unfaithful to the LORD.

The Philistines Attack Israel

[7]When the Philistine rulers found out about the meeting at Mizpah, they sent an army there to attack the people of Israel.

The Israelites were afraid when they heard that the Philistines were coming. [8]"Don't stop praying!" they told Samuel. "Ask the LORD our God to rescue us."

[9-10]Samuel begged the LORD to rescue Israel, then he sacrificed a young lamb to the LORD. Samuel had not even finished offering the sacrifice when the Philistines started to attack. But the LORD answered his prayer and made thunder crash all around them. The Philistines panicked and ran away. [11]The men of Israel left Mizpah and went

[g]6.18 *stone*: A few Hebrew manuscripts; most Hebrew manuscripts "meadow" or "stream."
[h]6.19 *70*: A few Hebrew manuscripts; most Hebrew manuscripts "70 men, 50,000 men."
[i]7.2 *Israel . . . help*: Or "Israel turned to the LORD and begged him for help."

6.19 *looked inside . . . killed 70:* Looking inside the sacred chest to see God was so disrespectful that those who did it were struck dead (see also 2 Sam 6.6,7). In the Bible, 70 often stands for a large number rather than an exact amount. **(See the chart Numbers in the Bible on pg 1844.)**

7.3,4 *foreign idols . . . Astarte . . . Baal:* Idols are objects made of wood, stone, metal, or baked clay that represent gods. Many places in the Jewish Scriptures claim that the God of Israel could not be contained in such a handmade image.

Astarte is also known as "Asherah," the goddess of fertility. Her worshipers believed that she made the land produce crops and gave them many children.

"Baal" means "owner" or "lord" and is used in the Bible as both a common and proper noun. Here it is used as the name of a weather god, who was worshiped from a number of locations in Canaan. Baal's worshipers believed he brought thunderstorms and fertility to the land.

Canaanite Gods and Goddesses

7.5-11 *Mizpah . . . Beth-Car:* At least five places were called "Mizpah" or "Mizpeh," a word that means watchtower. The Mizpah in this verse was probably near Kiriath-Jearim (6.21).

7.6 *went without eating:* Going without eating, or fasting, was a common way of showing sorrow or regret.

7.15,16 *leader . . . judge:* The Hebrew word translated as "leader" here could mean an army commander, a judge, or a religious leader. Samuel was all three. Judges in ancient Israel did more than just settle disputes. An Israelite judge guided people toward making the right decisions.

8.1-2 *Beersheba:* This could show how widespread Samuel's influence was among the tribes of Israel. Beersheba was an important city in the semi-desert area at the southern end of the Israelites' lands. Abraham had named Beersheba and lived there for a time. (See Map 3 on pg 1881.)

8.1-5 *leaders . . . king . . . leader:* Kings ruled most of Israel's neighbors. The Israelites hoped that a king would unite their tribes as a nation and protect them from the Philistines and Ammonites. They used Samuel's age and the behavior of his sons as an excuse to ask for a different kind of leader (8.19,20; 10.19; 12.12).

8.7 *I am really . . . as their king:* When the Israelites asked for a king, the LORD knew that they were breaking their promise to rely only on God to save and protect them. Years earlier, Moses had said they would reject God and ask for a king (Deut 17.14).

8.11 *If you have a king:* Samuel reminded the Israelites that it could cost them dearly to have a king. When he told them they would have to give up their sons and daughters, part of their property, and some of the food that they raise, Samuel hoped to make them think again about wanting a king.

after them as far as the hillside below Beth-Car, killing every enemy soldier they caught.

12-13 The Philistines were so badly beaten that it was quite a while before they attacked Israel again. After the battle, Samuel set up a monument between Mizpah and the rocky cliffs. He named it "Help Monument"[j] to remind Israel how much the LORD had helped them.

For as long as Samuel lived, the LORD helped Israel fight the Philistines. **14**The Israelites were even able to recapture their towns and territory between Ekron and Gath.

Israel was also at peace with the Amorites.[k]

Samuel Is a Leader in Israel

15Samuel was a leader[l] in Israel all his life. **16**Every year he would go around to the towns of Bethel, Gilgal, and Mizpah where he served as judge for the people. **17**Then he would go back to his home in Ramah and do the same thing there. He also had an altar built for the LORD at Ramah.

The People of Israel Want a King

8 **1-2**Samuel had two sons. The older one was Joel, and the younger one was Abijah. When Samuel was getting old, he let them be leaders[l] at Beersheba. **3**But they were not like their father. They were dishonest and accepted bribes to give unfair decisions.

4One day the nation's leaders came to Samuel at Ramah **5**and said, "You are an old man. You set a good example for your

sons, but they haven't followed it. Now we want a king to be our leader,[l] just like all the other nations. Choose one for us!"

6Samuel was upset to hear the leaders say they wanted a king, so he prayed about it. **7**The LORD answered:

Samuel, do everything they want you to do. I am really the one they have rejected as their king. **8**Ever since the day I rescued my people from Egypt, they have turned from me to worship idols. Now they are turning away from you. **9**Do everything they ask, but warn them and tell them how a king will treat them.

10Samuel told the people who were asking for a king what the LORD had said:

11If you have a king, this is how he will treat you. He will force your sons to join his army. Some of them will ride in his chariots, some will serve in the cavalry, and others will run ahead of his own chariot.[m] **12**Some of them will be officers in charge of 1,000 soldiers, and others will be in charge of 50. Still others will have to farm the king's land and harvest his crops, or make weapons and parts for his chariots. **13**Your daughters will have to make perfume or do his cooking and baking.

14The king will take your best fields, as well as your vineyards, and olive orchards and give them to his own officials. **15**He will also take a tenth of your grain and grapes and give it to his officers and officials.

16The king will take your slaves and your best young men and your donkeys and make them do his work. **17**He will also take a tenth of your sheep and goats. You will become the king's slaves,

---

[j]**7.12,13** *Help Monument:* Or "Ebenezer." [k]**7.14** *Amorites:* In this verse, the non-Israelite peoples of Canaan. [l]**7.15; 8.1,2,5** *leader(s):* The Hebrew word could mean an army commander, a judge, and a religious leader. [m]**8.11** *others . . . chariot:* These men were probably his bodyguards.

[18]and you will finally cry out for the LORD to save you from the king you wanted. But the LORD won't answer your prayers.

[19-20]The people would not listen to Samuel. "No!" they said. "We want to be like other nations. We want a king to rule us and lead us in battle."

[21]Samuel listened to them and then told the LORD exactly what they had said. [22]"Do what they want," the LORD answered. "Give them a king."

Samuel told the people to go back to their homes.

Saul Meets Samuel

9 Kish was a wealthy man who belonged to the tribe of Benjamin. His father was Abiel, his grandfather was Zeror, his great-grandfather was Becorath, and his great-great-grandfather was Aphiah. [2]Kish had a son named Saul, who was better looking and more than a head taller than anyone else in all Israel.

[3]Kish owned some donkeys, but they had run off. So he told Saul, "Take one of the servants and go look for the donkeys."

[4]Saul and the servant went through the hill country of Ephraim and the territory of Shalishah, but they could not find the donkeys. Then they went through the territories of Shaalim and Benjamin, but still there was no sign of the donkeys. [5]Finally they came to the territory where the clan of Zuph[n] lived. "Let's go back home," Saul told his servant. "If we don't go back soon, my father will stop worrying about the donkeys and start worrying about us!"

[6]"Wait!" the servant answered. "There's a man of God who lives in a town near here.

He's amazing! Everything he says comes true. Let's talk to him. Maybe he can tell us where to look."

[7]Saul said, "How can we talk to the prophet when I don't have anything to give him? We don't even have any bread left in our sacks. What can we give him?"

[8]"I have a small piece of silver," the servant answered. "We can give him that, and then he will tell us where to look for the donkeys."

[9-10]"Great!" Saul replied. "Let's go to the man who can see visions!" He said this because in those days God would answer questions by giving visions to prophets.

Saul and his servant went to the town where the prophet lived. [11]As they were going up the hill to the town, they met some young women coming out to get water,[o] and the two men said to them, "We're looking for the man who can see visions. Is he in town?"

[12]"Yes, he is," they replied. "He's in town today because there's going to be a sacrifice and a sacred meal at the place of worship. In fact, he's just ahead of you. Hurry [13]and you should find him right inside the town gate. He's on his way out to the place of worship to eat with the invited guests. They can't start eating until he blesses the sacrifice. If you go now, you should find him."

[14]They went to the town, and just as they were going through the gate, Samuel was coming out on his way to the place of worship.

[15]The day before Saul came, the LORD had told Samuel, [16]"I've seen how my people are suffering, and I've heard their call for help. About this time tomorrow I'll send you a man from the tribe of

[n]9.5 Zuph: Samuel's father Elkanah was from the Zuph clan.   [o]9.11 water: Towns were often built on a hill near a source of water, which would often be down in the valley outside of the town. It was usually the job of women to get water for their family.

● 9.2 Saul: Saul became the first king of Israel, and reigned from about 1030 to 1000 B.C.

■ 9.13 blesses: As the priest, Samuel had to bless the meat from the sacrifice before it could be eaten.

"We want to be like other nations. We want a king to rule us and lead us in battle." 1 SAM 8.19-20

9.16 *pour olive oil on his head:* Olive oil was poured on the head of someone who was chosen to perform special tasks to be a priest, a prophet, or a king. This was called "anointing.'

10.2 *Rachel:* Rachel was one of the wives of Jacob (whose sons were the ancestors of the twelve tribes of Israel) and the mother of Joseph and Benjamin.

10.3-5 *Tabor . . . Bethel . . . Gibeah:* Tabor was probably in the territory of Benjamin. For Bethel, see 7.16. Gibeah was a few miles north of Jerusalem. Archaeologists have suggested that Saul took over the Philistines' "army camp" at Gibeah and made it his palace.

Benjamin, who will rescue my people from
the Philistines. I want you to pour olive oil[p]
on his head to show that he will be their
leader."
17Samuel looked at Saul, and the LORD
told Samuel, "This is the man I told you
about. He's the one who will rule Israel."
18Saul went over to Samuel in the gateway and said, "A man who can see visions
lives here in town. Could you tell me the
way to his house?"
19"I am the one who sees visions!"
Samuel answered. "Go on up to the place
of worship. You will eat with me today, and
in the morning I'll answer your questions.
20Don't worry about your donkeys that
ran off three days ago. They've already
been found. Everything of value in Israel
now belongs to you and your family."[q]
21"Why are you telling me this?" Saul
asked. "I'm from Benjamin, the smallest
tribe in Israel, and my clan is the least important in the tribe."

Saul Eats with Samuel and Stays at His House

22Samuel took Saul and his servant into
the dining room at the place of worship.
About 30 people were there for the dinner,
but Samuel gave Saul and his servant the
places of honor. 23-24Then Samuel told the
cook, "I gave you the best piece of meat and
told you to set it aside. Bring it here now."
The cook brought the meat over and set
it down in front of Saul. "This is for you,"
Samuel told him. "Go ahead and eat it. I
had this piece saved especially for you, and
I invited these guests to eat with you."
After Saul and Samuel had finished eating, 25they went down from the place of
worship and back into town. A bed was set
up for Saul on the flat roof[r] of Samuel's
house, 26and Saul slept there.
About sunrise the next morning,[s] Samuel
called up to Saul on the roof, "Time to get
up! I'll help you get started on your way."
Saul got up. He and Samuel left together
27and had almost reached the edge of town
when Samuel stopped and said, "Tell your
servant go on. Stay here with me for a few
minutes, and I'll tell you what God has
told me."

Samuel Tells Saul He Will Be King

10 After the servant had gone, 1Samuel
took a small jar of olive oil and
poured it on Saul's head. Then he kissed[t]
Saul and told him:
The LORD has chosen you to be the
leader and ruler of his people.[u] 2When
you leave me today, you'll meet two
men near Rachel's tomb at Zelzah in
the territory of Benjamin. They'll tell
you, "The donkeys you've been looking for have been found. Your father
has forgotten about them, and now
he's worrying about you! He's wondering how he can find you."
3Go on from there until you reach
the big oak tree at Tabor, where you'll

[p]**9.16** *olive oil*: Olive oil was poured on the head of someone who was chosen to be a priest, a prophet, or a king. [q]**9.20** *Everything . . . family*: Or "You and your family are what all Israel wants." [r]**9.25** *roof*: Guests often slept on the flat roof of their host's house, where it was cool and breezy. [s]**9.25,26** *was set . . . morning*: One ancient translation; Hebrew "Samuel spoke with Saul on the flat roof of his house. They got up early the next morning, around sunrise, and . . ." [t]**10.1** *kissed*: Relatives or close friends often greeted one another with a kiss. But this may have been a ceremonial kiss after Samuel poured oil on Saul's head to show that he was to be the king. [u]**10.1** *people*: One ancient translation adds "You will rule the LORD's people and save them from their enemies who are all around them. These things will prove that what I say is true."

meet three men on their way to worship God at Bethel. One of them will be leading three young goats, another will be carrying three round loaves of bread, and the last one will be carrying a clay jar of wine. ⁴After they greet you, they'll give you two loaves of bread.

⁵Next, go to Gibeah,^v where the Philistines have an army camp. As you're going into the town, you'll meet a group of prophets coming down from the place of worship. They'll be going along prophesying while others are walking in front of them, playing small harps, small drums, and flutes. ⁶The Spirit of the Lord will suddenly take control of you.^w You'll become a different person and start prophesying right along with them. ⁷After these things happen, do whatever you think is right! God will help you.

⁸Then go to Gilgal. I'll come a little later, so wait for me. It may even take a week for me to get there, but when I come, I'll offer sacrifices to please the Lord and to ask for his blessings. I'll also tell you what to do next.

Saul Goes Back Home

⁹As Saul turned around to leave Samuel, God made Saul feel like a different person. That same day, everything happened just as Samuel had said. ¹⁰When Saul arrived at Gibeah, a group of prophets met him. The Spirit of God suddenly took control of him,^x and right there in the middle of the group he began prophesying. ¹¹Some people who had known Saul for a long time saw that he was speaking and behaving like a prophet. They said to each other, "What's happened? How can Saul be a prophet?"

¹²"Why not?" one of them answered. "Saul has as much right to be a prophet as anyone else!"^y That's why everyone started saying, "How can Saul be a prophet?"

¹³After Saul stopped prophesying, he went to the place of worship.

¹⁴Later, Saul's uncle asked him, "Where have you been?"

Saul answered, "Looking for the donkeys. We couldn't find them, so we went to talk with Samuel."

¹⁵"And what did he tell you?" Saul's uncle asked.

¹⁶Saul answered, "He told us the donkeys had been found." But Saul didn't mention that Samuel had chosen him to be king.

The Lord Shows Israel that Saul Will Be King

¹⁷Samuel sent messengers to tell the Israelites to come to Mizpah and meet with the Lord. ¹⁸When everyone had arrived, Samuel said:

The Lord God of Israel told me to remind you that he had rescued you from the Egyptians and from the other nations that abused you.

¹⁹God has rescued you from your troubles and hard times. But you have rejected your God and have asked for a king. Now each tribe and clan must come near the place of worship so the Lord can choose a king.

^v10.5 *Gibeah*: The Hebrew text has "Gibeah of God," which may or may not have been the same Gibeah as Saul's hometown. ^w10.6 *take . . . you*: Or "will take control of you in a powerful way." ^x10.10 *suddenly . . . him*: Or "came over him in a powerful way." ^y10.12 *Why not . . . anyone else*: Or "Sure he is! He's probably the leader of the prophets!" or "How can he be? Those prophets are nobodies!"

Samuel said, "God has rescued you from your troubles and hard times. But you have rejected your God and have asked for a king." 1 Sam 10.19

● 11.2 *poking out the right eye:* Since the shield was held in the left hand and covered the left eye, the loss of the right eye would make warriors useless, giving Nahash a military advantage.

²⁰Samuel brought each tribe, one after the other, to the altar, and the Lord chose the Benjamin tribe. ²¹Next, Samuel brought each clan of Benjamin there, and the Lord chose the Matri clan. Finally, Saul the son of Kish was chosen. But when they looked for him, he was nowhere to be found.

²²The people prayed, "Our Lord, is Saul here?"

"Yes," the Lord answered, "he is hiding behind the baggage."

²³The people ran and got Saul and brought him into the middle of the crowd. He was more than a head taller than anyone else. ²⁴"Look closely at the man the Lord has chosen!" Samuel told the crowd. "There is no one like him!"

The crowd shouted, "Long live the king!"

²⁵Samuel explained the rights and duties of a king and wrote them all in a book. He put the book in one of the shrines where the Lord was worshiped. Then Samuel sent everyone home.

²⁶God had encouraged some young men to become followers of Saul, and when he returned to his hometown of Gibeah, they went with him. ²⁷But some worthless fools said, "How can someone like Saul rescue us from our enemies?" They did not want Saul to be their king, and so they didn't bring him any gifts. But Saul kept calm.

Saul Rescues the Town of Jabesh in Gilead

11 About this time,ᶻ King Nahash of Ammon came with his army and surrounded the town of Jabesh in Gilead.

The people who lived there told Nahash, "If you will sign a peace treaty with us, you can be our ruler, and we will pay taxes to you."

²Nahash answered, "Sure, I'll sign a treaty! But not before I insult Israel by poking out the right eye of every man who lives in Jabesh."

³The town leaders said, "Give us seven days so we can send messengers everywhere in Israel to ask for help. If no one comes here to save us, we will surrender to you."

⁴Some of the messengers went to Gibeah, Saul's hometown. They told what was happening at Jabesh, and everyone in Gibeah started crying. ⁵Just then, Saul came in from the fields, walking behind his oxen.

"Why is everyone crying?" Saul asked.

They told him what the men from Jabesh had said. ⁶Then the Spirit of God suddenly took control of Saul and made him furious. ⁷Saul killed two of his oxen, cut them up in pieces, and gave the pieces to theᵃ messengers. He told them to show the pieces to everyone in Israel and say, "Saul and Samuel are getting an army together. Come and join them. If you don't, this is what will happen to your oxen!"

The Lord made the people of Israel terribly afraid. So all the men came together ⁸at Bezek. Saul had them organized and counted. There were 300,000 from Israel and 30,000ᵇ from Judah.

⁹Saul and his officers sent the messengers back to Jabesh with this promise: "We will rescue you tomorrow afternoon." The messengers went back to the people at

ᶻ10.27—11.1 *But Saul . . . time:* The Standard Hebrew Text; the Dead Sea Scrolls add "King Nahash of Ammon was making the people of Gad and Reuben miserable. He was poking out everyone's right eye, and no one in Israel could stop him. He had poked out the right eye of every Israelite man who lived east of the Jordan River. Only 7,000 men had escaped from the Ammonites, and they had gone into the town of Jabesh in Gilead. About a month later . . ." ᵃ11.7 *the:* Or "some other." ᵇ11.8 *300,000 . . . 30,000:* The Dead Sea Scrolls and some ancient translations have different numbers.

Jabesh and told them that they were going to be rescued.

Everyone was encouraged! **10**So they told the Ammonites, "We will surrender to you tomorrow, and then you can do whatever you want to."

11The next day, Saul divided his army into three groups and attacked before daylight. They started killing Ammonites and kept it up until afternoon. A few Ammonites managed to escape, but they were scattered far from each other.

12The Israelite soldiers went to Samuel and demanded, "Where are the men who said they didn't want Saul to be king? Bring them to us, and we will put them to death!"

13"No you won't!" Saul told them. "The LORD rescued Israel today, and no one will be put to death."

Saul Is Accepted as King

14"Come on!" Samuel said. "Let's go to Gilgal and make an agreement that Saul will continue to be our king."

15Everyone went to the place of worship at Gilgal, where they agreed that Saul would be their king. Saul and the people sacrificed animals to ask for the LORD's blessing,[c] and they had a big celebration.

Samuel's Farewell Speech

12 Samuel told the Israelites:
I have given you a king, just as you asked. **2**You have seen how I have led you ever since I was a young man. I'm already old. My hair is gray, and my own sons are grown. Now you must see how well your king will lead you.

3Let me ask this. Have I ever taken anyone's ox or donkey or forced you to give me anything? Have I ever hurt anyone or taken a bribe to give an unfair decision? Answer me so the LORD and his chosen king can hear you. And if I have done any of these things, I will give it all back.

4"No," the Israelites answered. "You've never cheated us in any way!"

5Samuel said, "The LORD and his chosen king are witnesses to what you have said."

"That's true," they replied.

6Then Samuel told them:

The LORD brought your ancestors out of Egypt and chose Moses and Aaron to be your leaders. **7**Now the LORD will be your judge. So stand here and listen, while I remind you how often the LORD has saved you and your ancestors from your enemies.

8After Jacob went to Egypt, your ancestors cried out to the LORD for help, and he sent Moses and Aaron. They brought your ancestors out of Egypt and led them here to settle this land. **9**But your ancestors forgot the LORD, so he let them be defeated by the Philistines, the king of Moab, and Sisera, the commander of Hazor's army.

10Again your ancestors cried out to the LORD for help. They said, "We have sinned! We stopped worshiping you, our LORD, and started worshiping Baal and Astarte. But now, if you rescue us from our enemies, we will worship you."

11The LORD sent Gideon,[d] Bedan, Jephthah, and Samuel to rescue you from your enemies, and you didn't have to worry about being attacked.

● **12.5** *witnesses to what you have said*: The law required at least two witnesses for proof (Deut 19.15). Samuel asked the Israelites if what he said about his service to God was true and, in front of witnesses, they said it was. This reminded the people that the rest of what he would say was also true.

● **12.6** *ancestors*: The people of Israel had been slaves in Egypt. Moses' brother Aaron was Israel's first high priest.

ᛟ   Moses

● **12.11** *Gideon, Bedan, Jephthah, and Samuel*: Samuel was reminding the Israelites that God had taken care of them, and that so far they had not needed a king. The people would have known these Israelite judges of the past. Gideon rescued Israel from the Midianites. Jephthah delivered Israel from the Ammonites. Samuel led the people against the Philistines. Bedan's contribution is not clear, but had to be important to be mentioned with the others. Some think that "Bedan" might be another name for "Jephthah."

---

[c]**11.15** *sacrificed . . . blessing*: This kind of sacrifice is described in Leviticus 3; 7.11-36; 19.5-8. People who offered these sacrifices were allowed to eat most of the meat, and they could invite others to share it with them.   [d]**12.11** *Gideon*: The Hebrew text has "Jerubbaal," another name for "Gideon."

"I have given you a king, just as you asked . . . Now you must see how well your king will lead you." 1 SAM 12.1,2

12.22 *the* LORD *has chosen you:* God promised Abraham that his descendants, the Israelites, would form a great nation (Gen 12.2).

Israel

13.3 *trumpet:* Here, probably a *shofar.* Made from the horn of a ram or other animal, it could make several different sounds. These were used to signal events, danger, or the death of important people. The shofar is still used as part of Jewish religious celebrations.

[12]Then you saw that King Nahash of Ammon was going to attack you. And even though the LORD your God is your king, you told me, "This time it's different. We want a king to rule us!"

[13]You asked for a king, and you chose one. Now he stands here where all of you can see him. But it was really the LORD who made him your king. [14]If you and your king want to be followers of the LORD, you must worship him[e] and do what he says. Don't be stubborn! [15]If you're stubborn and refuse to obey the LORD, he will turn against you and your king.[f]

[16]Just stand here and watch the LORD show his mighty power. [17]Isn't this the dry season?[g] I'm going to ask the LORD to send a thunderstorm. When you see it, you will realize how wrong you were to ask for a king.

[18]Samuel prayed, and that same day the LORD sent a thunderstorm. Everyone was afraid of the LORD and of Samuel. [19]They told Samuel, "Please, pray to the LORD your God for us! We don't want to die. We have sinned many times in the past, and we were very wrong to ask for a king."

[20]Samuel answered:

Even though what you did was wrong, you don't need to be afraid. But you must always follow the LORD and worship him with all your heart. [21]Don't worship idols! They don't have any power, and they can't help you or save you when you're in trouble. [22]But the LORD has chosen you to be his own people. He will always take care of you so that everyone will know how great he is.

[23]I would be disobeying the LORD if I stopped praying for you! I will always teach you how to live right. [24]You also must obey the LORD—you must worship him with all your heart and remember the great things he has done for you. [25]But if you and your king do evil, the LORD will wipe you out.

Saul Disobeys the LORD

13 Saul was a young man[h] when he became king, and he ruled Israel for two years. [2]Then[i] he chose 3,000 men from Israel to be full-time soldiers and sent everyone else[j] home. Two thousand of these troops stayed with him in the hills around Michmash and Bethel. The other 1,000 were stationed with Jonathan[k] at Gibeah[l] in the territory of Benjamin.

[3]Jonathan led an attack on the Philistine army camp at Geba.[m] The Philistine camp was destroyed, but[n] the other Philistines heard what had happened. Then Saul told his messengers, "Go to every village in the country. Give a signal with the trumpet, and when the people come together, tell them what has happened."

[e]12.14 *If . . . him:* Or "If you and your king want things to go well for you, then you must worship the LORD." [f]12.15 *and your king:* One ancient translation; Hebrew "and your ancestors" or "as he was against your ancestors." [g]12.17 *the dry season:* The Hebrew text has "time for wheat harvest," which was usually in the spring, the beginning of the dry season. [h]13.1 *a young man:* One possible meaning for the difficult Hebrew text; several manuscripts of one ancient translation have "thirty years old." [i]13.1,2 *for . . . Then:* One possible meaning for the difficult Hebrew text. [j]13.2 *everyone else:* People who were not full-time soldiers, but fought together with the army when the nation was in danger. [k]13.2 *Jonathan:* Saul's son (see verse 16). [l]13.2 *Michmash . . . Bethel . . . Gibeah:* These three towns form a triangle, with Bethel to the north. [m]13.3 *Geba:* Geba was between Gibeah and Michmash. [n]13.3 *led an attack . . . destroyed, but:* Or "killed the Philistine military governor who lived at Geba, and . . ."

[4]The messengers then said to the people of Israel, "Saul has destroyed the Philistine army camp at Geba.[o] Now the Philistines really hate Israel, so every town and village must send men to join Saul's army at Gilgal."

[5]The Philistines called their army together to fight Israel. They had 3,000[p] chariots, 6,000 cavalry, and as many foot soldiers as there are grains of sand on the beach. They went to Michmash and set up camp there east of Beth-Aven.[q]

[6]The Israelite army realized that they were outnumbered and were going to lose the battle. Some of the Israelite men hid in caves or in clumps of bushes,[r] and some ran to places where they could hide among large rocks. Others hid in tombs[s] or in deep dry pits. [7]Still others[t] went to Gad and Gilead on the other side of the Jordan River.

Saul stayed at Gilgal. His soldiers were shaking with fear, [8]and they were starting to run off and leave him. Saul waited there seven days, just as Samuel had ordered him to do,[u] but Samuel did not come. [9]Finally, Saul commanded, "Bring me some animals, so we can offer sacrifices to please the LORD and ask for his help."

Saul killed one of the animals, [10]and just as he placed it on the altar, Samuel arrived. Saul went out to welcome him.

[11]"What have you done?" Samuel asked.

Saul answered, "My soldiers were leaving in all directions, and you didn't come when you were supposed to. The Philistines were gathering at Michmash, [12]and I was worried that they would attack me here at Gilgal. I hadn't offered a sacrifice to ask for the LORD's help, so I forced myself to offer a sacrifice on the altar fire."

[13]"That was stupid!" Samuel said. "You didn't obey the LORD your God. If you had obeyed him, someone from your family would always have been king of Israel. [14]But no, you disobeyed, and so the LORD won't choose anyone else from your family to be king. In fact, he has already chosen the one he wants to be the next leader of his people." [15]Then Samuel left Gilgal.

Part of Saul's army had not deserted him, and he led them to Gibeah in Benjamin to join his other troops. Then he counted them[v] and found that he still had 600 men. [16]Saul, Jonathan, and their army set up camp at Geba in Benjamin.

Jonathan Attacks the Philistines

The Philistine army was camped at Michmash. [17]Each day they sent out patrols to attack and rob villages and then destroy them. One patrol would go north along the road to Ophrah in the region of Shual. [18]Another patrol would go west along the road to Beth-Horon. A third patrol would go east toward the desert on the road to the ridge that overlooks Zeboim Valley.

[19]The Philistines would not allow any Israelites to learn how to make iron tools. "If we allowed that," they said, "those

13.8-12 *Samuel had ordered . . . forced myself to offer a sacrifice:* As a king chosen by God, Saul was supposed to follow God's law and know that the prophet Samuel's word was God's word. Samuel had told Saul to wait—that he would tell Saul what to do after he came and offered sacrifices (10.8). Saul panicked, ignored Samuel's instructions, and went ahead on his own.

13.13 *would always have been king:* Because Saul broke his promise to obey God, his son Jonathan and all of Saul's other descendants lost the right to become kings of Israel.

[o]**13.4** *destroyed . . . Geba*: Or "killed the Philistine military governor who lived at Geba." [p]**13.5** *3,000*: Some ancient translations; Hebrew "30,000." [q]**13.5** *Beth-Aven*: This Beth-Aven was probably located about a mile southwest of Michmash, between Michmash and Geba. [r]**13.6** *in . . . bushes*: Or "in cracks in the rocks." [s]**13.6** *tombs*: The Hebrew word may mean a room cut into solid rock and used as a burial place, or it may mean a cellar. [t]**13.7** *Still others*: This translates a Hebrew word which may be used of wandering groups of people who sometimes became outlaws or hired soldiers (see also 14.21). [u]**13.8** *Samuel . . . to do*: See 10.8. [v]**13.15** *Then Samuel . . . counted them*: Two ancient translations; Hebrew "Then Samuel left Gilgal and went to Gibeah in Benjamin. Saul counted his army."

14.4-5 *Michmash . . . Geba:* Michmash and Geba guarded an important travel route between Jericho and the Mediterranean coast. That route went through the pass that Jonathan and the soldier crossed to surprise the Philistines.

worthless Israelites would make swords and spears."

20-21 Whenever the Israelites wanted to get an iron point put on a cattle prod,[w] they had to go to the Philistines. Even if they wanted to sharpen plow-blades, picks, axes, sickles,[x] and pitchforks[y] they still had to go to them. And the Philistines charged high prices. **22**So, whenever the Israelite soldiers had to go into battle, none of them had a sword or a spear except Saul and his son Jonathan.

23The Philistines moved their camp to the pass at Michmash, **1-3**and Saul was in Geba[z] with his 600 men. Saul's own tent was set up under a fruit tree[a] by the threshing place[b] at the edge of town. Ahijah was serving as priest, and one of his jobs was to get answers from the LORD for Saul. Ahijah's father was Ahitub, and his father's brother was Ichabod. Ahijah's grandfather was Phinehas, and his great-grandfather Eli had been the LORD's priest at Shiloh.

One day, Jonathan told the soldier who carried his weapons that he wanted to attack the Philistine camp on the other side of the valley. So they slipped out of the Israelite camp without anyone knowing it. Jonathan didn't even tell his father he was leaving.

4-5 Jonathan decided to get to the Philistine camp by going through the pass that led between Shiny Cliff and Michmash to the north and Thornbush Cliff[c] and Geba to the south.

6Jonathan and the soldier who carried his weapons talked as they went toward the Philistine camp. "It's just the two of us against all those godless men," Jonathan said. "But the LORD can help a few soldiers win a battle just as easily as he can help a whole army. Maybe the LORD will help us win this battle."

7"Do whatever you want," the soldier answered. "I'll be right there with you."

8"This is what we will do," Jonathan said. "We will go across and let them see us. **9**If they agree to come down the hill and fight where we are, then we won't climb up to their camp. **10**But we will go if they tell us to come up the hill and fight. That will mean the LORD is going to help us win."

11-12 Jonathan and the soldier stood at the bottom of the hill where the Philistines could see them. The Philistines said, "Look! Those worthless Israelites have crawled out of the holes where they've been hiding." Then they yelled down to Jonathan and the soldier, "Come up here, and we will teach you a thing or two!"

Jonathan turned to the soldier and said, "Follow me! The LORD is going to let us win."

13Jonathan crawled up the hillside with the soldier right behind him. When they got to the top, Jonathan killed the Philistines who attacked from the front, and the soldier killed those who attacked from behind.[d] **14**Before they had gone 100 feet,[e] they had killed about 20 Philistines.

15The whole Philistine army panicked— those in camp, those on guard duty, those

---

[w]**13.20,21** *cattle prod:* A pole used to poke cattle and make them move.   [x]**13.20,21** *sickles:* One ancient translation; Hebrew "plow-blades."   [y]**13.20,21** *pitchforks:* One possible meaning for the difficult Hebrew text.   [z]**14.1-3** *Geba:* Or "Gibeah." In 13.16 and 14.4,5 the name "Geba" is used, while 14.1-3,16 have "Gibeah." In ancient Hebrew writing there is only one letter different between the two words.   [a]**14.1-3** *fruit tree:* Hebrew "pomegranate tree." A pomegranate is a bright red fruit that looks like an apple.   [b]**14.1-3** *threshing place:* Or "in Migron."   [c]**14.4,5** *Shiny Cliff . . . Thornbush Cliff:* Or "Bozez Cliff . . . Seneh Cliff."   [d]**14.13** *Jonathan killed . . . from behind:* Or "Jonathan attacked the Philistines with his sword, and the soldier killed those who fell to the ground wounded."   [e]**14.14** *100 feet:* One possible meaning for the difficult Hebrew text.

in the fields, and those on raiding patrols. All of them were afraid and confused. Then God sent an earthquake, and the ground began to tremble.[f]

Israel Defeats the Philistines

[16]Saul's lookouts at Geba[g] saw that the Philistine army was running in every direction, like melted wax. [17]Saul told his officers, "Call the roll and find out who left our camp." When they had finished, they found out that Jonathan and the soldier who carried his weapons were missing. [18]At that time, Ahijah was serving as priest for the army of Israel, and Saul told him, "Come over here! Let's ask God what we should do."[h] [19]Just as Saul finished saying this, he could see that the Philistine army camp was getting more and more confused, and he said, "Ahijah, never mind!"

[20]Saul quickly called his army together, then led them to the Philistine camp. By this time the Philistines were so confused that they were killing each other. [21]There were also some hired soldiers[i] in the Philistine camp, who now switched to Israel's side and fought for Saul and Jonathan. [22]Many Israelites had been hiding in the hill country of Ephraim. And when they heard that the Philistines were running away, they came out of hiding and joined in chasing the Philistines. [23-24]So the LORD helped Israel win the battle that day.

Saul's Curse on Anyone Who Eats

Saul had earlier told his soldiers, "I want to get even with those Philistines by sunset. If any of you eat before then, you will be under a curse!" So he made them swear not to eat.

By the time the fighting moved past Beth-Aven,[j] the Israelite troops were weak from hunger. [25-26]The army and the people who lived nearby had gone into a forest, and they came to a place where honey was dripping on the ground.[k] But no one ate any of it, because they were afraid of being put under the curse.

[27]Jonathan did not know about Saul's warning to the soldiers. So he dipped the end of his walking stick in the honey and ate some with his fingers. He felt stronger and more alert. [28]Then a soldier told him, "Your father swore that anyone who ate food today would be put under a curse, and we agreed not to eat. That's why we're so weak."

[29]Jonathan said, "My father has caused you a lot of trouble. Look at me! I ate only a little of this honey, but already I feel strong and alert. [30]I wish you had eaten some of the food the Philistines left behind. We would have been able to kill a lot more of them."

[31]By evening the Israelite army was exhausted from killing Philistines all the way from Michmash to Aijalon.[l] [32]They grabbed the food they had captured from the Philistines and started eating. They

[f]14.15 *Then . . . tremble:* Or "Then the ground began to tremble, and everyone was in a terrible panic." Or "Then the ground began to tremble, and God made them all panic." [g]14.16 *Geba:* See the note at 14.1-3. [h]14.18 *At that time . . . should do:* One ancient translation; Hebrew "Saul told Ahijah, 'Bring the sacred chest,' because at that time it was with the army of Israel." [i]14.21 *hired soldiers:* See the note at 13.7. [j]14.23,24 *Beth-Aven:* See the note at 13.5. [k]14.25,26 *The army . . . ground:* One possible meaning for the difficult Hebrew text. [l]14.31 *Aijalon:* About 20 miles west of Michmash.

14.47-48 *Moabites . . . the Amalekites:* Israel's enemies had come from all directions. **(See Map 4 on pg 1882.)**

even killed sheep and cows and calves right on the spot and ate the meat without draining the blood.[m] 33Someone told Saul, "Look! The army is disobeying the LORD by eating meat before the blood drains out."

"You're right," Saul answered. "They are being unfaithful to the LORD! Hurry! Roll a big rock over here.[n] 34Then tell everyone in camp to bring their cattle and lambs to me. They can kill the animals on this rock,[o] then eat the meat. That way no one will disobey the LORD by eating meat with blood still in it."

That night the soldiers brought their cattle over to the big rock and killed them there. 35It was the first altar Saul had built for offering sacrifices to the LORD.[p]

The Army Rescues Jonathan

36Saul said, "Let's attack the Philistines again while it's still dark. We can fight them all night. Let's kill them and take everything they own!"

The people answered, "We will do whatever you want."

"Wait!" Ahijah the priest said. "Let's ask God what we should do."

37Saul asked God, "Should I attack the Philistines? Will you help us win?"

This time God did not answer. 38Saul called his army officers together and said, "We have to find out what sin has kept God from answering. 39I swear by the living LORD that whoever sinned must die, even if it turns out to be my own son Jonathan."

No one said a word.

40Saul told his army, "You stand on that side of the priest, and Jonathan and I will stand on the other side."

Everyone agreed.

41Then Saul prayed, "Our LORD, God of Israel, why haven't you answered me today? Please show us who sinned. Was it my son Jonathan and I, or was it your people Israel?"[q]

The answer came back that Jonathan or Saul had sinned, not the army. 42Saul told Ahijah, "Now ask the LORD to decide between Jonathan and me."

The answer came back that Jonathan had sinned. 43"Jonathan," Saul exclaimed, "tell me what you did!"

"I dipped the end of my walking stick in some honey and ate a little. Now you say I have to die!"

44"Yes, Jonathan. I swear to God that you must die."

45"No!" the soldiers shouted. "God helped Jonathan win the battle for us. We won't let you kill him. We swear to the LORD that we won't let you kill him or even lay a hand on him!" So the army kept Saul from killing Jonathan.

46Saul stopped hunting down the Philistines, and they went home.

Saul Fights His Enemies

47-48When Saul became king, the Moabites, the Ammonites, the Edomites, the kings of Zobah, the Philistines, and the Amalekites had all been robbing the Israelites. Saul fought back against these enemies and stopped them from robbing Israel. He was a brave commander and always won his battles.[r]

[m]14.32 *blood:* The Israelites were supposed to drain the blood from a butchered animal before the meat was cooked and eaten (see Genesis 9.4; Leviticus 17.11; Deuteronomy 12.23). [n]14.33 *over here:* One ancient translation; Hebrew "today." [o]14.34 *kill . . . rock:* That is, up off the ground so the blood could drain out. [p]14.35 *offering sacrifices to the LORD:* Even when animals were killed for food, it was often done as a sacrifice to the LORD. [q]14.41 *why . . . Israel:* One ancient translation; Hebrew "give me an answer." [r]14.47,48 *won his battles:* One ancient translation; Hebrew "hurt them."

Saul's Family

49-51 Saul's wife was Ahinoam, the daughter of Ahimaaz. They had three sons: Jonathan, Ishvi,**s** and Malchishua. They also had two daughters: The older one was Merab, and the younger one was Michal.

Abner, Saul's cousin, was the commander of the army. Saul's father Kish and Abner's father Ner were sons of Abiel.

War with the Philistines

52Saul was at war with the Philistines for as long as he lived. Whenever he found a good warrior or a brave man, Saul made him join his army.

Saul Disobeys the Lord

15
One day, Samuel told Saul:

The LORD told me to choose you to be king of his people, Israel. Now listen to this message from the LORD: **2**"When the Israelites were on their way out of Egypt, the nation of Amalek attacked them. I am the LORD All-Powerful, and now I am going to make Amalek pay!

3"Go and attack the Amalekites! Destroy them and all their possessions. Don't have any pity. Kill their men, women, children, and even their babies. Slaughter their cattle, sheep, camels, and donkeys."

4Saul sent messengers who told every town and village to send men to join the army at Telaim. There were 210,000 troops in all, and 10,000 of these were from Judah.

Saul organized them, **5**then led them to a valley near one of the towns in**t** Amalek, where they got ready to make a surprise attack. **6**Some Kenites lived nearby, and Saul told them, "Your people were kind to our nation when we left Egypt, and I don't want you to get killed when I wipe out the Amalekites. So stay away from them."

The Kenites left, **7**and Saul attacked the Amalekites from Havilah**u** to Shur, which is just east of Egypt. **8**Every Amalekite was killed except King Agag. **9**Saul and his army let Agag live, and they also spared the best sheep and cattle. They didn't want to destroy anything of value, so they only killed the animals that were worthless or weak.**v**

The LORD Rejects Saul

10The LORD told Samuel, **11**"Saul has stopped obeying me, and I'm sorry that I made him king."

Samuel was angry, and he cried out in prayer to the LORD all night. **12**Early the next morning he went to talk with Saul. Someone told him, "Saul went to Carmel, where he had a monument built so everyone would remember his victory. Then he left for Gilgal."

13Samuel finally caught up with Saul,**w** and Saul told him, "I hope the LORD will bless you! I have done what the LORD told me."

14"Then why," Samuel asked, "do I hear sheep and cattle?"

15"The army took them from the Amalekites," Saul explained. "They kept the best sheep and cattle, so they could

15.3 *Go and attack . . . Destroy:* This is what God required of the Israelites when they captured towns in the land God gave them.

Holy War (The LORD's Battles)

15.6 *Kenites:* The Kenites were a group of nomads in the southern part of the Israelites' land. They would later become part of the tribe of Judah (30.27-31).

15.12 *Carmel:* A city about seven miles south of Hebron near the Amalekite territory. (See Map 3 on pg 1881.)

---

s14.49-51 *Ishvi:* Also known as Eshbaal (see 1 Chronicles 8.33; 9.39) and Ishbosheth (see 2 Samuel 2.8-13; 3.8-15; 4.5-12). **t**15.5 *one . . . in:* Or "the town of." **u**15.7 *from Havilah:* Or "from the valley" (see 15.5). **v**15.9 *animals . . . weak:* One possible meaning for the difficult Hebrew text. **w**15.13 *Saul:* One ancient translation adds "Saul had sacrificed to the LORD the best animals they had taken from Amalek, when Samuel came up to him . . ."

■ *15.26-28 You disobeyed . . . The LORD has torn the kingdom:* Saul still didn't understand. He seemed to think that he could do what he wanted, as long as he gave sacrifices and offerings (15.22). Samuel's tearing of the robe was like taking the kingship away from Saul. Saul no longer measured up to God's rule that kings must obey God's law.

● *16.1 Jesse:* The son of Obed and grandson of Boaz and Ruth (Ruth 4.17-22). Bethlehem is only a few miles south of Jerusalem. **(See Map 3 on pg 1881.)**

sacrifice them to the LORD your God. But we destroyed everything else."

¹⁶"Stop!" Samuel said. "Let me tell you what the LORD told me last night."

"All right," Saul answered.

¹⁷Samuel continued, "You may not think you're very important, but the LORD chose you to be king, and you are in charge of the tribes of Israel. ¹⁸When the LORD sent you on this mission, he told you to wipe out those worthless Amalekites. ¹⁹Why didn't you listen to the LORD? Why did you keep the animals and make him angry?"

²⁰"But I did listen to the LORD!" Saul answered. "He sent me on a mission, and I went. I captured King Agag and destroyed his nation. ²¹All the animals were going to be destroyed[x] anyway. That's why the army brought the best sheep and cattle to Gilgal as sacrifices to the LORD your God."

²²"Tell me," Samuel said. "Does the LORD really want sacrifices and offerings? No! He doesn't want your sacrifices. He wants you to obey him. ²³Rebelling against God or disobeying him because you are proud is just as bad as worshiping idols or asking them for advice. You refused to do what God told you, so God has decided that you can no longer be king."

²⁴"I have sinned," Saul admitted. "I disobeyed both you and the LORD. I was afraid of the army, and I listened to them instead. ²⁵Please forgive me and come back with me so I can worship the LORD."

²⁶"No!" Samuel replied, "You disobeyed the LORD, and I won't go back with you. Now the LORD has said that you can't be king of Israel any longer."

²⁷As Samuel turned to go, Saul grabbed the edge of Samuel's robe. It tore! ²⁸Samuel said, "The LORD has torn the kingdom of Israel away from you today, and he will give it to someone who is better than you. ²⁹Besides, the eternal[y] God of Israel isn't a human being. He doesn't tell lies or change his mind."

³⁰Saul said, "I did sin, but please honor me in front of the leaders of the army and the people of Israel. Come back with me, so I can worship the LORD your God."

³¹Samuel followed Saul back, and Saul worshiped the LORD. ³²Then Samuel shouted, "Bring me King Agag of Amalek!"

Agag came in chains,[z] and he was saying to himself, "Surely they won't kill me now."[a]

³³But Samuel said, "Agag, you have snatched children from their mothers' arms and killed them. Now your mother will be without children." Then Samuel chopped Agag to pieces at the place of worship in Gilgal.

³⁴Samuel went home to Ramah, and Saul returned to his home in Gibeah. ³⁵Even though Samuel felt sad about Saul, Samuel never saw him again.

The LORD Chooses David To Be King

16 The LORD was sorry he had made Saul the king of Israel. ¹One day he said, "Samuel, I've rejected Saul, and I refuse to let him be king any longer. Stop feeling sad about him. Put some olive oil[b] in a small container[c] and go visit a man named Jesse, who lives in Bethlehem. I've chosen one of his sons to be my king."

[x]**15.21** *animals . . . destroyed:* The Hebrew means things that were set aside for God. They could not be used for anything else, so they had to be destroyed. [y]**15.29** *eternal:* Or "glorious." [z]**15.32** *in chains:* One possible meaning for the difficult Hebrew text. [a]**15.32** *Surely . . . now:* Hebrew; one ancient translation "It would have been better to die in battle!" [b]**16.1** *olive oil:* See the note at 9.16. [c]**16.1** *small container:* Hebrew "horn"; animal horns were sometimes hollowed out and used as containers.

Saul said, "I have sinned . . . I disobeyed both you and the LORD. I was afraid of the army, and I listened to them instead." 1 SAM 15.24

[2]Samuel answered, "If I do that, Saul will find out and have me killed."

"Take a calf with you," the LORD replied. "Tell everyone that you've come to offer it as a sacrifice to me, [3]then invite Jesse to the sacrifice.[d] When I show you which one of his sons I have chosen, pour the olive oil on his head."

[4]Samuel did what the LORD told him and went to Bethlehem. The town leaders went to meet him, but they were terribly afraid and asked, "Is this a friendly visit?"

[5]"Yes, it is!" Samuel answered. "I've come to offer a sacrifice to the LORD. Get yourselves ready[e] to take part in the sacrifice and come with me." Samuel also invited Jesse and his sons to come to the sacrifice, and he got them ready to take part.

[6]When Jesse and his sons arrived, Samuel noticed Jesse's oldest son, Eliab. "He has to be the one the LORD has chosen," Samuel said to himself.

[7]But the LORD told him, "Samuel, don't think Eliab is the one just because he's tall and handsome. He isn't the one I've chosen. People judge others by what they look like, but I judge people by what is in their hearts."

[8]Jesse told his son Abinadab to go over to Samuel, but Samuel said, "No, the LORD hasn't chosen him."

[9]Next, Jesse sent his son Shammah to him, and Samuel said, "The LORD hasn't chosen him either."

[10]One by one, Jesse told all seven of his sons to go over to Samuel. Finally, Samuel said, "Jesse, the LORD hasn't chosen any of these young men. [11]Do you have any other sons?"

"Yes," Jesse answered. "My youngest son David is out taking care of the sheep."

"Send for him!" Samuel said. "We won't start the ceremony until he gets here."

[12]Jesse sent for David. He was a healthy, good-looking boy with a sparkle in his eyes. As soon as David came, the LORD told Samuel, "He's the one! Get up and pour the olive oil on his head."[f]

[13]Samuel poured the oil on David's head while his brothers watched. At that moment, the Spirit of the LORD took control of David and stayed with him from then on.

Samuel returned home to Ramah.

David Plays the Harp for Saul

[14]The Spirit of the LORD had left Saul, and an evil spirit from the LORD was terrifying him. [15]"It's an evil spirit from God that's frightening you," Saul's officials told him. [16]"Your Majesty, let us go and look for someone who is good at playing the harp. He can play for you whenever the evil spirit from God bothers you, and you'll feel better."

[17]"All right," Saul answered. "Find me someone who is good at playing the harp and bring him here."

[18]"A man named Jesse who lives in Bethlehem has a son who can play the harp," one official said. "He's a brave warrior, he's good-looking, he can speak well, and the LORD is with him."

[19]Saul sent a message to Jesse: "Tell your son David to leave your sheep and come here to me."

[20]Jesse loaded a donkey with bread and a goatskin full of wine,[g] then he told David

---

16.3-5 *to the sacrifice . . . Get yourselves ready:* After a sacrifice, part of the animal might be eaten in a sacred meal, but only by people who were properly prepared. A number of things could make a person unfit to eat the meal.

Purity (Clean and Unclean)

16.11 *David . . . taking care of the sheep:* David's humble beginnings as a shepherd would later be understood as a symbol for his role as a kind of shepherd (leader) of God's chosen people.

David

16.12 *olive oil on his head:* Although David's brothers watched, they might not have known exactly what was happening. See, for example, Eliab's angry outburst at 17.28.

16.14 *an evil spirit from the LORD:* Saul probably was suffering from depression or a similar illness. People believed evil spirits caused such conditions, and that God sent both evil spirits and good spirits.

Wine

---

[d]**16.3** *sacrifice:* A sacrifice often involved a dinner where the meat from the sacrificed animal would be served.   [e]**16.5** *Get yourselves ready:* The people of Israel sometimes had to perform certain ceremonies to make themselves acceptable to God.   [f]**16.12** *olive oil on his head:* See the note at 9.16. [g]**16.20** *wine:* Wine was sometimes kept in bottles made of goatskin sewn up with the fur on the outside.

The LORD said, "People judge others by what they look like, but I judge people by what is in their hearts." 1 SAM 16.7

17.1-3 *Socoh and Azekah . . . Elah Valley:* This area was about 15 miles west of the hills of southern Judah. At the time, Socoh was controlled by the Israelites, and Azekah was controlled by the Philistines.

17.4-10 *hero . . . challenge:* The Hebrew word translated as "hero" means "the man between two (armies)." Goliath came out between the two armies to fight an Israelite soldier in one-on-one combat. The result of that fight would decide which army won the battle. This way of fighting kept the loss of life to a minimum.

17.5-7 *a bronze helmet . . . carry his shield:* Even though Goliath wore a heavy armor and carried a huge sword, David would be able to defeat him with a few stones because he had the LORD All-Powerful on his side.

to take the donkey and a young goat to Saul. [21]David went to Saul and started working for him. Saul liked him so much that he put David in charge of carrying his weapons. [22]Not long after this, Saul sent another message to Jesse: "I really like David. Please let him stay with me."

[23]Whenever the evil spirit from God bothered Saul, David would play his harp. Saul would relax and feel better, and the evil spirit would go away.

Goliath Challenges Israel's Army

17 The Philistines got ready for war and brought their troops together to attack the town of Socoh in Judah. They set up camp at Ephes-Dammim, between Socoh and Azekah.[h] [2-3]King Saul and the Israelite army set up camp on a hill overlooking Elah Valley, and they got ready to fight the Philistine army that was on a hill on the other side of the valley.

[4]The Philistine army had a hero named Goliath who was from the town of Gath and was over nine feet[i] tall. [5-6]He wore a bronze helmet and had bronze armor to protect his chest and legs. The chest armor alone weighed about 125 pounds. He carried a bronze sword strapped on his back, [7]and his spear was so big that the iron spearhead alone weighed more than 15 pounds. A soldier always walked in front of Goliath to carry his shield.

[8]Goliath went out and shouted to the army of Israel:

Why are you lining up for battle? I'm the best soldier in our army, and all of you are in Saul's army. Choose your best soldier to come out and fight me! [9]If he can kill me, our people will be

your slaves. But if I kill him, your people will be our slaves. [10]Here and now I challenge Israel's whole army! Choose someone to fight me!

[11]Saul and his men heard what Goliath said, but they were so frightened of Goliath that they couldn't do a thing.

David Decides To Challenge Goliath

[12]David's father Jesse was an old man, who belonged to the Ephrath clan and lived in Bethlehem in Judah. Jesse had eight sons: [13-14]the oldest was Eliab, the next was Abinadab, and Shammah was the third. The three of them had gone off to fight in Saul's army.

David was Jesse's youngest son. [15]He took care of his father's sheep, and he went back and forth between Bethlehem and Saul's camp.

[16]Goliath came out and gave his challenge every morning and every evening for 40 days.

[17]One day, Jesse told David, "Hurry and take this sack of roasted grain and these ten loaves of bread to your brothers at the army camp. [18]And here are ten large chunks of cheese to take to their commanding officer. Find out how your brothers are doing and bring back something that shows that they're all right. [19]They're with Saul's army, fighting the Philistines in Elah Valley."

[20]David obeyed his father. He got up early the next morning and left someone else in charge of the sheep; then he loaded the supplies and started off. He reached the army camp just as the soldiers were taking their places and shouting the battle cry.

[h]17.1 *Socoh and Azekah:* Socoh was controlled by the Israelites, while Azekah was in Philistine hands. [i]17.4 *over nine feet:* The Standard Hebrew Text; the Dead Sea Scrolls and some manuscripts of one ancient translation have "almost seven feet."

²¹The army of Israel and the Philistine army stood there facing each other.

²²David left his things with the man in charge of supplies and ran up to the battle line to ask his brothers if they were well. ²³While David was talking with them, Goliath came out from the line of Philistines and started boasting as usual. David heard him.

²⁴When the Israelite soldiers saw Goliath, they were scared and ran off. ²⁵They said to each other, "Look how he keeps coming out to insult us. The king is offering a big reward to the man who kills Goliath. That man will even get to marry the king's daughter, and no one in his family will ever have to pay taxes again."

²⁶David asked some soldiers standing nearby, "What will a man get for killing this Philistine and stopping him from insulting our people? Who does that worthless Philistine think he is? He's making fun of the army of the living God!"

²⁷The soldiers told David what the king would give the man who killed Goliath.

²⁸David's oldest brother Eliab heard him talking with the soldiers. Eliab was angry with him and said, "What are you doing here, anyway? Who's taking care of your little flock of sheep out in the desert? You spoiled brat! You came here just to watch the fighting, didn't you?"

²⁹"Now what have I done?" David answered. "Can't I even ask a question?" ³⁰Then he turned and asked another soldier the same thing he had asked the others, and he got the same answer.

³¹Some soldiers overheard David talking, so they told Saul what David had said. Saul sent for David, and David came. ³²"Your Majesty," he said, "this Philistine shouldn't turn us into cowards. I'll go out and fight him myself!"

³³"You don't have a chance against him," Saul replied. "You're only a boy, and he's been a soldier all his life."

³⁴But David told him:

Your Majesty, I take care of my father's sheep. And when one of them is dragged off by a lion or a bear, ³⁵I go after it and beat the wild animal until it lets the sheep go. If the wild animal turns and attacks me, I grab it by the throat and kill it.

³⁶Sir, I have killed lions and bears that way, and I can kill this worthless Philistine. He shouldn't have made fun of the army of the living God! ³⁷The LORD has rescued me from the claws of lions and bears, and he will keep me safe from the hands of this Philistine.

"All right," Saul answered, "go ahead and fight him. And I hope the LORD will help you."

³⁸Saul had his own military clothes and armor put on David, and he gave David a bronze helmet to wear. ³⁹David strapped on a sword and tried to walk around, but he was not used to wearing those things.

"I can't move with all this stuff on," David said. "I'm just not used to it."

David took off the armor ⁴⁰and picked up his shepherd's stick. He went out to a stream and picked up five smooth rocks and put them in his leather bag. Then with his sling in his hand, he went straight toward Goliath.

David Kills Goliath

⁴¹Goliath came toward David, walking behind the soldier who was carrying his shield. ⁴²When Goliath saw that David was just a healthy, good-looking boy, he made fun of him. ⁴³"Do you think I'm a dog?" Goliath asked. "Is that why you've come after me with a stick?" He cursed David in the name of the Philistine gods ⁴⁴and

17.34,35 *I take care of my father's sheep . . . and kill it:* Shepherds and shepherding are mentioned over 200 times in the Bible. Shepherds fed, watered, and protected their sheep day and night. The term "shepherd" is used to describe Israel's leaders and kings, as well as for describing God.

Shepherds

17.40 *shepherd's stick . . . rocks . . . leather bag . . . sling:* The shepherd used the wooden stick for support when walking in the hills and carried a few days' supply of food in the bag, which was worn over the shoulder.

This hand-held weapon was used to throw rocks. Leather strings or straps were attached to both sides of a wider leather band or pocket. A rock was put in the leather pocket, and the thrower held on to both straps while swinging it above his head. When the thrower let go of one strap, the rock would fly out of the sling at speeds of up to 100 miles per hour.

David asked, "Who does that worthless Philistine think he is? He's making fun of the army of the living God!" 1 SAM 17.26

17.52-54 *Shaaraim . . . Jerusalem:* Shaaraim was a town in Judah. The Jebusites still held Jerusalem at this time, so David probably would not have gone there. Perhaps he took Goliath's head to Jerusalem later, after he conquered and made it the capital of Israel.

17.55-58 *who is that:* It seems strange that Saul did not recognize David as the one who had played the harp for him (16.14-23). These verses may be part of another story of how Saul comes to know David. They also reflect (like 16.14-23) Saul's positive feelings about David when they first met. See also 18.5.

18.4 *Jonathan took off the robe . . . military clothes:* It was probably too soon for Jonathan to have recognized David as the future king. But David's taking the robe from Jonathan can be seen as a symbol of the transfer of royal power from Saul to David, rather than to his own son. The transfer of military gear indicates that David would soon surpass Saul and Jonathan in military skill and success.

shouted, "Come on! When I'm finished with you, I'll feed you to the birds and wild animals!"

⁴⁵David answered:

You've come out to fight me with a sword and a spear and a dagger. But I've come out to fight you in the name of the LORD All-Powerful. He is the God of Israel's army, and you have insulted him too!

⁴⁶Today the LORD will help me defeat you. I'll knock you down and cut off your head, and I'll feed the bodies of the other Philistine soldiers to the birds and wild animals. Then the whole world will know that Israel has a real God. ⁴⁷Everybody here will see that the LORD doesn't need swords or spears to save his people. The LORD always wins his battles, and he will help us defeat you.

⁴⁸When Goliath started forward, David ran toward him. ⁴⁹He put a rock in his sling and swung the sling around by its straps. When he let go of one strap, the rock flew out and hit Goliath on the forehead. It cracked his skull, and he fell facedown on the ground. ⁵⁰David defeated Goliath with a sling and a rock. He killed him without even using a sword.

⁵¹David ran over and pulled out Goliath's sword. Then he used it to cut off Goliath's head.

When the Philistines saw what had happened to their hero, they started running away. ⁵²But the soldiers of Israel and Judah let out a battle cry and went after them as far as Gath[j] and Ekron. The bodies of the Philistines were scattered all along the road from Shaaraim to Gath and Ekron. ⁵³When the Israelite army returned from chasing the Philistines, they took what they wanted from the enemy camp. ⁵⁴David took Goliath's head to Jerusalem, but he kept Goliath's weapons in his own tent.

David Becomes One of Saul's Officers

⁵⁵After King Saul had watched David go out to fight Goliath, Saul turned to the commander of his army and said, "Abner, who is that young man?"

"Your Majesty," Abner answered, "I swear by your life that I don't know."

⁵⁶"Then find out!" Saul told him.

⁵⁷When David came back from fighting Goliath, he was still carrying Goliath's head.

Abner took David to Saul, ⁵⁸and Saul asked, "Who are you?"

"I am David the son of Jesse, a loyal Israelite from Bethlehem."

18 David and Saul finished talking, and soon David and Jonathan[k] became best friends. Jonathan thought as much of David as he did of himself. ²From that time on, Saul kept David in his service and would not let David go back to his own family.

³Jonathan liked David so much that they promised to always be loyal friends. ⁴Jonathan took off the robe that he was wearing and gave it to David. He also gave him his military clothes,[l] his sword, his bow and arrows, and his belt.

⁵David was a success in everything that Saul sent him to do, and Saul made him a high officer in his army. That pleased everyone, including Saul's other officers.

Saul Becomes David's Enemy

⁶David had killed Goliath, the battle was over, and the Israelite army set out for

[j]17.52 *Gath*: One ancient translation; Hebrew "a valley."   [k]18.1 *Jonathan*: Saul's oldest son (see chapter 14).   [l]18.4 *military clothes*: Or "armor."

home. As the army went along, women came out of each Israelite town to welcome King Saul. They were celebrating by singing songs and dancing to the music of tambourines and harps. [7] They sang:

Saul has killed
a thousand enemies;
David has killed
ten thousand!

[8]This song made Saul very angry, and he thought, "They are saying that David has killed ten times more enemies than I ever did. Next they will want to make him king." [9]Saul never again trusted David.

[10]The next day the LORD let an evil spirit take control of Saul, and he began acting like a crazy man inside his house. David came to play the harp for Saul as usual, but this time Saul had a spear in his hand. [11]Saul thought, "I'll pin David to the wall." He threw the spear at David twice, but David dodged and got away both times.

[12]Saul was afraid of David, because the LORD was helping David and was no longer helping him. [13]Saul put David in charge of 1,000 soldiers and sent him out to fight. [14]The LORD helped David, and he and his soldiers always won their battles. [15]This made Saul even more afraid of David. [16]But everyone else in Judah and Israel was loyal to[m] David, because he led the army in battle.

[17]One day, Saul told David, "If you'll be brave and fight the LORD's battles for me, I'll let you marry my oldest daughter Merab." But Saul was really thinking, "I don't want to kill David myself, so I'll let the Philistines do it for me."

[18]David answered, "How could I possibly marry your daughter? I'm not very important, and neither is my family."

[19]But when the time came for David to marry Saul's daughter Merab, Saul told her to marry Adriel from the town of Meholah.

[20]Saul had another daughter. Her name was Michal, and Saul found out that she was in love with David. This made Saul happy, [21]and he thought, "I'll tell David he can marry Michal, but I'll set it up so that the Philistines will kill him." He told David, "I'm going to give you a second chance to marry one of my daughters."

[22-23]Saul ordered his officials to speak to David in private, so they went to David and said, "Look, the king likes you, and all of his officials are loyal to you. Why not ask the king if you can marry his daughter Michal?"

"I'm not rich[n] or famous enough to marry princess Michal!" David answered.

[24]The officials went back to Saul and told him exactly what David had said. [25]Saul was hoping that the Philistines would kill David, and he told his officials to tell David, "The king doesn't want any silver or gold. He only wants to get even with his enemies. All you have to do is to bring back proof that you have killed 100 Philistines!"[o] [26]The officials told David, and David wanted to marry the princess.

King Saul had set a time limit, and before it ran out, [27]David and his men left and killed 200 Philistines. David brought back the proof that Saul had demanded and showed it to him, so he could marry Michal. Saul agreed to let David marry Michal. [28]King Saul knew that she loved David,[p] and he also realized that the LORD

[m]18.16 was loyal to: Or "loved." [n]18.22,23 not rich: It was the custom for a man to give the bride's father some silver or gold in order to marry his daughter, and it would take a large amount to marry the daughter of the king. [o]18.25 proof . . . Philistines: Hebrew "100 Philistine foreskins." In ancient times soldiers would sometimes cut off body parts of their dead enemies to prove how many they had killed. [p]18.28 she . . . David: Hebrew; one ancient translation "all Israel was loyal to David."

■ 18.9,10 *Saul never again trusted David . . . let an evil spirit take control of Saul:* This marks an important turning point in the relationship between Saul and David. Saul's jealousy and crazy behavior are clear signs that he is no longer in God's favor. Similarly, David's military successes, the affection and loyalty shown to him by Saul's own children, and the honorable way David continues to respect Saul as God's chosen king, show that David is increasing in God's favor.

● 18.17-21 *I'll let you marry my oldest daughter Merab . . . he can marry Michal:* Kings in the ancient world often relied on political marriages as a way of cementing alliances and preventing rebellions. Even though Saul distrusted David (18.9), allowing this popular warrior to marry one of his daughters made it look like he trusted him. If Saul's subjects believed this they would be less likely to suspect the king of having arranged David's death, should David die in battle.

● 18.18 *I'm not very important:* Family ties and status were very important among the scattered Israelite tribes. It was common courtly practice to speak humbly to the king as David is doing here. Compare his statement to what Saul said to Samuel (9.21). Unlike Saul, however, David is in reality the son of a wealthy man who was respected by the community.

■ 19.9-10 *an evil spirit from the* LORD*:* Saul had promised in 16.6 not to have David killed. Saul's inability to keep the promises he made is further evidence that he had lost control of his faculties and no longer fit to be king.

was helping David. 29But knowing those things made Saul even more afraid of David, and he was David's enemy for the rest of his life.

30The Philistine rulers kept coming to fight Israel, but whenever David fought them, he won. He was famous because he won more battles against the Philistines than any of Saul's other officers.

Saul Tries To Have David Killed

19 One day, Saul told his son Jonathan and his officers to kill David. But Jonathan and David were best friends, 2-3and he warned David, "My father is trying to have you killed, so be very careful. Hide in a field tomorrow morning, and I'll bring him there. Then I'll talk to him about you, and if I find out anything, I'll let you know."

4-5The next morning, Jonathan reminded Saul about the many good things David had done for him. Then he said, "Why do you want to kill David? He hasn't done anything to you. He has served in your army and has always done what's best for you. He even risked his life to kill Goliath. The LORD helped Israel win a great victory that day, and it made you happy."

6Saul agreed and promised, "I swear by the living LORD that I won't have David killed!"

7Jonathan went to David and told him what Saul had said. Then he brought David to Saul, and David served in Saul's army just as he had done before.

8The next time there was a war with the Philistines, David fought hard and forced them to retreat.

Michal Helps David Escape

9-10One night, David was in Saul's home, playing the harp for him. Saul was sitting there, holding a spear, when an evil spirit from the LORD took control of him. Saul tried to pin David to the wall with the spear, but David dodged, and it stuck in the wall. David ran out of the house and escaped.

11Saul sent guards to watch David's house all night and then to kill him in the morning.

Michal, David's wife, told him, "If you don't escape tonight, they'll kill you tomorrow!" 12She helped David leave through a window and climb down to the ground.[q] As David ran off, 13Michal put a statue in his bed. She put goat hair on its head and dressed it in some of David's clothes.

14The next morning, Saul sent guards to arrest David. But Michal told them, "David is sick."

15Saul sent the guards back and told them, "Bring David to me—bed and all—so I can kill him."

16When the guards went in, all they found in the bed was the statue with the goat hair on its head.

17"Why have you tricked me this way?" Saul asked Michal. "You helped my enemy get away!"

She answered, "He said he would kill me if I didn't help him escape!"

Samuel Helps David Escape

18Meanwhile, David went to Samuel at Ramah and told him what Saul had done. Then Samuel and David went to Prophets Village[r] and stayed there.

[q]**19.12** *ground:* The house was probably built into the town wall, allowing David to come down outside the wall. [r]**19.18** *Prophets Village:* Or "Naioth."

¹⁹Someone told Saul, "David is at Prophets Village in Ramah."

²⁰Saul sent a few soldiers to bring David back. They went to Ramah and found Samuel in charge of a group of prophets who were all prophesying. Then the Spirit of God took control of the soldiers and they started prophesying too. ²¹When Saul heard what had happened, he sent some more soldiers, but they prophesied just like the first group. He sent a third group of soldiers, but the same thing happened to them. ²²Finally, Saul left for Ramah himself. He went as far as the deep pit^s at the town of Secu, and he asked, "Where are Samuel and David?"

"At Prophets Village in Ramah," the people answered.

²³Saul left for Ramah. But as he walked along, the Spirit of God took control of him, and he started prophesying. Then, when he reached Prophets Village, ²⁴he stripped off his clothes and prophesied in front of Samuel. He dropped to the ground and lay there naked all that day and night. That's how the saying started, "Is Saul now a prophet?"

Jonathan Helps David Escape

20 David escaped from Prophets Village. Then he ran to see Jonathan and asked, "Why does your father Saul want to kill me? What have I done wrong?"

²"My father can't be trying to kill you! He never does anything without telling me about it. Why would he hide this from me? It can't be true!"

³"Jonathan, I swear it's true! But your father knows how much you like me, and he didn't want to break your heart. That's why he didn't tell you. I swear by the living LORD and by your own life that I'm only one step ahead of death."

⁴Then Jonathan said, "Tell me what to do, and I'll do it."

⁵David answered:

Tomorrow is the New Moon Festival,^t and I'm supposed to eat dinner with your father. But instead, I'll hide in a field until the evening of the next day. ⁶If Saul wonders where I am, tell him, "David asked me to let him go to his hometown of Bethlehem, so he could take part in a sacrifice his family makes there every year."

⁷If your father says it's all right, then I'm safe. But if he gets angry, you'll know he wants to harm me. ⁸Be kind to me. After all, it was your idea to promise the LORD that we would always be loyal friends. If I've done anything wrong, kill me yourself, but don't hand me over to your father.

⁹"Don't worry," Jonathan said. "If I find out that my father wants to kill you, I'll certainly let you know."

¹⁰"How will you do that?" David asked.

¹¹"Let's go out to this field, and I'll tell you," Jonathan answered.

When they got there, ¹²Jonathan said:

I swear by the LORD God of Israel, that two days from now I'll know what my father is planning. Of course I'll let you know if he's friendly toward you. ¹³But if he wants to harm you, I promise to tell you and help you escape. And I ask the LORD to punish me severely if I don't keep my promise.

I pray that the LORD will bless you, just as he used to bless my father. ¹⁴⁻¹⁵Someday the LORD will wipe out

---

^s**19.22** *pit*: A cistern, a large pit dug down into the rock and used for storing rainwater.   ^t**20.5** *New Moon Festival*: The first day of the month, when Israelites offered special sacrifices to the LORD and had special sacred meals.

● 19.19 *Prophets Village*: Prophets in the ancient Near East may have lived together in large groups to help support one another's work and show their legitimacy as a prophet.

■ 19.24 *stripped off his clothes*: Prophets were said to be under God's control while they were prophesying, and they could no longer control their own actions. (See the article Prophets and Prophecy on pg 1791.)

● 20.14-15 *be as kind to me . . . be kind to my family*: Saul was Israel's first king, and Jonathan was his son. In the ancient world when a new ruler came to power, members of the old royal household were usually killed. Jonathan asked David not to do that in Israel. Even after Jonathan died in battle, David honored Jonathan's request by letting Jonathan's son live (2 Sam 9).

all of your enemies. Then if I'm still alive, please be as kind to me as the LORD has been. But if I'm dead, be kind to my family.

[16]Jonathan and David made an agreement that even David's descendants would have to keep.[u] Then Jonathan said, "I pray that the LORD will take revenge on your descendants if they break our promise."[v]

[17]Jonathan thought as much of David as he did of himself, so he asked David to promise once more that he would be a loyal friend. [18]After this Jonathan said:

Tomorrow is the New Moon Festival, and people will wonder where you are, because your place at the table will be empty. [19]By the day after tomorrow, everyone will think you've been gone a long time.[w] Then go to the place where you hid before and stay beside Going-Away Rock.[x] [20]I'll shoot three arrows at a target off to the side of the rock, [21]and send my servant to find the arrows.

You'll know if it's safe to come out by what I tell him. If it is safe, I swear by the living LORD that I'll say, "The arrows are on this side of you! Pick them up!" [22]But if it isn't safe, I'll say to the boy, "The arrows are farther away!" This will mean that the LORD wants you to leave, and you must go. [23]But he will always watch us to make sure that we keep the promise we made to each other.
[24]So David hid there in the field.

During the New Moon Festival, Saul sat down to eat [25]by the wall, just as he always did. Jonathan sat across from him,[y] and Abner sat next to him. But David's place was empty. [26]Saul didn't say anything that day, because he was thinking, "Something must have happened to make David unfit to be at the Festival.[z] Yes, something must have happened."

[27]The day after the New Moon Festival, when David's place was still empty, Saul asked Jonathan, "Why hasn't that son of Jesse come to eat with us? He wasn't here yesterday, and he still isn't here today!"

[28-29]Jonathan answered, "The reason David hasn't come to eat with you is that he begged me to let him go to Bethlehem. He said, 'Please let me go. My family is offering a sacrifice, and my brother told me I have to be there. Do me this favor and let me slip away to see my brothers.' "

[30]Saul was furious with Jonathan and yelled, "You're no son of mine, you traitor! I know you've chosen to be loyal to that son of Jesse. You should be ashamed of yourself! And your own mother should be ashamed that you were ever born. [31]You'll never be safe, and your kingdom will be in danger as long as that son of Jesse is alive. Turn him over to me now! He deserves to die!"

[32]"Why do you want to kill David?" Jonathan asked. "What has he done?"

[33]Saul threw his spear at Jonathan and tried to kill him. Then Jonathan was sure that his father really did want to kill David. [34]Jonathan was angry and hurt that his father had insulted David[a] so terribly. He got

[u]**20.16** *Jonathan . . . keep*: Or, continuing Jonathan's statement to David, "You and your descendants must not kill off my descendants." [v]**20.16** *I pray . . . promise*: Or "I pray that the LORD take revenge on you if you break our promise!" [w]**20.19** *By . . . time*: One possible meaning for the difficult Hebrew text. [x]**20.19** *Going-Away Rock*: Or "Ezel Rock"; one ancient translation "that mound" (see 20.41). [y]**20.25** *sat . . . him*: One ancient translation; Hebrew "stood up." [z]**20.26** *unfit . . . Festival*: During the New Moon Festival a sacred meal was served that could only be eaten by people who were properly prepared. Some of the things that could make a person unfit are listed in Leviticus 7.20,21; 15.2,31; 22.4-8; Deuteronomy 23.10,11. [a]**20.34** *insulted David*: Or "insulted him" (that is, Jonathan).

Jonathan asked his father, "*Why do you want to kill David? . . . What has he done?*" 1 SAM 20.32

up, left the table, and didn't eat anything all that day.

^{35}In the morning, Jonathan went out to the field to meet David. He took a servant boy along ^{36}and told him, "When I shoot the arrows, you run and find them for me."

The boy started running, and Jonathan shot an arrow so that it would go beyond him. ^{37}When the boy got near the place where the arrow had landed, Jonathan shouted, "Isn't the arrow on past you?" ^{38}Jonathan shouted to him again, "Hurry up! Don't stop!"

The boy picked up the arrows and brought them back to Jonathan, ^{39}but he had no idea about what was going on. Only Jonathan and David knew. ^{40}Jonathan gave his weapons to the boy and told him, "Take these back into town."

^{41}After the boy had gone, David got up from beside the mound^b and bowed very low three times. Then he and Jonathan kissed^c each other and cried, but David cried louder. ^{42}Jonathan said, "Take care of yourself. And remember, we each have asked the LORD to watch and make sure that we and our descendants keep our promise forever."

David left and Jonathan went back to town.

Ahimelech Helps David

21 David went to see Ahimelech, a priest who lived in the town of Nob. Ahimelech was trembling with fear as he came out to meet David. "Why are you alone?" Ahimelech asked. "Why isn't anyone else with you?"

^{2}"I'm on a mission for King Saul," David answered. "He ordered me not to tell anyone what the mission is all about, so I ordered my soldiers to stay somewhere else. ^{3}Do you have any food you can give me? Could you spare five loaves of bread?"

^{4}"The only bread I have is the sacred bread," the priest told David. "You can have it if your soldiers didn't sleep with women last night."^{d}

^{5}"Of course we didn't sleep with women," David answered. "I never let my men do that when we're on a mission. They have to be acceptable to worship God even when we're on a regular mission, and today we're on a special mission."

^{6}The only bread the priest had was the sacred bread that he had taken from the place of worship after putting out the fresh loaves. So he gave it to David.

^{7}It so happened that one of Saul's officers was there, worshiping the LORD that day. His name was Doeg the Edomite,^{e} and he was the strongest of^f Saul's shepherds.

^{8}David asked Ahimelech, "Do you have a spear or a sword? I had to leave so quickly on this mission for the king that I didn't bring along my sword or any other weapons."

^{9}The priest answered, "The only sword here is the one that belonged to Goliath the Philistine. You were the one who killed him in Elah Valley, and so you can take his sword if you want to. It's wrapped in a cloth behind the statue."

"It's the best sword there is," David said. "I'll take it!"

20.41 *kissed:* Although kissing was a common way of greeting or saying good-bye in ancient times, the kiss between David and Jonathan is a symbol of their deep friendship.

21.1 *Nob:* Nob was in Benjamin, not too far from Jerusalem (Isa 10.32).

21.4-6 *sacred bread . . . gave it to David:* In Israel, objects were considered to be either "common," "sacred," or "banned." Common objects could be used by anyone. Sacred objects were put aside for God, and people other than priests usually could not use them. Banned objects were totally dedicated to God and had to be destroyed.

The sacred bread (called showbread) was set out in the place of worship every week as a way of thanking God for providing the bread people needed each day. At the end of the week, the priests ate the bread; no one else was allowed to eat it (Lev 24.5-9). But Ahimelech made an exception and gave some of the sacred bread to David.

---

^{b}**20.41** *the mound:* One ancient translation; Hebrew "from the south side." ^{c}**20.41** *kissed:* A common way of greeting or saying goodbye in biblical times (see Mark 14.44). ^{d}**21.4** *night:* Having sex was one of the things that would make someone temporarily unfit to take part in worship or a sacred meal (see Exodus 19.15; Leviticus 15.18). ^{e}**21.7** *Edomite:* A person from the country of Edom, to the south of Israel. ^{f}**21.7** *the strongest of:* Or "in charge of."

● 22.1 *Adullam Cave:* Adullam was about eighteen miles southwest of Gibeah and nine miles southeast of Gath.

● 22.3 *Mizpeh in Moab:* The exact location of this Mizpeh is unknown. Moab was located east of the Dead Sea. The Moabites were enemies of Israel. David probably thought Moab's king would help him because both of them were now enemies of Saul, and also because David's great grandmother was a Moabite.

● 22.5 *Hereth Forest:* The exact location of Hereth Forest is not known, but it is thought to have been a few miles south of Adullam.

● 22.6 *Saul was sitting . . . in front of him:* Ancient rulers are sometimes described as sitting under a well-known tree to hold court and make important decisions. Saul is at the highest point of his hometown of Gibeah.

● 22.7 *You belong to the Benjamin tribe:* Saul warned that David would give the tribe of Judah special privileges if he became king. This echoed Samuel's warning about what a king would do (8.11-15). But Saul's words show that he has done the same thing by giving special favors to his own tribe, the tribe of Benjamin.

David Tries To Find Safety in Gath

10David kept on running from Saul that day until he came to Gath,^g where he met with King Achish. **11**The officers of King Achish were also there, and they asked Achish, "Isn't David a king back in his own country? Don't the Israelites dance and sing,

'Saul has killed
a thousand enemies;
David has killed
ten thousand'?"

12David thought about what they were saying, and it made him afraid of Achish. **13**So right there in front of everyone, he pretended to be insane. He acted confused and started making scratches on the doors of the town gate, while drooling in his beard. **14**"Look at him!" Achish said to his officers. "You can see he's crazy. Why did you bring him to me? **15**I have enough crazy people without your bringing another one here. Keep him away from my palace!"

People Join David

22 When David escaped from the town of Gath, he went to Adullam Cave. His brothers and the rest of his family found out where he was, and they followed him there. **2**A lot of other people joined him too. Some were in trouble, others were angry or in debt, and David was soon the leader of 400 men.

3David left Adullam Cave and went to the town of Mizpeh in Moab, where he talked with the king of Moab. "Please," David said, "let my father and mother stay with you until I find out what God will do with me." **4**So he brought his parents to the king of Moab, and they stayed with him while David was in hiding.

5One day the prophet Gad told David, "Don't stay here! Go back to Judah." David then left and went to Hereth Forest.

Saul Kills the Priests of the LORD

6Saul was sitting under a small tree on top of the hill at Gibeah when he heard that David and his men had been located. Saul was holding his spear, and his officers were standing in front of him. **7**He told them:

Listen to me! You belong to the Benjamin tribe,^h so if that son of Jesse ever becomes king, he won't give you fields or vineyards. He won't make you officers in charge of thousands or hundreds as I have done. **8**But you're all plotting against me! Not one of you told me that my own son Jonathan had made an agreement with him. Not one of you cared enough to tell me that Jonathan had helped one of my officersⁱ rebel. Now that son of Jesse is trying to ambush me.

9Doeg the Edomite was standing with the other officers and spoke up, "When I was in the town of Nob, I saw that son of Jesse. He was visiting the priest Ahimelech the son of Ahitub. **10**Ahimelech talked to the LORD for him, then gave him food and the sword that had belonged to Goliath the Philistine."

11Saul sent a message to Ahimelech and his whole family of priests at Nob, ordering

g21.10 *Gath:* One of the five main Philistine towns. h22.7 *You . . . Benjamin tribe:* David was from the Judah tribe and would have given special privileges to the people of his own tribe rather than to those of Benjamin. i22.7,8 *son of Jesse . . . officers:* That is, David. Saul avoids even saying David's name.

them to come to him. When they came, ¹²Saul told them, "Listen to me, you son of Ahitub."

"Certainly, Your Majesty," Ahimelech answered.

¹³Saul demanded, "Why did you plot against me with that son of Jesse? You helped him rebel against me by giving him food and a sword, and by talking with God for him. Now he's trying to ambush me!"

¹⁴"Your Majesty, none of your officers is more loyal than David!" Ahimelech replied. "He's your son-in-law and the captain of your bodyguard. Everyone in your family respects him. ¹⁵This isn't the first time I've talked with God for David, and it's never made you angry before! Please don't accuse me or my family like this. I have no idea what's going on!"

¹⁶"Ahimelech," Saul said, "you and your whole family are going to die."

¹⁷Saul shouted to his bodyguards, "These priests of the LORD helped David! They knew he was running away, but they didn't tell me. Kill them!"

But the king's officers would not attack the priests of the LORD.

¹⁸Saul turned to Doeg, who was from Edom, and said, "Kill the priests!"

On that same day, Doeg killed 85 priests. ¹⁹Then he attacked the town of Nob, where the priests had lived, and he killed everyone there—men, women, children, and babies. He even killed their cattle, donkeys, and sheep.

Only Abiathar Escapes from Nob

²⁰Ahimelech's son Abiathar was the only one who escaped. He ran to David ²¹and told him, "Saul has murdered the LORD's priests at Nob!"

²²David answered, "That day when I saw Doeg, I knew he would tell Saul! Your family died because of me. ²³Stay here. Isn't the same person trying to kill both of us? Don't worry! You'll be safe here with me."

David Rescues the Town of Keilah

23 One day some people told David, "The Philistines keep attacking the town of Keilah and stealing grain from the threshing place."

²David asked the LORD, "Should I attack these Philistines?"

"Yes," the LORD answered. "Attack them and rescue Keilah."

³But David's men said, "Look, even here in Judah we're afraid of the Philistines. We will be terrified if we try to fight them at Keilah!"^j

⁴David asked the LORD about it again. "Leave at once," the LORD answered. "I will give you victory over the Philistines at Keilah."

⁵David and his men went there and fiercely attacked the Philistines. They killed many of them, then led away their cattle, and rescued the people of Keilah.

⁶⁻⁸Meanwhile, Saul heard that David was in Keilah. "God has let me catch David," Saul said. "David is trapped inside a walled town where the gates can be locked." Saul decided to go there and surround the town, in order to trap David and his men. He sent messengers who told the towns and villages, "Send men to serve in Saul's army!"

By this time, Abiathar had joined David in Keilah and had brought along everything he needed to get answers from God.

⁹David heard about Saul's plan to capture him, and he told Abiathar, "Let's ask God what we should do."

^j**23.3** *Keilah:* Keilah was probably not controlled by Israelites at this time.

22.17,18 *Saul shouted . . . 85 priests:* Saul's men were still loyal to God and knew better than to strike his priests. Doeg was not an Israelite and was loyal only to Saul, so he was not afraid to kill the priests.

22.20 *Abiathar:* Abiathar would stay in David's life (23.6-8,9; 30.7). He served as a high priest in Israel until David's son Solomon removed him.

23.1 *stealing grain . . . threshing place:* The Philistines might have wanted the grain for their people, or they may have stolen the grain simply to keep the Israelites hungry and unable to fight.

23.1 *Keilah:* Keilah was just south of Adullam, where David was staying. It probably was not controlled by Israelites at this time.

23.14 *Ziph Desert:* A rocky area south of Hebron near the Southern Desert. (See Map 3 on pg 1881.)

23.16,17 *Jonathan . . . I'll be your highest official:* Jonathan is not jealous of the favor God is showing David, and he wishes to continue to show his loyalty by serving David as a trusted official.

23.23 *clans of Judah:* That is, the family groups that made up the tribe of Judah. Because David was from the tribe of Judah, Saul had good reason to suspect that the people from related clans would help hide David from him. It is not clear why the people of Ziph were willing to help Saul.

23.29 *En-Gedi:* A spring on the western shore of the Dead Sea. It was an important source of fresh water.

¹⁰David prayed, "Lord God of Israel, I was told that Saul is planning to come here. What should I do? Suppose he threatens to destroy the town because of me. ¹¹Would the leaders of Keilah turn me over to Saul? Or is he really coming? Please tell me, Lord."

"Yes, he will come," the Lord answered.

¹²David asked, "Would the leaders of Keilah hand me and my soldiers over to Saul?"

"Yes, they would," the Lord answered.

¹³David and his 600 men got out of there fast and started moving from place to place. Saul heard that David had left Keilah, and he decided not to go after him.

Jonathan Says David Will Be King

¹⁴David stayed in hideouts in the hill country of Ziph Desert. Saul kept searching, but God never let Saul catch him. ¹⁵One time, David was at Horesh in Ziph Desert. He was afraid because[k] Saul had come to the area to kill him. ¹⁶But Jonathan went to see David, and God helped him encourage David. ¹⁷"Don't be afraid," Jonathan said. "My father Saul will never get his hands on you. In fact, you're going to be the next king of Israel, and I'll be your highest official. Even my father knows it's true."

¹⁸They both promised the Lord that they would always be loyal to each other. Then Jonathan went home, but David stayed at Horesh.

David Escapes from Saul

¹⁹Some people from the town of Ziph went to Saul at Gibeah and said, "Your Majesty, David has a hideout not far from us! It's near Horesh, somewhere on Mount Hachilah south of Jeshimon.[l] ²⁰If you come, we will help you catch him."

²¹Saul told them:

You've done me a big favor, and I pray that the Lord will bless you. ²²Now please do just a little more for me. Find out exactly where David is, as well as where he goes, and who has seen him there. I've been told that he's very tricky. ²³Find out where all his hiding places are and come back when you're sure. Then I'll go with you. If he is still in the area, or anywhere among the clans of Judah, I'll find him.

²⁴The people from Ziph went back ahead of Saul, and they found out that David and his men were still south of Jeshimon in the Maon Desert. ²⁵Saul and his army set out to find David. But David heard that Saul was coming, and he went to a place called The Rock, one of his hideouts in Maon Desert.

Saul found out where David was and started closing in on him. ²⁶Saul was going around a hill on one side, and David and his men were on the other side, trying to get away. Saul and his soldiers were just about to capture David and his men, ²⁷when a messenger came to Saul and said, "Come quickly! The Philistines are attacking Israel and taking everything."

²⁸Saul stopped going after David and went back to fight the Philistines. That's why the place is called "Escape Rock." ²⁹David left and went to live in the hideouts at En-Gedi.

David Lets Saul Live

24 When Saul got back from fighting off the Philistines, he heard that

[k]**23.15** *He . . . because:* Or "He saw that." [l]**23.19** *Jeshimon:* A place in the desert near the southern border of Judah.

David was in the desert around En-Gedi. [2]Saul led 3,000 of Israel's best soldiers out to look for David and his men near Wild Goat Rocks at En-Gedi. [3] There were some sheep pens along the side of the road, and one of them was built around the entrance to a cave. Saul went into the cave to relieve himself.

David and his men were hiding at the back of the cave. [4]They whispered to David, "The LORD told you he was going to let you defeat your enemies and do whatever you want with them. This must be the day the LORD was talking about."

David sneaked over and cut off a small piece[m] of Saul's robe, but Saul didn't notice a thing. [5]Afterwards, David was sorry that he had even done that, [6-7]and he told his men, "Stop talking foolishly. We're not going to attack Saul. He's my king, and I pray that the LORD will keep me from doing anything to harm his chosen king."

Saul left the cave and started down the road. [8]Soon, David also got up and left the cave. "Your Majesty!" he shouted from a distance.

Saul turned around to look. David bowed down very low [9]and said:

Your Majesty, why do you listen to people who say that I'm trying to harm you? [10]You can see for yourself that the LORD gave me the chance to catch you in the cave today. Some of my men wanted to kill you, but I wouldn't let them do it. I told them, "I will not harm the LORD's chosen king!" [11]Your Majesty, look at what I'm holding. You can see that it's a piece of your robe. If I could cut off a piece of your robe, I could have killed you. But I let you live, and that should prove I'm not trying to harm you or to

rebel. I haven't done anything to you, and yet you keep trying to ambush and kill me.

[12]I'll let the LORD decide which one of us has done right. I pray that the LORD will punish you for what you're doing to me, but I won't do anything to you. [13]An old proverb says, "Only evil people do evil things," and so I won't harm you.

[14]Why should the king of Israel be out chasing me, anyway? I'm as worthless as a dead dog or a flea. [15]I pray that the LORD will help me escape and show that I am in the right.

[16]"David, my son—is that you?" Saul asked. Then he started crying [17]and said:

David, you're a better person than I am. You treated me with kindness, even though I've been cruel to you. [18]You've told me how you were kind enough not to kill me when the LORD gave you the chance. [19]If you really were my enemy, you wouldn't have let me leave here alive. I pray that the LORD will give you a big reward for what you did today.

[20]I realize now that you will be the next king, and a powerful king at that. [21]Promise me with the LORD as your witness, that you won't wipe out my descendants. Let them live to keep my family name alive.

[22]So David promised, and Saul went home. David and his men returned to their hideout.

Samuel Dies

25 Samuel died, and people from all over Israel gathered to mourn for him when he was buried at his home[n] in

[m]24.4 *small piece*: Hebrew "corner" or "lower hem."   [n]25.1 *at his home*: Hebrew "in his house." Family tombs were sometimes underneath the house or in the courtyard of the home.

● 24.16-20 *David, my son . . . crying . . . you will be the next king*: Saul was David's father-in-law. Moved by David's mercy, Saul finally admitted that David would be the next king (23.17). In spite of this realization, Saul's jealousy would again overtake him.

■ 24.21 *Let them live to keep my family name alive*: Jonathan had earlier asked David for the same favor (20.14, 15). Saul might have been worried that if his family died out, there would be no one left to remember him.

25.7,8 *nothing was ever stolen . . . be kind and share:* When the Philistines and Amalekites attacked walled towns (23.1; 30.1,2), the shepherds out in the fields had nowhere to go for protection and were in danger. David reminded Nabal that he and his men had protected Nabal's shepherds and sheep.

25.13 *"Everybody get your swords":* This might seem like a surprising reaction by David, since he had invited himself to Nabal's celebration. But the rules for hosts and guests were very rigid in the ancient Near East, where many people wandered from place to place. If strangers were not a threat, the host was expected to welcome them as guests. David proved he and his men were not threats to Nabal by reminding him how they protected the shepherds. Nabal's response was an insult, and refusing to let David's group eat with him was like calling them enemies.

Ramah. Meanwhile, David moved his camp
to Paran Desert.[o]

Abigail Keeps David from Killing Innocent People

2-3 Nabal was a very rich man who lived
in Maon. He owned 3,000 sheep and 1,000
goats, which he kept at Carmel.[p] His wife
Abigail was sensible and beautiful, but he
was from the Caleb clan[q] and was rough
and mean.
4 One day, Nabal was in Carmel where his
servants were cutting the wool from his
sheep. David was in the desert when he
heard about it. 5-6 So he sent ten men to
Carmel with this message for Nabal:

I hope that you and your family are
healthy and that all is going well for
you. 7 I've heard that you are cutting
the wool from your sheep.

When your shepherds were with us
in Carmel, we didn't harm them, and
nothing was ever stolen from them.
8 Ask your shepherds, and they'll tell
you the same thing.

My servants are your servants, and
you are like a father to me. This is a day
for celebrating,[r] so please be kind and
share some of your food with us.

9 David's men went to Nabal and gave
him David's message, then they waited for
Nabal's answer.
10 This is what he said:

Who does this David think he is?
That son of Jesse is just one more slave
on the run from his master, and there
are too many of them these days.
11 What makes you think I would take
my bread, my water, and the meat that
I've had cooked for my own servants[s]
and give it to you? Besides, I'm not sure
that David sent you![t]

12 The men returned to their camp and
told David everything Nabal had said.
13 "Everybody get your swords!" David
ordered.
They all strapped on their swords. Two
hundred men stayed behind to guard the
camp, but the other 400 followed David.
14-16 Meanwhile, one of Nabal's servants
told Abigail:

David's men were often nearby while
we were taking care of the sheep in the
fields. They were very good to us, they
never hurt us, and nothing was ever
stolen from us while they were nearby.
With them around day or night, we
were as safe as we would have been inside a walled city.

David sent some messengers from
the desert to wish our master well, but
he shouted insults at them. 17 He's a
bully who won't listen to anyone.

Isn't there something you can do?
Please think of something! Or else our
master and his family and everyone
who works for him are all doomed.

18 Abigail quickly got together 200 loaves
of bread, two large clay jars of wine, the
meat from five sheep, a large sack of roasted
grain, 100 handfuls of raisins, and 200 handfuls of dried figs. She loaded all the food on
donkeys 19 and told her servants, "Take this
on ahead, and I'll catch up with you." She
didn't tell her husband Nabal what she was
doing.
20 Abigail was riding her donkey on the

[o]**25.1** *Paran Desert:* Hebrew; some manuscripts of one ancient translation "Maon Desert." [p]**25.2,3** *Carmel:* About one mile north of Maon in the Southern Desert of Judah. [q]**25.2,3** *from the Caleb clan:* Or "behaved like a dog." [r]**25.8** *celebrating:* Cutting the wool from the sheep was a time for celebrating as well as for working. [s]**25.11** *servants:* Hebrew "shearers," the servants who cut the wool from the sheep. [t]**25.11** *I'm not sure . . . sent you:* Or "I don't know where you come from."

path that led around the hillside, when suddenly she met David and his men heading straight at her.

²¹David had just been saying, "I surely wasted my time guarding Nabal's things in the desert and keeping them from being stolen! I was good to him, and now he pays me back with insults. ²²I swear that by morning, there won't be a man or boy left from his family or his servants' families. I pray that God will punish me[u] if I don't do it!"

²³Abigail quickly got off her donkey and bowed down in front of David. ²⁴Then she said:

Sir, please let me explain! ²⁵Don't pay any attention to that good-for-nothing Nabal. His name means "fool," and it really fits him!

I didn't see the men you sent, ²⁶⁻²⁷but please take this gift of food that I've brought and share it with your followers. The LORD has kept you from taking revenge and from killing innocent people. But I hope your enemies and anyone else who wants to harm you will end up like Nabal. I swear this by the living LORD and by your life.

²⁸Please forgive me if I say a little more. The LORD will always protect you and your family, because you fight for him. I pray that you won't ever do anything evil as long as you live. ²⁹The LORD your God will keep you safe when your enemies try to kill you. But he will snatch away their lives quicker than you can throw a rock from a sling.

³⁰The LORD has promised to do many good things for you, even to make you the ruler of Israel. The LORD will keep his promises to you, ³¹and now your conscience will be clear, because you won't be guilty of taking revenge and killing innocent people.

When the LORD does all those good things for you, please remember me.

³²David told her:

I praise the LORD God of Israel! He must have sent you to meet me today. ³³And you should also be praised. Your good sense kept me from taking revenge and killing innocent people. ³⁴If you hadn't come to meet me so quickly, every man and boy in Nabal's family and in his servants' families would have been killed by morning. I swear by the living LORD God of Israel who protected you that this is the truth.

³⁵David accepted the food Abigail had brought. "Don't worry," he said. "You can go home now. I'll do what you asked."

³⁶Abigail went back home and found Nabal throwing a party fit for a king. He was very drunk and feeling good, so she didn't tell him anything that night. ³⁷But when he sobered up the next morning, Abigail told him everything that had happened. Nabal had a heart attack, and he lay in bed as still as a stone. ³⁸Ten days later, the LORD took his life.

³⁹⁻⁴⁰David heard that Nabal had died. "I praise the LORD!" David said. "He has judged Nabal guilty for insulting me. The LORD kept me from doing anything wrong, and he made sure that Nabal hurt only himself with his own evil."

David and Abigail Are Married

Abigail was still at Carmel. So David sent messengers to ask her if she would marry him.

[u]25.22 me: One ancient translation; Hebrew "my enemies."

25.25 *Nabal . . . fool:* This word play is a good example of how the Bible sometimes uses a person's name to reveal something about that person's character. When Abigail said Nabal was a fool, she meant he did not have any common sense.

25.41 *wash his servants' feet:* At that time, people walked almost everywhere and usually wore sandals. A traveler's feet became extremely tired and dirty after a day of walking on dirt roads and paths. Washing the feet both cleaned and comforted them, and seeing that a guest's feet were washed was an expected part of being a host. Since it was thought to be a lowly task, it was usually done by servants. Servants normally would not be treated to such hospitality, so Abigail was really telling David how deeply she appreciated his decision not to punish Nabal.

25.44 *Michal:* David's first wife. Taking Michal away from David and marrying her to someone else shows how much Saul distrusted and feared David. If Michal had a son by David, that child would have a legitimate claim to the throne. Later, David would demand her return.

26.6 *Ahimelech the Hittite:* This is not Ahimelech the priest (21.1). The Hittites came from what is now Turkey. They conquered much of the ancient Near East between 1600 and 1200 B.C. Some Hittites settled in areas that later belonged to the Israelites. The Hittites who remained by David's time had joined the Israelite community and taken Hebrew names, with "the Hittite" added to the end. **(See Map 1 on pg 1879.)**

26.11 *his spear and his water jar:* David will use these two personal items of Saul's to show that he could have killed the king to make himself king (26.16), just as he used a piece of Saul's robe before (24.11).

41She bowed down and said, "I would willingly be David's slave and wash his servants' feet."

42Abigail quickly got ready and went back with David's messengers. She rode on her donkey, while five of her servant women walked alongside. She and David were married as soon as she arrived.

43David had earlier married Ahinoam from the town of Jezreel, so both she and Abigail were now David's wives.[v] **44**Meanwhile, Saul had arranged for Michal[w] to marry Palti the son of Laish, who came from the town of Gallim.

David Again Lets Saul Live

26 Once again,[x] some people from Ziph went to Gibeah to talk with Saul. "David has a hideout on Mount Hachilah near Jeshimon out in the desert," they told him.

2Saul took 3,000 of Israel's best soldiers and went to look for David there in Ziph Desert. **3**Saul set up camp on Mount Hachilah, which is across the road from Jeshimon. But David was hiding out in the desert.

When David heard that Saul was following him, **4**he sent some spies to find out if it was true. **5**Then he sneaked up to Saul's camp. He noticed that Saul and his army commander Abner the son of Ner were sleeping in the middle of the camp, with soldiers sleeping all around them. **6**David asked Ahimelech the Hittite and Joab's brother Abishai,[y] "Which one of you will go with me into Saul's camp?"

"I will!" Abishai answered.

7That same night, David and Abishai crept into the camp. Saul was sleeping, and his spear was stuck in the ground not far from his head. Abner and the soldiers were sound asleep all around him.

8Abishai whispered, "This time God has let you get your hands on your enemy! I'll pin him to the ground with one thrust of his own spear."

9"Don't kill him!" David whispered back. "The Lord will punish anyone who kills his chosen king. **10**As surely as the Lord lives, the Lord will kill Saul, or Saul will die a natural death or be killed in battle. **11**But I pray that the Lord will keep me from harming his chosen king. Let's grab his spear and his water jar and get out of here!"

12David took the spear and the water jar, then left the camp. None of Saul's soldiers knew what had happened or even woke up—the Lord had made all of them fall sound asleep. **13**David and Abishai crossed the valley and went to the top of the next hill, where they were at a safe distance. **14**"Abner!" David shouted toward Saul's army. "Can you hear me?"

Abner shouted back. "Who dares disturb the king?"

15"Abner, what kind of a man are you?" David replied. "Aren't you supposed to be the best soldier in Israel? Then why didn't you protect your king? Anyone who went into your camp could have killed him tonight.[z] **16**You're a complete failure! I swear by the living Lord that you and your men deserve to die for not protecting the Lord's chosen king. Look and see if you can find the king's spear and the water jar that were near his head."

17Saul could tell it was David's voice,

[v]**25.43** *wives:* Having more than one wife was allowed in those times. [w]**25.44** *Michal:* David's first wife (see 18.20—19.17). [x]**26.1** *again:* See 23.19. [y]**26.6** *Abishai:* Hebrew "Abishai the son of Zeruiah." Zeruiah was David's older sister, so Abishai and Joab were David's nephews (see 1 Chronicles 2.12-17; 2 Samuel 17.25 and the note there). [z]**26.15** *Anyone . . . tonight:* Or "Someone went into your camp to kill him tonight."

and he called out, "David, my son! Is that you?"

"Yes it is, Your Majesty. [18]Why are you hunting me down? Have I done something wrong, or have I committed a crime? [19]Please listen to what I have to say. If the LORD has turned you against me, maybe a sacrifice will make him change his mind. But if some people have turned you against me, I hope the LORD will punish them! They have forced me to leave the land that belongs to the LORD and have told me to worship foreign gods.[a] [20]Don't let me die in a land far away from the LORD. I'm no more important than a flea! Why should the king of Israel hunt me down as if I were a bird in the mountains?"

[21]"David, you had the chance to kill me today. But you didn't. I was very wrong about you. It was a terrible mistake for me to try to kill you. I've acted like a fool, but I'll never try to harm you again. You're like a son to me, so please come back."

[22]"Your Majesty, here's your spear! Let one of your soldiers come and get it. [23]The LORD put you in my power today, but you are his chosen king and I wouldn't harm you. The LORD rewards people who are faithful and live right. [24]I spared your life today, and I pray that the LORD will spare my life and keep me safe."

[25]"David, my son, I pray that the Lord will bless you and make you successful!"

David in Philistia

27 Saul went back home. David also left, [1]but he thought to himself, "One of these days, Saul is going to kill me.

The only way to escape from him is to go to Philistia. Then I'll be outside of Israel, and Saul will give up trying to catch me."

[2-3]David and his 600 men went across the border to stay in Gath with King Achish the son of Maoch. His men brought their families with them. David brought his wife Ahinoam whose hometown was Jezreel, and he also brought his wife Abigail who had been married to Nabal from Carmel. [4]When Saul found out that David had run off to Gath, he stopped trying to catch him.

[5]One day, David was talking with Achish and said, "If you are happy with me, then let me live in one of the towns in the countryside. I'm not important enough to live here with you in the royal city."

[6]Achish gave David the town of Ziklag that same day, and Ziklag has belonged to the kings of Judah ever since.

[7]David was in Philistia for a year and four months. [8]The Geshurites, the Girzites, and the Amalekites lived in the area from Telam to Shur[b] and on as far as Egypt, and David often attacked their towns. [9]Whenever David and his men attacked a town, they took the sheep, cattle, donkeys, camels, and the clothing, and killed everyone who lived there.

After he returned from a raid, David always went to see Achish, [10]who would ask, "Where did you attack today?"[c]

David would answer, "Oh, we attacked some desert town that belonged to the Judah tribe." Sometimes David would say, "Oh, we attacked a town in the desert where the Jerahmeel clan lives" or "We attacked a town in the desert where the Kenites[d] live." [11]That's why David killed

---

[a]26.19 *gods*: In ancient times it was often believed that gods (even the God of Israel) could only be properly worshiped in their own countries, and only a country's gods should be worshiped in that country.   [b]27.8 *lived . . . Shur*: One ancient translation; Hebrew "had lived for a long time in Shur."   [c]27.10 *Where . . . today*: A few Hebrew manuscripts, the Dead Sea Scrolls, and three ancient translations; most Hebrew manuscripts "Didn't you make a raid today?"   [d]27.10 *Jerahmeel . . . Kenites*: These were clans of the Judah tribe.

● 27.1 *Philistia*: Saul probably did not have the military strength to risk going after David in Philistia. The Philistines were one of Israel's traditional enemies. It is ironic that David, who would one day be Israel's greatest king, should turn to them for protection.

● 27.6 *Ziklag*: The exact location is unknown. Many scholars believe it was near the Philistine border, about ten miles northeast of Beersheba in southern Judah. There is some question whether the Philistines ever controlled Ziklag. (See Map 4 on pg 1882.)

● 27.8,9 *David often attacked . . . killed everyone*: David wanted Achish to think he was raiding Israelite towns when he was really attacking towns belonging to Israel's enemies. David completely destroyed the towns he attacked, leaving no witnesses to let Achish know what he was really doing (27.11).

CR   Israel

28.4 *Shunem . . . Gilboa:* Gilboa was close to Mount Gilboa, and Shunem was about ten miles north of Gilboa. The armies faced each other across the Jezreel Valley. **(See Map 3 on pg 1881.)**

28.6,7 *in a dream or by a priest or by a prophet . . . I'll go to her:* Dreams or visions, priests, and prophets were ways in which God spoke to people and kings. None of these have worked for Saul, so he decided to break God's Law and ask someone to talk to the dead to try to find out what God wanted him to do.

everyone in the towns he attacked. He thought, "If I let any of them live, they might come to Gath and tell what I've really been doing."

David made these raids all the time he was in Philistia. [12]But Achish trusted David and thought, "David's people must be furious with him. From now on he will have to take orders from me."

Saul Asks To Talk with Samuel's Ghost

28 [1-3] Samuel had died some time earlier,[e] and people from all over Israel had attended his funeral in his hometown of Ramah.

Meanwhile, Saul had been trying to get rid of everyone who spoke with the spirits of the dead.[f] But one day the Philistines brought their soldiers together to attack Israel.

Achish told David, "Of course, you know that you and your men must fight as part of our Philistine army."

David answered, "That will give you a chance to see for yourself just how well we can fight!"

"In that case," Achish said, "you and your men will always be my bodyguards."

[4]The Philistines went to Shunem and set up camp. Saul called the army of Israel together, and they set up their camp in Gilboa. [5]Saul took one look at the Philistine army and started shaking with fear. [6]So he asked the LORD what to do. But the LORD would not answer, either in a dream or by a priest or a prophet. [7]Then Saul told his officers, "Find me a woman who can talk to the spirits of the dead. I'll go to her and find out what's going to happen."

His servants told him, "There's a woman at Endor who can talk to spirits of the dead."

[8]That night, Saul put on different clothing so nobody would recognize him. Then he and two of his men went to the woman, and asked, "Will you bring up the ghost of someone for us?"

[9]The woman said, "Why are you trying to trick me and get me killed? You know King Saul has killed everyone who talks to the spirits of the dead!"

[10]Saul replied, "I swear by the living LORD that nothing will happen to you because of this."

[11]"Who do you want me to bring up?" she asked.

"Bring up the ghost of Samuel," he answered.

[12]When the woman saw Samuel, she screamed. Then she turned to Saul and said, "You've tricked me! You're the king!"

[13]"Don't be afraid," Saul replied. "Just tell me what you see."

She answered, "I see a spirit rising up out of the ground."

[14]"What does it look like?"

"It looks like an old man wearing a robe."

Saul knew it was Samuel, so he bowed down low.

[15]"Why are you bothering me by bringing me up like this?" Samuel asked.

"I'm terribly worried," Saul answered. "The Philistines are about to attack me. God has turned his back on me and won't answer any more by prophets or by dreams. What should I do?"

[16]Samuel said:

If the LORD has turned away from you and is now your enemy, don't ask me what to do. [17]I've already told you:

[e]**28.1-3** *earlier:* See 25.1.   [f]**28.1-3** *dead:* Many people believed that it was possible to talk to spirits of the dead, and that these spirits could tell the future.

The LORD has sworn to take the kingdom from you and give it to David. And that's just what he's doing! ¹⁸When the LORD was angry with the Amalekites, he told you to destroy them, but you didn't do it. That's why the LORD is doing this to you. ¹⁹Tomorrow the LORD will let the Philistines defeat Israel's army, then you and your sons will join me down here in the world of the dead.

²⁰At once, Saul collapsed and lay stretched out on the floor, terrified at what Samuel had said. He was weak because he had not eaten anything since the day before.

²¹The woman came over to Saul, and when she saw that he was completely terrified, she said, "Your Majesty, I listened to you and risked my life to do what you asked. ²²Now please listen to me. Let me get you a little something to eat. It will give you strength for your walk back to camp."

²³"No, I won't eat!"

But his officers and the woman kept on urging Saul, until he finally agreed. He got up off the floor and sat on the bed. ²⁴At once the woman killed a calf that she had been fattening up. She cooked part of the meat and baked some thin bread.^g ²⁵Then she served the food to Saul and his officers, who ate and left before daylight.

The Philistines Send David Back

29 The Philistines had brought their whole army to Aphek,^h while Israel's army was camping near Jezreel Spring. ²⁻³The Philistine rulers and their troops were marching past the Philistine army commanders in groups of 100 and 1,000. When David and his men marched by at the end with Achish, the commanders said, "What are these worthless Israelites doing here?"

"They are David's men," Achish answered. "David used to be one of Saul's officers, but he left Saul and joined my army a long time ago. I've never had even one complaint about him."

⁴The Philistine army commanders were angry and shouted:

Send David back to the town you gave him. We won't have him going into the battle with us. He could turn and fight against us! Saul would take David back as an officer if David brought him the heads of our soldiers. ⁵The Israelites even dance and sing,

"Saul has killed
   a thousand enemies;
David has killed
   ten thousand!"

⁶Achish called David over and said:

I swear by the living LORD that you've been honest with me, and I want you to fight by my side. I don't think you've done anything wrong from the day you joined me until this very moment. But the other Philistine rulers don't want you to come along. ⁷Go on back home and try not to upset them.

⁸"But what have I done?" David asked. "Do you know of anything I've ever done that would keep me from fighting the enemies of my king?"ⁱ

⁹Achish said:

I believe that you're as good as an angel of God, but our army commanders

^g28.24 *thin bread*: Bread made without yeast, since there was no time for the bread to rise.
^h29.1 *Aphek*: The events of chapter 29 probably took place as the Philistine army was on its way to Shunem, which they reached in 28.4. ⁱ29.8 *my king*: David may be referring to either Saul or Achish.

29.8 *my king*: These words could refer to either Achish or King Saul. David was probably being unclear on purpose, so that Achish would believe David was being loyal to him.

30.1 *Ziklag:* This would have been an 80-mile march over rough land.

30.2-4 *taken away the women and children . . . too weak to cry any more:* The women and children most likely were to be sold into slavery. Loud, long crying was a normal way to express grief in this part of the world. Grieving this way can be emotionally and physically tiring, and the men were already exhausted from their difficult trip home.

30.6 *stoning David to death:* Dropping or piling heavy stones on a person until they died was a common form of capital punishment. Adultery, blasphemy, infant sacrifice, worshiping idols, failure to observe the Sabbath, witchcraft, and treason were among the crimes that were sometimes punished by stoning. David's men may have felt he had betrayed them by leaving the women and children without protection.

have decided that you can't fight in this battle. [10] You and your troops will have to go back to the town I gave you.[j] Get up and leave tomorrow morning as soon as it's light. I'm pleased with you, so don't let any of this bother you.[k]

[11] David and his men got up early in the morning and headed back toward Philistia, while the Philistines left for Jezreel.

David Rescues His Soldiers' Families

30 It took David and his men three days to reach Ziklag. But while they had been away, the Amalekites had been raiding in the desert around there. They had attacked Ziklag, burned it to the ground, [2] and had taken away the women and children. [3] When David and his men came to Ziklag, they saw the burned-out ruins and learned that their families had been taken captive. [4] They started crying and kept it up until they were too weak to cry any more. [5] David's two wives, Ahinoam and Abigail, had been taken captive with everyone else.

[6] David was desperate. His soldiers were so upset over what had happened to their sons and daughters that they were thinking about stoning David to death. But he felt the Lord God giving him strength, [7] and he said to the priest, "Abiathar, let's ask God what to do."

Abiathar brought everything he needed to get answers from God, and he went over to David. [8] Then David asked the Lord, "Should I go after the people who raided our town? Can I catch up with them?"

"Go after them," the Lord answered. "You will catch up with them, and you will rescue your families."

[9-10] David led his 600 men to Besor Gorge, but 200 of them were too tired to go across. So they stayed behind, while David and the other 400 men crossed the gorge.

[11] Some of David's men found an Egyptian out in a field and took him to David. They gave the Egyptian some bread, and he ate it. Then they gave him a drink of water, [12] some dried figs, and two handfuls of raisins. This was the first time in three days he had tasted food or water. Now he felt much better.

[13] "Who is your master?" David asked. "And where do you come from?"

"I'm from Egypt," the young man answered. "I'm the servant of an Amalekite, but he left me here three days ago because I was sick. [14] We had attacked some towns in the desert where the Cherethites live, in the area that belongs to Judah, and in the desert where the Caleb clan lives. And we burned down Ziklag."

[15] "Will you take me to those Amalekites?" David asked.

"Yes, I will, if you promise with God as a witness that you won't kill me or hand me over to my master."

[16] He led David to the Amalekites. They were eating and drinking everywhere, celebrating because of what they had taken from Philistia and Judah. [17] David attacked just before sunrise the next day and fought until sunset.[l] Four hundred Amalekites rode away on camels, but they were the only ones who escaped.

[18] David rescued his two wives and everyone else the Amalekites had taken from

Ziklag. [19]No one was missing—young or old, sons or daughters. David brought back everything that had been stolen, [20]including their livestock.

David also took the sheep and cattle that the Amalekites had with them, but he kept these separate from the others. Everyone agreed that these would be David's reward.

[21]On the way back, David went to the 200 men he had left at Besor Gorge, because they had been too tired to keep up with him. They came toward David and the people who were with him. When David was close enough, he greeted the 200 men and asked how they were doing.

[22]Some of David's men were good-for-nothings, and they said, "Those men didn't go with us to the battle, so they don't get any of the things we took back from the Amalekites. Let them take their wives and children and go!"

[23]But David said:

My friends, don't be so greedy with what the LORD has given us! The LORD protected us and gave us victory over the people who attacked. [24]Who would pay attention to you, anyway? Soldiers who stay behind to guard the camp get as much as those who go into battle.

[25]David made this a law for Israel, and it has been the same ever since.

[26]David went back to Ziklag with everything they had taken from the Amalekites. He sent some of these things as gifts to his friends who were leaders of Judah, and he told them, "We took these things from the LORD's enemies. Please accept them as a gift."

[27-31]This is a list of the towns where David sent gifts: Bethel,[m] Ramoth in the Southern Desert, Jattir, Aroer, Siphmoth, Eshtemoa, Racal, the towns belonging to the Jerahmeelites and the Kenites, Hormah, Bor-Ashan, Athach, and Hebron. He also sent gifts to the other towns where he and his men had traveled.

Saul and His Sons Die

31 Meanwhile, the Philistines were fighting Israel at Mount Gilboa. Israel's soldiers ran from the Philistines, and many of them were killed. [2]The Philistines closed in on Saul and his sons, and they killed his sons Jonathan, Abinadab, and Malchishua. [3]The fighting was fierce around Saul, and he was badly wounded by enemy arrows.

[4]Saul told the soldier who carried his weapons, "Kill me with your sword! I don't want these worthless Philistines to torture and make fun of me." But the soldier was afraid to kill him.

Saul then took out his own sword; he stuck the blade into his stomach, and fell on it. [5]When the soldier knew that Saul was dead, he killed himself in the same way.

[6]Saul was dead, his three sons were dead, and the soldier who carried his weapons was dead. They and all his soldiers died on that same day. [7]The Israelites on the other side of Jezreel Valley[n] and the other side of the Jordan learned that Saul and his sons were dead. They saw that the Israelite army had run away. So they ran away too, and the Philistines moved into the towns the Israelites had left behind.

[8]The day after the battle, when the Philistines returned to the battlefield to take the weapons of the dead Israelite soldiers, they found Saul and his three sons lying dead on Mount Gilboa. [9-10]The Philistines cut off Saul's head and pulled off

[m]30.27-31 *Bethel:* Or "Bethuel" (see Joshua 19.4).   [n]31.7 *Jezreel Valley:* Hebrew "valley." Shunem (see 28.4) and Gilboa (see verse 1) were across the Jezreel Valley from each other.

■ 30.23 *what the LORD has given us:* David reminded his men that the victory was the LORD's. Since even those who guarded the camp were serving the LORD, everyone should have a share in what had been taken from the Amalekites.

● 30.27-31 *the towns where David sent gifts . . . his men had traveled:* David probably hoped to win their favor and support by sharing the stolen goods that were taken back from the Amalekites. But since some of these things had been stolen from Judah, David could also have been returning things to their owners. Hebron was the most important of those towns. David made Hebron his capital when he became king of Judah. (See Map 3 on pg 1881.)

■ 31.3-5 *badly wounded . . . stuck the blade into his stomach . . . killed himself:* Saul was supposed to be the one who would rescue Israel from the Philistines (9.16). But in the final example of his failure, he died fighting them. Saul killed himself to avoid being humiliated and abused like Samson had been. It was common in the ancient world for a military leader's servant to kill himself when his master died in battle. David's reaction in similar situations was to gather strength from God (23.16; 30.6), but this was something Saul could no longer do. Suicide is extremely rare in the Bible. It is mentioned only three other times, and only in connection with the most serious betrayal or blatant disobedience of the LORD.

David said: "My friends, don't be so greedy with what the LORD has given us! The LORD protected us and gave us victory over the people who attacked." 1 SAM 30.23

31.11-13 *The people who lived in Jabesh . . . to show their sorrow:* One of the first things Saul had done as king was to rescue the people of Jabesh (11.1-13). They had not forgotten, and they showed their gratitude by bringing the bodies of Saul and his sons to Jabesh, in spite of the danger. David later moved the bones to Saul's family burial place in Benjamin (2 Sam 21.11-14).

his armor. Then they put his armor in the temple of the goddess Astarte, and they nailed his body to the city wall of Beth-Shan. They also sent messengers everywhere in Philistia to spread the good news in the temples of their idols and among their people.

¹¹The people who lived in Jabesh in Gilead heard what the Philistines had done to Saul's body. ¹²So one night, some brave men from Jabesh went to Beth-Shan. They took down the bodies of Saul and his sons, then brought them back to Jabesh and burned them. ¹³They buried the bones under a small tree in Jabesh, and for seven days, they went without eating to show their sorrow.

Reflection Questions About 1 Samuel 1.1—31.13

1. Samuel was an important figure in Israel's history, but most of the first two chapters tell his mother Hannah's story. Why do you think that is?

2. What were Eli's strengths and weaknesses as a priest and as a father? How did these affect the Israelites (1.1—2.35)?

3. The Philistines became afraid when they heard the sacred chest was in the Israelites' camp. If they were afraid, why do you think they captured it (4.6-11)? Why did they return it (5.1-13)? What was the importance of the sacred chest to the Israelites?

4. The behavior of Eli's sons led to his replacement as a leader (2.12-17,22-25; 3.11-18). By contrast, how did the behavior of Samuel's sons affect Samuel's leadership (8.1-5)?

5. The Israelites wanted to be like other nations and be led by a king (8.5,19,20). What reasons did they give? Why was it hard for them to trust in God alone (12.19,20)?

6. Saul offered a sacrifice to the LORD instead of waiting for Samuel (13.7-15). What did that say about Saul's character? How did Saul react to Samuel's angry response?

7. God told Samuel, "People judge others by what they look like, but I judge people by what is in their hearts" (16.7). According to 1 SAMUEL what was in David's heart that prepared him to be the future king (16.18)?

8. Describe in your own words the role David and Jonathan's friendship played in the up-and-down relationship of King Saul and David (18.1-4; 19.1-8; 20.1-42; and 23.14-18).

9. Jonathan put loyalty to David, the future king, above loyalty to his own father, the ruling king. Why do you think Jonathan acted in this way? What does loyalty mean to you? When is it justified? When is it misplaced?

10. What do you think were David's best qualities as a leader? What were his worst qualities? Describe the qualities you look for in a leader.

2 samuel

David is remembered as Israel's most powerful king and as a human being who made some terrible mistakes. Read about his struggles and see how one man's relationship with God affects the fate of the nation he rules.

WHAT MAKES 2 SAMUEL SPECIAL?

Some of the best stories about people in the Jewish Scriptures (Old Testament) are in 1 and 2 SAMUEL. In 2 SAMUEL the story of David, begun in the second half of 1 SAMUEL, is continued. It tells of David's triumphs and failures and shows how important one person's relationship with God is in shaping his life and the life of the nation he rules.

The second half of one long book that was split into two, 2 SAMUEL continues the story of Israel's first kings. FIRST SAMUEL ended with the death of King Saul. SECOND SAMUEL picks up with David's reign, from about 1010 to 970 B.C. The first dramatic section tells how David became king of Judah, then king of all Israel, in a series of military victories and with an extraordinary promise from God. Troubles followed his triumphs: David's life unraveled when he sinned with Bathsheba, arranged a murder, and watched his family come apart.

WHAT'S THE STORY BEHIND THE SCENE?

Instead of writing only about David's strengths, the author also needed to show David's weaknesses. JOSHUA, JUDGES, 1 and 2 SAMUEL, and 1 and 2 KINGS contain lessons for Israel that were brought together late in the seventh century B.C. They repeatedly describe what happens when individuals or groups of people don't live up to their agreements with God. Key to understanding 2 SAMUEL is the agreement God made with David (7.16). God promised David that one of his descendants would always be king. This promise led the people of Israel to expect a *messiah*, or "chosen one." Later, when

David's line was interrupted by the capture of Jerusalem (2 Kgs 25.7), people wondered how God would continue to keep the promise he made to David. In later generations, several of Israel's prophets would speak of a new king descended from David (Jer 33.15; Dan 9.25). In New Testament times Jesus' early apostles understood Jesus to be this new king (Acts 2.30; Rom 1.3,4).

HOW IS 2 SAMUEL CONSTRUCTED?

SECOND SAMUEL can be divided into two major sections—one for David's triumphs and one for his troubles. Added to these is a third section of other stories about David.

David's triumphs (1.1—10.19)
   David mourns for Saul and Jonathan (1.1-27)
   Israel's two kings (2.1—4.12)
   David unites all of Israel (5.1—6.23)
   God's promise to David (7.1-29)
   David defeats Israel's enemies (8.1—10.19)
David's troubles (11.1—20.26)
   David sins and suffers because of it (11.1—12.31)
   Violence tears David's family apart (13.1—14.33)
   Absalom challenges his father (15.1—19.43)
   Sheba's rebellion (20.1-26)
Other stories about David (21.1—24.25)
   A famine in Israel (21.1-14)
   Other victories (21.15-22)
   David's songs (22.1—23.7)
   David's warriors (23.8-39)
   David's sin brings an angel of destruction (24.1-25)

Second Samuel continues the story of David begun in 1 Samuel. It describes David's reign from about 1010 to 970 B.C. It shows both David's brilliant successes and his failures in a way intended to encourage and warn all who read his story. After being chosen by God, David experiences a series of military victories and becomes king of all Israel. He makes Jerusalem the capital of his kingdom, builds a palace there, and has the sacred chest brought there. The Lord gives David's kingdom a period of peace and promises him that one of his descendants would always be king. Yet troubles follow when David sins against the Lord by committing adultery with the wife of one of his trusted soldiers and arranging to have him murdered in order to cover up his sin. David's sin angers the Lord. As a result, David's family is torn apart by violence and rebellion. The final section of 2 Samuel contains a collection of stories about David—some favorable, others not—showing the strength that comes from trusting in the Lord and the troubles that result from disobedience.

Outline

David Finds Out about Saul's Death

1 Saul was dead.

Meanwhile, David had defeated the Amalekites and returned to Ziklag. [2]Three days later, a soldier came from Saul's army. His clothes were torn, and dirt was on his head.[a] He went to David and knelt down in front of him.

[3]David asked, "Where did you come from?"

The man answered, "From Israel's army. I barely escaped with my life."

[4]"Who won the battle?" David asked.

The man said, "Our army turned and ran, but many were wounded and died. Even King Saul and his son Jonathan are dead."

[5]David asked, "How do you know Saul and Jonathan are dead?"

[6] The young man replied:

I was on Mount Gilboa and saw King Saul leaning on his spear. The enemy's war chariots and cavalry were closing in on him. [7]When he turned around and saw me, he called me over. I went and asked what he wanted.

[8]Saul asked me, "Who are you?"

"An Amalekite," I answered.

[9]Then he said, "Kill me! I'm dying, and I'm in terrible pain."[b]

[10]So I killed him. I knew he was too badly wounded to live much longer. Then I took his crown and his armband, and I brought them to you, Your Majesty. Here they are.

[11]At once, David and his soldiers tore their clothes in sorrow. [12]They cried all day long and would not eat anything. Everyone was sad because Saul, his son Jonathan, and many of the LORD's people had been killed in the battle.

[13]David asked the young man, "Where is your home?"

The man replied, "My father is an Amalekite, but we live in Israel."

[a]**1.2** *His clothes . . . his head:* People tore their clothes and put dirt on their heads to show they were sad because someone had died.   [b]**1.9** *in terrible pain:* Or "very weak."

● **1.1** *Saul . . . David . . . Amalekites:* Saul was Israel's first king and ruled from about 1030 to 1010 B.C. David was king from about 1010 to 970 B.C. After Saul disobeyed God, God chose David to replace Saul. David had to wait over seven years to become king of all Israel, because Saul's family challenged David's right to rule. But in the end, David prevailed and God promised him that one of his descendants would always be king. The Amalekites were wandering tribes who lived mostly south and west of the Dead Sea. They were enemies of Israel that both Saul and David had fought. Even before the Israelites had settled in Canaan they had conflicts with the Amalekites.

꩜ David

● **1.1** *Ziklag:* King Achish of Philistia gave this town in Judah to David when Saul was chasing after David (1 Sam 27.5,6). Many scholars believe it was located close to the border of the Philistine territory, about ten miles northeast of Beersheba. **(See Map 4 on pg 1882.)**

● **1.9-16** *Then he said . . . kill this man:* 1 SAMUEL reports that Saul killed himself (1 Sam 31.1-13). Since Saul was David's enemy, the Amalekite may have hoped David would reward him if he said he killed Saul. But David was outraged that anyone would dare to kill God's chosen king (1 Sam 24.6,7; 26.9,23).

1.17-27 *David sang . . . weapons are destroyed:* David created many songs, which are included in Psalms. "The Song of the Bow" (1.19-27) is one of the earliest known pieces of Hebrew literature. David showed his own sadness as well as Israel's when he sang in memory of Saul and Jonathan.

1.21 *Don't let dew . . . offerings for God:* David cursed the place where Saul and Jonathan died. The Israelites believed the spoken word had a life and power of its own. Once spoken, a curse could not be taken back.

1.24 *Women of Israel, cry for Saul:* Women were often the ones who began the formal mourning in a community, just as they were usually the first to celebrate victories (verse 20).

LORD (YHWH)

2.1,2 *Judah . . . Hebron:* Before Saul became king, the Israelites were a loose collection of tribes. Each tribe had its own area. Hebron was the most important city in the area claimed by Judah and would be David's capital while he was king of Judah. It has been continuously occupied since 3300 B.C., making it one of the oldest cities in the world. **(See Maps 3 and 4 on pgs 1881 and 1882.)**

Israel

2.2 *Ahinoam . . . Abigail . . . Nabal:* At this time, men were allowed to have more than one wife. Ahinoam was David's second wife. Abigail was David's third wife and the mother of his second son, Chileab. Nabal was a rich sheep owner from Maon in southern Judah.

14-16 David said to him, "Why weren't you afraid to kill the LORD's chosen king? And you even told what you did. It's your own fault that you're going to die!"

Then David told one of his soldiers, "Come here and kill this man!"

David Sings in Memory of Saul

17David sang a song in memory of Saul and Jonathan, **18**and he ordered his men to teach the song to everyone in Judah. He called it "The Song of the Bow," and it can be found in *The Book of Jashar.*[c] This is the song:

19Israel, your famous hero
   lies dead on the hills,
and your mighty warriors
   have fallen!
20Don't tell it in Gath
   or spread the news
      on the streets of Ashkelon.
The godless Philistine women
will be happy
   and jump for joy.
21Don't let dew or rain fall
   on the hills of Gilboa.
Don't let its fields
   grow offerings for God.[d]
There the warriors' shields
   were smeared with mud,
and Saul's own shield
   was left unpolished.[e]

22The arrows of Jonathan struck,
   and warriors died.
The sword of Saul cut
   the enemy apart.

23It was easy to love Saul
   and Jonathan.

Together in life,
   together in death,
they were faster than eagles
   and stronger than lions.

24Women of Israel, cry for Saul.
He brought you fine red cloth
   and jewelry made of gold.
25Our warriors have fallen
   in the heat of battle,
and Jonathan lies dead
   on the hills of Gilboa.

26Jonathan, I miss you most!
I loved you
   like a brother.
You were truly loyal to me,
more faithful than a wife
   to her husband.[f]

27Our warriors have fallen,
   and their weapons[g]
      are destroyed.

David Becomes King of Judah

2 Later, David asked the LORD, "Should I go back to one of the towns of Judah?"
The LORD answered, "Yes."

David asked, "Which town should I go to?"

"Go to Hebron," the LORD replied.

2 David went to Hebron with his two wives, Ahinoam and Abigail. Ahinoam was from Jezreel, and Abigail was the widow of Nabal from Carmel. **3**David also told his men and their families to come and live in the villages near Hebron.

4 The people of Judah met with David at Hebron and poured olive oil on his head to

---

[c]**1.18** *The Book of Jashar:* This book may have been a collection of ancient war songs.   [d]**1.21** *Don't let its fields . . . for God:* One possible meaning for the difficult Hebrew text.   [e]**1.21** *unpolished:* Some shields were made of leather and were polished with olive oil.   [f]**1.26** *You . . . husband:* Or "You loved me more than a wife could possibly love her husband."   [g]**1.27** *weapons:* This may refer to Saul and Jonathan.

show that he was their new king. Then they told David, "The people from Jabesh in Gilead buried Saul."

⁵David sent messengers to tell them:

The Lord bless you! You were kind enough to bury Saul your ruler, ⁶and I pray that the Lord will be kind and faithful to you. I will be your friend because of what you have done. ⁷Saul is dead, but the tribe of Judah has made me their king. So be strong and have courage.

Ishbosheth Becomes King of Israel

⁸Abner the son of Ner[h] had been the general of Saul's army. He took Saul's son Ishbosheth[i] across the Jordan River to Mahanaim ⁹and made him king of Israel,[j] including the areas of Gilead, Asher,[k] Jezreel, Ephraim, and Benjamin. ¹⁰Ishbosheth was 40 years old at the time, and he ruled for two years. But the tribe of Judah made David their king, ¹¹and he ruled from Hebron for seven and a half years.

The War between David and Ishbosheth

¹²One day, Abner and the soldiers of Ishbosheth[l] left Mahanaim and went to Gibeon. ¹³Meanwhile, Joab the son of Zeruiah[m] was leading David's soldiers, and the two groups met at the pool in Gibeon.[n] Abner and his men sat down on one side of the pool, while Joab and his men sat on the other side. ¹⁴Abner yelled to Joab, "Let's get some of our best soldiers to stand up and fight each other!"

Joab agreed, ¹⁵and twelve of Ishbosheth's men from the tribe of Benjamin got up to fight twelve of David's men. ¹⁶They grabbed each other by the hair and stabbed each other in the side with their daggers. They all died right there! That's why the place in Gibeon is called "Field of Daggers."[o] ¹⁷Then everyone started fighting. Both sides fought very hard, but David's soldiers defeated Abner and the soldiers of Israel.

¹⁸Zeruiah's three sons were there: Joab, Abishai, and Asahel. Asahel could run as fast as a deer in an open field, ¹⁹and he ran straight after Abner, without looking to the right or to the left.

²⁰When Abner turned and saw him, he said, "Is that you, Asahel?"

Asahel answered, "Yes it is."

²¹Abner said, "There are soldiers all around. Stop chasing me and fight one of them! Kill him and take his clothes and weapons for yourself."

But Asahel refused to stop.

²²Abner said, "If you don't turn back, I'll have to kill you! Then I could never face your brother Joab again."

[h]2.8 son of Ner: Abner was Saul's cousin (see 1 Samuel 14.50). [i]2.8 Ishbosheth: One ancient translation has "Ishbaal" (see also 1 Chronicles 8.33). In Hebrew "baal" means "lord" and was used as the name of a Canaanite god. The people of Israel often changed "baal" to "bosheth" (which means "shame") in personal names. Ishbosheth was probably called Ishvi or Ishyo in 1 Samuel 14.49. [j]2.9 Israel: Sometimes "Israel" means the northern tribes and does not include the tribes of Judah and Simeon. That is how it is used in this verse. [k]2.9 Asher: The Hebrew text has "Ashur," which is the Hebrew name for the Assyrians. It may be another spelling for Asher (one of the tribes of Israel) or it may refer to Geshur (a small area between Gilead and Jezreel, east of Lake Galilee). [l]2.12 Ishbosheth: See the note at 2.8. [m]2.13 the son of Zeruiah: Zeruiah was David's older sister, so Joab was David's nephew (see 1 Chronicles 2.12-17 and the note at 2 Samuel 17.25). [n]2.13 pool in Gibeon: This pool was located just inside the city wall and was used for storing water. It was in the shape of a circle and was 36 feet wide and 36 feet deep. [o]2.16 Field of Daggers: Or "Field of Opponents" or "Battlefield."

● 2.8 son of Ner: Saul's cousin and faithful general. Abner was the real power behind the throne, since he proclaimed Ishbosheth as king.

● 2.8 Mahanaim: This was in the territory of Gad near where the Jabbok River flows into the Jordan. (See Map 3 on pg 1881.)

● 2.10,11 Ishbosheth was 40 . . . seven and a half years: The numbers for Ishbosheth's age and how long he ruled are puzzling. He apparently did not fight at the battle at Gilboa, which could mean he was too young to fight. But if he was too young, he could not have been 40 when he became king. David and Ishbosheth both became kings after Saul died. That means that Ishbosheth and David would have ruled separately for about the same length of time, around seven and a half years. David ruled in Hebron for seven and a half years, but some of that time might have been as king of all Israel.

● 2.13 Joab the son of Zeruiah: Joab was David's nephew, since Zeruiah was David's older sister. Joab became an important military leader for David, but Joab's brutality stood out against David's gentleness.

2.28 *trumpet:* Probably a *Shofar*, or ram's horn. Shofars can make several different sounds and were used to signal events, danger, or the death of important people (Judg 3.27,28; Neh 4.18-20). The shofar is still used today in Jewish meeting places (synagogues) for celebrating important holidays.

3.7 *wife:* This translates a Hebrew word for a woman who was legally bound to a man, but without the full privileges of a wife. As a kind of slave, these wives would pass to the next ruler because they were considered part of the property of the royal household. Ishbosheth accused Abner of trying to take the king's place by sleeping with Rizpah, who was one of these women.

3.8 *worthless dog:* To call someone a dog was an insult. Most dogs were considered filthy, unwanted animals. When dogs are mentioned in the Bible, it is usually in a negative way.

²³But Asahel would not turn back, so Abner struck him in the stomach with the back end of his spear. The spear went all the way through and came out of his back. Asahel fell down and died. Everyone who saw Asahel lying dead just stopped and stood still. ²⁴But Joab and Abishai went after Abner. Finally, about sunset, they came to the hill of Ammah, not far from Giah on the road to Gibeon Desert. ²⁵Abner brought the men of Benjamin together in one group on top of a hill, and they got ready to fight.

²⁶Abner shouted to Joab, "Aren't we ever going to stop killing each other? Don't you know that the longer we keep on doing this, the worse it's going to be when it's all over? When are you going to order your men to stop chasing their own relatives?"

²⁷Joab shouted back, "I swear by the living God, if you hadn't spoken, my men would have chased their relatives all night!" ²⁸Joab took his trumpet and blew the signal for his soldiers to stop chasing the soldiers of Israel. At once, the fighting stopped.

²⁹Abner and his troops marched through the Jordan River valley all that night. Then they crossed the river and marched all morning[P] until they arrived back at Mahanaim.

³⁰As soon as Joab stopped chasing Abner, he got David's troops together and counted them. There were 19 missing besides Asahel. ³¹But David's soldiers had killed 360 of Abner's men from the tribe of Benjamin. ³²Joab and his troops carried Asahel's body to Bethlehem and buried him in the family burial place. Then they marched all night and reached Hebron before sunrise.

3

This battle was the beginning of a long war between the followers of Saul and the followers of David. Saul's power grew weaker, but David's grew stronger.

David's Sons Born in Hebron
(1 Chronicles 3.1-4)

²⁻⁵Several of David's sons were born while he was living in Hebron. His oldest son was Amnon, whose mother was Ahinoam from Jezreel. David's second son was Chileab, whose mother was Abigail, who had been married to Nabal from Carmel. Absalom was the third. His mother was Maacah, the daughter of King Talmai of Geshur. The fourth was Adonijah, whose mother was Haggith. The fifth was Shephatiah, whose mother was Abital. The sixth was Ithream, whose mother was Eglah, another one of David's wives.

Abner Decides To Help David

⁶As the war went on between the families of David and Saul, Abner was gaining more power than ever in Saul's family. ⁷He had even slept with a wife[q] of Saul by the name of Rizpah the daughter of Aiah. But Saul's son Ishbosheth[r] told Abner, "You shouldn't have slept with one of my father's wives!"

⁸Abner was very angry because of what Ishbosheth had said, and he told Ishbosheth:

Am I some kind of worthless dog from Judah? I've always been loyal to your father's family and to his relatives and friends. I haven't turned you over to David. And yet you talk to me as

P2.29 *all morning:* One possible meaning for the difficult Hebrew text.   **q3.7** *wife:* This translates a Hebrew word for a woman who was legally bound to a man, but without the full privileges of a wife.   **r3.7** *Ishbosheth:* See the note at 2.8.

if I've committed a crime with this woman.

9I ask God to punish me if I don't help David get what the LORD promised him! **10**God said that he wouldn't let anyone in Saul's family ever be king again and that David would be king instead. He also said that David would rule both Israel and Judah, all the way from Dan in the north to Beersheba in the south.[s]

11Ishbosheth was so afraid of Abner that he could not even answer.

12Abner sent some of his men to David with this message: "You should be the ruler of the whole nation. If you make an agreement with me, I will persuade everyone in Israel to make you their king."

13David sent this message back: "Good! I'll make an agreement with you. But before I will even talk with you about it, you must get Saul's daughter Michal back for me."

14David sent a few of his officials to Ishbosheth to give him this message: "Give me back my wife Michal! I killed 100 Philistines so I could marry her."[t]

15Ishbosheth sent some of his men to take Michal away from her new husband, Paltiel the son of Laish. **16**Paltiel followed Michal and the men all the way to Bahurim, crying as he walked. But he went back home after Abner ordered him to leave.

17Abner talked with the leaders of the tribes of Israel and told them, "You've wanted to make David your king for a long time now. **18**So do it! After all, God said he would use his servant David to rescue his people Israel from their enemies, especially from the Philistines."

19Finally, Abner talked with the tribe of Benjamin. Then he left for Hebron to tell David everything that the tribe of Benjamin and the rest of the people of Israel wanted to do. **20**Abner took 20 soldiers with him, and when they got to Hebron, David gave a big feast for them.

21After the feast, Abner said, "Your Majesty, let me leave now and bring Israel here to make an agreement with you. You'll be king of the whole nation, just as you've been wanting."

David told Abner he could leave, and he left without causing any trouble.

Joab Kills Abner

22Soon after Abner had left Hebron, Joab and some of David's soldiers came back, bringing a lot of things they had taken from an enemy village. **23**Right after they arrived, someone told Joab, "Abner visited the king, and the king let him go. Abner even left without causing any trouble."

24Joab went to David and said, "What have you done? Abner came to you, and you let him go. Now he's long gone! **25**You know Abner—he came to trick you. He wants to find out how strong your army is and to know everything you're doing."

26Joab left David, then he sent some messengers to catch up with Abner. They brought him back from the well at Sirah,[u] but David did not know anything about it. **27**When Abner returned to Hebron, Joab pretended he wanted to talk privately with him. So he took Abner into one of the small rooms that were part of the town gate and stabbed him in the stomach. Joab killed him because Abner had killed Joab's brother Asahel.

3.17,19 *tribes of Israel . . . tribe of Benjamin:* In the Bible, Israel is made up of twelve tribes descended from Jacob. The tribe of Judah was mentioned in 2.1. Benjamin was Jacob's youngest son, and his descendants became the tribe of Benjamin. Jacob called Benjamin a "fierce wolf" when he blessed him (Gen 49.27), and the tribe of Benjamin became known as warriors. Approval from the tribe of Benjamin was important, because Saul was from the tribe of Benjamin.

   Israel

3.27 *rooms that were part of the town gate:* Most cities and towns in the ancient Near East had walls around them to keep out attackers. These had at least two gates in them so that the citizens could let in merchants, farmers with their produce, and friendly visitors. Gates usually had rooms for the guards who acted as lookouts.

s3.10 *from . . . south:* Hebrew "from Dan to Beersheba." This was one way of describing all of the Israelite land, from north to south.   **t3.14** *I killed . . . marry her:* See 1 Samuel 18.20-27.   **u3.26** *well at Sirah:* Or "oasis of Sirah" or "cistern at Sirah."

3.29 *I pray that ... starve to death:* David put a curse on Joab and his family. It would not be until shortly before his own death that David would command that Joab be punished for murdering Abner. Joab was guilty of murdering Abner. Killing during war was not seen as unlawful in ancient Israel, but Joab's killing of Abner was not an act of war, because David had just sent Abner away in peace (3.21). Also, Joab's act was not considered a kind of lawful blood revenge. Although Abner had killed Joab's brother Asahel, it was during battle and Abner had tried to avoid it. David's cursing of Joab would have shown the Israelites that he had not arranged to have Abner murdered for his own political gain.

Abner's Funeral

28David heard how Joab had killed Abner, and he said, "I swear to the LORD that I am completely innocent of Abner's death! 29Joab and his family are the guilty ones. I pray that Joab's family will always be sick with sores and other skin diseases. May they all be cowards,v and may they die in war or starve to death."

30Joab and his brother Abishai killed Abner because he had killed their brother Asahel in the battle at Gibeon.

31David told Joab and everyone with him, "Show your sorrow by tearing your clothes and wearing sackcloth!w Walk in front of Abner's body and cry!"

David walked behind the stretcher on which Abner's body was being carried. 32Abner was buried in Hebron, while David and everyone else stood at the tomb and cried loudly. 33Then the king sang a funeral song about Abner:

> Abner, why should you
>   have died like an outlaw?x
> 34No one tied your hands
>   or chained your feet,
>   yet you died as a victim
>   of murderers.

Everyone started crying again. 35Then they brought some food to David and told him he would feel better if he had something to eat. It was still daytime, and David said, "I swear to God that I won't take a bite of bread or anything else until sunset!"

36Everyone noticed what David did, and they liked it, just as they always liked what he did. 37Now the people of Judah and Israel were certain that David had nothing to do with killing Abner.

38David said to his officials, "Don't you realize that today one of Israel's great leaders has died? 39I am the chosen king, but Joab and Abishai have more power than I do. So God will have to pay them backy for the evil thing they did."

Ishbosheth Is Killed

4 Ishboshethz felt like giving up after he heard that Abner had died in Hebron. Everyone in Israel was terrified.

2Ishbosheth had put the two brothers Baanah and Rechab in charge of the soldiers who raided enemy villages. Rimmon was their father, and they were from the town of Beeroth, which belonged to the tribe of Benjamin. 3The people who used to live in Beeroth had run away to Gittaim, and they still livea there.

4 Saul's son Jonathan had a son named Mephibosheth,b who had not been able to walk since he was five years old. It happened when someone from Jezreel told his nurse that Saul and Jonathan had died.c She hurried off with the boy in her arms, but he fell and injured his legs.

5One day about noon, Rechab and Baanah went to Ishbosheth's house. It was a hot day, and he was resting 6-7in his bedroom. The two brothers went into the house, pre-

v3.29 *cowards:* One possible meaning for the difficult Hebrew text.   w3.31 *sackcloth:* Sackcloth was a rough, dark-colored cloth made from goat or camel hair and was used to make grain sacks. People wore sackcloth or tore their clothes in times of trouble or sorrow.   x3.33 *outlaw:* Or "fool."
y3.39 *God . . . back:* Or "I pray that God will pay them back."   z4.1 *Ishbosheth:* Hebrew "The Son of Saul."   a4.3 *live:* The Hebrew word means that they did not have the full legal rights of citizens.
b4.4 *Mephibosheth:* Some manuscripts of one ancient translation have "Mephibaal." In 1 Chronicles 8.34 and 9.40 he is called "Meribbaal." See the note on "baal" and "bosheth" at 2.8.   c4.4 *Saul . . . died:* See 1 Samuel 31.1-6.

tending to get some flour. But once they were inside, they stabbed Ishbosheth in the stomach and killed him. Then they cut off his head and took it with them.

Rechab and Baanah walked through the Jordan River valley all night long. **8**Finally they turned west and went to Hebron. They went in to see David and told him, "Your Majesty, here is the head of Ishbosheth, the son of your enemy Saul who tried to kill you! The LORD has let you get even with Saul and his family."

9David answered:

I swear that only the LORD rescues me when I'm in trouble! **10**When a man came to Ziklag and told me that Saul was dead, he thought he deserved a reward for bringing good news. But I grabbed him and killed him.

11You evil men have done something much worse than he did. You've killed an innocent man in his own house and on his own bed. I'll make you pay for that. I'll wipe you from the face of the earth!

12Then David said to his troops, "Kill these two brothers! Cut off their hands and feet and hang their bodies by the pool in Hebron. But bury Ishbosheth's head in Abner's tomb near Hebron." And they did.

David Becomes King of Israel
(1 Chronicles 11.1-3)

5 Israel's leaders met with David at Hebron and said, "We are your relatives. **2**Even when Saul was king, you led our nation in battle. And the LORD promised that someday you would rule Israel and take care of us like a shepherd."

3During the meeting, David made an agreement with the leaders and asked the LORD to be their witness. Then the leaders poured olive oil on David's head to show that he was now the king of Israel.

4David was 30 years old when he became king, and he ruled for 40 years. **5**He lived in Hebron for the first seven and a half years and ruled only Judah. Then he moved to Jerusalem, where he ruled both Israel and Judah for 33 years.

How David Captured Jerusalem
(1 Chronicles 11.4-9; 14.1,2)

6The Jebusites lived in Jerusalem, and David led his army there to attack them. The Jebusites did not think he could get in, so they told him, "You can't get in here! We could keep you out, even if we couldn't see or walk!"

7-9 David told his troops, "You will have to go up through the water tunnel to get those Jebusites. I hate people like them**d** who can't walk or see."

That's why there is still a rule that says, "Only people who can walk and see are allowed in the temple."**e**

David captured the fortress on Mount Zion, then he moved there and named it David's City. He had the city rebuilt, starting with the landfill to the east. **10**David became a great and strong ruler, because the LORD All-Powerful was on his side.

11King Hiram of Tyre sent some officials to David. Carpenters and stone workers came with them, and they brought cedar logs so they could build David a palace.

12David knew that the LORD had made him king of Israel and that he had made him a powerful ruler for the good of his people.

d5.7-9 *You will . . . them:* One possible meaning for the difficult Hebrew text. **e**5.7-9 *temple:* Or "palace."

4.6-7,12 *cut off his head . . . Cut off their hands and feet and hang their bodies:* Taking the head of a slain enemy was a common practice in the ancient Near East. Displaying the head was a way to announce the victory and to warn other enemies. David had done this after killing Goliath. David ordered that the criminals' bodies be displayed for similar reasons (4.12). Executing the killers also demonstrated that David did not approve of how they had eliminated his rival for the throne.

5.4 *40 years:* Forty stands for a large number or a long period of time in the Bible. (See the chart Numbers in the Bible on pg 1844.)

5.6 *Jebusites . . . Jerusalem:* Jebusites lived in Canaan long before the Israelites. Jerusalem, one of the towns of the Jebusites, was on the border between the tribes of Judah and Benjamin.

Jerusalem

5.7-9 *water tunnel:* Archaeologists have discovered a tunnel running under the city wall from the Gihon Spring to a storage pool inside the city wall. People could get water without going outside the walls for water. This was a true advantage when the city was under attack.

5.7-9 *Mount Zion . . . David's City:* Mount Zion was one of the hills on which Jerusalem was built.

Zion

LORD (YHWH)

Jerusalem

6.2 *sacred chest:* The sacred chest held the two flat stones that had the Ten Commandments written on them. Bringing the sacred chest to Jerusalem would make the city the religious as well as political center of Israel.

The Sacred Chest

David's Sons Born in Jerusalem
(1 Chronicles 14.3-7)

¹³After David left Hebron and moved to Jerusalem, he married many women^f from Jerusalem,^g and he had a lot of children. ¹⁴His sons who were born there were Shammua, Shobab, Nathan, Solomon, ¹⁵Ibhar, Elishua, Nepheg, Japhia, ¹⁶Elishama, Eliada,^h and Eliphelet.

David Fights the Philistines
(1 Chronicles 14.8-17)

¹⁷The Philistines heard that David was now king of Israel, and they came into the hill country to try and capture him. But David found out and went into his fortress.ⁱ ¹⁸So the Philistines camped in Rephaim Valley.^j ¹⁹David asked the Lord, "Should I attack the Philistines? Will you let me win?"

The Lord told David, "Attack! I will let you win."

²⁰David attacked the Philistines and defeated them. Then he said, "I watched the Lord break through my enemies like a mighty flood." So he named the place "The Lord Broke Through."^k ²¹David and his troops also carried away the idols that the Philistines had left behind.

²²Some time later, the Philistines came back into the hill country and camped in Rephaim Valley. ²³David asked the Lord what he should do, and the Lord answered:

Don't attack them from the front. Circle around behind and attack from among the balsam^l trees. ²⁴Wait until you hear a sound in the treetops like marching troops. Then attack quickly! That sound will mean I have marched out ahead of you to fight the Philistine army.

²⁵David obeyed the Lord and defeated the Philistines. He even chased them all the way from Geba to the entrance to Gezer.

David Brings the Sacred Chest Back to Jerusalem
(1 Chronicles 13.1-14; 15.1—16.3,43)

6 David brought together 30,000 of Israel's best soldiers and ²led them to Baalah in Judah, which was also called Kiriath-Jearim. They were going there^m to get the sacred chest and bring it back to Jerusalem. The throne of the Lord All-Powerful is above the winged creaturesⁿ on top of this chest, and he is worshiped there.^o

³They put the sacred chest on a new ox cart and started bringing it down the hill from Abinadab's house. Abinadab's sons Uzzah and Ahio were guiding the ox cart, ⁴with Ahio^p walking in front of it. ⁵Some of the people of Israel were playing music on small harps and other stringed instru-

^f**5.13** *married many women:* Some of these women were second-class wives (see the note at 3.7). ^g**5.13** *from Jerusalem:* Or "in Jerusalem." ^h**5.16** *Eliada:* See 1 Chronicles 3.6-8. First Chronicles 14.7 has "Beeliada." ⁱ**5.17** *fortress:* Probably the fortress of Adullam, which was David's former hideout (see 1 Samuel 22.1,4; 24.22). Or it could refer to the older walled city of Jerusalem, called the "fortress on Mount Zion" in verses 7-9. ^j**5.18** *Rephaim Valley:* A few miles southwest of Jerusalem. ^k**5.20** *The Lord Broke Through:* Or "Baal-Perazim." ^l**5.23** *balsam:* One possible meaning for the difficult Hebrew text. ^m**6.2** *to Baalah . . . there:* The Dead Sea Scrolls and 1 Chronicles 13.6; the Standard Hebrew Text "from Baalah in Judah. They had gone there." ⁿ**6.2** *winged creatures:* Two golden statues of winged creatures were on top of the sacred chest and were symbols of the Lord's throne on earth (see Exodus 25.18). ^o**6.2** *he is worshiped there:* Or "the chest belongs to him." ^p**6.3,4** *Ahio . . . Ahio:* Or "his brother . . . his brother."

ments, and on tambourines, castanets, and
cymbals. David and the others were happy,
and they danced for the LORD with all their
might.
6But when they came to Nacon's
threshing-floor, the oxen stumbled, so Uzzah reached out and took hold of the sacred chest. 7The LORD God was very angry
with Uzzah for doing this, and he killed
Uzzah right there beside the chest.
8David got angry with God for killing
Uzzah. He named that place "Bursting Out
Against Uzzah,"[q] and that's what it's still
called.
9David was afraid of the LORD and
thought, "Should I really take the sacred
chest to my city?" 10He decided not to take
it there. Instead, he turned off the road and
took it to the home of Obed Edom, who
was from Gath.[r]
11-12The chest stayed there for three
months, and the LORD greatly blessed Obed
Edom, his family, and everything he owned.
Then someone told King David, "The LORD
has done this because the sacred chest is in
Obed Edom's house."
At once, David went to Obed Edom's
house to get the chest and bring it to
David's City. Everyone was celebrating.
13The people carrying the chest walked six
steps, then David sacrificed an ox and a
choice cow. 14He was dancing for the LORD
with all his might, but he wore only a linen
cloth.[s] 15He and everyone else were celebrating by shouting and blowing horns
while the chest was being carried along.
16Saul's daughter Michal looked out
her window and watched the chest being
brought into David's City. But when she
saw David jumping and dancing for the
LORD, she was disgusted.
17They put the chest inside a tent that
David had set up for it. David worshiped
the LORD by sacrificing animals and burning them on an altar,[t] 18then he blessed
the people in the name of the LORD All-
Powerful. 19He gave all the men and
women in the crowd a small loaf of bread,
some meat, and a handful of raisins, then
everyone went home.

Michal Talks to David

20David went home so he could ask the
LORD to bless his family. But Saul's daughter Michal went out and started yelling at
him. "You were really great today!" she
said. "You acted like a dirty old man, dancing around half-naked in front of your servants' slave-girls."
21David told her, "The LORD didn't
choose your father or anyone else in your
family to be the leader of his people. The
LORD chose me, and I was celebrating in
honor of him. 22I'll show you just how
great I can be! I'll even be disgusting to myself. But those slave-girls you talked about
will still honor me!"
23Michal never had any children.

The LORD's Message to David

(1 Chronicles 17.1-15)

7 King David moved into his new palace,
and the LORD let his kingdom be at
peace. 2Then one day, as David was talking

[q]6.8 *Bursting . . . Uzzah*: Or "Perez-Uzzah." [r]6.10 *Gath*: Or perhaps, "Gittaim." [s]6.14 *only a linen cloth*: The Hebrew word is "ephod," which can mean either a piece of clothing like a skirt that went from the waist to the knee or a garment like a vest or a jacket that only the priests wore. [t]6.17 *sacrificing . . . altar*: The Hebrew mentions two kinds of sacrifices. In one kind of sacrifice, the whole animal was burned on the altar. In the other kind, only part was burned, and the worshipers ate the rest, as in verse 19 (see Leviticus 1.2-17; 3.1-17).

■ 6.7 *God . . . killed Uzzah right there:* The sacred chest was holy and no one but Levites (priests) were allowed to touch it. Although Uzzah's intentions were probably good, he was not a Levite and should not have touched the chest.

■ 6.16 *disgusted:* Michal seemed to be concerned that David was not behaving like a king. But David thought of himself as God's servant celebrating God's victories (7.18-20).

● 6.23 *Michal never had any children:* This could be because David stopped having sexual relations with her, or because God was punishing her for making fun of David (verse 20). Whatever the reason, the fact that Michal and David never had children means that none of David's children would also be descendant of Saul.

7.2,3 *Nathan the prophet . . . "do what you want"*: This is the first time Nathan is mentioned. Prophets received messages from God to pass on to other people. But here Nathan spoke before hearing God's word, and was wrong to tell David to go ahead with his building plans. He corrected that error after God appeared to him in a vision (7.4-16). (See the article Prophets and Prophecy on pg 1791.)

7.5-16 *David, you are . . . always be king*: In the Hebrew text, God's promise to David plays on different meanings of the word "house," which could mean temple or descendants (family). In a political sense, the "House of David" did not last, falling to the Babylonians in 587 B.C. But God's promise to David has been the basis of the hope for a new "chosen one" (*messiah*). Jesus' apostles understood that Jesus' claim to be bringing about the "kingdom of God" rested partly on the fact that Jesus was descended from David.

The Sacred Tent

7.22-28 *LORD All-Powerful . . . bless my family forever*: David's prayer of thanks recalled other promises that the LORD had made and kept with Israel. He asked the LORD to keep this promise, too. But David recognized that he and his descendants would have to continue to serve the LORD if they were to be the chosen kings.

Ten Commandments

Agreements (Covenants)

with Nathan the prophet, David said, "Look around! I live in a palace made of cedar, but the sacred chest has to stay in a tent."

³Nathan replied, "The LORD is with you, so do what you want!"

⁴That night, the LORD told Nathan ⁵to go to David and give him this message:

David, you are my servant, so listen to what I say. Why should you build a temple for me? ⁶I didn't live in a temple when I brought my people out of Egypt, and I don't live in one now. A tent has always been my home wherever I have gone with them. ⁷I chose leaders and told them to be like shepherds for my people Israel. But did I ever say anything to even one of them about building a cedar temple for me?

⁸David, this is what I, the LORD All-Powerful, say to you. I brought you in from the fields where you took care of sheep, and I made you the leader of my people. ⁹Wherever you went, I helped you and destroyed your enemies right in front of your eyes. I have made you one of the most famous people in the world.

¹⁰I have given my people Israel a land of their own where they can live in peace, and they won't have to tremble with fear any more. Evil nations won't bother them, as they did ¹¹when I let judges rule my people. And I have kept your enemies from attacking you.

Now I promise that you and your descendants will be kings. ¹²I'll choose one of your sons to be king when you reach the end of your life and are buried in the tomb of your ancestors. I'll make him a strong ruler, ¹³and no one will be able to take his kingdom

away from him. He will be the one to build a temple for me. ¹⁴I will be his father, and he will be my son.

When he does wrong, I'll see that he is corrected, just as children are corrected by their parents. ¹⁵But I will never put an end to my agreement with him, as I put an end to my agreement with Saul, who was king before you. ¹⁶I will make sure that one of your descendants will always be king.

¹⁷Nathan told David exactly what he had heard in the vision.

David Gives Thanks to the LORD
(1 Chronicles 17.16-27)

¹⁸David went into the tent he had set up for the sacred chest. Then he sat there and prayed:

LORD All-Powerful, my family and I don't deserve what you have already done for us, ¹⁹and yet you have promised to do even more. Is this the way you usually treat people?[u] ²⁰I am your servant, and you know my thoughts, so there is nothing more that I need to say. ²¹You have done this wonderful thing, and you have let me know about it, because you wanted to keep your promise.

²²LORD All-Powerful, you are greater than all others. No one is like you, and you alone are God. Everything we have heard about you is true. ²³And there is no other nation on earth like Israel, the nation you rescued from slavery in Egypt to be your own. You became famous by using great and wonderful miracles to force other nations and their gods out of your land, so your people could live here.[v] ²⁴You have

[u]7.19 *Is this . . . people*: One possible meaning for the difficult Hebrew text.   [v]7.23 *You . . . here*: One possible meaning for the difficult Hebrew text.

The LORD told David, "*Now I promise that you and your descendants will be kings.*" 2 SAM 7.11

chosen Israel to be your people forever, and you have become their God. ²⁵And now, LORD God, please do what you have promised me and my descendants. ²⁶Then you will be famous forever, and everyone will say, "The LORD God All-Powerful rules Israel, and David's descendants are his chosen kings." ²⁷After all, you really are Israel's God, the LORD All-Powerful. You've told me that you will let my descendants be kings. That's why I have the courage to pray to you like this, even though I am only your servant.

²⁸LORD All-Powerful, you are God. You have promised me some very good things, and you can be trusted to do what you promise. ²⁹Please bless my descendants and let them always be your chosen kings. You have already promised, and I'm sure that you will bless my family forever.

A List of David's Victories in War
(1 Chronicles 18.1-13)

8 Later, David attacked and badly defeated the Philistines. Israel was now free from their control.ʷ

²David also defeated the Moabites. Then he made their soldiers lie down on the ground, and he measured them off with a rope. He would measure off two lengths of the rope and have those men killed, then he would measure off one length and let

those men live. The people of Moab had to accept David as their ruler and pay taxes to him.

³David set out for the Euphrates River to build a monumentˣ there. On his way,ʸ he defeated the king of Zobah, whose name was Hadadezer the son of Rehob. ⁴In the battle, David captured 1,700 cavalryᶻ and 20,000 foot soldiers. He also captured war chariots, but he destroyed all but 100 of them.ᵃ ⁵When troops from the Aramean kingdom of Damascus came to help Hadadezer, David killed 22,000 of them. ⁶He left some of his soldiers in Damascus, and the Arameans had to accept David as their ruler and pay taxes to him.

Everywhere David went, the LORD helped him win battles.

⁷Hadadezer's officers had carried their arrows in gold cases hung over their shoulders, but David took these casesᵇ and brought them to Jerusalem. ⁸He also took a lot of bronze from the cities of Betah and Berothai, which had belonged to Hadadezer.

⁹⁻¹⁰King Toi of Hamath and King Hadadezer had been enemies. So when Toi heard that David had attacked and defeatedᶜ Hadadezer's whole army, he sent his son Joram to praise and congratulate David. Joram also brought him gifts made of silver, gold, and bronze. ¹¹David gave these to the LORD, just as he had done with the silver and gold that he had captured from ¹²Edom,ᵈ Moab, Ammon, Philistia,

8.3 *Euphrates River*: God promised to give Abraham's descendants the land between Egypt and the Euphrates River. The part of the river referred to here is the upper Euphrates, which rises in modern Turkey and flows through Syria. **(See Map 1 on pg 1879.)**

8.5 *Aramean kingdom of Damascus*: Damascus was the largest independent Aramean (Syrian) city-state. It is perhaps the world's oldest continuously occupied city and a major trading and transportation center. By defeating Damascus, David gained control over much of Syria.

ʷ8.1 *Israel . . . control*: Or "David also took the town of Metheg-Ammah away from them."
ˣ8.3 *monument*: Kings sometimes set up monuments in lands they had conquered. ʸ8.3 *David . . . way*: One possible meaning for the difficult Hebrew text. It may have been Hadadezer who was going to the Euphrates River. And he may have gone there either to build a monument or to put down a rebellion. ᶻ8.4 *1,700 cavalry*: Hebrew; one ancient translation and 1 Chronicles 18.4 "1,000 chariots and 7,000 cavalry." ᵃ8.4 *He also captured . . . them*: Or "He crippled all but 100 of the horses." ᵇ8.7 *Hadadezer's . . . cases*: Or "Hadadezer's soldiers carried gold shields, but David took these shields." ᶜ8.9,10 *defeated*: Or "killed." ᵈ8.12 *Edom*: Some Hebrew manuscripts and two ancient translations (see also 1 Chronicles 18.11); most Hebrew manuscripts "Aram." In Hebrew the words for "Edom" and "Aram" look almost alike.

8.13 *Salt Valley:* Probably located south and east of the Dead Sea in Edom. In one place Joab gets credit for the victory at Salt Valley (Ps 60 Title) and in another Abishai does (1 Chr 18.12). Many years later, one of David's descendants, Amaziah, the ninth king of Judah, would also defeat the Edomites at Salt Valley (2 Kgs 14.7).

8.18 *David's bodyguard:* David's bodyguard was made up of hired fighters (mercenaries) who were not Israelites. They were Cherethites, who were probably originally from Crete, and Pelethites, who were probably originally from somewhere around the Aegean Sea or Asia Minor. Since the Cherethites and Pelethites had settled in Philistia, David may have won their loyalty during the time he had offered his services to King Achish of Gath.

9.7 *always eat with me at my table:* David was honoring Mephibosheth with a place at his table, not offering charity. David might also have hoped to secure Mephibosheth's loyalty.

Amalek, and from King Hadadezer of Zobah.

[13]David fought the Edomite[e] army in Salt Valley and killed 18,000 of their soldiers. When he returned, he built a monument.[f] [14]David left soldiers all through Edom, and the people of Edom had to accept him as their ruler.

Wherever David went, the LORD helped him.

A List of David's Officials
(1 Chronicles 18.14-17)

[15]David ruled all Israel with fairness and justice.

[16]Joab the son of Zeruiah was the commander in chief of the army.

Jehoshaphat the son of Ahilud kept the government records.

[17]Zadok the son of Ahitub, and Abiathar the son of Ahimelech,[g] were the priests.

Seraiah was the secretary.

[18]Benaiah the son of Jehoiada was the commander of[h] David's bodyguard.[i]

David's sons were priests.

David Is Kind to Mephibosheth

9 One day, David thought, "I wonder if any of Saul's family are still alive. If they are, I will be kind to them, because I made a promise to Jonathan." [2]David called in Ziba, one of the servants of Saul's family. David said, "So you are Ziba."

"Yes, Your Majesty, I am."

[3]David asked, "Are any of Saul's family still alive? If there are, I want to be kind to them."

Ziba answered, "One of Jonathan's sons is still alive, but he can't walk."

[4]"Where is he?" David asked.

Ziba replied, "He lives in Lo-Debar with Machir the son of Ammiel."

[5-6]David sent some servants to bring Jonathan's son from Lo-Debar. His name was Mephibosheth,[j] and he was the grandson of Saul. He came to David and knelt down.

David asked, "Are you Mephibosheth?"

"Yes, I am, Your Majesty."

[7]David said, "Don't be afraid. I'll be kind to you because Jonathan was your father. I'm going to give you back the land that belonged to your grandfather Saul. Besides that, you will always eat with me at my table."

[8]Mephibosheth knelt down again and said, "Why should you care about me? I'm worth no more than a dead dog."

[9]David called in Ziba, Saul's chief servant, and told him, "Since Mephibosheth is Saul's grandson, I've given him back everything that belonged to your master Saul and his family. [10]You and your 15 sons and 20 servants will work for Mephibosheth. You will farm his land and bring in his crops, so that Saul's family and servants[k] will have food. But Mephibosheth will always eat with me at my table."

[11-13]Ziba replied, "Your Majesty, I will do exactly what you tell me to do." So Ziba's family and servants worked for Mephibosheth.

---

[e]8.13 *Edomite:* Some Hebrew manuscripts and two ancient translations (see also 1 Chronicles 18.12); most Hebrew manuscripts "Aramean." In Hebrew the words for "Edomite" and "Aramean" look almost alike. [f]8.13 *built a monument:* Or "was famous." [g]8.17 *Abiathar the son of Ahimelech:* One ancient translation and 1 Samuel 22.11-23; Hebrew "Ahimelech the son of Abiathar." [h]8.18 *was the commander of:* Not in the Hebrew text of this verse, but see 1 Chronicles 18.17. [i]8.18 *David's bodyguard:* The Hebrew text has "the Cherethites and the Pelethites," who were foreign soldiers hired by David to be his bodyguard. [j]9.5,6 *Mephibosheth:* Or "Mephibaal" (see the note at 4.4). [k]9.10 *Saul's family and servants:* Some manuscripts of one ancient translation; Hebrew "the son of your master."

Wherever David went, the LORD helped him. 2 SAM 8.14

Mephibosheth was lame, but he lived in Jerusalem and ate at David's[l] table, just like one of David's own sons. And he had a young son of his own, named Mica.

Israel Fights Ammon
(1 Chronicles 19.1-19)

10 Some time later, King Nahash of Ammon died, and his son Hanun became king. [2]David said, "Nahash was kind to me, and I will be kind to his son." So he sent some officials to the country of Ammon to tell Hanun how sorry he was that his father had died.

[3]But Hanun's officials told him, "Do you really believe David is honoring your father by sending these people to comfort you? He probably sent them to spy on our city, so he can destroy it." [4]Hanun arrested David's officials and had their beards shaved off on one side of their faces. He had their robes cut off just below the waist, and then he sent them away. [5]They were terribly ashamed.

When David found out what had happened to his officials, he sent a message and told them, "Stay in Jericho until your beards grow back. Then you can come home."

[6]The Ammonites realized that they had made David very angry, so they hired more foreign soldiers. Twenty thousand of them were foot soldiers from the Aramean cities of Beth-Rehob and Zobah, 1,000 were from the king of Maacah, and 12,000 were from the region of Tob. [7]David heard what they had done, and he sent out Joab with all of his well-trained soldiers.

[8]The Ammonite troops came out and got ready to fight in front of the gate to their city. The Arameans from Zobah and Rehob and the soldiers from Tob and Maacah formed a separate group in the nearby fields.

[9]Joab saw that he had to fight in front and behind at the same time, and he picked some of the best Israelite soldiers to fight the Arameans. [10]He put his brother Abishai in command of the rest of the army and gave them orders to fight the Ammonites. [11]Joab told his brother, "If the Arameans are too much for me to handle, you can come and help me. If the Ammonites are too strong for you, I'll come and help you. [12]Be brave and fight hard to protect our people and the cities of our God. I pray that the LORD will do whatever pleases him."

[13]Joab and his soldiers attacked the Arameans, and the Arameans ran from them. [14]When the Ammonite soldiers saw that the Arameans had run away, they ran from Abishai's soldiers and went back into their own city. Joab stopped fighting the Ammonites and returned to Jerusalem.

[15]The Arameans realized they had lost the battle, so they brought all their troops together again. [16]Hadadezer sent messengers to call in the Arameans who were on the other side of the Euphrates River. Then Shobach, the commander of Hadadezer's army, led them to the town of Helam.

[17]David found out what the Arameans were doing, and he brought Israel's whole army together. They crossed the Jordan River and went to Helam, where the Arameans were ready to meet them. [18]The Arameans attacked, but then they ran from Israel. David killed 700 chariot drivers and 40,000 cavalry.[m] He also killed Shobach, their commander.

[19]When the kings who had been under Hadadezer's rule saw that Israel had beaten

[l]**9.11-13** *David's*: Hebrew "my." [m]**10.18** *cavalry*: The Hebrew manuscripts and ancient translations differ as to how many and what kind of soldiers were killed.

● **10.1** *King Nahash of Ammon*: Most likely the same person who threatened the town of Jabesh in Gilead and whose army was defeated by Saul. It is not known what kindness Nahash had done for David, though it is possible that Nahash helped David in some way when David was fleeing from Saul.

● **10.5** *Jericho*: Located about five miles west of the Jordan River and seven miles north of the Dead Sea, Jericho was an important city on the trade routes from the east to Palestine. Joshua had a major victory here after the Israelites crossed the Jordan. It is one of the oldest cities in the world with evidence of building on the site as early as 9250 B.C. **(See Map 4 on pg 1882.)**

● **10.19** *they made peace with Israel*: This would be David's last major military campaign against two enemies working together. Though some Arameans accepted David as their ruler, other Arameans beyond the Euphrates River remained loyal to Hadadezer.

11.1 *spring . . . kings go to war:* This was probably about ten years after David took over Jerusalem. More men and food would be available for warfare after the spring rains and the grain harvest in April or May.

11.2-4 *Uriah the Hittite:* The Hittites came from what is now modern Turkey, and once controlled much of the ancient Near East. Some Hittites settled in areas that later belonged to the Israelites. The few who remained by David's time had joined the Israelite community and taken Hebrew names, with "the Hittite" added to the end. **(See Map 1 on pg 1879.)**

11.11 *sacred chest:* The sacred chest held the two flat stones with the Ten Commandments written on them. Even though David had brought the sacred chest to Jerusalem, it was apparently still taken by the Israelites into battle so that the LORD would be with the people and help them defeat their enemies.

The Sacred Chest

11.14,15 *David wrote a letter . . . wounded and die:* It is unclear why David would allow Uriah to deliver a letter that had instructions that meant certain death for Uriah. Perhaps Uriah could not read or perhaps David knew Uriah was too honest to open a letter intended for someone else.

them, they made peace with Israel and accepted David as their ruler. The Arameans were afraid to help Ammon any more.

David and Bathsheba
(1 Chronicles 20.1a)

11 It was now spring, the time when kings go to war.[n] David sent out the whole Israelite army under the command of Joab and his officers. They destroyed the Ammonite army and surrounded the capital city of Rabbah, but David stayed in Jerusalem.

2-4Late one afternoon, David got up from a nap and was walking around on the flat roof of his palace. A beautiful young woman was down below in her courtyard, bathing as her religion required.[o] David happened to see her, and he sent one of his servants to find out who she was.

The servant came back and told David, "Her name is Bathsheba. She is the daughter of Eliam, and she is the wife of Uriah the Hittite."

David sent some messengers to bring her to his palace. She came to him, and he slept with her. Then she returned home. 5But later, when she found out that she was going to have a baby, she sent someone to David with this message: "I'm pregnant!"

6David sent a message to Joab: "Send Uriah the Hittite to me."

Joab sent Uriah 7to David's palace, and David asked him, "Is Joab well? How is the army doing? And how about the war?" 8Then David told Uriah, "Go home and clean up."[p] Uriah left the king's palace, and David had dinner sent to Uriah's house. 9But Uriah didn't go home. Instead,

he slept outside the entrance to the royal palace, where the king's guards slept.

10Someone told David that Uriah had not gone home. So the next morning David asked him, "Why didn't you go home? Haven't you been away for a long time?"

11Uriah answered, "The sacred chest and the armies of Israel and Judah are camping out somewhere in the fields[q] with our commander Joab and his officers and troops. Do you really think I would go home to eat and drink and sleep with my wife? I swear by your life that I would not!"

12Then David said, "Stay here in Jerusalem today, and I will send you back tomorrow."

Uriah stayed in Jerusalem that day. Then the next day, 13David invited him for dinner. Uriah ate with David, who gave him so much to drink that he got drunk. But Uriah still did not go home. He went out and slept on his mat near the palace guards. 14Early the next morning, David wrote a letter and told Uriah to deliver it to Joab. 15The letter said: "Put Uriah on the front line where the fighting is the worst. Then pull the troops back from him, so that he will be wounded and die."

16Joab had been carefully watching the city of Rabbah, and he put Uriah in a place where he knew there were some of the enemy's best soldiers. 17When the men of the city came out, they fought and killed some of David's soldiers—Uriah the Hittite was one of them.

18Joab sent a messenger to tell David everything that was happening in the war. 19He gave the messenger these orders:

When you finish telling the king

[n]**11.1** *when . . . war:* Or "when the messengers had gone to Ammon" (see 10.2) or "the time when the kings had gone to war" (see 10.6-8). [o]**11.2-4** *as . . . required:* This bathing was often a requirement for worshiping God. [p]**11.8** *and clean up:* Or "and sleep with your wife." [q]**11.11** *somewhere in the fields:* Or "at Succoth."

everything that has happened, ²⁰he may get angry and ask, "Why did you go so near the city to fight? Didn't you know they would shoot arrows from the wall? ²¹Don't you know how Abimelech the son of Gideon[r] was killed at Thebez? Didn't a woman kill him by dropping a large rock from the top of the city wall? Why did you go so close to the city walls?"

Then tell him, "One of your soldiers who was killed was Uriah the Hittite."

²²The messenger went to David and reported everything Joab had told him. ²³He added, "The enemy chased us from the wall and out into the open fields. But we pushed them back as far as the city gate. ²⁴Then they shot arrows at us from the top of the wall. Some of your soldiers were killed, and one of them was Uriah the Hittite."

²⁵David replied, "Tell Joab to cheer up and not to be upset about what happened. You never know who will be killed in a war. Tell him to strengthen his attack against the city and break through its walls."[s]

²⁶When Bathsheba heard that her husband was dead, she mourned for him. ²⁷Then after the time for mourning was over, David sent someone to bring her to the palace. She became David's wife, and they had a son.

The LORD's Message for David

12 The LORD was angry because of what David had done, ¹ and he sent Nathan the prophet to tell this story to David:

A rich man and a poor man lived in the same town. ²The rich man owned a lot of sheep and cattle, ³but the poor man had only one little lamb that he had bought and raised. The lamb became a pet for him and his children. He even let it eat from his plate and drink from his cup and sleep on his lap. The lamb was like one of his own children.

⁴One day someone came to visit the rich man, but the rich man didn't want to kill any of his own sheep or cattle and serve it to the visitor. So he stole the poor man's lamb and served it instead.

⁵David was furious with the rich man and said to Nathan, "I swear by the living LORD that the man who did this deserves to die! ⁶And because he didn't have pity on the poor man, he will have to pay four times what the lamb was worth."

⁷Then Nathan told David:

You are that rich man! Now listen to what the LORD God of Israel says to you: "I chose you to be the king of Israel. I kept you safe from Saul ⁸and even gave you his house and his wives. I let you rule Israel and Judah, and if that had not been enough, I would have given you much more. ⁹Why did you disobey me and do such a horrible thing? You murdered Uriah the Hittite by letting the Ammonites kill him, so you could take his wife.

¹⁰"Because you wouldn't obey me and took Uriah's wife for yourself, your family will never live in peace. ¹¹Someone from your own family will cause you a lot of trouble, and I will take your wives and give them to another man before your very eyes. He will go to bed with them while

12.6 *pay four times what the lamb was worth:* God's law required this payment.

12.10,11 *never live in peace . . . while everyone looks on:* Three of David's sons would die violently, and one of his sons, Absalom, would steal David's throne and sleep openly with David's wives.

[r]11.21 *Gideon:* The Hebrew text has Jerubbesheth, which stands for "Jerubbaal," another name for Gideon. See Judges 6.32 and the note on "bosheth" at 2.8 ("besheth" means the same as "bosheth").
[s]11.25 *break . . . walls:* Or "destroy it."

everyone looks on. [12]What you did was in secret, but I will do this in the open for everyone in Israel to see."

[13-14]David said, "I have disobeyed the LORD."

"Yes, you have!" Nathan answered. "You showed you didn't care what the LORD wanted.[t] He has forgiven you, and you won't die. But your newborn son will." [15]Then Nathan went back home.

David's Young Son Dies

The LORD made David's young son very sick.

[16]So David went without eating to show his sorrow, and he begged God to make the boy well. David would not sleep on his bed, but spent each night lying on the floor. [17]His officials stood beside him and tried to talk him into getting up. But he would not get up or eat with them.

[18]After the child had been sick for seven days, he died, but the officials were afraid to tell David. They said to each other, "Even when the boy was alive, David wouldn't listen to us. How can we tell him his son is dead? He might do something terrible!"

[19]David noticed his servants whispering, and he knew the boy was dead. "Did my son die?" he asked his servants.

"Yes, he did," they answered.

[20]David got up off the floor; he took a bath, combed his hair, and dressed. He went into the LORD's tent and worshiped, then he went back home. David asked for something to eat, and when his servants brought him some food, he ate it.

[21]His officials said, "What are you doing? You went without eating and cried for your son while he was alive! But now that he's dead, you're up and eating."

[22]David answered:

While he was still alive, I went without food and cried because there was still hope. I said to myself, "Who knows? Maybe the LORD will have pity on me and let the child live." [23]But now that he's dead, why should I go without eating? I can't bring him back! Someday I will join him in death, but he can't return to me.

Solomon Is Born

[24]David comforted his wife Bathsheba and slept with her. Later on, she gave birth to another son and named him Solomon. The LORD loved Solomon [25]and sent Nathan the prophet to tell David, "The LORD will call him Jedidiah."[u]

The End of the War with Ammon
(1 Chronicles 20.1b-3)

[26]Meanwhile, Joab had been in the country of Ammon, attacking the city of Rabbah. He captured the royal fortress [27]and sent a messenger to tell David:

I have attacked Rabbah and captured the fortress guarding the city water supply. [28]Call the rest of the army together. Then surround the city, and capture it yourself. If you don't, everyone will remember that I captured the city.

[29]David called the rest of the army together and attacked Rabbah. He captured the city [30]and took the crown from the statue of their god Milcom.[v] The crown

was made of 75 pounds of gold, and there was a valuable jewel on it. David put the jewel on his own crown.[w] He also carried off everything else of value. [31]David made the people of Rabbah tear down the city walls[x] with iron picks and axes, and then he put them to work making bricks. He did the same thing with all the other Ammonite cities.

David went back to Jerusalem, and the people of Israel returned to their homes.

Amnon Disgraces Tamar

13 David had a beautiful daughter named Tamar, who was the sister of Absalom. She was also the half sister of Amnon,[y] who fell in love with her. [2]But Tamar was a virgin, and Amnon could not think of a way to be alone with her. He was so upset about it that he made himself sick.

[3]Amnon had a friend named Jonadab, who was the son of David's brother Shimeah. Jonadab always knew how to get what he wanted, [4]and he said to Amnon, "What's the matter? You're the king's son! You shouldn't have to go around feeling sorry for yourself every morning."

Amnon said, "I'm in love with Tamar, my brother Absalom's sister."

[5]Jonadab told him, "Lie down on your bed and pretend to be sick. When your father comes to see you, ask him to send Tamar, so you can watch her cook something for you. Then she can serve you the food."

[6]So Amnon went to bed and pretended to be sick. When the king came to see him, Amnon said, "Please, ask Tamar to come over. She can make some special bread[z]

while I watch, and then she can serve it to me."

[7]David told Tamar, "Go over to Amnon's house and fix him some food." [8]When she got there, he was lying in bed. She mixed the dough, made the loaves, and baked them while he watched. [9]Then she took the bread out of the pan and put it on his plate, but he refused to eat it.

Amnon said, "Send the servants out of the house." After they had gone, [10]he said to Tamar, "Serve the food in my bedroom."

Tamar picked up the bread that she had made and brought it into Amnon's bedroom. [11]But as she was taking it over to him, he grabbed her and said, "Come to bed with me!"

[12]She answered, "No! Please don't force me! This sort of thing isn't done in Israel. It's disgusting! [13]Think of me. I'll be disgraced forever! And think of yourself. Everyone in Israel will say you're nothing but trash! Just ask the king, and he will let you marry me."

[14]But Amnon would not listen to what she said. He was stronger than she was, so he overpowered her and raped her. [15]Then Amnon hated her even more than he had loved her before. So he told her, "Get up and get out!"

[16]She said, "Don't send me away! That would be worse than what you have already done."

But Amnon would not listen. [17]He called in his servant and said, "Throw this woman out and lock the door!"

[18]The servant made her leave, and he locked the door behind her.

The king's unmarried daughters used to wear long robes with sleeves.[a] [19]Tamar

● 12.31 *put them to work:* When towns were captured, often the people who lived there became slaves.

● 13.1 *Tamar ... Absalom ... Amnon:* See 3.2-5 for a list of David's sons who were born in Hebron. Tamar and Absalom's mother was Maacah and Amnon's mother was Ahinoam. Amnon was David's oldest son and heir to the throne (verse 21). Absalom was next in line to the throne. David's second son, Chileab, probably died young as he was only mentioned once.

■ 13.12,13 *This sort of thing isn't done ... he will let you marry me:* Tamar was not just talking about rape. Men were not permitted to have sex with a half sister. Also, women were expected to stay virgins until their wedding night. This would have been especially important for a king's daughter (princess) who would not have been able to find a suitable husband from another royal family if she were not a virgin.

■ 13.18,19 *The king's unmarried daughters ... she walked away:* Tamar's robe identified her both as royalty and as a virgin. Tamar tore her robe, wore ashes, covered her face, and cried because she was twice shamed—raped by her half brother, and no longer a virgin.

[w]**12.30** *David ... crown:* Or "and David wore the crown." [x]**12.31** *tear ... walls:* One possible meaning for the difficult Hebrew text. [y]**13.1** *Tamar ... Absalom ... Amnon:* David was their father, but Amnon had a different mother. [z]**13.6** *special bread:* Or "heart-shaped bread" or "dumplings." [a]**13.18** *long ... sleeves:* One possible meaning for the difficult Hebrew text.

13.29 *mules:* Mules are a cross between a mare (female horse) and a male donkey. Since cross-breeding was forbidden by the Law (Lev 19.19), the king's sons' mules were probably acquired from some other nation. At this time, mules seem to have been used mainly by royalty (1 Kgs 1.33), and horses mostly in warfare.

tore the robe she was wearing and put ashes on her head. Then she covered her face with her hands and cried loudly as she walked away.

Absalom Kills Amnon

²⁰Tamar's brother Absalom said to her, "How could Amnon have done such a terrible thing to you! But since he's your brother, don't tell anyone what happened. Just try not to think about it."

Tamar soon moved into Absalom's house, but she was always sad and lonely. ²¹When David heard what had happened to Tamar, he was very angry. But Amnon was his oldest son and also his favorite, and David would not do anything to make Amnon unhappy.^b

²²Absalom treated Amnon as though nothing had happened, but he hated Amnon for what he had done to his sister Tamar.

²³Two years later, Absalom's servants were cutting wool from his sheep in Baal-Hazor near the town of Ephraim, and Absalom invited all of the king's sons to be there.^c ²⁴Then he went to David and said, "My servants are cutting the wool from my sheep. Please come and join us!"

²⁵David answered, "No, my son, we won't go. It would be too expensive for you." Absalom tried to get him to change his mind, but David did not want to go. He only said that he hoped they would have a good time.

²⁶Absalom said, "If you won't go, at least let my brother Amnon come with us."

David asked, "Why should he go with you?" ²⁷But Absalom kept on insisting, and finally David let Amnon and all his other sons go with Absalom.

Absalom prepared a banquet fit for a king.^d ²⁸But he told his servants, "Keep an eye on Amnon. When he gets a little drunk from the wine and is feeling relaxed, I'll give the signal. Then kill him! I've commanded you to do it, so don't be afraid. Be strong and brave."

²⁹Absalom's servants killed Amnon, just as Absalom had told them. The rest of the king's sons quickly rode away on their mules to escape from Absalom.

³⁰While they were on their way to Jerusalem, someone told David, "Absalom has killed all of your sons! Not even one is left." ³¹David got up, and in his sorrow he tore his clothes and lay down on the ground. His servants remained standing, but they tore their clothes too.

³²Then David's nephew^e Jonadab said, "Your Majesty, not all of your sons were killed! Only Amnon is dead. On the day that Amnon raped Tamar, Absalom decided to kill him. ³³Don't worry about the report that all your sons were killed. Only Amnon is dead, ³⁴and Absalom has run away."

One of the guards noticed a lot of people coming along the hillside on the road to Horonaim.^f He went and told the king, "I saw some men coming along Horonaim Road."^g

³⁵Jonadab said, "Your Majesty, look! Here come your sons now, just as I told you."

³⁶No sooner had he said it, than David's sons came in. They were weeping out loud, and David and all his officials cried just as

^b**13.21** *But Amnon . . . unhappy:* The Dead Sea Scrolls and one ancient translation; these words are not in the Standard Hebrew Text. ^c**13.23** *invited . . . there:* Cutting the wool from sheep was a time for celebrating as well as working. ^d**13.27** *Absalom prepared . . . king:* One ancient translation; these words are not in the Hebrew text. ^e**13.32** *David's nephew:* The Hebrew text has "the son of David's brother Shimeah." ^f**13.34** *the road to Horonaim:* Or "the road behind him" or "the road to the west." ^g**13.34** *He . . . Road:* One ancient translation; these words are not in the Hebrew text.

loudly. ³⁷⁻³⁸ David was sad for a long time because Amnon was dead.

David Lets Absalom Come Home

Absalom had run away to Geshur, where he stayed for three years with King Talmai[h] the son of Ammihud. ³⁹David still felt so sad over the loss of Amnon that he wanted to take his army there and capture Absalom.[i]

14 Joab knew that David couldn't stop thinking about Absalom, ²⁻³and he sent someone to bring in the wise woman who lived in Tekoa. Joab told her, "Put on funeral clothes and don't use any makeup. Go to the king and pretend you have spent a long time mourning the death of a loved one." Then he told her what to say.

⁴The woman from Tekoa went to David. She bowed very low and said, "Your Majesty, please help me!"

⁵David asked, "What's the matter?"

She replied:

My husband is dead, and I'm a widow. ⁶I had two sons, but they got into a fight out in a field where there was no one to pull them apart, and one of them killed the other. ⁷Now all of my relatives have come to me and said, "Hand over your son! We're going to put him to death for killing his brother." But what they really want is to get rid of him, so they can take over our land.

Please don't let them put out my only flame of hope! There won't be anyone left on this earth to carry on my husband's name.

⁸"Go on home," David told her. "I'll take care of this matter for you."

⁹The woman said, "I hope your decision doesn't cause any problems for you. But if it does, you can blame me."[j]

¹⁰He said, "If anyone gives you trouble, bring them to me, and it won't happen again!"

¹¹"Please," she replied, "swear by the LORD your God that no one will be allowed to kill my son!"

He said, "I swear by the living LORD that no one will touch even a hair on his head!"

¹²Then she asked, "Your Majesty, may I say something?"

"Yes," he answered.

¹³The woman said:

Haven't you been hurting God's people? Your own son had to leave the country. And when you judged in my favor, it was the same as admitting that you should have let him come back. ¹⁴We each must die and disappear like water poured out on the ground. But God doesn't take our lives.[k] Instead, he figures out ways of bringing us back when we run away.

¹⁵Your Majesty, I came here to tell you about my problem, because I was afraid of what someone might do to me. I decided to come to you, because I thought you could help. ¹⁶In fact, I knew that you would listen and save my son and me from those who want to take the land that God gave us.[l]

¹⁷I can rest easy now that you have given your decision. You know the difference between right and wrong just like an angel of God, and I pray that the LORD your God will be with you.

● 14.2-3 *he told her what to say:* Joab used the woman and a made-up story to help David see his own situation more clearly. Nathan had also used a story to confront David about Bathsheba (12.1-15).

■ 14.7 *But what they . . . my husband's name:* Israelite law allowed a murder victim's closest relatives to put the murderer to death (Deut 19.12). But the law also recognized the importance of continuing a family line (Deut 25.5-10). David was being asked to decide between these two competing concepts.

---

[h]13.37,38 *King Talmai:* Absalom's grandfather (see 3.3). [i]13.39 *David . . . Absalom:* Or "David was comforted over the loss of Amnon, and he no longer wanted to take his army there and capture Absalom." [j]14.9 *I hope . . . me:* Or "May I speak some more?" [k]14.14 *take our lives:* Or "make any exceptions." [l]14.16 *take . . . us:* Or "make sure we have no part in God's people."

The wise woman of Tekoa told David, "*God doesn't take our lives. Instead, he figures out ways of bringing us back when we run away.*" 2 SAM 14.14

15.1-12 *Absalom . . . plot:* The title of Psalm 3 says it was "written by David when he was running from his son Absalom." Whether David wrote this psalm during Absalom's rebellion, or whether someone put it in a collection in memory of David is unclear.

David

[18]Then David said to the woman, "Now I'm going to ask you a question, and don't try to hide the truth!"

The woman replied, "Please go ahead, Your Majesty."

[19]David asked, "Did Joab put you up to this?"

The woman answered, "Your Majesty, I swear by your life that no one can hide the truth from you. Yes, Joab did tell me what to say, [20]but only to show you the other side of this problem. You must be as wise as the angel of God to know everything that goes on in this country."

[21]David turned to Joab and said, "It seems that I have already given my decision. Go and bring Absalom back."

[22]Joab bowed very low and said, "Your Majesty, I thank you for giving your permission. It shows that you approve of me."

[23]Joab went to Geshur to get Absalom. But when they came back to Jerusalem, [24]David told Joab, "I don't want to see my son Absalom. Tell him to stay away from me." So Absalom went to his own house without seeing his father.

Absalom Was Handsome

[25]No one in all Israel was as handsome and well-built as Absalom. [26]His hair grew so thick and heavy that when he got it cut once a year, it weighed about five pounds.

[27]Absalom had three sons. He also had a daughter named Tamar, who grew up to be very beautiful.

Absalom Finally Sees David

[28]Absalom lived in Jerusalem for two years without seeing his father. [29]He wanted Joab to talk to David for him. So one day he sent a message asking Joab to come over, but Joab refused. Absalom sent another message, but Joab still refused. [30]Finally, Absalom told his servants, "Joab's barley field is right next to mine. Go set it on fire!" And they did.

[31]Joab went to Absalom's house and demanded, "Why did your servants set my field on fire?"

[32]Absalom answered, "You didn't pay any attention when I sent for you. I want you to ask my father why he told me to come back from Geshur. I was better off there. I want to see my father now! If I'm guilty, let him kill me."

[33]Joab went to David and told him what Absalom had said. David sent for Absalom, and Absalom came. He bowed very low, and David leaned over and kissed him.

Absalom Rebels against David

15 Some time later, Absalom got himself a chariot with horses to pull it, and he had 50 men run in front. [2]He would get up early each morning and wait by the side of the road that led to the city gate.[m] Anyone who had a complaint to bring to King David would have to go that way, and Absalom would ask each of them, "Where are you from?"

If they said, "I'm from a tribe in the north," [3]Absalom would say, "You deserve to win your case. It's too bad the king doesn't have anyone to hear complaints like yours. [4]I wish someone would make me the judge around here! I would be fair to everyone."

[5]Whenever anyone came to Absalom and started bowing down, he would reach out and hug and kiss them. [6]That's how he treated everyone from Israel who brought

[m]15.2 *the city gate:* Or "the entrance to the king's palace."

a complaint to the king. Soon everyone in Israel liked Absalom better than they liked David.

[7]Four years[n] later, Absalom said to David, "Please, let me go to Hebron. I have to keep a promise that I made to the LORD, [8]when I was living with the Arameans in Geshur. I promised that if the LORD would bring me back to live in Jerusalem, I would worship him in Hebron."[o]

[9]David gave his permission, and Absalom went to Hebron. [10-12]He took 200 men from Jerusalem with him, but they had no idea what he was going to do. Absalom offered sacrifices in Hebron and sent someone to Gilo to tell David's advisor Ahithophel to come.

More and more people were joining Absalom and supporting his plot. Meanwhile, Absalom had secretly sent some messengers to the northern tribes of Israel. The messengers told everyone, "When you hear the sound of the trumpets, you must shout, 'Absalom now rules as king in Hebron!'"

David Has To Leave Jerusalem

[13]A messenger came and told David, "Everyone in Israel is on Absalom's side!"

[14]David's officials were in Jerusalem with him, and he told them, "Let's get out of here! We'll have to leave soon, or none of us will escape from Absalom. Hurry! If he moves fast, he could catch us while we're still here. Then he will kill us and everyone else in the city."

[15]The officials said, "Your Majesty, we'll do whatever you say."

[16-17]David left behind ten of his wives[p] to take care of the palace, but the rest of his family and his officials and soldiers went with him.

They stopped at the last house at the edge of the city. [18]Then David stood there and watched while his regular troops and his bodyguards[q] marched past. The last group was the 600 soldiers who had followed him from Gath.[r] Their commander was Ittai.

[19]David spoke to Ittai and said, "You're a foreigner from the town of Gath. You don't have to leave with us. Go back and join the new king! [20]You haven't been with me very long, so why should you have to follow me, when I don't even know where I'm going? Take your soldiers and go back. I pray that the Lord will be[s] kind and faithful to you."

[21]Ittai answered, "Your Majesty, just as surely as you and the LORD live, I will go where you go, no matter if it costs me my life."

[22]"Then come on!" David said.

So Ittai and all his men and their families walked on past David.

David Sends the Sacred Chest Back to Jerusalem

[23]The people of Jerusalem were crying and moaning as David and everyone with him passed by. He led them across Kidron Valley[t] and along the road toward the desert.

[24]Zadok and Abiathar the priests were there along with several men from the tribe of Levi who were carrying the sacred

[n]15.7 *Four years:* The Hebrew text has "Forty years." [o]15.8 *in Hebron:* Some manuscripts of one ancient translation; these words are not in the Hebrew text. [p]15.16,17 *wives:* See the note at 3.7. [q]15.18 *bodyguards:* See the note at 8.18. [r]15.18 *the 600 . . . Gath:* These were Philistine soldiers who were loyal to David. [s]15.20 *I pray . . . be:* One ancient translation; these words are not in the Hebrew text. [t]15.23 *Kidron Valley:* This was considered the eastern boundary of Jerusalem.

15.10-12 *Ahithophel:* It is not clear why one of David's advisors would join with Absalom, especially when Ahithophel's son Eliam was one of David's top warriors (23.24-39). But Bathsheba's husband, Uriah the Hittite, was also one of David's top warriors, and her father was named Eliam. If Ahithopel was Bathsheba's grandfather, that would explain why he wanted revenge against David (chapter 11).

15.18 *600 soldiers:* The 600 soldiers were the Philistine soldiers who were loyal to David.

15.24 *Zadok and Abiathar the priests:* Zadok, previously mentioned in 8.17, would continue to be loyal to David. Abiathar was David's priest and close friend. Later, David would choose Zadok over Abiathar to assist Nathan in making Solomon the next king.

15.30 *Mount of Olives:* A high hill just east of Jerusalem, across the Kidron Valley. Its peak is taller than the highest part of Jerusalem and so this Mount sometimes served as Jerusalem's "watchtower."

16.1-4 *Ziba . . . Mephibosheth:* Ziba had been a servant of Saul's family (9.9). Mephibosheth was Saul's grandson and Jonathan's son. David returned Saul's property to Mephibosheth and treated him like a son (9.10-13) because of a promise he had made to Jonathan (1 Sam 20.14,15).

chest. They set the chest down, and left it there until David and his followers had gone out of the city.

²⁵Then David said:

Zadok, take the sacred chest back to Jerusalem. If the LORD is pleased with me, he will bring me back and let me see it and his tent again. ²⁶But if he says he isn't pleased with me, then let him do what he knows is best.

²⁷Zadok, you are a good judge of things,ᵘ so return to the city and don't cause any trouble. Take your son Ahimaaz with you. Abiathar and his son Jonathan will also go back. ²⁸I'll wait at the river crossing in the desert until I hear from you.

²⁹Zadok and Abiathar took the sacred chest back into Jerusalem and stayed there. ³⁰David went on up the slope of the Mount of Olives. He was barefoot and crying, and he covered his head to show his sorrow. Everyone with him was crying, and they covered their heads too.

³¹Someone told David, "Ahithophel is helping Absalom plot against you!"

David said, "Please, LORD, keep Ahithophel's plans from working!"

David Sends Hushai Back as a Spy

³²When David reached the top of the Mount of Olives, he met Hushai the Architeᵛ at a place of worship. Hushai's robe was torn, and dust was on his head.ʷ ³³David told him:

If you come with me, you might slow us down.ˣ ³⁴Go back into the city and tell Absalom, "Your Majesty, I am

your servant. I will serve you now, just as I served your father in the past."

Hushai, if you do that, you can help me ruin Ahithophel's plans. ³⁵Zadok and Abiathar the priests will be there with you, and you can tell them everything you hear in the palace. ³⁶Then they can send their sons Ahimaaz and Jonathan to tell me what you've heard.

³⁷David's advisor Hushai slipped back into Jerusalem, at just about the same time Absalom was coming in.

Ziba Gives Food to David

16 David had started down the other side of the Mount of Olives, when he was met by Ziba, the chief servant of Mephibosheth.ʸ Ziba had two donkeys that were carrying 200 loaves of bread, 100 handfuls of raisins, 100 figs,ᶻ and some wine.

²"What's all this?" David asked.

Ziba said, "The donkeys are for your family to ride. The bread and fruit are for the people to eat, and the wine is for them to drink in the desert when they are tired out."

³"And where is Mephibosheth?" David asked.

Ziba answered, "He stayed in Jerusalem, because he thinks the people of Israel want him to rule the kingdom of his grandfather Saul."

⁴David then told him, "Everything that used to belong to Mephibosheth is now yours."

Ziba said, "Your Majesty, I am your humble servant, and I hope you will be pleased with me."

ᵘ15.27 *you . . . things:* Or "You are a prophet" or "You are not a prophet." ᵛ15.32 *Archite:* The Archites were part of the tribe of Benjamin (see Joshua 16.2). ʷ15.32 *Hushai's . . . head:* See the note at 1.2. ˣ15.33 *you might slow us down:* Hushai was probably very old. ʸ16.1 *chief servant of Mephibosheth:* See 9.1-13. ᶻ16.1 *figs:* Or "pomegranates," a bright red fruit that looks like an apple.

Shimei Curses David

⁵David was near the town of Bahurim when a man came out and started cursing him. The man was Shimei the son of Gera, and he was one of Saul's distant relatives. ⁶He threw stones at David, at his soldiers, and at everyone else, including the bodyguards who walked on each side of David.

⁷Shimei was yelling at David, "Get out of here, you murderer! You good-for-nothing, ⁸the Lord is paying you back for killing so many in Saul's family. You stole his kingdom, but now the Lord has given it to your son Absalom. You're a murderer, and that's why you're in such big trouble!"

⁹Abishai said, "Your Majesty, this man is as useless as a dead dog! He shouldn't be allowed to curse you. Let me go over and chop off his head."

¹⁰David replied, "What will I ever do with you and your brother Joab? If Shimei is cursing me because the Lord has told him to, then who are you to tell him to stop?"

¹¹Then David said to Abishai and all his soldiers:

My own son is trying to kill me! Why shouldn't this man from the tribe of Benjamin want me dead even more? Let him curse all he wants. Maybe the Lord did tell him to curse me. ¹²But if the Lord hears these curses and sees the trouble I'm in, maybe he will have pity on me instead.

¹³David and the others went on down the road. Shimei went along the hillside by the road, cursing and throwing rocks and dirt at them. ¹⁴When David and those with him came to the Jordan River, they were tired out. But after they rested, they[a] felt much better.

Hushai Meets Absalom

¹⁵By this time, Absalom, Ahithophel, and the others had reached Jerusalem. ¹⁶David's friend Hushai came to Absalom and said, "Long live the king! Long live the king!"

¹⁷But Absalom asked Hushai, "Is this how you show loyalty to your friend David? Why didn't you go with him?"

¹⁸Hushai answered, "The Lord and the people of Israel have chosen you to be king. I can't leave. I have to stay and serve the one they've chosen. ¹⁹Besides, it seems right for me to serve you, just as I served your father."

Ahithophel's Advice

²⁰Absalom turned to Ahithophel and said, "Give us your advice! What should we do?"

²¹Ahithophel answered, "Some of your father's wives[b] were left here to take care of the palace. You should have sex with them. Then everyone will find out that you have publicly disgraced your father. This will make you and your followers even more powerful."

²²Absalom had a tent set up on the flat roof of the palace, and everyone watched as he went into the tent with his father's wives.

²³Ahithophel gave such good advice in those days that both Absalom and David thought it came straight from God.

17 Ahithophel said to Absalom:
Let me choose 12,000 men and attack David tonight, ²while he is tired and discouraged. He will panic, and everyone with him will run away. I won't kill anyone except David, ³since he's the one you want to get rid of.

16.5 Bahurim: Located on the road from Jerusalem to Jericho, not far from the Mount of Olives.

16.21,22 wives... his father's wives: These were women who did not have the full privileges of wives (3.7). Nathan had told David that another man would openly have sex with David's wives (12.11,12). This prophecy was now being fulfilled.

17.3 *civil war:* Ahithophel's advice that Absalom kill only David seemed good, because Ahithophel knew that the nation was divided in its loyalties between David and Absalom. If, however, a civil war broke out it would be difficult for either side to win, and the victor would still not have the loyalty of all the people.

17.14 *the* LORD *had decided:* As good as Ahithophel's advice was perceived to be, it still did not come from God (16.23). David was still God's chosen king and it would be wrong for anyone to kill him.

17.17 *Rogel Spring . . . servant girl:* The spring is south of Jerusalem in the Kidron Valley on the border between lands belonging to the tribe of Judah and the tribe of Benjamin. Using a servant girl as a messenger would arouse little suspicion, because they were the ones who usually went for water. **(See Map 5 on pg 1883.)**

Then I'll bring the whole nation back to you like a bride coming home to her husband.[c] This way there won't be a civil war.

Hushai Fools Absalom

[4]Absalom and all the leaders of the tribes of Israel agreed that Ahithophel had a good plan. [5]Then Absalom said, "Bring in Hushai the Archite. Let's hear what he has to say."

[6]Hushai came in, and Absalom told him what Ahithophel had planned. Then Absalom said, "Should we do what he says? And if we shouldn't, can you come up with anything better?"

[7]Hushai said:

This time Ahithophel's advice isn't so good. [8]You know that your father and his followers are real warriors. Now they are as fierce as a mother bear whose cubs have just been killed. Besides, your father has a lot of experience in fighting wars, and he won't be spending the night with the others. [9]He has probably already found a hiding place in a cave or somewhere else.

As soon as anyone hears that some of your soldiers have been killed, everyone will think your whole army has been destroyed. [10]Then even those who are as brave as a lion will lose their courage. All Israel knows what a great warrior your father is and what brave soldiers he has.

[11]My advice is to gather all the fighting men of Israel from the town of Dan in the north down to the town of Beersheba in the south. You will have more soldiers than there are grains of sand on the seashore. Absalom, you should lead them yourself, [12]and we will all go to fight David wherever he is. We will fall on him just as dew falls and covers the ground. He and all his soldiers will die! [13]If they go into a walled town, we will put ropes around that town and drag it into the river. We won't leave even one small piece of a stone.

[14]Absalom and the others liked Hushai's plan better than Ahithophel's plan. This was because the LORD had decided to keep Ahithophel's plan from working and to cause trouble for Absalom.

Jonathan and Ahimaaz Tell David the News

[15]At once, Hushai went to Zadok and Abiathar. He told them what advice Ahithophel had given to Absalom and to the leaders of Israel. He also told them about the advice he had given. [16]Then he said, "Hurry! Send someone to warn David not to spend the night on this side of the Jordan. He must get across the river, so he and the others won't be wiped out!"

[17]Jonathan and Ahimaaz[d] had been waiting at Rogel Spring[e] because they did not want to be seen in Jerusalem. A servant girl went to the spring and gave them the message for David. [18]But a young man saw them and went to tell Absalom. So Jonathan and Ahimaaz left and hurried to the house of a man who lived in Bahurim. Then they climbed down into a well in the courtyard. [19]The man's wife put the cover on the well and poured grain on top of it, so the well could not be seen.[f]

[c]17.3 *back to you . . . husband:* One ancient translation; Hebrew "back to you. The man you are chasing is like bringing back the whole nation."   [d]17.17 *Jonathan and Ahimaaz:* See 15.27.
[e]17.17 *Rogel Spring:* South of Jerusalem in Kidron Valley.   [f]17.19 *The man's wife . . . seen:* Everyone would have thought that the woman was drying grain on a mat that she had spread on the ground.

[20] Absalom's soldiers came to the woman and demanded, "Where are Ahimaaz and Jonathan?"

The woman answered, "They went across that stream."

The soldiers went off to look for the two men. But when they did not find the men, they went back to Jerusalem. [21] After the soldiers had gone, Jonathan and Ahimaaz climbed out of the well. They went to David and said, "Hurry! Get ready to cross the river!" Then they told him about Ahithophel's plan. [22] David and the others got ready and started crossing the Jordan River. By sunrise all of them were on the other side.

Ahithophel Kills Himself

[23] When Ahithophel saw that Absalom and the leaders of Israel were not going to follow his advice, he saddled his donkey and rode back to his home in Gilo. He told his family and servants what to do. Then he hanged himself, and they buried him in his family's burial place.

Absalom Puts Amasa in Charge of the Army

[24] David went to the town of Mahanaim, and Absalom crossed the Jordan River with the army of Israel. [25] Absalom put Amasa in Joab's place as commander of the army. Amasa's father was Ithra[g] from the family of Ishmael,[h] and his mother was Abigal,[i] the daughter of Nahash and the sister of Joab's mother Zeruiah. [26] The Israelites under Absalom's command set up camp in the region of Gilead.

Friends Bring Supplies to David

[27] After David came to the town of Mahanaim, Shobi the son of Nahash came from Rabbah in Ammon,[j] Machir the son of Ammiel came from Lo-Debar, and Barzillai the Gileadite came from Rogelim. [28-29] Here is a list of what they brought: sleeping mats, blankets, bowls, pottery jars, wheat, barley, flour, roasted grain, beans, lentils, honey, yogurt, sheep, and cheese.

They brought the food for David and the others because they knew that everyone would be hungry, tired, and thirsty from being out in the desert.

David Gets Ready for Battle

18 David divided his soldiers into groups of 100 and groups of 1,000. Then he chose officers to be in command of each group. [2] He sent out one third of his army under the command of Joab, another third under the command of Abishai the son of Zeruiah, and the rest under the command of Ittai from Gath. He told the soldiers, "I'm going into battle with you."

[3] But the soldiers said, "No, don't go into battle with us! It won't matter to our enemies if they make us all run away, or even if they kill half of us. But you are worth 10,000 of us. It would be better for you to stay in town and send help if we need it."

[4-6] David said, "All right, if you think I should."

17.23 *family's burial place:* Many families showed respect for the dead by burying them in family tombs. These burial places could be natural caves or cut out of the side of a hill or dug into the ground.

Burial

17.25-27 *Amasa . . . Abigal . . . Shobi . . . Ammon:* Abigal and Zeruiah (Joab's mother) were full sisters, and David was evidently their half brother with the same mother, but a different father. This made Amasa one of David's nephews. Shobi, one of the sons of Nahash, had probably been appointed the new king of the Ammonites after David captured Rabbah.

---

[g]17.25 *Ithra:* Or "Jether." [h]17.25 *the family of Ishmael:* Some manuscripts of one ancient translation; other manuscripts of the same translation "the town of Jezreel"; Hebrew "the people of Israel." [i]17.25 *Amasa . . . Abigal:* Abigal and Zeruiah (Joab's mother) were full sisters, and David was evidently their half brother with the same mother, but a different father. This made Amasa one of David's nephews (see 1 Chronicles 2.12-17). [j]17.27 *Shobi . . . Ammon:* Shobi was probably the new king of the Ammonites that David had appointed after he captured Rabbah (see 2 Samuel 10.1-3; 12.26-31).

18.9 *his head caught in the branches:* The word "head" could also be translated "hair." Absalom had very thick, heavy hair (14.26). The writer seems to want to call attention to the fact that Absalom's most renowned feature is the one that brings about his death.

18.17 *pile of rocks:* This burial does not show the respect usually given to the dead, much less the respect deserved by a king's son. The pile of rocks might have been put there to keep the body from being moved easily, or to mock the monument Absalom had erected to himself (verse 18).

18.18 *King's Valley:* The exact location of this valley is unknown, but it may be the same as the Kidron Valley just east of Jerusalem.

Then in a voice loud enough for everyone to hear, he said, "Joab! Abishai! Ittai! For my sake, be sure that Absalom comes back unharmed."

David stood beside the town gate as his army marched past in groups of 100 and in groups of 1,000.

Joab Kills Absalom

The war with Israel took place in Ephraim Forest. [7-8]Battles were being fought all over the forest, and David's soldiers were winning. Twenty thousand soldiers were killed[k] that day, and more of them died from the dangers of the forest than from the fighting itself.

[9]Absalom was riding his mule under a huge tree when his head[l] caught in the branches. The mule ran off and left Absalom hanging in midair. Some of David's soldiers happened by, [10]and one of them went and told Joab, "I saw Absalom hanging in a tree!"

[11]Joab said, "You saw Absalom? Why didn't you kill him? I would have given you ten pieces of silver and a special belt."

[12]The man answered, "Even if you paid me 1,000 pieces of silver here and now, I still wouldn't touch the king's son. We all heard King David tell you and Abishai and Ittai not to harm Absalom. [13]He always finds out what's going on. I would have been risking my life to kill Absalom, because you would have let me take the blame."

[14]Joab said, "I'm not going to waste any more time on you!"

Absalom was still alive, so Joab took three spears and stuck them through Absalom's chest. [15]Ten of Joab's bodyguards came over and finished him off. [16]Then Joab blew a trumpet to signal his troops to stop chasing Israel's soldiers. [17]They threw Absalom's body into a deep pit in the forest and put a big pile of rocks over it.

Meanwhile, the people of Israel had all run back to their own homes.

[18]When Absalom was alive, he had set up a stone monument for himself in King's Valley. He explained, "I don't have any sons[m] to keep my name alive." He called it Absalom's Monument, and that is the name it still has today.[n]

Ahimaaz Wants To Tell David

[19]Ahimaaz the son of Zadok said, "Joab, let me run and tell King David that the LORD has rescued him from his enemies."

[20]Joab answered, "You're not the one to tell the king that his son is dead. You can take him a message some other time, but not today."

[21]Someone from Ethiopia[o] was standing there, and Joab told him, "Go and tell the king what you have seen." The man knelt down in front of Joab, then got up and started running.

[22]Ahimaaz spoke to Joab again, "No matter what happens, I still want to go. And besides, the Ethiopian has already left."

Joab said, "Why should you go? You won't get a reward for the news you have!"

[23]"I'll run no matter what!" Ahimaaz insisted.

[k]18.7,8 *Twenty . . . killed:* This may refer to the total number or to the number of Absalom's soldiers who were killed.   [l]18.9 *head:* Or "hair."   [m]18.18 *I don't have any sons:* According to 14.27, Absalom had three sons. But they could have died young or been put to death for Absalom's murder of Amnon.   [n]18.18 *today:* That is, at the time of writing. This monument is not the same as the structure now known as "Absalom's Tomb," which was built at least 600 years later.
[o]18.21 *Ethiopia:* The Hebrew text has "Cush," which was a region south of Egypt that included parts of the present countries of Ethiopia and Sudan.

"All right then, run!" Joab said.

Ahimaaz took the road through the Jordan Valley and outran the Ethiopian.

²⁴Meanwhile, David was sitting between the inner and outer gates[p] in the city wall. One of his soldiers was watching from the roof of the gate-tower. He saw a man running toward the town ²⁵and shouted down to tell David.

David answered, "If he's alone, he must have some news."

The runner was getting closer, ²⁶when the soldier saw someone else running. He shouted down to the gate, "Look! There's another runner!"

David said, "He must have some news too."

²⁷The soldier on the roof shouted, "The first one runs just like Ahimaaz the son of Zadok."

This time David said, "He's a good man. He must have some good news."

²⁸Ahimaaz called out, "We won! We won!" Then he bowed low to David and said, "Your Majesty, praise the LORD your God! He has given you victory over your enemies."

²⁹"Is my son Absalom all right?" David asked.

Ahimaaz said, "When Joab sent your personal servant and me, I saw a noisy crowd. But I don't know what it was all about."

³⁰David told him, "Stand over there and wait."

Ahimaaz went over and stood there. ³¹The Ethiopian came and said, "Your Majesty, today I have good news! The LORD has rescued you from all your enemies!"

³²"Is my son Absalom all right?" David asked.

The Ethiopian replied, "I wish that all Your Majesty's enemies and everyone who tries to harm you would end up like him!"

David Cries for Absalom

³³David started trembling. Then he went up to the room above the city gate to cry. As he went, he kept saying, "My son Absalom! My son, my son Absalom! I wish I could have died instead of you! Absalom, my son, my son!"[q]

19 Someone told Joab, "The king is crying because Absalom is dead."

²David's army found out he was crying because his son had died, and their day of victory suddenly turned into a day of sadness. ³The troops were sneaking into Mahanaim, just as if they had run away from a battle and were ashamed.

⁴David covered his face with his hands and kept on crying loudly, "My son, Absalom! Absalom, my son, my son!"

⁵Joab went to the house where David was staying and told him:

You've made your soldiers ashamed! Not only did they save your life, they saved your sons and daughters and wives as well. ⁶You're more loyal to your enemies than to your friends. What you've done today has shown your officers and soldiers that they don't mean a thing to you. You would be happy if Absalom was still alive, even if the rest of us were dead.

⁷Now get up! Go out there and thank them for what they did. If you don't, I swear by the LORD that you won't even have one man left on your side tomorrow morning. You may have had a lot of troubles in the past, but this will be the worst thing that has ever happened to you!

ᵖ18.24 *between . . . gates:* The city gate was often like a tower in the city wall, with one gate on the outside of the wall and another gate on the inside of the wall.   **ᵠ18.33** *son:* In Hebrew, this verse is 19.1.

● **18.27** *Ahimaaz . . . good man . . . good news:* Who was chosen to carry a message was a sign of whether the message contained good or bad news (see verse 20).

David kept saying, *"My son Absalom! My son, my son Absalom! I wish I could have died instead of you! Absalom, my son, my son!"* 2 SAM 18.33

19.13 *Amasa . . . commander . . . instead of Joab:* Joab had finally gone too far by murdering Absalom (18.4-6, 12-14). Considering the severity of the crime, it is surprising that all David did was replace him as army commander with someone else. Although Amasa was David's nephew, he had commanded Absalom's army.

19.16 *Shimei:* Earlier, after David left Jerusalem, Shimei had thrown stones at David (16.5-13).

19.24-29 *Mephibosheth . . . Ziba:* David had returned Saul's property to Mephibosheth and treated him like a son (9.1-13). But after the servant Ziba said Mephibosheth had stayed in Jerusalem so he could rule the kingdom that was once his grandfather's, David took the property away from Mephibosheth and gave it to Ziba (16.1-4).

[8]David got up and went to the town gate and sat down. When the people heard that he was sitting there, they came to see him.

Israel and Judah Want David Back

After Israel's soldiers had all returned home, [9-10]everyone in Israel started arguing. They were saying to each other, "King David rescued us from the Philistines and from our other enemies. But then we chose Absalom to be our new leader, and David had to leave the country to get away. Absalom died in battle, so why hasn't something been done to bring David back?"

[11]When David found out what they were saying, he sent a message to Zadok and Abiathar the priests. It said:

Say to the leaders of Judah, "Why are you the last tribe to think about bringing King David back home? [12]He is your brother, your own relative! Why haven't you done anything to bring him back?"

[13]And tell Amasa, "You're my nephew, and with God as a witness, I swear I'll make you commander of my army instead of Joab."

[14]Soon the tribe of Judah again became followers of David, and they sent him this message: "Come back, and bring your soldiers with you."

David Starts Back for Jerusalem

[15]David started back and had gone as far as the Jordan River when he met the people of Judah. They had gathered at Gilgal and had come to help him cross the river. [16]Shimei[r] the son of Gera was there with them. He had hurried from Bahurim to meet David. Shimei was from the tribe of Benjamin, and [17]1,000 others from Benjamin had come with him.

Ziba, the chief servant of Saul's family, also came to the Jordan River. He and his 15 sons and 20 servants waded across[s] to meet David. [18]Then they brought David's family and servants back across the river, and they did everything he wanted them to do.

Shimei Meets with David

Shimei crossed the Jordan River and bowed down in front of David. [19]He said, "Your Majesty, I beg you not to punish me! Please, forget what I did when you were leaving Jerusalem. Don't even think about it. [20]I know I was wrong. That's why I wanted to be the first one from the northern tribes to meet you."

[21]But Abishai shouted, "You should be killed for cursing the LORD's chosen king!"

[22]David said, "Abishai, what will I ever do with you and your brother Joab? Is it your job to tell me who has done wrong? I've been made king of all Israel today, and no one will be put to death!" [23]Then David promised Shimei that he would not be killed.

Mephibosheth Meets with David

[24-25]Mephibosheth, the grandson of Saul, also came to meet David. He had missed David so much that he had not taken a bath or trimmed his beard or washed his clothes the whole time David was gone. David asked him, "Why didn't you go with me?"

[26]He answered, "Your Majesty, you know I can't walk. I told my servant to saddle a donkey for me[t] so I could go with

---

[r]19.16 *Shimei:* See 16.5-13.   [s]19.17 *waded across:* Or "rushed."   [t]19.26 *I told . . . me:* Two ancient translations; Hebrew, "I said, 'I will saddle a donkey for myself.'"

you. But my servant left without me, and [27]then he lied about me. You're as wise as an angel of God, so do what you think is right. [28]After all, you could have killed my whole family and me. But instead, you let me eat at your own table. Your Majesty, what more could I ask?"

[29]David answered, "You've said enough! I've decided to divide the property[u] between you and Ziba."

[30]Mephibosheth replied, "He can have it all! I'm just glad you've come home safely."

Barzillai Returns Home

[31]Barzillai came from Rogelim in Gilead to meet David at the Jordan River and go across with him. [32]Barzillai was 80 years old. He was very rich and had sent food to David in Mahanaim.

[33]David said to him, "Cross the river and go to Jerusalem with me. I will take care of you."

[34]Barzillai answered:

Your Majesty, why should I go to Jerusalem? I don't have much longer to live. [35]I'm already 80 years old, and my body is almost numb. I can't taste my food or hear the sound of singing, and I would be nothing but a burden. [36]I'll cross the river with you, but I'll only go a little way on the other side. You don't have to be so kind to me. [37]Just let me return to my hometown, where I can someday be buried near my father and mother. My servant Chimham[v] can go with you, and you can treat him as your own.

[38]David said, "I'll take Chimham with me, and whatever you ask me to do for him, I'll do. And if there's anything else you want, I'll also do that."

[39]David's soldiers went on across the river, while he stayed behind to tell Barzillai goodbye and to wish him well. Barzillai returned home, but [40]Chimham crossed the river with David.

Israel and Judah Argue

All of Judah's army and half of Israel's army were there to help David cross the river. [41]The soldiers from Israel came to him and said, "Why did our relatives from Judah secretly take you and your family and your soldiers across the Jordan?"

[42]The people of Judah answered, "Why are you so angry? We are the king's relatives. He didn't give us any food, and we didn't take anything for ourselves!"

[43]Those from Israel said, "King David belongs to us ten times more than he belongs to you.[w] Why didn't you think we were good enough to help you? After all, we were the first ones to think of bringing him back!"

The people of Judah argued more strongly than the people of Israel.

Sheba Rebels against David

20 A troublemaker from the tribe of Benjamin was there. His name was Sheba the son of Bichri, and he blew a trumpet to get everyone's attention. Then he said, "People of Israel, David the son of Jesse doesn't belong to us! Let's go home."

[2]So they stopped following David and went off with Sheba. But the people of Judah stayed close to David all the way from the Jordan to Jerusalem.

---

[u]**19.29** *the property*: The property that had belonged to Saul (see 9.7; 16.4).   [v]**19.37** *My servant Chimham*: Or "My son Chimham."   [w]**19.43** *King David . . . you*: In this verse "Israel" stands for the ten northern tribes and does not include the tribe of Judah in the south.

Israel

19.31-38 *Barzillai . . . servant Chimham*: See CEV footnote. David refers to the "sons" of Barzillai who helped him during Absalom's rebellion in his message to Solomon, 1 Kings 2.7.

20.3 *ten of his wives . . . widows:* Absalom had slept with these wives. Perhaps David did not trust these wives and wanted to be sure they did not have any sons who would betray him as Absalom had done.

David's Ten Wives

³David had left ten of his wives in Jerusalem to take care of his palace. But when he came back, he had them taken to another house, and he placed soldiers there to guard them. He gave them whatever they needed, but he never slept with any of them again.ˣ They had to live there for the rest of their lives as if they were widows.

The Army Goes after Sheba

⁴David said to Amasa, "Three days from now I want you and all of Judah's army to be here!"

⁵Amasa started bringing the army together, but it was taking him more than three days. ⁶So David said to Abishai, "Sheba will hurt us more than Absalom ever did. Take my best soldiers and go after him. We don't want him to take over any walled cities and get away from us."ʸ

Joab Kills Amasa

⁷Abishai left Jerusalem to try and capture Sheba. He took along Joab and his soldiers, as well as David's bodyguardᶻ and best troops. ⁸They had gone as far as the big rock at Gibeon when Amasa caught up with them. Joab had a dagger strapped around his waist over his military uniform, but it fell out as he started toward Amasa. ⁹Joab said, "Amasa, my cousin, how are you?" Then Joab took hold of Amasa's beard with his right hand, so that he could greet him with a kiss. ¹⁰Amasa did not see the dagger in Joab's other hand. Joab stuck it in Amasa's stomach, and his insides spilled out on the ground. Joab only struck him once, but Amasa was dying.

Joab and his brother Abishai went off to chase Sheba. ¹¹One of Joab's soldiers stood by Amasa and shouted, "If any of you are for Joab and David, then follow Joab!" ¹²Amasa was still rolling in his own blood in the middle of the road. The soldier who had shouted noticed that everyone who passed by would stop, so he dragged Amasa off the road and covered him with a blanket. ¹³After this, no one else stopped. They all walked straight past him on their way to help Joab capture Sheba.

Sheba Hides Out in the Town of Abel

¹⁴Sheba had gone through all of the tribes of Israel when he came to the town of Abel Beth-Maacah. All of his best soldiersᵃ met him there and followed him into the town.

¹⁵Joab and his troops came and surrounded Abel, so that no one could go in or come out. They made a dirt ramp up to the town wall and then started to use a battering ram to knock the wall down.

A Wise Woman Saves the Town

¹⁶A wise woman shouted from the top of the wall,ᵇ "Listen to me! Listen to me! I have to talk to Joab! Tell him to come here!" ¹⁷When he came, the woman said, "Are you Joab?"

"Yes, I am," he answered.

ˣ20.3 *he . . . again:* Because of what Absalom had done (see 16.21,22).   ʸ20.6 *get . . . us:* One possible meaning for the difficult Hebrew text.   ᶻ20.7 *bodyguard:* See the note at 8.18.   ᵃ20.14 *best soldiers:* One ancient translation; the difficult Hebrew text may mean either "Berites" or "Bichrites," Sheba's relatives.   ᵇ20.16 *the top of the wall:* Or "the town."

She said, "Please, listen to what I have to say."

"All right," he said. "I'll listen."

[18]She said, "Long ago people used to say, 'If you want good advice, go to the town of Abel to get it.' The answers they got here were all that was needed to settle any problem. [19]We are Israelites, and we want peace! You can trust us. Why are you trying to destroy a town that's like a mother in Israel? Why do you want to wipe out the LORD's people?"

[20]Joab answered, "No, no! I'm not trying to wipe you out or destroy your town! [21]That's not it at all. There's a man in your town from the hill country of Ephraim. His name is Sheba, and he is the leader of a rebellion against King David. Turn him over to me, and we will leave your town alone."

The woman told Joab, "We will throw his head over the wall."

[22]She went to the people of the town and talked them into doing it. They cut off Sheba's head and threw it to Joab.

Joab blew a signal on his trumpet, and the soldiers returned to their homes. Joab went back to David in Jerusalem.

Another List of David's Officials[c]

[23]Joab was the commander of Israel's entire army.

Benaiah the son of Jehoiada was in command of David's bodyguard.[d]

[24]Adoram[e] was in charge of the slave-labor force.

Jehoshaphat the son of Ahilud kept government records.

[25]Sheva was the secretary.

Zadok and Abiathar were the priests.

[26]Ira from Jair was David's priest.

The Gibeonites Hang Saul's Descendants

21 While David was king, there were three years in a row when the nation of Israel could not grow enough food. So David asked the LORD for help, and the LORD answered, "Saul and his family are guilty of murder, because he had the Gibeonites killed."

[2] The Gibeonites were not Israelites; they were descendants of the Amorites. The people of Israel had promised not to kill them,[f] but Saul had tried to kill them because he wanted Israel and Judah to control all the land.

David had the Gibeonites come, and he talked with them. [3]He said, "What can I do to make up for what Saul did, so that you'll ask the LORD to be kind to his people again?"[g]

[4]The Gibeonites answered, "Silver and gold from Saul and his family are not enough. On the other hand, we don't have the right to put any Israelite to death."

David said, "I'll do whatever you ask."[h]

[5]They replied, "Saul tried to kill all our people so that none of us would be left in the land of Israel. [6]Give us seven of his descendants. We will hang[i] these men near the place where the LORD is worshiped in Gibeah, the hometown of Saul, the LORD's chosen king."

"I'll give them to you," David said.

[7]David had made a promise to Jonathan

[c]20.23 *Another List of David's Officials*: See also the list in 8.16,17.   [d]20.23 *David's bodyguard*: See the note at 8.18.   [e]20.24 *Adoram*: One ancient translation "Adoniram" (see 1 Kings 4.1-6; 5.14).
[f]21.2 *promised . . . them*: See Joshua 9.3-27.   [g]21.3 *ask . . . again*: Saul's guilt had become a curse on Israel that had resulted in famine. For the effects of this curse to be removed, the Gibeonites would have to ask the LORD to be kind to Israel.   [h]21.4 *I'll . . . ask*: Or "What are you asking me to do for you?"   [i]21.6 *hang*: One possible meaning for the difficult Hebrew text.

● 21.2 *The Gibeonites:* The people who lived in and around Gibeon, a town about five miles northwest of Jerusalem. Though Israel's promise to the Gibeonites is recorded in Josh 9.3-27, Saul's attempt to kill them is not recorded in the Bible.

21.10 *until it started to rain*: Normally bodies were buried within 24 hours of death. These were left unburied as a mark of dishonor. She protected the bodies from the additional dishonor of being picked at by buzzards, jackals, and crows. Unless the rains came early she would have done this for about six months, until the start of the rainy season in September or October.

21.11-12 *hung their bodies*: It was common practice in the ancient Near East to bring back at least the head and the armor of the slain enemy, perhaps as proof of victory. The head and other body parts were displayed to announce the victory and to serve as a warning to other enemies. David followed this custom after killing Goliath.

21.13-14 *had their bones taken . . . bless the land*: David was moved by the way Rizpah protected the bodies of Saul's sons and grandsons. He restored some of the honor to the fallen king and his descendants by having them all buried at Saul's family burial place. "God answered prayers to bless the land" indicates that justice has been done and the famine that had begun three years before (verse 1) is now over.

21.19 *Goliath*: According to 1 Sam 17, David killed a giant named Goliath who made fun of Israel. The Goliath mentioned here may be a different warrior, perhaps "the brother of Goliath" as indicated in 1 Chr 20.5.

with the LORD as his witness, so he spared Jonathan's son Mephibosheth, the grandson of Saul. [8]But Saul and Rizpah the daughter of Aiah had two sons named Armoni and Mephibosheth. Saul's daughter Merab[j] had five sons whose father was Adriel the son of Barzillai from Meholah.[k] David took Rizpah's two sons and Merab's five sons and [9]turned them over to the Gibeonites, who hanged[l] all seven of them on the mountain near the place where the LORD was worshiped. This happened right at the beginning of the barley harvest.[m]

Rizpah Takes Care of the Bodies

[10]Rizpah spread out some sackcloth[n] on a nearby rock. She wouldn't let the birds land on the bodies during the day, and she kept the wild animals away at night. She stayed there from the beginning of the harvest until it started to rain.[o]

The Burial of Saul and His Descendants

[11-12]Earlier the Philistines had killed Saul and Jonathan on Mount Gilboa and had hung their bodies in the town square at Beth-Shan. The people of Jabesh in Gilead had secretly taken the bodies away, but David found out what Saul's wife[p] Rizpah

had done, and he went to the leaders of Jabesh to get the bones of Saul and his son Jonathan. [13-14]David had their bones taken to the land of Benjamin and buried in a side room in Saul's family burial place. Then he gave orders for the bones of the men who had been hanged[q] to be buried there. It was done, and God answered prayers to bless the land.

The Descendants of the Rephaim
(1 Chronicles 20.4-8)

[15]One time David got very tired when he and his soldiers were fighting the Philistines. [16]One of the Philistine warriors was Ishbibenob, who was a descendant of the Rephaim,[r] and he tried to kill David. Ishbibenob was armed with a new sword,[s] and his bronze spearhead[t] alone weighed about seven and a half pounds. [17]But Abishai[u] came to the rescue and killed the Philistine.

David's soldiers told him, "We can't let you risk your life in battle anymore! You give light to our nation, and we want that flame to keep burning."

[18]There was another battle with the Philistines at Gob, where Sibbecai from Hushah killed a descendant of the Rephaim named Saph.

[19]There was still another battle with the Philistines at Gob. A soldier named Elhanan killed Goliath[v] from Gath, whose

[j]21.8 *Merab*: Some Hebrew manuscripts and some manuscripts of one ancient translation. Most other manuscripts have "Michal," Saul's daughter who was one of David's wives, but she never had any children (see 2 Samuel 6.23). According to 1 Samuel 18.19, Merab was Saul's daughter, and she married Adriel from Meholah.   [k]21.8 *Meholah*: Also known as Abel-Meholah.   [l]21.9 *hanged*: One possible meaning for the difficult Hebrew text.   [m]21.9 *This . . . harvest*: This would have been late in April.   [n]21.10 *sackcloth*: See the note at 3.31.   [o]21.10 *started to rain*: This may have been the beginning of the rainy season in September or October. It usually didn't rain from May to September. Or, it may have been a sign that now there would be enough rain again.   [p]21.11,12 *wife*: See the note at 3.7.   [q]21.13,14 *hanged*: One possible meaning for the difficult Hebrew text.   [r]21.16 *Rephaim*: This may refer to a group of people that lived in Palestine before the Israelites and who were famous for their large size.   [s]21.16 *new sword*: One possible meaning for the difficult Hebrew text.   [t]21.16 *spearhead*: Or "helmet."   [u]21.17 *Abishai*: David's nephew, the brother of Joab.   [v]21.19 *Goliath*: According to 1 Chronicles 20.5, Elhanan killed the brother of Goliath.

spear shaft was like a weaver's beam.[w] El-hanan's father was Jari[x] from Bethlehem.

20There was another war, this time in Gath. One of the enemy soldiers was a descendant of the Rephaim. He was as big as a giant and had six fingers on each hand and six toes on each foot. **21**But when he made fun of Israel, David's nephew Jonathan killed him. Jonathan was the son of David's brother Shimei.

22David and his soldiers killed these four men who were descendants of the Rephaim from Gath.

David Sings to the LORD
(Psalm 18.1-50)

22 David sang a song to the LORD after the LORD had rescued him from his enemies, especially Saul. These are the words to David's song:

2Our LORD and our God,
   you are my mighty rock,[y]
      my fortress, my protector.
3You are the rock
   where I am safe.
You are my shield,
   my powerful weapon,[z]
      and my place of shelter.

You rescue me and keep me
   safe from violence.
4I praise you, our LORD!
   I prayed to you,
   and you rescued me
      from my enemies.
5Death, like ocean waves,

   surrounded me,
and I was almost swallowed
   by its flooding waters.

6Ropes from the world
   of the dead
      had coiled around me,
and death had set a trap
   in my path.
7I was in terrible trouble
   when I called out to you,
but from your temple
you heard me
   and answered my prayer.
8Earth shook and shivered!
The columns supporting the sky[a]
   rocked back and forth.
You were angry
9   and breathed out smoke.
Scorching heat and fiery flames
   spewed from your mouth.

10You opened the heavens
   like curtains,
and you came down
with storm clouds
   under your feet.
11You rode on the backs
   of flying creatures.[b]
You appeared[c]
   with the wind as wings.
12Darkness was your tent!
Thunderclouds filled the sky,
   hiding you from sight.
13Fiery coals lit up the sky
   in front of you.

[w]**21.19** *weaver's beam:* A large wooden rod used by a weaver when making cloth. [x]**21.19** *Jari:* Or "Jaare." [y]**22.2** *mighty rock:* The Hebrew text has "rock," which is sometimes used in poetry to compare the LORD to a mountain where his people can run for protection from their enemies. [z]**22.3** *powerful weapon:* The Hebrew has "the horn," which refers to the horn of a bull, one of the most powerful animals in ancient Palestine. [a]**22.8** *columns . . . sky:* The sky was sometimes described as a dome that was held up by a foundation or pillars. [b]**22.11** *flying creatures:* These were supernatural beings (see the note at 6.2). [c]**22.11** *appeared:* Most Hebrew manuscripts; some Hebrew manuscripts "swooped down" (see Psalm 18.10).

22.1-51 *David sang . . . will never end:* David's victory song, one of the oldest major poems in the Jewish Scriptures was also collected, in a slightly different form, in PSALMS (Ps 18). In verses 21 to 25, David makes it clear that he thought the LORD supported him because he was innocent by God's standards and because he obeyed the LORD.

22.11 *flying creatures:* Most likely some kind of supernatural beings, like the ones represented by the "winged creatures" on the top of the sacred chest.

The Sacred Chest

David sang, "Our LORD and our God, you are my mighty rock, my fortress, my protector. You are the rock where I am safe." 2 SAM 22.2

22.29 *lamp . . . light:* These are symbols of life (see also Prov 13.9). "Light" also stands for the wisdom and truth that come from God, as opposed to the "darkness," which symbolized evil. David was remembered for giving "light" to his people (21.17). Here David shows humility by saying that his light and life come from God.

¹⁴Lord Most High, your voice
    thundered from the heavens.
¹⁵You scattered your enemies
    with arrows of lightning.
¹⁶You roared at the sea,
  and its deepest channels
    could be seen.
You snorted,
and the earth shook
  to its foundations.

¹⁷You reached down from heaven,
  and you lifted me
    from deep in the ocean.
¹⁸You rescued me from enemies
  who were hateful
    and too powerful for me.
¹⁹On the day disaster struck,
  they came and attacked,
    but you defended me.
²⁰When I was fenced in,
  you freed and rescued me
    because you love me.
²¹You are good to me, Lord,
  because I do right,
and you reward me
  because I am innocent.
²²I do what you want
  and never turn to do evil.
²³I keep your laws in mind
  and never turn away
    from your teachings.
²⁴I obey you completely
  and guard against sin.
²⁵You have been good to me
  because I do right;
you have rewarded me
  for being innocent
    by your standards.

²⁶You are always loyal
  to your loyal people,
    and you are faithful

to the faithful.
²⁷With all who are sincere
  you are sincere,
but you treat the unfaithful
  as their deeds deserve.
²⁸You rescue the humble,
  but you look for ways
    to put down the proud.

²⁹Our Lord and God,
  you are my lamp.
You turn darkness to light.
³⁰You help me defeat armies
  and capture cities.

³¹Your way is perfect, Lord,
  and your word is correct.
You are a shield for those
  who run to you for help.
³²You alone are God!
  Only you are a mighty rock.[d]
³³You are my strong fortress,
  and you set me free.
³⁴ You make my feet run as fast
  as those of a deer,
and you help me stand
  on the mountains.

³⁵You teach my hands to fight
  and my arms to use
    a bow of bronze.
³⁶You alone are my shield,
  and by coming to help me,
    you have made me famous.
³⁷You clear the way for me,
  and now I won't stumble.

³⁸I kept chasing my enemies
  until I caught them
    and destroyed them.
³⁹I destroyed them!
  I stuck my sword
    through my enemies,

[d]22.32 *mighty rock:* See the note at 22.2.

and they were crushed
  under my feet.
[40]You helped me win victories
  and forced my attackers
    to fall victim to me.

[41]You made my enemies run,
  and I killed them.
[42]They cried out for help,
  but no one saved them;
they called out to you,
  but there was no answer.
[43]I ground them to dust,
  and I squashed them
    like mud in the streets.

[44]You rescued me
  from my stubborn people
and made me the leader
  of foreign nations,
    who are now my slaves.
[45]They obey and come crawling.
[46] They have lost all courage
  and from their fortresses
    they come trembling.

[47]You are the living LORD!
  I will praise you!
You are a mighty rock.[e]
  I will honor you
    for keeping me safe.
[48]You took revenge for me,
  and you put nations
    in my power.
[49]You protected me
  from violent enemies,
and you made me much greater
  than all of them.

[50] I will praise you, LORD,
  and I will honor you

among the nations.
[51]You give glorious victories
  to your chosen king.
Your faithful love for David
  and for his descendants
    will never end.

David's Last Words

23 These are the last words
  of David the son of Jesse.
The God of Jacob chose David
  and made him a great king.
The Mighty God of Israel
  loved him.[f]
When God told him to speak,
  David said:
[2]The Spirit of the LORD
  has told me what to say.
[3]Our Mighty Rock,[g]
  the God of Jacob, told me,
"A ruler who obeys God
  and does right
[4]is like the sunrise
  on a cloudless day,
or like rain that sparkles
  on the grass."[h]

[5]I have ruled this way,
  and God will never break
    his promise to me.
God's promise is complete
  and unchanging;
he will always help me
  and give me what I hope for.
[6]But evil people are pulled up
  like thornbushes.
They are not dug up by hand,
[7]but with a sharp spear
  and are burned on the spot.

[e]**22.47** *mighty rock:* See the note at 22.2.   [f]**23.1** *The Mighty . . . him:* Or "He wrote Israel's favorite songs."   [g]**23.3** *Mighty Rock:* See the note at 22.2.   [h]**23.4** *sparkles . . . grass:* Or "makes the grass grow."

The God of Jacob told David, "A ruler who obeys God and does right is like the sunrise on a cloudless day, or like rain that sparkles on the grass." 2 SAM 23.3,4

23.8 *the Three Warriors:* The most honored group of warriors. They might have been part of the Thirty Warriors.

23.18 *the Thirty Warriors:* The second most honored group of warriors. They also may have been officers in the army (23.8).

23.20 *Benaiah:* Benaiah was the commander of David's bodyguard and one of David's army commanders. Later he would support Solomon, David's son who would inherit the throne, and become the commander of Solomon's army.

The Three Warriors
(1 Chronicles 11.10-19)

[8]These are the names of David's warriors: Ishbosheth[i] the son of Hachmon[j] was the leader of the Three Warriors.[k] In one battle, he killed 800 men with his spear.[l]

[9]The next one of the Three Warriors was Eleazar the son of Dodo the Ahohite. One time when the Philistines were at war with Israel, he and David dared the Philistines to fight them. Every one of the Israelite soldiers turned and ran, [10]except Eleazar. He killed Philistines until his hand was cramped, and he couldn't let go of his sword. When Eleazar finished, all the Israelite troops had to do was come back and take the enemies' weapons and armor. The LORD gave Israel a great victory that day.

[11]Next was Shammah the son of Agee the Hararite. One time the Philistines brought their army together to destroy a crop of peas growing in a field near Lehi. The rest of Israel's soldiers ran away from the Philistines, [12]but Shammah stood in the middle of the field and killed the Philistines. The crops were saved, and the LORD gave Israel a great victory.

[13]One year at harvest time, the Three Warriors[m] went to meet David at Adullam Cave.[n] The Philistine army had set up camp in Rephaim Valley [14]and had taken over Bethlehem. David was in his fortress,

[15]and he was very thirsty. He said, "I wish I had a drink from the well by the gate at Bethlehem."

[16]The Three Warriors[o] sneaked into the Philistine camp and got some water from the well near Bethlehem's gate. But after they brought the water back to David, he refused to drink it. Instead, he poured it out as a sacrifice [17]and said to the LORD, "I can't drink this water! It's like the blood of these men who risked their lives to get it for me."

The Three Warriors did these brave deeds.

The Thirty Warriors
(1 Chronicles 11.20-47)

[18]Joab's brother Abishai was the leader of the Thirty Warriors,[p] and in one battle he killed 300 men with his spear. He was as famous as the Three Warriors [19]and certainly just as famous as the rest of the Thirty Warriors. He was the commander of the Thirty Warriors, but he still did not become one of the Three Warriors.

[20]Benaiah the son of Jehoiada was a brave man from Kabzeel who did some amazing things. He killed two of Moab's best fighters,[q] and on a snowy day he went down into a pit and killed a lion. [21]Another time, he killed an Egyptian, as big as a giant.[r] The Egyptian was armed with a spear, but Benaiah only had a club. Benaiah grabbed the

[i]23.8 *Ishbosheth:* Hebrew "Josheb Bashebeth," which seems to be another spelling of Ishbosheth. See the note at 2.8, although this is a different Ishbosheth.   [j]23.8 *the son of Hachmon:* Or "the Tahchemonite" (see 1 Chronicles 11.11).   [k]23.8 *the Three Warriors:* The most honored group of warriors. They may have been part of the Thirty Warriors. "Three" and "thirty" are spelled almost the same in Hebrew, so there is some confusion in the manuscripts as to which group is being talked about in some places in the following lists.   [l]23.8 *with . . . spear:* One possible meaning for the difficult Hebrew text (see 1 Chronicles 11.11).   [m]23.13 *the Three Warriors:* Or "three warriors." Hebrew "three of the thirty most important."   [n]23.13 *Adullam Cave:* This may have happened during the time that David was an outlaw (see 1 Samuel 22.1-6).   [o]23.16 *the Three Warriors:* Or "three warriors."   [p]23.18 *the Thirty Warriors:* The second most honored group of warriors. They may have also been officers in the army (see the note at 23.8).   [q]23.20 *Moab's best fighters:* Or "big lions in Moab;" one ancient translation "sons of Ariel from Moab."   [r]23.21 *Egyptian . . . giant:* First Chronicles 11.23; in this verse the Hebrew text has "good-looking Egyptian."

spear from the Egyptian and killed him with it. **22-23**Benaiah did these things. He never became one of the Three Warriors, but he was just as famous as they were and certainly just as famous as the rest of the Thirty Warriors. David made him the leader of his bodyguard.

24-39 Some of the Thirty Warriors were:
Asahel the brother of Joab
Elhanan the son of Dodo from Beth-
lehem
Shammah from Harod
Elika from Harod
Helez the Paltite
Ira the son of Ikkesh from Tekoa
Abiezer from Anathoth
Mebunnai[s] the Hushathite
Zalmon the Ahohite
Maharai from Netophah
Heleb the son of Baanah from
Netophah
Ittai the son of Ribai from Gibeah of
the tribe of Benjamin
Benaiah from Pirathon
Hiddai from the streams on Mount
Gaash
Abialbon from Beth-Arabah
Azmaveth from Bahurim[t]
Eliahba from Shaalbon
Jashen[u]
Jonathan the son of Shammah the
Hararite[v]
Ahiam the son of Sharar the Hararite
Eliphelet the son of Ahasbai from
Maacah
Eliam the son of Ahithophel from Gilo
Hezro from Carmel
Paarai the Arbite

Igal the son of Nathan from Zobah
Bani the Gadite
Zelek from Ammon
Naharai from Beeroth, who carried
the weapons of Joab the son of
Zeruiah
Ira the Ithrite
Gareb the Ithrite
Uriah the Hittite
There were 37 in all.

David Counts the People
(1 Chronicles 21.1-6)

24 The LORD was angry with Israel again, and he made David think it would be a good idea to count the people in Israel and Judah. **2**So David told Joab and the army officers,[w] "Go to every tribe in Israel, from the town of Dan in the north all the way south to Beersheba, and count everyone who can serve in the army. I want to know how many there are."

3Joab answered, "I hope the LORD your God will give you 100 times more soldiers than you already have. I hope you will live to see that day! But why do you want to do a thing like this?"

4But when David refused to change his mind, Joab and the army officers went out and started counting the people. **5**They crossed the Jordan River and began with[x] Aroer and the town in the middle of the river valley. From there they went toward Gad and on as far as Jazer. **6**They went to Gilead and to Kadesh in Syria.[y] Then they went to Dan, Ijon,[z] and on toward Sidon. **7**They came to the fortress of Tyre, then

[s]**23.24-39** *Mebunnai:* Or "Sibbecai" (see 1 Chronicles 11.26-47).   [t]**23.24-39** *Bahurim:* Or "Barhum." [u]**23.24-39** *Jashen:* Hebrew "sons of Jashen."   [v]**23.24-39** *Jonathan . . . Hararite:* Some manuscripts of one ancient translation (see 1 Chronicles 11.26-47). In the Hebrew text Jonathan and Shammah are separate members of the list.   [w]**24.2** *Joab . . . officers:* Some manuscripts of one ancient translation (see 24.4); 1 Chronicles 21.2; Hebrew "Joab, the officer of the army."   [x]**24.5** *began with:* Some manuscripts of one ancient translation; Hebrew "set up camp in."   [y]**24.6** *Kadesh in Syria:* Or "the lower slopes of Mount Hermon."   [z]**24.6** *Dan, Ijon:* Or "Danjaan," an unknown place.

24.22 *sacrifice:* These gifts to God included certain animals, grains, fruits, and sweet-smelling spices. Israelites offered sacrifices to give thanks to God, to ask for God's forgiveness and blessing, and to express regret for a wrong. **(See the chart Sacrifices and Offerings on pg 1828.)**

went through every town of the Hivites and the Canaanites. Finally, they went to Beersheba in the Southern Desert of Judah. [8]After they had gone through the whole land, they went back to Jerusalem. It had taken them 9 months and 20 days.

[9]Joab came and told David, "In Israel there are 800,000 who can serve in the army, and in Judah there are 500,000."

The LORD Punishes David
(1 Chronicles 21.7-17)

[10]After everyone had been counted, David realized he had done wrong. He told the LORD, "What I did was stupid and terribly wrong. LORD, please forgive me."

[11]Before David even got up the next morning, the LORD had told David's prophet Gad [12-13]to take a message to David. Gad went to David and told him:

You must choose one of three ways for the LORD to punish you: Will there be seven[a] years when the land won't grow enough food for your people? Or will your enemies chase you and make you run from them for three months? Or will there be three days of horrible disease in your land? Think about it and decide, because I have to give your answer to God, who sent me.

[14]David was really frightened and said, "It's a terrible choice to make! But the LORD is kind, and I'd rather be punished by him than by anyone else."

[15-16]So that morning, the LORD sent an angel to spread a horrible disease everywhere in Israel, from Dan to Beersheba. And before it was over, 70,000 people had died.

When the angel was about to destroy Jerusalem, the LORD felt sorry for all the suffering he had caused and told the angel, "That's enough! Don't touch them." This happened at the threshing place that belonged to Araunah the Jebusite.

[17]David saw the angel killing everyone and told the LORD, "These people are like sheep with me as their shepherd.[b] I have sinned terribly, but they have done nothing wrong. Please, punish me and my family instead of them!"

David Buys Araunah's Threshing Place
(1 Chronicles 21.18—22.1)

[18-19]That same day the prophet Gad came and told David, "Go to the threshing place that belongs to Araunah and build an altar there for the LORD."

So David went.

[20]Araunah looked and saw David and his soldiers coming up toward him. He went over to David, bowed down low, [21]and said, "Your Majesty! Why have you come to see me?"

David answered, "I've come to buy your threshing place. I have to build the LORD an altar here, so this disease will stop killing the people."

[22]Araunah said, "Take whatever you want and offer your sacrifice. Here are some oxen for the sacrifice. You can use the threshing-boards[c] and the wooden yokes for the fire. [23]Take them—they're yours! I hope the LORD your God will be pleased with you."

[24]But David answered, "No! I have to pay

[a]24.12,13 *seven:* Hebrew; some manuscripts of one ancient translation "three" (see 1 Chronicles 21.12). [b]24.17 *as their shepherd:* The Dead Sea Scrolls, and some manuscripts of two ancient translations (see 1 Chronicles 21.17); these words are not in the Standard Hebrew Text of this verse. [c]24.22 *threshing-boards:* Heavy boards with bits of rock or metal on the bottom. They were dragged across the grain to separate the husks from the kernels.

you what they're worth. I can't offer the LORD my God a sacrifice that cost me nothing." So David bought the threshing place and the oxen for 50 pieces of silver. ²⁵Then he built an altar for the LORD. He offered sacrifices to please the LORD and to ask for his blessings.

The LORD answered the prayers of the people, and no one else died from the terrible disease.

24.25 *altar:* A raised structure where sacrifices and offerings could be presented to the LORD, or to pagan gods. Altars could be made of rocks, packed earth, metal, or pottery.

Reflection Questions About 2 Samuel 1.1—24.25

1. FIRST SAMUEL tells how God rejected Saul as king and chose David, rather than one of Saul's sons, to be the next king (1 Sam 16.1-13). After Saul died, what kept David from taking his place as God's chosen king (2 Sam 1—4)?

2. In chapters 5 and 6, David becomes king of Israel, captures Jerusalem, and brings the sacred chest to Jerusalem. How are these events related and what do they signify? How do the people react when the sacred chest is brought to Jerusalem? What important events do you celebrate? How do you celebrate them?

3. What important message does the LORD's prophet Nathan bring to David in chapter 7? How is the agreement the LORD is making with David different from the one the LORD made with Saul? What will the relationship be between the LORD and one of David's sons? What will this son do for the LORD?

4. Re-read the story of David and Bathsheba (chapter 11). What did David do wrong? How did he make things worse? How did the prophet get David to confess his guilt (12.1-15)? What happened as a result of David's sin?

5. Part of the LORD's message that Nathan delivered to David was, "Because you wouldn't obey me . . . your family will never live in peace" (12.10). What are David's "family problems" as described in chapters 13 through 16? How did David react to each of these problems? Do you agree with all the choices he made? Why or why not?

6. What happened because Saul broke a promise the Israelites had made to the Gibeonites (21.1-9)? What did David do to make things right? How do you feel about this? When someone does something that harms another person today, what kind of punishment do you think is appropriate? What can a society do to see that justice is done and all people are treated fairly?

7. Re-read the key passages in 2 SAMUEL that deal with mourning for the dead: (a) David mourns for Saul and Jonathan, 1.17-27, (b) David mourns for Abner, 3.28-39, (c) David mourns for his infant son, 12.16-23, (d) David mourns for Amnon, 13.30—14.24, (e) David mourns for Absalom, 18.33—19.8, (f) Rizpah mourns for her relatives who were executed, 21.10. How are these stories similar? How are they different?

8. Re-read 21.17. Make a list of David's qualities that you think led to the devotion and honor his soldiers give him. What do these qualities have to do with David's relationship with God? Read what David has to say about himself in 22.21-25. Does this sound like boasting? What qualities do you have that might inspire respect from other people? How can improving your relationship with God improve your relationships with friends, family, and co-workers?

9. Why did David want to count the people of Israel and Judah (24.1-17)? What did Joab say when David told him that he wanted to do this (verse 3)? How did David feel afterwards (verse 10)? What message did the prophet Gad bring to David and how did David respond? Look back through 2 SAMUEL for an example of David asking for, trusting, and following God's direction. How was this different from the time David counted the people?

10. David was a great leader of the people of Israel and a man who put his trust in God, yet he was guilty of many sins. Why do you think God continued to forgive David? What does this tell you about God?

1 kings

Israel experienced its "golden age" of peace and prosperity under King Solomon. But even Israel's wisest king wasn't perfect. Read 1 KINGS to see what happened to the peace Israel enjoyed because of Solomon's disobedience to the LORD.

WHAT MAKES 1 KINGS SPECIAL?

FIRST KINGS is the first half of a single book that was divided into two parts, 1 and 2 KINGS, because they were too long to fit on one scroll. Together the books continue the history of Israel that is begun in the books of SAMUEL, but 1 and 2 KINGS tell the history in a special way. The story moves back and forth between reports of the kings of Judah and reports of the kings of Israel so that we can always compare what was going on in the north (Israel) with what was going on in the south (Judah).

FIRST and SECOND KINGS retell the history of Israel by looking at each king and judging him according to his faithfulness. If a king of Judah was faithful and obeyed God's law, especially by worshiping in the place the LORD chose, that is, in Jerusalem (Deut 12.5-19), he was praised as being good. If he disobeyed by tolerating the worship of other gods or by allowing the people to worship from places other than Jerusalem, he was condemned as being evil. Some of the kings of Judah were judged to be good, especially Hezekiah and Josiah, because they enforced worship at the temple in Jerusalem. All the kings of Israel were judged to be evil, because they worshiped at the rival shrines of Bethel and Dan.

WHAT'S THE STORY BEHIND THE SCENE?

The books of 1 and 2 KINGS were perhaps finally put together in Babylon from a number of sources sometime during the exile (586–539 B.C.).

HOW IS 1 KINGS CONSTRUCTED?

The book may be divided into three major sections. The first (1–2) tells about the last years of David's life and how Solomon, his son, became king of Israel. The second (3–11) reports what Solomon did as king, especially the building and dedication of the temple in Jerusalem. The last section (12–22) begins with the story of the northern tribes' rejection of Rehoboam as king after Solomon's death and the splitting of the nation into two separate kingdoms—Israel in the north and Judah in the south. This section then goes on to report the activities of the various kings of both kingdoms through the middle of the ninth century B.C.

The book may be outlined in the following way:

Originally, 1 and 2 Kings were one book. Together, they describe Israel's history from the last years of King David's life to the fall of Jerusalem and the exile of the people to Babylonia. First and Second Kings not only continue the history of Israel started in 1 and 2 Samuel, they also show the degree to which each of the kings was faithful or disobedient to God. First Kings begins by describing the last years of David's life, then goes on to tell how his son Solomon became king and undertook the construction and dedication of the temple in Jerusalem. The second half of 1 Kings tells how the united kingdom of Israel split into two kingdoms, Israel in the north and Judah in the south. Within this section is a description of the activities of an important prophet, Elijah. The book compares the rulers of the northern and southern kingdoms up to the deaths of King Ahab of Israel and King Jehoshaphat of Judah, in the middle of the ninth century B.C.

Outline

David in His Old Age

1 King David was now an old man, and he always felt cold, even under a lot of blankets. [2]His officials said, "Your Majesty, we will look for a young woman to take care of you. She can lie down beside you and keep you warm." [3-4]They looked everywhere in Israel until they found a very beautiful young woman named Abishag, who lived in the town of Shunem.[a] They brought her to David, and she took care of him. But David did not have sex with her.

Adonijah Tries To Become King

[5-6]Adonijah was the son of David and Haggith. He was Absalom's younger brother[b] and was very handsome. One day,

Adonijah started bragging, "I'm going to make myself king!" So he got some chariots and horses, and he hired 50 men as bodyguards. David did not want to hurt his feelings, so he never asked Adonijah why he was doing these things.

[7]Adonijah met with Joab the son of Zeruiah and Abiathar the priest and asked them if they would help him become king. Both of them agreed to help. [8]But Zadok the priest, Benaiah the son of Jehoiada, Nathan the prophet, Shimei, Rei,[c] and David's bodyguards all refused.

[9]Adonijah invited his brothers and David's officials from Judah to go with him to Crawling Rock[d] near Rogel Spring, where he sacrificed some sheep, cattle, and fat calves.[e] [10]But he did not invite Nathan, Benaiah, David's bodyguards, or his own brother Solomon.

---

[a]1.3,4 *Shunem*: A town in northern Israel, just north of Jezreel Valley.   [b]1.5,6 *brother*: Since Absalom was dead, Adonijah was now David's oldest living son and would be next in line to be king.
[c]1.8 *Shimei, Rei*: Or "Shimei his advisor."   [d]1.9 *Crawling Rock*: Or "Zoheleth Rock."
[e]1.9 *sacrificed . . . calves*: This was part of a ceremony where Adonijah was made the new king.

David

1.1-4 *Abishag*: Abishag becomes another of David's wives. Having more than one wife was allowed at this time. Sometimes "wife" refers to a woman legally bound to a man, but without the full privileges of a wife. The fact that David does not have sexual relations with this wife is probably the author's way of indicating that David was no longer a powerful ruler.

1.5-6 *Absalom's younger brother*: 2 Samuel 13–18 tells the tragic story of David and his son, Absalom, who died in battle against his father.

1.7,8 *Joab the son of Zeruiah . . . Abiathar . . . Zadok . . . Benaiah . . . Nathan*: Zeruiah was David's older sister, so Joab was David's nephew. Joab was an important military leader who had served King David. He commanded the troops in the field during battle, but would not have had men at his immediate command to support Adonijah in his claim as the new king. Abiathar was the son of Ahimelech, a priest whom Saul had killed for helping David. Abiathar became David's close friend and was now David's priest. Zadok, a priest, is first mentioned in 2 Samuel 8.17, and was continually loyal to David. Benaiah was the commander of the standing army, a group of paid foreign soldiers who acted as David's bodyguards. The man Benaiah supports would have troops at his immediate command. Nathan was a prophet who advised David. (See the article Prophets and Prophecy on pg 1791.)

1.11 *Bathsheba, Solomon's mother:* David slept with the beautiful Bathsheba while she was still the wife of one of his soldiers, Uriah the Hittite. When she became pregnant, David arranged for Uriah to be killed in battle and then married Bathsheba (2 Sam 11.2-27). The baby from their union died as punishment for David's sin. Solomon was their second son.

Solomon

1.17 *you promised:* This promise is not recorded anywhere in the Bible, but may be suggested in 2 Sam 12.24,25. David either remembers making this promise or is convinced that if Nathan and Bathsheba believe he made this promise, then he surely must have.

1.33 *Gihon Spring:* This spring was Jerusalem's primary source of water. Archaeologists have discovered a tunnel running from the Gihon Spring outside Jerusalem's walls to a pool under the city. Water jugs were lowered down a vertical shaft to the pool, giving the city access to water without going outside its walls. This was a real advantage during times when the city was under attack.

1.38 *Zadok . . . bodyguards:* By sending his officials (1.33), a priest (Zadok), a prophet (Nathan), his military commander (Benaiah), and his bodyguard to participate in the ceremony to make Solomon king, David shows that he supports Solomon, not Adonijah.

[11]When Nathan heard what had happened, he asked Bathsheba, Solomon's mother:

Have you heard that Adonijah the son of Haggith has made himself king? But David doesn't know a thing about it. [12]You and your son Solomon will be killed, unless you do what I tell you. [13]Go say to David, "You promised me that Solomon would be the next king. So why is Adonijah now king?"

[14]While you are still talking to David, I'll come in and tell him that everything you said is true.

[15]Meanwhile, David was in his bedroom where Abishag was taking care of him because he was so old. Bathsheba went in [16]and bowed down.

"What can I do for you?" David asked.

[17]Bathsheba answered:

Your Majesty, you promised me in the name of the Lord your God that my son Solomon would be the next king. [18]But Adonijah has already been made king, and you didn't know anything about it. [19]He sacrificed a lot of cattle, calves, and sheep. And he invited Abiathar the priest, Joab your army commander, and all your sons to be there, except Solomon, your loyal servant.

[20]Your Majesty, everyone in Israel is waiting for you to announce who will be the next king. [21]If you don't, they will say that Solomon and I have rebelled. They will treat us like criminals and kill us as soon as you die.

[22]Just then, Nathan the prophet arrived. [23]Someone told David that he was there, and Nathan came in. He bowed with his face to the ground [24]and said:

Your Majesty, did you say that Adonijah would be king? [25]Earlier today, he sacrificed a lot of cattle, calves, and sheep. He invited the army command-

ers, Abiathar, and all your sons to be there. They are already eating and drinking and shouting, "Long live King Adonijah!" [26]But he didn't invite me or Zadok the priest or Benaiah or Solomon. [27]Did you say they could do this without telling the rest of us who would be the next king?

Solomon Becomes King

[28]David said, "Tell Bathsheba to come here." She came and stood in front of him. [29-30]Then he said, "The living Lord God of Israel has kept me safe. And so today, I will keep the promise I made to you in his name: Solomon will be the next king!"

[31]Bathsheba bowed with her face to the ground and said, "Your Majesty, I pray that you will live a long time!"

[32]Then David said, "Tell Zadok, Nathan, and Benaiah to come here."

When they arrived, [33]he told them:

Take along some of my officials and let Solomon ride my own mule to Gihon Spring. [34]When you get there, Zadok and Nathan will pour olive oil over Solomon's head to show that he is the new king of Israel. Then order someone to blow a trumpet and tell everyone to shout, "Long live King Solomon!" [35]Bring him back here, and he will take my place as king. He is the one I have chosen to rule Israel and Judah.

[36]Benaiah answered, "We will do it, Your Majesty. I pray that the Lord your God will let it happen. [37]The Lord has always watched over you, and I pray that he will now watch over Solomon. May the Lord help Solomon to be an even greater king than you."

[38]Zadok, Nathan, and Benaiah left and took along the two groups of David's spe-

cial bodyguards.[f] Solomon rode on David's mule as they led him to Gihon Spring. [39]Zadok the priest brought some olive oil from the sacred tent and poured it on Solomon's head to show that he was now king. A trumpet was blown and everyone shouted, "Long live King Solomon!" [40]Then they played flutes and celebrated as they followed Solomon back to Jerusalem. They made so much noise that the ground shook.

[41]Adonijah and his guests had almost finished eating when they heard the noise. Joab also heard the trumpet and asked, "What's all that noise about in the city?"

[42]Just then, Jonathan son of Abiathar came running up. "Come in," Adonijah said. "An important man like you must have some good news."

[43]Jonathan answered:

No, I don't! David has just announced that Solomon will be king. [44-45]Solomon rode David's own mule to Gihon Spring, and Zadok, Nathan, Benaiah, and David's special bodyguards[g] went with him. When they got there, Zadok and Nathan made Solomon king. Then everyone celebrated all the way back to Jerusalem. That's the noise you hear in the city. [46]Solomon is now king.

[47]And listen to this! David's officials told him, "We pray that your God will help Solomon to be an even greater king!"

David was in his bed at the time, but he bowed [48]and prayed, "I praise you, LORD God of Israel. You have made my son Solomon king and have let me live to see it."

[49]Adonijah's guests shook with fear when they heard this news, and they left as fast as they could. [50]Adonijah himself was afraid of what Solomon might do to him, so he ran to the sacred tent and grabbed hold of the corners of the altar for protection.[h]

[51]Someone told Solomon, "Adonijah is afraid of you and is holding onto the corners of the altar. He wants you to promise that you won't kill him."

[52]Solomon answered, "If Adonijah doesn't cause any trouble, I won't hurt him. But if he does, I'll have him killed." [53]Then he sent someone to the altar to get Adonijah.

After Adonijah came and bowed down, Solomon said, "Adonijah, go home."

David's Instructions to Solomon

2 Not long before David died, he told Solomon:

[2]My son, I will soon die, as everyone must. But I want you to be strong and brave. [3]Do what the LORD your God commands and follow his teachings. Obey everything written in the Law of Moses. Then you will be a success, no matter what you do or where you go. [4]You and your descendants must always faithfully obey the LORD. If you do, he will keep the solemn promise he made to me that someone from our family will always be king of Israel.

[5]Solomon, don't forget what Joab did to me by killing Abner son of Ner and Amasa son of Jether, the two commanders of Israel's army. He killed

[f]1.38 *the two . . . bodyguards*: The Hebrew text has "the Cherethites and the Pelethites," who were foreign soldiers hired by David to be part of his bodyguard. [g]1.44,45 *David's special bodyguards*: See the note at 1.38. [h]1.50 *the corners . . . for protection*: The four corners of some ancient altars looked like animal horns. Since the entire altar was sacred, anyone holding on to its corners was supposed to be safe from being killed.

1.39 *sacred tent:* The sacred tent is sometimes called the "tabernacle," which means "dwelling place."

The Sacred Tent

1.50 *the corners . . . for protection:* The four corners of some ancient altars looked like animal horns. Since the entire altar was sacred, anyone holding on to its corners was supposed to be safe from being killed. This protection, however, was not for people who intentionally committed murder (Exod 21.14).

2.3 *Law of Moses:* The Law, including the Ten Commandments, given to Moses on Mount Sinai (Exod 19.16—20.17; Deut 5.1-22).

Law

Ten Commandments

2.8 *cursed . . . me:* A curse is the opposite of a blessing. A person who curses another asks for harm or destruction to happen to that person. Once spoken, a curse (like a blessing) could not be taken back, because it was believed that the spoken word had a life and power of its own, with the ability to make happen what was spoken. Only a blessing or other special action is able to control the evil intent of a curse.

2.10-11 *Jerusalem:* From this time, "City of David" becomes another term for Jerusalem.

Jerusalem

2.17 *Abishag:* Whoever inherited the king's wives was considered to have inherited the throne. Abishag was one of David's wives (1 Kgs 1.3-4). Solomon considers Adonijah's request to marry her as another attempt to establish himself as the rightful king. Family history probably added to Solomon's suspicions, as his older brother Absalom had tried to establish his ownership of the throne by sleeping with David's wives (2 Sam 16.20-23).

2.26 *sacred chest:* The sacred chest was the acacia wood box that accompanied the Hebrews on their wilderness wanderings in the time of Moses and housed the two flat stones that had the Ten Commandments written on them. It was understood to be the throne of the LORD All-Powerful from which God ruled his people.

The Sacred Chest

them as if they were his enemies in a war, but he did it when there was no war.[i] He is guilty, and now it's up to you to punish him [6]in the way you think best. Whatever you do, don't let him die peacefully in his old age.

[7]The sons of Barzillai from Gilead helped me when I was running from your brother Absalom.[j] Be kind to them and let them eat at your table.

[8]Be sure to do something about Shimei son of Gera from Bahurim in the territory of Benjamin. He cursed and insulted me the day I went to Mahanaim. But later, when he came to meet me at the Jordan River, I promised that I wouldn't kill him.[k] [9]Now you must punish him. He's an old man, but you're wise enough to know that you must have him killed.

David Dies

[10-11]David was king of Israel 40 years. He ruled 7 years from Hebron and 33 years from Jerusalem. Then he died and was buried in Jerusalem.[l] [12]His son Solomon became king and took control of David's kingdom.

Adonijah Is Killed

[13]One day, Adonijah went to see Bathsheba, Solomon's mother, and she asked, "Is this a friendly visit?"

"Yes. [14]I just want to talk with you."

"All right," she told him, "go ahead."

[15]"You know that I was king for a little while," Adonijah replied. "And everyone in Israel accepted me as their ruler. But the LORD wanted my brother to be king, so

now things have changed. [16]Would you do me a favor?"

"What do you want?" Bathsheba asked.

[17]"Please ask Solomon to let me marry Abishag. He won't say no to you."

[18]"All right," she said. "I'll ask him."

[19]When Bathsheba went to see Solomon, he stood up to meet her, then bowed low. He sat back down and had another throne brought in, so his mother could sit at his right side.[m] [20]Bathsheba sat down and then asked, "Would you do me a small favor?"

Solomon replied, "Mother, just tell me what you want, and I will do it."

[21]"Allow your brother Adonijah to marry Abishag," she answered.

[22]Solomon said:

What? Let my older brother marry Abishag? You may as well ask me to let him rule the kingdom! And why don't you ask such favors for Abiathar and Joab?[n]

[23]I swear in the name of the LORD that Adonijah will die because he asked for this! If he doesn't, I pray that God will severely punish me. [24]The LORD made me king in my father's place and promised that the kings of Israel would come from my family. Yes, I swear by the living LORD that Adonijah will die today.

[25]"Benaiah," Solomon shouted, "go kill Adonijah." So Adonijah died.

Abiathar Is Sent Back Home

[26]Solomon sent for Abiathar the priest and said:

Abiathar, go back home to Anathoth! You ought to be killed too, but I won't

[i]2.5 *war:* See 2 Samuel 3.22-27 and 20.7-10. [j]2.7 *Absalom:* See 2 Samuel 17.27-29. [k]2.8 *him:* See 2 Samuel 16.5-14 and 19.16-23. [l]2.10,11 *Jerusalem:* Hebrew "the city of David." [m]2.19 *at his right side:* The place of honor. [n]2.22 *And why . . . Joab:* One possible meaning for the difficult Hebrew text.

do it now. When my father David was king, you were in charge of the sacred chest, and you went through a lot of hard times with my father. [27]But I won't let you be a priest of the LORD anymore.

And so the promise that the LORD had made at Shiloh about the family of Eli came true.[o]

Joab Is Killed

[28]Joab had not helped Absalom try to become king, but he had helped Adonijah. So when Joab learned that Adonijah had been killed, he ran to the sacred tent and grabbed hold of the corners of the altar for protection.[p] [29]When Solomon heard about this, he sent someone to ask Joab, "Why did you run to the altar?"

Joab sent back his answer, "I was afraid of you, and I ran to the LORD for protection."[q]

Then Solomon shouted, "Benaiah, go kill Joab!"

[30]Benaiah went to the sacred tent and yelled, "Joab, the king orders you to come out!"

"No!" Joab answered. "Kill me right here."

Benaiah went back and told Solomon what Joab had said.

[31-32]Solomon replied:

Do what Joab said. Kill him and bury him! Then my family and I won't be responsible for what he did to Abner the commander of Israel's army and to Amasa the commander of Judah's army. He killed those innocent men without my father knowing about it. Both of them were better men than Joab. Now the LORD will make him pay for those murders. [33]Joab's family will always suffer because of what he did, but the LORD will always bless David's family and his kingdom with peace.

[34]Benaiah went back and killed Joab. His body was taken away and buried near his home in the desert.

[35]Solomon put Benaiah in Joab's place as army commander, and he put Zadok in Abiathar's place as priest.

Shimei Is Killed

[36]Solomon sent for Shimei and said, "Build a house here in Jerusalem and live in it. But whatever you do, don't leave the city! [37]If you ever cross Kidron Valley and leave Jerusalem, you will be killed. And it will be your own fault."

[38]"That's fair, Your Majesty," Shimei answered. "I'll do that." So Shimei lived in Jerusalem from then on.

[39]About three years later, two of Shimei's servants ran off to King Achish in Gath. When Shimei found out where they were, [40]he saddled his donkey and went after them. He found them and brought them back to Jerusalem.

[41]Someone told Solomon that Shimei had gone to Gath and was back. [42]Solomon sent for him and said:

Shimei, you promised in the name of the LORD that you would never leave Jerusalem. I warned you that you would die if you did. You agreed that this was fair, didn't you? [43]You have disobeyed me and have broken the promise you made to the LORD.

[44]I know you remember all the cruel things you did to my father David. Now the LORD is going to punish you for what you did. [45]But the LORD will

[o]2.27 *the promise . . . came true*: See 1 Samuel 2.27-34. [p]2.28 *the corners . . . for protection*: See the note at 1.50. [q]2.29 *he sent someone . . . for protection*: One ancient translation; these words are not in the Hebrew text.

● 2.34,35 *killed Joab . . . put Zadok in Abiathar's place as priest:* Perhaps Joab is not given the protection of the altar because his killings were murder, not accidental (2.31-32). Joab was buried near his home in Bethlehem (2 Sam 2.18,32). A priest was a man who led the worship in the sacred tent or in the temple and who offered sacrifices to the LORD for the sake of the people. From this time on, only Zadok and his descendants are considered legitimate priests.

Israel's Priests

● 2.36,37 *Jerusalem . . . Kidron Valley:* Jerusalem was Israel's political capital and the place where people were to worship God. The Kidron Valley was considered the eastern boundary of Jerusalem. **(See Map 4 on pg 1882.)**

3.2 *local shrines:* Many of the Israelites' altars were on hills, at places where foreign gods once had been worshiped. God's law required that these altars be destroyed (Num 33.52; Deut 7.5; 12.3), and that worship take place only at place chosen by the LORD.

3.7 *your servant . . . made me king:* These words show that Solomon understands his place as king of Israel. The LORD God is the true king. Israel's earthly kings were chosen by God and were expected to carry out God's will.

Kingship in Israel

3.15 *sacrifices to please the Lord . . . sacrifices to ask his blessing:* Sacrifices to please the LORD are traditionally called "whole burnt offerings" because the whole animal was burned on the altar. While these sacrifices did involve forgiveness for sin, their main purpose was to please the LORD with the smell of the smoke from the sacrifice. Sacrifices to ask the LORD's blessing are traditionally called "peace offerings" or "offerings of well-being." A main purpose was to ask for the LORD's blessing. **(See the chart Sacrifices and Offerings on pg 1828.)**

bless me and make my father's kingdom strong forever.

46 "Benaiah," Solomon shouted, "kill Shimei." So Shimei died.

Solomon was now in complete control of his kingdom.

The LORD Makes Solomon Wise
(2 Chronicles 1.1-13)

3 Solomon signed a treaty with the king of Egypt and married his daughter. She lived in the older part of Jerusalem[r] until the palace, the LORD's temple, and the wall around Jerusalem were completed. **2** At that time, there was no temple for worshiping the LORD, and everyone offered sacrifices at the local shrines.[s] **3** Solomon loved the LORD and followed his father David's instructions, but Solomon also offered sacrifices and burned incense at the shrines.

4 The most important shrine was in Gibeon, and Solomon had offered more than 1,000 sacrifices on that altar. **5** One night while Solomon was in Gibeon, the LORD God appeared to him in a dream and said, "Solomon, ask for anything you want, and I will give it to you." **6** Solomon answered:

My father David, your servant, was honest and did what you commanded. You were always loyal to him, and you gave him a son who is now king. **7** LORD God, I'm your servant, and you've made me king in my father's place. But I'm very young and know so little about being a leader. **8** And now I must rule your chosen people, even though there are too many of them to count.

9 Please make me wise and teach me the difference between right and wrong. Then I will know how to rule your people. If you don't, there is no way I could rule this great nation of yours. **10-11** God said:

Solomon, I'm pleased that you asked for this. You could have asked to live a long time or to be rich. Or you could have asked for your enemies to be destroyed. Instead, you asked for wisdom to make right decisions. **12** So I'll make you wiser than anyone who has ever lived or ever will live.

13 I'll also give you what you didn't ask for. You'll be rich and respected as long as you live, and you'll be greater than any other king. **14** If you obey me and follow my commands, as your father David did, I'll let you live a long time.

15 Solomon woke up and realized that God had spoken to him in the dream. He went back to Jerusalem and stood in front of the sacred chest, where he offered sacrifices to please the Lord[t] and sacrifices to ask his blessing.[u] Then Solomon gave a feast for his officials.

Solomon Makes a Difficult Decision

16 One day two women[v] came to King Solomon, **17** and one of them said:

Your Majesty, this woman and I live in the same house. Not long ago my baby was born at home, **18** and three days later her baby was born. Nobody else was there with us.

19 One night while we were all asleep, she rolled over on her baby, and he

---

[r]**3.1** *the older . . . Jerusalem:* Hebrew "the city of David." [s]**3.2** *local shrines:* The Hebrew text has "high places," which were local places to worship God or foreign gods. [t]**3.15** *sacrifices to please the Lord:* See Leviticus 1.1-17. [u]**3.15** *sacrifices to ask his blessing:* See Leviticus 3.1-17. [v]**3.16** *women:* Hebrew "prostitutes."

Solomon said to God, *"Please make me wise and teach me the difference between right and wrong. Then I will know how to rule your people."* 1 Kgs 3.9

died. **20**Then while I was still asleep, she got up and took my son out of my bed. She put him in her bed, then she put her dead baby next to me.

21In the morning when I got up to feed my son, I saw that he was dead. But when I looked at him in the light, I knew he wasn't my son.

22"No!" the other woman shouted. "He was your son. My baby is alive!"

"The dead baby is yours," the first woman yelled. "Mine is alive!"

They argued back and forth in front of Solomon, **23**until finally he said, "Both of you say this live baby is yours. **24**Someone bring me a sword."

A sword was brought, and Solomon ordered, **25**"Cut the baby in half! That way each of you can have part of him."

26"Please don't kill my son," the baby's mother screamed. "Your Majesty, I love him very much, but give him to her. Just don't kill him."

The other woman shouted, "Go ahead and cut him in half. Then neither of us will have the baby."

27Solomon said, "Don't kill the baby." Then he pointed to the first woman, "She is his real mother. Give the baby to her."

28Everyone in Israel was amazed when they heard how Solomon had made his decision. They realized that God had given him wisdom to judge fairly.

Solomon's Officials

4 **1-6**Here is a list of Solomon's highest officials while he was king of Israel:
Azariah son of Zadok was the priest;
Elihoreph and Ahijah sons of Shisha were the secretaries;
Jehoshaphat son of Ahilud kept the government records;
Benaiah son of Jehoiada was the army commander;
Zadok and Abiathar were priests;
Azariah son of Nathan was in charge of the regional officers;
Zabud son of Nathan was a priest and the king's advisor;
Ahishar was the prime minister;
Adoniram son of Abda was in charge of the forced labor.

7Solomon chose twelve regional officers, who took turns bringing food for him and his household. Each officer provided food from his region for one month of the year. **8**These were the twelve officers:
The son of Hur was in charge of the hill country of Ephraim.

9The son of Deker was in charge of the towns of Makaz, Shaalbim, Beth-Shemesh, and Elon-Beth-Hanan.

10The son of Hesed was in charge of the towns of Arubboth and Socoh, and the region of Hepher.

11The son of Abinadab was in charge of Naphath-Dor and was married to Solomon's daughter Taphath.

12Baana son of Ahilud was in charge of the towns of Taanach and Megiddo. He was also in charge of the whole region of Beth-Shan near the town of Zarethan, south of Jezreel from Beth-Shan to Abel-Meholah to the other side of Jokmeam.

13The son of Geber was in charge of the town of Ramoth in Gilead and the villages in Gilead belonging to the family of Jair, a descendant of Manasseh. He was also in charge of the region of Argob in Bashan, which had 60 walled towns with bronze bars on their gates.

14Ahinadab son of Iddo was in charge of the territory of Mahanaim.

15Ahimaaz was in charge of the territory of Naphtali and was married to Solomon's daughter Basemath.

16Baana son of Hushai was in charge of

3.28 *wisdom:* The story in 3.16-28 reflects the Israelites' understanding that "wisdom" is the ability to understand the human mind and intentions in order to see that God's justice is carried out. Other understandings of "wisdom" are revealed in the spoken and written literature of the people of Israel, particularly in their proverbs, songs, and riddles.

Wisdom

4.7-19 *twelve regional officers... territory of Judah:* Solomon divided the kingdom into twelve districts, each to be governed by an official. The district boundaries are somewhat different from the boundaries that separated the twelve tribes. Solomon may have hoped that this would break old tribal loyalties and work toward creating a more united nation. In the end, it may have contributed to the revolt after his death, especially since Judah (Solomon's own tribal territory) appears to have been a thirteenth territory that was not required to support the king in the same way as the others.

4.20 *Judah and Israel:* Before David united the kingdom as a whole under the name of Israel, "Israel" referred to the ten northern tribes (led by the tribe of Ephraim), and "Judah" to the two southern tribes (Simeon and Judah, with the tribe of Judah leading). **(See Map 3 on pg 1881.)**

Israel

4.21 *Euphrates River:* The longest, largest river in Western Asia, originating in the Armenian Mountains and flowing to the Persian Gulf. **(See Map 1 on pg 1879.)**

4.21 *Philistines:* The Philistines were people from Philistia, a strip of land along the eastern coast of the Mediterranean Sea. It included five main cities, each with its own ruler: Ekron, Ashdod, Ashkelon, Gath, and Gaza. Israel fought many wars against the Philistines.

Egypt

5.1 *King Hiram:* King Hiram, who ruled the city state of Tyre from around 970 to 935 B.C., had sent lumber and workmen to help David build his palace (2 Sam 5.11). His strong trade and military relations with David and Solomon was an important reason why the Philistines ceased to be a major threat to Israel during Solomon's time as king.

Phoenicia

the territory of Asher and the town of Bealoth.

[17]Jehoshaphat son of Paruah was in charge of the territory of Issachar.

[18]Shimei son of Ela was in charge of the territory of Benjamin.

[19]Geber son of Uri was in charge of Gilead, where King Sihon of the Amorites and King Og of Bashan had lived.

And one officer was in charge of the territory of Judah.[w]

The Size of Solomon's Kingdom

[20]There were so many people living in Judah and Israel while Solomon was king that they seemed like grains of sand on a beach. Everyone had enough to eat and drink, and they were happy.

[21]Solomon ruled every kingdom between the Euphrates River and the land of the Philistines down to Egypt. These kingdoms paid him taxes as long as he lived.

[22]Every day, Solomon needed 150 bushels of fine flour, 300 bushels of coarsely-ground flour, [23]10 grain-fed cattle, 20 pasture-fed cattle, 100 sheep, as well as deer, gazelles, and geese.

[24]Solomon ruled the whole region west of the Euphrates River, from Tiphsah to Gaza, and he was at peace with all of the countries around him. [25]Everyone living in Israel, from the town of Dan in the north to Beersheba in the south, was safe as long as Solomon lived. Each family sat undisturbed beneath its own grape vines and fig trees.

[26]Solomon had 40,000 stalls of chariot horses and 12,000 chariot soldiers.

[27]Each of the twelve regional officers brought food to Solomon and his household for one month of the year. They pro-

vided everything he needed, [28]as well as barley and straw for the horses.

Solomon's Wisdom

[29]Solomon was brilliant. God had blessed him with insight and understanding. [30-31]He was wiser than anyone else in the world, including the wisest people of the east and of Egypt. He was even wiser than Ethan the Ezrahite, and Mahol's three sons, Heman, Calcol, and Darda. Solomon became famous in every country around Judah and Israel. [32]Solomon wrote 3,000 wise sayings and composed more than 1,000 songs. [33]He could talk about all kinds of plants, from large trees to small bushes, and he taught about animals, birds, reptiles, and fish. [34]Kings all over the world heard about Solomon's wisdom and sent people to listen to him teach.

Solomon Asks Hiram To Help Build the Temple
(2 Chronicles 2.1-16)

5 King Hiram of Tyre[x] had always been friends with Solomon's father David. When Hiram learned that Solomon was king, he sent some of his officials to meet with Solomon.

[2]Solomon sent a message back to Hiram:

[3]Remember how my father David wanted to build a temple where the LORD his God could be worshiped? But enemies kept attacking my father's kingdom, and he never had the chance. [4]Now, thanks to the LORD God, there is peace in my kingdom and no trouble or threat of war anywhere.

[5] The LORD God promised my father

---

[w]**4.19** *of Judah:* One ancient translation; these words are not in the Hebrew text.   [x]**5.1** *Tyre:* The most important city in Phoenicia. It was located on the coast of the Mediterranean Sea north of Israel, in what is today southern Lebanon.

Everyone living in Israel . . . was safe as long as Solomon lived. Each family sat undisturbed beneath its own grape vines and fig trees. 1 KGS 4.25

that when his son became king, he would build a temple for worshiping the LORD. So I've decided to do that.

[6] I'd like you to send your workers to cut down cedar trees in Lebanon for me. I will pay them whatever you say and will even have my workers help them. We both know that your workers are more experienced than anyone else at cutting lumber.

[7] Hiram was so happy when he heard Solomon's request that he said, "I am grateful that the LORD gave David such a wise son to be king of that great nation!" [8] Then he sent back his answer:

I received your message and will give you all the cedar and pine logs you need. [9] My workers will carry them down from Lebanon to the Mediterranean Sea. They will tie the logs together and float them along the coast to wherever you want them. Then they will untie the logs, and your workers can take them from there.

To pay for the logs, you can provide the grain I need for my household. [10] Hiram gave Solomon all the cedar and pine logs he needed. [11] In return, Solomon gave Hiram about 125,000 bushels of wheat and about 1,100 gallons of pure olive oil each year.

[12] The LORD kept his promise and made Solomon wise. Hiram and Solomon signed a treaty and never went to war against each other.

Solomon's Workers

[13] Solomon ordered 30,000 people from all over Israel to cut logs for the temple, [14] and he put Adoniram in charge of these workers. Solomon divided them into three groups of 10,000. Each group worked one month in Lebanon and had two months off at home.

[15] He also had 80,000 workers to cut stone in the hill country of Israel, 70,000 workers to carry the stones, [16] and over 3,000 assistants to keep track of the work and to supervise the workers. [17] He ordered the workers to cut and shape large blocks of good stone for the foundation of the temple.

[18] Solomon's and Hiram's men worked with men from the city of Gebal,[y] and together they got the stones and logs ready for the temple.

The Outside of the Temple Is Completed

6 Solomon's workers started building the temple during Ziv,[z] the second month of the year. It had been 4 years since Solomon became king of Israel, and 480 years since the people of Israel left Egypt.

[2] The inside of the LORD's temple was 90 feet long, 30 feet wide, and 45 feet high. [3] A 15-foot porch went all the way across the front of the temple. [4] The windows were narrow on the outside but wide on the inside.

[5-6] Along the sides and back of the temple, there were three levels of storage rooms. The rooms on the bottom level were just over seven and a half feet wide, the rooms on the middle level were nine feet wide, and those on the top level were just ten and a half feet wide. There were ledges on the outside of the temple that supported the beams of the storage rooms, so that nothing was built into the temple walls.

[7] Solomon did not want the noise of hammers and axes to be heard at the place

[y]5.18 *Gebal*: Later known as Byblos.   [z]6.1 *Ziv*: The second month of the Hebrew calendar, from about mid-April to mid-May.

● 5.6 *cedar*: Cedar is an extremely hard wood that resists dry rot and insects, has a close beautiful grain for carving, and is valued for its distinctive smell. At one time cedar forests covered most of the Lebanon mountain range that stretches for around one hundred miles along the Syrian coast between Tyre and Arvad. **(See Map 4 on pg 1882.)**

● 5.18 *Gebal*: A seaport later known as Byblos, famous for its skilled stonemasons and shipbuilders. **(See Map 4 on pg 1882.)**

● 6.1 *Ziv . . . Israel left Egypt*: Ziv is the second month of the Hebrew calendar, from about mid-April to mid-May. Historians have used this verse to establish a probable date for the exodus, the time when the Hebrew people were freed from its captivity in Egypt. **(See the chart Pilgrimage Festivals on pg 1799.)**

6.16-18 *most holy place*: The most holy place in the temple is its inner sanctuary. This, the holy place, and the outer courtyard were the three major areas of the temple. Only the high priest could enter the most holy place, and even he could enter it only once a year on the Great Day of Forgiveness. The most holy place traditionally has been called "the holy of holies."

6.23 *winged creatures*: The statues of winged creatures were symbols of the LORD's throne on earth. Also called "cherubim," similar statues are described as having human, lion, eagle, or ox heads, sometimes with more than one of these on the same winged body. They may have been similar to the human-headed bull and lions that guarded Mesopotamian temples. Such winged creatures guarding sacred objects or places are commonly seen in Egyptian and Phoenician art as well.

where the temple was being built. So he gave orders for the workers to shape the blocks of stone at the quarry.

[8]The entrance to the bottom storage rooms was on the south side of the building, and stairs to the other rooms were also there. [9]The roof of the temple was made out of beams and cedar boards.

The workers finished building the outside of the temple. [10]Storage rooms seven and a half feet high were all around the temple, and they were attached to the temple by cedar beams.

[11]The LORD told Solomon:

[12-13]If you obey my commands and do what I say, I will keep the promise I made to your father David. I will live among my people Israel in this temple you are building, and I will not desert them.

[14]So Solomon's workers finished building the temple.

The Inside of the Temple Is Furnished
(2 Chronicles 3.8-14)

[15]The floor of the temple was made out of pine, and the walls were lined with cedar from floor to ceiling.[a]

[16]The most holy place was in the back of the temple, and it was 30 feet square. Cedar boards standing from floor to ceiling[b] separated it from the rest of the temple. [17]The temple's main room was 60 feet, and it was in front of the most holy place.

[18]The inside walls were lined with cedar to hide the stones, and the cedar was decorated with carvings of gourds and flowers.

[19]The sacred chest was kept in the most holy place. [20-22]This room was 30 feet long, 30 feet wide, and 30 feet high, and it was lined with pure gold. There were also gold chains across the front of the most holy place. The inside of the temple, as well as the cedar altar in the most holy place, was covered with gold.

[23]Solomon had two statues of winged creatures[c] made from olive wood to put in the most holy place. Each creature was 15 feet tall [24-26]and 15 feet across. They had two wings, and the wings were seven and a half feet long. [27]Solomon put them next to each other in the most holy place. Their wings were spread out and reached across the room. [28]The creatures were also covered with gold.

[29]The walls of the two rooms were decorated with carvings of palm trees, flowers, and winged creatures. [30]Even the floor was covered with gold.

[31-32]The two doors to the most holy place were made out of olive wood and were decorated with carvings of palm trees, flowers, and winged creatures. The doors and the carvings were covered with gold. The door frame came to a point at the top.

[33-34]The two doors to the main room of the temple were made out of pine, and each one had two sections[d] so they could fold open. The door frame was shaped like a rectangle and was made out of olive wood. [35]The doors were covered with gold and were decorated with carvings of palm trees, flowers, and winged creatures.

[36]The inner courtyard of the temple had walls made out of three layers of cut stones with one layer of cedar beams.

[37]Work began on the temple during Ziv,[e] the second month of the year, four

---

[a]6.15 *from floor to ceiling*: One possible meaning for the difficult Hebrew text.   [b]6.16 *standing . . . ceiling*: One possible meaning for the difficult Hebrew text.   [c]6.23 *statues of winged creatures*: These were symbols of the LORD's throne on earth (see Exodus 25.18-22).   [d]6.33,34 *two sections*: One possible meaning for the difficult Hebrew text.   [e]6.37 *Ziv*: See the note at 6.1.

The LORD told Solomon: *"If you obey my commands . . . I will live among my people Israel in this temple you are building, and I will not desert them."* 1 KGS 6.12-13

years after Solomon became king of Israel. [38]Seven years later the workers finished building it during Bul,[f] the eighth month of the year. It was built exactly as it had been planned.

Solomon's Palace Is Built

7 Solomon's palace took 13 years to build.

[2-3]Forest Hall was the largest room in the palace. It was 150 feet long, 75 feet wide, and 45 feet high, and was lined with cedar from Lebanon. It had 4 rows of cedar pillars, 15 in a row, and they held up 45 cedar beams. The ceiling was covered with cedar. [4]Three rows of windows on each side faced each other, [5]and there were three doors on each side near the front of the hall.

[6]Pillar Hall was 75 feet long and 45 feet wide. A covered porch supported by pillars went all the way across the front of the hall.

[7]Solomon's throne was in Justice Hall, where he judged cases. This hall was completely lined with cedar.

[8]The section of the palace where Solomon lived was behind Justice Hall and looked exactly like it. He had a similar place built for his wife, the daughter of the king of Egypt.

[9]From the foundation all the way to the top, these buildings and the courtyard were made out of the best stones[g] carefully cut to size, then smoothed on every side with saws. [10]The foundation stones were huge, good stones—some of them 15 feet long and others 12 feet long. [11]The cedar beams and other stones that had been cut to size were on top of these foundation stones. [12]The walls around the palace courtyard were made out of three layers of cut stones with one layer of cedar beams, just like the front porch and the inner courtyard of the temple.

Hiram Makes the Bronze Furnishings

(2 Chronicles 3.15-17; 4.1-10)

[13-14]Hiram was a skilled bronze worker from the city of Tyre.[h] His father was now dead, but he also had been a bronze worker from Tyre, and his mother was from the tribe of Naphtali.

King Solomon asked Hiram to come to Jerusalem and make the bronze furnishings to use for worship in the LORD's temple, and he agreed to do it.

[15]Hiram made two bronze columns 27 feet tall and about 6 feet across. [16]For the top of each column, he also made a bronze cap just seven and a half feet high. [17]The caps were decorated with seven rows of designs that looked like chains,[i] [18]with two rows of designs that looked like pomegranates.[j]

[19]The caps for the columns of the porch were six feet high and were shaped like lilies.[k]

[20]The chain designs on the caps were right above the rounded tops of the two columns, and there were 200 pomegranates in rows around each cap. [21]Hiram placed the two columns on each side of the main door of the temple. The column on

● 7.13-14 *Hiram . . . city of Tyre:* This is not the same person as "King Hiram of Tyre" (see 5.1). The bronze furnishings were made near the Jordan River between Succoth and Zarethan, because the clay soil was needed to make the molds for the objects. Bronze itself is made by mixing copper and tin, minerals that were available in this area.

● 7.15 *columns:* These were not building supports, but freestanding columns. It was common at the time to have such columns at the entrance to a temple, although these seem to have been particularly large.

---

[f]**6.38** *Bul:* The eighth month of the Hebrew calendar, from about mid-October to mid-November. [g]**7.9** *From . . . best stones:* One possible meaning for the difficult Hebrew text. [h]**7.13,14** *Hiram . . . city of Tyre:* This is not the same person as "King Hiram of Tyre" (see 5.1). [i]**7.17** *seven rows . . . chains:* One possible meaning for the difficult Hebrew text. [j]**7.18** *pomegranates:* One possible meaning for the difficult Hebrew text of verse 18. A pomegranate is a bright red fruit that looks like an apple. In ancient times, it was a symbol of life. [k]**7.19** *lilies:* One possible meaning for the difficult Hebrew text of verse 19.

7.23 *the Sea:* It is possible the priests used the water in this huge basin for ritual cleansing. The Sea may have symbolized God's separation of the waters that covered the earth to make the sky, land, and ocean in the creation story (Gen 1.6-10). The symbolism of the large bowl may have had its beginnings in an ancient Mesopotamian creation myth in which the hero-god battles the sea monster of Chaos. The Hebrews then used this ancient story as a way of describing the fight between God and evil.

7.48-50 *altar . . . sacred loaves . . . ten lampstands . . . small sprinkling bowls; dishes for incense; fire pans:* The golden altar was used for burning incense (Exod 25.23-30; 30.1-10, 27,34-35). The sacred bread was offered to the LORD and was a symbol of the LORD's presence in the temple. It was put on a special table, and was replaced with fresh bread each week (Lev 24.5-9). The ten lampstands had a centerpiece with three branches on either side, each with a small saucer-like lamp attached to its end (Exod 25.31-40). The light from the lamps symbolized the glory of God (Exod 29.43). The small lamps probably were simple oil lamps that were filled with enough oil to burn from sunset to sunrise (Exod 27.20). Tongs and lamp snuffers were used to cover a flame to extinguish it or to trim the wicks. Sprinkling bowls were used in the preparation for an animal sacrifice. Fire pans were metal pans used to burn incense, carry hot coals, and clean up the ashes after sacrifices.

the south side was called Jachin,[l] and the one on the north was called Boaz.[m]

[22]The lily-shaped caps were on top of the columns.

This completed the work on the columns.

[23]Hiram also made a large bowl called the Sea. It was just seven and a half feet deep, about 15 feet across, and 45 feet around. [24]Two rows of bronze gourds were around the outer edge of the bowl, ten gourds to every 18 inches. [25]The bowl itself sat on top of twelve bronze bulls with three bulls facing outward in each of four directions. [26]The sides of the bowl were 4 inches thick, and its rim was like a cup that curved outward like flower petals. The bowl held about 11,000 gallons.

[27]Hiram made ten movable bronze stands, each one four and a half feet high, six feet long, and six feet wide. [28-29]The sides were made with panels attached to frames decorated with flower designs. The panels themselves were decorated with figures of lions, bulls, and winged creatures. [30-31]Each stand had four bronze wheels and axles and a round frame 27 inches across, held up by four supports 18 inches high. A small bowl rested in the frame. The supports were decorated with flower designs, and the frame with carvings.

The side panels of the stands were square, [32]and the wheels and axles were underneath them. The wheels were about 27 inches high [33]and looked like chariot wheels. The axles, rims, spokes, and hubs were made out of bronze.

[34-35]Around the top of each stand was a nine-inch strip, and there were four braces[n] attached to the corners of each stand. The panels and the supports were attached to the stands, [36]and the stands were decorated with flower designs and figures of lions, palm trees, and winged creatures. [37]Hiram made the ten bronze stands from the same mold, so they were exactly the same size and shape.

[38]Hiram also made ten small bronze bowls, one for each stand. The bowls were six feet across and could hold about 230 gallons.

[39]He put five stands on the south side of the temple, five stands on the north side, and the large bowl at the southeast corner of the temple.

[40]Hiram made pans for hot ashes, and also shovels and sprinkling bowls.

A List of Everything inside the Temple
(2 Chronicles 4.11—5.1)

This is a list of the bronze items that Hiram made for the LORD's temple: [41]two columns; two bowl-shaped caps for the tops of the columns; two chain designs on the caps; [42]400 pomegranates[o] for the chain designs; [43]ten movable stands; ten small bowls for the stands; [44]a large bowl; twelve bulls that held up the bowl; [45]pans for hot ashes, and also shovels and sprinkling bowls.

Hiram made these bronze things for Solomon [46]near the Jordan River between Succoth and Zarethan by pouring melted bronze into clay molds.

[47]There were so many bronze things that Solomon never bothered to weigh them, and no one ever knew how much bronze was used.

[48]Solomon gave orders to make the following temple furnishings out of gold: the altar; the table that held the sacred loaves

---

[l]7.21 *Jachin:* Or "He makes secure."   [m]7.21 *Boaz:* Or "He is strong."   [n]7.34,35 *braces:* Or "handles."
[o]7.42 *pomegranates:* A bright red fruit that looks like an apple. In ancient times, it was a symbol of life.

of bread;P [49]ten lampstands that went in front of the most holy place; flower designs; lamps and tongs; [50]cups, lamp snuffers, and small sprinkling bowls; dishes for incense; fire pans; and the hinges for the doors to the most holy place and the main room of the temple.

[51]After the LORD's temple was finished, Solomon put into its storage rooms everything that his father David had dedicated to the LORD, including the gold and the silver.

Solomon Brings the Sacred Chest to the Temple
(2 Chronicles 5.2—6.2)

[1-2]The sacred chest had been kept on Mount Zion, also known as the city of David. But Solomon decided to have the chest moved to the temple while everyone was in Jerusalem, celebrating the Festival of Shelters during Ethanim,q the seventh month of the year.

Solomon called together the important leaders of Israel. [3-4]Then the priests and the Levites carried to the temple the sacred chest, the sacred tent, and the objects used for worship. [5]Solomon and a crowd of people stood in front of the chest and sacrificed more sheep and cattle than could be counted.

[6]The priests carried the chest into the most holy place and put it under the winged creatures, [7]whose wings covered both the chest and the poles used for carrying it. [8]The poles were so long that they could be seen from right outside the most holy place, but not from anywhere else. And they stayed there from then on.

[9]The only things kept in the chest were the two flat stones Moses had put there when the LORD made his agreement with the people of Israel at Mount Sinai,r after bringing them out of Egypt.

[10]Suddenly a cloud filled the temple as the priests were leaving the most holy place. [11]The LORD's glory was in the cloud, and the light from it was so bright that the priests could not stay inside to do their work. [12]Then Solomon prayed:

"Our LORD, you said that you
would live in a dark cloud.
[13]Now I have built a glorious temple
where you can live forever."

Solomon Speaks to the People
(2 Chronicles 6.3-11)

[14]Solomon turned toward the people standing there. Then he blessed them [15-16]and said:

Praise the LORD God of Israel! Long ago he brought his people out of Egypt. He did not choose a city from any tribe in Israel where his temple would be built, but he kept his promise to make my father David the king of Israel.

[17]So when David wanted to build a temple for the LORD God of Israel, [18]the LORD said, "It's good that you want to build a temple where I can be worshiped. [19]But you're not the one to do it. Your son will build a temple to honor me."

[20]The LORD has done what he promised. I am the king of Israel like my

---

P7.48 *sacred loaves of bread*: This bread was offered to the LORD and was a symbol of the LORD's presence in the temple. It was put out on a special table, and was replaced with fresh bread each week (see Leviticus 24.5-9).   q8.1,2 *Ethanim*: The seventh month of the Hebrew calendar, from about mid-September to mid-October.   r8.9 *Sinai*: Hebrew "Horeb."

● 8.1-2 *Mount Zion...city of David*: Mount Zion was a hill in the southernmost part of Jerusalem. The Jebusite fortress on Mount Zion that David conquered was called the "City of David." Later, both "Zion" and "City of David" are used to mean all of Jerusalem. (See Map 5 on pg 1883.)

Zion

● 8.1-2 *Festival of Shelters*: one of three yearly celebrations. It took place at the end of the fall harvest and lasted for seven days. (See the chart Pilgrimage Festivals on pg 1799.)

● 8.3-4 *Levites*: Priests were Levites descended from Aaron. Later in the Israelites' history, during the period known as the exile, the Levites would lose the position of priesthood and would become only special temple servants.

Israel's Priests

Exile

■ 8.11-13 *The LORD's glory...live forever*: Here as elsewhere, a cloud surrounds and covers God's presence before the people. At other times, God appears under the cover of fire. Verse 12 notes that God lives in a dark cloud. It is for this reason that in this glorious temple, the most holy place is completely dark, and it is there that the sacred chest is placed. Though God's earthly home will be within the most holy place, heaven also is still God's home.

⊘ Locusts

■ 8.39 You know . . . in their hearts:
Here, Solomon's understanding is that
God looks at people's motives as well
as at their actions (outward behavior).
This is similar to the message the
prophet Jeremiah would later give the
people of Israel and Judah about a new
agreement, one in which the LORD
would write his laws on people's hearts
and minds.

father, and I've built a temple for the
LORD our God. ²¹I've also made a place
in the temple for the sacred chest. And
in that chest are the two flat stones on
which is written the solemn agreement the LORD made with our ancestors when he led them out of Egypt.

Solomon Prays at the Temple
(2 Chronicles 6.12-42)

²²Solomon stood facing the altar with
everyone standing behind him. Then he
lifted his arms toward heaven ²³and prayed:

LORD God of Israel, no other god in
heaven or on earth is like you!

You never forget the agreement you
made with your people, and you are
loyal to anyone who faithfully obeys
your teachings. ²⁴My father David was
your servant, and today you have kept
every promise you made to him.

²⁵LORD God of Israel, you promised
my father that someone from his family would always be king of Israel, if
they do their best to obey you, just as
he did. ²⁶Please keep this promise you
made to your servant David.

²⁷There's not enough room in all of
heaven for you, LORD God. How could
you possibly live on earth in this temple I have built? ²⁸But I ask you to answer my prayer. ²⁹This is the temple
where you have chosen to be worshiped. Please watch over it day and
night and listen when I turn toward it
and pray. ³⁰I am your servant, and the
people of Israel belong to you. So
whenever any of us look toward this
temple and pray, answer from your
home in heaven and forgive our sins.

³¹Suppose someone accuses a person of a crime, and the accused has to

stand in front of the altar in your temple and say, "I swear I am innocent!"
³²Listen from heaven and decide who
is right. Then punish the guilty person
and let the innocent one go free.

³³Suppose your people Israel sin
against you, and then an enemy defeats them. If they come to this temple
and beg for forgiveness, ³⁴listen from
your home in heaven. Forgive them
and bring them back to the land you
gave their ancestors.

³⁵Suppose your people sin against
you, and you punish them by holding
back the rain. If they turn toward this
temple and pray in your name and stop
sinning, ³⁶listen from your home in
heaven and forgive them. The people of
Israel are your servants, so teach them
to live right. And please send rain on the
land you gave them to be theirs forever.

³⁷Sometimes the crops may dry up
or rot or be eaten by locusts§ or grasshoppers, and your people will be starving. Sometimes enemies may surround
their towns, or your people will become sick with deadly diseases. ³⁸Lis-
ten when anyone in Israel truly feels
sorry and sincerely prays with arms
lifted toward your temple. ³⁹You know
what is in everyone's heart. So from
your home in heaven answer their
prayers, according to the way they live
and what is in their hearts. ⁴⁰Then
your people will worship and obey you
for as long as they live in the land you
gave their ancestors.

⁴¹⁻⁴²Foreigners will hear about you
and your mighty power, and some of
them will come to live among your
people Israel. If any of them pray toward this temple, ⁴³listen from your
home in heaven and answer their

§8.37 locusts: A type of grasshopper that comes in swarms and causes great damage to plant life.

Solomon prayed, "LORD God of Israel, no other god in heaven or
on earth is like you! . . . You are loyal to anyone who faithfully
obeys your teachings." 1 KGS 8.23

prayers. Then everyone on earth will worship you, just like your people Israel, and they will know that I have built this temple to honor you.

44Our Lord, sometimes you will order your people to attack their enemies. Then your people will turn toward this temple I have built for you in your chosen city, and they will pray to you. **45**Answer their prayers from heaven and give them victory.

46Everyone sins. But when your people sin against you, suppose you get angry enough to let their enemies drag them away to foreign countries. **47-49**Later, they may feel sorry for what they did and ask your forgiveness. Answer them when they pray toward this temple I have built for you in your chosen city, here in this land you gave their ancestors. From your home in heaven, listen to their sincere prayers and do what they ask. **50**Forgive your people no matter how much they have sinned against you. Make the enemies who defeated them be kind to them. **51**Remember, they are the people you chose and rescued from Egypt that was like a blazing fire to them.

52I am your servant, and the people of Israel belong to you. So listen when any of us pray and cry out for your help. **53**When you brought our ancestors out of Egypt, you told your servant Moses to say to them, "From all people on earth, the Lord God has chosen you to be his very own."

Solomon Blesses the People

54When Solomon finished his prayer at the altar, he was kneeling with his arms lifted toward heaven. He stood up, **55**turned toward the people, blessed them, and said loudly:

56Praise the Lord! He has kept his promise and given us peace. Every good thing he promised to his servant Moses has happened.

57The Lord our God was with our ancestors to help them, and I pray that he will be with us and never abandon us. **58**May the Lord help us obey him and follow all the laws and teachings he gave our ancestors.

59I pray that the Lord our God will remember my prayer day and night. May he help everyone in Israel each day, in whatever way we need it. **60**Then every nation will know that the Lord is the only true God.

61Obey the Lord our God and follow his commands with all your heart, just as you are doing today.

Solomon Dedicates the Temple
(2 Chronicles 7.4-10)

62-63 Solomon and the people dedicated the temple to the Lord by offering 22,000 cattle and 120,000 sheep as sacrifices to ask the Lord's blessing.[t] **64**On that day, Solomon dedicated the courtyard in front of the temple and made it acceptable for worship. He offered the sacrifices there because the bronze altar in front of the temple was too small.

65Solomon and the huge crowd celebrated the Festival of Shelters at the temple for seven days.[u] There were people from as far away as the Egyptian Gorge in the south and Lebo-Hamath in the north. **66**Then on the eighth day, he sent everyone home. They said goodbye and left, very happy,

---

CR   Lord (YHWH)

● **8.56** *Praise the Lord . . . has happened:* The completion of the temple fulfills two important promises that God made to the nation of Israel. The first is the promise to David that his son would follow him as king and be the one to build the temple. The second is that Israel would have a time of peace after conquering the promised land (Canaan) and establishing a central place of worship at a place God would choose.

● **8.65,66** *Egyptian Gorge in the south . . . in the north:* In other words, all of Israel. The temple was to unite the people religiously the way the success of the king was to unite them politically. **(See Map 2 on pg 1880.)**

---

[t]**8.62,63** *sacrifices to ask the Lord's blessing:* See Leviticus 3.1-17.   [u]**8.65** *seven days:* One ancient translation; Hebrew "seven days and seven more days, fourteen days in all."

Solomon said to the people, "Praise the Lord! He has kept his promise and given us peace. Every good thing he promised to his servant Moses has happened." 1 Kgs 8.56

9.15-17 *fill in the land . . . Lower Beth-Horon:* Solomon increased the size of Jerusalem by filling in the land on the east side and extending the wall around it. Other cities important to Israel's defense and economy also were fortified with strong walls and gates. Hazor, in northern Galilee, controlled the trade route that ran north and south between the Euphrates River and Egypt. Megiddo was an important business and military center located at the intersection of the north-south trade route, and controlled the pass through the Carmel mountain range between the Plains of Jezreel and Sharon. Gezer was at the crossroads of the north-south trade route and the east-west route between Jerusalem and the port at Joppa. Lower Beth-Horon also protected the route between Jerusalem and the sea. (See Maps 4 and 5 on pgs 1882 and 1883.)

because of all the good things the Lord had done for his servant David and his people Israel.

The Lord Appears to Solomon Again
(2 Chronicles 7.11-22)

9 The Lord's temple and Solomon's palace were now finished, and Solomon had built everything he wanted. **2**Some time later the Lord appeared to him again in a dream, just as he had done at Gibeon. **3**The Lord said:

I heard your prayer and what you asked me to do. This temple you have built is where I will be worshiped forever. It belongs to me, and I will never stop watching over it.

4You must obey me, as your father David did, and be honest and fair. Obey my laws and teachings, **5**and I will keep my promise to David that someone from your family will always be king of Israel.

6But if you or any of your descendants disobey my commands or start worshiping foreign gods, **7**I will no longer let my people Israel live in this land I gave them. I will desert this temple where I said I would be worshiped. Then people everywhere will think this nation is only a joke and will make fun of it. **8**This temple will become a pile of rocks!ᵛ Everyone who walks by will be shocked, and they will ask, "Why did the Lord do such a terrible thing to his people and to this temple?" **9**Then they will answer, "We know why the Lord did this. The peo-

ple of Israel rejected the Lord their God, who rescued their ancestors from Egypt, and they started worshiping other gods."

Other Things Solomon Did
(2 Chronicles 8.1-18)

10It took 20 years for the Lord's temple and Solomon's palace to be built. **11**Later, Solomon gave King Hiram of Tyre 20 towns in the region of Galilee to repay him for the cedar, pine, and gold he had given Solomon.

12When Hiram went to see the towns, he did not like them. **13**He said, "Solomon, my friend, are these the kind of towns you want to give me?" So Hiram called the region Cabul because he thought it was worthless.ʷ **14**He sent Solomon only five tons of gold in return.

15After Solomon's workers had finished the temple and the palace, he ordered them to fill in the land on the east side of Jerusalem,ˣ to build a wall around the city, and to rebuild the towns of Hazor, Megiddo, and Gezer.

16Earlier, the king of Egypt had captured the town of Gezer; he burned it to the ground and killed the Canaanite people living there. Then he gave it to his daughter as a wedding present when she married Solomon. **17**So Solomon had the town rebuilt.

Solomon ordered his workers to rebuild Lower Beth-Horon, **18**Baalath, and Tamar in the desert of Judah. **19**They also built towns where he could keep his supplies and his chariots and horses. Solomon ordered them to build whatever he wanted

ᵛ**9.8** *a pile of rocks:* Some ancient translations; Hebrew "high."   ʷ**9.13** *Cabul . . . worthless:* Cabul sounds like the Hebrew word for "worthless."   ˣ**9.15** *fill . . . Jerusalem:* The Hebrew text has "build the Millo," which probably refers to a landfill to strengthen and extend the hill where the city was built.

in Jerusalem, Lebanon, and anywhere in his kingdom.

20-22 Solomon did not force the Israelites to do his work. They were his soldiers, officials, leaders, commanders, chariot captains, and chariot drivers. But he did make slaves of the Amorites, Hittites, Perizzites, Hivites, and Jebusites who were living in Israel. These were the descendants of those foreigners the Israelites could not destroy, and they remained Israel's slaves.

23Solomon appointed 550 officers to be in charge of his workers and to watch over his building projects.

24Solomon's wife, the daughter of the king of Egypt, moved from the older part of Jerusalem[y] to her new palace. Then Solomon had the land on the east side of Jerusalem filled in.[z]

25Three times a year, Solomon burned incense and offered sacrifices to the LORD on the altar he had built.

Solomon had now finished building the LORD's temple.

26He also had a lot of ships at Ezion-Geber, a town in Edom near Eloth on the Red Sea.[a] **27-28**King Hiram let some of his experienced sailors go to the country of Ophir[b] with Solomon's own sailors, and they brought back about 16 tons of gold for Solomon.

The Queen of Sheba Visits Solomon
(2 Chronicles 9.1-12)

10 The Queen of Sheba heard how famous Solomon was, so she went to Jerusalem to test him with difficult ques-

tions. **2**She took along several of her officials, and she loaded her camels with gifts of spices, jewels, and gold. When she arrived, she and Solomon talked about everything she could think of. **3**He answered every question, no matter how difficult it was.

4-5 The Queen was amazed at Solomon's wisdom. She was breathless when she saw his palace, the food on his table, his officials, his servants in their uniforms, the people who served his food, and the sacrifices he offered at the LORD's temple. **6**She said:

Solomon, in my own country I had heard about your wisdom and all you've done. **7**But I didn't believe it until I saw it with my own eyes! And there's so much I didn't hear about. You are wiser and richer than I was told. **8**Your wives[c] and officials are lucky to be here where they can listen to the wise things you say.

9I praise the LORD your God. He is pleased with you and has made you king of Israel. The LORD has always loved Israel, so he has given them a king who will rule fairly and honestly.

10The Queen of Sheba gave Solomon almost five tons of gold, many jewels, and more spices than anyone had ever brought into Israel.

11-13 In return, Solomon gave her the gifts he would have given any other ruler, but he also gave her everything else she wanted. Then she and her officials went back to their own country.

9.25 *Three times a year:* Israelite men were required to worship at the temple three times a year: during the Festival of Thin Bread, the Harvest Festival, and the Festival of Shelters. Because this required travel to Jerusalem, these are sometimes called "pilgrimage festivals." **(See the chart Pilgrimage Festivals on pg 1799.)**

10.1 *Queen of Sheba:* The exact location of Sheba is not certain, though many believe it may be the same as place as Seba, a wealthy kingdom in southwest Arabia that traded luxury items from India and east Africa. The Queen's interest in Solomon may have been partially a concern that Israel's control of major land and sea trade routes posed a threat to the trade relationships she had already established. **(See the article Trade and Travel on pg 1806.)**

---

[y]**9.24** *the older . . . Jerusalem:* See the note at 3.1.   [z]**9.24** *the land . . . filled in:* See the note at 9.15.
[a]**9.26** *Red Sea:* Hebrew *yam suph,* here referring to the Gulf of Aqaba, since the term is extended to include the northeastern arm of the Red Sea (see also the note at Exodus 13.11).   [b]**9.27,28** *Ophir:* The location of this place is not known.   [c]**10.8** *wives:* Two ancient translations; Hebrew "men."

10.28-29 *Musri:* For "Musri" the Hebrew text has "Egypt." If this translation is preferred, Solomon is acting in direct contradiction of the instructions recorded in Deuteronomy, where the king is advised not to have horses from Egypt (Deut 17.16). The author of 1 Kings is showing that Solomon is no longer acting wisely and in obedience to the Lord.

11.1-2 *foreign gods:* Foreign gods were the gods worshiped by Israel's neighbors or by the Canaanites who lived in Israel. God chose Israel to be God's special people and gave them laws to set them apart from their neighbors who worshiped other gods.

ભ Canaanite Gods and Goddesses

11.3-4 *Seven hundred of his wives:* Israelite men were instructed not to marry women from other nations (11.1,2) because the men might be tempted to worship gods from their wives' homelands. Yet Solomon married hundreds of foreign women. Many of these marriages were for political reasons or to seal agreements with other kings.

11.6 *did what the Lord hated:* In other words, the worship of idols. Often in the Bible, the word "disgusting" is used in connection with foreign gods and the worship of these gods. In Hebrew that word, *toebhah,* means abomination and is the strongest word used in the Jewish Scriptures (Old Testament) for something that is unclean and very displeasing to God.

Solomon's Wealth

(2 Chronicles 9.13-28)

King Hiram's ships brought gold, juniper wood, and jewels from the country of Ophir. Solomon used the wood to make steps[d] for the temple and palace, and harps and other stringed instruments for the musicians. It was the best juniper wood anyone in Israel had ever seen.

[14]Solomon received about 25 tons of gold a year. [15]The merchants and traders, as well as the kings of Arabia and rulers from Israel, also gave him gold.

[16]Solomon made 200 gold shields and used about seven and a half pounds of gold for each one. [17]He also made 300 smaller gold shields, using four pounds for each one, and he put the shields in his palace in Forest Hall.

[18]His throne was made of ivory and covered with pure gold. [19-20]The back of the throne was rounded at the top, and it had armrests on each side. There was a statue of a lion on both sides of the throne, and there was a statue of a lion at both ends of each of the six steps leading up to the throne. No other throne in the world was like Solomon's.

[21]Since silver was almost worthless in those days, everything was made of gold, even the cups and dishes used in Forest Hall.

[22]Solomon had a lot of seagoing ships.[e] Every three years he sent them out with Hiram's ships to bring back gold, silver, and ivory, as well as monkeys and peacocks.[f]

[23]He was the richest and wisest king in the world. [24]People from every nation wanted to hear the wisdom God had given him. [25]Year after year people came and brought gifts of silver and gold, as well as clothes, weapons, spices, horses, or mules.

[26]Solomon had 1,400 chariots and 12,000 horses that he kept in Jerusalem and other towns.

[27]While he was king, there was silver everywhere in Jerusalem, and cedar was as common as ordinary sycamore trees in the foothills.

[28-29]Solomon's merchants bought his horses and chariots in the regions of Musri and Kue.[g] They paid about 15 pounds of silver for a chariot and almost 4 pounds of silver for a horse. They also sold horses and chariots to the Hittite and Syrian kings.

Solomon Disobeys the Lord

11 [1-2]The Lord did not want the Israelites to worship foreign gods, so he had warned them not to marry anyone who was not from Israel.

Solomon loved his wife, the daughter of the king of Egypt. But he also loved some women from Moab, Ammon, and Edom, and others from Sidon and the land of the Hittites. [3-4]Seven hundred of his wives were daughters of kings, but he also married 300 other women.[h]

As Solomon got older, some of his wives led him to worship their gods. He wasn't like his father David, who had worshiped only the Lord God. [5]Solomon also worshiped Astarte the goddess of Sidon, and Milcom the disgusting god of Ammon. [6]Solomon's father had obeyed the Lord with all his heart, but Solomon disobeyed and did what the Lord hated.

[d]10.11-13 *steps:* Or "stools" or "railings." [e]10.22 *seagoing ships:* The Hebrew text has "ships of Tarshish," which may have been a Phoenician city in Spain. "Ships of Tarshish" probably means large, seagoing ships. [f]10.22 *peacocks:* Or "baboons." [g]10.28,29 *Musri and Kue:* Hebrew "Egypt and Kue." Musri and Kue were regions located in what is today southeast Turkey. [h]11.3,4 *other women:* This translates a Hebrew word for a woman who was legally bound to a man, but without the full privileges of a wife.

7Solomon built shrines on a hill east of Jerusalem to worship Chemosh the disgusting god of Moab, and Molech the disgusting god of Ammon. **8**In fact, he built a shrine for each of his foreign wives, so all of them could burn incense and offer sacrifices to their own gods.

9-10 The Lord God of Israel had appeared to Solomon two times and warned him not to worship foreign gods. But Solomon disobeyed and did it anyway. This made the Lord very angry, **11**and he said to Solomon:

You did what you wanted and not what I told you to do. Now I'm going to take your kingdom from you and give it to one of your officials. **12**But because David was your father, you will remain king as long as you live. I will wait until your son becomes king, then I will take the kingdom from him. **13**When I do, I will still let him rule one tribe, because I have not forgotten that David was my servant and Jerusalem is my chosen city.

Hadad Becomes an Enemy of Solomon

14Hadad was from the royal family of Edom, and here is how the Lord made him Solomon's enemy:

15-16 Some time earlier, when David conquered the nation of Edom,[i] Joab his army commander went there to bury those who had died in battle. Joab and his soldiers stayed in Edom six months, and during that time they killed every man and boy who lived there. **17-19**Hadad was a boy at the time, but he escaped to Midian with some of his father's officials. At Paran some other men joined them, and they went to the king of Egypt.

The king liked Hadad and gave him food, some land, and a house, and even let him marry the sister of Queen Tahpenes. **20**Hadad and his wife had a son named Genubath, and the queen let the boy grow up in the palace with her own children.

21When Hadad heard that David and Joab were dead, he said to the king, "Your Majesty, please let me go back to my own country."

22"Why?" asked the king. "Do you want something I haven't given you?"

"No, I just want to go home."

Rezon Becomes an Enemy of Solomon

23Here is how God made Rezon son of Eliada an enemy of Solomon:

Rezon had run away from his master, King Hadadezer of Zobah. **24-25**He formed his own small army and became its leader after David had defeated Hadadezer's troops.[j] Then Rezon and his army went to Damascus, where he became the ruler of Syria and an enemy of Israel.

Both Hadad and Rezon were enemies of Israel while Solomon was king, and they caused him a lot of trouble.

The Lord Makes a Promise to Jeroboam

26Jeroboam was from the town of Zeredah in Ephraim. His father Nebat had died, but his mother Zeruah was still alive. Jeroboam was one of Solomon's officials, but even he rebelled against Solomon. **27**Here is how it happened:

While Solomon's workers were filling in the land on the east side of Jerusalem[k] and repairing the city walls, **28**Solomon noticed

[i]**11.15,16** *Edom:* See 2 Samuel 8.13,14. [j]**11.24,25** *troops:* See 2 Samuel 8.3-6. [k]**11.27** *filling . . . Jerusalem:* See the note at 9.15.

11.15-19 Edom . . . Midian . . . . Paran: Edom was the area directly south of the Dead Sea and stood between the Zin Desert and the Land of Moab. The people of Edom were descendants of Jacob's brother, Esau. The nation of Edom is usually described in the Bible as an enemy of Israel. Midian was an area to the east of Egypt including the Sinai Peninsula and extending into northern Arabia. The Midianites, also known as the Kenites (Judg 1.16), were descendants of Abraham and Keturah (Gen 25.1-4) who lived as desert wanderers and traders. The relationship between the Israelites and Midianites was sometimes described as good and peaceful, but at other times they are identified as enemies of Israel. Paran is a desert area west of Edom, north of Sinai, and south of Judah. **(See Map 2 on pg 1880.)**

11.26 Jeroboam: Jeroboam will become the king of ten of the tribes of Israel, known also as the northern kingdom or Israel. Jeroboam ruled from around 931 to 910 B.C. **(See the chart The Kings of Israel on pg 1788.)**

11.42,43 *40 years . . . Rehoboam
then became king:* While "40" is sometimes used in a symbolic way to express
a long and complete period of time, here
it is also probably the actual number
of years Solomon ruled, from approximately 970 to 931 B.C.

12.1 *Shechem:* Shechem was on
an important trade route and figured
repeatedly in the religious and political
history of Israel, making it a good place
to crown a new king. A sacred tree at
Shechem is where Abram (Abraham)
first worshiped God in the promised land
(Gen 12.6,7); Abraham's grandson Jacob
built an altar in Shechem (Gen 33.18-
20); and Joseph, one of Jacob's sons,
was buried there (Josh 24.32). In addition, Joshua called a meeting of the
tribes of Israel at Shechem in order to
renew the agreement the people made
with the LORD in the desert before entering Canaan (Josh 24).

that Jeroboam was a hard worker. So he
put Jeroboam in charge of the work force
from Manasseh and Ephraim.

29-30 One day when Jeroboam was leaving Jerusalem, he met Ahijah, a prophet
from Shiloh. No one else was anywhere
around. Suddenly, Ahijah took off his
new coat and ripped it into twelve pieces.
31Then he said:

Jeroboam, take ten pieces of this
coat and listen to what the LORD God
of Israel says to you. "Jeroboam, I am
the LORD God, and I am about to take
Solomon's kingdom from him and give
you ten tribes to rule. **32**But Solomon
will still rule one tribe,[1] since he is the
son of David my servant, and Jerusalem
is my chosen city.

33"Solomon and the Israelites are
not like their ancestor David. They will
not listen to me, obey me, or do what
is right. They have turned from me to
worship Astarte the goddess of Sidon,
Chemosh the god of Moab, and Milcom the god of Ammon.

34"Solomon is David's son, and David
was my chosen leader, who did what I
commanded. So I will let Solomon be
king until he dies. **35**Then I will give
you ten tribes to rule, **36**but Solomon's
son will still rule one tribe. This way,
my servant David will always have a
descendant ruling in Jerusalem, the
city where I have chosen to be worshiped.

37"You will be king of Israel and will
rule every nation you want. **38**I'll help
you if you obey me. And if you do what
I say, as my servant David did, I will always let someone from your family

rule in Israel, just as someone from
David's family will always rule in Judah. The nation of Israel will be yours.
39"I will punish the descendants of
David, but not forever."

40When Solomon learned what the LORD
had told Jeroboam, Solomon tried to kill
Jeroboam. But he escaped to King Shishak
of Egypt and stayed there until Solomon
died.

Solomon Dies
(2 Chronicles 9.29-31)

41Everything else Solomon did while he
was king is written in the book about him
and his wisdom. **42**After he had ruled 40
years from Jerusalem, **43**he died and was
buried there in the city of his father David.
His son Rehoboam then became king.

Some of the People Rebel
against Rehoboam
(2 Chronicles 10.1-19)

12 Rehoboam went to Shechem where
everyone was waiting to crown him
king.

2Jeroboam son of Nebat heard what was
happening, and he stayed in Egypt,[m] where
he had gone to hide from Solomon. **3**But
the people from the northern tribes of Israel sent for him. Then together they went
to Rehoboam and said, **4**"Your father
Solomon forced us to work very hard. But
if you make our work easier, we will serve
you and do whatever you ask."

5"Give me three days to think about it,"
Rehoboam replied, "then come back for
my answer." So the people left.

---

[1]**11.31,32** *ten tribes . . . one tribe:* By this time the tribe of Simeon had become part of the tribe of
Judah. "One tribe" refers to Judah. Instead of "one tribe," one ancient translation has "two tribes."
[m]**12.2** *he stayed in Egypt:* Hebrew; two ancient translations "he returned from Egypt" (see also
2 Chronicles 10.2).

⁶Rehoboam went to some leaders who had been his father's senior officials, and he asked them, "What should I tell these people?"

⁷They answered, "If you want them to serve and obey you, then you should do what they ask today. Tell them you will make their work easier."

⁸But Rehoboam refused their advice and went to the younger men who had grown up with him and were now his officials. ⁹He asked, "What do you think I should say to these people who asked me to make their work easier?"

¹⁰His younger advisors said:

Here's what we think you should say to them: "Compared to me, my father was weak.ⁿ ¹¹He made you work hard, but I'll make you work even harder. He punished you with whips, but I'll use whips with pieces of sharp metal!"

¹²Three days later, Jeroboam and the others came back. ¹³Rehoboam ignored the advice of the older advisors. ¹⁴He spoke bluntly and told them exactly what his own advisors had suggested: "My father made you work hard, but I'll make you work even harder. He punished you with whips, but I'll use whips with pieces of sharp metal!"

¹⁵⁻¹⁹When the people realized that Rehoboam would not listen to them, they shouted: "We don't have to be loyal to David's family. We can do what we want. Come on, people of Israel, let's go home! Rehoboam can rule his own people."

Adoniramᵒ was in charge of the forced labor, and Rehoboam sent him to talk to the people. But they stoned him to death. Then Rehoboam ran to his chariot and hurried back to Jerusalem.

So the people from the northern tribes of Israel went home, leaving Rehoboam to rule only the people from the towns in Judah. Ever since that day, the people of Israel have opposed David's family in Judah. All of this happened just as the LORD's prophet Ahijah had told Jeroboam.

²⁰When the Israelites heard that Jeroboam was back, they called everyone together. Then they sent for Jeroboam and made him king of Israel. Only the people from the tribe of Judahᵖ remained loyal to David's family.

Shemaiah Warns Rehoboam
(2 Chronicles 11.1-4)

²¹After Rehoboam returned to Jerusalem, he decided to attack Israel and take control of the whole country. So he called together 180,000 soldiers from the tribes of Judah and Benjamin.

²²Meanwhile, God told Shemaiah the prophet ²³to give Rehoboam and everyone from Judah and Benjamin this warning: ²⁴"Don't go to war against the people from Israel—they are your relatives. Go home! I am the LORD, and I made these things happen."

Rehoboam and his army obeyed the LORD and went home.

Jeroboam Makes Religious Changes

²⁵Jeroboam rebuilt Shechem in Ephraim and made it a stronger town, then he moved there. He also fortified the town of Penuel.

²⁶⁻²⁷One day, Jeroboam started thinking,

● 12.24 *they are your relatives:* Judah and Benjamin, like all the twelve tribes, were descended from Jacob whose name was changed to Israel.

ᙟ Israel

● 12.25 *Shechem . . . Ephraim . . . Penuel:* Although Shechem was originally part of the territory of Manasseh, apparently the boundary between Manasseh and Ephraim changed at some point in Israelite history. Ephraim was one of the largest and most important tribes of Israel. Two early religious sites, Bethel and Shiloh, were located here. Joshua, who led the people of Israel into the promised land, was an Ephraimite (Num 13.4-16); as was the prophet and judge Samuel (1 Sam 1.1,19,20). Penuel was located east of the Jordan River near the Jabbok River. **(See Maps 3 and 6 on pgs 1881 and 1884.)**

ⁿ12.10 *Compared . . . weak:* Hebrew "My little finger is bigger than my father's waist."
ᵒ12.15-19 *Adoniram:* Two ancient translations (see also 4.6 and 5.14); Hebrew "Adoram."
ᵖ12.20 *Israelites . . . Israel . . . Judah:* From this time on, "Israel" usually refers to the northern kingdom, and "Israelites" refers to the people who lived there. The southern kingdom is called "Judah."

12.29-30 *Bethel . . . Dan:* Bethel was in the area of Benjamin, close to the border of Ephraim. This placed it in the southernmost part of Israel, about twelve miles north of Jerusalem in Judah. It had been a special place of worship at several times in Israel's history. Dan was near Mount Hermon located in the far north of Israel. Worship of foreign gods was a problem here during the time of the judges. **(See Map 6 on pg 1884.)**

12.32-33 *just like the one in Judah:* This probably refers to the Festival of Shelters. Jeroboam appears to be reestablishing former customs of the northern tribes, perhaps in an attempt to build a national identity for the northern kingdom that will set it apart from the southern kingdom.

13.1-2 *Bethel . . . Judah:* The prophet from the southern kingdom brings a message to Jeroboam at Bethel in the northern kingdom to warn him about what will result because of his improper worship at Bethel's altar.

13.1-2 *Josiah . . . David's family:* Josiah would not become king of Judah until almost 300 years later. He ruled from 640 to 609 B.C. His dramatic reform is described in 2 Kings 22,23.

Josiah

"Everyone in Israel still goes to the temple in Jerusalem to offer sacrifices to the Lord. What if they become loyal to David's family again? They will kill me and accept Rehoboam as their king."

28Jeroboam asked for advice and then made two gold statues of calves. He showed them to the people and said, "Listen everyone! You won't have to go to Jerusalem to worship anymore. Here are your gods^q who rescued you from Egypt." 29Then he put one of the gold calves in the town of Bethel and the other in the town of Dan. 30The people sinned because they started going to these places to worship.

31Jeroboam built small places of worship at the shrines^r and appointed men who were not from the tribe of Levi to serve as priests. 32-33 He also decided to start a new festival for the Israelites on the fifteenth day of the eighth month, just like the one in Judah.^s On that day, Jeroboam went to Bethel and offered sacrifices on the altar to the gold calf he had put there. Then he assigned the priests their duties.

A Prophet Condemns the Altar at Bethel

13 1-2One day, Jeroboam was standing at the altar in Bethel, ready to make an offering. Suddenly one of God's prophets^t arrived from Judah and shouted:

The Lord sent me with a message about this altar. A child named Josiah will be born into David's family. He will sacrifice on this altar the priests who make offerings here, and human bones will be burned on it.

3You will know that the Lord has said these things when the altar splits in half, and the ashes on it fall to the ground.

4Jeroboam pointed at the prophet and shouted, "Grab him!" But at once, Jeroboam's hand became stiff, and he could not move it. 5The altar split in half, and the ashes fell to the ground, just as the prophet had warned.

6"Please pray to the Lord your God and ask him to heal my hand," Jeroboam begged.

The prophet prayed, and Jeroboam's hand was healed.

7"Come home with me and eat something," Jeroboam said. "I want to give you a gift for what you have done."

8"No, I wouldn't go with you, even if you offered me half of your kingdom. I won't eat or drink here either. 9The Lord said I can't eat or drink anything and that I can't go home the same way I came." 10Then he started home down a different road.

An Old Prophet from Bethel

11At that time an old prophet lived in Bethel, and one of his sons told him what the prophet from Judah had said and done. 12"Show me which way he went," the old prophet said, and his sons pointed out the road. 13"Put a saddle on my donkey," he told them. After they did, he got on the donkey 14and rode off to look for the prophet from Judah.

The old prophet found him sitting under an oak tree and asked, "Are you the prophet from Judah?"

"Yes, I am."

15"Come home with me," the old prophet said, "and have something to eat."

16"I can't go back with you," the prophet replied, "and I can't eat or drink anything

q12.28 *Here are your gods:* Or "Here is your God." r12.31 *shrines:* See the note at 3.2. s12.32,33 *the one in Judah:* This probably refers to the Festival of Shelters. t13.1,2 *one of God's prophets:* Hebrew "a man of God."

with you. [17]The Lord warned me not to eat or drink or to go home the same way I came."

[18]The old prophet said, "I'm a prophet too. One of the Lord's angels told me to take you to my house and give you something to eat and drink."

The prophet from Judah did not know that the old prophet was lying, [19]so he went home with him and ate and drank.

[20]During the meal the Lord gave the old prophet [21]a message for the prophet from Judah:

Listen to the Lord's message. You have disobeyed the Lord your God. [22]He told you not to eat or drink anything here, but you came home and ate with me. And so, when you die, your body won't be buried in your family tomb.

[23]After the meal the old prophet got a donkey ready, [24]and the prophet from Judah left. Along the way, a lion attacked and killed him, and the donkey and the lion stood there beside his dead body.

[25]Some people walked by and saw the body with the lion standing there. They ran into Bethel, telling everyone what they had seen.

[26]When the old prophet heard the news, he said, "That must be the prophet from Judah. The Lord warned him, but he disobeyed. So the Lord sent a lion to kill him."

[27]The old prophet told his sons to saddle his donkey, and when it was ready, [28]he left. He found the body lying on the road, with the donkey and lion standing there. The lion had not eaten the body or attacked the donkey. [29]The old prophet picked up the body, put it on his own donkey, and took it back to Bethel, so he could bury it and mourn for the prophet from Judah.

[30]He buried the body in his own family tomb and cried for the prophet. [31]He said to his sons, "When I die, bury my body next to this prophet. [32]I'm sure that everything he said about the altar in Bethel and the shrines in Samaria will happen."

[33]But Jeroboam kept on doing evil things. He appointed men to be priests at the local shrines, even if they were not Levites. In fact, anyone who wanted to be a priest could be one. [34]This sinful thing led to the downfall of his kingdom.

Jeroboam's Son Dies

14 About the same time, Abijah son of Jeroboam got sick. [2-3]Jeroboam told his wife:

Disguise yourself so no one will know you're my wife, then go to Shiloh, where the prophet Ahijah lives. Take him ten loaves of bread, some small cakes, and honey, and ask him what will happen to our son. He can tell you, because he's the one who told me I would become king.

[4]She got ready and left for Ahijah's house in Shiloh.

Ahijah was now old and blind, [5]but the Lord told him, "Jeroboam's wife is coming to ask about her son. I will tell you what to say to her."

Jeroboam's wife came to Ahijah's house, pretending to be someone else. [6]But when Ahijah heard her walking up to the door, he said:

Come in! I know you're Jeroboam's wife—why are you pretending to be someone else? I have some bad news for you. [7]Give your husband this message from the Lord God of Israel: "Jeroboam, you know that I, the Lord, chose you over anyone else to be the leader of my people Israel. [8]I even took David's kingdom away from his family and gave it to you. But you are not like my servant David. He always obeyed me and did what was right.

13.22 *not to eat or drink . . . body won't be buried:* Refusing to eat or drink at a place was a sign of disapproval (13.7-9). In the ancient world it was very important to people to be buried near their ancestors and other family members, because they believed that the only comfort a person had following death was to sleep alongside one's relatives.

Burial

13.24 *lion:* At this time, lions were still found in many parts of the Middle East. In 1 and 2 Kings, lions are shown as bringing punishment to people who make fun of the Lord or the Lord's prophets.

● **14.11** *Dogs will eat . . . vultures will eat:* This accurate description of what happened to bodies left in the open was thought to be a horrible ending to one's life. First, Jeroboam and his descendants' last contact will be with dogs, animals that were considered unclean because they fed on dead animals. Second, they will not be buried.

● Purity (Clean and Unclean)

● **14.25** *King Shishak of Egypt:* Shishak is the first Egyptian ruler actually named in the Old Testament. (See the chart Egyptian Kings (Pharaohs) in the Bible on pg 1825.)

● Egypt

⁹"You have made me very angry by rejecting me and making idols out of gold. Jeroboam, you have done more evil things than any king before you. ¹⁰"Because of this, I will destroy your family by killing every man and boy in it, whether slave or free. I will wipe out your family, just as fire burns up trash. ¹¹Dogs will eat the bodies of your relatives who die in town, and vultures will eat the bodies of those who die in the country. I, the LORD, have spoken and will not change my mind!"

¹²That's the LORD's message to your husband. As for you, go back home, and right after you get there, your son will die. ¹³Everyone in Israel will mourn at his funeral. But he will be the last one from Jeroboam's family to receive a proper burial, because he's the only one the LORD God of Israel is pleased with.

¹⁴The LORD will soon choose a new king of Israel, who will destroy Jeroboam's family. And I mean very soon.ᵘ ¹⁵The people of Israel have made the LORD angry by setting up sacred polesᵛ for worshiping the goddess Asherah. So the LORD will punish them until they shake like grass in a stream. He will take them out of the land he gave to their ancestors, then scatter them as far away as the Euphrates River. ¹⁶Jeroboam sinned and caused the Israelites to sin. Now the LORD will desert Israel.

¹⁷Jeroboam's wife left and went back home to the town of Tirzah. As soon as she set foot in her house, her son died. ¹⁸Every-one in Israel came and mourned at his funeral, just as the LORD's servant Ahijah had said.

Jeroboam Dies

¹⁹Everything else Jeroboam did while he was king, including the battles he won, is written in *The History of the Kings of Israel.* ²⁰He was king of Israel for 22 years, then he died, and his son Nadab became king.

King Rehoboam of Judah
(2 Chronicles 11.5—12.16)

²¹Rehoboam son of Solomon was 41 years old when he became king of Judah, and he ruled 17 years from Jerusalem, the city where the LORD had chosen to be worshiped. His mother Naamah was from Ammon.

²²The people of Judah disobeyed the LORD and made him even angrier than their ancestors had. ²³They also built their own local shrinesʷ and stone images of foreign gods, and they set up sacred polesˣ for worshiping the goddess Asherah on every hill and in the shade of large trees. ²⁴Even worse, they allowed prostitutesʸ at the shrines, and followed the disgusting customs of the foreign nations that the LORD had forced out of Canaan.

²⁵After Rehoboam had been king for four years, King Shishak of Egypt attacked Jerusalem. ²⁶He took everything of value from the temple and the palace, including Solomon's gold shields.

²⁷Rehoboam had bronze shields made to replace the gold ones, and he ordered the

---

ᵘ**14.14** *And I mean very soon:* One possible meaning for the difficult Hebrew text.   ᵛ**14.15** *sacred poles:* Or "trees," used as symbols of Asherah, the goddess of fertility.   ʷ**14.23** *local shrines:* See the note at 3.2.   ˣ**14.23** *sacred poles:* See the note at 14.15.   ʸ**14.24** *prostitutes:* Men and women sometimes served at the local shrines as prostitutes in the worship of Canaanite gods, but the LORD had forbidden the people of Israel to worship in this way (see Deuteronomy 23.17,18).

guards at the city gates to keep them safe. [28]Whenever Rehoboam went to the LORD's temple, the guards carried the shields. But they always took them back to the guard-room as soon as he was finished.

[29]Everything else Rehoboam did while he was king is written in *The History of the Kings of Judah.* [30]He and Jeroboam were constantly at war. [31]Rehoboam's mother Naamah was from Ammon, but when Re-hoboam died, he was buried beside his an-cestors in Jerusalem.[z] His son Abijam then became king.

King Abijam of Judah
(2 Chronicles 13.1-22)

15 Abijam became king of Judah in Jeroboam's eighteenth year as king of Israel, [2]and he ruled from Jerusalem for three years. His mother was Maacah the daughter of Abishalom.

[3]Abijam did not truly obey the LORD his God as his ancestor David had done. In-stead, he was sinful just like his father Re-hoboam. [4-5]David had always obeyed the LORD's commands by doing right, except in the case of Uriah.[a] And since Abijam was David's great-grandson, the LORD kept Jerusalem safe and let Abijam have a son who would be the next king.

[6-7]The war that had broken out between Rehoboam and Jeroboam continued dur-ing the time that Abijam was king.

Everything else Abijam did while he was king is written in *The History of the Kings of Judah.* [8]Abijam died and was buried in Jerusalem,[b] and his son Asa became king.

King Asa of Judah
(2 Chronicles 15.16—16.6,11-13)

[9]Asa became king of Judah in the twenti-eth year of Jeroboam's rule in Israel, [10]and he ruled 41 years from Jerusalem. His grandmother was Maacah the daughter of Abishalom.

[11]Asa obeyed the LORD, as David had done. [12]He forced the prostitutes[c] at the shrines to leave the country, and he got rid of the idols his ancestors had made. [13]His own grandmother Maacah had made an idol of Asherah, and Asa took it and burned it in Kidron Valley. Then he re-moved Maacah from her position as queen mother.[d]

[14]As long as Asa lived, he was completely faithful to the LORD, even though he did not destroy the local shrines. [15]He placed in the temple all the silver and gold objects that he and his father had dedicated to the LORD.

[16]Asa was always at war with King Baasha of Israel. [17]One time, Baasha invaded Judah and captured the town of Ramah. He started making the town stronger, so he could put troops there to stop people from going in and out of Judah.

[18]When Asa heard about this, he took the silver and gold from his palace and from the LORD's temple. He gave it to some of his officials and sent them to Damascus with this message for King Benhadad[e] of Syria: [19]"Our fathers signed a peace treaty. Why don't we do the same thing? This sil-ver and gold is a present for you. So, would you please break your treaty with Baasha and force him to leave my country?"

[20]Benhadad did what Asa asked and

● **15.4-5** *Uriah:* A man who served in David's army (see 2 Sam 11.1-27). Even though David sinned against Uriah, he is held up as a standard of obedience because he did not worship other gods.

● **15.17** *Baasha:* Baasha was king of Israel from around 909 to 886 B.C. His rule is described in 15.33—16.7.

● **15.17** *Ramah:* A city about five miles north of Jerusalem. This border fortress was important to Israel not just for defense, but as a way of seeing who from the northern kingdom might still be going to Jerusalem to make sacri-fices at the temple.

● **15.18** *King Benhadad of Syria:* This is the first of three kings with this name who are mentioned in the Bible. The other two are this man's son (1 Kgs 20.1) and the son of Hazael who seized the second Benhadad's crown (2 Kgs 13.24). Syria took over several cities and areas in the north of Israel, forcing Baasha to leave Ramah to defend the northern area of his kingdom.

---

[z]**14.31** *Jerusalem:* See the note at 2.10,11. [a]**15.4,5** *Uriah:* A Hittite who served in David's army; David had him killed so he could marry his wife Bathsheba (see 2 Samuel 11.1-27). [b]**15.8** *Jerusalem:* See the note at 2.10,11. [c]**15.12** *prostitutes:* See the note at 14.24. [d]**15.13** *queen mother:* Or "the mother of the king," an important position in biblical times (see 2.19). [e]**15.18** *Benhadad:* Hebrew "Benhadad son of Tabrimmon son of Hezion."

15.25,26 *Nadab . . . example of his father:* Nadab ruled Israel from about 910 to 909 B.C. Jeroboam, Nadab's father, made religious changes that led to idol worship. For doing this, God promised to destroy Jeroboam's entire family (1 Kgs 14.6-16).

15.29 *Not one man or boy . . . will be left alive:* Baasha carries out God's judgment against Jeroboam (1 Kgs 14.10), but not knowingly. Baasha is simply following the common practice of killing all members of a ruler's family after seizing that ruler's throne. This was done so that no one would be left to take revenge or lay claim to the throne.

16.1 *Jehu son of Hanani:* The author of CHRONICLES mentions Jehu as one of the authors of *The History of the Kings of Israel* (2 Chr 20.34).

16.5-7 *even worse . . . in Jeroboam's family:* Even though Baasha's actions fulfilled God's judgment against Jeroboam, Baasha did them for personal gain and with evil intentions.

sent the Syrian army into Israel. They captured the towns of Ijon, Dan, and Abel-Bethmaacah, and the territories of Chinneroth and Naphtali. **21**When Baasha heard about it, he left Ramah and went back to Tirzah.

22Asa ordered everyone in Judah to carry away the stones and wood Baasha had used to strengthen the town of Ramah. Then he used these same stones and wood to fortify the town of Geba in the territory of Benjamin and the town of Mizpah.

23Everything else Asa did while he was king, including his victories and the towns he rebuilt, is written in *The History of the Kings of Judah.* When he got older, he had a foot disease. **24**Asa died and was buried in the tomb of his ancestors in Jerusalem.[f] His son Jehoshaphat then became king.

King Nadab of Israel

25Nadab son of Jeroboam became king of Israel in Asa's second year as king of Judah, and he ruled two years. **26**Nadab disobeyed the LORD by following the evil example of his father, who had caused the Israelites to sin.

27-28 Baasha son of Ahijah was from the tribe of Issachar, and he made plans to kill Nadab. When Nadab and his army went to attack the town of Gibbethon in Philistia, Baasha killed Nadab there. So in the third year of Asa's rule, Baasha became king of Israel.

29The LORD's prophet Ahijah had earlier said, "Not one man or boy in Jeroboam's family will be left alive." And, as soon as Baasha became king, he killed everyone in Jeroboam's family, **30**because Jeroboam had made the LORD God of Israel angry by sinning and causing the Israelites to sin.

31Everything else Nadab did while he was king is written in *The History of the Kings of Israel.*

32King Asa of Judah and King Baasha of Israel were always at war.

King Baasha of Israel

33Baasha son of Ahijah became king of Israel in Asa's third year as king of Judah, and he ruled 24 years from Tirzah. **34**Baasha also disobeyed the LORD by acting like Jeroboam, who had caused the Israelites to sin.

16 The LORD sent Jehu son of Hanani to say to Baasha:

2Nobody knew who you were until I, the LORD, chose you[g] to be the leader of my people Israel. And now you're acting exactly like Jeroboam by causing the Israelites to sin. What you've done has made me so angry **3**that I will destroy you and your family, just as I did the family of Jeroboam. **4**Dogs will eat the bodies of your relatives who die in town, and vultures will eat the bodies of those who die in the country.

5-7 Baasha made the LORD very angry, and that's why the LORD gave Jehu this message for Baasha and his family. Baasha constantly disobeyed the LORD by following Jeroboam's sinful example—but even worse, he killed everyone in Jeroboam's family!

Everything else Baasha did while he was king, including his brave deeds, is written in *The History of the Kings of Israel.* Baasha died and was buried in Tirzah, and his son Elah became king.

King Elah of Israel

8Elah son of Baasha became king of Israel after Asa had been king of Judah for 25 years, and he ruled from Tirzah for two years.

[f]**15.24** *Jerusalem:* Hebrew "the city of David his ancestor."   [g]**16.2** *Nobody . . . you:* Hebrew "I pulled you up out of the dust."

9Zimri commanded half of Elah's chariots, and he made plans to kill Elah.

One day, Elah was in Tirzah, getting drunk at the home of Arza, his prime minister, **10**when Zimri went there and killed Elah. So Zimri became king in the twenty-seventh year of Asa's rule in Judah.

11As soon as Zimri became king, he killed everyone in Baasha's family. Not one man or boy in his family was left alive—even his close friends were killed. **12**Baasha's family was completely wiped out, just as the Lord's prophet Jehu had warned. **13**Baasha and Elah sinned and caused the Israelites to sin, and they made the Lord angry by worshiping idols.

14Everything else Elah did while he was king is written in *The History of the Kings of Israel*.

King Zimri of Israel

15-16 Zimri became king of Israel in Asa's twenty-seventh year as king of Judah, but he ruled only seven days from Tirzah.

Israel's army was camped near Gibbethon in Philistia under the command of Omri. The soldiers heard that Zimri had killed Elah, and they made Omri their king that same day. **17**At once, Omri and his army marched to Tirzah and attacked. **18**When Zimri saw that the town was captured, he ran into the strongest part of the palace and killed himself by setting it on fire. **19**Zimri had disobeyed the Lord by following the evil example of Jeroboam, who had caused the Israelites to sin.

20Everything else Zimri did while he was king, including his rebellion against Elah, is written in *The History of the Kings of Israel*.

King Omri of Israel

21After Zimri died, some of the Israelites wanted Tibni son of Ginath to be king, but others wanted Omri. **22**Omri's followers were stronger than Tibni's, so Tibni was killed, and Omri became king of Israel **23**in the thirty-first year of Asa's rule in Judah.

Omri ruled Israel for twelve years. The first six years he ruled from Tirzah, **24**then he bought the hill of Samaria from Shemer for about 150 pounds of silver. He built a town there and named it Samaria, after Shemer who had owned the hill.

25Omri did more evil things than any king before him. **26**He acted just like Jeroboam and made the Lord God of Israel angry by causing the Israelites to sin and to worship idols.

27Everything else Omri did while he was king, including his brave deeds, is written in *The History of the Kings of Israel*. **28**Omri died and was buried in Samaria, and his son Ahab became king.

King Ahab of Israel

29Ahab son of Omri became king of Israel in the thirty-eighth year of Asa's rule in Judah, and he ruled 22 years from Samaria.

30Ahab did more things to disobey the Lord than any king before him. **31**He acted just like Jeroboam. Even worse, he married Jezebel the daughter of King Ethbaal of Sidon^h and started worshiping Baal. **32**Ahab built an altar and temple for Baal in Samaria **33**and set up a sacred pole^i for worshiping the goddess Asherah. Ahab did more to make the Lord God of Israel angry than any king of Israel before him.

34While Ahab was king, a man from

16.21-23 *some . . . wanted Tibni . . . others wanted Omri:* While Judah was enjoying stability under Asa, Israel was going through a civil war that would last four years.

16.23 *Omri:* Omri was a much more successful leader than is indicated here. He conquered Moab, formed an alliance with Sidon, and built up Samaria as his capital. However, this brilliant administrator was a failure as a religious leader.

16.29-31 *Ahab . . . Jezebel:* Ahab's wife encouraged him to promote the worship of other gods.

16.31-33 *worshiping Baal . . . the goddess Asherah:* Baal, a weather god, was believed by the Canaanites to be the most powerful god.

      Canaanite Gods and Goddesses

16.34 a *man from Bethel . . . ago:* This event fulfills a statement Joshua made after the Israelites destroyed Jericho when they first entered Canaan (Josh 6.26).

---

^h**16.31** *Sidon:* One of the most important cities in Phoenicia. It was located on the coast of the Mediterranean Sea, north of Israel, in what is today southern Lebanon.   ^i**16.33** *sacred pole:* See the note at 14.15.

17.1 *Elijah was a prophet . . . a servant of the living* LORD: A prophet was someone who spoke God's message to the people or to their rulers. Some of the prophets in 1 KINGS are not named; others are named, but not mentioned in any other part of the Bible. Elijah, however, would continue to have significance for Jews many centuries after the events reported in these few chapters (1 Kgs 17–21; 2 Kgs 1–2). Many Jews in later centuries thought that Elijah would return to prepare for the day of judgment or for the coming of the Messiah.

Elijah

17.9 *Zarephath in Sidon:* Zarephath was on the Mediterranean coast about eight miles south of the city of Sidon, Queen Jezebel's hometown. The worship of Baal would have been strong in this area.

17.19-23 *Bring me your son . . . your son is alive:* Elijah's bringing the dead boy back to life not only proves that he is a true prophet (17.24), but shows that the LORD, not Baal, has power over life and death. Doing something "three times" was considered the "right number" in ancient rituals. **(See the article Miracles, Magic, and Medicine on pg 1820.)**

Resurrection

Bethel named Hiel rebuilt the town of Jericho. But while Hiel was laying the foundation for the town wall, his oldest son Abiram died. And while he was finishing the gates, his youngest son Segub died. This happened just as the LORD had told Joshua to say many years ago.[j]

Elijah Stops the Rain

17 Elijah was a prophet from Tishbe in Gilead.[k] One day he went to King Ahab and said, "I'm a servant of the living LORD, the God of Israel. And I swear in his name that it won't rain until I say so. There won't even be any dew on the ground."

²Later, the LORD said to Elijah, ³"Leave and go across the Jordan River so you can hide near Cherith Creek. ⁴You can drink water from the creek, and eat the food I've told the ravens to bring you."

⁵Elijah obeyed the LORD and went to live near Cherith Creek. ⁶Ravens brought him bread and meat twice a day, and he drank water from the creek. ⁷But after a while, it dried up because there was no rain.

Elijah Helps a Widow in Zarephath

⁸The LORD told Elijah, ⁹"Go to the town of Zarephath in Sidon and live there. I've told a widow in that town to give you food."

¹⁰When Elijah came near the town gate of Zarephath, he saw a widow gathering sticks for a fire. "Would you please bring me a cup of water?" he asked. ¹¹As she left to get it, he asked, "Would you also please bring me a piece of bread?"

¹²The widow answered, "In the name of the living LORD your God, I swear that I don't have any bread. All I have is a handful of flour and a little olive oil. I'm on my way home now with these few sticks to cook what I have for my son and me. After that, we will starve to death."

¹³Elijah said, "Everything will be fine. Do what you said. Go home and fix something for you and your son. But first, please make a small piece of bread and bring it to me. ¹⁴The LORD God of Israel has promised that your jar of flour won't run out and your bottle of oil won't dry up before he sends rain for the crops."

¹⁵The widow went home and did exactly what Elijah had told her. She and Elijah and her family had enough food for a long time. ¹⁶The LORD kept the promise that his prophet Elijah had made, and she did not run out of flour or oil.

Elijah Brings a Boy Back to Life

¹⁷Several days later, the son of the woman who owned the house[l] got sick, and he kept getting worse, until finally he died. ¹⁸The woman shouted at Elijah, "What have I done to you? I thought you were God's prophet. Did you come here to cause the death of my son as a reminder that I've sinned against God?"[m]

¹⁹"Bring me your son," Elijah said. Then he took the boy from her arms and carried him upstairs to the room where he was staying. Elijah laid the boy on his bed ²⁰and prayed, "LORD God, why did you do such a terrible thing to this woman? She's letting me stay here, and now you've let her son die." ²¹Elijah stretched himself out over

[j]16.34 *a man from Bethel . . . ago:* See Joshua 6.26. [k]17.1 *from Tishbe in Gilead:* Or "from the settlers in Gilead." [l]17.17 *the woman who owned the house:* This may or may not be the same woman as the widow in verses 8-16. [m]17.18 *Did you . . . God:* In ancient times people sometimes thought that if they sinned, something terrible would happen to them.

the boy three times, while praying, "Lord God, bring this boy back to life!"

²²The Lord answered Elijah's prayer, and the boy started breathing again. ²³Elijah picked him up and carried him downstairs. He gave the boy to his mother and said, "Look, your son is alive."

²⁴"You are God's prophet!" the woman replied. "Now I know that you really do speak for the Lord."

Elijah Proves He Is the Lord's Prophet

18 ¹⁻²For three years no rain fell in Samaria, and there was almost nothing to eat anywhere. The Lord said to Elijah, "Go and meet with King Ahab. I will soon make it rain." So Elijah went to see Ahab.

³⁻⁴At that time Obadiah was in charge of Ahab's palace, but he faithfully worshiped the Lord. In fact, when Jezebel was trying to kill the Lord's prophets, Obadiah hid 100 of them in two caves and gave them food and water.

Ahab sent for Obadiah ⁵and said, "We have to find something for our horses and mules to eat. If we don't, we will have to kill them. Let's look around every creek and spring in the country for some grass. ⁶You go one way, and I'll go the other." Then they left in separate directions.

⁷As Obadiah was walking along, he met Elijah. Obadiah recognized him, bowed down, and asked, "Elijah, is it really you?"

⁸"Yes. Go tell Ahab I'm here."

⁹Obadiah replied:

King Ahab would kill me if I told him that. And I haven't even done anything wrong. ¹⁰I swear to you in the name of the living Lord your God that the king has looked everywhere for you. He sent people to look in every country, and when they couldn't find

you, he made the leader of each country swear that you were not in that country. ¹¹Do you really want me to tell him you're here?

¹²What if the Lord's Spirit takes you away as soon as I leave? When Ahab comes to get you, he won't find you. Then he will surely kill me.

I have worshiped the Lord since I was a boy. ¹³I even hid 100 of the Lord's prophets in caves when Jezebel was trying to kill them. I also gave them food and water. ¹⁴Do you really want me to tell Ahab you're here? He will kill me!

¹⁵Elijah said, "I'm a servant of the living Lord All-Powerful, and I swear in his name that I will meet with Ahab today."

¹⁶Obadiah left and told Ahab where to find Elijah.

Ahab went to meet Elijah, ¹⁷and when he saw him, Ahab shouted, "There you are, the biggest troublemaker in Israel!"

¹⁸Elijah answered:

You're the troublemaker—not me! You and your family have disobeyed the Lord's commands by worshiping Baal.

¹⁹Call together everyone from Israel to meet me on Mount Carmel. Be sure to bring along the 450 prophets of Baal and the 400 prophets of Asherah who eat at Jezebel's table.

²⁰Ahab got everyone together, then they went to meet Elijah on Mount Carmel. ²¹Elijah stood in front of them and said, "How much longer will you try to have things both ways? If the Lord is God, worship him! But if Baal is God, worship him!" The people did not say a word.

²²Then Elijah continued:

I am the Lord's only prophet, but Baal has 450 prophets.

²³Bring us two bulls. Baal's prophets can take one of them, kill it, and cut it

● 18.1-2 *King Ahab:* Ahab's marriage to the Phoenician princess Jezebel most likely brought economic and political benefits to Israel: it would have opened new trade routes and brought assurance that the Phoenician king would not invade Israel. Nevertheless, it was more important that a king of Israel lead the people in faithfulness to God.

● 18.3-4 *Obadiah:* Many men named Obadiah appear in the Jewish Scriptures. The name means "Servant of the Lord." The official mentioned here is not the author of Obadiah.

■ 18.15 "Servant of the Lord" is a title that applied to the kings of Israel, who were expected to rule as servants of God and to lead God's people and keep them faithful to God's laws. Israel's kings were not being faithful to God, however, and many of God's people were worshiping foreign gods while those who remained faithful were being persecuted. Elijah's task as a prophet and servant of the Lord was to lead people back to God.

● 18.19 *Mount Carmel:* A tall mountain on the Mediterranean coast near the western entrance to the Jezreel Valley. **(See Map 6 on pg 1884.)**

● 18.21 *How much longer will you:* Elijah will challenge the people of Israel three times during this contest between the powers of Baal and God: he will accuse them of worshiping Baal rather than God (18.21); he will engage them in a demonstration of who is greater, God or Baal (18.22-24); and he will call them to destroy the prophets of Baal (18.39,40).

18.28 *cut themselves with swords and knives:* Cutting oneself as part of rituals like mourning or idol worship was common (Lev 19.27-28; 21.5; Hos 7.14). Ecstatic prophets often cut themselves to bring on a loss of consciousness due to lack of blood. **(See the article Prophets and Prophecy on pg 1791.)**

18.33 *large jars with water:* Due to the drought, this water was as precious as the blood shed by Baal's prophets (18.28). Pouring water on the altar was symbolic of the pouring rains the people desired. It also made the igniting of the fire more difficult, and the resulting miracle more amazing, proving the superiority of the LORD over Baal.

into pieces. Then they can put the meat on the wood without lighting the fire. I will do the same thing with the other bull, and I won't light a fire under it either.

24The prophets of Baal will pray to their god, and I will pray to the LORD. The one who answers by starting the fire is God.

"That's a good idea," everyone agreed.

25Elijah said to Baal's prophets, "There are more of you, so you go first. Pick out a bull and get it ready, but don't light the fire. Then pray to your god."

26They chose their bull, then they got it ready and prayed to Baal all morning, asking him to start the fire. They danced around the altar and shouted, "Answer us, Baal!" But there was no answer.

27At noon, Elijah began making fun of them. "Pray louder!" he said. "Baal must be a god. Maybe he's day-dreaming or using the toilet or traveling somewhere. Or maybe he's asleep, and you have to wake him up."

28The prophets kept shouting louder and louder, and they cut themselves with swords and knives until they were bleeding. This was the way they worshiped, **29**and they kept it up until time for the evening sacrifice. But there was no answer of any kind.

30Elijah told everyone to gather around him while he repaired the LORD's altar. **31-32**Then he used twelve stones to build an altar in honor of the LORD. Each stone stood for one of the tribes of Israel, which was the name the LORD had given to their ancestor Jacob. Elijah dug a ditch around the altar, large enough to hold about 13 quarts. **33**He placed the wood on the altar, then they cut the bull into pieces and laid the meat on the wood.

He told the people, "Fill four large jars with water and pour it over the meat and the wood." After they did this, **34**he told them to do it two more times. They did exactly as he said **35**until finally, the water ran down the altar and filled the ditch.

36When it was time for the evening sacrifice, Elijah prayed:

Our LORD, you are the God of Abraham, Isaac, and Israel. Now, prove that you are the God of this nation,[n] and that I, your servant, have done this at your command. **37**Please answer me, so these people will know that you are the LORD God, and that you will turn their hearts back to you.[o]

38The LORD immediately sent fire, and it burned up the sacrifice, the wood, and the stones. It scorched the ground everywhere around the altar and dried up every drop of water in the ditch. **39**When the crowd saw what had happened, they all bowed down and shouted, "The LORD is God! The LORD is God!"

40Just then, Elijah said, "Grab the prophets of Baal! Don't let any of them get away."

So the people captured the prophets and took them to Kishon River, where Elijah killed every one of them.

It Starts To Rain

41Elijah told Ahab, "Get something to eat and drink. I hear a heavy rain coming."

42Ahab left, but Elijah climbed back to the top of Mount Carmel. Then he stooped down with his face almost to the ground

[n]**18.36** *this nation:* Hebrew "Israel." [o]**18.37** *will turn . . . to you:* One possible meaning for the difficult Hebrew text.

43and said to his servant, "Look toward the sea."

The servant left. And when he came back, he said, "I looked, but I didn't see anything." Elijah told him to look seven more times.

44After the seventh time the servant replied, "I see a small cloud coming this way. But it's no bigger than a fist."

Elijah told him, "Tell Ahab to get his chariot ready and start home now. Otherwise, the rain will stop him."

45-46A few minutes later, it got very cloudy and windy, and rain started pouring down. So Elijah wrapped his coat around himself, and the LORD gave him strength to run all the way to Jezreel. Ahab followed in his chariot.

Elijah Runs Away from Ahab and Jezebel

19 Ahab told his wife Jezebel what Elijah had done and that he had killed the prophets. 2She sent a message to Elijah: "You killed my prophets. Now I'm going to kill you! I pray that the gods will punish me even more severely if I don't do it by this time tomorrow."

3Elijah was afraid when he got her message, and he ran to the town of Beersheba in Judah. He left his servant there, 4then walked another whole day into the desert. Finally, he came to a large bush and sat down in its shade. He begged the LORD, "I've had enough. Just let me die! I'm no better off than my ancestors." 5Then he lay down in the shade and fell asleep.

Suddenly an angel woke him up and said, "Get up and eat." 6Elijah looked around, and by his head was a jar of water and some baked bread. He sat up, ate and drank, then lay down and went back to sleep.

7Soon the LORD's angel woke him again and said, "Get up and eat, or else you'll get too tired to travel." 8So Elijah sat up and ate and drank.

The food and water made him strong enough to walk 40 more days. At last, he reached Mount Sinai,P the mountain of God, 9and he spent the night there in a cave.

The LORD Appears to Elijah

While Elijah was on Mount Sinai, the LORD asked, "Elijah, why are you here?"

10He answered, "LORD God All-Powerful, I've always done my best to obey you. But your people have broken their solemn promise to you. They have torn down your altars and killed all your prophets, except me. And now they are even trying to kill me!"

11"Go out and stand on the mountain," the LORD replied. "I want you to be there when I pass by."

All at once, a strong wind shook the mountain and shattered the rocks. But the LORD was not in the wind. Next, there was an earthquake, but the LORD was not in the earthquake. 12Then there was a fire, but the LORD was not in the fire.

Finally, there was a gentle breeze,q 13and when Elijah heard it, he covered his face with his coat. He went out and stood at the entrance to the cave.

A voice asked, "Elijah, why are you here?"

14Elijah answered, "LORD God All-Powerful, I've always done my best to obey you. But your people have broken their solemn promise to you. They have torn down your altars and killed all your prophets, except me. And now they are even trying to kill me!"

P19.8 *Sinai:* Hebrew "Horeb."   q19.12 *a gentle breeze:* Or "a soft whisper" or "hardly a sound."

18.45-46 *run all the way to Jezreel:* Ahab had a second royal home in Jezreel, a city about 17 miles northwest of Mount Gilboa. In yet another miraculous event, Elijah runs so fast that Ahab's chariots and horses only can follow behind. By saying that Ahab followed Elijah, the author is showing that the true leader is the prophet of the LORD, not the king. **(See Map 6 on pg 1884.)**

19.3 *Beersheba in Judah:* Beersheba was on the southern border of Judah, in the semi-desert area known as the Southern Desert (or Negev), and served as an important commercial center between Israel and Egypt. **(See Map 6 on pg 1884.)**

Angels

19.8 *Mount Sinai, the mountain of God:* Considered holy because this is where God gave the Law, including the Ten Commandments, to Moses and the people.

19.10-12 *LORD God All-Powerful . . . wind . . . earthquake . . . fire:* Wind, earthquakes, and fire often are associated with God's presence.

Names of God

19.10 *your people . . . solemn promise:* The agreement God made with the people on Mount Sinai (Exod 19.1-7; 20.1-17).

Ten Commandments

Agreements (Covenants)

19.15,16 *appoint Hazael...
Jehu... Elisha:* "Appointing" would
have included a ceremony in which
olive oil was poured on the head of a
person to show that he was now king
("chosen one"). The prophet Samuel
had been given a similar instruction by
the LORD when he was told to make
Saul, and later, David king (1 Sam
10–11; 16.1-13). Unlike Samuel, however,
Elijah, is called to appoint a leader for a
non-Israelite nation (Syria). This shows
that the LORD is not just a local deity,
but the God of all nations.

19.19 *put his own coat on Elisha:*
This was a sign that Elijah wanted Elisha
to follow him and become a prophet.

20.3 *wives:* Apparently Ahab had
other wives in addition to Jezebel. Having more than one wife was allowed in
these times and was common for
kings.

15 The LORD said:

Elijah, you can go back to the desert
near Damascus. And when you get
there, appoint[r] Hazael to be king of
Syria. **16**Then appoint Jehu son of
Nimshi to be king of Israel, and Elisha
son of Shaphat[s] to take your place as
my prophet.

17Hazael will start killing the people
who worship Baal. Jehu will kill those
who escape from Hazael, and Elisha
will kill those who escape from Jehu.
18But 7,000 Israelites have refused to
worship Baal, and they will live.

Elisha Becomes Elijah's Assistant

19Elijah left and found Elisha plowing a
field with a pair of oxen. There were eleven
other men in front of him, and each one
was also plowing with a pair of oxen. Elijah
went over and put his own coat on Elisha.[t]
20Elisha stopped plowing and ran after
him. "Let me kiss my parents goodbye,
then I'll go with you," he said.

"You can go," Elijah said. "But remember what I've done for you."

21Elisha left and took his oxen with him.
He killed them and boiled them over a fire
he had made with the wood from his plow.
He gave the meat to the people who were
with him, and they ate it. Then he left with
Elijah and became his assistant.

Syria Attacks Israel

20 King Benhadad of Syria[u] called his
army together. He was joined by 32
other kings with their horses and chariots,
and together they marched to Samaria and
attacked. **2**Benhadad sent a messenger to
tell King Ahab of Israel, **3**"Ahab, give me
your silver and gold, your wives,[v] and your
strongest sons!"

4"Your Majesty," Ahab replied, "everything I have is yours, including me."

5Later, Benhadad sent another messenger to say to Ahab, "I already told you to
give me your silver and gold, your wives,
and your children. **6**But tomorrow at this
time, I will send my officials into your city
to search your palace and the houses of
your officials. They will take everything
else that you[w] own."

7Ahab called a meeting with the leaders
of Israel and said, "Benhadad is causing real
trouble. He told me to give him my wives
and children, as well as my silver and gold.
And I agreed."

8"Don't listen to him!" they answered.
"You don't have to do what he says."

9So Ahab sent someone to tell Benhadad, "Your Majesty, I'll give you my silver
and gold, and even my wives and children.
But I won't let you have anything else."

When Benhadad got his answer, **10**he
replied, "I'll completely destroy Samaria!
There won't even be enough left for
my soldiers to carry back in their hands. If I
don't do it, I pray that the gods will punish
me terribly."

11Ahab then answered, "Benhadad, don't
brag before the fighting even begins. Wait
and see if you live through it."

12Meanwhile, Benhadad and the other
kings had been drinking in their tents. But
when Ahab's reply came, he ordered his

[r]**19.15** *appoint:* This would have included a ceremony in which olive oil would be poured on his
head to show that he was now king.　[s]**19.16** *Shaphat:* Hebrew "Shaphat from Abel-Meholah."
[t]**19.19** *put... Elisha:* This was a sign that Elijah wanted Elisha to follow him and become a prophet.
[u]**20.1** *King Benhadad of Syria:* This is probably not the same Benhadad mentioned in 15.18-21.
[v]**20.3** *wives:* Having more than one wife was allowed in those times.　[w]**20.6** *you:* Hebrew; three
ancient translations "they."

*Elijah left and found Elisha plowing a field with a pair of
oxen... Elijah went over and put his own coat on Elisha.*
1 KGS 19.19

soldiers to prepare to attack Samaria, and they all got ready.

[13] At that very moment, a prophet ran up to Ahab and said, "You can see that Benhadad's army is very strong. But the LORD has promised to help you defeat them today. Then you will know that the LORD is in control."

[14] "Who will fight the battle?" Ahab asked.

The prophet answered, "The young bodyguards who serve the district officials."

"But who will lead them into battle?" Ahab asked.

"You will!" the prophet replied.

[15] So Ahab called together the 232 young soldiers and the 7,000 troops in Israel's army, and he got them ready to fight the Syrians.

Israel Defeats the Syrians

[16-17] At noon, King Ahab and his Israelite army marched out of Samaria, with the young soldiers in front.

King Benhadad of Syria and the 32 kings with him were drunk when the scouts he had sent out ran up to his tent, shouting, "We just now saw soldiers marching out of Samaria!"

[18] "Take them alive!" Benhadad ordered. "I don't care if they have come out to fight or to surrender."

[19] The young soldiers led Israel's troops into battle, [20] and each of them attacked and killed an enemy soldier. The rest of the Syrian army turned and ran, and the Israelites went after them. Benhadad and some others escaped on horses, [21] but Ahab and his soldiers followed them and captured[x] their horses and chariots.

Ahab and Israel's army crushed the Syrians.

[22] Later, the prophet[y] went back and warned Ahab, "Benhadad will attack you again next spring. Build up your troops and make sure you have some good plans."

Syria Attacks Israel Again

[23] Meanwhile, Benhadad's officials went to him and explained:

Israel's gods are mountain gods. We fought Israel's army in the hills, and that's why they defeated us. But if we fight them on flat land, there's no way we can lose.

[24] Here's what you should do. First, get rid of those 32 kings and put army commanders in their places. [25] Then get more soldiers, horses, and chariots, so your army will be as strong as it was before. We'll fight Israel's army on flat land and wipe them out.

Benhadad agreed and did what they suggested.

[26] In the spring, Benhadad got his army together, and they marched to the town of Aphek to attack Israel. [27] The Israelites also prepared to fight. They marched out to meet the Syrians, and the two armies camped across from each other. The Syrians covered the whole area, but the Israelites looked like two little flocks of goats.

[28] The prophet went to Ahab and said, "The Syrians think the LORD is a god of the hills and not of the valleys. So he has promised to help you defeat their powerful army. Then you will know that the LORD is in control."

[29] For seven days the two armies stayed in their camps, facing each other. Then on the seventh day the fighting broke out, and before sunset the Israelites had killed 100,000 Syrian troops. [30] The rest of the Syrian army ran back to Aphek, but the town wall fell and crushed 27,000 of them.

---

[x]20.21 captured: One ancient translation; Hebrew "attacked." [y]20.22 the prophet: See verse 13.

● 20.22 next spring: In this part of the ancient world kings would wait until after the spring rains and grain harvest before going to war so that they would have enough food and soldiers to fight.

● 20.30 the town wall fell: Many ancient cities had tall walls built around them for protection. These were usually made of clay and bricks. Stone walls were more durable, but stones were not always plentiful. Some walls were extremely thick, such as those at Nineveh and Babylon. They were wide enough to support a roadway that allowed up to six rows of chariots to travel side by side. Guardrooms, towers, and gates were built into city walls so that the citizens could control who entered the city. Many scholars believe the walls at Aphek actually fell as described. However, to say a city's walls "fell" also was a way of saying the city was captured, so other scholars believe this verse simply describes the number of lives lost when the city was taken.

20.31 *sackcloth*: During their time as slaves in Egypt, the Israelites wore loincloths made of dark, coarse goat or camel hair called "saq." This garment, known as sackcloth, became a symbol of slavery, humiliation, and great sadness and was worn at times of trouble or sorrow.

21.1 *Jezreel*: The Jezreel mentioned here was about 20 miles southeast of Mount Carmel at the foot of Mount Gilboa. **(See Map 6 on pg 1884.)**

21.2 *Give it to me*: As an Israelite, Naboth had the right to own this piece of the promised land that he inherited from his father. It belonged to Naboth's past, present, and future family and so it was not his alone to sell or trade (Lev 25.25-31), and not even a king could take it. Ahab accepts this, but Jezebel, who comes from another culture, does not (16.30,31).

Benhadad also escaped to Aphek and hid in the back room of a house. **31**His officials said, "Your Majesty, we've heard that Israel's kings keep their agreements. We will wrap sackcloth around our waists, put ropes around our heads, and ask Ahab to let you live."

32They dressed in sackcloth and put ropes on their heads, then they went to Ahab and said, "Your servant Benhadad asks you to let him live."

"Is he still alive?" Ahab asked. "Benhadad is like a brother to me."

33Benhadad's officials were trying to figure out what Ahab was thinking, and when he said "brother," they quickly replied, "You're right! You and Benhadad are like brothers."

"Go get him," Ahab said.

When Benhadad came out, Ahab had him climb up into his chariot.

34Benhadad said, "I'll give back the towns my father took from your father. And you can have shops in Damascus, just as my father had in Samaria."

Ahab replied, "If you do these things, I'll let you go free." Then they signed a peace treaty, and Ahab let Benhadad go.

A Prophet Condemns Ahab

35About this time the LORD commanded a prophet to say to a friend, "Hit me!" But the friend refused, **36**and the prophet told him, "You disobeyed the LORD, and as soon as you walk away, a lion will kill you." The friend left, and suddenly a lion killed him.

37The prophet found someone else and said, "Hit me!" So this man beat him up.

38The prophet left and put a bandage over his face to disguise himself. Then he went and stood beside the road, waiting for Ahab to pass by.

39When Ahab went by, the prophet shouted, "Your Majesty, right in the heat of battle, someone brought a prisoner to me and told me to guard him. He said if the prisoner got away, I would either be killed or forced to pay 75 pounds of silver. **40**But I got busy doing other things, and the prisoner escaped."

Ahab answered, "You will be punished just as you have said."

41The man quickly tore the bandage off his face, and Ahab saw that he was one of the prophets. **42**The prophet said, "The LORD told you to kill Benhadad, but you let him go. Now you will die in his place, and your people will die in place of his people."

43Ahab went back to Samaria, angry and depressed.

Jezebel Has Naboth Killed

21 Naboth owned a vineyard in Jezreel near King Ahab's palace.

2One day, Ahab said, "Naboth, your vineyard is near my palace. Give it to me so I can turn it into a vegetable garden. I'll give you a better vineyard or pay whatever you want for yours."

3Naboth answered, "This vineyard has always been in my family. I won't let you have it."

4So Ahab went home, angry and depressed because of what Naboth had told him. He lay on his bed, just staring at the wall and refusing to eat a thing.

5Jezebel his wife came in and asked, "What's wrong? Why won't you eat?"

6"I asked Naboth to sell me his vineyard or to let me give him a better one," Ahab replied. "And he told me I couldn't have it."

7"Aren't you the king of Israel?" Jezebel asked. "Get out of bed and eat something! Don't worry, I'll get Naboth's vineyard for you."

8-10 Jezebel wrote a letter to each of the leaders of the town where Naboth lived. In the letters she said:

Call everyone together and tell them to go without eating[z] today. When they come together, give Naboth a seat at the front. Get two liars to sit facing him and swear that Naboth has cursed God and the king. Then take Naboth outside and stone him to death!

She signed Ahab's name to the letters and sealed them with his seal. Then she sent them to the town leaders.

[11]After receiving her letters, they did exactly what she had asked. [12]They told the people that it was a day to go without eating, and when they all came together, they seated Naboth at the front. [13]The two liars came in and sat across from Naboth. Then they accused him of cursing God and the king, so the people dragged Naboth outside and stoned him to death.

[14]The leaders of Jezreel sent a message back to Jezebel that said, "Naboth is dead."

[15]As soon as Jezebel got their message, she told Ahab, "Now you can have the vineyard Naboth refused to sell. He's dead." [16]Ahab got up and went to take over the vineyard.

Elijah Condemns Ahab

[17]The LORD said to Elijah the prophet, [18]"King Ahab of Israel is in Naboth's vineyard right now, taking it over. [19]Go tell him that I say, 'Ahab, you murdered Naboth and took his property. And so, in the very spot where dogs licked up Naboth's blood, they will lick up your blood.' "

When Elijah found him, [20]Ahab said, "So, my enemy, you found me at last."

Elijah answered:

Yes, I did! Ahab, you have managed to do everything the LORD hates.

[21]Now you will be punished. You and every man and boy in your family will die, whether slave or free. [22]Your whole family will be wiped out, just like the families of King Jeroboam and King Baasha. You've made the LORD very angry by sinning and causing the Israelites to sin.

[23]And as for Jezebel, dogs will eat her body there in Jezreel. [24]Dogs will also eat the bodies of your relatives who die in town, and vultures will eat the bodies of those who die in the country.

[25-29]When Ahab heard this, he tore his clothes in sorrow and wore sackcloth day and night. He was depressed and refused to eat.

Some time later, the LORD said, "Elijah, do you see how sorry Ahab is for what he did? I won't punish his family while he is still alive. I'll wait until his son is king."

No one was more determined than Ahab to disobey the LORD. And Jezebel encouraged him. Worst of all, he had worshiped idols, just as the Amorites[a] had done before the LORD forced them out of the land and gave it to Israel.

Micaiah Warns Ahab about Disaster
(2 Chronicles 18.2-27)

22 For the next three years there was peace between Israel and Syria. [2]During the third year King Jehoshaphat of Judah went to visit King Ahab of Israel.

[3]Ahab asked his officials, "Why haven't we tried to get Ramoth in Gilead back from the Syrians? It belongs to us." [4]Then he asked Jehoshaphat, "Would you go to Ramoth with me and attack the Syrians?"

[z]**21.8-10** *to go without eating*: People sometimes came together to worship and to go without eating to show that they were sorry for their sins.   [a]**21.25-29** *Amorites*: A name sometimes used of the people who lived in Palestine before the Israelites.

21.8-10 *has cursed God and the king . . . stone him*: The accusation that Naboth had cursed God and the king was serious. If the accusation had been true, it would have been impossible to stop the curse except by taking some special action like killing the one who had spoken the curse. According to 2 KINGS, Naboth's sons also were stoned to death, probably so that they could not carry out the curse Naboth was supposed to have made (2 Kgs 9.25-26).

21.20 *my enemy*: This harsh term recalls what Ahab had previously called Elijah—"the biggest troublemaker in Israel" (18.16-18). Elijah is Ahab's enemy, because Elijah serves the LORD while Ahab serves false gods.

21.22,23 *King Jeroboam . . . King Baasha*: Jeroboam was the first king of the northern kingdom. Baasha was the third king of Israel.

21.25-29 *I won't punish . . . until his son is king*: The body of Ahab's son, Joram, was thrown on Naboth's land (2 Kgs 9.25-26). Ahab was killed in battle and dogs licked the blood from the chariot that carried his body to Samaria.

22.2 *King Jehoshaphat . . . King Ahab*: Jehoshaphat, the son of King Asa of Judah, ruled Judah from 870 to 848 B.C. and maintained friendly relationships with Israel. King Ahab was the son of King Omri of Israel and ruled Israel from 874 to 853 B.C.

22.10 *threshing place . . . gate:* A threshing place was where harvested stalks of grain were beaten with hand tools or walked over by oxen to separate the seeds (kernels) from the stalks and husks (chaff). It would be done outdoors on a hard floor of packed clay, soil, or rock. Threshing-floors were often on hills so that the wind could more easily blow away the chaff. Many cities, particularly those important to a nation's defense, were walled and had a central gate through which people could enter and leave the city. This gate often had a room where guards kept watch. The area just inside the town gate was a very active place where people gathered to make agreements and settle disputes.

"Just tell me what to do," Jehoshaphat answered. "My army and horses are at your command. **5**But first, let's ask the LORD."

6Ahab sent for about 400 prophets and asked, "Should I attack the Syrians at Ramoth?"

"Yes!" the prophets answered. "The Lord will help you defeat them."

7But Jehoshaphat said, "Just to make sure, is there another of the LORD's prophets we can ask?"

8"We could ask Micaiah son of Imlah," Ahab said. "But I hate Micaiah. He always has bad news for me."

"Don't say that!" Jehoshaphat replied. **9**Then Ahab sent someone to bring Micaiah as soon as possible.

10All this time, Ahab and Jehoshaphat were dressed in their royal robes and were seated on their thrones at the threshing place near the gate of Samaria. They were listening to the prophets tell them what the LORD had said.

11Zedekiah son of Chenaanah was one of the prophets. He had made some horns out of iron and shouted, "Ahab, the LORD says you will attack the Syrians like a bull with iron horns and wipe them out!"

12All the prophets agreed that Ahab should attack the Syrians at Ramoth, and they promised that the LORD would help him defeat them.

13Meanwhile, the messenger who went to get Micaiah whispered, "Micaiah, all the prophets have good news for Ahab. Now go and say the same thing."

14"I'll say whatever the living LORD tells me to say," Micaiah replied.

15Then Micaiah went to Ahab, and Ahab asked, "Micaiah, should I attack the Syrians at Ramoth?"

"Yes!" Micaiah answered. "The LORD will help you defeat them."

16"Micaiah, I've told you over and over to tell me the truth!" Ahab shouted. "What does the LORD really say?"

17He answered, "In a vision[b] I saw Israelite soldiers walking around in the hills like sheep without a shepherd to guide them. The LORD said, 'This army has no leader. They should go home and not fight.'"

18Ahab turned to Jehoshaphat and said, "I told you he would bring bad news!"

19 Micaiah replied:

Listen to this! I also saw the LORD seated on his throne with every creature in heaven gathered around him. **20**The LORD asked, "Who can trick Ahab and make him go to Ramoth where he will be killed?"

They talked about it for a while, **21**then finally a spirit came forward and said to the LORD, "I can trick Ahab."

"How?" the LORD asked.

22"I'll make Ahab's prophets lie to him."

"Good!" the LORD replied. "Now go and do it."

23This is exactly what has happened, Ahab. The LORD made all your prophets lie to you, and he knows you will soon be destroyed.

24Zedekiah walked up to Micaiah and slapped him on the face. Then he asked, "Do you really think the LORD would speak to you and not to me?"

25Micaiah answered, "You'll find out on the day you have to hide in the back room of some house."

26Ahab shouted, "Arrest Micaiah! Take him to Prince Joash and Governor Amon of Samaria. **27**Tell them to put him in

[b]22.17 *vision:* In ancient times, prophets often told about future events from what they had seen in visions or dreams.

prison and to give him nothing but bread and water until I come back safely."

²⁸Micaiah said, "If you do come back, I was wrong about what the LORD wanted me to say." Then he told the crowd, "Don't forget what I said!"

Ahab Dies at Ramoth
(2 Chronicles 18.28-34)

²⁹Ahab and Jehoshaphat led their armies to Ramoth in Gilead. ³⁰Before they went into battle, Ahab said, "Jehoshaphat, I'll disguise myself, but you wear your royal robe." Then Ahab disguised himself and went into battle.

³¹The king of Syria had ordered his 32 chariot commanders to attack only Ahab. ³²So when they saw Jehoshaphat in his robe, they thought he was Ahab and started to attack him. But when Jehoshaphat shouted out to them, ³³they realized he wasn't Ahab, and they left him alone.

³⁴However, during the fighting a soldier shot an arrow without even aiming, and it hit Ahab where two pieces of his armor joined. He shouted to his chariot driver, "I've been hit! Get me out of here!"

³⁵The fighting lasted all day, with Ahab propped up in his chariot so he could see the Syrian troops. He bled so much that the bottom of the chariot was covered with blood, and by evening he was dead.

³⁶As the sun was going down, someone in Israel's army shouted to the others, "Retreat! Go back home!"

³⁷Ahab's body was taken to Samaria and buried there. ³⁸Some workers washed his chariot near a spring in Samaria, and prostitutes washed themselves in his blood.ᶜ

Dogs licked Ahab's blood off the ground, just as the LORD had warned.

³⁹Everything else Ahab did while he was king, including the towns he strengthened and the palace he built and furnished with ivory, is written in *The History of the Kings of Israel*. ⁴⁰Ahab died, and his son Ahaziah became king.

King Jehoshaphat of Judah
(2 Chronicles 20.31—21.1)

⁴¹Jehoshaphat son of Asa became king of Judah in Ahab's fourth year as king of Israel. ⁴²Jehoshaphat was 35 years old when he became king, and he ruled from Jerusalem for 25 years. His mother was Azubah daughter of Shilhi.

⁴³⁻⁴⁶Jehoshaphat obeyed the LORD, just as his father Asa had done, and during his rule he was at peace with the king of Israel.

He got rid of the rest of the prostitutesᵈ from the local shrines, but he did not destroy the shrines, and they were still used as places for offering sacrifices.

Everything else Jehoshaphat did while he was king, including his brave deeds and military victories, is written in *The History of the Kings of Judah*.

⁴⁷The country of Edom had no king at the time, so a lower official ruled the land.

⁴⁸Jehoshaphat had seagoing shipsᵉ built to sail to Ophir for gold. But they were wrecked at Ezion-Geber and never sailed. ⁴⁹Ahaziah son of Ahab offered to let his sailors go with Jehoshaphat's sailors, but Jehoshaphat refused.

⁵⁰Jehoshaphat died and was buried beside his ancestors in Jerusalem,ᶠ and his son Jehoram became king.

22.37 *Samaria*: Built on the hill of the same name, the city of Samaria stood 300 feet above the surrounding plain, giving it great defensive strength. It was approximately 40 miles north of Jerusalem and midway between the Jordan River and the Mediterranean Sea. Eventually it became known as the burial place for the kings of Israel. (See Map 6 on pg 1884.)

ᶜ22.38 *in his blood*: One ancient translation; these words are not in the Hebrew text.
ᵈ22.43-46 *prostitutes*: See the note at 14.24.   ᵉ22.48 *seagoing ships*: See the note at 10.22.
ᶠ22.50 *Jerusalem*: Hebrew "the city of his ancestor David."

22.53 *worshiped Baal:* Baal, a weather god, was believed by the Canaanites to be the most powerful god.

Canaanite Gods and Goddesses

King Ahaziah of Israel

⁵¹Ahaziah son of Ahab became king of Israel in the seventeenth year of Jehoshaphat's rule in Judah, and he ruled two years from Samaria.

⁵²Ahaziah disobeyed the LORD, just as his father, his mother, and Jeroboam had done. They all led Israel to sin. ⁵³Ahaziah worshiped Baal and made the LORD God of Israel very angry, just as his father had done.

Reflection Questions About 1 Kings 1.1—22.53

1. Which two of David's sons thought they should be the next king (1 Kgs 1,2)? How did each of them go about making his claim? Who did each one of them turn to for support? What were David's final instructions to Solomon (2.1-9)?

2. In the dream in 1 Kgs 3.5-15, what did Solomon ask the LORD for? What was the LORD's response? What would you have asked for?

3. How would you define "wisdom"? Does the example of the difficult decision Solomon made in 3.16-28 fit your definition? Why or why not?

4. Read Solomon's prayer at the temple (8.22-53). What does this prayer have to say about human nature? About what God is like? About forgiveness? About prayer?

5. Read 10.14—11.6 again. How is Solomon's behavior in these passages different from what it was like when he first became king? What seems to have brought about this change?

6. Re-read David's statement about obedience and success in 2.3. List some of the events or situations in these first chapters of 1 KINGS that point to the truth of this statement. Do you think this applies just to leaders? Do you think this instruction can also apply to you? If so, how does your answer depend on how you define success?

7. Why did the Israelites from the northern tribes decide to break away and choose their own king rather than follow Solomon's heir, Rehoboam (chapter 12)? Who did they choose to be their leader instead? What did this leader do that upset the LORD?

8. Which of the rulers in 1 KINGS is most memorable? Why? Does the author of 1 KINGS call this ruler "faithful" or "evil"? What are the reasons the author gives?

9. FIRST KINGS includes stories about prophets. Some of the prophets are named (like Nathan, Elijah, and Micaiah), but others are unnamed. How would you describe their relationships with people in power? Which is your favorite story concerning a prophet? Why? Read the feature article called "Prophets and Prophecy" on pg 1791. How does the information in this article change your understanding of what the prophets in 1 KINGS were trying to do in the situations they found themselves?

10. A major theme in 1 KINGS is that God rewards those who obey God's law and punishes those who disobey it. Compare this with what Jesus says in Luke 13.1-5.

2 kings

This book continues the story of those who ruled Israel and Judah. Read 2 KINGS to find out which rulers were faithful to God and which were not. And read about a real hero, Elisha the prophet.

WHAT MAKES 2 KINGS SPECIAL?

SECOND KINGS is the second half of a single book (1 and 2 KINGS) that was divided into two parts. As in 1 KINGS the story moves back and forth between reports of the kings in Judah (the southern kingdom) and reports of the kings in Israel (the northern kingdom).

The destruction of Jerusalem in 586 B.C. was the major event that prompted the writing of 2 KINGS. The smashing of the city walls, the burning of the temple, and the humiliation of the people resulted in a religious crisis among the survivors. God had promised to protect Judah and allow its kings to rule forever. But when Jerusalem was destroyed and the temple was burned, the line of rulers from David's family line also came to an end. Together, these events threatened to destroy the people's trust in God, who seemed to have abandoned them.

The history as recorded in 1 and 2 KINGS was completed after the destruction of Jerusalem, so the books are a response to this event. SECOND KINGS shows the people that their kings, and not God, had been unfaithful. Prophets were sent over and over to warn the people and their kings to stop worshiping other gods and turn back to him. Finally, the people were punished. The two kingdoms were destroyed, and the people were forced to live in foreign nations.

Nathan's promise to David that one of his descendants would always rule Israel (2 Sam 7) is repeated often in 1 and 2 KINGS. This repeated promise gives hope that one day in the future Israel's punish-

ment would end, and the nation would again be ruled by a king descended from David's family.

WHAT'S THE STORY BEHIND THE SCENE?

SECOND KINGS is presented as an historical account of 300 years of Israel's and Judah's monarchy. But it is important to realize that the authors were also writing this history as an interpretation of the events that led to the destruction of the nation. As a result, these pages are also filled with an emphasis on traditional values, with frequent warnings against unfaithfulness, and with calls for obedience to God's commandments.

HOW IS 2 KINGS CONSTRUCTED?

2 KINGS can be outlined in the following way:

The prophet Elisha (1.1—8.15)
    Elisha follows Elijah as prophet (1.1—2.25)
    Elisha and Joram (3.1-27)
    Elisha's miracles (4.1—8.15)
Kings of Judah and Israel (8.16—17.41)
    Jehu and his house (9.1—14.29)
    The last days of Israel (15.1—17.41)
Judah alone (18.1—25.30)
    King Hezekiah and the Assyrian invasion (18.1—20.21)
    Two evil kings: Manasseh and Amon (21.1-26)
    King Josiah and his reform (22.1—23.30)
    The fall of Jerusalem (23.31—25.30)

Originally, 1 and 2 Kings were one book. Together they describe Israel's history from the last years of David's life to the fall of Jerusalem and the exile of the people to Babylonia. The first section of 2 Kings describes the last days of the prophet Elijah and tells how the Lord took Elijah up into heaven. It then gives an account of the prophet Elisha, who was chosen by the Lord to carry on Elijah's work. The book then compares the rulers of the two kingdoms up through the year 722 B.C., when the Assyrians defeated the northern kingdom of Israel. After the fall of the northern kingdom, its people are led away as captives. Judah, the southern kingdom, is now the only independent Israelite nation. The book concludes by relating the history of Judah from 722 B.C. until 586 B.C. Key figures in the final section are Hezekiah and Josiah, two of Judah's greatest kings. Yet even the faithfulness of these rulers cannot offset the unfaithfulness of the people of Judah. In the end, Judah is conquered by the Babylonians, Jerusalem is captured, the temple burned, and the people are led away as captives.

Outline

The Lord Condemns Ahaziah

1 ¹⁻²Soon after King Ahab of Israel died, the country of Moab rebelled against his son King Ahaziah.ᵃ

One day, Ahaziah fell through the wooden slats around the porch on the flat roof of his palace in Samaria, and he was badly injured. So he sent some messengers to the town of Ekronᵇ with orders to ask the god Baalzebub if he would get well.

³About the same time, an angel from the Lord sent Elijah the prophet from Tishbe to say to the king's messengers, "Ahaziah has rejected Israel's own God by sending you to ask Baalzebub about his injury. ⁴Tell him that because he has done this, he's on his deathbed!" And Elijah did what he was told.

⁵When the messengers returned to Ahaziah, he asked, "Why are you back so soon?"

⁶"A man met us along the road with a message for you from the Lord," they answered. "The Lord wants to know why you sent us to ask Baalzebub about your injury and why you don't believe there's a God in Israel. The man also told us that the Lord says you're going to die."

⁷"What did the man look like?" Ahaziah asked.

⁸"He was hairyᶜ and had a leather belt around his waist," they answered.

"It must be Elijah!" replied Ahaziah. ⁹So at once he sent an army officer and 50 soldiers to meet Elijah.

Elijah was sitting on top of a hillᵈ at the time. The officer went up to him and said, "Man of God,ᵉ the king orders you to come down and talk with him."

¹⁰"If I am a man of God," Elijah answered, "God will send down fire on you and your 50 soldiers." Fire immediately

---

ᵃ**1.1,2** *the country . . . King Ahaziah:* The story of Moab's rebellion is in 3.4-27. ᵇ**1.1,2** *Ekron:* An important Philistine town about 40 miles southwest of Samaria. ᶜ**1.8** *hairy:* Or "wearing a furry coat." ᵈ**1.9** *a hill:* Probably Mount Carmel. ᵉ**1.9** *Man of God:* Another name for a prophet of the Lord.

2.1 *Elisha:* Elijah already had chosen Elisha to follow him as a prophet (1 Kgs 19.19). Elisha's story will continue through 2 Kgs 13.20. **(See the article Prophets and Prophecy on pg 1791.)**

2.6 *Jordan River:* The Jordan River is the longest and most important river in Palestine. **(See Map 6 on pg 1884.)**

2.8 *struck the water . . . on dry ground:* Elijah uses his rolled-up coat to part the water of the Jordan River much like Moses used his walking stick to part the waters of the Red Sea (Exod 14.15-22). After crossing to the east bank of the Jordan, Elijah comes to the area where Moses died and where his own life will end (2.11).

came down from heaven and burned up the officer and his men.

¹¹Ahaziah sent another officer and 50 more soldiers to Elijah. The officer said, "Man of God, the king orders you to come see him at once."

¹²"If I am a man of God," Elijah answered, "fire will destroy you and your 50 soldiers." And God sent down fire[f] from heaven on the officer and his men.

¹³Ahaziah sent a third army officer and 50 more soldiers. This officer went up to Elijah, then he got down on his knees and begged, "Man of God, please be kind to me and these 50 servants of yours. Let us live! ¹⁴Fire has already wiped out the other officers and their soldiers. Please don't let it happen to me."

¹⁵The angel from the LORD said to Elijah, "Go with him and don't be afraid." So Elijah got up and went with the officer.

¹⁶When Elijah arrived, he told Ahaziah, "The LORD wants to know why you sent messengers to Ekron to ask Baalzebub about your injury. Don't you believe there's a God in Israel? Ahaziah, because you did that, the LORD says you will die."

¹⁷Ahaziah died, just as the LORD had said. But since Ahaziah had no sons, Joram[g] his brother[h] then became king. This happened in the second year that Jehoram son of Jehoshaphat was king of Judah.[i] ¹⁸Everything else Ahaziah did while he was king is written in *The History of the Kings of Israel.*

The LORD Takes Elijah Away

2 Not long before the LORD took Elijah up into heaven in a strong wind, Elijah and Elisha were leaving Gilgal. ²Elijah said to Elisha, "The LORD wants me to go to Bethel, but you must stay here."

Elisha replied, "I swear by the living LORD and by your own life that I will stay with you no matter what!" And he went with Elijah to Bethel.

³A group of prophets who lived there asked Elisha, "Do you know that today the LORD is going to take away your master?"

"Yes, I do," Elisha answered. "But don't remind me of it."

⁴Elijah then said, "Elisha, now the LORD wants me to go to Jericho, but you must stay here."

Elisha replied, "I swear by the living LORD and by your own life, that I will stay with you no matter what!" And he went with Elijah to Jericho.

⁵A group of prophets who lived there asked Elisha, "Do you know that today the LORD is going to take away your master?"

"Yes, I do," Elisha answered. "But don't remind me of it."

⁶Elijah then said to Elisha, "Now the LORD wants me to go to the Jordan River, but you must stay here."

Elisha replied, "I swear by the living LORD and by your own life that I will never leave you!" So the two of them walked on together.

⁷Fifty prophets followed Elijah and Elisha from Jericho, then stood at a distance and watched as the two men walked toward the river. ⁸When they got there, Elijah took off his coat, then he rolled it up and struck the water with it. At once a path opened up through the river, and the two of them walked across on dry ground.

[f]**1.12** *God sent down fire:* Or "A mighty fire came down." [g]**1.17** *Joram:* The Hebrew text has "Jehoram," another spelling of the name. [h]**1.17** *his brother:* Some ancient translations (see also 3.1); these words are not in the Hebrew text. [i]**1.17** *This happened . . . Judah:* According to 3.1, this was also the eighteenth year of Jehoshaphat's rule in Judah. In biblical times, a father and son would sometimes rule as kings at the same time. This way, when the father died, the son would already have control of the kingdom (see also 8.16).

[9]After they had reached the other side, Elijah said, "Elisha, the LORD will soon take me away. What can I do for you before that happens?"

Elisha answered, "Please give me twice as much of your power as you give the other prophets, so I can be the one who takes your place as their leader."

[10]"It won't be easy," Elijah answered. "It can happen only if you see me as I am being taken away."

[11]Elijah and Elisha were walking along and talking, when suddenly there appeared between them a flaming chariot pulled by fiery horses. At once, a strong wind took Elijah up into heaven. [12]Elisha saw this and shouted, "Israel's cavalry and chariots have taken my master away!"[j] After Elijah had gone, Elisha tore his clothes in sorrow.

[13]Elijah's coat had fallen off, so Elisha picked it up and walked back to the Jordan River. [14]He struck the water with the coat and wondered, "Will the LORD perform miracles for me as he did for Elijah?" As soon as Elisha did this, a dry path opened up through the water, and he walked across.

[15]When the prophets from Jericho saw what happened, they said to each other, "Elisha now has Elijah's power."

They walked over to him, bowed down, [16]and said, "There are 50 strong men here with us. Please let them go look for your master. Maybe the Spirit of the LORD carried him off to some mountain or valley."

"No," Elisha replied, "they won't find him."

[17]They kept begging until he was embarrassed to say no. He finally agreed, and the prophets sent the men out. They looked three days for Elijah but never found him.

[18]They returned to Jericho, and Elisha said, "I told you that you wouldn't find him."

Elisha Makes the Water Pure at Jericho

[19]One day the people of Jericho said, "Elisha, you can see that our city is in a good spot. But the water from our spring is so bad that it even keeps our crops from growing."

[20]He replied, "Put some salt in a new bowl and bring it to me."

They brought him the bowl of salt, [21]and he carried it to the spring. He threw the salt into the water and said, "The LORD has made this water pure again. From now on you'll be able to grow crops, and no one will starve."

[22]The water has been fine ever since, just as Elisha said.

Some Boys Make Fun of Elisha

[23]Elisha left and headed toward Bethel. Along the way some boys started making fun of him by shouting, "Go away, baldy! Get out of here!"

[24]Elisha turned around and stared at the boys. Then he cursed them in the name of the LORD. At once two bears ran out of the woods and ripped to pieces 42 of the boys.

[25]Elisha went up to Mount Carmel, then returned to Samaria.

King Joram of Israel

3 Joram[k] son of Ahab became king of Israel in Jehoshaphat's eighteenth year as king of Judah.[l] Joram ruled twelve years from Samaria [2]and disobeyed the LORD by doing wrong. He tore down the stone

[j]2.12 *Israel's . . . away:* Or "Master, you were like cavalry and chariots for the people of Israel!"
[k]3.1 *Joram:* See the note at 1.17.　[l]3.1 *Joram . . . Judah:* See 1.17 and the note there; see also 8.16.

2.9 *"Please give me twice . . . their leader":* In Israel at this time, sons received a share of their father's possessions, but the first-born son was entitled to a double share. Much like a first-born son, Elisha asks Elijah for a double share of Elijah's power.

2.13 *coat:* Elijah's coat marked Elisha as the one who now had Elijah's powers (2.14,15).

2.16 *Spirit of the LORD carried him off:* Elijah had also mysteriously appeared and disappeared on other occasions (1 Kgs 18.9-16).

Holy Spirit

2.20 *salt:* While salt can purify water, the action here is purely the LORD's. It is the first of several events that show the miraculous power God gives Elisha.

2.23,24 *baldy . . . he cursed them:* Having no hair was considered a disgrace at this time, and shaving their heads was a means of humiliating criminals or captured soldiers. Elisha either was naturally bald or had shaved his head to set himself apart as a prophet. By using the term "baldy" to ridicule Elisha, they insulted and ridiculed God. A curse is the opposite of blessing. It calls for harm or destruction to happen to someone or something. Once spoken, a curse or blessing could not be taken back, because it was believed that the spoken word had a life and power of its own, and could make happen what was spoken.

A strong wind took Elijah up into heaven. 2 KGS 2.11

3.4 *Mesha rebelled*: This took place in 853 B.C. during Ahaziah's brief rule. Mesha was probably tired of having to pay such high taxes to Israel's kings.

3.8 *Edom Desert*: Mesha's forces had a firm hold in the north, so the combined forces of Israel and Judah could more easily attack Moab from the south. (See Map 6 on pg 1884.)

3.19 *walled cities*: Many cities, particularly those important to a nation's defense, were walled and had a central gate that could be closed. The area near the gate was also where city leaders heard and decided disputes.

3.20 *sacrifice*: This was a required daily sacrifice (Exod 29.38-43; Num 28.3, 4). (See the chart Sacrifices and Offerings on pg 1828.)

image his father had made to honor Baal, and so he wasn't as sinful as his parents. ³But he kept doing the sinful things that Jeroboam son of Nebat had led Israel to do.[m]

The Country of Moab Rebels against Israel

⁴For many years the country of Moab had been controlled by Israel and was forced to pay taxes to the kings of Israel. King Mesha of Moab raised sheep, so he paid the king of Israel 100,000 lambs and the wool from 100,000 rams. ⁵But soon after the death of Ahab, Mesha rebelled against Israel.

⁶One day, Joram left Samaria and called together Israel's army. ⁷He sent this message to King Jehoshaphat of Judah, "The king of Moab has rebelled. Will you go with me to attack him?"

"Yes, I will," Jehoshaphat answered. "I'm on your side, and my soldiers and horses are at your command. ⁸But which way should we go?"

"We will march through Edom Desert," Joram replied.

⁹So Joram, Jehoshaphat, and the king of Edom led their troops out. But seven days later, there was no drinking water left for them or their animals. ¹⁰Joram cried out, "This is terrible! The LORD must have led us out here to be captured by Moab's army."

¹¹Jehoshaphat said, "Which of the LORD's prophets is with us? We can find out from him what the LORD wants us to do."

One of Joram's officers answered, "Elisha son of Shaphat is here. He was one of Elijah's closest followers."

¹²Jehoshaphat replied, "He can give us the LORD's message."

The three kings went over to Elisha, ¹³and he asked Joram, "Why did you come to me? Go talk to the prophets of the foreign gods your parents worshiped."[n]

"No," Joram answered. "It was the LORD who led us out here, so that Moab's army could capture us."

¹⁴Elisha said to him, "I serve the LORD All-Powerful, and as surely as he lives, I swear I wouldn't even look at you if I didn't respect King Jehoshaphat." ¹⁵Then Elisha said, "Send for someone who can play the harp."

The harpist began playing, and the LORD gave Elisha this message for Joram:

¹⁶The LORD says that this dry riverbed will be filled with water.[o] ¹⁷You won't feel any wind or see any rain, but there will be plenty of water for you and your animals.

¹⁸That simple thing isn't all the LORD is going to do. He will also help you defeat Moab's army. ¹⁹You will capture all their walled cities and important towns. You will chop down every good tree and stop up every spring of water, then ruin their fertile fields by covering them with rocks.

²⁰The next morning, while the sacrifice was being offered, water suddenly started flowing from the direction of Edom, and it flooded the land.

²¹Meanwhile, the people of Moab had heard that the three kings were coming to attack them. They had called together all of their fighting men, from the youngest to the oldest, and these troops were now

---

[m]3.3 *the sinful things . . . to do*: When Jeroboam became king of Israel, he made two gold statues of calves and put them in the towns of Bethel and Dan, so the people of Israel could worship them (see 1 Kings 12.26-30). [n]3.13 *the prophets . . . worshiped*: These were prophets of the Canaanite god Baal and the goddess Asherah (see 1 Kings 16.30-33; 18.19). [o]3.16 *that . . . water*: Or "to dig holes everywhere in this riverbed."

standing at their border, ready for battle. 22When they got up that morning, the sun was shining across the water, making it look red. The Moabite troops took one look 23and shouted, "Look at that blood! The armies of those kings must have fought and killed each other. Come on, let's go take what's left in their camp."

24But when they arrived at Israel's camp, the Israelite soldiers came out and attacked them, until they turned and ran away. Israel's army chased them all the way back to Moab, and even there they kept up the attack.[p] 25The Israelites destroyed the Moabite towns. They chopped down the good trees and stopped up the springs of water, then covered the fertile fields with rocks.

Finally, the only city left standing was Kir-Hareseth, but soldiers armed with slings surrounded and attacked it. 26King Mesha of Moab saw that he was about to be defeated. So he took along 700 soldiers with swords and tried to break through the front line where the Edomite troops were positioned. But he failed. 27He then grabbed his oldest son who was to be the next king and sacrificed him as an offering on the city wall. The Israelite troops were so horrified that[q] they left the city and went back home.

Elisha Helps a Poor Widow

4 One day the widow of one of the LORD's prophets said to Elisha, "You know that before my husband died, he was a follower of yours and a worshiper of the LORD. But he owed a man some money, and now that man is on his way to take my two sons as his slaves."

2"Maybe there's something I can do to help," Elisha said. "What do you have in your house?"

"Sir, I have nothing but a small bottle of olive oil."

3Elisha told her, "Ask your neighbors for their empty jars. And after you've borrowed as many as you can, 4go home and shut the door behind you and your sons. Then begin filling the jars with oil and set each one aside as you fill it." 5The woman left.

Later, when she and her sons were back inside their house, the two sons brought her the jars, and she began filling them.

6At last, she said to one of her sons, "Bring me another jar."

"We don't have any more," he answered, and the oil stopped flowing from the small bottle.

7After she told Elisha what had happened, he said, "Sell the oil and use part of the money to pay what you owe the man. You and your sons can live on what is left."

Elisha Brings a Rich Woman's Son Back to Life

8Once, while Elisha was in the town of Shunem,[r] he met a rich woman who invited him to her home for dinner. After that, whenever he was in Shunem, he would have a meal there with her and her husband.

9Some time later the woman said to her husband, "I'm sure the man who comes here so often is a prophet of God. 10Why don't we build him a small room on the flat roof of our house? We can put a bed, a table and chair, and an oil lamp in it. Then whenever he comes, he can stay with us."

[p]3.24 *chased . . . attack*: One possible meaning for the difficult Hebrew text. [q]3.27 *The Israelite . . . that*: One possible meaning for the difficult Hebrew text. [r]4.8 *Shunem*: A town in Israel, about 25 miles north of Samaria.

3.25 *Kir-Hareseth:* Moab's capital city. (See Map 6 on pg 1884.)

3.27 *sacrificed him:* This was probably a sacrifice to Chemosh, one of the Moabite gods.

4.1 *his slaves:* If a loan could not be repaid, the law allowed the lender to take the borrower's children as payment. Such slaves were to be treated as servants, and the length of their slavery was limited (Lev 25.39-43).

4.2 *olive oil:* The oil that came from crushed olives was very valuable. It was used in cooking, medicine, grooming, and special anointing ceremonies (see 1 Chr 11.3). It was also burned in lamps for light and was part of the ingredients in certain offerings to God.

4.14 *her husband is old . . . she doesn't have a son:* Without a son, the family name would not continue, and the family line would be destroyed. Also, a woman depended on her son to protect her and provide for her if her husband died.

4.23 *Sabbath . . . New Moon Festival:* The Sabbath and the New Moon Festival were holy days, and probably were considered more appropriate times to consult a prophet. The Sabbath was the weekly day of rest that began at sunset on Friday and ended at sunset on Saturday. No work was to be done on the Sabbath, which means "rest" or to "stop working." The New Moon Festival was held on the day of the new moon. This day was always the first day of the month for the Hebrew calendar. This festival was a time for worship, sacrifices, celebration, eating, and rest from work.

4.27 *grabbed Elisha by the feet:* This was a sign of humility and respect.

¹¹The next time Elisha was in Shunem, he stopped at their house and went up to his room to rest. ¹²⁻¹³He said to his servant Gehazi, "This woman has been very helpful. Have her come up here to the roof for a moment." She came, and Elisha told Gehazi to say to her, "You've gone to a lot of trouble for us, and we want to help you. Is there something we can request the king or army commander to do?"ˢ

The woman answered, "With my relatives nearby, I have everything I need."

¹⁴"Then what can we do for her?" Elisha asked Gehazi.

Gehazi replied, "I do know that her husband is old, and that she doesn't have a son."

¹⁵"Ask her to come here again," Elisha told his servant. He called for her, and she came and stood in the doorway of Elisha's room.

¹⁶Elisha said to her, "Next year at this time, you'll be holding your own baby son in your arms."

"You're a man of God," the woman replied. "Please don't lie to me."

¹⁷But a few months later, the woman got pregnant. She gave birth to a son, just as Elisha had promised.

¹⁸One day while the boy was still young, he was out in the fields with his father, where the workers were harvesting the crops. ¹⁹Suddenly he shouted, "My head hurts. It hurts a lot!"

"Carry him back to his mother," the father said to his servant. ²⁰The servant picked up the boy and carried him to his mother. The boy lay on her lap all morning, and by noon he was dead. ²¹She carried him upstairs to Elisha's room and laid him across the bed. Then she walked out and shut the door behind her.

²²The woman called to her husband, "I need to see the prophet. Let me use one of the donkeys. Send a servant along with me, and let me leave now, so I can get back quickly."

²³"Why do you need to see him today?" her husband asked. "It's not the Sabbath or time for the New Moon Festival."

"That's all right," she answered. ²⁴She saddled the donkey and said to her servant, "Let's go. And don't slow down unless I tell you to." ²⁵She left at once for Mount Carmel to talk with Elisha.ᵗ

When Elisha saw her coming, he said, "Gehazi, look! It's the woman from Shunem. ²⁶Run and meet her. And ask her if everything is all right with her and her family."

"Everything is fine," she answered Gehazi. ²⁷But as soon as she got to the top of the mountain, she went over and grabbed Elisha by the feet.

Gehazi started toward her to push her away, when Elisha said, "Leave her alone! Don't you see how sad she is? But the LORD hasn't told me why."

²⁸The woman said, "Sir, I begged you not to get my hopes up, and I didn't even ask you for a son."

²⁹"Gehazi, get ready and go to her house," Elisha said. "Take along my walking stick, and when you get there, lay it on the boy's face. Don't stop to talk to anyone, even if they try to talk to you."

³⁰But the boy's mother said to Elisha, "I swear by the living LORD and by your own life that I won't leave without you." So Elisha got up and went with them.

³¹Gehazi ran on ahead and laid Elisha's walking stick on the boy's face, but the boy didn't move or make a sound. Gehazi ran back to Elisha and said, "The boy didn't wake up."

ˢ**4.12,13** *request the king . . . do:* Elisha may have meant that he could ask these leaders to lower her taxes.   ᵗ**4.25** *Elisha:* Mount Carmel is about 25 miles from Shunem.

³²Elisha arrived at the woman's house and went straight to his room, where he saw the boy's body on his bed. ³³He walked in, shut the door, and prayed to the LORD. ³⁴Then he got on the bed and stretched out over the dead body, with his mouth on the boy's mouth, his eyes on his eyes, and his hand on his hands. As he lay there, the boy's body became warm. ³⁵Elisha got up and walked back and forth in the room, then he went back and leaned over the boy's body. The boy sneezed seven times and opened his eyes.

³⁶Elisha called out to Gehazi, "Ask the boy's mother to come here." Gehazi did, and when she was at the door, Elisha said, "You can take your son."

³⁷She came in and bowed down at Elisha's feet. Then she picked up her son and left.

Elisha Makes Some Stew Taste Better

³⁸Later, Elisha went back to Gilgal, where there was almost nothing to eat, because the crops had failed.

One day while the prophets who lived there were meeting with Elisha, he said to his servant, "Prepare a big pot of stew for these prophets."

³⁹One of them went out into the woods to gather some herbs. He found a wild vine and picked as much of its fruit as he could carry, but he didn't know that the fruit was very sour. When he got back, he cut up the fruit and put it in the stew. ⁴⁰The stew was served, and when the prophets started eating it, they shouted, "Elisha, this stew tastes terrible! We can't eat it."

⁴¹"Bring me some flour," Elisha said. He sprinkled the flour in the stew and said, "Now serve it to them." And the stew tasted fine.

Elisha Feeds One Hundred People

⁴²A man from the town of Baal-Shalishah ͧ brought Elisha some freshly cut grain and 20 loaves of bread made from the first barley that was harvested. Elisha said, "Give it to the people so they can eat."

⁴³"There's not enough here for 100 people," his servant said.

"Just give it to them," Elisha replied. "The LORD has promised there will be more than enough."

⁴⁴So the servant served the bread and grain to the people. They ate and still had some left over, just as the LORD had promised.

Elisha Heals Naaman

5 Naaman was the commander of the Syrian army. The LORD had helped him and his troops defeat their enemies, so the king of Syria respected Naaman very much. Naaman was a brave soldier, but he had leprosy. ͮ

²One day while the Syrian troops were raiding Israel, they captured a girl, and she became a servant of Naaman's wife. ³Some time later the girl said, "If your husband Naaman would go to the prophet in Samaria, he would be cured of his leprosy."

⁴When Naaman told the king what the girl had said, ⁵the king replied, "Go ahead! I will give you a letter to take to the king of Israel."

Naaman left and took along 750 pounds

ͧ4.42 Baal-Shalishah: The exact location of this town is not known, but it was probably somewhere near Shechem. ͮ5.1 leprosy: The word translated "leprosy" was used for many different kinds of skin diseases.

● 4.34, 35 *with his mouth . . . seven times:* Elijah performed a similar miracle (1 Kgs 17.21). In both instances, the prophets stretch their bodies over the dead body in what seems to be a transfer of life force from one body to the other. The number "seven" symbolized perfection. The book's original readers would have seen the seven sneezes as indicating the boy was restored to full life and breath. **(See the chart Numbers in the Bible on pg 1844.)**

● 4.39 *wild vine:* This may refer to a colocynthis, a bitter orange-shaped fruit that can cause vomiting and is poisonous in large amounts.

● 4.42 *first barley that was harvested:* The first part of a harvest was to be brought to the place of worship and offered to God (Lev 2.14; Deut 18.3-5). It appears that prophets as well as priests could receive the offering at this time. The offering recognized that everything comes from and belongs to God. Once a portion of the first harvest was offered to God, the rest could be used by the people. It is not clear whether the offering here is a one-time event or part of the Harvest Festival (Exod 23.16; Lev 23.15-21; Num 28.26-31) or the Festival of Shelters (Lev 23.33-43; Num 29.12-39).

● 5.1 *Syrian:* Syria (Aram) was located to the north and west of Israel. The Syrians traditionally had been enemies of Israel. **(See Map 6 on pg 1884.)**

5.7 *tore his clothes . . . pick a fight with me:* Tearing one's clothes was a common way of showing fear or grief. The king's worry over the Syrian king trying to pick a fight, and the raids mentioned in 5.2, both indicate that Syria had power over Israel at this time.

5.12 *Abana River . . . Pharpar River . . . Damascus:* The Abana River's clean waters flowed from the Lebanon mountains to Damascus, while the Pharpar River flowed from east of Mount Hermon to south of Damascus. Both rivers were much cleaner than the muddy waters of the Jordan River. Damascus was Syria's capital and a major trading and transportation center. The two rivers flowing into it and feeding its orchards and gardens made it a beautiful oasis in the middle of the desert. (See Map 6 on pg 1884.)

5.18 *Rimmon:* Another name for Hadad, a chief god of the Syrians. As the Syrian king's servant, Naaman was required to go with the king to worship at the temple of Rimmon.

of silver, 150 pounds of gold, and 10 new outfits. **6**He also carried the letter to the king of Israel. It said, "I am sending my servant Naaman to you. Would you cure him of his leprosy?"

7When the king of Israel read the letter, he tore his clothes in fear and shouted, "That Syrian king believes I can cure this man of leprosy! Does he think I'm God with power over life and death? He must be trying to pick a fight with me."

8As soon as Elisha the prophet[w] heard what had happened, he sent the Israelite king this message: "Why are you so afraid? Send the man to me, so that he will know there is a prophet in Israel."

9Naaman left with his horses and chariots and stopped at the door of Elisha's house. **10**Elisha sent someone outside to say to him, "Go wash seven times in the Jordan River. Then you'll be completely cured."

11But Naaman stormed off, grumbling, "Why couldn't he come out and talk to me? I thought for sure he would stand in front of me and pray to the LORD his God, then wave his hand over my skin and cure me. **12**What about the Abana River[x] or the Pharpar River? Those rivers in Damascus are just as good as any river in Israel. I could have washed in them and been cured."

13His servants went over to him and said, "Sir, if the prophet had told you to do something difficult, you would have done it. So why don't you do what he said? Go wash and be cured."

14Naaman walked down to the Jordan; he waded out into the water and stooped down in it seven times, just as Elisha had told him. At once, he was cured, and his skin became as smooth as a child's.

15Naaman and his officials went back to Elisha. Naaman stood in front of him and announced, "Now I know that the God of Israel is the only God in the whole world. Sir, would you please accept a gift from me?"

16"I am a servant of the living LORD," Elisha answered, "and I swear that I will not take anything from you."

Naaman kept begging, but Elisha kept refusing. **17**Finally Naaman said, "If you won't accept a gift, then please let me take home as much soil as two mules can pull in a wagon. Sir, from now on I will offer sacrifices only to the LORD.[y] **18**But I pray that the LORD will forgive me when I go into the temple of the god Rimmon and bow down there with the king of Syria."

19"Go on home, and don't worry about that," Elisha replied. Then Naaman left.

Elisha Places a Curse on Gehazi

After Naaman had gone only a short distance, **20**Gehazi said to himself, "Elisha let that Syrian off too easy. He should have taken Naaman's gift. I swear by the living LORD that I will talk to Naaman myself and get something from him." **21**So he hurried after Naaman.

When Naaman saw Gehazi running after him, he got out of his chariot to meet him. Naaman asked, "Is everything all right?"

22"Yes," Gehazi answered. "But my master has sent me to tell you about two young prophets from the hills of Ephraim. They came asking for help, and now Elisha wants to know if you would give them about 75 pounds of silver and some new clothes?"

[w]**5.8** *the prophet:* Hebrew "the man of God."   [x]**5.12** *Abana River:* Most Hebrew manuscripts; some Hebrew manuscripts and two ancient translations "Amana River."   [y]**5.17** *let me take . . . the LORD:* It was believed that the LORD had to be worshiped in Israel or on soil taken from Israel.

Naaman said, "Now I know that the God of Israel is the only God in the whole world." 2 KGS 5.15

²³"Sure," Naaman replied. "But why don't you take twice that amount of silver?" He convinced Gehazi to take it all, then put the silver in two bags. He handed the bags and the clothes to his two servants, and they carried them for Gehazi.

²⁴When they reached the hill where Gehazi lived, he took the bags from the servants and placed them in his house, then sent the men away. After they had gone, ²⁵Gehazi went in and stood in front of Elisha, who asked, "Gehazi, where have you been?"

"Nowhere, sir," Gehazi answered.

²⁶Elisha asked, "Don't you know that my spirit was there when Naaman got out of his chariot to talk with you? Gehazi, you have no right to accept money or clothes, olive orchards or vineyards, sheep or cattle, or servants. ²⁷Because of what you've done, Naaman's leprosy^z will now be on you and your descendants forever!"

Suddenly, Gehazi's skin became white with leprosy, and he left.

Elisha Makes an Ax Head Float

6 One day the prophets said to Elisha, "The place where we meet with you is too small. ²Why don't we build a new meeting place near the Jordan River? Each of us could get some wood, then we could build it."

"That's a good idea," Elisha replied, "get started."

³"Aren't you going with us?" one of the prophets asked.

"Yes, I'll go," Elisha answered, ⁴and he left with them.

They went to the Jordan River and began chopping down trees. ⁵While one of the prophets was working, his ax head fell off and dropped into the water. "Oh!" he shouted. "Sir, I borrowed this ax."

⁶"Where did it fall in?" Elisha asked. The prophet pointed to the place, and Elisha cut a stick and threw it into the water at that spot. The ax head floated to the top of the water.

⁷"Now get it," Elisha told him. And the prophet reached in and grabbed it.

Elisha Stops an Invasion of the Syrian Army

⁸Time after time, when the king of Syria was at war against the Israelites, he met with his officers and announced, "I've decided where we will set up camp."

⁹Each time, Elisha^a would send this warning to the king of Israel: "Don't go near there. That's where the Syrian troops have set up camp."^b ¹⁰So the king would warn the Israelite troops in that place to be on guard.

¹¹The king of Syria was furious when he found out what was happening. He called in his officers and asked, "Which one of you has been telling the king of Israel our plans?"

¹²"None of us, Your Majesty," one of them answered. "It's an Israelite named Elisha. He's a prophet, so he can tell his king everything—even what you say in your own room."

¹³"Find out where he is!" the king ordered. "I'll send soldiers to bring him here."

They learned that Elisha was in the town of Dothan^c and reported it to the king. ¹⁴He ordered his best troops to go there with horses and chariots. They marched

6.4 *trees:* The trees common to this area (willow, tamarisk, and acacia) produced lightweight lumber that was used to build smaller buildings but not great palaces or temples.

6.8 *king of Syria:* This probably refers to Benhadad II. By leaving him unnamed, the author may be emphasizing how unimportant the kings are compared to God or God's prophets.

6.13 *Dothan:* This town was located north of Samaria and twelve miles south of Jezreel. It controlled a main mountain pass along the road that connected Damascus and Egypt. (See Map 6 on pg 1884.)

^z5.27 *leprosy:* See the note at 5.1.   ^a6.9 *Elisha:* Hebrew "the man of God."   ^b6.9 *have set up camp:* Or "are going."   ^c6.13 *Dothan:* About ten miles north of Samaria.

6.23 *huge meal:* In the ancient Near East, such a meal often was part of sealing an agreement or settlement.

6.25 *donkey's head:* There was so little food that even undesirable parts of "unclean" animals, such as donkeys, were sold for high prices.

Purity (Clean and Unclean)

6.26 *the king of Israel:* This refers to either Jehoahaz or Jehoash, but possibly even Joram. Once again, the writer emphasizes how insignificant the kings are by omitting the actual ruler's name.

6.28,29 *agreed to eat our sons ... eat her son:* The Israelites' situation is so desperate that the woman is not ashamed to admit she has eaten her own child. Instead, she is concerned only with getting her fair share of the meat from another woman's child.

out during the night and surrounded the town.

¹⁵When Elisha's servant got up the next morning, he saw that Syrian troops had the town surrounded. "Sir, what are we going to do?" he asked.

¹⁶"Don't be afraid," Elisha answered. "There are more troops on our side than on theirs." ¹⁷Then he prayed, "LORD, please help him to see." And the LORD let the servant see that the hill[d] was covered with fiery horses and flaming chariots all around Elisha.

¹⁸As the Syrian army came closer, Elisha prayed, "LORD, make those soldiers blind!" And the LORD blinded them with a bright light.

¹⁹Elisha told the enemy troops, "You've taken the wrong road and are in the wrong town. Follow me. I'll lead you to the man you're looking for." Elisha led them straight to the capital city of Samaria.

²⁰When all the soldiers were inside the city, Elisha prayed, "LORD, now let them see again." The LORD let them see that they were standing in the middle of Samaria.

²¹The king of Israel saw them and asked Elisha, "Should I kill them, sir?"

²²"No!" Elisha answered. "You didn't capture these troops in battle, so you have no right to kill them. Instead, give them something to eat and drink and let them return to their leader."

²³The king ordered a huge meal to be prepared for Syria's army, and when they finished eating, he let them go.

For a while, the Syrian troops stopped invading Israel's territory.

King Benhadad of Syria Attacks Samaria

²⁴Some time later, King Benhadad of Syria[e] called his entire army together, then they marched to Samaria and attacked. ²⁵They kept up the attack until there was nothing to eat in the city. In fact, a donkey's head cost about two pounds of silver, and a small bowl of pigeon droppings[f] cost about two ounces of silver.

²⁶One day as the king of Israel[g] was walking along the top of the city wall, a woman shouted to him, "Please, Your Majesty, help me!"

²⁷"Let the LORD help you!" the king said. "Do you think I have grain or wine to give you?" ²⁸Then he asked, "What's the matter anyway?"

The woman answered, "Another woman and I were so hungry that we agreed to eat our sons. She said if we ate my son one day, we could eat hers the next day. ²⁹ So yesterday we cooked my son and ate him. But today when I went to her house to eat her son, she had hidden him."

³⁰The king tore off his clothes in sorrow, and since he was on top of the city wall, the people saw that he was wearing sackcloth underneath. ³¹He said, "I pray that God will punish me terribly, if Elisha's head is still on his shoulders by this time tomorrow." ³²Then he sent a messenger to Elisha.

Elisha was home at the time, and the important leaders of Israel were meeting with him. Even before the king's messenger arrived, Elisha told the leaders, "That murderer[h] is sending someone to cut off my

[d]**6.17** *the hill:* The hill on which the town was built.   [e]**6.24** *King Benhadad of Syria:* This may or may not be the same Benhadad mentioned in 1 Kings 20.1. Several of the Syrian kings were named Benhadad.   [f]**6.25** *pigeon droppings:* This may have been used for food or to burn for fuel. It also may have been a popular name for roasted beans or the shells of certain seeds.   [g]**6.26** *the king of Israel:* Probably either Jehoahaz or Jehoash, but possibly even Joram.   [h]**6.32** *That murderer:* Hebrew "That murderer's son."

head. When you see him coming, shut the door and don't let him in. I'm sure the king himself will be right behind him."

[33]Before Elisha finished talking, the messenger[i] came up and said, "The LORD has made all these terrible things happen to us. Why should I think he will help us now?"

7 Elisha answered, "I have a message for you. The LORD promises that tomorrow here in Samaria, you will be able to buy a large sack of flour or two large sacks of barley for almost nothing."

[2]The chief officer there with the king replied, "I don't believe it! Even if the LORD sent a rainstorm, it couldn't produce that much grain by tomorrow."

"You will see it happen, but you won't eat any of the food," Elisha warned him.

The Syrian Army Stops Its Attack

[3]About the same time, four men with leprosy[j] were just outside the gate of Samaria. They said to each other, "Why should we sit here, waiting to die? [4]There's nothing to eat in the city, so we would starve if we went inside. But if we stay out here, we will die for sure. Let's sneak over to the Syrian army camp and surrender. They might kill us, but they might not." [5-8]That evening the four men got up and left for the Syrian camp.

As they walked toward the camp, the Lord caused the Syrian troops to hear what sounded like the roar of a huge cavalry. The soldiers said to each other, "Listen! The king of Israel must have hired Hittite and Egyptian troops to attack us. Let's get out of here!" So they ran out of their camp that night, leaving their tents and horses and donkeys.

When the four men with leprosy reached the edge of the Syrian camp, no one was there. They walked into one of the tents, where they ate and drank, before carrying off clothes, as well as silver and gold. They hid all this, then walked into another tent; they took what they wanted and hid it too.

[9]They said to each other, "This isn't right. Today is a day to celebrate, and we haven't told anyone else what has happened. If we wait until morning, we will be punished. Let's go to the king's palace at once and tell the good news."

[10]They went back to Samaria and shouted up to the guards at the gate, "We've just come from the Syrian army camp, and all the soldiers are gone! The tents are empty, and the horses and donkeys are still tied up. We didn't see or hear anybody."

[11]The guards reported the news to the king's palace. [12]The king got out of bed and said to his officers, "I know what those Syrians are doing. They know we're starving, so they're hiding in the fields, hoping we will go out to look for food. When we do, they can capture us and take over our city."

[13]One of his officers replied, "We have a few horses left—why don't we let some men take five of them and go to the Syrian camp and see what's happening? We're going to die anyway like those who have already died."[k] [14]They found two chariots, and the king commanded the men to find out what had happened to the Syrian troops.

[15]The men rode as far as the Jordan River. All along the way they saw clothes and equipment that the Syrians had thrown away as they escaped. Then they went back to the king and told him what they had seen.

[16]At once the people went to the Syrian

● 7.5-8 Hittite and Egyptian troops: The Hittites once had a vast empire in Asia Minor and threatened Syria from the north. Hittites are mentioned as being settled in Canaan before the people of Israel took over the land (Gen 23.3; Num 13.29; Josh 1.4). At various times in history, Egypt was a great military power and attacked areas of the ancient Near East as far north as Syria.

[i]6.33 messenger: Or "king" (see 7.2,18); the two Hebrew words are very similar. [j]7.3 leprosy: See the note at 5.1. [k]7.13 We're going . . . died: One possible meaning for the difficult Hebrew text.

8.2 *Philistine territory:* This area was west of Judah along the Mediterranean Sea. It included five main cities, each with its own ruler: Ashdod, Ashkelon, Ekron, Gath, and Gaza. The Philistines often had been at war with Israel. **(See Map 6 on pg 1884.)**

8.9 *best things made in Damascus:* The finest merchandise from all over the ancient Near East could be found in Damascus, because it was a major trade center. It was the custom to bring a gift to a prophet when asking about God's will (1 Sam 9.7; 1 Kgs 14.2,3).

8.11,13-15 *Elisha stared . . . the next king:* Elisha's stare may indicate he has gone into a trance. On Mount Sinai, God had told Elijah that three things must be done (1 Kgs 19.15,16). Elijah accomplished one when he appointed Elisha to take his place (1 Kgs 19.19,20). Here, Elisha carries out the second by telling Hazael he will be the next king. Soon Elisha will carry out the third when he appoints Jehu as king of Israel (2 Kgs 9.6-10). **(See the article Prophets and Prophecy on pg 1791.)**

camp and carried off what was left. They took so much that a large sack of flour and two large sacks of barley sold for almost nothing, just as the LORD had promised.

[17]The king of Israel had put his chief officer in charge of the gate, but he died when the people trampled him as they rushed out of the city. [18]Earlier, when the king was at Elisha's house, Elisha had told him that flour or barley would sell for almost nothing. [19]But the officer refused to believe that even the LORD could do that. So Elisha warned him that he would see it happen, but would not eat any of the food. [20]And that's exactly what happened—the officer was trampled to death.

The Woman from Shunem Is Given Back Her Land

8 Elisha told the woman whose son he had brought back to life,[l] "The LORD has warned that there will be no food here for seven years. Take your family and go live somewhere else for a while." [2]The woman did exactly what Elisha had said and went to live in Philistine territory.

She and her family lived there seven years. [3]Then she returned to Israel and immediately begged the king to give back her house and property.

[4]Meanwhile, the king was asking Gehazi the servant of Elisha about the amazing things Elisha had been doing. [5]While Gehazi was telling him that Elisha had brought a dead boy back to life, the woman and her son arrived.

"Here's the boy, Your Majesty," Gehazi said. "And this is his mother."

[6]The king asked the woman to tell her story, and she told him everything that had happened. He then said to one of his officials, "I want you to make sure that this woman gets back everything that belonged to her, including the money her crops have made since the day she left Israel."

Hazael Kills Benhadad

[7]Some time later Elisha went to the capital city of Damascus to visit King Benhadad of Syria, who was sick. And when Benhadad was told he was there, [8]he said to Hazael,[m] "Go meet with Elisha the man of God and get him to ask the LORD if I will get well. And take along a gift for him."

[9]Hazael left with forty camel loads of the best things made in Damascus as a gift for Elisha. He found the prophet and said, "Your servant, King Benhadad, wants to know if he will get well."

[10]"Tell him he will," Elisha said to Hazael. "But the LORD has already told me that Benhadad will definitely die." [11]Elisha stared at him until Hazael was embarrassed, then Elisha began crying.[n]

[12]"Sir, why are you crying?" Hazael asked.

Elisha answered, "Because I know the terrible things you will do to the people of Israel. You will burn down their walled cities and slaughter their young men. You will even crush the heads of their babies and rip open their pregnant women."

[13] "How could I ever do anything like that?" Hazael replied. "I'm only a servant and don't have that kind of power."

"Hazael, the LORD has told me that you will be the next king of Syria."

[14]Hazael went back to Benhadad and told him, "Elisha said that you will get well." [15]But the very next day, Hazael got a thick blanket; he soaked it in water and held it over Benhadad's face until he died. Hazael then became king.

[l]8.1 *Elisha . . . life:* See 4.8-37.   [m]8.8 *Hazael:* Probably one of Benhadad's officials.   [n]8.11 *Elisha stared . . . crying:* Or "Hazael stared at him until Elisha was embarrassed and began to cry."

King Jehoram of Judah
(2 Chronicles 21.2-20)

[16]Jehoram son of Jehoshaphat became king of Judah in Joram's fifth year as king of Israel, while Jehoshaphat was still king of Judah.[o] [17]Jehoram was 32 years old when he became king, and he ruled 8 years from Jerusalem.

[18]Jehoram disobeyed the LORD by doing wrong. He married Ahab's daughter and was as sinful as Ahab's family and the kings of Israel. [19]But the LORD refused to destroy Judah, because he had promised his servant David that someone from his family would always rule in Judah.

[20]While Jehoram was king, the people of Edom rebelled and chose their own king. [21]So Jehoram[p] and his cavalry marched to Zair, where the Edomite army surrounded him and his commanders. During the night he attacked the Edomites, but he was defeated, and his troops escaped to their homes.[q] [22]Judah was never able to regain control of Edom. Even the town of Libnah[r] rebelled at that time.

[23]Everything else Jehoram did while he was king is written in *The History of the Kings of Judah.* [24]Jehoram died and was buried beside his ancestors in Jerusalem.[s] His son Ahaziah then became king.

King Ahaziah of Judah
(2 Chronicles 22.1-6)

[25]Ahaziah son of Jehoram became king of Judah in the twelfth year of Joram's rule in Israel. [26]Ahaziah was 22 years old when he became king, and he ruled from Jerusalem for only one year. His mother was Athaliah, a granddaughter of King Omri of Israel. [27]Since Ahaziah was related to Ahab's family,[t] he acted just like them and disobeyed the LORD by doing wrong.

[28]Ahaziah went with King Joram of Israel to attack King Hazael and the Syrian troops at Ramoth in Gilead. Joram was wounded in that battle, [29]so he went to the town of Jezreel to recover. Ahaziah went there to visit him.

Jehu Becomes King of Israel

9 One day, Elisha called for one of the other prophets and said:

Take this bottle of olive oil and get ready to go to the town of Ramoth in Gilead. [2]When you get there, find Jehu son of Jehoshaphat and grandson of Nimshi. Take him to a place where the two of you can be alone, [3]then pour olive oil on his head to show that he is the new king. Say to him, "The LORD has chosen you to be king of Israel." Then leave quickly—don't wait around for anything!

[4]The young prophet left for Ramoth. [5]When he arrived, the army officers were meeting together. "Sir, I have a message for you," he said.

"For which one of us?" Jehu asked.

"You, sir," the prophet answered. [6]So Jehu got up and went inside.[u] The prophet

---

8.16 *while Jehoshaphat . . . Judah:* In biblical times, a father and son would sometimes rule as kings at the same time. That way, when the father died, his son would already have control of the kingdom. P8.21 *Jehoram:* The Hebrew text has "Joram," another spelling of the name.   q8.21 *he attacked . . . homes:* One possible meaning for the difficult Hebrew text.   r8.22 *Even the town of Libnah:* This was a town on the border between Philistia and Judah, which means that Jehoram was facing rebellion on two sides of his kingdom.   s8.24 *Jerusalem:* Hebrew "the city of David."   t8.27 *Since . . . family:* Ahaziah's mother was Ahab's daughter (see verse 18).   u9.6 *went inside:* The officers were probably meeting outside in an open courtyard of some building.

● 8.16-18 *Jehoram . . . Ahab's daughter:* Jehoram, Judah's fifth king, ruled alone from 848 to 841 B.C. Before that, he ruled for four years with his father, Jehoshaphat. Athaliah may have been the daughter of Israel's King Ahab and Queen Jezebel. But some believe she was the daughter of Omri, Ahab's father, but that Ahab raised her.

● 8.18 *Jehoram disobeyed . . . as sinful as Ahab's family:* Jehoram allowed Baal worship in Judah, just as Ahab had during his rule as king of Israel (see 1 Kgs 16.29-33).

✿   Jerusalem

● 8.25-27 *Ahaziah . . . was related to Ahab's family:* Ahaziah, Judah's sixth king, ruled for one year in 841 B.C. His mother was Athaliah, the daughter of Israel's former King Ahab. The reference to Omri in 8.26 is a tribute to his greatness. Omri conquered Moab, formed an alliance with Sidon, and wisely built up Samaria as Israel's capital. A hundred years after his reign, Assyrian kings still called Israel "the land of Omri." However, this brilliant civilian and military leader was a failure as a religious leader for God's people.

● 9.2 *Jehu:* Jehu, Israel's tenth king, ruled from 841 to 814 B.C. God told Elijah that Jehu would become king and kill anyone who worshiped Baal (1 Kgs 19.16,17).

9.7 *Jezebel:* This woman, King Ahab's wife, encouraged Ahab to allow the people of Israel to worship Baal and Asherah, the Canaanite god and goddess of fertility (see 1 Kgs 16.31-33). She also tried to destroy God's prophets (1 Kgs 18.3-4; 21.1-16).

9.13 *coats . . . spread them . . . "Jehu is king!":* The officers hold a ceremony, making a type of throne with their coats spread on the steps. They complete the ceremony with a trumpet call and the customary shouting of "Jehu is king!"

9.21-28 *land that had belonged to Naboth . . . throw Joram's body . . . shot Ahaziah:* Ahab and Jezebel had earlier plotted to kill Naboth so they could steal his land (1 Kgs 21.1-16). The prophet Elijah warned Ahab that his body would end up in Naboth's field, and his family would be wiped out (1 Kgs 21.17-22). Jehu's killing of Ahab's sons, Joram and Ahaziah, fulfills Elijah's prophecy in part.

poured olive oil on Jehu's head and told him:

The LORD God of Israel has this message for you: "I am the LORD, and I have chosen you to be king of my people Israel. [7]I want you to wipe out the family of Ahab, so Jezebel will be punished for killing the prophets and my other servants. [8]Every man and boy in Ahab's family must die, whether slave or free. [9]His whole family must be destroyed, just like the families of Jeroboam son of Nebat and Baasha son of Ahijah. [10] As for Jezebel, her body will be eaten by dogs in the town of Jezreel. There won't be enough left of her to bury."

Then the young prophet opened the door and ran out.

[11]Jehu went back to his officers, and one of them asked, "What did that crazy prophet want? Is everything all right?"

"You know him and how he talks," Jehu answered.

[12]"No, we don't. What did he say?" they asked.

"He had a message from the LORD," Jehu replied. "He said that the LORD has chosen me to be the next king of Israel."

[13]They quickly grabbed their coats and spread them out on the steps where Jehu was standing. Someone blew a trumpet, and everyone shouted, "Jehu is king!"

Jehu Kills Joram and Ahaziah

[14-16]King Joram[v] of Israel had been badly wounded in the battle at Ramoth, trying to defend it against King Hazael and the Syrian army. Joram was now recovering in Jezreel, and King Ahaziah of Judah was there, visiting him.

Meanwhile, Jehu was in Ramoth, making plans to kill Joram. He said to his officers, "If you want me to be king, then don't let anyone leave this town. They might go to Jezreel and tell Joram." Then Jehu got in his chariot and rode to Jezreel.

[17]When the guard in the watchtower at Jezreel saw Jehu and his men riding up, he shouted to the king, "I see a large group of men coming this way."

Joram ordered, "Send someone out to ask them if this is a friendly visit."

[18]One of the soldiers rode out and said to Jehu, "King Joram wants to know if this is a friendly visit."

"What's it to you?" Jehu asked. "Just stay behind me with the rest of my troops!"

About the same time the guard in the watchtower said, "Your Majesty, the rider got there, but he isn't coming back."

[19]So Joram sent out another rider, who rode up to Jehu and said, "The king wants to know if this is a friendly visit."

"What's it to you?" Jehu asked. "Just get behind me with the rest of my troops!"

[20]The guard in the watchtower said, "Your Majesty, the rider got there, but he isn't coming back either. Wait a minute! That one man is a reckless chariot driver—it must be Jehu!"

[21]Joram commanded, "Get my chariot ready." Then he and Ahaziah got in their chariots and rode out to meet Jehu. They all met on the land that had belonged to Naboth.[w] [22]Joram asked, "Jehu, is this a peaceful visit?"

"How can there be peace?" Jehu asked. "Your mother Jezebel has caused everyone to worship idols and practice witchcraft."

[23]"Ahaziah, let's get out of here!" Joram yelled. "It's a trap!" As Joram tried to escape, [24]Jehu shot an arrow. It hit Joram be-

tween his shoulders, then it went through his heart and came out his chest. He fell over dead in his chariot.

25-26 Jehu commanded his assistant Bidkar, "Get Joram's body and throw it in the field that Naboth once owned. Do you remember when you and I used to ride side by side behind Joram's father Ahab? It was then that the LORD swore to Ahab that he would be punished in the same field where he had killed Naboth and his sons. So throw Joram's body there, just as the LORD said."

27 Ahaziah saw all of this happen and tried to escape to the town of Beth-Haggan, but Jehu caught up with him and shouted, "Kill him too!" So his troops shot Ahaziah with an arrow while he was on the road to Gur near Ibleam. He went as far as Megiddo, where he died. **28** Ahaziah's officers put his body in a chariot and took it back to Jerusalem, where they buried him beside his ancestors.

29 Ahaziah had become king of Judah in the eleventh year of the rule of Ahab's son Joram.

Jehu Kills Jezebel

30 Jehu headed toward Jezreel, and when Jezebel heard he was coming, she put on eye shadow and brushed her hair. Then she stood at the window, waiting for him to arrive. **31** As he walked through the city gate, she shouted down to him, "Why did you come here, you murderer? To kill the king? You're no better than Zimri!"[x]

32 He looked up toward the window and asked, "Is anyone up there on my side?" A few palace workers stuck their heads out of a window, **33** and Jehu shouted, "Throw her out the window!" They threw her down, and her blood splattered on the walls and on the horses that trampled her body.[y]

34 Jehu left to get something to eat and drink. Then he told some workers, "Even though she was evil, she was a king's daughter,[z] so make sure she has a proper burial."

35 But when they went out to bury her body, they found only her skull, her hands, and her feet. **36** They reported this to Jehu, and he said, "The LORD told Elijah the prophet that Jezebel's body would be eaten by dogs right here in Jezreel. **37** And he warned that her bones would be spread all over the ground like manure, so that no one could tell who it was."

Jehu Kills All of Ahab's Descendants

10 Ahab still had 70 descendants living in Samaria. So Jehu wrote a letter to each of the important leaders and officials of the town,[a] and to those who supported Ahab. In the letters he wrote:

2 Your town is strong, and you're protected by chariots and an armed cavalry. And I know that King Ahab's descendants live there with you. So as soon as you read this letter, **3** choose the best person for the job and make him the next king. Then be prepared to defend Ahab's family.

4 The officials and leaders read the letters and were very frightened. They said to each other, "Jehu has already killed King Joram and King Ahaziah! We have to do what he says." **5** The prime minister, the mayor of

9.29 *Ahaziah . . . king of Judah:* He ruled Judah briefly in 841 B.C. before being killed by Jehu. He was the son of Athaliah, the daughter of Ahab. He ruled in Judah, because his mother had earlier married King Jehoram of Judah.

9.31 *Zimri:* This Israelite king killed King Elah and his family so that he could become king, but he ruled only seven days (1 Kgs 16.8-20). Jezebel compares Jehu to Zimri, implying that he isn't capable of ruling any longer than Zimri had.

10.1 *Ahab . . . descendants:* To please his wife Jezebel, Ahab built a temple to honor Baal and allowed Baal worship in Israel (1 Kgs 16.29-33). Ahab had many wives (1 Kgs 20.5), and so would have had many children. Here, 70 may be a symbolic number for all of Ahab's male "descendants" (his sons and grandsons). A new ruler often killed all the male descendants of a former ruler so that none of them would lay claim to the throne (Num 35.12, 16-19).

[x]**9.31** *Zimri:* An Israelite king who killed King Elah and his family so he could become king, but who ruled only seven days (see 1 Kings 16.8-20). [y]**9.33** *horses . . . her body:* Two ancient translations; Hebrew "horses. Then Jehu trampled her body." [z]**9.34** *she . . . daughter:* Her father was King Ethbaal of Sidon (see 1 Kings 16.31). [a]**10.1** *the town:* Two ancient translations; Hebrew "Jezreel."

10.15 *Jehonadab son of Rechab:* Ancient texts indicate that Jehu and Jehonadab were long-time friends. Jehonadab's father, Rechab, was one of the two men who murdered Saul's son Ishbosheth (2 Sam 4.1-12). Jehonadab was a faithful servant who obeyed God's laws. His descendants, the Rechabites, followed his example of faithfulness. Well over 200 years later, the prophet Jeremiah mentioned Jehonadab and the Rechabites as examples of faithfulness and loyalty in contrast to the unfaithful people of Judah (Jer 35).

the city, as well as the other leaders and Ahab's supporters, sent this answer to Jehu, "We are your servants, Your Majesty, and we will do whatever you tell us. But it's not our place to choose someone to be king. You do what you think is best."

⁶Jehu then wrote another letter which said, "If you are on my side and will obey me, then prove it. Bring me the heads of the descendants of Ahab! And be here in Jezreel by this time tomorrow."

The 70 descendants of King Ahab were living with some of the most important people of the city. ⁷And when these people read Jehu's second letter, they called together all 70 of Ahab's descendants. They killed them, put their heads in baskets, and sent them to Jezreel.

⁸When Jehu was told what had happened, he said, "Put the heads in two piles at the city gate, and leave them there until morning."

⁹The next morning, Jehu went out and stood where everyone could hear him, and he said, "You people are not guilty of anything. I'm the one who plotted against Joram and had him killed. But who killed all these men? ¹⁰Listen to me. Everything the LORD's servant Elijah promised about Ahab's family will come true."ᵇ

¹¹Then Jehu killed the rest of Ahab's relatives living in Jezreel, as well as his highest officials, his priests, and his closest friends. No one in Ahab's family was left alive in Jezreel.

¹²⁻¹³Jehu left for Samaria, and along the way, he met some relatives of King Ahaziah of Judah at a place where shepherds meet.ᶜ He asked, "Who are you?"

"We are relatives of Ahaziah," they answered. "We're going to visit his family."

¹⁴"Take them alive!" Jehu said to his offi-

cers. So they grabbed them and led them to the well near the shepherds' meeting place, where they killed all 42 of them.

¹⁵As Jehu went on, he saw Jehonadab son of Rechabᵈ coming to meet him. Jehu greeted him, then said, "Jehonadab, I'm on your side. Are you on mine?"

"Yes, I am."

"Then give me your hand," Jehu answered. He helped Jehonadab into his chariot ¹⁶and said, "Come with me and see how faithful I am to the LORD."

They rode together in Jehu's chariot ¹⁷to Samaria. Jehu killed everyone there who belonged to Ahab's family, as well as all his officials. Everyone in his family was now dead, just as the LORD had promised Elijah.

Jehu Kills All the Worshipers of Baal

¹⁸Jehu called together the people in Samaria and said:

King Ahab sometimes worshiped Baal, but I will be completely faithful to Baal. ¹⁹I'm going to offer a huge sacrifice to him. So invite his prophets and priests, and be sure everyone who worships him is there. Anyone who doesn't come will be killed.

But this was a trick—Jehu was really planning to kill the worshipers of Baal. ²⁰He said, "Announce a day of worship for Baal!" After the day had been announced, ²¹Jehu sent an invitation to everyone in Israel. All the worshipers of Baal came, and the temple was filled from one end to the other. ²²Jehu told the official in charge of the sacred robes to make sure that everyone had a robe to wear.

²³Jehu and Jehonadab went into the temple, and Jehu said to the crowd, "Look

ᵇ10.10 *Everything . . . come true:* See 1 Kings 21.17-24. ᶜ10.12,13 *at a place where shepherds meet:* Or "at Betheked of the Shepherds." ᵈ10.15 *Jehonadab son of Rechab:* Or "Jehonadab the chariot driver."

around and make sure that only the worshipers of Baal are here. No one who worships the LORD is allowed in." **24**Then they began to offer sacrifices to Baal.

Earlier, Jehu had ordered 80 soldiers to wait outside the temple. He had warned them, "I will get all these worshipers here, and if any of you let even one of them escape, you will be killed instead!"

25As soon as Jehu finished offering the sacrifice, he told the guards and soldiers, "Come in and kill them! Don't let anyone escape." They slaughtered everyone in the crowd and threw the bodies outside. Then they went back into the temple **26**and carried out the image of Baal. They burned it **27**and broke it into pieces, then they completely destroyed Baal's temple. And since that time, it's been nothing but a public toilet.**e**

28That's how Jehu stopped the worship of Baal in Israel. **29**But he did not stop the worship of the gold statues of calves at Dan and Bethel that Jeroboam had made for the people to worship.**f**

30Later the LORD said, "Jehu, you have done right by destroying Ahab's entire family, just as I had planned. So I will make sure that the next four kings of Israel will come from your own family."

31But Jehu did not completely obey the commands of the LORD God of Israel. Instead, he kept doing the sinful things that Jeroboam had caused the Israelites to do.

Jehu Dies

32In those days the LORD began to reduce the size of Israel's territory. King Hazael of Syria defeated the Israelites and took control **33**of the regions of Gilead and Bashan east of the Jordan River and north of the town of Aroer near the Arnon River. This was the land where the tribes of Gad, Reuben, and Manasseh had once lived.

34Everything else Jehu did while he was king, including his brave deeds, is written in *The History of the Kings of Israel*. **35**Jehu died and was buried in Samaria, and his son Jehoahaz became king. **36**Jehu had ruled Israel 28 years from Samaria.

Queen Athaliah of Judah
(2 Chronicles 22.10-12)

11 As soon as Athaliah heard that her son King Ahaziah was dead, she decided to kill any relative who could possibly become king. She would have done that, **2**but Jehosheba rescued Joash son of Ahaziah just as he was about to be murdered. Jehosheba, who was Jehoram's**g** daughter and Ahaziah's half sister, hid her nephew Joash and his personal servant in a bedroom in the LORD's temple where he was safe from Athaliah. **3**Joash hid in the temple with Jehosheba**h** for six years while Athaliah ruled as queen of Judah.

Jehoiada Makes Joash King of Judah
(2 Chronicles 23.1-21)

4Joash son of Ahaziah had hidden in the LORD's temple six years. Then in the seventh year, Jehoiada the priest sent for the commanders of the king's special bodyguards**i** and the commanders of the palace

---

e10.27 *public toilet:* Or "garbage dump." **f**10.29 *gold statues . . . to worship:* See 1 Kings 12.26-30. **g**11.2 *Jehoram's:* The Hebrew text has "Joram's," another spelling of the name. **h**11.3 *Jehosheba:* Jehosheba was the wife of Jehoiada the priest (see 2 Chronicles 22.11), which is why she could hide Joash in one of the private bedrooms used only by the priests. **i**11.4 *the king's special bodyguards:* The Hebrew text has "the Carites," who were probably foreign soldiers hired to serve as royal bodyguards.

11.1 *Athaliah:* Athaliah, Judah's only queen and seventh "ruler," ruled from 841 to 835 B.C. When her son was killed, she tried to kill her own nephews and others who might claim to be king.

11.2 *the LORD's temple:* The temple in Jerusalem that had been built by Solomon (1 Kgs 7). **(See the article People of the Law: The Religion of Israel on pg 1794.)**

Solomon

● 11.6 *Sur Gate* This may have been the gate that connected the temple with the palace.

● 11.10 *swords and shields . . . King David:* After defeating King Hadadezer of Zobah, David brought the things he took from Hadadezer and his soldiers to Jerusalem and dedicated them to God (2 Sam 8.3-12).

● 11.12 *crown . . . copy of instructions:* A crown was a headpiece worn by royalty and sometimes by other people in special positions, such as a high priest (Exod 29.4-6). Because a crown was a symbol of authority, a ruler wore it on the throne and when leading an army into battle. Metal crowns probably had their beginnings in the cloth headpieces or headbands that tribal leaders wore. The "copy of instructions" may have been official papers that dealt with the king's position and duties. Some scholars feel it included a copy of the Ten Commandments or the entire Law of Moses.

● 11.14 *columns:* These may have been the two large columns on each side of the front door of the temple (1 Kgs 7.15-21), or one of the pillars by the platform that Solomon built in the center of the outer courtyard (2 Chr 6.12-13).

● 11.18 *temple built to honor Baal:* Athaliah encouraged Baal worship in Judah, just as her mother Jezebel had encouraged it in Israel.

● 12.1 *Joash:* Joash was Judah's seventh king but eighth ruler. He ruled from 835 to 796 B.C.

guards. They met him at the temple, and he asked them to make a promise in the name of the LORD. Then he brought out Joash ⁵and said to them:

Here's what I want you to do. Three of your guard units will be on duty on the Sabbath. I want one unit to guard the palace. ⁶Another unit will guard Sur Gate, and the third unit will guard the palace gate and relieve the palace guards.

⁷The other two guard units are supposed to be off duty on the Sabbath. But I want both of them to stay here at the temple and protect King Joash. ⁸Make sure they follow him wherever he goes, and tell them to keep their swords ready to kill anyone who tries to get near him.

⁹The commanders followed Jehoiada's orders. Each one called together his guards—those coming on duty and those going off duty. ¹⁰Jehoiada brought out the swords and shields that had belonged to King David and gave them to the commanders. ¹¹Then they gave the weapons to their guards, who took their positions around the temple and the altar to protect Joash on every side.

¹²Jehoiada brought Joash outside, where he placed the crown on his head and gave him a copy of instructions for ruling the nation. Olive oil was poured on his head to show that he was now king, while the crowd clapped and shouted, "Long live the king!"

¹³Queen Athaliah heard the crowd and went to the temple. ¹⁴There she saw Joash standing by one of the columns, which was the usual place for the king. The singers[j] and the trumpet players were standing next to him, and the people were celebrat-

ing and blowing trumpets. Athaliah tore her clothes in anger and shouted, "You betrayed me, you traitors!"

¹⁵At once, Jehoiada said to the army commanders, "Kill her! But don't do it anywhere near the LORD's temple. Take her out in front of the troops and kill anyone who is with her!" ¹⁶So the commanders dragged her to the gate where horses are led into the palace, and they killed her there.

¹⁷Jehoiada the priest asked King Joash and the people to promise that they would be faithful to each other and to the LORD. ¹⁸Then the crowd went to the temple built to honor Baal and tore it down. They smashed the altars and idols and killed Mattan the priest of Baal right in front of the altars.

After Jehoiada had placed guards around the LORD's temple, ¹⁹he called together all the commanders, the king's special bodyguards,[k] the palace guards, and the people. They led Joash from the temple, through the Guards' Gate, and into the palace. He took his place on the throne and became king of Judah. ²⁰Everyone celebrated because Athaliah had been killed and Jerusalem was peaceful again. ²¹Joash was only seven years old when this happened.

King Joash of Judah
(2 Chronicles 24.1-16)

12 Joash[l] became king of Judah in Jehu's seventh year as king of Israel, and he ruled 40 years from Jerusalem. His mother Zibiah was from the town of Beersheba.

²Jehoiada the priest taught Joash what was right, and so for the rest of his life Joash obeyed the LORD. ³But even Joash did not

[j]11.14 *singers:* Two ancient translations; Hebrew "commanders." [k]11.19 *the king's special bodyguards:* See the note at verse 4. [l]12.1 *Joash:* The Hebrew text has "Jehoash," another spelling of the name.

destroy the local shrines,^m and they were still used as places for offering sacrifices.

4 One day, Joash said to the priests, "Collect all the money that has been given to the Lord's temple, whether from taxes or gifts, **5**and use it to repair the temple whenever you see the need."

6But the priests never started repairing the temple. So in the twenty-third year of his rule, **7**Joash called for Jehoiada and the other priests and said, "Why aren't you using the money to repair the temple? Don't take any more money for yourselves. It is only to be used to pay for the repairs." **8**The priests agreed that they would not collect any more money or be in charge of the temple repairs.

9Jehoiada found a wooden box; he cut a hole in the top of it and set it on the right side of the altar where people went into the temple. Whenever someone gave money to the temple, the priests guarding the entrance would put it into this box. **10**When the box was full of money, the king's secretary and the chief priest would count the money and put it in bags. **11**Then they would give it to the men supervising the repairs to the temple. Some of the money was used to pay the builders, the woodworkers, **12**the stonecutters, and the men who built the walls. And some was used to buy wood and stone and to pay any other costs for repairing the temple.

13While the repairs were being made, the money that was given to the temple was not used to make silver bowls, lamp snuffers, small sprinkling bowls, trumpets, or anything gold or silver for the temple. **14**It went only to pay for repairs. **15**The men in charge were honest, so no one had to keep track of the money.

16The fines that had to be paid along with the sacrifices to make things right and the sacrifices for sin did not go to the temple. This money belonged only to the priests.

17About the same time, King Hazael of Syria attacked the town of Gath and captured it. Next, he decided to attack Jerusalem. **18**So Joash collected everything he and his ancestors Jehoshaphat, Jehoram, and Ahaziah had dedicated to the Lord, as well as the gold in the storage rooms in the temple and palace. He sent it all to Hazael as a gift, and when Hazael received it, he ordered his troops to leave Jerusalem.

19Everything else Joash did while he was king is written in *The History of the Kings of Judah.* **20-21**At the end of his rule, some of his officers rebelled against him. Jozabad^n son of Shimeath and Jehozabad son of Shomer murdered him in a building where the land was filled in on the east side of Jerusalem,^o near the road to Silla. Joash was buried beside his ancestors in Jerusalem,^p and his son Amaziah became king.

King Jehoahaz of Israel

13 Jehoahaz son of Jehu became king of Israel in the twenty-third year of Joash's rule in Judah. Jehoahaz ruled 17 years from Samaria **2**and disobeyed the Lord by doing wrong. He never stopped following the example of Jeroboam, who had caused the Israelites to sin.

3The Lord was angry with the Israelites,

● *12.4 taxes or gifts:* Each male over 20 years of age was required to pay taxes for the work of the priests at the place of worship.

● *12.16 The fines . . . only to the priests:* This money provided an income for the priests and so it was not used to repair the temple.

● *13.1,2 Jehoahaz . . . Jeroboam:* Jehoahaz, Israel's eleventh king, ruled from 814 to 798 B.C. Jeroboam was Israel's first king and ruled from 931 to 910 B.C. The sin of idol worship that began with his rule continued through the reigns of all of Israel's kings.

^m**12.3** *local shrines:* The Hebrew text has "high places," which were local places to worship God or foreign gods.   ^n**12.20,21** *Jozabad:* Some manuscripts of the Hebrew text; other manuscripts "Jozacar."   ^o**12.20,21** *where . . . Jerusalem:* The Hebrew text has "on the Millo," which probably refers to a landfill to strengthen and extend the hill where the city was built.   ^p**12.20,21** *Jerusalem:* See the note at 8.24.

● 13.10-13 *Jehoash . . . Jeroboam:* Jehoash, Israel's twelfth king, ruled from 798 to 783 B.C. He is not to be confused with Joash (sometimes spelled Jehoash), Judah's king from 835 to 796 B.C. "Jeroboam" in 13.11 refers to the first king of Israel, whereas "Jeroboam" in verse 13.13 is Joash's son, Jeroboam II.

● 13.14 *Elisha:* Elisha was the prophet who was chosen to follow Elijah (1 Kgs 19.19-21; 2 Kgs 2.1-15).

● 13.18 *Aphek:* Aphek was located near the source of the Yarkon River in the Plain of Sharon. In the New Testament, this city is known as Antipatris.

● 13.19,21 *Syrians . . . Moabites:* Following the death of Solomon and the division of the united Israel into the northern and southern kingdoms (1 Kgs 11.41—12.20), Syria occupied a large area north of Israel.

so he let King Hazael of Syria and his son Benhadad rule over them for a long time. [4]Jehoahaz prayed to the LORD for help, and the LORD saw how terribly Hazael was treating the Israelites. He answered Jehoahaz [5]by sending Israel a leader who rescued them from the Syrians,[q] and the Israelites lived in peace as they had before. [6-7]But Hazael had defeated Israel's army so badly that Jehoahaz had only 10 chariots, 50 cavalry troops, and 10,000 regular soldiers left in his army.

The Israelites kept sinning and following the example of Jeroboam's family. They did not tear down the sacred poles[r] that had been set up in Samaria for the worship of the goddess Asherah.

[8]Everything else Jehoahaz did while he was king, including his brave deeds, is written in *The History of the Kings of Israel.* [9]Jehoahaz died and was buried in Samaria, and his son Jehoash became king.

King Jehoash of Israel

[10]Jehoash became king of Israel in the thirty-seventh year of Joash's rule in Judah, and he ruled 16 years from Samaria. [11]He disobeyed the LORD by doing just like Jeroboam, who had caused the Israelites to sin. [12]Everything else Jehoash did while he was king, including his war against King Amaziah of Judah, is written in *The History of the Kings of Israel.* [13]Jehoash died and was buried in Samaria beside the other Israelite kings. His son Jeroboam then became king.

Elisha the Prophet Dies

[14]Some time before the death of King Jehoash, Elisha the prophet was very sick and about to die. Jehoash went in and stood beside him, crying. He said, "Master, what will Israel's chariots and cavalry be able to do without you?"[s]

[15-16]"Grab a bow and some arrows," Elisha told him, "and hold them in your hand." Jehoash grabbed the bow and arrows and held them. Elisha placed his hand on the king's hand [17]and said, "Open the window facing east." When it was open, Elisha shouted, "Now shoot!" Jehoash shot an arrow and Elisha said, "That arrow is a sign that the LORD will help you completely defeat the Syrian army at Aphek."

[18]Elisha said, "Pick up the arrows and hit the ground with them." Jehoash grabbed the arrows and hit the ground three times, then stopped. [19]Elisha became angry with the king and exclaimed, "If you had struck it five or six times, you would completely wipe out the Syrians. Now you will defeat them only three times."

[20]Elisha died and was buried.

Every year in the spring, Moab's leaders sent raiding parties into Israel. [21]Once, while some Israelites were burying a man's body, they saw a group of Moabites. The Israelites quickly threw the body into Elisha's tomb and ran away. As soon as the man's body touched the bones of Elisha, the man came back to life and stood up.

Israel Defeats Syria

[22]Israel was under the power of King Hazael of Syria during the entire rule of Je-

[q]13.5 *by sending . . . the Syrians:* The name of this leader is not given, but it may refer to Elisha the prophet, King Jehoash of Israel, or his son King Jeroboam. [r]13.6,7 *sacred poles:* Or "trees," used as symbols of Asherah, the goddess of fertility. [s]13.14 *Master . . . without you:* Or "Master, you were like chariots and cavalry for Israel!"

The Israelites kept sinning and following the example of Jeroboam's family. 2 Kgs 13.6-7

hoahaz. **23**But the LORD was kind to the Israelites and showed them mercy because of his solemn agreement with their ancestors Abraham, Isaac, and Jacob. In fact, he has never turned his back on them or let them be completely destroyed.

24Hazael died, and his son Benhadad then became king of Syria. **25**King Jehoash of Israel attacked and defeated the Syrian army three times. He took back from Benhadad all the towns Hazael had captured in battle from his father Jehoahaz.

King Amaziah of Judah
(2 Chronicles 25.1-24)

14 Amaziah son of Joash became king of Judah in the second year of Jehoash's rule in Israel. **2**Amaziah was 25 years old when he became king, and he ruled 29 years from Jerusalem, which was also the hometown of his mother Jehoaddin.

3Amaziah followed the example of his father Joash by obeying the LORD and doing right. But he was not as faithful as his ancestor David. **4**Amaziah did not destroy the local shrines, and they were still used as places for offering sacrifices.

5As soon as Amaziah had control of Judah, he arrested and killed the officers who had murdered his father. **6**But the children of those officers were not killed. The LORD had commanded in the Law of Moses that only the people who sinned were to be punished, not their parents or children.[t]

7While Amaziah was king, he killed 10,000 Edomite soldiers in Salt Valley. He captured the town of Sela and renamed it Joktheel, which is still its name.

8One day, Amaziah sent a message to King Jehoash of Israel: "Come out and face me in battle!"

9Jehoash sent back this reply:

Once upon a time, a small thornbush in Lebanon announced that his son was going to marry the daughter of a large cedar tree. But a wild animal came along and trampled the small bush.

10Amaziah, you think you're so powerful because you defeated Edom. Go ahead and celebrate—but stay at home. If you cause any trouble, both you and your kingdom of Judah will be destroyed.

11But Amaziah refused to listen. So Jehoash and his troops marched to the town of Beth-Shemesh in Judah to attack Amaziah and his troops. **12**During the battle, Judah's army was crushed. Every soldier from Judah ran back home, **13**and Jehoash captured Amaziah.

Jehoash then marched to Jerusalem and broke down the city wall from Ephraim Gate to Corner Gate, a section about 600 feet long. **14**He took the gold and silver, as well as everything of value from the LORD's temple and the king's treasury. He took hostages, then returned to Samaria.

15Everything else Jehoash did while he was king, including his brave deeds and how he defeated King Amaziah of Judah, is written in *The History of the Kings of Israel.* **16**Jehoash died and was buried in Samaria beside the other Israelite kings. His son Jeroboam then became king.

17Fifteen years after Jehoash died, **18-20**some people in Jerusalem plotted against Amaziah. He was able to escape to the town of Lachish, but another group of people caught him and killed him there. His body was taken back to Jerusalem on horseback and buried beside his ancestors.

Everything else Amaziah did while he was king is written in *The History of the*

[t]**14.6** *The LORD had commanded . . . children:* See Deuteronomy 24.16.

13.23 *solemn agreement . . . Abraham, Isaac, and Jacob:* God promised Abraham that his descendants would form a great nation (Gen 12.1-3). The promise was repeated to Isaac, Abraham's son (Gen 26.2-4), and still again to Jacob, Abraham's grandson (Gen 35.9-12).

Agreements (Covenants)

David

14.7 *Salt Valley . . . Sela . . . Joktheel:* The Salt Valley was a passage south and east of the Dead Sea. Many scholars identify Sela (Joktheel) as Petra, Edom's capital city. Petra was carved out of the side of a mountain. **(See Map 4 on pg 1882.)**

14.11 *Beth-Shemesh:* A town west of Jerusalem.

14.18-20 *Lachish:* Lachish was the second largest city in Judah. **(See Map 6 on pg 1884.)**

14.18-20 *people caught . . . killed him:* Amaziah is killed by his own people, perhaps because they had suffered due to his pride (14.13,14).

14.23 *Jeroboam:* This is Jeroboam II, Israel's thirteenth king. He
ruled from 783 to 743 B.C., eleven years
alongside his father, Jehoash. Jeroboam II regained much of the land that
had been lost to Hazael and Benhadad
of Syria (10.32; 12.17; 13.3,22,25), and
brought Israel's boundaries close to
what they had been under Solomon's
glorious rule (1 Kgs 8.65; 2 Chr 8.4).

14.25 *Lebo-Hamath . . . Dead Sea:*
Lebo-Hamath was north of Damascus,
on the Orontes River. The Dead Sea is
also known as the Salt Sea because it is
four times saltier than ocean water and
so cannot support fish and many water
plants. It is located 1300 feet below sea
level. **(See Map 6 on pg 1884.)**

15.1-4 *Azariah . . . did not destroy
the local shrines:* Azariah (also known
as Uzziah) was Judah's ninth king. He
ruled from 781 to 740 B.C. Isaiah the
prophet began his ministry during
Azariah's reign (Isa 1.1). Azariah's reign
was a time of increased growth and
wealth for Judah. He successfully battled the Philistines to expand Judah's
territory, built new cities, secured trade
routes, and created new and successful
agricultural methods. However, he did
not destroy the local shrines where idol
worship took place.

15.8 *Zechariah:* Zechariah was Israel's fourteenth king and ruled for six
months in 743 B.C.

Kings of Judah. **21**After his death the people
of Judah made his son Azariah king, even
though he was only 16 at the time. **22**Azariah was the one who later recaptured and
rebuilt the town of Elath.

King Jeroboam the Second of Israel

23Jeroboam son of Jehoash became king
of Israel in the fifteenth year of Amaziah's
rule in Judah. Jeroboam ruled 41 years
from Samaria. **24**He disobeyed the LORD by
following the evil example of Jeroboam
son of Nebat, who had caused the Israelites
to sin.

25Jeroboam extended the boundaries of
Israel from Lebo-Hamath in the north to
the Dead Sea in the south, just as the LORD
had promised his servant Jonah son of
Amittai, who was a prophet from Gath-
Hepher. **26**The LORD helped Jeroboam do
this because he had seen how terribly the
Israelites were suffering, whether slave or
free, and no one was left to help them.
27And since the LORD had promised that he
would not let Israel be completely destroyed, he helped Jeroboam rescue them.
28Everything else Jeroboam did while he
was king, including his brave deeds and
how he recaptured the towns of Damascus
and Hamath,[u] is written in *The History of
the Kings of Israel.* **29**Jeroboam died and was
buried, and his son Zechariah became king.

King Azariah of Judah
(2 Chronicles 26.1-23)

15 Azariah son of Amaziah became
king of Judah in Jeroboam's twenty-

seventh year as king of Israel. **2**He was only
16 years old when he became king, and he
ruled 52 years from Jerusalem, which was
also the hometown of his mother Jecoliah.

3Azariah obeyed the LORD by doing
right, as his father Amaziah had done. **4**But
Azariah did not destroy the local shrines,[v]
and they were still used as places for offering sacrifices.

5The LORD punished Azariah with leprosy[w] for the rest of his life. He wasn't allowed to live in the royal palace, so his son
Jotham lived there and ruled in his place.

6Everything else Azariah did while he
was king is written in *The History of the
Kings of Judah.* **7**Azariah died and was buried
beside his ancestors in Jerusalem. His son
Jotham then became king.

King Zechariah of Israel

8Zechariah son of Jeroboam became king
of Israel in the thirty-eighth year of
Azariah's rule in Judah, but he ruled only
six months from Samaria. **9**Like his ancestors, Zechariah disobeyed the LORD by following the evil ways of Jeroboam son of
Nebat, who had caused the Israelites to sin.

10Shallum son of Jabesh plotted against
Zechariah and killed him in public.[x] Shallum then became king. **11-12**So the LORD
had kept his promise to Jehu that the next
four kings of Israel would come from his
family.[y]

Everything else Zechariah did while he
was king is written in *The History of the
Kings of Israel.*

---

[u]**14.28** *how he recaptured . . . Hamath*: One possible meaning for the difficult Hebrew text.   [v]**15.4** *local
shrines*: See the note at 12.3.   [w]**15.5** *leprosy*: See the note at 5.1.   [x]**15.10** *in public*: Hebrew; some
manuscripts of one ancient translation "in Ibleam."   [y]**15.11,12** *So the LORD . . . family*: See 10.28-31.

King Shallum of Israel

[13]Shallum became king of Israel in the thirty-ninth year of Azariah's[z] rule in Judah. But only one month after Shallum became king, [14-16]Menahem son of Gadi came to Samaria from Tirzah and killed him. Menahem then became king. The town of Tiphsah would not surrender to him, so he destroyed it and all the surrounding towns as far as Tirzah. He killed everyone living in Tiphsah, and with his sword he even ripped open pregnant women.

Everything else Shallum did while he was king, including his plot against Zechariah, is written in *The History of the Kings of Israel.*

King Menahem of Israel

[17]Menahem became king of Israel in Azariah's thirty-ninth year as king of Judah, and he ruled Israel ten years from Samaria. [18]He constantly disobeyed the LORD by following the example of Jeroboam son of Nebat, who had caused the Israelites to sin.

[19]During Menahem's rule, King Tiglath Pileser[a] of Assyria invaded Israel. He agreed to help Menahem keep control of his kingdom, if Menahem would pay him over 30 tons of silver. [20]So Menahem ordered every rich person in Israel to give him at least one pound of silver, and he gave it all to Tiglath Pileser, who stopped his attack and left Israel.

[21]Everything else Menahem did while he was king is written in *The History of the*

Kings of Israel. [22]Menahem died, and his son Pekahiah became king.

King Pekahiah of Israel

[23]Pekahiah became king of Israel in the fiftieth year of Azariah's rule in Judah, and he ruled two years from Samaria. [24]He disobeyed the LORD and caused the Israelites to sin, just as Jeroboam son of Nebat had done.

[25]Pekah son of Remaliah was Pekahiah's chief officer, but he made plans to kill the king. So he and 50 men from Gilead broke into the strongest part of the palace in Samaria and murdered Pekahiah, together with Argob and Arieh.[b] Pekah then became king.

[26]Everything else Pekahiah did while he was king is written in *The History of the Kings of Israel.*

King Pekah of Israel

[27]Pekah son of Remaliah became king of Israel in Azariah's fifty-second year as king of Judah, and he ruled 20 years from Samaria. [28]He disobeyed the LORD and followed the evil example of Jeroboam son of Nebat, who had caused the Israelites to sin.

[29]During Pekah's rule, King Tiglath Pileser of Assyria marched into Israel. He captured the territories of Gilead and Galilee, including the towns of Ijon, Abel-Bethmaacah, Janoah, Kedesh, and Hazor, as well as the entire territory of Naphtali. Then he took Israelites from those regions to Assyria as prisoners.[c]

[30]In the twentieth year of Jotham's rule

---

[z]**15.13** *Azariah's:* The Hebrew text has "Uzziah's," another spelling of the name. [a]**15.19** *Tiglath Pileser:* The Hebrew text has "Pul," another name for Tiglath Pileser, who ruled Assyria from 745 to 727 B.C. [b]**15.25** *together with Argob and Arieh:* One possible meaning for the difficult Hebrew text. [c]**15.29** *prisoners:* The events in this verse probably took place around 733 B.C.

● **15.13** *Shallum:* Shallum, Israel's fifteenth king, ruled for one month in 743 B.C.

● **15.14-16** *Tirzah . . . Tiphsah:* Tirzah had been the capital of the northern kingdom at one time (1 Kgs 14.17; 15.21, 33). Tiphsah was on the Euphrates River about 325 miles northeast of Samaria, leading scholars to believe that town meant here is actually Tappuah, a town about 15 miles southwest of Tirzah.

● **15.19** *Assyria:* Around 911 B.C. Assyria began to expand its power and continued to grow throughout the period of the Israelite kings (931–722 B.C.). Its expansion into Palestine had begun around 855 B.C. At this time, Tiglath Pileser III ruled Assyria. In expanding his empire, he gained control of conquered areas in part by exiling native people to other lands owned by Assyria. **(See Map 7 on pg 1885.)**

✆   Assyria

● **15.23** *Pekahiah:* Pekahiah, Israel's sixteenth king, ruled from 738 to 737 B.C.

● **15.27** *Pekah:* Pekah was Israel's seventeenth king and probably ruled from 737 to 732 B.C. It is not exactly clear why his reign is given here as 20 years. His time of rule may include being in charge of a rival government set up at the time that Shallum became king, but a 20-year reign still does not seem likely.

15.32-38 *Jotham . . . Zadok:* Jotham, Judah's tenth king, ruled from 740 to 736 B.C. Though he is said to have ruled 16 years (15.33), a number of these years were probably as a powerless ruler under Assyrian control. The Zadok here is not the loyal priest and friend of King David and who made Solomon king (1 Kgs 1.28-46).

16.1 *Ahaz:* Judah's eleventh king, he ruled from 736 to 716 B.C. Though said to have ruled only 16 years (16.2), there were additional years during which he ruled along with Azariah, Jotham, and Hezekiah. Ahaz is remembered as a particularly evil king. He restored Baal worship to Judah, participated in child sacrifice (16.3), and bought Assyria's help against Israel. He also stripped the temple at Jerusalem of its remaining treasures in order to pay Assyria for protection against the invasion of Israel and Syria (16.7,8).

16.5-9 *King Rezin . . . King Pekah . . . Tiglath Pileser . . . captured . . . Damascus:* The events in these verses probably took place around 734 B.C., before the events described in 15.29. Rezin of Syria and Pekah of Israel tried to force Ahaz out of Judah, so they could install a ruler of their choice in Jerusalem and force Judah's armies to join them against Assyria. But Ahaz saved Judah by taking money from the temple treasury and giving it to Assyria's leader, Tiglath Pileser. By taking over Damascus, Syria's capital, Tiglath Pileser began to put down the rebellion.

in Judah, Hoshea son of Elah plotted against Pekah and murdered him. Hoshea then became king of Israel.

[31]Everything else Pekah did while he was king is written in *The History of the Kings of Israel.*

King Jotham of Judah

(2 Chronicles 27.1-9)

[32]Jotham son of Azariah[d] became king of Judah in the second year of Pekah's rule in Israel. [33]Jotham was 25 years old when he became king, and he ruled 16 years from Jerusalem. His mother Jerusha was the daughter of Zadok.

[34]Jotham followed the example of his father by obeying the LORD and doing right. [35]It was Jotham who rebuilt the Upper Gate that led into the court around the LORD's temple. But the local shrines were not destroyed, and they were still used as places for offering sacrifices.

[36]Everything else Jotham did while he was king is written in *The History of the Kings of Judah.* [37]During his rule, the LORD let King Rezin of Syria and King Pekah of Israel start attacking Judah. [38]Jotham died and was buried beside his ancestors in Jerusalem, and his son Ahaz became king.

King Ahaz of Judah

(2 Chronicles 28.1-27)

16 Ahaz son of Jotham became king of Judah in the seventeenth year of Pekah's rule in Israel. [2]He was 20 years old at the time, and he ruled from Jerusalem for 16 years.

Ahaz wasn't like his ancestor David. In-

stead, he disobeyed the LORD [3]and was even more sinful than the kings of Israel. He sacrificed his own son, which was a disgusting custom of the nations that the LORD had forced out of Israel. [4]Ahaz offered sacrifices at the local shrines, as well as on every hill and in the shade of large trees.

[5-6]While Ahaz was ruling Judah, the king of Edom recaptured the town of Elath from Judah and forced out the people of Judah. Edomites[e] then moved into Elath, and they still live there.

About the same time, King Rezin of Syria and King Pekah of Israel marched to Jerusalem and attacked, but they could not capture it.

[7]Ahaz sent a message to King Tiglath Pileser of Assyria that said, "Your Majesty, King Rezin and King Pekah are attacking me, your loyal servant. Please come and rescue me." [8]Along with the message, Ahaz sent silver and gold from the LORD's temple and from the palace treasury as a gift for the Assyrian king.

[9]As soon as Tiglath Pileser received the message, he and his troops marched to Syria. He captured the capital city of Damascus, then he took the people living there to the town of Kir as prisoners and killed King Rezin.[f]

[10]Later, Ahaz went to Damascus to meet Tiglath Pileser. And while Ahaz was there, he saw an altar and sent a model of it back to Uriah the priest, along with the plans for building one. [11]Uriah followed the plans and built an altar exactly like the one in Damascus, finishing it just before Ahaz came back.

[12]When Ahaz returned, he went to see

the altar and to offer sacrifices on it. He walked up to the altar [13]and poured wine over it. Then he offered sacrifices to please the LORD, to give him thanks, and to ask for his blessings.[g] [14]After that, he had the bronze altar moved aside,[h] so his new altar would be right in front of the LORD's temple. [15]He told Uriah the priest:

From now on, the morning and evening sacrifices as well as all gifts of grain and wine are to be offered on this altar. The sacrifices for the people and for the king must also be offered here. Sprinkle the blood from all the sacrifices on it, but leave the bronze altar for me to use for prayer and finding out what God wants me to do.

[16]Uriah did everything Ahaz told him.

[17]Ahaz also had the side panels and the small bowls taken off the movable stands in the LORD's temple. He had the large bronze bowl, called the Sea, removed from the bronze bulls on which it rested and had it placed on a stand made of stone. [18]He took down the special tent that was used for worship on the Sabbath[i] and closed up the private entrance that the kings of Judah used for going into the temple. He did all these things to please Tiglath Pileser.

[19]Everything else Ahaz did while he was king is written in *The History of the Kings of Judah.* [20]Ahaz died and was buried beside his ancestors in Jerusalem,[j] and his son Hezekiah became king.

King Hoshea of Israel

17 Hoshea son of Elah became king of Israel in the twelfth year of Ahaz's rule in Judah, and he ruled nine years from Samaria. [2]Hoshea disobeyed the LORD and sinned, but not as much as the earlier Israelite kings had done.

[3]During Hoshea's rule, King Shalmaneser of Assyria[k] invaded Israel; he took control of the country and made Hoshea pay taxes. [4]But later, Hoshea refused to pay the taxes and asked King So of Egypt to help him rebel. When Shalmaneser found out, he arrested Hoshea and put him in prison.

Samaria Is Destroyed and the Israelites Are Taken to Assyria

[5]Shalmaneser invaded Israel and attacked the city of Samaria for three years, [6]before capturing it in the ninth year of Hoshea's rule. The Assyrian king[l] took the Israelites away to Assyria as prisoners. He forced some of them to live in the town of Halah, others to live near the Habor River in the territory of Gozan, and still others to live in towns where the Median people lived.

[7]All of this happened because the people of Israel had sinned against the LORD their God, who had rescued them from Egypt, where they had been slaves. They worshiped foreign gods, [8]followed the customs of the nations that the LORD had forced out of Israel, and were just as sinful as the

16.17,18 the Sea . . . special tent: The Sea was a huge basin that the priests may have used for ritual cleansing. The special tent may have been a canopy where the king stood during worship on the Sabbath.

17.1 Hoshea: Hoshea was Israel's nineteenth and last king and ruled from 732 to 723 B.C.

17.3 King Shalmaneser of Assyria: Tiglath Pileser's son, who ruled Assyria from 727 to 722 B.C.

17.6 The Assyrian king: This probably refers to Sargon II, who followed Shalmaneser as king of Assyria. Shalmaneser died after the city of Samaria was captured (722 B.C.), but before the people of Israel were taken away as prisoners (720 B.C.). Sargon ruled Assyria from 722 to 705 B.C.

Assyria

17.6 Halah . . . Habor River . . . where the Median people lived: Halah's exact location is unknown. The Habor River in Gozan was a northern branch of the Euphrates River. The Median peoples lived in an area east of the Tigris River. **(See Map 7 on pg 1885.)**

[g]16.13 *offered . . . blessings:* In traditional translations, these sacrifices are usually called "whole burnt offerings," "grain offerings," and "peace offerings." These are described in Leviticus 1–3. [h]16.14 *aside:* Hebrew "to the north." [i]16.18 *the special tent . . . Sabbath:* One possible meaning for the difficult Hebrew text. [j]16.20 *Jerusalem:* See the note at 8.24. [k]17.3 *King Shalmaneser of Assyria:* The son of Tiglath Pileser, who ruled Assyria from 727 to 722 B.C. [l]17.6 *The Assyrian king:* Probably Sargon, Shalmaneser's successor. Shalmaneser died after the city of Samaria was captured (722 B.C.) but before the people were taken away as prisoners (720 B.C.). Sargon ruled Assyria from 721 to 705 B.C.

All of this happened because the people of Israel had sinned against the LORD their God. 2 KGS 17.7

CR Law

CR Agreements (Covenants)

● 17.21-23 *LORD took northern tribes away from David's family . . . people kept on sinning*: David's son, Solomon, was the final king to rule over the united tribes of Israel. But he did not remain faithful and obey God, and so God split the tribes into the northern and southern kingdoms. David's family continued to rule in the southern kingdom of Judah where Jerusalem was located. After the fall of Samaria, the northern kingdom of Israel came to an end, and the people remained in other lands.

● 17.24 *Babylon, Cuthah, Avva, Hamath, and Sepharvaim . . . Samaria*: Babylon and Cuthah were in southern Mesopotamia. The locations of Avva and Sepharvaim are unknown. Hamath, also known as Lebo-Hamath, was about 120 miles north of Damascus, on the Orontes River. (See Map 7 on pg 1885.)

Israelite kings. [9]Even worse, the Israelites tried to hide their sins from the LORD their God. They built their own local shrines everywhere in Israel—from small towns to large, walled cities. [10]They also built stone images of foreign gods and set up sacred poles[m] for the worship of Asherah on every hill and under every shady tree. [11]They offered sacrifices at the shrines,[n] just as the foreign nations had done before the LORD forced them out of Israel. They did sinful things that made the LORD very angry.

[12]Even though the LORD had commanded the Israelites not to worship idols,[o] they did it anyway. [13]So the LORD made sure that every prophet warned Israel and Judah with these words: "I, the LORD, command you to stop doing sinful things and start obeying my laws and teachings! I gave them to your ancestors, and I told my servants the prophets to repeat them to you."

[14]But the Israelites would not listen; they were as stubborn as their ancestors who had refused to worship the LORD their God. [15]They ignored the LORD's warnings and commands, and they rejected the solemn agreement he had made with their ancestors. They worshiped worthless idols and became worthless themselves. The LORD had told the Israelites not to do the things that the foreign nations around them were doing, but Israel became just like them.

[16]The people of Israel disobeyed all the commands of the LORD their God. They made two gold statues of calves and set up a sacred pole for Asherah; they also worshiped the stars and the god Baal. [17]They used magic and witchcraft and even sacrificed their own children. The Israelites were determined to do whatever the LORD

hated. [18]The LORD became so furious with the people of Israel that he allowed them to be carried away as prisoners.

Only the people living in Judah were left, [19]but they also disobeyed the LORD's commands and acted like the Israelites. [20]So the LORD turned his back on everyone in Israel and let them be punished and defeated until no one was left.

[21]Earlier, when the LORD took the northern tribes away from David's family,[p] the people living in northern Israel chose Jeroboam son of Nebat as their king. Jeroboam caused the Israelites to sin and to stop worshiping the LORD. [22]The people kept on sinning like Jeroboam, [23]until the LORD got rid of them, just as he had warned his servants the prophets.

That's why the people of Israel were taken away as prisoners to Assyria, and that's where they remained.

Foreigners Are Resettled in Israel

[24]The king of Assyria took people who were living in the cities of Babylon, Cuthah, Avva, Hamath, and Sepharvaim, and forced them to move to Israel. They took over the towns where the Israelites had lived, including the capital city of Samaria.

[25]At first these people did not worship the LORD, so he sent lions to attack them, and the lions killed some of them. [26]A messenger told the king of Assyria, "The people you moved to Israel don't know how to worship the god of that country. So he sent lions that have attacked and killed some of them."

[27]The king replied, "Get one of the Israelite priests we brought here and send him back to Israel. He can live there and

---

[m]17.10 *sacred poles:* See the note at 13.6,7.   [n]17.11 *shrines:* See the note at 12.3.   [o]17.12 *the LORD . . . idols:* See Exodus 20.4,5.   [p]17.21 *when the LORD . . . family:* See 1 Kings 11.29-39.

teach them about the god of that country."
28One of the Israelite priests was chosen to go back to Israel. He lived in Bethel and taught the people how to worship the Lord.

29But in towns all over Israel, the different groups of people made statues of their own gods, then they placed these idols in local Israelite⁹ shrines. **30**The people from Babylonia made the god Succoth-Benoth; those from Cuthah made the god Nergal; those from Hamath made Ashima; **31**those from Avva made Nibhaz and Tartak; and the people from Sepharvaim sacrificed their children to their own gods Adrammelech and Anammelech. **32-33**They worshiped their own gods, just as they had before they were taken away to Israel. They also worshiped the Lord, but they chose their own people to be priests at the shrines. **34**Everyone followed their old customs. None of them worshiped only the Lord, and they refused to obey the laws and commands that the Lord had given to the descendants of Jacob, the man he named Israel. **35**At the time when the Lord had made his solemn agreement with the people of Israel, he told them:

Do not worship any other gods! Do not bow down to them or offer them a sacrifice. **36**Worship only me! I am the one who rescued you from Egypt with my mighty power. Bow down to me and offer sacrifices. **37**Never worship any other god, always obey my laws and teachings, **38**and remember the solemn agreement between us.

I will say it again: Do not worship any god **39**except me. I am the Lord your God, and I will rescue you from all your enemies.

40But the people living in Israel ignored that command and kept on following their old customs. **41**They did worship the Lord, but they also worshiped their own idols. Their descendants did the same thing.

King Hezekiah of Judah
(2 Chronicles 29.1,2; 31.1)

18 Hezekiah son of Ahaz became king of Judah in the third year of Hoshea's rule in Israel. **2**Hezekiah was 25 years old when he became king, and he ruled 29 years from Jerusalem. His mother Abi was the daughter of Zechariah.

3Hezekiah obeyed the Lord, just as his ancestor David had done. **4**He destroyed the local shrines, then tore down the images of foreign gods and cut down the sacred pole for worshiping the goddess Asherah. He also smashed the bronze snake Moses had made. The people had named it Nehushtanʳ and had been offering sacrifices to it.

5Hezekiah trusted the Lord God of Israel. No other king of Judah was like Hezekiah, either before or after him. **6**He was completely faithful to the Lord and obeyed the laws the Lord had given to Moses for the people. **7**The Lord helped Hezekiah, so he was successful in everything he did. He even rebelled against the king of Assyria, refusing to be his servant. **8**Hezekiah defeated the Philistine towns as far away as Gaza—from the smallest towns to the large, walled cities.

9During the fourth year of Hezekiah's rule, which was the seventh year of Hoshea's rule in Israel, King Shalmaneser of Assyria led his troops to Samaria, the capital city of Israel. They attacked **10**and

⁹**17.29** *Israelite*: The Hebrew text has "Samaritan," which is a later word to describe the people who lived in northern Israel at this time.   ʳ**18.4** *the bronze snake . . . Nehushtan*: See Numbers 21.8,9. "Nehushtan" is a nickname that sounds like the Hebrew words for "snake" and "bronze."

● 17.34 *descendants of Jacob*: Another name for the people of Israel. Jacob, the grandson of Abraham, became known as "Israel" after he wrestled with God (Gen 32.28 and 35.9-12). His descendants were the people of Israel. In the Bible, Israel is the nation made up of the twelve tribes descended from Jacob, but in 2 Kings, it most often refers to just the northern kingdom.

Israel

● 18.1,2 *Hezekiah . . . Zechariah*: Hezekiah, Judah's twelfth king, ruled from 716 to 687 B.C. Hezekiah's grandfather was Zechariah, a former king of Israel.

Hezekiah

● 18.7,8 *Assyria . . . Gaza*: Judah came under Assyrian control when Hezekiah's father, Ahaz, was king. Because Assyria was such a powerful army, Hezekiah's rebellion demanded that he have great faith and trust that the Lord would protect him and the people of Judah. Gaza was one of five main cities in Philistia, a nation along the Mediterranean Sea. The Philistines were often at war with Israel. **(See Map 6 on pg 1884.)**

● 18.9 *fourth year of Hezekiah's rule . . . Shalmaneser . . . led his troops to Samaria*: Though the beginning of Hezekiah's rule is given as 716 B.C., he probably had begun to rule beside his father Ahaz when Shalmaneser invaded Israel and finally captured Samaria in 722 B.C.

The Lord said, "Do not worship any god except me. I am the Lord your God." 2 Kgs 17.38,39

18.11 *The king of Assyria:* This probably refers to Sargon.

18.12 *rejected the solemn agreement . . . Moses:* The solemn agreement here refers to the agreement based on the laws and teachings God gave to Moses and the people at Mount Sinai (Exod 19–40). God promised to give them a land of their own (Canaan). The people were to hold up their part of the agreement by obeying God's laws and worshiping only God (Exod 24.3-7; Deut 7.12-15; 29.9-28).

captured it three years later,^{s} in the sixth year of Hezekiah's rule and the ninth year of Hoshea's rule. ^{11}The king of Assyria^t took the Israelites away as prisoners; he forced some of them to live in the town of Halah, others to live near the Habor River in the territory of Gozan, and still others to live in towns where the Median people lived. ^{12}All of that happened because the people of Israel had not obeyed the LORD their God. They rejected the solemn agreement he had made with them, and they ignored everything that the LORD's servant Moses had told them.

King Sennacherib of Assyria Invades Judah
(2 Chronicles 32.1-19; Isaiah 36.1-22)

^{13}In the fourteenth year of Hezekiah's rule in Judah, King Sennacherib of Assyria invaded the country and captured every walled city,^{u} except Jerusalem. ^{14}Hezekiah sent this message to Sennacherib, who was in the town of Lachish: "I know I am guilty of rebellion. But I will pay you whatever you want, if you stop your attack."

Sennacherib told Hezekiah to pay 11 tons of silver and a ton of gold. ^{15}So Hezekiah collected all the silver from the LORD's temple and the royal treasury. ^{16}He even stripped the gold that he had used to cover the doors and doorposts^v in the temple. He gave it all to Sennacherib.

^{17}The king of Assyria ordered his three highest military officers to leave Lachish and take a large army to Jerusalem. When they arrived, the officers stood on the road near the cloth makers' shops along the canal from the upper pool. ^{18}They called out to Hezekiah, and three of his highest officials came out to meet them. One of them was Hilkiah's son Eliakim, who was the prime minister. The other two were Shebna, assistant to the prime minister, and Joah son of Asaph, keeper of the government records.

^{19}One of the Assyrian commanders told them:

I have a message for Hezekiah from the great king of Assyria. Ask Hezekiah why he feels so sure of himself. ^{20}Does he think he can plan and win a war with nothing but words? Who is going to help him, now that he has turned against the king of Assyria? ^{21}Is he depending on Egypt and its king? That's the same as leaning on a broken stick, and it will go right through his hand.

^{22}Is Hezekiah now depending on the LORD your God? Didn't Hezekiah tear down all except one of the LORD's altars and places of worship?^{w} Didn't he tell the people of Jerusalem and Judah to worship at that one place?

^{23}The king of Assyria wants to make a bet with you people. He will give you 2,000 horses, if you have enough troops to ride them. ^{24}How could you even defeat our lowest ranking officer, when you have to depend on Egypt for chariots and cavalry? ^{25}Don't forget that it was the LORD who sent me here with orders to destroy your nation!

^{s}18.10 *three years later:* When the Israelites measured time, part of a year could be counted as a whole year. ^{t}18.11 *The king of Assyria:* Probably Sargon, Shalmaneser's successor (see the note at 17.6). ^{u}18.13 *King Sennacherib . . . walled city:* Sennacherib ruled Assyria 705–681 B.C., and this event probably took place in 701 B.C. ^{v}18.16 *doorposts:* One possible meaning for the difficult Hebrew text. ^{w}18.22 *worship:* Hezekiah actually had torn down the places where idols were worshiped, and he had told the people to worship the LORD at the one place of worship in Jerusalem. But the Assyrian leader was confused and thought these were also places where the LORD was supposed to be worshiped.

[26]Eliakim, Shebna, and Joah said, "Sir, we don't want the people listening from the city wall to understand what you are saying. So please speak to us in Aramaic instead of Hebrew."

[27]The Assyrian army commander answered, "My king sent me to speak to everyone, not just to you leaders. These people will soon have to eat their own body waste and drink their own urine! And so will the three of you."

[28]Then, in a voice loud enough for everyone to hear, he shouted in Hebrew:

Listen to what the great king of Assyria says! [29]Don't be fooled by Hezekiah. He can't save you. [30]Don't trust him when he tells you that the LORD will protect you from the king of Assyria. [31]Stop listening to Hezekiah! Pay attention to my king. Surrender to him. He will let you keep your own vineyards, fig trees, and cisterns [32]for a while. Then he will come and take you away to a country just like yours, where you can plant vineyards, raise your own grain, and have plenty of olive oil and honey. Believe me, you won't starve there.

Hezekiah claims the LORD will save you. But don't be fooled by him. [33]Were any other gods able to defend their land against the king of Assyria? [34]What happened to the gods of Hamath and Arpad? What about the gods of Sepharvaim, Hena, and Ivvah? Were the gods of Samaria able to protect their land against the Assyrian forces? [35]None of these gods kept their people safe from the king of Assyria. Do you think the LORD your God can do any better?

[36-37]Eliakim, Shebna, and Joah had been warned by King Hezekiah not to answer the Assyrian commander. So they tore their clothes in sorrow and reported to Hezekiah everything the commander had said.

Hezekiah Asks Isaiah the Prophet for Advice
(Isaiah 37.1-13)

19 As soon as Hezekiah heard the news, he tore off his clothes in sorrow and put on sackcloth. Then he went into the temple of the LORD. [2]He told Prime Minister Eliakim, Assistant Prime Minister Shebna, and the senior priests to dress in sackcloth and tell the prophet Isaiah:

[3]These are difficult and disgraceful times. Our nation is like a woman too weak to give birth, when it's time for her baby to be born. [4]Please pray for those of us who are left alive. The king of Assyria sent his army commander to insult the living God. Perhaps the LORD heard what he said and will do something, if you will pray.

[5]When these leaders went to Isaiah, [6]he told them that the LORD had this message for Hezekiah:

I am the LORD. Don't worry about the insulting things that have been said about me by these messengers from the king of Assyria. [7]I will upset him with rumors about what's happening in his own country. He will go back, and there I will make him die a violent death.

[8]Meanwhile, the commander of the Assyrian forces heard that his king had left the town of Lachish and was now attacking Libnah. So he went there.

[9]About this same time the king of Assyria learned that King Tirhakah of Ethiopia[x] was on his way to attack him.

[x]**19.9** *Ethiopia*: The Hebrew text has "Cush," which was a region south of Egypt that included parts of the present countries of Ethiopia and Sudan.

● **18.33-35** *other gods . . . of Hamath . . . Ivvah*: The Assyrians captured Hamath in 738 B.C. and again in 720 B.C. Tiglath Pileser captured Arpad in 740 B.C. The locations of Sepharvaim, Hena, and Ivvah are unknown. The point of the Assyrian officer is that these national gods didn't protect those nations from Assyria. He argues that Judah's LORD God would also do nothing to stop the Assyrians.

● **19.2** *Isaiah*: The prophet Isaiah had been bringing God's messages of judgment and hope to Judah since the last year of Azariah's reign, 40 years before this time. However, this is the first time he is mentioned in 1 and 2 KINGS. ISAIAH includes parallel accounts of the Hezekiah stories given here in 2 KINGS. Isaiah is mentioned in 2 Chronicles 26.22 as the writer of a history of King Azariah (also called Uzziah). **(See the article Prophets and Prophecy on pg 1791.)**

● 19.21-28 *make fun of you . . . send you back*: These verses were written in a song style that was used in songs of sadness (laments) or satire. Here the song is used to make fun of Assyrian king Sennacherib.

■ 19.22 *holy God of Israel*: This phrase is common in ISAIAH (Isa 1.4; 43.14). It refers to God as special and different from other nations' gods. It emphasizes that Israel's LORD God controls what happens (19.25,26,28) and saves those who are faithful.

Then the king of Assyria sent some messengers with this note for Hezekiah:

¹⁰Don't trust your God or be fooled by his promise to defend Jerusalem against me. ¹¹You have heard how we Assyrian kings have completely wiped out other nations. What makes you feel so safe? ¹²The Assyrian kings before me destroyed the towns of Gozan, Haran, Rezeph, and everyone from Eden who lived in Telassar. What good did their gods do them? ¹³The kings of Hamath, Arpad, Sepharvaim, Hena, and Ivvah have all disappeared.

Hezekiah Prays

(Isaiah 37.14-20)

¹⁴After Hezekiah had read the note from the king of Assyria, he took it to the temple and spread it out for the LORD to see. ¹⁵He prayed:

LORD God of Israel, your throne is above the winged creatures.ʸ You created the heavens and the earth, and you alone rule the kingdoms of this world. ¹⁶But just look how Sennacherib has insulted you, the living God. ¹⁷It is true, our LORD, that Assyrian kings have turned nations into deserts. ¹⁸They destroyed the idols of wood and stone that the people of those nations had made and worshiped. ¹⁹But you are our LORD and our God! We ask you to keep us safe from the Assyrian king. Then everyone in every kingdom on earth will know that you are the only God.

The LORD's Answer to Hezekiah

(Isaiah 37.21-35)

²⁰Isaiah went to Hezekiah and told him that the LORD God of Israel had said:

Hezekiah, I heard your prayer about King Sennacherib of Assyria. ²¹Now this is what I say to that king:

The people of Jerusalem
hate and make fun of you;
   they laugh
   behind your back.

²²Sennacherib, you cursed,
   shouted, and sneered at me,
   the holy God of Israel.
²³You let your officials
   insult me, the Lord.
And this is how you
   bragged about yourself:
"I led my chariots
to the highest heights
   of Lebanon's mountains.
I went deep into its forest,
cutting down the best cedar
   and cypress trees.
²⁴I dried up every stream
   in the land of Egypt,
and I drank water
   from wells I had dug."

²⁵Sennacherib, now listen
   to me, the Lord.
I planned all this long ago.
And you don't even realize
   that I alone am the one
who decided that you
   would do these things.
I let you make ruins
   of fortified cities.

ʸ**19.15** *winged creatures*: Two winged creatures made of gold were on the top of the sacred chest and were symbols of the LORD's throne on earth (see Exodus 25.18; 2 Samuel 6.2).

Hezekiah prayed, "LORD God of Israel, . . . you created the heavens and the earth, and you alone rule the kingdoms of this world." 2 KGS 19.15

²⁶Their people became weak,
    terribly confused.
They were like wild flowers
    or tender young grass
       growing on a flat roof,
    scorched before it matures.ᶻ

²⁷I know all about you,
    even how fiercely angry
       you are with me.
²⁸I have seen your pride
    and the tremendous hatred
       you have for me.
Now I will put a hook
    in your nose,
       a bit in your mouth,ᵃ
    then I will send you back
       to where you came from.

²⁹Hezekiah, I will tell you what's going to happen. This year you will eat crops that grow on their own, and the next year you will eat whatever springs up where those crops grew. But the third year you will plant grain and vineyards, and you will eat what you harvest. ³⁰Those who survive in Judah will be like a vine that puts down deep roots and bears fruit. ³¹I, the LORD All-Powerful, will see to it that some who live in Jerusalem will survive.

³²I promise that the king of Assyria won't get into Jerusalem, or shoot an arrow into the city, or even surround it and prepare to attack. ³³As surely as I am the LORD, he will return by the way he came and will never enter Jerusalem. ³⁴I will protect it for myself and for my servant David.

The Death of King Sennacherib
(Isaiah 37.36-38)

³⁵That same night the LORD sent an angel to the camp of the Assyrians, and he killed 185,000 of them. And so the next morning, the camp was full of dead bodies. ³⁶After this King Sennacherib went back to Assyria and lived in the city of Nineveh. ³⁷One day he was worshiping in the temple of his god Nisroch, when his sons, Adrammelech and Sharezer, killed him with their swords. They escaped to the land of Ararat, and his son Esarhaddon became king.ᵇ

Hezekiah Gets Sick and Almost Dies
(2 Chronicles 32.24-26; Isaiah 38.1-8,21,22)

20 About this time, Hezekiah got sick and was almost dead. Isaiah the prophet went in and told him, "The LORD says you won't ever get well. You are going to die, so you had better start doing what needs to be done."

²Hezekiah turned toward the wall and prayed, ³"Don't forget that I have been faithful to you, LORD. I have obeyed you with all my heart, and I do whatever you say is right." After this, he cried bitterly.

⁴Before Isaiah got to the middle court of the palace, ⁵the LORD sent him back to Hezekiah with this message:

Hezekiah, you are the ruler of my people, and I am the LORD God, who was worshiped by your ancestor David. I heard you pray, and I saw you cry. I will heal you, so that three days from now you will be able to worship in my

19.28 *put . . . a bit in your mouth:* A piece of metal or wood (bit) was attached to leather straps and put inside the mouth of a horse or donkey in order to control it and make it turn or stop. The Assyrians sometimes used metal hooks, rings, and bits to control their human prisoners. Now the LORD will treat Sennacherib the same way. The Assyrians will be steered to destruction.

19.30,31 *Judah . . . Jerusalem:* The tribe of Judah occupied the hill country west of the Dead Sea. Following the death of Solomon, the ten northern tribes of Israel broke away. The tribes of Judah and Benjamin were left to form the southern kingdom, which they also called "Judah." Here, God assures Hezekiah that Judah will not experience total destruction and that he will keep his promise to David (2 Sam 7). **(See Map 5 on pg 1883.)**

Jerusalem

19.36,37 *Nineveh . . . land of Ararat:* Nineveh was the capital city of Assyria. It was in northeastern Mesopotamia (now modern-day Iraq) on the Tigris River. The land of Ararat is a mountainous region about 200 miles north of Nineveh, in what is now eastern Turkey. Noah's boat is said to have settled on a mountain called Mount Ararat (Gen 8.4). **(See Maps 1 and 7 on pgs 1879 and 1885.)**

19.37 *Esarhaddon became king:* He ruled Assyria 681–669 B.C.

ᶻ**19.26** *tender young grass . . . matures:* Many of the houses had roofs made of packed earth. Grass would sometimes grow out of the roof, but would die quickly because of the sun and hot winds.
ᵃ**19.28** *I will put . . . your mouth:* This is how the Assyrians treated their prisoners, and now the LORD will treat Sennacherib the same way. ᵇ**19.37** *Esarhaddon became king:* Ruled Assyria 681–669 B.C.

20.12 *Merodach Baladan . . . Babylonia:* Merodach Baladan ruled Babylonia during 722 to 710 B.C. and again, briefly, from 704 to 703 B.C. Assyria was a constant threat during his reign. Here the king of Babylonia appears to be building an alliance with Hezekiah, since there would be little reason otherwise for Hezekiah to show where all his wealth and weapons were stored (20.13). **(See Map 7 on pg 1885.)**

Babylon

20.20 *upper pool and tunnel:* In A.D. 1838, archaeologists discovered a tunnel 1,700 feet long running from the Gihon Spring outside Jerusalem's walls to the pool of Siloam within the city. The tunnel was filled with rocks and other debris left by Jerusalem's destruction in 586 B.C. This tunnel was probably not the first to bring water into the city, since David had entered the city through a water tunnel 300 years earlier (2 Sam 5.6-9).

21.1-3 *Manasseh . . . rebuilt local shrines . . . worshiped stars:* Manasseh, Judah's thirteenth king, ruled from 687 to 642 B.C. His "55" year reign includes 10 years ruling with his father Hezekiah. Manasseh undid his father's reforms. He rebuilt local shrines, and he set up altars to honor Baal and sacred poles to honor Asherah, and worshiped the stars, sun, and moon as gods.

temple. **6**I will let you live 15 years more, while I protect you and your city from the king of Assyria. I will defend this city as an honor to me and to my servant David.

7Then Isaiah said to the king's servants, "Bring some mashed figs and place them on the king's open sore. He will then get well."

8Hezekiah asked Isaiah, "Can you prove that the LORD will heal me, so that I can worship in his temple in three days?"

9Isaiah replied, "The LORD will prove to you that he will keep his promise. Will the shadow made by the setting sun on the stairway go forward ten steps or back ten steps?"**c**

10"It's normal for the sun to go forward," Hezekiah answered. "But how can it go back?"

11Isaiah prayed, and the LORD made the shadow go back ten steps on the stairway built for King Ahaz.**d**

The LORD Is Still with Hezekiah
(Isaiah 39.1-8)

12Merodach**e** Baladan, the son of Baladan, was now king of Babylonia.**f** And when he learned that Hezekiah had been sick, he sent messengers with letters and a gift for him. **13**Hezekiah welcomed**g** the messengers and showed them all the silver, the gold, the spices, and the fine oils that were in his storehouse. He even showed them where he kept his weapons. Nothing in his palace or in his entire kingdom was kept hidden from them.

14Isaiah asked Hezekiah, "Where did these men come from? What did they want?"

"They came all the way from Babylonia," Hezekiah answered.

15"What did you show them?" Isaiah asked.

Hezekiah answered, "I showed them everything in my kingdom."

16Then Isaiah told Hezekiah:

I have a message for you from the LORD. **17**One day everything you and your ancestors have stored up will be taken to Babylonia. The LORD has promised that nothing will be left. **18**Some of your own sons will be taken to Babylonia, where they will be disgraced and made to serve in the king's palace.

19Hezekiah thought, "At least our nation will be at peace for a while." So he told Isaiah, "The message you brought me from the LORD is good."

Hezekiah Dies
(2 Chronicles 32.32,33)

20Everything else Hezekiah did while he was king, including his brave deeds and how he made the upper pool and tunnel bring water into Jerusalem, is written in *The History of the Kings of Judah.* **21**Hezekiah died, and his son Manasseh became king.

King Manasseh of Judah
(2 Chronicles 33.1-20)

21 Manasseh was 12 years old when he became king of Judah, and he ruled 55 years from Jerusalem. His mother was Hephzibah. **2**Manasseh disobeyed the LORD by following the disgusting customs of the nations that the LORD had forced

c20.9 *Will . . . steps:* One possible meaning for the difficult Hebrew text.   **d20.11** *the shadow . . . Ahaz:* One possible meaning for the difficult Hebrew text.   **e20.12** *Merodach:* The Hebrew text has "Berodach," another spelling of the name.   **f20.12** *Merodach Baladan . . . Babylonia:* Ruled Babylonia 722–710 and 704–703 B.C.   **g20.13** *welcomed:* Or "listened to."

out of Israel. ³He rebuilt the local shrines that his father Hezekiah had torn down. He built altars for the god Baal and set up a sacred pole for worshiping the goddess Asherah, just as King Ahab of Israel had done. And he faithfully worshiped the stars in heaven.

⁴In the temple, where only the LORD was supposed to be worshiped, Manasseh built altars for the worship of pagan gods ⁵and the stars. He placed these altars in both courts of the temple, ⁶⁻⁷and even set up the pole for Asherah there. Manasseh practiced magic and witchcraft; he asked fortunetellers for advice and sacrificed his own son. He did many sinful things and made the LORD very angry.

Years ago the LORD had told David and his son Solomon:

Jerusalem is the place I prefer above all others in Israel. It belongs to me, and there I will be worshiped forever. ⁸If my people will faithfully obey all the commands in the Law of my servant Moses, I will never make them leave the land I gave to their ancestors.

⁹But the people of Judah disobeyed the LORD. They listened to Manasseh and did even more sinful things than the nations the LORD had wiped out.

¹⁰One day the LORD said to some of his prophets:

¹¹King Manasseh has done more disgusting things than the Amorites,ʰ and he has led my people to sin by forcing them to worship his idols. ¹²Now I, the LORD God of Israel, will destroy both Jerusalem and Judah! People will hear about it but won't believe it. ¹³Jerusalem is as sinful as Ahab and the people of Samaria were. So I will wipe out Jerusalem and be done

with it, just as someone wipes water off a plate and turns it over to dry.

¹⁴I will even get rid of my people who survive. They will be defeated and robbed by their enemies. ¹⁵My people have done what I hate and have not stopped making me angry since their ancestors left Egypt.

¹⁶Manasseh was guilty of causing the people of Judah to sin and disobey the LORD. He also refused to protect innocent people—he even let so many of them be killedⁱ that their blood filled the streets of Jerusalem.

¹⁷Everything else Manasseh did while he was king, including his terrible sins, is written in *The History of the Kings of Judah.* ¹⁸He died and was buried in Uzza Garden near his palace, and his son Amon became king.

King Amon of Judah
(2 Chronicles 33.21-25)

¹⁹Amon was 22 years old when he became king of Judah, and he ruled from Jerusalem for 2 years. His mother Meshullemeth was the daughter of Haruz from Jotbah. ²⁰Amon disobeyed the LORD, just as his father Manasseh had done. ²¹Amon worshiped the idols Manasseh had made and ²²refused to be faithful to the LORD, the God his ancestors had worshiped.

²³Some of Amon's officials plotted against him and killed him in his palace. ²⁴⁻²⁶He was buried in Uzza Garden. Soon after that, the people of Judah killed the murderers of Amon, then they made his son Josiah king.

Everything else Amon did while he was king is written in *The History of the Kings of Judah.*

● 21.15 *left Egypt:* The Hebrew people ("their ancestors") left Egypt around 1290 B.C., or 650 years before this time.

● 21.19 *Amon:* Amon, Judah's fourteenth king, ruled from 642 to 640 B.C. He followed his father's evil example. He was murdered by his own officials, who were then murdered by the people so that Amon's son, Josiah, could become king. Murder plots and assassinations had been common in the northern kingdom, and now they were happening in Judah as well.

ʰ21.11 *Amorites:* Here used in the general sense of nations that lived in Canaan before the Israelites.
ⁱ21.16 *He also refused . . . killed:* Or "He killed so many innocent people."

● 22.1 *Josiah*: Josiah, Judah's fifteenth king, ruled from 640 to 609 B.C.

☙ Josiah

☙ Jerusalem

● 22.8 *The Book of God's Law*: Many scholars feel this may have been a portion of DEUTERONOMY that includes the law God gave to Moses. Some think it was Deut 5, which includes the Ten Commandments. Others believe it was Deut 28–30, which explains how God would bless the people for obedience and curse them for disobedience, and tells of the renewal of the agreement between God and the people at Moab. Still other scholars think it refers to all of the first five books of the Bible, but this is less likely, since Shaphan read it twice in one day (22.8,10).

● 22.14 *Huldah the prophet*: Huldah is one of the women prophets named in the Bible. Two other famous female prophets are Miriam (Exod 15.20,21) and Deborah (Judg 4.4). **(See the article Prophets and Prophecy on pg 1791.)**

● 22.20 *in peace*: Since Josiah died before Jerusalem was destroyed, it could be said that he died at peace with God. Josiah actually was killed in 609 B.C. by the Egyptians who attacked at Megiddo when he was trying to make plans for Judah to become independent from Assyria. His death in battle (see 2 Chr 35.23-25) put an end to reforms in Judah.

King Josiah of Judah
(2 Chronicles 34.1,2)

22 Josiah was 8 years old when he became king of Judah, and he ruled 31 years from Jerusalem. His mother Jedidah was the daughter of Adaiah from Bozkath. ²Josiah always obeyed the LORD, just as his ancestor David had done.

Hilkiah Finds
The Book of God's Law
(2 Chronicles 34.8-28)

³After Josiah had been king for 18 years, he told Shaphan,ʲ one of his highest officials:

Go to the LORD's temple ⁴and ask Hilkiah the high priest to collect from the guards all the money that the people have donated. ⁵Tell Hilkiah to give it to the men supervising the repairs to the temple. They can use some of the money to pay ⁶the workers, and with the rest of it they can buy wood and stone for the repair work. ⁷They are honest, so we won't ask them to keep track of the money.

⁸While Shaphan was at the temple, Hilkiah handed him a book and said, "Look what I found here in the temple—*The Book of God's Law*."

Shaphan read it, ⁹then went back to Josiah and reported, "Your officials collected the money in the temple and gave it to the men supervising the repairs. ¹⁰But there's something else, Your Majesty. The priest Hilkiah gave me this book." Then Shaphan read it out loud.

¹¹When Josiah heard what was in *The Book of God's Law*, he tore his clothes in sorrow. ¹²At once he called together Hilkiah, Shaphan, Ahikam son of Shaphan,

Achbor son of Micaiah, and his own servant Asaiah. He said, ¹³"The LORD must be furious with me and everyone else in Judah, because our ancestors did not obey the laws written in this book. Go find out what the LORD wants us to do."

¹⁴The five men left at once and went to talk with Huldah the prophet. Her husband was Shallum,ᵏ who was in charge of the king's clothes. Huldah lived in the northern part of Jerusalem, and when they met in her home, ¹⁵she said:

You were sent here by King Josiah, and this is what the LORD God of Israel says to him: ¹⁶"Josiah, I am the LORD! And I will see to it that this country and everyone living in it will be destroyed. It will happen just as this book says. ¹⁷The people of Judah have rejected me. They have offered sacrifices to foreign gods and have worshiped their own idols. I cannot stand it any longer. I am furious.

¹⁸"Josiah, listen to what I am going to do. ¹⁹I noticed how sad you were when you read that this country and its people would be completely wiped out. You even tore your clothes in sorrow, and I heard you cry. ²⁰So I will let you die in peace, before I destroy this place."

The men left and took Huldah's answer back to Josiah.

Josiah Reads
The Book of God's Law
(2 Chronicles 34.29-33)

23 King Josiah called together the older leaders of Judah and Jerusalem. ²Then he went to the LORD's temple, together with the people of Judah and Jerusalem, the priests, and the prophets. Finally, when everybody was there, he read aloud *The Book of God's Law*[l] that had been found in the temple.

[3]After Josiah had finished reading, he stood by one of the columns. He asked the people to promise in the LORD's name to faithfully obey the LORD and to follow his commands. The people agreed to do everything written in the book.

Josiah Follows the Teachings of God's Law
(2 Chronicles 34.3-7)

[4]Josiah told Hilkiah the priest, the assistant priests, and the guards at the temple door to go into the temple and bring out the things used to worship Baal, Asherah, and the stars. Josiah had these things burned in Kidron Valley just outside Jerusalem, and he had the ashes carried away to the town of Bethel.

[5]Josiah also got rid of the pagan priests at the local shrines in Judah and around Jerusalem. These were the men that the kings of Judah had appointed to offer sacrifices to Baal and to the sun, moon, and stars. [6]Josiah had the sacred pole[m] for Asherah brought out of the temple and taken to Kidron Valley, where it was burned. He then had its ashes ground into dust and scattered over the public cemetery there. [7]He had the buildings torn down where the male prostitutes[n] lived next to the temple, and where the women wove sacred robes[o] for the idol of Asherah.

[8]In almost every town in Judah, priests had been offering sacrifices to the LORD at local shrines.[p] Josiah brought these priests to Jerusalem and had their shrines made unfit for worship—every shrine from Geba just north of Jerusalem to Beersheba in the south. He even tore down the shrine at Beersheba that was just to the left of Joshua Gate, which was named after the highest official of the city. [9]Those local priests could not serve at the LORD's altar in Jerusalem, but they were allowed to eat sacred bread,[q] just like the priests from Jerusalem.

[10]Josiah sent some men to Hinnom Valley just outside Jerusalem with orders to make the altar there unfit for worship. That way, people could no longer use it for sacrificing their children to the god Molech. [11]He also got rid of the horses that the kings of Judah used in their ceremonies to worship the sun, and he destroyed the chariots along with them. The horses had been kept near the entrance to the LORD's temple, in a courtyard[r] close to where an official named Nathan-Melech lived.

[12]Some of the kings of Judah, especially Manasseh, had built altars in the two courts of the temple and in the room that Ahaz had built on the palace roof. Josiah had these altars torn down and smashed to pieces, and he had the pieces thrown into Kidron Valley, just outside Jerusalem. [13]After that, he closed down the shrines that Solomon had built east of Jerusalem and south of Spoil Hill to honor Astarte

23.8 *Geba . . . Beersheba:* Geba is believed to have been north of Jerusalem close to the border between Judah and Israel. Beersheba was on the southern border of Judah. **(See Map 6 on pg 1884.)**

23.9 *Those local priests . . . priests from Jerusalem:* Priests led worship and offered sacrifices.

23.13 *the shrines that Solomon had built:* See 1 Kgs 11.5-7. Astarte was a Canaanite fertility goddess. Chemosh was a god of the Moabites and most likely the god that Moab's king sacrificed his son to when facing defeat in battle (2 Kgs 3.26, 27). Milcom, also known as Molech, was the national god of the Ammonites and was worshiped with human sacrifice. See 2 Chr 33.6-7. Milcom, Molech, and Chemosh may all be names for Nergal, the Mesopotamian god of death and the underworld.

Canaanite Gods and Goddesses

---

[l]**23.2** *The Book of God's Law:* The Hebrew text has "The Book of God's Agreement," which is the same as "The Book of God's Law" in 22.8,11. In traditional translations this is called "The Book of the Covenant." [m]**23.6** *sacred pole:* See the note at 13.6,7. [n]**23.7** *male prostitutes:* Young men or boys sometimes served as prostitutes in the worship of Canaanite gods, but the LORD had forbidden the people of Israel and Judah to worship in this way (see Deuteronomy 23.17,18). [o]**23.7** *sacred robes:* Or "coverings." [p]**23.8** *local shrines:* See the note at 12.3. [q]**23.9** *sacred bread:* The Hebrew text has "thin bread," which may be either the pieces of thin bread made without yeast to be eaten during the Passover Festival (see verses 21-23) or the baked flour used in sacrifices to give thanks to the LORD (see Leviticus 2.4,5). [r]**23.11** *in a courtyard:* One possible meaning for the difficult Hebrew text.

23.21 *Passover . . . The Book of God's Law:* The "Passover" is related to the Hebrew word translated as "pass over" in Exod 12.12,13,23,27. Passover was celebrated as a remembrance of how God saved the people from the final disaster (plague) and acted to help them escape from slavery in Egypt. The kings of Israel and Judah were not faithful, and so Passover probably had not been celebrated properly since the time of the judges almost 400 years earlier.

Passover and the Festival of Thin Bread

23.24 *disgusting:* Often in the Bible, the word "disgusting" is used in connection with foreign gods and the worship of these gods. Its use is an indication that the worship of idols or other gods is the worst of sins.

the disgusting goddess of Sidon, Chemosh the disgusting god of Moab, and Milcom the disgusting god of Ammon.[s] [14]He tore down the stone images of foreign gods and cut down the sacred pole used in the worship of Asherah. Then he had the whole area covered with human bones.[t]

[15]But Josiah was not finished yet. At Bethel he destroyed the shrine and the altar that Jeroboam son of Nebat had built and that had caused the Israelites to sin. Josiah had the shrine and the Asherah pole burned and ground into dust. [16]As he looked around, he saw graves on the hillside. He had the bones in them dug up and burned on the altar, so that it could no longer be used. This happened just as God's prophet had said when Jeroboam was standing at the altar, celebrating a festival.[u]

Then Josiah saw the grave of the prophet who had said this would happen [17]and he asked,[v] "Whose grave is that?"

Some people who lived nearby answered, "It belongs to the prophet from Judah who told what would happen to this altar."

[18]Josiah replied, "Then leave it alone. Don't dig up his bones." So they did not disturb his bones or the bones of the old prophet from Israel who had also been buried there.[w]

[19]Some of the Israelite kings had made the LORD angry by building pagan shrines all over Israel. So Josiah sent troops to destroy these shrines just as he had done to the one in Bethel. [20]He killed the priests who served at them and burned their bones on the altars.

After all that, Josiah went back to Jerusalem.

Josiah and the People of Judah Celebrate Passover
(2 Chronicles 35.1-19)

[21]Josiah told the people of Judah, "Celebrate Passover in honor of the LORD your God, just as it says in *The Book of God's Law.*"[x]

[22]This festival had not been celebrated in this way since the time that tribal leaders ruled Israel or the kings ruled Israel and Judah. [23]But in Josiah's eighteenth year as king of Judah, everyone came to Jerusalem to celebrate Passover.

The LORD Is Still Angry with the People of Judah

[24]Josiah got rid of every disgusting person and thing in Judah and Jerusalem—including magicians, fortunetellers, and idols. He did his best to obey every law written in the book that the priest Hilkiah found in the LORD's temple. [25]No other king before or after Josiah tried as hard as he did to obey the Law of Moses.

[26]But the LORD was still furious with the people of Judah because Manasseh had done so many things to make him angry. [27]The LORD said, "I will desert the people of Judah, just as I deserted the people of Israel. I will reject Jerusalem, even though I chose it to be mine. And I will abandon this temple built to honor me."

Josiah Dies in Battle
(2 Chronicles 35.20—36.1)

[28]Everything else Josiah did while he was king is written in *The History of the Kings of*

[s]23.13 *the shrines . . . Ammon:* See 1 Kings 11.5-7. [t]23.14 *Then he . . . human bones:* This made the whole area unfit for the worship of any god. [u]23.16 *just . . . festival:* See 1 Kings 13.1,2. [v]23.16,17 *said when Jeroboam . . . asked:* One ancient translation; Hebrew "said. [17]Then Josiah asked." [w]23.18 *old prophet . . . there:* See 1 Kings 13.11-32. [x]23.21 *The Book of God's Law:* See the note at verse 2.

Judah. ²⁹During Josiah's rule, King Neco of Egypt led his army north to the Euphrates River to help the king of Assyria. Josiah led his troops north to fight Neco, but when they met in battle at Megiddo, Josiah was killed.^y ³⁰A few of Josiah's servants put his body in a chariot and took it back to Jerusalem, where they buried it in his own tomb. Then the people of Judah found his son Jehoahaz and poured olive oil on his head to show that he was their new king.

King Jehoahaz of Judah
(2 Chronicles 36.2-4)

³¹Jehoahaz was 23 years old when he became king of Judah, and he ruled from Jerusalem only 3 months. His mother Hamutal was the daughter of Jeremiah from Libnah. ³²Jehoahaz disobeyed the LORD, just as some of his ancestors had done.

³³King Neco of Egypt had Jehoahaz arrested and put in prison at Riblah^z near Hamath. Then he forced the people of Judah to pay him almost 4 tons of silver and about 75 pounds of gold as taxes. ³⁴Neco appointed Josiah's son Eliakim king of Judah, and changed his name to Jehoiakim. He took Jehoahaz as a prisoner to Egypt, where he died.

³⁵Jehoiakim forced the people of Judah to pay higher taxes, so he could give Neco the silver and gold he demanded.

King Jehoiakim of Judah
(2 Chronicles 36.5-8)

³⁶Jehoiakim was 25 years old when he was appointed king, and he ruled 11 years from Jerusalem. His mother Zebidah was the daughter of Pedaiah from Rumah. ³⁷Jehoiakim disobeyed the LORD by following the example of his ancestors.

24 During Jehoiakim's rule, King Nebuchadnezzar of Babylonia^a invaded and took control of Judah. Jehoiakim obeyed Nebuchadnezzar for three years, but then he rebelled.

²At that time, the LORD started sending troops to rob and destroy towns in Judah. Some of these troops were from Babylonia, and others were from Syria, Moab, and Ammon. The LORD had sent his servants the prophets to warn Judah about this, ³and now he was making it happen. The country of Judah was going to be wiped out, because Manasseh had sinned ⁴and caused many innocent people to die. The LORD would not forgive this.

⁵Everything else Jehoiakim did while he was king is written in *The History of the Kings of Judah*. ⁶Jehoiakim died, and his son Jehoiachin became king.

⁷King Nebuchadnezzar defeated King Neco of Egypt and took control of his land from the Egyptian Gorge all the way north to the Euphrates River. So Neco never invaded Judah again.^b

● 23.29 *Megiddo*: Megiddo was an important business and military center located on an important north-south trade route. Whoever controlled Megiddo also controlled the pass through the Carmel mountain range between the Plain of Jezreel and the Plain of Sharon. **(See Map 4 on pg 1882.)**

● 23.31 *Jehoahaz*: Jehoahaz, Judah's sixteenth king, ruled for only three months in 609 B.C.

● 23.33 *Riblah*: Neco of Egypt set up his military headquarters at this important town in Syria on the Orontes River. **(See Map 4 on pg 1882.)**

● 23.34-36 *Jehoiakim*: Neco of Egypt removed Jehoahaz from Judah's throne and took him prisoner (23.34). Then he set up Jehoiakim (609–598 B.C.) as Judah's seventeenth king. By changing the name of Eliakim ("God has established") to Jehoiakim ("the LORD has established"), Neco was claiming to be the LORD of Judah, displacing God. Now that Judah was controlled by Egypt, it faced a great threat of being attacked by Babylonia, Egypt's enemy.

● 24.1 *King Nebuchadnezzar of Babylonia . . . Jehoiakim . . . rebelled*: Nebuchadnezzar ruled Babylonia from 605 to 562 B.C.

^y23.29 *killed*: At this time, King Neco of Egypt (609–595 B.C.) was fighting on the side of the Assyrians. He marched north to fight the Babylonian army and help Assyria keep control of its land. Since Josiah considered Assyria an enemy, he set out to stop Neco and the Egyptian troops. ^z23.33 *Riblah*: An important town in Syria on the Orontes River. ^a24.1 *King Nebuchadnezzar of Babylonia*: Ruled Babylonia 605–562 B.C. ^b24.7 *again*: Nebuchadnezzar defeated the Egyptian army in 605 B.C. at the town of Carchemish. But a few years later, he was forced to retreat all the way back to Babylonia, which allowed Jehoiakim to rebel (see verse 1).

24.8,9 *Jehoiachin . . . disobeyed the LORD:* Jehoiachin, Judah's eighteenth king, ruled for only three months in 598 B.C. He also disobeyed God by worshiping other gods.

24.10-12 *Jehoiachin arrested . . . eighth year of Nebuchadnezzar's rule:* These events took place in 597 B.C. Soon the nation and land of the Israelites would be ruled by non-Israelites.

24.18-20 *Zedekiah . . . rebelled against Nebuchadnezzar:* Zedekiah, Judah's nineteenth king, ruled from 598 to 587 B.C. Like other kings before him, Zedekiah also disobeyed the LORD, meaning he allowed the worship of idols in Judah. Apries, King Neco's grandson, reclaimed the Egyptian crown from Babylonia in 588 B.C. He may have encouraged Zedekiah's rebellion.

25.1 *tenth month . . . attack Jerusalem:* Zedekiah's treaty with Egypt caused Nebuchadnezzar to launch a second major attack against Judah. This happened in Tebeth, the tenth month of the Hebrew calendar, from about mid-December to mid-January, in 588 B.C. The Babylonians surrounded Jerusalem, causing starvation in the city (25.2-3).

25.2-3 *fourth month:* Tammuz, the fourth month of the Hebrew calendar, from about mid-June to mid-July.

King Jehoiachin of Judah Is Taken to Babylon

(2 Chronicles 36.9,10)

[8]Jehoiachin was 18 years old when he became king of Judah, and he ruled only 3 months from Jerusalem. His mother Nehushta was the daughter of Elnathan from Jerusalem. [9]Jehoiachin disobeyed the LORD, just as his father Jehoiakim had done.

[10]King Nebuchadnezzar of Babylonia sent troops to attack Jerusalem soon after Jehoiachin became king. [11]During the attack, Nebuchadnezzar himself arrived at the city. [12]Jehoiachin immediately surrendered, together with his mother and his servants, as well as his army officers and officials. Then Nebuchadnezzar had Jehoiachin arrested. These things took place in the eighth year of Nebuchadnezzar's rule in Babylonia.[c]

[13]The LORD had warned[d] that someday the treasures would be taken from the royal palace and from the temple, including the gold objects that Solomon had made for the temple. And that's exactly what Nebuchadnezzar ordered his soldiers to do. [14]He also led away as prisoners the Jerusalem officials, the military leaders, and the skilled workers—10,000 in all. Only the very poorest people were left in Judah.

[15]Nebuchadnezzar took Jehoiachin to Babylon, along with his mother, his wives, his officials, and the most important leaders of Judah. [16]He also led away 7,000 soldiers and 1,000 skilled workers, all of them trained for battle.

[17]Then Nebuchadnezzar appointed Jehoiachin's uncle Mattaniah king of Judah and changed his name to Zedekiah.

King Zedekiah of Judah

(2 Chronicles 36.11-16; Jeremiah 52.1-3)

[18]Zedekiah was 21 years old when he was appointed king of Judah, and he ruled from Jerusalem for 11 years. His mother Hamutal was the daughter of Jeremiah from Libnah. [19]Zedekiah disobeyed the LORD, just as Jehoiakim had done. [20]It was Zedekiah who finally rebelled against Nebuchadnezzar.

The people of Judah and Jerusalem had made the LORD so angry that he turned his back on them. That's why these horrible things were happening.

Jerusalem Is Captured and Destroyed

(2 Chronicles 36.17-21; Jeremiah 52.3-30)

25 In Zedekiah's ninth year as king, on the tenth day of the tenth month,[e] King Nebuchadnezzar of Babylonia led his entire army to attack Jerusalem. The troops set up camp outside the city and built ramps up to the city walls.

[2-3]After a year and a half, all the food in Jerusalem was gone. Then on the ninth day of the fourth[f] month, [4]the Babylonian troops broke through the city wall.[g] That same night, Zedekiah and his soldiers tried to escape through the gate near the royal garden, even though they knew the enemy had the city surrounded. They headed toward the desert, [5]but the Babylonian troops caught up with them near Jericho. They arrested Zedekiah, but his soldiers scattered in every direction.

[6]Zedekiah was taken to Riblah, where Nebuchadnezzar put him on trial and

found him guilty. [7]Zedekiah's sons were killed right in front of him. His eyes were then poked out, and he was put in chains and dragged off to Babylon.

[8]About a month later,[h] in Nebuchadnezzar's nineteenth year as king, Nebuzaradan, who was his official in charge of the guards, arrived in Jerusalem. [9]Nebuzaradan burned down the LORD's temple, the king's palace, and every important building in the city, as well as all the houses. [10]Then he ordered the Babylonian soldiers to break down the walls around Jerusalem. [11]He led away as prisoners the people left in the city, including those who had become loyal to Nebuchadnezzar. [12]Only some of the poorest people were left behind to work the vineyards and the fields.

[13]The Babylonian soldiers took the two bronze columns that stood in front of the temple, the ten movable bronze stands, and the large bronze bowl called the Sea. They broke them into pieces so they could take the bronze to Babylonia. [14]They carried off the bronze things used for worship at the temple, including the pans for hot ashes, and the shovels, snuffers, and also the dishes for incense, [15]as well as the fire pans and the sprinkling bowls. Nebuzaradan ordered his soldiers to take everything made of gold or silver.

[16]The pile of bronze from the columns, the stands, and the large bowl that Solomon had made for the temple was too large to be weighed. [17]Each column had been 27 feet tall with a bronze cap four and a half feet high. These caps were decorated with bronze designs—some of them like chains and others like pomegranates.[i]

[18]Next, Nebuzaradan arrested Seraiah the chief priest, Zephaniah his assistant, and three temple officials. [19]Then he arrested one of the army commanders, the king's five personal advisors, and the officer in charge of gathering the troops for battle. He also found 60 more soldiers who were still in Jerusalem. [20]Nebuzaradan led them all to Riblah [21]near Hamath, where Nebuchadnezzar had them killed.

Most of the people of Judah had been carried away as captives from their own country.

Gedaliah Is Made Ruler of the People Left in Judah
(Jeremiah 40.7-9; 41.1-3)

[22]King Nebuchadnezzar appointed Gedaliah son of Ahikam[j] to rule the few people still living in Judah. [23]When the army officers and troops heard that Gedaliah was their ruler, the officers met with him at Mizpah. These men were Ishmael son of Nethaniah, Johanan son of Kareah, Seraiah son of Tanhumeth from Netophah, and Jaazaniah from Maacah.

[24]Gedaliah said to them, "Everything will be fine, I promise. We don't need to be afraid of the Babylonian rulers, if we live here peacefully and do what Nebuchadnezzar says."

[25]Ishmael[k] was from the royal family. And about two months after Gedaliah began his rule,[l] Ishmael and ten other men went to Mizpah. They killed Gedaliah and his officials, including those from Judah and those from Babylonia. [26]After that, the army officers and all the people in Mizpah, whether important or not, were afraid of

25.22 *Gedaliah:* Gedaliah already had social standing in Judah. His father (Ahikam) and grandfather (Shaphan) were trusted servants in Josiah's court (22.3-13). An identification seal found at Lachish indicates that Gedaliah was also an official in Zedekiah's court. His kind, peaceful nature won him support, but also may have led to his death.

25.23 *Mizpah:* Gedaliah probably set up headquarters in a new city because Jerusalem was destroyed and because keeping Jerusalem as the capital may have been unacceptable to the ruler of Babylon.

---

[h]25.8 *About a month later:* Hebrew "On the seventh day of the fifth month." [i]25.17 *pomegranates:* A bright red fruit that looks like an apple. [j]25.22 *Ahikam:* Hebrew "Ahikam son of Shaphan." [k]25.25 *Ishmael:* Hebrew "Ishmael son of Nethaniah son of Elishama." [l]25.25 *about two months . . . his rule:* Hebrew "in the seventh month."

25.27 *Jehoiachin . . . Evil-Meroach . . . Babylonia:* Jehoiachin had been captured and taken to Babylon during Nebuchadnezzar's first invasion of Judah in 597 B.C. Evil-Merodach was the son of Nebuchadnezzar and ruled Babylonia from 562 to 560 B.C. "Evil" was his actual name and is not a description of his personality.

25.29 *ate at the king's table:* This was a high honor. The freeing of Jehoiachin provided the people of Judah with some hope for the future during the dark days of the exile in Babylon.

Exile

what the Babylonians might do. So they left Judah and went to Egypt.

Jehoiachin Is Set Free
(Jeremiah 52.31-34)

[27]Jehoiachin was a prisoner in Babylon for 37 years. Then Evil-Merodach became king of Babylonia,[m] and in the first year of his rule, on the twenty-seventh day of the twelfth month,[n] he let Jehoiachin out of prison. [28]Evil-Merodach was kind to Jehoiachin and honored him more than any of the other kings held prisoner there. [29]Jehoiachin was even allowed to wear regular clothes, and he ate at the king's table every day. [30]As long as Jehoiachin lived, he was paid a daily allowance to buy whatever he needed.

[m]*25.27 Evil-Merodach . . . Babylonia:* The son of Nebuchadnezzar, who ruled Babylonia from 562 to 560 B.C. [n]*25.27 twelfth month:* Adar, the twelfth month of the Hebrew calendar, from about mid-February to mid-March.

Reflection Questions About 2 Kings 1.1—25.30

1. How are Elijah and Elisha alike? How are they different? What words or phrases would you say best describe Elisha? Who functions like an Elisha in our world today?

2. Elisha performed about twice as many miracles as Elijah. Do you think that is what he meant when he asked for "twice as much" of Elijah's power (2.9)?

3. What happened to the chief officer who doubted God's power (7.1,2,17-20)? Do you believe God finds all doubt unacceptable? Why or why not?

4. Why does the author often not mention the specific names of Israelite or foreign kings in the stories about Elisha?

5. Review the story of King Jehu's reign as king of the northern kingdom (9.1—10.36). What means did he use to come to power? What is your reaction to the killing of Ahab and the other acts of violence in these chapters? Compare the description of how the prophet Elisha commissioned Jehu to rescue Israel from the King Ahab (2 Kings 9.4-10) with the words of the prophet Hosea regarding King Jehu (Hos 1.4,5). What do you make of these passages?

6. The author of 2 Kings consistently condemns the kings of Israel for allowing the people to worship idols. Why do you think the people of Israel and their leaders were attracted to worshiping the Canaanite fertility gods?

7. Idols in 2 Kings are statues made of wood or stone. But idols can also be understood to be anything other than God that people turn to for comfort and protection. What are some idols that people worship today? How does this affect people's relationship with God?

8. Some historians have identified King Jeroboam II as one of Israel's most important political and military leaders. The Bible, however, has little to say about this king's accomplishments (2 Kgs 14.23-29). Why do you think that is so? What does the author of 2 Kings want the reader to understand about Jeroboam as a ruler of the Israelites?

9. Why were the reforms of the good kings Hezekiah and Josiah not enough to turn away God's anger and prevent the destruction of Jerusalem by Babylon (2 Kgs 23.26,27)?

10. Why do 1 and 2 Kings generally criticize the kings of the northern kingdom (Israel) more severely than those of the southern kingdom (Judah)?

1 chronicles

*Important stories are worth repeating. Although the
story of David is told in 1 and 2 SAMUEL, the author of
1 CHRONICLES offers another viewpoint on the life of
Israel's greatest king.*

WHAT MAKES 1 CHRONICLES SPECIAL?

The long family lists that begin 1 CHRONICLES make this book special. For the writer of 1 CHRONICLES and his audience, who had recently returned from exile in Babylon, these long family lists were reassuring. The people were worried about their relationship with God, and they wondered if the promises God made to their ancestors still applied to them. The writer uses these lists to connect his own generation to ancestors going all the way back to Adam (1 Chr 1.1). For those who were worried that God had lost interest in them, the lists showed that Israel was still special to, and loved by, God.

FIRST CHRONICLES retells the story of King David, already familiar from 2 SAMUEL, from a more uplifting point of view. This is done by linking David to the sacred chest, worship in Jerusalem, and above all, to the careful preparations for the building of the temple. Some stories from 2 SAMUEL that might present David in an unfavorable light are left out. His adultery with Bathsheba, David's arranging of the death of her husband Uriah, and Nathan's criticism of David (2 Sam 11,12) are all left out. The purpose of presenting David's story in this way is to show his strengths rather than his human weaknesses, and to present his faith and devotion to God as a model for Israel's leaders.

WHAT'S THE STORY BEHIND THE SCENE?

For many years there were reasons to think that 1 and 2 CHRONICLES formed a single work with the books of EZRA and NEHEMIAH, with Ezra as the possible author. For example, the same decree of Cyrus appears at the ending of 2 CHRONICLES and at the beginning of EZRA. But today, many scholars think that 1 and 2 CHRONICLES should be separated from EZRA and NEHEMIAH. These books are very different in significant ways. Differences include their handling of the identity of "Israel," the Sabbath, mixed marriages, God's promise that David's ancestors would always rule, the role of prophecy, the function of the Levites, and the importance of the exodus.

HOW IS 1 CHRONICLES CONSTRUCTED?

FIRST CHRONICLES falls into two major sections. The first section, 1 Chronicles 1–9, makes use of long family lists to trace the history of God's people from Adam to the end of the Babylonian exile. The second section, 1 Chronicles 10–29, is devoted to retelling the story of David in terms of his contributions to the worship life of Israel.

From Adam to the exile (1.1—9.34)
  From Adam to Jacob (1.1-54)
  Judah, David, and his family (2.1—4.23)
  The rest of the tribes of Israel (4.24—8.40)
  Lists of the families returning to Jerusalem
  (9.1-34)
David, founder of the temple (9.35—29.30)
  Introduction: The death of Saul (9.35—10.14)
  David rules in Jerusalem (11.1—17.27)
  David's wars (18.1—20.8)
  David plans the temple (21.1—29.30)

First and Second Chronicles are actually one long book. Together, they present a historical survey of God's people from Adam to the return of the exiled people from Babylonia in 538 B.C. The unknown author took information from Hebrew Scriptures and other ancient books, and used great literary skill to combine these sources into a single, unified history. (An alternative version of the story is told in 1 and 2 Samuel and 1 and 2 Kings.) The author focuses on King David and King Solomon and gives special importance to the temple in Jerusalem as the center of Israelite worship. A key theme of the two-volume work is that times may change, but the Lord remains with his people, always ready to help the faithful. The author of 1 Chronicles shows that, despite almost 70 years in exile, the people's connection to their land is unbroken. The first eight chapters contain long family lists tracing the heritage of God's people back to Adam. Chapter nine connects that list to a list of families who returned from captivity in Babylonia. The remaining chapters tell the story of King David, showing his strengths as an ideal ruler, and conclude with an account of David's death and the appointment of his son Solomon as the new king.

Outline

The Descendants of Adam

(Genesis 5.1-32; 10.1-32; 11.10-32)

1 [1-4]Adam was the father of Seth, and his descendants were Enosh, Kenan, Mahalalel, Jared, Enoch, Methuselah, Lamech, and Noah, who had three sons: Shem, Ham, and Japheth.

[5]Japheth was the father of Gomer, Magog, Madai, Javan, Tubal, Meshech, and Tiras, and they were the ancestors of the kingdoms named after them. [6]Gomer was the ancestor of Ashkenaz, Riphath,[a] and Togarmah. [7]Javan was the ancestor of Elishah, Tarshish, Kittim, and Dodanim.[b]

[8]Ham was the father of Ethiopia,[c] Egypt, Put, and Canaan, and they were the ancestors of the kingdoms named after them. [9]Ethiopia was the ancestor of Seba, Havilah, Sabta, Raamah, and Sabteca. Raamah was the ancestor of Sheba and Dedan. [10]Ethiopia was also the father of Nimrod, the world's first mighty warrior. [11]Egypt was the ancestor of Ludim, Anamim, Lehabim, Naphtuhim, [12]Pathrusim, Casluhim, and Caphtorim, the ancestor of the Philistines.[d] [13]Canaan's oldest son was Sidon; his other son was Heth. [14-16]Canaan was also the ancestor of the Jebusites, the Amorites, the Girgashites, the Hivites, and Arkites, the Sinites, the Arvadites, the Zemarites, and the Hamathites.

[17]Shem was the ancestor of Elam, Asshur, Arpachshad, Lud, Aram, Uz, Hul, Gether,

[a]1.6 *Riphath*: Most Hebrew manuscripts and two ancient translations (see also Genesis 10.2-5); some Hebrew manuscripts "Diphath." In Hebrew the letters "d" and "r" look almost exactly the same.
[b]1.7 *Dodanim*: Most Hebrew manuscripts and one ancient translation (see also Genesis 10.2-5); some Hebrew manuscripts "Rodanim." In Hebrew the letters "d" and "r" look almost exactly the same.
[c]1.8 *Ethiopia*: The Hebrew text has "Cush," which was a region south of Egypt that included parts of the present countries of Ethiopia and Sudan.   [d]1.12 *Casluhim, and Caphtorim, the ancestor of the Philistines*: The Hebrew text has "Casluhim, the ancestor of the Philistines, and Caphtorim"; but see Jeremiah 47.4 and Amos 9.7.

1.1-4 *Adam . . . Noah*: Adam was the name of the first human God created.

Noah and his family were saved from the great flood that God sent to destroy the earth's living creatures as punishment for man's sinfulness (Gen 6-9).

Agreements (Covenants)

1.5-7 *Japheth was the father . . . Dodanim*: The kingdoms of Japheth's descendants were located mostly in Asia Minor and the upper Euphrates River region. Elishah could refer to the island of Cyprus, whose ancient name was Alashia. Tarshish may refer to southern Spain, and the Dodanim may be the people of the island of Rhodes. **(See Map 1 on pg 1879.)**

1.8-16 *Ham was the father . . . the Hamathites*: The descendants of Ham, one of Noah's sons, ruled kingdoms located mainly in northeastern Africa and Canaan. **(See the article The Ancient World: Peoples, Powers, and Politics on pg 1780.)**

1.14-16 *Canaan*: In a curse, Noah declared that Canaan, Ham's son, would be his brothers' slave (Gen 9.18-27). This curse was fulfilled when Canaan (the land of Canaan's descendants) was taken over by the Israelites (descendants of Canaan's brother, Shem). It is the land that God promised to give to Abraham and his descendants (Gen 15.7; 17.7,8; Exod 3.8).

1.19 *earth was divided:* This division of the earth refers to Noah's sons being assigned tribal territories following the flood (Gen 10) and to how God scattered those tribes over all the earth by confusing their common language (Gen 11.1-9).

1.24-27 *Shem's descendants:* Shem's descendants were called "Shemites," which became the modern word "Semites." The people known as Israel descended from the Hebrews (children of "Eber"), one group of ancient Semitic peoples.

1.28-33 *Abraham:* God promised Abraham and his wife Sarah that they would have more descendants than could be counted (Gen 12.1-7; 17.1—18.15). Isaac was the son God promised Abraham and Sarah. Ishmael, the son of Abraham and Sarah's servant Hagar, was actually Abraham's oldest son. Ancient laws allowed a man to give a greater share of his property to his oldest son. Abraham gave most of his property to Isaac, even though he wasn't the oldest. God blessed Ishmael, however, by making him the ancestor of twelve tribes (Gen 17.20; 25.12-16), just as Israel was later organized into twelve tribes (Gen 49.1-28; Josh 13.14—19.51).

Abraham

1.34-37 *Abraham's son Isaac:* Isaac married Rebekah, and together they had twin sons, Esau and Jacob.

Birthright

Genealogies in the Bible

and Meshech;[e] they were the ancestors of the kingdoms named after them. [18]Arpachshad was Shelah's father and Eber's grandfather. [19]Eber named his first son Peleg,[f] because in his time the earth was divided into tribal regions. Eber's second son was Joktan, [20-23]the ancestor of Almodad, Sheleph, Hazarmaveth, Jerah, Hadoram, Uzal, Diklah, Ebal, Abimael, Sheba, Ophir, Havilah, and Jobab.

[24-27]Shem's descendants included Arpachshad, Shelah, Eber, Peleg, Reu, Serug, Nahor, Terah, and Abram, later renamed Abraham.

Abraham's Family
(Genesis 25.1-4,12-16)

[28]Abraham was the father of Isaac and Ishmael.

[29-31]Ishmael had twelve sons, who were born in the following order: Nebaioth, Kedar, Adbeel, Mibsam, Mishma, Dumah, Massa, Hadad, Tema, Jetur, Naphish, and Kedemah.

[32]Abraham and his slave woman Keturah had six sons: Zimran, Jokshan, Medan, Midian, Ishbak, and Shuah. Jokshan was the father of Sheba and Dedan. [33]Midian was the father of Ephah, Epher, Hanoch, Abida, and Eldaah.

Esau's Family
(Genesis 36.1-14)

[34]Abraham's son Isaac was the father of Esau and Jacob.[g] [35]Esau was the father of Eliphaz, Reuel, Jeush, Jalam, and Korah. [36]Eliphaz was the father of Teman, Omar, Zephi, Gatam, Kenaz, Timna, and Amalek. [37]Reuel was the father of Nahath, Zerah, Shammah, and Mizzah.

The First Edomites and Their Kings
(Genesis 36.20-43)

[38]Seir was the father of Lotan, Shobal, Zibeon, Anah, Dishon, Ezer, and Dishan. [39]Lotan was the father of Hori and Homam; Lotan's sister was Timna. [40]Shobal was the father of Alvan,[h] Manahath, Ebal, Shephi, and Onam. Zibeon was the father of Aiah and Anah.

[41]Anah was the father of Dishon and the grandfather of Hemdan,[i] Eshban, Ithran, and Cheran. [42]Ezer was the father of Bilhan, Zaavan, and Jaakan.[j] Dishan[k] was the father of Uz and Aran.

[43]Before kings ruled in Israel, Bela son of Beor ruled the country of Edom from its capital of Dinhabah. [44]After Bela's death, Jobab son of Zerah from Bozrah became king. [45]After Jobab's death, Husham from the land of Teman became king. [46]After Husham's death, Hadad son of Bedad became king and ruled from Avith. Earlier, Bedad had defeated the Midianites in the territory of Moab. [47]After Hadad's death, Samlah from Masrekah became king; [48]after Samlah's death, Shaul from the town of Rehoboth on the Euphrates River became king; [49]and after Shaul's death, Baal Hanan son of Achbor became king. [50]After Baal

[e]**1.17** *Meshech:* Most Hebrew manuscripts; a few Hebrew manuscripts and some manuscripts of one ancient translation "Mash" (see also Genesis 10.21-31). [f]**1.19** *Peleg:* In Hebrew "Peleg" means "divided." [g]**1.34** *Jacob:* The Hebrew text has "Israel," which was Jacob's name after God renamed him. [h]**1.40** *Alvan:* Or "Alian." [i]**1.41** *Hemdan:* Most Hebrew manuscripts and some manuscripts of one ancient translation (see also Genesis 36.26); other Hebrew manuscripts "Hamran." [j]**1.42** *Jaakan:* Or "Akan" (see Genesis 36.27). [k]**1.42** *Dishan:* The Hebrew text has "Dishon," another spelling of the name (see Genesis 36.28).

Hanan's death, Hadad ruled from Pai. His wife was Mehetabel, the daughter of Matred and granddaughter of Mezahab.

[51]The Edomite clans[l] were Timna, Alvah,[m] Jetheth, [52]Oholibamah, Elah, Pinon, [53]Kenaz, Teman, Mibzar, [54]Magdiel, and Iram.

The Descendants of Judah

2 [1-2]Jacob[n] was the father of twelve sons: Reuben, Simeon, Levi, Judah, Issachar, Zebulun, Dan, Joseph, Benjamin, Naphtali, Gad, and Asher.

[3]Judah and his Canaanite wife Bathshua had three sons: Er, Onan, and Shelah. But the LORD had Er put to death, because he disobeyed and did what the LORD hated. [4]Judah and his daughter-in-law Tamar also had two sons: Perez and Zerah.

[5]Perez was the father of Hezron and Hamul. [6]Zerah was the father of Zimri, Ethan, Heman, Calcol, and Darda.[o] [7]Achan,[p] who was a descendant of Zerah and the son of Carmi, caused trouble for Israel, because he kept for himself things that belonged only to the LORD.[q] [8]Ethan's son was Azariah.

The Ancestors of King David

[9]Hezron was the father of Jerahmeel, Ram, and Caleb.[r] [10]Ram was the father of Amminadab and the grandfather of Nahshon, a tribal leader of Judah. [11]Nahshon's descendants included Salma, Boaz, [12]Obed, and Jesse. [13-15]Jesse had seven sons, who were born in the following order: Eliab, Abinadab, Shimea, Nethanel, Raddai, Ozem, and David. [16]Jesse also had two daughters: Zeruiah and Abigail. Zeruiah was the mother of Abishai, Joab, and Asahel. [17]Abigail's husband was Jether, who was a descendant of Ishmael, and their son was Amasa.

The Descendants of Hezron

[18]Hezron's son Caleb married Azubah, and their daughter was Jerioth,[s] the mother of Jesher, Shobab, and Ardon. [19]After the death of Azubah, Caleb married Ephrath. Their son Hur [20]was the father of Uri and the grandfather of Bezalel.

[21]When Hezron was 60 years old, he married the daughter of Machir, who settled the region of Gilead. Their son Segub [22]was the father of Jair, who ruled 23 villages in the region of Gilead. [23]Some time later the nations of Geshur and Aram captured 60 towns in that region, including the villages that belonged to Jair, as well as the town of Kenath and the nearby villages. Everyone from the region of Gilead was a descendant of Machir.

[24]After the death of Hezron, Caleb married Ephrath, his father's wife. Their son was Ashhur,[t] who later settled the town of Tekoa.

The Descendants of Jerahmeel

[25]Jerahmeel, Hezron's oldest son, was the father of Ram, Bunah, Oren, Ozem,

[l]**1.51** *The Edomite clans*: Or "The leaders of the Edomite clans." [m]**1.51** *Alvah*: Or "Aliah." [n]**2.1,2** *Jacob*: See the note at 1.34. [o]**2.6** *Darda*: Most Hebrew manuscripts and two ancient translations (see also 1 Kings 4.30,31); some Hebrew manuscripts "Dara." [p]**2.7** *Achan*: The Hebrew text has "Achar," which means "trouble." [q]**2.7** *Achan . . . the LORD*: See Joshua 7.1-26. [r]**2.9** *Caleb*: The Hebrew text has "Chelubai," another form of the name. [s]**2.18** *married Azubah . . . Jerioth*: One possible meaning for the difficult Hebrew text. [t]**2.24** *After the death of Hezron . . . Ashhur*: Two ancient translations; Hebrew "After Hezron died in Caleb-Ephrathah, Abijah his wife gave birth to Ashhur."

● **2.1-2** *Jacob . . . Asher*: Jacob, the son of Isaac and grandson of Abraham, was Israel's third great ancestor. His name was changed to Israel when he struggled with God at Peniel near the Jabbok River (Gen 32.22-32). In Hebrew, one meaning of "Israel" is "a man who wrestles with God." Each of the twelve tribes of Israel traces its beginning to one of Jacob's twelve sons. **(See the chart Jacob's Children and Their Mothers on pg 1824.)**

⊗ Israel

● **2.3** *Judah*: The fourth son born to Jacob and Leah (Gen 29.35). The tribe of Judah eventually became the most important among the tribes of Israel (Gen 49.8-10). Judah's descendants included King David and Jesus (Matt 1.1-17; Luke 3.23-33).

● **2.9-15** *Hezron . . . David*: The writer of 1 CHRONICLES considers Hezron to be the most important of Judah's clans because David's ancestry is traced to Hezron's son, Ram.

● **2.21** *Gilead*: This area was east of the Jordan River between the Jabbok River in the south and the Yarmuk River in the north. **(See Map 6 on pg 1884.)**

2.54 *Bethlehem:* This town in the territory of Judah is a few miles south of Jerusalem. Bethlehem is where Jesus would be born. **(See Map 3 on pg 1881.)**

2.55 *Kenite:* The Kenites originally were not part of the Israelite people, but later many became part of Judah (Judg 1.16).

3.1-4 *King David . . . Absalom . . . Adonijah:* David, the most famous king Israel ever had, was king from about 1010 to 970 B.C. Many of the people of Israel hoped that one of his descendants would always be their king. The tragic story of David and his son, Absalom, who died in battle fighting against his father, is found in 2 Samuel 13–18. Adonijah attempted to take over David's kingship just prior to David's death but lost it to Solomon, his younger brother, who later had him killed (1 Kgs 1; 2.13-25).

David

3.1-4 *Hebron . . . Jerusalem:* Hebron was David's capital during the seven and a half years he was king of Judah but not yet king of all Israel. Hebron is located about 20 miles southwest of Jerusalem. Jerusalem is also known as "The City of David." When David conquered Jerusalem and brought the sacred chest to that city, he made it the political and religious center of the Israelite nation. **(See Map 4 on pg 1882.)**

Jerusalem

and Ahijah. [26]Jerahmeel had a second wife, Atarah, who gave birth to Onam. [27]Ram was the father of Maaz, Jamin, and Eker. [28]Onam was the father of Shammai and Jada.

Shammai was the father of Nadab and Abishur. [29]Abishur married Abihail, and their two sons were Ahban and Molid. [30]Nadab was the father of Seled and Appaim. Seled had no children; [31]Appaim's son was Ishi, the father of Sheshan and the grandfather of Ahlai.

[32]Jada was the father of Jether and Jonathan. Jether had no children, [33]but Jonathan had two sons: Peleth and Zaza.

[34-35]Sheshan had no sons, and so he let one of his daughters marry Jarha, his Egyptian slave. Their son was Attai, [36]the father of Nathan and the grandfather of Zabad. [37-41]Zabad's descendants included Ephlal, Obed, Jehu, Azariah, Helez, Eleasah, Sismai, Shallum, Jekamiah, and Elishama.

The Descendants of Caleb

[42]Caleb, Jerahmeel's brother, had the following descendants: Mesha,[u] Ziph, Mareshah,[v] Hebron, [43]and Hebron's four sons, Korah, Tappuah, Rekem, and Shema. [44]Shema was the father of Raham and the grandfather of Jorkeam. Rekem was the father of Shammai, [45]the grandfather of Maon, and the great-grandfather of Bethzur.

[46]Ephah was one of Caleb's wives,[w] and their sons were Haran, Moza, and Gazez. Haran named his son after his brother Gazez. [47]Ephah was the daughter of Jahdai,

who was also the father of Regem, Jotham, Geshan, Pelet, and Shaaph.[x]

[48]Maacah was another of Caleb's wives,[y] and their sons were Sheber and Tirhanah. [49]Later, they had two more sons: Shaaph the father of Madmannah, and Sheva the father of Machbenah and Gibea. Caleb's daughter was Achsah. [50-51]All of these were Caleb's descendants.

Hur, the oldest son of Caleb and Ephrath, had three sons: Shobal, Salma, and Hareph, who settled the town of Beth-Gader. [52]Shobal, who settled the town of Kiriath-Jearim, was the ancestor of Haroeh, half of the Menuhoth clan, [53]and the clans that lived near Kiriath-Jearim; they were the Ithrites, the Puthites, the Shumathites, and the Mishraites. The Zorathites and the Eshtaolites were descendants of the Mishraites.

[54]Salma settled the town of Bethlehem and was the ancestor of the Netophathites, the people of Atroth-Bethjoab, half of the Manahathite clan, and the Zorites. [55]Salma was also the ancestor of the clans in Jabez that kept the court and government records; they were the Tirathites, the Shimeathites, and the Sucathites. These clans were the descendants of Hammath the Kenite, who was also the ancestor of the Rechabites.

The Descendants of King David

3 [1-4]King David ruled from Hebron for seven years and six months, and during that time he had six sons, who were born in the following order: Amnon, Daniel, Absa-

---

[u]2.42 *Mesha:* Hebrew; one ancient translation "Mareshah."   [v]2.42 *following descendants . . . Mareshah:* One possible meaning for the difficult Hebrew text.   [w]2.46 *wives:* This translates a Hebrew word for women who were legally bound to a man, but without the full privileges of a wife.
[x]2.47 *Shaaph:* One possible meaning for the difficult Hebrew text of verse 47.   [y]2.48 *wives:* See the note at 2.46.

lom, Adonijah, Shephatiah, and Ithream. Ahinoam from Jezreel was the mother of Amnon; Abigail from Carmel was the mother of Daniel; Maacah daughter of King Talmai of Geshur was the mother of Absalom; Haggith was the mother of Adonijah; Abital was the mother of Shephatiah; and Eglah was the mother of Ithream.

David then ruled from Jerusalem for 33 years, [5]and during that time, he had 13 more sons. His wife Bathsheba[z] daughter of Ammiel gave birth to Shimea, Shobab, Nathan, and Solomon. [6-8]David's other sons included Ibhar, Elishua,[a] Eliphelet, Nogah, Nepheg, Japhia, Elishama, Eliada, and Eliphelet. [9]David's other wives[b] also gave birth to sons. Tamar was his daughter.

The Descendants of King Solomon

[10-15]Solomon's descendants included the following kings: Rehoboam, Abijah, Asa, Jehoshaphat, Jehoram,[c] Ahaziah, Joash, Amaziah, Azariah, Jotham, Ahaz, Hezekiah, Manasseh, Amon, and Josiah and his four sons, Johanan, Jehoiakim, Zedekiah, and Jehoahaz.[d] [16]Jehoiakim was the father of Jehoiachin and Zedekiah.

[17]Jehoiachin, who was taken to Babylon as a prisoner, had seven sons: Shealtiel, [18]Malchiram, Pedaiah, Shenazzar, Jekamiah, Hoshama, and Nedabiah. [19]Pedaiah had two sons: Zerubbabel and Shimei. Zerubbabel was the father of Meshullam, Hananiah, and Shelomith their sister. [20]He also had five other sons: Hashubah, Ohel, Berechiah, Hasadiah, and Jushabhesed. [21]Hananiah's descendants were Pelatiah, Jeshaiah, Rephaiah, Arnan, Obadiah, and Shecaniah,[e] [22]the father of Shemaiah and the grandfather of Hattush, Igal, Bariah, Neariah, and Shaphat. [23]Neariah was the father of Elioenai, Hizkiah, and Azrikam. [24]Elioenai was the father of Hodaviah, Eliashib, Pelaiah, Akkub, Johanan, Delaiah, and Anani.

The Descendants of Judah

4 Judah was the father of five sons: Perez, Hezron, Carmi, Hur, and Shobal. [2]Shobal was the father of Reaiah, the grandfather of Jahath, and the great-grandfather of Ahumai and Lahad. These men all belonged to the Zorathite clan.

[3-4]Hur was the oldest son of Caleb and Ephrath. Some of his descendants settled the town of Bethlehem. Hur's other descendants included Etam, Penuel, and Ezer. Etam's sons[f] were Jezreel, Ishma, and Idbash, and his daughter was Hazzelelponi. Penuel settled the town of Gedor, and Ezer settled the town of Hushah.

[5]Ashhur, who settled the town of Tekoa, had two wives: Helah and Naarah. [6]Ashhur and Naarah were the parents of Ahuzzam, Hepher, Temeni, and Haahashtari. [7]Ashhur and Helah were the parents of Zereth, Izhar, and Ethnan.

[8]Koz, the father of Anub and Zobebah, was also the ancestor of the clans of Aharhel, the son of Harum.

[z]3.5 *Bathsheba*: Two ancient translations (see also 2 Samuel 11); Hebrew "Bathshua." [a]3.6-8 *Elishua*: Some Hebrew manuscripts and some manuscripts of one ancient translation (see also 2 Samuel 5.14,15); most Hebrew manuscripts "Elishama." [b]3.9 *other wives*: See the note at 2.46. [c]3.10-15 *Jehoram*: The Hebrew text has "Joram," another spelling of the name. [d]3.10-15 *Jehoahaz*: The Hebrew text has "Shallum," probably another name for Jehoahaz (see also 2 Kings 23.30). [e]3.21 *Shecaniah*: One possible meaning for the difficult Hebrew text of verse 21. [f]4.3,4 *Etam's sons*: Some manuscripts of one ancient translation; Hebrew "Etam's ancestors."

3.5 *Bathsheba . . . Solomon*: David married Bathsheba after arranging to have her husband killed in battle (2 Sam 11.2-5,14-17,26,27). The baby from their affair died as punishment for David's sin (2 Sam 12.13-23). Solomon, David and Bathsheba's second son (2 Sam 12.24), followed his father as king of Israel.

Solomon

3.9 *other wives*: In the ancient world, an important man, such as a king, might have many wives. Some wives were considered true wives, meaning they and their children had special privileges, and their children were entitled to inherit a portion of the husband's wealth. Other "wives" were known as concubines. They were legally bound to their "husband," but they and their children did not have the same privileges. They were more like servants who could be bought and sold or easily sent away.

3.10-16 *Rehoboam . . . Zedekiah*: Rehoboam was the first and Zedekiah the last of Judah's kings after the division of Israel into the northern kingdom of Israel and the southern kingdom of Judah. They and the other kings named in these verses ruled Judah from 931 to 587 B.C. **(See the article From Joshua to the Exile: The People of Israel in the Promised Land on pg 1783.)**

3.17-19 *Shealtiel . . . Zerubbabel*: Elsewhere, Zerubbabel is called the son of Shealtiel (Ezra 3.2). The list here is of David's descendants following Israel's exile in Babylonia.

4.21-22 *Moabite women:* Moab was located to the east of the Dead Sea. The Moabites were enemies of Israel (Judg 3.12-30; 1 Sam 14.47-48). Omri, Israel's sixth king, conquered Moab. Moab remained under Israel's control for 40 years, until it rebelled during the reign of Ahaziah, Israel's eighth king, in 853 B.C. (See Map 4 on pg 1882.)

4.21-22 *weaving cloth:* Cloth was woven on a loom in a manner still used today. Linen from the flax plant, wool from sheep and goats, and camel hair were the most common fibers used (Exod 35.25,26; Prov 31.13,19,24).

4.28-33 *Simeon tribe . . . family records:* The Simeon tribe, descended from Jacob's second son (Gen 29.31-33), lost its normal position of leadership among the tribes because of the evil actions of Simeon and his older brother Reuben (Gen 49.3-7). The area described here is immediately southwest of Judah. Eventually the Simeon tribe was, for all practical purposes, absorbed into Judah. (See Map 3 on pg 1881.)

⁹Jabez was a man who got his name because of the pain he caused his mother during birth.ᵍ But he was still the most respected son in his family. ¹⁰One day he prayed to Israel's God, "Please bless me and give me a lot of land. Be with me so I will be safe from harm."ʰ And God did just what Jabez had asked.

¹¹Chelub was the brother of Shuhah and the father of Mehir. Later, Mehir had a son, Eshton, ¹²whose three sons were Bethrapha, Paseah, and Tehinnah. It was Tehinnah who settled the town of Nahash.ⁱ These men and their families lived in the town of Recah.

¹³Kenaz was the father of Othniel and Seraiah. Othniel had two sons: Hathath and Meonothai,ʲ ¹⁴who was the father of Ophrah. Seraiah was the father of Joab, who settled a place called "Valley of Crafts"ᵏ because the people who lived there were experts in making things.

¹⁵Caleb son of Jephunneh had three sons: Iru, Elah, and Naam. Elah was the father of Kenaz.

¹⁶Jehallelel was the father of Ziph, Ziphah, Tiria, and Asarel.

¹⁷-¹⁸Ezrah was the father of Jether, Mered, Epher, and Jalon. Mered was married to Bithiah the daughter of the king of Egypt. They had a daughter named Miriam and two sons: Shammai and Ishbah. It was Ishbah who settled the town of Eshtemoa. Mered was also married to a woman from the tribe of Judah, and their sons were Jered, Heber, and Jekuthiel. Jered settled the town of Gedor; Heber settled the town of Soco; and Jekuthiel settled the town of Zanoah.

¹⁹A man named Hodiah was married to the sister of Naham. Hodiah's descendants included Keilah of the Garmite clan and Eshtemoa of the Maacathite clan.

²⁰Shimon was the father of Amnon, Rinnah, Benhanan, and Tilon.

Ishi was the father of Zoheth and Benzoheth.

²¹-²²Judah also had a son named Shelah, whose descendants included Jokim and the people of the town of Cozeba, as well as Er who settled the town of Lecah and Laadah who settled the town of Mareshah. The people who lived in Beth-Ashbea were also descendants of Shelah, and they were experts in weaving cloth. Shelah was the ancestor of Joash and Saraph, two men who married Moabite women and then settled near Bethlehemˡ—but these family records are very old. ²³The members of these clans were the potters who lived in the towns of Netaim and Gederah and worked for the king.

The Descendants of Simeon

²⁴Simeon had five sons: Nemuel, Jamin, Jarib, Zerah, and Shaul. ²⁵The descendants of Shaul included his son Shallum, his grandson Mibsam, and his great-grandson Mishma. ²⁶The descendants of Mishma included his son Hammuel, his grandson Zaccur, and his great-grandson Shimei. ²⁷Shimei had 16 sons and 6 daughters. But his brothers did not have as many children, so the Simeon tribe was smaller than the Judah tribe.

²⁸-³¹Before David became king, the people of the Simeon tribe lived in the fol-

ᵍ4.9 *Jabez . . . pain . . . birth*: In Hebrew "Jabez" sounds like "pain."   ʰ4.10 *I . . . harm*: Or "keep me from harm, so I won't cause any pain."   ⁱ4.12 *who settled the town of Nahash*: Or "who was the father of Irnahash."   ʲ4.13 *and Meonothai*: Two ancient translations; these words are not in the Hebrew text.   ᵏ4.14 *Valley of Crafts*: Hebrew "Geharashim."   ˡ4.21,22 *who married Moabite women and then settled near Bethlehem*: Or "who ruled in Moab and Jashubi-Lahem" or "who ruled in Moab but then returned to Lahem."

Jabez prayed to Israel's God, *"Please bless me and give me a lot of land. Be with me so I will be safe from harm."*
1 CHR 4.10

lowing towns: Beersheba, Moladah, Hazar-Shual, Bilhah, Ezem, Tolad, Bethuel, Hormah, Ziklag, Beth-Marcaboth, Hazar-susim, Bethbiri, and Shaaraim. [32]They also lived in the five villages of Etam, Ain, Rimmon, Tochen, and Ashan, [33]as well as in the nearby villages as far as the town of Baal. These are the places where Simeon's descendants had settled, according to their own family records.

[34-38]As their families and clans became larger, the people of Simeon had the following leaders: Meshobab, Jamlech, Joshah son of Amaziah, Joel, Jehu,[m] Elioenai, Jaakobah, Jeshohaiah, Asaiah, Adiel, Jesimiel, Benaiah, and Ziza.[n] [39]When the people needed more pastureland for their flocks and herds, they looked as far as the eastern side of the valley where the town of Gerar[o] is located, [40]and they found a lot of good pastureland that was quiet and undisturbed. This had once belonged to the Hamites, [41]but when Hezekiah was king of Judah, the descendants of Simeon attacked and forced the Hamites and Meunites off the land, then settled there.

[42]Some time later, 500 men from the Simeon tribe went into Edom[p] under the command of Pelatiah, Neariah, Rephaiah, and Uzziel the sons of Ishi. [43]They killed the last of the Amalekites and lived there from then on.

The Descendants of Reuben

5 Reuben was the oldest son of Jacob,[q] but he lost his rights as the first-born son[r] because he slept with one of his father's wives.[s] The honor of the first-born son was then given to Joseph, [2]even though it was the Judah tribe that became the most powerful and produced a leader.

[3]Reuben had four sons: Hanoch, Pallu, Hezron, and Carmi.

[4-6]The descendants of Joel included Shemaiah, Gog, Shimei, Micah, Reaiah, Baal, and Beerah, a leader of the Reuben tribe. Later, King Tiglath Pileser of Assyria took Beerah away as prisoner.

[7-8]The family records also include Jeiel, who was a clan leader, Zechariah, and Bela son of Azaz and grandson of Shema of the Joel clan. They lived in the territory around the town of Aroer, as far north as Nebo and Baal-Meon, [9]and as far east as the desert just west of the Euphrates River. They needed this much land because they owned too many cattle to keep them all in Gilead.

[10]When Saul was king, the Reuben tribe attacked and defeated the Hagrites, then took over their land east of Gilead.

The Descendants of Gad

[11]The tribe of Gad lived in the region of Bashan, north of the Reuben tribe. Gad's territory extended all the way to the town of Salecah. [12]Some of the clan leaders were Joel, Shapham, Janai, and Shaphat. [13]Their relatives included Michael, Meshullam, Sheba, Jorai, Jacan, Zia, and Eber.

[14]They were all descendants of Abihail, whose family line went back through Huri, Jaroah, Gilead, Michael, Jeshishai, Jahdo, and Buz. [15]Ahi, the son of Abdiel and the grandson of Guni, was the leader of their clan.

---

[m]**4.34-38** *Jehu:* Hebrew "Jehu son of Joshibiah son of Seraiah son of Asiel." [n]**4.34-38** *Ziza:* Hebrew "Ziza son of Shiphi son of Allon son of Jedaiah son of Shimri son of Shemaiah." [o]**4.39** *Gerar:* One ancient translation; Hebrew "Gedor." [p]**4.42** *Edom:* The Hebrew text has "Mount Seir," a common name for the nation of Edom. [q]**5.1** *Jacob:* See the note at 1.34. [r]**5.1** *rights as the first-born son:* The first-born son inherited the largest amount of property, as well as the leadership of the family. [s]**5.1** *wives:* See Genesis 35.22; 49.3,4.

● **4.39-42** *Gerar . . . Edom:* Gerar is possibly Gedor on the Philistine border and was known for its rich pasturelands. Edom was a land directly south of the Dead Sea. (See Map 4 on pg 1882.)

● **5.1** *rights as the first-born son:* The first-born son inherited the largest amount of property and leadership of the family. Because Reuben sinned (Gen 35.22), he lost his birthright to Joseph and his descendants (Gen 49.3,4; Gen 48.19,20).

◯ℝ Birthright

● **5.4-6** *King Tiglath Pileser of Assyria:* From 745 to 727 B.C., Assyria threatened and invaded the northern kingdom of Israel. The event in this verse probably took place around 733 B.C.

◯ℝ Assyria

● **5.9** *Euphrates River:* The Euphrates River was one of the four rivers flowing out of Eden (Gen 2.14). (See Map 1 on pg 1879.)

● **5.10** *Reuben tribe . . . defeated the Hagrites:* The Reuben tribe is associated with the tribe of Judah (Gen 29.32,35). The Hagrites were nomads from northern Arabia. (See Map 3 on pg 1881.)

◯ℝ Nomads (Wandering Herders)

5.16 *Gad . . . Sharon:* The tribe of Gad (Gen 30.9,10) was larger and more important than Reuben (Deut 33.6,20, 21). Bashan was known for its rich pastures, forests, and herds of cattle. "Sharon" here probably means pasturelands east of the Jordan. **(See Map 4 on pg 1882.)**

5.20-22 *these soldiers . . . God was fighting this battle:* A favorite theme of the writer of 1 CHRONICLES: Those who trust God in battle will be victorious over their enemies.

Holy War (The LORD's Battles)

5.23 *East Manasseh:* Ephraim and Manasseh were the sons of Jacob's son Joseph. Each received a share of land in Canaan. **(See Map 3 on pg 1881.)**

6.1-30 *Levi . . . Merari's descendants:* This family list traces the ancestry of Israel's high priesthood from Levi to Aaron, from Aaron to Eleazar, and from Eleazar to Phinehas. God had promised that Phineas' descendants would always be priests (Num 25.11-13). See Num 4.1—5.33, which describes the specific duties of the Levite clans of Kohath, Gershon, and Merari.

Israel's Priests

6.4-14 *Zadok . . . Zadok:* It is not clear why Zadok is listed twice. Solomon appointed him high priest in Jerusalem because Zadok had favored Solomon over Adonijah as David's successor (1 Kgs 1.5-8,39; 2.35).

Nebuchadnezzar

[16]The people of Gad lived in the towns in the regions of Bashan and Gilead, as well as in the pastureland of Sharon. [17]Their family records were written when Jotham was king of Judah and Jeroboam was king of Israel.

[18]The tribes of Reuben, Gad, and East Manasseh had 44,760 soldiers trained to fight in battle with shields, swords, bows, and arrows. [19]They fought against the Hagrites and the tribes of Jetur, Naphish, and Nodab. [20]Whenever these soldiers went to war against their enemies, they prayed to God and trusted him to help. That's why the tribes of Reuben, Gad, and East Manasseh defeated the Hagrites and their allies. [21]These Israelite tribes captured 50,000 camels, 250,000 sheep, 2,000 donkeys, and 100,000 people. [22]Many of the Hagrites died in battle, because God was fighting this battle against them. The tribes of Reuben, Gad, and East Manasseh lived in that territory until they were taken as prisoners to Assyria.[t]

The Tribe of East Manasseh

[23]East Manasseh was a large tribe, so its people settled in the northern region of Bashan, as far north as Baal-Hermon,[u] Senir, and Mount Hermon. [24]Epher, Ishi, Eliel, Azriel, Jeremiah, Hodaviah, and Jahdiel were their clan leaders; they were well-known leaders and brave soldiers.

The Tribes of Reuben, Gad, and East Manasseh Are Defeated

[25]The people of the tribes of Reuben, Gad, and East Manasseh were unfaithful to the God their ancestors had worshiped, and they started worshiping the gods of the nations that God had forced out of Canaan. [26]So God sent King Tiglath Pileser[v] of Assyria to attack these Israelite tribes. The king led them away as prisoners to Assyria, and from then on, he forced them to live in Halah, Habor, Hara, and near the Gozan River.

The Descendants of Levi

6 Levi was the father of Gershon, Kohath, and Merari. [2]Kohath was the father of Amram, Izhar, Hebron, and Uzziel. [3]Amram was the father of Aaron, Moses, and Miriam.

Aaron had four sons: Nadab, Abihu, Eleazar, and Ithamar.

[4-14]Eleazar's descendants included Phinehas, Abishua, Bukki, Uzzi, Zerahiah, Meraioth, Amariah, Ahitub, Zadok, Ahimaaz, Azariah, Johanan, Azariah the priest who served in the temple built by King Solomon, Amariah, Ahitub, Zadok, Shallum, Hilkiah, Azariah, Seraiah, and Jehozadak. [15]King Nebuchadnezzar of Babylonia took Jehozadak to Babylon as prisoner when the LORD let the people of Judah and Jerusalem be dragged from their land.[w]

[16]Levi's three sons had sons of their own. [17]Gershon was the father of Libni and Shimei. [18]Kohath was the father of Amram, Izhar, Hebron, and Uzziel. [19]Merari was the father of Mahli and Mushi. These descendants of Levi each became leaders of their own clans.

[20-21]Gershon's descendants included Libni, Jahath, Zimmah, Joah, Iddo, Zerah, and Jeatherai.

[t]**5.22** *they were taken as prisoners to Assyria:* See 2 Kings 15.29; 17.5-23.   [u]**5.23** *Baal-Hermon:* The location of this place is unknown.   [v]**5.26** *King Tiglath Pileser:* The Hebrew text also includes "King Pul," another name by which he was known.   [w]**6.15** *King Nebuchadnezzar . . . dragged from their land:* See 2 Kings 24.8-17; 25.1-21.

22-24Kohath's descendants included Amminadab, Korah, Assir, Elkanah, Ebiasaph, Assir, Tahath, Uriel, Uzziah, and Shaul.

25Elkanah was the father of Amasai and Ahimoth. 26-27Ahimoth's descendants included Elkanah, Zophai, Nahath, Eliab, Jeroham, and Elkanah.

28Samuel was the father of Joel[x] and Abijah, born in that order.

29-30Merari's descendants included Mahli, Libni, Shimei, Uzzah, Shimea, Haggiah, and Asaiah.

The Temple Musicians

31After King David had the sacred chest moved to Jerusalem, he appointed musicians from the Levi tribe to be in charge of the music at the place of worship. 32These musicians served at the sacred tent and later at the LORD's temple that King Solomon built.

33-38Here is a list of these musicians and their family lines:

Heman from the Kohathite clan was the director. His ancestors went all the way back to Jacob and included Joel, Samuel, Elkanah, Jeroham, Eliel, Toah, Zuph, Elkanah, Mahath, Amasai, Elkanah, Joel, Azariah, Zephaniah, Tahath, Assir, Ebiasaph, Korah, Izhar, Kohath, Levi.

39-43Asaph was Heman's relative and served as his assistant. Asaph's ancestors included Berechiah, Shimea, Michael, Baaseiah, Malchijah, Ethni, Zerah, Adaiah, Ethan, Zimmah, Shimei, Jahath, Gershon, and Levi.

44-47Ethan was also Heman's relative and served as his assistant. Ethan belonged to the Merari clan, and his ancestors included Kishi, Abdi, Malluch, Hashabiah, Amaziah, Hilkiah, Amzi, Bani, Shemer, Mahli, Mushi, Merari, and Levi.

48The rest of the Levites were appointed to work at the sacred tent.

The Descendants of Aaron

49Only Aaron and his descendants were allowed to offer sacrifices and incense on the two altars at the sacred tent.[y] They were in charge of the most holy place and the ceremonies to forgive sins, just as God's servant Moses had commanded.

50-53Aaron's descendants included his son Eleazar, Phinehas, Abishua, Bukki, Uzzi, Zerahiah, Meraioth, Amariah, Ahitub, Zadok, and Ahimaaz.

The Towns for the Levites

(Joshua 21.1-42)

54Aaron's descendants belonged to the Levite clan of Kohath, and they were the first group chosen to receive towns to live in. 55They received the town of Hebron in the territory of Judah and the pastureland around it. 56But the farmland and villages around Hebron were given to Caleb son of Jephunneh. 57-59So Aaron's descendants received the following Safe Towns[z] and the pastureland around them: Hebron, Libnah, Jattir, Eshtemoa, Hilen, Debir, Ashan, and Beth-Shemesh. 60From the Benjamin tribe they were given the towns of Geba, Alemeth, and Anathoth and the pastureland around them. Thirteen towns were given to Aaron's descendants.

61The rest of the Levite clan of Kohath received ten towns from West Manasseh.

[x]6.28 *Joel*: Two ancient translations (see also verse 33 and 1 Samuel 8.1,2); this name is not in the Hebrew text.   [y]6.49 *the two altars at the sacred tent*: The Hebrew text mentions two different altars: A large altar for offering sacrifices, and a smaller altar for offering incense.   [z]6.57-59 *Safe Towns*: These were special towns set aside where a person who had accidentally killed someone could run for protection from the victim's relatives (see Numbers 35.9-15; Deuteronomy 19.1-13; Joshua 20.1-9).

Exile

6.28 *Samuel*: Elsewhere, Samuel is said to be of the tribe of Ephraim (1 Sam 1.1-19). Perhaps his role as priest and prophet led to the assumption that he had family ties to the Levites. Samuel also is listed as an ancestor of the temple musicians (1 Chr 6.33-38).

6.31 *musicians from the Levi tribe*: David is given credit for establishing the tradition of musicians for the temple. The Levites from the families listed here were given the duty of singing God's praises. Those families are listed in order of importance or rank in 6.33-47. In later times, the Levite musicians began the tradition of choosing and singing psalms that were suitable to particular occasions, sacrifices, or festivals, much as this is done today.

The Sacred Tent

6.49 *sacrifices*: These gifts to God included certain animals, grains, fruits, and sweet-smelling spices. Israelites offered sacrifices to give thanks to God, to ask for God's forgiveness and blessing, and to make a payment for doing wrong. (See the chart Sacrifices and Offerings on pg 1828.)

6.54-81 *Aaron's descendants . . . pastureland around them*: The Levites were not given complete ownership of the cities. Rather, they were given certain privileges and property rights within those cities (Lev 25.32-34; Num 35.1-8). (See Map 3 on pg 1881.)

Safe Towns

6.65 *with the LORD's help:* Pieces of wood or stone called "lots" were used to find out what God wanted his people to do. This is similar to drawing straws or flipping a coin today. However "casting lots" was not considered mere chance, since it was believed that God guided which lots were chosen and who chose them.

7.1-5 *Issachar . . . warriors:* Issachar was the fifth son of Jacob and Leah (Gen 30.16-18). The family listings of Israel's northern tribes begin with the descendants of Issachar. As the listing includes only four generations, the writer of 1 CHRONICLES probably had only limited family records and military census figures available. **(See Map 3 on pg 1881.)**

7.6-12 *Benjamin . . . Dan:* Benjamin was Jacob and Rachel's youngest son (Gen 35.16-18). It would be more logical for the family listing of Zebulun rather than Benjamin to follow the listing of Issachar (see 2.1; 12.23-27; 27.16-22). The small Benjamin tribe was in the south next to Judah. Benjamin's family list appears again in chapter 8, while there is no family listing for Zebulun in chapters 2–9. The list here does not match other lists of either Zebulun or Benjamin (Gen 46.8-22; Num 26.26-27,38-41). Dan was the first-born son of Jacob and Rachel's maid Bilhah (Gen 30.4-6). The Dan tribe eventually settled in the north.

[62] The Levite clan of Gershon received thirteen towns from the tribes of Issachar, Asher, Naphtali, and East Manasseh in Bashan. [63] The Levite clan of Merari received twelve towns from the tribes of Reuben, Gad, and Zebulun.

[64] So the people of Israel gave the Levites towns to live in and the pastureland around them. [65] All the towns were chosen with the LORD's help,[a] including those towns from the tribes of Judah, Simeon, and Benjamin.

[66] Some of the families of the Kohath clan received their towns from the tribe of Ephraim. [67-69] These families received the following Safe Towns and the pastureland around them: Shechem in the hill country, Gezer, Jokmeam, Beth-Horon, Aijalon, and Gath-Rimmon. [70] And from West Manasseh they received Aner and Bileam, together with their pastureland.

[71] The Gershonite clan received two towns from the tribe of East Manasseh: Golan in Bashan and Ashtaroth, including the pastureland around them. [72-73] The Gershonites also received four towns from the tribe of Issachar: Kedesh, Daberath, Ramoth, and Anem, including the pastureland around them. [74-75] The Gershonites received four towns from the tribe of Asher: Mashal, Abdon, Hukok, and Rehob, including the pastureland around them. [76] Finally, the Gershonites received three towns from the tribe of Naphtali: Kedesh in Galilee, Hammon, and Kiriathaim, including the pastureland around them.

[77] The rest of the Merari clan received the towns of Rimmono and Tabor and their pastureland from the tribe of Zebulun. [78-79] They also received four towns east of the Jordan River from the tribe of

Reuben: Bezer in the flatlands, Jahzah, Kedemoth, and Mephaath, including the pastures around them. [80-81] And from the tribe of Gad the Merarites received the towns of Ramoth in Gilead, Mahanaim, Heshbon, and Jazer, including the pastureland around them.

The Descendants of Issachar

7 Issachar was the father of four sons: Tola, Puah, Jashub, and Shimron. [2] Tola was the father of Uzzi, Rephaiah, Jeriel, Jahmai, Ibsam, and Shemuel, who were all brave soldiers and family leaders in their clan. There were 22,600 people in Tola's family by the time David became king.

[3] Uzzi was the father of Izrahiah and the grandfather of Michael, Obadiah, Joel, and Isshiah, who were also family leaders. [4] Their families were so large that they had 36,000 soldiers in their clans. [5] In fact, according to family records, the tribe of Issachar had a total of 87,000 warriors.

The Descendants of Benjamin and Dan

[6] Benjamin was the father of three sons: Bela, Becher, and Jediael.

[7] Bela was the father of Ezbon, Uzzi, Uzziel, Jerimoth, and Iri. They were all brave soldiers and family leaders in their father's clan. The number of soldiers in their clan was 22,034.

[8] Becher was the father of Zemirah, Joash, Eliezer, Elioenai, Omri, Jeremoth, Abijah, Anathoth, and Alemeth. [9] The official family records listed 20,200 soldiers in the families of this clan, as well as their family leaders.

[10] Jediael was the father of Bilhan and the

[a] **6.65** *with the LORD's help:* The Hebrew text has "by lot." Pieces of wood or stone (called "lots") were used to find out what God wanted his people to do.

grandfather of Jeush, Benjamin, Ehud, Chenaanah, Zethan, Tarshish, and Ahishahar. [11] They were family leaders in their clan, which had 17,200 soldiers prepared to fight in battle. [12] Ir was the father of Shuppim and Huppim, who also belonged to this clan.

Dan[b] was the father of Hushim.

The Descendants of Naphtali

[13] Naphtali's mother was Bilhah,[c] and he was the father of Jahziel, Guni, Jezer, and Shallum.

The Descendants of Manasseh

[14] Manasseh and his Syrian wife[d] were the parents of Asriel and Machir the father of Gilead. [15] Machir found a wife for Huppim and one for Shuppim. Machir had a sister named Maacah.

Zelophehad was also a descendant of Manasseh, and he had five daughters.[e]

[16] Machir and his wife Maacah were the parents of Peresh and Sheresh. Peresh was the father of Ulam and Rekem. [17] Ulam was the father of Bedan. These were all descendants of Gilead, the son of Machir and the grandson of Manasseh.

[18] Gilead's sister Hammolecheth was the mother of Ishhod, Abiezer, and Mahlah.

[19] Shemida, another descendant of Manasseh, was the father of Ahian, Shechem, Likhi, and Aniam.

The Descendants of Ephraim

[20] Ephraim was the father of Shuthelah and the ancestor of Bered, Tahath, Eleadah, Tahath, [21] Zabad, and Shuthelah.

Ephraim had two other sons, Ezer and Elead. But they were killed when they tried to steal livestock from the people who lived in the territory of Gath. [22] Ephraim mourned for his sons a long time, and his relatives came to comfort him. [23] Some time later his wife gave birth to another son, and Ephraim named him Beriah, because he was born during a time of misery.[f]

[24] Ephraim's daughter was Sheerah. She built the towns of Lower Beth-Horon, Upper Beth-Horon, and Uzzen-Sheerah.

[25] Ephraim also had a son named Rephah, and his descendants included Resheph, Telah, Tahan, [26] Ladan, Ammihud, Elishama, [27] Nun, and Joshua.

[28] The descendants of Ephraim took over the territory as far south as Bethel, as far east as Naaran, and as far west as Gezer. Their territory included all the villages around these towns, as well as Shechem, Ayyah, and the nearby villages.

[29] The descendants of Manasseh settled in the territory that included Beth-Shan, Taanach, Megiddo, Dor, and the nearby villages.

The descendants of Joseph[g] lived in these towns and villages.

The Descendants of Asher

[30] Asher had four sons, Imnah, Ishvah, Ishvi, and Beriah, and one daughter, Serah. [31] Beriah was the father of Heber and Malchiel the father of Birzaith. [32] Heber was the father of three sons, Japhlet, Shomer, and Hotham, and one daughter, Shua. [33] Japhlet was the father of Pasach, Bimhal, and Ashvath. [34] Shomer was the father of Ahi, Rohgah, Hubbah, and Aram.

[b]7.12 *Dan*: The Hebrew text has "Aher," which can mean "someone else" (see Genesis 46.23-25).
[c]7.13 *Bilhah*: One of Jacob's wives and the mother of Dan and Naphtali (see Genesis 46.23-25).
[d]7.14 *wife*: See the note at 2.46.   [e]7.15 *Zelophehad . . . daughters*: One possible meaning for the difficult Hebrew text (see also Numbers 26.28-33).   [f]7.23 *Beriah . . . misery*: In Hebrew "Beriah" sounds like "in misery."   [g]7.29 *Joseph*: Hebrew "Joseph son of Israel."

7.13,14 *Naphtali's mother . . . Bilhah . . . Manasseh*: Naphtali was the son of Jacob and Rachel's servant Bilhah. The Naphtali tribe settled the region north and west of Lake Galilee.

7.30-40 *Asher*: Asher was the second son of Jacob and his wife Leah's servant Zilpah (Gen 30.9-13). The Asher tribe settled in the north along the Mediterranean Coast. **(See Map 3 on pg 1881.)**

8.1-40 *Benjamin had five sons . . . grandfather of King Saul . . . tribe of Benjamin:* The family line of Benjamin is given extra attention, probably because it was the tribe of Saul, Israel's first king (8.33), and because Benjaminites were among those who helped in the rebuilding of Jerusalem under Nehemiah after the exile (Neh 11.7-9). Jerusalem is located in what was the original territory of the Benjamin tribe. Note that though Saul was Israel's first king, his family lists are given at the end of chapter 8 while David's family lists are given first in chapter 3. **(See the article From Joshua to the Exile: The People of Israel in the Promised Land on pg 1783.)**

8.28 *These were . . . lived in Jerusalem:* Many Benjaminites were probably living in Jerusalem at the time of the writing of 1 CHRONICLES.

8.33 *King Saul . . . Jonathan:* Saul, Israel's first king, ruled from about 1030 to 1010 B.C. Jonathan, Saul's son, was the best friend of David, the second king of Israel. The dramatic story of the loyal friendship between Jonathan and David is told in 1 Sam 18–20 and 2 Sam 1.26.

[35]And Japhlet's brother Hotham[h] was the father of Zophah, Imna, Shelesh, and Amal. [36]Zophah was the father of Suah, Harnepher, Shual, Beri, Imrah, [37]Bezer, Hod, Shamma, Shilshah, Ithran, and Beera. [38]Jether was the father of Jephunneh, Pispa, and Ara.

[39]Ulla was the father of Arah, Hanniel, and Rizia.

[40]These were the descendants of Asher, and they were all respected family leaders and brave soldiers. The tribe of Asher had a total of 26,000 soldiers.

More Descendants of Benjamin

8 Benjamin had five sons, who were born in the following order: Bela, Ashbel, Aharah, [2]Nohah, and Rapha. [3]Bela was the father of Addar, Gera, Abihud, [4]Abishua, Naaman, Ahoah, [5]Gera, Shephuphan, and Huram.

[6-7]Ehud was the father of Naaman, Ahijah, and Gera. They were clan leaders in the town of Geba, but were later forced to move to the town of Manahath, and Gera led the way. He had two sons: Uzza and Ahihud.

[8-11]Shaharaim and his wife Hushim had two sons: Abitub and Elpaal. But Shaharaim later divorced her and his other wife, Baara. Then he moved to the country of Moab and married Hodesh, and they had seven sons: Jobab, Zibia, Mesha, Malcam, Jeuz, Sachia, and Mirmah. They were all family leaders in his clan. [12]Elpaal was the father of Eber, Misham, and Shemed, who settled the towns of Ono and Lod, as well as the nearby villages.

[13]Beriah and Shema were family leaders in the clan that lived in the town of Aijalon and that forced out the people of Gath. [14-16]Beriah's descendants included Ahio, Shashak, Jeremoth, Zebadiah, Arad, Eder, Michael, Ishpah, and Joha. [17-18]Elpaal's descendants included Zebadiah, Meshullam, Hizki, Heber, Ishmerai, Izliah, and Jobab. [19-21]Shimei's descendants included Jakim, Zichri, Zabdi, Elienai, Zillethai, Eliel, Adaiah, Beraiah, and Shimrath. [22-25]Shashak's descendants included Ishpan, Eber, Eliel, Abdon, Zichri, Hanan, Hananiah, Elam, Anthothijah, Iphdeiah, and Penuel. [26-27]Jeroham's descendants included Shamsherai, Sheariah, Athaliah, Jaareshiah, Elijah, and Zichri. [28]These were the family leaders in their ancestor's clan, and they and their descendants lived in Jerusalem.

[29]Jeiel[i] settled the town of Gibeon. He and his wife Maacah lived there [30]along with their sons, who were born in the following order: Abdon, Zur, Kish, Baal, Ner,[j] Nadab, [31]Gedor, Ahio, Zecher, [32]and Mikloth the father of Shimeah. Some of them went to live in Jerusalem near their relatives.

The Descendants of King Saul

[33]Ner was the father of Kish and the grandfather of King Saul.

Saul had four sons: Jonathan, Malchishua, Abinadab, and Eshbaal.[k] [34]Jonathan was the father of Meribbaal,[l] the grandfather of Micah, [35]and the great-grandfather of Pithon, Melech, Tarea, and Ahaz. [36]Saul's other descendants were Jehoaddah, Alemeth, Azmaveth, Zimri, Moza, [37]Binea, Raphah, Eleasah, Azel, [38]as

---

[h]7.35 *Hotham:* The Hebrew text has "Helem," another spelling of the name.   [i]8.29 *Jeiel:* One ancient translation and 9.35; the Hebrew text does not have this name.   [j]8.30 *Ner:* One ancient translation and 9.36; the Hebrew text does not have this name.   [k]8.33 *Eshbaal:* Also called "Ishbosheth" (see 2 Samuel 2.8 and the note there).   [l]8.34 *Meribbaal:* Also called "Mephibosheth" (see 2 Samuel 4.4 and the note there).

well as Azel's six sons: Azrikam, Bocheru, Ishmael, Sheariah, Obadiah, and Hanan. [39]Azel's brother Eshek was the father of Ulam, Jeush, and Eliphelet. [40]Ulam's sons were brave soldiers who were experts at using a bow and arrows. They had a total of 150 children and grandchildren.

All of these belonged to the tribe of Benjamin.

The People Who Returned from Babylonia and Settled in Jerusalem

9 Everyone in Israel was listed in the official family records that were included in the history of Israel's kings.

The people of Judah were taken to Babylonia as prisoners because they sinned against the LORD. [2]And the first people to return to their towns included priests, Levites, temple workers, and other Israelites. [3]People from the tribes of Judah, Benjamin, Ephraim, and Manasseh settled in Jerusalem.

[4-6]There were 690 people from the Judah tribe who settled in Jerusalem. They were all descendants of Judah's three sons: Perez, Shelah, and Zerah. Their leaders were Uthai, Asaiah, and Jeuel. Uthai was the son of Ammihud and a descendant of Omri, Imri, Bani, and Perez. Asaiah was a descendant of Shelah; Jeuel was a descendant of Zerah.

[7-9]There were also 956 family leaders from the Benjamin tribe who settled in Jerusalem. They included: Sallu son of Meshullam, grandson of Hodaviah, and great-grandson of Hassenuah; Ibneiah son of Jeroham; Elah son of Uzzi and grandson of Michri; Meshullam son of Shephatiah, grandson of Reuel, and great-grandson of Ibnijah.

The Priests Who Settled in Jerusalem

[10-12]Here is a list of priests who settled in Jerusalem: Jedaiah; Jehoiarib; Jachin; Azariah, who was a temple official, and whose ancestors included Hilkiah, Meshullam, Zadok, Meraioth, and Ahitub; Adaiah son of Jeroham, whose ancestors included Pashhur and Malchijah; Maasai son of Adiel, whose ancestors included Jahzerah, Meshullam, Meshillemith, and Immer. [13]There was a total of 1,760 priests, all of them family leaders in their clan and trained in the work at the temple.

The Levites Who Settled in Jerusalem

[14-16]Here is a list of Levites who settled in Jerusalem: Shemaiah from the Merari clan, whose ancestors included Hasshub, Azrikam, and Hashabiah; Bakbakkar; Heresh; Galal; Mattaniah son of Mica, whose ancestors included Zichri and Asaph; Obadiah son of Shemaiah, whose ancestors included Galal and Jeduthun; Berechiah son of Asa and grandson of Elkanah, who had lived in the villages near the town of Netophah.

The Temple Guards Who Settled in Jerusalem

[17]Shallum, Akkub, Talmon, Ahiman, and their relatives were the guards at the temple gates. Shallum was the leader of this clan, [18]and for a long time they had been the guards at the King's Gate on the east side of the city. Before that, their ancestors guarded the entrance to the Levite camp. [19]Shallum son of Kore,[m] as well as the other men in the Korahite clan, guarded

[m]9.19 *Shallum son of Kore*: Hebrew "Shallum son of Kore, grandson of Ebiasaph, and great-grandson of Korah."

CR   Babylon

CR   Exile

● 9.2 *other Israelites:* Before David united the whole kingdom under the name "Israel," the name referred to the ten northern tribes led by the tribe of Ephraim. "Judah" referred to the two southern tribes led by the tribe of Judah. Following the death of David's son, Solomon, the nation of Israel was once again divided (1 Kgs 12.1-20). From that time on, "Israel" usually referred to the northern kingdom, and the people who lived there were called "Israelites," as is the case in this verse. The southern kingdom was called "Judah." Some of the people left the northern kingdom and became citizens of Jerusalem so that they could worship God in that city as God's law required. As a result, Judah had citizens from the northern tribes such as Ephraim and Manasseh (9.3) as well as from the southern tribes of Judah and Benjamin.

● 9.2-34 *And the first people . . . lived in Jerusalem:* These lists show the concern the writer of 1 CHRONICLES had for rank within the community that returned to Jerusalem. The common citizens among the Israelites are listed (9.4-9), followed by the priests (9.10-13), then the Levites (9.14-16), and finally, the temple guards (9.17-27).

● 9.18,19 *King's Gate:* Many cities, particularly those important to a nation's defense, were walled and had one or more gates. (See Map 5 on pg 1883.)

9.29,31,32 *incense . . . bread used for offerings . . . the sacred loaves . . . for each Sabbath:* Incense was made of frankincense, other gums and spices, and a seasoning of salt, which together produced a sweet smell when burned (Exod 30.34-38). The smoke from the burning incense represented the prayers that went up to God (Ps 141.2; Rev 5.8). The altar for burning incense (1 Chr 6.49) was in the holy place. Bread offerings could be prepared in several ways: oven-baked loaves, oven-baked wafers, bread made over the fire in a shallow pan, or bread fried in a covered pan. The dough for each was made of fine wheat and olive oil. No recipe was to include yeast, also known as leavening. Bread that has no yeast, or leaven, is flat and is called "thin bread" (unleavened bread). On each Sabbath, twelve loaves of fresh bread, representing the twelve tribes of Israel, were to be placed on the holy table in the temple. The loaves were an ongoing offering to God and a reminder of God's blessings.

Temple Offerings

Bread

10.1 *Philistines:* Philistia had five main cities, each with its own ruler: Ashdod, Ashkelon, Ekron, Gath, and Gaza. The Philistines were often at war with Israel. (See Map 4 on pg 1882.)

the entrance to the temple, just as their ancestors had guarded the entrance to the sacred tent. [20]Phinehas son of Eleazar had supervised their work because the LORD was with him.

[21]Zechariah son of Meshelemiah was also one of the guards at the temple.

[22]There was a total of 212 guards, all of them listed in the family records in their towns. Their ancestors had been chosen by King David and by Samuel the prophet to be responsible for this work, [23]and now they guarded the temple gates.

[24]There was one full-time guard appointed to each of the four sides of the temple. [25]Their assistants lived in the villages outside the city, and every seven days a group of them would come into the city and take their turn at guard duty. [26]The four full-time guards were Levites, and they supervised the other guards and were responsible for the rooms in the temple and the supplies kept there. [27]They guarded the temple day and night and opened its doors every morning.

The Duties of the Levites

[28]Some of the Levites were responsible for the equipment used in worship at the temple, and they had to count everything before and after it was used. [29]Others were responsible for the temple furnishings and its sacred objects, as well as the flour, wine, olive oil, incense, and spices. [30]But only the priests could mix the spices. [31]Mattithiah, Shallum's oldest son, was a member of the Levite clan of Korah, and he was in charge of baking the bread used for offerings.[n] [32]The Levites from the Kohath clan were

in charge of baking the sacred loaves of bread for each Sabbath.[o]

[33]The Levite family leaders who were the musicians also lived at the temple. They had no other responsibilities, because they were on duty day and night.

[34]All of these men were family leaders in the Levi tribe and were listed that way in their family records. They lived in Jerusalem.

King Saul's Family
(1 Chronicles 8.29-38)

[35]Jeiel had settled the town of Gibeon, where he and his wife Maacah lived. [36]They had ten sons, who were born in the following order: Abdon, Zur, Kish, Baal, Ner, Nadab, [37]Gedor, Ahio, Zechariah, and Mikloth [38]the father of Shimeam. Some of them went to live in Jerusalem near their relatives.

[39]Ner was the father of Kish and the grandfather of King Saul.

Saul had four sons: Jonathan, Malchishua, Abinadab, and Eshbaal.[p] [40-41]Jonathan was the father of Meribbaal,[q] the grandfather of Micah, and the great-grandfather of Pithon, Melech, Tahrea, and Ahaz.[r] [42-44]The descendants of Ahaz included Jarah, Alemeth, Azmaveth, Zimri, Moza, Binea, Rephaiah, Eleasah, and Azel and his six sons: Azrikam, Bocheru, Ishmael, Sheariah, Obadiah, and Hanan.

King Saul and His Sons Die
(1 Samuel 31.1-13)

10 The Philistines fought against Israel in a battle at Mount Gilboa. Israel's

[n]**9.31** *the bread used for offerings:* See Leviticus 2.4-7. [o]**9.32** *the sacred loaves of bread for each Sabbath:* See Leviticus 24.5-9. [p]**9.39** *Eshbaal:* See the note at 8.33. [q]**9.40,41** *Meribbaal:* See the note at 8.34. [r]**9.40,41** *and Ahaz:* Most ancient translations and 8.35; the Hebrew text does not have this name.

soldiers ran from the Philistines, and many of them were killed. [2]The Philistines closed in on Saul and his sons and killed three of them: Jonathan, Abinadab, and Malchishua. [3]The fighting was fierce around Saul, and he was badly wounded by enemy arrows.

[4]Saul told the soldier who carried his weapons, "Kill me with your sword! I don't want those godless Philistines to torture and make fun of me."

But the soldier was afraid to kill him. Then Saul stuck himself in the stomach with his own sword and fell on the blade. [5]When the soldier realized that Saul was dead, he killed himself in the same way.

[6]Saul, three of his sons, and all his male relatives were dead. [7]The Israelites who lived in Jezreel Valley[s] learned that their army had run away and that Saul and his sons were dead. They ran away too, and the Philistines moved into the towns the Israelites left behind.

[8]The next day the Philistines came back to the battlefield to carry away the weapons of the dead Israelite soldiers. When they found the bodies of Saul and his sons on Mount Gilboa, [9]they took Saul's weapons, pulled off his armor, and cut off his head. Then they sent messengers everywhere in Philistia to spread the news among their people and to thank the idols of their gods. [10]They put Saul's armor in the temple of their gods and hung his head in the temple of their god Dagon.

[11]When the people who lived in Jabesh in Gilead heard what the Philistines had done to Saul, [12]some brave men went to get his body and the bodies of his three sons. The men brought the bodies back to Jabesh, where they buried them under an oak tree. Then for seven days, they went without eating to show their sorrow.

[13]Saul died because he was unfaithful and disobeyed the LORD. He even asked advice from a woman who talked to spirits of the dead, [14]instead of asking the LORD. So the LORD had Saul killed and gave his kingdom to David, the son of Jesse.

David Becomes King of Israel
(2 Samuel 5.1-3)

11 Israel's leaders met with David at Hebron and said, "We are your relatives, [2]and we know that you have led our army into battle, even when Saul was still our king. The LORD God has promised that you would rule our country and take care of us like a shepherd. [3]So we have come to crown you king of Israel."

David made an agreement with the leaders and asked the LORD to be their witness. Then the leaders poured olive oil on David's head to show that he was now king of Israel. This happened just as the LORD's prophet Samuel had said.

David Captures Jerusalem
(2 Samuel 5.6-10)

[4]Jerusalem was called Jebus at the time, and David led Israel's army to attack the town. [5]The Jebusites said, "You won't be able to get in here!" But David captured the fortress of Mount Zion, which is now called the City of David.

[6]David had told his troops, "The first soldier to kill a Jebusite will become my army commander." And since Joab son of Zeruiah attacked first, he became commander.

[7]Later, David moved to the fortress—

[s]**10.7** *Jezreel Valley:* Hebrew "the valley."

10.4,6 *make fun of me . . . relatives were dead:* Saul killed himself (1 Sam 31.1-13) rather than be humiliated as Samson had been (Judg 16.23-25). Not all of Saul's male relatives died. His son Ishbosheth (Eshbaal) took over his father's rule following Saul's death (2 Sam 2.8-11).

10.10 *hung his head:* It was common practice in the ancient Near East to display the head and other body parts to announce the victory and to serve as a warning to other enemies.

10.12 *Jabesh:* A city east of the Jordan River. **(See Map 3 on pg 1881.)**

Burial

10.13 *talked to spirits of the dead:* Saul became impatient and broke God's Law by seeking advice from the dead in an attempt to know God's will (Lev 20.27; Deut 18.10,11; 1 Sam 28.7,8).

11.3 *Israel . . . poured olive oil on David's head:* Olive oil was poured on the head of someone who was chosen to be a priest, a prophet, or a king (Exod 28.41; 29.7; 2 Sam 2.4; 5.3). This process was called "anointing."

Israel

11.5 *fortress of Mount Zion . . . City of David:* Both "Zion" and "City of David" became alternative names for Jerusalem.

Jerusalem

Zion

11.9 *LORD All-Powerful:* Sometimes translated as "LORD of Hosts." The "hosts" here probably refers to the armies of Israel, which the LORD was said to command.

Names of God

11.10–12.40 *The LORD had promised . . . Everyone in Israel was very happy:* In this section, the writer of 1 CHRONICLES puts forth the idea that all of Israel united to make David their king, with God at David's side (11.9,10). The writer does so by listing the warriors of each tribe who fought with David in the conquest of Jerusalem and by pointing out that even while Saul was alive, men from Saul's own tribe of Benjamin and from the northern tribes of Gad and Manasseh supported David (12.1-23).

11.19 *like drinking the blood . . . risked their lives:* The men risked their own lives, or blood, to get the water for David. As a result, David may have poured out the water to make a drink offering of this precious gift back to God. Or he may have seen the water as being like blood, which God's laws would not allow him to touch. Blood was considered sacred and not to be eaten or drunk.

Purity (Clean and Unclean)

Blood

that's why it's called the City of David. [8]He had the city rebuilt, starting at the landfill on the east side.[t] Meanwhile, Joab supervised the repairs to the rest of the city.

[9]David became a great and strong ruler, because the LORD All-Powerful was on his side.

The Three Warriors
(2 Samuel 23.8-17)

[10]The LORD had promised that David would become king, and so everyone in Israel gave David their support. Certain warriors also helped keep his kingdom strong. [11]The first of these warriors was Jashobeam the son of Hachmoni, the leader of the Three Warriors.[u] In one battle he killed 300 men with his spear. [12]Another one of the Three Warriors was Eleazar son of Dodo the Ahohite. [13]During a battle against the Philistines at Pas-Dammim, all the Israelite soldiers ran away, [14]except Eleazar, who stayed with David. They took their positions in a nearby barley field and defeated the Philistines! The LORD gave Israel a great victory that day. [15]One time the Three Warriors[v] went to meet David among the rocks at Adullam Cave. The Philistine army had set up camp in Rephaim Valley [16]and had taken over Bethlehem. David was in a fortress, [17]and he said, "I'm very thirsty. I wish I had a drink of water from the well by the gate to Bethlehem."

[18]The Three Warriors sneaked through the Philistine camp and got some water from the well near Bethlehem's gate. They took it back to David, but he refused to drink it. Instead, he poured out the water as a sacrifice to the LORD [19]and said, "Drinking this water would be like drinking the blood of these men who risked their lives to get it for me."

The Three Warriors did these brave deeds.

The Thirty Warriors
(2 Samuel 23.18-39)

[20]Joab's brother Abishai was the leader of the Thirty Warriors,[w] and in one battle he killed 300 men with his spear. He was just as famous as the Three Warriors [21]and was more famous than the rest of the Thirty Warriors. He was their commander, but he never became one of the Three Warriors.[x] [22]Benaiah the son of Jehoiada was a brave man from Kabzeel who did some amazing things. One time he killed two of Moab's best fighters, and one snowy day he went into a pit and killed a lion. [23]Another time he killed an Egyptian who was seven and a half feet tall and was armed with a spear. Benaiah only had a club, so he grabbed the spear from the Egyptian and killed him with it. [24]Benaiah did things like that; he was just as brave as the Three Warriors, [25]even though he never became one of them. And he was certainly as famous as the rest of the Thirty Warriors. So David

[t]11.8 *the landfill on the east side:* The Hebrew text has "the Millo," which probably refers to a landfill to strengthen and extend the hill where the city was built.   [u]11.11 *the Three Warriors:* One ancient translation and 2 Samuel 23.8; Hebrew "the Thirty Warriors." The "Three Warriors" was the most honored group of warriors and may have been part of the "Thirty Warriors." "Three" and "thirty" are spelled almost the same in Hebrew, so there is some confusion in the manuscripts as to which group is being talked about in some places in the following lists.   [v]11.15 *the Three Warriors:* Hebrew "three of the thirty most important warriors."   [w]11.20 *the Thirty Warriors:* One ancient translation; Hebrew "the Three Warriors." The "Thirty Warriors" was the second most honored group of warriors and may have also been officers in the army.   [x]11.20,21 *Warriors:* One possible meaning for the difficult Hebrew text of these verses.

made him the leader of his own bodyguard.

26-47 Here is a list of the other famous warriors:

Asahel the brother of Joab; Elhanan the son of Dodo from Bethlehem; Shammoth from Haror; Helez from Pelon; Ira the son of Ikkesh from Tekoa; Abiezer from Anathoth; Sibbecai the Hushathite; Ilai[y] the Ahohite; Maharai from Netophah; Heled the son of Baanah from Netophah; Ithai the son of Ribai from Gibeah in Benjamin; Benaiah from Pirathon; Hurai[z] from near the streams on Mount Gaash; Abiel from Arbah; Azmaveth from Baharum; Eliahba from Shaalbon; Hashem[a] the Gizonite; Jonathan the son of Shagee from Harar; Ahiam the son of Sachar the Hararite; Eliphal the son of Ur; Hepher from Mecherah; Ahijah from Pelon; Hezro from Carmel; Naarai the son of Ezbai; Joel the brother of Nathan; Mibhar the son of Hagri; Zelek from Ammon; Naharai from Beeroth who carried Joab's weapons; Ira the Ithrite; Gareb the Ithrite; Uriah the Hittite; Zabad the son of Ahlai; Adina the son of Shiza, a leader in the Reuben tribe, and 30 of his soldiers; Hanan the son of Maacah; Joshaphat from Mithan; Uzzia from Ashterah; Shama and Jeiel the sons of Hotham from Aroer; Jediael and Joha the sons of Shimri from Tiz; Eliel from Mahavah; Jeribai and Joshaviah the sons of Elnaam; Ithmah from Moab; Eliel, Obed, and Jaasiel from Mezobah.

David's Men at Ziklag

12 Some time earlier, David had gone to live in the town of Ziklag to es-cape from King Saul. While David was there, several brave warriors joined him to help fight his battles.[b]

WARRIORS FROM THE BENJAMIN TRIBE

2Several of these warriors were from King Saul's own tribe of Benjamin. They were experts at using a bow and arrows, and they could shoot an arrow or sling a stone with either hand. **3-7**Their leaders were Ahiezer and Joash, the sons of Shemaah from Gibeah. Here is a list of those men from Benjamin: Jeziel and Pelet the sons of Azmaveth; Beracah and Jehu from Anathoth; Ishmaiah from Gibeon, who was the leader of the Thirty Warriors; Jeremiah, Jahaziel, Johanan, and Jozabad from Gederah; Eluzai, Jerimoth, Bealiah, Shemariah, and Shephatiah from Haruph; Elkanah, Isshiah, Azarel, Joezer, and Jashobeam from the Korah clan; Joelah and Zebadiah the sons of Jeroham from Gedor.

WARRIORS FROM THE GAD TRIBE

8Men from the tribe of Gad also joined David at his fortress in the desert and served as his warriors. They were also brave soldiers—fierce as lions and quick as gazelles. They were always prepared to fight with shields and spears. **9-13**There were eleven of them, ranked in the following order: Ezer the leader, then Obadiah, Eliab, Mishmannah, Jeremiah, Attai, Eliel, Johanan, Elzabad, Jeremiah, and Machbannai.

14All these men were army officers; some were high-ranking officers over a thousand troops, and others were officers over a hundred troops. **15**Earlier, they had crossed the Jordan River when it flooded,

● 12.2 *warriors . . . from . . . tribe of Benjamin:* The story emphasizes that warriors from King Saul's own Benjamin tribe abandoned Saul and joined David's army.

● 12.15 *when it flooded:* This may refer to March or April when the melting snow from the north can fill the Jordan River to overflowing. Or it may simply refer to a flood caused by heavy rains.

---

[y]11.26-47 *Ilai:* Or "Zalmon" (see 2 Samuel 23.24-39).   [z]11.26-47 *Hurai:* Or "Hiddai" (see 2 Samuel 23.24-39).   [a]11.26-47 *Hashem:* One ancient translation; Hebrew "the sons of Hashem."   [b]12.1 *David had gone . . . battles:* Ziklag was the Philistine town that King Achish of Gath gave David in return for his loyalty (see 1 Samuel 27.6). This happened during the time that David was living as an outlaw, so the events in this chapter actually took place before chapter 11 when David became king of Israel.

12.23-40 *The kingdom of Israel . . . was very happy:* David ruled from Hebron for seven and a half years before he was made king of all Israel and moved to Jerusalem (2 Sam 5.1-5). But here Israelites from the northern tribes come to Hebron to convince David to be king over all Israel. The celebration in 12.38-40 is in honor of David being made king.

and they chased out the people who lived in the valleys on each side of the river.

WARRIORS FROM THE BENJAMIN AND JUDAH TRIBES

¹⁶One time a group of men from the tribes of Benjamin and Judah went to the fortress where David was staying. ¹⁷David met them outside and said, "If you are coming as friends to fight on my side, then stay and join us. But if you try to turn me over to my enemies, the God our ancestors worshiped will punish you, because I have done nothing wrong."

¹⁸Amasai, who later became the leader of the Thirty Warriors, was one of these men who went to David. God's Spirit took control of him, and he said, "We will join you, David son of Jesse! You and your followers will always be successful, because God fights on your side."

So David agreed to let them stay, and he even put them in charge of his soldiers who raided enemy villages.

WARRIORS FROM THE MANASSEH TRIBE

¹⁹Some of the warriors who joined David were from the tribe of Manasseh. They had earlier gone with David when he agreed to fight on the side of the Philistines against King Saul. But as soon as the Philistine rulers realized that David might turn against them and rejoin Saul, they sent David away to the town of Ziklag. ²⁰That's when the following men from Manasseh joined him: Adnah, Jozabad, Jediael, Michael, Jozabad, Elihu, and Zillethai. They had all been commanders in Saul's army ²¹and brave soldiers, and so David made them officers in his army. They fought on his side when enemy troops attacked.

²²Day after day, new men came to join David, and soon he had a large, powerful army.

David's Men at Hebron

²³⁻³⁷The kingdom of Israel had been taken away from Saul, and it now belonged to David. He was ruling from Hebron, and thousands of well-trained soldiers from each tribe went there to crown David king of all Israel, just as the LORD had promised. These soldiers, who were always prepared for battle, included: 6,800 from Judah, who were armed with shields and spears; 7,100 from Simeon; 4,600 from Levi, including Jehoiada, who was a leader from Aaron's descendants, and his 3,700 men, as well as Zadok, who was a brave soldier, and 22 of his relatives, who were also officers; 3,000 from Benjamin, because this was Saul's own tribe and most of the men had remained loyal to him; 20,800 from Ephraim, who were not only brave, but also famous in their clans; 18,000 from West Manasseh, who had been chosen to help make David king; 200 leaders from Issachar, along with troops under their command—these leaders knew the right time to do what needed to be done; 50,000 from Zebulun, who were not only loyal, but also trained to use any weapon; 1,000 officers from Naphtali and 37,000 soldiers armed with shields and spears; 28,600 from Dan; 40,000 from Asher; and 120,000 from the tribes of Reuben, Gad, and East Manasseh, who were armed with all kinds of weapons.

³⁸All of these soldiers voluntarily came to Hebron because they wanted David to become king of Israel. In fact, everyone in Israel wanted the same thing. ³⁹The soldiers stayed in Hebron three days, eating and drinking what their relatives had prepared for them. ⁴⁰Other Israelites from as far away as the territories of Issachar, Zebulun, and Naphtali brought cattle and sheep to slaughter for food. They also brought donkeys, camels, mules, and oxen that

Amasai said, *"We will join you, David son of Jesse! You and your followers will always be successful, because God fights on your side."* 1 CHR 12.18

were loaded down with flour, dried figs and raisins, wine, and olive oil.

Everyone in Israel was very happy.

David Moves the Sacred Chest to Jerusalem
(2 Samuel 6.1-12a)

13 Some time later, David talked with his army commanders, [2-3]and then announced to the people of Israel:

While Saul was king, the sacred chest was ignored. But now it's time to bring the chest to Jerusalem. We will invite everyone in Israel to come here, including the priests and the Levites in the towns surrounded by pastureland. But we will do these things only if you agree, and if the LORD our God wants us to.

[4]The people agreed this was the right thing to do.

[5]David gathered everyone from the Shihor River in Egypt to Lebo-Hamath in the north. [6] Then he led them to Baalah in Judah, which was also called Kiriath-Jearim. They went there to get the sacred chest and bring it to Jerusalem, because it belonged to the LORD God, whose throne is above the winged creatures[c] on the lid of the chest.

[7]The sacred chest was still at Abinadab's house,[d] and when David and the crowd arrived there, they brought the chest outside and placed it on a new ox cart. Abinadab's sons[e] Uzzah and Ahio guided the cart, [8]while David and the crowd danced and sang praises to the LORD with all their might. They played music on small harps and other stringed instruments, and on tambourines, cymbals, and trumpets.

[9]But when they came to Chidon's threshing place, the oxen stumbled, and Uzzah reached out and took hold of the chest to stop it from falling. [10]The LORD God was very angry with Uzzah for doing this, and he killed Uzzah right there beside the chest.

[11]David then got angry with God for killing Uzzah. So he named that place "Attack on Uzzah,"[f] and it's been called that ever since.

[12]David was afraid what the LORD might do to him, and he asked himself, "Should I really be the one to take care of the sacred chest?" [13]So instead of taking it to Jerusalem, David decided to take it to the home of Obed-Edom, who lived in the town of Gath.

[14]The chest stayed there for three months, and the LORD blessed Obed-Edom, his family, and everything he owned.

David's Palace in Jerusalem
(2 Samuel 5.11-16)

14 King Hiram of Tyre sent some officials to David. They brought along carpenters and stone workers, and enough cedar logs to build David a palace. [2]David now knew that the LORD had made him a powerful king of Israel for the good of his people.

[3]After David moved to Jerusalem, he married more women and had more sons and daughters. [4-7]His children born there were Shammua, Shobab, Nathan, Solomon, Ibhar, Elishua, Elpelet, Nogah,

---

[c]**13.6** *winged creatures:* Two golden statues of winged creatures were on top of the sacred chest and were symbols of the LORD's throne on earth (see Exodus 25.18).   [d]**13.7** *The sacred chest . . . Abinadab's house:* See 1 Samuel 6.19—7.2.   [e]**13.7** *Abinadab's sons:* These words are not in the Hebrew text, but see 2 Samuel 6.3.   [f]**13.11** *Attack on Uzzah:* Or "Perez-Uzzah."

○ 13.5,6 *Shihor River in Egypt to Lebo-Hamath . . . Baalah in Judah:* The Shihor River and Lebo-Hamath represent the southern and northern boundaries of Israel. The Shihor may be the river that runs through the Egyptian Gorge in the northern Sinai Peninsula. Lebo-Hamath was somewhere to the north of Lebanon near the Orontes River. Baalah (Kiriath-Jearim) is where the ark was sent after the Philistines returned it to the Israelites (1 Sam 7.1,2). **(See Map 4 on pg 1882.)**

○ 14.1 *King Hiram of Tyre:* Tyre was an important Phoenician seaport on the Mediterranean coast. Good relationships with Israel were important to Tyre, because most of the inland trade routes Tyre used for transporting goods passed through territory controlled by Israel. Israel also supplied much of Tyre's food. According to 1 Kgs 5.1-18, Hiram of Tyre provided David's son Solomon with cedar and pine logs for building the temple. **(See the article Trade and Travel on pg 1806.)**

14.8-17 *When the Philistines . . . the LORD made all the nations afraid:* The Philistines may have hoped to destroy David before he had a chance to build Israel. In relating David's victory against the Philistines, the writer of 1 CHRONICLES clearly gives the credit for that victory to God (14.10,11,14-17). The victory also shows that David is indeed the one God supported as king of all Israel, especially since Saul's defense of Israel against the Philistines ended in defeat (1 Sam 28.16-25; 31.1-13).

Holy War (The LORD's Battles)

14.12 *idols:* The Philistines used "idols," images made of wood or stone, to worship their many gods. The Israelites were supposed to destroy captured idols (Deut 7.5; 12.3), but in another version of this battle, they do not (2 Sam 5.21).

Canaanite Gods and Goddesses

15.12 *make yourselves clean and acceptable to the LORD:* In Old Testament times, a person who was acceptable to worship God was called "clean." A person who had certain kinds of diseases, who had touched a dead body, or who had broken certain laws became "unclean," and was unacceptable to worship God. Becoming clean involved performing certain ceremonies that sometimes included sacrifices, special baths, and not having sex. Priests went through particular rituals to assure that they were "clean" and fit to perform their duties.

Purity (Clean and Unclean)

Nepheg, Japhia, Elishama, Beeliada,g and Eliphelet.

David Defeats the Philistines
(2 Samuel 5.17-25)

8When the Philistines heard that David had become king of Israel, they came to capture him. But David heard about their plan and marched out to meet them in battle. **9**The Philistines had already camped in Rephaim Valley and were raiding the nearby villages.

10David asked God, "Should I attack the Philistines? Will you help me win?"

The LORD told David, "Yes, attack them! I will give you victory."

11David and his army marched to Baal-Perazim, where they attacked and defeated the Philistines. He said, "I defeated my enemies because God broke through them like a mighty flood." So he named the place "The Lord Broke Through."h **12**Then David ordered his troops to burn the idols that the Philistines had left behind.

13Some time later, the Philistines came back into the hill country and camped in Rephaim Valley. **14**David asked God what he should do, and God answered, "Don't attack them from the front. Circle around behind them where the balsami trees are. **15**Wait there until you hear the treetops making the sound of marching troops. That sound will mean I have marched out ahead of you to fight the Philistine army. So you must then attack quickly!"

16David obeyed God and he defeated the Philistines. He even chased them all the way from Gibeon to the entrance to Gezer.

17From then on, David became even more famous, and the LORD made all the nations afraid of him.

David Gets Ready To Bring the Sacred Chest to Jerusalem

15 David had several buildings built in Jerusalem, and he had a tent set up where the sacred chest would be kept. **2**He said, "Only Levites will be allowed to carry the chest, because the LORD has chosen them to do that work and to serve him forever."

3Next, David invited everyone to come to Jerusalem and watch the sacred chest being carried to the place he had set up for it. **4**He also sent for Aaron's descendants and for the Levites. The Levites that came were: **5**Uriel, the leader of the Kohath clan, and 120 of his relatives; **6**Asaiah, the leader of the Merari clan, and 220 of his relatives; **7**Joel, the leader of the Gershon clan, and 130 of his relatives; **8**Shemaiah, the leader of the Elizaphan clan, and 200 of his relatives; **9**Eliel, the leader of the Hebron clan, and 80 of his relatives; and **10**Amminadab, the leader of the Uzziel clan, with 112 of his relatives.

11David called together these six Levites and the two priests, Zadok and Abiathar. **12**He said to them, "You are the leaders of the clans in the Levi tribe. You and your relatives must first go through the ceremony to make yourselves clean and acceptable to the LORD. Then you may carry the sacred chest that belongs to the LORD God of Israel and bring it to the place I have prepared for it. **13**The first time we tried to bring the chest to Jerusalem, we didn't ask the LORD what he wanted us to do. He was angry with us, because you Levites weren't there to carry the chest."

14The priests and the Levites made themselves clean. They were now ready to

g**14.4-7** *Beeliada:* Or "Eliada" (see 3.6-8).   h**14.11** *The Lord Broke Through:* Or "Baal-Perazim."
i**14.14** *balsam:* One possible meaning for the difficult Hebrew text.

The LORD told David, "Yes, attack them! I will give you victory." 1 CHR 14.10

carry the sacred chest [15]on poles that rested on their shoulders, just as the LORD had told Moses to do.

[16]David then told the leaders to choose some Levites to sing and play music on small harps, other stringed instruments, and cymbals. [17-21]The men chosen to play the cymbals were Heman the son of Joel, his relative Asaph the son of Berechiah, and Ethan the son of Kushaiah from the Merari clan. Some of their assistants played the smaller harps: they were Zechariah, Aziel, Shemiramoth, Jehiel, Unni, Eliab, Maaseiah, and Benaiah. Others played the larger harps: they were Mattithiah, Eliphelehu, Mikneiah, Azaziah, and two of the temple guards, Obed-Edom and Jeiel.

[22]Chenaniah was chosen to be the music director, because he was a skilled musician.

[23-24]Four Levites were then appointed to guard the sacred chest. They were Berechiah, Elkanah, Obed-Edom, and Jehiah.

Finally, David chose priests to walk in front of the sacred chest and blow trumpets. They were Shebaniah, Joshaphat, Nethanel, Amasai, Zechariah, Benaiah, and Eliezer.

The Sacred Chest Is Brought to Jerusalem
(2 Samuel 6.12-22)

[25]David, the leaders of Israel, and the army commanders were very happy as they went to Obed-Edom's house to get the sacred chest. [26]God gave the Levites the strength they needed to carry the chest, and so they sacrificed seven bulls and seven rams.

[27]David, the Levites, Chenaniah the music director, and all the musicians were wearing linen robes, and David was also wearing a linen cloth.[j] [28]While the sacred chest was being carried into Jerusalem, everyone was celebrating by shouting and playing music on horns, trumpets, cymbals, harps, and other stringed instruments.

[29]Saul's daughter Michal[k] looked out her window and watched the chest being brought into David's City. But when she saw David jumping and dancing in honor of the LORD, she was disgusted.

16 They put the sacred chest inside the tent that David had set up for it, then they offered sacrifices to please the LORD[l] and sacrifices to ask his blessing.[m] [2]After David had finished, he blessed the people in the name of the LORD [3]and gave every person in the crowd a small loaf of bread, some meat, and a handful of raisins.

[4]David appointed some of the Levites to serve at the sacred chest; they were to play music and sing praises to the LORD God of Israel. [5]Asaph was their leader, and Zechariah was his assistant. Jeiel, Shemiramoth, Jehiel, Mattithiah, Eliab, Benaiah, Obed-Edom, and another man named Jeiel were appointed to play small harps and stringed instruments. Asaph himself played the cymbals, [6]and the two priests Benaiah and Jahaziel were to blow trumpets every day in front of the sacred chest.

15.29 *Michal:* She was one of David's wives. Michal felt David's dancing and jumping was improper for one chosen to be king.

16.1-3 *offered sacrifices ... handful of raisins:* David supervises the sacrifices and performs the priestly tasks of blessing the people and giving them food (Lev 7.11-19; Num 6.22-27). (See the chart Sacrifices and Offerings on pg 1828.)

[j]15.27 *a linen cloth:* The Hebrew word is "ephod," which can mean either a piece of clothing like a skirt that went from the waist to the knee or a garment like a vest or jacket that only the priests wore. [k]15.29 *Michal:* One of David's wives. [l]16.1 *sacrifices to please the LORD:* These sacrifices have traditionally been called "whole burnt offerings" because the whole animal was burned on the altar. A main purpose of such sacrifices was to please the LORD with the smell of the sacrifice, and so in the CEV they are often called "sacrifices to please the LORD." [m]16.1 *sacrifices to ask his blessing:* These sacrifices have traditionally been called "peace offerings" or "offerings of well-being." A main purpose was to ask for the LORD's blessing, and so in the CEV they are sometimes called "sacrifices to ask the LORD's blessing."

16.7-36 *David instructed . . . Praise the LORD:* The writer of 1 CHRONI-CLES includes portions of three Psalms as part of the worshiping community's celebration.

16.14-18 *justice . . . his agreement:* The Law not only told the people what to avoid doing, it also told them how they were to treat others. God was concerned that they treat each other with justice and fairness.

CR   Justice

16.31-33 *The LORD is King . . . judge:* In addition to choosing Israel and saving it in times of trouble, the LORD God also rules the whole universe, which he created, and all the nations on earth (Ps 5.2). God is also often referred to as the one who will judge Israel and the nations.

CR   Day of the LORD

David's Song of Praise
(Psalms 105.1-15; 96.1-13; 106.1,47,48)

⁷That same day, David instructed Asaph and his relatives for the first time to sing these praises to the LORD:

⁸Praise the LORD
    and pray in his name!
Tell everyone
    what he has done.
⁹Sing praises to the LORD!
    Tell about his miracles.
¹⁰Celebrate and worship
    his holy name
    with all your heart.

¹¹Trust the LORD
    and his mighty power.
    Worship him always.
¹²Remember his miracles
    and all his wonders
    and his fair decisions.
¹³You belong to the family
    of Israel, his servant;
    you are his chosen ones,
    the descendants of Jacob.

¹⁴The LORD is our God,
    bringing justice
    everywhere on earth.
¹⁵We must never forget
    his agreement and his promises,
    not in thousands of years.
*¹⁶God made an eternal promise
¹⁷   to Abraham, Isaac, and Jacob
¹⁸when he said, "I'll give you
    the land of Canaan."

¹⁹At the time there were
    only a few of us,
    and we were homeless.
²⁰We wandered from nation
    to nation, from one country
    to another.

²¹God did not let anyone
    mistreat our people.
Instead he protected us
    by punishing rulers
²²and telling them,
    "Don't touch my chosen leaders
    or harm my prophets!"

²³Everyone on this earth,
    sing praises to the LORD.
Day after day announce,
    "The LORD has saved us!"
²⁴Tell every nation on earth,
    "The LORD is wonderful
    and does marvelous things!
²⁵The LORD is great and deserves
    our greatest praise!
He is the only God
    worthy of our worship.
²⁶Other nations worship idols,
    but the LORD created
    the heavens.
²⁷Give honor and praise
    to the LORD,
    whose power and beauty
    fill his holy temple."

²⁸Tell everyone of every nation,
    "Praise the glorious power
    of the LORD.
²⁹He is wonderful! Praise him
    and bring an offering
    into his temple.
Worship the LORD,
    majestic and holy.
³⁰Everyone on earth, now tremble!"

The world stands firm,
    never to be shaken.

³¹Tell the heavens and the earth
    to be glad and celebrate!
And announce to the nations,
    "The LORD is King!"
³²Command the ocean to roar
    with all of its creatures

Tell everyone of every nation, "Praise the glorious power of the LORD.*"   1* CHR *16.28*

and the fields to rejoice
  with all of their crops.
³³Then every tree in the forest
  will sing joyful songs
    to the LORD.
He is coming to judge
  all people on earth.

³⁴Praise the LORD
  because he is good to us,
    and his love never fails.
³⁵Say to him, "Save us, LORD God!
  Bring us back
    from among the nations.
Let us celebrate and shout
  in praise of your holy name.
³⁶LORD God of Israel,
  you deserve to be praised
    forever and ever."

After David finished, the people shouted,
"Amen! Praise the LORD!"

David Appoints Worship Leaders at Jerusalem and Gibeon

³⁷David chose Asaph and the Levites in his clan to be in charge of the daily worship at the place where the sacred chest was kept. ³⁸Obed-Edom and 68 of his relatives were their assistants, and Hosah and Obed-Edom the son of Jeduthun were the guards. ³⁹David also chose Zadok the priest and his relatives who were priests to serve at the LORD's sacred tent at Gibeon. ⁴⁰They were to offer sacrifices on the altar every morning and evening, just as the LORD had commanded in the Law he gave Israel. ⁴¹Heman and Jeduthun were their assistants, as well as the other men who had been chosen to praise the LORD for his never-ending love. ⁴²Heman and Jeduthun were also responsible for blowing the trumpets, and for playing the cymbals and other instruments during worship at the tent. The Levites in Jeduthun's clan were the guards at Gibeon. ⁴³After that, everyone went home, and David went home to his family.

The LORD's Message to David

(2 Samuel 7.1-17)

17 Soon after David moved into his new palace, he said to Nathan the prophet, "Look around! I live in a palace made of cedar, but the sacred chest is kept in a tent."

²Nathan replied, "The LORD is with you—do what you want."

³That night, the LORD told Nathan ⁴to go to David and tell him:

David, you are my servant, so listen carefully: You are not the one to build a temple for me. ⁵I didn't live in a temple when I brought my people out of Egypt, and I don't live in one now. A tent has always been my home wherever I have gone with them. ⁶I chose special leaders and told them to be like shepherds for my people Israel. But did I ever say anything to even one of them about building a cedar temple for me?

⁷David, this is what I, the LORD All-Powerful, say to you. I brought you in from the fields where you took care of sheep, and I made you the leader of my people. ⁸Wherever you went, I helped you and destroyed your enemies right in front of your eyes. I have made you one of the most famous people in the world. ⁹I have given my people Israel a land of their own where they can live in peace. They will no longer have to tremble with fear—evil nations won't bother them, as they did ¹⁰when I let

● 16.37,39 *sacred chest . . . sacred tent:* The sacred chest was in a tent in Jerusalem that David had set up for it (1 Chr 15.1; 16.1). The sacred tent stayed in Gibeon until Solomon finished building the temple in Jerusalem (2 Chr 1.2-5,13; 5.4-5).

CR The Sacred Chest

CR The Sacred Tent

● 16.39 *Gibeon:* This town was located in the area of Benjamin about six miles northwest of Jerusalem. It was at the shrine in Gibeon that God spoke to Solomon and gave him the gift of wisdom (1 Kgs 3.4-15). Gibeon was also known as Gibeah.

● 17.1 *Nathan the prophet:* A prophet was someone who spoke God's message. At first, Nathan speaks before hearing God's word and incorrectly advises David. He corrects that error after God appears to him in a vision (17.2-15). **(See the article Prophets and Prophecy on pg 1791.)**

■ 17.10-14 *Now I promise . . . my kingdom forever:* God promises that there always will be a descendant of David on the throne. This promise did remain true for about 400 years until 587 B.C. when the Babylonians conquered Jerusalem and took many of its people into exile. David's descendants no longer ruled over Israel. Christians believe that Jesus, who is of the line of David, restores David's kingdom.

Messiah (Chosen One)

17.17,20,22 *you have promised . . . you alone are God . . . become their God:* God's promise is for David and for all of Israel. David knows that there is only one true God, the God of Israel (17.20). David then repeats the agreement God made with Israel that they would be God's special people (17.22).

Agreements (Covenants)

18.1-6 *David attacked . . . the* Lord *helped him win battles:* David fights a series of battles that defeat Israel's enemies on all sides. Earlier, David had defeated the Amalekites to the south (1 Sam 30.16-20). Now he defeats the Philistines to the west (18.1), the Moabites to the east (18.2), and Hadadezer of Zobah and the Syrian kingdom of Damascus to the north (18.3,5). Zobah was an Aramean kingdom north of Damascus. The Arameans (Syrians), including Zobah, were controlled by Damascus, perhaps the world's oldest continually occupied city and a major trading and transportation center. Later, David's troops will further secure Israel's southern borders by defeating the Edomites (18.12,13). **(See Map 4 on pg 1882.)**

judges rule my people, and I will keep your enemies from attacking you.

Now I promise that like you, your descendants will be kings. [11] I'll choose one of your sons to be king when you reach the end of your life and are buried beside your ancestors. I'll make him a strong ruler, [12] and no one will be able to take his kingdom away from him. He will be the one to build a temple for me. [13] I will be like a father to him, and he will be like a son to me. I will never put an end to my agreement with him, as I put an end to my agreement with Saul, who was king before you. [14] I will make sure that your son and his descendants will rule my people and my kingdom forever.

[15] Nathan told David exactly what the Lord had said.

David Gives Thanks to the Lord
(2 Samuel 7.18-29)

[16] David went into the tent he had set up for the sacred chest. He sat there and prayed:

Lord God, my family and I don't deserve what you have already done for us, [17] and yet you have promised to do even more for my descendants. You are treating me as if I am a very important person.[n] [18] I am your servant, and you know my thoughts. What else can I say, except that you have honored me? [19] It was your choice to do these wonderful things for me and to make these promises.

[20] No other god is like you, Lord— you alone are God. Everything we have heard about you is true. [21] And there is no other nation on earth like Israel, the nation you rescued from

slavery in Egypt to be your own. You became famous by using great and wonderful miracles to force other nations and their gods out of your land, so that your people could live here. [22] You have chosen Israel to be your people forever, and you have become their God.

[23] Lord God, please do what you promised me and my descendants. [24] Then you will be famous forever, and everyone will say, "The Lord All-Powerful rules Israel and is their God."

My kingdom will be strong, [25] because you are my God, and you have promised that my descendants will be kings. That's why I have the courage to pray to you like this, even though I am only your servant.

[26] You are the Lord God, and you have made this good promise to me. [27] Now please bless my descendants forever, and let them always be your chosen kings. You have already blessed my family, and I know you will bless us forever.

A List of David's Victories in War
(2 Samuel 8.1-14)

18 Later, David attacked and defeated the Philistines. He captured their town of Gath and the nearby villages.

[2] David also defeated the Moabites, and so they had to accept him as their ruler and pay taxes to him.

[3] While King Hadadezer of Zobah was trying to gain control of the territory near the Euphrates River, David met him in battle at Hamath and defeated him. [4] David captured 1,000 chariots, 7,000 chariot drivers, and 20,000 soldiers. And he crippled all but 100 of the horses.

[n]17.17 *You are treating me . . . person:* One possible meaning for the difficult Hebrew text.

Everyone will say, "The Lord *All-Powerful rules Israel and is their God."* 1 Chr 17.24

5When troops from the Syrian kingdom of Damascus came to help Hadadezer, David killed 22,000 of them. 6Then David stationed some of his troops in Damascus, and the people there had to accept David as their ruler and pay taxes to him.

Everywhere David went, the LORD helped him win battles.

7Hadadezer's officers had carried gold shields, but David took these shields and brought them back to Jerusalem. 8He also took a lot of bronze from the cities of Tibhath and Cun, which had belonged to Hadadezer. Later, Solomon used this bronze to make the large bowl called the Sea, and to make the pillars and other furnishings for the temple.

9-10King Tou of Hamath and King Hadadezer had been enemies. So when Tou heard that David had defeated Hadadezer's whole army, he sent his son Hadoram to congratulate David on his victory. Hadoram also brought him gifts made of gold, silver, and bronze. 11David gave these gifts to the LORD, just as he had done with the silver and gold he had captured from Edom, Moab, Ammon, Philistia, and Amalek.

12Abishai the son of Zeruiah defeated the Edomite army in Salt Valley and killed 18,000 of their troops. 13Then he stationed troops in Edom, and the people there had to accept David as their ruler.

Everywhere David went, the LORD gave him victory in war.

A List of David's Officials
(2 Samuel 8.15-18)

14David ruled all Israel with fairness and justice.

15Joab the son of Zeruiah was the commander in chief of the army.

Jehoshaphat the son of Ahilud kept the government records.

16Zadok the son of Ahitub and Ahimelech the son of Abiathar were the priests.

Shavsha was the secretary.

17Benaiah the son of Jehoiada was the commander of David's bodyguard.o

David's sons were his highest-ranking officials.

Israel Fights Ammon and Syria
(2 Samuel 10.1-19)

19 Some time later, King Nahash of Ammon died, and his son Hanun became king. 2David said, "Nahash was kind to me, so I will be kind to his son." He sent some officials to Ammon to tell Hanun how sorry he was that his father had died.

But when David's officials arrived at Ammon, 3the Ammonite leaders said to Hanun, "Do you really believe King David is honoring your father by sending these men to comfort you? He probably sent them to spy on our country, so he can come and destroy it."

4Hanun arrested David's officials and had their beards shaved off and their robes cut off just below the waist, and then he sent them away. 5They were terribly ashamed.

When David found out what had happened to his officials, he sent a message that told them, "Stay in Jericho until your beards grow back. Then you can come home."

6The Ammonites realized they had made David furious. So they paid over 30 tons of silver to hire chariot troops from Mesopotamia and from the Syrian kingdoms of Maacah and Zobah. 7Thirty-two thousand troops, as well as the king of Maacah and

o 18.17 David's bodyguard: The Hebrew text has "the Cherethites and the Pelethites," who were foreign soldiers hired by David to be his bodyguard.

● 18.7,8 gold shields . . . the Sea: The gold shields were probably used for ceremonies rather than for battle. The "Sea" was a huge basin that held water that possibly was used by the priests for ritual cleansing. It may have symbolized God's separation of the waters that covered the earth to make the sky, land, and ocean in the creation story (Gen 1.6-10; 1 Kgs 7.23-26).

● 18.12,13 Salt Valley . . . Edom: "Salt Valley" probably refers to the area at the southern end of the Dead Sea, near where Edom's northern border meets Judah's southern border. (See Map 6 on pg 1884.)

● 19.4 beards shaved off . . . below the waist: In this culture, beards were a symbol of honor and manliness and were shaved only in times of mourning (Isa 15.2; Jer 41.5). Even plucking the beard was an insult, and so to shave a man's beard in this way was extremely humiliating. Exposing the body was also considered shameful. Cutting the garments so short that the lower body showed caused such great humiliation that it was normally done only to prisoners of war.

● 19.5 Jericho: Jericho was an important city on the trade routes from the east to Palestine. It is one of the oldest cities in the world with evidence of building on the site before 5000 B.C. It was the first city the people of Israel captured when they crossed into Canaan (Josh 5.13—6.26). (See Map 3 on pg 1881.)

19.17-19 *David found out . . . the Ammonites again:* This is the last time David leads a major military campaign against combined foreign powers. Though Hadadezer's subjects accept David as their ruler, we have no evidence that Hadadezer himself did so.

20.4 *Gezer:* Gezer was at the crossroads of the north-south trade route and the east-west route between Jerusalem and the port at Joppa. Lower Beth-Horon also protected the route between Jerusalem and the sea. (See Map 4 on pg 1882.)

his army, came and camped near Medeba. The Ammonite troops also left their towns and came to prepare for battle.

8David heard what was happening, and he sent out Joab with his army. **9**The Ammonite troops marched to the entrance of the city[P] and prepared for battle, while the Syrian troops took their positions in the open fields.

10Joab saw that the enemy troops were lined up on both sides of him. So he picked some of the best Israelite soldiers to fight the Syrians. **11**Then he put his brother Abishai in command of the rest of the army and told them to fight against the Ammonites. **12**Joab told his brother, "If the Syrians are too much for me to handle, come and help me. And if the Ammonites are too strong for you, I'll come and help you. **13**Be brave and fight hard to protect our people and the towns of our LORD God. I pray he will do whatever pleases him."

14Joab and his soldiers attacked the Syrians, and the Syrians ran from them. **15**When the Ammonite troops saw that the Syrians had run away, they ran from Abishai's soldiers and went back into their own city. Joab then returned to Jerusalem.

16As soon as the Syrians realized they had been defeated, they sent for their troops that were stationed on the other side of the Euphrates River. Shophach, the commander of Hadadezer's army, led these troops to Ammon.

17David found out what the Syrians were doing, and he brought Israel's entire army together. They crossed the Jordan River, and he commanded them to take their positions facing the Syrian troops.

Soon after the fighting began, **18**the Syrians ran from Israel. David killed 7,000 chariot troops and 40,000 regular soldiers. He also killed Shophach, their commander.

19When the kings who had been under Hadadezer's rule saw that Israel had defeated them, they made peace with David and accepted him as their new ruler. The Syrians never helped the Ammonites again.

The End of the War with Ammon
(2 Samuel 11.1; 12.26-31)

20 The next spring, the time when kings go to war, Joab marched out in command of the Israelite army and destroyed towns all over the country of Ammon. He attacked the capital city of Rabbah and left it in ruins. But David stayed in Jerusalem.

2Later, David himself went to Rabbah, where he took the crown from the statue of their god Milcom.[q] The crown was made of 75 pounds of gold, and there was a valuable jewel on it. David put the jewel on his crown,[r] then carried off everything else of value. **3**He forced the people of Rabbah to work with saws, iron picks, and axes. He also did the same thing with the people in all the other Ammonite towns.

David then led Israel's army back to Jerusalem.

The Descendants of the Rephaim
(2 Samuel 21.15-22)

4Some time later, Israel fought a battle against the Philistines at Gezer. During this battle, Sibbecai from Hushah killed Sippai, a descendant of the Rephaim,[s] and the Philistines were defeated.

P19.9 *the city:* Probably Rabbah, the capital city of Ammon. q20.2 *the statue of their god Milcom:* Or "their king." r20.2 *David put the jewel on his crown:* Or "David put the crown on his head." s20.4 *Rephaim:* This may refer to a group of people that lived in Palestine before the Israelites and who were famous for their large size.

⁵In another battle against the Philistines, Elhanan the son of Jair killed Lahmi the brother of Goliath from Gath, whose spear shaft was like a weaver's beam.ᵗ

⁶Another one of the Philistine soldiers who was a descendant of the Rephaim was as big as a giant and had six fingers on each hand and six toes on each foot. During a battle at Gath, ⁷he made fun of Israel, so David's nephew Jonathanᵘ killed him.

⁸David and his soldiers killed these three men from Gath who were descendants of the Rephaim.

David Counts the People
(2 Samuel 24.1-9)

21 Satan decided to cause trouble for Israel by making David think it was a good idea to find out how many people there were in Israel and Judah. ²David told Joab and the army commanders, "Count everyone in Israel, from the town of Beersheba in the south all the way north to Dan. Then I will know how many people can serve in my army."

³Joab answered, "Your Majesty, even if the LORD made your kingdom a hundred times larger, you would still rule everyone in it. Why do you need to know how many soldiers there are? Don't you think that would make the whole nation angry?"

⁴But David would not change his mind. And so Joab went everywhere in Israel and Judah and counted the people. He returned to Jerusalem ⁵and told David that the total number of men who could serve in the army was 1,100,000 in Israel and 470,000 in Judah. ⁶Joab refused to include anyone from the tribes of Levi and Benjamin, because he still disagreed with David's orders.

God Punishes Israel
(2 Samuel 24.10-17)

⁷David's order to count the people made God angry, and he punished Israel. ⁸David prayed, "I am your servant. But what I did was stupid and terribly wrong. Please forgive me."

⁹The LORD said to Gad, one of David's prophets, ¹⁰"Tell David that I will punish him in one of three ways. But he will have to choose which one it will be."

¹¹Gad went to David and told him:

You must choose how the LORD will punish you: ¹²Will there be three years when the land won't grow enough food for its people? Or will your enemies constantly defeat you for three months? Or will the LORD send a horrible disease to strike your land for three days? Think about it and decide, because I have to give your answer to God who sent me.

¹³David was miserable and said, "It's a terrible choice to make! But the LORD is kind, and I'd rather be punished by him than by anyone else."

¹⁴So the LORD sent a horrible disease on Israel, and 70,000 Israelites died. ¹⁵Then he sent an angel to destroy the city of Jerusalem. But just as the angel was about to do that, the LORD felt sorry for all the suffering he had caused the people, and he told the angel, "Stop! They have suffered enough." This happened at the threshing place that belonged to Araunahᵛ the Jebusite.

21.1 *Satan:* Here, Satan makes David count the people (compare to 2 Sam 24.1). But God allows Satan to do so, and David must bear the responsibility of his own actions (21.7-13).

Satan

21.5,6 *1,100,000 . . . disagreed with David's orders:* These numbers differ from those in 2 Sam 24.9. Levites did not have to serve in the military, because they were responsible for Israel's religious life (Num 1.47-51). Because the sacred tent was in Gibeon in Benjamin territory (21.29-30), the tribe of Benjamin may also have been excused from military service.

Angels

ᵗ**20.5** *weaver's beam:* When a weaver made cloth, one set of threads was tied onto a large wooden rod that was known as a weaver's beam. ᵘ**20.7** *David's nephew Jonathan:* Hebrew "Jonathan son of Shimea, David's brother." ᵛ**21.15** *Araunah:* The Hebrew text has "Ornan," another spelling of Araunah (see 2 Samuel 24.16).

21.18 *Araunah's threshing place:* This is believed to be the flat rock under the Dome of the Rock in present-day Jerusalem. At a threshing place, bundles of grain stalks were beaten or crushed in order to separate the kernels from the outer husk.

21.26 *fire . . . altar:* In the Bible, fire is often associated with God's presence. Here, it also signals God's acceptance of David's prayer and approval of the future site of the temple.

Fire

21.28 *sacrifices there at the threshing place:* With the Levites prepared for their work (chapter 15) and the sacred chest already in Jerusalem (chapter 16), this approval by God of a new site for the offering of sacrifices indicates that all is now ready for the building of the temple.

22.2 *foreigners:* Non-Israelites who were descendants of the Canaanites, or slaves taken in war.

Foreigners (Aliens)

22.3,4 *bronze . . . cedar logs:* Bronze is made by melting and mixing copper and tin. Ancient copper mines dating back at least to the time of Solomon have been discovered in the Arabah south of the Dead Sea. Cedar is an extremely hard wood that has a beautiful tight grain for carving, and is valued for its distinctive smell. At one time cedar forests covered most of the Lebanon mountain range. **(See Map 4 on pg 1882.)**

[16]David saw the Lord's angel in the air, holding a sword over Jerusalem. He and the leaders of Israel, who were all wearing sackcloth,[w] bowed with their faces to the ground, [17]and David prayed, "It's my fault! I sinned by ordering the people to be counted. They have done nothing wrong— they are innocent sheep. Lord God, please punish me and my family. Don't let the disease wipe out your people."

David Buys Araunah's Threshing Place
(2 Samuel 24.18-25)

[18]The Lord's angel told the prophet Gad to tell David that he must go to Araunah's threshing place and build an altar in honor of the Lord. [19]David followed the Lord's instructions.

[20]Araunah and his four sons were threshing wheat at the time, and when they saw the angel, the four sons ran to hide. [21]Just then, David arrived, and when Araunah saw him, he stopped his work and bowed down.

[22]David said, "Would you sell me your threshing place, so I can build an altar on it to the Lord? Then this disease will stop killing the people. I'm willing to pay whatever you say it's worth."

[23]Araunah answered, "Take it, Your Majesty, and do whatever you want with it. I'll even give you the oxen for the sacrifice and the wheat for the grain sacrifice. And you can use the threshing-boards[x] for the fire. It's all yours!"

[24]But David replied, "No! I want to pay you what they're worth. I can't just take

something from you and then offer the Lord a sacrifice that cost me nothing."

[25]So David paid Araunah 600 gold coins for his threshing place. [26]David built an altar and offered sacrifices to please the Lord[y] and sacrifices to ask his blessing.[z] David prayed, and the Lord answered him by sending fire down on the altar. [27]Then the Lord commanded the angel to put the sword away.[a]

[28]When David saw that the Lord had answered his prayer, he offered more sacrifices there at the threshing place, [29-30]because he was afraid of the angel's sword and did not want to go all the way to Gibeon. That's where the sacred tent that Moses had made in the desert was kept, as well as the altar where sacrifices were offered to the Lord.

22 David said, "The temple of the Lord God must be built right here at this threshing place. And the altar for offering sacrifices will also be here."

David Prepares To Build the Temple

[2]David ordered the foreigners living in Israel to come to Jerusalem. Then he assigned some to cut blocks of stone for building the temple. [3]He got a large supply of iron to make into nails and hinges for the doors, and he provided so much bronze that it could not be weighed. [4]He also brought an endless supply of cedar logs from the cities of Sidon and Tyre.

[5]He said, "The temple for the Lord must be great, so that everyone in the world will know about it. But since my son Solomon

---

[w]**21.16** *sackcloth:* A rough, dark-colored cloth made from goat or camel hair and used to make grain sacks. It was worn in times of trouble or sorrow.   [x]**21.23** *threshing-boards:* Heavy boards with bits of rock or metal on the bottom. They were dragged across the grain to separate the husks from the kernels.   [y]**21.26** *sacrifices to please the Lord:* See the note at 16.1.   [z]**21.26** *sacrifices to ask his blessing:* See the note at 16.1.   [a]**21.27** *the Lord commanded the angel to put the sword away:* See verse 16.

is young and has no experience, I will make sure that everything is ready for the temple to be built."

That's why David did all these things before he died.

David Instructs Solomon To Build the Temple

6David sent for his son Solomon and told him to build a temple for the LORD God of Israel. **7**He said:

My son, I wanted to build a temple where the LORD my God would be worshiped. **8**But some time ago, he told me, "David, you have killed too many people and have fought too many battles. That's why you are not the one to build my temple. **9**But when your son becomes king, I will give him peace throughout his kingdom. His name will be Solomon, because during his rule I will keep Israel safe and peaceful.[b] **10**Solomon will build my temple. He will be like a son to me, and I will be like a father to him. In fact, one of his descendants will always rule in Israel."

11Solomon, my son, I now pray that the LORD your God will be with you and keep his promise to help you build a temple for him. **12**May he give you wisdom and knowledge, so that you can rule Israel according to his Law. **13**If you obey the laws and teachings that the LORD gave Moses, you will be successful. Be strong and brave and don't get discouraged or be afraid of anything.

14I have all the supplies you'll need to build the temple: You have 4,000 tons of gold and 40,000 tons of silver. There's also plenty of wood, stone, and more bronze and iron than I could weigh. Ask for anything else you need. **15**I have also assigned men who will cut and lay the stone. And there are carpenters and people who are experts in working with **16**gold, silver, bronze, and iron. You have plenty of workers to do the job. Now get started, and I pray that the LORD will be with you in your work.

17David then gave orders for the leaders of Israel to help Solomon. **18**David said:

The LORD our God has helped me defeat all the people who lived here before us, and he has given you peace from all your enemies. Now this land belongs to the LORD and his people. **19**Obey the LORD your God with your heart and soul. Begin work on the temple to honor him, so that the sacred chest and the things used for worship can be kept there.

David Assigns the Levites Their Duties

23 David was old when he chose his son Solomon to be king of Israel. **2**Some time later, David called together all of Israel's leaders, priests, and Levites. **3**He then counted the Levite men who were at least 30 years old, and the total was 38,000. **4**He said, "Twenty-four thousand of the Levites will be in charge of the temple, 6,000 will be temple officials and judges, **5**4,000 will be guards at the temple, and 4,000 will praise the LORD by playing the musical instruments I have given them."

6David then divided the Levites into three groups according to the clans of Levi's sons, Gershon, Kohath, and Merari. **7**Gershon had two sons: Ladan and Shimei. **8**Ladan was the father of Jehiel,

b**22.9** *Solomon . . . safe and peaceful*: In Hebrew "Solomon" sounds like "peace."

22.9 *Solomon . . . safe and peaceful*: The Hebrew word for "Solomon" sounds like the word for "peace" (shalom). Solomon will rule in a time of peace, while David spent much of his time at war. The writer of 1 CHRONICLES suggests that it was not only the time spent in war that kept David from building the temple (1 Kgs 5.3,4), but that the blood shed by David made him unfit for the task.

Solomon

22.12,13 *give you wisdom . . . laws and teachings*: Solomon is given this wisdom by God (1 Kgs 3.5-14; 2 Chr 1.7-12). The wisdom that God gives is often closely related to God's Law or to obeying the Law (see Prov 1.7; 2.4-7). David tells Solomon that he will be successful as long as he obeys God's Law, which includes the Ten Commandments and the rest of the laws God gave to Moses and the people at Mount Sinai.

Wisdom

Law

23.3 *30 years old*: The age of the Levites who were considered able to serve in the temple varied from time to time even in Moses' day (Num 4.1-3; 8.24-25). David changes the age again (1 Chr 23.24).

David said, "Obey the LORD your God with your heart and soul. Begin work on the temple to honor him." 1 CHR 22.19

23.13-15 *Aaron . . . Moses:* Aaron's descendants were considered Israel's true priests (Exod 28.1; Num 3.5-8; 18.1), while Moses' descendants, the Levites, were to be assistants to the priests (23.28).

23.31 *New Moon Festivals:* This religious festival was held on the day of the new moon, the day when only a thin edge of the moon can be seen. This day was always the first day of the month for the Hebrew calendar. The New Moon Festival was a time of worship, sacrifices, celebration, feasting, and rest from work. (See the article People of the Law: The Religion of Israel on pg 1794.)

24.4 *16 . . . eight:* In addition to organizing the Levites (chapter 23), David organizes the priests by creating 24 divisions of duties. This allowed the priests to work in monthly shifts or for two-week shifts once a year as will be done in New Testament times (Luke 1.5-9).

Israel's Priests

Zetham, and Joel. [9]They were all family leaders among their father's descendants. Shimei was the father of Shelomoth, Haziel, and Haran. [10-11]Later, Shimei had four more sons, in the following order: Jahath, Ziza, Jeush, and Beriah. But Jeush and Beriah didn't have many children, so their descendants were counted as one family.

[12]Kohath had four sons: Amram, Izhar, Hebron, and Uzziel. [13]Amram was the father of Aaron and Moses. Aaron and his descendants were chosen to be in charge of all the sacred things. They served the LORD by offering sacrifices to him and by blessing the people in his name. [14-15]Moses, the man of God, was the father of Gershom and Eliezer, and their descendants were considered Levites. [16]Gershom's oldest son was Shebuel. [17]Rehabiah, who was Eliezer's only son, had many children. [18]The second son born to Kohath was Izhar, and his oldest son was Shelomith. [19]Hebron, the third son of Kohath, was the father of Jeriah, Amariah, Jahaziel, and Jekameam. [20]Kohath's youngest son, Uzziel, was the father of Micah and Isshiah.

[21]Merari had two sons: Mahli and Mushi. Mahli was the father of Eleazar and Kish. [22]Eleazar had no sons, only daughters, and they married their uncle's sons. [23]Mushi the second son of Merari, was the father of Mahli, Eder, and Jeremoth.

[24]These were the clans and families of the tribe of Levi. Those who were 20 years and older were assigned to work at the LORD's temple.

[25]David said:

The LORD God of Israel has given his people peace, and he will live in Jerusalem forever. [26]And so, the Levites won't need to move the sacred tent and the things used for worship from place to place. [27]From now on, all Levites at least 20 years old [28]will serve

the LORD by helping Aaron's descendants do their work at the temple, by keeping the courtyards and rooms of the temple clean, and by making sure that everything used in worship stays pure. [29]They will also be in charge of the sacred loaves of bread, the flour for the grain sacrifices, the thin wafers, any offerings to be baked, and the flour mixed with olive oil. These Levites will weigh and measure these offerings.

[30]Every morning and evening, the Levites are to give thanks to the LORD and sing praises to him. [31]They must also give thanks and sing praises when sacrifices are offered on each Sabbath, as well as during New Moon Festivals and other religious feasts. There must always be enough Levites on duty at the temple to do everything that needs to be done. [32]They were once in charge of taking care of the sacred tent; now they are responsible for the temple and for helping Aaron's descendants.

David Assigns the Priests Their Duties

24 Aaron's descendants were then divided into work groups. Aaron had four sons: Nadab, Abihu, Eleazar, and Ithamar. [2]But Nadab and Abihu died long before their father, without having any sons. That's why Eleazar and Ithamar served as priests.

[3]David divided Aaron's descendants into groups, according to their assigned work. Zadok, one of Eleazar's descendants, and Ahimelech, one of Ithamar's descendants, helped David.

[4]Eleazar's descendants were divided into 16 groups, and Ithamar's were divided into eight groups, because Eleazar's family included more family leaders. [5]However, both families included temple officials and

priests, and so to make sure the work was divided fairly, David asked God what to do.^c

6As each group was assigned their duties, Shemaiah the son of Nethanel the Levite wrote down the name of the family leader in charge of that group. The witnesses were David and his officials, as well as Zadok the priest, Ahimelech the son of Abiathar, and the family leaders from the clans of the priests and the Levites.

7-18 Each group of priests went by the name of its family leader, and they were assigned their duties in the following order: Jehoiarib, Jedaiah, Harim, Seorim, Malchijah, Mijamin, Hakkoz, Abijah, Jeshua, Shecaniah, Eliashib, Jakim, Huppah, Jeshebeab, Bilgah, Immer, Hezir, Happizzez, Pethahiah, Jehezkel, Jachin, Gamul, Delaiah, Maaziah. **19**These men were assigned their duties at the temple, just as the LORD God of Israel had commanded their ancestor Aaron.

The Rest of the Levites Are Assigned Their Duties

20Here is a list of the other descendants of Levi:

Amram was the ancestor of Shubael and Jehdeiah.

21Rehabiah was the ancestor of Isshiah, the oldest son in his family.

22Izhar was the father of Shelomoth and the grandfather of Jahath.

23Hebron had four sons, in the following order: Jeriah, Amariah, Jahaziel, and Jekameam.

24Uzziel was the father of Micah and the grandfather of Shamir.

25Isshiah, Micah's brother, was the father of Zechariah.

26Merari was the father of Mahli, Mushi, and Jaaziah.

27Jaaziah had three sons: Shoham, Zaccur, and Ibri.^d **28-29**Mahli was the father of Eleazar and Kish. Eleazar had no sons, but Kish was the father of Jerahmeel. **30**Mushi had three sons: Mahli, Eder, and Jerimoth.

These were the descendants of Levi, according to their clans. **31**Each one was assigned his duties in the same way that their relatives the priests had been assigned their duties. David, Zadok, Ahimelech, and the family leaders of the priests and Levites were the witnesses.

David Assigns the Temple Musicians Their Duties

25 David and the temple officials chose the descendants of Asaph, Heman, and Jeduthun to be in charge of music. They were to praise the LORD by playing cymbals, harps and other stringed instruments. Here is a list of the musicians and their duties:

2Asaph's four sons, Zaccur, Joseph, Nethaniah, and Asarelah, were under the direction of their father and played music whenever the king told them to.

3Jeduthun's six sons, Gedaliah, Zeri, Jeshaiah, Shimei,^e Hashabiah, and Mattithiah, were under the direction of their father and played harps and sang praises to the LORD.

4Heman had 14 sons: Bukkiah, Mattaniah, Uzziel, Shebuel, Jerimoth, Hananiah, Hanani, Eliathah, Giddalti, Romamtiezer, Joshbekashah, Mallothi, Hothir, Mahazioth. **5**Heman was one of the king's proph-

^c**24.5** *asked God what to do:* The Hebrew text has "cast lots" (see the note at 6.65). ^d**24.26,27** *Ibri:* One possible meaning for the difficult Hebrew text of verses 26,27. ^e**25.3** *Shimei:* One Hebrew manuscript and two ancient translations; other Hebrew manuscripts do not have this name.

26.14-16 *East Gate . . . West Gate:* The four main gates to the temple each faced a different direction. The East Gate was the main entrance and had six guard posts. The others had four. The South Gate was closest to David and Solomon's palaces. The honor of guarding it was probably given to Obed-Edom because he had taken care of the sacred chest (13.13,14). Particular laws governed how the people were to enter and leave by the gates (Ezek 46.1-10). **(See Map 5 on pg 1883.)**

ets, and God honored Heman by giving him 14 sons and 3 daughters. [6]His sons were under his direction and played cymbals, harps, and other stringed instruments during times of worship at the temple.

Asaph, Jeduthun, and Heman took their orders directly from the king.

[7]There were 288 of these men, and all of them were skilled musicians. [8]David assigned them their duties by asking the LORD what he wanted.[f] Everyone was responsible for something, whether young or old, teacher or student.

[9-31]The musicians were divided into 24 groups of twelve, and each group went by the name of their family leader. They were assigned their duties in the following order: Joseph, Gedaliah, Zaccur, Zeri, Nethaniah, Bukkiah, Asarelah, Jeshaiah, Mattaniah, Shimei, Uzziel, Hashabiah, Shebuel, Mattithiah, Jerimoth, Hananiah, Joshbekashah, Hanani, Mallothi, Eliathah, Hothir, Giddalti, Mahazioth, and Romamtiezer.

The Temple Guards Are Assigned Their Duties

26 The temple guards were also divided into groups according to clans.

Meshelemiah son of Kore was from the Korah clan and was a descendant of Asaph. [2]He had seven sons, who were born in the following order: Zechariah, Jediael, Zebadiah, Jathniel, [3]Elam, Jehohanan, and Eliehoenai.

[4-5]Obed-Edom had been blessed with eight sons: Shemaiah, Jehozabad, Joah, Sachar, Nethanel, Ammiel, Issachar, and Peullethai.

[6-7]Shemaiah was the father of Othni, Rephael, Obed, Elzabad, Elihu, and Semachiah. They were all respected leaders in their clan. [8]There were 62 descendants of Obed-Edom who were strong enough to be guards at the temple.

[9]Eighteen descendants of Meshelemiah were chosen for this work.

[10-11]Hosah, from the Merari clan, was the father of Shimri, Hilkiah, Tebaliah, and Zechariah. Hosah had made Shimri the family leader, even though he was not the oldest son. Thirteen men from Hosah's family were chosen to be temple guards.

[12]The guards were divided into groups, according to their family leaders, and they were assigned duties at the temple, just like the other Levites. [13]Each group, no matter how large or small, was assigned a gate to guard, and they let the LORD show them what he wanted done.[g]

[14]Shelemiah[h] was chosen to guard the East Gate. Zechariah his son was a wise man and was chosen to guard the North Gate. [15]Obed-Edom was then chosen to guard the South Gate, and his sons were chosen to guard the storerooms. [16]Shuppim and Hosah were chosen to guard the West Gate and the Shallecheth Gate on the upper road.

The guards were assigned the following work schedule: [17]Each day six guards were on duty on the east side of the temple, four were on duty on the north side, and four were on duty on the south side. Two guards were stationed at each of the two storerooms, [18]four were stationed along the road leading to the west courtyard,[i] and two guards stayed in the court itself.

[f]**25.8** *asking the* LORD *what he wanted:* The Hebrew text has "casting lots" (see the note at 6.65). [g]**26.13** *they let the* LORD *show them what he wanted done:* The Hebrew text has "they cast lots to find out what the* LORD *wanted done" (see the note at 6.65). [h]**26.14** *Shelemiah:* Another spelling for Meshelemiah. [i]**26.18** *courtyard:* One possible meaning for the difficult Hebrew text.

[19]These were the guard duties assigned to the men from the clans of Korah and Merari.

Guards Are Assigned to the Treasury

[20]The Levites who were relatives of the Korahites and the Merarites were[j] in charge of guarding the temple treasury and the gifts that had been dedicated to God. [21]Ladan was from the Gershon clan and was the father of Jehieli. Many of his other descendants were family leaders in the clan.[k] [22]Jehieli was the father of Zetham and Joel, and they were responsible for guarding the treasury.

[23]Other guards at the treasury were from the Kohathite clans of Amram, Izhar, Hebron, and Uzziel. [24]Shebuel was a descendant of Gershom the son of Moses. He was the chief official in charge of the temple treasury. [25]The descendants of Gershom's brother Eliezer included Rehabiah, Jeshaiah, Joram, Zichri, and Shelomoth.

[26]Shelomoth and his relatives were in charge of all the gifts that were dedicated to the LORD. These included the gifts that King David had dedicated, as well as those dedicated by the family leaders, army officers, and army commanders. [27]And whenever valuable things were captured in battle, these men brought back some of them to make repairs to the temple. [28]Shelomoth and his relatives were responsible for any gifts that had been given to the temple, including those from Samuel the prophet, King Saul the son of Kish, Abner the son of Ner,[l] and Joab the son of Zeruiah.

Other Officers Are Assigned Their Duties

[29]Chenaniah from the Izhar clan and his sons were government officials and judges. They did not work at the temple.

[30]Hashabiah from the Hebron clan and 1,700 of his skilled relatives were the officials in charge of all religious and government business in the Israelite territories west of the Jordan River.

[31-32]Jerijah was the leader of the Hebron clan. David assigned him and 2,700 of his relatives, who were all respected family leaders, to be the officials in charge of all religious and government business in the tribes of Reuben, Gad, and East Manasseh. David found out about these men during the fortieth year of his rule, when he had a list made of all the families in the Hebron clan. They were from the town of Jazer in the territory of Gilead.

David Assigns Army Commanders

27 Each month a group of 24,000 men served as soldiers in Israel's army. These men, which included the family leaders, army commanders, and officials of the king, were under the command of the following men, arranged by the month of their service:

[2]In the first month, Jashobeam the son of Zabdiel, [3]a descendant of Perez;

[4]in the second month, Dodai the Ahohite, whose assistant was Mikloth;[m]

[5]in the third month, Benaiah the son of Jehoiada the priest, [6]who was the leader of the Thirty Warriors, and

● 26.20 *temple treasury . . . gifts that had been dedicated:* These included the gifts the people brought, the precious furnishings and equipment, and those things taken in warfare (26.26,27; 2 Chr 5.1).

● 27.1-15 *following men:* The regular army of Israel was made up of twelve divisions of 24,000 men each. The commanders of these divisions are listed here, and they are also are named in the list of David's warriors (11.11-14,20-47). This may indicate that David rewarded those who were faithful to him when he ran away from Saul (1 Sam 21–24). Besides the regular monthly army, many other warriors were available if a full-scale war broke out (21.5).

[j]**26.20** *The Levites . . . were:* One ancient translation; Hebrew "Ahijah the Levite was." [k]**26.21** *Many of his other . . . clan:* One possible meaning for the difficult Hebrew text. [l]**26.28** *Abner the son of Ner:* Abner was King Saul's uncle (see 9.39). [m]**27.4** *whose . . . Mikloth:* One possible meaning for the difficult Hebrew text.

● 27.16-22 *leaders of each tribe*: The leaders of ten of the tribes are named along with the leaders of the Levites and the descendants of Aaron, but the tribes of Asher and Gad are not mentioned. (See the chart Jacob's Children and Their Mothers on pg 1824.)

ᴄ፝ᴇ Israel

● 27.25-31 *Azmaveth . . . royal property*: This and the earlier lists (chapters 22–24) are evidence of the great wealth David had in terms of people and property. As there is no evidence that David ever taxed the people of Israel, it appears he was able to finance the nation by way of trade, earnings on the land he held, valuables captured in wars, and taxes (tribute) paid by nations he conquered.

whose son Ammizabad was also an army commander;[n]

[7]in the fourth month, Asahel the brother of Joab, whose son Zebadiah took over command after him;

[8]in the fifth month, Shamhuth from the Izrah clan;

[9]in the sixth month, Ira the son of Ikkesh from Tekoa;

[10]in the seventh month, Helez from Pelon in the territory of Ephraim;

[11]in the eighth month, Sibbecai from Hushah of the Zerah clan;

[12]in the ninth month, Abiezer from Anathoth in the territory of Benjamin;

[13]in the tenth month, Maharai from Netophah of the Zerah clan;

[14]in the eleventh month, Benaiah from Pirathon in the territory of Ephraim;

[15]in the twelfth month, Heldai from Netophah, who was a descendant of Othniel.

David Assigns Tribal Leaders

[16-22]Here is a list of the leaders of each tribe in Israel:

Eliezer son of Zichri was over Reuben; Shephatiah son of Maacah was over Simeon; Hashabiah son of Kemuel was over the Levites, and Zadok the priest was over the descendants of Aaron; Elihu the brother of David was over Judah; Omri son of Michael was over Issachar; Ishmaiah son of Obadiah was over Zebulun; Jerimoth son of Azriel was over Naphtali; Hoshea son of Azaziah was over Ephraim; Joel son of Pedaiah was over West Manasseh; Iddo son of Zechariah was over East Manasseh; Jaasiel son of Abner was over Benjamin; Azarel son of Jeroham was over Dan.

[23]When David decided to count the people of Israel, he gave orders not to count anyone under 20 years of age, because the Lord had promised long ago that Israel would have as many people as there are stars in the sky. [24]Joab the son of Zeruiah had begun to count the people, but he stopped when the Lord began punishing Israel. So the total number was never included in David's official records.

Officials in Charge of the King's Property

[25]Azmaveth the son of Adiel was in charge of the king's personal storage rooms. Jonathan the son of Uzziah was in charge of the king's other storerooms that were in the towns, the villages, and the defense towers in Israel.

[26]Ezri the son of Chelub was in charge of the workers who farmed the king's land.

[27]Shimei from Ramah was in charge of the vineyards, and Zabdi from Shepham was in charge of storing the wine.

[28]Baal Hanan from Geder was in charge of the olive and sycamore trees in the western foothills, and Joash was in charge of storing the olive oil.

[29]Shitrai from Sharon was responsible for the cattle that were kept in Sharon Plain, and Shaphat son of Adlai was responsible for those kept in the valleys.

[30]Obil the Ishmaelite was in charge of the camels, Jehdeiah from Meronoth was in charge of the donkeys, and Jaziz the Hagrite was in charge of the sheep and goats.

[31]These were the men in charge of David's royal property.

---

[n]27.6 *whose son Ammizabad . . . army commander*: One possible meaning for the difficult Hebrew text.

David's Personal Advisors

³²David's uncle Jonathan was a wise and intelligent advisor. He and Jehiel the son of Hachmoni taught David's sons.

³³Ahithophel and Hushai the Archite were two of David's advisors. ³⁴Jehoiada the son of Benaiah was the king's advisor after Ahithophel, and later, Abiathar was his advisor.

Joab was commander of Israel's army.

David Gives Solomon the Plans for the Temple

28 David called a meeting in Jerusalem for all of Israel's leaders, including the tribal leaders, the government officials, the army commanders, the officials in charge of the royal property and livestock, the palace officials, and the brave warriors. ²After everyone was there, David stood up and said:

Listen to me, my people. I wanted to build a place where the sacred chest would be kept, so we could go there and worship the LORD our God. I have prepared all the supplies for building a temple, ³but the LORD has refused to let me build it, because he said I have killed too many people in battle.

⁴The LORD God chose Judah to be the leading tribe in Israel. Then from Judah, he chose my father's family, and from that family, he chose me to be the king of Israel, and he promised that my descendants will also rule as kings. ⁵The LORD has blessed me with many sons, but he chose my son Solomon to be the next king of Israel. ⁶The LORD said to me, "Your son Solomon will build my temple, and it will honor me. Solomon will be like a son to me, and I will be like a father to him. ⁷If he continues to obey my laws and commands, his kingdom will never end."

⁸My friends, you are the LORD's people. And now, with God as your witness, I want you to promise that you will do your best to obey everything the LORD God has commanded us. Then this land will always belong to you and your descendants.

⁹Solomon, my son, worship God and obey him with all your heart and mind, just as I have done. He knows all your thoughts and your reasons for doing things, and so if you turn to him, he will hear your prayers. But if you ignore him, he will reject you forever. ¹⁰The LORD has chosen you to build a temple for worshiping him. Be confident and do the work you have been assigned.

¹¹After David finished speaking, he gave Solomon the plans for building the main rooms of the temple, including the porch, the storerooms, the rooms upstairs and downstairs, as well as the most holy place. ¹²He gave Solomon his plans for the courtyards and the open areas around the temple, and for the rooms to store the temple treasures and gifts that had been dedicated to God.

¹³David also gave Solomon his plans for dividing the priests and the Levites into groups, as well as for the work that needed to be done at the temple and for taking care of the objects used for worship. ¹⁴He told Solomon how much gold and silver was to be used in making the sacred objects, ¹⁵including the lampstands and lamps, ¹⁶the gold table which held the sacred loaves of bread, the tables made of silver, ¹⁷the meat forks, the bowls and cups, ¹⁸the gold incense altar, and the gold statue of a chariot for the winged creatures which were on the lid of the sacred chest.

¹⁹David then said to Solomon:

28.8,9 *you are the LORD's people . . . reject you forever:* Just as the temple was to be God's permanent home on earth (28.2), Israel was to be the people's permanent home on earth. David reminds the people and Solomon that this promise and the promise of God's great blessing depend on their obedience to God's laws.

28.19 *The LORD showed . . . built:* Just as Moses was given God's Law, which showed the people how to live (Exod 20), David was given the plans for the temple where the people would worship God in the proper way.

David said, "Solomon, my son, worship God and obey him with all your heart and mind, just as I have done." 1 CHR 28.9

■ 29.1 *God chose my son Solomon:* The Hebrew word for "chosen" used here and in 28.5,10 is only used in reference to Solomon and to no other king after David.

The LORD showed me how his temple is to be built. **20**But you must see that everything is done according to these plans. Be confident, and never be afraid of anything or get discouraged. The LORD my God will help you do everything needed to finish the temple, so it can be used for worshiping him. **21**The priests and Levites have been assigned their duties, and all the skilled workers are prepared to do their work. The people and their leaders will do anything you tell them.

Gifts for Building the Temple

29 David told the crowd:
God chose my son Solomon to build the temple, but Solomon is young and has no experience. This is not just any building—this is the temple for the LORD God! **2**That's why I have done my best to get everything Solomon will need to build it—gold, silver, bronze, iron, wood, onyx, turquoise, colored gems, all kinds of precious stones, and marble.

3Besides doing all that, I have promised to give part of my own gold and silver as a way of showing my love for God's temple. **4**Almost 120 tons of my finest gold and over 250 tons of my silver will be used to decorate its walls **5**and to make the gold and silver objects. Now, who else will show their dedication to the LORD by giving gifts for building his temple?

6After David finished speaking, the family leaders, the tribal leaders, the army commanders, and the government officials voluntarily gave gifts **7**for the temple. These gifts included almost 200 tons of gold, 380 tons of silver, almost 700 tons of bronze, and 3,750 tons of iron. **8**Everyone who owned precious stones also donated them to the temple treasury, where Jehiel from the Levite clan of Gershon guarded them.

9David and the people were very happy that so much had been given to the LORD, and they all celebrated.

David Praises the LORD

10Then, in front of everyone, David sang praises to the LORD:

I praise you forever, LORD! You are the God our ancestor Jacob[o] worshiped. **11**Your power is great, and your glory is seen everywhere in heaven and on earth. You are king of the entire world, **12**and you rule with strength and power. You make people rich and powerful and famous. **13**We thank you, our God, and praise you.

14But why should we be happy that we have given you these gifts? They belong to you, and we have only given back what is already yours. **15**We are only foreigners living here on earth for a while, just as our ancestors were. And we will soon be gone, like a shadow that suddenly disappears.

16Our LORD God, we have brought all these things for building a temple to honor you. They belong to you, and you gave them to us. **17**But we are happy, because everyone has voluntarily given you these things. You know what is in everyone's heart, and you are pleased when people are honest. **18**Always make us eager to give, and help us be faithful to you, just as our ancestors Abraham, Isaac, and Jacob

---

[o]**29.10** *Jacob:* See the note at 1.34.

faithfully worshiped you. **19**And give Solomon the desire to completely obey your laws and teachings, and the desire to build the temple for which I have provided these gifts.

20David then said to the people, "Now it's your turn to praise the LORD, the God your ancestors worshiped!" So everyone praised the LORD, and they bowed down to honor him and David their king.

Solomon Is Crowned King

21The next day, the Israelites slaughtered 1,000 bulls, 1,000 rams, and 1,000 lambs, and they offered them as sacrifices to please the LORD,P along with offerings of wine. **22**The people were very happy, and they ate and drank there at the LORD's altar.

That same day, Solomon was again crowned king. The people celebrated and poured olive oil on Solomon's head to show that he would be their next king. They also poured oil on Zadok's head to show that he was their priest.

23So Solomon became king after David his father. Solomon was successful, and everyone in Israel obeyed him. **24**Every official and every soldier, as well as all of David's other sons, were loyal to him. **25**The LORD made Solomon a great king, and the whole nation was amazed at how famous he was. In fact, no other king of Israel was as great as Solomon.

David Dies

26David the son of Jesse was king of Israel **27**for 40 years. He ruled from Hebron for 7 years and from Jerusalem for 33 years. **28**David was rich and respected and lived to be an old man. Then he died, and his son Solomon became king.

29Everything David did while he was king is included in the history written by the prophets Samuel, Nathan, and Gad. **30**They wrote about his powerful rule and about the things that happened not only to him, but also to Israel and the other nations.

29.24 *Every official . . . loyal to him:* This ignores the events recorded in 1 Kgs 1, which describes Adonijah and others attempting to take the throne from David.

29.29,30 *Samuel, Nathan, and Gad . . . wrote about:* These three are given credit for writing the books of SAMUEL and KINGS, or some other separate unknown history of David.

P**29.21** *sacrifices to please the LORD*: See the note at 16.1.

No other king of Israel was as great as Solomon.
1 CHR 29.25

Reflection Questions About 1 Chronicles 1.1—29.30

1. The writer of 1 CHRONICLES was writing this history for those Israelites who had returned from exile in Babylonia. Why would the long family lists be important to them?

2. Why had the Israelites been in exile in Babylonia (9.1,2)? Why do you think the writer reminds the readers of this?

3. Why do you think the writer gave additional attention to the tribes of Judah and Levi? In the end, what do you think will be of greater importance to the Israelites, the continuation of the kingly line of David or the continuation of proper worship?

4. David was promised that when he became king, everyone in Israel would support him (11.10). When David is at Hebron, what evidence is given that David will receive unified support from Israel's tribes (12.1-40)?

5. Why was it so important for David to bring the sacred chest to Jerusalem (13.1—16.43)?

6. What is your reaction to God's severe punishment of Uzzah (13.9-11)? Why was God so angry? What is the positive lesson this story seeks to teach?

7. Read 5.20-22; 14.8-17. What does the Holy War concept have to do with David's kingship? Where have you heard of the concept of "holy war" in today's society? In your opinion, are any wars being fought today true "holy wars"? Why or why not?

8. What was God's promise to David (17.3-15)? How is this promise significant to David? To the people of Israel? To Christians today?

9. List at least five things David contributed toward the building and functioning of the temple (22.1—29.30).

10. "Solomon" is related to the Hebrew word for "peace." How does this help us to understand why God chose Solomon rather than David to build the temple (22.6-9)?

2 chronicles

Remembering a golden age from the past can give people strength and hope even when they are living in exile. Read 2 CHRONICLES and see how God's chosen people were encouraged by recalling their faithful leaders from the past.

WHAT MAKES 2 CHRONICLES SPECIAL?

The book of 2 CHRONICLES continues the story told in 1 CHRONICLES, and before that, in the books of SAMUEL and KINGS. But 2 CHRONICLES introduces a new point of view. The writer of 2 CHRONICLES is more concerned with the ways of proper worship than with political matters, focusing on encouraging the people who had returned from exile in Babylon to reestablish their religious practices and institutions in the tradition of those who had gone before them.

WHAT'S THE STORY BEHIND THE SCENE?

The book of 2 CHRONICLES repeats many stories that are found in 1 and 2 KINGS, but from the point of view of devotion to faith. The original readers of those earlier books had lived during the exile and had experienced the destruction of Jerusalem and the end of the rule by David's ancestors. Their lives were filled with questions, such as "Why did this happen to us?" and "Did God's plan fail?" The books of SAMUEL and KINGS answer these questions by showing that God did not fail. God fulfilled his warning that the people would be punished for their failure to live up to their agreement to obey God's word.

The books of CHRONICLES, on the other hand, are addressed to people who have returned from exile in Babylon. Their questions are different and require a different telling of the story. Instead of asking "Why did this happen to us?" the people want to ask: "Are we still the people of God?" and "What do God's

promises to David mean for us today?" The books of CHRONICLES retell the story of Israel's past in ways that speak to these questions.

HOW IS 2 CHRONICLES CONSTRUCTED?

The book of 2 CHRONICLES is told in three major sections. The first section (2 Chr 1–9) tells the story of Solomon, the builder of the temple. The second section (2 Chr 10–28) retells the story of the divided monarchy following the rebellion of the northern tribes, but it records only the history of the southern kingdom, Judah. The third section (2 Chr 29–36) presents the story of the monarchy from the conquest of the northern kingdom by the Assyrians until the exile of the people of Judah to Babylon. At the close of 2 CHRONICLES, King Cyrus of Persia declares the end of the exile, and the people are allowed to return to Judah.

Solomon, builder of the temple (1.1—9.31)
   Solomon's wisdom and wealth (1.1-17)
   Solomon builds the temple (2.1—5.1)
   Solomon dedicates the temple (5.2—7.22)
   Solomon's long rule (8.1—9.31)
The divided monarchy (10.1—28.27)
   Introduction: The North Revolts (10.1—11.4)
   Kings of Judah (11.5—28.27)
The end of the divided monarchy (29.1—36.23)
   Hezekiah's reform (29.1—32.33)
   Manasseh and Amon (33.1-25)
   Josiah's reform (34.1—35.27)
   Judah's defeat, exile, and return (36.1-23)

First and Second Chronicles are actually one long book. Together, they present a historical survey of God's people from Adam to the return of the exiled people from Babylonia in 538 B.C. The author's key theme is that times and circumstances may change, but the Lord remains with his people, always ready to help the faithful. Rather than give political details, 2 Chronicles shows history in terms of proper worship and the people's agreement with the Lord. The author pays particular attention to rulers of the southern kingdom (Judah) who were faithful to the Lord and ignores the history of the rebellious northern tribes. Much attention is given to Solomon and the construction of the temple in Jerusalem. The author goes on to recount the history of the divided kingdom and tells how Judah was defeated by the Babylonian Kingdom in 586 B.C. and its people taken into exile. Second Chronicles concludes by noting that King Cyrus of Persia allowed the people to return home to Judah.

Outline

The LORD Makes Solomon Wise

(1 Kings 3.1-15)

1 King Solomon, the son of David, was now in complete control of his kingdom, because the LORD God had blessed him and made him a powerful king.

2-5 At that time, the sacred tent that Moses the servant of the LORD had made in the desert was still kept at Gibeon, and in front of the tent was the bronze altar that Bezalel[a] had made.

One day, Solomon told the people of Israel, the army commanders, the officials, and the family leaders, to go with him to the place of worship at Gibeon, even though his father King David had already moved the sacred chest from Kiriath-Jearim to the tent that he had set up for it in Jerusalem. Solomon and the others went to Gibeon to worship the LORD, **6**and

there at the bronze altar, Solomon offered a thousand animals as sacrifices to please the LORD.[b]

7God appeared to Solomon that night in a dream and said, "Solomon, ask for anything you want, and I will give it to you."

8Solomon answered:

LORD God, you were always loyal to my father David, and now you have made me king of Israel. **9**I am supposed to rule these people, but there are as many of them as there are specks of dust on the ground. So keep the promise you made to my father **10**and make me wise. Give me the knowledge I'll need to be the king of this great nation of yours.

11God replied:

Solomon, you could have asked me to make you rich or famous or to let you live a long time. Or you could

---

a1.2-5 *Bezalel*: Hebrew "Bezalel son of Uri son of Hur."   **b**1.6 *sacrifices to please the* LORD: These sacrifices have traditionally been called "whole burnt offerings," because the whole animal was burned on the altar. A main purpose of such sacrifices was to please the LORD with the smell of the sacrifice, and so in the CEV they are often called "sacrifices to please the LORD."

● 1.1 *Solomon . . . David:* Solomon was the second son of David and Bathsheba (2 Sam 12.24). He followed his father as king and was chosen by God to build the temple in Jerusalem (1 Chr 28.1—29.2). The writer of 2 CHRONICLES is primarily concerned with Solomon's greatness as king and builder of the temple, and so ignores the violence that was part of his path to the throne (1 Kgs 1,2). David was king of Israel from about 1010 to 970 B.C., and was the most famous king Israel ever had. Many of the people of Israel hoped that one of his descendants would always be their king.

☙ Solomon

☙ David

■ 1.7,8 *in a dream . . . you have made me king:* God spoke to people in dreams and visions. Solomon's words "you have made me king" show his proper understanding of kingship in Israel. God chooses Israel's earthly kings, who then carry out God's will.

have asked for your enemies to be destroyed. Instead, you asked for wisdom and knowledge to rule my people. ¹²So I will make you wise and intelligent. But I will also make you richer and more famous than any king before or after you.

¹³Solomon then left Gibeon and returned to Jerusalem, the capital city of Israel.

Solomon's Wealth
(1 Kings 10.26-29)

¹⁴ Solomon had a force of 1,400 chariots and 12,000 horses that he kept in Jerusalem and other towns.

¹⁵While Solomon was king of Israel, there was silver and gold everywhere in Jerusalem, and cedar was as common as ordinary sycamore trees in the foothills.

¹⁶⁻¹⁷ Solomon's merchants bought his horses and chariots in the regions of Musri and Kue.ᶜ They paid about 15 pounds of silver for a chariot and almost 4 pounds of silver for a horse. They also sold horses and chariots to the Hittite and Syrian kings.

Solomon Asks Hiram
To Help Build the Temple
(1 Kings 5.1-12)

2 Solomon decided to build a temple where the LORD would be worshiped, and also to build a palace for himself. ²He assigned 70,000 men to carry building supplies and 80,000 to cut stone from the hills. And he chose 3,600 men to supervise these workers.

³Solomon sent the following message to King Hiram of Tyre:

Years ago, when my father David was building his palace, you supplied him with cedar logs. Now will you send me supplies? ⁴I am building a temple where the LORD my God will be worshiped. Sweet-smelling incense will be burned there, and sacred bread will be offered to him. Worshipers will offer sacrifices to the LORD every morning and evening, every Sabbath, and on the first day of each month, as well as during all our religious festivals. These things will be done for all time, just as the LORD has commanded.

⁵This will be a great temple, because our God is greater than all other gods. ⁶ No one can ever build a temple large enough for God—even the heavens are too small a place for him to live in! All I can do is build a place where we can offer sacrifices to him.

⁷Send me a worker who can not only carve, but who can work with gold, silver, bronze, and iron, as well as make brightly colored cloth. The person you send will work here in Judah and Jerusalem with the skilled workers that my father has already hired.

⁸I know that you have workers who are experts at cutting lumber in Lebanon. So would you please send me some cedar, pine, and juniper logs? My workers will be there to help them, ⁹because I'll need a lot of lumber to build such a large and glorious temple. ¹⁰I will pay your woodcutters 125,000 bushels of wheat, the same amount of barley, 115,000 gallons of wine, and that same amount of olive oil.

¹¹Hiram sent his answer back to Solomon:

I know that the LORD must love his people, because he has chosen you to be their king. ¹²Praise the LORD God of

Side notes

1.13 *Jerusalem:* Jerusalem was Israel's political and religious capital. **(See Map 4 on pg 1882.)**

Jerusalem

1.16-17 *Hittite and Syrian kings:* The Hittite nation had its capital in what is now modern-day Turkey. At one time its empire included part of the land the Israelites now occupied. Syria occupied a large area north of Israel. **(See Map 1 on pg 1879.)**

2.3 *King Hiram of Tyre:* Tyre was the most important city in Phoenicia. It was located north of Israel on the coast of the Mediterranean Sea, in modern south Lebanon. **(See Map 6 on pg 1884.)**

2.7 *Send me . . . brightly colored cloth:* The Phoenicians were well known in the ancient world for their skills in many crafts.

Phoenicia

2.8 *cedar, pine, and juniper:* Cedar is an extremely hard wood that resists dry rot and insects, has a beautiful tight grain for carving, and is valued for its distinctive smell. At one time, cedar forests covered most of the Lebanon mountain range that runs north of Tyre for about 100 miles along the Syrian coast. In general, however, large forests were not common in this part of the world, and so all wood was precious. **(See Map 4 on pg 1882.)**

ᶜ1.16,17 *Musri and Kue:* Hebrew "Egypt and Kue." Musri and Kue were regions located in what is today southeast Turkey.

Hiram said to Solomon, "*I know that the LORD must love his people, because he has chosen you to be their king.*" 2 CHR 2.11

Israel who made heaven and earth! He has given David a son who isn't only wise and smart, but who has the knowledge to build a temple for the LORD and a palace for himself.

[13]I am sending Huram Abi to you. He is wise and very skillful. [14]His mother was from the Israelite tribe of Dan, and his father was from Tyre. Not only is Huram an expert at working with gold, silver, bronze, iron, stone, and wood, but he can also make colored cloth and fine linen. And he can carve anything if you give him a pattern to follow. He can help your workers and those hired by your father King David.

[15]Go ahead and send the wheat, barley, olive oil, and wine you promised to pay my workers. [16]I will tell them to start cutting down trees in Lebanon. They will cut as many as you need, then tie them together into rafts, and float them down along the coast to Joppa. Your workers can take them to Jerusalem from there.

Solomon's Work Force

[17]Solomon counted all the foreigners who were living in Israel, just as his father David had done when he was king, and the total was 153,600. [18]He assigned 70,000 of them to carry building supplies and 80,000 of them to cut stone from the hills. He chose 3,600 others to supervise the workers and to make sure the work was completed.

The Temple Is Built
(1 Kings 6.1-38)

3 [1-2]Solomon's workers began building the temple in Jerusalem on the second day of the second month,[d] four years after Solomon had become king of Israel. It was built on Mount Moriah where the LORD had appeared to David at the threshing place that had belonged to Araunah[e] from Jebus.

[3]The inside of the temple was 90 feet long and 30 feet wide, according to the older standards.[f] [4]Across the front of the temple was a porch 30 feet wide and 30 feet[g] high. The inside walls of the porch were covered with pure gold.

[5]Solomon had the inside walls of the temple's main room paneled first with pine and then with a layer of gold, and he had them decorated with carvings of palm trees and designs that looked like chains. [6]He used precious stones to decorate the temple, and he used gold imported from Parvaim[h] [7]to decorate the ceiling beams, the doors, the door frames, and the walls. Solomon also told the workers to carve designs of winged creatures into the walls.

[8]The most holy place was 30 feet square, and its walls were covered with almost 25 tons of fine gold. [9]More than a pound of gold was used to cover the heads of the nails. The walls of the small storage rooms were also covered with gold.[i]

[10]Solomon had two statues of winged creatures[j] made to put in the most holy place, and he covered them with gold.

● 2.13,14 *Huram Abi . . . tribe of Dan:* Huram is called Hiram in 1 KINGS. There it says that Huram's mother was from the tribe of Naphtali (1 Kgs 7.13-14). Perhaps one of his mother's parents was of the Naphtali tribe, and the other of the Dan tribe. Or perhaps it was Huram's father who was from the tribe of Dan. Either of these circumstances would allow Huram to claim to be from Naphtali or Dan. The relationship to the Israelite community is what is important.

● 2.16 *Joppa:* This major port city is on the coast of the Mediterranean Sea. (See Map 4 on pg 1882 and the article Trade and Travel on pg 1806.)

[d]3.1,2 *second month*: Ziv, the second month of the Hebrew calendar, from about mid-April to mid-May.   [e]3.1,2 *Araunah*: The Hebrew text has "Ornan," another spelling of the name (see 2 Samuel 24.18-25; 1 Chronicles 21.18—22.1).   [f]3.3 *according to the older standards*: There were possibly two different standards of measurement during Israel's history.   [g]3.4 *30 feet*: Some manuscripts of two ancient translations; Hebrew "180 feet."   [h]3.6 *Parvaim*: An unknown place.   [i]3.9 *The walls . . . gold*: One possible meaning for the difficult Hebrew text.   [j]3.10 *statues of winged creatures*: These were symbols of the LORD's throne on earth (see Exodus 25.18-22).

4.1,2 *bronze altar . . . the Sea:* The bronze altar was the main altar where sacrifices were offered. This bronze altar outside the entrance to the temple was solid bronze while the one inside the sacred tent and the earlier altar were bronze over wood. The Sea was possibly used by the priests for ritual cleansing. It may have symbolized God's separation of the waters that covered the earth to make the sky, land, and ocean in the creation story (Gen 1.6-10; 1 Kgs 7.23-26; 1 Chr 18.8). The symbolism of the basin may have had its beginnings in an ancient Mesopotamian creation myth in which the hero-god battles the sea monster of Chaos. The Hebrews turned the story into a fight between God and evil.

11-13Each creature had two wings and was 15 feet from the tip of one wing to the tip of the other wing. Solomon set them next to each other in the most holy place, facing the doorway. Their wings were spread out and reached all the way across the 30 foot room.

14 A curtain[k] was made of fine linen woven with blue, purple, and red wool, and embroidered with designs of winged creatures.

The Two Columns
(1 Kings 7.15-22)

15Two columns were made for the entrance to the temple. Each one was 52 feet tall and had a cap on top that was seven and a half feet. 16The top of each column was decorated with designs that looked like chains[l] and with 100 carvings of pomegranates.[m] 17Solomon had one of the columns placed on the south side of the temple's entrance; it was called Jachin.[n] The other one was placed on the north side of the entrance; it was called Boaz.[o]

The Furnishings for the Temple
(1 Kings 7.23-51)

4 Solomon had a bronze altar made that was 30 feet square and 15 feet high. 2He also gave orders to make a large metal bowl called the Sea. It was 15 feet across, about seven and a half feet deep, and 45 feet around. 3Its outer edge was decorated with two rows of carvings of bulls, ten bulls to about every 18 inches, all made from the same piece of metal as the bowl. 4The bowl itself sat on top of twelve bronze bulls, with three bulls facing outward in each of four directions. 5The sides of the bowl were 4 inches thick, and its rim was in the shape of a cup that curved outward like flower petals. The bowl held about 15,000 gallons.

6 He also made ten small bowls and put five on each side of the large bowl. The small bowls were used to wash the animals that were burned on the altar as sacrifices, and the priests used the water in the large bowl to wash their hands.

7 Ten gold lampstands were also made according to the plans. Solomon placed these lampstands inside the temple, five on each side of the main room. 8 He also made ten tables and placed them in the main room, five on each side. And he made 100 small gold sprinkling bowls.

9Solomon gave orders to build two courtyards: a smaller one that only priests could use and a larger one. The doors to these courtyards were covered with bronze. 10The large bowl called the Sea was placed near the southeast corner of the temple.

11Huram made shovels, sprinkling bowls, and pans for hot ashes. Here is a list of the other furnishings he made for God's temple: 12two columns, two bowl-shaped caps for the tops of these columns, two chain designs on the caps, 13400 pomegranates[p] in two rows for the chain designs, 14the stands and the small bowls, 15the large bowl and the twelve bulls that held it up, 16pans for hot ashes, as well as shovels and meat forks.

Huram made all these things out of polished bronze 17by pouring melted bronze into the clay molds he had set up near

[k]3.14 *A curtain:* To separate the most holy place from the main room of the temple.   [l]3.16 *designs that looked like chains:* One possible meaning for the difficult Hebrew text.   [m]3.16 *pomegranates:* A pomegranate is a small red fruit that looks like an apple. In ancient times, it was a symbol of life.   [n]3.17 *Jachin:* Or "He (God) makes secure."   [o]3.17 *Boaz:* Or "He (God) is strong."   [p]4.13 *pomegranates:* See the note at 3.16.

the Jordan River, between Succoth and Zeredah.

18There were so many bronze furnishings that no one ever knew how much bronze it took to make them.

19Solomon also gave orders to make the following temple furnishings out of gold: the altar, the tables that held the sacred loaves of bread,⁹ **20**the lampstands and the lamps that burned in front of the most holy place, **21**flower designs, lamps and tongs, **22**lamp snuffers, small sprinkling bowls, ladles, fire pans, and the doors to the most holy place and the main room of the temple.

5 After the Lord's temple was finished, Solomon put in its storage rooms everything that his father David had dedicated to the Lord, including the gold and silver, and the objects used in worship.

Solomon Brings the Sacred Chest to the Temple
(1 Kings 8.1-13)

2-3 The sacred chest had been kept on Mount Zion, also known as the city of David. But Solomon decided to have the chest moved to the temple while everyone was in Jerusalem to celebrate the Festival of Shelters during the seventh month.ʳ

Solomon called together all the important leaders of Israel. **4-5**Then the priests and the Levites picked up the sacred chest, the sacred tent, and the objects used for worship, and they carried them to the temple. **6**Solomon and a crowd of people stood in front of the chest and sacrificed more sheep and cattle than could be counted.

7The priests carried the chest into the most holy place and put it under the winged creatures, **8**whose wings covered both the chest and the poles used for carrying it. **9**The poles were so long that they could be seen from just outside the most holy place, but not from anywhere else. And they stayed there from then on.

10The only things kept in the chest were the two flat stones Moses had put there when the Lord made his agreement with the people of Israel at Mount Sinai,ˢ after bringing them out of Egypt.

11-13 The priests of every group had gone through the ceremony to make themselves clean and acceptable to the Lord. The Levite musicians, including Asaph, Heman, Jeduthun, and their sons and relatives, were wearing robes of fine linen. They were standing on the east side of the altar, playing cymbals, small harps, and other stringed instruments. One hundred and twenty priests were with these musicians, and they were blowing trumpets.

They were praising the Lord by playing music and singing:

"The Lord is good,
and his love never ends."

Suddenly a cloud filled the temple as the priests were leaving the holy place. **14**The Lord's glory was in that cloud, and the light from it was so bright that the priests could not stay inside to do their work.

6 Solomon prayed:
"Our Lord, you said that you would live in a dark cloud.
2Now I've built a glorious temple where you can live forever."

---

⁹4.19 *sacred loaves of bread*: This bread was offered to the Lord and was a symbol of the Lord's presence in the temple. It was put out on special tables, and was replaced with fresh bread every week (see Leviticus 24.5-9). **ʳ5.2,3** *seventh month*: Tishri (also called Ethanim), the seventh month of the Hebrew calendar, from about mid-September to mid-October. **ˢ5.10** *Sinai*: Hebrew "Horeb."

● **4.17** *Jordan River, between Succoth and Zeredah*: The bronze furnishings were made here because the clay soil was needed to make the molds for the objects. Bronze is made by mixing copper and tin.

● **5.1** *temple was finished*: The temple took seven and a half years to build and was completed in Solomon's eleventh year as king, or about 959 B.C.

● **5.1** *everything that . . . dedicated*: Foreign kings offered gifts to David, and David collected valuable things from enemies he defeated (2 Sam 8.9-12; 1 Chr 18.11). These things were dedicated to the Lord (1 Chr 29.1-8).

● **5.2-3** *Mount Zion . . . city of David*: Mount Zion was a hill in Jerusalem. The City of David was the Jebusite fortress on Mount Zion that David conquered. **(See Map 5 on pg 1883.)**

◌﹅ Zion

● **5.2-3** *Festival of Shelters . . . seventh month*: The Festival of Shelters took place at the end of the fall harvest (Exod 23.16; Lev 23.33-36) and lasted for seven days.

▩ **5.14** *The Lord's glory*: Here as elsewhere, a cloud surrounds and covers God's appearance before the people (Exod 14.19,20; 33.9-11; 40.34-37; Ps 18.11; Isa 6.4; Mark 9.7). At other times, God appears under the cover of fire (Exod 3.2-4; 2 Chr 7.3; Ezek 1.27).

6.11 *solemn agreement:* This refers to the agreement God made with the people of Israel on Mount Sinai (Exod 19.1-7; 20.1-17).

⚭   Agreements (Covenants)

6.12-14 *bronze platform . . . prayed:* It was common for kings or priests to offer prayers from a special raised platform they had made (34.31). The platform was in the courtyard near the altar used for sacrifice, not inside the temple itself.

Solomon Speaks to the People
(1 Kings 8.14-21)

[3]Solomon turned toward the people standing there. Then he blessed them [4-6]and said:

Praise the LORD God of Israel! He brought his people out of Egypt long ago and later kept his promise to make my father David the king of Israel. The LORD also promised him that Jerusalem would be the city where his temple will be built, and now that promise has come true. [7]When my father wanted to build a temple for the LORD God of Israel, [8]the LORD said, "It's good that you want to build a temple where I can be worshiped. [9]But you're not the one to do it. Your son will build the temple to honor me."

[10]The LORD has done what he promised. I am now the king of Israel, and I've built a temple for the LORD our God. [11]I've also put the sacred chest in the temple. And in that chest are the two flat stones on which is written the solemn agreement the LORD made with our ancestors when he rescued them from Egypt.

Solomon Prays at the Temple
(1 Kings 8.22-53)

[12-13]Earlier, Solomon had a bronze platform made that was eight feet square and five feet high, and he put it in the center of the outer courtyard near the altar. Solomon stood on the platform facing the altar with everyone standing behind him. Then he lifted his arms toward heaven; he knelt down [14]and prayed:

LORD God of Israel, no other god in heaven or on earth is like you!

You never forget the agreement you made with your people, and you are loyal to anyone who faithfully obeys your teachings. [15]My father David was your servant, and today you have kept every promise you made to him. [16]You promised that someone from his family would always be king of Israel, if they do their best to obey you, just as he did. [17]Please keep this promise you made to your servant David. [18]There's not enough room in all of heaven for you, LORD God. How could you possibly live on earth in this temple I have built? [19]But I ask you to answer my prayer. [20]This is the temple where you have chosen to be worshiped. Please watch over it day and night and listen when I turn toward it and pray. [21]I am your servant, and the people of Israel belong to you, and so whenever any of us look toward this temple and pray, answer from your home in heaven and forgive our sins.

[22]Suppose someone accuses a person of a crime, and the accused has to stand in front of the altar in your temple and say, "I swear I am innocent!" [23]Listen from heaven and decide who is right. Then punish the guilty person and let the innocent one go free.

[24]Suppose your people Israel sin against you, and then an enemy defeats them. If they come to this temple and beg for forgiveness, [25]listen from your home in heaven. Forgive them and bring them back to the land you gave their ancestors.

[26]Suppose your people sin against you, and you punish them by holding back the rain. If they stop sinning and turn toward this temple to pray in your name, [27]listen from your home in heaven and forgive them. The peo-

ple of Israel are your servants, so teach them to live right. And send rain on the land you promised them forever.

²⁸Sometimes the crops may dry up or rot or be eaten by locusts^t or grasshoppers, and your people will be starving. Sometimes enemies may surround their towns, or your people will become sick with deadly diseases. ²⁹Please listen when anyone in Israel truly feels sorry and sincerely prays with arms lifted toward your temple. ³⁰You know what is in everyone's heart. So from your home in heaven answer their prayers, according to what they do and what is in their hearts. ³¹Then your people will worship you and obey you for as long as they live in the land you gave their ancestors.

³²Foreigners will hear about you and your mighty power, and some of them will come to live among your people Israel. If any of them pray toward this temple, ³³listen from your home in heaven and answer their prayers. Then everyone on earth will worship you, just as your own people Israel do, and they will know that I have built this temple in your honor.

³⁴Sometimes you will order your people to attack their enemies. Then your people will turn toward this temple I have built for you in your chosen city, and they will pray to you. ³⁵Answer their prayers from heaven and give them victory.

³⁶Everyone sins. But when your people sin against you, suppose you get angry enough to let their enemies drag them away to foreign countries. ³⁷⁻³⁹Later, they may feel sorry for what they did and ask your forgiveness. Answer them when they pray toward this temple I have built for you in your chosen city, here in this land you gave their ancestors. From your home in heaven, listen to their sincere prayers and forgive your people who have sinned against you.

⁴⁰Lord God, hear us when we pray in this temple. ⁴¹Come to your new home, where we have already placed the sacred chest, which is the symbol of your strength. I pray that when the priests announce your power to save people, those who are faithful to you will celebrate what you've done for them. ⁴²Always remember the love you had for your servant David,^u so that you will not reject your chosen kings.

Solomon Dedicates the Temple
(1 Kings 8.62-66)

7 As soon as Solomon finished praying, fire came down from heaven and burned up the offerings. The Lord's dazzling glory then filled the temple, ²and the priests could not go in.

³When the crowd of people saw the fire and the Lord's glory, they knelt down and worshiped the Lord. They prayed:

"The Lord is good,
  and his love never ends."

⁴⁻⁵Solomon and the people dedicated the temple to the Lord by sacrificing 22,000 cattle and 120,000 sheep. ⁶Everybody stood up during the ceremony. The priests were in their assigned places, blowing their trumpets. And the Levites faced them, playing

6.36-39 *Everyone sins . . . drag them away . . . forgive your people:* Solomon's prayer includes prophetic words about Israel's future. The people did sin by turning their backs on God, disobeying God's law, and worshiping idols. Many people in Israel were dragged away into exile by the Assyrians around 721 B.C. and later by the Babylonians in 587 B.C. after they destroyed Jerusalem and Solomon's temple. The exile was seen as God's punishment for the sins of the people of Israel. **(See the article From Joshua to the Exile: The People of Israel in the Promised Land on pg 1783.)**

7.1 *fire came down . . . burned up the offerings:* Fire coming down and burning up the offerings is a sign of God's presence and approval. Fire can also be a sign of God's disapproval for an improper offering (see Lev 10.2).

---

^t**6.28** *locusts:* A type of grasshopper that comes in swarms and causes great damage to crops.
^u**6.42** *the love you had for your servant David:* Or "how loyal your servant David was to you."

"You know what is in everyone's heart. So from your home in heaven answer their prayers." 2 Chr 6.30

7.8-10 *For 7 days . . . Festival of Shelters . . . seventh month:* It appears that the temple dedication was celebrated on the eighth to fourteenth days of the month and the Festival of Shelters on the fifteenth to twenty-second days of the month. The Great Day of Forgiveness fell on the tenth day of the month. On the Great Day of Forgiveness, the sins of the priests and the people were forgiven. Today this festival is known as Yom Kippur (Day of Atonement).

8.1,2 *20 years . . . towns that Hiram had given him:* The completion of both the temple and palace would have been about 946 B.C. (1 Kgs 6.38; 7.1). In 1 Kgs 9.10-14, Solomon gave these towns to Hiram, who rejected them because of their poor condition.

the musical instruments that David had made for them to use when they praised the LORD for his never-ending love.

[7] On that same day, Solomon dedicated the courtyard in front of the temple and got it ready to be used for worship. The bronze altar he had made was too small, so he used the courtyard to offer sacrifices to please the LORD[v] and grain sacrifices, and also to send up in smoke the fat from the other offerings.

[8] For 7 days, Solomon and the crowd celebrated the Festival of Shelters, and people came from as far away as the Egyptian Gorge in the south and Lebo-Hamath in the north. [9] Then on the next day, everyone came together for worship. They had celebrated a total of 14 days, 7 days for the dedication of the altar and 7 more days for the festival. [10] Then on the twenty-third day of the seventh month,[w] Solomon sent everyone home. They left very happy because of all the good things the LORD had done for David and Solomon, and for his people Israel.

The LORD Appears to Solomon Again
(1 Kings 9.1-9)

[11] The LORD's temple and Solomon's palace were now finished. In fact, everything Solomon had planned to do was completed.

[12] Some time later, the LORD appeared to Solomon in a dream and said:

I heard your prayer, and I have chosen this temple as the place where sacrifices will be offered to me.

[13] Suppose I hold back the rain or send locusts[x] to eat the crops or make

my people suffer with deadly diseases. [14] If my own people will humbly pray and turn back to me and stop sinning, then I will answer them from heaven. I will forgive them and make their land fertile once again. [15] I will hear the prayers made in this temple, [16] because it belongs to me, and this is where I will be worshiped forever. I will never stop watching over it.

[17] Your father David obeyed me, and now, Solomon, you must do the same. Obey my laws and teachings, [18] and I will keep my solemn promise to him that someone from your family will always be king of Israel.

[19] But if you or any of the people of Israel disobey my laws or start worshiping foreign gods, [20] I will pull you out of this land I gave you. I will desert this temple where I said I would be worshiped, so that people everywhere will think it is only a joke and will make fun of it. [21] This temple is now magnificent. But when these things happen, everyone who walks by it will be shocked and will ask, "Why did the LORD do such a terrible thing to his people and to this temple?" [22] Then they will answer, "It was because the people of Israel rejected the LORD their God, who rescued their ancestors from Egypt, and they started worshiping other gods."

Other Things Solomon Did
(1 Kings 9.10-28)

8 It took 20 years for the LORD's temple and Solomon's palace to be built. [2] After that, Solomon had his workers rebuild

---

[v]**7.7** *sacrifices to please the LORD:* See the note at 1.6.
[x]**7.13** *locusts:* See the note at 6.28.
[w]**7.10** *seventh month:* See the note at 5.2,3.

the towns that Hiram had given him. Then Solomon sent Israelites to live in those towns.

³Solomon attacked and captured the town of Hamath-Zobah. ⁴He ordered his workers to build the town of Tadmor in the desert and some towns in Hamath where he could keep his supplies. ⁵He strengthened Upper Beth-Horon and Lower Beth-Horon by adding walls and gates that could be locked. ⁶He did the same thing to the town of Baalath and to the cities where he kept supplies, chariots, and horses. Solomon ordered his workers to build whatever he wanted in Jerusalem, Lebanon, and anywhere else in his kingdom.

⁷⁻⁹Solomon did not force the Israelites to do his work. Instead, they were his soldiers, officers, army commanders, and cavalry troops. But he did make slaves of the Hittites, Amorites, Perizzites, Hivites, and Jebusites who were living in Israel. These were the descendants of those foreigners the Israelites did not destroy, and they remained Israel's slaves.

¹⁰Solomon appointed 250 officers to be in charge of his workers.

¹¹Solomon's wife, the daughter of the king of Egypt, moved from the part of Jerusalem called David's City to her new palace that Solomon had built. The sacred chest had been kept in David's City, which made his palace sacred, and so Solomon's wife could no longer live there.

¹²Solomon offered sacrifices to the LORD on the altar he had built in front of the temple porch. ¹³He followed the requirements that Moses had given for sacrifices offered on the Sabbath, on the first day of each month, the Festival of Thin Bread, the Harvest Festival, and the Festival of Shelters.

¹⁴Solomon then assigned the priests and the Levites their duties at the temple, and he followed the instructions that his father, the man of God, had given him. Some of the Levites were to lead music and help the priests in their duties, and others were to guard the temple gates ¹⁵and the storage rooms. The priests and Levites followed these instructions exactly.

¹⁶Everything Solomon had planned to do was now finished—from the laying of the temple's foundation to its completion.

¹⁷Solomon went to Ezion-Geber and Eloth, two Edomite towns on the Red Sea.ʸ ¹⁸Hiram sent him ships and some of his experienced sailors. They went with Solomon's own sailors to the country of Ophirᶻ and brought back about 17 tons of gold for Solomon.

The Queen of Sheba Visits Solomon
(1 Kings 10.1-13)

9 The Queen of Sheba heard how famous Solomon was, so she went to Jerusalem to test him with difficult questions. She took along several of her officials, and she loaded her camels with gifts of spices, jewels, and gold. When she arrived, she and Solomon talked about everything she could think of. ²He answered every question, no matter how difficult it was.

³⁻⁴The Queen was amazed at Solomon's wisdom. She was breathless when she saw his palace,ᵃ the food on his table, his officials, all his servants in their uniforms, and the sacrifices he offered at the LORD's temple. ⁵She said:

Solomon, in my own country I had

ʸ8.17 *Red Sea*: Hebrew *yam suph*, here referring to the Gulf of Aqaba, since the term is extended to include the northeastern arm of the Red Sea (see also the note at Exodus 13.18). ᶻ8.18 *Ophir*: The location of this place is not known. ᵃ9.3,4 *his palace*: Or "the temple."

9.15,16 *gold shields:* These were probably used for ceremonies, as were the smaller round shields. Large shields that covered the whole body were the type normally used in battle.

9.25 *stalls for his horses and chariots:* Horses and chariots were an important part of a king's wealth in the ancient Near East. Archaeologists believe that the stables at Megiddo could have housed 450 horses.

heard about your wisdom and all you've done. **6**But I didn't believe it until I saw it with my own eyes! And there's so much I didn't hear about. You are greater than I was told. **7**Your people and officials are lucky to be here where they can listen to the wise things you say.

8I praise the LORD your God. He is pleased with you and has made you king of Israel. God loves the people of this country and will never desert them, so he has given them a king who will rule fairly and honestly.

9The Queen of Sheba gave Solomon almost five tons of gold, a large amount of jewels, and the best spices anyone had ever seen.

10-12 In return, Solomon gave her everything she wanted—even more than she had given him. Then she and her officials went back to their own country.

Solomon's Wealth
(1 Kings 10.14-29)

Hiram's and Solomon's sailors brought gold, juniper wood, and jewels from the country of Ophir. Solomon used the wood to make steps[b] for the temple and palace, and harps and other stringed instruments for the musicians. Nothing like these had ever been made in Judah.

13Solomon received about 25 tons of gold each year, **14**not counting what the merchants and traders brought him. The kings of Arabia and the leaders of Israel also gave him gold and silver.

15Solomon made 200 gold shields that weighed about seven and a half pounds

each. **16**He also made 300 smaller gold shields that weighed almost four pounds, and he put these shields in his palace in Forest Hall.

17His throne was made of ivory and covered with pure gold. **18**It had a gold footstool attached to it and armrests on each side. There was a statue of a lion on each side of the throne, **19**and there were two lion statues on each of the six steps leading up to the throne. No other throne in the world was like Solomon's.

20Solomon's cups and dishes in Forest Hall were made of pure gold, because silver was almost worthless in those days.

21Solomon had a lot of seagoing ships.[c] Every three years he sent them out with Hiram's ships to bring back gold, silver, and ivory, as well as monkeys and peacocks.[d]

22Solomon was the richest and wisest king in the world. **23-24**Year after year, other kings came to hear the wisdom God had given him. And they brought gifts of silver and gold, as well as clothes, weapons, spices, horses, and mules.

25 Solomon had 4,000 stalls for his horses and chariots, and he owned 12,000 horses that he kept in Jerusalem and other towns.

26 He ruled all the nations from the Euphrates River in the north to the land of Philistia in the south, as far as the border of Egypt.

27While Solomon was king, there was silver everywhere in Jerusalem, and cedar was as common as the sycamore trees in the western foothills. **28** Solomon's horses were brought in from other countries, including Musri.[e]

[b]**9.10-12** *steps:* Or "stools" or "railings."   [c]**9.21** *seagoing ships:* The Hebrew text has "ships of Tarshish," which may have been a Phoenician city in Spain. "Ships of Tarshish" probably means large, seagoing ships.   [d]**9.21** *peacocks:* Or "baboons."   [e]**9.28** *Musri:* See the note at 1.16,17.

Solomon Dies
(1 Kings 11.41-43)

29Everything else Solomon did while he was king is written in the records of Nathan the prophet, Ahijah the prophet from Shiloh, and Iddo the prophet who wrote about Jeroboam son of Nebat. **30**After Solomon had ruled 40 years from Jerusalem, **31**he died and was buried in the city of his father David. His son Rehoboam then became king.

Some of the People Rebel against Rehoboam
(1 Kings 12.1-20)

10 Rehoboam went to Shechem where everyone was waiting to crown him king.

2Jeroboam son of Nebat heard what was happening, and he returned from Egypt, where he had gone to hide from Solomon. **3**The people from the northern tribes of Israel sent for him. Then together they went to Rehoboam and said, **4**"Your father Solomon forced us to work very hard. But if you make our work easier, we will serve you and do whatever you ask."

5Rehoboam replied, "Come back in three days for my answer." So the people left.

6Rehoboam went to some leaders who had been his father's senior officials, and he asked them, "What should I tell these people?"

7They answered, "If you want them to serve and obey you, then you should be kind and promise to make their work easier."

8But Rehoboam refused their advice and went to the younger men who had grown up with him and were now his officials. **9**He asked, "What do you think I should say to these people who asked me to make their work easier?"

10His younger advisors said:

Here's what we think you should say to them: "Compared to me, my father was weak.**f** **11**He made you work hard, but I'll make you work even harder. He punished you with whips, but I'll use whips with pieces of sharp metal!"

12Three days later, Jeroboam and the others came back. **13**Rehoboam ignored the advice of the older advisors. He spoke bluntly **14**and told them exactly what his own advisors had suggested. He said: "My father made you work hard, but I'll make you work even harder. He punished you with whips, but I'll use whips with pieces of sharp metal!"

15-19 When the people realized that Rehoboam would not listen to them, they shouted: "We don't have to be loyal to David's family. We can do what we want. Come on, people of Israel, let's go home! Rehoboam can rule his own people."

Adoniram**g** was in charge of the work force, and Rehoboam sent him to talk to the people. But they stoned him to death. Then Rehoboam ran to his chariot and hurried back to Jerusalem.

Everyone from Israel's northern tribes went home, leaving Rehoboam to rule only the people from Judah. And since that day, the people of Israel have been opposed to David's descendants in Judah.**h** All of this happened just as Ahijah the LORD's prophet from Shiloh had told Jeroboam.

f10.10 *Compared . . . weak*: Hebrew "My little finger is bigger than my father's waist." **g10.15-19** *Adoniram*: The Hebrew text has "Hadoram," another spelling of the name. **h10.15-19** *the people of Israel have been opposed . . . Judah*: From this time on, "Israel" usually refers only to the northern kingdom. The southern kingdom is called "Judah."

● 9.29 *Everything else Solomon did*: In keeping with his desire to emphasize the greatness of Solomon, the writer of 2 CHRONICLES chooses not to include Solomon's failings (1 Kgs 11.1-13; 33–40).

● 9.30,31 *40 years . . . Rehoboam then became king*: While the number 40 is often used in a symbolic sense, here it can be taken literally. Solomon is believed to have reigned from approximately 970 to 931 B.C. Rehoboam ruled from 931 to 913 B.C. Almost as soon as he came to power, the people of the northern tribes revolted and formed the northern kingdom (Israel) under the rule of Jeroboam. Rehoboam was left as ruler only of the tribes of Judah and Benjamin in what became known as the southern kingdom (Judah). **(See the chart Numbers in the Bible on pg 1844.)**

● 10.19 *Ahijah the LORD's prophet*: A prophet is one who delivers God's messages. The writer of 2 CHRONICLES assumes the reader is familiar with the prophet Ahijah's message for Jeroboam prior to Solomon's death. Ahijah predicted that Jeroboam would become king of the north because of Solomon's disobedience to God (1 Kgs 11.29-40). The writer claims this revolt fulfilled these prophetic words from God. **(See the article Prophets and Prophecy on pg 1791.)**

Shemaiah the Prophet Warns Rehoboam

(1 Kings 12.21-24)

11 After Rehoboam returned to Jerusalem, he decided to attack Israel and regain control of the whole country. So he called together 180,000 soldiers from the tribes of Judah and Benjamin.

[2]Meanwhile, the Lord had told Shemaiah the prophet [3]to tell Rehoboam and everyone from Judah and Benjamin, [4]"The Lord warns you not to go to war against the people from the northern tribes—they are your relatives. Go home! The Lord is the one who made these things happen."

Rehoboam and his army obeyed the Lord's message and did not attack Jeroboam and his troops.

Rehoboam Fortifies Cities in Judah

[5]Rehoboam ruled from Jerusalem, and he had several cities in Judah turned into fortresses so he could use them to defend his country. These cities included [6]Bethlehem, Etam, Tekoa, [7]Beth-Zur, Soco, Adullam, [8]Gath, Mareshah, Ziph, [9]Adoraim, Lachish, Azekah, [10]Zorah, Aijalon, and Hebron. After he had fortified these cities in the territories of Judah and Benjamin, [11]he assigned an army commander to each of them and stocked them with supplies of food, olive oil, and wine, [12]as well as with shields and spears. He used these fortified cities to keep control of Judah and Benjamin.

The Priests and the Levites Support Rehoboam

[13]The priests and Levites from the northern tribes of Israel gave their support to King Rehoboam. [14]And since Jeroboam and the kings of Israel that followed him would not allow any Levites to serve as priests, most Levites left their towns and pasturelands in Israel and moved to Jerusalem and other towns in Judah. [15]Jeroboam chose his own priests to serve at the local shrines[i] in Israel and at the places of worship where he had set up statues of goat-demons and of calves.

[16]But some of the people from Israel wanted to worship the Lord God, just as their ancestors had done. So they followed the priests and Levites to Jerusalem, where they could offer sacrifices to the Lord. [17]For the next three years, they lived in Judah and were loyal to Rehoboam and his kingdom, just as they had been loyal to David and Solomon.

Rehoboam's Family

[18]Rehoboam married Mahalath, whose father was Jerimoth son of David, and whose mother was Abihail the daughter of Eliab and granddaughter of Jesse. [19]Rehoboam and Mahalath had three sons: Jeush, Shemariah, and Zaham. [20]Then Rehoboam married Maacah the daughter of Absalom. Their sons were Abijah, Attai, Ziza, and Shelomith.

[21]Rehoboam had 18 wives, but he also married 60 other women,[j] and he was the father of 28 sons and 60 daughters. Rehoboam loved his wife Maacah the most, [22]so he chose their oldest son Abijah to be

[i]**11.15** *local shrines:* The Hebrew text has "high places," which were local places to worship foreign gods. [j]**11.21** *other women:* This translates a Hebrew word for women who were legally bound to a man, but without the full privileges of a wife.

the next king. ²³Rehoboam was wise enough to put one of his sons in charge of each fortified city in his kingdom. He gave them all the supplies they needed and found wives for every one of them.

King Shishak of Egypt Invades Judah
(1 Kings 14.25-28)

12 Soon after Rehoboam had control of his kingdom, he and everyone in Judah stopped obeying the LORD. ²So in the fifth year of Rehoboam's rule, the LORD punished them for their unfaithfulness and allowed King Shishak of Egypt to invade Judah. ³Shishak attacked with his army of 1,200 chariots and 60,000 cavalry troops, as well as countless Egyptian soldiers from Libya, Sukkoth, and Ethiopia.ᵏ ⁴He captured every one of the fortified cities in Judah and then marched to Jerusalem.

⁵Rehoboam and the leaders of Judah had gone to Jerusalem to escape Shishak's invasion. And while they were there, Shemaiah the prophet told them, "The LORD says that because you have disobeyed him, he has now abandoned you. The LORD will not help you against Shishak!"

⁶Rehoboam and the leaders were sorry for what they had done and admitted, "The LORD is right. We have deserted him."

⁷When the LORD heard this, he told Shemaiah:

The people of Judah are truly sorry for their sins, and so I won't let Shishak completely destroy them. But because I am still angry, ⁸he will conquer and rule them.

Then my people will know what it's like to serve a foreign king instead of serving me.

⁹Shishak attacked Jerusalem and took all the valuable things from the temple and from the palace, including Solomon's gold shields.

¹⁰Rehoboam had bronze shields made to replace the gold ones, and he ordered the guards at the city gates to keep them safe. ¹¹Whenever Rehoboam went to the LORD's temple, the guards carried the shields. But they always took them back to the guardroom as soon as he had finished worshiping.

¹²Rehoboam turned back to the LORD, and so the LORD did not let Judah be completely destroyed, and Judah was prosperous again.

Rehoboam's Rule in Judah
(1 Kings 14.21,29-31)

¹³Rehoboam was 41 years old when he became king, and he ruled 17 years from Jerusalem, the city where the LORD had chosen to be worshiped. His mother Naamah was from Ammon. Rehoboam was a powerful king, ¹⁴but he still did wrong and refused to obey the LORD.

¹⁵Everything else Rehoboam did while he was king, including a history of his family, is written in the records of the two prophets, Shemaiah and Iddo. During Rehoboam's rule, he and King Jeroboam of Israel were constantly at war. ¹⁶When Rehoboam died, he was buried beside his ancestors in Jerusalem, and his son Abijah became king.

King Abijah of Judah
(1 Kings 15.1-8)

13 Abijahˡ became king of Judah in Jeroboam's eighteenth year as king of Israel, ²and he ruled from Jerusalem for

---

ᵏ**12.3** *Ethiopia:* The Hebrew text has "Cush," which was a region south of Egypt that included parts of the present countries of Ethiopia and Sudan.   ˡ**13.1** *Abijah:* In 1 Kings 15.1-8 his name is spelled "Abijam."

● 12.2 *Shishak:* Shishak ruled Egypt from about 945 to 924 B.C. According to Shishak's own inscription on the wall of the temple of Amun at Karnak (Thebes), this attack went as far north as Megiddo, putting Judah and several important trade routes in both Judah and Israel under Egypt's control. **(See Map 6 on pg 1884.)**

● 13.1,3 *Abijah . . . Jeroboam:* In 1 Kgs 15.1-8 Abijah's name is spelled "Abijam." There too, as in 2 Chr 11.21, 22, he is said to be the son of Maacah, not Micaiah. The reason for this difference is not known. He ruled Judah from 913 to 911 B.C. Jeroboam was the first king of the northern kingdom (Israel) and ruled from 931 to 910 B.C. (1 Kgs 11.26—14.20).

13.3 *400,000 . . . 800,000:* These high numbers fit with David's census (1 Chr 21.5). Each nation was prepared for a major effort. Since Judah was outnumbered by two to one, the writer of 2 Chronicles stresses God's ability to give victory against all odds.

13.4-12 *Listen Jeroboam . . . ancestors worshiped:* In this passage and elsewhere, the message is repeated that the southern kingdom will keep God's favor by obeying God's laws and keeping itself separate from the sinful northern kingdom (16.7-9; 19.2-11; 25.7-9). The northern kingdom will not be able to defeat the southern kingdom, because one of David's ancestors remains on Judah's throne (1 Chr 17.13,14; 2 Chr 7.17,18). Further, Jeroboam set up altars in honor of the Canaanite god Baal and appointed non-Levites as priests.

13.20,21 *Abijah became more powerful . . . 16 daughters:* 2 Chronicles stresses the good rather than the negative aspects (1 Kgs 15.3) of Abijah's rule. Abijah was blessed by God with many children, though not as many Rehoboam.

14.1 *Asa:* Asa, Judah's third king, ruled from 911 to 870 B.C. The book of 2 Chronicles gives a much more detailed account of Asa's reign than that in 1 Kings 15.9-24. Three examples in this account (14.1-15; 15.1-19; 16.1-13) again point out the idea that obedience brings blessing and disobedience brings punishment.

three years. His mother was Micaiah the daughter of Uriel from Gibeah.

Some time later, Abijah and King Jeroboam of Israel went to war against each other. [3]Abijah's army had 400,000 troops, and Jeroboam met him in battle with 800,000 troops.

[4]Abijah went to the top of Mount Zemaraim[m] in the hills of Ephraim and shouted:

Listen, Jeroboam and all you Israelites! [5]The Lord God of Israel has made a solemn promise that every king of Israel will be from David's family. [6]But Jeroboam, you were King Solomon's official, and you rebelled. [7]Then right after Rehoboam became king, you and your bunch of worthless followers challenged Rehoboam, who was too young to know how to stop you.

[8]Now you and your powerful army think you can stand up to the kingdom that the Lord has given to David's descendants. The only gods you have are those gold statues of calves that Jeroboam made for you. [9]You don't even have descendants of Aaron on your side, because you forced out the Lord's priests and Levites. In their place, you appoint ordinary people to be priests, just as the foreign nations do. In fact, anyone who brings a bull and seven rams to the altar can become a priest of your so-called gods.

[10]But we have not turned our backs on the Lord God! Aaron's own descendants serve as our priests, and the Levites are their assistants. [11]Two times every day they offer sacrifices and burn incense to the Lord. They set out the sacred loaves of bread on a table that has been purified, and they light the lamps in the gold lampstand

every day at sunset. We follow the commands of the Lord our God—you have rejected him! [12]That's why God is on our side and will lead us into battle when the priests sound the signal on the trumpets. It's no use, Israelites. You might as well give up. There's no way you can defeat the Lord, the God your ancestors worshiped.

[13]But while Abijah was talking, Jeroboam had sent some of his troops to attack Judah's army from behind, while the rest attacked from the front. [14]Judah's army realized they were trapped, and so they prayed to the Lord. The priests blew the signal on the trumpet, [15]and the troops let out a battle cry. Then with Abijah leading them into battle, God defeated Jeroboam and Israel's army. [16]The Israelites ran away, and God helped Judah's soldiers slaughter [17]500,000 enemy troops. [18]Judah's army won because they had trusted the Lord God of their ancestors.

[19]Abijah kept up his attack on Jeroboam's army and captured the Israelite towns of Bethel, Jeshanah, and Ephron, as well as the villages around them.

[20]Jeroboam never regained his power during the rest of Abijah's rule. The Lord punished Jeroboam, and he died, but Abijah became more powerful.

[21]Abijah had a total of 14 wives, 22 sons, and 16 daughters. [22]Everything Abijah said and did while he was king is written in the records of Iddo the prophet.

King Asa of Judah

14 Abijah died and was buried in Jerusalem. Then his son Asa became king, and Judah had ten years of peace.

[2]Asa obeyed the Lord his God and did

[m]13.4 *Mount Zemaraim:* Probably located on the northern border of the territory of Benjamin.

right. [3]He destroyed the local shrines[n] and the altars to foreign gods. He smashed the stone images of gods and cut down the sacred poles[o] used in worshiping the goddess Asherah. [4]Then he told everyone in Judah to worship the LORD God, just as their ancestors had done, and to obey his laws and teachings. [5]He destroyed every local shrine and incense altar in Judah.

[6]The LORD blessed Judah with peace while Asa was king, and so during that time, Asa fortified many of the towns. [7]He said to the people, "Let's build walls and defense towers for these towns, and put in gates that can be locked with bars. This land still belongs to us, because we have obeyed the LORD our God. He has given us peace from all our enemies." The people did everything Asa had suggested.

[8]Asa had a large army of brave soldiers: 300,000 of them were from the tribe of Judah and were armed with shields and spears; 280,000 were from Benjamin and were armed with shields and bows.

Judah Defeats Ethiopia's Army

[9]Zerah from Ethiopia[p] led an army of 1,000,000 soldiers and 300 chariots to the town of Mareshah[q] in Judah. [10]Asa met him there, and the two armies prepared for battle in Zephathah Valley.

[11]Asa prayed:

LORD God, only you can help a powerless army defeat a stronger one. So we depend on you to help us. We will fight against this powerful army to honor your name, and we know that you won't be defeated. You are the LORD our God.

[12]The LORD helped Asa and his army defeat the Ethiopians. The enemy soldiers ran away, [13]but Asa and his troops chased them as far as Gerar. It was a total defeat—the Ethiopians could not even fight back![r]

The soldiers from Judah took everything that had belonged to the Ethiopians. [14]The people who lived in the villages around Gerar learned what had happened and were afraid of the LORD. So Judah's army easily defeated them and carried off everything of value that they wanted from these towns. [15]They also attacked the camps where the shepherds lived and took a lot of sheep, goats, and camels. Then they went back to Jerusalem.

Asa Destroys the Idols in Judah

15 Some time later, God spoke to Azariah son of Oded. [2]At once, Azariah went to Asa and said:

Listen to me, King Asa and you people of Judah and Benjamin. The LORD will be with you and help you, as long as you obey and worship him. But if you disobey him, he will desert you.

[3]For a long time, the people of Israel did not worship the true God or listen to priests who could teach them about God. They refused to obey God's Law. [4]But whenever trouble came, Israel turned back to the LORD their God and worshiped him.

[5]There was so much confusion in those days that it wasn't safe to go anywhere in Israel. [6]Nations were destroying each other, and cities were wiping out other cities, because God was causing trouble and unrest everywhere.

[7]So you must be brave. Don't give up! God will honor you for obeying him.

14.9,10,13   *Ethiopia . . . Gerar:* Ethiopia was a region south of Egypt that included parts of the present countries of Ethiopia and Sudan. Mareshah was about 25 miles southwest of Jerusalem. The Zephathah Valley led to the hills of Jerusalem. Gerar was located south of Gaza near the Mediterranean coast. **(See Maps 4 and 8 on pgs 1882 and 1886.)**

[n]14.3 *local shrines:* See the note at 11.15.   [o]14.3 *sacred poles:* Or "trees," used as symbols of Asherah, the goddess of fertility.   [p]14.9 *Ethiopia:* See the note at 12.3.   [q]14.9 *Mareshah:* About 25 miles southwest of Jerusalem.   [r]14.13 *the Ethiopians could not even fight back:* Or "not one of the Ethiopians survived!"

15.9 *Ephraim, West Manasseh, and Simeon:* These tribes were among those that formed the northern kingdom, but some of their people moved to Jerusalem so that they could worship God properly.

15.10 *In the third month:* Sivan, which ran from about mid-May to mid-June. During Sivan, the Harvest Festival was celebrated.

16.1 *King Baasha:* Baasha was king of Israel from 909 to 886 B.C.

16.2 *King Benhadad of Syria:* This is the first of at least three Syrian kings with this name. Another attacked Israel during King Ahab's rule (1 Kgs 20.1). A third was the son of Hazael who seized the second Benhadad's crown (2 Kgs 8.7-15; 13.24). Syria was north of Israel. Benhadad begins by capturing several cities in northern Israel (16.4), forcing Baasha to leave Ramah in the south in order to defend the northern area of his kingdom. **(See Map 4 on pg 1882.)**

16.4-6 *Ijon, Dan, Abel-Maim . . . Naphtali . . . Geba . . . Mizpah:* Ijon was in the area of the tribe of Naphtali. Dan was on a fertile plain southwest of Mount Hermon. In earlier times, it was known as Leshem (Josh 19.47-48) or Laish (Judg 18.7). Abel-Maim (known in 1 Kgs 15.20 as Abel-Bethmaacah) was near Dan, but in the territory of the tribe of Naphtali. The listing of these cities and areas indicates that Benhadad had taken all of Israel's northwest territory. Geba and Mizpah are believed to have been north of Jerusalem. **(See Maps 3 and 4 on pgs 1881 and 1882.)**

⁸As soon as Asa heard what Azariah the prophet said, he gave orders for all the idols in Judah and Benjamin to be destroyed, including those in the towns he had captured in the territory of Ephraim. He also repaired the LORD's altar that was in front of the temple porch.

⁹Asa called together the people from Judah and Benjamin, as well as the people from the territories of Ephraim, West Manasseh, and Simeon who were living in Judah. Many of these people were now loyal to Asa, because they had seen that the LORD was with him.

¹⁰In the third month of the fifteenth year of Asa's rule, they all met in Jerusalem. ¹¹That same day, they took 700 bulls and 7,000 sheep and goats from what they had brought back from Gerar and sacrificed them as offerings to the LORD. ¹²They made a solemn promise to faithfully worship the LORD God their ancestors had worshiped, ¹³and to put to death anyone who refused to obey him. ¹⁴The crowd solemnly agreed to keep their promise to the LORD, then they celebrated by shouting and blowing trumpets and horns. ¹⁵Everyone was happy because they had made this solemn promise, and in return, the LORD blessed them with peace from all their enemies.

¹⁶Asa's grandmother Maacah had made a disgusting idol of the goddess Asherah, so he cut it down, crushed it, and burned it in Kidron Valley. Then he removed Maacah from her position as queen mother.ˢ ¹⁷As long as Asa lived, he was faithful to the LORD, even though he did not destroy the local shrinesᵗ in Israel. ¹⁸He placed in the temple all the silver and gold objects that he and his father had dedicated to God.

¹⁹There was peace in Judah until the thirty-fifth year of Asa's rule.

King Baasha of Israel Invades Judah
(1 Kings 15.16-22)

16 In the thirty-sixth year of Asa's rule, King Baasha of Israel invaded Judah and captured the town of Ramah. He started making the town stronger, and he put troops there to stop people from going in and out of Judah.

²When Asa heard about this, he took the silver and gold from his palace and from the LORD's temple. Then he sent it to Damascus with this message for King Benhadad of Syria: ³"I think we should sign a peace treaty, just as our fathers did. This silver and gold is a present for you. Would you please break your treaty with King Baasha of Israel and force him to leave my country?"

⁴Benhadad did what Asa asked and sent the Syrian army into Israel. They captured the towns of Ijon, Dan, Abel-Maim,ᵘ and all the towns in Naphtali where supplies were kept. ⁵When Baasha heard about it, he stopped his work on the town of Ramah.

⁶Asa ordered everyone in Judah to carry away the stones and wood Baasha had used to fortify Ramah. Then he fortified the towns of Geba and Mizpah with these same stones and wood.

Hanani the Prophet Condemns Asa

⁷Soon after that happened, Hanani the prophet went to Asa and said:
 You depended on the king of Syria

ˢ**15.16** *queen mother:* Or "the mother of the king," which was an important position in biblical times (see 1 Kings 2.19).   ᵗ**15.17** *local shrines:* See the note at 11.15.   ᵘ**16.4** *Abel-Maim:* Also called "Abel-Bethmaacah" (see 1 Kings 15.20).

instead of depending on the LORD your God. And so, you will never defeat the Syrian army. **8**Remember how powerful the Ethiopian[v] and Libyan army was, with all their chariots and cavalry troops! You trusted the LORD to help you then, and you defeated them. **9**The LORD is constantly watching everyone, and he gives strength to those who faithfully obey him. But you have done a foolish thing, and your kingdom will never be at peace again. **10**When Asa heard this, he was so angry that he put Hanani in prison. Asa was also cruel to some of his people.[w]

Asa Dies
(1 Kings 15.23,24)

11Everything Asa did while he was king is written in *The History of the Kings of Judah and Israel.* **12**In the thirty-ninth year of his rule, he got a very bad foot disease, but he relied on doctors and refused to ask the LORD for help. **13**He died two years later. **14**Earlier, Asa had his own tomb cut out of a rock hill in Jerusalem. So he was buried there, and the tomb was filled with spices and sweet-smelling oils. Then the people built a bonfire in his honor.

King Jehoshaphat of Judah

17 Jehoshaphat son of Asa became king and strengthened his defenses against Israel. **2**He assigned troops to the fortified cities in Judah, as well as to other towns in Judah and to those towns in Ephraim that his father Asa had captured. **3-4**When Jehoshaphat's father had first become king of Judah, he was faithful to the LORD and refused to worship the god Baal as the kings of Israel did. Jehoshaphat followed his father's example and obeyed and worshiped the LORD. And so the LORD blessed Jehoshaphat **5**and helped him keep firm control of his kingdom. The people of Judah brought gifts to Jehoshaphat, but even after he became very rich and respected, **6**he remained completely faithful to the LORD. He destroyed all the local shrines[x] in Judah, including the places where the goddess Asherah was worshiped.

7In the third year of Jehoshaphat's rule, he chose five officials and gave them orders to teach the LORD's Law in every city and town in Judah. They were Benhail, Obadiah, Zechariah, Nethanel, and Micaiah. **8**Their assistants were the following nine Levites: Shemaiah, Nethaniah, Zebadiah, Asahel, Shemiramoth, Jehonathan, Adonijah, Tobijah, and Tob-Adonijah. Two priests, Elishama and Jehoram, also went along. **9**They carried with them a copy of the LORD's Law wherever they went and taught the people from it.

10The nations around Judah were afraid of the LORD's power, so none of them attacked Jehoshaphat. **11**Philistines brought him silver and other gifts to keep peace. Some of the Arab people brought him 7,700 rams and the same number of goats. **12**As Jehoshaphat became more powerful, he built fortresses and cities **13**where he stored supplies. He also kept in Jerusalem some experienced soldiers **14**from the Judah and Benjamin tribes. These soldiers were grouped according to their clans.

Adnah was the commander of the troops from Judah, and he had 300,000 soldiers under his command. **15**Jehohanan was second in command, with 280,000 soldiers

---

16.14 *his own tomb . . . bonfire in his honor:* Tombs cut into rock or hillsides were common burial places. Asa's long reign and many accomplishments earned him the honor of a bonfire despite his sinful later years (in contrast to Jehoram's burial at 21.19).

Burial

17.1 *Jehoshaphat:* Jehoshaphat, the son of King Asa of Judah, ruled Judah from 870 to 848 B.C.

17.7 *the LORD's Law:* Religious and state law were the same for God's people.

Law

17.11 *Philistines:* The Philistines were people from Philistia, an area on the eastern coast of the Mediterranean Sea. Israel fought many wars against the Philistines. **(See Map 6 on pg 1884.)**

17.14 *clans:* A "clan" was a group of families who were related to each other. A group of clans made up a tribe. Ten of the twelve tribes of Israel formed the northern kingdom (Israel), while the other two formed the southern kingdom (Judah).

---

[v]**16.8** *Ethiopian:* See the note at 12.3.　[w]**16.10** *Asa was also cruel . . . people:* Or "Asa also started being cruel to some of his people."　[x]**17.6** *local shrines:* See the note at 11.15.

18.1 *King Ahab . . . Ahab's daughter:* King Ahab ruled the northern kingdom (Israel) from 874 to 853 B.C. Ahab's daughter here refers to Athaliah, the daughter of Ahab and Jezebel. The marriage between Jehoram and Athaliah was a military alliance and therefore a sin, because it showed a lack of trust in God's ability to protect Judah. Athaliah later became Judah's seventh ruler and only queen. During her rule (841–835 B.C.), she killed almost all of David's descendants (22.10) and helped bring the worship of foreign gods back to Judah. This eventually led to the destruction of the nation (36.17-21).

18.2 *Samaria . . . Ramoth in Gilead:* Ramoth was east of the Jordan River and south of the Yarmuk River. It had been an Israelite city since the time of Moses. The Syrians had taken control of Ramoth (1 Kgs 22.3,4). Samaria was Israel's capital. Built on the hill of the same name, the city stood 300 feet above the surrounding plain, giving it great defensive strength. It was approximately 40 miles north of Jerusalem and midway between the Jordan River and the Mediterranean Sea. Eventually it became known as the burial place for the kings of Israel. **(See Map 6 on pg 1884.)**

18.5 *400 prophets:* Ahab's false prophets told the kings what they wanted to hear, unlike true prophets who spoke God's message.

under him. ¹⁶Amasiah son of Zichri, who had volunteered to serve the LORD, was third in command, with 200,000 soldiers under him.

¹⁷Eliada was a brave warrior who commanded the troops from Benjamin. He had 200,000 soldiers under his command, all of them armed with bows and shields. ¹⁸Jehozabad was second in command, with 180,000 soldiers under him. ¹⁹These were the troops who protected the king in Jerusalem, not counting those he had assigned to the fortified cities throughout the country.

Micaiah Warns King Ahab of Israel
(1 Kings 22.1-28)

18 Jehoshaphat was now very rich and famous. He signed a treaty with King Ahab of Israel by arranging the marriage of his son and Ahab's daughter.

²One day, Jehoshaphat went to visit Ahab in his capital city of Samaria. Ahab slaughtered sheep and cattle and prepared a big feast to honor Jehoshaphat and the officials with him. Ahab talked about attacking the city of Ramoth in Gilead,ʸ ³and finally asked, "Jehoshaphat, would you go with me to attack Ramoth?"

"Yes," Jehoshaphat answered. "My army is at your command. ⁴But first let's ask the LORD what to do."

⁵Ahab sent for 400 prophets and asked, "Should I attack the city of Ramoth?"

"Yes!" the prophets answered. "God will help you capture the city."

⁶But Jehoshaphat said, "Just to make sure, is there another of the LORD's prophets we can ask?"

⁷"We could ask Micaiah son of Imlah,"

Ahab said. "But I hate Micaiah. He always has bad news for me."

"Don't say that!" Jehoshaphat replied. ⁸Then Ahab sent someone to bring Micaiah as soon as possible.

⁹All this time, Ahab and Jehoshaphat were dressed in their royal robes and were seated on their thrones at the threshing place near the gate of Samaria, listening to the prophets tell them what the LORD had said.

¹⁰Zedekiah son of Chenaanah was one of the prophets. He had made some horns out of iron and shouted, "Ahab, the LORD says you will attack the Syrians like a bull with iron horns and wipe them out!"

¹¹All the prophets agreed that Ahab should attack the Syrians at Ramoth and promised that the LORD would help him defeat them.

¹²Meanwhile, the messenger who went to get Micaiah whispered, "Micaiah, all the prophets have good news for Ahab. Now go and say the same thing."

¹³"I'll say whatever the living LORD my God tells me to say," Micaiah replied.

¹⁴Then Micaiah went up to Ahab, who asked, "Micaiah, should we attack Ramoth?"

"Yes!" Micaiah answered. "The LORD will help you capture the city."

¹⁵Ahab shouted, "Micaiah, I've told you over and over to tell me the truth! What does the LORD really say?"

¹⁶Micaiah answered, "In a visionᶻ I saw Israelite soldiers wandering around, lost in the hills like sheep without a shepherd. The LORD said, 'These troops have no leader. They should go home and not fight.'"

¹⁷Ahab turned to Jehoshaphat and said, "I told you he would bring me bad news!"

ʸ**18.2** *attacking the city of Ramoth in Gilead:* The Syrians had taken control of Ramoth (see 1 Kings 22.3,4).   ᶻ**18.16** *vision:* In ancient times, prophets often told about future events from what they had seen in visions or dreams.

[18]Micaiah replied:

I then saw the LORD seated on his throne with every creature in heaven gathered around him. [19]The LORD asked, "Who can trick Ahab and make him go to Ramoth where he will be killed?"

They talked about it for a while, [20]then finally a spirit came forward and said to the LORD, "I can trick Ahab."

"How?" the LORD asked.

[21]"I'll make Ahab's prophets lie to him."

"Good!" the LORD replied. "Now go and do it. You will be successful."

[22]Ahab, this is exactly what has happened. The LORD made all your prophets lie to you, and he knows you will soon be destroyed.

[23]Zedekiah walked over and slapped Micaiah on the face. Then he asked, "Do you really think the LORD would speak to you and not to me?"

[24]Micaiah answered, "You'll find out on the day you have to hide in the back room of some house."

[25]Ahab shouted, "Arrest Micaiah! Take him to Prince Joash and Governor Amon of Samaria. [26]Tell them to put him in prison and to give him nothing but bread and water until I come back safely."

[27]Micaiah said, "If you do come back, I was wrong about what the LORD wanted me to say." Then he told the crowd, "Don't forget what I said!"

Ahab Dies at Ramoth
(1 Kings 22.29-35)

[28]Ahab and Jehoshaphat led their armies to Ramoth in Gilead. [29]Before they went into battle, Ahab said, "Jehoshaphat, I'll disguise myself, but you wear your royal robe." Ahab disguised himself and went into battle.

[30]The king of Syria had ordered his chariot commanders to attack only Ahab. [31]So when they saw Jehoshaphat in his robe, they thought he was Ahab and started to attack him. But Jehoshaphat prayed, and the LORD made the Syrian soldiers stop. [32]And when they realized he wasn't Ahab, they left him alone.

[33]However, during the fighting a soldier shot an arrow without even aiming, and it hit Ahab between two pieces of his armor. He shouted to his chariot driver, "I've been hit! Get me out of here!"

[34]The fighting lasted all day, with Ahab propped up in his chariot so he could see the Syrian troops. He stayed there until evening, and by sundown he was dead.

19 Jehoshaphat returned safely to his palace in Jerusalem. [2]But the prophet Jehu son of Hanani met him and said:

By helping that wicked Ahab, you have made friends with someone who hates the LORD. Now the LORD God is angry with you! [3]But not everything about you is bad. You destroyed the sacred poles[a] used in worshiping the goddess Asherah—that shows you have tried to obey the LORD.

Jehoshaphat Appoints Judges To Settle Cases

[4]Jehoshaphat lived in Jerusalem, but he often traveled through his kingdom, from Beersheba in the south to the edge of the hill country of Ephraim in the north. He talked with the people and convinced them to turn back to the LORD God and worship him, just as their ancestors had done.

[a]**19.3** *sacred poles*: See the note at 14.3.

■   18.33 *it hit Ahab:* Ahab's death by an unaimed arrow makes it seem like God's doing (18.19).

■   19.2 *helping that wicked Ahab:* Jehoshaphat's treaty with Ahab was considered sinful, but most of what Jehoshaphat did was considered good.

19.5 judges: Jehoshaphat, whose name means "the LORD judges," reformed the justice system by placing godly judges throughout the country and by establishing a "court of appeals," or higher court, in Jerusalem (19.8-11).

19.7 bribes: Payments given to influence someone else's acts or decisions. The practice of giving and taking bribes was often criticized by Israel's prophets. Bribing officials kept God's true justice from being carried out.

19.8 family leaders: Family leaders were the elders of the tribes and traditionally helped to settle disputes and make economic and political decisions. A judicial system was not new to Israel or to other nations. Israel's system was based on God's command to treat all people equally, without regard to their standing in society (Lev 19.15; Deut 16.18-20).

Justice

20.1 Moab and Ammon . . . Meunites: Moab was located to the east of the Dead Sea. The Moabites were long-time enemies of Israel. Ammon was a nation east of the northern kingdom (Israel). Like the Moabites, the Ammonites were related to the Israelites through Lot (Gen 19.36-38), but refused to help Israel and often warred against them. The Meunites lived in Edom near Mount Seir. **(See Map 6 on pg 1884.)**

⁵He assigned judges to each of the fortified cities in Judah ⁶and told them:

Be careful when you make your decisions in court, because you are judging by the LORD's standards and not by human standards, and he will know what you decide. ⁷So do your work in honor of him and know that he won't allow you to be unfair to anyone or to take bribes.

⁸Jehoshaphat also chose some Levites, some priests, and some of the family leaders, and he appointed them to serve as judges in Jerusalem. ⁹He told them:

Faithfully serve the LORD! ¹⁰The people of Judah will bring you legal cases that involve every type of crime, including murder. You must settle these cases and warn the people to stop sinning against the LORD, so that he won't get angry and punish Judah. Remember, if you follow these instructions, you won't be held responsible for anything that happens.

¹¹Amariah the high priest will have the final say in any religious case. And Zebadiah, the leader[b] of the Judah tribe, will have the final say in all other cases. The rest of the Levites will serve as your assistants. Be brave, and I pray that the LORD will help you do right.

Moab and Ammon Are Defeated

20 Some time later, the armies of Moab and Ammon, together with the Meunites,[c] went to war against Jehoshaphat. ²Messengers told Jehoshaphat, "A large army from Edom[d] east of the Dead Sea has invaded our country. They have already reached En-Gedi."[e]

³Jehoshaphat was afraid, so he asked the LORD what to do. He then told the people of Judah to go without eating to show their sorrow. ⁴They immediately left for Jerusalem to ask for the LORD's help.

⁵After everyone from Judah and Jerusalem had come together at the LORD's temple, Jehoshaphat stood in front of the new courtyard ⁶and prayed:

You, LORD, are the God our ancestors worshiped, and from heaven you rule every nation in the world. You are so powerful that no one can defeat you. ⁷Our God, you forced out the nations who lived in this land before your people Israel came here, and you gave it to the descendants of your friend Abraham forever. ⁸Our ancestors lived in this land and built a temple to honor you. ⁹They believed that whenever this land is struck by war or disease or famine, your people can pray to you at the temple, and you will hear their prayer and save them.

¹⁰You can see that the armies of Ammon, Moab, and Edom are attacking us! Those are the nations you would not let our ancestors invade on their way from Egypt, so these nations were not destroyed. ¹¹Now they are coming to take back the land you gave us. ¹²Aren't you going to punish them? We won't stand a chance when this army attacks. We don't know what to do—we are begging for your help.

¹³While every man, woman, and child of Judah was standing there at the temple,

[b]**19.11** *Zebadiah, the leader*: Hebrew "Zebadiah son of Ishmael, who is the leader."   [c]**20.1** *Meunites*: One ancient translation (see also 26.7); Hebrew "Ammonites."   [d]**20.2** *Edom*: The Hebrew text has "Syria"; in Hebrew there is only one letter difference between "Edom" and "Aram," which is the usual Hebrew name for Syria in the Bible.   [e]**20.2** *En-Gedi*: The Hebrew text has "Hazazon-Tamar, also known as En-Gedi," a city on the west shore of the Dead Sea, about 25 miles southeast of Jerusalem.

[14]the LORD's Spirit suddenly spoke to Jahaziel, a Levite from the Asaph clan.[f] [15]Then Jahaziel said:

Your Majesty and everyone from Judah and Jerusalem, the LORD says that you don't need to be afraid or let this powerful army discourage you. God will fight on your side! [16]So here's what you must do. Tomorrow the enemy armies will march through the desert around the town of Jeruel. March down and meet them at the town of Ziz as they come up the valley. [17]You won't even have to fight. Just take your positions and watch the LORD rescue you from your enemy. Don't be afraid. Just do as you're told. And as you march out tomorrow, the LORD will be there with you.

[18]Jehoshaphat bowed low to the ground and everyone worshiped the LORD. [19]Then some Levites from the Kohath and Korah clans stood up and shouted praises to the LORD God of Israel.

[20]Early the next morning, as everyone got ready to leave for the desert near Tekoa, Jehoshaphat stood up and said, "Listen my friends, if we trust the LORD God and believe what these prophets have told us, the LORD will help us, and we will be successful." [21]Then he explained his plan and appointed men to march in front of the army and praise the LORD for his holy power by singing:[g]

"Praise the LORD!
His love never ends."

[22]As soon as they began singing, the LORD confused the enemy camp, [23]so that the Ammonite and Moabite troops attacked and completely destroyed those from Edom. Then they turned against each other and fought until the entire camp was wiped out!

[24]When Judah's army reached the tower that overlooked the desert, they saw that every soldier in the enemy's army was lying dead on the ground. [25]So Jehoshaphat and his troops went into the camp to carry away everything of value. They found a large herd of livestock,[h] a lot of equipment, clothes,[i] and other valuable things. It took them three days to carry it all away, and there was still some left over.

[26]Then on the fourth day, everyone came together in Beracah Valley and sang praises to the LORD. That's why that place was called Praise Valley.[j]

[27-28]Jehoshaphat led the crowd back to Jerusalem. And as they marched, they played harps and blew trumpets. They were very happy because the LORD had given them victory over their enemies, so when they reached the city, they went straight to the temple.

[29]When the other nations heard how the LORD had fought against Judah's enemies, they were too afraid [30]to invade Judah. The LORD let Jehoshaphat's kingdom be at peace.

Jehoshaphat Dies

(1 Kings 22.41-50)

[31]Jehoshaphat was 35 years old when he became king of Judah, and he ruled from Jerusalem for 25 years. His mother was Azubah daughter of Shilhi. [32]Jehoshaphat

20.16 *through the desert . . . up the valley:* This is an area between En-Gedi on the Dead Sea and and Tekoa (20.20), fewer than 20 miles northwest of En-Gedi and about ten miles south of Jerusalem. It includes the pass that leads from En-Gedi to Jerusalem. (See Map 3 on pg 1881.)

20.21-24 *march in front of the army and praise the LORD . . . lying dead on the ground:* The people's trust in God's power was so great that they were given victory by God without even having to fight.

Holy War (The LORD's Battles)

---

[f]**20.14** *Jahaziel, a Levite from the Asaph clan:* Hebrew "Jahaziel son of Zechariah son of Benaiah son of Jeiel son of Mattaniah, who was a Levite from the Asaph clan." [g]**20.21** *to march in front . . . singing:* Or "to put on their sacred robes, lead the army into battle, and praise the LORD by singing." [h]**20.25** *a large herd of livestock:* One ancient translation; Hebrew "among the bodies a large herd of." [i]**20.25** *clothes:* One ancient translation; Hebrew "dead bodies." [j]**20.26** *Beracah Valley . . . sang praises . . . Praise Valley:* In Hebrew the name "Beracah" means "praise."

Jehoshaphat said, "*Praise the LORD! His love never ends.*" 2 CHR 20.21

20.33 *local shrines:* This verse contradicts 17.6. Perhaps Jehoshaphat destroyed the shrines initially, but could not keep the people from rebuilding them.

21.1 *Jehoram:* Jehoram was Judah's fifth king and ruled alone from 848 to 841 B.C. Before that, he ruled for four years with his father, Jehoshaphat. In biblical times, a father and son would sometimes rule as kings at the same time. That way, when the father died, his son would already have control of the kingdom.

21.2-4 *Jehoshaphat had seven sons . . . had his brothers killed:* Having many children was a sign of God's blessing (1 Chr 25.5; 2 Chr 11.18-21). Eventually, only one of Jehoram's children would be left after Judah was invaded (21.17). It was not unusual for a new king to remove or kill anyone who might try to take the throne from him, but Jehoram's murder of his own brothers is particularly evil (21.13). Later, Athaliah acts in a similar way (22.10).

21.8 *Edom rebelled:* Edom is usually described in the Bible as Israel's enemy. The Edomites were descendants of Esau (Gen 25.24-26; 36.1). David had conquered Edom about 250 years prior to this time (2 Sam 8.13,14). Esau's father had said that Esau's descendants would be ruled by Jacob's descendants, but that one day they would rebel and be free (Gen 27.40).

21.12 *Elijah the prophet:* The name Elijah means "the LORD is my God."

obeyed the LORD, just as his father Asa had done, ³³but he did not destroy the local shrines.^k So the people still worshiped foreign gods, instead of faithfully serving the God their ancestors had worshiped.

³⁴Everything else Jehoshaphat did while he was king is written in the records of Jehu son of Hanani that are included in *The History of the Kings of Israel.*

³⁵While Jehoshaphat was king, he signed a peace treaty with Ahaziah the wicked king of Israel. ³⁶They agreed to build several seagoing ships^l at Ezion-Geber. ³⁷But the prophet Eliezer^m warned Jehoshaphat, "The LORD will destroy these ships because you have supported Ahaziah." The ships were wrecked and never sailed.

21 Jehoshaphat died and was buried beside his ancestors in Jerusalem, and his son Jehoram became king.

King Jehoram of Judah
(2 Kings 8.16-24)

²King Jehoshaphat had seven sons: Jehoram, Azariah, Jehiel, Zechariah, Azariah, Michael, and Shephatiah. ³Jehoshaphat gave each of them silver and gold, as well as other valuable gifts. He also put them in charge of the fortified cities in Judah, but he had chosen his oldest son Jehoram to succeed him as king.

⁴After Jehoram had taken control of Judah, he had his brothers killed, as well as some of the nation's leaders. ⁵He was 32 years old when he became king, and he ruled eight years from Jerusalem.

⁶Jehoram married Ahab's daughter and followed the sinful example of Ahab's family and the other kings of Israel. He dis-

obeyed the LORD by doing wrong, ⁷but because the LORD had made a solemn promise to King David that someone from his family would always rule in Judah, he refused to wipe out David's descendants.

⁸While Jehoram was king, the people of Edom rebelled and chose their own king. ⁹Jehoram, his officers, and his cavalry marched to Edom, where the Edomite army surrounded them. He escaped during the night, ¹⁰but Judah was never able to regain control of Edom. Even the town of Libnahⁿ rebelled at that time.

Those things happened because Jehoram had turned away from the LORD, the God his ancestors had worshiped. ¹¹Jehoram even built local shrines^o in the hills of Judah and let the people sin against the LORD by worshiping foreign gods.

¹²One day, Jehoram received a letter from Elijah the prophet that said:

I have a message for you from the LORD God your ancestor David worshiped. He knows that you have not followed the example of Jehoshaphat your father or Asa your grandfather. ¹³Instead you have acted like those sinful kings of Israel and have encouraged the people of Judah to stop worshiping the LORD, just as Ahab and his descendants did. You even murdered your own brothers, who were better men than you.

¹⁴Because you have done these terrible things, the LORD will severely punish the people in your kingdom, including your own family, and he will destroy everything you own. ¹⁵You will be struck with a painful stomach disease and suffer until you die.

^k**20.33** *local shrines:* See the note at 11.15. ^l**20.36** *seagoing ships:* See the note at 9.21. ^m**20.37** *Eliezer:* Hebrew "Eliezer son of Dodavahu from Mareshah." ⁿ**21.10** *Even the town of Libnah:* This was a town on the border between Philistia and Judah, which means that Jehoram was facing rebellion on both sides of his kingdom. ^o**21.11** *local shrines:* See the note at 11.15.

[16]The LORD later caused the Philistines and the Arabs who lived near the Ethiopians[P] to become angry with Jehoram. [17]They invaded Judah and stole the royal property from the palace, and they led Jehoram's wives and sons away as prisoners. The only one left behind was Ahaziah,[q] his youngest son.

[18]After this happened, the LORD struck Jehoram with an incurable stomach disease. [19]About two years later, Jehoram died in terrible pain. No bonfire was built to honor him, even though the people had done this for his ancestors.

[20]Jehoram was 32 years old when he became king, and he ruled 8 years from Jerusalem. He died, and no one even felt sad. He was buried in Jerusalem, but not in the royal tombs.

King Ahaziah of Judah
(2 Kings 8.25-29; 9.21,27,28)

22 Earlier, when the Arabs led a raid against Judah, they killed all of Jehoram's sons, except Ahaziah, the youngest one. So the people of Jerusalem crowned him their king. [2]He was 22[r] years old at the time, and he ruled only one year from Jerusalem.

Ahaziah's mother was Athaliah, a granddaughter of King Omri of Israel, [3]and she encouraged her son to sin against the LORD. He followed the evil example of King Ahab and his descendants. [4]In fact, after his father's death, Ahaziah sinned against the LORD by appointing some of Ahab's relatives to be his advisors.

Their advice led to his downfall. [5]He listened to them and went with King Joram of Israel to attack King Hazael and the Syrian troops at Ramoth in Gilead. Joram was wounded in that battle, [6]and he went to the town of Jezreel to recover. And Ahaziah later went there to visit him. [7]It was during that visit that God had Ahaziah put to death.

When Ahaziah arrived at Jezreel, he and Joram went to meet with Jehu grandson of Nimshi. The LORD had already told Jehu to kill every male in Ahab's family, [8]and while Jehu was doing that, he saw some of Judah's leaders and Ahaziah's nephews who had come with Ahaziah. Jehu killed them on the spot, [9]then gave orders to find Ahaziah. Jehu's officers found him hiding in Samaria. They brought Ahaziah to Jehu, who immediately put him to death. They buried Ahaziah only because they respected Jehoshaphat his grandfather, who had done his best to obey the LORD.

There was no one from Ahaziah's family left to become king of Judah.

Queen Athaliah of Judah
(2 Kings 11.1-3)

[10]As soon as Athaliah heard that her son King Ahaziah was dead, she decided to kill any relative who could possibly become king. She would have done just that, [11]but Jehosheba[s] rescued Joash son of Ahaziah just as the others were about to be murdered. Jehosheba, who was Jehoram's daughter and Ahaziah's half sister, was married to Jehoiada the priest. So she was able to hide her nephew Joash and his personal servant in a bedroom in the LORD's temple where he was safe from Athaliah. [12]Joash hid in the temple with them for six years while Athaliah ruled as queen of Judah.

● 22.1 *Ahaziah:* Ahaziah was Judah's sixth king and ruled for one year in 841 B.C. His mother was Athaliah, whose father (Ahab) and brothers (Ahaziah and Joram) were kings of Israel (1 Kgs 16.29; 22.51; 2 Kgs 1.17).

● 22.5 *King Joram . . . King Hazael:* Joram was ninth king of Israel's northern kingdom and ruled from 852 to 841 B.C. He was the brother of Ahaziah, Israel's eighth king (2 Kgs 1.17), and Athaliah, making him the uncle of Ahaziah, Judah's sixth king. Hazael became Syria's king by killing King Benhadad (2 Kgs 8.7-15). He went on to fulfill the words of Elisha the prophet by bringing oppression and pain to Israel (2 Kgs 10.32; 12.17,18; 13.3,22).

● 22.7 *Jehu:* Jehu was Israel's tenth king and ruled from 841 to 814 B.C. God told Elijah that Jehu would become king and kill the worshipers of Baal (1 Kgs 19.16,17).

● 22.10-12 *Joash:* Joash became Judah's seventh king. He ruled from 835 to 796 B.C.

[P]21.16 *Ethiopians:* See the note at 12.3.   [q]21.17 *Ahaziah:* The Hebrew text has "Jehoahaz," another spelling of the name.   [r]22.2 *22:* One ancient translation (see also 2 Kings 8.26); Hebrew "42."
[s]22.11 *Jehosheba:* The Hebrew text has "Jehoshabeath," another spelling of the name.

23.1,2 *Jehoiada ... Levites ... clan leaders:* Jehoiada, the high priest, provides religious leadership by leading the revolt against Athaliah and establishing Joash as the rightful ruler.

23.5 *Foundation Gate:* This may have been the gate that connected the temple with the palace.

23.6 *make themselves clean:* In Old Testament times, a person who was acceptable to worship God was called "clean." Priests went through particular rituals to assure that they were "clean" and fit to perform their duties.

Purity (Clean and Unclean)

23.13 *columns:* The two large columns on each side of the front door of the temple (1 Kgs 7.15-21), or one of the pillars by the platform that Solomon built in the center of the outer courtyard (2 Chr 6.12-13).

23.14 *Don't kill ... near the* LORD's *temple:* Killing was not allowed at the LORD's temple (2 Chr 24.21-22). Interestingly, Athaliah was killed near the horse gate, while years earlier her mother Jezebel's body was trampled by horses (2 Kgs 9.33).

Jehoiada Makes Joash King of Judah
(2 Kings 11.4-21)

23 After Ahaziah's son Joash had hidden in the temple for six years, Jehoiada the priest knew that something had to be done. So he made sure he had the support of several army officers. They were Azariah son of Jeroham, Ishmael son of Jehohanan, Azariah son of Obed, Maaseiah son of Adaiah, and Elishaphat son of Zichri. ²These five men went to the towns in Judah and called together the Levites and the clan leaders. They all came to Jerusalem ³and gathered at the temple, where they agreed to help Joash.

Jehoiada said to them:

Joash will be our next king, because long ago the LORD promised that one of David's descendants would always be king. ⁴Here is what we will do. Three groups of priests and Levites will be on guard duty on the Sabbath—one group will guard the gates of the temple, ⁵one will guard the palace, and the other will guard Foundation Gate. The rest of you will stand guard in the temple courtyards. ⁶Only the priests and Levites who are on duty will be able to enter the temple, because they will be the only ones who have gone through the ceremony to make themselves clean and acceptable. The others must stay outside in the courtyards, just as the LORD has commanded. ⁷You Levites must protect King Joash. Don't let him out of your sight! And keep your swords ready to kill anyone who comes into the temple.

⁸The Levites and the people of Judah followed Jehoiada's orders. The guards going off duty were not allowed to go home, and so each commander had all his guards available—those going off duty as well as those coming on duty. ⁹Jehoiada went into the temple and brought out the swords and shields that had belonged to King David, and he gave them to the commanders. ¹⁰They gave the weapons to the guards, and Jehoiada then made sure that the guards took their positions around the temple and the altar to protect the king on every side.

¹¹Jehoiada and his sons brought Joash outside, where they placed the crown on his head and gave him a copy of the instructions for ruling the nation. Olive oil was poured on his head to show that he was now king, and the crowd cheered and shouted, "Long live the king!"

¹²As soon as Queen Athaliah heard the crowd cheering for Joash, she went to the temple. ¹³There she saw Joash standing by one of the columns near the entrance, which was the usual place for the king. The commanders and the trumpet players were standing next to him, and the musicians were playing instruments and leading the people as they celebrated and blew trumpets. Athaliah tore her clothes in anger and shouted, "You betrayed me, you traitors!"

¹⁴At once, Jehoiada said to the army commanders, "Don't kill her near the LORD's temple. Take her out in front of the troops, and be sure to kill all of her followers!" ¹⁵She tried to escape, but the commanders caught and killed her near the gate where horses are led into the palace.

¹⁶Jehoiada asked King Joash and the people to join with him in being faithful to the LORD. They agreed, ¹⁷then rushed to the temple of the god Baal and tore it down. They smashed the altars and the idols and killed Mattan the priest of Baal in front of the altars.

¹⁸Jehoiada assigned the priests and Levites their duties at the temple, just as

David had done. They were in charge of offering sacrifices to the LORD according to the Law of Moses, and they were responsible for leading the celebrations with singing. [19]Jehoiada ordered the guards at the temple gates to keep out anyone who was unclean.

[20]Finally, Jehoiada called together the army commanders, the most important citizens of Judah, and the government officials. The crowd of people followed them as they led Joash from the temple, through the Upper Gate, and into the palace, where he took his place as king of Judah. [21]Everyone celebrated because Athaliah had been killed and Jerusalem was peaceful again.

King Joash of Judah
(2 Kings 12.1-16)

24 Joash was only 7 years old when he became king of Judah, and he ruled 40 years from Jerusalem. His mother Zibiah was from the town of Beersheba.

[2]While Jehoiada the priest was alive, Joash obeyed the LORD by doing right. [3]Jehoiada even chose two women for Joash to marry so he could have a family.

[4]Some time later, Joash decided it was time to repair the temple. [5]He called together the priests and Levites and said, "Go everywhere in Judah and collect the annual tax from the people. I want this done at once—we need that money to repair the temple."

But the Levites were in no hurry to follow the king's orders. [6]So he sent for Jehoiada the high priest and asked, "Why didn't you send the Levites to collect the taxes? The LORD's servant Moses and the people agreed long ago that this tax would be collected and used to pay for the upkeep of the sacred tent. [7]And now we need it to repair the temple because the sons of that evil woman Athaliah came in and wrecked it. They even used some of the sacred objects to worship the god Baal."

[8]Joash gave orders for a wooden box to be made and had it placed outside, near the gate of the temple. [9]He then sent letters everywhere in Judah and Jerusalem, asking everyone to bring their taxes to the temple, just as Moses had required their ancestors to do.

[10]The people and their leaders agreed, and they brought their money to Jerusalem and placed it in the box. [11]Each day, after the Levites took the box into the temple, the king's secretary and the high priest's assistant would dump out the money and count it. Then the empty box would be taken back outside.

This happened day after day, and soon a large amount of money was collected. [12]Joash and Jehoiada turned the money over to the men who were supervising the repairs to the temple. They used the money to hire stonecutters, carpenters, and experts in working with iron and bronze.

[13]These workers went right to work repairing the temple, and when they were finished, it looked as good as new. [14]They did not use all the tax money for the repairs, so the rest of it was handed over to Joash and Jehoiada, who then used it to make dishes and other gold and silver objects for the temple.

Sacrifices to please the LORD[t] were offered regularly in the temple for as long as Jehoiada lived. [15]He died at the ripe old age of 130 years, [16]and he was buried in the royal tombs in Jerusalem, because he had done so much good for the people of Israel, for God, and for the temple.

[t]**24.14** *Sacrifices to please the LORD:* See the note at 1.6.

24.1 *Beersheba:* Beersheba served as an important commercial center between Israel and Egypt. **(See Map 6 on pg 1884.)**

24.2,3 *doing right:* "Doing right" meant to obey God's laws and worship only God. CHRONICLES differs from KINGS on whether Joash did what was "right" all through his life (compare 2 Kgs 12.2 and 2 Chr 24.17-24).

24.15,16 *130 years . . . buried in the royal tombs:* A long life was seen as God's reward for a godly life. Jehoiada's burial reflects his faithful leadership of God's people and is used by the writer of 2 CHRONICLES to divide Joash's reign into two periods. While Jehoiada was alive, Joash was faithful. After the death of the priest, Joash turned away from God.

24.21-22 *I pray . . . punish all of you*: Zechariah's words reflect the belief that God blesses those who are faithful and punishes those who are not.

25.1 *Amaziah*: Amaziah was Judah's eighth king. Though he is said to have ruled 29 years, the actual length of his rule is uncertain. During many of the years, 796–766 B.C., his son Uzziah ruled with him. Uzziah also ruled in his father's place when Amaziah was a prisoner in Israel, so that Amaziah's active rule is thought to have been from 796 to 781 B.C.

25.5,6 *Three hundred thousand . . . 100,000*: Jehoshaphat's army (17.14-19) numbered over one million soldiers. Amaziah's much smaller army shows how much power Judah had lost in 80 years.

Joash Turns Away from the LORD

[17]After the death of Jehoiada the priest, the leaders of Judah went to Joash and talked him into doing what they wanted. [18]The people of Judah soon stopped worshiping in the temple of the LORD God and started worshiping idols and the symbols of the goddess Asherah. These sinful things made the LORD God angry with the people of Judah and Jerusalem, [19]but he still sent prophets who warned them to turn back to him. The people refused to listen.

[20]God's Spirit spoke to Zechariah son of Jehoiada the priest, and Zechariah told everyone that God was saying: "Why are you disobeying me and my laws? This will only bring punishment! You have deserted me, so now I will desert you."

[21-22]King Joash forgot that Zechariah's father had always been a loyal friend. So when the people of Judah plotted to kill Zechariah, Joash joined them and gave orders for them to stone him to death in the courtyard of the temple. As Zechariah was dying, he said, "I pray that the LORD will see this and punish all of you."

Joash Is Killed

[23]In the spring of the following year, the Syrian army invaded Judah and Jerusalem, killing all of the nation's leaders. They collected everything of value that belonged to the people and took it back to their king in Damascus. [24]The Syrian army was very small, but the LORD let them defeat Judah's large army, because he was punishing Joash and the people of Judah for turning away from him.

[25-26]Joash was severely wounded during the battle, and as soon as the Syrians left Judah, two of his officials, Zabad and Jehozabad,[u] decided to revenge the death of Zechariah. They plotted and killed Joash while he was in bed, recovering from his wounds. Joash was buried in Jerusalem, but not in the royal tombs. [27]*The History of the Kings* also tells more about the sons of Joash, what the prophets said about him, and how he repaired the temple. Amaziah son of Joash became king after his father's death.

King Amaziah of Judah
(2 Kings 14.1-6)

25 Amaziah was 25 years old when he became king, and he ruled 29 years from Jerusalem, the hometown of his mother Jehoaddin.[v]

[2]Even though Amaziah obeyed the LORD by doing right, he refused to be completely faithful. [3]For example, as soon as he had control of Judah, he arrested and killed the officers who had murdered his father. [4]But the children of those officers were not killed; the LORD had commanded in the Law of Moses that only the people who sinned were to be punished.[w]

Edom Is Defeated
(2 Kings 14.7)

[5]Amaziah sent a message to the tribes of Judah and Benjamin and called together all the men who were 20 years old and older. Three hundred thousand men went to Jerusalem, all of them ready for battle and able to fight with spears and shields. Amaziah grouped these soldiers according to their clans and put them under the

[u]24.25,26 *Zabad and Jehozabad*: Hebrew "Zabad son of Shimeath from Ammon and Jehozabad son of Shimrith from Moab." [v]25.1 *Jehoaddin*: The Hebrew text has "Jehoaddan," another spelling of the name. [w]25.4 *the LORD had commanded . . . punished*: See Deuteronomy 24.16.

command of his army officers. **6**Amaziah also paid almost 4 tons of silver to hire 100,000 soldiers from Israel.

7One of God's prophets said, "Your Majesty, don't let these Israelite soldiers march into battle with you. The Lord has refused to help anyone from the northern kingdom of Israel, **8**and so he will let your enemies defeat you, even if you fight hard. He is the one who brings both victory and defeat."

9Amaziah replied, "What am I supposed to do about all the silver I paid those troops?"

"The Lord will give you back even more than you paid," the prophet answered.

10Amaziah ordered the troops from Israel to go home, but when they left, they were furious with the people of Judah.

11After Amaziah got his courage back, he led his troops to Salt Valley, where he killed 10,000 Edomite soldiers in battle. **12**He captured 10,000 more soldiers and dragged them to the top of a high cliff. Then he pushed them over the side, and they all were killed on the rocks below.

13Meanwhile, the Israelite troops that Amaziah had sent home, raided the towns in Judah between Samaria and Beth-Horon. They killed 3,000 people and carried off their possessions.

14After Amaziah had defeated the Edomite army, he returned to Jerusalem. He took with him the idols of the Edomite gods and set them up. Then he bowed down and offered them sacrifices. **15**This made the Lord very angry, and he sent a prophet to ask Amaziah, "Why would you worship these foreign gods that couldn't even save their own people from your attack?"

16But before the prophet finished speaking, Amaziah interrupted and said, "You're not one of my advisors! Don't say another word, or I'll have you killed."

The prophet stopped. But then he added, "First you sinned and now you've ignored my warning. It's clear that God has decided to punish you!"

Israel Defeats Judah
(2 Kings 14.8-14)

17King Amaziah of Judah talked with his officials, then sent a message to King Jehoash[x] of Israel: "Come out and face me in battle!"

18Jehoash sent back a reply that said:

Once upon a time, a small thornbush in Lebanon arranged the marriage between his son and the daughter of a large cedar tree. But a wild animal came along and trampled the small bush.

19Amaziah, you think you're so powerful because you defeated Edom. But stay at home and do your celebrating. If you cause any trouble, both you and your kingdom of Judah will be destroyed.

20God made Amaziah stubborn because he was planning to punish him for worshiping the Edomite gods. Amaziah refused to listen to Jehoash's warning, **21**so Jehoash led his army to the town of Beth-Shemesh in Judah to attack Amaziah and his troops. **22**During the battle, Judah's army was crushed. Every soldier from Judah ran back home, **23**and Jehoash captured Amaziah.

Jehoash took Amaziah with him when he went to attack Jerusalem. Jehoash broke down the city wall from Ephraim Gate to

---

[x]**25.17** *King Jehoash:* The Hebrew text has "King Joash son of Jehoahaz son of Jehu"; Jehoash is another spelling for the name Joash.

● 25.11,13 *Salt Valley. . . . Samaria and Beth-Horon:* The Salt Valley was a passage south and east of the Dead Sea between Jerusalem and Edom.

● 25.17 *Jehoash:* Jehoash was the twelfth king of the northern kingdom of Israel. He ruled from 798 to 783 B.C. He should not be confused with Joash (sometimes spelled Jehoash), Judah's prior king, and Amaziah's father.

Corner Gate, a section about 600 feet long. ²⁴He carried away the gold, the silver, and all the valuable furnishings from God's temple where the descendants of Obed-Edom stood guard. He robbed the king's treasury, took hostages, then returned to Samaria.

Amaziah Is Killed
(2 Kings 14.15-20)

²⁵Amaziah lived 15 years after Jehoash died. ²⁶Everything else Amaziah did while he was king is written in *The History of the Kings of Judah and Israel.*

²⁷As soon as Amaziah started disobeying the LORD, some people in Jerusalem plotted against Amaziah. He was able to escape to the town of Lachish, but another group of people caught him and killed him there. ²⁸His body was taken to Jerusalem on horseback and buried beside his ancestors.

King Uzziah of Judah
(2 Kings 14.21,22; 15.1-7)

26 ¹⁻³After the death of King Amaziah, the people of Judah crowned his son Uzziah[y] king, even though he was only 16 at the time. Uzziah ruled 52 years from Jerusalem, the hometown of his mother Jecoliah. During his rule, he recaptured and rebuilt the town of Elath.

⁴He obeyed the LORD by doing right, as his father Amaziah had done. ⁵Zechariah was Uzziah's advisor and taught him to obey God. And so, as long as Zechariah was alive, Uzziah was faithful to God, and God made him successful.

⁶While Uzziah was king, he started a war against the Philistines. He smashed the walls of the cities of Gath, Jabneh, and Ashdod, then rebuilt towns around Ashdod and in other parts of Philistia. ⁷God helped him defeat the Philistines, the Arabs living in Gur-Baal, and the Meunites. ⁸Even the Ammonites paid taxes to Uzziah. He became very powerful, and people who lived as far away as Egypt heard about him.

⁹In Jerusalem, Uzziah built fortified towers at the Corner Gate, the Valley Gate, and the place where the city wall turned inward.[z] ¹⁰He also built defense towers out in the desert.

He owned such a large herd of livestock in the western foothills and in the flatlands, that he had cisterns dug there to catch the rainwater. He loved farming, so he had crops and vineyards planted in the hill country wherever there was fertile soil, and he hired farmers to take care of them.

¹¹Uzziah's army was always ready for battle. Jeiel and Maaseiah were the officers who kept track of the number of soldiers, and these two men were under the command of Hananiah, one of Uzziah's officials. ¹²⁻¹³There were 307,500 trained soldiers, all under the command of 2,600 clan leaders. These powerful troops protected the king against any enemy. ¹⁴Uzziah supplied his army with shields, spears, helmets, armor, bows, and stones used for slinging. ¹⁵Some of his skilled workers invented machines that could shoot arrows and sling large stones. Uzziah set these up in Jerusalem at his defense towers and at the corners of the city wall.

God helped Uzziah become more and more powerful, and he was famous all over the world.

[y]**26.1-3** *Uzziah:* In the parallel passages in 2 Kings, he is called "Azariah" (see also 1 Chronicles 3.10-15). He is also called "Uzziah" in 2 Kings 15.13; Isaiah 1.1; Hosea 1.1; and Amos 1.1. One of these names was probably his birth name, while the other was his name after he became king. [z]**26.9** *the place where the city wall turned inward:* One possible meaning for the difficult Hebrew text.

Uzziah Becomes Too Proud

16Uzziah became proud of his power, and this led to his downfall.

One day, Uzziah disobeyed the LORD his God by going into the temple and burning incense as an offering to him.[a] **17**Azariah the priest and 80 other brave priests followed Uzziah into the temple **18**and said, "Your Majesty, this isn't right! You are not allowed to burn incense to the LORD. That must be done only by priests who are descendants of Aaron. You will have to leave! You have sinned against the LORD, and so he will no longer bless you."

19Uzziah, who was standing next to the incense altar at the time, was holding the incense burner, ready to offer incense to the LORD. He became very angry when he heard Azariah's warning, and leprosy[b] suddenly appeared on his forehead! **20**Azariah and the other priests saw it and immediately told him to leave the temple. Uzziah realized that the LORD had punished him, so he hurried to get outside.

21Uzziah had leprosy the rest of his life. He was no longer allowed in the temple or in his own palace. That's why his son Jotham lived there and ruled in his place. **22**Everything else Uzziah did while he was king is in the records written by the prophet Isaiah son of Amoz. **23**Since Uzziah had leprosy, he could not be buried in the royal tombs. Instead, he was buried in a nearby cemetery that the kings owned. His son Jotham then became king.

King Jotham of Judah
(2 Kings 15.32-38)

27 Jotham was 25 years old when he became king of Judah, and he ruled from Jerusalem for 16 years. Jerushah his mother was the daughter of Zadok.

2Jotham obeyed the LORD and did right. He followed the example of his father Uzziah, except he never burned incense in the temple as his father had done. But the people of Judah kept sinning against the LORD.

3Jotham rebuilt the Upper Gate of the temple and did a lot of work to repair the wall near Mount Ophel. **4**He built towns in the mountains of Judah and built fortresses and defense towers in the forests.

5During his rule he attacked and defeated the Ammonites. Then every year for the next three years, he forced them to pay 4 tons of silver, 60,000 bushels of wheat, and 60,000 bushels of barley.

6Jotham remained faithful to the LORD his God and became a very powerful king.

7Everything else Jotham did while he was king, including the wars he fought, is written in *The History of the Kings of Israel and Judah*. **8**After he had ruled Judah 16 years, he died at the age of 41. **9**He was buried in Jerusalem, and his son Ahaz became king.

King Ahaz of Judah
(2 Kings 16.1-4)

28 Ahaz was 20 years old when he became king of Judah, and he ruled from Jerusalem for 16 years.

Ahaz was nothing like his ancestor David. Ahaz disobeyed the LORD **2**and was as sinful as the kings of Israel. He made idols of the god Baal, **3**and he offered sacrifices in Hinnom Valley. Worst of all, Ahaz sacrificed his own sons, which was a disgusting custom of the nations that the LORD had forced out of Israel. **4**Ahaz offered sacrifices at the

26.16 *going into the temple and burning incense as an offering to him:* Only the priests were to enter the holy place to offer the incense sacrifice (Exod 30.1-10; Num 16.39,40). Uzziah disobeyed God's Law by making such an offering.

Israel's Priests

Purity (Clean and Unclean)

27.1 *Jotham:* Jotham was Judah's tenth king. He ruled from 740 to 736 B.C. Though he is said to have ruled 16 years, a number of these years were probably as a powerless ruler under Assyrian control.

28.1 *Ahaz:* Ahaz was Judah's eleventh king. He ruled from 736 to 716 B.C. Though he is said to have ruled only 16 years, there were additional years when he ruled along with Azariah, Jotham, and Hezekiah. Ahaz restored Baal worship to Judah, participated in child sacrifice (28.3), and bought Assyria's help against Israel and Syria with treasures taken from the temple in Jerusalem (28.20,21).

28.3 *Hinnom Valley:* This burning and dumping ground southwest of Jerusalem had been used to offer human sacrifice to the god Molech (2 Kgs 23.10). This earned it the name "Slaughter Valley" (Jer 19.6).

---

[a]**26.16** *going into the temple and burning incense as an offering to him:* This was to be done only by priests (see Exodus 30.1-10; Numbers 16.39,40). [b]**26.19** *leprosy:* The word translated "leprosy" was used for many different kinds of skin diseases.

● 28.15 *Jericho:* Jericho was an important city on the trade routes from the east (See Map 6 on pg 1884.)

local shrines,[c] as well as on every hill and in the shade of large trees.

Syria and Israel Attack Judah
(2 Kings 16.5,6)

5-6 Ahaz and the people of Judah sinned and turned away from the LORD, the God their ancestors had worshiped. So the LORD punished them by letting their enemies defeat them.

The king of Syria attacked Judah and took many of its people to Damascus as prisoners. King Pekah[d] of Israel later defeated Judah and killed 120,000 of its bravest soldiers in one day. **7**During that battle, an Israelite soldier named Zichri killed three men from Judah: Maaseiah the king's son; Azrikam, the official in charge of the palace; and Elkanah, the king's second in command. **8**The Israelite troops captured 200,000 women and children and took them back to their capital city of Samaria, along with a large amount of their possessions. They did these things even though the people of Judah were their own relatives.

Oded the Prophet Condemns Israel

9Oded lived in Samaria and was one of the LORD's prophets. He met Israel's army on their way back from Judah and said to them:

The LORD God of your ancestors let you defeat Judah's army only because he was angry with them. But you should not have been so cruel! **10**If you make slaves of the people of Judah and Jerusalem, you will be as guilty as they are of sinning against the LORD. **11**Send these prisoners back home—

they are your own relatives. If you don't, the LORD will punish you in his anger.

12About the same time, four of Israel's leaders arrived. They were Azariah son of Johanan, Berechiah son of Meshillemoth, Jehizkiah son of Shallum, and Amasa son of Hadlai. They agreed with Oded that the Israelite troops were wrong, **13**and they said:

If you bring these prisoners into Samaria, that will be one more thing we've done to sin against the LORD. And he is already angry enough with us.

14So in front of the leaders and the crowd, the troops handed over their prisoners and the property they had taken from Judah. **15**The four leaders took some of the stolen clothes and gave them to the prisoners who needed something to wear. They later gave them all a new change of clothes and shoes, then fixed them something to eat and drink, and cleaned their wounds with olive oil. They gave donkeys to those who were too weak to walk, and led all of them back to Jericho, the city known for its palm trees. The leaders then returned to Samaria.

Ahaz Asks the King of Assyria for Help
(2 Kings 16.7-9)

16-18 Some time later, the Edomites attacked the eastern part of Judah again and carried away prisoners. And at the same time, the Philistines raided towns in the western foothills and in the Southern Desert. They conquered the towns of Beth-Shemesh, Aijalon, Gederoth, Soco, Timnah, and Gimzo, including the villages around them. Then some of the Philistines went to live in these places.

[c]**28.4** *local shrines:* See the note at 11.15.   [d]**28.5,6** *Pekah:* Hebrew "Pekah son of Remaliah."

Ahaz sent a message to King Tiglath Pileser of Assyria and begged for help. [19]But God was punishing Judah with these disasters, because Ahaz had disobeyed him and refused to stop Judah from sinning. [20]So Tiglath Pileser came to Judah, but instead of helping, he made things worse. [21]Ahaz gave him gifts from the LORD's temple and the king's palace, as well as from the homes of Israel's other leaders. The Assyrian king still refused to help Ahaz.

The Final Sin of Ahaz and His Death

[22]Even after all these terrible things happened to Ahaz, he sinned against the LORD even worse than before. [23]He said to himself, "The Syrian gods must have helped their kings defeat me. Maybe if I offer sacrifices to those gods, they will help me." That was the sin that finally led to the downfall of Ahaz, as well as to the destruction of Judah.

[24]Ahaz collected all the furnishings of the temple and smashed them to pieces. Then he locked the doors to the temple and set up altars to foreign gods on every street corner in Jerusalem. [25]In every city and town in Judah he built local shrines[e] to worship foreign gods. All of this made the LORD God of his ancestors very angry.

[26]Everything else Ahaz did while he was king is written in *The History of the Kings of Judah and Israel*. [27]Ahaz died and was buried in Jerusalem, but not in the royal tombs. His son Hezekiah then became king.

King Hezekiah of Judah
(2 Kings 18.1-3)

29 Hezekiah was 25 years old when he became king of Judah, and he ruled 29 years from Jerusalem. His mother was Abijah daughter of Zechariah. [2]Hezekiah obeyed the LORD by doing right, just as his ancestor David had done.

The Temple Is Purified

[3]In the first month[f] of the first year of Hezekiah's rule, he unlocked the doors to the LORD's temple and had them repaired.[g] [4]Then he called the priests and Levites to the east courtyard of the temple [5]and said:

It's time to purify the temple of the LORD God of our ancestors. You Levites must first go through the ceremony to make yourselves clean, then go into the temple and bring out everything that is unclean and unacceptable to the LORD. [6]Some of our ancestors were unfaithful and disobeyed the LORD our God. Not only did they turn their backs on the LORD, but they also completely ignored his temple. [7]They locked the doors, then let the lamps go out and stopped burning incense and offering sacrifices to him. [8]The LORD became terribly angry with the people of Judah and Jerusalem, and everyone was shocked and horrified at what he did to punish them. Not only were [9]our ancestors killed in battle, but our own children and wives were taken captive.

[10]So I have decided to renew our agreement with the LORD God of Israel.

[e]28.25 *local shrines:* See the note at 11.15. [f]29.3 *first month:* Abib (also called Nisan), the first month of the Hebrew calendar, from about mid-March to mid-April. [g]29.3 *he unlocked the doors . . . repaired:* King Ahaz had locked the doors and stopped everyone from worshiping the LORD (see 28.24,25).

28.18 *Tiglath Pileser of Assyria:* Assyria began to expand its power and continued to do so throughout the period of the Israelite kings (931–722 B.C.) Its expansion into Israel had begun around 855 B.C. During the rule of Tiglath Pileser III (745–727 B.C.), the Assyrian expansion continued, gaining control of conquered areas in part by forcing native people to leave their homelands and move to other lands owned by Assyria. (See Map 7 on pg 1885.)

Assyria

28.20,21 *Tiglath Pileser came . . . refused to help Ahaz:* This is somewhat different from the account in 2 KINGS (2 Kgs 15.29; 16.5-9). The writer of 2 CHRONICLES stresses the end result: because they put trust in the Assyrian king instead of in God, Ahaz and the people of Judah are severely punished.

29.1 *Hezekiah:* Hezekiah was Judah's twelfth king, ruling from 716 to 687 B.C. One of Judah's greatest kings, he struggled to free his people from Assyrian domination and was the first king to eliminate the local shrines. His grandfather was Zechariah, a former king of Israel. In 2 CHRONICLES, Hezekiah shares many similarities with Solomon: his attention to the temple as a place of worship, his celebration of Passover, and his wealth.

Hezekiah

■ 29.21,22 *seven bulls . . . splattered their blood on the altar:* Seven is a number that symbolized perfection and is often not meant literally, though here it probably is. Because blood carried the life force, it was considered sacred (Gen 4.10,11; Lev 17.14). It was not to be eaten (Lev 7.26,27; 17.10-14; 19.26; Deut 12.23-24; 15.23). It also has power to protect (Exod 4.25; 12.7). Blood splattered or smeared on the altar or on the people had cleansing power and showed that something or someone was dedicated to God (Exod 29.10-21). (See the chart Numbers in the Bible on pg 1844.)

∝ Blood

■ 29.23,24 *laid their hands . . . all the people of Israel:* The laying on of hands was to connect the offerer to the animal in order to get rid of the person's sins through the animal (Lev 4.15; 16.21; Num 8.12). Hezekiah demands that the sacrifices are for all of Israel, meaning both the northern and southern kingdoms.

Maybe then he will stop being so angry with us. [11]Let's not waste any time, my friends. You are the ones who were chosen to be the LORD's priests and to offer him sacrifices.

[12-14]When Hezekiah finished talking, the following Levite leaders went to work:

Mahath son of Amasai and Joel son of Azariah from the Kohath clan; Kish son of Abdi and Azariah son of Jehallelel from the Merari clan; Joah son of Zimmah and Eden son of Joah from the Gershon clan; Shimri and Jeuel from the Elizaphan clan; Zechariah and Mattaniah from the Asaph clan; Jehuel and Shimei from the Heman clan; Shemaiah and Uzziel from the Jeduthun clan.

[15]These leaders gathered together the rest of the Levites, and they all went through the ceremony to make themselves clean. Then they began to purify the temple according to the Law of the LORD, just as Hezekiah had commanded.

[16]The priests went into the temple and carried out everything that was unclean. They put these things in the courtyard, and from there, the Levites carried them outside the city to Kidron Valley.

[17]The priests and Levites began their work on the first day of the first month.[h] It took them one week to purify the courtyards of the temple and another week to purify the temple. So on the sixteenth day of that same month [18]they went back to Hezekiah and said:

Your Majesty, we have finished our work. The entire temple is now pure again, and so is the altar and its utensils, as well as the table for the sacred loaves of bread and its utensils. [19]And we have brought back all the things that King Ahaz took from the temple during the time he was unfaithful to God. We purified them and put them back in front of the altar.

Worship in the Temple

[20]At once, Hezekiah called together the officials of Jerusalem, and they went to the temple. [21]They brought with them seven bulls, seven rams, seven lambs, and seven goats[i] as sacrifices to take away the sins of Hezekiah's family and of the people of Judah, as well as to purify the temple. Hezekiah told the priests, who were descendants of Aaron, to sacrifice these animals on the altar.

[22]The priests killed the bulls, the rams, and the lambs, then splattered the blood on the altar. [23]They took the goats to Hezekiah and the worshipers, and they laid their hands on the animals. [24]The priests then killed the goats and splattered the blood on the altar as a sacrifice to take away the sins of everyone in Israel, because Hezekiah had commanded that these sacrifices be made for all the people of Israel.

[25]Next, Hezekiah assigned the Levites to their places in the temple. He gave them cymbals, harps, and other stringed instruments, according to the instructions that the LORD had given King David and the two prophets, Gad and Nathan. [26]The Levites were ready to play the instruments that had belonged to David; the priests were ready to blow the trumpets.

[27]As soon as Hezekiah gave the signal for the sacrifices to be burned on the altar, the musicians began singing praises to the LORD and playing their instruments, [28]and everyone worshiped the LORD. This continued until the last animal was sacrificed.

[29]After that, Hezekiah and the crowd of worshipers bowed down and worshiped the LORD. [30]Then Hezekiah and his officials

[h]29.17 *first month:* See the note at 29.3.   [i]29.21 *goats:* Hebrew "male goats."

ordered the Levites to sing the songs of praise that David and Asaph the prophet had written. And so they bowed down and joyfully sang praises to the Lord. [31]Hezekiah said to the crowd, "Now that you are once again acceptable to the Lord, bring sacrifices and offerings to give him thanks."

The people did this, and some of them voluntarily brought animals to be offered as sacrifices. [32]Seventy bulls, 100 rams, and 200 lambs were brought as sacrifices to please the Lord;[j] [33]600 bulls and 3,000 sheep were brought as sacrifices to ask the Lord's blessing.[k] [34]There were not enough priests to skin all these animals, because many of the priests had not taken the time to go through the ceremony to make themselves clean. However, since all the Levites had made themselves clean, they helped the priests until the last animal was skinned. [35]Besides all the sacrifices that were burned on the altar, the fat from the other animal sacrifices was burned, and the offerings of wine were poured over the altar.

So the temple was once again used for worshiping the Lord. [36]Hezekiah and the people of Judah celebrated, because God had helped them make this happen so quickly.

Hezekiah Prepares To Celebrate Passover

30 [1-4]Passover wasn't celebrated in the first month,[l] which was the usual time, because many of the priests were still unclean and unacceptable to serve, and be-cause not everyone in Judah had come to Jerusalem for the festival. So Hezekiah, his officials, and the people agreed to celebrate Passover in the second month.[m]

Hezekiah sent a message to everyone in Israel and Judah, including those in the ter-ritories of Ephraim and West Manasseh, inviting them to the temple in Jerusalem for the celebration of Passover in honor of the Lord God of Israel. [5]Everyone from Beersheba in the south to Dan in the north was invited. This was the largest crowd of people that had ever celebrated Passover, according to the official records.

[6]Hezekiah's messengers went every-where in Israel and Judah with the follow-ing letter:

People of Israel, now that you have survived the invasion of the Assyrian kings,[n] it's time for you to turn back to the Lord God our ancestors Abraham, Isaac, and Jacob worshiped. If you do this, he will stop being angry. [7]Don't follow the example of your ancestors and your Israelite relatives in the north. They were unfaithful to the Lord, and he punished them horribly. [8]Don't be stubborn like your ances-tors. Decide now to obey the Lord our God! Come to Jerusalem and worship him in the temple that will belong to him forever. Then he will stop being angry, [9]and the enemies that have cap-tured your families will show pity and send them back home. The Lord God is kind and merciful, and if you turn back to him, he will no longer turn his back on you.

[10]The messengers went to every town in

---

[j]**29.32** *sacrifices to please the Lord:* See the note at 1.6.   [k]**29.33** *sacrifices to ask the Lord's blessing:* These sacrifices have traditionally been called "peace offerings" or "offerings of well-being." A main purpose was to ask for the Lord's blessing, and so in the CEV they are sometimes called "sacrifices to ask the Lord's blessing."   [l]**30.1-4** *first month:* See the note at 29.3.   [m]**30.1-4** *second month:* See the note at 3.1,2.   [n]**30.6** *the invasion of the Assyrian kings:* See 2 Kings 17.1-22.

30.26 *since the days of King Solomon:* Like Solomon more than 215 years earlier, Hezekiah brings the people together in proper worship.

Ephraim and West Manasseh as far north as the territory of Zebulun, but people laughed and insulted them. [11]Only a few people from the tribes of Asher, West Manasseh, and Zebulun were humble and went to Jerusalem. [12]God also made everyone in Judah eager to do what Hezekiah and his officials had commanded.

Passover Is Celebrated

[13]In the second month,[o] a large crowd of people gathered in Jerusalem to celebrate the Festival of Thin Bread.[P] [14]They took all the foreign altars and incense altars in Jerusalem and threw them into Kidron Valley.

[15-17]Then, on the fourteenth day of that same month, the Levites began killing the lambs for Passover, because many of the worshipers were unclean and were not allowed to kill their own lambs. Meanwhile, some of the priests and Levites felt ashamed because they had not gone through the ceremony to make themselves clean. They immediately went through that ceremony and went to the temple, where they offered sacrifices to please the LORD.[9] Then the priests and Levites took their positions, according to the Law of Moses, the servant of God.

As the Levites killed the lambs, they handed some of the blood to the priests, who splattered it on the altar.

[18-19]Most of the people that came from Ephraim, West Manasseh, Issachar, and Zebulun had not made themselves clean, but they ignored God's Law and ate the Passover lambs anyway. Hezekiah found out what they had done and prayed, "LORD God, these people are unclean according to the laws of holiness. But they are worshiping you, just as their ancestors did. So, please be kind and forgive them." [20]The LORD answered Hezekiah's prayer and did not punish them.

[21]The worshipers in Jerusalem were very happy and celebrated the Festival for seven days. The Levites and priests sang praises to the LORD every day and played their instruments. [22]Hezekiah thanked the Levites for doing such a good job, leading the celebration.

The worshipers celebrated for seven days by offering sacrifices, by eating the sacred meals, and by praising the LORD God of their ancestors. [23]Everyone was so excited that they agreed to celebrate seven more days.

[24]So Hezekiah gave the people 1,000 bulls and 7,000 sheep to be offered as sacrifices and to be used as food for the sacred meals. His officials gave 1,000 bulls and 10,000 sheep, and many more priests agreed to go through the ceremony to make themselves clean. [25]Everyone was very happy, including those from Judah and Israel, the priests and Levites, and the foreigners living in Judah and Israel. [26]It was the biggest celebration in Jerusalem since the days of King Solomon, the son of David. [27]The priests and Levites asked God to bless the people, and from his home in heaven, he did.

The People Destroy the Local Shrines

(2 Kings 18.4)

31 After the Festival, the people went to every town in Judah and smashed the stone images of foreign gods and cut

[o]**30.13** *second month:* See the note at 3.1,2.   [P]**30.13** *the Festival of Thin Bread:* The celebration of this Festival began one day after Passover. And so these two festivals were often referred to as one.
[9]**30.15-17** *sacrifices to please the LORD:* See the note at 1.6.

down the sacred poles[r] for worshiping the goddess Asherah. They destroyed all the local shrines[s] and foreign altars in Judah, as well as those in the territories of Benjamin, Ephraim, and West Manasseh. Then everyone went home.

Offerings for the Priests and Levites

[2]Hezekiah divided the priests and Levites into groups, according to their duties. Then he assigned them the responsibilities of offering sacrifices to please the Lord[t] and sacrifices to ask his blessing.[u] He also appointed people to serve at the temple and to sing praises at the temple gates. [3]Hezekiah provided animals from his own herds and flocks to use for the morning and evening sacrifices, as well as for the sacrifices during the Sabbath celebrations, the New Moon Festivals, and the other religious feasts required by the Law of the Lord.

[4]He told the people of Jerusalem to bring the offerings that were to be given to the priests and Levites, so that they would have time to serve the Lord with their work. [5]As soon as the people heard what the king wanted, they brought a tenth of everything they owned, including their best grain, wine, olive oil, honey, and other crops. [6]The people from the other towns of Judah brought a tenth of their herds and flocks, as well as a tenth of anything they had dedicated to the Lord. [7]The people started bringing their offerings to Jerusalem in the third month,[v] and the last ones arrived four months later. [8]When Hezekiah and his officials saw these offerings, they thanked the Lord and the people.

[9]Hezekiah asked the priests and Levites about the large amount of offerings. [10]The high priest at the time was Azariah, a descendant of Zadok, and he replied, "Ever since the people have been bringing us their offerings, we have had more than enough food and supplies. The Lord has certainly blessed his people. Look at how much is left over!"

[11]So the king gave orders for storerooms to be built in the temple, and when they were completed, [12-13]all the extra offerings were taken there. Hezekiah and Azariah then appointed Conaniah the Levite to be in charge of these storerooms. His brother Shimei was his assistant, and the following Levites worked with them: Jehiel, Azaziah, Nahath, Asahel, Jerimoth, Jozabad, Eliel, Ismachiah, Mahath, and Benaiah. [14]Kore son of Imnah was assigned to guard the East Gate, and he was put in charge of receiving the offerings voluntarily given to God and of dividing them among the priests and Levites. [15-16]He had six assistants who were responsible for seeing that all the priests in the other towns of Judah also got their share of these offerings. They were Eden, Miniamin, Jeshua, Shemaiah, Amariah, and Shecaniah.

Every priest and every Levite over 30[w] years old who worked daily in the temple received part of these offerings, according to their duties. [17]The priests were listed in the official records by clans, and the Levites 20 years old and older were listed by their duties. [18]The official records also included their wives and children, because they had also been faithful in keeping themselves clean and acceptable to serve the Lord.

[19]Hezekiah also appointed other men to

31.3 *New Moon Festivals . . . other religious feasts:* The New Moon Festival was held on the day of the new moon, the day when only a thin edge of the moon can be seen. This day was always the first day of the month for the Hebrew calendar. The festival was a time for worship, sacrifices, celebration, eating, and rest from work. **(See the article People of the Law: The Religion of Israel on pg 1794.)**

31.7 *third month:* This is Sivan, the third month of the Hebrew calendar, from about mid-May to mid-June.

31.14 *receiving the offerings . . . dividing them among the priests and Levites:* Because the tribe of Levi was set apart for priestly service to all the tribes, they were not given their own land in Canaan. Instead, they were scattered throughout the land belonging to the other tribes and were supported with a portion of the offerings brought by the people.

Israel's Priests

---

[r]31.1 *sacred poles:* See the note at 14.3. [s]31.1 *local shrines:* See the note at 11.15. [t]31.2 *sacrifices to please the Lord:* See the note at 1.6. [u]31.2 *sacrifices to ask his blessing:* See the note at 29.33. [v]31.7 *third month:* Sivan, the third month of the Hebrew calendar, from about mid-May to mid-June. [w]31.15,16 30: The Hebrew text has "3" instead of "30"; in Hebrew, these two words look almost exactly the same (see also Numbers 4.3; 1 Chronicles 23.3).

The high priest Azariah said, *"The Lord has certainly blessed his people. Look at how much is left over!"* 2 Chr 31.10

32.1 *King Sennacherib . . . fortified cities*: Sennacherib ruled Assyria from 705 to 681 B.C. This event probably took place in 701 B.C.

take food and supplies to the priests and Levites whose homes were in the pastureland around the towns of Judah. But the priests had to be descendants of Aaron, and the Levites had to be listed in the official records.

²⁰⁻²¹Everything Hezekiah did while he was king of Judah, including what he did for the temple in Jerusalem, was right and good. He was a successful king, because he obeyed the LORD God with all his heart.

King Sennacherib of Assyria Invades Judah
(2 Kings 18.13-37; Isaiah 36.1-22)

32 After King Hezekiah had faithfully obeyed the LORD's instructions by doing these things, King Sennacherib of Assyria invaded Judah. He attacked the fortified cities and thought he would capture every one of them.

²As soon as Hezekiah learned that Sennacherib was planning to attack Jerusalem, ³⁻⁴he and his officials worked out a plan to cut off the supply of water outside the city, so that the Assyrians would have no water when they came to attack. The officials got together a large work force that stopped up the springs and streams near Jerusalem.

⁵Hezekiah's workers also repaired the broken sections of the city wall. Then they built defense towers and an outer wall to help protect the one already there. The landfill on the east side of David's City was also strengthened.

He gave orders to make a large supply of weapons and shields, ⁶and he appointed army commanders over the troops. Then he gathered the troops together in the open area in front of the city gate and said to them:

⁷Be brave and confident! There's no reason to be afraid of King Sennacherib and his powerful army. We are much more powerful, ⁸because the LORD our God fights on our side. The Assyrians must rely on human power alone.

These words encouraged the army of Judah.

⁹When Sennacherib and his troops were camped at the town of Lachish, he sent a message to Hezekiah and the people in Jerusalem. It said:

¹⁰I am King Sennacherib of Assyria, and I have Jerusalem surrounded. Do you think you can survive my attack? ¹¹Hezekiah your king is telling you that the LORD your God will save you from me. But he is lying, and you'll die of hunger and thirst. ¹²Didn't Hezekiah tear down all except one of the LORD's altars and places of worship?^x And didn't he tell you people of Jerusalem and Judah to worship at that one place?

¹³You've heard what my ancestors and I have done to other nations. Were the gods of those nations able to defend their land against us? ¹⁴None of those gods kept their people safe from the kings of Assyria. Do you really think your God can do any better? ¹⁵Don't be fooled by Hezekiah! No god of any nation has ever been able to stand up to Assyria. Believe me, your God cannot keep you safe!

¹⁶The Assyrian officials said terrible things about the LORD God and his servant Hezekiah. ¹⁷Sennacherib's letter even made

^x**32.12** *worship*: Hezekiah actually had torn down the places where idols were worshiped, and he had told the people to worship the LORD at the one place of worship in Jerusalem. But the Assyrian leader was confused and thought these were also places where the LORD was supposed to be worshiped.

fun of the LORD. It said, "The gods of other nations could not save their people from Assyria's army, and neither will the God that Hezekiah worships." [18]The officials said all these things in Hebrew, so that everyone listening from the city wall would understand and be terrified and surrender. [19]The officials talked about the LORD God as if he were nothing but an ordinary god or an idol that someone had made.

The Death of King Sennacherib
(2 Kings 19.14-19,35-37; Isaiah 37.14-20; 37.36-38)

[20]Hezekiah and the prophet Isaiah son of Amoz begged the LORD for help, [21]and he sent an angel that killed every soldier and commander in the Assyrian camp.

Sennacherib returned to Assyria, completely disgraced. Then one day he went into the temple of his god where some of his sons killed him. [22]The LORD rescued Hezekiah and the people of Jerusalem from Sennacherib and also protected them from other enemies. [23]People brought offerings to Jerusalem for the LORD and expensive gifts for Hezekiah, and from that day on, every nation on earth respected Hezekiah.

Hezekiah Gets Sick and Almost Dies
(2 Kings 20.1-11; Isaiah 38.1-8)

[24]About this same time, Hezekiah got sick and was almost dead. He prayed, and the LORD gave him a sign that he would recover. [25]But Hezekiah was so proud that he refused to thank the LORD for everything he had done for him. This made the LORD angry, and he punished Hezekiah and the people of Judah and Jerusalem.

[26]Hezekiah and the people later felt sorry and asked the LORD to forgive them. So the LORD did not punish them as long as Hezekiah was king.

Hezekiah's Wealth
(2 Kings 20.12-19; Isaiah 39.1-8)

[27]Hezekiah was very rich, and everyone respected him. He built special rooms to store the silver, the gold, the precious stones and spices, the shields, and the other valuable possessions. [28]Storehouses were also built for his supply of grain, wine, and olive oil; barns were built for his cattle, and pens were put up for his sheep. [29]God made Hezekiah extremely rich, so he bought even more sheep, goats, and cattle. And he built towns where he could keep all these animals.

[30]It was Hezekiah who built a tunnel that carried the water from Gihon Spring into the city of Jerusalem. In fact, everything he did was successful! [31]Even when the leaders of Babylonia sent messengers to ask Hezekiah about the sign God had given him, God let Hezekiah give his own answer to test him and to see if he would remain faithful.

Hezekiah Dies
(2 Kings 20.20,21)

[32]Everything else Hezekiah did while he was king, including how faithful he was to the LORD, is included in the records kept by Isaiah the prophet. These are written in *The History of the Kings of Judah and Israel.* [33]When Hezekiah died, he was buried in the section of the royal tombs that was reserved for the most respected kings,[y] and everyone in Judah and Jerusalem honored him. His son Manasseh then became king.

[y]**32.33** *in the section . . . reserved for the most respected kings*: One possible meaning for the difficult Hebrew text.

33.1 *Manasseh:* Manasseh was Judah's thirteenth king, ruling from 687 to 642 b.c. The "55" year reign mentioned in this verse is the longest reign in the Bible, though it includes an extra 10 years during which he ruled alongside his father.

33.2-7 *Manasseh disobeyed the* Lord . . . *made the* Lord *very angry:* Manasseh brought the worship of the Canaanite gods back to Judah. He built altars honoring these gods right in the temple area and rebuilt local shrines that his father had torn down. Manasseh also built altars honoring the stars, sun, and moon. He allowed the practice of magic and witchcraft, as well as the practice of trying to talk to the spirits of the dead. Both were forbidden by the Law of Moses. He even sacrificed his own son to the god Molech in the Hinnom Valley, a practice that was also forbidden.

33.8 *the land I gave to their ancestors:* God gave Canaan to Abraham and his descendents (Gen 17.7,8). But the people could only keep the land if they continued to be faithful to the Lord alone.

King Manasseh of Judah
(2 Kings 21.1-9,17,18)

33 Manasseh was 12 years old when he became king of Judah, and he ruled 55 years from Jerusalem. **2**Manasseh disobeyed the Lord by following the disgusting customs of the nations that the Lord had forced out of Israel. **3**He rebuilt the local shrines[z] that his father Hezekiah had torn down. He built altars for the god Baal and set up sacred poles[a] for worshiping the goddess Asherah. And he continued to worship the stars.

4In the temple, where only the Lord was supposed to be worshiped, Manasseh built altars for the worship of pagan gods **5**and the stars. He placed these altars in both courtyards of the temple **6-7**and even set up a stone image of a foreign god. Manasseh practiced magic and witchcraft; he asked fortunetellers for advice and sacrificed his own sons in Hinnom Valley. He did many other sinful things and made the Lord very angry.

Years ago, God had told David and Solomon:

Jerusalem is the place I prefer above all others in Israel. It belongs to me, and there in the temple I will be worshiped forever. **8**If my people will faithfully obey all the laws and teaching I gave to my servant Moses, I will never again force them to leave the land I gave to their ancestors.

9But the people of Judah and Jerusalem listened to Manasseh and did even more sinful things than the nations the Lord had wiped out.

10The Lord tried to warn Manasseh and the people about their sins, but they ignored the warning. **11**So he let Assyrian army commanders invade Judah and capture Manasseh. They put a hook in his nose and tied him up in chains, and they took him to Babylon. **12**While Manasseh was held captive there, he asked the Lord God to forgive him and to help him. **13**The Lord listened to Manasseh's prayer and saw how sorry he was, and so he let him go back to Jerusalem and rule as king. Manasseh knew from then on that the Lord was God.

14Later, Manasseh rebuilt the eastern section of Jerusalem's outer wall and made it taller. This section went from Gihon Valley north to Fish Gate and around the part of the city called Mount Ophel. He also assigned army officers to each of the fortified cities in Judah.[b]

15Manasseh also removed the idols and the stone image of the foreign god from the temple, and he gathered the altars he had built near the temple and in other parts of Jerusalem. He threw all these things outside the city. **16**Then he repaired the Lord's altar and offered sacrifices to thank him and sacrifices to ask his blessing.[c] He gave orders that everyone in Judah must worship the Lord God of Israel. **17**The people obeyed Manasseh, but they worshiped the Lord at their own shrines.

18Everything else Manasseh did while he was king, including his prayer to the Lord God and the warnings from his prophets, is written in *The History of the Kings of Israel.* **19**Hozai[d] wrote a lot about Manasseh, including his prayer and God's answer. But Hozai also recorded the evil things Ma-

[z]**33.3** *local shrines:* See the note at 11.15. [a]**33.3** *sacred poles:* See the note at 14.3. [b]**33.14** *fortified cities in Judah:* At this time, Judah was under the control of Assyria. The fortifications mentioned in this verse may have been done under orders from Assyrian officials, hoping to strengthen their southern border against the rising power of Egypt. [c]**33.16** *sacrifices to ask his blessing:* See the note at 29.33. [d]**33.19** *Hozai:* Or "The prophets."

nasseh did before turning back to God, as well as a list of places where Manasseh set up idols, and where he built local shrines and places to worship Asherah. **20**Manasseh died and was buried near the palace, and his son Amon became king.

King Amon of Judah
(2 Kings 21.19-26)

21Amon was 22 years old when he became king of Judah, and he ruled from Jerusalem for 2 years. **22**Amon disobeyed the LORD, just as his father Manasseh had done, and he worshiped and offered sacrifices to the idols his father had made. **23**Manasseh had turned back to the LORD, but Amon refused to do that. Instead, he sinned even more than his father.

24Some of Amon's officials plotted against him and killed him in his palace. **25**But the people of Judah killed the murderers of Amon and made his son Josiah king.

King Josiah of Judah
(2 Kings 22.1,2)

34 Josiah was 8 years old when he became king of Judah, and he ruled 31 years from Jerusalem. **2**He followed the example of his ancestor David and always obeyed the LORD.

Josiah Stops the Worship of Foreign Gods
(2 Kings 23.4-20)

3When Josiah was only 16 years old he began worshiping God, just as his ancestor David had done. Then, 4 years later, he decided to destroy the local shrines[e] in Ju-

dah and Jerusalem, as well as the sacred poles[f] for worshiping the goddess Asherah and the idols of foreign gods. **4**He watched as the altars for the worship of the god Baal were torn down, and as the nearby incense altars were smashed. The Asherah poles, the idols, and the stone images were also smashed, and the pieces were scattered over the graves of their worshipers. **5**Josiah then had the bones of the pagan priests burned on the altars.[g]

And so Josiah got rid of the worship of foreign gods in Judah and Jerusalem. **6**He did the same things in the towns and ruined villages[h] in the territories of West Manasseh, Ephraim, and Simeon, as far as the border of Naphtali. **7**Everywhere in the northern kingdom of Israel, Josiah tore down pagan altars and Asherah poles; he crushed idols to dust and smashed incense altars.

Then Josiah went back to Jerusalem.

Hilkiah Finds
The Book of God's Law
(2 Kings 22.3-20)

8In the eighteenth year of Josiah's rule in Judah, after he had removed all the sinful things from the land and from the LORD's temple, he sent three of his officials to repair the temple. They were Shaphan son of Azaliah, Governor Maaseiah of Jerusalem, and Joah son of Joahaz, who kept the government records.

9These three men went to Hilkiah the high priest. They gave him the money that the Levite guards had collected from the people of West Manasseh, Ephraim, and the rest of Israel, as well as those living in Judah, Benjamin, and Jerusalem. **10**Then the money was turned over to the men

---

[e]**34.3** *local shrines:* See the note at 11.15.   [f]**34.3** *sacred poles:* See the note at 14.3.   [g]**34.5** *the bones of the pagan priests burned on the altars:* This made the altars unclean, so that they could not be used in worshiping any god.   [h]**34.6** *ruined villages:* One possible meaning for the difficult Hebrew text.

33.20 *buried near the palace:* In 2 Kgs 21.18, Manasseh is said to be buried in the Uzza Garden near the palace. Since Uzza was a foreign god, the writer of 2 CHRONICLES may not have given the name of the garden—feeling that this was not a proper place to bury a king who had returned to a proper faith in God.

33.21 *Amon:* Amon was Judah's fourteenth king, ruling from 642 to 640 B.C.

33.24 *killed him:* The writer of 2 CHRONICLES does not add the typical burial notice that ends his histories of the other kings. Amon was buried near his father in the Uzza Garden by the palace (2 Kgs 21.17,18,23-26).

34.1 *Josiah:* Josiah was Judah's fifteenth king, ruling from 640 to 609 B.C.

Josiah

34.6 *West Manasseh, Ephraim, and Simeon, . . . Naphtali:* Josiah's reforms reach into the northern kingdom of Israel and cover a territory similar to that ruled by David and Solomon. The writer of 2 CHRONICLES compares Josiah and Hezekiah to kings David and Solomon, who had ruled when Judah and Israel were united as one kingdom of Israel. The people of both nations shared common ancestors who had made a special agreement with God. **(See Map 3 on pg 1881.)**

34.9 *Hilkiah . . . the money:* King Joash also had collected money for repairing the temple during his rule approximately 200 years earlier.

34.15 *The Book of God's Law:* Many scholars feel this may have been a portion of DEUTERONOMY, which includes the laws given to Moses. Some point to Deut 5, which gives the Ten Commandments. Others suggest Deut 28–30, which tells how God would bless the people for obedience and curse them for disobedience, and includes the renewal of the agreement between God and the people at Moab. Others think this "Book" may have been the text of all of the first five books of the Bible.

34.22 *Huldah the prophet:* Huldah is one of several female prophets names in the Bible. Miriam (Exod 15.20), Deborah (Judg 4.4) and Noadiah (Neh 6.14) are other women who served as prophets. **(See the article Prophets and Prophecy on pg 1791.)**

who supervised the repairs to the temple. They used some of it to pay the workers, [11]and they gave the rest of it to the carpenters and builders, who used it to buy the stone and wood they needed to repair the other buildings that Judah's kings had not taken care of.

[12]The workers were honest, and their supervisors were Jahath and Obadiah from the Levite clan of Merari, and Zechariah and Meshullam from the Levite clan of Kohath. Other Levites, who were all skilled musicians, [13]were in charge of carrying supplies and supervising the workers. Other Levites were appointed to stand guard around the temple.

[14]While the money was being given to these supervisors, Hilkiah found the book that contained the laws that the LORD had given to Moses. [15]Hilkiah handed the book to Shaphan the official and said, "Look what I found here in the temple—*The Book of God's Law.*"

[16]Shaphan took the book to Josiah and reported, "Your officials are doing everything you wanted. [17]They have collected the money from the temple and have given it to the men supervising the repairs. [18]But there's something else, Your Majesty. The priest Hilkiah gave me this book." Then Shaphan read it aloud.

[19]When Josiah heard what was in *The Book of God's Law,* he tore his clothes in sorrow. [20]At once he called together Hilkiah, Shaphan, Ahikam son of Shaphan, Abdon son of Micah,[i] and his own servant Asaiah. He said, [21]"The LORD must be furious with me and everyone else in Israel and Judah, because our ancestors did not obey the laws written in this book. Go find out what the LORD wants us to do."

[22]Hilkiah and the four other men left at once and went to talk with Huldah the prophet. Her husband was Shallum,[j] who was in charge of the king's clothes. Huldah lived in the northern part of Jerusalem, and when they met in her home, [23]she said:

You were sent here by King Josiah, and this is what the LORD God of Israel says to him: [24]"Josiah, I am the LORD! And I intend to punish this country and everyone in it, just as this book says. [25]The people of Judah and Israel have rejected me. They have offered sacrifices to foreign gods and have worshiped their own idols. I can't stand it any longer. I am furious.

[26-27]"Josiah, listen to what I am going to do. I noticed how sad you were when you heard that this country and its people would be completely wiped out. You even tore your clothes in sorrow, and I heard you cry. [28]So before I destroy this place, I will let you die in peace."

The men left and reported to Josiah what Huldah had said.

Josiah Reads
The Book of God's Law
(2 Kings 23.1-3)

[29]King Josiah called together the leaders of Judah and Jerusalem. [30]Then he went to the LORD's temple, together with all the people of Judah and Jerusalem, the priests, and the Levites.

Finally, when everybody was there, he read aloud *The Book of God's Law*[k] that had been found in the temple.

[31]After Josiah had finished reading, he stood in the place reserved for the king. He

[i]**34.20** *Abdon son of Micah:* Also called "Achbor son of Micaiah" (see 2 Kings 22.12).   [j]**34.22** *Shallum:* Hebrew "Shallum son of Tokhath son of Hasrah."   [k]**34.30** *The Book of God's Law:* The Hebrew text has "The Book of God's Agreement," which is the same as "The Book of God's Law" in verses 15 and 19. In traditional translations this is called "The Book of the Covenant."

promised in the LORD's name to faithfully obey the LORD and to follow his laws and teachings that were written in the book. [32]Then he asked the people of Jerusalem and Benjamin to make that same promise and to obey the God their ancestors had worshiped.

[33]Josiah destroyed all the idols in the territories of Israel, and he commanded everyone in Israel to worship only the LORD God. The people did not turn away from the LORD God of their ancestors for the rest of Josiah's rule as king.

Passover Is Celebrated

(2 Kings 23.21-23)

35 Josiah commanded that Passover be celebrated in Jerusalem to honor the LORD. So, on the fourteenth day of the first month,[1] the lambs were killed for the Passover celebration.

[2]On that day, Josiah made sure the priests knew what duties they were to do in the temple. [3]He called together the Levites who served the LORD and who taught the people his laws, and he said:

No longer will you have to carry the sacred chest from place to place. It will stay in the temple built by King Solomon son of David, where you will serve the LORD and his people Israel. [4]Get ready to do the work that David and Solomon assigned to you, according to your clans. [5]Divide yourselves into groups, then arrange yourselves throughout the temple so that each family of worshipers will be able to get help from one of you.[m] [6]When the people bring you their Passover lamb, you must kill it and prepare it to be sacrificed to the LORD. Make sure the

people celebrate according to the instructions that the LORD gave Moses, and don't do anything to make yourselves unclean and unacceptable.

[7]Josiah donated 30,000 sheep and goats, and 3,000 bulls from his own flocks and herds for the people to offer as sacrifices. [8]Josiah's officials also voluntarily gave some of their animals to the people, the priests, and the Levites as sacrifices. Hilkiah, Zechariah, and Jehiel, who were the officials in charge of the temple, gave the priests 2,600 sheep and lambs and 300 bulls to sacrifice during the Passover celebration. [9]Conaniah, his two brothers Shemaiah and Nethanel, as well as Hashabiah, Jeiel, and Jozabad were leaders of the Levites, and they gave the other Levites 5,000 sheep and goats, and 500 bulls to offer as sacrifices.

[10]When everything was ready to celebrate Passover, the priests and the Levites stood where Josiah had told them. [11]Then the Levites killed and skinned the Passover lambs, and they handed some of the blood to the priests, who splattered it on the altar. [12]The Levites set aside the parts of the animal that the worshipers needed for their sacrifices to please the LORD,[n] just as the Law of Moses required. They also did the same thing with the bulls. [13]They sacrificed the Passover animals on the altar and boiled the meat for the other offerings in pots, kettles, and pans. Then they quickly handed the meat to the people so they could eat it.

[14]All day long, the priests were busy offering sacrifices and burning the animals' fat on the altar. And when everyone had finished, the Levites prepared Passover animals for themselves and for the priests.

[15]During the celebration some of the Levites prepared Passover animals for the

● 35.1 *Passover . . . first month:* Passover was celebrated as a remembrance of how God saved the people from disaster in Egypt. It was to be celebrated beginning at twilight on the fourteenth day of Nisan/Abib, the first month of the Hebrew calendar (from about mid-March to mid-April), not in the second month.

○g Passover

● 35.2-3 *priests . . . Levites:* Priests led worship and offered sacrifices. They were Levites descended from Levi's grandson, Aaron (Num 3.1-13). Other Levites were assigned positions as temple servants. They took care of the temple and assisted the priests.

○g Israel's Priests

---

[1]35.1 *first month:* See the note at 29.3. [m]35.5 *each family of worshipers . . . you:* One possible meaning for the difficult Hebrew text. [n]35.12 *sacrifices to please the LORD:* See the note at 1.6.

Josiah destroyed all the idols in the territories of Israel, and he commanded everyone in Israel to worship only the LORD God. 2 CHR 34.33

35.18 *Passover had not been ob-served:* The Passover celebration under Hezekiah had been held a month late, and many of the people had not made themselves clean (30.1-4,18-19).

35.22 *Megiddo:* Megiddo was an important business and military center located at the intersection of the north-south trade route. Whoever controlled Megiddo also controlled the pass through the Carmel mountain range between the Plain of Jezreel and the Plain of Sharon. This is also the place called Armagedon (Rev 16.16). **(See Map 6 on pg 1884.)**

36.1 *Jehoahaz:* Jehoahaz was Ju-dah's sixteenth king and ruled for three months in 609 B.C., even though he was not Josiah's oldest son.

36.4,6,12 *Eliakim . . . changed his name to Jehoiakim . . . Nebuchadnezzar . . . Jeremiah:* Jehoiakim was Ju-dah's seventeenth king, and ruled from 609 to 598 B.C. The meaning of a name was very important during this period. By changing Jehoahaz's older brother's name from Eliakim ("God has established") to Jehoiakim ("the LORD has established"), Neco was claiming to be the LORD of Judah, displacing God. Now that Judah was controlled politically by Egypt, it faced the threat of being attacked by Babylonia, Egypt's enemy. Nebuchadnezzar ruled Babylonia from 605 to 562 B.C. and ordered the attacks on Jerusalem in 597 and 587 B.C. The prophet Jeremiah began bringing God's message to the people during Amon's rule (642–640 B.C.).

musicians and the guards, so that the Levite musicians would not have to leave their places, which had been assigned to them according to the instructions of David, Asaph, Heman, and Jeduthun the king's prophet. Even the guards at the temple gates did not have to leave their posts. ¹⁶So on that day, Passover was celebrated to honor the LORD, and sacrifices were offered on the altar to him, just as Josiah had commanded. ¹⁷The worshipers then celebrated the Festival of Thin Bread for the next seven days.

¹⁸People from Jerusalem and from towns all over Judah and Israel were there. Passover had not been observed like this since the days of Samuel the prophet. In fact, this was the greatest Passover celebration in Israel's history! ¹⁹All these things happened in the eighteenth year of Josiah's rule in Judah.

Josiah Dies in Battle
(2 Kings 23.28-30)

²⁰Some time later, King Neco of Egypt led his army to the city of Carchemish on the Euphrates River. And Josiah led his troops north to meet the Egyptians in battle.°
²¹Neco sent the following message to Josiah:

I'm not attacking you, king of Judah! We're not even at war. But God has told me to quickly attack my enemy. God is on my side, so if you try to stop me, he will punish you.

²²But Josiah ignored Neco's warning, even though it came from God! Instead, he disguised himself and marched into battle against Neco in the valley near Megiddo.
²³During the battle an Egyptian soldier shot Josiah with an arrow. Josiah told his

servants, "Get me out of here! I've been hit." ²⁴They carried Josiah out of his chariot, then put him in the other chariot he had there and took him back to Jerusalem, where he soon died. He was buried beside his ancestors, and everyone in Judah and Jerusalem mourned his death.
²⁵Jeremiah the prophet wrote a funeral song in honor of Josiah. And since then, anyone in Judah who mourns the death of Josiah sings that song. It is included in the collection of funeral songs.
²⁶Everything else Josiah did while he was king, including how he faithfully obeyed the LORD, ²⁷is written in *The History of the Kings of Israel and Judah.*

King Jehoahaz of Judah
(2 Kings 23.30-35)

36 After the death of Josiah, the people of Judah crowned his son Jehoahaz their new king. ²He was 23 years old at the time, and he ruled only 3 months from Jerusalem. ³King Neco of Egypt captured Jehoahaz and forced Judah to pay almost 4 tons of silver and 75 pounds of gold as taxes. ⁴Then Neco appointed Jehoahaz's brother Eliakim king of Judah and changed his name to Jehoiakim. He led Jehoahaz away to Egypt as his prisoner.

King Jehoiakim of Judah
(2 Kings 23.36—24.7)

⁵Jehoiakim was 25 years old when he was appointed king, and he ruled 11 years from Jerusalem. Jehoiakim disobeyed the LORD his God by doing evil.
⁶During Jehoiakim's rule, King Nebuchadnezzar of Babylonia invaded Judah. He arrested Jehoiakim and put him in

°**35.20** *battle:* At this time, King Neco of Egypt (609–595 B.C.) was fighting on the side of the Assyrians. He marched north to fight the Babylonian army and help Assyria keep control of its land. Since Josiah considered Assyria an enemy, he set out to stop Neco and the Egyptian troops.

chains, and he sent him to the capital city of Babylon. **7**Nebuchadnezzar also carried off many of the valuable things in the LORD's temple, and he put them in his palace in Babylon.

8Everything else Jehoiakim did while he was king, including all the disgusting and evil things, is written in *The History of the Kings of Israel and Judah*. His son Jehoiachin then became king.

King Jehoiachin of Judah
(2 Kings 24.8-17)

9Jehoiachin was 18 years^P old when he became king of Judah, and he ruled only 3 months and 10 days from Jerusalem. Jehoiachin also disobeyed the LORD by doing evil. **10**In the spring of the year, King Nebuchadnezzar of Babylonia had Jehoiachin arrested and taken to Babylon, along with more of the valuable items in the temple. Then Nebuchadnezzar appointed Zedekiah king of Judah.

King Zedekiah of Judah
(2 Kings 24.18-20; Jeremiah 52.1-3)

11Zedekiah was 21 years old when he was appointed king of Judah, and he ruled from Jerusalem for 11 years. **12**He disobeyed the LORD his God and refused to change his ways, even after a warning from Jeremiah, the LORD's prophet.

13King Nebuchadnezzar of Babylonia had forced Zedekiah to promise in God's name that he would be loyal. Zedekiah was stubborn and refused to turn back to the LORD God of Israel, so he rebelled against Nebuchadnezzar. **14**The people of Judah and even the priests who were their leaders became more unfaithful. They followed the disgusting example of the nations around them and made the LORD's holy temple unfit for worship. **15**But the LORD God felt sorry for his people, and instead of destroying the temple, he sent prophets who warned the people over and over about their sins. **16**But the people only laughed and insulted these prophets. They ignored what the LORD God was trying to tell them, until he finally became so angry that nothing could stop him from punishing Judah and Jerusalem.

Jerusalem Is Destroyed
(2 Kings 25.1-21; Jeremiah 52.3-30)

17The LORD sent King Nebuchadnezzar of Babylonia to attack Jerusalem. Nebuchadnezzar killed the young men who were in the temple, and he showed no mercy to anyone, whether man or woman, young or old. God let him kill everyone in the city. **18**Nebuchadnezzar carried off everything that was left in the temple; he robbed the treasury and the personal storerooms of the king and his officials. He took everything back to Babylon. **19**Nebuchadnezzar's troops burned down the temple and destroyed every important building in the city. Then they broke down the city wall. **20**The survivors were taken to Babylonia as prisoners, where they were slaves of the king and his sons, until Persia became a powerful nation.

21Judah was an empty desert, and it stayed that way for 70 years, to make up for all the years it was not allowed to rest.^q These things happened just as Jeremiah the LORD's prophet had said.^r

Nebuchadnezzar

36.9 *Jehoiachin . . . disobeyed the LORD*: Jehoiachin was Judah's eighteenth king, and ruled for three months in 598 B.C. He disobeyed God by worshiping other gods.

36.11 *Zedekiah*: Zedekiah was Judah's nineteenth king, ruling from 598 to 587 B.C. Nebuchadnezzar changed Zedekiah's name from Mattaniah ("gift of the LORD") to Zedekiah ("righteousness of the LORD"). Nebuchadnezzar was showing that he was lord over Zedekiah.

36.13 *Zedekiah . . . rebelled against Nebuchadnezzar*: Hophra (also known as Apries), the king of Egypt from 589 to 570 B.C., may have encouraged Zedekiah's rebellion.

36.17-20 *The LORD sent King Nebuchadnezzar . . . they were slaves*: The writer says that the LORD sent Nebuchadnezzar to show that the defeat of Jerusalem was punishment for the sins of the leaders and people of Judah. The city and temple were destroyed in 586 B.C.

36.21 *Judah was an empty desert . . . not allowed to rest . . . prophet had said*: Jeremiah the prophet warned the people of Judah that they would spend 70 years in captivity in Babylon (Jer 25.11). He also said that later they would be set free (Jer 29.10). The actual length of the exile was about 50 years.

Exile

● **36.22** *the first year that Cyrus was king:* This probably refers to 538 B.C., after Cyrus captured Babylonia. He had actually ruled Persia since 549 B.C.

● **36.22** *Cyrus:* Cyrus II, "the Great," founded the Achaemenid dynasty and the Persian Empire and ruled it from 549 to 530 B.C. The capture of Babylon in 539 B.C. was his greatest military victory. The prophet Isaiah praises Cyrus as God's "chosen one," since he was the one God used to allow the people of Judah to go back to its own land and worship God there (Isa 45.1-4).

● **36.22** *Persia:* See Map 8 on pg 1886.

○8 Persia

● **36.23** *He has also chosen me to build a temple:* The Assyrians and Babylonians reorganized their empires by forcing conquered peoples to move to other areas. After defeating the Babylonians, the Persians tried to win the loyalty of those conquered peoples by encouraging them to return to their own lands. Cyrus' actions, then, may have been politically motivated. (**See the article After the Exile: God's People Return to Judea on pg 1789.**)

Cyrus Lets the Jews Return Home
(Ezra 1.1-4)

²²In the first year that Cyrus was king of Persia,ˢ the LORD had Cyrus send a message to all parts of his kingdom. This happened just as Jeremiah the LORD's prophet had promised. ²³The message said:

I am King Cyrus of Persia.

The LORD God of heaven has made me the ruler of every nation on earth. He has also chosen me to build a temple for him in Jerusalem, which is in Judah. The LORD God will watch over any of his people who want to go back to Judah.

ˢ**36.22** *the first year that Cyrus was king of Persia:* Probably 538 B.C., when Cyrus captured Babylonia. He had actually ruled Persia since 549 B.C.

Reflection Questions About 2 Chronicles 1.1—36.23

1. Solomon is known for his wisdom, wealth, and worship. Find two examples of each of these qualities.

2. When David brought the sacred chest to Jerusalem, he made the city the central place for both the political and religious lives of the people. How did Solomon's building of the temple complete this process and make it permanent (6.1—7.22)?

3. How did the people celebrate the dedication of the temple (7.4-10)? Why was the completion of the temple such an important event in the lives of the people of Israel?

4. Why did the northern tribes rebel (10.1—19.11)? Name something Judah gained and something Judah lost as a result of this.

5. Read the introduction to the section at 11.5. Which kings provide examples of how God rewards faithful kings and punishes the unfaithful? Is this concept of reward and punishment true in your experience? Why or why not?

6. Why do you think the writer of 2 CHRONICLES seems to judge the kings only on the basis of their religious faithfulness and not on their political achievements? In your opinion, what would the writer say about our leaders today?

7. Jehoshaphat's prayer (20.6-12) has been described as a "model" prayer. Why do you think this is? Compare this prayer to your own prayers and those you hear offered in worship.

8. What might the words of 2 Chronicles 20.20 have meant to those living at the time this history was written? What do these words mean to you?

9. Compare Hezekiah and Josiah (see chapters 29–32 and 34,35). Which one do you think was more important and why?

10. A number of the Old Testament prayers are found in 1 and 2 CHRONICLES. They tend to be group prayers for worship, rather than private or devotional prayers. What is the place of private prayer in the life of faith?

ezra

Going home can be an exciting time. As you read Ezra,
look for the different experiences God's people had when
they returned with Zerubbabel, Ezra, and Nehemiah.

WHAT MAKES EZRA SPECIAL?

Ezra and the next book in the Bible, Nehemiah, were originally one book. Together they make up the most important source for the history of 538 to 430 B.C. This period saw the formation of the Jewish religious community following the Babylonian exile. Ezra the priest, as the main religious leader of this time, and Nehemiah, as appointed governor, were largely responsible for the shape that community was to take.

Ezra was written to help the Jewish community in Jerusalem understand who they were as God's people. It does this by remembering how the community began and by describing how some of them returned home to Judah and struggled to obey the Law of Moses, rebuild the city and the temple, and keep themselves pure in the midst of foreign peoples.

WHAT'S THE STORY BEHIND THE SCENE?

A number of historical and literary questions surround Ezra and Nehemiah. The traditional view sees Ezra beginning his mission in the seventh year of the reign of Artaxerxes I (458 B.C.; Ezra 7.8) and Nehemiah arriving 13 years later in the twentieth year of Artaxerxes' reign (445 B.C.; Neh. 1.1). Others suggest the opposite order is more accurate, because it better explains certain difficulties in the text. In this view, Nehemiah still arrives at Jerusalem in 445 B.C., but Ezra comes later, in the seventh year of Artaxerxes II (398 B.C.). Still others place Ezra's arrival before Nehemiah's but insist that their ministries overlapped. This view must change the text of Ezra 7.8,9 from "seventh" to either "twenty-seventh" or "thirty-seventh." There is no agreement as to which order is most accurate.

The author of Ezra and Nehemiah probably used several different sources in writing these books. The most important ones are the first-person accounts called the "Memoirs of Ezra" that form the basis of Ezra 8–10 and Nehemiah 8–9, and the "Memoirs of Nehemiah" which lie behind Nehemiah 1–7; 11.1,2; 12.31-43; and 13.4-31. The author also draws upon a number of Persian documents written in Aramaic (Ezra 1.2-4; 4.8—6.18; 7.12-28), and many lists of people.

HOW IS EZRA CONSTRUCTED?

Originally, Ezra and Nehemiah were one book that told the story of God restoring the Jewish people to their homeland in Israel. It is structured around the decrees of two Persian kings, Cyrus and Artaxerxes. Cyrus' decree that allowed the Jews to return home and rebuild the temple (Ezra 1.2-4) is followed by the story of their homecoming and the rebuilding of the temple (Ezra 1–6). In Ezra 7.12-26, Artaxerxes calls for all Jews to obey the Law of Moses. This is followed by Ezra's mission. His reading of the Law to the people becomes the basis for several changes he makes in response to various problems he finds in the community (Ezra 7–10; Neh. 8–10, 13). Artaxerxes also authorizes Nehemiah to return to Jerusalem (Neh 2) to rebuild and dedicate the city's walls (Neh. 2–7, 12).

Ezra can be outlined in the following way:

God's people return from exile and begin
    rebuilding the temple (1.1—6.22)
        God's people come home (1.1—4.24)
        Work on the temple continues (5.1—6.22)
Ezra returns and restores the people (7.1—10.44)
        Ezra and his mission (7.1—8.36)
        Ezra deals with problems in the community
        (9.1—10.44)

Originally, Ezra and Nehemiah were one book. Together, they form the main historical record of the period when God's people, having returned from exile in Babylonia, rebuilt the temple, restored Jerusalem, and rededicated themselves to obeying God's Law. The first six chapters of Ezra describe the return of the people from exile, the rebuilding of the altar in Jerusalem, and the first sacrifices offered there to please the Lord. Cyrus, the Persian king who had allowed the Israelites to return to Judah, encourages them to rebuild the Jerusalem temple. Construction on the temple is delayed by political and social problems, and eventually halted until a new Persian king, Darius, takes power and orders the work to continue. The temple is completed and it is dedicated to the Lord with great celebration in about 515 B.C. Later the Persian king Artaxerxes sends Ezra, a priest and teacher of God's Law living in Babylonia, to Jerusalem to restore the religion of Israel and instruct the people in the Law of Moses. Ezra selects religious leaders and promises to purify the Jewish people, ordering an end to the practice of Jewish men marrying foreign women.

Outline

Cyrus Lets the Jews Return Home

1 Years ago the LORD sent Jeremiah with a message about a promise[a] for the people of Israel. Then in the first year that Cyrus was king of Persia,[b] the LORD kept his promise by telling Cyrus to send this official message to all parts of his kingdom:

2-3 I am King Cyrus of Persia.

The LORD God of heaven, who is also the God of Israel, has made me the ruler of all nations on earth. And he has chosen me to build a temple for him in Jerusalem, which is in Judah. The LORD God will watch over and encourage any of his people who want to go back to Jerusalem and help build the temple.

4 Everyone else must provide what is needed. They must give money, supplies, and animals, as well as gifts for rebuilding God's temple.

5 Many people felt that the LORD God wanted them to help rebuild his temple, and they made plans to go to Jerusalem. Among them were priests, Levites, and leaders of the tribes of Judah and Benjamin. 6 The others helped by giving silver articles, gold, personal possessions, cattle, and other valuable gifts, as well as offerings for the temple.

7 King Cyrus gave back the things that Nebuchadnezzar[c] had taken from the LORD's temple in Jerusalem and had put in the temple of his own gods. 8 Cyrus placed Mithredath, his chief treasurer, in charge of these things. Mithredath counted them and gave a list to Sheshbazzar, the governor of Judah. 9-10 Included among them were: 30 large gold dishes; 1,000 large silver

---

[a]1.1 *a promise:* That the people of Israel would be set free from Babylonia after 70 years (see Jeremiah 25.11; 29.10). [b]1.1 *the first year that Cyrus was king of Persia:* Probably 539 B.C., when Cyrus captured Babylonia. He had actually ruled Persia since 549 B.C. [c]1.7 *Nebuchadnezzar:* Known as Nebuchadnezzar II, who ruled Babylonia from 605 to 562 B.C. In 586 B.C. he destroyed Jerusalem and took many of its people to Babylonia.

1.1-3 *Years ago . . . help build the temple:* These verses are nearly the same as the final verses of 2 CHRONICLES. This may indicate that the same person wrote 1 and 2 CHRONICLES, EZRA, and NEHEMIAH. Since EZRA and NEHEMIAH come before 1 and 2 CHRONICLES in the Hebrew Bible, the repetition of the verses is probably a way to connect these works.

1.2-3 *King Cyrus of Persia:* Cyrus II ("Cyrus the Great") founded the Achaemenid dynasty and the Kingdom of Persia, and ruled it from 539 to 530 B.C. The capture of Babylonia in 539 B.C. was his greatest military victory. The prophet Isaiah praised Cyrus as God's "chosen one," which in the Hebrew text means the "anointed one" or "Messiah" (Isa 45.1-4), since he was the one God used to allow the Israelites to go back to their own land in Judea and to worship God there. Isaiah also said Cyrus would lead Israel in the rebuilding of the temple (Isa 44.28).

1.2-3 *he has chosen me to build a temple:* After defeating the Babylonians, the Persians tried to win the loyalty of these displaced people by encouraging them to return to their own lands. Though Cyrus' actions may have been politically motivated, Ezra says that God caused Cyrus to be kind toward the people of Israel.

1.2-3 *Jerusalem:* This was the Israelites' religious and political capital. (See Maps 4 and 5 on pgs 1882 and 1883.)

Jerusalem

Nebuchadnezzar

2.2-20 *Zerubbabel . . . Baanah:* If the first eleven names in verses 2-20 are a listing of those who, at various times, had led groups back to Jerusalem, then Zerubbabel and Joshua may be the governor and priest mentioned in Ezra 3.2. NEHEMIAH is perhaps the governor named in Nehemiah 1.1, but may be simply a leader of the people who returned with Sheshbazzar. Seraiah is Ezra's father (Ezra 7.1-6), and Bigvai was a later governor of Judah.

dishes; 29 other dishes;[d] 30 gold bowls; 410 silver bowls; and 1,000 other articles.

[11] Altogether, there were 5,400 gold and silver dishes, bowls, and other articles. Sheshbazzar took them with him when he and the others returned to Jerusalem from Babylonia.

A List of People Who Returned from Exile
(Nehemiah 7.4-73)

2 King Nebuchadnezzar[e] of Babylonia had captured many of the people of Judah and had taken them as prisoners to Babylonia. Now they were on their way back to Jerusalem and to their own towns everywhere in Judah.

[2-20] Zerubbabel, Joshua,[f] Nehemiah, Seraiah, Reelaiah, Mordecai, Bilshan, Mispar, Bigvai, Rehum, and Baanah were in charge of the ones who were coming back. And here is a list of how many returned from each family group: 2,172 from Parosh; 372 from Shephatiah; 775 from Arah; 2,812 descendants of Jeshua and Joab[g] from Pahath Moab; 1,254 from Elam; 945 from Zattu; 760 from Zaccai; 642 from Bani; 623 from Bebai; 1,222 from Azgad; 666 from Adonikam; 2,056 from Bigvai; 454 from Adin; 98 from Ater, also known as Hezekiah; 323 from Bezai; 112 from Jorah; 223 from Hashum; and 95 from Gibbar.

[21-35] Here is how many people returned whose ancestors had come from the following towns: 123 from Bethlehem; 56 from Netophah; 128 from Anathoth; 42 from Azmaveth; 743 from Kiriatharim, Chephirah, and Beeroth; 621 from Ramah and Geba; 122 from Michmas; 223 from Bethel and Ai; 52 from Nebo; 156 from Magbish; 1,254 from the other Elam; 320 from Harim; 725 from Lod, Hadid, and Ono; 345 from Jericho; and 3,630 from Senaah.

[36-39] Here is a list of how many returned from each family of priests: 973 descendants of Jeshua from the family of Jedaiah; 1,052 from the family of Immer; 1,247 from the family of Pashhur; and 1,017 from the family of Harim.

[40-42] And here is a list of how many returned from the families of Levites: 74 descendants of Hodaviah from the families of Jeshua and Kadmiel; 128 descendants of Asaph from the temple musicians; and 139 descendants of Shallum, Ater, Talmon, Akkub, Hatita, and Shobai from the temple guards.

[43-54] Here is a list of the families of temple workers whose descendants returned: Ziha, Hasupha, Tabbaoth, Keros, Siaha, Padon, Lebanah, Hagabah, Akkub, Hagab, Shamlai, Hanan, Giddel, Gahar, Reaiah, Rezin, Nekoda, Gazzam, Uzza, Paseah, Besai, Asnah, Meunim, Nephisim, Bakbuk, Hakupha, Harhur, Bazluth, Mehida, Harsha, Barkos, Sisera, Temah, Neziah, and Hatipha.

[55-57] Here is a list of Solomon's servants whose descendants returned: Sotai, Hassophereth, Peruda, Jaalah, Darkon, Giddel, Shephatiah, Hattil, Pochereth Hazzebaim, and Ami.

[58] A total of 392 descendants of temple workers and of Solomon's servants returned.

[59-60] There were 652 who returned from the families of Delaiah, Tobiah, and Nekoda, though they could not prove that they were Israelites. They had lived in the Baby-

[d] 1.9,10 *other dishes:* Or "knives." [e] 2.1 *Nebuchadnezzar:* See the note at 1.7. [f] 2.2-20 *Joshua:* Hebrew "Jeshua." In this translation the name "Joshua" is used of the descendant of Jozadak, the last chief priest before the exile; this same Joshua is often mentioned together with Zerubbabel (2.2-20; 3.2,8,9; 4.3; 5.2; 10.18,19). In other places the name "Jeshua" is used (2.2-20,36-39,40-42; 8.33). [g] 2.2-20 *Jeshua and Joab:* Hebrew "Jeshua Joab."

lonian towns of Tel-Melah, Tel-Harsha, Cherub, Addan, and Immer. **61-62**The families of Habaiah, Hakkoz, and Barzillai could not prove that they were priests. The ancestor of the family of Barzillai had married the daughter of Barzillai from Gilead and had taken his wife's family name. But the records of these three families could not be found, and none of them were allowed to serve as priests. **63**In fact, the governor[h] told them, "You cannot eat the food offered to God until we find out if you really are priests."[i]

64-67 There were 42,360 who returned, in addition to 7,337 servants and 200 musicians, both women and men. They brought with them 736 horses, 245 mules, 435 camels, and 6,720 donkeys.

68When the people came to where the LORD's temple had been in Jerusalem, some of the family leaders gave gifts so it could be rebuilt in the same place. **69**They gave all they could, and it came to a total of 1,030 pounds of gold, 5,740 pounds of silver, and 100 robes for the priests.

70Everyone returned to the towns from which their families had come, including the priests, the Levites, the musicians, the temple guards, and the workers.[j]

The First Offering on the New Altar

3 During the seventh month[k] of the year, the Israelites who had settled in their towns went to Jerusalem. **2**The priest Joshua son of Jozadak, together with the other priests, and Zerubbabel son of Shealtiel and his relatives rebuilt the altar of Israel's God. Then they were able to offer sacrifices there by following the instructions God had given to Moses, the man of God. **3**And they built the altar where it had stood before,[l] even though they were afraid of the people who were already living around there. Then every morning and evening they burned sacrifices and offerings to the LORD.

4The people followed the rules for celebrating the Festival of Shelters and offered the proper sacrifices each day. **5**They offered sacrifices to please the LORD,[m] sacrifices at each New Moon Festival, and sacrifices at the rest of the LORD's festivals. Every offering the people had brought voluntarily was also presented to the LORD.

6Although work on the temple itself had not yet begun, the people started offering sacrifices on the LORD's altar on the first day of the seventh month of that year.

The Rebuilding of the Temple Begins

7King Cyrus of Persia had said the Israelites could have cedar trees brought from Lebanon to Joppa by sea. So they sent grain, wine, and olive oil to the cities of Tyre and Sidon as payment for these trees, and they gave money to the stoneworkers and carpenters.

8During the second month[n] of the second year after the people had returned from Babylonia, they started rebuilding the

3.1 *seventh month of the year:* This could mean the seventh month after the people left Babylonia, but probably means the seventh month of the Hebrew calendar, Tishri. It lasts from about mid-September to mid-October and included many important religious festivals. The year may be either 538 B.C., the first year of Cyrus' reign, or 520 B.C. during the second year of Darius' reign. (See the chart Pilgrimage Festivals on pg 1799.)

3.2 *The priest Joshua son of Jozadak . . . Moses:* It is possible that Joshua is listed first here because this is a religious occasion. Jozadak was the high priest at the time of the exile, 587 B.C. (1 Chr 6.15, Jehozadak).

Moses

3.3 *people:* Foreigners or other non-Israelites who had been forced by the Assyrians to move to the area around Jerusalem.

3.4,5 *Festival of Shelters . . . New Moon Festival . . . LORD's festivals:* The Festival of Shelters was celebrated as a reminder of how God protected the people of Israel in the wilderness (see Lev 23.33-36; Num 29.12-38). The new moon marked the beginning of the month and was a holy day. (See the chart Pilgrimage Festivals on pg 1799.)

[h]**2.63** *governor:* In Nehemiah 8.9; 10.1, this same title is used of Nehemiah, though it is doubtful if he is the one referred to here. [i]**2.63** *until . . . priests:* The Hebrew text has "until a priest comes with the urim and thummin," sacred objects which were used in some way to receive answers from God. [j]**2.70** *workers:* One possible meaning for the difficult Hebrew text of verse 70. [k]**3.1** *seventh month:* Tishri (also called Ethanim), the seventh month of the Hebrew calendar, from about mid-September to mid-October. [l]**3.3** *where it had stood before:* One possible meaning for the difficult Hebrew text. [m]**3.5** *sacrifices to please the LORD:* In traditional translations these sacrifices are usually called "whole burnt offerings" (see Leviticus 1.1-16). [n]**3.8** *second month:* Ziv, the second month of the Hebrew calendar, from about mid-April to mid-May.

3.11,12 *gave thanks . . . singing . . . wept bitterly:* The song of thanksgiving recalls the song of praise sung at the dedication of Solomon's temple (2 Chr 5.11-13; 7.3; Ps 136.1). The people were reminded of the destruction of Solomon's temple in 586 B.C., and wept (3.12) because they knew the new smaller and simpler temple never could compare with the glory of the one Solomon had built (Hag 2.3).

King David

4.1,2 *enemies of the tribes of Judah and Benjamin . . . King Esarhaddon of Assyria:* The enemies were the people who had been captured by Assyrian and Babylonian kings and forced to settle in Palestine when the northern kingdom (Israel) fell in 722 B.C. Esarhaddon, the son of Sennacherib, ruled Assyria from 681 to 669 B.C. He continued the policy of relocating conquered people to other lands.

4.4,5 *Jews . . . Darius:* The name "Jews" comes from "Judah," the one of the tribes of Israel. Darius I ruled from 522 to 486 B.C.

Israel

4.5 *slow down the work:* Constant problems caused by neighboring people halted the rebuilding of the temple, from 536 to 520 B.C.

4.6 *Xerxes was king:* The "first year that Xerxes was king" was either the end of 486 B.C. or early in 485 B.C. The Hebrew text has the king's Persian name, "Ahasuerus."

LORD's temple. Zerubbabel son of Shealtiel, Joshua son of Jozadak, the priests, the Levites, and everyone else who had returned started working. Every Levite over 20 years of age was put in charge of some part of the work. [9]The Levites in charge of the whole project were Joshua and his sons and relatives and Kadmiel and his sons from the family of Hodaviah.[o] The family of Henadad worked along with them.

[10]When the builders had finished laying the foundation of the temple, the priests put on their robes and blew trumpets in honor of the LORD, while the Levites from the family of Asaph praised God with cymbals. All of them followed the instructions given years before by King David.[p] [11]They praised the LORD and gave thanks as they took turns singing:

"The LORD is good!
His faithful love for Israel
will last forever."

Everyone started shouting and praising the LORD because work on the foundation of the temple had begun. [12]Many of the older priests and Levites and the heads of families wept bitterly because they remembered seeing the first temple years before. But others were so happy that they celebrated with joyful shouts. [13]Their shouting and crying were so noisy that it all sounded alike and could be heard a long way off.

Foreigners[q] Want To Help Rebuild the Temple

4 The enemies of the tribes of Judah and Benjamin heard that the people had come back to rebuild the temple of the LORD God of Israel. [2]So they went to Zerubbabel and to the family leaders and said, "Let us help! Ever since King Esarhaddon of Assyria[r] brought us here, we have worshiped your God and offered sacrifices to him."

[3]But Zerubbabel, Joshua, and the family leaders answered, "You cannot take part in building a temple for the LORD our God! We will build it ourselves, just as King Cyrus of Persia commanded us."

[4]Then the neighboring people began to do everything possible to frighten the Jews[s] and to make them stop building. [5]During the time that Cyrus was king and even until Darius[t] became king, they kept bribing government officials to slow down the work.

Trouble Rebuilding Jerusalem[u]

[6]In the first year that Xerxes was king,[v] the neighboring people brought written charges against the people of Judah and Jerusalem.

[7]Later, Bishlam, Mithredath, Tabeel, and their advisors got together and wrote a letter to Artaxerxes when he was king of Per-

[o]**3.9** *Hodaviah:* Or "Yehudah" or "Hodiah." [p]**3.10** *King David:* Ruled from about 1010 to 970 B.C. [q]**4.1** *Foreigners:* People from foreign countries who had been captured by Assyrian and Babylonian kings and forced to settle in Palestine. [r]**4.2** *King Esarhaddon of Assyria:* Ruled from 681 to 669 B.C. These people may have been brought to Palestine in 677 or 676 B.C., when Esarhaddon invaded Syria. [s]**4.4** *Jews:* This was the name given to those Israelites who settled in Judah after returning from Babylonia. [t]**4.5** *Cyrus . . . Darius:* Cyrus ruled 539–530 B.C. (see the note at 1.1); Darius I, known as Darius the Great, ruled 522–486 B.C. [u]**4.6** *Jerusalem:* Verses 6-23, which tell about the events of a later period, are placed here because they are also concerned with the problem of stopping or slowing down work on the temple. [v]**4.6** *first year that Xerxes was king:* Either the end of 486 or the beginning of 485 B.C. The Hebrew has the king's Persian name "Ahasuerus," but he is better known as "Xerxes," the Greek form of the name.

sia.[w] It was written in Aramaic and had to be translated.[x]

[8-10]A letter was also written to Artaxerxes about Jerusalem by Governor Rehum, Secretary Shimshai, and their advisors, including the judges, the governors, the officials, and the local leaders. They were joined in writing this letter by people from Erech and Babylonia, the Elamites from Susa,[z] and people from other foreign nations that the great and famous Ashurbanipal[a] had forced to settle in Samaria and other parts of Western Province.[b]

[11]This letter said:

Your Majesty King Artaxerxes, we are your servants from everywhere in Western Province, and we send you our greetings.

[12]You should know that the Jews who left your country have moved back to Jerusalem and are now rebuilding that rebellious city. In fact, they have almost finished rebuilding the walls and repairing the foundations. [13]You should also know that if the walls are completed and the city is rebuilt, the Jews won't pay any kind of taxes, and there will be less money in your treasury.

[14]We are telling you this, because you have done so much for us, and we want everyone to respect you. [15]If you look up the official records of your ancestors, you will find that Jerusalem has constantly rebelled and has led others to rebel against kings and provinces. That's why the city was destroyed in the first place. [16]If Jerusalem is rebuilt and its walls completed, you will no longer have control over Western Province.

[17]King Artaxerxes answered:

Greetings to Governor Rehum, Secretary Shimshai, and to your advisors in Samaria and other parts of Western Province.

[18]After your letter was translated and read to me, [19]I had the old records checked. It is true that for years Jerusalem has rebelled and caused trouble for other kings and nations. [20]And powerful kings have ruled Western Province from Jerusalem and have collected all kinds of taxes.

[21]I want you to command the people to stop rebuilding the city until I give further notice. [22]Do this at once, so that no harm will come to the kingdom.

[23]As soon as this letter was read, Governor Rehum, Secretary Shimshai, and their advisors went to Jerusalem and forced everyone to stop rebuilding the city.

Work on the Temple Starts Again

[24]The Jews were forced to stop work on the temple and were not able to do any more building until the year after Darius became king of Persia.[c] 5 [1]Then the LORD God of Israel told the prophets Haggai and Zechariah[d] to speak in his name to the people of Judah and Jerusalem. And

4.8-10 *Samaria:* Omri, the sixth king of Israel (885–874 B.C.), made Samaria the capital of the northern kingdom (Israel). Eventually, Samaria became the name used for the entire northern kingdom. (See Map 8 on pg 1886.)

Persia

4.14 *you have done so much for us:* In Aramaic, the phrase reads, "because we eat the salt of the palace" and may indicate that there had been a treaty or special agreement between the Samaritan officials and the Persian authorities. Sharing salt with another person in the ancient world symbolized friendship, support, and alliance.

4.24 *year after . . . king of Persia:* This verse resumes the story of the rebuilding of the temple that was interrupted at 4.5. That interruption (verses 6-23) told of the later rebuilding of the city.

5.1,3 *Haggai and Zechariah . . . Tattenai . . . Shethar Bozenai:* The story of Haggai and Zechariah urging the people to complete the rebuilding of the temple is found throughout the book of HAGGAI and the first eight chapters of ZECHARIAH. A Babylonian record dated 502 B.C. mentions Tattenai as governor of the Western Province (Syria-Palestine). Shethar Bozenai probably held a lower office.

[w]4.7 *Artaxerxes . . . Persia:* Artaxerxes I (465–425 B.C.). [x]4.7 *It was . . . translated:* One possible meaning for the difficult Hebrew text. [y]4.8-10 Ezra 4.8—6.18 was written in Aramaic, instead of Hebrew like most of the Old Testament. [z]4.8-10 *the judges . . . Susa:* One possible translation for the names and titles. [a]4.8-10 *Ashurbanipal:* King of Assyria 669–633 (or possibly 627) B.C. In Aramaic the king's name is "Osnapper," but he is better known as Ashurbanipal. [b]4.8-10 *Western Province:* The land from the Euphrates River west to the Mediterranean Sea. [c]4.24 *year after . . . king of Persia:* 520 B.C. [d]5.1 *Zechariah:* Aramaic "Zechariah son of Iddo."

5.11 *one of Israel's greatest kings:* Refers to Solomon, King David's son, who ruled from about 970 to 931 B.C. It took Solomon seven years to build Israel's first temple (1 Kgs 6.37-38).

6.2 *scroll:* Long rolls made of smaller pieces of papyrus or leather that were glued or sewn together into long strips (Isa 34.4; Jer 36.20-25; Ezek 2.9,10).

Scrolls

6.2 *Ecbatana:* The Persian kings spent their summers in this city.

they did. **2**So Zerubbabel the governor and Joshua the priest urged the people to start working on the temple again, and God's prophets encouraged them.

3Governor Tattenai of Western Province and his assistant Shethar Bozenai got together with some of their officials. Then they went to Jerusalem and said to the people, "Who told you to rebuild this temple? **4**Give us the names of the workers!"

5But God was looking after the Jewish leaders. So the governor and his group decided not to make the people stop working on the temple until they could report to Darius and get his advice.

6Governor Tattenai, Shethar Bozenai, and their advisors sent a report to Darius, **7**which said:

King Darius, we wish you the best! **8**We went to Judah, where the temple of the great God is being built with huge stones and wooden beams set in the walls. Everyone is working hard, and the building is going up quickly.

9We asked those in charge to tell us who gave them permission to rebuild the temple. **10**We also asked for the names of their leaders, so that we could write them down for you.

11They claimed to be servants of the God who rules heaven and earth. And they said they were rebuilding the temple that was built many years ago by one of Israel's greatest kings.**e**

12We were told that their people had made God angry, and he let them be captured by Nebuchadnezzar,**f** the Babylonian king**g** who took them

away as captives to Babylonia. Nebuchadnezzar tore down their temple, **13-15**took its gold and silver articles, and put them in the temple of his own god in Babylon.

They also said that during the first year Cyrus was king of Babylonia,**h** he gave orders for God's temple to be rebuilt in Jerusalem where it had stood before. So Cyrus appointed Sheshbazzar governor of Judah and sent these gold and silver articles for him to put in the temple. **16**Sheshbazzar then went to Jerusalem and laid the foundation for the temple, and the work is still going on.

17Your Majesty, please order someone to look up the old records in Babylonia and find out if King Cyrus really did give orders to rebuild God's temple in Jerusalem. We will do whatever you think we should.

King Cyrus' Order Is Rediscovered

6 King Darius ordered someone to go through the old records kept in Babylonia. **2**Finally, a scroll**i** was found in Ecbatana, the capital of Media Province, and it said:

This official record will show **3**that in the first year Cyrus was king, he gave orders to rebuild God's temple in Jerusalem, so that sacrifices and offerings could be presented there.**j** It is to be built 90 feet high and 90 feet wide, **4**with one**k** row of wooden beams for each three rows of large stones. The

e5.11 *one of Israel's greatest kings:* Solomon (ruled from about 970 to 931 B.C.).   **f**5.12 *Nebuchadnezzar:* See the note at 1.7.   **g**5.12 *the Babylonian king:* Aramaic "the Babylonian king from Chaldea," but Chaldea is another name for Babylonia.   **h**5.13-15 *Cyrus was king of Babylonia:* King Cyrus of Persia became king of Babylonia when the Persians conquered the city of Babylon in 539 B.C.   **i**6.2 *scroll:* A roll of paper or special leather used for writing on.   **j**6.3 *so that . . . there:* One possible meaning for the difficult Aramaic text.   **k**6.4 *one:* One possible meaning for the difficult Aramaic text.

royal treasury will pay for everything. [5]Then the gold and silver things that Nebuchadnezzar took from the temple and brought to Babylonia are to be returned to their proper places.

King Darius Orders the Work To Continue

[6]King Darius sent this message:

Governor Tattenai of Western Province and Shethar Bozenai, you and your advisors must stay away from the temple. [7]Let the Jewish governor and leaders rebuild it where it stood before. And stop slowing them down!

[8]Starting at once, I am ordering you to help the leaders by paying their expenses from the tax money collected in Western Province. [9]And don't fail to let the priests in Jerusalem have whatever they need each day so they can offer sacrifices to the God of heaven. Give them young bulls, rams, sheep, as well as wheat, salt, wine, and olive oil. [10]I want them to be able to offer pleasing sacrifices to God and to pray for me and my family.

[11]If any of you don't obey this order, a wooden beam will be taken from your house and sharpened on one end. Then it will be driven through your body,[l] and your house will be torn down and turned into a garbage dump. [12]I ask the God who is worshiped in Jerusalem to destroy any king or nation who tries either to change what I have said or to tear down his temple. I,

Darius, give these orders, and I expect them to be followed carefully.

The Temple Is Dedicated

[13]Governor Tattenai, Shethar Bozenai, and their advisors carefully obeyed King Darius. [14]With great success the Jewish leaders continued working on the temple, while Haggai and Zechariah encouraged them by their preaching. And so, the temple was completed at the command of the God of Israel and by the orders of kings Cyrus, Darius, and Artaxerxes of Persia.[m] [15]On the third day of the month of Adar[n] in the sixth year of the rule of Darius,[o] the temple was finished.

[16]The people of Israel, the priests, the Levites, and everyone else who had returned from exile were happy and celebrated as they dedicated God's temple. [17]One hundred bulls, two hundred rams, and four hundred lambs were offered as sacrifices at the dedication. Also twelve goats were sacrificed as sin offerings for the twelve tribes of Israel. [18]Then the priests and Levites were assigned their duties in God's temple in Jerusalem, according to the instructions Moses had written.[p]

The Passover

[19]Everyone who had returned from exile celebrated Passover on the fourteenth day of the first month.[q] [20]The priests and Levites had gone through a ceremony to make themselves acceptable to lead in worship. Then some of them killed Passover

---

6.10 *pleasing sacrifices:* Literally, this means "sweet smelling sacrifices." Pagan religions often regarded sacrifices as food for the gods. For the Israelites, the important thing was that the smell of the sacrifices pleased God.

6.14 *Artaxerxes of Persia:* This possibly refers to Artaxerxes II (405–358 B.C.), who ruled in the next century.

6.15,16 *Adar . . . sixth year . . . exile:* Adar is the twelfth month of the Hebrew calendar, from about mid-February to about mid-March. The "sixth year" would be 515 B.C. The exile lasted until 538 B.C.

Exile

6.17 *twelve tribes of Israel:* A sacrificial goat was offered for each of the original twelve tribes of Israel, even the ten northern tribes that had largely disappeared after most of them were taken into exile by the Assyrians in 722 B.C.

6.19-22 *Passover . . . Festival of Thin Bread:* (See the chart Pilgrimage Festivals on pg 1799.)

Passover and the Festival of Thin Bread

---

[k]6.11 *driven through your body:* A well-known punishment in the ancient Near East.   [m]6.14 *Artaxerxes of Persia:* See the note at 4.7.   [n]6.15 *Adar:* The twelfth month of the Hebrew calendar, from about mid-February to about mid-March.   [o]6.15 *sixth year . . . Darius:* 515 B.C.   [p]6.18 Ezra 4.8—6.18 was written in Aramaic instead of Hebrew like most of the Old Testament.   [q]6.19 *the first month:* Nisan, the first month of the Hebrew calendar, from about mid-March to mid-April.

7.1-6 *Much later:* If Artaxerxes I is the king intended here, this story jumps from the completion of the temple toward the end of the sixth century (516 B.C.) to the middle of the fifth century (458 B.C.). The opposition to the rebuilding of Jerusalem (4.6) occurred during the 57-year gap between the events of chapters 6 and 7.

7.1-6 *Ezra:* Ezra had three different jobs. One of his jobs was as a priest. Ezra's long family history proves he is a descendant of priests and so is qualified to be a priest himself.

Ezra also was an "expert in the Law." In the Hebrew, those words literally mean "ready scribe" or "capable writer." Scribes were experts in reading and writing. Before the exile, they functioned as royal secretaries responsible for letter writing and accounting. During and after the exile, their duties became copying, studying, and teaching the Scriptures. Eventually they became the official interpreters of the Law.

Lastly, Ezra was in a position of high favor at the court of Artaxerxes, during the time following the Babylonian captivity when Jerusalem was rebuilt. With Artaxerxes' blessing, he led 1,500 Jewish settlers and 258 Levites back to Jerusalem. After restoring the proper worship of God and ending the marriages between Jewish men and foreign women, he helped to reestablish Israel's special relationship with God by reading and teaching the Law of Moses to the people.

lambs for those who had returned, including the other priests and themselves. **21**The sacrifices were eaten by the Israelites who had returned and by the neighboring people who had given up the sinful customs of other nations in order to worship the LORD God of Israel. **22**For seven days they celebrated the Festival of Thin Bread. Everyone was happy because the LORD God of Israel had made sure that the king of Assyria[r] would be kind to them and help them build the temple.

Ezra Comes to Jerusalem

7 **1-6**Much later, when Artaxerxes[s] was king of Persia, Ezra came to Jerusalem from Babylonia. Ezra was the son of Seraiah and the grandson of Azariah. His other ancestors were Hilkiah, Shallum, Zadok, Ahitub, Amariah, Azariah, Meraioth, Zerahiah, Uzzi, Bukki, Abishua, Phinehas, Eleazar, and Aaron, the high priest.

Ezra was an expert in the Law that the LORD God of Israel had given to Moses, and the LORD made sure that the king gave Ezra everything he asked for. **7**Other Jews, including priests, Levites, musicians, the temple guards, and servants, came to Jerusalem with Ezra. This happened during the seventh year that Artaxerxes[t] was king. **8-9**God helped Ezra, and he arrived in Jerusalem on the first day of the fifth month[u] of that seventh year, after leaving Babylonia on the first day of the first month.[v] **10**Ezra had spent his entire life

studying and obeying the Law of the LORD and teaching it to others.

Artaxerxes Gives a Letter to Ezra

11Ezra was a priest and an expert in the laws and commands that the LORD had given to Israel. One day King Artaxerxes gave Ezra a letter which said:

12[w]Greetings from the great King Artaxerxes to Ezra the priest and expert in the teachings of the God of heaven.

13-14 Any of the people of Israel or their priests or Levites in my kingdom may go with you to Jerusalem if they want to. My seven advisors and I agree that you may go to Jerusalem and Judah to find out if[x] the laws of your God are being obeyed.

15When you go, take the silver and gold that I and my advisors are freely giving to the God of Israel, whose temple is in Jerusalem. **16**Take the silver and gold that you collect from everywhere in Babylonia. Also take the gifts that your own people and priests have so willingly contributed for the temple of your God in Jerusalem. **17**Use the money carefully to buy the best bulls, rams, lambs, grain, and wine. Then sacrifice them on the altar at God's temple in Jerusalem. **18**If any silver or gold is left, you and your people may use it for whatever pleases your God. **19**Give your God the other articles that have been contributed for

[r]**6.22** *king of Assyria:* Meaning the king of Persia, because Assyria was now part of the Persian Empire. [s]**7.1-6** *Artaxerxes:* Either Artaxerxes I (ruled from 465 to 425 B.C.) or Artaxerxes II (ruled from 405–358 B.C.). [t]**7.7** *seventh year . . . Artaxerxes:* 458 B.C. if this is Artaxerxes I; 398 B.C., if this is Artaxerxes II (see the note at 7.1-6). [u]**7.8,9** *fifth month:* Ab, the fifth month of the Hebrew calendar, from about mid-July to mid-August. [v]**7.8,9** *first month:* See the note at 6.19. [w]**7.12-26:** Ezra 7.12-26 was written in Aramaic, instead of Hebrew like most of the Old Testament. [x]**7.13,14** *find out if:* Or "make sure that."

Ezra had spent his entire life studying and obeying the Law of the LORD and teaching it to others.
EZRA 7.10

use in his temple. ²⁰If you need to get anything else for the temple, you may have the money you need from the royal treasury.

²¹Ezra, you are a priest and an expert in the laws of the God of heaven, and I order all treasurers in Western Province to do their very best to help you. ²²They will be allowed to give as much as 7,500 pounds of silver, 500 bushels of wheat, 550 gallons of wine, 550 gallons of olive oil, and all the salt you need.

²³They must provide whatever the God of heaven demands for his temple, so that he won't be angry with me and with the kings who rule after me. ²⁴We want you to know that no priests, Levites, musicians, guards, temple servants, or any other temple workers will have to pay any kind of taxes.

²⁵Ezra, use the wisdom God has given you and choose officials and leaders to govern the people of Western Province. These leaders should know God's laws and have them taught to anyone who doesn't know them. ²⁶Everyone who fails to obey God's Law or the king's law will be punished without pity. They will either be executed or put in prison or forced to leave their country, or have all they own taken away.

Ezra Praises God

²⁷Because King Artaxerxes was so kind, Ezra said:

Praise the LORD God of our ancestors! He made sure that the king honored the LORD's temple in Jerusalem.

²⁸God has told the king, his advisors, and his powerful officials to treat me with kindness. The LORD God has helped me, and I have been able to bring many Jewish leaders back to Jerusalem.

The Families Who Came Back with Ezra

8 Artaxerxes was king of Persia when I^y led the following chiefs of the family groups from Babylonia to Jerusalem: ²⁻¹⁴Gershom of the Phinehas family;
Daniel of the Ithamar family;
Hattush son of Shecaniah of the David family;
Zechariah and 150 other men of the Parosh family, who had family records;
Eliehoenai son of Zerahiah with 200 men of the Pahath Moab family;
Shecaniah son of Jahaziel with 300 men of the Zattu family;^z
Ebed son of Jonathan with 50 men of the Adin family;
Jeshaiah son of Athaliah with 70 men of the Elam family;
Zebadiah son of Michael with 80 men of the Shephatiah family;
Obadiah son of Jehiel with 218 men of the Joab family;
Shelomith son of Josiphiah with 160 men of the Bani family;^a
Zechariah son of Bebai with 28 men of the Bebai family;
Johanan son of Hakkatan with 110 men of the Azgad family;
Eliphelet, Jeuel, and Shemaiah who returned sometime later with 60 men of the Adonikam family;

7.23-26 *They must provide . . . will be punished*: According to the king's decree, Ezra is to function as a kind of governor, and the Law of Moses is to be the law of the land for the Jews. The Persian king offered Ezra and the Jewish people remarkable privileges and religious protection.

7.28 *kindness*: The Hebrew word translated here as "kindness" refers to the special love God promised his people. This love was based on God's loyalty, commitment, and faithfulness to the promises that he had made with the people. As a result, God's people were to respond in the same way.

8.1 *I*: Ezra. Beginning here and continuing through chapter 9 is a passage that scholars have called the "Memoirs of Ezra." Its beginning is marked by a switch to first person speech ("I").

^y**8.1** *I*: Ezra. ^z**8.2-14** *of the Zattu family*: One ancient translation; these words are not in the Hebrew text, but see 2.2-20, where Zattu is mentioned. ^a**8.2-14** *of the Bani family*: One ancient translation; these words are not in the Hebrew text, but see 2.2-20.

8.15 *Not one Levite could be found*: This may be because they preferred to stay in Babylonia where they had greater position and importance than they expected to have in Jerusalem and Judah.

8.22 *ashamed . . . soldiers*: Ezra does not mean he felt sorry or guilty. Rather, he means he did not want to show a lack of faith in God by asking for human help. However, the mention of the soldiers and cavalry shows that Ezra was aware of the dangerous nature of the journey he was asking the people to take with him.

8.24 *I chose twelve*: Ezra chose twelve because there were twelve tribes of Israel. **(See the chart Numbers in the Bible on pg 1844.)**

8.25-27 *25 tons . . . 270 ounces*: The huge amounts given here would be equal to tens of millions of dollars today. This may have been an intentional exaggeration to emphasize the importance of the temple, or an accidental misrepresentation of the actual numbers by a scribe who copied the text.

8.28 *belong to*: The Hebrew here is, "are holy to," which means set aside for God's own use. Both the gifts and those in charge of them were set aside for God's use.

Uthai and Zaccur with 70 men of the Bigvai family.

Ezra Finds Levites for the Temple

[15]I[b] brought everyone together by the river[c] that flows to the town of Ahava[d] where we camped for three days. Not one Levite could be found among the people and priests. [16]So I sent for the leaders Eliezer, Ariel, Shemaiah, Elnathan, Jarib, Elnathan, Nathan, Zechariah, and Meshullam. I also sent for Joiarib and Elnathan, who were very wise counselors. [17]Then I sent them to Iddo, the leader at Casiphia,[e] and I told them to ask him and his temple workers to send people to serve in God's temple.

[18]God was kind to us and caused them to send a skillful man named Sherebiah, who was a Levite from the family of Mahli. Eighteen of his relatives came with him. [19]We were also sent Hashabiah and Jeshaiah from the family of Merari along with 20 of their relatives. [20]In addition, 220 others came to help the Levites in the temple. The ancestors of these workers had been chosen years ago by King David[f] and his officials, and they were all listed by name.

Ezra Asks the People To Go without Eating and To Pray

[21]Beside the Ahava River,[g] I[h] asked the people to go without eating[i] and to pray. We humbled ourselves and asked God to bring us and our children safely to Jerusalem with all of our possessions. [22]I was ashamed to ask the king to send soldiers and cavalry to protect us against enemies

along the way. After all, we had told the king that our God takes care of everyone who truly worships him, but that he gets very angry and punishes anyone who refuses to obey. [23]So we went without food and asked God himself to protect us, and he answered our prayers.

The Gifts for the Temple

[24]I[j] chose twelve of the leading priests—Sherebiah, Hashabiah and ten of their relatives. [25-27]Then I weighed the gifts that had been given for God's temple, and I divided them among the twelve priests I had chosen. There were gifts of silver and gold, as well as the articles that the king, his advisors and officials, and the people of Israel had contributed. In all there were: 25 tons of silver; 100 silver articles weighing 150 pounds; 7,500 pounds of gold; 20 gold bowls weighing 270 ounces; and 2 polished bronze articles as valuable as gold.

[28]I said to the priests:

You belong to the LORD, the God of your ancestors, and these things also belong to him. The silver and gold were willingly given as gifts to the LORD. [29]Be sure to guard them and keep them safe until you reach Jerusalem. Then weigh them inside God's temple in the presence of the chief priests, the Levites, and the heads of the Israelite families.

[30]The priests and Levites then took charge of the gifts that had been weighed, so they could take them to the temple of our God in Jerusalem.

[b]**8.15** *I*: See the note at 8.1.   [c]**8.15** *river*: Or "canal."   [d]**8.15** *town of Ahava*: A town (or place) in Babylonia, but the exact location is unknown.   [e]**8.17** *Casiphia*: The location is not known.   [f]**8.20** *King David*: See the note at 3.10.   [g]**8.21** *River*: See the note at 8.15.   [h]**8.21** *I*: See the note at 8.1.   [i]**8.21** *to go without eating*: The Jews often went without eating as a way of worshiping God. This is sometimes called "fasting."   [j]**8.24** *I*: See the note at 8.1.

The Return to Jerusalem

[31]On the twelfth day of the first month,[k] we left the Ahava River[l] and started for Jerusalem. Our God watched over us, and as we traveled along, he kept our enemies from ambushing us.

[32]After arriving in Jerusalem, we rested for three days. [33]Then on the fourth day we went to God's temple, where the silver, the gold, and the other things were weighed and given to the priest Meremoth son of Uriah. With him were Eleazar son of Phinehas and the two Levites, Jozabad son of Jeshua and Noadiah son of Binnui. [34]Everything was counted, weighed, and recorded.

[35]Those who had returned from exile offered sacrifices on the altar to the God of Israel. Twelve bulls were offered for all Israel. Ninety-six rams and 77 lambs[m] were offered on the altar, and 12 goats were sacrificed for the sins of the people. [36]Some of those who had returned took the king's orders to the governors and officials in Western Province. Then the officials did what they could for the people and for the temple of God.

Ezra Condemns Mixed Marriages

9 Later the Jewish leaders came to me[n] and said:

Many Israelites, including priests and Levites, are living just like the people around them. They are even guilty of some of the horrible sins of the Canaanites, the Hittites, the Perizzites, the Jebusites, the Ammonites, the Moabites, the Egyptians, and the Amorites. [2]Some Israelite men have married foreign women and have let their sons

do the same thing. Our own officials and leaders were the first to commit this disgusting sin, and now God's holy people are mixed with foreigners. [3]This news made me so angry that I ripped my clothes and tore hair from my head and beard. Then I just sat in shock [4]until the time for the evening sacrifice. Many of our people were greatly concerned and gathered around me, because the God of Israel had warned us to stay away from foreigners.

Ezra's Prayer

[5]At the time of the evening sacrifice, I was still sitting there in sorrow with my clothes all torn. So I got down on my knees, then lifted my arms, [6]and prayed:

I am much too ashamed to face you, LORD God. Our sins and our guilt have swept over us like a flood that reaches up to the heavens. [7]Since the time of our ancestors, all of us have sinned. That's why we, our kings, and our priests have often been defeated by other kings. They have killed some of us and made slaves of others; they have taken our possessions and made us ashamed, just as we are today.

[8]But for now, LORD God, you have shown great kindness to us. You made us truly happy by letting some of us settle in this sacred place and by helping us in our time of slavery. [9]We are slaves, but you have never turned your back on us. You love us, and because of you, the kings of Persia have helped us. It's as though you have given us new life! You let us rebuild your temple and live safely in Judah and Jerusalem.

[10]Our God, what can we say now?

---

[k]8.31 *first month:* See the note at 6.19.   [l]8.31 *River:* See the note at 8.15.   [m]8.35 *77 lambs:* Or "72 lambs."   [n]9.1 *me:* Ezra.

● 9.1 *Canaanites . . . Amorites:* These eight groups were among the original inhabitants of Canaan before the Israelites conquered the land. They were included on a list of groups the Israelites were forbidden to marry. The Moabites, Ammonites, and Egyptians were still present in Ezra's time. The Phoenicians, who were linked to the ancient Canaanites by a common religion and culture, continued to live in the north coastal areas of Palestine.

■ 9.2 *God's holy people are mixed with foreigners:* This phrase means that God's special people had mixed with foreigners by marrying them. The sin was not that Jewish men married women of a different race or culture, but that by doing so they married women who did not follow the God of Israel. Such marriages could lead to the adoption of sinful religious practices and the worship of foreign gods.

■ 9.6-8 *Our sins . . . some of us:* After beginning his prayer with "I" (9.6), Ezra immediately shifts to "our" and "we," to show that he includes himself as one of the people, although he was innocent. Since the nation as a whole was bound together in the agreement made with God, all the people were threatened by this sin. "Some of us" refers to the prophecy that a faithful portion of the Israelites would survive God's judgment and continue God's work in the world.

● 9.9 *We are slaves:* The Persians did not treat the Israelites as actual slaves, but because Israelites were subjects of the Persian Empire, they lacked national independence.

10.1 *Ezra:* The "Memoirs of Ezra" that began at 8.1 ends at the conclusion of his prayer (9.15). From 10.1 on, EZRA continues in the third person.

10.5 *swear:* To say, "I swear" was like saying, "If I don't keep my promise, I accept a curse upon myself." To make a person swear to do something was a way to be certain that the person kept his or her promise. The first five verses of this chapter emphasize that the most important thing the people can do in their situation is to renew their agreement with God.

10.6 *did not eat . . . a thing:* Here, going without food (fasting) is not a sign of worshiping God, but rather a sign of sorrow. David went without food after hearing about the death of Saul and Jonathan (2 Sam 1.12) , and Nehemiah fasted upon hearing that Jerusalem remained in ruins (Neh 1.4).

10.9 *ninth month:* Chislev, the ninth month of the Hebrew calendar, from about mid-November to mid-December. **(See the chart Pilgrimage Festivals on pg 1799.)**

Even after all this, we have disobeyed the commands [11]that were given to us by your servants the prophets. They said the land you are giving us is full of sinful and wicked people, who never stop doing disgusting things.[o] [12]And we were warned not to let our daughters and sons marry their sons and daughters.

Your prophets also told us never to help those foreigners or even let them live in peace. You wanted us to become strong and to enjoy the good things in the land, then someday to leave it to our children forever.

[13]You punished us because of our terrible sins. But you did not punish us nearly as much as we deserve, and you have brought some of us back home. [14]Why should we disobey your commands again by letting our sons and daughters marry these foreigners who do such disgusting things? That would make you angry enough to destroy us all! [15]LORD God of Israel, you have been more than fair by letting a few of us survive. But once again, our sins have made us ashamed to face you.

The Plan for Ending Mixed Marriages

10 While Ezra was down on his knees in front of God's temple, praying with tears in his eyes and confessing the sins of the people of Israel, a large number of men, women, and children gathered around him and cried bitterly.

[2]Shecaniah son of Jehiel from the family of Elam said:

Ezra, we have disobeyed God by marrying these foreign women. But there is still hope for the people of Israel, [3]if we follow your advice and the advice of others who truly respect the laws of God. We must promise God that we will divorce our foreign wives and send them away, together with their children.

[4]Ezra, it's up to you to do something! We will support whatever you do. So be brave!

[5]Ezra stood up and made the chief priests, the Levites, and everyone else in Israel swear that they would follow the advice of Shecaniah. [6]Then Ezra left God's temple and went to spend the night in the living quarters of Jehohanan son of Eliashib. He felt sorry because of what the people had done, and he did not eat or drink a thing.

[7-8]The officials and leaders sent a message to all who had returned from Babylonia and were now living in Jerusalem and Judah. This message told them to meet in Jerusalem within three days, or else they would lose everything they owned and would no longer be considered part of the people that had returned from Babylonia.

[9]Three days later, on the twentieth day of the ninth month,[P] everyone from Judah and Benjamin came to Jerusalem and sat in the temple courtyard. It was a serious meeting, and they sat there, trembling in the rain.

[10]Ezra the priest stood up and said:

You have broken God's Law by marrying foreign women, and you have made the whole nation guilty! [11]Now you must confess your sins to the LORD God of your ancestors and obey him. Divorce your foreign wives and don't

[o]9.11 *doing disgusting things:* Probably worshiping idols.   [P]10.9 *ninth month:* Chislev, the ninth month of the Hebrew calendar, from about mid-November to mid-December.

have anything to do with the rest of the foreigners who live around here. [12]Everyone in the crowd shouted:

You're right! We will do what you say. [13]But there are so many of us, and we can't just stay out here in this downpour. A lot of us have sinned by marrying foreign women, and the matter can't be settled in only a day or two.

[14]Why can't our officials stay on in Jerusalem and take care of this for us? Let everyone who has sinned in this way meet here at a certain time with leaders and judges from their own towns. If we take care of this problem, God will surely stop being so terribly angry with us.

[15]Jonathan son of Asahel and Jahzeiah son of Tikvah were the only ones who objected, except for the two Levites, Meshullam and Shabbethai.

[16]Everyone else who had returned from exile agreed with the plan. So Ezra the priest chose men[q] who were heads of the families, and he listed their names. They started looking into the matter on the first day of the tenth month,[r] [17]and they did not finish until the first day of the first month[s] of the next year.

The Men Who Had Foreign Wives

[18-19]Here is a list of the priests who had agreed to divorce their foreign wives and to sacrifice a ram as a sin offering:

Maaseiah, Eliezer, Jarib, and Gedaliah from the family of Joshua son of Jozadak and his brothers; [20]Hanani and Zebadiah from the family of Immer; [21]Maaseiah, Eli-jah, Shemaiah, Jehiel, and Uzziah from the family of Harim; [22]Elioenai, Maaseiah, Ishmael, Nethanel, Jozabad, and Elasah from the family of Pashhur.

[23]Those Levites who had foreign wives were: Jozabad, Shimei, Kelaiah (also known as Kelita), Pethahiah, Judah, and Eliezer.

[24]Eliashib, the musician, had a foreign wife.

These temple guards had foreign wives: Shallum, Telem, and Uri.

[25]Here is a list of the others from Israel who had foreign wives:

Ramiah, Izziah, Malchijah, Mijamin, Eleazar, Hashabiah,[t] and Benaiah from the family of Parosh;

[26]Mattaniah, Zechariah, Jehiel, Abdi, Jeremoth, and Elijah from the family of Elam;

[27]Elioenai, Eliashib, Mattaniah, Jeremoth, Zabad, and Aziza from the family of Zattu;

[28]Jehohanan, Hananiah, Zabbai, and Athlai from the family of Bebai;

[29]Meshullam, Malluch, Adaiah, Jashub, Sheal, and Jeremoth from the family of Bani;

[30]Adna, Chelal, Benaiah, Maaseiah, Mattaniah, Bezalel, Binnui, and Manasseh from the family of Pahath Moab;

[31-32]Eliezer, Isshijah, Malchijah, Shemaiah, Shimeon, Benjamin, Malluch, and Shemariah from the family of Harim;

[33]Mattenai, Mattattah, Zabad, Eliphelet, Jeremai, Manasseh, and Shimei from the family of Hashum;

[34-37]Maadai, Amram, Uel, Benaiah, Bedeiah, Cheluhi, Vaniah, Meremoth, Eliashib, Mattaniah, Mattenai, and Jaasu from the family of Bani;

[38-42]Shimei, Shelemiah, Nathan, Adaiah, Machnadebai, Shashai, Sharai, Azarel,

10.13 *sinned:* The Hebrew word translated "sinned" means "rebelled" here. The same word is used to describe the revolt of the northern tribes against Rehoboam, Solomon's son (1 Kgs 12.19).

10.14 *leaders:* The elders or older men of the various villages usually formed a council that made decisions for governing the community. They were gathered from all the towns to represent God's people as a whole.

10.16,17 *tenth month:* Tebeth, the tenth month of the Hebrew calendar, from about mid-December to mid-January. (See the chart Pilgrimage Festivals on pg 1799.)

10.18-19 *agreed:* In Hebrew, this reads "they all gave their hands." To seal an agreement with a handshake was quite common.

[q]10.16 *So . . . men:* One possible meaning for the difficult Hebrew text.   [r]10.16 *tenth month:* Tebeth, the tenth month of the Hebrew calendar, from about mid-December to mid-January.   [s]10.17 *first month:* See the note at 6.19.   [t]10.25 *Hashabiah:* One ancient translation; Hebrew "Malchijah."

10.44 *divorced their foreign wives:* This extreme action was taken in order to preserve the "purity" of the small group of Jewish people who had returned to Judah to rebuild the peoples' cities and renew their commitment to living as God's people. This meant being loyal to the LORD God alone.

Shelemiah, Shemariah, Shallum, Amariah, and Joseph from the family of Binnui;[u]

43Jeiel, Mattithiah, Zabad, Zebina, Jaddai, Joel, and Benaiah from the family of Nebo.

44These men divorced their foreign wives, then sent them and their children away.[v]

[u]10.38-42 *from the family of Binnui:* One possible meaning for the difficult Hebrew text.   [v]10.44 *away:* One possible meaning for the difficult Hebrew text of verse 44.

Reflection Questions About Ezra 1.1—10.44

1. Why did Cyrus allow the Jews to return to Jerusalem (1.1-3)?

2. Why were foreigners not allowed to help rebuild the temple? What problems did these people cause for the returning Jews (4.1-23)?

3. What does this book reveal about Ezra and his personality? How does God help Ezra to use the gifts he has been given? What does this tell you about how God can use you?

4. How did Artaxerxes assist Ezra and the Jewish people (7.11-26)? According to Ezra, why did Artaxerxes do these things (7.27,28)?

5. The book of EZRA is about how the Jews tried to start over in their relationship with God. Many forces from both inside and outside the community tested the Jew's faith in God and tempted them to abandon God's Law. What things in your life threaten your relationship with God?

nehemiah

Nehemiah faced great opposition to the task God gave him. Yet, with God's help, he succeeded. Read his book to find out how.

WHAT MAKES NEHEMIAH SPECIAL?

NEHEMIAH, together with EZRA (they were originally one book), is special because it is our only biblical source for this period of Israelite history. In addition, Nehemiah himself is a wonderful example of leadership and of how to live one's faith in the face of difficulties.

NEHEMIAH continues the story that began in EZRA: the history of the Israelites after their return from Babylonia to Jerusalem. In particular, it provides a written history of the rebuilding of the walls of Jerusalem, lists those who returned to Jerusalem, and describes the people's commitment to worship and remain faithful to the God of Israel.

WHAT'S THE STORY BEHIND THE SCENE?

Just as EZRA is not complete without NEHEMIAH, NEHEMIAH is not complete without EZRA. Indeed, Ezra the scribe not only appears in the book of NEHEMIAH, but his reading of the Law to the Jews in Jerusalem is vital to the story and action of NEHEMIAH. As with the book of EZRA, biblical editors of NEHEMIAH were less concerned with exact historical dates than with simply presenting the Jews' activity following their return to Jerusalem.

Nehemiah was a trusted personal servant to King Artaxerxes and had attained high rank in the Persian court. He was a man of great ability and persuasiveness. Most importantly, he was a Jew who loved and obeyed the God of Israel. When he heard that the walls and gates of the holy city, Jerusalem, were in ruins, Nehemiah returned to Jerusalem, and despite much opposition, supervised the rebuilding of the city's walls and gates.

The first part of NEHEMIAH (the third section of EZRA-NEHEMIAH as a whole) deals with Nehemiah's mission to return to Jerusalem and rebuild its walls. Like the missions of Sheshbazzar (Ezra 1–6) and Ezra (Ezra 7–10), this mission was authorized by the Persian king. Nehemiah's capable leadership, faith, and courage were tested as he worked to overcome the tricks and schemes of his enemies.

HOW IS NEHEMIAH CONSTRUCTED?

NEHEMIAH can be outlined in the following way:

Nehemiah returns and rebuilds the walls
  (1.1—7.73)
    Nehemiah and his mission (1.1—2.10)
    Nehemiah supervises the rebuilding (2.11—7.73)
A new community based on old agreements
  (8.1—10.39)
    Ezra teaches the people (8.1—8.18)
    The people respond (9.1—10.39)
Nehemiah's work continues (11.1—13.31)
    Jerusalem is repopulated (11.1—12.26)
    Joyful dedication (12.27—12.43)
    Nehemiah's final reforms (12.44—13.31)

Originally, Ezra and Nehemiah were one book. Together, they form the main historical record of the period when God's people, having returned from exile in Babylonia, rebuilt the temple, restored Jerusalem, and re-dedicated themselves to obeying God's Law. Nehemiah, a court official to the Persian king Artaxerxes, learns that the people who have returned to Jerusalem from exile in Babylonia are suffering all kinds of troubles. Jerusalem's city gates have been burned and the city's defensive walls are in ruins. Praying to the Lord for forgiveness and guidance, Nehemiah is able to win Artaxerxes' permission to return to Jerusalem as its governor, and rebuild the city. Though opposed by other local governors who want Jerusalem to remain weak, Nehemiah succeeds in organizing workers to rebuild the city's walls and repair its gates. Ezra the priest reads the Law of Moses to the people, who confess their sins, pray together, and once again celebrate the Lord's sacred festivals. Nehemiah continues his bold work of reforming the Jewish faith by sending away foreigners, restoring the laws requiring the observance of the Sabbath, and outlawing mixed marriages.

Outline

Nehemiah's Prayer

1 I am Nehemiah son of Hacaliah, and in this book I tell what I have done.

During the month of Chislev[a] in the twentieth year that Artaxerxes[b] ruled Persia, I was in his fortress city of Susa,[c] ²when my brother Hanani came with some men from Judah. So I asked them about the Jews who had escaped[d] from being captives in Babylonia. I also asked them about the city of Jerusalem.

³They told me, "Those captives who have come back are having all kinds of troubles. They are terribly disgraced, Jerusalem's walls are broken down, and its gates have been burned."

⁴When I heard this, I sat down on the ground and cried. Then for several days, I mourned; I went without eating to show my sorrow, and I prayed:

⁵Lord God of heaven, you are great and fearsome. And you faithfully keep your promises to everyone who loves you and obeys your commands. ⁶I am your servant, so please have mercy on me and answer the prayer that I make day and night for these people of Israel who serve you. I, my family, and the rest of your people have sinned ⁷by choosing to disobey you and the laws and teachings you gave to your servant Moses.

⁸Please remember the promise you made to Moses. You told him that if we were unfaithful, you would scatter us among foreign nations. ⁹But you also said that no matter how far away we were, we could turn to you and start obeying your laws. Then you would bring us back to the place where you have chosen to be worshiped.

¹⁰Our Lord, I am praying for your servants—those you rescued by your

ᵃ1.1 *Chislev:* The ninth month of the Hebrew calendar, from about mid-November to mid-December. ᵇ1.1 *Artaxerxes:* Probably Artaxerxes I, who ruled Persia 465–425 B.C. ᶜ1.1 *Susa:* Capital of Elam Province, the winter home of Persian kings. ᵈ1.2 *escaped:* Or "returned."

1.1,2 *Artaxerxes . . . Hanani . . . Jews who had escaped:* This is probably Artaxerxes I, who ruled Persia from 465 to 424 B.C. Hanani was later put in charge of Jerusalem (see 7.2). "Jews who had escaped" (verse 2) most likely refers to both those who had returned from exile in Babylon and those who had not been forced to go to Babylonia and remained in Judah during the exile.

Exile

1.5,6 *keep your promises . . . I . . . have sinned:* If the people of Israel obeyed God's commands (Deut 5.1-21, 28-33; 6.1-9), then God promised to give them their own land, make them a great nation (see Gen 12.1-3), and give them blessings (Deut 7.12-15). God's love for Israel is demonstrated throughout the Old Testament even though Israel sinned and rebelled. Like Ezra before him (Ezra 9.6-15), Nehemiah admits that he and his family share in the sins of the people of Israel.

1.7 *Moses:* God gave Moses the laws and commandments that showed the Israelites they were God's special people and taught them how to live their lives (Exodus 19–40).

Moses

2.3 *the city*: Nehemiah does not mention Jerusalem by name because of the city's reputation for rebellion (see Ezra 4.12,15).

2.7 *Euphrates River*: The Euphrates is the longest (1,700 miles) and most important river in western Asia. **(See Map 1 on pg 1879.)**

2.8 *the king did everything I asked*: In doing so, the king reverses his earlier decision to stop the rebuilding of the city (Ezra 4.21).

2.9,10 *Sanballat . . . Tobiah*: Sanballat was the governor of Samaria, Judah's neighbor to the north. He probably was a native of Beth-Horon. Tobiah is called "the Ammonite" because he was a leader from Ammon. Tobiah was probably an Israelite but worked with Sanballat and Geshem to try to stop Nehemiah's attempts to rebuild Jerusalem's walls. **(See Map 6 on pg 1884.)**

2.11 *Jerusalem*: Around 1010 B.C., King David captured the walled city of Jerusalem from a Canaanite tribe called the Jebusites. He rebuilt the city and made it the capital of Israel (2 Sam 5.6-9). So Jerusalem is sometimes called "David's City." **(See Map 5 on pg 1883.)**

Jerusalem

2.15 *Kidron Valley*: The Kidron Valley formed the city's eastern boundary. **(See Map 5 on page 1883.)**

great strength and mighty power. [11]Please answer my prayer and the prayer of your other servants who gladly honor your name. When I serve the king his wine today, make him pleased with me and let him do what I ask.

Nehemiah Goes to Jerusalem

2 During the month of Nisan[e] in the twentieth year that Artaxerxes was king, I served him his wine, as I had done before. But this was the first time I had ever looked depressed. [2]So the king said, "Why do you look so sad? You're not sick. Something must be bothering you."

Even though I was frightened, [3]I answered, "Your Majesty, I hope you live forever! I feel sad because the city where my ancestors are buried is in ruins, and its gates have been burned down."

[4]The king asked, "What do you want me to do?"

I prayed to the God who rules from heaven. [5]Then I told the king, "Sir, if it's all right with you, please send me back to Judah, so that I can rebuild the city where my ancestors are buried."

[6]The queen was sitting beside the king when he asked me, "How long will it take, and when will you be back?" The king agreed to let me go, and I told him when I would return.

[7]Then I asked, "Your Majesty, would you be willing to give me letters to the governors of the provinces west of the Euphrates River, so that I can travel safely to Judah? [8]I will need timber to rebuild the gates of the fortress near the temple and more timber to construct the city wall and to build a

place for me to live. And so, I would appreciate a letter to Asaph, who is in charge of the royal forest." God was good to me, and the king did everything I asked.

[9]The king sent some army officers and cavalry troops along with me, and as I traveled through the Western Provinces, I gave the letters to the governors. [10]But when Sanballat from Horon[f] and Tobiah the Ammonite official heard about what had happened, they became very angry, because they didn't want anyone to help the people of Israel.

Nehemiah Inspects the Wall of Jerusalem

[11]Three days after arriving in Jerusalem, [12]I got up during the night and left my house. I took some men with me, without telling anyone what I thought God wanted me to do for the city. The only animal I took was the donkey I rode on. [13]I went through Valley Gate on the west, then south past Dragon Spring, before coming to Garbage Gate. As I rode along, I took a good look at the crumbled walls of the city and the gates that had been torn down and burned. [14]On the east side of the city, I headed north to Fountain Gate and King's Pool, but then the trail became too narrow for my donkey. [15]So I went down to Kidron Valley and looked at the wall from there. Then before daylight I returned to the city through Valley Gate.

[16]None of the city officials knew what I had in mind. And I had not even told any of the Jews—not the priests, the leaders, the officials, or any other Jews who would be helping in the work. [17]But when I got back, I said to them, "Jerusalem is truly in a

[e]2.1 *Nisan*: Or Abib, the first month of the Hebrew calendar, from about mid-March to mid-April.
[f]2.10 *Horon*: Possibly meaning that Sanballat was the official in charge of Beth-Horon, an important town on the road from Jerusalem to Lydda and the Mediterranean Sea.

mess! The gates have been torn down and burned, and everything is in ruins. We must rebuild the city wall so that we can again take pride in our city."

[18] Then I told them how kind God had been and what the king had said.

Immediately, they replied, "Let's start building now!" So they got everything ready.

[19] When Sanballat, Tobiah, and Geshem the Arab heard about our plans, they started insulting us and saying, "Just look at you! Do you plan to rebuild the walls of the city and rebel against the king?"

[20] I answered, "We are servants of the God who rules from heaven, and he will make our work succeed. So we will start rebuilding Jerusalem, but you have no right to any of its property, because you have had no part in its history."

Rebuilding the Wall of Jerusalem

3 These are the people who helped rebuild the wall and gates of Jerusalem:

The high priest Eliashib and the other priests rebuilt Sheep Gate and hung its doors. Then they dedicated Sheep Gate and the section of the wall as far as Hundred Tower and Hananel Tower.

[2] The people of Jericho rebuilt the next section of the wall, and Zaccur son of Imri rebuilt the section after that.

[3] The family of Hassenaah built Fish Gate. They put the beams in place and hung the doors, then they added metal bolts and wooden beams as locks.

[4] Meremoth, son of Uriah and grandson of Hakkoz, completed the next section of the wall.

Meshullam, son of Berechiah and grandson of Meshezabel, rebuilt the next section, and Zadok son of Baana rebuilt the section beside that.

[5] The next section was to be repaired by the men of Tekoa, but their town leaders refused to do the hard work they were assigned.[g]

[6] Joiada son of Paseah and Meshullam son of Besodeiah restored Ancient Gate. They put the beams in place, hung the doors, and added metal bolts and wooden beams as locks. [7] Melatiah from Gibeon, Jadon from Meronoth, and the men from Gibeon and Mizpah rebuilt the next section of the wall. This section reached as far as the house of the governor of West Euphrates Province.[h]

[8] Uzziel son of Harhaiah the goldsmith rebuilt the next section.

Hananiah the perfume maker rebuilt the section next after that, and it went as far as Broad Wall.

[9] Rephaiah son of Hur ruled half of the Jerusalem District, and he rebuilt the next section of the wall.

[10] The section after that was close to the home of Jedaiah son of Harumaph, and he rebuilt it.

Hattush son of Hashabneiah constructed the next section of the wall.

[11] Malchijah son of Harim and Hasshub son of Pahath Moab rebuilt the section after that, and they also built Oven Tower.

[12] Shallum son of Hallohesh ruled the other half of the Jerusalem District, and he rebuilt the next section of the wall. Shallum's daughters also worked with him.

[13] Hanun and the people who lived

● **2.19** *Geshem the Arab:* Geshem was kept in power by the Persians and had their authority to rule over a large number of Arab tribes. These tribes were located to the south and east of Judah in Edom and Idumaea. Nehemiah's enemies were coming at him from north, east, and south.

● **3.1,3** *Sheep Gate . . . Hundred Tower and Hananel Tower . . . Fish Gate:* The Sheep Gate was located in the northeastern part of the wall. John 5.2 locates it beside the pool Bethzatha. To this day, this gate is the place where sheep are bought and sold. The name of the Hundred Tower may refer to the tower's height or may indicate that it housed a military unit of 100 men. Jeremiah 31.38 and Zechariah 14.10,11 suggest that the Hananel Tower was the northernmost point in the city. Fish Gate was the site of the city's fish markets and was located near the northwest corner of the city. This gate opened to the road that led to the Mediterranean Sea, a main source of fish for the city. (See Map 4 on pg 1882.)

● **3.6,8** *Ancient Gate . . . Broad Wall:* The Ancient Gate (known later as the Ephraim Gate) was located in the western section of the wall. The Broad Wall may have been the western wall built by Hezekiah to enclose the city and its water supply (2 Chr 32.3-5). (See Map 5 on pg 1883.)

● **3.12** *Shallum's daughters:* This is the only reference to women helping with the rebuilding of Jerusalem's walls, although others were most likely involved.

Nehemiah told his opponents, "We are servants of the God who rules from heaven, and he will make our work succeed." NEH 2.20

3.17,22 *Levites . . . priests:* While both Levites and priests were members of the tribe of Levi, the Levites were not descended from Aaron and so could not serve as priests. The Levites who had been in exile in Babylonia were thought to have worshiped the Canaanite gods and so were considered unfit to do anything except work as janitors in the temple. The priests worked on the parts of the wall near where they and the high priest had lived before the city was destroyed.

Israel's Priests

3.26 *Water Gate:* This gate led into the area of the royal palace from the Kidron Valley on the east. The large area in front of the Water Gate was where Ezra read the Law of Moses to the Jewish people (Neh 8.1,2). (See Map 5 on pg 1883.)

3.26 *Ophel:* The southern part of the hill between the Kidron and Tyropoeon Valleys. Solomon built the temple and the royal palace there.

3.27 *men from Tekoa:* The town leaders of Tekoa refused to work, but the citizens made up for their leaders' refusal by working on two sections of the wall.

3.28,29 *Horse Gate . . . East Gate:* Since the Horse Gate was near where the priests lived, it was possibly on the east wall between the temple and the royal palace. The East Gate was most likely a gate in the eastern wall of the city. (See Map 5 on pg 1883.)

in the town of Zanoah rebuilt Valley Gate. They hung the doors and added metal bolts and wooden beams as locks. They also rebuilt the wall for 1,500 feet, all the way to Garbage Gate.

[14]Malchijah son of Rechab ruled the district of Beth-Haccherem, and he rebuilt Garbage Gate. He hung the doors and added metal bolts and wooden beams as locks.

[15]Shallum[i] son of Colhozeh ruled the district of Mizpah, and he rebuilt Fountain Gate. He put a cover over the gateway, then hung the doors and added metal bolts and wooden beams as locks. He also rebuilt the wall at Shelah Pool. This section was next to the king's garden and went as far as the stairs leading down from David's City.

[16]Nehemiah son of Azbuk ruled half of the district of Beth-Zur, and he rebuilt the next section of the wall. It went as far as the royal cemetery,[j] the artificial pool, and the army barracks.

Levites Who Worked on the Wall

[17]The Levites who worked on the next sections of the wall were Rehum son of Bani; Hashabiah, who ruled half of the district of Keilah and did this work for his district; [18]Binnui[k] son of Henadad, who ruled the other half of the district of Keilah; [19]Ezer son of Jeshua, who ruled Mizpah, rebuilt the section of the wall that was in front of the armory and reached to the corner of the wall; [20]Baruch son of Zabbai eagerly rebuilt the section of the wall that went all the way to the door of the house of Eliashib the high priest; [21]Meremoth,

son of Uriah and grandson of Hakkoz, built up to the far end of Eliashib's house.

Priests Who Worked on the Wall

[22]Here is a list of the priests who worked on the wall:

Priests from the region around Jerusalem rebuilt the next section of the wall.

[23]Benjamin and Hasshub rebuilt the wall in front of their own houses.

Azariah, who was the son of Maaseiah and the grandson of Ananiah, rebuilt the section in front of his house.

[24]Binnui son of Henadad rebuilt the section of the wall from Azariah's house to the corner of the wall.

[25]Palal son of Uzai rebuilt the next section, which began at the corner of the wall and the tower of the upper palace near the court of the guard.

Pedaiah son of Parosh rebuilt the next section of the wall. [26]He stopped at a place near the Water Gate on the east and the tower guarding the temple. This was close to a section in the city called Ophel, where the temple workers lived.[l]

Other Builders Who Worked on the Wall

[27]The men from Tekoa rebuilt the next section of the wall, and it was their second section.[m] It started at a place across from the large tower that guarded the Temple, and it went all the way to the wall near Ophel.

[28]Some priests rebuilt the next sec-

[i]3.15 *Shallum:* A few Hebrew manuscripts and one ancient translation; most Hebrew manuscripts "Shallun"; one ancient translation "Solomon." [j]3.16 *royal cemetery:* Hebrew "David's tombs." [k]3.18 *Binnui:* Two ancient translations; Hebrew "Bavvai." [l]3.26 *This . . . lived:* One possible meaning for the difficult Hebrew text. [m]3.27 *second section:* See verse 5.

tion of the wall. They began working north of Horse Gate, and each one worked on a section in front of his own house.

²⁹Zadok son of Immer rebuilt the wall in front of his house.

Shemaiah son of Shecaniah, who looked after the East Gate, rebuilt the section after that.

³⁰Hananiah and Hanun[n] rebuilt the next section, which was the second section[o] for them.

Meshullam son of Berechiah rebuilt the next section, which happened to be in front of his house.

³¹Malchijah, a goldsmith, rebuilt the next section, as far as the house used by the temple workers and merchants. This area was across from Gathering Gate, near the room on top of the wall at the northeast corner.

³²The goldsmiths and merchants rebuilt the last section of the wall, which went from the corner room all the way to Sheep Gate.

Nehemiah's Enemies

4 When Sanballat, the governor of Samaria, heard that we were rebuilding the walls of Jerusalem, he became angry and started insulting our people. ²In front of his friends and the Samaritan army he said, "What is this feeble bunch of Jews trying to do? Are they going to rebuild the wall and offer sacrifices all in one day? Do they think they can make something out of this pile of scorched stones?"

³Tobiah from Ammon was standing beside Sanballat and said, "Look at the wall

they are building! Why, even a fox could knock over this pile of stones."

⁴But I prayed, "Our God, these people hate us and have wished horrible things for us. Please answer our prayers and make their insults fall on them! Let them be the ones to be dragged away as prisoners of war. ⁵Don't forgive the mean and evil way they have insulted the builders."

⁶The people worked hard, and we built the walls of Jerusalem halfway up again. ⁷But Sanballat, Tobiah, the Arabs, the Ammonites, and the people from the city of Ashdod saw the walls going up and the holes being repaired. So they became angry ⁸and decided to stir up trouble, and to fight against the people of Jerusalem. ⁹But we kept on praying to our God, and we also stationed guards day and night.

¹⁰Meanwhile, the people of Judah were singing a sorrowful song:

"So much rubble for us to haul!
    Worn out and weary,
  will we ever finish this wall?"

¹¹Our enemies were saying, "Before those Jews know what has happened, we will sneak up and kill them and put an end to their work."

¹²On at least ten different occasions, the Jews living near our enemies warned us against attacks from every side,[p] ¹³and so I sent people to guard the wall at its lowest places and where there were still holes in it. I placed them according to families, and they stood guard with swords and spears and with bows and arrows. ¹⁴Then I looked things over and told the leaders, the officials, and the rest of the people, "Don't be afraid of your enemies! The Lord is great

[n]3.30 *Hananiah and Hanun:* Hebrew "Hananiah son of Shelemiah and Hanun, Zalaph's sixth son."
[o]3.30 *second section:* See verses 8,13.   [p]4.12 *against . . . side:* One possible meaning for the difficult Hebrew text.

● 3.31 *Gathering Gate:* Located near the northern part of the eastern temple area, Gathering Place was probably where Solomon's palace and center of government had been. This may also have been the "special place" where a sin-offering should be made (Ezek 43.21). **(See Map 5 on pg 1883.)**

● 4.1 *Sanballat, the governor:* Nehemiah never uses the title "governor" for Sanballat, though he is identified as the governor of Samaria in other ancient sources.

● 4.1 *Samaria:* Samaria, meaning "mountain of watching," was the name of a prominent hill, a city, and a region in ancient Israel. Omri, the sixth king of Israel (885–874 B.C.), bought the hill of Samaria as the site for his palace and the new capital of Israel. Eventually, Samaria became synonymous with the entire northern kingdom (Israel). **(See Maps 6 and 8 on pgs 1884 and 1886.)**

■ 4.4,5 *make . . . them . . . the builders:* Nehemiah's prayer is known as a "curse." The Bible has many examples of such prayers (see, for example, Ps 10; 35; 58; 109; and 137).

● 4.7 *people . . . Ashdod:* Nehemiah is surrounded by enemies. These include Sanballat and the Samaritans on the north, Tobiah and the Ammonites on the east, Geshem and the Arabs on the south, and "people from the city of Ashdod," the most important city of Philistia. **(See Map 3 on pg 1881.)**

● 5.1 *Jews in power:* These made up a privileged minority that was working with the Persian government. The shortage of food and the burden of the heavy Persian taxes had led to hunger for most people (5.2) and debts for the poor (5.3,4). The Jews in power had taken advantage of the situation by loaning money at very high rates of interest.

● 5.5 *sell . . . slaves . . . raped:* Often, when a family could not pay its debts, the children were forced to become slaves until the debt was paid (see 2 Kgs 4.1). Though the Law allowed the practice, it also limited how long these "debt slaves" could be required to serve their masters (Exod 21.1-11; Lev 25.39,40).

■ 5.7,8 *interest . . . exile:* Though charging interest was not permitted by the Law (Lev 25.36,37; Deut 23.19-20), taking a "guarantee" was acceptable (Deut 24.10-13). Nehemiah also had lent money in this way (5.10). Nehemiah warns that this practice, while not illegal, is "wrong" (5.9). The Hebrew for the word translated as "exile" here can mean more than one thing. It is uncertain whether Nehemiah means those sold into "debt slavery," or those who had returned from the Babylonian captivity. Nehemiah seems to be encouraging those who have returned from exile to buy these other Jews out of slavery. Instead, they continued to sell their own people into slavery. As a result, Nehemiah and his supporters must buy them back.

CR   Redeemer (Redemption)

and fearsome. So think of him and fight for your relatives and children, your wives and homes!"

¹⁵Our enemies found out that we knew about their plot against us, but God kept them from doing what they had planned. So we went back to work on the wall.

¹⁶From then on, I let half of the young men work while the other half stood guard. They wore armor and had spears and shields, as well as bows and arrows. The leaders helped the workers ¹⁷who were rebuilding the wall. Everyone who hauled building materials kept one hand free to carry a weapon. ¹⁸Even the workers who were rebuilding the wall strapped on a sword. The worker who was to blow the signal trumpet stayed with me.

¹⁹I told the people and their officials and leaders, "Our work is so spread out, that we are a long way from one another. ²⁰If you hear the sound of the trumpet, come quickly and gather around me. Our God will help us fight."

²¹Every day from dawn to dark, half of the workers rebuilt the walls, while the rest stood guard with their spears.

²²I asked the men in charge and their workers to stay inside Jerusalem and stand guard at night. So they guarded the city at night and worked during the day. ²³I even slept in my work clothes at night; my relatives, the workers, and the guards slept in theirs as well. And we always kept our weapons close by.�q

Nehemiah's Concern for the Poor

5 Some of the men and their wives complained about the Jews in power ²and said, "We have large families, and it takes a lot of grain merely to keep us alive."

³Others said, "During the famine we even had to mortgage our fields, vineyards, and homes to them in order to buy grain."

⁴Then others said, "We had to borrow money from those in power to pay the government tax on our fields and vineyards. ⁵We are Jews just as they are, and our children are as good as theirs. But we still have to sell our children as slaves, and some of our daughters have already been raped. We are completely helpless; our fields and vineyards have even been taken from us."

⁶When I heard their complaints and their charges, I became very angry. ⁷So I thought it over and said to the leaders and officials, "How can you charge your own people interest?"

Then I called a public meeting and accused the leaders ⁸by saying, "We have tried to buy back all of our people who were sold into exile. But here you are, selling more of them for us to buy back!" The officials and leaders did not say a word, because they knew this was true.

⁹I continued, "What you have done is wrong! We must honor our God by the way we live, so the Gentiles can't find fault with us. ¹⁰My relatives, my friends, and I are also lending money and grain, but we must no longer demand payment in return. ¹¹Now give back the fields, vineyards, olive orchards, and houses you have taken and also the interest you have been paid."

¹²The leaders answered, "We will do whatever you say and return their property, without asking to be repaid."

So I made the leaders promise in front of the priests to give back the property. ¹³Then I emptied my pockets and said, "If you don't keep your promise, that's what God will do to you. He will empty out everything you own, even taking away your houses."

q4.23 *And . . . by:* One possible meaning for the difficult Hebrew text.

The people answered, "We will keep our promise." Then they praised the LORD and did as they had promised.

Nehemiah Is Generous

[14]I was governor of Judah from the twentieth year that Artaxerxes[r] was king until the thirty-second year. And during these entire twelve years, my relatives and I refused to accept the food that I was allowed. [15]Each governor before me had been a burden to the people by making them pay for his food and wine and by demanding forty silver coins a day. Even their officials had been a burden to the people. But I respected God, and I didn't think it was right to be so hard on them. [16]I spent all my time getting the wall rebuilt and did not buy any property. Everyone working for me did the same thing. [17]I usually fed 150 of our own Jewish people and their leaders, as well as foreign visitors from surrounding lands. [18]Each day one ox, six of the best sheep, and lots of chickens were prepared. Then every ten days, a large supply of wine was brought in. I knew what a heavy burden this would have been for the people, and so I did not ask for my food allowance as governor.

[19]I pray that God will bless me for everything I have done for my people.

Plots against Nehemiah

6 Sanballat, Tobiah, Geshem, and our other enemies learned that I had completely rebuilt the wall. All I lacked was hanging the doors in the gates. [2]Then Sanballat and Geshem sent a message, asking me to meet with them in one of the villages in Ono Valley. I knew they were planning to harm me in some way. [3]So I sent messengers to tell them, "My work is too important to stop now and go there. I can't afford to slow down the work just to visit with you." [4]They invited me four times, but each time I refused to go.

[5]Finally, Sanballat sent an official to me with an unsealed letter, [6]which said:

A rumor is going around among the nations that you and the other Jews are rebuilding the wall and planning to rebel, because you want to be their king. And Geshem[s] says it's true! [7]You even have prophets in Jerusalem, claiming you are now the king of Judah. You know the Persian king will hear about this, so let's get together and talk it over.

[8]I sent a message back to Sanballat, saying, "None of this is true! You are making it all up."

[9]Our enemies were trying to frighten us and to keep us from our work. But I asked God to give me strength.

[10]One day I went to visit Shemaiah.[t] He wasn't supposed to leave his house, but he said, "Let's hurry to the holy place of the temple and hide there.[u] We will lock the temple doors, because your enemies are planning to kill you tonight."

[11]I answered, "Why should someone like me have to run and hide in the temple to save my life? I won't go!"

[12]Suddenly I realized that God had not given Shemaiah this message. But Tobiah and Sanballat had paid him to trick me [13]and to frighten me into doing something wrong, because they wanted to ruin my good name.

[14]Then I asked God to punish Tobiah

[r]5.14 Artaxerxes: See the note at 1.1. [s]6.6 Geshem: Hebrew "Gashmu" (see verse 1 and 2.19). [t]6.10 Shemaiah: Hebrew "Shemaiah son of Delaiah son of Mehetabel." [u]6.10 holy place . . . hide there: Only priests were allowed to enter the holy place; anyone else could be put to death.

5.13 *The people:* This does not refer to the community as a whole, but to those who had been lending money.

5.14 *twentieth year . . . thirty-second year:* In the modern calendar, 445 B.C. and 433 B.C. respectively.

5.14 *refused . . . allowed:* As governor, Nehemiah was allowed to require the local people to supply him with food, and to make them pay heavy taxes.

6.2 *Ono Valley:* This broad valley was on the coastal plain a few miles southeast of the city of Joppa. **(See Map 6 on pg 1884.)**

6.5 *unsealed letter:* By leaving the letter unsealed, Sanballat hoped others would learn that Nehemiah was accused of working against his Persian superiors.

Scrolls

6.13 *something wrong:* Since Nehemiah was not a priest, it would have been wrong for him to enter the holy place.

6.14 *Then I asked God to punish . . . had done . . . punish the prophet:* Rather than getting his own revenge, Nehemiah left vengeance to God and did not strike back at those who had tried to hurt him. This woman and others who claimed to be prophets were not messengers of God. Instead their aim was to silence the one who was: Nehemiah.

6.15 *Elul:* The sixth month of the Hebrew calendar, from about mid-August to mid-September.

6.15 *the wall . . . 52 days:* Archaeologists have determined that the wall was almost three yards thick and had a rough finish outside that shows it was built in a hurry. Fifty-two days is a very short time for so big a project.

7.1 *temple guards:* The temple guards (literally, "gatekeepers") usually patrolled the entrance to the temple. Nehemiah stationed them at the city gates because of the danger.

7.3 *Don't let . . . own houses:* These were safety measures. Usually, the gates were opened at sunrise. Keeping them shut until later in the day would make certain that everyone was awake. Having people guard the portions of the wall that were near their own homes encouraged them to do their jobs well.

7.4-73 *people . . . towns of Judah:* This list is like the one in Ezra 2, though there are many differences, partly in the names but especially in the numbers, which seem to be rounded off in Ezra. Here, the list is used to make sure that those who live within the city are of Jewish descent.

7.5-6 *Nebuchadnezzar:* Known as Nebuchadnezzar II, he ruled Babylonia from 605 to 562 B.C. In 586 B.C., he destroyed Jerusalem and took many of its people to Babylonia.

Nebuchadnezzar

and Sanballat for what they had done. I prayed that God would punish the prophet Noadiah and the other prophets who, together with her, had tried to frighten me.

The Work Is Finished

[15]On the twenty-fifth day of the month Elul,[v] the wall was completely rebuilt. It had taken 52 days. [16]When our enemies in the surrounding nations learned that the work was finished, they felt helpless, because they knew that our God had helped us rebuild the wall.

[17]All this time the Jewish leaders and Tobiah had been writing letters back and forth. [18]Many people in Judah were loyal to Tobiah for two reasons: Shecaniah son of Arah was his father-in-law, and Tobiah's son Jehohanan had married the daughter of Meshullam son of Berechiah.[w] [19]The people would always tell me about the good things Tobiah had done, and then they would tell Tobiah everything I had said. So Tobiah kept sending letters, trying to frighten me.

7 After the wall had been rebuilt and the gates hung, then the temple guards, the singers, and the other Levites were assigned their work. [2]I put my brother Hanani in charge of Jerusalem, along with Hananiah, the commander of the fortress, because Hananiah could be trusted, and he respected God more than most people did. [3]I said to them, "Don't let the gates to the city be opened until the sun has been up for a while. And make sure that they are closed and barred before the guards go off duty at sunset. Choose people from Jeru-

salem to stand guard at different places around the wall and others to stand guard near their own houses."

A List of Exiles Who Returned
(Ezra 2.1-70)

[4]Although Jerusalem covered a large area, not many people lived there, and no new houses had been built. [5-6]So God gave me the idea to bring together the people, their leaders, and officials and to check the family records of those who had returned from captivity in Babylonia, after having been taken there by King Nebuchadnezzar.[x] About this same time, I found records of those who had been the first to return to Jerusalem from Babylon Province.[y] By reading these records, I learned that they settled in their own hometowns, [7]and that they had come with Zerubbabel, Joshua, Nehemiah, Azariah, Raamiah, Nahamani, Mordecai, Bilshan, Mispereth, Bigvai, Nehum, and Baanah.

[8-25]This is a list of how many returned from each family group: 2,172 from Parosh; 372 from Shephatiah; 652 from Arah; 2,818 from Pahath Moab, who were all descendants of Jeshua and Joab; 1,254 from Elam; 845 from Zattu; 760 from Zaccai; 648 from Binnui; 628 from Bebai; 2,322 from Azgad; 667 from Adonikam; 2,067 from Bigvai; 655 from Adin; 98 from Ater, also known as Hezekiah; 328 from Hashum; 324 from Bezai; 112 from Hariph; and 95 from Gibeon.

[26-38]This is a list of how many returned whose ancestors had come from the following towns: 188 from Bethlehem and Netophah; 128 from Anathoth; 42 from

[v]**6.15** *Elul:* The sixth month of the Hebrew calendar, from about mid-August to mid-September.
[w]**6.18** *Shecaniah . . . Berechiah:* Jews who had helped rebuild the Jerusalem wall (see 3.4,29,30).
[x]**7.5,6** *Nebuchadnezzar:* Known as Nebuchadnezzar II, who ruled Babylonia from 605 to 562 B.C. In 586 B.C. he destroyed Jerusalem and took many of its people to Babylonia. [y]**7.5,6** *first to return . . . Province:* Probably 539 B.C., when Cyrus, the ruler of Persia, captured the city of Babylon.

Beth-Azmaveth; 743 from Kiriath-Jearim, Chephirah, and Beeroth; 621 from Ramah and Geba; 122 from Michmas; 123 from Bethel and Ai; 52 from Nebo;[z] 1,254 from Elam;[a] 320 from Harim; 345 from Jericho; 721 from Lod, Hadid, and Ono; and 3,930 from Senaah.

39-42 This is a list of how many returned from each family of priests: 973 descendants of Jeshua from Jedaiah; 1,052 from Immer; 1,247 from Pashhur; and 1,017 from Harim.

43-45 This is a list of how many returned from the families of Levites: 74 descendants of Hodevah from the families of Jeshua and Kadmiel; 148 descendants of Asaph from the temple musicians; and 138 descendants of Shallum, Ater, Talmon, Akkub, Hatita, and Shobai from the temple guards.

46-56 These are the names of the families of temple workers whose descendants returned: Ziha, Hasupha, Tabbaoth, Keros, Sia, Padon, Lebana, Hagaba, Shalmai, Hanan, Giddel, Gahar, Reaiah, Rezin, Nekoda, Gazzam, Uzza, Paseah, Besai, Meunim, Nephushesim, Bakbuk, Hakupha, Harhur, Bazlith, Mehida, Harsha, Barkos, Sisera, Temah, Neziah, and Hatipha.

57-59 Here are the names of Solomon's servants whose descendants returned: Sotai, Sophereth, Perida, Jaala, Darkon, Giddel, Shephatiah, Hattil, Pochereth Hazzebaim, and Amon.

60A total of 392 descendants of temple workers and of Solomon's servants returned.

61-62 There were 642 who returned from the families of Delaiah, Tobiah, and Nekoda,

though they could not prove they were Israelites. They had lived in the Babylonian towns of Tel-Melah, Tel-Harsha, Cherub, Addon, and Immer.

63-64 The families of Hobaiah, Hakkoz, and Barzillai could not prove they were priests. The ancestor of the family of Barzillai had married the daughter of Barzillai from Gilead and had taken his wife's family name. But the records of these three families could not be found, and none of them were allowed to serve as priests. **65**In fact, the governor told them, "You cannot eat the food offered to God until he lets us know if you really are priests."[b]

66-69 There were 42,360 who returned, in addition to 7,337 servants and 245 musicians, counting both men and women. Altogether, they brought with them 736 horses, 245 mules,[c] 435 camels, and 6,720 donkeys.

70-72 Many people gave gifts to help pay for the materials to rebuild the temple. The governor himself gave 17 pounds of gold, 50 bowls to be used in the temple, and 530 robes for the priests. Family leaders gave 337 pounds of gold and 3,215 pounds of silver. The rest of the people gave 337 pounds of gold, 2,923 pounds of silver, and 67 robes for the priests.

73And so, by the seventh month,[d] priests, Levites, temple guards, musicians, workers, and many of the ordinary people had settled in the towns of Judah.

7.57-59 *Solomon's servants:* Refers to those descended from Israel's King Solomon, the king who built the first temple in Jerusalem about 500 years earlier.

7.73 *seventh month:* Tishri (also called Ethanim), the seventh month of the Hebrew calendar, from about mid-September to mid-October. **(See the chart Pilgrimage Festivals on pg 1799.)**

[z]**7.26-38** *Nebo:* Hebrew "the other Nebo."   [a]**7.26-38** *Elam:* Hebrew "the other Elam."
[b]**7.65** *until . . . priests:* The Hebrew text has "until a priest comes with the urim and thummim," sacred objects which were used in some way to receive answers from God.   [c]**7.66-69** *736 horses, 245 mules:* A few Hebrew manuscripts; this is not found in most Hebrew manuscripts of verse 68.
[d]**7.73** *seventh month:* Tishri (also called Ethanim), the seventh month of the Hebrew calendar, from about mid-September to mid-October.

Ezra Reads God's Law to the People

8 [1-2]On the first day of the seventh month,[e] the people came together in the open area in front of the Water Gate. Then they asked Ezra, who was a teacher of the Law of Moses, to read to them from this Law that the LORD had given his people. Ezra the priest came with the Law and stood before the crowd of men, women, and the children who were old enough to understand. [3]From early morning till noon, he read the Law of Moses to them, and they listened carefully. [4]Ezra stood on a high wooden platform that had been built for this occasion. Mattithiah, Shema, Anaiah, Uriah, Hilkiah, and Maaseiah were standing to his right, while Pedaiah, Mishael, Malchijah, Hashum, Hash Baddanah, Zechariah, and Meshullam were standing to his left.

[5]Ezra was up on the high platform, where he could be seen by everyone, and when he opened the book, all the people stood up. [6]Ezra praised the great LORD God, and they lifted their hands, shouting "Amen! Amen!" Then they bowed with their faces to the ground and worshiped the LORD.

[7-8]After this, the Levites Jeshua, Bani, Sherebiah, Jamin, Akkub, Shabbethai, Hodiah, Maaseiah, Kelita, Azariah, Jozabad, Hanan, and Pelaiah went among the people, explaining the meaning of what Ezra had read.

[9]The people started crying when God's Law was read to them. Then Nehemiah the governor, Ezra the priest and teacher, and the Levites who had been teaching the people all said, "This is a special day for the LORD your God. So don't be sad and don't cry!"

[10]Nehemiah told the people, "Enjoy your good food and wine and share some with those who didn't have anything to bring. Don't be sad! This is a special day for the LORD, and he will make you happy and strong."

[11]The Levites encouraged the people by saying, "This is a sacred day, so don't worry or mourn!" [12]When the people returned to their homes, they celebrated by eating and drinking and by sharing their food with those in need, because they had understood what had been read to them.

Celebrating the Festival of Shelters

[13]On the second day of the seventh month,[f] the leaders of all the family groups came together with the priests and the Levites, so Ezra could teach them the Law [14]that the LORD had given to Moses. They learned from the Law that the people of Israel were to live in shelters when they celebrated the festival in the seventh month of the year. [15]They also learned that they were to go into the woods and gather branches of leafy trees such as olives, myrtles, and palms for making these shelters.

[16]So the people gathered branches and made shelters on the flat roofs of their houses, in their yards, in the courtyard of the temple, and in the open areas around the Water Gate and Ephraim Gate. [17]Everyone who had returned from Babylonia built shelters. They lived in them and joyfully celebrated the Festival of Shelters for the first time since the days of Joshua son of Nun. [18]On each of the first seven days of the festival, Ezra read to the people from God's Law. Then on the eighth day, everyone gathered for worship, just as the Law had said they must.

[e]8.1,2 *seventh month:* Tishri (also called Ethanim), the seventh month of the Hebrew calendar, from about mid-September to mid-October. [f]8.13 *seventh month:* Hebrew "same month."

The People Confess Their Sins

9 On the twenty-fourth day of the seventh month,[g] the people of Israel went without eating, and they dressed in sackcloth and threw dirt on their heads to show their sorrow. [2] They refused to let foreigners join them, as they met to confess their sins and the sins of their ancestors. [3] For three hours they stood and listened to the Law of the LORD their God, and then for the next three hours they confessed their sins and worshiped the LORD.

[4] Jeshua, Bani, Kadmiel, Shebaniah, Bunni, Sherebiah, Bani, and Chenani stood on the special platform for the Levites and prayed aloud to the LORD their God. [5] Then the Levites Jeshua, Kadmiel, Bani, Hashabneiah, Sherebiah, Hodiah, Shebaniah, and Pethahiah said:

"Stand and shout praises
to your LORD,
the eternal God![h]
Praise his wonderful name,
though he is greater
than words can express."

The People Pray

[6] You alone are the LORD,
Creator of the heavens
and all the stars,
Creator of the earth
and those who live on it,
Creator of the ocean
and all its creatures.
You are the source of life,
praised by the stars
that fill the heavens.

[7] You are the LORD our God,
the one who chose Abram—
you brought him from Ur
in Babylonia
and named him Abraham.
[8] Because he was faithful,
you made an agreement
to give his descendants
the land of the Canaanites
and Hittites,
of the Amorites and Perizzites,
and of the Jebusites
and Girgashites.
Now you have kept your promise,
just as you always do.

[9] When our ancestors
were in Egypt,
you saw their suffering;
when they were at the Red Sea,[i]
you heard their cry for help.
[10] You knew that the King of Egypt
and his officials and his nation
had mistreated your people.
So you worked fearsome miracles
against the Egyptians
and earned a reputation
that still remains.
[11] You divided the deep sea,
and your people walked through
on dry land.
But you tossed their enemies in,
and they sank down
like a heavy stone.
[12] Each day you led your people
with a thick cloud,
and at night you showed the way
with a flaming fire.
[13] At Sinai you came down

9.1 *twenty-fourth day:* The Festival of Shelters ended on the twenty-second day of the month, so there was only one day between the joyous celebration of Shelters and this serious and sorrowful time of confession.

9.6 *You . . . the LORD:* This confirms that, in a world where many gods and goddesses were worshiped, Israel trusted only in the one true God (Deut 5.6,7; 6.4).

9.7 *Abram:* Also known as Abraham. He was the son of Terah (Gen 11.26-28) and the founder of the Hebrew nation.

Abraham

9.8 *agreement:* God's promise to Abraham in Genesis 15.18-21.

Agreements (Covenants)

9.9 *Red Sea:* The Hebrew text reads *yam suph,* "Sea of Reeds." It is one of the marshes and fresh-water lakes near the eastern part of the Nile River delta. This identification is based on Exodus 13.17—14.9, which lists the towns on the route of the Israelites before crossing the sea. In the Greek translation of the Scriptures, made about 200 B.C., the "Sea of Reeds" was called "Red Sea." **(See Map 3 on pg 1881.)**

---

[g]8.13; 9.1 *seventh month:* Hebrew "same month." [h]9.5 *shout . . . God:* Or "shout eternal praises to the LORD your God." [i]9.9 *Red Sea:* Hebrew *yam suph,* "Sea of Reeds," one of the marshes of fresh water lakes near the eastern part of the Nile Delta. This identification is based on Exodus 13.17—14.9, which lists the towns on the route of the Israelites before crossing the sea. In the Greek translation of the Scriptures made about 200 B.C., the "Sea of Reeds" was named "Red Sea."

For three hours they stood and listened to the Law of the LORD their God, and then for the next three hours they confessed their sins and worshiped the LORD. NEH 9.3

9.14 *Sabbath:* This Jewish day of rest began at sunset on Friday when a ram's horn (shofar) was blown. It ended with a blessing at sunset on Saturday. The Sabbath was the seventh day of the week, the day that God rested after the work of creation (Gen 2.2,3). Observing the Sabbath, which means "rest" or "stop working," was required of all Jewish people. In the period following the exile, keeping the Sabbath became a major symbol of faithfulness to the Law of Moses.

9.20 *manna:* When the people of Israel were wandering through the desert, the Lord gave them a special kind of food to eat called "manna." In Hebrew this means, "What is this?" (Exod 16.1-36; Num 11.7-9).

from heaven,
and you gave your people
good laws and teachings
that are fair and honest.
¹⁴You commanded them to respect
your holy Sabbath,
and you instructed
your servant Moses
to teach them your laws.
¹⁵When they were hungry,
you sent bread from heaven,
and when they were thirsty,
you let water flow
from a rock.
Then you commanded them
to capture the land
that you had solemnly promised.

*¹⁶Our stubborn ancestors
refused to obey—
they forgot about the miracles
you had worked for them,
and they were determined
to return to Egypt
and become slaves again.
¹⁷But, our God, you are merciful
and quick to forgive;
you are loving, kind,
and very patient.
So you never turned away
from them—
¹⁸not even when they made
an idol shaped like a calf
and insulted you by claiming,
"This is the god who rescued us
from Egypt."

¹⁹Because of your great mercy,
you never abandoned them
in the desert.

And you always guided them
with a cloud by day
and a fire at night.
²⁰Your gentle Spirit
instructed them,[j]
and you gave them manna[k] to eat
and water to drink.
²¹You took good care of them,
and for forty years
they never lacked a thing.
Their clothes didn't wear out,
and their feet were never swollen.

²²You let them conquer kings
and take their land,
including King Sihon of Heshbon
and King Og of Bashan.[l]
²³You brought them into the land
that you had promised
their ancestors,
and you blessed their nation
with people that outnumbered
the stars in the sky.

²⁴Then their descendants
conquered the land.
You helped them defeat
the kings and nations
and treat their enemies
however they wished.
²⁵They captured strong cities
and rich farmland;
they took furnished houses,
as well as cisterns,[m]
vineyards, olive orchards,
and numerous fruit trees.
They ate till they were satisfied,
and they celebrated
your abundant blessings.

[j]9.20 *Your gentle Spirit instructed them:* Or "You gently instructed them." [k]9.20 *manna:* This was something like a thin wafer (see Exodus 16.1-36). [l]9.22 *Bashan:* One possible meaning for the difficult Hebrew text of verse 22. [m]9.25 *cisterns:* Pits dug into the ground to hold water.

"*Our God, you are merciful and quick to forgive; you are loving, kind, and very patient.*" Neh 9.17

²⁶In spite of this, they rebelled
  and disobeyed your laws.
They killed your prophets,
  who warned them
to turn back to you,
  and they cursed your name.
²⁷So you handed them over
to their enemies,
  who treated them terribly.
But in their sufferings,
  they begged you to help.
From heaven you listened
  to their prayers
and because of your great mercy,
you sent leaders to rescue them.

²⁸But when they were at peace,
  they would turn against you,
and you would hand them over
  to their enemies.
Then they would beg for help,
and because you are merciful,
  you rescued them
  over and over again.
²⁹You warned them to turn back
  and discover true life
  by obeying your laws.
But they stubbornly refused
  and continued to sin.
³⁰For years, you were patient,
  and your Spirit[n] warned them
with messages spoken
  by your prophets.
Still they refused to listen,
and you handed them over
  to their enemies.
³¹But you are merciful and kind,
  and so you never forgot them
  or let them be destroyed.

³²Our God, you are powerful,
  fearsome, and faithful,
  always true to your word.

So please keep in mind
  the terrible sufferings
of our people, kings, leaders,
  priests, and prophets,
from the time Assyria ruled
  until this very day.
³³You have always been fair
  when you punished us
  for our sins.

³⁴Our kings and leaders,
  our priests and ancestors
have never obeyed your commands
  or heeded your warnings.
³⁵You blessed them with a kingdom
  and with an abundance
  of rich, fertile land,
but they refused to worship you
  or turn from their evil.
³⁶Now we are slaves
  in this fruitful land
  you gave to our ancestors.
³⁷Its plentiful harvest is taken
  by kings you placed over us
  because of our sins.
Our suffering is unbearable,
because they do as they wish
  to us and our livestock.

The People Make an Agreement

³⁸And so, a firm agreement was made
that had the official approval of the leaders,
the Levites, and priests. **10** ¹As governor, I[o] signed the agreement together with Zedekiah and the following
priests: ²⁻⁸Seraiah, Azariah, Jeremiah, Pashhur, Amariah, Malchijah, Hattush, Shebaniah, Malluch, Harim, Meremoth, Obadiah,
Daniel, Ginnethon, Baruch, Meshullam,
Abijah, Mijamin, Maaziah, Bilgai, and Shemaiah.
⁹The Levites who signed were: Jeshua son

ⁿ**9.30** *your Spirit*: Or "you." ᵒ**10.1** *I*: Hebrew "Nehemiah son of Hacaliah."

9.32 *from . . . day*: The Assyrians defeated the northern kingdom (Israel) in 722 B.C. and took most of the people into exile in Assyria. "This very day" means the time of Nehemiah.

Assyria

10.35-37 *first part of our harvest . . . first-born sons . . . ten percent:* The first crops harvested were brought to the temple. They were used to provide for the needs of the priests and the Levites (Num 18.12,13). This offering acknowledged that the crops were God's gift and showed thankfulness for them. The dedication of first-born sons (10.36) recalled how God killed the first-born sons of the Egyptians when they refused to release the Israelites from slavery. The custom of giving God ten percent of one's possessions recognized that God was the ruler of the land and showed that the people were grateful for God's blessings.

10.38 *temple storeroom:* This was where the sacred objects used for worship in the temple were kept (10.39), but it was also where the Levites kept the gifts the people had given to God.

of Azaniah, Binnui from the clan of Henadad, Kadmiel, [10]Shebaniah, Hodiah, Kelita, Pelaiah, Hanan, [11]Mica, Rehob, Hashabiah, [12]Zaccur, Sherebiah, Shebaniah, [13]Hodiah, Bani, and Beninu.

[14]The leaders who signed were: Parosh, Pahath Moab, Elam, Zattu, Bani, [15]Bunni, Azgad, Bebai, [16]Adonijah, Bigvai, Adin, [17]Ater, Hezekiah, Azzur, [18]Hodiah, Hashum, Bezai, [19]Hariph, Anathoth, Nebai, [20]Magpiash, Meshullam, Hezir, [21]Meshezabel, Zadok, Jaddua, [22]Pelatiah, Hanan, Anaiah, [23]Hoshea, Hananiah, Hasshub, [24]Hallohesh, Pilha, Shobek, [25]Rehum, Hashabnah, Maaseiah, [26]Ahiah, Hanan, Anan, [27]Malluch, Harim, and Baanah.

The Agreement

[28-29]All of us, including priests, Levites, temple guards, singers, temple workers and leaders, together with our wives and children, have separated ourselves from the foreigners in this land and now enter into an agreement with a complete understanding of what we are doing. And so, we now place ourselves under the curse of the LORD our God, if we fail to obey his laws and teachings that were given to us by his servant Moses.

[30]We won't let our sons and daughters marry foreigners.

[31]We won't buy goods or grain on the Sabbath or on any other sacred day, not even from foreigners.

Every seven years we will let our fields rest, and we will cancel all debts.

[32]Once a year we will each donate a small amount of silver to the temple of our God. [33]This is to pay for the sacred bread, as well as for the daily sacrifices and special sacrifices such as those offered on the Sabbath and during the New Moon Festival and the other festivals. It will also pay for the sacrifices to forgive our sins and for all expenses connected with the worship of God in the temple.

[34]We have decided that the families[P] of priests, Levites, and ordinary people will supply firewood for the temple each year, so that sacrifices can be offered on the altar, just as the LORD our God has commanded.

[35]Each year we will bring to the temple the first part of our harvest of grain and fruit.

[36]We will bring our first-born sons and the first-born males of our herds and flocks and offer them to the priests who serve in the temple, because this is what is written in God's Law.[q]

[37]To the priests in the temple of our God, we will bring the bread dough from the first harvest, together with our best fruit, and an offering of new wine and olive oil.

We will bring ten percent of our grain harvest to those Levites who are responsible for collecting it in our towns. [38]A priest from the family of Aaron must be there when we give this to the Levites. Then the Levites will put one tenth of this part in the temple storeroom, [39]which is also the place for the sacred objects used by the priests, the temple guards, and the singers.

Levites and everyone else must bring their gifts of grain, wine, and olive oil to this room.

We will not neglect the temple of our God.

P10.34 *that the families:* Or "which families." q10.36 *first-born sons . . . God's Law:* See Exodus 13.2, 12-15; 34.19,20.

People Who Settled in Jerusalem

11 The nation's leaders and their families settled in Jerusalem. But there was room for only one out of every ten of the remaining families, and so they asked God to show them[r] who would live there. [2]Then everyone else asked God to bless those who were willing to live in Jerusalem.

[3] Some of the people of Israel, the priests, the Levites, the temple workers, and the descendants of Solomon's servants lived on their own property in the towns of Judah. But the leaders of the province lived in Jerusalem with their families.

The Judah Tribe

[4-6]From the Judah tribe, two leaders settled in Jerusalem with their relatives. One of them was Athaiah son of Uzziah. His ancestors were Zechariah, Amariah, Shephatiah, Mahalalel, and Perez, the son of Judah. From the descendants of Perez, 468 of the best men lived in Jerusalem.

The other leader from Judah was Maaseiah the son of Baruch. His ancestors were Colhozeh, Hazaiah, Adaiah, Joiarib, Zechariah, and Shelah, the son of Judah.

The Benjamin Tribe

[7-8]From the Benjamin tribe, three leaders settled in Jerusalem. The first was Sallu son of Meshullam, and the others were Gabbai and Sallai. Sallu's ancestors were Joed, Pedaiah, Kolaiah, Maaseiah, Ithiel, and Jeshaiah. Altogether, there were 928 men of the Benjamin tribe living in Jerusalem. [9]Joel son of Zichri was their

leader, and Judah son of Hassenuah was second in command.

Priests

[10]Four priests settled in Jerusalem. The first was Jedaiah; he was the son of Joiarib and the uncle of Jachin.[s] [11]The second priest to settle there was Seraiah son of Hilkiah. His ancestors were Meshullam, Zadok, Meraioth, and Ahitub, who had been a high priest. [12]Altogether, there were 822 from his clan who served in the temple.

The third priest to settle there was Adaiah son of Jeroham. His ancestors were Pelaliah, Amzi, Zechariah, Pashhur, and Malchijah. [13]Altogether, there were 242 clan leaders among his relatives.

The fourth priest to settle there was Amashsai son of Azarel. His ancestors were Ahzai, Meshillemoth, and Immer. [14]Altogether, there were 128 brave warriors from their clans, and their leader was Zabdiel son of Haggedolim.

Levites

[15]Several Levites settled in Jerusalem. First, there was Shemaiah son of Hasshub. His ancestors were Azrikam, Hashabiah, and Bunni.

[16]Next, there were Shabbethai and Jozabad, the Levite leaders in charge of the work outside the temple.

[17]Then there was Mattaniah son of Mica. His ancestors were Zabdi and Asaph. Mattaniah led the temple choir in the prayer of praise. Bakbukiah, who also settled in Jerusalem, was his assistant.

[r]**11.1** *asked God to show them*: The Hebrew text has "cast lots." These were made of wood or stone and were thrown on the ground by a priest or official to find out how and when to do something.
[s]**11.10** *son of Joiarib and the uncle of Jachin*: See 1 Chronicles 9.10-12; the Hebrew text has "son of Joiarib, Jachin."

11.1 *asked God to show them*: The Hebrew text has "cast lots." Lots were made of wood or stone and were thrown on the ground by a priest or official to find out how and when to do something. The outcome was not considered luck or simple chance, since the people believed that God guided which lot was chosen.

11.18,21 *holy city:* The temple mount in Jerusalem was known as the holy hill, mountain, or city after the exile. All of Ezra's and Nehemiah's work had been directed toward establishing Jerusalem as a city set apart for God.

11.23 *decided . . . king:* A reminder that the Jews were not politically free, but were ruled by the Persians, who had allowed them to return from exile in Babylonia.

Finally, there was Abda son of Shammua; his grandfather was Galal, and his great-grandfather was Jeduthun. ¹⁸Altogether, 284 Levites settled in the holy city.

Temple Guards and Others

¹⁹One hundred seventy-two temple guards settled in Jerusalem; their leaders were Akkub and Talmon. ²⁰The rest of the Israelites, including priests and Levites, lived on their own property in the other towns of Judah. ²¹But the temple workers lived in the section of Jerusalem known as Ophel, and the two men in charge of them were Ziha and Gishpa. ²²Uzzi son of Bani was the leader of the Levites in Jerusalem. His grandfather was Hashabiah, his great-grandfather was Mattaniah, and his great-great-grandfather was Mica. He belonged to the Asaph clan that was in charge of the music for the temple services, ²³though the daily choice of music and musicians was decided by royal decree of the Persian king. ²⁴The people of Israel were represented at the Persian court by Pethahiah son of Meshezabel from the Zerah clan of the Judah tribe.

The People in the Other Towns and Villages

²⁵Some of the people of Judah lived in the following towns near their farms: Kiriath-Arba, Dibon, Jekabzeel, ²⁶Jeshua, Moladah, Beth-Pelet, ²⁷Hazar-Shual, Beersheba, ²⁸Ziklag, Meconah, ²⁹Enrimmon, Zorah, Jarmuth, ³⁰Zanoah, Adullam, Lachish, and Azekah. In fact, they settled the towns from Beersheba in the south to Hinnom Valley in the north. ³¹The people of Benjamin lived in the towns of Geba, Michmash, Aija, Bethel with its nearby villages, ³²Anathoth, Nob, Ananiah, ³³Hazor, Ramah, Gittaim, ³⁴Hadid, Zeboim, Neballat, ³⁵Lod, and Ono, as well as in Craft Valley. ³⁶Several groups of Levites from the territory of Judah were sent to live among the people of Benjamin.

A List of Priests and Levites

12 Many priests and Levites had returned from Babylonia with Zerubbabel^t and Joshua as their leaders. Those priests were Seraiah, Jeremiah, Ezra, ²Amariah, Malluch, Hattush, ³Shecaniah, Rehum, Meremoth, ⁴Iddo, Ginnethoi, Abijah, ⁵Mijamin, Maadiah, Bilgah, ⁶Shemaiah, Joiarib, Jedaiah, ⁷Sallu, Amok, Hilkiah, and another Jedaiah. These were the leading priests and their assistants during the time of Joshua.^u

⁸The Levites who returned were Jeshua, Binnui, Kadmiel, Sherebiah, Judah, and Mattaniah. They and their assistants were responsible for the songs of praise, ⁹while Bakbukiah and Unno, together with their assistants, were responsible for the choral responses.

Descendants of Joshua the High Priest

¹⁰Joshua was the father of Joiakim, the grandfather of Eliashib, and the great-grandfather of Joiada. ¹¹Joiada was the father of Jonathan and the grandfather of Jaddua.

^t**12.1** *Zerubbabel:* Hebrew "Zerubbabel son of Shealtiel."   ^u**12.7** *Joshua:* Joshua the high priest and friend of Zerubbabel (see verse 1 and Haggai 1.1; 2.2).

Leaders of the Priestly Clans

[12]When Joiakim was high priest, the following priests were leaders of their clans: Meraiah of the Seraiah clan, Hananiah of Jeremiah, [13]Meshullam of Ezra, Jehohanan of Amariah, [14]Jonathan of Malluchi, Joseph of Shebaniah, [15]Adna of Harim, Helkai of Meraioth, [16]Zechariah of Iddo, Meshullam of Ginnethon, [17]Zichri of Abijah,[v] Piltai of Moadiah, [18]Shammua of Bilgah, Jehonathan of Shemaiah, [19]Mattenai of Joiarib, Uzzi of Jedaiah, [20]Kallai of Sallai, Eber of Amok, [21]Hashabiah of Hilkiah, and Nethanel of Jedaiah.

The Priestly and Levite Families

[22]During the time of the high priests Eliashib, Joiada, Johanan, and Jaddua, and including the time that Darius was king of Persia, a record was kept of the heads of the Levite and priestly families. [23]However, no official record was kept of the heads of the Levite clans after the death of Johanan,[w] the grandson of Eliashib.

[24]Hashabiah, Sherebiah, Jeshua son of Kadmiel,[x] and their assistants organized two choirs of Levites to offer praises to God, just as King David, the man of God, had commanded.

[25]Mattaniah, Bakbukiah, Obadiah, Meshullam, Talmon, and Akkub were responsible for guarding the storerooms near the temple gates.

[26]All of these men lived during the time of Joiakim[y] and during the time that I was governor and Ezra, a teacher of the Law of Moses, was priest.

Nehemiah Dedicates the City Wall

[27]When the city wall was dedicated, Levites from everywhere in Judah were invited to join in the celebration with songs of praise and with the music of cymbals, small harps, and other stringed instruments. [28-29]The Levite singers lived in villages around Jerusalem, and so they came from there, as well as from the villages around Netophah, Beth-Gilgal, Geba, and Azmaveth. [30]The priests and Levites held special ceremonies to make themselves holy, and then they did the same for the rest of the people and for the gates and walls of the city.

[31]I brought the leaders of Judah to the top of the city wall and put them in charge of the two groups that were to march around on top of the wall, singing praises to God. One group marched to the right in the direction of Garbage Gate. [32]Hoshaiah and half of the leaders followed them. [33]Then came the priests Azariah, Ezra, Meshullam, [34]Judah, Benjamin, Shemaiah, and Jeremiah, [35]all of them blowing trumpets. Next, there was Zechariah of the Asaph clan[z] [36]and his relatives, Shemaiah, Azarel, Milalai, Gilalai, Maai, Nethanel, Judah, and Hanani. They played musical instruments like those that had been played by David, the man of God. And they marched behind Ezra, the teacher of the Law. [37]When they reached Fountain Gate, they climbed the steps to David's City and went past his palace, before stopping at the Water Gate near the eastern wall of the city.

[38]The second group of singers marched

12.27 *When . . . dedicated:* It is not clear how long after the completion of the walls that this joyful dedication took place.

12.31 *wall:* The wall that Tobiah said would not support a fox now supports the joyful procession of two groups. One group marched counterclockwise on the southern and eastern wall. A second group marched clockwise. The two groups joined at the Gate of the Guard.

12.36 *Ezra:* The mention of Ezra in this verse may suggest that Nehemiah and Ezra were at work in the same period, but some scholars believe it is more likely that Ezra came several years later and finished the work Nehemiah had begun. A later editor of the text may have added Ezra's name in this verse to connect the work of these two reformers.

---

[v]**12.17** *of Abijah:* The Hebrew text adds " . . . of Miniamin." [w]**12.23** *death of Johanan:* Probably between 408 and 405 B.C., when Darius II died. [x]**12.24** *son of Kadmiel:* Or possibly "Binnui, Kadmiel" (see 10.9; 12.8). [y]**12.26** *Joiakim:* Hebrew "Joiakim son of Joshua son of Jozadak." [z]**12.35** *Zechariah of the Asaph clan:* Hebrew "Zechariah son of Jonathan son of Shemaiah son of Mattaniah son of Micaiah son of Zaccur son of Asaph."

● **12.45** *instructions . . . Solomon:* Reported as given by David in 1 Chronicles 23–26 and carried out by Solomon in 2 Chronicles 8.14.

● **13.1,2** *Ammonites . . . Moabites:* The Ammonites and Moabites were descendants of Lot, Abraham's nephew, and were frequent enemies of Israel (Num 22.2-11; 2 Sam 8.2,11,12; 12.26-31; 2 Kgs 3.4-27; 13.20; 1 Chr 20.1-3). Both nations were located east of Israel. **(See Map 3 on pg 1881.)**

● **13.2** *Balaam . . . curse:* See Num 22.1-6. King Balak of Moab hired Balaam to bring curses on the people of Israel. God, however, did not allow Balaam to deliver the curses (Num 22.12; 23.11; 24.10).

● **13.6** *thirty-second year:* Therefore, Nehemiah's term as governor lasted twelve years, from 445 to 433 B.C.

● **13.6** *ruled Babylonia:* Artaxerxes was actually the king of Persia. After they conquered the Babylonian Empire, the Persian kings adopted this grander title as well.

ᴄℝ Babylon

ᴄℝ Persia

along the wall in the opposite direction, and I followed them, together with the other half of the leaders of Judah. We went past Oven Tower, Broad Wall, [39]Ephraim Gate, Old Gate, Fish Gate, Hananel Tower, Hundred Tower, and on to Sheep Gate. Finally, we stopped at Gate of the Guard, [40]where we stood in front of the temple with the other group, praising God. In the group with me were half of the leaders, [41]as well as the priests Eliakim, Maaseiah, Miniamin, Micaiah, Elioenai, Zechariah, and Hananiah, who were blowing trumpets. [42]Maaseiah, Shemaiah, Eleazar, Uzzi, Jehohanan, Malchijah, Elam, and Ezer also stood there, as Jezrahiah led the singers. [43]God had made the people very happy, and so on that day they celebrated and offered many sacrifices. The women and children joined in the festivities, and joyful shouts could be heard far from the city of Jerusalem.

Preparation for Worship

[44]On that same day, some leaders were appointed to be responsible for the safekeeping of gifts for the temple and to be in charge of receiving the first part of the harvest and the ten percent of the crops and livestock that was offered to God. These same leaders also collected the part of crops that the Law of Moses taught was to be given to the Levites.

Everyone was pleased with the work of the priests and Levites, [45]when they performed the ceremonies to make people acceptable to worship God. And the singers and the temple guards did their jobs according to the instructions given by David and his son Solomon. [46]In fact, ever since the days of David and Asaph, there had been song leaders and songs of praise and worship. [47]During the time that Zerubbabel and I were in charge, everyone in Israel gave what they were supposed to give for the daily needs of the singers and temple guards from the Levi tribe. Then the Levites would give the priests their share from what they had received.

Foreigners Are Sent Away

13 On that day when the Law of Moses was read aloud to everyone, it was discovered that Ammonites and Moabites were forbidden to belong to the people of God. [2]This was because they had refused to give food and water to Israel and had hired Balaam[a] to call down a curse on them. However, our God turned the curse into a blessing. [3]Following the reading of the Law of Moses, the people of Israel started sending away anyone who had any foreign ancestors.

Nehemiah Makes Other Changes

[4]The priest Eliashib was a relative of Tobiah and had earlier been put in charge of the temple storerooms. [5]So he let Tobiah live in one of these rooms, where all kinds of things had been stored—the grain offerings, incense, utensils for the temple, as well as the tenth of the grain, wine, and olive oil that had been given for the use of the Levites, singers, and temple guards, and the gifts for the priests.

[6]This happened in the thirty-second year that Artaxerxes[b] ruled Babylonia. I was away from Jerusalem at the time, because I was visiting him. Later I received permission from the king [7]to return to Jerusalem. Only then did I find out that Eliashib had done this terrible thing of letting Tobiah have a room in the temple. [8]It

[a]**13.2** *Balaam:* See Numbers 22.1-6.   [b]**13.6** *Artaxerxes:* See the note at 1.1.

God had made the people very happy . . . and joyful shouts could be heard far from the city of Jerusalem. NEH 12.43

upset me so much that I threw out every bit of Tobiah's furniture. ⁹Then I ordered the room to be cleaned and the temple utensils, the grain offerings, and the incense to be brought back into the room.

¹⁰I also found out that the temple singers and several other Levites had returned to work on their farms, because they had not been given their share of the harvest. ¹¹I called the leaders together and angrily asked them, "Why is the temple neglected?" Then I told them to start doing their jobs. ¹²After this, everyone in Judah brought a tenth of their grain, wine, and olive oil to the temple storeroom. ¹³Finally, I appointed three men with good reputations to be in charge of what was brought there and to distribute it to the others. They were Shelemiah the priest, Zadok the teacher of the Law, and Pedaiah the Levite. Their assistant was Hanan, the son of Zaccur and the grandson of Mattaniah.

¹⁴I pray that my God will remember these good things that I have done for his temple and for those who worship there.

The Sabbath

¹⁵ I also noticed what the people of Judah were doing on the Sabbath. Not only were they trampling grapes to make wine, but they were harvesting their grain, grapes, figs, and other crops, and then loading these on donkeys to sell in Jerusalem. So I warned them not to sell food on the Sabbath. ¹⁶People who had moved to Jerusalem from the city of Tyre were bringing in fish and other things to sell there on the Sabbath. ¹⁷I got angry and said to the leaders of Judah, "This evil you are doing is an insult to the Sabbath! ¹⁸Didn't God punish us and this city because our ancestors did

these very same things? And here you are, about to make God furious again by disgracing the Sabbath!"

¹⁹I ordered the gates of Jerusalem to be closed on the eve of the Sabbath[c] and not to be opened until after the Sabbath had ended. Then I put some of my own men in charge of the gates to make certain that nothing was brought in on the Sabbath. ²⁰Once or twice some merchants spent the night outside Jerusalem with their goods. ²¹But I warned them, "If you do this again, I'll have you arrested." From then on, they did not come on the Sabbath. ²²I ordered the Levites to make themselves holy and to guard the gates on the Sabbath, so that it would be kept holy.

God is truly merciful, and I pray that he will treat me with kindness and bless me for doing this.

Mixed Marriages

²³I discovered that some Jewish men had married women from Ashdod, Ammon, and Moab. ²⁴About half of their children could not speak Hebrew—they spoke only the language of Ashdod or some other foreign language. ²⁵So in my anger, I called down curses on those men. I had them beaten and even pulled out the hair of some of them. Then I made them promise:

In the name of God we solemnly promise not to let our sons and daughters marry foreigners. ²⁶God dearly loved King Solomon of Israel and made him the greatest king on earth, but Solomon's foreign wives led him into sin. ²⁷So we will obey you and not rebel against our God by marrying foreign women.

²⁸Jehoiada, the son of the high priest

c13.19 *eve of the Sabbath:* The Jewish day began at sunset.

13.19 *eve of the Sabbath:* In the Jewish calendar, days begin at sunset, not at midnight or at sunrise as in other cultures.

13.26 *King Solomon:* Solomon, King David's son, who ruled from about 960 to 931 B.C.

Solomon

13.28 *Sanballat:* Sanballat was the governor of Samaria, Judah's neighbor to the north. He probably was a native of Beth-Horon. **(See Map 6 on pg 1884.)**

Eliashib, had a son who had married a daughter of Sanballat from Horon,[d] and I forced his son to leave.

²⁹I pray that God will punish them for breaking their priestly vows and disgracing the Levi tribe.

³⁰Then I made sure that the people were free from every foreign influence, and I as-signed duties for the priests and Levites. ³¹I also arranged for the people to bring fire-wood to the altar each day and for them to bring the first part of their harvest to the temple.

I pray that God will bless me for the good I have done.

[d]13.28 *Horon:* See the note at 2.10.

Reflection Questions About Nehemiah 1.1—13.31

1. What did Nehemiah do when he heard that the Israelites who had returned to Jerusalem had not begun to fix the walls and gates of the city (Neh 1.3,4; 2.4,5)?

2. After arriving in Jerusalem, what steps did Nehemiah take to see that work on the walls began (Neh 2.11-18)? How did he handle the trouble nearby enemies tried to stir up in order to stop the work on the walls (Neh 2.11-20; 4.6-23)?

3. What were some of the problems with the community itself in Jerusalem, and how did Nehemiah work to solve them (Neh 1.5-9; 5.1-19)?

4. What part did Ezra play in helping the community return to faithful worship and obedience to God (Neh 8)? How did the people show that they were truly sorry for their sins and meant to keep their promises to God (Neh 9.1-5,38; 10.28-39)?

5. What leadership qualities do you see in Nehemiah? When choosing or evaluating leaders in your own life, are these the qualities you look for? Why or why not?

6. Nehemiah had to face serious opposition at each stage of his mission. How might Nehemiah's example help you face the forces of opposition in your life?

esther

*Fancy dinners both begin and end this story, and no
less than eight other banquets play a role in the middle.
Read this "feast for the eyes" to learn why Jewish people
still celebrate the exciting party of Purim.*

WHAT MAKES ESTHER SPECIAL?

ESTHER is one of the most dramatic stories in the Bible—full of plot twists and interesting characters. The hero of the story is a woman, which was un-usual for the time this story was written. In this tale, Esther is able to hide her Jewish identity from the Persian court, and risks her own life to save her people.

The author's use of names, dates, and ideas shows that ESTHER is more like a modern historical novel than a history book. For example, the Persians were well known for accepting other religions, not for giving orders to kill people for their beliefs. Curi-ously, ESTHER is the only biblical book that does not mention God directly. God's presence, however, may be seen as the guiding force that makes Esther queen and protects the Jewish people.

ESTHER was written primarily to explain the Jewish festival of Purim celebrated in the month of Adar, which is in mid-February/mid-March. Purim is a lively party where celebrants are encouraged to let themselves go in carefree enjoyment of the moment. The Talmud, one of Judaism's central religious books, dating from the fifth century A.D., instructs faithful Jews to, "Drink wine until you can no longer distinguish between 'Blessed be Mordecai' and 'Cursed be Haman.'" Mordecai and Haman are two of the main characters in the story. ESTHER tells the story of Jews who triumphed in spite of plots against them. The book of ESTHER survives in its original He-brew and in a Greek version that made additions to the story. This Greek version is often found in the Apocrypha, or secondary books of the Bible.

WHAT'S THE STORY BEHIND THE SCENE?

King Cyrus the Great of Persia defeated Babylonia in 538 B.C. He gave Jews, who had been forced to live in Babylonia for 70 years, a chance to go home. Yet many of the Jews liked their new home better than the ruins of Jerusalem and decided to stay where they were. In this story, Mordecai and his cousin Es-ther represent those who stayed. Some scholars have suggested that the experiences of Esther and Mordecai during the reign of Ahasuerus (also called Xerxes I, 485–465 B.C.), retell an old Babylonian myth for a new purpose. In the old story, Marduk, the Babylonian god who is the hero of the myth (re-named Mordecai here), and Ishtar, the Babylonian goddess of love (renamed Esther in this story), de-feat the evil gods that oppose them (Haman and his followers in the story). Of course, the biblical book carefully avoids calling Mordecai, Haman, or Esther "gods," but it still emphasizes the triumph of good over evil.

HOW IS ESTHER CONSTRUCTED?

Esther can be outlined in the following way:

The queen disobeys the king (1.1-22)
Mordecai, Esther, and Haman (2.1—3.6)
The Jews are in danger (3.7—4.17)
Esther uses her influence (5.1—7.10)
The Jews destroy their enemies (8.1—9.19)
The Festival of Purim (9.20—10.3)

The story of Esther resembles a historical novel or wisdom story. It tells how the beautiful young Jewish woman Esther, who becomes Queen of Persia, is able to use her position to stop a plot to kill all the Jews in the Persian Kingdom. Other characters who play important roles in this exciting story are Xerxes, the easily influenced and quick-tempered king of Persia; Mordecai, Esther's cousin, who saves the king's life only to find his own life in jeopardy; and Haman, the king's highest official, who plots the death of every Jew in the kingdom. The story explains the reason for the Jewish festival of Purim. Although some scholars have pointed out some historical inconsistencies in the book of Esther, they acknowledge that it demonstrates significant understanding of Persian customs. The book also reflects the experience of Jews who had lived in exile in foreign lands, trying to maintain their religion and customs while avoiding persecution. Although the book of Esther doesn't mention God, the story suggests the constant presence of a protecting God, who guides his people through times of severe ethnic hatred.

Outline

Queen Vashti
Disobeys King Xerxes

1 ¹⁻²King Xerxes[a] of Persia lived in his capital city of Susa[b] and ruled 127 provinces from India to Ethiopia.[c] ³During the third year of his rule, Xerxes gave a big dinner for all his officials and officers. The governors and leaders of the provinces were also invited, and even the commanders of the Persian and Median armies came. ⁴For 180 days he showed off his wealth and spent a lot of money to impress his guests with the greatness of his kingdom.

⁵At the end of this time, King Xerxes gave another dinner and invited everyone in the city of Susa, no matter who they were. The eating and drinking lasted seven days in the beautiful palace gardens. ⁶The area was decorated with blue and white cotton curtains tied back with purple linen cords that ran through silver rings fastened to marble columns. Couches of gold and silver rested on pavement that had all kinds of designs made from costly bright-colored stones and marble and mother-of-pearl.

⁷The guests drank from gold cups, and each cup had a different design. The king was generous ⁸and said to them, "Drink all you want!" Then he told his servants, "Keep their cups full."

⁹While the men were enjoying themselves, Queen Vashti gave the women a big dinner inside the royal palace.

¹⁰By the seventh day, King Xerxes was feeling happy because of so much wine. And he asked his seven personal servants, Mehuman, Biztha, Harbona, Bigtha, Abagtha, Zethar, and Carkas, ¹¹to bring Queen Vashti to him. The king wanted her to wear her crown and let his people and his

[a]1.1,2 *Xerxes*: The Hebrew text has "Ahasuerus," who was better known as King Xerxes I (485–465 B.C.).   [b]1.1,2 *in his capital city of Susa*: Or "in his royal fortress in the city of Susa." Susa was a city east of Babylon and a winter home for Persian kings.   [c]1.1,2 *Ethiopia*: The Hebrew text has "Cush," which was a region south of Egypt that included parts of the present countries of Ethiopia and Sudan.

1.17 *The women in the kingdom will hear about this:* In biblical times, life was very difficult for women and children who did not have the support of a husband or father. At this time, the custom was that wives, even queens, had to obey their husbands without question. Queen Vashti's punishment for refusing to appear before the king would have seemed logical to the first readers of ESTHER, who were used to this status of women. It is not clear whether Persian laws could never be changed, and this is not the only book of the Bible where the idea is mentioned (Dan 6.8).

2.5 *Mordecai . . . Jair . . . Shimei:* Mordecai is a Jew whose name may refer to the Babylonian god, Marduk, the original character in this story. Mordecai's father, Jair, and his grandfather, Shimei, are named so that readers will know that Mordecai was connected to the twelve tribes of Israel.

Israel

2.7 *Esther:* Esther is a Jew whose name may refer to the Babylonian goddess of love, Ishtar, the Persian word for star. Her Hebrew name, Hadassah, means "myrtle." The myrtle tree is an evergreen shrub with fragrant leaves and beautiful white flowers. In ancient times, evergreens were symbols of fertility and renewal.

Nebuchadnezzar

officials see how beautiful she was. **12**The king's servants told Queen Vashti what he had said, but she refused to go to him, and this made him terribly angry.

13-14 The king called in the seven highest officials of Persia and Media. They were Carshena, Shethar, Admatha, Tarshish, Meres, Marsena, and Memucan. These men were very wise and understood all the laws and customs of the country, and the king always asked them what they thought about such matters.

15The king said to them, "Queen Vashti refused to come to me when I sent my servants for her. What does the law say I should do about that?"

16Then Memucan told the king and the officials:

Your Majesty, Queen Vashti has not only embarrassed you, but she has insulted your officials and everyone else in all the provinces.

17The women in the kingdom will hear about this, and they will refuse to respect their husbands. They will say, "If Queen Vashti doesn't obey her husband, why should we?" **18**Before this day is over, the wives of the officials of Persia and Media will find out what Queen Vashti has done, and they will refuse to obey their husbands. They won't respect their husbands, and their husbands will be angry with them.

19Your Majesty, if you agree, you should write for the Medes and Persians a law that can never be changed. This law would keep Queen Vashti from ever seeing you again. Then you could let someone who respects you be queen in her place.

20When the women in your great kingdom hear about this new law,

they will respect their husbands, no matter if they are rich or poor.

21King Xerxes and his officials liked what Memucan had said, **22**and he sent letters to all of his provinces. Each letter was written in the language of the province to which it was sent, and it said that husbands should be in charge of their wives and children.

Esther Becomes Queen

2 After a while, King Xerxes got over being angry. But he kept thinking about what Vashti had done and the law that he had written because of her. **2**Then the king's personal servants said:

Your Majesty, a search must be made to find you some beautiful young women. **3**You can select officers in every province to bring them to the place where you keep your wives in the capital city of Susa. Put your servant Hegai in charge of them since that is his job. He can see to it that they are given the proper beauty treatments. **4**Then let the young woman who pleases you most take Vashti's place as queen.

King Xerxes liked these suggestions, and he followed them.

5At this time a Jew named Mordecai was living in Susa. His father was Jair, and his grandfather Shimei was the son of Kish from the tribe of Benjamin. **6**Kish^d was one of the people that Nebuchadnezzar had taken from Jerusalem, when he took King Jeconiah of Judah to Babylonia. **7**Mordecai had a very beautiful cousin named Esther, whose Hebrew name was Hadassah. He had raised her as his own daughter, after her father and mother died. **8**When the king ordered the search

^d**2.6** *Kish:* Or "Mordecai." The Hebrew text has "He."

for beautiful women, many were taken to the king's palace in Susa, and Esther was one of them.

Hegai was put in charge of all the women, [9]and from the first day, Esther was his favorite. He began her beauty treatments at once. He also gave her plenty of food and seven special maids from the king's palace, and they had the best rooms.

[10]Mordecai had warned Esther not to tell anyone that she was a Jew, and she obeyed him. [11]He was anxious to see how Esther was getting along and to learn what had happened to her. So each day he would walk back and forth in front of the court where the women lived.

[12]The young women were given beauty treatments for one whole year. The first six months their skin was rubbed with olive oil and myrrh, and the last six months it was treated with perfumes and cosmetics. Then each of them spent the night alone with King Xerxes. [13]When a young woman went to the king, she could wear whatever clothes or jewelry she chose from the women's living quarters. [14]In the evening she would go to the king, and the following morning she would go to the place where his wives stayed after being with him. There a man named Shaashgaz was in charge of the king's wives.[e] Only the ones the king wanted and asked for by name could go back to the king.

[15-16]Xerxes had been king for seven years when Esther's turn came to go to him during Tebeth,[f] the tenth month of the year. Everyone liked Esther. The king's personal servant Hegai was in charge of the women, and Esther trusted Hegai and asked him what she ought to take with her.[g]

[17]Xerxes liked Esther more than he did any of the other young women. None of them pleased him as much as she did, and he immediately fell in love with her and crowned her queen in place of Vashti. [18]In honor of Esther he gave a big dinner for his leaders and officials. Then he declared a holiday[h] everywhere in his kingdom and gave expensive gifts.

Mordecai Saves the King's Life

[19]When the young women were brought together again, Esther's cousin Mordecai had become a palace official. [20]He had told Esther never to tell anyone that she was a Jew, and she obeyed him, just as she had always done.

[21]Bigthana and Teresh were the two men who guarded King Xerxes' rooms, but they got angry with the king and decided to kill him. [22]Mordecai found out about their plans and asked Queen Esther to tell the king what he had found out. [23]King Xerxes learned that Mordecai's report was true, and he had the two men hanged. Then the king had all of this written down in his record book as he watched.

Haman Plans To Destroy the Jews

3 Later, King Xerxes promoted Haman the son of Hammedatha to the highest position in his kingdom. Haman was a

---

[e]**2.14** *wives:* This translates a Hebrew word for women who were legally bound to a man, but without the full privileges of a wife. [f]**2.15,16** *Tebeth:* The tenth month of the Hebrew calendar, from about mid-December to mid-January. [g]**2.15,16** *her:* The Hebrew text adds, "Esther was the daughter of Abihail and was the cousin of Mordecai, who had adopted her after her parents died" (see verse 7). [h]**2.18** *holiday:* The Hebrew expression refers to a certain amount of time when the people did not have to pay their regular taxes.

2.9,10 *gave her plenty of food . . . not to tell anyone that she was a Jew:* Esther does not tell anyone she is Jewish, probably for fear of being persecuted. The Jewish faith had many laws about how to worship and what to eat that would have made it difficult for Esther to hide her faith. It is likely she may not have openly practiced these laws.

Purity (Clean and Unclean)

2.21 *King Xerxes' rooms . . . decided to kill him:* These would be the king's private rooms, including his bedroom. That meant that the guards, Bigthana and Teresh, could easily get to the king. This plan failed but years later a similar plan was actually used to kill Xerxes.

2.23 *hanged:* Hanging was a common form of execution in ancient Persia. In some ways, it resembled a crucifixion because when hanged, a person was impaled on a stake or nailed to a tree and left hanging from it.

3.7 *twelfth year:* Esther was crowned queen in the seventh year of King Xerxes' rule, so she has been queen for more than four years.

3.8 *some people:* Haman means the Jews, but it is not clear that the king knows that. Haman is bending the truth about the Jews, who did indeed have customs that were different from those of other groups in Xerxes' kingdom. The Jewish religion required that the Jews follow the law that God gave to Moses above all other laws. This did not necessarily mean that the Jews refused to obey all of Xerxes' laws.

Law

3.10 *official ring:* When a king gave his official ring to someone it was the same thing as giving his official signature or permission.

4.1 *put on sackcloth:* Sometimes people wore sackcloth or sat in dust or ashes to show how sorry they were for their sins or to show their grief. A person wearing sackcloth could only go as far as the city gate (outside the palace gate) because they were considered unclean.

Purity (Clean and Unclean)

descendant of Agag,[i] [2]and the king had given orders for his officials at the royal gate to honor Haman by kneeling down to him. All of them obeyed except Mordecai. [3]When the other officials asked Mordecai why he disobeyed the king's command, [4]he said, "Because I am a Jew." They spoke to him for several days about kneeling down, but he still refused to obey. Finally, they reported this to Haman, to find out if he would let Mordecai get away with it.

[5]Haman was furious to learn that Mordecai refused to kneel down and honor him. [6]And when he found out that Mordecai was a Jew, he knew that killing only Mordecai was not enough. Every Jew in the whole kingdom had to be killed.

[7]It was now the twelfth year of the rule of King Xerxes. During Nisan,[j] the first month of the year, Haman said, "Find out the best time for me to do this."[k] The time chosen was Adar,[l] the twelfth month.

[8]Then Haman went to the king and said:

Your Majesty, there are some people who live all over your kingdom and won't have a thing to do with anyone else. They have customs that are different from everyone else's, and they refuse to obey your laws. We would be better off to get rid of them! [9]Why not give orders for all of them to be killed? I can promise that you will get tons of silver for your treasury.

[10]The king handed his official ring to Haman, who hated the Jews, and the king told him, [11]"Do what you want with those people! You can keep their money."

[12]On the thirteenth day of Nisan, Haman called in the king's secretaries and ordered them to write letters in every language used in the kingdom. The letters were written in the name of the king and sealed by using the king's own ring.[m] At once they were sent to the king's highest officials, the governors of each province, and the leaders of the different nations in the kingdom of Xerxes.

[13]The letters were taken by messengers to every part of the kingdom, and this is what was said in the letters:

On the thirteenth day of Adar, the twelfth month, all Jewish men, women, and children are to be killed. And their property is to be taken.

[14-15]King Xerxes gave orders for these letters to be posted where they could be seen by everyone all over the kingdom. The king's command was obeyed, and one of the letters was read aloud to the people in the walled city of Susa. Then the king and Haman sat down to drink together, but no one in the city[n] could figure out what was going on.

Mordecai Asks for Esther's Help

4 When Mordecai heard about the letter, he tore his clothes in sorrow and put on sackcloth. Then he covered his head with ashes and went through the city, crying and weeping. [2]But he could go only as far as the palace gate, because no one wearing sackcloth was allowed inside the palace. [3]In every province where the king's orders

[i]**3.1** *Agag:* Agag was a king who had fought against the Jews long before the time of Esther (see 1 Samuel 15.1-33). [j]**3.7** *Nisan:* The first month of the Hebrew calendar, from about mid-March to mid-April. [k]**3.7** *Find out . . . do this:* The Hebrew text has "cast lots," which were pieces of wood or stone used to find out how and when to do something. For "lots" the Hebrew text uses the Babylonian word "purim." [l]**3.7** *Adar:* The twelfth month of the Hebrew calendar, from about mid-February to mid-March. [m]**3.12** *king's own ring:* Melted wax was used to seal a letter, and while the wax was still soft, the king's ring was pressed in the wax to show that the letter was official. [n]**3.14,15** *walled city . . . city:* Or "royal fortress . . . rest of the city."

were read, the Jews cried and mourned, and they went without eating.º Many of them even put on sackcloth and sat in ashes.

⁴When Esther's servant girls and her other servants told her what Mordecai was doing, she became very upset and sent Mordecai some clothes to wear in place of the sackcloth. But he refused to take them.

⁵Esther had a servant named Hathach, who had been given to her by the king. So she called him in and said, "Find out what's wrong with Mordecai and why he's acting this way."

⁶Hathach went to Mordecai in the city square in front of the palace gate, ⁷and Mordecai told him everything that had happened. He also told him how much money Haman had promised to add to the king's treasury, if all the Jews were killed.

⁸Mordecai gave Hathach a copy of the orders for the murder of the Jews and told him that these had been read in Susa. He said, "Show this to Esther and explain what it means. Ask her to go to the king and beg him to have pity on her people, the Jews!"

⁹Hathach went back to Esther and told her what Mordecai had said. ¹⁰She answered, "Tell Mordecai ¹¹there is a law about going in to see the king, and all his officials and his people know about this law. Anyone who goes in to see the king without being invited by him will be put to death. The only way that anyone can be saved is for the king to hold out the gold scepter to that person. And it's been thirty days since he has asked for me."

¹²When Mordecai was told what Esther had said, ¹³he sent back this reply, "Don't think that you will escape being killed with the rest of the Jews, just because you live in the king's palace. ¹⁴If you don't speak up now, we will somehow get help, but you and your family will be killed. It could be that you were made queen for a time like this!"

¹⁵Esther sent a message to Mordecai, saying, ¹⁶"Bring together all the Jews in Susa and tell them to go without eating for my sake! Don't eat or drink for three days and nights. My servant girls and I will do the same. Then I will go in to see the king, even if it means I must die."

¹⁷Mordecai did everything Esther told him to do.

Esther Invites the King and Haman to a Dinner

5 Three days later, Esther dressed in her royal robes and went to the inner court of the palace in front of the throne. The king was sitting there, facing the open doorway. ²He was happy to see Esther, and he held out the gold scepter to her.

When Esther came up and touched the tip of the scepter, ³the king said, "Esther, what brings you here? Just ask, and I will give you as much as half of my kingdom."

⁴Esther answered, "Your Majesty, please come with Haman to a dinner I will prepare for you later today."

⁵The king said to his servants, "Hurry and get Haman, so we can accept Esther's invitation."

The king and Haman went to Esther's dinner, ⁶and while they were drinking wine, the king asked her, "What can I do for you? Just ask, and I will give you as much as half of my kingdom."

⁷⁻⁸Esther replied, "Your Majesty, if you really care for me and are willing to do what I want, please come again tomorrow with Haman to the dinner I will prepare

º4.3 *went without eating*: The Israelites would sometimes go without eating (also called "fasting") in times of great sorrow or danger.

● 4.4 *she . . . sent Mordecai some clothes*: Esther sent Mordecai clothes so that he could enter the palace and talk to her. He showed his distress to her by wearing the sackcloth and urged her to help the Jews from her special position at court.

● 4.11 *gold scepter*: A scepter is the official staff of a king or queen and symbolizes his or her authority. Esther is afraid that if she tries to see the king without being invited by him, she will be suspected of putting him in danger and will be killed.

■ 4.14 *If you don't speak*: Mordecai warns Esther that she cannot avoid danger by avoiding the king. He suggests that God may have made Esther queen so that she could help her people, the Jews.

Queen Esther sent a message saying, *"I will go in to see the king, even if it means I must die."* ESTH 4.16

5.14 *gallows:* Usually a person would be hung from a tree or stake. If a very tall gallows is used to hang Mordecai, many people will see it from a distance, and everyone will know that Haman has had his revenge.

6.8 *one of your own robes . . . horses with a fancy headdress:* To put one's own robe or fine clothes on a person was a sign of honor in ancient times. Likewise, the horse was a highly valued symbol of royal authority, and the horse's fancy headdress was intended to impress crowds.

6.10 *Mordecai the Jew:* The fact that King Xerxes would choose to honor a Jew in this way suggests that he may not have realized that it was the Jews he had ordered killed.

for you. At that time I will answer Your Majesty's question."

Haman Plans To Kill Mordecai

[9]Haman was feeling great as he left. But when he saw Mordecai at the palace gate, he noticed that Mordecai did not stand up or show him any respect. This made Haman really angry, [10]but he did not say a thing.

When Haman got home, he called together his friends and his wife Zeresh [11]and started bragging about his great wealth and all his sons. He told them the many ways that the king had honored him and how all the other officials and leaders had to respect him. [12]Haman added, "That's not all! Besides the king himself, I'm the only person Queen Esther invited for dinner. She has also invited the king and me to dinner tomorrow. [13]But none of this makes me happy, as long as I see that Jew Mordecai serving the king."

[14]Haman's wife and friends said to him, "Have a gallows built about 75 feet high, and tomorrow morning ask the king to hang Mordecai there. Then later, you can have dinner with the king and enjoy yourself."

This seemed like a good idea to Haman, and he had the gallows built.

The King Honors Mordecai

6 That night the king could not sleep, and he had a servant read him the records of what had happened since he had been king. [2]When the servant read how Mordecai had kept Bigthana and Teresh from killing the king, [3]the king asked, "What has been done to reward Mordecai for this?"

"Nothing, Your Majesty!" the king's servants replied.

[4]About this time, Haman came in to ask the king to have Mordecai hanged on the gallows he had built. The king saw him and asked, "Who is that man waiting in front of the throne room?"

[5]The king's servants answered, "Your Majesty, it is Haman."

"Tell him to come in," the king commanded.

[6]When Haman entered the room, the king asked him, "What should I do for a man I want to honor?"

Haman was sure that he was the one the king wanted to honor. [7]So he replied, "Your Majesty, if you wish to honor a man, [8]get someone to bring him one of your own robes and one of your own horses with a fancy headdress. [9]Tell one of your highest officials place your robe on this man and lead him through the streets on your horse, while someone shouts, 'This is how the king honors a man!'"

[10]The king replied, "Hurry and do just what you have said! Don't forget a thing. Get the robe and the horse for Mordecai the Jew, who serves as one of the king's officials!"

[11]Haman got the king's robe and put it on Mordecai. He led him through the city on the horse and shouted as he went, "This is how the king honors a man!"

[12]Afterwards, Mordecai returned to his duties in the king's palace, and Haman hurried home, hiding his face in shame. [13]Haman told his wife and friends what had happened. Then his wife and his advisors said, "If Mordecai is a Jew, this is just the beginning of your troubles! You will end up a ruined man." [14]They were still talking, when the king's servants came and quickly took Haman to the dinner that Esther had prepared.

Haman Is Punished

7 The king and Haman were dining with Esther [2]and drinking wine during the second dinner, when the king again said, "Esther, what can I do for you? Just ask, and I will give you as much as half of my kingdom!"

[3]Esther answered, "Your Majesty, if you really care for me and are willing to help, you can save me and my people. That's what I really want, [4]because a reward has been promised to anyone who kills my people. Your Majesty, if we were merely going to be sold as slaves, I would not have bothered you."P

[5]"Who would dare to do such a thing?" the king asked.

[6]Esther replied, "That evil Haman is the one out to get us!"

Haman was terrified, as he looked at the king and the queen.

[7]The king was so angry that he got up, left his wine, and went out into the palace garden.

Haman realized that the king had already decided what to do with him, and he stayed and begged Esther to save his life.

[8]Just as the king came back into the room, Haman got down on his knees beside Esther, who was lying on the couch. The king shouted, "Now you're even trying to rape my queen here in my own palace!"

As soon as the king said this, his servants covered Haman's head. [9]Then Harbona, one of the king's personal servants, said, "Your Majesty, Haman built a gallows 75 feet high beside his house, so he could hang Mordecai on it. And Mordecai is the very one who spoke up and saved your life."

"Hang Haman from his own gallows!"

the king commanded. [10]At once, Haman was hanged on the gallows he had built to hang Mordecai, and the king calmed down.

A Happy Ending for the Jews

8 Before the end of the day, King Xerxes gave Esther everything that had belonged to Haman, the enemy of the Jews. Esther told the king that Mordecai was her cousin. So the king made Mordecai one of his highest officials [2]and gave him the royal ring that Haman had worn. Then Esther put Mordecai in charge of Haman's property.

[3]Once again Esther went to speak to the king. This time she fell down at his feet, crying and begging, "Please stop Haman's evil plan to have the Jews killed!" [4]King Xerxes held out the golden scepter to Esther, [5]and she got up and said, "Your Majesty, I know that you will do the right thing and that you really love me. Please stop what Haman has planned. He has already sent letters demanding that the Jews in all your provinces be killed, [6]and I can't bear to see my people and my own relatives destroyed."

[7]King Xerxes then said to Esther and Mordecai, "I have already ordered Haman to be hanged and his house given to Esther, because of his evil plans to kill the Jews. [8]I now give you permission to make a law that will save the lives of your people. You may use my ring to seal the law, so that it can never be changed."

[9]On the twenty-third day of Sivan,q the third month, the king's secretaries wrote the law. They obeyed Mordecai and wrote to the Jews, the rulers, the governors, and the officials of all 127 provinces from India

7.8 got down on his knees . . . covered Haman's head: It was a common custom in the ancient world to bow down at someone's feet when asking for mercy. It was also the custom to lie on one's side while eating, as Esther does. When Haman falls down by Esther's couch, the king interprets it as an assault on the queen.

7.9 gallows: Haman's plan to destroy Mordecai is now used to destroy Haman instead. ESTHER contains many such "ironies" and changes in fortune.

8.1 King Xerxes gave Esther everything that had belonged to Haman: The king had the power to take all the property of any criminal who, like Haman, was sentenced to death.

8.1,2 Mordecai: Mordecai's new position allows him to see and talk to the king without being called on first. Mordecai now has the privileges and the ring that the king had given Haman.

8.5-8 He has already sent . . . I have already ordered . . . never be changed: Out of respect for the king Esther suggests that Haman was the only one responsible for the letters ordering the killing of all the Jews, and appeals to him to do the right thing by her and her people. He then allows Esther and Mordecai to write a new law to save the Jews. This new law will be as harsh as Haman's since the first law is still in effect. Only with this second law will the Jews be able to stop their enemies.

P7.4 *I would . . . bothered you:* One possible meaning for the difficult Hebrew text.   q8.9 *Sivan:* The third month of the Hebrew calendar, from about mid-May to mid-June.

8.14-15 *purple cloth:* At this time, a person's clothes were a sign of that person's place in society. Some colors, like purple, were rare and expensive to produce, and were only worn by the privileged.

9.1 *Adar:* The thirteenth day of Adar is noted because it will be important to the dating of the festival of Purim.

9.13-19 *let the Jews in Susa . . . a joyful holiday:* It seems odd that there would be so many enemies for the Jews to destroy in Susa. Earlier, the story says that the citizens of Susa "shouted and cheered" when they heard the law that saved the Jews. The writer may have been trying to find a way to explain why during his time the Jews in the villages were celebrating Purim on one day (the fourteenth day of Adar, 9.16-17) and the Jews in Susa were celebrating it on another day (the fifteenth day of Adar, 9.18).

to Ethiopia.ᵣ The letters were written in every language used in the kingdom, including the Jewish language. **10**They were written in the name of King Xerxes and sealed with his ring. Then they were taken by messengers who rode the king's finest and fastest horses.

11-13 In these letters the king said:

On the thirteenth day of Adar,ˢ the twelfth month, the Jews in every city and province will be allowed to get together and defend themselves. They may destroy any army that attacks them, and they may kill all of their enemies, including women and children. They may also take everything that belongs to their enemies.

A copy of this law is to be posted in every province and read by everyone.

14-15 Then the king ordered his messengers to take their fastest horses and deliver the law as quickly as possible to every province. When Mordecai left, he was wearing clothes fit for a king. He wore blue and white robes, a large gold crown, and a cape made of fine linen and purple cloth.

After the law was announced in Susa, everyone shouted and cheered, **16**and the Jews were no longer afraid. In fact, they were very happy and felt that they had won a victory.

17In every province and city where the law was sent, the Jews had parties and celebrated. Many of the people in the provinces accepted the Jewish religion, because they were now afraid of the Jews.

The Jews Destroy Their Enemies

9 The first law that the king had made was to be followed on the thirteenth day of Adar,ᵗ the twelfth month. This was the very day that the enemies of the Jews had hoped to do away with them. But the Jews turned things around, **2**and in the cities of every province they came together to attack their enemies. Everyone was afraid of the Jews, and no one could do anything to oppose them.

3The leaders of the provinces, the rulers, the governors, and the court officials were afraid of Mordecai and took sides with the Jews. **4**Everyone in the provinces knew that the king had promoted him and had given him a lot of power.

5The Jews took their swords and did away with their enemies, without showing any mercy. **6-10**They killed 500 people in Susa,ᵘ but they did not take anything that belonged to the ones they killed. Haman had been one of the worst enemies of the Jews, and ten of his sons were among those who were killed. Their names were Parshandatha, Dalphon, Aspatha, Poratha, Adalia, Aridatha, Parmashta, Arisai, Aridai, and Vaizatha.

11Later that day, someone told the king how many people had been killed in Susa.ᵛ **12**Then he told Esther, "Five hundred people, including Haman's ten sons, have been killed in Susa alone. If that many were killed here, what must have happened in the provinces? Is there anything else you want done? Just tell me, and it will be done."

13Esther answered, "Your Majesty, please let the Jews in Susa fight to defend themselves tomorrow, just as they did today. And order the bodies of Haman's ten sons to be hanged in public."

14King Xerxes did what Esther had requested, and the bodies of Haman's sons

ᵣ**8.9** *Ethiopia:* See the note at 1.1,2.   ˢ**8.11-13** *Adar:* See the note at 3.7.   ᵗ**9.1** *Adar:* See the note at 3.7.   ᵘ**9.6-10** *in Susa:* Or "in the royal fortress in Susa."   ᵛ**9.11** *in Susa:* Or "in the royal fortress in Susa."

were hung in Susa. **15**Then on the fourteenth day of Adar the Jews of the city got together and killed 300 more people. But they still did not take anything that belonged to their enemies.

16-17 On the thirteenth day of Adar, the Jews in the provinces had come together to defend themselves. They killed 75,000 of their enemies, but the Jews did not take anything that belonged to the ones they killed. Then on the fourteenth day of the month the Jews celebrated with a feast.

18On the fifteenth day of the month the Jews in Susa held a holiday and celebrated, after killing their enemies on the thirteenth and the fourteenth. **19**This is why the Jews in the villages now celebrate on the fourteenth day of the month. It is a joyful holiday that they celebrate by feasting and sending gifts of food to each other.

The Festival of Purim

20Mordecai wrote down everything that had happened. Then he sent letters to the Jews everywhere in the provinces **21**and told them:

Each year you must celebrate on both the fourteenth and the fifteenth of Adar, **22**the days when we Jews defeated our enemies. Remember this month as a time when our sorrow was turned to joy, and celebration took the place of crying. Celebrate by having parties and by giving to the poor and by sharing gifts of food with each other.

23They followed Mordecai's instructions and set aside these two days every year as a time of celebration.

The Reason for the Festival of Purim

24Haman was the son of Hammedatha and a descendant of Agag. He hated the Jews so much that he planned to destroy them, but he wanted to find out the best time to do it. So he cast lots.**w**

25Esther went to King Xerxes and asked him to save her people. Then the king gave written orders for Haman and his sons to be punished in the same terrible way that Haman had in mind for the Jews. So they were hanged. **26**Mordecai's letter had said that the Jews must celebrate for two days because of what had happened to them. This time of celebration is called Purim,**x** which is the Hebrew word for the lots that were cast. **27**Now every year the Jews set aside these two days for having parties and celebrating, just as they were told to do. **28**From now on, all Jewish families must remember to celebrate Purim on these two days each year.

29Queen Esther, daughter of Abihail, wanted to give full authority to Mordecai's letter about the Festival of Purim, and with his help she wrote a letter about the feast. **30**Copies of this letter were sent to Jews in the 127 provinces of King Xerxes. In the letter they said:

We pray that all of you will live in peace and safety.

31You and your descendants must always remember to celebrate Purim at the time and in the way that we have said. You must also follow the instructions that we have given you about mourning and going without eating.**y**

9.26 *Purim*: The Jewish festival of Purim got its name from "purim," which is the Babylonian term for the lots that Haman used to determine on which day he should have the Jews killed. Instead, fortunes changed in favor of the Jews, so the Jews survived and their enemies were destroyed. Purim is celebrated each year on the 14th and 15th of Adar, which is about March 1. Purim is a lively festival that is still celebrated by Jews around the world today. It is preceded by a day of fasting. On Purim, ESTHER is read in synagogues. Whenever the villain Haman's name is read out, children are encouraged to drown out the sound of it with noisemakers. **(See the chart Pilgrimage Festivals on pg 1799.)**

---

w9.24 *cast lots*: See the note at 3.7.   **x**9.26 *Purim*: The Jewish festival of Purim got its name from "purim," which is the Babylonian name for the lots that Haman used. Purim is celebrated each year on the fourteenth and fifteenth of Adar, which is about the first of March.   **y**9.31 *going without eating*: See the note at 4.3.

Mordecai sent a letter to his fellow Jews saying, "Remember . . . when our sorrow was turned to joy, and celebration took the place of crying." ESTH 9.22

10.2 *record books:* We do not know if the writer had such records to use in writing the book of ESTHER.

³²These laws about Purim are written by the authority of Queen Esther.

The Greatness of Xerxes and Mordecai

10 King Xerxes made everyone in his kingdom pay taxes, even those in lands across the sea. ²All the great and famous things that King Xerxes did are written in the record books of the kings of Media and Persia. These records also tell about the honors that the king gave to Mordecai. ³Next to the king himself, Mordecai was the highest official in the kingdom. He was a popular leader of the Jews, because he helped them in many ways and would even speak to the king on their behalf.

Reflection Questions About Esther 1.1—10.3

1. What role do dinners, banquets, and luxury play in the story? What role do their opposites have: Mordecai's sackcloth, Esther's fasting?

2. In this story two women, Esther and Vashti, gain and lose their crowns. One is originally an orphan who ends up queen. The other starts out as queen, but returns to the harem. How does each use her position to get what she wants? Where in the book do you see women thinking for themselves, influencing and even disobeying their husbands?

3. What events in modern history or situations in today's society did you think of when you read the story of Esther? What groups of people in our times do you think have had to fight off prejudices to keep their identity?

4. ESTHER tells about the origins of the Jewish holiday of Purim (9.20-28). Do you know anyone who celebrates this holiday? If so, ask them what this festival means to them. How does understanding the holiday help to understand the book that inspired it?

5. There is no reference to God in the entire book of ESTHER. Why do you think, then, that it is included in the Bible?

job

Where does suffering come from? Why do good people suffer? Read how Job and his friends try to answer these big questions.

WHAT MAKES JOB SPECIAL?

JOB tells the story of one man's suffering and deliverance from suffering. It is told as a series of conversations written in the form of poetry. These conversations between Job, Job's friends, and the LORD focus on difficult life questions. In the story section of JOB and when the LORD speaks (chapters 38–41), the Hebrew name for the LORD (Yahweh) is used. In the poetry sections, various names for God are used.

The main character, Job, is described as "a truly good person, who respected God and refused to do evil" (1.1). He trusted God and was blessed with many children, good health, and much wealth. Yet Job loses everything and suffers terribly, and the book seems to focus directly on the question of why a good and faithful person like Job has to suffer. The different characters in the story try to answer this and other questions. Is all suffering caused by human sin? Does God cause people to suffer, and if so, why? JOB invites readers to struggle with these age-old questions along with the characters and, in the end, discover that although the mysterious power and ways of God are beyond human understanding, God's presence with us can give us the strength to endure hardship and face the future.

WHAT'S THE STORY BEHIND THE SCENE?

JOB is set in a time before the nation of Israel existed. Job is mentioned in EZEKIEL (14.14,20), along with Noah, as a faithful man of ancient times. In Job's day, wealth was based on the number of cattle and servants a person owned, rather than on money, which was not commonly used in ancient times.

It is impossible to give a clear date for the writing of JOB. Scholars have argued for dating the book anywhere from the time of Moses (about 1300 B.C.) all the way to the time when the Greeks replaced the Persians as rulers of Palestine (333 B.C.).

HOW IS JOB CONSTRUCTED?

JOB consists of a series of poems contained inside a prose story. The Introduction (chapters 1 and 2) and the conclusion (42.7-17) are written in prose, while the chapters in-between (3.1—42.6) are in poetic form. The prose section tells a story of a man named Job who lost his children and everything he owned, but later recovered his riches and started a new family. The poetic section consists of speeches by Job, his three friends, another observer named Elihu, and the LORD. The following outline is one way JOB can be divided.

The story of Job begins (1.1—2.13)
Job speaks with his friends about his suffering
   (3.1—31.40)
     The first round of the debate (3.1—14.22)
     The second round of the debate (15.1—21.34)
     The third round of the debate (22.1—31.40)
Elihu speaks to Job and Job's friends (32.1—37.24)
The LORD speaks to Job, and Job replies (38.1—42.6)
The story of Job ends (42.7-17)

The story of Job deals with age-old questions about human suffering: whether suffering is the result of sin and whether God causes people to suffer. The core of the book is a series of interrelated speeches written in poetic form framed within a prose narrative. The book of Job is among the wisdom writings of the Old Testament. It tells the story of Job, a good person who respects God and refuses to do evil, but who nevertheless is tested by personal disasters and suffering. Job questions God's justice and challenges God either to judge him or to end his suffering. Several of Job's friends offer their views of Job's troubles. When, at last, the Lord speaks, Job learns that the mysterious power and ways of God are beyond human understanding, and that God is present in times of suffering. The story concludes with the Lord blessing Job with new children and wealth greater that what he had lost.

Outline

Job and His Family

1 Many years ago, a man named Job lived in the land of Uz.[a] He was a truly good person, who respected God and refused to do evil.

² Job had 7 sons and 3 daughters. ³ He owned 7,000 sheep, 3,000 camels, 500 pair of oxen, 500 donkeys, and a large number of servants. He was the richest person in the East.

⁴ Job's sons took turns having feasts in their homes, and they always invited their three sisters to join in the eating and drinking. ⁵ After each feast, Job would send for his children and perform a ceremony, as a way of asking God to forgive them of any wrongs they may have done. He would get up early the next morning and offer a sacrifice for each of them, just in case they had sinned or silently cursed God.

Angels, the Lord, and Satan

⁶ One day, when the angels[b] had gathered around the Lord, and Satan[c] was there with them, ⁷ the Lord asked, "Satan, where have you been?"

Satan replied, "I have been going all over the earth."

⁸ Then the Lord asked, "What do you think of my servant Job? No one on earth is like him—he is a truly good person, who respects me and refuses to do evil."

⁹ "Why shouldn't he respect you?" Satan remarked. ¹⁰ "You are like a wall protecting not only him, but his entire family and all his property. You make him successful in whatever he does, and his flocks and herds are everywhere. ¹¹ Try taking away everything he owns, and he will curse you to your face."

¹² The Lord replied, "All right, Satan, do

● 1.1 *Job*: Job was a good man, meaning he refused to do evil and respected God. Other books of the Bible call this the most important kind of wisdom (Ps 119.99-101; Prov 1.7; Eccl 12.13). In ancient times, people often believed that riches, a large family, and good health were signs of God's favor. Job certainly had all these. He was the richest man for miles around.

● 1.5 *ceremony . . . asking God to forgive them . . . sacrifice:* In ancient times, the head of each family offered burned sacrifices as a way to worship God and to maintain, restore, or celebrate the relationship between the giver and God. Later, the laws that the Lord gave to Moses and the Israelite people included instructions for offering sacrifices to ask for forgiveness.

■ 1.6,7 *angels . . . Satan:* In Hebrew the word for "angel" means "messenger." Here, angels make up part of God's heavenly court. In Hebrew, "Satan" means "the accuser."

🕮 Angels

🕮 Satan

■ 1.10 *You make him successful:* In ancient times, it was believed that God provided health and wealth for good people, and punished those who did evil by bringing sickness and poverty. These beliefs affect much of the conversations in JOB.

1.15-17 *Sabeans . . . Chaldeans:* "Sabeans" may refer to caravan traders from Sheba in southwest Arabia. The Chaldeans were from the region of Babylonia. **(See Map 1 on pg 1879.)**

1.16-19 *fire . . . windstorm:* In the Bible, God's presence often is revealed by fire, and God uses fire to punish evil people. Wind or windstorms also signal God's presence.

⟳ Fire

1.20 *tore his clothes and shaved his head:* In ancient times, people did these things to show their sadness or to show that they were sorry for their sins.

1.22 *Job did not sin:* "Sin" is turning away from God and refusing to obey God's laws. Job did not turn away from God when he lost everything. He kept on praising God (1.21) instead of cursing him, as Satan said he would do (1.11).

2.1 *angels gathered around the* LORD *. . . Satan:* "LORD" is often used in the CEV for the Hebrew word *Yahweh,* the name of the Israel's one true God.

⟳ LORD (YHWH)

2.10 *accept blessings . . . trouble:* Job expresses the belief that all things, whether good or bad, come from God.

what you want with anything that belongs to him, but don't harm Job."

Then Satan left.

Job Loses Everything

[13]Job's sons and daughters were having a feast in the home of his oldest son, [14]when someone rushed up to Job and said, "While your servants were plowing with your oxen, and your donkeys were nearby eating grass, [15]a gang of Sabeans[d] attacked and stole the oxen and donkeys! Your other servants were killed, and I am the only one who escaped to tell you."

[16]That servant was still speaking, when a second one came running and said, "God sent down a fire that killed your sheep and your servants. I am the only one who escaped to tell you."

[17]Before that servant finished speaking, a third one raced up and said, "Three gangs of Chaldeans[e] attacked and stole your camels! All of your other servants were killed, and I am the only one who escaped to tell you."

[18]That servant was still speaking, when a fourth one dashed up and said, "Your children were having a feast and drinking wine at the home of your oldest son, [19]when suddenly a windstorm from the desert blew the house down, crushing all of your children. I am the only one who escaped to tell you."

[20]When Job heard this, he tore his clothes and shaved his head because of his great sorrow. He knelt on the ground, then worshiped God [21]and said:

"We bring nothing at birth;
we take nothing

with us at death.
The LORD alone gives and takes.
Praise the name of the LORD!"

[22]In spite of everything, Job did not sin or accuse God of doing wrong.

Job Loses His Health

2 When the angels[f] gathered around the LORD again, Satan[g] was there with them, [2]and the LORD asked, "Satan, where have you been?"

Satan replied, "I have been going all over the earth."

[3]Then the LORD asked, "What do you think of my servant Job? No one on earth is like him—he is a truly good person, who respects me and refuses to do evil. And he hasn't changed, even though you persuaded me to destroy him for no reason."

[4]Satan answered, "There's no pain like your own.[h] People will do anything to stay alive. [5]Try striking Job's own body with pain, and he will curse you to your face."

[6]"All right!" the LORD replied. "Make Job suffer as much as you want, but just don't kill him." [7]Satan left and caused painful sores to break out all over Job's body—from head to toe.

[8]Then Job sat on the ash-heap to show his sorrow. And while he was scraping his sores with a broken piece of pottery, [9]his wife asked, "Why do you still trust God? Why don't you curse him and die?"

[10]Job replied, "Don't talk like a fool! If we accept blessings from God, we must accept trouble as well." In all that happened, Job never once said anything against God.

[d]**1.15** *Sabeans:* Perhaps the people of Sheba in what is now southwest Arabia (see Isaiah 60.6). [e]**1.17** *Chaldeans:* People from the region of Babylonia, northeast of Palestine. [f]**2.1** *angels:* See the note at 15.8. [g]**2.1** *Satan:* See the note at 1.6. [h]**2.4** *There's no pain like your own:* The Hebrew text has "Skin for skin," which was probably a popular saying.

Then the LORD asked, *"What do you think of my servant Job? No one on earth is like him—he is a truly good person, who respects me and refuses to do evil."* JOB 2.3

Job's Three Friends

[11]Eliphaz from Teman, Bildad from Shuah, and Zophar from Naamah[i] were three of Job's friends, and they heard about his troubles. So they agreed to visit Job and comfort him. [12]When they came near enough to see Job, they could hardly recognize him. And in their great sorrow, they tore their clothes, then sprinkled dust on their heads and cried bitterly. [13]For seven days and nights, they sat silently on the ground beside him, because they realized what terrible pain he was in.

JOB'S FIRST SPEECH
Blot Out the Day of My Birth

3 Finally, Job cursed the day
of his birth
2 by saying to God:
[3]Blot out the day of my birth
and the night when my parents
created a son.
[4]Forget about that day,
cover it with darkness,
[5]and send thick, gloomy shadows
to fill it with dread.
[6]Erase that night from the calendar
and conceal it with darkness.
[7]Don't let children be created
or joyful shouts be heard
ever again in that night.
[8]Let those with magic powers[j]
place a curse on that day.

[9]Darken its morning stars
and remove all hope of light,
[10]because it let me be born
into a world of trouble.

Why Didn't I Die at Birth?

[11]Why didn't I die at birth?
[12]Why was I accepted[k]
and allowed to nurse
at my mother's breast?
[13]Now I would be at peace
in the silent world below
[14]with kings and their advisors
whose palaces lie in ruins,
[15]and with rulers once rich
with silver and gold.
[16]I wish I had been born dead
and then buried, never to see
the light of day.
[17]In the world of the dead,
the wicked and the weary rest
without a worry.
*[18]Everyone is there—
[19]where captives and slaves
are free at last.

Why Does God Let Me Live?

[20]Why does God let me live
when life is miserable
and so bitter?
[21]I keep longing for death
more than I would seek

---

[i]2.11 *Teman . . . Shuah . . . Naamah:* Teman was a place in northern Edom; Shuah may have been a town on the Euphrates River or else further south, near the towns of Dedan and Sheba; Naamah may have been located on the road between Beirut and Damascus, though its exact location is unknown. [j]3.8 *those with magic powers:* The Hebrew text has "those who can place a curse on the day and rouse up Leviathan," which was some kind of sea monster. God's victory over this monster sometimes stood for God's power over all creation and sometimes for his defeat of his enemies (see Isaiah 27.1). In Job 41.1, Leviathan is either a sea monster or a crocodile with almost supernatural powers. [k]3.12 *Why was I accepted:* The Hebrew text has "Why were there knees to receive me," which may refer either to Job's mother or to his father, who would have placed Job on his knees to show that he had accepted him as his child.

● 2.11 *Teman . . . Naamah:* The three friends who come to give Job comfort are from Teman (a place in northern Edom), Shuah (possibly a town on the Euphrates River or else further south near the towns of Dedan and Sheba), and Naamah (possibly located on the road between Beirut, Lebanon, and Damascus in Syria). **(See Map 1 on pg 1879.)**

● 2.13 *seven days:* Seven days was a common time for someone to mourn (Gen 50.10). Note that Job's friends did not say anything to Job during this seven-day period.

■ 3.13-17 *silent world below . . . world of the dead:* This refers to the underground world of the dead, known as Sheol. Sheol is usually described as being totally silent, where no one knows or feels anything. Punishment and torture are not connected with Sheol. Job wants to go to this place where he can rest peacefully with kings and heroes (Isa 14.9-11), and be free from his pain, as a slave becomes free from his master when he dies.

4.12-15 *secret was told to me:* God revealed a message to Eliphaz in his dreams. His message is that all humans are sinful when compared to God. Though he is a good and faithful man, Job cannot be perfect, because no human being is. According to Eliphaz, Job's suffering and punishment come from some wrong Job has done, even though it is not clear exactly what that wrong is.

a valuable treasure.
²²Nothing could make me happier
than to be in the grave.
²³Why do I go on living
when God has me surrounded,
and I can't see the road?
²⁴Moaning and groaning
are my food and drink,
²⁵and my worst fears
have all come true.
²⁶I have no peace or rest—
only troubles and worries.

ELIPHAZ'S FIRST SPEECH
Please Be Patient and Listen

4 Eliphaz from Teman[1] said:
²Please be patient and listen
to what I have to say.
*³Remember how your words
⁴have guided and encouraged
many in need.
⁵But now you feel discouraged
when struck by trouble.
⁶You respect God and live right,
so don't lose hope!
⁷No truly innocent person
has ever died young.
⁸In my experience, only those
who plant seeds of evil
harvest trouble,
⁹and then they are swept away
by the angry breath of God.
¹⁰They may roar and growl
like powerful lions.
But when God breaks their teeth,
¹¹they starve, and their children
are scattered.

[1]**4.1** *Teman:* See the note at 2.11.

A Secret Was Told to Me

¹²A secret was told to me
in a faint whisper—
¹³I was overcome by sleep,
but disturbed by dreams;
¹⁴I trembled with fear,
¹⁵and my hair stood on end,
as a wind blew past my face.
¹⁶It stopped and stood still.
Then a form appeared—
a shapeless form.
And from the silence,
I heard a voice say,
¹⁷"No humans are innocent
in the eyes of God
their Creator.
¹⁸He finds fault with his servants
and even with his angels.
¹⁹Humans are formed from clay
and are fragile as moths,
so what chance do you have?
²⁰Born after daybreak,
you die before nightfall
and disappear forever.
²¹Your tent pegs are pulled up,
and you leave this life,
having gained no wisdom."

ELIPHAZ CONTINUES
Call Out for Help

5 Job, call out for help
and see if an angel comes!

²Envy and jealousy
will kill a stupid fool.
³I have seen fools take root.
But God sends a curse,
suddenly uprooting them
⁴and leaving their children
helpless in court.

⁵Then hungry and greedy people
  gobble up their crops
    and grab their wealth.ᵐ
⁶Our suffering isn't caused
  by the failure of crops;
⁷it's all part of life,
  like sparks shooting skyward.

⁸Job, if I were you,
  I would ask God for help.
⁹His miracles are marvelous,
  more than we can count.
¹⁰God sends showers on earth
  and waters the fields.
¹¹He protects the sorrowful
  and lifts up those
    who have been disgraced.
*¹²God swiftly traps the wicked
¹³in their own evil schemes,
  and their wisdom fails.
¹⁴Darkness is their only companion,
  hiding their path at noon.
¹⁵God rescues the needy
  from the words of the wicked
    and the fist of the mighty.
¹⁶The poor are filled with hope,
  and injustice is silenced.

Consider Yourself Fortunate

¹⁷Consider yourself fortunate
  if God All-Powerful
    chooses to correct you.
¹⁸He may cause injury and pain,
  but he will bandage and heal
    your cuts and bruises.
¹⁹God will protect you from harm,
  no matter how often
    trouble may strike.

²⁰In times of war and famine,
  God will keep you safe.

²¹You will be sheltered,
  without fear of hurtful words
    or any other weapon.
²²You will laugh at the threat
  of destruction and famine.
  And you won't be afraid
    of wild animals—
²³they will no longer be fierce,
  and your rocky fields
    will become friendly.
²⁴Your home will be secure,
  and your sheep will be safe.
²⁵You will have more descendants
  than there are blades of grass
    on the face of the earth.
²⁶You will live a very long life,
  and your body will be strong
    until the day you die.
²⁷Our experience has proven
  these things to be true,
    so listen and learn.

JOB'S REPLY TO ELIPHAZ
It's Impossible

6 Job said:
²It's impossible to weigh
  my misery and grief!
³They outweigh the sand
  along the beach,
  and that's why I have spoken
    without thinking first.
⁴The fearsome arrows
  of God All-Powerful
  have filled my soul
    with their poison.
⁵Do oxen and wild donkeys
  cry out in distress
    unless they are hungry?
⁶What is food without salt?
  What is more tasteless
    than the white of an egg?ⁿ

ᵐ**5.5** *wealth*: One possible meaning for the difficult Hebrew text of verse 5.   ⁿ**6.6** *What is more tasteless . . . egg*: One possible meaning for the difficult Hebrew text.

5.6,7 *suffering . . . part of life, like sparks*: In Hebrew, the word for "ground," where crops grow, is similar to the word for human being ("life" in 5.7.) Eliphaz's words may be a kind of pun, meaning that troubles do not just pop up from the ground by chance. Rather, they fly up like sparks from human beings, which would agree with his message in 4.17. The word translated here as "sparks" is similar to the name of the Canaanite god who was believed to bring sickness and crop failure.

5.17,18 *God All-Powerful*: "All-Powerful" here is used for the Hebrew *Shaddai*. This name for God is used 31 times in JOB, over half the total number of times it appears in the Hebrew Scriptures. Its meaning is not certain, but it may be related to the word for "mountain," so "God, the one of the Mountains." Eliphaz tells Job that he should feel fortunate that God cares enough about Job to discipline ("correct") him. God does punish but will also heal those who ask for help (5.8).

5.25-26 *more descendants . . . long life*: These are two important signs of God's blessing in the ancient world. See also Gen 15.13-15; Ps 112.1,2; Prov 9.10,11.

Job said: "It's impossible to weigh my misery and grief!" JOB 6.1,2

6.18 *caravan, lost in the desert:* In the Middle East, traveling caravans of traders and animal herders had to use travel routes that took them right through deserts. Because desert land has few landmarks, it is easy to lose one's way or to miss a watering spot. Job's disappointment with God is like the frustration of those looking for water in the desert.

6.29 *Stop accusing me falsely:* Job continues to argue that he has not done anything wrong. If his friends cannot say exactly how he has offended God, their charges against him are false.

7.1 *Why do we suffer:* This is Job's main question and a key question for all human beings.

⁷That's how my food tastes,
   and my appetite is gone.

*⁸How I wish that God
  would answer my prayer
⁹ and do away with me.
¹⁰Then I would be comforted,
  knowing that in all of my pain
  I have never disobeyed God.
¹¹Why should I patiently hope
  when my strength is gone?
¹²I am not strong as stone
  or bronze,
¹³and I have finally reached
  the end of my rope.

My Friends, I Am Desperate

¹⁴My friends, I am desperate,
  and you should help me,
  even if I no longer respect
  God All-Powerful.ᵒ
*¹⁵But you are treacherous
¹⁶like streams that swell
  with melting snow,
¹⁷then suddenly disappear
  in the summer heat.
¹⁸I am like a caravan,
  lost in the desert
  while searching for water.
¹⁹Caravans from Tema and Shebaᴾ
²⁰ thought they would find water.
  But they were disappointed,
²¹ just as I am with you.ᑫ
  Only one look at my suffering,
  and you run away scared.

What Have I Done Wrong?

²²Have I ever asked any of you
  to give me a gift

²³or to purchase my freedom
  from brutal enemies?
²⁴What have I done wrong?
  Show me,
  and I will keep quiet.
²⁵The truth is always painful,
  but your arguments
  prove nothing.
²⁶Here I am desperate,
  and you consider my words
  as worthless as wind.
²⁷Why, you would sell an orphan
  or your own neighbor!
²⁸Look me straight in the eye;
  I won't lie to you.
²⁹Stop accusing me falsely;
  my reputation is at stake.
³⁰I know right from wrong,
  and I am not telling lies.

Job Continues
Why Is Life So Hard?

7 Why is life so hard?
  Why do we suffer?
²We are slaves in search of shade;
  we are laborers longing
  for our wages.
³God has made my days drag on
  and my nights miserable.
⁴I pray for night to end,
  but it stretches out
  while I toss and turn.
⁵My parched skin is covered
  with worms, dirt, and sores,
⁶and my days are running out
  quicker than the thread
  of a fast-moving needle.

ᵒ**6.14** *and you should help me . . . God All-Powerful:* Or "and if you don't help me, you no longer respect God All-Powerful."   ᴾ**6.19** *Tema and Sheba:* Tema was a region in northwest Arabia, and Sheba was probably a region in southwest Arabia.   ᑫ**6.21** *just . . . you:* One possible meaning for the difficult Hebrew text.

Don't Forget!

⁷I beg you, God, don't forget!
My life is just a breath,
and trouble lies ahead.
⁸I will vanish from sight,
and no one, including you,
will ever see me again.
⁹I will disappear in the grave
or vanish from sight
like a passing cloud.
¹⁰Never will I return home;
soon I will be forgotten.

¹¹And so, I cry out to you
in agony and distress.
¹²Am I the sea or a sea monster?
Is that why you imprison me?ʳ
¹³I go to bed, hoping for rest,
¹⁴but you torture me
with terrible dreams.
*¹⁵I'd rather choke to death
than live in this body.
¹⁶Leave me alone and let me die;
my life has no meaning.ˢ
¹⁷What makes you so concerned
about us humans?
¹⁸Why do you test us
from sunrise to sunset?
¹⁹Won't you look away
just long enough
for me to swallow?
²⁰Why do you watch us so closely?
What's it to you, if I sin?
Why am I your target
and such a heavy burden?
²¹Why do you refuse to forgive?
Soon you won't find me,
because I'll be dead.

ʳ7.12 sea monster . . . imprison me: "Sea monster" translates the Hebrew word "Tannin," which was possibly a sea monster similar to Leviathan (3.8), Rahab (9.13), and Behemoth (40.15). According to 38.8-11, God makes the sea his prisoner by setting its boundaries. ˢ7.16 my life . . . meaning: Or "my life will soon be over." ᵗ8.1 Shuah: See the note at 2.11.

BILDAD'S FIRST SPEECH
How Long Will You Talk?

8 Bildad from Shuahᵗ said:
²How long will you talk
and keep saying nothing?
³Does God All-Powerful
stand in the way of justice?
⁴He made your children pay
for their sins.
⁵So why don't you turn to him
6 and start living right?
Then he will decide
to rescue and restore you
to your place of honor.
⁷Your future will be brighter
by far than your past.

Our Ancestors Were Wise

⁸Our ancestors were wise,
so learn from them.
⁹Our own time has been short,
like a fading shadow,
and we know very little.
¹⁰But they will instruct you
with great understanding.

¹¹Papyrus reeds grow healthy
only in a swamp,
¹²and if the water dries up,
they die sooner than grass.
¹³Such is the hopeless future
of all who turn from God
¹⁴and trust in something as frail
as a spider's web—
¹⁵they take hold and fall
because it's so flimsy.
¹⁶Sinful people are like plants

7.20,21 *sin . . . forgive:* God forgives, that is, "takes away" the guilt and punishment brought on by the sin. Job asks God to forgive him, so he isn't claiming to have never sinned against God. He may have sinned without knowing it.

8.3 *God All-Powerful . . . justice:* Justice in the Bible is not simply obeying the law, but also includes living out God's love and caring, especially for those who are poor or in need.

∞ Justice

8.8 *ancestors were wise:* Bildad is probably referring to the ancient ones who first taught the meaning of true wisdom. While Eliphaz received his wisdom and insights from his vision, Bildad's insights come from ancient wisdom passed on through generations.

8.11-19 *Papyrus reeds . . . Sinful people . . . other plants grow:* Bildad's words can be interpreted in a number of ways. He may be comparing the papyrus reed to the person who turns away from God. Sinful people who do not recognize their sins and do not turn to God for help are like weeds that grow in a garden. Even though they scatter everywhere and attach even to rocks, they are soon pulled up and destroyed. Compare this to Eliphaz's description of evil springing up from the ground.

∞ Scrolls

9.3,4 *win our case:* Job argues that taking God to court would be useless, since human beings can neither win an argument against God nor answer all God's questions.

9.6-9 *God can shake . . . foundations . . . stars:* These verses may be part of an ancient hymn praising God who created the universe. The heavens and the earth were covered by dark waters of chaos (Gen 1.1-19). In ancient times, the sea was seen as a monster that God had to step on and tame in order to create land. The ancient Israelites believed that the earth was flat and was built on solid pillars (2 Sam 22.8; Ps 75.3). God could upset this natural order of creation by shaking the pillars. Even in ancient times, people studied and named the stars.

with spreading roots and plenty
   of sun and water.
¹⁷They wrap their roots tightly
   around rocks.^u
¹⁸But once they are pulled up,
   they have no more place;
¹⁹their life slips away,^v
   and other plants grow there.

²⁰We know God doesn't reject
   an innocent person
   or help a sinner.
²¹And so, he will make you happy
   and give you something
   to smile about.
²²But your evil enemies
   will be put to shame
   and disappear forever.

Job's Reply to Bildad
What You Say Is True

9 Job said:
²What you say is true.
   No human is innocent
   in the sight of God.
³Not once in a thousand times
   could we win our case
   if we took him to court.
⁴God is wise and powerful—
   who could possibly
   oppose him and win?
⁵When God becomes angry,
   he can move mountains
   before they even know it.
⁶God can shake the earth loose
   from its foundations
⁷or command the sun and stars
   to hold back their light.

⁸God alone stretched out the sky,
   stepped on the sea,^w
⁹and set the stars in place—
   the Big Dipper and Orion,
   the Pleiades and the stars
   in the southern sky.
¹⁰Of all the miracles God works,
   we cannot understand a one.
¹¹God walks right past me,
   without making a sound.
¹²And if he grabs something,
   who can stop him
   or raise a question?

¹³When God showed his anger,
   the servants of the sea monster^x
   fell at his feet.
¹⁴How, then, could I possibly
   argue my case with God?

Though I Am Innocent

¹⁵Even though I am innocent,
   I can only beg for mercy.
¹⁶And if God came into court
   when I called him,
   he would not hear my case.
¹⁷He would strike me with a storm^y
   and increase my injuries
   for no reason at all.
¹⁸Before I could get my breath,
   my miseries would multiply.
¹⁹God is much stronger than I am,
   and who would call me into court
   to give me justice?

²⁰Even if I were innocent,
   God would prove me wrong.^z
²¹I am not guilty,

---

^u**8.17** *rocks:* One possible meaning for the difficult Hebrew text of verse 17.   ^v**8.19** *their . . . away:* One possible meaning for the difficult Hebrew text.   ^w**9.8** *sea:* Or "sea monster" (see verse 13 and the note there).   ^x**9.13** *the sea monster:* The Hebrew text has "Rahab," which was some kind of sea monster with supernatural powers (see the notes at 3.8 and 26.12).   ^y**9.17** *strike . . . storm:* One possible meaning for the difficult Hebrew text.   ^z**9.20** *God . . . wrong:* Or "my own words would prove me wrong."

but I no longer care
  what happens to me.
²²What difference does it make?
  God destroys the innocent
  along with the guilty.
²³When a good person dies
  a sudden death,
  God sits back and laughs.
²⁴And who else but God
  blindfolds the judges,
  then lets the wicked
  take over the earth?

My Life Is Speeding By

²⁵My life is speeding by,
  without a hope of happiness.
²⁶Each day passes swifter
  than a sailing ship
  or an eagle swooping down.
²⁷Sometimes I try to be cheerful
  and to stop complaining,
²⁸but my sufferings frighten me,
  because I know that God
  still considers me guilty.
²⁹So what's the use of trying
  to prove my innocence?
³⁰Even if I washed myself
  with the strongest soap,
³¹God would throw me into a pit
  of stinking slime, leaving me
  disgusting to my clothes.

³²God isn't a mere human like me.
  I can't put him on trial.
³³Who could possibly judge
  between the two of us?
³⁴Can someone snatch away
  the stick God carries
  to frighten me?
³⁵Then I could speak up

without fear of him,
  but for now, I cannot speak.^a

JOB COMPLAINS TO GOD
I Am Sick of Life!

10 I am sick of life!
  And from my deep despair,
  I complain to you, my God.
²Don't just condemn me!
  Point out my sin.
³Why do you take such delight
  in destroying those you created
  and in smiling on sinners?
⁴Do you look at things
  the way we humans do?
⁵Is your life as short as ours?
⁶Is that why you are so quick
  to find fault with me?
⁷ You know I am innocent,
  but who can defend me
  against you?
⁸Will you now destroy
  someone you created?
⁹Remember that you molded me
  like a piece of clay.
  So don't turn me back
  into dust once again.
¹⁰As cheese is made from milk,
  you created my body
  from a tiny drop.
¹¹Then you tied my bones together
  with muscles and covered them
  with flesh and skin.
¹²You, the source of my life,
  showered me with kindness
  and watched over me.

You Have Not Explained

¹³You have not explained
  all of your mysteries,

---

^a**9.35** *but . . . speak*: One possible meaning for the difficult Hebrew text.

9.33 *judge between the two of us*: Job wonders if a third person could listen to Job's arguments and God's arguments and decide between them, but Job quickly realizes that no one can judge God.

10.13-16 *mysteries . . . hunting me down*: Job realizes he cannot understand all of God's mysteries or escape from God's watchful eye. God sees everything Job does.

11.1 *Zophar from Naamah:* Zophar is the third friend to speak.

11.4-6 *claim to be innocent . . . deserve:* Zophar claims that Job has argued that he is pure and without sin. Job did claim to be innocent of doing something that deserved God's strict punishment, but he never claimed to be pure, that is, acceptable to God because he was free of all sin. Having heard Job reply to his other friends, Zophar criticizes him even more and says he deserves to be punished.

11.13 *Surrender your heart to God:* Zophar repeats the advice of Eliphaz and Bildad, that Job should return to God and confess his sins. Then he can sleep without fear. In ancient times, the heart was considered the source of a person's emotions and behavior.

¹⁴but you catch and punish me
  each time I sin.
¹⁵Guilty or innocent,
  I am condemned and ashamed
    because of my troubles.
¹⁶No matter how hard I try,
  you keep hunting me down
    like a powerful lion.ᵇ
¹⁷You never stop accusing me;
  you become furious and attack
    over and over again.

¹⁸Why did you let me be born?
  I would rather have died
    before birth
¹⁹and been carried to the grave
  without ever breathing.
²⁰I have only a few days left.
  Why don't you leave me alone?ᶜ
  Let me find some relief,
*²¹before I travel to the land
²²of darkness and despair,
  the place of no return.

Zophar's First Speech
So Much Foolish Talk

11 Zophar from Naamahᵈ said:
²So much foolish talk
  cannot go unanswered.
³Your words have silenced others
  and made them ashamed;
  now it is only right for you
    to be put to shame.
⁴You claim to be innocent
  and argue that your beliefs
    are acceptable to God.
⁵But I wish God would speak
⁶and let you know that wisdom
  has many different sides.

You would then discover
  that God has punished you
    less than you deserve.

⁷Can you understand the mysteries
  surrounding God All-Powerful?
⁸They are higher than the heavens
  and deeper than the grave.
So what can you do
  when you know so little,
⁹and these mysteries outreach
  the earth and the ocean?

¹⁰If God puts you in prison
  or drags you to court,
    what can you do?
¹¹God has the wisdom to know
  when someone is worthless
    and sinful,
¹²but it's easier to tame
a wild donkey
    than to make a fool wise.ᵉ

Surrender Your Heart to God

¹³Surrender your heart to God,
  turn to him in prayer,
¹⁴and give up your sins—
  even those you do in secret.
¹⁵Then you won't be ashamed;
  you will be confident
    and fearless.
¹⁶Your troubles will go away
  like water beneath a bridge,
¹⁷and your darkest night
  will be brighter than noon.
¹⁸You will rest safe and secure,
  filled with hope
    and emptied of worry.
¹⁹You will sleep without fear

ᵇ10.16 *lion:* One possible meaning for the difficult Hebrew text of verse 16.   ᶜ10.20 *I have only . . . alone:* One possible meaning for the difficult Hebrew text.   ᵈ11.1 *Naamah:* See the note at 2.11.   ᵉ11.12 *it's . . . wise:* One possible meaning for the difficult Hebrew text.

and be greatly respected.
²⁰But those who are evil
  will go blind and lose their way.
    Their only escape is death!

Job's Reply to Zophar
You Think You Are So Great

12 ^{*1}Job said to his friends:
  ²You think you are so great,
    with all the answers.
³But I know as much as you do,
  and so does everyone else.
⁴I have always lived right,
  and God answered my prayers;
    now friends make fun of me.
⁵It's easy to condemn
  those who are suffering,
    when you have no troubles.
⁶Robbers and other godless people
  live safely at home and say,
    "God is in our hands!"^f

If You Want To Learn

⁷If you want to learn,
    then go and ask
  the wild animals and the birds,
⁸ the flowers and the fish.
⁹Any of them can tell you
  what the Lord has done.^g
¹⁰Every living creature
  is in the hands of God.

¹¹We hear with our ears,
    taste with our tongues,
¹²and gain some wisdom from those
  who have lived a long time.
¹³But God is the real source
  of wisdom and strength.

¹⁴No one can rebuild
  what he destroys, or release
    those he has imprisoned.
¹⁵God can hold back the rain
  or send a flood,
¹⁶just as he rules over liars
  and those they lie to.

¹⁷God shames counselors,
  turns judges into fools,
¹⁸ and makes slaves of kings.
¹⁹God removes priests and others
  who have great power—
²⁰he confuses wise,
  experienced advisors,
²¹puts mighty kings to shame,
  and takes away their power.
²²God turns darkness to light;
²³he makes nations strong,
  then shatters their strength.
²⁴God strikes their rulers senseless,
  then leaves them to roam
    through barren deserts,
²⁵lost in the dark, staggering
  like someone drunk.

Job Continues
I Know and Understand

13 I know and understand
    every bit of this.
²None of you are smarter
    than I am;
  there's nothing you know
    that I don't.
³But I prefer to argue my case
  with God All-Powerful—
⁴you are merely useless doctors,
  who treat me with lies.
⁵The wisest thing you can do
  is to keep quiet ⁶and listen

---

^f**12.6** *God is in our hands:* One possible meaning for the difficult Hebrew text.   ^g**12.9** *Any . . . done:* One possible meaning for the difficult Hebrew text.

■ **12.9** *Lord:* This is the only time this name for Israel's God is used in the poetry sections of Job.

■ **12.13** *wisdom:* Job says that wisdom can be discovered by looking at God's creation and can be passed on by earlier generations and those with experience. However, true wisdom comes from God.

❧ Wisdom

■ **12.17-24** *God shames counselors . . . strikes their rulers senseless:* Job claims that God has power to make and destroy earthly rulers and other powerful people, just as God can shake up the earth and the stars that he created (9.5-10). Because he believes this, Job thinks his suffering must be caused by God. This brings him back again to his original question of what he may have done to cause God to make him suffer so much.

Job said, "It's easy to condemn those who are suffering,
when you have no troubles." Job 12.5

13.16 *what saves me:* Since no guilty person could come into God's court without being punished, Job believes he may be able to face God and be saved from punishment, because he is not guilty.

14.4 *no way a human . . . pure:* This phrase appears to agree with earlier statements by Eliphaz and Job himself, but this phrase can also mean that nothing pure can come from what is impure. If Job is speaking about being pure in a legal sense, he could mean that if he is truly guilty, he will not be found innocent. He seems to leave the door open for the unspoken question: "If I am not guilty, then will God stop making me suffer?"

to my argument.
⁷Are you telling lies for God
⁸and not telling the whole truth
when you argue his case?
⁹If he took you to court,
could you fool him,
just as you fool others?
¹⁰If you were secretly unfair,
he would correct you,
¹¹and his glorious splendor
would make you terrified.
¹²Your wisdom and arguments
will blow away like dust.

Be Quiet While I Speak

¹³Be quiet while I speak,
and we'll see what happens.
¹⁴I will be responsible
for what happens to me.
¹⁵God may kill me, but still
I will trust him^h
and offer my defense.
¹⁶This may be what saves me,
because no guilty person
would come to his court.
¹⁷Listen carefully to my words!
¹⁸I have prepared my case well,
and I am certain to win.
¹⁹If you can prove me guilty,
I will give up and die.

JOB PRAYS
I Ask Only Two Things

²⁰I ask only two things
of you, my God,
and I will no longer
hide from you—
²¹stop punishing
and terrifying me!

²²Then speak, and I will reply;
or else let me speak,
and you reply.
²³Please point out my sins,
so I will know them.
²⁴Why have you turned your back
and count me your enemy?
²⁵Do you really enjoy
frightening a fallen leaf?
²⁶Why do you accuse me
of horrible crimes
and make me pay for sins
I did in my youth?
²⁷You have tied my feet down
and keep me surrounded;
²⁸I am rotting away like cloth
eaten by worms.

JOB CONTINUES HIS PRAYER
Life Is Short and Sorrowful

14 Life is short and sorrowful
for every living soul.
²We are flowers that fade
and shadows that vanish.
³And so, I ask you, God,
why pick on me?
⁴There's no way a human
can be completely pure.
⁵Our time on earth is brief;
the number of our days
is already decided by you.
⁶Why don't you leave us alone
and let us find some happiness
while we toil and labor?

When a Tree Is Chopped Down

⁷When a tree is chopped down,
there is always the hope
that it will sprout again.
⁸Its roots and stump may rot,

^h**13.15** *God . . . trust him:* Or "God will surely kill me; I have lost all hope."

"When a tree is chopped down, there is always the hope that it will sprout again. Its roots and stump may rot, but at the touch of water, it sprouts once again." JOB 14.7-9

9but at the touch of water,
  it sprouts once again.
10Humans are different—
  we die, and that's the end.
11We are like streams and lakes
  after the water has gone;
12we fall into the sleep of death,
  never to rise again,
  until the sky disappears.
13Please hide me, God,
  deep in the ground—
  and when you are angry no more,
  remember to rescue me.

Will We Humans Live Again?

14Will we humans live again?
  I would gladly suffer
  and wait for my time.
15My Creator, you would want me;
  you would call out,
  and I would answer.
16You would take care of me,
  but not count my sins—
17you would put them in a bag,
  tie it tight,
  and toss them away.
18But in the real world,
  mountains tumble,
  and rocks crumble;
19streams wear away stones
  and wash away soil.
  And you destroy our hopes!
20You change the way we look,
  then send us away,
  wiped out forever.
21We never live to know
  if our children are praised
  or disgraced.
22We feel no pain but our own,
  and when we mourn,
  it's only for ourselves.

ELIPHAZ'S SECOND SPEECH
If You Had Any Sense

15 Eliphaz from Teman[i] said:
*2Job, if you had any sense,
3you would stop spreading
  all of this hot air.
4Your words are enough
  to make others turn from God
  and lead them to doubt.
5And your sinful, scheming mind
  is the source of all you say.
6I am not here as your judge;
  your own words are witnesses
  against you.

7Were you the first human?
  Are you older than the hills?
8Have you ever been present
  when God's council[j] meets?
  Do you alone have wisdom?
9Do you know and understand
  something we don't?
10We have the benefit of wisdom
  older than your father.
11And you have been offered
  comforting words from God.
  Isn't this enough?

12Your emotions are out of control,
  making you look fierce;
13that's why you attack God
  with everything you say.
14No human is pure and innocent,
15and neither are angels—
  not in the sight of God.
  If God doesn't trust his angels,
16 what chance do humans have?
  We are so terribly evil
  that we thirst for sin.

14.10-12 that's the end . . . never to rise again: A common understanding of death in ancient Israel was that it was simply the end of life. After death, there was nothing more.

⊂⊃   Eternal Life

14.14-22 Will we humans live again? . . . . we mourn: Job seems to be wondering if people can live again after they have died. This idea is suggested in a few Hebrew Scripture passages (Isa 26.19; Dan 12.2). Job's hope for life after death is balanced by his knowledge that in the "real world" God has the power to destroy hopes.

15.7,8 first human . . . God's council: Eliphaz sarcastically asks Job if he was present when God created the world. Eliphaz also asks if Job sits in on God's council, which is a gathering of angels and others who meet to discuss matters with God.

---

i15.1 Teman: See the note at 2.11. j15.8 God's council: The angels and others who gather to discuss matters with God (see 1.6; 2.1).

15.19 *Those who gained . . . the land*: It is not clear what people or which land is being described in this verse. It does not seem possible that it refers to the ancient Israelites taking over Canaan, because they were influenced by the traditions and religion of the Canaanites and others. It may refer to very ancient and wise ancestors who had not yet been influenced by foreign people and their teachings.

Just Listen to What I Know

17Just listen to what I know,
and you will learn
18wisdom known by others
since ancient times.
19Those who gained such insights
also gained the land,
and they were not influenced
by foreign teachings.
20But suffering is in store
each day for those who sin.
21Even in times of success,
they constantly hear
the threat of doom.
22Darkness, despair, and death
are their destiny.
23They scrounge around for food,
all the while dreading
the approaching darkness.
24They are overcome with despair,
like frightened soldiers facing
a fearsome king in battle.
25This is because they rebelled
against God All-Powerful
26and have attacked him
with their weapons.

27They may be rich and fat,
28but they will live in the ruins
of deserted towns.
29Their property and wealth
will shrink and disappear.
30They won't escape the darkness,
and the blazing breath of God
will set their future aflame.
*31They have put their trust
in something worthless;
now they will become worthless
32like a date palm tree
without a leaf.**k**
33Or like vineyards or orchards
whose blossoms and unripe fruit

drop to the ground.
34Yes, the godless and the greedy
will have nothing but flames
feasting on their homes,
35because they are the parents
of trouble and vicious lies.

Job's Reply to Eliphaz
I Have Often Heard This

16 Job said:
2I have often heard this,
and it offers no comfort.
3So why don't you keep quiet?
What's bothering you?
4If I were in your place,
it would be easy to criticize
or to give advice.
5But I would offer hope
and comfort instead.

6If I speak, or if I don't,
I hurt all the same.
My torment continues.
7God has worn me down
and destroyed my family;
8my shriveled up skin proves
that I am his prisoner.
9God is my hateful enemy,
glaring at me and attacking
with his sharp teeth.
10Everyone is against me;
they sneer and slap my face.
11And God is the one
who handed me over
to this merciless mob.

Everything Was Going Well

12Everything was going well,
until God grabbed my neck
and shook me to pieces.

k15.32 *leaf*: One possible meaning for the difficult Hebrew text of verse 32.

God set me up as the target
13 for his arrows,
and without showing mercy,
he slashed my stomach open,
spilling out my insides.
14God never stops attacking,
15 and so, in my sorrow
I dress in sackcloth[l]
and sit in the dust.
16My face is red with tears,
and dark shadows
circle my eyes,
17though I am not violent,
and my prayers are sincere.

18If I should die,
I beg the earth not to cover
my cry for justice.
19Even now, God in heaven
is both my witness
and my protector.
20My friends have rejected me,
but God is the one I beg[m]
21to show that I am right,
just as a friend should.
22Because in only a few years,
I will be dead and gone.

JOB COMPLAINS TO GOD
My Hopes Have Died

17 My hopes have died,
my time is up,
and the grave is ready.
2All I can see are angry crowds,
making fun of me.
3If you, LORD, don't help,
who will pay the price
for my release?

4My friends won't really listen,
all because of you,
and so you must be the one
to prove them wrong.
5They have condemned me,
just to benefit themselves;
now blind their children.

6You, God, are the reason
I am insulted and spit on.
7I am almost blind with grief;
my body is a mere shadow.

8People who are truly good
would feel so alarmed,
that they would become angry
with my worthless friends.
9They would do the right thing
and because they did,
they would grow stronger.[n]
10But none of my friends
show any sense.

11My life is drawing to an end;
hope has disappeared.
12But all my friends can do
is offer empty hopes.[o]
13I could tell the world below
to prepare me a bed.
14Then I could greet the grave
as my father
and say to the worms,
"Hello, mother and sisters!"

15But what kind of hope is that?
16Will it keep me company
in the world of the dead?

16.18 *cry for justice:* In the Hebrew text of this verse Job is literally asking the earth not to "cover his blood" when he soon dies. He wants the blood he shed in his suffering to cry out for justice, just as Abel's blood called out for justice because Cain murdered him (Gen 4.1-10). The Israelites believed that the blood of an innocent victim cried out for justice until someone took revenge against the one who killed the victim.

17.3 *pay the price:* Since his friends won't help him, Job asks God to pay a down payment as a guarantee that he is innocent. This kind of a pledge was often sealed with a handshake and an exchange of money or property. Job offers his life as the pledge of his innocence.

[l]16.15 *sackcloth:* A rough, dark-colored cloth made from goat hair and used to make grain sacks. It was worn in times of trouble or sorrow.   [m]16.20 My *friends . . . beg:* Or "God is my friend, and he is the one I beg."   [n]17.9 *stronger:* One possible meaning for the difficult Hebrew text of verses 8,9. [o]17.12 *hopes:* One possible meaning for the difficult Hebrew text of verse 12.

Job said, "*Even now, God in heaven is both my witness and my protector.*" JOB 16.19

18.5,6 *lamps of sinful people:* The light of lamps is often used as a symbol for life and goodness in the Bible, while darkness is often an image for evil and death.

19.6,7 *God . . . at fault . . . justice:* Bildad argues that Job is responsible for his own "torment" and that God would never "stand in the way of justice," but Job complains that God is being unjust toward him. It's as if he is already behind prison walls (19.8), even before he gets a fair trial.

BILDAD'S SECOND SPEECH
How Long Will You Talk?

18 Bildad from ShuahP said:
² How long will you talk?
Be sensible! Let us speak.
³ Or do you think that we
are dumb animals?
⁴ You cut yourself in anger.
Will that shake the earth
or even move the rocks?

*⁵ The lamps of sinful people
soon are snuffed out,
6 leaving their tents dark.
⁷ Their powerful legs become weak,
and they stumble on schemes
of their own doing.
*⁸ Before they know it,
⁹ they are trapped in a net,
10 hidden along the path.
¹¹ Terror strikes and pursues
from every side.
¹² Starving, they run,
only to meet disaster,
¹³ then afterwards to be eaten alive
by death itself.

¹⁴ Those sinners are dragged
from the safety of their tents
to die a gruesome death.
¹⁵ Then their tents and possessions
are burned to ashes,
¹⁶ and they are left like trees,
dried up from the roots.
¹⁷ They are gone and forgotten,
¹⁸ thrown far from the light
into a world of darkness,
¹⁹ without any children
to carry on their name.
²⁰ Everyone, from east to west,
is overwhelmed with horror.

P18.1 *Shuah:* See the note at 2.11.

²¹ Such is the fate of sinners
and their families
who don't know God.

JOB'S REPLY TO BILDAD
How Long Will You Torture Me?

19 Job said:
² How long will you torture me
with your words?
³ Isn't ten times enough
for you to accuse me?
Aren't you ashamed?
⁴ Even if I have sinned,
you haven't been harmed.
⁵ You boast of your goodness,
claiming I am suffering
because I am guilty.
⁶ But God is the one at fault
for finding fault with me.

⁷ Though I pray to be rescued
from this torment,
no whisper of justice
answers me.
⁸ God has me trapped
with a wall of darkness
9 and stripped of respect.
¹⁰ God rips me apart,
uproots my hopes,
¹¹ and attacks with fierce anger,
as though I were his enemy.
¹² His entire army advances,
then surrounds my tent.

I Am Forgotten

*¹³ God has turned relatives
and friends against me,
14 and I am forgotten.
¹⁵ My guests and my servants
consider me a stranger,
¹⁶ and when I call my servants,

they pay no attention.
¹⁷My breath disgusts my wife;
   everyone in my family
      turns away.
¹⁸Young children can't stand me,
   and when I come near,
      they make fun.
¹⁹My best friends and loved ones
   have turned from me.
²⁰I am skin and bones—
   just barely alive.
²¹My friends, I beg you for pity!
   God has made me his target.
²²Hasn't he already done enough?
   Why do you join the attack?

²³I wish that my words
   could be written down
²⁴   or chiseled into rock.
²⁵I know that my Protector[q] lives,
   and at the end
      he will stand on this earth.
²⁶My flesh may be destroyed,
   yet from this body
      I will see God.[r]
²⁷Yes, I will see him for myself,
   and I long for that moment.

²⁸My friends, you think up ways
   to blame and torment me, saying
      I brought it on myself.
²⁹But watch out for the judgment,
   when God will punish you!

ZOPHAR'S SECOND SPEECH
Your Words Are Disturbing

20 Zophar from Naamah[s] said:
²Your words are disturbing;
   now I must speak.

³You have accused
   and insulted me,
      and reason requires a reply.
⁴Since the time of creation,
   everyone has known
⁵that sinful people are happy
   for only a while.
⁶Though their pride and power
   may reach to the sky,
⁷they will disappear like dust,
   and those who knew them
      will wonder what happened.
⁸They will be forgotten
   like a dream
⁹and vanish from the sight
   of family and friends.
¹⁰Their children will have to repay
   what the parents took
      from the poor.
¹¹Indeed, the wicked will die
   and go to their graves
      in the prime of life.

Sinners Love the Taste of Sin

¹²Sinners love the taste of sin;
   they relish every bite
¹³   and swallow it slowly.
¹⁴But their food will turn sour
   and poison their stomachs.
¹⁵Then God will make them lose
   the wealth they gobbled up.
¹⁶They will die from the fangs
   of poisonous snakes
¹⁷and never enjoy rivers flowing
   with milk and honey.
¹⁸Their hard work will result
   in nothing gained,
¹⁹because they cheated the poor
   and took their homes.

■ 19.25 *Protector:* The Hebrew word (*goel*) translated here as "Protector" is often translated as "Savior" or "Defender." The identity of the Protector has been widely debated. Some believe Job is referring to God, though up to this point, Job has described God as his enemy and accuser. Others believe Job is referring to a "redeemer" or "defender" who will argue Job's case in court against God.

ඟ   Redeemer (Redemption)

■ 19.29 *the judgment:* This refers to a time when God would punish evildoers.

ඟ   Day of the LORD

■ 20.3 *accused and insulted me:* By reminding Job that God punishes the wicked, Zophar and his friends think they are doing Job a favor. When Job states that his friends will also be judged by God, Zophar is insulted.

---

[q]**19.25** *Protector:* Or "Defender" or "Savior."   [r]**19.26** *God:* One possible meaning for the difficult Hebrew text of verses 25,26.   [s]**20.1** *Naamah:* See the note at 2.11.

Job said, "I know that my Protector lives, and at the end he will stand on this earth." JOB 19.25

21.7,8 *Why do evil people live . . . gain such power?*: Even though his friends all say that the wicked are punished by God and lose their wealth, Job knows that life is not so simple. Sometimes evil people get more wealth, live long enough to see their children grow up, and celebrate.

²⁰Greedy people want everything
  and are never satisfied.ᵗ
²¹But when nothing remains
  for them to grab,
    they will be nothing.
²²Once they have everything,
  distress and despair
    will strike them down,
²³and God will make them swallow
  his blazing anger.ᵘ

²⁴While running from iron spears,
  they will be killed
    by arrows of bronze,
²⁵whose shining tips go straight
  through their bodies.
  They will be trapped by terror,
²⁶and what they treasure most
    will be lost in the dark.
  God will send flames
  to destroy them in their tents
    with all their property.
²⁷The heavens and the earth
    will testify against them,
²⁸and all their possessions
  will be dragged off
    when God becomes angry.
²⁹This is what God has decided
    for those who are evil.

Job's Reply to Zophar
If You Want To Offer Comfort

21 Job said:
²If you want to offer comfort,
    then listen to me.
³And when I have finished,
  you can start your insults
    all over again.
⁴My complaint is against God;
    that's why I am impatient.

⁵Just looking at me is enough
    to make you sick,
⁶and the very thought of myself
  fills me with disgust.

⁷Why do evil people live so long
    and gain such power?
⁸Why are they allowed to see
    their children grow up?ᵛ
⁹They have no worries at home,
  and God never punishes them.
¹⁰Their cattle have lots of calves
    without ever losing one;
¹¹their children play and dance
    safely by themselves.
¹²These people sing and celebrate
  to the sound of tambourines,
    small harps, and flutes,
¹³and they are successful,
  without a worry,
    until the day they die.

Leave Us Alone!

¹⁴Those who are evil say
  to God All-Powerful,
"Leave us alone! Don't bother us
  with your teachings.
¹⁵What do we gain from praying
  and worshiping you?
¹⁶We succeeded all on our own."
  And so, I keep away from them
    and their evil schemes.

¹⁷How often does God become angry
  and send disaster and darkness
    to punish sinners?
¹⁸How often does he strike them
  like a windstorm
    that scatters straw?

ᵗ**20.20** *are never satisfied*: One possible meaning for the difficult Hebrew text.   ᵘ**20.23** *anger*: One possible meaning for the difficult Hebrew text of verse 23.   ᵛ**21.8** *up*: One possible meaning for the difficult Hebrew text of verse 8.

¹⁹You say, "God will punish
those sinners' children
in place of those sinners."
But I say, "Let him punish
those sinners themselves
until they really feel it.
²⁰Let God All-Powerful force them
to drink their own destruction
from the cup of his anger.
²¹Because after they are dead,
they won't care what happens
to their children."

Who Can Tell God What To Do?

²²Who can tell God what to do?
He judges powerful rulers.
*²³Some of us die prosperous,
²⁴ enjoying good health,
²⁵while others die in poverty,
having known only pain.
²⁶But we all end up dead,
beneath a blanket of worms.

²⁷My friends, I know that you
are plotting against me.
²⁸You ask, "Where is the home
of that important person
who does so much evil?"

²⁹Everyone, near and far, agrees
³⁰ that those who do wrong
never suffer disaster,
when God becomes angry.
³¹No one points out their sin
or punishes them.
³²Then at their funerals,
they are highly praised;
³³the earth welcomes them home,
while crowds mourn.

³⁴But empty, meaningless words
are the comfort you offer me.

Eliphaz's Third Speech
What Use Are We Humans to God?

22 ¹Eliphaz from Teman^w said:
²What use are we humans
to God,
even the wisest of us?
³If you were completely sinless,
that would still mean nothing
to God All-Powerful.
⁴Is he correcting you
for worshiping him?
⁵No! It's because of
your terrible and endless sins.
⁶To guarantee payment of a debt,
you have taken clothes
from innocent people.
⁷And you refused bread and water
to the hungry and thirsty,
⁸although you were rich,
respected, and powerful.
⁹You have turned away widows
and have broken the arms
of orphans.
¹⁰That's why you were suddenly
trapped by terror,
¹¹blinded by darkness,
and drowned in a flood.

God Lives in the Heavens

¹²God lives in the heavens
above the highest stars,
where he sees everything.
¹³Do you think the deep darkness
hides you from God?
¹⁴Do thick clouds cover his eyes,
as he walks around heaven's dome

^w**22.1** *Teman:* See the note at 2.11.

21.20 *the cup of his anger:* Drinking the cup of God's anger means to receive God's punishment.

21.34 *empty, meaningless words:* Because the arguments of Job's friends are not supported by what happens in real life, Job considers their advice meaningless.

22.5 *sins:* Eliphaz presents a specific list of Job's sins, which center on his failure to act according to God's justice. A number of Israel's prophets accused the Israelite people of similar sins.

Justice

22.12-14 *heavens . . . heaven's dome:* Eliphaz describes God as being distant, living at the highest point of the heavens (above "the highest stars"), where he can watch what everyone on earth is doing. Ancient people understood the sky to be like a solid bowl set over the flat earth, and they believed that high mountains held up the sky like columns. This bowl or dome held back the flood of water above. Rain and snow were said to come through the dome when God opened windows or doors in the sky (Gen 7.11-12; Ps 78.23).

23.8 *cannot find God anywhere:* The directions are based on a person facing the rising sun. Front is east, back is west, left is north, and right is south.

high above the earth?
¹⁵Give up those ancient ideas
    believed by sinners,
¹⁶who were swept away
    without warning.
¹⁷They rejected God All-Powerful,
    feeling he was helpless,
¹⁸although he had been kind
    to their families.
The beliefs of these sinners
    are truly disgusting.
¹⁹When God's people see
    the godless swept away,
    they celebrate, ²⁰saying,
"Our enemies are gone,
    and fire has destroyed
    their possessions."

Surrender to God All-Powerful

²¹Surrender to God All-Powerful!
    You will find peace
    and prosperity.
²²Listen to his teachings
    and take them to heart.
²³If you return to God
    and turn from sin,
    all will go well for you.
²⁴So get rid of your finest gold,
    as though it were sand.
²⁵Let God All-Powerful
    be your silver and gold,
²⁶and you will find happiness
    by worshiping him.
²⁷God will answer your prayers,
    and you will keep the promises
    you made to him.
²⁸He will do whatever you ask,
    and life will be bright.
²⁹When others are disgraced,
    God will clear their names
    in answer to your prayers.

³⁰Even those who are guilty
    will be forgiven,
    because you obey God.^x

Job's Reply to Eliphaz
Today I Complain Bitterly

23 Job said:
²Today I complain bitterly,
    because God has been cruel
    and made me suffer.
³If I knew where to find God,
    I would go there
⁴   and argue my case.
⁵Then I would discover
    what he wanted to say.
⁶Would he overwhelm me
    with his greatness?
No! He would listen
⁷   because I am innocent,
    and he would say,
    "I now set you free!"

⁸I cannot find God anywhere—
    in front or back of me,
⁹   to my left or my right.
God is always at work,
    though I never see him.
¹⁰But he knows what I am doing,
    and when he tests me,
    I will be pure as gold.
^{*11}I have never refused to follow
    any of his commands,
¹²and I have always treasured
    his teachings.^y
¹³But he alone is God,
    and who can oppose him?
God does as he pleases,
¹⁴and he will do exactly
    what he intends with me.
^{*15}Merely the thought
    of God All-Powerful

^x**22.30** *God:* One possible meaning for the difficult Hebrew text of verses 29,30.   ^y**23.12** *treasured his teachings:* One possible meaning for the difficult Hebrew text.

Eliphaz said to Job, "Let God All-Powerful be your silver and gold, and you will find happiness by worshiping him."
Job 22.25,26

16   makes me tremble with fear.
17God has covered me
with darkness,
but I refuse to be silent.[z]

JOB CONTINUES
Why Doesn't God Set a Time?

24 Why doesn't God
set a time for court?
Why don't his people know
where he can be found?
2Sinners remove boundary markers
and take care of sheep
they have stolen.
3They cheat orphans and widows
by taking their donkeys
and oxen.
4The poor are trampled
and forced to hide
5   in the desert,
where they and their children
must live like wild donkeys
and search for food.
6If they want grain or grapes,[a]
they must go to the property
of these sinners.
7They sleep naked in the cold,
because they have no cover,
8and during a storm
their only shelters are caves
among the rocky cliffs.

9Children whose fathers have died
are taken from their mothers
as payment for a debt.
10Then they are forced to work
naked in the grain fields
because they have no clothes,
and they go hungry.
11They crush olives to make oil
and grapes to make wine—

but still they go thirsty.
12And along the city streets,
the wounded and dying cry out,
yet God does nothing.

Some Reject the Light

13Some rebel and refuse
to follow the light.
14Soon after sunset they murder
the poor and the needy,
and at night they steal.

15Others wait for the dark,
thinking they won't be seen
if they sleep with the wife
or husband of someone else.
16Robbers hide during the day,
then break in after dark
because they reject the light.
17They prefer night to day,
since the terrors of the night
are their friends.

Sinners Are Filthy Foam

18Those sinners are filthy foam
on the surface of the water.
And so, their fields and vineyards
will fall under a curse
and won't produce.
19Just as the heat of summer
swallows the snow,
the world of the dead
swallows those who sin.
20Forgotten here on earth,
and with their power broken,
they taste sweet to worms.

21Sinners take advantage of widows
and other helpless women.[b]
22But God's mighty strength

[z]23.17 silent: One possible meaning for the difficult Hebrew text of verse 17.   [a]24.6 If they want grain
or grapes: Poor people were allowed to gather what was left in the fields and vineyards after the
harvest.   [b]24.21 women: One possible meaning for the difficult Hebrew text of verse 21.

● 24.2-7 boundary markers . . . sleep naked in the cold: Job mentions a number of ways sinners disobey God's laws and reject God's concern for justice. Moving boundary markers was a crime forbidden in Israel's law, because it was the same as stealing. Widows and children had few rights and were powerless to defend themselves against those who wanted to steal their property. It was the custom at harvest time to leave some stalks of grain in the field for poor people, widows, orphans, and foreigners to pick up and eat.

● 24.9 Children . . . taken from their mothers: An Israelite who kidnapped another could be punished by death. Taking a child as guarantee to make sure a loan was paid back was an especially terrible crime, because a poor woman's child was likely her only real possession. These children were sometimes forced to work as slaves (crushing olives and grapes), but were not allowed to eat or drink their masters' food and wine.

26.2-4 *helpful . . . understanding:* Job's reply to Bildad is probably intended to be sarcastic. Bildad hasn't told Job anything he doesn't already know, so his words do not comfort Job.

26.10,11 *boundary line . . . columns:* Ancient Israelites believed that the horizon was the boundary where light and darkness meet. Human beings couldn't travel beyond this point to find God, since God lives beyond the horizon. The columns probably refer to high mountains in the north.

26.12,13 *mighty ocean . . . sea monster:* In these verses, the sea monster Rahab stands for the fearsome power of the ocean. By conquering these powerful forces of chaos, God brought all heaven and earth under his control.

destroys those in power.
Even if they seem successful,
 they are doomed to fail.
²³God may let them feel secure,
 but they are never
  out of his sight.
²⁴Great for a while; gone forever!
 Sinners are mowed down
  like weeds,
 then they wither and die.
²⁵If I haven't spoken the truth,
 then prove me wrong.

BILDAD'S THIRD SPEECH
God Is the One To Fear

25 Bildad from Shuah[c] said:
 ²God is the one to fear,
because God is in control
 and rules the heavens.
³Who can count his army of stars?
 Isn't God the source of light?
⁴How can anyone be innocent
 in the sight of God?
⁵To him, not even the light
 of the moon and stars
  can ever be pure.
⁶So how can we humans,
 when we are merely worms?

JOB'S REPLY TO BILDAD
You Have Really Been Helpful

26 Job said:
 ²You have really been helpful
  to someone weak and weary.
³You have given great advice
 and wonderful wisdom
  to someone truly in need.
⁴How can anyone possibly speak
 with such understanding?

⁵Remember the terrible trembling
 of those in the world of the dead
  below the mighty ocean.
⁶Nothing in that land
 of death and destruction
  is hidden from God,
⁷who hung the northern sky
 and suspended the earth
  on empty space.
⁸God stores water in clouds,
 but they don't burst,
⁹and he wraps them around
 the face of the moon.
¹⁰On the surface of the ocean,
 God has drawn a boundary line
  between light and darkness.
¹¹And columns supporting the sky
 tremble at his command.

¹²By his power and wisdom,
 God conquered the force
  of the mighty ocean.[d]
¹³The heavens became bright
 when he breathed,
and the escaping sea monster[e]
 died at his hands.
¹⁴These things are merely a whisper
 of God's power at work.
How little we would understand
if this whisper
 ever turned into thunder!

JOB CONTINUES
I Am Desperate

27 Job said:
 ²I am desperate because
God All-Powerful refuses
 to do what is right.
As surely as God lives,

[c]**25.1** *Shuah:* See the note at 2.11. [d]**26.12** *the force of the mighty ocean:* The Hebrew text has "the ocean . . . Rahab." In this passage the sea monster Rahab stands for the fearsome power of the ocean (see the notes at 3.8 and 9.13). [e]**26.13** *sea monster:* The Hebrew text has "snake," which probably stands for some kind of fearsome sea monster, such as Leviathan (see Isaiah 27.1).

3and while he gives me breath,
4 I will tell only the truth.
5Until the day I die,
I will refuse to do wrong
by saying you are right,
6because each day my conscience
agrees that I am innocent.

7I pray that my enemies
will suffer no less
than the wicked.
8Such people are hopeless,
and God All-Powerful
will cut them down,
9without listening
when they beg for mercy.
10And that is what God should do,
because they don't like him
or ever pray.
11Now I will explain in detail
what God All-Powerful does.
12All of you have seen these things
for yourselves.
So you have no excuse.

How God Treats the Wicked

13Here is how God All-Powerful
treats those who are wicked
and brutal.
14They may have many children,
but most of them will go hungry
or suffer a violent death.
15Others will die of disease,
and their widows
won't be able to weep.
16The wicked may collect riches
and clothes in abundance
as easily as clay.
17But God's people will wear
clothes taken from them
and divide up their riches.
18No homes built by the wicked
will outlast a cocoon
or a shack.
19Those sinners may go to bed rich,
but they will wake up poor.[f]
20Terror will strike at night
like a flood or a storm.
21Then a scorching wind
will sweep them away
22without showing mercy,
as they try to escape.
23At last, the wind will celebrate
because they are gone.

Job Continues

Gold and Silver Are Mined

28 Gold and silver are mined,
then purified;
2the same is done
with iron and copper.
3Miners carry lanterns
deep into the darkness
to search for these metals.
4They dig tunnels
in distant, unknown places,
where they dangle by ropes.
5Far beneath the grain fields,
fires are built
to break loose those rocks
6 that have jewels or gold.[g]

7Miners go to places unseen
by the eyes of hawks;
8they walk on soil unknown
to the proudest lions.
9With their own hands
they remove sharp rocks
and uproot mountains.
10They dig through the rocks
in search of jewels
and precious metals.
11They also uncover

[f]27.19 *poor*: Or "dead." [g]28.6 *gold*: One possible meaning for the difficult Hebrew text of verses 5,6.

27.7-23 *the wicked:* This passage about how God will punish the wicked sounds more like words that have been spoken earlier by Job's friends rather than by Job, who doesn't trust God to act in this way (9.22-24; 12.6; 21.7-13). That is why some scholars think that these verses might have originally been a speech by Zophar, who doesn't speak a third time as Eliphaz and Bildad do. If Job is speaking, his words are filled with sarcasm and bitterness.

28.1-6 *Gold and silver . . . purified . . . jewels:* Gold and silver were made more pure by a process called refining, or smelting. The metal was heated until it melted into a liquid; then the hot metal was poured through a sieve to strain out particles that were not silver or gold. Jewels and gold were discovered by mining and examining rocks. The point of this opening section is that valuable metals and gems can be found by looking for them, by mining.

28.12 *wisdom:* Precious metals and gems can be found by searching, but wisdom is harder to discover. The kind of wisdom Job is referring to is wisdom that comes from God. Here Job says that only God knows the way to wisdom, and that wisdom means respecting the LORD and turning away from sin.

Wisdom

29.7,8 *city council:* In ancient times, trials and important business took place near the city gate. Job apparently was a highly respected member of the city council.

the sources of[h] rivers
  and discover secret places.

Where Is Wisdom Found?

12But where is wisdom found?
13   No human knows the way.[i]
14Nor can it be discovered
  in the deepest sea.
*15It is worth much more
  than silver or pure gold
16   or precious stones.
17Nothing is its equal—
  not gold or costly glass.[j]
18Wisdom is worth much more than
  coral, jasper,[k] or rubies.
19All the topaz[l] of Ethiopia[m]
  and the finest gold
  cannot compare with it.
20Where then is wisdom?
21It is hidden from human eyes
  and even from birds.
22Death and destruction
  have merely heard rumors
  about where it is found.
23God is the only one who knows
  the way to wisdom;
24he alone sees everything
  beneath the heavens.
25When God divided out
  the wind and the water,
26and when he decided the path
  for rain and lightning,
27he also determined the truth
  and defined wisdom.
28God told us, "Wisdom means
  that you respect me, the Lord,
  and turn from sin."

JOB CONTINUES
I Long for the Past

29 Job said:
2I long for the past,
  when God took care of me,
3and the light from his lamp
  showed me the way
  through the dark.
4I was in the prime of life,
  God All-Powerful
  was my closest friend,
5and all of my children
  were nearby.
6My herds gave enough milk
  to bathe my feet,
  and from my olive harvest
  flowed rivers of oil.
*7When I sat down at the meeting
  of the city council,
8the young leaders stepped aside,
*9while the older ones stood
10   and remained silent.

Everyone Was Pleased

11Everyone was pleased
  with what I said and did.
12When poor people or orphans
  cried out for help,
  I came to their rescue.
13And I was highly praised
  for my generosity to widows
  and others in poverty.
14Kindness and justice
  were my coat and hat;
15I was helpful to the blind
  and to the lame.
16I was a father to the needy,

[h]28.11 *uncover the sources of:* Two ancient translations; Hebrew "dam up." [i]28.13 *the way:* Or "its worth." [j]28.17 *costly glass:* In the ancient world, objects made of glass were costly. [k]28.18 *jasper:* A valuable stone, usually green or clear. [l]28.19 *topaz:* A valuable, yellow stone. [m]28.19 *Ethiopia:* The Hebrew text has "Cush," which was a region south of Egypt that included parts of the present countries of Ethiopia and Sudan.

God told us, "Wisdom means that you respect me, the Lord, and turn from sin." JOB 28.28

and I defended them in court,
even if they were strangers.
17When criminals attacked,
I broke their teeth
and set their victims free.

18I felt certain that I would live
a long and happy life,
then die in my own bed.
19In those days I was strong
like a tree with deep roots
and with plenty of water,
20 or like an archer's new bow.
21Everyone listened in silence
to my welcome advice,
22and when I finished speaking,
nothing needed to be said.
23My words were eagerly accepted
like the showers of spring,
24and the smile on my face
renewed everyone's hopes.
25My advice was followed
as though I were a king
leading my troops,
or someone comforting
those in sorrow.

JOB CONTINUES
Young People Now Insult Me

30 Young people now insult me,
although their fathers
would have been a disgrace
to my sheep dogs.
2And those who insult me
are helpless themselves.
3They must claw the desert sand
in the dark for something
to satisfy their hunger.n

4They gather tasteless shrubs
for food and firewood,
5and they are run out of towns,
as though they were thieves.
6Their only homes are ditches
or holes between rocks,
7where they bray like donkeys
gathering around shrubs.
8And like senseless donkeys
they are chased away.

Those Worthless Nobodies

9Those worthless nobodies
make up jokes and songs
to disgrace me.
10They are hateful
and keep their distance,
even while spitting
in my direction.
11God has destroyed me,
and so they don't care
what they do.o
12Their attacks never stop,
though I am defenseless,
and my feet are trapped.p
13Without any help,
they prevent my escape,
destroying me completelyq
14 and leaving me crushed.
15Terror has me surrounded;
my reputation and my riches
have vanished like a cloud.

I Am Sick at Heart

16I am sick at heart!
Pain has taken its toll.
17Night chews on my bones,
causing endless torment,

n30.3 hunger: One possible meaning for the difficult Hebrew text of verse 3. o30.11 God . . . do: Or "They have destroyed me, and so they don't care what else they do." p30.12 trapped: One possible meaning for the difficult Hebrew text of verse 12. q30.13 destroying . . . completely: One possible meaning for the difficult Hebrew text.

29.20 archer's new bow: Bows for shooting arrows are one of the oldest weapons used for hunting and warfare. A strong archer using a good bow could shoot arrows up to a distance of 400 yards. Biblical authors often use bows as a symbol of power and strength.

30.4 tasteless shrubs: This may refer to the roots of the large bush known as the broom tree that grows in the desert areas of Palestine and Arabia (1 Kgs 19.4).

30.29 *jackals:* These desert animals are related to wolves and have a very sad-sounding howl.

18and God has shrunk my skin,
  choking me to death.ʳ
19I have been thrown in the dirt
  and now am dirt myself.
20I beg God for help,
  but there is no answer;
and when I stand up,
  he simply stares.
21God has turned brutal,
22stirring up a windstorm
  to toss me about.
23Soon he will send me home
  to the world of the dead,
  where we all must go.

24No one refuses help to others,
  when disaster strikes.ˢ
25I mourned for the poor
  and those who suffered.
26But when I beg for relief
  and light,
all I receive are disaster
  and darkness.
27My stomach is tied in knots;
  pain is my daily companion.
28My days are dark and gloomy
  and in the city council
  I stand and cry out,
29making mournful sounds
  like jackalsᵗ and owls.
30My skin is so parched,
  that it peels right off,
  and my bones are burning.
31My only songs are sorrow
  and sadness.

Job Continues
I Promised Myself

31 I promised myself
  never to stare with desire

at a young woman.
2God All-Powerful punishes
  men who do that.
3In fact, God sends disaster
  on all who sin,
4and he keeps a close watch
  on everything I do.

5I am not dishonest or deceitful,
6and I beg God to prove
  my innocence.
7If I have disobeyed him
  or even wanted to,
8then others can eat my harvest
  and uproot my crops.
9If I have desired someone's wife
  and chased after her,
10then let some stranger
  steal my wife from me.
11If I took someone's wife,
  it would be a horrible crime,
12sending me to destruction
  and my crops to the flames.ᵘ

13When my servants
  complained against me,
  I was fair to them.
14Otherwise, what answer
  would I give to God
  when he judges me?
15After all, God is the one
  who gave life to each of us
  before we were born.

I Have Never Cheated Anyone

16I have never cheated widows
  or others in need,
17and I have always shared
  my food with orphans.
18Since the time I was young,

ʳ**30.18** *death:* One possible meaning for the difficult Hebrew text of verse 18.   ˢ**30.24** *strikes:* One possible meaning for the difficult Hebrew text of verse 24.   ᵗ**30.29** *jackals:* Desert animals related to wolves, but smaller.   ᵘ**31.12** *flames:* One possible meaning for the difficult Hebrew text of verse 12.

Job said, *"My only songs are sorrow and sadness."*
Job 30.31

I have cared for orphans
and helped widows.^v
¹⁹I provided clothes for the poor,
²⁰   and I was praised
for supplying woolen garments
to keep them warm.
²¹If I have ever raised my arm
to threaten an orphan
when the power was mine,
²²I hope that arm will fall
from its socket.
²³I could not have been abusive;
I was terrified at the thought
that God might punish me.
²⁴ I have never trusted
the power of wealth,
²⁵or taken pride in owning
many possessions.
^{*26}I have never openly or secretly
²⁷   worshiped the sun or moon.
²⁸Such horrible sins
would have deserved
punishment from God.

²⁹I have never laughed
when my enemies
were struck by disaster.
³⁰Neither have I sinned
by asking God
to send down on them
the curse of death.
³¹No one ever went hungry^w
at my house,
³²and travelers
were always welcome.
³³Many have attempted to hide
their sins from others—

but I refused.
³⁴And the fear of public disgrace
never forced me to keep silent
about what I had done.

Why Doesn't God Listen?

³⁵Why doesn't God All-Powerful
listen and answer?
If God has something against me,
let him speak up
or put it in writing!
³⁶Then I would wear his charges
on my clothes and forehead.
³⁷And with my head held high,
I would tell him everything
I have ever done.

³⁸I have never mistreated
the land I farmed
and made it mourn.^x
³⁹Nor have I cheated
my workers
and caused them pain.^y
⁴⁰If I had, I would pray
for weeds instead of wheat
to grow in my fields.
After saying these things,
Job was silent.

Elihu Is Upset with Job's Friends

32 Finally, these three men stopped arguing with Job, because he refused to admit he was guilty.
²Elihu from Buz^z was there, and he had

^v**31.18** *widows*: One possible meaning for the difficult Hebrew text of verse 18.   ^w**31.31** *ever went hungry*: Or "was ever sexually abused" (see Genesis 19.1-11; Judges 19.10-30). In ancient Israel, the lives of one's guests were sacred and had to be protected at any cost.   ^x**31.38** *mourn*: In biblical times there were strict regulations for proper use of the land, and land that was abused was said to "mourn" and become no longer productive.   ^y**31.39** *pain*: One possible meaning for the difficult Hebrew text of verse 39.   ^z**32.2** *Elihu from Buz*: The Hebrew text has "Elihu son of Barachel from Buz of the family of Ram." Buz may have been somewhere in the territory of Edom; in Jeremiah 25.23 it is mentioned along with Dedan and Tema (see 6.19).

31.27 *worshiped the sun or moon*: The people of Israel were to worship God alone and not worship the sun and moon as gods, as some of their neighbors did. Job worshiped Israel's one true God, though according to the story, he lived at a time long before Moses and the people received God's laws concerning worship and daily living.

32.2 *Elihu from Buz*: The name of Elihu's father (Barachel) in Hebrew means "El (God) has blessed," and Elihu's own name means "He is my God." Elihu is a descendant of Buz, nephew of Abraham and brother of Uz. Buz may have been an area in the territory of Edom.

32.21 *be unfair . . . flatter anyone:* Elihu claims that he is so completely fair that he is not able to give special honor to anyone. His attitude seems overly boastful, especially since he has not experienced the kind of suffering that Job has.

33.4 *Spirit:* The Hebrew word *ruah,* translated here as "Spirit," is the same word used to describe God's creating power in Genesis 1.2. Elihu may also be comparing this Spirit to the source of wisdom that comes from God.

become upset with Job for blaming God instead of himself. [3]He was also angry with Job's three friends for not being able to prove that Job was wrong. [4]Elihu was younger than these three, and he let them speak first. [5]But he became irritated when they could not answer Job, [6]and he said to them:

I am much younger than you,
so I have shown respect
by keeping silent.
[7]I once believed age
was the source of wisdom;
[8]now I truly realize
wisdom comes from God.
[9]Age is no guarantee of wisdom
and understanding.
[10]That's why I ask you
to listen to me.

I Eagerly Listened

*[11]I eagerly listened
to each of your arguments,
[12]but not one of you proved
Job to be wrong.
[13]You shouldn't say,
"We know what's right!
Let God punish him."
[14]Job hasn't spoken against me,
and so I won't answer him
with your arguments.

[15]All of you are shocked;
you don't know what to say.
[16]But am I to remain silent,
just because you
have stopped speaking?
[17]No! I will give my opinion,
[18]because I have so much to say,

that I can't keep quiet.
[19]I am like a swollen wineskin,
and I will burst[a]
[20] if I don't speak.
*[21]I don't know how to be unfair
or to flatter anyone—
[22]if I did, my Creator
would quickly destroy me!

ELIHU SPEAKS
Job, Listen to Me!

33 Job, listen to me!
Pay close attention.
*[2]Everything I will say
[3] is true and sincere,
[4]just as surely as the Spirit
of God All-Powerful[b]
gave me the breath of life.
[5]Now line up your arguments
and prepare to face me.
[6]We each were made from clay,
and God has no favorites,
[7]so don't be afraid of me
or what I might do.

I Have Heard You Argue

[8]I have heard you argue
[9]that you are innocent,
guilty of nothing.
[10]You claim that God
has made you his enemy,
[11]that he has bound your feet
and blocked your path.
[12]But, Job, you're wrong—
God is greater
than any human.
[13]So why do you challenge God
to answer you?[c]

[a]**32.19** *swollen wineskin . . . burst:* While the juice from grapes was becoming wine, it would swell and stretch the skins in which it had been stored; sometimes the swelling would burst the wineskins. [b]**33.4** *the Spirit of God All-Powerful:* Or "God All-Powerful." [c]**33.13** *answer you:* One possible meaning for the difficult Hebrew text of verse 13.

Elihu said, *"I once believed age was the source of wisdom; now I truly realize wisdom comes from God."* JOB 32.7,8

¹⁴God speaks in different ways,
   and we don't always
      recognize his voice.
*¹⁵Sometimes in the night,
   he uses terrifying dreams
¹⁶   to give us warnings.
¹⁷God does this to make us turn
      from sin and pride
¹⁸and to protect us
   from being swept away
      to the world of the dead.

¹⁹Sometimes we are punished
   with a serious illness
      and aching joints.
²⁰Merely the thought
   of our favorite food
      makes our stomachs sick,
²¹and we become so skinny
      that our bones stick out.
²²We feel death and the grave
      taking us in their grip.

²³One of a thousand angels
   then comes to our rescue
      by saying we are innocent.
²⁴The angel shows kindness,
   commanding death to release us,
      because the price was paid.
²⁵Our health is restored,
   we feel young again,
²⁶   and we ask God to accept us.
   Then we joyfully worship God,
   and we are rewarded
      because we are innocent.
²⁷When that happens,
   we tell everyone,
   "I sinned and did wrong,
      but God forgave me
²⁸and rescued me from death!
   Now I will see the light."

²⁹God gives each of us
   chance after chance
³⁰to be saved from death

and brought into the light
   that gives life.
³¹So, Job, pay attention
   and don't interrupt,
³²though I would gladly listen
   to anything you say
      that proves you are right.
³³Otherwise, listen in silence
   to my wisdom.

Elihu Continues
You Men Think You Are Wise

34 Elihu said:
   ²You men think you are wise,
      but just listen to me!
   ³Think about my words,
      as you would taste food.
   ⁴Then we can decide the case
      and give a just verdict.
   ⁵Job claims he is innocent
   and God is guilty
      of mistreating him.
   ⁶Job also argues that God
      considers him a liar
   and that he is suffering severely
      in spite of his innocence.
   ⁷But to tell the truth,
      Job is shameless!
   ⁸He spends his time with sinners,
   ⁹because he has said,
      "It doesn't pay to please God."

If Any of You Are Smart

¹⁰If any of you are smart,
   you will listen and learn
   that God All-Powerful
      does what is right.
¹¹God always treats everyone
   the way they deserve,
¹²   and he is never unfair.
¹³From the very beginning,
   God has been in control
      of all the world.

■   33.30 *saved from death . . . light that gives life:* The word translated as "death" here can also be translated as "pit" or "grave." The pit stands for the dark world of the dead. Light is a symbol of life. Elihu is saying that the suffering God has given to Job is an act of love, since Job and all other human beings actually deserve worse.

■   34.9 *doesn't pay to please God:* Elihu says that Job's sin is giving up on trying to do what God wants. Like Job's other friends, Elihu pays little attention to how much Job's suffering may be affecting his thinking.

Elihu said, "God gives each of us chance after chance to be saved from death and brought into the light that gives life."
Job 33.29,30

34.23 *time for judgment:* Elihu argues that God can judge a person at any time and in any place, so Job's request for a formal trial in God's court is unnecessary and disrespectful.

¹⁴If God took back the breath
  that he breathed into us,
¹⁵we humans would die
  and return to the soil.
¹⁶ So be smart and listen!
¹⁷The mighty God is the one
  who brings about justice,
    and you are condemning him.
¹⁸Indeed, God is the one
  who condemns unfair rulers.
¹⁹And God created us all;
  he has no favorites,
    whether rich or poor.
²⁰Even powerful rulers die
  in the darkness of night
    when they least expect it,
      just like the rest of us.

God Watches Everything We Do

²¹God watches everything we do.
²²No evil person can hide
  in the deepest darkness.
²³And so, God doesn't need
  to set a time for judgment.
²⁴Without asking for advice,
  God removes mighty leaders
    and puts others in their place.
²⁵He knows what they are like,
  and he wipes them out
    in the middle of the night.
²⁶And while others look on,
  he punishes them
    because they were evil
²⁷ and refused to obey him.
²⁸The persons they mistreated
  had prayed for help,
    until God answered
      their prayers.
²⁹When God does nothing,
  can any person or nation
    find fault with him?

³⁰But still, he punishes rulers
  who abuse their people.ᵈ
³¹Job, you should tell God
  that you are guilty
    and promise to do better.
³²Then ask him to point out
  what you did wrong,
    so you won't do it again.
³³Do you make the rules,
  or does God?
    You have to decide—
    I can't do it for you;
      now make up your mind.
³⁴Job, anyone with good sense
  can easily see
³⁵that you are speaking nonsense
  and lack good judgment.
³⁶So I pray for you to suffer
  as much as possible
    for talking like a sinner.
³⁷You have rebelled against God,
  time after time,
    and have even insulted us.

ELIHU CONTINUES
Are You Really Innocent?

35 Elihu said:
²Job, are you really innocent
  in the sight of God?ᵉ
³Don't you honestly believe
  it pays to obey him?
⁴I will give the answers
  to you and your friends.
*⁵Look up to the heavens
 ⁶ and think!
  Do your sins hurt God?
⁷Is any good you may have done
  at all helpful to him?
⁸The evil or good you do
  only affects other humans.

ᵈ34.30 *people:* One possible meaning for the difficult Hebrew text of verses 29,30.   ᵉ35.2 *are . . . God:* Or "is it right for you to accuse God?"

⁹In times of trouble,
   everyone begs the mighty God
      to have mercy.
¹⁰But after their Creator
   helps them through hard times,
      they forget about him,
¹¹though he makes us wiser
   than animals or birds.
¹²God won't listen to the prayers
   of proud and evil people.
¹³If God All-Powerful refuses
   to answer their empty prayers,
¹⁴   he will surely deny
   your impatient request
      to face him in court.
¹⁵Job, you were wrong to say
   God doesn't punish sin.
¹⁶Everything you have said
   adds up to nonsense.

Elihu Continues
Be Patient a While Longer

36 Elihu said:
²Be patient a while longer;
I have something else to say
   in God's defense.
³God always does right—
   and this knowledge
      comes straight from God.ᶠ
⁴You can rest assured
   that what I say is true.
⁵Although God is mighty,
   he cares about everyone
      and makes fair decisions.

⁶The wicked are cut down,
   and those who are wronged
      receive justice.
⁷God watches over good people
   and places them in positions

of power and honor forever.
⁸But when people are prisoners
   of suffering and pain,
*⁹God points out their sin
   and their pride,
¹⁰then he warns them
   to turn back to him.
¹¹And if they obey,
   they will be successful
      and happy from then on.
¹²But if they foolishly refuse,
   they will be rewarded
      with a violent death.

Godless People Are Too Angry

¹³Godless people are too angry
   to ask God for help
      when he punishes them.
¹⁴So they die young
   in shameful disgrace.
¹⁵Hard times and trouble
   are God's way
      of getting our attention!
¹⁶And at this very moment,
   God deeply desires
      to lead you from trouble
   and to spread your table
      with your favorite food.

¹⁷Now that the judgment
   for your sins
      has fallen upon you,
¹⁸don't let your anger
   and the pain you endured
      make you sneer at God.
¹⁹Your reputation and riches
   cannot protect you
      from distress,
²⁰nor can you find safety
   in the dark world below.ᵍ
²¹Be on guard! Don't turn to evil

ᶠ**36.3** *comes straight from God*: The Hebrew text has "comes from a distant place," which refers to the place where God lives; Elihu is claiming that he learned this from God.   ᵍ**36.20** *below*: One possible meaning for the difficult Hebrew text of verses 18-20.

35.9-14 *In times of trouble . . . impatient request*: Elihu is arguing that when people in trouble cry out to God for help, their prayers are usually selfish. And when help comes, they soon forget about God. Elihu says that Job's prayers and his request to face God in court are selfish and impatient, and that Job is unwilling to trust and understand God or God's wisdom (33.10-14; Prov 8.12-36).

Elihu said, *"Hard times and trouble are God's way of getting our attention!"* Job 36.15

37.2,3 *roaring voice of God . . . lightning*: Fire and smoke and thunder and lightning often signal the presence of God in the Bible (Gen 15.17,18; Exod 3.2; 13.21-22; 19.16-19; Judg 13.20; Matt 24.27). When God is revealed in this way, it is sometimes called a "theophany."

37.17 *desert winds . . . brass*: High winds in the desert blow lots of sand and dust into the air, giving the sky a gold hue, like the color of brass, when the sun is shining (see also Deut 28.21-23).

as a way of escape.
²²God's power is unlimited.
He needs no teachers
²³ to guide or correct him.

Others Have Praised God

²⁴Others have praised God
for what he has done,
so join with them.
²⁵From down here on earth,
everyone has looked up and seen
²⁶ how great God is—
God is more than we imagine;
no one can count the years
he has lived.
*²⁷God gathers moisture
into the clouds
²⁸ and supplies us with rain.
²⁹Who can understand
how God scatters the clouds
and speaks from his home
in the thunderstorm?
³⁰And when God sends lightning,
it can be seen
at the bottom of the sea.[h]
³¹By producing such rainstorms,
God rules the world
and provides us with food.
³²Each flash of lightning
is one of his arrows
striking its target,
³³and the thunder tells
of his anger against sin.[i]

ELIHU CONTINUES
I Am Frightened

37 I am frightened
and tremble all over,

²when I hear the roaring voice
of God in the thunder,
³and when I see his lightning
flash across the sky.
⁴God's majestic voice
thunders his commands,[j]
⁵creating miracles too marvelous
for us to understand.
⁶Snow and heavy rainstorms
⁷make us stop and think
about God's power,[k]
⁸and they force animals
to seek shelter.
⁹The windstorms of winter strike,
¹⁰and the breath of God
freezes streams and rivers.
¹¹Rain clouds filled with lightning
appear at God's command,
¹²traveling across the sky
¹³ to release their cargo—
sometimes as punishment for sin,
sometimes as kindness.

Consider Carefully

¹⁴Job, consider carefully
the many wonders of God.
¹⁵Can you explain why lightning
flashes at the orders
¹⁶ of God who knows all things?
Or how he hangs the clouds
in empty space?
¹⁷You almost melt in the heat
of fierce desert winds
when the sky is like brass.
¹⁸God can hammer out the clouds
in spite of the oppressive heat,
but can you?

¹⁹Tell us what to say to God!
Our minds are in the dark,

[h]36.30 *sea*: One possible meaning for the difficult Hebrew text of verse 30.   [i]36.33 *sin*: One possible meaning for the difficult Hebrew text of verse 33.   [j]37.4 *commands*: One possible meaning for the difficult Hebrew text of verse 4.   [k]37.7 *God's power*: One possible meaning for the difficult Hebrew text of verse 7.

and we don't know how
  to argue our case.
²⁰Should I risk my life
  by telling God
    that I want to speak?
²¹No one can stare at the sun
  after a breeze has blown
    the clouds from the sky.
²²Yet the glorious splendor
  of God All-Powerful
    is brighter by far.
²³God cannot be seen—
  but his power is great,
    and he is always fair.
²⁴And so we humans fear God,
  because he shows no respect
  for those who are proud
    and think they know so much.

THE LORD SPEAKS
From Out of a Storm

38 From out of a storm,
    the LORD said to Job:
²Why do you talk so much
  when you know so little?
³Now get ready to face me!
  Can you answer
    the questions I ask?
⁴How did I lay the foundation
  for the earth?
    Were you there?
⁵Doubtless you know who decided
  its length and width.
⁶What supports the foundation?
  Who placed the cornerstone,
⁷ while morning stars sang,
    and angels rejoiced?

⁸When the ocean was born,
  I set its boundaries
⁹and wrapped it in blankets
  of thickest fog.
¹⁰Then I built a wall around it,
  locked the gates, ¹¹and said,

"Your powerful waves stop here!
  They can go no farther."

Did You Ever Tell the Sun To Rise?

¹²Did you ever tell the sun to rise?
  And did it obey?
¹³Did it take hold of the earth
  and shake out the wicked
    like dust from a rug?
¹⁴Early dawn outlines the hills
  like stitches on clothing
    or sketches on clay.
¹⁵But its light is too much
  for those who are evil,
    and their power is broken.

¹⁶Job, have you ever walked
  on the ocean floor?
¹⁷Have you seen the gate
  to the world of the dead?
¹⁸And how large is the earth?
  Tell me, if you know!

¹⁹Where is the home of light,
  and where does darkness live?
²⁰ Can you lead them home?
²¹I'm certain you must be able to,
  since you were already born
    when I created everything.

²²Have you been to the places
  where I keep snow and hail,
²³until I use them to punish
  and conquer nations?
²⁴From where does lightning leap,
  or the east wind blow?
²⁵Who carves out a path
  for thunderstorms?
  Who sends torrents of rain
²⁶on empty deserts
  where no one lives?
²⁷Rain that changes barren land
  to meadows green with grass.
²⁸Who is the father of the dew

37.24 *fear:* The word translated as "fear" does not refer simply to being afraid, but to respecting, obeying, and honoring God.

38.1 *storm:* Sometimes this word is translated as "whirlwind." A storm is a common way to describe how God appears in the Bible (Ps 18.7-15; 50.3; Ezek 1.4; Zech 9.14). The power and effects of a windstorm can be felt and seen, but the wind itself is invisible.

38.4 *How did I lay . . . earth:* The LORD's questions in this passage focus on how the LORD created and still controls the world and the universe.

38.5 *you know:* Job's earlier comments provide an answer to the LORD's questions (see 9.6-10).

38.16-21 *ocean floor . . . world of the dead . . . already born:* Of course, Job cannot answer "yes" to these questions. Light and darkness are described as two distinct parts of God's created universe (Gen 1.3,4).

38.31,32 *Orion . . . Little Dipper:*
Only God has the power to rearrange
the stars, so once again the questions
remind Job that he is merely a human
being. He is nothing compared to the
Lord, the powerful creator of the whole
universe.

39.1 *mountain goats and deer:*
The Hebrew word translated as "mountain goat" may refer to an ibex, a kind of
wild goat that has shorter hair than a
common goat and has horns that are
slender and curve back. These animals
live in the rugged hills and mountains
and usually avoid people.

39.5-9 *wild donkeys . . . wild ox:*
Wild donkeys in the Middle East are
larger and livelier than European donkeys. Oxen were often used to pull
loads and do work, but some oxen remained wild. Wild oxen probably were
not easily tamed to do farm work.

and of the rain?
²⁹Who gives birth to the sleet
  and the frost
³⁰that fall in winter,
  when streams and lakes
  freeze solid as a rock?

Can You Arrange Stars?

³¹Can you arrange stars in groups
  such as Orion
    and the Pleiades?
³²Do you control the stars
  or set in place the Big Dipper
    and the Little Dipper?
³³Do you know the laws
    that govern the heavens,
  and can you make them rule
    the earth?
³⁴Can you order the clouds
  to send a downpour,
³⁵or will lightning flash
  at your command?
³⁶Did you teach birds to know
  that rain or floods
  are on their way?[1]
³⁷Can you count the clouds
  or pour out their water
³⁸ on the dry, lumpy soil?

³⁹When lions are hungry,
  do you help them hunt?
⁴⁰Do you send an animal
  into their den?
⁴¹And when starving young ravens
  cry out to me for food,
    do you satisfy their hunger?

THE LORD CONTINUES
When Do Mountain Goats
Give Birth?

39 When do mountain goats
    and deer give birth?
Have you been there
    when their young are born?
*²How long are they pregnant
³ before they deliver?
⁴Soon their young grow strong
  and then leave
    to be on their own.

⁵Who set wild donkeys free?
⁶I alone help them survive
  in salty desert sand.
⁷They stay far from crowded cities
  and refuse to be tamed.
⁸Instead, they roam the hills,
  searching for pastureland.

⁹Would a wild ox agree
  to live in your barn
  and labor for you?
¹⁰Could you force him to plow
  or to drag a heavy log
  to smooth out the soil?
¹¹Can you depend on him
  to use his great strength
  and do your heavy work?
¹²Can you trust him
  to harvest your grain
  or take it to your barn
  from the threshing place?

An Ostrich Proudly Flaps
Her Wings

¹³An ostrich proudly
  flaps her wings,
  but not because

[1]**38.36** *way:* One possible meaning for the difficult Hebrew text of verse 36.

The LORD asked Job, "Do you know the laws that govern
the heavens, and can you make them rule the earth?"
JOB 38.33

she loves her young.[m]

14She abandons her eggs
and lets the dusty ground
keep them warm.

15And she doesn't seem to worry
that the feet of an animal
could crush them all.

16She treats her eggs as though
they were not her own,
unconcerned that her work
might be for nothing.

17I myself made her foolish
and without common sense.

18But once she starts running,[n]
she laughs at a rider
on the fastest horse.

Did You Give Horses Their Strength?

19Did you give horses their strength
and the flowing hair
along their necks?

20Did you make them able
to jump like grasshoppers
or to frighten people
with their snorting?

21Before horses are ridden
into battle,
they paw at the ground,
proud of their strength.

22Laughing at fear, they rush
toward the fighting,

23while the weapons of their riders
rattle and flash in the sun.

24Unable to stand still,
they gallop eagerly into battle
when trumpets blast.

25Stirred by the distant smells

and sounds of war, they snort
in reply to the trumpet.

26Did you teach hawks to fly south
for the winter?

*27Did you train eagles[o] to build

28   their nests on rocky cliffs,

29where they can look down
to spot their next meal?

30Then their young gather to feast
wherever the victim lies.

The Lord Continues
I Am the Lord All-Powerful

40 *1I am the Lord All-Powerful,
2but you have argued
that I am wrong.
Now you must answer me.

3Job said to the Lord:

4   Who am I to answer you?

5I did speak once or twice,
but never again.

6Then out of the storm
the Lord said to Job:

7Face me and answer
the questions I ask!

8Are you trying to prove
that you are innocent
by accusing me of injustice?

9Do you have a powerful arm
and a thundering voice
that compare with mine?

10If so, then surround yourself
with glory and majesty.

*11Show your furious anger!
Throw down and crush

12   all who are proud and evil.

13Wrap them in grave clothes

39.20 *grasshoppers:* Winged insects that move by jumping or flying.

Locusts

39.26,27 *hawks . . . eagles:* Hawks and eagles are praised for protecting their eggs in nests built high where enemies cannot reach them. They also provide food for their young. Job had earlier described God as watching him closely and hunting him, just as the eagle and hawk fly high above the earth looking for prey.

40.1 Lord *All-Powerful:* Three names for Israel's God appear in these verses. "Lord" is a translation of the name *Yahweh.* "All-Powerful" is a translation of the names *El* and *Shaddai.*

40.5 *never again:* Job recognizes how hopeless it is to argue with the Lord, so he vows to stop questioning the Lord's actions.

---

[m]39.13 *young:* One possible meaning for the difficult Hebrew text of verse 13.   [n]39.18 *starts running:* One possible meaning for the difficult Hebrew text.   [o]39.27 *eagles:* Or "vultures."

The Lord asked Job, "Do you have a powerful arm and a thundering voice that compare with mine? If so, then surround yourself with glory and majesty." Job 40.9,10

40.23 *Jordan River:* The animal described in 40.15-24 is the hippopotamus. The hippopotamus and the crocodile are found in Egypt, but not in the Jordan River, which flows from Lake Galilee to the Dead Sea. The Jordan River may have been mentioned here as an example of fast-moving water, which doesn't frighten or panic the hippopotamus. **(See Map 2 on pg 1880.)**

41.1-34 *sea monster . . . king of all proud creatures:* In the Old Testament, the term translated here as "sea monster" is a symbol for powerful forces that only God can control. Such a monster can also be a symbol of evil and stand for God's enemies (Job 3.8; Ps 74.14; 104.26; Isa 27.1). The point is that no human could attack and defeat the monster, which God defeated, so how could a human like Job hope to attack God?

and bury them together
in the dusty soil.
[14]Do this, and I will agree
that you have won
this argument.

I Created You

[15]I created both you
and the hippopotamus.[P]
It eats only grass like an ox,
[16]but look at the mighty muscles
in its body [17]and legs.
Its tail is like a cedar tree,
and its thighs are thick.
[18]The bones in its legs
are like bronze or iron.

[19]I made it more powerful
than any other creature,
yet I am stronger still.
[20]Undisturbed, it eats grass
while the other animals
play nearby.[q]
*[21]It rests in the shade of trees
along the riverbank
[22]or hides among reeds
in the swamp.
[23]It remains calm and unafraid
with the Jordan River rushing
and splashing in its face.
[24]There is no way to capture
a hippopotamus—
not even by hooking its nose
or blinding its eyes.

THE LORD CONTINUES
Can You Catch a Sea Monster?

41 Can you catch a sea monster[r]
by using a fishhook?
Can you tie its mouth shut
with a rope?
[2]Can it be led around
by a ring in its nose
or a hook in its jaw?
[3]Will it beg for mercy?
[4]Will it surrender
as a slave for life?
[5]Can it be tied by the leg
like a pet bird
for little girls?
[6]Is it ever chopped up
and its pieces bargained for
in the fish-market?
[7]Can it be killed
with harpoons or spears?
[8]Wrestle it just once—
that will be the end.
[9]Merely a glimpse of this monster
makes all courage melt.
[10]And if it is too fierce
for anyone to attack,
who would dare oppose me?
[11]I am in command of the world
and in debt to no one.

[12]What powerful legs,
what a stout body
this monster possesses!
[13]Who could strip off its armor
or bring it under control
with a harness?
[14]Who would try to open its jaws,

P40.15 *the hippopotamus:* The Hebrew text has "Behemoth," which was sometimes understood to be a sea monster like Rahab (9.13; 26.12), Leviathan (3.8; 41.1), and Tannin (7.12).   **q40.20** *nearby:* One possible meaning for the difficult Hebrew text of verse 20.   **r41.1** *sea monster:* The Hebrew text has "Leviathan," which may refer to a sea monster or possibly to a crocodile in this verse (see the note at 3.8).

full of fearsome teeth?
*15Its back[s] is covered
  with shield after shield,
16firmly bound and closer together
17   than breath to breath.

When This Monster Sneezes

18When this monster sneezes,
  lightning flashes, and its eyes
    glow like the dawn.
19Sparks and fiery flames
    explode from its mouth.
20And smoke spews from its nose
  like steam
    from a boiling pot,
21while its blazing breath
    scorches everything in sight.

22Its neck is so tremendous
    that everyone trembles,
23the weakest parts of its body
  are harder than iron,
24   and its heart is stone.
25When this noisy monster appears,
  even the most powerful[t]
    turn and run in fear.
26No sword or spear can harm it,
27and weapons of bronze or iron
  are as useless as straw
    or rotten wood.
28Rocks thrown from a sling
  cause it no more harm
    than husks of grain.
This monster fears no arrows,
29   it simply smiles at spears,
  and striking it with a stick
    is like slapping it with straw.

30As it crawls through the mud,
  its sharp and spiny hide
    tears the ground apart.
31And when it swims down deep,
  the sea starts churning
    like boiling oil,
32and it leaves behind a trail
  of shining white foam.
33No other creature on earth
  is so fearless.
34It is king of all proud creatures,
  and it looks upon the others
    as nothing.

Job's Reply to the Lord
No One Can Oppose You

42 Job said:
  2No one can oppose you,
  because you have the power
    to do what you want.
3 You asked why I talk so much
    when I know so little.
I have talked about things
  that are far beyond
    my understanding.
4 You told me to listen
    and answer your questions.[u]
5I heard about you from others;
  now I have seen you
    with my own eyes.
6That's why I hate myself
  and sit here in dust and ashes
    to show my sorrow.

The Lord Corrects Job's Friends

7The Lord said to Eliphaz:
  What my servant Job has said about
me is true, but I am angry with you
and your two friends for not telling
the truth. 8So I want you to go over to
Job and offer seven bulls and seven

42.2-6 *you have the power... I hate myself:* The experience of facing the Lord and the Lord's questions has made Job realize just how powerful the Lord is. The Lord is beyond Job's understanding. Job had heard about the Lord, but seeing the Lord face to face appears to have turned the questioning Job into a more trusting Job.

---

[s]41.15 *back*: Two ancient translations; Hebrew "pride."   [t]41.25 *most powerful*: Or "gods."
[u]42.4 *questions*: One possible meaning for the difficult Hebrew text of verse 4.

42.8 *sacrifice to please me:* These sacrifices have traditionally been called "whole burnt offerings" because the whole animal was burned on the altar. A main purpose of such a sacrifice was to please the LORD with the smell of the sacrifice, and so in the CEV they are called "sacrifices to please the LORD." **(See the chart Sacrifices and Offerings on pg 1828.)**

42.13-15 *three daughters . . . gave them shares of his property:* In ancient times, it was unusual for daughters to inherit a share of their father's possessions and property, unless the man had no sons (Num 27.1-11).

goats on an altar as a sacrifice to please me.[v] After this, Job will pray, and I will agree not to punish you for your foolishness. [9]Eliphaz, Bildad, and Zophar obeyed the LORD, and he answered Job's prayer.

A Happy Ending

[10]After Job had prayed for his three friends, the LORD made Job twice as rich as he had been before. [11]Then Job gave a feast for his brothers and sisters and for his old friends. They expressed their sorrow for the suffering the LORD had brought on him, and they each gave Job some silver and a gold ring.

[12]The LORD now blessed Job more than ever; he gave him 14,000 sheep, 6,000 camels, 1,000 pair of oxen, and 1,000 donkeys.

[13]In addition to seven sons, Job had three daughters, [14]whose names were Jemimah, Keziah, and Keren Happuch. [15]They were the most beautiful women in that part of the world, and Job gave them shares of his property, along with their brothers.

[16]Job lived for another 140 years—long enough to see his great-grandchildren have children of their own—[17]and when he finally died, he was very old.

[v]**42.8** *sacrifice to please me:* These sacrifices have traditionally been called "whole burnt offerings" because the whole animal was burned on the altar. A main purpose of such sacrifices was to please the LORD with the smell of the sacrifice, and so in the CEV they are often called "sacrifices to please the LORD."

Reflection Questions About Job 1.1—42.17

1. What picture does Job 1,2 give of Satan? Of God?

2. List the four ways that Job lost everything (1.13-19). What did Job do after he lost these things (1.20-22)? Who was especially surprised at Job's reaction? Why?

3. What did Satan ask for next (2.4-7)? Again, what was Job's reaction (2.10)?

4. What is the first thing Job's friends did when they saw him (2.12,13)? In your opinion, was their action helpful to Job or not? Why?

5. What are some ways we can respond to people who are in great sorrow or suffering a great loss? If you were hurting like Job, what help would you want? Where would you mostly likely turn for help or comfort?

6. Summarize the advice given to Job by each of his friends—Eliphaz (chapters 4,5; 15; 22), Bildad (8; 18; 25), and Zophar (11; 20). How did Job respond to each friend?

7. According to JOB, what is true wisdom and where does it come from (28.12-28)? Does modern society define wisdom the same way as it is defined in JOB? If not, what are the differences?

8. What does Elihu tell Job to do (34.31; 36.17-23; 37.14)? Do you think Elihu's advice is any better or any worse than that of Job's other friends? Why or why not?

9. Based on the LORD's conversations with Job in chapters 38–41, how would you describe who the LORD is and what the LORD does? What effect does the LORD's response have on Job (40.3-5; 42.1-6)?

10. The book of JOB forces the reader to consider difficult questions, such as:
    a. Where does suffering come from?
    b. Why do good people suffer and evil people prosper?
    c. Where does evil come from?
    In your opinion, does the book give clear answers to these questions? Explain.

psalms

Read this ancient book of songs and prayers to discover what it has to say about life, about God, and about living as a person of faith.

WHAT MAKES PSALMS SPECIAL?

PSALMS is the longest book in the Bible, and it expresses many of the Bible's main ideas. It contains songs of praise, prayers for God's help, and poems that express trust in God. The psalms express every possible human feeling, including sorrow and joy, doubt and trust, pain and comfort, despair and hope, anger and contentment, the desire for revenge and the willingness to forgive. As models of prayer and praise, the psalms invite people to share every part of their lives with God.

The individual psalms in the book were composed and collected over hundreds of years. Though some psalms probably date from early in Israel's history, others were probably written after the time of the exile in Babylon. The titles of 73 psalms mention Israel's King David, who ruled Israel from about 1010 to 970 B.C. David may have written some of these psalms, but others were written after David's time. The persons who collected the psalms put David's name in the titles of many psalms as a way of honoring David—presenting him as a model of how a person can depend upon God in difficult times. PSALMS became the hymnbook or prayer book used in the temple in Jerusalem, then in Jewish meeting places (synagogues), and later in Christian churches.

Jesus used the psalms when he preached and taught, and the writers of the New Testament often quote PSALMS. For example, a verse from Psalm 118 is mentioned six times in the New Testament.

WHAT'S THE STORY BEHIND THE SCENE?

PSALMS is traditionally divided into five sections, or books. Some psalms have music notations (12; 22; 67; 76) or tell how and when the psalm is to be used (38; 92; 120–134).

For more information on the different types of psalms that appear in the Bible, **see the chart Kinds of Psalms on pg 1833.**

HOW IS PSALMS CONSTRUCTED?

Because PSALMS is a collection of 150 separate songs, prayers, and poems, it may appear that the book has no structure. Yet there are smaller collections within the larger whole. In addition, a similar concluding "amen" verse appears to divide PSALMS into five smaller books (see 41.13; 72.19; 89.52; and 106.48). This five-book structure may have been meant to remind the people that the five "books" of psalms had the same purpose as the five books of Moses (GENESIS—DEUTERONOMY), namely to teach them about God and what it means to follow God.

The five "books" that provide the outline of PSALMS are:

Book I (1.1—41.13)
Book II (42.1—72.20)
Book III (73.1—89.52)
Book IV (90.1—106.48)
Book V (107.1—150.6)

Psalms is a collection of songs, hymns, poems, and prayers written over a period of at least five hundred years and intended for use in public and private worship. The wide range of feelings expressed in the psalms—sorrow and joy, despair and hope, doubt and trust, pain and consolation, anger and contentment—has made them the most-quoted literature in the Bible. A large number of the psalms are expressions of praise and thanks to God; many are pleas for God's help in a time of crisis; some celebrate an important event such as a military victory or the enthronement of a king; and others are expressions of trust in God or delight in the wisdom God provides. Psalms traditionally is divided into five collections or "books" and the last verse of the last psalm in each book concludes with an expression of praise and a double "amen."

One of the most noteworthy aspects of Hebrew poetry is its use of parallelism, in which one verse echoes, modifies, expands, or contradicts statements made in an adjacent verse. Paying attention to the psalmists' use of parallelism is helpful in discovering the key themes of psalms and enriching an understanding of this still vital, ancient literature.

Some psalms are preceded by "superscriptions." These appear in parentheses under the psalm number in CEV and can indicate a number of different things: (1) the name of the person who wrote the psalm or the person it was dedicated to, (2) information about the occasion for which the psalm was written, or (3) instructions for performing the psalm as part of worship.

Outline

BOOK I
(Psalms 1–41)

PSALM 1
The Way to Happiness

[1]God blesses those people
   who refuse evil advice
   and won't follow sinners
   or join in sneering at God.
[2]Instead, they find happiness
   in the Teaching of the LORD,
   and they think about it
   day and night.

[3]They are like trees
   growing beside a stream,
trees that produce
fruit in season
   and always have leaves.
Those people succeed
   in everything they do.

[4]That isn't true of those
   who are evil—
they are like straw
blown by the wind.
[5]Sinners won't have an excuse
   on the day of judgment,
and they won't have a place
   with the people of God.
[6]The LORD protects everyone
   who follows him,
but the wicked follow a road
   that leads to ruin.

PSALM 2
The LORD's Chosen King

[1]Why do the nations plot,[a]
   and why do their people
   make useless plans?[b]
[2]The kings of this earth
   have all joined together
to turn against the LORD
   and his chosen king.
[3]They say, "Let's cut the ropes
   and set ourselves free!"

[4]In heaven the LORD laughs
   as he sits on his throne,

---

[a]2.1 *Why . . . plot*: Or "Why are the nations restless?" [b]2.1 *make useless plans*: Or "grumble uselessly."

1.1,2 *God blesses . . . find happiness in the Teaching of the LORD.* To be blessed and happy means more than just feeling good. It means doing what God wants. Blessings and happiness come from being constantly open to God's "teaching."

Law

1.3 *trees*: Trees growing beside a stream put down deep roots that allow them to be healthy and bear fruit even in times of little rain (Jer 17.8).

1.4,5 *That . . . day of judgment*: Those who are "evil," sinful, or "wicked" turn away from God and disobey God's Teaching. Such self-centered persons are like "straw." They have no roots. They will not survive the "day of judgment."

Day of the LORD

Enemies (The Wicked)

2.2 *his chosen king*: "His chosen king" refers to the one chosen by God to lead Israel. This psalm was used when new kings took office, a time when the nation was vulnerable to attack by other nations or when rival leaders were likely to plot rebellion. Those chosen to serve God in a special way were "anointed," meaning they had oil poured over their heads as a sign that God would be with them. The English word "Messiah" comes from the Hebrew word for "anointed one."

Messiah (Chosen One)

making fun of the nations.
[5]The LORD becomes furious
and threatens them.
His anger terrifies them
as he says,
[6]"I've put my king on Zion,
my sacred hill."

[7]I will tell the promise
that the LORD made to me:
"You are my son, because today
I have become your father.
[8]Ask me for the nations,
and every nation on earth
will belong to you.
[9]You will smash them
with an iron rod
and shatter them
like dishes of clay."

[10]Be smart, all you rulers,
and pay close attention.
[11]Serve and honor the LORD;
be glad and tremble.
[12]Show respect to his son
because if you don't,
the LORD might become furious
and suddenly destroy you.[c]
But he blesses and protects
everyone who runs to him.

PSALM 3
(Written by David when he was running
from his son Absalom.)
An Early Morning Prayer

[1]I have a lot of enemies, LORD.
Many fight against [2]me and say,
"God won't rescue you!"

[3]But you are my shield,
and you give me victory

and great honor.
[4]I pray to you, and you answer
from your sacred hill.

[5]I sleep and wake up refreshed
because you, LORD,
protect me.
[6]Ten thousand enemies attack
from every side,
but I am not afraid.

[7]Come and save me, LORD God!
Break my enemies' jaws
and shatter their teeth,
[8]because you protect
and bless your people.

PSALM 4
(A psalm by David for the music leader. Use stringed
instruments.)
An Evening Prayer

[1]You are my God and protector.
Please answer my prayer.
I was in terrible distress,
but you set me free.
Now have pity and listen
as I pray.

[2]How long will you people
refuse to respect me?[d]
You love foolish things,
and you run after
what is worthless.[e]

[3]The LORD has chosen
everyone who is faithful
to be his very own,[f]
and he answers my prayers.
[4]But each of you
had better tremble
and turn from your sins.

[c]**2.11,12** *Serve . . . you:* One possible meaning for the difficult Hebrew text of verses 11,12. [d]**4.2** *me:* Or "my God." [e]**4.2** *foolish . . . worthless:* This may refer to idols and false gods. [f]**4.3** *has chosen . . . very own:* Some Hebrew manuscripts have "work miracles for his faithful people."

Silently search your heart
as you lie in bed.
[5]Offer the proper sacrifices
and trust the LORD.

[6]There are some who ask,
"Who will be good to us?"
Let your kindness, LORD,
shine brightly on us.
[7]You brought me more happiness
than a rich harvest
of grain and grapes.
[8]I can lie down
and sleep soundly
because you, LORD,
will keep me safe.

PSALM 5

(A psalm by David for the music leader. Use flutes.)

A Prayer for Help

[1]Listen, LORD, as I pray!
Pay attention when I groan.[g]
[2]You are my King and my God.
Answer my cry for help
because I pray to you.
[3]Each morning you listen
to my prayer,
as I bring my requests[h] to you
and wait for your reply.

[4]You are not the kind of God
who is pleased with evil.
Sinners can't stay with you.
[5]No one who boasts can stand
in your presence, LORD,
and you hate evil people.
[6]You destroy every liar,
and you despise violence
and deceit.

[7]Because of your great mercy,
I come to your house, LORD,

and I am filled with wonder
as I bow down to worship
at your holy temple.
[8]You do what is right,
and I ask you to guide me.
Make your teaching clear
because of my enemies.

[9]Nothing they say is true!
They just want to destroy.
Their words are deceitful
like a hidden pit,
and their tongues are good
only for telling lies.
[10]Punish them, God,
and let their own plans
bring their downfall.
Get rid of them!
They keep committing crimes
and turning against you.

[11]Let all who run to you
for protection
always sing joyful songs.
Provide shelter for those
who truly love you
and let them rejoice.
[12]Our LORD, you bless those
who live right,
and you shield them
with your kindness.

PSALM 6

(A psalm by David for the music leader. Use stringed
instruments.[i])

A Prayer in Time of Trouble

[1]Don't punish me, LORD,
or even correct me
when you are angry!
[2]Have pity on me and heal

---

[g]5.1 *when I groan*: Or "to my thoughts" or "to my words."   [h]5.3 *requests*: Or "sacrifices."
[i]**Psalm 6** *instruments*: The Hebrew text adds "according to the sheminith," which may refer to a
musical instrument with eight strings.

■ 4.6 *There are some who ask*: The
question is asked by the enemies, who
desire material gain. The psalmist is
content to depend upon God.

■ 5.2 *King*: This title is often used
for God in PSALMS.

■ 5.7 *your house . . . holy temple*:
The Hebrew word for "temple" also can
mean "palace." Because it was the
"house" of God "my King" (5.2), it is
fitting that the psalmist would "bow
down" to show his loyalty.

■ 5.10-12 *Punish them . . . bless
those who live right*: The psalmist asks
for God's justice. Those who lie and destroy are to be punished because of
their own evil plans and crimes. Those
who love God, obey his commands ("live
right"), and turn to him for protection
will be blessed. That the enemies can
"keep committing crimes" means that
God's power does not take the form of
immediate enforcement. This is why
the psalmist has to "wait." God does
not only use his power to destroy liars
and people who do evil. He also uses it
to extend his mercy to people who suffer and need God's protection. God's
"mercy" offers true security.

■ 6.1-4 *Don't punish . . . come to
my rescue*: These verses suggest that
this is a prayer for healing. Even if the
psalmist views his sickness as punishment that comes from the LORD, the
psalmist trusts that the LORD will save
him, and that God's "wonderful love"
will be stronger than God's anger.

6.5 *If I die, I cannot . . . remember you:* For most of the Old Testament period, people believed that death cut a person off from God.

Eternal Life

Enemies (The Wicked)

7 (Title) *Cush . . . tribe of Benjamin:* It is not clear who Cush is, since no one by this name appears in the stories about David in 1 and 2 SAMUEL. The tribe of Benjamin was named for Jacob and Rachel's youngest son (Gen 35.16-18). They settled in the area just north of the lands settled by the tribe of Judah. **(See Map 3 on pg 1881.)**

7.3-5 *I . . . dirt:* The psalmist seems to have been falsely accused of something by his "enemies." In response to the false charges, he offers his innocence in the form of an oath, a very serious promise made to God.

Making Promises (Vows)

7.6,7 *See that justice is done . . . as you sit on your throne:* These verses suggest that God is king over all. One of the major responsibilities of a king was to settle disputes and to see that justice was done.

Justice

my feeble body.
My bones tremble with fear,
³and I am in deep distress.
How long will it be?

⁴Turn and come to my rescue.
Show your wonderful love
and save me, LORD.
⁵If I die, I cannot praise you
or even remember you.
⁶My groaning has worn me out.
At night my bed and pillow
are soaked with tears.
⁷Sorrow has made my eyes dim,
and my sight has failed
because of my enemies.

⁸You, LORD, heard my crying,
and those hateful people
had better leave me alone.
⁹You have answered my prayer
and my plea for mercy.
¹⁰My enemies will be ashamed
and terrified,
as they quickly run away
in complete disgrace.

PSALM 7
(Written by David.[j] He sang this to the LORD because
of Cush from the tribe of Benjamin.)
The LORD Always Does Right

¹You, LORD God,
are my protector.
Rescue me and keep me safe
from all who chase me.
²Or else they will rip me apart
like lions attacking a victim,
and no one will save me.

³I am innocent, LORD God!
⁴I have not betrayed a friend
or had pity on an enemy[k]
who attacks for no reason.
⁵If I have done any of this,
then let my enemies
chase and capture me.
Let them trample me to death
and leave me in the dirt.

⁶Get angry, LORD God!
Do something!
Attack my furious enemies.
See that justice is done.
⁷Make the nations come to you,
as you sit on your throne[l]
above them all.

⁸Our LORD, judge the nations!
Judge me and show that I
am honest and innocent.
⁹You know every heart and mind,
and you always do right.
Now make violent people stop,
but protect all of us
who obey you.

¹⁰You, God, are my shield,
the protector of everyone
whose heart is right.
¹¹You see that justice is done,
and each day
you take revenge.
¹²Whenever your enemies refuse
to change their ways,
you sharpen your sword
and string your bow.
¹³Your deadly arrows are ready
with flaming tips.

[j]**Psalm 7** *Written by David:* The Hebrew text has "a shiggaion by David," which may refer to a psalm of mourning.   [k]**7.4** *had pity on an enemy:* Or "failed to have pity on an enemy."   [l]**7.7** *sit . . . throne:* Or "return to your place."

[14]An evil person is like a woman
    about to give birth
to a hateful, deceitful,
    and rebellious child.
[15]Such people dig a deep hole,
    then fall in it themselves.
[16]The trouble they cause
    comes back on them,
and their heads are crushed
    by their own evil deeds.

[17]I will praise you, LORD!
    You always do right.
I will sing about you,
    the LORD Most High.

PSALM 8
(A psalm by David for the music leader.[m])
The Wonderful Name of the LORD

[1]Our LORD and Ruler,
your name is wonderful
    everywhere on earth!
You let your glory be seen[n]
    in the heavens above.
[2]With praises from children
    and from tiny infants,
    you have built a fortress.
It makes your enemies silent,
and all who turn against you
    are left speechless.

[3]I often think of the heavens
    your hands have made,
and of the moon and stars
    you put in place.
[4]Then I ask, "Why do you care
    about us humans?
Why are you concerned
    for us weaklings?"
[5]You made us a little lower

than you yourself,[o]
and you have crowned us
    with glory and honor.

[6]You let us rule everything
    your hands have made.
And you put all of it
    under our power—
[7]the sheep and the cattle,
    and every wild animal,
[8]the birds in the sky,
    the fish in the sea,
    and all ocean creatures.

[9]Our LORD and Ruler,
your name is wonderful
    everywhere on earth!

PSALM 9
(A psalm by David for the music leader. To the tune
"The Death of the Son.")
Sing Praises to the LORD

[1]I will praise you, LORD,
    with all my heart
and tell about the wonders
    you have worked.
[2]God Most High, I will rejoice;
I will celebrate and sing
    because of you.

[3]When my enemies face you,
    they run away and stumble
    and are destroyed.
[4]You take your seat as judge,
    and your fair decisions prove
    that I was in the right.
[5]You warn the nations
    and destroy evil people;
you wipe out their names
    forever and ever.

7.14-16 *evil person . . . trouble . . . comes back on them:* A common belief in ancient times was that evildoers would eventually be punished while those who turned to God and "lived right" would be blessed. This concept—that a person always gets what he or she deserves—is referred to as "just retribution." However, a more complicated view is found in other examples of Hebrew wisdom literature.

8.1 *Ruler:* "Ruler" is a title that describes God's kingship. The rest of the psalm tells how God rules by sharing power with human beings.

9.1 *wonders:* God's "wonders" included delivering the people out of their slavery in Egypt (Exod 5–14) and sending bread ("manna") to the Israelites starving in the wilderness (Exod 16.1-36). These and God's many other wonders provide help for people in need or danger.

9.3 *enemies:* These are people who oppose God and who selfishly make victims of others. They are mentioned often in Psalms 9 and 10, which may have originally been one psalm. In Hebrew, every other verse of the two psalms begins with a successive letter of the Hebrew alphabet, making an acrostic.

Enemies (The Wicked)

9.7 *your throne:* God's throne can mean God's place in heaven, but the sacred chest in the temple was also viewed as God's throne on earth.

The Sacred Chest

9.8,9 *You judge . . . with justice . . . poor can run to you:* A king's main responsibility was to "judge" in order to establish "justice," especially for victims of injustice. Because God rules justly, victims "can run to" God for help. The so-called "victims" are the poor, those in need, the homeless, helpless, and those who suffer.

Justice

The Poor

9.13 *the gates that lead to death:* For most of the Old Testament period, people believed that everyone who died went to the dark underground place known as "the world of the dead," or "Sheol." Sheol is usually described as being totally silent, a place where no one knows or feels anything.

Resurrection

Hell

Eternal Life

10.1 *Why . . . I am in trouble:* These kinds of questions appear often in the prayers for help. They are usually balanced by the confidence that God is or will be present.

⁶Our enemies are destroyed
  completely for all time.
Their cities are torn down,
and they will never
  be remembered again.

⁷You rule forever, Lord,
and you are on your throne,
  ready for judgment.
⁸You judge the world fairly
and treat all nations
  with justice.
⁹The poor can run to you
because you are a fortress
  in times of trouble.
¹⁰Everyone who honors your name
  can trust you,
because you are faithful
  to all who depend on you.

¹¹You rule from Zion, Lord,
  and we sing about you
to let the nations know
  everything you have done.
¹²You did not forget
  to punish the guilty
or listen to the cries
  of those in need.

¹³Please have mercy, Lord!
  My enemies mistreat me.
Keep me from the gates
  that lead to death,
¹⁴and I will sing about you
  at the gate to Zion.
I will be happy there
  because you rescued me.

¹⁵Our Lord, the nations fell
  into their own pits,
and their feet were caught
  in their own traps.
¹⁶You showed what you are like,
  and you made certain
    that justice is done,

but evil people are trapped
  by their own evil deeds.
¹⁷The wicked will go down
  to the world of the dead
to be with those nations
  that forgot about you.

¹⁸The poor and the homeless
  won't always be forgotten
  and without hope.

¹⁹Do something, Lord!
  Don't let the nations win.
Make them stand trial
  in your court of law.
²⁰Make the nations afraid
  and let them all discover
    just how weak they are.

PSALM 10
A Prayer for Help

¹Why are you far away, Lord?
Why do you hide yourself
  when I am in trouble?
²Proud and brutal people
  hunt down the poor.
But let them get caught
  by their own evil plans!

³The wicked brag about
  their deepest desires.
Those greedy people hate
  and curse you, Lord.
⁴The wicked are too proud
  to turn to you
or even think about you.
⁵They are always successful,
though they can't understand
  your teachings,
and they keep sneering
  at their enemies.

⁶In their hearts they say,
  "Nothing can hurt us!

The poor and the homeless won't always be forgotten and without hope. Ps 9.18

We'll always be happy
and free from trouble."
⁷They curse and tell lies,
and all they talk about
is how to be cruel
or how to do wrong.

⁸They hide outside villages,
waiting to strike and murder
some innocent victim.
⁹They are hungry lions
hiding in the bushes,
hoping to catch
some helpless passerby.
They trap the poor in nets
and drag them away.
¹⁰They crouch down and wait
to grab a victim.
¹¹They say, "God can't see!
He's got on a blindfold."

¹²Do something, Lord God,
and use your powerful arm
to help those in need.
¹³The wicked don't respect you.
In their hearts they say,
"God won't punish us!"

¹⁴But you see the trouble
and the distress,
and you will do something.
The poor can count on you,
and so can orphans.
¹⁵Now break the power
of all merciless people.
Punish them for doing wrong
and make them stop.

¹⁶Our Lord, you will always rule,
but every godless nation
will vanish from the earth.
¹⁷You listen to the longings
of those who suffer.

P11.6 *fiery coals:* Or "trouble, fire."

You offer them hope,
and you pay attention
to their cries for help.
¹⁸You defend orphans
and everyone else in need,
so that no one on earth
can terrify others again.

PSALM 11
(A psalm by David for the music leader.)
Trusting the Lord

¹The Lord is my fortress!
Don't say to me,
"Escape like a bird
to the mountains!"
²You tell me, "Watch out!
Those evil people have put
their arrows on their bows,
and they are standing
in the shadows,
aiming at good people.
³What can an honest person do
when everything crumbles?"

⁴The Lord is sitting
in his sacred temple
on his throne in heaven.
He knows everything we do
because he sees us all.
⁵The Lord tests honest people,
but despises those
who are cruel
and love violence.
⁶He will send fiery coalsP
and flaming sulfur
down on the wicked,
and they will drink nothing
but a scorching wind.

⁷The Lord always does right
and wants justice done.

13.2 *enemies:* Even when the "enemies" (13.4) are not the direct cause of the distress, they are present to take advantage of the situation.

Enemies (The Wicked)

13.5,6 *I trust ... about you:* The sudden move to trust and celebration is not unusual in the prayers for help. It is possible that these verses were written later than 13.1-4, after a cure or rescue took place. They also may be a response to a promise delivered by a priest. In this case, the psalmist looks forward with certain "trust" in God's goodness and "love." In either case, trust in God means both suffering and celebration at the same time.

14.1 *fool:* This is another name for the wicked. "A fool" does not lack intelligence, though he may lack wisdom. Most importantly, a fool lacks trust in God and love for others.

Everyone who does right
will see his face.

Psalm 12

(A psalm by David for the music leader.[q])

A Prayer for Help

[1]Please help me, LORD!
All who were faithful
and all who were loyal
have disappeared.
[2]Everyone tells lies,
and no one is sincere.
[3]Won't you chop off
all flattering tongues
that brag so loudly?
[4]They say to themselves,
"We are great speakers.
No one else has a chance."

[5]But you, LORD, tell them,
"I will do something!
The poor are mistreated
and helpless people moan.
I'll rescue all who suffer."

[6]Our LORD, you are true
to your promises,
and your word is like silver
heated seven times
in a fiery furnace.[r]
[7]You will protect us
and always keep us safe
from those people.
[8]But all who are wicked
will keep on strutting,
while everyone praises
their shameless deeds.[s]

Psalm 13

(A psalm by David for the music leader.)

A Prayer for the LORD's Help

[1]How much longer, LORD,
will you forget about me?
Will it be forever?
How long will you hide?
[2]How long must I be confused
and miserable all day?
How long will my enemies
keep beating me down?

[3]Please listen, LORD God,
and answer my prayers.
Make my eyes sparkle again,
or else I will fall
into the sleep of death.
[4]My enemies will say,
"Now we've won!"
They will be greatly pleased
when I am defeated.

[5]I trust your love,
and I feel like celebrating
because you rescued me.
[6]You have been good to me, LORD,
and I will sing about you.

Psalm 14

(A psalm by David for the music leader.)

No One Can Ignore the LORD

[1]Only a fool would say,
"There is no God!"
People like that are worthless;
they are heartless and cruel
and never do right.

[2]From heaven the LORD
looks down to see

[q]**Psalm 12** *leader:* The Hebrew text adds "according to the sheminith," which may be a musical instrument with eight strings.   [r]**12.6** *in a fiery furnace:* The Hebrew text has "in a furnace to the ground," which may describe part of a process for refining silver in Old Testament times.
[s]**12.8** *while ... deeds:* One possible meaning for the difficult Hebrew text.

if anyone is wise enough
   to search for him.
3But all of them are corrupt;
   no one does right.

4Won't you evil people learn?
   You refuse to pray,
and you gobble up
   the Lord's people.
5But you will be frightened,
because God is on the side
   of every good person.
6You may spoil the plans
of the poor,
   but the Lord protects them.

7I long for someone from Zion
   to come and save Israel!
Our Lord, when you bless
   your people again,
Jacob's family will be glad,
   and Israel will celebrate.

Psalm 15

(A psalm by David.)

Who May Worship the Lord?

1Who may stay in God's temple
or live on the holy mountain
   of the Lord?

2Only those who obey God
   and do as they should.
They speak the truth
3 and don't spread gossip;
they treat others fairly
   and don't say cruel things.

4They hate worthless people,
but show respect for all
   who worship the Lord.
And they keep their promises,

no matter what the cost.
5They lend their money
   without charging interest,
and they don't take bribes
   to hurt the innocent.

Those who do these things
   will always stand firm.

Psalm 16

(A special psalm by David.)

The Best Choice

1Protect me, Lord God!
   I run to you for safety,
2and I have said,
   "Only you are my Lord!
Every good thing I have
   is a gift from you."

3Your people are wonderful,
   and they make me happy,[t]
4but worshipers of other gods
   will have much sorrow.[u]
I refuse to offer sacrifices
of blood to those gods
   or worship in their name.

5You, Lord, are all I want!
You are my choice,
   and you keep me safe.
6You make my life pleasant,
   and my future is bright.

7I praise you, Lord,
   for being my guide.
Even in the darkest night,
   your teachings fill my mind.
8I will always look to you,
as you stand beside me
   and protect me from fear.
9With all my heart,

15.1 *holy mountain:* The holy mountain is Mount Zion in Jerusalem where the temple, God's earthly house, was built. This psalm may have been used in a ceremony as worshipers entered the temple. Worshipers asked the question in 15.1 as they approached the temple, and the priest answered with 15.2-5.

16.4 *sacrifices of blood:* Throughout the ancient Near East, blood was used in ceremonies honoring various gods, either by pouring it over the altar or by drinking it as an offering. Unlike the people of other nations, the people of Israel were forbidden to eat or drink blood. (See the chart Sacrifices and Offerings on pg 1828.)

   Blood

---

t16.3 *Your people . . . happy:* Or "I was happy worshiping gods I thought were powerful."
u16.4 *but . . . sorrow:* One possible meaning for the difficult Hebrew text.

You, Lord, are all I want! You are my choice, and you keep me safe. Ps 16.5

17.8 *wings:* The mention of God's "wings" suggests that the prayer was offered originally in the temple. The sacred chest, God's earthly throne, was kept in the temple. On its lid were carved two winged creatures (Exod 25.18-22; Isa 6.1,2). They were symbols of protection for the sacred chest. This may explain why God sometimes is pictured with "wings" that protect people.

The Sacred Chest

17.15 *see your face . . . When I awake:* Seeing God's "face" is a way for the psalmist to say that he experienced God's presence and protection in the temple. It is possible that the psalmist spent the night at the temple because he sought protection there or to show his dependence upon God's help.

I will celebrate,
and I can safely rest.

¹⁰ I am your chosen one.
You won't leave me in the grave
or let my body decay.
¹¹You have shown me
the path to life,
and you make me glad
by being near to me.
Sitting at your right side,ᵛ
I will always be joyful.

PSALM 17
(A prayer by David.)
The Prayer of an Innocent Person

¹I am innocent, LORD!
Won't you listen as I pray
and beg for help?
I am honest!
Please hear my prayer.
²Only you can say
that I am innocent,
because only your eyes
can see the truth.

³You know my heart,
and even during the night
you have tested me
and found me innocent.
I have made up my mind
never to tell a lie.
⁴I don't do like others.
I obey your teachings
and am not cruel.
⁵I have followed you,
without ever stumbling.

⁶I pray to you, God,
because you will help me.

Listen and answer my prayer!
⁷ Show your wonderful love.
Your mighty arm protects those
who run to you for safety
from their enemies.
⁸Protect me as you would
your very own eyes;
hide me in the shadow
of your wings.

⁹Don't let my brutal enemies
attack from all sides
and kill me.
¹⁰They refuse to show mercy,
and they keep bragging.

¹¹They have caught up with me!
My enemies are everywhere,
eagerly hoping to smear me
in the dirt.
¹²They are like hungry lions
hunting for food,
or like young lions
hiding in ambush.

¹³Do something, LORD!
Attack and defeat them.
Take your sword and save me
from those evil people.
¹⁴Use your powerful arm
and rescue me
from the hands of mere humans
whose world won't last.ᵂ

You provide food
for those you love.
Their children have plenty,
and their grandchildren
will have more than enough.

¹⁵I am innocent, LORD,
and I will see your face!

ᵛ**16.11** *right side:* The place of power and honor. ᵂ**17.14** *Use . . . last:* One possible meaning for the difficult Hebrew text.

When I awake, all I want
is to see you as you are.

Psalm 18

(For the music leader. A psalm by David, the LORD's
servant. David sang this to the LORD after the LORD
had rescued him from his enemies, but especially
from Saul.)

David's Song of Thanks

¹I love you, LORD God,
and you make me strong.
²You are my mighty rock,ˣ
my fortress, my protector,
the rock where I am safe,
my shield, my powerful weapon,ʸ
and my place of shelter.

³I praise you, LORD!
I prayed, and you rescued me
from my enemies.
⁴Death had wrapped
its ropes around me,
and I was almost swallowed
by its flooding waters.

⁵Ropes from the world
of the dead
had coiled around me,
and death had set a trap
in my path.
⁶I was in terrible trouble
when I called out to you,
but from your temple
you heard me
and answered my prayer.

⁷The earth shook and shivered,
and the mountains trembled
down to their roots.
You were angry

⁸and breathed out smoke.
Scorching heat and fiery flames
spewed from your mouth.

⁹You opened the heavens
like curtains,
and you came down
with storm clouds
under your feet.
¹⁰You rode on the backs
of flying creatures
and swooped down
with the wind as wings.
¹¹Darkness was your robe;
thunderclouds filled the sky,
hiding you from sight.
¹²Hailstones and fiery coals
lit up the sky
in front of you.

¹³LORD Most High, your voice
thundered from the heavens,
as hailstones and fiery coals
poured down like rain.
¹⁴You scattered your enemies
with arrows of lightning.
¹⁵You roared at the sea,
and its deepest channels
could be seen.
You snorted,
and the earth shook
to its foundations.

¹⁶You reached down from heaven,
and you lifted me
from deep in the ocean.
¹⁷You rescued me from enemies,
who were hateful
and too powerful for me.
¹⁸On the day disaster struck,
they came and attacked,

18 (Title) *David sang . . . from
Saul:* Psalm 18 is almost exactly the
same as 2 Samuel 22. Centuries after
the time of David, this psalm was used
to express the hope that God would
rescue the people of Israel from their
enemies.

18.7-15 *The earth shook . . . its
foundations:* In the Canaanite religion,
the god Baal was considered to control
rain and wind. Yet here that power is
recognized as belonging to God.

18.13 *LORD Most High:* "Most
High" was a term used for the main
Canaanite god in ancient times. The
psalmist uses this title of honor along
with "LORD," the name of Israel's one
true God.

Names of God

ˣ18.2 *mighty rock:* The Hebrew text has "rock," which is sometimes used in poetry to compare the
Lord to a mountain where his people can run for protection from their enemies. ʸ18.2 *my powerful
weapon:* The Hebrew text has "the horn," which refers to the horn of a bull, one of the most powerful animals in ancient Palestine.

18.28 *lamp . . . light:* These are symbols of life. "Light" also stands for the wisdom and truth that come from God, as opposed to the "darkness," which symbolized evil. David was re-membered for giving "light" to his people (2 Sam 21.17). Here David shows humility by saying that his light and life come from God.

18.34-48 *You teach my hands to fight . . . protected me from violent enemies:* These verses are a victory celebration. The king thanks God for preparing him for battle and giving him victory. God teaches the king "to fight" so he can defend Israel against "violent enemies." Nations are put under the king's power, not for the king's personal benefit, but so that the nations will honor Israel's God, and God's justice and peace can be established in all the earth.

Holy War (The LORD's Battles)

but you defended me.
¹⁹When I was fenced in,
   you freed and rescued me
   because you love me.

²⁰You are good to me, LORD,
   because I do right,
   and you reward me
   because I am innocent.
²¹I do what you want
   and never turn to do evil.
²²I keep your laws in mind
   and never look away
   from your teachings.
²³I obey you completely
   and guard against sin.
²⁴You have been good to me
   because I do right;
   you have rewarded me
   for being innocent
   by your standards.

²⁵You are always loyal
   to your loyal people,
   and you are faithful
   to the faithful.
²⁶With all who are sincere,
   you are sincere,
   but you treat the unfaithful
   as their deeds deserve.
²⁷You rescue the humble,
   but you put down all
   who are proud.

²⁸You, the LORD God,
   keep my lamp burning
   and turn darkness to light.
²⁹You help me defeat armies
   and capture cities.

³⁰Your way is perfect, LORD,
   and your word is correct.
   You are a shield for those

who run to you for help.
³¹You alone are God!
   Only you are a mighty rock.ᶻ
³²You give me strength
   and guide me right.
³³You make my feet run as fast
   as those of a deer,
   and you help me stand
   on the mountains.

³⁴You teach my hands to fight
   and my arms to use
   a bow of bronze.
³⁵You alone are my shield.
   Your right hand supports me,
   and by coming to help me,
   you have made me famous.
³⁶You clear the way for me,
   and now I won't stumble.

³⁷I kept chasing my enemies,
   until I caught them
   and destroyed them.
³⁸I stuck my sword
   through my enemies,
   and they were crushed
   under my feet.
³⁹You helped me win victories,
   and you forced my attackers
   to fall victim to me.

⁴⁰You made my enemies run,
   and I killed them.
⁴¹They cried out for help,
   but no one saved them;
   they called out to you,
   but there was no answer.
⁴²I ground them to dust
   blown by the wind,
   and I poured them out
   like mud in the streets.

⁴³You rescued me
   from stubborn people,

ᶻ**18.31** *mighty rock:* See the note at 18.2.

and you made me the leader
of foreign nations,
who are now my slaves.
44They obey and come crawling.
45 They have lost all courage,
and from their fortresses,
they come trembling.

46You are the living LORD!
I will praise you.
You are a mighty rock.[a]
I will honor you
for keeping me safe.
47You took revenge for me,
and you put nations
in my power.
48You protected me
from violent enemies
and made me much greater
than all of them.

49I will praise you, LORD,
and I will honor you
among the nations.
50You give glorious victories
to your chosen king.
Your faithful love for David
and for his descendants
will never end.

PSALM 19

(A psalm by David for the music leader.)
The Wonders of God
and the Goodness of His Law

1The heavens keep telling
the wonders of God,
and the skies declare
what he has done.
2Each day informs
the following day;
each night announces
to the next.

[a]**18.46** *mighty rock*: See the note at 18.2.

3They don't speak a word,
and there is never
the sound of a voice.
4Yet their message reaches
all the earth,
and it travels
around the world.

In the heavens a tent
is set up for the sun.
5It rises like a bridegroom
and gets ready like a hero
eager to run a race.
6It travels all the way
across the sky.
Nothing hides from its heat.

7The Law of the LORD is perfect;
it gives us new life.
His teachings last forever,
and they give wisdom
to ordinary people.
8The LORD's instruction is right;
it makes our hearts glad.
His commands shine brightly,
and they give us light.

9Worshiping the LORD is sacred;
he will always be worshiped.
All his decisions
are correct and fair.
10They are worth more
than the finest gold
and are sweeter than honey
from a honeycomb.

11By your teachings, Lord,
I am warned;
by obeying them,
I am greatly rewarded.
12None of us know our faults.
Forgive me when I sin
without knowing it.

18.46 *mighty rock*: "Mighty rock" is a symbol of God's strength and ability to protect people.

18.50 *David and . . . his descendants*: God promised David that one of David's descendants always would be on the throne.

David

Messiah (Chosen One)

19.1 *The heavens . . . the skies declare*: In PSALMS, songs of praise often invite the whole creation to praise God.

19.7,8 *Law of the LORD . . . give wisdom . . . give us light*: The Hebrew word for "Law" means "teaching." God's "teaching" included written commandments given in the Torah (EXODUS through DEUTERONOMY), but prophets and priests were constantly reinterpreting this material. Just as the sun's heat makes life possible on the earth, so God's teaching "gives new life" to God's people, and is a source of wisdom, guidance, understanding, and insight.

Law

Wisdom

You are the living LORD! I will praise you. Ps 18.46

20.1 *you:* "You" is the king. Verses 1 to 5 are spoken not to God but to the king, perhaps upon coming to the temple to pray for help in battle.

21.3-6 *blessed the king . . . blessings that will last forever:* God's people viewed the king as God's "Son" (2 Sam 7.14; Ps 2.7) and God's "chosen one." "Life that never ends" here probably refers to the promise that the king's family line would continue and that the king would live on through his descendants. In New Testament times, people came to believe that anyone could become a child of God and be raised to life after death (have eternal life).

Son of God

Messiah (Chosen One)

Kingship in Israel

13Don't let me do wrong
  on purpose, Lord,
  or let sin have control
  over my life.
Then I will be innocent,
  and not guilty
  of some terrible fault.

14Let my words and my thoughts
  be pleasing to you, Lord,
because you are my mighty rock[b]
  and my protector.

PSALM 20
(A psalm by David for the music leader.)
A Prayer for Victory

1I pray that the LORD
  will listen when you
  are in trouble,
  and that the God of Jacob
  will keep you safe.
2May the LORD send help
  from his temple
  and come to your rescue
  from Mount Zion.
3May he remember your gifts
  and be pleased
  with what you bring.

4May God do what you want most
  and let all go well for you.
5Then you will win victories,
  and we will celebrate,
  while raising our banners
  in the name of our God.
May the LORD answer
  all your prayers!

6I am certain, Lord,
  that you will help
  your chosen king.

You will answer my prayers
  from your holy place
  in heaven,
and you will save me
  with your mighty arm.

7Some people trust the power
  of chariots or horses,
  but we trust you, LORD God.
8Others will stumble and fall,
  but we will be strong
  and stand firm.

9Give the king victory, LORD,
  and answer our prayers.[c]

PSALM 21
(A psalm by David for the music leader.)
Thanking the LORD for Victory

1Our LORD, your mighty power
  makes the king glad,
and he celebrates victories
  that you have given him.
2You did what he wanted most
  and never told him "No."
3You truly blessed the king,
  and you placed on him
  a crown of finest gold.
4He asked to live a long time,
  and you promised him life
  that never ends.

5The king is highly honored.
  You have let him win victories
  that have made him famous.
6You have given him blessings
  that will last forever,
and you have made him glad
  by being so near to him.
7LORD Most High,
  the king trusts you,

b19.14 *mighty rock:* See the note at 18.2.   c20.9 *victory . . . prayers:* Or "victory. He (God or the king) answers us."

and your kindness
  keeps him from defeat.

[8]With your mighty arm, LORD,
  you will strike down all
    of your hateful enemies.
[9]They will be destroyed by fire
  once you are here,
  and because of your anger,
    flames will swallow them.
[10]You will wipe their families
  from the earth,
  and they will disappear.
[11]All their plans to harm you
  will come to nothing.
[12]You will make them run away
  by shooting your arrows
    at their faces.

[13]Show your strength, LORD,
  so that we may sing
  and praise your power.

PSALM 22

(A psalm by David for the music leader. To the tune
"A Deer at Dawn.")

Suffering and Praise

[1]My God, my God, why have you
  deserted me?
Why are you so far away?
Won't you listen to my groans
  and come to my rescue?
[2]I cry out day and night,
  but you don't answer,
  and I can never rest.

[3]Yet you are the holy God,
  ruling from your throne
  and praised by Israel.
[4]Our ancestors trusted you,
  and you rescued them.

[5]When they cried out for help,
  you saved them,
and you did not let them down
  when they depended on you.

[6]But I am merely a worm,
  far less than human,
and I am hated and rejected
  by people everywhere.
[7]Everyone who sees me
  makes fun and sneers.
They shake their heads,
[8] and say, "Trust the LORD!
If you are his favorite,
let him protect you
  and keep you safe."

[9]You, LORD, brought me
  safely through birth,
and you protected me
when I was a baby
  at my mother's breast.
[10]From the day I was born,
  I have been in your care,
and from the time of my birth,
  you have been my God.

[11]Don't stay far off
when I am in trouble
  with no one to help me.
[12]Enemies are all around
  like a herd of wild bulls.
Powerful bulls from Bashan[d]
  are everywhere.
[13]My enemies are like lions
roaring and attacking
  with jaws open wide.

[14]I have no more strength
  than a few drops of water.
All my bones are out of joint;
  my heart is like melted wax.

[d]22.12 *Bashan:* A land east of the Jordan River, where there were pastures suitable for raising fine cattle.

22.4,5 *our ancestors . . . depended on you:* The psalmist remembers how God rescued the people from slavery in Egypt (Exod 2.23-25).

22.12,13 *Enemies . . . wide:* The "enemies" oppose God and the psalmist. Here and in 22.16,20-22, they are compared to vicious animals. Animals sometimes symbolized demons, suggesting that the opposition seems more than human.

Enemies (The Wicked)

22.12 *Bashan:* This land, east of the Jordan River, was known for its rich pastures and strong cattle. **(See Map 4 on pg 1882.)**

22.21 *You rescued . . . bulls:* The Hebrew text reads "answered" instead of "rescued." This suggests that the praise that follows in verses 22 to 31 is not to be separated from the suffering expressed in 22.1-21.

22.28 *ruler of all nations:* The hope that all nations would recognize Israel's God as ruler is expressed by the prophets (Isa 56.6,7; Zeph 3.8,9; Zech 14.16). Much later, Jesus told his followers to gather a kingdom from "all over the world" (compare Ps 22.27 and Matt 28.19,20).

23.1-3 *shepherd . . . paths:* God's kingship is a frequent subject in the PSALMS. Kings were known as the shepherds of their people. Their responsibility was to feed and protect their people (Ezek 34.1-16).

¹⁵My strength has dried up
 like a broken clay pot,
and my tongue sticks
 to the roof of my mouth.
You, God, have left me
 to die in the dirt.

¹⁶Brutal enemies attack me
 like a pack of dogs,
 tearing at[e] my hands
 and my feet.
¹⁷I can count all my bones,
 and my enemies just stare
 and sneer at me.
¹⁸They took my clothes
 and gambled for them.

¹⁹Don't stay far away, LORD!
 My strength comes from you,
 so hurry and help.
²⁰Rescue me from enemy swords
 and save me from those dogs.
²¹ Don't let lions eat me.

You rescued me from the horns
 of wild bulls,
²²and when your people meet,
I will praise you, LORD.

²³All who worship the LORD,
 now praise him!
You belong to Jacob's family
 and to the people of Israel,
 so fear and honor the LORD!
²⁴The LORD doesn't hate
or despise the helpless
 in all of their troubles.
When I cried out, he listened
 and did not turn away.

²⁵When your people meet,
 you will fill my heart

with your praises, LORD,
 and everyone will see me
 keep my promises to you.
²⁶The poor will eat and be full,
 and all who worship you
 will be thankful
 and live in hope.

²⁷Everyone on this earth
 will remember you, LORD.
People all over the world
 will turn and worship you,
²⁸because you are in control,
 the ruler of all nations.

²⁹All who are rich
 and have more than enough
 will bow down to you, Lord.
Even those who are dying
 and almost in the grave
 will come and bow down.
³⁰In the future, everyone
 will worship and learn
 about you, our Lord.
³¹People not yet born
 will be told,
 "The Lord has saved us!"

PSALM 23

(A psalm by David.)

The Good Shepherd

¹You, LORD, are my shepherd.
 I will never be in need.
²You let me rest in fields
 of green grass.
You lead me to streams
 of peaceful water,
³ and you refresh my life.

You are true to your name,
 and you lead me

[e]22.16 *tearing at:* One possible meaning for the difficult Hebrew text.

along the right paths.
[4]I may walk through valleys
as dark as death,
but I won't be afraid.
You are with me,
and your shepherd's rod[f]
makes me feel safe.

[5]You treat me to a feast,
while my enemies watch.
You honor me as your guest,
and you fill my cup
until it overflows.
[6]Your kindness and love
will always be with me
each day of my life,
and I will live forever
in your house, Lord.

Psalm 24
(A psalm by David.)
Who Can Enter the Lord's Temple?

[1]The earth and everything on it,
including its people,
belong to the Lord.
The world and its people
belong to him.
[2]The Lord placed it all
on the oceans and rivers.

[3]Who may climb the Lord's hill[g]
or stand in his holy temple?
[4]Only those who do right
for the right reasons,
and don't worship idols
or tell lies under oath.
[5]The Lord God, who saves them,
will bless and reward them,

[6]because they worship and serve
the God of Jacob.[h]
[7]Open the ancient gates,
so that the glorious king
may come in.

[8]Who is this glorious king?
He is our Lord, a strong
and mighty warrior.

[9]Open the ancient gates,
so that the glorious king
may come in.

[10]Who is this glorious king?
He is our Lord,
the All-Powerful!

Psalm 25
(By David.)
A Prayer for Guidance and Help

[1]I offer you my heart, Lord God,
[2] and I trust you.
Don't make me ashamed
or let enemies defeat me.
[3]Don't disappoint any
of your worshipers,
but disappoint all
deceitful liars.
[4]Show me your paths
and teach me to follow;
[5]guide me by your truth
and instruct me.
You keep me safe,
and I always trust you.

[6]Please, Lord, remember,
you have always
been patient and kind.

[f]**23.4** *shepherd's rod*: The Hebrew text mentions two objects carried by the shepherd: a club to defend against wild animals and a long pole to guide and control the sheep. [g]**24.3** *the Lord's hill*: The hill in Jerusalem where the temple was built. [h]**24.6** *worship . . . Jacob*: Two ancient translations; Hebrew "worship God and serve the descendants of Jacob."

23.6 *I will live . . . in your house*: The Lord's "house" originally may have meant the temple where people went for protection, but it also can be a symbol for God's presence.

24.3 *the Lord's hill . . . holy temple*: The "hill" is Mount Zion. This psalm may have been used in a ceremony as worshipers entered the temple.

24.7-10 *Open the ancient gates . . . Who is this glorious king*: The questions and responses in these verses probably were part of an ancient liturgy (religious service) that was spoken as worshipers and Israel's priests brought the sacred chest into the temple. The sacred chest was seen as the earthly throne of God, the King. The title "All-Powerful" often appears when the sacred chest is mentioned. It refers to God's rule over all creation.

Names of God

25.4 *your paths*: God's "paths" refer to the "right way," that is, living and worshiping according to God's Law. Note how the very first psalm begins by inviting people to be open to God's teaching.

Your kindness and love will always be with me each day of my life, and I will live forever in your house, Lord. Ps 23.6

25.10 *who keeps our agreement with you:* "Agreement" here probably refers to the agreement based on God's Law. God will bless those who obey God's Law.

25.13 *receive the land:* Because the land meant the opportunity to make a living, it became a symbol for life. Also, obedience to the Law meant being able to keep the promised land that God gave to Israel (Deut 7.6-15).

26.8 *the temple where you live . . . glory shines:* God was said to live in the temple in Jerusalem. God's "glory" refers to God's powerful presence.

⁷Forget each wrong I did
  when I was young.
Show how truly kind you are
  and remember me.
⁸You are honest and merciful,
  and you teach sinners
  how to follow your path.

⁹You lead humble people
  to do what is right
  and to stay on your path.
¹⁰In everything you do,
  you are kind and faithful
  to everyone who keeps
  our agreement with you.

¹¹Be true to your name, Lord,
  by forgiving each one
  of my terrible sins.
¹²You will show the right path
  to all who worship you.
¹³Then they will have plenty,
  and their children
  will receive the land.

¹⁴Our Lord, you are the friend
  of your worshipers,
  and you make an agreement
  with all of us.
¹⁵I always look to you,
  because you rescue me
  from every trap.
¹⁶I am lonely and troubled.
  Show that you care
  and have pity on me.
¹⁷My awful worries keep growing.
  Rescue me from sadness.
¹⁸See my troubles and misery
  and forgive my sins.

¹⁹Look at all my enemies!
  See how much they hate me.

²⁰I come to you for shelter.
  Protect me, keep me safe,
  and don't disappoint me.
²¹I obey you with all my heart,
  and I trust you, knowing
  that you will save me.

²²Our God, please save Israel
  from all its troubles.

Psalm 26
(By David.)
The Prayer of an Innocent Person

¹Show that I am right, Lord!
  I stay true to myself,
  and I have trusted you
  without doubting.
²Test my thoughts and find out
  what I am like.
³I never forget your kindness,
  and I am always faithful
  to you.[i]
⁴I don't spend my time
  with worthless liars
⁵ or go with evil crowds.

⁶I wash my hands, Lord,
  to show my innocence,
  and I worship at your altar,
⁷while gratefully singing
  about your wonders.
⁸I love the temple
  where you live, and where
  your glory shines.
⁹Don't sweep me away,
  as you do sinners.
Don't punish me with death
  as you do those people
  who are brutal
¹⁰ or full of meanness

---

[i]26.3 *I am . . . to you:* Or "I trust your faithfulness."

or who bribe others.
[11] I stay true to myself.
 Be kind and rescue me.

[12] Now I stand on solid ground!
 And when your people meet,
  I will praise you, LORD.

PSALM 27
(By David.)
A Prayer of Praise

[1] You, LORD, are the light
 that keeps me safe.
I am not afraid of anyone.
 You protect me,
  and I have no fears.
[2] Brutal people may attack
 and try to kill me,
  but they will stumble.
Fierce enemies may attack,
  but they will fall.
[3] Armies may surround me,
  but I won't be afraid;
war may break out,
  but I will trust you.

[4] I ask only one thing, LORD:
Let me live in your house
 every day of my life
to see how wonderful you are
 and to pray in your temple.

[5] In times of trouble, LORD,
 you will protect me.
You will hide me in your tent
and keep me safe
 on top of a mighty rock.[j]
[6] You will let me defeat
 all my enemies.
Then I will celebrate,
 as I enter your tent

with animal sacrifices
 and songs of praise.

[7] Please listen when I pray!
 Have pity. Answer my prayer.
[8] My heart tells me to pray.
I am eager to see your face,
[9] so don't hide from me.
I am your servant, LORD,
and you have helped me.
 Don't turn from me in anger.
You alone keep me safe.
 Don't reject or desert me.
[10] Even if my father and mother
should desert me,
 you will take care of me.

[11] Teach me to follow, LORD,
 and lead me on the right path
  because of my enemies.
[12] Don't let them do to me
 what they want.
People tell lies about me
 and make violent threats,
[13] but I know I will live
 to see how kind you are.

[14] Trust the LORD!
Be brave and strong
 and trust the LORD.

PSALM 28
(By David.)
A Prayer for Help

[1] Only you, LORD,
 are a mighty rock![k]
Don't refuse to help me
 when I pray.
If you don't answer me,
 I will soon be dead.
[2] Please listen to my prayer

[j] 27.5 *mighty rock:* See the note at 18.2. [k] 28.1 *mighty rock:* See the note at 18.2.

27.5,6 *your tent . . . mighty rock:* When the people were in the desert, they worshiped God in a tent (Exod 25.1-9). The temple was sometimes called God's "tent."

The Sacred Tent

28.2 *as I lift my hands:* In ancient times, people lifted their hands when they prayed to the gods above, and lowered their hands when praying to the gods below.

28.8 *your chosen ones:* The "chosen ones" could refer to the kings that God chose, or it may refer to the whole people of God, who also could be called "chosen ones" (Gen 12.1-3; Deut 7.6; Ps 105.6; Isa 41.8,9).

29.1,2 *angels . . . worship the* LORD: Those who live in heaven are invited to recognize God's kingship over all things.

Angels

29.5-8 *Mount Lebanon . . . Mount Hermon . . . Kadesh:* Mount Lebanon is a tall peak in the Lebanon Mountain range north of Palestine, though exactly which peak is uncertain. Mount Hermon is the tallest peak (9,100 feet) in the Anti-Lebanon Mountains, a range to the east of the Lebanon Mountains. It was known for its abundant dew, and it was probably viewed as a home of Canaanite gods and goddesses. Lebanon was renowned for its cedar forests. The strong and aromatic timber from tall cedar trees was ideal for building palaces and was used to build the temple in Jerusalem. Kadesh may be Kadesh-Barnea, a city about 50 miles south of Beersheba, or it may be the Syrian city of Kadesh on the Orontes River. **(See Map 3 on pg 1881.)**

and my cry for help,
    as I lift my hands
    toward your holy temple.

[3]Don't drag me away, LORD,
    with those cruel people,
who speak kind words,
    while planning trouble.
[4]Treat them as they deserve!
    Punish them for their sins.
[5]They don't pay any attention
    to your wonderful deeds.
Now you will destroy them
    and leave them in ruin.

[6]I praise you, LORD,
    for answering my prayers.
[7]You are my strong shield,
    and I trust you completely.
You have helped me,
and I will celebrate
    and thank you in song.

[8]You give strength
    to your people, LORD,
and you save and protect
    your chosen ones.
[9]Come save us and bless us.
Be our shepherd and always
    carry us in your arms.

PSALM 29
(A psalm by David.)
The Voice of the LORD in a Storm

[1]All you angels[l] in heaven,
    honor the glory and power
    of the LORD!
[2]Honor the wonderful name
    of the LORD,

and worship the LORD
    most holy and glorious.[m]

[3]The voice of the LORD
    echoes over the oceans.
The glorious LORD God
    thunders above the roar
    of the raging sea,
[4]and his voice is mighty
    and marvelous.
[5]The voice of the LORD
    destroys the cedar trees;
    the LORD shatters cedars
    on Mount Lebanon.
[6]God makes Mount Lebanon
    skip like a calf
and Mount Hermon
    jump like a wild ox.

[7]The voice of the LORD
    makes lightning flash
[8]   and the desert tremble.
And because of the LORD,
    the desert near Kadesh
    shivers and shakes.

[9]The voice of the LORD
    makes deer give birth
    before their time.[n]
Forests are stripped of leaves,
    and the temple is filled
    with shouts of praise.

[10]The LORD rules on his throne,
    king of the flood[o] forever.
[11]Pray that our LORD
    will make us strong
    and give us peace.

[l]29.1 *angels:* Or "supernatural beings" or "gods."   [m]29.2 *most . . . glorious:* Or "in his holy place" or "and wear your glorious clothes."   [n]29.9 *makes . . . time:* Or "twists the oak trees around."
[o]29.10 *king of the flood:* In ancient times the people of Israel believed that a mighty ocean surrounded all of creation, and that God could release the water to flood the earth.

PSALM 30

(A psalm by David for the dedication of the temple.)

A Prayer of Thanks

[1]I will praise you, LORD!
   You saved me from the grave
and kept my enemies
   from celebrating my death.
[2]I prayed to you, LORD God,
   and you healed me,
[3]saving me from death
   and the grave.

[4]Your faithful people, LORD,
will praise you with songs
   and honor your holy name.
[5]Your anger lasts a little while,
but your kindness lasts
   for a lifetime.
At night we may cry,
but when morning comes
   we will celebrate.

[6]I felt secure and thought,
   "I'll never be shaken!"
[7]You, LORD, were my friend,
and you made me strong
   as a mighty mountain.
But when you hid your face,
   I was crushed.

[8]I prayed to you, LORD,
   and in my prayer I said,
[9]"What good will it do you
   if I am in the grave?
Once I have turned to dust,
   how can I praise you
or tell how loyal you are?
[10] Have pity, LORD! Help!"

[11]You have turned my sorrow
   into joyful dancing.
No longer am I sad
   and wearing sackcloth.P
[12]I thank you from my heart,
   and I will never stop
singing your praises,
   my LORD and my God.

PSALM 31

(A psalm by David for the music leader.)

A Prayer for Protection

[1]I come to you, LORD,
for protection.
   Don't let me be ashamed.
Do as you have promised
   and rescue me.
[2]Listen to my prayer
   and hurry to save me.
Be my mighty rockq
and the fortress
   where I am safe.

[3]You, LORD God,
are my mighty rock
   and my fortress.
Lead me and guide me,
so that your name
   will be honored.
[4]Protect me from hidden traps
   and keep me safe.
[5]You are faithful,
and I trust you
   because you rescued me.

[6]I hate the worshipers
of worthless idols,
   but I trust you, LORD.
[7]I celebrate and shout
   because you are kind.
You saw all my suffering,
   and you cared for me.
[8]You kept me from the hands

30.9 *turned to dust:* Meaning died. Since the dead cannot praise God, the psalmist uses this familiar argument to bargain for his life.

31.4 *hidden traps:* Traps, snares, and pits were used to catch animals. They are used symbolically here and throughout PSALMS to refer to a variety of plots and schemes used by enemies to hurt God's people.

31.5 *I trust you:* Traditionally, this phrase has been translated "Into your hand I commit my spirit." LUKE reports Jesus speaking the words of Psalm 31.5 from the cross (see Luke 23.46).

31.6 *I hate … worthless idols:* Those who worshiped idols were enemies of God and a threat to God's people. "Idols" were wooden, stone, or metal images of the gods worshiped by other nations. Above everything else, the people of Israel were to trust in and worship only the LORD God (Exod 20.1-6; Isa 44.6-20).

Enemies (The Wicked)

P30.11 *sackcloth:* A rough, dark-colored cloth made from goat or camel hair and used to make grain sacks. It was worn in times of trouble or sorrow.   q31.2 *mighty rock:* See the note at 18.2.

of my enemies,
and you set me free.

⁹Have pity, Lord!
I am hurting and almost blind.
My whole body aches.
¹⁰I have known only sorrow
all my life long, and I suffer
year after year.
I am weak from sin,
and my bones are limp.

¹¹My enemies insult me.
Neighbors are even worse,
and I disgust my friends.
People meet me on the street,
and they turn and run.
¹²I am completely forgotten
like someone dead.
I am merely a broken dish.
¹³I hear the crowds whisper,
"Everyone is afraid!"
They are plotting and scheming
to murder me.

¹⁴But I trust you, Lord,
and I claim you as my God.
¹⁵My life is in your hands.
Save me from enemies
who hunt me down.
¹⁶Smile on me, your servant.
Have pity and rescue me.

¹⁷I pray only to you.
Don't disappoint me.
Disappoint my cruel enemies
until they lie silent
in their graves.
¹⁸Silence those proud liars!
Make them stop bragging
and insulting your people.

¹⁹You are wonderful,
and while everyone watches,

you store up blessings for all
who honor and trust you.
²⁰You are their shelter
from harmful plots,
and you are their protection
from vicious gossip.

²¹I will praise you, Lord,
for showing great kindness
when I was like a city
under attack.
²²I was terrified and thought,
"They've chased me
far away from you!"
But you answered my prayer
when I shouted for help.

²³All who belong to the Lord,
show how you love him.
The Lord protects the faithful,
but he severely punishes
everyone who is proud.
²⁴All who trust the Lord,
be cheerful and strong.

Psalm 32
(A special psalm by David.)
The Joy of Forgiveness

¹Our Lord, you bless everyone
whose sins you forgive
and wipe away.
²You bless them by saying,
"You told me your sins,
without trying to hide them,
and now I forgive you."

³Before I confessed my sins,
my bones felt limp,
and I groaned all day long.
⁴Night and day your hand
weighed heavily on me,
and my strength was gone
as in the summer heat.

⁵So I confessed my sins
   and told them all to you.
I said, "I'll tell the LORD
   each one of my sins."
Then you forgave me
   and took away my guilt.

⁶We worship you, Lord,
   and we should always pray
whenever we find out
   that we have sinned.ʳ
Then we won't be swept away
   by a raging flood.
⁷You are my hiding place!
   You protect me from trouble,
and you put songs in my heart
   because you have saved me.

⁸You said to me,
"I will point out the road
   that you should follow.
I will be your teacher
   and watch over you.
⁹Don't be stupid
   like horses and mules
that must be led with ropes
   to make them obey."

¹⁰All kinds of troubles
   will strike the wicked,
but your kindness shields those
   who trust you, LORD.
¹¹And so your good people
   should celebrate and shout.

PSALM 33
Sing Praises to the LORD

¹You are the LORD's people.
   Obey him and celebrate!
   He deserves your praise.
²Praise the LORD with harps!
   Use harps with ten strings

to make music for him.
³Sing a new song. Shout!
   Play beautiful music.

⁴The LORD is truthful;
   he can be trusted.
⁵He loves justice and fairness,
   and he is kind to everyone
   everywhere on earth.

⁶The LORD made the heavens
   and everything in them
   by his word.
⁷He scooped up the ocean
   and stored the water.
⁸Everyone in this world
   should worship and honor
   the LORD!
⁹As soon as he spoke
   the world was created;
at his command,
   the earth was formed.

¹⁰The LORD destroys the plans
   and spoils the schemes
   of the nations.
¹¹But what the LORD has planned
   will stand forever.
   His thoughts never change.
¹²The LORD blesses each nation
   that worships only him.
   He blesses his chosen ones.
¹³The LORD looks at the world
¹⁴from his throne in heaven,
   and he watches us all.
¹⁵The LORD gave us each a mind,
   and nothing we do
   can be hidden from him.

¹⁶Mighty armies alone
   cannot win wars for a king;
great strength by itself
   cannot keep a soldier safe.

ʳ**32.6** *whenever . . . sinned:* Hebrew "at a time of finding only."

33.2 *harps with ten strings:* The psalmist encourages worshipers to use a musical instrument in singing praises to the LORD. Many PSALMS were sung as music was played.

33.6 *The LORD made . . . by his word:* This verse, as well as 33.9, reflects the creation story of Genesis 1 where God creates everything by speaking commands.

You are my hiding place! You protect me from trouble, and you put songs in my heart because you have saved me.
Ps 32.7

34 (Title) *David . . . Abimelech*: Psalm 34 is another of the "acrostic" psalms. There is no one named Abimelech in the stories about David in 1 and 2 Samuel. A similar name, Ahimelech, does appear.

David

34.7 *angel*: The Hebrew word means "messenger." Mysterious messengers sometimes appear in human form to do God's work.

Angels

[17]In war the strength of a horse
cannot be trusted
to take you to safety.
[18]But the Lord watches over
all who honor him
and trust his kindness.
[19]He protects them from death
and starvation.

[20]We depend on you, Lord,
to help and protect us.
[21]You make our hearts glad
because we trust you,
the only God.
[22]Be kind and bless us!
We depend on you.

PSALM 34

(Written by David when he pretended to be crazy in front of Abimelech, so that Abimelech would send him away, and David could leave.)

Honor the Lord

[1]I will always praise the Lord.
[2]With all my heart,
I will praise the Lord.
Let all who are helpless,
listen and be glad.
[3]Honor the Lord with me!
Celebrate his great name.

[4]I asked the Lord for help,
and he saved me
from all my fears.
[5]Keep your eyes on the Lord!
You will shine like the sun
and never blush with shame.
[6]I was a nobody, but I prayed,
and the Lord saved me
from all my troubles.

[7]If you honor the Lord,
his angel will protect you.
[8]Discover for yourself
that the Lord is kind.
Come to him for protection,
and you will be glad.

[9]Honor the Lord!
You are his special people.
No one who honors the Lord
will ever be in need.
[10]Young lions[s] may go hungry
or even starve,
but if you trust the Lord,
you will never miss out
on anything good.

[11]Come, my children, listen
as I teach you
to respect the Lord.
[12]Do you want to live
and enjoy a long life?
[13]Then don't say cruel things
and don't tell lies.
[14]Do good instead of evil
and try to live at peace.

[15]If you obey the Lord,
he will watch over you
and answer your prayers.
[16]But God despises evil people,
and he will wipe them all
from the earth,
till they are forgotten.
[17]When his people pray for help,
he listens and rescues them
from their troubles.
[18]The Lord is there to rescue
all who are discouraged
and have given up hope.

[19]The Lord's people
may suffer a lot,
but he will always
bring them safely through.
[20]Not one of their bones
will ever be broken.

[s]**34.10** *Young lions*: In the Psalms wild animals often stand for God's enemies.

The Lord is there to rescue all who are discouraged and have given up hope. Ps 34.18

21 Wicked people are killed
   by their own evil deeds,
and if you hate God's people
   you will be punished.
22 The LORD saves the lives
   of his servants.
Run to him for protection,
   and you won't be punished.

PSALM 35

(A psalm by David.)

A Prayer for Protection from Enemies

1 Fight my enemies, LORD!
Attack my attackers!
2   Shield me and help me.
3 Aim your spear at everyone
who hunts me down,
   but promise to save me.

4 Let all who want to kill me
be disgraced
   and put to shame.
Chase away and confuse
   all who plan to harm me.
5 Send your angel after them
and let them be like straw
   in the wind.
6 Make them run in the dark
on a slippery road,
   as your angel chases them.
7 I did them no harm,
but they hid a net
   to trap me,
and they dug a deep pit
   to catch and kill me.
8 Surprise them with disaster!
   Trap them in their own nets
and let them fall and rot
   in the pits they have dug.

9 I will celebrate and be joyful
because you, LORD,
   have saved me.
10 Every bone in my body
will shout:
   "No one is like the LORD!"
You protect the helpless
   from those in power;
you save the poor and needy
   from those who hurt them.

11 Liars accuse me of crimes
   I know nothing about.
12 They repay evil for good,
   and I feel all alone.
13 When they were sick,
I wore sackcloth[t]
   and went without food.[u]
I truly prayed for them,[v]
14 as I would for a friend
   or a relative.
I was in sorrow and mourned,
   as I would for my mother.

15 I have stumbled,
   and worthless liars
I don't even know
   surround me and sneer.
16 Worthless people make fun[w]
   and never stop laughing.
17 But all you do is watch!
   When will you do something?
Save me from the attack
   of those vicious lions.
18 And when your people meet,
   I will praise you
and thank you, Lord,
   in front of them all.

19 Don't let my brutal enemies
   be glad because of me.
They hate me for no reason.

35.5 *your angel . . . like straw in the wind:* God's angels are sometimes sent to carry out God's punishment (1 Chr 21.14-17; Isa 37.36).

35.19 *hate me for no reason:* This is the psalmist's way of saying that his enemies' accusations are false. Centuries later, when Jesus was falsely accused and unfairly opposed, this and other psalms were recalled.

[t]35.13 *sackcloth:* See the note at 30.11.   [u]35.13 *went without food:* People sometimes went without food (called "fasting") to show sorrow.   [v]35.13 *I . . . them:* Or "My prayer wasn't answered, but I prayed."   [w]35.16 *Worthless . . . fun:* One possible meaning for the difficult Hebrew text.

36.1 *Sinners:* "Sinners" refers to those who never think about God, and so never ask for forgiveness. They are enemies of God and God's people.

℞ Sin

36.5,6 *Your love . . . decisions:* These verses begin a celebration of God's love for the whole world, mentioning each major part of the world—sky, land (mountains), and sea. Because God loves the whole world, God's care extends beyond humanity. In keeping with this understanding, the final psalm invites "every living creature" to praise God.

Don't let them wink
  behind my back.
²⁰They say hurtful things,
  and they lie to people
  who want to live in peace.
²¹They are quick to accuse me.
  They say, "You did it!
  We saw you ourselves."

²²You see everything, LORD!
  Please don't keep silent
  or stay so far away.
²³Fight to defend me, Lord God,
²⁴and prove that I am right
  by your standards.
  Don't let them laugh at me
²⁵ or say to each other,
  "Now we've got what we want!
  We'll gobble him up!"

²⁶Disappoint and confuse
  all who are glad
  to see me in trouble;
  disgrace and embarrass
  my proud enemies who say to me,
  "You are nothing!"

²⁷Let all who want me to win
  be happy and joyful.
  From now on let them say,
  "The LORD is wonderful!
  God is glad when all goes well
  for his servant."
²⁸Then I will shout all day,
  "Praise the LORD God!
  He did what was right."

PSALM 36
(For the music leader by David, the LORD's servant.)
Human Sin and God's Goodness

¹Sinners don't respect God;
  sin is all they think about.

²They like themselves too much
  to hate their own sins
  or even to see them.
³They tell deceitful lies,
  and they don't have the sense
  to live right.
⁴Those people stay awake,
  thinking up mischief,
  and they follow the wrong road,
  refusing to turn from sin.

⁵Your love is faithful, LORD,
  and even the clouds in the sky
  can depend on you.
⁶Your decisions are always fair.
  They are firm like mountains,
  deep like the sea,
  and all people and animals
  are under your care.

⁷Your love is a treasure,
  and everyone finds shelter
  in the shadow of your wings.
⁸You give your guests a feast
  in your house,
  and you serve a tasty drink
  that flows like a river.
⁹The life-giving fountain
  belongs to you,
  and your light gives light
  to each of us.

¹⁰Our LORD, keep showing love
  to everyone who knows you,
  and use your power to save all
  whose thoughts please you.
¹¹Don't let those proud
  and merciless people
  kick me around
  or chase me away.

¹²Look at those wicked people!
  They are knocked down,
  never to get up again.

PSALM 37
(By David.)
Trust the LORD

¹Don't be annoyed by anyone
who does wrong,
and don't envy them.
²They will soon disappear
like grass without rain.

³Trust the LORD and live right!
The land will be yours,
and you will be safe.
⁴Do what the LORD wants,
and he will give you
your heart's desire.

⁵Let the LORD lead you
and trust him to help.
⁶Then it will be as clear
as the noonday sun
that you were right.

⁷Be patient and trust the LORD.
Don't let it bother you
when all goes well for those
who do sinful things.
⁸Don't be angry or furious.
Anger can lead to sin.
⁹All sinners will disappear,
but if you trust the LORD,
the land will be yours.

¹⁰Sinners will soon disappear,
never to be found,
¹¹but the poor will take the land
and enjoy a big harvest.

¹²Merciless people make plots
against good people
and snarl like animals,
¹³but the Lord laughs and knows
their time is coming soon.
¹⁴The wicked kill with swords
and shoot arrows to murder

the poor and the needy
and all who do right.
¹⁵But they will be killed
by their own swords,
and their arrows
will be broken.

¹⁶It is better to live right
and be poor
than to be sinful and rich.
¹⁷The wicked will lose all
of their power,
but the LORD gives strength
to everyone who is good.

¹⁸Those who obey the LORD
are daily in his care,
and what he has given them
will be theirs forever.
¹⁹They won't be in trouble
when times are bad,
and they will have plenty
when food is scarce.

²⁰Wicked people are enemies
of the LORD
and will vanish like smoke
from a field on fire.

²¹An evil person borrows
and never pays back;
a good person is generous
and never stops giving.
²²Everyone the LORD blesses
will receive the land;
everyone the LORD curses
will be destroyed.

²³If you do what the LORD wants,
he will make certain
each step you take is sure.
²⁴The LORD will hold your hand,
and if you stumble,
you still won't fall.

■ 37.1 *anyone who does wrong*: This acrostic psalm deals with the question of why "all goes well" for those who do wrong, while God's people suffer.

● 37.11 *the poor will take the land*: God's people are regularly called "the poor" and "the needy." The promise of land is also a promise of life. Centuries later, Jesus made a similar promise (Matt 5.5).

⁂℞ The Land

⁂℞ The Poor

37.33 *trial:* The Hebrew word for "on trial" also means "justice." God's actions show that God "loves justice."

38 *offering:* The Hebrew means "to cause to remember." It may refer to a type of offering. (See the chart Sacrifices and Offerings on pg 1828.)

38.5-10 *covered with sores . . . eyes are red:* The description given here suggest the psalmist is suffering from leprosy, a word used for various skin diseases that were greatly feared at this time. Because leprosy was highly contagious, those who had it were forced to live outside the community.

²⁵As long as I can remember,
good people have never
been left helpless,
and their children have never
gone begging for food.
²⁶They gladly give and lend,
and their children
turn out good.

²⁷If you stop sinning
and start doing right,
you will keep living
and be secure forever.
²⁸The LORD loves justice,
and he won't ever desert
his faithful people.
He always protects them,
but destroys the children
of the wicked.
²⁹God's people will own the land
and live here forever.

³⁰Words of wisdom come
when good people speak
for justice.
³¹They remember God's teachings,
and they never take
a wrong step.

³²The wicked try to trap
and kill good people,
³³but the LORD is on their side,
and he will defend them
when they are on trial.

³⁴Trust the LORD and follow him.
He will give you the land,
and you will see
the wicked destroyed.

³⁵I have seen brutal people
abuse others and grow strong

like trees in rich soil.ˣ
³⁶Suddenly they disappeared!
I looked, but they were gone
and no longer there.

³⁷Think of the bright future
waiting for all the families
of honest, innocent,
and peace-loving people.
³⁸But not a trace will be left
of the wicked
or their families.

³⁹The LORD protects his people,
and they can come to him
in times of trouble.
⁴⁰The LORD helps his people
and saves them from the wicked
because they run to him.

PSALM 38

(A psalm by David to be used
when an offering is made.)

A Prayer in Times of Trouble

¹When you are angry, LORD,
please don't punish me
or even correct me.
²You shot me with your arrows,
and you struck me
with your hand.

³My body hurts all over
because of your anger.
Even my bones are in pain,
and my sins ⁴are so heavy
that I am crushed.

⁵Because of my foolishness,
I am covered with sores
that stink and spread.
⁶My body is twisted and bent,
and I groan all day long.

ˣ37.35 *like . . . soil:* One possible meaning for the difficult Hebrew text.

Words of wisdom come when good people speak for justice. Ps 37.30

⁷Fever has my back in flames,
   and I hurt everywhere.
⁸I am worn out and weak,
   moaning and in distress.

⁹You, Lord, know every one
   of my deepest desires,
  and my noisy groans
   are no secret to you.
¹⁰My heart is beating fast.
  I feel weak all over,
   and my eyes are red.

¹¹Because of my sickness,
   no friends or neighbors
   will come near me.
¹²All who want me dead
   set traps to catch me,
  and those who want
  to harm and destroy me
   plan and plot all day.

¹³I am not able to hear
   or speak a word;
¹⁴I am completely deaf
   and can't make a sound.

¹⁵I trust you, Lord God,
   and you will do something.
¹⁶I said, "Don't let them laugh
   or brag when I slip and fall."

¹⁷I am about to collapse
   from constant pain.
¹⁸I told you my sins,
   and I am sorry for them.
¹⁹Many deadly and powerful
   enemies hate me,
²⁰and they repay evil for good
   because I try to do right.

²¹You are the Lord God!
  Stay nearby

and don't desert me.
²²You are the one who saves me.
   Please hurry and help.

PSALM 39

(A psalm by David for Jeduthun, the music leader.)

A Prayer for Forgiveness

¹I told myself, "I'll be careful
   not to sin by what I say,
  and I'll muzzle my mouth
   when evil people are near."
²I kept completely silent,
  but it did no good,ʸ
   and I hurt even worse.

³I felt a fire burning inside,
   and the more I thought,
  the more it burned,
   until at last I said:
⁴"Please, Lord,
  show me my future.
  Will I soon be gone?
⁵You made my life short,
  so brief that the time
   means nothing to you.

"Human life is but a breath,
⁶and it disappears
  like a shadow.
Our struggles are senseless;
  we store up more and more,
   without ever knowing
   who will get it all.

⁷"What am I waiting for?
   I depend on you, Lord!
⁸Save me from my sins.
   Don't let fools sneer at me.
⁹You treated me like this,
  and I kept silent,
   not saying a word.

ʸ**39.2** *but . . . good:* One possible meaning for the difficult Hebrew text.

■ 38.21,22 *You . . . help:* The psalmist trusts that his suffering is not God's last word. Instead, it will be what leads God to help him.

● 39 (Title) *Jeduthun:* Jeduthun, a member of the Levite clan of Asaph, was appointed by David to play musical instruments during worship in the sacred tent (1 Chr 16.37-42; 25.1-3). The title may also mean that the music was to be played according to the style of Jeduthun of the Asaph clan.

■ 39.4-6 *soon be gone . . . get it all:* The psalmist does not complain about his sufferings but about the shortness of all human life. The words "breath" and "senseless" come from the same Hebrew word.

39.12 *a stranger visiting in your home:* Non-Israelites living in the land were considered strangers.

Foreigners (Aliens)

40.2 *pit:* The word is probably meant to be a symbol of danger and distress, but the word is also sometimes used for a grave or for the land of the dead.

40.6 *Sacrifices . . . not what you demand:* To say that the LORD "does not demand" sacrifices may seem confusing, since sacrifices were a regular, required part of worship at the temple. They were clearly described in God's Law (see especially LEVITICUS). However, true obedience is not simply a matter of performing a ceremony. It is trusting God alone, being truly sorry for sins, and living as God wants, including treating others with justice (1 Sam 15.22; Ps 50.23; 51.16,17; Isa 1.12-17; Hos 6.6; Amos 5.21-24).

40.7 *the book:* The Bible refers to "books" that contain the names of those who belong to God, or to a list of their deeds (Exod 32.32,33; Ps 69.28; 87.6; 139.16; Isa 34.16; Dan 12.1,4; Phil 4.3; Rev 3.5; 13.8; 17.8; 20.12,15; 21.27). The symbolism of a record book expresses that God knows everything about people.

10"Won't you stop punishing me?
You have worn me down.
11You punish us severely
because of our sins.
Like a moth, you destroy
what we treasure most.
We are as frail as a breath.

12"Listen, LORD, to my prayer!
My eyes are flooded with tears,
as I pray to you.
I am merely a stranger
visiting in your home
as my ancestors did.
13Stop being angry with me
and let me smile again
before I am dead and gone."

PSALM 40
(A psalm by David for the music leader.)
A Prayer for Help

1I patiently waited, LORD,
for you to hear my prayer.
You listened 2and pulled me
from a lonely pit
full of mud and mire.
You let me stand on a rock
with my feet firm,
3and you gave me a new song,
a song of praise to you.
Many will see this,
and they will honor and trust
you, the LORD God.

4You bless all of those
who trust you, LORD,
and refuse to worship idols
or follow false gods.
5You, LORD God, have done
many wonderful things,
and you have planned
marvelous things for us.
No one is like you!

I would never be able to tell
all you have done.

6Sacrifices and offerings
are not what please you;
gifts and payment for sin
are not what you demand.
But you made me willing
to listen and obey.
7And so, I said, "I am here
to do what is written
about me in the book,
where it says,
8'I enjoy pleasing you.
Your Law is in my heart.'"

9When your people worshiped,
you know I told them,
"Our LORD always helps!"
10When all your people met,
I did not keep silent.
I said, "Our LORD is kind.
He is faithful and caring,
and he saves us."

11You, LORD, never fail
to have pity on me;
your love and faithfulness
always keep me secure.

12I have more troubles
than I can count.
My sins are all around me,
and I can't find my way.
My sins outnumber
the hairs on my head,
and I feel weak.
13Please show that you care
and come to my rescue.
Hurry and help me!

14Disgrace and confusion
all who want me dead;
turn away and disgrace

all who want to hurt me.
¹⁵Embarrass and shame
everyone who says,
"Just look at you now!"

¹⁶Our LORD, let your worshipers
rejoice and be glad.
They love you for saving them,
so let them always say,
"The LORD is wonderful!"

¹⁷I am poor and needy,
but, LORD God,
you care about me,
and you come to my rescue.
Please hurry and help.

PSALM 41
(A psalm by David for the music leader.)

A Prayer in Time of Sickness

¹You, LORD God, bless everyone
who cares for the poor,
and you rescue those people
in times of trouble.
²You protect them
and keep them alive.
You make them happy here
in this land,
and you don't hand them over
to their enemies.
³You always heal them
and restore their strength
when they are sick.
⁴I prayed, "Have pity, LORD!
Heal me, though I have sinned
against you."

⁵My vicious enemies ask me,
"When will you die
and be forgotten?"
⁶When visitors come,
all they ever bring
are worthless words,

and when they leave,
they spread gossip.

⁷My enemies whisper about me.
They think the worst,
⁸ and they say,
"You have some fatal disease!
You'll never get well."
⁹My most trusted friend
has turned against me,
though he ate at my table.

¹⁰Have pity, LORD! Heal me,
so I can pay them back.
¹¹Then my enemies
won't defeat me,
and I will know
that you really care.
¹²You have helped me
because I am innocent,
and you will always
be close to my side.

¹³You, the LORD God of Israel,
will be praised forever!
Amen and amen.

BOOK II
(Psalms 42–72)

PSALM 42
(A special psalm by the clan of Korah and for the
music leader.)

Longing for God

¹As a deer gets thirsty
for streams of water,
I truly am thirsty
for you, my God.
²In my heart, I am thirsty
for you, the living God.
When will I see your face?
³Day and night my tears
are my only food,

41.1,2 *bless . . . happy:* Like the first psalm in "Book I," this last one also begins with the ideas of blessing and happiness.

Blessed (Happy)

42 (Title) *Korah:* Korah was a Levite whose family served in areas of music and worship at the temple (1 Chr 6.33-38). Psalms 42 and 43 were originally one psalm with three stanzas that were united by the same refrain at 42.5; 42.11; and 43.5.

42.6 *the Jordan . . . Mount Hermon . . . Mount Mizar:* The Jordan River begins to the north of Palestine near Mount Hermon. It runs through Lake Galilee and south to the Dead Sea. The location of Mount Mizar is unknown. **(See Map 3 on pg 1881.)**

as everyone keeps asking,
  "Where is your God?"

⁴Sorrow floods my heart,
  when I remember
leading the worshipers
  to your house.ᶻ
I can still hear them shout
  their joyful praises.
⁵Why am I discouraged?
Why am I restless?
  I should trust you, Lᴏʀᴅ.
I will praise you again
because you help me,
⁶ and you are my God.

I am deeply discouraged,
  and so I think about you
here where the Jordan begins
at Mount Hermon
  and at Mount Mizar.ᵃ
⁷Your vicious waves
  have swept over me
like an angry ocean
  or a roaring waterfall.

⁸Every day, you are kind,
  and at night
you give me a song
as my prayer to you,
  the God of my life.

⁹You are my mighty rock.ᵇ
  Why have you forgotten me?
Why must enemies mistreat me
  and make me sad?
¹⁰Even my bones are in pain,
  while all day long
my enemies sneer and ask,
  "Where is your God?"

¹¹Why am I discouraged?
Why am I restless?
  I trust you, Lᴏʀᴅ!
And I will praise you again
because you help me,
  and you are my God.

Psᴀʟᴍ 43
A Prayer in Times of Trouble

¹Show that I am right, God!
Defend me against everyone
  who doesn't know you;
rescue me from each
  of those deceitful liars.
²I run to you for protection.
Why do you turn me away?
Why must enemies mistreat me
  and make me sad?

³Send your light and your truth
  to guide me.
Let them lead me to your house
  on your sacred mountain.
⁴Then I will worship
at your altar because you
  make me joyful.
You are my God,
  and I will praise you.
Yes, I will praise you
  as I play my harp.

⁵Why am I discouraged?
Why am I restless?
  I trust you, Lᴏʀᴅ!
And I will praise you again
because you help me,
  and you are my God.

ᶻ42.4 *leading . . . house:* One possible meaning for the difficult Hebrew text.   ᵃ42.6 *Mount Mizar:* The location is not known.   ᵇ42.9 *mighty rock:* See the note at 18.2.

Why am I discouraged? Why am I restless? I trust you, Lᴏʀᴅ! And I will praise you again because you help me, and you are my God. Ps 43.5

PSALM 44

(A special psalm by the clan of Korah and for the
music leader.)

A Prayer for Help

¹Our God, our ancestors told us
what wonders you worked
and we listened carefully.
²You chased off the nations
by causing them trouble
with your powerful arm.
Then you let our ancestors
take over their land.
³Their strength and weapons
were not what won the land
and gave them victory!
You loved them and fought
with your powerful arm
and your shining glory.

⁴You are my God and King,
and you give victory^c
to the people of Jacob.
⁵By your great power,
we knocked our enemies down
and trampled on them.
⁶I don't depend on my arrows
or my sword to save me.
⁷But you saved us
from our hateful enemies,
and you put them to shame.
⁸We boast about you, our God,
and we are always grateful.

⁹But now you have rejected us;
you don't lead us into battle,
and we look foolish.
¹⁰You made us retreat,
and our enemies have taken
everything we own.
¹¹You let us be slaughtered
like sheep,
and you scattered us
among the nations.
¹²You sold your people
for little or nothing,
and you earned no profit.

¹³You made us look foolish
to our neighbors;
people who live nearby
insult us and sneer.
¹⁴Foreigners joke about us
and shake their heads.
¹⁵I am embarrassed every day,
and I blush with shame.
¹⁶But others mock and sneer,
as they watch my enemies
take revenge on me.

¹⁷All this happened to us,
though we didn't forget you
or break our agreement.
¹⁸We always kept you in mind
and followed your teaching.
¹⁹But you crushed us,
and you covered us
with deepest darkness
where wild animals live.

²⁰We did not forget you
or lift our hands in prayer
to foreign gods.
²¹You would have known it
because you discover
every secret thought.
²²We face death all day for you.
We are like sheep on their way
to be slaughtered.

²³Wake up! Do something, Lord!
Why are you sleeping?
Don't desert us forever.
²⁴Why do you keep looking away?
Don't forget our sufferings

^c44.4 *and . . . victory:* One ancient translation; Hebrew "please give victory."

44.1-3 *wonders . . . powerful
arm . . . shining glory:* God's "wonders"
include rescuing the people from slavery in Egypt and leading them to the
land of Canaan. According to NUMBERS,
the LORD led and cared for the people in
the desert. JOSHUA tells how the LORD
fought for the people and helped them
defeat powerful armies and "win the
land." The image of God's powerful or
mighty arm is often used to describe
the LORD's protection or power, especially in battle.

Holy War (The LORD's Battles)

44.9-11 *rejected us . . . scattered
us:* Verses 10 and 11 suggest that the
psalm was written in response to the
destruction of Jerusalem in 586 B.C. In
586, the people were "scattered," and
many were taken into exile in Babylon.

Exile

45.1 *My . . . king:* This psalm is unusual, because it is spoken to "the king" instead of to God. The psalm was written for a royal wedding.

45.6,7 *You are God . . . God chose you:* Israel worshiped only one God, but the people understood the king to be related to God in a special way. As God's "chosen" one, the king would uphold God's concern for justice.

45.12 *Tyre:* Many luxury items were imported through this important Mediterranean port city. **(See Map 4 on pg 1882 and the article Trade and Travel on pg 1806.)**

45.13 *wedding gown . . . threads of gold:* The gown was probably woven from the finest wool and linen and embroidered with golden threads.

and all our troubles.
25We are flat on the ground,
    holding on to the dust.
26Do something! Help us!
    Show how kind you are
    and come to our rescue.

PSALM 45

(A special psalm by the clan of Korah and for the music leader. To the tune "Lilies." A love song.)

For a Royal Wedding

1My thoughts are filled
with beautiful words
    for the king,
    and I will use my voice
    as a writer would use
    pen and ink.

2No one is as handsome as you!
    Your words are always kind.
    That is why God
    will always bless you.
3Mighty king, glorious ruler,
    strap on your sword
4   and ride out in splendor!
    Win victories for truth
    and mercy and justice.
    Do fearsome things
    with your powerful arm.
5Send your sharp arrows
    through enemy hearts
    and make all nations fall
    at your feet.

6You are God, and you will rule
    forever as king.d
    Your royal power
    brings about justice.
7You love justice and hate evil.
    And so, your God chose you

and made you happier
    than any of your friends.
8The sweet aroma of the spices
    myrrh, aloes, and cassia
    covers your royal robes.
    You enjoy the music of harps
    in palaces decorated
    with ivory.
9Daughters of kings are here,
    and your bride stands
    at your right side,
    wearing a wedding gown
    trimmed with pure gold.e

10Bride of the king,
    listen carefully to me.
    Forget your own people
    and your father's family.
11The king adores you.
    He is your master,
    so do what he desires.
12All of the richest people
    from the city of Tyre
    will try to influence you
13   with precious treasures.

Your bride, my king,
    has inward beauty,f
and her wedding gown is woven
    with threads of gold.
14Wearing the finest garments,
    she is brought to you,
    followed by her young friends,
    the bridesmaids.
15Everyone is excited,
    as they follow you
    to the royal palace.

16Your sons and your grandsons
    will also be kings
    as your ancestors were.

d45.6 *You . . . king:* Or "God has made you king, and you will rule forever." e45.9 *trimmed with pure gold:* Hebrew has "with gold from Ophir," which may have been in Africa or India. Gold from there was considered the very best. f45.13 *has inward beauty:* Or "is dressed in her room."

You will make them rulers
     everywhere on earth.

[17]I will make your name famous
     from now on,
     and you will be praised
     forever and ever.

PSALM 46

(A special song by the clan of Korah and for
the music leader.)

God Is Our Mighty Fortress

[1]God is our mighty fortress,
     always ready to help
     in times of trouble.
[2]And so, we won't be afraid!
     Let the earth tremble
     and the mountains tumble
     into the deepest sea.
[3]Let the ocean roar and foam,
     and its raging waves
     shake the mountains.

[4]A river and its streams
     bring joy to the city,
     which is the sacred home
     of God Most High.
[5]God is in that city,
     and it won't be shaken.
     He will help it at dawn.

[6]Nations rage! Kingdoms fall!
     But at the voice of God
     the earth itself melts.
[7]The LORD All-Powerful
     is with us.
     The God of Jacob
     is our fortress.

[8]Come! See the fearsome things
     the LORD has done on earth.
[9]God brings wars to an end

[g]46.9 *shields:* Or "chariots."

all over the world.
     He breaks the arrows,
     shatters the spears,
     and burns the shields.[g]
[10]Our God says, "Calm down,
     and learn that I am God!
     All nations on earth
     will honor me."

[11]The LORD All-Powerful
     is with us.
     The God of Jacob
     is our fortress.

PSALM 47

(A psalm by the clan of Korah and for
the music leader.)

God Rules the Nations

[1]All of you nations,
     clap your hands and shout
     joyful praises to God.
[2]The LORD Most High is fearsome,
     the ruler of all the earth.
[3]God has put every nation
     under our power,
[4]and he chose for us the land
     that was the pride of Jacob,
     his favorite.

[5]God goes up to his throne,
     as people shout
     and trumpets blast.
[6]Sing praises to God our King,
[7]the ruler of all the earth!
     Praise God with songs.

[8]God rules the nations
     from his sacred throne.
[9]Their leaders come together
     and are now the people
     of Abraham's God.

46.6,7 *the earth itself melts . . . LORD All-Powerful:* The word "melts" does not mean destruction. Instead, it suggests that the whole world realizes God's power and its own powerlessness by comparison. The title "All-Powerful" often is used for God when the sacred chest is mentioned. It refers to God's rule over all creation.

47.2 *LORD Most High . . . ruler of all the earth:* God's universal rule is a major idea in the PSALMS, and it is especially celebrated in this psalm.

47.9 *Abraham's God:* God chose Abraham to be the father of the people of God (Gen 12.1-3).

Abraham

48.4-8 *Kings . . . attack the city . . . stand forever:* Jerusalem and its people did withstand many attacks by enemy armies and even destruction by the Babylonians (586 B.C.). Still, the people believed that the city would "stand forever" as the place where God rules.

48.11 *Mount Zion . . . Judah:* In this passage Mount Zion means Jerusalem. Following the death of King Solomon, Israel split into two kingdoms: the northern kingdom, called Israel, and the southern kingdom, called Judah after one of the twelve sons of Jacob.

Israel

49.3,4 *wisdom . . . a mystery:* Unlike most psalms, this one is neither a prayer nor a song of praise. Instead, it teaches a lesson by exploring the question of poverty and wealth. Its message is similar to sayings found in other books of Hebrew Wisdom (Job 22.25; Prov 11.28; Eccl 5.10-17).

All rulers on earth
surrender their weapons,
   and God is greatly praised!

PSALM 48
(A song and a psalm by the clan of Korah.)
The City of God

[1]The LORD God is wonderful!
He deserves all praise
   in the city where he lives.
His holy mountain,
[2]beautiful and majestic,
   brings joy to all on earth.
Mount Zion, truly sacred,
   is home for the Great King.
[3]God is there to defend it
and has proved to be
   its protector.

[4]Kings joined forces
   to attack the city,
[5]but when they saw it,
they were terrified
   and ran away.
[6]They trembled all over
   like women giving birth
[7]or like seagoing ships[h]
   wrecked by eastern winds.
[8]We had heard about it,
and now we have seen it
   in the city of our God,
   the LORD All-Powerful.
This is the city that God
   will let stand forever.

[9]Our God, here in your temple
   we think about your love.
[10]You are famous and praised
   everywhere on earth,
as you win victories
   with your powerful arm.

[11]Mount Zion will celebrate,
   and all Judah will be glad,
   because you bring justice.

[12]Let's walk around Zion
   and count its towers.
[13]We will see its strong walls
   and visit each fortress.
Then you can say
   to future generations,
[14]"Our God is like this forever
   and will always[i] guide us."

PSALM 49
(A psalm by the clan of Korah and for the music leader.)
Don't Depend on Wealth

[1]Everyone on this earth,
   now listen to what I say!
[2]Listen, no matter who you are,
   rich or poor.
[3]I speak words of wisdom,
   and my thoughts make sense.
[4]I have in mind a mystery
   that I will explain
   while playing my harp.

[5]Why should I be afraid
   in times of trouble,
when I am surrounded
   by vicious enemies?
[6]They trust in their riches
   and brag about
   all their wealth.
[7]You cannot buy back your life
   or pay off God!
[8]It costs far too much
   to buy back your life.
You can never pay God enough
[9]to stay alive forever
   and safe from death.

[h]**48.7** *seagoing ships:* The Hebrew text has "ships of Tarshish," which probably means large, seagoing ships.   [i]**48.14** *always:* One possible meaning for the difficult Hebrew text.

¹⁰We see that wise people die,
and so do stupid fools.
Then their money is left
for someone else.
¹¹The grave^j will be their home
forever and ever,
although they once had land
of their own.
¹²Our human glory disappears,
and, like animals, we die.

¹³Here is what happens to fools
and to those who trust
the words of fools:^k
¹⁴They are like sheep
with death as their shepherd,
leading them to the grave.
In the morning God's people
will walk all over them,^l
as their bodies lie rotting
in their home, the grave.
¹⁵But God will rescue me
from the power of death.

¹⁶Don't let it bother you
when others get rich
and live in luxury.
¹⁷Soon they will die
and all their wealth
will be left behind.

¹⁸We humans are praised
when we do well,
and all of us are glad
to be alive.
¹⁹But we each will go down
to our ancestors,
never again to see
the light of day.
²⁰Our human glory disappears,
and, like animals, we die.

PSALM 50
(A psalm by Asaph.)
What Pleases God

¹From east to west,
the powerful LORD God
has been calling together
everyone on earth.
²God shines brightly from Zion,
the most beautiful city.

³Our God approaches,
but not silently;
a flaming fire comes first,
and a storm surrounds him.
⁴God comes to judge his people.
He shouts to the heavens
and to the earth,
⁵"Call my followers together!
They offered me a sacrifice,
and we made an agreement."

⁶The heavens announce,
"God is the judge,
and he is always honest."

⁷My people, I am God!
Israel, I am your God.
Listen to my charges
against you.
⁸Although you offer sacrifices
and always bring gifts,
⁹I won't accept your offerings
of bulls and goats.

¹⁰Every animal in the forest
belongs to me,
and so do the cattle
on a thousand hills.
¹¹I know all the birds
in the mountains,

■ 49.20 *we die:* The Hebrew of 49.20 suggests that people who do not "understand" will die like animals. Those who "understand" will still die, but they know that God's power is greater than the power of death.

● 50 (Title) *Asaph:* Asaph was from the tribe of Levi and was appointed by David to provide music and lead worship at the sacred tent and later at the temple (1 Chr 6.39-43; 16.4-7,37).

■ 50.4,5 *God comes to judge . . . agreement:* As ruler of the world, God is concerned with justice. When God's people do not do God's will, they are called to account. The "agreement" here recalls Exodus 24.1-8, the ceremony where the people agree to obey God and live according to God's Law.

℞ Agreements (Covenants)

℞ Day of the LORD

^j49.11 *The grave:* Some ancient translations; Hebrew "Their inward thoughts." ^k49.13 *and to those . . . fools:* One possible meaning for the difficult Hebrew text. ^l49.14 *as their shepherd . . . over them:* One possible meaning for the difficult Hebrew text.

and every wild creature
is in my care.

¹²If I were hungry,
I wouldn't tell you,
because I own the world
and everything in it.
¹³I don't eat the meat of bulls
or drink the blood of goats.
¹⁴I am God Most High!
The only sacrifice I want
is for you to be thankful
and to keep your word.
¹⁵Pray to me in time of trouble.
I will rescue you,
and you will honor me.

¹⁶But to the wicked I say:
"You don't have the right
to mention my laws or claim
to keep our agreement!
¹⁷You refused correction
and rejected my commands.
¹⁸You made friends
with every crook you met,
and you liked people who break
their wedding vows.
¹⁹You talked only about violence
and told nothing but lies;
²⁰you sat around gossiping,
ruining the reputation
of your own relatives."

²¹When you did all this,
I didn't say a word,
and you thought,
"God is just like us!"
But now I will accuse you.
²²You have ignored me!
So pay close attention

or I will tear you apart,
and no one can help you.

²³The sacrifice that honors me
is a thankful heart.
Obey me,ᵐ and I, your God,
will show my power to save.

Psalm 51

(For the music leader. A psalm by David when the prophet Nathan came to him after David had been with Bathsheba.)

A Prayer for Forgiveness

¹You are kind, God!
Please have pity on me.
You are always merciful!
Please wipe away my sins.
²Wash me clean from all
of my sin and guilt.
³I know about my sins,
and I cannot forget
the burden of my guilt.
⁴You are really the one
I have sinned against;
I have disobeyed you
and have done wrong.
So it is right and fair for you
to correct and punish me.

⁵I have sinned and done wrong
since the day I was born.
⁶But you want complete honesty,
so teach me true wisdom.
⁷Wash me with hyssopⁿ
until I am clean
and whiter than snow.
⁸Let me be happy and joyful!
You crushed my bones,
now let them celebrate.

ᵐ50.23 *Obey me:* One possible meaning for the difficult Hebrew text.   ⁿ51.7 *hyssop:* A small bush with bunches of small, white flowers. It was sometimes used as a symbol for making a person clean from sin.

The sacrifice that honors me is a thankful heart. Obey me, and I, your God, will show my power to save.   Ps 50.23

⁹Turn your eyes from my sin
and cover my guilt.
¹⁰Create pure thoughts in me
and make me faithful again.
¹¹Don't chase me away from you
or take your Holy Spirit
away from me.

¹²Make me as happy as you did
when you saved me;
make me want to obey!
¹³I will teach sinners your Law,
and they will return to you.
¹⁴Keep me from any deadly sin.
Only you can save me!
Then I will shout and sing
about your power to save.

¹⁵Help me to speak,
and I will praise you, Lord.
¹⁶Offerings and sacrifices
are not what you want.
¹⁷The way to please you
is to be truly sorry
deep in our hearts.
This is the kind of sacrifice
you won't refuse.

¹⁸Please be willing, Lord,
to help the city of Zion
and to rebuild its walls.
¹⁹Then you will be pleased
with the proper sacrifices,
and we will offer bulls
on your altar once again.

PSALM 52

(A special psalm by David for the music leader. He
wrote this when Doeg from Edom went to Saul and
said, "David has gone to Ahimelech's house.")

God Is in Control

¹You people may be strong
and brag about your sins,

but God can be trusted
day after day.
²You plan brutal crimes,
and your lying words cut
like a sharp razor.
³You would rather do evil
than good, and tell lies
than speak the truth.
⁴You love to say cruel things,
and your words are a trap.

⁵God will destroy you forever!
He will grab you and drag you
from your homes.
You will be uprooted
and left to die.
⁶When good people see
this fearsome sight,
they will laugh and say,
7   "Just look at them now!
Instead of trusting God,
they trusted their wealth
and their cruelty."

⁸But I am like an olive tree
growing in God's house,
and I can count on his love
forever and ever.
⁹I will always thank God
for what he has done;
I will praise his good name
when his people meet.

PSALM 53

(A special psalm by David for the music leader. To the
tune "Mahalath."ᵒ)

No One Can Ignore God

¹Only a fool would say,
"There is no God!"
People like that are worthless!

ᵒPsalm 53 *Mahalath*: Or "For flutes," one possible meaning for the difficult Hebrew text.

■ 51.11 *Holy Spirit*: God's Spirit can create new things and is God's enduring presence.

❧   Holy Spirit

❧   God's Saving Love (Salvation)

●   51.18 *city of Zion . . . rebuild its walls*: This is Jerusalem. Verses 18 and 19 may have been added to the psalm after the destruction of Jerusalem in 586 B.C. and before the rebuilding of its walls was completed in about 445 B.C. **(See the article After the Exile: God's People Return to Judea on pg 1789.)**

●   52 (Title) *Doeg . . . Saul . . . David . . . Ahimelech's house*: Doeg the Edomite was one of King Saul's army officers. While trying to help Saul capture David, Doeg killed Ahimelech and many of Israel's priests and their families (1 Sam 22.9-19). The Edomites were descendants of Esau, Jacob's brother (Gen 36.1,9-14,40-43). The nation of Edom is usually described in the Bible as an enemy of Israel (Num 24.18; 1 Sam 14.47-48; 2 Sam 8.13,14). David, a shepherd boy from Judah, entered the court of King Saul after defeating the Philistine giant Goliath in combat (1 Sam 17.55—18.5). He became king of Israel after Saul died, and is remembered as Israel's greatest king. **(See Map 6 on pg 1884.)**

❧   David

●   52.8 *olive tree*: Olive trees live a long time, and even when cut down, they sprout from the root. They are a good symbol for people whose foundation for life is their trust in God's love.

54 (Title) *the people of Ziph...*
Saul: The people of Ziph tried to help
King Saul kill David (1 Sam 23.19; 26.1).

David

Enemies (The Wicked)

They are heartless and cruel
　and never do right.

2From heaven God
　looks down to see
if anyone is wise enough
　to search for him.
3But all of them
are crooked and corrupt.
　Not one of them does right.

4Won't you lawbreakers learn?
　You refuse to pray,
and you gobble up
　the people of God.
5But you will be terrified
　worse than ever before.
God will scatter the bones
　of his enemies,
and you will be ashamed
　when God rejects you.

6I long for someone from Zion
　to come and save Israel!
Our God, when you bless
　your people again,
Jacob's family will be glad,
　and Israel will celebrate.

Psalm 54

(For the music leader. Use with stringed instruments. A
special psalm that David wrote when the people of Ziph
went to Saul and said, "David is hiding here with us.")

Trusting God in Times of Trouble

1Save me, God, by your power
　and prove that I am right.
2Listen to my prayer
　and hear what I say.
3Cruel strangers have attacked
　and want me dead.
Not one of them cares
　about you.

4You will help me, Lord God,
　and keep me from falling;

5you will punish my enemies
　for their evil deeds.
Be my faithful friend
　and destroy them.

6I will bring a gift
and offer a sacrifice
　to you, LORD.
I will praise your name
　because you are good.
7You have rescued me
　from all my troubles,
and my own eyes have seen
　my enemies fall.

Psalm 55

(A special psalm by David for the music leader. Use
with stringed instruments.)

Betrayed by a Friend

1Listen, God, to my prayer!
　Don't reject my request.
2Please listen and help me.
My thoughts are troubled,
　and I keep groaning
3because my enemies attack
　with loud shouts.
They treat me terribly
　and hold angry grudges.
4My heart is racing fast,
　and I am afraid of dying.
5I am trembling with fear,
　completely terrified.

6I wish I had wings
　like a dove,
so I could fly far away
　and be at peace.
7I would go and live
　in some distant desert.
8I would quickly find shelter
　from howling winds
　and raging storms.

9Confuse my enemies, Lord!
　Upset their plans.

Cruelty and violence
are all I see in the city,
10and they are like guards
on patrol day and night.
The city is full of trouble,
evil, 11and corruption.
Troublemakers and liars
freely roam the streets.

12My enemies are not the ones
who sneer and make fun.
I could put up with that
or even hide from them.
13But it was my closest friend,
the one I trusted most.
14We enjoyed being together,
when we went with others
to your house, our God.

15All who hate me are controlled
by the power of evil.
Sentence them to death
and send them down alive
to the world of the dead.

16I ask for your help, LORD God,
and you will keep me safe.
17Morning, noon, and night
you hear my concerns
and my complaints.
18I am attacked from all sides,
but you will rescue me
unharmed by the battle.
19You have always ruled,
and you will hear me.
You will defeat my enemies
because they won't turn
and worship you.

20My friend turned against me
and broke his promise.
21His words were smoother
than butter, and softer
than olive oil.
But hatred filled his heart,
and he was ready to attack
with a sword.

22Our LORD, we belong to you.
We tell you what worries us,
and you won't let us fall.
23But what about those people
who are cruel and brutal?
You will throw them down
into the deepest pit
long before their time.
I trust you, LORD!

PSALM 56

(For the music leader. To the tune "A Silent Dove in the Distance."[p] A special psalm by David when the Philistines captured him in Gath.)

A Prayer of Trust in God

1Have pity, God Most High!
My enemies chase me all day.
2Many of them are pursuing
and attacking me,
3but even when I am afraid,
I keep on trusting you.
4I praise your promises!
I trust you and am not afraid.
No one can harm me.

5Enemies spend the whole day
finding fault with me;
all they think about
is how to do me harm.
6They attack from ambush,
watching my every step
and hoping to kill me.
7They won't get away[q]
with these crimes, God,

[p]**Psalm 56** *A Silent . . . Distance*: One possible meaning for the difficult Hebrew text.
[q]**56.7** *They . . . away*: One possible meaning for the difficult Hebrew text.

55.10 *The city:* The "city" may be Jerusalem, but this is not certain. The concern about a violent and troubled city makes the psalm apply to many places and times.

56 (Title) *David . . . Philistines . . . Gath:* David ran to the Philistine city of Gath to get away from Saul (1 Sam 21.10-15), but he was not really "captured." The Philistines who lived to the west of Judah were traditional enemies of Israel from before the time of David and continued to be enemies long after David's death. **(See Map 4 on pg 1882.)**

57.3 *help from heaven:* God sees everything from "his throne in heaven" and acts to oppose "the wicked."

57.8 *wake up the sun:* This phrase may be a poetic way of saying that the psalmist will get an early start or sing praises early in the morning.

because when you get angry,
  you destroy people.

⁸You have kept record
  of my days of wandering.
You have stored my tears
in your bottle
  and counted each of them.

⁹When I pray, LORD God,
  my enemies will retreat,
because I know for certain
  that you are with me.
¹⁰I praise your promises!
¹¹I trust you and am not afraid.
  No one can harm me.

¹²I will keep my promises
to you, my God,
  and bring you gifts.
¹³You protected me from death
  and kept me from stumbling,
so that I would please you
and follow the light
  that leads to life.

PSALM 57

(For the music leader. To the tune "Don't Destroy."ʳ A special psalm by David when he was in the cave while running from Saul.)

Praise and Trust in Times of Trouble

¹God Most High, have pity on me!
Have mercy. I run to you
  for safety.
In the shadow of your wings,
I seek protection
  till danger dies down.
²I pray to you, my protector.
³You will send help from heaven

and save me,
  but you will bring trouble
  on my attackers.
You are faithful,
  and you can be trusted.

⁴My enemies are fierce,
  much worse than lions!
They have spears and arrows
  instead of teeth,
and they have sharp swords
  instead of tongues.

⁵May you, my God, be honored
  above the heavens;
may your glory be seen
  everywhere on earth.

⁶Enemies set traps for my feet
  and struck me down.
They dug a pit in my path,
  but fell in it themselves.
⁷I am faithful to you,
  and you can trust me.
I will sing and play music
  for you, my God.
⁸I feel wide awake!
I will wake up my harp
  and wake up the sun.
⁹I will praise you, Lord,
  for everyone to hear,
and I will sing hymns to you
  in every nation.
¹⁰Your love reaches higher
  than the heavens;
your loyalty extends
  beyond the clouds.

¹¹May you, my God, be honored
  above the heavens;
may your glory be seen
  everywhere on earth.

ʳ**Psalm 57** *Don't Destroy:* One possible meaning for the difficult Hebrew text.

PSALM 58

(A special psalm by David for the music leader. To the tune "Don't Destroy."[S])

A Prayer When All Goes Wrong

[1]Do you mighty people[t] talk
  only to oppose justice?[u]
    Don't you ever judge fairly?
[2]You are always planning evil,
  and you are brutal.
[3]You have done wrong and lied
  from the day you were born.
[4]Your words spread poison
  like the bite of a cobra
[5]that refuses to listen
  to the snake charmer.

[6]My enemies are fierce
  as lions, LORD God!
Shatter their teeth.
  Snatch out their fangs.
[7]Make them disappear
  like leaking water,
    and make their arrows miss.
[8]Let them dry up like snails
  or be like a child that dies
    before seeing the sun.
[9]Wipe them out quicker
  than a pot can be heated
    by setting thorns on fire.[v]

[10]Good people will be glad
  when they see the wicked
    getting what they deserve,
  and they will wash their feet
    in their enemies' blood.
[11]Everyone will say, "It's true!
  Good people are rewarded.
  God does indeed rule the earth
    with justice."

PSALM 59

(For the music leader. To the tune "Don't Destroy."[W]
A special psalm by David when Saul had David's house
watched so that he could kill him.)

A Prayer for Protection

[1]Save me, God! Protect me
  from enemy attacks!
[2]Keep me safe from brutal people
  who want to kill me.

[3]Merciless enemies, LORD,
  are hiding and plotting,
    hoping to kill me.
I have not hurt them
  in any way at all.
[4]But they are ready to attack.
Do something! Help me!
  Look at what's happening.
[5]LORD God All-Powerful,
  you are the God of Israel.
Punish the other nations
and don't pity those terrible
  and rebellious people.

[6]My enemies return at evening,
  growling like dogs
    roaming the city.
[7]They curse, and their words
  cut like swords,
as they say to themselves,
  "No one can hear us!"

[8]You, LORD, laugh at them
  and sneer at the nations.
[9]You are my mighty fortress,
  and I depend on you.
[10]You love me and will let me
  see my enemies defeated.
[11]Don't kill them,

58.11 *Good . . . rewarded:* The Hebrew word for "are rewarded" means "are fruitful." If there is a "reward," it is the experience of being protected by God.

59 (Title) *Saul had David's house watched:* This probably refers to the night Saul tried to kill David (1 Sam 19.9-11).

[S]**Psalm 58** *Don't Destroy:* One possible meaning for the difficult Hebrew text.   [t]**58.1** *mighty people:* Or "mighty rulers" or "mighty gods."   [u]**58.1** *Do . . . justice:* One possible meaning for the difficult Hebrew text.   [v]**58.9** *Wipe . . . fire:* One possible meaning for the difficult Hebrew text.
[W]**Psalm 59** *Don't Destroy:* See the note at Psalm 57.

59.11 *You are a shield:* Ancient warriors relied on shields for protection in close combat. They were made of wood covered by leather or metal. In this psalm, God is called a shield because of the protection he gives to his people.

60 (Title) *wars with the Arameans . . . Joab . . . Edomites:* The title describes the events of 2 Samuel 8.3-8,13; 10.16-18; 1 Chronicles 18.3-11. "Arameans" is another name for the people of Syria, Israel's traditional enemy to the northeast. Joab, David's nephew, was one of David's army commanders. Joab's defeat of the Edomites is described in 2 Samuel 8.13; 1 Chronicles 18.12. "Salt Valley" probably refers to the area at the southern end of the Dead Sea. **(See Map 6 on pg 1884.)**

60.3 *gave us wine:* Drinking from the LORD's "cup of anger" is a common symbol for God's punishment (Jer 25.15-29; Rev 16.19).

or everyone may forget!
Just use your mighty power
to make them tremble
and fall.

You are a shield
for your people.
¹²My enemies are liars!
So let them be trapped
by their boastful lies.
¹³Get angry and destroy them.
Leave them in ruin.
Then all the nations will know
that you rule in Israel.

¹⁴Those liars return at evening,
growling like dogs
roaming the city.
¹⁵They search for scraps of food,
and they snarl
until they are stuffed.

¹⁶But I will sing about
your strength, my God,
and I will celebrate
because of your love.
You are my fortress,
my place of protection
in times of trouble.
¹⁷I will sing your praises!
You are my mighty fortress,
and you love me.

PSALM 60

(For the music leader. To the tune "Lily of the Promise." A special psalm by David for teaching. He wrote it during his wars with the Arameans of northern Syria,ˣ when Joab came back and killed twelve thousand Edomitesʸ in Salt Valley.)

You Can Depend on God

¹You, God, are angry with us!
We are rejected and crushed.
Make us strong again!
²You made the earth shake
and split wide open;
now heal its wounds
and stop its trembling.
³You brought hard times
on your people,
and you gave us wine
that made us stagger.

⁴You gave a signal to those
who worship you,
so they could escape
from enemy arrows.ᶻ
⁵Answer our prayers, God!
Use your powerful arm
and give us victory.
Then the people you love
will be safe.

⁶Our God, you solemnly promised,
"I would gladly divide up
the city of Shechem
and give away Succoth Valley
piece by piece.
⁷The lands of Gilead
and Manasseh are mine.
Ephraim is my war helmet,
and Judah is the symbol
of my royal power.
⁸Moab is merely my washbasin.
Edom belongs to me,
and I shout in triumph
over the Philistines."

⁹Our God, who will bring me
to the fortress,
or lead me to Edom?
¹⁰Have you rejected us
and deserted our armies?
¹¹Help us defeat our enemies!

ˣPsalm 60 *wars . . . Syria:* See 2 Samuel 8.3-8; 10.16-18; 1 Chronicles 18.3-11; 19.6-19. ʸPsalm 60 *killed . . . Edomites:* See 2 Samuel 8.13; 1 Chronicles 18.12. ᶻ60.4 *so . . . arrows:* Some ancient translations and one possible meaning for the difficult Hebrew text.

No one else can rescue us.
¹²You will give us victory
   and crush our enemies.

PSALM 61

(A psalm by David for the music leader. Use with
stringed instruments.)

Under the Protection of God

¹Please listen, God,
   and answer my prayer!
²I feel hopeless,
   and I cry out to you
      from a faraway land.

Lead me to the mighty rock[a]
   high above me.
³You are a strong tower,
   where I am safe
      from my enemies.

⁴Let me live with you forever
   and find protection
      under your wings, my God.
⁵You heard my promises,
   and you have blessed me,
just as you bless everyone
   who worships you.

⁶Let the king have a long
   and healthy life.
⁷May he always rule
   with you, God, at his side;
may your love and loyalty
   watch over him.

⁸I will sing your praises
   forever, God, and will always
      keep my promises.

PSALM 62

(A psalm by David for Jeduthun, the music leader.)

God Is Powerful and Kind

¹Only God can save me,
   and I calmly wait for[b] him.
²God alone is the mighty rock[c]
   that keeps me safe
and the fortress
   where I am secure.

³I feel like a shaky fence
   or a sagging wall.
How long will all of you
   attack and assault me?
⁴You want to bring me down
   from my place of honor.
You love to tell lies,
and when your words are kind,
   hatred hides in your heart.

⁵Only God gives inward peace,
   and I depend on him.
⁶God alone is the mighty rock
   that keeps me safe,
and he is the fortress
   where I feel secure.
⁷God saves me and honors me.
   He is that mighty rock
      where I find safety.

⁸Trust God, my friends,
   and always tell him
each of your concerns.
   God is our place of safety.

⁹We humans are only a breath;
   none of us are truly great.
All of us together weigh less
   than a puff of air.
¹⁰Don't trust in violence

● **61.3** *strong tower:* Towers were important features built into the protective walls surrounding many ancient cities.

● **61.6,7** *Let . . . him:* This prayer for the king's health comes either from the king himself or from a representative of the community.

■ **62.8-10** *Trust God . . . Don't trust in violence . . . wealth:* The psalmists regularly show their trust in God, even as they suffer. The wicked regularly trust in themselves or in their wealth.

[a]**61.2** *mighty rock:* See the note at 18.2.   [b]**62.1** *calmly wait for:* Or "am at peace with."   [c]**62.2** *mighty rock:* See the note at 18.2.

Let me live with you forever and find protection under your wings, my God. Ps 61.4

63 (Title) *in the desert of Judah:* This may refer either to Saul's attempt to kill David (1 Sam 23.14) or to Absalom's revolt (2 Sam 15–17).

or depend on dishonesty
    or rely on great wealth.

¹¹I heard God say two things:
    "I am powerful,
¹²   and I am very kind."
    The Lord rewards each of us
    according to what we do.

Psalm 63

(A psalm by David when he was in the desert of Judah.)

God's Love Means More than Life

¹You are my God. I worship you.
    In my heart, I long for you,
as I would long for a stream
    in a scorching desert.

²I have seen your power
and your glory
    in the place of worship.
³Your love means more
    than life to me,
    and I praise you.
⁴As long as I live,
    I will pray to you.
⁵I will sing joyful praises
    and be filled with excitement
        like a guest at a banquet.

⁶I think about you, God,
    before I go to sleep,
and my thoughts turn to you
    during the night.
⁷You have helped me,
    and I sing happy songs
        in the shadow of your wings.
⁸I stay close to you,
    and your powerful arm
        supports me.

⁹All who want to kill me
    will end up in the ground.
¹⁰Swords will run them through,
    and wild dogs will eat them.

¹¹Because of you, our God,
    the king will celebrate
with your faithful followers,
    but liars will be silent.

Psalm 64

(A psalm by David for the music leader.)

Celebrate because of the Lord

¹Listen to my concerns, God,
    and protect me
        from my enemies' threats.
²Keep me safe from secret plots
    of corrupt and evil gangs.
³Their words cut like swords,
    and their cruel remarks
        sting like sharp arrows.
⁴They fearlessly ambush
    and shoot innocent people.

⁵They are determined to do evil,
    and they tell themselves,
"Let's set traps!
    No one can see us."ᵈ
⁶They make evil plans and say,
    "We'll commit a perfect crime.
    No one knows our thoughts."ᵉ

⁷But God will shoot his arrows
    and quickly wound them.
⁸They will be destroyed
    by their own words,
and everyone who sees them
    will tremble with fear.ᶠ
⁹They will be afraid and say,
    "Look at what God has done
        and keep it all in mind."

ᵈ**64.5** *us:* One ancient translation; Hebrew "them." ᵉ**64.6** *thoughts:* One possible meaning for the difficult Hebrew text of verse 6. ᶠ**64.8** *tremble with fear:* Or "turn and run."

[10]May the LORD bless his people
with peace and happiness
and let them celebrate.

PSALM 65

(A psalm by David and a song for the music leader.)

God Answers Prayer

[1]Our God, you deserve[g] praise
in Zion, where we keep
our promises to you.
[2]Everyone will come to you
because you answer prayer.
[3]When our sins get us down,
you forgive us.
[4]You bless your chosen ones,
and you invite them
to live near you
in your temple.
We will enjoy your house,
the sacred temple.

[5]Our God, you save us,
and your fearsome deeds answer
our prayers for justice!
You give hope to people
everywhere on earth,
even those across the sea.
[6]You are strong,
and your mighty power
put the mountains in place.
[7]You silence the roaring waves
and the noisy shouts
of the nations.
[8]People far away marvel
at your fearsome deeds,
and all who live under the sun
celebrate and sing
because of you.

[9]You take care of the earth
and send rain to help the soil
grow all kinds of crops.

Your rivers never run dry,
and you prepare the earth
to produce abundant grain.
[10]You water all its fields
and level the lumpy ground.
You send showers of rain
to soften the soil
and help the plants sprout.
[11]Wherever your footsteps
touch the earth,
a rich harvest is gathered.
[12]Desert pastures blossom,
and mountains celebrate.
[13]Meadows are filled
with sheep and goats;
valleys overflow with grain
and echo with joyful songs.

PSALM 66

(A song and a psalm for the music leader.)

Shout Praises to God

[1]Tell everyone on this earth
to shout praises to God!
[2]Sing about his glorious name.
Honor him with praises.
[3]Say to God, "Everything you do
is fearsome,
and your mighty power makes
your enemies come crawling.
[4]You are worshiped by everyone!
We all sing praises to you."

[5]Come and see the fearsome things
our God has done!
[6]When God made the sea dry up,
our people walked across,
and because of him,
we celebrated there.
[7]His mighty power rules forever,
and nothing the nations do
can be hidden from him.
So don't turn against God.

[g]65.1 *deserve*: One possible meaning for the difficult Hebrew text.

■ 64.10 *LORD bless . . . happiness*: To find protection in God even while suffering means "happiness."

■ 65.1 *our promises to you*: The people kept their promises with correct worship, including offering prayers of thanks and bringing gifts and sacrifices.

● 65.9-13 *You take care of the earth . . . valleys overflow*: At this time Israel's neighbors, the Canaanites, believed that the god Baal sent the rain that made the crops grow. However, this psalm says that it is God who sends the rain that brings rich harvests and fertile pastures where sheep and goats can graze.

Tell everyone on this earth to shout praises to God!
Ps 66.1

66.10-12 *as silver is tested . . . plenty:* To "test" silver or gold means to "refine" it. Gold and silver were melted in a hot fire, which burned off unwanted impurities such as dust. The events recall the troubles faced by the people in the desert after leaving Egypt and before entering Canaan. Those who survived the "testing" would be like the pure silver or gold that remains after being refined by fire. What the people experienced as a testing resulted in the gift of the promised land.

67.1,2 *bless us . . . all nations:* God's blessing means that God provides everything needed for life, including teaching, forgiveness, and material blessings. When other nations see how God has blessed Israel, they will honor Israel's God. The psalmist also has in mind here the promise that God made to Abraham in Genesis 12.1-3. The blessings that Abraham's descendants receive will make them a blessing to others.

68.1,2 *Scatter your hateful enemies . . . fire:* Moses prays a similar prayer to ask God to lead the people from Sinai to the promised land (Num 10.35).

68.4 *rides on the clouds:* The Canaanites believed that the god Baal brought rain to make crops grow. But this psalm says that God "rides on the clouds," meaning provides needed rain.

8All of you people,
  come praise our God!
  Let his praises be heard.
9God protects us from death
  and keeps us steady.

10Our God, you tested us,
  just as silver is tested.
11You trapped us in a net
  and gave us heavy burdens.
12You sent war chariots
  to crush our skulls.
  We traveled through fire
  and through floods,
  but you brought us
  to a land of plenty.

13I will bring sacrifices
  into your house, my God,
  and I will do what I promised
14 when I was in trouble.
15I will sacrifice my best sheep
  and offer bulls and goats
  on your altar.

16All who worship God,
  come here and listen;
  I will tell you everything
  God has done for me.
17I prayed to the Lord,
  and I praised him.
18If my thoughts had been sinful,
  he would have refused
  to hear me.
19But God did listen
  and answered my prayer.
20Let's praise God!
  He listened when I prayed,
  and he is always kind.

Psalm 67

(A psalm and a song for the music leader. Use with stringed instruments.)

Tell the Nations To Praise God

1Our God, be kind and bless us!
  Be pleased and smile.
2Then everyone on earth
  will learn to follow you,
  and all nations will see
  your power to save us.

3Make everyone praise you
  and shout your praises.
4Let the nations celebrate
  with joyful songs,
  because you judge fairly
  and guide all nations.
5Make everyone praise you, God,
  and shout your praises.

6Our God has blessed the earth
  with a wonderful harvest!
7Pray for his blessings
  to continue
  and for everyone on earth
  to worship our God.

Psalm 68

(A psalm and a song by David for the music leader.)

God Will Win the Battle

1Do something, God!
  Scatter your hateful enemies.
  Make them turn and run.
2Scatter them like smoke!
  When you come near,
  make them melt
  like wax in a fire.
3But let your people be happy
  and celebrate because of you.

4Our God, you are the one
  who rides on the clouds,h

h**68.4** *on the clouds:* Or "across the desert."

and we praise you.
Your name is the LORD,
and we celebrate
    as we worship you.

⁵Our God, from your sacred home
you take care of orphans
    and protect widows.
⁶You find families
    for those who are lonely.
You set prisoners free
    and let them prosper,ⁱ
but all who rebel will live
    in a scorching desert.

⁷You set your people free,
and you led them
    through the desert.
⁸ God of Israel,
the earth trembled,
    and rain poured down.
You alone are the God
    who rules from Mount Sinai.
⁹When your land was thirsty,
you sent showers
    to refresh it.
¹⁰Your people settled there,
and you were generous
    to everyone in need.

¹¹You gave the command, LORD,
and a chorus of women told
    what had happened:
¹²"Kings and their armies
    retreated and ran,
and everything they left
    is now being divided.
¹³And for those who stayed back
    to guard the sheep,
there are metal doves

with silver-coated wings
    and shiny gold feathers."

¹⁴God All-Powerful, you scattered
the kings like snow falling
    on Mount Zalmon.ʲ

¹⁵Our LORD and our God,
Bashan is a mighty mountain
    covered with peaks.
¹⁶Why is it jealous of Zion,
the mountain you chose
    as your home forever?

¹⁷When you, LORD God, appeared
    to your peopleᵏ at Sinai,
you came with thousands
    of mighty chariots.
¹⁸When you climbed
    the high mountain,
you took prisoners with you
    and were given gifts.
Your enemies didn't want you
to live there,
    but they gave you gifts.

¹⁹We praise you, Lord God!
You treat us with kindness
    day after day,
    and you rescue us.
²⁰You always protect us
    and save us from death.

²¹Our Lord and our God,
your terrible enemies
    are ready for war,ˡ
but you will crush
    their skulls.
²²You promised to bring them

ⁱ**68.6** *and let them prosper*: Or "and give them a song."   ʲ**68.14** *Mount Zalmon*: The location of this mountain is not known.   ᵏ**68.17** *to your people*: Or "in all your holiness" or "in your holy place."
ˡ**68.21** *are ready for war*: The Hebrew text has "have long hair," which probably refers to the ancient custom of wearing long hair on special occasions, such as a "holy war."

● **68.9-14** *your land . . . Mount Zalmon*: After 40 years of wandering, the people of Israel entered the land of Canaan ("your land"). Verses 12 to 14 refer to the battles described in JOSHUA and JUDGES. The location of Mount Zalmon is not known.

● **68.13** *metal doves . . . gold feathers*: This may refer to a valuable object left by the retreating Canaanite armies. The Canaanite goddess Astarte was represented by a dove.

⌘   Canaanite Gods and Goddesses

68.27 *Benjamin . . . Judah . . . Zebulun and Naphtali:* These are four of the twelve tribes of Israel. Perhaps the tribes were to march to the temple in this particular order for the celebration of God's kingship. **(See Map 3 on pg 1881.)**

68.30,31 *Punish that animal . . . wild bulls . . . offer presents:* The "swamp animal" probably refers to Egypt, which had much marshy land near the Nile River. The prophets of Israel also said that Egypt, Ethiopia, and other nations would bring gifts to honor Israel's God (Isa 18.7; 60.4-9; Zeph 3.10).

69.1,2 *drown . . . mighty flood:* Drowning is a symbol of severe distress, and flooding was a major danger in ancient times and often a symbol of chaos and death.

from Bashan
and from the deepest sea.
[23] Then we could wash our feet
in their blood,
and our dogs could chew
on their bones.

[24] We have seen crowds marching
to your place of worship,
our God and King.
[25] Singers come first,
and then the musicians,
surrounded by young women
playing tambourines.
[26] They come shouting,
"People of Israel,
praise the LORD God!"
[27] The small tribe of Benjamin
leads the way,
followed by the leaders
from Judah.
Then come the leaders
from Zebulun and Naphtali.

[28] Our God, show your strength!
Show us once again.
[29] Then kings will bring gifts
to your temple
in Jerusalem.[m]

[30] Punish that animal
that lives in the swamp![n]
Punish that nation
whose leaders and people
are like wild bulls.
Make them come crawling
with gifts of silver.
Scatter those nations
that enjoy making war.[o]

[31] Force the Egyptians to bring
gifts of bronze;
make the Ethiopians[p] hurry
to offer presents.[q]

[32] Now sing praises to God!
Every kingdom on earth,
sing to the Lord!
[33] Praise the one who rides
across the ancient skies;
listen as he speaks
with a mighty voice.
[34] Tell about God's power!
He is honored in Israel,
and he rules the skies.
[35] The God of Israel is fearsome
in his temple,
and he makes us strong.
Let's praise our God!

PSALM 69
(By David for the music leader. To the tune "Lilies.")
God Can Be Trusted

[1] Save me, God!
I am about to drown.
[2] I am sinking deep in the mud,
and my feet are slipping.
I am about to be swept under
by a mighty flood.
[3] I am worn out from crying,
and my throat is dry.
I have waited for you
till my eyes are blurred.

[4] There are more people
who hate me for no reason
than there are hairs

[m]**68.28,29** *Our God . . . Jerusalem:* One possible meaning for the difficult Hebrew text of verses 28,29. [n]**68.30** *animal . . . swamp:* Probably Egypt. [o]**68.30** *war:* One possible meaning for the difficult Hebrew text of verse 30. [p]**68.31** *the Ethiopians:* The Hebrew text has "the people of Cush," which was a region south of Egypt that included parts of the present countries of Ethiopia and Sudan. [q]**68.31** *presents:* One possible meaning for the difficult Hebrew text of verse 31.

on my head.
Many terrible enemies
want to destroy me, God.
Am I supposed to give back
something I didn't steal?
⁵You know my foolish sins.
Not one is hidden from you.

⁶Lᴏʀᴅ God All-Powerful,
ruler of Israel,
don't let me embarrass anyone
who trusts and worships you.
⁷It is for your sake alone
that I am insulted
and blush with shame.
⁸I am like a stranger
to my relatives
and like a foreigner
to my own family.

⁹My love for your house
burns in me like a fire,
and when others insult you,
they insulted me as well.
¹⁰I cried and went without food,ʳ
but they still insulted me.
¹¹They sneered at me
for wearing sackclothˢ
to show my sorrow.
¹²Rulers and judges gossip
about me,
and drunkards make up songs
to mock me.

¹³But I pray to you, Lᴏʀᴅ.
So when the time is right,
answer me and help me
with your wonderful love.
¹⁴Don't let me sink in the mud,
but save me from my enemies
and from the deep water.
¹⁵Don't let me be
swept away by a flood

or drowned in the ocean
or swallowed by death.

¹⁶Answer me, Lᴏʀᴅ!
You are kind and good.
Pay attention to me!
You are truly merciful.
¹⁷Don't turn away from me.
I am your servant,
and I am in trouble.
Please hurry and help!
¹⁸Come and save me
from my enemies.

¹⁹You know how I am insulted,
mocked, and disgraced;
you know every one
of my enemies.
²⁰I am crushed by insults,
and I feel sick.
I had hoped for mercy and pity,
but there was none.
²¹Enemies poisoned my food,
and when I was thirsty,
they gave me vinegar.

²²Make their table a trap
for them and their friends.
²³Blind them with darkness
and make them tremble.
²⁴Show them how angry you are!
Be furious and catch them.
²⁵Destroy their camp
and don't let anyone live
in their tents.

²⁶They cause trouble for people
you have already punished;
their gossip hurts those
you have wounded.
²⁷Make them guiltier than ever
and don't forgive them.
²⁸Wipe their names from the book

ʳ**69.10** *went without food:* See the note at 35.13. ˢ**69.11** *sackcloth:* See the note at 30.11.

69.7 *It . . . shame:* The psalmist does not view his suffering as punishment. Instead, he suffers for God's sake (69.9). This probably explains why parts of the psalm are used in the New Testament to suggest that Jesus lived out the experiences described here.

69.21 *poisoned my food . . . gave me vinegar:* These symbolize the deadly threats of the enemies. Vinegar is wine that has gone sour. The writers of the Gospels used this verse to describe the opposition to Jesus (see Matt 27.48; Mark 15.36; Luke 23.36; John 19.28,29).

71.2 *what is right:* For those who are faithful to God, "what is right" always involves doing justice and includes help and protection for people who are victims.

☙   Enemies (The Wicked)

of the living;
remove them from the list
of the innocent.
²⁹I am mistreated and in pain.
Protect me, God,
and keep me safe!

³⁰I will praise the Lord God
with a song
and a thankful heart.
³¹This will please the Lord
better than offering an ox
or a full-grown bull.
³²When those in need see this,
they will be happy,
and the Lord's worshipers
will be encouraged.
³³The Lord will listen
when the homeless cry out,
and he will never forget
his people in prison.

³⁴Heaven and earth
will praise our God,
and so will the oceans
and everything in them.
³⁵God will rescue Jerusalem,
and he will rebuild
the towns of Judah.
His people will live there
on their own land,
³⁶and when the time comes,
their children will inherit
the land.
Then everyone who loves God
will also settle there.

PSALM 70

(By David for the music leader. To be used when an offering is made.)

God Is Wonderful

¹Save me, Lord God!
Hurry and help.

ᵗ71.3 *mighty rock:* See the note at 18.2.

²Disappoint and confuse
all who want to kill me.
Turn away and disgrace
all who want to hurt me.
³Embarrass and shame those
who say, "We told you so!"

⁴Let your worshipers celebrate
and be glad because of you.
They love your saving power,
so let them always say,
"God is wonderful!"
⁵I am poor and needy,
but you, the Lord God,
care about me.

You are the one who saves me.
Please hurry and help!

PSALM 71
A Prayer for God's Protection

¹I run to you, Lord,
for protection.
Don't disappoint me.
²You do what is right,
so come to my rescue.
Listen to my prayer
and keep me safe.
³Be my mighty rock,ᵗ the place
where I can always run
for protection.
Save me by your command!
You are my mighty rock
and my fortress.

⁴Come and save me, Lord God,
from vicious and cruel
and brutal enemies!
⁵I depend on you,
and I have trusted you
since I was young.

⁶I have relied on you^u
from the day I was born.
You brought me safely
through birth,
and I always praise you.

⁷Many people think of me
as something evil.
But you are my mighty protector,
⁸and I praise and honor you
all day long.
⁹Don't throw me aside
when I am old;
don't desert me
when my strength is gone.
¹⁰My enemies are plotting
because they want me dead.
¹¹They say, "Now we'll catch you!
God has deserted you,
and no one can save you."
¹²Come closer, God!
Please hurry and help.
¹³Embarrass and destroy
all who want me dead;
disgrace and confuse
all who want to hurt me.
¹⁴I will never give up hope
or stop praising you.
¹⁵All day long I will tell
the wonderful things you do
to save your people.
But you have done much more
than I could possibly know.
¹⁶I will praise you, Lord God,
for your mighty deeds
and your power to save.

¹⁷You have taught me
since I was a child,
and I never stop telling about
your marvelous deeds.
¹⁸Don't leave me when I am old
and my hair turns gray.

Let me tell future generations
about your mighty power.
¹⁹Your deeds of kindness
are known in the heavens.
No one is like you!

²⁰You made me suffer a lot,
but you will bring me
back from this deep pit
and give me new life.
²¹You will make me truly great
and take my sorrow away.

²²I will praise you, God,
the Holy One of Israel.
You are faithful.
I will play the harp
and sing your praises.
²³You have rescued me!
I will celebrate and shout,
singing praises to you
with all my heart.
²⁴All day long I will announce
your power to save.
I will tell how you disgraced
and disappointed those
who wanted to hurt me.

Psalm 72
(By Solomon.)
A Prayer for God To Guide and Help the King

¹Please help the king
to be honest and fair
just like you, our God.
²Let him be honest and fair
with all your people,
especially the poor.
³Let peace and justice rule
every mountain and hill.
⁴Let the king defend the poor,

^u71.6 *I . . . you:* One possible meaning for the difficult Hebrew text.

71.22 *Holy One:* To be holy means to be set apart. To call God "the Holy One" suggests God's greatness, and it is especially fitting after the psalmist has said, "No one is like you!" (71.19).

Holiness

72 (Title) *Solomon:* Solomon was David's son. For the account of his life and kingship, see 1 Kings 3–11.

Solomon

72.1-3 *help the king to be honest . . . justice rule:* The king was to serve God by being honest and fair and by taking care of the poor. Honesty and fairness are also called "justice." It is what God always wants, and there can be no "peace" without it.

Justice

Peace

72.8-11 *kingdom reach from sea to sea . . . nations serve him:* Because God wants justice and peace for "everyone" (72.2), the king needs to be recognized by "all nations" all over the world. The Euphrates River was located in Assyria and Mesopotamia to the north and east of Israel. "Desert tribes" probably refers to tribes to the south and southeast. Tarshish probably refers to a city far to the west in Spain. The "islands" may refer to the Greek islands, Crete, or Cyprus. Sheba may have been a place in what is now southwest Arabia, and Seba may have been in southern Arabia (1 Kgs 10.1-13). **(See Map 7 on pg 1885.)**

72.16 *Mount Lebanon:* The name "Lebanon" comes from the Hebrew word for "white" and refers to the snow that caps the mountain peaks of this range.

72.20 *This ends the prayers of David, the son of Jesse:* For Jesse, see 1 Sam 16.1-22. This verse was probably added sometime after the psalm was written. When the PSALMS were being collected, it served as a way to identify Books I and II as the prayers of David.

73.1 *pure heart:* In Hebrew thought, the heart was not understood to be the seat of emotions so much as the place where a person's thoughts and intentions resided (see 51.10, where CEV translates "pure heart" as "pure thoughts"). To have a "pure heart," then, is to be obedient and loyal to God.

rescue the homeless, and crush
    everyone who hurts them.
⁵Let the king liveᵛ forever
    like the sun and the moon.
⁶Let him be as helpful as rain
    that refreshes the meadows
    and the ground.
⁷Let the king be fair
    with everyone,
and let there be peace
until the moon
    falls from the sky.

⁸Let his kingdom reach
    from sea to sea,
from the Euphrates River
    across all the earth.
⁹Force the desert tribes
    to accept his rule,
and make his enemies
    crawl in the dirt.
¹⁰Force the rulers of Tarshishʷ
    and of the islands
    to pay taxes to him.
Make the kings of Sheba
    and of Sebaˣ bring gifts.
¹¹Make other rulers bow down
    and all nations serve him.

¹²Do this because the king
    rescues the homeless
    when they cry out,
and he helps everyone
    who is poor and in need.
¹³The king has pity
    on the weak and the helpless
    and protects those in need.
¹⁴He cares when they hurt,
    and he saves them from cruel
    and violent deaths.

¹⁵Long live the king!
    Give him gold from Sheba.
Always pray for the king
    and praise him each day.
¹⁶Let cities overflow with food
    and hills be covered with grain,
    just like Mount Lebanon.
Let the people in the cities
    prosper like wild flowers.
¹⁷May the glory of the king
    shine brightly forever
    like the sun in the sky.
Let him make nations prosper
    and learn to praise him.

¹⁸LORD God of Israel,
    we praise you.
    Only you can work miracles.
¹⁹We will always praise
    your glorious name.
Let your glory be seen
everywhere on earth.
    Amen and amen.

²⁰This ends the prayers
    of David, the son of Jesse.

BOOK III
(Psalms 73–89)

PSALM 73
(A psalm by Asaph.)
God Is Good

¹God is truly good to Israel,ʸ
especially to everyone
    with a pure heart.
²But I almost stumbled and fell,
³ because it made me jealous
to see proud and evil people
    and to watch them prosper.

ᵛ72.5 *Let the king live:* One ancient translation; Hebrew "Let them worship you."   ʷ72.10 *Tarshish:* Possibly a city in Spain.   ˣ72.10 *Sheba . . . Seba:* Sheba may have been a place in what is now southwest Arabia, and Seba may have been in southern Arabia.   ʸ73.1 *to Israel:* Or "to those who do right."

4They never have to suffer,^z
  they stay healthy,
5and they don't have troubles
  like everyone else.

6Their pride is like a necklace,
  and they commit sin more often
    than they dress themselves.
7Their eyes bulge with fat,
  and their minds are flooded
    with foolish thoughts.
8They sneer and say cruel things,
  and because of their pride,
    they make violent threats.
9They dare to speak against God
  and to order others around.

10God will bring his people back,
  and they will drink the water
    he so freely gives.^a

11Only evil people would say,
  "God Most High cannot
    know everything!"
12Yet all goes well for them,
  and they live in peace.
13What good did it do me
  to keep my thoughts pure
    and refuse to do wrong?
14I am sick all day,
  and I am punished
    each morning.
15If I had said evil things,
  I would not have been loyal
    to your people.

16It was hard for me
  to understand all this!
17Then I went to your temple,
  and there I understood
  what will happen

to my enemies.
18You will make them stumble,
  never to get up again.
19They will be terrified,
  suddenly swept away
  and no longer there.
20They will disappear, Lord,
  despised like a bad dream
  the morning after.

21Once I was bitter
  and brokenhearted.
22I was stupid and ignorant,
  and I treated you
    as a wild animal would.
23But I never really left you,
  and you hold my right hand.
24Your advice has been my guide,
  and later you will welcome me
    in glory.^b
25In heaven I have only you,
  and on this earth
    you are all I want.
26My body and mind may fail,
  but you are my strength
  and my choice forever.

27All-Powerful Lord God,
  those who stay far from you
    will be lost,
  and you will destroy those
    who are unfaithful.
28It is good for me
  to be near you.
  I choose you as my protector,
  and I will tell about
    your wonderful deeds.

73.23 *hold my right hand:* To be held by the "right hand" means that God is always present, even during times of suffering.

---

^z**73.4** *They . . . suffer:* Or "They die a painless death." ^a**73.10** *gives:* One possible meaning for the difficult Hebrew text of verse 10. ^b**73.24** *in glory:* Or "with honor."

74.2,3 *Mount Zion, your home:* The temple built on Mount Zion in Jerusalem was viewed as God's "home."

74.3-7 *temple left in ruins... burned down your temple:* This suggests that the psalm was written shortly after the temple and the city of Jerusalem were destroyed by the Babylonians in 586 B.C. (see 2 Kgs 25.1-17; 2 Chr 36.17-21). The people took this as a sign of rejection by God and as a punishment for their sins (Jer 25.1-11).

74.9 *no more prophets:* True prophets brought God's messages and helped to interpret God's will to the people, but they are silent at this time (see Lam 2.9). **(See the article Prophets and Prophecy on pg 1791.)**

74.13,14 *sea monsters... Leviathan:* The sea and its creatures represent the forces of chaos and opposition to God. God's defeat of the monsters and Leviathan show God's power over all creation (Job 41.1; Ps 104.26; Isa 27.1), as does God's victory over the Egyptians at the exodus.

PSALM 74

(A special psalm by Asaph.)

A Prayer for the Nation in Times of Trouble

[1]Our God, why have you
completely rejected us?
Why are you so angry
with the ones you care for?
[2]Remember the people
you rescued long ago,
the tribe you chose
for your very own.

Think of Mount Zion,
your home;
[3]walk over to the temple
left in ruins forever
by those who hate us.

[4]Your enemies roared like lions
in your holy temple,
and they have placed
their banners there.
[5]It looks like a forest
chopped to pieces.[c]
[6]They used axes and hatchets
to smash the carvings.
[7]They burned down your temple
and badly disgraced it.
[8]They said to themselves,
"We'll crush them!"
Then they burned every one
of your meeting places
all over the country.
[9]There are no more miracles
and no more prophets.
Who knows how long
it will be like this?

[10]Our God, how much longer
will our enemies sneer?

Won't they ever stop
insulting you?
[11]Why don't you punish them?
Why are you holding back?

[12]Our God and King,
you have ruled
since ancient times;
you have won victories
everywhere on this earth.
[13]By your power you made a path
through the sea,
and you smashed the heads
of sea monsters.
[14]You crushed the heads
of the monster Leviathan,[d]
then fed him to wild creatures
in the desert.
[15]You opened the ground
for streams and springs
and dried up mighty rivers.
[16]You rule the day and the night,
and you put the moon
and the sun in place.
[17]You made summer and winter
and gave them to the earth.[e]

[18]Remember your enemies, LORD!
They foolishly sneer
and won't respect you.
[19]You treat us like pet doves,
but they mistreat us.
Don't keep forgetting us
and letting us be fed
to those wild animals.
[20]Remember the agreement
you made with us.
Violent enemies are hiding
in every dark corner
of the earth.
[21]Don't disappoint those in need
or make them turn from you,

[c]**74.5** *pieces:* One possible meaning for the difficult Hebrew text of verse 5. [d]**74.14** *Leviathan:* God's victory over this monster sometimes stands for his power over all creation and sometimes for his defeat of Egypt. [e]**74.17** *gave . . . earth:* Or "made boundaries for the earth."

but help the poor and homeless
    to shout your praises.
²²Do something, God!
    Defend yourself.
Remember how those fools
    sneer at you all day long.
²³Don't forget the loud shouts
    of your enemies.

PSALM 75

(A psalm and a song by Asaph for the music leader. To
the tune "Don't Destroy."ᶠ)

Praise God for All He Has Done

¹Our God, we thank you
    for being so near to us!
Everyone celebrates
    your wonderful deeds.

²You have set a time
    to judge with fairness.
³The earth trembles,
    and its people shake;
you alone keep
    its foundations firm.
⁴You tell every bragger,
    "Stop bragging!"
And to the wicked you say,
    "Don't boast of your power!
⁵Stop bragging! Quit telling me
    how great you are."

⁶Our LORD and our God,
    victory doesn't come
from the east or the west
    or from the desert.
⁷You are the one who judges.
    You can take away power
    and give it to others.
⁸You hold in your hand
    a cup filled with wine,ᵍ

strong and foaming.
You will pour out some
    for every sinful person
    on this earth,
and they will have to drink
    until it is gone.
⁹But I will always tell about
    you, the God of Jacob,
    and I will sing your praise.

¹⁰Our Lord, you will destroy
    the power of evil people,
but you will give strength
    to those who are good.

PSALM 76

(A song and a psalm by Asaph for the music leader.
Use stringed instruments.)

God Always Wins

¹You, our God,
    are famous in Judah
    and honored in Israel.
²Your home is on Mount Zion,
    the city of peace.
³There you destroyed
    fiery arrows, shields, swords,
    and all the other weapons.

⁴You are more glorious than
    the eternal mountains.ʰ
⁵Brave warriors were robbed
    of what they had taken,
and now they lie dead,
    unable to lift an arm.
⁶God of Jacob, when you roar,
    enemy chariots and horses
    drop dead in their tracks.

⁷Our God, you are fearsome,
    and no one can oppose you

● 75.1 *wonderful deeds*: These include helping the Hebrew people escape from slavery in Egypt and cross the Red Sea on dry land (Exod 14.1—15.21), feeding the people in the wilderness (Exod 16), helping them cross the Jordan River (Josh 3.14-17), and helping them win many victories over their enemies.

■ 75.8 *a cup filled with wine*: In the Bible, "a cup filled with wine" sometimes stands for God's anger or judgment to be poured on evildoers.

ᶠ**Psalm 75** *Don't Destroy*: See the note at Psalm 57. ᵍ**75.8** *a cup . . . wine*: In the Old Testament "a cup
filled with wine" sometimes stands for God's anger. ʰ**76.4** *the eternal mountains*: One ancient
translation; Hebrew "the mountains of victims (of wild animals)."

77.7-10 *Have you rejected . . . no longer help:* In the past God helped the people by choosing leaders such as Moses and Aaron and by rescuing Israel. The psalmist wonders if God has forgotten about the people. Such questions may suggest that this psalm comes from the time of the exile in Babylon or some other time of severe national distress.

77.15 *Jacob and Joseph:* Joseph was one of Jacob's twelve sons.

when you are angry.
⁸From heaven you announced
   your decisions as judge!
And all who live on this earth
   were terrified and silent
⁹when you took over as judge,
   ready to rescue
     everyone in need.
¹⁰Even the most angry people
   will praise you
     when you are furious.ⁱ

¹¹Everyone, make your promises
   to the LORD your God
     and do what you promise.
The LORD is fearsome,
  and all his servants
     should bring him gifts.
¹²God destroys the courage
   of rulers and kings
     and makes cowards of them.

PSALM 77
(A psalm by Asaph for Jeduthun, the music leader.)
In Times of Trouble
God Is with His People

¹I pray to you, Lord God,
   and I beg you to listen.
²In days filled with trouble,
   I search for you.
And at night I tirelessly
  lift my hands in prayer,
     refusing comfort.
³When I think of you,
   I feel restless and weak.

⁴Because of you, Lord God,
   I can't sleep.
I am restless
   and can't even talk.

⁵I think of times gone by,
   of those years long ago.
⁶Each night my mind
   is flooded with questions:ʲ
⁷"Have you rejected me forever?
   Won't you be kind again?
⁸Is this the end of your love
   and your promises?
⁹Have you forgotten
   how to have pity?
Do you refuse to show mercy
   because of your anger?"
¹⁰Then I said, "God Most High,
   what hurts me most
is that you no longer help us
   with your mighty arm."

¹¹Our LORD, I will remember
   the things you have done,
     your miracles of long ago.
¹²I will think about each one
   of your mighty deeds.
¹³Everything you do is right,
   and no other god
     compares with you.
¹⁴You alone work miracles,
   and you have let nations
     see your mighty power.
¹⁵With your own arm you rescued
   your people, the descendants
     of Jacob and Joseph.

¹⁶The ocean looked at you, God,
   and it trembled deep down
     with fear.
¹⁷Water flowed from the clouds.
   Thunder was heard above
as your arrows of lightning
   flashed about.
¹⁸Your thunder roared
   like chariot wheels.
The world was made bright

ⁱ**76.10** *furious:* One possible meaning for the difficult Hebrew text of verse 10.   ʲ**77.6** *my mind . . . questions:* One ancient translation; Hebrew "I remember my music."

by lightning,
and all the earth trembled.

¹⁹You walked through the water
of the mighty sea,
but your footprints
were never seen.
²⁰You guided your people
like a flock of sheep,
and you chose Moses and Aaron
to be their leaders.

PSALM 78
(A special psalm by Asaph.)
What God Has Done
for His People

¹My friends, I beg you
to listen as I teach.
²I will give instruction
and explain the mystery
of what happened long ago.
³These are things we learned
from our ancestors,
⁴and we will tell them
to the next generation.
We won't keep secret
the glorious deeds
and the mighty miracles
of the LORD.

⁵God gave his Law
to Jacob's descendants,
the people of Israel.
And he told our ancestors
to teach their children,
⁶so that each new generation
would know his Law
and tell it to the next.
⁷Then they would trust God
and obey his teachings,
without forgetting anything
God had done.

⁸They would be different
from their ancestors,
who were stubborn, rebellious,
and unfaithful to God.

⁹The warriors from Ephraim
were armed with arrows,
but they ran away
when the battle began.
¹⁰They broke their agreement
with God,
and they turned their backs
on his teaching.
¹¹They forgot all he had done,
even the mighty miracles
¹²he did for their ancestors
near Zoan^k in Egypt.

¹³God made a path in the sea
and piled up the water
as he led them across.
¹⁴He guided them during the day
with a cloud,
and each night he led them
with a flaming fire.
¹⁵God made water flow
from rocks he split open
in the desert,
and his people drank freely,
as though from a lake.
¹⁶He made streams gush out
like rivers from rocks.

¹⁷But in the desert,
the people of God Most High
kept sinning and rebelling.
¹⁸They stubbornly tested God
and demanded from him
what they wanted to eat.
¹⁹They challenged God by saying,
"Can God provide food
out here in the desert?
²⁰It's true God struck the rock

^k78.12 *Zoan*: A city in the eastern part of the Nile Delta.

77.20 *Moses and Aaron:* These two brothers led the people out of slavery in Egypt (Exod 3–15).

Moses

78.1-4 *listen as I teach . . . next generation:* This psalm is neither a prayer for help nor a song of praise. Instead, it tells the story of God's people from the exodus to the time of David. Its purpose is to "teach" present and future generations about the past, so they will faithfully obey God.

78.5-7 *Law . . . teachings:* The Law was given to Moses on Mount Sinai where the people stopped on their way from Egypt to the promised land. "Law" means "teaching."

Law

78.9 *Ephraim:* Ephraim was Joseph's youngest son. One of the twelve tribes was named after him, and the northern kingdom was sometimes known as Ephraim. It is not known what specific battle is being described here.

78.12 *Zoan in Egypt:* Zoan is not mentioned in Exodus 7.8—12.32, which tells about God's miracles leading up to the exodus. Zoan is often identified with the city of Rameses that is mentioned in Exodus 1.11. **(See Map 2 on pg 1880.)**

78.15,16 *water flow from rocks:* When the people complained of thirst, God provided water. See Exod 17.1-7; Num 20.2-13.

78.31-34 *God became angry and . . . killed some of them:* The people were to take only as much food as they needed each day as a sign of their ongoing trust in God. But they took more than they needed, so many were killed by disease (Exod 16.14-20; Num 11.32-34). The people rebelled and sinned against God in many other ways while in the desert, so they received punishment (Exod 32; Num 14.1-30; 16; 25).

and water gushed out
   like a river,
but can he give his people
   bread and meat?"

²¹When the Lord heard this,
   he was angry and furious
with Jacob's descendants,
   the people of Israel.
²²They had refused to trust him,
   and they had doubted
   his saving power.

²³But God gave a command
   to the clouds,
and he opened the doors
   in the skies.
²⁴ From heaven he sent grain
   that they called manna.[l]
²⁵He gave them more than enough,
   and each one of them ate
   this special food.

²⁶God's mighty power
   sent a strong wind
   from the southeast,
²⁷and it brought birds
   that covered the ground,
   like sand on the beach.
²⁸Then God made the birds fall
   in the camp of his people
   near their tents.

²⁹God gave his people
   all they wanted,
and each of them ate
   until they were full.
³⁰But before they had swallowed
   the last bite,
³¹God became angry and killed

the strongest and best
   from the families of Israel.

³²But the rest kept on sinning
   and would not trust
   God's miracles.
³³So he cut their lives short
   and made them terrified.
³⁴After he killed some of them,
   the others turned to him
   with all their hearts.
³⁵They remembered God Most High,
   the mighty rock[m]
   that kept them safe.
³⁶But they tried to flatter God,
   and they told him lies;
³⁷they were unfaithful
   and broke their promises.

³⁸Yet God was kind.
   He kept forgiving their sins
   and didn't destroy them.
He often became angry,
   but never lost his temper.
³⁹God remembered that they
   were made of flesh
and were like a wind
   that blows once
   and then dies down.

⁴⁰While they were in the desert,
   they often rebelled
   and made God sad.
⁴¹They kept testing him
   and caused terrible pain
   for the Holy One of Israel.
⁴²They forgot about his power
   and how he had rescued them
   from their enemies.

[l]78.24 *manna:* When the people of Israel were wandering through the desert, the Lord gave them a special kind of food to eat. It tasted like a wafer and was called "manna," which in Hebrew means, "What is this?" [m]78.35 *mighty rock:* See the note at 18.2.

^{43}God showed them all kinds
of wonderful miracles
near Zoan^n in Egypt.
^{44}He turned the rivers of Egypt
into blood,
and no one could drink
from the streams.
^{45}He sent swarms of flies
to pester the Egyptians,
and he sent frogs
to cause them trouble.

^{46}God let worms and grasshoppers
eat their crops.
^{47}He destroyed their grapevines
and their fig trees
with hail and floods.^{o}
^{48}Then he killed their cattle
with hail
and their other animals
with lightning.

^{49}God was so angry and furious
that he went into a rage
and caused them great trouble
by sending swarms
of destroying angels.
^{50}God released his anger
and slaughtered them
in a terrible way.
^{51}He killed the first-born son
of each Egyptian family.

^{52}Then God led his people
out of Egypt
and guided them in the desert
like a flock of sheep.
^{53}He led them safely along,
and they were not afraid,
but their enemies drowned
in the sea.

^{54}God brought his people
to the sacred mountain
that he had taken
by his own power.
^{55}He made nations run
from the tribes of Israel,
and he let the tribes
take over their land.

^{56}But the people tested
God Most High,
and they refused
to obey his laws.
^{57}They were as unfaithful
as their ancestors,
and they were as crooked
as a twisted arrow.
^{58}God demanded all their love,
but they made him angry
by worshiping idols.

^{59}So God became furious
and completely rejected
the people of Israel.
^{60}Then he deserted his home
at Shiloh, where he lived
here on earth.
^{61} He let enemies capture
the sacred chest^p
and let them dishonor him.

^{62}God took out his anger
on his chosen ones
and let them be killed
by enemy swords.
^{63}Fire destroyed the young men,
and the young women were left
with no one to marry.
^{64}Priests died violent deaths,
but their widows
were not allowed to mourn.

78.43-53 *God showed . . . wonderful miracles near Zoan*: The "miracles" are the events that led up to the exodus, especially the terrible disasters (plagues).

Disasters (Plagues)

78.60 *Shiloh*: Before Jerusalem became the center for worshiping God and before the temple was built on Mount Zion in Jerusalem, the people worshiped God in a sacred tent that was considered God's "home." The tent was once at Shiloh in the territory of Ephraim. (See Map 3 on pg 1881.)

^{n}**78.43** *Zoan*: See the note at 78.12. ^{o}**78.47** *floods*: Or "frost." ^{p}**78.61** *sacred chest*: The Hebrew text has "his power," which refers to the sacred chest. In Psalm 132.8 it is called "powerful."

79.1 *foreign nations . . . Jerusalem in ruins*: The psalm was written after the Babylonians destroyed Jerusalem in 586 B.C.

⁶⁵Finally the Lord woke up,
  like a soldier
    startled from a drunken sleep.
⁶⁶God scattered his enemies
  and made them ashamed
    forever.

⁶⁷Then the Lord decided
  not to make his home
  with Joseph's descendants
  in Ephraim.⁹
⁶⁸Instead he chose the tribe
  of Judah,
  and he chose Mount Zion,
    the place he loves.
⁶⁹There he built his temple
  as lofty as the mountains
  and as solid as the earth
  he made to last forever.

⁷⁰The Lord God chose David
  to be his servant and took him
    from tending sheep
⁷¹ and from caring for lambs.
  Then God made him the leader
  of Israel, his own nation.
⁷²David treated the people fairly
  and guided them with wisdom.

PSALM 79
(A psalm by Asaph.)
Have Pity on Jerusalem

¹Our God, foreign nations
  have taken your land,
  disgraced your temple,
  and left Jerusalem in ruins.
²They have fed the bodies
  of your servants

to flesh-eating birds;
  your loyal people are food
  for savage animals.
³All Jerusalem is covered
  with their blood,
  and there is no one left
    to bury them.
⁴Every nation around us
  sneers and makes fun.

⁵Our LORD, will you keep on
  being angry?
  Will your angry feelings
    keep flaming up like fire?
⁶Get angry with those nations
  that don't know you
  and won't worship you!
⁷They have gobbled up
  Jacob's descendants
  and left the land in ruins.

⁸Don't make us pay for the sins
  of our ancestors.
  Have pity and come quickly!
  We are completely helpless.
⁹Our God, you keep us safe.
  Now help us! Rescue us.
  Forgive our sins
  and bring honor to yourself.

¹⁰Why should nations ask us,
  "Where is your God?"
  Let us and the other nations
    see you take revenge
  for your servants who died
  a violent death.

¹¹Listen to the prisoners groan!
  Let your mighty power save all
  who are sentenced to die.

⁹78.67 *with . . . Ephraim*: Ephraim was Joseph's youngest son. One of the twelve tribes was named after him, and sometimes the northern kingdom of Israel was also known as Ephraim. The town of Shiloh was in the territory of Ephraim, but the place where God was worshiped was moved from there to Zion (Jerusalem) in the territory of Judah.

¹²Each of those nations sneered
at you, our Lord.
Now let others sneer at them,
seven times as much.
¹³Then we, your people,
will always thank you.
We are like sheep
with you as our shepherd,
and all generations
will hear us praise you.

PSALM 80

(A psalm by Asaph for the music leader. To the tune
"Lilies of the Agreement.")

Help Our Nation

¹Shepherd of Israel, you lead
the descendants of Joseph,
and you sit on your throne
above the winged creatures.ʳ
Listen to our prayer
and let your light shine
²for the tribes of Ephraim,
Benjamin, and Manasseh.
Save us by your power.

³Our God, make us strong again!
Smile on us and save us.

⁴LORD God All-Powerful,
how much longer
will the prayers of your people
make you angry?
⁵You gave us tears for food,
and you made us drink them
by the bowlful.
⁶Because of you,
our enemies who live nearby
laugh and joke about us.
⁷Our God, make us strong again!
Smile on us and save us.

⁸We were like a grapevine
you brought out of Egypt.
You chased other nations away
and planted us here.
⁹Then you cleared the ground,
and we put our roots deep,
spreading over the land.
¹⁰Shade from this vine covered
the mountains.
Its branches climbed
the mighty cedars
¹¹ and stretched to the sea;
its new growth reached
to the river.ˢ

¹²Our Lord, why have you
torn down the wall
from around the vineyard?
You let everyone who walks by
pick the grapes.
¹³Now the vine is gobbled up
by pigs from the forest
and other wild animals.

¹⁴God All-Powerful,
please do something!
Look down from heaven
and see what's happening
to this vine.
¹⁵With your own hands
you planted its roots,
and you raised it
as your very own.

¹⁶Enemies chopped the vine down
and set it on fire.
Now show your anger
and destroy them.
¹⁷But help the one who sits
at your right side,ᵗ
the one you raised

80.1,2 *descendants of Joseph . . . Manasseh*: Ephraim and Manasseh were Joseph's sons. Two of Israel's tribes were named for them. Because the northern kingdom was sometimes called "Ephraim," Psalm 80 may have been written shortly before or after its destruction in 722 B.C.

80.8-11 *grapevine . . . river*: The grapevine represents the people of Israel. The "sea" in 80.11 is the Mediterranean Sea, the "mountains" refer to Lebanon, and the "river" is probably the Euphrates. These formed the ideal western and northern boundaries for Israel. (See Map 4 on pg 1882.)

ʳ80.1 *winged creatures*: Two winged creatures made of gold were on the top of the sacred chest and were symbols of the LORD's throne on earth (see Exodus 25.18). ˢ80.11 *the sea . . . the river*: The Mediterranean Sea and the Euphrates River were part of the ideal boundaries for Israel. ᵗ80.17 *right side*: See the note at 16.11.

81.4,5 *the law in Israel . . . obey:* There are festival instructions in Leviticus 23.1-44; Numbers 28,29; and Deuteronomy 16.1-15. **(See the chart Pilgrimage Festivals on pg 1799.)**

81.6,7 *took the heavy basket . . . tested you at Meribah Spring:* A priest or prophet may have spoken 81.6-16 during a festival. Removing the heavy basket probably refers to rescuing the people from slavery in Egypt. The thunderclouds may refer to the events at Mount Sinai (Exod 19.16). When the people complained of thirst in the desert, God told Moses to strike a rock with his walking stick and water came out. The place was called Massah ("test") and Meribah ("complaining").

to be your very own.
¹⁸Then we will never turn away.
Put new life into us,
    and we will worship you.

¹⁹Lord God All-Powerful,
make us strong again!
    Smile on us and save us.

Psalm 81

(By Asaph for the music leader.[u])

God Makes Us Strong

¹Be happy and shout to God
    who makes us strong!
Shout praises to the God
    of Jacob.
²Sing as you play tambourines
and the lovely sounding
    stringed instruments.
³Sound the trumpets and start
    the New Moon Festival.[v]
We must also celebrate
    when the moon is full.
⁴This is the law in Israel,
and it was given to us
    by the God of Jacob.
⁵The descendants of Joseph
    were told to obey it,
when God led them out
    from the land of Egypt.

In a voice unknown to me,
    I heard someone say:
⁶"I lifted the burden
    from your shoulder
and took the heavy basket
    from your hands.

⁷When you were in trouble,
    I rescued you,
and from the thunderclouds,
    I answered your prayers.
Later I tested you
    at Meribah Spring.[w]

⁸"Listen, my people,
    while I, the Lord,
    correct you!
Israel, if you would only
    pay attention to me!
⁹Don't worship foreign gods
or bow down to gods
    you know nothing about.
¹⁰I am the Lord your God.
    I rescued you from Egypt.
Just ask, and I will give you
    whatever you need.

¹¹"But, my people, Israel,
    you refused to listen,
and you would have nothing
    to do with me!
¹²So I let you be stubborn
and keep on following
    your own advice.

¹³"My people, Israel,
if only you would listen
    and do as I say!
¹⁴I, the Lord, would quickly
    defeat your enemies
    with my mighty power.
¹⁵Everyone who hates me
    would come crawling,
and that would be the end
    of them.

[u]**Psalm 81** *leader:* See the note at Psalm 8.   [v]**81.3** *New Moon Festival:* Celebrated on the first day of each new moon, which was the beginning of the month. But this may refer to either the New Year celebration or the Harvest Festival. "The moon is full" suggests a festival in the middle of the month.   [w]**81.7** *Meribah Spring:* When the people of Israel complained to Moses about the need for water, God commanded Moses to strike a rock with his walking stick, and water came out. The place was then named Massah ("test") and Meribah ("complaining").

¹⁶But I would feed you
  with the finest bread
and with the best honey^x
  until you were full."

PSALM 82

(A psalm by Asaph.)

Please Do Something, God!

¹When all the other gods^y
  have come together,
the Lord God judges them
  and says:
²"How long will you
  keep judging unfairly
  and favoring evil people?
³Be fair to the poor
  and to orphans.
Defend the helpless
  and everyone in need.
⁴Rescue the weak and homeless
  from the powerful hands
  of heartless people.

⁵"None of you know
  or understand a thing.
You live in darkness,
  while the foundations
  of the earth tremble.^z

⁶"I, the Most High God, say
  that all of you are gods^a
  and also my own children.
⁷But you will die,
  just like everyone else,
  including powerful rulers."

⁸Do something, God!
  Judge the nations of the earth;
  they belong to you.

PSALM 83

(A song and a psalm by Asaph.)

God Rules All the Earth

¹Our God, don't just sit there,
  silently doing nothing!
²Your hateful enemies
  are turning against you
  and rebelling.
³They are sly, and they plot
  against those you treasure.
⁴They say, "Let's wipe out
  the nation of Israel
and make sure that no one
  remembers its name!"

⁵All of them fully agree
  in their plans against you,
  and among them are
⁶Edom and the Ishmaelites;
  Moab and the Hagrites;
⁷Gebal, Ammon, and Amalek;
  Philistia and Phoenicia.^b
⁸Even Assyria has joined forces
  with Moab and Ammon.^c

⁹Our Lord, punish all of them
  as you punished Midian.
Destroy them, as you destroyed
  Sisera and Jabin
at Kishon Creek ¹⁰near Endor,
  and let their bodies rot.

● **82.5** *foundations . . . tremble:* In ancient times, it was believed that the earth was flat and supported by columns. These "foundations" are the mountains. When injustice exists, the whole world is threatened.

● **83.9** *punished Midian:* God's defeat of Midian is described in Judges 6–8. Midian lies to the south of Edom.

● **83.9** *Sisera and Jabin:* Jabin was the King of Hazor (Judg 4.2), and Sisera was his army commander. Jabin and Sisera's army was defeated by Deborah and Barak, and Sisera was killed by Jael (Judg 4.1-24; 7.1-23).

● **83.9,10** *Kishon Creek near Endor:* Sisera's defeat was just south of Mount Tabor "near Endor." **(See Map 3 on pg 1881.)**

^x**81.16** *the best honey:* The Hebrew text has "honey from rocks," referring to honey taken from beehives in holes or cracks in large rocks.   ^y**82.1** *the other gods:* This probably refers to the gods of the nations that God defeated, but it could refer to God's servants (angels) in heaven or even to human rulers.   ^z**82.5** *foundations . . . tremble:* In ancient times it was believed that the earth was flat and supported by columns.   ^a**82.6** *all of you are gods:* See the note at 82.1.   ^b**83.7** *Phoenicia:* The Hebrew text has "Tyre," the main city in Phoenicia.   ^c**83.8** *Moab and Ammon:* The Hebrew text has "the descendants of Lot," whose older daughter was the mother of the Moabites and whose younger daughter was the mother of the Ammonites (see Genesis 19.30-38).

83.11 *Oreb . . . Zalmunna:* Midianite leaders defeated by Gideon. See Judg 7.25; 8.4-21.

83.13-15 *whirlwind . . . flames . . . storms:* God's appearance in these forces usually signals a time of judgment (see Isa 66.15,16; Amos 1.14; Nah 1.3).

Fire

Enemies (The Wicked)

¹¹Treat their leaders as you did
Oreb and Zeeb,
Zebah and Zalmunna.
¹²All of them said, "We'll take
God's valuable land!"

¹³Our God, scatter them around
like dust in a whirlwind.
¹⁴Just as flames destroy forests
on the mountains,
¹⁵pursue and terrify them
with storms of your own.
¹⁶Make them blush with shame,
until they turn and worship
you, our Lord.
¹⁷Let them be forever ashamed
and confused.
Let them die in disgrace.
¹⁸Make them realize that you
are the Lord Most High,
the only ruler of earth!

PSALM 84

(For the music leader.^d A psalm by the clan of Korah.)

The Joy of Worship

¹Lord God All-Powerful,
your temple is so lovely!
²Deep in my heart I long
for your temple,
and with all that I am
I sing joyful songs to you.

³Lord God All-Powerful,
my King and my God,
sparrows find a home
near your altars;
swallows build nests there
to raise their young.

⁴You bless everyone
who lives in your house,
and they sing your praises.
⁵You bless all who depend
on you for their strength
and all who deeply desire
to visit your temple.
⁶When they reach Dry Valley,^e
springs start flowing,
and the autumn rain fills it
with pools of water.^f
⁷Your people grow stronger,
and you, the God of gods,
will be seen in Zion.

⁸Lord God All-Powerful,
the God of Jacob,
please answer my prayer!
⁹You are the shield
that protects your people,
and I am your chosen one.
Won't you smile on me?

¹⁰One day in your temple
is better than a thousand
anywhere else.
I would rather serve
in your house,
than live in the homes
of the wicked.

¹¹Our Lord and our God,
you are like the sun
and also like a shield.
You treat us with kindness
and with honor,
never denying any good thing
to those who live right.

¹²Lord God All-Powerful,
you bless everyone
who trusts you.

^d**Psalm 84** *leader:* See the note at Psalm 8.   ^e**84.6** *Dry Valley:* Or "Balsam Tree Valley." The exact location is not known.   ^f**84.6** *and . . . water:* One possible meaning for the difficult Hebrew text.

PSALM 85

(A psalm by the clan of Korah for the music leader.)

A Prayer for Peace

¹Our LORD, you have blessed
your land
and made all go well
for Jacob's descendants.
²You have forgiven the sin
and taken away the guilt
of your people.
³Your fierce anger is no longer
aimed at us.

⁴Our LORD and our God,
you save us!
Please bring us back home
and don't be angry.
⁵Will you always be angry
with us and our families?
⁶Won't you give us fresh life
and let your people be glad
because of you?
⁷Show us your love
and save us!

⁸I will listen to you, LORD God,
because you promise peace
to those who are faithful
and no longer foolish.
⁹You are ready to rescue
everyone who worships you,
so that you will live with us
in all your glory.

¹⁰Love and loyalty
will come together;
goodness and peace
will unite.
¹¹Loyalty will sprout
from the ground;
justice will look down
from the sky above.

¹²Our LORD, you will bless us;
our land will produce
wonderful crops.
¹³Justice will march in front,
making a path
for you to follow.

PSALM 86

(A prayer by David.)

A Prayer for Help

¹Please listen, LORD,
and answer my prayer!
I am poor and helpless.
²Protect me and save me
because you are my God.
I am your faithful servant,
and I trust you.
³Be kind to me!
I pray to you all day.
⁴Make my heart glad!
I serve you,
and my prayer is sincere.
⁵You willingly forgive,
and your love is always there
for those who pray to you.
⁶Please listen, LORD!
Answer my prayer for help.
⁷When I am in trouble, I pray,
knowing you will listen.

⁸No other gods are like you;
only you work miracles.
⁹You created each nation,
and they will all bow down
to worship and honor you.
¹⁰You perform great wonders
because you alone are God.

¹¹Teach me to follow you,
and I will obey your truth.
Always keep me faithful.
¹²With all my heart I thank you.
I praise you, LORD God.
¹³Your love for me is so great

85.1-4 *blessed your land . . . bring us back home:* These verses suggest that the psalm was written about the time the people of Israel returned home to Judah from exile in Babylon (after 539 B.C.). See Isa 40.1-11.

87.4 *Egypt . . . Ethiopia:* These nations are usually presented as Israel's enemies. Here, God claims them, and they claim God's city as their hometown, indicating that God rules over and cares for all persons. It is also possible that this refers to Israelite people who have been scattered to these nations because of wars. Ethiopia was a region south of Egypt that included parts of the present countries of Ethiopia and Sudan. The people of Phoenicia, located along the Mediterranean Sea north of Israel, were known for their sea travel and trading. **(See Maps 6 and 8 on pgs 1884 and 1886.)**

88 (Title) *Heman the Ezrahite:* Heman was appointed by David to help in leading worship in the sacred tent and later at the temple (1 Chr 16.41,42; 25.1-8).

that you protected me
   from death and the grave.

14Proud and violent enemies,
   who don't care about you,
have ganged up to attack
   and kill me.
15But you, the Lord God,
   are kind and merciful.
You don't easily get angry,
   and your love
   can always be trusted.
16I serve you, Lord,
   and I am the child
   of one of your servants.
Look on me with kindness.
   Make me strong and save me.
17Show that you approve of me!
Then my hateful enemies
   will feel like fools,
because you have helped
   and comforted me.

PSALM 87
(A psalm and a song by the clan of Korah.)
The Glory of Mount Zion

1Zion was built by the Lord
   on the holy mountain,
2and he loves that city
   more than any other place
   in all of Israel.
3Zion, you are the city of God,
   and wonderful things
   are told about you.

4Egypt,g Babylonia, Philistia,
   Phoenicia,h and Ethiopiai
are some of those nations
   that know you,

and their people all say,
   "I was born in Zion."

5God Most High will strengthen
   the city of Zion.
Then everyone will say,
   "We were born here too."
6The Lord will make a list
   of his people,
and all who were born here
   will be included.

7All who sing or dance will say,
   "I too am from Zion."

PSALM 88
(A song and a psalm by the clan of Korah for the music leader. To the tune "Mahalath Leannoth."j A special psalm by Heman the Ezrahite.)
A Prayer When You Can't Find the Way

1You keep me safe, Lord God.
   So when I pray at night,
2please listen carefully
   to each of my concerns.

3I am deeply troubled
   and close to death;
4I am as good as dead
   and completely helpless.
5I am no better off
   than those in the grave,
   those you have forgotten
   and no longer help.

6You have put me in the deepest
   and darkest grave;
7your anger rolls over me
   like ocean waves.

g**87.4** *Egypt:* The Hebrew text has "Rahab," the name of a monster that stands for Egypt (see Isaiah 30.7).   h**87.4** *Phoenicia:* See the note at 83.7.   i**87.4** *Ethiopia:* The Hebrew text has "Cush," which was a region south of Egypt that included parts of the present countries of Ethiopia and Sudan.
j**Psalm 88** *To . . . Leannoth:* Or "For the flutes," one possible meaning for the difficult Hebrew text.

You keep me safe, Lord God. So when I pray at night, please listen carefully to each of my concerns. Ps 88.1,2

⁸You have made my friends turn
   in horror from me.
I am a prisoner
   who cannot escape,
⁹and I am almost blind
   because of my sorrow.

Each day I lift my hands
   in prayer to you, LORD.
¹⁰Do you work miracles
   for the dead?
Do they stand up
   and praise you?
¹¹Are your love and loyalty
   announced in the world
   of the dead?
¹²Do they know of your miracles
   or your saving power
in the dark world below
   where all is forgotten?

¹³Each morning I pray
   to you, LORD.
¹⁴Why do you reject me?
   Why do you turn from me?
¹⁵Ever since I was a child,
I have been sick
   and close to death.
You have terrified me
   and made me helpless.ᵏ

¹⁶Your anger is like a flood!
And I am shattered
   by your furious attacks
¹⁷that strike each day
   and from every side.
¹⁸My friends and neighbors
   have turned against me
   because of you,
and now darkness
   is my only companion.

PSALM 89

(A special psalm by Ethan the Ezrahite.)

The LORD's Agreement with David

¹Our LORD, I will sing
   of your love forever.
Everyone yet to be born
   will hear me praise
   your faithfulness.
²I will tell them, "God's love
   can always be trusted,
and his faithfulness lasts
   as long as the heavens."

³You said, "David, my servant,
   is my chosen one,
and this is the agreement
   I made with him:
⁴David, one of your descendants
   will always be king."

⁵Our LORD, let the heavens
   now praise your miracles,
and let all your angels
   praise your faithfulness.

⁶None who live in the heavens
   can compare with you.
⁷You are the most fearsome
   of all who live in heaven;
all the others fear
   and greatly honor you.
⁸You are LORD God All-Powerful!
No one is as loving
   and faithful as you are.
⁹You rule the roaring sea
   and calm its waves.
¹⁰You crushed the monster Rahab,ˡ
   and with your powerful arm
   you scattered your enemies.

● 89 (Title) *Ethan the Ezrahite:*
Ethan was known for his great wisdom
(1 Kgs 4.30-31).

■ 89.3,4 *agreement . . . king:* God's
"agreement" with David is found in
2 Sam 7.8-16; 1 Chr 17.9-14; Ps 132.11.
Years after the disappearance of the
kingdom of David, Christians claimed
that Jesus fulfilled this promise
(Acts 2.30).

○ⵣ David

■ 89.5 *angels:* The Hebrew for this
is "holy ones," which may be "angels"
or perhaps "other gods."

● 89.10 *scattered your enemies:* May
refer to Rahab, or to people and nations
that oppose God.

ᵏ**88.15** *and made me helpless:* One possible meaning for the difficult Hebrew text. ˡ**89.10** *Rahab:* Many
people in the ancient world thought that the world was controlled by this sea monster that the
Lord destroyed at the time of creation (see Isaiah 51.9).

89.12 *Mount Tabor:* Tabor is located just southeast of Lake Galilee. (See Map 3 on pg 1881.)

89.15 *bless those who join in:* The "festival" probably refers to the celebration of the LORD's kingship over Israel (see 2 Sam 6.13-15).

89.19-37 *mighty hero . . . chosen David . . . his kingdom last:* This long passage recalls 2 Samuel 7.10-16, which tells of God's promise to David that one of his descendants would always rule Israel. This message was delivered by Nathan, the prophet who may have received God's word in a "vision."

89.28 *my agreement:* Though a descendant of David continued on the throne for many years, the fall of Jerusalem put an end to the promise, at least until years later when a descendant of David (Joshua the High Priest) ruled alongside the governor Zerubbabel (Zech 6.9-14). Because Jesus was from the family of David (Matt 1.1), Christians said the agreement with David continued in Jesus, the Messiah.

[11] The heavens and the earth
belong to you.
And so does the world
with all its people
because you created them
[12] and everything else.[m]

Mount Tabor and Mount Hermon
gladly praise you.
[13] You are strong and mighty!
[14] Your kingdom is ruled
by justice and fairness
with love and faithfulness
leading the way.

[15] Our LORD, you bless those
who join in the festival
and walk in the brightness
of your presence.
[16] We are happy all day
because of you,
and your saving power
brings honor to us.
[17] Your own glorious power
makes us strong,
and because of your kindness,
our strength increases.
[18] Our LORD and our King,
the Holy One of Israel,
you are truly our shield.

[19] In a vision, you once said
to your faithful followers:
"I have helped a mighty hero.
I chose him from my people
and made him famous.
[20] David, my servant, is the one
I chose to be king,
[21] and I will always be there
to help and strengthen him.

[22] "No enemy will outsmart David,
and he won't be defeated
by any hateful people.
[23] I will strike down and crush
his troublesome enemies.
[24] He will always be able
to depend on my love,
and I will make him strong
with my own power.
[25] I will let him rule the lands
across the rivers and seas.
[26] He will say to me,
'You are my Father
and my God,
as well as the mighty rock[n]
where I am safe.'

[27] "I have chosen David
as my first-born son,
and he will be the ruler
of all kings on earth.
[28] My love for him will last,
and my agreement with him
will never be broken.

[29] "One of David's descendants
will always be king,
and his family will rule
until the sky disappears.
[30] Suppose some of his children
should reject my Law
and refuse my instructions.
[31] Or suppose they should disobey
all of my teachings.
[32] Then I will correct
and punish them
because of their sins.
[33] But I will always love David
and faithfully keep all
of my promises to him.

[m]**89.12** *and everything else:* The Hebrew text has "Zaphon and Yamin," which may either be the names of mountains or refer to the directions "north and south," with the meaning "everything from north to south."   [n]**89.26** *mighty rock:* See the note at 18.2.

The LORD said, "One of David's descendants will always be king, and his family will rule until the sky disappears." Ps 89.29

³⁴"I won't break my agreement
    or go back on my word.
³⁵I have sworn once and for all
    by my own holy name,
    and I won't lie to David.
³⁶His family will always rule.
    I will let his kingdom last
    as long as the sun ³⁷and moon
    appear in the sky."

³⁸You are now angry, LORD,
    and you have turned your back
    on your chosen king.
³⁹You broke off your agreement
    with your servant, the king,
    and you completely destroyed
    his kingdom.
⁴⁰The walls of his city
    have been broken through,
    and every fortress
    now lies in ruins.
⁴¹All who pass by
    take what they want,
    and nations everywhere
    joke about the king.

⁴²You made his enemies powerful
    and let them celebrate.
⁴³But you forced him to retreat
    because you did not fight
    on his side.
⁴⁴You took his crown°
    and threw his throne
    in the dirt.
⁴⁵You made an old man of him
    and put him to shame.

⁴⁶How much longer, LORD?
    Will you hide forever?
    How long will your anger
    keep burning like fire?
⁴⁷Remember, life is short!ᴾ

Why did you empty our lives
    of all meaning?
⁴⁸No one can escape the power
    of death and the grave.

⁴⁹Our Lord, where is the love
    you have always shown
    and that you promised
    so faithfully to David?
⁵⁰Remember your servant, Lord!
    People make jokes about me,
    and I suffer many insults.
⁵¹I am your chosen one,
    but your enemies chase
    and make fun of me.

⁵²Our LORD, we praise you
    forever. Amen and amen.

BOOK IV
(Psalms 90–106)

PSALM 90
(A prayer by Moses, the man of God.)
God Is Eternal

¹Our Lord, in all generations
    you have been our home.
²You have always been God—
    long before the birth
    of the mountains,
    even before you created
    the earth and the world.

³At your command we die
    and turn back to dust,
⁴but a thousand years
    mean nothing to you!
    They are merely a day gone by
    or a few hours in the night.

⁵You bring our lives to an end
    just like a dream.

°89.44 *You took . . . crown:* One possible meaning for the difficult Hebrew text.
ᴾ89.47 *Remember . . . short:* One possible meaning for the difficult Hebrew text.

▪ **89.38-44** *turned your back . . . threw his throne in the dirt:* These verses mark a major shift in the psalm. The "agreement" that could "never be broken" (89.28) has now been broken. This reflects the crisis of 586 B.C., when Jerusalem's city walls were broken through and the kingdom of David and his descendants ended. See 2 Kgs 24,25.

◈   Messiah (Chosen One)

● **90** (Title) *Moses:* Moses led God's people out of Egypt, received God's teaching at Mount Sinai, and led the people to the borders of their new land. Psalm 90 was probably written in response to the destruction of the temple in 586 B.C. Note how the psalmist calls the LORD "our home." In previous psalms, "home" usually referred to the LORD's temple. By assigning Psalm 90 to Moses, the collectors of the PSALMS suggest that Moses' prayers of long ago will still be helpful as the people face new troubles.

◈   Moses

91.7 *though thousands fall:* This could be from disease or from military conflict. The language is probably symbolic.

We are merely tender grass
6 that sprouts and grows
in the morning,
but dries up by evening.
7Your furious anger frightens
and destroys us,
8and you know all our sins,
even those we do in secret.

9Your anger is a burden
each day we live,
then life ends like a sigh.
10We can expect seventy years,
or maybe eighty,
if we are healthy,
but even our best years
bring trouble and sorrow.
Suddenly our time is up,
and we disappear.
11No one knows the full power
of your furious anger,
but it is as great as the fear
that we owe to you.
12Teach us to use wisely
all the time we have.

13Help us, Lord! Don't wait!
Pity your servants.
14When morning comes,
let your love satisfy
all our needs.
Then we can celebrate
and be glad for what time
we have left.
15Make us happy for as long
as you caused us trouble
and sorrow.
16Do wonderful things for us,
your servants,
and show your mighty power
to our children.
17Our Lord and our God,

treat us with kindness
and let all go well for us.
Please let all go well!

Psalm 91
The Lord Is My Fortress

1Live under the protection
of God Most High
and stay in the shadow
of God All-Powerful.
2Then you will say to the Lord,
"You are my fortress,
my place of safety;
you are my God,
and I trust you."

3The Lord will keep you safe
from secret traps
and deadly diseases.
4He will spread his wings
over you
and keep you secure.
His faithfulness is like
a shield or a city wall.q

5You won't need to worry
about dangers at night
or arrows during the day.
6And you won't fear diseases
that strike in the dark
or sudden disaster at noon.

7You will not be harmed,
though thousands fall
all around you.
8And with your own eyes
you will see the punishment
of the wicked.
9The Lord Most High
is your fortress.

q91.4 *city wall:* One possible meaning for a difficult Hebrew word; it may possibly mean some kind of shield or weapon.

Our Lord and our God, treat us with kindness and let all go well for us. Ps 90.17

Run to him for safety,
10and no terrible disasters
    will strike you
    or your home.

11God will command his angels
  to protect you
    wherever you go.
12They will carry you
    in their arms,
  and you won't hurt your feet
    on the stones.
13You will overpower
  the strongest lions
    and the most deadly snakes.

14The Lord says, "If you love me
    and truly know who I am,
  I will rescue you
    and keep you safe.
15When you are in trouble,
    call out to me.
  I will answer and be there
    to protect and honor you.
16You will live a long life
    and see my saving power."

Psalm 92

(A psalm and a song for the Sabbath.)

Sing Praises to the Lord

1It is wonderful to be grateful
  and to sing your praises,
    Lord Most High!
2It is wonderful each morning
    to tell about your love
  and at night to announce
    how faithful you are.
3I enjoy praising your name
    to the music of harps,
4because everything you do

makes me happy,
    and I sing joyful songs.

5You do great things, Lord.
    Your thoughts are too deep
6for an ignorant fool
    to know or understand.
7Though the wicked sprout
    and spread like grass,
  they will be pulled up
    by their roots.
8But you will rule
    over all of us forever,
9and your hateful enemies
  will be scattered
    and then destroyed.

10You have given me
    the strength of a wild ox,
  and you have chosen me
    to be your very own.
11My eyes have seen,
    and my ears have heard
  the doom and destruction
    of my evil enemies.

12Good people will prosper
    like palm trees,
  and they will grow strong
    like the cedars of Lebanon.
13They will take root
  in your house, Lord God,
    and they will do well.
14They will be like trees
    that stay healthy and fruitful,
  even when they are old.
15And they will say about you,
  "The Lord always does right!
    God is our mighty rock."r

r92.15 mighty rock: See the note at 18.2.

91.10 no . . . home: The promise is not that nothing bad will ever happen, but rather that God's protection will always be present for those who turn to God for help.

91.11 angels: In the Bible, angels act as both messengers and servants of God.

Angels

92 (Title) the Sabbath: The Sabbath was the seventh day of the week. It was a day for rest and worship. See Exod 20.8-11; Deut 5.12-15. (See the chart Pilgrimage Festivals on pg 1799.)

93.1,2 *King . . . You have always ruled*: Psalms 93 and 95–99 may have been used in the temple to celebrate God's kingship.

94.5 *your chosen nation*: This refers to the people of Israel (Exod 19.3-6; Deut 7.6-8). In this psalm, the whole people of God are suffering.

94.20,21 *dishonest lawmakers . . . innocent victims*: The prophets of Israel often condemned those in power who ignored God's concern for justice and took advantage of the poor (see Isa 1.21-23; 5.8-24; Amos 2.6,7; 5.10-12; Mic 2.1,2).

PSALM 93
The LORD Is King

¹Our LORD, you are King!
Majesty and power
  are your royal robes.
You put the world in place,
  and it will never be moved.
²You have always ruled,
  and you are eternal.

³The ocean is roaring, LORD!
  The sea is pounding hard.
⁴Its mighty waves are majestic,
 but you are even more majestic,
  and you rule over all.
⁵Your decisions are firm,
 and your temple will always
  be beautiful and holy.

PSALM 94
The LORD Punishes the Guilty

¹LORD God, you punish
  the guilty.
Show what you are like
  and punish them now.
²You judge the earth.
  Come and help us!
Pay back those proud people
  for what they have done.
³How long will the wicked
  celebrate and be glad?

⁴All of those cruel people
  strut and boast,
⁵and they crush and wound
  your chosen nation, LORD.
⁶They murder widows,
  foreigners, and orphans.
⁷Then they say,
 "The LORD God of Jacob
  doesn't see or know."

⁸Can't you fools see?
  Won't you ever learn?
⁹God gave us ears and eyes!
  Can't he hear and see?
¹⁰God instructs the nations
  and gives knowledge to us all.
  Won't he also correct us?
¹¹The LORD knows how useless
  our plans really are.

¹²Our LORD, you bless everyone
  that you instruct and teach
  by using your Law.
¹³You give them rest
  from their troubles,
until a pit can be dug
  for the wicked.
¹⁴You won't turn your back
  on your chosen nation.
¹⁵Justice and fairness
  will go hand in hand,
  and all who do right
  will follow along.

¹⁶Who will stand up for me
  against those cruel people?
¹⁷If you had not helped me, LORD,
  I would soon have gone
  to the land of silence.ˢ
¹⁸When I felt my feet slipping,
  you came with your love
  and kept me steady.
¹⁹And when I was burdened
  with worries,
you comforted me
  and made me feel secure.
²⁰But you are opposed
  to dishonest lawmakers
²¹who gang up to murder
  innocent victims.

²²You, LORD God, are my fortress,
  that mighty rockᵗ

ˢ**94.17** *land of silence*: The grave or the world of the dead.   ᵗ**94.22** *mighty rock*: See the note at 18.2.

where I am safe.
²³You will pay back my enemies,
and you will wipe them out
for the evil they did.

PSALM 95
Worship and Obey the LORD

¹Sing joyful songs to the LORD!
Praise the mighty rock^u
where we are safe.
²Come to worship him
with thankful hearts
and songs of praise.

³The LORD is the greatest God,
king over all other gods.
⁴He holds the deepest part
of the earth in his hands,
and the mountain peaks
also belong to him.
⁵The ocean is the Lord's
because he made it,
and with his own hands
he formed the dry land.

⁶Bow down and worship
the LORD our Creator!
⁷The LORD is our God,
and we are his people,
the sheep he takes care of
in his own pasture.

Listen to God's voice today!
⁸Don't be stubborn and rebel
as your ancestors did
at Meribah and Massah^v
out in the desert.
⁹For forty years
they tested God and saw
the things he did.

¹⁰Then God got tired of them
and said,
"You never show good sense,
and you don't understand
what I want you to do."
¹¹In his anger, God told them,
"You people will never enter
my place of rest."

PSALM 96
Sing a New Song to the LORD

¹Sing a new song to the LORD!
Everyone on this earth,
sing praises to the LORD,
² sing and praise his name.

Day after day announce,
"The LORD has saved us!"
³Tell every nation on earth,
"The LORD is wonderful
and does marvelous things!
⁴The LORD is great and deserves
our greatest praise!
He is the only God
worthy of our worship.
⁵Other nations worship idols,
but the LORD created
the heavens.
⁶Give honor and praise
to the LORD,
whose power and beauty
fill his holy temple."

⁷Tell everyone of every nation,
"Praise the glorious power
of the LORD.
⁸He is wonderful! Praise him
and bring an offering
into his temple.
⁹Everyone on earth, now tremble
and worship the LORD,
majestic and holy."

95.7 *Listen to God's voice today:* Sheep normally listen to their shepherd (John 10.4), but 95.8-11 tells how God's people did not listen. The psalmist uses this memory to call people to obey God "today." These verses may have been spoken in a worship service by a priest or prophet.

95.9-11 *forty years . . . my place of rest:* What happened at Meribah and Massah was not unusual. Because of the people's disobedience, God did not let the older generation of Israelites enter their "place of rest," the promised land of Canaan (Num 14.20-30; Deut 1.34-36; Heb 4.3,5).

96.1 *a new song:* New songs celebrate new acts of deliverance by God. This "new song" could certainly have been sung in celebration of how God eventually restored the people following the crisis of 586 B.C.

^u**95.1** *mighty rock:* See the note at 18.2.   ^v**95.8** *Meribah and Massah:* See the note at 81.7.

96.11,12 *heavens and the earth . . . celebrate . . . sing:* All parts of the universe join humankind in praising God. This shows God's kingship over all things.

97.2-5 *Dark clouds . . . Fire leaps from his throne . . . Mountains melt:* God's appearance in these natural forces is meant to symbolize God's powerful presence.

98.1 *worked miracles . . . powerful arm:* The word "miracles" here probably is meant to recall what God did to free the people from their life of slavery in Egypt. The people's return to Judah after the crisis of the exile in Babylon was also seen as a miracle of God's saving power (see Isa 43.14-20; 49.19-23).

¹⁰Announce to the nations,
  "The LORD is King!
The world stands firm,
  never to be shaken,
and he will judge its people
  with fairness."

¹¹Tell the heavens and the earth
  to be glad and celebrate!
Command the ocean to roar
  with all its creatures,
¹²and the fields to rejoice
  with all their crops.
Then every tree in the forest
  will sing joyful songs
¹³ to the LORD.
He is coming to judge
  all people on earth
  with fairness and truth.

PSALM 97
The LORD Brings Justice

¹The LORD is King!
Tell the earth to celebrate
  and all islands to shout.
²Dark clouds surround him,
  and his throne is supported
  by justice and fairness.
³Fire leaps from his throne,
  destroying his enemies,
⁴and his lightning is so bright
  that the earth sees it
  and trembles.
⁵Mountains melt away like wax
  in the presence of the LORD
  of all the earth.

⁶The heavens announce,
  "The LORD brings justice!"
  Everyone sees God's glory.
⁷Those who brag about
  the useless idols they worship
  are terribly ashamed,
and all the false gods
  bow down to the LORD.

⁸When the people of Zion
  and of the towns of Judah
hear that God brings justice,
  they will celebrate.
⁹The LORD rules the whole earth,
  and he is more glorious
  than all the false gods.

¹⁰Love the LORD
  and hate evil!
God protects his loyal people
  and rescues them
  from violence.
¹¹If you obey and do right,
  a light will show you the way
  and fill you with happiness.
¹²You are the LORD's people!
So celebrate and praise
  the only God.

PSALM 98
The LORD Works Miracles

¹Sing a new song to the LORD!
  He has worked miracles,
and with his own powerful arm,
  he has won the victory.
²The LORD has shown the nations
  that he has the power to save
  and to bring justice.
³God has been faithful
  in his love for Israel,
and his saving power is seen
  everywhere on earth.

⁴Tell everyone on this earth
  to sing happy songs
  in praise of the LORD.
⁵Make music for him on harps.
  Play beautiful melodies!
⁶Sound the trumpets and horns
  and celebrate with joyful songs
  for our LORD and King!

⁷Command the ocean to roar
  with all its creatures,

The heavens announce, "The LORD brings justice!" Everyone sees God's glory. Ps 97.6

and the earth to shout
with all its people.
⁸Order the rivers
to clap their hands,
and all the hills
to sing together.
⁹Let them worship the LORD!
He is coming to judge
everyone on the earth,
and he will be honest
and fair.

PSALM 99
Our LORD Is King

¹Our LORD, you are King!
You rule from your throne
above the winged creatures,ʷ
as people tremble
and the earth shakes.
²You are praised in Zion,
and you control all nations.
³Only you are God!
And your power alone,
so great and fearsome,
is worthy of praise.
⁴You are our mighty King,ˣ
a lover of fairness,
who sees that justice is done
everywhere in Israel.
⁵Our LORD and our God,
we praise you
and kneel down to worship you,
the God of holiness!

⁶Moses and Aaron were two
of your priests.
Samuel was also one of those
who prayed in your name,
and you, our LORD,
answered their prayers.

⁷You spoke to them
from a thick cloud,
and they obeyed your laws.

⁸Our LORD and our God,
you answered their prayers
and forgave their sins,
but when they did wrong,
you punished them.
⁹We praise you, LORD God,
and we worship you
at your sacred mountain.
Only you are God!

PSALM 100
(A psalm of praise.)
The LORD Is God

¹Shout praises to the LORD,
everyone on this earth.
²Be joyful and sing
as you come in
to worship the LORD!

³You know the LORD is God!
He created us,
and we belong to him;
we are his people,
the sheep in his pasture.

⁴Be thankful and praise the LORD
as you enter his temple.
⁵The LORD is good!
His love and faithfulness
will last forever.

PSALM 101
(A psalm by David.)
A King and His Promises

¹I will sing to you, LORD!
I will celebrate your kindness

ʷ99.1 winged creatures: See the note at 80.1. ˣ99.4 You . . . King: One possible meaning for the difficult Hebrew text.

99.6 *Moses . . . Aaron . . . priests . . . Samuel:* Samuel led the people of God after the time of the judges until Israel got its first king. See 1 Sam 1.1—12.25.

Israel's Priests

99.9 *your sacred mountain:* This refers to Mount Zion in Jerusalem.

100.5 *love . . . will last forever:* This verse gives the basic reasons for praising God, and it is found in several other places in the Jewish Scriptures (Old Testament). See 1 Chr 16.34; 2 Chr 5.11-13; 7.3; Ezra 3.11; Ps 106.1; 107.1; 118.1; 136.1; Jer 33.11.

102.9 *ashes to eat:* This probably refers to acts of mourning. People sometimes put dirt or ashes on themselves as a sign of deep sadness (see Esth 4.1-3; Job 2.8; Jer 6.26).

102.13-16 *Zion . . . rebuild the city:* Verses 14 and 16 suggest that the psalm was written after Jerusalem was destroyed in 586 B.C.

and your justice.

²Please help me learn
 to do the right thing,
and I will be honest and fair
 in my own kingdom.

³I refuse to be corrupt
 or to take part
 in anything crooked,
⁴and I won't be dishonest
 or deceitful.

⁵Anyone who spreads gossip
 will be silenced;
no one who is conceited
 will be my friend.

⁶I will find trustworthy people
 to serve as my advisors;
only an honest person
 will serve as an official.

⁷No one who cheats or lies
 will have a position
 in my royal court.
⁸Each morning I will silence
 any lawbreakers I find
in the countryside
 or in the city of the LORD.

PSALM 102

(A prayer for someone who hurts and needs to ask the
LORD for help.)

A Prayer in Time of Trouble

¹I pray to you, LORD!
 Please listen.
²Don't hide from me
 in my time of trouble.
Pay attention to my prayer
 and quickly give an answer.

³My days disappear like smoke,
 and my bones are burning
 as though in a furnace.

⁴I am wasting away like grass,
 and my appetite is gone.
⁵My groaning never stops,
 and my bones can be seen
 through my skin.
⁶I am like a lonely owl
 in the desert
⁷or a restless sparrow
 alone on a roof.

⁸My enemies insult me all day,
 and they use my name
 for a curse word.
⁹Instead of food,
 I have ashes to eat
 and tears to drink,
¹⁰because you are furious
 and have thrown me aside.
¹¹My life fades like a shadow
 at the end of day
 and withers like grass.

¹²Our LORD, you are King forever
 and will always be famous.
¹³You will show pity to Zion
 because the time has come.
¹⁴We, your servants,
 love each stone in the city,
and we are sad to see them
 lying in the dirt.

¹⁵Our LORD, the nations
 will honor you,
and all kings on earth
 will praise your glory.
¹⁶You will rebuild
 the city of Zion.
Your glory will be seen,
¹⁷and the prayers of the homeless
 will be answered.

¹⁸Future generations must also
 praise the LORD,
 so write this for them:
¹⁹"From his holy temple,

the LORD looked down
  at the earth.
[20]He listened to the groans
  of prisoners,
and he rescued everyone
  who was doomed to die."

[21]All Jerusalem should praise
  you, our LORD,
[22]when people from every nation
  meet to worship you.

[23]I should still be strong,
  but you, LORD, have made
  an old person of me.
[24]You will live forever!
  Years mean nothing to you.
  Don't cut my life in half!

[25]In the beginning, LORD,
  you laid the earth's foundation
  and created the heavens.
[26]They will all disappear
  and wear out like clothes.
You change them,
  as you would a coat,
  but you last forever.
[27]You are always the same.
  You are God for all time.
[28]Every generation of those
  who serve you
  will live in your presence.

PSALM 103
(By David.)
The LORD's Wonderful Love

[1]With all my heart
  I praise the LORD,
and with all that I am
  I praise his holy name!
[2]With all my heart
  I praise the LORD!

I will never forget
  how kind he has been.

[3]The LORD forgives our sins,
  heals us when we are sick,
[4]   and protects us from death.
His kindness and love
  are a crown on our heads.
[5]Each day that we live,[y]
  he provides for our needs
and gives us the strength
  of a young eagle.

[6]For all who are mistreated,
  the LORD brings justice.
[7]He taught his Law to Moses
  and showed all Israel
  what he could do.

[8]The LORD is merciful!
  He is kind and patient,
  and his love never fails.
[9]The LORD won't always be angry
  and point out our sins;
[10]he doesn't punish us
  as our sins deserve.

[11]How great is God's love for all
  who worship him?
Greater than the distance
  between heaven and earth!
[12]How far has the LORD taken
  our sins from us?
Farther than the distance
  from east to west!

[13]Just as parents are kind
  to their children,
  the LORD is kind
  to all who worship him,
[14]because he knows
  we are made of dust.
[15]We humans are like grass

[y]103.5 Each . . . live: One possible meaning for the difficult Hebrew text.

● 102.22 *every nation*: Some of Israel's prophets said that when Jerusalem and the temple were rebuilt after the exile, people from all nations would meet there to worship God (Isa 2.1-4; 56.6-8; Mic 4.1-3). The "second temple" was built in Jerusalem between 520 and 515 B.C.

■ 102.25 *laid the earth's foundation . . . created the heavens*: This brief description of the creation of the world recalls the longer account in GENESIS (see Gen 1.3-10).

■ 103.8-10 *The LORD is merciful . . . sins deserve*: See Exodus 34.6, which tells what God said when he appeared to Moses after the people had sinned (Exod 32.1-14). The LORD's "mercy" means that people will not be punished as their "sins deserve."

■ 103.14-16 *made of dust . . . quickly wither*: The psalmist comments on how short human life is when compared with the timeless God.

104.16-18 *Lebanon ... tall mountains ... small animals:* The Lebanon mountains were well-known in ancient times for their tall cedars used for building palaces and temples, and as a home for many types of animals (2 Kgs 19.23; Isa 60.13; Song 4.8). The "small animals" mentioned in 104.18 probably are rock badgers, also called coneys.

or wild flowers
    that quickly bloom.
¹⁶But a scorching wind blows,
  and they quickly wither
    to be forever forgotten.

¹⁷The Lord is always kind
    to those who worship him,
  and he keeps his promises
    to their descendants
¹⁸who faithfully obey him.

¹⁹God has set up his kingdom
  in heaven, and he rules
    the whole creation.
²⁰All of you mighty angels,
  who obey God's commands,
    come and praise your Lord!
²¹All of you thousands
  who serve and obey God,
    come and praise your Lord!
²²All of God's creation
  and all that he rules,
    come and praise your Lord!
With all my heart
  I praise the Lord!

PSALM 104
The Lord Takes Care
of His Creation

¹I praise you, Lord God,
  with all my heart.
You are glorious and majestic,
dressed in royal robes
² and surrounded by light.
You spread out the sky
  like a tent,
³and you built your home
  over the mighty ocean.
The clouds are your chariot
  with the wind as its wings.
⁴The winds are your messengers,

and flames of fire
  are your servants.

⁵You built foundations
  for the earth, and it
    will never be shaken.
⁶You covered the earth
  with the ocean that rose
    above the mountains.
⁷Then your voice thundered!
And the water flowed
⁸ down the mountains
  and through the valleys
    to the place you prepared.
⁹Now you have set boundaries,
  so that the water will never
    flood the earth again.

¹⁰You provide streams of water
  in the hills and valleys,
¹¹so that the donkeys
  and other wild animals
    can satisfy their thirst.
¹²Birds build their nests nearby
  and sing in the trees.
¹³From your home above
  you send rain on the hills
    and water the earth.
¹⁴You let the earth produce
    grass for cattle,
    plants for our food,
¹⁵ wine to cheer us up,
    olive oil for our skin,
    and grain for our health.

¹⁶Our Lord, your trees
  always have water,
  and so do the cedars
    you planted in Lebanon.
¹⁷Birds nest in those trees,
  and storks make their home
    in the fir trees.
¹⁸Wild goats find a home

in the tall mountains,
and small animals can hide
between the rocks.

¹⁹You created the moon
to tell us the seasons.
The sun knows when to set,
20 and you made the darkness,
so the animals in the forest
could come out at night.
²¹Lions roar as they hunt
for the food you provide.
²²But when morning comes,
they return to their dens,
²³then we go out to work
until the end of day.

²⁴Our LORD, by your wisdom
you made so many things;
the whole earth is covered
with your living creatures.
²⁵But what about the ocean
so big and wide?
It is alive with creatures,
large and small.
26 And there are the ships,
as well as Leviathan,ᶻ
the monster you created
to splash in the sea.

²⁷All of these depend on you
to provide them with food,
²⁸and you feed each one
with your own hand,
until they are full.
²⁹But when you turn away,
they are terrified;
when you end their life,
they die and rot.
³⁰You created all of them
by your Spirit,

and you give new life
to the earth.

³¹Our LORD, we pray
that your glory
will last forever
and that you will be pleased
with what you have done.
³²You look at the earth,
and it trembles.
You touch the mountains,
and smoke goes up.
³³As long as I live,
I will sing and praise you,
the LORD God.
³⁴I hope my thoughts
will please you,
because you are the one
who makes me glad.

³⁵Destroy all wicked sinners
from the earth
once and for all.
With all my heart
I praise you, LORD!
I praise you!

PSALM 105
The LORD Can Be Trusted

¹Praise the LORD
and pray in his name!
Tell everyone
what he has done.
²Sing praises to the LORD!
Tell about his miracles.
³Celebrate and worship
his holy name
with all your heart.

⁴Trust the LORD
and his mighty power.

ᶻ104.26 *Leviathan:* See the note at 74.14.

104.19 *the moon . . . sun:* In ancient times, people often worshiped the moon and the sun. Here it is clear that God "created" them, and so only God deserves to be worshiped.

104.24 *by your wisdom:* The word "wisdom" means both knowledge and creative power. In both senses of the word, God's creation shows God's wisdom.

104.30 *Spirit . . . give new life:* The "Spirit of God" was present as the creative force at creation (Gen 1.1,2). God's Spirit inspired Israel's prophets and their messages (Isa 48.16; Ezek 2.2; Mic 3.8). And God's Spirit was with those special "chosen ones" who were to lead Israel (Judg 6.34; 1 Sam 16.13; Isa 11.1-3).

⊗   Holy Spirit

105.1-15 *Praise the LORD:* According to 1 Chronicles 16.7, "David instructed Asaph and his relatives" to sing a song of praise that is similar to these verses.

105.6 *family of Abraham . . . chosen ones . . . descendants of Jacob:* These all are names for the people of Israel. "Chosen one" usually refers to special leaders of the people, but here it refers to the whole people.

Agreements (Covenants)

105.16-22 *food was scarce . . . Joseph:* Joseph, one of Jacob's twelve sons, was sold into slavery by his brothers (Gen 37.12-28). He ended up in Egypt where he earned his freedom and a position of authority by interpreting the dreams of the Egyptian king (Gen 39.20—41.36). He was put in charge of Egypt's grain storage (Gen 41.39-49). When food became scarce in the region, including Canaan, Jacob sent his sons to Egypt to buy grain (Gen 41.53—42.8).

105.23-36 *Jacob and his family . . . Moses . . . took the life of every first-born son:* These verses tell what happened to the descendants of Jacob, who settled as foreigners in Egypt (Gen 46.1-7; 47.11). When the Hebrews (Israelites) grew "stronger," that is, more numerous, the Egyptians became "their enemies" and enslaved them (Exod 1.7-14). In response to the oppression of the Hebrew people, God chose Moses and his brother Aaron to speak to Egypt's king and ask him to let the Hebrew people go (Exod 3.1—4.17). When the king refused, God sent a number of disasters (plagues) upon Egypt. These disasters are listed in a different order here than in EXODUS.

Disasters (Plagues)

⁵Remember his miracles
 and all his wonders
  and his fair decisions.
⁶You belong to the family
 of Abraham, his servant;
you are his chosen ones,
 the descendants of Jacob.

⁷The LORD is our God,
 bringing justice
  everywhere on earth.
⁸He will never forget
 his agreement or his promises,
  not in thousands of years.
*⁹God made an eternal promise
¹⁰ to Abraham, Isaac, and Jacob,
¹¹when he said, "I'll give you
 the land of Canaan."

¹²At the time there were
 only a few of us,
  and we were homeless.
¹³We wandered from nation
 to nation, from one country
  to another.
¹⁴God did not let anyone
 mistreat our people.
Instead he protected us
 by punishing rulers
¹⁵and telling them,
 "Don't touch my chosen leaders
  or harm my prophets!"

¹⁶God kept crops from growing
 until food was scarce
  everywhere in the land.
¹⁷But he had already sent Joseph,
 sold as a slave into Egypt,
¹⁸with chains of iron
 around his legs and neck.

¹⁹Joseph remained a slave
 until his own words
  had come true,

and the LORD had finished
 testing him.
²⁰Then the king of Egypt
 set Joseph free
²¹and put him in charge
 of everything he owned.
²²Joseph was in command
 of the officials,
and he taught the leaders
 how to use wisdom.

²³Jacob and his family
 came and settled in Egypt
  as foreigners.
²⁴They were the LORD's people,
 so he let them grow stronger
  than their enemies.
²⁵They served the LORD,
 and he made the Egyptians plan
  hateful things against them.
²⁶God sent his servant Moses.
 He also chose and sent Aaron
²⁷ to his people in Egypt,
 and they worked miracles
  and wonders there.
²⁸Moses and Aaron obeyed God,
 and he sent darkness
  to cover Egypt.
²⁹God turned their rivers
 into streams of blood,
  and the fish all died.
³⁰Frogs were everywhere,
 even in the royal palace.
³¹When God gave the command,
 flies and gnats
  swarmed all around.

³²In place of rain,
 God sent hailstones
  and flashes of lightning.
³³He destroyed their grapevines
 and their fig trees,
and he made splinters
 of all the other trees.
³⁴God gave the command,

and more grasshoppers came
than could be counted.
35 They ate every green plant
and all the crops that grew
in the land of Egypt.
36 Then God took the life
of every first-born son.

37 When God led Israel from Egypt,
they took silver and gold,
and no one was left behind.
38 The Egyptians were afraid
and gladly let them go.
39 God hid them under a cloud
and guided them by fire
during the night.

40 When they asked for food,
he sent more birds
than they could eat.
41 God even split open a rock,
and streams of water
gushed into the desert.
42 God never forgot
his sacred promise
to his servant Abraham.

43 When the Lord rescued
his chosen people from Egypt,
they celebrated with songs.
44 The Lord gave them the land
and everything else
the nations had worked for.
45 He did this so that his people
would obey all his laws.
Shout praises to the Lord!

Psalm 106
A Nation Asks for Forgiveness

1 We will celebrate
and praise you, Lord!
You are good to us,
and your love never fails.
2 No one can praise you enough
for all the mighty things
you have done.
3 You bless those people
who are honest and fair
in everything they do.

4 Remember me, Lord,
when you show kindness
by saving your people.
5 Let me prosper with the rest
of your chosen ones,
as they celebrate with pride
because they belong to you.

6 We and our ancestors
have sinned terribly.
7 When they were in Egypt,
they paid no attention
to your marvelous deeds
or your wonderful love.
And they turned against you
at the Red Sea.[a]

8 But you were true to your name,
and you rescued them to prove
how mighty you are.
9 You said to the Red Sea,[b]
"Dry up!"
Then you led your people across

[a] **106.7** *Red Sea:* Hebrew *yam suph,* "Sea of Reeds," one of the marshes or fresh water lakes near the eastern part of the Nile Delta. This identification is based on Exodus 13.17—14.9, which lists the towns on the route of the Israelites before crossing the sea. In the Greek translation of the Scriptures made about 200 B.C., the "Sea of Reeds" was named "Red Sea." [b] **106.9** *Red Sea:* Hebrew *yam suph,* "Sea of Reeds," one of the marshes or fresh water lakes near the eastern part of the Nile Delta. This identification is based on Exodus 13.17—14.9, which lists the towns on the route of the Israelites before crossing the sea. In the Greek translation of the Scriptures made about 200 B.C., the "Sea of Reeds" was named "Red Sea."

105.37-41 *God led Israel from Egypt . . . streams of water:* These verses describe the days immediately after the Hebrew people left Egypt.

105.44,45 *gave them the land . . . obey . . . laws:* After 40 years of wandering in the desert, the Lord helped the people enter Canaan, the land God promised to give their ancestor Abraham. The people received God's "laws" at Mount Sinai in the desert. To keep their new land, the people were to obey the laws and worship God alone.

106.2 *mighty things you have done:* Like Psalm 105, this psalm retells Israel's story. Unlike Psalm 105, Psalm 106 calls attention to Israel's disobedience.

106.7-12 *marvelous deeds . . . sang your praises:* Even as God was preparing to deliver them from the Egyptians at the Red Sea, the people were complaining (Exod 14.10-12). The story of the crossing of the sea and God's defeat of the people's "enemies," the Egyptians, is found in Exodus 14.21-29. The people respond with trust (Exod 14.30,31) and praise (Exod 15.1-21). **(See Map 2 on pg 1880.)**

106.13-15 *soon forgot . . . greedy for food:* Despite the rescue at the Red Sea, the people began to grumble about being thirsty and hungry (Exod 15.1—16.3). God gave them water and food (Exod 16.4-34). Still, the people complained, so God destroyed some of the people with a disease (Num 11.4-34).

106.16-18 *jealous . . . fire:* The rebellion of Dathan and Abiram against Moses and Aaron is described in Numbers 16.1-35.

106.19-20 *At Horeb your people . . . worshiped the statue of a bull:* Horeb is another name for Mount Sinai where Moses received God's Law. While Moses was on Mount Sinai, the people angered God by making and worshiping a golden statue of a bull. Moses talked God out of destroying all the people (Exod 32.1-14).

106.24-26 *would not trust you:* The people became afraid of entering Canaan, even though Joshua and Caleb gave a good report of the land. So, the people had to wander in the wilderness another 39 years (see Num 14.1-35).

106.28-31 *became followers of . . . Baal Peor . . . Phinehas helped:* At the Acacia camp in Moab, some Israelite men had sex with Moabite women and worshiped the Moabite gods, including Baal Peor. Phinehas, grandson of Aaron, put to death two people who had been unfaithful. This led God to forgive the rest of the people and to honor Phinehas (Num 25.1-15).

on land as dry as a desert.
10You saved all of them
11and drowned every one
   of their enemies.
12Then your people trusted you
   and sang your praises.

13But they soon forgot
   what you had done
   and rejected your advice.
14They became greedy for food
   and tested you there
   in the desert.
15So you gave them
   what they wanted,
   but later you destroyed them
   with a horrible disease.

16Everyone in camp was jealous
   of Moses and of Aaron,
   your chosen priest.
17Dathan and Abiram rebelled,
   and the earth opened up
   and swallowed them.
18Then fire broke out
   and destroyed all
   of their followers.

19At Horeb your people
   made and worshiped the statue
20 of a bull, instead of you,
   their glorious God.
21You worked powerful miracles
   to save them from Egypt,
   but they forgot about you
22and the fearsome things
   you did at the Red Sea.c

23You were angry and started
   to destroy them,
   but Moses, your chosen leader,
   begged you not to do it.

24They would not trust
   you, Lord,
   and they did not like
   the promised land.
25They would not obey you,
   and they grumbled
   in their tents.
26So you threatened them
   by saying, "I'll kill you
   out here in the desert!
27I'll scatter your children
   everywhere in the world."

28Your people became followers
   of a god named Baal Peor,
   and they ate sacrifices
   offered to the dead.d
29They did such terrible things
   that you punished them
   with a deadly disease.
30But Phinehase helped them,
   and the sickness stopped.
31Now he will always
   be highly honored.

32At Meribah Springf
   they turned against you
   and made you furious.
33Then Moses got into trouble
   for speaking in anger.

c106.22 *Red Sea:* Hebrew *yam suph,* "Sea of Reeds," one of the marshes or fresh water lakes near the eastern part of the Nile Delta. This identification is based on Exodus 13.17—14.9, which lists the towns on the route of the Israelites before crossing the sea. In the Greek translation of the Scriptures made about 200 B.C., the "Sea of Reeds" was named "Red Sea." d106.28 *the dead:* Or "lifeless idols." e106.30 *Phinehas:* The grandson of Aaron, who put two people to death and kept the Lord from being angry with the rest of his people (see Numbers 25.1-13). f106.32 *Meribah Spring:* See the note at 81.7.

34Our Lord, they disobeyed you
   by refusing to destroy
      the nations.
35Instead they were friendly
   with those foreigners
      and followed their customs.
36Then they fell into the trap
   of worshiping idols.
37They sacrificed their sons
   and their daughters to demons
38   and to the gods of Canaan.
   Then they poured out the blood
   of these innocent children
      and made the land filthy.
39By doing such gruesome things,
   they also became filthy.

40Finally, Lord, you were angry
   and terribly disgusted
      with your people.
41So you put them in the power
   of nations that hated them.
42They were mistreated and abused
   by their enemies,
43but you saved them
   time after time.
   They were determined to rebel,
   and their sins caused
      their downfall.

44You answered their prayers
   when they were in trouble.
45You kept your agreement
   and were so merciful
46that their enemies
   had pity on them.

47Save us, Lord God!
   Bring us back
   from among the nations.
   Let us celebrate and shout
   in praise of your holy name.

48Lord God of Israel,
   you deserve to be praised
      forever and ever.
   Let everyone say, "Amen!
   Shout praises to the Lord!"

BOOK V
(Psalms 107–150)

PSALM 107
The Lord Is Good to His People

1Shout praises to the Lord!
   He is good to us,
      and his love never fails.
2Everyone the Lord has rescued
   from trouble
      should praise him,
3everyone he has brought
   from the east and the west,
      the north and the south.g

4Some of you were lost
   in the scorching desert,
      far from a town.
5You were hungry and thirsty
   and about to give up.
6You were in serious trouble,
   but you prayed to the Lord,
      and he rescued you.
7At once he brought you
   to a town.
8You should praise the Lord
   for his love
   and for the wonderful things
   he does for all of us.
9To everyone who is thirsty,
   he gives something to drink;
   to everyone who is hungry,
   he gives good things to eat.

● 106.34-39 *destroy the nations . . . followed their customs . . . became filthy:* The people's disobedience continued after they entered the promised land. They adopted the ways of the Canaanites, including worshiping their gods (see Judg 2.1-3; 3.5-6). Sacrificing children was against God's instruction (Lev 18.21), but the people sometimes disobeyed (2 Kgs 17.17). The shedding of innocent blood was said to "pollute" the land (Num 35.33-34).

⊛ Holy War (The Lord's Battles)

■ 106.40-46 *Finally . . . them:* These verses describe a pattern found in JUDGES. The pattern is introduced in Judg 2.11-18. The other historical books (JUDGES through 2 CHRONICLES) also give many examples of Israel's sin and tell about the threats that came from neighboring nations. The prophets of Israel warned them of punishment if they turned away from God and God's Law (Isa 1.2-20,27-31).

● 106.47-48 *Save us . . . Bring us back:* These verses end the song that David told Asaph and his relatives to sing.

● 107.2,3 *rescued . . . brought from . . . south:* These verses suggest that the prayer of 106.47 has been answered and that the exile is over. People had been scattered not only to Babylon to the east, but to other nations as well.

g107.3 *south:* The Hebrew text has "sea," probably referring to the Mediterranean Sea.

107.10-16 *prisoners . . . bound by chains . . . shatters iron locks:* This is the second example of how God rescues people in "trouble" (107.13). It recalls the rescue from the "chains" of slavery in Egypt as well as the rescue from exile in Babylon. See also Isa 40.2; 49.7-12. "Deepest darkness" (107.10,14) symbolizes serious "trouble."

107.17-22 *committed a lot of sins . . . saved you:* This third example of how God rescues people in "trouble" (107.19) involves healing from sickness, which may be a symbol for other kinds of distress, including "spiritual sickness" (sins). See the note at 38.11. Those who are healed and saved are to praise the LORD and offer sacrifices (107.21,22). See the notes at 22.24-26; 27.6; and 40.6.

107.23-32 *sailing the mighty sea . . . worship:* This fourth example of how God rescues people in "trouble" (107.28) involves rescue from distress at sea. The sea and the ocean often were symbols for the deadly forces of chaos (see the notes at 18.16 and 69.1-2; see also Jonah 1.10—2.10). Again, those who are saved are encouraged to praise the LORD.

107.33-42 *doing wrong . . . hungry . . . crushed by troubles . . . in need:* These verses review the four examples in 107.4-32. They recall especially 107.4-9.

10Some of you were prisoners
  suffering in deepest darkness
  and bound by chains,
11because you had rebelled
  against God Most High
  and refused his advice.
12You were worn out
  from working like slaves,
  and no one came to help.
13You were in serious trouble,
  but you prayed to the LORD,
  and he rescued you.
14He brought you out
  of the deepest darkness
  and broke your chains.

15You should praise the LORD
  for his love
  and for the wonderful things
  he does for all of us.
16He breaks down bronze gates
  and shatters iron locks.

17Some of you had foolishly
  committed a lot of sins
  and were in terrible pain.
18The very thought of food
  was disgusting to you,
  and you were almost dead.
19You were in serious trouble,
  but you prayed to the LORD,
  and he rescued you.
20By the power of his own word,
  he healed you and saved you
  from destruction.

21You should praise the LORD
  for his love
  and for the wonderful things
  he does for all of us.
22You should celebrate
  by offering sacrifices
  and singing joyful songs
  to tell what he has done.

23Some of you made a living
  by sailing the mighty sea,
24and you saw the miracles
  the LORD performed there.
25At his command a storm arose,
  and waves covered the sea.
26You were tossed to the sky
  and to the ocean depths,
  until things looked so bad
  that you lost your courage.
27You staggered like drunkards
  and gave up all hope.
28You were in serious trouble,
  but you prayed to the LORD,
  and he rescued you.
29He made the storm stop
  and the sea be quiet.
30You were happy because of this,
  and he brought you to the port
  where you wanted to go.

31You should praise the LORD
  for his love
  and for the wonderful things
  he does for all of us.
32Honor the LORD
  when you and your leaders
  meet to worship.

33If you start doing wrong,
  the LORD will turn rivers
  into deserts,
34flowing streams
  into scorched land,
  and fruitful fields
  into beds of salt.

35But the LORD can also turn
  deserts into lakes
  and scorched land
  into flowing streams.
36If you are hungry,
  you can settle there
  and build a town.

³⁷You can plant fields
and vineyards that produce
a good harvest.
³⁸The LORD will bless you
with many children
and with herds of cattle.

³⁹Sometimes you may be crushed
by troubles and sorrows,
until only a few of you
are left to survive.
⁴⁰But the LORD will take revenge
on those who conquer you,
and he will make them wander
across desert sands.
⁴¹When you are suffering
and in need,
he will come to your rescue,
and your families will grow
as fast as a herd of sheep.
⁴²You will see this because
you obey the LORD,
but everyone who is wicked
will be silenced.

⁴³Be wise! Remember this
and think about the kindness
of the LORD.

PSALM 108
(A song and a psalm by David.)
With God on Our Side

¹Our God, I am faithful to you
with all my heart,
and you can trust me.
I will sing
and play music for you
with all that I am.
²I will start playing my harps
before the sun rises.
³I will praise you, LORD,
for everyone to hear;
I will sing hymns to you
in every nation.

⁴Your love reaches higher
than the heavens,
and your loyalty extends
beyond the clouds.

⁵Our God, may you be honored
above the heavens;
may your glory be seen
everywhere on earth.
⁶Answer my prayers
and use your powerful arm
to give us victory.
Then the people you love
will be safe.

⁷Our God, from your holy place
you made this promise:
"I will gladly divide up
the city of Shechem
and give away Succoth Valley
piece by piece.
⁸The lands of Gilead
and Manasseh are mine.
Ephraim is my war helmet,
and Judah is my symbol
of royal power.
⁹Moab is merely my washbasin,
and Edom belongs to me.
I shout with victory
over the Philistines."

¹⁰Our God, who will bring me
to the fortress
or lead me to Edom?
¹¹Have you rejected us?
You don't lead our armies.
¹²Help us defeat our enemies!
No one else can rescue us.
¹³Only you give us victory
and crush our enemies.

107.42,43 *because you obey the LORD . . . Be wise:* To obey the LORD and live according to the Law of the LORD is wisdom (Prov 1.7; 9.10,11).

Your love reaches higher than the heavens, and your loyalty extends beyond the clouds. Ps 108.4

109.6 *My enemies said:* These three words do not appear in the Hebrew text. Their addition to the CEV suggests that the speech in 109.6-19 contains the "hateful things" that the enemies "said for no reason" (109.3). However, these verses could be understood as the psalmist's speech about one of his accusers. Even if the psalmist does not speak the words in verses 109.6-19, he claims them as his own when he says in 109.20, "Let it all happen to them!"

Enemies (The Wicked)

109.7-19 *Try him . . . curses surround him:* Whether these words were spoken by the psalmist, or whether they were claimed by him after they were spoken by his enemies, they sound like a prayer for revenge. Such prayers appear often in the prayers for help. They show how people naturally respond when they are victims of injustice.

PSALM 109

(A psalm by David for the music leader.)

A Prayer for the LORD's Help

¹I praise you, God!
 Don't keep silent.
²Destructive and deceitful lies
 are told about me,
³and hateful things are said
 for no reason.
⁴I had pity and prayed[h]
 for my enemies,
but their words to me
 were harsh and cruel.
⁵For being friendly and kind,
they paid me back
 with meanness and hatred.

⁶My enemies said,
 "Find some worthless fools
 to accuse him of a crime.
⁷Try him and find him guilty!
 Consider his prayers a lie.
⁸Cut his life short
 and let someone else
 have his job.
⁹Make orphans of his children
 and a widow of his wife;
¹⁰make his children beg for food
 and live in the slums.

¹¹"Let the people he owes
 take everything he owns.
 Give it all to strangers.
¹²Don't let anyone be kind to him
 or have pity on the children
 he leaves behind.
¹³Bring an end to his family,
 and from now on let him be
 a forgotten man.

¹⁴"Don't let the LORD forgive
 the sins of his parents

and his ancestors.
¹⁵Don't let the LORD forget
 the sins of his family,
 or let anyone remember
 his family ever lived.
¹⁶He was so cruel to the poor,
 homeless, and discouraged
 that they died young.

¹⁷"He cursed others.
 Now place a curse on him!
 He never wished others well.
 Wish only trouble for him!
¹⁸He cursed others more often
 than he dressed himself.
 Let his curses strike him deep,
 just as water and olive oil
 soak through to our bones.
¹⁹Let his curses surround him,
 just like the belt and clothes
 he wears each day."

²⁰Those are the cruel things
 my enemies wish for me.
 Let it all happen to them!
²¹Be true to your name, LORD God!
 Show your great kindness
 and rescue me.

²²I am poor and helpless,
 and I have lost all hope.
²³I am fading away
 like an evening shadow;
I am tossed aside
 like a crawling insect.
²⁴I have gone without eating,[i]
 until my knees are weak,
 and my body is bony.
²⁵When my enemies see me,
 they say cruel things
 and shake their heads.

[h]**109.4** *and prayed:* One possible meaning for the difficult Hebrew text.   [i]**109.24** *without eating:* See the note at 35.13.

[26]Please help me, LORD God!
Come and save me
because of your love.
[27]Let others know that you alone
have saved me.
[28]I don't care if they curse me,
as long as you bless me.
You will make my enemies fail
when they attack,
and you will make me glad
to be your servant.
[29]You will cover them with shame,
just as their bodies
are covered with clothes.

[30]I will sing your praises
and thank you, LORD,
when your people meet.
[31]You help everyone in need,
and you save them from death.

PSALM 110
(A psalm by David.)
The LORD Gives Victory

[1]The LORD said to my Lord,
"Sit at my right side,[j]
until I make your enemies
into a footstool for you."

[2]The LORD will let your power
reach out from Zion,
and you will rule
over your enemies.
[3]Your glorious power
will be seen on the day
you begin to rule.
You will wear the sacred robes
and shine like the morning sun
in all of your strength.[k]
[4]The LORD has made a promise

that will never be broken:
"You will be a priest forever,
just like Melchizedek."

[5]The Lord is at your right side,
and when he gets angry
he will crush
the other kings.
[6]He will judge the nations
and crack their skulls,
leaving piles of dead bodies
all over the earth.
[7]He will drink from any stream
that he chooses, while winning
victory after victory.[l]

PSALM 111
Praise the LORD
for All He Has Done

[1]Shout praises to the LORD!
With all my heart
I will thank the LORD
when his people meet.
[2]The LORD has done
many wonderful things!
Everyone who is pleased
with God's marvelous deeds
will keep them in mind.
[3]Everything the LORD does
is glorious and majestic,
and his power to bring justice
will never end.

[4]The LORD God is famous
for his wonderful deeds,
and he is kind and merciful.
[5]He gives food to his worshipers
and always keeps his agreement
with them.
[6]He has shown his mighty power

● 110.1 *right side . . . footstool:* The "right side" is the side of power and authority. Footstools probably were commonly used with a throne (see 2 Chr 9.18). Some ancient throne footstools have been discovered with the pictures of defeated enemies painted on them. This may be what is behind the idea of a king making his enemies a footstool.

■ 110.4 *a promise . . . You will be a priest . . . like Melchizedek:* God promised that one of David's descendants would always rule Israel. Here the king also is called "priest." The kings of Israel were responsible for helping the priesthood provide for Israel's worship life (see 1 Kings 5–7; 1 Chr 15.11-16; Neh 12.24,45). After the exile, the royal throne of David was not restored. Instead, the High Priest named Joshua, one of David's descendants, was chosen to rule (see Zech 6.9-14). Melchizedek was king of Salem and he is called a priest (Gen 14.18-20).

[j]**110.1** *right side:* See the note at 16.11.   [k]**110.3** *You will . . . strength:* One possible meaning for the difficult Hebrew text.   [l]**110.7** *while . . . victory:* Or "God will give him victory after victory."

111.9 *fearsome and holy:* This does not mean that God scares people, but rather that God deserves respect.

112.1 *Shout praises:* Psalms 111 and 112 are probably meant as a pair. Psalm 111 tells what God has done, and Psalm 112 describes the lives of those who follow the advice of 111.10. Psalms 111 and 112 are acrostic poems.

112.1,2 *LORD blesses . . . who do right:* Those who obey God's Law will be blessed.

113.7 *dust and ashes:* These are symbols of oppression.

to his people
and has given them the lands
of other nations.

[7]God is always honest and fair,
and his laws can be trusted.
[8]They are true and right
and will stand forever.
[9]God rescued his people,
and he will never break
his agreement with them.
He is fearsome and holy.

[10]Respect and obey the LORD!
This is the first step
to wisdom and good sense.[m]
God will always be respected.

PSALM 112
God Blesses His Worshipers

[1]Shout praises to the LORD!
The LORD blesses everyone
who worships him and gladly
obeys his teachings.
[2]Their descendants will have
great power in the land,
because the LORD blesses
all who do right.
[3]They will get rich and prosper
and will always be remembered
for their fairness.
[4]They will be so kind
and merciful and good,
that they will be a light
in the dark for others
who do the right thing.

[5]Life will go well for those
who freely lend
and are honest in business.
[6]They won't ever be troubled,

and the kind things they do
will never be forgotten.
[7]Bad news won't bother them;
they have decided
to trust the LORD.
[8]They are dependable
and not afraid,
and they will live to see
their enemies defeated.
[9]They will always be remembered
and greatly praised,
because they were kind
and freely gave to the poor.
[10]When evil people see this,
they angrily bite their tongues
and disappear.
They will never get
what they really want.

PSALM 113
The LORD Helps People in Need

[1]Shout praises to the LORD!
Everyone who serves him,
come and praise his name.

[2]Let the name of the LORD
be praised now and forever.
[3]From dawn until sunset
the name of the LORD
deserves to be praised.
[4]The LORD is far above
all of the nations;
he is more glorious
than the heavens.

[5]No one can compare
with the LORD our God.
His throne is high above,
[6]and he looks down to see
the heavens and the earth.
[7]God lifts the poor and needy
from dust and ashes,

[m]**111.10** *This . . . sense:* Or "This is what wisdom and good sense are all about."

Let the name of the LORD be praised now and forever.
Ps 113.2

8and he lets them take part
  in ruling his people.
9When a wife has no children,
  he blesses her with some,
and she is happy.
    Shout praises to the LORD!

PSALM 114
The LORD Works Wonders

1God brought his people
out of Egypt, that land
  with a strange language.
2He made Judah his holy place
  and ruled over Israel.

3When the sea looked at God,
  it ran away,
and the Jordan River
  flowed upstream.
4The mountains and the hills
  skipped around like goats.

5Ask the sea why it ran away
or ask the Jordan
  why it flowed upstream.
6Ask the mountains and the hills
  why they skipped like goats!

7Earth, you will tremble,
when the Lord God of Jacob
  comes near,
8because he turns solid rock
into flowing streams
  and pools of water.

PSALM 115
The LORD Deserves To Be Praised

1We don't deserve praise!
The LORD alone deserves
  all of the praise,
because of his love
  and faithfulness.

2Why should the nations ask,
  "Where is your God?"

3Our God is in the heavens,
  doing as he chooses.
4 The idols of the nations
  are made of silver and gold.
5They have a mouth and eyes,
  but they can't speak or see.
6Their ears can't hear,
  and their noses can't smell.
7Their hands have no feeling,
  their legs don't move,
  and they can't make a sound.
8Everyone who made the idols
  and all who trust them
are just as helpless
  as those useless gods.

9People of Israel,
  you must trust the LORD
    to help and protect you.
10Family of Aaron the priest,
  you must trust the LORD
    to help and protect you.
11All of you worship the LORD,
  so you must trust him
    to help and protect you.

12The LORD will not forget
  to give us his blessing;
he will bless all of Israel
  and the family of Aaron.
13All who worship the LORD,
  no matter who they are,
    will receive his blessing.

14I pray that the LORD
  will let your family
and your descendants
  always grow strong.
15May the LORD who created
  the heavens and the earth
    give you his blessing.

■ 113.9 *children . . . blesses her:* Children are viewed in the Bible as a gift from God and a sign of God's blessing.

● 114.1,2 *out of Egypt . . . made Judah his holy place:* God chose Moses to lead the Hebrew people out of slavery in Egypt (see Exod 12.51; Ps 105.37-41). Later, the people entered Canaan, the land God promised to give them. Still later, David made Jerusalem in Judah the capital of all Israel. Because the temple (God's house) was there, Judah is called a "holy place."

● 114.3 *sea . . . Jordan River flowed upstream . . . mountains . . . skipped:* These verses tell in poetic terms of God's miraculous acts on behalf of Israel.

■ 114.8 *rock . . . flowing streams:* This recalls God's providing for the people in the desert on their way to the promised land (Exod 17.1-7; Num 20.2-13).

■ 115.2 *Where is your God:* In the ancient world, each nation had its own god or gods. When things went poorly for a nation, or if they were defeated in battle, it was thought to be a sign that the gods were angry or punishing them. Nations sometimes mocked the nations they defeated by asking this question.

116.3 *Death attacked:* "Death" is described as a power that invades life.

116.10 *faithful . . . suffering:* The psalmist realizes that suffering does not separate him from God.

116.13 *offering of wine:* "Wine" was part of the daily "offering" to God (Exod 29.40-41; Num 28.7). Many cultures in the ancient Near East practiced some sort of drink offering (also called a "libation").

117.1 *All . . . praise the LORD:* The psalm invites "everyone" to praise God. Paul uses this verse in Romans 15.11 to support his claim that the good news of Jesus Christ is for all people.

16The LORD has kept the heavens
for himself,
but he has given the earth
to us humans.
17The dead are silent
and cannot praise the LORD,
18but we will praise him
now and forevermore.
Shout praises to the LORD!

PSALM 116
When the LORD Saves You from Death

1I love you, LORD!
You answered my prayers.
2You paid attention to me,
and so I will pray to you
as long as I live.
3Death attacked from all sides,
and I was captured
by its painful chains.
But when I was really hurting,
4I prayed and said, "LORD,
please don't let me die!"

5You are kind, LORD,
so good and merciful.
6You protect ordinary people,
and when I was helpless,
you saved me
7and treated me so kindly
that I don't need
to worry anymore.

8You, LORD, have saved
my life from death,
my eyes from tears,
my feet from stumbling.
9Now I will walk at your side
in this land of the living.
10I was faithful to you
when I was suffering,
11though in my confusion I said,
"I can't trust anyone!"

12What must I give you, LORD,
for being so good to me?
13I will pour out an offering
of wine to you,
and I will pray in your name
because you
have saved me.
14I will keep my promise to you
when your people meet.
15You are deeply concerned
when one of your loyal people
faces death.

16I worship you, LORD,
just as my mother did,
and you have rescued me
from the chains of death.
17I will offer you a sacrifice
to show how grateful I am,
and I will pray.
18I will keep my promise to you
when your people
19gather at your temple
in Jerusalem.
Shout praises to the LORD!

PSALM 117
Come Praise the LORD

1All of you nations,
come praise the LORD!
Let everyone praise him.
2God's love for us is wonderful;
his faithfulness never ends.
Shout praises to the LORD!

PSALM 118
The LORD Is Always Merciful

1Tell the LORD
how thankful you are,
because he is kind
and always merciful.

²Let Israel shout,
  "God is always merciful!"
³Let the family of Aaron
  the priest shout,
  "God is always merciful!"
⁴Let every true worshiper
  of the LORD shout,
  "God is always merciful!"

⁵When I was really hurting,
  I prayed to the LORD.
He answered my prayer,
  and took my worries away.
⁶The LORD is on my side,
and I am not afraid
  of what others can do to me.
⁷With the LORD on my side,
I will defeat
  my hateful enemies.
⁸It is better to trust the LORD
  for protection
than to trust anyone else,
⁹   including strong leaders.

¹⁰Nations surrounded me,
  but I got rid of them
  by the power of the LORD.
¹¹They attacked from all sides,
  but I got rid of them
  by the power of the LORD.
¹²They swarmed around like bees,
  but by the power of the LORD,
  I got rid of them
  and their fiery sting.
¹³Their attacks were so fierce
  that I nearly fell,
  but the LORD helped me.
¹⁴My power and my strength
  come from the LORD,
  and he has saved me.

¹⁵From the tents of God's people
  come shouts of victory:
  "The LORD is powerful!

¹⁶With his mighty arm
  the LORD wins victories!
  The LORD is powerful!"

¹⁷And so my life is safe,
  and I will live to tell
  what the LORD has done.
¹⁸He punished me terribly,
  but he did not let death
  lay its hands on me.

¹⁹Open the gates of justice!
  I will enter and tell the LORD
  how thankful I am.

²⁰Here is the gate of the LORD!
  Everyone who does right
  may enter this gate.

²¹I praise the LORD
  for answering my prayers
  and saving me.
²²The stone that the builders
  tossed aside
has now become
  the most important stone.

²³The LORD has done this,
  and it is amazing to us.
²⁴This day belongs to the LORD!
  Let's celebrate
  and be glad today.
²⁵We'll ask the LORD to save us!
  We'll sincerely ask the LORD
  to let us win.

²⁶God bless the one who comes
  in the name of the LORD!
  We praise you from here
  in the house of the LORD.

²⁷The LORD is our God,
  and he has given us light!

118.19,20 *gates of justice . . . gate of the LORD:* The references are to the entrance to the temple. Because God wants people to do "right," the entrance to the temple is called "the gates of justice." These verses and those that follow may have been spoken during a ceremonial entry into the temple, "the house of the LORD."

118.22 *most important stone:* The "most important stone" refers to a cornerstone put in the building's foundation. This cornerstone had been thrown away by builders constructing another project. Because the early Christians viewed Jesus as the most important example of a person saved from death by God, they claimed that Jesus fulfills the meaning of 118.22,23. See Matt 21.42; Mark 12.10,11; Luke 20.17; Acts 4.11; 1 Pet 2.7.

118.25,26 *let us win . . . praise you:* Having seen the psalmist saved by God, the people now ask for help. When Jesus entered Jerusalem, the crowds repeated 118.26 (see Matt 21.9; 23.39; Mark 11.9; Luke 13.35; 19.38; John 12.13).

Let every true worshiper of the LORD shout, "God is always merciful!" Ps 118.4

118.27 *March with palm branches*: The use of "palm branches" may suggest that the psalm was used originally during the Festival of Shelters (Lev 23.40).

119.1 *bless everyone who . . . obeys your Law*: The word "Law" and other related words ("commands," "teachings," "laws," "word," "instructions," and "rules") are repeated several times in Psalm 119. The repetition of these words makes the point that God's "Law" is all-important. In Hebrew, each eight-line stanza of Psalm 119 begins with the same letter. Verses 1 to 8 each begin with the first letter of the Hebrew alphabet; verses 9 to 16 each begins with the second letter of the Hebrew alphabet; and so forth. This kind of patterning supports the author's claim that God's Law applies to everything (from "A to Z," as we would say in English).

119.9 *a clean life*: God's Law contains instructions about persons, animals, things, and situations that are "clean" or "unclean." Here "clean" is a symbol for a life that is in keeping with God's will and remains pure.

Purity (Clean and Unclean)

Law

Start the celebration!
March with palm branches
all the way to the altar.[n]

28The LORD is my God!
I will praise him and tell him
how thankful I am.

29Tell the LORD
how thankful you are,
because he is kind
and always merciful.

PSALM 119
In Praise of the Law of the LORD

1Our LORD, you bless everyone
who lives right
and obeys your Law.
2You bless all those
who follow your commands
from deep in their hearts
3and who never do wrong
or turn from you.
4You have ordered us always
to obey your teachings;
5I don't ever want to stray
from your laws.
6Thinking about your commands
will keep me from doing
some foolish thing.
7I will do right and praise you
by learning to respect
your perfect laws.
8I will obey all of them!
Don't turn your back on me.

9Young people can live
a clean life
by obeying your word.

10I worship you
with all my heart.
Don't let me walk away
from your commands.
11I treasure your word
above all else;
it keeps me from sinning
against you.
12I praise you, LORD!
Teach me your laws.
13With my own mouth,
I tell others the laws
that you have spoken.
14Obeying your instructions
brings as much happiness
as being rich.
15I will study your teachings
and follow your footsteps.
16I will take pleasure
in your laws
and remember your words.

17Treat me with kindness, LORD,
so that I may live
and do what you say.
18Open my mind
and let me discover
the wonders of your Law.
19I live here as a stranger.
Don't keep me from knowing
your commands.
20What I want most
and at all times
is to honor your laws.
21You punish those boastful,
worthless nobodies who turn
from your commands.
22Don't let them sneer
and insult me
for following you.
23I keep thinking about

[n]**118.27** *Start . . . altar*: One possible meaning for the difficult Hebrew text.

Open my mind and let me discover the wonders of your Law. Ps 119.18

your teachings, LORD,
even if rulers plot
against me.
²⁴Your laws are my greatest joy!
I follow their advice.

²⁵I am at the point of death.
Let your teachings
breathe new life into me.
²⁶When I told you my troubles,
you answered my prayers.
Now teach me your laws.
²⁷Help me to understand
your teachings,
and I will think about
your marvelous deeds.
²⁸I am overcome with sorrow.
Encourage me,
as you have promised to do.
²⁹Keep me from being deceitful,
and be kind enough
to teach me your Law.
³⁰I am determined to be faithful
and to respect your laws.
³¹I follow your rules, LORD.
Don't let me be ashamed.
³²I am eager to learn all
that you want me to do;
help me to understand more.

³³Point out your rules, LORD,
and I won't disobey
even one of them.
³⁴Help me to understand your Law;
I promise to obey it
with all my heart.
³⁵Direct me by your commands!
I love to do what you say.
³⁶Make me want to obey you,
rather than to be rich.
³⁷Take away my foolish desires,
and let me find life
by walking with you.
³⁸I am your servant!

Do for me what you promised
to those who worship you.
³⁹Your wonderful teachings
protect me from the insults
that I hate so much.
⁴⁰I long for your teachings.
Be true to yourself
and let me live.

⁴¹Show me your love
and save me, LORD,
as you have promised.
⁴²Then I will have an answer
for everyone who insults me
for trusting your word.
⁴³I rely on your laws!
Don't take away my chance
to speak your truth.
⁴⁴I will keep obeying your Law
forever and ever.
⁴⁵I have gained perfect freedom
by following your teachings,
⁴⁶and I trust them so much
that I tell them to kings.
⁴⁷I love your commands!
They bring me happiness.
⁴⁸I love and respect them
and will keep them in mind.

⁴⁹Don't forget your promise
to me, your servant.
I depend on it.
⁵⁰When I am hurting,
I find comfort in your promise
that leads to life.
⁵¹Conceited people sneer at me,
but I obey your Law.
⁵²I find true comfort, LORD,
because your laws have stood
the test of time.
⁵³I get furious when evil people
turn against your Law.
⁵⁴No matter where I am,
your teachings

119.25-28 *point of death . . . Encourage me:* These verses are like the complaints in the prayers for help. The psalmist's "troubles" (119.26) show that blessing is not a matter of material reward. He calls on God's teachings (Law) to breathe new life into him.

119.45 *perfect freedom:* God gave the Law to Moses shortly after God had set the people free from slavery in Egypt. The Law was intended to help people stay free by worshiping the LORD and living right, including treating one another with justice. This is what it means to "serve" God. The psalmist realizes that "perfect freedom" is to be a servant of God (119.38,49,65).

Blessed (Happy)

Wisdom

Show me your love and save me, LORD. Ps 119.41

119.83 *a dried-up wineskin:* In ancient times, bags made from animal skins were used to hold wine, but when the bags dried up they cracked and could no longer be used.

fill me with songs.
55 Even in the night
  I think about you, LORD,
  and I obey your Law.
56 You have blessed me
  because I have always followed
    your teachings.

57 You, LORD, are my choice,
  and I will obey you.
58 With all my heart
  I beg you to be kind to me,
    just as you have promised.
59 I pay careful attention
  as you lead me,
    and I follow closely.
60 As soon as you command,
  I do what you say.
61 Evil people may set a trap,
  but I obey your Law.
62 Your laws are so fair
  that I wake up and praise you
    in the middle of the night.
63 I choose as my friends
  everyone who worships you
    and follows your teachings.
64 Our LORD, your love is seen
  all over the world.
    Teach me your laws.

65 I am your servant, LORD,
  and you have kept your promise
    to treat me with kindness.
66 Give me wisdom and good sense.
  I trust your commands.
67 Once you corrected me
  for not obeying you,
    but now I do obey.
68 You are kindhearted,
  and you do good things,
    so teach me your laws.
69 My reputation is being ruined
  by conceited liars,
    but with all my heart

I follow your teachings.
70 Those liars have no sense,
  but I find happiness
    in your Law.
71 When you corrected me,
  it did me good
  because it taught me
    to study your laws.
72 I would rather obey you
  than to have a thousand pieces
    of silver and gold.

73 You created me
  and put me together.
  Make me wise enough to learn
    what you have commanded.
74 Your worshipers will see me,
  and they will be glad
    that I trust your word.
75 Your decisions are correct,
  and you were right
    to punish me.
76 I serve you, LORD.
  Comfort me with your love,
    just as you have promised.
77 I love to obey your Law!
  Have mercy and let me live.
78 Put down those proud people
  who hurt me with their lies,
  because I have chosen
    to study your teachings.
79 Let your worshipers come to me,
  so they will learn
    to obey your rules.
80 Let me truly respect your laws,
  so I won't be ashamed.

81 I long for you to rescue me!
  Your word is my only hope.
82 I am worn out from waiting
  for you to keep your word.
    When will you have mercy?
83 My life is wasting away

I would rather obey you than to have a thousand pieces of silver and gold. Ps 119.72

like a dried-up wineskin,[o]
but I have not forgotten
    your teachings.
[84]I am your servant!
    How long must I suffer?
When will you punish
    those troublemakers?
[85]Those proud people reject
    your teachings,
and they dig pits
    for me to fall in.
[86]Your laws can be trusted!
    Protect me from cruel liars.
[87]They have almost killed me,
but I have been faithful
    to your teachings.
[88]Show that you love me
    and let me live,
so that I may obey
    your commands.

[89]Our LORD, you are eternal!
    Your word will last as long
    as the heavens.[P]
[90]You remain faithful
    in every generation,
and the earth you created
    will keep standing firm.
[91]All things are your servants,
    and the laws you made
    are still in effect today.
[92]If I had not found happiness
    in obeying your Law,
    I would have died in misery.
[93]I won't ever forget
    your teachings,
because you give me new life
    when I follow them.
[94]I belong to you,
    and I have respected your laws,

so keep me safe.
[95]Brutal enemies are waiting
    to ambush and destroy me,
    but I obey your rules.
[96]Nothing is completely perfect,
    except your teachings.

[97]I deeply love your Law!
    I think about it all day.
[98]Your laws never leave my mind,
    and they make me much wiser
    than my enemies.
[99]Thinking about your teachings
    gives me better understanding
    than my teachers,
[100]and obeying your laws
    makes me wiser than those
    who have lived a long time.
[101]I obey your word
    instead of following a way
    that leads to trouble.
[102]You have been my teacher,
    and I won't reject
    your instructions.
[103]Your teachings are sweeter
    than honey.
[104]They give me understanding
    and make me hate all lies.

[105]Your word is a lamp
    that gives light
    wherever I walk.
[106]Your laws are fair,
    and I have given my word
    to respect them all.
[107]I am in terrible pain!
    Save me, LORD,
    as you have promised.
[108]Accept my offerings of praise
    and teach me your laws.

119.98-100 *wiser . . . lived a long time:* Those who has grown old were considered wise because of their experience. But the psalmist suggests that true wisdom comes from studying God's Law.

[o]119.83 *a dried-up wineskin:* The Hebrew text has "a wineskin in the smoke." In ancient times bags were made from animal skins to hold wine, but when the bags dried up they cracked and could no longer be used.   [P]119.89 *Our . . . heavens:* Or "Our LORD your word is eternal. It will last as long as the heavens."

Our LORD, you are eternal! Your word will last as long as the heavens. Ps 119.89

119.110 *trying to trap me:* Traps, snares, and pits were used to catch animals. They are used symbolically here and throughout PSALMS to refer to a variety of plots and schemes used by enemies to hurt God's people.

119.123 *waiting:* The psalmist's many complaints (119.25-28, 84-87, 109, 110) show that God does not use his power to enforce his will immediately. So the psalmist is "waiting."

109I never forget your teachings,
    although my life is always
        in danger.
110Some merciless people
    are trying to trap me,
    but I never turn my back
        on your teachings.
111They will always be
    my most prized possession
        and my source of joy.
112I have made up my mind
    to obey your laws forever,
        no matter what.

113I hate anyone
    whose loyalty is divided,
        but I love your Law.
114You are my place of safety
    and my shield.
        Your word is my only hope.

115All you worthless people,
    get away from me!
    I am determined to obey
        the commands of my God.

116Be true to your word, LORD.
    Keep me alive and strong;
    don't let me be ashamed
        because of my hope.
117Keep me safe and secure,
    so that I will always
        respect your laws.
118You reject all deceitful liars
    because they refuse
        your teachings.
119As far as you are concerned,
    evil people are⁹ garbage,
        and so I follow your rules.

120I tremble all over
    when I think of you
        and the way you judge.

121I did what was fair and right!
    Don't hand me over to those
        who want to mistreat me.
122Take good care of me,
    your servant,
    and don't let me be harmed
        by those conceited people.
123My eyes are weary from waiting
    to see you keep your promise
        to come and save me.
124Show your love for me,
    your servant,
        and teach me your laws.
125I serve you,
    so let me understand
        your teachings.
126Do something, LORD!
    They have broken your Law.
127Your laws mean more to me
        than the finest gold.
128I follow all your commands,ʳ
    but I hate anyone
        who leads me astray.

129Your teachings are wonderful,
        and I respect them all.
130Understanding your word
    brings light to the minds
        of ordinary people.
131I honestly want to know
    everything you teach.
132Think about me and be kind,
    just as you are to everyone
        who loves your name.
133Keep your promise
    and don't let me stumble

⁹119.119 *As far as . . . are:* A few Hebrew manuscripts and ancient translations. Most Hebrew manuscripts have "You get rid of evil people as if they were."   ʳ119.128 *I . . . commands:* One possible meaning for the difficult Hebrew text.

or let sin control my life.
134Protect me from abuse,
   so I can obey your laws.
135Smile on me, your servant,
   and teach me your laws.
136When anyone disobeys you,
   my eyes overflow with tears.

137Our LORD, you always do right,
   and your decisions are fair.
138All your teachings are true
   and trustworthy.
139It upsets me greatly
   when my enemies neglect
   your teachings.
140Your word to me, your servant,
   is like pure gold;
   I treasure what you say.
141Everyone calls me a nobody,
   but I remember your laws.
142You will always do right,
   and your teachings are true.
143I am in deep distress,
   but I love your teachings.
144Your rules are always fair.
   Help me to understand them
   and live.

145I pray to you, LORD!
   Please answer me.
   I promise to obey your laws.
146I beg you to save me,
   so I can follow your rules.
147Even before sunrise,
   I pray for your help,
   and I put my hope
   in what you have said.
148I lie awake at night,
   thinking of your promises.
149Show that you love me, LORD,
   and answer my prayer.
   Please do the right thing
   and save my life.
150People who disobey your Law

have made evil plans
   and want to hurt me,
151but you are with me,
   and all your commands
   can be trusted.
152From studying your laws,
   I found out long ago
   you made them to last forever.

153I have not forgotten your Law!
   Look at the trouble I am in,
   and rescue me.
154Be my defender and protector!
   Remember your promise
   and save my life.
155Evil people won't obey you,
   and so they have no hope
   of being saved.
156You are merciful, LORD!
   Please do the right thing
   and save my life.
157I have a lot of brutal enemies,
   but still I never turn
   from your laws.
158Those unfaithful people
   who refuse to obey you
   are disgusting to me.
159Remember how I love your laws,
   and show your love for me
   by keeping me safe.
160All you say can be trusted;
   your teachings are true
   and will last forever.

161Rulers are cruel to me
   for no reason.
   But with all my heart
   I respect your words,
162because they bring happiness
   like treasures taken in war.
163I can't stand liars,
   but I love your Law.
164I praise you seven times a day
   because your laws are fair.

119.134 *Protect me from abuse:* "Abuse" results from injustice, which in turn results from failing to do God's will. The psalmist is asking for protection from his enemies.

Your word to me, your servant, is like pure gold; I treasure what you say. Ps 119.140

120 (Title) *A song for worship:* The Hebrew word that the CEV translates "for worship" means "for going up," and it appears in the titles of Psalms 120–134. Jerusalem is built on hills, and the temple was located on the hill called Zion. This collection was probably used by worshipers as they were "going up" to Jerusalem for one of the three festivals that all Israelite men were supposed to attend (Deut 16.16). Except for Psalm 132, all the psalms are very short and would have been easy to memorize. They often mention Jerusalem or Zion, the place where the people were going to celebrate the festival (122.2,3,6; 125.1; 126.1; 128.5; 129.5; 132.13,15; 133.3; 134.3). The order of the psalms also suggests their use by worshipers traveling to Jerusalem. Psalm 120 is spoken by someone who lives outside the land (120.5); Psalm 121 is about a journey; Psalm 122 talks about arriving at the temple in Jerusalem; Psalms 123–133 are prayers that could have been used at a festival; and Psalm 134 sounds like a blessing for the trip back home.

120.5 *Meshech . . . Kedar:* Meshech and Kedar may be symbols for "people who hate peace" (120.6). **(See Map 7 on pg 1885.)**

120.6,7 *peace:* Peace results when justice is done.

Peace

121.3 *your protector . . . won't go to sleep:* The LORD is the protector of those who travel to Jerusalem to celebrate the holy festivals.

---

165 You give peace of mind
  to all who love your Law.
    Nothing can make them fall.
166 You are my only hope
  for being saved, LORD,
    and I do all you command.
167 I love and obey your laws
  with all my heart.
168 You know everything I do.
  You know I respect every law
    you have given.

169 Please, LORD, hear my prayer
  and give me the understanding
    that comes from your word.
170 Listen to my concerns
  and keep me safe,
    just as you have promised.
171 If you will teach me your laws,
  I will praise you 172 and sing
    about your promise,
  because all your teachings
    are what they ought to be.
173 Be ready to protect me
  because I have chosen
    to obey your laws.
174 I am waiting for you
  to save me, LORD.
    Your Law makes me happy.
175 Keep me alive,
    so I can praise you,
  and let me find help
    in your teachings.
176 I am your servant,
  but I have wandered away
    like a lost sheep.
  Please come after me,
  because I have not forgotten
    your teachings.

PSALM 120
(A song for worship.)
A Prayer for the LORD's Help

1 When I am in trouble, I pray,
2 "Come and save me, LORD,
  from deceitful liars!"

3 What punishment is fitting
  for you deceitful liars?
4 Your reward should be
  sharp and flaming arrows!

5 But I must live as a foreigner
  among the people of Meshech
    and in the tents of Kedar.[s]
6 I have spent too much time
  living among people
    who hate peace.
7 I am in favor of peace,
  but when I speak of it,
    all they want is war.

PSALM 121
(A song for worship.)
The LORD Will Protect His People

1 I look to the hills!
  Where will I find help?
2 It will come from the LORD,
  who created heaven and earth.

3 The LORD is your protector,
  and he won't go to sleep
    or let you stumble.
4 The protector of Israel
  doesn't doze
    or ever get drowsy.

5 The LORD is your protector,
  there at your right side

---

[s]**120.5** *Meshech . . . Kedar:* Meshech was a country near the Black Sea, and Kedar was a tribe of the Syrian desert.

to shade you from the sun.
⁶You won't be harmed
by the sun during the day
or by the moon^t at night.

⁷The Lord will protect you
and keep you safe
from all dangers.
⁸The Lord will protect you
now and always
wherever you go.

Psalm 122
(A song by David for worship.)
A Song of Praise

¹It made me glad when they said,
"Let's go to the house
of the Lord!"
²Jerusalem, we are standing
inside your gates.

³Jerusalem, what a strong
and beautiful city you are!
⁴Every tribe of the Lord
obeys him and comes to you
to praise his name.
⁵David's royal throne is here
where justice rules.

⁶Jerusalem, we pray
that you will have peace,
and that all will go well
for those who love you.
⁷May there be peace
inside your city walls
and in your palaces.
⁸Because of my friends
and my relatives,
I will pray for peace.

⁹And because of the house
of the Lord our God,
I will work for your good.

Psalm 123
(A song for worship.)
A Prayer for Mercy

¹Our Lord and our God,
I turn my eyes to you,
on your throne in heaven.
²Servants look to their master,
but we will look to you,
until you have mercy on us.

³Please have mercy, Lord!
We have been insulted
more than we can stand,
⁴and we can't take more abuse
from those proud,
conceited people.

Psalm 124
(A song by David for worship.)
Thanking the Lord for Victory

¹The Lord was on our side!
Let everyone in Israel say:
² "The Lord was on our side!
Otherwise, the enemy attack
³would have killed us all,
because it was furious.
⁴We would have been swept away
in a violent flood
⁵ of high and roaring waves."

⁶Let's praise the Lord!
He protected us from enemies
who were like wild animals,
⁷and we escaped like birds
from a hunter's torn net.

---

^t121.6 harmed . . . sun . . . moon: In ancient times people saw the harmful effects of the rays of the sun, and they thought that certain illnesses (especially mental disorders) were also caused by the rays of the moon.

122.1-3 the house of the Lord . . . Jerusalem: The "house of the Lord" was the temple in Jerusalem. Travelers to Jerusalem probably used the psalm as they passed the city's gates or as they arrived in the temple area. (See Map 5 on pg 1883.)

122.4 Every tribe: All Israelite men were supposed to go to Jerusalem for the three major festivals of the year. See Deut 16.16. (See the chart Pilgrimage Festivals on pg 1799.)

122.5 David's royal throne . . . justice rules: The royal palace of King David and his descendants was in Jerusalem. As king of the universe, God wills "justice." It was the responsibility of the earthly kings, David and his descendants, to establish justice on earth.

123.3,4 have mercy . . . conceited people: This prayer for help for the whole people probably fits well into the period after the exile. Although the people had returned to the land, other nations still ruled over them and caused them problems (123.4; also Neh 2.19; 4.4).

126.2,3 *miracles:* The psalmist considers Israel's return from exile in Babylonia and the rebuilding of Jerusalem as "miracles" of God. Likewise, the people of Israel spoke of their escape from Egypt and safe crossing of the Red Sea as God's "miracles."

126.4 *streams in the Southern Desert:* In the rainy season, dry stream beds can suddenly become flowing streams, a wonderful and seemingly miraculous occurrence in the desert. **(See Map 3 on pg 1881.)**

127.3-5 *children are . . . a gift:* In ancient times, having many children meant parents would have lots of help with daily tasks and would be cared for in old age. All parts of daily life—home, town, job, and family—find their meaning as they are related to God.

[8]The Lord made heaven and earth,
and he is the one
who sends us help.

PSALM 125
(A song for worship.)
The Lord's People Are Safe

[1]Everyone who trusts the Lord
is like Mount Zion
that cannot be shaken
and will stand forever.
[2]Just as Jerusalem is protected
by mountains on every side,
the Lord protects his people
by holding them in his arms
now and forever.
[3]He won't let the wicked
rule his people
or lead them to do wrong.
[4]Let's ask the Lord to be kind
to everyone who is good
and completely obeys him.

[5]When the Lord punishes
the wicked,
he will punish everyone else
who lives an evil life.
Pray for peace in Israel!

PSALM 126
(A song for worship.)
Celebrating the Harvest

[1]It seemed like a dream
when the Lord brought us back
to the city of Zion.[u]
[2]We celebrated with laughter
and joyful songs.
In foreign nations it was said,
"The Lord has worked miracles
for his people."

[3]And so we celebrated
because the Lord had indeed
worked miracles for us.

[4]Our Lord, we ask you to bless
our people again,
and let us be like streams
in the Southern Desert.
[5]We cried as we went out
to plant our seeds.
Now let us celebrate
as we bring in the crops.
[6]We cried on the way
to plant our seeds,
but we will celebrate and shout
as we bring in the crops.

PSALM 127
(A song by Solomon for worship.)
Only the Lord Can Bless a Home

[1]Without the help of the Lord
it is useless to build a home
or to guard a city.
[2]It is useless to get up early
and stay up late
in order to earn a living.
God takes care of his own,
even while they sleep.[v]

[3]Children are a blessing
and a gift from the Lord.
[4]Having a lot of children
to take care of you
in your old age
is like a warrior
with a lot of arrows.
[5]The more you have,
the better off you will be,
because they will protect you
when your enemies
attack you in court.

[u]**126.1** *brought . . . Zion:* Or "made the city of Zion prosperous again." [v]**127.2** *God . . . sleep:* One possible meaning for the difficult Hebrew text.

Without the help of the Lord it is useless to build a home or to guard a city. Ps 127.1

PSALM 128

(A song for worship.)

The LORD Rewards
His Faithful People

[1] The LORD will bless you
if you respect him
and obey his laws.
[2] Your fields will produce,
and you will be happy—
all will go well.
[3] Your wife will be as fruitful
as a grapevine,
and just as an olive tree
is rich with olives,
your home will be rich
with healthy children.
[4] This is how the LORD will bless
everyone who respects him.

[5] I pray that the LORD
will bless you from Zion
and let Jerusalem prosper
as long as you live.
[6] May you live long enough
to see your grandchildren.
Let's pray for peace in Israel!

PSALM 129

(A song for worship.)

A Prayer for Protection

[1] Since the time I was young,
enemies have often attacked!
Let everyone in Israel say:
[2] "Since the time I was young,
enemies have often attacked!
But they have not defeated me,
[3] though my back is like a field
that has just been plowed."

[4] The LORD always does right,
and he has set me free
from the ropes

of those cruel people.
[5] I pray that all who hate
the city of Zion
will be made ashamed
and forced to turn and run.
[6] May they be like grass
on the flat roof of a house,
grass that dries up
as soon as it sprouts.
[7] Don't let them be like wheat
gathered in bundles.
[8] And don't let anyone
who passes by say to them,
"The LORD bless you!"
I give you my blessing
in the name of the LORD."

PSALM 130

(A song for worship.)

Trusting the LORD
in Times of Trouble

[1] From a sea of troubles
I cry out to you, LORD.
[2] Won't you please listen
as I beg for mercy?

[3] If you kept record of our sins,
no one could last long.
[4] But you forgive us,
and so we will worship you.

[5] With all my heart,
I am waiting, LORD, for you!
I trust your promises.
[6] I wait for you more eagerly
than a soldier on guard duty
waits for the dawn.
Yes, I wait more eagerly
than a soldier on guard duty
waits for the dawn.

[7] Israel, trust the LORD!
God is always merciful
and has the power to save you.

■ **128.1-4** *bless you . . . everyone who respects him:* The LORD's blessings are for those who obey the LORD and respect the LORD's Law. The blessings include good harvests and many healthy children. The promise that "all will go well" should not be understood to mean that those who obey God will never have troubles.

⊗ Promises (Vows)

■ **130.7,8** *always merciful . . . save you from all your sins:* The understanding of God as "always merciful" is in keeping with God's message to Moses in Exodus 34.6,7. See also Matt 1.21; Titus 2.14.

131.2,3 *mother's arms . . . trust the LORD:* Some scholars think Psalm 131 may have been written by a woman, perhaps one of the travelers to Jerusalem who brought her young child with her.

132 (Title) *A song for worship:* Psalm 132 celebrates the key reason that people traveled to Jerusalem, to visit God's "chosen . . . home" (132.13) where David had ruled Israel.

132.2-5 *how . . . Jacob:* This promise refers either to David's goal of taking the sacred chest to Jerusalem or to David's desire to build a house (temple) for God (2 Sam 7.1,2).

132.6 *Ephrath . . . Jaar:* Ephrath probably refers to the region around Bethlehem. Jaar may be a poetic way of referring to Kiriath-Jearim where the sacred chest was located in 1 Samuel 6.19—7.2.

The Sacred Chest

---

[8]Israel, the LORD will save you
  from all your sins.

PSALM 131
(A song by David for worship.)
Trust the LORD!

[1]I am not conceited, LORD,
  and I don't waste my time
    on impossible schemes.
[2]But I have learned to feel safe
  and satisfied,
like a young child
  in its mother's arms.

[3]People of Israel,
  you must trust the LORD
    now and forever.

PSALM 132
(A song for worship.)
The LORD Is Always with His People

[1]Our LORD, don't forget David
  and how he suffered.
[2]Mighty God of Jacob,
  remember how he promised:
[3]"I won't go home
  or crawl into bed
[4] or close my eyelids,
[5]until I find a home for you,
  the mighty LORD God of Jacob."

[6]When we were in Ephrath,
  we heard that the sacred chest
    was somewhere near Jaar.
[7]Then we said, "Let's go
  to the throne of the LORD
    and worship at his feet."

[8]Come to your new home, LORD,
  you and the sacred chest

---

with all its power.
[9]Let victory be like robes
  for the priests;
let your faithful people
  celebrate and shout.
[10]David is your chosen one,
  so don't reject him.
[11]You made a solemn promise
  to David, when you said,
"I, the LORD, promise
  that someone in your family
    will always be king.
[12]If they keep our agreement
  and follow my teachings,
then someone in your family
  will rule forever."

[13]You have gladly chosen Zion
  as your home, our LORD.
[14]You said, "This is my home!
  I will live here forever.
[15]I will bless Zion with food,
  and even the poor will eat
    until they are full.
[16]Victory will be like robes
  for the priests,
and its faithful people
  will celebrate and shout.
[17]I will give mighty power
  to the kingdom of David.
Each of my chosen kings
  will shine like a lamp
[18] and wear a sparkling crown.
But I will disgrace
  their enemies."

PSALM 133
(A song for worship.)
Living Together in Peace

[1]It is truly wonderful
  when the people of God
    live together in peace.
[2]It is as beautiful as olive oil

poured on Aaron's head[w]
and running down his beard
and the collar of his robe.
[3]It is like the dew
from Mount Hermon,
   falling on Zion's mountains,
where the Lord has promised
to bless his people
   with life forevermore.

Psalm 134
(A song for worship.)
Praising the Lord at Night

[1]Everyone who serves the Lord,
   come and offer praises.
Everyone who has gathered
   in his temple tonight,
[2]lift your hands in prayer
toward his holy place
   and praise the Lord.

[3]The Lord is the Creator
   of heaven and earth,
and I pray that the Lord
   will bless you from Zion.

Psalm 135
In Praise of the Lord's Kindness

[1]Shout praises to the Lord!
You are his servants,
   so praise his name.
[2]All who serve in the temple
of the Lord our God,
[3]   come and shout praises.
Praise the name of the Lord!
   He is kind and good.
[4]He chose the family of Jacob
and the people of Israel
   for his very own.

[5]The Lord is much greater
   than any other god.
[6]He does as he chooses
in heaven and on earth
   and deep in the sea.
[7]The Lord makes the clouds rise
   from far across the earth,
and he makes lightning
   to go with the rain.
Then from his secret place
   he sends out the wind.

[8]The Lord killed the first-born
of people and animals
   in the land of Egypt.
[9]God used miracles and wonders
to fight the king of Egypt
   and all of his officials.
[10]He destroyed many nations
   and killed powerful kings,
[11]including King Sihon
of the Amorites
   and King Og of Bashan.
He conquered every kingdom
   in the land of Canaan
[12]and gave their property
   to his people Israel.

[13]The name of the Lord
   will be remembered forever,
and he will be famous
   for all time to come.
[14]The Lord will bring justice
and show mercy to all
   who serve him.

[15] Idols of silver and gold
are made and worshiped
   in other nations.
[16]They have a mouth and eyes,

135.11 *King Sihon . . . Og of Bashan:* Sihon refused to let the people pass through his land (Num 21.21-33; Deut 2.26-37). After defeating Sihon, the people also defeated Og (Num 21.33-35; Deut 3.1-11).

135.11,12 *conquered . . . Canaan . . . Israel:* God helped the people enter Canaan (Josh 3.14-17), and take it over (Josh 4.1—11.23).

---

[w]133.2 *head*: Olive oil was poured on Aaron's head to show that God had chosen him to be the high priest.

136.10-16 *God struck down . . . through the desert*: These verses describe events connected with the time God rescued the Hebrew people from their life of slavery in Egypt (Exod 3–19).

but they can't speak or see.
¹⁷They are completely deaf,
and they can't breathe.
¹⁸Everyone who makes idols
and all who trust them
will end up as helpless
as their idols.

¹⁹Everyone in Israel,
come praise the LORD!
All the family of Aaron
²⁰and all the tribe of Levi,^x
come praise the LORD!
All of his worshipers,
come praise the LORD.
²¹Praise the LORD from Zion!
He lives here in Jerusalem.
Shout praises to the LORD!

PSALM 136
God's Love Never Fails

¹Praise the LORD! He is good.
God's love never fails.
²Praise the God of all gods.
God's love never fails.
³Praise the Lord of lords.
God's love never fails.

⁴Only God works great miracles.^y
God's love never fails.
⁵With wisdom he made the sky.
God's love never fails.
⁶The Lord stretched the earth
over the ocean.
God's love never fails.
⁷He made the bright lights
in the sky.
God's love never fails.
⁸He lets the sun rule each day.

God's love never fails.
⁹He lets the moon and the stars
rule each night.
God's love never fails.

¹⁰God struck down the first-born
in every Egyptian family.
God's love never fails.
¹¹He rescued Israel from Egypt.
God's love never fails.
¹²God used his great strength
and his powerful arm.
God's love never fails.
¹³He split the Red Sea^z apart.
God's love never fails.

¹⁴The Lord brought Israel safely
through the sea.
God's love never fails.
¹⁵He destroyed the Egyptian king
and his army there.
God's love never fails.
¹⁶The Lord led his people
through the desert.
God's love never fails.

¹⁷Our God defeated mighty kings.
God's love never fails.
¹⁸And he killed famous kings.
God's love never fails.
¹⁹One of them was Sihon,
king of the Amorites.
God's love never fails.
²⁰Another was King Og of Bashan.
God's love never fails.
²¹God took away their land.
God's love never fails.
²²He gave their land to Israel,
the people who serve him.
God's love never fails.

^x**135.19,20** *Aaron . . . Levi*: Aaron was from the tribe of Levi, and all priests were from his family. The temple helpers, singers, and musicians were also from the tribe of Levi. ^y**136.4** *great miracles*: One Hebrew manuscript and one ancient translation have "miracles." ^z**136.13** *Red Sea*: See the note at 106.7.

²³God saw the trouble we were in.
  God's love never fails.
²⁴He rescued us from our enemies.
  God's love never fails.
²⁵He gives food to all who live.
  God's love never fails.

²⁶Praise God in heaven!
  God's love never fails.

PSALM 137
A Prayer for Revenge

¹Beside the rivers of Babylon
  we thought about Jerusalem,
    and we sat down and cried.
²We hung our small harps
  on the willow^a trees.
³Our enemies had brought us here
  as their prisoners;
now they wanted us to sing
  and entertain them.
They insulted us and shouted,
  "Sing about Zion!"

⁴Here in a foreign land,
  how can we sing
    about the LORD?
⁵Jerusalem, if I forget you,
  let my right hand go limp.
⁶Let my tongue stick
  to the roof of my mouth,
if I don't think about you
  above all else.

⁷Our LORD, punish the Edomites!
On the day Jerusalem fell,
  they shouted,
"Completely destroy the city!
  Tear down every building!"

⁸Babylon, you are doomed!
  I pray the Lord's blessings
on anyone who punishes you
  for what you did to us.
⁹May the Lord bless everyone
  who beats your children
    against the rocks!

PSALM 138
(By David.)
Praise the LORD
with All Your Heart

¹With all my heart
  I praise you, LORD.
In the presence of angels^b
  I sing your praises.
²I worship at your holy temple
  and praise you for your love
    and your faithfulness.
You were true to your word
  and made yourself more famous
    than ever before.^c
³When I asked for your help,
  you answered my prayer
    and gave me courage.^d

⁴All kings on this earth
  have heard your promises, LORD,
    and they will praise you.
⁵You are so famous
  that they will sing about
    the things you have done.
⁶Though you are above us all,
  you care for humble people,
and you keep a close watch
  on everyone who is proud.

⁷I am surrounded by trouble,
  but you protect me

137.1 *the rivers of Babylon:* The psalm probably was written between 586 and 539 B.C. while the people were in exile in Babylon. The "rivers" probably refer to the canals that ran between the Tigris and the Euphrates Rivers. (See Map 7 on pg 1885.)

Babylon

137.2 *willow trees:* The tree is probably the Euphrates poplar that often grows along streams in the Middle East.

137.7 *Edomites:* The Edomites seem to have rejoiced when the Babylonians destroyed Jerusalem. See Ezek 35.5-15; Obad 10-14.

137.8,9 *Babylon, you are doomed:* This disturbing prayer for revenge is also a cry for justice. Verse 9 reflects the cruelty of war that God's people had already experienced themselves. See 2 Kgs 8.12; Isa 13.16; Hos 10.14; Rev 18.6.

^a137.2 *willow:* Or "poplar." ^b138.1 *angels:* Or "gods" or "supernatural beings" who worship and serve God in heaven; or possibly "rulers" or "leaders." ^c138.2 *You were . . . before:* One possible meaning for the difficult Hebrew text. ^d138.3 *and gave me courage:* One possible meaning for the difficult Hebrew text.

Here in a foreign land, how can we sing about the LORD? Ps 137.4

139.1-3 *know all about me . . . notice everything I do:* The theme of this psalm is the psalmist's insight that God knows him completely.

139.8 *highest heavens . . . world of the dead:* The psalmist refers to the two most distant places in the universe to declare that there is nowhere he could go where God could not care for him.

139.15 *secretly woven . . . out of human sight:* "Out of human sight" may mean in the mother's womb, or this may be a poetic way of describing God as a weaver.

against my angry enemies.
With your own powerful arm
　　you keep me safe.

⁸You, Lord, will always
treat me with kindness.
　Your love never fails.
You have made us what we are.
　Don't give up on us now!ᵉ

Psalm 139
(A psalm by David for the music leader.)
The Lord Is Always Near

¹You have looked deep
into my heart, Lord,
　　and you know all about me.
²You know when I am resting
　　or when I am working,
and from heaven
　　you discover my thoughts.

³You notice everything I do
　　and everywhere I go.
⁴Before I even speak a word,
　　you know what I will say,
⁵and with your powerful arm
　you protect me
　　from every side.
⁶I can't understand all of this!
Such wonderful knowledge
　　is far above me.

⁷Where could I go to escape
　from your Spirit
　　or from your sight?
⁸If I were to climb up
　to the highest heavens,
　　you would be there.
If I were to dig down
　to the world of the dead
　　you would also be there.

⁹Suppose I had wings
　like the dawning day
　　and flew across the ocean.
¹⁰Even then your powerful arm
　　would guide and protect me.
¹¹Or suppose I said, "I'll hide
　in the dark until night comes
　　to cover me over."
¹²But you see in the dark
　because daylight and dark
　　are all the same to you.

¹³You are the one
　who put me together
　　inside my mother's body,
¹⁴and I praise you because of
　the wonderful way
　　you created me.
Everything you do is marvelous!
　Of this I have no doubt.

¹⁵Nothing about me
　is hidden from you!
I was secretly woven together
　　out of human sight,
¹⁶but with your own eyes you saw
　　my body being formed.
Even before I was born,
　you had written in your book
　　everything about me.

¹⁷Your thoughts are far beyond
　　my understanding,
much more than I
　　could ever imagine.
¹⁸I try to count your thoughts,
　but they outnumber the grains
　　of sand on the beach.
And when I awake,
　I will find you nearby.

¹⁹How I wish that you would kill
　all cruel and heartless people

ᵉ**138.8** *You have . . . now:* Or "Please don't desert your people."

You have looked deep into my heart, Lord, and you know all about me. Ps 139.1

and protect me from them!
²⁰They are always rebelling
and speaking evil of you.ᶠ
²¹You know I hate anyone
who hates you, LORD,
and refuses to obey.
²²They are my enemies too,
and I truly hate them.

²³Look deep into my heart, God,
and find out everything
I am thinking.
²⁴Don't let me follow evil ways,
but lead me in the way
that time has proven true.

PSALM 140

(A psalm by David for the music leader.)

A Prayer for the LORD's Help

¹Rescue me from cruel
and violent enemies, LORD!
²They think up evil plans
and always cause trouble.
³Their words bite deep
like the poisonous fangs
of a snake.

⁴Protect me, LORD, from cruel
and brutal enemies,
who want to destroy me.
⁵Those proud people have hidden
traps and nets
to catch me as I walk.

⁶You, LORD, are my God!
Please listen to my prayer.
⁷You have the power to save me,
and you keep me safe
in every battle.

⁸Don't let the wicked succeed
in doing what they want,
or else they might never
stop planning evil.
⁹They have me surrounded,
but make them the victims
of their own vicious lies.ᵍ
¹⁰Dump flaming coals on them
and throw them into pits
where they can't climb out.
¹¹Chase those cruel liars away!
Let trouble hunt them down.

¹²Our LORD, I know that you
defend the homeless
and see that the poor
are given justice.
¹³Your people will praise you
and will live with you
because they do right.

PSALM 141

(A psalm by David.)

A Prayer for the LORD's Protection

¹I pray to you, LORD!
Please listen when I pray
and hurry to help me.
² Think of my prayer
as sweet-smelling incense,
and think of my lifted hands
as an evening sacrifice.

³Help me to guard my words
whenever I say something.
⁴Don't let me want to do evil
or waste my time doing wrong
with wicked people.
Don't let me even taste
the good things they offer.

141.2 *my prayer as . . . incense:* In Exodus 30.1, God instructs Moses to build an altar for burning incense, and Aaron is told to "burn sweet-smelling incense" each evening (Exod 30.7-8). Incense was made of frankincense, other gums and spices, and a seasoning of salt, which together produced a sweet smell when burned. The smoke from the burning incense represented the prayers that went up to God.

ᶠ**139.20** *you:* One possible meaning for the difficult Hebrew text of verse 20.　ᵍ**140.8,9** *or else . . . lies:* One possible meaning for the difficult Hebrew text.

142 (Title) *by David . . . cave:* David hid in caves to escape his enemies (1 Sam 22.1; 24.3).

David

143.3 *total darkness:* Since God and God's Word are described as "light," then "darkness" stands for evil and for times of deep despair.

⁵Let your faithful people
correct and punish me.
My prayers condemn the deeds
of those who do wrong,
so don't let me be friends
with any of them.
⁶Everyone will admit
that I was right
when their rulers are thrown
down a rocky cliff,
⁷and their bones lie scattered
like crushed rocks
on top of a grave.[h]

⁸You are my LORD and God,
and I look to you for safety.
Don't let me be harmed.
⁹Protect me from the traps
of those violent people,
¹⁰and make them fall
into their own traps
while you help me escape.

PSALM 142
(A special psalm and a prayer by David when he was in the cave.)

A Prayer for Help

¹I pray to you, LORD.
I beg for mercy.
²I tell you all my worries
and my troubles,
³and whenever I feel low,
you are there to guide me.

A trap has been hidden
along my pathway.
⁴Even if you look,
you won't see anyone
who cares enough
to walk beside me.
There is no place to hide,
and no one who really cares.

⁵I pray to you, LORD!
You are my place of safety,
and you are my choice
in the land of the living.
Please answer my prayer.
I am completely helpless.

⁶Help! They are chasing me,
and they are too strong.
⁷Rescue me from this prison,
so I can praise your name.
And when your people notice
your wonderful kindness to me,
they will rush to my side.

PSALM 143
(A psalm by David.)

A Prayer in Time of Danger

¹Listen, LORD, as I pray!
You are faithful and honest
and will answer my prayer.
²I am your servant.
Don't try me in your court,
because no one is innocent
by your standards.
³My enemies are chasing me,
crushing me in the ground.
I am in total darkness,
like someone long dead.
⁴I have given up hope,
and I feel numb all over.

⁵I remember to think about
the many things you did
in years gone by.
⁶Then I lift my hands in prayer,
because my soul is a desert,
thirsty for water from you.

⁷Please hurry, LORD,
and answer my prayer.
I feel hopeless.

[h]141.5-7 *Let . . . grave:* One possible meaning for the difficult Hebrew text of verses 5-7.

Don't turn away
and leave me here to die.
[8]Each morning let me learn
more about your love
because I trust you.
I come to you in prayer,
asking for your guidance.

[9]Please rescue me
from my enemies, LORD!
I come to you for safety.[i]
[10]You are my God. Show me
what you want me to do,
and let your gentle Spirit
lead me in the right path.

[11]Be true to your name, LORD,
and keep my life safe.
Use your saving power
to protect me from trouble.
[12]I am your servant.
Show how much you love me
by destroying my enemies.

PSALM 144
(By David.)
A Prayer for the Nation

[1]I praise you, LORD!
You are my mighty rock,[j]
and you teach me
how to fight my battles.
[2]You are my friend, my fortress,
where I am safe.
You are my shield,
and you made me the ruler
of our people.[k]

[3]Why do we humans mean anything
to you, our LORD?
Why do you care about us?

[4]We disappear like a breath;
we last no longer
than a faint shadow.

[5]Open the heavens like a curtain
and come down, LORD.
Touch the mountains
and make them send up smoke.
[6]Use your lightning as arrows
to scatter my enemies
and make them run away.
[7]Reach down from heaven
and set me free.
Save me from the mighty flood
[8]of those lying foreigners
who never tell the truth.

[9]In praise of you, our God,
I will sing a new song,
while playing my harp.
[10]By your power, kings win wars,
and your servant David is saved
from deadly swords.
[11]Won't you keep me safe
from those lying foreigners
who never tell the truth?

[12]Let's pray that our young sons
will grow like strong plants
and that our daughters
will be as lovely as columns
in the corner of a palace.
[13]May our barns be filled
with all kinds of crops.
May our fields be covered
with sheep by the thousands,
[14]   and every cow have calves.[l]
Don't let our city be captured
or any of us be taken away,
and don't let cries of sorrow
be heard in our streets.

144.1,2 *mighty rock . . . fortress:*
The beginning of Psalm 144 is like the beginning of Psalm 18. There are other similarities as well. Psalm 144 seems to be a new version of Psalm 18 that takes into account the end of the kingdom of David and his descendants.

144.3,4 *Why do we humans . . . We disappear:* The end of the kingdom of David called into question the meaning of life. Verse 3 recalls Psalm 8. Verse 4 recalls Psalm 89.

144.5-8 *Open . . . truth:* Verse 5 recalls 18.9; verse 6 recalls 18.14; and verses 7,8 recall 18.16-17,43-45. What Psalm 18 describes as God's actions on David's behalf, in Psalm 144 have become requests for God to act. This change suggests the new situation after the end of the kingdom of David. In this new situation, the "enemies" and "lying foreigners" are the nations that oppressed God's people during the exile and after their return.

144.10 *David is saved:* This verse recalls the title of Psalm 18.

144.12-14 *Let's pray . . . cries of sorrow:* This prayer for the nation looks back on the events of 586 B.C. when Jerusalem was "captured," many people were "taken away," and there was much "sorrow." The year 586 B.C. also marked the end of the kingdom of David. It is important that Psalm 144 ends with a prayer for and a promise to the nation. This suggests that it is the responsibility of the whole people to establish justice.

[i]143.9 *I . . . safety:* Or "You are my hiding place." [j]144.1 *mighty rock:* See the note at 18.2. [k]144.2 *of our people:* Some Hebrew manuscripts and ancient translations have "of the nations." [l]144.14 *have calves:* Or "grow fat."

145.11-13 *marvelous kingdom . . . rule forever:* The word "kingdom" appears three times. God's kingdom is where God "rules" and where God's will and purposes are carried out.

146.1 *Shout praises to the Lord:* Psalms 146–150 all begin and end with this line.

15Our Lord and our God,
  you give these blessings
    to all who worship you.

Psalm 145
(By David for praise.)
The Lord Is Kind and Merciful

1I will praise you,
  my God and King,
    and always honor your name.
2I will praise you each day
  and always honor your name.
3You are wonderful, Lord,
  and you deserve all praise,
    because you are much greater
      than anyone can understand.

4Each generation will announce
  to the next your wonderful
    and powerful deeds.
5I will keep thinking about
  your marvelous glory
    and your mighty miracles.m
6Everyone will talk about
  your fearsome deeds,
    and I will tell all nations
      how great you are.
7They will celebrate and sing
  about your matchless mercy
    and your power to save.

8You are merciful, Lord!
  You are kind and patient
    and always loving.
9You are good to everyone,
  and you take care
    of all your creation.

10All creation will thank you,
  and your loyal people

will praise you.
11They will tell about
  your marvelous kingdom
    and your power.
12Then everyone will know about
  the mighty things you do
    and your glorious kingdom.
13Your kingdom will never end,
  and you will rule forever.

Our Lord, you keep your word
  and do everything you say.n
14When someone stumbles or falls,
  you give a helping hand.
15Everyone depends on you,
  and when the time is right,
    you provide them with food.
16By your own hand you satisfy
  the desires of all who live.

17Our Lord, everything you do
  is kind and thoughtful,
18and you are near to everyone
  whose prayers are sincere.
19You satisfy the desires
  of all your worshipers,
    and you come to save them
      when they ask for help.
20You take care of everyone
  who loves you,
    but you destroy the wicked.

21I will praise you, Lord,
  and everyone will respect
    your holy name forever.

Psalm 146
Shout Praises to the Lord

1Shout praises to the Lord!
  With all that I am,

m145.5 *and . . . miracles:* One Hebrew manuscript and two ancient translations have "as others tell about your mighty miracles." n145.13 *Our . . . say:* These words are found in one Hebrew manuscript and two ancient translations.

You are merciful, Lord! You are kind and patient and always loving. You are good to everyone, and you take care of all your creation. Ps 145.8,9

I will shout his praises.
²I will sing and praise
the LORD God
as long as I live.

³You can't depend on anyone,
not even a great leader.
⁴Once they die and are buried,
that will be the end
of all their plans.

⁵The LORD God of Jacob blesses
everyone who trusts him
and depends on him.
⁶ God made heaven and earth;
he created the sea
and everything else.
God always keeps his word.
⁷He gives justice to the poor
and food to the hungry.

The LORD sets prisoners free
⁸ and heals blind eyes.
He gives a helping hand
to everyone who falls.
The LORD loves good people
⁹ and looks after strangers.
He defends the rights
of orphans and widows,
but destroys the wicked.

¹⁰The LORD God of Zion
will rule forever!
Shout praises to the LORD!

PSALM 147
Sing and Praise the LORD

¹Shout praises to the LORD!
Our God is kind,
and it is right and good
to sing praises to him.
²The LORD rebuilds Jerusalem
and brings the people of Israel

back home again.
³He renews our hopes
and heals our bodies.
⁴He decided how many stars
there would be in the sky
and gave each one a name.
⁵Our LORD is great and powerful!
He understands everything.
⁶The LORD helps the oppressed,
but he smears the wicked
in the dirt.

⁷Celebrate and sing!
Play your harps
for the LORD our God.
⁸He fills the sky with clouds
and sends rain to the earth,
so that the hills
will be green with grass.
⁹He provides food for cattle
and for the young ravens,
when they cry out.
¹⁰The LORD doesn't care about
the strength of horses
or powerful armies.
¹¹The LORD is pleased only
with those who worship him
and trust his love.

¹²Everyone in Jerusalem,
come and praise
the LORD your God!
¹³He makes your city gates strong
and blesses your people.
¹⁴God lets you live in peace,
and he gives you
the very best wheat.

¹⁵As soon as God speaks,
the earth obeys.
¹⁶He covers the ground with snow
like a blanket of wool,
and he scatters frost
like ashes on the ground.

■ 146.3 *can't depend on anyone:* This verse reflects the strong message of Israel's prophets and the Law that the people were to place their trust in the LORD God and not in earthly leaders, wealth, foreign powers, or idols. For example, see Exod 20.2-6; Isa 31.1-5; Hos 4.17-19; 14.1-3.

● 147.2,3 *rebuilds Jerusalem . . . renews our hopes:* These verses suggest that the psalm was written after the exile in Babylon was over. The people of Israel were allowed to return home after Cyrus of Persia defeated the Babylonians in 539 B.C.

Shout praises to the LORD! With all that I am, I will shout his praises. Ps 146.1

148.3,4 *Sun and moon . . . stars . . . water above:* Some of Israel's neighbors worshiped the sun, moon, and stars as gods. Here these heavenly bodies worship the God who created them. It was believed that the sky was a dome that covered the flat earth. Above the sky were heavenly waters. It was also believed that an ocean of water was under the earth. See Gen 1.6-10.

148.7-12 *All . . . praise the LORD:* These verses invite everyone and everything "on earth" to praise God as creator. The list recalls the parts of creation in Genesis 1,2. Because the LORD is "King" all earthly rulers will also praise and honor the LORD God.

148.14 *bull with mighty horns:* Bull horns were a symbol of power. Israel's altars had horns on them. A person accused of a crime punishable by death could run to an altar of the LORD for protection until proven guilty (Exod 21.14; 1 Kgs 1.50,51; Amos 3.14).

¹⁷God sends down hailstones
   like chips of rocks.
      Who can stand the cold?
¹⁸At his command the ice melts,
   the wind blows,
      and streams begin to flow.

¹⁹God gave his laws and teachings
   to the descendants of Jacob,
      the nation of Israel.
²⁰But he has not given his laws
   to any other nation.
      Shout praises to the LORD!

PSALM 148
Come Praise the LORD

¹Shout praises to the LORD!
   Shout the LORD's praises
      in the highest heavens.
²All of you angels,
   and all who serve him above,
      come and offer praise.

³Sun and moon,
   and all of you bright stars,
      come and offer praise.
⁴Highest heavens, and the water
   above the highest heavens,^o
      come and offer praise.

⁵Let all things praise
   the name of the LORD,
      because they were created
      at his command.
⁶He made them to last forever,
   and nothing can change
      what he has done.^P

⁷All creatures on earth,
   you obey his commands,
      so come praise the LORD!

⁸Sea monsters and the deep sea,
   fire and hail, snow and frost,
      and every stormy wind,
         come praise the LORD!

⁹All mountains and hills,
   fruit trees and cedars,
¹⁰every wild and tame animal,
   all reptiles and birds,
      come praise the LORD!

¹¹Every king and every ruler,
   all nations on earth,
¹²every man and every woman,
   young people and old,
      come praise the LORD!

¹³All creation, come praise
   the name of the LORD.
      Praise his name alone.
      The glory of God is greater
         than heaven and earth.

¹⁴Like a bull with mighty horns,
   the LORD protects
      his faithful nation Israel,
   because they belong to him.
      Shout praises to the LORD!

PSALM 149
A New Song of Praise

¹Shout praises to the LORD!
   Sing him a new song of praise
      when his loyal people meet.
²People of Israel, rejoice
   because of your Creator.
   People of Zion, celebrate
      because of your King.
³Praise his name by dancing
   and playing music on harps
      and tambourines.

^o**148.4** *the water . . . heavens:* It was believed that the earth and the heavens were surrounded by water. ^P**148.6** *nothing . . . done:* Or "his laws will never change."

⁴The Lord is pleased
  with his people,
and he gives victory
  to those who are humble.
⁵All of you faithful people,
  praise our glorious Lord!
    Celebrate and worship.
⁶Praise God with songs
  on your lips
    and a sword in your hand.
⁷Take revenge and punish
  the nations.
⁸Put chains of iron
  on their kings and rulers.
⁹Punish them as they deserve;
  this is the privilege
of God's faithful people.
  Shout praises to the Lord!

Psalm 150
The Lord Is Good to His People

¹Shout praises to the Lord!
  Praise God in his temple.

Praise him in heaven,
  his mighty fortress.
²Praise our God!
His deeds are wonderful,
  too marvelous to describe.

³Praise God with trumpets
  and all kinds of harps.
⁴Praise him with tambourines
  and dancing,
with stringed instruments
  and woodwinds.
⁵Praise God with cymbals,
  with clashing cymbals.
⁶Let every living creature
praise the Lord.
  Shout praises to the Lord!

● 150.3,4 *trumpets . . . harps . . . woodwinds:* Trumpets were used to welcome rulers and at festival times. "Stringed instruments" probably refers to the lyre. "Woodwinds" probably meant some kind of wooden flute.

■ 150.6 *every living creature:* The full orchestra of musical instruments is to be joined by a full choir of voices, as "-every living creature" joins the song of praise. There is no better way to express the message that is found throughout Psalms—God, the creator and ruler of the world, deserves the praise of everything and everybody.

Reflection Questions About Psalms 1.1—150.6

1. A number of psalms in "Book I" are prayers for help (for example, Psalms 3; 5; 10; 13; 28; 35; 38). In what situations do the psalmists ask for God's help? What "enemies" oppose God and God's people? How can the psalms help people today deal with opposition and trouble?

2. In many prayers for help, the psalmists ask God to punish or destroy their enemies (3.7; 5.10; 10.15; 28.4; 35.4-6,8; 41.10). How are these prayers more than simple requests for personal revenge? What do you make of the fact that God opposes evil, but evil still exists?

3. The "titles" of many psalms (51; 52; 54; 56; 57; 59; 60; and 63) mention David and things that happened in David's life. What do many of these events have in common? What do these "titles" add to the meaning of the psalms?

4. Read Psalm 63 again (see also 57.1). What does it mean when the psalmist says to God that he finds help "in the shadow of your wings"?

5. Read Psalm 82 again. What are "the other gods" that are mentioned in verse 1? How does God's purpose differ from the behavior of the gods? How do people today sometimes worship what might be called "other gods?"

6. According to a number of psalms in Psalms 90 to 106 (93; 95–99), God is King. What sort of things does a king typically do for the people he rules? What sort of things does a king have a right to expect from his people? In what ways does God rule your life? How do you honor him in return?

7. What are some common ideas found in the collection of psalms made up of Psalms 120 through 134? How were these psalms probably used in ancient times? What ideas found in these psalms may be important for people today?

8. Read Psalms 140 and 142 again. What situations might have prompted these prayers for help? Our world today has its share of brutality, violence, and loneliness. How can "prayers for help" make a difference in dealing with such things?

9. Read Psalms 148 and 150 again. How are they alike? Why is it important that these psalms invite not only people but also "every living creature" (150.6) and "All creation" (148.13) to praise God?

10. What images of God stand out for you in PSALMS? Name at least three important themes you discovered in your reading and study of PSALMS. Do these themes affect your life and your faith? If so, how?

proverbs

Where does wisdom come from? How can a person be truly "wise"? Read PROVERBS *to discover the answer to these questions and much more.*

WHAT MAKES PROVERBS SPECIAL?

PROVERBS was originally included in that part of Hebrew Scriptures known as the Writings, which contains other "wisdom" books such as ECCLESIASTES and JOB. Along with SONG OF SONGS and ECCLESIASTES, PROVERBS has traditionally been credited to Israel's wise king Solomon. Like other wisdom books, PROVERBS says little about the history, laws, or religious life of Israel. Instead it provides a picture of the kind of practical teaching and instruction done in families, schools, and the royal palace.

WHAT'S THE STORY BEHIND THE SCENE?

PROVERBS is said to be a collection of wise sayings—primarily from Israel's King Solomon (1.1; 10.1; 25.1), though other authors are quoted as well. The collection as we have it now probably was edited and put in its final form between 300 and 400 years after Solomon died.

A number of wise sayings probably came from a group known as Israel's "wise people" (Jer 18.18). They were teachers of practical wisdom and were familiar with similar kinds of wisdom writings found in the literature of Israel's neighbors.

The wise sayings in PROVERBS share a view of wisdom commonly held in the ancient world, but they differ from other wisdom literature of the day on the key point of where wisdom comes from. PROVERBS states that wisdom comes from the LORD God, and was with the LORD at the beginning of time (8.22-31).

HOW IS PROVERBS CONSTRUCTED?

The first nine chapters of PROVERBS have a number of short two-line sayings or "truth statements" and include instructions of a parent to a child. Wisdom is pictured as a "woman" who invites all to live according to good sense and sound judgment (8.1—9.6). The wise sayings in Proverbs 10.1—22.16 are credited to Solomon (10.1). Thirty wise sayings credited to an unknown group of wise people (22.17—24.22) and further sayings of an unknown author (24.23-34) form another section. These are followed by a group of proverbs (25.1—29.27) credited to Solomon but copied in the time of Judah's King Hezekiah (715–687 B.C.). The final two chapters provide wise sayings of Agur (30.1) and the mother of King Lemuel (31.1). The final section (31.10-31) has been described as the book's ending (epilogue). It is an acrostic poem, which means the first word of each verse begins with a different letter of the Hebrew alphabet.

PROVERBS can be outlined in the following way:

Wisdom, advice, and instruction (1–9)
    Introduction (1.1-7)
    Seek wisdom and run away from foolishness
    (1.8—7.27)
    Wisdom's invitation to find life (8,9)
Many of Solomon's wise sayings (10.1—22.16)
Sayings of people with wisdom (22.17—24.34)
Solomon's proverbs copied by Hezekiah (25–29)
The wise sayings of Agur and of Lemuel's Mother
    (30,31)

ike Job and Ecclesiastes, Proverbs is among the major works of Jewish Wisdom literature, a type of writing which tries to show God's order in the universe, and help people live according to God's plan. The book is a collection of instructional material and wise sayings from many periods of Israel's history. Many sections of the book offer practical moral advice to help people build character, develop qualities of leadership, foster healthy family life, and keep a good reputation in the community. Above all, Proverbs teaches the importance of wisdom and the value of staying away from foolish or evil actions. Those with wise attitudes will experience a full life and live in ways that show their deep respect for the Lord. People with evil or foolish attitudes will be led to death and destruction. Wisdom is shown as God's gift to the faithful, a guide to help people understand and follow the Lord.

Outline

How Proverbs Can Be Used

1 These are the proverbs
of King Solomon of Israel,
the son of David.
²Proverbs will teach you
wisdom and self-control
and how to understand
sayings with deep meanings.
³You will learn what is right
and honest and fair.
⁴From these, an ordinary person
can learn to be smart,
and young people can gain
knowledge and good sense.

⁵If you are already wise,
you will become even wiser.
And if you are smart,
you will learn to understand
⁶ proverbs and sayings,
as well as words of wisdom,
and all kinds of riddles.

⁷Respect and obey the LORD!
This is the beginning
of knowledge.^a
Only a fool rejects wisdom
and good advice.

Warnings against Bad Friends

⁸My child, obey the teachings
of your parents,
⁹and wear their teachings
as you would a pretty hat
or a lovely necklace.
¹⁰Don't be tempted by sinners
or listen ¹¹when they say,
"Come on! Let's gang up
and kill somebody,
just for the fun of it!
¹²They're well and healthy now,
but we'll finish them off
once and for all.
¹³We'll take their valuables
and fill our homes

^a**1.7** *the beginning of knowledge*: Or "what knowledge is all about."

1.1 *proverbs*: Ancient proverbs are usually short statements that give advice or express some truth about human behavior. **(See the chart Kinds of Proverbs on pg 1834.)**

◌ℛ   Solomon

◌ℛ   David

◌ℛ   Wisdom

1.3 *what is right . . . fair*: What is "right" means what is acceptable to God. According to Israel's Law and Prophets, those who do what is right are living according to God's commands. Right living includes treating others with justice and fairness.

◌ℛ   Justice

1.7 *Respect and obey the LORD*: Wisdom and common sense were important in all ancient cultures. In PROVERBS, wisdom is seen as directly related to the LORD's instruction. The truly wise person is the one who worships and honors the LORD and lives according to the LORD's commands.

◌ℛ   LORD (YHWH)

1.8,9 *My child, obey . . . wear their teachings*: Wisdom is passed to the young by older generations, especially from parent to child.

1.10 *sinners*: Those who turn their backs on God or refuse to obey God's teachings. Such people are often called "fools" in PROVERBS, because their sins lead to death (1.32; 9.13-18).

1.17 *a bird . . . trap:* Birds and small animals were often caught in traps made of netting. These were especially effective in capturing waterfowl that nested in marshes. Foolish or evil people are often compared to animals blindly walking into traps (7.23; Eccl 9.12).

1.21 *marketplaces . . . city gates:* These are places in ancient cities where large crowds were most likely to gather. City leaders judged court cases and made important decisions next to the city gates.

1.31,32 *eat the fruit . . . death to stupid fools:* Those who reject Wisdom's warnings and advice will get what they deserve—destruction and death. Those who listen to Wisdom will be safe and live a happy life.

with stolen goods.
¹⁴If you join our gang,
   you'll get your share."

¹⁵Don't follow anyone like that
   or do what they do.
¹⁶They are in a big hurry
   to commit some crime,
      perhaps even murder.
¹⁷They are like a bird
   that sees the bait,
      but ignores the trap.^b
¹⁸They gang up to murder someone,
   but they are the victims.
¹⁹The wealth you get from crime
   robs you of your life.

Wisdom Speaks

²⁰ Wisdom^c shouts in the streets
   wherever crowds gather.
²¹She shouts in the marketplaces
   and near the city gates
      as she says to the people,
²²"How much longer
will you enjoy
   being stupid fools?
Won't you ever stop sneering
   and laughing at knowledge?
²³Listen as I correct you
   and tell you what I think.
²⁴You completely ignored me
   and refused to listen;
²⁵you rejected my advice
   and paid no attention
      when I warned you.

²⁶"So when you are struck
   by some terrible disaster,
²⁷or when trouble and distress

surround you like a whirlwind,
   I will laugh and make fun.
²⁸You will ask for my help,
   but I won't listen;
you will search,
   but you won't find me.
²⁹No, you would not learn,
   and you refused
      to respect the Lord.
³⁰You rejected my advice
   and paid no attention
      when I warned you.

³¹"Now you will eat the fruit
   of what you have done,
until you are stuffed full
   with your own schemes.
³²Sin and self-satisfaction
   bring destruction and death
      to stupid fools.
³³But if you listen to me,
   you will be safe and secure
      without fear of disaster."

Wisdom and Bad Friends

2 My child, you must follow
   and treasure my teachings
      and my instructions.
²Keep in tune with wisdom
   and think what it means
      to have common sense.
³Beg as loud as you can
   for good common sense.
⁴Search for wisdom
   as you would search for silver
      or hidden treasure.
⁵Then you will understand
   what it means to respect
      and to know the Lord God.

^b**1.17** *They are . . . trap:* Or "Be like a bird that won't go for the bait, if it sees the trap."
^c**1.20** *Wisdom:* In the book of Proverbs the word "wisdom" is sometimes used as though wisdom were a supernatural being who was with God at the time of creation.

⁶All wisdom comes from the Lord,
and so do common sense
and understanding.
⁷God gives helpful advice^d
to everyone who obeys him
and protects those
who live as they should.
⁸God sees that justice is done,
and he watches over everyone
who is faithful to him.
⁹With wisdom you will learn
what is right
and honest and fair.

¹⁰Wisdom will control your mind,
and you will be pleased
with knowledge.
¹¹Sound judgment and good sense
will watch over you.
¹²Wisdom will protect you
from evil schemes
and from those liars
¹³who turned from doing good
to live in the darkness.
¹⁴Most of all they enjoy
being mean and deceitful.
¹⁵They are dishonest themselves,
and so are all their deeds.

Wisdom and Sexual Purity

¹⁶Wisdom will protect you
from the smooth talk
of a sinful woman,
¹⁷who breaks her wedding vows
and leaves the man she married
when she was young.
¹⁸The road to her house leads
down to the dark world
of the dead.
¹⁹Visit her, and you will never
find the road to life again.

^d2.7 *helpful advice*: Or "wisdom."

²⁰Follow the example
of good people
and live an honest life.
²¹If you are honest and innocent,
you will keep your land;
²²if you do wrong
and can never be trusted,
you will be rooted out.

Trust God

3 My child, remember
my teachings and instructions
and obey them completely.
²They will help you live
a long and prosperous life.
³Let love and loyalty
always show like a necklace,
and write them in your mind.
⁴God and people will like you
and hold you in high esteem.

⁵With all your heart
you must trust the Lord
and not your own judgment.
⁶Always let him lead you,
and he will clear the road
for you to follow.
⁷Don't ever think that you
are wise enough,
but respect the Lord
and stay away from evil.
⁸This will make you healthy,
and you will feel strong.
⁹Honor the Lord by giving him
your money and the first part
of all your crops.
¹⁰Then you will have
more grain and grapes
than you will ever need.

¹¹My child, don't turn away
or become bitter

2.7 *God gives helpful advice . . . protects:* People are encouraged to search for wisdom, and those who obey its teachings will be protected by the Lord.

2.13 *live in the darkness:* In the ancient world, the night was an especially frightening time. So, darkness often is used in the Bible to describe evil, stupidity, or death. Compare this to the life of good (wise) people, whose lifestyle is like sunlight, and to the Law of the Lord, which is like a lamp.

2.16,17 *sinful woman, who breaks her wedding vows:* Having sex with an unfaithful woman (adulteress) is often used in the Bible as a symbol for being unfaithful to the Lord (Ezek 23; Hos 1.2; Mal 2.10-16).

2.21,22 *keep your land . . . rooted out:* This may simply refer to losing one's blessings (including land and possessions) because of foolish actions. It could also refer to Israel's being able to keep the land that the Lord had given them (Canaan). The people were warned that being disobedient or unfaithful to the Lord might cause them to lose the land (Deut 28.63).

3.6 *clear the road for you to follow:* Being wise and obeying the Lord's teachings is often described as taking the right road (4.10,11; 15.19,24; Ps 143.10).

3.14-18 *Wisdom . . . life-giving tree:* These verses are a hymn that summarizes the benefits of Wisdom—long life, wealth, honor, safety, and happiness. Life-giving trees are a symbol of the LORD's blessing (Gen 2.9; Ezek 47.12; Rev 22.2). Those who follow the LORD's Law are also described as trees growing beside a stream (Ps 1.1-3).

3.20 *ocean break loose . . . rain:* The ancient Israelites believed the earth was flat. Under the earth was a huge ocean, and over the earth was a solid dome ("sky") that held back the flood of water above. Rain and snow were said to fall when God opened windows in the sky (Gen 7.11,12; Ps 78.23). God's wisdom is compared to water, which is essential for sustaining life.

3.33-35 *curse . . . blesses . . . praised . . . disgraced:* This is a series of three sayings comparing positive and negative. The LORD will bless the home of the one who is wise but curse the home of the evil or foolish person. A wise person who is humble will be praised by neighbors, but the fool who sneers at the LORD will end up being disgraced.

when the LORD corrects you.
12The LORD corrects
    everyone he loves,
just as parents correct
    a child they dearly love.

The Value of Wisdom

13God blesses everyone
    who has wisdom
    and common sense.
14Wisdom is worth more
    than silver;
it makes you much richer
    than gold.
15Wisdom is more valuable
    than precious jewels;
nothing you want
    compares with her.

16In her right hand
    Wisdom holds a long life,
and in her left hand
    are wealth and honor.
17Wisdom makes life pleasant
    and leads us safely along.
18Wisdom is a life-giving tree,
    the source of happiness
    for all who hold on to her.

19By his wisdom and knowledge
    the LORD created
    heaven and earth.
20By his understanding
    he let the ocean break loose
    and clouds release the rain.
21My child, use common sense
    and sound judgment!
    Always keep them in mind.
22They will help you to live
    a long and beautiful life.
23You will walk safely
    and never stumble;
24you will rest without a worry

and sleep soundly.
25So don't be afraid
    of sudden disasters
or storms that strike
    those who are evil.
26You can be sure that the LORD
    will protect you from harm.

27Do all you can for everyone
    who deserves your help.
28Don't tell your neighbor
    to come back tomorrow,
    if you can help today.
29Don't try to be mean
    to neighbors who trust you.
30Don't argue just to be arguing,
    when you haven't been hurt.
31Don't be jealous
    of cruel people
    or follow their example.

32The LORD doesn't like
    anyone who is dishonest,
but he lets good people
    be his friends.
33He places a curse on the home
    of everyone who is evil,
but he blesses the home
    of every good person.
34 The LORD sneers at those
    who sneer at him,
but he is kind to everyone
    who is humble.
35You will be praised
    if you are wise,
but you will be disgraced
    if you are a stubborn fool.

Advice to Young People

4 My child, listen closely
    to my teachings
    and learn common sense.
2My advice is useful,

so don't turn away.
³When I was still very young
and my mother's favorite child,
my father ⁴said to me:
"If you follow my teachings
and keep them in mind,
you will live.
⁵Be wise and learn good sense;
remember my teachings
and do what I say.

⁶If you love Wisdom
and don't reject her,
she will watch over you.
⁷The best thing about Wisdom
is Wisdom herself;
good sense is more important
than anything else.
⁸If you value Wisdom
and hold tightly to her,
great honors will be yours.
⁹It will be like wearing
a glorious crown
of beautiful flowers.

The Right Way and the Wrong Way

¹⁰My child, if you listen
and obey my teachings,
you will live a long time.
¹¹I have shown you the way
that makes sense;
I have guided you
along the right path.
¹²Your road won't be blocked,
and you won't stumble
when you run.
¹³Hold firmly to my teaching
and never let go.
It will mean life for you.
¹⁴Don't follow the bad example
of cruel and evil people.
¹⁵Turn aside and keep going.
Stay away from them.

¹⁶They can't sleep or rest
until they do wrong or harm
some innocent victim.
¹⁷Their food and drink
are cruelty and wickedness.

¹⁸The lifestyle of good people
is like sunlight at dawn
that keeps getting brighter
until broad daylight.
¹⁹The lifestyle of the wicked
is like total darkness,
and they will never know
what makes them stumble.

²⁰My child, listen carefully
to everything I say.
²¹Don't forget a single word,
but think about it all.
²²Knowing these teachings
will mean true life
and good health for you.
²³Carefully guard your thoughts
because they are the source
of true life.
²⁴Never tell lies or be deceitful
in what you say.
²⁵Keep looking straight ahead,
without turning aside.
²⁶ Know where you are headed,
and you will stay
on solid ground.
²⁷Don't make a mistake by turning
to the right or the left.

Be Faithful to Your Wife

5 My son, if you listen closely
to my wisdom and good sense,
²you will have sound judgment,
and you will always know
the right thing to say.
³The words of an immoral woman
may be as sweet as honey

4.6 *love Wisdom:* Loving Wisdom, like faithfully obeying the LORD's teachings, is compared to the committed love of a husband for his wife.

4.17 *food and drink are cruelty and wickedness:* In the Bible, drinking from the LORD's cup of anger means experiencing God's judgment and punishment (Job 21.20; Ps 60.3; Isa 51.22; Rev 14.10). On the other hand, those who eat Wisdom's feast will live (9.1-6).

4.25 *Keep looking straight ahead:* Another way of saying "stay on the right road."

5.5 *world of the dead:* Sheol, the dark underground world of the dead, where the souls of the dead were thought to go (Job 30.23; Ps 139.7,8; Ezek 31.16-18; Acts 2.27). Sheol is usually described as being a totally silent place where no one knows or feels anything (Ps 88.12; 94.17).

5.10 *Strangers:* Being unable to pass one's wealth to family members was considered a great tragedy (Eccl 5.13-16). Losing wealth to foreigners is a symbol for the Israelite people giving up their customs and worship for the customs of other nations and the worship of foreign gods.

5.15-18 *your own well . . . the wife you married:* Taking water from another person's well was a serious crime.

6.1-3 *pay the debt . . . call off the agreement:* These verses warn against co-signing a loan, meaning promising to pay off someone else's debt. This is dangerous, because the person who does this may lose his own money or may have to become the lender's slave.

and as smooth as olive oil.
⁴But all that you really get
  from being with her
  is bitter poison and pain.
⁵If you follow her,
  she will lead you down
    to the world of the dead.
⁶She has missed the path
  that leads to life
    and doesn't even know it.

⁷My son, listen to me
  and do everything I say.
⁸Stay away from a bad woman!
  Don't even go near the door
    of her house.
⁹You will lose your self-respect
  and end up in debt
  to some cruel person
    for the rest of your life.
¹⁰Strangers will get your money
  and everything else
    you have worked for.
¹¹When it's all over,
  your body will waste away,
    as you groan ¹²and shout,
  "I hated advice and correction!
¹³I paid no attention
    to my teachers,
¹⁴and now I am disgraced
    in front of everyone."

¹⁵You should be faithful
    to your wife,
  just as you take water
    from your own well.ᵉ
¹⁶And don't be like a stream
  from which just any woman
    may take a drink.
¹⁷Save yourself for your wife
  and don't have sex
    with other women.

¹⁸Be happy with the wife
  you married
    when you were young.
¹⁹She is beautiful and graceful,
    just like a deer;
  you should be attracted to her
    and stay deeply in love.

²⁰Don't go crazy over a woman
  who is unfaithful
    to her own husband!
²¹The LORD sees everything,
  and he watches us closely.
²²Sinners are trapped and caught
  by their own evil deeds.
²³They get lost and die
  because of their foolishness
    and lack of self-control.

Don't Be Foolish

6 My child, suppose you agree
  to pay the debt of someone,
    who cannot repay a loan.
²Then you are trapped
  by your own words,
³and you are now in the power
    of someone else.
  Here is what you should do:
  Go and beg for permission
    to call off the agreement.
⁴Do this before you fall asleep
    or even get sleepy.
⁵Save yourself, just as a deer
  or a bird tries to escape
    from a hunter.

⁶You lazy people can learn
  by watching an anthill.
⁷Ants don't have leaders,
⁸but they store up food
    during harvest season.

ᵉ**5.15** *own well:* In biblical times water was scarce and wells were carefully guarded.

[9]How long will you lie there
doing nothing at all?
When are you going to get up
and stop sleeping?
[10]Sleep a little. Doze a little.
Fold your hands
and twiddle your thumbs.
[11]Suddenly, everything is gone,
as though it had been taken
by an armed robber.

[12]Worthless liars go around
[13]winking and giving signals
to deceive others.
[14]They are always thinking up
something cruel and evil,
and they stir up trouble.
[15]But they will be struck
by sudden disaster
and left without a hope.

[16]There are six or seven
kinds of people
the LORD doesn't like:
[17]Those who are too proud
or tell lies or murder,
[18]those who make evil plans
or are quick to do wrong,
[19]those who tell lies in court
or stir up trouble
in a family.

[20]Obey the teaching
of your parents—
[21]always keep it in mind
and never forget it.
[22]Their teaching will guide you
when you walk,
protect you when you sleep,
and talk to you
when you are awake.

[23]The Law of the Lord is a lamp,
and its teachings
shine brightly.
Correction and self-control
will lead you through life.
[24]They will protect you
from the flattering words
of someone else's wife.[f]
[25]Don't let yourself be attracted
by the charm and lovely eyes
of someone like that.
[26]A woman who sells her love
can be bought for as little
as the price of a meal.
But making love
to another man's wife
will cost you everything.
[27]If you carry burning coals,
you burn your clothes;
[28]if you step on hot coals,
you burn your feet.
[29]And if you go to bed
with another man's wife,
you pay the price.

[30]We don't put up with thieves,
not even[g] with one who steals
for something to eat.
[31]And thieves who get caught
must pay back
seven times what was stolen
and lose everything.
[32]But if you go to bed
with another man's wife,
you will destroy yourself
by your own stupidity.
[33]You will be beaten
and forever disgraced,
[34]because a jealous husband
can be furious and merciless
when he takes revenge.

[f]6.24 someone else's wife: Or "an evil woman."   [g]6.30 not even: Or "except."

■ 6.10,11 twiddle your thumbs . . . everything is gone: This is a warning about being lazy or careless about work that needs to be done In contrast, hard work will be rewarded (12.11; 28.19).

■ 6.12,13 Worthless liars . . . winking and giving signals: This may refer to the deceitful attitude of liars and cheaters, or to specific hand or eye signals that business partners used to cheat a customer.

■ 6.23 Law: The Law of the LORD refers to the commandments and laws given to Moses and the people. The word translated here as "Law" could also refer to the command of a parent.

Law

● 6.26 sells her love . . . cost you everything: Having sex with another person's wife or husband was punishable by death (Lev 20.10). Jewish society was built on a man being able to pass on his inheritance to his children by his legal wife. If she had sex with another man, she might get pregnant, and her husband might end up passing on part of his inheritance to a child that was not really his.

Prostitution in the Bible

● 6.31 must pay back seven times: The number "seven" stood for completeness. Here, seven is meant to symbolize full repayment, since the Law said a thief was to pay back no more than five times what he or she had stolen (Exod 22.1-9).

7.4,5 *wisdom be your sister . . . someone else's wife:* The Hebrew word translated here as "sister" may refer to a lover or bride rather than a biological sister. Those who have a close, intimate relationship with wisdom will not be tempted to chase after "another woman."

7.14 *offer a sacrifice . . . meat left over:* The sacrifice offered may have been given as part of an ancient Canaanite fertility ritual. That would mean that the woman's invitation also includes eating meat offered to an idol. More likely the leftover meat is from a regular sacrifice to ask the LORD's blessing (Lev 7.11-36). Depending on the kind of sacrifice, the meat had to be eaten the same day (Lev 7.15) or by the end of the day after the sacrifice (7.16-18).

7.16,17 *bright-colored cloth . . . myrrh, aloes:* The cloth is expensive linen, a fine cloth woven out of the dried fibers of the flax plant. Egyptian linen was considered very valuable (Ezek 27.7). Myrrh and aloes had to be imported to Israel, so they were expensive. (See the chart Spices and Perfumes on pg 1835.)

7.22 *ox:* This large animal was used for heavy work, such as plowing fields and pulling carts. They were also slaughtered and used for food.

³⁵He won't let you pay him off,
  no matter what you offer.

The Foolishness of Unfaithfulness

7 My son, pay close attention
  and don't forget
    what I tell you to do.
²Obey me, and you will live!
  Let my instructions be
    your greatest treasure.
³Keep them at your fingertips
  and write them
    in your mind.
⁴Let wisdom be your sister
  and make common sense
    your closest friend.
⁵They will protect you
  from the flattering words
    of someone else's wife.

⁶From the window of my house,
  I once happened to see
⁷ some foolish young men.
⁸It was late in the evening,
  sometime after dark.
⁹One of these young men
  turned the corner
    and was walking by the house
    of an unfaithful wife.
¹⁰She was dressed fancy
  like a woman of the street
    with only one thing in mind.
¹¹She was one of those women
  who are loud and restless
    and never stay at home,
¹²who walk street after street,
  waiting to trap a man.

¹³She grabbed him and kissed him,
  and with no sense of shame,
    she said:
¹⁴"I had to offer a sacrifice,
  and there is enough meat

left over for a feast.
¹⁵So I came looking for you,
  and here you are!
¹⁶The sheets on my bed
  are bright-colored cloth
    from Egypt.
¹⁷And I have covered it
  with perfume made of myrrh,
    aloes, and cinnamon.

¹⁸"Let's go there
  and make love all night.
¹⁹My husband is traveling,
  and he's far away.
²⁰He took a lot of money along,
  and he won't be back home
    before the middle
    of the month."

²¹And so, she tricked him
  with all of her sweet talk
    and her flattery.
²²At once he followed her
  like an ox on the way
    to be slaughtered,
    or like a fool on the way
  to be punished^h
²³ and killed with arrows.
  He was no more than a bird
    rushing into a trap,
  without knowing
    it would cost him his life.

²⁴My son, pay close attention
  to what I have said.
²⁵Don't even think about
    that kind of woman
  or let yourself be misled
    by someone like her.
²⁶Such a woman has caused
  the downfall and destruction
    of a lot of men.
²⁷Her house is a one-way street

^h7.22 *a fool . . . punished:* One possible meaning for the difficult Hebrew text.

leading straight down
   to the world of the dead.

In Praise of Wisdom

8 With great understanding,
      Wisdom[i] is calling out
²as she stands at the crossroads
   and on every hill.
³She stands by the city gate
   where everyone enters the city,
      and she shouts:
⁴"I am calling out
   to each one of you!
⁵Good sense and sound judgment
   can be yours.
⁶Listen, because what I say
   is worthwhile and right.
⁷I always speak the truth
   and refuse to tell a lie.
⁸Every word I speak is honest,
   not one is misleading
      or deceptive.

⁹"If you have understanding,
   you will see that my words
      are just what you need.
¹⁰Let instruction and knowledge
   mean more to you than silver
      or the finest gold.
¹¹Wisdom is worth much more
   than precious jewels
      or anything else you desire."

Wisdom Speaks

¹²I am Wisdom[j]—Common Sense
   is my closest friend;
I possess knowledge
   and sound judgment.

¹³If you respect the LORD,
   you will hate evil.
I hate pride and conceit
   and deceitful lies.
¹⁴I am strong, and I offer
   sensible advice
      and sound judgment.
¹⁵By my power kings govern,
   and rulers make laws
      that are fair.
¹⁶Every honest leader rules
   with help from me.

¹⁷I love everyone who loves me,
   and I will be found by all
      who honestly search.
¹⁸I can make you rich and famous,
   important and successful.
¹⁹What you receive from me
   is more valuable
than even the finest gold
   or the purest silver.
²⁰I always do what is right,
²¹and I give great riches
   to everyone who loves me.

²²From the beginning,
   I was with the LORD.[k]
I was there before he began
²³   to create the earth.
At the very first,
   the LORD gave life to[l] me.
²⁴When I was born,
   there were no oceans
      or springs of water.
²⁵My birth was before
   mountains were formed
      or hills were put in place.
²⁶It happened long before God
   had made the earth

i**8.1** *Wisdom:* See the note at 1.20.   j**8.12** *Wisdom:* See the note at 1.20.   k**8.22** *From the beginning . . . with the* LORD: Or "In the very beginning, the LORD created me."   l**8.23** *gave life to:* Or "formed."

"*Wisdom is worth much more than precious jewels or anything else you desire.*" PROV 8.11

8.32-34 *Pay attention, my children . . . Come to my home:* Wisdom continues the invitation that began in Proverbs 8.1, but this time Wisdom uses the same words that have been used by human parents instructing their children. Wisdom's house is a place to find happiness and blessing, in contrast to the house of the bad woman, which leads to death.

9.1 *seven columns:* The seven columns may be a reference to the foundation or pillars that the LORD God in wisdom built at creation. On the other hand, because seven was considered a perfect or complete number, this may mean that Wisdom's house is perfect, unlike the house of Stupidity (9.14).

9.2 *Her feast:* The food of Wisdom is life-giving and provides strength for right living.

9.6 *your foolishness:* This includes laughing at knowledge (1.22); self-satisfaction (1.32); refusing to respect and obey the LORD (2.7); following an immoral woman (5.3-6; 7.6-23); and making evil plans, including stirring up trouble in a family (6.18,19).

9.10 *Holy God:* This title describes how God is set apart from human beings and how God's wisdom is far greater than human understanding. Israel's LORD was also a personal God who chose them (Isa 41.8,9) and lived among them (Exod 25.18-22; 1 Kgs 8.6-13; Isa 6.1-8).

or any of its fields
or even the dust.

^{27}I was there when the LORD
put the heavens in place
and stretched the sky
over the surface of the sea.
^{28}I was with him when he placed
the clouds in the sky
and created the springs
that fill the ocean.
^{29}I was there when he set
boundaries for the sea
to make it obey him,
and when he laid foundations
to support the earth.

^{30}I was right beside the LORD,
helping him plan and build.^{m}
I made him happy each day,
and I was happy at his side.
^{31}I was pleased with his world
and pleased with its people.

^{32} Pay attention, my children!
Follow my advice,
and you will be happy.
^{33}Listen carefully
to my instructions,
and you will be wise.

^{34}Come to my home each day
and listen to me.
You will find happiness.
^{35}By finding me, you find life,
and the LORD will be pleased
with you.
^{36}But if you don't find me,
you hurt only yourself,
and if you hate me,
you are in love with death.

Wisdom Gives a Feast

9 Wisdom has built her house
with its seven columns.
^{2}She has prepared the meat
and set out the wine.
Her feast is ready.

^{3}She has sent her servant women
to announce her invitation
from the highest hills:
^{4}"Everyone who is ignorant
or foolish is invited!
^{5}All of you are welcome
to my meat and wine.
^{6}If you want to live,
give up your foolishness
and let understanding
guide your steps."

True Wisdom

^{7}Correct a worthless bragger,
and all you will get
are insults and injuries.
^{8}Any bragger you correct
will only hate you.
But if you correct someone
who has common sense,
you will be loved.
^{9}If you have good sense,
instruction will help you
to have even better sense.
And if you live right,
education will help you
to know even more.

^{10}Respect and obey the LORD!
This is the beginning
of wisdom.^{n}
To have understanding,
you must know the Holy God.

^{m}**8.30** *helping . . . build:* Or "like his own child." ^{n}**9.10** *the beginning of wisdom:* Or "what wisdom is all about."

¹¹I am Wisdom. If you follow me,
you will live a long time.
¹²Good sense is good for you,
but if you brag,
you hurt yourself.

A Foolish Invitation

¹³Stupidity^o is reckless,
senseless, and foolish.
¹⁴She sits in front of her house
and on the highest hills
in the town.
¹⁵She shouts to everyone
who passes by,
¹⁶"If you are stupid,
come on inside!"
And to every fool she says,
¹⁷ "Stolen water tastes best,
and the food you eat in secret
tastes best of all."
¹⁸None who listen to Stupidity
understand that her guests
are as good as dead.

Solomon's Wise Sayings

10 Here are some proverbs
of Solomon:
Children with good sense
make their parents happy,
but foolish children
make them sad.
²What you gain by doing evil
won't help you at all.
Obeying God is the only way
to be saved from death.

³If you obey the LORD,
you won't go hungry;
if you are wicked,

God won't let you have
what you want.
⁴Laziness leads to poverty;
hard work makes you rich.
⁵At harvest season
it's smart to work hard,
but stupid to sleep.

⁶Everyone praises good people,
but evil hides behind
the words of the wicked.
⁷Good people are remembered
long after they are gone,
but the wicked
are soon forgotten.

⁸If you have good sense,
you will listen and obey;
if all you do is talk foolishly,
you will destroy yourself.
⁹You will be safe,
if you always do right,
but you will get caught,
if you are dishonest.
¹⁰Deceit causes trouble,
and foolish talk
will bring you to ruin.^P
¹¹The words of good people
are a source of life,
but evil hides behind
the words of the wicked.

¹²Hatred stirs up trouble;
love overlooks the wrongs
that others do.
¹³If you have good sense,
it will show when you speak.
But if you are stupid,
you will be beaten
with a stick.
¹⁴If you have good sense,

9.13-18 *Stupidity . . . sits in front of her house . . . her guests are . . . dead:* Like Wisdom, Stupidity invites people into her house to eat her food, her foolish or evil actions.

10.4 *Laziness:* Many proverbs praise effort but condemn laziness.

10.5 *harvest season:* Crops, fruits, and vegetables need to be picked when they are ripe, so harvest time is a very busy time. If crops are not picked in time, they will become too ripe to store or eat.

10.7 *are remembered:* Having a good reputation is highly prized in Hebrew wisdom.

10.8-14 *if all you do is talk . . . foolish talk:* This group of sayings draws attention to the foolishness of pointless or evil talk. Words have the power to be a source of good or evil. Good words spoken wisely show a person has good sense, but wicked words may lead to the speaker's punishment.

^o**9.13** *Stupidity:* Or "A foolish woman." **P10.10** *and foolish . . . ruin:* One ancient translation "but you can help people by correcting them."

10.15,16 *wealth . . . poverty . . . reward:* Wealth was considered a blessing or reward for good living.

10.17 *Accept correction:* This may refer to the LORD's correction, but more likely refers to parental instruction or wise teaching.

11.1 *cheats . . . honest:* In the Hebrew, this verse refers to the use of false and true balances when weighing goods to be bought or sold. Some merchants and traders used incorrect weights and balances to cheat people.

11.2 *pride . . . humble:* Pride is dangerous. It can cause a person to mock the LORD (3.34), disregard the LORD's commands, or trust in wealth (16.18,19) or one's own power instead of trusting in God (Isa 14.11-14). Being humble and being wise go hand in hand. To be humble is to recognize that wisdom is a gift from God.

you will learn all you can,
but foolish talk
will soon destroy you.

15 Great wealth can be a fortress,
but poverty
is no protection at all.
16 If you live right,
the reward is a good life;
if you are evil,
all you have is sin.

17 Accept correction,
and you will find life;
reject correction,
and you will miss the road.
18 You can hide your hatred
by telling lies,
but you are a fool
to spread lies.
19 You will say the wrong thing
if you talk too much—
so be sensible and watch
what you say.
20 The words of a good person
are like pure silver,
but the thoughts
of an evil person
are almost worthless.
21 Many are helped
by useful instruction,
but fools are killed
by their own stupidity.

22 When the LORD blesses you
with riches,
you have nothing to regret.q
23 Fools enjoy doing wrong,
but anyone with good sense
enjoys acting wisely.
24 What evil people dread most
will happen to them,
but good people will get

what they want most.
25 Those crooks will disappear
when a storm strikes,
but God will keep safe
all who obey him.
26 Having a lazy person on the job
is like a mouth full of vinegar
or smoke in your eyes.

27 If you respect the LORD,
you will live longer;
if you keep doing wrong,
your life will be cut short.
28 If you obey the Lord,
you will be happy,
but there is no future
for the wicked.
29 The LORD protects everyone
who lives right,
but he destroys anyone
who does wrong.
30 Good people will stand firm,
but the wicked will disappear
from the land.
31 Honest people speak sensibly,
but deceitful liars
will be silenced.
32 If you obey the Lord,
you will always know
the right thing to say.
But no one will trust you
if you tell lies.

Watch What You Say and Do

11 The LORD hates anyone
who cheats,
but he likes everyone
who is honest.
2 Too much pride
can put you to shame.
It's wiser to be humble.
3 If you do the right thing,

q 10.22 *When . . . regret:* Or "No matter how hard you work, your riches really come from the LORD."

honesty will be your guide.
But if you are crooked,
    you will be trapped
        by your own dishonesty.

⁴When God is angry,
    money won't help you.
Obeying God is the only way
    to be saved from death.
⁵If you are truly good,
    you will do right;
if you are wicked,
you will be destroyed
    by your own sin.
⁶Honesty can keep you safe,
but if you can't be trusted,
    you trap yourself.
⁷When the wicked die,
    their hopes die with them.
⁸Trouble goes right past
    the Lord's people
        and strikes the wicked.

⁹Dishonest people use gossip
    to destroy their neighbors;
good people are protected
    by their own good sense.
¹⁰When honest people prosper
and the wicked disappear,
    the whole city celebrates.
¹¹Good people bring prosperity
    to their city,
but deceitful liars
    can destroy a city.

¹²It's stupid to say bad things
    about your neighbors.
If you are sensible,
    you will keep quiet.
¹³A gossip tells everything,
but a true friend
    will keep a secret.

¹⁴A city without wise leaders
    will end up in ruin;
a city with many wise leaders
    will be kept safe.

¹⁵It's a dangerous thing
    to guarantee payment
for someone's debts.
    Don't do it!
¹⁶A gracious woman
    will be respected,
but a ruthless man
    will only get rich.
¹⁷Kindness is rewarded—
but if you are cruel,
    you hurt yourself.
¹⁸Meanness gets you nowhere,
    but goodness is rewarded.
¹⁹Always do the right thing,
    and you will live;
keep on doing wrong,
    and you will die.

²⁰The Lord hates sneaky people,
but he likes everyone
    who lives right.
²¹You can be sure of this:
    All crooks will be punished,
        but God's people won't.
²²A beautiful woman
    who acts foolishly
is like a gold ring
    on the snout of a pig.
²³Good people want what is best,
but troublemakers
    hope to stir up trouble.ʳ

²⁴Sometimes you can become rich
    by being generous
        or poor by being greedy.
²⁵Generosity will be rewarded:
    Give a cup of water,

ʳ**11.23** *Good people . . . trouble*: Or "Good people do what is best, but troublemakers just stir up trouble."

■   11.4 *Obeying God . . . saved from death*: God's wisdom and commands show the path to life (3.1,2; 6.23; 10.2). This is not a reference to life after death but a warning about unwise living that leads to the kind of death the wicked face.

■   11.24,25 *being generous*: Giving to others is rewarded, perhaps because a generous giver is remembered by those he or she helps. But a greedy person does not make friends and is cursed by the poor.

A gossip tells everything, but a true friend will keep a secret. Prov 11.13

11.26 *Charge too much:* Dishonest business practices eventually make people angry. This verse likely refers to merchants hoarding grain in order to cause a shortage. Then they can charge higher prices.

12.4 *helpful wife:* For a full description of such a wife, see Proverbs 31.10-31. In ancient Hebrew society, the behavior of a man's wife and children affected his reputation and standing within the community.

and you will receive
  a cup of water in return.
²⁶Charge too much for grain,
  and you will be cursed;
sell it at a fair price,
  and you will be praised.
²⁷Try hard to do right,
  and you will win friends;
go looking for trouble,
  and you will find it.
²⁸Trust in your wealth,
  and you will be a failure,
but God's people will prosper
  like healthy plants.

²⁹Fools who cause trouble
  in the family
won't inherit a thing.
They will end up as slaves
  of someone with good sense.
³⁰Live right, and you will eat
  from the life-giving tree.
And if you act wisely,
  others will follow.^s
³¹If good people are rewarded^t
  here on this earth,
all who are cruel and mean
  will surely be punished.

You Can't Hide behind Evil

12 To accept correction is wise,
  to reject it is stupid.
²The LORD likes everyone
  who lives right,
but he punishes everyone
  who makes evil plans.
³Sin cannot offer security!
  But if you live right,
you will be as secure
  as a tree with deep roots.

⁴A helpful wife is a jewel
  for her husband,
but a shameless wife
  will make his bones rot.

⁵Good people have kind thoughts,
  but you should never trust
  the advice of someone evil.
⁶Bad advice is a deadly trap,
  but good advice
  is like a shield.
⁷Once the wicked are defeated,
  they are gone forever,
but no one who obeys God
  will ever be thrown down.
⁸Good sense is worthy of praise,
  but stupidity is a curse.
⁹It's better to be ordinary
  and have only one servant^u
than to think you are somebody
  and starve to death.
¹⁰Good people are kind
  to their animals,
  but a mean person is cruel.

¹¹Hard working farmers have more
  than enough food;
daydreamers are nothing more
  than stupid fools.
¹²An evil person tries to hide
  behind evil;^v
good people are like trees
  with deep roots.
¹³We trap ourselves
  by telling lies,
but we stay out of trouble
  by living right.
¹⁴We are rewarded or punished
  for what we say and do.
¹⁵Fools think they know
  what is best,

^s**11.30** *act . . . follow:* Hebrew; one ancient translation "but violence leads to death." ^t**11.31** *rewarded:* Or "punished." ^u**12.9** *It's . . . servant:* Or "It is better just to have an ordinary job." ^v**12.12** *An evil . . . evil:* Or "Evil people love what they get from being evil."

but a sensible person
 listens to advice.

¹⁶Losing your temper is foolish;
 ignoring an insult is smart.
¹⁷An honest person
 tells the truth in court,
 but a dishonest person
 tells nothing but lies.
¹⁸Sharp words cut like a sword,
 but words of wisdom heal.
¹⁹Truth will last forever;
 lies are soon found out.
²⁰An evil mind is deceitful,
 but gentle thoughts
 bring happiness.
²¹Good people never have trouble,
 but troublemakers
 have more than enough.
²²The LORD hates every liar,
 but he is the friend of all
 who can be trusted.
²³Be sensible and don't tell
 everything you know—
 only fools spread
 foolishness everywhere.

²⁴Work hard, and you
 will be a leader;
 be lazy, and you
 will end up a slave.
²⁵Worry is a heavy burden,
 but a kind word
 always brings cheer.
²⁶You are better off to do right,
 than to lose your way
 by doing wrong.^w
²⁷Anyone too lazy to cook
 will starve,
 but a hard worker
 is a valuable treasure.^x
²⁸Living right is a pathway

that leads to life
 and away from death.

Wise Friends Make You Wise

13 Children with good sense
 accept correction
 from their parents,
 but stubborn children
 ignore it completely.
²You will be well rewarded
 for saying something kind,
 but all some people think about
 is how to be cruel and mean.
³Keep what you know to yourself,
 and you will be safe;
 talk too much,
 and you are done for.
⁴No matter how much you want,
 laziness won't help a bit,
 but hard work will reward you
 with more than enough.
⁵A good person hates deceit,
 but those who are evil
 cause shame and disgrace.
⁶Live right, and you are safe!
 But sin will destroy you.

⁷Some who have nothing
 may pretend to be rich,
 and some who have everything
 may pretend to be poor.
⁸The rich may have
 to pay a ransom,
 but the poor don't have
 that problem.
⁹The lamp of a good person
 keeps on shining;
 the lamp of an evil person
 soon goes out.
¹⁰Too much pride causes trouble.
 Be sensible and take advice.

12.23 *don't tell everything you know:* A common theme in PROVERBS is the importance of choosing words carefully when speaking. A wise person does not say more than is necessary and does not speak too quickly (Prov 10.13; 18.2,21).

13.9 *lamp:* This image is used here as a symbol for a person's life.

^w**12.26** *wrong:* One possible meaning for the difficult Hebrew text of verse 26. ^x**12.27** *but . . . treasure:* One possible meaning for the difficult Hebrew text.

Sharp words cut like a sword, but words of wisdom heal. PROV 12.18

13.14 *life-giving fountain:* Living things cannot survive without water. Sensible instruction (wisdom) is compared to a fountain of water, which was highly prized in the dry climate of the Middle East.

13.17 *Whoever delivers your message:* A bad messenger may cause problems by giving incorrect information or by treating the hearer with disrespect. A good messenger's gentle words and patience can help smooth out hard feelings and cause people, including rulers, to listen (12.18; 25.13).

14.1 *her wisdom . . . foolishness:* Some have suggested that this verse may refer to the houses built by Wisdom and Stupidity (9.1,13), but it may also refer to the important role a woman plays in teaching her family good values and respect for the LORD (14.2; 31.10-31).

[11]Money wrongly[y] gained
    will disappear bit by bit;
money earned little by little
    will grow and grow.
[12]Not getting what you want
    can break your heart,
but a wish that comes true
    is a life-giving tree.
[13]If you reject God's teaching,
    you will pay the price;
if you obey his commands,
    you will be rewarded.

[14]Sensible instruction
    is a life-giving fountain
that helps you escape
    all deadly traps.
[15]Sound judgment is praised,
    but people without good sense
    are on the way to disaster.[z]
[16]If you have good sense,
    you will act sensibly,
    but fools act like fools.
[17]Whoever delivers your message
    can make things better
    or worse for you.

[18]All who refuse correction
    will be poor and disgraced;
all who accept correction
    will be praised.
[19]It's a good feeling
    to get what you want,
but only a stupid fool
    hates to turn from evil.
[20] Wise friends make you wise,
    but you hurt yourself
    by going around with fools.
[21]You are in for trouble
    if you sin,
but you will be rewarded
    if you live right.

[22]If you obey God,
    you will have something
    to leave your grandchildren.
If you don't obey God,
    those who live right
    will get what you leave.

[23]Even when the land of the poor
    produces good crops,
    they get cheated
    out of what they grow.[a]
[24]If you love your children,
    you will correct them;
if you don't love them,
    you won't correct them.
[25]If you live right,
    you will have plenty to eat;
if you don't live right,
    you will go away empty.

Wisdom Makes Good Sense

14 A woman's family
    is held together
        by her wisdom,
but it can be destroyed
    by her foolishness.
[2]By living right, you show
    that you respect the LORD;
by being deceitful, you show
    that you despise him.
[3]Proud fools are punished
    for their stupid talk,
but sensible talk
    can save your life.
[4]Without the help of an ox
    there can be no crop,
but with a strong ox
    a big crop is possible.
[5]An honest witness
    tells the truth;

[y]**13.11** *wrongly:* Or "quickly."   [z]**13.15** *people . . . disaster:* One possible meaning for the difficult Hebrew text.   [a]**13.23** *grow:* One possible meaning for the difficult Hebrew text of verse 23.

Wise friends make you wise, but you hurt yourself by going around with fools. PROV 13.20

a dishonest witness
  tells nothing but lies.

⁶Make fun of wisdom,
    and you will never find it.
  But if you have understanding,
    knowledge comes easily.
⁷Stay away from fools,
    or you won't learn a thing.
⁸Wise people have enough sense
    to find their way,
    but stupid fools get lost.
⁹Fools don't care
    if they are wrong,^b
  but God is pleased
    when people do right.

¹⁰No one else can really know
    how sad or happy you are.
¹¹The tent of a good person
    stands longer than the house
    of someone evil.
¹² You may think you are
    on the right road
    and still end up dead.
¹³Sorrow may hide
    behind laughter,
  and happiness may end
    in sorrow.
¹⁴You harvest what you plant,
    whether good or bad.

¹⁵Don't be stupid
    and believe all you hear;
  be smart and know
    where you are headed.
¹⁶Only a stupid fool
    is never cautious—
  so be extra careful
    and stay out of trouble.
¹⁷Fools have quick tempers,
    and no one likes you

if you can't be trusted.
¹⁸Stupidity leads to foolishness;
    be smart and learn.

¹⁹The wicked will come crawling
    to those who obey God.
²⁰You have no friends
    if you are poor,
  but you have lots of friends
    if you are rich.
²¹It's wrong to hate others,
    but God blesses everyone
    who is kind to the poor.
²²It's a mistake
    to make evil plans,
  but you will have loyal friends
    if you want to do right.
²³Hard work is worthwhile,
    but empty talk
    will make you poor.
²⁴Wisdom can make you rich,
    but foolishness leads
    to more foolishness.
²⁵An honest witness
  can save your life,
    but liars can't be trusted.

²⁶If you respect the LORD,
    you and your children
    have a strong fortress
²⁷ and a life-giving fountain
    that keeps you safe
    from deadly traps.

²⁸Rulers of powerful nations
    are held in honor;
  rulers of weak nations
    are nothing at all.
²⁹It's smart to be patient,
    but it's stupid
    to lose your temper.
³⁰It's healthy to be content,

^b**14.9** *Fools . . . wrong*: One possible meaning for the difficult Hebrew text.

14.11 *tent . . . house:* Permanent houses made of brick and wood were meant to stand up to rain, wind, and heat better than tents. But the evil person's house (life) is more likely to be swept away because of the way he lives.

14.14 *what you plant:* Meaning what one does and how one lives.

14.26 *respect the LORD:* Respecting the LORD is closely connected to wisdom.

It's wrong to hate others, but God blesses everyone who is kind to the poor. PROV 14.21

14.31 *insult your Creator:* Meaning Israel's LORD God.

15.3 *LORD sees everything:* Those who are foolish and evil cannot hide what they are doing.

15.8 *gifts from the wicked:* This probably refers to the sacrifices offered in worship by those who do not live right.

15.15-17 *a hard life . . . simple meal:* Riches may help make one's life go easier, but they are no substitute for being content and obeying the LORD. Here the rich are depicted as people who live difficult and complicated lives and who are forced to take their meals with people they cannot trust.

but envy can eat you up.
³¹If you mistreat the poor,
  you insult your Creator;
if you are kind to them,
  you show him respect.
³²In times of trouble
  the wicked are destroyed,
but even at death
  the innocent have faith.ᶜ

³³Wisdom is found in the minds
  of people with good sense,
  but fools don't know it.ᵈ
³⁴Doing right brings honor
  to a nation,
  but sin brings disgrace.
³⁵Kings reward servants
  who act wisely,
but they punish those
  who act foolishly.

The LORD Sees Everything

15 A kind answer
  soothes angry feelings,
but harsh words
  stir them up.
²Words of wisdom
come from the wise,
  but fools speak foolishness.

³The LORD sees everything,
  whether good or bad.
⁴Kind words are good medicine,
  but deceitful words
  can really hurt.
⁵Don't be a fool
and disobey your parents.
  Be smart! Accept correction.
⁶Good people become wealthy,
but those who are evil

will lose what they have.
⁷Words of wisdom
  make good sense;
the thoughts of a fool
  make no sense at all.

⁸The LORD is disgusted
  by gifts from the wicked,
but it makes him happy
  when his people pray.
⁹The LORD is disgusted
  with all who do wrong,
but he loves everyone
  who does right.
¹⁰If you turn from the right way,
  you will be punished;
if you refuse correction,
  you will die.

¹¹If the LORD can see everything
  in the world of the dead,
  he can see in our hearts.
¹²Those who sneer at others
  don't like to be corrected,
and they won't ask help
  from someone with sense.
¹³Happiness makes you smile;
  sorrow can crush you.
¹⁴Anyone with good sense
  is eager to learn more,
but fools are hungry
  for foolishness.

¹⁵The poor have a hard life,
  but being content is as good
  as an endless feast.
¹⁶It's better to obey the LORD
  and have only a little,
than to be very rich
  and terribly anxious.
¹⁷A simple meal with love

ᶜ**14.32** *but even . . . faith:* One possible meaning for the difficult Hebrew text. Some ancient translations "but good people trust their innocence." ᵈ**14.33** *but . . . it:* One possible meaning for the difficult Hebrew text; some ancient translations "but not in the mind of a fool."

is better than a feast
  where there is hatred.

18Losing your temper
  causes a lot of trouble,
but staying calm
  settles arguments.
19A lazy person refuses
  to clear a thorny path,
but everyone who does right
  walks on a smooth road.
20Children with good sense
  make their parents happy,
but foolish children
  despise them.
21Stupidity brings happiness
  to senseless fools,
but everyone with good sense
  follows the straight path.

22Without good advice
  everything goes wrong—
it takes careful planning
  for things to go right.
23Giving the right answer
  at the right time
  makes everyone happy.
24All who are wise follow a road
  that leads upward to life
  and away from death.

25The Lord destroys the homes
  of those who are proud,
but he protects the property
  of widows.
26The Lord hates evil thoughts,
  but kind words please him.
27Being greedy causes trouble
  for your family,
but you protect yourself
  by refusing bribes.
28Good people think
  before they answer,
but the wicked speak evil
  without ever thinking.

29The Lord never even hears
  the prayers of the wicked,
but he answers the prayers
  of all who obey him.
30A friendly smile
  makes you happy,
and good news
  makes you feel strong.
31Healthy correction is good,
  and if you accept it,
  you will be wise.
32You hurt only yourself
  by rejecting instruction,
but it makes good sense
  to accept it.
33Showing respect to the Lord
  will make you wise,
and being humble
  will bring honor to you.

The Lord Has the Final Word

16 We humans make plans,
  but the Lord
    has the final word.
2We may think we know
  what is right,
but the Lord is the judge
  of our motives.
3Share your plans with the Lord,
  and you will succeed.

4The Lord has a reason
  for everything he does,
and he lets evil people live
  only to be punished.
5The Lord doesn't like
  anyone who is conceited—
you can be sure
  they will be punished.
6If we truly love God,
  our sins will be forgiven;
if we show him respect,
  we will keep away from sin.

16.1 *Lord has the final word:* The idea that the Lord controls all that happens in life is a common theme in wisdom literature (Prov 16.4,9; Eccl 3.11-15; 8.6).

16.4 *a reason for everything:* Compare to Ecclesiastes 3.1-15. Those reasons may not always be clear to human minds.

16.6 *sins will be forgiven:* To "truly love God" here means to be faithful and loyal to God. Those who turn away from evil and turn back to God can be forgiven.

16.10 *Rulers . . . are never wrong:* While modern readers can agree that leaders have authority, it is difficult to believe that they are "never wrong." In ancient Israel, the king functioned as God's chosen representative. This meant that his actions and words were considered to have come from God and therefore were "correct." However, the record of Israel's rulers shows that many of them were wrong and acted against the Lord's commands.

16.26 *hungrier . . . work:* Physical hunger can motivate a person to work hard at growing and harvesting food or earning money to buy it.

16.31 *Gray hair is a glorious crown . . . lived right:* Meaning that someone who has followed wisdom has lived right and has been blessed with a long life.

16.33 *Lord alone determines:* In Hebrew, this verse refers to the practice of casting lots in order to make a decision. The lots could be sticks of different lengths or various kinds of stones. A decision was made based on which stick or stone was chosen. But this verse makes the point that even if lots are cast, the Lord determines which one is chosen, and so the Lord is in control of what happens.

⁷When we please the Lord,
  even our enemies
    make friends with us.
⁸It's better to be honest
  and poor
  than to be dishonest
  and rich.

⁹We make our own plans,
  but the Lord decides
    where we will go.
¹⁰Rulers speak with authority
  and are never wrong.
¹¹The Lord watches to see
  if we are fair
  or if we cheat others.
¹²Justice makes rulers powerful.
  They should hate evil
¹³ and like honesty and truth.
¹⁴An angry ruler
  can put you to death.
  So be wise!
    Don't make one angry.
¹⁵When a ruler is happy
  and pleased with you,
  it's like refreshing rain,
  and you will live.

¹⁶It's much better to be wise
  and sensible
    than to be rich.
¹⁷God's people avoid evil ways,
  and they protect themselves
    by watching where they go.
¹⁸Too much pride
  will destroy you.
¹⁹You are better off
  to be humble and poor
  than to get rich
    from what you take by force.
²⁰If you know what you're doing,^e
  you will prosper.
  God blesses everyone

who trusts him.
²¹Good judgment proves
  that you are wise,
  and if you speak kindly,
  you can teach others.
²²Good sense is a fountain
  that gives life,
  but fools are punished
  by their foolishness.
²³You can persuade others
  if you are wise
  and speak sensibly.

²⁴Kind words are like honey—
  they cheer you up
  and make you feel strong.
²⁵Sometimes what seems right
  is really a road to death.
²⁶The hungrier you are,
  the harder you work.
²⁷Worthless people plan trouble.
  Even their words burn
  like a flaming fire.
²⁸Gossip is no good!
  It causes hard feelings
  and comes between friends.

²⁹Don't trust violent people.
  They will mislead you
  to do the wrong thing.
³⁰When someone winks
  or grins behind your back,
  trouble is on the way.
³¹Gray hair is a glorious crown
  worn by those
  who have lived right.
³²Controlling your temper
  is better than being a hero
  who captures a city.
³³We make our own decisions,
  but the Lord alone
  determines what happens.

^e**16.20** *know what . . . doing:* Or "do what you're taught."

Our Thoughts Are Tested
by the LORD

17 A dry crust of bread eaten
in peace and quiet
is better than a feast eaten
where everyone argues.
² A wise slave
will be placed in charge
of a no-good child,
and that slave will be given
the same inheritance
that each child receives.
³ Silver and gold are tested
by flames of fire;
our thoughts are tested
by the LORD.
⁴ Troublemakers listen
to troublemakers,
and liars listen to liars.
⁵ By insulting the poor,
you insult your Creator.
You will be punished
if you make fun
of someone in trouble.
⁶ Grandparents are proud
of their grandchildren,
and children should be proud
of their parents.

⁷ It sounds strange for a fool
to talk sensibly,
but it's even worse
for a ruler to tell lies.
⁸ A bribe works miracles
like a magic charm
that brings good luck.
⁹ You will keep your friends
if you forgive them,
but you will lose your friends
if you keep talking about
what they did wrong.
¹⁰ A sensible person
accepts correction,
but you can't beat sense
into a fool.

¹¹ Cruel people want to rebel,
and so vicious attackers
will be sent against them.
¹² A bear robbed of her cubs
is far less dangerous
than a stubborn fool.
¹³ You will always have trouble
if you are mean to those
who are good to you.
¹⁴ The start of an argument
is like a water leak—
so stop it before
real trouble breaks out.
¹⁵ The LORD doesn't like those
who defend the guilty
or condemn the innocent.
¹⁶ Why should fools have money
for an education
when they refuse to learn?

¹⁷ A friend is there to help,
in any situation,
and relatives are born
to share our troubles.
¹⁸ It's stupid to guarantee
someone else's loan.
¹⁹ The wicked and the proud
love trouble and keep begging
to be hurt.
²⁰ Dishonesty does you no good,
and telling lies
will get you in trouble.
²¹ It's never pleasant
to be the parent of a fool
and have nothing but pain.
²² If you are cheerful,
you feel good;
if you are sad,
you hurt all over.

²³ Crooks accept secret bribes
to keep justice
from being done.
²⁴ Anyone with wisdom knows
what makes good sense,

● **17.2** *wise slave . . . same inheritance:* Israelite law did not provide for slaves to receive an inheritance. But a wise slave may receive more favorable treatment than a disobedient child.

● **17.3** *tested by flames of fire:* Precious metals such as silver and gold were made more pure by a refining process called smelting. Metal ore was heated in a furnace at very high temperatures. When the ore melted, the precious metal could easily be separated from the impure materials (called slag) because they were different weights. In a similar way, the LORD tests the thoughts of his people.

■ **17.8** *bribe works . . . like a magic charm:* This verse probably is not meant to encourage secret bribes (as described in 17.23), but rather makes the point that the common practice of giving a gift in order to receive a favor in return was very effective.

● **17.23** *secret bribes:* It may have been common for those with money to bribe judges so they could escape punishment for a crime they committed or to get a ruling in their favor.

18.10 *LORD is a mighty tower:* The LORD is often described as a fortress or tower of protection.

18.18 *Drawing straws:* This is another way of describing the practice of casting lots.

but fools can never
    make up their minds.
²⁵Foolish children bring sorrow
    and pain to their parents.
²⁶It isn't fair
    to punish the innocent
    and those who do right.
²⁷It makes a lot of sense
    to be a person of few words
    and to stay calm.
²⁸Even fools seem smart
    when they are quiet.

It's Wrong To Favor the Guilty

18 It's selfish and stupid
    to think only of yourself
and to sneer at people
    who have sense.[f]
²Fools have no desire to learn,
instead they would rather
    give their own opinion.
³Wrongdoing leads to shame
    and disgrace.
⁴Words of wisdom
are a stream that flows
    from a deep fountain.
⁵It's wrong to favor the guilty
and keep the innocent
    from getting justice.

⁶Foolish talk will get you
    into a lot of trouble.
⁷Saying foolish things
is like setting a trap
    to destroy yourself.
⁸There's nothing so delicious
as the taste of gossip!
    It melts in your mouth.

⁹Being lazy is no different
    from being a troublemaker.

¹⁰The LORD is a mighty tower
    where his people can run
    for safety—
¹¹the rich think their money
    is a wall of protection.

¹²Pride leads to destruction;
    humility leads to honor.
¹³It's stupid and embarrassing
    to give an answer
    before you listen.
¹⁴Being cheerful helps
    when you are sick,
but nothing helps
    when you give up.
¹⁵Everyone with good sense
    wants to learn.
¹⁶A gift will get you in
    to see anyone.
¹⁷You may think you have won
your case in court,
    until your opponent speaks.
¹⁸Drawing straws is one way
    to settle a difficult case.
¹⁹Making up with a friend
    you have offended[g]
is harder than breaking
    through a city wall.

²⁰Make your words good—
    you will be glad you did.
²¹Words can bring death or life!
    Talk too much, and you will eat
    everything you say.
²² A man's greatest treasure
is his wife—
    she is a gift from the LORD.

[f]**18.1** *sense:* One possible meaning for the difficult Hebrew text of verse 1. [g]**18.19** *Making . . . offended:* One possible meaning for the difficult Hebrew text.

Make your words good—you will be glad you did.
PROV 18.20

²³The poor must beg for help,
  but the rich can give
     a harsh reply.
²⁴Some friends don't help,ʰ
  but a true friend is closer
     than your own family.

It's Wise To Be Patient

19 It's better to be poor
  and live right
     than to be a stupid liar.
²Willingness and stupidity
  don't go well together.
If you are too eager,
  you will miss the road.
³We are ruined
  by our own stupidity,
     though we blame the Lord.

⁴The rich have many friends;
  the poor have none.
⁵Dishonest witnesses and liars
  won't escape punishment.
⁶Everyone tries to be friends
  of those who can help them.
⁷If you are poor,
  your own relatives reject you,
     and your friends are worse.
When you really need them,
  they are not there.ⁱ

⁸Do yourself a favor
  by having good sense—
     you will be glad you did.
⁹Dishonest witnesses and liars
  will be destroyed.
¹⁰It isn't right for a fool
  to live in luxury
     or for a slave to rule
        in place of a king.
¹¹It's wise to be patient

and show what you are like
  by forgiving others.
¹²An angry king roars
  like a lion,
but when a king is pleased,
  it's like dew on the crops.

¹³Foolish children bring disgrace
  to their fathers.
A nagging wife goes on and on
like the drip, drip, drip
  of the rain.
¹⁴You may inherit all you own
  from your parents,
but a sensible wife
  is a gift from the Lord.
¹⁵If you are lazy
and sleep your time away,
  you will starve.

¹⁶Obey the Lord's teachings
  and you will live—
     disobey and you will die.
¹⁷Caring for the poor
  is lending to the Lord,
     and you will be well repaid.
¹⁸Correct your children
  before it's too late;
if you don't punish them,
  trouble will come their way.ʲ
¹⁹People with bad tempers
  are always in trouble,
and they need help
  over and over again.ᵏ
²⁰Pay attention to advice
  and accept correction,
     so you can live sensibly.

²¹We may make a lot of plans,
  but the Lord will do
     what he has decided.

ʰ**18.24** *Some . . . help:* One possible meaning for the difficult Hebrew text.   ⁱ**19.7** *When . . . there:* One possible meaning for the difficult Hebrew text.   ʲ**19.18** *if . . . way:* Or "but be careful not to punish them too harshly."   ᵏ**19.19** *and they . . . again:* One possible meaning for the difficult Hebrew text.

19.4 *rich have many friends:* Some people become friends with rich people only because they hope that the rich people will give them something.

19.7 *poor:* The poor were at or near the bottom of the social ladder in ancient Israel. People did not want to make friends with someone who had very little.

The Poor

19.10 *fool . . . slave to rule:* Neither fit with what was expected in Israelite society. A slave would not rule in place of a king, unless that king had foolishly given up his authority or mistreated others so that they rebelled.

19.17 *Caring for the poor:* This was expected of those who wanted to "live right."

20.9 *thoughts are pure . . . sins are gone:* This form of question in Hebrew assumes a negative answer.

20.20 *go to the land of darkness:* In Hebrew, this literally is "their lamp will go out," meaning they will die prematurely.

²²What matters most is loyalty.
   It's better to be poor
      than to be a liar.
²³Showing respect to the LORD
   brings true life—
if you do it, you can relax
   without fear of danger.

²⁴Some people are too lazy
   to lift a hand
      to feed themselves.
²⁵Stupid fools learn good sense
   by seeing others punished;
a sensible person learns
   by being corrected.
²⁶Disgraceful children
   rob their father
      and chase their mother away.
²⁷If you stop learning,
   you will forget
      what you already know.
²⁸A lying witness makes fun
   of the court system,
and criminals think crime
   is really delicious.
²⁹A stupid fool should expect
   to be punished.

Words of Wisdom Are Better than Gold

20 It isn't smart to get drunk!
   Drinking makes a fool of you
      and leads to fights.
²An angry ruler
   is like a roaring lion—
make either one angry,
   and you are dead.
³It makes you look good
   when you avoid a fight—
      only fools love to quarrel.
⁴If you are too lazy to plow,
   don't expect a harvest.
⁵Someone's thoughts may be
   as deep as the ocean,

but if you are smart,
   you will discover them.

⁶There are many who say,
   "You can trust me!"
      But can they be trusted?
⁷Good people live right,
   and God blesses the children
      who follow their example.
⁸When rulers decide cases,
   they weigh the evidence.
⁹Can any of us really say,
   "My thoughts are pure,
      and my sins are gone"?

¹⁰Two things the LORD hates
   are dishonest scales
      and dishonest measures.
¹¹The good or bad
   that children do
      shows what they are like.
¹²Hearing and seeing
   are gifts from the LORD.
¹³If you sleep all the time,
   you will starve;
if you get up and work,
   you will have enough food.
¹⁴Everyone likes to brag
   about getting a bargain.
¹⁵Sensible words are better
   than gold or jewels.

¹⁶You deserve to lose your coat
   if you loan it to someone
to guarantee payment
   for the debt of a stranger.
¹⁷The food you get by cheating
   may taste delicious,
      but it turns to gravel.
¹⁸Be sure you have sound advice
   before making plans
      or starting a war.
¹⁹Stay away from gossips—
   they tell everything.
²⁰Children who curse their parents

If you stop learning, you will forget what you already know. PROV 19.27

will go to the land of darkness
  long before their time.
²¹Getting rich quick[l]
  may turn out to be a curse.
²²Don't try to get even.
  Trust the Lord,
  and he will help you.

²³The Lord hates dishonest scales
  and dishonest weights.
  So don't cheat!
²⁴How can we know
  what will happen to us
  when the Lord alone decides?
²⁵Don't fall into the trap
  of making promises to God
  before you think!
²⁶A wise ruler severely punishes
  every criminal.
²⁷Our inner thoughts are a lamp
  from the Lord,
  and they search our hearts.
²⁸Rulers are protected
  by God's mercy and loyalty,
  but[m] they must be merciful
  for their kingdoms to last.
²⁹Young people take pride
  in their strength,
  but the gray hairs of wisdom
  are even more beautiful.
³⁰A severe beating can knock all
  of the evil out of you!

The Lord Is In Charge

21 The Lord controls rulers,
  just as he determines
  the course of rivers.
²We may think we are doing
  the right thing,
  but the Lord always knows

what is in our hearts.
³Doing what is right and fair
  pleases the Lord
  more than an offering.
⁴Evil people are proud
  and arrogant,
  but sin is the only crop
  they produce.[n]
⁵If you plan and work hard,
  you will have plenty;
  if you hurry to get rich,
  you will end up poor.

⁶Cheating to get rich
  is a foolish dream
  and no less than suicide.[o]
⁷You destroy yourself
  by being cruel and violent
  and refusing to live right.
⁸All crooks are liars,
  but anyone who is innocent
  will do right.
⁹It's better to stay outside
  on the roof of your house
  than to live inside
  with a nagging wife.
¹⁰Evil people want to do wrong,
  even to their friends.
¹¹An ignorant fool learns
  by seeing others punished;
  a sensible person learns
  by being instructed.

¹²God is always fair!
  He knows what the wicked do
  and will punish them.
¹³If you won't help the poor,
  don't expect to be heard
  when you cry out for help.
¹⁴A secret bribe will save you
  from someone's fierce anger.

20.25 *making promises to God:* Making a promise to God or in God's name was a serious commitment. This saying warns against making promises that one could not or did not intend to keep.

Making Promises (Vows)

20.27 *a lamp from the Lord . . . hearts:* The Law of the Lord was also called a lamp.

21.1 *Lord controls rulers . . . rivers:* Israel's Lord, the Creator of all things (14.31), is said to control the actions of rulers just as he controls the direction a river will flow. Not only did the Lord control Israel's rulers but the rulers of other nations as well.

---

[l]20.21 *quick:* Or "the wrong way." [m]20.28 *by God's mercy . . . but:* Or "by their mercy . . . and."
[n]21.4 *but sin . . . produce:* Or "but sin is the only light they ever follow." [o]21.6 *and . . . suicide:* One possible meaning for the difficult Hebrew text.

21.30 *No matter how much you know*: It is impossible to trick or out-guess the LORD, who knows what is in every heart and mind.

21.31 *horses ready for battle*: Ancient armies that used horses for cavalry and chariots had an advantage in battle. When Israel first settled in Canaan, they did not have horses to use in battle. Instead, they were expected to rely on the LORD's help.

Holy War (The LORD's Battles)

22.7 *slaves of moneylenders*: Some moneylenders charged high interest on loans, which made it hard for people to repay their debts in full. Sometimes people had to become slaves of the people they owed money to in order to work off their debts.

¹⁵When justice is done,
   good citizens are glad
      and crooks are terrified.
¹⁶If you stop using good sense,
   you will find yourself
      in the grave.
¹⁷Heavy drinkers and others
   who live only for pleasure
      will lose all they have.

¹⁸God's people will escape,
   but all who are wicked
      will pay the price.
¹⁹It's better out in the desert
   than at home with a nagging,
      complaining wife.
²⁰Be sensible and store up
   precious treasures—
don't waste them
   like a fool.
²¹If you try to be kind and good,
   you will be blessed with life
      and goodness and honor.
²²One wise person can defeat
   a city full of soldiers
      and capture their fortress.
²³Watching what you say
   can save you
      a lot of trouble.
²⁴If you are proud and conceited,
   everyone will say,
      "You're a snob!"

²⁵If you want too much
   and are too lazy to work,
      it could be fatal.
²⁶But people who obey God
   are always generous.

²⁷The Lord despises the offerings
   of wicked people
      with evil motives.
²⁸If you tell lies in court,
   you are done for;
      only a reliable witness

can do the job.
²⁹Wicked people bluff their way,
   but God's people think
      before they take a step.

³⁰No matter how much you know
   or what plans you make,
      you can't defeat the LORD.
³¹Even if your army has horses
   ready for battle,
      the LORD will always win.

The Value of a Good Reputation

22 A good reputation and respect
   are worth much more
      than silver and gold.
²The rich and the poor
   are all created
      by the LORD.
³When you see trouble coming,
   don't be stupid
and walk right into it—
   be smart and hide.

⁴Respect and serve the LORD!
   Your reward will be wealth,
      a long life, and honor.
⁵Crooks walk down a road
   full of thorny traps.
      Stay away from there!
⁶Teach your children
   right from wrong,
and when they are grown
   they will still do right.
⁷The poor are ruled by the rich,
   and those who borrow
      are slaves of moneylenders.
⁸Troublemakers get in trouble,
   and their terrible anger
      will get them nowhere.

⁹The LORD blesses everyone
   who freely gives food
      to the poor.

When you see trouble coming, don't be stupid and walk right into it—be smart and hide. PROV 22.3

¹⁰Arguments and fights
    will come to an end,
if you chase away those
    who insult others.
¹¹The king is the friend of all
    who are sincere
    and speak with kindness.

¹²The Lord watches over everyone
    who shows good sense,
but he frustrates the plans
    of deceitful liars.
¹³Don't be so lazy that you say,
    "If I go to work,
    a lion will eat me!"
¹⁴The words of a bad woman
    are like a deep pit;
if you make the Lord angry,
    you will fall right in.
¹⁵All children are foolish,
    but firm correction
    will make them change.
¹⁶Cheat the poor to make profit
or give gifts to the rich—
    either way you lose.

Thirty Wise Sayings

¹⁷Here are some sayings
    of people with wisdom,
so listen carefully
    as I teach.
¹⁸You will be glad
    that you know these sayings
    and can recite them.
¹⁹I am teaching them today,
    so that you
    may trust the Lord.
²⁰I have written thirty sayings
    filled with sound advice.
²¹You can trust them completely

to give you the right words
    for those in charge of you.

(1)
²²Don't take advantage
    of the poor
    or cheat them in court.
²³The Lord is their defender,
    and what you do to them,
    he will do to you.

(2)
²⁴Don't make friends with anyone
    who has a bad temper.
²⁵You might turn out like them
    and get caught in a trap.

(3)
²⁶Don't guarantee to pay
    someone else's debt.
²⁷If you don't have the money,
    you might lose your bed.

(4)
²⁸Don't move a boundary markerᴾ
    set up by your ancestors.

(5)
²⁹If you do your job well,
    you will work for a ruler
    and never be a slave.

(6)
23 When you are invited
    to eat with a king,
    use your best manners.
²Don't go and stuff yourself!
    That would be just the same
    as cutting your throat.
³Don't be greedy for all
of that fancy food!
    It may not be so tasty.

22.17 *people with wisdom:* Exactly who these "people with wisdom" may be is uncertain. This phrase functions like a title for the section.

22.20,21 *thirty sayings . . . trust them . . . those in charge of you:* The Egyptian *Instruction of Amenemope* also had thirty sections, or "houses." The purpose of that Egyptian work is similar to the purpose stated here. The introduction to *Amenemope* says the wise sayings are given to help the listener answer the one who has spoken, or to report to the one who has sent him and to show him the paths of life.

23.1 *eat with a king . . . best manners:* Using good manners included eating only what was offered and not more. How one acted at the table would be watched closely. Verse three may also be a warning about how a fancy feast might be used as a form of bribery to influence the guest.

P22.28 *marker:* In ancient Israel boundary lines were sacred because all property was a gift from the Lord (see Deuteronomy 19.14).

23.11 *God All-Powerful . . . defend:* According to Israelite law, a relative was supposed to step in and help a person who was having money trouble. This was done to make sure family land or property was not sold to or taken by outsiders (Lev 25.25). A close relative could also take revenge for a relative's death (Num 35.16-19). In the same way, Israel's God would defend those who had no one else to stand up for them, including widows, orphans, and the poor (Ps 68.5; 109.31; Joel 3.21).

(7)

4Give up trying so hard
to get rich.
5Your money flies away
before you know it,
just like an eagle
suddenly taking off.

(8)

6Don't accept an invitation
to eat a selfish person's food,
no matter how good it is.
7People like that take note
of how much you eat.[q]
They say, "Take all you want!"
But they don't mean it.
8Each bite will come back up,
and all your kind words
will be wasted.

(9)

9Don't talk to fools—
they will make fun of you.

(10)

10Don't move a boundary marker[r]
or take the land
that belongs to orphans.
11God All-Powerful is there
to defend them against you.

(11)

12Listen to instruction
and do your best to learn.

(12)

13Don't fail to correct
your children.
You won't kill them
by being firm,
14and it may even
save their lives.

(13)

15My children,
if you show good sense,
I will be happy,
16and if you are truthful,
I will really be glad.

(14)

17Don't be jealous of sinners,
but always honor the LORD.
18Then you will truly have hope
for the future.

(15)

19Listen to me, my children!
Be wise and have enough sense
to follow the right path.
20Don't be a heavy drinker
or stuff yourself with food.
21It will make you feel drowsy,
and you will end up poor
with only rags to wear.

(16)

22Pay attention to your father,
and don't neglect your mother
when she grows old.
23Invest in truth and wisdom,
discipline and good sense,
and don't part with them.
24Make your father truly happy
by living right and showing
sound judgment.
25Make your parents proud,
especially your mother.

(17)

26My son, pay close attention,
and gladly follow
my example.
27Bad women and unfaithful wives

[q]**23.7** *People . . . eat*: One possible meaning for the difficult Hebrew text. [r]**23.10** *marker*: See the note at 22.28.

Invest in truth and wisdom, discipline and good sense, and don't part with them. PROV 23.23

are like a deep pit—
²⁸they are waiting to attack you
   like a gang of robbers
     with victim after victim.

(18)

²⁹Who is always in trouble?
   Who argues and fights?
   Who has cuts and bruises?
   Whose eyes are red?
³⁰Everyone who stays up late,
   having just one more drink.
³¹Don't even look
   at that colorful stuff
     bubbling up in the glass!
   It goes down so easily,
³²but later it bites
   like a poisonous snake.
³³You will see weird things,
   and your mind
     will play tricks on you.
³⁴You will feel tossed about
   like someone trying to sleep
     on a ship in a storm.
³⁵You will be bruised all over,
   without even remembering
     how it all happened.
   And you will lie awake asking,
   "When will morning come,
     so I can drink some more?"

(19)

24 Don't be jealous of crooks
     or want to be their friends.
²All they think about
   and talk about
     is violence and cruelty.

(20)

³Use wisdom and understanding
   to establish your home;
⁴let good sense fill the rooms
   with priceless treasures.

(21)

⁵Wisdom brings strength,
   and knowledge gives power.
⁶Battles are won
   by listening to advice
     and making a lot of plans.

(22)

⁷Wisdom is too much for fools!
   Their advice is no good.

(23)

⁸No one but troublemakers
   think up trouble.
⁹Everyone hates senseless fools
   who think up ways to sin.

(24)

¹⁰Don't give up and be helpless
   in times of trouble.

(25)

¹¹Don't fail to rescue those
   who are doomed to die.
¹²Don't say, "I didn't know it!"
   God can read your mind.
   He watches each of us
     and knows our thoughts.
   And God will pay us back
     for what we do.

(26)

¹³Honey is good for you,
   my children,
     and it tastes sweet.
¹⁴Wisdom is like honey
   for your life—
   if you find it,
     your future is bright.

(27)

¹⁵Don't be a cruel person
   who attacks good people
     and hurts their families.
¹⁶Even if good people

■ **23.29-35** *always in trouble . . . drink some more:* This section provides a graphic description of the effects of drinking too much. Wine may look good in the glass and taste good going down, but too much of it can cause a person to get sick or feel pain that's as bad as the effects of a snake bite. Drunkenness can cause a person to sleep as if on a rolling boat and to be bruised from bumping into things or falling down. Despite these bad effects, a person addicted to alcohol wants to start drinking again in the morning (23.35).

■ **24.3** *establish your home:* Compare this verse to the description of Wisdom building her house.

Use wisdom and understanding to establish your home; let good sense fill the rooms with priceless treasures. PROV 24.3,4

24.16 *seven times:* Seven was considered a complete or perfect number. Here it stands for a very large number of times. Even good people, meaning those who obey the Lord, fall or experience hardship.

24.23 *more sayings:* The sayings in 24.23-34 are related to the sayings described in 22.17-21, but exactly who created these sayings is unclear.

24.27 *Get your fields ready:* This may refer to a young farmer working to build a livelihood before building a home, but it probably has the more general meaning of doing things in the proper order. A similar modern saying might be, "First things first."

25.1 *Solomon's proverbs . . . Hezekiah of Judah:* After Solomon died, the united Israel divided into two separate kingdoms. The southern kingdom was named Judah, which Hezekiah ruled from 715 to 687 B.C., or over 200 years after the time of Solomon. Hezekiah was responsible for a religious reform in the country (2 Kgs 18.1-7). Such a time may have awakened interest in ancient wisdom, so that court officials and teachers researched ancient wisdom sayings and perhaps edited them or even added new ones of their own.

25.2,3 *God is . . . mysterious . . . thoughts of a ruler:* Human beings are to praise God, because God is beyond human understanding (Job 26.12-14; 37.14-24; Isa 40.12-26; Rom 11.33-36). The wise ruler who can explain certain mysteries is also to be highly respected.

fall seven times,
    they will get back up.
But when trouble strikes
the wicked,
    that's the end of them.

(28)

17Don't be happy
    to see your enemies trip
    and fall down.
18The Lord will find out
    and be unhappy.
Then he will stop
    being angry with them.

(29)

19Don't let evil people
    worry you
    or make you jealous.
20They will soon be gone
    like the flame of a lamp
    that burns out.

(30)

21My children, you must respect
    the Lord and the king,
    and you must not make friends
    with anyone who rebels
    against either of them.
22Who knows what sudden disaster
    the Lord or a ruler
    might bring?

More Sayings That Make Good Sense

23Here are some more sayings
    that make good sense:
When you judge,
    you must be fair.
24If you let the guilty
    go free,
people of all nations
    will hate and curse you.

25But if you punish the guilty,
    things will go well for you,
    and you will prosper.
26Giving an honest answer
    is a sign
    of true friendship.
27Get your fields ready
    and plant your crops
    before starting a home.
28Don't accuse anyone
    who isn't guilty.
Don't ever tell a lie
29   or say to someone,
    "I'll get even with you!"

30I once walked by the field
    and the vineyard
    of a lazy fool.
31Thorns and weeds
    were everywhere,
    and the stone wall
    had fallen down.
32When I saw this,
    it taught me a lesson:
33 Sleep a little. Doze a little.
    Fold your hands
    and twiddle your thumbs.
34Suddenly poverty hits you
    and everything is gone!

More of Solomon's Wise Sayings

25 Here are some more
    of Solomon's proverbs.
They were copied by the officials
    of King Hezekiah of Judah.
2God is praised
    for being mysterious;
rulers are praised
    for explaining mysteries.
3Who can fully understand
    the thoughts of a ruler?
They reach beyond the sky
    and go deep in the earth.

⁴Silver must be purified
  before it can be used
    to make something of value.
⁵Evil people must be removed
  before anyone can rule
    with justice.

⁶Don't try to seem important
  in the court of a ruler.
⁷It's better for the ruler
  to give you a high position
than for you to be embarrassed
  in front of royal officials.
Be sure you are right
8 before you sue someone,
or you might lose your case
  and be embarrassed.

⁹When you and someone else
  can't get along,
    don't gossip about it.ˢ
¹⁰Others will find out,
  and your reputation
    will then be ruined.

¹¹The right word
    at the right time
  is like precious gold
    set in silver.
¹²Listening to good advice
  is worth much more
    than jewelry made of gold.
¹³A messenger you can trust
  is just as refreshing
    as cool water in summer.
¹⁴Broken promises
  are worse than rain clouds
    that don't bring rain.
¹⁵Patience and gentle talk
  can convince a ruler
    and overcome any problem.

¹⁶Eating too much honey
    can make you sick.
¹⁷Don't visit friends too often,
  or they will get tired of it
    and start hating you.
¹⁸Telling lies about friends
    is like attacking them
  with clubs and swords
    and sharp arrows.
¹⁹A friend you can't trust
    in times of trouble
  is like having a toothache
    or a sore foot.
²⁰Singing to someone
    in deep sorrow
  is like pouring vinegar
    in an open cut.ᵗ

²¹If your enemies are hungry,
    give them something to eat.
And if they are thirsty,
  give them something
    to drink.
²²This will be the same
  as piling burning coals
    on their heads.
And the LORD
    will reward you.
²³As surely as rain blows in
    from the north,
  anger is caused
    by cruel words.
²⁴It's better to stay outside
    on the roof of your house
  than to live inside
    with a nagging wife.

²⁵Good news from far away
  refreshes like cold water
    when you are thirsty.
²⁶When a good person gives in
    to the wicked,

25.21 *enemies... something to drink:* The opposite of taking revenge or getting even (Lev 24.20), this saying shows the importance of being kind to one's enemy, or "turning the other cheek" (Matt 5.38-41). In an ancient Egyptian ritual, a person who had done wrong was to carry a bowl of hot coals on his head to show that he was sorry for what he had done. Perhaps this saying means that kindness will cause a guilty person to be sorry for the hurt he or she may have caused.

25.23 *rain blows in... north:* North winds do not normally bring rain to Israel, but cruel words do cause anger.

ˢ25.9 *When... it:* Or "Settle a problem privately between you and your neighbor and don't involve others." ᵗ25.20 *cut:* One possible meaning for the difficult Hebrew text of verse 20.

25.28 *city without a wall:* Many ancient cities were surrounded by walls as a protection against enemies.

26.1 *dry season:* In the Near East, it usually rains very little in the months of June through September. **(See the chart Pilgrimage Festivals on pg 1799.)**

26.3 *beaten and bridled:* Sticks or whips were sometimes used to get horses and donkeys to move faster, just as rods were sometimes used to beat fools (10.13). Then, as today, bridles made of strips of leather were placed over a horse's head, nose, and mouth as a way of guiding the animal. The bridle was attached to a wooden or metal bit that went in the horse's mouth. The rider controlled the horse by pulling on the reins that were attached to the bit.

26.8 *slingshot . . . tied tight:* A rock tied tightly in the loading area of a slingshot will not fly when the slingshot is released. Instead, it could return and hit the one who shot it.

26.9 *thornbush . . . in the hand of a drunkard:* A drunken person's uncontrolled and unpredictable movements could easily cause harm to himself or others, especially if he is wildly waving a thorny bush.

it's like dumping garbage
  in a stream of clear water.
²⁷Don't eat too much honey
  or always want praise.ᵘ
²⁸Losing self-control
  leaves you as helpless
  as a city without a wall.

Don't Be a Fool

26 Expecting snow in summer
  and rain in the dry season
makes more sense
  than honoring a fool.
²A curse you don't deserve
  will take wings and fly away
  like a sparrow or a swallow.
³Horses and donkeys
  must be beaten and bridled—
  and so must fools.
⁴Don't make a fool of yourself
  by answering a fool.
⁵But if you answer any fools,
  show how foolish they are,
  so they won't feel smart.

⁶Sending a message by a fool
  is like chopping off your foot
  just to spite yourself.
⁷A fool with words of wisdom
  is like an athlete
  with legs that can't move.ᵛ
⁸Are you going to honor a fool?
  Why not shoot a slingshot
  with the rock tied tight?
⁹A thornbush waved around
  in the hand of a drunkard
  is no worse than a proverb
  in the mouth of a fool.

¹⁰It's no smarter to shoot arrows
  at every passerby
than it is to hire a bunch
  of worthless nobodies.ʷ
¹¹ Dogs return to eat their vomit,
  just as fools repeat
  their foolishness.
¹²There is more hope for a fool
  than for someone who says,
  "I'm really smart!"

¹³Don't be lazy and keep saying,
  "There's a lion outside!"
¹⁴A door turns on its hinges,
  but a lazy person
  just turns over in bed.
¹⁵Some of us are so lazy
  that we won't lift a hand
  to feed ourselves.
¹⁶A lazy person says,
  "I am smarter
  than everyone else."

¹⁷It's better to take hold
  of a mad dog by the ears
  than to take part
  in someone else's argument.
¹⁸It's no crazier to shoot
  sharp and flaming arrows
¹⁹than to cheat someone and say,
  "I was only fooling!"

²⁰Where there is no fuel
  a fire goes out;
where there is no gossip
  arguments come to an end.
²¹Troublemakers start trouble,
  just as sparks and fuel
  start a fire.
²²There is nothing so delicious

ᵘ**25.27** *or . . . praise:* One possible meaning for the difficult Hebrew text.   ᵛ**26.7** *with . . . move:* One possible meaning for the difficult Hebrew text.   ʷ**26.10** *nobodies:* One possible meaning for the difficult Hebrew text of verse 10.

as the taste of gossip!
   It melts in your mouth.

23Hiding hateful thoughts
   behind smooth[x] talk
is like coating a clay pot
   with a cheap glaze.
24The pleasant talk
   of an enemy
hides more evil plans
25than can be counted—
   so don't believe a word!
26Everyone will see through
   those evil plans.
27If you dig a pit,
   you will fall in;
if you start a stone rolling,
   it will roll back on you.
28Watch out for anyone
   who tells lies and flatters—
   they are out to get you.

Don't Brag about Tomorrow

27 Don't brag about tomorrow!
   Each day brings
      its own surprises.
2Don't brag about yourself—
   let others praise you.
3Stones and sand are heavy,
   but trouble caused by a fool
   is a much heavier load.
4An angry person is dangerous,
   but a jealous person
   is even worse.

5A truly good friend
   will openly correct you.
6You can trust a friend
   who corrects you,
but kisses from an enemy
are nothing but lies.
7If you have had enough to eat,
   honey doesn't taste good,
but if you are really hungry,
   you will eat anything.

8When you are far from home,
   you feel like a bird
   without a nest.
9The sweet smell of incense
   can make you feel good,
but true friendship
   is better still.[y]
10Don't desert an old friend
   of your family
or visit your relatives
   when you are in trouble.
A friend nearby is better
   than relatives far away.

11My child, show good sense!
   Then I will be happy
and able to answer anyone
   who criticizes me.
12Be cautious and hide
   when you see danger—
don't be stupid and walk
   right into trouble.
13You deserve to lose your coat
   if you loan it to someone
to guarantee payment
   for the debt of a stranger.
14A loud greeting
   early in the morning
   is the same as a curse.
15The steady dripping of rain
   and the nagging of a wife
   are one and the same.
16It's easier to catch the wind
   or hold olive oil in your hand
   than to stop a nagging wife.

26.23 *cheap glaze:* Clay pots were sometimes made smoother or fancier by a covering of transparent glaze, but the pot itself was not changed underneath. Smooth talk may be used as a cover-up for evil thoughts or plans.

27.9 *incense:* A sweet-scented substance that is burned or used in ointments and perfumes. Incense was burned to cover unpleasant odors and as a part of Israelite worship in the sacred tent and temple. Because the spices and resins used in making incense had to be imported from far-off lands, incense was a luxury item. **(See the chart Spices and Perfumes on pg 1835.)**

27.10 *relatives . . . friend:* This is a caution about depending only on the help of family members, especially if a nearby friend can provide help more quickly.

27.11 *show good sense:* Parents' reputations were judged by the behavior of their children.

27.13 *loan . . . guarantee:* Lending money to a stranger was considered risky. To reduce the risk, some item was given as a guarantee against the loan.

27.16 *easier to catch the wind . . . hold olive oil:* The difference between a nagging wife and good wife is a common theme in PROVERBS. "Catching the wind" is a phrase used to mean something that is impossible. Olive oil is very slippery.

---

[x]**26.23** *smooth:* One ancient translation; Hebrew "hateful."   [y]**27.9** *still:* One possible meaning for the difficult Hebrew text of verse 9.

27.17 *iron sharpens iron:* A coarse piece of iron was often used to sharpen an iron blade.

27.20 *Death . . . never satisfied:* The Hebrew words here translated as "death" and "grave" refer to the dark world of the dead known by the names "Sheol" and "Abaddon."

28.8 *charging high interest rates:* Moneylenders made a living by charging interest on loans. This proverb warns that those who charge an unfairly high interest rate will lose business to those who are charging a fair interest rate.

¹⁷Just as iron sharpens iron,
friends sharpen the minds
of each other.
¹⁸Take care of a tree,
and you will eat its fruit;
look after your master,
and you will be praised.
¹⁹You see your face in a mirror
and your thoughts
in the minds of others.
²⁰Death and the grave
are never satisfied,
and neither are humans.
²¹Gold and silver are tested
in a red-hot furnace,
but we are tested by praise.
²²No matter how hard
you beat a fool,
you can't pound out
the foolishness.

²³You should take good care
of your sheep and goats,
²⁴because wealth and honor
don't last forever.
²⁵After the hay is cut
and the new growth appears
and the harvest is over,
²⁶you can sell lambs and goats
to buy clothes and land.
²⁷From the milk of the goats,
you can make enough cheese
to feed your family
and all your servants.

The Law of God Makes Sense

28 Wicked people run away
when no one chases them,
but those who live right
are as brave as lions.
²In time of civil war
there are many leaders,

but a sensible leader
restores law and order.^z
³When someone poor takes over
and mistreats the poor,
it's like a heavy rain
destroying the crops.

⁴Lawbreakers praise criminals,
but law-abiding citizens
always oppose them.
⁵Criminals don't know
what justice means,
but all who respect the LORD
understand it completely.
⁶It's better to be poor
and live right,
than to be rich
and dishonest.

⁷It makes good sense
to obey the Law of God,
but you disgrace your parents
if you make friends
with worthless nobodies.
⁸If you make money by charging
high interest rates,
you will lose it all to someone
who cares for the poor.
⁹God cannot stand the prayers
of anyone who disobeys
his Law.
¹⁰By leading good people to sin,
you dig a pit for yourself,
but all who live right
will have a bright future.

¹¹The rich think highly
of themselves,
but anyone poor and sensible
sees right through them.
¹²When an honest person wins,
it's time to celebrate;
when crooks are in control,

^z**28.2** *but . . . order:* One possible meaning for the difficult Hebrew text.

it's best to hide.
¹³If you don't confess your sins,
  you will be a failure.
But God will be merciful
  if you confess your sins
  and give them up.
¹⁴The LORD blesses everyone
  who is afraid to do evil,
but if you are cruel,
  you will end up in trouble.

¹⁵A ruler who mistreats the poor
  is like a roaring lion
  or a bear hunting for food.
¹⁶A heartless leader is a fool,
  but anyone who refuses
  to get rich by cheating others
  will live a long time.
¹⁷Don't give help to murderers!
  Make them stay on the run
  for as long as they live.^a

¹⁸Honesty will keep you safe,
  but everyone who is crooked
  will suddenly fall.
¹⁹Work hard, and you will have
  a lot of food;
waste time, and you will have
  a lot of trouble.

²⁰God blesses his loyal people,
  but punishes all who want
  to get rich quick.
²¹It isn't right to be unfair,
  but some people can be bribed
  with only a piece of bread.
²²Don't be selfish
  and eager to get rich—
you will end up worse off
  than you can imagine.

²³Honest correction
  is appreciated

more than flattery.
²⁴If you cheat your parents
  and don't think it's wrong,
  you are a common thief.
²⁵Selfish people cause trouble,
  but you will live a full life
  if you trust the LORD.
²⁶Only fools would trust
  what they alone think,
but if you live by wisdom,
  you will do all right.

²⁷Giving to the poor
  will keep you from poverty,
but if you close your eyes
  to their needs,
  everyone will curse you.
²⁸When crooks are in control,
  everyone tries to hide,
but when they lose power,
  good people are everywhere.

Use Good Sense

²⁹ If you keep being stubborn
  after many warnings,
you will suddenly discover
  you have gone too far.
²When justice rules a nation,
  everyone is glad;
when injustice rules,
  everyone groans.
³If you love wisdom
  your parents will be glad,
but chasing after bad women
  will cost you everything.
⁴An honest ruler
  makes the nation strong;
a ruler who takes bribes
  will bring it to ruin.

⁵Flattery is nothing less
  than setting a trap.

^a**28.17** *live:* One possible meaning for the difficult Hebrew text of verse 17.

■ **28.13** *don't confess your sins . . . failure:* This proverb warns that those who keep on doing evil things or who try to cover them up will end up losing what they have.

Honest correction is appreciated more than flattery.
PROV 28.23

29.8 *Sneering . . . is a spark:* Attitudes and actions that create anger can spread quickly, but wise words and actions can stop anger from spreading.

29.18 *guidance . . . Law:* These are two ways that God's message and purposes are communicated to people. The message of God's prophets was guided by God's Spirit, while the Law was given to Moses and the people of Israel.

30.1 *message of Agur son of Jakeh:* The Hebrew word here translated as "message" may also be a place name (*Massa*). If so, this could connect Agur with the ancestors of Ishmael who lived in northern Arabia (Gen 25.12-18). Exactly which or how many sayings are to be credited to this wise man is unclear.

⁶Your sins will catch you,
  but everyone who lives right
    will sing and celebrate.
⁷The wicked don't care
  about the rights of the poor,
    but good people do.
⁸Sneering at others is a spark
    that sets a city on fire;
  using good sense can put out
    the flames of anger.

⁹Be wise and don't sue a fool.
    You won't get satisfaction,
  because all the fool will do
    is sneer and shout.
¹⁰A murderer hates everyone
  who is honest
    and lives right.ᵇ
¹¹Don't be a fool
  and quickly lose your temper—
    be sensible and patient.

¹²A ruler who listens to lies
    will have corrupt officials.
¹³The poor and all who abuse them
  must each depend on God
    for light.
¹⁴Kings who are fair to the poor
    will rule a long time.

¹⁵Correct your children,
    and they will be wise;
  children out of control
    disgrace their mothers.
¹⁶Crime increases
    when crooks are in power,
  but law-abiding citizens
    will see them fall.
¹⁷If you correct your children,
  they will bring you peace
    and happiness.

¹⁸Without guidance from God
    law and order disappear,
  but God blesses everyone
    who obeys his Law.
¹⁹Even when servants are smart,
    it takes more than words
      to make them obey.
²⁰There is more hope for a fool
    than for someone who speaks
      without thinking.
²¹Slaves that you treat kindly
    from their childhood
      will cause you sorrow.ᶜ
²²A person with a quick temper
    stirs up arguments
  and commits a lot of sins.

²³Too much pride brings disgrace;
    humility leads to honor.
²⁴If you take part in a crime
    you are your worst enemy,
  because even under oath
    you can't tell the truth.
²⁵Don't fall into the trap
    of being a coward—
  trust the LORD,
    and you will be safe.
²⁶Many try to make friends
    with a ruler,
  but justice comes
    from the LORD.
²⁷Good people and criminals
    can't stand each other.

The Sayings of Agur

30 These are the sayings
    and the message
      of Agur son of Jakeh.
  Someone cries out to God,
    "I am completely worn out!

ᵇ**29.10** *and lives right*: Or "and those who live right are friends of honest people."   ᶜ**29.21** *will . . . sorrow*: One possible meaning for the difficult Hebrew text.

Too much pride brings disgrace; humility leads to honor. PROV 29.23

How can I last?[d]
²I am far too stupid
    to be considered human.
³I never was wise,
    and I don't understand
        what God is like."

⁴Has anyone gone up to heaven
    and come back down?
Has anyone grabbed hold
    of the wind?
Has anyone wrapped up the sea
or marked out boundaries
    for the earth?
If you know of any
    who have done such things,
then tell me their names
    and their children's names.

⁵Everything God says is true—
    and it's a shield for all
        who come to him for safety.
⁶Don't change what God has said!
He will correct you and show
    that you are a liar.

⁷There are two things, Lord,
I want you to do for me
    before I die:
⁸Make me absolutely honest
and don't let me be too poor
    or too rich.
Give me just what I need.
⁹If I have too much to eat,
    I might forget about you;
if I don't have enough,
    I might steal
        and disgrace your name.

¹⁰Don't tell a slave owner
    something bad about one

of the slaves.
That slave will curse you,
    and you will be in trouble.

¹¹Some people curse their father
    and even their mother;
¹²others think they are perfect,
    but they are stained by sin.
¹³Some people are stuck-up
    and act like snobs;
¹⁴others are so greedy
    that they gobble up
        the poor and homeless.

¹⁵Greed[e] has twins,
    each named "Give me!"
There are three or four things
    that are never satisfied:
¹⁶The world of the dead
    and a childless wife,
the thirsty earth
    and a flaming fire.

¹⁷Don't make fun of your father
    or disobey your mother—
crows will peck out your eyes,
    and buzzards will eat
        the rest of you.

¹⁸There are three or four things
    I cannot understand:
¹⁹How eagles fly so high
    or snakes crawl on rocks,
how ships sail the ocean
    or people fall in love.

²⁰An unfaithful wife says,
    "Sleeping with another man
        is as natural as eating."

²¹There are three or four things
    that make the earth tremble

30.2,3 *I am . . . stupid . . . don't understand what God is like:* Agur says that his wisdom and understanding are nothing when compared to the wisdom and mystery of God. Compare his comments to Job 42.1-6.

30.4 *Has anyone:* A series of questions that expect a negative answer. No human can do these things, but the LORD can.

30.8 *too poor or too rich:* Both can present problems.

30.9 *have too much:* God's people are to give the LORD credit for the things they have been given and for the help they have received (Deut 8.7-20; Ps 44).

30.11-14 *Some people curse . . . gobble up the poor:* Four types of people who are considered especially bad: those who curse their parents (Exod 20.12; Deut 27.14-26; Matt 15.4-6); those who do not recognize that they sin (16.2; Isa 65.1-7; Luke 18.9-14); those who are overly proud (11.2; 13.10; 16.5); and those who mistreat or rob the poor (28.3).

30.17 *crows . . . buzzards:* Such disobedience will result in death and the further humiliation of not being properly buried. Unburied dead were eaten by scavenger birds.

---

[d]**30.1** *last:* One possible meaning for the difficult Hebrew text of verse 1.   [e]**30.15** *Greed:* Or "A leech."

30.25-28 *Ants . . . lizards:* Four small animals admired for particular abilities: ants for their ability to work hard (6.6-8); badgers for being able to survive among the rocks in the wilderness (Ps 104.18); locusts for their ability to swarm in large numbers (Joel 1.4); and lizards (or spiders) for their ability to sneak over a king's guarded palace walls.

30.33 *churn milk:* Milk or cream poured into a barrel or a clay pot was stirred or beaten until it turned into butter.

31.1 *King Lemuel of Massa . . . mother:* Literature offering advice for young princes or kings is common in the ancient wisdom writings of Egypt and Mesopotamia. Here, advice comes from a mother. This follows the theme of the wise woman introduced earlier (see 1.20-33). The words of a good wife and mother are "sensible, and her advice is thoughtful" (31.26).

31.3 *chasing after women:* For the potential problems that come from chasing after many women, see 5.1-23; 7.6-27. Some women may use their relationship to spy on the king and discover some important national secrets.

31.4-7 *not get drunk . . . Let them drink:* Nations suffer when their leaders get drunk and can't handle their responsibilities (Eccl 10.16, 17; Isa 5.21-24; 28.7-13).

and are unbearable:
²²A slave who becomes king,
  a fool who eats too much,
²³a hateful woman
  who finds a husband,
  and a slave who takes the place
  of the woman who owns her.

²⁴On this earth four things
  are small but very wise:
²⁵Ants, who seem to be feeble,
  but store up food
  all summer long;
²⁶badgers, who seem to be weak,
  but live among the rocks;
²⁷locusts, who have no king,
  but march like an army;
²⁸lizards,ᶠ which can be caught
  in your hand,
  but sneak into palaces.

²⁹Three or four creatures
  really strut around:
³⁰Those fearless lions
  who rule the jungle,
³¹those proud roosters,
  those mountain goats,
  and those rulers
  who have no enemies.ᵍ

³²If you are foolishly bragging
  or planning something evil,
  then stop it now!
³³If you churn milk
  you get butter;
  if you pound on your nose,
  you get blood—
  and if you stay angry,
  you get in trouble.

What King Lemuel's Mother Taught Him

31 These are the sayings
  that King Lemuel of Massa
  was taught by his mother.
²My son Lemuel, you were born
  in answer to my prayers,
  so listen carefully.
³Don't waste your life
  chasing after women!
  This has ruined many kings.

⁴Kings and leaders
  should not get drunk
  or even want to drink.
⁵Drinking makes you forget
  your responsibilities,
  and you mistreat the poor.
⁶Beer and wine are only
  for the dying or for those
  who have lost all hope.
⁷Let them drink and forget
  how poor and miserable
  they feel.
⁸But you must defend
  those who are helpless
  and have no hope.
⁹Be fair and give justice
  to the poor and homeless.

In Praise of a Good Wife

¹⁰A truly good wife
  is the most precious treasure
  a man can find!
¹¹Her husband depends on her,
  and she never
  lets him down.
¹²She is good to him

ᶠ**30.28** *lizards:* Or "spiders."   ᵍ**30.31** *enemies:* One possible meaning for the difficult Hebrew text of verse 31.

every day of her life,
[13] and with her own hands
  she gladly makes clothes.

[14] She is like a sailing ship
  that brings food
  from across the sea.
[15] She gets up before daylight
  to prepare food for her family
  and for her servants.[h]
[16] She knows how to buy land
  and how to plant a vineyard,
[17]   and she always works hard.
[18] She knows when to buy or sell,
  and she stays busy
  until late at night.
[19] She spins her own cloth,
[20] and she helps the poor
  and the needy.
[21] Her family has warm clothing,
  and so she doesn't worry
  when it snows.
[22] She does her own sewing,
  and everything she wears
  is beautiful.

[23] Her husband is a well-known
  and respected leader

in the city.
[24] She makes clothes to sell
  to the shop owners.
[25] She is strong and graceful,[i]
  as well as cheerful
  about the future.
[26] Her words are sensible,
  and her advice
  is thoughtful.
[27] She takes good care
  of her family
  and is never lazy.
[28] Her children praise her,
  and with great pride
  her husband says,
[29] "There are many good women,
  but you are the best!"

[30] Charm can be deceiving,
  and beauty fades away,
  but a woman
  who honors the LORD
  deserves to be praised.
[31] Show her respect—
  praise her in public
  for what she has done.

31.13,14 *makes clothes . . . brings food:* In most families, the mother and older daughters made clothing and prepared meals. These activities started early in the morning and continued throughout the day.

31.16-20 *buy land . . . works hard . . . helps the poor:* The good wife and mother displays in her life many of the things connected with wisdom.

31.23 *respected leader:* Her husband's work is public and visible for all to see, but a woman's work in the home and family setting is equally important and will bring her praise and respect (31.31).

31.26 *words are sensible:* Because she follows the wisdom that comes from the LORD (2.6,7).

[h] **31.15** *and . . . servants:* Or "and to tell her servants what to do."   [i] **31.25** *She . . . graceful:* Or "The clothes she makes are attractive and of good quality."

Reflection Questions About Proverbs 1.1—31.31

1. What kinds of things are proverbs meant to teach (1.1-6)? What are some wise sayings or proverbs you heard as a child? How are they similar to or different from the proverbs you have read in the book of PROVERBS? What is the source of true wisdom (1.7; 2.4-7)?

2. Wisdom teaches what is right and honest and fair (2.9). Explain what this statement means in your own words. In contrast, "stupid fools" are described as living in darkness and headed for death (1.32; 2.13; 9.13,17). What does this mean?

3. Who or what is Woman Wisdom (1.20-33; 3.16-18; 4.6-9; 8.1—9.12)? Who or what is the opposite of Wisdom (2.16; 5.3-6; 7.6-27; 9.13-18)?

4. To have wisdom means taking the path or road that leads to life (4.10-13). When people have the option of going in many directions or taking many paths through life, how do they know which path to take? How do you find guidance when making important "life decisions"?

5. According to Wisdom, how can riches be both a blessing (10.22) and a curse (13.8; 11.28)? What does it mean that one can become rich by being generous, or poor by being greedy (11.24)?

6. The sayings in PROVERBS are over 2,000 years old. It has been said that true wisdom is time-less. What does that mean? Give two or three examples of proverbs that may be described as "timeless wisdom." Explain. Which proverbs, if any, do you believe are not timeless, that do not make sense today?

7. Choose at least one of the 30 sayings in 22.17—24.22 and explain what it means in your own words. How does the saying apply to modern circumstances?

8. Modern society puts a great deal of emphasis on wealth. What do you think of the prayer in Proverbs 30.7-9? What do you ask God for when you pray?

9. Why is the description of a good wife and mother (31.10-31) a fitting ending for PROVERBS? List some of the book's themes which can be found in this description.

10. Name two new things you discovered while reading and studying PROVERBS. How can these things be applied to your life?

ecclesiastes

What can people do to find satisfaction and happiness?
Read ECCLESIASTES to find out what one wise author
says about the meaning of life.

WHAT MAKES ECCLESIASTES SPECIAL?

The book's title comes from the ancient Greek translation of the Hebrew word *Qoheleth,* which means "preacher" or "one who assembles." The unknown author may have been a teacher, preacher, or philosopher. The author is not telling a story, but is sharing his thoughts on the meaning of life. He uses sayings, proverbs, and poems to illustrate his point. A key phrase, "nothing makes sense," begins and ends the book (1.2; 12.8), and is repeated throughout the book, emphasizing that the answers to many of life's questions are not easy to find.

This book is a search for meaning in life. The writer sees that from the human viewpoint life is full of contradictions and mysteries. Wisdom is better than foolishness, but whether a person is wise or foolish, everyone dies (2.13-16; 3.20), and knowing too much can be painful (1.18). Above all, human wisdom cannot help people understand the ways of God (8.17), who makes everything happen (3.11; 6.10; 7.13,14; 9.1). People are to respect and obey God (5.7; 8.12,13; 12.13), for God will judge what they do (12.4; 3.17). Nevertheless, the same thing happens to all people, whether they live right or whether they sin (9.2).

With life being so full of contradictions, where do humans find meaning? Some readers think the message of ECCLESIASTES lacks hope and gives no answers regarding the meaning of life. Others see hope and answers in the author's repeated invitations to enjoy life as a gift from God (2.24-26).

WHAT'S THE STORY BEHIND THE SCENE?

The author is identified in 1.1 as being a son of David and a king in Jerusalem. While Solomon is not mentioned by name anywhere in ECCLESIASTES, he is the only one of David's sons who was a king in Jerusalem (1 Kgs 1). Solomon was known for his wisdom and was given credit for writing many wise sayings and songs (1 Kgs 3.5-12; 4.29-34; Prov 1.1).

It was not uncommon in ancient times to write "in the name" of an important person such as Solomon, and most scholars now agree that Solomon did not write ECCLESIASTES. The Hebrew language of this book appears to come from a period many centuries after the time of Solomon, who ruled around 970 to 931 B.C. Also the writer speaks as though he is not a king, but a subject (5.8,9; 8.2-5; 10.5-7,16,17,20).

HOW IS ECCLESIASTES CONSTRUCTED?

The following is just one of the dozens of different outlines that have been suggested for ECCLESIASTES.

A wise person and the search for the meaning in
    life (1.1—2.26)
      One known to be very wise (1.1)
      The search for meaning in life (1.2—2.26)
Life is puzzling, but it's a gift from God (3.1—11.6)
Enjoy life and remember God while you are young
    (11.7—12.8)
Conclusion (12.9-14)

Ecclesiastes is an example of Jewish Wisdom literature that uses a variety of methods to convey its message. It employs personal reflections, examples, parables (stories), poems, and proverbs to describe the search for meaning in life. The Hebrew title of the book, *Qoheleth*, meaning "somebody who takes part in an assembly," suggests the author was a teacher, preacher, or philosopher of some kind. Like Job, Ecclesiastes discusses the limits of human wisdom. Only God knows what will happen in the future and people cannot control the mystery of God's creation. No matter how people try to understand life, it is too complicated for human understanding alone. Throughout the book, the author states that "nothing makes sense," and that individual human actions and possessions cannot offer protection from injustice, suffering, or death. Everything that happens in life is controlled by God. The author concludes that all teachings can be summed up in the words, "Respect and obey God! This is what life is all about."

Outline

Nothing Makes Sense

1 When the son of David was king in
Jerusalem, he was known to be very
wise,[a] and he said:

²Nothing makes sense!
Everything is nonsense.
  I have seen it all—
  nothing makes sense!
³What is there to show
for all of our hard work
  here on this earth?
⁴People come, and people go,
but still the world
  never changes.

⁵The sun comes up,
  the sun goes down;
it hurries right back
  to where it started from.
⁶The wind blows south,

the wind blows north;
round and round it blows
  over and over again.
⁷All rivers empty into the sea,
  but it never spills over;
one by one the rivers return
  to their source.[b]

⁸All of life is far more boring
  than words could ever say.
Our eyes and our ears
are never satisfied
  with what we see and hear.
⁹Everything that happens
  has happened before;
nothing is new,
  nothing under the sun.
¹⁰Someone might say,
  "Here is something new!"
But it happened before,
  long before we were born.
¹¹No one who lived in the past

---

[a]**1.1** *known to be very wise*: This stands for the Hebrew word often translated "preacher" or "teacher."
The word may refer to someone who was a very wise leader or to someone who had become wise
from collecting sayings about wisdom.   [b]**1.7** *return to their source*: Or "flow into the sea."

1.1 *When the son of David . . . was
known to be very wise:* David, Israel's
greatest king, ruled in Jerusalem as king
of Israel from about 1010 to 970 B.C.
His son Solomon followed him as king
and ruled from about 970 to 931 B.C.
Solomon was known for his great wisdom (1 Kgs 4.29-34). The lives of David
and Solomon are described in detail in
1 Samuel 16—1 Kings 11. The opening
verse, called a superscription, provides
the title for the book, and credits the
words of the book to David's son,
which probably means Solomon. This
connects ECCLESIASTES with the "wisdom" literature of Solomon, who was
called Israel's wisest person.

David

Solomon

1.3-9 *here on this earth . . . under
the sun:* These phrases, meaning "from
a human perspective" and "apart from
God," provide balance to the seemingly
hopeless attitude that "nothing makes
sense" (1.2; 12.8).

1.8-11 *life is . . . boring . . . everyone . . . forgotten:* The author's observation that the cycles of nature and life
are boring and unsatisfying may grow
out of his frustration at not understanding how God works. The author believes that God does make "everything
happen at the right time" (3.11), and
that God decided long ago what will
happen in the world. But even these beliefs seem to make the author feel powerless.

1.13,14 *God . . . senseless as chasing the wind:* The only Hebrew word used for God in this book is *Elohim,* the name of God used in the creation story (Gen 1.1—2.4). The Hebrew verb translated as "chasing" (1.14) also may be related to a Hebrew word for taking care of sheep. "Shepherding" the wind would be even more impossible than catching it.

Names of God

1.17 *wisdom:* Wisdom often refers to common sense and practical skill needed to solve everyday problems, but sometimes it involves trying to find answers to hard questions about the meaning of life. According to PROVERBS, true wisdom comes from God and is given to those who obey God.

Wisdom

2.3 *I:* It is not certain who this is. Some say that it is Solomon. Others think that it is the author imagining himself as a king like Solomon. In 2.3-11, the "king" tells of trying to find pleasure and enjoyment in the things he did and the wealth he owned. Like the king in these verses, Solomon was known for his great wealth, huge flocks of sheep and cattle, and for having many wives.

2.9 *Jerusalem:* Jerusalem was Israel's political and religious capital.

Jerusalem

2.12 *next king:* After Solomon's death, his son Rehoboam became king (1 Kgs 11.42).

is remembered anymore,
and everyone yet to be born
will be forgotten too.

It Is Senseless To Be Wise

¹²I said these things when I lived in Jerusalem as king of Israel. ¹³With all my wisdom I tried to understand everything that happens here on earth. And God has made this so hard for us humans to do. ¹⁴I have seen it all, and everything is just as senseless as chasing the wind.[c]

¹⁵If something is crooked,
it can't be made straight;
if something isn't there,
it can't be counted.

¹⁶I said to myself, "You are by far the wisest person who has ever lived in Jerusalem. You are eager to learn, and you have learned a lot." ¹⁷Then I decided to find out all I could about wisdom and foolishness. Soon I realized that this too was as senseless as chasing the wind.[d]

¹⁸The more you know,
the more you hurt;
the more you understand,
the more you suffer.

It Is Senseless To Be Selfish

2 I said to myself, "Have fun and enjoy yourself!" But this didn't make sense. ²Laughing and having fun is crazy. What good does it do? ³I wanted to find out what was best for us during the short time we have on this earth. So I decided to make myself happy with wine and find out what it means to be foolish, without really being foolish myself.

⁴I did some great things. I built houses and planted vineyards. ⁵I had flower gardens and orchards full of fruit trees. ⁶And I had pools where I could get water for the trees. ⁷I owned slaves, and their sons and daughters became my slaves. I had more sheep and goats than anyone who had ever lived in Jerusalem. ⁸Foreign rulers brought me silver, gold, and precious treasures. Men and women sang for me, and I had many wives[e] who gave me great pleasure.

⁹I was the most famous person who had ever lived in Jerusalem, and I was very wise. ¹⁰I got whatever I wanted and did whatever made me happy. But most of all, I enjoyed my work. ¹¹Then I thought about everything I had done, including the hard work, and it was simply chasing the wind.[f] Nothing on earth is worth the trouble.

Wisdom Comes from God

¹²I asked myself, "What can the next king do that I haven't done?" Then I decided to compare wisdom with foolishness and stupidity. ¹³And I discovered that wisdom is better than foolishness, just as light is better than darkness. ¹⁴Wisdom is like having two good eyes; foolishness leaves you in the dark. But wise or foolish, we all end up the same.

¹⁵Finally, I said to myself, "Being wise got me nowhere! The same thing will happen to me that happens to fools. Nothing makes sense. ¹⁶Wise or foolish, we all die and are soon forgotten." ¹⁷This made me hate life. Everything we do is painful; it's just as senseless as chasing the wind.[g]

¹⁸Suddenly I realized that others would someday get everything I had worked for so hard, then I started hating it all. ¹⁹Who

[c]**1.14** *chasing the wind:* Or "eating the wind."   [d]**1.17** *chasing the wind:* See the note at verse 14.   [e]**2.8** *many wives:* One possible meaning for the difficult Hebrew text.   [f]**2.11** *chasing the wind:* See the note at 1.14.   [g]**2.17** *chasing the wind:* See the note at 1.14.

knows if those people will be sensible or stupid? Either way, they will own everything I have earned by hard work and wisdom. It doesn't make sense.

20I thought about all my hard work, and I felt depressed. 21When we use our wisdom, knowledge, and skill to get what we own, why do we have to leave it to someone who didn't work for it? This is senseless and wrong. 22What do we really gain from all of our hard work? 23Our bodies ache during the day, and work is torture. Then at night our thoughts are troubled. It just doesn't make sense.

24The best thing we can do is to enjoy eating, drinking, and working.h I believe these are God's gifts to us, 25and no one enjoys eating and living more than I do. 26If we please God, he will make us wise, understanding, and happy. But if we sin, God will make us struggle for a living, then he will give all we own to someone who pleases him. This makes no more sense than chasing the wind.i

Everything Has Its Time

3 Everything on earth has its own time and its own season.
2There is a time
for birth and death,
planting and reaping,
3for killing and healing,
destroying and building,
4for crying and laughing,
weeping and dancing,
5for throwing stones
and gathering stones,
embracing and parting.
6There is a time

for finding and losing,
keeping and giving,
7for tearing and sewing,
listening and speaking.
8There is also a time
for love and hate,
for war and peace.

What God Has Given Us To Do

9What do we gain by all our hard work? 10I have seen what difficult things God demands of us. 11God makes everything happen at the right time. Yet none of us can ever fully understand all he has done, and he puts questions in our minds about the past and the future. 12I know the best thing we can do is to always enjoy life, 13because God's gift to us is the happiness we get from our food and drink and from the work we do. 14Everything God has done will last forever; nothing he does can ever be changed. God has done all this, so that we will worship him.

15Everything that happens
has happened before,
and all that will be
has already been—
God does everything
over and over again.j

The Future Is Known Only to God

16Everywhere on earth I saw violence and injustice instead of fairness and justice. 17So I told myself that God has set a time and a place for everything. He will judge everyone, both the wicked and the good. 18I know God is testing us to show us that we are merely animals. 19Like animals we breathe and die, and we are no better off

2.24-26 best thing we can do . . . please God . . . sin: The author gives a common understanding of reward and punishment that can be found in many places in the Bible. God rewards those who are faithful and punishes those who are evil. Those who were wealthy were assumed to be favored by God. Later, however, the author says that good people are not always rewarded and that bad people sometimes live long and prosperous lives.

3.1 its own time: This phrase means that God controls what happens and when.

3.11 right time . . . he puts questions in our minds: The author says that God's actions and timing are always correct. But human beings cannot fully understand God's actions, because God has put "questions" in their minds. The author's point is that people have limited knowledge, and this leads to questions that cannot be answered.

3.16,17 justice . . . judge everyone: The author seems to struggle with the fact that violence and injustice happen so often on the earth that God controls (3.11). Though life does not appear to be fair to humans (3.16), justice will be carried out when God judges the good and wicked (12.4).

Justice

Enemies (The Wicked)

Day of the LORD

h2.24 The best . . . working: One possible meaning for the difficult Hebrew text.   i2.26 chasing the wind: See the note at 1.14.   j3.15 God does . . . again: One possible meaning for the difficult Hebrew text.

Everything on earth has its own time and its own season. ECCL 3.1

than they are. It just doesn't make sense. [20]All living creatures go to the same place. We are made from earth, and we return to earth. [21]Who really knows if our spirits go up and the spirits of animals go down into the earth? [22]We were meant to enjoy our work, and that's the best thing we can do. We can never know the future.

4 I looked again and saw people being mistreated everywhere on earth. They were crying, but no one was there to offer comfort, and those who mistreated them were powerful. [2]I said to myself, "The dead are better off than the living. [3]But those who have never been born are better off than anyone else, because they have never seen the terrible things that happen on this earth."

[4]Then I realized that we work and do wonderful things just because we are jealous of others. This makes no more sense than chasing the wind.[k]

[5]Fools will fold their hands
    and starve to death.
[6]Yet a very little food
    eaten in peace
is better than twice as much
earned from overwork
    and chasing the wind.[l]

[7]Once again I saw that nothing on earth makes sense. [8]For example, some people don't have friends or family. But they are never satisfied with what they own, and they never stop working to get more. They should ask themselves, "Why am I always working to have more? Who will get what I leave behind?" What a senseless and miserable life!

It Is Better To Have a Friend

[9]You are better having a friend than to be all alone, because then you will get more enjoyment out of what you earn. [10]If you fall, your friend can help you up. But if you fall without having a friend nearby, you are really in trouble. [11]If you sleep alone, you won't have anyone to keep you warm on a cold night. [12]Someone might be able to beat up one of you, but not both of you. As the saying goes, "A rope made from three strands of cord is hard to break."

[13]You may be poor and young, but if you are wise, you are better off than a foolish old king who won't listen to advice. [14]Even if you were not born into the royal family and have been a prisoner and poor, you can still be king. [15]I once saw everyone in the world follow a young leader who came to power after the king was gone. [16]His followers could not even be counted. But years from now, no one will praise him— this makes no more sense than chasing the wind.[m]

Be Careful How You Worship

5 Be careful what you do when you enter the house of God. Fools go there to offer sacrifices, because all they do is sin.[n] But it's best just to listen when you go to worship. [2]Don't talk before you think or make promises to God without thinking them through. God is in heaven, and you are on earth, so don't talk too much. [3]If you keep thinking about something, you will dream about it. If you talk too much, you will say the wrong thing.

[4]God doesn't like fools. So don't be slow to keep your promises to God. [5]It's better

[k]**4.4** *chasing the wind:* See the note at 1.14.   [l]**4.6** *chasing the wind:* See the note at 1.14.   [m]**4.16** *chasing the wind:* See the note at 1.14.   [n]**5.1** *because . . . sin:* One possible meaning for the difficult Hebrew text.

not to make a promise at all than to make one and not keep it. **6**Don't let your mouth get you in trouble! And don't say to the worship leader,[o] "I didn't mean what I said." God can destroy everything you have worked for, so don't say something that makes God angry.

7Respect and obey God! Daydreaming leads to a lot of senseless talk.[p]

8Don't be surprised if the poor of your country are abused, and injustice takes the place of justice. After all, the lower officials must do what the higher ones order them to do. **9**And since the king is the highest official, he benefits most from the taxes paid on the land.[q]

10If you love money and wealth, you will never be satisfied with what you have. This doesn't make a bit of sense. **11**The more you have, the more everyone expects from you. Your money won't do you any good—others will just spend it for you. **12**If you have to work hard for a living, you can rest well at night, even if you don't have much to eat. But if you are rich, you can't even sleep.

13I have seen something terribly unfair. People get rich, but it does them no good. **14**Suddenly they lose everything in a bad business deal, then have nothing to leave for their children. **15**They came into this world naked, and when they die, they will be just as naked. They can't take anything with them, and they won't have anything to show for all their work. **16**That's terribly unfair. They leave the world just as they came. They gained nothing from running after the wind. **17**Besides all this, they are always gloomy at mealtime, and they are troubled, sick, and bitter.[r]

18What is the best thing to do in the short life God has given us? I think we should enjoy eating, drinking, and working hard. This is what God intends for us to do. **19**Suppose you are very rich and able to enjoy everything you own. Then go ahead and enjoy working hard—this is God's gift to you. **20**God will keep you so happy that you won't have time to worry about each day.

Don't Depend on Wealth

6 There is something else terribly unfair, and it troubles everyone on earth. **2**God may give you everything you want—money, property, and wealth. Then God doesn't let you enjoy it, and someone you don't even know gets it all. That's senseless and terribly unfair!

3You may live a long time and have a hundred children. But a child born dead is better off than you, unless you enjoy life and have a decent burial. **4-5**That child will never live to see the sun or to have a name, and it will go straight to the world of darkness. But it will still find more rest than you, **6**even if you live two thousand years and don't enjoy life. As you know, we all end up in the same place.

7We struggle just to have enough to eat, but we are never satisfied. **8**We may be sensible, yet we are no better off than a fool. And if we are poor, it still doesn't do us any good to try to live right. **9**It's better to enjoy what we have than to always want something else, because that makes no more sense than chasing the wind.[s]

10Everything that happens was decided long ago. We humans know what we are like, and we can't argue with God, because

5.8,9 *poor . . . officials . . . taxes:* In Israelite society, the king's officials collected taxes from everyone, including the poor. People were also expected to pay temple taxes to support those who were in charge of the temple. The author makes the point that dishonest officials, who make it difficult for the poor to receive fair treatment, often run these systems.

The Poor

Justice

6.2 *give you everything . . . doesn't let you enjoy it:* God may give people wealth, but some who have received riches may not be allowed to enjoy them. The author calls this situation senseless and unfair, but probably thinks that this is just one more example of how human beings cannot fully understand God's ways.

6.3-5 *have a hundred children . . . decent burial . . . world of darkness:* Having children was considered a great gift from God. The more the children, the greater the blessing. But life is not worth living, and having many children and great wealth aren't important, if one doesn't enjoy life or receive a decent burial (Jer 16.4-7; 22.18,19).

---

[o]**5.6** *worship leader:* Or "messenger." [p]**5.7** *Daydreaming . . . talk:* One possible meaning for the difficult Hebrew text. [q]**5.9** *land:* One possible meaning for the difficult Hebrew text of verse 9. [r]**5.17** *bitter:* One possible meaning for the difficult Hebrew text of verse 17. [s]**6.9** *chasing the wind:* See the note at 1.14.

If you love money and wealth, you will never be satisfied with what you have. ECCL 5.10

6.11 *The more we talk:* The author may be repeating the idea that talking too much and talking without thinking are foolish.

7.2-4 *better to go to a funeral . . . sensible person mourns:* The author makes the point that it is better to face life and death in a realistic way. Life is meant to be enjoyed (2.24), but people are not to ignore the reality of death.

7.16 *too good . . . too smart:* The advice in this verse has been interpreted in various ways. The author may be saying that a person shouldn't try to be too good or too wise, because it may not be worth the effort, and besides, no one in the world always does the right thing anyway (7.20). Or, the author may be warning against pretending to be wiser or better than one really is, because that can lead to disaster (Prov 16.18).

7.18 *middle of the road . . . respect God:* The author encourages living life in a realistic way. Avoid evil and be good, but do not claim to be perfect. Avoid foolishness and be wise, but do not pretend to be wiser than you are.

7.26 *bad woman:* On one level, the bad woman is one who tries to tempt a man to commit adultery (Prov 2.16-19; 5.7-18; 9.13-18; 23.27,28). But the bad woman here also stands for anything that tempts people to disobey God. In the Bible, both Wisdom and Stupidity are sometimes compared to a woman (Prov 3.15-18; 9.1-6, 13-18). Wisdom, like God's Law, is something to be followed. But unfaithfulness to God's Law, like a bad woman, is to be avoided.

he is[t] too strong for us. [11]The more we talk, the less sense we make, so what good does it do to talk? [12]Life is short and meaningless, and it fades away like a shadow. Who knows what is best for us? Who knows what will happen after we are gone?

The Best in Life

7 A good reputation
  at the time of death
is better than loving care
  at the time of birth.[u]
[2]It's better to go to a funeral
  than to attend a feast;
funerals remind us
  that we all must die.
[3]Choose sorrow over laughter
because a sad face
  may hide a happy heart.
[4]A sensible person mourns,
  but fools always laugh.
[5]Correction from someone wise
is better by far
  than praise from fools.
[6]Foolish laughter is stupid.
It sounds like thorns
  crackling in a fire.
[7]Corruption[v] makes fools
of sensible people,
  and bribes can ruin you.
[8]Something completed is better
  than something just begun;
patience is better
  than too much pride.
[9]Only fools get angry quickly
  and hold a grudge.
[10]It isn't wise to ask,
"Why is everything worse
  than it used to be?"
[11]Having wisdom is better
  than an inheritance.

[12]Wisdom will protect you
  just like money;
knowledge with good sense
  will lead you to life.
[13]Think of what God has done!
If God makes something crooked,
  can you make it straight?

[14]When times are good,
  you should be cheerful;
when times are bad,
  think about what it means.
God makes them both
  to keep us from knowing
  what will happen next.

Some of Life's Questions

[15]I have seen everything during this senseless life of mine. I have seen good citizens die for doing the right thing, while criminals live and prosper. [16]So don't destroy yourself by being too good or acting too smart! [17]Don't die before your time by being too evil or acting like a fool. [18]Keep to the middle of the road. You can do this if you truly respect God.
[19]Wisdom will make you stronger than the ten most powerful leaders in your city.
[20]No one in this world always does right.
[21]Don't listen to everything that everyone says, or you might hear your servant cursing you. [22]Haven't you cursed many others?
[23]I told myself that I would be smart and try to understand all this, but it was too much for me. [24]The truth is beyond us. It's far too deep. [25]So I decided to learn everything I could and become wise enough to discover what life is all about. At the same time, I wanted to understand why it's stupid and senseless to be an evil fool.
[26]Here is what I discovered: A bad woman

[t]**6.10** *with God, because he is:* Or "with anyone who is."   [u]**7.1** *birth:* One possible meaning for the difficult Hebrew text of verse 1.   [v]**7.7** *Corruption:* Or "Oppression."

is worse than death. She is a trap, reaching out with body and soul to catch you. But if you obey God, you can escape. If you don't obey, you are done for. ²⁷With all my wisdom I have tried to find out how everything fits together, ²⁸but so far I have not been able to. I do know there is one good man in a thousand, but never have I found a good woman. ²⁹I did learn one thing: We were completely honest when God created us, but now we have twisted minds.

8 Who is smart enough
    to explain everything?
   Wisdom makes you cheerful
    and gives you a smile.

Obey the King

²If you promised God that you would be loyal to the king, I advise you to keep that promise. ³Don't quickly oppose the king or argue when he has already made up his mind. ⁴The king's word is law. No one can ask him, "Why are you doing this?" ⁵If you obey the king, you will stay out of trouble. So be wise and learn what to do and when to do it. ⁶Life is hard, but there is a time and a place for everything, ⁷though no one can tell the future. ⁸We cannot control the wind[w] or determine the day of our death. There is no escape in time of war, and no one can hide behind evil. ⁹I noticed all this and thought seriously about what goes on in the world. Why does one person have the power to hurt another?

Who Can Understand the Ways of God?

¹⁰I saw the wicked buried with honor, but God's people had to leave the holy city

and were forgotten.[x] None of this makes sense. ¹¹When we see criminals commit crime after crime without being punished, it makes us want to start a life of crime. ¹²They commit hundreds of crimes and live a long time, in spite of the saying:

   Everyone who lives right
    and respects God
      will prosper,
   ¹³but no one who sins
    and rejects God
   will prosper or live very long.

¹⁴There is something else that doesn't make sense to me. Good citizens are treated as criminals, while criminals are honored as though they were good citizens. ¹⁵So I think we should get as much out of life as we possibly can. There is nothing better than to enjoy our food and drink and have a good time. Then we can make it through this troublesome life that God has given us here on earth.

¹⁶Day and night I went without sleep, trying to understand what goes on in this world. ¹⁷I saw everything God does, and I realized no one can really understand what happens. We may be very wise, but no matter how much we try or how much we claim to know, we cannot understand it all.

One Day at a Time

9 I thought about these things. Then I understood that God has power over everyone, even those who are wise and live right. Anything can happen to any one of us, and so we never know if life will be good or bad.[y] ²But exactly[z] the same thing will finally happen to all of us, whether we live

[w]8.8 *control the wind*: Or "escape from death." [x]8.10 *but . . . forgotten*: One possible meaning for the difficult Hebrew text. [y]9.1 *or bad*: Three ancient translations; the Hebrew text does not have these words. [z]9.2 *But exactly*: One possible meaning for the difficult Hebrew text.

7.28 *one good man . . . woman*: The author says that finding a good man or woman is difficult. Some scholars suggest that this refers to Solomon and his hundreds of wives. King Solomon could not find one woman who was as good and precious as the one described in Proverbs 31.10-31.

8.2-4 *be loyal to the king . . . word is law*: Respecting the king's power and authority are stressed in Israelite wisdom, but keeping a promise made to God is commanded as well.

8.10-14 *wicked buried with honor . . . criminals are honored*: A common belief in ancient times, supported by certain Bible passages, was that God provides health and wealth for everyone who lives right, but God punishes those who do evil (Job 4.7-9; Ps 94.1-3; Prov 10.27-29). The author is trying to figure out how God's justice works, but recognizes that there are certain situations he cannot understand.

We may be very wise, but no matter how much we try or how much we claim to know, we cannot understand it all. ECCL 8.17

CR   Eternal Life

CR   Hell

■ 9.11,12 *fastest runners . . . birds in a trap:* A fish net or bird trap is quickly closed before the prey is aware of the danger. The author uses a wise saying (9.11) to say once again that life is unpredictable and often does not fit with human expectations. Here he seems to say that chance (good or bad luck) determines what happens, though earlier he stated that God determines everything (3.1-17; 7.14).

■ 9.13-18 *wisdom . . . poor . . . one mistake can destroy:* Teaching stories (parables) and wise sayings (proverbs) show the value of wisdom. The Hebrew of 9.15 can have different meanings: (1) the poor person offered wisdom that saved the town from attack, but he was soon forgotten because he was poor; or (2) the poor person gave wise advice that was ignored because he was poor. The second meaning seems to fit better with the conclusion in 9.16. An attitude of disrespect toward the poor can be found in other wisdom sayings (Prov 14.20; 18.23; 19.7). The "yet" in both 9.16 and 9.18 shows the "yes, but" style used in many ancient wisdom sayings. A wise person can outsmart a stronger opponent, but the actions of one fool can undo the good work someone else has done.

right and respect God or sin and don't respect God. Yes, the same thing will happen if we offer sacrifices to God or if we don't, if we keep our promises or are afraid to make them.

³It's terribly unfair for the same thing to happen to each of us. We are mean and foolish while we live, and then we die. ⁴As long as we are alive, we still have hope, just as a live dog is better off than a dead lion. ⁵We know we will die, but the dead don't know a thing. Nothing good will happen to them—they are gone and forgotten. ⁶Their loves, their hates, and their jealous feelings have all disappeared with them. They will never again take part in anything that happens on this earth.

⁷So be happy and enjoy eating and drinking! God decided long ago that this is what you should do. ⁸Dress up, comb your hair, and look your best. ⁹Life is short, and you love your wife, so enjoy being with her. This is what you are supposed to do as you struggle through life on this earth. ¹⁰Work hard at whatever you do. You will soon go to the world of the dead, where no one works or thinks or reasons or even knows anything.

¹¹Here is something else I have learned:
The fastest runners
  and the greatest heroes
don't always win races
  and battles.
Wisdom, intelligence, and skill
don't always make you healthy,
  rich, or popular.
We each have our own share
  of misfortune.

¹²None of us know when we might fall victim to a sudden disaster and find ourselves like fish in a net or birds in a trap.

Better To Be Wise than Foolish

¹³Once I saw what people really think of wisdom, and it made an impression on me. ¹⁴It happened when a powerful ruler surrounded and attacked a small city where only a few people lived. The enemy army was getting ready to break through the city walls. ¹⁵But the city was saved by the wisdom of a poor person who was soon forgotten. ¹⁶So I decided that wisdom is better than strength. Yet if you are poor, no one pays any attention to you, no matter how smart you are.

¹⁷Words of wisdom spoken softly
  make much more sense
than the shouts of a ruler
  to a crowd of fools.
¹⁸Wisdom is more powerful
  than weapons,
yet one mistake can destroy
  all the good you have done.

10 A few dead flies in perfume
  make all of it stink,
and a little foolishness
  outweighs a lot of wisdom.
²Sensible thoughts lead you
  to do right;
foolish thoughts lead you
  to do wrong.
³Fools show their stupidity
  by the way they live;
it's easy to see
  they have no sense.
⁴Don't give up your job
  when your boss gets angry.
If you stay calm,
  you'll be forgiven.

⁵Rulers do some things that are terribly unfair: ⁶They honor fools, but dishonor the rich; ⁷they let slaves ride on horses, but force slave owners to walk.

⁸ If you dig a pit,
  you might fall in;

if you break down a wall,
    a snake might bite you.[a]
[9]You could even get hurt
    by chiseling a stone
    or chopping a log.
[10]If you don't sharpen your ax,
    it will be harder to use;
if you are wise,
    you'll know what to do.[b]
[11]The power to charm a snake
    does you no good
    if it bites you anyway.

[12]If you talk sensibly,
    you will have friends;
if you talk foolishly,
    you will destroy yourself.
[13]Fools begin with nonsense,
    and their stupid chatter
    ends with disaster.
[14]They never tire of talking,
    but none of us really know
    what the future will bring.
[15]Fools wear themselves out—
    they don't know enough
    to find their way home.[c]

[16]A country is in for trouble
    when its ruler is childish,
    and its leaders
    party all day long.
[17]But a nation will prosper
    when its ruler is mature,
    and its leaders
    don't party too much.
[18]Some people are too lazy
    to fix a leaky roof—
    then the house collapses.
[19]Eating and drinking

make you feel happy,
    and money can buy
    everything you need.
[20]Don't let yourself think about
    cursing the king;
don't curse the rich,
    not even in secret.
A little bird might hear
    and tell everything.

It Pays To Work Hard

11 Be generous, and someday
    you will be rewarded.[d]
[2]Share what you have
    with seven or eight others,
because you never know
    when disaster may strike.
[3]Rain clouds always bring rain;
trees always stay
    wherever they fall.
[4]If you worry about the weather
and don't plant seeds,
    you won't harvest a crop.

[5]No one can explain how a baby breathes before it is born.[e] So how can anyone explain what God does? After all, God created everything.
[6]Plant your seeds early in the morning and keep working in the field until dark. Who knows? Your work might pay off, and your seeds might produce.

Youth and Old Age

[7]Nothing on earth is more beautiful than the morning sun. [8]Even if you have a very long life, you should try to enjoy each

[a]**10.8** *a snake might bite you*: Walls of houses were often made of stones with mud to fill in the cracks between them. If some of the mud washed out, a snake could be living inside the wall. [b]**10.10** *do*: One possible meaning for the difficult Hebrew text of verse 10. [c]**10.15** *home*: One possible meaning for the difficult Hebrew text of verse 15. [d]**11.1** *Be generous . . . rewarded*: Or "Don't be afraid to invest. Someday it will pay off." [e]**11.5** *how . . . born*: Or "what makes the wind blow or how a baby grows inside its mother."

10.11 *charm a snake*: Snake-charming was common in the ancient world (see Ps 58.4,5). Poisonous cobras were tamed by charmers, a practice that continues to this day. The word for "charmer" means "controller of the tongue." Either this may refer to how the charmer used his voice to control the snake and make it move, or it may refer to the snake's tongue, which was thought to be the source of its poison.

10.19 *Eating and drinking*: The first part of this verse restates a common theme of the book.

11.1 *Be generous*: Verse 1 is the translation of a difficult Hebrew phrase that literally means "Send out your bread on the waters." Some have taken this phrase to refer to giving gifts (alms) to the poor.

11.4 *worry about the weather*: In ancient times, weather was much more difficult to predict than it is today. Since both life and the weather are unpredictable and under God's control (3.11, 15,17; 6.10; 8.6-8; 9.1), a farmer must plant his crops and not worry about ideal weather conditions (11.6).

11.7-10 *the morning sun . . . darkness . . . youth quickly disappear*: The author acknowledges that there is great beauty in life (11.7). Whether the "morning sun" refers to the sun itself or to youth, the author says that it should be enjoyed when it is present, because death ("darkness") comes all too soon.

11.9 *Do what you want . . . God will judge:* The first part of this verse sounds like the author's general philosophy of life. Some scholars believe that the last part of the verse may have been added by a later editor, so readers would not use the earlier part of the verse as an excuse to live in a selfish way or to disobey God.

12.2 *light . . . dim . . . Rain clouds:* The author compares old age to a gloomy and rainy day.

12.6 *silver cord:* Light and water were important symbols of life. The author uses the spilling of oil and water to symbolize death. Oil was burned in a clay or metal bowl to make a lamp. Sometimes, these lamps were hung by metal cords. Only the wealthy could afford a golden bowl held by a silver cord. The author is stating again that the wealthy have to face death just like everyone else.

12.8 *Nothing makes sense:* The book's major theme, first stated in chapter 1, is repeated here. This forms a kind of "frame" around the rest of the author's thoughts.

12.13,14 *Respect and obey God . . . will judge:* In Hebrew wisdom, obeying God is often the best evidence that one is wise. These statements bring the author's often conflicting observations more into line with the common viewpoint of Hebrew wisdom: Because human understanding is so limited and "nothing makes sense," it is okay to go ahead and enjoy life; but the most important thing for a person to do is to respect and obey God.

day, because darkness will come and will last a long time. Nothing makes sense.[f]

⁹Be cheerful and enjoy life while you are young! Do what you want and find pleasure in what you see. But don't forget that God will judge you for everything you do.

¹⁰Rid yourself of all worry and pain, because the wonderful moments of youth quickly disappear.

12 Keep your Creator in mind while you are young! In years to come, you will be burdened down with troubles and say, "I don't enjoy life anymore."

²Someday the light of the sun
and the moon and the stars
    will all seem dim to you.
Rain clouds will remain
    over your head.
³Your body will grow feeble,
your teeth will decay,
    and your eyesight fail.
⁴The noisy grinding of grain
    and the voices of singers
will be shut out
    by your deaf ears,
but even the song of a bird
    will keep you awake.[g]

⁵You will be afraid
    to climb up a hill
    or walk down a road.
Your hair will turn as white
    as almond blossoms.
You will feel lifeless
and drag along
    like an old grasshopper.

We each go to our eternal home,
and the streets here are filled

with those who mourn.
⁶The silver cord snaps,
    the golden bowl breaks;
the water pitcher is smashed,
and the pulley at the well
    is shattered.
⁷So our bodies return
    to the earth,
and the life-giving breath[h]
    returns to God.
⁸Nothing makes sense.
I have seen it all—
    nothing makes sense.

Respect and Obey God

⁹I was a wise teacher with much understanding, and I collected a number of proverbs that I had carefully studied. ¹⁰Then I tried to explain these things in the best and most accurate way.

¹¹Words of wisdom are like the stick a farmer uses to make animals move. These sayings come from a shepherd,[i] and they are like nails that fasten things together.[j] ¹²My child, I warn you to stay away from any teachings except these.

There is no end to books,
    and too much study
    will wear you out.

¹³Everything you were taught can be put into a few words:
    Respect and obey God!
    This is what life
    is all about.
¹⁴God will judge
    everything we do,
    even what is done in secret,
    whether good or bad.

[f]11.8 *Nothing makes sense:* Or "There's nothing to look forward to!"   [g]12.4 *but even the song . . . awake:* One possible meaning for the difficult Hebrew text.   [h]12.7 *life-giving breath:* Or "spirit."   [i]12.11 *a shepherd:* This may be a reference to God as shepherd (see also Psalm 23.1).   [j]12.11 *These sayings . . . together:* One possible meaning for the difficult Hebrew text.

Reflection Questions About Ecclesiates 1.1—12.14

1. How would you describe the author of
   ECCLESIASTES?

2. How does the author describe life (1.8-11)?
   What do you think of this view?

3. Think about the statement in 1.18. Can you
   think of experiences in your own life or in the
   lives of others that show this to be true?

4. How did the author try to find out "what was
   best for us" and make himself happy (2.1-10)?
   What did he discover (2.10,11)?

5. How does the author describe "wisdom"
   (2.13,14)? According to the author, did "being
   wise" seem to make a difference (2.15-19)?
   Why or why not?

6. What conclusion does the author come to in
   2.24,25?

7. The author believes that everything on earth
   has its own time and season (3.1-8). According

to the author, who controls everything that
happens and when (3.11,15)? How might such
a philosophy affect how a person lives his or
her life?

8. What kinds of "terrible things" is the author
   describing in 4.1-3? The author suggests that it
   would be better not to be born than to have
   seen these terrible things. How might those
   who have been born respond to evil and injustice in the world?

9. What does the author say about proper worship and respect for God (5.1-7)?

10. For you, which of the following statements
    seems to be a better summary of the author's
    view of life in ECCLESIASTES?

    "Nothing makes sense." (12.8)

    "Respect and obey God!" (12.13)

    Explain your choice.

song of songs

Why is ancient love poetry included in the Holy Scriptures? Read this book that describes love as being "more powerful than death."

WHAT MAKES SONG OF SONGS SPECIAL?

The title of this book means "the most beautiful of songs," and in some translations it is called "The Song of Solomon" (see 1.1). In the Jewish Scriptures, this book is found in the section known as "The Writings." **(See the article What Books Belong in the Bible on pg 1764.)**

On the surface, SONG OF SONGS is love poetry that celebrates the powerful love between a man and a woman. Some scholars consider the book to be a unified poem written by one author. Others describe it as a collection of love songs or poems put together by an editor. God is not mentioned in the book, and the poems seem only to provide a description of romantic love.

If SONG OF SONGS is simply a collection of poems that express human love, why is it included in the Bible? Though this was long debated, eventually Jewish teachers determined the book symbolized God's love for the people of Israel. This interpretation may be based on passages from HOSEA (1–3) and JEREMIAH (2.20—3.5), which describe the relationship between God and Israel in terms of a marriage. Many Christian interpreters came to a similar conclusion, saying that the book symbolizes the kind of relationship that Jesus Christ (the bridegroom) has with the church (his bride).

WHAT'S THE STORY BEHIND THE SCENE?

Scholars do not agree on who wrote this book or when. The first verse of the book (1.1) connects the book with King Solomon, who ruled Israel from 970 to 931 B.C. But the Hebrew in this verse can be translated various ways. The book may be "by," "according to," or "for" Solomon; or it may "belong to," or be "dedicated to" him. All that is clear is that the book was in some way owned by (or connected to) Solomon, who was known in ancient Israel as the author of many wise sayings and poems (1 Kgs 4.32). As in the case of ECCLESIASTES, having Solomon's name connected with the book added to its authority as true Israelite Wisdom.

HOW IS SONG OF SONGS CONSTRUCTED?

If the book is a collection of poems, an editor probably arranged them so that they would relate to each other as a whole. The romance between two lovers is the focus of the poem and provides a kind of connection between its various scenes or sections. But at some points it is hard to know who exactly is speaking. When a new poem or speech begins, the CEV inserts a phrase in italics (such as "She speaks" or "He speaks") as a way of indicating who might be the speaker in the section that follows. The following outline suggests just one of many ways the book's sections may be grouped:

Solomon's Song (1.1)
Love blossoms (1.2—2.7)
Love dreams (2.8—3.5)
Love plans (3.6—6.10)
Love dances (6.11—8.4)
Powerful love is not for sale (8.5-14)

S ong of Songs means "the most beautiful of all songs" or "the greatest of all songs." The book is a collection of beautiful love poems which have been arranged to create a single dramatic narrative or literary unit. In Song of Songs, a woman and a man tell of their love for each other, and their beautiful words are sometimes answered by the words of their friends. Rich in metaphor and images of the natural world, bursting with vitality and desire, Song of Songs celebrates the passion of love. Because these poems express so many levels of love, the book is often understood theologically by Jews as an allegory (moral story) of God's love for Israel, and by Christians as an allegory of Jesus' loving relationship to the church.

Outline

Love Is Better than Wine

1 This is Solomon's
   most beautiful song.

She Speaks:
   [2] Kiss me tenderly!
   Your love is better than wine,
   [3] and you smell so sweet.
   All the young women adore you;
   the very mention of your name
   is like spreading perfume.
   *[4] Hurry, my king! Let's hurry.
   Take me to your home.

The Young Women Speak:
   We are happy for you!
   And we praise your love
   even more than wine.

She Speaks:
   Young women of Jerusalem,
   it is only right
   that you should adore him.

[5] My skin is dark and beautiful,
   like a tent in the desert
   or like Solomon's curtains.
[6] Don't stare at me
   just because the sun
   has darkened my skin.
   My brothers were angry with me;
   they made me work in the vineyard,
   and so I neglected
   my complexion.

[7] My darling, I love you!
   Where do you feed your sheep
   and let them rest at noon?
   Don't let the other shepherds
   think badly of me.
   I'm not one of those women
   who shamelessly follow
   after shepherds.[a]

He Speaks:
[8] My dearest, if you don't know,
   just follow the path
   of the sheep.

[a] **1.7** *Don't let . . . after shepherds*: One possible meaning for the difficult Hebrew text.

1.13 *perfume . . . flower blossoms:* "Perfume" refers to "myrrh," and the flower blossoms are the strongly scented henna flowers. (See the chart Spices and Perfumes on pg 1835.)

1.14 *En-Gedi:* En-Gedi was an oasis on the western shore of the Dead Sea. Its fresh running water and many green plants contrasted sharply with the surrounding desert. (See Map 3 on pg 1881.)

1.16,17 *wedding bed . . . cedar and cypress:* Ancient Near Eastern love songs mention beds made of or decorated with fresh-cut branches. The cedar tree, which was highly valued throughout the ancient Near East, was used to build royal palaces, including the temple and palace of King Solomon (1 Kgs 5.3-9; 7.1-12). Cypress, a form of pine, also was used for building. Perhaps the young woman is expressing a desire to meet her lover in a royal bedroom, or she is imagining their meeting place in the fields as a palace bedroom.

2.4 *banquet room:* This literally means a "house of wine." Wine symbolizes the joy of love (5.1).

2.6 *left hand . . . right arm:* In some parts of the world, the right hand is used for special purposes, such as eating, preparing food, greeting with a handshake, and caressing someone.

Then feed your young goats
    near the shepherds' tents.
⁹You move as gracefully
    as the pony that leads
        the chariot of the king.
¹⁰Earrings add to your beauty,
    and you wear a necklace
        of precious stones.
¹¹Let's make you some jewelry
    of gold, woven with silver.

She Speaks:
¹²My king, while you
    were on your couch,
        my aroma was a magic charm.ᵇ
¹³My darling, you are perfume
    between my breasts;
¹⁴you are flower blossoms
    from the gardens of En-Gedi.ᶜ

He Speaks:
¹⁵My darling, you are lovely,
    so very lovely—
        your eyes are those of a dove.

She Speaks:
¹⁶My love, you are handsome,
    truly handsome—
        the fresh green grass
            will be our wedding bed
¹⁷in the shade of cedar
    and cypress trees.

Love Makes Everything Beautiful

She Speaks:
2 I am merely a roseᵈ
    from the land of Sharon,
        a lily from the valley.

He Speaks:
²My darling, when compared
    with other young women,
        you are a lily among thorns.

She Speaks:
³And you, my love,
    are an apple tree
        among trees of the forest.
    Your shade brought me pleasure;
        your fruit was sweet.
⁴You led me to your banquet room
    and showered me with love.
⁵Refresh and strengthen me
    with raisins and apples.
    I am hungry for love!
⁶Put your left hand under my head
    and embrace me
        with your right arm.

⁷Young women of Jerusalem,
    promise me by the power
        of deer and gazellesᵉ
    never to awaken love
        before it is ready.

Winter Is Past

She Speaks:
⁸I hear the voice
    of the one I love,
    as he comes leaping
        over mountains and hills
⁹   like a deer or a gazelle.
    Now he stands outside our wall,
        looking through the window
¹⁰   and speaking to me.

ᵇ**1.12** *magic charm:* The Hebrew text has "spikenard" (or "nard"), a sweet-smelling ointment made from a plant that comes from India. The ointment was sometimes used as a love charm.   ᶜ**1.14** *En-Gedi:* An oasis west of the Dead Sea.   ᵈ**2.1** *rose:* The traditional translation. The exact variety of the flower is not known, though it may have been a crocus.   ᵉ**2.7** *deer and gazelles:* Deer and gazelles were sacred animals in some religions of Old Testament times, and they were thought to have special powers.

He Speaks:
    My darling, I love you!
        Let's go away together.
    [11] Winter is past,
        the rain has stopped;
    [12] flowers cover the earth,
        it's time to sing.[f]
    The cooing of doves
        is heard in our land.
    [13] Fig trees are bearing fruit,
        while blossoms on grapevines
            fill the air with perfume.
    My darling, I love you!
        Let's go away together.
    [14] You are my dove
        hiding among the rocks
            on the side of a cliff.
    Let me see how lovely you are!
    Let me hear the sound
        of your melodious voice.
    [15] Our vineyards are in blossom;
        we must catch the little foxes
            that destroy the vineyards.[g]

She Speaks:
    [16] My darling, I am yours,
        and you are mine,
    as you feed your sheep
        among the lilies.
    [17] Pretend to be a young deer
        dancing on mountain slopes[h]
    until daylight comes
        and shadows fade away.

Beautiful Dreams

She Speaks:
3 While in bed at night,
    I reached for the one I love
        with heart and soul.

I looked for him,
    but he wasn't there.
[2] So I searched through the town
    for the one I love.
I looked on every street,
    but he wasn't there.
[3] I even asked the guards
    patrolling the town,
"Have you seen the one
    I love so much?"
[4] Right after that, I found him.
    I held him and would not let go
        until I had taken him
            to the home of my mother.
[5] Young women of Jerusalem,
    promise me by the power
        of deer and gazelles,[i]
never to awaken love
    before it is ready.

The Groom
and the Wedding Party

Their Friends Speak:
    [6] What do we see approaching
        from the desert
            like a cloud of smoke?
    With it comes the sweet smell
        of spices, including myrrh
            and frankincense.
    [7] It is King Solomon
        carried on a throne,
    surrounded by sixty
        of Israel's best soldiers.
    [8] Each of them wears a sword.
        They are experts at fighting,
            even in the dark.
    [9] The throne is made of trees
        from Lebanon.
    [10] Its posts are silver,

2.11,12 *Winter . . . cooing of doves:*
The winter is a rainy season in the Near East. In spring, flowers bloom and doves that have flown away during winter return. The "singing" may refer to the cooing song of turtledoves, or it may be translated as "pruning." Grapevines were cut back (pruned) in both early and late spring.

2.15 *little foxes . . . destroy the vineyards:* Here, vineyards refer to the lovers' own physical bodies. Foxes were known for damaging vineyards. No one really knows what these foxes refer to, though many think they represent other young men who hope to win the woman for themselves.

3.1-4 *in bed . . . home of my mother:* The young woman appears to be describing a dream. A young woman usually avoided being alone on the street after dark because she might be attacked, or people might think she was looking for men in order to have sex with them (see Prov 7.6-12). Little is known about the "guards" who patrolled the city at night. The mother's home may refer to the mother's protective relationship with her unmarried daughter.

---

[f]**2.12** *sing:* Or "trim the vines." [g]**2.15** *vineyards:* One possible meaning for the difficult Hebrew text of verse 15. [h]**2.17** *mountain slopes:* One possible meaning for the difficult Hebrew text. [i]**3.5** *deer and gazelles:* See the note at 2.7.

3.11 *crown:* Probably a wedding crown made of flowers, rather than a royal crown.

4.1 *eyes . . . hair:* The woman's hair flows like a flock of black goats moving down a hillside. The hills of Gilead had good pastures for raising sheep. **(See Map 6 on pg 1884.)**

4.3 *rosy cheeks:* Pomegranate fruit has red seeds surrounded by sweet-tasting pulp. If the round, red fruit were cut in half, each piece would look like a rosy cheek.

4.4 *tower of David:* What or where this "tower" may have been is unknown. The image suggests a neck that is made to look longer by adding rows of necklaces.

4.5,6 *twin deer . . . hills:* The man describes the graceful curves of the young woman's body.

4.8 *Lebanon . . . Hermon:* Mount Hermon is over 9,000 feet high. These rugged Lebanon mountains were difficult to climb and dangerous lions and leopards lived in them. This poetic image may mean that for now—before they are married—the woman's body seems as unapproachable as these mountains. **(See Map 3 on pg 1881.)**

4.11 *tongue . . . cedar trees from Lebanon:* May refer to her kisses or to the sweet words that come from her mouth.

the back is gold,
and the seat is covered
with purple cloth.
You women of Jerusalem
have taken great care
to furnish the inside.[j]
¹¹Now come and see the crown
given to Solomon by his mother
on his happy wedding day.

What a Beautiful Bride

He Speaks:

4 My darling, you are lovely,
so very lovely—
as you look through your veil,
your eyes are those of a dove.
Your hair tosses about
as gracefully as goats
coming down from Gilead.
²Your teeth are whiter
than sheep freshly washed;
they match perfectly,
not one is missing.
³Your lips are crimson cords,
your mouth is shapely;
behind your veil are hidden
beautiful rosy cheeks.[k]
⁴Your neck is more graceful
than the tower of David,
decorated with thousands
of warriors' shields.

⁵Your breasts are perfect;
they are twin deer
feeding among lilies.
⁶I will hasten to those hills
sprinkled with sweet perfume
and stay there till sunrise.

⁷My darling, you are lovely
in every way.
⁸My bride, together
we will leave Lebanon!
We will say goodbye
to the peaks of Mount Amana,
Senir, and Hermon,
where lions and leopards
live in the caves.

⁹My bride, my very own,
you have stolen my heart!
With one glance from your eyes
and the glow of your necklace,
you have stolen my heart.
¹⁰Your love is sweeter than wine;
the smell of your perfume
is more fragrant than spices.
¹¹Your lips are a honeycomb;
milk and honey
flow from your tongue.
Your dress has the aroma
of cedar trees from Lebanon.

¹²My bride, my very own,
you are a garden, a fountain
closed off to all others.
¹³Your arms[l] are vines,
covered with delicious fruits
and all sorts of spices—
henna, nard, ¹⁴saffron,
calamus, cinnamon,
frankincense, myrrh, and aloes—
all the finest spices.
¹⁵You are a spring in the garden,
a fountain of pure water,
and a refreshing stream
from Mount Lebanon.

[j]3.10 *inside:* One possible meaning for the difficult Hebrew text. [k]4.3 *beautiful rosy cheeks:* One possible meaning for the difficult Hebrew text. [l]4.13 *Your arms:* One possible meaning for the difficult Hebrew text.

She Speaks:

16 Let the north wind blow,
    the south wind too!
Let them spread the aroma
    of my garden,
so the one I love
    may enter and taste
    its delicious fruits.

He Speaks:

5 My bride, my very own,
    I come to my garden
    and enjoy its spices.
I eat my honeycomb and honey;
    I drink my wine and milk.

Their Friends Speak:

Eat and drink until
    you are drunk with love.

Another Dream

She Speaks:

2 I was asleep, but dreaming:
The one I love was at the door,
    knocking and saying,
"My darling, my very own,
    my flawless dove,
    open the door for me!
My head is drenched
    with evening dew."

3 But I had already undressed
    and bathed my feet.
Should I dress again
    and get my feet dirty?
4 Then my darling's hand
    reached to open the latch,
    and my heart stood still.
5 When I rose to open the door,
    my hands and my fingers
    dripped with perfume.

6 And I yearned for him
    while he spoke to me,
but when I opened the door,
    my darling had disappeared.
I searched and shouted,
    but I could not find him—
    there was no answer.
7 Then I was found by the guards
    patrolling the town
    and guarding the wall.
They beat me up
    and stripped off my robe.

8 Young women of Jerusalem,
    if you find the one I love,
please say to him,
    "She is weak with desire."

Their Friends Speak:

9 Most beautiful of women,
    why is the one you love
    more special than others?
Why do you ask us
    to tell him how you feel?

She Speaks:

10 He is handsome and healthy,
    the most outstanding
    among ten thousand.
11 His head is purest gold;
    his hair is wavy,
    black as a raven.
12 His eyes are a pair of doves
    bathing in a stream
    flowing with milk.**m**
13 His face is a garden
    of sweet-smelling spices;
his lips are lilies
    dripping with perfume.

m **5.12** *milk:* One possible meaning for the difficult Hebrew text of verse 12.

● **4.16** *my garden:* The young woman invites her lover into her "garden," her fragrant body, to enjoy the "fruit" of love. In 5.1, he claims this "garden" belongs to him alone.

● **5.7** *guards . . . beat me up:* The young woman is so anxious to find her lover that she is willing to risk running through the dark streets, a very dangerous thing for a young woman to do.

■ **5.8,9** *weak with desire . . . how you feel:* The young woman may not want her friends to tell the one she loves about her search for him through the dark streets or about the way the guards treated her. Nevertheless, she does want them to give him the message that she is still "weak with desire."

■ **5.10** *healthy . . . among ten thousand:* The same Hebrew word used to describe the healthy and good-looking young David (1 Sam 16.12; 17.42) is used here. "Ten thousand" is meant to symbolize a very large number.

● **5.11-15** *purest gold . . . cedar trees:* A "gold" head may refer to one that shines and stands out above all others. The eyes like doves in milk could mean that his eyes are bright and clear. His face (or beard) smells like spices and his lips like lilies. The water lily (lotus) was a flower that was connected with the pleasures of love. The dripping perfume (myrrh) probably refers to his sweet and wet kisses.

6.4 *Tirzah and Jerusalem:* Jerusalem was the capital city of all Israel under kings David and Solomon, and of the southern kingdom (Judah) after the kingdom divided. Tirzah was chosen by Jeroboam (ruled 931–910 B.C.) as the first capital city of the northern kingdom (1 Kgs 14.17; 16.23,24). Tirzah means "beauty."

6.8 *sixty queens . . . thousands:* This refers to Solomon's many wives and mistresses (his harem), but the numbers are smaller than those mentioned in 1 Kings 11.3.

6.13 *woman from Shulam:* This phrase is difficult. "Shulamite" is a feminine form of "Solomon," and it has been suggested that "Shulam" was a word that meant "Solomon's girl." Another suggestion is that she is "a woman from Shunem," a "Shunammite" (see 1 Kgs 1.3,4). Still others suggest the name may be connected with Shulmanitu, a Semitic goddess of war and love.

[14]His arms are branches of gold
    covered with jewels;
his body is ivory[n]
    decorated with sapphires.
[15]His legs are columns of marble
    on feet of gold.
He stands there majestic
    like Mount Lebanon
    and its choice cedar trees.
[16]His kisses are sweet.
    I desire him so much!
Young women of Jerusalem,
    he is my lover and friend.

Their Friends Speak:

6 Most beautiful of women,
    tell us where he has gone.
    Let us help you find him.

She Speaks:
    [2]My darling has gone down
        to his garden of spices,
    where he will feed his sheep
        and gather lilies.
    [3]I am his, and he is mine,
        as he feeds his sheep
        among the lilies.

He Speaks:
    [4]My dearest, the cities of Tirzah
        and Jerusalem
        are not as lovely as you.
    Your charms are more powerful
        than all of the stars
        in the heavens.[o]
    [5]Turn away your eyes—
        they make me melt.
    Your hair tosses about
        as gracefully as goats
        coming down from Gilead.

[6]Your teeth are whiter
    than sheep freshly washed;
they match perfectly,
    not one is missing.
[7]Behind your veil are hidden
    beautiful rosy cheeks.[P]

[8]What if I could have
    sixty queens, eighty wives,
    and thousands of others!
[9]You would be my only choice,
    my flawless dove,
    the favorite child
    of your mother.
The young women, the queens,
    and all the others
tell how excited you are
    as they sing your praises:
[10]"You are as majestic
    as the morning sky—
glorious as the moon—
    blinding as the sun!
Your charms are more powerful
    than all the stars above."[q]

She Speaks:
    [11]I went down to see if blossoms
        were on the walnut trees,
        grapevines, and fruit trees.
    [12]But in my imagination
        I was suddenly riding
        on a glorious chariot.[r]

Their Friends Speak:
    [13]Dance! Dance!
    Beautiful woman from Shulam,
        let us see you dance!

She Speaks:
    Why do you want to see

[n]5.14 *his . . . ivory:* One possible meaning for the difficult Hebrew text.   [o]6.4 *all . . . heavens:* Or "a mighty army ready for war."   [P]6.7 *cheeks:* One possible meaning for the difficult Hebrew text of verse 7.   [q]6.10 *all . . . above:* Or "a mighty army ready for war."   [r]6.12 *chariot:* One possible meaning for the difficult Hebrew text of verse 12.

He said, "Your charms are more powerful than all the stars above." SONG 6.10

this woman from Shulam
    dancing with the others?[s]

The Wedding Dance

He Speaks:

7 You are a princess,
  and your feet are graceful
    in their sandals.
  Your thighs are works of art,
    each one a jewel;
2your navel is a wine glass
    filled to overflowing.
  Your body is full and slender
  like a bundle of wheat
    bound together by lilies.
3Your breasts are like twins
    of a deer.
4Your neck is like ivory,
  and your eyes sparkle
  like the pools of Heshbon
    by the gate of Bath-Rabbim.
  Your nose is beautiful
  like Mount Lebanon
    above the city of Damascus.
5Your head is held high
    like Mount Carmel;
  your hair is so lovely
    it holds a king prisoner.[t]

6You are very beautiful,
    so desirable!
7You are tall and slender
  like a palm tree,
    and your breasts are full.
8I will climb that tree
  and cling to its branches.
  I will discover that your breasts
    are clusters of grapes,

and that your breath
  is the aroma of apples.
9Kissing you is more delicious
  than drinking the finest wine.
  How wonderful and tasty![u]

She Speaks:

10My darling, I am yours,
  and you desire me.
11Let's stroll through the fields
  and sleep in the villages.
12At dawn let's slip out and see
  if grapevines and fruit trees
    are covered with blossoms.
  When we are there,
    I will give you my love.
13Perfume from the magic flower[v]
  fills the air, my darling.
  Right at our doorstep
  I have stored up for you
    all kinds of tasty fruits.

If Only You and I . . .

She Speaks:

8 If you were my brother,
   I could kiss you
  whenever we happen to meet,
  and no one would say
   I did wrong.
2I could take you to the home
  of my mother,
   who taught me all I know.[w]
  I would give you delicious wine
   and fruit juice as well.
3Put your left hand under my head
  and embrace me
   with your right arm.

● **7.7-9** *palm tree . . . finest wine:* The palm tree here is the tall date palm, whose fruit grows in clusters in the leafy tops of the tree. The dates and clusters of grapes describe the woman's breasts. Her breath smelling like apples and her kisses tasting like wine are both images connected to sexual pleasure.

● **7.11** *fields . . . villages:* The Hebrew word for village is similar to the word for "henna." Her desire to "sleep in the villages," then, could mean "sleep in beds of henna flowers" (see 1.13,14).

● **7.13** *magic flower:* SONG OF SONGS is rich in animal and plant imagery. One plant, called a "magic flower" in the CEV, is the mandrake. The flowers, fruit, and root of this plant were used in medicines. This plant was also thought to give sexual powers to people who possessed it (see Gen 30.14-16).

● **8.1,2** *brother . . . mother:* A sister could kiss her brother in public, but kissing a man who was not a close relative would have been shameful. She certainly does not want their relationship to be that of a brother and sister, but she does want their love to be publicly recognized. To bring her beloved to the home of her mother would be another step in making their relationship public.

---

[s]**6.13** *dancing . . . others:* One possible meaning for the difficult Hebrew text.   [t]**7.5** *it . . . prisoner:* One possible meaning for the difficult Hebrew text.   [u]**7.9** *How . . . tasty:* One possible meaning for the difficult Hebrew text.   [v]**7.13** *magic flower:* The Hebrew text has "mandrake," a plant that was thought to give sexual powers.   [w]**8.2** *who . . . know:* One possible meaning for the difficult Hebrew text.

8.6 *heart . . . bracelet:* Her bracelet may have had a personalized design to be used as a seal. A seal was used to imprint a person's initials in wax on legal documents or to mark possessions to prove ownership (Jer 32.10,11).

8.6,7 *grave . . . floods:* In Hebrew "grave" refers to "Sheol," the underground world of the dead (Job 10.21,22; Ps 88.12; 94.17). The "flood" waters refer to the dark waters of chaos that God brought under control at creation (Gen 1.2; Ps 33.6,7; Job 38.8-10).

8.8,9 *little sister . . . wooden door:* Most scholars interpret these verses to be the words of the young woman's brothers. They shared the family responsibility of protecting her and for approving the one she married.

8.10 *I am a wall . . . towers:* "Wall" may refer to her virginity or to her loyalty to her beloved. By describing her breasts as being like towers, she seems to be refuting her brothers who think she is too young to get married.

8.12 *My vineyard:* Most likely, this refers to her own body. Verse 12 seems to imply that she will not give herself even to the richest man in the world, no matter what is offered.

[4]Young women of Jerusalem,
   promise me never to awaken love
   before it is ready.

Their Friends Speak:
   [5]Who is this young woman
      coming in from the desert
   and leaning on the shoulder
      of the one she loves?

She Speaks:
   I stirred up your passions
      under the apple tree
      where you were born.
   [6]Always keep me in your heart
      and wear this bracelet
      to remember me by.
   The passion of love
      bursting into flame
   is more powerful than death,
      stronger than the grave.
   [7]Love cannot be drowned
      by oceans or floods.
   It cannot be bought—
      any offer would be scorned
      no matter how great.

Their Friends Speak:
   [8]We have a little sister
      whose breasts
      are not yet formed.
   If someone asks to marry her,

   what should we do?
   [9]She isn't a wall
      that we can defend
      behind a silver shield.
   Neither is she a room
      that we can protect
      behind a wooden door.

She Speaks:
   [10]I am a wall around a city,
      my breasts are towers,
   and just looking at me
      brings him great pleasure.
   [11]Solomon has a vineyard
      at Baal-Hamon,
   which he rents to others
      for a thousand pieces
      of silver each.
   [12]My vineyard is mine alone!
      Solomon can keep his silver
   and the others can keep
      their share of the profits.

He Speaks:
   [13]You are in the garden
      with friends all around.
      Let me hear your voice!

She Speaks:
   [14]Hurry to me, my darling!
      Run faster than a deer
      to mountains of spices.

Reflection Questions About Song of Songs 1.1—8.14

1. SONG OF SONGS has been described as a collection of loosely-related love poems, a drama, or a long poem that tells a story. Which of these descriptions, if any, best describes this book for you? Why? How else might this book be described?

2. If SONG OF SONGS is one long poem, who do you imagine the main characters in the poem to be? What can be known about the woman's relationships to people other than the man she loves? Her mother? Her brothers? The other young women of her town?

3. The man and the woman in this book use many images from nature (plants, animals, hills, etc.) to describe themselves and one another. Which "word pictures" did you find most interesting? Which were difficult for you to understand or relate to? Try describing yourself (or a friend) using "word pictures."

4. What does SONG OF SONGS have to say about love? About commitment? About God? What does it mean to say that love is "more powerful than death," "cannot be drowned," and "cannot be bought"?

5. Some Jews have interpreted SONG OF SONGS as God's love for the people of Israel, and some Christians have seen it as Jesus' love for the church ("his bride"). Which verses, if any, seem to support this kind of interpretation? What do you think is the main purpose of this book?

isaiah

It's a familiar phrase: "I have some good news and some bad news." Read this book to discover what the prophet Isaiah has to say about the bad news of God's judgment and the good news of God's love.

WHAT MAKES ISAIAH SPECIAL?

ISAIAH contains some of the most beautiful poetry and some of the best-known words of hope in the entire Bible. ISAIAH's message shows a deep understanding of God's Law as it relates to the history of God's chosen people, Israel. The people and their leaders disobeyed the Law of the LORD and so were punished. They were taken into exile in Babylon, but they returned home to Judah. Their temple was rebuilt, as God had promised it would be, and the people looked forward to a brighter future.

The New Testament writers often quote from ISAIAH to show that Jesus Christ is the Messiah, the long-awaited king from the family of David. His coming fulfills God's promise to save all people and to create a future filled with promise. This Messiah is described as the one who will rule David's kingdom forever and bring everlasting peace (Isa 9.6,7; 11.1-9). Christian teachers also interpreted the suffering and death of Jesus as a fulfillment of the passages in ISAIAH that describe the work of God's special "Servant" (Isa 49.1-6; 50.1-11; 52.13—53.12).

WHAT'S THE STORY BEHIND THE SCENE?

The meaning of Isaiah's own name reveals one of the key themes in the book. In Hebrew, Isaiah means "The LORD (Yahweh) saves." A major theme in the center section of the book (Isa 40–55) is comfort and hope for God's chosen people, who have been living in exile in Babylonia. The LORD, the Holy One of Israel, will open a pathway for the people to return home to Judah and will restore the temple on God's holy Mount Zion in Jerusalem. There, God will once again live among the people (Exod 25.8; 2 Sam 6.1,2; 1 Kgs 8.1,2,10-13).

HOW IS ISAIAH CONSTRUCTED?

Here is one way ISAIAH can be outlined:

ISAIAH, part 1: Before the exile (1.1—39.8)
Introduction (1.1-31)
Prophecies concerning Judah and Jerusalem (2.1—12.6)
Prophecies concerning foreign nations (13.1—23.18)
A view of God's future judgment (24.1—27.13)
Those who rebel against God will be punished (28.1—33.24)
Visions of judgment and joy (34.1—35.10)
In the days of King Hezekiah (36.1—39.8)
ISAIAH, part 2: Good News for God's people in exile (40.1—55.13)
Babylonia is defeated and God's people are set free (40.1—48.22)
Jerusalem will be rebuilt (49.1—55.13)
ISAIAH, part 3: Warnings and promises for God's new people after the exile (56.1—66.24)
Do right and obey God's Laws (56.1—59.21).
Celebrate, Jerusalem, for I have saved you (60.1—62.12)
I will bless my servants but punish sinners (63.1—66.24)

saiah is the longest prophetic book in the Jewish Scriptures (Old Testament), and contains some of the Bible's most powerful poetry and strongest words of hope. The prophet Isaiah lived in Judah, the southern kingdom, and spoke the Lord's messages from about 742 to about 698 B.C. Some of Isaiah's prophecies probably were written after the Jewish people returned from exile in 538 B.C., and are best understood as having been written in the prophet's name by one or more Jewish sages who wished to continue the prophet's message of God's justice and mercy. Isaiah can be divided into three parts. The first part warns about God's coming judgment against his people. Because they disobeyed the Law of Moses and did not trust in the Lord's protection, the prophet declares that the Lord will punish them by allowing their enemies to conquer them. The second part offers hope to God's people living in exile. With poetry of joyful praise, the author promises that the Lord will allow his people to return home and rebuild the temple in Jerusalem. The final part of Isaiah pictures the restored nation. In a vision of renewal, Isaiah announces to the people of Jerusalem a new day when the glory of the Lord will shine brightly on them.

Outline

1 I am Isaiah, the son of Amoz.
And this is the message[a] that I was given about Judah and Jerusalem when Uzziah, Jotham, Ahaz, and Hezekiah were the kings of Judah:[b]

A Guilty Nation

[2] The LORD has said,
"Listen, heaven and earth!
The children I raised
have turned against me.
[3] Oxen and donkeys know
who owns and feeds them,
but my people won't ever learn."

[4] Israel, you are a sinful nation
loaded down with guilt.
You are wicked and corrupt
and have turned from the LORD,
the holy God of Israel.

[5] Why be punished more?
Why not give up your sin?
Your head is badly bruised,
and you are weak all over.
[6] From your head to your toes
there isn't a healthy spot.
Bruises, cuts, and open sores
go without care
or oil to ease the pain.

A Country in Ruins

[7] Your country lies in ruins;
your towns are in ashes.
Foreigners and strangers
take and destroy your land
while you watch.
[8] Enemies surround Jerusalem,
alone like a hut
in a vineyard[c]
or in a cucumber field.

[a] **1.1** *message:* Or "vision." [b] **1.1** *kings of Judah:* Uzziah (783–742 B.C.); Jotham (742–735 B.C.); Ahaz (735–715 B.C.); Hezekiah (715–687 B.C.). [c] **1.8** *a hut in a vineyard:* When it was almost time for grapes to ripen, farmers would put up a temporary shelter or hut in the field or vineyard and stay there to keep thieves and wild animals away.

1.1 *Judah and Jerusalem:* Jerusalem was the capital city of the southern kingdom (Judah). The temple of the people of Israel was located there. After the death of King Solomon, the Israelites were a divided nation consisting of the northern kingdom (Israel) and the southern kingdom (Judah). (See Maps 5 and 6 on pgs 1883 and 1884 and the article From Joshua to the Exile: The People of Israel in the Promised Land on pg 1783.)

Jerusalem

Hezekiah

LORD (YHWH)

1.2 *children I raised:* "Children" refers to the people of Israel. The LORD calls heaven and earth to be witnesses to Israel's sin.

1.4 *Israel . . . sinful nation:* Here "Israel" probably refers to all God's people, not simply the northern kingdom.

Israel

1.9 *Zion:* Here, "Zion" is another name for the city of Jerusalem.

Zion

1.9 *the LORD All-Powerful:* The Hebrew, *Yahweh Sebaoth*, is also translated as "LORD of hosts." This term for Israel's God is used often in the first main part of ISAIAH (1–39). See for instance 5.16; and 10.33. The "hosts" in this ancient name are either the armies of Israel, which the LORD led into battle (1 Sam 4.4), or the heavenly stars, which God created. Isaiah makes it clear throughout the book that the powerful LORD of creation is also the God who has chosen Israel to be his special people.

1.13 *Sabbaths:* The Sabbath is the weekly day of rest. **(See the chart Pilgrimage Festivals on pg 1799.)**

1.17 *widows and orphans:* These were often treated unfairly in ancient Near Eastern societies. The Law of Moses commanded the people of Israel to protect widows and orphans (Exod 22.22,23; Deut 24.17; 27.14-26).

1.21 *unfaithful wife:* When the people of Judah turned their backs on God's Law and lived as they pleased, they were acting like an unfaithful wife, a description used by other prophets of Israel as well (Jer 3.6-10; Ezek 16; 23; Hos 1–3).

⁹Zion would have disappeared
  like Sodom and Gomorrah,ᵈ
if the LORD All-Powerful
had not let a few
  of its people survive.

Justice, Not Sacrifices

¹⁰You are no better
  than the leaders and people
of Sodom and Gomorrah!
  So listen to the LORD God:
¹¹"Your sacrifices
  mean nothing to me.
I am sick of your offerings
  of rams and choice cattle;
I don't like the blood
  of bulls or lambs or goats.

¹²"Who asked you to bring all this
  when you come to worship me?
  Stay out of my temple!
¹³Your sacrifices are worthless,
  and your incense disgusting.
I can't stand the evil you do
  on your New Moon Festivals
or on your Sabbaths
  and other times of worship.
¹⁴I hate your New Moon Festivals
  and all others as well.
They are a heavy burden
  I am tired of carrying.

¹⁵"No matter how much you pray,
  I won't listen.
  You are too violent.
¹⁶Wash yourselves clean!
  I hate your filthy deeds.
Stop doing wrong
¹⁷ and learn to live right.
  See that justice is done.

Defend widows and orphans
  and help the oppressed."ᵉ

An Invitation from the LORD

¹⁸I, the LORD, invite you
  to come and talk it over.
Your sins are scarlet red,
  but they will be whiter
  than snow or wool.
¹⁹If you willingly obey me,
  the best crops in the land
  will be yours.
²⁰But if you turn against me,
  your enemies will kill you.
  I, the LORD, have spoken.

The LORD Condemns Jerusalem

²¹Jerusalem, you are like
  an unfaithful wife.
Once your judges were honest
  and your people lived right;
now you are a city
  full of murderers.
²²Your silver is fake,
  and your wine
  is watered down.
²³Your leaders have rejected me
  to become friends of crooks;
your rulers are looking
  for gifts and bribes.
Widows and orphans
  never get a fair trial.

²⁴I am the LORD All-Powerful,
  the mighty ruler of Israel,
  and I make you a promise:
You are now my enemy,
  and I will show my anger
  by taking revenge on you.

ᵈ1.9 *Sodom and Gomorrah:* Two ancient cities of Palestine that God destroyed because the people were so wicked (see Genesis 19.1-29).   ᵉ1.17 *and help the oppressed:* Or "and punish cruel people."

²⁵I will punish you terribly
and burn away everything
that makes you unfit
to worship me.
²⁶Jerusalem, I will choose
judges and advisors
like those you had before.
Your new name will be
"Justice and Faithfulness."

The LORD Will Save Jerusalem

²⁷Jerusalem, you will be saved
by showing justice;[f]
Zion's people who turn to me
will be saved
by doing right.
²⁸But those rebellious sinners
who turn against me, the LORD,
will all disappear.

²⁹You will be made ashamed
of those groves of trees
where you worshiped idols.
³⁰You will be like a grove of trees
dying in a drought.
³¹Your strongest leaders
will be like dry wood
set on fire by their idols.[g]
No one will be able to help,
as they all go up in flames.

Peace That Lasts Forever

2 This is the message[h] I was given about
Judah and Jerusalem:

²In the future, the mountain
with the LORD's temple
will be the highest of all.

It will reach above the hills;
every nation will rush to it.
³Many people will come and say,
"Let's go to the mountain
of the LORD God of Jacob
and worship in his temple."

The LORD will teach us his Law
from Jerusalem,
and we will obey him.
⁴He will settle arguments
between nations.
They will pound their swords
and their spears
into rakes and shovels;
they will never make war
or attack one another.
⁵People of Israel, let's live
by the light of the LORD.

Following Sinful Customs

⁶Our LORD, you have deserted
your people, Israel,
because they follow customs
of nations from the east.
They worship Philistine gods
and are close friends
of foreigners.[i]
⁷They have endless treasures
of silver and gold;
they have countless horses
and war chariots.
⁸Everywhere in the country
they worship the idols
they have made.
⁹And so, all of them
will be ashamed and disgraced.
Don't forgive them!

1.26 *judges and advisors like those you had before*: This probably refers to the days of King David, when Jerusalem first became the capital city of Israel (2 Sam 5.1-12).

1.29-31 *groves . . . idols . . . flames*: Canaanite places of worship were usually built on a high place near a grove of trees (Deut 12.2; 1 Kgs 14.23; Jer 2.20).

Canaanite Gods and Goddesses

Fire

2.2 *mountain with the LORD's temple*: This refers to Zion. Zion is the "highest" because the temple of the LORD God of Israel is there, and the LORD will be recognized as the supreme judge of all the nations.

2.3 *LORD God of Jacob . . . Law*: The people of Israel were descendants of Jacob, the grandson of Abraham. God changed Jacob's name to Israel (Gen 32.22-28) and chose the Israelites to be his own people (Deut 7.6-8; Isa 41.8,9; 43.1). God gave the Law to Moses and the people of Israel at Mount Sinai (see Exod 19–40), so they would know how God wanted them to live their lives.

Law

2.5 *the light of the LORD*: In the Bible, "light" often symbolizes God or God's word (Law).

2.11,12 *When the* LORD *comes . . . a day:* On such a day of judgment, the LORD will reward the faithful and punish those who have opposed him.

Day of the LORD

2.13-16 *cedars of Lebanon . . . seagoing ships:* The tall cedar trees of Lebanon's forests were valued for their hardwood. Bashan, a region east of the Jordan River was famous for its oak trees. These impressive trees, high mountains, ships, and fortresses were all symbols of worldly strength.

2.18,19 *Idols . . . caves:* Isaiah often makes the point that Israel's LORD is stronger than the worthless idols made by people (30.22; 40.18-20,25,26; 44.9-20). Palestine has a number of limestone caves that people used as hiding places.

3.1-4 *take away . . . soldiers . . . children:* The powerful people in Judah would one day be taken away from the land. As punishment, the LORD promises to one day give lowly children power to rule over the evil adult leaders.

Exile

A Day of Judgment

¹⁰Every one of you,
  go hide among the rocks
    and in the ground,
  because the LORD is fearsome,
    marvelous, and glorious.
¹¹When the LORD comes,
  everyone who is proud
    will be made humble,
  and the LORD alone
    will be honored.
¹²The LORD All-Powerful
    has chosen a day
  when those who are proud
  and conceited
    will be put down.

¹³The tall and towering
  cedars of Lebanon
    will be destroyed.
  So will the oak trees of Bashan,
¹⁴all high mountains and hills,
¹⁵ every strong fortress,
¹⁶all the seagoing ships,ʲ
  and every beautiful boat.
¹⁷When that day comes,
  everyone who is proud
    will be put down.
  Only the LORD will be honored.
¹⁸ Idols will be gone for good.

¹⁹You had better hide
  in caves and holes—
  the LORD will be fearsome,
    marvelous, and glorious
  when he comes to terrify
    people on earth.

²⁰On that day everyone will throw
  to the moles and bats

their idols of silver and gold
  they made to worship.
²¹The LORD will be fearsome,
  marvelous, and glorious
  when he comes to terrify
    people on earth—
  they will hide in caves
    and in the hills.

²²Stop trusting the power
    of humans.
  They are all going to die,
    so how can they help?

Judgment on Jerusalem and Judah

3 The mighty LORD All-Powerful
  is going to take away
    from Jerusalem and Judah
  everything you need—
    your bread and water,
*²soldiers and heroes,
  judges and prophets,
    leaders and army officers,
³officials and advisors,
  fortunetellers and others
    who tell the future.
⁴He will let children and babiesᵏ
  become your rulers.
⁵You will each be cruel
    to friends and neighbors.
  Young people will insult
    their elders;
  no one will show respect
    to those who deserve it.

⁶Some of you will grab hold
    of a relative and say,
  "You still have a coat.
  Be our leader and rule

ʲ2.16 *seagoing ships:* The Hebrew text has "ships of Tarshish," which may have been a Phoenician city in Spain. "Ships of Tarshish" probably means large, seagoing ships. ᵏ3.4 *babies:* Or "worthless nobodies."

this pile of ruins."
⁷But the answer will be,
"I can't do you any good.
　Don't make me your leader.
There's no food or clothing
　left in my house."

⁸Jerusalem and Judah,
you rebelled against
　your glorious LORD—
your words and your actions,
　made you stumble and fall.
⁹The look on your faces shows
that you are sinful as Sodom,
　and you don't try to hide it.
You are in for trouble,
and you have brought it all
　on yourselves.

The Wrong Kind of Leaders

¹⁰Tell those who obey God,
"You're very fortunate—
　you will be rewarded
　for what you have done."
¹¹Tell those who disobey,
"You're in big trouble—
　what you did to others
　will come back to you."
¹²Though you are God's people,
you are ruled and abused
　by women and children.
You are confused by leaders
who guide you
　down the wrong path.

¹³The LORD is ready to accuse
　and judge all nations.
¹⁴He will even judge
you rulers and leaders
　of his own nation.
You destroyed his vineyard[l]

[l]3.14 *his vineyard*: The nation Israel (see 5.1-7).

and filled your houses
　by robbing the poor.
¹⁵The LORD All-Powerful says,
"You have crushed my people
　and rubbed in the dirt
　the faces of the poor."

The Women of Jerusalem

¹⁶The LORD says:
The women of Jerusalem
are proud and strut around,
　winking shamelessly.
They wear anklets that jingle
and call attention
　to the way they walk.
¹⁷But I, the LORD, will cover
　their heads with sores,
and I will uncover
　their private parts.

¹⁸⁻²³When that day comes, I will take
away from those women all the fine jewelry they wear on their ankles, heads, necks,
ears, arms, noses, fingers, and on their
clothes. I will remove their veils, their
belts, their perfume, their magic charms,
their royal robes, and all their fancy
dresses, hats, and purses.
²⁴In place of perfume,
　there will be a stink;
in place of belts,
　there will be ropes;
in place of fancy hairdos,
　they will have bald heads.
Instead of expensive clothes,
　they will wear sackcloth;
instead of beauty,
　they will have ugly scars.
²⁵The fighting men of Jerusalem
　will be killed in battle.
²⁶The city will mourn

■　3.10,11 *those who obey . . . dis-obey*: These verses are like many of the ancient Israelite wisdom sayings about what will happen to those who are good (obey God) and to those who are evil (disobey God).

●　3.12 *women and children*: Like children, women had less power or sta-tus in many ancient Near Eastern soci-eties, including Israel. By turning away from the LORD, Judah's male leaders caused the usual social order to be turned upside down.

●　3.16-24 *women of Jerusalem . . . anklets . . . fine jewelry . . . magic charms . . . sackcloth*: "Women" probably refers to the wives of Jerusalem's powerful and wealthy men. Their fine jewelry would have included necklaces and rings. Some of the necklaces may have been in the shape of a crescent moon, which suggested worship of a popular moon-god. Other necklaces may have had charms with magic sayings written on them. Small boxes containing per-fumed flower petals also may have been worn along with very fancy clothes. Sackcloth (3.24) was dark, coarse cloth made from goat's wool. People wore sackcloth as a way of showing their deep sadness.

3.26—4.1 *sit in the dirt:* People sometimes rubbed dust on themselves or sat in dirt to show their sorrow or to show that they were sorry for their sins (Job 2.8,12; Lam 4.5; Jon 3.5,6).

4.4 *fiery judgment:* Fire is often connected with the LORD's judgment against those who are evil or disobedient (Gen 19.23-29; Joel 2.1-3). Fire is also a symbol of purification.

Fire

5.1,2 *vineyard:* The vineyard is Israel (5.7), but it is not clear whether this means the northern kingdom, or if it refers to all God's people, including those in Judah.

5.4 *bitter grapes:* A "fertile hill" (5.1) that is well taken care of should produce sweet grapes. Here, God compares Israel with such a hill. Israel's sins were like bitter grapes to the LORD and were described in detail by many of Israel's prophets, including Amos, Hosea, and Micah.

5.5 *vineyard will be trampled:* This may refer to Israel's fall to Assyria, but the warning also applies to Judah, whose leaders were not being honest or fair.

and sit in the dirt,
    emptied of its people.

4 When this happens, seven women will grab the same man, and each of them will say, "I'll buy my own food and clothes! Just marry me and take away my disgrace."[m]

The LORD Will Bless His People Who Survive

[2]The time is coming when the LORD will make his land fruitful and glorious again, and the people of Israel who survive will take great pride in what the land produces. [3]Everyone who is left alive in Jerusalem will be called special, [4]after the LORD sends a fiery judgment to clean the city and its people of their violent deeds.

[5]Then the LORD will cover the whole city and its meeting places with a thick cloud each day and with a flaming fire[n] each night. God's own glory will be like a huge tent that covers everything. [6]It will provide shade from the heat of the sun and a place of shelter and protection from storms and rain.

A Song about a Vineyard

The LORD said:

5 I will sing a song
    about my friend's vineyard
  that was on the side
    of a fertile hill.
[2]My friend dug the ground,
  removed the stones,
    and planted the best vines.
He built a watchtower

and dug a pit in rocky ground
    for pressing the grapes.
He hoped they would be sweet,
  but bitter grapes
    were all it produced.

[3]Listen, people of Jerusalem
    and of Judah!
You be the judge of me
  and my vineyard.
[4]What more could I have done
    for my vineyard?
I hoped for sweet grapes,
  but bitter grapes
    were all that grew.

[5]Now I will let you know
    what I am going to do.
I will cut down the hedge
    and tear down the wall.
My vineyard will be trampled
    and left in ruins.
[6]It will turn into a desert,
    neither pruned nor hoed;
it will be covered
    with thorns and briars.
I will command the clouds
    not to send rain.

[7]I am the LORD All-Powerful!
    Israel is the vineyard,
and Judah is the garden
    I tended with care.
I had hoped for honesty
    and for justice,
but dishonesty
  and cries for mercy
    were all I found.

[m]**4.1** *take away my disgrace:* If a woman did not have a husband or children, it was thought that God was punishing her.   [n]**4.5** *thick . . . fire:* This is how the LORD led the people of Israel during the 40 years they were in the desert (see Exodus 13.20-22; 40.36-38).

Isaiah Condemns Social Injustice

⁸You are in for trouble! You take over house after house and field after field, until there is no room left for anyone else in all the land. ⁹But the LORD All-Powerful has made this promise to me:

Those large and beautiful homes will be left empty, with no one to take care of them. ¹⁰Ten acres of grapevines will produce only six gallons of juice, and five bushels of seed will produce merely a half-bushel of grain.

¹¹You are in for trouble! You get up early to start drinking, and you keep it up late into the night. ¹²At your drinking parties you have the music of stringed instruments, tambourines, and flutes. But you never even think about all the LORD has done, ¹³and so his people know nothing about him. That's why many of you will be dragged off to foreign lands. Your leaders will starve to death, and everyone else will suffer from thirst.

¹⁴The world of the dead has opened its mouth wide and is eagerly waiting for the leaders of Jerusalem and for its noisy crowds, especially for those who take pride in that city. ¹⁵Its citizens have been put down, and its proud people have been brought to shame. ¹⁶But the holy LORD God All-Powerful is praised, because he has shown who he is by bringing justice. ¹⁷His people will be like sheep grazing in their own pasture, and they will take off what was left by others.ᵒ

¹⁸You are in for trouble! The lies you tell are like ropes by which you drag along sin and evil. ¹⁹And you say, "Let the holy God of Israel hurry up and do what he has promised, so we can see it for ourselves." ²⁰You are headed for trouble! You say wrong is right, darkness is light, and bitter is sweet.

²¹You think you are clever and smart. ²²And you are great at drinking and mixing drinks. But you are in for trouble. ²³You accept bribes to let the guilty go free, and you cheat the innocent out of a fair trial.

²⁴You will go up in flames like straw and hay! You have rejected the teaching of the holy LORD God All-Powerful of Israel. Now your roots will rot, and your blossoms will turn to dust.

²⁵You are the LORD's people, but you made him terribly angry, and he struck you with his mighty arm. Mountains shook, and dead bodies covered the streets like garbage. The LORD is still angry, and he is ready to strike you again.ᴾ

Foreign Nations Will Attack

²⁶The LORD has signaled for the foreign nations to come and attack you. He has already whistled, and they are coming as fast as they can. ²⁷None of them are tired. They don't sleep or get drowsy, and they run without stumbling. Their belts don't come loose; their sandal straps don't break. ²⁸Their arrows are sharp, and their bows are ready. The hoofs of their horses are hard as flint; the wheels of their war chariots turn as fast as a whirlwind. ²⁹They roar and growl like fierce young lions as they grab their victims and drag them off where no one can rescue them. ³⁰On the day they attack, they will roar like the ocean. And across the land you will see nothing but darkness and trouble, because the light of day will be covered by thick clouds.

ᵒ5.17 *and they . . . others*: One possible meaning for the difficult Hebrew text.   ᴾ5.25 *is ready . . . again*: Or "hasn't given up on you yet."

■ 5.8 *You are in for trouble*: This phrase occurs a number of times in this chapter (5.8,11,18,20,22). Isaiah announces judgments known as "woes."

● 5.8 *take over house . . . field*: In ancient Israel, land was given or assigned to tribes and families. The ownership rights to these lands were to be passed on within the tribes, so every family could work the land and harvest crops or fruit. Land could be leased, but not bought or sold (Lev 25.23-28; Num 27.5-11; 1 Kgs 21.1-3). Isaiah describes some people in Israel buying or taking land away from the original family owners. This especially affected poor landowners.

● 5.11-13 *You . . . will be dragged*: This refers to wealthy persons. Instead of using their wealth to help others, they wasted it on parties. Eventually, these people would lose the land that the LORD gave them and be taken off to exile.

■ 5.18,19 *drag along sin . . . holy God of Israel*: The leaders, harnessed to their sins, drag the punishment for their lies behind them like a farmer forced to drag a cart by leather ropes. Isaiah uses the name "Holy God of Israel" to show that God is both "set apart from human beings" (holy), but also close and personal. God chose Israel (41.8,9) and lives among them (Exod 25.18-22; 1 Kgs 8.6-13; Isa 6.1-8).

● 5.25,26 *Mountains shook*: The shaking mountains may refer to a violent earthquake that struck Israel in 760 B.C. (see Amos 1.1).

6.5 *I'm doomed . . . seen the King:* Isaiah thought he was doomed to die, because humans, being sinful, were not supposed to see God's face.

6.6,7 *burning coal . . . metal tongs . . . touched your lips:* On the Great Day of Forgiveness (Lev 16.11-14), the high priest took burning coals into the most holy place as part of a ceremony to forgive the sins of the priest and the people. The "tongs" were probably a bronze tool used by the priests to offer sacrifices at the bronze altar (Exod 27.1-3).

6.11,12 *towns are destroyed . . . sent them far away:* The Assyrians destroyed the northern kingdom (Israel) and took many of its people into exile in 721 B.C. Later, the Babylonians defeated and destroyed the southern kingdom (Judah) and its capital Jerusalem, and took many of its people into exile.

7.1-2 *Ahaz . . . Pekah:* Ahaz ruled Judah from 735 to 715 B.C., and Pekah ruled the northern kingdom of Israel from 752 to 732 B.C. Between 735 and 732 B.C., Israel and Syria invaded Judah during what is known as the Syro-Ephraimite War (2 Kgs 15.27—16.20; 2 Chr 28.1-27). At first, Pekah and Rezin of Syria tried to force Ahaz to join them in their battles against Assyria. When Ahaz did not cooperate, Pekah and Rezin tried to replace him with a king more friendly to their purpose (7.6). Against Isaiah's advice, Ahaz turned to the Assyrians for help, which later made things worse for Judah (2 Chr 28.16-20).

A Vision of the Lord in the Temple

6 In the year that King Uzziah died,[q] I had a vision of the Lord. He was on his throne high above, and his robe filled the temple. [2]Flaming creatures with six wings each were flying over him. They covered their faces with two of their wings and their bodies with two more. They used the other two wings for flying, [3]as they shouted,

"Holy, holy, holy,
   Lord All-Powerful!
The earth is filled
   with your glory."

[4]As they shouted, the doorposts of the temple shook, and the temple was filled with smoke. [5]Then I cried out, "I'm doomed! Everything I say is sinful, and so are the words of everyone around me. Yet I have seen the King, the Lord All-Powerful."

[6]One of the flaming creatures flew over to me with a burning coal that it had taken from the altar with a pair of metal tongs. [7]It touched my lips with the hot coal and said, "This has touched your lips. Your sins are forgiven, and you are no longer guilty."

[8]After this, I heard the Lord ask, "Is there anyone I can send? Will someone speak for us?"

"I'll go," I answered. "Send me!"

[9] Then the Lord told me to go and speak this message to the people:

"You will listen and listen,
   but never understand.
You will look and look,
   but never see."

The Lord also said,
[10]"Make these people stubborn!
Make them stop up
   their ears,
cover their eyes,
   and fail to understand.
Don't let them turn to me
   and be healed."

[11]Then I asked the Lord, "How long will this last?"

The Lord answered:

Until their towns are destroyed and their houses are deserted, until their fields are empty, [12]and I have sent them far away, leaving their land in ruins. [13]If only a tenth of the people are left, even they will be destroyed. But just as stumps remain after trees have been cut down,[r] some of my chosen ones will be left.

Isaiah Offers Hope to King Ahaz

7 Ahaz, the son of Jotham and the grandson of Uzziah, was king of Judah when King Rezin of Syria and King Pekah son of Remaliah of Israel went to attack Jerusalem. But they were not able to do what they had planned.[s] [2]When news reached the royal palace that Syria had joined forces with Israel, King Ahaz and everyone in Judah were so terrified that they shook like trees in a windstorm.

[3]Then the Lord said to me:

Take your son Shearjashub[t] and go see King Ahaz. You will find him on the road near the cloth makers' shops at the end of the canal that brings water from the upper pool. [4]Tell Ahaz to stop worrying. There's no need for him to be afraid of King Rezin and King Pekah. They are very angry, but they are nothing more than a dying fire. Ahaz doesn't need to fear [5]their evil threats [6]to invade and defeat Judah and Jerusalem and to let the son of Tabeel be king in his place.

[7]I, the LORD, promise that this will never happen. [8-9]Damascus is just the capital of Syria, and King Rezin rules only in Damascus. Samaria is just the capital of Israel, and King Pekah rules only in Samaria. But in less than 65 years, Israel will be destroyed. And if Ahaz and his officials don't trust me, they will be defeated.

A Son Named Immanuel

[10]Once again the LORD God spoke to King Ahaz. This time he said, [11]"Ask me for proof that my promise will come true. Ask for something to happen deep in the world of the dead or high in the heavens above."

[12]"No, LORD," Ahaz answered. "I won't test you!"

[13]Then I said:

Listen, every one of you in the royal family of David. You have already tried my patience. Now you are trying God's patience by refusing to ask for proof. [14]But the LORD will still give you proof. A virgin[u] is pregnant; she will have a son and will name him Immanuel.[v] [15-16]Even before the boy is old enough to know how to choose between right and wrong, he will eat yogurt and honey,[w] and the countries of the two kings you fear will be destroyed. [17]But the LORD will make more trouble for your people and your kingdom than any of you have known since Israel broke away from Judah. He will even bring the king of Assyria to attack you.

The Threat of an Invasion

[18]When that time comes, the LORD will whistle, and armies will come from Egypt like flies and from Assyria like bees. [19]They will settle everywhere—in the deep valleys and between the rocks, on every thornbush and all over the pastureland.

[20]The Lord will pay the king of Assyria to bring a razor from across the Euphrates River and shave your head and every hair on your body, including your beard.[x]

[21]Anyone who is able to save only one young cow and two sheep, [22]will have enough milk to make yogurt. In fact, everyone left in the land will eat yogurt and honey.[y]

[23]Vineyards that had 1,000 vines and were worth 1,000 pieces of silver will turn into thorn patches. [24]You will go there to hunt with your bow and arrows, because the whole country will be covered with thornbushes. [25]The hills where you once planted crops will be overgrown with thorns and thistles.

---

[u]**7.14** *virgin:* Or "young woman." In this context the difficult Hebrew word did not imply a virgin birth. However, in the Greek translation made about 200 B.C. and used by the early Christians, the word *parthenos* had a double meaning. While the translator took it to mean "young woman," Matthew understood it to mean "virgin" and quoted the passage (Matthew 1.23) because it was the appropriate description of Mary, the mother of Jesus. [v]**7.14** *Immanuel:* In Hebrew "Immanuel" means "God is with us." [w]**7.15,16** *yogurt and honey:* This may refer either to expensive foods eaten in a time of plenty or to a limited diet eaten in times of a food shortage. [x]**7.20** *shave . . . head . . . body . . . beard:* This would have been a terrible insult. [y]**7.22** *yogurt and honey:* See the note at 7.15,16.

8.1 *MAHER-SHALAL-HASH-BAZ*: This means "suddenly attacked, quickly taken," and was the name of one of Isaiah's sons.

8.2 *Uriah . . . Zechariah*: Uriah served as priest under King Ahaz (2 Kgs 16.10-16). Zechariah may be Ahaz's father-in-law (2 Kgs 18.2).

8.3 *my wife . . . son*: Isaiah's "wife" may be the same person as the "young woman" mentioned in 7.14. If this is so, the births of Immanuel (7.14) and Maher-Shalal-Hash-Baz (8.3) were not far apart, and their names refer to the same invasion of Israel and Syria by the Assyrians around 732 B.C.

8.6 *Shiloah*: Shiloah was the canal that brought water from Gihon Spring to Jerusalem. (**See Map 7 on pg 1885.**)

8.11 *The LORD took hold of me*: Meaning the prophet was about to receive a special message from the LORD.

8.16 *teachings . . . sealed*: Isaiah's prophecies were written on scrolls and sealed with wax. The scrolls were to be kept sealed as long as the people remained disobedient.

You will be afraid to go there, and your cattle, sheep, and goats will be turned loose on those hills.

A Warning and a Hope

8 The LORD said, "Isaiah, get something to write on. Then write in big clear letters[z] the name, MAHER-SHALAL-HASH-BAZ.[a] ²I will tell Uriah the priest and Zechariah son of Jeberechiah to serve as witnesses to this."

³Sometime later, my wife and I had a son, and the LORD said, "Name him Maher-Shalal-Hash-Baz. ⁴Because before he can say 'Mommy' or 'Daddy,' the king of Assyria will attack and take everything of value from Damascus and Samaria."

⁵The LORD spoke to me again and said:

⁶These people have refused the gentle waters of Shiloah[b] and have gladly gone over to the side of King Rezin and King Pekah. ⁷Now I will send the king of Assyria against them with his powerful army, which will attack like the mighty Euphrates River overflowing its banks. ⁸Enemy soldiers will cover Judah like a flood reaching up to your neck.

But God is with us.[c]
He will spread his wings
    and protect our land.[d]
⁹All of you foreign nations,
    go ahead and prepare for war,
    but you will be crushed.
¹⁰Get together and make plans,
    but you will fail
    because God is with us.

¹¹The LORD took hold of me with his powerful hand and said:

I'm warning you! Don't act like these people. ¹²Don't call something a rebellious plot, just because they do, and don't be afraid of something, just because they are. ¹³I am the one you should fear and respect. I am the holy God, the LORD All-Powerful! ¹⁴⁻¹⁵Run to me for protection. I am a rock that will make both Judah and Israel stumble and break their bones. I am a trap that will catch the people of Jerusalem—they will be captured and dragged away.

Isaiah and His Followers

¹⁶My message and my teachings are to be sealed and given to my followers. ¹⁷Meanwhile, I patiently trust the LORD, even though he is no longer pleased with Israel. ¹⁸My children and I are warning signs to Israel from the LORD All-Powerful, who lives on Mount Zion.

¹⁹Someone may say to you, "Go to the fortunetellers who make soft chirping sounds or ask the spirits of the dead. After all, a nation ought to be able to ask its own gods ²⁰what it should do."

None of those who talk like that will live to see the light of day! ²¹They will go around in great pain and will become so hungry that they will angrily curse their king and their gods. And when they try to find help in heaven ²²and on earth, they will find only trouble and darkness, terrible trouble and deepest darkness.

---

[z]**8.1** *in big clear letters*: Or "in letters everyone can understand."   [a]**8.1** *MAHER-SHALAL-HASH-BAZ*: In Hebrew "Maher-Shalal-Hash-Baz" means "suddenly attacked, quickly taken."   [b]**8.6** *Shiloah*: The canal that brought water from Gihon Spring to Jerusalem.   [c]**8.8** *God is with us*: Here and in verse 10 this translates the Hebrew word "Immanuel" (see 7.14).   [d]**8.8** *But . . . land*: One possible meaning for the difficult Hebrew text.

9 But those who have suffered will no longer be in pain.[e] The territories of Zebulun and Naphtali in Galilee were once hated. But this land of the Gentiles across the Jordan River and along the Mediterranean Sea will be greatly respected.

War Is Over

[2] Those who walked in the dark
have seen a bright light.
And it shines upon everyone
who lives in the land
of darkest shadows.
[3] Our LORD, you have made
your nation stronger.[f]
Because of you, its people
are glad and celebrate
like workers at harvest time
or like soldiers dividing up
what they have taken.

[4] You have broken the power
of those who abused
and enslaved your people.
You have rescued them
just as you saved your people
from Midian.[g]
[5] The boots of marching warriors
and the blood-stained uniforms
have been fed to flames
and eaten by fire.

A Child Has Been Born

[6] A child has been born for us.
We have been given a son
who will be our ruler.
His names will be
Wonderful Advisor

and Mighty God,
Eternal Father
and Prince of Peace.
[7] His power will never end;
peace will last forever.
He will rule David's kingdom
and make it grow strong.
He will always rule
with honesty and justice.
The LORD All-Powerful
will make certain
that all of this is done.

God Will Punish Israel

[8] The Lord had warned the people of Israel, [9] and all of them knew it, including everyone in the capital city of Samaria. But they were proud and stubborn and said,
[10] "Houses of brick and sycamore
have fallen to the ground,
but we will build houses
with stones and cedar."

[11] The LORD made their enemies[h] attack them. [12] He sent the Arameans from the east and the Philistines from the west, and they swallowed up Israel. But even this did not stop him from being angry, so he kept on punishing them.[i] [13] The people of Israel still did not turn back to the LORD All-Powerful and worship him. [14] In one day he cut off their head and tail, their leaves and branches. [15] Their rulers and leaders were the head, and the lying prophets were the tail. [16] They had led the nation down the wrong path, and the people were confused. [17] The Lord was angry with his people and kept punishing them, because they had turned against

● 9.1 *Zebulun and Naphtali . . . land of the Gentiles:* Zebulun (Gen 30.19, 20) and Naphtali (Gen 30.7,8) were the names of two of Israel's northern tribes (Josh 19.10-16,32-39). In 733/32 B.C. Tiglath Pileser of Assyria turned their lands into the Assyrian province known as Galilee. Gilead, the land east of the Jordan, and Dor, the land along the Mediterranean Sea, also were made into Assyrian provinces.

■ 9.2 *who walked in the dark . . . light:* Those living in the areas threatened or captured by Assyria. The "bright light" that gives them hope has to do with God's saving help, perhaps in the form of a new king.

● 9.6 *Prince of Peace:* A king of Israel was compared to God's son (Ps 2.7). The titles were similar to those given to an Egyptian king. "Wonderful Advisor" refers to a political leader; "Mighty God" to a warrior; "Eternal Father" to one who cares for his people; and "Prince of Peace" to one who brings prosperity.

● 9.10 *brick and sycamore . . . stones and cedar:* Mud bricks and sycamore wood were common building materials. Cut stones and cedar wood were more expensive and were used in building palaces.

[e]9.1 *will . . . pain:* One possible meaning for the difficult Hebrew text.   [f]9.3 *stronger:* Or "happy" or "larger."   [g]9.4 *rescued . . . from Midian:* The time when Gideon defeated the people of Midian in Jezreel Valley (see Judges 6–8).   [h]9.11 *their enemies:* Hebrew "the enemies of Rezin."   [i]9.12 *so . . . them:* Or "but he hasn't given up on them yet."

9.21 *Ephraim and Manasseh:* These two northern tribes were named after the sons of Joseph (Gen 48.5,6).

10.5 *king of Assyria:* Various kings of Assyria invaded and captured parts of Israel, Judah, and surrounding countries. The invasions took place from 738 to 701 B.C.

10.9-12 *Calno . . . Damascus:* Assyrian king Tiglath Pileser captured Calno twice, in 740 and in 738 B.C. He also captured Carchemish, which Sargon II of Assyria later recaptured in 717 B.C. The Assyrians captured Hamath in 738 B.C. and 720 B.C. Tiglath Pileser captured Arpad in 740 B.C. Israel's capital, Samaria, fell to Assyria in 721 B.C. (2 Kgs 17.3-6). Damascus, capital of Syria, was captured by Tiglath Pileser in 732 B.C.

10.12 *punish . . . boastful king of Assyria:* This refers to destruction of Sennacherib and his army (see 2 Kgs 19; Isa 36,37).

him.[j] They were evil and spoke foolishly. That's why he did not have pity on their young people or on their widows and orphans. [18]Evil had spread like a raging forest fire sending thornbushes up in smoke. [19]The LORD All-Powerful was angry and used the people as fuel for a fire that scorched the land. They turned against each other [20]like wild animals attacking and eating everyone around them, even their own relatives.[k] But still they were not satisfied. [21]The tribes of Ephraim and Manasseh turned against each other, then joined forces to attack Judah. But the LORD was still angry and ready to punish the nation even more.

10 You people are in for trouble! You have made cruel and unfair laws [2]that let you cheat the poor and needy and rob widows and orphans. [3]But what will you do when you are fiercely attacked and punished by foreigners? Where will you run for help? Where will you hide your valuables? [4]How will you escape being captured[l] or killed? The Lord is still angry, and he isn't through with you yet![m]

The Lord's Purpose and the King of Assyria

[5] The Lord says:

I am furious! And I will use the king of Assyria[n] as a club [6]to beat down you godless people. I am angry with you, and I will send him to attack you. He will take what he wants and walk on you like mud in the streets. [7]He has

even bigger plans in mind, because he wants to destroy many nations. [8]The king of Assyria says:

My army commanders are kings! [9]They have already captured[o] the cities of Calno, Carchemish, Hamath, Arpad, Samaria, and Damascus. [10-11]The gods of Jerusalem and Samaria are weaker than the gods of those powerful nations. And I will destroy Jerusalem, together with its gods and idols, just as I did Samaria.

[12]The Lord will do what he has planned against Jerusalem and Mount Zion. Then he will punish the proud and boastful king of Assyria, [13]who says:

I did these things by my own power because I am smart and clever. I attacked kings like a wild bull, and I took the land and the treasures of their nations. [14]I have conquered the whole world! And it was easier than taking eggs from an unguarded nest. No one even flapped a wing or made a peep.

[15]King of Assyria, can an ax or a saw overpower the one who uses it? Can a wooden pole lift whoever holds it? [16]The mighty LORD All-Powerful will send a terrible disease to strike down your army, and you will burn with fever under your royal robes. [17]The holy God, who is the light of Israel, will turn into a fire, and in one day you will go up in flames, just like a thornbush. [18]The Lord will make your beautiful forests and fertile fields slowly rot. [19]There will be so few trees that even a young child can count them.

[j]**9.17** *and kept . . . against him*: Or "but even though they had turned against him, he still had not given up on them." [k]**9.20** *their own relatives*: One possible meaning for the difficult Hebrew text. [l]**10.4** *escape being captured*: One possible meaning for the difficult Hebrew text. [m]**10.4** *and he . . . yet*: Or "but he hasn't given up on you yet!" [n]**10.5** *king of Assyria*: Probably King Sennacherib who invaded Israel in 701 B.C. [o]**10.9** *already captured*: Calno (in northern Syria), Carchemish (on the Euphrates River), Hamath (on the Orontes River), Arpad (near Aleppo in northern Syria), Samaria, and Damascus had already been captured by Assyrian kings (738–717 B.C.).

Only a Few Will Come Back

20A time is coming when the survivors from Israel and Judah will completely depend on the holy LORD of Israel, instead of the nation[p] that defeated them. 21-22There were as many people as there are grains of sand along the seashore, but only a few will survive to come back to Israel's mighty God. This is because he has threatened to destroy their nation, just as they deserve. 23The LORD All-Powerful has promised that everyone on this earth[q] will be punished.

24Now the LORD God All-Powerful says to his people in Jerusalem:

The Assyrians will beat you with sticks and abuse you, just as the Egyptians did. But don't be afraid of them. 25Soon I will stop being angry with you, and I will punish them for their crimes.[r] 26I will beat the Assyrians with a whip, as I did the people of Midian near the rock at Oreb. And I will show the same mighty power that I used when I made a path through the sea in Egypt. 27Then they will no longer rule your nation. All will go well for you,[s] and your burden will be lifted.

28Enemy troops have reached the town of Aiath.[t] They have gone through Migron, and they stored their supplies at Michmash, 29before crossing the valley and spending the night at Geba.[u] The people of Ramah are terrified; everyone in Gibeah, the hometown of Saul, has run away. 30Loud crying can be heard in the towns of Gallim, Laishah, and sorrowful Anathoth. 31No one is left in Madmenah or Gebim. 32Today the enemy will camp at Nob[v] and shake a threatening fist at Mount Zion in Jerusalem.

33But the LORD All-Powerful
    will use his fearsome might
to bring down the tallest trees
    and chop off every branch.
34With an ax, the glorious Lord
    will destroy every tree
in the forests of Lebanon.[w]

Peace at Last

11 Like a branch that sprouts
        from a stump,
someone from David's family[x]
    will someday be king.
2The Spirit of the LORD
    will be with him
to give him understanding,
    wisdom, and insight.
He will be powerful,
    and he will know
    and honor the LORD.
3His greatest joy will be
    to obey the LORD.

This king won't judge
    by appearances
    or listen to rumors.
4The poor and the needy
    will be treated with fairness
    and with justice.
His word will be law
    everywhere in the land,
    and criminals
    will be put to death.

P10.20 *nation*: That is, Assyria.   q10.23 *on this earth*: Or "in this land."   r10.25 *punish . . . crimes*: Or "completely destroy them."   s10.27 *All . . . you*: One possible meaning for the difficult Hebrew text.   t10.28 *Aiath*: Probably Ai (Joshua 7.2).   u10.29 *Geba*: Only six miles from Jerusalem.   v10.32 *Nob*: Perhaps within two miles of Jerusalem.   w10.34 *Lebanon*: One possible meaning for the difficult Hebrew text of verse 34.   x11.1 *David's family*: Hebrew "Jesse's family." Jesse was the father of King David.

10.21-22 *grains of sand . . . few will survive*: The grains of sand refer to the many descendants that God promised to Abraham, Israel's ancestor (Gen 12.2; 22.17). Because of their sins, however, Isaiah warned that the LORD would punish the people of Israel and Judah and allow many to be carried off to foreign lands. Afterwards, a much smaller number would return to Judah.

10.33 LORD *All-Powerful will . . . tallest trees*: The LORD will protect Zion by cutting down the proud and powerful Assyrians like lumberjacks cut down trees.

11.1 *branch . . . someone from David's family will . . . be king*: The text actually names Jesse, the father of King David (1 Sam 16.1-20). The image of the stump may mean that David's royal dynasty (2 Sam 7) has been threatened and reduced in power, as in the time of Ahaz and the Syro-Ephraimite War.

11.2 *Spirit of the LORD*: Just as the Spirit came to David when he was chosen to be king of Israel (1 Sam 16.13), so this new king will receive the Spirit.

Holy Spirit

11.2-5 *understanding . . . fairness*: The new king will be wise in his political dealings and wise in his respect of the LORD. In Israel, true wisdom came from the LORD, and the wise person obeyed the LORD's teachings (Prov 2.6,7; 1.7). The new king also would rule with justice and fairness, which God's law demanded.

11.6-8 *Leopards . . . poisonous snakes:* Dangerous animals no longer will be a threat. The poisonous snakes (11.8) are the small, but deadly snakes known as adders.

11.14 *Philistines . . . Ammonites:* Once the Israelite people are reunited, they will defeat their old, traditional enemies and regain the lands captured during David's reign. (See Map 6 on pg 1884.)

11.15 *Red Sea:* The arm of the Red Sea is the Gulf of Suez. (See Map 7 on pg 1885.)

12.3 *water . . . well of victory:* This phrase may come from an ancient Israelite rite of worship. In it, water was taken from the spring of Gihon in Jerusalem and poured out on the altar in the temple in thanksgiving for the LORD's blessings. On the other hand, it simply may be meant to compare the LORD's life-giving power to a well, a very important source of life and well-being.

Water

⁵Honesty and fairness
   will be his royal robes.

⁶Leopards will lie down
   with young goats,
and wolves will rest
   with lambs.
Calves and lions
   will eat together
and be cared for
   by little children.
⁷Cows and bears will share
   the same pasture;
their young will rest
   side by side.
Lions and oxen
   will both eat straw.

⁸Little children will play
   near snake holes.
They will stick their hands
into dens of poisonous snakes
   and never be hurt.

⁹Nothing harmful will take place
   on the LORD's holy mountain.
Just as water fills the sea,
   the land will be filled
with people who know
   and honor the LORD.

God's People Will Come Back Home

¹⁰The time is coming when one of David's descendants[y] will be the signal for the people of all nations to come together. They will follow his advice, and his own nation will become famous.
¹¹When that day comes, the Lord will again reach out his mighty arm and bring home his people who have survived in Assyria, Egypt, Pathros, Ethiopia,[z] Elam, Shinar, Hamath, and the land along the coast.[a] ¹²He will give a signal to the nations, and he will bring together the refugees from Judah and Israel, who have been scattered all over the earth. ¹³Israel will stop being jealous of Judah, and Judah will no longer be the enemy of Israel. ¹⁴Instead, they will get together and attack the Philistines in the west. Then they will defeat the Edomites, the Moabites, and the Ammonites in the east. They will rule those people and take from them whatever they want.
¹⁵The Lord will dry up the arm of the Red Sea near Egypt,[b] and he will send a scorching wind to divide the Euphrates River into seven streams that anyone can step across. ¹⁶Then for his people who survive, there will be a good road from Assyria, just as there was a good road for their ancestors when they left Egypt.

A Song of Praise

12 At that time you will say,
   "I thank you, LORD!
     You were angry with me,
but you stopped being angry
   and gave me comfort.
²I trust you to save me,
   LORD God,
     and I won't be afraid.
My power and my strength[c]
   come from you,
     and you have saved me."

³With great joy, you people
   will get water

[y]**11.10** *David's descendants:* Hebrew "Jesse's descendants" (see the note at 11.1). [z]**11.11** *Ethiopia:* The Hebrew text has "Cush," which was a region south of Egypt that included parts of the present countries of Ethiopia and Sudan. [a]**11.11** *land along the coast:* Or "islands." [b]**11.15** *arm of the Red Sea near Egypt:* Gulf of Suez. [c]**12.2** *strength:* Or "song."

from the well of victory.
⁴At that time you will say,
  "Our Lord, we are thankful,
    and we worship only you.
  We will tell the nations
  how glorious you are
    and what you have done.
⁵Because of your wonderful deeds
  we will sing your praises
    everywhere on earth."

⁶Sing, people of Zion!
  Celebrate the greatness
    of the holy Lord of Israel.
  God is here to help you.

Babylon Will Be Punished

13 This is the message[d] that I was given about Babylon:

²From high on a barren hill
  give a signal, shout the orders,
    and point the way
  to enter the gates
    of Babylon's proud rulers.
³The Lord has commanded
  his very best warriors
  and his proud heroes
    to show how angry he is.

⁴Listen to the noisy crowds
  on the mountains!
  Kingdoms and nations
  are joining forces.
  The Lord All-Powerful
  is bringing together
    an army for battle.
⁵From a distant land
  the Lord is coming
    fierce and furious—
  he brings his weapons
    to destroy the whole earth.

⁶Cry and weep!
  The day is coming
  when the mighty Lord
    will bring destruction.
*⁷All people will be terrified.
  Hands will grow limp;
    courage will melt away.
⁸Everyone will tremble with pain
  like a woman giving birth;
  they will stare at each other
    with horror on their faces.

There Will Be No Mercy

⁹I, the Lord,
  will show no mercy or pity
    when that time comes.
  In my anger I will destroy
  the earth and every sinner
    who lives on it.
¹⁰Light will disappear
    from the stars in the sky;
  the dawning sun will turn dark,
  and the moon
    will lose its brightness.

¹¹I will punish this evil world
  and its people
    because of their sins.
  I will crush the horrible pride
    of those who are cruel.
¹²Survivors will be harder to find
    than the purest gold.
¹³I, the Lord All-Powerful,
    am terribly angry—
  I will make the sky tremble
    and the earth shake loose.

¹⁴Everyone will run
    to their homelands,
  just as hunted deer run,

---

d 13.1 *message:* See the note at 1.1.

13.1 *This is the message:* This phrase is often used to introduce a prophetic saying. The word translated as "message" is traditionally translated as "oracle," which in Hebrew means "to lift up the voice" or "to carry a burden." Here the message is a warning against Babylonia/Assyria.

13.1 *Babylon:* It is difficult to give the exact date and historical situation concerning this message about Babylon. In Isaiah's day, Babylon was under the Assyrian Empire's control. Between 708 and 689 B.C. Assyria had to put down four different rebellions led by Babylon's rulers. However, many argue that this message against Babylon points to the historical situation over 100 years later in the middle of the sixth century B.C. after the Neo-Babylonian Empire had captured Judah and had taken many of the Israelite people into exile. In 550 B.C., the Persian ruler Cyrus became king of the Medes and threatened Babylon. In 539 B.C. Cyrus defeated Babylon, but the city was not destroyed, because its rulers surrendered peacefully.

Babylon

13.17 *Medes . . . attack Babylonia:* The Medes were from Media, a nation northeast of Babylonia. In Isaiah's day, the Medes were under the control of the Assyrians. Later, they joined the Babylonians in defeating Assyria (612–609 B.C.). Still later, they joined the Persians in defeating Babylon.

13.22 *Hyenas:* Hyenas are scavengers, eating dead things that they find or that have been killed by other animals. They usually hunt in packs at night. This verse pictures hyenas coming in from the desert to hunt the ruins of Babylon looking for dead bodies.

14.4 *King of Babylonia:* If this poem is from Isaiah's time, this king may be either Assyrian King Sargon II, who died in battle against Tabal in Turkey in 705 B.C., or Sennacherib, whose Assyrian army suffered great losses in 701 B.C. while threatening Jerusalem (Isa 37.36). During Isaiah's time, these Assyrian kings were considered kings of Babylonia, since Babylonia was under Assyrian control. The poem probably refers to Nebuchadnezzar, the Babylonian king who later forced the people of Judah to go into exile in Babylonia.

14.8 *cypress trees . . . cedars of Lebanon:* Cypress, a form of evergreen, and the tall cedar trees, which grew in the forests of Lebanon, were used to build royal palaces, including the temple and palace of King Solomon (1 Kgs 5.3-9; 7.1-12). Assyrian and Babylonian kings also used cedars for building (37.24).

and sheep scatter
    when they have no shepherd.
15Those men who are captured
    will be killed by a sword.
16They will see their children
    beaten against rocks,
    their homes robbed,
    and their wives abused.

17The Medes[e] can't be bought off
    with silver or gold,
and I'm sending them
    to attack Babylonia.
18Their arrows will slaughter
    the young men;
no pity will be shown
    to babies and children.

The LORD Will Destroy Babylon

19The city of Babylon
is glorious and powerful,
    the pride of the nation.
But it will be like the cities
    of Sodom and Gomorrah
after I, the Lord,
    destroyed them.
20No one will live in Babylon.
Even nomads won't camp nearby,
    and shepherds won't let
    their sheep rest there.
21Only desert creatures,
    hoot owls, and ostriches
will live in its ruins,
    and goats[f] will leap about.
22Hyenas and wolves will howl
from Babylon's fortresses
    and beautiful palaces.
Its time is almost up!

The LORD's People Will Come Home

14 The LORD will have mercy on Israel and will let them be his chosen people once again. He will bring them back to their own land, and foreigners will join them as part of Israel. 2Other nations will lead them home, and Israel will make slaves of them in the land that belongs to the Lord. Israel will rule over those who once governed and mistreated them.

Death to the King of Babylonia!

3The LORD will set you free from your sorrow, suffering, and slavery. 4Then you will make fun of the King of Babylonia by singing this song:

That cruel monster is done for!
    He won't attack us again.[g]
5The LORD has crushed the power
    of those evil kings,
6who were furious
    and never stopped abusing
    the people of other nations.

7Now all the world is at peace;
its people are celebrating
    with joyful songs.
8King of Babylonia,
    even the cypress trees
and the cedars of Lebanon
    celebrate and say,
"Since you were put down,
no one comes along
    to chop us down."

9The world of the dead
    eagerly waits for you.
With great excitement,

[e]**13.17** *Medes:* People of a nation northeast of Babylonia, which became part of the Persian Empire. [f]**13.21** *goats:* Or "demons."   [g]**14.4** *He . . . again:* One possible meaning for the difficult Hebrew text.

the spirits of ancient rulers
hear about your coming.
[10] Each one of them will say,
"Now you are just as weak
as any of us!
[11] Your pride and your music
have ended here
in the world of the dead.
Worms are your blanket,
maggots are your bed."

[12] You, the bright morning star,
have fallen from the sky!
You brought down other nations;
now you are brought down.
[13] You said to yourself,
"I'll climb to heaven
and place my throne
above the highest stars.
I'll sit there with the gods
far away in the north.
[14] I'll be above the clouds,
just like God Most High."

[15] But now you are deep
in the world of the dead.
[16] Those who see you will stare
and wonder, "Is this the man
who made the world tremble
and shook up kingdoms?
[17] Did he capture every city
and make earth a desert?
Is he the one who refused
to let prisoners go home?"

[18] When kings die, they are buried
in glorious tombs.
[19] But you will be left unburied,
just another dead body
lying underfoot
like a broken branch.

You will be one of many
killed in battle and gone down
to the deep rocky pit.[h]
[20] You won't be buried with kings;
you ruined your country
and murdered your people.

You evil monster!
We hope that your family
will be forgotten forever.
[21] We will slaughter your sons
to make them pay for the crimes
of their ancestors.
They won't take over the world
or build cities
anywhere on this earth.

[22] The Lord All-Powerful has promised to attack Babylonia and destroy everyone there, so that none of them will ever be remembered again. [23] The Lord will sweep out the people, and the land will become a swamp for wild animals.

Assyria Will Be Punished

[24] The Lord All-Powerful
has made this promise:
Everything I have planned
will happen just as I said.
[25] I will wipe out every Assyrian
in my country,
and I will crush those
on my mountains.
I will free my people
from slavery
to the Assyrians.
[26] I have planned this
for the whole world,
and my mighty arm
controls every nation.
[27] I, the Lord All-Powerful,

[h]**14.19** *deep rocky pit*: The world of the dead.

■ **14.12** *bright morning star:* The "bright morning star" that falls from the sky may refer to the Babylonian king and his descent into the world of the dead. The image would have reminded ancient readers of the Canaanite myth about "Day Star, son of Dawn." In it, Day Star tries to climb above all the stars in the heavens to overthrow the Most High, who was said to live on Mount Zaphon in Syria. Day Star makes his move at daybreak, but the rays of the sun-god Shamash chase him and throw him back down to earth. Some later writers interpreted this morning star as Satan, perhaps based on Jesus' words in Luke 10.18. In the Latin Vulgate Bible, the Hebrew for "Morning star" is translated "Lucifer," which in modern times has come to mean Satan.

● **14.18,19** *glorious tombs . . . left unburied:* The great pyramids in Egypt were tombs built to honor and provide a place of rest for those earthly leaders who had been servants of the gods, or were considered to be gods themselves. The spirit of a person left unburied was believed to wander around forever, unable to rest in peace. Both Sargon II and Sennacherib fit the description of kings who died but did not receive proper royal burial. Sargon's body was not found after he died in battle. Sennacherib was murdered by his own sons, and so did not receive a royal funeral.

⟨R Burial

have made these plans.
No one can stop me now!

The Philistines Will Be Punished

28 This message came from the LORD in the year King Ahaz died:[i]

29Philistines, don't be happy
just because the rod
that punished you
is broken.
That rod will become
a poisonous snake, and then
a flying fiery dragon.

30The poor and needy will find
pastures for their sheep
and will live in safety.
But I will starve some of you,
and others will be killed.

31Cry and weep in the gates
of your towns,
you Philistines!
Smoke blows in from the north,[j]
and every soldier is ready.
32If a messenger comes
from a distant nation,
you must say:
"The LORD built Zion.
Even the poorest of his people
will find safety there."

Moab Will Be Punished

15 This is a message about Moab:

The towns of Ar and Kir
were destroyed in a night.

Moab is left in ruins!
2Everyone in Dibon has gone up
to the temple[k] and the shrines
to cry and weep.
All of Moab is crying.
Heads and beards are shaved[l]
because of what happened
at Nebo and Medeba.
3In the towns and at home,
everyone wears sackcloth
and cries loud and long.
4From Heshbon and Elealeh,
weeping is heard in Jahaz;
Moab's warriors scream
while trembling with fear.

Pity Moab

5I pity Moab!
Its people are running to Zoar
and to Eglath-Shelishiyah.
They cry on their way up
to the town of Luhith;
on the road to Horonaim
they tell of disasters.
6The streams of Nimrim
and the grasslands
have dried up.
Every plant is parched.

7The people of Moab are leaving,
crossing over Willow Creek,
taking everything they own
and have worked for.
8In the towns of Eglaim
and of Beerelim
and everywhere else in Moab
mournful cries are heard.
9The streams near Dimon
are flowing with blood.
But the Lord will bring

i14.28 *King Ahaz died*: 715 B.C. j14.31 *north*: The Assyrian and Babylonian attacks came from the north. k15.2 *Everyone . . . temple*: One possible meaning for the difficult Hebrew text.
l15.2 *Heads . . . shaved*: As a sign of sorrow and mourning.

even worse trouble to Dimon,[m]
because all in Moab who escape
   will be attacked by lions.[n]

More Troubles for Moab

16 Send lambs[o] as gifts
      to the ruler of the land.
   Send them across the desert
      from Sela[p] to Mount Zion.
[2] The women of Moab
      crossing the Arnon River
   are like a flock of birds
      scattered from their nests.
[3] Moab's messengers say
      to the people of Judah,
   "Be kind and help us!
   Shade us from the heat
      of the noonday sun.
   Hide our refugees!
      Don't turn them away.
[4] Let our people live
   in your country
      and find safety here."

   Moab, your cruel enemies
      will disappear;
   they will no longer attack
      and destroy your land.
[5] Then a kingdom of love
      will be set up,
   and someone from David's family
      will rule with fairness.
   He will do what is right
      and quickly bring justice.

Moab's Pride Is Destroyed

[6] We have heard of Moab's pride.
   Its people strut and boast,

but without reason.
[7] Tell everyone in Moab
   to mourn for their nation.
   Tell them to cry and weep
   for those fancy raisins[q]
      of Kir-Hareseth.

[8] Vineyards near Heshbon
and Sibmah
   have turned brown.
   The rulers of nations
      used to get drunk
   on wine from those vineyards[r]
      that spread to Jazer,
   then across the desert
      and beyond the sea.

[9] Now I mourn like Jazer
   for the vineyards
      of Sibmah.
   I shed tears for Heshbon
      and for Elealeh.
   There will be no more
      harvest celebrations
[10] or joyful and happy times,
      while bringing in the crops.
   Singing and shouting are gone
      from the vineyards.
   There are no joyful shouts
   where grapes were pressed.
      God has silenced them all.

[11] Deep in my heart I hurt
   for Moab and Kir-Heres.
[12] It's useless for Moab's people
      to wear themselves out
   by going to their altars
      to worship and pray.

[m]15.9 *Dimon . . . Dimon:* The Standard Hebrew Text; the Dead Sea Scrolls and one ancient translation have Dibon . . . Dibon.   [n]15.9 *lions:* One possible meaning for the difficult Hebrew text of verse 9.   [o]16.1 *lambs:* The main product of Moab.   [p]16.1 *Sela:* A town in Edom.   [q]16.7 *fancy raisins:* The Hebrew text has "raisin-cakes," which could mean either the rich produce or the prosperous farmers.   [r]16.8 *The rulers . . . vineyards:* Or "The rulers of nations have destroyed those vineyards."

● 16.1 *lambs as gifts:* Lambs were the main product of Moab. See 2 Kgs 3.4. Now, Judah's ruler will be offered lambs in the hope that he will then allow refugees from Moab to come into Judah.

● 16.1,2 *from Sela to Mount Zion . . . Arnon River:* Sela, the capital of the Edomites, was located on a high plateau near the southern end of the Dead Sea. The Arnon River flows west into the Dead Sea, so the women were probably wading through the river from south to north in order to escape.

● 16.7-9 *of Kir-Hareseth . . . Heshbon:* Kir-Hareseth is probably the same as Kir (15.1,2-9) and Kir-Heres (16.11). Heshbon was located about 18 miles east of the northern end of the Dead Sea.

17.1 *Damascus:* Damascus was the capital city of Aram (Syria). The Arameans had been enemies of Israel in the past (2 Sam 8.3-6; 1 Kgs 22.29-38), but in 735 B.C. they joined with Israel to invade Judah and to stand up to the Assyrians.

17.3-5 *Israel . . . Rephaim Valley:* Here meaning the northern kingdom.

17.8,9 *captured powerful cities:* For the powerful Canaanite cities that were captured, see Deut 7.1-5; Josh 10.5-13; 11.1—12.24.

Canaanite Gods and Goddesses

17.12-14 *nations . . . are destroyed:* "Nations" refers to those who attack God's people in Judah (5.30; 7.1—8.8; 29.1-4).

¹³The Lord has already said all of this about Moab. ¹⁴Now he says, "The contract of a hired worker is good for three years, but Moab's glory and greatness won't last any longer than that. Only a few of its people will survive, and they will be left helpless."

Damascus Will Be Punished

17 This is a message about Damascus:

Damascus is doomed!
  It will end up in ruins.
²The villages around Aroer[s]
  will be deserted,
with only sheep living there
  and no one to bother them.
³Israel[t] will lose its fortresses.
  The kingdom of Damascus
    will be destroyed;
its survivors will suffer
  the same fate as Israel.
The Lord All-Powerful
  has promised this.

Sin and Suffering

⁴When that time comes,
  the glorious nation of Israel
    will be brought down;
its prosperous people
  will be skin and bones.
⁵Israel will be like wheat fields
  in Rephaim Valley
    picked clean of grain.
⁶It will be like an olive tree
  beaten with a stick,
leaving two or three olives
  or maybe four or five

on the highest
  or most fruitful branches.
The Lord God of Israel
  has promised this.

⁷At that time the people will turn and trust their Creator, the holy God of Israel. ⁸They have built altars and places for burning incense to their goddess Asherah, and they have set up sacred poles[u] for her. But they will stop worshiping at these places. ⁹Israel captured powerful cities and chased out the people who lived there. But these cities will lie in ruins, covered over with weeds and underbrush.[v]

¹⁰Israel, you have forgotten
  the God who saves you,
the one who is the mighty rock[w]
  where you find protection.
You plant the finest flowers
  to honor a foreign god.
¹¹The plants may sprout
  and blossom
    that very same morning,
but it will do you no good,
because you will suffer
  endless agony.

God Defends His People

¹²The nations are a noisy,
  thunderous sea.
¹³But even if they roar
  like a fearsome flood,
God will give the command
  to turn them back.
They will be like dust,

---

[s]**17.2** *Aroer:* Either a city near Damascus with the same name as the Moabite city or the Moabite city itself, here used as an example of what will happen to Damascus.   [t]**17.3** *Israel:* The Hebrew text has "Ephraim," another name for the northern kingdom.   [u]**17.8** *sacred poles:* Or "trees," used as symbols of Asherah, the goddess of fertility.   [v]**17.9** *covered . . . underbrush:* Hebrew; one ancient translation "like the cities of the Hivites and the Amorites."   [w]**17.10** *mighty rock:* The Hebrew text has "rock," which is sometimes used in poetry to compare the Lord to a mountain where his people can run for protection from their enemies.

or like a tumbleweed
blowing across the hills
in a windstorm.
¹⁴In the evening
their attack is fierce,
but by morning
they are destroyed.
This is what happens to those
who raid and rob us.

Ethiopia Will Be Punished

18 Downstream from Ethiopiaˣ
lies the country of Egypt,
swarming with insects.ʸ
²Egypt sends messengers
up the Nile River
on ships made of reeds.ᶻ
Send them fast to Ethiopia,
whose people are tall
and have smooth skin.
Their land is divided by rivers;
they are strong and brutal,
feared all over the world.ᵃ

³Everyone on this earth,
listen with care!
A signal will be given
on the mountains,
and you will hear a trumpet.
⁴The LORD said to me,
"I will calmly look down
from my home above—
as calmly as the sun at noon
or clouds in the heat
of harvest season."

⁵Before the blossoms
can turn into grapes,
God will cut off the sprouts
and hack off the branches.

⁶Ethiopians will be food
for mountain vultures
during the summer
and for wild animals
during the winter.

⁷Those Ethiopians are tall and their skin is smooth. They are feared all over the world, because they are strong and brutal. But at that time they will come from their land divided by rivers, and they will bring gifts to the LORD All-Powerful, who is worshiped on Mount Zion.

Egypt Will Be Punished

19 This is a message about Egypt:

The LORD comes to Egypt,
riding swiftly on a cloud.
The people are weak from fear.
Their idols tremble
as he approaches and says,
²"I will punish Egypt
with civil war—
neighbors, cities, and kingdoms
will fight each other.

³"Egypt will be discouraged
when I confuse their plans.
They will try to get advice
from their idols,
from the spirits of the dead,
and from fortunetellers.
⁴I will put the Egyptians
under the power of a cruel,
heartless king.
I, the LORD All-Powerful,
have promised this."

ˣ**18.1** *Ethiopia*: See the note at 11.11.   ʸ**18.1** *insects*: Or "sailing ships."   ᶻ**18.2** *reeds*: Ancient Egypt was famous for the papyrus reeds that grew in the Nile Delta.   ᵃ**18.2** *world*: One possible meaning for the difficult Hebrew text of verse 2.

19.5 *Nile River:* During the yearly rainy season, the Nile River overflows its banks, and the floodwaters fertilize fields of crops near the river. In Isaiah's time, a year or more without flooding was disastrous for ancient Egypt. Poor crops meant low food supplies and fewer plants that could be made into cloth.

19.11,13 *Zoan . . . Memphis:* Zoan, also called Tanis, was an important city in the northeastern delta region of Egypt (Num 13.22; Ps 78.9-12). Memphis, located on the Nile River about 15 miles south of the delta, was the capital city of Egypt's Old Kingdom (2686–2160 B.C.). It is not clear what kind of "stupid advice" Egypt's leaders gave.

19.17-22 *Judah . . . healed:* Why Egypt will fear Judah is not clear, nor is the identity of four of the five Egyptian cities. The "City of the Sun," is probably Heliopolis (Jer 43.13). In the time when Babylonia threatened Judah, a number of Israelites migrated to Egypt to escape the coming destruction (Jer 44.1,15). These cities near the eastern boundaries of Egypt may have been strongly influenced by the language and religion of the migrant Israelites (19.18-21).

Trouble along the Nile

[5]The Nile River will dry up
and become parched land.
[6]Its streams will stink,
Egypt will have no water,
and the reeds and tall grass
will dry up.
[7]Fields along the Nile
will be completely barren;
every plant will disappear.

[8]Those who fish in the Nile
will be discouraged
and mourn.
[9]None of the cloth makers[b]
will know what to do,
and they will turn pale.[c]
[10]Weavers will be confused;
paid workers will cry and mourn.

Egypt's Helpless Leaders

[11]The king's officials in Zoan[d]
are foolish themselves
and give stupid advice.
How can they say to him,
"We are very wise,
and our families go back
to kings of long ago?"
[12]Where are those wise men now?
If they can, let them say
what the Lord All-Powerful
intends for Egypt.

[13]The royal officials in Zoan
and in Memphis
are foolish and deceived.
The leaders in every state

have given bad advice
to the nation.
[14]The Lord has confused Egypt;
its leaders have made it stagger
and vomit like a drunkard.
[15]No one in Egypt can do a thing,
no matter who they are.

[16]When the Lord All-Powerful punishes Egypt with his mighty arm, the Egyptians will become terribly weak and will tremble with fear. [17]They will be so terrified of Judah that they will be frightened by the very mention of its name. This will happen because of what the Lord All-Powerful is planning against Egypt.

The Lord Will Bless Egypt, Assyria, and Israel

[18]The time is coming when Hebrew will be spoken in five Egyptian cities, and their people will become followers of the Lord. One of these cities will be called City of the Sun.[e]

[19]In the heart of Egypt an altar will be set up for the Lord; at its border a shrine will be built to honor him. [20]These will remind the Egyptians that the Lord All-Powerful is with them. And when they are in trouble and ask for help, he will send someone to rescue them from their enemies. [21]The Lord will show the Egyptians who he is, and they will know and worship the Lord. They will bring him sacrifices and offerings, and they will keep their promises to him. [22]After the Lord has punished Egypt, the people will turn to him. Then he will answer their prayers, and the Egyptians will be healed.

[b]**19.9** *cloth makers:* Cloth was made from several kinds of plants that grew in the fields along the Nile.   [c]**19.9** *turn pale:* One possible meaning for the difficult Hebrew text.   [d]**19.11** *Zoan:* The city of Tanis in the Nile delta.   [e]**19.18** *City of the Sun:* Some manuscripts of the Standard Hebrew Text, the Dead Sea Scrolls, and one ancient translation; most manuscripts of the Standard Hebrew Text have "City of Destruction." This probably refers to Heliopolis which means "City of the Sun" (see Jeremiah 43.13).

23At that time a good road will run from Egypt to Assyria. The Egyptians and the Assyrians will travel back and forth from Egypt to Assyria, and they will worship together. **24**Israel will join with these two countries. They will be a blessing to everyone on earth, **25**then the LORD All-Powerful will bless them by saying,

> "The Egyptians are my people.
> I created the Assyrians
>   and chose the Israelites."

Isaiah Acts Out the Defeat of Egypt and Ethiopia

20 King Sargon of Assyria gave orders for his army commander to capture the city of Ashdod.**f** **2**About this same time the LORD had told me, "Isaiah, take off everything, including your sandals!" I did this and went around naked and barefoot **3**for three years.

Then the LORD said:

What Isaiah has done is a warning to Egypt and Ethiopia.**g** **4**Everyone in these two countries will be led away naked and barefoot by the king of Assyria. Young or old, they will be taken prisoner, and Egypt will be disgraced. **5**They will be confused and frustrated, because they depended on Ethiopia and bragged about Egypt. **6**When this happens, the people who live along the coast**h** will say, "Look what happened to them! We ran to them for safety, hoping they would protect us from the king of Assyria. But now, there is no escape for us."

The Fall of Babylonia**i**

21 This is a message about a desert beside the sea:**j**

> Enemies from a hostile nation
> attack like a whirlwind
>   from the Southern Desert.
> **2**What a horrible vision
>   was shown to me—
> a vision of betrayal
>   and destruction.
> Tell Elam and Media**k**
> to surround and attack
>   the Babylonians.
> The LORD has sworn to end
>   the suffering they caused.

> **3**I'm in terrible pain
>   like a woman giving birth.
> I'm shocked and hurt so much
>   that I can't hear or see.
> **4**My head spins; I'm horrified!
> Early evening, my favorite time,
>   has become a nightmare.

> **5**In Babylon the high officials
>   were having a feast.
> They were eating and drinking,
>   when someone shouted,
> "Officers, take your places!
>   Grab your shields."

> **6**The LORD said to me,
> "Send guards to find out
>   what's going on.
> **7**When they see cavalry troops

f20.1 *Ashdod:* King Sargon II of Assyria captured this Philistine city in 711 B.C. **g20.3** *Ethiopia:* See the note at 11.11. **h20.6** *people . . . coast:* Probably the Philistines. **i21.1** *Babylonia:* King Cyrus and his army of Medes and Persians captured the city of Babylon in 539 B.C. **j21.1** *This . . . sea:* One possible meaning for the difficult Hebrew text. The prophet may be speaking of Babylonia as a desert, because of the terrible punishment God will bring on it. The southern part of Babylonia on the Persian Gulf was sometimes called "the land beside the sea." **k21.2** *Elam and Media:* People from the Iranian highlands; the capital of Elam was Susa, in the hill country east of Babylon.

20.1-3 *King Sargon . . . Ashdod . . . warning to Egypt and Ethiopia:* King Sargon II, who ruled Assyria from 721 to 705 B.C., captured the Philistine city of Ashdod in 711 B.C. after it had rebelled against Assyria in 713 B.C. A number of Israel's prophets were told to act out the LORD's messages by doing something dramatic (see Hos 1–3; Jer 27; Ezek 24.15-27). Isaiah's nakedness (20.2) demonstrated how Egypt and Ethiopia would be stripped of their power and taken prisoner. It gave the same warning to King Hezekiah and the leaders of Judah, who apparently decided to join Ashdod and the Ethiopians in their rebellion against Assyria.

20.6 *people . . . coast:* This refers to the Philistines, whose land was along the Mediterranean Sea coast. "Them" may be Egypt and Ethiopia. However, it also could be a warning to Judah against putting trust in political treaties and leaders instead of the LORD.

21.1 *desert beside the sea . . . Southern Desert:* The dry flatlands south of Babylon near the Persian Gulf were sometimes called "the land beside the sea." The Southern Desert refers to a desert area between Egypt and southern Canaan. The attack on Babylon would be as sudden and destructive as the hot windstorms that blew in from the desert.

21.2 *Elam . . . Media:* Elam and Media were located in the hill country to the east and northeast of Babylon. The Elamites and Medians battled Assyria in 691–689 B.C. before Assyria destroyed Babylon in 689 B.C. (See Map 7 on pg 1885.)

21.11 *Dumah . . . Seir:* Dumah was an oasis in the Arabian Desert. Seir was a mountainous region of Edom southwest of the Dead Sea. The Assyrian army of Sennacherib probably went through these locations about the time it attacked Babylon.

21.13-17 *Dedan . . . Kedar:* The peoples living in the Arabian regions of Dedan (northwest), Tema (oasis in north), and Kedar (desert area) were told to provide food and shelter for the Edomite refugees who were running away from the advancing army. Note the phrase "A year from now," and compare it to Isa 16.14. If the Babylonian attack is meant, this prophecy was fulfilled at least a century after Isaiah lived.

22.1 *Vision Valley:* The exact location of Vision Valley is not known. It may refer to the Babylonian land beside the sea (21.1) or to one of the many valleys surrounding Jerusalem.

and columns of soldiers
on donkeys and camels,
  tell them to be ready!"

[8]Then a guard[l] said,
"I have stood day and night
  on this watchtower, Lord.
[9]Now I see column after column
  of cavalry troops."

At once someone shouted,
  "Babylon has fallen!
Every idol in the city
  lies broken on the ground."

[10]Then I said, "My people,
  you have suffered terribly,
but I have a message for you
from the LORD All-Powerful,
  the God of Israel."

How Much Longer?

[11]This is a message about Dumah:

From the country of Seir,[m]
  someone shouts to me,
"Guard, how much longer
  before daylight?"

[12]From my guard post, I answered,
"Morning will soon be here,
  but night will return.
If you want to know more,
  come back later."

[13]This is a message for Arabs who live in the barren desert in the region of Dedan:[n]

You must order your caravans
[14]to bring water for those
  who are thirsty.
You people of Tema[o]
  must bring food
  for the hungry refugees.
[15]They are worn out and weary
  from being chased by enemies
  with swords and arrows.

[16]The Lord said to me:
A year from now the glory of the people of Kedar[p] will all come to an end, just as a worker's contract ends after a year. [17]Only a few of their warriors will be left with bows and arrows. This is a promise that I, the LORD God of Israel, have made.

Trouble in Vision Valley

22 This is a message about Vision Valley:[q]

Why are you celebrating
on the flat roofs[r]
  of your houses?
[2]Your city is filled
  with noisy shouts.
Those who lie drunk
in your streets
  were not killed in battle.

[l]**21.8** *guard:* The Dead Sea Scrolls and one ancient translation; the Standard Hebrew Text has "lion."
[m]**21.11** *Dumah . . . Seir:* Dumah was an oasis in the Arabian desert. One ancient translation has "Edom," which may be what is meant. Seir is a mountainous region of Edom southwest of the Dead Sea.   [n]**21.13** *Dedan:* A region in northwest Arabia.   [o]**21.14** *Tema:* A region in north Arabia.
[p]**21.16** *Kedar:* A region in the Arabian desert.   [q]**22.1** *Vision Valley:* The exact location is not known. In Hebrew the name sounds something like "Hinnom Valley," where the people of Jerusalem sometimes offered human sacrifices to the gods of Canaan.   [r]**22.1** *flat roofs:* In Palestine the houses usually had a flat roof. Stairs on the outside led up to the roof, which was made of beams and boards covered with packed earth.

³Your leaders ran away,
  but they were captured
    without a fight.
  No matter how far they ran,
    they were found and caught.ˢ

⁴Then I said, "Leave me alone!
  Let me cry bitter tears.
  My people have been destroyed,
    so don't try to comfort me."

⁵The LORD All-Powerful
  had chosen a time
  for noisy shouts and confusion
    to fill Vision Valley,
  and for everyone to beg
    the mountains for help.ᵗ
⁶The people of Elam and Kirᵘ
  attacked with chariotsᵛ
    and carried shields.
⁷Your most beautiful valleys
    were covered with chariots;
  your cities were surrounded
    by cavalry troops.
⁸ Judah was left defenseless.

At that time you trusted in the weapons you had stored in Forest Palace.ʷ ⁹You saw the holes in the outer wall of Jerusalem, and you brought water from the lower pool.ˣ ¹⁰You counted the houses in Jerusalem and tore down some of them, so you could get stones to repair the city wall. ¹¹Then you built a large tank between the wallsʸ to store the water. But you refused to trust the God who planned this long ago and made it happen.

A Time To Weep

¹²When all of this happened,
  the LORD All-Powerful told you
    to weep and mourn,
    to shave your heads,
    and wear sackcloth.
¹³But instead, you celebrated
  by feasting on beef and lamb
    and by drinking wine,
  because you said,
  "Let's eat and drink today!
    Tomorrow we may die."

¹⁴The LORD All-Powerful
  has spoken to me
    this solemn promise:
  "I won't forgive them for this,
    not as long as they live."

Selfish Officials Are Doomed

¹⁵The LORD All-Powerful is sending me with this message for Shebna, the prime minister:
  ¹⁶Shebna, what gives you the right to have a tomb carved out of rock in this burial place of royalty? None of your relatives are buried here. ¹⁷You may be powerful, but the LORD is about to snatch you up and throw you away. ¹⁸He will roll you into a ball and throw you into a wide open country, where you will die and your chariots will be destroyed. You're a disgrace to those you serve.

ˢ22.3 No matter . . . caught: One possible meaning for the difficult Hebrew text.   ᵗ22.5 and for . . . help: One possible meaning for the difficult Hebrew text.   ᵘ22.6 Elam and Kir: Regions in the Iranian highlands.   ᵛ22.6 chariots: One possible meaning for the difficult Hebrew text.   ʷ22.8 Forest Palace: Built by Solomon (1 Kings 7.2) and used as a place for storing weapons.   ˣ22.9 the lower pool: Mentioned only here; probably in the southern part of the Central Valley (Tyropoean Valley) of Jerusalem. ʸ22.11 between the walls: Some cities had two walls with a space between them. If the enemy broke through the outer wall, the city was still protected by the inner wall. The houses that were torn down to repair the outer wall were probably squatters' huts that had been built between the two walls.

22.3-6 leaders . . . captured . . . Elam and Kir attacked: These verses may be describing Assyria's attacks on Babylon under Sennacherib. Some scholars suggest that these verses are describing the Babylonian King Nebuchadnezzar's attack on Jerusalem in 587 B.C. His army would likely have included warriors from Elam.

22.13 instead, you celebrated: Judah's leaders did not mourn the disaster that was about to come upon their city. Instead, they decided to have one last big party, in case they died the next day. This was seen as a lack of trust in the LORD's ability to protect them.

22.15-21 Shebna . . . Eliakim: Shebna is mentioned only here and in 2 Kgs 18.18 and Isa 36.3, where he is called an "assistant to the prime minister." He apparently overstepped his position of authority by ordering a tomb for himself to be carved out of the rocks where Judah's royalty had been buried. Eliakim, whose name means "God will approve," would receive royal robes symbolizing his authority.

Commentary

23.1-4 *Tyre... in ruins... Sidon... disgraced:* Tyre was an important Phoenician seaport city built on the Mediterranean coast and on two islands near the shore. Sidon was a seacoast city about 25 miles north of Tyre. The Assyrians did invade Phoenicia in 734 B.C. and again in 701 B.C. King Nebuchadnezzar of Babylon captured the mainland part of Tyre in 572 B.C. (Ezek 26.7-11), and Alexander the Great of Macedonia captured the whole city in 332 B.C. (See Map 4 on pg 1882.)

Phoenicia

23.5-10 *When Egypt hears... become farmers:* Egypt's leaders probably worried about what might happen to their economy, if they could no longer rely on Phoenician sailors to trade their crops and goods. Enemy attacks forced some Phoenicians to leave their cities and become farmers to make a living (23.10).

[19]The LORD is going to take away your job! [20-21]He will give your official robes and your authority to his servant Eliakim son of Hilkiah.

Eliakim will be like a father to the people of Jerusalem and to the royal family of Judah. [22]The LORD will put him in charge of the key that belongs to King David's family. No one will be able to unlock what he locks, and no one will be able to lock what he unlocks. [23]The LORD will make him as firm in his position as a tent peg hammered in the ground, and Eliakim will bring honor to his family.

[24]His children and relatives will be supported by him, like pans hanging from a peg on the wall. [25]That peg is fastened firmly now, but someday it will be shaken loose and fall down. Then everything that was hanging on it will be destroyed. This is what the LORD All-Powerful has promised.

The City of Tyre Will Be Punished

23 This is a message from distant islands about the city of Tyre:[z]

Cry, you seagoing ships![a]
Tyre and its houses
   lie in ruins.[b]
[2]Mourn in silence,
you shop owners of Sidon,[c]
   you people on the coast.

Your sailors crossed oceans,
   making your city rich.
[3]Your merchants sailed the seas,
   making you wealthy by trading
   with nation after nation.
They brought back grain
   that grew along the Nile.[d]
[4]Sidon, you are a mighty fortress
   built along the sea.
But you will be disgraced
like a married woman
   who never had children.[e]

[5]When Egypt hears about Tyre,
   it will tremble.
[6]All of you along the coast
   had better cry and sail
   far across the ocean.[f]
[7]Can this be the happy city
   that has stood for centuries?
Its people have spread
   to distant lands;
[8]its merchants were kings
   honored all over the world.
Who planned to destroy Tyre?
[9]The LORD All-Powerful planned it
   to bring shame and disgrace
   to those who are honored
   by everyone on earth.
[10]People of Tyre,[g]
   your harbor is destroyed!
You will have to become farmers
   just like the Egyptians.[h]

[z]23.1 *Tyre:* A fortress city built on an island in the Mediterranean Sea off the coast of what is now Lebanon. [a]23.1 *seagoing ships:* See the note at 2.16. [b]23.1 *Tyre... ruins:* One possible meaning for the difficult Hebrew text. [c]23.2 *Sidon:* A coastal city just north of Tyre. [d]23.3 *along the Nile:* The Hebrew text has "grain of Shihor, the harvest of the Nile," but Shihor is probably a name for a region near the lower part of the Nile. [e]23.4 *children:* One possible meaning for the difficult Hebrew text. [f]23.6 *far across the ocean:* The Hebrew text has "to Tarshish," probably meaning a long distance. [g]23.10 *People of Tyre:* The Hebrew text has "the people of Tarshish," which stands for the colonies of Tyre. [h]23.10 *Egyptians:* One possible meaning for the difficult Hebrew text of verse 10.

Tyre Will Be Forgotten

[11]The Lord's hand has reached
across the sea,
    upsetting the nations.
He has given a command
to destroy fortresses
    in the land of Canaan.
[12]The Lord has said
to the people of Sidon,
"Your celebrating is over—
    you are crushed.
Even if you escape to Cyprus,
    you won't find peace."

[13]Look what the Assyrians have done to
Babylonia! They have attacked, destroying
every palace in the land. Now wild animals
live among the ruins.[i] [14]Not a fortress will
be left standing, so tell all the seagoing
ships[j] to mourn.

[15]The city of Tyre will be forgotten for 70
years, which is the lifetime of a king. Then
Tyre will be like that evil woman in the
song:
[16]You're gone and forgotten,
    you evil woman!
So strut through the town,
    singing and playing
    your favorite tune
    to be remembered again.

[17]At the end of those 70 years, the Lord
will let Tyre get back into business. The city
will be like a woman who sells her body to
everyone of every nation on earth, [18]but
none of what is earned will be kept in the
city. That money will belong to the Lord,
and it will be used to buy more than enough
food and good clothes for those who worship the Lord.

The Earth Will Be Punished

24 The Lord is going to twist the earth
out of shape and turn it into a
desert. Everyone will be scattered, [2]including ordinary people and priests, slaves and
slave owners, buyers and sellers, lenders
and borrowers, the rich and the poor. [3]The
earth will be stripped bare and left that
way. This is what the Lord has promised.

[4]The earth wilts away;
    its mighty leaders melt
      to nothing.[k]
[5]The earth is polluted
    because its people
    disobeyed the laws of God,
    breaking their agreement
      that was to last forever.

[6]The earth is under a curse;
    its people are dying out
      because of their sins.
[7]Grapevines have dried up:
    wine is almost gone—
    mournful sounds are heard
      instead of joyful shouts.

[8]No one plays tambourines
    or stringed instruments;
    all noisy celebrating
      has come to an end.
[9]They no longer sing
    as they drink their wine,
      and it tastes sour.

[10]Towns are crushed and in chaos;
    houses are locked tight.
[11]Happy times have disappeared
    from the earth,
and people shout in the streets,
    "We're out of wine!"

23.15 *70 years*: This may be a symbolic number, meaning a long time or a lifetime. Compare this to the time the prophet Jeremiah said Judah would be in exile in Babylon (Jer 25.11). **(See the chart Numbers in the Bible on pg 1844.)**

23.17,18 *woman . . . money will belong to the Lord*: Tyre's merchants, who would do anything to make a profit, are compared to a prostitute. But some day Tyre's wealth would be dedicated to the Lord God of Israel (60.5-13; 61.6).

---

[i]**23.13** *ruins*: One possible meaning for the difficult Hebrew text of verse 13.   [j]**23.14** *seagoing ships*: See the note at 2.16.   [k]**24.4** *its . . . to nothing*: One possible meaning for the difficult Hebrew text.

24.18-20 *sky . . . earth . . . sin:* Ancient people believed the sky was like a solid bowl set over the flat earth, and that high mountains held up the sky like columns (Job 9.5-10). This bowl or dome held back the flood of water above. Rain and snow were said to come through the dome when God opened windows or doors in the sky (Gen 7.11, 12; Ps 78.23). God had the power to shake the foundations of the earth, probably meaning cause an earthquake. Natural disasters like floods and earthquakes were thought to be brought on by human sin.

¹²Cities are destroyed;
  their gates are torn down.
¹³Nations will be stripped bare,
  like olive trees or vineyards
  after the harvest season.

Praise the God of Justice

¹⁴People in the west shout;
  they joyfully praise
  the majesty of the LORD.
¹⁵And so, everyone in the east
  and those on the islands
  should praise the LORD,
  the God of Israel.
¹⁶From all over the world
  songs of praise are heard
  for the God of justice.[l]
But I feel awful,
  terribly miserable.
Can anyone be trusted?
  So many are treacherous!

There's No Escape

¹⁷Terror, traps, and pits
  are waiting for everyone.
¹⁸If you are terrified and run,
  you will fall into a pit;
if you crawl out of the pit,
  you will get caught in a trap.

The sky has split apart
  like a window thrown open.
The foundations of the earth
  have been shaken;
¹⁹the earth is shattered,
  ripped to pieces.
²⁰It staggers and shakes
  like a drunkard
  or a hut in a windstorm.

It is burdened down with sin;
  the earth will fall,
  never again to get up.

²¹On that day the LORD
  will punish the powers
in the heavens[m]
  and the kings of the earth.
²²He will put them in a pit
  and keep them prisoner.
Then later on,
  he will punish them.
²³Both the moon and sun will
  be embarrassed and ashamed.
The LORD All-Powerful will rule
  on Mount Zion in Jerusalem,
where he will show its rulers
  his wonderful glory.

A Prayer of Thanks to God

25 You, LORD, are my God!
  I will praise you
for doing the wonderful things
  you had planned and promised
  since ancient times.
²You have destroyed the fortress
  of our enemies,
  leaving their city in ruins.
Nothing in that foreign city
  will ever be rebuilt.
³Now strong and cruel nations
  will fear and honor you.

⁴You have been a place of safety
  for the poor and needy
  in times of trouble.
Brutal enemies pounded us
  like a heavy rain
or the heat of the sun at noon,
  but you were our shelter.
⁵Those wild foreigners struck

[l]**24.16** *God of justice:* Or "people who do right."   [m]**24.21** *the powers in the heavens:* In ancient times the stars were thought of as powerful spiritual beings, and sometimes they stood for pagan gods.

like scorching desert heat.
But you were like a cloud,
    protecting us from the sun.
You kept our enemies from singing
    songs of victory.

The LORD Has Saved Us

[6]On this mountain
    the LORD All-Powerful
will prepare for all nations
    a feast of the finest foods.
Choice wines and the best meats
    will be served.
[7]Here the LORD will strip away
    the burial clothes
        that cover the nations.
[8]The LORD All-Powerful
will destroy the power of death
    and wipe away all tears.
No longer will his people
be insulted everywhere.
    The LORD has spoken!

[9]At that time, people will say,
    "The LORD has saved us!
        Let's celebrate.
We waited and hoped—
    now our God is here."
[10]The powerful arm of the LORD
    will protect this mountain.

The Moabites will be put down
    and trampled on like straw
        in a pit of manure.
[11]They will struggle to get out,
    but God will humiliate them
        no matter how hard they try.[n]
[12]The walls of their fortresses
    will be knocked down
        and scattered in the dirt.

A Song of Victory

26 The time is coming when the peo-
    ple of Judah will sing this song:

"Our city[o] is protected.
The LORD is our fortress,
    and he gives us victory.
[2]Open the city gates
for a law-abiding nation
    that is faithful to God.
[3]The LORD gives perfect peace
    to those whose faith is firm.
[4]So always trust the LORD
because he is forever
    our mighty rock.[p]
[5]God has put down our enemies
in their mountain city[q]
    and rubbed it in the dirt.
[6]Now the poor and abused
    trample all over that city."

The LORD Can Be Trusted

[7]Our LORD, you always do right,
    and you make the path smooth
        for those who obey you.
[8]You are the one we trust
    to bring about justice;
above all else we want
    your name to be honored.
[9]Throughout the night,
    my heart searches for you,
because your decisions
show everyone on this earth
    how to live right.

[10]Even when the wicked
    are treated with mercy
        in this land of justice,

[n]25.11 no matter . . . try: One possible meaning for the difficult Hebrew text.   [o]26.1 city: Probably Jerusalem.   [p]26.4 mighty rock: See the note at 17.10.   [q]26.5 our enemies . . . city: One possible meaning for the difficult Hebrew text.

25.6 *this mountain . . . wines:* Mount Zion is the place where Israel's LORD will give a royal banquet for the nations. Zion, which represents both the people of God and the place where God will live among his people, is the source of the LORD's blessings (Ps 22.24-28; Ezek 47.1,2,12; Rev 22.1,2). Certain New Testament texts also describe life in God's kingdom as a banquet (Matt 3.2; 22.1-4; Luke 14.15-24; 22.14-17; 1 John 2.17; Rev 19.6-10).

25.7 *strip away the burial clothes:* The "burial clothes" may refer to clothes worn by those who are in mourning, or to the strips of linen cloth used to wrap a dead body. If the people are in burial clothes, it is because Israel has been defeated by other nations (25.8).

Eternal Life

26.1,2 *Our city . . . law-abiding nation:* This means Jerusalem, when the people have returned to the LORD and are obeying the laws of the LORD.

26.3 *perfect peace:* The kind of inner peace that comes from confidence in God's promise.

Peace

26.7 *do right . . . path smooth:* The path of right living is laid out by the LORD, who determines what is right and wrong. Those who obey the LORD (live right and do justice) will walk on the LORD's smooth path.

26.15-18 *more land . . . punished our people . . . no descendants:* God promised to give Abraham's descendants, the people of Israel, their own land (Gen 15.18-21; 17.1-8). The promise of regaining their land provided great hope to the people of Israel and Judah who had been forced to leave.

Land

26.19; 27.1 *rise to life . . . Leviathan:* The phrase "rise to life" has been taken by some to refer to the rebirth of the Israelite nation from the dark period of the exile (Ezek 37.1-14). Others think it describes the promise of rising from death to new life (resurrection), and suggest that this part of Isaiah's message must be from a later time in Israel's history. Leviathan (27.1) is the sea monster of chaos God conquered at the time of creation. In the Bible, it often symbolizes evil.

they do wrong and are blind
    to your glory, our LORD.
¹¹Your hand is raised and ready
    to punish them,
but they don't see it.
    Put them to shame!
Show how much you care for us
and throw them into the fire
    intended for your enemies.

¹²You will give us peace, LORD,
    because everything we have done
        was by your power.
¹³Others have ruled over us
    besides you, our LORD God,
        but we obey only you.
¹⁴Those enemies are now dead
    and can never live again.
You have punished them—
    they are destroyed,
        completely forgotten.
¹⁵Our nation has grown
    because of you, our LORD.
We have more land than before,
    and you are honored.

The LORD Gives Life to the Dead

¹⁶When you punished our people,
    they turned and prayed
        to you, our LORD.^r
¹⁷Because of what you did to us,
    we suffered like a woman
        about to give birth.
¹⁸But instead of having a child,
    our terrible pain
        produced only wind.
We have won no victories,
    and we have no descendants
        to take over the earth.

¹⁹Your people will rise to life!
    Tell them to leave their graves
        and celebrate with shouts.
You refresh the earth
    like morning dew;
        you give life to the dead.

²⁰Go inside and lock the doors,
    my people.
Hide there for a little while,
    until the LORD
        is no longer angry.

The Earth and the Sea Will Be Punished

²¹The LORD will come out
    to punish everyone on earth
        for their sins.
And when he does,
    those who did violent crimes
        will be known and punished.

27 On that day, Leviathan,^s
    the sea monster,
will squirm and try to escape,
    but the LORD will kill him
        with a cruel, sharp sword.

Protection and Forgiveness

The LORD said:
²At that time you must sing
    about a fruitful^t vineyard.
³I, the LORD, will protect it
    and always keep it watered.
I will guard it day and night
    to keep it from harm.
⁴I am no longer angry.
    But if it produces thorns,

^r**26.16** *LORD:* One possible meaning for the difficult Hebrew text of verse 16.   ^s**27.1** *Leviathan:* God's victory over this monster sometimes stands for God's power over all creation and sometimes for his defeat of his enemies, especially Egypt.   ^t**27.2** *fruitful:* Some Hebrew manuscripts have "lovely."

I will go to war against it
and burn it to the ground.
⁵Yet if the vineyard depends
on me for protection,
it will become my friend
and be at peace with me.

⁶Someday Israel will take root
like a vine.
It will blossom and bear fruit
that covers the earth.

⁷I, the LORD, didn't punish and kill
the people of Israel
as fiercely as I punished
and killed their enemies.
⁸I carefully measured out
Israel's punishmentᵘ
and sent the scorching heat
to chase them far away.

⁹There's only one way
that Israel's sin and guilt
can be completely forgiven:
They must crush the stones
of every pagan altar
and place of worship.

The LORD Will Bring His People Together

¹⁰Fortress cities are left
like a desert
where no one lives.
Cattle walk through the ruins,
stripping the trees bare.
¹¹When broken branches
fall to the ground,
women pick them up
to feed the fire.

But these people are so stupid
that the God who created them
will show them no mercy.

¹²The time is coming when the LORD will shake the land between the Euphrates River and the border of Egypt, and one by one he will bring all of his people together. ¹³A loud trumpet will be heard. Then the people of Israel who were dragged away to Assyria and Egypt will return to worship the LORD on his holy mountain in Jerusalem.

Samaria Will Be Punished

28 The city of Samaria
above a fertile valley
is in for trouble!
Its leaders are drunkards,
who stuff themselves
with food and wine.
But they will be like flowers
that dry up and wilt.
²Only the Lord is strong
and powerful!
His mighty hand
will strike them down
with the force of a hailstorm
or a mighty whirlwind
or an overwhelming flood.

³Every drunkard in Ephraimᵛ
takes pride in Samaria,
but it will be crushed.
⁴Samaria above a fertile valley
will quickly lose its glory.
It will be gobbled up
like the first ripe fig
at harvest season.

28.1-3 *Samaria:* The first message of judgment is against Samaria, the capital of the northern kingdom of Israel.

ᵘ27.8 *I . . . punishment:* One possible meaning for the difficult Hebrew text.   ᵛ28.3 *Ephraim:* The northern kingdom of Israel; Samaria was its capital.

28.7-9 *Priests and prophets... drunken leaders:* Priests and prophets were to be spiritual leaders, but Isaiah says the priests and leaders of Jerusalem are foolish and drunken, just like the leaders of Samaria.

28.11 *strange sounds and foreign languages:* This probably refers to the language of the Assyrian invaders. Because Judah's leaders treated Isaiah's message from the LORD as sound with no meaning, they will hear the language of Assyrian invaders, but not understand it (28.13).

28.15 *an agreement with ... world of the dead:* This may refer to a treaty (agreement) made with Egypt (30.1-5). Egypt's religion had a cult of the dead. This interest in the world of the dead would have been known in Judah.

28.16,17 *cornerstone:* The new people of Jerusalem will look to the LORD as their "cornerstone," their "mighty rock."

⁵When this time comes,
  the LORD All-Powerful
will be a glorious crown
  for his people who survive.
⁶He will see that justice rules
  and that his people are able
  to defend their cities.

Corrupt Leaders Will Be Punished

⁷Priests and prophets stumble
  because they are drunk.
Their minds are too confused
  to receive God's messages
  or give honest decisions.
⁸Their tables are covered,
  completely covered,
    with their stinking vomit.

⁹You drunken leaders
  are like babies!
How can you possibly understand
  or teach the LORD's message?
¹⁰You don't even listen—
  all you hear is senseless sound
  after senseless sound.ᵂ

¹¹So, the Lord will speak
  to his people
in strange sounds
  and foreign languages.ˣ
¹²He promised you
  perfect peace and rest,
  but you refused to listen.
¹³Now his message to you
  will be senseless sound
  after senseless sound.ʸ
Then you will fall backwards,
  injured and trapped.

False Security Is Fatal

¹⁴You rulers of Jerusalem
  do nothing but sneer;
now you must listen
  to what the LORD says.
¹⁵ Do you think you have
  an agreement with death
  and the world of the dead?
Why do you trust in your lies
  to keep you safe from danger
  and the mighty flood?

¹⁶And so the LORD says,
"I'm laying a firm foundation
  for the city of Zion.
It's a valuable cornerstone
  proven to be trustworthy;
no one who trusts it
  will ever be disappointed.
¹⁷Justice and fairness
  will be the measuring lines
  that help me build."

Hailstones and floods
  will destroy and wash away
  your shelter of lies.
¹⁸Your agreement with death
  and the world of the dead
  will be broken.
Then angry, roaring waves
  will sweep over you.
¹⁹Morning, noon, and night
  an overwhelming flood
  will wash you away.
The terrible things that happen
  will teach you this lesson:
²⁰Your bed is too short,
  your blanket too skimpy.ᶻ

ᵂ**28.10** *sound:* One possible meaning for the difficult Hebrew text of verses 9,10.   ˣ**28.11** *in . . . foreign languages:* This probably refers to the language of the Assyrians.   ʸ**28.13** *Now . . . sound:* One possible meaning for the difficult Hebrew text.   ᶻ**28.20** *Your bed . . . skimpy:* Isaiah quotes a popular saying to teach that the treaty made with Egypt (verse 18) cannot give the nation security from its enemies.

²¹The LORD will fiercely attack
    as he did at Mount Perazim[a]
    and in Gibeon Valley.[b]
But this time the LORD
    will do something surprising,
    not what you expect.
²²So you had better stop sneering
    or you will be in worse shape
    than ever before.
I heard the LORD All-Powerful
    threaten the whole country
    with destruction.

All Wisdom Comes from the LORD

²³Pay close attention
    to what I am saying.
²⁴Farmers don't just plow
    and break up the ground.
²⁵When a field is ready,
    they scatter the seeds
    of dill and cumin;
    they plant the seeds
    of wheat and barley
    in the proper places
    and sow other grains
    around the edges.
²⁶They learn this from their God.

²⁷After dill and cumin
    have been harvested,
    the stalks are pounded,
    not run over with a wagon.
²⁸Wheat and barley are pounded,
    but not beaten to pulp;
    they are run over with a wagon,
    but not ground to dust.
²⁹This wonderful knowledge comes

from the LORD All-Powerful,
    who has such great wisdom.

Jerusalem Will Suffer

The LORD said:

29 Jerusalem, city of David,
    the place of my altar,[c]
    you are in for trouble!
Celebrate your festivals
    year after year.
²I will still make you suffer,
    and your people will cry
    when I make an altar of you.[d]
³I will surround you and prepare
    to attack from all sides.[e]
⁴From deep in the earth,
    you will call out for help
    with only a faint whisper.

⁵Then your cruel enemies
    will suddenly be swept away
    like dust in a windstorm.
⁶I, the LORD All-Powerful,
    will come to your rescue
    with a thundering earthquake
    and a fiery whirlwind.

⁷Every brutal nation
    that attacks Jerusalem
    and makes it suffer
    will disappear like a dream
    when night is over.
⁸Those nations that attack
    Mount Zion
will suffer from hunger
    and thirst.
They will dream of food and drink

---

[a]**28.21** *Mount Perazim*: This may refer to David's defeat of the Philistines at Baal Perazim (2 Samuel 5.17-21).   [b]**28.21** *Gibeon Valley*: This refers to Joshua's victory at Gibeon (Joshua 10.1-11).   [c]**29.1** *the place of my altar*: One possible meaning for "ariel, ariel" of the Hebrew text. In Hebrew "ariel" can mean "God's hero" or "God's lion" or "God's altar."   [d]**29.2** *when . . . you*: One possible meaning for the difficult Hebrew text.   [e]**29.3** *from all sides*: One possible meaning for the difficult Hebrew text. One ancient translation has "like David."

28.21 *attack . . . Mount Perazim . . . Gibeon Valley . . . surprising*: The LORD helped Israel at these places in the past: David defeated the Philistines at Baal Perazim (2 Sam 5.17-21; 1 Chr 14.11), and Joshua defeated the Amorites at Gibeon Valley (Josh 10.1-11). The "something surprising" is that the LORD will attack Jerusalem (see 29.1-3).

28.25-28 *dill and cumin . . . wheat and barley*: These crops were grown in various types of soil at different times. After harvest, the spices dill and cumin were pounded to remove the seeds. The heavier wheat and barley stalks had to be placed on a stone threshing floor and run over by something heavy in order to remove the husks from the grain. In the same way, Judah will face the LORD's "harvest," meaning they will be attacked (29.3) but not completely destroyed.

Zion

29.1 *altar*: This may refer to the altar of sacrifice at the temple in Jerusalem, or it may mean that Jerusalem itself will be like a burning altar.

29.1 *Celebrate your festivals*: For more about Israel's religious festivals, see the article People of the Law: The Religion of Israel on pg 1794.

29.4-8 *deep in the earth*: "Deep in the earth" is the place of the dead called Sheol.

29.13 *praise . . . worship me:* Judah's priests and people appeared to be following the laws and rituals of worship, but their devotion was false. Their show of faith did not come from the heart, and so they were not living right.

■ 29.14 *wisdom:* In Israel, true wisdom came from the LORD. The truly wise person was one who obeyed the LORD's teachings (Prov 2.6,7; 1.7). Judah's priests and leaders have not been obeying the LORD, so their wisdom is called into question.

ℭℜ   Wisdom

29.17 *forest of Lebanon:* This may represent how the whole creation will be fertile once again when the LORD brings a new future. Or this may represent God's people. They will be cut down like Assyria (see 10.15-19,33,34), but one day they will again be a thick field.

29.21 *tells lies in court:* Some people in Judah were using their power or wealth to bribe court officials to keep certain people, especially the poor, from getting a fair hearing.

29.22 *rescued Abraham . . . Jacob's descendants:* Abraham's "rescue" probably refers to the LORD's choosing him to be the father of God's chosen people (Gen 12.1-3; 41.8,9; Isa 51.2). Jacob was Abraham's grandson, and the tribes of Israel were named after Jacob's sons.

but wake up weary and hungry
and thirsty as ever.

Prophets Who Fool Themselves

⁹Be shocked and stunned,
   you prophets!
Refuse to see.
Get drunk and stagger,
   but not from wine.
¹⁰The LORD has made you drowsy;
he put you into a deep sleep
   and covered your head.

¹¹Now his message is like a sealed letter to you. Some of you say, "We can't read it, because it's sealed." ¹²Others say, "We can't read it, because we don't know how to read." ¹³The Lord has said:

"These people praise me
   with their words,
but they never really
   think about me.
They worship me by repeating
   rules made up by humans.
¹⁴ So once again I will do things
   that shock and amaze them,
and I will destroy the wisdom
of those who claim to know
   and understand."

¹⁵You are in for trouble,
if you try to hide your plans
   from the LORD!
Or if you think what you do
   in the dark can't be seen.
¹⁶You have it all backwards.
A clay dish doesn't say
   to the potter,
"You didn't make me.
   You don't even know how."

Hope for the Future

¹⁷Soon the forest of Lebanon
will become a field with crops,
   thick as a forest.ᶠ
¹⁸The deaf will be able to hear
   whatever is read to them;
the blind will be freed
   from a life of darkness.
¹⁹The poor and the needy
   will celebrate and shout
because of the LORD,
   the holy God of Israel.

²⁰All who are cruel and arrogant
   will be gone forever.
Those who live by crime
   will disappear,
²¹together with everyone
   who tells lies in court
and keeps innocent people
   from getting a fair trial.

²²The LORD who rescued Abraham
   has this to say
   about Jacob's descendants:
"They will no longer
   be ashamed and disgraced.
²³When they see how great
   I have made their nation,
they will praise and honor me,
   the holy God of Israel.
²⁴Everyone who is confused
   will understand,
and all who have complained
   will obey my teaching."

Don't Expect Help from Egypt

30 This is the LORD's message for his rebellious people:

"You follow your own plans
   instead of mine;

ᶠ**29.17** *with . . . forest:* Or "and Mount Carmel will be covered with forests."

you make treaties
without asking me,
    and you keep on sinning.
2You trust Egypt for protection.
    So you refuse my advice
and send messengers to Egypt
    to beg their king for help.

3"You will be disappointed,
completely disgraced
    for trusting Egypt.
4The king's power reaches
from the city of Zoan
    as far south as Hanes.**g**
5But Egypt can't protect you,
    and to trust that nation
        is useless and foolish."

6This is a message
about the animals
    of the Southern Desert:
"You people carry treasures
    on donkeys and camels.
You travel to a feeble nation
through a troublesome desert
    filled with lions
    and flying fiery dragons.
7Egypt can't help you!
That's why I call that nation
    a helpless monster."**h**

Israel Refuses To Listen

8The LORD told me to write down his
message for his people, so that it would be
there forever. **9**They have turned against
the LORD and can't be trusted. They have
refused his teaching **10**and have said to his
messengers and prophets:
    Don't tell us what God has shown
    you and don't preach the truth. Just
    say what we want to hear, even if it's
false. **11**Stop telling us what God has
said! We don't want to hear any more
about the holy One of Israel.

12Now this is the answer
    of the holy One of Israel:
"You rejected my message,
and you trust in violence
    and lies.
13This sin is like a crack
    that makes a high wall
quickly crumble **14**and shatter
    like a crushed bowl.
There's not a piece left
big enough to carry hot coals
    or to dip out water."

Trust the LORD

15The holy LORD God of Israel
    had told all of you,
"I will keep you safe
if you turn back to me
    and calm down.
I will make you strong
    if you quietly trust me."

Then you stubbornly **16**said,
"No! We will safely escape
    on speedy horses."

But those who chase you
    will be even faster.
17As few as five of them,
or even one, will be enough
    to chase a thousand of you.
Finally, all that will be left
    will be a few survivors
as lonely as a flag pole
    on a barren hill.

g30.4 *Zoan . . . Hanes:* Or "Your messengers have reached the city of Zoan and gone as far as Hanes."
Zoan was in northeast Egypt; Hanes was to the south.   **h**30.7 *a helpless monster:* One possible meaning for the difficult Hebrew text.

● 30.2 *trust Egypt:* This message
probably was directed toward the leaders of Judah in 703–701 B.C. During
that time, Sennacherib of Assyria was
threatening to capture Jerusalem. By
asking Egypt for help, Isaiah said that
Judah's leaders showed a lack of trust
in the LORD.

● 30.6,7 *flying fiery dragons . . .
helpless monster:* The fiery dragon may
be a reference to poisonous snakes or
to some mythical creature that was
thought to live in the frightening desert
(Deut 8.15). The "helpless monster"
may refer to "Rahab," the sea monster.
God was said to have defeated Rahab at
the time of creation (Job 9.13; 26.12,13;
Ps 89.9,10; Isa 51.9).

● 30.8 *his people:* Refers to people
of Judah who have rebelled against
the LORD (30.1) by trusting in foreign
powers.

---

*The holy LORD God of Israel had told all of you, "I will keep you
safe if you turn back to me and calm down. I will make you
strong if you quietly trust me."* ISA 30.15

30.19 *Jerusalem, you don't need to cry:* This message of promise regarding Jerusalem's future (30.18-26) interrupts Isaiah's messages of judgment (compare 29.17-24).

30.25-27 *slaughtered . . . light of seven days . . . LORD is coming . . . fire:* The reference to people slaughtered may refer to Assyria's defeat. Then Judah's people will have a future filled with great brightness and joy. The LORD's coming judgment against Assyria (30.31) is described as a punishment by fire, smoke, and flood.

30.28 *bridle:* Ropes or leather straps are attached to a piece of metal or wood that fits inside the mouth of a horse or donkey. By pulling on the ropes, a rider or driver makes the animal turn or stop. In the same way the LORD will bridle the Assyrians and steer them to destruction.

Passover and the Festival of Thin Bread

30.33 *place . . . for burning:* In Hebrew, the place is called Topheth, where children were burned as sacrifices to the god Molech (2 Kgs 23.10; Jer 7.31; 19.4-7). The Hebrew word for "king" is similar to the name Molech.

The LORD Will Show Mercy

¹⁸The LORD God is waiting
  to show how kind he is
    and to have pity on you.
  The LORD always does right;
    he blesses those who trust him.

¹⁹People of Jerusalem, you don't need to cry anymore. The Lord is kind, and as soon as he hears your cries for help, he will come. ²⁰The Lord has given you trouble and sorrow as your food and drink. But now you will again see the Lord, your teacher, and he will guide you. ²¹Whether you turn to the right or to the left, you will hear a voice saying, "This is the road! Now follow it." ²²Then you will treat your idols of silver and gold like garbage; you will throw them away like filthy rags.

²³The Lord will send rain to water the seeds you have planted—your fields will produce more crops than you need, and your cattle will graze in open pastures. ²⁴Even the oxen and donkeys that plow your fields will be fed the finest grain.[i]

²⁵On that day people will be slaughtered and towers destroyed, but streams of water will flow from high hills and towering mountains. ²⁶Then the LORD will bandage his people's injuries and heal the wounds he has caused. The moon will shine as bright as the sun, and the sun will shine seven times brighter than usual. It will be like the light of seven days all at once.

Assyria Will Be Punished

²⁷The LORD is coming
  from far away

with his fiery anger
  and thick clouds of smoke.[j]
His angry words flame up
  like a destructive fire;
²⁸he breathes out a flood
  that comes up to the neck.
He sifts the nations
  and destroys them.
Then he puts a bridle
  in every foreigner's mouth
  and leads them to doom.

²⁹The LORD's people will sing as they do when they celebrate a religious festival[k] at night. The LORD is Israel's mighty rock,[l] and his people will be as happy as they are when they follow the sound of flutes to the mountain where he is worshiped.

³⁰The LORD will get furious. His fearsome voice will be heard, his arm will be seen ready to strike, and his anger will be like a destructive fire, followed by thunderstorms and hailstones. ³¹When the Assyrians hear the LORD's voice and see him striking with his iron rod, they will be terrified. ³²He will attack them in battle, and each time he strikes them, it will be to the music of tambourines and harps.

³³Long ago the LORD got a place ready for burning the body of the dead king.[m] The place for the fire is deep and wide, the wood is piled high, and the LORD will start the fire by breathing out flaming sulfur.

Don't Trust the Power of Egypt

31 You are in for trouble
  if you go to Egypt for help,
  or if you depend on
    an army of chariots

---

[i]**30.24** *the finest grain:* The Hebrew text refers to grain with the husks removed.   [j]**30.27** *with . . . smoke:* One possible meaning for the difficult Hebrew text.   [k]**30.29** *a religious festival:* Probably Passover.   [l]**30.29** *mighty rock:* See the note at 17.10.   [m]**30.33** *burning . . . king:* Or "sacrificing the king" or "sacrificing to Molech." Human sacrifices were sometimes offered to Molech, a god whose name sounds like the Hebrew word for "king" (see 2 Kings 23.10; Jeremiah 32.35).

or a powerful cavalry.
Instead you should depend on
and trust the holy LORD God
of Israel.
²The LORD isn't stupid!
He does what he promises,
and he can bring doom.
If you are cruel yourself,
or help those who are evil,
you will be destroyed.

³The Egyptians are mere humans.
They aren't God.
Their horses are made of flesh;
they can't live forever.
When the LORD shows his power,
he will destroy the Egyptians
and all who depend on them.
Together they will fall.

⁴The LORD All-Powerful
said to me,
"I will roar and attack
like a fearless lion
not frightened by the shouts
of shepherds trying to protect
their sheep.
That's how I will come down
and fight on Mount Zion.
⁵I, the LORD All-Powerful,
will protect Jerusalem
like a mother bird circling
over her nest."

Come Back to the LORD

⁶People of Israel, come back!
You have completely turned
from the LORD.
⁷The time is coming
when you will throw away

your idols of silver and gold,
made by your sinful hands.

⁸The Assyrians will be killed,
but not by the swords
of humans.
Their young men will try
to escape,
but they will be captured
and forced into slavery.
⁹Their fortress[n] will fall
when terror strikes;
their army officers
will be frightened
and run from the battle.
This is what the LORD has said,
the LORD whose fiery furnace
is built on Mount Zion.

Justice Will Rule

32 A king and his leaders
will rule with justice.
²They will be a place of safety
from stormy winds,
a stream in the desert,
and a rock that gives shade
from the heat of the sun.
³Then everyone who has eyes
will open them and see,
and those who have ears
will pay attention.
⁴All who are impatient
will take time to think;
everyone who stutters
will talk clearly.

⁵Fools will no longer
be highly respected,
and crooks won't be given
positions of honor.

[n]**31.9** *fortress:* The Hebrew text has "rock," which may refer to the Assyrian god or king, or to their army.

● 31.8,9 *Assyrians . . . will fall:* The Assyrian army under Sennacherib suffered great losses in 701 B.C. (See 37.36-38.) In 612 B.C. the Assyrians were defeated, and their capital city of Nineveh was destroyed by the combined armies of the Medes and Babylonians.

32.9-11 *you women . . . put on sackcloth:* "You women" refers to the women of Jerusalem. This message of judgment against the women of Jerusalem (32.9-14) breaks up the message of promise begun in 32.1 and continued in 32.15.

⁶Fools talk foolishness.
They always make plans
  to do sinful things,
  to lie about the LORD,
  to let the hungry starve,
and to keep water from those
  who are thirsty.
⁷Cruel people tell lies—
they do evil things,
  and make cruel plans
to destroy the poor and needy,
even when they beg
  for justice.
⁸But helpful people
can always be trusted
  to make helpful plans.

Punishment for the Women of Jerusalem

⁹Listen to what I say,
you women who are carefree
  and careless!
¹⁰You may not have worries now,
  but in about a year,
the grape harvest will fail,
  and you will tremble.

¹¹Shake and shudder,
  you women without a care!
Strip off your clothes—
  put on sackcloth.
¹²Slap your breasts in sorrow
  because of what happened
to the fruitful fields
  and vineyards,
¹³and to the happy homes
  in Jerusalem.
The land of my people
  is covered with thorns.

¹⁴The palace will be deserted,
  the crowded city empty.
Fortresses and towers
will forever become
playgrounds for wild donkeys
  and pastures for sheep.

God's Spirit Makes the Difference

¹⁵When the Spirit is given to us
  from heaven,
deserts will become orchards
  thick as fertile forests.
¹⁶Honesty and justice
  will prosper there,
¹⁷and justice will produce
  lasting peace and security.

¹⁸You, the LORD's people,
will live in peace,
  calm and secure,
¹⁹even if hailstones flatten
  forests and cities.
²⁰You will have God's blessing,
as you plant your crops
  beside streams,
while your donkeys and cattle
  roam freely about.

Jerusalem Will Be Safe

33 You defeated my people.
  Now you're in for trouble!
You've never been destroyed,
  but you will be destroyed;
you've never been betrayed,
  but you will be betrayed.
When you have finished
  destroying and betraying,
you will be destroyed
  and betrayed in return.

²Please, LORD, be kind to us!
  We depend on you.
Make us strong each morning,
and come to save us
  when we are in trouble.

³Nations scatter when you roar
    and show your greatness.°
⁴We attack our enemies
    like swarms of locusts;ᴾ
we take everything
    that belongs to them.ᵠ

⁵You, Lord, are above all others,
    and you live in the heavens.
You have brought justice
    and fairness to Jerusalem;
⁶you are the foundation
    on which we stand today.
You always save us and give
    true wisdom and knowledge.
Nothing means more to usʳ
    than obeying you.

The Lord Will Do Something

⁷Listen! Our bravest soldiers
are running through the streets,
    screaming for help.ˢ
Our messengers hoped for peace,
    but came home crying.
⁸No one travels anymore;
    every road is empty.
Treaties are broken,
and no respect is shown
    to any who keep promises.ᵗ
⁹Fields are dry and barren;
Mount Lebanon wilts
    with shame.
Sharon Valley is a desert;
the forests of Bashan and Carmel
    have lost their leaves.

¹⁰But the Lord says,
    "Now I will do something

and be greatly praised.
¹¹Your deeds are straw
    that will be set on fire
        by your very own breath.
¹²You will be burned to ashes
    like thorns in a fire.
¹³Everyone, both far and near,
    come look at what I have done.
        See my mighty power!"

Punishment and Rewards

¹⁴Those terrible sinners
    on Mount Zion tremble
        as they ask in fear,
"How can we possibly live
where a raging fire
    never stops burning?"

¹⁵But there will be rewards
    for those who live right
        and tell the truth,
for those who refuse
        to take money by force
        or accept bribes,
for all who hate murder
    and violent crimes.
¹⁶They will live in a fortress
    high on a rocky cliff,
where they will have food
    and plenty of water.

The Lord Is Our King

¹⁷With your own eyes
    you will see the glorious King;
        you will see his kingdom
            reaching far and wide.

■   **33.6** *true wisdom and knowledge:*
For the people of Israel, true wisdom is
based on understanding and obeying
God's law.

●   **33.7,8** *messengers . . . Treaties are
broken:* This sorrowful prayer (lament)
follows the prayer for help in 33.2-6. It
describes the terrible conditions caused
by the enemy invasion (33.1). The identity of the messengers who hoped for
peace (33.7) is not certain. It could refer
to those who met the Assyrian commander (Isa 36.2, 3,21,22; 2 Kgs 18.13-37).
The broken treaties could be military
treaties, or they could be business agreements that had to be canceled because
of war.

●   **33.9** *Lebanon . . . Carmel:* These
areas of Canaan were known for their
beauty and rich pastures. Mount Carmel
was located near the Mediterranean
Sea. It was just south of Phoenicia and
just north of the fertile Sharon Valley
that ran along the Mediterranean coast
north of Philistia and west of Samaria.
(See Map 3 on pg 1881.)

●   **33.17** *glorious King:* This may be
the Lord himself, who lives with and
rules the people on Zion (33.22). Or it
may mean the king that the Lord will
choose to rule in Zion.

°**33.3** *greatness:* One possible meaning for the difficult Hebrew text of verse 3.   ᴾ**33.4** *locusts:* Insects
like grasshoppers that travel in swarms and cause great damage to crops.   ᵠ**33.4** *them:* One possible
meaning for the difficult Hebrew text of verse 4.   ʳ**33.6** *Nothing . . . us:* One possible meaning for
the difficult Hebrew text.   ˢ**33.7** *Listen . . . help:* Or "The Lord heard our shouts and will come to
help us."   ᵗ**33.8** *to any . . . promises:* The Dead Sea Scrolls; the Standard Hebrew Text "to those in the
cities."

33.18,19 *heavy taxes . . . foreign language:* These heavy taxes may actually be the huge amounts of silver and gold that Judah's King Hezekiah paid to Assyria's Sennacherib in 701 B.C. to keep him from attacking Jerusalem (2 Kgs 18.13-16). Alternatively, the payment of taxes may symbolize any enemy that terrified the people of Jerusalem and made them suffer (29.7,8). When the "King" rules Zion, this "taxation" will end, and those who speak a strange language will no longer rule God's people.

33.21,23 *deep rivers . . . ships . . . your nation is a ship:* Jerusalem did not have any deep rivers running by or through it. The image in 33.21 promises that Jerusalem will have plenty of "water" (spiritual blessings; see Ezek 47.1-12), and that it will be protected from the danger of attack by enemy ships.

34.5 *Edom . . . doomed:* The Edomites were descendants of Esau, Jacob's brother (Gen 36.1,9-14,40-43). The nation of Edom is usually described in the Bible as an enemy of Israel (Num 24.18; 1 Sam 14.47,48; 2 Sam 8.13,14). **(See Map 6 on pg 1884.)**

34.6 *blood . . . fat:* The LORD's blood-covered sword is used to make a holy sacrifice of the Edomites in Bozrah. They are compared to the lambs and goats that were sacrificed by Israel's priests. The fat, which was considered the best part of the meat, was to be burned as an offering to the LORD (Lev 3.6-17).

18 Then you will ask yourself,
    "Where are those officials
who terrified us and forced us
    to pay such heavy taxes?"
19 You will never again have to see
    the proud people who spoke
a strange and foreign language
    you could not understand.

20 Look to Mount Zion
    where we celebrate
    our religious festivals.
You will see Jerusalem,
    secure as a tent with pegs
that cannot be pulled up
and fastened with ropes
    that can never be broken.
21 Our wonderful LORD
    will be with us!
There will be deep rivers
and wide streams
    safe from enemy ships.[u]

The LORD Is Our Judge

22 The LORD is our judge
    and our ruler;
the LORD is our king
    and will keep us safe.
23 But your nation[v] is a ship
    with its rigging loose,
its mast shaky,
    and its sail not spread.

Someday even you that are lame
will take everything you want
    from your enemies.
24 The LORD will forgive your sins,

and none of you will say,
    "I feel sick."

The Nations Will Be Judged

34 Everyone of every nation,
    the entire earth,
and all its creatures,
    come here and listen!
2 The LORD is terribly angry
    with the nations;
he has condemned them
    to be slaughtered.
3 Their dead bodies will be left
    to rot and stink;
their blood will flow
    down the mountains.
4 Each star[w] will disappear—
the sky will roll up
    like a scroll.[x]
Everything in the sky
    will dry up and wilt
like leaves on a vine
    or fruit on a tree.

Trouble for Edom

5 After the sword of the LORD
    has done what it wants
    to the skies above,[y]
it will come down on Edom,
    the nation that the LORD
    has doomed for destruction.

6 The sword of the LORD
    is covered with blood
    from lambs and goats,
together with fat
    from kidneys of rams.

[u]**33.21** *safe . . . ships:* This probably means that Jerusalem will have a lot of water, without the danger of attacks from enemy ships.   [v]**33.23** *your nation:* Possibly Judah or Assyria.   [w]**34.4** *star:* Stars were worshiped as gods.   [x]**34.4** *scroll:* A roll of paper or specially prepared leather used for writing on.   [y]**34.5** *has done . . . above:* The Standard Hebrew Text; the Dead Sea Scrolls "appears in the skies above."

This is because the LORD
 will slaughter many people
and make a sacrifice of them
 in the city of Bozrah
and everywhere else
 in Edom.
[7]Edom's leaders are wild oxen.
 They are powerful bulls,
 but they will die
 with the others.
 Their country will be soaked
 with their own blood,
 and its soil made fertile
 with their own fat.

[8]The LORD has chosen
 the year and the day,
 when he will take revenge
 and come to Zion's defense.
[9]Edom's streams will turn into tar
 and its soil into sulfur—
 then the whole country
 will go up in flames.
[10]It will burn night and day
 and never stop smoking.
 Edom will be a desert,
 generation after generation;
 no one will ever travel
 through that land.
[11]Owls, hawks, and wild animals[z]
 will make it their home.
 God will leave it in ruins,
 merely a pile of rocks.

The End of Edom

[12]Edom will be called
 "Kingdom of Nothing."
 Its rulers will also be nothing.
[13]Its palaces and fortresses
 will be covered with thorns;

only wolves and ostriches
 will make their home there.
[14]Wildcats and hyenas
 will hunt together,
 demons will scream to demons,
 and creatures of the night
 will live among the ruins.
[15]Owls will nest there
 to raise their young
 among its shadows,[a]
 while families of vultures
 circle around.

[16]In *The Book of the* LORD[b]
 you can search and find
 where it is written,
 "The LORD brought together
 all of his creatures
 by the power of his Spirit.
 Not one is missing."
[17]The LORD has decided
 where they each should live;
 they will be there forever,
 generation after generation.

God's Splendor Will Be Seen

35 Thirsty deserts will be glad;
 barren lands will celebrate
 and blossom with flowers.
[2]Deserts will bloom everywhere
 and sing joyful songs.
 They will be as majestic
 as Mount Lebanon,
 as glorious as Mount Carmel
 or Sharon Valley.
 Everyone will see
 the wonderful splendor
 of the LORD our God.

- 34.6 *Bozrah:* This main city of Edom was located about 25 miles south of the Dead Sea. Its name means "grape gathering" (Isa 63.1-13). **(See Map 4 on pg 1882.)**

- 34.16 *The Book of the* LORD: This book is unknown. It may refer to a scroll that included the judgment against Babylon (13.19-22). Or it may refer to a larger collection of prophetic books that include warning messages against Edom.

- 34.16,17 *creatures . . . should live:* Meaning the wild animals will inherit the land of Edom forever.

- 35.1 *barren lands will celebrate and blossom:* The land of God's people is pictured as blooming and rejoicing, because the LORD will bring his people back from exile to live in Zion (35.10). This image of a blooming wilderness is also found in parts of Isaiah 40–55, which dates to the time of exile in Babylon (41.18-20; 43.19,20; 51.30).

---

[z]**34.11** *Owls . . . animals:* One possible meaning for the difficult Hebrew text.   [a]**34.15** *Owls . . . shadows:* One possible meaning for the difficult Hebrew text.   [b]**34.16** *The Book of the* LORD: The book that Isaiah refers to is unknown.

35.5,6 *The blind . . . ears . . . tongue:* This may refer to the healing of physical disabilities, or to God's opening of people's eyes, ears, and hearts to spiritual understanding (29.18; 32.3; 42.16,18-20).

35.6,7 *Water . . . fountains:* Water was the most precious natural resource in the dry lands where God's people lived. The image of desert turning into wetland symbolizes abundance (41.17-19; Num 20.2-11).

35.8 *God's Sacred Highway:* See also 11.16 and 40.3-5, which tell of a path or road that the LORD will make for his people to return to Judah following their time in exile. Here, the road is not just a path, but a "holy," or sacred, way. Only the people the LORD has saved can take this highway, which leads to Zion (35.10).

Redeemer (Redemption)

36.1 *Hezekiah . . . 14 years . . . Sennacherib:* Ancient Assyrian records show that King Sennacherib of Assyria invaded Judah in 705 B.C. His army camped outside of Jerusalem in 701 B.C. This would mean Hezekiah became Judah's king in 715 B.C. However, other passages list the beginning of his reign as 729 B.C., or the third year of Hoshea's reign (see 2 Kgs 18.1).

36.1 *every walled city:* Many towns had walls built around them for protection. According to Assyrian records, there were 46 walled cities in Judah.

God Changes Everything

*[3] Here is a message for all
  who are weak, trembling,
    and worried:
[4] "Cheer up! Don't be afraid.
  Your God is coming
    to punish your enemies.
  God will take revenge on them
    and rescue you."

[5] The blind will see,
  and the ears of the deaf
    will be healed.
[6] Those who were lame
    will leap around like deer;
  tongues once silent
    will shout for joy.
  Water will rush
    through the desert.
[7] Scorching sand
    will turn into a lake,
  and thirsty ground
    will flow with fountains.
  Grass will grow in deserts,
  where packs of wild dogs
    once made their home.[c]

God's Sacred Highway

[8] A good road will be there,
  and it will be named
    "God's Sacred Highway."
  It will be for God's people;
  no one unfit to worship God
    will walk on that road.
  And no fools can travel
    on that highway.[d]
[9] No lions or other wild animals
  will come near that road;

only those the LORD has saved
    will travel there.

[10] The people the LORD has rescued
  will come back singing
    as they enter Zion.
  Happiness will be a crown
    everyone will always wear.
  They will celebrate and shout
  because all sorrows and worries
    will be gone far away.

The Assyrians Surround Jerusalem
(2 Kings 18.13-27; 2 Chronicles 32.1-19)

36 Hezekiah had been king of Judah for 14 years when King Sennacherib of Assyria invaded the country and captured every walled city [2] except Jerusalem. The Assyrian king ordered his army commander to leave the city of Lachish and to take a large army to Jerusalem.

The commander went there and stood on the road near the cloth makers' shops along the canal from the upper pool. [3] Three of the king's highest officials came out of Jerusalem to meet him. One of them was Hilkiah's son Eliakim, who was the prime minister. The other two were Shebna, assistant to the prime minister, and Joah son of Asaph, keeper of the government records.

[4] The Assyrian commander told them:
  I have a message for Hezekiah from the great king of Assyria. Ask Hezekiah why he feels so sure of himself. [5] Does he think he can plan and win a war with nothing but words? Who is going to help him, now that he has

[c]**35.7** *Grass . . . home:* One possible meaning for the difficult Hebrew text.   [d]**35.8** *And . . . highway:* Or "And not even a fool can miss that highway."

turned against the king of Assyria? **6**Is he depending on Egypt and its king? That's the same as leaning on a broken stick, and it will go right through his hand.

7Is Hezekiah now depending on the LORD, your God? Didn't Hezekiah tear down all except one of the LORD's altars and places of worship?**e** Didn't he tell the people of Jerusalem and Judah to worship at that one place?

8The king of Assyria wants to make a bet with you people! He will give you 2,000 horses, if you have enough troops to ride them. **9**How could you even defeat our lowest ranking officer, when you have to depend on Egypt for chariots and cavalry? **10**Don't forget that it was the LORD who sent me here with orders to destroy your nation!

11Eliakim, Shebna, and Joah said, "Sir, we don't want the people listening from the city wall to understand what you are saying. So please speak to us in Aramaic instead of Hebrew."

12The Assyrian army commander answered, "My king sent me to speak to everyone, not just to you leaders. These people will soon have to eat their own body waste and drink their own urine! And so will the three of you!"

13Then, in a voice loud enough for everyone to hear, he shouted out in Hebrew:

Listen to what the great king of Assyria says! **14**Don't be fooled by Hezekiah. He can't save you. **15**Don't trust him when he tells you that the LORD will protect you from the king of Assyria. **16**Stop listening to Hezekiah.

Pay attention to my king. Surrender to him. He will let you keep your own vineyards, fig trees, and cisterns **17**for a while. Then he will come and take you away to a country just like yours, where you can plant vineyards and raise your own grain.

18Hezekiah claims the LORD will save you. But don't be fooled by him. Were any other gods able to defend their land against the king of Assyria? **19**What happened to the gods of Hamath, Arpad, and Sepharvaim? Were the gods of Samaria able to protect their land against the Assyrian forces? **20**None of those gods kept their people safe from the king of Assyria. Do you think the LORD, your God, can do any better?

21-22 Eliakim, Shebna, and Joah had been warned by King Hezekiah not to answer the Assyrian commander. So they tore their clothes in sorrow and reported to Hezekiah everything the commander had said.

Hezekiah Asks Isaiah for Advice
(2 Kings 19.1-13)

37 As soon as Hezekiah heard the news, he tore off his clothes in sorrow and put on sackcloth. Then he went into the temple of the LORD. **2**He told Prime Minister Eliakim, Assistant Prime Minister Shebna, and the senior priests to dress in sackcloth and tell me:

3Isaiah, these are difficult and disgraceful times. Our nation is like a woman too weak to give birth, when it's time for her baby to be born. **4**Please pray for those of us who are left

36.11 *Aramaic . . . Hebrew:* Aramaic was spoken by government officials and merchants throughout the region at this time. Hebrew, however, was the language spoken in Judah. Most of the people in Judah did not understand Aramaic.

36.13-17 *shouted out in Hebrew . . . take you away:* The Assyrian commander ignored Hezekiah's officials (36.11) and yelled out in Hebrew, so all the people of Jerusalem could understand and be convinced to surrender. He promised that Sennacherib would let the people keep their land and water for a time before they were sent away to live in other lands held by the Assyrians. The Assyrian policy was to remove the peoples they defeated from their native lands and make them resettle in other places.

36.21,22—37.1 *tore their clothes in sorrow . . . put on sackcloth:* Tearing one's clothes and wearing sackcloth were ways people showed sadness or sorrow.

37.1 *temple:* This refers to the temple in Jerusalem, where Israel's priests offered sacrifices to the LORD.

e36.7 *worship*: Hezekiah actually had torn down the places where idols were worshiped, and he had told the people to worship the LORD at the one place of worship in Jerusalem. But the Assyrian leader was confused and thought these were also places where the LORD was supposed to be worshiped.

37.7-9 *die a violent death...
Tirhakah:* Sennacherib's sons stabbed him to death (37.38) in 682 B.C., nearly 20 years after Sennacherib's siege of Jerusalem. Tirhakah did not become the king of Upper (Ethiopia) and Lower Egypt until 689 B.C., but he may have taken part in fighting against Assyria around the time of Sennacherib's invasion of Judah.

37.16 *winged creatures:* These "cherubim" sat on top of the sacred chest in the most holy place in the temple.

37.19 *destroyed the idols:* The Assyrians destroyed the wood and metal idols worshiped by the peoples they defeated. Hezekiah asks the LORD to protect Jerusalem, to show that Israel's God is more powerful than the gods of the other nations.

37.24 *insult me, the Lord:* This refers to the message Sennacherib's commander shouted to the people outside the walls of Jerusalem (36.12-20).

alive. The king of Assyria sent his army commander to insult the living God. Perhaps the LORD heard what he said and will do something, if you will pray. **5**When these leaders came to me, **6**I told them that the LORD had this message for Hezekiah:

I am the LORD. Don't worry about the insulting things that have been said about me by these messengers from the king of Assyria. **7**I will upset him with rumors about what's happening in his own country. He will go back, and there I will make him die a violent death. **8**Meanwhile the commander of the Assyrian forces heard that his king had left the town of Lachish and was now attacking Libnah. So he went there.

9About this same time, the king of Assyria learned that King Tirhakah of Ethiopia[f] was on his way to attack him. Then the king of Assyria sent some messengers with this note for Hezekiah:

10Don't trust your God or be fooled by his promise to defend Jerusalem against me. **11**You have heard how we Assyrian kings have completely wiped out other nations. What makes you feel so safe? **12**The Assyrian kings before me destroyed the towns of Gozan, Haran, Rezeph, and everyone from Eden who lived in Telassar. What good did their gods do them? **13**The kings of Hamath, Arpad, Sepharvaim, Hena, and Ivvah have all disappeared.

Hezekiah Prays
(2 Kings 19.14-19)

14After Hezekiah had read the note from the king of Assyria, he took it to the temple and spread it out for the LORD to see. **15**Then he prayed:

16 LORD God All-Powerful of Israel, your throne is above the winged creatures.[g] You created the heavens and the earth, and you alone rule the kingdoms of this world. **17**Just look and see how Sennacherib has insulted you, the living God.

18It is true, our LORD, that Assyrian kings have turned nations into deserts. **19**They destroyed the idols of wood and stone that the people of those nations had made and worshiped. **20**But you are our LORD and our God! We ask you to keep us safe from the Assyrian king. Then everyone in every kingdom on earth will know that you are the only LORD.

Isaiah Gives the LORD's Answer to Hezekiah
(2 Kings 19.20-34)

21-22I went to Hezekiah and told him that the LORD God of Israel had said:

Hezekiah, you prayed to me about King Sennacherib of Assyria.[h] Now this is what I say to that king:

The people of Jerusalem
hate and make fun of you;
   they laugh behind your back.

23Sennacherib, you cursed,
   shouted and sneered at me,
      the holy One of Israel.
24You let your officials
   insult me, the Lord.
And here is what you
   have said about yourself,

[f]**37.9** *Ethiopia:* See the note at 11.11. [g]**37.16** *winged creatures:* Two winged creatures made of gold were on the top of the sacred chest and were symbols of the LORD's throne on earth (see Exodus 25.18; 2 Samuel 6.2). [h]**37.21,22** *Hezekiah, you prayed . . . Assyria:* One possible meaning for the difficult Hebrew text.

"I led my chariots
to the highest heights
of Lebanon's mountains.
I went deep into its forest,
cutting down the best cedar
and cypress trees.
25I dried up every stream
in the land of Egypt,
and I drank water
from wells I had dug."

26Sennacherib, now listen
to me, the LORD.
I planned all of this long ago.
And you don't even know
that I alone am the one
who decided that you
would do these things.
I let you make ruins
of fortified cities.
27Their people became weak,
terribly confused.
They were like wild flowers
or like tender young grass
growing on a flat roof
or like a field of grain
before it matures.i

28I know all about you,
even how fiercely angry
you are with me.
29I have seen your pride
and the tremendous hatred
you have for me.
Now I will put a hook
in your nose,
a bit in your mouth,j
then I will send you back
to where you came from.

30Hezekiah, I will tell you what's going to happen. This year you will eat
crops that grow on their own, and the
next year you will eat whatever springs
up where those crops grew. But the
third year, you will plant grain and
vineyards, and you will eat what you
harvest. 31Those who survive in Judah
will be like a vine that puts down deep
roots and bears fruit. 32I, the LORD All-
Powerful, will see to it that some who
live in Jerusalem will survive.

33I promise that the king of Assyria
won't get into Jerusalem, or shoot an
arrow into the city, or even surround
it and prepare to attack. 34As surely as
I am the LORD, he will return by the
way he came and will never enter
Jerusalem. 35I will protect it for the
sake of my own honor and because of
the promise I made to my servant
David.

The Death of King Sennacherib
(2 Kings 19.35-37)

36The LORD sent an angel to the camp of
the Assyrians, and he killed 185,000 of them
all in one night. The next morning, the
camp was full of dead bodies. 37After this,
King Sennacherib went back to Assyria and
lived in the city of Nineveh. 38One day he
was worshiping in the temple of his god
Nisroch, when his sons, Adrammelech and
Sharezer, killed him with their swords.
They escaped to the land of Ararat, and his
son Esarhaddon became king.k

i37.27 tender young grass . . . matures: The Standard Hebrew Text; the Dead Sea Scrolls and some
Hebrew manuscripts "tender young grass, growing on a flat roof and scorched by the heat." Many
of the houses had roofs made of packed earth. Grass would sometimes grow on the roof, but would
die quickly because of the sun and hot winds.   j37.29 I will put . . . your mouth: This is how the
Assyrians treated their prisoners, and now the LORD will treat Sennacherib the same way.
k37.38 Esarhaddon became king: He ruled Assyria 681–669 B.C.

37.26 I planned all of this: Though
Sennacherib and other Assyrian leaders
took credit for their many victories, it
was Israel's LORD God who allowed
them to happen.

37.30 This year . . . third year: The
Assyrian army controlled the farmland
around Jerusalem for about three years,
probably meaning 703–701 B.C. This
caused hunger in Jerusalem.

37.36 angel . . . killed: The Hebrew word for "angel" means "messenger." In the Bible, angels act both as
messengers and as servants of God.
Sometimes they serve God's purpose
by bringing plagues or disaster (Exod
12.23; 2 Sam 24.15-17). The death of the
Assyrian soldiers relates to Isaiah's earlier prophecies.

Angels

37.37,38 Sennacherib . . . his god
Nisroch . . . his sons: In 701 B.C., after
the disaster in Judah, Sennacherib and
his army returned to Assyria. There, he
continued to rule in the capital city of
Nineveh until 682 B.C. when his own sons
killed him (probably in an argument
over which son would follow his father
on the throne). The murdering sons escaped to Ararat north of Assyria, so another son, Esarhaddon, became king.
He ruled Assyria from 681 to 669 B.C.
The identity and significance of the god
Nisroch is uncertain.

38.5 *your ancestor David:* Like the other rulers of Judah, Hezekiah was a descendant of King David.

38.9 *Hezekiah wrote:* Hezekiah's song does not appear in 2 KINGS or 2 CHRONICLES. It is similar to a number of psalms that give thanks for God's saving help (see Ps 18; 22; 30; 41).

Hezekiah

Hezekiah Gets Sick and Almost Dies

(2 Kings 20.1-11; 2 Chronicles 32.24-26)

38 About this time, Hezekiah got sick and was almost dead. So I went in and told him, "The LORD says you won't ever get well. You are going to die, and so you had better start doing what needs to be done."

2 Hezekiah turned toward the wall and prayed, 3 "Don't forget that I have been faithful to you, LORD. I have obeyed you with all my heart, and I do whatever you say is right." After this, he cried hard.

4 Then the LORD sent me 5 with this message for Hezekiah:

I am the LORD God, who was worshiped by your ancestor David. I heard you pray, and I saw you cry. I will let you live 15 more years, 6 while I protect you and your city from the king of Assyria.

7 Now I will prove to you that I will keep my promise. 8 Do you see the shadow made by the setting sun on the stairway built for King Ahaz? I will make the shadow go back ten steps. Then the shadow went back ten steps.[l]

King Hezekiah's Song of Praise

9 This is what Hezekiah wrote after he got well:

10 I thought I would die
    during my best years
    and stay as a prisoner forever
    in the world of the dead.
11 I thought I would never again
    see you, my LORD,
    or any of the people
    who live on this earth.

12 My life was taken from me
    like the tent that a shepherd
    pulls up and moves.
You cut me off like thread
    from a weaver's loom;
you make a wreck of me
    day and night.

13 Until morning came, I thought
    you would crush my bones
    just like a hungry lion;
both night and day
    you make a wreck of me.[m]
14 I cry like a swallow;
    I mourn like a dove.
My eyes are red
    from looking to you, LORD.
I am in terrible trouble.
    Please come and help me.[n]
15 There's nothing I can say
    in answer to you,
since you are the one
    who has done this to me.[o]
My life has turned sour;
    I will limp until I die.

16 Your words and your deeds
    bring life to everyone,
    including me.[p]
Please make me healthy
    and strong again.
17 It was for my own good
    that I had such hard times.
But your love protected me
    from doom in the deep pit,[q]
and you turned your eyes
    away from my sins.

18 No one in the world of the dead
    can thank you or praise you;

[l]38.8 *steps:* One possible meaning for the difficult Hebrew text of verse 8.   [m]38.13 *of me:* One possible meaning for the difficult Hebrew text of verse 13.   [n]38.14 *help me:* One possible meaning for the difficult Hebrew text of verse 14.   [o]38.15 *There's . . . me:* One possible meaning for the difficult Hebrew text.   [p]38.16 *Your . . . me:* One possible meaning for the difficult Hebrew text.   [q]38.17 *deep pit:* The world of the dead, as in verse 18.

none of those in the deep pit
can hope for you
  to show them
  how faithful you are.
[19]Only the living can thank you,
  as I am doing today.
Each generation tells the next
  about your faithfulness.[r]

[20]You, Lord, will save me,
  and every day that we live
we will sing in your temple
  to the music
  of stringed instruments.

Isaiah's Advice to Hezekiah

[21]I had told King Hezekiah's servants to put some mashed figs on the king's open sore, and he would get well. [22]Then Hezekiah asked for proof that he would again worship in the Lord's temple.

Isaiah Speaks
the Lord's Message to Hezekiah
(2 Kings 20.12-19)

39 Merodach Baladan, the son of Baladan, was now king of Babylonia. And when he learned that Hezekiah was well, he sent messengers with letters and a gift for him. [2]Hezekiah welcomed the messengers and showed them all the silver, the gold, the spices, and the fine oils that were in his storehouse. He even showed them where he kept his weapons. Nothing in his palace or in his entire kingdom was kept hidden from them.

[3]I asked Hezekiah, "Where did these men come from? What did they want?"

"They came all the way from Babylonia," Hezekiah answered.

[4]"What did you show them?" I asked.

Hezekiah answered, "I showed them everything in my kingdom."

[5]Then I told Hezekiah:

I have a message for you from the Lord All-Powerful. [6]One day everything you and your ancestors have stored up will be taken to Babylonia. The Lord has promised that nothing will be left. [7]Some of your own sons will be taken to Babylonia, where they will be disgraced and made to serve in the king's palace.

[8]Hezekiah thought, "At least our nation will be at peace for a while." So he told me, "The message you brought from the Lord is good."

Encourage God's People

40 Our God has said:
  "Encourage my people!
    Give them comfort.
[2]Speak kindly to Jerusalem
  and announce:
Your slavery is past;
  your punishment is over.
I, the Lord, made you pay
  double for your sins."

[3]Someone is shouting:
  "Clear a path in the desert!
  Make a straight road
    for the Lord our God.
[4]Fill in the valleys;
  flatten every hill
    and mountain.
Level the rough
  and rugged ground.
[5]Then the glory of the Lord
  will appear for all to see.
The Lord has promised this!"

[6]Someone told me to shout,
and I asked,

[r]**38.19** *about your faithfulness:* One possible meaning for the difficult Hebrew text.

Babylon

39.2 *silver . . . oils:* It is not clear why Hezekiah showed the Babylonian messengers these treasures. Perhaps he saw the Babylonians as a possible ally against the Assyrians who were threatening Jerusalem.

39.6,7 *taken to Babylonia . . . own sons . . . disgraced:* Isaiah likely refers to the events that were to occur about 100 years later.

39.8 *message you brought . . . is good:* Hezekiah's response seems shortsighted and unfeeling. However, taken positively, Hezekiah's response shows that he accepts the disturbing prophecy about Judah's future while hoping for peace in his lifetime.

Exile

40.3 *path in the desert:* The Babylonians were known for their parades during religious celebrations. Isaiah uses the imagery of such a parade to describe the Lord's victory march back to Judah. Those traveling from Babylon to Judah usually followed the river valleys north through Mesopotamia. They then headed east to Syria and then south from there. This path allowed them to avoid the hazards of the great Arabian Desert that lay directly between Babylon and Judah. But here the Lord leads the parade right through the desert. The New Testament uses Isaiah's prophecy to describe John the Baptist, who came from the desert to prepare the way for the Lord's Messiah (Matt 3.3; Mark 1.3; John 1.23; Luke 3.4-6). **(See Map 7 on pg 1885.)**

40.15,16 *dust on balance scales . . . cattle on the mountains of Lebanon:* Balance scales were used to weigh precious metals or grain. Dust would be too light to make a scale move at all. The message then is that no amount of cattle or even valuable cedar would be enough to equal God's greatness.

"What should I shout?"
We humans are merely grass,
and we last no longer
    than wild flowers.
[7]At the Lord's command,
flowers and grass disappear,
    and so do we.
[8]Flowers and grass fade away,
but what our God has said
    will never change.

Your God Is Here!

[9]There is good news
    for the city of Zion.
Shout it as loud as you can[s]
    from the highest mountain.
Don't be afraid to shout
to the towns of Judah:
    "Your God is here!"
[10]Look! The powerful Lord God
is coming to rule
    with his mighty arm.
He brings with him
what he has taken in war,
    and he rewards his people.
[11]The Lord cares for his nation,
just as shepherds care
    for their flocks.
He carries the lambs
    in his arms,
while gently leading
    the mother sheep.

Who Compares with God?

[12]Did any of you measure
    the ocean by yourself
or stretch out the sky

with your own hands?
Did you put the soil
    of the earth in a bucket
or weigh the hills and mountains
    on balance scales?

[13]Has anyone told the Lord[t]
    what he must do
or given him advice?
[14]Did the Lord ask anyone
to teach him wisdom
    and justice?
Who gave him knowledge
    and understanding?
[15]To the Lord, all nations
are merely a drop in a bucket
    or dust on balance scales;
all of the islands
    are but a handful of sand.
[16]The cattle on the mountains
    of Lebanon
would not be enough to offer
    as a sacrifice to God,
and the trees would not
    be enough for the fire.
[17]God thinks of the nations
    as far less than nothing.

[18]Who compares with God?
    Is anything like him?
[19]Is an idol at all like God?
    It is made of bronze
with a thin layer of gold,
    and decorated with silver.
[20]Or special wood may be chosen[u]
    because it doesn't rot—
then skilled hands
    take care to make an idol
    that won't fall on its face.

[s]**40.9** *There . . . can:* Or "City of Jerusalem, you have good news. Shout it as loud as you can."
[t]**40.13** *the* Lord: Or "the Lord's Spirit." [u]**40.20** *Or . . . chosen:* One possible meaning for the difficult Hebrew text. Two kinds of idols seem to be described: bronze idols covered with gold (verse 19) and wooden idols (verse 20).

God Rules the Whole Earth

21Don't you know?
   Haven't you heard?
Hasn't it been clear
   since the time of creation?[v]
22God is the one who rules
   the whole earth,
and we that live here
   are merely insects.
He spread out the heavens
like a curtain or an open tent.

23God brings down rulers
   and turns them into nothing.
24They are like flowers
freshly sprung up
   and starting to grow.
But when God blows on them,
they wilt and are carried off
   like straw in a storm.

25The holy God asks,
   "Who compares with me?
   Is anyone my equal?"

26Look at the evening sky!
   Who created the stars?
Who gave them each a name?
   Who leads them like an army?
The Lord is so powerful
that none of the stars
   are ever missing.

The Lord Gives Strength

27You people of Israel, say,
   "God pays no attention to us!
   He doesn't care if we
   are treated unjustly."

But how can you say that?
28Don't you know?
   Haven't you heard?
The Lord is the eternal God,
   Creator of the earth.
He never gets weary or tired;
his wisdom cannot be measured.

29The Lord gives strength
   to those who are weary.
30Even young people get tired,
   then stumble and fall.
31But those who trust the Lord
   will find new strength.
They will be strong like eagles
   soaring upward on wings;
they will walk and run
   without getting tired.

The Lord Controls Human Events

41 Be silent and listen,
      every island in the sea.
Have courage and come near,
   every one of you nations.
Let's settle this matter!
2Who appointed this ruler
   from the east?[w]
Who puts nations and kings
   in his power?[x]
His sword and his arrows
turn them to dust
   blown by the wind.
3He goes after them so quickly
that his feet
   barely touch the ground—
he doesn't even get hurt.

4Who makes these things happen?
Who controls human events?
   I do! I am the Lord.

40.28 *eternal God, Creator:* Compare God, who never gets weary, to the human being who makes idols in 44.12.

41.1 *Let's settle this matter:* The nations are called into God's court to hear evidence concerning who controls human events (41.4).

[v]**40.21** *Hasn't . . . creation:* Or "Isn't it clear that God created the world?" [w]**41.2** *ruler from the east:* Probably Cyrus (see 44.28; 45.1; 48.14). [x]**41.2** *Who puts . . . power:* One possible meaning for the difficult Hebrew text.

Those who trust the Lord will find new strength. They will be strong like eagles soaring upward on wings; they will walk and run without getting tired. Isa 40.31

■ *41.8 Israel . . . my servant . . . Abraham:* The LORD's chosen "servant" is the whole people of Israel. As the LORD's "servant," the people were to trust only in the LORD and live according to his teachings (Exod 20.1-6; Deut 6.4-25). In the second section of Isaiah (40–55) "servant" sometime refers to the whole people of Israel and sometimes just to one person.

■ *41.14 only a worm . . . holy God of Israel:* Other nations referred to Israel as a lowly worm because of the people's defeat and exile in Babylonia (Ps 22.6-8).

● *41.15 log covered with sharp spikes:* In ancient times, this type of log or other heavy object was dragged over wheat or barley to separate the grain from the husk. The mountains and hills stand for the power and pride of Israel's enemies. So, like Cyrus (41.2), Israel will crush its enemies to dust.

I was there at the beginning;
    I will be there at the end.
[5]Islands and foreign nations
saw what I did and trembled
    as they came near.

What Can Idols Do?

[6]Worshipers of idols
comfort each other,
    saying, "Don't worry!"
[7]Woodcarvers, goldsmiths,
    and other workers[y]
encourage one another and say,
    "We've done a great job!"
Then they nail the idol down,
    so it won't fall over.

The LORD's Chosen Servant

[8]Israel, you are my servant.
I chose you, the family
    of my friend Abraham.
[9]From far across the earth
    I brought you here and said,
"You are my chosen servant.
    I haven't forgotten you."

[10]Don't be afraid. I am with you.
Don't tremble with fear.
    I am your God.
I will make you strong,
as I protect you with my arm
    and give you victories.
[11]Everyone who hates you
    will be terribly disgraced;
those who attack
    will vanish into thin air.
[12]You will look around

for those brutal enemies,
but you won't find them—
    they will be gone.

[13]I am the LORD your God.
I am holding your hand,
    so don't be afraid.
I am here to help you.

[14]People of Israel, don't worry,
though others may say,
    "Israel is only a worm!"
I am the holy God of Israel,
    who saves and protects you.
[15]I will let you be like a log
    covered with sharp spikes.[z]
You will grind and crush
every mountain and hill[a]
    until they turn to dust.
[16]A strong wind will scatter them
    in all directions.
Then you will celebrate
and praise me, your LORD,
    the holy God of Israel.

The LORD Helps the Poor

[17]When the poor and needy
are dying of thirst
    and cannot find water,
I, the LORD God of Israel,
will come to their rescue.
    I won't forget them.
[18]I will make rivers flow
    on mountain peaks.
I will send streams
    to fill the valleys.
Dry and barren land
    will flow with springs

[y]**41.7** *and other workers:* One possible meaning for the difficult Hebrew text.   [z]**41.15** *I will let . . . sharp spikes:* In ancient times a heavy object was sometimes dragged over wheat or barley to separate the grain from the husk. This was called threshing.   [a]**41.15** *mountain and hill:* These stand for the power and pride of Israel's enemies.

and become a lake.
[19]I will fill the desert
  with all kinds of trees—
cedars, acacias, and myrtles;
olive and cypress trees;
  fir trees and pines.
[20]Everyone will see this
  and know that I,
the holy Lord God of Israel,
  created it all.

Idols Are Useless

[21]I am the Lord,
  the King of Israel!
Come argue your case with me.
  Present your evidence.
[22]Come near me, you idols.[b]
Tell us about the past,
  and we will think about it.
Tell us about the future,
so we will know
  what is going to happen.
[23]Prove that you are gods
by making your predictions
  come true.
Do something good or evil,
so we can be amazed
  and terrified.[c]
[24]You idols are nothing,
  and you are powerless.[d]
To worship you
  would be disgusting.

[25]I, the Lord, appointed a ruler
  in the north;
now he comes from the east
  to honor my name.

He tramples[e] kings like mud,
  as potters trample clay.[f]
[26]Did any of you idols predict
  what would happen?
Did any of you get it right?
None of you told about this
  or even spoke a word.
[27]I was the first to tell
the people of Jerusalem,
  "Look, it's happening!"[g]
I was the one who announced
  this good news to Zion.

[28]None of these idols
are able to give advice
  or answer questions.
[29]They are nothing,[h]
  and they can do nothing—
they are merely
  a passing breeze.

The Lord's Servant

42 Here is my servant!
     I have made him strong.
He is my chosen one;
  I am pleased with him.
I have given him my Spirit,
and he will bring justice
  to the nations.
[2]He won't shout or yell
  or call out in the streets.
[3]He won't break off a bent reed
  or put out a dying flame,
but he will make sure
  that justice is done.
[4]He won't quit or give up
until he brings justice
everywhere on earth,

---

[b]41.22 *Come near . . . idols*: One possible meaning for the difficult Hebrew text.   [c]41.23 *and terrified*: Or "when we see it."   [d]41.24 *powerless*: One possible meaning for the difficult Hebrew text.
[e]41.25 *tramples*: One possible meaning for the difficult Hebrew text.   [f]41.25 *trample clay*: This was done to soften the clay and make it easier to shape.   [g]41.27 *Look . . . happening*: One possible meaning for the difficult Hebrew text.   [h]41.29 *nothing*: One possible meaning for the difficult Hebrew text.

● 41.22,23 *idols . . . predictions*: God challenges the idols to tell what will happen in the future or to do something amazing, but they cannot. Only the Lord, who is in control of history, can tell what will happen and then make it come true.

● 41.25 *trample clay*: This was done to soften the clay and make it easier to shape.

■ 41.27 *good news to Zion*: The Lord announced that the people of Judah and Jerusalem (Zion) would return home from exile (40.9-11; 52.7-10).

■ 42.1 *my servant . . . chosen one . . . justice*: Isaiah 42.1-7 is the first of four "servant songs." Scholars usually identify the "servant" in this song as Israel (41.8; 44.1,2; 45.4). But the servant may also be a ruler such as the one mentioned in 9.6,7 and 11.1-5. This ruler from the family of David will also receive the Lord's spirit. Whether the servant is Israel or one chosen to lead Israel, the task of the servant is to bring "justice" to the nations.

⊘ The Servant Songs in Isaiah

⊘ Justice

■ 42.3-6 *bent reed . . . dying flame*: The "bent reed and dying flame" are symbols of those who are weak. In contrast to a warrior who crushes enemies (41.15), the just servant will not cut down or snuff out the weak but bring them help and healing.

42.10 *ocean . . . those who live far away:* The "ocean" is the Mediterranean Sea. "Those who live far away" may refer to the people of Tarshish (southern Spain).

42.18,19 *You people . . . chosen servant:* The LORD's people and their leaders were blind and deaf to the warnings of the prophets (1.2; 5.7; 6.9,10; 28.7-13; 29.9-14).

42.21,22 *wanted his Law . . . people were trapped:* As the LORD's chosen people, Israel is to be an example to all other nations by living according to the Law that God gave Moses at Sinai. But because they had turned away from God, the Israelites were now trapped in exile in Babylonia, and all their wealth had been taken away.

Law

and people in foreign nations
    long for his teaching.

⁵I am the LORD God.
 I created the heavens
    like an open tent above.
 I made the earth and everything
    that grows on it.
 I am the source of life
 for all who live on this earth,
    so listen to what I say.
⁶ I chose you to bring justice,
    and I am here at your side.
 I selected you and sent you[i]
    to bring light
 and my promise of hope
    to the nations.
⁷You will give sight
    to the blind;
 you will set prisoners free
    from dark dungeons.

⁸My name is the LORD!
 I won't let idols or humans
    share my glory and praise.
⁹Everything has happened
    just as I said it would;
 now I will announce
    what will happen next.

Sing Praises to the LORD

¹⁰Tell the whole world to sing
    a new song to the LORD!
 Tell those who sail the ocean
 and those who live far away
    to join in the praise.
¹¹Tell the tribes of the desert
 and everyone in the mountains[j]
    to celebrate and sing.
¹²Let them announce
    his praises everywhere.

¹³The LORD is marching out
    like an angry soldier,
 shouting with all his might
    while attacking his enemies.

The LORD Will Help His People

¹⁴For a long time, I, the LORD,
    have held my temper;
 now I will cry out and groan
    like a woman giving birth.
¹⁵I will destroy the mountains
    and what grows on them;
 I will dry up rivers and ponds.

¹⁶I will lead the blind on roads
    they have never known;
 I will guide them on paths
    they have never traveled.
 Their road is dark and rough,
    but I will give light
 to keep them from stumbling.
    This is my solemn promise.

¹⁷Everyone who worships idols
    as though they were gods
    will be terribly ashamed.

God's People Won't Obey

¹⁸You people are deaf and blind,
    but the LORD commands you
    to listen and to see.
¹⁹No one is as blind or deaf
    as his messenger,
    his chosen servant,
²⁰who sees and hears so much,
    but pays no attention.

²¹The LORD always does right,
    and so he wanted his Law
    to be greatly praised.[k]

[i]**42.6** *I selected . . . you:* One possible meaning for the difficult Hebrew text. [j]**42.11** *desert . . . mountains:* The Hebrew text includes the place names of Kedar in the desert and Sela in the mountains.
[k]**42.21** *greatly praised:* One possible meaning for the difficult Hebrew text of verse 21.

22But his people were trapped
  and imprisoned in holes
    with no one to rescue them.
All they owned had been taken,
and no one was willing
    to give it back.
23Why won't his people
  ever learn to listen?

24Israel sinned and refused
  to obey the LORD
    or follow his instructions.
So the LORD let us be robbed
  of everything we owned.
25He was furious with us
  and punished our nation
    with the fires of war.
Still we paid no attention.
  We didn't even care
when we were surrounded
  and scorched by flames.

The LORD Has Rescued His People

43 Descendants of Jacob,
   I, the LORD, created you
     and formed your nation.
Israel, don't be afraid.
  I have rescued you.
  I have called you by name;
    now you belong to me.
2When you cross deep rivers,
I will be with you,
    and you won't drown.
When you walk through fire,
you won't be burned
    or scorched by the flames.

3I am the LORD, your God,
  the Holy One of Israel,
    the God who saves you.

I gave up Egypt, Ethiopia,l
  and the region of Sebam
    in exchange for you.
4To me, you are very dear,
  and I love you.
That's why I gave up nations
  and people to rescue you.

5Don't be afraid! I am with you.
From both east and west
  I will bring you together.
6I will say to the north
  and to the south,
"Free my sons and daughters!
Let them return
  from distant lands.
7They are my people—
I created each of them
  to bring honor to me."

The LORD Alone Is God

The LORD said:
8Bring my people together.
They have eyes and ears,
  but they can't see or hear.
9Tell everyone of every nation
  to gather around.
None of them can honestly say,
  "We told you so!"
If someone heard them say this,
  then tell us about it now.

10My people, you are my witnesses
  and my chosen servant.
I want you to know me,
to trust me, and understand
  that I alone am God.
I have always been God;
  there can be no others.

43.3 *gave up Egypt . . . Seba:* The Persians allowed the people of Judah to return home from exile and to rebuild their temple and their cities. Yet this did not mean that Judah was a free and independent country. Persia continued to control Judah as one of its provinces. Persia helped Judah in order to gain the favor of its leaders, so Judah would support Persia in its efforts to take over Egypt, Ethiopia, and Seba, a region in southwest Arabia.

43.6 *return from distant lands:* The return from Babylonia is most important here. But God's people returned from other places as well after the Persians allowed Jerusalem and Judah to be resettled. (See the article After the Exile: God's People Return to Judea on pg 1789.)

l43.3 *Ethiopia:* See the note at 11.11.   m43.3 *Seba:* A region in southwest Arabia. Egypt, Ethiopia, and Seba probably stood for all that was known of Africa in biblical times.

43.15 *Israel's Creator and King:* The LORD allowed the people of Israel to have kings (1 Sam 8.1-22). Still, the LORD was to be considered Israel's ruler.

43.16,17 *cut a path . . . an army . . . unable to move:* This refers to the Egyptian army, which was destroyed in the waters of the Red Sea while chasing after the Israelites (Exod 14).

43.19,20 *something new . . . roads . . . water in deserts:* The LORD will help the people escape from exile in Babylonia and return to Judah. The most direct path back to Judah from Babylonia was through the desert.

43.23,24 *sacrificing sheep . . . incense . . . spices:* God's Law called for Israel's priests to offer sacrifices to honor the LORD (Lev 1–7). These included animal sacrifices, grain sacrifices, and sacrifices mixed with incense and spices ("calamus," or "sweet cane" in 43.24) that gave a pleasing smell when burned. Rather than these sacrifices, the LORD prefers the people trust and serve him by doing right (Isa 1.12-17,27; Mic 6.6-8). **(See the chart Sacrifices and Offerings on pg 1828.)**

43.26 *Meet me in court:* The LORD invites Israel to court, just as the nations were invited in 41.21-23. However, Israel has no case. The people were guilty of sinning against God, so they were disgraced (43.28).

¹¹I alone am the LORD;
  only I can rescue you.
¹²I promised to save you,
  and I kept my promise.
 You are my witnesses
  that no other god did this.
  I, the LORD, have spoken.
¹³I am God now and forever.
  No one can snatch you from me
  or stand in my way.

The LORD Will Prepare the Way

¹⁴I, the LORD, will rescue you!
 I am Israel's holy God,
  and this is my promise:
 For your sake, I will send
  an army against Babylon
 to drag its people away,
  crying as they go.[n]

¹⁵I am the LORD, your holy God,
  Israel's Creator and King.
¹⁶I am the one who cut a path
  through the mighty ocean.
¹⁷I sent an army to chase you
  with chariots and horses;
 now they lie dead,
  unable to move.
 They are like an oil lamp
  with the flame snuffed out.

Forget the Past

The LORD said:
¹⁸Forget what happened long ago!
  Don't think about the past.
¹⁹I am creating something new.
  There it is! Do you see it?
 I have put roads in deserts,

 streams[o] in thirsty lands.
²⁰Every wild animal honors me,
  even jackals[p] and owls.
 I provide water in deserts—
  streams in thirsty lands
  for my chosen people.
²¹I made them my own nation,
  so they would praise me.

²²I, the LORD, said to Israel:
 You have become weary of me,
  but not from worshiping me.
²³You have not honored me
  by sacrificing sheep
  or other animals.
 And I have not burdened you
  with demands for sacrifices
  or sweet-smelling incense.

²⁴You have not brought
  delicious spices for me
 or given me the best part
  of your sacrificed animals.
 Instead, you burden me down
  with your terrible sins.
²⁵But I wipe away your sins
  because of who I am.
 And so, I will forget
  the wrongs you have done.

²⁶Meet me in court!
 State your case and prove
  that you are right.
²⁷Your earliest ancestor[q]
 and all your leaders[r]
  rebelled against me.
²⁸That's why I don't allow
  your priests to serve me;
 I let Israel be destroyed
  and your people disgraced.

[n]**43.14** *crying as they go:* Or "in their glorious ships." [o]**43.19** *streams:* The Standard Hebrew Text; the Dead Sea Scrolls "paths." [p]**43.20** *jackals:* Desert animals related to wolves, but smaller. [q]**43.27** *earliest ancestor:* Jacob, also known as Israel. [r]**43.27** *leaders:* Probably prophets, but perhaps also priests and kings.

The Lord's Promise to Israel

44 People of Israel,
I have chosen you
        as my servant.
²I am your Creator.
You were in my care
    even before you were born.
Israel, don't be terrified!
You are my chosen servant,
    my very favorite.ˢ

³I will bless the thirsty land
    by sending streams of water;
I will bless your descendants
    by giving them my Spirit.
⁴They will spring up like grassᵗ
or like willow trees
    near flowing streams.
⁵They will worship me
    and become my people.
They will write my name
    on the back of their hands.ᵘ

⁶I am the Lord All-Powerful,
the first and the last,
    the one and only God.
Israel, I have rescued you!
    I am your King.
⁷Can anyone compare with me?
If so, let them speak up
    and tell me now.
Let them say what has happened
since I made my nation
    long ago,
and let them tell
    what is going to happen.ᵛ
⁸Don't tremble with fear!
Didn't I tell you long ago?
    Didn't you hear me?

I alone am God—
    no one else is a mighty rock.ʷ

Idols Can't Do a Thing

The Lord said:
⁹Those people who make idols
    are nothing themselves,
and the idols they treasure
    are just as worthless.
Worshipers of idols are blind,
    stupid, and foolish.
¹⁰Why make an idol or an image
    that can't do a thing?
¹¹Everyone who makes idols
    and all who worship them
        are mere humans,
who will end up
    sadly disappointed.
Let them face me in court
    and be terrified.

Idols and Firewood

¹²A metalworker shapes an idol
by using a hammerˣ
    and heat from the fire.
In his powerful hand
    he holds a hammer,
as he pounds the metal
    into the proper shape.
But he gets hungry and thirsty
    and loses his strength.

¹³Some woodcarver measures
a piece of wood,
    then draws an outline.
The idol is carefully carved
    with each detail exact.
At last it looks like a person

● 44.5 *write my name . . . hands:* An owner's name was sometimes tattooed or branded on a slave's hand. Israel belongs to the Lord.

● 44.9-20 *Those . . . who make idols . . . metalworker:* These verses make fun of people who make and worship idols, because idols are powerless. Idol worship was against God's Law because Israel was to trust in the Lord God alone. Archaeologists believe that the craft of metalworking began in the ancient Near East around 9000 B.C. The earliest evidence of metalworking, found at Shanidar cave in Iraq, are pieces of pure copper that have been shaped by hammers. Metalworking is mentioned many times in the Bible. In Genesis 4.22, Tubal Cain is described as having "made tools out of bronze and iron."

ˢ**44.2** *my very favorite:* Or "Jeshurun." ᵗ**44.4** *like grass:* One possible meaning for the difficult Hebrew text. ᵘ**44.5** *write . . . hands:* To show that they belong to the Lord and to Israel. ᵛ**44.7** *Let them say . . . happen:* One possible meaning for the difficult Hebrew text. ʷ**44.8** *mighty rock:* See the note at 17.10. ˣ**44.12** *by using a hammer:* One possible meaning for the difficult Hebrew text.

and is placed in a temple.
¹⁴Either cedar, cypress, oak,
    or any tree from the forest
        may be chosen.
    Or even a pine tree planted
    by the woodcarver
        and watered by the rain.

¹⁵Some of the wood is used
    to make a fire for heating
        or for cooking.
    One piece is made into an idol,
    then the woodcarver bows down
        and worships it.
¹⁶He enjoys the warm fire
    and the meat that was roasted
        over the burning coals.
¹⁷Afterwards, he bows down
        to worship the wooden idol.
    "Protect me!" he says.
        "You are my god."

¹⁸Those who worship idols are stupid and blind! ¹⁹They don't have enough sense to say to themselves, "I made a fire with half of the wood and cooked my bread and meat on it. Then I made something worthless with the other half. Why worship a block of wood?"

²⁰How can anyone be stupid enough to trust something that can be burned to ashes?ʸ No one can save themselves like that. Don't they realize that the idols they hold in their hands are not really gods?

The Lord Won't Forget His People

²¹People of Israel,
    you are my servant,
        so remember all of this.
    Israel, I created you,

and you are my servant.
    I won't forget you.ᶻ
²²Turn back to me!
    I have rescued you
    and swept away your sins
        as though they were clouds.

Sing Praises to the Lord

²³Tell the heavens and the earth
        to start singing!
    Tell the mountains
    and every tree in the forest
        to join in the song!
    The Lord has rescued his people;
        now they will worship him.

The Lord Created Everything

²⁴Israel, I am your Lord,
    the source of your life,
        and I have rescued you.
    I created everything
    from the sky above
        to the earth below.

²⁵I make liars of false prophets
        and fools of fortunetellers.
    I take human wisdom
        and turn it into nonsense.
²⁶I will make the message
        of my prophets come true.
    They are saying, "Jerusalem
        will be filled with people,
    and the Lord will rebuild
        the towns of Judah."

²⁷I am the one who commands
    the sea and its streams
        to run dry.
²⁸I am also the one who says,
    "Cyrus will lead my people

ʸ**44.20** *How . . . ashes:* One possible meaning for the difficult Hebrew text.   ᶻ**44.21** *I won't forget you:* One possible meaning for the difficult Hebrew text.

and obey my orders.
Jerusalem and the temple
will be rebuilt."

Cyrus Obeys
the Lord's Commands

45 The Lord said to Cyrus, his chosen
one:

I have taken hold
of your right hand
to help you capture nations
and remove kings from power.
City gates will open for you;
not one will stay closed.
[2] As I lead you,
I will level mountains[a]
and break the iron bars
on bronze gates of cities.

[3] I will give you treasures
hidden in dark
and secret places.
Then you will know that I,
the Lord God of Israel,
have called you by name.
[4] Cyrus, you don't even know me!
But I have called you by name
and highly honored you[b]
because of Israel,
my chosen servant.

[5] Only I am the Lord!
There are no other gods.
I have made you strong,
though you don't know me.
[6] Now everyone from east to west
will learn that I am the Lord.
No other gods are real.
[7] I create light and darkness,

happiness and sorrow.
I, the Lord, do all this.

[8] Tell the heavens
to send down justice
like showers of rain.
Prepare the earth
for my saving power
to sprout and produce justice
that I, the Lord, create.[c]

The Lord's Mighty Power

The Lord said:
[9] Israel, you have no right
to argue with your Creator.
You are merely a clay pot
shaped by a potter.
The clay doesn't ask,
"Why did you make me this way?
Where are the handles?"
[10] Children don't have the right
to demand of their parents,
"What have you done
to make us what we are?"

[11] I am the Lord, the Creator,
the holy God of Israel.
Do you dare question me
about my own nation
or about what I have done?
[12] I created the world
and covered it with people;
I stretched out the sky
and filled it with stars.
[13] I have done the right thing
by placing Cyrus in power,
and I will make the roads easy
for him to follow.
I am the Lord All-Powerful!

---

[a] **45.2** *mountains:* The Dead Sea Scrolls and one ancient translation; the Standard Hebrew Text "rising waves."   [b] **45.4** *But . . . you:* One possible meaning for the difficult Hebrew text.   [c] **45.8** *Prepare . . . create:* One possible meaning for the difficult Hebrew text.

⬤   45.1 *Cyrus . . . chosen one:* The word translated as "chosen one" in 45.1 is the Hebrew word for messiah, or anointed one. Cyrus is the only non-Israelite in the Bible to be called the Lord's chosen messiah. The title was usually given only to certain Israelite leaders.

↗   Messiah (Chosen One)

⬤   45.13 *placing Cyrus in power:* God used Cyrus to free the Israelite people from exile in Babylonia so they could rebuild Jerusalem ("my city").

46.1,2 *gods Bel and Nebo:* Bel, meaning "lord," became another name for Marduk, the chief god of Babylon. Nebo is "Nabu," the son of Bel-Marduk and the chief god of the city of Borsippa. Just before the invasion of Cyrus, King Nabonidus of Babylonia had many images of the Babylonian gods brought from outlying areas in order to protect them. The writer of ISAIAH mocks Babylon, saying that rather than the people bowing down to the images, the images bowed down to get out of the city. The Babylonian gods are helpless to protect their own images.

Cyrus will rebuild my city
and set my people free
without being paid a thing.
I, the LORD, have spoken.

The LORD Alone Can Save

¹⁴My people, I, the LORD, promise
that the riches of Egypt
and the treasures of Ethiopia^d
will belong to you.
You will force into slavery
those tall people of Seba.^e

They will bow down and say,
"The only true God is with you;
there are no other gods."
¹⁵People of Israel,
your God is a mystery,
though he alone can save.
¹⁶Anyone who makes idols
will be confused
and terribly disgraced.
¹⁷But Israel, I, the LORD,
will always keep you safe
and free from shame.

Everyone Is Invited

¹⁸The LORD alone is God!
He created the heavens
and made a world
where people can live,
instead of creating
an empty desert.
The LORD alone is God;
there are no others.
¹⁹The LORD did not speak
in a dark secret place
or command Jacob's descendants
to search for him in vain.

The LORD speaks the truth,
and this is what he says
²⁰to every survivor
from every nation:
"Gather around me!
Learn how senseless it is
to worship wooden idols
or pray to helpless gods.

²¹"Why don't you get together
and meet me in court?
Didn't I tell you long ago
what would happen?
I am the only God!
There are no others.
I bring about justice,
and have the power to save.

²²"I invite the whole world
to turn to me and be saved.
I alone am God!
No others are real.
²³I have made a solemn promise,
one that won't be broken:
Everyone will bow down
and worship me.
²⁴They will admit that I alone
can bring about justice.
Everyone who is angry with me
will be terribly ashamed
and will turn to me.
²⁵I, the LORD, will give
victory and great honor
to the people of Israel."

Babylonia's Gods Are Helpless

The LORD said:

46 The gods Bel and Nebo^f
are down on their knees,
as wooden images of them

^d**45.14** *Ethiopia:* See the note at 11.11.   ^e**45.14** *Seba:* See the note at 43.3.   ^f**46.1** *Bel and Nebo:* Bel was another name for Marduk, the chief god of the Babylonians. Nebo was the son of Marduk and also an important god.

"I am the only God! There are no others. I bring about justice, and have the power to save." ISA 45.21

are carried away
on weary animals.g
²They are down on their knees
to rescue the heavy load,
but the images are still taken
to a foreign country.

³You survivors in Israel,
listen to me, the LORD.
Since the day you were born,
I have carried you along.
⁴I will still be the same
when you are old and gray,
and I will take care of you.
I created you. I will carry you
and always keep you safe.

⁵Can anyone compare with me?
Is anyone my equal?
⁶Some people hire a goldsmith
and give silver and gold
to be formed into an idol
for them to worship.
⁷They carry the idol
on their shoulders,
then put it on a stand,
but it cannot move.

They call out to the idol
when they are in trouble,
but it doesn't answer,
and it cannot help.
⁸Now keep this in mind,h
you sinful people.
And don't ever forget it.

The LORD Alone Is God

⁹I alone am God!
There are no other gods;

no one is like me.
Think about what happened
many years ago.
¹⁰From the very beginning,
I told what would happen
long before it took place.

I kept my word ¹¹and brought
someone from a distant land
to do what I wanted.
He attacked from the east,
like a hawk swooping down.
Now I will keep my promise
and do what I planned.

¹²You people are stubborn
and far from being safe,
so listen to me.
¹³I will soon come to save you.
I am not far away
and will waste no time;
I take pride in Israel
and will save Jerusalem.

Babylon Will Fall

The LORD said:

47 City of Babylon,
You are delicate
and untouched,
but that will change.
Surrender your royal power
and sit in the dirt.
²Start grinding grain!
Take off your veil.
Strip off your fancy clothes
and wade across rivers.i
³You will suffer the shame
of going naked,
because I will take revenge,

---

g**46.1** *as . . . animals:* One possible meaning for the difficult Hebrew text.   h**46.8** *Now . . . mind:* One possible meaning for the difficult Hebrew text.   i**47.2** *Strip . . . rivers:* This may be a command to get ready for work that requires wading in the river, or it may be a warning that they are going to be taken away as slaves.

● 46.13 *Israel . . . Jerusalem:* God will free the people of Israel from exile in Babylon and help them rebuild Jerusalem.

47.9-15 *magic powers and charms . . . wisdom . . . fortunetellers:* The Babylonian leaders had advisors who used various means to predict the future, including reading drops of fluid in a cup, examining the inner organs of dead animals, and studying the movement of the stars. They also cast evil spells on their enemies, and performed special ceremonies to protect themselves. The wisdom and knowledge of Babylon was well known in the ancient world. However, "wisdom" here refers to advice and information given by these Babylonian magician-priests. Present-day astrology is based in part on the ancient Babylonian study of the stars and planets. Fortunetellers would observe the positions of the stars and planets, and then would use them to predict Babylon's future. God says that trusting in such information is useless. It is like trying to stay warm with a fire fueled by straw (47.14), which burns quickly and then goes out.

48.1 *Israel . . . Jacob's family . . . tribe of Judah:* Those Israelites who returned from exile in Babylon were mainly from the southern tribes of Judah and Benjamin. **(See the article After the Exile: God's People Return to Judea on pg 1789.)**

and no one can escape.[j]
⁴I am the Lord All-Powerful,
   the holy God of Israel.
   I am their Savior.

⁵Babylon, be silent!
   Sit in the dark.
No longer will nations
   accept you as their queen.
⁶I was angry with my people.
So I let you take their land
   and bring disgrace on them.
You showed them no mercy,
but were especially cruel
   to those who were old.
⁷You thought that you
   would be queen forever.
You didn't care what you did;
it never entered your mind
   that you might get caught.

⁸You think that you alone
   are all-powerful,
that you won't be a widow
   or lose your children.
All you care about is pleasure,
   but listen to what I say.
⁹Your magic powers and charms
   will suddenly fail,
then you will be a widow
   and lose your children.

¹⁰You hid behind evil
   like a shield and said,
   "No one can see me!"
You were fooled by your wisdom
   and your knowledge;
you felt sure that you alone
   were in full control.
¹¹But without warning,
   disaster will strike—
and your magic charms
   won't help at all.

¹²Keep using your magic powers
   and your charms
   as you have always done.
Maybe—just maybe—
   you will frighten somebody!
¹³You have worn yourself out,
   asking for advice
from those who study the stars
   and tell the future
   month after month.
Go ask them how to be saved
   from what will happen.
¹⁴People who trust the stars
   are as helpless as straw
   in a flaming fire.
No one can even keep warm,[k]
sitting by a fire
   that feeds only on straw.
¹⁵These are the fortunetellers
   you have done business with
   all of your life.
But they don't know
   where they are going,
   and they can't save you.

The Lord Corrects His People

48 People of Israel,
   you come from Jacob's family
      and the tribe[l] of Judah.
You claim to worship me,
   the Lord God of Israel,
      but you are lying.
²You call Jerusalem your home
   and say you depend on me,
the Lord All-Powerful,
   the God of Israel.

³Long ago I announced
   what was going to be,
then without warning,
   I made it happen.

[j]47.3 *escape:* Or "oppose me."   [k]47.14 *keep warm:* Or "cook food."   [l]48.1 *tribe:* Hebrew "waters."

[4]I knew you were stubborn
and hardheaded.
[5]And I told you these things,
so that when they happened
you would not say,
"The idols we worship did this."

[6]You heard what I said,
and you have seen it happen.
Now admit it's true!
I will show you secrets
you have never known.
[7]Today I am doing something new,
something you cannot say
you have heard before.
[8]You have never been willing
to listen to what I say;
from the moment of your birth,
I knew you would rebel.

The LORD Warns Israel

[9]I, the LORD, am true to myself;
I will be praised for not punishing
and destroying you.
[10]I tested you in hard times
just as silver is refined
in a heated furnace.[m]
[11]I did this because of who I am.
I refuse to be dishonored[n]
or share my praise
with any other god.

[12]Israel, my chosen people,
listen to me.
I alone am the LORD,
the first and the last.
[13]With my own hand
I created the earth
and stretched out the sky.
They obey my every command.

The LORD Speaks to the Nations

[14]Gather around me, all of you!
Listen to what I say.
Did any of your idols
predict this would happen?
Did they say that my friend[o]
would do what I want done
to Babylonia?[p]
[15]I was the one who chose him.
I have brought him this far,
and he will be successful.
[16]Come closer and listen!
I have never kept secret
the things I have said,
and I was here
before time began.

It Is Best To Obey the LORD

By the power of his Spirit
the LORD God has sent me
[17]   with this message:
People of Israel,
I am the holy LORD God,
the one who rescues you.
For your own good,
I teach you, and I lead you
along the right path.
[18]How I wish that you
had obeyed my commands!
Your success and good fortune
would then have overflowed
like a flooding river.
[19]Your nation would be blessed
with more people
than there are grains of sand
along the seashore.
And I would never have let
your country be destroyed.

[m]**48.10** *furnace*: One possible meaning for the difficult Hebrew text of verse 10.   [n]**48.11** *I refuse to be dishonored*: One possible meaning for the difficult Hebrew text.   [o]**48.14** *my friend*: Probably Cyrus (see 44.28; 45.1).   [p]**48.14** *Babylonia*: One possible meaning for the difficult Hebrew text of verse 14.

■ **48.10** *tested …. as silver is refined*: The LORD tested and refined Israel's faith by allowing Babylon to defeat them and make them live in exile.

■ **48.18** *my commands*: The "commands" were the Law. Becoming a great nation was only one of the LORD's blessings that would have resulted from obeying God's commands (48.19; Gen 17.1-8; Deut 6.4-25; Ps 1).

49.1 *foreign nations:* This probably means those Gentile (non-Israelite) peoples who lived along the coastlands of the Mediterranean Sea, Red Sea, and Persian Gulf. This verse repeats the theme introduced in the first servant song (42.1-7). Israel was chosen to bring justice, light, and hope to the nations (compare to 49.6).

The Servant Songs in Isaiah

49.7,8 *slaves of rulers . . . rebuild the country:* The exile in Babylon is compared to the slavery the people's ancestors faced in Egypt (Exod 1.1-14). As long as the people of Israel are in exile, they are despised by the nations (53.2,3). But God promises that those who despise and enslave Israel will honor Israel's people and bring them gifts (49.23; 60.10-18). The people of Israel would rebuild the cities of Judah (49.8). **(See the article After the Exile: God's People Return to Judea on pg 1789.)**

20 Now leave Babylon!
Celebrate as you go.
Be happy and shout
for everyone to hear,
"The LORD has rescued
his servant Israel!
21 He led us through the desert
and made water flow from a rock
to satisfy our thirst.
22 But the LORD has promised
that none who are evil
will live in peace."

The Work of the LORD's Servant

49 Everyone, listen,
even you foreign nations
across the sea.
The LORD chose me
and gave me a name
before I was born.
2 He made my words pierce
like a sharp sword
or a pointed arrow;
he kept me safely hidden
in the palm of his hand.
3 The LORD said to me,
"Israel, you are my servant;
and because of you
I will be highly honored."

4 I said to myself,
"I'm completely worn out;
my time has been wasted.
But I did it for the LORD God,
and he will reward me."

5 Even before I was born,
the LORD God chose me
to serve him and to lead back
the people of Israel.
So the LORD has honored me
and made me strong.

6 Now the LORD says to me,
"It isn't enough for you
to be merely my servant.
You must do more than lead back
survivors from the tribes
of Israel.
I have placed you here as a light
for other nations;
you must take my saving power
to everyone on earth."

The LORD Will Rescue His People

7 Israel, I am the holy LORD God,
the one who rescues you.
You are slaves of rulers
and of a nation
who despises you.[q]
Now this is what I promise:
Kings and rulers will honor you
by kneeling at your feet.
You can trust me! I am your LORD,
the holy God of Israel,
and you are my chosen ones.

The LORD Will Lead His People Home

8 This is what the LORD says:
I will answer your prayers
because I have set a time
when I will help
by coming to save you.
I have chosen you
to take my promise of hope
to other nations.[r]
You will rebuild the country

[q] **49.7** *You . . . you:* One possible meaning for the difficult Hebrew text. [r] **49.8** *my . . . nations:* One possible meaning for the difficult Hebrew text.

from its ruins,
then people will come
and settle there.
⁹You will set prisoners free
from dark dungeons
to see the light of day.

On their way home,
they will find plenty to eat,
even on barren hills.
¹⁰They won't go hungry
or get thirsty;
they won't be bothered
by the scorching sun
or hot desert winds.
I will be merciful
while leading them along
to streams of water.
¹¹I will level the mountains
and make roads.
¹²Then my people will return
from distant lands
in the north and the west
and from the city of Syene.ˢ

The LORD's Mercy

¹³Tell the heavens and the earth
to celebrate and sing;
command every mountain
to join in the song.
The LORD's people have suffered,
but he has shown mercy
and given them comfort.

¹⁴The people of Zion said,
"The LORD has turned away
and forgotten us."

¹⁵The LORD answered,
"Could a mother forget a child
who nurses at her breast?
Could she fail to love an infant
who came from her own body?
Even if a mother could forget,
I will never forget you.
¹⁶A picture of your city
is drawn on my hand.
You are always in my thoughts!

¹⁷"Your city will be built faster
than it was destroyedᵗ—
those who attacked it
will retreat and leave.
¹⁸Look around! You will see
your people coming home.
As surely as I live,
I, the LORD, promise
that your city with its people
will be as lovely as a bride
wearing her jewelry."

Jerusalem's Bright Future

¹⁹Jerusalem is now in ruins!
Nothing is left of the city.
But it will be rebuilt
and soon overcrowded;
its cruel enemies
will be gone far away.

²⁰Jerusalem is a woman
whose children were born
while she was in deep sorrowᵘ
over the loss of her husband.
Now those children
will come and seek room

49.17 *city will be built faster:* The Israelite exiles began to return to Jerusalem in 538 B.C. In 515 B.C. the newly built temple was dedicated. It took many more years before Jerusalem's city walls were rebuilt (Neh 1.1—2.6; 6.15,16).

ˢ**49.12** *Syene:* The Dead Sea Scrolls; the Standard Hebrew Text "Sinim." This city was located at the first cataract of the Nile near the site of modern-day Aswan.   ᵗ**49.17** *Your city . . . destroyed:* One possible meaning for the difficult Hebrew text.   ᵘ**49.20** *whose children . . . sorrow:* These "children" are Jews who were born in foreign countries during the time that Jerusalem was in ruins. Jerusalem probably stands for all the cities in Judah that were destroyed by the Babylonians.

50.1 *divorced . . . because of your sins:* The LORD seems to be answering an unspoken question from Israel: "Why did you divorce our mother?" God's Law did allow divorce under certain circumstances (Deut 24.1-4; Jer 3.1), and a husband could send his wife away. Israel is reminded that the LORD sent them away because of their sins. Israel, and not God, was responsible for the "divorce."

50.2,3 *rivers turn into deserts . . . sky turn dark:* The LORD called out to the people of Israel through the prophets, but many ignored the prophets' warnings. The dried up waters and darkened sky may be reminders of how the LORD rescued the Israelites from slavery in Egypt (Exod 14; 10.21-23).

50.4-10 *LORD God gives me . . . his servant:* This is the third "servant song."

50.5,6 *not rebel . . . beat my back . . . spit in my face:* Unlike Israel, the servant (prophet) listened to God's teaching and did not rebel. The servant was beaten like a criminal or a fool (see Prov 10.13; 19.30). Pulling out a man's beard and spitting in someone's face were both acts of extreme disrespect (2 Sam 10.4,5; Neh 13.25; Job 30.9,10; Matt 26.67).

in the crowded city,
²¹and Jerusalem will ask,
    "Am I really their mother?
How could I have given birth
when I was still mourning
    in a foreign land?
Who raised these children?
Where have they come from?"

²² The LORD God says:
"I will soon give a signal
    for the nations
to return your sons
and your daughters
    to the arms of Jerusalem.
²³The kings and queens
    of those nations
where they were raised
    will come and bow down.
They will take care of you
just like a slave
    taking care of a child.
Then you will know
    that I am the LORD.
You won't be disappointed
    if you trust me."

The LORD Is on Our Side

²⁴Is it possible to rescue victims
from someone strong
    and cruel?ᵛ
²⁵But the LORD has promised
    to fight on our side
and to rescue our children
from those strong
    and violent enemies.
²⁶He will make those cruel people
    dine on their own flesh
and get drunk from drinking
    their own blood.
Then everyone will know
    that the LORD is our Savior;

the powerful God of Israel
    has rescued his people.

The LORD's Power To Punish

50 The LORD says, "Children,
    I didn't divorce your mother
        or sell you to pay debts;
I divorced her and sold you
    because of your sins.
²I came and called out,
    but you didn't answer.
Have I lost my power
    to rescue and save?
At my command oceans and rivers
    turn into deserts;
fish rot and stink
    for lack of water.
³I make the sky turn dark
like the sackcloth
    you wear at funerals."

God's Servant Must Suffer

⁴The LORD God gives me
    the right words
    to encourage the weary.
Each morning he awakens me
    eager to learn his teaching;
⁵he made me willing to listen
    and not rebel or run away.

⁶I let them beat my back
    and pull out my beard.
I didn't turn aside
when they insulted me
    and spit in my face.
⁷But the LORD God keeps me
    from being disgraced.
So I refuse to give up,
because I know
    God will never let me down.

ᵛ**49.24** *cruel:* The Dead Sea Scrolls and two ancient translations; the Standard Hebrew Text "good."

⁸My protector is nearby;
no one can stand here
to accuse me of wrong.
⁹The Lord God will help me
and prove I am innocent.
My accusers will wear out
like moth-eaten clothes.

¹⁰None of you respect the Lord
or obey his servant.
You walk in the dark
instead of the light;
you don't trust the name
of the Lord your God.ʷ
¹¹Go ahead and walk in the light
of the fires you have set.ˣ
But with his own hand,
the Lord will punish you
and make you suffer.

The Lord Will Bring Comfort

51 If you want to do right
and obey the Lord,
follow Abraham's example.
He was the rock from which
you were chipped.
²God chose Abraham and Sarah
to be your ancestors.
The Lord blessed Abraham,
and from that one man
came many descendants.

³Though Zion is in ruins,
the Lord will bring comfort,
and the city will be as lovely
as the garden of Eden
that he provided.
Then Zion will celebrate;
it will be thankful
and sing joyful songs.

The Lord's Victory Will Last

⁴The Lord says:
You are my people and nation!
So pay attention to me.
My teaching will cause justice
to shine like a light
for every nation.
⁵Those who live across the sea
are eagerly waiting
for me to rescue them.
I am strong and ready;
soon I will come to save
and to rule all nations.

⁶Look closely at the sky!
Stare at the earth.
The sky will vanish like smoke;
the earth will wear out
like clothes.
Everyone on this earth
will die like flies.
But my victory will last;
my saving power never ends.

⁷If you want to do right
and obey my teaching
with all your heart,
then pay close attention.
Don't be discouraged
when others insult you
and say hurtful things.
⁸They will be eaten away
like a moth-eaten coat.
But my victory will last;
my saving power
will never end.

A Prayer for the Lord's Help

⁹Wake up! Do something, Lord.
Be strong and ready.

50.10,11 *walk in the dark . . . fires:* Most of God's people did not listen to the prophet. They chose to turn away from the Lord (walk in darkness). They will be "burned" by their own evil ways and will face the Lord's judgment.

51.2 *Abraham and Sarah:* Abraham and Sarah obeyed the Lord, who told them to leave their homeland and go to Canaan. Later generations would use Abraham's obedient action as an example of "doing right" (Gen 12.1-5; 15.6; Hab 2.4; Rom 4.1-3; Gal 3.6).

Abraham

51.6 *sky will vanish . . . saving power never ends:* Though the earth and sky will change, God's saving power will go on forever (Isa 65.17-19; 2 Pet 3.10-13).

God's Saving Love (Salvation)

ʷ**50.10** *God:* One possible meaning for the difficult Hebrew text of verse 10.   ˣ**50.11** *Go . . . set:* One possible meaning for the difficult Hebrew text.

51.9,10 *Rahab the monster . . . dry up the deep sea*: Rahab was said to be the chaos monster God defeated at creation.

51.17,18 *cup filled with the LORD's anger . . . children*: The people of Jerusalem have been punished for their sins. Drinking from the LORD's "cup of anger" is a symbol for God's judgment and punishment. Jerusalem is pictured as a mother who has lost her children.

Wake up! Do what you did
  for our people long ago.
Didn't you chop up
  Rahab[y] the monster?
¹⁰Didn't you dry up the deep sea
  and make a road for your people
    to follow safely across?
¹¹Now those you have rescued
  will return to Jerusalem,
    singing on their way.
They will be crowned
  with great happiness,
never again to be burdened
  with sadness and sorrow.

The LORD Gives Hope

¹²I am the LORD, the one
  who encourages you.
Why are you afraid
  of mere humans?
They dry up and die like grass.

¹³I spread out the heavens
  and laid foundations
    for the earth.
But you have forgotten me,
  your LORD and Creator.
All day long you were afraid
  of those who were angry
    and hoped to oppress you.
Where are they now?

¹⁴Everyone crying out in pain
  will be quickly set free;
they will be rescued
from the power of death
  and never go hungry.
¹⁵I will help them
  because I am your God,

the LORD All-Powerful,
  who makes the ocean roar.

¹⁶I have told you what to say,
  and I will keep you safe
    in the palm of my hand.
I spread out the heavens
  and laid foundations
    for the earth.
Now I say, "Jerusalem,
  your people are mine."

A Warning to Jerusalem

¹⁷Jerusalem, wake up! Stand up!
  You've drunk too much
    from the cup filled
      with the LORD's anger.
You have swallowed every drop,
  and you can't walk straight.
¹⁸Not one of your many children
  is there to guide you
    or to offer a helping hand.
¹⁹You have been destroyed
  by war and by famine;
    I cannot comfort you.[z]
²⁰The LORD your God is angry,
  and on every street corner
your children lie helpless,
  like deer trapped in nets.

²¹You are in trouble and drunk,
  but not from wine.
So pay close attention
²²to the LORD your God,
  who defends you and says,
"I have taken from your hands
the cup filled with my anger
  that made you drunk.
You will never be forced
  to drink it again.

[y]**51.9** *Rahab*: This may refer to Egypt at the time of the exodus. [z]**51.19** *I . . . you*: One possible meaning for the difficult Hebrew text.

²³Instead I will give it
   to your brutal enemies,
who treated you like dirt
   and walked all over you."

Jerusalem Can Celebrate

52 Jerusalem, wake up!
   Stand up and be strong.
Holy city of Zion,
   dress in your best clothes.
Those foreigners who ruined
your sacred city
   won't bother you again.
²Zion, rise from the dirt!
Free yourself from the rope
   around your neck.

Suffering Will End

³The LORD says:
My people, you were sold,
   but not for money;
now you will be set free,
   but not for a payment.
⁴Long ago you went to Egypt
where you lived
   as foreigners.
Then Assyria was cruel to you,
⁵ and now another nation[a]
has taken you prisoner
   for no reason at all.
Your leaders groan with pain,[b]
and day after day
   my own name is cursed.
⁶My people, you will learn
who I am and who is speaking
   because I am here.

A Message of Hope for Jerusalem

⁷ What a beautiful sight!
On the mountains a messenger
   announces to Jerusalem,
"Good news! You're saved.
There will be peace.
   Your God is now King."
⁸Everyone on guard duty,
   sing and celebrate!
Look! You can see the LORD
   returning to Zion.
⁹Jerusalem, rise from the ruins!
   Join in the singing.
The LORD has given comfort
to his people;
   he comes to your rescue.
¹⁰The LORD has shown all nations
   his mighty strength;
now everyone will see
   the saving power of our God.

A Command To Leave Babylon

¹¹Leave the city of Babylon!
   Don't touch anything filthy.
Wash yourselves. Be ready
to carry back everything sacred
   that belongs to the LORD.
¹²You won't need to run.
   No one is chasing you.
The LORD God of Israel
will lead and protect you
   from enemy attacks.

The Suffering Servant

¹³The LORD says:
   My servant will succeed!
   He will be given great praise

[a]**52.5** *another nation:* Babylonia.   [b]**52.5** *groan with pain:* One possible meaning for the difficult Hebrew text.

52.4,5 *went to Egypt:* Around 1,000 years earlier, Israel's ancestors (the family of Jacob) had gone to live in Egypt (Gen 46.1-4). The Israelite people were treated as slaves in Egypt, but the LORD saved them (Exod 1–15). Centuries later, Assyria defeated the northern kingdom of Israel.

52.7 *messenger:* In ancient times, messengers ran carrying news from place to place. They were especially important in times of battle (2 Sam 18.24-28).

52.13—53.12 *My servant:* This is the fourth and last "servant song" in ISAIAH. The servant could be the whole people of Israel.

53.2-5 *wasn't some handsome king . . . crushed because of our sins:* It is not clear who is speaking these lines. Perhaps it is the other nations who are surprised to find out that Israel's suffering did not mean that the LORD had turned away from Israel forever. The LORD intended the suffering to be a step in God's plan to restore Israel and draw all people to worship Israel's God.

53.8,9 *life was taken away . . . tomb:* How the servant died is a mystery. Some have suggested this refers to someone who had a disease such as leprosy that eats away at the skin on a person's face and hands. His death is described as the result of the sins of others.

Burial

53.10 *sacrifice to take away the sin:* The Law of Moses included instructions to Israel's priests for presenting burned offerings (sacrifices) to the LORD to remove guilt and sin (see Lev 4.1— 6.7; 6.24—7.10). **(See the chart Sacrifices and Offerings on pg 1828.)**

and the highest honors.
¹⁴Many were horrified
    at what happened to him.ᶜ
But everyone who saw him
    was even more horrified
because he suffered until
    he no longer looked human.ᵈ
¹⁵My servant will make
    nations worthy to worship me;ᵉ
    kings will be silent
    as they bow in wonder.ᶠ
They will see and think about
    things they have never seen
    or thought about before.

What God's Servant Did for Us

53 Has anyone believed us
    or seen the mighty power
    of the LORD in action?
²Like a young plant or a root
    that sprouts in dry ground,
    the servant grew up
    obeying the LORD.
He wasn't some handsome king.
Nothing about the way he looked
    made him attractive to us.
³He was hated and rejected;
his life was filled with sorrow
    and terrible suffering.
No one wanted to look at him.
We despised him and said,
    "He is a nobody!"

⁴He suffered and endured
    great pain for us,
but we thought his suffering
    was punishment from God.
⁵He was wounded and crushed
because of our sins;
by taking our punishment,
    he made us completely well.
⁶All of us were like sheep
    that had wandered off.
We had each gone our own way,
but the LORD gave him
    the punishment we deserved.

⁷He was painfully abused,
    but he did not complain.
He was silent like a lamb
    being led to the butcher,
as quiet as a sheep
    having its wool cut off.

⁸He was condemned to death
    without a fair trial.
Who could have imagined
    what would happen to him?
His life was taken away
because of the sinful things
    my peopleᵍ had done.
⁹He wasn't dishonest or violent,
but he was buried in a tomb
    among cruel, rich people.ʰ

¹⁰The LORD decided his servant
    would suffer as a sacrifice
    to take away the sin
    and guilt of others.
Now the servant will live
    to see his own descendants.ⁱ
He did everything
    the LORD had planned.

¹¹By suffering, the servant
    will learn the true meaning

ᶜ**52.14** *him:* One ancient translation; Hebrew "you." ᵈ**52.14** *human:* One possible meaning for the difficult Hebrew text of verse 14. ᵉ**52.15** *My . . . me:* Hebrew; one ancient translation "The nations will be amazed at him." ᶠ**52.15** *kings . . . wonder:* One possible meaning for the difficult Hebrew text. ᵍ**53.8** *my people:* Or "his people." ʰ**53.9** *but he . . . people:* One possible meaning for the difficult Hebrew text. ⁱ**53.10** *The LORD . . . descendants:* One possible meaning for the difficult Hebrew text.

of obeying the LORD.
Although he is innocent,
he will take the punishment
for the sins of others,
so that many of them
will no longer be guilty.
¹²The LORD will reward him
with honor and power
for sacrificing his life.
Others thought he was a sinner,
but he suffered for our sins
and asked God to forgive us.

A Promise
of the LORD's Protection

54 Sing and shout,
even though you have never
had children!
The LORD has promised that you
will have more children
than someone married
for a long time.
²Make your tents larger!
Spread out the tent pegs;
fasten them firmly.
³You and your descendants
will take over the land
of other nations.
You will settle in towns
that are now in ruins.

⁴Don't be afraid or ashamed
and don't be discouraged.
You won't be disappointed.
Forget how sinful you were
when you were young;
stop feeling ashamed
for being left a widow.
⁵The LORD All-Powerful,
the Holy God of Israel,
rules all the earth.

He is your Creator and husband,
and he will rescue you.

⁶You were like a young wife,
brokenhearted and crying
because her husband
had divorced her.
But the LORD your God says,
"I am taking you back!
⁷I rejected you for a while,
but with love and tenderness
I will embrace you again.
⁸For a while, I turned away
in furious anger.
Now I will have mercy
and love you forever!
I, your protector and LORD,
make this promise."

The LORD Promises Lasting Peace

⁹I once promised Noah that I
would never again destroy
the earth by a flood.
Now I have promised that I
will never again get angry
and punish you.
¹⁰Every mountain and hill
may disappear.
But I will always be kind
and merciful to you;
I won't break my agreement
to give your nation peace.

The New Jerusalem

¹¹Jerusalem, you are sad
and discouraged,
tossed around in a storm.
But I, the LORD,
will rebuild your city
with precious stones;ʲ

ʲ**54.11** *with precious stones:* One possible meaning for the difficult Hebrew text.

54.3 *take over the land . . . settle in towns:* Not only will Israel's people return to rebuild the towns of Judah, their descendants will occupy even more territory (26.15-18).

54.6-8 *young wife:* The prophets often portrayed Israel as the LORD's wife. See Hos 1–3, for example.

54.10 *my agreement:* The LORD's relationship with the people is Israel was based on a number of agreements.

Agreements (Covenants)

54.11,12 *Jerusalem . . . walls of gems:* Jerusalem was left in ruins when the Babylonian armies destroyed the city. Now the LORD will help the people build a new Jerusalem even more beautiful than the old one.

54.16 *metalworkers:* Metalworkers melted metal over hot coal fires and then poured the hot liquid metal into molds. After the metal cooled, the molded objects were pounded or trimmed into shape. This method was used to make weapons of iron, bronze or copper.

for your foundation
    I will use blue sapphires.
[12]Your fortresses[k]
    will be built of rubies,
your gates of jewels,
    and your walls of gems.
[13]I will teach your children
    and make them successful.

[14]You will be built on fairness
    with no fears of injustice;
every one of your worries
    will be taken far from you.
[15]I will never send anyone
    to attack your city,
and you will make prisoners
    of those who do attack.
[16]Don't forget that I created
    metalworkers who make weapons
    over burning coals.
I also created armies
    that can bring destruction.
[17]Weapons made to attack you
    won't be successful;
words spoken against you
    won't hurt at all.

My servants, Jerusalem is yours!
I, the LORD, promise
    to bless you with victory.

The LORD's Invitation

55 If you are thirsty,
    come and drink water!
If you don't have any money,
    come, eat what you want!
Drink wine and milk
    without paying a cent.
[2]Why waste your money
    on what really isn't food?
Why work hard for something

that doesn't satisfy?
Listen carefully to me,
    and you will enjoy
    the very best foods.

[3]Pay close attention!
    Come to me and live.
I will promise you
    the eternal love and loyalty
    that I promised David.
[4]I made him the leader and ruler
    of the nations;
    he was my witness to them.
[5]You will call out to nations
    you have never known.
And they have never known you,
    but they will come running
    because I am the LORD,
the holy God of Israel,
    and I have honored you.

God's Words Are Powerful

[6]Turn to the LORD!
    He can still be found.
    Call out to God! He is near.
[7]Give up your evil ways
    and your evil thoughts.
    Return to the LORD our God.
    He will be merciful
    and forgive your sins.

[8]The LORD says:
    "My thoughts and my ways
    are not like yours.
[9]Just as the heavens
    are higher than the earth,
my thoughts and my ways
    are higher than yours.

[10]"Rain and snow fall from the sky.
    But they don't return
    without watering the earth

[k]**54.12** *fortresses:* One possible meaning for the difficult Hebrew text.

that produces seeds to plant
  and grain to eat.
¹¹That's how it is with my words.
  They don't return to me
without doing everything
  I send them to do."

God's People Will Celebrate

¹²When you are set free,
  you will celebrate
    and travel home in peace.
Mountains and hills will sing
  as you pass by,
    and trees will clap.
¹³Cypress and myrtle trees
  will grow in fields
    once covered by thorns.
And then those trees will stand
  as a lasting witness
    to the glory of the LORD.

All Nations Will Be Part of God's People

56 The LORD said:
    Be honest and fair!
  Soon I will come to save you;
  my saving power will be seen
    everywhere on earth.

²I will bless everyone
  who respects the Sabbath
    and refuses to do wrong.

³Foreigners who worship me
    must not say,
  "The LORD won't let us
    be part of his people."
Men who are unable
    to become fathers
must no longer say,
    "We are dried-up trees."

⁴To them, I, the LORD, say:
    Respect the Sabbath,

obey me completely,
  and keep our agreement.
⁵Then you will be like monuments
  in my temple with your names
    written on them.
This will be much better
  than having children,
because these monuments
  will stand there forever.

⁶Foreigners will follow me.
  They will love me and worship
    in my name;
they will respect the Sabbath
  and keep our agreement.
⁷I will bring them
  to my holy mountain,
where they will celebrate
  in my house of worship.
Their sacrifices and offerings
  will always be welcome
    on my altar.
Then my house will be known
  as a house of worship
    for all nations.
⁸I, the LORD, promise
  to bring together my people
    who were taken away,
and let them join the others.

God Promises To Punish Israel's Leaders

⁹Come from the forest,
  you wild animals!
Attack and gobble up
  your victims.
¹⁰You leaders of Israel
  should be watchdogs,
    protecting my people.
But you can't see a thing,
  and you never warn them.
Dozing and daydreaming
  are all you ever do.
¹¹You stupid leaders are a pack

■ 55.11 *my words:* The LORD's "words" have power to create (Gen 1) and to save (Ps 107.20). Here the LORD's words promise to bring the people out of exile in Babylonia (46.10) and to help them build a new Jerusalem (54.11-14).

● 55.13 *Cypress and myrtle trees:* These trees will grow in areas that had earlier been turned into thorny desert by the LORD's judgment (Isa 5.5-7).

● 56.2-6 *respects the Sabbath . . . keep our agreement:* Foreigners (non-Israelites) are welcome in the new Jerusalem. However, they must follow the same rules as the Israelites. They must respect the Sabbath (Exod 20.8-11; 31.12-17; Deut 5.12-15). They must refuse to worship idols or do other "wrong." Finally, they must obey the Law of Moses.

● 56.5 *monuments:* If a person had no children to carry on his family name, a small sign or plaque could be placed in the temple so their name might be remembered (2 Sam 18.18).

● 56.8 *my people . . . others:* The Israelites who were brought back to Jerusalem from exile would be joined by non-Israelites ("others") in worshiping the LORD.

57.8 *pagan symbols . . . lovers . . . them:* The "symbols" were small idols or good luck charms believed to provide protection and fertility. "Lovers" here are the foreign gods and the idols that represented them. The people have not literally "gone to bed" with these idols. The peoples' unfaithfulness to God is like a person being unfaithful in marriage.

of hungry and greedy dogs
  that never get enough.
You are shepherds
  who mistreat your own sheep
  for selfish gain.
[12] You say to each other,
  "Let's drink till we're drunk!
  Tomorrow we'll do it again.
  We'll really enjoy ourselves."

God's Faithful People Suffer

57 God's faithful people
  are dragged off and killed,
    and no one even cares.
  Evil sweeps them away,
[2] but in death they find peace
  for obeying God.[l]

The LORD Condemns Idolatry

[3] You people are unfaithful!
  You go to fortunetellers,
    and you worship idols.
  Now pay close attention!
[4] Who are you making fun of?
  Who are you sneering at?
  Look how your sins
    have made fools of you.

[5] All you think about is sex
  under those green trees
    where idols are worshiped.
  You sacrifice your children
  on altars built in valleys
    under rocky slopes.
[6] You have chosen to worship
    idols made of stone;[m]
  you have given them offerings

of wine and grain.
  Should I be pleased?

[7] You have spread out your beds
  on the tops of high mountains,
    where you sacrifice to idols.
[8] Even in your homes
  you have placed pagan symbols
    all around your huge beds.
  Yes, you have rejected me,
  sold yourselves to your lovers,
    and gone to bed with them.[n]

[9] You smear on olive oil
  and all kinds of perfume
    to worship the god Molech.[o]
  You even seek advice
    from spirits of the dead.
[10] Though you tired yourself out
  by running after idols,
    you refused to stop.
  Your desires were so strong
    that they kept you going.

[11] Did you forget about me
  and become unfaithful
  because you were more afraid
    of someone else?
  Have I been silent so long[p]
    that you no longer fear me?
[12] You think you're so good,
    but I'll point out the truth.
[13] Ask your idols to save you
  when you are in trouble.
  Be careful though—
  it takes only a faint breath
    to blow them over.
  But if you come to me
    for protection,

[l]57.1,2 *Evil . . . God:* One possible meaning for the difficult Hebrew text.   [m]57.6 *You have . . . stone:* One possible meaning for the difficult Hebrew text.   [n]57.8 *them:* One possible meaning for the difficult Hebrew text of verse 8.   [o]57.9 *the god Molech:* Or "the king." In Hebrew "Molech" and "king" sound alike.   [p]57.11 *so long:* One possible meaning for the difficult Hebrew text.

this land and my holy mountain
    will always belong to you.

The Lord Helps the Helpless

14 The Lord says,
"Clear the road!
    Get it ready for my people."

15 Our holy God lives forever
in the highest heavens,
    and this is what he says:
Though I live high above
    in the holy place,
I am here to help those
who are humble
    and depend only on me.

16 My people, I won't stay angry
    and keep on accusing you.
After all, I am your Creator.
I don't want you to give up
    in complete despair.
17 Your greed made me furious.
That's why I punished you
    and refused to be found,
while you kept returning
    to your old sinful ways.

18 I know what you are like!
But I will heal you, lead you,
    and give you comfort,
until those who are mourning
19   start singing my praises.q
No matter where you are,
I, the Lord, will heal your
    and give you peace.

20 The wicked are a restless sea
    tossing up mud.
21 But I, the Lord, have promised

that none who are evil
    will live in peace.

True Religion

58 Shout the message!
    Don't hold back.
Say to my people Israel:
You've sinned! You've turned
    against the Lord.
2 Day after day, you worship him
and seem eager to learn
    his teachings.
You act like a nation
that wants to do right
    by obeying his laws.
You ask him about justice,
and say you enjoy
    worshiping the Lord.

3 You wonder why the Lord
    pays no attention
when you go without eating
    and act humble.
But on those same days
    that you give up eating,
you think only of yourselvess
    and abuse your workers.
4 You even get angry
    and ready to fight.
No wonder God won't listen
    to your prayers!

5 Do you think the Lord
    wants you to give up eating
and to act as humble
    as a bent-over bush?
Or to dress in sackcloth
    and sit in ashes?
Is this really what he wants
    on a day of worship?

● **57.13,14** *this land and my holy mountain:* "This land" and "my holy mountain" refer to Judah and Jerusalem's Mount Zion.

■ **57.15** *live high above in the holy place:* The Lord's home was pictured as being in the heavens, far removed from human beings (18.4). However, God also promised to be near the people by living above the sacred chest in the most holy place of the temple.

● **58.2-5** *worship . . . obeying . . . give up eating . . . dress in sackcloth:* Outwardly, the people had continued to worship the Lord. They brought the required sacrifices and offerings. They went without eating (fasted) on special holy festival days. They even wore coarse sackcloth made of goat hair and rubbed ashes on themselves to show that they were sorry for their sins.

---

q57.18,19 *until . . . praises:* One possible meaning for the difficult Hebrew text. r57.19 *heal you:* One possible meaning for the difficult Hebrew text. s58.3 *you think . . . yourselves:* One possible meaning for the difficult Hebrew text.

58.6,7 *what it really means to worship:* True worship was more than rituals and acts of honor or praise. Here, worship also means treating others with justice and fairness.

58.8 *glory of the LORD:* This probably refers to how the LORD protected the people of ancient Israel as they ran away from Egypt (Exod 13.21,22). The LORD's glory is often described as coming in thunder and lightning (see Exod 19.16-19, for example).

58.10 *your light will shine in the dark:* They will live according to the "light" of God's truth and justice, making the dark places of evil and injustice disappear.

59.5 *poisonous snakes:* This refers to "adders" or to "vipers." In the Bible, wicked people or evil in general is often represented by poisonous snakes (Ps 58.4; 140.1-3; Matt 3.7; 23.33; Jas 3.8).

⁶I'll tell you
  what it really means
    to worship the LORD.
Remove the chains of prisoners
  who are bound unjustly.
Free those who are abused!
⁷Share your food with everyone
  who is hungry;
share your home
  with the poor and homeless.
Give clothes to those in need;
  don't turn away your relatives.

⁸Then your light will shine
  like the dawning sun, and you
    will quickly be healed.
Your honesty† will protect you
  as you advance,
and the glory of the LORD
  will defend you from behind.
⁹When you beg the LORD for help,
  he will answer, "Here I am!"

Don't mistreat others
  or falsely accuse them
    or say something cruel.
¹⁰Give your food to the hungry
  and care for the homeless.
Then your light will shine
  in the dark;
your darkest hour will be
  like the noonday sun.

¹¹The LORD will always guide you
  and provide good things to eat
    when you are in the desert.
He will make you healthy.
You will be like a garden
  that has plenty of water
or like a stream
  that never runs dry.
¹²You will rebuild those houses

†**58.8** *honesty:* Or "honest leader."

left in ruins for years;
you will be known
  as a builder and repairer
    of city walls and streets.

¹³But first, you must start
  respecting the Sabbath
    as a joyful day of worship.
You must stop doing and saying
  whatever you please
    on this special day.
¹⁴Then you will truly enjoy
  knowing the LORD.
He will let you rule
  from the highest mountains
and bless you with the land
  of your ancestor Jacob.
  The LORD has spoken!

Social Injustice Is Condemned

59 The LORD hasn't lost
    his powerful strength;
he can still hear
  and answer prayers.
²Your sins are the roadblock
  between you and your God.
That's why he doesn't answer
  your prayers
or let you see his face.

³Your talk is filled with lies
  and plans for violence;
every finger on your hands
  is covered with blood.
⁴You falsely accuse others
  and tell lies in court;
sin and trouble are the names
  of your children.
⁵You eat the deadly eggs
  of poisonous snakes,
and more snakes crawl out
  from the eggs left to hatch.

You weave spider webs,
⁶but you can't make clothes
with those webs
or hide behind them.

You're sinful and brutal.
⁷You hurry off to do wrong
or murder innocent victims.
All you think about is sin;
you leave ruin and destruction
wherever you go.
⁸You don't know how
to live in peace
or to be fair with others.
The roads you make are crooked;
your followers cannot find peace.

The People Confess Their Sins

⁹No one has come to defend us
or to bring about justice.
We hoped for a day of sunshine,
but all we found
was a dark, gloomy night.
¹⁰We feel our way along,
as if we were blind;
we stumble at noon,
as if it were night.
We can see no better
than someone dead.ᵘ

¹¹We growl like bears
and mourn like doves.
We hope for justice and victory,
but they escape us.
¹²How often have we sinned
and turned against you,
the Lord God?
Our sins condemn us!
We have done wrong.
¹³We have rebelled and refused
to follow you.
Our hearts were deceitful,

and so we lied;
we planned to abuse others
and turn our backs on you.

¹⁴Injustice is everywhere;
justice seems far away.
Truth is chased out of court;
honesty is shoved aside.
¹⁵Everyone tells lies;
those who turn from crime
end up ruined.

The Lord Will Rescue His People

When the Lord noticed
that justice had disappeared,
he became very displeased.
¹⁶It disgusted him even more
to learn that no one
would do a thing about it.
So with his own powerful arm,
he won victories for truth.
¹⁷Justice was the Lord's armor;
saving power was his helmet;
anger and revenge
were his clothes.

¹⁸Now the Lord will get furious
and do to his enemies,
both near and far,
what they did to his people.
¹⁹He will attack like a flood
in a mighty windstorm.
Nations in the west and the east
will then honor and praise
his wonderful name.
²⁰The Lord has promised to rescue
the city of Zion
and Jacob's descendants
who turn from sin.

²¹The Lord says: "My people,
I promise to give you my Spirit

ᵘ**59.10** *We can . . . dead*: One possible meaning for the difficult Hebrew text.

59.18-20 *Lord . . . will . . . attack . . . rescue . . . Zion and Jacob's descendants*: The Lord will punish Israel's enemies and bring his people back to Zion (Jerusalem) from distant lands. When Zion is rebuilt and repopulated, foreign nations will see what has happened and honor Israel's Lord (see 56.2-6).

59.21 *my Spirit*: Prophets like Isaiah, who have received the Lord's Spirit will bring the Lord's message to the people.

60.1 *new day is dawning . . . glory of the* LORD *shines:* The future that the LORD has promised for Jerusalem is like a new day that dawns with a bright sunrise.

60.7 *my temple:* This refers to the new temple that was rebuilt after the exile. It was rededicated in 515 B.C.

60.9 *distant islands:* This likely refers to Greek islands in the Mediterranean Sea, where some of the people of Judah had been sold as slaves.

60.10 *Jerusalem . . . city walls . . . rebuilt:* After many of the Israelite people returned from exile, Kings Cyrus and Darius of Persia helped them rebuild the temple (Ezra 3.7; 4.24—6.15). Later, King Artaxerxes of Persia helped the Israelite people rebuild the city walls (Neh 2.1-8).

and my message.
These will be my gifts to you
  and your families forever.
I, the LORD, have spoken."

A New Day for Jerusalem

60 Jerusalem, stand up! Shine!
  Your new day is dawning.
The glory of the LORD
  shines brightly on you.
[2] The earth and its people
  are covered with darkness,
but the glory of the LORD
  is shining upon you.
[3] Nations and kings
will come to the light
  of your dawning day.

Crowds Are Coming to Jerusalem

The LORD *said:*
  [4] Open your eyes! Look around!
    Crowds are coming.
  Your sons are on their way
    from distant lands;
  your daughters are being carried
    like little children.
[5] When you see this,
  your faces will glow;
your hearts will pound
  and swell with pride.[v]
Treasures from across the sea
and the wealth of nations
  will be brought to you.
[6] Your country will be covered
  with caravans of young camels

from Midian and Ephah.[w]
The people of Sheba[x]
will bring gold and spices
  in praise of me, the LORD.
[7] Every sheep of Kedar
  will come to you;
rams from Nebaioth[y]
  will be yours as well.
I will accept them as offerings
  and bring honor to my temple.

[8] What is that sailing by
like clouds
  or like doves flying home?
[9] On those distant islands
your people are waiting
  for me, the LORD.[z]
Seagoing ships[a] lead the way
to bring them home
  with their silver and gold.
I, the holy LORD God of Israel,
do this to honor your people,
  so they will honor me.

Jerusalem Will Be Rebuilt

The LORD *said:*
[10] Jerusalem, your city walls
  will be rebuilt by foreigners;
their rulers will become
  your slaves.
I punished you in my anger;
now I will be kind
  and treat you with mercy.

[11] Your gates will be open
  day and night

---

[v]**60.5** *swell with pride:* One possible meaning for the difficult Hebrew text.   [w]**60.6** *Midian . . . Ephah:* Midian was the ancestor of a nomadic tribe of the Arabian desert, east of the Gulf of Aqaba. Ephah was a clan within the tribe of Midian.   [x]**60.6** *Sheba:* Perhaps a place in what is now southwest Arabia. The Queen of Sheba brought gifts to Solomon (1 Kings 10.1-13).   [y]**60.7** *Kedar . . . Nebaioth:* Regions in northern Arabia.   [z]**60.9** *On . . .* LORD: One possible meaning for the difficult Hebrew text.   [a]**60.9** *Seagoing ships:* See the note at 2.16.

to let the rulers of nations
lead their people to you
with all their treasures.
¹²Any nation or kingdom
that refuses to serve you
will be wiped out.
¹³Wood from Lebanon's best trees
will be brought to you—
the pines, the firs,
and the cypress trees.
It will be used in my temple
to make beautiful the place
where I rest my feet.

¹⁴The descendants of enemies
who hated and mistreated you
will kneel at your feet.
They will say, "You are Zion,
the city of the Lord,
the holy One of Israel."

¹⁵You were hated and deserted,
rejected by everyone.
But I will make you beautiful,
a city to be proud of
for all time to come.
¹⁶You will drain the wealth
of kings and foreign nations.
You will know that I,
the mighty Lord God of Israel,
have saved and rescued you.

¹⁷I will bring bronze and iron
in place of wood and stone;
in place of bronze and iron,
I will bring gold and silver.
I will appoint peace and justice
as your rulers and leaders.
¹⁸Violence, destruction, and ruin
will never again be heard of
within your borders.
"Victory" will be the name
you give to your walls;

"Praise" will be the name
you give to your gates.

¹⁹You won't need the light
of the sun or the moon.
I, the Lord your God,
will be your eternal light
and bring you honor.
²⁰Your sun will never set
or your moon go down.
I, the Lord, will be
your everlasting light,
and your days of sorrow
will come to an end.
²¹Your people will live right
and always own the land;
they are the trees I planted
to bring praise to me.
²²Even the smallest family
will be a powerful nation.
I am the Lord,
and when the time comes,
I will quickly do all this.

The Good News of Victory

61 The Spirit of the Lord God
has taken control of me!
The Lord has chosen and sent me
to tell the oppressed
the good news,
to heal the brokenhearted,
and to announce freedom
for prisoners and captives.
²This is the year
when the Lord God
will show kindness to us
and punish our enemies.

The Lord has sent me
to comfort those who mourn,
³ especially in Jerusalem.
He sent me to give them flowers
in place of their sorrow,

■ 60.21 *live right . . . own the land:*
The Lord's ancient agreement with Israel's ancestor Abraham (Gen 17.7,8) included a promise of land. But Israel could only keep the land if they "lived right," that is, obeyed the Law and worshiped only the Lord God. God "planted" Israel in the land, so the people could be examples of the Lord's justice (5.2,7).

∞   Land

61.4 *rebuild cities:* Meaning those cities destroyed when the armies of Assyria and Babylon invaded the land.

61.6 *priests and servants:* The people of Israel will have a special place as the LORD's priests among the nations (Exod 19.6).

61.8,9 *eternal agreement . . . blessed:* This agreement could be the new one the LORD promised to make with Israel (55.3-5; 59.21; also Jer 31.31-37). The very first agreement the LORD made with Israel's ancestor Abraham said that natioins would be blessed by Abraham's descendants.

62.4,5 *Your name . . . a bride:* The imagery here promises that the LORD will give Israel the attention a new husband gives his bride. The LORD's people will once again occupy the land they had been promised.

olive oil in place of tears,
and joyous praise
    in place of broken hearts.
They will be called
    "Trees of Justice,"
planted by the LORD
    to honor his name.
4 Then they will rebuild cities
that have been in ruins
    for many generations.

5 They will hire foreigners
to take care of their sheep
    and their vineyards.
6 But they themselves will be
priests and servants
    of the LORD our God.
The treasures of the nations
will belong to them,
    and they will be famous.**b**
7 They were terribly insulted
    and horribly mistreated;
now they will be greatly blessed
    and joyful forever.

The LORD Loves Justice

8 I, the LORD, love justice!
But I hate robbery
    and injustice.**c**
My people, I solemnly promise
to reward you
    with an eternal agreement.
9 Your descendants will be known
    in every nation.
All who see them will realize
that they have been blessed,
    by me, the LORD.

Celebrate and Shout

10 I celebrate and shout
    because of my LORD God.
His saving power and justice
    are the very clothes I wear.
They are more beautiful
than the jewelry worn
    by a bride or groom.
11 The LORD will bring about
justice and praise
    in every nation on earth,
like flowers blooming
    in a garden.

Jerusalem Will Be Saved

62 Jerusalem, I will speak up
    for your good.
I will never be silent
till you are safe and secure,
    sparkling like a flame.
2 Your great victory will be seen
    by every nation and king;
the LORD will even give you
    a new name.
3 You will be a glorious crown,
a royal headband
    for the LORD your God.

4 Your name will no longer be
"Deserted and Childless,"
    but "Happily Married."
You will please the LORD;
your country
    will be his bride.
5 Your people will take the land,**d**
just as a young man
    takes a bride.
The LORD will be pleased
    because of you,

b 61.6 *and . . . famous:* One possible meaning for the difficult Hebrew text.   **c** 61.8 *But . . . injustice:* One possible meaning for the difficult Hebrew text.   **d** 62.5 *Your . . . land:* One possible meaning for the difficult Hebrew text.

The LORD will bring about justice and praise in every nation on earth, like flowers blooming in a garden. ISA 61.11

just as a husband is pleased
with his bride.

⁶Jerusalem, on your walls
I have stationed guards,
whose duty it is
to speak out day and night,
without resting.
They must remind the Lord
⁷ and not let him rest
till he makes Jerusalem strong
and famous everywhere.

⁸The Lord has given his word
and made this promise:
"Never again will I give
to your enemies
the grain and grapes
for which you struggled.
⁹As surely as you harvest
your grain and grapes,
you will eat your bread
with thankful hearts,
and you will drink your wine
in my temple."

¹⁰People of Jerusalem,
open your gates!
Repair the road to the city
and clear it of stones;
raise a banner to help
the nations find their way.
¹¹Here is what the Lord has said
for all the earth to hear:
"Soon I will come to save
the city of Zion
and to reward you.
¹²Then you will be called,
'The Lord's Own People,
The Ones He Rescued!'
Your city will be known
as a good place to live
and a city full of people."

The Lord's Victory over the Nations

63 Who is this coming
from Bozrah[e] in Edom
with clothes stained red?
Who is this hero marching
in his glorious uniform?

"It's me, the Lord!
I have won the battle,
and I can save you!"

²What are those red spots?
Your clothes look stained
from trampling on grapes.[f]

³"I alone trampled the grapes!
None of the nations helped.
I trampled nations in my anger
and stained my clothes
with their blood.
⁴I did this because I wanted
to take revenge—
the time had come
to rescue my people.
⁵No one was there to help me
or to give support;
my mighty arm won the battle,
strengthened by my anger.
⁶In my fury I trampled on nations
and made them drunk;
their blood poured out
everywhere on earth."

The Lord's Goodness to His People

⁷I will tell about the kind deeds
the Lord has done.
They deserve praise!
The Lord has shown mercy

[e]63.1 *Bozrah*: The main city of Edom. [f]63.2 *trampling on grapes*: This is one way that grapes were crushed to make them into juice.

63.9 *angel saved them:* This may refer to the death angel that passed over the homes of Israelites in Egypt (Exod 12.23), or to the presence of the LORD who went with the Israelites in the wilderness (Exod 33.14).

63.10 *people turned against him:* This probably refers to the times the people rebelled while they were in the wilderness (Exod 32; Num 20.1-13; 25.1-9).

63.17 *make us turn away:* Some passages claim that Israel's rebellion was caused by the LORD making them stubborn (see Exod 4.21; Isa 6.10).

63.18 *your temple belonged to us:* Israel's first temple was built while Solomon was king of Israel (970–931 B.C.). In 587 B.C., the Babylonians destroyed the temple and much of the city of Jerusalem. A second temple was rebuilt and rededicated in 515 B.C.

to the people of Israel;
    he has been kind and good.

⁸The LORD rescued his people,
    and said, "They are mine.
    They won't betray me."
⁹It troubled the LORD
    to see them in trouble,
    and his angel saved them.ᵍ
The LORD was truly merciful,
    so he rescued his people.
He took them in his arms
    and carried them all those years.

¹⁰Then the LORD's people
    turned against him and made
    his Holy Spirit sad.
So he became their enemy
    and attacked them.
¹¹But his people remembered
    what had happened
    during the time of Moses.ʰ
Didn't the LORDⁱ bring them
    and their leaders
    safely through the sea?
Didn't heʲ give them
    his Holy Spirit?
¹²The glorious power of the LORD
    marched beside Moses.
The LORD will be praised forever
    for dividing the sea.
¹³He led his people across
    like horses running wild
    without stumbling.
¹⁴His Spirit gave them rest,
    just as cattle find rest
    when led into a valley.ᵏ
The name of the LORD was praised
    for doing these things.

A Prayer for Mercy and Help

¹⁵Please, LORD, look down
    from your holy and glorious
home in the heavens
    and see what's going on.
Have you lost interest?
    Where is your power?
Show that you care about usˡ
    and have mercy!
¹⁶Our ancestors Abraham and Jacob
    have both rejected us.
But you are still our Father;
    you have been our protector
    since ancient times.

¹⁷Why did you make us turn away
    from you, our LORD?
Why did you make us want
    to disobey you?
Please change your mind!
    We are your servants,
    your very own people.
¹⁸For a little while,
    your temple belonged to us;ᵐ
and now our enemies
    have torn it down.
¹⁹We act as though you
    had never ruled us
    or called us your people.

64 Rip the heavens apart!
    Come down, LORD;
        make the mountains tremble.
²Be a spark that starts a fire
    causing water to boil.ⁿ
Then your enemies will know
    who you are;

ᵍ**63.9** *It . . . them:* One possible meaning for the difficult Hebrew text.   ʰ**63.11** *But . . . Moses:* One possible meaning for the difficult Hebrew text.   ⁱ**63.11** *the* LORD: Or "Moses."   ʲ**63.11** *he:* Or "Moses."   ᵏ**63.14** *His . . . valley:* One possible meaning for the difficult Hebrew text.   ˡ**63.15** *us:* Hebrew "me."   ᵐ**63.18** *For . . . us:* One possible meaning for the difficult Hebrew text.   ⁿ**64.2** *Be . . . boil:* One possible meaning for the difficult Hebrew text.

Please, LORD, look down from your holy and glorious home in the heavens and see what's going on. Have you lost interest?
ISA 63.15

all nations will tremble
    because you are nearby.

³Your fearsome deeds
    have completely amazed us;
even the mountains shake
    when you come down.
⁴You are the only God
    ever seen or heard of
who works miracles
    for his followers.

⁵You help all who gladly obey
and do what you want,
    but sin makes you angry.
Only by your help
    can we ever be saved.^o
⁶We are unfit to worship you;
each of our good deeds
    is merely a filthy rag.
We dry up like leaves;
    our sins are storm winds
    sweeping us away.
⁷No one worships in your name
    or remains faithful.
You have turned your back on us
    and let our sins melt us away.^P

⁸You, Lord, are our Father.
    We are nothing but clay,
but you are the potter
    who molded us.
⁹Don't be so furious
    or keep our sins
    in your thoughts forever!
Remember that all of us
    are your people.
¹⁰Every one of your towns
    has turned into a desert,
    especially Jerusalem.

¹¹Zion's glorious and holy temple
    where our ancestors praised you
    has been destroyed by fire.
Our beautiful buildings
    are now a pile of ruins.
¹²When you see these things,
    how can you just sit there
    and make us suffer more?

The Lord Will Punish the Guilty

65 I, the Lord, was ready
    to answer even those
        who were not asking
and to be found by those
        who were not searching.
To a nation that refused
    to worship me,^q
        I said, "Here I am!"

²All day long I have reached out
    to stubborn and sinful people
        going their own way.
³They keep making me angry
        by sneering at me,
while offering sacrifices
        to idols in gardens
and burning incense
        to them on bricks.
⁴They spend their nights
        hiding in burial caves;
they eat the meat of pigs,^r
cooked in sauces
        made of stuff unfit to eat.
⁵And then they say to others,
"Don't come near us!
    We're dedicated to God."
Such people are like smoke,
    irritating my nose all day.
⁶I have written this down;

64.8 *our Father . . . the potter:* The Lord created and formed Israel (43.1) as a potter shapes a piece of clay into something useful or beautiful.

64.10,11 *your towns . . . temple . . . destroyed:* This is another reference to the Babylonian army's destruction of Jerusalem and other towns of Judah.

65.4,5 *burial caves . . . meat of pigs . . . dedicated to God:* People sometimes went to burial caves to try to speak to the spirits of the dead. This was forbidden in the Law (Lev 19.26; Deut 18.11; 1 Sam 28.3; 2 Kgs 23.4). Some animals, such as pigs, were considered unclean, according to the Law of Moses, and could not be touched or eaten (Deut 14.7,8). Those who did these things claimed to be holy, perhaps so holy that they were actually above the Law.

Purity (Clean and Unclean)

^o**64.5** *saved:* One possible meaning for the difficult Hebrew text of verse 5.   ^P**64.7** *and let . . . away:* One possible meaning for the difficult Hebrew text.   ^q**65.1** *refused . . . me:* One possible meaning for the difficult Hebrew text.   ^r**65.4** *burial . . . pigs:* Coming in contact with the dead or eating the meat of pigs made a person unacceptable to God.

65.9,10 *land of mountains...Achor Valley:* The "land of mountains" is Canaan. Canaan stretched from the plain of Sharon on the Mediterranean coast in the west to the Achor Valley near Jericho in the east. These two places stand for the whole country.

65.11 *my holy mountain:* Meaning Mount Zion in Jerusalem. **(See Map 3 on pg 1881.)**

65.11 *gods... "Good Luck" and "Fate":* This probably refers to two Syrian and Arabian gods of fortune. Trusting in these gods and their "good luck charms" would lead to disaster (65.12).

65.13-15 *servants... sinners... new names to my servants:* "Sinners" refers to all who have turned away from the LORD, including many of the Israelites. The "servants" are those who worship and obey the LORD. These servants will be given new names, as though they were beginning a new life.

65.16 *in my name:* Prayers and promises were to be made in the name of the LORD, who alone is the source of all blessings. To make a promise in the name of another god would be a sin.

Making Promises (Vows)

I won't keep silent.
  I'll pay them back
    just as their sins deserve.
⁷I, the LORD, will make them pay
  for their sins and for those
    of their ancestors—
they have disgraced me
  by burning incense
    on mountains.

⁸Here is what the LORD says:
  A cluster of grapes
    that produces wine
      is worth keeping!
So, because of my servants,
  I won't destroy everyone.
⁹I have chosen the people
  of Israel and Judah,
and I will bless them
  with many descendants.
They will settle here
  in this land of mountains,
    and it will be theirs.
¹⁰My people will worship me.
Then the coastlands of Sharon
  and the land as far
    as Achor Valley^s
will turn into pastureland
  where cattle and sheep
    will feed and rest.

¹¹What will I, the LORD, do
  if any of you reject me
    and my holy mountain?
What will happen to you
  for offering food and wine
to the gods you call
  "Good Luck" and "Fate"?
¹²Your luck will end!

I will see to it that you
  are slaughtered with swords.
You refused to answer
  when I called out;
you paid no attention
  to my instructions.
Instead, you did what I hated,
  knowing it was wrong.

¹³I, the LORD God, will give
  food and drink to my servants,
    and they will celebrate.
But all of you sinners
  will go hungry and thirsty,
    overcome with disgrace.
¹⁴My servants will laugh and sing,
  but you will be sad
    and cry out in pain.
¹⁵I, the LORD God, promise
  to see that you are killed
and that my chosen servants use
  your names as curse words.
But I will give new names^t
  to my servants.^{u}
¹⁶I am God! I can be trusted.
Your past troubles are gone;
  I no longer think of them.
When you pray for someone
  to receive a blessing,
or when you make a promise,
  you must do it in my name.
I alone am the God
  who can be trusted.

The LORD's New Creation

¹⁷I am creating new heavens
  and a new earth;
everything of the past

^{s}**65.10** *coastlands of Sharon . . . Achor Valley:* Sharon is the coastal plain on the west, and Achor Valley is in the east near Jericho. These two places stand for the whole country. ^{t}**65.15** *new names:* The giving of a new name suggests the beginning of a new life. ^{u}**65.15** *But I . . . servants:* One possible meaning for the difficult Hebrew text.

The LORD says, "I am creating new heavens and a new earth; everything of the past will be forgotten." ISA 65.17

will be forgotten.

¹⁸Celebrate and be glad forever!
I am creating a Jerusalem,
full of happy people.
¹⁹I will celebrate with Jerusalem
and all its people;
there will be no more crying
or sorrow in that city.

²⁰No child will die in infancy;
everyone will live
a very long life.
Anyone a hundred years old
will be considered young,
and to die younger than that
will be considered a curse.

²¹My people will live
in the houses they build;
they will enjoy grapes
from their own vineyards.
²²No one will take away
their homes or vineyards.
My chosen people will live
to be as old as trees,
and they will enjoy
what they have earned.
²³Their work won't be wasted,
and their children won't die
of dreadful diseases.^v
I will bless their children
and their grandchildren.
²⁴I will answer their prayers
before they finish praying.

²⁵Wolves and lambs
will graze together;
lions and oxen
will feed on straw.
Snakes will eat only dirt!
They won't bite or harm anyone
on my holy mountain.
I, the Lord, have spoken!

True Worship

66 The Lord said:
Heaven is my throne;
the earth is my footstool.
What kind of house
could you build for me?
In what place will I rest?
²I have made everything;
that's how it all came to be.^w
I, the Lord, have spoken.

The people I treasure most
are the humble—
they depend only on me
and tremble when I speak.

³You sacrifice oxen to me,
and you commit murder;
you sacrifice lambs to me
and dogs to other gods;
you offer grain to me
and pigs' blood to idols;
you burn incense to me
and praise your idols.^x
You have made your own choice
to do these disgusting things
that you enjoy so much.
⁴You refused to answer
when I called out;
you paid no attention
to my instructions.

^v**65.23** *their children . . . diseases*: One possible meaning for the difficult Hebrew text. ^w**66.2** *that's . . . be*: One possible meaning for the difficult Hebrew text. ^x**66.3** *You sacrifice oxen . . . idols*: Or "Sacrificing oxen to me is the same as murder; sacrificing lambs to me is the same as sacrificing dogs to other gods; offering grain to me is the same as offering pigs' blood to idols; and burning incense to me is the same as praising idols."

65.20-23 *No child . . . dreadful diseases*: The new Jerusalem will be a place of good health, long life, and prosperity. All these are signs of God's blessing and presence.

Heaven

66.4 *my instructions*: Meaning the Lord's Law or the words of the prophets.

66.8 *Jerusalem is like a mother:* Jerusalem is again pictured as a mother. With the LORD's help, she will give birth to new sons and daughters, and her labor will be short and nearly painless. The city will be a place of comfort.

Instead, you did what I hated,
    knowing it was wrong.
Now I will punish[y] you
    in a way you dread the most.

The LORD Will Help Jerusalem

⁵If you tremble
when the LORD speaks,
    listen to what he says:
"Some of your own people hate
and reject you because of me.
    They make fun and say,
'Let the LORD show his power!
Let us see him
    make you truly happy.'[z]
But those who say these things
    will be terribly ashamed."

⁶Do you hear that noise
in the city and those shouts
    coming from the temple?
It is the LORD shouting
    as he punishes his enemies.

⁷Have you ever heard of a woman
who gave birth to a child
    before having labor pains?
⁸Who ever heard of such a thing
    or imagined it could happen?
Can a nation be born in a day
    or come to life in a second?
Jerusalem is like a mother
who gave birth to her children
    as soon as she was in labor.
⁹The LORD is the one
    who makes birth possible.
And he will see that Zion
has many more children.
    The LORD has spoken.

¹⁰If you love Jerusalem,
    celebrate and shout!
If you were in sorrow
because of the city,
    you can now be glad.
¹¹She will nurse and comfort you,
    just like your own mother,
until you are satisfied.
You will fully enjoy
    her wonderful glory.

¹²The LORD has promised:
    "I will flood Jerusalem
with the wealth of nations
    and make the city prosper.
Zion will nurse you at her breast,
carry you in her arms,
    and hold you in her lap.
¹³I will comfort you there
like a mother
    comforting her child."

¹⁴When you see this happen,
    you will celebrate;
your strength will return
    faster than grass can sprout.
Then everyone will know
that the LORD provides help
    for his servants,
but he is angry
    with his enemies.
¹⁵The LORD will come down
like a whirlwind
    with his flaming chariots.
He will be furiously angry
and punish his enemies
    with fire.
¹⁶The LORD's fiery sword
    will bring justice
everywhere on this earth
    and execute many people.

ʸ**66.4** *punish:* One possible meaning for the difficult Hebrew text.   ᶻ**66.5** *Some . . . happy:* One possible meaning for the difficult Hebrew text.

A Threat and a Promise

17Some of you get yourselves ready and go to a garden to worship a foreign goddess.[a] You eat the meat of pigs, lizards, and mice. But I, the LORD, will destroy you for this.

18I know everything you do and think! The time has now come[b] to bring together the people of every language and nation and to show them my glory **19**by proving what I can do.[c] I will send the survivors to Tarshish, Pul,[d] Lud, Meshech,[e] Tubal, Javan,[f] and to the distant islands. I will send them to announce my wonderful glory to nations that have never heard about me.

20They will bring your relatives from the nations as an offering to me, the LORD. They will come to Jerusalem, my holy mountain, on horses, chariots, wagons, mules, and camels.[g] It will be like the people of Israel bringing the right offering to my temple. **21**I promise that some of them will be priests and others will be helpers in my temple. I, the LORD, have spoken.

22I also promise that you will always have descendants and will never be forgotten, just as the new heavens and the new earth that I create will last forever. **23**On the first day of each month and on each Sabbath, everyone will worship me. I, the LORD, have spoken.

24 My people will go out and look at the dead bodies of those who turned against me. The worms there never die, the fire never stops burning, and the sight of those bodies will be disgusting to everyone.

● 66.19 *Tarshish . . . Javan*: These locations were meant to represent the entire known world.

● 66.23 *first day . . . Sabbath*: Trumpets were blown on the first day of every month, which began with the "new moon" (Ps 81.3; Num 28.11-15). Special sacrifices were offered on this day, also known as the New Moon Festival.

■ 66.24 *worms . . . fire*: The book ends with a picture of the LORD's eternal punishment for those who have turned against him (see 1.2; 1.31). Worms are constant companions in the world of the dead (14.11), and fire often appears as God's punishment of evildoers. In Mark 9.48, this verse is quoted in part as a description of "hell."

∞ Hell

[a]**66.17** *Some . . . goddess*: One possible meaning for the difficult Hebrew text. [b]**66.18** *I . . . come*: One possible meaning for the difficult Hebrew text. [c]**66.19** *by . . . do*: One possible meaning for the difficult Hebrew text. [d]**66.19** *Pul*: Hebrew; one ancient translation "Put," a country in Africa, but neither the location of Pul or Put is known for certain. [e]**66.19** *Meshech*: One ancient translation; Hebrew "those who use bows and arrows." [f]**66.19** *Tarshish . . . Javan*: Tarshish may have been a Phoenician city in Spain; Put (see note on Pul) and Lud were African people; Meshech and Tubal were regions south or southeast of the Black Sea; the Javan were people of Asia Minor and the Greek islands. [g]**66.20** *camels*: One possible meaning for the difficult Hebrew text.

Reflection Questions About Isaiah 1.1—66.24

1. When and where did Isaiah bring the LORD's message to the people (1.1)?

2. ISAIAH 1 introduces some themes that will be repeated throughout the whole book. What are some of these key themes?

3. Who was "Immanuel" (7.13-16)? What, if any, connection do you think there is between Immanuel, the "child" (9.6,7), and the "sprout" from the stump of David's family (11.1-9)?

4. Chapters 13–23 provide messages about many of the neighboring nations. How would you describe the news given in most of these messages?

5. Name two or three reasons why Isaiah 24–27 is often referred to as "apocalyptic."

6. How does the end of chapter 39 serve as a kind of "bridge" between the first main section of ISAIAH (1–39) and the second main section (40–55)?

7. Isaiah 40–55 often describes a "servant" chosen by the LORD. In the following passages decide who the servant could be and describe what the servant is chosen to do:

a. 41.8-11   **e.** 49.1-6
b. 42.1-7,19   **f.** 50.4-11
c. 44.1-5,21   **g.** 52.1—53.12
d. 44.28—45.4

8. According to 58.6-10 and 61.1-3, what is true worship of the LORD?

9. Describe the "new heaven and new earth" the LORD was creating (65.17-25). If our world today could have a fresh new start, what would need to be different?

10. Isaiah's prophecies are based on the belief that the LORD of Israel has acted and will act at various times, using earthly rulers and armies to punish or to save. What do you think of the idea that God can or may be directing earthly events today? Choose a favorite passage from ISAIAH and explain why it is meaningful to you.

jeremiah

*Imagine you were chosen to speak God's word to the nations.
How would you respond? Read this book to find out how the
young prophet Jeremiah responded when God chose him. And
discover the plans God has for God's people.*

WHAT MAKES JEREMIAH SPECIAL?

The message of JEREMIAH is one of doom before the fall of Judah, and one of hope after the fall. Jeremiah began to serve as God's prophet in 627 B.C. when he was a young man, possibly less than 20 years old, and continued until shortly after the Babylonians captured Jerusalem in 586 B.C. During Jeremiah's time as prophet, he warned the kings, priests, and people of Judah of their coming doom.

WHAT'S THE STORY BEHIND THE SCENE?

Jeremiah's message was delivered during the reign of the last five kings of Judah, beginning in the "thirteenth year that Josiah was king of Judah" (627 B.C.). Josiah made a series of reforms that were based on a scroll containing parts of the book of DEUTERONOMY. This scroll, discovered in the Jerusalem temple around 621 B.C., prompted Josiah to get rid of foreign gods in the Jerusalem temple and to encourage the people to turn back to the LORD.

After Josiah was killed by the Egyptians in battle in 609 B.C., there was political upheaval. Josiah's son Jehoahaz was replaced on the throne by Jehoiakim, who brought back the worship of foreign gods and burned Jeremiah's message. In 598 B.C., the Babylonian king Nebuchadnezzar invaded Judah and put puppet king Zedekiah on the throne; 12 years later, in 586 B.C., Nebuchadnezzar returned and destroyed Jerusalem and took many of the Jewish people back to exile in Babylon. Jeremiah, however, remained in Jerusalem. His message changed from doom and destruction to hope and the promise of a new agreement between the LORD and his people. He was later forced to flee to Egypt, which is the last we know of this great prophet.

HOW IS JEREMIAH CONSTRUCTED?

JEREMIAH does not describe events in chronological order. The book is roughly grouped by subjects, not dates.

The following is one way that JEREMIAH can be outlined:

Introducing Jeremiah, the LORD's prophet (1.1-19)
Words of warning and punishment (2.1—25.38)
    Jeremiah's early messages (2.1—6.30)
    Scenes from Jeremiah's life (7.1—13.27)
    A time of great sadness (14.1—17.27)
    Plots on Jeremiah's life and warnings to Judah (18.1—25.38)
Jeremiah against the lying prophets (26.1—29.32)
A homecoming and a new beginning (30.1—33.26)
Disaster for Judah and Jerusalem (34.1—44.30)
    Scenes from Jeremiah's ministry (34.1—38.28)
    The fall of Jerusalem and the escape to Egypt (39.1—44.30)
The LORD's judgment against the nations (45.1—51.64)
Another account of the fall of Jerusalem (52.1-34)

eremiah includes prophecies, autobiography, history, and sermons. The book is arranged by themes rather than according to a historical timeline. Chapter 36 may contain the story of how this book was composed. It provides a vivid portrait of the prophet being called as a young man to speak God's message. Jeremiah accepts this task and remains a faithful messenger of God, even during his nation's greatest crisis. Jeremiah began his ministry as a prophet sometime around 627 B.C. and remained active even after 586 B.C., when Jerusalem was captured by the Babylonians. Throughout his career as the Lord's prophet, Jeremiah urged the people to remain faithful to the Lord, and warned the people of Judah, the southern Israelite kingdom, that their nation would be conquered. Speaking the Lord's message to powerful people in Judah who had turned away from God brought Jeremiah suffering. Considered a traitor, he was arrested, imprisoned, beaten, and finally forced to flee his own land. Jeremiah proclaimed a hopeful message for the people taken into captivity: the Lord's promise to set the people free and to make a new agreement with the people of Israel and Judah.

Outline

1

My name is Jeremiah. I am a priest, and my father Hilkiah and everyone else in my family are from Anathoth in the territory of the Benjamin tribe. This book contains the things that the LORD told me to say. [2]The LORD first spoke to me in the thirteenth year that Josiah[a] was king of Judah, [3]and he continued to speak to me during the rule of Josiah's son Jehoiakim.[b] The last time the LORD spoke to me was in the fifth month[c] of the eleventh year that Josiah's son Zedekiah[d] was king. That was also when the people of Jerusalem were taken away as prisoners.

The LORD Chooses Jeremiah

[4]The LORD said:

[5]"Jeremiah, I am your Creator,
    and before you were born,
I chose you to speak for me
    to the nations."

[6]I replied, "I'm not a good speaker, LORD, and I'm too young."

[7]"Don't say you're too young," the LORD answered. "If I tell you to go and speak to someone, then go! And when I tell you what to say, don't leave out a word! [8]I promise to be with you and keep you safe, so don't be afraid."

[9]The LORD reached out his hand, then he touched my mouth and said, "I am giving you the words to say, [10]and I am sending you with authority to speak to the nations for me. You will tell them of doom and destruction, and of rising and rebuilding again."

[11]The LORD showed me something in a vision. Then he asked, "What do you see, Jeremiah?"

I answered, "A branch of almonds that ripen early."

[12]"That's right," the LORD replied, "and I always rise early[e] to keep a promise."

---

[a]1.2 *Josiah*: Ruled 640–609 B.C.   [b]1.3 *Jehoiakim*: Ruled 609–598 B.C.   [c]1.3 *fifth month*: Ab, the fifth month of the Hebrew calendar, from about mid-July to mid-August.   [d]1.3 *Zedekiah*: Ruled 598–586 B.C.   [e]1.11,12 *almonds . . . rise early*: In Hebrew "almonds that ripen early" sounds like "always rise early."

● 1.1 *Jeremiah*: Jeremiah was a descendant of Abiathar, one of the chief priests in the time of King David (1 Sam 22.20; 2 Sam 20.25). Abiathar was a Levite priest, while David's other chief priest was Zadok. The descendants of these two priests struggled with each other to be in charge of Israel's religious life.

Jeremiah's strong criticism of the rulers from David's family and the Jerusalem temple probably can be traced, in part, to his family's ancient struggle with the Zadokite priests. In addition, Jeremiah argues that God's Law, given to the Moses and the people of Israel at Mount Sinai, should guide the life of God's people, more so than the royal family or proper worship at the temple.

● 1.1 *Anathoth . . . Benjamin tribe*: Anathoth, Jeremiah's hometown, was over two miles northeast of Jerusalem. Benjamin was the youngest son of Jacob and Rachel (Gen 35.16-18). The Benjamin tribe, the smallest of Israel's tribes, was located in an area to the north of Judah. Together the tribes of Judah and Benjamin formed Israel's southern kingdom, also known as Judah. **(See Maps 3 and 6 on pgs 1881 and 1884.)**

■ 1.6 *I'm too young*: It is not clear just how old Jeremiah was. Compare his response to that of Moses (Exod 4.10) and Isaiah (Isa 6.8).

■ 1.10 *tell them of doom . . . and rebuilding again*: Jeremiah's message is twofold: God will destroy and overthrow Judah, and then God will restore and rebuild God's people.

The LORD said: "Jeremiah, I am your Creator, and before you were born, I chose you to speak for me to the nations."
JER 1.4,5

1.13 *pot of boiling water in the north:* The boiling pot stands for invading armies that will attack Judah and Jerusalem from the north. The exact identity of this enemy is not clear, though the Babylonians eventually did capture Jerusalem a few years after defeating the Assyrians, who had controlled the area to the north of Judah. **(See Map 7 on pg 1885.)**

2.2,3 *Jerusalem . . . my young bride . . . the first part of the harvest:* Jerusalem was the capital city of Judah, and the center of the religious life of the people of Israel. The LORD is often described as Israel's husband (Isa 54.5; Hos 2.16-20). God chose Israel, and Israel was to be devoted to God alone, just as a husband and wife promise to be faithful to one another. The people of Israel were supposed to offer the first part of the harvest as a gift to the LORD (Lev 23.10,11). Like this best "first part" Israel was considered the LORD's best.

Israel

2.8 *priests . . . leaders . . . prophets:* The priests have ignored the terms of the agreement with God, which included obedience to God's commandments. Some false prophets claimed to get messages from Baal, the Canaanite god of rain and fertility. Jeremiah will oppose all these people in power (1.18,19). **(See the article Prophets and Prophecy on pg 1791.)**

Israel's Priests

Canaanite Gods and Goddesses

13Then the LORD showed me something else and asked, "What do you see now?"

I answered, "I see a pot of boiling water in the north, and it's about to spill out toward us."

14The LORD said:

I will pour out destruction
all over the land.
15Just watch while I send
for the kings of the north.
They will attack and capture
Jerusalem and other towns,
then set up their thrones
at the gates of Jerusalem.

16I will punish my people,
because they are guilty
of turning from me
to worship idols.

17Jeremiah, get ready!
Go and tell the people
what I command you to say.
Don't be frightened by them,
or I will make you terrified
while they watch.

18My power will make you strong
like a fortress
or a column of iron
or a wall of bronze.
You will oppose all of Judah,
including its kings and leaders,
its priests and people.
19They will fight back,
but they won't win.
I, the LORD, give my word—
I won't let them harm you.

Israel's Unfaithfulness

2 The LORD told me 2to go to Jerusalem and tell everyone that he had said:

When you were my young bride,
you loved me and followed me
through the barren desert.
3You belonged to me alone,
like the first part of the harvest,
and I severely punished
those who mistreated you.

4Listen, people of Israel,f
5 and I, the LORD, will speak.
I was never unfair
to your ancestors,
but they left me
and became worthless
by following worthless idols.
6Your ancestors refused
to ask for my help,
though I had rescued them
from Egypt
and led them through
a treacherous, barren desert,
where no one lives
or dares to travel.

7I brought you here to my land,
where food is abundant,
but you made my land filthy
with your sins.
8The priests who teach my laws
don't care to know me.
Your leaders rebel against me;
your prophets
give messages from Baal
and worship false gods.

f2.4 *Israel:* After the nation was divided, the northern kingdom was called "Israel," and the southern kingdom was called "Judah" (see 1 Kings 12.1-20). In 722 B.C. the Assyrians conquered the northern kingdom, and Judah was all that was left. And so in the book of Jeremiah the name "Israel" is most often used of the southern kingdom.

The Lord Accuses His People

⁹I will take you to court
and accuse you
and your descendants
*¹⁰of a crime that no nation
has ever committed before.
Just ask anyone, anywhere,
from the eastern deserts
to the islands in the west.
¹¹You will find that no nation
has ever abandoned its gods
even though they were false.
I am the true and glorious God,
but you have rejected me
to worship idols.
¹²Tell the heavens
to tremble with fear!
¹³You, my people, have sinned
in two ways—
you have rejected me, the source
of life-giving water,
and you've tried to collect water
in cracked and leaking pits
dug in the ground.

¹⁴People of Israel,
you weren't born slaves;
you were captured in war.
¹⁵Enemies roared like lions
and destroyed your land;
towns lie burned and empty.
¹⁶Soldiers from the Egyptian towns
of Memphis and Tahpanhes
have cracked your skulls.
¹⁷It's all your own fault!
You stopped following me,
the Lord your God,
¹⁸and you trusted the power

of Egypt and Assyria.ᵍ
¹⁹Your own sins will punish you,
because it was a bitter mistake
for you to reject me
without fear of punishment.
I, the Lord All-Powerful,
have spoken.

²⁰Long ago you left me
and broke all ties between us,
refusing to be my servant.
Now you worship other gods
by having sex
on hilltops or in the shade
of large trees.ʰ
²¹You were a choice grapevine,
but you have become
a wild, useless vine.

Israel Is Stained with Guilt

²²The Lord said:

People of Israel,
you are stained with guilt,
and no soap or bleach
can wash it away.
²³You deny your sins
and say, "We aren't unclean.
We haven't worshiped Baal."ⁱ
But think about what you do
in Hinnom Valley.ʲ
You run back and forth
like young camels,
as you rush to worship one idol
after another.
²⁴You are a female donkey
sniffing the desert air,
wanting to mate

2.13 *water . . . leaking pits:* In Judah, rainfall was scarce during the dry part of the year, so the people made cisterns, or pits in the ground, for holding water. A cracked cistern was useless because it could not hold water. The idols are like cracked cisterns.

2.16 *Memphis and Tahpanhes:* Israelite leaders met with Egyptians in these cities to discuss a military alliance against the Assyrians (2.15). The Egyptian ruler Neco killed Judah's King Josiah at the Battle of Megiddo in 609 B.C. Judah remained under Egyptian control until the Battle of Carchemish in 605 B.C. when Egypt fell to Babylon. **(See Map 2 on pg 1880.)**

2.18 *trusted the power of Egypt and Assyria:* Israel's leaders begged for help from one of these two powerful empires.

2.19 *LORD All-Powerful:* This Hebrew name, *Yahweh Sebaoth*, is also translated as "LORD of hosts." The "hosts" in this ancient name refer to the armies of Israel (1 Sam 4.4), or to the heavenly stars, which God created.

Prostitution in the Bible

2.23 *Hinnom Valley:* This narrow valley, located south of Jerusalem, is mentioned in the Old Testament as a place where children were sometimes sacrificed to the god Molech by burning them to death (Lev 18.21; 20.1-5; 2 Kgs 23.10; Jer 7.30,31; 19.1-6). **(See Map 5 on pg 1883.)**

ᵍ2.18 *trusted . . . Assyria:* Hebrew "went to Egypt and drank from the Shihor River, and you went to Assyria and drank from the Euphrates River." ʰ2.20 *having sex . . . trees:* In some Canaanite religions, worshipers had sex with temple prostitutes, who represented their gods; many of the Canaanite places of worship were on hilltops or under large trees. ⁱ2.23 *Baal:* The Hebrew text has "the Baals," probably because the god Baal was believed to be present in different forms at different places of worship. ʲ2.23 *Hinnom Valley:* Hebrew "the valley" (see 7.31-32; 19.1-6).

2.27,28 *stone idols and sacred poles . . . gods you made:* These sacred stones and carved wooden poles represented the male (stone) and female (wood) fertility gods of Canaan. People were praying to these idols, which could be found in every city. They ignored the LORD God who alone could help Israel.

Canaanite Gods and Goddesses

2.31-34 *Did I abandon you . . . killed innocent people:* Though God saved the people from slavery in Egypt and did not abandon them in the desert, Israel worshiped idols and asked for help from foreign powers. In this way, they were like an unfaithful bride who acted like a prostitute. The people and their leaders also were guilty of treating others unfairly, especially the poor (see Isa 1.15-17; Amos 2.6-8; 5.10-12).

Justice

2.35 *take you to court:* God's judgment of Israel and other nations sometimes is described by the prophets in terms of a hearing or trial (Deut 30.19; Jer 2.9; Mic 6.1,2).

3.1 *If a divorced woman marries:* According to the Law of Moses, a woman could never return to the husband who had divorced her, even if she remarried and her second husband died or divorced her also (see Deut 24.1-4). This would cause the land to be polluted (not acceptable to God). Yet, God was willing to be more merciful than this law and invited Israel to come back to him (Jer 3.12-14).

with just anyone.
    You are an easy catch!
[25]Your shoes are worn out,
    and your throat is parched
from running here and there
    to worship foreign gods.
"Stop!" I shouted,
but you replied, "No!
    I love those gods too much."

[26]You and your leaders
are more disgraceful
    than thieves—
you and your kings,
    your priests and prophets
[27]worship stone idols
    and sacred poles
as if they had created you
    and had given you life.
You have rejected me,
but when you're in trouble,
    you cry to me for help.
[28]Go cry to the gods you made!
There should be enough of them
    to save you,
because Judah has as many gods
    as it has towns.

Israel Rebels against the LORD

[29]The LORD said to Israel:

You accuse me of not saving you,
    but I say you have rebelled.
[30]I tried punishing you,
but you refused
    to come back to me,
and like fierce lions
    you killed my prophets.

[31]Now listen to what I say!
Did I abandon you in the desert
    or surround you with darkness?
You are my people,

yet you have told me,
    "We'll do what we want,
and we refuse
    to worship you!"
[32]A bride could not forget
to wear her jewelry
    to her wedding,
but you have forgotten me
    day after day.
[33]You are so clever
at finding lovers
that you could give lessons
    to a prostitute.
[34]You killed innocent people
    for no reason at all.
And even though their blood
    can be seen on your clothes,
[35]you claim to be innocent,
    and you want me to stop
    being angry with you.
So I'll take you to court,
    and we'll see who is right.

[36]When Assyria let you down,
    you quickly ran to Egypt,
but you'll find no help there,
[37]and you will leave
    in great sadness.[k]
I won't let you find help
    from those you trust.

Sin and Shame

3   The LORD said to the people of Israel:
    If a divorced woman marries,
can her first husband
    ever marry her again?
No, because this
    would pollute the land.
But you have more gods
than a prostitute has lovers.
    Why should I take you back?
[2]Just try to find one hilltop

[k]**2.37** *in great sadness:* Or "as prisoners."

where you haven't gone
  to worship other gods
    by having sex.[l]
You sat beside the road
  like a robber in ambush,
except you offered yourself
  to every passerby.
Your sins of unfaithfulness
  have polluted the land.
[3]So I, the Lord, refused
  to let the spring rains fall.
But just like a prostitute,
  you still have no shame
    for what you have done.
[4]You call me your father
  or your long-lost friend;
[5]you beg me to stop being angry,
  but you won't stop sinning.

The Lord Asks Israel To Come Back to Him

[6] When Josiah[m] was king, the Lord said: Jeremiah, the kingdom of Israel[n] was like an unfaithful wife who became a prostitute on the hilltops and in the shade of large trees.[o] [7-8]I knew that the kingdom of Israel had been unfaithful and committed many sins, yet I still hoped she might come back to me. But she didn't, so I divorced her and sent her away.

Her sister, the kingdom of Judah, saw what happened, but she wasn't worried in the least, and I watched her become unfaithful like her sister. [9]The kingdom of Judah wasn't sorry for being a prostitute, and she didn't care that she had made both herself and the land unclean by worshiping idols of stone and wood. [10]And worst of all,

the people of Judah pretended to come back to me. [11]Even the people of Israel were honest enough not to pretend.

[12]Jeremiah, shout toward the north:

Israel, I am your Lord—
  come back to me!
You were unfaithful
  and made me furious,
but I am merciful,
  and so I will forgive you.
[13]Just admit that you rebelled
  and worshiped foreign gods
    under large trees everywhere.
[14]You are unfaithful children,
  but you belong to me.
    Come home!
I'll take one or two of you
  from each town and clan
    and bring you to Zion.
[15]Then I'll appoint wise rulers
  who will obey me,
and they will care for you
  like shepherds.

[16]You will increase in numbers,
  and there will be no need
    to remember the sacred chest
      or to make a new one.[p]
[17]The whole city of Jerusalem
  will be my throne.[q]
All nations will come here
  to worship me,
and they will no longer follow
  their stubborn, evil hearts.
[18]Then, in countries to the north,
  you people of Judah and Israel
    will be reunited,
and you will return to the land

---

[l]**3.2** *hilltop . . . sex:* See the note at 2.20.   [m]**3.6** *Josiah:* Ruled 640–609 B.C.   [n]**3.6** *Israel:* The northern kingdom (see the note at 2.4).   [o]**3.6** *prostitute . . . trees:* See the note at 2.20.   [p]**3.16** *make a new one:* The sacred chest was probably destroyed or taken away by the Babylonians when they captured Jerusalem in 586 B.C.   [q]**3.16,17** *sacred chest . . . throne:* The sacred chest was thought to be God's throne on earth.

● **3.6-10** *Israel . . . Her sister . . . Judah:* This refers to the northern kingdom of Israel, which fell to Assyria in 722 B.C. Jeremiah uses the image of the unfaithful wife when speaking of Israel. Many in Judah also worshiped idols, even while pretending to return to the Lord. This "pretending" may refer to Jeremiah's disappointment that Josiah's reforms weren't taken to heart by the people of Judah.

■ **3.12** *I am merciful:* God's kindness here is like the love of a parent who forgives a disobedient child.

● **3.14** *Zion:* Zion is the name of a hill in Jerusalem where God's temple was built.

ଓଆ   Zion

● **3.15** *like shepherds:* Israel's leaders did not live up to their responsibilities (Isa 56.10,11; Jer 23.1,2).

ଓଆ   Shepherds

● **3.16,17** *sacred chest . . . throne:* The sacred chest was kept in the most holy place of the temple (1 Kgs 8.1-13). It was thought to be God's throne on earth, the place where God lived among his people (Exod 25.22; 1 Sam 4.4; 2 Sam 6.2; Isa 6.1-5).

ଓଆ   The Sacred Chest

● **3.18** *reunited:* The ten northern tribes of Israel broke away from the two southern tribes after the death of King Solomon (1 Kgs 12.1-19).

4.1 *get rid of . . . disgusting idols:* Getting rid of the worship places and objects connected to other gods was the only way to remove Israel's past guilt and sins (Isa 27.9).

4.2 *Make promises . . . I will bless them:* If a promise was made in the name of the LORD, it was to be kept. Making vows in the name of other gods was forbidden. The idea of Israel being a blessing to other nations is first found in the promises to Abraham (Gen 12.1-3).

☞ Making Promises (Vows)

4.6 *disaster from the north:* It is not clear who is meant. Assyria, Egypt, and Babylonia are all possibilities. Most invasions of Israel came through the northern part of the country. Jeremiah knows that this disaster is an agent of God, sent by God to punish the people for their sins. **(See Map 7 on pg 1885.)**

I gave your ancestors.
¹⁹I have always wanted
     to treat you as my children
and give you the best land,
     the most beautiful on earth.
I wanted you to call me "Father"
     and not turn from me.
²⁰But instead, you are like a wife
     who broke her wedding vows.
You have been unfaithful to me.
     I, the LORD, have spoken.

The People Confess Their Sins

The LORD said:
²¹Listen to the noise
     on the hilltops!
It's the people of Israel,
     weeping and begging me
     to answer their prayers.
They forgot about me
     and chose the wrong path.
²²I will tell them, "Come back,
and I will cure you
     of your unfaithfulness."

They will answer,
     "We will come back, because you
     are the LORD our God.
²³On hilltops, we worshiped idols
     and made loud noises,
but it was all for nothing-
     only you can save us.
²⁴Since the days of our ancestors
     when our nation was young,
     that shameful god Baal[r] has taken
our crops and livestock,
     our sons and daughters.
²⁵We have rebelled against you
     just like our ancestors,
and we are ashamed of our sins."

How Israel Can Return to the LORD

4 The LORD said:
Israel, if you really want
     to come back to me, get rid
     of those disgusting idols.
²Make promises only in my name,
     and do what you promise!
Then all nations will praise me,
     and I will bless them.
³People of Jerusalem and Judah,
     don't be so stubborn!
Your hearts have become hard,
     like unplowed ground
     where thornbushes grow.
⁴With all your hearts,
     keep the agreement
     I made with you.
But if you are stubborn
     and keep on sinning,
my anger will burn like a fire
     that cannot be put out.

Disaster Is Coming

The LORD said:
*⁵"Sound the trumpets, my people.
Warn the people of Judah,[s]
     'Run for your lives!
⁶Head for Jerusalem
     or another walled town!'

"Jeremiah, tell them I'm sending
     disaster from the north.
⁷An army will come out,
     like a lion from its den.
It will destroy nations
     and leave your towns empty
     and in ruins."

---

[r]**3.24** *that shameful god Baal:* The Hebrew text has "The Shame," which was sometimes used as a way of making fun of the Canaanite god Baal.   [s]**4.5** *Judah:* Hebrew "Judah and Jerusalem."

8Then I told the people
of Israel,
"Put on sackcloth!t
Mourn and cry out,
'The LORD is still angry
with us.'"

9The LORD said,
"When all this happens,
the king and his officials,
the prophets and the priests
will be shocked and terrified."

10I said, "You are the LORD God. So why have you fooled everyone, especially the people of Jerusalem? Why did you promise peace, when a knife is at our throats?"

The Coming Disaster

11-12When disaster comes, the LORD will tell you people of Jerusalem,

"I am sending a windstorm
from the desert—
not a welcome breeze.u
And it will sweep you away
as punishment for your sins.
13Look! The enemy army
swoops down like an eagle;
their cavalry and chariots
race faster than storm clouds
blown by the wind."

Then you will answer,
"We are doomed!"

14But Jerusalem, there is still time
for you to be saved.

Wash the evil from your hearts
and stop making sinful plans,
15before a message of disaster
arrives from the hills of Ephraim
and the town of Dan.v

16-17The LORD said,

"Tell the nations that my people
have rebelled against me.
And so an army will come
from far away
to surround Jerusalem
and the towns of Judah.
I, the LORD, have spoken.

18"People of Judah,
your hearts will be in pain,
but it's your own fault
that you will be punished."

Jeremiah's Vision of the Coming Punishment

19I can't stand the pain!
My heart pounds,
as I twist and turn in agony.
I hear the signal trumpet
and the battle cry of the enemy,
and I cannot be silent.
20I see the enemy defeating us
time after time,
leaving everything in ruins.
Even my own home
is destroyed in a moment.
21How long will I see enemy flags
and hear their trumpets?

● 4.14 *making sinful plans:* This probably refers to the treaties made with foreign powers, especially Egypt.

● 4.15 *Ephraim . . . Dan:* News of an invasion would travel from Dan in the far north to the hills of Ephraim, which were about 20 miles north of Jerusalem. Then the bad news would reach Jerusalem. **(See Map 3 on pg 1881.)**

● 4.16-17 *an army . . . from far away:* The Babylonian army under King Nebuchadnezzar surrounded Jerusalem for 18 months, from 588 to 586 B.C., and destroyed the surrounding towns and villages. When they finally left, the temple was robbed and destroyed, and the city was devastated (2 Kgs 25.1-21; 2 Chr 36.17-21). Many of the Jewish people and their leaders were taken away into exile in Babylon. Jeremiah predicts this destruction, which is Judah's punishment for repeatedly disobeying the agreement made with the LORD.

■ 4.19 *My heart pounds:* Jeremiah feels the pain of his people (4.18; 10.19) and the pain of God. The anguish of Jeremiah is too deep to hold back. All will suffer—prophet, people, God—and everyone will be hurt. This shared heartache is a major theme of the poetic messages in JEREMIAH.

---

t4.8 *sackcloth:* A rough, dark-colored cloth made from goat or camel hair and used to make grain sacks. It was worn in times of trouble or sorrow. u4.11,12 *a welcome breeze:* Hebrew "a wind to blow away the husks." Farmers used a special shovel to pitch grain and husks into the air. Wind would blow away the light husks, and the grain would fall back to the ground, where it could be gathered up. v4.15 *Ephraim . . . Dan:* The hills of Ephraim were to the north of Jerusalem, and Dan was even farther north. They would be reached by the invading army first.

But Jerusalem, there is still time for you to be saved. Wash the evil from your hearts and stop making sinful plans.
JER 4.14

4.22 *foolish . . . how to sin:* The people are morally stupid and too foolish to recognize that their sinful actions will lead to punishment.

Sin

4.23 *The earth was barren:* This vision is the creation story in reverse. Jeremiah sees a world that has no life and no light (Gen 1.2). Darkness and destruction are commonly found in other prophetic visions of God's judgment (Joel 2.1-3,10,11; Amos 5.18-20; Zeph 1.14-18).

Day of the Lord

4.27-28 *destroyed, although not completely:* God will bring something new out of this destruction. Devastation is not the last word.

5.1 *Search Jerusalem:* God looked for ten people who were righteous in the evil city of Sodom (Gen 18.22-32). Here, Jeremiah searches for just one honest person but cannot find any. The leaders of the people are no better (5.5). The entire city and its people choose to disobey God. They are content with their rebellion and rottenness.

²²I heard the Lord say,
    "My people ignore me.
They are foolish children
    who do not understand
    that they will be punished.
All they know is how to sin."

²³After this, I looked around.
The earth was barren,
    with no form of life.
The sun, moon, and stars
    had disappeared.
²⁴The mountains were shaking;
²⁵no people could be seen,
    and all the birds
    had flown away.
²⁶Farmland had become a desert,
    and towns were in ruins.
The Lord's fierce anger
    had done all of this.

The Death of Jerusalem

²⁷⁻²⁸The Lord said:

I have made my decision,
    and I won't change my mind.
This land will be destroyed,
    although not completely.
The sky will turn dark,
    and the earth will mourn.

²⁹Enemy cavalry and archers
    shout their battle cry.
People run for their lives
and try to find safety
    among trees and rocks.
Every town is empty.

³⁰Jerusalem, your land
    has been wiped out.
But you act like a prostitute
and try to win back your lovers,
    who now hate you.
You can put on a red dress,
gold jewelry, and eye shadow,

but it's no use—
    your lovers are out to kill you!

³¹I heard groaning and crying.
Was it a woman giving birth
    to her first child?
No, it was Jerusalem,
    gasping for breath
    and begging for help.
"I'm dying!" she said.
    "They have murdered me."

Is Anyone Honest and Faithful?

The Lord said to me:

5 "Search Jerusalem
    for honest people
    who try to be faithful.
If you can find even one,
    I'll forgive the whole city.
²Everyone breaks promises
    made in my name."

³I answered, "I know
    that you look for truth.
You punished your people
    for their lies,
but in spite of the pain,
    they became more stubborn
and refused to turn back
    to you."
⁴Then I thought to myself,
"These common people
    act like fools,
and they have never learned
what the Lord their God
    demands of them.
⁵So I'll go and talk to the leaders.
They know what God demands."
    But even they had decided
    not to obey the Lord.

⁶The people have rebelled
and rejected the Lord
    too many times.

So enemies will attack
like lions from the forest
    or wolves from the desert.
Those enemies will watch
    the towns of Judah,
and like leopards
they will tear to pieces
    whoever goes outside.

Enemies Will Punish Judah

The LORD said:
7People of Judah,
    how can I forgive you?
I gave you everything,
but you abandoned me
    and worshiped idols.
You men go to prostitutes
and are unfaithful
    to your wives.
8You are no better than animals,
and you always want sex
    with someone else's wife.

9Why shouldn't I punish
    the people of Judah?
10I will tell their enemies,
    "Go through my vineyard.
Don't destroy the vines,
    but cut off the branches,
because they are the people
    who don't belong to me."

11In every way, Judah and Israel
    have been unfaithful to me.
*★**12**Their prophets lie and say,
    "The LORD won't punish us.
We will have peace
    and plenty of food."
13They tell these lies in my name,
    so now they will be killed in war
    or starve to death.

14I am the LORD God All-Powerful.
Jeremiah, I will tell you

exactly what to say.
Your words will be a fire;
Israel and Judah
    will be the fuel.

15People of Israel,
    I have made my decision.
An army from a distant country
    will attack you.
I've chosen an ancient nation,
and you won't understand
    their language.
16All of them are warriors,
    and their arrows bring death.
17This nation will eat your crops
    and livestock;
they will leave no fruit
    on your vines or fig trees.
And although you feel safe
    behind thick walls,
your towns will be destroyed
    and your children killed.

Israel Refused
To Worship the LORD

18The LORD said:
Jeremiah, the enemy army won't kill everyone in Judah. **19**And the people who survive will ask, "Why did the LORD our God do such terrible things to us?" Then tell them:

I am the LORD,
    but you abandoned me
and worshiped other gods
    in your own land.
Now you will be slaves
    in a foreign country.
20Tell these things to each other,
you people of Judah,
    you descendants of Jacob.

21You fools! Why don't you listen
    when I speak?
Why can't you understand

5.10 *vineyard:* Vineyards, where grapes are grown, are often used by the prophets as a symbol for Israel (Isa 5.1-7; Ezek 17.1-10). The vine branches are cut (pruned), but the main vine stalks are not destroyed, so the destruction is not final.

5.12 *Their prophets lie:* Lying prophets deny that God will bring disaster, so the people get a false sense of security. As God's true prophet, Jeremiah will offer words like a fire burning the false calm in Judah and Jerusalem (5.14). **(See the article Prophets and Prophecy on pg 1791.)**

5.15 *An army from a distant country:* This probably refers to Babylonia.

5.19 *people who survive . . . slaves in a foreign country:* After Babylon destroyed Jerusalem, some survivors, including Jeremiah, stayed in Jerusalem and the surrounding area. Others were taken away. Two or three different groups from Judah went to Babylon as prisoners: one group in 598 B.C.; another in 586 B.C.; and possibly a third in 582 B.C.

Exile

5.22 *I'm the one:* The idols that the people were worshiping were useless, but the LORD God is the powerful living God of creation who created the shores to hold back the earth's waters (Gen 1.9,10; Job 38.8-11; Ps 104.5-9), which were viewed as dangerous and sometimes compared to a monster (Job 26.12,13).

5.26 *hunter traps birds:* Bird catchers used large nets to catch birds. When a bird landed or flew close to where they were lying, the bird catcher threw the net over the bird and closed it by pulling on the cords. The birds were then placed in a basket or cage. The caging of birds is compared to the way some Israelites treated their neighbors unjustly and enslaved them.

5.28 *prosperous . . . justice:* Moses had warned of the dangers of prosperity in Deuteronomy 8.10-20. When they became successful, the people forgot that their ancestors had once been slaves in Egypt and they abandoned God's concern for justice to the poor.

6.4 *Kings will tell their troops:* Invading kings decide that the midday time of rest or the cover of darkness are the best times to attack Jerusalem's walls.

6.6 *I will command these armies:* God's judgment against the people of Judah includes guiding their enemies to victory.

²²that you should worship me
  with fear and trembling?
I'm the one who made the shore
  to hold back the ocean.
Waves may crash on the beach,
  but they can come no farther.
²³You stubborn people have rebelled
  and turned your backs on me.
²⁴You refuse to say,
  "Let's worship the LORD!
He's the one who sends rain
in spring and autumn
  and gives us a good harvest."
²⁵That's why I cannot bless you!

*²⁶A hunter traps birds
  and puts them in a cage,
but some of you trap humans
  and make them your slaves.
²⁷You are evil, and you lie and cheat
  to make yourselves rich.
You are powerful
²⁸ and prosperous,
but you refuse to help[w] the poor
  get the justice they deserve.
²⁹You need to be punished,
  and so I will take revenge.
³⁰Look at the terrible things
going on in this country.
  I am shocked!
³¹Prophets give their messages
  in the name of a false god,[x]
my priests don't want
  to serve me,[y]
and you—my own people—
  like it this way!
But on the day of disaster,
  where will you turn for help?

A Warning for the People of Jerusalem

The LORD said:

6 Run for your lives,
  people of Benjamin.
    Get out of Jerusalem.
Sound a trumpet in Tekoa
  and light a signal fire
    in Beth-Haccherem.
Soon you will be struck
  by disaster from the north.
*²Jerusalem is a lovely pasture,
³but shepherds will surround it
  and divided up,
    then let their flocks
      eat all the grass.[z]
⁴Kings will tell their troops,
  "If we reach Jerusalem
in the morning,
  we'll attack at noon.
But if we arrive later,
⁵we'll attack after dark
  and destroy its fortresses."

⁶I am the LORD All-Powerful,
  and I will command these armies
    to chop down trees
and build a ramp up to the walls
  of Jerusalem.

People of Jerusalem,
I must punish you
  for your injustice.
⁷Evil pours from your city
  like water from a spring.
Sounds of injustice and violence
  echo within your walls;
victims are everywhere,
  wounded and dying.

---

[w]**5.28** *refuse to help:* One possible meaning for the difficult Hebrew text.   [x]**5.31** *give . . . god:* Or "tell lies."   [y]**5.31** *don't . . . me:* Or "don't care what I want."   [z]**6.2,3** *Jerusalem . . . grass:* One possible meaning for the difficult Hebrew text.

⁸Listen to me,
  you people of Jerusalem
    and Judah.
  I will abandon you,
    and your land will become
      an empty desert.
⁹I will tell your enemies
  to leave your nation bare
    like a vine stripped of grapes.
  I, the LORD All-Powerful,
    have spoken.

Jeremiah's Anger

¹⁰I have told the people
  that you, LORD,
    will punish them,
  but they just laugh
    and refuse to listen.
¹¹Your anger against Judah
    flames up inside me,
  and I can't hold it in
    much longer.

The LORD's Anger Will Sweep Everyone Away

The LORD answered:
  Don't hold back my anger!
  Let it sweep away everyone—
    the children at play
  and all adults,
    young and old alike.
¹²I'll punish the people of Judah
    and give to others
  their houses and fields,
    as well as their wives.
  I, the LORD, have spoken.

¹³Everyone is greedy and dishonest,
    whether poor or rich.
  Even the prophets and priests
    cannot be trusted.
¹⁴All they ever offer
  to my deeply wounded people

are empty hopes for peace.
¹⁵They should be ashamed
  of their disgusting sins,
    but they don't even blush.
  And so, when I punish Judah,
    they will end up on the ground,
      dead like everyone else.
  I, the LORD, have spoken.

The People of Judah Rejected God's Way of Life

¹⁶The LORD said:

My people, when you stood
    at the crossroads,
  I told you, "Follow the road
    your ancestors took,
  and you will find peace."
    But you refused.
¹⁷I also sent prophets
    to warn you of danger,
  but when they sounded the alarm,
    you paid no attention.
*¹⁸So I tell all nations on earth,
  "Watch what I will do!
¹⁹My people ignored me
    and rejected my laws.
  They planned to do evil,
    and now the evil they planned
      will happen to them."

²⁰People of Judah,
  you bring me incense from Sheba
    and spices from distant lands.
  You offer sacrifices of all kinds.
  But why bother?
    I hate these gifts of yours!
²¹So I will put stumbling blocks
    in your path,
  and everyone will die,
    including parents and children,
      neighbors and friends.

6.11 *anger:* Jeremiah feels God's anger, and neither God nor the prophet can hold the fury back any longer. The LORD is not "above" or beyond these very real emotions. God is deeply wounded by his disobedient children.

6.13,14 *prophets and priests . . . empty hopes:* These leaders deceive the people with peaceful words when peace is not at hand.

6.20 *incense from Sheba . . . sacrifices:* Sheba was located in southwest Arabia. It was famous for the spices and incense it exported. Incense here probably is frankincense, which was burned to make a sweet smell. It was also an ingredient in ointments and in the holy incense burned at Israel's holy tent of meeting and was mixed with sacrifices offered by the priests (Exod 30.34-38; Lev 6.14,15). "Spices" probably refers to calamus, a sweet-smelling reed or cane that was used in making sweet-smelling oil used by Israel's holy priests (Exod 30.23; Isa 43.24). These sacrifices are not satisfying to God, and cannot cover up the fact that the people have continued to disobey God. God desires a true change of heart that results in obedience and justice rather than meaningless ceremonies and rituals (Amos 5.21-24; Isa 1.12-17).

The LORD said: My people, when you stood at the crossroads, I told you, "Follow the road your ancestors took, and you will find peace." But you refused. JER 6.16

6.27-29 *test my people . . . Silver can be purified:* Jeremiah's testing is compared to the process of refining silver to make it more pure. In ancient times, lead or iron was placed in a container with silver ore. When taken to a white-hot heat, the lead oxidized and carried off impurities in the silver ore, leaving behind silver that is more pure. The people are like hopelessly impure metal that cannot be purified by the refining process.

7.1-4 *stand by the gate of the temple . . . in Jerusalem:* Chapter 7 has been described as a series of sermons. The first sermon (7.1-20) warns that the temple in Jerusalem will be destroyed just like the sanctuary that was built in the north at Shiloh, if the people of Judah continue to worship false gods. It was after this temple sermon that Jeremiah's enemies began to oppose his message and persecute the prophet.

7.4 *temple:* Because of the promises made to David in 2 Samuel 7, the people felt that the Jerusalem temple would never be destroyed, and it would keep them safe no matter what (7.10).

7.10,11 *protect you . . . hideout:* The people are using the temple and worship there as a kind of "good-luck" charm. They are living immoral lives and not living up to God's laws (7.5-9). They go to the temple where they use worship as a cover-up for the way they are really living.

An Army from the North

²²The Lord said,
"Look toward the north,
   where a powerful nation
   has prepared for war.
²³Its well-armed troops are cruel
   and never show mercy.
Their galloping horses sound
   like ocean waves
   pounding on the shore.
This army will attack you,
   lovely Jerusalem."

²⁴Then the people said,
"Just hearing about them
   makes us tremble with fear,
and we twist and turn in pain
   like a woman giving birth."

²⁵The Lord said,
"Don't work in your fields
   or walk along the roads.
It's too dangerous.
The enemy is well armed
²⁶   and attacks without warning.
So mourn, my people, as though
   your only child had died.
Wear clothes made of sackcloth^a
   and roll in the ash pile."

The Lord's People Must Be Tested

The Lord said:
²⁷Jeremiah, test my people
   as though they were metal.
²⁸And you'll find they are hard
   like bronze and iron.
They are stubborn rebels,
   always spreading lies.
*²⁹⁻³⁰Silver can be purified

in a fiery furnace,
but my people are too wicked
   to be made pure,
and so I have rejected them.

Jeremiah Speaks in the Temple
(Jeremiah 26.1-6)

7 ¹⁻³The Lord told me to stand by the gate of the temple^b and tell the people who were going in that the Lord All-Powerful, the God of Israel, had said:

Pay attention, people of Judah! Change your ways and start living right, then I will let you keep on living in your own country.^c ⁴Don't fool yourselves! My temple is here in Jerusalem, but that doesn't mean I will protect you. ⁵I will keep you safe only if you change your ways and are fair and honest with each other. ⁶Stop taking advantage of foreigners, orphans, and widows. Don't kill innocent people. And stop worshiping other gods. ⁷Then I will let you enjoy a long life in this land I gave your ancestors.

⁸But just look at what is happening! You put your trust in worthless lies. ⁹You steal and murder; you lie in court and are unfaithful in marriage. You worship idols and offer incense to Baal, when these gods have never done anything for you. ¹⁰And then you come into my temple and worship me! Do you think I will protect you so that you can go on sinning? ¹¹You are thieves, and you have made my temple your hideout. But I've seen everything you have done.

¹²Go to Shiloh, where my sacred tent once stood. Take a look at what I did there. My people Israel sinned, and so I destroyed Shiloh!

¹³While you have been sinning, I have been trying to talk to you, but you refuse

^a**6.26** *sackcloth:* See the note at 4.8.   ^b**7.1-3** *temple:* The Hebrew text has "house of the Lord," another name for the temple.   ^c**7.1-3** *let you . . . own country:* Or "live here with you."

to listen. **14**Don't think this temple will protect you. Long ago I told your ancestors to build it and worship me here, but now I have decided to tear it down, just as I destroyed Shiloh. **15**And as for you, people of Judah, I'm going to send you away from my land, just as I sent away the people of Ephraim and the other northern tribes.

Punishment for Worshiping Other Gods

16Jeremiah, don't pray for these people! I, the Lord, would refuse to listen. **17**Do you see what the people of Judah are doing in their towns and in the streets of Jerusalem? **18**Children gather firewood, their fathers build fires, and their mothers mix dough to bake bread for the goddess they call the Queen of Heaven.**d** They even offer wine sacrifices to other gods, just to insult me. **19**But they are not only insulting me; they are also harming themselves by doing these shameful things.

20And now, I, the Lord All-Powerful, will flood Judah with my fiery anger until nothing is left—no people or animals, no trees or crops.

It Is Useless To Offer Sacrifices

21The Lord told me to say to the people of Judah:

I am the Lord All-Powerful, the God of Israel, but I won't accept sacrifices from you. So don't even bother bringing them to me. You might as well just cook the meat for yourselves. **22**At the time I brought your ancestors out of Egypt, I didn't command them to offer sacrifices to me. **23**Instead, I told them, "If you listen to me and do what I tell you, I will be your God, you will be my people,

and all will go well for you." **24**But your ancestors refused to listen. They were stubborn, and whenever I wanted them to go one way, they always went the other. **25**Ever since your ancestors left Egypt, I have been sending my servants the prophets to speak for me. **26**But you have ignored me and become even more stubborn and sinful than your ancestors ever were!

Slaughter Valley

The Lord said:

27Jeremiah, no matter what you do, the people won't listen. **28**So you must say to them:

People of Judah, I am the Lord your God, but you have refused to obey me, and you didn't change when I punished you. And now, you no longer even pretend to be faithful to me.

29Shave your head bald
      and throw away the hair.
   Sing a funeral song
      on top of a barren hill.
   You people have made me angry,
      and I have abandoned you.

30You have disobeyed me by putting your disgusting idols in my temple, and now the temple itself is disgusting to me. **31**At Topheth in Hinnom Valley you have built altars where you kill your children and burn them as sacrifices to other gods. I would never think of telling you to do this. **32**So watch out! Someday that place will no longer be called Topheth or Hinnom Valley. It will be called Slaughter Valley, because you will bury your dead there until you run out of room, **33**and then bodies will lie scattered on the ground. Birds and wild animals will come and eat, and no one will be around to scare them off. **34**When I am finished

d7.18 *Queen of Heaven:* Probably another name for the goddess Astarte.

7.21 *cook the meat:* Certain animal sacrifices called "whole burnt offerings" were burned on the altar by the priests to send up a pleasing smell to the Lord (Lev 1.1-17). Because the people have been so sinful, the Lord will not accept the burned offerings of the priests. **(See the chart Sacrifices and Offerings on pg 1828.)**

7.27 *no matter what you do:* Jeremiah persisted in trying to make the people hear the words of the Lord, even though he knew they would not listen and change their ways. He also continued to pray for his people, as we can gather from God's repeated protests in Jeremiah 6.14; 7.16; 11.14; 14.11.

7.29 *Shave your head bald . . . Sing a funeral song:* Shaving the head was sometimes done as a sign of mourning or grief (Job 1.20; Ezek 7.18). A funeral song is also known as a "lament."

7.31 *Topheth in Hinnom Valley:* Topheth probably comes from an Aramaic word meaning "fireplace." It was likely at Topheth that Israel's kings Ahaz (2 Kgs 16.2,3) and Manasseh (2 Kgs 21.1, 6-7) sacrificed their sons to the god Molech. The practice of child sacrifice was forbidden by the Law of Moses (Lev 18.21; Deut 18.10,11).

8.1,2 *bones of the dead . . . sun, moon, and stars:* Some of Judah's neighbors worshiped the sun, moon, and stars as gods. A number of God's people, including some of the leaders of Judah, followed these forbidden worship practices. The digging up and scattering of human bones was considered a terrible insult. That is what Jeremiah warns will happen to the bones of the "moon worshipers."

8.7 *Storks . . . thrushes:* These migratory birds have a strong homing instinct. The stork spends winters in southeast Africa and summers in Europe and Asia. Jeremiah is criticizing Israel for not being as smart as the simple birds named here. The people have lost the instinct of self-preservation and their ability to obey the LORD.

8.9 *wise men . . . have no wisdom:* The wise men are scribes, or professional interpreters of the Law. In Israel, true wisdom came from respecting and obeying the LORD God (Prov 1.7), so it is ironic that the very ones who know God's Law the best do not live according to it.

Wisdom

with your land, there will be deathly silence in the empty ruins of Jerusalem and the towns of Judah—no happy voices, no sounds of parties or wedding celebrations.

8 Then the bones of the dead kings of Judah and their officials will be dug up, along with the bones of the priests, the prophets, and everyone else in Jerusalem
2 who loved and worshiped the sun, moon, and stars. These bones will be scattered and left lying on the ground like trash, where the sun and moon and stars can shine on them.
3 Some of you people of Judah will be left alive, but I will force you to go to foreign countries, and you will wish you were dead. I, the LORD God All-Powerful, have spoken.

The People Took the Wrong Road

4 The LORD said:

People of Jerusalem,
when you stumble and fall,
you get back up,
and if you take a wrong road,
you turn around and go back.[e]
5 So why do you refuse
to come back to me?
Why do you hold so tightly
to your false gods?

6 I listen carefully,
but none of you admit
that you've done wrong.
Without a second thought,
you run down the wrong road[f]
like horses running blindly
into battle.

7 Storks, doves, swallows,
and thrushes
all know when it's time
to fly away for the winter
and when to come back.
But you, my people,
don't know what I demand.
8 You say, "We are wise
because we have the teachings
and laws of the LORD."
But I say that your teachers
have turned my words
into lies!
9 Your wise men
have rejected what I say,
and so they have no wisdom.
Now they will be trapped
and put to shame;
they won't know what to do.
10 I'll give their wives and fields
to strangers.

Everyone is greedy and dishonest,
whether poor or rich.
Even the prophets and priests
cannot be trusted.
11 All they ever offer
to my deeply wounded people
are empty hopes for peace.
12 They should be ashamed
of the way they live,
but they don't even blush.
And so, when I punish Judah,
they will end up on the ground,
dead like everyone else.
13 I will wipe them out.[g]
They are vines without grapes;
fig trees without figs or leaves.
They have not done a thing
that I told them![h]
I, the LORD, have spoken.

[e] **8.4** *if you take . . . go back:* One possible meaning for the difficult Hebrew text. [f] **8.6** *you run down the wrong road:* One possible meaning for the difficult Hebrew text. [g] **8.13** *I will wipe them out:* One possible meaning for the difficult Hebrew text. [h] **8.13** *They have not . . . them:* One possible meaning for the difficult Hebrew text.

The People and Their Punishment

¹⁴The people of Judah
   say to each other,
"What are we waiting for?
Let's run to a town with walls
   and die there.
We rebelled against the LORD,
and we were sentenced to die
   by drinking poison.
¹⁵We had hoped for peace
and a time of healing,
   but all we got was terror.
¹⁶Our enemies have reached
   the town of Dan in the north,
and the snorting of their horses
   makes us tremble with fear.
The enemy will destroy Jerusalem
and our entire nation.
   No one will survive."

¹⁷"Watch out!" the LORD says.
"I'm sending poisonous snakes
   to attack you,
and no one can stop them."

Jeremiah Mourns for His People

¹⁸I'm burdened with sorrow
   and feel like giving up.
¹⁹In a foreign land
   my people are crying.
Listen! You'll hear them say,
"Has the LORD deserted Zion?
   Is he no longer its king?"

I hear the LORD reply,
"Why did you make me angry
   by worshiping useless idols?"

²⁰The people complain,
"Spring and summer
   have come and gone,
but still the LORD
   hasn't rescued us."

²¹My people are crushed,
   and so is my heart.
   I am horrified and mourn.
²²If medicine and doctors
   may be found in Gilead,
   why aren't my people healed?

9 I wish that my eyes
   were fountains of tears,
so I could cry day and night
for my people
   who were killed.
²I wish I could go into the desert
   and find a hiding place
from all who are treacherous
   and unfaithful to God.

The LORD Answers Jeremiah

³The LORD replied:

Lies come from the mouths
of my people,
   like arrows from a bow.
With each dishonest deed
   their power increases,
and not one of them will admit
   that I am God.

⁴Jeremiah, all your friends
   and relatives
tell lies about you,
   so don't trust them.
⁵They wear themselves out,
   always looking for a new way
   to cheat their friends.
⁶Everyone takes advantage
   of everyone else,
and no one will admit
   that I am God.

⁷And so I will purify
   the hearts of my people
just as gold is purified
in a furnace.
   I have no other choice.

8.14 *die by drinking poison:* The people will not actually "drink" poison, but rather they will drink the poison of God's punishment.

8.18-21 *I'm burdened . . . horrified and mourn:* In this poem, Jeremiah identifies with the sorrow and suffering of his people. It appears as though the LORD has left Zion.

8.22 *medicine . . . Gilead:* Trees in this region east of the Jordan River produced a resin that was used to make an ointment for wounds, but no medicine or ointment can heal Israel's deep wounds.

9.1 *cry day and night for my people:* Jeremiah's sorrowful poem (8.18—9.2) expresses the heartache of God as well. God is not distant from the people's suffering. The people's pain is God's pain. Both Jeremiah and God are heartbroken over the spiritual illness that is killing and causing misery for the people of Judah.

9.8 *arrow:* The lie of peace is as deadly as an arrow, because those who think peace will come are likely to be caught off guard when invading armies attack.

9.11 *jackals:* Jackals survive by being scavengers, eating the flesh of dead animals or human beings. When Jerusalem and other cities are destroyed, the jackals will move in from the desert to feast on the dead.

9.17 *women . . . weep at funerals:* Two different practices may be in mind here: (1) Mourning was part of the ceremony of worshiping Baal. (2) Professional mourners, usually women, were hired to sing sad songs and wail in order to inspire grieving at funerals. The tears of these women were not a substitute for the tears of others, but a means of stirring the mourning process.

Burial

9.21 *death sneaked in:* Mot, the Canaanite god of death, was believed to sneak in through windows to claim his victims. In this funeral song, death is pictured as a person.

Canaanite Gods and Goddesses

⁸They say they want peace,
  but this lie is deadly,
like an arrow that strikes
  when you least expect it.
⁹Give me one good reason
  not to punish them
  as they deserve.
I, the Lord All-Powerful,
  have spoken.

Jeremiah Weeps for His People

¹⁰I weep for the pastureland
  in the hill country.
It's so barren and scorched
  that no one travels there.
No cattle can be found there,
  and birds and wild animals
  have all disappeared.

¹¹I heard the Lord reply,
  "When I am finished,
Jerusalem and the towns of Judah
  will be piles of ruins
  where only jackals^i live."

Why the Land Was Destroyed

¹²I said to the Lord, "None of us can understand why the land has become like an uncrossable desert. Won't you explain why?" ¹³The Lord said:
  I destroyed the land because the people disobeyed me and rejected my laws and teachings. ¹⁴They were stubborn and worshiped Baal,^j just as their ancestors did. ¹⁵So I, the Lord All-Powerful, the God of Israel, promise them poison to eat and drink.^k ¹⁶I'll scatter them in foreign countries that they

and their ancestors have never even heard of. Finally, I will send enemy soldiers to kill every last one of them.

The Women Who Are Paid To Weep

¹⁷The Lord All-Powerful said,
  "Make arrangements now
for the women who are paid
  to weep at funerals,^l
especially the women
  who can cry the loudest."

¹⁸The people answered,
  "Let them come quickly
  and cry for us,
until our own eyes
  are flooded with tears.
¹⁹Now those of us on Zion cry,
  'We are ruined!
  We can't stand the shame.
Our homes have been destroyed,
  and we must leave our land.'

²⁰"We ask you women
  to pay attention
  to what the Lord says.
We will teach you a funeral song
  that you can teach
  your daughters and friends:
²¹"We were in our fortress,
  but death sneaked in
  through our windows.
It even struck down
  children at play
  and our strongest young men.'

²²"The Lord has told us
  the ground will be covered

^i**9.11** *jackals:* Desert animals related to wolves, but smaller. ^j**9.14** *Baal:* See the note at 2.23.
^k**9.15** *poison to eat and drink:* Or "bitter disappointment to eat, and tears to drink." ^l**9.17** *women . . . weep at funerals:* Or "the women who weep for Baal"; the god Baal was believed to have died and come back to life, and some women would go to places of worship and weep over the death of Baal.

with dead bodies,
like ungathered stalks of grain
or manure in a field."

What the LORD Likes Best

23The LORD says:
Don't brag about your wisdom
or strength or wealth.
24If you feel you must brag,
then have enough sense
to brag about worshiping me,
the LORD.
What I like best
is showing kindness,
justice, and mercy
to everyone on earth.

25-26Someday I will punish the nations
of Egypt, Edom, Ammon, and Moab, and
the tribes of the desert.m The men of these
nations are circumcised, but they don't
worship me. And it's the same with you
people of Judah. Your bodies are circumcised, but your hearts are unchanged.

The LORD Talks about Idols

10 *1-2The LORD said:

Listen to me,
you people of Israel.
Don't follow the customs
of those nations
who become frightened
when they see something strange
happen in the sky.
3Their religion is worthless!
They chop down a tree,
carve the wood into an idol,
4cover it with silver and gold,
and then nail it down
so it won't fall over.

5An idol is no better
than a scarecrow.
It can't speak,
and it has to be carried,
because it can't walk.
Why worship an idol
that can't help or harm you?

Jeremiah Praises the LORD

6Our LORD, great and powerful,
you alone are God.
7You are King of the nations.
Everyone should worship you.
No human anywhere on earth
is wiser than you.
8Idols are worthless,
and anyone who worships them
is a fool!
9Idols are made by humans.
A carver shapes the wood.
A metalworker hammers out
a covering of gold from Uphaz
or of silver from Tarshish.
Then the idol is dressed
in blue and purple clothes.

10You, LORD, are the only true
and living God.
You will rule for all time.
When you are angry
the earth shakes,
and nations are destroyed.

11You told me to say
that idols did not create
the heavens and the earth,
and that you, the LORD,
will destroy every idol.

12With your wisdom and power
you created the earth

m9.25,26 the tribes of the desert: One possible meaning for the difficult Hebrew text.

9.24 *What I like best:* Worshiping the LORD alone is the only kind of worship that one can brag about. Even this worship is meaningless unless the people show their respect for the LORD by treating others with fairness and justice (Isa 1.16,17; Amos 5.21-24; Mic 6.8; 1 Cor 1.31; 2 Cor 10.17).

9.25-26 *Egypt . . . tribes of the desert:* Jeremiah preached the LORD's judgment against these nations. The "tribes of the desert" probably refers to tribes who lived in the Arabian Desert. **(See Map 7 on pg 1885.)**

9.25-26 *circumcised:* Circumcision was a common rite among many people in the ancient Near East. God commanded Abraham's male descendants to be circumcised as a physical sign that they were God's chosen people (see Gen 17.9-14; 34.21-23; Lev 12.3). The people of Judah continued to circumcise their sons as an outward sign of devotion to God, but the people were not spiritually devoted to God on the inside.

Circumcision

10.2-5 *something strange . . . in the sky:* Some of ancient Israel's neighbors explained lunar and solar eclipses and comets as signs from the gods.

10.12-16 *With your wisdom . . . created all things:* This hymn to the one true God is very close in thought to Psalm 135.

Wisdom

10.20 *Our homes . . . our children:* The nation mourns the loss of its homes and children. Compare to Isaiah 49.14-23.

10.25 *So get angry:* Except for chapters 46–51, this prayer for God to punish neighboring nations is rarely found in Jeremiah. Compare to Psalm 79.

and spread out the heavens.
¹³The waters in the heavens roar
   at your command.
You make clouds appear—
you send the winds
   from your storehouse
and make lightning flash
   in the rain.

¹⁴People who make idols
   are so stupid!
They will be disappointed,
because their false gods
   are not alive.
¹⁵Idols are merely a joke,
   and when the time is right,
   they will be destroyed.

¹⁶But you, Israel's God,
   created all things,
and you chose Israel
   to be your very own.
Your name is the Lord
   All-Powerful.

Judah Will Be Thrown from Its Land

¹⁷I said to the people of Judah,
   "Gather your things;
   you are surrounded.
¹⁸The Lord said these troubles
   will lead to your capture,
and he will throw you
   from this land
   like a rock from a sling."[n]

¹⁹The people answered,
   "We are wounded
   and doomed to die.
Why did we say
   we could stand the pain?

²⁰Our homes are destroyed;
   our children are dead.
No one is left
   to help us find shelter."

²¹But I told them,
   "Our leaders were stupid failures,
   because they refused
   to listen to the Lord.
And so we've been scattered
   like sheep.

²²"Sounds of destruction
rumble from the north
   like distant thunder.
Soon our towns will be ruins
   where only jackals[o] live."

Jeremiah Prays

²³I know, Lord, that we humans
   are not in control
   of our own lives.
²⁴Correct me, as I deserve,
   but not in your anger,
   or I will be dead.
²⁵Our enemies refuse
   to admit that you are God
   or to worship you.
They have wiped out our people
and left our nation
   lying in ruins.
So get angry
   and sweep them away!

Judah Has Broken the Lord's Agreement

11 ¹⁻³The Lord God told me to say to the people of Judah and Jerusalem: I, the Lord, am warning you that I will put a curse on anyone who

---

[n]**10.18** *like a rock from a sling:* One possible meaning for the difficult Hebrew text.   [o]**10.22** *jackals:* See the note at 9.11.

doesn't keep the agreement I made with Israel. So pay attention to what it says. **4**My commands haven't changed since I brought your ancestors out of Egypt, a nation that seemed like a blazing furnace where iron ore is melted. I told your ancestors that if they obeyed my commands, I would be their God, and they would be my people. **5**Then I did what I had promised and gave them this wonderful land, where you now live.

"Yes, Lord," I replied, "that's true."

6Then the Lord told me to say to everyone on the streets of Jerusalem and in the towns of Judah:

Pay attention to the commands in my agreement with you. **7**Ever since I brought your ancestors out of Egypt, I have been telling your people to obey me. But you and your ancestors **8**have always been stubborn. You have refused to listen, and instead you have done whatever your sinful hearts have desired.

You have not kept the agreement we made, so I will make you suffer every curse that goes with it.

9The Lord said to me:

Jeremiah, the people of Judah and Jerusalem are plotting against me. **10**They have sinned in the same way their ancestors did, by turning from me and worshiping other gods. The northern kingdom of Israel broke the agreement I made with your ancestors, and now the southern kingdom of Judah*P* has done the same.

11Here is what I've decided to do. I will bring suffering on the people of Judah and Jerusalem, and no one will escape. They will beg me to help, but I won't listen to their prayers. **12-13**Then they will offer sacrifices to their other gods and ask them for help. After all, the people of Judah have more gods than towns, and more shameful altars for Baal than there are streets in Jerusalem. But those gods won't be able to rescue the people of Judah from disaster.

14Jeremiah, don't pray for these people or beg me to rescue them. If you do, I won't listen, and I certainly won't listen if they pray!

15Then the Lord told me to say to the people of Judah:

You are my chosen people,
but you have no right
to be here in my temple,
doing such evil things.
The sacrifices you offer me
won't protect you from disaster,
so stop celebrating.*q*
16Once you were like an olive tree
covered with fruit.
But soon I will send a noisy mob
to break off your branches
and set you on fire.

17I am the Lord All-Powerful. You people of Judah were like a tree that I had planted, but you have made me angry by offering sacrifices to Baal, just as the northern kingdom did. And now I'm going to pull you up by the roots.

The Plot To Kill Jeremiah

*****18**Some people plotted to kill me.
And like a lamb
being led to the butcher,
I knew nothing
about their plans.

11.1-5 *keep the agreement... gave them this wonderful land:* This entire chapter belongs to the time following Josiah's reforms, which were based on *The Book of God's Law* found by Josiah's assistants in the temple (2 Kgs 22,23). The laws in this scroll were based on the agreement (covenant) God made with Moses and the Israelite people at Sinai (see Exod 19–23). In this agreement, God promised to be Israel's God and to give them "this wonderful land" of Canaan (Exod 23.20-31; Deut 1.6-8). In return, the people were to obey God's commands. God did give the land of Canaan to the people, but by Jeremiah's day, many had turned their backs on God. Jeremiah saw that Josiah's reforms were completely dropped by Jehoiakim, the king who followed Josiah.

11.18-23 *people plotted to kill me . . . no one . . . will be left alive:* This passage is the first of Jeremiah's personal laments. In this first lament (11.18-23), Jeremiah describes the plot on his life by some men from his hometown of Anathoth. It is not clear why they are plotting to kill him. It may be because he has criticized the priesthood, which would have included his own family. It may just be that Jeremiah's hometown folk are embarrassed by his message of doom against Judah and want to silence him. However, the Lord's response is one of doom for the men of Anathoth. Families will be completely wiped out, making it impossible for children to carry on the family name.

¹⁹But then the LORD told me
that they had planned
to chop me down like a tree—
fruit and all—
so that no one would ever
remember me again.
²⁰ I prayed, "LORD All-Powerful,
you always do what is right,
and you know every thought.
So I trust you to help me
and to take revenge."

²¹Then the LORD said:
Jeremiah, some men from Anathoth[r]
say they will kill you, if you keep on
speaking for me. ²²But I will punish
them. Their young men will die in battle, and their children will starve to
death. ²³And when I am finished, no
one from their families will be left
alive.

Jeremiah Complains to the LORD

12 Whenever I complain
to you, LORD,
you are always fair.
But now I have questions
about your justice.
Why is life easy for sinners?
Why are they successful?
²You plant them like trees;
you let them prosper
and produce fruit.
Yet even when they praise you,
they don't mean it.

³But you know, LORD,
how faithful I've always been,
even in my thoughts.
So drag my enemies away
and butcher them like sheep!

⁴How long will the ground be dry
and the pasturelands parched?
The birds and animals
are dead and gone.
And all of this happened because
the people are so sinful.
They even brag, "God can't see
the sins we commit."[s]

The LORD Answers Jeremiah

⁵Jeremiah, if you get tired
in a race against people,
how can you possibly run
against horses?
If you fall in open fields,
what will happen in the forest
along the Jordan River?
⁶Even your own family
has turned against you.
They act friendly,
but don't trust them.
They're out to get you,
and so is everyone else.

The LORD Is Furious with His People

⁷I loved my people and chose them
as my very own.
But now I will reject them
and hand them over
to their enemies.
⁸My people have turned against me
and roar at me like lions.
That's why I hate them.

⁹My people are like a hawk
surrounded and attacked
by other hawks.[t]
Tell the wild animals

[r]**11.21** *Anathoth:* Jeremiah's hometown (see 1.1).   [s]**12.4** *God can't see the sins we commit:* One ancient translation; Hebrew "He won't live to see what happens to us."   [t]**12.9** *My people . . . other hawks:* Or "My land has become a hyena's den with vultures circling above."

to come and eat their fill.
¹⁰My beautiful land is ruined
like a field or a vineyard
trampled by shepherds
and stripped bare
by their flocks.
¹¹Every field I see lies barren,
and no one cares.

¹²A destroying army
marches along desert roads
and attacks everywhere.
They are my deadly sword;
no one is safe from them.

¹³My people, you planted wheat,
but because I was furious,
I let only weeds grow.
You wore yourselves out
and gained only shame!

The LORD Will Have Pity on Other Nations

¹⁴The LORD said:

I gave this land to my people Israel, but enemies around it have attacked and robbed it. So I will uproot them from their own countries just as I will uproot Judah from its land. ¹⁵But later, I will have pity on these nations and bring them back to their own lands. ¹⁶They once taught my people to worship Baal. But if they admit I am the only true God, and if they let my people teach them how to worship me, these nations will also become my people. ¹⁷However, if they don't listen to me, I will uproot them from their lands and completely destroy them. I, the LORD, have spoken.

Jeremiah's Linen Shorts

13 The LORD told me, "Go and buy a pair of linen shorts. Wear them for a while, but don't wash them." ²So I bought a pair of shorts and put them on.

³Then the LORD said, ⁴"Take off the shorts. Go to Parahᵘ and hide the shorts in a crack between some large rocks." ⁵And that's what I did.

⁶Some time later the LORD said, "Go back and get the shorts." ⁷I went back and dug the shorts out of their hiding place, but the cloth had rotted, and the shorts were ruined.

⁸Then the LORD said:

⁹Jeremiah, I will use Babylonia toᵛ destroy the pride of the people of Judah and Jerusalem. ¹⁰The people of Judah are evil and stubborn. So instead of listening to me, they do whatever they want and even worship other gods. When I am finished with these people, they will be good for nothing, just like this pair of shorts. ¹¹These shorts were tight around your waist, and that's how tightly I held onto the kingdoms of Israel and Judah. I wanted them to be my people. I wanted to make them famous, so that other nations would praise and honor me, but they refused to obey me.

Wine Jars

The LORD said:

¹²Jeremiah, tell the people of Judah, "The LORD God of Israel orders you to fill your wine jars with wine."

They will answer, "Of course we fill our wine jars with wine! Why are you telling us something we already know?"

ᵘ**13.4** *Parah:* Or "the Euphrates River." Parah was a village about five and a half miles northeast of Jerusalem.   ᵛ**13.9** *I will use Babylonia to:* Or "that's how I'm going to."

12.15 *pity on these nations:* Destruction is not the last word, even for the enemies of Israel, if they give up their worship of other gods and turn to the LORD God of Israel. God's people will teach the foreigners how to worship.

13.1 *linen shorts:* This underwear, also known as a "loincloth," was wrapped around the hips and reached about halfway down the thighs. Linen is fabric woven from yarn made from the flax plant. Here the LORD gets the message across to Jeremiah by having him do something (13.3-11).

13.4 *Parah:* Parah was a village northeast of Jerusalem, close to Jeremiah's hometown of Anathoth.

13.9 *destroy the pride of the people:* God's people were supposed to cling to the LORD as tightly as the LORD held on to them. But the people left God behind, trusting in other gods and in their own resources. So the LORD would use the exile to destroy their pride, just as Jeremiah's linen shorts rotted and became good for nothing.

13.12-14 *we fill our wine jars . . . I will smash them:* Someone who has drunk too much wine becomes wobbly and can't think straight. In the same way the people of Judah and Jerusalem have drunk from the cup of unfaithfulness, so they can no longer see straight. Note that Jeremiah singles out the rulers who descended from King David. The LORD will destroy Judah's people like wine jars being smashed against each other, unless they return to God and confess their sins (13.16).

13.16 *light . . . darkness:* Light is often used as a symbol for life and goodness in the Bible, while darkness is often an image for evil and death (Job 18.15, 18; Prov 13.9; 20.20; John 8.12).

13.18 *king and his mother:* This probably refers to Jehoiachin, the young king who ruled for only three months in 598 B.C. Jehoiachin and his mother Nehushta were sent into exile (2 Kgs 24.8-16). The king's mother usually had an important position in the royal court as the "First Lady."

13.19 *the Southern Desert:* This refers to the Negev region, south of Judah. (See Map 3 on pg 1881.)

13.23 *Can people change:* The question expects a negative answer. Judah has sinned so long that they are unable to change themselves.

¹³Then say to them:

I am the LORD, and what I'm going to do will make everyone in Judah and Jerusalem appear to be full of wine. And the worst ones will be the kings of David's family and the priests and the prophets. ¹⁴Then I will smash them against each other like jars. I will have no pity on the young or the old, and they will all be destroyed. I, the LORD, have spoken.

The People of Judah Will Be Taken Away

¹⁵People of Judah,
    don't be too proud to listen
        to what the LORD has said.
¹⁶You hope for light,
    but God is sending darkness.
    Evening shadows already deepen
        in the hills.
    So return to God
    and confess your sins to him
        before you trip and fall.
¹⁷If you are too proud to listen,
    I will weep alone.
    Tears will stream from my eyes
    when the LORD's people
        are taken away as prisoners.

¹⁸The LORD told me to tell you
    that your king and his mother[w]
        must surrender their thrones
        and remove their crowns.[x]
¹⁹The cities in the Southern Desert
    are surrounded;
        no one can get in or out.
    Everyone in Judah
        will be taken away.
²⁰Jerusalem, you were so proud

of ruling the people of Judah.
    But where are they now?

Look north, and you will see
    your enemies approaching.
²¹You once trusted them to help,
    but now I'll let them rule you.[y]
    What do you say about that?
    You will be in pain
    like a woman giving birth.

²²Do you know why
    your clothes were torn off
        and you were abused?
    It was because
        of your terrible sins.
²³Can you ever change
        and do what's right?
    Can people change the color
        of their skin,
    or can a leopard
        remove its spots?
    If so, then maybe you can change
        and learn to do right.

²⁴I will scatter you,
    just as the desert wind
    blows husks from grain
        tossed in the air.
²⁵I won't change my mind.
    I, the LORD, have spoken.

You rejected me
    and worshiped false gods.
*²⁶You were married to me,
    but you were unfaithful.
    You even became a prostitute[z]
    by worshiping disgusting gods
        on hilltops and in fields.
²⁷So I'll rip off your clothes
    and leave you naked and ashamed

[w]**13.18** *mother:* The king's mother usually had an important position in the royal court.   [x]**13.18** *and remove their crowns:* One possible meaning for the difficult Hebrew text.   [y]**13.21** *You once . . . rule you:* One possible meaning for the difficult Hebrew text.   [z]**13.26** *prostitute:* See the note at 2.20.

Can you ever change and do what's right? Can people change the color of their skin, or can a leopard remove its spots? JER 13.23

for everyone to see.
You are doomed!
Will you ever be worthy
to worship me again?

The Land Dries Up

14 When there had been no rain for a
long time, the LORD told me to say
to the people:

²Judah and Jerusalem weep
as the land dries up.
³Rulers send their servants
to the storage pits for water.ᵃ
But there's none to be found;
they return in despair
with their jars still empty.

⁴There has been no rain,
and farmers feel sick
as they watch cracks appear
in the dry ground.ᵇ

⁵A deer gives birth in a field,
then abandons her newborn fawn
and leaves in search of grass.
⁶Wild donkeys go blind
from starvation.
So they stand on barren hilltops
and sniff the air,ᶜ
hoping to smell green grass.

The LORD's People Pray

⁷We rejected you and did evil,
so we deserve to be punished.

But if you rescue us, LORD,
everyone will see
how great you are.
⁸You're our only hope;
you alone can save us now.
You help us one day,
but you're gone the next.
⁹Did this disaster
take you by surprise?
Are you a warrior
with your hands tied?
You have chosen us,
and your temple is here.
Don't abandon us!

The LORD's Answer

¹⁰My people,
you love to wander away;
you don't even try
to stay close to me.
So now I will reject you
and punish you for your sins.
I, the LORD, have spoken.

Lying Prophets

¹¹The LORD said, "Jeremiah, don't ask me
to help these people. ¹²They may even go
without eatingᵈ and offer sacrifices to please
meᵉ and to give thanks.ᶠ But when they
cry out for my help, I won't listen, and I
won't accept their sacrifices. Instead, I'll
send war, starvation, and disease to wipe
them out."

ᵃ**14.3** *storage pits for water:* Since water was scarce, pits were dug into solid rock for collecting and
storing rainwater. These pits were called "cisterns." ᵇ**14.4** *cracks . . . ground:* One possible meaning
for the difficult Hebrew text. ᶜ**14.6** *sniff the air:* The Hebrew text has "sniff the air, like jackals" (see
the note at 9.11). ᵈ**14.12** *go without eating:* The people of Israel sometimes went without eating to
show sorrow for their sins. ᵉ**14.12** *sacrifices to please me:* These sacrifices have traditionally been called
"whole burnt offerings" because the whole animal was burned on the altar. A main purpose of such
sacrifices was to please the LORD with the smell of the sacrifice, and so in the CEV they are sometimes
called "sacrifices to please the LORD." ᶠ**14.12** *sacrifices . . . to give thanks:* These sacrifices have traditionally been called "grain offerings." A main purpose of such sacrifices was to thank the LORD with a
gift of grain, and so in the CEV they are sometimes called "sacrifices to give thanks to the LORD."

14.7 *rescue us . . . see how great
you are:* If the LORD allows Judah to be
destroyed, Jeremiah argues, Judah's enemies will think that the LORD God is
powerless. But if the LORD saves Judah,
the nations will declare the LORD's
greatness.

14.13 *The other prophets:* Lying prophets say "All is well" (1 Kgs 22.1-28) and give the people words they want to hear (Isa 30.8-11).

14.16 *dead bodies . . . bury them:* Both the lying prophets and those who listen to them will suffer the double disgrace of dying and being left unburied.

15.1 *Moses and Samuel:* Moses and Samuel were great leaders who successfully prayed to God on behalf of the people of Israel (Exod 32.11-14; Num 14.13-20; 1 Sam 7.5-10; 12.19-25; Ps 99.6). The urgent prayer of 14.19-22 is rejected. Judah will go into exile.

¹³I replied, "The other prophets keep telling everyone that you won't send starvation or war, and that you're going to give us peace."

¹⁴The Lord answered:

They claim to speak for me, but they're lying! I didn't even speak to them, much less choose them to be my prophets. Their messages come from worthless dreams, useless fortune-telling, and their own imaginations. ¹⁵Those lying prophets say there will be peace and plenty of food. But I say that those same prophets will die from war and hunger. ¹⁶And everyone who listens to them will be killed, just as they deserve. Their dead bodies will be thrown out into the streets of Jerusalem, because their families will also be dead, and no one will be left to bury them.ᵍ

¹⁷Jeremiah, go and tell the people how you feel about all this.

So I told them:

"Tears will flood my eyes
    both day and night,
because my nation suffers
    from a deadly wound.
¹⁸In the fields I see the bodies
    of those killed in battle.
And in the towns I see crowds
    dying of hunger.
But the prophets and priests
    go about their business,
without understanding
    what has happened."ʰ

Jeremiah Prays to the Lord

¹⁹Have you rejected Judah, Lord?
    Do you hate Jerusalem?
Why did you strike down Judah

with a fatal wound?
We had hoped for peace
    and a time of healing,
        but all we got was terror.
²⁰We and our ancestors are guilty
    of rebelling against you.
²¹If you save us, it will show
        how great you are.
Don't let our enemies
    disgrace your temple,
        your beautiful throne.
Don't forget that you promised
    to rescue us.
²²Idols can't send rain,
    and showers don't fall
        by themselves.
Only you control the rain,
    so we put our trust in you,
        the Lord our God.

The People of Judah Will Die

15 The Lord said to me:
    Even if Moses and Samuel were here, praying with you, I wouldn't change my mind. So send the people of Judah away. ²And when they ask where they are going, tell them that I, the Lord, have said:

Some of you are going to die
    of horrible diseases.
Others are going to die in war
    or from starvation.
The rest will be led away
    to a foreign country.
³I will punish you
    in four different ways:
You will be killed in war
and your bodies dragged off
    by dogs,
your flesh will be eaten by birds,
and your bones will be chewed on
    by wild animals.

ᵍ**14.16** *dead bodies . . . bury them:* A proper burial was considered very important.   ʰ**14.18** *go about . . . has happened:* One possible meaning for the difficult Hebrew text.

⁴This punishment will happen
   because of the horrible thingsⁱ
      your King Manasseh^j did.
   And you will be disgusting
      to all nations on earth.
⁵People of Jerusalem,
      who will feel sorry for you?
   Will anyone bother
      to ask if you are well?

⁶My people, you abandoned me
      and walked away.
   I am tired of showing mercy;
      that's why I'll destroy you
⁷by scattering you like straw
      blown by the wind.
   I will punish you with sorrow
      and death,
   because you refuse
      to change your ways.
⁸There will be more widows
      in Judah
   than grains of sand on a beach.

   A surprise attack at noon!
   And the mothers in Jerusalem
      mourn for their children.
⁹A mother is in deep despair
      and struggles for breath.
   Her daylight has turned
      to darkness—
   she has suffered the loss
      of her seven sons.

   I will kill anyone who survives.
      I, the LORD, have spoken.

Jeremiah Complains

¹⁰I wish I had never been born!
   I'm always in trouble

with everyone in Judah.
   I never lend or borrow money,
   but everyone curses me
      just the same.

¹¹Then the LORD replied,
   "I promise to protect you,
      and when disaster comes,
   even your enemies
      will beg you for help."^k

The Enemy Cannot Be Defeated

The LORD told me to say:
   ¹²People of Judah,
      just as you can't break iron
         mixed with bronze,
      you can't defeat the enemies
         that will attack
            from the north.
   ¹³I will give them
         everything you own,
      because you have sinned
         everywhere in your country.
   ¹⁴My anger is a fire
         that cannot be put out,^l
      so I will make you slaves
         of your enemies
            in a foreign land.^m

Jeremiah Complains Again

¹⁵You can see how I suffer
      insult after insult,
         all because of you, LORD.
   Don't be so patient
      with my enemies;
   take revenge on them
      before they kill me.

ⁱ**15.4** *the horrible things:* See 2 Kings 21.1-16.   ^j**15.4** *Manasseh:* Hebrew "Manasseh son of Hezekiah"; he ruled 687–642 B.C.   ^k**15.11** *help:* One possible meaning for the difficult Hebrew text of verse 11.   ^l**15.14** *that cannot be put out:* Some Hebrew manuscripts; most Hebrew manuscripts "against you."   ^m**15.14** *I will make . . . land:* Many Hebrew manuscripts; most Hebrew manuscripts "I will make your enemies go through to a land you don't know about."

15.4 *horrible things your King Manasseh did:* Manasseh ruled Judah from 687 to 642 B.C. and died just two years before Josiah became king. Judah sank to an all-time low under Manasseh, who built altars to foreign gods and even sacrificed his own son (2 Kgs 21.1-16; 2 Chr 33.1-9).

15.6 *I am tired:* As with the northern kingdom of Israel (Amos 7.1-9), God's patience has given out.

15.8 *more widows . . . than grains of sand on a beach:* Israel's sins will lead to a complete reversal of God's promise to Abraham (Gen 22.14-18).

15.9 *seven sons:* Having seven sons is a sign of God's favor (Ruth 4.15; 1 Sam 2.5). In ancient times "seven" also symbolized completeness or perfection. The loss of seven sons emphasizes how severe and complete will be the loss of Jerusalem's mothers.

15.10 *I wish:* Another of Jeremiah's laments.

15.13 *sinned everywhere . . . anger is a fire:* Fire is often connected with the LORD's judgment against those who are evil or disobedient (Gen 19.23-29; Lev 10.1,2; Isa 4.4; Jer 17.4; Joel 2.1-3; Matt 13.36-42).

15.15-18 *see how I suffer . . . constant pain:* Jeremiah complains bitterly about God's mistreatment of him. His task has made him an outcast, because he can't help speaking about the LORD's anger when he is with others. So he is ridiculed, hated, and alone.

15.20,21 *I am making you strong . . . I will be there:* The LORD repeats the promise to keep Jeremiah safe from those who dislike his message.

16.1-9 *Don't get married . . . celebrations:* Like the prophets of the eighth century B.C., Jeremiah is to be a living symbol of God's message (Isa 8.3,4; Hos 1.2-9). Jeremiah was a young man of marriageable age, but he is told to remain single, a status almost unheard of during his time. By remaining single, Jeremiah will draw attention to God's warnings: In the near future all family life will be disrupted. The usual traditions regarding mourning for the dead will be useless now. There will be no need for ritual cutting of the flesh and head-shaving, customs practiced in some Canaanite religions and by some Israelites (Jer 41.5; Amos 8.10), though such rituals were forbidden by the Law of Moses (Lev 21.5; Deut 14.1-2). Finally, Jeremiah is told not to attend feasts and joyful celebrations, as these too will end. All these actions are signs of the terrible future that awaits Judah. Jeremiah's task and the message he delivers make him a man set apart, and ultimately alone. (See the article Prophets and Prophecy on pg 1791.)

16.14,15 *A time will come . . . you will call me the Living LORD:* Doom is not the last word. Just as God rescued Israel's ancestors from Egypt, God will again rescue the people of Judah from the exile in Babylon.

[16]When you spoke to me,
   I was glad to obey,
because I belong to you,
   the LORD All-Powerful.
[17]I don't go to parties
   and have a good time.
Instead, I keep to myself,
because you have filled me
   with your anger.

[18]I am badly injured
   and in constant pain.
Are you going to disappoint me,
like a stream that goes dry
   in the heat of summer?

The LORD Replies

[19]Then the LORD told me:
   Stop talking like a fool!
If you turn back to me
   and speak my message,
I will let you be my prophet
   once again.
I hope the people of Judah
   will accept what you say.
But you can ignore their threats,
*[20]because I am making you strong,
   like a bronze wall.
They are evil and violent,
   but when they attack,
[21]I will be there to rescue you.
   I, the LORD, have spoken.

Jeremiah Must Live His Message

16 The LORD said to me: [2]Jeremiah, don't get married and have children—Judah is no place to raise a family. [3]I'll tell you what's going to happen to children and their parents here. [4]They will die of horrible diseases and of war and starvation. No one will give them a funeral or bury them, and their bodies will be food for the birds and wild animals. And what's left will lie on the ground like manure.

[5]When someone dies, don't visit the family or show any sorrow. I will no longer love or bless or have any pity on the people of Judah. [6]Rich and poor alike will die and be left unburied. No one will mourn and show their sorrow by cutting themselves or shaving their heads.[n] [7]No one will bring food and wine to help comfort those who are mourning the death of their father or mother.

[8]Don't even set foot in a house where there is eating and drinking and celebrating. [9]Warn the people of Judah that I, the LORD All-Powerful, will put an end to all their parties and wedding celebrations. [10]They will ask, "Why has the LORD our God threatened us with so many disasters? Have we done something wrong or sinned against him?"

[11]Then tell them I have said:
   People of Judah, your ancestors turned away from me; they rejected my laws and teachings and started worshiping other gods. [12]And you have done even worse! You are stubborn, and instead of obeying me, you do whatever evil comes to your mind. [13]So I will throw you into a land that you and your ancestors know nothing about, a place where you will have to worship other gods both day and night. And I won't feel the least bit sorry for you.

[14]A time will come when you will again worship me. But you will no longer call me the Living LORD who rescued Israel from Egypt. [15]Instead, you will call me the Living LORD who rescued you from that country in the

[n]16.6 *mourn and show their sorrow by cutting themselves or shaving their heads:* A custom in some Canaanite religions.

north and from the other countries where I had forced you to go.

Someday I will bring you back to this land that I gave your ancestors. **16**But for now, I am sending enemies who will catch you like fish and hunt you down like wild animals in the hills and the caves.

17I can see everything you are doing, even if you try to hide your sins from me. **18**I will punish you double for your sins, because you have polluted my own land. You have filled it with lifeless idols that remind me of dead bodies.

The Lord Gives Strength

I prayed to the Lord:

19Our Lord, you are the one
    who gives me strength
and protects me like a fortress
    when I am in trouble.
People will come to you
    from distant nations and say,
"Our ancestors worshiped
    false and useless gods,
20worthless idols
    made by human hands."

21Then the Lord replied,
"That's why I will teach them
    about my power,
and they will know that I
    truly am the Lord."

The Lord Will Punish Judah

The Lord said:

17 People of Judah,
        your sins cannot be erased.

They are written on your hearts
    like words chiseled in stone
or carved on the corners
    of your altars.**o**
***2**One generation after another
    has set up pagan altars
and worshiped the goddess Asherah
    everywhere in your country—
    on hills and mountains,
    and under large trees.
3So I'll take everything you own,
    including your altars,
and give it all
    to your enemies.**P**
4You will lose**q** the land
    that I gave you,
and I will make you slaves
    in a foreign country,
because you have made my anger
    blaze up like a fire
    that won't stop burning.

Trust the Lord

5I, the Lord, have put a curse
    on those who turn from me
    and trust in human strength.
6They will dry up like a bush
    in salty desert soil,
    where nothing can grow.

7But I will bless those
    who trust me, the Lord.
8They will be like trees
    growing beside a stream—
trees with roots that reach
    down to the water,
and with leaves
    that are always green.
They bear fruit every year

---

o17.1 *carved on the corners of your altars:* When sacrifices were offered to the Lord to ask him to forgive sins, some of the blood was smeared on the corners of the altar (see Leviticus 4.7,18-20,25,26,30,31,34,35; 16.18). But now the Lord refuses to accept these sacrifices. **P17.3** *enemies:* One possible meaning for the difficult Hebrew text of verses 2,3.   **q17.4** *You will lose:* One possible meaning for the difficult Hebrew text.

● 17.2 *the goddess Asherah:* This goddess was also known by the name Astarte. Asherah was represented by wooden poles called "Asherim."

■ 17.5-8 *trust in human strength . . . worried by a lack of rain:* Those who trust in God, the life-giving spring of water (2.13), will flourish, while those who do not trust in God will become dry as dust and be blown away.

Our Lord, you are the one who gives me strength and protects me like a fortress when I am in trouble. Jer 16.19

17.14 *heal me and rescue me:* Another of Jeremiah's personal laments.

17.18 *make my enemies fail:* If his enemies succeed, Jeremiah will not be alive to preach the second part of his message.

17.19-20 *each city gate:* Traders and visitors came and went through these busy entrances. City leaders met and held court hearings there. It was the most likely place for Jeremiah to get a large and influential audience.

17.21-24 *Keep the Sabbath day sacred:* The Sabbath day of rest began at sunset Friday and ended at sunset Saturday. The Sabbath law was to be obeyed (Exod 20.8-11; 23.12; Deut 5.12-14). Ignoring the Sabbath affected not only worship but also the people's fair treatment of their hired workers and animals.

17.25 *kings from David's family:* The promises made to David in 2 Samuel 7 seemed to ensure the continuation of his kingly line forever.

and are never worried
    by a lack of rain.

⁹You people of Judah
    are so deceitful
that you even fool yourselves,
    and you can't change.
¹⁰But I know your deeds
    and your thoughts,
and I will make sure
    you get what you deserve.
¹¹You cheated others,
    but everything you gained
will fly away, like birds
    hatched from stolen eggs.
Then you will discover
    what fools you are.

Jeremiah Prays to the Lord

¹²Our Lord, your temple
    is a glorious throne
that has stood on a mountain
    from the beginning.
¹³You are a spring of water
    giving Israel life and hope.
But if the people reject
    what you have told me,
they will be swept away
    like words written in dust.ʳ

¹⁴You, Lord, are the one I praise.
    So heal me and rescue me!
Then I will be completely well
    and perfectly safe.

¹⁵The people of Judah say to me,
    "Jeremiah, you claimed to tell us
    what the Lord has said.
So why hasn't it come true?"

¹⁶Our Lord, you chose me
    to care for your people,
    and that's what I have done.
You know everything I have said,
    and I have never once
    asked you to punish them.ˢ
¹⁷I trust you for protection
    in times of trouble,
    so don't frighten me.
¹⁸Keep me from failure
    and disgrace,
but make my enemies fail
    and be disgraced.
Send destruction to make
    their worst fears come true.

Resting on the Sabbath

¹⁹⁻²⁰The Lord said:
Jeremiah, stand at each city gate in Jerusalem, including the one the king uses, and speak to him and everyone else. Tell them I have said:

I am the Lord, so pay attention. ²¹⁻²⁴If you value your lives, don't do any work on the Sabbath. Don't carry anything through the city gates or through the door of your house, or anywhere else. Keep the Sabbath day sacred!

I gave this command to your ancestors, but they were stubborn and refused to obey or to be corrected. But if you obey, ²⁵then Judah and Jerusalem will always be ruled by kings from David's family. The king and his officials will ride through these gates on horses or in chariots, and the people of Judah and Jerusalem will be with them. There will always be people living in Jerusalem, ²⁶and others will come

ʳ17.13 *reject . . . dust:* One possible meaning for the difficult Hebrew text.   ˢ17.16 *you chose . . . punish them:* One possible meaning for the difficult Hebrew text.

here from the nearby villages, from the towns of Judah and Benjamin,[t] from the hill country and the foothills to the west, and from the Southern Desert. They will bring sacrifices to please me and to give me thanks,[u] as well as offerings of grain and incense.

²⁷But if you keep on carrying things through the city gates on the Sabbath and keep treating it as any other day, I will set fire to these gates and burn down the whole city, including the fortresses.

Jeremiah Goes to the Pottery Shop

18 The LORD told me, ²"Jeremiah, go to the pottery shop, and when you get there, I will tell you what to say to the people."

³I went there and saw the potter making clay pots on his pottery wheel. ⁴And whenever the clay would not take the shape he wanted, he would change his mind and form it into some other shape.

⁵Then the LORD told me to say:

⁶People of Israel, I, the LORD, have power over you, just as a potter has power over clay. ⁷If I threaten to uproot and shatter an evil nation, ⁸and that nation turns from its evil, I will change my mind.

⁹If I promise to make a nation strong, ¹⁰but its people start disobeying me and doing evil, then I will change my mind and not help them at all.

¹¹So listen to me, people of Judah and Jerusalem! I have decided to strike you with disaster, and I won't change my mind unless you stop sinning and start living right.

¹²But I know you won't listen. You might as well answer, "We don't care what you say. We have made plans to sin, and we are going to be stubborn and do as we please!"

¹³So I, the LORD, command you to ask the nations, and find out if they have ever heard of such a horrible sin as what you have done.

¹⁴The snow
on Lebanon's mountains
never melts away,
and the streams there
never run dry.[v]
¹⁵But you, my people,
have turned from me
to burn incense
to worthless idols.
You have left the ancient road
to follow an unknown path
where you stumble over idols.

¹⁶Your land will be ruined,
and every passerby
will look at it with horror
and make insulting remarks.
¹⁷When your enemies attack,
I will scatter you like dust
blown by an eastern wind.
Then, on that day of disaster,
I will turn my back on you.

The Plot against Jeremiah

¹⁸Some of the people said, "Let's get rid of Jeremiah! We will always have priests to teach us God's laws, as well as wise people to give us advice, and prophets to speak the LORD's messages. So, instead of listening to Jeremiah any longer, let's accuse him of a crime."

[t]**17.26** *Judah and Benjamin:* These two tribes made up the southern kingdom of Judah.
[u]**17.26** *sacrifices to please me and to give me thanks:* See the notes at 14.12.   [v]**18.14** *dry:* One possible meaning for the difficult Hebrew text of verse 14.

17.27 *treating it as any other day:* This probably refers to trading and selling on the Sabbath. Compare to Amos 8.4-6.

18.3-6 *clay pots . . . power over clay:* The LORD can change his creation (Israel) and even destroy it and start over (18.4), just as a potter can quickly change the shape of a clay object on the wheel.

18.14 *Lebanon's mountains:* Mount Hermon in Lebanon, to the north of Israel, is 9,000 feet above sea level. Its melting snows form part of the source of the Jordan River. Streams fed by mountain snows never run dry, but Israel will be scattered like dust (18.17). **(See Map 6 on pg 1884.)**

18.15 *the ancient road . . . unknown path:* The ancient road is the good road that the people's ancestors took. This road of obedience is compared to the wrong ("unknown") path of disobedience.

18.17 *eastern wind:* Hot, dry sirocco winds came from the desert areas to the east of Judah.

18.18 *Let's get rid of Jeremiah:* Jeremiah's enemies are tired of hearing his warnings. Besides, they already have plenty of other religious leaders who are willing to tell them what they want to hear. Jeremiah's enemies' plan is to tell lies about him and have him put away. They believe that if they silence him, his irritating message will go away.

19.3-6 *trouble on this valley:* The most gruesome of Israel's sins (child sacrifice) took place on a burning platform in Topheth.

19.9 *eat the flesh:* A common tactic in ancient warfare was surrounding a city until food and water supplies ran out. Before Nebuchadnezzar of Babylonia attacked Jerusalem, his army surrounded the city for a year and a half, until all the food had run out (2 Kgs 25.1-5).

Nebuchadnezzar

19.10 *smash the jar:* Jeremiah again takes action to dramatize God's message. Jeremiah's breaking of the jar was terrifying because it was understood as actually setting in motion God's destruction of Judah and Jerusalem.

Jeremiah Prays about His Enemies

¹⁹Please, LORD, answer my prayer.
 Make my enemies stop
  accusing me of evil.
²⁰I tried to help them,
 but they are paying me back
  by digging a pit to trap me.
I even begged you
 not to punish them.
²¹But now I am asking you
 to let their children starve
  or be killed in war.
Let women lose
 their husbands and sons
  to disease and violence.
²²These people have dug pits
 and set traps for me, LORD.
Make them scream in fear
 when you send enemy troops
  to attack their homes.
²³You know they plan to kill me.
 So get angry and punish them!
Don't ever forgive
 their terrible crimes.

Jeremiah and the Clay Jar

19 The LORD said:
 Jeremiah, go to the pottery shop and buy a clay jar. Then take along some of the city officials and leading priests ²and go to Hinnom Valley, just outside Potsherd^w Gate. Tell the people that I have said:

³I am the LORD All-Powerful, the God of Israel, and you kings of Judah and you people of Jerusalem had better pay attention. I am going to bring so much trouble on this valley that everyone who hears about it will be shocked. ⁴⁻⁵The people of Judah stopped worshiping me and made this valley into a place of worship for Baal and other gods that have never helped them or their ancestors or their kings. And they have committed murder here, burning their young, innocent children as sacrifices to Baal. I have never even thought of telling you to do that. ⁶So watch out! Someday this place will no longer be called Topheth or Hinnom Valley. It will be called Slaughter Valley!

⁷You people of Judah and Jerusalem may have big plans, but here in this valley I'll ruin^x those plans. I'll let your enemies kill you, and I'll tell the birds and wild animals to eat your dead bodies. ⁸I will turn Jerusalem into a pile of rubble, and every passerby will be shocked and horrified and will make insulting remarks. ⁹And while your enemies are trying to break through your city walls to kill you, the food supply will run out. You will become so hungry that you will eat the flesh of your friends and even of your own children.

¹⁰Jeremiah, as soon as you have said this, smash the jar while the people are watching. ¹¹Then tell them that I have also said:

I am the LORD All-Powerful, and I warn you that I will shatter Judah and Jerusalem just like this jar that is broken beyond repair. You will bury your dead here in Topheth, but so many of you will die that there won't be enough room.

¹²⁻¹³I will make Jerusalem as unclean as Topheth, by filling the city with your dead bodies. I will do this because you and your kings have gone up to the roofs of your houses and burned

^w**19.2** *Potsherd:* A piece of broken pottery. ^x**19.7** *ruin:* In Hebrew "ruin" sounds like "jar" (see verse 1).

incense to the stars in the sky, as though they were gods. And you have given sacrifices of wine to foreign gods.

Jeremiah Speaks in the Temple Courtyard

14I went to Topheth, where I told the people what the Lord had said. Then I went to the temple courtyard and shouted to the people, **15**"Listen, everyone! Some time ago, the Lord All-Powerful, the God of Israel, warned you that he would bring disaster on Jerusalem and all nearby villages. But you were stubborn and refused to listen. Now the Lord is going to bring the disaster he promised."

Pashhur Arrests Jeremiah

20 Pashhur son of Immer was a priest and the chief of temple security. He heard what I had said, **2**and so he hit me.ʸ Then he had me arrested and put in chainsᶻ at the Benjamin Gate in the Lord's temple.ᵃ **3**The next day, when Pashhur let me go free, I told him that the Lord had said:

No longer will I call you Pashhur. Instead, I will call you Afraid-of-Everything.ᵇ **4**You will be afraid, and you will bring fear to your friends as well. You will see enemies kill them in battle. Then I will let the king of Babylonia take everyone in Judah prisoner, killing some and dragging the rest away to Babylonia. **5**He will clean out the royal treasury and take everything else of value from Jerusalem. **6**Pashhur, you are guilty of telling

lies and claiming they were messages from me. That's why I will let the Babylonians take you, your family, and your friends as prisoners to Babylonia, where you will all die and be buried.

Jeremiah Complains to the Lord

7You tricked me, Lord,
and I was really fooled.
You are stronger than I am,
and you have defeated me.
People never stop sneering
and insulting me.
8You have let me announce
only injustice and death.
Your message has brought me
nothing but insults
and trouble.
9Sometimes I tell myself
not to think about you, Lord,
or even mention your name.
But your message burns
in my heart and bones,
and I cannot keep silent.

10I heard the crowds whisper,
"Everyone is afraid.
Now's our chance
to accuse Jeremiah!"
All of my so-called friends
are just waiting
for me to make a mistake.
They say, "Maybe Jeremiah
can be tricked.
Then we can overpower him
and get even at last."

11But you, Lord,
are a mighty soldier,

19.15 *Some time ago:* In the eighth century B.C. the prophet Micah first delivered the message of doom to Jerusalem (Mic 3.12). This message was shocking because of God's promise that one of David's descendants would always be king. An eternal kingship implied that Jerusalem, where Israel's rulers lived, would always be safe from attack. Any prophecy of disaster aimed against Jerusalem was thought to be a direct challenge to God's promise to David. Jeremiah points out that this message is not new, nor did he invent it.

20.1,2 *Passhur...had me arrested:* The temple police were to make sure that non-Israelites did not enter the holy temple. Passhur, the chief of temple security, punishes Jeremiah for the message given in Jeremiah 19.15. This beating and public humiliation lasted until the next day.

Israel's Priests

20.7-18 *You tricked me, Lord... Why did I have to be born?:* This section (20.7-18) probably is made up of two different personal laments—20.7-13 and 20.14-18. Jeremiah expresses his deep pain. How difficult it was to be a prophet of doom to his own people, a people he loved! It hurt to be hated and ridiculed. Jeremiah's mood swings between confident faith in God (20.11,13) and utter misery, cursing the day he was born. Not to live at all is better than the life he must lead as God's prophet.

20.16 *the towns you destroyed:* This probably refers to the ancient cities Sodom and Gomorrah (Gen 19.23-29).

21.3-7 *I will stretch out my mighty arm:* The LORD's outstretched arm is an image often used to describe the LORD's protection or power, especially in battle (Exod 14.21; 15.12,16; Deut 5.15; Isa 14.27; 19.16; 40.10). Here, the LORD is fighting against Judah, using the Babylonian army as an instrument of punishment against his sinful people.

standing at my side.
Those troublemakers
will fall down and fail—
    terribly embarrassed,
    forever ashamed.

¹²LORD All-Powerful,
    you test those who do right,
and you know every heart
    and mind.
I have told you my complaints,
so let me watch you
    take revenge on my enemies.
¹³I sing praises to you, LORD.
You rescue the oppressed
    from the wicked.

¹⁴Put a curse on the day I was born!
    Don't bless that day.
¹⁵Put a curse on the man
    who told my father, "Good news!
    You have a son."
¹⁶May that man be like the towns
    you destroyed without pity.
Let him hear shouts of alarm
    in the morning
    and battle cries at noon.
¹⁷He deserves to die
    for not killing me
    before I was born.
Then my mother's body
    would have been my grave.
¹⁸Why did I have to be born?
    Was it just to suffer
    and die in shame?

The LORD Will Fight against Jerusalem

21 King Zedekiah^c of Judah sent for Pashhur son of Malchiah and for a priest named Zephaniah son of Maaseiah.

Then he told them, "Talk with Jeremiah for me."

So they came to me and said, ²"King Nebuchadnezzar^d of Babylonia has attacked Judah. Please ask the LORD to work miracles for our people, as he has done in the past, so that Nebuchadnezzar will leave us alone."

³⁻⁷I told them that the LORD God of Israel had told me to say to King Zedekiah:

The Babylonians have surrounded Jerusalem and want to kill you and your people. You are asking me to save you, but you have made me furious. So I will stretch out my mighty arm and fight against you myself. Your army is using spears and swords to fight the Babylonians, but I will make your own weapons turn and attack you. I will send a horrible disease to kill many of the people and animals in Jerusalem, and there will be nothing left to eat. Finally, I will let King Nebuchadnezzar and his army fight their way to the center of Jerusalem and capture everyone who is left alive, including you and your officials. But Nebuchadnezzar won't be kind or show any mercy—he will have you killed! I, the LORD, have spoken.

⁸Then I told them that the LORD had said:

People of Jerusalem, I, the LORD, give you the choice of life or death. ⁹The Babylonian army has surrounded Jerusalem, so if you want to live, you must go out and surrender to them. But if you want to die because of hunger, disease, or war, then stay here in the city. ¹⁰I have decided not to rescue Jerusalem. Instead, I am going to let the king of Babylonia burn it to the ground. I, the LORD, have spoken.

^c**21.1** *Zedekiah:* See the note at 1.3.   ^d**21.2** *Nebuchadnezzar:* Ruled 605–562 B.C.

The Lord Warns the King of Judah

*[11]Pay attention, you that belong
    to the royal family.
[12]Each new day, make sure
    that justice is done,
and rescue those
    who are being robbed.
Or else my anger will flame up
    like a fire that never goes out.

[13]Jerusalem,
    from your mountaintop
you look out over the valleys[e]
    and think you are safe.
But I, the Lord, am angry,
[14]and I will punish you
    as you deserve.
I'll set your palace[f] on fire,
    and everything around you
    will go up in smoke.

The Lord Will Punish
the King of Judah

22 [1-3]The Lord sent me to the palace
of the king of Judah to speak to the
king, his officials, and everyone else who
was there. The Lord told me to say:

I am the Lord, so pay attention! You have
been allowing people to cheat, rob, and
take advantage of widows, orphans, and
foreigners who live here. Innocent people
have become victims of injustice, and some
of them have even been killed. But now I
command you to do what is right and see
that justice is done. Rescue everyone who
has suffered from injustice.

[4]If you obey me, the kings from David's
family will continue to rule Judah from
this palace. They and their officials will ride
in and out on their horses or in their chariots. [5]But if you ignore me, I promise in my
own name that this palace will lie in ruins.
[6]Listen to what I think about it:

The palace of Judah's king
    is as glorious as Gilead
    or Lebanon's highest peaks.
But it will be as empty
    as a ghost-town
    when I'm through with it.
[7]I'll send troops to tear it apart,
    and its beautiful cedar beams
    will be used for firewood.

[8]People from different nations will pass
by and ask, "Why did the Lord do this to
such a great city as Jerusalem?" [9]Others will
answer, "It's because the people worshiped
foreign gods and broke the agreement that
the Lord their God had made with them."

King Jehoahaz

The Lord said:
[10]King Josiah is dead,
    so don't mourn for him.[g]
Instead, mourn for his son
    King Jehoahaz,
    dragged off to another country,[h]
    never to return.

[11-12]Jehoahaz[i] became king of Judah after his father King Josiah died. But Jehoahaz was taken as a prisoner to a foreign
country. Now I, the Lord, promise that he
will die there without ever seeing his own
land again.

---

[e]**21.13** *Jerusalem . . . valleys:* One possible meaning for the difficult Hebrew text.   [f]**21.14** *your palace:*
The Hebrew text has "the forest"; the largest room in the king's palace was known as Forest Hall (see
1 Kings 7.2,3).   [g]**22.10** *King Josiah . . . him:* The Hebrew text has "don't mourn for the dead one,"
meaning King Josiah, who ruled 640–609 B.C.   [h]**22.10** *his son King Jehoahaz . . . country:* The Hebrew text
has "the one who was dragged off to another country," meaning King Jehoahaz, who ruled for three
months in 609 B.C.   [i]**22.11,12** *Jehoahaz:* The Hebrew text has "Shallum," another name for Jehoahaz.

● **21.11,12** *royal family . . . Each new
day:* The first part of each day was to be
given to matters of justice (2 Sam 15.1-
3). Israel's rulers were to defend the
poor and rescue the homeless (Ps 72.1-
4; Prov 16.11,12; Isa 11.1-5).

◑ **Justice**

● **21.13** *Jerusalem . . . valleys:* Three
deep valleys were in or just outside Jerusalem's walls. The temple was built
on a hill (Zion). It was believed that the
valleys helped protect the city by providing a good view of armies attacking
Jerusalem's high walls. **(See Map 5 on
pg 1883.)**

● **22.1-3** *king of Judah:* This probably refers to Zedekiah.

● **22.6,7** *Gilead . . . Lebanon . . .
cedar beams:* Gilead was a forest-rich
region east of the Jordan, and Lebanon,
to the north of Israel, was famous for its
magnificent tall cedar trees. King Solomon had imported cedar wood to make
the temple and palace (1 Kgs 5.1—7.12).
That is why the palace is compared to
the tree-covered hills of Gilead and
Lebanon. **(See Map 6 on pg 1884.)**

● **22.10-12** *Josiah . . . Jehoahaz:* The
lament in these verses concerns the
death of Josiah, who ruled from 640 to
609 B.C. Because Josiah was a good king
who ruled a long time, his death is not to
be mourned. The one to weep for instead
is Josiah's son, Jehoahaz, who ruled only
three months before being arrested by
Egypt's King Neco. He was sent away
to Egypt, where he died. See 2 Kgs 23.28-
34; 2 Chr 35.20—36.4; Ezek 19.1-4.

22.13-18 *King Jehoiakim:* Jehoiakim may have been assassinated by members of his own royal court in 598 B.C. because of his rebellion against Nebuchadnezzar in 602 B.C. See 2 Kgs 23.36—24.6; 2 Chr 36.5-7.

22.20 *Lebanon . . . Bashan . . . Moab:* These areas to the north (Lebanon), northeast (Bashan), and southeast (Moab) have mountain ranges. From these high places, the people of Jerusalem could look down on their land and mourn its destruction. These regions were also defeated and taken over by the Babylonians. **(See Map 6 on pg 1884.)**

22.24 *King Jehoiachin:* Jehoiachin was 18 years old when he followed Jehoiakim as ruler of Judah. But he ruled for only three months before being taken prisoner by Nebuchadnezzar in 598 B.C. He lived in Babylonia the rest of his life, being made a "royal guest" of Babylon by Evil Merodach after the death of Nebuchadnezzar in 562 B.C.

King Jehoiakim

The LORD told me to say:

⋆**13**King Jehoiakim,[j] you are doomed!
　You built a palace
　　with large rooms upstairs.
14You put in big windows
　and used cedar paneling
　　and red paint.
　But you were unfair
　and forced the builders to work
　　without pay.

⋆**15**More cedar in your palace
　doesn't make you a better king
　　than your father Josiah.
　He always did right—
　he gave justice to the poor
　　and was honest.
16That's what it means
　　to truly know me.
　So he lived a comfortable life
　and always had enough
　　to eat and drink.

17But all you think about
　is how to cheat
　or abuse or murder
　　some innocent victim.
18Jehoiakim, no one will mourn
　at your funeral.
　They won't turn to each other
　and ask,
　"Why did our great king
　　have to die?"
19You will be given a burial
　fit for a donkey;
　your body will be dragged

outside the city gates
　and tossed in the dirt.
I, the LORD, have spoken.

King Jehoiachin and the People of Jerusalem

The LORD told me to say:

20People of Jerusalem,
　the nations[k] you trusted
　　have been crushed.
　Go to Lebanon and weep;
　cry in the land of Bashan
　　and in Moab.
21When times were good,
　I warned you.
　But you ignored me,
　just as you have done
　　since Israel was young.
22Now you will be disgraced
　　because of your sins.
　Your leaders will be swept away
　　by the wind,
　and the nations you trusted
　will be captured and dragged
　　to a foreign country.
23Those who live in the palace
　　paneled with cedar[l]
　will groan with pain
　　like women giving birth.

24King Jehoiachin,[m] son of Jehoiakim,[n] even if you were the ring I wear as the sign of my royal power, I would still pull you from my finger. **25**I would hand you over to the enemy you fear, to King Nebuchadnezzar[o] and his army, who want to kill

[j]22.13 *Jehoiakim:* See the note at 1.3. 　[k]22.20 *nations:* Or "gods." 　[l]22.23 *who live in the palace paneled with cedar:* The Hebrew text has "who live in Lebanon and who nest among the cedars," which probably means Forest Hall in the royal palace at Jerusalem, which was paneled with cedar and had cedar columns and a cedar ceiling, all from Lebanon (see 1 Kings 7.2,3). 　[m]22.24 *Jehoiachin:* The Hebrew text has "Coniah," another form of Jehoiachin's name; he ruled for three months in 598 B.C. 　[n]22.24 *Jehoiakim:* See the note at 1.3. 　[o]22.25 *Nebuchadnezzar:* See the note at 21.2.

you. **26**You and your mother[p] were born in Judah, but I will throw both of you into a foreign country, where you will die, **27**longing to return home.

28Jehoiachin, you are unwanted
    like a broken clay pot.
So you and your children
    will be thrown into a country
    you know nothing about.

29Land of Judah, I am the Lord.
    Now listen to what I say!
30Erase the names
    of Jehoiachin's children
    from the royal records.
He is a complete failure,
    and so none of them
    will ever be king.
I, the Lord, have spoken.

A Message of Hope

The Lord said:

23 You leaders of my people are like shepherds that kill and scatter the sheep. **2**You were supposed to take care of my people, but instead you chased them away. So now I'll punish you severely and make you pay for your crimes!

3I will bring the rest of my people home from the lands where I have scattered them, and they will grow into a mighty nation. **4**I promise to choose leaders who will care for them like real shepherds. All of my people will be there, and they will never again be frightened.

5Someday I will appoint
    an honest king
    from the family of David,
    a king who will be wise
    and rule with justice.

6As long as he is king,
    Israel will have peace,
    and Judah will be safe.
The name of this king will be
    "The Lord Gives Justice."

7A time will come when you will again worship me. But you will no longer call me the Living God who rescued Israel from Egypt. **8**Instead, you will call me the Living God who rescued you from the land in the north and from all the other countries where I had forced you to go. And you will once again live in your own land.

Jeremiah Thinks about Unfaithful Prophets

9When I think of the prophets,
    I am shocked, and I tremble[q]
    like someone drunk,
because of the Lord
    and his sacred words.
10Those unfaithful prophets
    misuse their power
    all over the country.
So God turned the pasturelands
    into scorching deserts.[r]

The Lord Will Punish Unfaithful Prophets

11The Lord told me to say:

You prophets and priests
    think so little of me, the Lord,
    that you even sin
    in my own temple!
12Now I will punish you
    with disaster,
and you will slip and fall
    in the darkness.
I, the Lord, have spoken.

22.30 *Erase the names:* None of Jehoiachin's seven sons (1 Chr 3.17,18) ever became king of Judah. He was considered as good as childless, since his sons could not carry on his name as royalty. Though Jehoiachin's sons were disqualified from becoming king of Judah, his grandson Zerubbabel, son of Shealtiel, became governor of Judah after the time of the exile.

23.3 *bring . . . my people home:* This refers to the time after the people have been in exile. The Persian King Cyrus defeated Babylon in 539 B.C. and began to let the Jewish people return home in 538 B.C. (Isa 40.1-11; 45.1-8; Jer 50.4-9; Ezek 37.20-28).

23.5 *king from the family of David:* These verses tell of the coming of an ideal king from the line of David, who will rule with justice.

Messiah (The Chosen One)

23.7,8 *A time will come . . . live in your own land:* These verses date from the time of the exile. The living God will rescue the people from Babylon and restore them to the land of Israel.

---

[p]**22.26** *mother:* See the note at 13.18.   [q]**23.9** *tremble:* Or "become weak."   [r]**23.10** *deserts:* One possible meaning for the difficult Hebrew text of verse 10.

I will bring the rest of my people home from the lands where I have scattered them, and they will grow into a mighty nation. Jer 23.3

23.13,14 *prophets in Samaria . . . prophets in Jerusalem:* The city of Samaria was the capital of the northern kingdom of Israel for many years. Israel's King Ahab built an altar and temple to the Canaanite god Baal there (see 1 Kgs 16.29-33). A number of prophets of the northern kingdom served Baal (1 Kgs 18.1-40). Other prophets complained about the idol worship taking place in Israel (Hos 4.4-19; Mic 1.1-7). Like the prophets of Samaria before them, the prophets of Jerusalem in Jeremiah's day sinned against God and would suffer the LORD's punishment (23.15). **(See Map 6 on pg 1884.)**

23.23 *I am everywhere:* The LORD is not a small local god, as were the Canaanite idols, but rather the God of heaven and all the earth. God cannot be contained or confined to a single place. Therefore, nothing can be kept secret from the LORD.

23.28 *dreams . . . straw and wheat:* The dreams of the false prophets are one thing; God's word is another. The false prophets confuse the two, putting forth their dreams as God's truth. But these dreams are like worthless straw compared to God's real message (nutritious wheat). Such is the difference between pleasing the people and declaring the truth. **(See the article Prophets and Prophecy on pg 1791.)**

¹³The prophets in Samaria
were repulsive to me,
because they preached
in the name of Baal
and led my people astray.
¹⁴And you prophets in Jerusalem
are even worse.
You're unfaithful in marriage[s]
and never tell the truth.[t]
You even lead others to sin
instead of helping them
turn back to me.
You and the people of Jerusalem
are evil like Sodom
and Gomorrah.[u]
¹⁵You prophets in Jerusalem
have spread evil everywhere.
That's why I, the LORD, promise
to give you bitter poison
to eat and drink.

The LORD Gives a Warning

The LORD said:
¹⁶Don't listen to the lies
of these false prophets,
you people of Judah!
The message they preach
is something they imagined;
it did not come from me,
the LORD All-Powerful.
¹⁷These prophets go to people
who refuse to respect me
and who are stubborn
and do whatever they please.
The prophets tell them,
"The LORD has promised
everything will be fine."

¹⁸But I, the LORD, tell you
that these prophets
have never attended a meeting
of my council in heaven[v]
or heard me speak.
¹⁹They are evil! So in my anger
I will strike them
like a violent storm.
²⁰I won't calm down,
until I have finished
what I have decided to do.
Someday you will understand
exactly what I mean.
²¹I did not send these prophets
or speak to them,
but they ran to find you
and to preach their message.
²²If they had been in a meeting
of my council in heaven,
they would have told
you people of Judah
to give up your sins
and come back to me.

²³I am everywhere—
both near and far,
²⁴ in heaven and on earth.
There are no secret places
where you can hide from me.

²⁵These unfaithful prophets claim that I have given them a dream or a vision, and then they tell lies in my name. ²⁶But everything they say comes from their own twisted minds. How long can this go on? ²⁷They tell each other their dreams and try to get my people to reject me, just as their ancestors left me and worshiped Baal. ²⁸Their dreams and my truth are as differ-

[s]**23.14** *in marriage:* Or "to me."   [t]**23.14** *never tell the truth:* Or "worship other gods."   [u]**23.14** *Sodom and Gomorrah:* Two cities that the LORD destroyed because their people were so evil (see Genesis 18.16—19.29).   [v]**23.18** *a meeting of my council in heaven:* Sometimes, prophets had visions of the LORD meeting with his angels (see 1 Kings 22.19-23).

I am everywhere—both near and far, in heaven and on earth. There are no secret places where you can hide from me. JER 23.23,24

ent as straw and wheat. But when prophets speak for me, they must say only what I have told them. ²⁹My words are a powerful fire; they are a hammer that shatters rocks.

³⁰⁻³²These unfaithful prophets claim I give them their dreams, but it isn't true. I didn't choose them to be my prophets, and yet they babble on and on, speaking in my name, while stealing words from each other. And when my people hear these liars, they are led astray instead of being helped. So I warn you that I am now the enemy of these prophets. I, the LORD, have spoken.

News and Nuisance

The LORD said to me:

³³Jeremiah, when a prophet or a priest or anyone else comes to you and asks, "Does the LORD have news for us?" tell them, "You people are a nuisance[w] to the LORD, and he[x] will get rid of you."

³⁴If any of you say, "Here is news from the LORD," I will punish you and your families, even if you are a prophet or a priest. ³⁵Instead, you must ask your friends and relatives, "What answer did the LORD give?" or "What has the LORD said?" ³⁶It seems that you each have your own news! So if you say, "Here is news from the LORD," you are twisting my words into a lie. Remember that I am your God, the LORD All-Powerful.

³⁷If you go to a prophet, it's all right to ask, "What answer did the LORD give to my question?" or "What has the LORD said?" ³⁸But if you disobey me and say, "Here is news from the LORD," ³⁹I will pick you up[y] and throw you far away. And I will abandon this city of Jerusalem that I gave to your ancestors. ⁴⁰You will never be free from your shame and disgrace.

Jeremiah Has a Vision of Two Baskets of Figs

24 The LORD spoke to me in a vision after King Nebuchadnezzar[z] of Babylonia had come to Judah and taken King Jehoiachin,[a] his officials, and all the skilled workers back to Babylonia. In this vision I saw two baskets of figs in front of the LORD's temple. ²One basket was full of very good figs that ripened early, and the other was full of rotten figs that were not fit to eat.

³"Jeremiah," the LORD asked, "what do you see?"

"Figs," I said. "Some are very good, but the others are too rotten to eat."

⁴Then the LORD told me to say:

⁵People of Judah, the good figs stand for those of you I sent away as exiles to Babylonia, ⁶where I am watching over them. Then someday I will bring them back to this land. I will plant them, instead of uprooting them, and I will build them up, rather than tearing them down. ⁷I will give them a desire to know me and to be my people. They will want me to be their God, and they will turn back to me with all their heart.

⁸The rotten figs stand for King Zedekiah[b] of Judah, his officials, and

---

23.33 *news . . . nuisance:* The Hebrew words translated as "news" and "nuisance" in 23.33 were meant as a kind of wordplay. The people expect to hear good news—words of peace and prosperity—so the lying prophets give them what they want to hear. Their "news" has made them a nuisance to God because they fill the people with their false optimism.

24.1 *two baskets of figs:* The people of Israel were to honor the LORD God by bringing the "first fruits" of their harvest, not the leftovers (Lev 23.10,11; Deut 18.4). The two baskets represent two different groups (Jer 24.5-10).

24.5-8 *good figs . . . rotten figs:* The future of Israel lies with the prisoners of war in Babylon. The "good figs" stood for those who would remain faithful to God while living in Babylon. They or their descendants would one day return to Judah (29.10-14) and return to the LORD with all their heart (31.31-34). Many who were left behind in Judah after Nebuchadnezzar's first invasion in 598 B.C. thought that they were favored by God. They were wrong. These "rotten figs" included Jehoiachin's uncle, King Zedekiah, and his royal officials. Some of these officials convinced Zedekiah to rebel against Nebuchadnezzar, which brought on the second invasion and destruction of Jerusalem in 586 B.C.

Nebuchadnezzar

---

[w]23.33 *news . . . nuisance:* The Hebrew word for "news" in verses 33-38 is the same as "nuisance" and is related to "pick up" in verse 39.   [x]23.33 *You people are a nuisance to the LORD, and he:* Two ancient translations; Hebrew "Does the LORD have news for us? He."   [y]23.39 *pick you up:* A few Hebrew manuscripts and three ancient translations; most Hebrew manuscripts "forget you completely."   [z]24.1 *Nebuchadnezzar:* See the note at 21.2.   [a]24.1 *Jehoiachin:* The Hebrew text has "Jeconiah," another form of Jehoiachin's name; he ruled for three months in 598 B.C.   [b]24.8 *Zedekiah:* Ruled 598–586 B.C.

25.1-2 *In the fourth year:* The date is 605 B.C., when the newly enthroned Nebuchadnezzar defeated the Egyptians at the Battle of Carchemish. Egypt's King Neco, who had placed Jehoiakim on the Judean throne four years earlier, was defeated at this battle. This was the same year that Jehoiakim burned Jeremiah's scroll (book) mentioned in 25.13 (see Jer 36).

25.5 *Change your ways:* This is the heart of Jeremiah's message: turn back to God (repent), and God may allow you to stay in your own land.

25.11,12 *70 years . . . punish the king of Babylonia:* Seventy stands for a normal life span (Ps 90.10). The point is that few can expect to witness the punishment of Babylonia. The Babylonian exile actually lasted 50 years (586–538 B.C.), or at most 60 years.

Exile

25.13 *this book:* This scroll contained what is now JEREMIAH, chapters 1–25. It was burned by Jehoiakim and then rewritten by Baruch (see Jer 36).

all the others who were not taken away to Babylonia, whether they stayed here in Judah or went to live in Egypt. [9]I will punish them with a terrible disaster, and everyone on earth will tremble when they hear about it. I will force the people of Judah to go to foreign countries, where they will be cursed and insulted. [10]War and hunger and disease will strike them, until they finally disappear from the land that I gave them and their ancestors.

Seventy Years of Exile

25 [1-2]In the fourth year that Jehoiakim was king of Judah,[c] which was the first year that Nebuchadnezzar[d] was king of Babylonia, the LORD told me to speak to the people of Judah and Jerusalem. So I told them:

[3]For 23 years now, ever since the thirteenth year that Josiah[e] was king, I have been telling you what the LORD has told me. But you have not listened.

[4]The LORD has sent prophets to you time after time, but you refused to listen. [5]They told you that the LORD had said:

Change your ways! If you stop doing evil, I will let you stay forever in this land that I gave your ancestors. [6]I don't want to harm you. So don't make me angry by worshiping idols and other gods.

[7]But you refused to listen to my prophets. So I, the LORD, say that you have made me angry by worshiping idols, and you are the ones who were hurt by what you did. [8]You refused to listen to me, [9]and now I will let you be attacked by nations from the north, and especially by my servant, King

Nebuchadnezzar of Babylonia. You and other nearby nations will be destroyed and left in ruins forever. Everyone who sees what has happened will be shocked, but they will still make fun of you. [10]I will put an end to your parties and wedding celebrations; no one will grind grain or be here to light the lamps at night. [11]This country will be as empty as a desert, because I will make all of you the slaves of the king of Babylonia for 70 years.

[12]When that time is up, I will punish the king of Babylonia and his people for everything they have done wrong, and I will turn that country into a wasteland forever. [13]My servant Jeremiah has told you what I said I will do to Babylonia and to the other nations, and he wrote it all down in this book. I will do everything I threatened. [14]I will pay back the Babylonians for every wrong they have done. Great kings from many other nations will conquer the Babylonians and force them to be slaves.

The Cup Full of God's Anger

[15]The LORD God of Israel showed me a vision in which he said, "Jeremiah, here is a cup filled with the wine of my anger. Take it and make every nation drink some. [16]They will vomit and act crazy, because of the war this cup of anger will bring to them."

[17]I took the cup from the LORD's hand, and I went to the kings of the nations and made each of them drink some. [18]I started with Jerusalem and the towns of Judah, and the king and his officials were removed from power in disgrace. Everyone still

[c]*25.1,2 Jehoiakim . . . Judah:* See the note at 1.3.   [d]*25.1,2 Nebuchadnezzar:* See the note at 21.2.
[e]*25.3 Josiah:* Hebrew "Josiah son of Amon"; Josiah ruled 640–609 B.C.

makes insulting jokes about them and uses their names as curse words. **19**The second place I went was Egypt, where everyone had to drink from the cup, including the king and his officials, the other government workers, the rest of the Egyptians, **20**and all the foreigners who lived in the country.

Next I went to the king of Uz, and then to the four kings of Philistia, who ruled from Ashkelon, Gaza, Ekron, and what was left of Ashdod.**f** **21**Then I went to the kings of Edom, Moab, Ammon, **22**and to the kings of Tyre, Sidon, and their colonies across the sea. **23-24**After this, I went to the kings of Dedan, Tema, Buz, the tribes of the Arabian Desert,**g** **25**Zimri, Elam, Media, **26**and the countries in the north, both near and far.

I went to all the countries on earth, one after another, and finally to Babylonia.**h**

27The LORD had said to tell each king, "The LORD All-Powerful, the God of Israel, commands you to drink from this cup that is full of the wine of his anger. It will make you so drunk that you will vomit. And when the LORD sends war against the nations, you will be completely defeated."

28The LORD told me that if any of them refused to drink from the cup, I must tell them that he had said, "I, the LORD All-Powerful, command you to drink. **29**Starting with my own city of Jerusalem, everyone on earth will suffer from war. So there is no way I will let you escape unharmed."

30The LORD told me to say:
From my sacred temple
   I will roar like thunder,
   while I trample my people

and everyone else
   as though they were grapes.
31My voice will be heard
   everywhere on earth,
accusing nations of their crimes
and sentencing the guilty
   to death.

Disaster Is Coming

32The LORD All-Powerful says:
You can see disaster spreading
   from far across the earth,
from nation to nation
   like a horrible storm.

33When it strikes, I will kill so many people that their bodies will cover the ground like manure. No one will be left to bury them or to mourn.

The Leaders of Judah Will Be Punished

34The LORD's people are his flock,
   and you leaders
   were the shepherds.
But now it's your turn
   to be butchered like sheep.
You'll shatter like fine pottery
   dropped on the floor.**i**
So roll on the ground,
   crying and mourning.
35You have nowhere to run,
   nowhere to hide.

*36-37*Listen to the cries
   of the shepherds,
   as the LORD's burning anger
turns**j** peaceful meadows

f25.20 *what was left of Ashdod*: It was defeated by the king of Egypt after being surrounded for 29 years.   **g25.23,24** *the tribes of the Arabian Desert*: One possible meaning for the difficult Hebrew text.   **h25.26** *Babylonia*: The Hebrew text has "Sheshach," a secret way of writing "Babylonia."   **i25.34** *You'll shatter . . . floor*: One possible meaning for the difficult Hebrew text.   **j25.36,37** *anger turns*: Or "anger and enemy armies turn."

25.19-26 *Egypt . . . Babylonia*: All nations must drink from the cup of God's anger, beginning with Judah and including Egypt and Babylonia. Egypt was defeated by Babylon in 605 B.C. Uz (25.20), the land where Job lived (Job 1.1), was probably east of Judah. The four key cities of Philistia (Ashkelon . . . Ashdod) were defeated by the Egyptians and by the Babylonians. Tyre and Sidon were Phoenician cities on the coast of the Mediterranean Sea. King Nebuchadnezzar of Babylon captured the mainland of Tyre in 572 B.C. (Ezek 26.7-11), and Alexander the Great captured the city in 332 B.C. **(See Map 7 on pg 1885.)**

25.30 *I will roar . . . grapes*: For the image of God as the lion of judgment, see Amos 1.2. Trampling grapes is used elsewhere as a symbol for God's judgment (Isa 63.3; Joel 3.11-13; Rev 14.18-20).

My voice will be heard everywhere on earth, accusing nations of their crimes and sentencing the guilty to death. JER 25.31

Left column notes:

26.1 *Soon after Jehoiakim:* The date is 609 B.C. The nation is still in a state of shock following the death of Jehoiakim's father, the good King Josiah.

26.8-9 *put to death:* The priests and prophets demand that Jeremiah be put to death for the message he proclaimed in the LORD's name. Messages spoken in the LORD's name were to be taken seriously, since they were considered powerful enough to make the events they described actually happen.

26.10 *new gate . . . trial:* Next, the city leaders and officers of the royal court set up a trial for Jeremiah. Public trials were often held in an open area near the gate of a city, palace, or temple.

26.11 *the death penalty:* According to Deuteronomy 18.20, a prophet who lied or delivered a false message deserved death.

26.16 *judges . . . people:* The town officials did not find Jeremiah guilty of a crime punishable by death.

26.18 *Hezekiah . . . Micah:* Hezekiah made many religious reforms (2 Kgs 18.1-4). Like Jeremiah, the prophet Micah had preached against Jerusalem, especially its unjust rulers and lying prophets (Mic 3.1-12).

into barren deserts.
³⁸Like a lion leaving its den,
the LORD has abandoned his people
to the destruction of war.

Jeremiah's Message in the Temple
(Jeremiah 7.1-15)

26 Soon after Jehoiakim[k] became king of Judah, the LORD said:

²Jeremiah, I have a message for everyone who comes from the towns of Judah to worship in my temple. Go to the temple courtyard and speak every word that I tell you. ³Maybe the people will listen this time. And if they stop doing wrong, I will change my mind and not punish them for their sins. ⁴Tell them that I have said:

You have refused to listen to me and to obey my laws and teachings. ⁵Again and again I have sent my servants the prophets to preach to you, but you ignored them as well. Now I am warning you that if you don't start obeying me at once, ⁶I will destroy this temple, just as I destroyed the town of Shiloh.[l] Then everyone on earth will use the name "Jerusalem" as a curse word.

Jeremiah on Trial

⁷The priests, the prophets, and everyone else in the temple heard what I said, ⁸⁻⁹and as soon as I finished, they all crowded around me and started shouting, "Why did you preach that the LORD will destroy this temple, just as he destroyed Shiloh? Why did you say that Jerusalem will be empty and lie in ruins? You ought to be put to death for saying such things in the LORD's name!" Then they had me arrested.

¹⁰The royal officers heard what had happened, and they came from the palace to the new gate of the temple to be the judges at my trial.[m] ¹¹While they listened, the priests and the prophets said to the crowd, "All of you have heard Jeremiah prophesy that Jerusalem will be destroyed. He deserves the death penalty."

¹²⁻¹³Then I told the judges and everyone else:

The LORD himself sent me to tell you about the terrible things he will do to you, to Jerusalem, and to the temple. But if you change your ways and start obeying the LORD, he will change his mind.

¹⁴You must decide what to do with me. Just do whatever you think is right. ¹⁵But if you put me to death, you and everyone else in Jerusalem will be guilty of murdering an innocent man, because everything I preached came from the LORD.

¹⁶The judges and the other people told the priests and prophets, "Since Jeremiah only told us what the LORD our God had said, we don't think he deserves to die."

¹⁷Then some of the leaders from other towns stepped forward. They told the crowd that ¹⁸years ago when Hezekiah[n] was king of Judah, a prophet named Micah from the town of Moresheth had said:

"I, the LORD All-Powerful, say
Jerusalem will be plowed under
and left in ruins.
Thorns will cover the mountain
where the temple
now stands."[o]

¹⁹Then the leaders continued:
No one put Micah to death for say-

[k]26.1 *Jehoiakim:* See the note at 1.3. [l]26.6 *Shiloh:* The sacred tent had once stood at Shiloh. [m]26.10 *new gate . . . trial:* Public trials were often held in an open area at a gate of a city, palace, or temple. [n]26.18 *Hezekiah:* Ruled 716–687 B.C. [o]26.18 *Jerusalem . . . stands:* See Micah 3.12.

ing that. Instead, King Hezekiah prayed to the LORD with fear and trembling and asked him to have mercy. Then the LORD decided not to destroy Jerusalem, even though he had already said he would.

People of Judah, if Jeremiah is killed, we will bring a terrible disaster on ourselves.

²⁰⁻²⁴After these leaders finished speaking, an important man named Ahikam son of Shaphan spoke up for me as well. And so, I wasn't handed over to the crowd to be killed.

Uriah the Prophet

While Jehoiakim[p] was still king of Judah, a man named Uriah son of Shemaiah left his hometown of Kiriath-Jearim and came to Jerusalem. Uriah was one of the LORD's prophets, and he was saying the same things about Judah and Jerusalem that I had been saying. And when Jehoiakim and his officials and military officers heard what Uriah said, they tried to arrest him, but he escaped to Egypt. So Jehoiakim sent Elnathan son of Achbor and some other men after Uriah, and they brought him back. Then Jehoiakim had Uriah killed and his body dumped in a common burial pit.

Slaves of Nebuchadnezzar

27 ¹⁻²Not long after Zedekiah became king of Judah,[q] the LORD told me:
Jeremiah, make a wooden yoke[r] with leather straps, and place it on your neck. ³Then send a message[s] to the kings of

Edom, Moab, Ammon, Tyre, and Sidon. Some officials from these countries are in Jerusalem, meeting with Zedekiah. ⁴So have them tell their kings that I have said:

I am the All-Powerful LORD God of Israel, ⁵and with my power I created the earth, its people, and all animals. I decide who will rule the earth, ⁶⁻⁷and I have chosen my servant King Nebuchadnezzar[t] of Babylonia to rule all nations, including yours. I will even let him rule the wild animals. All nations will be slaves of Nebuchadnezzar, his son, and his grandson. Then many nations will join together, and their kings will make slaves of the Babylonians.

⁸This yoke stands for the power of King Nebuchadnezzar, and I will destroy any nation that refuses to obey him. Nebuchadnezzar will attack, and many will die in battle or from hunger and disease. ⁹You might have people in your kingdom who claim they can tell the future by magic or by talking with the dead or by dreams or messages from a god. But don't pay attention if any of them tell you not to obey Nebuchadnezzar. ¹⁰If you listen to such lies, I will have you dragged far from your country and killed. ¹¹But if you and your nation are willing to obey Nebuchadnezzar, I will let you stay in your country, and your people will continue to live and work on their farms.

¹²After I had spoken to the officials from the nearby kingdoms, I went to King Zedekiah and told him the same thing. Then I said:

Zedekiah, if you and the people of

26.20-24 *Ahikam . . . Uriah:* Ahikam and his father Shaphan were leaders of the reform under Josiah (2 Kgs 22.3,12,14). His son Gedaliah was appointed governor of Judah after the fall of Jerusalem (40.5—41.3). The prophet Uriah is mentioned only here in the Bible. His story shows how the situation might have turned out differently for Jeremiah. Jehoiakim showed no mercy toward Uriah.

27.1-2 *wooden yoke:* The ox yoke is a wooden collar that fits around the neck of an ox. Using leather straps attached to the yoke, a driver can make the ox pull a cart or plow. Jeremiah is told to put on a yoke as a way of symbolizing the power of Nebuchadnezzar (27.8).

27.11 *obey Nebuchadnezzar:* Jeremiah's advice went against those who believed the lying prophets who said that the LORD would protect Judah no matter what. Jeremiah saw a way for his nation and its neighbors to be spared total destruction.

27.12 *King Zedekiah . . . told him the same thing:* Zedekiah did not carry out his revolt at this time (594 B.C.) and Jerusalem was spared.

P**26.20-24** *Jehoiakim:* See the note at 1.3.   q**27.1,2** *Not long after Zedekiah became king of Judah:* A few manuscripts and one ancient translation; most Hebrew manuscripts "Not long after Jehoiakim became king of Judah"; most manuscripts of another ancient translation do not have these words. Jehoiakim ruled 609–598 B.C., and Zedekiah ruled 598–586 B.C.   r**27.1,2** *yoke:* A wooden collar that fits around the neck of an ox, so the ox can be made to pull a plow or a cart.   s**27.3** *a message:* Hebrew "them."   t**27.6,7** *Nebuchadnezzar:* See the note at 21.2.

27.19-21 *bronze pillars . . . valuable things:* The pillars stood in front of the Jerusalem temple. The Sea was a huge bowl in the temple court (see Exod 30.17-21). The stands were objects on wheels.

28.1 *Later that same year:* As in chapter 27, the date is 594 B.C. King Zedekiah of Judah was on the verge of revolting against King Nebuchadnezzar.

28.1 *Hananiah son of Azzur:* Nothing else is known about the prophet Hananiah. Hananiah's prophecy in the temple (28.2-4) is nearly the opposite of Jeremiah's (27.1-15). So, Judah's leaders have to try to determine which prophet is false and which is true (see Deut 18.21,22).

28.6-9 *I hope . . . wait and see:* Jeremiah hopes for good news and wishes for peace for his beloved country. But his and Hananiah's messages can't both be right—only one is truly from the LORD.

28.8 *prophets were saying:* Jeremiah is probably referring to Amos, Hosea, Micah, and Isaiah.

Judah want to stay alive, you must obey Nebuchadnezzar and the Babylonians. [13]But if you refuse, then you and your people will die from war, hunger, and disease, just as the LORD has warned. [14]Your prophets have told you that you don't need to obey Nebuchadnezzar, but don't listen to their lies. [15]Those prophets claim to be speaking for the LORD, but he didn't send them. They are lying! If you do what they say, he will have both you and them dragged off to another country and killed. The LORD has spoken.

[16]When I finished talking to the king, I told the priests and everyone else that the LORD had said:

Don't listen to the prophets when they say that very soon the Babylonians will return the things they took from my temple. Those prophets are lying! [17]If you choose to obey the king of Babylonia, you will live. But if you listen to those prophets, this whole city will be nothing but a pile of rubble.

[18]If I really had spoken to those prophets, they would know what I am going to do. Then they would be begging me not to let everything else be taken from the temple and the king's palace and the rest of Jerusalem. [19-21]After all, when Nebuchadnezzar took King Jehoiachin[u] to Babylonia as a prisoner, he didn't take everything of value from Jerusalem. He left the bronze pillars, the huge bronze bowl called the Sea, and the movable bronze stands in the temple, and he left a lot of other valuable things in the palace and in the rest of Jerusalem.

But now I, the LORD All-Powerful, the God of Israel, say that all these things [22]will be taken to Babylonia, where they will remain until I decide to bring them back to Jerusalem. I, the LORD, have spoken.

Jeremiah Accuses Hananiah of Being a False Prophet

28 Later that same year, in the fifth month of the fourth year that Zedekiah[v] was king,[w] the prophet Hananiah son of Azzur from Gibeon came up to me in the temple. And while the priests and others in the temple were listening, [2]he told me that the LORD had said:

I am the LORD All-Powerful, the God of Israel, and I will smash the yoke[x] that Nebuchadnezzar[y] put on the necks of the nations to make them his slaves. [3]And within two years, I will bring back to Jerusalem everything that he took from my temple and carried off to Babylonia. [4]King Jehoiachin[z] and the other people who were taken from Judah to Babylonia will be allowed to come back here as well. All this will happen because I will smash the power of the king of Babylonia!

[5]The priests and the others were still standing there, so I said:

[6]Hananiah, I hope the LORD will do exactly what you said. I hope he does bring back everything the Babylonians took from the temple, and that our people who were taken to Babylonia will be allowed to return home. [7]But let me remind you and everyone else [8]that long before we were born, proph-

[u]27.19-21 *Jehoiachin:* Hebrew "Jeconiah" (see the note at 24.1). [v]28.1 *Zedekiah:* See the note at 1.3. [w]28.1 *Later . . . king:* One possible meaning for the difficult Hebrew text. [x]28.2 *yoke:* See the note at 27.1,2. [y]28.2 *Nebuchadnezzar:* See the note at 21.2. [z]28.4 *Jehoiachin:* Hebrew "Jeconiah" (see the note at 24.1).

ets were saying powerful kingdoms would be struck by war, disaster, and disease. **9**Now you are saying we will have peace. We will just have to wait and see if that is really what the LORD has said.[a]

10Hananiah grabbed the wooden yoke from my neck and smashed it. **11**Then he said, "The LORD says this is the way he will smash the power Nebuchadnezzar has over the nations, and it will happen in less than two years."

I left the temple, **12**and a little while later, the LORD told me **13-14**to go back and say to Hananiah:

I am the LORD All-Powerful, the God of Israel. You smashed a wooden yoke, but I will replace it with one made of iron. I will put iron yokes on all the nations, and they will have to do what King Nebuchadnezzar commands. I will even let him rule the wild animals.

15-16 Hananiah, I have never sent you to speak for me. And yet you have talked my people into believing your lies and rebelling against me. So now I will send you—I'll send you right off the face of the earth! You will die before this year is over.

17Two months later, Hananiah died.

Jeremiah's Letter to the People of Judah in Babylonia

29 **1-2**I had been left in Jerusalem when King Nebuchadnezzar[b] took many of the people of Jerusalem and Judah to Babylonia as prisoners, including King Jehoiachin,[c] his mother, his officials, and the metal workers and others in Jerusalem who were skilled in making things. So I wrote a letter to the priests, the prophets, the leaders, and the rest of our people in Babylonia. **3**I gave the letter to Elasah and Gemariah,[d] two men that King Zedekiah[e] of Judah was sending to Babylon to talk with Nebuchadnezzar. In the letter, I wrote **4**that the LORD All-Powerful, the God of Israel, had said:

I had you taken from Jerusalem to Babylonia. Now I tell you **5**to settle there and build houses. Plant gardens and eat what you grow in them. **6**Get married and have children, then help your sons find wives and help your daughters find husbands, so they can have children as well. I want your numbers to grow, not to get smaller.

7Pray for peace in Babylonia and work hard to make it prosperous. The more successful that nation is, the better off you will be.

8-9 Some of your people there in Babylonia are fortunetellers, and you have asked them to tell you what will happen in the future. But they will only lead you astray with their dreams.[f] And don't let the prophets fool you, either. They speak in my name, but they are liars. I have not spoken to them.

10After Babylonia has been the strongest nation for 70 years, I will be kind and bring you back to Jerusalem, just as I have promised. **11**I will bless you with a future filled with hope—a future of success, not of suffering. **12**You will turn back to me and ask for help, and I will answer your prayers.

[a]**28.9** *We will . . . said*: See Deuteronomy 18.21,22. [b]**29.1,2** *Nebuchadnezzar*: See the note at 21.2.
[c]**29.1,2** *Jehoiachin*: Hebrew "Jeconiah" (see the note at 24.1). [d]**29.3** *Elasah and Gemariah*: Hebrew "Elasah son of Shaphan and Gemariah son of Hilkiah." [e]**29.3** *Zedekiah*: See the note at 1.3.
[f]**29.8,9** *their dreams*: Hebrew "your dreams."

29.21-23 *Ahab . . . Zedekiah:* These Jewish prophets living in exile in Babylon were making the same false claims that Hananiah made.

29.21-23 *burned . . . to death:* They were probably executed because they predicted Babylon's destruction. Their deaths show the LORD's judgment on them for their lies and immorality.

29.24-25 *Shemaiah . . . Zephaniah:* This is the only mention of Shemaiah, whose letters from Babylon are aimed at getting Jeremiah arrested.

29.28 *a letter:* This refers to Jeremiah's letter (29.3-23).

29.30 *a second letter:* In response to Shemaiah's letter, Jeremiah writes a second letter.

[13]You will worship me with all your heart, and I will be with you [14]and accept your worship. Then I will gather you from all the nations where I scattered you, and you will return to Jerusalem.

[15]You feel secure, because you think I have sent prophets to speak for me in Babylonia.

[16-19]But I have been sending prophets to the people of Judah for a long time, and the king from David's family and the people who are left in Jerusalem and Judah still don't obey me. So I, the LORD All-Powerful, will keep attacking them with war and hunger and disease, until they are as useless as rotten figs. I will force them to leave the land, and all nations will be disgusted and shocked at what happens to them. The nations will sneer and make fun of them and use the names "Judah" and "Jerusalem" as curse words.

And you have not obeyed me, even though [20]I had you taken from Jerusalem to Babylonia. But you had better listen to me now. [21-23]You think Ahab son of Kolaiah and Zedekiah son of Maaseiah are prophets because they claim to speak for me. But they are lying! I haven't told them anything. They are also committing other horrible sins in your community, such as sleeping with the wives of their friends. So I will hand them over to King Nebuchadnezzar, who will put them to death while the rest of you watch. And in the future, when you want to put a curse on someone, you will say, "I pray that the LORD will kill you in the same way the king of Babylonia burned Zedekiah and Ahab to death!"

A Message for Shemaiah

[24-25]The LORD All-Powerful, the God of Israel, told me what would happen to Shemaiah,[g] who was one of our people in Babylonia. After my letter reached Babylonia, Shemaiah wrote letters to the people of Jerusalem, including the priest Zephaniah son of Maaseiah, and the other priests. The letter to Zephaniah said:

[26]After the death of Jehoiada the priest, the LORD chose you to be the priest in charge of the temple security force. You know that anyone who acts crazy and pretends to be a prophet should be arrested and put in chains[h] and iron collars. [27]Jeremiah from the town of Anathoth is pretending to be a prophet there in Jerusalem, so why haven't you punished him? [28]He even wrote a letter to the people here in Babylonia, saying we would be here a long time. He told us to build homes and to plant gardens and grow our own food.

[29]When Zephaniah received Shemaiah's letter, he read it to me. [30]Then the LORD told me what to write in a second letter [31]to the people of Judah who had been taken to Babylonia. In this letter, I wrote that the LORD had said:

I, the LORD, have not chosen Shemaiah to be one of my prophets, and he has misled you by telling lies in my name. [32]He has even talked you into disobeying me. So I will punish Shemaiah. He and his descendants won't live to see the good things I will do for my people. I, the LORD, have spoken.

[g]29.24,25 *Shemaiah:* Hebrew "Shemaiah, who came from the town of Nehelam."   [h]29.26 *in chains:* See the note at 20.2.

The Lord Will Rescue Israel and Judah

30 ¹⁻²The Lord God of Israel said, "Jeremiah, get a scroll[i] and write down everything I have told you. ³Someday I will let my people from both Israel[j] and Judah return to the land I gave their ancestors."

⁴⁻⁵Then the Lord told me to say to Israel and Judah:

Screams of terror are heard,
    with no word of peace.
⁶Can men give birth?
Then why do I see them
    looking so pale
and clutching their stomachs
    like women in labor?
⁷My people, soon you will suffer
    worse than ever before,
    but I will save you.

⁸Now you are slaves
    of other nations,
but I will break the chains
    and smash the yokes[k]
    that keep you in slavery.
⁹Then you will be my servants,
    and I will choose a king for you
    from the family of David.

*¹⁰Israel,[l] you belong to me,
    so don't be afraid.
You deserved to be punished;
    that's why I scattered you
    in distant nations.
But I am with you,
    and someday I will destroy
    those nations.
¹¹Then I will bring you
    and your descendants
    back to your land,

where I will protect you
    and give you peace.
Then your fears will be gone.
    I, the Lord, have spoken.

The Lord Will Heal Israel and Judah

¹²The Lord said:

My people, you are wounded
    and near death.
¹³You are accused of a crime
    with no one to defend you,
and you are covered with sores
    that no medicine can cure.
*¹⁴Your friends have forgotten you;
    they don't care anymore.
Even I have acted like an enemy.
And because your sins
    are horrible and countless,
I will be cruel
    as I punish you.
¹⁵So don't bother to cry out
    for relief from your pain.

¹⁶But if your enemies try to rob
    or destroy you,
I will rob and destroy them,
    and they will be led as captives
    to foreign lands.
¹⁷No one wants you as a friend
    or cares what happens to you.
But I will heal your injuries,
    and you will get well.

The Lord Will Rescue Israel and Judah

¹⁸The Lord said:

Israel, I will be kind to you
    and let you come home.

---

[i]**30.1,2** *scroll:* A roll of paper or special leather used for writing on.   [j]**30.3** *Israel:* The northern kingdom.   [k]**30.8** *yokes:* See the note at 27.1,2.   [l]**30.10** *Israel:* The people of the northern and southern kingdoms.

30.1-2 *scroll:* This scroll was written just after Jerusalem fell to Babylon in 586 B.C. At last, Jeremiah can fulfill the second part of his twofold task (1.10): to preach rescue and rebuilding.

Scrolls

30.3 *Israel and Judah:* Here, Israel refers to the northern kingdom. (See Map 6 on pg 1884.)

30.4-7 *terror:* The suffering and destruction of Jerusalem and Judah will complete God's judgment.

30.8,9 *you are slaves . . . you will be my servants:* The people of Judah and Israel are like slaves in exile, but the Lord will end their exile and free them from the yoke of Babylon.

30.18 *I will be kind:* The Hebrew word translated as "kind" can also be translated as "mercy" or "compassion."

30.18-21 *come home . . . your ruler:* Because the people of Israel and Judah disobeyed the Lord, the promises made to their ancestors were endangered. The Lord will renew these promises in the future, which include reclaiming their land and having many children (see Gen 12.1-3; 15.4-6; Exod 3.7-10). They are also promised that their new ruler will be an Israelite, not a foreigner (see 30.9). When the people returned to Judah, they were ruled by a governor and the high priest working together (Hag 1,2).

■ 31.2 *In the desert I was kind:* God recalls Israel's days of wilderness wandering. God will rescue God's people from Babylonia, just as they were rescued from Egypt. See Exod 33.12-17; Jer 23.7,8.

■ 31.3 *I will always love you:* The patience of God has its limits and the judgment of God is sure, but the love of God cannot be exhausted.

Jerusalem now lies in ruins,
but you will rebuild it,
    complete with a new palace.[m]
[19]Other nations will respect
    and honor you.
Your homes will be filled
    with children,
and you will celebrate,
    singing praises to me.

[20]It will be just like old times.
Your nation will worship me,
    and I will punish anyone
    who abuses you.
[21]One of your own people
    will become your ruler.
And when I invite him
    to come near me
at the place of worship,
    he will do so.
No one would dare to come near
    without being invited.
[22]You will be my people,
and I will be your God.
    I, the LORD, have spoken.

[23]I am furious!
And like a violent storm
    I will strike those
    who do wrong.
[24]I won't calm down
until I have finished
    what I have decided to do.
Someday, you will understand
    what I mean.

Israel Will Return to God

31 The LORD said:
Israel, I promise

that someday all your tribes
will again be my people,
    and I will be your God.
[2]In the desert I was kind
    to those who escaped death.
I gave them peace,
    and when the time is right,
I'll do the same for you.[n]
    I, the LORD, have spoken.

The LORD Will Rebuild Israel

[3]Some time ago, the LORD appeared to me[o] and told me to say:
    Israel, I will always love you;
    that's why I've been so patient
        and kind.
[4]You are precious to me,
    and so I will rebuild
        your nation.
Once again you will dance for joy
    and play your tambourines.
[5]You will plant vineyards
    on the hills of Samaria
        and enjoy the grapes.
[6]Someday those who guard
    the hill country of Ephraim
will shout, "Let's go to Zion
and worship the LORD our God."

Israel Will Return to Its Own Land

[7]The LORD says:

Celebrate and sing for Israel,
    the greatest of nations.
Offer praises and shout,
    "Come and rescue
    your people, LORD!
Save what's left of Israel."

[m]30.18 *Jerusalem . . . palace:* Or "Your towns lie in ruins, but you will rebuild them, and your homes will be where they were before." [n]31.2 *In the desert . . . same for you:* One possible meaning for the difficult Hebrew text. [o]31.3 *Some time . . . me:* Or "The LORD appeared to me from far away."

⁸I, the Lord, will bring
my people back from Babylonia^p
and everywhere else on earth.
The blind and the lame
will be there.
Expectant mothers
and women about to give birth
will come and be part
of that great crowd.
⁹They will weep and pray
as I bring them home.
I will lead them
to streams of water.
They will walk on a level^q road
and not stumble.
I am a father to Israel,^r
my favorite children.

¹⁰Listen to me, you nations
nearby or across the sea.
I scattered the people of Israel,
but I will gather them again.
I will protect them like a shepherd
guarding a flock;
¹¹I will rescue them from enemies
who could overpower them.
¹²My people will come
to Mount Zion
and celebrate;
their faces will glow
because of my blessings.
I'll give them grain, grapes,
and olive oil,
as well as sheep and cattle.
Israel will be prosperous
and grow like a garden
with plenty of water.

¹³Young women and young men,
together with the elderly,
will celebrate and dance,
because I will comfort them
and turn their sorrow
into happiness.
¹⁴I will bless my people
with more food
than they need,
and the priests will enjoy
the choice cuts of meat.
I, the Lord, have spoken.

The Lord Offers Hope

¹⁵In Ramah^s a voice is heard,
crying and weeping loudly.
Rachel mourns for her children^t
and refuses to be comforted,
because they are dead.
*¹⁶But I, the Lord, say
to dry your tears.
Someday your children
will come home
from the enemy's land.
Then all you have done for them
will be greatly rewarded.
¹⁷So don't lose hope.
I, the Lord, have spoken.

¹⁸The people of Israel^u moan
and say to me,
"We were like wild bulls,
but you, Lord, broke us,
and we learned to obey.
You are our God—

---

^p31.8 *Babylonia*: The Hebrew text has "that country in the north," referring to Babylonia.
^q31.9 *level*: Or "straight."   ^r31.9 *Israel*: The Hebrew text also has "Ephraim," the leading tribe of
the northern kingdom of Israel, which sometimes stands for the whole northern kingdom.
^s31.15 *In Ramah*: Or "In the hills."   ^t31.15 *Rachel . . . children*: Rachel was one of the wives of Jacob,
the ancestor of the nation of Israel. She was the mother of Joseph and Benjamin. Joseph's two sons
Ephraim and Manasseh were the ancestors of the leading tribes of the northern kingdom of Israel.
^u31.18 *Israel*: Hebrew "Ephraim" (see the note at 31.9).

● **31.8,9** *back from Babylon . . . on a level road:* In 539 B.C. Cyrus of Persia defeated Babylon and soon after allowed the people of Judah to return home (Ezra 1.1-3; Isa 45.1-4). Jeremiah pictures God bringing his people back to their homeland (Canaan) from all over the earth in a "new exodus." The later chapters of Isaiah also echo this joyful theme (Isa 35.5-10; 40.3-5; 42.16; 43.1-7; 48.20-22; 49.8-12).

● **31.14** *priests . . . choice cuts:* Priests were to take a portion of the choice meats and grains brought by the people to be offered as sacrifices (Lev 7.7-10; 27.30; Deut 14.22-29).

● **31.15** *In Ramah . . . Rachel mourns:* Rachel was one of the wives of Jacob and the mother of Joseph and Benjamin (Gen 30.22-24; 35.16-19). She was buried near Ramah, a village to the north of Jerusalem (Gen 35.16-20; 1 Sam 10.2). Rachel's spirit weeps from the grave for her descendants, but God tells her that the people of these tribes will come back to her.

■ **31.18** *like wild bulls . . . we strayed and sinned . . . want to return:* Wild bulls or oxen had to be broken (tamed) in order to be used as work animals. Israel acted like a wild bull, but the Lord tamed them by punishing them. Now, like the prodigal son (Luke 15.17-19), the people of Israel want to come home, so they admit their sin and beg for God's forgiveness.

31.20 *my own dear children . . . I will have mercy:* God loves Rachel's children as strongly as their mother does. God is attached to the child (Israel) with unbreakable bonds of love.

31.21 *rock piles and signposts:* The first people who leave Babylon will set up stone markers on the road leading back home to Israel so that others can more easily find their way back.

31.29 *Sour grapes:* In ancient times, children were thought to suffer because of their parents' evil actions. Applied to the situation in Judah and Israel, innocent children did suffer because of the disobedience of adults. But this new day for Israel means a new way of looking at sin: Children cannot suffer for the sins of their parents, and the nation will not be punished for the sins of earlier generations (see Ezek 18.2,3; also Deut 24.16).

31.31 *a new agreement:* This is the high point of Jeremiah's message. God's new agreement with the people of Israel and Judah will not replace the earlier agreement made with Moses, which the people broke. In the new agreement, God will write the laws directly on the hearts and minds of the people. The people will obey the LORD because they will realize that it is for their own good (Jer 32.29-41). Also, in this new agreement, God will forgive and forget sins. See also Jer. 32.37-42; Hos 2.16-20; Heb 8.7-12; 10.16,17.

Agreements (Covenents)

please let us come home.
[19]When we were young,
    we strayed and sinned,
but then we realized
    what we had done.
We are ashamed and disgraced
    and want to return to you."

[20]People of Israel,
you are my own dear children.
    Don't I love you best of all?
Though I often make threats,
I want you to be near me,
    so I will have mercy on you.
I, the LORD, have spoken.

[21]With rock piles and signposts,
    mark the road well,
    my dear people.
The road by which you left
    by will now lead you home.
[22]Will you ever decide
    to be faithful?
I will make sure that someday
    things will be different,
as different as a woman
    protecting a man.[v]

The LORD Will Bring Judah Home

[23]The LORD All-Powerful, the God of Israel, said:

I promise to set the people of Judah free and to lead them back to their hometowns. And when I do, they will once again say,
    "We pray that the LORD
        will bless his home,
    the sacred hill in Jerusalem
        where his temple stands."

[24]The people will live in Jerusalem and in the towns of Judah. Some will be farmers, and others will be shepherds. [25]Those who feel tired and worn out will find new life and energy, [26]and when they sleep, they will wake up refreshed.[w]

[27]Someday, Israel and Judah will be my field where my people and their livestock will grow. [28]In the past, I took care to uproot them, to tear them down, and to destroy them. But when that day comes, I will take care to plant them and help them grow. [29] No longer will anyone go around saying,
    "Sour grapes eaten by parents
        leave a sour taste in the mouths
        of their children."
[30]When that day comes, only those who eat sour grapes will get the sour taste, and only those who sin will be put to death.

The New Agreement with Israel and Judah

[31]The LORD said:

The time will surely come when I will make a new agreement with the people of Israel and Judah. [32]It will be different from the agreement I made with their ancestors when I led them out of Egypt. Although I was their God, they broke that agreement. [33]Here is the new agreement that I, the LORD, will make with the people of Israel:
    "I will write my laws
        on their hearts and minds.
    I will be their God,
        and they will be my people.

[34]"No longer will they have to teach one another to obey me. I, the LORD, promise that all of them will obey me, ordinary people and rulers alike. I will forgive their sins and forget the evil things they have done."

[v]**31.22** *I will make sure . . . a woman protecting a man:* One possible meaning for the difficult Hebrew text.   [w]**31.26** *and when they sleep . . . refreshed:* One possible meaning for the difficult Hebrew text.

"I will write my laws on their hearts and minds. I will be their God, and they will be my people . . . I will forgive their sins and forget the evil things they have done." JER 31.33,34

35I am the Lord All-Powerful.
I command the sun
    to give light each day,
the moon and stars
to shine at night,
    and ocean waves to roar.
36I will never forget
    to give those commands,
and I will never let Israel
    stop being a nation.
I, the Lord, have spoken.

37Can you measure the heavens?
Can you explore
    the depths of the earth?
That's how hard it would be
for me to reject Israel forever,
    even though they have sinned.
I, the Lord, have spoken.

Jerusalem Will Be Rebuilt

38The Lord said:

Someday, Jerusalem will truly belong to me. It will be rebuilt with a boundary line running from Hananel Tower to Corner Gate. **39**From there, the boundary will go in a straight line to Gareb Hill, then turn toward Goah. **40**Even that disgusting Hinnom Valley[x] will be sacred to me, and so will the eastern slopes that go down from Horse Gate into Kidron Valley. Jerusalem will never again be destroyed.

Jeremiah Buys a Field

32 The Lord spoke to me in the tenth year that Zedekiah[y] was king of Judah, which was the eighteenth year that Nebuchadnezzar[z] was king of Babylonia.
2At that time, the Babylonian army had surrounded Jerusalem, and I was in the prison at the courtyard of the palace guards. **3**Zedekiah had ordered me to be held there because I told everyone that the Lord had said:

I am the Lord, and I am about to let the king of Babylonia conquer Jerusalem. **4**King Zedekiah will be captured and taken to King Nebuchadnezzar, who will speak with him face to face. **5**Then Zedekiah will be led away to Babylonia, where he will stay until I am finished with him. So, if you people of Judah fight against the Babylonians, you will lose. I, the Lord, have spoken.

6Later, when I was in prison, the Lord said:

7Jeremiah, your cousin Hanamel, the son of your uncle Shallum, will visit you. He must sell his field near the town of Anathoth, and because you are his nearest relative, you have the right and the responsibility to buy it and keep it in the family.[a]

8Hanamel came, just as the Lord had promised. And he said, "Please buy my field near Anathoth in the territory of the Benjamin tribe. You have the right to buy it, and if you do, it will stay in our family."

The Lord had told me to buy it **9**from Hanamel, and so I did. The price was 17 pieces of silver, and I weighed out the full amount on a scale. **10-11**I had two copies of the bill of sale written out: an official copy containing the details of our agreement and another copy, without the details. Some witnesses and I signed the official copy, which was folded and tied, before being

---

[x]**31.40** *that disgusting Hinnom Valley:* The Hebrew text has "the whole valley of the dead bodies and of the fatty ashes," which probably refers to Hinnom Valley, just southwest of Jerusalem, where human sacrifices had been offered to foreign gods.   [y]**32.1** *Zedekiah:* See the note at 1.3.   [z]**32.1** *Nebuchadnezzar:* See the note at 21.2.   [a]**32.7** *you have the right . . . in the family:* See Leviticus 25.25-32.

■ **31.35,36** *I command the sun . . . I will never forget:* Just as God controls nature and makes sure the cycle of days and nights continues, so God will ensure Israel's future.

● **31.38-40** *Hananel Tower . . . Kidron Valley:* Hananel Tower was at the northeast corner of the city; Corner Gate was at the northwest. Gareb Hill and Goah probably indicate the southwest and southeast corners. **(See Map 5 on pg 1883.)**

● **32.7** *He must sell . . . nearest relative:* When a person was forced to sell land to pay a debt, the law required family members to have the first right to purchase or refuse the land (see Lev 25.25-32; Ruth 4.1-6). Jeremiah's cousin is selling at a terrible time. Why would anyone be so foolish as to invest in real estate near Jerusalem in 587 B.C. when the Babylonians might steal the land at any moment?

● **32.9-11** *17 pieces of silver . . . hot wax:* An ancient business transaction is described. The silver pieces were not coins, but bars or rings known as shekels, which weighed about four-tenths of an ounce each. Two copies of the bill of sale were made and signed, probably on papyrus sheets. Then one copy was rolled, tied, and fastened shut with hot wax.

32.12 *Baruch:* Baruch was Jeremiah's friend and secretary (see chapter 36). Baruch "wrote down everything," both the messages from the LORD (36.1-32) and the stories about Jeremiah's life in Judah and Egypt.

32.13-14 *put them in a clay jar:* Certain items could be kept safe and would not decay in a sealed clay jar. In 1949, jars discovered in caves at Qumran in Palestine were found to contain readable scrolls dating back about 1900 years to the first century A.D.

32.15 *I promise you:* Jeremiah's purchase of land at such an unsettled time was a symbol of God's promise (32.43,44) and a sign of hope for Judah's future.

32.20-23 *worked miracles in Egypt . . . punished Israel:* Though the LORD God saved the people of Israel from slavery in Egypt and gave them the rich land of Canaan, the people did not obey God or remain faithful to him alone.

32.24,25 *Jerusalem is under attack . . . why did you tell me:* With Jerusalem under attack, Jeremiah wonders if he can really believe God's promise that things will return to normal in Judah in the future.

sealed shut with hot wax.[b] Then I gave Hanamel the silver. [12]And while he, the witnesses, and all the other Jews sitting in the courtyard were still watching, I gave both copies to Baruch son of Neriah.[c]

[13-14]I told Baruch that the LORD had said:

Take both copies of this bill of sale, one sealed shut and the other open, and put them in a clay jar so they will last a long time. [15]I am the LORD All-Powerful, the God of Israel, and I promise you that people will once again buy and sell houses, farms, and vineyards in this country.

Jeremiah Questions the LORD

[16]Then I prayed:

[17]LORD God, you stretched out your mighty arm and made the sky and the earth. You can do anything. [18]You show kindness for a thousand generations,[d] but you also punish people for the sins of their parents. You are the LORD All-Powerful. [19]With great wisdom you make plans, and with your great power you do all the mighty things you planned. Nothing we do is hidden from your eyes, and you reward or punish us as we deserve.

[20]You are famous because you worked miracles in Egypt, and you are still working them in Israel and in the rest of the world as well. [21]You terrified the Egyptians with your miracles, and you reached out your mighty arm and rescued your people Israel from Egypt. [22]Then you gave Israel this land rich with milk and honey, just as you had promised our ancestors.

[23]But when our ancestors took over the land, they did not obey you. And now you have punished Israel with disaster. [24]Jerusalem is under attack, and we suffer from hunger and disease. The Babylonians have already built dirt ramps up to the walls of our city, and you can see that Jerusalem will be captured just as you said.

[25]So why did you tell me to get some witnesses and buy a field with my silver, when Jerusalem is about to be captured by the Babylonians?

The LORD Explains about the Field

[26]The LORD explained:

[27]Jeremiah, I am the LORD God. I rule the world, and I can do anything!

[28]It is true that I am going to let King Nebuchadnezzar[e] of Babylonia capture Jerusalem. [29]The Babylonian army is already attacking, and they will capture the city and set it on fire. The people of Jerusalem have made me angry by going up to the flat roofs of their houses and burning incense to Baal and offering wine sacrifices to other gods. Now these houses will be burned to the ground!

[30-33]The kings and the officials, the priests and the prophets, and everyone else in Israel and Judah have turned from me and made me angry by worshiping idols. Again and again I have tried to teach my people to obey me, but they refuse to be corrected.

I am going to get rid of Jerusalem, because its people have done nothing but evil. [34]They have set up repulsive idols in my temple, and now it isn't a fit place to

[b]32.10,11 *signed the official copy, which was folded and tied, before being sealed shut with hot wax:* The signing was actually done by pressing a carved clay stamp (called a "seal") into the hot wax, leaving the design in the wax. [c]32.12 *Baruch son of Neriah:* Hebrew "Baruch son of Neriah and grandson of Mahseiah." [d]32.18 *for a thousand generations:* Or "to thousands of people." [e]32.28 *Nebuchadnezzar:* See the note at 21.2.

worship me. ³⁵And they led Judah into sin by building places to worship Baal in Hinnom Valley, where they also sacrificed their sons and daughters to the god Molech. I have never even imagined they would commit such disgusting sins.

³⁶Jeremiah, what you said is true. The people of Jerusalem are suffering from hunger and disease, and so the king of Babylonia will be able to capture Jerusalem. ³⁷I am angry with the people of Jerusalem, and I will scatter them in foreign countries. But someday I will bring them back here and let them live in safety. ³⁸They will be my people, and I will be their God. ³⁹⁻⁴¹I will make their thoughts and desires pure. Then they will realize that, for their own good and the good of their children, they must worship only me. They will even be afraid to turn away from me. I will make an agreement with them that will never end, and I won't ever stop doing good things for them. With all my heart I promise that they will be planted in this land once again. ⁴²Even though I have brought disaster on the people, I will someday do all these good things for them.

⁴³Jeremiah, when you bought the field, you showed that fields will someday be bought and sold again. You say that this land has been conquered by the Babylonians and has become a desert, emptied of people and animals. ⁴⁴But someday, people will again spend their silver to buy fields everywhere—in the territory of Benjamin, the region around Jerusalem and the towns of Judah, and in the hill country, the foothills to the west, and the Southern Desert. Buyers and sellers and witnesses will sign and seal the bills of sale for the fields. It will happen, because I will give this land back to my people. I, the Lord, have spoken.

The Lord Promises To Give the Land Back to His People

33 ¹⁻²I was still being held prisoner in the courtyard of the palace guards when the Lord told me:

I am the Lord, and I created the whole world.^f ³Ask me, and I will tell you things that you don't know and can't find out.

⁴⁻⁵Many of the houses in Jerusalem and some of the buildings at the royal palace have been torn down to be used in repairing the walls to keep out the Babylonian attackers.^g Now there are empty spaces where the buildings once stood. But I am furious, and these spaces will be filled with the bodies of the people I kill. The people of Jerusalem will cry out to me for help, but they are evil, and I will ignore their prayers. ⁶Then someday, I will heal this place and my people as well, and let them enjoy unending peace.^h ⁷I will give this land to Israel and Judah once again, and I will make them as strong as they were before. ⁸They sinned and rebelled against me, but I will forgive them and take away their guilt. ⁹When that happens, all nations on earth will see the good things I have done for Jerusalem, and how I have given it complete peace. The nations will celebrate and praise and honor me, but they will also tremble with fear because of the powerful things I have done.

¹⁰Jeremiah, you say that this land is a desert without people or animals, and for now, you are right. The towns of Judah and

* **32.36,37** *suffering from hunger . . . I will scatter them:* The people were starving and sick, because the Babylonian army had surrounded the city for months.

* **33.4-5** *houses . . . have been torn down:* Some houses and buildings on the palace grounds have been demolished and used for barricades and to plug gaps in the wall. Perhaps the Babylonian army has actually started to break through the outer walls of the city.

* **33.4-6** *I am furious . . . I will heal:* The destruction predicted in 21.3-7 and 37.6-10 is about to take place, but the Lord will not allow this destruction to be the last word. The Lord will eventually heal the people by forgiving them and heal the city by rebuilding it.

* **33.9** *all nations . . . tremble with fear:* The destruction of Jerusalem will lead to Israel's enemies insulting and making fun of the Lord and his people (Jer 8.19; 33.24). But when the Lord helps the people of Judah rebuild their land and gives them prosperity and peace, other nations will have respect for Israel's God.

* **33.10,11** *desert without people . . . happy voices:* Verse 11 promises a reversal of the total destruction predicted in 7.34. The uninhabited places will one day be the sites for joyful occasions and grateful worship, and the land will once again produce crops.

^f**33.1,2** *the whole world:* One ancient translation; Hebrew "it." ^g**33.4,5** *have been torn down . . . Babylonian attackers:* One possible meaning for the difficult Hebrew text. ^h**33.6** *let them enjoy unending peace:* One possible meaning for the difficult Hebrew text.

33.16 *"The LORD Gives Justice"*: Jerusalem is given a new name that emphasizes its concern for fair treatment of all people, especially the poor and homeless.

33.21 *agreements . . . with David's family . . . Levi tribe:* The agreements made with David (2 Sam 7) and with the true priests (Deut 8.1-5) will never again be broken. The promise of many descendants in 33.22 echoes the agreement the LORD made with Abraham (Gen 15.5; Gen 22.17).

Agreements (Covenants)

33.26 *the descendants of Abraham, Isaac, and Jacob:* The eternal promises are applied to all the people of Israel who descended from Abraham, his son Isaac, and his grandson Jacob.

the streets of Jerusalem are deserted, and people and animals are nowhere to be seen. But someday you will hear [11]happy voices and the sounds of parties and wedding celebrations. And when people come to my temple to offer sacrifices to thank me, you will hear them say:

"We praise you,
LORD All-Powerful!
You are good to us,
and your love never fails."

The land will once again be productive. [12-13]Now it is empty, without people or animals. But when that time comes, shepherds will take care of their flocks in pastures near every town in the hill country, in the foothills to the west, in the Southern Desert, in the land of the Benjamin tribe, and around Jerusalem and the towns of Judah.

I, the LORD, have spoken.

The LORD's Wonderful Promise

[14]The LORD said:

I made a wonderful promise to Israel and Judah,[i] and the days are coming when I will keep it.

[15]I promise that the time will come
when I will appoint a king
from the family of David,
a king who will be honest
and rule with justice.
[16]In those days,
Judah will be safe;
Jerusalem will have peace
and will be named,
"The LORD Gives Justice."

[17]The king of Israel will be one of David's descendants, [18] and there will always be

priests from the Levi tribe serving at my altar and offering sacrifices to please me and to give thanks.[j]

[19]Then the LORD told me:

[20]I, the LORD, have an agreement with day and night, so they always come at the right time. You can't break the agreement I made with them, [21]and you can't break the agreements I have made with David's family and with the priests from the Levi tribe who serve at my altar. A descendant of David will always rule as king of Israel, [22]and there will be more descendants of David and of the priests from the Levi tribe than stars in the sky or grains of sand on the beach.

[23]The LORD also said:

[24]You've heard foreigners insult my people by saying, "The LORD chose Israel and Judah, but now he has rejected them, and they are no longer a nation."

[25]Jeremiah, I will never break my agreement with the day and the night or let the sky and the earth stop obeying my commands. [26]In the same way, I will never reject the descendants of Abraham, Isaac, and Jacob or break my promise that they will always have a descendant of David as their king. I will be kind to my people Israel, and they will be successful again.

Jeremiah Warns Zedekiah

34 King Nebuchadnezzar[k] had a large army made up of people from every kingdom in his empire. He and his army were attacking Jerusalem and all the nearby towns, when the LORD told me [2]to say to King Zedekiah:[l]

I am the LORD, and I am going to let Nebuchadnezzar capture this city and burn it down. [3]You will be taken pris-

[i]**33.14** *Israel and Judah:* See the note at 2.4.   [j]**33.18** *sacrifices to please me and to give thanks:* See the notes at 14.12.   [k]**34.1** *Nebuchadnezzar:* See the note at 21.2.   [l]**34.2** *Zedekiah:* See the note at 1.3.

oner and brought to Nebuchadnezzar, and he will speak with you face to face. Then you will be led away to Babylonia.

[4]Zedekiah, I promise that you won't die in battle. [5]You will die a peaceful death. People will mourn when you die, and they will light bonfires in your honor, just as they did for your ancestors, the kings who ruled before you.

[6]I went to Zedekiah and told him what the Lord had said. [7]Meanwhile, the king of Babylonia was trying to break through the walls of Lachish, Azekah, and Jerusalem, the only three towns of Judah that had not been captured.

The People Break a Promise

[8-10]King Zedekiah,[m] his officials, and everyone else in Jerusalem made an agreement to free all Hebrew[n] men and women who were slaves. No Jew would keep another as a slave. And so, all the Jewish slaves were given their freedom.

[11]But those slave owners changed their minds and forced their former slaves back into slavery.

[12]That's when the Lord told me to say to the people:

[13]I am the Lord God of Israel, and I made an agreement with your ancestors when I brought them out of Egypt, where they had been slaves. [14]As part of this agreement, you must let a Hebrew slave go free after six years of service.

Your ancestors did not obey me, [15-16]but you decided to obey me and do the right thing by setting your Hebrew slaves completely free. You even went to my temple, and in my name you made an agreement to set them free. But you have abused my name, because you broke that agreement and forced your former slaves back into slavery.

[17]You have disobeyed me by not giving your slaves their freedom. So I will give you freedom—the freedom to die in battle or from disease or hunger. I will make you disgusting to all other nations on earth.

[18]You asked me to be a witness when you made the agreement to set your slaves free. And as part of the ceremony you cut a calf into two parts, then walked between the parts. But you people of Jerusalem have broken that agreement as well as my agreement with Israel. So I will do to you what you did to that calf. [19-20]I will let your enemies take all of you prisoner, including the leaders of Judah and Jerusalem, the royal officials, the priests, and everyone else who walked between the two parts of the calf. These enemies will kill you and leave your bodies lying on the ground as food for birds and wild animals.

[21-22]These enemies are King Nebuchadnezzar[o] of Babylonia and his army. They have stopped attacking Jerusalem, but they want to kill King Zedekiah and his high officials. So I will command them to return and attack again. This time they will conquer the city and burn it down, and they will capture Zedekiah and his officials. I will also let them destroy the towns of Judah, so that no one can live there any longer.

34.4 *you won't die in battle:* Zedekiah is promised a peaceful death and a funeral fit for a king (see 2 Chr 16.14) if he surrenders. But Zedekiah did not surrender, and he tried to sneak away before Jerusalem fell. He was captured, and sent to prison in Babylon where he died (Jer 52.6-11).

34.8-10 *Jewish slaves . . . given their freedom:* The law called for the release of Hebrew slaves after six years of service (Exod 21.2; Deut 15.12; also Jer 34.14). It is not clear if Zedekiah called for the release of all slaves, or if he was enforcing the law that was being ignored by slave owners. Most likely, the slaves were freed in order to make more people available to defend the city.

34.18 *the ceremony . . . cut a calf:* The ceremony involved cutting a calf in two and walking between the two parts to make a lasting agreement (see Gen 15.7-17). The point of the ceremony was to say: "May God do to me as has been done to this calf if I break the terms of this agreement."

34.21-22 *I will command them to return:* The Egyptians pulled back, so the Babylonian army once again surrounded Jerusalem in January 587 B.C.

[m]34.8-10 *Zedekiah:* See the note at 1.3. [n]34.8-10 *Hebrew:* An earlier term for Israelite and Jewish.
[o]34.21,22 *Nebuchadnezzar:* See the note at 21.2.

35.1 *When Jehoiakim was king:* The book now goes back in time to the last year of Jehoiakim's reign (598 B.C.) when the Babylonians first invaded Judah. The faithful Rechabite clan (35.1-19) provides a clear contrast to the story of the unfaithful people of Judah in chapter 34.

35.6 *Jonadab son of Rechab:* This founder of the Rechabite clan helped King Jehu kill the wicked descendants of Israel's King Ahab around 840 B.C. (see 2 Kgs 10.15-23).

35.11 *now we have to live inside Jerusalem:* The Rechabites refused Jeremiah's wine, but they feel they must explain why they are living in the city, which also went against their clan rules. They are in Jerusalem because Nebuchadnezzar's army is taking over the countryside.

35.12-16 *learn a lesson . . . Rechabites have obeyed . . . but you have not:* The point is not to become a Rechabite (Jeremiah certainly was not one), but to be faithful to one's vows. It has been over two centuries since Jonadab's day, yet the Rechabites have remained obedient. While they are faithful, Judah is not. Jeremiah's warning about disobedience fits equally as well in 598 B.C. as it does later, in 586 B.C.

35.18,19 *Lord All-Powerful . . . promise:* Because of their faithfulness, the Lord promises that the Rechabite clan will always exist in Israel. But their faithfulness remains an example for future generations.

Learn a Lesson from the Rechabites

35 When Jehoiakim[P] was king of Judah, the Lord told me, [2]"Go to the Rechabite clan and invite them to meet you in one of the side rooms[q] of the temple. When they arrive, offer them a drink of wine."

[3]So I went to Jaazaniah,[r] the leader of the clan, and I invited him and all the men of his clan. [4]I brought them into the temple courtyard and took them upstairs to a room belonging to the prophets who were followers of Hanan son of Igdaliah. It was next to a room belonging to some of the officials, and that room was over the one belonging to Maaseiah, a priest who was one of the high officials in the temple.[s]

[5]I set out some large bowls full of wine together with some cups, and then I said to the Rechabites, "Have some wine!"

[6]But they answered:

No! The ancestor of our clan, Jonadab son of Rechab,[t] made a rule that we must obey. He said, "Don't ever drink wine [7]or build houses or plant crops and vineyards. Instead, you must always live in tents and move from place to place. If you obey this command, you will live a long time."

[8-10]Our clan has always obeyed Jonadab's command. To this very day, we and our wives and sons and daughters don't drink wine or build houses or plant vineyards or crops. And we have lived in tents, [11]except now we have to live inside Jerusalem because Nebuchadnezzar[u] has taken over the countryside with his army from Babylonia and Syria.

[12-13]Then the Lord told me to say to the people of Judah and Jerusalem:

I, the Lord All-Powerful, the God of Israel, want you to learn a lesson [14]from the Rechabite clan. Their ancestor Jonadab told his descendants never to drink wine, and to this very day they have obeyed him. But I have spoken to you over and over, and you haven't obeyed me! [15]You refused to listen to my prophets, who kept telling you, "Stop doing evil and worshiping other gods! Start obeying the Lord, and he will let you live in this land he gave your ancestors."

[16]The Rechabites have obeyed the command of their ancestor Jonadab, but you have not obeyed me, [17]your God. I am the Lord All-Powerful, and I warned you about the terrible things that would happen to you if you did not listen to me. But you have ignored me, so now disaster will strike you. I, the Lord, have spoken.

The Lord Makes a Promise to the Rechabites

[18]Then the Lord told me to say to the Rechabite clan:

"I am the Lord All-Powerful, the God of Israel. You have obeyed your ancestor Jonadab, [19]so I promise that your clan will be my servants and will never die out."

[P]35.1 *Jehoiakim:* See the note at 1.3.   [q]35.2 *side rooms:* Probably a room with walls on three sides, and open to the courtyard on the fourth side.   [r]35.3 *Jaazaniah:* The Hebrew text has "Jaazaniah son of Jeremiah son of Habazziniah"; this is a different Jeremiah than the author of the book. [s]35.4 *Maaseiah . . . temple:* Hebrew "Maaseiah son of Shallum, the keeper of the temple door." [t]35.6 *Jonadab son of Rechab:* See 2 Kings 10.15-23. In the Hebrew of this chapter, "Jonadab" is sometimes spelled "Jehonadab."   [u]35.11 *Nebuchadnezzar:* See the note at 21.2.

King Jehoiakim Burns Jeremiah's First Scroll

36 During the fourth year that Jehoiakim[v] son of Josiah[w] was king of Judah, the Lord said to me, "Jeremiah, [2]since the time Josiah was king, I have been speaking to you about Israel, Judah, and the other nations. Now, get a scroll[x] and write down everything I have told you, [3]then read it to the people of Judah. Maybe they will stop sinning when they hear what terrible things I plan for them. And if they turn back to me, I will forgive them."

[4]I sent for Baruch son of Neriah and asked him to help me. I repeated everything the Lord had told me, and Baruch wrote it all down on a scroll. [5]Then I said,

Baruch, the officials refuse to let me go into the Lord's temple, [6]so you must go instead. Wait for the next holy day when the people of Judah come to the temple to pray and to go without eating.[y] Then take this scroll to the temple and read it aloud. [7]The Lord is furious, and if the people hear how he is going to punish them, maybe they will ask to be forgiven.

[8-10]In the ninth month[z] of the fifth year that Jehoiakim was king, the leaders set a day when everyone who lived in Jerusalem or who was visiting there had to pray and go without eating. So Baruch took the scroll to the upper courtyard of the temple. He went over to the side of the courtyard and stood in a covered area near New Gate, where he read the scroll aloud.

This covered area belonged to Gemariah,[a] one of the king's highest officials. [11]Gemariah's son Micaiah was there and heard Baruch read what the Lord had said. [12]When Baruch finished reading, Micaiah went down to the palace. His father Gemariah was in the officials' room, meeting with the rest of the king's officials, including Elishama, Delaiah, Elnathan, and Zedekiah.[b] [13]Micaiah told them what he had heard Baruch read to the people. [14]Then the officials sent Jehudi and Shelemiah[c] to tell Baruch, "Bring us that scroll."

When Baruch arrived with the scroll, [15]the officials said, "Please sit down and read it to us," which he did. [16]After they heard what was written on the scroll, they were worried and said to each other, "The king needs to hear this!" Turning to Baruch, they asked, [17]"Did someone tell you what to write on this scroll?"

[18]"Yes, Jeremiah did," Baruch replied. "I wrote down just what he told me."

[19]The officials said, "You and Jeremiah must go into hiding, and don't tell anyone where you are going."

[20-22]The officials put the scroll in Elishama's room and went to see the king, who was in one of the rooms where he lived and worked during the winter. It was the ninth month[d] of the year, so there was a fire burning in the fireplace,[e] and the king was sitting nearby. After the officials told the king about the scroll, he sent Jehudi to get it. Then Jehudi started reading the scroll to the king and his officials.

36.4 *Baruch*: Jeremiah's friend and secretary (scribe) will read the scroll, because the prophet is not allowed to enter the temple courtyard (36.5).

Scrolls

36.8-10 *fifth year*: The year is 604 B.C.

36.8-10 *courtyard of the temple . . . New Gate*: Baruch read this first scroll in an area belonging to Gemariah, whose brother Ahikam had earlier protected Jeremiah (26.20-24).

[v]**36.1** *Jehoiakim*: See the note at 1.3. [w]**36.1** *Josiah*: See the note at 3.6. [x]**36.2** *scroll*: See the note at 30.1,2. [y]**36.6** *to go without eating*: As a way of asking for God's help. [z]**36.8-10** *ninth month*: Chislev, the ninth month of the Hebrew calendar, from about mid-November to mid-December. [a]**36.8-10** *Gemariah*: Hebrew "Gemariah son of Shaphan"; Gemariah's brother Ahikam had earlier protected Jeremiah (see 26.20-24). [b]**36.12** *Delaiah, Elnathan, and Zedekiah*: Hebrew "Delaiah son of Shemaiah, Elnathan son of Achbor, and Zedekiah son of Hananiah." [c]**36.14** *Jehudi and Shelemiah*: Hebrew "Jehudi son of Nethaniah and Shelemiah son of Cushi." [d]**36.20-22** *ninth month*: See the note at 36.8-10. [e]**36.20-22** *fireplace*: Probably a large metal or clay pot on a movable stand, with the fire burning inside.

36.23-25 *Jehudi . . . penknife . . . he ignored them:* The first scroll is read a third time. Jehudi, probably one of the king's scribes, reads aloud to the king while the officials stand nearby.

36.23-25 *they did not tear their clothes in sorrow:* The same Hebrew word is used for both "tear" and "cut." The king had the scroll "cut" to pieces, but he did not "tear" his clothes in distress, though this would have been the proper response to Jeremiah's message.

36.26 *go arrest Baruch and me:* King Jehoiakim had executed the prophet Uriah for his message (26.20-23). He likely would have executed Jeremiah as well if God, with human help (36.19), had not hidden him safely.

36.27,28 *first scroll . . . another scroll:* See 36.2 (first scroll). This "second scroll" (36.32) will replace the first scroll, which was burned (36.23-25). It contains everything the first scroll contained, and more! The text of JEREMIAH grew from this second scroll dictated to Baruch.

37.3-5 *Later, the Babylonian army attacked:* Zedekiah broke his treaty with Nebuchadnezzar in 588 B.C., hoping for support from the new Egyptian king, Hophra (also known as Apries). Nebuchadnezzar immediately sent an army to surround Jerusalem. In the summer of 588 B.C. the Egyptian army started marching east, so Nebuchadnezzar pulled his troops away from Jerusalem to face the Egyptians. It was at this time that King Zedekiah sent messengers to Jeremiah.

23-25 But every time Jehudi finished reading three or four columns, the king would tell him to cut them off with his penknife and throw them in the fire. Elnathan, Delaiah, and Gemariah begged the king not to burn the scroll, but he ignored them, and soon there was nothing left of it.

The king and his servants listened to what was written on the scroll, but they were not the least bit afraid, and they did not tear their clothes in sorrow.[f]

26The king told his son Jerahmeel to take Seraiah and Shelemiah[g] and to go arrest Baruch and me.[h] But the LORD kept them from finding us.

Jeremiah's Second Scroll

27I had told Baruch what to write on that first scroll,[i] but King Jehoiakim[j] had burned it. So the LORD told me **28**to get another scroll and write down everything that had been on the first one. **29**Then he told me to say to King Jehoiakim:

Not only did you burn Jeremiah's scroll, you had the nerve to ask why he had written that the king of Babylonia would attack and ruin the land, killing all the people and even the animals. **30**So I, the LORD, promise that you will be killed and your body thrown out on the ground. The sun will beat down on it during the day, and the frost will settle on it at night. And none of your descendants will ever be king of Judah. **31**You, your children, and your ser-

vants are evil, and I will punish everyone of you. I warned you and the people of Judah and Jerusalem that I would bring disaster, but none of you have listened. So now you are doomed!

32After the LORD finished speaking to me, I got another scroll and gave it to Baruch. Then I told him what to write, so this second scroll would contain even more than was on the scroll Jehoiakim had burned.

King Zedekiah Asks Jeremiah To Pray

37 King Nebuchadnezzar[k] of Babylonia had removed Jehoiachin[l] son of Jehoiakim[m] from being the king of Judah and had made Josiah's[n] son Zedekiah[o] king instead.[p] **2**But Zedekiah, his officials, and everyone else in Judah ignored everything the LORD had told me.

3-5 Later, the Babylonian army attacked Jerusalem, but they left after learning that the Egyptian army[q] was headed in this direction.

One day, Zedekiah sent Jehucal and the priest Zephaniah[r] to talk with me. At that time, I was free to go wherever I wanted, because I had not yet been put in prison. Jehucal and Zephaniah said, "Jeremiah, please pray to the LORD our God for us."

6-7 Then the LORD told me to send them back to Zedekiah with this message:

Zedekiah, you wanted Jeremiah to ask me, the LORD God of Israel, what is

---

[f]**36.23-25** *they did not tear their clothes in sorrow:* Such actions would have shown that they were sorry for disobeying the LORD and were turning back to him.   [g]**36.26** *Seraiah and Shelemiah:* Hebrew "Seraiah son of Azriel and Shelemiah son of Abdeel."   [h]**36.26** *me:* Jeremiah.   [i]**36.27** *scroll:* See the note at 30.1,2.   [j]**36.27** *Jehoiakim:* See the note at 1.3.   [k]**37.1** *Nebuchadnezzar:* See the note at 21.2.   [l]**37.1** *Jehoiachin:* Hebrew "Coniah" (see the note at 22.24).   [m]**37.1** *Jehoiakim:* See the note at 1.3.   [n]**37.1** *Josiah's:* Josiah was the father of both Jehoiakim and Zedekiah. Josiah ruled 640–609 B.C.   [o]**37.1** *Zedekiah:* See the note at 1.3.   [p]**37.1** *King Nebuchadnezzar . . . instead:* See 2 Kings 24.10-17.   [q]**37.3-5** *Egyptian army:* Led by King Apries, also known as Hophra.   [r]**37.3-5** *Jehucal and the priest Zephaniah:* Hebrew "Jehucal son of Shelemiah, and the priest Zephaniah son of Maaseiah."

going to happen. So I will tell you. The king of Egypt and his army came to your rescue, but soon they will go back to Egypt. [8]Then the Babylonians will return and attack Jerusalem, and this time they will capture the city and set it on fire. [9]Don't fool yourselves into thinking that the Babylonians will leave as they did before. [10]Even if you could defeat their entire army, their wounded survivors would still be able to leave their tents and set Jerusalem on fire.

Jeremiah Is Put in Prison

[11]The Babylonian army had left because the Egyptian army was on its way to help us. [12]So I decided to leave Jerusalem and go to the territory of the Benjamin tribe to claim my share of my family's land. [13]I was leaving Jerusalem through Benjamin Gate, when I was stopped by Irijah,[s] the officer in charge of the soldiers at the gate. He said, "Jeremiah, you're under arrest for trying to join the Babylonians."

[14]"I'm not trying to join them!" I answered. But Irijah wouldn't listen, and he took me to the king's officials. [15-16]They were angry and ordered the soldiers to beat me. Then I was taken to the house that belonged to Jonathan, one of the king's officials. It had been turned into a prison, and I was kept in a basement room.

After I had spent a long time there, [17]King Zedekiah secretly had me brought to his palace, where he asked, "Is there any message for us from the LORD?"

"Yes, there is, Your Majesty," I replied.

"The LORD is going to let the king of Babylonia capture you."

[18]Then I continued, "Your Majesty, why have you put me in prison? Have I committed a crime against you or your officials or the nation? [19]Have you locked up the prophets who lied to you and said that the king of Babylonia would never attack Jerusalem? [20]Please, don't send me back to that prison at Jonathan's house. If you do, I will die there."

[21]King Zedekiah had me taken to the prison cells in the courtyard of the palace guards. He told the soldiers to give me a loaf of bread[t] from one of the bakeries every day until the city ran out of grain.

Jeremiah Is Held Prisoner in a Dry Well

38 One day, Shephatiah, Gedaliah, Jehucal,[u] and Pashhur[v] heard me tell the people of Judah [2-3]that the LORD had said, "If you stay here in Jerusalem, you will die in battle or from disease or hunger, and the Babylonian army will capture the city anyway. But if you surrender to the Babylonians, they will let you live."

[4]So the four of them went to the king and said, "You should put Jeremiah to death, because he is making the soldiers and everyone else lose hope. He isn't trying to help our people; he's trying to harm them."

[5]Zedekiah replied, "Do what you want with him. I can't stop you."

[6]Then they took me back to the courtyard of the palace guards and let me down with ropes into the well that belonged to

---

[s]**37.13** *Irijah*: Hebrew "Irijah son of Shelemiah and grandson of Hananiah." [t]**37.21** *a loaf of bread*: Bread was the main food of the Israelites. During this time of emergency in Jerusalem, everyone probably received the same amount each day. [u]**38.1** *Jehucal*: The Hebrew text has "Jucal," another form of the name. [v]**38.1** *Shephatiah, Gedaliah, Jehucal, and Pashhur*: Hebrew "Shephatiah son of Mattan, Gedaliah son of Pashhur, Jucal son of Shelemiah, and Pashhur son of Malchiah."

■ **37.8** *Babylonians will return . . . set it on fire*: While everyone else is hopeful, Jeremiah is not. The Babylonians will return, and this time they won't leave until they capture and destroy the city.

● **37.12,13** *territory of the Benjamin tribe . . . Benjamin Gate*: Jeremiah's hometown of Anathoth was there. Jeremiah's share of the family land is probably not the field he bought from a family member. The Benjamin Gate was in the north wall of Jerusalem. **(See Map 3 on pg 1881.)**

● **37.21** *prison cells . . . loaf of bread*: The palace prison cells were not as bad as the dungeon in Jonathan's house, where he surely would have died (37.20). This house arrest was the setting of 32.1-15.

■ **38.1** *Shephatiah . . . Pashhur*: This is a very different group than the officials who supported Jeremiah in the time of Jehoiakim (36.11-19,23-25). The earlier group probably had been forced to leave Jerusalem during the first exile of 598 B.C. What was left in Jerusalem were the "rotten figs" (see 24.8), men who hated Jeremiah and disregarded his message from the LORD. King Zedekiah was unable to stop their plot against Jeremiah (38.5).

● **38.5** *Zedekiah replied*: Nebuchadnezzar placed this puppet king on the throne in 598 B.C., probably because he knew Zedekiah was a weak leader and able to be controlled. Here in 587 B.C. these qualities show, as he is unable to stop his own men from doing whatever they wish.

38.7-8 *Ebedmelech from Ethiopia:* This court official came from the African region south of Egypt that included parts of the present countries of Ethiopia and Sudan. Jeremiah is delivered from his own fellow citizens by a foreigner, who recognizes their act as "wrong."

38.19 *I'm too afraid:* Zedekiah wants to hear the truth, but he cannot act on it. He fears that the Jewish people who have joined the Babylonians will torture him if Babylon gains control of Jerusalem. Some Jews had already taken Jeremiah's advice and surrendered to the Babylonians (39.9; 52.15). Perhaps these traitors think they will be put in power once Zedekiah is out of the way, or perhaps they will take their anger out on Zedekiah because he did not listen to Jeremiah's warnings.

38.21-23 *the Lord has shown me . . . trapped in mud:* Jeremiah reports that he has seen the capture of Zedekiah's royal household. The women of the palace speak of Zedekiah (38.6) as the one stuck in the mud. The "friends" Zedekiah trusts (38.22) probably are the Egyptians.

Nebuchadnezzar

38.24,25 *if my officials hear . . . threaten to kill you:* The king has no real authority; he fears his own officials. By protecting Jeremiah, the king puts his own life at risk as well.

Malchiah, the king's son. There was no water in the well, but I sank down in the mud.

7-8 Ebedmelech from Ethiopia[w] was an official at the palace, and he heard what they had done to me. So he went to speak with King Zedekiah, who was holding court at Benjamin Gate. **9**Ebedmelech said, "Your Majesty, Jeremiah is a prophet, and those men were wrong to throw him into a well. And when Jerusalem runs out of food, Jeremiah will starve to death down there."

10Zedekiah answered, "Take 30[x] of my soldiers and pull Jeremiah out before he dies."

11Ebedmelech and the soldiers went to the palace and got some rags from the room under the treasury. He used ropes to lower them into the well. **12**Then he said, "Put these rags under your arms so the ropes won't hurt you." After I did, **13**the men pulled me out. And from then on, I was kept in the courtyard of the palace guards.

King Zedekiah Questions Jeremiah

14King Zedekiah[y] had me brought to his private entrance[z] to the temple, and he said, "I'm going to ask you something, and I want to know the truth."

15"Why?" I replied. "You won't listen, and you might even have me killed!"

16He said, "I swear in the name of the living Lord our Creator that I won't have you killed. No one else can hear what we say, and I won't let anyone kill you."

17Then I told him that the Lord had said: "Zedekiah, I am the Lord God All-Powerful, the God of Israel. I promise that if you surrender to King Nebuchadnezzar's[a] officers, you and your family won't be killed, and Jerusalem won't be burned down. **18**But if you don't surrender, I will let the Babylonian army capture Jerusalem and burn it down, and you will be taken prisoner."

19Zedekiah answered, "I can't surrender to the Babylonians. I'm too afraid of the people of Judah who have already joined them. The Babylonians might hand me over to them, and they would torture me."

20I said, "If you will just obey the Lord, the Babylonians won't hand you over to those Jews. You will be allowed to live, and all will go well for you. **21**But the Lord has shown me that if you refuse to obey, **22**then the women of your palace will be taken prisoner by Nebuchadnezzar's officials. And those women will say to you:

Friends you trusted led you astray.
  Now you're trapped in mud,
  and those friends you trusted
  have all turned away.

23The Babylonian army will take your wives and children captive, you will be taken as a prisoner to the King of Babylonia, and Jerusalem will be burned down."[b]

24Zedekiah said, "Jeremiah, if you tell anyone what we have talked about, you might lose your life. **25**And I'm sure that if my officials hear about our meeting, they will ask you what we said to each other. They might even threaten to kill you if you don't tell them. **26**So if they question you,

---

[w]**38.7,8** *Ethiopia:* The Hebrew text has "Cush," a region south of Egypt that included parts of the present countries of Ethiopia and Sudan.   [x]**38.10** *30:* Most Hebrew manuscripts; one Hebrew manuscript "three."   [y]**38.14** *Zedekiah:* See the note at 1.3.   [z]**38.14** *his private entrance:* One possible meaning for the difficult Hebrew text.   [a]**38.17** *Nebuchadnezzar's:* See the note at 21.2.   [b]**38.23** *Jerusalem will be burned down:* A few Hebrew manuscripts and three ancient translations; most Hebrew manuscripts "you will burn Jerusalem down"; one ancient translation "he will burn Jerusalem down."

tell them you were begging me not to send you back to the prison at Jonathan's house, because going back there would kill you."

27The officials did come and question me about my meeting with the king, and I told them exactly what he had ordered me to say. They never spoke to me about the meeting again, since no one had heard us talking.

28I was held in the courtyard of the palace guards until the day Jerusalem was captured.

Jerusalem Is Captured by the Babylonians
(Jeremiah 52.4-16; 2 Kings 25.1-12)

39 1-3In the tenth month[c] of the ninth year that Zedekiah[d] was king of Judah, King Nebuchadnezzar[e] and the Babylonian army began their attack on Jerusalem. They kept the city surrounded for a year and a half. Then, on the ninth day of the fourth month[f] of the eleventh year that Zedekiah was king, they broke through the city walls.

After Jerusalem was captured,[g] Nebuchadnezzar's highest officials,[h] including Nebo Sarsechim[i] and Nergal Sharezer from Simmagir,[j] took their places at Middle Gate to show they were in control of the city.[k]

4When King Zedekiah and his troops saw that Jerusalem had been captured, they tried to escape from the city that same night. They went to the king's garden, where they slipped through the gate between the two city walls[l] and headed toward the Jordan River valley. 5But the Babylonian troops caught up with them near Jericho. They arrested Zedekiah and took him to the town of Riblah in the land of Hamath, where Nebuchadnezzar put him on trial, then found him guilty, 6and gave orders for him to be punished. Zedekiah's sons were killed there in front of him, and so were the leaders of Judah's ruling families. 7Then his eyes were poked out, and he was put in chains, so he could be dragged off to Babylonia.

8Meanwhile, the Babylonian army had burned the houses in Jerusalem, including[m] the royal palace, and they had broken down the city walls. 9Nebuzaradan, the Babylonian officer in charge of the guards, led away everyone from the city as prisoners, even those who had deserted to Nebuchadnezzar. 10Only the poorest people who owned no land were left behind in Judah, and Nebuzaradan gave them fields and vineyards.

11Nebuchadnezzar had given the following orders to Nebuzaradan: 12"Find Jeremiah and keep him safe. Take good care of him and do whatever he asks."

13Nebuzaradan, Nebushazban, Nergal

---

[c]39.1-3 *the tenth month*: Tebeth, the tenth month of the Hebrew calendar, from about mid-December to mid-January.   [d]39.1-3 *Zedekiah*: See the note at 1.3.   [e]39.1-3 *Nebuchadnezzar*: See the note at 21.2.
[f]39.1-3 *fourth month*: Tammuz, the fourth month of the Hebrew calendar, from about mid-June to mid-July.   [g]39.1-3 *After Jerusalem was captured*: This phrase is from 38.28.   [h]39.1-3 *highest officials*: The Hebrew text gives Nergal Sharezer's title as "the Rabmag," and Nebo Sarsechim's title as "the Rabsaris," but the exact meaning of the titles and the duties of these offices are not known.
[i]39.1-3 *Nebo Sarsechim*: Probably another form of the name Nebushazban (see verse 13).
[j]39.1-3 *Nergal Sharezer from Simmagir*: One possible meaning for the difficult Hebrew text. Probably Nebuchadnezzar's son-in-law, who was king of Babylonia 560–556 B.C. It is also possible that the Hebrew text mentions a second official named Nergal Sharezer.   [k]39.1-3 *took their places . . . control of the city*: The rulers and leaders often sat in the broad open area at the gate of a city to take care of official business and hold trials.   [l]39.4 *the gate between the two city walls*: The construction of the city walls at this point is not known.   [m]39.8 *the houses in Jerusalem, including*: Or "the temple and."

39.14 *Gedaliah:* Gedaliah's family members had befriended Jeremiah in 26.20 (his father Ahikam) and 36.10 (his uncle Gemariah). Gedaliah's ancestors are mentioned in 2 Kings 22.12, where they helped King Josiah with reforms in Jerusalem. Judah was made a province of the Babylonian Empire, and Gedaliah was made its first governor (40.7-12). His family was not part of the royal family of David, however.

39.15,16 *Ebedmelech from Ethiopia:* These verses continue the story from 38.27. In 38.7-13, this African official helped Jeremiah. Either Jeremiah sent the message to him, or Ebedmelech came to see him while he was still being held prisoner.

40.5 *you can live anywhere:* Jeremiah chooses his beloved homeland. He is old, and the future lies with the exiled Jews.

40.6 *Mizpah:* Mizpah became the new capital after the fall of Jerusalem. Gedaliah, the newly appointed governor of the Judah province, lived in Mizpah.

40.7-8 *Ishmael . . . Johanan . . . and their troops:* Some Judean troops that were stationed outside of Jerusalem were not captured by the Babylonians. They went to see Gedaliah, perhaps to work out a military strategy to get rid of the Babylonians. Of the list of names in these verses, the two that stand out are Ishmael, who acts with deceit (41.1-3) and Johanan, who tries to stop Ishmael's plan to kill Gedaliah (40.13-16).

Sharezer, and the other officers of King Nebuchadnezzar [14]sent some of their troops to bring me from the courtyard of the royal palace guards. They put me in the care of Gedaliah son of Ahikam[n] and told him to take me to my home. And so I was allowed to stay with the people who remained in Judah.

The LORD Promises To Protect Ebedmelech

[15]While I was a prisoner in the courtyard of the palace guard, the LORD told me to say [16]to Ebedmelech from Ethiopia:[o]

I am the LORD All-Powerful, the God of Israel. I warned everyone that I would bring disaster, not prosperity, to this city. Now very soon I will do what I said, and you will see it happen. [17-18]But because you trusted me,[P] I will protect you from the officials of Judah, and when Judah is struck by disaster, I will rescue you and keep you alive. I, the LORD, have spoken.

Jeremiah Is Set Free

40 I was led away in chains along with the people of Judah and Jerusalem who were being taken to Babylonia. Nebuzaradan was the officer in charge of the guard, and while we were stopped at Ramah, the LORD caused him to set me free. [2]Nebuzaradan said:

Jeremiah, the LORD your God warned your people that he would bring disaster on this land. [3]But they continued to rebel against him, and now he has punished them just as he threatened. [4]Today I am taking the chains off

your wrists and setting you free! If you want to, you can come with me to Babylonia, and I will see that you are taken care of. Or if you decide to stay here, you can go wherever you wish. [5]King Nebuchadnezzar[q] has chosen Gedaliah to rule Judah. You can live near Gedaliah, and he will provide for you, or you can live anywhere else you choose.

Nebuzaradan gave me a supply of food, then let me leave. [6]I decided to stay with the people of Judah, and I went to live near Gedaliah in Mizpah.

The Harvest Is Brought In

[7-8]Ishmael the son of Nethaniah, together with Johanan and Jonathan, the two sons of Kareah, had been officers in Judah's army. And so had Seraiah the son of Tanhumeth, the sons of Ephai the Netophathite, and Jezaniah from Maacah. They and their troops had been stationed outside Jerusalem and had not been captured. They heard that Gedaliah had been chosen to rule Judah, and that the poorest men, women, and children had not been taken away to Babylonia. So they went to Mizpah and met with their new ruler.

[9]Gedaliah told them, "There's no need to be afraid of the Babylonians. Everything will be fine, if we live peacefully and obey King Nebuchadnezzar.[r] [10]I will stay here at Mizpah and meet with the Babylonian officials on each of their visits. But you must go back to your towns and bring in the harvest, then store the wine, olive oil, and dried fruit."

[11-12]Earlier, when the Babylonians had invaded Judah, many of the Jews escaped to

[n]**39.14** *son of Ahikam:* Hebrew "son of Ahikam and grandson of Shaphan." [o]**39.16** *Ethiopia:* See the note at 38.7,8. [P]**39.17,18** *you trusted me:* See 38.7-13, where Ebedmelech helped Jeremiah. [q]**40.5** *Nebuchadnezzar:* See the note at 21.2. [r]**40.9** *Nebuchadnezzar:* See the note at 21.2.

Moab, Ammon, Edom, and several other countries. But these Jews heard that the king of Babylonia had appointed Gedaliah as ruler of Judah, and that only a few people were left there. So the Jews in these other countries came back to Judah and helped with the grape and fruit harvest, which was especially large that year.

Gedaliah Is Murdered

[13]One day, Johanan got together with some of the other men who had been army officers, and they came to Mizpah and met with Gedaliah. [14]They said, "Gedaliah, we came to warn you that King Baalis of Ammon hired Ishmael to murder you!"

Gedaliah refused to believe them, [15]so Johanan went to Gedaliah privately and said, "Let me kill Ishmael. No one will find out who did it. There are only a few people left in Judah, but they are depending on you. And if you are murdered, they will be scattered or killed."

[16]Gedaliah answered, "Don't kill Ishmael! What you've said about him can't be true."

41 But in the seventh month,[s] Ishmael[t] came to Mizpah with ten of his soldiers. He had been one of the king's officials and was a member of the royal family. Ishmael and his men were invited to eat with Gedaliah. [2]During the meal, Ishmael and his soldiers killed Gedaliah, the man chosen as ruler of Judah by the king of Babylonia. [3]Then they killed the Jews who were with Gedaliah, and they also killed the Babylonian soldiers who were there.

[4]The next day, the murders had still not been discovered, [5]when 80 men came down the road toward Mizpah from the towns of Shechem, Shiloh, and Samaria. They were on their way to the temple to offer gifts of grain and incense to the LORD. They had shaved off their beards, torn their clothes, and cut themselves, because they were mourning.

[6]Ishmael went out the town gate to meet them. He pretended to be weeping, and he asked them to come into Mizpah to meet with Gedaliah, the ruler of Judah. [7]But after they were inside the town, Ishmael ordered his soldiers to kill them and throw their bodies into a well. [8]He let ten of the men live, because they offered to give him supplies of wheat, barley, olive oil, and honey they had hidden in a field. [9]The well that he filled with bodies[u] had been dug by King Asa[v] of Judah to store rainwater, because he was afraid that King Baasha[w] of Israel might surround Mizpah and keep the people from getting to their water supply.

[10]Nebuzaradan, King Nebuchadnezzar's[x] officer in charge of the guard, had left King Zedekiah's[y] daughters and many other people at Mizpah, and he had put Gedaliah in charge of them. But now Ishmael took them all prisoner and led them toward Ammon, on the other side of the Jordan River.

[11]Johanan and the other army officers heard what Ishmael had done. [12]So they and their troops chased Ishmael and caught up with him at the large pit at Gibeon. [13]When Ishmael's prisoners saw Johanan and the officers, they were happy [14]and

---

[s]**41.1** *seventh month*: Tishri, also called Ethanim, the seventh month of the Hebrew calendar, from about mid-September to mid-October.   [t]**41.1** *Ishmael*: Hebrew "Ishmael son of Nethaniah and grandson of Elishama."   [u]**41.9** *with bodies*: One ancient translation; Hebrew "with bodies of those killed by Gedaliah."   [v]**41.9** *Asa*: Ruled 911–870 B.C.   [w]**41.9** *Baasha*: Ruled 909–886 B.C.   [x]**41.10** *Nebuchadnezzar's*: See the note at 21.2.   [y]**41.10** *Zedekiah's*: See the note at 1.3.

40.11-12 *Moab, Ammon, Edom*: During the Babylonian invasion of Judah, which lasted a year and a half, many of the people of Judah ran away to these surrounding countries. When Gedaliah was made ruler these refugees felt safe enough to return to Judah and help with that year's abundant grape harvest. (See Map 6 on pg 1884.)

40.13,14 *Johanan . . . met with Gedaliah . . . King Baalis of Ammon hired Ishmael*: According to 2 Kings 25.25, the plot against Gedaliah occurred only two months after he was appointed governor. Baalis, king of Ammon, hired Ishmael, a Judean army officer, to kill Gedaliah. Baalis of Ammon probably thought that a successful revolt by Judah would weaken Babylonian authority over the region, including his own country of Ammon. Ishmael came from the royal family of Zedekiah (2 Kgs 25.25), so he might have had some standing with the people of Judah.

41.1-3 *in the seventh month Ishmael . . . killed Gedaliah*: Ishmael and his small rebel army came to Mizpah in the month of Tishri. As Gedaliah's dinner guest, Ishmael took advantage of the situation and killed Gedaliah.

41.7-9 *a well . . . supplies . . . King Asa*: Ishmael makes a mass grave out of the well that had originally been dug in the time of Asa of Judah (911–870 B.C.).

41.11,12 *large pit at Gibeon*: Gibeon was about six miles northwest of Jerusalem. The large pit (41.12) was probably a cistern.

41.17,18 *toward Egypt... we stopped at... Geruth Chimham:* Afraid of what will happen when Nebuchadnezzar hears of Gedaliah's assassination, Johanan's group heads to Egypt to get as far as possible from any Babylonian retaliation. The location of Geruth is unknown. Bethlehem is a few miles south of Jerusalem. **(See Map 6 on pg 1884.)**

42.3 *Ask the LORD:* The refugees are in a real dilemma and sincerely ask Jeremiah what the LORD wants them to do. If they stay in Judah and are accused of the rebellion (41.1-15), they might be killed or they might be cleared of any wrongdoing. If they flee to Egypt, it may look like they are admitting guilt, but they might be safe there. They promise to do whatever the LORD tells Jeremiah.

42.7 *Ten days later:* God's word cannot be summoned at will. Ten days pass before Jeremiah has an answer.

42.10 *I am sorry... stay here in Judah:* This is a new message. Jeremiah had preached that the hope of Judah's future lay with the prisoners in Babylon (see 24.5), but now God is saying that this small group of survivors will also be part of God's plan to rebuild Judah. And God will keep them safe from Nebuchadnezzar's revenge.

42.18 *if you go to Egypt:* A large Jewish population eventually settled in Egypt. Alexandria, a major port, became an important center for Jewish literature and study until the second century A.D.

turned around and ran toward Johanan. [15]But Ishmael and eight of his men escaped and went to Ammon.

Johanan Decides To Take the People to Egypt

[16]Johanan and the officers had rescued the women, children, and royal officials that Ishmael had taken prisoner after killing Gedaliah. Johanan led the people from Gibeon [17-18]toward Egypt. They wanted to go there, because they were afraid of what the Babylonians would do when they found out that Ishmael had killed Gedaliah, the ruler appointed by King Nebuchadnezzar.[z]

The People Ask Jeremiah To Pray for Them

On the way to Egypt, we[a] stopped at the town of Geruth Chimham near Bethlehem.

42 [1]Johanan, Jezaniah,[b] the other army officers, and everyone else in the group, came to me [2]and said, "Please, Jeremiah, pray to the LORD your God for us. Judah used to have many people, but as you can see, only a few of us are left. [3]Ask the LORD to tell us where he wants us to go and what he wants us to do."

[4]"All right," I answered, "I will pray to the LORD your God, and I will tell you everything he says."

[5]They answered, "The LORD himself will be our witness that we promise to do whatever he says, [6]even if it isn't what we want to do. We will obey the LORD so that all will go well for us."

[7]Ten days later, the LORD gave me an an-

swer for [8]Johanan, the officers, and the other people. So I called them together [9]and told them that the LORD God of Israel had said:

You asked Jeremiah to pray and find out what you should do. [10]I am sorry that I had to punish you, and so I now tell you to stay here in Judah, where I will plant you and build you up, instead of tearing you down and uprooting you. [11]Don't be afraid of the King of Babylonia. I will protect you from him, [12]and I will even force him to have mercy on you and give back your farms.

[13]But you might keep on saying, "We won't stay here in Judah, and we won't obey the LORD our God. [14]We are going to Egypt, where there is plenty of food and no danger of war."

[15]People of Judah, you survived when the Babylonian army attacked. Now you are planning to move to Egypt, and if you do go, this is what will happen. [16-17]You are afraid of war, starvation, and disease here in Judah, but they will follow you to Egypt and kill you there. None of you will survive the disasters I will send.

[18]I, the LORD, was angry with the people of Jerusalem and punished them. And if you go to Egypt, I will be angry and punish you the same way. You will never again see your homeland. People will be horrified at what I do to you, and they will use the name of your city as a curse word.

[z]41.17,18 *Nebuchadnezzar:* See the note at 21.2. [a]41.17,18 *we:* The group of people included Jeremiah, since he had been staying with Gedaliah near Mizpah (see 40.6). [b]42.1 *Jezaniah:* Hebrew "Jezaniah son of Hoshaiah"; one ancient translation "Azariah son of Hoshaiah" (see also 43.2 and the note there).

Jeremiah Gives a Warning

19 I told the people:

You escaped the disaster that struck Judah, but now the LORD warns you to stay away from Egypt. **20** You asked me to pray and find out what the LORD our God wants you to do, and you promised to obey him. But that was a terrible mistake, **21** because now that I have given you the LORD's answer, you refuse to obey him. **22** And so, you will die in Egypt from war, hunger, and disease.

The People Go to Egypt

43 I told the people everything the LORD had told me. **2** But Azariah, Johanan[c] and some other arrogant men said to me, "You're lying! The LORD didn't tell you to say that we shouldn't go to Egypt. **3** Baruch son of Neriah must have told you to say that. He wants the Babylonians to capture us, so they can take us away to Babylonia or even kill us."

4 Johanan, the other army officers, and everyone else refused to stay in Judah in spite of the LORD's command. **5** So Johanan and the officers led us away toward Egypt. The group that left Judah included those who had been scattered in other countries and who had then come back to live in Judah. **6** Baruch and I and others in the group had been staying with Gedaliah, because Nebuzaradan, the Babylonian officer in charge of the guard, had ordered him to take care of the king's daughters and quite a few men, women, and children.

7 The people disobeyed the LORD and went to Egypt. The group had settled in Tahpanhes, **8** when the LORD told me:

9 Jeremiah, carry some large stones to the entrance of the government building in Tahpanhes. Bury the stones underneath the brick pavement[d] and be sure the Jews are watching.

10 Then tell them that I, the LORD All-Powerful, the God of Israel, have sent for my servant, Nebuchadnezzar[e] of Babylonia. I will bring him here and have him set up his throne and his royal tent over these stones that I told you to bury. **11** He will attack Egypt and kill many of its people; others will die of disease or be dragged away as prisoners. **12-13** I will let him set Egypt's temples on fire, and he will either burn or carry off their idols. He will destroy the sacred monuments at the temple of the sun-god.[f] Then Nebuchadnezzar will pick the land clean, just like a shepherd picking the lice off his clothes. And he will return safely home.

The LORD Will Destroy the People of Judah

44 The LORD told me to speak with the Jews who were living in the towns of Migdol, Tahpanhes, and Memphis in northern Egypt, and also to those living in southern Egypt. He told me to tell them:

2 I am the LORD All-Powerful, the God of Israel. You saw how I destroyed Jerusalem and the towns of Judah. They lie empty and in ruins today, **3** because the people of Judah made me angry by worshiping gods that had never helped them or their ancestors. **4** Time after time I sent my servants the prophets to tell the people of

---

c43.2 *Azariah, Johanan:* Hebrew "Azariah son of Hoshaiah, Johanan son of Kareah."   **d43.9** *underneath the brick pavement:* One possible meaning for the difficult Hebrew text.   **e43.10** *Nebuchadnezzar:* See the note at 21.2.   **f43.12,13** *at the temple of the sun-god:* Or "in the city of Heliopolis."

42.19-22 *You escaped . . . you will die:* Jeremiah warns the people that running away from Judah to Egypt is a mistake, outright disobedience to God's will. Perhaps, in the ten-day wait for this message, the group had already made up their minds to take the safe way out (43.1-5).

43.5 *led us away toward Egypt:* Jeremiah and Baruch probably had no choice but to go along with the group to Egypt. Perhaps he felt responsible to continue preaching the LORD's messages, or perhaps the group wished to use Jeremiah as a "good luck charm" in Egypt. See 2 Kgs 25.26.

43.6 *staying with Gedaliah:* After the fall of Jerusalem, Nebuzaradan allowed Jeremiah and Baruch to live at Mizpah under the protection of Gedaliah (40.1-6).

43.10,11 *Nebuchadnezzar . . . will attack Egypt:* Babylon's Nebuchadnezzar did invade Egypt in 568 B.C. as a warning to keep the Egyptians from trying to undermine Babylon's control over the region. This invasion did not lead to a decisive defeat of the Egyptians, and Nebuchadnezzar left the Egyptian king on the throne.

44.1 *Egypt:* Jewish colonies already existed in Egypt before the fall of Jerusalem. Jews were scattered there after the fall of the northern kingdom to Assyria in 722 B.C. (See Maps 2 and 7 on pgs 1880 and 1885.)

44.7,8 *Why do you insist . . . worshiping idols:* The Jewish people who escaped to Egypt were beginning to worship and burn incense to honor Egyptian gods and goddesses. This clearly violated the Law commanding people to worship the LORD alone (Exod 20.3-6). It was as if they had not learned a lesson from the recent events of 586 B.C. (Jer 39.1-14).

44.17 *the goddess Astarte, the Queen of Heaven:* The fertility goddess Astarte may have been especially popular among women, who offered wine and incense to her and made special loaves of bread in hopes of having many children.

44.19 *special loaves of bread:* The loaves were made in the shape of a crescent moon or stamped with a star shape for the "star" Venus, both images for the goddess Astarte.

44.23 *This disaster:* Jeremiah offers his counter-argument for the disasters that have fallen on Judah. It matches his earlier prophecies of warning (2.1-8; 4.1-4,11-18; 17.1-4).

Judah how much I hated their disgusting sins. The prophets warned them to stop sinning, **5**but they refused to listen and would not stop worshiping other gods. **6**Finally, my anger struck like a raging flood, and today Jerusalem and the towns of Judah are nothing but empty ruins.

7Why do you now insist on heading for another disaster? A disaster that will destroy not only you, but also your children and babies. **8**You have made me angry by worshiping idols and burning incense to other gods after you came here to Egypt. You will die such a disgusting death, that other nations will use the name of Judah as a curse word. **9**When you were living in Jerusalem and Judah, you followed the example of your ancestors in doing evil things, just like your kings and queens. **10**Even now, your pride keeps you from respecting me and obeying the laws and teachings I gave you and your ancestors.

11I, the LORD All-Powerful, have decided to wipe you out with disasters. **12**There were only a few of you left in Judah, and you decided to go to Egypt. But you will die such horrible deaths in war or from starvation, that people of other countries will use the name of Judah as a curse word. **13**I punished Jerusalem with war, hunger, and disease, and that's how I will punish you. **14**None of you will survive. You may hope to return to Judah someday, but only a very few of you will escape death and be able to go back.

The People Refuse To Worship the LORD

15A large number of Jews from both northern and southern Egypt listened to me as I told them what the LORD had said. Most of the men in the crowd knew that their wives often burned incense to other gods. So they and their wives shouted:

16Jeremiah, what do we care if you speak in the LORD's name? We refuse to listen! **17**We have promised to worship the goddess Astarte, the Queen of Heaven,**g** and that is exactly what we are going to do. We will burn incense and offer sacrifices of wine to her, just as we, our ancestors, our kings, and our leaders did when we lived in Jerusalem and the other towns of Judah. We had plenty of food back then. We were well off, and nothing bad ever happened to us. **18**But since the time we stopped burning incense and offering wine sacrifices to her, we have been dying from war and hunger.

19Then the women said, "When we lived in Judah, we worshiped the Queen of Heaven and offered sacrifices of wine and special loaves of bread shaped like her. Our husbands knew what we were doing, and they approved of it."

20Then I told the crowd:

21Don't you think the LORD knew that you and your ancestors, your leaders and kings, and the rest of the people were burning incense to other gods in Jerusalem and everywhere else in Judah? **22**And when he could no longer put up with your disgusting sins, he placed a curse on your land and turned it into a desert, as it is today. **23**This disaster happened because

g44.17 *the goddess Astarte, the Queen of Heaven:* The Hebrew text has "the queen of heaven," which probably refers to the goddess Astarte.

you worshiped other gods and rebelled against the LORD by refusing to obey him or follow his laws and teachings. ²⁴⁻²⁵Then I told the men and their wives, that the LORD All-Powerful, the God of Israel, had said:

Here in Egypt you still keep your promises to burn incense and offer sacrifices of wine to the so-called Queen of Heaven. ²⁶Keep these promises! But let me tell you what will happen. As surely as I am the LORD God, I swear that I will never again accept any promises you make in my name. ²⁷Instead of watching over you, I will watch for chances to harm you. Some of you will die in war, and others will starve to death. ²⁸Only a few will escape and return to Judah. Then everyone who went to live in Egypt will know that when I say something will happen, it will—no matter what you say.

²⁹And here is how you will know that I will keep my threats to punish you in Egypt. ³⁰I will hand over King Hophra of Egypt to those who want to kill him,ʰ just as I handed Zedekiahⁱ over to Nebuchadnezzar,ʲ who wanted to kill him.

The LORD Will Not Let Baruch Be Killed

45 In the fourth year that Jehoiakimᵏ was king of Judah, Baruch wrote down everything I had told him.ˡ ²Then later, the LORD God of Israel told me to say to Baruch:

³You are moaning and blaming me, the LORD, for your troubles and sorrow, and for being so tired that you can't even rest. ⁴But all over the earth I am tearing down what I built and pulling up what I planted. ⁵I am bringing disaster everywhere, so don't even think about making any big plans for yourself. However, I promise that wherever you go, I will at least protect you from death. I, the LORD, have spoken.

The LORD Speaks to Jeremiah about the Nations

46 The LORD often told me what to say about the different nations of the world.

What the LORD Says about Egypt

² In the fourth year that Jehoiakimᵐ was king of Judah, King Nebuchadnezzarⁿ of Babylonia defeated King Neco of Egyptᵒ in a battle at the city of Carchemish near the Euphrates River. And here is what the LORD told me to say about the Egyptian army:

³It's time to go into battle!
　So grab your shields,
⁴　saddle your horses,
　and polish your spears.
Put on your helmets and armor,
　then take your positions.

⁵I can see the battle now—
　you are defeated
and running away,

ʰ**44.30** *King Hophra . . . kill him*: Hophra, also known as Apries, ruled Egypt from 589 to 570 B.C., when he was killed by Ahmosis II, who then became king of Egypt and ruled until 526 B.C. ⁱ**44.30** *Zedekiah*: See the note at 1.3. ʲ**44.30** *Nebuchadnezzar*: See the note at 21.2. ᵏ**45.1** *Jehoiakim*: See the note at 1.3. ˡ**45.1** *Baruch wrote down everything I had told him*: See 36.1-32. ᵐ**46.2** *Jehoiakim*: See the note at 1.3. ⁿ**46.2** *King Nebuchadnezzar*: Ruled 605–562 B.C. At the time of the battle in 605 B.C., he was crown prince, but his father died a few months later, and he became king. ᵒ**46.2** *King Neco of Egypt*: Neco II, ruled 609–594 B.C.

44.26 *Keep these promises*: Jeremiah appears to "wash his hands" of his people's continuing desire to worship Astarte and other gods. He tells them to go ahead and worship these gods, but be prepared to suffer the consequences (44.28). The people apparently keep hoping that they can worship God alongside other gods. But idol worship is unacceptable, even fatal.

45.1 *the fourth year that Jehoiakim was king*: This message to Baruch is from 605 B.C., when Jehoiakim burned the first scroll (see chapter 36).

46.1 *about the different nations*: This verse provides a heading for the prophecies against the nations in chapters 46–51. While Jeremiah was a prophet of Judah, he was sent to speak to all the nations (1.10). This was also true of Isaiah (chapters 13–23), Ezekiel (chapters 25–32), and Amos (chapters 1,2).

46.2 *In the fourth year . . . Carchemish*: The date is the summer of 605 B.C. Judah is caught in the middle of a power struggle between Egypt to their west and the rising power Babylon to their east. While Judah's King Jehoiakim trusted in Egypt as an ally, the Babylonians shattered the Egyptian forces at Carchemish on the Euphrates River (46.6) and later at Hamath in Syria. (See Map 7 on pg 1885 and the article The Ancient World: Peoples, Powers, and Politics on pg 1780.)

46.15 *Apis:* A sacred bull idol representing the fertility god Apis (later, Osiris) was kept in a temple in Memphis, Egypt, and worshiped there. God is pictured "butting" the bull Apis aside (as in Ezek 34.21).

46.17 *this new name:* The king of Egypt brags but never acts.

46.18 *Mount Tabor . . . Carmel:* These mountains in northern Israel are not especially tall, but both have steep slopes that rise above plains. Babylonia will tower over (dominate) Egypt like mountains towering over the plains. **(See Map 3 on pg 1881.)**

never once looking back.
Terror is all around.
6You are strong and run fast,
but you can't escape.
You fall in battle
near the Euphrates River.

7What nation is this,
that rises like the Nile River
overflowing its banks?
8It is Egypt, rising with a roar
like a raging river
and saying,
"I'll flood the earth,
destroying cities, and killing
everyone in them."

9Go ahead, Egypt.
Tell your chariots and cavalry
to attack and fight hard.
Order your troops to march out,
with Ethiopians[p] and Libyans
carrying shields,
and the Lydians[q] armed with bows
and arrows.

10But the LORD All-Powerful
will win this battle
and take revenge
on his enemies.
His sword will eat them
and drink their blood
until it is full.
They will be killed in the north
near the Euphrates River,
as a sacrifice to the LORD.

11Egypt, no medicine can heal you,
not even the soothing lotion
from Gilead.

12All nations have heard you weep;
you are disgraced,
and they know it.
Your troops fall to the ground,
stumbling over each other.

A Warning for Egypt

13-14When King Nebuchadnezzar[r] of Babylonia was on his way to attack Egypt, the LORD sent me with a warning for every Egyptian town, but especially for Migdol, Memphis, and Tahpanhes. He said to tell them:

Prepare to defend yourselves!
Everywhere in your nation,
people are dying in war.
15I have struck down
your mighty god Apis[s]
and chased him away.[t]
16Your soldiers stumble
over each other
and say, "Get up!
The enemy will kill us,
unless we can escape
to our own land."

17Give the king of Egypt
this new name,
"Talks-Big-Does-Nothing."

18Egypt, I am the true king,
the LORD All-Powerful,
and as surely as I live,
those enemies who attack
will tower over you
like Mount Tabor among the hills
or Mount Carmel by the sea.

[p]**46.9** *Ethiopians*: See the note at 38.7,8. [q]**46.9** *Lydians*: Probably hired soldiers from Lydia, an area in west-central Asia minor. [r]**46.13,14** *Nebuchadnezzar*: See the note at 21.2. [s]**46.15** *Apis*: A sacred bull, kept in a temple at Memphis, Egypt, and worshiped as a god. [t]**46.15** *I have . . . him away*: One possible meaning for the difficult Hebrew text.

¹⁹You will be led away captive,
   so pack a few things
      to bring with you.
   Your capital, Memphis,
      will lie empty and in ruins.

²⁰An enemy from the north
   will attack you, beautiful Egypt,
      like a fly biting a cow.
²¹The foreign soldiers you hired
   will turn and run.
   But they are doomed,
   like well-fed calves
      being led to the butcher.

*²²The enemy army will go forward
   like a swarm of locusts.ᵘ
   Your troops will feel helpless,
      like a snake in a forest
²³when men with axes
      start chopping down trees.
   It can only hiss
      and try to escape.
²⁴Your people will be disgraced
   and captured by the enemy
      from the north.

²⁵I am the LORD All-Powerful, the God
of Israel. Soon I will punish the god Amon
of Thebesᵛ and the other Egyptian gods,
the Egyptian kings, the people of Egypt,
and everyone who trusts in the Egyptian
power. ²⁶I will hand them over to King
Nebuchadnezzar and his army. But I also
promise that Egypt will someday have people living here again, just as it had before. I,
the LORD, have spoken.

The LORD Will Bring Israel Home

The LORD said:
   ²⁷Israel,ʷ don't be afraid.
   Someday I will bring you home
      from foreign lands.
   You and your descendants
   will live in peace and safety,
      with nothing to fear.
²⁸So don't be afraid,
   even though now
      you deserve to be punished
   and have been scattered
      among other nations.
   But when I destroy them,
      I will protect you.
   I, the LORD, have spoken.

What the LORD Says about the Philistines

47 Before the king of Egypt attacked
the town of Gaza,ˣ the LORD told
me to say to the Philistines:

   ²I, the LORD, tell you
      that your land will be flooded
         with an army from the north.
   It will destroy your towns
   and sweep you away,
      moaning and screaming.
   ³When you hear the thunder
      of horses and chariots,
         your courage will vanish,
   and parents will even abandon
      their own children.

   ⁴You refugees from Crete,ʸ
      your time has now come,
         and I will destroy you.
   None of you will be left

ᶜᴿ   Locusts

■   46.27 *Israel, don't be afraid:* "Israel" here refers to all God's people,
both northern and southern kingdoms.

●   47.4 *Crete . . . Tyre and Sidon:*
Crete is an island south of Greece and
the original homeland of the ancestors
of the Philistines. Tyre and Sidon were
Phoenician cities on the Mediterranean
Sea coast north of Judah. The leaders of
these city-states rebelled against Babylonia in 594 B.C., and in 587 B.C. they
formed an alliance with the Philistine
cities against Babylonia. **(See Map 7 on
pg 1885.)**

ᵘ**46.22** *locusts:* A type of grasshopper that comes in swarms and causes great damage to plant life.
ᵛ**46.25** *the god Amon of Thebes:* Amon was the king of the Egyptian gods and was the special god of
the Egyptian kings.   ʷ**46.27** *Israel:* See the note at 30.10,11.   ˣ**47.1** *attacked the town of Gaza:* One of
the major Philistine towns; nothing is known about this attack.   ʸ**47.4** *Crete:* Hebrew "Caphtor,"
another name for Crete, the original homeland of the ancestors of the Philistines.

48.1 *Moab:* The people of Moab are often described as enemies of the Israelite people (Num 22–24; Judg 10.11-18; 1 Sam 14.47,48; 2 Kgs 3.21-27; 2 Chr 20.11). The defeat of Moabite cities probably refers to the invasion by Babylonian troops.

48.7 *your god Chemosh:* Chemosh, the national god of the Moabites, is mentioned in various Old Testament passages (1 Kgs 11.7,33; 2 Kgs 23.13; Jer 48.45,46). The national gods of Moab and other nations are useless against the living God of Israel (48.13)

48.9 *Spread salt on the ground:* This may have been part of a ceremony to put a curse on a town (see Judg 9.45). Crops cannot grow in soil that contains too much salt.

48.11 *wine . . . never poured from jar to jar:* Moab was famous for its vineyards (Isa 16.8-10). When bottled wine was not disturbed, some particles would settle to the bottom of the bottle. This "aging" process actually improved the quality of the wine. Unlike Judah, Moab was not destroyed by the Babylonians in 586 B.C. But eventually Moab was "poured out" (48.12) after it was invaded by Nebuchadnezzar's troops. Moab ceased to exist as a nation after an invasion of Arab tribes in the sixth century B.C.

to help the cities
   of Tyre and Sidon.
*⁵The Anakim who survive[z]
   in Gaza and Ashkelon
will mourn for you
by shaving their heads
   and sitting in silence.
⁶You ask how long will I continue
   to attack you with my sword,
then you tell me to put it away
   and leave you alone.
⁷But how can my sword rest,
when I have commanded it
   to attack Ashkelon
   and the seacoast?

What the Lord Says about Moab

48 The Lord All-Powerful, the God of Israel, told me to say to the nation of Moab:

   The town of Nebo is doomed;
   Kiriathaim will be captured
      and disgraced,
   and even its fortress
      will be left in ruins.
²No one honors you, Moab.
   In Heshbon, enemies make plans
      to end your life.
   My sword will leave only silence
      in your town named "Quiet."[a]
³The people of Horonaim
   will cry for help,
   as their town is attacked
      and destroyed.

⁴Moab will be shattered!
   Your children will sob

⁵and cry on their way up
   to the town of Luhith;
on the road to Horonaim
   they will tell of disasters.

⁶Run for your lives!
Head into the desert
   like a wild donkey.[b]
⁷You thought you could be saved
   by your power and wealth,
but you will be captured
along with your god Chemosh,
   his priests, and officials.
⁸Not one of your towns
   will escape destruction.

I have told your enemies,
   "Wipe out the valley
      and the flatlands of Moab.
⁹Spread salt on the ground
   to kill the crops.[c]
Leave its towns in ruins,
   with no one living there.
¹⁰I want you to kill the Moabites,
and if you let them escape,
   I will put a curse on you."

¹¹Moab, you are like wine
   left to settle undisturbed,
      never poured from jar to jar.
And so, your nation continues
   to prosper and improve.[d]
¹²But now, I will send enemies
   to pour out the wine
      and smash the jars!
¹³Then you will be ashamed,
   because your god Chemosh
      cannot save you,

---

[z]**47.5** *Anakim who survive:* One ancient translation; Hebrew "people in the valley who survive." The Anakim may have been a group of very large people that lived in Palestine before the Israelites (see Numbers 13.33; Deuteronomy 2.10,11,20,21; and Joshua 11.21,22).   [a]**48.2** *silence . . . Quiet:* In Hebrew the name of the town was "Madmen," which sounds like the word for "silence."   [b]**48.6** *like a wild donkey:* One ancient translation; Hebrew "like (the town of) Aroer" (see verse 19).   [c]**48.9** *Spread salt . . . crops:* One possible meaning for the difficult Hebrew text.   [d]**48.11** *continues . . . improve:* Or "remains as evil as ever."

just as Bethel[e] could not help
the Israelites.

[14]You claim that your soldiers
are strong and brave.
[15]But I am the LORD,
the all-powerful King,
and I promise that enemies
will overpower your towns.
Even your best warriors
will die in the battle.
[16]It won't be long now—
disaster will hit Moab!

[17]I will order the nearby nations
to mourn for you and say,
"Isn't it sad? Moab ruled others,
but now its glorious power
has been shattered."

[18]People in the town of Dibon,[f]
you will be honored no more,
so have a seat in the dust.
Your walls will be torn down
when the enemies attack.

[19]You people of Aroer,[g]
go wait beside the road,
and when refugees run by,
ask them, "What happened?"
[20]They will answer,
"Moab has been defeated!
Weep with us in shame.
Tell everyone at the Arnon River
that Moab is destroyed."

*[21]I will punish every town
that belongs to Moab,
but especially Holon,

Jahzah, Mephaath,
[22] Dibon, Nebo,
Beth-Diblathaim, [23]Kiriathaim,
Beth-Gamul, Beth-Meon,
[24] Kerioth, and Bozrah.[h]
[25]My decision is final—
your army will be crushed,
and your power broken.

[26]People of Moab, you claim
to be stronger than I am.
Now I will tell other nations
to make you drunk
and to laugh while you collapse
in your own vomit.
[27]You made fun of my people
and treated them like criminals
caught in the act.
[28]Now you must leave your towns
and live like doves
in the shelter of cliffs
and canyons.

[29]I know about your pride,
and how you strut and boast.
[30]But I also know bragging
will never save you.
[31]So I will cry and mourn
for Moab
and its town of Kir-Heres.

[32]People of Sibmah,
you were like a vineyard
heavy with grapes,
and with branches reaching
north to the town of Jazer
and west to the Dead Sea.[i]
But you have been destroyed,
and so I will weep for you,

48.21 *I will punish every town:* The complete destruction of Moab is described. Many of the places mentioned here are unknown. Bozrah is not the same Bozrah as in 49.13, where it is the capital of Edom.

48.26 *nations . . . laugh while you collapse:* Moab assisted Babylonia in the attack on Judah in 598 B.C. (2 Kgs 24.1,2). While once Moab had made fun of Judah, now Moab will be laughed at.

48.28 *doves:* Like doves that made their nests in the rocks of high mountains, the Moabites will leave their lowland towns and take to the hills.

48.31-34 *Kir-Heres . . . Nimrim Creek:* More Moabite locations will be destroyed. Kir-Heres was probably located about 17 miles south of Ar. Sibmah is compared to a lush vineyard, heavy with riches and prosperity. The wine trade reached to Jazer, which was a center for the god Tammuz. Worship of Tammuz involved weeping over his death. Jazer was probably north of the Dead Sea near the southern border of Ammon. Elealeh was about one mile from Heshbon (see Num 32.3). Zoar was in southern Moab near the south end of the Dead Sea. The location of Nimrim Creek may refer to Wadi Nimrim, which flows east into the Jordan River about eight miles north of the Dead Sea.

[e]48.13 *Bethel:* It may refer to the Phoenician or Canaanite god of that name; or it may refer to the town where people of the northern kingdom worshiped at a local shrine (see 1 Kings 12.26-30). [f]48.18 *Dibon:* The capital city of Moab. [g]48.19 *Aroer:* A Moabite town located just north of the Arnon River. [h]48.24 *Bozrah:* Not the same Bozrah as in 49.13. [i]48.32 *reaching north . . . Dead Sea:* One possible meaning for the difficult Hebrew text.

48.38 *shattered Moab like a jar:* Compare this picture of Moab's destruction with the destruction of Judah (13.12-14) and of King Jehoiachin and his family (22.28).

48.45 *Sihon once ruled:* Sihon was the Amorite king who refused to let the Israelites pass through his country on their way to the promised land. (Num 21.21-30).

48.47 *someday, I will bring:* Compare to the last line of Jeremiah's message to Egypt (46.26).

as the people of Jazer weep
for the vineyards.
³³Harvest celebrations are gone
from the orchards and farms
of Moab.
I have silenced the shouts
of people making wine.
³⁴Weeping from Heshbon
can be heard as far
as Elealeh and Jahaz;
cries from Zoar are heard
in Horonaim
and Eglath-Shelishiyah.
And Nimrim Creek has run dry.

³⁵I will get rid of anyone
who burns incense
to the gods of Moab
or offers sacrifices
at their shrines.
I, the Lord, have spoken.

³⁶In my heart I moan for Moab,
like a funeral song
played on a flute.
I mourn for the people
of the town of Kir-Heres,
because their wealth is gone.

*³⁷⁻³⁸The people of Moab
mourn on the rooftops
and in the streets.
Men cut off their beards,
people shave their heads;
they make cuts on their hands
and wear sackcloth.ʲ
And it's all because I, the Lord,
have shattered Moab like a jar
that no one wants.
³⁹Moab lies broken!
Listen to its people cry

as they turn away in shame.
Other nations are horrified
at what happened,
but still they mock her.

⁴⁰Moab, an enemy swoops down
like an eagle spreading its wings
over your land.
⁴¹Your citiesᵏ and fortresses
will be captured,
and your warriors as fearful
as women giving birth.ˡ
⁴²You are finished as a nation,
because you dared oppose me,
the Lord.
⁴³Terror, pits, and traps
are waiting for you.
⁴⁴If you are terrified and run,
you will fall into a pit;
and if you crawl out of the pit,
you'll get caught in a trap.
The time has come
for you to be punished.
I, the Lord, have spoken.

⁴⁵Near the city of Heshbon,
where Sihon once ruled,
tired refugees stand in shadows
cast by the flames
of their burning city.
Soon, the towns on other hilltops,
where those warlike people live,
will also go up in smoke.

⁴⁶People of Moab, you worshiped
Chemosh, your god,
but now you are done for,
and your children are prisoners
in a foreign country.
⁴⁷Yet someday, I will bring
your people back home.
I, the Lord, have spoken.

ʲ**48.37,38** *sackcloth:* See the note at 4.8.   ᵏ**48.41** *Your cities:* Or "Kerioth."   ˡ**48.41** *as fearful . . . birth:* One possible meaning for the difficult Hebrew text.

What the LORD Says about Ammon

49 The LORD has this to say about the nation of Ammon:

The people of Israel
have plenty of children
    to inherit their lands.
So why have you worshipers
    of the god Milcom[m]
taken over towns and land
    belonging to the tribe of Gad?
[2]Someday I will send an army
to attack you in Rabbah,
    your capital city.
It will be left in ruins,
and the surrounding villages
    will lie in ashes.
You took some of Israel's land,
but on that day
    Israel will take yours!

[3]Cry, people of Heshbon;[n]
your town will become
    a pile of rubble.[o]
You will turn here and there,
    but your path will be blocked.[p]

Put on sackcloth[q] and mourn,
    you citizens of Rabbah,
because the idol you worship[r]
will be taken
    to a foreign country,

along with its priests
    and temple officials.
[4]You rebellious Ammonites
trust your wealth and ask,
    "Who could attack us?"
But I warn you not to boast
    when your strength is fading.[s]
[5]I, the LORD All-Powerful,
will send neighboring nations
    to strike you with terror.
You will be scattered,
with no one to care
    for your refugees.
[6]Yet someday, I will bring
    your people back home.
I, the LORD, have spoken.

What the LORD Says about Edom

[7]The LORD All-Powerful says about Edom:
    Wisdom and common sense
        have vanished from Teman.[t]
[8]I will send disaster to punish
    you descendants of Esau,[u]
so anyone from Dedan[v]
    had better turn around
    and run back home.[w]
[9]People who harvest grapes
    leave some for the poor.
Thieves who break in at night
    take only what they want.
[10]But I will take everything
    that belongs to you,
        people of Edom,

---

[m]**49.1** *Milcom*: The national god of Ammon, probably the same as the god Molech in 32.35. [n]**49.3** *Heshbon*: See also 48.45; since Heshbon was near the border of Moab and Ammon, it was probably ruled by the country that was stronger at the time. [o]**49.3** *your town will become a pile of rubble*: Or "because the town of Ai has been destroyed"; referring to an Ammonite town named Ai, not the town of that name near Bethel in the land of Israel. [p]**49.3** *You will turn . . . blocked*: One possible meaning for the difficult Hebrew text. [q]**49.3** *sackcloth*: See the note at 4.8. [r]**49.3** *the idol you worship*: Hebrew "Milcom" (see verse 1 and the note there). [s]**49.4** *when . . . fading*: One possible meaning for the difficult Hebrew text. [t]**49.7,8** *Teman*: The name of a town in Edom, sometimes used as the name of the northern half of the nation of Edom; here it probably stands for the whole nation. [u]**49.7,8** *Esau*: The ancestor of the nation of Edom. [v]**49.7,8** *Dedan*: The name of a town in northwest Arabia, also used of the northwest region of Arabia along the Red Sea. [w]**49.7,8** *anyone . . . home*: One possible meaning for the difficult Hebrew text.

49.1 *Ammon*: Ammon and the people of Israel often battled (Judg 10.6—11.40; 1 Sam 11; 2 Sam 12.26-31). After the collapse of the northern kingdom of Israel in 722 B.C., Ammonites invaded portions of the territory of the Gad tribe. Finally, in Jeremiah's time, the Ammonite king Baalis hired Ishmael to assassinate the Jewish governor Gedaliah in 586 B.C. (Jer 40.13,14). **(See Map 6 on pg 1884.)**

49.5 *You will be scattered*: The Ammonites came under Babylonian control when Babylon defeated Assyria (612 B.C.). They helped Babylon attack Judah during the rule of Jehoiakim (2 Kgs 24.2). But later they rebelled against Babylon (Jer 27.3; Ezek 21.18-23). Even after Judah fell, Ammon continued to support the Jewish rebel Ishmael (Jer 40.7-16). Because of their disloyalty to Babylonia, Nebuchadnezzar invaded in 582 B.C.

49.7-8 *Edom . . . Esau*: The land of Edom, sometimes called Seir, was located south and southeast of the Dead Sea, which put it next to Judah's southwestern border. The people of Edom were descendants of Jacob's brother Esau (Gen 25.24-26; 36.1). The nation of Edom is usually described in the Bible as an enemy of Israel (Num 20.14-21; 24.18; 1 Sam 14.47,48; 2 Sam 8.13,14). The Edomites joined Nebuchadnezzar in defeating Jerusalem in 587 B.C. and is reported to have rejoiced when the city fell (Ps 137.7; Lam 4.21; Obad 10-16). The Edomites took advantage of Judah's defeat by settling in southern Judah. **(See Map 6 on pg 1884.)**

49.16 *cliffs . . . mountains*: Edom was noted for its rock fortresses built high in mountainous cliffs.

49.19-21 *attack you like a lion . . . cause the earth to shake*: In 50.44-46, this same wording is used to describe Babylonia.

49.21 *Red Sea*: The term for Red Sea here may refer to the marshy area ("Sea of Reeds") that the Hebrew people crossed to escape the Egyptian army (Exod 13.17—14.31). However, the Red Sea is also understood as referring to the Gulf of Aqaba, the northeastern arm of the Red Sea. (See Map 2 on pg 1880.)

49.22 *like an eagle . . . as fearful as women giving birth*: Compare to 30.6 and 48.40. Note that there is no prophecy of the restoration of Edom as there is with other nations in this section (46.26,27; 48.47; 49.6). The hatred between "brothers" Edom and Israel was deep and persistent.

49.23 *Damascus . . . Arpad*: The modern day capital of Syria, Damascus, fell to the Assyrian king Tiglath-pileser II in 732 B.C., and little is known of its history in the next few centuries. Arpad was captured by the Assyrians in 740 B.C., and Hamath in 738 B.C. (See Map 7 on pg 1885.)

and I will uncover every place
　where you try to hide.
Then you will die,
and so will your children,
　relatives, and neighbors.
¹¹But I can be trusted
　to care for your orphans
　and widows.

¹²Even those nations that don't deserve to be punished will have to drink from the cup of my anger. So how can you possibly hope to escape? ¹³I, the LORD, swear in my own name that your city of Bozrah[x] and all your towns will suffer a horrible fate. They will lie in ruins forever, and people will use the name "Bozrah" as a curse word.

¹⁴I have sent a messenger
　to command the nations
　to prepare for war
　against you people of Edom.
¹⁵Your nation will be small,
　yet hated by other nations.
¹⁶Pride tricks you into thinking
　that other nations
　look at you with fear.[y]
You live along the cliffs
and high in the mountains
　like the eagles,
but I am the LORD,
　and I will bring you down.
¹⁷People passing by your country
　will be shocked and horrified
　to see a disaster
¹⁸as bad as the destruction
　of Sodom and Gomorrah

and towns nearby.
The towns of Edom will be empty.

¹⁹I, the LORD, will attack you
　like a lion from the forest,
attacking sheep in a meadow
　along the Jordan.
In a moment the flock runs,
　and the land is empty.
Who will I choose to attack you?
　I will do it myself!
No one can force me to fight
　or chase me away.
²⁰Listen to my plans for you,
　people of Edom.[z]
Your children will be dragged off
　and your country destroyed.
²¹The sounds of your destruction
　will reach the Red Sea[a]
　and cause the earth to shake.
²²An enemy will swoop down
　to attack you,
like an eagle spreading its wings
　and circling over Bozrah.
Your warriors will be as fearful
　as women giving birth.[b]

What the LORD Says about Damascus

²³The LORD says about Damascus:

The towns of Hamath and Arpad[c]
　have heard your bad news.
They have lost hope,
and worries roll over them
　like ocean waves.[d]
²⁴You people of Damascus

[x]**49.13** *Bozrah*: The main city and capital of Edom. [y]**49.16** *Pride . . . fear*: One possible meaning for the difficult Hebrew text. [z]**49.20** *Edom*: The Hebrew text also uses the name "Teman" (see the note at verses 7,8). [a]**49.21** *Red Sea*: Hebrew *yam suph*, here referring to the Gulf of Aqaba, since the term is extended to include the northeastern arm of the Red Sea (see also the note at Exodus 13.18). [b]**49.22** *as fearful . . . birth*: One possible meaning for the difficult Hebrew text. [c]**49.23** *Hamath and Arpad*: Two towns in Syria that had been the capitals of small kingdoms allied with the more powerful kingdom whose capital was Damascus. [d]**49.23** *worries . . . waves*: One possible meaning for the difficult Hebrew text.

have lost your courage,
and in panic you turn to run,
gripped by fear and pain.[e]

25Once I was pleased
with your famous city.
But now I warn you, "Escape
while you still can!"[f]
26Soon, even your best soldiers
will lie dead in your streets.
I, the LORD All-Powerful,
have spoken.

27I will set fire to your city walls
and burn down the fortresses
King Benhadad built.

Nebuchadnezzar and the People of the Desert

28Here is what the LORD says about the Kedar tribe and the desert villages[g] that were conquered by King Nebuchadnezzar[h] of Babylonia:

Listen, you people of Kedar
and the other tribes
of the eastern desert.
I have told Nebuchadnezzar
to attack and destroy you.
29His fearsome army
will surround you,
taking your tents and possessions,
your sheep and camels.

30Run and hide,
you people of the desert
who live in villages![i]

Nebuchadnezzar has big plans
for you.
31You have no city walls
and no neighbors to help,
yet you think you're safe—
so I told him to attack.
32Then your camels
and large herds
will be yours no longer.

People of the Arabian Desert,[j]
disaster will strike you
from every side,
and you will be scattered
everywhere on earth.
33Only jackals[k] will live
where your villages[l] once stood.
I, the LORD, have spoken.

What the LORD Says about Elam

34-35Not long after Zedekiah[m] became king of Judah, the LORD told me to say:

People of Elam,[n]
I, the LORD All-Powerful,
will kill the archers
who make your army strong.
36Enemies will attack
from all directions,
and you will be led captive
to every nation on earth.
37Their armies will crush
and kill you,
and you will face the disaster
that my anger brings.
38Your king and his officials

[e]49.24 gripped by fear and pain: One possible meaning for the difficult Hebrew text. [f]49.25 can: One possible meaning for the difficult Hebrew text of verse 25. [g]49.28 desert villages: The Hebrew text has "kingdoms of Hazor," which probably refers to several kingdoms of desert peoples who were not nomads, but who lived in small villages. [h]49.28 Nebuchadnezzar: See the note at 21.2. [i]49.30 villages: See the note at 49.28. [j]49.32 People of the Arabian Desert: One possible meaning for the difficult Hebrew text. [k]49.33 jackals: See the note at 9.11. [l]49.33 villages: See the note at 49.28. [m]49.34,35 Zedekiah: See the note at 1.3. [n]49.34,35 Elam: A nation east of Babylonia, attacked by Nebuchadnezzar about 596 B.C.

49.27 *King Benhadad:* This was the name of several rulers of Damascus (1 Kgs 15.18-20; 20.1; 2 Kgs 6.24; 8.7; 13.24).

49.28 *Kedar tribe . . . desert villages:* The Kedar tribe probably refers to the leading tribe of a group of nomadic tribes (wandering herders) in the north Arabian desert east of Syria. Other desert peoples lived in villages and were not nomads. Neither the tent-dwelling tribes nor the desert villagers had cities with walls, so they were vulnerable to attack (49.31). Bedouin herders today live in tents made of animal skins much like the Kedir tribe described by Jeremiah.

49.34 *after Zedekiah:* Zedekiah became king in March 598 B.C.

49.34-35 *Elam:* This nation east of Babylonia in modern southwest Iran was attacked by Nebuchadnezzar about 596 B.C. The Elamites later played a role in the overthrow of Babylonia in 540 B.C. (Isa 21.2). **(See Map 7 on pg 1885.)**

● 50.2 *Marduk:* Marduk was the great cosmic god of the heavens and father of the family of gods in Babylonia. He was worshiped with elaborate rituals and ceremonies led by priests, who carried images of Marduk through the streets in the New Year's procession. Marduk was also known by the names "Bel" and "Merodach." He is sometimes represented in art as a dragon or bull.

● 50.3 *attack on the Babylonians:* Elsewhere in Jeremiah, Babylon and its king Nebuchadnezzar are called the LORD's "servant," chosen to be the instrument of God's judgment against the people of Judah and surrounding nations (25.9; 27.6,7; 29.7). But now the tone of the prophecies turns bitterly against Babylon. Babylon fell to the Persian king Cyrus in October 539 B.C., but without a battle and with little damage to the city. The powerful priests of Marduk actually opened the city gates to Cyrus, because they were furious with their king, Nabonidus (556–539 B.C.), who tried to replace Marduk with the moon-god Sin.

ⓒ⃥　Babylon

ⓒ⃥　Persia

will die, and I will rule
in their place.
I, the LORD, have spoken.

³⁹But I promise that someday
I will bring your people
back to their land.

Babylon Will Be Captured

50 ^{*1} The LORD told me to say:

Announce what will happen
and don't leave anything out.
²　Raise the signal flags;
shout so all nations can hear—
Babylon will be captured!

Marduk,[o] Babylon's god,
will be ashamed and terrified,
and his idols broken.
³The attack on the Babylonians
will come from the north;
they and their animals will run,
leaving the land empty.

Israel and Judah Will Return to Their Land

⁴The LORD said:

People of Israel and Judah,
when these things happen
you will weep, and together
you will return to your land
and worship me,
the LORD your God.
⁵You will ask the way to Zion
and then come and join with me
in making an agreement
you won't break or forget.

⁶My people, you are lost sheep
abandoned in the mountains
by their shepherds.
You don't even remember
your resting place.
⁷I am your true pastureland,
the one who gave hope
to your ancestors.
But you abandoned me,
so when your enemies found you,
they felt no guilt
as they gobbled you up.

⁸Escape from Babylonia,
my people.
Get out of that country!
Don't wait for anyone else.
⁹In the north I am bringing
great nations together.
They will attack Babylon
and capture it.
The arrows they shoot
are like the best soldiers,[P]
always finding their target.
¹⁰Babylonia will be conquered,
and its enemies will carry off
everything they want.

Babylon Will Be Disgraced

The LORD said:
¹¹People of Babylonia,
you were glad
to rob my people.
You had a good time,
making more noise
than horses
and jumping around
like calves threshing grain.[q]
¹²The city of Babylon

---

[o]**50.2** *Marduk:* The Hebrew text has "Bel" and "Marduk," two names for the same god. 　[P]**50.9** *the best soldiers:* Some Hebrew manuscripts and two ancient translations; most Hebrew manuscripts "soldiers that kill children." 　[q]**50.11** *threshing grain:* Hebrew; two ancient translations "in a pasture."

was like a mother to you.
But it will be disgraced
and become nothing
but a barren desert.
¹³My anger will destroy Babylon,
and no one will live there.
Everyone who passes by
will be shocked to see
what has happened.

¹⁴Babylon has rebelled against me.
Archers, take your places.
Shoot all your arrows at Babylon.
¹⁵ Attack from every side!

Babylon surrenders!
The enemy tears down
its walls and towers.
I am taking my revenge
by doing to Babylon what it did
to other cities.
¹⁶There is no one in Babylonia
to plant or harvest crops.
Even foreigners who lived there
have left for their homelands,
afraid of the enemy armies.

¹⁷Israel is a flock of sheep
scattered by hungry lions.
The king of Assyria^r
first gobbled Israel up.
Then Nebuchadnezzar,^s
king of Babylonia,
crunched on Israel's bones.
¹⁸I, the LORD All-Powerful,
the God of Israel,
punished the king of Assyria,
and I will also punish

the king of Babylonia.
¹⁹But I will bring Israel
back to its own land.
The people will be like sheep
eating their fill
on Mount Carmel
and in Bashan,
in the hill country of Ephraim
and in Gilead.
²⁰I will rescue a few people
from Israel and Judah.
I will forgive them so completely
that their sin and guilt
will disappear,
never to be found.

The LORD's Commands to the Enemies of Babylonia

²¹The LORD said:

I have told
the enemies of Babylonia,
"Attack the people of Merathaim
and Pekod.^t
Kill them all!
Destroy their possessions!"

²²Sounds of war
and the noise of destruction
can be heard.
²³Babylonia was a hammer
pounding every country,
but now it lies broken.
What a shock to the nations
of the world!

²⁴Babylonia challenged me,
the LORD God All-Powerful,

50.13 *Everyone who passes by:* The Hebrew has "they will hiss." Hissing was thought to be a way to ward off the evil witnessed by those passing by.

50.16 *foreigners who lived there:* This refers to foreigners who willingly settled in Babylon or those brought there by force. After Persia captured Babylon, many Jewish people returned home to Judah. But a number stayed on in Babylonia.

50.21 *Merathaim . . . Pekod:* Merathaim probably referred to lagoons near the mouth of the Tigris and Euphrates rivers or to the Persian Gulf, but in Hebrew it means "Twice as Rebellious." Pekod referred to a tribe of southeastern Babylonia, but in Hebrew, it means "Punishment." Thus, "Double Rebellion" will get its reward, and "Punishment" will see its own. The invitation to "kill them all" and destroy all their possessions was part of the "ban" called for in Israel's "holy wars."

Holy War (The LORD's Battles)

---

^r**50.17** *king of Assyria:* Either Shalmaneser V, who ruled 726–722 B.C., conquered most of the northern kingdom, and surrounded its capital city Samaria; or Sargon II, who ruled 721–705 B.C. and took thousands of prisoners back to Assyria. ^s**50.17** *Nebuchadnezzar:* See the note at 21.2.
^t**50.21** *Merathaim . . . Pekod:* Hebrew forms of two Babylonian names that refer to the land of Babylonia. Merathaim probably referred to lagoons near the mouth of the Tigris and Euphrates rivers or to the Persian Gulf, but in Hebrew it means "Twice as Rebellious." Pekod referred to a tribe of southeastern Babylonia, but in Hebrew it means "Punishment."

50.28 *my temple . . . Zion:* Those exiled in Babylonia, set free at last, will tell how God took revenge on their captors in response to the destruction of the temple in Jerusalem.

50.32 *proud . . . stumble and fall:* Babylon was an impressive and powerful city. But the pride of its people and leaders has turned into arrogance. So they will stumble and fall from their high position.

50.33,34 *You took them captive . . . But I . . . will rescue:* In 586 B.C., thousands of Judeans were deported to Babylonia. Now God will bring peace to Israel (Isa 32.18) and unrest for Babylonia.

50.36 *your prophets:* Babylonian prophets and fortunetellers tried to predict the future by examining fluid in a cup, looking at the livers of animals, or trying to contact the spirits of the dead. The priests of Babylon also used astrology to chart a person's future based on the position of the stars and planets at the time of his or her birth. These prophets are called fools because they did not correctly predict Babylon's destruction.

50.37 *foreigners in your army:* When the defense of Babylon is necessary, these foreign soldiers will refuse to risk their lives.

50.38 *Your . . . canals:* Babylon had two major rivers (Tigris and Euphrates), and it had developed a system of canals for transportation and irrigating crops.

but that nation doesn't know
　　it is caught in a trap
　　　that I set.
25I've brought out my weapons,
　　and with them I will put a curse
　　　on Babylonia.

26Come from far away,
　　you enemies of Babylon!
Pile up the grain
　　from its storehouses,
and destroy it completely,
　　along with everything else.
27Kill the soldiers of Babylonia,
because the time has come
　　for them to be punished.

28The Babylonian army
destroyed my temple,
　　but soon I will take revenge.
Then refugees from Babylon
　　will tell about it in Zion.

29Attack Babylon, enemy archers;
set up camp around the city,
　　and don't let anyone escape.
It challenged me, the holy God,
so do to it
　　what it did to other cities.

Proud Babylon Will Fall

30People of Babylon,
　　I, the LORD, promise
that even your best soldiers
　　will lie dead in the streets.

31Babylon, you should be named,
　"The Proud One."
But the time has come when I,
　the LORD All-Powerful,

u50.39 *jackals:* See the note at 9.11.

will punish you.
32You are proud,
　　but you will stumble and fall,
　　　and no one will help you up.
I will set your villages on fire,
　　and everything around you
　　　will go up in flames.

33You Babylonians were cruel
　　to Israel and Judah.
You took them captive, and now
　　you refuse to let them go.
34But I, the LORD All-Powerful,
　　will rescue and protect them.
I will bring peace to their land
　　and trouble to yours.
35I have declared war on you,
　　your officials, and advisors.
36This war will prove
　　that your prophets
　　are liars and fools.
And it will frighten
　　your warriors.
37Then your chariot horses
　　and the foreigners in your army
　　　will refuse to go into battle,
and the enemy will carry away
　　everything you treasure.
38Your rivers and canals
　　will dry up.

All of this will happen,
because your land
　　is full of idols,
and they have made fools
　　of you.
39Never again will people live
　　in your land—
only desert animals, jackals,u
　　and unclean birds.
40I destroyed Sodom and Gomorrah
　　and the nearby towns,

and I will destroy Babylon
    just as completely.
No one will live there again.

Babylonia Is Invaded

The LORD said:

41Far to the north,
    a nation and its allies
    have been awakened.
They are powerful
    and ready for war.
42Bows and arrows and swords
    are in their hands.
The soldiers are cruel
    and show no pity.
The hoofbeats of their horses
    echo like ocean waves
    crashing against the shore.
The army has lined up for battle
    and is coming to attack you,
    people of Babylonia!

43Ever since your king heard
    about this army,
he has been weak with fear;
    he twists and turns in pain
    like a woman giving birth.
44Babylonia, I will attack you
    like a lion from the forest,
attacking sheep in a meadow
    along the Jordan.
In a moment the flock runs,
    and the land is empty.
Who will I choose to attack you?
    I will do it myself!
No one can force me to fight
    or chase me away.
45Listen to my plans for you,

people of Babylonia.
Your children will be dragged off,
    and your country destroyed.
46The sounds of your destruction
    will be heard among the nations,
    and the earth will shake.

Babylon Will Be Destroyed

51 I, the LORD, am sending
    a wind[v] to destroy
the people of Babylonia[w]
    and Babylon, its capital.
2Foreign soldiers will come
    from every direction,
and when the disaster is over,
    Babylonia will be empty
    and worthless.
3I will tell these soldiers,
    "Attack quickly,
before the Babylonians
    can string their bows
    or put on their armor.[x]
Kill their best soldiers
    and destroy their army!"
4Their troops will fall wounded
    in the streets of Babylon.

5Everyone in Israel and Judah
    is guilty.
But I, the LORD All-Powerful,
    their holy God,
    have not abandoned them.

6Get out of Babylon!
    Run for your lives!
If you stay, you will be killed
    when I take revenge on the city
    and punish it for its sins.

[v]**51.1** *wind:* Or "spirit." [w]**51.1** *Babylonia:* The Hebrew text has "Leb-Qamai," a secret way of writing "Babylonia." [x]**51.3** *I will tell . . . armor:* Or "Attack quickly! String your bows and put on your armor."

■ 50.41-43 *Far to the north . . . woman giving birth:* These verses echo 6.22-24, where they were addressed to Judah; here they are applied to Babylonia. The enemy from the north here is Persia. **(See Map 8 on pg 1886.)**

● 51.1 *Babylon, its capital:* The theme of this chapter, and chapter 50 before it, is the end of Babylon's history. The Hebrew of 51.1 uses a code name for Babylon. Codes (ciphers) were used as a means of protecting the writer and readers from punishment at the hands of an enemy. These codes were developed during the time of exile in Babylon. Code language was used frequently in REVELATION in New Testament times, when persecution of the churches in the Roman Empire was widespread. In REVELATION, "Babylon" is the code name for the mighty Roman Empire. **(See Map 7 on pg 1885.)**

Babylon

■ 51.5 *Israel and Judah is guilty . . . not abandoned:* Jeremiah's two-fold task is restated. Israel and Judah turned away from the LORD, and so they were punished. Babylonia was the instrument of God's judgment. Babylon crushed Judah, reduced Jerusalem to rubble, stole Israel's sacred objects while tearing down the temple, and took many of Judah's citizens into exile in Babylon. But this humiliating and dark time in the history of God's people will end with the defeat of Babylon, and the Jewish people will go home and be restored.

51.11 *kings of Media:* Media was the ancient kingdom northeast of Babylonia. The Median king Astyges was overthrown by Cyrus of Persia in 550 B.C. Then, Media was part of a coalition headed by Cyrus that brought Babylonia down in 539 B.C.

Persia

⁷Babylon was my golden cup,
filled with the wine
    of my anger.
The nations of the world
got drunk on this wine
    and went insane.
⁸But suddenly, Babylon will fall
    and be destroyed.

I, the LORD, told the foreigners^y
    who lived there,
"Weep for the city!
Get medicine for its wounds;
    maybe they will heal."

⁹The foreigners answered,
    "We have already tried
to treat Babylon's wounds,
    but they would not heal.
Come on, let's all go home
    to our own countries.
Nothing is left in Babylonia;
    everything is destroyed."

¹⁰The people of Israel said,
    "Tell everyone in Zion!
The LORD has taken revenge
    for what Babylon did to us."

The LORD Wants Babylon Destroyed

¹¹I, the LORD,
    want Babylon destroyed,
because its army
    destroyed my temple.
So, you kings of Media,^z
sharpen your arrows
    and pick up your shields.
¹²Raise the signal flag
    and attack the city walls.

Post more guards.
Have soldiers watch the city
    and set up ambushes.
I have made plans
to destroy Babylon,
    and nothing will stop me.

¹³People of Babylon, you live
along the Euphrates River
    and are surrounded by canals.
You are rich,
but now the time has come
    for you to die.^a
¹⁴I, the LORD All-Powerful,
    swear by my own life
that enemy soldiers
will fill your streets
    like a swarm of locusts.^b
They will shout
    and celebrate their victory.

A Hymn of Praise

(Jeremiah 10.12-16)

¹⁵God used his wisdom and power
    to create the earth
    and spread out the heavens.
¹⁶The waters in the heavens roar
    at his command.
He makes clouds appear;
he sends the wind
    from his storehouse
and makes lightning flash
    in the rain.

¹⁷People who make idols
    are stupid!
They will be disappointed,
because their false gods
    cannot breathe.
¹⁸Idols are merely a joke,

^y51.8 *the foreigners:* Or "my people."   ^z51.11 *kings of Media:* Probably kings of smaller kingdoms that were part of the Median Empire (see also verse 27 and the note there).   ^a51.13 *for you to die:* One possible meaning for the difficult Hebrew text.   ^b51.14 *locusts:* See the note at 46.22.

and when the time is right,
  they will be destroyed.
[19]But the Lord, Israel's God,
  is all-powerful.
He created everything,
  and he chose Israel
  to be his very own.

God's Hammer

The Lord said:
[20]Babylonia, you were my hammer;
  I used you to pound nations
  and break kingdoms,
[21]to shatter cavalry and chariots,
[22]as well as men and women,
  young and old,
[23]shepherds and their flocks,
  farmers and their oxen,
  and governors and leaders.

[24]But now, my people will watch,
  while I repay you
  for what you did to Zion.

[25]You destroyed the nations
  and seem strong as a mountain,
  but I am your enemy.
I might even grab you
  and roll you off a cliff.
When I am finished,
  you'll only be a pile
  of scorched bricks.
[26]Your stone blocks won't be reused
  for cornerstones
  or foundations,
and I promise that forever
  you will be a desert.
I, the Lord, have spoken.

The Nations Will Attack Babylon

The Lord said:
[27]Signal the nations
  to get ready to attack.
Raise a flag and blow a trumpet.
Send for the armies of Ararat,
  Minni, and Ashkenaz.[c]
Choose a commander;
  let the cavalry attack
  like a swarm of locusts.
[28]Tell the kings and governors,
  the leaders and the people
of the kingdoms of the Medes
  to prepare for war!

[29]The earth twists and turns
  in torment,
because I have decided
  to make Babylonia a desert
  where no one can live,
and I won't change my mind.

[30]The Babylonian soldiers
  have lost their strength
  and courage.[d]
They stay in their fortresses,
  unable to fight,
while the enemy breaks through
  the city gates,
  then sets their homes on fire.
[31]One messenger after another
  announces to the king,
  "Babylon has been captured!"
[32]The enemy now controls
  the river crossings!
The marshes[e] are on fire!
  Your army has panicked!"

[33]I am the Lord All-Powerful,
  the God of Israel,

---

[c]**51.27** *Ararat, Minni, and Ashkenaz:* Kingdoms to the north of Babylonia that were part of the Median Empire (see also verse 28).   [d]**51.30** *have lost their strength and courage:* Hebrew "have lost their strength and have become like women."   [e]**51.32** *marshes:* The tall grass in the marshes could have provided hiding places for people trying to escape from Babylon.

■ 51.19 *Lord, Israel's God . . . chose Israel:* The powerful God of creation is also Israel's personal God, who chose them (Isa 41.8,9).

■ 51.20 *you were my hammer:* Once the Lord's chosen agent of judgment (25.9; 27.6,7; 29.7), Babylonia will soon be judged.

● 51.25 *pile of scorched bricks:* Ancient Babylon was known for its towering brick temple (ziggurat) to the god Marduk and for beautiful cut stone palaces, walls, and roadways. The pile of bricks may refer to the destruction of the towering temple of Marduk, which rose above the plains of Babylon like a mountain (51.25).

● 51.27,28 *Ararat, Minni, Ashkenaz . . . kingdoms of the Medes:* These small kingdoms were defeated by the Medes between 600 and 575 B.C. and became part of the Median Empire. They joined the Medes in the battle against Babylon (51.28). Ararat (Urartu) peoples probably came from southeast Turkey, and the Minni from northern Iraq. The Ashkenaz, later called Scythians, came from the area of present-day Armenia. **(See Map 7 on pg 1885.)**

■ 51.30-32 *breaks through the city gates . . . marshes are on fire:* The Babylonian king receives one message of doom after another. Once Babylon's important waterways have been captured, the country is in deep trouble (see 51.36 and 50.38). The tall grass is set on fire to cut off escape and to smoke out enemy troops.

51.33 *threshing place*: In preparation for harvest, a dirt surface for threshing the grain was made level and packed down to make it hard and smooth. After the grain was threshed (separated from the stalk), the place was swept clean. So will Babylon be pounded and then swept away by war.

51.36 *water supply . . . stream*: The stream is probably the Euphrates River. Cutting off the water supply is cutting off Babylon's life, as the city depended on the river and canals.

51.44 *Marduk*: The fall of Babylon is described as a cosmic battle between Israel's LORD God and Babylon's god Marduk.

51.45-50 *run for your lives . . . Leave Babylon*: Many political upheavals and changes on the throne occurred in Babylonia after Nebuchadnezzar's death in 562 B.C. These changes and the rumors of the Persian advance on Babylon around 540 B.C. would make the Judean prisoners living there fearful. God's people are told to run away, because Babylon's destruction is coming. But God will protect the people of Judah when the Persians attack Babylon. In reality, the Persian takeover of Babylon was not violent. And Cyrus of Persia allowed the people of Judah to return home in peace. **(See the article After the Exile: God's People Return to Judea on pg 1789.)**

Exile

and I make this promise—
"Soon Babylon will be leveled
    and packed down
like a threshing place
    at harvest time."[f]

Babylonia Will Pay!

[34]The people of Jerusalem say,
"King Nebuchadnezzar[g]
    made us panic.
That monster stuffed himself
    with us and our treasures,
    leaving us empty—
he gobbled up
    what he wanted
    and spit out the rest.
[35]The people of Babylonia
    harmed some of us[h]
    and killed others.
Now, LORD, make them pay!"

The LORD Will Take Revenge on Babylon

[36]My people, I am on your side,
    and I will take revenge
    on Babylon.
I will cut off its water supply,
    and its stream[i] will dry up.
[37]Babylon will be a pile of rubble
    where only jackals[j] live,
and everyone will be afraid
    to walk among the ruins.
[38]The Babylonians roar and growl
    like young lions.
[39]And since they are hungry,
    I will give them a banquet.
They will celebrate, get drunk,
    then fall asleep,

never to wake up!
[40]I will lead them away to die,
    like sheep, lambs, and goats
    being led to the butcher.
[41]All nations now praise Babylon,[k]
    but when it is captured,
    those same nations
    will be horrified.
[42]Babylon's enemies will rise
    like ocean waves
    and flood the city.
[43]Horrible destruction will strike
    the nearby towns.
The land will become
    a barren desert,
where no one can live
    or even travel.
[44]I will punish Marduk,[l]
    the god of Babylon,
and make him vomit out
    everything he gobbled up.
Then nations will no longer
    bring him gifts,
and Babylon's walls will crumble.

The LORD Offers Hope to His People

[45]Get out of Babylon, my people,
    and run for your lives,
before I strike the city
    in my anger!
[46]Don't be afraid or lose hope,
    though year after year
    there are rumors
of leaders fighting for control
    in the city of Babylon.
[47]The time will come
    when I will punish
    Babylon's false gods.

[f]**51.33** *leveled . . . harvest time*: A threshing place with a dirt surface had to be leveled and packed down before it could be used. [g]**51.34** *Nebuchadnezzar*: See the note at 21.2. [h]**51.35** *harmed some of us*: One possible meaning for the difficult Hebrew text. [i]**51.36** *stream*: Probably the Euphrates River. [j]**51.37** *jackals*: See the note at 9.11. [k]**51.41** *Babylon*: The Hebrew text has "Sheshach," a secret way of writing the name "Babylon." [l]**51.44** *Marduk*: Hebrew "Bel" (see the note at 50.2).

Everyone there will die,
and the whole nation
will be disgraced,
[48]when an army attacks
from the north
and brings destruction.
Then the earth and the heavens
and everything in them
will celebrate.
[49]Babylon must be overthrown,
because it slaughtered
the people of Israel
and of many other nations.

[50]My people, you escaped death
when Jerusalem fell.
Now you live far from home,
but you should trust me
and think about Jerusalem.
Leave Babylon! Don't stay!

[51]You feel ashamed and disgraced,
because foreigners have entered
my sacred temple.
[52]Soon I will send a war
to punish Babylon's idols
and leave its wounded people
moaning everywhere.
[53]Although Babylon's walls
reach to the sky,
the army I send
will destroy that city.
I, the LORD, have spoken.

Babylon Will Be Destroyed

The LORD said:
[54]Listen to the cries for help
coming from Babylon.
Everywhere in the country

the sounds of destruction
can be heard.
[55]The shouts of the enemy,
like crashing ocean waves,
will drown out Babylon's cries
as I level the city.

[56]An enemy will attack
and destroy Babylon.
Its soldiers will be captured
and their weapons broken,
because I am a God
who takes revenge against nations
for what they do.
[57]I, the LORD All-Powerful,
the true King, promise
that the officials and advisors,
the governors and leaders,
and the soldiers of Babylon
will get drunk, fall asleep,
and never wake up.
[58]The thick walls of that city
will be torn down,
and its huge gates burned.
Everything that nation
worked so hard to gain
will go up in smoke.

Jeremiah Gives Seraiah a Scroll

[59]During Zedekiah's[m] fourth year as
king of Judah, he went to Babylon. And
Baruch's brother Seraiah[n] went along as
the officer in charge of arranging for places
to stay overnight.[o]
[60]Before they left, I wrote on a scroll[p] all
the terrible things that would happen to
Babylon. [61]I gave the scroll to Seraiah and
said:
   When you get to Babylon, read this

51.58 huge gates: A wide avenue known as the Processional Way led through the heart of ancient Babylon. Its entrance was the famous Ishtar Gate, made of brick and decorated with some 575 bulls and serpent-headed dragons. It was an impressive entryway into a proud city. All the effort that Nebuchadnezzar put into building projects to beautify and fortify the city would become as nothing.

   Babylon

---

[m]51.59 Zedekiah's: See the note at 1.3.   [n]51.59 Baruch's brother Seraiah: Hebrew "Seraiah son of Neriah and grandson of Mahseiah"; Baruch helped Jeremiah write down his messages (see 32.12; 36.4-10).
[o]51.59 arranging for places to stay overnight: Hebrew and one ancient translation; two ancient translations, "the tax money."   [p]51.60 scroll: See the note at 30.1,2.

51.63 *tie the scroll to a rock:* The prophecy is acted out as in 13.1-11. The message is given emphasis by the action. Compare this action also to the purchase of the field in 32.1-14. There the message is hope for Judah; here the message is doom for Babylon.

51.64 *Jeremiah's writing ends here:* This is probably an editor's comment to show that what follows in Jeremiah 52 was added to the end of the book by another editor to give further background for the events described in Jeremiah's prophecies and in the episodes from his life.

52.7-11 *Zedekiah . . . escape . . . dragged off to Babylon:* See 39.6,7. The last thing Zedekiah saw was the execution of his own sons. See 2 Kgs 25.7; Ezek 12.13.

52.17-20 *take everything . . . used for worship . . . large bowl called the Sea:* Nebuzaradan had his men take from the temple the sacred objects that Israel's priests used to offer sacrifices to the LORD. For detailed descriptions of these objects, see 1 Kings 7.15-47.

scroll aloud, **62**then pray, "Our LORD, you promised to destroy this place and make it into a desert where no people or animals will ever live."

63When you finish praying, tie the scroll to a rock and throw it in the Euphrates River. Then say, **64**"This is how Babylon will sink when the LORD destroys it. Everyone in the city will die, and it won't have the strength to rise again."

The End of Jeremiah's Writing

Jeremiah's writing ends here.

Jerusalem Is Captured
(2 Kings 24.18—25.30; 2 Chronicles 36.11-21)

52 Zedekiah was 21 years old when he was appointed king of Judah,**q** and he ruled from Jerusalem for eleven years.**r** His mother Hamutal was the daughter of Jeremiah from the town of Libnah.**s 2**Zedekiah disobeyed the LORD, just as Jehoiakim had done, **3**and it was Zedekiah who finally rebelled against Nebuchadnezzar.**t**

The people of Judah and Jerusalem had made the LORD so angry that he finally turned his back on them. That's why horrible things were happening there.

4 In Zedekiah's ninth year as king, on the tenth day of the tenth month,**u** King Nebuchadnezzar of Babylonia led his entire army to attack Jerusalem. The troops set up camp outside the city and built ramps up to the city walls.

5-6 After a year and a half,**v** all the food in

Jerusalem was gone. Then on the ninth day of the fourth month,**w 7**the Babylonian troops broke through the city wall. That same night, Zedekiah and his soldiers tried to escape through the gate near the royal garden, even though they knew the enemy had the city surrounded. They headed toward the Jordan River valley, **8**but the Babylonian troops caught up with them near Jericho. The Babylonians arrested Zedekiah, but his soldiers scattered in every direction. **9**Zedekiah was taken to Riblah in the land of Hamath, where Nebuchadnezzar put him on trial and found him guilty. **10**Zedekiah's sons and the officials of Judah were killed while he watched, **11**then his eyes were poked out. He was put in chains, then dragged off to Babylon and kept in prison until he died.

12Jerusalem was captured during Nebuchadnezzar's nineteenth year as king of Babylonia.

About a month later,**x** Nebuchadnezzar's officer in charge of the guards arrived in Jerusalem. His name was Nebuzaradan, **13**and he burned down the LORD's temple, the king's palace, and every important building in the city, as well as all the houses. **14**Then he ordered the Babylonian soldiers to break down the walls around Jerusalem. **15**He led away the people left in the city, including everyone who had become loyal to Nebuchadnezzar, the rest of the skilled workers,**y** and even some of the poor people of Judah. **16**Only the very poorest were left behind to work the vineyards and the fields.

17-20 Nebuzaradan ordered his soldiers to

q52.1 *appointed king of Judah:* By Nebuchadnezzar (see 37.1). **r52.1** *he ruled . . . years:* Ruled 598–586 B.C. **s52.1** *Jeremiah from the town of Libnah:* Not the same Jeremiah as the author of this book (see 1.1). **t52.3** *Nebuchadnezzar:* See the note at 21.2. **u52.4** *tenth month:* See the note at 39.1-3. **v52.5,6** *After a year and a half:* Jerusalem was captured in 586 B.C. **w52.5,6** *fourth month:* See the note at 39.1-3. **x52.12** *About a month later:* Hebrew "On the seventh day of the fifth month." **y52.15** *the rest of the skilled workers:* Nebuchadnezzar had taken away some of the skilled workers eleven years before (see 2 Kings 24.14-16).

go to the temple and take everything made of gold or silver, including bowls, fire pans, sprinkling bowls, pans, lampstands, dishes for incense, and the cups for wine offerings. The Babylonian soldiers took all the bronze things used for worship at the temple, including the pans for hot ashes, and the shovels, lamp snuffers, sprinkling bowls, and dishes for incense. The soldiers also took everything else made of bronze, including the two columns that stood in front of the temple, the large bowl called the Sea, the twelve bulls that held it up, and the movable stands.[z] The soldiers broke these things into pieces so they could take them to Babylonia. There was so much bronze that it could not be weighed. [21]For example, the columns were 27 feet high and 18 feet around. They were hollow, but the bronze was about three inches thick. [22]Each column had a bronze cap over seven feet high that was decorated with bronze designs. Some of these designs were like chains and others were like pomegranates.[a] [23]There were 96 pomegranates evenly spaced[b] around each column, and a total of 100 pomegranates were located above the chains.

[24]Next, Nebuzaradan arrested Seraiah the chief priest, Zephaniah his assistant, and three temple officials. [25]Then he arrested one of the army commanders, seven of King Zedekiah's personal advisors, and the officer in charge of gathering the troops for battle. He also found 60 more soldiers who were still in Jerusalem. [26-27]Nebu-

zaradan led them to Riblah in the land of Hamath, where Nebuchadnezzar had them killed.

The people of Judah no longer lived in their own country.

People of Judah Taken Prisoner

[28-30]Here is a list of the number of the people of Judah that Nebuchadnezzar[c] took to Babylonia as prisoners:
In his seventh year as king, he took 3,023 people.
In his eighteenth year as king, he took 832 from Jerusalem.
In his twenty-third year as king, his officer Nebuzaradan took 745 people.
So, Nebuchadnezzar took a total of 4,600 people from Judah to Babylonia.

Jehoiachin Is Set Free
(2 Kings 25.27-30)

[31]Jehoiachin was a prisoner in Babylon for 37 years. Then Evil Merodach[d] became king of Babylonia, and in the first year of his rule, on the twenty-fifth day of the twelfth month,[e] he let Jehoiachin out of prison. [32]Evil Merodach was kind to Jehoiachin and honored him more than any of the other kings held prisoner there. [33]Jehoiachin was allowed to wear regular clothes instead of a prison uniform, and he even ate at the king's table every day. [34]As long as Jehoiachin lived, he was paid a daily allowance to buy whatever he needed.

● 52.24 *Seraiah . . . Zephaniah:* This Seraiah may be the same as the one mentioned in 36.26 but not the one in 52.59. Seraiah was the grandfather of Joshua, the high priest when the temple was rebuilt after the exile. See 21.1; 29.29; 37.3-5 (Zephaniah).

● 52.25-27 *soldiers . . . Riblah . . . killed:* The 74 arrested men are taken to the Babylonian camp at Riblah and killed as a representative punishment and warning to the rest who survived.

● 52.28-30 *list of the number:* Nebuchadnezzar's seventh year was 598 B.C., when Jehoiachin was king of Judah (compare the number in 2 Kgs 24.14). His eighteenth year (compare 52.12) was 586 B.C., when Zedekiah reigned and Jerusalem was destroyed. The twenty-third year would have been 582 B.C., which probably refers to the time of troubles following the assassination of Gedaliah (41.1-3). These numbers for exiled Jews are not found in 2 Kings; perhaps they come from a Babylonian record. What happened to the rest of the people? The poorest were left behind (52.16); others chose to relocate to Egypt and nearby lands.

● 52.31-34 *Jehoiachin . . . Evil Merodach:* Jehoiachin was sent into exile after the first rebellion in 598 B.C. After Nebuchadnezzar died in 562, his son Evil Merodach succeeded him. After 37 years of imprisonment, Jehoiachin was set free by Evil Merodach who treated him as a royal guest. Jehoiachin's freedom was a hopeful sign of the coming restoration of Judah.

---

[z]52.17-20 *the large bowl called the Sea, the twelve bulls that held it up, and the movable stands:* One ancient translation; Hebrew "the large bowl called the Sea, and the twelve bulls under the movable stands." [a]52.22 *pomegranates:* A small red fruit that looks like an apple.   [b]52.23 *evenly spaced:* One possible meaning for the difficult Hebrew text.   [c]52.28-30 *Nebuchadnezzar:* See the note at 21.2.   [d]52.31 *Evil Merodach:* The son of Nebuchadnezzar who ruled Babylonia from 562–560 B.C.   [e]52.31 *twelfth month:* Adar, the twelfth month of the Hebrew calendar, from about mid-February to mid-March.

Reflection Questions About Jeremiah 1.1—52.34

1. How does Jeremiah try to excuse himself from being the prophet that the LORD wants him to be? How does God respond to Jeremiah (1.4-8)?

2. What is the twofold message that Jeremiah is told to preach (1.10,15,16)? How will the people respond to Jeremiah's message (1.17,19)?

3. The vision of the LORD's day of judgment in 4.23-26 is a powerful one. What in this description gets your attention the most? Why?

4. In his "Confessions," Jeremiah shows that prayer means talking to God (1.18-23; 12.1-6). This can include complaining to God and questioning God's ways. Does Jeremiah help you think differently about prayer? If so, in what ways? When have you had similar questions?

5. Review Jeremiah's personal laments in 15.15-18 and 17.12-18. Note his honesty. Where do you see signs of his struggle with the LORD? Where do you see signs of his sadness?

6. What was it about Jeremiah's message in the temple (chapter 26) that put him in such danger? What was it that made the angry crowds change their mind about arresting and killing him?

7. Read the promise made to the Jewish people living in exile (Jer 29.10-14). What is important about this message, especially regarding worshiping the LORD? What made this message "good" news for the exiles? Why do you think some considered it bad news?

8. Chapters 30–33 are full of remarkable and wonderful promises made to the people by God. What words of comfort do you think the exiled people would most cherish? What promises do you find most significant? Most comforting? Why?

9. Review what the LORD says about the Egyptians, Philistines, and Moabites in chapters 46–48. Why do you think these foreign nations are included in Jeremiah's prophecy? What images do you find particularly powerful? What hope is given in a number of these prophecies?

10. Choose two or three images from the book of JEREMIAH that especially help you remember and understand the book's message. Explain your choices.

lamentations

Grief and sadness are part of life, sometimes forcing us to find meaning in tragedy. Read LAMENTATIONS to see how eyewitnesses responded to the destruction of God's city, Jerusalem, and its temple.

WHAT MAKES LAMENTATIONS SPECIAL?

LAMENTATIONS is a collection of five separate poems, printed here as chapters. The five poems are presented as eyewitness accounts to one of the greatest tragedies in Jewish history. God's special city (Jerusalem) and God's special place (the temple) were robbed and destroyed by Israel's enemies. The poems are written to lament this destruction, but also to show how the tragedy reveals God's purpose. God punished the people for their sins but did not abandon them completely.

In synagogues today, LAMENTATIONS is read aloud on the ninth day of Ab (late July), a day of fasting that commemorates the destruction of the Jerusalem temple in 586 B.C., and of the second temple in A.D. 70. Many Christian churches include readings from LAMENTATIONS in their worship services during Holy Week, the week before Easter.

WHAT'S THE STORY BEHIND THE SCENE?

Following an unsuccessful rebellion in 597 B.C., the small southern kingdom of Judah fell to the powerful forces of Babylonia in 586 B.C. The capture and destruction, described in 2 Kings 25, was swift, terrible, and total. King Zedekiah, who ruled Judah from 598 to 586 B.C., was taken prisoner and exiled to Babylon along with many of Jerusalem and Judah's leading citizens, priests, and craftsmen. Only the poor and the peasants were left behind.

The poems—whether composed by the people of Judah who had been taken into captivity by the Bab-

ylonians or by those who were left behind—were no doubt written by eyewitnesses to this terrible tragedy. Though the authors are unknown, the expression of the people's grief and agony is timeless, as is the hope for a restoration and renewal based on God's mercy.

HOW IS LAMENTATIONS CONSTRUCTED?

The careful structure of these five poems shows an expression of grief that is measured and conscious, and the book is well-suited to public worship services where it would be read aloud. Chapters 1, 2, and 4 are public expressions of grief over the loss of Jerusalem. Chapter 3 is a personal lament, which ends in a prayer of thanksgiving and trust. Chapter 5 is a public prayer for mercy.

The poems in chapters 1 through 4 are called "alphabetic acrostics," meaning that each stanza (verse) begins with a letter of the Hebrew alphabet and follows the order of the alphabet. Chapters 1, 2, and 4 have 22 stanzas, one for each of the 22 letters of the alphabet. Chapter 3 has 66 stanzas, 3 for each letter. Chapter 5 also has 22 stanzas, but is not an acrostic.

First lament: Lonely Jerusalem (1.1-22)
Second lament: The LORD was like an enemy (2.1-22)
Third lament: There is still hope (3.1-66)
Fourth lament: The punishment of Jerusalem (4.1-22)
Fifth lament: A prayer for mercy (5.1-22)

amentations contains five deeply moving poems (called laments) about the destruction of Jerusalem and its temple in 586 B.C. The poems do not tell the story of the destruction. Instead, they offer glimpses of the horrible conditions in the ruined city, ponder the reasons for its destruction, and beg for God's mercy. The speakers of these laments are: an unnamed prophet, the city of Jerusalem (depicted as a ruined widow), and the collective people of Jerusalem. In the third poem, the writer discovers hope in the depth of his sorrow, recognizes that the Lord has mercy and love, and expresses heartfelt belief that the pain of the Lord's punishment will end. The fourth poem, however, returns to a depiction of horror, loss, humiliation, and exhaustion. The final poem is a prayer for mercy, spoken by the people of Jerusalem, who beg the Lord to see their suffering and give them a fresh start.

Outline

Lonely Jerusalem

The Prophet Speaks:

1 Jerusalem, once so crowded,
    lies deserted and lonely.
This city that was known
    all over the world
is now like a widow.
This queen of the nations
    has been made a slave.
2 Each night, bitter tears
    flood her cheeks.
None of her former lovers
    are there to offer comfort;
her friends[a] have betrayed her
    and are now her enemies.

3 The people of Judah are slaves,
    suffering in a foreign land,
    with no rest from sorrow.
Their enemies captured them
    and were terribly cruel.[b]
4 The roads to Zion mourn
because no one travels there
    to celebrate the festivals.
The city gates are deserted;
    priests are weeping.
Young women are raped;[c]
    Zion is in sorrow!
5 Enemies now rule the city
    and live as they please.
The LORD has punished Jerusalem
    because of her awful sins;
he has let her people
    be dragged away.

6 Zion's glory has disappeared.
Her leaders are like deer
    that cannot find pasture;
they are hunted down
    till their strength is gone.
7 Her people recall the good life
    that once was theirs;
now they suffer
    and are scattered.
No one was there to protect them

---

[a]1.2 *lovers . . . friends*: Israel's former allies.   [b]1.3 *Their . . . cruel*: One possible meaning for the difficult Hebrew text.   [c]1.4 *raped*: One possible meaning for the difficult Hebrew text.

1.1 *Jerusalem*: Jerusalem was the capital of the united Israelite kingdom under Kings David and Solomon (from around 1010 to 931 B.C.). It became the capital of the southern kingdom (Judah) when the kingdom divided after the death of Solomon.

Jerusalem

1.2 *lovers . . . friends*: The poet speaks of Judah's former allies as "lovers" and "friends" who were not trustworthy; Judah relied on other nations, in particular Egypt, for support in its rebellion against Babylonia, rather than relying on the LORD. **(See Map 7 on pg 1885.)**

1.3 *Their enemies*: The Babylonian army.

1.4 *Zion*: The hill where the temple stood; also used as a name for the city of Jerusalem.

Zion

1.7 *now they suffer and are scattered*: Many Judeans fled to the neighboring nations of Edom, Moab, and Ammon for safety in the turbulent years between the "first exile" of 597 B.C. and the "last exile" of 586 B.C. Large numbers of people from Judah also settled in Egypt during this period. Edom and Moab did not come to Judah's aid; instead, these nations assisted Babylonia in the destruction of Judah.

The LORD has punished Jerusalem because of her awful sins; he has let her people be dragged away. LAM 1.5

Purity (Clean and Unclean)

■ 1.13 *you sent a fire . . . you set a trap*: The author of this lament states that the destruction is God's doing. Jerusalem is painfully learning what the prophets Jeremiah and Ezekiel had been trying to tell her: Sin has consequences, and it is God who does the punishing.

● 1.14 *enemies too strong for me*: The Babylonian forces invaded Judah and leveled the towns surrounding Jerusalem in 587 B.C., then proceeded to lay siege to Jerusalem with a blockade that lasted a year and a half. In 586 B.C., the walls of Jerusalem fell. The temple was robbed and its treasure sent back to Babylon (2 Kgs 25.9-17; Jer 52.17-23). King Zedekiah was blinded after seeing his sons put to death.

Nebuchadnezzar

Exile

Enemies (The Wicked)

■ 1.15 *like grapes in a wine pit*: Other prophets were also drawn to this vivid image of God's punishment.

Wine

● 1.17 *Jacob's descendants*: Jacob was the grandson of Abraham and father to twelve sons who are named as the ancestors of the twelve tribes of Israel.

Israel

from their enemies who sneered
    when their city was taken.

⁸Jerusalem's horrible sins
    have made the city a joke.
Those who once admired her
    now hate her instead—
she has been disgraced;
    she groans and turns away.

⁹Her sins had made her filthy,
but she wasn't worried
    about what could happen.
And when Jerusalem fell,
    it was so tragic.
No one gave her comfort
    when she cried out,
"Help! I'm in trouble, LORD!
    The enemy has won."

¹⁰Zion's treasures were stolen.
Jerusalem saw foreigners
    enter her place of worship,
though the LORD
had forbidden them
    to belong to his people.ᵈ
¹¹Everyone in the city groans
    while searching for food;
they trade their valuables
for barely enough scraps
    to stay alive.

Jerusalem Speaks:
Jerusalem shouts to the LORD,
"Please look and see
    how miserable I am!"
¹²No passerby even cares.ᵉ
Why doesn't someone notice
    my terrible sufferings?

You were fiercely angry, LORD,
and you punished me
    worst of all.
¹³From heaven you sent a fire
    that burned in my bones;
you set a trap for my feet
    and made me turn back.
All day long you leave me
    in shock from constant pain.
¹⁴You have tied my sins
    around my neck,ᶠ
and they weigh so heavily
    that my strength is gone.
You have put me in the power
    of enemies too strong for me.

¹⁵You, LORD, have turned back
my warriors and crushed
    my young heroes.
Judah was a woman untouched,
but you let her be trampled
    like grapes in a wine pit.
¹⁶Because of this, I mourn,
    and tears flood my eyes.
No one is here to comfort
    or to encourage me;
we have lost the war—
    my people are suffering.

The Prophet Speaks:
¹⁷Zion reaches out her hands,
    but no one offers comfort.
The LORD has turned
the neighboring nations
    against Jacob's descendants.
Jerusalem is merely a filthy rag
    to her neighbors.

ᵈ**1.10** *to . . . people*: Or "to enter his temple."   ᵉ**1.12** *No . . . cares*: One possible meaning for the difficult Hebrew text.   ᶠ**1.14** *You . . . neck*: One possible meaning for the difficult Hebrew text.

Jerusalem Speaks:

¹⁸The Lord was right,
  but I refused to obey him.
Now I ask all of you to look
  at my sufferings—
even my young people
  have been dragged away.
¹⁹I called out to my lovers,
  but they betrayed me.
My priests and my leaders died
while searching the city
  for scraps of food.

²⁰Won't you look and see
  how upset I am, our Lord?
My stomach is in knots,
  and my heart is broken
  because I betrayed you.
In the streets and at home,
  my people are slaughtered.

²¹Everyone heard my groaning,
  but no one offered comfort.
My enemies know of the trouble
that you have brought on me,
  and it makes them glad.
Hurry and punish them,
  as you have promised.
²²Don't let their evil deeds
  escape your sight.
Punish them as much
as you have punished me
  because of my sins.
I never stop groaning—
  I've lost all hope!

The Lord Was Like an Enemy

The Prophet Speaks:

2 The Lord was angry!
  So he disgraced^g Zion
  though it was Israel's pride
  and his own place of rest.
In his anger he threw Zion down
  from heaven to earth.
²The Lord had no mercy!
He destroyed the homes
  of Jacob's descendants.
In his anger he tore down
  every walled city in Judah;
he toppled the nation
together with its leaders,
  leaving them in shame.

³The Lord was so furiously angry
  that he wiped out
    the whole army^h of Israel
by not supporting them
  when the enemy attacked.
He was like a raging fire
that swallowed up
  the descendants of Jacob.
⁴He attacked like an enemy
with a bow and arrows,
  killing our loved ones.
He has burned to the ground
  the homes on Mount Zion.ⁱ

⁵The Lord was like an enemy!
  He left Israel in ruins
with its palaces
  and fortresses destroyed,
and with everyone in Judah
  moaning and weeping.
⁶He shattered his temple

^g**2.1** *disgraced:* One possible meaning for the difficult Hebrew text. ^h**2.3** *army:* The Hebrew text has "horn," which refers to the horn of a bull, one of the most powerful animals in ancient Palestine. ⁱ**2.4** *the homes on Mount Zion:* Or "the temple on Mount Zion."

1.20 *my heart is broken:* The author of this lament continues to speak of Jerusalem as if it were a woman. After listing the terrible hardships she has experienced, Jerusalem is able to confess her guilt to God. This is the first step toward turning back to the Lord.

2.1 *The Lord was angry:* God's anger at the people was justified. God's people are finally realizing that what happened to them was not an accident, but an expression of God's righteous character.

2.1 *threw Zion down from heaven to earth:* An image applied to enemy rulers in Isaiah 14.12 and Ezekiel 28.17. Here it is used to describe God's anger toward the people.

2.2 *every walled city in Judah:* In the ancient Near East almost all cities were enclosed by a wall for protection.

2.3 *wiped out the whole army of Israel:* This refers to the Assyrian victory over the northern kingdom, also called Israel, resulting in its fall in 722 B.C.

2.6 *temple . . . festivals and Sabbaths:* The temple, God's own "place of rest," is destroyed as if it were a temporary shelter set up at harvest time. Everything that God is destroying here was originally given to the people of Israel as something holy and good. Because of the people's sins God is now punishing them and taking these good things away from them, including the monarchy and priesthood.

2.7 *Noisy shouts:* The roar of battle replaces the happy shouts of giving thanks to God.

2.9 *king . . . priests . . . prophets:* The leadership of God's people. The Babylonians took King Zedekiah into exile in Babylon in 586 B.C. The main function of priests was to offer sacrifices for the people, but they were also responsible for teaching the people the Law. Like the priests described here, the prophets also have failed to look after the needs of God's people.

Israel's Priests

2.13 *wounds, gaping as wide as the sea:* No one can comfort Zion; her pain is too enormous.

2.14 *Your prophets deceived you:* Jeremiah and Ezekiel were obedient prophets who spoke for the LORD, but there were many other prophets in Judah in the sixth century B.C. who did not. These false prophets told the kings and people what they wanted to hear, giving them false hopes. (See the article Prophets and Prophecy on pg 1791.)

like a hut in a garden;[j]
he completely wiped out
    his meeting place,
and did away with festivals
and Sabbaths
    in the city of Zion.
In his fierce anger he rejected
    our king and priests.

7 The Lord abandoned his altar
    and his temple;
he let Zion's enemies
    capture her fortresses.
Noisy shouts were heard
    from the temple,
as if it were a time
    of celebration.

8 The LORD had decided
to tear down the walls of Zion
    stone by stone.
So he started destroying
    and did not stop
until walls and fortresses
    mourned and trembled.
9 Zion's gates have fallen
    facedown on the ground;
the bars that locked the gates
    are smashed to pieces.
Her king and royal family
are prisoners
    in foreign lands.
Her priests don't teach,
and her prophets don't have
    a message from the LORD.

10 Zion's leaders are silent.
    They just sit on the ground,
tossing dirt on their heads
    and wearing sackcloth.
Her young women can do nothing
    but stare at the ground.

11 My eyes are red from crying,
my stomach is in knots,
    and I feel sick all over.
My people are being wiped out,
    and children lie helpless
    in the streets of the city.
12 A child begs its mother
    for food and drink,
then blacks out
like a wounded soldier
    lying in the street.
The child slowly dies
    in its mother's arms.

13 Zion, how can I comfort you?
    How great is your pain?[k]
Lovely city of Jerusalem,
    how can I heal your wounds,
    gaping as wide as the sea?
14 Your prophets deceived you
    with false visions
    and lying messages—
they should have warned you
to leave your sins
    and be saved from disaster.
15 Those who pass by
    shake their heads and sneer
    as they make fun and shout,
"What a lovely city you were,
    the happiest on earth,
    but look at you now!"

16 Zion, your enemies curse you
    and snarl like wild animals,
    while shouting,
"This is the day
    we've waited for!
    At last, we've got you!"

17 The LORD has done everything
that he had planned
    and threatened long ago.

---

[j] 2.6 *He . . . garden:* Or "He shattered the temple walls, as if they were the walls of a garden."
[k] 2.13 *How great . . . pain:* Or "What are you really like?" or "What can I say about you?"

He destroyed you without mercy
and let your enemies boast about
   their powerful forces.[l]

[18]Zion, deep in your heart
   you cried out to the Lord.
Now let your tears overflow
   your walls day and night.
Don't ever lose hope
   or let your tears stop.
[19]Get up and pray for help
   all through the night.
Pour out your feelings
   to the Lord,
as you would pour water
   out of a jug.
Beg him to save your people,
who are starving to death
   at every street crossing.

Jerusalem Speaks:
[20]Think about it, LORD!
Have you ever been this cruel
   to anyone before?
Is it right for mothers
   to eat their children,
or for priests and prophets
   to be killed in your temple?
[21]My people, both young and old,
   lie dead in the streets.
Because you were angry,
my young men and women
   were brutally slaughtered.
[22]When you were angry, LORD,
you invited my enemies
   like guests for a party.
No one survived that day;
enemies killed my children,
   my own little ones.

There Is Still Hope

The Prophet Speaks:

3 I have suffered much
      because God was angry.
[2]He chased me into a dark place,
   where no light could enter.
[3]I am the only one he punishes
   over and over again,
      without ever stopping.
[4]God caused my skin and flesh
   to waste away,
      and he crushed my bones.
[5]He attacked and surrounded me
   with hardships and trouble;
[6]he forced me to sit in the dark
   like someone long dead.

[7]God built a fence around me
   that I cannot climb over,
      and he chained me down.
[8]Even when I shouted
   and prayed for help,
      he refused to listen.
[9]God put big rocks in my way
   and made me follow
      a crooked path.
[10]God was like a bear or a lion
   waiting in ambush for me;
[11]he dragged me from the road,
   then tore me to shreds.[m]
[12]God took careful aim
   and shot his arrows
[13]   straight through my heart.

[14]I am a joke to everyone—
   no one ever stops
      making fun of me.
[15]God has turned my life sour.
[16]He made me eat gravel
   and rubbed me in the dirt.

2.20 *Is it right . . . children:* The disaster of 586 B.C. caused starvation, a punishment predicted in Leviticus 26.29 and Ezekiel 5.10.

2.22 *that day:* For many of the prophets in the Bible, "that day" or "the day of the LORD" means a future time when God will punish the enemies of the LORD and save the people who have been faithful (Isa 24.21-23).

Day of the LORD

3.1 *I have suffered much:* The deep personal sense of anguish in this poem has much in common with psalms of lamentation, such as Ps 6; 56; 140.

3.10 *like a bear or a lion:* The LORD is compared to a predatory animal, who waits patiently for the prey and then attacks fiercely.

3.14 *I am a joke to everyone:* Being mocked by neighbors or enemies is another kind of pain frequently addressed in the Bible.

Enemies (The Wicked)

---

[l]**2.17** *powerful forces:* The Hebrew text has "horn," which refers to the horn of a bull, one of the most powerful animals in ancient Palestine.   [m]**3.11** *shreds:* One possible meaning for the difficult Hebrew text of verse 11.

Pour out your feelings to the Lord, as you would pour water out of a jug. LAM 2.19

3.21 *Then I remember:* It is not until after the prophet has finished describing his suffering that he is able to say what it is that fills the heart with hope. The shift from anguish to hope is based on the prophet's trust and faith in God. Once he acknowledges this for himself, the prophet can then proclaim it to other suffering people.

3.24 *The Lord is all I need:* The prophet ends his personal lament confident that God has heard him and can be trusted. The prophet's words apply as well to all the people of Judah who have experienced loss. Though they too will raise their voices in sad cries of lamentation, the people will also find hope. God will act to save as surely as God has acted to punish.

3.29,30 *Being rubbed in the dirt . . . hard knocks:* The Hebrew can be read "mouth in the dust." To accept the reality of the situation is the important first step. Like a loving parent, God punishes the people to teach them valuable lessons, not merely to inflict pain.

3.40 *we should think:* Honest self-examination is the first step in turning back to the Lord (repentance).

Prayer

¹⁷I cannot find peace
   or remember happiness.
¹⁸I tell myself, "I am finished!
   I can't count on the Lord
   to do anything for me."
¹⁹Just thinking of my troubles
   and my lonely wandering
   makes me miserable.
²⁰That's all I ever think about,
   and I am depressed.[n]
²¹Then I remember something
   that fills me with hope.
²²The Lord's kindness never fails!
   If he had not been merciful,
   we would have been destroyed.[o]
²³The Lord can always be trusted
   to show mercy each morning.
²⁴Deep in my heart I say,
   "The Lord is all I need;
   I can depend on him!"

²⁵The Lord is kind to everyone
   who trusts and obeys him.
²⁶It is good to wait patiently
   for the Lord to save us.
²⁷When we are young,
   it is good to struggle hard
²⁸and to sit silently alone,
   if this is what
   the Lord intends.
²⁹Being rubbed in the dirt
   can teach us a lesson;[P]
³⁰we can also learn from insults
   and hard knocks.

³¹The Lord won't always reject us!
³²   He causes a lot of suffering,
   but he also has pity
   because of his great love.
³³The Lord doesn't enjoy
   sending grief or pain.

³⁴Don't trample prisoners
   under your feet
³⁵or cheat anyone out of
   what is rightfully theirs.
   God Most High sees everything,
³⁶and he knows when you refuse
   to give someone a fair trial.
³⁷No one can do anything
   without the Lord's approval.
³⁸Good and bad each happen
   at the command
   of God Most High.
³⁹We're still alive!
   We shouldn't complain
   when we are being punished
   for our sins.
⁴⁰Instead, we should think
   about the way we are living,
   and turn back to the Lord.

⁴¹When we lift our hands
   in prayer to God in heaven,
   we should offer him our hearts
   and say, ⁴²"We've sinned!
   We've rebelled against you,
   and you haven't forgiven us!
⁴³Anger is written all over you,
   as you pursue and slaughter us
   without showing pity.
⁴⁴You are behind a wall of clouds
   that blocks out our prayers.
⁴⁵You allowed nations
   to treat us like garbage;
⁴⁶   our enemies curse us.
⁴⁷We are terrified and trapped,
   caught and crushed."

⁴⁸My people are destroyed!
   Tears flood my eyes,
⁴⁹   and they won't stop
⁵⁰until the Lord looks down

[n]3.20 *I am depressed:* One possible meaning for the difficult Hebrew text.   [o]3.22 *destroyed:* One possible meaning for the difficult Hebrew text of verse 22.   [P]3.29 *lesson:* One possible meaning for the difficult Hebrew text of verse 29.

The Lord's kindness never fails! If he had not been merciful, we would have been destroyed. The Lord can always be trusted to show mercy each morning. Lam 3.22,23

from heaven and helps.
[51] I am horrified when I see
      what enemies have done
      to the young women of our city.

[52] No one had reason to hate me,
      but I was hunted down
      like a bird.
[53] Then they tried to kill me
      by tossing me into a pit
      and throwing stones at me.
[54] Water covered my head—
      I thought I was gone.

[55] From the bottom of the pit,
      I prayed to you, LORD.
[56] I begged you to listen.
      "Help!" I shouted. "Save me!"
      You answered my prayer
[57] and came when I was in need.
      You told me, "Don't worry!"
[58] You rescued me
      and saved my life.
[59] You saw them abuse me, LORD,
      so make things right.
[60] You know every plot
      they have made against me.
[61] Yes, you know their insults
      and their evil plans.
[62] All day long they attack
      with words and whispers.
[63] No matter what they are doing,
      they keep on mocking me.

[64] Pay them back for everything
      they have done, LORD!
[65] Put your curse on them
      and make them suffer.[q]
[66] Get angry and go after them
      until not a trace is left
      under the heavens.

The Punishment of Jerusalem

The Prophet Speaks:

4 The purest gold is ruined
      and has lost its shine;
   jewels from the temple
      lie scattered in the streets.
[2] These are Zion's people,
      worth more than purest gold;
   yet they are counted worthless
      like dishes of clay.

[3] Even jackals[r] nurse their young,
      but my people are like ostriches
      that abandon their own.
[4] Babies are so thirsty
      that their tongues are stuck
      to the roof of the mouth.
   Children go begging for food,
      but no one gives them any.
[5] All who ate expensive foods
      lie starving in the streets;
   those who grew up in luxury
      now sit on trash heaps.

[6] My nation was punished worse
      than the people of Sodom,
   whose city was destroyed
      in a flash without the help
      of human hands.[s]
[7] The leaders of Jerusalem
      were purer than snow
      and whiter than milk;
   their bodies were healthy
      and glowed like jewels.[t]
[8] Now they are blacker than tar,
      and no one recognizes them;
   their skin clings to their bones
      and is drier than firewood.
[9] Being killed with a sword
      is better than slowly

[q]3.65 *make them suffer:* One possible meaning for the difficult Hebrew text.   [r]4.3 *jackals:* Desert animals related to wolves, but smaller.   [s]4.6 *hands:* One possible meaning for the difficult Hebrew text of verse 6.   [t]4.7 *jewels:* One possible meaning for the difficult Hebrew text of verse 7.

3.53 *pit:* This was a cistern or deep well for holding fresh water. In Judah, rainfall was scarce, and the people dug deep pits for holding water and preventing it from evaporating too quickly in the hot sun.

Water

4.1,2 *purest gold . . . Zion's people:* The temple treasures have been thrown into the streets by the enemy. God's people living in Zion (Jerusalem) are thrown out of their homes.

4.3 *jackals . . . ostriches:* Jackals are desert animals related to wolves. They were seen as pests because they ate crops and killed livestock. Ostriches are large birds that run swiftly but cannot fly. They were thought to be foolish and neglectful of their young.

4.5 *starving in the streets:* A horrible famine occurred in Jerusalem as a result of the long siege by the Babylonians in 587–586 B.C. The prophet's other references to eating human flesh are further evidence of the horror of the famine.

4.6 *Sodom:* This ancient city was destroyed along with its sister city Gomorrah because of the sin of its inhabitants (Gen 19.24,25).

4.11,12 *burned the city of Zion . . . Not a king on this earth:* In the eighth century B.C. the prophet Micah first delivered the message of doom to Jerusalem (Mic 3.12). God promised David, "I will make sure that one of your descendants will always be king" (2 Sam 7.16). Thus to promise disaster on Jerusalem, David's city, was blasphemy. Jeremiah echoed this prophecy and was beaten and arrested for it (Jer 19.15). The poem repeats an idea popular in Judah—that no earthly power could overcome the great capital.

⊗   Blood

⊗   Purity (Clean and Unclean)

4.17 *a nation that could not save us:* Egypt had been an ally of Judah against their common enemy, the Babylonians.

starving to death.
¹⁰Life in the city is so bad
    that loving mothers have boiled
    and eaten their own children.

¹¹The Lord was so fiercely angry
    that he burned the city of Zion
    to the ground.
¹²Not a king on this earth
    or the people of any nation
    believed enemies could break
    through her gates.

¹³Jerusalem was punished because
    her prophets and her priests
    had sinned and caused the death
    of innocent victims.
¹⁴Yes, her prophets and priests
    were covered with blood;
no one would come near them,
    as they wandered
    from street to street.
¹⁵Instead, everyone shouted,
    "Go away! Don't touch us!
You're filthy and unfit
    to belong to God's people!"

So they had to leave
    and become refugees.
But foreign nations told them,
    "You can't stay here!"ᵁ
¹⁶The Lord is the one
    who sent them scattering,
    and he has forgotten them.
No respect or kindness
    will be shown
    to the priests or leaders.
¹⁷Our eyes became weary,
    hopelessly looking
for help from a nationⱽ

that could not save us.
¹⁸Enemies hunted us down
    on every public street.
Our time was up;
    our doom was near.
¹⁹They swooped down faster
    than eagles from the sky.
They hunted for us in the hills
    and set traps to catch us
    out in the desert.
²⁰The Lord's chosen leaderᵂ
    was our hope for survival!
We thought he would keep us safe
    somewhere among the nations,
but even he was caught
    in one of their traps.

²¹You people of Edom
    can celebrate now!
But your time will come
    to suffer and stagger
    around naked.
²²The people of Zion
    have paid for their sins,
and the Lord will soon
    let them return home.
But, people of Edom,
    you will be punished,
    and your sins exposed.

A Prayer for Mercy

*The People of Jerusalem Pray:*ˣ
5 Our Lord, don't forget
    how we have suffered
    and been disgraced.
²Foreigners and strangers
    have taken our land
    and our homes.
³We are like children

ᵁ**4.15** *here:* One possible meaning for the difficult Hebrew text of verse 15. ⱽ**4.17** *nation:* Egypt, a former ally of Judah. ᵂ**4.20** *chosen leader:* Probably Zedekiah, the last king of Judah, taken away to Babylonia in 586 B.C. ˣ**5.1** *The People of Jerusalem Pray:* Or "The Prophet Prays."

whose mothers are widows.
⁴The water we drink
  and the wood we burn
    cost far too much.
⁵We are terribly mistreated;ʸ
  we are worn out
    and can find no rest.
⁶We had to surrender
  toᶻ Egypt and Assyria
    because we were hungry.

⁷Our ancestors sinned,
  but they are dead,
and we are left to pay
    for their sins.
⁸Slaves are now our rulers,
  and there is no one
    to set us free.
⁹We are in danger
  from brutal desert tribes;
we must risk our lives
    just to bring in our crops.ᵃ
¹⁰Our skin is scorched
    from fever and hunger.

¹¹On Zion and everywhere in Judah
  our wives and daughters
    are being raped.
¹²Our rulers are strung up
  by their arms,

and our nation's advisors
    are treated shamefully.
¹³Young men are forced
  to do the work of slaves;
boys must carry
    heavy loads of wood.
¹⁴Our leaders are not allowed
  to decide cases in court,
and young people
    no longer play music.

¹⁵Our hearts are sad;
  instead of dancing,
    we mourn.
¹⁶Zion's glory has disappeared!
  And we are doomed
    because of our sins.
¹⁷We feel sick all over
  and can't even see straight;
¹⁸our city is in ruins,
    overrun by wild dogs.

¹⁹You will rule forever, Lord!
  You are King for all time.
²⁰Why have you forgotten us
  for so long?
²¹Bring us back to you!
  Give us a fresh start.
²²Or do you despise us so much
  that you don't want us?

⌘   Egypt

⌘   Assyria

◼ **5.7** *ancestors sinned . . . we are left to pay:* It was a common understanding in the ancient world that God not only punished people for the sins they committed, but he also punished the descendants of these sinners. The prophet Ezekiel announced that God would not punish children for the sins of their parents (Ezek 18.19,20).

⌘   Sin

● **5.8** *Slaves are now our rulers:* Important jobs were sometimes given to high-ranking slaves of foreign kings. The Israelites, the ancestors of the people of Judah, were once slaves in Egypt, but now they were being ruled by slaves. This situation is devastating to the people of Judah who were left behind after 586 B.C.

◼ **5.21,22** *a fresh start . . . you don't want us:* The fifth lament ends on a note of hope mixed with doubts about the future.

ʸ**5.5** *We . . . mistreated:* One possible meaning for the difficult Hebrew text.   ᶻ**5.6** *surrender to:* Or "make treaties with."   ᵃ**5.9** *crops:* One possible meaning for the difficult Hebrew text of verse 9.

Young men are forced to do the work of slaves; boys must carry heavy loads of wood. Our leaders are not allowed to decide cases in court, and young people no longer play music. Lam 5.13,14

Reflection Questions About Lamentations 1.1—5.22

1. The poems in LAMENTATIONS were written not simply to lament the destruction of Jerusalem, but to interpret its meaning for God's people. What did the people of Judah learn about themselves and God from this tragic event (1.5; 3.39,40; 4.13)?

2. The poems in LAMENTATIONS contain three speakers, the city of Jerusalem itself, the collective people of Jerusalem, and a writer (called "the prophet" in the CEV translation). What purpose does this serve?

3. Re-read 3.21-24. Which statements in this short passage give you hope? What is the relationship between hope and depending on the LORD?

4. What seem to be some of the key characteristics and themes of the five poems (laments) that make up this book? What is the relationship of sadness and hope in a lament?

5. If you were to write a lament, what key ideas would you include?

ezekiel

*Visions of God's bright glory, dry bones that come back
to life, and a life-giving river that flows out of God's
new temple—read about these and other messages from
the prophet Ezekiel.*

WHAT MAKES EZEKIEL SPECIAL?

EZEKIEL is unique among the prophetic books because the Hebrew text is written completely in the
first person from Ezekiel's own point of view. The
book has traditionally been thought to be difficult to
interpret, and even dangerous. Some early Jewish
teachers were troubled by Ezekiel's vision of the new
temple (40–48) because it seemed to contradict
parts of the Law of Moses. They also feared that
Ezekiel's graphic visions of God's glory (1.1-28; 10.1-
22) might lead to controversial beliefs about the
mystery of God.

WHY WAS EZEKIEL WRITTEN?

In 587 B.C., after years of upheaval, King Nebuchadnezzar of Babylonia destroyed Jerusalem and its
temple, and took people into exile.

Ezekiel's visions and prophecies were meant to
explain why the LORD God of Israel had allowed such
a terrible thing to happen. The people had sinned
against God, and made their land and God's temple
impure. Because of their sins, the "glory of the LORD"
left the temple in Jerusalem. Yet Ezekiel's message
also included promises of hope. The LORD would free
the people from exile and lead them back to Jerusalem where they would worship the LORD in a new
temple and again live according to God's Law.

WHAT'S THE STORY BEHIND THE SCENE?

Some prophetic books give little or no information
that helps place the time of the prophet or the

prophet's message, but many of Ezekiel's messages
(oracles) begin with specific dates (for example, see
1.1-3; 8.1; and 40.1). According to these dates,
Ezekiel's work as a prophet probably began in late
June or early July of 593 B.C.

Most of Ezekiel's prophecies date to the time between 593 and 586 B.C. and provide warnings to the
people of Judah about the LORD's coming judgment—their defeat at the hands of the Babylonians
because of their sin and unfaithfulness.

HOW IS EZEKIEL CONSTRUCTED?

Here is one way EZEKIEL can be outlined:

The LORD will judge Judah and Jerusalem
    (1.1—24.27)
    Ezekiel is chosen to be a prophet (1.1—3.27)
    Disaster is coming (4.1—7.27)
    The LORD's glory leaves Jerusalem (8.1—11.25)
    Messages of doom for Judah and Jerusalem
    (12.1—24.27)
Messages of judgment on foreign nations
    (25.1—32.32)
The LORD will restore Jerusalem and Israel
    (33.1—39.29)
    Watchman and shepherd (33.1—34.31)
    Preparing the way for Judah's new future (35.1—
    39.29)
The LORD's glory returns to Judah and Jerusalem
    (40.1—48.35)
    A new temple (40.1—44.3)
    Laws and rules for God's people (44.4—46.24)
    Dividing the land (47.1—48.34)

When Babylonia conquered Jerusalem in 597 B.C., many important people were taken to live in exile in Babylonia. Ezekiel, a priest from Jerusalem, was sent to Babylonia with the first group of exiles. In 593 B.C., he responded to the Lord's call to watch over the people of Israel as a prophet. The first section of Ezekiel describes the Lord's coming judgment against God's people, condemning the sinful nation's wicked leaders and lying prophets. These visions are followed by judgments against foreign nations. When the Lord first takes control of Ezekiel, the prophet loses his ability to speak, making him unable to warn people directly of the terrible punishment the Lord had commanded. However, when a refugee brings news of the final destruction of Jerusalem and its temple, the Lord restores Ezekiel's ability to speak, and the nature of Ezekiel's prophecies change. Ezekiel speaks of a new agreement between God and his people, and says that the Lord will breathe new life into the people and let them live safely again in their own land. The Lord gives Ezekiel a detailed vision of the new temple and tells him that a day is coming when the Lord's glory will return to the temple, just rule will be restored, and the people and land will be refreshed.

Outline

Ezekiel Sees the Lord's Glory

1 ¹⁻³I am Ezekiel—a priest and the son of Buzi.^a

Five years after King Jehoiachin of Judah had been led away as a prisoner to Babylonia, I was living near the Chebar River among those who had been taken there with him. Then on the fifth day of the fourth month^b of the thirtieth year,^c the heavens suddenly opened. The Lord placed his hand upon me^d and showed me some visions.

⁴I saw a windstorm blowing in from the north. Lightning flashed from a huge cloud and lit up the whole sky with a dazzling brightness. The fiery center of the cloud was as shiny as polished metal, ⁵and in that center I saw what looked like four living creatures. They were somewhat like humans, ⁶except that each one had four faces and four wings. ⁷Their legs were straight, but their feet looked like the hoofs of calves and sparkled like bronze. ⁸Under each of their wings, these creatures had a human hand. ⁹The four creatures were standing back to back with the tips of their wings touching. They moved together in every direction, without turning their bodies.

¹⁰Each creature had the face of a human in front, the face of a lion on the right side, the face of a bull on the left, and the face of an eagle in back. ¹¹Two wings^e of each creature were spread out and touched the wings of the creatures on either side. The other two wings of each creature were folded against its body.

¹²The four living creatures went wherever the Spirit led them, and they moved together without turning their bodies, because each creature faced straight ahead.

---

^a**1.1-3** *a priest and the son of Buzi:* Or "the son of Buzi the priest." ^b**1.1-3** *Five years . . . prisoner . . . fourth month:* Probably July of 593 B.C. ^c**1.1-3** *thirtieth year:* The event from which this date is figured is unknown. ^d**1.1-3** *The Lord placed his hand upon me:* This was a sign that the Lord had chosen Ezekiel to be his prophet. ^e**1.11** *Two wings:* One possible meaning for the difficult Hebrew text.

● 1.1-3 *Ezekiel—a priest:* Ezekiel was not only a prophet, but also a priest, most likely from the Zadokite clan. He was probably serving in Jerusalem's temple when the Babylonian army first invaded the city in 597 B.C. Ezekiel was among those forced to leave Jerusalem in 597 B.C.

○ Israel's Priests

● 1.5-9 *four living creatures:* These creatures probably looked something like the man-beast statues that guarded some ancient Near Eastern temples and palaces. In Ezekiel 10, these creatures are called "winged creatures," also known as "cherubim."

■ 1.10-12 *face of a human . . . eagle:* The creatures and their faces were arranged so that they could see in all directions at all times. Christian sculpture and art used the human, bull, lion, and eagle faces to represent each of the four Gospels.

1.18 *wheels:* The wheels could move with the "creatures" in any direction much more easily than any chariot or wagon made by human hands. The "eyes all the way around" these wheels are probably meant to symbolize God's all-seeing nature.

1.22-23 *dome:* Ancient Hebrews understood the sky to be like a solid bowl or dome set over the flat earth (Gen 1.6-8; Job 9.5-10; 26.11) that held back the waters above.

1.24 *God All-Powerful:* Translation for *Shaddai,* one of the ancient names for Israel's God.

Names of God

1.27,28 *like the flames . . . brightness of the LORD's glory:* God's glory is often connected with bright light or fire. The "rainbow" is a reminder of God's promise in Genesis 9.9-11 that God would not destroy humankind. Also important here is the location of Ezekiel's vision. According to traditions connected to Israel's priests, the LORD's glory or presence was to be found in the sacred tent or in the most holy place in the temple (Exod 25.22; 40.34; Lev 9.22-24; Num 14.10; 1 Kgs 8.11). But here the LORD's glory is seen outside the temple and in a foreign land (Babylonia).

Holy Spirit

2.3 *people of Israel:* Here "Israel" refers to both the northern and southern kingdoms of Israel.

Israel

---

[13]The creatures were glowing like hot coals, and I saw something like a flaming torch moving back and forth among them. Lightning flashed from the torch every time its flame blazed up.[f] [14]The creatures themselves moved as quickly as sparks jumping from a fire.[g]

[15] I then noticed that on the ground beside each of the four living creatures was a wheel,[h] [16]shining like chrysolite.[i] Each wheel was exactly the same and had a second wheel that cut through the middle of it,[j] [17]so that they could move in any direction without turning. [18]The rims of the wheels were large and frightening, and they had eyes all the way around them.[k] [19-21]The creatures controlled when and where the wheels moved—the wheels went wherever the four creatures went and stopped whenever they stopped. Even when the creatures flew in the air, the wheels were beside them.

[22-23]Above the living creatures, I saw something that was sparkling like ice, and it reminded me of a dome. Each creature had two of its wings stretched out toward the creatures on either side, with the other two wings folded against its body. [24]Whenever the creatures flew, their wings roared like an ocean or a large army or even the voice of God All-Powerful. And whenever the creatures stopped, they folded their wings against their bodies.

[25]When the creatures stopped flapping their wings, I heard a sound coming from above the dome. [26]I then saw what looked like a throne made of sapphire,[l] and sitting on the throne was a figure in the shape of a human. [27]From the waist up, it was glowing like metal in a hot furnace, and from the waist down it looked like the flames of a fire. The figure was surrounded by a bright light, [28]as colorful as a rainbow that appears after a storm.

I realized I was seeing the brightness of the LORD's glory! So I bowed with my face to the ground, and just then I heard a voice speaking to me.

The LORD Chooses Ezekiel

2 The LORD[m] said, "Ezekiel, son of man,[n] I want you to stand up and listen." [2]After he said this, his Spirit took control of me and lifted me to my feet. Then the LORD said:

[3]Ezekiel, I am sending you to the people of Israel. They are just like their ancestors who rebelled against me and refused to stop. [4]They are stubborn and hardheaded. But I, the LORD God, have chosen you to tell them what I say. [5]Those rebels may not even listen, but at least they will know that a prophet has come to them.

[6]Don't be afraid of them or of anything they say. You may think you're in the middle of a thorn patch or a bunch of scorpions. But be brave [7]and preach my message to them, whether they choose to listen or not. [8]Ezekiel, don't rebel against me, as they have

---

[f]1.13 *up:* One possible meaning for the difficult Hebrew text of verse 13.   [g]1.14 *as sparks jumping from a fire:* Or "as flashes of lightning."   [h]1.15 *wheel:* One possible meaning for the difficult Hebrew text of verse 15.   [i]1.16 *chrysolite:* A precious stone that has an olive green color.   [j]1.16 *a second wheel that cut through the middle of it:* Or "a smaller wheel inside it."   [k]1.18 *them:* One possible meaning for the difficult Hebrew text of verse 18.   [l]1.26 *sapphire:* A precious stone that has a blue color.   [m]2.1 *The LORD:* Hebrew "The voice."   [n]2.1 *Ezekiel, son of man:* The Hebrew text has "Son of man," which is often used in this book when the LORD speaks directly to Ezekiel. It means that Ezekiel is a mere human, yet he is the one the LORD has chosen to be his prophet who speaks for him to the people of Israel.

done. Instead, listen to everything I tell you.

And now, Ezekiel, open your mouth and eat what I am going to give you. ⁹Just then, I saw a hand stretched out toward me. And in it was a scroll.^o ¹⁰The hand opened the scroll, and both sides of it were filled with words of sadness, mourning, and grief.

³ The LORD said, "Ezekiel, son of man, after you eat this scroll, go speak to the people of Israel."

²⁻³He handed me the scroll and said, "Eat this and fill up on it." So I ate the scroll, and it tasted sweet as honey.

⁴The LORD said:

Ezekiel, I am sending you to your own people. ⁵⁻⁶They are Israelites, not some strangers who speak a foreign language you can't understand. If I were to send you to foreign nations, they would listen to you. ⁷But the people of Israel will refuse to listen, because they have refused to listen to me. All of them are stubborn and hardheaded, ⁸so I will make you as stubborn as they are. ⁹You will be so determined to speak my message that nothing will stop you. I will make you hard like a diamond, and you'll have no reason to be afraid of those arrogant rebels.

¹⁰Listen carefully to everything I say and then think about it. ¹¹Then go to the people who were brought here to Babylonia with you and tell them you have a message from me, the LORD God. Do this, whether they listen to you or not.

¹²The Spirit^P lifted me up, and as the glory of the LORD started to leave,^q I heard a loud, thundering noise behind me. ¹³It was the sound made by the creatures' wings as they brushed against each other, and by the rumble of the wheels beside them. ¹⁴Then the Spirit carried me away.

The LORD's power had taken complete control of me, and I was both annoyed and angry.

¹⁵When I was back with the others living at Abib Hill near the Chebar River, I sat among them for seven days, shocked at what had happened to me.

The LORD Appoints Ezekiel To Stand Watch
(Ezekiel 33.1-9)

¹⁶Seven days after I had seen the brightness of the LORD's glory, the LORD said:

¹⁷Ezekiel, son of man, I have appointed you to stand watch for the people of Israel. So listen to what I say, then warn them for me. ¹⁸When I tell wicked people they will die because of their sins, you must warn them to turn from their sinful ways so they won't be punished. If you refuse, you are responsible for their death. ¹⁹However, if you do warn them, and they keep on sinning, they will die because of their sins, and you will be innocent.

²⁰Now suppose faithful people start sinning, and I decide to put stumbling blocks in their paths to make them fall. They deserve to die because of their sins. So if you refuse to warn them, I will forget about the times they were faithful, and I will hold you responsible for their death. ²¹But if you do warn them, and they listen to you and stop sinning, I will let them live. And you will be innocent.

2.8—3.3 *eat . . . the scroll:* The scroll, a roll of papyrus or special leather used for writing, contained the LORD's message. Touching the mouth was an important symbolic part of being chosen as a prophet of the LORD, but only Ezekiel actually ate God's words. Even though these words were filled with bad news, they tasted sweet to Ezekiel.

3.9 *nothing will stop you:* Ezekiel's message would not be popular, especially to those who had rebelled against the LORD (2.5-7). Also, those living in exile in Babylonia were probably convinced that God had forgotten about them.

3.11 *people who were brought here to Babylonia with you:* Refers to the first group of Israelites who had been taken away into exile in Babylonia.

Babylon

3.15 *sat . . . for seven days . . . shocked:* Ezekiel was made speechless by the experience of seeing the LORD's glory. Compare this to the experiences of Job (Job 2.11-13) and Saul (Acts 9.1-9).

3.17-21 *Ezekiel . . . stand watch . . . innocent:* Ezekiel is appointed to be a watchman for the people of Israel. This includes warning the people to turn away from their sins. If Ezekiel doesn't warn the people, he will be responsible for their death.

---

^o2.9 *scroll:* A roll of paper or special leather used for writing on.   ^P3.12 *The Spirit:* Or "A wind."
^q3.12 *as the glory of the LORD started to leave:* One possible meaning for the difficult Hebrew text.

3.24-27 *lock yourself in your house . . . unable to talk . . . speak my message:* These verses have been difficult for interpreters. Why is Ezekiel to be locked in his house and made not to speak right after he has been told to warn the Israelite people? If his silence is meant to last until the city of Jerusalem is destroyed about seven years later, why does he tell the people many messages of doom beginning in chapter 4? Some have suggested that Ezekiel wrote down his messages or acted them out, rather than speaking them out loud. Others believe his inability to speak was only temporary or symbolic. Still others think that Ezekiel's silence meant that during this time he was not supposed to pray for his people, but could only deliver his messages of doom.

4.1 *son of man:* This phrase is often used in this book when the LORD speaks directly to Ezekiel. It means that Ezekiel is a mere human, yet he is the one the LORD has chosen to speak for him to the people of Israel.

4.4-5 *390 days . . . suffering:* It is unclear exactly what period of time the 390 years refers to. Israel's "suffering" possibly refers to the time when the northern and southern kingdoms first split apart after the death of King Solomon. **(See the article From Joshua to the Exile: The People of Israel in the Promised Land on pg 1783.)**

⊗   Israel

⊗   Purity (Clean and Unclean)

Ezekiel Cannot Talk

²²The LORD took control of me and said, "Stand up! Go into the valley, and I will talk with you there."

²³I immediately went to the valley, where I saw the brightness of the LORD's glory, just as I had seen it near the Chebar River, and I bowed with my face to the ground. ²⁴His Spirit took control of me and lifted me to my feet. Then the LORD said:

Go back and lock yourself in your house! ²⁵You will be tied up to keep you inside, ²⁶and I will make you unable to talk or to warn those who have rebelled against me. ²⁷But the time will come, when I will tell you what to say, and you will again be able to speak my message.ʳ Some of them will listen; others will be stubborn and refuse to listen.

Ezekiel Acts Out an Attack on Jerusalem

The LORD said:

4 Ezekiel, son of man, find a brick and sketch a picture of Jerusalem on it. ²Then prepare to attack the brick as if it were a real city. Build a dirt mound and a ramp up to the top and surround the brick with enemy camps. On every side put large wooden poles as though you were going to break down the gate to the city. ³Set up an iron pan like a wall between you and the brick. All this will be a warning for the people of Israel.

⁴⁻⁵After that, lie down on your left side and stay there for 390 days as a sign of Israel's punishmentˢ—one day for each year of its suffering. ⁶Then turn over and lie on your right side 40 more days. That will be a sign of Judah's punishment—one day for each year of its suffering.

⁷The brick stands for Jerusalem, so attack it! Stare at it and shout angry warnings. ⁸I will tie you up, so you can't leave until your attack has ended.

⁹Get a large bowl. Then mix together wheat, barley, beans, lentils, and millet, and make some bread. This is what you will eat for the 390 days you are lying down. ¹⁰Eat only a small loaf of bread each day ¹¹and drink only two large cups of water. ¹²Use dried human waste to start a fire, then bake the bread on the coals where everyone can watch you. ¹³When I scatter the people of Israel among the nations, they will also have to eat food that is unclean, just as you must do.ᵗ

¹⁴I said, "LORD God, please don't make me do that! Never in my life have I eaten food that would make me unacceptable to you. I've never eaten anything that died a natural death or was killed by a wild animal or that you said was unclean."

¹⁵The LORD replied, "Instead of human waste, I will let you bake your bread on a fire made from cow manure. ¹⁶Ezekiel, the people of Jerusalem will starve. They will have so little food and water that they will be afraid and hopeless. ¹⁷Everyone will be shocked at what is happening, and, because of their sins, they will die a slow death."

ʳ3.27 *again . . . , speak my message:* See 33.21,22.   ˢ4.4,5 *Israel's punishment:* Israel here refers to the northern kingdom that was destroyed in 722 B.C.   ᵗ4.13 *have to eat food that is unclean, just as you must do:* The LORD had forbidden the people of Israel to mix certain things (see Deuteronomy 22.9-11), and so the people would not have been allowed to eat this bread under normal conditions. It is used here to show that when a city is under attack, people eat whatever food is left, even if the LORD had said it was unclean.

Jerusalem's Coming Destruction

The LORD said:

5 Ezekiel, son of man, get a sharp sword and use it to cut off your hair and beard. Weigh the hair and divide it into three equal piles. ²After you attack the brick that stands for Jerusalem, burn one pile of your hair on the brick. Chop up the second pile and let the small pieces of hair fall around the brick. Throw the third pile into the wind, and I will strike it with my own sword.

³Keep a few of the hairs and wrap them in the hem of your clothes. ⁴Then pull out a few of those hairs and throw them in the fire, so they will also burn. This fire will spread, destroying everyone in Israel.

⁵I am the LORD God, and I have made Jerusalem the most important place in the world, and all other nations admire it. ⁶But the people of Jerusalem rebelled and refuse to obey me. They ignored my laws and have become even more sinful than the nations around them.

⁷So tell the people of Jerusalem:

I am the LORD God! You have refused to obey my laws and teachings, and instead you have obeyed the laws of the surrounding nations. You have become more rebellious than any of them! ⁸Now all those nations will watch as I turn against you and punish you ⁹for your sins. Your punishment will be more horrible than anything I've ever done or will ever do again. ¹⁰Parents will be so desperate for food that they will eat their own children, and children will eat their parents. Those who survive this horror will be scattered in every direction. ¹¹Your sins have disgusted me and

made my temple unfit as a place to worship me. So I swear by my own life that I will cut you down[u] and show you no pity. ¹²A third of you will die here in Jerusalem from disease or starvation. Another third will be killed in war. And I will scatter the last third of you in every direction, then track you down and kill you.

¹³You will feel my fierce anger until I have finished taking revenge. Then you will know that I, the LORD, was furious because of your disobedience. ¹⁴Every passerby will laugh at your destruction. Foreign nations ¹⁵will insult you and make fun of you, but they will also be shocked and terrified at what I did in my anger. ¹⁶I will destroy your crops until you starve to death, and disasters will strike you like arrows. ¹⁷Starvation and wild animals will kill your children. I'll punish you with horrible diseases, and your enemies will strike you down with their swords. I, the LORD, have spoken.

Israel Is Doomed

6 The LORD God said:
²Ezekiel, son of man, face the hills of Israel and tell them:

³Listen, you mountains and hills, and every valley and gorge! I, the LORD, am about to turn against you and crush all the places where foreign gods are worshiped. ⁴Every altar will be smashed, and in front of the idols I will put to death the people who worship them. ⁵Dead bodies and bones will be lying around the idols and the altars. ⁶Every town in Israel will be destroyed to make sure that each shrine, idol,

u5.11 *cut you down*: Or "turn my back on you."

5.1-4 *cut off your hair and beard*: Having one's hair or beard cut off was considered a great embarrassment and a loss of personal identity. Ezekiel's haircut with a sword was meant to symbolize Jerusalem's embarrassment when they are defeated in battle. Next the hair was divided into three piles to show that a third of Jerusalem's people would die by fire, a third would be killed by the sword, and a third would be scattered, that is, sent away into exile. The few hairs Ezekiel kept in the hem of his clothes symbolized those in exile in Babylonia.

5.5 *Jerusalem*: In the traditions connected to Israel's priests, Jerusalem and the LORD's holy temple there were the center of all the other nations of the world.

5.6,7 *ignored my laws . . . teachings*: See the article People of the Law: The Religion of Israel on pg 1794.

Law

5.8-17 *Your punishment*: These verses explain the scene that Ezekiel was supposed to draw and act out (4.1-3; 5.1-4). Because of their sins against the LORD, some of the people of Jerusalem would suffer starvation; others would be killed in battle; and still others would be scattered, that is, sent into exile in foreign lands.

7.2 *Israel:* Ezekiel is primarily speaking to the people of Judah and Jerusalem.

Justice

7.12 *The time is coming:* The LORD's coming day of judgment is described by many of Israel's prophets. Here Ezekiel is referring to the day when Babylonia will capture and destroy Jerusalem.

Day of the LORD

and altar is smashed—everything the Israelites made will be a pile of ruins.ᵛ ⁷All over the country, your people will die. And those who survive will know that I, the LORD, did these things. ⁸I will let some of the people live through this punishment, but I will scatter them among the nations, ⁹where they will be prisoners. And when they think of me, they will realize that they disgraced me by rebelling and by worshiping idols. They will hate themselves for the evil things they did, ¹⁰and they will know that I am the LORD and that my warnings must be taken seriously.

¹¹The LORD God then said:

Ezekiel, beat your fists together and stomp your feet in despair! Moan in sorrow, because the people of Israel have done disgusting things and now will be killed by enemy troops, or they will die from starvation and disease. ¹²Those who live far away will be struck with deadly diseases. Those who live nearby will be killed in war. And the ones who are left will starve to death. I will let loose my anger on them! ¹³These people used to offer incense to idols at altars built on hills and mountaintops and in the shade of large oak trees. But when they see dead bodies lying around those altars, they will know that I am the LORD. ¹⁴I will make their country a barren wasteland, from the Southern Desert to the town of Diblah in the north. Then they will know that I, the LORD, have done these things.

Disaster Is Near

7 The LORD God said:

²Ezekiel, son of man, tell the people of Israel that I am saying:

Israel will soon come to an end! Your whole country is about to be destroyed ³as punishment for your disgusting sins. I, the LORD, am so angry ⁴that I will show no pity. I will punish you for the evil you've done, and you will know that I am the LORD.

⁵There's never been anything like the coming disaster.ʷ ⁶And when it comes, your life will be over. ⁷You people of Israel are doomed! Soon there will be panic on the mountaintops instead of celebration.ˣ ⁸I will let loose my anger and punish you for the evil things you've done. You'll get what you deserve. ⁹Your sins are so terrible, that you'll get no mercy from me. Then you will know that I, the LORD, have punished you.

¹⁰Disaster is near! Injustice and arrogance are everywhere, ¹¹and violent criminals run free. None of you will survive the disaster, and everything you own and value will be shattered.ʸ ¹²The time is coming when everyone will be ruined. Buying and selling will stop, ¹³and people who sell property will never get it back, because all of you must be punished for your sins. And I won't change my mind!ᶻ

¹⁴A signal has been blown on the trumpet, and weapons are prepared for battle. But no one goes to war, because in my anger I will strike down everyone in Israel.

ᵛ**6.6** *will be a pile of ruins:* Three ancient translations; Hebrew "will become guilty."   ʷ**7.5** *disaster:* One possible meaning for the difficult Hebrew text of verse 5.   ˣ**7.7** *celebration:* One possible meaning for the difficult Hebrew text of verse 7.   ʸ**7.11** *shattered:* One possible meaning for the difficult Hebrew text of verses 10,11.   ᶻ**7.13** *mind:* One possible meaning for the difficult Hebrew text of verse 13.

Israel Is Surrounded

The LORD said to the people of Israel:

[15]War, disease, and starvation are everywhere! People who live in the countryside will be killed in battle, and those who live in towns will die from starvation or deadly diseases. [16]Anyone who survives will escape into the hills, like doves who leave the valleys to find safety.

All of you will moan[a] because of your sins. [17]Your hands will tremble, and your knees go limp. [18]You will put on sackcloth[b] to show your sorrow, but terror will overpower you. Shame will be written all over your faces, and you will shave your heads in despair. [19]Your silver and gold will be thrown into the streets like garbage, because those are the two things that led you into sin, and now they cannot save you from my anger. They are not even worth enough to buy food. [20]You took great pride in using your beautiful jewelry to make disgusting idols of foreign gods. So I will make your jewelry worthless.

[21]Wicked foreigners will rob and disgrace you. [22]They will break into my temple[c] and leave it unfit as a place to worship me, but I will look away and let it happen.

[23]Your whole country is in confusion![d] Murder and violence are everywhere in Israel, [24]so I will tell the most wicked nations to come and take over your homes. They will put an end to the pride you have in your strong army, and they will make your places of worship unfit to use. [25]You will be terrified and will desperately look for peace—but there will be no peace. [26]One tragedy will follow another, and you'll hear only bad news. People will beg prophets to give them a message from me. Priests will stop teaching my Law, and wise leaders won't be able to give advice. [27]Even your king and his officials will lose hope and cry in despair. Your hands will tremble with fear.

I will punish you for your sins and treat you the same way you have treated others. Then you will know that I am the LORD.

Ezekiel Sees the Terrible Sins of Jerusalem

8 Six years after King Jehoiachin and the rest of us had been led away as prisoners to Babylonia, the leaders of Judah were meeting with me in my house. On the fifth day of the sixth month,[e] the LORD God suddenly took control of me, [2]and I saw something in the shape of a human.[f] This figure was like fire from the waist down, and it was bright as polished metal from the waist up. [3]It reached out what seemed to be a hand and grabbed my hair. Then in my vision the LORD's Spirit lifted me into the sky and carried me to Jerusalem.

The Spirit took me to the north gate of the temple's inner courtyard, where there was an idol that disgusted the LORD and made him furious. [4]Then I saw the brightness of the glory of the God of Israel, just as I had seen it near the Chebar River.

[5]God said to me, "Ezekiel, son of man, look north." And when I did, I saw that repulsive idol by the altar near the gate.

[6]God then said, "Do you see the terrible

7.18 *sackcloth . . . shave your heads:* Wearing sackcloth and shaving one's head were done in times of trouble or sorrow.

7.19-20 *silver and gold . . . thrown . . . jewelry:* Some people in Israel may have made jewelry and necklaces in the shape of a crescent moon, which suggested worship of a popular moon-god. Other necklaces may have had sayings written on them that were supposed to protect the wearer.

7.22 *break into my temple:* The Babylonians destroyed much of the temple area in Jerusalem and took many of its holy furnishings and treasures back to Babylonia (2 Kgs 25.8-17; Dan 1.2; 5.1,2). The people were likely surprised that the LORD allowed foreigners to enter the holy temple and make it unfit for worship.

8.2 *shape of a human . . . fire:* This figure is similar to the one described in Ezekiel's first vision.

---

[a]7.16 *will moan:* Hebrew; two ancient translations "will die." [b]7.18 *sackcloth:* A rough, dark-colored cloth made from goat or camel hair and used to make grain sacks. It was worn in times of trouble or sorrow. [c]7.22 *my temple:* The Hebrew text has "my treasure," which may refer to the temple, to Jerusalem, or to Israel itself. [d]7.23 *Your whole country is in confusion:* One ancient translation; Hebrew "Get chains ready to drag away the dead bodies of your people." [e]8.1 *Six years . . . sixth month:* Probably September of 592 B.C. [f]8.2 *a human:* One ancient translation; Hebrew "a fiery figure."

8.10 *pictures of reptiles . . . unclean animals:* Pictures of animals that were considered ritually impure (see Lev 11.9-19) were placed in the temple along with idols.

8.16 *temple's inner courtyard . . . rising sun:* Ezekiel is in the temple courtyard, near the doorway to the temple. The men bowing toward the rising sun may have been worshiping the Babylonian sun god Shamash. By turning their backs on the temple and facing east to worship this god, they were showing that they believed the LORD was helpless against the sun god of Babylonia.

9.1,2 *men chosen to destroy the city . . . linen robe:* These six figures may have been angels the LORD had sent to bring about destruction (see Exod 12.23; 2 Sam 24.15,16; Isa 37.36). Israel's priests wore linen robes (Exod 29.39-42), so the seventh figure "in a linen robe" was perhaps meant to be a priest or an angel (see Dan 10.4-9).

9.3 *brightness of God's glory . . . above . . . winged creatures:* Winged creatures (cherubim) were placed on the lid of the sacred chest, which was kept in the most holy place in the temple (Exod 25.10-22; 1 Kgs 6.19-28). The LORD's glory now moves out of the most holy place to the door of the temple.

9.4 *mark the forehead:* These allowed the destroyers to know which people to kill and which not to harm.

sins of the people of Israel? Their sins are making my holy temple unfit as a place to worship me. Yet you will see even worse things than this."

⁷Next, I was taken to the entrance of the courtyard, where I saw a hole in the wall. ⁸God said, "Make this hole bigger." And when I did, I realized it was a doorway. ⁹"Go in," God said, "and see what horrible and evil things these people are doing."

¹⁰Inside, I saw that the walls were covered with pictures of reptiles and disgusting, unclean animals,ᵍ as well as with idols that the Israelites were worshiping. ¹¹Seventy Israelite leaders were standing there, including Jaazaniah son of Shaphan. Each of these leaders was holding an incense burner, and the smell of incense filled the room.

¹²God said, "Ezekiel, do you see what horrible things Israel's leaders are doing in secret? They have filled their rooms with idols. And they say I can't see them, because they think I have already deserted Israel. ¹³But I will show you something even worse than this."

¹⁴He took me to the north gate of the temple, where I saw women mourning for the god Tammuz.ʰ ¹⁵God asked me, "Can you believe what these women are doing? But now I want to show you something even worse."

¹⁶I was then led into the temple's inner courtyard, where I saw about 25 men standing near the entrance, between the porch and the altar. Their backs were to the LORD's temple, and they were bowing down to the rising sun.

¹⁷God said, "Ezekiel, it's bad enough that the people of Judah are doing these dis-

gusting things. But they have also spread violence and injustice everywhere in Israel and have made me very angry. They have disgraced and insulted me in the worst possible way.ⁱ ¹⁸So in my fierce anger, I will punish them without mercy and refuse to help them when they cry out to me."

The LORD Gives the Command To Punish Jerusalem

9 After that, I heard the LORD shout, "Come to Jerusalem, you men chosen to destroy the city. And bring your weapons!"

²I saw six men come through the north gate of the temple, each one holding a deadly weapon. A seventh man dressed in a linen robe was with them, and he was carrying things to write with. The men went into the temple and stood by the bronze altar.

³The brightness of God's glory then left its place above the statues of the winged creaturesʲ inside the temple and moved to the entrance. The LORD said to the man in the linen robe, ⁴"Walk through the city of Jerusalem and mark the forehead of anyone who is truly upset and sad about the terrible things that are being done here."

⁵⁻⁶He turned to the other six men and said, "Follow him and put to death everyone who doesn't have a mark on their forehead. Show no mercy or pity! Kill men and women, parents and children. Begin here at my temple, but be sure not to harm those who are marked."

The men immediately killed the leaders who were standing there.

ᵍ**8.10** *disgusting, unclean animals:* See, for example, Leviticus 11.9-19.   ʰ**8.14** *the god Tammuz:* A god of vegetation who was thought to die in the dry season. During the Hebrew month of Tammuz (from about mid-June to mid-July), women mourned the death of this god, hoping to bring him back to life.   ⁱ**8.17** *disgraced and insulted me . . . way:* One possible meaning for the difficult Hebrew text.   ʲ**9.3** *the statues of the winged creatures:* These were symbols of the LORD's throne on earth (see Exodus 25.18-22; 1 Kings 6.23-28).

[7]Then the LORD said, "Pollute the temple by piling the dead bodies in the courtyards. Now get busy!" They left and started killing the people of Jerusalem.

[8]I was then alone, so I bowed down and cried out to the LORD, "Why are you doing this? Are you so angry with the people of Jerusalem that everyone must die?"

[9]The LORD answered, "The people of Israel and Judah have done horrible things. Their country is filled with murderers, and Jerusalem itself is filled with violence. They think that I have deserted them, and that I can't see what they are doing. [10]And so I will not have pity on them or forgive them. They will be punished for what they have done."

[11]Just then, the man in the linen robe returned and said, "I have done what you commanded."

The LORD's Glory Leaves the Temple

10 I saw the dome that was above the four winged creatures,[k] and on it was the sapphire[l] throne.[m] [2]The LORD said to the man in the linen robe, "Walk among the four wheels beside the creatures and pick up as many hot coals as you can carry. Then scatter them over the city of Jerusalem." I watched him as he followed the LORD's instructions.

[3]The winged creatures were standing south of the temple when the man walked among them. A cloud filled the inner courtyard, [4]and the brightness of the LORD's glory moved from above the creatures and stopped at the entrance of the temple. The entire temple was filled with his glory, and the courtyard was dazzling bright. [5]The sound of the creatures' wings was as loud as the voice of God All-Powerful and could even be heard in the outer courtyard.

[6]The man in the robe was now standing beside a wheel. [7]One of the four creatures reached its hand into the fire among them and gave him some of the hot coals. The man took the coals and left.

[8]I noticed again that each of the four winged creatures had what looked like human hands under their wings, [9]and I saw the four wheels near the creatures. These wheels were shining like chrysolite.[n] [10]Each wheel was exactly the same and had a second wheel that cut through the middle of it,[o] [11]so that they could move in any direction without turning. The wheels moved together whenever the creatures moved. [12]I also noticed that the wheels and the creatures' bodies, including their backs, their hands, and their wings, were covered with eyes. [13]And I heard a voice calling these "the wheels that spin."

[14]Each of the winged creatures had four faces: the face of a bull,[p] the face of a human, the face of a lion, and the face of an eagle. [15-17]These were the same creatures I had seen near the Chebar River. They controlled when and where the wheels moved—the wheels went wherever the creatures went and stopped whenever they stopped. Even when the creatures flew in the air, the wheels stayed beside them.

[18]Then I watched the brightness of the LORD's glory move from the entrance of the temple and stop above the winged creatures. [19]They spread their wings and flew into the air with the wheels at their

[k]10.1 *winged creatures:* See the note at 9.3. [l]10.1 *sapphire:* See the note at 1.26. [m]10.1 *dome ... creatures ... throne:* See 1.22-26. [n]10.9 *chrysolite:* See the note at 1.16. [o]10.10 *a second wheel that cut through the middle of it:* See the note at 1.16. [p]10.14 *a bull:* The Hebrew text has "a winged creature," but see 1.10.

11.1-3 *cooking pot:* The men promise that the city walls will protect them from enemy attacks, just as a cooking pot protects meat from a blazing fire.

11.5 *Spirit took control . . . tell:* In the middle of his vision, the LORD's Spirit gives Ezekiel a message that he is to tell the leaders.

11.12 *laws . . . my laws:* "The laws of nearby nations" refers to following their religious practices. "My laws and teachings" refers to the Law that the LORD gave to Moses and the Israelite people.

11.13 *Pelatiah:* Though Ezekiel had said the leaders would die when their nation was invaded, Pelatiah died immediately, as if to put an exclamation point on Ezekiel's words. This causes Ezekiel to act in the role of a priest and speak in defense of his people.

11.15-21 *people living in Jerusalem . . . worship idols:* Some who were left in Judah after the Babylonians' first attack on Jerusalem thought that the land of Judah belonged to them. Some leaders, both in Jerusalem and living in exile in Babylonia, believed that the LORD could not be worshiped properly outside of Judah. But the LORD tells those in exile that he is with them so they can worship him even if they are far away from the temple.

Exile

side. They stopped at the east gate of the temple, and the LORD's glory was above them. ²⁰I knew for sure that these were the same creatures I had seen beneath the LORD's glory near the Chebar River. ²¹⁻²²They had four wings with hands beneath them, and they had the same four faces as those near the River. Each creature moved straight ahead without turning.

Ezekiel Condemns Jerusalem's Wicked Leaders

11 The LORD's Spirit⁹ lifted me up and took me to the east gate of the temple, where I saw 25 men, including the two leaders, Jaazaniah son of Azzur and Pelatiah son of Benaiah. ²The LORD said, "Ezekiel, son of man, these men are making evil plans and giving dangerous advice to the people of Jerusalem. ³They say things like, 'Let's build more houses.ʳ This city is like a cooking pot over a fire, and we are the meat, but at least the pot keeps us from being burned in the fire.'ˢ ⁴So, Ezekiel, condemn them!"

⁵The LORD's Spirit took control of me and told me to tell these leaders:

I, the LORD God, know what you leaders are saying. ⁶You have murdered so many people that the city is filled with dead bodies! ⁷This city is indeed a cooking pot, but the bodies of those you killed are the meat. And so I will force you to leave Jerusalem, ⁸and I'll send armies to attack you, just as you fear. ⁹Then you will be captured and punished by foreign enemies.ᵗ ¹⁰You will be killed in your own coun-

try, but not before you realize that I, the LORD, have done these things.

¹¹You leaders claim to be meat in a cooking pot, but you won't be protected by this city. No, you will die at the border of Israel. ¹²You will realize that while you were following the laws of nearby nations, you were disobeying my laws and teachings. And I am the LORD!

¹³Before I finished speaking, Pelatiah dropped dead. I bowed down and cried out, "Please, LORD God, don't kill everyone left in Israel."

A Promise of Hope

¹⁴The LORD replied:

¹⁵Ezekiel, son of man, the people living in Jerusalem claim that you and the other Israelites who were taken to Babylonia are too far away to worship me. They also claim that the land of Israel now belongs only to them. ¹⁶But here is what I want you to tell the Israelites in Babylonia:

It's true that I, the LORD God, have forced you out of your own country and made you live among foreign nations. But for now, I will be with you wherever you are, so that you can worship me. ¹⁷And someday, I will gather you from the nations where you are scattered and let you live in Israel again. ¹⁸When that happens, I want you to clear the land of all those idols I hate so much. ¹⁹Then I will take away your stubbornness and make you eager to be completely faithful to me. You will want to obey me ²⁰and all my laws and teachings. You will be my

⁹11.1 *The LORD's Spirit:* Or "A wind."   ʳ11.3 *Let's . . . houses:* One possible meaning for the difficult Hebrew text.   ˢ11.3 *the pot keeps us from being burned in the fire:* These leaders were trying to convince the people of Jerusalem that they were secure, and that their future was bright.   ᵗ11.9 *foreign enemies:* That is, the Babylonians.

people, and I will be your God. [21]But those who worship idols will be punished and get what they deserve. I, the LORD God, have spoken.

The LORD's Glory Leaves Jerusalem

[22]After the LORD had finished speaking, the winged creatures spread their wings and flew into the air, and the wheels were beside them. The brightness of the LORD's glory above them [23]left Jerusalem and stopped at a hill east of the city.

[24]Then in my vision, the LORD's Spirit[u] lifted me up and carried me back to the other exiles in Babylonia. The vision faded away, [25]and I told them everything the LORD had shown me.

Ezekiel Acts Out Israel's Captivity

12 The LORD said: [2]Ezekiel, son of man, you are living among rebellious people. They have eyes, but refuse to see; they have ears, but refuse to listen. [3]So before it gets dark, here is what I want you to do. Pack a few things as though you were going to be taken away as a prisoner. Then go outside where everyone can see you and walk around from place to place. Maybe as they watch, they will realize what rebels they are. [4]After you have done this, return to your house.

Later that evening leave your house as if you were going into exile. [5]Dig through the wall of your house[v] and crawl out, carrying the bag with you.

Make sure everyone is watching. [6]Lift the bag to your shoulders, and with your face covered, take it into the darkness, so that you cannot see the land you are leaving. All this will be a warning for the people of Israel.

[7]I did everything the LORD had said. I packed a few things. Then as the sun was going down, and while everyone was watching, I dug a hole through one of the walls of my house. I pulled out my bag, then lifted it to my shoulders and left in the darkness.

[8]The next morning, the LORD [9]reminded me that those rebellious people didn't even ask what I was doing. [10]So he sent me back to tell them:

The LORD God has a message for the leader of Jerusalem and everyone living there! [11]I have done these things to show them what will happen when they are taken away as prisoners.

[12]The leader of Jerusalem will lift his own bag to his shoulders at sunset and leave through a hole that the others have dug in the wall of his house. He will cover his face, so he can't see the land he is leaving. [13]The LORD will spread out a net and trap him as he leaves Jerusalem. He will then be led away to the city of Babylon, but will never see that place,[w] even though he will die there. [14]His own officials and troops will scatter in every direction, and the LORD will track them down and put them to death.

[15]The LORD will force the rest of the people in Jerusalem to live in foreign nations, where they will realize that he

11.24 *my vision:* At the time that Ezekiel was carried to Jerusalem (8.1-3). When he comes back to himself at home in Babylonia, he explains his vision to his visitors.

12.3-7 *Pack . . . darkness:* Ezekiel is told to act out a night-time escape, as one might do to avoid being taken prisoner. Though many watched Ezekiel's strange pantomime, no one asked what it meant.

12.10-13 *leader of Jerusalem . . . led away . . . die there:* Ezekiel's pantomime was intended to show what was going to happen to Zedekiah, the leader that Nebuchadnezzar had put in charge of Judah after Judah's King Jehoiachin. When Zedekiah rebelled against Babylonia, Nebuchadnezzar's army returned to Jerusalem and surrounded the city (587/6 B.C.). Zedekiah and his family managed to escape, but they were captured on the plains near Jericho and taken to Nebuchadnezzar at Riblah. Zedekiah's sons were killed, and Zedekiah's eyes were poked out before he was taken away as a prisoner to Babylonia (2 Kgs 24.18—25; Jer 52.1-11). About a month later, the Babylonians burned down the temple and king's palace in Jerusalem, tore down the city's walls, and took all but the poorest people away into exile.

---

[u]11.24 *the LORD's Spirit:* See the note at 11.1.   [v]12.5 *Dig through the wall of your house:* The walls of most houses in Babylonia were made of mud bricks that had been dried in the sun. A hole could easily have been dug through these bricks.   [w]12.13 *He will then be led away . . . that place:* According to 2 Kings 25.6,7, King Zedekiah of Judah was blinded before he was taken to Babylon.

12.22-28 *prophets are proved wrong . . . true:* Perhaps rival prophets gave opposite messages, or perhaps messages about Jerusalem's coming destruction had been spoken so often and for so long that the people had come to think that it wouldn't really happen, or that it would happen in the distant future. So the people probably felt they had no reason to believe Ezekiel's messages and pantomimes of doom. **(See the article Prophets and Prophecy on pg 1791.)**

13.10-16 *prophets refuse to be honest . . . there was no peace:* The lying prophets are deceiving the people by claiming that the city will soon have peaceful times, but the Babylonian threat is real. They are like builders who try to cover dangerous cracks in a wall by painting over them. But cracked walls, especially those made with mud bricks, will fall apart when they are hit with hard rain, hail, and wind.

has done all these things. [16]Some of them will survive the war, the starvation, and the deadly diseases. That way, they will be able to tell foreigners how disgusting their sins were, and that it was the LORD who punished them in this way.

A Sign of Fear

[17]The LORD said:

[18]Ezekiel, son of man, shake with fear when you eat, and tremble when you drink. [19]Tell the people of Israel that I, the LORD, say that someday everyone in Jerusalem will shake when they eat and tremble when they drink. Their country will be destroyed and left empty, because they have been cruel and violent. [20]Every town will lie in ruins, and the land will be a barren desert. Then they will know that I am the LORD.

The Words of the LORD Will Come True

[21]The LORD said:

[22]Ezekiel, son of man, you've heard people in Israel use the saying, "Time passes, and prophets are proved wrong." [23]Now tell the people that I, the LORD, am going to prove that saying wrong. No one will ever be able to use it again in Israel, because very soon everything I have said will come true! [24]The people will hear no more useless warnings and false messages. [25]I will give them my message, and what I say will certainly happen. Warn those rebels that the time has come for them to be punished. I, the LORD, make this promise.

[26-27]Ezekiel, the people of Israel are also saying that your visions and messages are only about things in the future. [28]So tell them that my words will soon come true, just as I have warned. I, the LORD, have spoken.

Lying Prophets

13 The LORD said:

[2]Ezekiel, son of man, condemn the prophets of Israel who say they speak in my name, but who preach messages that come from their own imagination. Tell them it's time to hear my message.

[3]I, the LORD God, say those lying prophets are doomed! They don't see visions—they make up their own messages! [4]Israel's prophets are no better than jackals[x] that hunt for food among the ruins of a city. [5]They don't warn the people about coming trouble or tell them how dangerous it is to sin against me. [6]Those prophets lie by claiming they speak for me, but I have not even chosen them to be my prophets. And they still think their words will come true. [7]They say they're preaching my messages, but they are full of lies—I did not speak to them!

[8]So I am going to punish those lying prophets for deceiving the people of Israel with false messages. [9]I will turn against them and no longer let them belong to my people. They will not be allowed to call themselves Israelites or even to set foot in Israel. Then they will realize that I am the LORD God.

[10]Those prophets refuse to be honest. They tell my people there will be peace, even though there's no peace to be found. They are like workers who think they can fix a shaky wall by covering it with paint. [11]But when I send rainstorms, hailstones, and strong winds, the wall will surely collapse. [12]People will then ask the workers why the paint didn't hold it up.

[x]**13.4** *jackals:* Desert animals related to wolves, but smaller.

[13]That wall is the city of Jerusalem. And I, the LORD God, am so angry that I will send strong winds, rainstorms, and hailstones to destroy it. [14]The lying prophets have tried to cover up the evil in Jerusalem, but I will tear down the city, all the way to its foundations. And when it collapses, those prophets will be killed, and everyone will know that I have done these things.

[15]The city of Jerusalem and its lying prophets will feel my fierce anger. Then I will announce that the city has fallen and that the lying prophets are dead, [16]because they promised my people peace, when there was no peace. I, the LORD God, have spoken.

Women Who Wear Magic Charms

The LORD said:

[17]Ezekiel, son of man, now condemn the women of Israel who preach messages that come from their own imagination. [18]Tell them they're doomed! They wear magic charms on their wrists and scarves on their heads, then trick others into believing they can predict the future.[y] They won't get away with telling those lies. [19]They charge my people a few handfuls of barley and a couple pieces of bread, and then give messages that are insulting to me. They use lies to sentence the innocent to death and to help the guilty go free. And my people believe them!

[20]I hate the magic charms they use to trick people into believing their lies. I will rip those charms from their wrists and set free the people they have trapped like birds.[z] [21]I will tear the scarves from their heads and rescue my people from their power once and for all. Then they will know that I am the LORD God.

[22]They do things I would never do. They lie to good people and encourage them to do wrong, and they convince the wicked to ruin their own lives by not turning from sin. [23]I will no longer let these women give false messages and use magic, and I will free my people from their control. Then they will know that I, the LORD, have done these things.

Ezekiel Encourages the People To Turn Back to the LORD

14 One day, some of Israel's leaders came to me and asked for a message from the LORD. [2]While they were there, the LORD said:

[3]Ezekiel, son of man, these men have started worshiping idols, though they know it will cause them to sin even more. So I refuse to give them a message!

[4]Tell the people of Israel that if they sin by worshiping idols and then go to a prophet to find out what I say, I will give them the answer their sins deserve. [5]When they hear my message, maybe they will see that they need to turn back to me and stop worshiping those idols.

[6]Now, Ezekiel, tell everyone in Israel:

I am the LORD God. Stop worshiping those idols I hate so much and come back to me.

[7]Suppose one of you Israelites or a foreigner living in Israel rejects me and starts worshiping idols. If you then go to a prophet to find out what I say, I will answer [8]by turning against you. I will make you a warning to anyone who might think of doing the same thing, and you will no longer belong to my people. Then you will know that I am the LORD and that you have sinned against me.

● 13.17-23 *women of Israel . . . free my people:* Some women were also giving false prophecies while claiming their messages came from the LORD. They apparently made and wore charm bracelets and special scarves that were supposed to give them power to predict the future. They may have sold these charms and their messages to people for a few handfuls of barley or a couple of pieces of bread. This "price" would have seemed very cheap for such important information. Perhaps these lying prophetesses also were asked to hear cases and decide whether a person should go free or be punished. Because the people believed the women had special powers, their decisions were accepted, no matter what the actual evidence was.

● 14.1 *Israel's leaders . . . asked for a message:* These are leaders of the Jewish people living in exile in Babylonia. Once again they come to Ezekiel for a message from the LORD.

---

[y]**13.18** *They wear . . . the future*: One possible meaning for the difficult Hebrew text.   [z]**13.20** *like birds*: One possible meaning for the difficult Hebrew text.

14.14 *Noah, Daniel, and Job:* These men were known in the ancient Near East for being faithful to God even though they and their children suffered under difficult circumstances. See Genesis 6–9, Noah; Job 1; 2; 42. Daniel may refer to an ancient hero or ruler named Dan'el described in the tale of Aqhat, (the Ugaritic legend from about 1500 B.C.) or to the Daniel in the Bible. Even the presence of such faithful men could not save a sinful nation from the LORD's destruction.

14.21,22 *war . . . disease . . . Babylonia:* Ezekiel repeats the four ways the people of Jerusalem will be punished for their sins.

15.2 *wood of a grapevine:* Grapevines are thin and flexible, so they are not strong enough to use as pegs to hang things on. When they no longer grow fruit, grapevines are cut down and burned.

[9]If a prophet gives a false message, I am the one who caused that prophet to lie. But I will still reject him and cut him off from my people, [10]and anyone who goes to that prophet for a message will be punished in the same way. [11]I will do this, so that you will come back to me and stop destroying yourselves with these disgusting sins. So turn back to me! Then I will be your God, and you will be my people. I, the LORD God, make this promise.

Judgment on a Sinful Nation

[12]The LORD God said:
[13]Ezekiel, son of man, suppose an entire nation sins against me, and I punish it by destroying the crops and letting its people and livestock starve to death. [14]Even if Noah, Daniel,[a] and Job were living in that nation, their faithfulness would not save anyone but themselves.

[15]Or suppose I punish a nation by sending wild animals to eat people and scare away every passerby, so that the land becomes a barren desert. [16]As surely as I live, I promise that even if these three men lived in that nation, their own children would not be spared. The three men would live, but the land would be an empty desert.

[17]Or suppose I send an enemy to attack a sinful nation and kill its people and livestock. [18]If these three men were in that nation when I punished it, not even their children would be spared. Only the three men would live.

[19]And suppose I am so angry that I send a deadly disease to wipe out the people and livestock of a sinful nation. [20]Again, even if Noah, Daniel, and Job were living there, I,

the LORD, promise that the children of these faithful men would also die. Only the three of them would be spared.

[21]I am the LORD God, and I promise to punish Jerusalem severely. I will send war, starvation, wild animals, and deadly disease to slaughter its people and livestock. [22]And those who survive will be taken from their country and led here to Babylonia. Ezekiel, when you see how sinful they are, you will know why I did all these things to Jerusalem. [23]You will be convinced that I, the LORD God, was right in doing what I did.

Jerusalem Is a Useless Vine

15 Some time later, the LORD said:
[2]Ezekiel, son of man, what happens to the wood of a grapevine after the grapes have been picked? It isn't like other trees in the forest, [3]because the wood of a grapevine can't be used to make anything, not even a small peg to hang things on. [4]It can only be used as firewood. But after its ends are burnt and its middle is charred, it can't be used for anything. [5]The wood is useless before it is burned, and afterwards, it is completely worthless.

[6]I, the LORD God, promise that just as the wood of a grapevine is burned as firewood, [7]I will punish the people of Jerusalem with fire. Some of them have escaped one destruction, but soon they will be completely burned. And when that happens, you, Ezekiel, will know that I am the LORD. [8]I will make their country an empty wasteland, because they have not been loyal to me. I, the LORD God, have spoken.

[a]14.14 *Daniel:* Or "Danel," possibly a well-known hero or wise man.

Jerusalem Is Unfaithful

16 The Lord said:
²Ezekiel, son of man, remind the people of Jerusalem of their disgusting sins ³and tell them that I, the Lord God, am saying:

Jerusalem, you were born in the country where Canaanites lived. Your father was an Amorite, and your mother was a Hittite.ᵇ ⁴When you were born, no one cut you loose from your mother or washed your body. No one rubbed your skin with salt and olive oil,ᶜ and wrapped you in warm blankets. ⁵Not one person loved you enough to do any of these things, and no one even felt sorry for you. You were despised, thrown into a field, and forgotten.

⁶I saw you lying there, rolling around in your own blood, and I couldn't let you die. ⁷I took care of you, like someone caring for a tender, young plant. You grew up to be a beautiful young woman with mature breasts and hair, but you were still naked.

⁸When I saw you again, you were old enough to have sex. So I covered your naked body with my own robe.ᵈ Then I solemnly promised that you would belong to me and that I, the Lord God, would take care of you.

⁹I washed the blood off you and rubbed your skin with olive oil. ¹⁰I gave you the finest clothes and the most expensive robes,ᵉ as well as sandals made from the best leather. ¹¹I gave you bracelets, a necklace, ¹²a ring for your nose, some earrings, and a beautiful crown. ¹³Your jewelry was gold and silver, and your clothes were made of only the finest material and embroidered linen. Your bread was baked from fine flour, and you ate honey and olive oil. You were as beautiful as a queen, ¹⁴and everyone on earth knew it. I, the Lord God, had helped you become a lovely young woman.

¹⁵You learned that you were attractive enough to have any man you wanted, so you offered yourself to every passerby.ᶠ ¹⁶You made shrines for yourself and decorated them with some of your clothes. That's where you took your visitors to have sex with them. These things should never have happened!ᵍ ¹⁷You made idols out of the gold and silver jewelry I gave you, then you sinned by worshiping those idols. ¹⁸You dressed them in the clothes you got from me, and you offered them the olive oil and incense I gave you. ¹⁹I supplied you with fine flour, olive oil, and honey, but you sacrificed it all as offerings to please those idols. I, the Lord God, watched this happen.

²⁰But you did something even worse than that—you sacrificed your own children to those idols! ²¹You slaughtered my children, so you could offer them as sacrifices. ²²You were so busy sinning and being a prostitute that you refused to think about the days when you were young and were rolling around naked in your own blood.

²³Now I, the Lord God, say you are doomed! Not only did you do these evil things, ²⁴but you also built places on every street corner ²⁵where you disgraced your-

16.3 *Canaanites . . . Amorite . . . Hittite:* The Canaanites, descendants of Noah's son Ham, settled mainly in cities or villages near the Jordan River and the Mediterranean Sea northwest of Jerusalem. The Amorites lived in the hill country of Canaan at the time the Israelites invaded it. The Hittites were a powerful people descended from Heth, grandson of Ham. They established an empire in Asia Minor and were a dominant force in Canaan from the time of Abraham to the twelfth century B.C. These names would remind the people of Jerusalem that as descendants of foreigners, they were also foreigners in the land.

16.8 *I covered . . . my own robe:* When a man spread his robe over a woman, he was showing his intention to marry her. The Lord here promises to make Jerusalem his bride and take care of her.

16.20 *sacrificed your own children:* Child sacrifice was forbidden, but some Israelites did this anyway in and near Jerusalem (see 2 Kgs 21.4-7; 23.10; Jer 7.31; 32.35).

16.22 *being a prostitute:* Jerusalem is pictured as a prostitute having "sex" with foreign nations and their gods, meaning its people worshiped those gods and Jerusalem's leaders made treaties with foreign nations (16.26-29), instead of trusting in the Lord for help.

ᵇ**16.3** *Amorite . . . Hittite:* People who lived in Canaan before the Israelites and who worshiped idols.
ᶜ**16.4** *rubbed your skin with salt and olive oil:* People believed this toughened the skin of the babies.
ᵈ**16.8** *I covered your naked body with my own robe:* To show that he would protect and take care of her.
ᵉ**16.10** *most expensive robes:* One possible meaning for the difficult Hebrew text.   ᶠ**16.15** *so you offered yourself to every passerby:* One possible meaning for the difficult Hebrew text.   ᵍ**16.16** *These things should never have happened:* One possible meaning for the difficult Hebrew text.

● **16.38** *sentence you to . . . death:* According to the Law of Moses, the penalty for having sex with another's wife or husband could be death by stoning (Lev 20.10; Deut 23.22-27). Jerusalem's coming punishment (see 5.11-17; 14.21-23) is here described as that kind of punishment, because its people have been unfaithful to their husband, the LORD.

● **16.46-52** *sister was Samaria . . . Sodom . . . be disgraced:* Shortly after King Solomon died (931 B.C.), the northern kingdom of Israel was formed when ten of Israel's tribes broke away from the southern tribes. The southern tribes were known as Judah (see 1 Kgs 12). King Omri of Israel built the city of Samaria and made it the capital of the northern kingdom of Israel (1 Kgs 16.24). Samaria became known as an evil place, because many of its kings allowed and even encouraged the people to worship Baal, the Canaanite god of rain and fertility. Because of this sin, the LORD allowed Samaria and the northern kingdom to be destroyed by the Assyrians (see 2 Kgs 17.1-23). The ancient city of Sodom was destroyed because of its wicked people (Gen 18.16—19.29), and it became a symbol of evil for Israel (Isa 3.8,9; 13.19). Ezekiel says that Jerusalem's wickedness is even greater than that of these two evil cities.

self by having sex with anyone who walked by. And you did that more and more every day! **26**To make me angry, you even offered yourself to Egyptians, who were always ready to sleep with you.

27So I punished you by letting those greedy Philistine enemies take over some of your territory. But even they were offended by your repulsive behavior.

28You couldn't get enough sex, so you chased after Assyrians and slept with them. You still weren't satisfied, **29**so you went after Babylonians. But those merchants could not satisfy you either.

30I, the LORD God, say that you were so disgusting that you would have done anything to get what you wanted.^h **31**You had sex on every street corner, and when you finished, you refused to accept money. That's worse than being a prostitute! **32**You are nothing but an unfaithful wife who would rather have sex with strangers than with your own husband. **33**Prostitutes accept money for having sex, but you bribe men from everywhere to have sex with you. **34**You're not like other prostitutes. Men don't ask you for sex—you offer to pay them!

Jerusalem Must Be Punished

The LORD said:

35Jerusalem, you prostitute, listen to me. **36**You chased after lovers, then took off your clothes and had sex. You even worshiped disgusting idols and sacrificed your own children as offerings to them. **37**So I, the LORD God, will gather every one of your lovers, those you liked and those you hated. They will stand around you, and I will rip off your clothes and let all of those lovers stare at your nakedness. **38**I will find

you guilty of being an unfaithful wife and a murderer, and in my fierce anger I will sentence you to a violent death! **39**Then I will hand you over to your lovers, who will tear down the places where you had sex. They will take your clothes and jewelry, leaving you naked and empty-handed.

40Your lovers and an angry mob will stone you to death; they will cut your dead body into pieces **41**and burn down your houses. Other women will watch these terrible things happen to you. I promise to stop you from being a prostitute and paying your lovers for sex.

42Only then will I calm down and stop being angry and jealous. **43**You made me furious by doing all these disgusting things and by forgetting how I took care of you when you were young. Then you made things worse by acting like a prostitute. You must be punished! I, the LORD God, have spoken.

Jerusalem's Two Sisters

The LORD said:

44People will use this saying about you, Jerusalem: "If the mother is bad, so is her daughter." **45**You are just like your mother, who hated her husband and her own children. You are also like your sisters, who hated their husbands and children. Your father was an Amorite, and your mother was a Hittite.^i **46**Your older sister was Samaria, that city to your north with her nearby villages. Your younger sister was Sodom, that city to your south with her nearby villages. **47**You followed their way of life and their wicked customs, and soon you were more repulsive than they were.

48As surely as I am the living LORD God, the people of Sodom and its nearby villages

^h**16.30** *wanted:* One possible meaning for the difficult Hebrew text of verse 30.   ^i**16.45** *Amorite . . . Hittite:* See the note at 16.3.

were never as sinful as you. **49**They were arrogant and spoiled; they had everything they needed and still refused to help the poor and needy. **50**They thought they were better than everyone else, and they did things I hate. And so I destroyed them.

51You people of Jerusalem have sinned twice as much as the people of Samaria. In fact, your evil ways have made both Sodom and Samaria look innocent. **52**So their punishment will seem light compared to yours. You will be disgraced and put to shame because of your disgusting sins.

Jerusalem Will Be Ashamed

The LORD said to Jerusalem:
53Someday I will bless Sodom and Samaria and their nearby villages. I will also bless you, Jerusalem. **54**Then you will be ashamed of how you've acted, and Sodom and Samaria will be relieved that they weren't as sinful as you. **55**When that day comes, you and Sodom and Samaria will once again be well-off, and all nearby villages will be restored.

56Jerusalem, you were so arrogant that you sneered at Sodom. **57**But now everyone has learned how wicked you really are. The countries of Syria and Philistia, as well as your other neighbors, hate you and make insulting remarks. **58**You must pay for all the vulgar and disgusting things you have done. I, the LORD, have spoken.

The LORD Makes a Promise to Jerusalem

The LORD said:
59Jerusalem, you deserve to be punished, because you broke your promises and ig-

nored our agreement. **60**But I remember the agreement I made with you when you were young,[j] and so I will make you a promise that will last forever. **61**When you think about how you acted, you will be ashamed, especially when I return your sisters[k] to you as daughters, even though this was not part of our agreement.[l] **62**I will keep this solemn promise, and you will know that I am the LORD. **63**I will forgive you, but you will think about your sins and be too ashamed to say a word. I, the LORD God, have spoken.

A Story about Two Eagles and a Vine

17 The LORD said:
2Ezekiel, son of man, tell the people of Israel the following story, **3**so they will understand what I am saying to them:

A large eagle with strong wings and beautiful feathers once flew to Lebanon. It broke the top branch off a cedar tree, **4**then carried it to a nation of merchants and left it in one of their cities. **5**The eagle also took a seed from Israel and planted it in a fertile field with plenty of water, like a willow tree beside a stream.[m] **6**The seed sprouted and grew into a grapevine that spread over the ground. It had lots of leaves and strong, deep roots, and its branches grew upward toward the eagle.

7There was another eagle with strong wings and thick feathers. The roots and branches of the grapevine soon turned toward this eagle, hoping it would bring water for the soil. **8**But the vine was already growing in fertile soil, where there was plenty of water to produce healthy leaves and large grapes.

[j]*16.60 the agreement . . . when you were young:* See verse 8.   [k]*16.61 sisters:* Sodom and Samaria (see verses 44-52).   [l]*16.61 even though this was not part of our agreement:* One possible meaning for the difficult Hebrew text.   [m]*17.5 like a willow tree beside a stream:* One possible meaning for the difficult Hebrew text.

16.57 *Syria and Philistia:* These traditional enemies of Israel and Judah will join other countries in making fun of Jerusalem, even after it is restored.

16.59-63 *agreement . . . promise that will last forever . . . too ashamed:* The agreement (covenant) mentioned in verses 59 and 60 may refer to the ancient agreement the LORD made with Moses and the people of Israel at Sinai (Exod 19–40), or it may refer to the marriage agreement described in Ezekiel 16.8.

Agreements (Covenants)

17.2 *story:* The story is an allegory, in which the actions of animals and plants are compared to historical human actions or events.

17.3-6 *eagle . . . Lebanon . . . top branch off a cedar tree . . . branches grew:* The large eagle is Nebuchadnezzar, the king of Babylonia, who put down a rebellion in Jerusalem in 597 B.C. The cedar is a majestic tree that grew in the forests of Lebanon. Israel's King Solomon used cedars to build the temple and his palace in Jerusalem. The "top branch" refers to Judah's King Jehoiachin, who was taken captive to Babylonia, ("the nation of merchants.") The "seed" planted by the eagle refers to Zedekiah.

17.7-10 *another eagle . . . grapevine:* This second eagle refers to the ruler of Egypt (probably Pharaoh Psammetichus II). The seed (Zedekiah of Israel) turned into a grapevine and turned toward this new eagle for help. This represents Zedekiah's rebellion against the Babylonians.

Jerusalem, you deserve to be punished, because you broke your promises and ignored our agreement. EZEK 16.59

17.16-21 *king of Judah will die in Babylon:* Refers to Zedekiah, who made a sacred promise in the name of Israel's LORD to keep his treaty with Babylonia. When he asked for Egypt's help, he broke this promise and disgraced the LORD's name.

17.22-24 *the LORD . . . will cut a tender twig . . . green trees:* Meaning that the LORD will choose someone from Judah's royal family (cedar tree) and put him back on the throne in Jerusalem. Jerusalem's Mount Zion was not Israel's tallest mountain, but it was more important than all the others because the LORD's holy temple was located there.

Zion

18.2-4 *Sour grapes . . . Only those who sin:* This popular saying meant that children suffered because of the actions of their parents. However, that old saying will no longer be true. Each person will be judged by his or her sins, and not the sins of another generation.

[9]Now tell me, Ezekiel, do you think this grapevine will live? Or will the first eagle pull it up by its roots and pluck off the grapes and let its new leaves die? The eagle could easily kill it without the help of a large and powerful army. [10]The grapevine is strong and healthy, but as soon as the scorching desert wind blows, it will quickly wither.

The LORD Explains the Story

[11]The LORD said:

[12] Ezekiel, ask the rebellious people of Israel if they know what this story means.

Tell them that the king of Babylonia came to Jerusalem, then he captured the king of Judah[n] and his officials, and took them back to Babylon as prisoners. [13]He chose someone from the family of Judah's king[o] and signed a treaty with him, then made him swear to be loyal. He also led away other important citizens, [14]so that the rest of the people of Judah would obey only him and never gain control of their own country again.

[15]But this new king of Judah later rebelled against Babylonia and sent officials to Egypt to get horses and troops. Will this king be successful in breaking the treaty with Babylonia? Or will he be punished for what he's done?

[16] As surely as I am the living LORD God, I swear that the king of Judah will die in Babylon, because he broke the treaty with the king of Babylonia, who appointed him king. [17]Even the king of Egypt and his powerful army will be useless to Judah when the Babylonians attack and build towers and dirt ramps to destroy the cities of Judah and its people. [18]The king of Judah broke his own promises and ignored

the treaty with Babylonia. And so he will be punished!

[19]He made a promise in my name and swore to honor the treaty. And now that he has broken that promise, my name is disgraced. He must pay for what he's done. [20]I will spread out a net to trap him. Then I will drag him to Babylon and see that he is punished for his unfaithfulness to me. [21]His best troops[P] will be killed in battle, and the survivors will be scattered in every direction. I, the LORD, have spoken.

[22]Someday, I, the LORD,
  will cut a tender twig
    from the top of a cedar tree,
    then plant it on the peak
      of Israel's tallest mountain,
  [23]where it will grow
  strong branches
    and produce large fruit.
  All kinds of birds will find
    shelter under the tree,
  and they will rest in the shade
    of its branches.
[24]Every tree in the forest
  will know that I, the LORD,
  can bring down tall trees
    and help short ones grow.
I dry up green trees
  and make dry ones green.
I, the LORD, have spoken,
  and I will keep my word.

Those Who Sin Will Die

18 The LORD said:
[2]Ezekiel, I hear the people of Israel using the old saying,
  "Sour grapes eaten by parents
  leave a sour taste in the mouths
    of their children."

[n]17.12 *king of Judah:* Probably King Jehoiachin (see 2 Kings 24.10-12,15,16).   [o]17.13 *someone from the family of Judah's king:* Probably King Zedekiah (see 2 Kings 24.17).   [P]17.21 *best troops:* Two ancient translations; Hebrew "troops that ran away."

³Now tell them that I am the Lord God, and as surely as I live, that saying will no longer be used in Israel. ⁴The lives of all people belong to me—parents as well as children. However, only those who sin will be put to death.

⁵Suppose there is a truly good man who always does what is fair and right. ⁶He refuses to eat meat sacrificed to foreign gods at local shrines or to worship Israel's idols. He doesn't have sex with someone else's wife or with a woman having her monthly period. ⁷He never cheats or robs anyone and always returns anything taken as security for a loan; he gives food and clothes to the poor ⁸and doesn't charge interest when lending money. He refuses to do anything evil; he is fair to everyone ⁹and faithfully obeys my laws and teachings. This man is good, and I promise he will live.

¹⁰But suppose this good man has an evil son who is violent and commits sins ¹¹his father never did. He eats meat at local shrines, has sex with someone else's wife, ¹²cheats the poor, and robs people. He keeps what is given to him as security for a loan. He worships idols, does disgusting things, ¹³and charges high interest when lending money. An evil man like that will certainly not live. He is the one who has done these horrible sins, so it's his own fault that he will be put to death.

¹⁴But suppose this evil man has a son who sees his father do these things and refuses to act like him. ¹⁵He doesn't eat meat at local shrines or worship Israel's idols, and he doesn't have sex with someone else's wife. ¹⁶He never cheats or robs anyone and doesn't even demand security for a loan. He gives food and clothes to the poor ¹⁷and refuses to do anything evil⁹ or to charge interest. And he obeys all my laws and teachings. Such a man will live. His own father sinned, but this good man will not be put to death for the sins of his father. ¹⁸It is his father who will die for cheating and robbing and doing evil.

¹⁹You may wonder why a son isn't punished for the sins of his father. It is because the son does what is right and obeys my laws. ²⁰Only those who sin will be put to death. Children won't suffer for the sins of their parents, and parents won't suffer for the sins of their children. Good people will be rewarded for what they do, and evil people will be punished for what they do.

²¹Suppose wicked people stop sinning and start obeying my laws and doing right. They won't be put to death, ²²All their sins will be forgiven, and they will live because they did right. ²³I, the Lord God, don't like to see wicked people die. I had much rather see them turn back from their sins and live.

²⁴But when good people start sinning and doing disgusting things, will they live? No! All their good deeds will be forgotten, and they will be put to death because of their sins.

²⁵You people of Israel accuse me of being unfair! But listen—I'm not unfair; you are! ²⁶If good people start doing evil, they must be put to death, because they have sinned. ²⁷And if wicked people start doing right, they will save themselves from punishment. ²⁸They will think about what they've done and stop sinning, and so they won't be put to death. ²⁹But you still say that I am unfair. You are the ones who have done wrong and are unfair!

³⁰I will judge each of you for what you've done. So stop sinning, or else you will certainly be punished. ³¹Give up your evil ways and start thinking pure thoughts. And be faithful to me! Do you really want to be put to death for your sins? ³²I, the

⁹18.17 evil: One ancient translation; Hebrew "for the poor."

18.30-32 *stop sinning . . . and live:* Though most of Ezekiel's messages predict destruction and death for the people of Israel, this message opens the door for the people to come back to the Lord and receive forgiveness. To turn away from sin is sometimes called "repenting."

I, the Lord God, don't like to see wicked people die. I had much rather see them turn back from their sins and live. EZEK 18.23

19.1 *funeral song:* Though the verses in chapter 19 are in the form of a Hebrew funeral song, they are really a story (allegory) used to explain historical events.

19.1-4 *two of Israel's leaders . . . brave lioness . . . to Egypt:* The first of the two leaders (cubs) probably refers to Jehoahaz, the son of King Josiah and wife Hamutal (2 Kgs 23.28-32). The "lioness" may refer to Hamutal the mother of Zedekiah, or more likely to the tribe of Judah. Judah is elsewhere symbolized as a lion (Gen 49.8-10).

19.5-9 *another cub . . . to Babylonia:* The second lion cub may refer to Jehoiachin (grandson of King Josiah), who ruled Judah for only three months before he was taken as a prisoner to Babylonia. It may also mean Zedekiah (son of King Josiah and Hamutal), who was captured and taken prisoner to Babylonia in 587/6 B.C.

19.10-14 *Your mother was a vine . . . stripped bare:* This second allegory is probably meant to be related to the lion allegory (19.1-9) and the eagle and vine allegory in chapter 17. The vine probably refers to Judah or more generally to the line of kings descended from King David. Transplanting the vine in a hot, dry desert refers to the Israelite people being forced to live in exile in Babylonia or to the capture of Judah's kings.

LORD God, don't want to see that happen to anyone. So stop sinning and live!

A Funeral Song for Israel's Leaders

The LORD said:

19 Ezekiel, sing a funeral song for two of Israel's leaders:[r]

²Your mother was a brave lioness
    who raised her cubs
        among lions.
³She taught one of them to hunt,
    and he learned to eat people.
⁴When the nations heard of him,
    they trapped him in a pit,
then they used hooks
    to drag him to Egypt.

⁵His mother waited
    for him to return.
But soon she lost all hope
    and raised another cub,
    who also became fierce.
⁶He hunted with other lions
    and learned to eat people.
⁷He destroyed fortresses[s]
    and ruined towns;
his mighty roar
    terrified everyone.
⁸Nations plotted to kill him,
    and people came from all over
        to spread out a net
        and catch him in a trap.
⁹They put him in a cage
    and took him to Babylonia.
The lion was locked away,
    so that his mighty roar
would never again be heard
    on Israel's hills.

¹⁰Your mother was a vine like you,[t]
    growing near a stream.
There was plenty of water,
    so she was filled with branches
    and with lots of fruit.
¹¹Her strong branches
    became symbols of authority,
and she was taller
    than all other trees—
everyone could see how strong
    and healthy she was.
¹²But in anger, I pulled her up
    by the roots
and threw her to the ground,
    where the scorching desert wind
        dried out her fruit.
Her strong branches wilted
    and burned up.
¹³Then she was planted
    in a hot, dry desert,
¹⁴where her stem caught fire,
    and flames burned
        her branches and fruit.
Not one strong branch is left;
    she is stripped bare.

This funeral song must be sung with sorrow.

Israel Keeps On Rebelling

20 Seven years after King Jehoiachin and the rest of us had been led away as prisoners to Babylonia, some of Israel's leaders came to me on the tenth day of the fifth month.[u] They sat down and asked for a message from the LORD. ²Just then, the LORD God said:
³Ezekiel, son of man, these leaders have come to find out what I want them to do.

[r]**19.1** *two of Israel's leaders:* Probably Jehoahaz (ruled three months in 609 B.C.) and Jehoiachin (ruled three months in 598 B.C.) or Zedekiah (598–586 B.C.). [s]**19.7** *He destroyed fortresses:* One possible meaning for the difficult Hebrew text. [t]**19.10** *Your mother . . . like you:* One possible meaning for the difficult Hebrew text. [u]**20.1** *Seven years . . . fifth month:* Probably August of 591 B.C.

As surely as I live, I will not give them an answer of any kind.

⁴Are you willing to warn them, Ezekiel? Then remind them of the disgusting sins of their ancestors.

⁵Tell them that long ago I, the LORD God, chose Israel to be my own. I appeared to their ancestors in Egypt and made a solemn promise that I would be their God and the God of their descendants. ⁶I swore that I would rescue them from Egypt and lead them to a land I had already chosen. This land was rich with milk and honey and was the most splendid land of all. ⁷I told them to get rid of their disgusting idols and not to sin by worshiping the gods of Egypt. I reminded them that I was the LORD their God, ⁸but they still rebelled against me. They refused to listen and kept on worshiping their idols and foreign gods.

In my anger, I decided to punish the Israelites in Egypt. ⁹But that would have made me look like a liar, because I had already promised in front of everyone that I would lead them out of Egypt. ¹⁰So I brought them out and led them into the desert. ¹¹I gave them my laws and teachings, so they would know how to live right. ¹²And I commanded them to respect the Sabbath as a way of showing that they were holy and belonged to me. ¹³But the Israelites rebelled against me in the desert. They refused to obey my laws and teachings, and they treated the Sabbath like any other day.

Then in my anger, I decided to destroy the Israelites in the desert once and for all. ¹⁴But that would have disgraced me, because many other nations had seen me bring the Israelites out of Egypt. ¹⁵Instead, I told them in the desert that I would not lead them into the beautiful, fertile land I had promised. ¹⁶I said this because they

had not only ignored my laws and teachings, but had disgraced my Sabbath and worshiped idols.

¹⁷Yet, I felt sorry for them and could not let them die in the desert. ¹⁸So I warned the children not to act like their parents or follow their evil ways or worship their idols. ¹⁹I reminded them that I was the LORD their God and that they should obey my laws and teachings. ²⁰I told them to respect my Sabbath to show that they were my people and that I was the LORD their God. ²¹But the children also rebelled against me. They refused to obey my laws and teachings, and they treated the Sabbath as any other day.

I became angry and decided to punish them in the desert. ²²But I did not. That would have disgraced me in front of the nations that had seen me bring the Israelites out of Egypt. ²³So I solemnly swore that I would scatter the people of Israel across the nations, ²⁴because they had disobeyed my laws and ignored my teachings; they had disgraced my Sabbath and worshiped the idols their ancestors had made. ²⁵I gave them laws that bring punishment instead of life, ²⁶and I let them offer me unacceptable sacrifices, including their firstborn sons. I did this to horrify them and to let them know that I, the LORD, was punishing them.

²⁷Ezekiel, tell the people of Israel that their ancestors also rejected and insulted me ²⁸by offering sacrifices, incense, and wine to gods on every hill and under every large tree. I was very angry, because they did these things in the land I had given them! ²⁹I asked them where they went to worship those gods, and they answered, "At the local shrines."ᵛ And those places of worship are still called shrines.

ᵛ**20.29** *where they went to worship those gods . . . local shrines:* In Hebrew "where they went" sounds like "local shrines." These were places to worship foreign gods.

20.12 *Sabbath:* The Sabbath is the weekly day of rest that began at sunset on Friday when a ram's horn (shofar) was blown. It ended with a blessing (benediction) at sunset on Saturday. No work was to be done on the Sabbath, which means to "rest" or "stop working."

20.18-22 *warned the children . . . disgraced:* Though the second generation of Hebrews who came out of Egypt were allowed to enter Canaan, they and their descendants also rebelled. This rebellion took many forms in the centuries between the time the people entered the land and the time of the prophets, including Ezekiel.

20.33 *living LORD God . . . power-ful arm*: Israel's LORD was "living," and not like the idols made of wood and stone, which were lifeless and could not help the people. The LORD's powerful or outstretched arm is an image often used to describe the LORD's protection or power.

20.40-44 *When that day comes . . . know that I am the LORD*: The time of judgment (exile) would not last forever. Some of the Israelite people who had been scattered among the nations would be allowed to return to rebuild the temple on Mount Zion in Jerusalem. Then the people and their priests could once again offer holy sacrifices to honor the LORD. The restoration did begin in 538 B.C. when the Persian ruler named Cyrus defeated Babylonia and allowed the Israelite people living in exile to return home to Judah. The rebuilt temple was dedicated in 515 B.C. **(See the article After the Exile: God's People Return to Judea on pg 1789.)**

20.45-47 *turn toward the south . . . fire*: The locations in this short message about the burning forests are unclear. In Hebrew, the region known as the Negeb is mentioned, but it is a dry area to the south of Judah with few trees. Perhaps the far southern and northern borders of Israel are intended to emphasize the LORD's complete destruction of the land.

30Then ask the Israelites why they are following the example of their wicked ancestors 31by worshiping idols and by sacrificing their own children as offerings. They commit these sins and still think they can ask me for a message. As surely as I am the living LORD God, I will give them no answer. 32They may think they can be like other nations and get away with worshiping idols made of wood and stone. But that will never happen!

The LORD Promises To Restore Israel

The LORD said to the people of Israel:
33As surely as I am the living LORD God, I will rule over you with my powerful arm. You will feel my fierce anger 34and my power, when I gather you from the places where you are scattered 35and lead you into a desert surrounded by nations. I will meet you there face to face. Then I will pass judgment on you 36and punish you, just as I punished your ancestors in the desert near Egypt.[w] 37I will force each of you to obey the regulations of our solemn agreement. 38I will separate the sinful rebels from the rest of you, and even though I will bring them from the nations where they live in exile, they won't be allowed to return to Israel. Then you will know that I am the LORD.

39Go ahead and worship your idols for now, you Israelites, because soon I will no longer let you dishonor me by offering gifts to them. You will have no choice but to obey me![x] 40When that day comes, everyone in Israel will worship me on Mount Zion, my holy mountain in Jerusalem. I will once again call you my own, and I will accept your sacred offerings and sacrifices.

41When I bring you home from the places where you are now scattered, I will be pleased with you, just as I am pleased with the smell of the smoke from your sacrifices. Every nation on earth will see that I am holy, 42and you will know that I, the LORD, am the one who brought you back to Israel, the land I promised your ancestors. 43Then you will remember your wicked sins, and you will hate yourselves for doing such horrible things. They have made you unacceptable to me, 44so you deserve to be punished. But I will treat you in a way that will bring honor to my name, and you will know that I am the LORD God.

Fire from the South

45The LORD said, 46"Ezekiel, son of man, turn toward the south and warn the forests 47that I, the LORD God, will start a fire that will burn up every tree, whether green or dry. Nothing will be able to put out the blaze of that fire as it spreads to the north and burns everything in its path. 48Everyone will know that I started it, and that it cannot be stopped."

49But I complained, "LORD God, I don't want to do that! People already say I confuse them with my messages."

The LORD Will Punish Jerusalem

21 The LORD said: 2Ezekiel, son of man, condemn the places in Jerusalem where people worship. Warn everyone in Israel 3that I am about to punish them. I will pull out my sword and have it ready to kill everyone, whether good or evil. 4From south to north, people will die, 5knowing that my sword will never be put away.

[w]**20.36** *the desert near Egypt*: The Sinai Desert.   [x]**20.39** *me*: One possible meaning for the difficult Hebrew text of verse 39.

⁶Ezekiel, groan in sorrow and despair so that everyone can hear you. ⁷When they ask why you are groaning, tell them you have terrifying news that will make them faint and tremble in fear and lose all courage. These things will happen soon. I, the Lord God, make this promise!

A Sword Is Ready To Attack Israel

⁸The Lord said:

⁹⁻¹⁰Ezekiel, son of man, tell the people of Jerusalem:

I have sharpened my sword
to slaughter you;
it is shiny and will flash
like lightning!
Don't celebrate—
punishment is coming,
because everyone has ignored
my warnings.^y
¹¹My sword has been polished;
it's sharp and ready to kill.

¹²Groan in sorrow, Ezekiel;
the sword is drawn against
my people and their leaders.
They will die!
So give up all hope.
¹³I am testing my people,
and they can do nothing
to stop me.^z
I, the Lord, have spoken.

¹⁴Ezekiel, warn my people,
then celebrate my victory
by clapping your hands.
My vicious sword will attack
again and again,

killing my people
with every stroke.
¹⁵They will lose all courage
and stumble with fear.
My slaughtering sword
is waiting at every gate,
flashing and ready to kill.^a
¹⁶It will slash right and left,
wherever the blade is pointed.
¹⁷Then I will stop being angry,
and I will clap my hands
in victory.
I, the Lord, have spoken.

The King of Babylonia and His Sword

¹⁸The Lord said:

¹⁹Ezekiel, son of man, mark two roads for the king of Babylonia to follow when he comes with his sword. The roads will begin at the same place, but be sure to put up a signpost where the two roads separate and go in different directions. ²⁰Clearly mark where the two roads lead. One goes to Rabbah, the capital of Ammon, and the other goes to Jerusalem, the fortified capital of Judah. ²¹When the Babylonian king stands at that signpost, he will decide which way to go by shaking his arrows, by asking his idols, and by carefully looking at the liver of a sacrificed animal.^b ²²His right hand will pull out the arrow marked "Jerusalem." Then he will immediately give the signal to shout the battle cry, to build dirt ramps up to the top of the city walls, to break down its walls and gates with large wooden poles, and to kill the people. ²³Everyone in Jerusalem had promised to be loyal to Babylonia, and so none of them

21.6 *groan in sorrow:* Ezekiel was told to wail loudly, the way mourners did during funeral processions in ancient Israel. His wailing was meant to attract attention so he could give a message about the Lord's coming judgment against Judah, which would happen soon or in about four years.

21.19 *mark two roads:* Next, Ezekiel is to draw a map in the dirt showing two roads leading west from Babylonia, one going to Rabbah in Ammon and the other going to Jerusalem in Judah.

21.21,22 *shaking his arrows . . . shout the battle cry:* Babylonia's leaders often tried to find out what their gods wanted them to do by divining (examining fluid in a cup or looking at the liver of a sacrificed animal), by astrology (telling the future by observing the movement of the stars and planets), or by trying to contact the spirits of the dead. Here Nebuchadnezzar puts the names "Rabbah" and "Jerusalem" on different arrows. The direction he went also would be determined by the luck of the draw, though the Lord is actually directing Nebuchadnezzar to choose the Jerusalem arrow.

^y**21.9,10** *Don't celebrate . . . my warnings:* One possible meaning for the difficult Hebrew text. ^z**21.13** *I am testing . . . me:* One possible meaning for the difficult Hebrew text. ^a**21.15** *My slaughtering sword . . . ready to kill:* One possible meaning for the difficult Hebrew text. ^b**21.21** *shaking . . . animal:* These were ways the Babylonians found out what their gods wanted them to do.

21.25 *wicked ruler of Israel:* Meaning Zedekiah, who was Israel's ruler at the time of Ezekiel's prophecy.

21.27 *my chosen one:* King Nebuchadnezzar of Babylonia, Israel's enemy, is also the LORD's "chosen" one to punish Jerusalem.

22.7-12 *None . . . charge high interest:* The people of Jerusalem had disobeyed many of the Laws of Moses, including: dishonoring parents; cheating foreigners, widows, and orphans, who were protected by the Law; not respecting the temple by worshiping idols in the temple area; ignoring the Sabbath; eating meat sacrificed to idols; improper sexual behavior; accepting murder payoffs, and charging high interest.

will believe that this could happen to them. But Babylonia's king will remind them of their sinful ways and warn them of their coming captivity. ²⁴Ezekiel, tell the people of Jerusalem and their ruler that I, the LORD God, am saying:

Everything you do is wicked and shows how sinful you are. You are guilty and will be taken away as prisoners.

²⁵And now, you evil and wicked ruler of Israel, your day of final punishment is almost here. ²⁶I, the LORD God, command you to take off your royal turban and your crown, because everything will be different. Those who had no power will be put in charge, and those who now rule will become nobodies. ²⁷I will leave Jerusalem in complete ruins like no one has ever seen until my chosen one comes to punish this city.

Judgment against Ammon

²⁸The LORD God said:
Ezekiel, son of man, the Ammonites have insulted Israel, so condemn them and tell them I am saying:

A sword is drawn,
    ready to slaughter;
it is polished and prepared
    to kill as fast as lightning.

²⁹You wicked Ammonites see false visions and believe untrue messages. But your day of punishment is coming soon, and my sword will slaughter you!
³⁰Your days to punish others are over, so put your swords away.ᶜ You will be punished in the land of your birth. ³¹My furious anger will scorch you like fire, and I

will hand you over to cruel men who are experts in killing. ³²You will be burned and will die in your own land. Then you will be forgotten forever. I, the LORD, have spoken.

Jerusalem Is Condemned

22 Some time later, the LORD said:
²Ezekiel, son of man, are you ready to condemn Jerusalem? That city is filled with murderers, so remind the people of their sins ³and tell them I am saying:

Jerusalem, you have murdered many of your own people and have worshiped idols. You will soon be punished! ⁴Those crimes have made you guilty, and the idols have made you unacceptable to me. So your final punishment is near. Other nations will laugh at you and make insulting remarks, ⁵and people far and near will make fun of your misery.

⁶Your own leaders use their power to murder. ⁷None of you honor your parents, and you cheat foreigners, orphans, and widows. ⁸You show no respect for my sacred places and treat the Sabbath just like any other day. ⁹Some of your own people tell lies, so that others will be put to death. Some of you eat meat sacrificed to idols at local shrines, and others never stop doing vulgar things. ¹⁰Men have sex with their father's wife or with women who are having their monthly period ¹¹or with someone else's wife. Some men even sleep with their own daughter-in-law or half sister. ¹²Others of you accept money to murder someone. Your own people charge high interest when making a loan to other Israelites, and they get rich by cheating. Worst of all, you have forgotten me, the LORD God.

¹³I will shake my fist in anger at your violent crimes. ¹⁴When I'm finished with

ᶜ**21.30** *Your days . . . put your swords away:* One possible meaning for the difficult Hebrew text.

you, your courage will disappear, and you will be so weak that you won't be able to lift your hands. I, the LORD, have spoken and will not change my mind. [15]I will scatter you throughout every nation on earth and put a stop to your sinful ways. [16]You[d] will be humiliated in the eyes of other nations. Then you will know that I, the LORD God, have done these things.

Jerusalem Must Be Purified

[17]The LORD said:

[18]Ezekiel, son of man, I consider the people of Israel as worthless as the leftover metal in a furnace after silver has been purified. [19]So I am going to bring them together in Jerusalem. [20-21]I will be like a metalworker who collects that metal from the furnace and melts it down. I will collect the Israelites and blow on them with my fiery anger. They will melt inside the city of Jerusalem [22]like silver in a furnace. Then they will know that I, the LORD, have punished them in my anger.

Everyone in Jerusalem Is Guilty

[23]The LORD said:

[24]Ezekiel, son of man, tell the people of Israel that their country is full of sin, and that I, the LORD, am furious! [25]Their leaders are like[e] roaring lions, tearing apart their victims. They put people to death, then steal everything of value. Husbands are killed, and many women are left as widows.

[26]The priests of Israel ignore my Law! Not only do they refuse to respect any of my sacred things, but they don't even teach the difference between what is sacred and what is ordinary or between what is clean and what is unclean. They treat my Sabbath like any other day, and so my own people no longer honor me.

[27]Israel's officials are like ferocious wolves, ripping their victims apart. They make a dishonest living by injuring and killing people.

[28]And then the prophets in Israel cover up these sins by giving false visions. I have never spoken to them, but they lie and say they have a message from me. [29]The people themselves cheat and rob; they abuse the poor and take advantage of foreigners.

[30]I looked for someone to defend the city and to protect it from my anger, as well as to stop me from destroying it. But I found no one. [31]So in my fierce anger, I will punish the Israelites for what they have done, and they will know that I am furious. I, the LORD, have spoken.

Two Sinful Sisters

23 The LORD said:
[2]Ezekiel, son of man, listen to this story about two sisters. [3]While they were young and living in Egypt, they became prostitutes. [4]The older one was named Oholah, which stands for Samaria; the younger one was Oholibah, which stands for Jerusalem.[f] They became my wives and gave birth to my children.

[5]Even though Oholah was my wife, she continued to be a prostitute and chased after Assyrian lovers. [6]She offered herself to soldiers in purple uniforms: handsome, high-ranking officers and cavalry troops. [7]She had sex with all the important

---

[d]22.16 You: Hebrew; two ancient translations "Because of you, I." [e]22.25 Their leaders are like: One ancient translation; Hebrew "Their prophets are like herds of." [f]23.4 Samaria . . . Jerusalem: After the nation of Israel was divided, the northern kingdom was called "Israel," and the southern kingdom was called "Judah." Samaria was the capital of the northern kingdom, and Jerusalem was the capital of the southern kingdom.

22.18-22 *leftover metal . . . silver in a furnace:* Precious metals such as silver were purified by a process called refining or smelting. Metal ore was melted into a liquid, and the particles that were not pure silver (22.20-22) were separated out. This leftover metal (dross) was thrown away (22.18).

22.26 *priests of Israel ignore my Law:* The priests mentioned here were not keeping the temple area free of impure or unclean things.

Israel's Priests

Purity (Clean and Unclean)

23.2-4 *two sisters . . . Samaria . . . Jerusalem:* Ezekiel uses the image of the two cities as prostitutes to describe their unfaithfulness and their worship of foreign gods and idols.

23.5-10 *Oholah . . . killed her:* During the time of Assyria's control in the ancient Near East, they threatened Israel and its capital Samaria. Some of the northern kingdom's rulers made treaties with and paid bribe money to Assyria to keep from being attacked. Even worse, however, was the fact that Samaria's leaders allowed the people to worship foreign gods. Ezekiel is saying that Israel's dependence on Assyria (her "lovers") instead of on the LORD is as bad as the worst sexual sins. Eventually, Assyria's army destroyed Samaria (722–721 B.C.) and forced many people in Israel to leave their homes and live in foreign lands.

23.11-18 *Oholibah . . . chased af-*
ter . . . Assyrian officers . . . her older sis-
ter: To protect themselves, the southern
kingdom of Israel (Judah) also made
treaties with foreign countries, such as
Assyria and Babylonia.

23.20 *Egyptian men . . . sexual*
powers: Another reference to being attracted to the gods of Egypt. The danger in Ezekiel's day was that the people
of Judah who had been taken into exile
in Babylonia would start worshiping the
gods of the Babylonians.

23.23 *Babylonia and Assyria . . .*
Chaldean tribes: The Babylonians were
sometimes referred to as Chaldeans.
The Pekod tribe lived east of Babylonia,
but the exact identity of the Shoa and
Koa tribes is unknown. Babylonian and
Assyrian armies attacked Judah and Jerusalem from the north, using the best
routes from Mesopotamia.

23.25 *kill . . . burn alive:* Because
Jerusalem had acted like a prostitute
and was not a faithful wife to the LORD,
it would be put to death, the usual
penalty for adultery, according to the
Law of Moses.

23.31-34 *drink from the cup . . .*
every drop: Drinking from the LORD's
cup of anger is a common symbol for
God's judgment and punishment. Drinking every drop means receiving the full
amount of God's anger.

Assyrian officials and even worshiped their
disgusting idols. ⁸Once she started doing
these things in Egypt, she never stopped.
Men slept with her, and she was always
ready for sex.

⁹So I gave Oholah to the Assyrian lovers
she wanted so badly. ¹⁰They ripped off her
clothes, then captured her children and
killed her. Women everywhere talked about
what had happened to Oholah.

¹¹Oholibah saw all this, but she was
more sinful and wanted sex more than her
sister Oholah ever did. ¹²Oholibah also
chased after good-looking Assyrian officers,
uniformed soldiers, and cavalry troops.
¹³Just like her sister, she did vulgar things.

¹⁴But Oholibah behaved worse than her
sister. Oholibah saw images of Babylonian
men carved into walls and painted red.
¹⁵They had belts around their waists and
large turbans on their heads, and they reminded her of Babylonian cavalry officers.
¹⁶As soon as she looked at them, she
wanted to have sex with them. And so, she
sent messengers to bring them to her.
¹⁷Men from Babylonia came and had sex
with her so many times that she got disgusted with them. ¹⁸She let everyone see
her naked body and didn't care if they
knew she was a prostitute. That's why I
turned my back on her, just as I had done
with her older sister.

¹⁹Oholibah didn't stop there, but became even more immoral and acted as she
had back in Egypt. ²⁰She eagerly wanted to
go to bed with Egyptian men, who were famous for their sexual powers. ²¹And she
longed for the days when she was a young
prostitute, when men enjoyed caressing
her body.

The LORD Will Punish Oholibah

²²The LORD God said:

Oholibah,ᵍ though you no longer want
to be around your lovers, they will surround you like enemies, when I turn them
against you. ²³I will gather all the handsome young officials and the high-ranking
cavalry officers from Babylonia and Assyria, as well as from the Chaldean tribes of
Pekod, Shoa, and Koa. ²⁴Their large armies
will come from the northʰ with chariots
and wagons carrying weapons. They will
wear shields and helmets and will surround you, and I will let them judge and
sentence you according to their own laws.
²⁵I am angry with you, so I will let them be
very cruel. They will cut off your nose and
ears; they will kill your children and burn
alive anyone in your family who survives.
²⁶Your clothes and jewelry will be torn off.
²⁷I will stop your wickedness and the prostitution you started back in Egypt. You will
never want to think about those days again.

²⁸I, the LORD God, am ready to hand you
over to those hateful enemies that you find
so disgusting. ²⁹They will cruelly take
away everything you have worked for and
strip you naked. Then everyone will see
you for the prostitute you really are. Your
own vulgar sins ³⁰have led to this. You
were the one determined to have sex with
men from other nations and to worship
their idols. ³¹You have turned out no better than your older sister, and now you
must drink from the cup filled with my
anger.

³²I, the LORD God, gave your sister a
large, deep cup filled with my anger. And
when you drink from that cup, you will be
mocked and insulted. ³³You will end up
drunk and devastated, because that cup is

ᵍ23.22 *Oholibah:* That is, Jerusalem (see verse 4).   ʰ23.24 *from the north:* One ancient translation;
Hebrew "with weapons."

filled with horror and ruin. **34**But you must drink every drop! Then smash the cup and chew on its broken pieces. Use them to cut your breasts in sorrow. I, the LORD God, have spoken.

35You have completely rejected me, and so I promise that you will be punished for the disgusting things you did as a prostitute.

The Two Sisters Are Condemned

36The LORD said:

Ezekiel, son of man, it's time for you to tell Oholah and Oholibah[i] that they are guilty. Remind them of their evil ways! **37**They have been unfaithful by worshiping idols, and they have committed murder by sacrificing my own children as offerings to idols. **38-39**They came into my temple that same day, and that made it unfit as a place to worship me. They have even stopped respecting the Sabbath.

40They sent messengers to attract men from far away. When those men arrived, the two sisters bathed themselves and put on eye shadow and jewelry. **41**They sat on a fancy couch, and in front of them was a table for the olive oil and incense that had belonged to me. **42**Their room was always filled with a noisy crowd of drunkards brought in from the desert. These men gave the women bracelets and beautiful crowns, **43**and I noticed that the men were eager to have sex with these women, though they were exhausted from being prostitutes.[j] **44**In fact, the men had sex over and over with Oholah and Oholibah, the two sinful sisters. **45**But honest judges will someday accuse those two of murder

and of being unfaithful, because they are certainly guilty.

46So I, the LORD God, now say to these sisters:

I will call together an angry mob that will abuse and rob you. **47**They will stone you to death and cut you to pieces; they will kill your children and burn down your houses. **48**I will get rid of sinful prostitution in this country, so that women everywhere will be warned not to act as you have. **49**You will be punished for becoming prostitutes and for worshiping idols. Then you will know that I am the LORD God.

A Cooking Pot

24 Nine years after King Jehoiachin and the rest of us had been led away as prisoners to Babylonia, the LORD spoke to me on the tenth day of the tenth month.[k] He said:

2 Ezekiel, son of man, write down today's date, because the king of Babylonia has just begun attacking the city of Jerusalem. **3**Then tell my rebellious people:

"Pour water in a cooking pot
    and set it over a fire.
* **4**Throw[l] in the legs and shoulders
    of your finest sheep
    and put in the juicy bones.
5"Pile wood[m] underneath the pot,
    and let the meat and bones
        boil until they are done."

6These words mean that Jerusalem is doomed! The city is filled with murderers and is like an old, rusty pot. The meat is taken out piece by piece, and no one cares

[i]**23.36** *Oholah and Oholibah:* That is, Samaria and Jerusalem (see verse 4).   [j]**23.43** *prostitutes:* One possible meaning for the difficult Hebrew text of verse 43.   [k]**24.1** *Nine years . . . tenth month:* Probably January of 588 B.C.   [l]**24.4** *Throw:* When an asterisk (*) occurs before a verse number, it indicates that this verse and the following have been combined.   [m]**24.5** *Pile wood:* Or "Stack the bones."

24.16 *the person you love most:* Ezekiel's wife (24.19), who had suddenly become so sick that she was close to death.

24.20-25 *destroy the temple . . . their children:* The Babylonians returned to destroy Jerusalem and its temple in 587/6 B.C. By not mourning in the "expected" way, Ezekiel got the attention of his neighbors. He warned that they would soon mourn for Jerusalem the way he mourned for his wife. The people living in exile in Babylonia would be so shocked when they heard about the temple's destruction and about the deaths of the children they had left behind in 597 B.C. that they would only be able to walk around and groan. They would realize that their sins had caused this terrible tragedy.

24.26,27 *someone will escape . . . speak again:* The LORD told Ezekiel that one of the people who escapes Jerusalem's destruction in 587/6 B.C. will reach Babylonia with the bad news. When Ezekiel heard the news, he would be able to speak again. Ezekiel's prophecies and actions in the first part of the book have focused on the coming destruction of Jerusalem. After the Jerusalem tragedy is reported, Ezekiel continues to warn his people, but the focus of his message changes.

what happens to it.[n] [7]The people of Jerusalem murdered innocent people in the city and didn't even try to cover up the blood that flowed out on the hard ground. [8]But I have seen that blood, and it cries out for me to take revenge.

[9]I, the LORD God, will punish that city of violence! I will make a huge pile of firewood, [10]so bring more wood and light it. Cook the meat and boil away the broth[o] to let the bones scorch. [11]Then set the empty pot over the hot coals until it is red-hot. That will clean the pot and burn off the rust. [12]I've tried everything else. Now the rust must be burned away.[p]

[13]Jerusalem is so full of sin and evil that I can't get it clean, even though I have tried. It will stay filthy until I let loose my fierce anger against it. [14]That time will certainly come! And when it does, I won't show the people of Jerusalem any pity or change my mind. They must be punished for the evil they have done. I, the LORD God, have spoken.

Ezekiel's Wife Dies

[15]The LORD said, [16]"Ezekiel, son of man, I will suddenly take the life of the person you love most. But I don't want you to complain or cry. [17]Mourn in silence and don't show that you are grieving. Don't remove your turban or take off your sandals; don't cover your face to show your sorrow, or eat the food that mourners eat."[q]

[18]One morning, I was talking with the people as usual, and by sunset my wife was dead. The next day I did what the LORD had told me, [19]and when people saw me, they asked, "Why aren't you mourning for your wife?"

[20]I answered:

The LORD God says [21]he is ready to destroy the temple in which you take such pride and which makes you feel so safe. Your children who now live in Jerusalem will be killed. [22]Then you will do the same things I have done. You will leave your face uncovered and refuse to eat the food that mourners usually eat. [23]You won't take off your turbans and your sandals.[r] You won't cry or mourn, but all day long you will go around groaning because of your sins.

[24]I am a warning sign—everything I have done, you will also do. And then you will know the LORD God has made these things happen.

[25]The LORD said, "Ezekiel, I will soon destroy the temple that makes everyone feel proud and safe, and I will take away their children as well. [26]On that same day, someone will escape from the city and come to tell you what has happened. [27]Then you will be able to speak again,[s] and the two of you will talk. You will be a warning sign to the people, and they will know that I am the LORD."

[n]**24.6** *and no one cares what happens to it:* One possible meaning for the difficult Hebrew text. [o]**24.10** *boil away the broth:* One ancient translation; Hebrew "mix the spices." [p]**24.12** *away:* One possible meaning for the difficult Hebrew text of verse 12. [q]**24.17** *Don't remove your turban . . . take off your sandals . . . cover your face . . . eat the food that mourners eat:* The usual way people mourned was to remove anything worn on the head, to go barefoot, to cover their faces, and to eat special food to show they were grieving. [r]**24.22,23** *You will leave your face uncovered . . . refuse to eat the food . . . won't take off your turbans and your sandals:* See the note at 24.17. [s]**24.27** *you will be able to speak again:* See 3.25-27; 33.21,22.

Judgment on Ammon

25 The Lord God said: ²Ezekiel, son of man, condemn the people of Ammon ³and tell them:

You celebrated when my temple was destroyed, when Israel was defeated, and when my people were taken away as prisoners. ⁴Now I am going to let you be conquered by tribes from the eastern desert. They will set up their camps in your land and eat your fruit and drink your milk. ⁵Your capital city of Rabbah will be nothing but pasture-land for camels, and the rest of the country will be pastures for sheep. Then you will know that I am the Lord God.

⁶You hated Israel so much that you clapped and shouted and celebrated. ⁷And so I will hand you over to enemies who will rob you. I will completely destroy you. There won't be enough of your people left to be a nation ever again, and you will know that I, the Lord, have done these things.

Judgment on Moab

⁸The Lord God said, "The people of Moab[t] thought Judah was no different from any other nation. ⁹So I will let Moab's fortress towns along its border be attacked, including Beth-Jeshimoth, Baal-Meon, and Kiriathaim. ¹⁰The same eastern desert tribes that invade Ammon will invade Moab, and just as Ammon will be forgotten forever, ¹¹Moab will be punished. Then the people there will know that I am the Lord."

Judgment on Edom

¹²The Lord God then said, "The people of Edom are guilty of taking revenge on Judah. ¹³So I will punish Edom by killing all its people and livestock. It will be an empty wasteland all the way from Teman to Dedan. ¹⁴I will send my own people to take revenge on the Edomites by making them feel my fierce anger. And when I punish them, they will know that I am the Lord God."

Judgment on Philistia

¹⁵The Lord God said, "The cruel Philistines have taken revenge on their enemies over and over and have tried to destroy them. ¹⁶Now it's my turn to treat the Philistines as my enemies and to kill everyone[u] living in their towns along the seacoast. ¹⁷In my fierce anger, I will take revenge on them. And when I punish them, they will know that I am the Lord."

Judgment on the City of Tyre

26 Eleven years[v] after King Jehoiachin and the rest of us had been led away as prisoners to Babylonia, the Lord spoke to me on the first day of the month. He said: ²Ezekiel, son of man, the people of the city of Tyre[w] have celebrated Jerusalem's defeat by singing,

"Jerusalem has fallen!
It used to be powerful,
   a center of trade.
Now the city is shattered,
   and we will take its place."

[t]25.8 *Moab:* One ancient translation; Hebrew "Moab and Edom." [u]25.16 *kill everyone:* The Hebrew text also has the name "Cherethites," which was a group of people that lived just southeast of Philistia, and was often identified with the Philistines. [v]26.1 *Eleven years:* Probably late in 587 B.C. [w]26.2 *Tyre:* One of the two major cities of Phoenicia; Sidon was the other.

25.2 *Ammon:* Ammon would be punished by "tribes from the eastern desert" (meaning Babylonia or Persia), because Ammon celebrated when the Babylonians destroyed the temple in Jerusalem. According to 2 Kings 24.2 some troops from Ammon and Moab joined the Babylonian troops when they first invaded Judah in 597 B.C.

25.8-11 *Moab:* Like the Ammonites, the people of Moab were traditional enemies of Israel. In Ezekiel's day, the Moabites were to be punished because they said that Judah and its people were not really special to the Lord.

25.12,13 *Edom:* The nation of Edom is usually described in the Bible as an enemy of Israel.

25.15 *Philistines:* People who lived on a strip of land bordered by the Mediterranean Sea on the west and Judah on the east. The Philistine people often battled the people of Israel. It is not clear how, but it is possible that the Philistines profited in some way from the destruction of Judah and Jerusalem.

26.2 *city of Tyre:* Tyre was an important seaport city in Phoenicia. Tyre celebrated Jerusalem's destruction for economic reasons. If Jerusalem was no longer a major center for trade, more nations would come to Tyre to do business.

Phoenicia

26.3-14 *nations to attack . . . dry their nets*: The Assyrians had invaded Phoenicia in 734 B.C. and again in 701 B.C. King Nebuchadnezzar of Babylonia surrounded and tried to blockade the city for 13 years. He finally captured the mainland part of the city of Tyre in 572 B.C. The long Babylonian invasion caused many deaths and the loss of much property. Alexander the Great of Macedonia captured Tyre in 332 B.C.

26.19-20 *ocean depths . . . the world of the dead*: The ocean itself will cover the city and take its people to the "world of the dead," also known as *Sheol*, the underground world inhabited by the dead. This is a place of total silence where no one knows or feels anything (Job 10.21,22; Ps 88.12; 94.17; Isa 44.23). Tyre's destruction was not as complete as Ezekiel's prophecy suggests, but its power and freedom were greatly reduced.

[3]Because the people of Tyre have sung that song, I have the following warning for them: I am the LORD God, and I am now your enemy! I will send nations to attack you, like waves crashing against the shore. [4]They will tear down your city walls and defense towers. I will sweep away the ruins until all that's left of you is a bare rock, [5]where fishermen can dry their nets along the coast. I promise that you will be robbed [6]and that the people who live in your towns along the coast will be killed. Then you will know that I am the LORD.

[7]King Nebuchadnezzar of Babylonia is the world's most powerful king, and I will send him to attack you. He will march from the north with a powerful army, including horses and chariots and cavalry troops. [8]First, he will attack your towns along the coast and kill the people who live there. Then he will build dirt ramps up to the top of your city walls and set up rows of shields around you. [9]He will command some of his troops to use large wooden poles to beat down your walls, while others use iron rods to knock down your watchtowers. [10]He will have so many horses that the dust they stir up will seem like a thick fog. And as his chariots and cavalry approach, even the walls will shake, especially when he proudly enters your ruined city. [11]His troops will ride through your streets, killing people left and right, and your strong columns will crumble to the ground. [12]The troops will steal your valuable possessions; they will break down your walls, and crush your expensive houses. Then the stones and wood and all the remains will be dumped into the sea. [13]You will have no reason to sing or play music on harps, [14]because I will turn you into a bare rock where fishermen can dry their nets. And you will never rebuild your city. I, the LORD God, make this promise.

[15]The people of the nations up and down the coast will shudder when they hear your screams and moans of death. [16]The kings will step down from their thrones, then take off their royal robes and fancy clothes, and sit on the ground, trembling. They will be so shocked at the news of your defeat that they will shake in fear [17]and sing this funeral song:

"The great city beside the sea
  is destroyed![x]
Its people once ruled the coast
  and terrified everyone there.
 [18]But now Tyre is in ruins,
  and the people on the coast
  stare at it in horror
  and tremble in fear."

[19]I, the LORD God, will turn you into a ghost-town. The ocean depths will rise over you [20]and carry you down to the world of the dead, where you will join people of ancient times and towns ruined long ago. You will stay there and never again be a city filled with people.[y] [21]You will die a horrible death! People will come looking for your city, but it will never be found. I, the LORD, have spoken.

A Funeral Song for Tyre

27 The LORD said:
   [2]Ezekiel, son of man, sing a funeral song for Tyre,[z] [3]the city that is built along the sea and that trades with nations along the coast. Tell the people of Tyre that the following message is from me:

[x]**26.17** *The great city . . . is destroyed*: One possible meaning for the difficult Hebrew text. [y]**26.20** *You will stay there . . . with people*: One possible meaning for the difficult Hebrew text. [z]**27.2** *Tyre*: See the note at 26.2.

Tyre, you brag about
your perfect beauty,
⁴ and your control of the sea.^a

You are a ship
built to perfection.
⁵Builders used cypress trees
from Mount Hermon
to make your planks
and a cedar tree from Lebanon
for your tall mast.
⁶Oak trees from Bashan
were shaped into oars;
pine trees from Cyprus^b
were cut for your deck,
which was then decorated
with strips of ivory.
⁷The builders used fancy linen
from Egypt for your sails,
so everyone could see you.
Blue and purple cloth
from Cyprus was used
to shade your deck.
⁸Men from Sidon and Arvad
did the rowing,
and your own skilled workers
were the captains.
⁹Experienced men from Byblos
repaired any damages.
Sailors from all over
shopped at the stores
in your port.

¹⁰Brave soldiers from Persia,
Lydia, and Libya
served in your navy,
protecting you with shields

and helmets,
and making you famous.
¹¹Your guards came from
Arvad and Cilicia,
and men from Gamad
stood watch in your towers.
With their weapons
hung on your walls,
your beauty was complete.

¹²Merchants from southern Spain^c traded silver, iron, tin, and lead for your products. ¹³The people of Greece, Tubal, and Meshech traded slaves and things made of bronze, ¹⁴and those from Beth-Togarmah traded work horses, war horses, and mules. ¹⁵You also did business with people from Rhodes,^d and people from nations along the coast gave you ivory and ebony^e in exchange for your goods. ¹⁶Edom^f traded emeralds, purple cloth, embroidery, fine linen, coral, and rubies. ¹⁷Judah and Israel gave you their finest wheat, fancy figs,^g honey, olive oil, and spices in exchange for your merchandise. ¹⁸The people of Damascus saw what you had to offer and brought you wine from Helbon and wool from Zahar. ¹⁹Vedan and Javan near Uzal^h traded you iron and spices. ²⁰The people of Dedan supplied you with saddle blankets, ²¹while people from Arabia and the rulers of Kedar traded lambs, sheep, and goats. ²²Merchants from Sheba and Raamah gave you excellent spices, precious stones, and gold in exchange for your products. ²³You also did business with merchants from the cities of Haran, Canneh, Eden, Sheba, Asshur, and Chilmad, ²⁴and they gave you

^a**27.4** *and your control of the sea*: One possible meaning for the difficult Hebrew text.   ^b**27.6** *pine trees from Cyprus*: One possible meaning for the difficult Hebrew text.   ^c**27.12** *southern Spain*: The Hebrew text has "Tarshish," which may have been a Phoenician city in southern Spain.   ^d**27.15** *Rhodes*: One ancient translation; Hebrew "Dedan."   ^e**27.15** *ebony*: A valuable black wood.   ^f**27.16** *Edom*: Some Hebrew manuscripts and one ancient translation; most Hebrew manuscripts "Syria."   ^g**27.17** *their finest wheat, fancy figs*: One possible meaning for the difficult Hebrew text.   ^h**27.19** *Vedan and Javan near Uzal*: One possible meaning for the difficult Hebrew text.

27.5,6 *trees*: The ships built in Tyre used the best woods from all over the ancient Near East. Cypress (a form of pine) and the tall cedar trees which grew in the forests of Lebanon were used to build royal palaces, including the temple and palace of King Solomon (1 Kgs 5.3-9; 7.1-12). Assyrian and Babylonian kings also cut down cedars and used them for building (Isa 37.24). Mount Hermon was located in the far north of Israel near the border of southern Lebanon. Bashan, a region east of the Jordan River and north of Gilead, was famous for its many large oak trees, which were a source of solid and valuable wood. Cyprus is a large island in the Mediterranean Sea to the northwest of Tyre.

27.7 *fancy linen from Egypt . . . purple cloth*: The ships of Tyre made their sails out of linen, a fine cloth woven out of the dried fibers of the flax plant, and cloth from the island of Cyprus that had been dyed purple, using "ink" from the crushed shells of large sea snails.

27.8-11 *Sidon and Arvad . . . Gamad*: Tyre's merchant navy also attracted workers, sailors, and soldiers from all over. Sidon, Arvad, and Byblos (also known as Gebal) were important coastal cities of Phoenicia, located north of Tyre. Soldiers came from the northeast (Persia, or modern-day Iraq), the north (Lydia, a province in Asia Minor), and the southwest (Libya, a province in northern Africa). Cilicia is a region in southeast Asia Minor. The location of Gamad is uncertain, but may be in northern Asia Minor.

27.29-31 *Every ship is deserted . . . dress in sackcloth:* The crew members from Tyre's sunken ships mourn in the traditional way by putting dust on their heads, smearing themselves with ashes, cutting their hair, and wearing sackcloth.

28.2-10 *king of Tyre . . . think you're a god . . . don't worship me:* Tyre had its own king, but just which ruler is meant here is not clear. The king will be punished because he is arrogant and acts like a god. The people of Tyre worshiped the Canaanite gods, including the chief god known as El, who was described as living in a place where rivers and deep waters come together. Tyre comes close to fitting such a description. The king will drown in a watery grave, just the way the city will be covered by the ocean's depths (26.19-21). Some think this judgment message also has to do with Israel's LORD overthrowing the gods of Tyre.

expensive clothing, purple and embroidered cloth, brightly colored rugs, and strong rope. [i]25Large, seagoing ships carried your goods wherever they needed to go.

You were like a ship
loaded with heavy cargo
26   and sailing across the sea,
but you were wrecked
by strong eastern winds.
27Everything on board was lost—
your valuable cargo,
your sailors and carpenters,
merchants and soldiers.
28The shouts of your drowning crew
were heard on the shore.

29Every ship is deserted;
rowers and sailors and captains
all stand on shore,
30   mourning for you.
They show their sorrow
by putting dust on their heads
and rolling in ashes;
31they shave their heads
and dress in sackcloth[j]
as they cry in despair.
32In their grief they sing
a funeral song for you:
"Tyre, you were greater
than all other cities.
But now you lie in silence
at the bottom of the sea.[k]

33"Nations that received
your merchandise
were always pleased;
kings everywhere got rich
from your costly goods.
34But now you are wrecked
in the deep sea,
with your cargo and crew
scattered everywhere.
35People living along the coast
are shocked at the news.
Their rulers are horrified,
and terror is written
across their faces.
36The merchants of the world
can't believe what happened.
Your death was gruesome,
and you are gone forever."

Judgment on the King of Tyre

28 The LORD God said: 2Ezekiel, son of man, tell the king of Tyre[l] that I am saying:

You are so arrogant that you think you're a god and that the city of Tyre is your throne. You may claim to be a god, though you're nothing but a mere human. 3You think you're wiser than Daniel[m] and know everything.[n]

4Your wisdom has certainly made you rich, because you have storehouses filled with gold and silver. 5You're a clever businessman and are extremely wealthy, but your wealth has led to arrogance!

6You compared yourself to a god, so now I, the LORD God, 7will make you the victim of cruel enemies. They will destroy all the possessions you've worked so hard to get. 8Your enemies will brutally kill you, and the sea will be your only grave.

9When you face your enemies, will you still claim to be a god? They will at-

[i]27.25 *Large, seagoing ships:* The Hebrew text has "Ships of Tarshish," which may have been a Phoenician city in Spain. "Ships of Tarshish" probably means large, seagoing ships.   [j]27.31 *sackcloth:* See the note at 7.18.   [k]27.32 *Tyre, you were greater . . . the bottom of the sea:* One possible meaning for the difficult Hebrew text.   [l]28.2 *Tyre:* See the note at 26.2.   [m]28.3 *Daniel:* See the note at 14.14.   [n]28.3 *and know everything:* One possible meaning for the difficult Hebrew text.

tack, and you will suffer like any other human. [10]Foreigners will kill you, and you will die the death of those who don't worship me. I, the Lord, have spoken.

A Funeral Song for the King of Tyre

[11]The Lord said: [12]Ezekiel, son of man, sing a funeral song for the king of Tyre[o] and tell him I am saying:

At one time, you were perfect,[p] intelligent, and good-looking. [13]You lived in the garden of Eden and wore jewelry made of brightly colored gems and precious stones. They were all set in gold[q] and were ready for you on the day you were born. [14]I appointed a winged creature to guard your home[r] on my holy mountain, where you walked among gems that dazzled like fire.

[15]You were truly good from the time of your birth, but later you started doing wicked things. [16]You traded with other nations and became more and more cruel and evil. So I forced you to leave my mountain, and the creature that had been your protector now chased you away from the jewels.

[17]It was your good looks that made you arrogant, and you were so famous that you started acting like a fool. That's why I threw you to the ground and let other kings sneer at you. [18]You have cheated so many other merchants that your places of worship are corrupt. So I set your city on fire and

burned it down. Now everyone sees only ashes where your city once stood, [19]and the people of other nations are shocked. Your punishment was horrible, and you are gone forever.

Judgment on Sidon and Peace for Israel

[20]The Lord said: [21]Ezekiel, son of man, condemn the city of Sidon[s] [22]and tell its people:

I, the Lord God, am your enemy! People will praise me when I punish you, and they will see that I am holy. [23]I will send deadly diseases to wipe you out, and I will send enemies to invade and surround you. Your people will be killed, and you will know that I am the Lord.

[24]When that happens, the people of Israel will no longer have cruel neighbors that abuse them and make them feel as though they are in a field of thorns and briers. And the Israelites will know that I, the Lord God, have done these things.

A Blessing for Israel

[25]The Lord God said:

Someday I will gather the people of Israel from the nations where they are now scattered, and every nation will see that I am holy. The Israelites will once again live in the land I gave to my servant Jacob. [26]They will be safe and will build houses and plant vineyards. They will no longer be in danger, because I will punish their hateful

---

[o]28.12 *Tyre*: See the note at 26.2.   [p]28.12 *you were perfect*: One possible meaning for the difficult Hebrew text.   [q]28.13 *They were all set in gold*: One possible meaning for the difficult Hebrew text.   [r]28.14 *I appointed a winged creature to guard your home*: One possible meaning for the difficult Hebrew text.   [s]28.21 *Sidon*: See the note at 26.2.

■ 28.12-19 *a funeral song for the king of Tyre . . . gone forever*: The downfall of Tyre's king is described in a way that recalls the way the first human beings sinned and were forced to leave the Garden of Eden. Though he was good at birth, he started doing evil things, so he was forced to leave the Lord's "holy mountain," a phrase that described the home of the gods in the Canaanite religion. Some believe that Ezekiel meant this allegory about Tyre's fallen ruler to have a double meaning. In the Hebrew text of 28.13, all the brightly-colored gems and precious stones are named individually, and they match the stones in the breastpiece worn by Israel's high priest (see Exod 28.15-21). The "winged creature" is similar to the creatures that guarded the Garden of Eden (Gen 3.24), but it also is similar to the winged creatures on the sacred chest in the most holy place in the temple. Finally, because the Lord's "holy mountain" could also be Zion, some think this allegory is also about the downfall of Israel's high priest in Jerusalem. Taken this way, Ezekiel's Jewish neighbors living in exile may have heard this message about Tyre's king and recognized their own sins and resulting downfall.

● 28.25 *my servant Jacob*: Another name for the people of Israel. Jacob's name was changed to Israel after he wrestled with God (Gen 32.22-28). The people of Israel were descendants of Jacob's sons and two of his grandsons. The God of Jacob is the Lord (*Yahweh*), who chose the Israelite people to be his own people (Deut 7.6-8; Isa 2.3; 41.8,9; 43.1).

King of Egypt (Pharaoh)

29.3-5 *giant crocodile . . . fish . . . left unburied:* Egypt's ruler is compared to one of the large crocodiles that lived along the banks of the Nile River. The "fish" that stick to the crocodile probably refer to the king's officials and priests who will be removed from power and destroyed along with the king. Ancient Egyptian kings were usually honored as gods with big funerals, and placed in huge tombs, such as the pyramids. But this king would suffer the terrible humiliation of being left unburied.

29.8-12 *troops to attack you . . . Egypt will lie in ruins . . . 40 years:* Probably refers to the Babylonian troops under the command of Nebuchadnezzar. Though the Babylonians likely battled and won a victory over the Egyptians around the time of Jerusalem's fall, there is no record of a full-scale invasion and destruction of Egypt by the Babylonians. But the idea of Egypt's destruction from Migdol in the northern delta region to Aswan in Ethiopia in the far south compares to the total destruction that was to occur in Israel.

29.13,14 *bring your people back . . . weak kingdom:* It is not clear if a major exile occurred in Egypt. War in ancient times often caused defeated people to be captured as slaves or to become refugees.

neighbors. Israel will know that I am the LORD their God.

Judgment on the King of Egypt

29 Ten years after King Jehoiachin and the rest of us had been led away as prisoners to Babylonia, the LORD spoke to me on the twelfth day of the tenth month.[t] He said: [2]Ezekiel, son of man, condemn the king of Egypt. Tell him and his people [3]that I am saying:

King of Egypt, you were like a giant crocodile lying in a river. You acted as though you owned the Nile and made it for yourself. But now I, the LORD God, am your enemy! [4]I will put a hook in your jaw and pull you out of the water, and all the fish in your river will stick to your scaly body.[u] [5]I'll throw you and the fish into the desert, and your body will fall on the hard ground. You will be left unburied,[v] and wild animals and birds will eat your flesh. [6]Then everyone in Egypt will know that I am the LORD.

You and your nation refused to help the people of Israel and were nothing more than a broken stick. [7]When they reached out to you for support, you broke in half, cutting their arms and making them fall.[w]

[8]So I, the LORD God, will send troops to attack you, king of Egypt. They will kill your people and livestock, [9]until your land is a barren desert. Then you will know that I have done these things.

You claimed that you made the Nile River and control it. [10]Now I am turning against you and your river. Your nation will be nothing but an empty wasteland all the way from the town of Migdol in the north to Aswan in the south, and as far as the border of Ethiopia.[x] [11]No human or animal will even dare travel through Egypt, because no sign of life will be found there for 40 years. [12]It will be the most barren place on earth. Every city in Egypt will lie in ruins during those 40 years, and I will scatter your people throughout the nations of the world.

[13]Then after those 40 years have passed, I will bring your people back from the places where I scattered them. [14]They will once again live in their homeland in southern Egypt. But they will be a weak kingdom [15]and won't ever be strong enough to rule nations, as they did in the past. [16]My own people Israel will never again depend on your nation. In fact, when the Israelites remember what happened to you Egyptians, they will realize how wrong they were to turn to you for help. Then the Israelites will know that I, the LORD God, did these things.

King Nebuchadnezzar of Babylonia Will Conquer Egypt

[17]Twenty-seven years after King Jehoiachin and the rest of us had been led away as prisoners to Babylonia, the LORD spoke to

[t]**29.1** *Ten years . . . tenth month:* Probably January of 587 B.C. [u]**29.4** *all the fish in your river will stick to your scaly body:* All the king's officials will be removed from power and destroyed along with the king himself. [v]**29.5** *You will be left unburied:* A proper burial in a royal tomb was extremely important to Egyptian kings, because they often thought of themselves as gods. [w]**29.7** *making them fall:* One possible meaning for the difficult Hebrew text. [x]**29.10** *Ethiopia:* The Hebrew text has "Cush," which was a region south of Egypt that included parts of the present countries of Ethiopia and Sudan.

me on the first day of the first month.ʸ He said:

¹⁸King Nebuchadnezzar of Babylonia has attacked the city of Tyre. He forced his soldiers to carry so many heavy loads that their heads were rubbed bald, and their shoulders were red and sore. Nebuchadnezzar and his army still could not capture the city. ¹⁹So now I will hand over the nation of Egypt to him. He will take Egypt's valuable treasures and give them to his own troops. ²⁰Egypt will be his reward, because he and his army have been following my orders. I, the LORD God, have spoken.

²¹Ezekiel, when Egypt is defeated, I will make the people of Israel strong, and I will give you the power to speak to them. Then they will know that I, the LORD, have done these things.

Egypt Will Be a Barren Desert

30 The LORD said: ²Ezekiel, son of man, tell the people of Egypt that I am saying:

Cry out in despair,
³because you will soon
be punished!
That will be a time
of darkness and doom
for all nations.
⁴Your own nation of Egypt
will be attacked,
and Ethiopiaᶻ will suffer.
You will be killed in battle,
and your land will be robbed
and left in ruins.

⁵Soldiers hired from Ethiopia, Libya, Lydia, Arabia, Kub, as well as from Israel,ᵃ

will die in that battle. ⁶All of your allies will be killed, and your proud strength will crumble. People will die from Migdol in the north to Aswan in the south. I, the LORD, have spoken.

⁷Your nation of Egypt will be the most deserted place on earth, and its cities will lie in complete ruin. ⁸I will set fire to your land, and anyone who defended your nation will die. Then you will know that I am the LORD.

⁹On the same day I destroy Egypt, I will send messengers to the Ethiopians to announce their coming destruction. They think they are safe, but they will be terrified.

¹⁰Your Egyptian army is very strong, but I will send King Nebuchadnezzar of Babylonia to completely defeat that army. ¹¹He and his cruel troops will invade and destroy your land and leave your dead bodies piled everywhere.

¹²I will dry up the Nile River, then sell the land to evil buyers. I will send foreigners to turn your entire nation into a barren desert. I, the LORD, have spoken.

Egypt's Proud Cities Will Lie in Ruins

The LORD said to the people of Egypt:

¹³All the idols and images you Egyptians worship in the city of Memphisᵇ will be smashed. No one will be left to rule your nation, and terror will fill the land. ¹⁴The city of Pathros will be left in ruins, and Zoan will be burned to the ground. Thebes,ᶜ your capital city, will also be destroyed! ¹⁵The fortress city of Pelusium will feel my fierce anger, and all the troops stationed at Thebes will be slaughtered.

29.18-20 *Nebuchadnezzar . . . attacked . . . Tyre . . . Egypt will be his reward:* This prophecy takes place just a year or two after Nebuchadnezzar's attack on Tyre. Nebuchadnezzar did send raids into Egypt, but Babylonia did not destroy all of Egypt. Egypt's defeat opened the way for Israel to become strong again (29.21). Ezekiel apparently did not live to see Jerusalem and its temple rebuilt.

30.3 *a time of darkness and doom:* The day of the LORD's coming judgment is often accompanied by darkness. The judgment day of the LORD is a common theme in many of the prophets.

Day of the LORD

30.5 *Ethiopia . . . Kub . . . Israel:* These countries may refer to Egypt's allies in battle against the enemy Babylonia.

30.10-12 *I will send King Nebuchadnezzar . . . dry up the Nile River:* Nebuchadnezzar of Babylonia is the one who was to bring destruction to Egypt. But the death caused by his troops won't be any worse than the death and starvation that will occur when the Nile River dries up.

30.13-18 *Memphis . . . Tahpanhes:* A number of Egypt's major cities will be destroyed. **(See Map 7 on pg 1885.)**

Egypt

ʸ**29.17** *Twenty-seven . . . first month:* Probably March of 571 B.C.   ᶻ**30.4** *Ethiopia:* See the note at 29.10.
ᵃ**30.5** *as well as from Israel:* One possible meaning for the difficult Hebrew text.   ᵇ**30.13** *Memphis:* Hebrew "Noph."   ᶜ**30.14** *Thebes:* Hebrew "No."

30.21-26 *LORD . . . defeated the king of Egypt:* When the Babylonian army surrounded Jerusalem in 588 B.C., King Hophra of Egypt sent troops to help Judah rebel against Babylonia, but the powerful Babylonian army overpowered the Egyptian troops. The Egyptian king's "broken arm" is a symbol for his army's total defeat.

31.2-9 *king of Egypt . . . a cedar tree:* Ezekiel's message to the Egyptian king and people begins as a story (allegory) about a tall cedar tree that grew in the forests of Lebanon. Verse 9 makes it clear that it was the LORD who made the tree beautiful and strong.

[16]I will set fire to your nation of Egypt! The city of Pelusium will be in anguish. Thebes will fall, and the people of Memphis will live in constant fear.[d] [17]The young soldiers in the cities of Heliopolis and Bubastis[e] will die in battle, and the rest of the people will be taken prisoner. [18]You were so proud of your nation's power, but when I crush that power and kill that pride, darkness will fall over the city of Tahpanhes. A dark, gloomy cloud will cover the land as you are being led away into captivity. [19]When I'm through punishing Egypt, you will know that I am the LORD.

Egypt's King Is Powerless

[20]Eleven years after King Jehoiachin and the rest of us had been led away as prisoners to Babylonia, the LORD spoke to me on the seventh day of the first month.[f] He said: [21]Ezekiel, son of man, I, the LORD, have defeated the king of Egypt! I broke his arm, and no one has wrapped it or put it in a sling, so that it could heal and get strong enough to hold a sword. [22]So tell him that I am now his worst enemy. I will break both his arms—the good one and the broken one! His sword will drop from his hand forever, [23]and I will scatter the Egyptians all over the world.

[24-25]I will strengthen the power of Babylonia's king and give him my sword to use against Egypt. I will also make the wounded king of Egypt powerless, and he will moan in pain and die in front of the Babylonian king. Then everyone on earth will know that I am the LORD. [26]I will force the Egyptians to live as prisoners in foreign nations, and they will know that I, the LORD, have punished them.

Egypt's King Will Be Chopped Down like a Cedar Tree

31 Eleven years after King Jehoiachin and the rest of us had been led away as prisoners to Babylonia, the LORD spoke to me on the first day of the third month.[g] He said:

[2]Ezekiel, son of man, tell the king of Egypt and his people that I am saying:

You are more powerful
    than anyone on earth.
    Now listen to this.
[3]There was once a cedar tree
    in Lebanon
with large, strong branches
    reaching to the sky.[h]
[4]This tree had plenty of water
    to help it grow tall,
and nearby streams watered
    the other trees
    in the forest.
[5]But this tree towered over
    those other trees,
    and its branches
    grew long and thick.
[6]Birds built nests
    in its branches,
and animals were born
    beneath it.
People from all nations
    lived in the shade
    of this strong tree.

[7]It had beautiful,
    long branches,
and its roots found water
    deep in the soil.
[8]None of the cedar trees
    in my garden of Eden

[d]**30.16** *the people of Memphis . . . constant fear:* One possible meaning for the difficult Hebrew text. [e]**30.17** *Heliopolis and Bubastis:* Hebrew "On and Pi-Beseth." [f]**30.20** *Eleven years . . . first month:* Probably March of 587 B.C. [g]**31.1** *Eleven years . . . third month:* Probably May of 587 B.C. [h]**31.3** *sky:* One possible meaning for the difficult Hebrew text of verse 3.

were as beautiful
   as this tree;
no tree of any kind
   had such long branches.
⁹I, the Lord, gave this tree
   its beauty,
and I helped the branches
   grow strong.
All other trees in Eden
   wanted to be just like it.

¹⁰King of Egypt, now listen to what I, the Lord God, am saying about that tree:

The tree grew so tall that it reached the sky[i] and became very proud and arrogant. ¹¹So I, the Lord God, will reject the tree and hand it over to a foreign ruler, who will punish it for its wickedness. ¹²Cruel foreigners will chop it down and leave it wherever it falls. Branches and broken limbs will be scattered over the mountains and in the valleys. The people living in the shade of those branches will go somewhere else. ¹³Birds will then nest on the stump of the fallen tree, and wild animals will trample its branches.

¹⁴Never again will any tree dare to grow as tall as this tree, no matter how much water it has. Every tree must die, just as humans die and go down to the world of the dead.

¹⁵On the day this tree dies and goes to the world below, I, the Lord God, will command rivers and streams to mourn its death. Every underground spring of water and every river will stop flowing.[j] The mountains in Lebanon will be covered with darkness as a sign of their sorrow, and all the trees in the forest will wither. ¹⁶This tree will crash

to the ground, and I will send it to the world below. Then the nations of the earth will tremble.

The trees from Eden and the choice trees from Lebanon are now in the world of the dead, and they will be comforted when this tree falls. ¹⁷Those people who found protection in its shade will also be sent to the world below, where they will join the dead.[k]

¹⁸King of Egypt, all these things will happen to you and your people! You were like this tree at one time—taller and stronger than anyone on earth. But now you will be chopped down, just as every tree in the garden of Eden must die. You will be sent down to the world of the dead, where you will join the godless and the other victims of violent death. I, the Lord God, have spoken.

A Funeral Song for the King of Egypt

32 Twelve years after King Jehoiachin and the rest of us had been led away as prisoners to Babylonia, the Lord spoke to me on the first day of the twelfth month.[l] He said:

²Ezekiel, son of man, condemn the king of Egypt and tell him I am saying:

You act like a lion
   roaming the earth;
but you are nothing more than
   a crocodile in a river,
churning up muddy water
   with your feet.

³King of Egypt, listen to me. I, the Lord God, will catch you in my net and let a crowd of foreigners drag you to shore. ⁴I

31.10-13 *tree . . . became . . . proud . . . chop it down:* The cedar tree corresponds to Egypt and its arrogant and proud king. The Lord allowed a foreign ruler to chop it down. The birds nesting in the tree and the people in the tree's shade probably stand for Egypt's allies, who relied on Egypt's army for help.

31.14-17 *world of the dead . . . below:* The dark underground place also known as *Sheol*. The Lord would send the tree down to the world of the dead along with those who relied on the tree for protection.

31.18 *King of Egypt . . . your people . . . to the world of the dead:* Egypt's destruction will be complete. The Egyptian king, who was considered a god in Egyptian religion, would end up in the world of the dead, where he would discover that he was human after all.

୦୪   Hell

32.2 *crocodile:* The Hebrew word translated "crocodile" is *tannin,* a great sea monster like Leviathan (Isa 27.1) or Rahab (Job 7.12). The image of the Lord catching the water monster in a net is similar to battle scenes of Babylonian mythology in which Marduk, the Babylonian god of creation, catches the great sea monster Tiamat in a net, kills her, and then chops her up.

[i]31.10 *the sky:* One ancient translation; Hebrew "over the thick branches." [j]31.15 *rivers and streams . . . stop flowing:* One possible meaning for the difficult Hebrew text. [k]31.17 *dead:* One possible meaning for the difficult Hebrew text of verse 17. [l]32.1 *Twelve years . . . twelfth month:* Probably February of 585 b.c.

32.22-23 *soldiers from Assyria:* Assyria was the most powerful nation in the Near East for over 200 years until it was defeated at Nineveh in 612 B.C. by the Babylonians, who then took over as the main power in the region.

32.24-27 *soldiers from Elam . . . Meshech and Tubal . . . proper burial:* Elam was a kingdom to the east of Babylonia and the Tigris River. It was defeated by the Assyrians around 650 B.C. Meshech and Tubal probably refer to areas of Asia Minor. Soldiers from all these warring countries would die in battle and not receive proper burial. To be unburied was considered a terrible thing. Some believed the spirits of the unburied dead could never rest in peace.

will throw you into an open field, where birds and animals will come to feed on your flesh. [5]I will spread your rotting flesh[m] over the mountains and in the valleys, [6]and your blood will flow throughout the land and fill up the streams. [7]I will cover the whole sky and every star with thick clouds, so that the sun and moon will stop shining. [8]The heavens will become black, leaving your country in total darkness. I, the Lord God, have spoken.

[9]Foreign nations you have never heard of will be shocked when I tell them how I destroyed you.[n] [10]They will be horrified, and when I flash my sword in victory on the day of your death, their kings will tremble in the fear of what could happen to them.

[11]The king of Babylonia is coming to attack you, king of Egypt! [12]Your soldiers will be killed by the cruelest army in the world, and everything you take pride in will be crushed. [13]I will slaughter your cattle that graze by the river,[o] and no people or livestock will be left to muddy its water. [14]The water will be clear, and streams will be calm. I, the Lord God, have spoken.

[15]Egypt will become a barren wasteland, and no living thing will ever survive there. Then you and your people will know that I am the Lord.

[16]This is your warning, and it will be used as a funeral song by foreign women to mourn the death of your people. I, the Lord God, have spoken.

A Sad Ending for Egypt

[17]On the fifteenth day of that same month,[p] the Lord said:

[18]Ezekiel, son of man, mourn for the Egyptians and condemn them to the world of the dead, where they will be buried alongside the people of other powerful nations.[q] [19]Say to them:

You may be more beautiful
than the people
    of other nations,
but you will also die
and join the godless
    in the world below.

[20]You cannot escape! The enemy's sword is ready to slaughter every one of you.[r] [21]Brave military leaders killed in battle will gladly welcome you and your allies into the world of the dead.

[22-23]The graves of soldiers from Assyria are there. They once terrified people, but they were killed in battle and now lie deep in the world of the dead.[s]

[24-25]The graves of soldiers from Elam are there. The very sight of those godless soldiers once terrified their enemies and made them panic. But now they are disgraced and ashamed as they lie in the world of the dead, alongside others who were killed in battle.

[26]The graves of soldiers from Meshech and Tubal are there. These godless soldiers who terrified people were all killed in battle. [27]They were not given a proper burial like the heroes of long ago,[t] who were

[m]32.5 *rotting flesh:* One possible meaning for the difficult Hebrew text.   [n]32.9 *when I tell them how I destroyed you:* Hebrew; one ancient translation "when I scatter you like prisoners among them."   [o]32.13 *the river:* This possibly refers to the Nile River.   [p]32.17 *that same month:* See verse 1.   [q]32.18 *where they will be buried . . . powerful nations:* One possible meaning for the difficult Hebrew text.   [r]32.20 *The enemy's sword . . . you:* One possible meaning for the difficult Hebrew text.   [s]32.22,23 *deep in the world of the dead:* The place of greatest dishonor.   [t]32.27 *heroes of long ago:* One ancient translation; Hebrew "godless heroes."

buried with their swords under their heads and with their shields[u] over their bodies. These were the heroes who made their enemies panic.

28 You Egyptians will be cruelly defeated, and you will be buried alongside these other godless soldiers who died in battle.

29 The graves of kings and leaders from Edom are there. They were powerful at one time. Now they are buried in the world of the dead with other godless soldiers killed in battle.

30 The graves of the rulers of the north[v] are there, as well as those of the Sidonians. Their powerful armies once terrified enemies. Now they lie buried in the world of the dead, where they are disgraced like other soldiers killed in battle.

31 The Lord God says:

When your king of Egypt sees all of these graves, he and his soldiers will be glad they are not the only ones suffering. 32 I sent him to terrify people all over the earth. But he and his army will be killed and buried alongside other godless soldiers in the world of the dead. I, the Lord God, have spoken.

The Lord Appoints Ezekiel To Stand Watch
(Ezekiel 3.16-21)

33 The Lord said:
2 Ezekiel, son of man, warn your people by saying:

Someday, I, the Lord, may send an enemy to invade a country. And suppose its people choose someone to stand watch 3 and to sound a warning signal when the enemy is seen coming.

4-5 If any of these people hear the signal and ignore it, they will be killed in battle. But it will be their own fault, because they could have escaped if they had paid attention.

6 But suppose the person watching fails to sound the warning signal. The enemy will attack and kill some of the sinful people in that country, and I, the Lord, will hold that person responsible for their death.

7 Ezekiel, I have appointed you to stand watch for the people of Israel. So listen to what I say, then warn them for me. 8 When I tell wicked people they will die because of their sins, you must warn them to turn from their sinful ways. But if you refuse to warn them, you are responsible for their death. 9 If you do warn them, and they keep sinning, they will die because of their sins, and you will be innocent.

The Lord Is Always Fair
(Ezekiel 18.21-30)

10 The Lord said:

Ezekiel, son of man, the people of Israel are complaining that the punishment for their sins is more than they can stand. They have lost all hope for survival, and they blame me. 11 Tell them that as surely as I am the living Lord God, I don't like to see wicked people die. I enjoy seeing them turn from their sins and live. So if the Israelites want to live, they must stop sinning and turn back to me.

12 Tell them that when good people start sinning, all the good they did in the past cannot save them from being punished. And remind them that when wicked people stop sinning, their past sins will be

● 33.2-7 *someone to stand watch . . . for the people*: Watchmen stood on the walls of cities and warned people if they saw an enemy approaching. The Lord appointed Ezekiel as Israel's watchman, to warn the people of their sins.

■ 33.11 *turn from their sins and live*: The people of Israel living in exile have already suffered for their sins, but Ezekiel is told to continue telling the present generation to turn back to the Lord.

[u] 32.27 *shields*: One possible meaning for the difficult Hebrew text.   [v] 32.30 *the rulers of the north*: Probably the Phoenicians.

33.24 *Abraham . . . whole land of Israel:* The LORD made an agreement with Israel's first ancestor, Abraham. If Abraham trusted and obeyed the LORD, he and his descendants would receive their own land, namely Canaan (Gen 12.1-3; 17.1-8). This promise was repeated to Moses (Exod 6.2-8).

Land

completely forgiven, and they won't be punished.

¹³Suppose I promise good people that they will live, then later they start sinning and believe they will be saved by the good they did in the past. These people will certainly be put to death because of their sins. Their good deeds will be forgotten. ¹⁴Suppose I warn wicked people that they will die because of their sins, and they stop sinning and start doing right. ¹⁵For example, they need to return anything they have taken as security for a loan and anything they have stolen. Then if they stop doing evil and start obeying my Law, they will live. ¹⁶Their past sins will be forgiven, and they will live because they have done right.

¹⁷Ezekiel, your people accuse me of being unfair. But they are the ones who are unfair. ¹⁸If good people start doing evil, they will be put to death, because they have sinned. ¹⁹And if wicked people stop sinning and start doing right, they will save themselves from punishment. ²⁰But the Israelites still think I am unfair. So warn them that they will be punished for what they have done.

The News of Jerusalem's Fall

²¹ Twelve years after King Jehoiachin and the rest of us had been led away as prisoners to Babylonia, a refugee who had escaped from Jerusalem came to me on the fifth day of the tenth month.ʷ He told me that the city had fallen. ²²The evening before this man arrived at my house, the LORD had taken control of me. So when the man came to me the next morning, I could once again speak.ˣ

What Will Happen to Those Left in Israel?

²³Then the LORD said:

²⁴Ezekiel, son of man, the people living in the ruined cities of Israel are saying, "Abraham was just one man, and the LORD gave him this whole land of Israel. There are many of us, and so this land must be ours." ²⁵So, Ezekiel, tell them I am saying:

How can you think the land is still yours? You eat meat with blood in it and worship idols. You commit murder ²⁶and spread violence throughout the land. Everything you do is wicked; you are even unfaithful in marriage. And you claim the land is yours!

²⁷As surely as I am the living LORD God, you people in the ruined cities will be killed in battle. Those of you living in the countryside will be eaten by wild animals, and those hiding in caves and on rocky cliffs will die from deadly diseases. ²⁸I will make the whole country an empty wasteland and crush the power in which you take such pride. Even the mountains will be bare, and no one will try to cross them. ²⁹I will punish you because of your sins, and I will turn your nation into a barren desert. Then you will know that I am the LORD.

The People Listen, but Don't Change

The LORD said:

³⁰Ezekiel, son of man, the people with you in Babylonia talk about you when they meet by the city walls or in the doorways of their houses. They say, "Let's ask Ezekiel

ʷ**33.21** *Twelve years . . . tenth month:* Probably December of 586 B.C.　　ˣ**33.22** *I could once again speak:* See 3.27.

what the LORD has said today." [31]So they all come and listen to you, but they refuse to do what you tell them. They claim to be faithful, but they are forever trying to cheat others out of their money. [32]They treat you as though you were merely singing love songs or playing music. They listen, but don't do anything you say.

[33]Soon they will be punished, just as you warned, and they will know that a prophet has been among them.

Israel's Leaders Are Worthless Shepherds

34 The LORD God said:
[2]Ezekiel, son of man, Israel's leaders are like shepherds taking care of my sheep, the people of Israel. But I want you to condemn these leaders and tell them:

I, the LORD God, say you shepherds of Israel are doomed! You take care of yourselves while ignoring my sheep. [3]You drink their milk and use their wool to make your clothes. Then you butcher the best ones for food. But you don't take care of the flock! [4]You have never protected the weak ones or healed the sick ones or bandaged those that get hurt. You let them wander off and never look for those that get lost. You are cruel and mean to my sheep. [5]They strayed in every direction, and because there was no shepherd to watch them, they were attacked and eaten by wild animals. [6]So my sheep were scattered across the earth. They roamed on hills and mountains, without anyone even bothering to look for them.

[7-8]Now listen to what I, the living LORD God, am saying to you shepherds. My sheep have been attacked and eaten by wild animals, because you refused to watch them. You never went looking for the lost ones, and you fed yourselves without feeding my sheep. [9-10]So I, the LORD, will punish you! I will rescue my sheep from you and never let you be their shepherd again or butcher them for food. I, the LORD, have spoken.

The LORD Is the Good Shepherd

[11]The LORD God then said:
I will look for my sheep and take care of them myself, [12]just as a shepherd looks for lost sheep. My sheep have been lost since that dark and miserable day when they were scattered throughout the nations.[y] But I will rescue them [13]and bring them back from the foreign nations where they now live. I will be their shepherd and will let them graze on Israel's mountains and in the valleys and fertile fields. [14]They will be safe as they feed on grassy meadows and green hills. [15]I promise to take care of them and keep them safe, [16]to look for those that are lost and bring back the ones that wander off, to bandage those that are hurt and protect the ones that are weak. I will also slaughter[z] those that are fat and strong, because I always do right.

Judgment on the Strong Sheep

[17]The LORD God said to his sheep, the people of Israel:
I will carefully watch each one of you to decide which ones are the strong sheep and which ones are weak. [18]Some of you eat

---

[y]**34.12** *dark and miserable day . . . nations:* That is, the day the Babylonians defeated Jerusalem and led its people away as prisoners.   [z]**34.16** *slaughter:* Hebrew; three ancient translations "take care of."

● **34.2-10** *Israel's leaders are like shepherds . . . butcher them:* Shepherds protected their flocks. Many of Israel's leaders had not been good shepherds, and because of their evil and neglectful ways, the sheep (the people of Israel) were killed or scattered across the earth. The LORD will punish those shepherds (leaders) who failed to be good shepherds.

● **34.13:** *I will be their shepherd:* The image of the LORD as a shepherd repeats throughout the Bible (see also Gen 49.24; Ps 23; 80.1; Isa 40.11; John 10.11; Heb 13.20).

The LORD God then said: I will look for my sheep and take care of them myself, just as a shepherd looks for lost sheep.
EZEK 34.11,12

34.25 *they will live in peace:* The Hebrew word here translated as "peace" is *shalom,* which means "well-being." It means the absence of war, but also includes good health and blessings.

Peace

34.26-30 *I will bless them . . . everyone will know:* Ezekiel's promise of a time of peace and blessing contrasts with his earlier prophecies of doom and punishment. Once again, the Lord will protect Israel in order to show other nations that the Lord is Israel's shepherd.

the greenest grass, then trample down what's left when you finish. Others drink clean water, then step in the water to make the rest of it muddy. ¹⁹That means my other sheep have nothing fit to eat or drink.

²⁰So I, the Lord God, will separate you strong sheep from the weak. ²¹You strong ones have used your powerful horns to chase off those that are weak, ²²but I will rescue them and no longer let them be mistreated. I will separate the good from the bad.

²³After that, I will give you a shepherd from the family of my servant King David. All of you, both strong and weak, will have the same shepherd, and he will take good care of you. ²⁴He will be your leader, and I will be your God. I, the Lord, have spoken.

A Bright Future for the Lord's Sheep

The Lord God said:

²⁵The people of Israel are my sheep, and I solemnly promise that they will live in peace. I will chase away every wild animal from the desert and the forest, so my sheep will not be afraid. ²⁶They will live around my holy mountain,ᵃ and I will bless them by sending more than enough rain ²⁷to make their trees produce fruit and their crops to grow. I will set them free from slavery and let them live safely in their own land. Then they will know that I am the Lord. ²⁸Foreign nations will never again rob them, and wild animals will no longer kill and eat them. They will have nothing to fear. ²⁹I will make their fields produce large amounts of crops, so they will never again go hungry or be laughed at by foreigners. ³⁰Then everyone will know that I protect my people Israel. I, the Lord, make

this promise. ³¹They are my sheep; I am their God, and I take care of them.

Edom Will Be a Wasteland

35 The Lord said:
²Ezekiel, son of man, condemn the people of Edomᵇ ³and say to them:
I, the Lord God,
am now your enemy!
And I will turn your nation
into an empty wasteland,
⁴ leaving your towns in ruins.
Your land will be a desert,
and then you will know
that I am the Lord.

⁵People of Edom, not only have you been Israel's longtime enemy, you simply watched when disaster wiped out its people as punishment for their sins. ⁶And so, as surely as I am the living Lord God, you are guilty of murder and must be put to death. ⁷I will destroy your nation and kill anyone who travels through it. ⁸Dead bodies will cover your mountains and fill up your valleys, ⁹and your land will lie in ruins forever. No one will live in your towns ever again. You will know that I am the Lord.

¹⁰You thought the nations of Judah and Israel belonged to you, and that you could take over their territory. But I am their God, ¹¹and as surely as I live, I will punish you for treating my people with anger and hatred. Then they will know that I, the Lord, am punishing you! ¹²And you will finally realize that I heard you laugh at their destruction and say their land was yours to take. ¹³You even insulted me, but I heard it all.

¹⁴Everyone on earth will celebrate when

ᵃ**34.26** *my holy mountain:* That is, Mount Zion in Jerusalem. ᵇ**35.2** *Edom:* The Hebrew text has "Mount Seir," another name for Edom.

I destroy you, ¹⁵just as you celebrated when Israel was destroyed. Your nation of Edom will be nothing but a wasteland. Then everyone will know that I am the Lord.

A Message for Israel's Mountains

36 The Lord said:
Ezekiel, son of man, tell the mountains of Israel ²that I, the Lord God, am saying:

Your enemies sneered and said that you mountains belonged to them. ³They ruined and crushed you from every side, and foreign nations captured and made fun of you. ⁴So all you mountains and hills, streams and valleys, listen to what I will do. Your towns may now lie in ruins, and nations may laugh and insult you. ⁵But in my fierce anger, I will turn against those nations, and especially the Edomites, because they laughed at you the loudest and took over your pasturelands. ⁶You have suffered long enough, and, I, the Lord God, am very angry! Nations have insulted you, ⁷so I will now insult and disgrace them. That is my solemn promise.

⁸Trees will grow on you mountains of Israel and produce fruit for my people, because they will soon come home. ⁹I will take care of you by plowing your soil and planting crops on your fertile slopes. ¹⁰The people of Israel will return and rebuild your ruined towns and live in them. ¹¹Children will be born, and animals will give birth to their young. You will no longer be deserted as you are now, but you will be covered with people and treated better than ever. Then you will know that I am the Lord.

¹²I will bring my people Israel home, and they will live on you mountains, because you belong to them, and your fertile slopes will never again let them starve. ¹³It's true

that you have been accused of not producing enough food and of letting your people starve. ¹⁴⁻¹⁵But I, the Lord, promise that you won't hear other nations laugh and sneer at you ever again. From now on, you will always produce plenty of food for your people. I, the Lord God, have spoken.

The Lord Will Be Honored

¹⁶The Lord said:
¹⁷Ezekiel, son of man, when the people of Israel were living in their own country, they made the land unclean by the way they behaved, just as a woman's monthly period makes her unclean. ¹⁸They committed murders and worshiped idols, which made the land even worse. So in my anger, I punished my people ¹⁹and scattered them throughout the nations, just as they deserved. ²⁰Wherever they went, my name was disgraced, because foreigners insulted my people by saying I had forced them out of their own land.

²¹I care what those foreigners think of me, ²²so tell the Israelites that I am saying:

You have disgraced my holy name among the nations where you now live. So you don't deserve what I'm going to do for you. I will lead you home to bring honor to my name ²³and to show foreign nations that I am holy. Then they will know that I am the Lord God. I have spoken.

²⁴I will gather you from the foreign nations and bring you home. ²⁵I will sprinkle you with clean water, and you will be clean and acceptable to me. I will wash away everything that makes you unclean, and I will remove your disgusting idols. ²⁶I will take away your stubborn heart and give you a new heart and a desire to be faithful. You will have only pure thoughts, ²⁷because I will put my Spirit in you

35.15 *a wasteland:* After the Babylonians defeated Israel, some Edomites seized land that belonged to the people of Israel. Just as Edom celebrated when Israel was destroyed, so everyone on earth will celebrate the destruction of Edom.

36.22-24 *my holy name:* The sinful actions of the people of Israel made the land unclean. For these sins, they were defeated and sent into exile. This humiliation of the Lord's people disgraced the name of the Lord. Israel's enemies believed that their Lord was not powerful enough to save them. Yet the Lord now promises to bring the people home so that the Lord's name can once again be honored among the nations.

Purity (Clean and Unclean)

36.25 *sprinkle you with clean water:* In ancient Israel, water was used in a ceremony to wash away sin and in other cleansing rituals. The Lord promised to make the people ritually clean again, especially by removing the idols they had been worshiping.

36.27 *put my Spirit in you:* The Lord's Spirit would help the people obey the Lord's teachings. Their obedience would help the land from becoming ritually unclean again.

"I will take away your stubborn heart and give you a new heart and a desire to be faithful." Ezek 36.26

36.33-38 *made you clean . . . rebuild . . . sacrifices during a festival:* The cleansing of Israel begins the process of restoring the people and renewing the land. Fields and trees will grow plenty of food, and cities will be rebuilt and repopulated. Then God's people will once again be able to bring sacrifices to honor the LORD during regular festivals, such as the New Moon festival. (See the charts Sacrifices and Offerings on pg 1828 and Pilgrimage Festivals on pg 1799, and the article People of the Law: The Religion of Israel on pg 1794.)

Holiness

37.1 *valley full of bones:* The valley of dry bones may be the same valley where Ezekiel had his first vision (1.1—3.15). An important word that occurs in the following verses is the Hebrew word *ruach*. This word means either "wind," "breath," or "Spirit." These three meanings are all used in the vision of dry bones coming back to life.

37.11-14 *they are dried up . . . will bring you home:* These verses interpret the vision. The people of Israel living in exile are feeling as if their hopes have dried up. But the LORD offers hopeful news. Like the army of dry bones that rose from death, the people of Israel will stand up and return home.

and make you eager to obey my laws and teachings. **28**You will once again live in the land I gave your ancestors; you will be my people, and I will be your God.

29I will protect you from anything that makes you unclean. Your fields will overflow with grain, and no one will starve. **30**Your trees will be filled with fruit, and crops will grow in your fields, so that you will never again feel ashamed for not having enough food. **31**You will remember your evil ways and hate yourselves for what you've done. **32**People of Israel, I'm not doing these things for your sake. You sinned against me, and you must suffer shame and disgrace for what you have done. I, the LORD God, have spoken.

33After I have made you clean, I will let you rebuild your ruined towns and let you live in them. **34**Your land will be plowed again, and nobody will be able to see that it was once barren. **35**Instead, they will say that it looks as beautiful as the garden of Eden. They won't see towns lying in ruins, but they will see your strong cities filled with people. **36**Then the nearby nations that survive will know that I am the one who rebuilt the ruined places and replanted the barren fields. I, the LORD, make this promise.

37I will once again answer your prayers, and I will let your nation grow until you are like a large flock of sheep. **38**The towns that now lie in ruins will be filled with people, just as Jerusalem was once filled with sheep to be offered as sacrifices during a festival. Then you will know that I am the LORD.

Dry Bones Live Again

37 Some time later, I felt the LORD's power take control of me, and his Spirit carried me to a valley full of bones. **2**The LORD showed me all around, and everywhere I looked I saw bones that were dried out. **3**He said, "Ezekiel, son of man, can these bones come back to life?"

I replied, "LORD God, only you can answer that."

4He then told me to say:

Dry bones, listen to what the LORD is saying to you, **5**"I, the LORD God, will put breath in you, and once again you will live. **6**I will wrap you with muscles and skin and breathe life into you. Then you will know that I am the LORD."

7I did what the LORD said, but before I finished speaking, I heard a rattling noise. The bones were coming together! **8**I saw muscles and skin cover the bones, but they had no life in them.

9The LORD said:

Ezekiel, now say to the wind,[c] "The LORD God commands you to blow from every direction and to breathe life into these dead bodies, so they can live again."

10As soon as I said this, the wind blew among the bodies, and they came back to life! They all stood up, and there were enough to make a large army.

11The LORD said:

Ezekiel, the people of Israel are like dead bones. They complain that they are dried up and that they have no hope for the future. **12**So tell them, "I, the LORD God, promise to open your graves and set you free. I will bring you back to Israel, **13**and when that happens, you will realize that I am the

[c]**37.9** *wind:* Or "breath." The Hebrew word may mean either.

LORD. ¹⁴My Spirit will give you breath, and you will live again. I will bring you home, and you will know that I have kept my promise. I, the LORD, have spoken."

Judah and Israel Together Again

¹⁵The LORD said:

¹⁶Ezekiel, son of man, get a stick and write on it, "The kingdom of Judah." Then get another stick and write on it, "The kingdom of Israel."d ¹⁷Hold these two sticks end to end, so they look like one stick. ¹⁸And when your people ask you what this means, ¹⁹tell them that I, the LORD, will join together the stick of Israel and the stick of Judah. I will hold them in my hand, and they will become one.

²⁰Hold these two sticks where they can be seen by everyone ²¹and then say:

I, the LORD God, will gather the people of Israel and bring them home from the foreign nations where they now live. ²²I will make them into one nation and let them once again live in the land of Israel. Only one king will rule them, and they will never again be divided into two nations. ²³They will no longer worship idols and do things that make them unacceptable to me. I will wash away their sin and make them clean, and I will protect them from everything that makes them unclean. They will be my people, and I will be their God.

²⁴⁻²⁵Their king will always come from the family of my servant King David and will care for them like a shepherd. The people of Israel will faithfully obey my laws. They and their descendants will live in the land I gave

my servant Jacob, just as their ancestors did. ²⁶I solemnly promise to bless the people of Israel with unending peace. I will protect them and let them become a powerful nation. My temple will stand in Israel for all time, ²⁷and I will live among my people and be their God. ²⁸Every nation on earth will know that my temple is in Israel and that I have chosen the Israelites to be my people.

Gog Invades Israel

38 The LORD said:

²Ezekiel, son of man, condemn Gog, that wicked ruler of the kingdoms of Meshech and Tubal in the land of Magog. Tell him:

³I, the LORD God, am your enemy, ⁴and I will make you powerless! I will put a hook in your jaw and drag away both you and your large army. You command cavalry troops that wear heavy armor and carry shields and swords. ⁵Your army includes soldiers from Persia, Ethiopia,e and Libya, ⁶as well as from Gomer and Beth-Togarmah in the north. Your army is enormous!

⁷So keep your troops prepared to fight, ⁸because in a few years, I will command you to invade Israel, a country that was ruined by war. It was deserted for a long time, but its people have returned from the foreign nations where they once lived. The Israelites now live in peace in the mountains of their own land. ⁹But you and your army will attack them like a fierce thunderstorm and surround them like a cloud.

37.26 *solemnly promise to bless . . . peace:* The LORD repeats his new agreement with the people of Israel (see also 36.24-38).

37.28 *my temple:* The first temple built by Solomon was destroyed by the Babylonians in 587/6 B.C. The people who returned to Jerusalem from exile built a new temple, dedicated in 515 B.C.

38.2 *Gog . . . ruler of . . . land of Magog:* The exact identity of Gog is unknown, though the name has been linked with King Gyges, who ruled the kingdom of Lydia in Asia Minor around 600 B.C. Meshech and Tubal probably refer to areas of Asia Minor, so Magog may refer to Asia Minor, north of Israel. In Genesis 10.2, Magog was the name of one of Japheth's sons.

38.5 *Persia:* The Persians defeated the Babylonians in 539 B.C.

Persia

---

d**37.16** *Israel:* The Hebrew text has "Joseph, that is, Ephraim," the leading tribe in the northern kingdom.   e**38.5** *Ethiopia:* See the note at 29.10.

38.16 *attack my people . . . invade my country:* The LORD allows Gog's army to invade Israel so that Gog's defeat (38.21-23) will show that the LORD is holy. Gog's army is defeated by earthquakes, Israel's mountains, disease, hail, and burning sulfur rain, all sent by the LORD.

Holiness

39.6 *set fire to the land of Magog:* Fire is often used as a weapon of the LORD's judgment against those who are evil or disobedient (Gen. 19.23-29; Lev 10.1,2; Ezek 5.1-5;10.2; 20.45-47; Joel 2.1-3; Matt 13.36-42).

[10]When that day comes, I know that you will have an evil plan [11]to take advantage of Israel, that weak and peaceful country where people live safely inside towns that have no walls or gates or locks. [12]You will rob the people in towns that were once a pile of rubble. These people lived as prisoners in foreign nations, but they have returned to Israel, the most important place in the world, and they own livestock and property. [13]The people of Sheba and Dedan, along with merchants from villages in[f] southern Spain,[g] will be your allies. They will want some of the silver and gold, as well as the livestock and property that your army takes from Israel.

[14]I, the LORD God, know that when you see[h] my people Israel living in peace, [15]you will lead your powerful cavalry from your kingdom in the north. [16]You will attack my people like a storm-cloud that covers their land. I will let you invade my country Israel, so that every nation on earth will know that I, the LORD, am holy.

Judgment on Gog

[17]The LORD said to Gog:

Long ago, I ordered my prophets to warn the people of Israel that someday I would send an enemy to attack them. You, Gog, are that enemy, and that day is coming. [18]When you invade Israel, I will become furious, [19]and in my anger I will send a terrible earthquake to shake Israel. [20]Every living thing on earth will tremble in fear of me—every fish and bird, every wild animal and reptile, and every human. Mountains

will crumble, cliffs will fall, and cities will collapse. [21]I, the LORD, will make the mountains of Israel turn against you.[i] Your troops will be so terrified that they will attack each other. [22]I will strike you with diseases and punish you with death. You and your army will be pounded with rainstorms, hailstones, and burning sulfur. [23]I will do these things to show the world that I, the LORD, am holy.

Gog Is Defeated

The LORD said:

39 Ezekiel, son of man, condemn Gog and tell him:

You are the ruler of Meshech and Tubal, but I, the LORD, am your enemy! [2]I will turn you around and drag you from the north until you reach the mountains of Israel. [3]I will knock the bow out of your left hand and the arrows out of your right hand, [4]and you and your army will die on those mountains. Then birds and wild animals will eat the flesh [5]of your dead bodies left lying in open fields. I, the LORD, have spoken.

[6]I will set fire to the land of Magog and to those nations along the seacoast that think they are so secure, and they will know that I am the LORD.

[7]My people Israel will know me, and they will no longer disgrace my holy name. Everyone on earth will know that I am the holy LORD God of Israel. [8]The day is coming when these things will happen, just as I have promised.

[9]When that day comes, the people in the towns of Israel will collect the weapons of their dead enemies. They will use these shields, bows and arrows, spears, and clubs

[f]**38.13** *from villages in:* One ancient translation; Hebrew "and soldiers from."   [g]**38.13** *southern Spain:* See the note at 27.12.   [h]**38.14** *when you see:* One possible meaning for the difficult Hebrew text.
[i]**38.21** *I, the LORD . . . against you:* One possible meaning for the difficult Hebrew text.

as firewood, and there will be enough to last for seven years. [10]They will burn these weapons instead of gathering sticks or chopping down trees. That's how the Israelites will take revenge on those who robbed and abused them. I, the LORD, have spoken.

The Burial of Gog

The LORD said:

[11]After Gog has been destroyed, I will bury him and his army in Israel, in Travelers'[j] Valley, east of the Dead Sea. That graveyard will be so large that it will block the way of anyone who tries to walk through the valley,[k] which will then be known as "The Valley of Gog's Army."[l] [12]The Israelites will spend seven months burying dead bodies and cleaning up their land. [13]Everyone will help with the burial, and they will be honored for this on the day the brightness of my glory is seen. [14]After those seven months, the people will appoint a group of men to look for any dead bodies left unburied. This must be done for seven months to make sure that the land is no longer unclean. [15]Whenever they find a human bone, they will set up a marker next to it. Then the gravediggers will bury it in "The Valley of Gog's Army" [16]near the town of "Gog's Army." After that, the land will be pure again.

[17]Ezekiel, son of man, I am going to hold a feast on Israel's mountains and offer sacrifices there. So invite all the birds and wild animals to come from every direction and eat the meat of sacrifices and drink the blood. The birds and animals [18]will feast on the bodies of warriors and foreign rulers that I will sacrifice like sheep, goats, and bulls. [19]I want the birds and animals to eat until they are full and drink until they are drunk. [20]They will come to my table and stuff themselves with the flesh of horses and warriors of every kind. I, the LORD God, have spoken.

Israel Will Be Restored

The LORD said:

[21]When I punish the nations of the earth, they will see the brightness of my glory. [22]The people of Israel will know from then on that I am the LORD their God. [23]Foreign nations will realize that the Israelites were forced to leave their own land because they sinned against me. I turned my back on my people and let enemies attack and kill them. [24]Their lives were wicked and corrupt, and they deserved to be punished.

[25]Now I will show mercy to the people of Israel and bring them back from the nations where they are living. They are Jacob's descendants, so I will bless them and show that I am holy. [26]They will live safely in their own land, but will be ashamed when they remember their evil ways and how they disgraced me.[m] [27]Foreign nations will watch as I take the Israelites from enemy lands and bring them back home, and those nations will see that I am holy.

[28]My people will realize that I, the LORD their God, sent them away as prisoners and now will bring them back to their own land. [29]Never again will I turn my back on the people of Israel, and my Spirit will live in them. I, the LORD, have spoken.

39.9 *firewood . . . seven years:* So many weapons will be collected from Gog's dead soldiers that they can be burned as firewood for seven years. In the ancient world, the number "seven" symbolized completion or perfection.

39.12-15 *cleaning up their land . . . gravediggers:* According to the Law of Moses, touching the body or bones of a corpse could make a person ritually unclean (Lev 21.1,11; Num 6.6-12) and the blood of dead bodies could make the land itself ritually unclean (Num 35.33,34). To make the land clean again, the bodies had to be buried. Burying the bodies of Gog's army outside the land was a way to make certain the land was purified.

[j]39.11 *Travelers':* Hebrew "Abarim." [k]39.11 *That graveyard . . . the valley:* One possible meaning for the difficult Hebrew text. [l]39.11 *Gog's Army:* Hebrew "Hamon-Gog." [m]39.26 *me:* One possible meaning for the difficult Hebrew text of verse 26.

40.1-2 *high mountain in Jerusalem:* Probably meaning Mount Zion. Ezekiel is carried to Jerusalem from Babylonia.

40.5-7 *outer wall . . . east gate:* The temple area was surrounded completely by a wall that was about ten feet high and ten feet thick. Steps led up to the east gate entrance to the temple area. In the passage way connecting the outer entrance and inner entrance to the temple area were six guard rooms, three on each side and each ten feet square.

Ezekiel Sees the Future Temple in Jerusalem

40 [1-2]Twenty-five years after King Jehoiachin and the rest of us had been led away as prisoners to Babylonia, and 14 years after the Babylonians had captured Jerusalem, the LORD's power took control of me on the tenth day of the first month.[n] The LORD showed me some visions in which I was carried to the top of a high mountain in Jerusalem. I looked to the south and saw what looked like a city full of buildings. [3]In my vision the LORD took me closer, and I saw a man who was sparkling like polished bronze. He was standing near one of the gates and was holding a tape measure in one hand and a measuring stick in the other. [4]The man said, "Ezekiel, son of man, pay close attention to everything I'm going to show you—that's why you've been brought here. Listen carefully, because you must tell the people of Israel what you see."

The East Gate

[5]The first thing I saw was an outer wall that completely surrounded the temple area. The man took his measuring stick, which was ten feet long, and measured the wall; it was ten feet high and ten feet thick. [6-7]Then he went to the east gate, where he walked up steps that led to a long passageway. On each side of this passageway were three guardrooms, which were ten feet square, and they were separated by walls over eight feet thick. The man measured the distance between the opening of the gate and the first guardroom, and it was ten feet, the thickness of the outer wall.

At the far end of this passageway, I saw an entrance room that faced the courtyard of the temple itself. There was also a distance of ten feet between the last guardroom and the entrance room [8-9]at the end of the passageway. The man measured this room: It was 13 feet from the doorway to the opposite wall, and the distance from the doorway to the wall on either side was three feet. [10]The three guardrooms on each side of the passageway were the same size, and the walls that separated them were the same thickness.

[11]Next, the man measured the width of the passageway, and it was 22 feet, but the two doors of the gate were only 16 feet wide.[o] [12]In front of the guardrooms, which were ten feet square, was a railing about 20 inches high and 20 inches thick. [13]The man measured the distance from the back wall[p] of one of these rooms to the same spot in the room directly across the passageway, and it was 42 feet. [14]He measured the entrance room at the far end of the passageway, and it was 34 feet wide.[q] [15]Finally, he measured the total length of the passageway, from the outer wall to the entrance room, and it was 85 feet. [16]The three walls in the guardrooms had small windows in them, just like the ones in the entrance room.[r] The walls along the passageway were decorated with carvings of palm trees.

The Outer Courtyard

[17]The man then led me through the passageway and into the outer courtyard of

[n]**40.1,2** *Twenty-five years . . . first month:* Probably March of 573 B.C.   [o]**40.11** *the width of the passageway . . . 22 feet . . . the two doors of the gate . . . 16 feet wide:* The doors themselves probably were hung on stone sockets, which could explain the six-foot difference in width between the passageway and the doors.   [p]**40.13** *back wall:* One ancient translation; Hebrew "roof."   [q]**40.14** *wide:* One possible meaning for the difficult Hebrew text of verse 14.   [r]**40.16** *just like the ones in the entrance room:* One possible meaning for the difficult Hebrew text.

the temple, where I saw 30 rooms built around the outside of the courtyard.[s] These side rooms were built against the outer wall, and in front of them was a sidewalk that circled the courtyard. [18]This was known as the lower sidewalk, and it was 85 feet wide.

[19]I saw the gates that led to the inner courtyard of the temple and noticed that they were higher than those leading to the outer courtyard. The man measured the distance between the outer and inner gates, and it was 170 feet.[t]

The North Gate

[20]Next, the man measured the north gate that led to the outer courtyard. [21]This gate also had three guardrooms on each side of a passageway. The measurements of these rooms, the walls between them, and the entrance room at the far end of the passageway were exactly the same as those of the east gate. The north gate was also 85 feet long and 42 feet wide, [22]and the windows, the entrance room, and the carvings of palm trees were just like those in the east gate. The entrance room also faced the courtyard of the temple and had seven steps leading up to it. [23]Directly across the outer courtyard was a gate that led to the inner courtyard, just as there was for the east gate. The man measured the distance between the outer and inner gate, and it was 170 feet.

The South Gate

[24]The man then took me to the south gate. He measured the walls and the entrance room of this gate, and the measurements were exactly the same as those of the other two gates. [25]There were windows in the guardrooms of this gate and in the entrance room, just like the others, and this gate was also 85 feet long and 42 feet wide. [26]Seven steps led up to the gate; the entrance room was at the far end of the passageway and faced the courtyard of the temple. Carvings of palm trees decorated the walls along the passageway. [27]And directly across the outer courtyard was a gate on the south side of the inner courtyard. The man measured the distance between the outer and inner gate, and it was also 170 feet.

The Gates Leading to the Inner Courtyard

[28]We then went into the inner courtyard, through the gate on the south side of the temple. The man measured the gate, and it was the same size as the gates in the outer wall. [29-30]In fact, everything along the passageway was also the same size, including the guardrooms, the walls separating them, the entrance room at the far end, and the windows. This gate, like the others, was 85 feet long and 42 feet wide. [31]The entrance room of this gate faced the outer courtyard, and carvings of palm trees decorated the walls of the passageway. Eight steps led up to this gate.

[32]Next, we went through the east gate to the inner courtyard. The man measured this gate, and it was the same size as the others. [33]The guardrooms, the walls separating them, and its entrance room had the same measurements as the other gates. The guardrooms and the entrance room had windows, and the gate was 85 feet long

40.19 *gates . . . to the inner courtyard:* Three gated entrances leading to the inner courtyard that surrounded the sanctuary. These gated entrances were located directly across from the three gated entrances that opened onto the outer courtyard.

---

[s]**40.17** *30 rooms built around the outside of the courtyard:* These were probably used by worshipers as places to meet and share sacrificial meals (see, for example, Jeremiah 35.2). [t]**40.19** *feet:* The Hebrew text adds "the east and the north."

40.38-39 *sacrifices for sin:* Different sacrifices to purify intentional sin were used for different individuals and for the whole people. **(See the chart Sacrifices and Offerings on pg 1828.)**

40.38-39 *sacrifices to make things right:* This kind of sacrifice was like a sacrifice to ask forgiveness, except that the offender also paid a fine for the damages. This payment included the cost of fixing or replacing the broken object plus 20 percent extra. Sacrifices to make things right were sometimes called "guilt" offerings.

40.45,46 *priests . . . descendants of Zadok:* Only priests of the Levi tribe were allowed to serve in the temple area, preparing and making sacrifices. Zadok was a priest at the time of King David. The Zadok family was in charge of Israel's priests from the time of Solomon until the time of the exile. Ezekiel's vision supported the Zadok family of priests continuing to serve in the temple.

Israel's Priests

and 42 feet wide. ³⁴The entrance room faced the outer courtyard, and the walls in the passageway were decorated with carvings of palm trees. Eight steps also led up to this gate.

³⁵Then the man took me to the north gate. He measured it, and it was the same size as the others, ³⁶including the guardrooms, the walls separating them, and the entrance room. There were also windows in this gate. It was 85 feet long and 42 feet wide, ³⁷and like the other inner gates, its entrance room faced the outer courtyard, and its walls were decorated with carvings of palm trees. Eight steps also led up to this gate.

The Rooms for Sacrificing Animals

³⁸⁻³⁹Inside the entrance room of the north gate, I saw four tables, two on each side of the room, where the animals to be sacrificed were killed. Just outside[u] this room was a small building used for washing the animals before they were offered as sacrifices to please the LORD[v] or sacrifices for sin[w] or sacrifices to make things right.[x] ⁴⁰Four more tables were in the outer courtyard, two on each side of the steps leading into the entrance room. ⁴¹So there was a total of eight tables, four inside and four outside, where the animals were killed, ⁴²⁻⁴³and where the meat was placed until it was sacrificed on the altar.[y]

Next to the tables in the entrance room were four stone tables 20 inches high and 30 inches square; the equipment used for killing the animals was kept on top of these tables. All around the walls of this room was a 3 inch shelf.[z]

The Rooms Belonging to the Priests

⁴⁴The man then took me to the inner courtyard, where I saw two buildings, one beside the inner gate on the north and the other beside the inner gate on the south.[a] ⁴⁵He said, "The building beside the north gate belongs to the priests who serve in the temple, ⁴⁶and the building beside the south gate belongs to those who serve at the altar. All of them are descendants of Zadok and are the only Levites allowed to serve as the LORD's priests."

The Inner Courtyard and the Temple

⁴⁷Now the man measured the inner courtyard; it was 170 feet square. I also saw an altar in front of the temple.

⁴⁸We walked to the porch of the temple, and the man measured the doorway of the porch: It was 24 feet long,[b] 8 feet wide, and the distance from the doorway to the wall on either side was 5 feet. ⁴⁹The porch itself was 34 feet by 20[c] feet, with steps[d] leading up to it. There was a column on each side of these steps.

[u]**40.38,39** *Just outside:* Or "Inside." [v]**40.38,39** *sacrifices to please the LORD:* These sacrifices have traditionally been called "whole burnt offerings" because the whole animal was burned on the altar. A main purpose of such sacrifices was to please the LORD with the smell of the sacrifice, and so in the CEV they are often called "sacrifices to please the LORD." [w]**40.38,39** *sacrifices for sin:* See Leviticus 4.1,2; 6.24-30. [x]**40.38,39** *sacrifices to make things right:* See Leviticus 5.14-19; 7.1-10. [y]**40.42,43** *where the meat . . . altar:* One possible meaning for the difficult Hebrew text. [z]**40.42,43** *was a 3 inch shelf:* Or "were 3 inch pegs." [a]**40.44** *south:* One possible meaning for the difficult Hebrew text of verse 44. [b]**40.48** *24 feet long:* One ancient translation; these words are not in the Hebrew text of this verse. [c]**40.49** *20:* One ancient translation; Hebrew "18." [d]**40.49** *steps:* Hebrew; one ancient translation "ten steps."

41 Next we went into the main room of the temple. The man measured the doorway of this room: It was 10 feet wide,[e] [2]17 feet long, and the distance from the doorway to the wall on either side was 8 feet. The main room itself was 68 feet by 34 feet.

[3-4]Then the man walked to the far end of the temple's main room and said, "Beyond this doorway is the most holy place." He first measured the doorway: It was 3 feet wide, 10 feet long, and the distance from the doorway to the wall on either side was 12 feet. Then he measured the most holy place, and it was 34 feet square.

The Storage Rooms of the Temple

[5]The man measured the wall of the temple, and it was ten feet thick. Storage rooms seven feet wide were built against the outside of the wall. [6]There were three levels of rooms, with 30 rooms on each level, and they rested on ledges that were attached to the temple walls, so that nothing was built into the walls. [7]The walls of the temple were thicker at the bottom than at the top, which meant that the storage rooms on the top level were wider than those on the bottom level.[f] Steps led from the bottom level, through the middle level, and into the top level.

[8]The temple rested on a stone base ten feet high, which also served as the foundation for the storage rooms. [9]The outside walls of the storage rooms were eight feet thick; there was nothing between these walls [10]and the nearest buildings 34 feet away. [11]One door led into the storage rooms on the north side of the temple, and another door led to those on the south side. The stone base extended eight feet beyond the outside wall of the storage rooms.

The West Building and the Measurements of the Temple

[12]I noticed another building: It faced the west end of the temple and was 117 feet wide, 150 feet long, and had walls over 8 feet thick. [13]The man measured the length of the temple, and it was 170 feet. He then measured from the back wall of the temple, across the open space behind the temple, to the back wall of the west building; it was 170 feet. [14]The distance across the front of the temple, including the open space on either side, was also 170 feet.

[15]Finally, the man measured the length of the west building, including the side rooms on each end, and it was also 170 feet.

The Inside of the Temple

The inside walls of the temple's porch and main room[g] [16]were paneled with wood all the way from the floor to the windows, while the doorways, the small windows, and the three side rooms were trimmed in wood.[h] [17]The paneling stopped just above the doorway. These walls were decorated[i] [18-20]with carvings of winged creatures and had a carving of a palm tree between the creatures. Each winged creature had two faces: A human face looking at the palm tree on one side, and a lion's

41.3-4 *most holy place:* This area, separated from the main room of the temple sanctuary, contained Israel's sacred chest and was considered God's dwelling place among the people (Exod 25.22). Ezekiel does not enter the most holy place. Only Israel's high priest was allowed to enter, and only on the Great Day of Forgiveness. (Lev 16.1-28; Heb 9.7) .

41.17-20 *decorated with carvings:* The winged creatures carved into the walls probably were intended to be heavenly guards. These winged creatures only had two faces, unlike the creatures in Ezekiel's earlier vision, which had four faces.

[e]41.1 *It was 10 feet wide:* One possible meaning for the difficult Hebrew text. [f]41.7 *which meant that . . . on the bottom level:* One possible meaning for the difficult Hebrew text. [g]41.15 *The inside walls of the temple's porch and main room:* One possible meaning for the difficult Hebrew text. [h]41.16 *were trimmed in wood:* One possible meaning for the difficult Hebrew text. [i]41.17 *decorated:* One possible meaning for the difficult Hebrew text of verse 17.

42.13 *where the* LORD's *priests will eat the most holy offerings . . . sacrifices:* The priests who served in the temple were allowed to eat a portion of the grain and meat offerings sacrificed to the LORD.

42.14 *sacred clothes:* The priests and the high priests wore special clothes that were to be worn while they were performing their sacred duties.

face looking at the palm tree on the other side. These designs were carved into the paneling all the way around the two rooms.

[21]The doorframe to the temple's main room was in the shape of a rectangle.

The Wooden Altar

In front of the doorway to the most holy place was something that looked like [22]a wooden altar. It was five feet high and four feet square,[j] and its corners, its base,[k] and its sides were made of wood. The man said, "This is a reminder that the LORD is constantly watching over his temple."

The Doors in the Temple

[23]Both the doorway to the main room of the temple and the doorway to the most holy place had two doors, [24]and each door had two sections that could fold open. [25]The doors to the main room were decorated with carvings of winged creatures and palm trees just like those on the walls, and there was a wooden covering over the porch just outside these doors. [26]The walls on each side of this porch had small windows and were also decorated with carvings of palm trees.

The Sacred Rooms for the Priests

42 [1-2]After the man and I left the temple and walked back to the outer courtyard, he showed me a set of rooms on the north side of the west building.[l] This set of rooms was 170 feet long and 85 feet wide. [3]On one side of them was the 34 feet of open space that ran alongside the temple,[m] and on the other side was the sidewalk that circled the outer courtyard.[n] The rooms were arranged in three levels [4]with doors that opened toward the north, and in front of them was a walkway 17 feet wide and 170 feet long.[o] [5]The rooms on the top level were narrower than those on the middle level, and the rooms on the middle level were narrower than those on the bottom level. [6]The rooms on the bottom level supported those on the two upper levels, and so these rooms did not have columns like other buildings in the courtyard. [7-8]To the north was a privacy wall 85 feet long,[p] [9-10]and at the east end of this wall was the door leading from the courtyard to these rooms.

There was also a set of rooms on the south[q] side of the west building. [11]These rooms were exactly like those on the north side, and they also had a walkway in front of them. [12]The door to these rooms was at the east end of the wall that stood in front of them.

[13]The man then said to me:

These rooms on the north and south sides of the temple are the sacred rooms where the LORD's priests will eat the most holy offerings. These offerings include the grain sacrifices, the sacrifices for sin, and the sacrifices to make things right. [14]When the priests are ready to leave the temple, they must go through these rooms before they return to the outer courtyard. They must leave their sacred clothes in these rooms and put on reg-

---

[j]**41.22** *four feet square:* One ancient translation; Hebrew "four feet wide."   [k]**41.22** *base:* One ancient translation; Hebrew "length."   [l]**42.1,2** *he showed me . . . the west building:* One possible meaning for the difficult Hebrew text.   [m]**42.3** *the 34 feet of open space . . . the temple:* See 41.10.   [n]**42.3** *the sidewalk that circled the outer courtyard:* See 40.17.   [o]**42.4** *170 feet long:* Two ancient translations; Hebrew "20 inches long."   [p]**42.7,8** *long:* One possible meaning for the difficult Hebrew text of verses 5-8.   [q]**42.9,10** *south:* One ancient translation; Hebrew "east."

ular clothes before going anywhere near other people.

The Size of the Temple Area

¹⁵After the man had finished measuring the buildings inside the temple area, he took me back through the east gate and measured the wall around this area. ¹⁶He used his measuring stick to measure the east side of this wall; it was 840 feet long. ¹⁷⁻¹⁹Then he measured the north side, the south side, and the west side of the wall, and they were each 840 feet long, ²⁰and so the temple area was a perfect square. The wall around this area separated what was sacred from what was ordinary.

The Lord's Glory Returns to the Temple

43 The man took me back to the east gate of the temple, ²where I saw the brightness of the glory of Israel's God coming from the east. The sound I heard was as loud as ocean waves, and everything around was shining with the dazzling brightness of his glory. ³This vision was like the one I had seen when God came to destroy Jerusalem and like the one I had seen near the Chebar River.

I immediately bowed with my face to the ground, ⁴and the Lord's glory came through the east gate and into the temple.ʳ ⁵The Lord's Spirit lifted me to my feet and carried me to the inner courtyard, where I saw that the Lord's glory had filled the temple.

⁶The man was standing beside me, and I heard the Lordˢ say from inside the temple:

⁷Ezekiel, son of man, this temple is my throne on earth. I will live here among the people of Israel forever. They and their kings will never again disgrace me by worshiping idols at local shrines or by setting up memorials to their dead kings.ᵗ ⁸Israel's kings built their palaces so close to my holy temple that only a wall separated them from me. Then these kings disgraced me with their evil ways, and in my fierce anger I destroyed them. ⁹But if the people and their kings stop worshiping other gods and tear down those memorials, I will live among them forever.

¹⁰The people of Israel must suffer shame for sinning against me, so tell them about my holy temple. Let them think about it, ¹¹then if they are truly sorry, describe for them the design and shape of the temple, the gates, the measurements, and how the buildings are arranged. Explain the regulations about worshiping there, then write down these things, so they can study and obey them.

¹²The temple area on my holy mountain must be kept sacred! This is the most important law about the temple.

The Altar

¹³According to the official standards, the altar in the temple had the following measurements: Around the bottom of the altar was a gutter 20 inches wide and 20 inches deep, with a 10 inch ledge on the outer rim. ¹⁴⁻¹⁷The altar rested on a base and had three sections, each one of them square. The bottom section was 27 feet on each side and 3 feet high. The middle sec-

43.18 *splattering it with blood*: Blood splattered or smeared on the altar or on the people had cleansing power and showed that something or someone was dedicated to God.

Blood

tion was 24 feet on each side and 7 feet high, and it had a 10 inch rim around its outer edge. The top section, which was 20 feet on each side and 7 feet high, was the place where sacrifices were burned, and the four corners of the top section looked like the horns of a bull. The steps leading up to the altar were on the east side.

The Dedication of the Altar

18 The LORD God said:

Ezekiel, son of man, after the altar is built, it must be dedicated by offering sacrifices on it and by splattering it with blood. Here is what you must do: 19The priests of the Levi tribe from the family of Zadok the priest are the only ones who may serve in my temple—this is my law. So give them a young bull to slaughter as a sacrifice for sin. 20Take some of the animal's blood and smear it on the four corners of the altar, some on the corners of the middle section, and some more on the rim around its edge. That will purify the altar and make it fit for offering sacrifices to me. 21Then take the body of the bull outside the temple area and burn it at the special place.

22The next day, a goat[u] that has nothing wrong with it must be offered as a sacrifice for sin. Purify the altar with its blood, just as you did with the blood of the bull. 23Then choose a young bull and a young ram that have nothing wrong with them, 24and bring them to my temple. The priests will sprinkle salt on them[v] and offer them as sacrifices to please me.[w]

25Each day for the next seven days, you must offer a goat and a bull and a ram as sacrifices for sin. These animals must have nothing wrong with them. 26The priests will purify the altar during those days, so that it will be acceptable to me and ready to use. 27From then on, the priests will use this altar to offer sacrifices to please me and sacrifices to ask my blessing.[x] Then I will be pleased with the people of Israel. I, the LORD God, have spoken.

The East Gate Must Remain Closed

44 The man took me back to the outer courtyard, near the east gate of the temple area. I saw that the doors to this gate were closed. 2The LORD said:

I, the LORD God of Israel, came through this gate, so it must remain closed forever! No one must ever use it. 3The ruler of Israel may come here to eat a sacrificial meal that has been offered to me, but he must use only the entrance room of this gate.

People Who Are Not Allowed in the Temple

4Then the man took me through the north gate to the front of the temple. I saw that the brightness of the LORD's glory had filled the temple, and I immediately bowed with my face to the ground.

5The LORD said:

Ezekiel, son of man, I am going to give you the laws for my temple. So pay attention and listen carefully to what kind of people are allowed to come in the temple, and what kind are not. 6Tell those rebellious people of Israel:

I, the LORD God, command you to

---

[u]43.22 *goat*: Hebrew "male goat."   [v]43.24 *The priests will sprinkle salt on them*: See Leviticus 2.13.
[w]43.24 *sacrifices to please me*: See the note at 40.38,39.   [x]43.27 *sacrifices to ask my blessing*: These sacrifices have traditionally been called "peace offerings" or "offerings of well-being." A main purpose was to ask for the LORD's blessing, and so in the CEV they are sometimes called "sacrifices to ask the LORD's blessing."

stop your evil ways! [7]My temple has been disgraced, because you have let godless, stubborn foreigners come here when sacrifices are being offered to me. You have sinned and have broken our solemn agreement. [8]Instead of following the proper ways to worship me, you have put foreigners in charge of worship at my temple.

[9]And so I, the LORD God, say that no godless foreigner who disobeys me will be allowed in my temple. This includes any foreigner living in Israel.

The Levites Are Punished

The LORD said:

[10]Some of the Levites turned their backs on me and joined the other people of Israel in worshiping idols. So these Levites must be punished! [11]They will still be allowed to serve me as temple workers by guarding the gates and by killing the animals to be sacrificed and by helping the worshipers. [12]But because these Levites served the people of Israel when they worshiped idols, I, the LORD God, promise that the Levites will be punished. They did not stop the Israelites from sinning, [13]and now I will no longer let the Levites serve as my priests or come near anything sacred to me. They must suffer shame and disgrace for their disgusting sins. [14]They will be responsible for all the hard work that must be done in the temple.

Rules for Priests

The LORD said:

[15]The priests of the Levi tribe who are descendants of Zadok the priest were faithful to me, even when the rest of the Israelites turned away. And so, these priests will continue to serve as my priests and to offer the fat and the blood of sacrifices. [16]They will come into my temple, where they will offer sacrifices at my altar and lead others in worship.

[17]When they come to the inner courtyard, they must wear their linen priestly clothes. My priests must never wear anything made of wool when they are on duty in this courtyard or in the temple. [18]Even their turbans and underwear must be made of linen to keep my priests from sweating when they work. [19]And before they leave to join the other people in the outer courtyard, they must take off their priestly clothes, then place them in the sacred rooms and put on their regular clothes.[y] That way, no one will touch their sacred clothes and be harmed.[z]

[20]Priests must never shave their heads when they are mourning. But they must keep their hair properly trimmed and not let it grow too long. [21]They must not drink wine before going to the inner courtyard.

[22]A priest must not marry a divorced woman; he can marry only a virgin from Israel or the widow of another priest.

[23]Priests must teach my people the difference between what is sacred and what is ordinary, and between what is clean and what is unclean. [24]They will make decisions in difficult legal cases, according to my own laws. They must also observe the religious festivals my Law requires and must always respect the Sabbath.

[25]Touching a dead body will make a person unclean. So a priest must not go near a dead body, unless it is one of his parents or

● **44.7-9** *temple . . . disgraced . . . no godless foreigner:* In the past, Israel's priests had apparently allowed foreigners (non-Jews) to help in the temple area. This increased the chance that the temple and sacrifices to the LORD might be polluted by those who did not fully understand Israel's laws, especially those laws regarding ritual purity.

● **44.10-14** *Levites . . . temple workers:* God chose the men of one Levite family, the descendants of Aaron, to be Israel's priests

◻ Israel's Priests

[y]**44.19** *take off their priestly clothes . . . put on their regular clothes:* See 42.14.   [z]**44.19** *no one will touch . . . and be harmed:* Ordinary people were forbidden to touch anything that was sacred. If they did, it was believed they would somehow be harmed.

44.29 *completely dedicated to me:* This translates a Hebrew word that describes property and things that were taken from humans and given to God. In the early history of Israel, such things had to be destroyed. Now the priests were to receive these things along with a part of other offerings.

Holy War (The Lord's Battles)

45.1-5 *land of Israel is divided ... twelve tribes ... the Levites:* The tribes of Israel were named for the sons of Jacob (also known as "Israel," Gen 32.27, 28). Ephraim and Manasseh were the sons of Jacob's son Joseph. Each received a share of land in Canaan (see Josh 12–24). The new division of the land for the exiles who have returned to the land was to include a large sacred area. One half of the area included the temple and space for the priests' houses, while the other half was reserved for the Levite towns (see Num 35.1-8; Josh 21.1-42).

children, or his brother or unmarried sister. **26**If a priest touches a dead body, he is unclean and must go through a ceremony to make himself clean. Then seven days later, **27**he must go to the inner courtyard of the temple and offer a sacrifice for sin. After that, he may once again serve as my priest. I, the Lord God, have spoken.

28I myself will provide for my priests, and so they won't receive any land of their own. **29**Instead, they will receive part of the grain sacrifices, as well as part of the sacrifices for sin and sacrifices to make things right. They will also be given everything in Israel that has been completely dedicated to me.[a] **30**The first part of every harvest will belong to the priests. They will also receive part of all special gifts and offerings the Israelites bring to me. And whenever any of my people bake bread, they will give their first loaf as an offering to the priests, and I will bless the homes of the people when they do this.

31Priests must not eat any bird or animal that dies a natural death or that has been killed by a wild animal.

The Lord's Sacred Land

The Lord said:

45 When the land of Israel is divided among the twelve tribes, you must set aside an area that will belong to me. This sacred area will be eight miles long and six[b] miles wide. **2**The temple will be on a piece of land 840 feet square, and the temple will be completely surrounded by an open space 84 feet wide.

3-4I will give half of my sacred land, a section eight miles long and three miles wide, to the priests who serve in the temple. Their houses will be in this half, as well as my temple, which is the most sacred place of all.

5I will give the other half of my land to the Levites who work in my temple, and the towns[c] where they will live will be there.

6Next to my sacred land will be an area eight miles long and two miles wide. This will belong to the people of Israel and will include the city of Jerusalem.

Land for Israel's Ruler

The Lord said:

7-8 The regions west and east of my sacred land and the city of Jerusalem will belong to the ruler of Israel. He will be given the region between the western edge of my land and the Mediterranean Sea, and between the eastern edge of my land and the Jordan River. This will mean that the length of his property will be the same as the sections of land given to the tribes.

This property will belong to every ruler of Israel, so they will always be fair to my people and will let them live peacefully in the land given to their tribes.

Israel's Rulers Must Be Honest

9The Lord God said:

You leaders of Israel have cheated and abused my people long enough! I want you to stop sinning and start doing what is right and fair. You must never again force my people off their own land. I, the Lord, have spoken.

10So from now on, you must use honest weights and measures. **11**The *ephah* will be

---

[a]**44.29** *that has been completely dedicated to me:* This translates a Hebrew word that describes property and things that were taken away from humans and given to God. In the early history of Israel, such things often had to be destroyed (see Joshua 6.15-19).   [b]**45.1** *six:* One ancient translation; Hebrew "three."   [c]**45.5** *the towns:* One ancient translation; Hebrew "the 20 rooms."

the standard dry measure, and the *bath* will be the standard liquid measure. Their size will be based on the *homer*, which will equal ten *ephahs* or ten *baths*.[d]

¹²The standard unit of weight will be the *shekel*.[e] One *shekel* will equal 20 *gerahs*, and 60 *shekels* will equal one *mina*.

¹³Leaders of Israel, the people must bring you one sixtieth of their grain harvests as offerings to me. ¹⁴They will also bring one percent of their olive oil. These things will be measured according to the *bath*, and ten *baths* is the same as one *homer* or one *cor*. ¹⁵Finally, they must bring one sheep out of every 200 from their flocks.

These offerings will be used as grain sacrifices, as well as sacrifices to please me[f] and those to ask my blessing.[g] I, the LORD, will be pleased with these sacrifices and will forgive the sins of my people.

¹⁶The people of Israel will bring you these offerings. ¹⁷But during New Moon Festivals, Sabbath celebrations, and other religious feasts, you leaders will be responsible for providing animals for the sacrifices, as well as the grain and wine. All these will be used for the sacrifices for sin, the grain sacrifices, the sacrifices to please me, and those to ask my blessing. I will be pleased and will forgive the sins of my people.

The Festivals
(Exodus 12.1-20; Leviticus 23.33-43)

¹⁸The LORD God said:

On the first day of the first month,[h] a young bull that has nothing wrong with it must be offered as a sacrifice to purify the temple. ¹⁹The priest will take some blood from this sacrifice and smear it on the doorposts of the temple, as well as on the four corners of the altar and on the doorposts of the gates that lead into the inner courtyard.

²⁰The same ceremony must also be done on the seventh day of the month, so that anyone who sins accidentally or without knowing it will be forgiven, and so that my temple will remain holy.

²¹Beginning on the fourteenth day of the first month, and continuing for seven days, everyone will celebrate Passover and eat bread made without yeast. ²²On the first day, the ruler will bring a bull to offer as a sacrifice for his sins and for the sins of the people. ²³Each day of the festival he is to bring seven bulls and seven rams as sacrifices to please me,[i] and he must bring a goat[j] as a sacrifice for sin. These animals must have nothing wrong with them. ²⁴He will also provide 20 pounds of grain and four quarts of olive oil to be offered with each bull and each ram.

²⁵The Festival of Shelters will begin on the fifteenth day of the seventh month[k] and will continue for seven days. On each day of this festival, the ruler will provide the same number of animals that he did each day during Passover, as well as the same amount of grain and olive oil for the sacrifices.

45.17 *New Moon Festivals:* Special sacrifices were offered on the first day of a new month, known as the New Moon festival (Ps 81.3; Num 28.11-15). **(See the article People of the Law: The Religion of Israel on pg 1794.)**

45.21 *celebrate Passover and eat bread made without yeast:* The "Passover" festival was a celebration of how God acted to save the Israelite people in Egypt, and the thin bread was eaten as a reminder that the people had to leave Egypt so quickly they did not have time to let the dough for their bread rise.

Passover and the Festival of Thin Bread

45.25 *Festival of Shelters:* The Festival of Shelters took place at the end of the fall harvest (Exod 23.16; Deut 16.13-17). In addition to giving thanks to God for the fall harvest, the people were to build and live in shelters made of tree branches to remember the temporary shelters they lived in after they left Egypt and wandered in the wilderness (Lev 23.33-36,42,43).

[d]**45.11** *the homer . . . ten ephahs . . . ten baths:* A *homer* was either a dry or a liquid measure and equaled about five bushels or 55 gallons; an *ephah* would be about a half bushel, and a *bath* would be about five and a half gallons.   [e]**45.12** *the shekel:* The *shekel* was about four-tenths of an ounce.
[f]**45.15** *sacrifices to please me:* See the note at 40.38,39.   [g]**45.15** *sacrifices . . . to ask my blessing:* See the note at 43.27.   [h]**45.18** *the first month:* Abib (also called Nisan), the first month of the Hebrew calendar, from about mid-March to mid-April.   [i]**45.23** *sacrifices to please me:* See the note at 40.38,39.
[j]**45.23** *goat:* See the note at 43.22.   [k]**45.25** *seventh month:* Tishri (also called Ethanim), the seventh month of the Hebrew calendar, from about mid-September to mid-October.

46.16,17 *land . . . Year of Celebration:* Land could be sold or given away in Israel, but during the sacred Year of Celebration (also called the "Year of Jubilee") property was to be returned to its original owners (see Lev 25.8-34). This was done so that each Israelite tribe could hold on to the land they were given when they first entered the land of Canaan.

Various Laws for the Ruler and the People

46 The LORD said:

The east gate of the inner courtyard must remain closed during the six working days of each week. But on the Sabbath and on the first day of the month, this gate will be opened. [2]Israel's ruler will go from the outer courtyard into the entrance room of this gate and stand in the doorway while the priest offers sacrifices to ask my blessing[l] and sacrifices to please me.[m] The ruler will bow with his face to the ground to show that he has worshiped me. Then he will leave, and the gate will remain open until evening.

[3]Each Sabbath and on the first day of each month, the people of Israel must also come to the east gate and worship me. [4]On the Sabbath, the ruler will bring six lambs and one ram to be offered as sacrifices to please me. There must be nothing wrong with any of these animals. [5]With the ram, he is to offer 20 pounds of grain, and with each of the lambs, he can offer as much as he wants. He must also offer four quarts of olive oil with every 20 pounds of grain.

[6]The ruler is to bring six lambs, a bull, and a ram to be offered as sacrifices at the New Moon Festival. There must be nothing wrong with any of these animals. [7]With the bull and the ram, he is to offer 20 pounds of grain, and with each of the lambs, he can offer as much as he wants. He must also offer four quarts of olive oil with every 20 pounds of grain. [8]The ruler must come through the entrance room of the east gate and leave the same way.

[9]When my people come to worship me during any festival, they must always leave by the opposite gate from which they came: Those who come in the north gate must leave by the south gate, and those who come in the south gate must leave by the north gate. [10]Their ruler will come in at the same time they do and leave at the same time they leave.

[11]At all other festivals and celebrations, 20 pounds of grain will be offered with a bull, and 20 pounds will be offered with a ram. The worshipers can offer as much grain as they want with each lamb. Four quarts of olive oil must be offered with every 20 pounds of grain.

[12]If the ruler voluntarily offers a sacrifice to please me or to ask my blessing, the east gate of the inner courtyard will be opened for him. He will offer his sacrifices just as he does on each Sabbath; then he will leave, and the gate will be closed.

[13]Each morning a year-old lamb that has nothing wrong with it must be offered as a sacrifice to please me. [14]Along with it, three pounds of fine flour mixed with a quart of olive oil must be offered as a grain sacrifice. This law will never change—[15]the lamb, the flour, and the olive oil will be offered to me every morning for all time.

Laws about the Ruler's Land

[16]The LORD God said:

If the ruler of Israel gives some of his land to one of his children, it will belong to the ruler's child as part of the family property. [17]But if the ruler gives some of his land to one of his servants, the land will belong to the servant until the Year of Celebration, when it will be returned to the ruler.[n]

[l]**46.2** *sacrifices to ask my blessing:* See the note at 43.27.   [m]**46.2** *sacrifices to please me:* See the note at 40.38,39.   [n]**46.17** *the Year of Celebration . . . to the ruler:* This was a sacred year for Israel, traditionally called the "Year of Jubilee." During this year, all property had to go back to its original owner (see Leviticus 25.8-34).

Only the ruler's children can keep what is given to them. ¹⁸The ruler must never abuse my people by taking land from them. Any land he gives his children must already belong to him.

The Sacred Kitchens

¹⁹The man who was showing me the temple^o then took me back to the inner courtyard. We walked to the south side of the courtyard and stopped at the door to the sacred rooms that belonged to the priests. He showed me more rooms at the western edge of the courtyard ²⁰and said, "These are the kitchens where the priests must boil the meat to be offered as sacrifices to make things right^p and as sacrifices for sin.^q They will also bake the grain for sacrifices in these kitchens. That way, these sacred offerings won't have to be carried through the outer courtyard, where someone could accidentally touch them and be harmed."^r

²¹We went back to the outer courtyard and walked past the four corners. ²²At each corner I saw a smaller courtyard, 68 feet long and 50 feet wide. ²³Around the inside of these smaller courtyards was a low wall of stones, and against the wall were places to build fires.^s ²⁴The man said, "These are the kitchens where the temple workers will boil the meat that worshipers offer as sacrifices."

The Stream Flowing from the Temple

47 The man took me back to the temple, where I saw a stream flowing from under the entrance. It began in the south part of the temple, where it ran past the altar and continued east through the courtyard. ²We walked out of the temple area through the north gate and went around to the east gate. I saw the small stream of water flowing east from the south side of the gate.

³The man walked east, then took out his measuring stick and measured 560 yards downstream. He told me to wade through the stream there, and the water came up to my ankles. ⁴Then he measured another 560 yards downstream, and told me to wade through it there. The water came up to my knees. Another 560 yards downstream the water came up to my waist. ⁵Another 560 yards downstream, the stream had become a river that could be crossed only by swimming. ⁶The man said, "Ezekiel, son of man, pay attention to what you've seen."

We walked to the riverbank, ⁷where I saw dozens of trees on each side. ⁸The man said:

This water flows eastward to the Jordan River valley and empties into the Dead Sea, where it turns the salt water into fresh water. ⁹Wherever this water flows, there will be all kinds of animals and fish, because it will bring life and fresh water to the Dead Sea. ¹⁰From En-Gedi to Eneglaim, people will fish in the sea and dry their nets along the coast. There will be as many kinds of fish in the Dead Sea as there are in the Mediterranean Sea. ¹¹But the marshes along the shore will remain salty, so that people can use the salt from them.

¹²Fruit trees will grow all along this river and produce fresh fruit every month. The leaves will never dry out, because they will always have water

47.1-5 *a stream . . . a river:* The stream may refer to the LORD as the source of life and fertility. Compare the water springing up out of the temple to the river that watered God's garden in Eden (Gen 2.10-14).

47.8-10 *Jordan River valley . . . Mediterranean Sea:* The Jordan River flowed south from Lake Galilee and emptied into the Dead Sea. The stream from the temple would purify the salty water of the Dead Sea so that fish could live in it. **(See Map 3 on pg 1881.)**

ᗆ   Water

---

^o**46.19** *The man . . . temple:* See 40.3.   ^p**46.20** *sacrifices to make things right:* See the note at 40.38,39.
^q**46.20** *sacrifices for sin:* See the note at 40.38,39.   ^r**46.20** *someone . . . touch them and be harmed:* See the note at 44.19.   ^s**46.23** *fires:* One possible meaning for the difficult Hebrew text of verse 23.

47.15-21 *northern border . . . the land:* For many of the key locations listed in this passage, **see Map 4 on pg 1882.**

48.8-20 *special section of land:* The special section of land running through the middle of the tribal lands included a section for the temple and the priests, land for the Levites, and Jerusalem and its adjoining farmland.

from the stream that flows from the temple, and they will be used for healing people.

The Borders of the Land

13-14 The LORD God said to the people of Israel:

When the land is divided among the twelve tribes of Israel, the Joseph tribe[t] will receive two shares. Divide the land equally, because I promised your ancestors that this land would someday belong to their descendants. These are the borders of the land:
15The northern border will begin at the Mediterranean Sea, then continue eastward to Hethlon, to Lebo-Hamath, then across to Zedad, **16**Berothah,[u] and Sibraim, which is on the border between the two kingdoms of Damascus and Hamath. The border will end at Hazar-Hatticon, which is on the border of Hauran. **17**So the northern border will run between the Mediterranean Sea and Hazar-Enon, which is on the border between Damascus and Hamath.[v]
18The eastern border will begin on the border between the two kingdoms of Hauran and Damascus. It will run south along the Jordan River, which separates the territories of Gilead and Israel, and it will end at the Dead Sea near the town of Tamar.[w]
19The southern border will begin at Tamar, then run southwest to the springs near Meribath-Kadesh. It will continue along the Egyptian Gorge and will end at the Mediterranean Sea.
20The western border will run north along the Mediterranean Sea to a point just west of Lebo-Hamath.

21That is the land to be divided among the tribes of Israel. **22**It will belong to the Israelites and to any foreigners living among them whose children were born in Israel. These foreigners must be treated like any other Israelite citizen, and they will receive **23**a share of the land given to the tribe where they live. I, the LORD God, have spoken.

The Division of Land among Tribes in the North

The LORD said:

48 **1-7**Each tribe will receive a section of land that runs from the eastern border of Israel west to the Mediterranean Sea. The northern border of Israel will run along the towns of Hethlon and Lebo-Hamath, and will end at Hazar-Enon, which is on the border between the kingdoms of Damascus and Hamath. The tribes will receive their share of land in the following order, from north to south: Dan, Asher, Naphtali, Manasseh, Ephraim, Reuben, and Judah.

The Special Section of Land

The LORD said:

8South of Judah's territory will be a special section of land. Its length will be eight miles, and its width will run from the eastern border of Israel west to the Mediterranean Sea. My temple will be located in this section of land.
9An area in the center of this land will belong to me. It will be eight miles long and six[x] miles wide.
10I, the LORD, will give half of my sacred

[t]**47.13,14** *the Joseph tribe:* That is, the two tribes of Manasseh and Ephraim, Joseph's sons. [u]**47.15,16** *to Lebo-Hamath, then across to Zedad,* **16***Berothah:* One ancient translation; Hebrew "to Lebo-Zedad, **16**then across to Hamath, Berothah." [v]**47.17** *which is on the border between Damascus and Hamath:* One possible meaning for the difficult Hebrew text. [w]**47.18** *near the town of Tamar:* One possible meaning for the difficult Hebrew text. [x]**48.9** *six:* The Hebrew text has "three" (but see 45.1 and the note there).

land to the priests. Their share will be eight miles long and three miles wide, and my temple will be right in the middle. [11]Only priests who are descendants of Zadok will receive a share of this sacred land, because they remained faithful to me when the Levites and the rest of the Israelites started sinning. [12]The land belonging to the priests will be the most sacred area and will lie south of the area that belongs to the Levites.

[13]I will give the other half of my sacred land to the Levites. Their share will also be eight miles long and three miles wide, [14]and they must never sell or trade any of this land—it is the best land and belongs to me.

[15]South of my sacred land will be a section eight miles long and two miles wide. It will not be sacred, but will belong to the people of Israel and will include the city of Jerusalem, together with its houses and pastureland. [16]The city will be a square: Each side will be a mile and a half long, [17]and an open area 420 feet wide will surround the city. [18]The land on the east and west sides of the city limits will be farmland for the people of Jerusalem; both sections will be three miles long and two miles wide. [19]People from the city will farm the land, no matter which tribe they belong to.

[20]And so the center of this special section of land will be for my sacred land, as well as for the city and its property. The land will be a square, eight miles on each side.

[21]The regions east and west of this square of land will belong to the ruler of Israel. His property will run east to the Jordan River and west to the Mediterranean Sea. In the very center of his property will be my sacred land, as well as the temple, [22]together with the share belonging to the Levites and the city of Jerusalem. The northern border of the ruler's property will be the land that belongs to Judah, and the southern border will be the land that belongs to Benjamin.

The Division of Land among Tribes in the South

The LORD God said:

[23-27]South of this special section will be the land that belongs to the rest of Israel's tribes. Each tribe will receive a section of land that runs from the eastern border of Israel west to the Mediterranean Sea. The tribes will receive their share of land in the following order, from north to south: Benjamin, Simeon, Issachar, Zebulun, and Gad.

[28]Gad's southern border is also the southern border of Israel. It will begin at the town of Tamar, then run southwest to the springs near Meribath-Kadesh. It will continue along the Egyptian Gorge and end at the Mediterranean Sea.

[29]That's how the land of Israel will be divided among the twelve tribes. I, the LORD God, have spoken.

The Gates of Jerusalem

The LORD said:

[30-34]The city of Jerusalem will have twelve gates, three on each of the four sides of the city wall. These gates will be named after the twelve tribes of Israel. The gates of Reuben, Judah, and Levi will be in the north; Joseph, Benjamin, and Dan will be in the east; Simeon, Issachar, and Zebulun will be in the south; Gad, Asher, and Naphtali will be in the west. Each side of the city wall will be a mile and a half long, [35]and so the total length of the wall will be six miles. The new name of the city will be "The-LORD-Is-Here!"

48.35 *new name . . . "The-LORD-Is-Here!":* A translation of the Hebrew *Yahweh-Shammah* which emphasizes the return of the LORD's glory to Jerusalem and ends the book on a very hopeful note.

Reflection Questions About Ezekiel 1.1—48.35

1. Where and when did Ezekiel receive his first vision (1.1-4)? What was the historical situation in Israel at this time?

2. Why was Ezekiel chosen, and what did the LORD want him to do (2.3—3.11; 3.16-21)?

3. Where was Ezekiel taken in his second vision (8.1—11.23)? What terrible things did he see there? Where did the LORD's glory "live" (9.3)? Why did the LORD's glory leave that place?

4. Who were the "lying" prophets (13.1-16)? What was false about their messages?

5. According to chapter 18, who is responsible for a person's sins? What is the good news about sin in this chapter?

6. What important news came to Ezekiel (33.21)? What happened to Ezekiel after he heard this news (33.22)?

7. Explain why it was important that the land and the people of Israel be "cleaned" at the time they returned from exile (36.16-38). What does the modern phrase "clean up your act" mean? How might this modern saying apply to Ezekiel's message to his Israelite neighbors?

8. How was the vision of the dry bones coming to life again related to the people of Israel returning home from exile (chapter 37)?

9. Explain the difference between what was sacred and ordinary, clean and unclean, especially as they relate to the temple, the priests, and the people of Israel.

10. Why was the stream flowing from the temple such a hopeful vision (47.1-12)?

daniel

*How does the message of Daniel bring hope to God's
faithful people in times of hardship and persecution?*

WHAT MAKES DANIEL SPECIAL?

In the Hebrew Scriptures, DANIEL is listed in the section called the Writings. In the Greek translation of
the Old Testament during the third and second centuries B.C. (called the *Septuagint*), it is listed among
the prophetical books. DANIEL has been described
both as prophecy and as an apocalypse, a kind of literature that uses symbols, signs, and interpretations of the underlying meaning of events in current
history in order to describe how God will triumph
over his enemies and the enemies of God's people.
(See the chart Apocalyptic Writings on pg 1836.)
DANIEL is a strong testimony to the strength God
gives to people of faith during times of difficulty and
persecution.

One other fact makes DANIEL unique. Just over
half the book (2.4—7.28) is written in Aramaic; the
rest is in Hebrew. Why this is so is not clear, though
it is a factor that has led some scholars to conclude
that DANIEL was written at a date much later than the
time of the historic events described in DANIEL 1–6.
The traditional view, however, holds that the prophet
Daniel received the visions described in this book
and wrote them down during the time of the exile
some time in the sixth century B.C.

WHAT'S THE STORY BEHIND THE SCENE?

At various times in their history, the Jewish people
were tempted to turn away from God and abandon
the religious practices that were based on the Law
of Moses. During the exile in Babylon (from around
587 to 538 B.C.), the people were forced to live
among people who had different gods and observed
different religious practices. Under Cyrus II of Persia, in 538 B.C. many Jews began to return to Judah,
the area around Jerusalem. Hundreds of years later,
they suffered severe persecution under Antiochus IV
Epiphanes (ruled 175–164 B.C.). These horrible events
are described in the books of 1 and 2 *Maccabees*,
which are included in some editions of the Bible.
(See the article What Books Belong in the Bible? on
pg 1764.)

Though scholars are divided as to when DANIEL
was most likely written, most agree that much of
what is described in its visions applies to the cruel
treatment of the Jewish people by Antiochus IV, who
pressured the Jews to abandon their faith in God.

HOW IS DANIEL CONSTRUCTED?

DANIEL can be divided into two main parts: chapters
1–6 include the stories of Daniel and his friends set
during the time of the Babylonian exile. Chapters
7–12 describe a number of Daniel's visions. The outline of DANIEL below shows how these stories and visions are collected and arranged. Note that the final
vision spans three chapters.

The stories of Daniel in Babylon (1.1—6.28)
    God is with Daniel and his friends (1.1—3.30)
    The dream, the strange writing, and the pit of
    lions (4.1—6.28)
The visions of Daniel (7.1—12.13)
    Two visions and a prayer (7.1—9.27)
    The final vision (10.1—12.13)

Daniel is a form of wisdom writing that contains elements of prophecy, folk-tale, and apocalyptic writing. The first six chapters of Daniel are a third-person narrative that tells the story of Daniel and his three friends, young Hebrew men living in exile in Babylonia. Daniel and his friends—who are faithful to the Lord and under God's protection—train to be court officials for King Nebuchadnezzar. Daniel, already known for his wisdom, becomes famous as an interpreter of dreams and mysterious writings. God saves Daniel's friends from Nebuchadnezzar's flaming furnace. Others in the king's court become jealous of Daniel's success and seek to undermine him, even trying to use Daniel's faith to destroy him. The enemies succeed in having Daniel thrown into a pit of lions, but God sends an angel to protect him. At chapter seven, the narrative abruptly changes to a series of first-person accounts of Daniel's visions and dreams, which are explained to him by an angel. Together, the first and second parts of Daniel clearly celebrate God as the one who controls the universe and all of human events. For this reason the book offers hope and consolation to God's people living under foreign rule.

Outline

Daniel and His Friends

1 In the third year that Jehoiakim was king of Judah,[a] King Nebuchadnezzar of Babylonia attacked Jerusalem. [2]The Lord let Nebuchadnezzar capture Jehoiakim and take away some of the things used in God's temple. And when the king returned to Babylonia,[b] he put these things in the temple of his own god.

[3]One day the king ordered Ashpenaz, his highest palace official, to choose some young men from the royal family of Judah and from other leading Jewish families. [4]The king said, "They must be healthy, handsome, smart, wise, educated, and fit to serve in the royal palace. Teach them how to speak and write our language [5]and give them the same food and wine that I am served. Train them for three years, and then they can become court officials."

[6]Four of the young Jews chosen were Daniel, Hananiah, Mishael, and Azariah, all from the tribe of Judah. [7]But the king's chief official gave them Babylonian names: Daniel became Belteshazzar, Hananiah became Shadrach, Mishael became Meshach, and Azariah became Abednego.

[8]Daniel made up his mind to eat and drink only what God had approved for his people to eat. And he asked the king's chief official for permission not to eat the food and wine served in the royal palace. [9]God had made the official friendly and kind to Daniel. [10]But the man still told him, "The king has decided what you must eat and drink. And I am afraid he will kill me, if you eat something else and end up looking worse than the other young men."

[11]The king's official had put a guard in charge of Daniel and his three friends. So Daniel said to the guard, [12]"For the next ten days, let us have only vegetables and water at mealtime. [13]When the ten days are up, compare how we look with the other young men, and decide what to do

[a]1.1 *Jehoiakim . . . king of Judah:* Ruled 609–598 B.C. another name for Babylonia.

[b]1.2 *Babylonia:* The Hebrew text has "Shinar,"

with us." ¹⁴The guard agreed to do what Daniel had asked.

¹⁵Ten days later, Daniel and his friends looked healthier and better than the young men who had been served food from the royal palace. ¹⁶After this, the guard let them eat vegetables instead of the rich food and wine.

¹⁷God made the four young men smart and wise. They read a lot of books and became well educated. Daniel could also tell the meaning of dreams and visions.

¹⁸At the end of the three-year period set by King Nebuchadnezzar, his chief palace official brought all the young men to him. ¹⁹The king interviewed them and discovered that none of the others were as outstanding as Daniel, Hananiah, Mishael, and Azariah. So they were given positions in the royal court. ²⁰From then on, whenever the king asked for advice, he found their wisdom was ten times better than that of any of his other advisors and magicians. ²¹Daniel served there until the first year of King Cyrus.ᶜ

Nebuchadnezzar's Dream

2 During the second year that Nebuchadnezzar was king, he had such horrible nightmares that he could not sleep. ²So he called in his counselors, advisors, magicians, and wise men, ³and said, "I am disturbed by a dream that I don't understand, and I want you to explain it."

⁴They answered in Aramaic,ᵈ "Your Majesty, we hope you live forever! We are your servants. Please tell us your dream, and we will explain what it means."

⁵But the king replied, "No! I have made up my mind. If you don't tell me both the dream and its meaning, you will be

chopped to pieces and your houses will be torn down. ⁶However, if you do tell me both the dream and its meaning, you will be greatly rewarded and highly honored. Now tell me the dream and explain what it means."

⁷"Your Majesty," they said, "if you will only tell us your dream, we will interpret it for you."

⁸The king replied, "You're just stalling for time, ⁹because you know what's going to happen if you don't come up with the answer. You've decided to make up a bunch of lies, hoping I might change my mind. Now tell me the dream, and that will prove that you can interpret it."

¹⁰His advisors explained, "Your Majesty, you are demanding the impossible! No king, not even the most famous and powerful, has ever ordered his advisors, magicians, or wise men to do such a thing. ¹¹It can't be done, except by the gods, and they don't live here on earth."

¹²⁻¹³This made the king so angry that he gave orders for every wise man in Babylonia to be put to death, including Daniel and his three friends.

God Tells Nebuchadnezzar's Dream to Daniel

¹⁴Arioch was the king's official in charge of putting the wise men to death. He was on his way to have it done, when Daniel very wisely went to him ¹⁵and asked, "Why did the king give such cruelᵉ orders?" After Arioch explained what had happened, ¹⁶Daniel rushed off and said to the king, "If you will just give me some time, I'll explain your dream."

¹⁷Daniel returned home and told his three friends. ¹⁸Then he said, "Pray that

the God who rules from heaven will be merciful and explain this mystery, so that we and the others won't be put to death." ¹⁹In a vision one night, Daniel was shown the dream and its meaning. Then he praised the God who rules from heaven:

²⁰"Our God, your name
    will be praised
        forever and forever.
You are all-powerful,
    and you know everything.
²¹You control human events—
    you give rulers their power
        and take it away,
    and you are the source
        of wisdom and knowledge.

²²"You explain deep mysteries,
    because even the dark
        is light to you.
²³You are the God
    who was worshiped
        by my ancestors.
Now I thank you and praise you
    for making me wise
    and telling me the king's dream,
        together with its meaning."

Daniel Interprets the Dream

²⁴Daniel went back to Arioch, the official in charge of executing the wise men. Daniel said, "Don't kill those men! Take me to the king, and I will explain the meaning of his dream."

²⁵Arioch rushed Daniel to the king and announced, "Your Majesty, I have found out that one of the men brought here from Judah can explain your dream."

²⁶The king asked Daniel,ᶠ "Can you tell me my dream and what it means?"

²⁷Daniel answered:

Your Majesty, not even the smartest person in all the world can do what you are demanding. ²⁸⁻²⁹But the God who rules from heaven can explain mysteries. And while you were sleeping, he showed you what will happen in the future. ³⁰However, you must realize that these mysteries weren't explained to me because I am smarter than everyone else. Instead, it was done so that you would understand what you have seen.

³¹Your Majesty, what you saw standing in front of you was a huge and terrifying statue, shining brightly. ³²Its head was made of gold, its chest and arms were silver, and from its waist down to its knees, it was bronze. ³³From there to its ankles it was iron, and its feet were a mixture of iron and clay. ³⁴As you watched, a stone was cut from a mountain—but not by human hands. The stone struck the feet, completely shattering the iron and clay. ³⁵Then the iron, the clay, the bronze, the silver, and the gold were crushed and blown away without a trace, like husks of wheat at threshing time. But the stone became a tremendous mountain that covered the entire earth.

³⁶That was the dream, and now I'll tell you what it means. ³⁷Your Majesty, you are the greatest of kings, and God has highly honored you with power ³⁸over all humans, animals, and birds. You are the head of gold. ³⁹After you are gone, another kingdom will rule, but it won't be as strong. Then it will be followed by a kingdom of bronze that will rule the whole world. ⁴⁰Next, a kingdom of iron will come to power, crushing and shattering everything.ᵍ

ᶠ2.26 *Daniel*: Aramaic "Daniel whose name was Belteshazzar" (see 1.7).   ᵍ2.40 *crushing . . . everything*: Three ancient translations; Aramaic adds "and like iron crushing."

2.18 *God who rules from heaven*: This name for God is common in writings from the Persian period, about 539 to 333 B.C. Of the 22 uses of this name in the Old Testament, 17 come from Ezra, Nehemiah, and Daniel.

Names of God

2.21,22 *wisdom*: Proverbs stresses that true wisdom comes from God and that God's Law offers wisdom and guidance for daily life.

Law

2.30 *mysteries*: The word for "mysteries" came into the Aramaic from the Persian language and means something secret that can only be revealed by God, not by human wisdom. This particular word is found only in Daniel and in the writings known as the Dead Sea Scrolls, which date from the third century B.C. to the first century A.D.

2.36-45 *kingdom*: Some scholars have suggested that the first kingdom, represented by the gold head, was the Babylonian kingdom ruled by Nebuchadnezzar II and that this kingdom was followed by the Media-Persian, Greek, and Roman Empires. Other scholars believe the first kingdom (Babylonia) was followed by the kingdoms of Media, Persia, and Greece. Whichever understanding is preferred, the rule of the mysterious "Darius the Mede" (5.31) falls between the rules of Babylonia's Nebuchadnezzar and Persia's Cyrus.

"Our God, your name will be praised forever and forever. You are all-powerful, and you know everything." Dan 2.20

3.1 *gold statue:* According to the Babylonian measuring system, the statue was 60 cubits high and 6 cubits wide. Sources outside the Bible dating to both the first and fifth centuries B.C. report a golden statue of Zeus in Babylon. This statue may have originally represented the Babylonian god Bel.

3.6 *Anyone who refuses:* As faithful Jews, Daniel and his friends lived by the laws Moses received from the LORD. When the king asked them to worship the statue, he was really asking them to turn their back on their faith.

41-42 This fourth kingdom will be divided—it will be both strong and brittle, just as you saw that the feet and toes were a mixture of iron and clay. **43**This kingdom will be the result of a marriage between kingdoms, but it will crumble, just as iron and clay don't stick together. **44-45**During the time of those kings, the God who rules from heaven will set up an eternal kingdom that will never fall. It will be like the stone that was cut from the mountain, but not by human hands—the stone that crushed the iron, bronze, clay, silver, and gold. Your Majesty, in your dream the great God has told you what is going to happen, and you can trust this interpretation.

Daniel Is Promoted

46King Nebuchadnezzar bowed low to the ground and worshiped Daniel. Then he gave orders for incense to be burned and a sacrifice of grain to be offered in honor of Daniel. **47**The king said, "Now I know that your God is above all other gods and kings, because he gave you the power to explain this mystery." **48**The king then presented Daniel with a lot of gifts; he promoted him to governor of Babylon Province and put him in charge of the other wise men. **49**At Daniel's request, the king appointed Shadrach, Meshach, and Abednego to high positions in Babylon Province, and he let Daniel stay on as a palace official.

King Nebuchadnezzar's Gold Statue

3 King Nebuchadnezzar ordered a gold statue to be built 90 feet high and 9 feet wide. He had it set up in Dura Valley near the city of Babylon, **2**and he commanded

his governors, advisors, treasurers, judges, and his other officials to come from everywhere in his kingdom to the dedication of the statue. **3**So all of them came and stood in front of it.

4Then an official stood up and announced:

People of every nation and race, now listen to the king's command! **5**Trumpets, flutes, harps, and all other kinds of musical instruments will soon start playing. When you hear the music, you must bow down and worship the statue that King Nebuchadnezzar has set up. **6**Anyone who refuses will at once be thrown into a flaming furnace.

7As soon as the people heard the music, they bowed down and worshiped the gold statue that the king had set up.

8Some Babylonians used this as a chance to accuse the Jews to King Nebuchadnezzar. **9**They said, "Your Majesty, we hope you live forever! **10**You commanded everyone to bow down and worship the gold statue when the music played. **11**And you said that anyone who did not bow down and worship it would be thrown into a flaming furnace. **12**Sir, you appointed three men to high positions in Babylon Province, but they have disobeyed you. Those Jews, Shadrach, Meshach, and Abednego, refuse to worship your gods and the statue you have set up."

13King Nebuchadnezzar was furious. So he sent for the three young men and said, **14**"I hear that you refuse to worship my gods and the gold statue I have set up. **15**Now I am going to give you one more chance. If you bow down and worship the statue when you hear the music, everything will be all right. But if you don't, you will at once be thrown into a flaming furnace. No god can save you from me."

16The three men replied, "Your Majesty, we don't need to defend ourselves. **17**The

God we worship can save us from you and your flaming furnace. [18]But even if he doesn't, we still won't worship your gods and the gold statue you have set up."

[19]Nebuchadnezzar's face twisted with anger at the three men. And he ordered the furnace to be heated seven times hotter than usual. [20]Next, he commanded some of his strongest soldiers to tie up the men and throw them into the flaming furnace. [21-23]The king wanted it done at that very moment. So the soldiers tied up Shadrach, Meshach, and Abednego and threw them into the flaming furnace with all of their clothes still on, including their turbans. The fire was so hot that flames leaped out and killed the soldiers.

[24]Suddenly the king jumped up and shouted, "Weren't only three men tied up and thrown into the fire?"

"Yes, Your Majesty," his officers answered.

[25]"But I see four men walking around in the fire," the king replied. "None of them is tied up or harmed, and the fourth one looks like a god."[h]

[26]Nebuchadnezzar went closer to the flaming furnace and said to the three young men, "You servants of the Most High God, come out at once!"

They came out, [27]and the king's high officials, governors, and advisors all crowded around them. The men were not burned, their hair wasn't scorched, and their clothes didn't even smell like smoke. [28]King Nebuchadnezzar said:

Praise their God for sending an angel to rescue his servants! They trusted their God and refused to obey my commands. Yes, they chose to die rather than to worship or serve any god except their own. [29]And I won't allow people of any nation or race to say anything against their God. Anyone who does will be chopped up and their houses will be torn down, because no other god has such great power to save.

[30]After this happened, the king appointed Shadrach, Meshach, and Abednego to even higher positions in Babylon Province.

King Nebuchadnezzar's Letter about His Second Dream

4 King Nebuchadnezzar sent the following letter to the people of all nations and races on the earth:

Greetings to all of you!
[2]I am glad to tell about
    the wonderful miracles
God Most High
    has done for me.
[3]His miracles are mighty
    and marvelous.
He will rule forever,
    and his kingdom
    will never end.

[4]I was enjoying a time of peace and prosperity, [5]when suddenly I had some horrifying dreams and visions. [6]Then I commanded every wise man in Babylonia to appear in my court, so they could explain the meaning of my dream. [7]After they arrived, I told them my dream, but they were not able to say what it meant. [8]Finally, a young man named Daniel came in, and I told him the dream. The holy gods had given him special powers, and I had renamed him Belteshazzar after my own god.
[9]I said, "Belteshazzar, not only are you the wisest of all advisors and counselors,

[h]3.25 *a god*: Aramaic "a son of the gods" or "a son of God."

King Nebuchadnezzar said, *"They chose to die rather than to worship or serve any god except their own . . . no other god has such great power to save."* DAN 3.28,29

4.22 *kingdom covers the earth:* The Babylonian kingdom covered a large area of the ancient Near East. The language is exaggerated to emphasize just how powerful Nebuchadnezzar was. (See Map 7 on pg 1885.)

but the holy gods have given you special powers to solve the most difficult mysteries. So listen to what I dreamed and tell me what it means:

[10]In my sleep I saw
a very tall tree
in the center of the world.
[11]It grew stronger and higher,
until it reached to heaven
and could be seen
from anywhere on earth.
[12]It was covered with leaves
and heavy with fruit—
enough for all nations.
Wild animals enjoyed its shade,
birds nested in its branches,
and all creatures on earth
lived on its fruit.

[13]"While I was in bed, having this vision, a holy angel[i] came down from heaven [14]and shouted:

'Chop down the tree
and cut off its branches;
strip off its leaves
and scatter its fruit.
Make the animals leave its shade
and send the birds flying
from its branches.
[15]But leave its stump and roots
in the ground,
surrounded by grass
and held by chains
of iron and bronze.

'Make sure that this ruler
lives like the animals
out in the open fields,
unprotected from the dew.
[16]Give him the mind

of a wild animal
for seven long years.[j]
[17]This punishment is given
at the command
of the holy angels.[k]
It will show to all who live
that God Most High
controls all kingdoms
and chooses for their rulers
persons of humble birth.'

[18]"Daniel,[l] that was the dream that none of the wise men in my kingdom were able to understand. But I am sure that you will understand what it means, because the holy gods have given you some special powers."

[19]For a while, Daniel[l] was terribly confused and worried by what he was thinking. But I said, "Don't be bothered either by the dream or by what it means."

Daniel replied:

Your Majesty, I wish the dream had been against your enemies. [20]You saw a tree that grew so big and strong that it reached up to heaven and could be seen from anywhere on earth. [21]Its leaves were beautiful, and it produced enough fruit for all living creatures; animals lived in its shade, and birds nested in its branches. [22]Your Majesty, that tree is you. Your glorious reputation has reached heaven, and your kingdom covers the earth.

[23]Then you saw a holy angel[i] come down from heaven and say, "Chop down the tree and destroy it! But leave its stump and roots in the ground, fastened there by a chain of iron and bronze. Let it stay for seven years[m] out in the field with the wild animals, unprotected from the dew."

[i]**4.13** *angel:* The Aramaic text has "watcher," which may be some special class of angel.   [j]**4.16** *long years:* Aramaic "times."   [k]**4.17** *angels:* See the note at 4.13.   [l]**4.18,19** *Daniel:* See the note at 2.26.   [m]**4.23** *years:* Aramaic "times."

²⁴Your Majesty, God Most High has sent you this message, and it means ²⁵that you will be forced to live with the wild animals, far away from humans. You will eat grass like a wild animal and live outdoors for seven years,[n] until you learn that God Most High controls all earthly kingdoms and chooses their rulers. ²⁶But he gave orders not to disturb the stump and roots. This is to show that you will be king once again, after you learn that the God who rules from heaven is in control. ²⁷Your Majesty, please be willing to do what I say. Turn from your sins and start living right; have mercy on those who are mistreated. Then all will go well with you for a long time.

The Rest of Nebuchadnezzar's Letter about His Second Dream

²⁸⁻³⁰About twelve months later, I was walking on the flat roof of my royal palace and admiring the beautiful city of Babylon, when these things started happening to me. I was saying to myself, "Just look at this wonderful capital city that I have built by my own power and for my own glory!" ³¹But before I could finish speaking, a voice from heaven interrupted:

King Nebuchadnezzar, this kingdom is no longer yours. ³²You will be forced to live with the wild animals, away from people. For seven years[n] you will eat grass, as though you were an ox, until you learn that God Most High is in control of all earthly kingdoms and that he is the one who chooses their rulers.

³³This was no sooner said than done—I was forced to live like a wild animal; I ate grass and was unprotected from the dew. As time went by, my hair grew longer than eagle feathers, and my fingernails looked like the claws of a bird.

³⁴Finally, I prayed to God in heaven, and my mind was healed. Then I said:

"I praise and honor
   God Most High.
God lives forever,
and his kingdom
   will never end.
³⁵To him the nations
   are far less than nothing;
God controls the stars in the sky
   and everyone on this earth.
When God does something,
   we cannot change it
   or even ask why."

³⁶At that time my mind was healed, and once again I became the ruler of my glorious kingdom. My advisors and officials returned to me, and I had greater power than ever before. ³⁷That's why I say:

"Praise and honor the King
   who rules from heaven!
Everything he does
   is honest and fair,
and he can shatter the power
   of those who are proud."

King Belshazzar's Banquet

5 One evening, King Belshazzar gave a great banquet for a thousand of his highest officials, and he drank wine with them. ²He got drunk and ordered his servants to bring in the gold and silver cups his father Nebuchadnezzar[o] had taken

---

[n]4.25,32 *years*: Aramaic "times."   [o]5.2 *his father Nebuchadnezzar*: Belshazzar was actually the son of King Nabonidus, who was from another family. But in ancient times, it was possible to refer to a previous king as the "father" of the present king.

■ 4.27 *Turn from your sins . . . have mercy*: The king's repentance was to be carried out in acts of justice and mercy.

Sin

● 4.28-30 *royal palace . . . Babylon*: Nebuchadnezzar rebuilt the great city of Babylon and dedicated it to the god, Marduk. The huge palace and a large temple were protected by a double wall so wide that a chariot team four-horses across could ride on top of it. Ancient Babylon also had one of the Seven Wonders of the ancient world, the Hanging Gardens, and a temple tower known as the Tower of Babel that was nearly 300 feet high.

● 5.1,2 *King Belshazzar . . . father . . . wives*: Belshazzar's name in Babylonian means "Bel, protect the king." Bel was another name for Marduk, Babylon's chief god. No Babylonian records say that Belshazzar was a "full king," but some ancient inscriptions have been discovered which tell of King Nabonidus being away from Babylon for long periods. While he was gone, his son Belshazzar acted as king on his behalf. Following ancient customs Belshazzar had many wives, and many of them were at the banquet. The "wives" probably included women called "concubines," who, though legally bound to a man, did not have the full privileges of a primary wife.

5.7 advisors . . . spirits of the dead: Some of the king's advisors claimed to have the power to speak to the spirits of the dead who were said to have special knowledge about coming events. Others claimed to predict the future based on the movement of the stars.

5.16 third most powerful . . . purple robes: Daniel would be third most powerful after Belshazzar and the king. Purple dye was so expensive that only very wealthy people, like kings, could afford it.

from the temple in Jerusalem. Belshazzar wanted the cups, so that he and all his wives and officials could drink from them.

3-4 When the gold cups were brought in, everyone at the banquet drank from them and praised their idols made of gold, silver, bronze, iron, wood, and stone.

5Suddenly a human hand was seen writing on the plaster wall of the palace. The hand was just behind the lampstand, and the king could see it writing. **6**He was so frightened that his face turned pale, his knees started shaking, and his legs became weak.

7The king called in his advisors, who claimed they could talk with the spirits of the dead and understand the meanings found in the stars. He told them, "The man who can read this writing and tell me what it means will become the third most powerful man in my kingdom. He will wear robes of royal purple and a gold chain around his neck."

8All of King Belshazzar's highest officials came in, but not one of them could read the writing or tell what it meant, **9**and they were completely puzzled. Now the king was more afraid than ever before, and his face turned white as a ghost.

10When the queen heard the king and his officials talking, she came in and said:

Your Majesty, I hope you live forever! Don't be afraid or look so pale. **11**In your kingdom there is a man who has been given special powers by the holy gods. When your father Nebuchadnezzar was king, this man was known to be as smart, intelligent, and wise as the gods themselves. Your father put him in charge of all who claimed they could talk with the spirits or understand the meanings in the stars or tell about the future. **12**He also changed the man's name from Daniel to Belteshazzar. Not only is he wise

and intelligent, but he can explain dreams and riddles and solve difficult problems. Send for Daniel, and he will tell you what the writing means.

13When Daniel was brought in, the king said:

So you are Daniel, one of the captives my father brought back from Judah! **14**I was told that the gods have given you special powers and that you are intelligent and very wise. **15**Neither my advisors nor the men who talk with the spirits of the dead could read this writing or tell me what it means. **16**But I have been told that you understand everything and that you can solve difficult problems. Now then, if you can read this writing and tell me what it means, you will become the third most powerful man in my kingdom. You will wear royal purple robes and have a gold chain around your neck.

17Daniel answered:

Your Majesty, I will read the writing and tell you what it means. But you may keep your gifts or give them to someone else. **18**Sir, the Most High God made your father a great and powerful man and brought him much honor and glory. **19**God did such great things for him that people of all nations and races shook with fear.

Your father had the power of life or death over everyone, and he could honor or ruin anyone he chose. **20**But when he became proud and stubborn, his glorious kingdom was taken from him. **21**His mind became like that of an animal, and he was forced to stay away from people and live with wild donkeys. Your father ate grass like an ox, and he slept outside where his body was soaked with dew. He was forced to do this until he learned that the Most

High God rules all kingdoms on earth and chooses their kings.

²²King Belshazzar, you knew all of this, but you still refused to honor the Lord who rules from heaven. ²³Instead, you turned against him and ordered the cups from his temple to be brought here, so that you and your wives and officials could drink wine from them. You praised idols made of silver, gold, bronze, iron, wood, and stone, even though they cannot see or hear or think. You refused to worship the God who gives you breath and controls everything you do. ²⁴That's why he sent the hand to write this message on the wall.

²⁵⁻²⁸The words written there are *mene*, which means "numbered," *tekel*, which means "weighed," and *parsin*,^P which means "divided." God has numbered the days of your kingdom and has brought it to an end. He has weighed you on his balance scales, and you fall short of what it takes to be king. So God has divided your kingdom between the Medes and the Persians.

²⁹Belshazzar gave a command for Daniel to be made the third most powerful man in his kingdom and to be given a purple robe and a gold chain. ³⁰That same night, the king was killed. ³¹Then Darius the Mede, who was 62 years old, took over his kingdom.

Daniel in a Pit of Lions

6 Darius divided his kingdom into 120 states and placed a governor in charge of each one. ²In order to make sure that his government was run properly, Darius put three other officials in charge of the governors. One of these officials was Daniel. ³And he did his work so much better than the other governors and officials that the king decided to let him govern the whole kingdom.

⁴The other men tried to find something wrong with the way Daniel did his work for the king. But they could not accuse him of anything wrong, because he was honest and faithful and did everything he was supposed to do. ⁵Finally, they said to one another, "We will never be able to bring any charge against Daniel, unless it has to do with his religion."

⁶They all went to the king and said:

"Your Majesty, we hope you live forever! ⁷All of your officials, leaders, advisors, and governors agree that you should make a law forbidding anyone to pray to any god or human except you for the next 30 days. Everyone who disobeys this law must be thrown into a pit of lions. ⁸Order this to be written and then sign it, so it cannot be changed, just as no written law of the Medes and Persians can be changed."

⁹So King Darius made the law and had it written down.

¹⁰Daniel heard about the law, but when he returned home, he went upstairs and prayed in front of the window that faced Jerusalem. In the same way that he had always done, he knelt down in prayer three times a day, giving thanks to God.

¹¹The men who had spoken to the king watched Daniel and saw him praying to his God for help. ¹²They went back to the king and said, "Didn't you make a law that

5.25-28 *Medes and the Persians:* The Medes came from Media, a land about 400 miles north of the Persian Gulf. The Medes helped Babylon defeat the Assyrians in 612 B.C. Media became a province of the Persian Empire in 549 B.C. The Persians came from the area that corresponds to modern-day Iran. After defeating the Medes in 549 B.C. they defeated Babylon in 539 B.C. Their empire influenced much of the ancient Near East until they were defeated by Alexander the Great of Macedonia (Greece) in 331 B.C. **(See Map 8 on pg 1886.)**

5.31 *Darius the Mede:* There is no mention of this Darius outside of the Bible. Darius I was a Persian king who ruled from 522 to 486 B.C. and may not be the ruler intended here.

6.8 *cannot be changed:* Once signed, an official decree must be carried out. Note that Darius does not want Daniel to be killed, although it is Darius' own decree that puts Daniel in danger.

6.10 *prayer three times a day:* During and after the time of the exile, facing west towards Jerusalem during prayer was important for the Jewish people (2 Chr 6.37-39; 1 Kgs 8.38-45). Prayers were not required three times a day, but the Law of Moses did call for morning and evening prayer (1 Chr 23.30).

Prayer

P5.25-28 *mene . . . tekel . . . parsin:* In the Aramaic text of verse 25, the words "mene, tekel, parsin," are used, and in verses 26-28 the words "mene, tekel, peres" (the singular of "parsin") are used. "Parsin" means "divided," but "peres" can mean either "divided" or "Persia."

6.28 *Cyrus the Persian:* Cyrus of Persia defeated Babylon and brought it under Persian rule in 539 B.C. He ruled from 539 to 530 B.C. The prophet Isaiah spoke of Cyrus as God's "chosen one" (Isa 45.1,4) who would help the Jewish people to be released from captivity in Babylon. An ancient Persian document, called the *Cyrus Cylinder,* describes how Cyrus defeated the Babylonians and treated foreign captives there with generosity. (See the article After the Exile: God's People Return to Judea on pg 1789.)

7.1,2 *first year of King Belshazzar:* 554 or 553 B.C. The events described in chapter 7 happened before the events in chapter 5.

7.1-2 *winds . . . mighty sea:* The four winds and the sea are characters in an ancient Babylonian myth about Marduk.

7.3-7 *four powerful beasts:* The beasts that come from the sea are different ancient kingdoms. The first refers to the Babylonian Empire. The second beast represents the kingdom of Media. The Medes' attack on Babylon had been predicted but did not happen. The third beast represents Persia. The fourth beast refers to the empire founded by Alexander the Great, who defeated the Persians in 331 B.C. Some scholars suggest that the second kingdom was that of Media-Persia, the third, Greek, and the fourth, Roman.

forbids anyone to pray to any god or human except you for the next 30 days? And doesn't the law say that everyone who disobeys it will be thrown into a pit of lions?"

"Yes, that's the law I made," the king agreed. "And just like all written laws of the Medes and Persians, it cannot be changed."

[13]The men then told the king, "That Jew named Daniel, who was brought here as a captive, refuses to obey you or the law that you ordered to be written. And he still prays to his god three times a day." [14]The king was really upset to hear about this, and for the rest of the day he tried to think how he could save Daniel.

[15]At sunset the men returned and said, "Your Majesty, remember that no written law of the Medes and Persians can be changed, not even by the king."

[16]So Darius ordered Daniel to be brought out and thrown into a pit of lions. But he said to Daniel, "You have been faithful to your God, and I pray that he will rescue you."

[17]A stone was rolled over the pit, and it was sealed. Then Darius and his officials stamped the seal to show that no one should let Daniel out. [18]All night long the king could not sleep. He did not eat anything, and he would not let anyone come in to entertain him.

[19]At daybreak the king got up and ran to the pit. [20]He was anxious and shouted, "Daniel, you were faithful and served your God. Was he able to save you from the lions?"

[21]Daniel answered, "Your Majesty, I hope you live forever! [22]My God knew that I was innocent, and he sent an angel to keep the lions from eating me. Your Majesty, I have never done anything to hurt you."

[23]The king was relieved to hear Daniel's voice, and he gave orders for him to be taken out of the pit. Daniel's faith in his God had kept him from being harmed. [24]And the king ordered the men who had brought charges against Daniel to be thrown into the pit, together with their wives and children. But before they even reached the bottom, the lions ripped them to pieces.

[25]King Darius then sent this message to all people of every nation and race in the world:

"Greetings to all of you!
[26]I command everyone
in my kingdom
to worship and honor
the God of Daniel.
He is the living God,
the one who lives forever.
His power and his kingdom
will never end.
[27]He rescues people
and sets them free
by working great miracles.
Daniel's God has rescued him
from the power of the lions."

[28]All went well for Daniel while Darius was king, and even when Cyrus the Persian ruled.⁋

Daniel's Vision of the Four Beasts

7 [1-2]Daniel wrote:
In the first year of King Belshazzar[r] of Babylonia, I had some dreams and visions while I was asleep one night, and I wrote them down.

The four winds were stirring up the mighty sea, [3]when suddenly four powerful beasts came out of the sea. Each beast was different. [4] The first was like a lion with the wings of an eagle. As I watched, its wings were pulled off. Then it was lifted to an upright position and made to stand on two feet, just like a human, and it was given a human mind.

⁵The second beast looked like a bear standing on its hind legs.ˢ It held three ribs in its teeth, and it was told, "Attack! Eat all the flesh you want."

⁶The third beast was like a leopard—except that it had four wings and four heads. It was given authority to rule.

⁷The fourth beast was stronger and more terrifying than the others. Its huge teeth were made of iron, and what it didn't grind with its teeth, it smashed with its feet. It was different from the others, and it had horns on its head—ten of them. ⁸Just as I was thinking about these horns, a smaller horn appeared, and three of the other horns were pulled up by the roots to make room for it. This horn had the eyes of a human and a mouth that spoke with great arrogance.

Judgment

Daniel wrote:
> ⁹Thrones were set up
>   while I was watching,
> and the Eternal Godᵗ
>   took his place.
> His clothing and his hair
>   were white as snow.
> His throne was a blazing fire
>   with fiery wheels,
> ¹⁰and flames were dashing out
>   from all around him.

> Countless thousands
>   were standing there
>   to serve him.
> The time of judgment began,
>   and the booksᵘ were opened.

¹¹I watched closely to see what would happen to this smaller horn because of the arrogant things it was saying. Then before my very eyes, the fourth beast was killed and its body destroyed by fire. ¹²The other three beasts had their authority taken from them, but they were allowed to live a while longer.ᵛ ¹³As I continued to watch the vision that night,
> I saw what looked like
>   a son of manʷ
> coming with the clouds of heaven,
> and he was presented
>   to the Eternal God.ˣ
> ¹⁴He was crowned king
>   and given power and glory,
> so that all people
> of every nation and race
>   would serve him.
> He will rule forever,
> and his kingdom is eternal,
>   never to be destroyed.

The Meaning of Daniel's Vision

¹⁵Daniel wrote:
I was terrified by these visions, and I didn't know what to think. ¹⁶So I asked one of those standing there,ʸ and he explained, ¹⁷"The four beasts are four earthly kingdoms. ¹⁸But God Most High will give his

● **7.8** *smaller horn:* Probably Antiochus IV Epiphanes, the Seleucid ruler who controlled Palestine from 175 to 164 B.C. He tried to get the Jewish people to abandon their worship and customs and adopt the Greek lifestyle. Some traditions interpret the smaller horn as the antichrist.

■ **7.10** *books:* Books of judgment containing the record of good and evil that each person has done. God is depicted as a judge.

■ **7.13** *son of man:* The human being is contrasted with the beasts representing the earthly kingdoms. The "son" is crowned as king over an eternal kingdom. In the New Testament, Jesus refers to himself as the son of man, to emphasize his humanity and his role as the one who will save all of God's people (see Matt 24.30; 26.64; Mark 13.26; 14.62; Luke 21.27; Rev 1.7,13; 14.14).

❧   Son of Man

ˢ**7.5** *standing on its hind legs:* Or "higher on one side than the other" or "with a paw lifted up." ᵗ**7.9** *Eternal God:* Aramaic "Ancient of Days." ᵘ**7.10** *books:* Containing the record of the good and evil that each person has done. ᵛ**7.12** *a while longer:* Aramaic "for a time and a season." ʷ**7.13** *son of man:* Or "human." In Aramaic "son of man" may mean a human or even "oneself" ("I" or "me"). Jesus often used the phrase "the Son of Man" when referring to himself. ˣ**7.13** *Eternal God:* See the note at 7.9. ʸ**7.16** *one of those standing there:* Possibly an angel sent to interpret the visions or one of those thousands mentioned in verse 10.

7.25 *king will speak evil . . . try to change God's Law:* Antiochus IV Epiphanes banned the Jewish people from observing the Sabbath and from celebrating the yearly Jewish festivals (see Rev 12.14; 13.5,6; and 1 Maccabees 1.41-53 in the *Apocrypha*).

8.1 *third year:* With this verse, the rest of DANIEL is written in Hebrew.

8.2 *Susa:* Susa was a fortress-city located east of Babylon in the province of Elam. **(See Map 8 on pg 1886.)**

8.3-7 *ram . . . with two horns . . . goat:* The ram with two horns refers to the Medes and Persians who were pictured as being together in one kingdom. The longer horn stands for Persia, which controlled lands to its west, north, and south, including Palestine. The goat from the west represents the Macedonians, led by Alexander the Great, who conquered Persia in 331 B.C.

kingdom to his chosen ones, and it will be theirs forever and ever."

¹⁹I wanted to know more about the fourth beast,ᶻ because it was so different and much more terrifying than the others. What was the meaning of its iron teeth and bronze claws and of its feet that smashed what the teeth and claws had not ground and crushed? ²⁰I also wanted to know more about all ten of those horns on its head. I especially wanted to know more about the one that took the place of three of the others—the horn that had eyes and spoke with arrogance and seemed greater than the others. ²¹While I was looking, this horn attacked God's chosen ones and was winning the battle. ²²Then God Most High, the Eternal God,ᵃ came and judged in favor of his chosen ones, because the time had arrived for them to be given the kingdom.

²³Then I was told
by the one standing there:
"The fourth beast
will be a fourth kingdom
to appear on earth.
It will be different
from all the others—
it will trample the earth
and crush it to pieces.
²⁴All ten of those horns are kings
who will come from this kingdom,
and one more will follow.
This horn will be different
from the others,
and it will conquer
three other kings.

²⁵"This king will speak evil
of God Most High,

and he will be cruel
to God's chosen ones.
He will try to change God's Law
and the sacred seasons.
And he will be able to do this
for a time, two times,
and half a time.ᵇ
²⁶But he will finally be judged,
and his kingdom
completely destroyed.

²⁷"Then the greatest kingdom of all
will be given to the chosen ones
of God Most High.
His kingdom will be eternal,
and all others will serve
and obey him."

²⁸That was what I saw and heard. I turned pale with fear and kept it all to myself.

Vision of a Ram and a Goat

8 Daniel wrote:
In the third year of King Belshazzar of Babylonia,ᶜ I had a second vision ²in which I was in Susa, the chief city of Babylonia's Elam Province. I was beside the Ulai River,ᵈ ³when I looked up and saw a ram standing there with two horns on its head—both of them were long, but the second one was longer than the first. ⁴The ram went charging toward the west, the north, and the south. No other animals were strong enough to oppose him, and nothing could save them from his power. So he did as he pleased and became even more powerful.

⁵I kept on watching and saw a goat come from the west and charge across the entire

ᶻ7.19 *fourth beast:* See verses 7,8.   ᵃ7.22 *Eternal God:* See the note at 7,9.   ᵇ7.25 *for . . . time:* Or "for a year, two years, and half a year."   ᶜ8.1 *third year . . . Babylonia:* 552 B.C., two years after the first vision (see 7.1,2).   ᵈ8.2 *River:* Or "Gate."

earth, without even touching the ground. Between his eyes was a powerful horn,[e] [6]and with tremendous anger the goat started toward the ram that I had seen beside the river.[f] [7]The goat was so fierce that its attack broke both horns of the ram, leaving him powerless. Then the goat stomped on the ram, and no one could do anything to help. [8]After this, the goat became even more powerful. But at the peak of his power, his mighty horn was broken, and four other mighty horns took its place— one pointing to the north and one to the east, one to the south and one to the west.

[9]A little horn came from one of these, and its power reached to the south, the east, and even to the holy land.[g] [10]It became so strong that it attacked the stars in the sky, which were heaven's army.[h] Then it threw some of them down to the earth and stomped on them. [11-12]It humiliated heaven's army and dishonored its leader[i] by keeping him from offering the daily sacrifices. In fact, it was so terrible that it even disgraced the temple and wiped out true worship. It also did everything else it wanted to do.

[13]Then one of the holy angels asked another, "When will the daily sacrifices be offered again? What about this horrible rebellion? When will the temple and heaven's army no longer be trampled in the dust?"

[14]The other answered, "It will be 2,300 evenings and mornings before the temple is dedicated and in use again."

Gabriel Interprets the Vision

[15]Daniel wrote:

I was trying to figure out the meaning of the vision, when someone suddenly appeared there beside me. [16]And from beside the Ulai River,[j] a voice like that of a human said, "Gabriel, help him understand the vision."

[17]Gabriel came over, and I fell to the ground in fear. Then he said, "You are merely a human, but you need to understand that this vision is about the end of time."

[18]While he was speaking, I fell facedown in a deep sleep. But he lifted me to my feet [19]and said:

Listen, and I will tell you what will happen at the end of time, when God has chosen to show his anger. [20]The two horns of the ram are the kings of Media and Persia, [21]the goat is the kingdom of Greece, and the powerful horn between his eyes is the first of its kings. [22]After this horn is broken, four other kingdoms will appear, but they won't be as strong.

[23]When these rulers have become as evil as possible, their power will end, and then a king who is dangerous and cannot be trusted will appear. [24]He will gain strength, but not on his own, and he will cause terrible destruction. He will wipe out powerful leaders and God's people as well. [25]His deceitful lies will make him so successful, that he will think he is really great. Suddenly he will kill many people, and he will even attack God, the Supreme Ruler. But God will crush him!

[26]This vision about the evenings and mornings is true, but these things won't happen for a long time, so don't tell it to others.

[27]After this, I was so worn out and weak

8.8 *mighty horn was broken:* Alexander the Great died in 323 B.C. His large empire was divided among four generals. The four horns most likely refer to these four men. The descendants of Ptolemy and Seleucus fought each other for control of the Near East and Egypt.

8.9-12 *little horn . . . attacked . . . heaven's army:* The little horn is Antiochus IV Epiphanes.

8.14 *2,300:* Or 1,150 days. There were to be two daily sacrifices in the temple, one in the morning and one at dusk (Exod 29.38-42). Antiochus IV stopped these sacrifices and set up the foreign altar in 167 B.C. The Jewish people led by Judas Maccabeus eventually defeated Antiochus and rededicated the temple on Chislev 25, 164 B.C. (around mid-December). The 1,150 days roughly correspond to the three and a half years mentioned in 1 Maccabees 1.54—4.52.

8.16 *Gabriel:* An angel whose name means "God is Mighty."

8.17 *end of time:* Here this phrase refers to the end of the persecution of God's people, not to the final end of time.

8.23 *a king who is dangerous:* Antiochus IV Epiphanes. Record of Antiochus' sneak attack on Jerusalem is reported in the *Apocrypha,* 1 Maccabees 1.29,30.

---

[e]**8.5** *powerful horn:* Hebrew "horn of vision." [f]**8.6** *river:* See the note at 8.2. [g]**8.9** *holy land:* Hebrew "the lovely land." [h]**8.10** *heaven's army:* In verses 10-13 the Hebrew word translated "heaven's army" may also mean "God's people." [i]**8.11,12** *leader:* Hebrew "prince." [j]**8.16** *River:* See the note at 8.2.

9.1-2 *70 years:* The rebuilt temple was dedicated in 515 B.C. Most likely, the "70 years" here symbolizes a whole lifetime.

9.12-14 *worst disaster . . . horrible disaster:* Refers either to the destruction of Jerusalem and the temple and the exile that followed in Babylon in the sixth century B.C., or the pollution of the Jerusalem temple under Antiochus in the second century B.C.

9.16 *holy mountain:* The temple in Jerusalem was built on an area of high ground known as Mount Zion.

Zion

that it was several days before I could get out of bed and go about my duties for the king. I was disturbed by this vision that made no sense to me.

Daniel Prays for the People

9 [1-2] Daniel wrote:
.   Some years later, Darius the Mede,[k] who was the son of Xerxes,[l] had become king of Babylonia. And during his first year as king, I found out from studying the writings of the prophets that the LORD had said to Jeremiah, "Jerusalem will lie in ruins for 70 years."[m] [3-4]Then, to show my sorrow, I went without eating and dressed in sackcloth[n] and sat in ashes. I confessed my sins and earnestly prayed to the LORD my God:

Our Lord, you are a great and fearsome God, and you faithfully keep your agreement with those who love and obey you. [5]But we have sinned terribly by rebelling against you and rejecting your laws and teachings. [6]We have ignored the message your servants the prophets spoke to our kings, our leaders, our ancestors, and everyone else.

[7]Everything you do is right, our Lord. But still we suffer public disgrace because we have been unfaithful and have sinned against you. This includes all of us, both far and near—the people of Judah, Jerusalem, and Israel, as well as those you dragged away to foreign lands, [8]and even our kings, our officials, and our ancestors. [9]LORD God, you are merciful and forgiving, even though we have rebelled against

you [10]and rejected your teachings that came to us from your servants the prophets.

[11]Everyone in Israel has stubbornly refused to obey your laws, and so those curses written by your servant Moses have fallen upon us. [12]You warned us and our leaders that Jerusalem would suffer the worst disaster in human history, and you did exactly as you had threatened. [13]We have not escaped any of the terrible curses written by Moses, and yet we have refused to beg you for mercy and to remind ourselves of how faithful you have always been. [14]And when you finally punished us with this horrible disaster, that was also the right thing to do, because we deserved it so much.

[15]Our Lord God, with your own mighty arm you rescued us from Egypt and made yourself famous to this very day, but we have sinned terribly. [16]In the past, you treated us with such kindness, that we now beg you to stop being so terribly angry with Jerusalem. After all, it is your chosen city built on your holy mountain, even though it has suffered public disgrace because of our sins and those of our ancestors.

[17]I am your servant, Lord God, and I beg you to answer my prayers and bring honor to yourself by having pity on your temple that lies in ruins. [18]Please show mercy to your chosen city, not because we deserve it, but because of your great kindness. [19]Forgive us! Hurry and do something, not only for your city and your chosen people, but to bring honor to yourself.

[k]9.1,2 *Darius the Mede:* See 5.31. [l]9.1,2 *Xerxes:* Hebrew "Ahasuerus." [m]9.1,2 *70 years:* See Jeremiah 25.11-13; 29.10. [n]9.3,4 *sackcloth:* A rough, dark-colored cloth made from goat or camel hair and used to make grain sacks. It was worn in times of trouble or sorrow.

The Seventy Weeks

Daniel wrote:

[20]I was still confessing my sins and those of all Israel to the LORD my God, and I was praying for the good of his holy mountain,[o] [21]when Gabriel suddenly came flying in at the time of the evening sacrifice. This was the same Gabriel I had seen in my vision, [22]and he explained:

Daniel, I am here to help you understand the vision. [23]God thinks highly of you, and at the very moment you started praying, I was sent to give you the answer. [24]God has decided that for 70 weeks,[p] your people and your holy city must suffer as the price of their sins. Then evil will disappear, and justice will rule forever; the visions and words of the prophets will come true, and a most holy place will be dedicated.[q]

[25]You need to realize that from the command to rebuild Jerusalem until the coming of the Chosen Leader,[r] it will be 7 weeks and another 62 weeks.[s] Streets will be built in Jerusalem, and a trench will be dug around the city for protection, but these will be difficult times.[t] [26]At the end of the 62 weeks,[u] the Chosen Leader[v] will be killed and left with nothing.[w]

A foreign ruler and his army will sweep down like a mighty flood, leaving both the city and the temple in ruins, and war and destruction will continue until the end, just as God has decided. [27]For one week[x] this foreigner[y] will make a firm agreement with many people, and halfway through this week,[z] he will end all sacrifices and offerings. Then the "Horrible Thing" that causes destruction will be put there. And it will stay there until the time God has decided to destroy this one who destroys.

Daniel's Vision beside the Tigris River

10 In the third year[a] of Cyrus the king of Persia, a message came to Daniel[b] from God, and it was explained in a vision. The message was about a dreadful war, and it was true. [2]Daniel wrote:

For three weeks I was in sorrow. [3]I ate no fancy food or meat, I drank no wine, and I put no olive oil on my face or hair.[c] [4]Then, on the twenty-fourth day of the first month,[d] I was standing on the banks of the

---

9.24 *70 weeks ... most holy place ... dedicated:* This time of suffering is also translated as 70 weeks of years, or 490 years. Daniel may be describing the restoration of the temple completed in 515 B.C.

9.26 *Chosen Leader ... foreign ruler:* This refers to another "chosen leader" many years after the one mentioned in 9.25. Most likely it is Onias III, the high priest when Antiochus IV came to power. For those who identify Jesus Christ as the "chosen leader," the killing refers to the death of Jesus on a cross. The "foreign ruler" refers to Antiochus IV.

9.27 *"Horrible Thing":* The "Horrible Thing" has been identified as an altar used to make sacrifices to foreign gods or as some kind of statue honoring one of the Greek gods (see the *Apocrypha,* 1 Maccabees 1.11,15,54). It remained in the temple for the three and a half years till 25 Chislev 164 B.C. when the temple was purified and rededicated.

10.4 *Tigris River:* A river in Babylonia that joined the Euphrates River and formed a wide fertile area. **(See Map 8 on pg 1886.)**

---

[o]**9.20** *holy mountain:* Jerusalem (see verse 16) or the temple. [p]**9.24** *70 weeks:* Or "70 times 7 years." [q]**9.24** *a most holy place will be dedicated:* Or "God's Holy One will appear." [r]**9.25** *the Chosen Leader:* Or "a chosen leader." In Hebrew the word "chosen" means "to pour oil (on someone's head)." In Old Testament times it was the custom to pour oil on a person's head when that person was chosen to be a priest or a king. [s]**9.25** *7 weeks and another 62 weeks:* Or "7 times 7 years and another 62 times 7 years." [t]**9.25** *it will be 7 . . . difficult times:* Or "it will be 7 weeks. Then streets will be built in Jerusalem, and a trench will be dug around the city for protection. But Jerusalem will have difficult times for 62 weeks." [u]**9.26** *62 weeks:* Or "62 times 7 years." [v]**9.26** *the Chosen Leader:* See the note at 9.25. [w]**9.26** *left with nothing:* Or "no one will take his place." [x]**9.27** *one week:* Or "7 years." [y]**9.27** *this foreigner:* Or "the Chosen Leader." [z]**9.27** *halfway through this week:* Or "for half of this week of 7 years." [a]**10.1** *third year:* 536 B.C. [b]**10.1** *Daniel:* See the note at 2.26. [c]**10.3** *olive oil . . . hair:* On special occasions, it was the custom to put olive oil on one's face and hair. [d]**10.4** *first month:* Nisan (also known as Abib), the first month of the Hebrew calendar, from about mid-March to mid-April.

10.13 *guardian angel of Persia . . . Michael:* In ancient Near Eastern stories, battles between the gods or angel-princes who represented different countries were common. Michael was the guardian angel of the Jewish people.

Persia

11.5 *king of the south . . . one of his generals:* This may refer to Ptolemy I of Egypt and Seleucus I, who established an even greater empire to the north in Syria.

great Tigris River, ⁵when I looked up and saw someone dressed in linen and wearing a solid gold belt.ᵉ ⁶His body was like a precious stone,ᶠ his face like lightning, his eyes like flaming fires, his arms and legs like polished bronze, and his voice like the roar of a crowd. ⁷Although the people who were with me did not see the vision, they became so frightened that they scattered and hid. ⁸Only I saw this great vision. I became weak and pale, ⁹and at the sound of his voice, I fell facedown in a deep sleep.

¹⁰He raised me to my hands and knees ¹¹and then said, "Daniel, your God thinks highly of you, and he has sent me. So stand up and pay close attention." I stood trembling, while the angel said:

¹²Daniel, don't be afraid! God has listened to your prayers since the first day you humbly asked for understanding, and he has sent me here. ¹³But the guardian angelᵍ of Persia opposed me for 21 days. Then Michael, who is one of the strongest guardian angels,ʰ came to rescue me from the kings of Persia.ⁱ ¹⁴Now I have come here to give you another vision about what will happen to your people in the future.

¹⁵While this angel was speaking to me, I stared at the ground, speechless. ¹⁶Then he appeared in human form and touched my lips. I said, "Sir, this vision has brought me great pain and has drained my strength. ¹⁷I am merely your servant. How can I possibly speak with someone so powerful, when I am almost too weak to get my breath?"

¹⁸⁻¹⁹The angel touched me a second time and said, "Don't be frightened! God thinks highly of you, and he intends this for your good, so be brave and strong."

At this, I regained my strength and replied, "Please speak! You have already made me feel much better."

²⁰Then the angel said:

Now do you understand why I have come? Soon I must leave to fight against the guardian angel of Persia. Then after I have defeated him, the guardian angel of Greece will attack me. ²¹I will tell you what is written in *The Book of Truth.* But first, you must realize that no one except Michael, the guardian angel of Israel, is on my side.

11 ¹You also need to know that I protected and helped Darius the Medeʲ in his first year as king.

The Angel's Message to Daniel

Part One: The Four Kings and Their Successors

²What I am going to tell you is certain to happen. Four kings will rule Persia, one after the other, but the fourth one will become much richer than the others. In fact, his wealth will make him so powerful that he will turn everyone against the kingdom of Greece. ³Then a mighty king will come to power and will be able to do whatever he pleases. ⁴But suddenly his kingdom will be crushed and scattered to the four corners of the earth, where four more kingdoms will rise. But these won't be ruled by his descendants or be as powerful as his kingdom.

⁵The king of the south will grow powerful. Then one of his generals will rebel and will rule an even larger kingdom. ⁶Years later the southern kingdom and the northern kingdom will make a treaty, and the

ᵉ**10.5** *solid gold belt:* Hebrew "belt of gold from Uphaz." ᶠ**10.6** *a precious stone:* The Hebrew text has "beryl," which is green or bluish-green. ᵍ**10.13** *guardian angel:* Hebrew "prince." ʰ**10.13** *one of the strongest guardian angels:* Hebrew "chief prince." ⁱ**10.13** *came . . . Persia:* One possible meaning for the difficult Hebrew text. ʲ**11.1** *Darius the Mede:* See 5.30.

daughter of the king of the south will marry the king of the north. But she will lose her power. Then she, her husband, their child,[k] and the servants who came with her will all be killed.

After this, **7**one of her relatives will become the ruler of the southern kingdom. He will attack the army of the northern kingdom and capture its fortresses. **8**Then he will carry their idols to Egypt, together with their precious treasures of silver and gold, but it will be a long time before he attacks the northern kingdom again. Some years later **9**the king of the north will invade the southern kingdom, but he will be forced back to his own country.

10The sons of the king of the north will gather a huge army that will sweep down like a roaring flood, reaching all the way to the fortress of the southern kingdom. **11**But this will make the king of the south angry, and he will defeat this large army from the north. **12**The king of the south will feel proud because of the many thousands he has killed. But his victories won't last long, **13**because the king of the north will gather a larger and more powerful army than ever before. Then in a few years, he will start invading other countries.

14At this time many of your own people will try to make this vision come true by rebelling against the king of the south, but their rebellion will fail. **15**Then the army from the north will surround and capture a fortress in the south, and not even the most experienced troops of the southern kingdom will be able to make them retreat. **16**The king who invaded from the north will do as he pleases, and he will even capture and destroy the holy land.[l] **17**In fact, he will decide to invade the south with his entire army. Then he will attempt

to make peace by giving the king of the south a bride from the northern kingdom, but this won't be successful.

18Afterwards, this proud king of the north will invade and conquer many of the nations along the coast, but a military leader will defeat him and make him lose his pride. **19**He will retreat to his fortresses in his own country, but on the way he will be defeated and never again be seen.

20The next king of the north will try to collect taxes for the glory of his kingdom. However, he will come to a sudden end in some mysterious way, instead of in battle or because of someone's anger.

Part Two: The Evil King from the North

21The successor of this king of the north will be a worthless nobody, who doesn't even come from a royal family. He will suddenly appear and gain control of the kingdom by treachery. **22**Then he will destroy armies and remove God's chosen high priest. **23**He will make a treaty, but he will be deceitful and break it, even though he has only a few followers. **24**Without warning, he will successfully invade a wealthy province, which is something his ancestors never did. Then he will divide among his followers all of its treasures and property. But none of this will last very long.

25He will gather a large and powerful army, and with great courage he will attack the king of the south. The king of the south will meet him with a much stronger army, but he will lose the battle, because he will be betrayed **26**by members of the royal court. He will be ruined, and most of his army will be slaughtered.

27The two kings will meet around a table

---

k11.6 *their child:* One Hebrew manuscript and two ancient translations; most Hebrew manuscripts "her father." **l**11.16 *the holy land:* See the note at 8.9.

● 11.9,10 *king of the north . . . sons:* Seleucus II Callinicus (246–226 B.C.) tried to invade the southern kingdom but was defeated. His sons, Seleucus III (226–223 B.C.) and Antiochus III (called "the Great"; 223–187 B.C.) could not defeat the southern kingdom either.

● 11.11 *king of the south . . . north:* Ptolemy IV Philopator (221–203 B.C.), king of the south, defeated Antiochus III, king of the north, in 217 B.C. at Raphia. Later Antiochus III was joined by some of the Jewish people to fight against Ptolemy V Epiphanes (203–181 B.C.), king of the south.

● 11.20 *next king of the north:* Antiochus III's son Seleucus IV Philopator (187–175 B.C.). He sent his finance minister Heliodorus to take money from the treasury of the Jewish temple in Jerusalem (see the *Apocrypha,* 1 Maccabees 3.1-40). Seleucus IV was assassinated by supporters of Heliodorus.

● 11.22-24 *remove . . . high priest . . . make a treaty . . . invade a wealthy province:* Antiochus IV removed the Jewish high priest Onias III and made a treaty with Pergamum, which allowed Antiochus to take it over with a small force. The "wealthy province" may refer to Egypt.

● 11.25-27 *attack the king of the south . . . tell evil lies:* Antiochus IV attacked Egypt, which was ruled by the young Ptolemy VI Philometor. The "evil lies" may refer to Antiochus IV trying to trick Ptolemy VI into giving Antiochus control over Egypt.

11.28 *return . . . attack:* Before Antiochus left Egypt, the city of Alexandria declared its support for Ptolemy Euergetes and Cleopatra (brother and sister of Philometor). Antiochus tried to take the city but couldn't, so he returned home by way of Palestine in 169 B.C. He entered the temple in Jerusalem and stole large amounts of gold (see the *Apocrypha,* 1 Maccabees 1.20).

11.29,30 *invade the southern kingdom . . . Ships from the west:* Antiochus IV's next invasion of Egypt in 168 B.C. was stopped by Roman troops that came on ships from the west.

11.37,38 *god preferred by women . . . god of fortresses:* It is unclear which gods Antiochus IV rejected, but the god preferred by women probably is Tammuz (Adonis), the Mesopotamian god of vegetation. The "god of fortresses" likely refers to the Greek god Zeus. Antiochus rewarded those who worshiped Zeus and encouraged the spread of the Zeus cult.

11.40-45 *king of the south . . . Ammon . . . King of the north:* Daniel 11.40-45 describes the hoped-for end of Antiochus IV, but the historical records apart from the Bible do not clearly show the details mentioned here. The king of the northern kingdom is identified as Antiochus IV. Edom, Moab, and Ammon escape the northern king's massacre, but the people of the holy land do not. Verse 44 shows a reaction similar to that of Antiochus IV in 11.30,31. The destruction of the evil king is said to come in a battle taking place between the Mediterranean Sea and Mount Zion.

and tell evil lies to each other. But their plans will fail, because God has already decided what will happen. [28]Then the king of the north will return to his country with great treasures. But on the way, he will attack the religion of God's people and do whatever else he pleases.

[29]At the time God has decided, the king of the north will invade the southern kingdom again, but this time, things will be different. [30]Ships from the west will come to attack him, and he will be discouraged. Then he will start back to his own country and take out his anger on the religion of God's faithful people, while showing kindness to those who are unfaithful. [31]He will send troops to pollute the temple and the fortress, and he will stop the daily sacrifices. Then he will set up that "Horrible Thing" that causes destruction. [32]The king will use deceit to win followers from those who are unfaithful to God, but those who remain faithful will do everything possible to oppose him.

[33]Wise leaders will instruct many of the people. But for a while, some of these leaders will either be killed with swords or burned alive, or else robbed of their possessions and thrown into prison. [34]They will receive only a little help in their time of trouble, and many of their followers will be treacherous. [35]Some of those who are wise will suffer, so that God will make them pure and acceptable until the end, which will still come at the time he has decided.

[36]This king will do as he pleases. He will proudly claim to be greater than any god and will insult the only true God. Indeed, he will be successful until God is no longer angry with his people. [37]This king will reject the gods his ancestors worshiped and the god preferred by women.[m] In fact, he will put himself above all gods [38]and worship only the so-called god of fortresses, who was unknown to his ancestors. And he will honor it with gold, silver, precious stones, and other costly gifts. [39]With the help of this foreign god, he will capture the strongest fortresses. Everyone who worships this god will be put in a position of power and rewarded with wealth and land.

Part Three: The Time of the End

[40]At the time of the end, the king of the south will attack the kingdom of the north. But its king will rush out like a storm with war chariots, cavalry, and many ships. Indeed, his forces will flood one country after another, [41]and when they reach the holy land,[n] tens of thousands will be killed. But the countries of Edom and Moab and the ruler of Ammon[o] will escape.

[42]The king of the north will invade many countries, including Egypt, [43]and he will take its rich treasures of gold and silver. He will also conquer Libya and Ethiopia.[P] [44]But he will be alarmed by news from the east and the north, and he will become furious and cause great destruction. [45]After this, he will set up camp between the Mediterranean Sea and Mount Zion. Then he will be destroyed, and no one will be able to save him.

Part Four: The Dead Will Rise to Life

12 Michael, the chief of the angels, is the protector of your people, and he will come at a time of terrible suffering, the worst in all of history. And your people

[m]11.37 *god preferred by women:* Perhaps Tammuz or Adonis, which were popular among the women of that time.   [n]11.41 *the holy land:* See the note at 8.9.   [o]11.41 *the ruler of Ammon:* Or "what is left of Ammon."   [P]11.43 *Ethiopia:* The Hebrew text has "Cush," which was a region south of Egypt that included parts of the present countries of Ethiopia and Sudan.

who have their names written in *The Book* will be protected. ² Many of those who lie dead in the ground will rise from death. Some of them will be given eternal life, and others will receive nothing but eternal shame and disgrace. ³Everyone who has been wise will shine as bright as the sky above, and everyone who has led others to please God will shine forever like the stars.

⁴Daniel, I now command you to keep the message of this book secret until the end of time, even though many people will go everywhere, searching for the knowledge to be found in it.

The End of Time

⁵Daniel wrote:

I looked around and saw two other people—one on this side of the river and one on the other side. ⁶The angel who had spoken to me was dressed in linen and was standing upstream from them. So one of the two beside the river asked him, "How long before these amazing things happen?"

⁷The angel then raised both hands toward heaven and said, "In the name of the God who lives forever, I solemnly promise that it will be a time, two times, and half a time. Everything will be over, when the suffering of God's holy people comes to an end."

⁸I heard what the angel said, but I didn't understand. So I asked, "Sir, how will it all end?"

The angel in my vision then replied:

⁹Daniel, go about your business, because the meaning of this message will remain secret until the end of time. ¹⁰Many people will have their hearts and lives made pure and clean, but those who are evil will keep on being evil and never understand. Only the wise will understand. ¹¹There will be 1,290 days from the time that the daily sacrifices are stopped, until someone sets up the "Horrible Thing" that causes destruction. ¹²God will bless everyone who patiently waits until 1,335 days have gone by.

¹³So, Daniel, be faithful until the end! You will rest, and at the end of time, you will rise from death to receive your reward.

12.5,6 *two other people ... angel*: The two people witness the angel's proclamation. According to the Law of Moses, two witnesses were needed to confirm an event.

12.11 *days ... sacrifices ... "Horrible Thing"*: This number of days may refer to the number of days that Antiochus IV's persecutions will continue, or they may refer to some other future time connected with the end.

12.13 *rise from death*: This one of only a few references to "resurrection" in the Old Testament.

Resurrection

Eternal Life

^q12.1 *The Book*: Either the book with the names of God's people in it or the book with the record of the good and evil that people have done. ^r12.4 *even though ... in it*: One possible meaning for the difficult Hebrew text. ^s12.6 *angel ... upstream from them*: See 10.4-6. ^t12.7 *a time, two times, and half a time*: Or "a year, two years, and half a year," that is, about 1,260 days.

The angel said, "So, Daniel, be faithful until the end! You will rest, and at the end of time, you will rise from death to receive your reward." DAN 12.13

Reflection Questions About Daniel 1.1–12.13

1. Why were Daniel and his friends chosen by the king's official (1.3-5)? Why did Daniel object to eating the king's food? What do you think it took for Daniel and his friends to avoid this food (1.9-16)?

2. What special power or gift was Daniel given? According to Daniel, where did that power come from (1.17,20; 2.27-29)? What opportunities did Daniel have to use this special gift (2; 4; 5)? What was the result of Daniel using this power successfully (2.46; 5.29; 6.2)?

3. What was the meaning of Nebuchadnezzar's two dreams (2.26-45 and 4.18-37)? What did they help him to understand about Daniel's God?

4. Who was Belshazzar, and how did he and his party guests mock the God of Israel? What strange event occurred at the party? What role did Daniel play in the story?

5. On what grounds did Daniel's fellow officials try to get the king to get rid of Daniel (6.1-13)? What was King Darius' reaction to the news that Daniel had broken his new decree (6.14-20)? What was his reaction to Daniel being saved in the pit of lions (6.23-27)?

6. Summarize the meaning of Daniel's vision in 7.1-27. What would such a vision mean to people who were going through a time of persecution and suffering?

7. Who are the "ram," the "goat," and the "little horn"? How will the little horn attack God and God's people (8.1-14)?

8. What was the main purpose behind Daniel's prayer for his people (9.1-20)? What are some of the reasons God has allowed his people to endure suffering, such as the exile or later persecutions?

9. How did Daniel prepare to receive the vision given in chapters 11 and 12? How can we receive God's messages today?

10. What great promise is given in Daniel's final vision (12.1-13)? Who will benefit from this promise?

hosea

*A strong marriage is built on trust and commitment.
But trust is broken when one partner is unfaithful. Keep
this image in mind as you read the prophet Hosea's
message to Israel.*

WHAT MAKES HOSEA SPECIAL?

Hosea is a short version of the Hebrew name Hoshaiah, which means, "the LORD has saved." Hosea lived and wrote in the northern kingdom (Israel). Many believe that when the Assyrians invaded Israel, Hosea may have escaped to the southern kingdom (Judah), taking his prophecies with him.

Hosea told the people of Israel and Judah to be faithful to the LORD, who had brought them out of slavery in Egypt and kept his promise to give them a land of their own. But the people sinned by worshiping other gods. Their leaders trusted in their own military strength and in the power of allied foreign countries rather than depending on the LORD to protect their nation. Hosea told the people of Israel that they were to be punished because they had not been loyal to the LORD. However, he also offered the hope that God would forgive them and give them a fresh start as God's chosen people.

WHAT'S THE STORY BEHIND THE SCENE?

Why would the people turn away from the LORD God after becoming rich and wealthy in the land of promise (Canaan)? When the people of Israel settled in Canaan, they did not force all of the Canaanite people out the land. Instead, they settled among the Canaanites and began to adopt some of their ways. Israel was also threatened by the powerful Assyrian Empire. Various kings of Israel bribed Assyrian leaders to keep them from taking over the land. At other times, they asked countries such as Egypt to help them stand up against the Assyrians. Eventually, these political attempts backfired. Assyria defeated the northern kingdom (Israel) in 722 B.C. and forced many of its people to leave their homeland.

Most of the prophecies in the book are directed toward the northern kingdom (Israel). But the southern kingdom (Judah) is also named in a few places (5.5,10-15; 6.4-11; 12.2). Some scholars have suggested that the prophecies naming Judah may have been added at a later time, so that HOSEA's strong message could apply to all God's people.

HOW IS HOSEA CONSTRUCTED?

HOSEA has two clear sections. The first section (chapters 1–3) compares Hosea's marriage with the LORD's relationship with the people of Israel. The second section contains Hosea's messages to the people and leaders of Israel and Judah. His words describe God's anger and judgment as well as God's promise to forgive the people.

Hosea's family compared to unfaithful Israel
  (1.1—3.5)
Hosea's message to Israel, Judah, and their leaders
  (4.1—14.9)
  Israel and Judah are unfaithful to the LORD
  (4.1—5.15)
  The people try to trust the LORD but fail
  (6.1—8.14)
  The LORD will punish Israel (9.1—13.16)
  Those who return to the LORD will be forgiven
  (14.1-9)

osea lived at about the same time as the prophet Isaiah, during the last years of the northern kingdom of Israel, before it was conquered by the Assyrians in 721 B.C. Israel's sins against God had brought them great punishment and suffering. But Hosea uses the image of human marriage as a way of describing God's relationship with and unending love for his people. The first part of Hosea describes Hosea's marriage to Gomer, an unfaithful wife. The prophet uses this sad and humiliating situation as a way of depicting the people's unfaithfulness to the Lord. Hosea argues that because of their unfaithfulness, the people deserve God's punishment. But he follows this up with words of hope: even though the people of Israel have rejected God, God will acknowledge their repentance and forgive them. The second part of Hosea is a collection of Hosea's prophecies. Hosea describes the sins of the people, including the sins of their kings, priests, and prophets. Hosea warns of the punishment God is ready to impose, urges the people to come back to the Lord, and offers hope for the mercy and forgiveness of God.

Outline

1

I am Hosea son of Beeri. When Uzziah, Jotham, Ahaz, and Hezekiah were the kings of Judah, and when Jeroboam son of Jehoash[a] was king of Israel,[b] the LORD spoke this message to me.

Hosea's Family

[2]The LORD said, "Hosea, Israel has betrayed me like an unfaithful wife.[c] Marry such a woman and have children by her." [3]So I married Gomer the daughter of Diblaim, and we had a son.

[4]Then the LORD said, "Hosea, name your son Jezreel,[d] because I will soon punish the descendants of King Jehu of Israel for the murders he committed in Jezreel Valley.[e] I will destroy his kingdom, [5]and in Jezreel Valley I will break the power of Israel."

[6]Later, Gomer had a daughter, and the LORD said, "Name her Lo-Ruhamah,[f] because I will no longer have mercy and forgive Israel. [7]But I am the LORD God of Judah, and I will have mercy and save Judah by my own power—not by wars and arrows or swords and cavalry."

[8]After Gomer had stopped nursing Lo-Ruhamah, she had another son. [9]Then the LORD said, "Name him Lo-Ammi,[g] because

[a]**1.1** *Jehoash:* The Hebrew text has "Joash," another spelling of the name. [b]**1.1** *kings of Judah . . . king of Israel:* Uzziah (781–740 B.C.), Jotham (740–736), Ahaz (736–716), Hezekiah (716–687), and Jeroboam II (783–743). [c]**1.2** *unfaithful wife:* In some Canaanite religions of Old Testament times, young women were expected to have sex with the worshipers of their god before marriage. Such women were called "temple prostitutes." Many of the Israelite women did this same thing, and Hosea is told to marry one of them to show that the nation has turned from the LORD to worship idols. [d]**1.4** *Jezreel:* In Hebrew "Jezreel" means "God scatters (seed)." Here the name is used as a threat (meaning the LORD will punish Israel by scattering its people), while in verse 11 it is used as a promise (meaning the LORD will bless Israel by giving their nation many people, just as a big harvest comes when many seeds are scattered in a field). [e]**1.4** *murders . . . Valley:* Jehu murdered the wife and relatives of King Ahab (see 2 Kings 9.15—10.14). [f]**1.6** *Lo-Ruhamah:* In Hebrew "Lo-Ruhamah" means "No Mercy." [g]**1.9** *Lo-Ammi:* In Hebrew "Lo-Ammi" means "Not My People."

1.1 *Hosea:* Little is known about the prophet Hosea except what is told in the first three chapters of this book about his wife and children. Hosea's work as a prophet began around 750 B.C.

1.2 *Israel . . . unfaithful wife:* Israel here refers to the northern kingdom, which broke away from the southern tribes known as Judah. The Canaanite worship of the fertility god Baal included ritual prostitution. People believed that this practice would bring rain and make their crops grow. It's not clear whether the woman Hosea was told to marry was a temple prostitute or a woman who had been unfaithful to her husband. Either way, Hosea's marriage was to draw attention to Israel's own unfaithfulness. When nation turned from the LORD to worship idols, they were like a wife who is being unfaithful to her husband.

Israel

Prostitution in the Bible

■ 1.10,11 *as many . . . one leader . . . Jezreel:* Hosea foresees a time when God will restore Israel and Judah and bring them together under one leader. This promise echoes the ancient promise the Lord had made to the Israelite ancestors, Abraham and Jacob (Gen 22.17; 32.12).

■ 2.8 *gifts from me . . . worshiping Baal:* Israel was to celebrate the Harvest Festival to thank the Lord for a good harvest. In Hosea's time, many of the people were honoring Baal instead, because he was believed to fertilize the earth with rain.

☙ Canaanite Gods and Goddesses

● 2.11 *New Moon Festivals, Sabbaths:* The New Moon Festival was celebrated on the first day of each month when the new moon came out. The Sabbath began at sunset on Friday and ended at sunset on Saturday. No work was to be done on the Sabbath, which means "rest" or to "stop working." (See the chart Pilgrimage Festivals on pg 1799.)

these people are not mine, and I am not their God."

Hope for Israel

¹⁰Someday it will be impossible to count the people of Israel, because there will be as many of them as there are grains of sand along the seashore. They are now called "Not My People," but in the future they will be called "Children of the Living God." ¹¹Israel and Judah will unite and choose one leader. Then they will take back their land, and this will be a great day for Jezreel.ʰ

2 ¹So let your brothers be called "My People" and your sisters be called "Shown Mercy."ⁱ

The Lord Promises To Punish Israel

²Accuse! Accuse your mother!
   She is no longer my wife,
and now I, the Lord,
   am not her husband.
Beg her to give up prostitution
   and stop being unfaithful.ʲ
³or I will strip her naked
   like the day she was born.
I will make her barren
like a desert,
   and she will die of thirst.
⁴You children are the result
of her unfaithfulness,
   and I'll show you no pity.
⁵Your mother was unfaithful.
She was disgraceful and said,
   "I'll run after my lovers.
Everything comes from them—

my food and drink,
my linen and wool,
my olive oil and wine."

⁶I, the Lord, will build
a fence of thorns
   to block her path.
⁷She will run after her lovers,
   but not catch them;
she will search,
   but not find them.
Then she will say, "I'll return
to my first husband.
   Life was better then."
⁸She didn't know that her grain,
wine, and olive oil
   were gifts from me,
as were the gold and silver
   she used in worshiping Baal.ᵏ

⁹So I'll hold back the harvest
   of grain and grapes.
I'll take back
my wool and my linen
   that cover her body.
¹⁰Then I'll strip her naked
   in the sight of her lovers.ˡ
   No one can rescue her.

¹¹I'll stop Israel's celebrations—
   no more New Moon Festivals,
   Sabbaths, or other feasts.
¹²She said, "My lovers gave me
vineyards and fig trees
   as paymentᵐ for sex."

Now I, the Lord, will ruin
   her vineyards and fig trees;
they will become clumps of weeds
   eaten by wild animals.

ʰ1.11 *Jezreel:* See the note at verse 4.   ⁱ2.1 *My People . . . Shown Mercy:* In Hebrew "My People" is "Ammi" and "Shown Mercy" is "Ruhamah" (see Lo-Ruhamah in 1.6 and Lo-Ammi in 1.9).   ʲ2.2 *prostitution . . . unfaithful:* See the note at 1.2.   ᵏ2.8 *Baal:* A Canaanite god of fertility.   ˡ2.10 *I'll strip . . . lovers:* Or "I'll show her lovers how disgusting she is."   ᵐ2.12 *fig trees . . . payment:* Hosea uses an unusual word for "fig tree," which is spelled something like the word for "payment."

¹³I'll punish her for the days
  she worshiped Baal
    and burned incense to him.
I'll punish her for the times
    she forgot about me
and wore jewelry and rings
  to attract her lovers.
    I, the LORD, have spoken!

The LORD Will Help Israel

¹⁴Israel, I, the LORD,
  will lure you into the desert
    and speak gently to you.
¹⁵I will return your vineyards,
  and then Trouble Valleyⁿ
    will become Hopeful Valley.
  You will say "Yes" to me
    as you did in your youth,
      when leaving Egypt.

¹⁶I promise from that day on, you will call me your husband instead of your master.^o ¹⁷I will no longer even let you mention the names of those pagan gods that you called "Master." ¹⁸And I will agree to let you live in peace—you will no longer be attacked by wild animals and birds or by weapons of war. ¹⁹I will accept you as my wife forever, and instead of a bride price^p I will give you justice, fairness, love, kindness, ²⁰and faithfulness. Then you will truly know who I am.

²¹I will command the sky to send rain on the earth, ²²and it will produce grain, grapes, and olives in Jezreel Valley. ²³ I will scatter the seeds and show mercy to Lo-Ruhamah.^q I will say to Lo-Ammi,^r "You are my people," and they will answer, "You are our God."

God's Love Offers Hope

3 Once again the LORD spoke to me. And this time he said, "Hosea, fall in love with an unfaithful woman^s who has a lover. Do this to show that I love the people of Israel, even though they worship idols and enjoy the offering cakes made with fruit."

²So I paid 15 pieces of silver and about ten bushels of grain for such a woman. ³Then I said, "Now you are mine! You will have to remain faithful to me, though it will be a long time before we sleep together."

⁴It will also be a long time before Israel has a king or before sacrifices are offered at the temple or before there is any way to get guidance from God. ⁵But later, Israel will turn back to the LORD their God and to David their king. At that time they will come to the LORD with fear and trembling, and he will be good to them.

Israel Is Unfaithful

4 Israel, listen
  as the LORD accuses
    everyone in the land!
  No one is faithful or loyal
    or truly cares about God.
²Cursing, dishonesty, murder,

2.16 *your master:* "Master" probably refers to Baal. In ancient Israel, a man could have, in addition to a wife who had full legal rights, a wife known as a "concubine." A concubine was legally bound to the man but did not have the full privileges of the primary wife. The LORD will be Israel's true husband and not merely her master.

2.19 *bride price:* It was customary in the ancient Near East for a man to pay a "bride price" to the father of his proposed wife. If accepted, the exchange marked the beginning of the couple's betrothal. The LORD tells Hosea how much more than a bride price he is willing to give to show the people the kind of husband he intends to be.

3.5 *David their king:* David ruled over the united Israelite kingdom (1010–970 B.C.).

David

ⁿ**2.15** *Trouble Valley:* Or "Achor Valley." The exact location of the valley is unknown, but in Hebrew "Achor" sounds like "Achan," who brought trouble on Israel by disobeying the Lord (see Joshua 7.24-26). ^o**2.16** *husband . . . master:* In Hebrew the word "master" is the same as the name of the god Baal. But the LORD promises that his people will have a deep personal relationship with him (like a devoted wife and husband) rather than merely a legal tie (like a wife and her "master"). ^p**2.19** *bride price:* It was the custom for the husband to pay his wife's parents a bride price. Instead of money, the LORD will give much better benefits to Israel. ^q**2.23** *Lo-Ruhamah:* See the note at 1.6. ^r**2.23** *Lo-Ammi:* See the note at 1.9. ^s**3.1** *unfaithful woman:* This may refer to Gomer, the woman Hosea married (see 1.3), or it may refer to another woman.

4.4,5 *priests . . . prophets:* Israel's priests served as God's representatives for all the people. The prophets of the Bible observed what was happening around them and then delivered God's message for that situation. (**See the article Prophets and Prophecy on pg 1791.**)

Israel's Priests

4.13,14 *offer sacrifices . . . men are to blame:* Ancient Canaanite worship places were usually built on a high place near a grove of trees. The people of Israel did not destroy all these places when they settled in Canaan, so the fertility rituals honoring the Canaanite gods continued. Some Israelite men and women joined in these rituals.

4.15 *Bethel:* Bethel was a sacred place to the people of Israel because their ancestor Jacob received a special dream from the LORD there, and named the place "Beth-El," which means "house of God." Hosea calls this same place "Beth-Aven," meaning "house of sin" or "house of nothing."

robbery, unfaithfulness—
these happen all the time.
Violence is everywhere.
³And so your land is a desert.
Every living creature is dying—
people and wild animals,
birds and fish.

The LORD Warns the Priests

⁴Don't accuse just anyone!
Not everyone is at fault.
My case is against you,
the priests.ᵗ
⁵You and the prophets
will stumble day and night;
I'll silence your mothers.
⁶You priests have rejected me,
and my people are destroyed
by refusing to obey.
Now I'll reject you and forget
your children, because you
have forgotten my Law.

⁷By adding more of you priests,
you multiply the number
of people who sin.
Now I'll change your pride
into shame.
⁸You encourage others to sin,
so you can stuff yourselves
on their sin offerings.

⁹That's why I will punish
the people for their deeds,
just as I will punish
you priests.
¹⁰Their food won't satisfy,

and having sex at pagan shrines
won't produce children.
My people have rebelled
¹¹and have been unfaithful
to me, their LORD.

God Condemns Israel's Idolatry

My people, you are foolish
because of too much pleasure
and too much wine.
¹²You expect wooden idols
and other objects of wood
to give you advice.
Lusting for sex at pagan shrines
has made you unfaithful
to me, your God.
¹³You offer sacrifices
on mountaintops and hills,
under oak trees, and wherever
good shade is found.

Your own daughters
and daughters-in-law
sell themselves for sex.
¹⁴But I won't punish them.
You men are to blame,
because you go to prostitutes
and offer sacrifices with them
at pagan shrines.
Your own foolishness
will lead to your ruin.
¹⁵Israel, you are unfaithful,
but don't lead Judah to sin.
Stop worshiping at Gilgal
or at sinful Bethel.ᵘ
And quit making promises
in my name— the name

ᵗ**4.4** *priests:* One possible meaning for the difficult Hebrew text of verse 4. Hosea may have had in mind only one priest, possibly the chief priest.   ᵘ**4.15** *sinful Bethel:* The Hebrew text has "Beth-Aven," which means "house of sin" or "house of nothing," referring to "Bethel," which means "house of God."

of the living Lord.
¹⁶You are nothing more
    than a stubborn cow—
so stubborn that I, the Lord,
cannot feed you like lambs
    in an open pasture.

¹⁷You people of Israel^v
are charmed by^w idols.
    Leave those people alone!
¹⁸You get drunk, then sleep
    with prostitutes;
you would rather be vulgar
    than lead a decent life.^x
¹⁹And so you will be swept away^y
in a whirlwind
    for sacrificing to idols.

Israel and Judah Will Be Judged

The Lord said:

5 Listen, you priests!
    Pay attention, Israel!^z
Listen, you members
    of the royal family.
Justice was your duty.
But^a at Mizpah and Mount Tabor
    you trapped the people.
²At the place of worship
you were a treacherous pit,^b
    and I will punish you.

³Israel, I know all about you,
and because of your unfaithfulness,

I find you unacceptable.
⁴Your evil deeds are the reason
you won't return to me,
    your Lord God.
And your constant craving for sex
    keeps you from knowing me.

⁵Israel, your pride
    testifies to your guilt;
it makes you stumble,
    and Judah stumbles too.
⁶You offer sheep and cattle
    as sacrifices to me,
but I have turned away
    and refuse to be found.
⁷You have been unfaithful
    to me, your Lord;
you have had children
    by prostitutes.^c
So at the New Moon Festival,
you and your crops
    will be destroyed.^d

The Lord Warns Israel and Judah

⁸Give a warning on the trumpet!
Let it be heard in Gibeah,
    Ramah, and sinful Bethel.^e
Benjamin, watch out!^f
⁹I, the Lord, will punish
    and wipe out Israel.
This is my solemn promise
    to every tribe of Israel.
¹⁰Judah's leaders are like crooks

● 5.1 *Mizpah and Mount Tabor:* Jacob and Laban made an agreement at Mizpah (Gen 31.43-49), perhaps because it was an ancient holy place. Mount Tabor was located between Nazareth and Lake Galilee near the Valley of Jezerel. **(See Map 6 on pg 1884.)**

^v**4.17** *Israel:* The Hebrew text has "Ephraim," the leading tribe of the northern kingdom of Israel, which sometimes stands for the whole kingdom.   ^w**4.17** *charmed by:* Or "joined to."   ^x**4.18** *life:* One possible meaning for the difficult Hebrew text of verse 18.   ^y**4.19** *And so...swept away:* Or "And so you will be ashamed."   ^z**5.1** *Israel:* Probably meaning the tribal leaders of Israel.   ^a**5.1** *Justice ... duty. But:* Or "You are doomed, because."   ^b**5.2** *At ... pit:* One possible meaning for the difficult Hebrew text.   ^c**5.7** *prostitutes:* See 4.14, and the note at 1.2.   ^d**5.7** *So ... destroyed:* One possible meaning for the difficult Hebrew text.   ^e**5.8** *sinful Bethel:* See the note at 4.15. Gibeah is three miles north of Jerusalem, Ramah is five miles north, and Bethel is eleven miles north. The attack comes from the south, and all the land of Benjamin (belonging to Israel) is in danger.   ^f**5.8** *watch out:* Or "lead the way."

5.13 *asked help from Assyria:* This passage may refer to King Menahem's attempt to buy an alliance with the Assyrian king, Tiglath Pileser, in 738 B.C. Alternatively, it may refer to King Hoshea of Israel paying taxes to King Shalmaneser of Assyria and then asking King So of Egypt to help him rebel against Assyria.

5.15 *return to my temple:* The word translated as "temple" in this verse can also refer to the LORD's place in the heavens.

6.7-8 *Adam . . . Gilead:* Which of God's laws the people broke at Adam is not clear (Josh 3.14-17). Gilead most likely refers to the mountainous region southeast of Lake Galilee. The blood may refer to child sacrifices, or it may refer to a political revolt (see 2 Kgs 15.25). **(See Map 3 on pg 1881.)**

who move boundary markers;
    that's why I will flood them
    with my anger.

¹¹Israel was brutally crushed.
    They got what they deserved
    for worshiping useless idols.^g
¹²Now I, the LORD,
    will fill Israel with maggots
    and make Judah rot.
¹³When Israel and Judah saw
    their sickness and wounds,
    Israel asked help from Assyria
    and its mighty king.^h

But the king cannot cure them
    or heal their wounds.
¹⁴So I'll become a fierce lion
    attacking Israel and Judah.
    I'll snatch and carry off
    what I want,
    and no one can stop me.
¹⁵Then I'll return to my temple
    until they confess their guilt
    and worship me,
    until they are desperate
    and beg for my help.

The LORD's People Speak

6 Let's return to the LORD.
    He has torn us to shreds,
    but he will bandage our wounds
    and make us well.
²In two or three days
    he will heal us
    and restore our strength
    that we may live with him.

³Let's do our best
    to know the LORD.
    His coming is as certain
    as the morning sun;
    he will refresh us like rain
    renewing the earth
    in the springtime.

The LORD Speaks to Israel and Judah

⁴People of Israel and Judah,
    what can I do with you?
    Your love for me disappears
    more quickly than mist
    or dew at sunrise.
⁵That's why I slaughtered you
    with the words
    of my prophets.
    That's why my judgments blazed
    like the dawning sun.ⁱ
⁶I'd rather for you to be faithful
    and to know me
    than to offer sacrifices.

⁷At a place named Adam,
    you^j betrayed me
    by breaking our agreement.
⁸Everyone in Gilead is evil;
    your hands are stained
    with the blood of victims.^k
⁹You priests are like a gang
    of robbers in ambush.^l
    On the road to Shechem^m
    you murder and commit
    other horrible crimes.
¹⁰I have seen a terrible thing
    in Israel—

^g5.11 *for . . . idols:* One possible meaning for the difficult Hebrew text.   ^h5.13 *and . . . king:* One possible meaning for the difficult Hebrew text.   ⁱ6.5 *That's why my . . . sun:* One possible meaning for the difficult Hebrew text.   ^j6.7 *At . . . you:* Or "Like Adam, you" or "Each one of you."   ^k6.8 *your hands . . . victims:* This may refer to child sacrifice.   ^l6.9 *You . . . ambush:* One possible meaning for the difficult Hebrew text.   ^m6.9 *Shechem:* This was one of the towns where people could run for safety, if they had accidentally killed someone (see Joshua 20.1-9).

you are unfaithful
and unfit to worship me.
[11] People of Judah,
your time is coming too.

The LORD Wants To Help Israel

7 [1] I, the LORD, would like to make
my nation prosper again
and to heal its wounds.
But then I see the crimes
in Israel[n] and Samaria.
Everyone is deceitful;
robbers roam the streets.
[2] No one realizes
that I have seen their sins
surround them like a flood.

[3] The king and his officials
take great pleasure
in their sin and deceit.
[4] Everyone burns with desire—
they are like coals in an oven,
ready to burst into flames.
[5] On the day their king
was crowned,
his officials got him drunk,
and he joined
in their foolishness.[o]

[6] Their anger is a fire
that smolders all night,
then flares up at dawn.
[7] They are flames
destroying their leaders.
And their kings are powerless;
none of them trust me.

[8] The people of Israel[p]
have mixed with foreigners;
they are a thin piece of bread
scorched on one side.
[9] They don't seem to realize
how weak and feeble they are;
their hair has turned gray,
while foreigners rule.
[10] I am the LORD, their God,
but in all of their troubles
their pride keeps them
from returning to me.

No Help
from Foreign Nations

The LORD said:
[11] Israel[q] is a senseless bird,
fluttering back and forth
between Egypt and Assyria.
[12] But I will catch them in a net
as hunters trap birds;
I threatened to punish them,
and indeed I will.[r]
[13] Trouble and destruction
will be their reward
for rejecting me.
I would have rescued them,
but they told me lies.

[14] They don't really pray to me;
they just howl in their beds.
They have rejected me for Baal
and slashed themselves,[s]
in the hope that Baal
will bless their crops.
[15] I taught them what they know,
and I made them strong.

---

[n]**7.1** *Israel:* See the note at 4.17. Samaria was the capital city of Israel.   [o]**7.5** *foolishness:* One possible meaning for the difficult Hebrew text of verse 5.   [p]**7.8** *Israel:* Hebrew "Ephraim" (see the note at 4.17).   [q]**7.11** *Israel:* Hebrew "Ephraim" (see the note at 4.17).   [r]**7.12** *I threatened . . . will:* One possible meaning for the difficult Hebrew text.   [s]**7.14** *slashed themselves:* One ancient translation and some Hebrew manuscripts; other Hebrew manuscripts "gather together." Slashing themselves was one way of worshiping Baal (see 1 Kings 18.28).

● **6.11** *Judah:* The southern kingdom is warned that its people will also turn to idol worship, and their leaders will rely on the protection of foreign kings.

● **7.1** *Samaria:* King Omri (ruled 885–874 B.C.) built the city of Samaria and made it the capital of the northern kingdom of Israel. **(See Map 6 on pg 1884.)**

● **7.3** *king:* This may refer to King Hoshea. He took Israel's throne by murdering King Pekah (2 Kgs 15.30) and ruled for nine years.

● **7.5** *On the day . . . got him drunk:* The "day" here probably refers to the day Hoshea's friends got King Pekah drunk and killed him, and then crowned Hoshea king.

● **7.7** *flames destroying . . . leaders:* During a twelve-year period (745–732 B.C.), four of Israel's kings were murdered by those who replaced them in power (2 Kgs 15.8-30).

8.1 *eagle:* Probably refers to Assyria. The Bible often compares enemies to attacking birds (Deut 28.49; Jer 4.13; Lam 4.18,19; Hab 1.6-8).

8.3 *our good agreement:* This refers to the agreement that the LORD made with Moses and the people at Sinai (Exod 19–40; Lev 26.1-13).

8.13 *return to Egypt:* This may refer to going to Egypt to find help against Assyria, or it may refer to being slaves there as Israel's ancestors had been in the past (Exod 1.8-14).

Now they plot against me
16 and refuse to obey.[t]
They are more useless
than a crooked arrow.
Their leaders will die in war
for saying foolish things.
Egyptians will laugh at them.

Israel Rejects the LORD

The LORD said:

8 Sound a warning!
Israel, you broke our agreement
and ignored my teaching.
Now an eagle[u] is swooping down
to attack my land.
²Israel, you say, "We claim you,
the LORD, as our God."
³But your enemies
will chase you for rejecting
our good agreement.[v]

⁴You chose kings and leaders
without consulting me;
you made silver and gold idols
that led to your downfall.
⁵City of Samaria, I'm angry
because of your idol
in the shape of a calf.
When will you ever
be innocent again?
⁶Someone from Israel built
that idol for you,
but only I am God.
And so it will be smashed
to pieces.[w]

⁷If you scatter wind
instead of wheat,
you will harvest a whirlwind
and have no wheat.
Even if you harvest grain,
enemies will steal it all.

⁸Israel, you are ruined,
and now the nations
consider you worthless.
⁹You are like a wild donkey
that goes its own way.
You've run off to Assyria
and hired them as allies.
¹⁰You can bargain with nations,
but I'll catch you anyway.
Soon you will suffer abuse
by kings and rulers.

¹¹Israel, you have built
many altars where you offer
sacrifices for sin.
But these altars have become
places for sin.
¹²My instructions for sacrifices
were written in detail,
but you ignored them.
¹³You sacrifice your best animals
and eat the sacrificial meals,[x]
but I, the LORD,
refuse your offerings.
I will remember your sins
and punish you.
Then you will return to Egypt.[y]

¹⁴Israel, I created you,
but you forgot me.

[t]**7.16** *and . . . obey:* One possible meaning for the difficult Hebrew text.   [u]**8.1** *an eagle:* Or "a vulture."   [v]**8.3** *our good agreement:* Or "me, the Good One" (referring to God).   [w]**8.6** *smashed to pieces:* Or "destroyed by fire."   [x]**8.13** *sacrifice . . . sacrificial meals:* One possible meaning for the difficult Hebrew text. Two kinds of sacrifices are referred to: Those in which the whole animal is burned on the altar ("whole burnt offerings" in traditional translations) and those in which part is eaten by the worshipers ("fellowship offerings" in traditional translations).   [y]**8.13** *return to Egypt:* Either as slaves or to find help against Assyria.

You and Judah built palaces
  and many strong cities.[z]
Now I will send fire to destroy
  your towns and fortresses.

Israel Will Be Punished

9 Israel, don't celebrate
or make noisy shouts[a]
  like other nations.
You have been unfaithful
  to your God.
Wherever grain is threshed,
  you behave like prostitutes
because you enjoy
  the money you receive.[b]
[2]But you will run short
  of grain and wine,
[3]and you will have to leave
  the land of the LORD.
Some of you will go to Egypt;
  others will go to Assyria
  and eat unclean food.

[4]You won't be able to offer
  sacrifices of wine
    to the LORD.
None of your sacrifices
  will please him—
they will be unclean
  like food offered to the dead.
Your food will only be used
  to satisfy your hunger;
none of it will be brought
  to the LORD's temple.
[5]You will no longer be able
  to celebrate the festival
of the LORD.[c]
[6]Even if you escape alive,
  you will end up in Egypt
    and be buried in Memphis.[d]
Your silver treasures
  will be lost among weeds;[e]
thorns will sprout in your tents.

[7]Israel, the time has come.
You will get what you deserve,
  and you will know it.
"Prophets are fools," you say.
"And God's messengers
  are crazy."
Your terrible guilt
  has filled you with hatred.

[8]Israel, the LORD sent me
  to look after you.[f]
But you trap his prophets
and flood his temple
  with your hatred.
[9]You are brutal and corrupt,
  as were the men of Gibeah.[g]
But God remembers your sin,
  and you will be punished.

Sin's Terrible Results

[10]Israel, when I, the LORD,
  found you long ago
it was like finding
  grapes in a barren desert
  or tender young figs.
Then you worshiped Baal Peor,
  that disgusting idol,

● **9.1** *Wherever grain is threshed . . . like prostitutes:* In threshing grain, stalks of grain were beaten by hand or walked on by large animals in order to separate the kernels from the husks. Threshing was done on hills or other windy places. People also met at these places to worship Baal, the god they thought had given them the grain harvest.

● **9.3** *the land:* Meaning Canaan, the land the LORD gave to the Israelites. By 733 B.C. some of the people of Israel had already been taken into exile in Assyria. Others ran away to hide in Egypt. When they worshiped Baal as the lord of the land, they gave up their rights as God's chosen people.

∝ Purity (Clean and Unclean)

■ **9.10** *Baal Peor:* Some Israelites had worshiped the idol Baal Peor even before entering Canaan (Num 25.1-5).

[z]**8.14** *built palaces . . . cities:* They did this because they no longer trusted the LORD to protect them. "Palaces" may also mean "temples." [a]**9.1** *or . . . shouts:* One possible meaning for the difficult Hebrew text. [b]**9.1** *Wherever . . . receive:* Grain was threshed on hills or other places where the wind could blow away the husks. People also met at these places to worship Baal, the god they thought had given them the grain harvest. [c]**9.5** *festival of the LORD:* Probably the Festival of Shelters. [d]**9.6** *Memphis:* An Egyptian city with a famous cemetery. [e]**9.6** *Your silver . . . weeds:* One possible meaning for the difficult Hebrew text. [f]**9.8** *Israel . . . you:* One possible meaning for the difficult Hebrew text. [g]**9.9** *the men of Gibeah:* They raped and murdered a woman (see Judges 19).

9.15 *my house:* Meaning the land of Canaan.

9.17 *roam from nation to nation:* The people of Israel will lose their identity as God's people when they are forced to leave the land that the LORD has given them.

and you became as disgusting
as the idol you loved.
[11] And so, Israel, your glory
will fly away like birds—
your women will no longer
be able to give birth.
[12] Even if you do have children,
I will take them all
and leave you to mourn.
I will turn away,
and you will sink down
in deep trouble.
[13] Israel, when I first met you,
I thought of you as palm trees
growing in fertile ground.[h]
Now you lead your people out,
only to be slaughtered.

Hosea's Advice

[14] Our LORD, do just one thing
for your people—
make their women unable
to have children
or to nurse their babies.

The LORD's Judgment on Israel

[15] Israel, I first began
to hate you because
you did evil at Gilgal.[i]
Now I will chase you
out of my house.
No longer will I love you;
your leaders betrayed me.
[16] Israel, you are a vine
with dried-up roots
and fruitless branches.

Even if you had more children
and loved them dearly,
I would slaughter them all.

Hosea Warns Israel

[17] Israel, you disobeyed my God.
Now he will force you to roam
from nation to nation.

10 You were a healthy vine
covered with grapes.
But the more grapes you grew,
the more altars you built;
the better off you became,
the better shrines you set up
for pagan gods.
[2] You are deceitful and disloyal.
So you will pay
for your sins,
because the LORD will destroy
your altars and images.

[3] "We don't have a king,"
you will say.
"We don't fear the LORD.
And what good are kings?"
[4] Israel, you break treaties
and don't keep promises;
you turn justice
into poisonous weeds
where healthy plants should grow.[j]

[5] All who live in Samaria tremble
with concern for the idols[k]
at sinful Bethel.[l]
The idol there was the pride
of the priests,
but it has been put to shame;
now everyone will cry.

[h]9.13 *Israel, when . . . ground:* One possible meaning for the difficult Hebrew text. [i]9.15 *Gilgal:* See 4.15. [j]10.4 *you turn . . . grow:* One possible meaning for the difficult Hebrew text. [k]10.5 *idols:* The Hebrew text has "calves," referring to the idols made in the shape of calves. [l]10.5 *sinful Bethel:* See the note at 4.15.

[6]It will be taken to Assyria
and given to the great king.
Then Israel will be disgraced
for worshiping that idol.

[7]Like a twig in a stream,
the king of Samaria
will be swept away.
[8]The altars at sinful Bethel
will be destroyed
for causing Israel to sin;
they will be grown over
with thorns and thistles.
Then everyone will beg
the mountains and hills
to cover and protect them.

The LORD Promises To Punish Israel

[9]Israel, you have never
stopped sinning[m]
since that time at Gibeah.[n]
That's why you
will be attacked at Gibeah.[o]
[10]Your sins have doubled,
and you are rebellious.
Now I have decided
to send nations to attack
and put you in chains.

[11]Once you were obedient
like a calf
that loved to thresh grain.
But I will put a harness
on your beautiful neck;
you and Judah must plow
and cultivate the ground.
[12]Plow your fields,

scatter seeds of justice,
and harvest faithfulness.
Worship me, the LORD,
and I will send my saving power
down like rain.
[13]You have planted evil,
harvested injustice, and eaten
the fruit of your lies.
You trusted your own strength
and your powerful forces.
[14]So war will break out,
and your fortresses
will be destroyed.
Your enemies will do to you
what Shalman[p] did to the people
of Beth-Arbel—
mothers and their children
will be beaten to death
against rocks.
[15]Bethel, this will be your fate
because of your evil.
Israel, at dawn your king
will be killed.

God's Love for His People

11 When Israel was a child,
I loved him, and I called
my son out of Egypt.
[2]But as the saying goes,
"The more they were called,
the more they rebelled."[q]
They never stopped offering
incense and sacrifices
to the idols of Baal.

[3]I took Israel by the arm
and taught them to walk.
But they would not admit

10.6,7 *taken to Assyria . . . king of Samaria*: Pekah was king of Israel from 737 to 732 B.C. During Pekah's reign, the Assyrian king Tiglath Pileser invaded Israel and forced a number of Israelites into exile in Assyria (2 Kgs 15.27-29). Pekah's palace was in the city of Samaria, the capital of Israel. In 722 B.C. the Assyrian king Shalmaneser captured Samaria (2 Kgs 17.5-23). Sargon, the king who followed Shalmaneser, took many of the remaining people of Israel as prisoners to Assyria.

10.14 *war will break out . . . Shalman*: Israel was threatened by the Assyrians. There is no other record in the Bible of what happened at Beth-Arbel. "Shalman" may refer to the Moabite king known as Salamanu, who paid taxes to Tiglath Pileser III of Assyria around 735–733 B.C. It could also be a shortened version of Shalmaneser, an Assyrian king by this name.

---

[m]10.9 *never stopped sinning*: One possible meaning for the difficult Hebrew text.   [n]10.9 *Gibeah*: See the note at 9.9.   [o]10.9 *That's why . . . Gibeah*: One possible meaning for the difficult Hebrew text.   [p]10.14 *Shalman*: Perhaps a Moabite king, also known as Salamanu.   [q]11.2 *But . . . rebelled*: One possible meaning for the difficult Hebrew text.

12.2-4 *people of Judah . . . Jacob:* In Hebrew, "Jacob" sounds like the words for "cheat" and "heel" (Gen 25.26). The Israelites who heard Hosea's prophecy would have recalled the stories about their sometimes sneaky ancestor Jacob (Gen 25.29-34; 27.1-40; 32.22-28).

Israel

that I was the one
who had healed them.
⁴I led them with kindness
and with love,
not with ropes.
I held them close to me;^r
I bent down to feed them.

⁵But they rejected me,
and so must return to Egypt;
now Assyria will rule them.
⁶War will visit their cities,
and their plans will fail.^s
⁷My people are determined
to reject me for a god
they think is stronger,
but he can't help.^t

⁸Israel, I can't let you go.
I can't give you up.
How could I possibly destroy you
as I did the towns of Admah
and Zeboiim?^u
I just can't do it.
My feelings for you
are much too strong.
⁹Israel, I won't lose my temper
and destroy you again.
I am the Holy God—
not merely some human,
and I won't stay angry.

¹⁰I, the LORD, will roar like a lion,
and my children will return,
trembling from the west.
¹¹They will come back,

fluttering like birds from Egypt
or like doves from Assyria.
Then I will bring them
back to their homes.
I, the LORD, have spoken!

Israel and Judah Compared

¹²Israel is deceitful to me,
their loyal and holy God;
they surround me with lies,
and Judah worships
other gods.^v

12 All day long Israel chases
wind from the desert;
deceit and violence
are found everywhere.
Treaties are made with Assyria;
olive oil is taken to Egypt.

Israel and Judah Condemned

²The LORD also brings charges
against the people of Judah,
the descendants of Jacob.
He will punish them
for what they have done.
³Even before Jacob was born,
he cheated his brother,^w
and when he grew up,
he fought against God.^x

⁴At Bethel, Jacob wrestled
with an angel and won;
then with tears in his eyes,

^r11.4 *I held . . . to me:* One possible meaning for the difficult Hebrew text. ^s11.6 *fail:* One possible meaning for the difficult Hebrew text of verse 6. ^t11.7 *help:* One possible meaning for the difficult Hebrew text of verse 7. ^u11.8 *Admah and Zeboiim:* When the LORD destroyed Sodom and Gomorrah, he also destroyed these two towns (see Deuteronomy 29.23). ^v11.12 *and Judah worships other gods:* Or "but Judah remains faithful." ^w12.3 *Jacob . . . cheated . . . brother:* In Hebrew "Jacob" sounds like "cheat" and also like "heel." Jacob grabbed his twin brother Esau by the heel at the time of their birth (see Genesis 25.26). Later he cheated him out of his rights and blessings as the firstborn son (see Genesis 25.29-34; 27.1-40). ^x12.3 *fought against God:* See Genesis 32.22-32.

he asked for a blessing,
  and God spoke to us[y] there.
[5]God's name is the Lord,
  the Lord God All-Powerful.
[6]So return to your God.
Patiently trust him,
  and show love and justice.

[7]Israel, you enjoy cheating
and taking advantage
  of others.
[8]You say to yourself, "I'm rich!
I earned it all on my own,
  without committing a sin."[z]

The Lord Is Still the God of Israel

[9]Israel, I, the Lord,
am still your God,
  just as I have been
since the time
  you were in Egypt.
Now I will force you
to live in tents once again,
  as you did in the desert.[a]
[10]I spoke to the prophets—
  often I spoke in visions.
And so, I will send my prophets
  with messages of doom.
[11]Gilead is terribly sinful
  and will end up ruined.
Bulls are sacrificed in Gilgal
  on altars made of stones,
but those stones will be scattered
  in every field.

[12]Jacob[b] escaped to Syria[c]
where he tended sheep
  to earn himself a wife.
[13]I sent the prophet Moses
to lead Israel from Egypt
  and to keep them safe.
[14]Israel, I will make you pay
for your violent crimes
  and for insulting me.

Israel Is Doomed

The Lord said:

13 When your leaders[d] spoke,
  everyone in Israel trembled
    and showed great respect.
But you sinned by worshiping Baal,
  and you were destroyed.
[2]Now you continue to sin
  by designing and making
idols of silver
  in the shape of calves.
You are told to sacrifice
to these idols[e] —
  yes, even to kiss them.
[3]And so, all of you will vanish
like the mist or the dew
  of early morning,
or husks of grain in the wind
  or smoke from a chimney.

[4]I, the Lord, have been your God
since the time
  you were in Egypt.

12.5 *Lord God All-Powerful*: "Lord" is a translation of *Yahweh,* the Hebrew word used as God's personal name. The Hebrew word translated here as "God" is *Elohim.*

Names of God

Lord (YHWH)

13.4-6 *in Egypt . . . thirsty desert . . . fed you*: The Lord helped the Israelites escape slavery in Egypt (Exod 12–14). During the 40 years that Israel wandered through the desert, the Lord fed them (Exod 16; Num 11.7-9,31,32) and provided water (Exod 17.1-7; Num 20.1-13). The people of Hosea's generation have forgotten how the Lord saved their ancestors.

[y]12.4 *us*: Hebrew; two ancient translations "him." [z]12.8 *without . . . sin*: One possible meaning for the difficult Hebrew text. [a]12.9 *as . . . desert*: One possible meaning for the difficult Hebrew text. This probably refers to the 40 years of wandering through the desert after leaving Egypt, though it could refer to the "tents" (or "shelters") in which the Israelites lived during the Festival of Shelters (see 9.5,6). [b]12.12 *Jacob*: His name was later changed to Israel (see Genesis 32.28), and he became the ancestor of the nation by that name. [c]12.12 *Syria*: The Hebrew text has "Aram," probably referring to northern Syria in the region of Haran. [d]13.1 *your leaders*: The Hebrew text has "Ephraim," here meaning Mount Ephraim, where the royal palace of Samaria (capital of the northern kingdom of Israel) was located. [e]13.2 *You are told . . . idols*: One possible meaning for the difficult Hebrew text.

I, the Lord, have been your God since the time you were in Egypt. I am the only God you know, the only one who can save. Hosea 13.4

13.10,11 *wanted a king:* When the people of Israel begged for a king, God granted their request (1 Sam 8.4-22; 10.17-26). The king who has been "taken away" may refer to Israel's king Hoshea who was arrested by Shalmaneser when the Assyrians captured Samaria, the capital of Israel (2 Kgs 17.1-9).

Kingship in Israel

13.12 *terrible sins . . . stored away:* The sins here refer to Israel's worshipping Canaanite gods and trusting in foreign powers rather than trusting the LORD. Ancient documents were rolled and stored in a dry place.

Scrolls

13.15 *desert wind . . . precious treasures:* The translation of this verse is difficult. The desert wind may refer to the Assyrians who will invade from the desert to the east of Canaan. They will kill and capture many Israelites and take Israel's jewels and gold from the royal treasury.

14.3 *Assyria . . . chariots:* The Assyrian army's skillful use of its many chariots made it the leading military force of the period. Although Israel's army also used chariots, Hosea declares that winning a military battle was not the way out of Israel's troubles.

I am the only God you know,
the only one who can save.
5 I took care of you
in a thirsty desert.[f]
6 I fed you till you were satisfied,
then you became proud
and forgot about me.
7 Now I will attack like a lion,
ambush you like a leopard,
8 and rip you apart like a bear
robbed of her cubs.
I will gnaw on your bones,
as though I were a lion
or some other wild animal.
9 Israel, you are done for.
Don't expect help from me.[g]
10 You wanted a king and rulers.
Where is your king now?
What cities have rulers?
11 In my anger, I gave you a king;
in my fury, I took him away.

Israel's Terrible Fate

The LORD said:

12 Israel, your terrible sins
are written down
and stored away.
13 You are like a senseless child
who refuses to be born
at the proper time.
14 Should I, the LORD, rescue you
from death and the grave?
No! I call death and the grave
to strike you like a plague.
I refuse to show mercy.

15 No matter if you prosper
more than the other tribes,[h]
I, the LORD, will wipe you out,
just as a scorching desert wind
dries up streams of water.
I will take away
your precious treasures.
16 Samaria[i] will be punished
for turning against me.
It will be destroyed in war—
children will be beaten
against rocks,
and pregnant women
will be ripped open.

Turn Back to the LORD

14 Israel, return! Come back
to the LORD, your God.
Sin has made you fall.
2 Return to the LORD and say,
"Please forgive our sins.
Accept our good sacrifices
of praise instead of bulls.[j]
3 Assyria can't save us,
and chariots can't help.
So we will no longer worship
the idols we have made.
Our LORD, you show mercy
to orphans."

The LORD Promises To Forgive

4 Israel, you have rejected me,
but my anger is gone;
I will heal you and love you
without limit.
5 I will be like the dew—
then you will blossom like lilies
and have roots like a tree.[k]
6 Your branches will spread

[f] **13.5** *thirsty desert*: The 40 years that Israel wandered through the desert, after leaving Egypt. [g] **13.9** *Don't . . . me*: Or "You are against me, the one who helps you." [h] **13.15** *more . . . tribes*: One possible meaning for the difficult Hebrew text. [i] **13.16** *Samaria*: The capital of the northern kingdom of Israel. [j] **14.2** *Accept . . . bulls*: One possible meaning for the difficult Hebrew text. [k] **14.5** *like a tree*: The Hebrew text has "like Lebanon," probably referring to the famous cedar trees on Mount Lebanon.

with the beauty
  of an olive tree
and with the aroma
  of Lebanon Forest.
⁷You will rest in my shade,
  and your grain will grow.
You will blossom
  like a vineyard
and be famous as the wine
  from Lebanon.

⁸Israel, give up your idols!
  I will answer your prayers

and take care of you.^l
I am that glorious tree,
  the source of your fruit.^m

⁹If you are wise, you will know
  and understand what I mean.
I am the Lord, and I lead you
  along the right path.
If you obey me,
  we will walk together,
but if you are wicked,
  you will stumble.

14.7 *vineyard:* A vineyard filled with grapes was considered a sign of God's blessing.

14.8 *I am that glorious tree:* This is the only place in the Old Testament where the Lord is compared to a tree. Hosea reminds the people that the Lord is the source of life, rather than the Canaanite gods and goddesses that are worshiped under trees at the local shrine.

---

^l**14.8** *Israel . . . you:* One possible meaning for the difficult Hebrew text.   ^m**14.8** *I am . . . fruit:* This is the only place in the Old Testament where the Lord is compared to a tree. Hosea reminds the people that it is the Lord who is the source of life, rather than the Canaanite gods and goddesses that are worshiped under trees at the local shrines.

Reflection Questions About Hosea 1.1—14.9

1. Who was Hosea, and what did the LORD tell him to do (1.2; 3.1)? Who was Gomer? What did the names of Hosea's children have to do with the relationship between the LORD and Israel at this time (1.3-9)?

2. Why did the LORD promise to punish Israel (2.2-13)?

3. Why is King David mentioned in 3.5?

4. Of what specific sins did the LORD accuse Israel? What role did Israel's priests play in Israel's sins (4.1—5.7)?

5. How did the people respond to Hosea's warnings (6.1-3)? Was their response honest and sincere? Why or why not?

6. In terms of Israel's history, what is the meaning of Hosea 7.11?

7. Why were the Israelites drawn toward worshiping Baal and the other Canaanite gods and goddesses (7.14-16)?

8. Why are Judah and Israel compared to their ancestor Jacob (12.1-8)?

9. How were the people of Israel supposed to return to the LORD (14.1-3)? For you, what does the phrase "return to the LORD" mean?

10. HOSEA describes idols as images made of wood, metal, or stone that represent gods. What or who might be considered "idols" in society today? How could these "idols" challenge faithfulness or trust in God?

joel

*The prophet Joel watched a hungry swarm of locusts cover
the land of Israel, destroying crops and causing starvation.
Read his vivid description and see why he compares this
disaster to the Lord's coming day of judgment.*

WHAT MAKES JOEL SPECIAL?

The book of JOEL belongs to the writings in the Bible
called the books of the prophets. All we know for
certain about the prophet Joel is his name, which in
Hebrew means, "The LORD (*Yahweh*) is God." JOEL
describes in very lively language the effects of a locust plague—an attack by so many locusts flying
over the land that they block out the sun. JOEL goes
on to compare the resulting darkness with the day of
the LORD, a special event he refers to several more
times. On that day God will judge and punish the
nations that have hurt Israel.

Joel prays to God and warns the people that the
LORD will send his army to fight for justice. He compares the locusts to horses in battle that make loud
noises as they charge and are frightening to look at.
But, there is hope if people will turn to the LORD with
all their hearts. The LORD will listen to them and save
them from the destruction, not only by restoring the
harvest, but by assuring everyone that he is indeed
their God. The LORD will even help them to understand the future through his Spirit (prophecy). **(See
the article Prophets and Prophecy on pg 1791.)**

WHAT'S THE STORY BEHIND THE SCENE?

A number of books of prophecy in the Bible tell who
was king at the time the prophet preached (for example, see Hos 1.1; Amos 1.1; Mic 1.1). This gives
modern readers a sense of when the prophet was
most active by matching what the prophet said with
specific historical situations. Since JOEL does not
mention any specific king or ruler, the exact dating
of the book continues to be a mystery.

There are a few clues in the book about who Joel
was and when he preached. He speaks of Judah and
Jerusalem and the LORD's temple. He mentions no
king, but refers to the priests and elders as Israel's
"leaders." The invading army mentioned in the book
is sometimes thought to be from Assyria, which defeated Israel (northern kingdom) in 721 B.C., or
Babylonia, which defeated Judah (southern kingdom) in 586 B.C. and took many of its leading citizens into exile. Some scholars suggest that Joel
lived and preached in Judah sometime after the
people returned from exile and rebuilt the temple in
515 B.C.

HOW IS JOEL CONSTRUCTED?

Although JOEL has been divided into the three chapters, it has two main parts: The first (1.1—2.17) tells
of an invasion of locusts, the invasion of the LORD's
unstoppable army, and includes Joel's message
telling the people to return to the LORD. The second
part (2.18—3.21) describes how the LORD will rescue
the people of Israel and bring a future day of judgment when the enemies of Israel will be punished.

The LORD's invitation to Israel (1.1—2.17)
The LORD's blessings and judgment of nations
   (2.18—3.21)

The prophet Joel's vision moves from punishment for sin to repentance, and from forgiveness to renewal. Joel watches swarms of locusts cover the land. Locusts are a species of grasshopper that travels in enormous swarms which can darken the sky. They eat all the plants and crops wherever they land. Joel sees the locusts as God's punishment for the people's unfaithfulness, and compares the locusts to a powerful army that has destroyed the nation. The land is barren, the priests mourn—even the land itself mourns. In distress, Joel cries out to the Lord and sees a vision of the coming judgment day of the Lord. The Lord tells Joel that if the people turn back to him, he will treat them with mercy. In the end, the Lord takes pity on his people, announces that he will restore the damage done by the locusts, and save everyone who worships him. Joel is given a vision of the day when the nations who conquered and occupied Israel and Judah will be punished. The land will be restored to its people and made safe under the rule of God.

Outline

1

I am Joel the son of Pethuel.
And this is the message
    the LORD gave to me.

Locusts Cover the Land

[2]Listen, you leaders
and everyone else
    in the land.
Has anything like this
    ever happened before?
[3]Tell our children!
Let it be told
    to our grandchildren
    and their children too.

[4]Swarm after swarm of locusts[a]
has attacked our crops,
    eating everything in sight.
[5]Sober up, you drunkards!
Cry long and loud;
your wine supply is gone.
[6]A powerful nation[b]
with countless troops
    has invaded our land.
They have the teeth and jaws
    of powerful lions.
[7]Our grapevines and fig trees
are stripped bare;
    only naked branches remain.

[8]Grieve like a young woman
mourning for the man
    she was to marry.
[9]Offerings of grain and wine
are no longer brought
    to the LORD's temple.
His servants, the priests,
    are deep in sorrow.
[10]Barren fields mourn;
grain, grapes, and olives
    are scorched and shriveled.

[a]1.4 Swarm . . . locusts: The Hebrew text lists either four kinds of locusts or locusts in four stages of their development. Locusts are a type of grasshopper that comes in swarms and causes great damage to plant life.   [b]1.6 A powerful nation: The swarms of locusts.

1.2 *Listen:* Compare Joel's invitation to "listen" to similar invitations at the beginning of other prophetic books (Isa 1.2; Hos 4.1; Mic 1.2). Here everyone is asked to listen to the words of the prophet, not just one specific leader or a king. After they understand his message, everyone in the nation will have the LORD's Spirit.

1.5 *Sober up, you drunkards:* The abundance of wine in the ancient world was seen as evidence of God's blessings. But drunkenness was viewed as a sign of foolishness that could lead to a person's destruction. The prophet's warning is also a blunt statement of fact. Those who often got drunk, he says, would have no choice but to sober up. The locust swarm would eat all the grapevines, and there would be no new grapes for making wine.

1.9 *Offerings . . . LORD's temple:* The LORD's temple refers to the temple in Jerusalem, where Israel's priests made offerings. (See the chart Sacrifices and Offerings on pg 1828.)

Israel's Priests

Names of God

1.17 *Our barns . . . no grain:* If enough grain was stored, a community could survive one or two years of bad harvests. Grain was stored in large clay jars in storehouses, and in grain silos (pits).

2.1 *Zion:* Another name for Jerusalem.

2.1 *judgment day of the* LORD: This is an important theme in JOEL. In the future, the LORD will interrupt history and judge the nations. This day is often described as being accompanied by destruction, darkness, and unusual natural events. Joel sees the locust invasion as a sign of the coming day of judgment. Besides Joel, other prophets spoke about a judgment day of the LORD.

Day of the LORD

Zion

2.2 *Troops . . . army this powerful:* Refers to another swarm of locusts, an enemy of Israel, or a "supernatural army" sent by the LORD.

2.3 *Eden:* The beautiful and fertile garden of Eden (Gen 2.4-15).

2.4,5 *cavalry . . . chariots:* In ancient warfare, soldiers on horses or driving chariots at high speeds were a frightening sight in battle. Chariots were fast enough to gain on fleeing enemy armies or to quickly change positions and attack their enemies from behind.

11Mourn for our farms
  and our vineyards!
There's no wheat or barley
  growing in our fields.
12Grapevines have dried up
  and so has every tree—
  figs and pomegranates,c
  date palms and apples.
All happiness has faded away.

Return to God

13Mourn, you priests who serve
  at the altar of my God.
Spend your days and nights
  wearing sackcloth.d
Offerings of grain and wine
  are no longer brought
  to the LORD's temple.

14Tell the leaders and people
  to come together
  at the temple.
Order them to go without eatinge
  and to pray sincerely.
15We are in for trouble!
  Soon the LORD All-Powerful
  will bring disaster.
16Our food is already gone;
  there's no more celebrating
  at the temple of our God.

17Seeds dry up in the ground;f
  no harvest is possible.
Our barns are in bad shape,
  with no grain
  to store in them.
18Our cattle wander aimlessly,
  moaning for lack of pasture,

and sheep are suffering.g
19I cry out to you, LORD.
  Grasslands and forests are eaten
  by the scorching heat.
20Wild animals have no water
  because of you;
  rivers and streams are dry,
  and pastures are parched.

Locusts and an Enemy Army

2 Sound the trumpet on Zion,
  the LORD's sacred hill.
Warn everyone to tremble!
The judgment day of the LORD
  is coming soon.
2It will be dark and gloomy
  with storm clouds overhead.
Troops will cover the mountains
  like thunderclouds.
No army this powerful
  has ever been gathered before
  or will be gathered again.
3Fiery flames surround them;
  no one escapes.
Before they invaded,
  the land was like Eden;
  now only a desert remains.

4They look like horses
  and charge like cavalry.
5They roar over mountains
  like noisy chariots,
or a mighty army
  ready for battle.
They are a forest fire
  that feasts on straw.
6The very sight of them
  is frightening.h

c1.12 *pomegranates:* A bright red fruit that looks like an apple.   d1.13 *sackcloth:* A rough, dark-colored cloth made from goat or camel hair and used to make grain sacks. It was worn in times of trouble or sorrow.   e1.14 *go without eating:* As a way of showing sorrow for their sins.   f1.17 *Seeds . . . ground:* One possible meaning for the difficult Hebrew text.   g1.18 *sheep are suffering:* One possible meaning for the difficult Hebrew text.   h2.6 *The very . . . frightening:* One possible meaning for the difficult Hebrew text.

⁷They climb over walls
   like warriors;
they march in columns
   and never turn aside.ⁱ
⁸They charge straight ahead,
   without pushing each other;
even arrows and spears
   cannot make them retreat.
⁹They swarm over city walls
   and enter our homes;
they crawl in through windows,
   just like thieves.

¹⁰They make the earth tremble
   and the heavens shake;
the sun and moon turn dark,
   and stars stop shining.
¹¹The Lord God leads this army
   of countless troops,
   and they obey his commands.
The day of his judgment
   is so terrible
   that no one can stand it.

The Lord's Invitation

¹²The Lord said:

It isn't too late.
You can still return to me
   with all your heart.
Start crying and mourning!
   Go without eating.
¹³Don't rip your clothes
   to show your sorrow.
Instead, turn back to me
   with broken hearts.
I am merciful, kind, and caring.
I don't easily lose my temper,
   and I don't like to punish.

¹⁴I am the Lord your God.
   Perhaps I will change my mind
   and treat you with mercy.
Then you will be blessed
   with enough grain and wine
   for offering sacrifices to me.

¹⁵Sound the trumpet on Zion!
   Call the people together.
Show your sorrow
   by going without food.
¹⁶Make sure that everyone
   is fit to worship me.^j
Bring adults, children, babies,
   and even bring newlyweds
   from their festivities.

¹⁷Tell my servants, the priests,
   to cry inside the temple
and to offer this prayer
   near the altar.^k
"Save your people, Lord God!
Don't let foreign nations
   make jokes about us.
Don't let them laugh and ask,
   'Where is your God?'"

The Lord Will Bless the Land

¹⁸The Lord was deeply concerned
   about his land
   and had pity on his people.
¹⁹In answer to their prayers
   he said,
"I will give you enough grain,
wine, and olive oil
   to satisfy your needs.
No longer will I let you
   be insulted by the nations.

2.10 *sun and moon turn dark*: May be a reference to the swarms of locusts blocking out the sun during the day and the moon and stars at night. The Bible frequently uses images of darkness to describe what happens when the judgment day of the Lord is near (Isa 13.9,10; Amos 5.18-20; Zeph 1.14-16; Mark 13.24-25; Rev 8.12).

Locusts

2.12,13 *return to me . . . broken hearts*: Though the judgment day is coming, the Lord says that it is not too late for the people of Israel to return to obeying him. Joel doesn't say what the people's specific sins are, but in order to be forgiven, they need to show an honest attitude of sadness (broken hearts) and admit that they are guilty. The people are to show their sadness by performing acts of mourning.

2.14 *offering sacrifices*: Turning back to the Lord will cause the Lord to restore the land and its crops. With plenty of food, the people can again make sacrifices at the temple.

2.16 *fit to worship me*: The people of Israel performed certain rituals in order to be "clean" enough for worship.

Purity (Clean and Unclean)

Israel's Priests

ⁱ**2.7** *and never turn aside*: One possible meaning for the difficult Hebrew text.   ^j**2.16** *fit to worship me*: This required going through certain kinds of ceremonies.   ^k**2.17** *inside . . . altar*: The Hebrew text has "between the porch and the altar," which is the place where the priests usually prayed for the people.

The Lord said: It isn't too late. You can still return to me with all your heart. Joel 2.12

2.20 *army . . . from the north:* It is not clear what army is being described here. If it is the locust "army," the smell of rotting locusts covers the whole land. If it is one of Israel's enemies, it is not clear which one, since even enemies from the east and the west would have used the trade routes from the north to attack Israel.

2.20 *Dead Sea . . . Mediterranean:* These large bodies of water served as boundaries for Israel. (See Map 6 on pg 1884.)

2.24 *threshing places:* Harvested grain was carried to dry, open places called threshing floors. There, the dried stalks were beaten with something like a whip or crushed by a heavy board with sharp stones in it. The board was dragged across the threshing floor by an ox or a donkey to loosen the chaff (husks) from the grain. Then the grain and husks were thrown into the air. Wind blew away the light husks, while the heavier grain kernels fell to the ground and were gathered up.

2.28 *Spirit:* The Spirit brings the LORD's power and special gifts.

Holy Spirit

2.30,31 *wonders . . . terrible day:* These wonders are common in the "apocalyptic" writings of the Bible. The "terrible day" is the judgment day of the LORD.

Apocalyptic Writings

²⁰An army attacked from the north,
  but I will chase it
    into a scorching desert.
  There it will rot and stink
  from the Dead Sea
    to the Mediterranean."

The LORD works wonders
²¹ and does great things.
  So tell the soil to celebrate
²²and wild animals
    to stop being afraid.
  Grasslands are green again;
  fruit trees and fig trees
    are loaded with fruit.
  Grapevines are covered
    with grapes.

²³People of Zion,[l]
  celebrate in honor
    of the LORD your God!
  He is generous and has sent
  the autumn and spring rains
  in the proper seasons.[m]
²⁴Grain will cover
    your threshing places;
  jars will overflow
    with wine and olive oil.

The LORD Will Rescue His People

²⁵I, the LORD your God,
  will make up for the losses
    caused by those swarms
  and swarms of locusts[n]
    I sent to attack you.
²⁶My people, you will eat
    until you are satisfied.
  Then you will praise me
  for the wonderful things
    I have done.

Never again will you
  be put to shame.

²⁷Israel, you will know
    that I stand at your side.
  I am the LORD your God—
    there are no other gods.
  Never again will you
  be put to shame.

The LORD Will Work Wonders

The LORD said:
²⁸Later, I will give my Spirit
    to everyone.
  Your sons and daughters
    will prophesy.
  Your old men
    will have dreams,
  and your young men
    will see visions.
²⁹In those days I will even give
  my Spirit to my servants,
    both men and women.

³⁰I will work wonders
  in the sky above
    and on the earth below.
  There will be blood and fire
    and clouds of smoke.
³¹The sun will turn dark,
  and the moon
    will be as red as blood
  before that great
  and terrible day
    when I appear.

³²Then I, the LORD, will save everyone who faithfully worships me. I have promised there will be survivors on Mount Zion and in Jerusalem, and among them will be my chosen ones.

[l]2.23 *Zion:* Jerusalem.   [m]2.23 *in . . . seasons:* Or "as he used to do."   [n]2.25 *swarms . . . locusts:* See the note at 1.4.

The Lord Will Judge the Nations

3 At that time I, the Lord, will make Judah and Jerusalem prosperous again. ²Then in Judgment Valley° I will bring together the nations that scattered my people Israel everywhere in the world, and I will bring charges against those nations. They divided up my land ³and gambled to see who would get my people; they sold boys and girls to pay for prostitutes and wine.

⁴You people of Tyre and Sidonᴾ and you Philistines, why are you doing this? Are you trying to get even with me? I'll strike back before you know what's happened. ⁵You've taken my prized possessions, including my silver and gold, and carried them off to your temples.�q ⁶You have dragged the people of Judah and Jerusalem from their land and sold them to the Greeks.

⁷But I'll make the people of Judah determined to come home, and what happened to them will happen to you. ⁸I'll hand over your sons and daughters to the people of Judah, and they will sell them to the Sabeans,ʳ who live far away. I, the Lord, have spoken!

Judgment in Judgment Valley

⁹Say to the nations:

"Get ready for war!
  Be eager to fight.
Line up for battle
  and prepare to attack.
¹⁰Make swords out of plows

and spears out of garden tools.
  Strengthen every weakling."

¹¹Hurry, all you nations!
  Come quickly.
Ask the Lord to bring
  his warriors along.ˢ
¹²You must come now
  to Judgment Valley,ᵗ
where the Lord will judge
  the surrounding nations.

¹³They are a field of ripe crops.
  Bring in the harvest!
They are grapes piled high.
  Start trampling them now!ᵘ
If our enemy's sins were wine,
  every jar would overflow.
¹⁴Crowds fill Decision Valley.
  The judgment day of the Lord
  will soon be here—
¹⁵no light from the sun or moon,
  and stars no longer shine.
¹⁶From the heart of Jerusalem
  the Lord roars like a lion,
  shaking the earth and sky.
But the Lord is a fortress,
a place of safety
  for his people Israel.

God Will Bless His People

¹⁷I am the Lord your God.
  And you will know I live on Zion,
  my sacred hill,
because Jerusalem will be sacred,
  untouched by foreign troops.

○3.2 *Judgment Valley:* The Hebrew text has "Jehoshaphat Valley," which means "Valley of the Lord's Judgment." This valley is mentioned here and in verse 12, but nowhere else in the Bible.   ᴾ3.4 *Tyre and Sidon:* Two Phoenician coastal cities.   q3.5 *temples:* Or "palaces."   ʳ3.8 *Sabeans:* The people of Seba, a region in southwest Arabia.   ˢ3.11 *Ask . . . along:* One possible meaning for the difficult Hebrew text.   ᵗ3.12 *Judgment Valley:* See the note at 3.2.   ᵘ3.13 *grapes . . . now:* People trampled grapes with their bare feet to squeeze out the juice.

● 3.1,2 *Judah and Jerusalem . . . Judgment Valley:* Joel's mention of Judah and Jerusalem is another clue that his prophecy was given after the rebuilding of the temple, when the people of Israel's future and hopes were centered on Jerusalem. The location of Judgment Valley is unknown.

● 3.2-8 *nations . . . Sabeans:* Babylon and Assyria, who had defeated Israel and Judah, are not named here. Tyre and Sidon were important coastal cities in Phoenicia. The Philistines were ancient enemies of Israel; the Greeks lived on the western coast of Asia Minor; and the Sabeans were people from southwest Arabia.

⊕ Exile

⊕ Phoenicia

⊕ Wine

▪ 3.14 *Decision Valley:* The Valley of Decision is not mentioned anywhere else in the Bible. It may be another name for the Valley of Judgment (3.2,12).

▪ 3.16 *From . . . Jerusalem the Lord roars:* This phrase is nearly identical to one used by the prophet Amos (Amos 1.2). If Joel preached after the people returned from their exile in Babylonia (538 B.C.), then he is most likely quoting Amos, whose prophecy dates from 760 to 750 B.C.

"That day" follows the LORD's
day of judgment, when the LORD has restored the people of Judah. They will
have plenty to eat and trade with others, and won't be bothered by enemies.
The everflowing stream that comes
from the LORD's house (the temple) is
like the river that runs from the temple
in Ezekiel 47.1-12.

18On that day, fruitful vineyards
    will cover the mountains.
And your cattle and goats
that graze on the hills
    will produce a lot of milk.
Streams in Judah
    will never run dry;
a stream from my house
    will flow in Acacia Valley.v

19Egypt and Edom were cruel
and brutal to Judah,

without a reason.
    Now their countries will become
        a barren desert,
20but Judah and Jerusalem
    will always have people.
21I, the LORD, live on Mount Zion.
    I will punish the guilty
    and defend the innocent.w

v3.18 Acacia Valley: In the plains of Moab, northeast of the Dead Sea.   w3.21 I will . . . innocent: One
possible meaning for the difficult Hebrew text.

Reflection Questions About Joel 1.1—3.21

1. What astonishing event did Joel witness? Why was this event so devastating for the people? Why did the people and the temple priests mourn (1.4-20)?

2. What is the "judgment day of the LORD," and what hints does nature give that this day is about to happen (2.1-12)?

3. Who or what are the troops and army compared to (2.2-11)? Do you think knowing about Joel's message in advance could have helped the people? How?

4. What important thing does the LORD invite the people to do (2.12-17)? What does the LORD promise if the people do what he asks (2.18-27; 3.17-21)? Can you think of someone you might want to make things right with? How would the person respond to an apology?

5. Why does the LORD judge the nations (3.1-13)?

amos

"No more of your noisy songs! . . . But let justice and fairness flow like a river" (Amos 5.23,24). Read Amos to find out why God told the prophet to speak these powerful words to the people of Israel.

WHAT MAKES AMOS SPECIAL?

Amos wasn't a professional prophet like the members of a prophetic guild (1 Sam 19.18-24) or those who served the king (1 Chr 21.9; 25.5). He was a farmer who raised sheep and tended fig trees. Though Amos lived near the small town of Tekoa, located south of Jerusalem in the southern kingdom (Judah), the LORD gave Amos messages to preach to the people and leaders of the northern kingdom (Israel). Although Israel had many prophets before the time of Amos (1 Sam 9.9-13; 2 Sam 12), his prophecies are thought to be the first to be written down and preserved as a book of the Bible.

Amos was sent to tell the people of Israel that the LORD was going to punish them because the rich and powerful were robbing the poor and treating them unjustly. Many of the people and their priests worshiped other gods besides the LORD at new worship places built by Israel's kings. Amos preached his messages at the city of Bethel, where Israel's Jeroboam I had built a worship place. Amos' message also included words of judgment against several countries that were neighbors of Israel and Judah.

WHAT'S THE STORY BEHIND THE SCENE?

The first verse of the book says that Amos preached during the time Uzziah was king in Judah (781–740 B.C.) and Jeroboam II was king of Israel (786–746 B.C.). It is not clear which earthquake he is referring to in the same verse, but it may be one that happened in 760 B.C. So, Amos likely preached his message for about one year sometime between 762 and 750 B.C.

Jeroboam II ruled Israel during a prosperous and peaceful time. Israel became a wealthy nation. Many people became rich, built fancy homes, and had all they wanted to eat and drink. But the rich people did not use their wealth or influence to help others. Instead, driven by endless greed, they cheated honest people and made the poor pay heavy taxes. Though many people continued to celebrate the religious festivals, the LORD grew tired of their insincere rituals. What the LORD really wanted them to do was to treat others with justice and fairness, and to be faithful to the LORD alone.

HOW IS AMOS CONSTRUCTED?

Amos can be divided into two main sections: The first section (1.1—6.14) includes Amos' messages of judgment against Israel and neighboring nations. The second section (7.1—9.15) includes the visions of Amos, which tell of the LORD's coming judgment against Israel, and also describe a future time when the LORD will help Israel rebuild its kingdom and prosper (9.11-15).

Messages of judgment against Israel and its
   neighbors (1.1—6.14)
    Amos preaches against Israel's neighbors
    (1.1—2.5)
    Amos announces the LORD's judgment against
    Israel (2.6—6.14)
Visions of Israel's punishment and renewal
   (7.1—9.15)
    The Punishment Visions (7.1—9.10)
    The LORD will rebuild Israel (9.11-15)

Amos was a shepherd who spoke the Lord's message around 760 B.C. Though Amos was born in the southern kingdom of Judah, the Lord tells him to travel to Bethel and preach in Israel, the northern kingdom, and to announce that the nations of Syria, Philistia, Phoenicia, Edom, Ammon, Moab, and Judah will be punished. However, the longest message of punishment Amos delivers is for Israel itself because the wealthy people there were mistreating those who were poor and helpless. The message of judgment against Israel is in the form of five visions: locusts that will destroy all the food; fire that will burn everything on earth; a measuring line that shows the Israelites they do not meet God's standards of faithfulness; a basket of ripe fruit that shows that the people are ready for destruction; and the collapse of the Bethel temple and death of the people worshiping there. The Lord promises to scatter the people of Israel among other nations. But the final message in Amos is one of hope; it promises that the Lord will rebuild the kingdom and its people will once again prosper.

Outline

1

I am Amos. And I raised sheep near the town of Tekoa[a] when Uzziah was king of Judah and Jeroboam[b] son of Jehoash[c] was king of Israel.

Two years before the earthquake,[d] the LORD gave me several messages[e] about Israel, 2 and I said:

When the LORD roars
    from Jerusalem,
pasturelands and Mount Carmel
    dry up and turn brown.

Judgment on Syria

3The LORD said:
    I will punish Syria[f]
for countless crimes,
    and I won't change my mind.
They dragged logs with spikes[g]
    over the people of Gilead.
4Now I will burn down the palaces
    and fortresses of King Hazael
    and of King Benhadad.[h]
5I will break through
    the gates of Damascus.
I will destroy the people[i]
    of Wicked Valley[j]
    and the ruler of Beth-Eden.[k]
Then the Syrians will be dragged
    as prisoners to Kir.[l]
I, the LORD, have spoken!

---

a1.1 *Tekoa:* In the hill country of Judah about five miles south of Bethlehem.   b1.1 *Uzziah . . . Jeroboam:* Uzziah was king of Judah 781–740 B.C., and Jeroboam II was king of Israel 783–743 B.C.   c1.1 *Jehoash:* The Hebrew text has "Joash," another spelling of the name.   d1.1 *Two years . . . earthquake:* Possibly the earthquake of 760 B.C., which seems to have been especially violent.   e1.1 *messages:* Or "visions."   f1.3 *Syria:* The Hebrew text has "Damascus," the leading city of Syria.   g1.3 *logs with spikes:* These were dragged over grain to thresh it.   h1.4 *Hazael . . . Benhadad:* Two Syrian kings.   i1.5 *people:* Or "king."   j1.5 *Wicked Valley:* The Hebrew text has "Aven Valley," probably the fertile valley between the Lebanon and the anti-Lebanon mountains.   k1.5 *I will . . . Beth-Eden:* Or "I will destroy the people of Wicked Valley and the king who rules from Beth-Eden." Beth-Eden was a city-state on the banks of the Euphrates River.   l1.5 *Kir:* The exact location of this country is not known; in 9.7 Amos refers to Kir as the original home of the Syrians, and so the verse probably means that the Syrians will lose everything they have gained as a people.

● 1.1 *Amos:* All that we now know about Amos is what is mentioned in this book of the Bible. Amos lived in the town of Tekoa in the Judean hills. He made his living by raising sheep and taking care of fig trees. Though Amos was from the south (Judah), his message was for the people of the northern kingdom (Israel). Amos preached his messages just a few years before the prophets Isaiah, Hosea, and Micah began their work. **(See the article Prophets and Prophecy on pg 1791.)**

● 1.1,2 *Tekoa . . . Mount Carmel:* Tekoa was in the hill country of Judah south of Jerusalem (2 Sam 14.1-4; 2 Chr 11.5,6). When King Solomon died (about 931 B.C.), Israel's ten northern tribes broke away from the two remaining southern tribes (1 Kgs 12). Two kingdoms were formed—Israel (the northern kingdom) and Judah (the southern kingdom). Jerusalem remained the capital of Judah and its traditional center of worship. Mount Carmel was located in Israel about 70 miles northwest of Jerusalem. **(See Map 6 on pg 1884.)**

● 1.4 *Hazael . . . Benhadad:* Hazael became king of Syria by murdering a king named Benhadad (2 Kgs 8.7-15), and ruled from about 842 to 806 B.C.

1.6-8 *Philistia . . . Ekron:* The people of Philistia often battled the people of Israel. The Philistines probably kidnapped people in border towns of Judah and sold them to the Edomites.

1.9,10 *Phoenicia . . . Tyre:* What treaty the Phoenicians broke is not clear, but their other crime is similar to that of the Philistines. Tyre was the leading city of Phoenicia at the time of Amos.

Phoenicia

1.13,14 *Ammon . . . Gilead . . . Rabbah:* The event mentioned in 1.13 probably refers to a border war Ammon fought to try to take over some of Israel's land in Gilead. Rabbah was the capital city of Ammon.

Judgment on Philistia

[6]The LORD said:

I will punish Philistia[m]
for countless crimes,
    and I won't change my mind.
They dragged off my people[n]
    from town after town
to sell them as slaves
    to the Edomites.

[7]That's why I will burn down
    the walls and fortresses
    of the city of Gaza.
[8]I will destroy the king[o] of Ashdod
    and the ruler of Ashkelon.
I will strike down Ekron,[p]
and that will be the end
    of the Philistines.
I, the LORD, have spoken!

Judgment on Phoenicia

[9]The LORD said:
I will punish Phoenicia[q]
for countless crimes,
    and I won't change my mind.
They broke their treaty
and dragged off my people[r]
    from town after town
to sell them as slaves
    to the Edomites.
[10]That's why I will send flames
    to burn down the city of Tyre
    along with its fortresses.

Judgment on Edom

[11]The LORD said:
I will punish Edom
for countless crimes,
    and I won't change my mind.
They killed their own relatives[s]
and were so terribly furious
    that they showed no mercy.
[12]Now I will send fire to wipe out
    the fortresses of Teman
    and Bozrah.[t]

Judgment on Ammon

[13]The LORD said:

I will punish Ammon
for countless crimes,
    and I won't change my mind.
In Gilead they ripped open
    pregnant women,
    just to take the land.

[14]Now I will send fire to destroy
    the walls and fortresses
    of Rabbah.[u]
Enemies will shout and attack
    like a whirlwind.
[15]Ammon's king and leaders
    will be dragged away.
I, the LORD, have spoken!

[m]1.6 *Philistia:* The Hebrew text has "Gaza," one of the main Philistine cities. [n]1.6 *my people:* The people of Israel. [o]1.8 *king:* Or "people." [p]1.8 *Ashdod . . . Ashkelon . . . Ekron:* Philistine cities. [q]1.9 *Phoenicia:* The Hebrew text has "Tyre," which was one of the two Phoenician cities; the other was Sidon, which is not mentioned by Amos. [r]1.9 *my people:* See the note at 1.6. [s]1.11 *their own relatives:* The Edomites were descendants of Esau, the brother of Jacob, the ancestor of the Israelites. [t]1.12 *Teman and Bozrah:* These stand for all of Edom; Teman may have been a city or a district. Bozrah, the chief city of northern Edom, was 30 miles southeast of the Dead Sea. [u]1.14 *Rabbah:* The capital city of Ammon.

Judgment on Moab

2 The LORD said:
I will punish Moab
    for countless crimes,
        and I won't change my mind.
    They made lime from the bones[v]
        of the king of Edom.
² Now I will send fire to destroy
        the fortresses of Kerioth.[w]
    Battle shouts and trumpet blasts
    will be heard as I destroy Moab
³   with its king and leaders.
    I, the LORD, have spoken!

Judgment on Judah

⁴ The LORD said:
    I will punish Judah
    for countless crimes,
        and I won't change my mind.
    They have rejected my teachings
        and refused to obey me.
    They were led astray
    by the same false gods
        their ancestors worshiped.
⁵ Now I will send fire on Judah
    and destroy the fortresses
        of Jerusalem.

Judgment on Israel

⁶ The LORD said:

    I will punish Israel
    for countless crimes,
        and I won't change my mind.
    They sell honest people for money,

and the needy are sold
    for the price of sandals.
⁷ They smear the poor in the dirt
    and push aside
        those who are helpless.

My holy name is dishonored,
because fathers and sons sleep
    with the same young women.
⁸ They lie down beside altars
on clothes taken
    as security for loans.
And they drink wine in my temple,
wine bought with the money
    they received from fines.

⁹ Israel, the Amorites[x] were there
    when you entered Canaan.
They were tall as cedars
    and strong as oaks.
But I wiped them out—
    I destroyed their branches
    and their roots.
¹⁰ I had rescued you from Egypt,
    and for forty years I had led you
        through the desert.
    Then I gave you the land
        of the Amorites.

¹¹ I chose some of you
to be prophets
    and others to be Nazirites.[y]
People of Israel,
you know this is true.
    I, the LORD, have spoken!
¹² But you commanded the prophets
    not to speak their message,

[v]**2.1** *They . . . bones:* They dug up the bodies of kings and made lime out of them to use as whitewash on their houses and walls. [w]**2.2** *Kerioth:* A leading city of Moab and a center for the worship of Chemosh, the chief god of Moab. [x]**2.9** *Amorites:* This word is used for all the people who lived in Canaan at the time Israel took over the land. [y]**2.11** *Nazirites:* People who promised the LORD that they would never drink wine or cut their hair or come in contact with a dead body.

● **2.4,5** *Judah . . . Jerusalem:* Over 150 years after Amos preached, the LORD's judgment against Judah took place when the armies of Babylon destroyed Jerusalem (587 or 586 B.C.). The phrase, "rejected my teachings," is similar to language used in DEUTERONOMY, which was completed in its final form sometime after the people returned to Jerusalem from exile. Some scholars conclude that these words of judgment may have been added well after the time of Amos.

◈ Israel

● **2.6,7** *sell honest people . . . push aside . . . helpless:* Honest people who owed debts were being sold as slaves when they could not pay their debts on time. Pushing aside the helpless probably refers to bribing court officials to keep certain people from getting a fair hearing.

◈ Justice

● **2.11** *prophets . . . Nazirites:* Nazirites showed their dedication to the LORD by refusing to eat or drink certain things, and by promising not to cut their hair or touch a dead body (Num 6.1-8). **(See the article Prophets and Prophecy on pg 1791.)**

3.2 *chosen . . . your sins:* The people of Israel were chosen to have a special relationship with the LORD, and they were chosen for a purpose—to be living examples of the LORD's justice and goodness. But many in Israel turned their backs on the LORD and refused to live according to this purpose. Being the LORD's chosen people did not protect Israel from being judged for these sins. Rather, the LORD judged them even more strictly.

3.3-8 *Can two people walk . . . lion roars:* Amos asks a series of questions about events that don't happen simply by chance. These lead to the final key point of his argument: The LORD can do whatever the LORD wants to do, including bringing disaster on a city. The LORD's voice is like a lion's terrifying roar that can turn ordinary people—including Amos himself—into prophets.

3.9 *Egypt . . . Samaria:* The ancestors of the Israelite people had once been slaves in Egypt. The Egyptians saw the LORD work miracles and lead the people out of slavery (Exod 6–14; Amos 3.1). Now, because of Israel's lawlessness, the leaders of Egypt and Philistia were going to see the LORD punish Samaria, Israel's capital city. The northern kingdom of Israel was also known as Samaria.

and you pressured the Nazirites
  into drinking wine.
¹³And so I will crush you,
  just as a wagon full of grain
    crushes the ground.ᶻ
¹⁴No matter how fast you run,
  you won't escape.
No matter how strong you are,
  you will lose your strength
    and your life.
¹⁵Even if you are an expert
  with a bow and arrow,
    you will retreat.
And you won't get away alive,
  not even if you run fast
    or ride a horse.
¹⁶You may be brave and strong,
  but you will run away,
    stripped naked.
I, the LORD, have spoken!

3 People of Israel,
  I rescued you from Egypt.
Now listen to my judgment
  against you.
²Of all nations on earth,
  you are the only one
    I have chosen.
That's why I will punish you
  because of your sins.

The Work of a Prophet

³Can two people walk together
  without agreeing to meet?
⁴Does a lion roar in the forest
  unless it has caught
    a victim?
Does it growl in its den
  unless it is eating?
⁵How can anyone catch a bird

without using a net?
Does a trap spring shut
  unless something is caught?

⁶Isn't the whole city frightened
  when the trumpet
    signals an attack?
Isn't the LORD the one who brings
  disaster on a city?
⁷Whatever the LORD God
  plans to do,
he tells his servants,
  the prophets.
⁸Everyone is terrified
  when a lion roars—
and ordinary people
  become prophets
    when the LORD God speaks.

Samaria Is Doomed

⁹Here is a message
  for the leaders
    of Philistiaᵃ and Egypt—
tell everyone to come together
  on the hills of Samaria.
Let them see the injustice
  and the lawlessness
    in that city.
¹⁰The LORD has said
  that they don't even know how
    to do right.
They have become rich
  from violence and robbery.
¹¹And so the LORD God has sworn
  that they will be surrounded.
Enemies will break through
  their defenses
    and steal their treasures.

¹²The LORD has promised
  that only a few from Samaria

ᶻ2.13 *ground:* One possible meaning for the difficult Hebrew text of verse 13.   ᵃ3.9 *Philistia:* The Hebrew text has "Ashdod," one of the leading cities of Philistia.

will escape with their lives
and with some broken pieces
of their beds and couches.[b]
It will be like when a shepherd
rescues two leg bones
and part of a sheep's ear
from the jaws of a lion.[c]

The Altars at Bethel

[13]The LORD God All-Powerful
told me to speak this message
against Jacob's descendants:
[14]When I, the LORD, punish Israel
for their sins,
I will destroy the altars
at Bethel.
Even the corners of the altar[d]
will be left in the dirt.
[15]I will tear down winter homes
and summer homes.
Houses decorated with ivory
and all other mansions
will be gone forever.
I, the LORD, have spoken!

The Women of Samaria

The LORD said:

4 You women of Samaria
are fat cows![e]
You mistreat and abuse
the poor and needy,

then you say to your husbands,
"Bring us more drinks!"
[2]I, the LORD God, have sworn
by my own name
that your time is coming.
Not one of you will be left—
you will be taken away
by sharp hooks.[f]
[3]You will be dragged through holes
in your city walls,
and you will be thrown
toward Harmon.[g]
I, the LORD, have spoken!

Israel Refuses To Obey

The LORD said:
[4]Come to Bethel and Gilgal.[h]
Sin all you want!
Offer sacrifices the next morning
and bring a tenth of your crops
on the third day.[i]
[5]Bring offerings to show me
how thankful you are.
Gladly bring more offerings
than I have demanded.
You really love to do this.
I, the LORD God, have spoken!

How the LORD Warned Israel

[6]I, the LORD, took away the food
from every town and village,

[b]3.12 *some . . . couches:* One possible meaning for the difficult Hebrew text. [c]3.12 *lion:* When a wild animal attacked and killed a sheep, the shepherd had to rescue part of the sheep and take it to the owner as proof that it had been killed by an animal. Otherwise, the shepherd had to pay the owner the cost of the sheep. [d]3.14 *altar:* Altars were places of worship but also places of protection. People whose lives were in danger could grab hold of the corners of an altar, and no one was allowed to kill them. [e]4.1 *fat cows:* The Hebrew text has "cows of Bashan," a fertile plain famous for its rich pastures and well-fed cattle. [f]4.2 *taken . . . hooks:* One possible meaning for the difficult Hebrew text. [g]4.3 *Harmon:* Hebrew; some manuscripts of one ancient translation "Mount Hermon," a mountain in the north of Palestine, on the way to Assyria. [h]4.4 *Bethel and Gilgal:* These were two of the most important centers of worship in northern Israel. Amos mentions these together again in 5.5. [i]4.4 *Offer . . . day:* Or "Offer sacrifices each morning and bring a tenth of your crops every three days." In verses 4,5 God is condemning the people for meaningless acts of worship.

Shepherds

3.13 LORD *God All-Powerful:* "LORD" is a translation of *Yahweh,* the Hebrew word used as God's personal name (see Exod 3.14,15). The Hebrew word translated here as "God" is *Elohim.* Used together, these names describe Israel's one true God, the powerful ruler of all creation.

Names of God

LORD (YHWH)

3.13 *Jacob's descendants:* Meaning all the Israelite people.

3.14,15 *destroy the altars at Bethel . . . mansions:* Canaanite gods were worshiped at the altars of Bethel, a religious shrine built by Jeroboam I (1 Kgs 12.25—13.10). Bethel's altars represented Israel's unfaithfulness to the LORD, and the mansions represented Israel's greed.

4.4-5 *sacrifices . . . offerings:* The things mentioned here are simply things the LORD expected the Israelites to do, such as offering sacrifices to ask the LORD's blessing (Lev 3; 7.11-38), bringing a tenth of their harvest and the first-born of their flocks to celebrate the LORD's blessings (Deut 14.22-29). But Amos is saying that these outward acts of worship have no meaning because the people are ignoring what the LORD really wants them to do—stop worshiping other gods and start treating all people with justice.

5.1 mournful message: Songs of mourning were sung at funerals in ancient Israel. Amos is trying to shock the Israelites by singing a funeral song (5.2,3) even before Israel had fallen and been defeated.

5.5 Beersheba: Beersheba was an ancient place of worship in the southern part of Judea going back to the days of Israel's ancestors, Abraham (Gen 21.30-33), Isaac (Gen 26.23-25), and Jacob (Gen 46.1-4). The LORD warns the people not to go to these places, because they will be destroyed. Rather they are to turn to the LORD (5.4,6) in true prayer and by living according to the LORD's purpose for them.

5.6 descendants of Joseph: Two of Israel's tribes were named after Joseph's sons, Ephraim and Manasseh (Gen 48). By the time of Amos, Ephraim was the most influential tribe in the northern kingdom and so "descendants of Joseph" is here used as another name for "Israel."

but still you rejected me.
⁷Three months before harvest,
  I kept back the rain.
Sometimes I would let it fall
  on one town or field
but not on another,
  and pastures dried up.
⁸People from two or three towns
  would go to a town
that still had water,
  but it wasn't enough.
Even then you rejected me.
  I, the LORD, have spoken!

⁹I dried up your grain fields;
your gardens and vineyards
  turned brown.
Locusts[j] ate your fig trees
  and olive orchards,
but even then you rejected me.
  I, the LORD, have spoken!

¹⁰I did terrible things to you,
  just as I did to Egypt—
I killed your young men in war;
  I let your horses be stolen,
and I made your camp stink
  with dead bodies.
Even then you rejected me.
  I, the LORD, have spoken!

¹¹I destroyed many of you,
  just as I did the cities
    of Sodom and Gomorrah.
You were a burning stick
  I rescued from the fire.
But even then you rejected me.
  I, the LORD, have spoken!

¹²Now, Israel, I myself
  will deal with you.
    Get ready to face your God!

¹³I created the mountains
  and the wind.
I let humans know
  what I am thinking.[k]
I bring darkness at dawn
  and step over hills.
I am the LORD God All-Powerful!

Turn Back to the LORD

5 Listen, nation of Israel,
  to my mournful message:
²You, dearest Israel, have fallen,
  never to rise again—
you lie deserted in your own land,
  with no one to help you up.

³The LORD God has warned,
  "From every ten soldiers
    only one will be left;
from a thousand troops,
  only a hundred will survive."

⁴The LORD keeps saying,
  "Israel, turn back to me
    and you will live!
⁵Don't go to Gilgal or Bethel
  or even to Beersheba.[l]
Gilgal will be dragged away,
  and Bethel will end up
    as nothing."[m]

⁶Turn back to the LORD,
  you descendants of Joseph,[n]

[j]**4.9** *Locusts:* A type of grasshopper that comes in swarms and causes great damage to plant life. [k]**4.13** *I let . . . thinking:* Or "No one's secret thoughts are hidden from me." [l]**5.5** *Gilgal . . . Bethel . . . Beersheba:* These were ancient places of worship, but the LORD had warned his people to stay away from them. [m]**5.5** *Gilgal . . . nothing:* In Hebrew "Gilgal" and "dragged away" sound something alike. Bethel (meaning "house of God") is sometimes called "house of nothing" or "house of sin" by the prophets (see Hosea 4.15; 5.8; 10.5-8). [n]**5.6** *descendants of Joseph:* Another name for the people of the northern kingdom of Israel.

The LORD said, "I created the mountains and the wind. I let humans know what I am thinking. I bring darkness at dawn and step over hills. I am the LORD God All-Powerful!" AMOS 4.13

and you will live.
If you don't, the LORD
    will attack like fire.
Bethel will burn to the ground,
    and no one can save it.
⁷You people are doomed!
You twist the truth
    and trample on justice.

⁸But the LORD created the stars
    and put them in place.ᵒ
He turns darkness to dawn
    and daylight to darkness;
he scoops up the ocean
    and empties it on the earth.
⁹God destroys mighty soldiers
    and strong fortresses.

Choose Good Instead of Evil!

The LORD said:
¹⁰You people hate judges
    and honest witnesses;
¹¹you abuse the poor and demand
    heavy taxes from them.
You have built expensive homes,
    but you won't enjoy them;
you have planted vineyards,
    but you will get no wine.
¹²I am the LORD, and I know
    your terrible sins.
You cheat honest people
and take bribes;
    you rob the poor of justice.
¹³Times are so evil
that anyone with good sense
    will keep quiet.

¹⁴If you really want to live,
    you must stop doing wrong
        and start doing right.
I, the LORD God All-Powerful,
    will then be on your side,
        just as you claim I am.
¹⁵Choose good instead of evil!
    See that justice is done.
Maybe I, the LORD All-Powerful,
    will be kind to what's left
        of your people.ᴾ

Judgment Is Coming

¹⁶This is what the LORD has sworn:
    Noisy crying will be heard
        in every town and street.
Even farmers will be told
    to mourn for the dead,
together with those
    who are paid to mourn.�q
¹⁷Your vineyards will be filled
with crying and weeping,ʳ
    because I will punish you.
I, the LORD, have spoken!

When the LORD Judges

¹⁸You look forward to the day
    when the LORD comes to judge.
        But you are in for trouble!
It won't be a time of sunshine;
    all will be darkness.
¹⁹You will run from a lion,
    only to meet a bear.
You will escape to your house,
    rest your hand on the wall,

◌ Burial

▪ 5.18-20 *the day . . . LORD comes to judge:* Amos is the first prophet to speak about a specific day in the future when the LORD would come to judge.

◌ The Day of the LORD

ᵒ5.8 *the stars . . . place:* The Hebrew text mentions two groups of stars, Pleiades and Orion. Since the LORD is the Creator of the stars, he controls the seasons that are signaled by the different positions of the stars. Moreover, the stars are created objects and should not be worshiped.   ᴾ5.15 *your people:* Hebrew "Joseph's descendants" (see the note at verse 6).   �q5.16 *paid to mourn:* In ancient times some people were paid to mourn and make loud cries at funerals.   ʳ5.17 *Your vineyards . . . weeping:* Instead of happy celebrations that were often held in vineyards after the harvest.

and be bitten by a snake.
20The day when the LORD judges
     will be dark, very dark,
        without a ray of light.

What the LORD Demands

21I, the LORD, hate and despise
     your religious celebrations
        and your times of worship.
22I won't accept your offerings
     or animal sacrifices—
        not even your very best.
23No more of your noisy songs!
     I won't listen
        when you play your harps.
24But let justice and fairness
     flow like a river
        that never runs dry.

25Israel, for forty years
     you wandered in the desert,
without bringing offerings
     or sacrifices to me.
26Now you will have to carry
     the two idols you made—
Sakkuth, the one you call king,
and Kaiwan, the one you built
     in the shape of a star.^{s}
27I will force you to march
     as captives beyond Damascus.
I, the LORD God All-Powerful,
     have spoken!^{t}

Israel Will Be Punished

6 Do you rulers in Jerusalem
     and in the city of Samaria
        feel safe and at ease?
Everyone bows down to you,
     and you think you are better
        than any other nation.
But you are in for trouble!
2Look what happened
     to the cities of Calneh,
        powerful Hamath,
        and Gath^{u} in Philistia.
Are you greater than any
     of those kingdoms?
3You are cruel, and you forget
     the coming day of judgment.

4You rich people lounge around
     on beds with ivory posts,
while dining on the meat
     of your lambs and calves.
5You sing foolish songs
     to the music of harps,
and you make up new tunes,
     just as David used to do.
6You drink all the wine you want
     and wear expensive perfume,
but you don't care about
     the ruin of your nation.^{v}
7So you will be the first
     to be dragged off as captives;
        your good times will end.

8The LORD God All-Powerful
     has sworn by his own name:
"You descendants of Jacob

---

^{s}**5.26** *star*: One possible meaning for the difficult Hebrew text of verse 26. ^{t}**5.27** *I, the LORD . . .
spoken*: Israel did not offer sacrifices and gifts to the LORD during the time they wandered through
the desert. But now they have made idols to carry during their ceremonies. So the LORD warns
that he will make them "march" away as captives beyond Damascus, where Israel had extended its
borders by victories in war (see 2 Kings 14.28). ^{u}**6.2** *Calneh . . . Hamath . . . Gath*: City-states
captured by the Assyrians: Calneh in 738 B.C., Hamath in 720, and Gath in 711. ^{v}**6.6** *your nation*:
Hebrew "Joseph's descendants" (see the note at 5.6).

make me angry by your pride,
and I hate your fortresses.
And so I will surrender your city
and possessions
to your enemies."

⁹If only ten of you survive
by hiding in a house
you will still die.
¹⁰As you carry out a corpse
to prepare it for burial,ʷ
your relative in the house
will ask, "Are there others?"
You will answer, "No!"
Then your relative will reply,
"Be quiet! Don't dare mention
the name of the LORD."ˣ
¹¹At the LORD's command,
houses great and small
will be smashed to pieces.

¹²Horses can't gallop on rocks;
oceansʸ can't be plowed.
But you have turned justice
and fairness
into bitter poison.
¹³You celebrate the defeat
of Lo-Debar and Karnaim,ᶻ
and you boast by saying,
"We did it on our own."

¹⁴But the LORD God All-Powerful
will send a nation to attack

you people of Israel.
They will capture Lebo-Hamath
in the north,
Arabah Creekᵃ in the south,
and everything in between.

A Vision of Locusts

7 The LORD God showed me that he is going to send locustsᵇ to attack your crops. It will happen after the king has already been given his share of the grain and before the rest of the grain has been harvested.ᶜ ²In my vision the locusts ate every crop in the land, and I said to the LORD, "Please forgive your nation. It's so weak. How can it survive?"

³Then the LORD felt sorry and answered, "I won't let it be destroyed."

A Vision of Fire

⁴The LORD showed me that he is going to send a ball of fire to burn up everything on earth, including the ocean.ᵈ ⁵Then I said, "Won't you please stop? How can our weak nation survive?"

⁶Again the LORD felt sorry and answered, "I won't let it be destroyed."

A Vision of a Measuring Line

⁷The LORD showed me a vision of himself standing beside a wall and holding a string

ʷ6.10 prepare . . . burial: Or "burn it" or "burn incense for it." ˣ6.10 the name of the LORD: Two relatives seem to be carrying out corpses for burial. One of them warns the other to be careful not even to say "Thank the LORD!" for fear that the mention of his name may cause something worse to happen. ʸ6.12 oceans: Or "rocky fields." ᶻ6.13 Lo-Debar and Karnaim: Two cities east of the Jordan River that were captured by Jeroboam II (see 2 Kings 14.25). In Hebrew "Lo-Debar" can mean "nothing," and "Karnaim" means "two horns (of a bull)." Horns were symbols of strength, and so the people are bragging about their military power (defeat of "two horns"), which Amos says is "nothing" (Lo-Debar). ᵃ6.14 Lebo-Hamath . . . Arabah Creek: The northern and southern boundaries of the northern kingdom. ᵇ7.1 locusts: See the note at 4.9. ᶜ7.1 harvested: This would have been an especially bad time for a locust attack. The non-grain crops such as vegetables and onions were just beginning to sprout, and the grain crops were almost ready to be harvested. ᵈ7.4 to burn up everything . . . ocean: One possible meaning for the difficult Hebrew text.

7.1 *his share . . . harvested:* The king may have had first choice of the grain to feed his troops and animals. A swarm of hungry locusts would have been especially bad at the time described. The non-grain crops such as vegetables and onions were just beginning to sprout, and the spring grain harvest was beginning. The people needed the food produced by this first harvest to survive until the second harvest in the fall.

7.4 *ball of fire:* The LORD's judgment fire is described as being so huge that it burns up the whole earth and dries up the oceans, which here means more than waters on the surface of the earth. They are also the waters that many ancient peoples called the "great deep," which was believed to run under the surface of the earth and feed the earth's rivers and springs (Gen 1.2; 7.11,12; Isa 51.10).

7.7,8 *string and weight . . . measuring line:* Amos sees a long string with a weight tied to it. Builders used such a measuring line, sometimes called a "plumb line," to make sure walls were being built straight up and down. The LORD is using the measuring device to see if the people of Israel are measuring up to their role as the LORD's chosen people.

7.10 *Amaziah the priest:* Amaziah was probably the head priest of Israel's temple at Bethel.

7.17 *prostitute:* Two kinds of prostitutes were common during Amos' time—those paid for sex and those who had sex as part of religious rituals.

Prostitution in the Bible

8.5 *New Moon Festival . . . Sabbath:* Selling grain and other kinds of work were forbidden on the first day of every month, which began with the "new moon" (Ps 81.3; Num 28.11-15). This was also true on the weekly day of rest called the Sabbath, which means "rest" or to "stop working" (Exod 20.8-11; 31.12-17; Deut 5.12-15).

with a weight tied to the end of it. The string and weight had been used to measure the straightness of the wall. **8**Then he asked, "Amos, what do you see?"

"A measuring line," I answered.

The LORD said, "I'm using this measuring line to show that my people Israel don't measure up, and I won't forgive them any more. **9**Their sacred places will be destroyed, and I will send war against the nation of King Jeroboam."[e]

Amos and Amaziah

10Amaziah the priest at Bethel sent this message to King Jeroboam of Israel, "Amos is plotting against you in the very heart of Israel. Our nation cannot put up with his message for very long. **11**Here is what he is saying:

'Jeroboam will be put to death,
and the people will be taken
to a foreign country.' "

12Then Amaziah told me, "Amos, take your visions and get out! Go back to Judah and earn your living there as a prophet. **13**Don't do any more preaching at Bethel. The king worships here at our national temple."

14I answered:

I'm not a prophet! And I wasn't trained to be a prophet. I am a shepherd, and I take care of fig trees. **15**But the LORD told me to leave my herds and preach to the people of Israel. **16**And here you are, telling me not to preach! **17**Now, listen to what the LORD says about you:

Your wife will become
a prostitute in the city,

your sons and daughters
will be killed in war,
and your land will be divided
among others.
You will die in a country
of foreigners,
and the people of Israel
will be dragged
from their homeland.

A Basket of Fruit

8 The LORD God showed me a basket of ripe fruit **2**and asked, "Amos, what do you see?"

"A basket of ripe fruit," I replied.

Then he said,
"This is the end[f]
for my people Israel.
I won't forgive them again.
3Instead of singing
in the temple,
they will cry and weep.
Dead bodies will be everywhere.
So keep silent!
I, the LORD, have spoken!"

Israel Is Doomed

The LORD said:
4You people crush those in need
and wipe out the poor.
5You say to yourselves,
"How much longer before the end
of the New Moon Festival?
When will the Sabbath[g] be over?
Our wheat is ready,
and we want to sell it now.
We can't wait to cheat
and charge high prices
for the grain we sell.

[e]**7.9** *Jeroboam:* Jeroboam II, who ruled Israel 783–743 B.C. [f]**8.2** *end:* In Hebrew "ripe fruit" and "end" sound alike. [g]**8.5** *New Moon Festival . . . Sabbath:* Selling grain at these times was forbidden by the Law of Moses.

We will use dishonest scales
6   and mix dust in the grain.
Those who are needy and poor
    don't have any money.
We will make them our slaves
for the price
    of a pair of sandals."

7I, the LORD, won't forget
    any of this,
though you take great pride
    in your ancestor Jacob.**h**
8Your country will tremble,
    and you will mourn.
It will be like the Nile River
    that rises and overflows,
        then sinks back down.

9On that day, I, the LORD God,
will make the sun
    go down at noon,
and I will turn daylight
    into darkness.
10Your festivals and joyful singing
    will turn into sorrow.
You will wear sackcloth**i**
    and shave your heads,
as you would at the death
of your only son.
    It will be a horrible day.

11I, the LORD, also promise you
a terrible shortage,
    but not of food and water.
You will hunger and thirst
    to hear my message.
12You will search everywhere—
    from north to south,
        from east to west.

You will go all over the earth,
    seeking a message
from me, the LORD.
    But you won't find one.

13Your beautiful young women
    and your young men
        will faint from thirst.
14You made promises
to the goddess Ashimah
    at Samaria;
you made vows to other gods
at the shrines
    of Dan and Beersheba.**j**
So now you will fall
    and never get up.

Judgment on Israel

9 I saw a vision of the LORD
standing by the temple altar,**k**
    and he said,
"Shake the columns
until the tops fall loose,
    and the doorposts crumble.
Then make the pieces fall
    on the people below.
I will take a sword and kill
    anyone who escapes.

2"If they dig deep into the earth
or climb to the sky,
    I'll reach out and get them.
3If they escape to the peaks
of Mount Carmel,
    I'll search and find them.
And if they hide from me
    at the bottom of the ocean,
I'll command a sea monster

● 8.8 *tremble . . . Nile River:* This probably refers to an earthquake. The Nile River flooded over its banks each year (like ground pushed up and down by an earthquake). This comparison seems unusual, since the Nile floods were welcomed because they made the land fertile.

● 8.9 *sun go down at noon:* This probably refers to some kind of eclipse, an event that often caused great fear for ancient people. An eclipse had been seen in this region of the world in both 784 and 763 B.C.

● 8.14 *Dan and Beersheba:* Jeroboam I built a shrine for worshiping the LORD at Dan in the northern part of Israel.

■ 8.14 *Ashimah:* Ashimah probably refers to one of the Syrian or Canaanite goddesses that some Israelites worshiped.

■ 9.2 *dig deep into the earth:* Meaning down to the world of the dead underground, known as *Sheol* (Job 30.23; Ps 139.7,8; Ezek 31.16-18; Acts 2.27).

h8.7 *though . . . Jacob:* Or "though I am the God that Jacob proudly worshiped."   **i**8.10 *sackcloth:* A rough, dark-colored cloth made from goat or camel hair and used to make grain sacks. It was worn in times of trouble or sorrow.   **j**8.14 *You made . . . Beersheba:* Or "You made promises to the goddess Ashimah at Samaria, and you made vows in the names of other gods at the shrines of Dan and Beersheba."   **k**9.1 *the temple altar:* The one at Bethel.

9.7 *Ethiopians . . . Philistines . . . Arameans:* Ethiopia was a region south of Egypt that included parts of the present-day countries of Ethiopia and Sudan. In the twelfth century B.C., the people who came to be known as Philistines migrated from the island of Crete to the area west of Canaan. The Arameans migrated from Kir.

9.11 *David's fallen kingdom:* David, Israel's great king, ruled the united kingdom of Israel from around 1010 to 970 B.C.. Later, around 931 B.C., the kingdom split in two. Eventually the northern kingdom (Israel) was defeated by the Assyrians. Afterward, Judah was defeated by the Babylonians, as Amos had warned. Amos 9.11-15 seems to imply that both Israel and Judah have already been defeated. This vision of a reunited Israel has led some scholars to suggest that these final verses of AMOS were added to the book during the time of the Babylonian exile (597–539 B.C.), a number of years after Amos lived. (See the articles From Joshua to the Exile: The People of Israel in the Promised Land on pg 1783 and After the Exile: God's People Return to Judea on pg 1789).

to bite them.
⁴I'll send a sword to kill them,
wherever their enemies
     drag them off as captives.
I'm determined to hurt them,
     not to help them."

His Name Is the LORD

⁵When the LORD God All-Powerful
touches the earth, it melts,
     and its people mourn.
God makes the earth rise
and then fall,
     just like the Nile River.
⁶He built his palace in the heavens
and let its foundations
     rest on the earth.[l]
He scoops up the ocean
and empties it on the earth.
     His name is the LORD.

The LORD Is God

⁷Israel, I am the LORD God,
     and the Ethiopians[m]
are no less important to me
     than you are.
I brought you out of Egypt,
     but I also brought
the Philistines from Crete[n]
     and the Arameans from Kir.[o]
⁸My eyes have seen
what a sinful nation you are,
     and I'll wipe you out.
But I will leave a few

of Jacob's descendants.
     I, the LORD, have spoken!

⁹At my command, all of you
     will be sifted like grain.
Israelites who remain faithful
will be scattered
     among the nations.
And the others will be trapped
     like trash in a sifter.
¹⁰Some of you are evil,
     and you deny
that you will ever get caught.
     But you will be killed.

The LORD's Promise to Israel

¹¹In the future, I will rebuild
     David's fallen kingdom.
I will build it from its ruins
and set it up again,
     just as it used to be.
¹²Then you will capture Edom
and the other nations
     that are mine.
I, the LORD, have spoken,
     and my words will come true.

¹³You will have such a harvest
     that you won't be able
to bring in all of your wheat
     before plowing time.
You will have grapes left over
     from season to season;
your fruitful vineyards
     will cover the mountains.

[l]**9.6** *He built . . . earth:* One possible meaning for the difficult Hebrew text.   [m]**9.7** *Ethiopians:* The Hebrew text has "people of Cush," which was a region south of Egypt that included parts of the present countries of Ethiopia and Sudan.   [n]**9.7** *Crete:* Hebrew "Caphtor."   [o]**9.7** *Philistines . . . Arameans from Kir:* The Philistines were Israel's enemies to the west, and the Arameans were enemies to the northeast. For Kir, see the note at 1.5.

14I'll make Israel prosper again.
  You will rebuild your towns
    and live in them.
  You will drink wine
  from your own vineyards
    and eat the fruit you grow.

15I'll plant your roots deep
  in the land I have given you,
    and you won't ever
    be uprooted again.
  I, the Lord God, have spoken!

9.15 *Lord God:* "Lord" is a translation of *Yahweh*, the Hebrew word used as God's personal name (see Exod 3.14, 15). The Hebrew word translated here as "God" is *Elohim*. Used together these names describe Israel's one true God, the powerful ruler of all creation.

Names of God

Lord (YHWH)

Reflection Questions About Amos 1.1—9.15

1. What does 1.1 tell about who Amos was? What was Amos supposed to do with what the LORD gave him? What was unusual about Amos being chosen by the LORD? Some additional information about Amos is given in 7.12-15. How does this add to your understanding of who Amos was?

2. For what reasons did the LORD judge many of the nations bordering Israel (1.3—2.3)?

3. What was the relationship between Israel and Judah at the time of Amos' preaching?

4. For what reasons did Amos preach the LORD's words of judgment against Israel (2.6—6.14)? How would Israel be punished?

5. After reading the first six chapters of AMOS, how would you define the kind of "justice" the LORD wants? What pictures of this kind of justice come to mind?

6. Where do you see examples of true justice in today's world? Where do you see injustice?

7. What did Amos see in the first four visions of the LORD's judgment against Israel (7.1—8.3)? How did the first two visions differ from the last two visions?

8. Who was Amaziah, and why did he tell Amos to stop preaching in Israel (7.10-13)? How did Amos respond to Amaziah's request (7.14-17)?

9. Why were the rich grain merchants impatient during the Sabbath and New Moon Festival (8.4-6)? What affect did their dishonest business practices have on their country and its people? How did the LORD respond to these practices (8.7-14; 9.1-4)?

10. What, if anything, is surprising about the last verses of the book (9.11-15)? Why is it difficult to live without hope?

obadiah

Injustice! Betrayal! Tragedy! Even if you don't cause it, should you still be blamed if you watch it and do nothing to prevent it? Read OBADIAH's prophecy about Edom to find out.

WHAT MAKES OBADIAH SPECIAL?

OBADIAH is the shortest book in the Old Testament—so short that it has no chapter divisions. The name "Obadiah" was a common one in ancient Israel and means "worshiper of the LORD." All that we know about Obadiah the person comes from this book, which was probably written sometime after the Babylonians invaded Jerusalem in 587 B.C. Other prophetic books, such as ISAIAH and JEREMIAH, have passages condemning the sins of many nations (see Isa 13, 15–21; Jer 46–51), but OBADIAH singles out the sins of just one nation. That nation is Edom, which bordered the land of Judah on the south near the Dead Sea.

Obadiah condemns Edom, the descendants of Esau, because of the way they mistreated their own relatives (Israel), descendants of Esau's brother Jacob. More than that, Obadiah speaks out against Edom's pride. Even though Edom was a small nation it felt confident that no enemy could destroy its fortress cities built high on rocky, mountainous land. But Obadiah made it clear that no nation which disobeyed God, including Edom, could be protected against God's judgment. Obadiah's prophecy also describes a future victory for the LORD's people, who will capture and rule over many neighboring lands, including Edom.

WHAT'S THE STORY BEHIND THE SCENE?

OBADIAH is part of the story of a long-lasting bitterness between two families: the family of Jacob (the ancestor of the Israelites) and the family of Esau (the ancestor of the Edomites). Hundreds of years before Obadiah's time, Jacob had cheated his brother Esau out of his inheritance (Gen 25.27-34; 27.1-41; 36.1,9-14). Esau hated Jacob, but forgave him in later life (Gen 33.1-16). Conflict between the descendants of Jacob and Esau resumed in the time of Moses (Num 20.14-21). It continued in the time of King David when Edom was conquered by Israel (2 Sam 8.13-14), and in the time of King Ahaz (736–716 B.C.), when the Edomites regained their independence from Judah.

The invasion of Jerusalem mentioned in verse 11 is most likely the Babylonian invasion of Jerusalem in 587 or 586 B.C. The Edomites did nothing to help Judah, but stood by and celebrated the enemy's victory. The Edomites moved north into southern Judah, and seized land and property. When they captured Judean refugees, the Edomites handed them over to the Babylonians. Obadiah declared that no natural defenses or treaties with friends could preserve Edom from God's coming judgment. One day Edom would be destroyed, and Israel would capture Edom's land. By the fourth century B.C., the land of Edom had been taken over by the Nabateans, an Arab people who lived in the northwestern Arabian Desert.

HOW IS OBADIAH CONSTRUCTED?

This short book can be divided into two main sections:

God's judgment on Edom and the nations (1-16)
Israel's expansion and victory (17-21)

The book of Obadiah is a prophecy of punishment against Edom, a nation south of the Dead Sea. The Edomites were descended from Isaac's son Esau, and so would have been relatives of the Israelites, who claim Esau's brother Jacob as their ancestor. The Lord accuses the Edomites of pride and cruelty toward their relatives, the people of Judah. When the Babylonian army destroyed Jerusalem in 586 B.C., the people of Edom celebrated, looted the towns in Judah, and turned refugees over to the Babylonians. Obadiah announces that a day of judgment is approaching when the Edomites will be defeated, vanish without a trace, and the people of a restored Israel will rule their land.

Outline

Edom's Pride and Punishment

The LORD God gave Obadiah
a message[a] about Edom,
   and this is what we heard:
"I, the LORD, have sent
   a messenger
with orders for the nations
   to attack Edom."

[2]The LORD said to Edom:
I will make you the weakest
   and most despised nation.
[3]You live in a mountain fortress,[b]
   because your pride
makes you feel safe from attack,
   but you are mistaken.
[4]I will still bring you down,
   even if you fly higher
     than an eagle

or nest among the stars.
   I, the LORD, have spoken!

[5]If thieves break in at night,
   they steal
     only what they want.
And people who harvest grapes
   always leave some unpicked.
But, Edom, you are doomed!
[6]Everything you treasure most
   will be taken from you.
[7]Your allies can't be trusted.
They will force you out
   of your own country.
And your best friends
will trick and trap you,
   even before you know it.

[8]Edom, when this happens,
   I, the LORD, will destroy

---

[a]1 *message:* Or "vision."   [b]3 *mountain fortress:* The Hebrew text has "rocky cliff," which sounds like "Sela," the capital of Edom, a fortress city built on a mountain.

9 *Teman:* With Bozrah (Amos 1.12), Teman was one of the two main cities in Edom. Teman was fortified and controlled the fertile region of Edom.

11 *foreigners entered Jerusalem:* The story of Babylonia's capture of Jerusalem is told in 2 Kgs 24.15—25.21 and 2 Chr 36.17-21. Edom reportedly rejoiced when the city fell (Ps 137.7; Lam 4.21; Obad 12).

15 *day:* The "day" Obadiah mentions is a coming day of judgment. Edom's punishments fit the sins its people committed.

Day of the LORD

16 *Judah . . . the wine of my anger:* God's judgment on Judah came in 587 B.C. when the Babylonian army destroyed Jerusalem. Drinking from the LORD's wine or cup of anger is a symbol for God's judgment and punishment (Ps 60.3; Isa 51.22; Jer 25.15-29; Rev 14.10; 16.19).

17 *escape . . . to Mount Zion:* Those "who escape" probably refers to those who will be freed from captivity in Babylon. They will return to Zion, because it is their holy mountain.

Zion

18 *Israel will be a fire . . . Edom will be straw:* Obadiah believed that God would use Israel as his instrument to destroy Edom as easily as fire destroys straw.

Fire

all your marvelous wisdom.
⁹Warriors from the city of Teman[c]
    will be terrified,
and you descendants of Esau[d]
    will be wiped out.

The LORD Condemns Edom's Cruelty

¹⁰You were cruel to your relatives,
    the descendants of Jacob.[e]
Now you will be destroyed,
    disgraced forever.
¹¹You stood there and watched
    as foreigners entered Jerusalem
    and took what they wanted.
In fact, you were no better
    than those foreigners.

¹²Why did you celebrate
    when such a dreadful disaster
        struck your relatives?
Why were you so pleased
    when everyone in Judah
        was suffering?
¹³They are my people,
    and you were cruel to them.
You went through their towns,
sneering and stealing
    whatever was left.
¹⁴In their time of torment,
    you ambushed refugees
and handed them over
    to their attackers.

The LORD Will Judge the Nations

¹⁵The day is coming
    when I, the LORD,
        will judge the nations.
And, Edom, you will pay in full
    for what you have done.

¹⁶I forced the people of Judah[f]
    to drink the wine of my anger
        on my sacred mountain.
Soon the neighboring nations
must drink their fill—
    then vanish without a trace.

Victory for Israel

¹⁷The LORD's people who escape
    will go to Mount Zion,
        and it will be holy.
Then Jacob's descendants
    will capture the land of those
        who took their land.
¹⁸Israel[g] will be a fire,
    and Edom will be straw
        going up in flames.
The LORD has spoken!

¹⁹The people of Israel
    who live in the Southern Desert
        will take the land of Edom.
Those who live in the hills
    will capture Philistia,
        Ephraim, and Samaria.
And the tribe of Benjamin
    will conquer Gilead.

²⁰Those who return from captivity
    will control Phoenicia
        as far as Zarephath.[h]

[c]**9** *Teman:* A famous city in Edom.   [d]**9** *descendants of Esau:* The people of Edom were descendants of Esau, the brother of Jacob (Israel).   [e]**10** *descendants of Jacob:* Jacob and Esau were brothers (see the note on Esau at verse 9).   [f]**16** *I forced . . . Judah:* Or "I will force the people of Edom."   [g]**18** *Israel:* Hebrew "The descendants of Jacob and of Joseph."   [h]**20** *Those who return . . . Zarephath:* One possible meaning for the difficult Hebrew text.

Captives from Jerusalem
   who were taken to Sepharad[i]
will capture the towns
   of the Southern Desert.
21 Those the LORD has saved

will live on Mount Zion
   and rule over Edom.[j]
Then the kingdom will belong
   to the LORD.

■   21 *the kingdom:* Obadiah looked for the day when God's rule would be restored on Zion, and the suffering and shame that God's people had suffered would be reversed. The LORD would rule over all people, including Edom.

[i]**20** *Sepharad:* Possibly the city of Sardis, the capital of Lydia, a country north and west of Media. This would refer to those captives from Judah who had been taken beyond the kingdom of Babylonia.
[j]**21** *Those the* LORD . . . *Edom:* Or "Leaders on (from) Mount Zion will save the people and rule over Edom."

Reflection Questions About Obadiah 1-21

1. What did Edom do (or not do) to God's people that was worthy of judgment (10-14)?

2. Why did Edom think that it was safe from any harm (4,8)? Why did Obadiah say that Edom was not safe at all?

3. The Babylonians defeated Judah, destroyed Jerusalem, and took many of Judah's people away into exile. According to OBADIAH, how would this situation be reversed?

4. What would happen to God's people (Israel) and to their enemies, such as Edom (17-21)?

5. Summarize the key message of OBADIAH in one or two sentences.

jonah

God chooses prophets to deliver messages of doom and hope. But what happens if the prophet disobeys God and fails to deliver these important messages? Read JONAH *and find out.*

WHAT MAKES JONAH SPECIAL?

All the other prophetic books primarily contain speeches of the prophets they are named after. JONAH has only one verse of prophecy (3.4). A few prophetic books also contain historical information about the prophets. But JONAH reads more like a story from beginning to end.

Many scholars think that the message of Jonah reflects the situation for Israel during or after the time of the exile in Babylon, which lasted from 597 to 539 B.C. The exile was considered a time of punishment, because the people had turned away from the LORD. After the exile, Israel struggled with how they could keep their identity as God's chosen people. Some suggested that the best way to do this was to separate themselves from people of other nations. This led to a self-centered and unforgiving attitude toward those who were not Jewish. Many forgot that God had chosen the people of Israel to be a blessing to everyone on earth (Gen 12.3) and a light to other nations (Isa 49.6). JONAH challenges this attitude by showing the people how foolish it is to try to keep God to themselves, because God is the God of all, and can show mercy to everyone, even to enemies.

WHAT'S THE STORY BEHIND THE SCENE?

Assyria was an aggressive and destructive power in the ancient Near East. When it conquered nations, families were often split apart and sent to different regions of the empire. As a result, Assyria was hated by many of the peoples of the ancient world. This was especially true for the people of Israel who had been defeated by the Assyrians in 722 B.C. The ten tribes of Israel that were taken from their homes by Assyria were completely destroyed, never to be heard from again. By sending Jonah to Nineveh, the capital of Assyria, God's overwhelming love and mercy are revealed. Jonah's anger at God for forgiving Israel's hated enemy is probably meant to reflect a similar attitude in Israel. Israel was jealous of its special relationship with God and was unwilling to allow this relationship be extended to other nations, especially nations that were clearly enemies of God and God's people.

HOW IS JONAH CONSTRUCTED?

Jonah tries to run away from the LORD (1.1-16)
The LORD saves Jonah (1.17—2.10)
Jonah in Nineveh (3.1—4.11)

Unlike most of the prophetic books in the Bible, Jonah is not a collection of a prophet's sayings. It is best understood as a story about how one prophet responded to God's call. The key theme of this story is that the Lord wants to show mercy to everyone—even those who are hated enemies. God tells Jonah to go to the Assyrian city of Nineveh and announce that the Lord will punish Nineveh for its sins. Instead of obeying the Lord, Jonah boards a ship headed for Spain. God sends a powerful storm that threatens to sink the ship. When the crew of the ship, who worship foreign gods, discover that Jonah's disobedience to the Lord has caused the storm, they throw Jonah overboard. The storm stops and the sailors make a sacrifice to the Lord, Jonah's God. The Lord sends a big fish to swallow Jonah. Inside the fish, Jonah prays to the Lord, who makes the fish spit out Jonah on the shore. Again, the Lord tells Jonah to go to Nineveh. This time, Jonah obeys. Instead of rejecting Jonah's message, as might be expected of Israel's enemies, the people of Nineveh pray to the Lord and are forgiven. In the final chapter, the Lord uses an unexpected event to teach Jonah the meaning of his mercy.

Outline

Jonah Runs from the Lord

1 One day the Lord told Jonah, the son of Amittai, ²to go to the great city of Nineveh[a] and say to the people, "The Lord has seen your terrible sins. You are doomed!"

³Instead, Jonah ran from the Lord. He went to the seaport of Joppa and found a ship that was going to Spain. So he paid his fare, then got on the ship and sailed away to escape.

⁴But the Lord made a strong wind blow, and such a bad storm came up that the ship was about to be broken to pieces. ⁵The sailors were frightened, and they all started praying to their gods. They even threw the ship's cargo overboard to make the ship lighter.

All this time, Jonah was down below deck, sound asleep. ⁶The ship's captain went to him and said, "How can you sleep at a time like this? Get up and pray to your God! Maybe he will have pity on us and keep us from drowning."

⁷Finally, the sailors got together and said, "Let's ask our gods to show us[b] who caused all this trouble." It turned out to be Jonah.

⁸They started asking him, "Are you the one who brought all this trouble on us? What business are you in? Where do you come from? What is your country? Who are your people?"

⁹Jonah answered, "I'm a Hebrew, and I worship the Lord God of heaven, who made the sea and the dry land."

¹⁰When the sailors heard this, they were frightened, because Jonah had already told them he was running from the Lord. Then they said, "Do you know what you have done?"

¹¹The storm kept getting worse, until finally the sailors asked him, "What should we do with you to make the sea calm down?"

[a]1.2 *Nineveh:* Capital city of Assyria, a hated enemy of Israel.   [b]1.7 *ask . . . show us:* The Hebrew text has "cast lots," which were pieces of wood or stone used to find out how and when to do something. In this case, the lots would show who was the guilty person.

● 1.1-3 *Nineveh, Joppa, and Spain:* By naming Nineveh and Spain in the opening of Jonah, the author is preparing the reader to learn one of the key messages of this short book—that God rules the entire world from one end to the other. **(See Map 1 on pg 1879 and Map 10 on pg 1888.)**

CR   Assyria

■ 1.1 *Lord:* "Lord" is used for the Hebrew *Yahweh*, which is God's personal name in the Jewish Scriptures (Old Testament). These verses clearly show God's power over all of creation. In Jonah's time, many people believed there was more than one god.

CR   Lord (YHWH)

● 1.1 *Jonah, the son of Amittai:* A prophet with this name lived at the time of Jeroboam II, who ruled the northern kingdom of Israel from 783 to 743 B.C. (see 2 Kgs 14.25). Jonah's name means "dove, senseless bird."

● 1.5,6 *sailors . . . ship's captain:* The Hebrew text refers to the sailors as "salts" and the captain as the "chief rope puller." Notice that when the storm comes up, it is the sailors who pray to their gods, while Jonah, God's prophet, is fast asleep.

■ 1.9 *Hebrew:* Israelites called themselves "Hebrews" when identifying themselves to foreigners.

1.16 *sailors . . . offered a sacrifice to the* LORD: Fearing that they will be punished for throwing Jonah overboard, the sailors offer a sacrifice to Jonah's LORD. **(See the chart Sacrifices and Offerings on pg 1828.)**

1.17 *big fish:* The type of fish is unknown.

2.2-6 *deep in the world of the dead . . . that pit:* The ancient Hebrews believed that a deep sea was located under the surface of the earth. The world of the dead, the "pit," lay beneath this great sea. The Hebrew name for the underground world of the dead was *Sheol,* described in the Bible as a totally silent place where no one knows or feels anything (Job 10.21,22; Ps 88.12; 94.17). Jonah uses this imagery to show that he felt both physically and spiritually separated from God.

2.4 *your holy temple:* Jonah believed God was present in a special way in the temple in Jerusalem (Exod 25.10-22; 2 Sam 6.2; 1 Kgs 8.6-13; Ezek 10.1-5). Jonah was tossed into the "pit" below the deepest part of the sea, and far from God's temple. But no physical distance was great enough to keep God from hearing Jonah's prayers.

2.9 *power to save:* When Jonah is the one being saved, he is happy to state his belief in God's ability to do so. Later in the story, Jonah will not be so happy to witness God's mercy (see 4.1-3).

3.4 *Forty days:* This period of time can be found in other times of testing in the Bible. (See Gen 6.17; Exod 34.28).

[12]Jonah told them, "Throw me into the sea, and it will calm down. I'm the cause of this terrible storm."
[13]The sailors tried their best to row to the shore. But they could not do it, and the storm kept getting worse every minute. [14]So they prayed to the LORD, "Please don't let us drown for taking this man's life. Don't hold us guilty for killing an innocent man. All of this happened because you wanted it to." [15]Then they threw Jonah overboard, and the sea calmed down. [16]The sailors were so terrified that they offered a sacrifice to the LORD and made all kinds of promises.
[17]The LORD sent a big fish to swallow Jonah, and Jonah was inside the fish for three days and three nights.

Jonah's Prayer

2 From inside the fish, Jonah prayed to the LORD his God:

[2]When I was in trouble, LORD,
  I prayed to you,
    and you listened to me.
From deep in the world
  of the dead,
I begged for your help,
  and you answered my prayer.

[3]You threw me down
  to the bottom of the sea.
The water was churning
  all around;
I was completely covered
  by your mighty waves.
[4]I thought I was swept away
  from your sight,
never again to see
  your holy temple.

[5]I was almost drowned
  by the swirling waters
    that surrounded me.

Seaweed had wrapped
  around my head.
[6]I had sunk down deep
  below the mountains
    beneath the sea.
I knew that forever,
  I would be a prisoner there.

But, you, LORD God,
  rescued me from that pit.
[7]When my life was slipping away,
  I remembered you—
and in your holy temple
  you heard my prayer.

[8]All who worship worthless idols
  turn from the God
    who offers them mercy.
[9]But with shouts of praise,
  I will offer a sacrifice
    to you, my LORD.
I will keep my promise,
  because you are the one
    with power to save.

[10]The LORD commanded the fish to vomit up Jonah on the shore. And it did.

Jonah Goes to Nineveh

3 Once again the LORD told Jonah [2]to go to that great city of Nineveh and preach his message of doom.
[3]Jonah obeyed the LORD and went to Nineveh. The city was so big that it took three days just to walk through it. [4]After walking for a day, Jonah warned the people, "Forty days from now, Nineveh will be destroyed!"
[5]They believed God's message and set a time when they would go without eating to show their sorrow. Then everyone in the city, no matter who they were, dressed in sackcloth.
[6]When the king of Nineveh heard what

was happening, he also dressed in sackcloth; he left the royal palace and sat in dust.[c] **7-9**Then he and his officials sent out an order for everyone in the city to obey. It said:

> None of you or your animals may eat or drink a thing. Each of you must wear sackcloth, and you must even put sackcloth on your animals.
>
> You must also pray to the Lord God with all your heart and stop being sinful and cruel. Maybe God will change his mind and have mercy on us, so we won't be destroyed.

10When God saw that the people had stopped doing evil things, he had pity and did not destroy them as he had planned.

Jonah Gets Angry with the Lord

4 Jonah was really upset and angry. **2**So he prayed:

> Our Lord, I knew from the very beginning that you wouldn't destroy Nineveh. That's why I left my own country and headed for Spain. You are a kind and merciful God, and you are very patient. You always show love, and you don't like to punish anyone. **3**Now let me die! I'd be better off dead.

4The Lord replied, "What right do you have to be angry?"

5Jonah then left through the east gate of the city and made a shelter to protect himself from the sun. He sat under the shelter, waiting to see what would happen to Nineveh.

6The Lord made a vine grow up to shade Jonah's head and protect him from the sun. Jonah was very happy to have the vine, **7**but early the next morning the Lord sent a worm to chew on the vine, and the vine dried up. **8**During the day the Lord sent a scorching wind, and the sun beat down on Jonah's head, making him feel faint. Jonah was ready to die, and he shouted, "I wish I were dead!"

9But the Lord asked, "Jonah, do you have the right to be angry about the vine?"

"Yes, I do," he answered, "and I'm angry enough to die."

10But the Lord said:

> You are concerned about a vine that you did not plant or take care of, a vine that grew up in one night and died the next. **11**In that city of Nineveh there are more than 120,000 people who cannot tell right from wrong, and many cattle are also there. Don't you think I should be concerned about that big city?

4.1-3 *Jonah was really upset . . . Now let me die:* Now it becomes clearer why Jonah wanted to run away from the Lord. He knew that the Lord was merciful and may forgive the people of Nineveh. But like many in Israel, Jonah probably thought the Assyrians deserved the Lord's punishment, not the Lord's forgiveness.

4.6 *vine:* The Hebrew word translated here as "vine" is *kikayon,* which would indicate a plant with wide leaves, such as a castor bean or cucumber plant.

4.6 *protect him from the sun:* Once again God protects Jonah, in spite of his anger at God.

4.11 *cannot tell right from wrong . . . many cattle:* This phrase may refer to infants and young children. If so, that would mean that there were many more than 120,000 people in Nineveh. Even the cattle of Nineveh wore sackcloth. The fact that the Lord was concerned about the cattle further drove home the point that the Lord's mercy was not just for the people of Israel.

---

[c]**3.5,6** *dressed in sackcloth . . . sat in dust:* Sackcloth was a rough, dark-colored cloth made from goat or camel hair and used to make grain sacks. Sometimes people wore sackcloth and sat in dust to show how sorry they were for their sins.

"You are a kind and merciful God, and you are very patient. You always show love, and you don't like to punish anyone."
Jon 4.2

Reflection Questions About Jonah 1.1—4.11

1. Why did Jonah find going to Nineveh such an undesirable task? Have you ever felt that way about something you had to do? Did you do it? Why or why not? What happened?

2. Compare the attitudes and actions of the non-Israelites (the sailors, ship captain, and people of Nineveh) to the actions of Jonah. How do they differ? How does the contrast between these characters support the overall theme of the book?

3. How is Jonah's personality revealed in the story? What do you admire about Jonah? What are Jonah's less admirable qualities? In what ways does Jonah remind you of yourself?

4. What aspects of God are revealed in the story? Which ones give you comfort or strength? Which ones trouble you?

5. What can the story of Jonah teach us about trying to understand God's will for the world?

micah

What does God want more than anything else? Read
MICAH to find out what happened to the people of Israel
when they forgot the answer to this important question.

WHAT MAKES MICAH SPECIAL?

The prophet Micah proclaims that no one is as powerful as the LORD God of Israel. God judges earthly
leaders and nations who oppose God and ignore
God's concern for justice, but God also saves those
who confess their sins and return to him. It did not
matter to Micah that he came from a small town in
the country. He dared to criticize leaders in the capital cities of Israel and Judah.

The LORD God had made agreements with the ancestors of the people of Israel, promising to bless
Israel with land and many descendants if they worshiped him alone and obeyed his Law. Micah said
that many of God's people had turned their backs
on God's Law and were in danger of losing out on
God's promises.

Micah also announced that God would lead the
people home to worship once again in Jerusalem
and choose a leader who would care for the people
like a shepherd and bring them peace. Micah shared
a hope with the prophet Isaiah that one day the
LORD's Law would be obeyed by all nations, and all
weapons of war would be remade into "rakes and
shovels" (Isa 2.1-5; Mic 4.1-5).

One brief passage in MICAH (5.2-5) has become
an important passage for Christians. It tells of a
shepherd from Bethlehem who will take care of his
sheep (his people) and bring peace to the world.
MATTHEW identifies this "shepherd" with Jesus of
Nazareth (Matt 2.1-6).

WHAT'S THE STORY BEHIND THE SCENE?

Micah's warnings were fulfilled in 722–21 B.C. when
Assyria invaded Israel and conquered Samaria. Many
of the people of Israel's northern kingdom were
forced to leave their land and live in other parts of
the Assyrian kingdom. Micah warned the leaders of
Jerusalem that they would suffer a similar punishment, because they were doing the same evil things.
In 539 B.C., however, the Persians conquered Babylon and allowed many of Judah's people to return
home and rebuild Jerusalem and the temple (2 Chr
36.22,23). The new temple was dedicated in 515 B.C.
(Ezra 6.13-18). Micah's words of hope echo the
great promises of a number of Israel's prophets
(Isa 45.1-13; 52.1-12; 59.9-21; Jer 46.27,28; Ezek 37;
Zech 9.9-17).

HOW IS MICAH CONSTRUCTED?

The prophecies in MICAH alternate between doom
and hope.

The book can be outlined as follows:

Messages of judgment against Israel and Judah
  (1.1—3.12)
Messages of hope for God's people (4.1—5.15)
The LORD puts the people of Israel on trial for their
  sins (6.1—7.7)
The LORD forgives those who confess their sins
  (7.8-20)

Micah lived during the eighth century B.C. The speeches collected in this book were warnings of the Lord's judgment against two cities: Samaria, the capital of the northern kingdom of Israel, and Jerusalem, the capital of the southern kingdom of Judah. Micah courageously speaks out against injustice. He accuses the rich of oppressing the poor and condemns the worship of pagan idols, the cruelty of rulers, and the lies told by priests and prophets who care more for money than for God. He prophesies that Jerusalem will be left in ruins and the temple will become a barren mountain. But Micah also announces a future time of peace and prosperity, when the Lord will lead his people home and bring to power a new ruler who will bring peace and who will be known and honored throughout the world. In the book's concluding poems, Micah says that God's people will praise the Lord for keeping the agreement he made with their ancestor Abraham.

Outline

1

I am Micah from Moresheth.[a] And this is the message about Samaria and Jerusalem[b] that the LORD gave to me when Jotham, Ahaz, and Hezekiah[c] were the kings of Judah.

Judgment on Samaria

[2]Listen, all of you!
Earth and everything on it,
    pay close attention.
The LORD God accuses you
    from his holy temple.[d]
[3]And he will come down
to crush underfoot
    every pagan altar.
[4]Mountains will melt
beneath his feet
    like wax beside a fire.

Valleys will vanish like water
    rushing down a ravine.
[5]This will happen because of
    the terrible sins of Israel,
    the descendants of Jacob.
Samaria has led Israel to sin,
and pagan altars at Jerusalem
    have made Judah sin.

[6]So the LORD will leave Samaria
    in ruins—
merely an empty field
    where vineyards are planted.
He will scatter its stones
    and destroy its foundations.
[7]Samaria's idols will be smashed,
    and the wages
of temple prostitutes[e]
    will be destroyed by fire.

---

[a]1.1 *Moresheth*: A town in southern Judah not far from Gath. In verse 14 it is called Moresheth-Gath.   [b]1.1 *Samaria and Jerusalem*: Samaria was the capital of the northern kingdom (Israel), and Jerusalem was the capital of the southern kingdom (Judah).   [c]1.1 *Jotham, Ahaz, and Hezekiah*: Jotham, the son of Uzziah, ruled Judah 740–736 B.C.; Ahaz, the son of Jotham, ruled 736–716 B.C.; Hezekiah, the son of Ahaz, ruled 716–687 B.C.   [d]1.2 *holy temple*: Possibly the one in heaven, though it may be the Jerusalem temple.   [e]1.7 *wages of temple prostitutes*: At pagan temples, people had sex with prostitutes as a way of worshiping the idols, and the money earned in this way was used to support the pagan religion.

1.2 *holy temple*: Here "temple" may mean God's throne in heaven (Ps 11.4), or may refer to the Jerusalem temple, where God was said to live (1 Kgs 8.1-13; Isa 6.1-4). If the "temple" here refers to heaven, then Micah may be saying that the Jerusalem temple is no longer the center of God's rule on earth. It has become a center of idolatry, and God will judge and purify it until it is fit to be used again.

1.4 *Mountains . . . Valleys*: God's presence and power are often described in terms of their effect on the world's land and waters (Exod 19.18; Judg 5.4,5; Ps 18.6-15).

1.5 *descendants of Jacob*: "Jacob" is used as a name for the people of Israel. Here Micah is probably referring to the northern kingdom rather than to the entire nation of Israel. However, he also uses the name "Jacob" for the southern kingdom of Judah (2.7) or for the whole people of Israel (5.7).

☙   Israel

1.10-12 *Gath . . . Beth-Leaphrah . . . Maroth:* Gath was a Philistine city; Beth-Leaphrah is unknown. Shaphir, Bethezel, Zaanan and Maroth are mentioned only here in the Hebrew Scriptures. These towns form the path of an invading army approaching Jerusalem from the coastal plain. The punishments these towns face are related in some way to the meaning of their names. In Hebrew "Shaphir" means "beautiful"; "Bethezel" means "house next door"; "Zaanan" means "one who goes out"; and "Maroth" means "bitter."

1.13 *Lachish:* This important fortified city of southwest Judah was the base for the Assyrian attack on Jerusalem about 701 B.C. (2 Kgs 18.13-17).

Silver and gold from those idols
    will then be used by foreigners
    as payment for prostitutes.

Judah Is Doomed

8Because of this tragedy,f
    I go barefoot and naked.
My crying and weeping
    sound like howling wolves
    or ostriches.
9The nation is fatally wounded.
Judah is doomed.
    Jerusalem will fall.

10Don't tell it in Gath!
    Don't even cry.
Instead, roll in the dust
    at Beth-Leaphrah.g
11Depart naked and ashamed,
    you people of Shaphir.h
The town of Bethezeli mourns
because no one from Zaananj
    went out to help.k

12Everyone in Marothl
    hoped for the best,
but the LORD sent disaster
    down on Jerusalem.

13Get the war chariots ready,
    you people of Lachish.m
You led Jerusalem into sin,
    just as Israel did.n
14Now you will have to give
    a going-away gifto
    to Moresheth.p
Israel's kings will discover
    that they cannot trust
    the town of Achzib.q

15People of Mareshah,r
    the LORD will send someone
    to capture your town.
Then Israel's glorious king
    will be forced to hide
    in Adullam Cave.s
16Judah, shave your head
    as bald as a vulture
    and start mourning.

f1.8 *this tragedy:* Either the destruction of Samaria (verses 6,7) or the coming destruction of Judah and Jerusalem. g1.10 *Gath . . . Beth-Leaphrah:* Gath was a Philistine city; Beth-Leaphrah is unknown, but in Hebrew it sounds like "House of Dust." h1.11 *Shaphir:* Mentioned only here in the Old Testament; in Hebrew "Shaphir" means "beautiful." i1.11 *Bethezel:* Mentioned only here in the Old Testament; in Hebrew "Bethezel" means "house next door." j1.11 *Zaanan:* Mentioned only here in the Old Testament; in Hebrew "Zaanan" means "one who goes out." k1.11 *The town . . . help:* Or "No one from Zaanan refused to desert their town, and Bethezel mourns because it is left undefended." l1.12 *Maroth:* Mentioned only here in the Old Testament; in Hebrew "Maroth" means "bitter." m1.13 *Lachish:* The chief city of southwest Judah, about 30 miles from Jerusalem. n1.13 *led . . . sin . . . did:* Or "You led Jerusalem and Israel into sin." In Hebrew "Lachish" sounds like "a team of horses (that pulls a war chariot)." And the sin may be that Lachish led the nation to trust the power of war chariots instead of the LORD. But the sin could be idolatry or some false teachings that were brought in from Egypt by way of Lachish. o1.14 *going-away gift:* The gift (dowry) that a bride's father gave her when she left the home of her parents to live with the family of her husband. In Hebrew the word for "bride" or "fiancee" sounds like "Moresheth." p1.14 *Moresheth:* Hebrew "Moresheth-Gath"; the home of Micah (see verse 1). q1.14 *Achzib:* Meaning "lie" or "deception" was near Adullam Cave (verse 15), where David hid from King Saul (see 1 Samuel 22.1,2). Micah probably means that the people of Israel (including their king) will have to run for their lives, but will find that all hope for escape is merely a "lie" (see verse 15). r1.15 *Mareshah:* Sounds something like the Hebrew word for "conqueror" and was only a few miles northeast of Lachish. s1.15 *Adullam Cave:* See the note at 1.14.

Your precious children[t]
will be dragged off
    to a foreign country.

Punishment for Those Who Abuse Their Power

2 Doomed! You're doomed!
At night you lie in bed,
    making evil plans.
And when morning comes,
you do what you've planned
    because you have the power.
[2]You grab any field or house
    that you want;
you cheat families
    out of homes and land.

[3]But here is what the LORD says:
"I am planning trouble for you.
Your necks will be caught
    in a noose,
and you will be disgraced
    in this time of disaster."

[4]When that happens,
this sorrowful song
    will be sung about you:
"Ruined! Completely ruined!
The LORD has taken our land
    and given it to traitors."[u]
[5]And so you will never again
own property
    among the LORD's people.

[6]"Enough of your preaching!"
    That's what you tell me.
"We won't be disgraced,
    so stop preaching!"

[7]Descendants of Jacob,
    is it right for you to claim
that the LORD did what he did
    because he was angry?
Doesn't he always bless
    those who do right?
[8]My people, you have turned against
    one another!
You have even stolen
    clothes right off the backs
of innocent neighbors
    who pass by in peace.[v]
[9]You take over lovely homes
    that belong to the women
    of my nation.
Then you cheat their children
out of the inheritance
    that comes from the LORD.[w]

[10]Get out of here, you crooks!
    You'll find no rest here.
You're not fit to belong
    to the LORD's people,
    and you will be destroyed.[x]
[11]The only prophet you want
    is a liar who will say,
    "Drink and get drunk!"

A Promise of Hope

[12]I, the LORD, promise
    to bring together
the people of Israel
    who have survived.
I will gather them,
    just as a shepherd
brings sheep together,
    and there will be many.

---

[t]1.16 precious children: The towns mentioned in verses 10-15.   [u]2.4 The LORD . . . traitors: One possible meaning for the difficult Hebrew text.   [v]2.8 of innocent neighbors . . . peace: Or "of your unsuspecting soldiers returning home from battle."   [w]2.9 inheritance . . . LORD: The Hebrew text has "my glory," which refers to the inheritance of land that the LORD had promised his people.
[x]2.10 destroyed: One possible meaning for the difficult Hebrew text.

1.16 precious children . . . foreign country: The smaller towns were like children to the "mother" city of Jerusalem. This prophecy was fulfilled when many of Judah's citizens were forced to live in exile after the Babylonians destroyed Jerusalem in 586 B.C.

⊂℞ Exile

2.4 sorrowful song: This means the kind of song (lament) sung by professional mourners at funerals.

2.7 those who do right: It is unclear exactly who is speaking. It may be Micah's enemies challenging those who agree with Micah. They may have thought of themselves as "those who do right." However the questions may be the prophet's. In verse 2.8, Micah clearly is presenting the LORD's case again.

2.9 homes . . . inheritance: In ancient Israel, land ownership rights were to be passed on within families.

⊂℞ Land

2.12,13 promise to . . . gather them . . . as a shepherd . . . king: Micah adds a hopeful promise. God will gather together those who "survive" the difficult days ahead as a shepherd gathers his flock. God will be a good shepherd and take care of the faithful ones who return to Judah.

3.5-7 *lying prophets . . . fortunetellers:* The prophets were to remind the people how God wanted them to live. The priests and prophets could receive money or goods in return for doing their religious duties (Num 18.8-13; 1 Sam 9.6-8; Amos 7.12). Some prophets took payments but were not willing to speak out against injustice or encourage the leaders to do what was right. For not speaking out against the evil in Israel, they would be silenced.

3.8 *filled me with . . . Spirit:* In contrast to the prophets who preached what people wanted to hear in order to get paid, Micah's prophecies came directly from the LORD's "Spirit," which is God's presence and power.

   Holy Spirit

4.1 *In the future:* The prophet describes a future time when Judah's people will return home and rebuild Jerusalem and the temple (2 Chr 36.22, 23). The new temple was dedicated in 515 B.C.

4.1 *mountain with the LORD's temple:* The temple in Jerusalem was located on a hill known as Mount Zion.

   Zion

4.2 *Law:* Here "Law" probably refers to the Law of Moses.

   Law

   Wisdom

¹³I will break down the gate
  and lead them out—
   then I will be their king.

Evil Rulers and Lying Prophets

3 Listen to me,
  you rulers of Israel!
You know right from wrong,
²but you prefer to do evil
  instead of what is right.
You skin my people alive.
You strip off their flesh,
³ break their bones,
  cook it all in a pot,
  and gulp it down.

⁴Someday you will beg the LORD
  to help you,
but he will turn away
  because of your sins.

⁵You lying prophets promise
security for anyone
  who gives you food,
but disaster for anyone
  who refuses to feed you.
Here is what the LORD says
  to you prophets:
⁶"You will live in the dark,
far from the sight of the sun,
  with no message from me.
⁷You prophets and fortunetellers
will all be disgraced,
  with no message from me."

⁸But the LORD has filled me
  with power and his Spirit.
I have been given the courage
  to speak about justice
and to tell you people of Israel
  that you have sinned.
⁹So listen to my message,
  you rulers of Israel!

You hate justice
  and twist the truth.
¹⁰You make cruelty and murder
  a way of life in Jerusalem.
¹¹You leaders accept bribes
  for dishonest decisions.
You priests and prophets
teach and preach,
  but only for money.

Then you say,
"The LORD is on our side.
  No harm will come to us."
¹²And so, because of you,
Jerusalem will be plowed under
  and left in ruins.
Thorns will cover the mountain
  where the temple now stands.

Peace and Prosperity

4 In the future, the mountain
  with the LORD's temple
   will be the highest of all.
It will reach above the hills,
and every nation
  will rush to it.
²People of many nations
  will come and say,
"Let's go up to the mountain
of the LORD God of Jacob
  and worship in his temple."

The LORD will teach us his Law
from Jerusalem,
  and we will obey him.
³He will settle arguments
between distant
  and powerful nations.
They will pound their swords
and their spears
  into rakes and shovels;
they will never again make war
  or attack one another.

⁴Everyone will find rest
    beneath their own fig trees
        or grape vines,
and they will live in peace.
This is a solemn promise
    of the Lord All-Powerful.

⁵Others may follow their gods,
but we will always follow
    the Lord our God.

The Lord Will Lead His People Home

⁶The Lord said:
At that time
    I will gather my people—
the lame and the outcasts,
and all others into whose lives
    I have brought sorrow.
⁷Then the lame and the outcasts
will belong to my people
    and become a strong nation.
I, the Lord, will rule them
    from Mount Zion forever.
⁸Mount Zion in Jerusalem,
guardian of my people,
    you will rule again.

⁹Jerusalem, why are you crying?
Don't you have a king?
    Have your advisors gone?
Are you suffering
    like a woman in childbirth?
¹⁰Keep on groaning with pain,
    you people of Jerusalem!
If you escape from your city
    to the countryside,
you will still be taken
    as prisoners to Babylonia.

But later I will rescue you
    from your enemies.

¹¹Zion, because of your sins
you are surrounded
    by many nations who say,
"We can hardly wait
    to see you disgraced."ʸ
¹²But they don't know
    that I, the Lord,
have gathered them here
    to grind them like grain.
¹³Smash them to pieces, Zion!
I'll let you be like a bull
    with iron horns
    and bronze hoofs.
Crush those nations
and bring their wealth to me,
    the Lord of the earth.

A Promised Ruler

5 Jerusalem, enemy troops
        have surrounded you;ᶻ
they have struck Israel's ruler
    in the face with a stick.

²Bethlehem Ephrath,
you are one of the smallest towns
    in the nation of Judah.
But the Lord will choose
one of your people
    to rule the nation—
someone whose family
    goes back to ancient times.ᵃ
³The Lord will abandon Israel
    only until this ruler is born,
and the rest of his familyᵇ
    returns to Israel.
⁴Like a shepherd
    taking care of his sheep,

☜ Justice

■ 4.12,13 *grind them like grain:* The Lord will punish the nations who made fun of Judah's fall.

● 4.13 *bring their wealth to me:* When God's people defeated an enemy, it was understood that all wealth gained in battle belonged to God, who gave them the victory. This is why the wealth of defeated nations is to be given to the Lord. See Lev 27.28,29; Deut 20.16-18; Isa 23.18.

☜ Holy War (The Lord's Battles)

● 5.2 *Bethlehem Ephrath:* Bethlehem was a small town located in the farming region five miles south of Jerusalem. Ephrath is the name of a tribe that lived in Bethlehem or the region around it and may have been another name for the town. Bethlehem was the hometown of Israel's King David. In the New Testament, Jesus' birth in Bethlehem is seen as the fulfillment of Micah's prophecy in 5.2-5 (Matt 2.1-6; Luke 2.4-7; John 7.42). **(See Map 6 on pg 1884.)**

● 5.3,4 *this ruler . . . shepherd:* The exact identity of this ruler is not certain. He will come from the hometown of Israel's greatest king, David (2 Sam 16.1). He will rule like the ideal shepherd-king, bringing justice and peace to his people (Ps 72.1-4,12-14; see also Isa 9.6,7; 11.1-5). New Testament writers interpret this ruler to be a description of God's Messiah, Jesus Christ (Matt 2.6-17; John 7.40-42).

☜ Messiah (Chosen One)

ʸ4.11 *We . . . disgraced:* Or "We'll pull up your skirt and expose your nakedness!" ᶻ5.1 *Jerusalem . . . you:* Or "Jerusalem, you are slashing yourself in sorrow, because of the enemy troops." ᵃ5.2 *family . . . times:* Or "kingdom is eternal." ᵇ5.3 *family:* Or "people."

Like a shepherd taking care of his sheep, this ruler will lead and care for his people by the power and glorious name of the Lord his God. Mic 5.4

5.7 *cover the earth like dew:* When the northern kingdom of Israel was defeated, many of its people were scattered throughout the Assyrian Empire. The same thing happened to many people in Judah when the Babylonians captured Jerusalem over 100 years later. Here, Micah pictures the descendants of the exiled survivors growing in numbers (covering the ground like dew) and then returning in the future to defeat their enemies.

5.10-13 *wipe out . . . chariots . . . idols:* When God's people return to their land, God will do away with witchcraft, idol worship, and battle chariots, which are symbols of Israel's trust in things other than God.

6.2 *my witnesses:* In this court scene, God calls on mountains and earth to be witnesses in the trial against Israel (compare to Isa 1.2; Ezek 6.3).

6.4,5 *rescued you from Egypt . . . King Balak:* God rescued Israel repeatedly, beginning in the time of the exodus from Egypt (Exod 3–15; Num 21.24; 31.7). Moses' brother Aaron was appointed the first high priest of Israel (Exod 28.1-4), and his sister Miriam was called a prophet (Exod 15.20). King Balak of Moab wanted to get rid of the people of Israel who were passing through his land, so, he hired Balaam the prophet to place a curse on them (Num 22.2—24.25).

this ruler will lead
   and care for his people
by the power and glorious name
   of the LORD his God.
His people will live securely,
   and the whole earth will know
   his true greatness,
⁵because he will bring peace.

Assyria Will Be Defeated

Let Assyria attack our country
   and our palaces.
We will counterattack,
   led by a number of rulers
⁶whose strong army will defeat
   the nation of Assyria.ᶜ
Yes, our leaders will rescue us,
if those Assyrians
   dare to invade our land.

The Survivors Will Be Safe

⁷A few of Jacob's descendants
   survived and are scattered
   among the nations.
But the LORD will let them
cover the earth like dew and rain
   that refreshes the soil.
⁸At present they are scattered,
   but later they will attack,
as though they were fierce lions
   pouncing on sheep.
Their enemies will be torn
to shreds,
   with no one to save them;
⁹they will be helpless,
   completely destroyed.

Idols Will Be Destroyed in Israel

¹⁰The LORD said:
   At that time I will wipe out
   your cavalry and chariots,
¹¹as well as your cities
   and your fortresses.
¹²I will stop you
   from telling fortunes
   and practicing witchcraft.
¹³You will no longer worship
   the idols or stone images
   you have made—
I will destroy them,
¹⁴together with the sacred polesᵈ
   and even your towns.
¹⁵I will become furious
   and take revenge on the nations
   that refuse to obey me.

The LORD's Challenge
to His People

6 The LORD said to his people:
   Come and present your case
   to the hills and mountains.
²Israel, I am bringing charges
   against you—
I call upon the mountains
   and the earth's firm foundation
   to be my witnesses.

³My people, have I wronged you
in any way at all?
   Please tell me.
⁴I rescued you from Egypt,
   where you were slaves.
I sent Moses, Aaron, and Miriam
   to be your leaders.
⁵Don't forget the evil plans

ᶜ5.6 *the nation of Assyria:* The Hebrew text uses both "land of Assyria" and "land of Nimrod," which was a poetic name for Assyria.   ᵈ5.14 *sacred poles:* Used in the worship of Asherah, the fertility goddess.

of King Balak of Moab
or what Balaam son of Beor[e]
    said to him.
Remember how I, the LORD,
    saved you many times
on your way from Acacia
    to Gilgal.[f]

True Obedience

6 What offering should I bring
when I bow down to worship
    the LORD God Most High?
Should I try to please him[g]
by sacrificing
    calves a year old?
7 Will thousands of sheep
or rivers of olive oil
    make God satisfied with me?
Should I sacrifice to the LORD
my first-born child as payment
    for my terrible sins?
8 The LORD God has told us
what is right
    and what he demands:
"See that justice is done,
let mercy be your first concern,
    and humbly obey your God."

Cheating and Violence

9 I am the LORD,
and you are wise to respect
    my power to punish.
So listen to my message

for the city of Jerusalem:[h]
10 You store up stolen treasures
    and use dishonest scales.[i]
11 But I, the LORD, will punish you
for cheating with weights
    and with measures.
12 You rich people are violent,
    and everyone tells lies.

13 Because of your sins,
I will wound you and leave you
    ruined and defenseless.
14 You will eat,
    but still be hungry;
you will store up goods,
    but lose everything—
I, the LORD, will let it all
    be captured in war.
15 You won't harvest what you plant
or use the oil
    from your olive trees
or drink the wine
    from grapes you grow.

16 Jerusalem, this will happen
    because you followed
the sinful example
    of kings Omri and Ahab.[j]
Now I will destroy you
    and your property.
Then the people of every nation
    will make fun and insult you.

[e]6.5 Balak . . . Beor: See Numbers 22–24. [f]6.5 Acacia to Gilgal: Acacia was where the Israelites camped after the experience with Balaam (see Numbers 25.1; Joshua 2.1; 3.1); Gilgal was where they camped while waiting to attack Jericho (see Joshua 4.19—5.12). [g]6.6 try to please him: This refers to what are traditionally called "burnt sacrifices," which were offered as a way of pleasing the LORD. [h]6.9 Jerusalem: One possible meaning for the difficult Hebrew text of verse 9. [i]6.10 scales: One possible meaning for the difficult Hebrew text of verse 10. [j]6.16 Omri and Ahab: King Ahab was the son of Omri and the husband of the evil Jezebel. Almost two centuries before Micah, the prophet Elijah had spoken against the idolatry and the other sinful practices that Ahab had encouraged in Israel (see 1 Kings 16.21-34; 18.1-18; 21.1-26).

6.6,7 offering . . . sacrifice . . . first-born child: The people of Israel assume that they can restore the broken relationship with God by offering some kind of sacrifice to please God. The numbers of sheep and the amount of oil go far beyond the amount required in the Law and reflect what only a king might be able to afford (1 Kgs 3.4; 8.62-64). The ultimate suggestion, child-sacrifice, was forbidden in the Law (Lev 18.21; 20.2-5; Deut 18.10) and was condemned by the prophets (Isa 57.5; Jer 19.5; Ezek 16.20). The suggested sacrifices reveal a sense of panic or desperation. (See the chart Sacrifices and Offerings on pg 1828.)

6.8 justice: Micah reminds the people that God doesn't want their sacrifices if people refuse to do what's most important—treat each other with justice and love. (See 1 Sam 15.22; Isa 1.10-17; Hos 6.6; Amos 5.21-24. See also Mark 12.28-31; Rom 12.1.)

Justice

6.10-12 dishonest scales: These dishonest practices were forbidden by the Law of Moses (Exod 20.15; Lev 19.35, 36; Deut 25.13-16; Prov 20.10).

6.16 Omri and Ahab: Omri encouraged the people of Israel to worship idols (1 Kgs 16.25-28). His son Ahab also encouraged the worship of idols (1 Kgs 16.29-33) and plotted with his wife Jezebel to kill Naboth so they could steal his vineyard (1 Kgs 21.1-16).

Israel Is Corrupt

7 I feel so empty inside—
  like someone starving
  for grapes or figs,
  after the vines and trees
  have all been picked clean.
² No one is loyal to God;
  no one does right.
  Everyone is brutal
  and eager to deceive
  everyone else.
³ People cooperate to commit crime.
  Judges and leaders demand bribes,
  and rulers cheat in court.[k]
⁴ The most honest of them
  is worse than a thorn patch.

  Your doom has come!
  Lookouts sound the warning,
  and everyone panics.
⁵ Don't trust anyone,
  not even your best friend,
  and be careful what you say
  to the one you love.

⁶ Sons refuse to respect
  their own fathers,
  daughters rebel against
  their own mothers,
  and daughters-in-law despise
  their mothers-in-law.
  Your family is now your enemy.
⁷ But I trust the LORD God
  to save me,
  and I will wait for him
  to answer my prayer.

The Nation Turns to God

⁸ My enemies, don't be glad
  because of my troubles!
  I may have fallen,
  but I will get up;
  I may be sitting in the dark,
  but the LORD is my light.
⁹ I have sinned against the LORD.
  And so I must endure his anger,
  until he comes to my defense.
  But I know that I will see him
  making things right for me
  and leading me to the light.

¹⁰ You, my enemies, said,
  "The LORD God is helpless."
  Now each of you
  will be disgraced
  and put to shame.
  I will see you trampled
  like mud in the street.

A Bright Future

¹¹ Towns of Judah, the day is coming
  when your walls will be rebuilt,
  and your boundaries enlarged.
¹² People will flock to you
  from Assyria and Egypt,
  from Babylonia[l]
  and everywhere else.
¹³ Those nations will suffer disaster
  because of what they did.

Micah's Prayer and the LORD's Answer

¹⁴ Lead your people, LORD!
  Come and be our shepherd.

[k]7.3 *court:* One possible meaning for the difficult Hebrew text of verse 3. [l]7.12 *Babylonia:* The Hebrew text has "the river," meaning the Euphrates River, which stood for Babylonia.

Grasslands surround us,
    but we live in a forest.
So lead us to Bashan and Gilead,[m]
and let us find pasture
    as we did long ago.

¹⁵I, the LORD, will work miracles
just as I did when I led you
    out of Egypt.
¹⁶Nations will see this
and be ashamed because
    of their helpless armies.
They will be in shock,
    unable to speak or hear,
¹⁷because of their fear of me,
    your LORD and God.
Then they will come trembling,
crawling out of their fortresses
    like insects or snakes,
    lapping up the dust.

No One Is Like God

The people said:
¹⁸Our God, no one is like you.
    We are all that is left
        of your chosen people,
    and you freely forgive
        our sin and guilt.
    You don't stay angry forever;
    you're glad to have pity
¹⁹   and pleased to be merciful.
    You will trample on our sins
        and throw them in the sea.
²⁰You will keep your word
    and be faithful to Jacob
        and to Abraham,
    as you promised our ancestors
        many years ago.

7.14 *Bashan and Gilead:* These two regions had belonged to Israel "long ago" in the days of King David. **(See Map 6 on pg 1884.)**

7.20 *keep your word . . . to Jacob . . . Abraham:* Starting with forgiveness, God will completely restore the people of Israel by helping them return to the land God promised to give their ancestors so they can rebuild it (Gen 22.16; 26.3; 50.24; Exod 13.5,11; Deut 7.1-15; Jer 32.22).

[m]**7.14** *Bashan and Gilead:* Two regions east of the Jordan River, known for their fertile pasturelands.

Reflection Questions About Micah 1.1—7.20

1. What kind of sins committed in Israel and Judah led to God's judgment (1.3-7,13; 2.8-11; 3.1-11)? Where do you see evidence of such sins in society today?

2. According to Micah, who was going to suffer God's punishment (1–3; 5.10—6.16)? Do God's judgments seem fair or unfair? Why?

3. In what ways would God show mercy to and restore the people of Israel (4.1—5.5; 7.11-20)?

4. Micah speaks a great deal about good and bad rulers. How does Micah think a ruler influences people? Micah uses the image of "shepherd" to describe a leader. How can leaders in government and the church be more like shepherds?

5. Read Micah 6.6-8 and Amos 5.21-24. In your own words, describe what God "wants" more than anything else. How easy or difficult is it to do this? Why?

nahum

You've probably heard it said: "I hope that bully gets what's coming to him (or her)!" Read NAHUM to find out what harsh words God's prophet had for a powerful nation that "bullied" God's people and many other nations as well.

WHAT MAKES NAHUM SPECIAL?

Little is known about the prophet Nahum. Even the location of his hometown of Elkosh is not known for certain, though it was somewhere in the nation of Judah. NAHUM's severe message of judgment against Assyria's capital, Nineveh, is often compared and contrasted with JONAH, which describes the people of Nineveh giving up their wicked ways and being forgiven by God.

NAHUM announces the coming downfall of the Assyrian Empire and its capital city, Nineveh. The powerful Assyrians caused great suffering for a number of other nations, including the people of Israel. In fact, Assyria invaded and defeated the northern kingdom of Israel in 722 B.C., taking many of its people into exile. During the following 100 years, Assyria continued to be a threat to the southern kingdom of Judah as well. But Nahum reassures the people of Judah that God will soon set them free from the "chains" of the Assyrians, so they can once again enjoy peace and celebrate their festivals. The LORD "protects those who trust him in times of trouble" (1.7). NAHUM's message of doom for Assyria repeated a theme that was common in the message of Israel's prophets: the LORD is concerned with justice and will punish those nations or individuals who use their power to mistreat others.

WHAT'S THE STORY BEHIND THE SCENE?

In 853 B.C. Assyria attacked and won a victory over a group of allied nations that included the northern kingdom of Israel.

It is uncertain when the prophet Nahum lived and preached. But it was sometime after 663 B.C., when Assyria defeated the Egyptian city of Thebes, and before 612 B.C., when Assyria's capital city Nineveh was destroyed by a group of nations that included the Babylonians and Medes. Most likely, Nahum's message comes from the time of Judah's king Josiah (640–609 B.C.), which means he lived and preached at the same time as the prophets Zephaniah and the young Jeremiah.

HOW IS NAHUM CONSTRUCTED?

NAHUM can be divided into two main sections: the first is a psalm describing the power of LORD God and how the LORD will deliver Judah from the chains of Assyrian influence; the second part of the book includes prophecies announcing the downfall of Nineveh, the capital of Assyria.

Hope for Judah: The LORD will break the power of Assyria (1.1-15)

Nahum's strong words of judgment for Nineveh (2.1—3.19)

n the book of Nahum, the Lord promises to help his people by destroying the Assyrian Empire and Nineveh, its beautiful and wealthy capital. In 721 B.C., the Assyrian army had defeated the northern kingdom of Israel and forced much of the Israelite population to resettle in distant lands. But the Lord tells Nahum he is going to set God's people free of Assyrian domination, and the evil enemies will never invade Israel again. Nahum is considered a masterpiece of ancient Hebrew poetry. It consists of a psalm that describes the fierce anger and invincible power of God followed by rich poetic sections that declare the end of Nineveh, describe its defeat, and celebrate the end of the cruel nation.

Outline

1 I am Nahum from Elkosh.[a] And this is the message[b] that I wrote down about Nineveh.[c]

The Fierce Anger of the LORD

²The LORD God demands loyalty.
  In his anger, he takes revenge
    on his enemies.
³The LORD is powerful,
    yet patient;
  he makes sure that the guilty
    are always punished.
He can be seen in storms
    and in whirlwinds;
  clouds are the dust from his feet.

⁴At the LORD's command,
    oceans and rivers dry up.
  Bashan, Mount Carmel,
    and Lebanon[d] wither,
    and their flowers fade.

⁵At the sight of the LORD,
  mountains and hills
    tremble and melt;
  the earth and its people
    shudder and shake.
⁶Who can stand the heat
    of his furious anger?
  It flashes out like fire
    and shatters stones.

The Power of Assyria Will Be Broken

⁷The LORD is good.
  He protects those who trust him
    in times of trouble.
⁸But like a roaring flood,
    the LORD chases his enemies
      into dark places
      and destroys them.[e]
⁹So don't plot against the LORD!
  He wipes out his enemies,

---

[a]**1.1** *Elkosh:* The location of Elkosh is not known.   [b]**1.1** *message:* Or "vision."   [c]**1.1** *Nineveh:* The capital of Assyria, the hated enemy of Israel.   [d]**1.4** *Bashan, Mount Carmel, and Lebanon:* Three regions noted for their trees and flowers.   [e]**1.8** *the LORD chases his enemies . . . and destroys them:* Or "the LORD chases Nineveh . . . and destroys her."

1.1 *Nineveh:* The ancient city of Nineveh was located on the Tigris River in northern Mesopotamia. People probably lived on the site of Nineveh even before 3000 B.C. It was rebuilt and resettled many times in the centuries before Sennacherib made Nineveh the capital of the growing Assyrian Empire in 705 B.C. When Akkadian kings ruled Assyria (about 1750 B.C.), the city of Nineveh was dedicated to the fertility goddess known as "Ishtar." As goddess of fertility, Ishtar is similar to the Canaanite goddess "Astarte" (see 1 Kgs 11.5). **(See Map 7 on pg 1885.)**

Assyria

LORD (YHWH)

1.3-6 *powerful, yet patient . . . shatters stones:* NAHUM uses a number of images found elsewhere in the Hebrew Scriptures to describe the LORD's patience, power, and anger. No doubt some people in Judah wondered why it was taking the LORD so long to free them from the power of Assyria, but Nahum assured the people the LORD would act when the time was right, and the "guilty" would be punished.

The LORD is good. He protects those who trust him in time of trouble. NAH 1.7

1.11 *one of your rulers*: Exactly which ruler Nahum had in mind is uncertain. It could refer to Sennacherib, who surrounded Jerusalem in 701 B.C. (2 Kgs 18.13—19.37), but any of the kings that followed Sennacherib would also have been regarded as a threat to God's people in Judah.

1.12,13 *Judah . . . set you free*: Judah was the name for the southern kingdom of Israel. When the Assyrians destroyed Samaria in 722 B.C., they forced many people from Israel's northern kingdom to leave their homeland and live as servants in other parts of the Assyrian Empire (2 Kgs 17.6). The "chains" may refer to this captivity, or they may represent the heavy taxes Judah was forced to pay Assyria (2 Kgs 15.19,20,29; 16.5-11).

1.15 *peace . . . festivals*: Nahum is the messenger of peace. When Assyria threatened Judah, the yearly festivals may not have been celebrated because of the threat of invasion. This verse may refer to renewing the Passover celebration in the "eighteenth year" (622 B.C.) of the reign of Judah's king Josiah (2 Kgs 23.21-23), ten years before the downfall of Nineveh in 612 B.C.

2.5 *rocks thrown . . . from the city wall*: When enemies tried to climb over the walls around the city, the people often threw large rocks down on them. It is unclear here who is throwing rocks, those attacking Nineveh or those defending it.

and they never revive.
¹⁰They are like drunkards
  overcome by wine,
  or like twisted thornbushes
  burning in a fire.^f
¹¹Assyria, one of your rulers
  has made evil plans
  against the LORD.

¹²But the LORD says, "Assyria,
  no matter how strong you are,
  you will be cut down!
My people Judah,
I have troubled you before,
  but I won't do it again.
¹³I'll snap your chains
and set you free
  from the Assyrians."

¹⁴Assyria, this is what else
  the LORD says to you:
"Your name will be forgotten.
I will destroy every idol
  in your temple,
and I will send you to the grave,
  because you are worthless."

¹⁵ Look toward the mountains,
  people of Judah!
Here comes a messenger
  with good news of peace.
Celebrate your festivals.
  Keep your promises to God.
Your evil enemies are destroyed
and will never again
  invade your country.

Nineveh Will Fall

2 Nineveh, someone is coming
  to attack and scatter you.
Guard your fortresses!
Watch the road! Be brave!
  Prepare for battle!
²Judah and Israel are like trees
  with branches broken
  by their enemies.
But the LORD is going to restore
  their power and glory.

*³Nineveh, on this day of attack,
  your enemies' shields are red;
  their uniforms are crimson.
⁴Their horses^g prance,
  and their armored^h chariots
  dart around like lightning
  or flaming torches.
⁵An officer gives a command.
But his soldiers stumble,
  as they hasten to build
a shelter to protect themselves
against rocks thrown down
  from the city wall.ⁱ

⁶The river gates^j fly open,
  and panic floods the palace.
⁷Nineveh is disgraced.
  The queen is dragged off.
Her servant women mourn;
  they moan like doves,
and they beat their breasts
  in sorrow.^k
⁸Nineveh is like a pond
  with leaking water.

^f**1.10** *fire*: One possible meaning for the difficult Hebrew text of verse 10.   ^g**2.4** *horses*: Two ancient translations; Hebrew "spears."   ^h**2.4** *armored*: One possible meaning for the difficult Hebrew text.   ⁱ**2.5** *to build . . . city wall*: One possible meaning for the difficult Hebrew text.   ^j**2.6** *river gates*: Nineveh was protected by a moat filled with water from the nearby Tigris River.   ^k**2.7** *sorrow*: One possible meaning for the difficult Hebrew text of verse 7.

Shouts of "Stop! Don't go!"
can be heard everywhere.
But everyone is leaving.

[9]Enemy soldiers shout,
"The city is full of treasure
and all kinds of wealth.
Steal her silver! Grab her gold!"

[10]Nineveh is doomed! Destroyed!
Her people tremble with fear;
their faces turn pale.[l]
[11]What happened to this city?
They were safer there
than powerful lions in a den,
with no one to disturb them.
[12]These are the same lions
that ferociously attacked
their victims,
then dragged away the flesh
to feed their young.

[13]The LORD All-Powerful
is against you, Nineveh.
God will burn your chariots
and send an army to kill
those young lions of yours.
You will never again
make victims of others
or send messengers to threaten
everyone on this earth.

Punishment for Nineveh

The LORD said:

3 Doom to the crime capital!
Nineveh, city of murder
and treachery,

[2]here is your fate—
cracking whips,
churning wheels;
galloping horses,
roaring chariots;
[3]cavalry attacking,
swords and spears flashing;
soldiers stumbling
over piles of dead bodies.
[4]You were nothing more
than a prostitute
using your magical charms
and witchcraft
to attract and trap nations.

[5]But I, the LORD All-Powerful,
am now your enemy.
I will pull up your skirt
and let nations and kingdoms
stare at your nakedness.
[6]I will cover you with garbage,
treat you like trash,
and rub you in the dirt.
[7]Everyone who sees you
will turn away and shout,
"Nineveh is done for!
Is anyone willing to mourn
or to give her comfort?"

Nineveh's Fate Is Sealed

[8]Nineveh, do you feel safer
than the city of Thebes?[m]
The Nile River
was its wall of defense.[n]
[9]Thebes trusted the mighty power
of Ethiopia[o] and Egypt;
the nations of Put[p] and Libya

2.13 *LORD All-Powerful*: In Hebrew this name for God is *Yahweh Sabaoth*, also translated as "LORD of hosts." The "hosts" in this ancient name may refer to the armies of Israel, which the LORD led into battle (1 Sam 4.4), or to the heavenly stars, which God created.

3.4 *prostitute . . . witchcraft*: Nineveh is pictured as a prostitute, attracting nations to itself so it can steal their treasures. The reference to magic and witchcraft may be a reference to the influence of Assyrian religion and gods upon those nations they defeated.

Prostitution in the Bible

3.8 *Thebes*: Thebes was the prosperous capital of Egypt for over 1,000 years until 663 B.C. when the Assyrian king Ashurbanipal captured it. The city was built on the River Nile with magnificent temples and palaces on both sides of the river.

[l]2.10 *faces turn pale*: Or "ashes cover their faces." [m]3.8 *Thebes*: In 663 B.C., the Assyrian King Ashurbanipal captured this Egyptian city, which seems to have been built with protection similar to that of Nineveh. [n]3.8 *was its . . . defense*: One possible meaning for the difficult Hebrew text. [o]3.9 *Ethiopia*: The Hebrew text has "Cush," which was a region south of Egypt that included parts of the present countries of Ethiopia and Sudan. [p]3.9 *Put*: A region in Africa, possibly part of the present country of Libya.

3.12-17 *fortresses . . . guards and your officials*: Nahum lists many aspects of Assyrian life that made the nation great: its fortresses, its army, its city gates, its water supply and defenses, its ability to build, its many merchants, and its efficient government leaders. But none of these, Nahum believes, will be of any value when the enemy comes.

3.15-17 *locusts*: Locusts are flying insects that are known for their ability to move in and devour crops quickly.

Locusts

3.18 *sound sleep*: This probably refers to the death of the Assyrian leaders.

3.18 *sheep without a shepherd*: In the Bible, kinds and rulers are often compared to shepherds because they are responsible for leading and protecting the people of their nation. See also Num 27.17; Ps 78.70-72; Ezek 34; John 10.1-18.

Shepherds

were her allies.
¹⁰But she was captured and taken
    to a foreign country.
Her children were murdered
    at every street corner.
The members of her royal family
    were auctioned off,
and her high officials
    were bound in chains.

¹¹Nineveh, now it's your turn!
    You will get drunk and try to hide
    from your enemy.
¹²Your fortresses are fig trees
    with ripe figs.
Merely shake the trees,
and fruit will fall
    into every open mouth.
¹³Your army is weak.
    Fire has destroyed the crossbars
    on your city gates;
now they stand wide open
    to your enemy.

¹⁴Your city is under attack.
    Haul in extra water!
        Strengthen your defenses!
    Start making bricks!
        Stir the mortar!
¹⁵You will still go up in flames
    and be cut down by swords
    that will wipe you out like a field

attacked by grasshoppers.
So, go ahead and increase
    like a swarm of locusts!⁹

¹⁶More merchants are in your city
    than there are stars
        in the sky—
but they are like locusts
that eat everything,
    then fly away.
¹⁷Your guards and your officials
    are swarms of locusts.
On a chilly day
    they settle on a fence,
but when the sun comes out,
they take off
    to who-knows-where.

¹⁸King of Assyria,
    your officials and leaders
    are sound asleep,
while your people are scattered
    in the mountains.
Yes, your people are sheep
    without a shepherd.
¹⁹You're fatally wounded.
    There's no hope for you.
But everyone claps
    when they hear this news,
because your constant cruelty
    has caused them pain.

---

⁹3.15 *locusts*: A type of grasshopper that comes in swarms and causes great damage to plant life.

Reflection Questions About Nahum 1.1—3.19

1. Most of NAHUM speaks about God's judgment. In which verses does Nahum speak about God's kindness and mercy? What is the message of these verses, and who are they directed toward?

2. In the years before and during the time of Nahum, why was Assyria hated and feared by other nations in the ancient Near East? (See the Introduction to Nahum.)

3. According to the prophet, why will Assyria and its capital city Nineveh fall (1.11,14; 2.12,13; 3.1-4,10)? Describe the city's destruction.

4. According to NAHUM, what does God "demand" (1.2) of people?

5. What can people expect from God (1.3,7)?

habakkuk

How do you keep trusting in God when it seems that God's ways make no sense? That's what the prophet Habakkuk wondered. Read this book to find out how God answered Habakkuk's questions.

WHAT MAKES HABAKKUK SPECIAL?

This short book records a conversation between the prophet Habakkuk and the LORD God. Habakkuk complained that the LORD had not acted to stop cruelty and injustice in Judah. When the LORD told him that Judah's punishment would be carried out by the army of Babylon, Habakkuk became even more upset. To Habakkuk, this solution was worse than the crime, because the cruelty of the Babylonians was worse than the behavior of the leaders and people of Judah. Comments on HABAKKUK were discovered among the Dead Sea Scrolls, written during the century before Christ. New Testament writers, such as Paul (Rom 1.17; Gal 3.11) and the writer to the Hebrews (10.38), quoted Habakkuk 2.4.

HABAKKUK shows how the prayers of a faithful person can include both complaint and praise, and combine questioning with trust. The Babylonians may punish Judah, but Babylon will eventually fall because its leaders worship their own strength. The LORD does not accept the proud but rather accepts those who live by faith. HABAKKUK shows the importance of continuing to praise God, who is the one true source of strength and the one who "saves."

WHAT'S THE STORY BEHIND THE SCENE?

Little is known about Habakkuk except what we learn from his book. He calls himself a prophet, a person who speaks for God. Some ancient traditions suggest that Habakkuk was also a priest who served in the Jerusalem temple. Certain terms or directions ("Use stringed instruments," 3.19) suggest to many scholars that the prayer in chapter 3 was a formal prayer used in Israel's worship.

Habakkuk wrote during a time of violence, terrible injustice, and lawlessness among God's people (1.2-4)—a situation often repeated in Israel's history. However, the reference to "sending the Babylonians" (1.6) may indicate that Habakkuk wrote shortly before or after 600 B.C., when the Babylonians became the strongest power in the ancient Near East. In 586 B.C., the Babylonians captured and destroyed the city of Jerusalem and its temple. Habakkuk's book may have been used for worship in the temple before it was destroyed. In Jewish tradition, chapter 3 of HABAKKUK is one of the readings for the second day of the Harvest Festival (*Shavuoth*), which celebrates God's giving of the Law at Mount Sinai.

HOW IS HABAKKUK CONSTRUCTED?

HABAKKUK has two major sections. The first section (1.1—2.20) contains two conversations between Habakkuk and God. In the second section (3.1-19), Habakkuk's formal prayer or hymn praises God for helping the people of Israel in the past, and the prophet declares his trust in God.

Habakkuk's conversations with God
 (1.1—2.20)
Habakkuk's prayer of praise and trust (3.1-19)

The prophet Habakkuk lived in a time of chaos. There was lawlessness and corruption in Judah, and bloody wars of conquest between the powerful nations of Assyria and Babylonia. Like the book of Job, Habakkuk depicts a human being questioning God on the matter of justice. Habakkuk asks the Lord to end the violence and injustice in Judah. God replies that he will send the Babylonians to punish Judah. A shocked Habakkuk asks God how he can use the sinful Babylonians to destroy people who are better than they are. God responds by telling Habakkuk that he does not tolerate the proud, and the Babylonians will eventually be punished. Terrified of the coming judgment against Judah, Habakkuk nevertheless submits to God's will, assured that the Lord will save his people and give them the strength to endure the troubles to come.

Outline

1

I am Habakkuk the prophet. And this is the message[a] that the LORD gave me.

Habakkuk Complains to the LORD

[2]Our LORD, how long must I beg
for your help
  before you listen?
How long before you save us
  from all this violence?
[3]Why do you make me watch
  such terrible injustice?
Why do you allow violence,
lawlessness, crime, and cruelty
  to spread everywhere?
[4]Laws cannot be enforced;
  justice is always the loser;
criminals crowd out honest people
  and twist the laws around.

The LORD Answers Habakkuk

[5]Look and be amazed
  at what's happening
    among the nations!
Even if you were told,
  you would never believe
    what's taking place now.
[6]I am sending the Babylonians.
They are fierce and cruel—
  marching across the land,
    conquering cities and towns.

[7]How fearsome and frightening.
Their only laws and rules
  are the ones they make up.
[8]Their cavalry troops are faster
  than leopards,
more ferocious than wolves
  hunting at sunset,
and swifter than hungry eagles
  suddenly swooping down.

[a]**1.1** *message*: Or "vision."

1.1. *Habakkuk the prophet:* Nothing is known about the prophet Habakkuk. He probably lived in the southern kingdom (Judah) and may have served in the temple, perhaps as a priest, but this is uncertain. A short book called *Bel and the Dragon,* listed in the *Apocrypha* as an addition to DANIEL, claims to be a "prophecy of Habakkuk . . . of the tribe of Levi." Another Jewish tradition says Habakkuk lived during the reign of King Manasseh of Judah (687–642 B.C.), but it is most likely that Habakkuk served as a prophet in Judah during the reign of Jehoiakim, who ruled from 609 to 598 B.C. **(See the article What Books Belong in the Bible? on pg 1764.)**

1.2-4 *violence . . . injustice . . . twist the laws:* Habakkuk is likely complaining about violence and lawlessness in his own nation of Judah. According to the Law of Moses, the people of Israel were to treat each other with honesty and fairness. Yet many of the LORD's prophets accused the people and their leaders of being unjust in their treatment of others (Isa 1.4, 15-17; 5.7-25; Hos 4.1-3; Amos 5.10-13). For many years, God's Law had been ignored in the nation of Judah.

ᴄᴿ Justice

1.5-8 *be amazed . . . sending the Babylonians:* The LORD "amazes" Habakkuk by sending the Babylonians to conquer "cities and towns," including those of Judah.

ᴄᴿ Babylon

1.12 *Holy Lord God:* "Lord" is frequently used in English translations of the Old Testament for the Hebrew term *Yahweh.* When combined with "God," this name refers to the God of Israel who is holy but who also is Israel's personal God, who chose them.

Lord (YHWH)

1.13 *can't stand sin or wrong:* Habakkuk wonders how the "Holy Lord God," who hates sin, can use the sinful Babylonians to punish God's people. From Habakkuk's perspective, the sin of the ones who attack God's chosen people will always be greater than the sins of Israel.

1.14 *like fish:* Habakkuk compares the people of Judah to fish or reptiles who are easily captured in the nets of the enemy (the Babylonians).

2.1 *watchtower:* Watchtowers were placed on city walls to help watch for enemies, or built in fields to protect crops from thieves and wild animals at harvest time. Habakkuk pictures himself as a watchtower guard waiting for the Lord's answer to his questions (2.1). See also Ezek 3.17-21.

2.4 *anyone who is proud . . . faith:* The "proud" likely refers to the Babylonians, who "worship their own strength" (1.11). In general, it also refers to those who take pride in their own abilities, power, or wealth above trusting in God.

9They are eager to destroy,[b]
and they gather captives
like handfuls of sand.
10They make fun of rulers
and laugh at fortresses,
while building dirt mounds
so they can capture cities.[c]
11Then suddenly they disappear
like a gust of wind—
those sinful people who worship
their own strength.

Habakkuk Complains Again

12Holy Lord God, mighty rock,[d]
you are eternal,
and we[e] are safe from death.
You are using those Babylonians
to judge and punish others.[f]
13But you can't stand sin or wrong.
So don't sit by in silence
while they gobble up people
who are better than they are.

14The people you put on this earth
are like fish or reptiles
without a leader.
15Then an enemy comes along
and takes them captive
with hooks and nets.
It makes him so happy
16that he offers sacrifices
to his fishing nets,
because they make him rich
and provide choice foods.
17Will he keep hauling in his nets

and destroying nations
without showing mercy?

The Lord Answers Habakkuk Again

2 While standing guard
on the watchtower,
I waited for the Lord's answer,
before explaining the reason
for my complaint.[g]
2Then the Lord told me:
"I will give you my message
in the form of a vision.
Write it clearly enough
to be read at a glance.
3At the time I have decided,
my words will come true.
You can trust what I say
about the future.
It may take a long time,
but keep on waiting—
it will happen!

4"I, the Lord, refuse to accept
anyone who is proud.
Only those who live by faith
are acceptable to me."[h]

Trouble for Evil People

5Wine[i] is treacherous,
and arrogant people
are never satisfied.
They are no less greedy
than death itself—

[b]**1.9** *eager to destroy:* One possible meaning for the difficult Hebrew text. [c]**1.10** *dirt mounds . . . cities:* Attacking armies often build dirt mounds against city walls to make it easier for them to climb the wall and capture the city. [d]**1.12** *mighty rock:* The Hebrew text has "rock," which is sometimes used in poetry to compare the Lord to a mountain where his people can run for protection from their enemies. [e]**1.12** *we:* Hebrew; one ancient Jewish tradition "you." [f]**1.12** *You . . . others:* Or "You will judge and punish those Babylonians." [g]**2.1** *I . . . complaint:* One possible meaning for the difficult Hebrew text. [h]**2.4** *Only . . . me:* Or "But those who are acceptable to me will live because of their faithfulness." [i]**2.5** *Wine:* The Standard Hebrew Text; the Dead Sea Scrolls "Wealth."

they open their mouths as wide
    as the world of the dead
        and swallow everyone.

⁶But they will be mocked
    with these words:
        You're doomed!
You stored up stolen goods
    and cheated others
        of what belonged to them.
⁷But without warning,
    those you owe
        will demand payment.
Then you will become
    a frightened victim.
⁸You robbed cities and nations
    everywhere on earth
        and murdered their people.
Now those who survived
    will be as cruel to you.

⁹You're doomed!
    You made your family rich
        at the expense of others.
You even said to yourself,
    "I'm above the law."
¹⁰But you will bring shame
    on your family
        and ruin to yourself
            for what you did to others.
¹¹The very stones and wood
    in your home
        will testify against you.

¹²You're doomed! You built a city
    on crime and violence.
¹³But the LORD All-Powerful
    sends up in flames
        what nations and people
            work so hard to gain.

¹⁴Just as water fills the sea,
    the land will be filled
        with people who know
            and honor the LORD.

¹⁵You're doomed!
    You get your friends drunk,
        just to see them naked.
¹⁶Now you will be disgraced
    instead of praised.
The LORD will make you drunk,
    and when others see you naked,
        you will lose their respect.
¹⁷You destroyed trees and animals
    on Mount Lebanon;
you were ruthless to towns
    and people everywhere.
Now you will be terrorized.

Idolatry Is Foolish

¹⁸What is an idol worth?
    It's merely a false god.
Why trust a speechless image
    made from wood or metal
        by human hands?
¹⁹What can you learn from idols
    covered with silver or gold?
        They can't even breathe.
Pity anyone who says to an idol
    of wood or stone,
        "Get up and do something!"

²⁰Let all the world be silent—
    the LORD is present
        in his holy temple.

Habakkuk's Prayer

3 This is my prayer:ʲ
²I know your reputation, LORD,
    and I am amazed
        at what you have done.
Please turn from your anger
    and be merciful;

ʲ3.1 *prayer:* The Hebrew text adds "according to the shigionoth," which may mean a prayer of request or a prayer to be accompanied by a special musical instrument.

2.6 *You're doomed:* This phrase is used to introduce a prophetic message known as a "woe." The messages of doom in chapter 2 are likely aimed at the arrogant Babylonians, who will be punished according to how they have treated others.

☞ Babylon

☞ Nebuchadnezzar

2.10 *ruin to yourself:* The Babylonians destroyed Jerusalem in 586 B.C. and stole the treasures of Israel's temple. By 539 B.C., the Babylonian leaders had become so weak that King Cyrus of Persia was able to capture the city of Babylon without a fight. The city itself was never destroyed in battle, but its population grew smaller until it turned into ruins.

2.13 *LORD All-Powerful sends up in flames:* The title "All-Powerful" is used in the Old Testament to describe God as the commander, either of the armies of Israel or of all the angels in heaven.

2.20 *silent . . . in his holy temple:* This verse could be an ending to the final "woe" (2.18,19). All people who trust in lifeless idols should remain silent and worship before the holy LORD who is present in Israel's temple in Jerusalem. This verse also looks ahead to Habakkuk's psalm of praise in chapter 3: The LORD has not abandoned his people and will save them from the present trouble.

3.4 *glory shone . . . light flashed:* Fire, thunder, and lightning are often connected with the appearance of God in the Bible (Exod 3.1-6; 13.20-22; 24.15-18; Isa 4.5). God's appearance to Moses and the people in the past at Sinai is probably the event described in this verse (Exod 19.16-19; 24.15-18).

3.8 *monsters of the deep:* God's control over the forces of nature is compared to a victory over chaos monsters believed to live in the oceans (see also Job 3.8; Ps 74.12-17; Isa 27.1). Habakkuk may also have in mind the Lord's parting of the waters, to let the people of Israel escape from the Egyptian army (Exod 14). This event is the focus of Psalm 77, which is very similar to Habakkuk 3.8-15.

3.12,13 *trampled on nations . . . save your chosen one:* A number of God's acts on behalf of Israel may be in mind here: the Lord's victory over Egypt (Exod 7-14); Israel's victories when they entered Canaan (Josh 3-12); or even the victories of God's chosen ruler King David over many surrounding nations (2 Sam 5-8).

3.16 *weak from fear:* Habakkuk's "fear" does not mean he is afraid of God but rather shows his deep respect for God and for God's power to defeat evil.

do for us what you did
   for our ancestors.

³You are the same Holy God
   who came from Teman
   and Paran[k] to help us.
The brightness of your glory
   covered the heavens,
and your praises were heard
   everywhere on earth.
⁴Your glory shone like the sun,
   and light flashed from your hands,
   hiding your mighty power.
⁵Dreadful diseases and plagues
   marched in front
   and followed behind.
⁶When you stopped,
   the earth shook;
when you stared,
   nations trembled;
when you walked
   along your ancient paths,
eternal mountains and hills
   crumbled and collapsed.
⁷The tents of desert tribes
in Cushan and Midian[l]
   were ripped apart.

⁸Our Lord, were you angry
   with the monsters
   of the deep?[m]
You attacked in your chariot
   and wiped them out.
⁹Your arrows were ready
   and obeyed your commands.[n]

You split the earth apart
   with rivers and streams;
¹⁰mountains trembled
   at the sight of you;
rain poured from the clouds;
   ocean waves roared and rose.
¹¹The sun and moon stood still,
   while your arrows and spears
   flashed like lightning.

¹²In your furious anger,
   you trampled on nations
¹³to rescue your people
   and save your chosen one.[o]
You crushed a nation's ruler
   and stripped his evil kingdom
   of its power.[p]
¹⁴His troops had come like a storm,
   hoping to scatter us
   and glad to gobble us up.
To them we were refugees
   in hiding—
but you smashed their heads
   with their own weapons.[q]
¹⁵Then your chariots churned
   the waters of the sea.

Habakkuk's Response to God's Message

¹⁶When I heard this message,[r]
   I felt weak from fear,
   and my lips quivered.
My bones seemed to melt,
   and I stumbled around.

[k]3.3 *Teman . . . Paran:* Teman is a district in Edom, but the name is sometimes used of the whole country of Edom; Paran is the hill country along the western border of the Gulf of Aqaba. In Judges 5.4, the Lord is said to have marched from Edom to help his people; in Deuteronomy 33.2, Paran is mentioned in connection with the Lord's appearance at Sinai. [l]3.7 *Cushan and Midian:* Tribes of the Arabian desert who were enemies of Israel. [m]3.8 *monsters of the deep:* The Hebrew text has "rivers and oceans," which may stand for the powerful monsters that were thought to have lived there before the Lord defeated them. [n]3.9 *obeyed your commands:* One possible meaning for the difficult Hebrew text. [o]3.13 *chosen one:* Or "chosen ones." [p]3.13 *You crushed . . . power:* One possible meaning for the difficult Hebrew text. [q]3.14 *but you . . . weapons:* One possible meaning for the difficult Hebrew text. [r]3.16 *heard this message:* Or "saw this vision."

But I will patiently wait.
Someday those vicious enemies
  will be struck by disaster.[s]

Trust in a Time of Trouble

[17]Fig trees may no longer bloom,
  or vineyards produce grapes;
olive trees may be fruitless,
  and harvest time a failure;
sheep pens may be empty,
  and cattle stalls vacant—

[18]but I will still celebrate
  because the Lord God
    is my Savior.
[19] The Lord gives me strength.
  He makes my feet as sure
    as those of a deer,
and he helps me stand
  on the mountains.[t]

To the music director:
Use stringed instruments.

■ 3.18,19 *still celebrate . . . stand on the mountains:* Even though judgment would bring suffering to God's people, Habakkuk trusted that not all would be lost. This trust allows him to celebrate in the midst of defeat and have confidence like that of a sure-footed deer climbing on a dangerous rocky mountain slope. Though he questioned God, Habakkuk did not stop trusting in God's power to save. This kind of "faith" makes one acceptable to God.

[s]**3.16** *I will . . . disaster*: One possible meaning for the difficult Hebrew text.　　[t]**3.19** *stand on the mountains*: One possible meaning for the difficult Hebrew text.

The Lord gives me strength. He makes my feet as sure as those of a deer, and he helps me stand on the mountains. Hab 3.19

Reflection Questions About Habakkuk 1.1—3.19

1. What is Habakkuk's first complaint (1.2-4)? What is the LORD's surprising response to this complaint (1.5-11)? The LORD's response leads to Habakkuk's second complaint. What is it (1.12-17)?

2. In chapter 1, who seems to be weak (the "losers"), and who seems to be strong (the "winners")? What warning is given to the so-called winners, the "proud" (1.11)?

3. Habakkuk 2.4 is used by a number of New Testament writers (see Rom 1.17; Gal 3.11; Eph 2.8; Heb 10.38). The translation of 2.4 is uncertain. What do you think Habakkuk most likely meant by this verse? Why?

4. Habakkuk speaks about those who are "doomed" (2.6,9). In a column, list the actions that lead to the "doom." Next to these, make a second column listing the punishments for each of the evil actions. How do the punishments fit the actions?

5. In your opinion, does Habakkuk's view of God change from the beginning of the book to the end? Why or why not? What have you learned about God by reading and studying HABAKKUK?

zephaniah

*What can one person say or do to change the hearts,
minds, and actions of society's most powerful people?
Armed with God's Word, a young prophet named
Zephaniah faced this question.*

WHAT MAKES ZEPHANIAH SPECIAL?

ZEPHANIAH has two key messages. The first is that a "great day of the LORD" is coming soon. The people of Judah believed that one day the LORD would make them powerful and destroy their enemies; however, Zephaniah stated that when the day of the LORD did come, the LORD would punish those who had not obeyed him—including the people of Judah. Zephaniah described how the people had disobeyed the LORD. He also told the people that they could still avoid God's terrible punishment if they would be humble, obey the LORD, and worship only God (2.3; 3.12).

The second message of ZEPHANIAH is that the LORD also wants to create a new people who will "live right" (3.13) and will "celebrate and shout" (3.14), because the LORD has given them victory and refreshes their lives with his love (3.15-17). The LORD will bring home to Judah those who have been scattered or exiled by war. They will once again worship the LORD in Jerusalem, and other nations will see how the LORD has blessed them (3.18-20).

WHAT'S THE STORY BEHIND THE SCENE?

Zephaniah probably preached his message from the LORD near the beginning of the reign of Judah's King Josiah (640–609 B.C.). The people of Judah were greatly influenced by the Assyrians during the reigns of Manasseh (687–642 B.C.) and Amon (642–640 B.C.). Kings and other royal leaders of Judah followed Assyrian customs and dressed in Assyrian clothing (1.8). People were allowed to worship the stars and foreign gods, such as Baal and Milcom (1.4,5). Zephaniah's message was clear: Judah must reform and turn back to the LORD. King Josiah would later repeat this message in 621 B.C. after *The Book of God's Law* was discovered in the Jerusalem temple (see 2 Kgs 22,23). Josiah banned foreign gods in the temple and encouraged the people to live according to the Law of Moses. Yet after Josiah's death in a battle in 609 B.C., Jerusalem's leaders returned to their old ways.

After Josiah died, ZEPHANIAH reports that the people were "eager to start sinning again" (3.7). Eventually, Zephaniah's warnings of a day of punishment came true when the Babylonians captured and destroyed Jerusalem in 587 or 586 B.C. It took nearly 50 years before the people taken as prisoners to Babylon were allowed to return home to Judah and begin to rebuild Jerusalem and the temple, a hopeful time that seems to be described in 3.18-20.

HOW IS ZEPHANIAH CONSTRUCTED?

ZEPHANIAH has three main sections. The first two focus on God's judgment. The final section focuses on a time of celebration after the day of judgment has passed.

A day of judgment for Judah (1.1—2.3)
A day of judgment for all people (2.4—3.13)
A new day of celebration promised (3.14-20)

The prophet Zephaniah warns of the great day of the Lord, a future time of God's punishment for everyone who has not obeyed him. The Lord's message to Zephaniah begins with overwhelming images of God's destructive power whereby all life on earth—people and animals, birds and fish—will be destroyed in the opposite order in which they were created. Even though the great day of the Lord is coming quickly and unannounced, those who humbly obey the Lord and worship him may survive that terrible day when it does finally arrive. The concluding section of Zephaniah depicts the faithful people returning to Jerusalem and Judah. They celebrate the Lord's victory and the Lord celebrates the renewal of his people.

Outline

1

I am Zephaniah, the son of Cushi, the grandson of Gedaliah, the great-grandson of Amariah, and the great-great-grandson of Hezekiah.[a]

When Josiah son of Amon was king of Judah,[b] the LORD gave me this message.

Judgment on Judah

[2]I, the LORD, now promise
to destroy everything
on this earth—
[3]people and animals,
birds and fish.
Everyone who is evil
will crash to the ground,[c]
and I will wipe out
the entire human race.
[4]I will reach out to punish
Judah and Jerusalem—
nothing will remain
of the god Baal;[d]

nothing will be remembered
of his pagan priests.
[5]Not a trace will be found
of those who worship stars
from their rooftops,
or bow down to the god Milcom,[e]
while claiming loyalty
to me, the LORD.
[6]Nothing will remain of anyone
who has turned away
and rejected me.

[7]Be silent! I am the LORD God,
and the time is near.
I am preparing
to sacrifice my people
and to invite my guests.
[8]On that day I will punish
national leaders
and sons of the king,
along with all who follow
foreign customs.[f]

---

[a]1.1 *Hezekiah*: Ruled 716–687 B.C.   [b]1.1 *Josiah . . . king of Judah*: Ruled 640–609 B.C.   [c]1.3 *Everyone . . . ground*: One possible meaning for the difficult Hebrew text.   [d]1.4 *Baal*: A Caananite fertility god.   [e]1.5 *Milcom*: An Ammonite fertility god.   [f]1.8 *follow foreign customs*: Hebrew "wear foreign clothes."

1.1 *Hezekiah . . . Josiah . . . king of Judah:* Hezekiah was 25 years old when he became king (2 Kgs 18.2). Figuring about 25 years for each generation from the beginning of Hezekiah's rule, Zephaniah would have been born around 666 B.C. That means Zephaniah would have been in his mid-twenties when King Josiah began to rule Judah in 640 B.C., when he was only eight years old (2 Kgs 22.1). At that time, Judah and its capital city Jerusalem were badly in need of reform.

Eighteen years after Josiah became king, a great event occurred. The high priest Hilkiah found *The Book of God's Law* in the temple in Jerusalem (2 Kgs 22). Josiah read this book and reformed Judah by tearing down shrines built to honor pagan gods. But the kings who followed Josiah did not continue the reforms he had begun, so Judah was punished (2 Kgs 23.31—25.21). It was during and, perhaps, after Josiah's reign that Zephaniah preached his messages.

LORD (YHWH)

1.4 *Judah and Jerusalem:* After the death of King Solomon about 931 B.C., the united kingdom of Israel divided into two nations. The northern kingdom was named Israel, and the southern kingdom was called Judah. (See Map 6 on pg 1884.)

1.7,8 *the time is near . . . On that day:* The "day" Zephaniah mentions is "the great day of the LORD" when the LORD will judge all the nations.

Justice

1.10,11 *Fish Gate, New Town, and Upper Hills . . . Lower Hollow:* These sections of Jerusalem were probably centers of the city's business activity. The cries heard from these places are probably meant to be the cries of the merchants and wealthy people who had been cheating their neighbors. Zephaniah is warning these people that their possessions, homes, and vineyards will be destroyed.

1.14-18 *great day of the LORD . . . furious fire:* Zephaniah describes a time when the LORD will act like a great warrior who was not going to fight for his own people. God's judgment is also compared to a raging fire.

Fire

Day of the LORD

⁹I will punish worshipers
   of pagan gods[g]
and cruel palace officials
   who abuse their power.

¹⁰I, the LORD, promise
   that on that day
noisy crying will be heard
   from Fish Gate, New Town,
   and Upper Hills.
¹¹Everyone in Lower Hollow[h]
   will mourn loudly,
because merchants
   and money changers
   will be wiped out.
¹²I'll search Jerusalem with lamps
   and punish those people
who sit there unworried
   while thinking,
"The LORD won't do anything,
   good or bad."
¹³Their possessions will be taken,
   their homes left in ruins.
They won't get to live
   in the houses they build,
or drink wine from the grapes
   in their own vineyards.

A Terrible Day

¹⁴The great day of the LORD
   is coming soon, very soon.
On that terrible day,
   fearsome shouts of warriors
   will be heard everywhere.
¹⁵It will be a time of anger—
   of trouble and torment,
   of disaster and destruction,
   of darkness and despair,
   of storm clouds and shadows,

¹⁶of trumpet calls
   and battle cries
against fortified cities
   and mighty fortresses.

¹⁷The LORD warns everyone
   who has sinned against him,
"I'll strike you blind!
Then your blood and your insides
   will gush out like vomit.
¹⁸Not even your silver or gold
can save you on that day
   when I, the LORD, am angry.
My anger will flare up
   like a furious fire
scorching the earth
   and everyone on it."

Turn to the LORD

2 ¹You disgraceful nation,
   gather around,
²   before it's too late.
The LORD has set a time
   when his fierce anger
will strike like a storm
   and sweep you away.
³If you humbly obey the LORD,
   then come and worship him.
If you do right and are humble,
   perhaps you will be safe
on that day when the LORD
   turns loose his anger.

Judgment on Philistia

⁴Gaza and Ashkelon
will be deserted
   and left in ruins.

[g]**1.9** *worshipers . . . gods:* The Hebrew text has "all who jump over the threshold," which was a Philistine religious practice (see 1 Samuel 5.5).   [h]**1.10,11** *Fish Gate, New Town, and Upper Hills . . . Lower Hollow:* Names for different sections of Jerusalem: Fish Gate was probably the main gate on the north side of the city; New Town was a newer section; Upper Hills may have been a suburb north of the city; Lower Hollow was probably on the southern edge of town.

Ashdod will be emptied
in broad daylight,
and Ekron[i] uprooted.
[5]To you people of Philistia[j]
who live along the coast,
the LORD has this to say:
"I am now your enemy,
and I'll wipe you out!"

[6]Your seacoast will be changed
into pastureland
and sheep pens.[k]
[7]The LORD God hasn't forgotten
those survivors in Judah,
and he will help them—
his people will take your land
to use for pasture.
And when evening comes,
they will rest
in houses at Ashkelon.[l]

Judgment on Moab and Ammon

*[8]The LORD All-Powerful,
the God of Israel, said:
I've heard Moab and Ammon
insult my people
and threaten their nation.[m]
[9]And so, I swear by my very life
that Moab and Ammon will end up
like Sodom and Gomorrah—
covered with thornbushes
and salt pits forever.
Then my people who survive
will take their land.
[10]This is how Moab and Ammon

will at last be repaid
for their pride—
and for sneering at the nation
that belongs to me,
the LORD All-Powerful.
[11]I will fiercely attack.
Then every god on this earth
will shrink to nothing,
and everyone of every nation
will bow down to me,
right where they are.

Judgment on Ethiopia

[12]People of Ethiopia,[n]
the sword of the LORD
will slaughter you!

Judgment on Assyria

[13]The LORD will reach to the north
to crush Assyria
and overthrow Nineveh.[o]
[14]Herds of wild animals
will live in its rubble;
all kinds of desert owls
will perch on its stones
and hoot in the windows.
Noisy ravens will be heard
inside its buildings,
stripped bare of cedar.[p]
[15]This is the glorious city
that felt secure and said,
"I am the only one!"
Now it's merely ruins,
a home for wild animals.

2.8 LORD All-Powerful: This name for God is sometimes translated as "LORD of hosts." The "hosts" in this name refers either to the armies of Israel (1 Sam 4.4) or to the heavenly stars, which God created. Here it is used to show the superiority of the God of Israel.

2.8,9 Moab and Ammon; Sodom and Gomorrah: The people of Moab and Ammon had been enemies of Israel in the past. Zephaniah warns that Moab and Ammon will end up like the cities of Sodom and Gomorrah, which God destroyed because of the evil people who lived there (Gen 19.23-29). (See Map 4 on pg 1882.)

2.12,13 Ethiopia and Assyria: The prophet Isaiah had once warned Judah's King Hezekiah not to make a treaty with Ethiopia and Egypt against Assyria, Judah's enemy to the north (Isa 20.1-6; 30.1-7; 31.1-3).
For many years, Assyria was the most powerful nation in ancient Near East. It defeated the northern kingdom of Israel in 721 B.C. and threatened the southern kingdom of Judah during Zephaniah's lifetime.

Assyria

2.14 desert owls . . . Noisy ravens: Owls and ravens were considered unclean animals because they eat raw flesh. Because owls live in ruins, their presence in cities indicates that the Assyrian capital that once thrived is now a lonely and abandoned place.

[i]2.4 Gaza . . . Ekron: Gaza, Ashkelon, Ashdod, Ekron, and Gath (not mentioned because it was already destroyed) were the five major Philistine towns. [j]2.5 people of Philistia: The Hebrew text also mentions "Canaan" and "Cherethites," which are other ways of referring to the Philistines. [k]2.6 pens: One possible meaning for the difficult Hebrew text of verse 6. [l]2.7 Ashkelon: A Philistine town; see the note at 2.4. [m]2.8 threaten their nation: Or "boast about their own nation." [n]2.12 Ethiopia: The Hebrew text has "Cush," which was a region south of Egypt that included parts of the present countries of Ethiopia and Sudan. [o]2.13 Nineveh: The capital of Assyria; Nineveh was protected by a moat filled with water from the nearby Tigris River. [p]2.14 stripped . . . cedar: One possible meaning for the difficult Hebrew text.

3.1 *lawless city:* Zephaniah's message of judgment now turns to Jerusalem.

3.6 *wiped out nations:* This may refer to the defeat of Nineveh, the Assyrian capital city.

3.7 *God felt certain . . . sinning again:* Some scholars have suggested that the prophecy in 3.1-7 follows the reforms of King Josiah. The discovery of *The Book of God's Law* in the temple and Josiah's reforms may have given hope that Jerusalem would turn away from evil and once again obey the Law of Moses. But after Josiah died in battle against the Egyptians in 609 B.C., the leaders and people abandoned Josiah's reforms.

3.9,10 *purify each language . . . scattered people:* Compare the purifying of languages, which brings unity, to the story of Genesis 11.1-9, where God punishes proud people by confusing their languages and scattering the people all over the earth. Zephaniah sees both the ancient scattering and the exile of God's people being reversed.

3.11 *my holy mountain:* This refers to Mount Zion in Jerusalem.

Every passerby simply sneers
and makes vulgar signs.

Sinful Jerusalem

3 Too bad for that disgusting,
corrupt, and lawless city!
2 Forever rebellious
and rejecting correction,
Jerusalem refuses to trust
or obey the LORD God.
3 Its officials are roaring lions,
its judges are wolves;
in the evening they attack,
by morning nothing is left.
4 Jerusalem's prophets are proud
and not to be trusted.
The priests have disgraced
the place of worship
and abused God's Law.
5 All who do evil are shameless,
but the LORD does right
and is always fair.
With the dawn of each day,
God brings about justice.

6 The LORD wiped out nations
and left fortresses
crumbling in the dirt.
Their streets and towns
were reduced to ruins
and emptied of people.
7 God felt certain that Jerusalem
would learn to respect
and obey him.
Then he would hold back
from punishing the city
and not wipe it out.
But everyone there was eager
to start sinning again.

Nations Will Turn to the LORD

8 The LORD said:
Just wait for the day
when I accuse you nations.
I have decided on a day,
when I will bring together
every nation and kingdom
and punish them all
in my fiery anger.
I will become furious
and destroy the earth.

9 I will purify each language
and make those languages
acceptable for praising me.[q]
Then, with hearts united,
everyone will serve
only me, the LORD.
10 From across the rivers
of Ethiopia,[r]
my scattered people,
my true worshipers,
will bring offerings to me.

11 When that time comes,
you won't rebel against me
and be put to shame.
I'll do away with those
who are proud and arrogant.
Never will any of them
strut around
on my holy mountain.
12 But I, the LORD, won't destroy
any of your people
who are truly humble
and turn to me for safety.
13 The people of Israel who survive
will live right
and refuse to tell lies.
They will eat and rest
with nothing to fear.

[q] **3.9** *I will . . . praising me*: Or "I will change the hearts of all people and make them fit for praising me." [r] **3.10** *Ethiopia*: See the note at 2.12.

A Song of Celebration

¹⁴Everyone in Jerusalem and Judah,
  celebrate and shout
    with all your heart!
¹⁵Zion, your punishment is over.
  The Lord has forced your enemies
    to turn and retreat.
  Your Lord is King of Israel
    and stands at your side;
  you don't have to worry
    about any more troubles.

¹⁶Jerusalem, the time is coming,
    when it will be said to you:
  "Don't be discouraged
    or grow weak from fear!
¹⁷The Lord your God
  wins victory after victory
    and is always with you.
  He celebrates and sings
    because of you,
  and he will refresh your life
    with his love."^s

The Lord's Promise to His People

¹⁸The Lord has promised:
  Your sorrow has ended,
    and you can celebrate.^t
¹⁹I will punish those
  who mistreat you.
  I will bring together the lame
    and the outcasts,
  then they will be praised,
  instead of despised,
    in every country on earth.
²⁰I will lead you home,
  and with your own eyes
  you will see me bless you
    with all you once owned.
  Then you will be famous
    everywhere on this earth.
  I, the Lord, have spoken!

Zion

3.19 *lame and the outcasts:* The Lord is concerned for the "lame and the outcasts," not only in Judah but also in the entire world. One sign of God's future rule will be that the lame, the outcasts, and other persons needing help will receive it. But the outcasts may also refer specifically to the people of Judah who had been "cast out" of their homeland during the Babylonian invasion. They will receive the Lord's blessings once again and be restored to a place of honor in the world.

^s**3.17** *refresh . . . love:* Two ancient translations; Hebrew "silently show you his love." ^t**3.18** *celebrate:* One possible meaning for the difficult Hebrew text of verse 18.

"The Lord your God wins victory after victory and is always with you. He celebrates and sings because of you, and he will refresh your life with his love." Zeph 3.17

Reflection Questions About Zephaniah 1.1—3.20

1. What sins described in 1.2-13 led to Judah being punished by the LORD?

2. How could the people escape the LORD's anger (2.3)?

3. According to Zephaniah, how will Judah's neighbors be affected by the LORD's day of judgment? Why (2.4-15)?

4. What does Zephaniah say about the people's leaders and how they have misused their powers? What will happen to Jerusalem as a result (3.1-7)?

5. Why will Jerusalem and the people of Judah celebrate once again (3.11-20)?

haggai

Life is filled with choices. As you read HAGGAI, think about the choices the people of Jerusalem made and how this affected their relationship with God. What can you learn about the choices you make?

WHAT MAKES HAGGAI SPECIAL?

Haggai is the first prophet God sent to the Jewish people after they returned to Judah from exile in Babylon. His language is plain and direct, not poetic like many of the prophets. While his name means "festive," Haggai's message is serious.

This book was written to record Haggai's tireless activity in encouraging the people of Judah to rebuild the temple in Jerusalem. Haggai told the people that they were experiencing hard times because they stopped working on the temple (1.6-11). However, if they began to work again to rebuild the temple, God would once again fill the temple and bless the people with peace (2.7-9). Haggai also prophesied that Governor Zerubbabel of Judah would rule over a restored kingdom (2.21-23). These promises were especially meaningful to the Jewish people, who had suffered through a time of exile in Babylon and were now living under Persian rule.

WHAT'S THE STORY BEHIND THE SCENE?

In 538 B.C., King Cyrus of Persia gave an order that allowed the Jews who had been captive in Babylon for 70 years to return home to Jerusalem (Ezra 1.2-4). About 40,000 people returned with Governor Zerubbabel and High Priest Joshua, and they began to rebuild Jerusalem and the temple that had been destroyed in 587 B.C. The foundations of the temple were laid right away. However, a group of neighboring peoples opposed the rebuilding of the temple and interfered with its construction, because they did not want the people of Judah to become a strong nation again (Ezra 3.1—4.23). Fifteen years later, no progress had been made on the temple.

In 522 B.C., Darius, the next Persian king, encouraged the Jews to begin building again (Ezra 4.24). But the people complained that they couldn't continue rebuilding because of poor harvests, little food, and lack of money (Hag 1.1-6). In 520 B.C., the prophet Haggai warned the people that time was running out. God's people had delayed rebuilding the LORD's temple long enough. Haggai and the prophet Zechariah (Ezra 5.1,2) challenged and encouraged the people to complete the rebuilding of the temple. Construction started up again, and in 515 B.C. the newly rebuilt temple was dedicated (Ezra 6.13-15). It is not clear whether Haggai was alive to see the new temple completed.

HOW IS HAGGAI CONSTRUCTED?

Haggai can be divided into two sections:

Neglect and rebuilding of the temple (1.1-15)
The LORD will bless Judah and its leader,
    Zerubbabel (2.1-23)

King Cyrus of Persia had allowed the Jewish people who had been captive in Babylonia to return to Jerusalem to rebuild the temple there. When the people built their own houses before rebuilding the temple, the Lord gave Haggai a message for Zerubbabel, the governor of Judah, and Joshua, the high priest. Unless God's people began work on the temple, Haggai warned, conditions in Judah would never improve. But if they rebuilt the temple, the Lord would help the people prosper and bless them with peace. When the people of Jerusalem finally begin work on the temple, Haggai tells the governor that God has chosen Zerubbabel to rule over a restored kingdom, even as other kingdoms are destroyed.

Outline

Rebuild the Temple

1 On the first day of the sixth month of the second year that Darius was king of Persia,[a] the LORD told Haggai the prophet to speak his message to the governor of Judah and to the high priest. So Haggai told Governor Zerubbabel and High Priest Joshua[b] **2-5** that the LORD All-Powerful had said to them and to the people:

You say this isn't the right time to build a temple for me. But is it right for you to live in expensive houses,[c] while my temple is a pile of ruins? Just look at what's happening. **6** You harvest less than you plant, you never have enough to eat or drink, your clothes don't keep you warm, and your wages are stored in bags full of holes.

7 Think about what I have said! **8** But first, go to the hills and get wood for my temple, so I can take pride in it and be worshiped there. **9** You expected much, but received only a little. And when you brought it home, I made that little disappear. Why have I done this? It's because you hurry off to build your own houses, while my temple is still in ruins. **10** That's also why the dew doesn't fall and your harvest fails. **11** And so, at my command everything will become barren—your farmland and pastures, your vineyards and olive trees, your animals and you yourselves. All your hard work will be for nothing.

12 Zerubbabel and Joshua, together with the others who had returned from exile in Babylonia, obeyed the LORD's message spoken by his prophet Haggai, and they started showing proper respect for the LORD.

---

[a]**1.1** *sixth month . . . king of Persia*: Elul, the sixth month of the Hebrew calendar, from about mid-August to mid-September; the second year of the rule of Darius was 520 B.C. [b]**1.1** *Governor . . . Joshua*: Hebrew "Governor Zerubbabel son of Shealtiel and High Priest Joshua son of Jehozadak." [c]**1.2-5** *expensive houses*: Either houses with paneled interiors or with roofs; the temple was not yet completely rebuilt at this time.

"You say this isn't the right time to build a temple for me. But is it right for you to live in expensive houses, while my temple is a pile of ruins?" HAG 1.2-5

2.3 *temple used to be:* The first temple was built when Solomon was king of Israel. It took seven years to build (1 Kgs 6.38) and was finished in 951 B.C. (1 Kgs 5.1—8.13). The Babylonians destroyed the temple in 587 B.C. Some older people living in 520 B.C. may have been alive when the first temple was destroyed. They would have remembered what it looked like and mourned its loss.

2.11 *priests:* Israel's priests were responsible for offering sacrifices to the LORD and for blessing the people. In addition, they taught the people God's Law and how they should live according to it.

Israel's Priests

2.12-14 *acceptable for sacrifice . . . unacceptable:* The rules that defied ritual purity and right sacrifices were especially important in Jewish worship and culture. The example Haggai presents to the priests is a reminder that it is much easier to pass on uncleanness than cleanness (Num 19.11-22). In times past, the sacrifices of Judah's priests were sometimes unacceptable to the LORD because of all the evil things the people were doing (Isa 1.10-17,21-25; Mic 6.6-16).

Purity (Clean and Unclean)

13Haggai then told them that the LORD had promised to be with them. 14So the LORD God All-Powerful made everyone eager to work on his temple, especially Zerubbabel and Joshua. 15And the work began on the twenty-fourth day of that same month.

The Glorious New Temple

2 1-2On the twenty-first day of the next month,[d] the LORD told Haggai the prophet to speak this message to Governor Zerubbabel, High Priest Joshua, and everyone else:

3Does anyone remember how glorious this temple used to be? Now it looks like nothing. 4But cheer up! Because I, the LORD All-Powerful, will be here to help you with the work, 5 just as I promised your ancestors when I brought them out of Egypt. Don't worry. My Spirit is[e] right here with you.

6Soon I will again shake the heavens and the earth, the sea and the dry land. 7I will shake the nations, and their treasures[f] will be brought here. Then the brightness of my glory will fill this temple. 8All silver and gold belong to me, 9and I promise that this new temple will be more glorious than the first one. I will also bless this city[g] with peace.

The Past and the Future

10On the twenty-fourth day of the ninth month,[h] the LORD God All-Powerful told the prophet Haggai 11to ask the priests for their opinion on the following matters:

12Suppose meat ready to be sacrificed to God is being carried in the folds of someone's clothing, and the clothing rubs against some bread or stew or wine or olive oil or any other food. Would those foods that were touched then become acceptable for sacrifice?

"Of course not," the priests answered.

13Then Haggai said, "Suppose someone has touched a dead body and is considered unacceptable to worship God. If that person touches these foods, would they become unclean?"

"Of course they would," the priests answered.

14So the LORD told Haggai to say:

That's how it is with this entire nation. Everything you do and every sacrifice you offer is unacceptable to me. 15But from now on, things will get better. Before you started laying the foundation for the temple, 16you recalled what life was like in the past.[i] When you wanted 20 bushels of wheat, there were only 10, and when you wanted 50 jars of wine, there were only 20. 17I made all of your hard work useless by sending mildew, mold, and hail—but you still did not return to me, your LORD.

18Today you have completed the foundation for my temple, so listen to what your future will be like. 19Although you have not yet harvested any grain, grapes, figs, pomegranates,[j]

[d]**2.1,2** *the next month:* Tishri (also called Ethanim), the seventh month of the Hebrew calendar, from about mid-September to mid-October (see the note at 1.1). [e]**2.5** *My Spirit is:* Or "I am." [f]**2.7** *their treasures:* Hebrew "what they most desire." [g]**2.9** *city:* Or "temple." [h]**2.10** *ninth month:* Chislev, the ninth month of the Hebrew calendar, from about mid-November to mid-December. [i]**2.16** *you recalled . . . past:* One possible meaning for the difficult Hebrew text. [j]**2.19** *pomegranates:* A bright red fruit that looks like an apple.

or olives, I will richly bless you in the days ahead.

God's Promise to Zerubbabel

20That same day the LORD spoke to Haggai again and said:
21Tell Governor Zerubbabel of Judah that I am going to shake the heavens and the earth 22and wipe out kings and their kingdoms. I will overturn war chariots, and then cavalry troops will start slaughtering each other. 23But tell my servant Zerubbabel that I, the LORD All-Powerful, have chosen him, and he will rule in my name.k

2.23 *my servant . . . rule in my name:* The words "my servant" mean someone God has chosen for a special role or task (Num 12.7,8; Isa 22.20; Jer 27.6,7). God had once called Israel's King David his "servant" and promised that someone from his family would always rule over Israel (2 Sam 7.4,10-16). The prophets said that a special chosen leader would come from the line of David (Isa 11.1-9; Mic 5.2-5), bringing justice and peace. Zerubbabel was a descendant of David.

Messiah (Chosen One)

k2.23 *rule in my name:* The Hebrew text has "be my signet ring," which signified authority.

Reflection Questions About Haggai 1.1—2.23

1. When Haggai preached his messages in 520 B.C. many of the Jewish people had been back in Jerusalem for almost 20 years. Why hadn't they finished rebuilding God's temple (1.1-11)?

2. What encouraging promises did Haggai give to the people and their leader, Zerubbabel (2.3-9,18-23)?

3. What important "unfinished work" do you have to do? What stops your work? What or who encourages you to keep going?

4. Most of us will never be involved in building a temple, cathedral, or church. Nevertheless, what other things can we "build" for God?

5. What can you do to make sure that God's work has top priority in your life?

zechariah

A person with "vision" understands how to make plans for a better future. The prophet Zechariah was a person of "vision." In fact, he actually had visions about Israel's future. Read ZECHARIAH *to find out what he had to say.*

WHAT MAKES ZECHARIAH SPECIAL?

ZECHARIAH is made up of a number of different kinds of writings found in prophetic literature, including visions, speeches of prophets (oracles), and apocalyptic writings. Apocalyptic writings often focus on the "end of time" when God will defeat evil and bring about a new creation. This type of writing commonly includes visions and symbolic imagery using animals, angels, demons, and numbers.

New Testament Gospel writers quote ZECHARIAH (Matt 21.5; Mark 14.27; John 12.15) or refer to certain passages indirectly (compare, for instance, Matt 26.15 and Zech 11.12; Matt 26.28 and Zech 9.11) to show that Jesus is the fulfillment of prophecies of a coming Messiah. Many references to ZECHARIAH also appear in REVELATION, because both books have visions of God's victory over all enemies and the creation of a new Jerusalem where God will bless and give new life to all who are faithful (compare Rev 22.1 and Zech 14.8; Rev 22.3 and Zech 14.10-11).

Zechariah joined the prophet Haggai in encouraging the people of Jerusalem to complete the work of rebuilding the temple. In addition, ZECHARIAH focuses on other concerns that the people of Judah had after the exile. What kind of political leadership could they expect? What about God's promise to King David that one of his descendants would rule over Israel (2 Sam 7.12-16)—was this still to be expected? Would God continue to protect them now that they were back in their homeland? God had punished them in the past by letting their enemies take over their land and send many of them into exile. Would God punish them in this way again? What could they expect to happen in the near future? Where did they fit in God's plans for the rest of the world?

WHAT'S THE STORY BEHIND THE SCENE?

ZECHARIAH is really two books rolled into one. The first book (chapters 1–8) was written by the prophet Zechariah who preached to the people of Judah from 520 to 518 B.C. Like the prophet Haggai, Zechariah encouraged the people to trust in God and rebuild the temple. Zechariah's message comes through eight visions, as well as prophetic speeches. The visions describe who will end up ruling Judah. What seems to come out of these visions is a partnership between the civil leader, Governor Zerubbabel, and the religious leader, High Priest Joshua.

Jerusalem and Judah will be attacked by all nations, and many of Jerusalem's people will die. However, the LORD will come to the rescue and create a new holy Jerusalem where the LORD will rule as King.

HOW IS ZECHARIAH CONSTRUCTED?

ZECHARIAH can be divided as follows:

Zechariah preaches to the people of Israel in the days of Darius, King of Persia (1.1—8.23)
    Introduction (1.1-6)
    Zechariah's eight visions (1.7—6.8)
    Joshua is made high priest (6.9-15)
    Questions and promises (7.1—8.23)
Visions of Israel's future (9.1—14.21)
Punishment and victory (9.1—11.17)
The LORD will rule as King in Jerusalem (12.1—14.21)

The prophet Zechariah preached the Lord's message to the Jews who had returned from exile in Babylonia. Like his contemporary Haggai, he urged the people to trust the Lord and rebuild the temple. Like many of Israel's prophets before him, Zechariah was concerned about the religious purity of the returning Jews and the fairness of their leaders. Hoping to encourage the people, Zechariah described eight visions he had received from the Lord, affirming God's love and protection for Jerusalem and its people, and anticipating a return of Israel's former glory and power. The visions also identified who was to govern Judah: Zerubbabel would rule as governor and Joshua would serve as high priest. The second part of the book of Zechariah consists of prophecies detailing a future day when the Lord would punish Israel's enemies, rescue and reunite the people, strengthen Israel's leaders, and transform Jerusalem once again into the holy dwelling place of the Lord.

Outline

Turn to the LORD

1 I am the prophet Zechariah, the son of Berechiah and the grandson of Iddo.

In the eighth month of the second year that Darius was king of Persia,[a] the LORD told me to say:

[2-3]Israel, I, the LORD All-Powerful, was very angry with your ancestors. But if you people will return to me, I will turn and help you. [4]Don't be stubborn like your ancestors. They were warned by the earlier prophets[b] to give up their evil and turn back to me, but they paid no attention.

[5]Where are your ancestors now? Not even prophets live forever. [6]But my warnings and my words spoken by the prophets caught up with your ancestors. So they turned back to me and said, "LORD All-Powerful, you have punished us for our sins, just as you had planned."

First Vision: Horses and Riders

[7-8] On the twenty-fourth day of Shebat,[c] which was the eleventh month of that same year,[d] the LORD spoke to me in a vision during the night: In a valley among myrtle trees,[e] I saw someone on a red horse, with riders on red, brown, and white horses behind him. [9]An angel was there to explain things to me, and I asked, "Sir, who are these riders?"

"I'll tell you," the angel answered.

[10]At once, the man standing among the myrtle trees said, "These are the ones the LORD has sent to find out what's happening on earth."

[a]1.1 eighth month . . . second year . . . king of Persia: Bul, the eighth month of the Hebrew calender, from about mid-October to mid-November; the second year of the rule of Darius was 520 B.C.
[b]1.4 the earlier prophets: Those who preached before the fall of Jerusalem in either 587 or 586 B.C.
[c]1.7,8 Shebat: The eleventh month of the Hebrew calendar, from about mid-January to mid-February. [d]1.7,8 that same year: See verse 1 and the note there. [e]1.7,8 myrtle trees: Evergreen shrubs, which in ancient times were symbols of fertility and renewal.

Jerusalem

Zion

1.18-21 *Next, I saw . . . crush those horns:* In this second vision, four animal horns symbolize four major enemies that threatened Israel and Judah from the time of King David (about 1000 B.C.) to the time of Zechariah. These powerful nations probably are Egypt, Assyria, Babylonia, and Medo-Persia. The blacksmiths symbolize the power God will use to crush those enemies.

2.1-5 *This time I saw . . . heart of the city:* In this vision someone is about to measure the city of Jerusalem so that walls can be built to protect it. The angel says that Jerusalem will grow too large to stay within its walls, but that God promises to live in and protect the city. God's promise to be Jerusalem's "shining glory in the heart of the city" could refer to the rebuilt temple.

2.6,7 *land in the north . . . Babylonia:* The land to the north is often the location of Israel's enemies. Here, the enemy is Babylon, which is east of Judah. The Babylonians and other enemies from the east could not easily cross the Arabian Desert, but had to follow the Euphrates River Valley and then attack Israel and Judah from the north. (See Map 7 on pg 1885.)

¹¹Then the riders spoke to the LORD's angel, who was standing among the myrtle trees, and they said, "We have gone everywhere and have discovered that the whole world is at peace."

¹²At this, the angel said, "LORD All-Powerful, for 70 years you have been angry with Jerusalem and the towns of Judah. When are you ever going to have mercy on them?"

¹³The LORD's answer was kind and comforting. ¹⁴So the angel told me to announce:

I, the LORD All-Powerful, am very protective of Jerusalem. ¹⁵For a while I was angry at the nations, but now I am furious, because they have made things worse for Jerusalem and are not the least bit concerned. ¹⁶And so, I will have pity on Jerusalem. The city will be completely rebuilt, and my temple will stand again. ¹⁷I also promise that my towns will prosper—Jerusalem will once again be my chosen city, and I will comfort the people of Zion.

Second Vision: Animal Horns

¹⁸Next, I saw four animal horns.[f] ¹⁹⁻²¹The angel who was sent to explain was there, and so I asked, "What do these mean?"

His answer was, "These horns are the nations that scattered the people of Judah, Israel, and Jerusalem, and took away their freedom."

Then the LORD showed me four blacksmiths, and I asked, "What are they going to do?"

He replied, "They are going to terrify and crush those horns."

Third Vision: A Measuring Line

2 This time I saw someone holding a measuring line, ²and I asked, "Where are you going?"

"To measure Jerusalem," was the answer. "To find out how wide and long it is."

³The angel who had spoken to me came toward me, when another angel came up to him ⁴and said, "Hurry! Tell that man with the measuring line that Jerusalem won't have any boundaries. It will be too full of people and animals even to have a wall. ⁵The LORD himself has promised to be a protective wall of fire surrounding Jerusalem, and he will be its shining glory in the heart of the city."

A Call to Action

⁶The LORD says to his people, "Run! Escape from the land in the north, where I scattered you to the four winds. ⁷Leave Babylonia and hurry back to Zion."

⁸Then the glorious LORD All-Powerful ordered me to say to the nations that had raided and robbed Zion:

Zion is as precious to the LORD as are his eyes. Whatever you do to Zion, you do to him. ⁹And so, he will put you in the power of your slaves, and they will raid and rob you. Then you will know that I am a prophet of the LORD All-Powerful.

¹⁰City of Zion, sing and celebrate! The LORD has promised to come and live with you. ¹¹When he does, many nations will turn to him and become his people. At that time you will know that I am a prophet of the LORD All-Powerful. ¹²Then Judah will be his

[f]**1.18** *animal horns:* Horns, especially those of a bull, were symbols of power in ancient times. The number "four" would signal completeness, one representing each of the four directions.

part of the holy land, and Jerusalem will again be his chosen city.

¹³Everyone, be silent!
The LORD is present
and moving about
in his holy place.

Fourth Vision: Joshua and Satan

3 I was given another vision. This time Joshua the high priest was standing in front of the LORD's angel. And there was Satan, standing at Joshua's right side, ready to accuse him. ²But the LORD said, "Satan, you are wrong. Jerusalem is my chosen city, and this man was rescued like a stick from a flaming fire."

³Joshua's clothes were filthy. ⁴So the angel told some of the people to remove Joshua's filthy clothes. Then he said to Joshua, "This means you are forgiven. Now I will dress you in priestly clothes."

⁵I spoke up and said, "Also put a clean priestly turban on his head." Then they dressed him in priestly clothes and put the turban on him, while the LORD's angel stood there watching.

⁶After this, the angel encouraged Joshua by telling him that the LORD All-Powerful had promised:

⁷If you truly obey me, I will put you in charge of my temple, including the courtyard around it, and you will be allowed to speak at any time with the angels standing beside me.^g ⁸Listen carefully, High Priest Joshua and all of you other priests. You are a sign of things to come, because I am going to bring my servant, the Chosen King.^h

⁹Joshua, I have placed in front of you a stone with seven sides.ⁱ I will engrave something on that stone, and in a single day I will forgive this guilty country. ¹⁰Then each of you will live at peace and entertain your friends in your own vineyard and under your own fig trees.

Fifth Vision: A Lampstand and Olive Trees

4 The angel who explained the visions woke me from what seemed like sleep. ²Then he asked, "What do you see?"

"A solid gold lampstand with an oil container above it," I answered. "On the stand are seven lamps, each with seven flames. ³One olive tree is on the right side and another on the left of the oil container. ⁴But, sir, what do these mean?"

⁵Then he asked, "Don't you know?"
"No sir," I replied.

⁶ So the angel explained that it was the following message of the LORD to Zerubbabel:^j

I am the LORD All-Powerful. So don't depend on your own power or strength, but on my Spirit. ⁷Zerubbabel, that mountain in front of you will be leveled to the ground. Then you will bring out the temple's most important stone and shout, "God has been very kind."^k

⁸The LORD spoke to me again and said:
⁹Zerubbabel laid the foundation for the temple, and he will complete it. Then everyone will know that you were sent by me, the LORD All-Powerful.

^g3,7 *with the angels . . . me:* Or "with me." The angels are members of God's Council, who stand beside the throne of God in heaven and are allowed to speak with him and for him.   ^h3.8 *Chosen King:* The Hebrew text has "Sprout" or "Branch," a term used of royalty (see Isaiah 11.1).   ⁱ3.9 *seven sides:* Or "seven eyes."   ^j4.6 *Zerubbabel:* Governor of Judah (see Haggai 1.1).   ^k4.7 *God . . . kind:* Or "What a beautiful stone."

3.1 *Joshua:* As the high priest, Joshua was the spiritual leader of the people. He was one of the leaders in charge of the people who returned to Judah from Babylon in 538 B.C. (Ezra 2.1-20).

Israel's Priests

3.1,2 *another vision . . . LORD's angel . . . Satan:* In this vision, Joshua stands before God's council of angels, which includes Satan, whose role is pointing out people's weaknesses.

Satan

3.8 *Chosen King:* This may refer to Zerubbabel.

Messiah (Chosen One)

4.2-14 *gold lampstand . . . olive tree . . . chosen leaders:* In this vision, the lampstand symbolizes the eyes of the LORD watching over the earth. The two olive trees most likely represent the chosen leaders, Joshua and Zerubbabel. Because of its use in the temple, the lampstand (*menorah*) is a very ancient symbol for the Jewish people.

4.7 *that mountain . . . most important stone:* The "mountain" that Zerubbabel faced may have been opposition from outsiders, or the apathy of the people of Judah. The "most important stone" may refer to the final stone to be put in place in the rebuilt temple, or it may refer to a stone taken from the rubble of the old temple that would be placed in the new temple.

5.1 *scroll:* The scroll described here is much wider than normal scrolls.

Scrolls

5.1-.4 *When I looked . . . that house crumbles:* In this vision, the scroll is a record of those who steal and lie. God warns that anyone named on the scroll is cursed.

5.5-11 *Now the angel . . . set it down inside:* This vision continues the ideas of the last vision. The woman in the basket represents all the sins of the people of Judah. She is taken to Babylonia, the same country where the people of Judah were exiled because of their sins (2 Kgs 25.8-21).

6.1-5 *bronze mountains . . . horses . . . four winds:* Compare this to Zechariah's first vision (1.7-11). The chariots come from an opening between two bronze mountains, which some scholars think represents the opening to the place where God lives. In Zechariah's first vision, things were calm. In this vision, God begins to act.

[10]Those who have made fun of this day of small beginnings will celebrate when they see Zerubbabel holding this important stone.[l]

Those seven lamps represent my eyes—the eyes of the Lord—and they see everything on this earth. [11]Then I asked the angel, "What about the olive trees on each side of the lampstand? What do they represent? [12]And what is the meaning of the two branches from which golden olive oil[m] flows through the two gold pipes?"

[13]"Don't you know?" he asked.

"No sir, I don't," was my answer.

[14]Then he told me, "These branches are the two chosen leaders[n] who stand beside the Lord of all the earth."

Sixth Vision: A Flying Scroll

5 When I looked the next time, I saw a flying scroll,[o] [2]and the angel asked, "What do you see?"

"A flying scroll," I answered. "About 30 feet long and 15 feet wide."

[3]Then he told me:

This scroll puts a curse on everyone in the land who steals or tells lies. The writing on one side tells about the destruction of those who steal, while the writing on the other side tells about the destruction of those who lie.

[4]The Lord All-Powerful has said, "I am sending this scroll into the house of everyone who is a robber or tells lies in my name, and it will remain there until every piece of wood and stone in that house crumbles."

Seventh Vision: A Woman in a Basket

[5]Now the angel who was there to explain the visions came over and said, "Look up and tell me what you see coming."

[6]"I don't know what it is," was my reply.

"It's a big basket," he said. "And it shows what everyone in the land has in mind."[p]

[7]The lead cover of the basket was opened, and in the basket was a woman. [8]"This woman represents evil," the angel explained. Then he threw her back into the basket and slammed the heavy cover down tight.

[9]Right after this I saw two women coming through the sky with wings outstretched like a stork in the wind. Suddenly they lifted the basket into the air, [10]and I asked the angel, "Where are they taking the basket?"

[11]"To Babylonia,"[q] he answered, "where they will build a house for the basket and set it down inside."

Eighth Vision: Four Chariots

6 Finally, I looked up and saw four chariots coming from between two bronze mountains. [2]The first chariot was pulled by red horses, and the second by black horses; [3]the third chariot was pulled by white horses, and the fourth by spotted gray[r] horses.

[l]**4.10** *important stone:* Or "measuring line (with a stone attached to the end)."   [m]**4.12** *golden olive oil:* The Hebrew text has "gold," which possibly refers to the color of the olive oil as it flows through the gold pipe.   [n]**4.14** *chosen leaders:* The Hebrew text has "people of oil." In ancient times prophets, priests, and kings had olive oil poured over their heads to show that they had been chosen (see 1 Samuel 10.1; 16.13).   [o]**5.1** *scroll:* A roll of paper or special leather used for writing on. [p]**5.6** *what . . . mind:* Hebrew; one ancient translation "the sin of everyone in the land." [q]**5.11** *Babylonia:* The Hebrew text has "Shinar," an ancient name for Babylonia.   [r]**6.3** *spotted gray:* Or "strong."

[4]"Sir," I asked the angel. "What do these stand for?"

[5] Then he explained, "These are the four winds[s] of heaven, and now they are going out, after presenting themselves to the Lord of all the earth. [6]The chariot with black horses goes toward the north, the chariot with white horses goes toward the west,[t] and the one with spotted horses goes toward the south."

[7]The horses came out eager to patrol the earth, and the angel told them, "Start patrolling the earth."

When they had gone on their way, [8]he shouted to me, "Those that have gone to the country in the north will do what the Lord's Spirit[u] wants them to do there."[v]

The Chosen Leader

[9]The Lord said to me:

[10-11]Heldai, Tobijah, and Jedaiah have returned from Babylonia. Collect enough silver and gold from them to make a crown.[w] Then go with them to the house of Josiah son of Zephaniah and put the crown on the head of the high priest Joshua son of Jehozadak.[x] [12-13]Tell him that I, the Lord All-Powerful, say, "Someone will reach out from here like a branch and build a temple for me. I will name him 'Branch,' and he will rule with royal honors. A priest will stand beside his throne,[y] and the two of them will be good friends. [14]This crown will be kept in my temple as a reminder and will be taken care of by Heldai,[z] Tobijah, Jedaiah, and Josiah."[a]

[15]When people from distant lands come and help build the temple of the Lord All-Powerful, you will know that the Lord is the one who sent me. And this will happen, if you truly obey the Lord your God.

A Question about Going without Eating

7 On the fourth day of Chislev, the ninth month of the fourth year that Darius was king of Persia,[b] the Lord again spoke to me. [2-3]It happened after the people of Bethel had sent Sharezer with Regem-Melech and his men to ask the priests in the Lord's temple and the prophets to pray for them. So they prayed, "Should we mourn and go without eating during the fifth month,[c] as we have done for many years?"

[4-5]It was then that the Lord All-Powerful told me to say to everyone in the country, including the priests:

For 70 years you have gone without eating during the fifth and seventh months of the year. But did you really do it for me? [6]And when you eat and drink, isn't it for your own enjoyment? [7]My message today is the same one I

---

[s]6.5 *winds:* Or "spirits." The Hebrew word may mean either. [t]6.6 *goes toward the west:* Or "follows behind." [u]6.8 *Lord's Spirit:* Or "Lord." [v]6.8 *will do . . . to do there:* One possible meaning for the difficult Hebrew text. [w]6.10,11 *a crown:* Two ancient translations; Hebrew "some crowns." [x]6.10,11 *Heldai . . . Jehozadak:* Or "Go to the house of Josiah son of Zephaniah, where you will find Heldai, Tobijah, and Jedaiah, who have returned from Babylonia. Collect enough silver and gold from them to make a crown. Then put it on the head of the high priest Joshua son of Jehozadak." [y]6.12,13 *stand beside his throne:* Or "sit on a throne." [z]6.14 *Heldai:* One ancient translation; Hebrew "Helem." [a]6.14 *Josiah:* One ancient translation; Hebrew "Hen." [b]7.1 *Chislev . . . fourth year . . . king of Persia:* Chislev, the ninth month of the Hebrew calendar, from about mid-November to mid-December; the fourth year of the rule of Darius was 518 B.C. [c]7.2,3 *fifth month:* Ab, the fifth month of the Hebrew calendar, from about mid-July to mid-August. The temple was destroyed by the Babylonians in the year 587 or 586 B.C.

● 6.10-11 *Heldai, Tobijah, and Jedaiah . . . Joshua son of Jehozadak:* Nothing more is known about the first three men, who are told to make a crown to put on Joshua's head. Josiah most likely was a wealthy homeowner in Jerusalem. Josiah's father Zephaniah should not be confused with the prophet of the same name.

■ 6.12-15 *I will name him 'Branch,' . . . Lord your God:* Although earlier, Zerubbabel was identified as the one to complete the rebuilding of the temple, these verses suggest that Joshua the high priest would wear the crown. The term "branch" was used to show that the Lord had chosen Joshua to be a ruler. This passage may reflect the growing importance of priests after the rebuilding of the temple.

● 7.2-3 *Bethel:* Bethel was an important city in the religious history of the Israelites. Abraham built an altar there when he entered Canaan. Jacob, Abraham's grandson, built an altar at Bethel after God appeared to him there at two different times. The sacred chest was kept in Bethel for a period of time (Judg 20.27). Deborah (Judg 4.5) and Samuel (1 Sam 7.16) served as judges in Bethel. People worshiped God properly in Bethel until Jeroboam built two golden calf statues and began worshiping idols there (1 Kgs 12.29-33). Bethel was destroyed during the exile, but some Israelites returned there after being released by the Persians. **(See Map 6 on pg 1884.)**

7.9 *See that justice is done:* The people of Judah had observed a time of fasting (going without eating) during the fifth and seventh months of every year since the temple in Jerusalem was destroyed. The men from Bethel ask Zechariah whether they need to continue this custom, and Zechariah answers that fasting does not take the place of obeying God's law and treating each other with justice and kindness.

Justice

8.9,10 *the foundation of my temple was laid . . . that time:* These verses seem to describe the situation in 520 B.C. The foundation of the temple had been laid soon after the people returned to Jerusalem from exile in Babylon in about 538 B.C., but work on the temple stopped, so harvests went bad and everyone suffered.

8,13 *People of Judah and Israel:* Israel was defeated by the Assyrians in 722 B.C., and Judah was defeated by the Babylonians in 586 B.C., because the people had made the LORD angry. Now, the LORD promises to save those who survived the time of punishment and to make them a blessing to the same nations that had cursed them (see also Gen 12.3). **(See Map 6 on pg 1884.)**

commanded the earlier prophets[d] to speak to Jerusalem and its villages when they were prosperous, and when all of Judah, including the Southern Desert and the hill country, was filled with people.

⁸⁻⁹So once again, I, the LORD All-Powerful, tell you, "See that justice is done and be kind and merciful to one another! ¹⁰Don't mistreat widows or orphans or foreigners or anyone who is poor, and stop making plans to hurt each other."

¹¹⁻¹²But everyone who heard those prophets, stubbornly refused to obey. Instead, they turned their backs on everything my Spirit[e] had commanded the earlier prophets to preach. So I, the LORD, became angry ¹³and said, "You people paid no attention when I called out to you, and now I'll pay no attention when you call out to me."

¹⁴That's why I came with a whirlwind and scattered them among foreign nations, leaving their lovely country empty of people and in ruins.[f]

The LORD's Promises to Zion

8 The LORD All-Powerful said to me: ²I love Zion so much that her enemies make me angry. ³I will return to Jerusalem and live there on Mount Zion. Then Jerusalem will be known as my faithful city, and Zion will be known as my holy mountain.

⁴Very old people with walking sticks will once again sit around in Jerusalem, ⁵while boys and girls play in the streets. ⁶This may seem impossible for my people who are left, but it isn't impossible for me, the LORD All-Powerful. ⁷I

will save those who were taken to lands in the east and the west, ⁸and I will bring them to live in Jerusalem. They will be my people, and I will be their God, faithful to bring about justice.

⁹I am the LORD All-Powerful! So don't give up. Think about the message my prophets spoke when the foundation of my temple was laid. ¹⁰Before that time, neither people nor animals were rewarded for their work, and no one was safe anywhere, because I had turned them against each other.

¹¹My people, only a few of you are left, and I promise not to punish you as I did before. ¹²Instead, I will make sure that your crops are planted in peace and your vineyards are fruitful, that your fields are fertile, and the dew falls from the sky. ¹³People of Judah and Israel, you have been a curse to the nations, but I will save you and make you a blessing to them. So don't be afraid or lose courage.

¹⁴When your ancestors made me angry, I decided to punish you with disasters, and I didn't hold back. ¹⁵Now you no longer need to be afraid. I have decided to treat Jerusalem and Judah with kindness. ¹⁶But you must be truthful with each other, and in court you must give fair decisions that lead to peace. ¹⁷Don't ever plan evil things against others or tell lies under oath. I, the LORD, hate such things.

A Time of Celebration

¹⁸The LORD All-Powerful told me to say: ¹⁹People of Judah, I, the LORD, demand that whenever you go without food as a way of worshiping me, it

[d]7.7 *the earlier prophets:* See the note at 1.4.   [e]7.11,12 *my Spirit:* Or "I."   [f]7.14 *leaving their . . . in ruins:* Or "because they had ruined their lovely country."

should become a time of celebration. No matter if it's the fourth month, the fifth month, the seventh month, or the tenth month, you should have a joyful festival. So love truth and live at peace.

20I tell you that people will come here from cities everywhere. 21Those of one town will go to another and say, "We're going to ask the Lord All-Powerful to treat us with kindness. Come and join us."

22Many people from strong nations will come to Jerusalem to worship me and to ask me to treat them with kindness. 23When this happens, ten people from nations with different languages will grab a Jew by his clothes and say, "Let us go with you. We've heard that God is on your side." I, the Lord All-Powerful, have spoken!

Israel's Enemies Will Be Punished

9   This is a message
       from the Lord:
His eyes are on everyone,
especially the tribes
    of Israel.g
So he pronounces judgment
against the cities
    of Hadrach and Damascus.h
2Judgment will also fall
on the nearby city
    of Hamath,
as well as on Tyre and Sidon,i
whose people are clever.

3Tyre has built a fortress
    and piled up silver and gold,
as though they were dust
    or mud from the streets.
4Now the Lord will punish Tyre
    with poverty;
he will sink its ships
    and send it up in flames.

5Both Ashkelon and Gaza
will tremble with fear;
    Ekron will lose all hope.
Gaza's king will be killed,
and Ashkelon emptied
    of its people.
6A mob of half-breeds
    will settle in Ashdod,j
and the Lord himself
    will rob Philistia of pride.

7No longer will the Philistines
eat meat with blood in it
    or any unclean food.k
They will become part
of the people of our God
    from the tribe of Judah.
And God will accept
the people of Ekron,
    as he did the Jebusites.l

8God says, "I will stand guard
to protect my temple from those
    who come to attack.
I know what's happening,
and no one will mistreat
    my people ever again."

● 9.1 *tribes of Israel:* The nation of Israel was divided into twelve tribes, which were descended from the twelve sons of Jacob (Gen 48,49).

● 9.1-6 *Hadrach and Damascus . . . Philistia:* The cities and nations mentioned in these verses had been enemies of Israel and Judah. Hadrach was located north of both Damascus and Hamath. Tyre and Sidon were Phoenician cities. Other prophets also spoke of the Lord's judgment against these cities (Isa 23.1-18; Ezek 26.1—28.26; Joel 3.4-8; Amos 1.9,10). Ashkelon, Gaza, Ekron, and Ashdod were Philistine cities. The Philistines settled in the area west of Judah and often battled with the people of Israel.

■ 9.6 *half-breeds:* The term "half-breeds" may refer to a group of half-Jewish people, or it may refer to settlers from other nations who will come to Ashdod and take the place of its citizens after God has destroyed it.

Oℛ   Blood

---

g9.1 *His . . . Israel:* One possible meaning for the difficult Hebrew text.   h9.1 *Hadrach and Damascus:* Hadrach was north of both Damascus (the main city of Syria) and Hamath (verse 2).   i9.2 *Tyre and Sidon:* Phoenician cities.   j9.5,6 *Ashkelon and Gaza . . . Ekron . . . Ashdod:* Philistine cities.
k9.7 *eat . . . food:* The Philistines will become part of Judah and no longer eat meat with blood in it (see Genesis 9.4) or any other forbidden foods (see Leviticus 11.1-23; Deuteronomy 14.3-21).
l9.7 *Jebusites:* The original people of Canaan, who lived in Jerusalem before it was captured by David (see 2 Samuel 5.6-10) and were later accepted as part of Israel.

9.9,10 *Your king...across the earth:* Israel's new king rides a donkey rather than war chariot. This is a sign of the peace that he will bring to Jerusalem and the nations. The exact identity of this king is not certain, but he sounds like the chosen king (Messiah) described by other prophets (Isa 9.6,7; 11.1-9; Mic 5.2-5). In reality, Judah and its leader never again ruled over a large nation that stretched from the Mediterranean Sea east to the Euphrates River. New Testament writers understood Jesus to be the one God chose to bring peace and to restore Israel and the nations (Matt 21.5; John 12.15).

Agreements (Covenants)

9.13 *Greeks:* After Alexander the Great conquered the region in 333 B.C., the Greeks ruled the land of Israel. At the time of Zechariah, Judah was not threatened by the Greeks, so some scholars believe this message refers to this future time. Other scholars suggest that mentioning the Greeks means the later chapters of ZECHARIAH (9–14) were written long after Zechariah lived.

10.1,2 *LORD...sends...rain... can't believe idols:* The people are to pray to God if they need rain, instead of offering sacrifices to idols or relying on fortunetellers and witchcraft. The people are compared to sheep without a shepherd, because they have not looked to God for help.

The LORD Tells about the Coming King

⁹Everyone in Jerusalem,
 celebrate and shout!
Your king has won a victory,
 and he is coming to you.
He is humble
 and rides on a donkey;
he comes on the colt
 of a donkey.
¹⁰I, the LORD, will take away
 war chariots and horses
 from Israel[m] and Jerusalem.
Bows that were made for battle
 will be broken.
I will bring peace to nations,
and your king will rule
 from sea to sea.
His kingdom will reach
from the Euphrates River
 across the earth.

The LORD Promises To Rescue Captives

¹¹When I made a sacred agreement
 with you, my people,
 we sealed it with blood.[n]
Now some of you are captives
 in waterless pits,
but I will come to your rescue
¹² and offer you hope.
Return to your fortress,
because today I will reward you
 with twice what you had.
¹³I will use Judah as my bow
 and Israel[o] as my arrow.
I will take the people of Zion
 as my sword
 and attack the Greeks.

The LORD Will Protect His People

¹⁴Like a cloud, the LORD God
 will appear over his people,
and his arrows will flash
 like lightning.
God will sound his trumpet
 and attack in a whirlwind
 from the south.
¹⁵The LORD All-Powerful
 will protect his people,
and they will trample down
 the sharpshooters
 and their slingshots.
They will drink and get rowdy;
they will be as full as a bowl
 at the time of sacrifice.

¹⁶The LORD God will save them
 on that day,
 because they are his people,
and they will shine on his land
 like jewels in a crown.
¹⁷How lovely they will be.
Young people will grow there
 like grain in a field
 or grapes in a vineyard.

A Bright Future for Judah and Israel

10 I, the LORD, am the one
 who sends storm clouds
and showers of rain
 to make fields produce.
So when the crops need rain,
 you should pray to me.

²You can't believe idols
 and fortunetellers,
or depend on the hope

[m]9.10 *Israel:* The Hebrew text has "Ephraim," the leading tribe of the northern kingdom of Israel, which sometimes stands for the whole kingdom.   [n]9.11 *agreement...blood:* The agreement at Mount Sinai (see Exodus 24.7,8).   [o]9.13 *Israel:* Hebrew "Ephraim" (see the note at 9.10).

you receive from witchcraft
    and interpreters of dreams.
But you have tried all of these,
and now you are like sheep
    without a shepherd.

³I, the LORD All-Powerful,
    am fiercely angry
with you leaders,
    and I will punish you.
I care for my people,
    the nation of Judah,
and I will change
this flock of sheep
    into charging war horses.

⁴From this flock will come leaders
    who will be strong
like cornerstones and tent pegs
    and weapons of war.
⁵They will join in the fighting,
and together they will trample
    their enemies like mud.
They will fight,
because I, the LORD,
    will be on their side.
And they will crush
    the enemy cavalry.

⁶I will strengthen
the kingdoms of Judah
    and Israel.^P
And I will show mercy
because I am the LORD,
    their God.
I will answer their prayers
    and bring them home.
Then it will seem as though
    I had never rejected them.
⁷Israel^q will be like
a tribe of warriors

celebrating with wine.
When their children see this,
they will also be happy
    because of me, the LORD.

⁸I will give a signal
for them to come together
    because I have rescued them.
And there will be as many
    as ever before.
⁹Although I scattered my people
in distant countries,
    they won't forget me.
Once their children are raised,^r
    they will return—
¹⁰I will bring them home
from Egypt and Assyria,
    then let them settle
as far as Gilead and Lebanon,
until the land overflows
    with them.
¹¹My people will go through
    an ocean of troubles,
but I will overcome the waves
and dry up the deepest part
    of the Nile.
Assyria's great pride
    will be put down,
and the power of Egypt
    will disappear.
¹²I'll strengthen my people
because of who I am,
    and they will follow me.
I, the LORD, have spoken!

Trouble for Israel's Enemies

11 Lebanon, open your gates!
    Let the fire come in
        to destroy your cedar trees.
²Cry, you cypress trees!

10.3 *leaders:* The leaders may be the leaders of enemy nations or the leaders of Judah who have failed to be good shepherds of the people.

10.9,10 *distant countries . . . Egypt and Assyria:* The people of Israel and Judah were scattered to distant countries, including Egypt and Assyria, after being defeated by the Assyrians and Babylonians.

10.10 *Gilead and Lebanon:* Gilead bordered Israel on the east across the Jordan River. Lebanon was along Israel's northern border. **(See Map 6 on pg 1884.)**

10.11 *ocean of troubles . . . dry up the . . . Nile:* This probably refers to the period of punishment that led to the exile. But the LORD would punish Israel's enemies, symbolized by the drying up of Egypt's main source of fresh water, the Nile River, and by the eventual defeat of Assyria.

^P**10.6** *Israel:* The Hebrew text has "family of Joseph," the ancestor of Ephraim and Manasseh, the leading tribes of the northern kingdom (Israel).   ^q**10.7** *Israel:* Hebrew "Ephraim" (see the note at 9.10).   ^r**10.9** *Once . . . raised:* One possible meaning for the difficult Hebrew text.

11.4-17 *me . . . shepherds . . . sheep dealers . . . worthless shepherd:* This difficult passage appears to be a warning to the people and their leaders to obey God, so that God will not abandon them. The people are in danger of being destroyed because the sheep dealers (perhaps community leaders) care more about money than they do about the people. The shepherd names the sticks he uses to tend the sheep "Mercy" and "Unity." These names represent the kind of relationships God wanted the people to have with God and with each other. The warning is made clear when the shepherd breaks the two sticks. The people see that the breaking of "Mercy" is a sign that God is breaking the agreement with them. The breaking of "Unity" may suggest a despair that a united kingdom of Judah and Israel will never come about. The final verses of this passage tell how the same shepherd will then become a "worthless" leader who will be cursed for his mistreatment of the sheep.

12.1 *stretched out the heavens . . . gave breath to humans:* The LORD God of Israel is the creator of the earth (Gen 1.1-31; Isa 42.5; Jer 10.12).

The glorious cedars have fallen
    and are rotting.
Cry, you oak trees of Bashan!
The dense forest
    has been chopped down.
³Listen! Shepherds are crying.
Their glorious pastures
    have been ruined.
Listen! Lions are roaring.
The forests of the Jordan Valley
    are no more to be found.

Worthless Shepherds

⁴The LORD my God said to me:
Tend those sheep doomed for slaughter! ⁵The people who buy and butcher them go unpunished, while everyone who sells them says, "Praise the LORD! I'm rich." Not even their shepherds have pity on them.

⁶Tend those sheep because I, the LORD, will no longer have pity on the people of this earth. I'll turn neighbor against neighbor and make them slaves of a king. They will bring disaster on the earth, and I'll do nothing to rescue any of them.

⁷So I became a shepherd of those sheep doomed to be slaughtered by the sheep dealers.^s And I gave names to the two sticks I used for tending the sheep: One of them was named "Mercy" and the other "Unity." ⁸In less than a month, I became impatient with three shepherds who didn't like me, and I got rid of them. ⁹Then I said, "I refuse to be your shepherd. Let the sheep that are going to die, go on and die, and those that are going to be destroyed, go on and be destroyed. Then let the others eat one another alive."

¹⁰On that same day, I broke the stick named "Mercy" to show that the LORD had canceled his agreement with all people. ¹¹The sheep dealers who saw me knew at once that this was a message from the LORD. ¹²⁻¹³ I told them, "Pay me my wages, if you think you should; otherwise, forget it." So they handed me my wages, a measly 30 pieces of silver.

Then the LORD said, "Throw the money into the treasury."^t So I threw the money into the treasury at the LORD's temple. ¹⁴Then I broke the stick named "Unity" and canceled the ties between Judah and Israel.

¹⁵Next, the LORD said to me, "Act like a shepherd again—this time a worthless shepherd. ¹⁶Once more I am going to let a worthless nobody rule the land—one who won't care for the strays or search for the young or heal the sick or feed the healthy. He will just dine on the fattest sheep, leaving nothing but a few bones."

¹⁷You worthless shepherd,
    deserting the sheep!
I hope a sword
    will cripple your arm
    and blind your right eye.

Victory for Jerusalem

12 This is a message from the LORD about Israel:

I am the LORD! I stretched out the heavens; I put the earth on its foundations and gave breath to humans. ²I have decided that Jerusalem will become a bowl of wine that makes the neighboring nations drunk. And when Jerusalem is attacked, Judah will also be attacked.^u ³But I will turn Jeru-

^s**11.7** *by the sheep dealers:* One ancient translation; Hebrew "especially the weak ones."
^t**11.12,13** *Throw . . . treasury:* Hebrew "Throw the money to the potter."   ^u**12.2** *Judah . . . attacked:* One possible meaning for the difficult Hebrew text.

salem into a heavy stone that crushes anyone who tries to lift it.

When all nations on earth surround Jerusalem, **4**I will blind every horse and make them panic, and every rider will be confused. But at the same time, I will watch over Judah. **5**Then every clan in Judah will realize that I, the LORD All-Powerful, am their God, and that I am the source of their strength.

6At that time I will let the clans of Judah be like a ball of fire in a wood pile or a fiery torch in a hay stack. Then Judah will send the surrounding nations up in smoke. And once again the city of Jerusalem will be filled with people.

7But I will first give victory to Judah, so the kingdom of David and the city of Jerusalem in all of their glory won't be thought of more highly than Judah itself. **8**I, the LORD God, will protect Jerusalem. Even the weakest person there will be as strong as David, and David's kingdom will rule as though my very own angel were its leader. **9**I am determined to wipe out every nation that attacks Jerusalem.

Mourning for the One Pierced with a Spear

10I, the LORD, will make the descendants of David and the people of Jerusalem feel deep sorrow and pray when they see the one they pierced with a spear. They will mourn and weep for him, as parents weep over the death of their only child or their first-born. **11**On that day the people of Jerusalem will mourn as much as everyone did for Hadad Rimmon**v** on the flatlands near Megiddo. **12**Everyone of each family in the land will mourn, and the men will mourn separately from the women. This includes those from the family of David, and the families of Nathan, **13**Levi, Shimei,**w** **14**and all other families as well.

Getting Rid of Idols and False Prophets

13 In the future there will be a fountain, where David's descendants and the people of Jerusalem can wash away their sin and guilt.

2The LORD All-Powerful says:

When that time comes, I will get rid of every idol in the country, and they will be forgotten forever. I will also do away with their prophets and those evil spirits that control them. **3**If any such prophets ever appear again, their own parents must warn them that they will die for telling lies in my name—the name of the LORD. If those prophets don't stop speaking, their parents must then kill them with a sword.

4Those prophets will be ashamed of their so-called visions, and they won't deceive anyone by dressing like a true prophet. **5**Instead, they will say, "I'm no prophet. I've been a farmer all my life."**x**

6And if any of them are asked why they are wounded,**y** they will answer, "It happened at the house of some friends."

Fire

12.7 *kingdom of David*: David was Israel's greatest king. The LORD promised David that one of his descendants would always rule Israel (2 Sam 7.11-16). In this vision, David's kingdom won't simply be led by an earthly ruler. God and God's angel will rule.

12.10 *the one they pierced*: The identity of "the one they pierced" is not certain and neither is it clear who killed him. It may refer to the prophet Zechariah. New Testament writers saw the suffering and death of Jesus as a fulfillment of the death of this unknown person (John 19.37; Rev 1.7).

12.11 *Hadad Rimmon*: Hadad Rimmon is a foreign god who is not mentioned anywhere else in the Old Testament. In some ancient religions, it was believed that certain gods died and could be brought back to life if people cried and mourned for them.

Canaanite Gods and Goddesses

12.11 *Megiddo*: Because of its strategic location along trade and military routes, Megiddo was a famous battle site (Judg 5.19; 2 Kgs 23.29). **(See Map 3 on pg 1881.)**

13.7 *My sword . . . sheep:* The sword is used as a weapon to bring about God's justice. The "shepherd and friend" appears to be a faithful leader who suffers even though he has been faithful. The sheep are God's people. Only a third of them will survive the time of testing. (See also Matt 26.31; Mark 14.27.)

13.9 *gold and silver are purified:* Around 1000 B.C. the people in the ancient world had discovered a process of refining metals known as "smelting." In smelting, gold and silver are melted in a hot fire, which burns off unwanted metals and impurities such as dust. Zechariah is saying that the survivors of the destruction will be like the pure silver and gold that remain after being tested (smelted) by fire.

14.1-7 *LORD . . . his day . . . attack . . . unending day:* Here, the LORD's day brings an attack against Jerusalem and its people. Though many will die or be dragged off, this final attack is not a dark day, because the LORD will take charge and turn the battle around, just as he has done in the past.

Day of the LORD

14.5 *earthquake . . . time of King Uzziah:* Uzziah was king of Judah from 781 to 740 B.C. The earthquake is probably the earthquake of 760 B.C., which seems to have been very destructive (Amos 1.1).

A Wounded Shepherd and Scattered Sheep

⁷The LORD All-Powerful said:
    My sword, wake up! Attack
        my shepherd and friend.
    Strike down the shepherd!
    Scatter the little sheep,
        and I will destroy them.
⁸Nowhere in the land
    will more than a third of them
        be left alive.
⁹Then I will purify them
        and put them to the test,
    just as gold and silver
        are purified and tested.
    They will pray in my name,
        and I will answer them.
    I will say, "You are my people,"
        and they will reply,
        "You, LORD, are our God!"

War and Victory

14 The LORD will have his day. And when it comes, everything that was ever taken from Jerusalem will be returned and divided among its people. ²But first, he will bring many nations to attack Jerusalem—homes will be robbed, women raped, and half of the population dragged off, though the others will be allowed to remain.

³The LORD will attack those nations like a warrior fighting in battle. ⁴He will take his stand on the Mount of Olives east of Jerusalem, and the mountain will split in half, forming a wide valley that runs from east to west. ⁵Then you people will escape from the LORD's mountain, through this valley, which reaches to Azal.ᶻ You will run in all directions, just as everyone did when the earthquake struckᵃ in the time of King Uzziah of Judah. Afterwards, the LORD my God will appear with his holy angels.

⁶It will be a bright day that won't turn cloudy or cold.ᵇ ⁷And the LORD has decided when it will happen—this time of unending day.

⁸ In both summer and winter, life-giving streams will flow from Jerusalem, half of them to the Dead Sea in the east and half to the Mediterranean Sea in the west. ⁹Then there will be only one LORD who rules as King and whose name is worshiped everywhere on earth.

¹⁰⁻¹¹From Geba down to Rimmonᶜ south of Jerusalem, the entire country will be turned into flatlands, with Jerusalem still towering above. Then the city will be full of people, from Benjamin Gate, Old Gate Place, and Hananel Tower in the northeast part of the city over to Corner Gate in the northwest and down to King's Wine Press in the south. Jerusalem will always be secure and will never again be destroyed.

¹²Here is what the LORD will do to those who attack Jerusalem: While they are standing there, he will make their flesh rot and their eyes fall from their sockets and their tongues drop out. ¹³The LORD will make them go into a frenzy and start attacking each other, ¹⁴⁻¹⁵until even the people of Judah turn against those in Jerusalem.ᵈ This same terrible disaster will

---

ᶻ**14.5** *to Azal:* One possible meaning for the difficult Hebrew text. The location of Azal is unknown. ᵃ**14.5** *earthquake struck:* See Amos 1.1. ᵇ**14.6** *a bright . . . cold:* One possible meaning for the difficult Hebrew text. ᶜ**14.10** *From Geba down to Rimmon:* Approximately the northern and southern borders of Judah before the exile (see 2 Kings 23.8); Geba is about ten miles north of Jerusalem, and Rimmon is about ten miles north of Beersheba. ᵈ**14.13-15** *each other . . . Jerusalem:* Or "each other. ¹⁴⁻¹⁵ But the people of Judah will fight on the side of Jerusalem."

also strike every animal nearby, including horses, mules, camels, and donkeys. Finally, everything of value in the surrounding nations will be collected and brought to Jerusalem—gold, silver, and piles of clothing.

¹⁶Afterwards, the survivors from those nations that attacked Jerusalem will go there each year to worship the King, the LORD All-Powerful, and to celebrate the Festival of Shelters. ¹⁷No rain will fall on the land of anyone in any country who refuses to go to Jerusalem to worship the King, the LORD All-Powerful. ¹⁸⁻¹⁹This horrible disaster will strike the Egyptians and everyone else who refuses to go there for the celebration.

²⁰⁻²¹At that time the words "Dedicated to the LORD" will be engraved on the bells worn by horses. In fact, every ordinary cooking pot in Jerusalem will be just as sacred to the LORD All-Powerful as the bowls used at the altar. Any one of them will be acceptable for boiling the meat of sacrificed animals, and there will no longer be a need to sell special pots and bowls.^e

14.16 *worship the King . . . Festival of Shelters:* The whole world will worship the LORD and recognize the LORD as King. The Festival of Shelters took place at the end of the fall harvest (Exod 23.16; Deut 16.13-7). In addition to giving thanks to God for the fall harvest, the people were to build and live in shelters made of tree branches during the celebration.

14.20.-21 *cooking pot . . . special pots:* Merchants sold special metal pots that were acceptable for offering sacrifices to the LORD. However, after the LORD's victory purifies Jerusalem, all pots and bowls will be considered acceptable for use in the temple. All of God's people will truly be a "holy nation" and serve the LORD as priests.

^e14.20,21 *special pots and bowls:* Since all pots and bowls will be considered acceptable for use in the temple, there will be no more need for merchants to sell special ones to those people who come to offer sacrifices.

Reflection Questions About Zechariah 1.1—14.21

1. What was the situation in Judah at the time of Zechariah's visions (1.1—6.8)? Take a moment to read the short book of HAGGAI. What parts of Zechariah's message are like the message of the prophet Haggai?

2. Who were Joshua and Zerubbabel (3.1—4.14; 6.9-14)? What roles were they to play in the future of the people of Israel, according to Zechariah's visions and messages?

3. How might our society be different today if religious leaders were in charge of leading our country and government? In your opinion, would this be a good change or not? Explain your answer.

4. Summarize what Zechariah says will happen to Jerusalem and its people in the future (9.1—14.21). What part will the LORD play in future events? How will the nations of the earth respond to the LORD (14.9,16)?

5. Choose one vision or image from ZECHARIAH and explain why it was particularly meaningful to you.

malachi

How does the LORD respond to those who grow careless about how they worship, break important promises, fail to make proper gifts to God, and ignore the needs of their neighbors? Read MALACHI to find out.

WHAT MAKES MALACHI SPECIAL?

MALACHI is the last book of the "Scroll of the Twelve" (which Christians sometimes call the "Minor Prophets") in the Hebrew Scriptures. In Hebrew, the name "Malachi" means "my messenger." This may be the name of the author or a description of the author as a "messenger" of God. This is how the word is used in the Hebrew text of Malachi 3.1.

MALACHI takes the form of an argument, with charges and responses being traded back and forth between God and the people of Judah. In love, God chose the people of Israel to be his precious children, promising to bless them if they would obey his commands. God wanted the people to respond to his love with joyful obedience. But the people kept forgetting that God loved them, so God's rules and rituals seemed to be hard and demanding. The priests and the people simply ignored some of them and were careless about the way they carried out others. MALACHI was written to remind the people of God's love, and to call them back to a joyful obedience to God.

WHAT'S THE STORY BEHIND THE SCENE?

In 586 B.C., Jerusalem and its temple were destroyed by the Babylonians. Many citizens of Judah were taken as captives to Babylon. In 538 B.C., after the Persians defeated the Babylonians, some of the Israelites who had been taken into captivity returned Jerusalem. The prophets Haggai and Zechariah encouraged the people to rebuild the temple in Jerusalem, promising that a new day of success and prosperity would follow. The new temple in Jerusalem was completed and dedicated in 515 B.C. Yet Judah did not win independence from Persia, nor did it become prosperous.

MALACHI was probably written around 470–440 B.C., after the rebuilding of the temple and around the time of Ezra and Nehemiah. At this time, Judah was under Persian control. Life was very difficult. Many people in Judah, including the spiritual leaders, began to question whether the LORD God really was concerned about them.

HOW IS MALACHI CONSTRUCTED?

MALACHI is a series of questions and responses between God and the people of Israel. The message can only be understood clearly if the reader keeps asking "what is the question?" and "who is speaking now?" Some questions are stated clearly in the text, but sometimes the reader has to figure out the questions that prompt Malachi's messages. The following outline is a general overview of the book:

Malachi declares God's love for Israel (1.1-5)
Unfaithful priests and broken promises (1.6—2.16)
God promises to judge evil and reward good
   (2.17—4.6)

The book of Malachi describes a time of doubt and misery for the Jewish people. Although the temple in Jerusalem had been rebuilt in 515 B.C., the promise of God's blessings seemed more remote than ever. In response to this despair, the prophet Malachi tells of the Lord's anger at the priests for being disrespectful and not properly performing their duties. Likewise the people have fallen away from God and do not present the proper offerings. Malachi makes it clear that the troubles people are experiencing are a direct result of their unfaithfulness. But he also lets them know that God's love for his people does not change, and those who truly respect the Lord and honor his name will someday be rewarded. Malachi concludes with a warning of the coming day of the Lord, a day when God will punish the wicked and restore the faithful. Before that day comes, however, God promises to send the prophet Elijah as a messenger. Elijah will lead the people to love one another more, assuring that the faithful will escape any punishment.

Outline

1

I am Malachi. And this is the message that the Lord gave me for Israel.

The Lord's Love for Israel

²Israel, I, the Lord, have loved you. And yet you ask in what way have I loved you. Don't forget that Esau was the brother of your ancestor Jacob, but I chose Jacob ³instead of Esau. And I turned Esau's hill country into a barren desert where jackals[a] roam. ⁴Esau's descendants may say, "Although our nation Edom is in ruins, we will rebuild it."

But I, the Lord All-Powerful, promise to tear down whatever they build. Then everyone will know that I will never stop being angry with them as long as they are so sinful.

⁵Israel, when you see this, you will shout, "The Lord's great reputation reaches beyond our borders."

---

[a]1.3 *jackals*: Desert animals related to wolves, but smaller.

Judgment against Priests

⁶I, the Lord All-Powerful, have something to say to you priests. Children respect their fathers, and servants respect their masters. I am your father and your master, so why don't you respect me? You priests have insulted me, and now you ask, "How did we insult you?"

⁷You embarrass me by offering worthless food on my altar. Then you ask, "How have we embarrassed you?" You have done it by saying, "What's so great about the Lord's altar?"

⁸ But isn't it wrong to offer animals that are blind, lame, or sick? Just try giving those animals to your governor. That certainly wouldn't please him or make him want to help you. ⁹I am the Lord God All-Powerful, and you had better try to please me. You have sinned. Now see if I will have mercy on any of you.

¹⁰I wish someone would lock the doors of my temple, so you would stop wasting

1.11 *every nation . . . proper sacrifices:* Malachi tries to shame the people of Israel into action by comparing them with other nations who have no special relationship with God. Malachi says that other nations make "proper sacrifices," while God's people bring offerings that are far from perfect. The LORD's altar is the altar of sacrifice at the temple in Jerusalem.

2.4 *agreement with your ancestor Levi:* The Bible does not mention an agreement between God and Levi. "Levi" may refer to the whole tribe of Levi (Num 3.11-13;8.20-26; Deut 33.8-11). On the other hand, it may refer to Phinehas, a descendant of Levi, who had been loyal to the LORD (Num 25.10-13; Ps 106.30,31).

2.9 *failed to treat all people alike:* The priests were to support themselves and their families by keeping a portion of the offerings the people made to God (Exod 29.27,28; Lev 7.34,35; 22.10-16; Num 5.9,10; 18.8-24). The priests may have been giving preference to those who could afford large offerings rather than small ones.

2.11 *Judah and Jerusalem:* Jerusalem was the capital city of Judah, the name given to the southern part of Israel and to the people who returned there from exile in Babylon in the sixth century B.C. (See Map 6 on pg 1884.)

time building fires on my altar. I am not pleased with you priests, and I refuse to accept any more of your offerings. [11]From dawn until dusk my name is praised by every nation on this earth, as they burn incense and offer the proper sacrifices to me. [12]But even you priests insult me by saying, "There's nothing special about the LORD's altar, and these sacrifices are worthless."

[13]You get so disgusted that you even make vulgar signs at me.[b] And for an offering, you bring stolen[c] animals or those that are lame or sick. Should I accept these? [14]Instead of offering the acceptable animals you have promised, you bring me those that are unhealthy. I will punish you for this, because I am the great King, the LORD All-Powerful, and I am worshiped by nations everywhere.

True and False Priests

2 I, the LORD All-Powerful, have something else to say to you priests. [2]You had better take seriously the need to honor my name. Otherwise, when you give a blessing, I will turn it into a curse. In fact, I have already done this, because you haven't taken to heart your duties as priests. [3]I will punish your descendants and rub your faces in the manure from your animal sacrifices, and then be done with you.[d]

[4]I am telling you this, so I can continue to keep my agreement with your ancestor Levi. [5]I blessed him with a full life, as I had promised, and he kept his part of the agreement by honoring me and respecting my name. [6]He taught the truth and never told lies, and he led a lot of people to turn from sin, because he obeyed me and lived right.

[7]You priests should be eager to spread knowledge, and everyone should come to you for instruction, because you speak for me, the LORD All-Powerful. [8]But you have turned your backs on me. Your teachings have led others to do sinful things, and you have broken the agreement I made with your ancestor Levi. [9]So I caused everyone to hate and despise you, because you disobeyed me and failed to treat all people alike.

A Broken Agreement

[10]Don't you know that we all have God as our Father? Didn't the one God create each of us? Then why do you cheat each other by breaking the agreement God made with your ancestors? [11]You people in Judah and Jerusalem have been unfaithful to the LORD. You have disgraced the temple that he loves, and you have committed the disgusting sin of marrying the worshipers of other gods. [12]I pray that the LORD will no longer let those who are guilty belong to his people, even if they eagerly decide to offer the LORD a gift.[e]

[13]And what else are you doing? You cry noisily and flood the LORD's altar with your tears, because he isn't pleased with your offerings and refuses to accept them. [14]And why isn't God pleased? It's because he knows that each of you men has been unfaithful to the wife you married when you were young. You promised that she would be your partner, but now you have broken that promise. [15]Didn't God create you and your wife to become like one person?[f] And why did he do this? It was so you would have children, and then lead them to become God's people. Don't ever be unfaithful to your wife. [16]The LORD God All-Powerful of

[b]1.13 *me:* Or "the altar." [c]1.13 *stolen:* Or "injured." [d]2.3 *and then be done with you:* One possible meaning for the difficult Hebrew text. [e]2.12 *even if . . . gift:* One possible meaning for the difficult Hebrew text. [f]2.15 *Didn't . . . person:* One possible meaning for the difficult Hebrew text.

Israel hates anyone who is cruel enough to divorce his wife. So take care never to be unfaithful!

17You have worn out the LORD with your words. And yet, you ask, "How did we do that?"

You did it by saying, "The LORD is pleased with evil and doesn't care about justice."

The Promised Messenger

3 I, the LORD All-Powerful,
will send my messenger
   to prepare the way for me.
Then suddenly the Lord
you are looking for
   will appear in his temple.
The messenger you desire
is coming with my promise,
   and he is on his way.

A Day of Change

2On the day the Lord comes, he will be like a furnace that purifies silver or like strong soap in a washbasin. No one will be able to stand up to him. **3**The LORD will purify the descendants of Levi,**g** as though they were gold or silver. Then they will bring the proper offerings to the LORD, **4**and the offerings of the people of Judah and Jerusalem will please him, just as they did in the past.

Don't Cheat God

5The LORD All-Powerful said:
   I'm now on my way to judge you. And I will quickly condemn all who practice witchcraft or cheat in mar-riage or tell lies in court or rob workers of their pay or mistreat widows and orphans or steal the property of foreigners or refuse to respect me.

6Descendants of Jacob, I am the LORD All-Powerful, and I never change. That's why you haven't been wiped out, **7**even though you have ignored and disobeyed my laws ever since the time of your ancestors. But if you return to me, I will return to you.

And yet you ask, "How can we return?"

8You people are robbing me, your God. And, here you are, asking, "How are we robbing you?"

You are robbing me of the offerings and of the ten percent that belongs to me.**h 9**That's why your whole nation is under a curse. **10**I am the LORD All-Powerful, and I challenge you to put me to the test. Bring the entire ten percent into the storehouse, so there will be food in my house. Then I will open the windows of heaven and flood you with blessing after blessing.**i 11**I will also stop locusts**j** from destroying your crops and keeping your vineyards from producing. **12**Everyone of every nation will talk about how I have blessed you and about your wonderful land. I, the LORD All-Powerful, have spoken!

13You have said horrible things about me, and yet you ask, "What have we said?"

14Here is what you have said: "It's foolish to serve the LORD God All-Powerful. What do we get for obeying God and from going around looking

g3.3 *descendants of Levi*: The priests.   **h**3.8 *the ten percent . . . to me*: The people of Israel were supposed to give a tenth of their harvests and of their flocks and herds to the LORD (see Leviticus 27.30-33; Deuteronomy 14.22-29).   **i**3.10 *open the windows . . . blessing*: This may refer to rain, since there seems to have been a terrible drought at this time.   **j**3.11 *locusts*: A kind of grasshopper that comes in swarms and causes great damage to plant life.

■ 2.16 *divorce his wife*: Malachi sees marriage as the same kind of permanent agreement as the agreement that united God and the people of Israel.

● 3.1 *my messenger*: For Malachi, the "messenger" is a person who would prepare the people for the LORD's coming or return. Many years later, the early Christians described John the Baptist as this "messenger" (Matt 11.10; Mark 1.2; Luke 1.76; 7.27).

∞ Day of the LORD

■ 3.8 *the ten percent . . . to me:*. The ten percent belonged to God, meaning it was to be used in temple sacrifices and to support the temple priests and their families. Choosing not to give the required offerings was like "robbing" God and failing to support God's priests.

∞ Locusts

3.16 *in his book:* The Bible often refers to "books" that contain the names of those who belong to God or to a list of their deeds (see Exod 32.32, 33; Ps 40.7,8; 69.28; 87.6; 139.16; Isa 34.16; Dan 12.1,4; Phil 4.3; Rev 3.5; 13.8; 17.8; 20.12,15; 21.27). The "book" mentioned by Malachi probably refers to the book that records good deeds.

4.3 *trample those who are evil:* Malachi and other prophets believed that the faithful people of Israel would be God's helpers on the day of judgment (Isa 11.10-14; Amos 9.12; Mic 4.13; see also 1 Cor 6.2).

4.4 *Mount Sinai:* God gave the Law to Moses and the people of Israel while they camped at Sinai (Exod 19.1—20.17; 31.18; 34.29-32; Lev 26.46; 27.34; Neh 9.13). **(See Map 2 on pg 1880.)**

4.5 *Elijah:* A prophet who lived in Israel from around 899 to 850 b.c. According to 2 Kings 2.11, Elijah did not die but ascended into heaven. This led many to believe that Elijah would return.

Elijah

sad? [15]See how happy those arrogant people are. Everyone who does wrong is successful, and when they put God to the test, they always get away with it."

Faithfulness Is Rewarded

[16]All those who truly respected the LORD and honored his name started discussing these things, and when God saw what was happening, he had their names[k] written as a reminder in his book. [17]Then the LORD All-Powerful said:

You people are precious to me, and when I come to bring justice, I will protect you, just as parents protect an obedient child. [18]Then everyone will once again see the difference between those who obey me by doing right and those who reject me by doing wrong.

The Day of Judgment

The LORD said:

4 The day of judgment is certain to come. And it will be like a red-hot furnace with flames that burn up proud and sinful people, as though they were straw. Not a branch or a root will be left. I, the LORD All-Powerful, have spoken! [2]But for you that honor my name, victory will shine like the sun with healing in its rays, and you will jump around like calves at play. [3]When I come to bring justice, you will trample those who are evil, as though they were ashes under your feet. I, the LORD All-Powerful, have spoken!

[4]Don't ever forget the laws and teachings I gave my servant Moses on Mount Sinai.[l]

[5]I, the LORD, promise to send the prophet Elijah before that great and terrible day comes. [6]He will lead children and parents to love each other more, so that when I come, I won't bring destruction to the land.

[k]**3.16** *names:* Or "deeds."   [l]**4.4** *Sinai:* Hebrew "Horeb."

"Everyone will once again see the difference between those who obey me by doing right and those who reject me by doing wrong." MAL 3.17,18

Reflection Questions About Malachi 1.1—4.6

1. Some of God's people doubted God's love for them (1.2). What did Malachi say to respond to their doubts?

2. What were the priests doing wrong that made God wish that all their acts of worship would stop (1.6—2.12)?

3. What did Malachi say about divorce (2.14-16)? How is marriage like the relationship that the people were to have with God?

4. Keeping promises is an important theme in MALACHI. List all references to "promises" that you can find. What promises does God make? How are these promises related to the behavior of God's people?

5. Choose one passage from MALACHI and explain why it is meaningful to you.

the new testament

The "New Testament" is the second part of the Christian Bible. Its twenty-seven books continue the story of God's people begun in the Old Testament (the Jewish Scriptures). The Old Testament describes the agreement God made with the people of Israel. Those who obeyed God and lived according to this Law were God's people. But about six hundred years before Jesus, the prophet Jeremiah announced a "new agreement" based on an inward relationship with God (Jer 31.31-34). Christian writers of the New Testament used the language of a "new agreement" to describe what God had done in Jesus (1 Cor 8.7-13; 9.15-17; 11.25; 12.24-27). The apostle Paul says that this new agreement is not based on written law but comes from God's Spirit and brings new life (2 Cor 3.6-15; Gal 3.10-14).

Though Jesus and his disciples spoke Aramaic, the New Testament was first written in the "everyday" Greek of that time. The New Testament writers also were familiar with the Greek translation of the Jewish Scriptures (called the Septuagint). A number of quotations found in the New Testament come directly from this Greek translation, while others were translated into Greek from the Hebrew of the Jewish Scriptures.

THE GOSPELS AND ACTS

The word "Gospel" comes from an Old English word that means "good news." The four Gospels—MATTHEW, MARK, LUKE, and JOHN—present various accounts of the life and teachings of Jesus Christ. ACTS gives a detailed report of what happened to some of Jesus' early followers as they carried the message about Jesus from Jerusalem to the other areas of the Roman Empire.

The Gospels were probably written down in their present form between thirty and sixty years after Jesus' crucifixion. As Jesus' first followers and eyewitnesses grew older and died, it became more important to have a written record of what Jesus did and taught—to describe his death, and tell how God brought him back to life. Although other "gospels" about Jesus were written and circulated, the only ones accepted as reliable by the whole church were MATTHEW, MARK, LUKE, and JOHN. It is not certain who actually wrote these Gospels. Most likely, they were written by early followers of Christ who heard about Jesus from one or more of Jesus' first disciples.

The Gospels are based on many sources. These sources probably included various collections of Jesus' sayings and stories that were available to the Gospel writers. For example, a number of Jesus' sayings are similar in MATTHEW and LUKE, so they may have been working with the same source. Both of them also appear to have used MARK for their basic outlines. But MATTHEW and LUKE also used different sources to describe the events surrounding Jesus' birth, since MARK has nothing to say about Jesus' childhood. MATTHEW, MARK, and LUKE have so much material in common and follow the same basic outline that they are sometimes referred to as the "Synoptic" Gospels (from the Greek word synopsis, which means, "seeing together").

The three Synoptic Gospels are more like each other than any of them is like JOHN. While MATTHEW, MARK, and LUKE focus on Jesus' public teaching and miracle working in Galilee, JOHN contains information about Jesus' early work in Judea. JOHN also contains some of Jesus' sayings that are not found in the other Gospels. These include the so-called "I am" sayings, such as "I am the bread that gives life!" (John 6.35) and "I am the light for the world!" (John 8.12). The order of events in JOHN does not follow the order shared by the Synoptic Gospels. JOHN does not include any of Jesus' stories (parables) that are found in the other three Gospels.

Although the author of ACTS is unknown, scholars agree that the same person who wrote LUKE wrote ACTS. Besides being addressed to someone known as Theophilus (Luke 1.1-4; Acts 1.1), these books share a written style of Greek that is more formal than the Greek used in the other Gospels or in any other book of the New Testament. A number of common themes also tie these two books together as the work of one author.

LETTERS OF PAUL

The Letters of Paul include some of the oldest writings in the New Testament. The dates of his earliest letters most likely fall in the period A.D. 50–60 and were written before the Gospels, ACTS, and other New Testament writings.

Paul was one of the most important leaders of early Christianity. He taught the good news about Jesus Christ in many of the regions bordering the Mediterranean Sea. The Letters of Paul provide a picture of life among the early Christians who struggled to understand what Jesus and his teachings meant for life in this world and in the world to come. Paul studied the Jewish Scriptures and was a member of the Pharisees, a group devoted to teaching and living according to God's Law (Gal 1.14; Phil 3.5). However, when God showed Paul who Jesus really was (Gal 1.15,16), Paul began to preach and teach the good news about Jesus.

The Letters of Paul address key issues of Christian faith. Paul taught that God sent "Christ to be our sacrifice" and to set us "free from our sins" (Rom 3.24-26). He also said that no one could please God or become acceptable to God by obeying the Law (Gal 3.11; Rom 3.23) but that "God accepts only those who have faith in Jesus Christ" (Gal 2.16). Those who put their trust in Jesus benefit not only from the sacrifice Christ made, but also by sharing in the new life Jesus received when he was raised from death (Rom 6.5-11). Paul told Christians to live according to God's Spirit, who gives gifts for serving others (Rom 12.6-21; 1 Cor 12–13; Gal 5.16-25). He looked forward to Christ's return (Phil 3.20; 4.5; 1 Thes 4.13-18), and encouraged Jesus' followers to live as if Jesus might return any day (1 Thes 5.1-8; 1 Cor 7.29-39).

GENERAL LETTERS AND REVELATION

The final nine books of the New Testament were written in a number of styles by different writers. Some of these are written in ancient letter form, similar in style to Paul's letters.

The first eight (HEBREWS through JUDE) are often referred to as the General Letters. The General Letters include warnings against following false teachers (2 Pet 2.1-3; 1 John 2.18-26; 4.1,2; Jude 3-13), as well as encouragement to live holy lives (Jas 2.14-26; 1 Pet 1.13-16; 2 Pet 1.5-11) and to love one another (Heb 13.1,2; 1 John 3.11-19; 2 John 5,6). Christians are called God's chosen people (Heb 3.1; 1 Pet 2.9,10), but they are also warned that being chosen will not shield them from suffering or from having their faith tested (Heb 13.3; Jas 1.12; 1 Pet 1.5-7; 3.13-17; 4.12-14).

REVELATION records the visions of John of Patmos and includes a number of letters written to churches in Asia Minor (Rev 2,3). REVELATION is an example of apocalyptic writing, which is based, in part, on earlier Jewish apocalyptic writings such as DANIEL and EZEKIEL. Such writings describe an ongoing battle between God and the forces of evil, and tell how God achieves final victory in the end.

matthew

Promises are meant to be kept. Read the book of
Matthew to find out how God kept an ancient promise
by sending Jesus to be the Savior of the entire world.

WHAT MAKES MATTHEW SPECIAL?

Like the other Gospels, Matthew tells about the life and teachings of Jesus. It also describes what it means to be part of God's people and includes instructions on how God expects them to live.

The writer of Matthew was writing for people who knew the Jewish Scriptures, which Christians call the Old Testament. The writer often points out how these earlier texts look forward to Jesus as the Messiah sent from God.

WHAT'S THE STORY BEHIND THE SCENE?

Matthew shows that the message Jesus taught was based on the laws and teachings found in the Old Testament. On Mount Sinai, God gave Moses the laws that the people of Israel were to live by. In the Sermon on the Mount found in Matthew's Gospel, Jesus goes up on a mountain and tells his followers how God wants them to live.

The section of Matthew that tells about Jesus' work and teachings is arranged in five parts, just as the Law of Moses contains five parts in the Hebrew Scriptures—Genesis, Exodus, Leviticus, Numbers, and Deuteronomy. Matthew also wanted to show that much of what Jesus said and did was predicted hundreds of years earlier by the prophets of Israel, and that Jesus expresses in a new way the hope that all nations will share the faith of Israel (for example, Isaiah 2.2,3). Jesus' message was new, and it was offered to all people, not just to those who lived by the Law of Moses. Jesus invited everyone to trust and serve God and to love their neighbors.

HOW IS MATTHEW CONSTRUCTED?

Matthew can be outlined in the following way:

God sends Jesus, the Messiah (1.1—4.11)
   Where Jesus came from (1.1—2.23)
   Preparing the way for Jesus (3.1—4.11)
Jesus teaches the Good News in Galilee and Judea
   (4.12—25.46)
   Jesus preaches and chooses his first followers
   (4.12-25)
   Jesus teaches the crowds from a mountain
   (5.1—7.29)
   Jesus heals many and works miracles
   (8.1—9.38)
   Jesus instructs the twelve apostles (10.1-42)
   Jesus faces opponents and their questions
   (11.1—12.50)
   Jesus tells stories about the kingdom of heaven
   (13.1—58)
   Jesus is the Messiah (14.1—17.27)
   Jesus instructs his followers (18.1-34)
   Jesus faces opponents in Judea (19.1—23.39)
   Jesus teaches about God's coming kingdom
   (24.1—25.46)
Jesus dies and is raised to life to fulfill God's plan
   (26.1—28.20)

From the very beginning, Matthew celebrates Jesus as the Messiah who fulfills the Jewish Scriptures. Some scholars have called Matthew "the most Jewish" of the Gospels. The teachings of Jesus are presented in five speeches. This way of organizing Jesus' teachings would have made Jewish readers think of Moses, because their tradition taught that Moses wrote the five books of the Law (Torah). This similarity suggests that the author of Matthew is presenting Jesus as "the new Moses." The book also constantly refers to the Jewish Scriptures, uses a Jewish literary style, and employs number symbolism common in some Jewish circles at that time. Scholars also call Matthew "the Gospel of the church" because of the book's focus on Jesus as the risen Lord, on the kingdom of heaven, and on the church itself. In fact, Matthew is the only Gospel to use the Greek word for "church." Matthew often shows Jesus standing "outside of time," presenting both Jesus' ministry in the context of history and his glory as the eternal, resurrected Lord.

Outline

The Ancestors of Jesus

(Luke 3.23-38)

1 Jesus Christ came from the family of King David and also from the family of Abraham. And this is a list of his ancestors. **2-6a**From Abraham to King David, his ancestors were:

Abraham, Isaac, Jacob, Judah and his brothers (Judah's sons were Perez and Zerah, and their mother was Tamar), Hezron;

Ram, Amminadab, Nahshon, Salmon, Boaz (his mother was Rahab), Obed (his mother was Ruth), Jesse, and King David.

6b-11 From David to the time of the exile in Babylonia, the ancestors of Jesus were:

David, Solomon (his mother had been Uriah's wife), Rehoboam, Abijah, Asa, Jehoshaphat, Jehoram;

Uzziah, Jotham, Ahaz, Hezekiah, Manasseh, Amon, Josiah, and Jehoiachin and his brothers.

12-16 From the exile to the birth of Jesus, his ancestors were:

Jehoiachin, Shealtiel, Zerubbabel, Abiud, Eliakim, Azor, Zadok, Achim;

Eliud, Eleazar, Matthan, Jacob, and Joseph, the husband of Mary, the mother of Jesus, who is called the Messiah.

17There were 14 generations from Abraham to David. There were also 14 from David to the exile in Babylonia and 14 more to the birth of the Messiah.

The Birth of Jesus

(Luke 2.1-7)

18This is how Jesus Christ was born. A young woman named Mary was engaged to Joseph from King David's family. But before they were married, she learned that she was going to have a baby by God's Holy Spirit. **19**Joseph was a good man[a] and did not want to embarrass Mary in front of everyone. So he decided to quietly call off the wedding.

---

[a]**1.19** *good man:* Or "kind man," or "man who always did the right thing."

1.1 *family of King David and . . . Abraham:* King David was considered Israel's greatest ruler. Some prophets said that the Messiah would come from David's family (Isa 11.1-5). Abraham lived hundreds of years before David. Abraham obeyed God, and so God promised Abraham and Sarah that their descendants would become a great nation. Their descendants were called Israelites.

David

Abraham

1.17 *Messiah: Messiah* comes from the Hebrew word that means "the chosen one," or "anointed one." Anointing was done by putting oil on someone's head to show that the person was chosen for a special duty, like a high office (1 Sam 10.1). Anointing was also considered a sign that God's power had come upon the person. In Greek, the word for "anointed one" is *christos* (Christ).

1.18 *Holy Spirit:* The Holy Spirit is God's power at work in the world.

Holy Spirit

2.1 *Bethlehem in Judea:* Bethlehem was known as King David's hometown (Luke 2.4) and the village where Jesus was born (Matt 2.1). A similar connection between King David and Jesus is made by including David in the list of Jesus' ancestors (1.1).

2.1 *Herod:* Also known as Herod the Great, he was appointed governor of Galilee when the Romans occupied Palestine. About 37 B.C., Herod became king of Judea, Galilee, Samaria and the area east of the Jordan River.

2.1 *wise men:* These men, who are identified in Greek as *magoi*, may have been astrologers who came from a land to the east. Like others who studied the stars, they believed that when a great leader was about to be born, a new star would appear in the sky.

Dates in B.C. and A.D.

2.4 *chief priests and the teachers of the Law of Moses:* Chief priests were members of the group in charge of the temple in Jerusalem. The teachers of the Law of Moses were Jewish scholars who studied the first five books of the Jewish Scriptures, and explained how to live by what they taught.

Law

²⁰While Joseph was thinking about this, an angel from the Lord appeared to him in a dream. The angel said, "Joseph, the baby that Mary will have is from the Holy Spirit. Go ahead and marry her. ²¹Then after her baby is born, name him Jesus,[b] because he will save his people from their sins."

²²So the Lord's promise came true, just as the prophet had said, ²³"A virgin will have a baby boy, and he will be called Immanuel," which means "God is with us."

²⁴After Joseph woke up, he and Mary were soon married, just as the Lord's angel had told him to do. ²⁵But they did not sleep together before her baby was born. Then Joseph named him Jesus.

The Wise Men

2 When Jesus was born in the village of Bethlehem in Judea, Herod was king. During this time some wise men[c] from the east came to Jerusalem ²and said, "Where is the child born to be king of the Jews? We saw his star in the east[d] and have come to worship him."

³When King Herod heard about this, he was worried, and so was everyone else in Jerusalem. ⁴Herod brought together the chief priests and the teachers of the Law of Moses and asked them, "Where will the Messiah be born?"

⁵They told him, "He will be born in Bethlehem, just as the prophet wrote,

⁶'Bethlehem in the land
   of Judea,
you are very important
   among the towns of Judea.
From your town
   will come a leader,

who will be like a shepherd
   for my people Israel.'"

⁷Herod secretly called in the wise men and asked them when they had first seen the star. ⁸He told them, "Go to Bethlehem and search carefully for the child. As soon as you find him, let me know. I also want to go and worship him."

⁹The wise men listened to what the king said and then left. And the star they had seen in the east went on ahead of them until it stopped over the place where the child was. ¹⁰They were thrilled and excited to see the star.

¹¹When the men went into the house and saw the child with Mary, his mother, they knelt down and worshiped him. They took out their gifts of gold, frankincense, and myrrh[e] and gave them to him. ¹²Later they were warned in a dream not to return to Herod, and they went back home by another road.

The Escape to Egypt

¹³After the wise men had gone, an angel from the Lord appeared to Joseph in a dream and said, "Get up! Hurry and take the child and his mother to Egypt! Stay there until I tell you to return, because Herod is looking for the child and wants to kill him."

¹⁴That night, Joseph got up and took his wife and the child to Egypt, ¹⁵where they stayed until Herod died. So the Lord's promise came true, just as the prophet had said, "I called my son out of Egypt."

[b]**1.21** *name him Jesus:* In Hebrew the name "Jesus" means "the Lord saves."   [c]**2.1** *wise men:* People famous for studying the stars.   [d]**2.2** *his star in the east:* Or "his star rise."   [e]**2.11** *frankincense, and myrrh:* Frankincense was a valuable powder that was burned to make a sweet smell. Myrrh was a valuable sweet-smelling powder often used in perfume.

The prophet had said, "A virgin will have a baby boy, and he will be called Immanuel," which means "God is with us."
MATT 1.23

The Killing of the Children

[16]When Herod found out that the wise men from the east had tricked him, he was very angry. He gave orders for his men to kill all the boys who lived in or near Bethlehem and were two years old and younger. This was based on what he had learned from the wise men.

[17]So the Lord's promise came true, just as the prophet Jeremiah had said,

[18]"In Ramah a voice was heard
    crying and weeping loudly.
Rachel was mourning
    for her children,
and she refused
to be comforted,
    because they were dead."

The Return from Egypt

[19]After King Herod died, an angel from the Lord appeared in a dream to Joseph while he was still in Egypt. [20]The angel said, "Get up and take the child and his mother back to Israel. The people who wanted to kill him are now dead."

[21]Joseph got up and left with them for Israel. [22]But when he heard that Herod's son Archelaus was now ruler of Judea, he was afraid to go there. Then in a dream he was told to go to Galilee, [23]and they went to live there in the town of Nazareth. So the Lord's promise came true, just as the prophet had said, "He will be called a Nazarene."[f]

The Preaching of John the Baptist

(Mark 1.1-8; Luke 3.1-18; John 1.19-28)

3 Years later, John the Baptist started preaching in the desert of Judea. [2]He said, "Turn back to God! The kingdom of heaven[g] will soon be here."[h]

[3]John was the one the prophet Isaiah was talking about, when he said,

"In the desert someone
    is shouting,
'Get the road ready
    for the Lord!
Make a straight path
    for him.' "

[4]John wore clothes made of camel's hair. He had a leather strap around his waist and ate grasshoppers and wild honey. [5]From Jerusalem and all Judea and from the Jordan River Valley crowds of people went to John. [6]They told how sorry they were for their sins, and he baptized them in the river.

[7]Many Pharisees and Sadducees also came to be baptized. But John said to them:

You bunch of snakes! Who warned you to run from the coming judgment? [8]Do something to show you have really given up your sins. [9]And don't start telling yourselves that you belong to Abraham's family. I tell you that God can turn these stones into children for Abraham. [10]An ax is ready to cut the trees down at their roots. Any tree that doesn't produce good fruit will be chopped down and thrown into a fire.

[f]2.23 *He will be called a Nazarene:* The prophet who said this is not known.   [g]3.2 *kingdom of heaven:* In the Gospel of Matthew "kingdom of heaven" is used with the same meaning as "God's kingdom" in Mark and Luke.   [h]3.2 *will soon be here:* Or "is already here."

2.22 *Archelaus:* Archelaus had no authority in Galilee, so Joseph could live there safely with Mary and Jesus.

2.22,23 *Galilee . . . Nazareth:* Galilee was the area west of the Jordan River and Lake Galilee. The area was once part of the Northern Kingdom of Israel. Later, it was ruled by the Assyrians, Babylonians, Persians, Greeks, and Syrians. In 63 B.C., the Romans made it part of their empire and ruled it during the time Jesus lived. Nazareth was a small town that is never mentioned in the Old Testament. (See Map 12 on pg 1890.)

2.23 *Nazarene:* The exact meaning of the Greek word is unclear. It may come from the Hebrew word meaning "branch" or "root" (Isa 11.1). The author of MATTHEW could have been saying that Jesus would be known as a "branch of Jesse" the father of David.

3.1 *desert of Judea:* This area stretched about 20 miles eastward from the Jerusalem-Bethlehem plateau down to the Jordan River and the Dead Sea. (See Map 12 on pg 1890.)

3.2 *kingdom of heaven:* This term refers to the eternal rule of God, who lives in heaven, but whose kingdom will include everything that happens on earth. Jesus talks about how God's rule will be complete at some time in the future (24.14,30).

3.11 *carry his sandals:* Carrying another person's sandals was one of the duties of a servant or slave. John wanted to let the people know that he was not good enough to serve Jesus even by carrying his sandals.

John the Baptist

3.16 *Jesus was baptized:* John preached and baptized in order to encourage people to turn back to God and to be forgiven for their sins (Luke 3.3). Even though John insisted that Jesus didn't need this, Jesus said he should be baptized because God wanted him to be.

Baptism

4.1 *devil:* The devil is the leader of the evil forces that are against God and God's people.

Satan

4.1 *desert:* This was probably the Desert of Judea.

4.3 *tell these stones to turn into bread:* The devil was trying to take advantage of Jesus' hunger and make him act disloyally toward God.

¹¹I baptize you with water so you will give up your sins.ⁱ But someone more powerful is going to come, and I am not good enough even to carry his sandals.ʲ He will baptize you with the Holy Spirit and with fire. ¹²His threshing fork is in his hand, and he is ready to separate the wheat from the husks.ᵏ He will store the wheat in a barn and burn the husks in a fire that never goes out.

The Baptism of Jesus
(Mark 1.9-11; Luke 3.21,22)

¹³Jesus left Galilee and went to the Jordan River to be baptized by John. ¹⁴But John kept objecting and said, "I ought to be baptized by you. Why have you come to me?"

¹⁵Jesus answered, "For now this is how it should be, because we must do all God wants us to do." Then John agreed.

¹⁶So Jesus was baptized. And as soon as he came out of the water, the sky opened, and he saw the Spirit of God coming down on him like a dove. ¹⁷Then a voice from heaven said, "This is my own dear Son, and I am pleased with him."

Jesus and the Devil
(Mark 1.12,13; Luke 4.1-13)

4 The Holy Spirit led Jesus into the desert, so that the devil could test him. ²After Jesus had gone without eatingˡ for 40 days and nights, he was very hungry. ³Then the devil came to him and said, "If you are God's Son, tell these stones to turn into bread."

⁴Jesus answered, "The Scriptures say:
'No one can live only on food.
People need every word
    that God has spoken.' "

⁵Next, the devil took Jesus into the holy city to the highest part of the temple. ⁶The devil said, "If you are God's Son, jump off. The Scriptures say:
'God will give his angels
    orders about you.
They will catch you
    in their arms,
and you won't hurt
    your feet on the stones.' "

⁷Jesus answered, "The Scriptures also say, 'Don't try to test the Lord your God!' "

⁸Finally, the devil took Jesus up on a very high mountain and showed him all the kingdoms on earth and their power. ⁹The devil said to him, "I will give all this to you, if you will bow down and worship me."

¹⁰Jesus answered, "Go away Satan! The Scriptures say:
'Worship the Lord your God
    and serve only him.' "

¹¹Then the devil left Jesus, and angels came to help him.

Jesus Begins His Work
(Mark 1.14,15; Luke 4.14,15)

¹²When Jesus heard that John had been put in prison, he went to Galilee. ¹³But in-

---

ⁱ3.11 *so you will give up your sins:* Or "because you have given up your sins." ʲ3.11 *carry his sandals:* This was one of the duties of a slave. ᵏ3.12 *His threshing fork is in his hand, and he is ready to separate the wheat from the husks:* After Jewish farmers had trampled out the grain, they used a large fork to pitch the grain and the husks into the air. Wind would blow away the light husks, and the grain would fall back to the ground, where it could be gathered up. ˡ4.2 *without eating:* The Jewish people sometimes went without eating (also called "fasting") to show their love for God or to show sorrow for their sins.

stead of staying in Nazareth, Jesus moved to Capernaum. This town was beside Lake Galilee in the territory of Zebulun and Naphtali.[m] [14]So God's promise came true, just as the prophet Isaiah had said,

[15]"Listen, lands of Zebulun
and Naphtali,
lands along the road
to the sea
and across the Jordan.
Listen Galilee,
land of the Gentiles!
[16]Although your people
live in darkness,
they will see
a bright light.
Although they live
in the shadow of death,
a light will shine
on them."

[17]Then Jesus started preaching, "Turn back to God! The kingdom of heaven will soon be here."[n]

Jesus Chooses Four Fishermen
(Mark 1.16-20; Luke 5.1-11)

[18]While Jesus was walking along the shore of Lake Galilee, he saw two brothers. One was Simon, also known as Peter, and the other was Andrew. They were fishermen, and they were casting their net into the lake. [19]Jesus said to them, "Follow me! I will teach you how to bring in people instead of fish." [20]Right then the two brothers dropped their nets and went with him. [21]Jesus walked on until he saw James and John, the sons of Zebedee. They were in a

boat with their father, mending their nets. Jesus asked them to come with him. [22]At once they left the boat and their father and went with Jesus.

Jesus Teaches, Preaches, and Heals
(Luke 6.17-19)

[23]Jesus went all over Galilee, teaching in their synagogues and preaching the good news about God's kingdom. He also healed every kind of disease and sickness. [24]News about him spread all over Syria, and people with every kind of sickness or disease were brought to him. Some of them had a lot of demons in them, others were thought to be crazy,[o] and still others could not walk. But Jesus healed them all. [25]Large crowds followed Jesus from Galilee and the region around the ten cities known as Decapolis.[P] They also came from Jerusalem, Judea, and from across the Jordan River.

The Sermon on the Mount

5 When Jesus saw the crowds, he went up on the side of a mountain and sat down.[q]

Blessings
(Luke 6.20-23)

Jesus' disciples gathered around him, [2]and he taught them:
[3]God blesses those people
who depend only on him.

[m]**4.13** *Zebulun and Naphtali:* In Old Testament times these tribes were in northern Palestine, and in New Testament times many Gentiles lived where these tribes had once been. [n]**4.17** *The kingdom of heaven will soon be here:* See the two notes at 3.2. [o]**4.24** *thought to be crazy:* In ancient times people with epilepsy were thought to be crazy. [P]**4.25** *the ten cities known as Decapolis:* A group of ten cities east of Samaria and Galilee, where the people followed the Greek way of life. [q]**5.1** *sat down:* Teachers in the ancient world, including Jewish teachers, usually sat down when they taught.

4.13 *Capernaum . . . Lake Galilee:* An important fishing town on the northern shore of Lake Galilee, Capernaum was located on a major trade route between Egypt and Syria. In Jesus' day, Capernaum was a base for Roman soldiers who enforced the collection of taxes. Lake Galilee is also known as Lake Gennesaret (Luke 5.1) and the Sea of Tiberias (John 6.1; 21.1). (See Map 12 on pg 1890.)

4.18 *fishermen . . . casting their net:* Fishing on Lake Galilee was often done by spinning a circular net overhead and throwing (casting) it into shallow water. The outside of the net had weights tied to it so the net would sink in the shape of a dome. When the fish swam into this dome, the fisherman would pull the net closed with a line attached to its center. (See the article How People Made a Living in the Time of Jesus on pg 1813.)

Fish and Fishing

Synagogues

5.1 *mountain:* In MATTHEW, Jesus often went up on the side of a mountain to teach or to pray or to be alone (14.23; 15.29; 17.1,2; 24.3; 28.16). This makes him like Moses, who went up on Mount Sinai to learn from God what he should teach the people of Israel (see Exod 19).

5.13 *salt:* Salt was used to flavor food and to keep it from spoiling. Jesus was telling his followers to help others, just as salt helps the taste of food.

5.14,15 *light . . . lamp:* In Jesus' day, people used small clay lamps that burned olive oil. In the Jewish Scriptures, God's Word is compared to a "lamp that gives light" (Ps 119.105). See also John 8.12; 9.5.

5.17 *the Law and the Prophets:* The "Law" refers to the first five books of the Jewish Scriptures: GENESIS, EXODUS, LEVITICUS, NUMBERS, and DEUTERONOMY. The "Prophets" refers to the books of JOSHUA, JUDGES, SAMUEL, KINGS, ISAIAH, JEREMIAH, EZEKIEL, and "The Twelve," which Christians usually refer to as. "The Minor Prophets." **(See the article What Books Belong in the Bible? on pg 1764.)**

They belong to the kingdom
  of heaven!ʳ
⁴God blesses those people
  who grieve.
    They will find comfort!
⁵God blesses those people
  who are humble.
  The earth will belong
    to them!
⁶God blesses those people
  who want to obey himˢ
    more than to eat or drink.
  They will be given
    what they want!
⁷God blesses those people
  who are merciful.
  They will be treated
    with mercy!
⁸God blesses those people
  whose hearts are pure.
    They will see him!
⁹God blesses those people
  who make peace.
  They will be called
    his children!
¹⁰God blesses those people
  who are treated badly
    for doing right.
  They belong to the kingdom
    of heaven.ᵗ

¹¹God will bless you when people insult you, mistreat you, and tell all kinds of evil lies about you because of me. ¹²Be happy and excited! You will have a great reward in heaven. People did these same things to the prophets who lived long ago.

Salt and Light
(Mark 9.50; Luke 14.34,35)

¹³You are the salt for everyone on earth. But if salt no longer tastes like salt, how can it make food salty? All it is good for is to be thrown out and walked on.

¹⁴You are the light for the whole world. A city built on top of a hill cannot be hidden, ¹⁵and no one lights a lamp and put it under a clay pot. Instead, it is placed on a lampstand, where it can give light to everyone in the house. ¹⁶Make your light shine, so others will see the good you do and will praise your Father in heaven.

The Law of Moses

¹⁷Don't suppose I came to do away with the Law and the Prophets.ᵘ I did not come to do away with them, but to give them their full meaning. ¹⁸Heaven and earth may disappear. But I promise you not even a period or comma will ever disappear from the Law. Everything written in it must happen.

¹⁹If you reject even the least important command in the Law and teach others to do the same, you will be the least important person in the kingdom of heaven. But if you obey and teach others its commands, you will have an important place in the kingdom. ²⁰You must obey God's commands better than the Pharisees and the teachers of the Law obey them. If you don't, I promise you will never get into the kingdom of heaven.

ʳ5.3 *They belong to the kingdom of heaven:* Or "The kingdom of heaven belongs to them." ˢ5.6 *who want to obey him:* Or "who want to do right" or "who want everyone to be treated right." ᵗ5.10 *They belong to the kingdom of heaven:* See the note at 5.3. ᵘ5.17 *the Law and the Prophets:* The Jewish Scriptures, that is, the Old Testament.

Jesus said, "Make your light shine, so others will see the good you do and will praise your Father in heaven."
MATT 5.16

Anger

²¹You know our ancestors were told, "Do not murder" and "A murderer must be brought to trial." ²²But I promise you if you are angry with someone,ᵛ you will have to stand trial. If you call someone a fool, you will be taken to court. And if you say that someone is worthless, you will be in danger of the fires of hell.

²³So if you are about to place your gift on the altar and remember that someone is angry with you, ²⁴leave your gift there in front of the altar. Make peace with that person, then come back and offer your gift to God.

²⁵Before you are dragged into court, make friends with the person who has accused you of doing wrong. If you don't, you will be handed over to the judge and then to the officer who will put you in jail. ²⁶I promise you will not get out until you have paid the last cent you owe.

Marriage

²⁷You know the commandment which says, "Be faithful in marriage." ²⁸But I tell you if you look at another woman and want her, you are already unfaithful in your thoughts. ²⁹If your right eye causes you to sin, poke it out and throw it away. It is better to lose one part of your body, than for your whole body to end up in hell. ³⁰If your right hand causes you to sin, chop it off and throw it away! It is better to lose one part of your body, than for your whole body to be thrown into hell.

Divorce

(Matthew 19.9; Mark 10.11,12; Luke 16.18)

³¹You have been taught that a man who divorces his wife must write out divorce papers for her.ʷ ³²But I tell you not to divorce your wife unless she has committed some terrible sexual sin.ˣ If you divorce her, you will cause her to be unfaithful, just as any man who marries her is guilty of taking another man's wife.

Promises

³³You know our ancestors were told, "Don't use the Lord's name to make a promise unless you are going to keep it." ³⁴But I tell you not to swear by anything when you make a promise! Heaven is God's throne, so don't swear by heaven. ³⁵The earth is God's footstool, so don't swear by the earth. Jerusalem is the city of the great king, so don't swear by it. ³⁶Don't swear by your own head. You cannot make one hair white or black. ³⁷When you make a promise, say only "Yes" or "No." Anything else comes from the devil.

5.22 *fires of hell:* In Greek, the word for hell is *gehenna,* from the Hebrew words that mean "Valley of Hinnom," a valley near Jerusalem where children were once burned as sacrifices to the god Molech (Jer 32.35; Lev 20.2-5); it was later used for burning garbage. In the century before Jesus, some Jewish teachers taught that when wicked people die, they go to a place like the burning Hinnom Valley. New Testament writers picture the place of judgment as one of fiery torture (Luke 16.23, 24; Rev 20.14).

⚭ Hell

5.24 *gift there in front of the altar:* While the temple in Jerusalem was still standing, Jewish people offered to God gifts called "sacrifices." Jesus told people not to offer their gifts to God until after they have made peace with others who might be angry with them.

5.27 *marriage:* As head of the family, the father chose the wife for his son and the husband for his daughter. If two families could reach an agreement, then the engagement would be final, and the bride might go to live at the groom's house. Or she might stay at her father's house for up to a year before going to live with the groom.

ᵛ5.22 *someone:* In verses 22-24 the Greek text has "brother," which may refer to people in general or to other followers.   ʷ5.31 *write out divorce papers for her:* Jewish men could divorce their wives, but the women could not divorce their husbands. The purpose of writing these papers was to make it harder for a man to divorce his wife. Before this law was made, all a man had to do was to send his wife away and say that she was no longer his wife.   ˣ5.32 *some terrible sexual sin:* This probably refers to the laws about the wrong kinds of marriages that are forbidden in Leviticus 18.6-18 or to some serious sexual sin.

5.46 *tax collectors:* The Romans hired local people to collect taxes for them. These tax collectors often became wealthy by collecting much more than they needed to pay the Romans. Jewish tax collectors in Palestine were hated by their own people, who considered them traitors to their country and to their religion.

6.1 *deeds:* This refers to giving money to the poor. The Jewish people thought that three things were most important: giving gifts to the poor, praying, and fasting (not eating during certain periods of time). In 6.1-18, Jesus teaches people not to misuse their good deeds by doing them in order to show off or look good to other people.

6.2 *show-offs:* The Greek word used here is *hypocrites,* which has become an English word that means "show-offs" or "fakers."

6.6 *pray:* The Jewish people usually prayed in public at the temple or in their meetings (synagogues), normally while standing with their arms raised. They also prayed while kneeling or lying down. Jesus wanted people to see that it was wrong to pray just to be seen by others.

Prayer

Revenge
(Luke 6.29,30)

[38]You know you have been taught, "An eye for an eye and a tooth for a tooth." [39]But I tell you not to try to get even with a person who has done something to you. When someone slaps your right cheek,[y] turn and let that person slap your other cheek. [40]If someone sues you for your shirt, give up your coat as well. [41]If a soldier forces you to carry his pack one mile, carry it two miles.[z] [42]When people ask you for something, give it to them. When they want to borrow money, lend it to them.

Love
(Luke 6.27,28,32-36)

[43]You have heard people say, "Love your neighbors and hate your enemies." [44]But I tell you to love your enemies and pray for anyone who mistreats you. [45]Then you will be acting like your Father in heaven. He makes the sun rise on both good and bad people. And he sends rain for the ones who do right and for the ones who do wrong. [46]If you love only those people who love you, will God reward you for this? Even tax collectors[a] love their friends. [47]If you greet only your friends, what's so great about this? Don't even unbelievers do that? [48]But you must always act like your Father in heaven.

Giving

6 When you do good deeds, don't try to show off. If you do, you won't get a reward from your Father in heaven.

[2]When you give to the poor, don't blow a loud horn. That's what show-offs do in the synagogues and on the street corners, because they are always looking for praise. I can assure you that they already have their reward.

[3]When you give to the poor, don't let anyone know about it.[b] [4]Then your gift will be given in secret. Your Father knows what is done in secret and will reward you.

Prayer
(Luke 11.2-4)

[5]When you pray, don't be like those show-offs who love to stand up and pray in the synagogues and on the street corners. They do this just to look good. I can assure you that they already have their reward.

[6]When you pray, go into a room alone and close the door. Pray to your Father in private. He knows what is done in private and will reward you.

[7]When you pray, don't talk on and on as people do who don't know God. They think God likes to hear long prayers. [8]Don't be like them. Your Father knows what you need even before you ask.

[9]You should pray like this:
  Our Father in heaven,
  help us to honor

[y]**5.39** *right cheek:* A slap on the right cheek was a bad insult.   [z]**5.41** *two miles:* A Roman soldier had the right to force a person to carry his pack as far as one mile.   [a]**5.46** *tax collectors:* These were usually Jewish people who paid the Romans for the right to collect taxes. They were hated by other Jews who thought of them as traitors to their country and to their religion.   [b]**6.3** *don't let anyone know about it:* The Greek text has, "Don't let your left hand know what your right hand is doing."

your name.
¹⁰Come and set up
   your kingdom,
so that everyone on earth
   will obey you,
as you are obeyed
   in heaven.
¹¹Give us our food for today.ᶜ
¹²Forgive us for doing wrong,
   as we forgive others.
¹³Keep us from being temptedᵈ
   and protect us from evil.ᵉ

¹⁴If you forgive others for the wrongs they do to you, your Father in heaven will forgive you. ¹⁵But if you don't forgive others, your Father will not forgive your sins.

Worshiping God by Going without Eating

¹⁶When you go without eating,ᶠ don't try to look gloomy as those show-offs do when they go without eating. I can assure you that they already have their reward. ¹⁷Instead, comb your hair and wash your face. ¹⁸Then others won't know you are going without eating. But your Father sees what is done in private, and he will reward you.

Treasures in Heaven
(Luke 12.33,34)

¹⁹Don't store up treasures on earth! Moths and rust can destroy them, and thieves can break in and steal them. ²⁰Instead, store up your treasures in heaven, where moths and rust cannot destroy them, and thieves cannot break in and steal them. ²¹Your heart will always be where your treasure is.

Light
(Luke 11.34-36)

²²Your eyes are a window for your body. When they are good, you have all the light you need. ²³But when your eyes are bad, everything is dark. If the light inside you is dark, you surely are in the dark.

Money
(Luke 16.13)

²⁴You cannot be the slave of two masters! You will like one more than the other or be more loyal to one than the other. You cannot serve both God and money.

Worry
(Luke 12.22-31)

²⁵I tell you not to worry about your life. Don't worry about having something to eat, drink, or wear. Isn't life more than food or clothing? ²⁶Look at the birds in the sky! They don't plant or harvest. They don't even store grain in barns. Yet your Father in heaven takes care of them. Aren't you worth much more than birds? ²⁷Can worry make you live longer?ᵍ ²⁸Why worry about clothes? Look how the wild flowers grow. They don't work hard to make their clothes. ²⁹But I tell

6.16 *go without eating*: On special occasions the Jewish people went without eating (called "fasting") to show sorrow for their sins.

6.20 *heaven*: Living under God's rule in heaven will be the reward for those who are faithful.

∞ Heaven

6.26 *your Father*: Jesus is referring to God.

ᶜ**6.11** *our food for today*: Or "the food that we need" or "our food for the coming day."
ᵈ**6.13** *tempted*: Or "tested." ᵉ**6.13** *evil*: Or "the evil one," that is, the devil. Some manuscripts add, "The kingdom, the power, and the glory are yours forever. Amen." ᶠ**6.16** *without eating*: See the note at 4.2. ᵍ**6.27** *live longer*: Or "grow taller."

Jesus taught, "If you forgive others for the wrongs they do to you, your Father in heaven will forgive you." MATT 6.14

6.29 *Solomon with all his wealth:* Solomon, son of the great King David, ruled Israel at a time when the country was very rich. Solomon collected taxes from his own people to train a large army, to build the first temple in Jerusalem, and to construct a huge palace for himself. He had dealings with the leaders of many of Israel's neighbors. According to Jewish tradition, Solomon was the wisest and richest person who had ever lived.

7.15 *false prophets:* Those who claim to speak for God but actually lead God's people away from the truth into trouble.

you that Solomon with all his wealth[h] wasn't as well clothed as one of them. [30]God gives such beauty to everything that grows in the fields, even though it is here today and thrown into a fire tomorrow. God will surely do even more for you! Why do you have such little faith?

[31]Don't worry and ask yourselves, "Will we have anything to eat? Will we have anything to drink? Will we have any clothes to wear?" [32]Only people who don't know God are always worrying about such things. Your Father in heaven knows you need all of these. [33]But more than anything else, put God's work first and do what he wants. Then the other things will be yours as well.

[34]Don't worry about tomorrow. It will take care of itself. You have enough to worry about today.

Judging Others
(Luke 6.37,38,41,42)

7 Don't condemn others, and God won't condemn you. [2]God will be as hard on you as you are on others! He will treat you exactly as you treat them. [3]You can see the speck in your friend's eye, but you don't notice the log in your own eye. [4]How can you say, "My friend, let me take the speck out of your eye," when you don't see the log in your own eye? [5]You're nothing but show-offs! First, take the log out of your own eye; then you can see how to take the speck out of your friend's eye.

[6]Don't give to dogs what belongs to God. They will only turn and attack

you. Don't throw pearls down in front of pigs. They will trample all over them.

Ask, Search, Knock
(Luke 11.9-13)

[7]Ask, and you will receive. Search, and you will find. Knock, and the door will be opened for you. [8]Everyone who asks will receive. Everyone who searches will find. And the door will be opened for everyone who knocks. [9]Would any of you give your hungry child a stone, if the child asked for some bread? [10]Would you give your child a snake if the child asked for a fish? [11]As bad as you are, you still know how to give good gifts to your children. But your heavenly Father is even more ready to give good things to people who ask.

[12]Treat others as you want them to treat you. This is what the Law and the Prophets[i] are all about.

The Narrow Gate
(Luke 13.24)

[13]Go in through the narrow gate. The gate to destruction is wide, and the road that leads there is easy to follow. A lot of people go through that gate. [14]But the gate to life is very narrow. The road that leads there is so hard to follow that only a few people find it.

A Tree and Its Fruit
(Luke 6.43-45)

[15]Watch out for false prophets! They dress up like sheep, but inside they are

[h]**6.29** *Solomon with all his wealth:* The Jewish people thought that Solomon was the richest person who had ever lived. [i]**7.12** *the Law and the Prophets:* See the note at 5.17.

Jesus said, "Don't worry about tomorrow. It will take care of itself. You have enough to worry about today." MATT 6.34

wolves who have come to attack you. [16]You can tell what they are by what they do. No one picks grapes or figs from thornbushes. [17]A good tree produces good fruit, and a bad tree produces bad fruit. [18]A good tree cannot produce bad fruit, and a bad tree cannot produce good fruit. [19]Every tree producing bad fruit will be chopped down and burned. [20]You can tell who the false prophets are by their deeds.

A Warning
(Luke 13.26,27)

[21]Not everyone who calls me their Lord will get into the kingdom of heaven. Only the ones who obey my Father in heaven will get in. [22]On the day of judgment many will call me their Lord. They will say, "We preached in your name, and in your name we forced out demons and worked many miracles." [23]But I will tell them, "I will have nothing to do with you! Get out of my sight, you evil people!"

Two Builders
(Luke 6.47-49)

[24]Anyone who hears and obeys these teachings of mine is like a wise person who built a house on solid rock. [25]Rain poured down, rivers flooded, and winds beat against that house. But it was built on solid rock, and so it did not fall. [26]Anyone who hears my teachings and doesn't obey them is like a foolish person who built a house on sand.

[27]Rain poured down, rivers flooded, and the winds blew and beat against that house. Finally, it fell with a crash. [28]When Jesus finished speaking, the crowds were surprised at his teaching. [29]He taught them like someone with authority, and not like their teachers of the Law of Moses.

Jesus Heals a Man
(Mark 1.40-45; Luke 5.12-16)

8 As Jesus came down the mountain, he was followed by large crowds. [2]Suddenly a man with leprosy[j] came and knelt in front of Jesus. He said, "Lord, you have the power to make me well, if only you wanted to."

[3]Jesus put his hand on the man and said, "I want to! Now you are well." At once the man's leprosy disappeared. [4]Jesus told him, "Don't tell anyone about this, but go and show the priest that you are well. Then take a gift to the temple just as Moses commanded, and everyone will know that you have been healed."[k]

Jesus Heals an Army Officer's Servant
(Luke 7.1-10; John 4.43-54)

[5]When Jesus was going into the town of Capernaum, an army officer came up to him and said, [6]"Lord, my servant is at home in such terrible pain that he can't even move."

[7]"I will go and heal him," Jesus replied. [8]But the officer said, "Lord, I'm not good enough for you to come into my house. Just give the order, and my servant will get

[j]8.2 *leprosy*: In biblical times the word "leprosy" was used for many different kinds of skin diseases.
[k]8.4 *everyone will know that you have been healed*: People with leprosy had to be examined by a priest and told that they were well (that is "clean") before they could once again live a normal life in the Jewish community. The gift that Moses commanded was the sacrifice of some lambs together with flour mixed with olive oil.

7.16 *figs*: Figs are sweet fruits that grow on bushy trees related to the mulberry tree. A fig tree can produce two crops each year. Early fig crops ripen in June and are eaten fresh. The second crop is harvested in August or September. Many families covered the roofs of their homes with this second crop of figs so they could dry in the sun, and be eaten during the winter months.

7.22 *day of judgment*: Refers to the time when God will examine how people have lived and judge whether they have been faithful and obedient to God. This is an important theme in MATTHEW.

Day of the LORD

7.28 *When Jesus finished speaking*: This phrase, or one like it, is repeated five times in MATTHEW (7.28; 11.1; 13.53; 19.1; 26.1), and is used to organize the book. Matthew 4–25 can be divided into five sections that end with this phrase. Each section has two smaller parts: one telling what Jesus did, and the other giving some of Jesus' teachings.

8.5 *army officer*: A Roman centurion who commanded and trained 100 men who were ready to fight and die at his command. Centurions were expected to serve in the army for 25 years.

8.11 *feast in the kingdom of heaven:* This feast refers to a future event when God will bring together people who trust in Jesus, not only from the family of Israel but also from every nation. Jesus compares this event to a feast, a time of celebration. See also Isa 25.6-8; Luke 13.29.

8.12 *dark:* This is another word for the place of punishment for those who do evil.

8.16 *demons:* Demons are evil spirits that work for the devil.

8.19 *teacher of the Law of Moses:* Another name for this kind of teacher was scribe, which means one who was an expert in the sacred writings. These scribes studied the Jewish Scriptures and interpreted the Law in order to help people know how they should live.

8.20 *Son of Man:* When Jesus calls himself the Son of Man, he may be drawing attention to the fact that he is a human being.

Son of Man

Burial

8.28 *Gadara:* Gadara (sometimes called Gerasa) was located east of the Jordan River and to the south of Lake Galilee. Its population, architecture, and style of life were mostly Greek. **(See Map 12 on pg 1890.)**

well. [9]I have officers who give orders to me, and I have soldiers who take orders from me. I can say to one of them, 'Go!' and he goes. I can say to another, 'Come!' and he comes. I can say to my servant, 'Do this!' and he will do it."

[10]When Jesus heard this, he was so surprised that he turned and said to the crowd following him, "I tell you in all of Israel I've never found anyone with this much faith! [11]Many people will come from everywhere to enjoy the feast in the kingdom of heaven with Abraham, Isaac, and Jacob. [12]But the ones who should have been in the kingdom will be thrown out into the dark. They will cry and grit their teeth in pain."

[13]Then Jesus said to the officer, "You may go home now. Your faith has made it happen."

Right then his servant was healed.

Jesus Heals Many People
(Mark 1.29-34; Luke 4.38-41)

[14]Jesus went to the home of Peter, where he found that Peter's mother-in-law was sick in bed with fever. [15]He took her by the hand, and the fever left her. Then she got up and served Jesus a meal.

[16]That evening many people with demons in them were brought to Jesus. And with only a word he forced out the evil spirits and healed everyone who was sick. [17]So God's promise came true, just as the prophet Isaiah had said,

"He healed our diseases
and made us well."

Some Who Wanted To Go with Jesus
(Luke 9.57-62)

[18]When Jesus saw the crowd,[l] he went across Lake Galilee. [19]A teacher of the Law of Moses came up to him and said, "Teacher, I'll go anywhere with you!"

[20]Jesus replied, "Foxes have dens, and birds have nests. But the Son of Man doesn't have a place to call his own."

[21]Another disciple said to Jesus, "Lord, let me wait till I bury my father."

[22]Jesus answered, "Follow me, and let the dead bury their dead."[m]

A Storm
(Mark 4.35-41; Luke 8.22-25)

[23]After Jesus left in a boat with his disciples, [24]a terrible storm suddenly struck the lake, and waves started splashing into their boat.

Jesus was sound asleep, [25]so the disciples went over to him and woke him up. They said, "Lord, wake up! Save us before we drown!"

[26]But Jesus replied, "Why are you so afraid? You surely don't have much faith." Then he got up and ordered the wind and the waves to calm down. And everything was calm.

[27]The men in the boat were amazed and said, "Who is this? Even the wind and the waves obey him."

Two Men with Demons in Them
(Mark 5.1-20; Luke 8.26-39)

[28]After Jesus had crossed the lake, he came to shore near the town of Gadara[n]

[l]8.18 *saw the crowd:* Some manuscripts have "large crowd." Others have "large crowds."   [m]8.22 *let the dead bury their dead:* For the Jewish people a proper burial of their dead was a very important duty. But Jesus teaches that following him is even more important.   [n]8.28 *Gadara:* Some manuscripts have "Gergesa." Others have "Gerasa."

and started down the road. Two men with demons in them came to him from the tombs.º They were so fierce that no one could travel that way. ²⁹Suddenly they shouted, "Jesus, Son of God, what do you want with us? Have you come to punish us before our time?"

³⁰Not far from there a large herd of pigs was feeding. ³¹So the demons begged Jesus, "If you force us out, please send us into those pigs!" ³²Jesus told them to go, and they went out of the men and into the pigs. All at once the pigs rushed down the steep bank into the lake and drowned.

³³The people taking care of the pigs ran to the town and told everything, especially what had happened to the two men. ³⁴Everyone in town came out to meet Jesus. When they saw him, they begged him to leave their part of the country.

Jesus Heals a Man Who Could Not Walk

(Mark 2.1-12; Luke 5.17-26)

9 Jesus got into a boat and crossed back over to the town where he lived.P ²Some people soon brought to him a man lying on a mat because he could not walk. When Jesus saw how much faith they had, he said to the man, "My friend, don't worry! Your sins are forgiven."

³Some teachers of the Law of Moses said to themselves, "Jesus must think he is God!"

⁴But Jesus knew what was in their minds, and he said, "Why are you thinking such evil things? ⁵Is it easier for me to tell this man his sins are forgiven or to tell him to get up and walk? ⁶But I will show you that the Son of Man has the right to forgive sins here on earth." So Jesus said to the man, "Get up! Pick up your mat and go on home." ⁷The man got up and went home. ⁸When the crowds saw this, they were afraidᑫ and praised God for giving such authority to people.

Jesus Chooses Matthew

(Mark 2.13-17; Luke 5.27-32)

⁹As Jesus was leaving, he saw a tax collectorʳ named Matthew sitting at the place for paying taxes. Jesus said to him, "Follow me." Matthew got up and went with him.

¹⁰Later, Jesus and his disciples were having dinner at Matthew's house.ˢ Many tax collectors and other sinners were also there. ¹¹Some Pharisees asked Jesus' disciples, "Why does your teacher eat with tax collectors and other sinners?"

¹²Jesus heard them and answered, "Healthy people don't need a doctor, but sick people do. ¹³Go and learn what the Scriptures mean when they say, 'Instead of offering sacrifices to me, I want you to be merciful to others.' I didn't come to invite good people to be my followers. I came to invite sinners."

People Ask about Going without Eating

(Mark 2.18-22; Luke 5.33-39)

¹⁴Some followers of John the Baptist came and asked Jesus, "Why do we and the Pharisees often go without eating,ᵗ while your disciples never do?"

¹⁵Jesus answered:

The friends of a bridegroom aren't

º**8.28** *tombs*: It was thought that demons and evil spirits lived in tombs and in caves that were used for burying the dead. P**9.1** *where he lived*: Capernaum (see 4.13). ᑫ**9.8** *afraid*: Some manuscripts have "amazed." ʳ**9.9** *tax collector*: See the note at 5.46. ˢ**9.10** *Matthew's house*: Or "Jesus' house." ᵗ**9.14** *without eating*: See the note at 4.2.

8.28 *tombs*: In Palestine, tombs were usually carved into soft limestone hillsides. Most tombs had more than one room and a number of burial chambers.

Burial

8.30 *large herd of pigs*: According to the Law of Moses, pigs were "unclean" animals and could not be eaten (Lev 11.4-8; Deut 14.8). That a large herd of pigs was feeding near Gadara makes it clear that this was a Gentile area where few Jews lived.

Purity (Clean and Unclean)

9.1 *where he lived*: At this time, Jesus lived in Capernaum (see 4.13).

9.2 *Your sins are forgiven*: Sin occurs when people rebel against God and disobey God's Law. The Law of Moses taught that sins could be taken away by the sacrifice of a young goat on the Great Day of Forgiveness (Lev 16.1-22). In Jesus' day, the teachers of the Law taught that only God could forgive sins. When Jesus told the man that his sins were forgiven, the teachers were shocked and angry. They thought Jesus had no respect for God or God's power.

9.9 *Matthew*: Matthew was one of Jesus' twelve closest disciples. Though tradition says Matthew is the author of the Gospel bearing his name, most scholars believe it is not possible to identify the author.

Jesus said, "I didn't come to invite good people to be my followers. I came to invite sinners." MATT 9.13

9.17 *swell and burst the old skins:* Grape juice turns to wine during a process called fermentation. Fermenting grape juice produces a gas that swells and stretches the fresh skins where the wine is stored. If new wine was put into old skins that had become stiff, the skins could burst when the new wine began to ferment.

9.23 *crowd of mourners:* The family of a dead person often hired mourners for funerals. A few hours before a body was to be brought to a tomb, family members, neighbors, relatives, and hired mourners would begin to wail (cry out loud). They often beat on their chests or tore their clothes to express their sadness. Mourners would follow the body as it was carried to the tomb.

9.34 *leader of the demons:* Also known as Beelzebul or Beelzebub (see Matt 10.25; 12.24; Mark 3.22; Luke 11.15). The first title is from the name of the Canaanite god Baal. The second is from a Hebrew pun on that title, which means "lord of the flies." The leader of the demons was also known as Satan or the devil.

sad while he is still with them. But the time will come when he will be taken from them. Then they will go without eating.

[16]No one uses a new piece of cloth to patch old clothes. The patch would shrink and tear a bigger hole. [17]No one pours new wine into old wineskins. The wine would swell and burst the old skins.[u] Then the wine would be lost, and the skins would be ruined. New wine must be put into new wineskins. Both the skins and the wine will then be safe.

A Dying Girl and a Sick Woman
(Mark 5.21-43; Luke 8.40-56)

[18]While Jesus was still speaking, an official came and knelt in front of him. The man said, "My daughter has just now died! Please come and place your hand on her. Then she will live again." [19]Jesus and his disciples got up and went with the man.

[20]A woman who had been bleeding for twelve years came up behind Jesus and barely touched his clothes. [21]She had said to herself, "If I can just touch his clothes, I will be healed."

[22]Jesus turned. He saw the woman and said, "Don't worry! You are now healed because of your faith." At that moment she was healed.

[23]When Jesus went into the home of the official and saw the musicians and the crowd of mourners,[v] [24]he said, "Get out of here! The little girl isn't dead. She is just asleep." Everyone started laughing at Jesus. [25]But after the crowd had been sent out of

the house, Jesus went to the girl's bedside. He took her by the hand and helped her up. [26]News about this spread all over that part of the country.

Jesus Heals Two Blind Men

[27]As Jesus was leaving that place, two blind men began following him and shouting, "Son of David,[w] have pity on us!" [28]After Jesus had gone indoors, the two blind men came up to him. He asked them, "Do you believe I can make you well?"

"Yes, Lord," they answered.

[29]Jesus touched their eyes and said, "Because of your faith, you will be healed." [30]They were able to see, and Jesus strictly warned them not to tell anyone about him. [31]But they left and talked about him to everyone in that part of the country.

Jesus Heals a Man Who Could Not Talk

[32]As Jesus and his disciples were on their way, some people brought to him a man who could not talk because a demon was in him. [33]After Jesus had forced the demon out, the man started talking. The crowds were so amazed they began saying, "Nothing like this has ever happened in Israel!" [34]But the Pharisees said, "The leader of the demons gives him the power to force out demons."

Jesus Has Pity on People

[35]Jesus went to every town and village. He taught in their synagogues and preached the good news about God's kingdom. Jesus

[u]**9.17** *swell and burst the old skins:* While the juice from grapes was becoming wine, it would swell and stretch the skins in which it had been stored. If the skins were old and stiff, they would burst. [v]**9.23** *the crowd of mourners:* The Jewish people often hired mourners for funerals. [w]**9.27** *Son of David:* The Jewish people expected the Messiah to be from the family of King David, and for this reason the Messiah was often called the "Son of David."

also healed every kind of disease and sickness. **36**When he saw the crowds, he felt sorry for them. They were confused and helpless, like sheep without a shepherd. **37**He said to his disciples, "A large crop is in the fields, but there are only a few workers. **38**Ask the Lord in charge of the harvest to send out workers to bring it in."

Jesus Chooses His Twelve Apostles
(Mark 3.13-19; Luke 6.12-16)

10 Jesus called together his twelve disciples. He gave them the power to force out evil spirits and to heal every kind of disease and sickness. **2**The first of the twelve apostles was Simon, better known as Peter. His brother Andrew was an apostle, and so were James and John, the two sons of Zebedee. **3**Philip, Bartholomew, Thomas, Matthew the tax collector,[x] James the son of Alphaeus, and Thaddaeus were also apostles. **4**The others were Simon, known as the Eager One,[y] and Judas Iscariot,[z] who later betrayed Jesus.

Instructions for the Twelve Apostles
(Mark 6.7-13; Luke 9.1-6)

5Jesus sent out the twelve apostles with these instructions:

Stay away from the Gentiles and don't go to any Samaritan town. **6**Go only to the people of Israel, because they are like a flock of lost sheep. **7**As you go, announce that the kingdom of heaven will soon be here.[a] **8**Heal the sick, raise the dead to life, heal people who have leprosy,[b] and force out demons. You received without paying, now give without being paid. **9**Don't take along any gold, silver, or copper coins. **10**And don't carry[c] a traveling bag or an extra shirt or sandals or a walking stick.

Workers deserve their food. **11**So when you go to a town or a village, find someone able and willing to have you as their guest and stay with them until you leave. **12**When you go to a home, give it your blessing of peace. **13**If the home is deserving, let your blessing remain with them. But if the home doesn't accept you, take back your blessing of peace. **14**If someone won't welcome you or listen to your message, leave their home or town. And shake the dust from your feet at them.[d] **15**I promise you the day of judgment will be easier for the towns of Sodom and Gomorrah[e] than for that town.

Warning about Trouble
(Mark 13.9-13; Luke 21.12-17)

16I am sending you like lambs into a pack of wolves. So be as wise as snakes and as innocent as doves. **17**Watch out for people who will take you to court

---

[x]**10.3** *tax collector*: See the note at 5.46.   [y]**10.4** *known as the Eager One*: The Greek text has "Cananaean," which probably comes from a Hebrew word meaning "zealous" (see Luke 6.15). "Zealot" was the name later given to the members of a Jewish group that resisted and fought against the Romans.   [z]**10.4** *Iscariot*: This may mean "a man from Kerioth" (a place in Judea). But more probably it means "a man who was a liar" or "a man who was a betrayer."   [a]**10.7** *will soon be here*: Or "is already here."   [b]**10.8** *leprosy*: See the note at 8.2.   [c]**10.9,10** *Don't take along . . . don't carry*: Or "Don't accept . . . don't accept."   [d]**10.14** *shake the dust from your feet at them*: This was a way of showing rejection (see Acts 13.51).   [e]**10.15** *Sodom and Gomorrah*: During the time of Abraham the Lord destroyed these towns because the people there were so evil.

● **10.1,2** *twelve disciples . . . apostles*: A "disciple" means a follower who learns from a master teacher, and the term "apostle" refers to those who carry to others the teacher's actions and message. The disciples were later called apostles, as were a few others such as Paul. Jesus gave his disciples the power to heal people and force out evil spirits. A list of disciples is also given, with slight changes, in Mark 3.16-19 and Luke 6.13-16. **(See the chart Jesus' Twelve Disciples on pg 1837.)**

● **10.2** *Peter*: This is Simon, who was the first disciple Jesus chose (4.18-22). The Greek form of his name, *Petros*, and the Aramaic form, *Cephas*, both mean "rock." In Matthew 8.14, Jesus heals Peter's mother-in-law. MARK and LUKE also tell about the healing of Peter's mother-in-law. In those accounts, Peter is called Simon.

● **10.5** *Samaritan*: Samaritans lived in the area of Palestine near the city of Samaria. Some Jews in Jesus' day believed they should have nothing to do with Gentiles and disliked Samaritans. **(See Map 11 on pg 1889.)**

Gentiles

● **10.8** *leprosy*: According to Leviticus 13–14, certain skin diseases made a person unclean. Anyone who touched an unclean person had to go through a cleansing ritual to be fit to rejoin the worshiping community. When Jesus touched the man with leprosy, he was making himself unclean according to the Law of Moses.

10.41 *Anyone who welcomes:* According to the Law of Moses, the Jewish people were expected to be kind and generous to strangers and to welcome them into their homes to rest or to eat. One way people showed hospitality to guests was to wash their feet, because most people went barefoot or wore open sandals.

and have you beaten in their synagogues. ¹⁸Because of me, you will be dragged before rulers and kings to tell them and the Gentiles about your faith. ¹⁹But when someone arrests you, don't worry about what you will say or how you will say it. At that time you will be given the words to say. ²⁰But you will not really be the one speaking. The Spirit from your Father will tell you what to say.

²¹Brothers and sisters will betray one another and have each other put to death. Parents will betray their own children, and children will turn against their parents and have them killed. ²²Everyone will hate you because of me. But if you remain faithful until the end, you will be saved. ²³When people mistreat you in one town, hurry to another one. I promise you before you have gone to all the towns of Israel, the Son of Man will come.

²⁴Students are not better than their teacher, and slaves are not better than their master. ²⁵It is enough for students to be like their teacher and for slaves to be like their master. If people call the head of the family Satan, what will they say about the rest of the family?

The One To Fear
(Luke 12.2-7)

²⁶Don't be afraid of anyone! Everything is hidden will be found out, and every secret will be known. ²⁷Whatever I say to you in the dark, you must tell in the light. And you must announce from the housetops whatever I have whispered to you. ²⁸Don't be afraid of people. They can kill you, but they cannot harm your soul. Instead, you should fear God who can destroy both your body and your soul in hell.

²⁹Aren't two sparrows sold for only a penny? But your Father knows when any one of them falls to the ground. ³⁰Even the hairs on your head are counted. ³¹So don't be afraid! You are worth much more than many sparrows.

Telling Others about Christ
(Luke 12.8,9)

³²If you tell others you belong to me, I will tell my Father in heaven you are my followers. ³³But if you reject me, I will tell my Father in heaven you don't belong to me.

Not Peace, but Trouble
(Luke 12.51-53; 14.26,27)

³⁴Don't think I came to bring peace to the earth! I came to bring trouble, not peace. ³⁵I came to turn sons against their fathers, daughters against their mothers, and daughters-in-law against their mothers-in-law. ³⁶Your worst enemies will be in your own family.

³⁷If you love your father or mother or even your sons and daughters more than me, you are not fit to be my disciples. ³⁸And unless you are willing to take up your cross and follow me, you are not fit to be my disciples. ³⁹If you try to save your life, you will lose it. But if you give it up for me, you will surely find it.

Rewards
(Mark 9.41)

⁴⁰Anyone who welcomes you welcomes me. And anyone who welcomes me also welcomes the one who sent me. ⁴¹Anyone who welcomes a

Jesus said, "Don't be afraid of people. They can kill you, but they cannot harm your soul." MATT 10.28

prophet, just because that person is a prophet, will be given the same reward as a prophet. Anyone who welcomes a good person, just because that person is good, will be given the same reward as a good person. **42**And anyone who gives one of my most humble followers a cup of cool water, just because that person is my follower, will be rewarded.

John the Baptist
(Luke 7.18-35)

11 After Jesus had finished instructing his twelve disciples, he left and began teaching and preaching in the towns.**f**

2John was in prison when he heard what Christ was doing. So John sent some of his followers **3**to ask Jesus, "Are you the one we should be looking for? Or must we wait for someone else?"

4Jesus answered, "Go and tell John what you have heard and seen. **5**The blind are now able to see, and the lame can walk. People with leprosy**g** are being healed, and the deaf can hear. The dead are raised to life, and the poor are hearing the good news. **6**God will bless everyone who doesn't reject me because of what I do."

7As John's followers were going away, Jesus spoke to the crowds about John:

What sort of person did you go out into the desert to see? Was he like tall grass blown about by the wind? **8**What kind of man did you go out to see? Was he someone dressed in fine clothes? People who dress like that live in the king's palace. **9**What did you really go out to see? Was he a prophet? He certainly was. I tell you that he was more than a prophet. **10**In the Scriptures God says about him, "I am sending my messenger ahead to get things ready for you." **11**I tell you no one ever born on this earth is greater than John the Baptist. But whoever is least in the kingdom of heaven is greater than John.

12From the time of John the Baptist until now, violent people have been trying to take over the kingdom of heaven by force. **13**All the Books of the Prophets and the Law of Moses**h** told what was going to happen up to the time of John. **14**And if you believe them, John is Elijah, the prophet you are waiting for. **15**If you have ears, pay attention!

16You people are like children sitting in the market and shouting to each other,

17"We played the flute,
    but you would not dance!
We sang a funeral song,
    but you would not mourn!"

18John the Baptist did not go around eating and drinking, and you said, "That man has a demon in him!" **19**But the Son of Man goes around eating and drinking, and you say, "That man eats and drinks too much! He is even a friend of tax collectors**i** and sinners." Yet Wisdom is shown to be right by what it does.

The Unbelieving Towns
(Luke 10.13-15)

20In the towns where Jesus had worked most of his miracles, the people refused to

11.2 *John:* This refers to John the Baptist.

    John the Baptist

11.2 *Christ:* This is the Greek word, *Christos,* that translates the Hebrew word *Messiah.* The Jewish people believed that God would give power to a leader who would renew the faith of the people and fulfill God's purposes for them.

11.14 *Elijah:* Elijah was a prophet in Israel over 800 years before Jesus was born. Some later prophets expected God to send Elijah back to earth to warn people of God's judgment (Mal 3.1-4; 4.5,6). Some people thought John the Baptist was Elijah (Matt 17.10-13; Mark 9.11-13). By saying that "John is Elijah," Jesus meant that John was like Elijah, a person sent from God with power and an important message.

11.19 *Wisdom:* True wisdom was said to come from obeying God's Law (Ps 19.7). But Jesus seems to be saying that wisdom is more than this. Wisdom finds a way to help a neighbor, even if that person is a Gentile or someone who doesn't live by the Law of Moses.

    Wisdom

f11.1 *the towns:* The Greek text has "their towns," which may refer to the towns of Galilee or to the towns where Jesus' disciples had lived. **g11.5** *leprosy:* See the note at 8.2. **h11.13** *the Books of the Prophets and the Law of Moses:* The Jewish Scriptures, that is, the Old Testament. **i11.19** *tax collectors:* See the note at 5.46.

11.21 *Chorazin . . . Bethsaida . . . Tyre and Sidon:* Chorazin was a Jewish town just north of Lake Galilee. Bethsaida was a Jewish town just east of the Jordan River. Tyre and Sidon were important Phoenician port cities on the Mediterranean Sea. While the people in the Jewish towns often did not respond to Jesus' message and miracles, Jesus says that non-Jewish people in cities like Tyre and Sidon were more willing to turn to God. (See Map 12 on pg 1890.)

12.1 *Sabbath:* In Hebrew, *Sabbath* means to rest or to stop working. Sabbath is the Jewish day of rest that begins at sunset on Friday and ends at sunset on Saturday. In this story, some Pharisees considered picking grain to be work, and therefore a violation of the Sabbath law.

12.3 *what David did:* Jesus is referring to a time when David and his followers received special bread from the priests in the temple because they were hungry (Lev 24.5-9; 1 Sam 21.1-6).

Son of Man

turn to God. So Jesus was upset with them and said:

²¹You people of Chorazin are in for trouble! You people of Bethsaida are in for trouble too! If the miracles that took place here had happened in Tyre and Sidon, the people there would have turned to God long ago. They would have dressed in sackcloth and put ashes on their heads.ʲ ²²I tell you on the day of judgment the people of Tyre and Sidon will get off easier than you will.

²³People of Capernaum, do you think you will be honored in heaven? You will go down to hell! If the miracles that took place in your town had happened in Sodom, would still be standing. ²⁴So I tell you on the day of judgment the people of Sodom will get off easier than you.

Come to Me and Rest
(Luke 10.21,22)

²⁵At that moment Jesus said:

My Father, Lord of heaven and earth, I am grateful that you hid all this from wise and educated people and showed it to ordinary people. ²⁶Yes, Father, this is what pleased you.

²⁷My Father has given me everything, and he is the only one who knows the Son. The only one who truly knows the Father is the Son. But the Son wants to tell others about the Father, so they can know him too.

²⁸If you are tired from carrying heavy burdens, come to me and I will give you rest. ²⁹Take the yokeᵏ I give you. Put it on your shoulders and learn from me. I am gentle and humble, and you will find rest. ³⁰This yoke is easy to bear, and this burden is light.

A Question about the Sabbath
(Mark 2.23-28; Luke 6.1-5)

12 One Sabbath, Jesus and his disciples were walking through some wheat fields.ˡ His disciples were hungry and began picking and eating grains of wheat. ²Some Pharisees noticed this and said to Jesus, "Why are your disciples picking grain on the Sabbath? They are not supposed to do this!"

³Jesus answered:

You surely must have read what David did when he and his followers were hungry. ⁴He went into the house of God, and then they ate the sacred loaves of bread that only priests are supposed to eat. ⁵Haven't you read in the Law of Moses that the priests are allowed to work in the temple on the Sabbath? But no one says they are guilty of breaking the law of the Sabbath. ⁶I tell you there is something here greater than the temple. ⁷Don't you know what the Scriptures mean when they say, "Instead of offering sacrifices to me, I want you to be merciful to others?" If you knew what this means, you would not condemn these innocent disciples of mine. ⁸So the Son of Man is Lord over the Sabbath.

A Man with a Paralyzed Hand
(Mark 3.1-6; Luke 6.6-11)

⁹Jesus left and went into one of their synagogues, ¹⁰where there was a man whose

ʲ11.21 *sackcloth . . . ashes on their heads:* This was one way that people showed how sorry they were for their sins.   ᵏ11.29 *yoke:* Yokes were put on the necks of animals, so that they could pull a plow or wagon. A yoke was a symbol of obedience and hard work.   ˡ12.1 *walking through some wheat fields:* It was the custom to let hungry travelers pick grains of wheat.

hand was paralyzed. Some Pharisees wanted to accuse Jesus of doing something wrong, so they asked him, "Is it right to heal someone on the Sabbath?"

¹¹Jesus answered, "If one of your sheep fell into a ditch on the Sabbath, wouldn't you lift it out? ¹²People are worth much more than sheep, and so it is right to do good on the Sabbath." ¹³Then Jesus told the man, "Hold out your hand." The man did, and it became as healthy as the other one.

¹⁴The Pharisees left and started making plans to kill Jesus.

God's Chosen Servant

¹⁵When Jesus found out what was happening, he left there and large crowds followed him. He healed all of their sick, ¹⁶but warned them not to tell anyone about him. ¹⁷So God's promise came true, just as Isaiah the prophet had said,

¹⁸"Here is my chosen servant!
    I love him,
        and he pleases me.
    I will give him my Spirit,
    and he will bring justice
        to the nations.
¹⁹He won't shout or yell
        or call out in the streets.
²⁰He won't break off a bent reed
        or put out a dying flame,
    but he will make sure
        that justice is done.
²¹All nations will place
        their hope in him."

Jesus and the Ruler of the Demons

(Mark 3.20-30; Luke 11.14-23; 12.10)

²²Some people brought to Jesus a man who was blind and could not talk because he had a demon in him. Jesus healed the man, and then he was able to talk and see. ²³The crowds were so amazed they asked, "Could Jesus be the Son of David?"ᵐ

²⁴When the Pharisees heard this, they said, "He forces out demons by the power of Beelzebul, the ruler of the demons!"

²⁵Jesus knew what they were thinking, so he said to them:

Any kingdom where people fight each other will end up ruined. And a town or family that fights will soon destroy itself. ²⁶So if Satan fights against himself, how can his kingdom last? ²⁷If I use the power of Beelzebul to force out demons, whose power do your own followers use to force them out? Your followers are the ones who will judge you. ²⁸But when I force out demons by the power of God's Spirit, it proves that God's kingdom has already come to you. ²⁹How can anyone break into a strong man's house and steal his things, unless he first ties up the strong man? Then he can take everything.

³⁰If you are not on my side, you are against me. If you don't gather in the harvest with me, you scatter it. ³¹⁻³²I tell you any sinful thing you do or say can be forgiven. Even if you speak against the Son of Man, you can be forgiven. But if you speak against the Holy Spirit, you can never be forgiven, either in this life or in the life to come.

A Tree and Its Fruit

(Luke 6.43-45)

³³A good tree produces good fruit, and a bad tree produces bad fruit. You can tell what a tree is like by the fruit it produces. ³⁴You are a bunch of evil

ᵐ12.23 Could Jesus be the Son of David: Or "Does Jesus think he is the Son of David?" See the note at 9.27.

● 12.14 Pharisees . . . making plans to kill Jesus: The Pharisees were respected by many of the Jewish people because they studied God's Law and helped the people see how to live according to it. When Jesus challenged their teachings and authority, some Pharisees tried to get rid of him, because they thought he was becoming a threat to their position and power.

■ 12.16 warned them not to tell anyone about him: When Jesus healed people, he often told them not to tell what he had done for them. He probably said this so that others would not come to him simply for miracles of healing and nothing more.

◎◎ Heaven

12.39-41 *prophet Jonah . . . Nineveh:* God chose the prophet Jonah to go to Nineveh, the capital of Assyria, and tell the people of Nineveh to ask for God's forgiveness. Jonah did not want God to forgive Israel's Assyrian enemies, so he tried to escape from God. Jonah boarded a ship heading for Spain, but God sent a storm. Jonah was thrown into the water, and a big fish swallowed him (Jonah 1.12-17). He stayed inside the fish for three days before being spit out (Jonah 2.10). Jesus is comparing the time he would spend in the grave with the time Jonah spent inside the big fish. See also Matt 16.4; Mark 8.12; Jonah 3.5.

12.42 *The Queen of the South . . . to hear Solomon's wisdom:* This refers to the Queen of Sheba, a country in southern Arabia. The queen traveled north to listen to the wisdom of Israel's King Solomon (see 1 Kgs 10.1-10; 2 Chr 9.1-12). Jesus is making the point that if a Gentile like the Queen of Sheba could learn from a Jewish king in the past, why can't the leaders of the Jewish people recognize God's message from one of their own people, namely Jesus?

13.1-3 *Jesus . . . sat down to teach . . . by using stories:* Jewish teachers usually sat down when they taught. Jesus often used stories called "parables" to teach something important.

Stories (Parables)

snakes, so how can you say anything good? Your words show what is in your hearts. [35]Good people bring good things out of their hearts, but evil people bring evil things out of their hearts. [36]I promise you on the day of judgment, everyone will have to account for every careless word they have spoken. [37]On that day they will be told they are either innocent or guilty because of the things they have said.

A Sign from Heaven
(Mark 8.11,12; Luke 11.29-32)

[38]Some Pharisees and teachers of the Law of Moses said, "Teacher, we want you to show us a sign from heaven."

[39]But Jesus replied:

You want a sign because you are evil and won't believe! But the only sign you will get is the sign of the prophet Jonah. [40]He was in the stomach of a big fish for three days and nights, just as the Son of Man will be deep in the earth for three days and nights. [41]On the day of judgment the people of Nineveh[n] will stand there with you and condemn you. They turned to God when Jonah preached, and yet here is something far greater than Jonah. [42]The Queen of the South[o] will also stand there with you and condemn you. She traveled a long way to hear Solomon's wisdom, and yet here is something much greater than Solomon.

Return of an Evil Spirit
(Luke 11.24-26)

[43]When an evil spirit leaves a person, it travels through the desert, looking for a place to rest. But when the demon doesn't find a place, [44]it says, "I will go back to the home I left." When it gets there and finds the place empty, clean, and neat, [45]it goes off and finds seven other evil spirits even worse than itself. They all come and make their home there, and the person ends up in worse shape than before. That's how it will be with you evil people of today.

Jesus' Mother and Brothers
(Mark 3.31-35; Luke 8.19-21)

[46]While Jesus was still speaking to the crowds, his mother and brothers came and stood outside because they wanted to talk with him. [47]Someone told Jesus, "Your mother and brothers are standing outside and want to talk with you."[P]

[48]Jesus answered, "Who is my mother and who are my brothers?" [49]Then he pointed to his disciples and said, "These are my mother and my brothers! [50]Anyone who obeys my Father in heaven is my brother or sister or mother."

A Story about a Farmer
(Mark 4.1-9; Luke 8.4-8)

13 That same day Jesus left the house and went out beside Lake Galilee, where he sat down to teach.[q] [2]Such large crowds gathered around him that he had

[n]12.41 *Nineveh:* During the time of Jonah this city was the capital of the Assyrian Empire, which was Israel's worst enemy. But Jonah was sent there to preach, so that the people would turn to the Lord and be saved. [o]12.42 *South:* Sheba, probably a country in southern Arabia. [P]12.47 *with you:* Some manuscripts do not have verse 47. [q]13.1 *sat down to teach:* See the note at 5.1.

Jesus said, "Anyone who obeys my Father in heaven is my brother or sister or mother." MATT 12.50

to sit in a boat, while the people stood on the shore. ³Then he taught them many things by using stories. He said:

A farmer went out to scatter seed in a field. ⁴While the farmer was scattering the seed, some of it fell along the road and was eaten by birds. ⁵Other seeds fell on thin, rocky ground and quickly started growing because the soil wasn't very deep. ⁶But when the sun came up, the plants were scorched and dried up, because they did not have deep roots. ⁷Some other seeds fell where thornbushes grew up and choked the plants. ⁸But a few seeds did fall on good ground where the plants produced 100 or 60 or 30 times as much as was scattered. ⁹If you have ears, pay attention!

Why Jesus Used Stories
(Mark 4.10-12; Luke 8.9,10)

¹⁰Jesus' disciples came to him and asked, "Why do you use stories to speak to the people?"

¹¹Jesus answered:

I have explained the secrets about the kingdom of heaven to you, but not to others. ¹²Everyone who has something will be given more. But people who don't have anything will lose even what little they have. ¹³I use stories when I speak to them because when they look, they cannot see, and when they listen, they cannot hear or understand. ¹⁴So God's promise came true, just as the prophet Isaiah had said,

"These people will listen
  and listen,
    but never understand.
They will look and look,
    but never see.
¹⁵All of them have

stubborn minds!
They refuse to listen;
  they cover their eyes.
They cannot see or hear
  or understand.
If they could,
  they would turn to me,
    and I would heal them."

¹⁶But God has blessed you, because your eyes can see and your ears can hear! ¹⁷Many prophets and good people were eager to see what you see and to hear what you hear. But I tell you they did not see or hear.

Jesus Explains the Story about the Farmer
(Mark 4.13-20; Luke 8.11-15)

¹⁸Now listen to the meaning of the story about the farmer:

¹⁹The seeds that fell along the road are the people who hear the message about the kingdom, but don't understand it. Then the evil one comes and snatches the message from their hearts. ²⁰The seeds that fell on rocky ground are the people who gladly hear the message and accept it at once. ²¹But they don't have deep roots, and they don't last very long. As soon as life gets hard or the message gets them in trouble, they give up.

²²The seeds that fell among the thornbushes are also people who hear the message. But they start worrying about the needs of this life and are fooled by the desire to get rich. So the message gets choked out, and they never produce anything. ²³The seeds that fell on good ground are the people who hear and understand the message. They produce as much as 100 or 60 or 30 times what was planted.

13.4 *farmer was scattering the seed:* After breaking up the ground, a farmer planted seeds by scattering them a handful at a time. Birds quickly ate some seeds. Other seeds dried in the sun or landed among weeds. After sowing the seeds, the farmer would plow the seed into the ground along with the stubble from the previous crop, which would act as fertilizer as it decayed.

Stories (Parables)

Jesus explained, "The seeds that fell on good ground are the people who hear and understand the message." Matt 13.23

13.31 *mustard seed:* Since ancient times, this tiny black seed has been used to flavor food and to keep it fresh. It contained an oil that was used as a medicine. The sturdy mustard plant grows quickly, requires little cultivation, and can grow taller than a human being.

13.33 *yeast:* Yeast is mixed with water and flour to cause the dough to rise, so the bread will not be flat when baked. Yeast is also called leaven. Bread that has no yeast, or leaven, is flat and is called "thin bread" (unleavened bread). Thin bread was served at special times, such as Passover.

13.39 *end of time:* MATTHEW describes it as a future time when God will judge and separate the faithful ones from the ones who have not been faithful.

Stories (Parables)

Weeds among the Wheat

24Jesus then told them this story:

The kingdom of heaven is like what happened when a farmer scattered good seed in a field. 25But while everyone was sleeping, an enemy came and scattered weed seeds in the field and then left. 26When the plants came up and began to mature, the farmer's servants could see the weeds. 27The servants came and asked, "Sir, didn't you scatter good seed in your field? Where did these weeds come from?"

28"An enemy did this," he replied.

His servants then asked, "Do you want us to go out and pull up the weeds?"

29"No!" he answered. "You might also pull up the wheat. 30Leave the weeds alone until harvest time. Then I'll tell my workers to gather the weeds and tie them up and burn them. But I'll order them to store the wheat in my barn."

Stories about a Mustard Seed and Yeast
(Mark 4.30-32; Luke 13.18-21)

31Jesus told them another story:

The kingdom of heaven is like what happens when a farmer plants a mustard seed in a field. 32Although it is the smallest of all seeds, it grows larger than any garden plant and becomes a tree. Birds even come and nest on its branches.

33Jesus also said:

The kingdom of heaven is like what happens when a woman mixes a little yeast into three big batches of flour. Finally, all the dough rises.

The Reason for Teaching with Stories
(Mark 4.33,34)

34Jesus used stories when he spoke to the people. In fact, he did not tell them anything without using stories. 35So God's promise came true, just as the prophet[r] had said,

"I will use stories
   to speak my message
and to explain things hidden
   since the creation
   of the world."

Jesus Explains the Story about the Weeds

36After Jesus left the crowd and went inside,[s] his disciples came to him and said, "Explain to us the story about the weeds in the wheat field."

37Jesus answered:

The one who scattered the good seed is the Son of Man. 38The field is the world, and the good seeds are the people who belong to the kingdom. The weeds are those who belong to the evil one, 39and the one who scattered them is the devil. The harvest is the end of time, and angels are the ones who bring in the harvest.

40Weeds are gathered and burned. That's how it will be at the end of time. 41The Son of Man will send out his angels, and they will gather from his kingdom everyone who does wrong or causes others to sin. 42Then he will throw them into a flaming furnace,

[r]13.35 *the prophet:* Some manuscripts have "the prophet Isaiah." [s]13.36 *went inside:* Or "went home."

where people will cry and grit their teeth in pain. **43**But everyone who has done right will shine like the sun in their Father's kingdom. If you have ears, pay attention!

A Hidden Treasure

44The kingdom of heaven is like what happens when someone finds a treasure hidden in a field and buries it again. Such a person is happy and goes and sells everything in order to buy that field.

A Valuable Pearl

45The kingdom of heaven is like what happens when a shop owner is looking for fine pearls. **46**After finding a very valuable one, the owner goes and sells everything in order to buy that pearl.

A Fish Net

47The kingdom of heaven is like what happens when a net is thrown into a lake and catches all kinds of fish. **48**When the net is full, it is dragged to the shore, and the fishermen sit down to separate the fish. They keep the good ones, but throw the bad ones away. **49**That's how it will be at the end of time. Angels will come and separate the evil people from the ones who have done right. **50**Then those evil people will be thrown into a flaming furnace, where they will cry and grit their teeth in pain.

New and Old Treasures

51Jesus asked his disciples if they understood all these things. They said, "Yes, we do."

52So he told them, "Every student of the Scriptures who becomes a disciple in the kingdom of heaven is like someone who brings out new and old treasures from the storeroom."

The People of Nazareth Turn against Jesus
(Mark 6.1-6; Luke 4.16-30)

53When Jesus had finished telling these stories, he left **54**and went to his hometown. He taught in their synagogue, and the people were so amazed that they asked, "Where does he get all this wisdom and the power to work these miracles? **55**Isn't he the son of the carpenter? Isn't Mary his mother, and aren't James, Joseph, Simon, and Judas his brothers? **56**Don't his sisters still live here in our town? How can he do all this?" **57**So the people were upset because of what he was doing.

But Jesus said, "Prophets are honored by everyone, except the people of their hometown and their own family." **58**And because the people did not have any faith, Jesus did not work many miracles there.

The Death of John the Baptist
(Mark 6.14-29; Luke 9.7-9)

14 About this time Herod the ruler[t] heard the news about Jesus **2**and told his officials, "This is John the Baptist! He has come back from death, and that's why he has the power to work these miracles."

3-4 Herod had earlier arrested John and

● 13.50 *flaming furnace:* Another way of describing the place of punishment for evildoers.

● 13.54 *his hometown:* Nazareth.

CR   Synagogues

● 14.1 *Herod the ruler:* This is Herod Antipas, one of the sons of Herod the Great. After Herod the Great died in 4 B.C., the area he had ruled was divided among his four sons. Herod Antipas ruled over Galilee and Perea from 4 B.C. to A.D. 39. His formal title was Tetrarch, which meant someone who ruled part of a province. Sometimes people also called him a king (see 14.9).

---

[t]**14.1** *Herod the ruler:* Herod Antipas, the son of Herod the Great (see 2.1).

Jesus said, "Every student of the Scriptures who becomes a disciple in the kingdom of heaven is like someone who brings out new and old treasures from the storeroom." MATT 13.52

14.3-4 *Herodias . . . brother Philip:* Herodias was a granddaughter of Herod the Great. She married Herod's son, Philip, who was her uncle. When Herod Antipas was visiting in Philip's house in Rome, he talked Herodias into leaving Philip and marrying him. The Law of Moses did not allow a man to marry his brother's wife, while the brother was still living (see Lev 18.16; 20.21). That's why John the Baptist told Herod Antipas that marrying Herodias was wrong.

14.9 *did not want to break the promise he had made:* Rulers were especially expected to follow through on what they said they would do, even if their promise could cause problems. So when Herod made his promise in the presence of important guests, he could not take it back.

14.13 *he crossed Lake Galilee:* Lake Galilee is located in the northern part of the Jordan River Valley. Storms often sweep across the lake, because it is surrounded by mountains. **(See Map 12 on pg 1890.)**

had him chained and put in prison. He did this because John had told him, "It isn't right for you to take Herodias, the wife of your brother Philip." [5]Herod wanted to kill John. But the people thought John was a prophet, and Herod was afraid of what they might do.

[6]When Herod's birthday came, the daughter of Herodias danced for the guests. She pleased Herod [7]so much he swore to give her whatever she wanted. [8]But the girl's mother told her to say, "Here on a serving plate I want the head of John the Baptist!"

[9]Herod was sorry for what he had said. But he did not want to break the promise he had made in front of his guests. So he ordered a guard [10]to go to the prison and cut off John's head. [11]It was taken on a serving plate to the girl, and she gave it to her mother. [12]John's followers took his body and buried it. Then they told Jesus what had happened.

Jesus Feeds Five Thousand
(Mark 6.30-44; Luke 9.10-17; John 6.1-14)

[13]After Jesus heard about John, he crossed Lake Galilee[u] to go to some place where he could be alone. But the crowds found out and followed him on foot from the towns. [14]When Jesus got out of the boat, he saw the large crowd. He felt sorry for them and healed everyone who was sick.

[15]That evening the disciples came to Jesus and said, "This place is like a desert, and it's already late. Let the crowds leave, so they can go to the villages and buy some food."

[16]Jesus replied, "They don't have to leave. Why don't you give them something to eat?"

[17]But they said, "We have only five small loaves of bread[v] and two fish." [18]Jesus asked his disciples to bring the food to him, [19]and he told the crowd to sit down on the grass. Jesus took the five loaves and the two fish. He looked up toward heaven and blessed the food. Then he broke the bread and handed it to his disciples, and they gave it to the people.

[20]After everyone had eaten all they wanted, Jesus' disciples picked up twelve large baskets of leftovers.

[21]There were about 5,000 men who ate, not counting the women and children.

Jesus Walks on the Water
(Mark 6.45-52; John 6.15-21)

[22]At once, Jesus made his disciples get into a boat and start back across the lake.[w] But he stayed until he had sent the crowds away. [23]Then he went up on a mountain where he could be alone and pray. Later in the evening, he was still there.

[24]By this time the boat was a long way from the shore. It was going against the wind and was being tossed around by the waves. [25]A little while before morning, Jesus came walking on the water toward his disciples. [26]When they saw him, they thought he was a ghost. They were terrified and started screaming.

[27]At once, Jesus said to them, "Don't worry! I am Jesus. Don't be afraid."

[28]Peter replied, "Lord, if it really is you, tell me to come to you on the water."

[29]"Come on!" Jesus said. Peter then got out of the boat and started walking on the water toward him.

[30]But when Peter saw how strong the wind was, he was afraid and started sinking. "Save me, Lord!" he shouted.

[u]14.13 *crossed Lake Galilee:* To the east side.   [v]14.17 *small loaves of bread:* These would have been flat and round or in the shape of a bun.   [w]14.22 *back across the lake:* To the west side.

³¹At once, Jesus reached out his hand. He helped Peter up and said, "You surely don't have much faith. Why do you doubt?"

³²When Jesus and Peter got into the boat, the wind died down. ³³The men in the boat worshiped Jesus and said, "You really are the Son of God!"

Jesus Heals Sick People in Gennesaret
(Mark 6.53-56)

³⁴Jesus and his disciples crossed the lake and came to shore near the town of Gennesaret. ³⁵The people found out he was there, and they sent word to everyone who lived in this part of the country. So they brought all the sick people to Jesus. ³⁶They begged him just to let them touch his clothes, and everyone who did was healed.

The Teaching of the Ancestors
(Mark 7.1-13)

15 About this time some Pharisees and teachers of the Law of Moses came from Jerusalem. They asked Jesus, ²"Why don't your disciples obey what our ancestors taught us to do? They don't even wash their hands[x] before they eat."

³Jesus answered:

Why do you disobey God and follow your own teaching? ⁴ Didn't God command you to respect your father and mother? Didn't he tell you to put to death all who curse their parents? ⁵But you let people get by without helping their parents when they should. You let them say that what they have has been offered to God.[y] ⁶Is this any way

to show respect to your parents? You ignore God's commands in order to follow your own teaching. ⁷And you are nothing but show-offs! Isaiah the prophet was right when he wrote that God had said,

⁸"All of you praise me
    with your words,
    but you never really
    think about me.
⁹It is useless for you
    to worship me,
when you teach rules
    made up by humans."

What Really Makes People Unclean
(Mark 7.14-23)

¹⁰Jesus called the crowd together and said, "Pay attention and try to understand what I mean. ¹¹The food you put into your mouth doesn't make you unclean and unfit to worship God. The bad words that come out of your mouth are what make you unclean."

¹²Then his disciples came over to him and asked, "Do you know you insulted the Pharisees by what you said?"

¹³Jesus answered, "Every plant that my Father in heaven did not plant will be pulled up by the roots. ¹⁴Stay away from those Pharisees! They are like blind people leading other blind people, and all of them will fall into a ditch."

¹⁵Peter replied, "What did you mean when you talked about the things that make people unclean?"

¹⁶Jesus then said:

Don't any of you know by now what

● 14.34 *Gennesaret:* This town was located on the northwestern side of Lake Galilee, south of Capernaum, where Jesus lived. It was probably located on a narrow plain, also known as Gennesaret, which was about four miles long and about two miles wide. This plain's rich soil and abundant rainfall made it excellent farmland. **(See Map 14 on pg 1892.)**

● 15.2 *wash their hands:* According to the Law of Moses, if people touched something impure before they ate, any food they touched would also be ritually impure.

■ 15.5 *has been offered to God:* According to Jewish custom, when people said something was offered to God, it belonged to God and could not be used for anyone else. The teachers said that they had offered to God many of the things they owned. That is why they would not use these things, even to help their parents.

● 15.11 *unclean and unfit:* The Law of Moses taught that what people ate and touched could make them unfit to worship God. The Jewish people tried to keep their relationship with God clean and pure by eating only foods that the Law allowed. However, Jesus taught that it is what people think and say that makes them unclean, not what they eat or touch.

15.21 *Tyre and Sidon:* Non-Jewish people like the Phoenicians and Canaanites lived in these cities.

15.22 *Canaanite woman:* This woman was not Jewish. Her Canaanite ancestors had lived in the area before the tribes of Israel took it over and settled there hundreds of years earlier.

15.26 *feed it to dogs:* Jewish people considered dogs to be unclean animals because they ate garbage and the carcasses of dead animals. They did not keep them as pets.

I am talking about? [17]Don't you know that the food you put into your mouth goes into your stomach and then out of your body? [18]But the words that come out of your mouth come from your heart. And they are what make you unfit to worship God. [19]Out of your heart come evil thoughts, murder, unfaithfulness in marriage, vulgar deeds, stealing, telling lies, and insulting others. [20]These are what make you unclean. Eating without washing your hands will not make you unfit to worship God.

A Woman's Faith
(Mark 7.24-30)

[21]Jesus left and went to the territory near the towns of Tyre and Sidon. [22]Suddenly a Canaanite woman[z] from there came out shouting, "Lord and Son of David,[a] have pity on me! My daughter is full of demons." [23]Jesus did not say a word. But the woman kept following along and shouting, so his disciples came up and asked him to send her away.

[24]Jesus said, "I was sent only to the people of Israel! They are like a flock of lost sheep."

[25]The woman came closer. Then she knelt down and begged, "Please help me, Lord!"

[26]Jesus replied, "It isn't right to take food away from children and feed it to dogs."[b]

[27]"Lord, this is true," the woman said, "but even puppies get the crumbs that fall from their owner's table."

[28]Jesus answered, "Dear woman, you really do have a lot of faith, and you will be given what you want." At that moment her daughter was healed.

Jesus Heals Many People

[29]From there, Jesus went along Lake Galilee. Then he climbed a hill and sat down. [30]Large crowds came and brought many people who were paralyzed or blind or lame or unable to talk. They placed them, and many others, in front of Jesus, and he healed them all. [31]Everyone was amazed at what they saw and heard. People who had never spoken could now speak. The lame were healed, the paralyzed could walk, and the blind were able to see. Everyone was praising the God of Israel.

Jesus Feeds Four Thousand
(Mark 8.1-10)

[32]Jesus called his disciples together and told them, "I feel sorry for these people. They have been with me for three days, and they don't have anything to eat. I don't want to send them away hungry. They might faint on their way home."

[33]His disciples said, "This place is like a desert. Where can we find enough food to feed such a crowd?"

[34]Jesus asked them how much food they had. They replied, "Seven small loaves of bread[c] and a few little fish."

[35]After Jesus had told the people to sit down, [36]he took the seven loaves of bread and the fish and gave thanks. He then broke them and handed them to his disciples, who passed them around to the crowds.

[37]Everyone ate all they wanted, and the leftovers filled seven large baskets. [38]There were 4,000 men who ate, not counting the women and children. [39]After Jesus had sent the crowds away,

---

[z]**15.22** *Canaanite woman:* This woman was not Jewish.   [a]**15.22** *Son of David:* See the note at 9.27.
[b]**15.26** *feed it to dogs:* Some Jewish people referred to Gentiles as dogs.   [c]**15.34** *small loaves of bread:* See the note at 14.17.

he got into a boat and sailed across the lake. He came to shore near the town of Magadan.[d]

A Demand for a Sign from Heaven
(Mark 8.11-13; Luke 12.54-56)

16 The Pharisees and Sadducees came to Jesus and tried to test him by asking for a sign from heaven. [2]He told them:

If the sky is red in the evening, you say the weather will be good. [3]But if the sky is red and gloomy in the morning, you say it is going to rain. You can tell what the weather will be like by looking at the sky. But you don't understand what is happening now.[e] [4]You want a sign because you are evil and won't believe! But the only sign you will be given is what happened to Jonah.[f]

Then Jesus left.

The Yeast of the Pharisees and Sadducees
(Mark 8.14-21)

[5]The disciples had forgotten to bring any bread when they crossed the lake.[g] [6]Jesus then warned them, "Watch out! Guard against the yeast of the Pharisees and Sadducees."

[7]The disciples talked this over and said to each other, "He must be saying this because we didn't bring along any bread."

[8]Jesus knew what they were thinking and said:

You surely don't have much faith! Why are you talking about not having any bread? [9]Don't you understand? Have you forgotten about the 5,000 people and all those baskets of leftovers from just five loaves of bread? [10]And what about the 4,000 people and all those baskets of leftovers from only seven loaves of bread? [11]Don't you know by now that I am not talking to you about bread? Watch out for the yeast of the Pharisees and Sadducees!

[12]Finally, the disciples understood that Jesus wasn't talking about the yeast used to make bread, but about the teaching of the Pharisees and Sadducees.

Who Is Jesus?
(Mark 8.27-30; Luke 9.18-21)

[13]When Jesus and his disciples were near the town of Caesarea Philippi, he asked them, "What do people say about the Son of Man?"

[14]The disciples answered, "Some people say you are John the Baptist or maybe Elijah[h] or Jeremiah or some other prophet."

[15]Then Jesus asked, "But who do you say I am?"

[16]Simon Peter spoke up, "You are the Messiah, the Son of the living God."

[17]Jesus told him:

Simon, son of Jonah, you are blessed! You didn't discover this on your own. It was shown to you by my Father in heaven. [18]So I will call you Peter, which means "a rock." On this rock I will build my church, and death itself will not have any power over it. [19]I will give you the keys to the kingdom of heaven, and God in heaven will allow whatever you allow on earth. But he

---

[d]15.39 *Magadan:* The location is unknown.   [e]16.2,3 *If the sky is red . . . what is happening now:* The words of Jesus in verses 2 and 3 are not in some manuscripts.   [f]16.4 *what happened to Jonah:* Jonah was in the stomach of a big fish for three days and nights (see 12.40).   [g]16.5 *crossed the lake:* To the east side.   [h]16.14 *Elijah:* Many of the Jewish people expected the prophet Elijah to come and prepare the way for the Messiah.

● 16.1 *Pharisees and Sadducees:* The name Pharisee comes from Hebrew words that may mean "separate ones" or "pure ones," though the exact meaning is not clear. Pharisees dedicated themselves to studying and teaching the Jewish Scriptures. The Sadducees were a wealthy group of Jews whose name probably comes from Zadok, a major priestly family (see 2 Sam 20.25; 1 Kgs 1.39-45). They taught that the most important thing was going to the temple and offering sacrifices there. (See the article The World of Jesus: Peoples, Powers, and Politics on pg 1801.)

● 16.6-12 *yeast of the Pharisees and Sadducees:* When yeast is put in a batch of bread dough, it makes the whole batch rise and expand. Jesus was saying that the dishonest teaching of the Pharisees and Sadducees affected the whole people of Israel the way a little bit of yeast makes a whole batch of bread dough rise.

● 16.13 *Caesarea Philippi:* This city was located about 25 miles north of Lake Galilee. (See Map 11 on pg 1889.)

● 16.14 *Jeremiah:* Jeremiah served as a prophet in Judah from about 626 to 586 B.C.

● 16.18 *church:* MATTHEW is the only Gospel that uses the word "church." The Greek word for church means "a group of people who are called together," that is to say, they have a common purpose. The "church" refers to the new people of God that Jesus was "building."

16.21 *Jerusalem:* The capital city of Judea, the area where the Israelites who belonged to the tribe of Judah had settled. From the time of King David, Jerusalem was the center of the Jewish religion. In Jesus' day, the Romans controlled Jerusalem, but the Jewish people were allowed to worship at the temple, which had been rebuilt twice since the days of Solomon. Jesus went to Jerusalem to preach his message, knowing that he would face the Jewish religious leaders.

Jerusalem

16.23 *Satan:* This word means "adversary." Satan was also known as the devil ("accuser") and the leader of the demons.

17.3 *Moses and Elijah:* Two of Israel's most important leaders. They called God's people to live a new way of life, and are used here to represent the two main sections of the Hebrew Scriptures. Moses represents the Law, while Elijah represents the Prophets. MATTHEW seems to suggest that Jesus is the fulfillment of the Hebrew Scriptures.

Moses

Elijah

17.10 *Elijah must come before the Messiah does:* Many Jews in Jesus' day believed that the prophet Elijah must return before the Messiah could appear. This belief was based on the Old Testament prophecy in Malachi 4.5,6. They wondered: If Jesus was the Messiah, why hadn't they seen Elijah?

will not allow anything you don't allow.

²⁰Jesus told his disciples not to tell anyone he was the Messiah.

Jesus Speaks about His Suffering and Death

(Mark 8.31—9.1; Luke 9.22-27)

²¹From then on, Jesus began telling his disciples what would happen to him. He said, "I must go to Jerusalem. There the nation's leaders, the chief priests, and the teachers of the Law of Moses will make me suffer terribly. I will be killed, but three days later I will rise to life."

²²Peter took Jesus aside and told him to stop talking like that. He said, "God would never let this happen to you, Lord!"

²³Jesus turned to Peter and said, "Satan, get away from me! You're in my way because you think like everyone else and not like God."

²⁴Then Jesus said to his disciples:

If any of you want to be my followers, you must forget about yourself. You must take up your cross and follow me. ²⁵If you want to save your life,[i] you will destroy it. But if you give up your life for me, you will find it. ²⁶What will you gain, if you own the whole world but destroy yourself? What would you give to get back your soul?

²⁷The Son of Man will soon come in the glory of his Father and with his angels to reward all people for what they have done. ²⁸I promise you some of those standing here will not die before they see the Son of Man coming with his kingdom.

The True Glory of Jesus

(Mark 9.2-13; Luke 9.28-36)

17 Six days later Jesus took Peter and the brothers James and John with him. They went up on a very high mountain where they could be alone. ²There in front of the disciples, Jesus was completely changed. His face was shining like the sun, and his clothes became white as light.

³All at once Moses and Elijah were there talking with Jesus. ⁴So Peter said to him, "Lord, it is good for us to be here! Let us make three shelters, one for you, one for Moses, and one for Elijah."

⁵While Peter was still speaking, the shadow of a bright cloud passed over them. From the cloud a voice said, "This is my own dear Son, and I am pleased with him. Listen to what he says!" ⁶When the disciples heard the voice, they were so afraid they fell flat on the ground. ⁷But Jesus came over and touched them. He said, "Get up and don't be afraid!" ⁸When they opened their eyes, they saw only Jesus.

⁹On their way down from the mountain, Jesus warned his disciples not to tell anyone what they had seen until after the Son of Man had been raised from death.

¹⁰The disciples asked Jesus, "Don't the teachers of the Law of Moses say Elijah must come before the Messiah does?"

¹¹Jesus told them, "Elijah certainly will come and get everything ready. ¹²In fact, he has already come. But the people did not recognize him and treated him just as they wanted to. They will soon make the Son of Man suffer in the same way." ¹³Then the disciples understood Jesus was talking to them about John the Baptist.

---

[i]**16.25** *life:* In verses 25 and 26 the same Greek word is translated "life," "yourself," and "soul."

Jesus Heals a Boy
(Mark 9.14-29; Luke 9.37-43a)

[14]Jesus and his disciples returned to the crowd. A man knelt in front of him [15]and said, "Lord, have pity on my son! He has a bad case of epilepsy and often falls into a fire or into water. [16]I brought him to your disciples, but none of them could heal him."

[17]Jesus said, "You people are too stubborn to have any faith! How much longer must I be with you? Why do I have to put up with you? Bring the boy here." [18]Then Jesus spoke sternly to the demon. It went out of the boy, and right then he was healed.

[19]Later the disciples went to Jesus in private and asked him, "Why couldn't we force out the demon?"

[20-21]Jesus replied:

It is because you don't have enough faith! But I can promise you this. If you had faith no larger than a mustard seed, you could tell this mountain to move from here to there. And it would. Everything would be possible for you.[j]

Jesus Again Speaks about His Death
(Mark 9.30-32; Luke 9.43b-45)

[22]While Jesus and his disciples were going from place to place in Galilee, he told them, "The Son of Man will be handed over to people [23]who will kill him. But three days later he will rise to life." All of this made the disciples very sad.

Paying the Temple Tax

[24]When Jesus and the others arrived in Capernaum, the collectors for the temple tax came to Peter and asked, "Does your teacher pay the temple tax?"

[25]"Yes, he does," Peter answered.

After they had returned home, Jesus went up to Peter and asked him, "Simon, what do you think? Do the kings of this earth collect taxes and fees from their own people or from foreigners?"[k]

[26]Peter answered, "From foreigners."

Jesus replied, "Then their own people[l] don't have to pay. [27]But we don't want to cause trouble. So go cast a line into the lake and pull out the first fish you hook. Open its mouth, and you will find a coin. Use it to pay your taxes and mine."

Who Is the Greatest?
(Mark 9.33-37; Luke 9.46-48)

18 About this time the disciples came to Jesus and asked him who would be the greatest in the kingdom of heaven. [2]Jesus called for a child to come over and stand near him. [3]Then he said:

I promise you this. If you don't change and become like a child, you will never get into the kingdom of heaven. [4]But if you are as humble as this child, you are the greatest in the kingdom of heaven. [5]And when you welcome one of these children because of me, you welcome me.

[j]17.20,21 *for you*: Some manuscripts add, "But the only way to force out that kind of demon is by praying and going without eating." [k]17.25 *from their own people or from foreigners*: Or "from their children or from others." [l]17.26 *From foreigners . . . their own people*: Or "From other people . . . their children."

17.15 *epilepsy*: A disease of the nervous system that sometimes causes a person to fall down and begin to shake uncontrollably for several minutes.

17.18 *demon*: In Jesus' day, it was believed that epilepsy was caused by demons.

17.24 *temple tax*: The temple tax was required according to the Law of Moses (Exod 30.11-16; 38.26). The tax was half a shekel, which amounted on average to what a laborer earned for working two days.

18.5 *children*: Children were considered a gift from God, because they cared for older parents and carried on the family name when the parents died. Yet children had little power and were to obey their parents completely and do as they were told. Jesus used children as an example to show that being powerful is not the way to get into God's kingdom. What God wants is obedience.

18.8,9 *your hand . . . your eye . . . get rid of it*: Sometimes Jesus used very difficult and unpopular sayings to emphasize the truth. He wanted to make it clear that the physical pain of losing a hand or an eye is nothing compared to the pain of being in the fires of hell.

Temptations To Sin
(Mark 9.42-48; Luke 17.1,2)

[6]It will be terrible for people who cause even one of my little followers to sin. Those people would be better off thrown into the deepest part of the ocean with a heavy stone tied around their necks! [7]The world is in for trouble because of the way it causes people to sin. There will always be something to cause people to sin, but anyone who does this will be in for trouble.

[8]If your hand or foot causes you to sin, chop it off and throw it away! You would be better off to go into life paralyzed or lame than to have two hands or two feet and be thrown into the fire that never goes out. [9]If your eye causes you to sin, poke it out and get rid of it. You would be better off to go into life with only one eye than to have two eyes and be thrown into the fires of hell.

The Lost Sheep
(Luke 15.3-7)

[10-11]Don't be cruel to any of these little ones! I promise you their angels are always with my Father in heaven.[m] [12]Let me ask you this. What would you do if you had 100 sheep and one of them wandered off? Wouldn't you leave the 99 on the hillside and go look for the one that had wandered away? [13]I am sure that finding it would make you happier than having the 99 that never wandered off. [14]That's how it is with your Father in heaven. He doesn't want any of these little ones to be lost.

When Someone Sins
(Luke 17.3)

[15]If one of my followers[n] sins against you, go and point out what was wrong. But do it in private, just between the two of you. If that person listens, you have won back a follower. [16]But if that one refuses to listen, take along one or two others. The Scriptures teach that every complaint must be proven true by two or more witnesses. [17]If the follower refuses to listen to them, report the matter to the church. Anyone who refuses to listen to the church must be treated like an unbeliever or a tax collector.[o]

Allowing and Not Allowing

[18]I promise you God in heaven will allow whatever you allow on earth, but God will not allow anything you don't allow. [19]I promise that when any two of you on earth agree about something you are praying for, my Father in heaven will do it for you. [20]Whenever two or three of you come together in my name,[p] I am there with you.

An Official Who Refused To Forgive

[21]Peter came up to the Lord and asked, "How many times should I forgive someone[q] who does something wrong to me? Is seven times enough?"

[m]18.10,11 *in heaven*: Some manuscripts add, "The Son of Man came to save people who are lost." [n]18.15 *followers*: The Greek text has "brother," which is used here and elsewhere in this chapter to refer to a follower of Christ. [o]18.17 *tax collector*: See the note at 5.46. [p]18.20 *in my name*: Or "as my followers." [q]18.21 *someone*: Or "a follower." See the note at 18.15.

Jesus told his disciples, *"Whenever two or three of you come together in my name, I am there with you."* MATT 18.20

²²Jesus answered:

Not just 7 times, but 77 times!ʳ ²³This story will show you what the kingdom of heaven is like:

One day a king decided to call in his officials and ask them to give an account of what they owed him. ²⁴As he was doing this, one official was brought in who owed him 50,000,000 silver coins. ²⁵But he didn't have any money to pay what he owed. The king ordered him to be sold, along with his wife and children and all he owned, in order to pay the debt.

²⁶The official got down on his knees and began begging, "Have pity on me, and I will pay you every cent I owe!" ²⁷The king felt sorry for him and let him go free. He even told the official that he did not have to pay back the money.

²⁸But as this official was leaving, he happened to meet another official, who owed him 100 silver coins. So he grabbed the man by the throat. He started choking him and said, "Pay me what you owe!"

²⁹The man got down on his knees and began begging, "Have pity on me, and I will pay you back." ³⁰But the first official refused to have pity. Instead, he went and had the other official put in jail until he could pay what he owed.

³¹When some other officials found out what had happened, they felt sorry for the man who had been put in jail. Then they told the king what had happened. ³²The king called the first official back in and said, "You're an evil man! When you begged for mercy, I said you did not have to pay back a cent. ³³Don't you think you should show pity to someone else, as I did to you?" ³⁴The king was so angry that he ordered the official to be tortured until he could pay back everything he owed. ³⁵That is how my Father in heaven will treat you, if you don't forgive each of my followers with all your heart.

Teaching about Divorce
(Mark 10.1-12)

19 When Jesus finished teaching, he left Galilee and went to the part of Judea east of the Jordan River. ²Large crowds followed him, and he healed their sick.

³Some Pharisees wanted to test Jesus. They came up to him and asked, "Is it right for a man to divorce his wife for just any reason?"

⁴Jesus answered, "Don't you know in the beginning the Creator made a man and a woman? ⁵That's why a man leaves his father and mother and gets married. He becomes like one person with his wife. ⁶Then they are no longer two people, but one. And no one should separate a couple God has joined together."

⁷The Pharisees asked Jesus, "Why did Moses say a man could write out divorce papers and send his wife away?"

⁸Jesus replied, "You are so heartless! That's why Moses allowed you to divorce your wife. But from the beginning God did not intend it to be that way. ⁹I say if your wife has not committed some terrible sexual sin,ˢ you must not divorce her to marry someone else. If you do, you are unfaithful."

¹⁰The disciples said, "If that's how it is between a man and a woman, it's better not to get married."

¹¹Jesus told them, "Only those people

● 18.22 *77*: The large number means that one follower should never stop forgiving another. **(See the chart Numbers in the Bible on pg 1844.)**

● 19.1 *Judea east of the Jordan River*: This area was later known as Transjordan or Perea. Today this area is in Jordan.

ʳ**18.22** *77 times*: Or "70 times 7." The large number means that one follower should never stop forgiving another.   ˢ**19.9** *some terrible sexual sin*: See the note at 5.32.

19.16 *eternal life:* By the time of Jesus, many Jewish people had come to believe in life after death. Some, like the Sadducees, did not accept the concept of eternal life, because it was not described in the Law of Moses. Others thought that life after death would be like life on earth. Jesus compares the future kingdom of God to a feast.

Eternal Life

19.24 *camel:* Because of their ability to go long periods of time, camels were used for transporting goods over long desert trade routes. Camels are about six feet tall, ten feet long, and often weigh over 1,000 pounds.

19.28 *twelve thrones to judge the twelve tribes of Israel:* Israel is the name that God gave to Jacob, the grandson of Abraham and Sarah (see Gen 32.22-30). Israel's twelve tribes are named for Jacob's twelve sons.

who have been given the gift of staying single can accept this teaching. ¹²Some people are unable to marry because of birth defects or because of what someone has done to their bodies. Others stay single in order to serve God better. Anyone who can accept this teaching should do so."

Jesus Blesses Little Children
(Mark 10.13-16; Luke 18.15-17)

¹³Some people brought their children to Jesus, so he could place his hands on them and pray for them. His disciples told the people to stop bothering him. ¹⁴But Jesus said, "Let the children come to me, and don't try to stop them! People who are like these children belong to God's kingdom."ᵗ ¹⁵After Jesus had placed his hands on the children, he left.

A Rich Young Man
(Mark 10.17-31; Luke 18.18-30)

¹⁶A man came to Jesus and asked, "Teacher, what good thing must I do to have eternal life?"

¹⁷Jesus said to him, "Why do you ask me about what is good? Only God is good. If you want to have eternal life, you must obey his commandments."

¹⁸"Which ones?" the man asked.

Jesus answered, "Do not murder. Be faithful in marriage. Do not steal. Do not tell lies about others. ¹⁹Respect your father and mother. And love others as much as you love yourself." ²⁰The young man said, "I have obeyed all of these. What else must I do?"

²¹Jesus replied, "If you want to be perfect, go sell everything you own! Give the money to the poor, and you will have riches in heaven. Then come and be my follower." ²²When the young man heard this, he went away sad, because he was very rich.

²³Jesus said to his disciples, "I tell you, it's terribly hard for rich people to get into the kingdom of heaven! ²⁴In fact, it's easier for a camel to go through the eye of a needle than for a rich person to get into God's kingdom."

²⁵When the disciples heard this, they were greatly surprised and asked, "How can anyone ever be saved?"

²⁶Jesus looked straight at them and said, "There are some things people cannot do, but God can do anything."

²⁷Peter replied, "Remember, we have left everything to be your followers! What will we get?"

²⁸Jesus answered:

Yes, all of you have become my followers. And so in the future world, when the Son of Man sits on his glorious throne, I promise you will sit on twelve thrones to judge the twelve tribes of Israel. ²⁹All who have given up home or brothers and sisters or father and mother or children or land for me will be given 100 times as much. They will also have eternal life. ³⁰But many who are now first will be last, and many who are last will be first.

Workers in a Vineyard

20 As Jesus was telling what the kingdom of heaven would be like, he said:

Early one morning a man went out to hire some workers for his vineyard. ²After he had agreed to pay them the usual amount for a day's work, he sent them off to his vineyard.

ᵗ19.14 *People who are like these children belong to God's kingdom:* Or "God's kingdom belongs to people who are like these children."

³About nine that morning, the man saw some other people standing in the market with nothing to do. ⁴He promised to pay them what was fair, if they would work in his vineyard. ⁵So they went.

At noon and again about three in the afternoon he returned to the market. And each time he made the same agreement with others who were loafing around with nothing to do.

⁶Finally, about five in the afternoon the man went back and found some others standing there. He asked them, "Why have you been standing here all day long doing nothing?"

⁷"Because no one has hired us," they answered. Then he told them to go work in his vineyard.

⁸That evening the owner of the vineyard told the man in charge of the workers to call them in and give them their money. He also told the man to begin with the ones who were hired last. ⁹When the workers arrived, the ones who had been hired at five in the afternoon were given a full day's pay.

¹⁰The workers who had been hired first thought they would be given more than the others. But when they were given the same, ¹¹they began complaining to the owner of the vineyard. ¹²They said, "The ones who were hired last worked for only one hour. But you paid them the same that you did us. And we worked in the hot sun all day long!"

¹³The owner answered one of them, "Friend, I didn't cheat you. I paid you exactly what we agreed on. ¹⁴Take your money now and go! What business is it of yours if I want to pay them the same that I paid you? ¹⁵Don't I have the right to do what I want with my own money? Why should you be jealous, if I want to be generous?"

¹⁶Jesus then said, "So it is. Everyone who is now last will be first, and everyone who is first will be last."

Jesus Again Tells about His Death
(Mark 10.32-34; Luke 18.31-34)

¹⁷As Jesus was on his way to Jerusalem, he took his twelve disciples aside and told them in private:

¹⁸We are now on our way to Jerusalem, where the Son of Man will be handed over to the chief priests and the teachers of the Law of Moses. They will sentence him to death, ¹⁹and then they will hand him over to foreignersᵘ who will make fun of him. They will beat him and nail him to a cross. But on the third day he will rise from death.

A Mother's Request
(Mark 10.35-45)

²⁰The mother of James and Johnᵛ came to Jesus with her two sons. She knelt down and started begging him to do something for her. ²¹Jesus asked her what she wanted, and she said, "When you come into your kingdom, please let one of my sons sit at your right side and the other at your left."ʷ

²²Jesus answered, "Not one of you knows what you are asking. Are you able to drink from the cupˣ that I must soon drink from?" James and John said, "Yes, we are!"

ᵘ**20.19** *foreigners:* The Romans, who ruled Judea at this time. ᵛ**20.20** *mother of James and John:* The Greek text has "mother of the sons of Zebedee" (see 26.37). ʷ**20.21** *right side . . . left:* The most powerful people in a kingdom sat at the right and left side of the king. ˣ**20.22** *drink from the cup:* In the Scriptures a cup is sometimes used as a symbol of suffering. To "drink from the cup" is to suffer.

At the Market

20.18 *chief priests:* These men were assigned special duties connected to the temple and to worship, like preparing sacrifices, collecting donations, blessing the people, and taking care of the building itself. For most of the first century A.D., the Romans appointed one priest to be in charge of the others; he was called the high priest. **(See the article People of the Law: The Religion of Israel on pg 1794.)**

21.7 *donkey:* The Israelite people rode on donkeys and used them to carry and move things much more often than they used horses or camels. Sometimes donkeys were used for farm work, like pulling a grinding wheel that crushed grain into flour.

23Jesus replied, "You certainly will drink from my cup! But it isn't for me to say who will sit at my right side and at my left. This is for my Father to say."

24When the ten other disciples heard this, they were angry with the two brothers. **25**But Jesus called the disciples together and said:

You know foreign rulers like to order their people around. And their great leaders have full power over everyone they rule. **26**But don't act like them. If you want to be great, you must be the servant of all the others. **27**And if you want to be first, you must be the slave of the rest. **28**The Son of Man did not come to be a slave master, but a slave who will give his life to rescue[y] many people.

Jesus Heals Two Blind Men

(Mark 10.46-52; Luke 18.35-43)

29Jesus was followed by a large crowd as he and his disciples were leaving Jericho. **30**Two blind men were sitting beside the road. And when they heard that Jesus was coming their way, they shouted, "Lord and Son of David,[z] have pity on us!"

31The crowd told them to be quiet, but they shouted even louder, "Lord and Son of David, have pity on us!"

32When Jesus heard them, he stopped and asked, "What do you want me to do for you?"

33They answered, "Lord, we want to see!"

34Jesus felt sorry for them and touched their eyes. At once they could see, and they became his followers.

Jesus Enters Jerusalem

(Mark 11.1-11; Luke 19.28-38; John 12.12-19)

21 When Jesus and his disciples came near Jerusalem, he went to Bethphage on the Mount of Olives and sent two of them on ahead. **2**He told them, "Go into the next village, where you will at once find a donkey and her colt. Untie the two donkeys and bring them to me. **3**If anyone asks why you are doing this, just say, 'The Lord[a] needs them.' He will at once let you have the donkeys."

4So God's promise came true, just as the prophet had said,

5"Announce to the people
of Jerusalem:
'Your king is coming to you!
He is humble
and rides on a donkey.
He comes on the colt
of a donkey.'"

6The disciples left and did what Jesus had told them to do. **7**They brought the donkey and its colt and laid some clothes on their backs. Then Jesus got on.

8Many people spread clothes in the road, while others put down branches[b] which they had cut from trees. **9**Some people walked ahead of Jesus and others followed behind. They were all shouting,

"Hooray[c] for the Son of David![d]
God bless the one who comes
in the name of the Lord.
Hooray for God
in heaven above!"

10When Jesus came to Jerusalem, everyone in the city was excited and asked, "Who can this be?"

[y]20.28 *rescue:* The Greek word often, though not always, means the payment of a price to free a slave or a prisoner.   [z]20.30 *Son of David:* See the note at 9.27.   [a]21.3 *The Lord:* Or "The master of the donkeys."   [b]21.8 *spread clothes . . . put down branches:* This was one way that the Jewish people welcomed a famous person.   [c]21.9 *Hooray:* This translates a word that can mean "please save us." But it is most often used as a shout of praise to God.   [d]21.9 *Son of David:* See the note at 9.27.

Jesus said, "*If you want to be great, you must be the servant of all the others.*" MATT 20.26

[11]The crowds answered, "This is Jesus, the prophet from Nazareth in Galilee."

Jesus in the Temple
(Mark 11.15-19; Luke 19.45-48; John 2.13-22)

[12]Jesus went into the temple and chased out everyone who was selling or buying. He turned over the tables of the money-changers and the benches of the ones who were selling doves. [13]He told them, "The Scriptures say, 'My house should be called a place of worship.' But you have turned it into a place where robbers hide."

[14]Blind and lame people came to Jesus in the temple, and he healed them. [15]But the chief priests and the teachers of the Law of Moses were angry when they saw his miracles and heard the children shouting praises to the Son of David.[e] [16]The men said to Jesus, "Don't you hear what those children are saying?"

"Yes, I do!" Jesus answered. "Don't you know that the Scriptures say, 'Children and infants will sing praises'?" [17]Then Jesus left the city and went out to the village of Bethany, where he spent the night.

Jesus Puts a Curse on a Fig Tree
(Mark 11.12-14,20-24)

[18]When Jesus got up the next morning, he was hungry. He started out for the city, [19]and along the way he saw a fig tree. But when he came to it, he found only leaves and no figs. So he told the tree, "You will never again grow any fruit!" Right then the fig tree dried up.

[20]The disciples were shocked when they saw how quickly the tree had dried up. [21]But Jesus said to them, "If you have faith and don't doubt, I promise you can do what I did to this tree. And you will be able

to do even more. You can tell this mountain to get up and jump into the sea, and it will. [22]If you have faith when you pray, you will be given whatever you ask for."

A Question about Jesus' Authority
(Mark 11.27-33; Luke 20.1-8)

[23]Jesus had gone into the temple and was teaching when the chief priests and the leaders of the people came up to him. They asked, "What right do you have to do these things? Who gave you this authority?"

[24]Jesus answered, "I have just one question to ask you. If you answer it, I will tell you where I got the right to do these things. [25]Who gave John the right to baptize? Was it God in heaven or merely some human being?"

They thought it over and said to each other, "We can't say God gave John this right. Jesus will ask us why we didn't believe John. [26]On the other hand, these people think John was a prophet, and we are afraid of what they might do to us. That's why we can't say it was merely some human who gave John the right to baptize." [27]So they told Jesus, "We don't know."

Jesus said, "Then I won't tell you who gave me the right to do what I do."

A Story about Two Sons

[28]Jesus said:

I will tell you a story about a man who had two sons. Then you can tell me what you think. The father went to the older son and said, "Go work in the vineyard today!" [29]His son told him he would not do it, but later he changed his mind and went. [30]The man then told his younger son to go work in the vineyard. The boy said he

[e]21.15 *Son of David:* See the note at 9.27.

21.11 *Nazareth in Galilee:* Jesus' hometown in northern Palestine.

Money Changing in the Temple

21.17 *village of Bethany:* This is a small town about two miles east of Jerusalem, below the slope of the Mount of Olives. Jesus' friends Mary, Martha, and their brother Lazarus lived in Bethany where Jesus raised Lazarus back to life (see John 11). Today it is known as El-'Azariyeh, named after Lazarus, whose tomb is still said to be there.

21.25 *John:* John the Baptist.

John the Baptist

22.2 *wedding banquet:* Wedding feasts most often took place in the home of the groom, where food and wine would be served, and people would celebrate with music and dancing.

would, but he didn't go. [31]Which one of the sons obeyed his father?

"The older one," the chief priests and leaders answered.

Then Jesus told them:

You can be sure tax collectors[f] and prostitutes will get into the kingdom of God before you ever will! [32]When John the Baptist showed you how to do right, you would not believe him. But these evil people did believe. And even when you saw what they did, you still would not change your minds and believe.

Renters of a Vineyard
(Mark 12.1-12; Luke 20.9-19)

[33]Jesus told the chief priests and leaders to listen to this story:

A land owner once planted a vineyard. He built a wall around it and dug a pit to crush the grapes in. He also built a lookout tower. Then he rented out his vineyard and left the country. [34]When it was harvest time, the owner sent some servants to get his share of the grapes. [35]But the renters grabbed those servants. They beat up one, killed one, and stoned one of them to death. [36]He then sent more servants than he did the first time. But the renters treated them in the same way. [37]Finally, the owner sent his own son to the renters, because he thought they would respect him. [38]But when they saw the man's son, they said, "Someday he will own the vineyard. Let's kill him! Then we can have it all for ourselves." [39]So they grabbed him, threw him out of the vineyard, and killed him.

[40]Jesus asked, "When the owner of that

vineyard comes, what do you suppose he will do to those renters?"

[41]The chief priests and leaders answered, "He will kill them in some horrible way. Then he will rent out his vineyard to people who will give him his share of grapes at harvest time."

[42]Jesus replied, "You surely know that the Scriptures say,

'The stone the builders
    tossed aside
is now the most important
    stone of all.
This is something
    the Lord has done,
    and it is amazing to us.'

[43]I tell you God's kingdom will be taken from you and given to people who will do what he demands. [44]Anyone who stumbles over this stone will be crushed, and anyone it falls on will be smashed to pieces."[g]

[45]When the chief priests and the Pharisees heard these stories, they knew Jesus was talking about them. [46]So they looked for a way to arrest Jesus. But they were afraid to, because the people thought he was a prophet.

The Great Banquet
(Luke 14.15-24)

22 Once again Jesus used stories to teach the people:

[2]The kingdom of heaven is like what happened when a king gave a wedding banquet for his son. [3]The king sent some servants to tell the invited guests to come to the banquet, but the guests refused. [4]He sent other servants to say to the guests, "The banquet is ready! My cattle and prize calves have all been prepared. Everything is ready. Come to the banquet!"

[f]21.31 *tax collectors:* See the note at 5.46.   [g]21.44 *pieces:* Verse 44 is not in some manuscripts.

Jesus said, "The stone the builders tossed aside is now the most important stone of all." MATT 21.42

[5]But the guests did not pay any attention. Some of them left for their farms, and some went to their places of business. [6]Others grabbed the servants, then beat them up and killed them.

[7]This made the king so furious that he sent an army to kill those murderers and burn down their city. [8]Then he said to the servants, "It is time for the wedding banquet, and the invited guests don't deserve to come. [9]Go out to the street corners and tell everyone you meet to come to the banquet." [10]They went out on the streets and brought in everyone they could find, good and bad alike. And the banquet room was filled with guests.

[11]When the king went in to meet the guests, he found that one of them wasn't wearing the right kind of clothes for the wedding. [12]The king asked, "Friend, why didn't you wear proper clothes for the wedding?" But the guest had no excuse. [13]So the king gave orders for this person to be tied hand and foot and to be thrown outside into the dark. That's where people will cry and grit their teeth in pain. [14]Many are invited, but only a few are chosen.

Paying Taxes
(Mark 12.13-17; Luke 20.20-26)

[15]The Pharisees got together and planned how they could trick Jesus into saying something wrong. [16]They sent some of their followers and some of Herod's followers[h] to say to him, "Teacher, we know that you are honest. You teach the truth about what God wants people to do. And you treat everyone with the same respect, no matter who they are. [17]Tell us what you think! Should we pay taxes to the Emperor or not?"

[18]Jesus knew their evil thoughts and said, "Why are you trying to test me? You show-offs! [19]Let me see one of the coins used for paying taxes." They brought him a silver coin, [20]and he asked, "Whose picture and name are on it?"

[21]"The Emperor's," they answered.

Then Jesus told them, "Give the Emperor what belongs to him and give God what belongs to God." [22]His answer surprised them so much that they walked away.

Life in the Future World
(Mark 12.18-27; Luke 20.27-40)

[23]The Sadducees did not believe people would rise to life after death. So that same day some of the Sadducees came to Jesus and said:

[24]Teacher, Moses wrote that if a married man dies and has no children, his brother should marry the widow. Their first son would then be thought of as the son of the dead brother. [25]Once there were seven brothers who lived here. The first one married, but died without having any children. So his wife was left to his brother. [26]The same thing happened to the second and third brothers and finally to all seven of them. [27]At last the woman died. [28]When God raises people from death, whose wife will this woman be? She had been married to all seven brothers.

[29]Jesus answered:

You are completely wrong! You don't know what the Scriptures teach. And you don't know anything about the

22.11,12 *right kind of clothes for the wedding*: It was customary to wear the finest clothes for a wedding.

22.13 *dark*: This is another word for the place where those who do evil will be punished. See also Matt 8.12; 25.30; Luke 13.38.

22.17 *taxes to the Emperor*: Jewish people had to pay taxes to the Roman government that controlled their land. The highest Roman leader was called the Emperor (Caesar). Had Jesus said that people should not pay taxes, the Jewish leaders could have accused him of being disloyal to the Roman rulers.

22.19 *silver coin*: This coin was probably a denarius. In the time of Jesus, a denarius had a picture of Emperor Tiberius on one side. This coin was used to pay taxes to Caesar.

22.23 *Sadducees*: The Sadducees did not believe that God brought people back to life after they had died, because they did not think that was directly taught in the Law of Moses. They thought their question to Jesus would show how foolish it was to believe that people came back to life after they died.

[h]22.16 *Herod's followers*: People who were political followers of the family of Herod the Great (see 2.1) and his son Herod Antipas (see 14.1), and who wanted Herod to be king in Jerusalem.

22.32 *I am the God worshiped by Abraham, Isaac, and Jacob:* Jesus argues that if God is still worshiped by these three, who entered into an agreement (covenant) with God in ancient times, then they must in some way still be alive, because he is the God of the living.

22.45 *David . . . Messiah:* Jesus asked a question that the Pharisees could not answer. That is, how could a person be both David's son and David's Lord? In other words, how could the Messiah be descended from David and be more important than David? In asking this question, Jesus contrasts the Pharisees' traditional view of God's Law with the good news that Jesus is bringing.

23.4 *pile heavy burdens on people's shoulders:* The Pharisees and teachers of the Law of Moses taught people how to follow the Law as the way to serve God. Jesus was saying that these teachers liked to lay down rules but were not willing to help others keep them.

power of God. [30]When God raises people to life, they won't marry. They will be like the angels in heaven. [31]And as for people being raised to life, God was speaking to you when he said, [32]"I am the God worshiped by Abraham, Isaac, and Jacob."[i] He isn't the God of the dead, but of the living.

[33]The crowds were surprised to hear what Jesus was teaching.

The Most Important Commandment
(Mark 12.28-34; Luke 10.25-28)

[34]After Jesus had made the Sadducees look foolish, the Pharisees heard about it and got together. [35]One of them was an expert in the Jewish Law. So he tried to test Jesus by asking, [36]"Teacher, what is the most important commandment in the Law?"

[37]Jesus answered:

Love the Lord your God with all your heart, soul, and mind. [38]This is the first and most important commandment. [39]The second most important commandment is like this one. And it is, "Love others as much as you love yourself." [40]All the Law of Moses and the Books of the Prophets[j] are based on these two commandments.

About David's Son
(Mark 12.35-37; Luke 20.41-44)

[41]While the Pharisees were still there, Jesus asked them, [42]"What do you think

about the Messiah? Whose family will he come from?"

They answered, "He will be a son of King David."[k]

[43]Jesus replied, "How then could the Spirit lead David to call the Messiah his Lord? David said,

[44]'The Lord said to my Lord:
Sit at my right side[l]
until I make your enemies
into a footstool for you.'

[45]If David called the Messiah his Lord, how can the Messiah be a son of King David?" [46]No one was able to give Jesus an answer, and from that day on, no one dared ask him any more questions.

Jesus Condemns the Pharisees and the Teachers of the Law of Moses
(Mark 12.38-40; Luke 11.37-52; 20.45-47)

23 Jesus said to the crowds and to his disciples:

[2]The Pharisees and the teachers of the Law are experts in the Law of Moses. [3]So obey everything they teach you, but don't do as they do. After all, they say one thing and do something else.

[4]They pile heavy burdens on people's shoulders and won't lift a finger to help. [5]Everything they do is just to show off in front of others. They even make a big show of wearing Scripture verses on their foreheads and arms, and they wear big tassels[m] for every-

[i]**22.32** *I am the God worshiped by Abraham, Isaac, and Jacob:* Jesus argues that if God is worshiped by these three, they must still be alive, because he is the God of the living.   [j]**22.40** *the Law of Moses and the Books of the Prophets:* The Jewish Scriptures, that is, the Old Testament.   [k]**22.42** *son of King David:* See the note at 9.27.   [l]**22.44** *right side:* The place of power and honor.   [m]**23.5** *wearing Scripture verses on their foreheads and arms . . . tassels:* As a sign of their love for God and his teachings, the Jewish people often wore Scripture verses in small leather boxes. But the Pharisees tried to show off by making the boxes bigger than necessary. The Jewish people were also taught to wear tassels on the four corners of their robes to show their love for God.

Jesus said, "Love the Lord your God with all your heart, soul, and mind . . . 'Love others as much as you love yourself.'" MATT 22.37,39

one to see. [6]They love the best seats at banquets and the front seats in the synagogues. [7]And when they are in the market, they like to have people greet them as their teachers.

[8]But none of you should be called a teacher. You have only one teacher, and all of you are like brothers and sisters. [9]Don't call anyone on earth your father. All of you have the same Father in heaven. [10]None of you should be called the leader. The Messiah is your only leader. [11]Whoever is the greatest should be the servant of the others. [12]If you put yourself above others, you will be put down. But if you humble yourself, you will be honored.

[13-14]You Pharisees and teachers of the Law of Moses are in for trouble! You're nothing but show-offs. You lock people out of the kingdom of heaven. You won't go in yourselves, and you keep others from going in.[n]

[15]You Pharisees and teachers of the Law of Moses are in for trouble! You're nothing but show-offs. You travel over land and sea to win one follower. And when you have done so, you make that person twice as fit for hell as you are.

[16]You are in for trouble! You are supposed to lead others, but you are blind. You teach that it doesn't matter if a person swears by the temple. But you say it does matter if someone swears by the gold in the temple. [17]You blind fools! Which is greater, the gold or the temple that makes the gold sacred? [18]You also teach that it doesn't matter if a person swears by the altar. But you say it does matter if someone swears by the gift on the altar. [19]Are you blind? Which is more important, the gift or the altar that makes the gift sacred? [20]Anyone who swears by the altar also swears by everything on it. [21]And anyone who swears by the temple also swears by God, who lives there. [22]To swear by heaven is the same as swearing by God's throne and by the one who sits on that throne.

[23]You Pharisees and teachers are show-offs, and you're in for trouble! You give God a tenth of the spices from your garden, such as mint, dill, and cumin. Yet you neglect the more important matters of the Law, such as justice, mercy, and faithfulness. These are the important things you should have done, though you should not have left the others undone either. [24]You blind leaders! You strain out a small fly but swallow a camel.

[25]You Pharisees and teachers are show-offs, and you're in for trouble! You wash the outside of your cups and dishes, while inside there is nothing but greed and selfishness. [26]You blind Pharisee! First clean the inside of a cup, and then the outside will also be clean.

[27]You Pharisees and teachers are in for trouble! You're nothing but show-offs. You're like tombs that have been whitewashed.[o] On the outside they are beautiful, but inside they are full of bones and filth. [28]That's what you are like. Outside you look good, but inside you are evil and only pretend to be good.

[29]You Pharisees and teachers are

[n]23.13,14 *from going in:* Some manuscripts add, "You Pharisees and teachers are in for trouble! And you're nothing but show-offs! You cheat widows out of their homes and then pray long prayers just to show off. So you will be punished most of all."   [o]23.27 *whitewashed:* Tombs were whitewashed to keep anyone from accidentally touching them. A person who touched a dead body or a tomb was considered unclean and could not worship with the rest of the Jewish people.

23.37 *stoned the messengers:* It is unclear what prophets Jesus had in mind. Dropping or placing heavy stones on a criminal was a common form of capital punishment in Israelite society.

24.1,2 *temple . . . Not one stone will be left in place:* The temple that Herod built in Jerusalem. was made of large blocks of stone. Its foundation was nearly a mile around at the base, set on the same bedrock where King Solomon had built the first temple 900 years earlier. In A.D. 70, the Romans defeated the first Jewish revolt against them, captured Jerusalem, and destroyed Herod's temple. **(See the article People of the Law: The Religion of Israel on pg 1794.)**

24.3 *Mount of Olives:* The Mount of Olives is a ridge located just east of the temple area in Jerusalem. **(See Map 13 on pg 1891.)**

nothing but show-offs, and you're in for trouble! You build monuments for the prophets and decorate the tombs of good people. ³⁰And you claim you would not have taken part with your ancestors in killing the prophets. ³¹But you prove you really are the relatives of the ones who killed the prophets. ³²So keep on doing everything they did. ³³You are nothing but snakes and the children of snakes! How can you escape going to hell?

³⁴I will send to you prophets and wise people and experts in the Law of Moses. You will kill them or nail them to a cross or beat them in your synagogues or chase them from town to town. ³⁵That's why you will be held guilty for the murder of every good person, beginning with the good man Abel. This also includes Barachiah's son Zechariah,P the man you murdered between the temple and the altar. ³⁶I can promise that you people living today will be punished for all these things!

Jesus Loves Jerusalem
(Luke 13.34,35)

³⁷Jerusalem, Jerusalem! Your people have killed the prophets and have stoned the messengers who were sent to you. I have often wanted to gather your people, as a hen gathers her chicks under her wings. But you wouldn't let me. ³⁸And now your temple will be deserted. ³⁹You won't see me again until you say,

"Blessed is the one who comes
in the name of the Lord."

The Temple Will Be Destroyed
(Mark 13.1,2; Luke 21.5,6)

24 After Jesus left the temple, his disciples came over and said, "Look at all these buildings!"

²Jesus replied, "Do you see these buildings? They will certainly be torn down! Not one stone will be left in place."

Warning about Trouble
(Mark 13.3-13; Luke 21.7-19)

³Later, as Jesus was sitting on the Mount of Olives, his disciples came to him in private and asked, "When will this happen? What will be the sign of your coming and of the end of the world?"

⁴Jesus answered:

Don't let anyone fool you. ⁵Many will come and claim to be me. They will say they are the Messiah, and they will fool many people.

⁶You will soon hear about wars and threats of wars, but don't be afraid. These things will have to happen first, but that isn't the end. ⁷Nations and kingdoms will go to war against each other. People will starve to death, and in some places there will be earthquakes. ⁸But this is just the beginning of troubles.

⁹You will be arrested, punished, and even killed. Because of me, you will be hated by people of all nations. ¹⁰Many will give up and will betray and hate each other. ¹¹Many false prophets will come and fool a lot of people. ¹²Evil will spread and cause many people to stop loving others. ¹³But if you keep on being faithful right to the end, you

P23.35 *Zechariah:* Genesis is the first book in the Jewish Scriptures, and it tells that Abel was the first person to be murdered. Second Chronicles is the last book in the Jewish Scriptures, and the last murder that it tells about is that of Zechariah.

will be saved. [14]When the good news about the kingdom has been preached all over the world and told to all nations, the end will come.

The Horrible Thing
(Mark 13.14-23; Luke 21.20-24)

[15]Someday you will see that "Horrible Thing" in the holy place, just as the prophet Daniel said. Everyone who reads this must try to understand! [16]If you are living in Judea at that time, run to the mountains. [17]If you are on the roof[q] of your house, don't go inside to get anything. [18]If you are out in the field, don't go back for your coat. [19]It will be a terrible time for women who are expecting babies or nursing young children. [20]And pray that you won't have to escape in winter or on a Sabbath.[r] [21]This will be the worst time of suffering since the beginning of the world, and nothing this terrible will ever happen again. [22]If God doesn't make the time shorter, no one will be left alive. But because of God's chosen ones, he will make the time shorter. [23]Someone may say, "Here is the Messiah!" or "There he is!" But don't believe it. [24]False messiahs and false prophets will come and work great miracles and signs. They will even try to fool God's chosen ones. [25]But I have warned you ahead of time. [26]If you are told the Messiah is out in the desert, don't go there! And if you are told he is in some secret place, don't believe it! [27]The coming of the Son of Man will be like lightning that can be seen from east to west. [28]Where there is a corpse, there will always be vultures.[s]

When the Son of Man Appears
(Mark 13.24-27; Luke 21.25-28)

[29]Right after those days of suffering,
"The sun will become dark,
    and the moon
        will no longer shine.
The stars will fall,
    and the powers in the sky[t]
        will be shaken."

[30]Then a sign will appear in the sky. And there will be the Son of Man.[u] All nations on earth will weep when they see the Son of Man coming on the clouds of heaven with power and great glory. [31]At the sound of a loud trumpet, he will send his angels to bring his chosen ones together from all over the earth.

A Lesson from a Fig Tree
(Mark 13.28-31; Luke 21.29-33)

[32]Learn a lesson from a fig tree. When its branches sprout and start putting out leaves, you know summer is near.

[q]24.17 *roof*: In Palestine the houses usually had a flat roof. Stairs on the outside led up to the roof, which was made of beams and boards covered with packed earth. [r]24.20 *in winter or on a Sabbath*: In Palestine the winters are cold and rainy and make travel difficult. The Jewish people were not allowed to travel much more than half a mile on the Sabbath. For these reasons it was hard for them to escape from their enemies in the winter or on a Sabbath. [s]24.28 *Where there is a corpse, there will always be vultures*: This saying may mean that when anything important happens, people soon know about it. Or the saying may mean that whenever something bad happens, curious people gather around and stare. But the word translated "vulture" also means "eagle" and may refer to the Roman army, which had an eagle as its symbol. [t]24.29 *the powers in the sky*: In ancient times people thought that the stars were spiritual powers. [u]24.30 *And there will be the Son of Man*: Or "And it will be the Son of Man."

⬤ 24.15 *"Horrible Thing"*: Jesus repeated Daniel's prophecy (see Dan 9.27; 11.31; 12.11). In 168 B.C., a Syrian ruler named Antiochus IV Epiphanes set up an altar to the Greek god Zeus in the temple. Within three years, the people of Judea got rid of this altar and reclaimed the temple. This event is still celebrated in the Temple Festival, also known as Hanukkah.

⬤ 24.17 *roof*: In Palestine the houses usually had a flat roof. Stairs or a ladder on the outside led up to the roof, which was made of beams and boards covered with packed earth. When people wanted to get fresh air, they often went out into their courtyard or up on the roof.

24.37 *Noah:* Noah was a good and faithful man. God chose him and his family to build a big boat (ark) that would save humanity and other living things from the flood (see Gen 6.5-8).

25.1-4 *ten young women took their oil lamps. . . . to meet the groom:* It was the custom for the groom to go to the home of the bride's parents to get the bride. Young women and other guests would then go with them to the home of the groom's parents, where the wedding feast would take place. Since lamps needed oil to burn, some of the young women were prepared, because they brought extra oil.

³³So when you see all these things happening, you will know the time has almost come.ᵛ ³⁴I can promise you that some of the people of this generation will still be alive when all this happens. ³⁵The sky and the earth won't last forever, but my words will.

No One Knows the Day or Time
(Mark 13.32-37; Luke 17.26-30,34-36)

³⁶No one knows the day or hour. The angels in heaven don't know, and the Son himself doesn't know.ʷ Only the Father knows. ³⁷When the Son of Man appears, things will be just as they were when Noah lived. ³⁸People were eating, drinking, and getting married right up to the day the flood came and Noah went into the big boat. ³⁹They didn't know anything was happening until the flood came and swept them all away. This is how it will be when the Son of Man appears.

⁴⁰Two men will be in the same field, but only one will be taken. The other will be left. ⁴¹Two women will be together grinding grain, but only one will be taken. The other will be left. ⁴²So be on your guard! You don't know when your Lord will come. ⁴³Homeowners never know when a thief is coming, and they are always on guard to keep one from breaking in. ⁴⁴Always be ready! You don't know when the Son of Man will come.

Faithful and Unfaithful Servants
(Luke 12.35-48)

⁴⁵Who are faithful and wise servants? Who are the ones the master will put in charge of giving the other servants their food supplies at the proper time? ⁴⁶Servants are fortunate if their master comes and finds them doing their job. ⁴⁷You may be sure a servant who is always faithful will be put in charge of everything the master owns. ⁴⁸But suppose one of the servants thinks the master won't return until late. ⁴⁹Suppose this evil servant starts beating the other servants and eats and drinks with people who are drunk. ⁵⁰If that happens, the master will surely come on a day and at a time when the servant least expects him. ⁵¹This servant will then be punished and thrown out with the ones who only pretended to serve their master. There they will cry and grit their teeth in pain.

A Story about Ten Young Women

25 The kingdom of heaven is like what happened one night when ten young women took their oil lamps and went to a wedding to meet the groom.ˣ ²Five of them were foolish and five were wise. ³The foolish ones took their lamps, but no extra oil. ⁴The ones who were wise took along extra oil for their lamps.

⁵The groom was late arriving, and the young women became drowsy and fell asleep. ⁶Then in the middle of the

ᵛ**24.33** *the time has almost come:* Or "he (that is, the Son of Man) will soon be here." ʷ**24.36** *and the Son himself doesn't know:* These words are not in some manuscripts. ˣ**25.1** *to meet the groom:* Some manuscripts add "and the bride." It was the custom for the groom to go to the home of the bride's parents to get his bride. Young women and other guests would then go with them to the home of the groom's parents, where the wedding feast would take place.

Jesus taught, "*Always be ready! You don't know when the Son of Man will come.*" MATT 24.44

night someone shouted, "Here's the groom! Come to meet him!"

7 When the women got up and started getting their lamps ready, **8** the foolish ones said to the others, "Let us have some of your oil! Our lamps are going out."

9 Those who were wise answered, "There's not enough oil for all of us! Go and buy some for yourselves."

10 While the foolish ones were on their way to get some oil, the groom arrived. The five who were ready went into the wedding, and the doors were closed. **11** Later the others returned and shouted, "Sir, sir! Open the door for us!"

12 But the groom replied, "I don't even know you!"

13 So, my disciples, always be ready! You don't know the day or the time when all this will happen.

A Story about Three Servants
(Luke 19.11-27)

14 The kingdom is also like what happened when a man went away and put his three servants in charge of all he owned. **15** The man knew what each servant could do. So he handed 5,000 coins to the first servant, 2,000 to the second, and 1,000 to the third. Then he left the country.

16 As soon as the man had gone, the servant with the 5,000 coins used them to earn 5,000 more. **17** The servant who had 2,000 coins did the same with his money and earned 2,000 more. **18** But the servant with 1,000 coins dug a hole and hid his master's money in the ground.

19 Some time later the master of those servants returned. He called them in and asked what they had done with his money. **20** The servant who had been given 5,000 coins brought them in with the 5,000 that he had earned. He said, "Sir, you gave me 5,000 coins, and I have earned 5,000 more."

21 "Wonderful!" his master replied. "You are a good and faithful servant. I left you in charge of only a little, but now I will put you in charge of much more. Come and share in my happiness!"

22 Next, the servant who had been given 2,000 coins came in and said, "Sir, you gave me 2,000 coins, and I have earned 2,000 more."

23 "Wonderful!" his master replied. "You are a good and faithful servant. I left you in charge of only a little, but now I will put you in charge of much more. Come and share in my happiness!"

24 The servant who had been given 1,000 coins then came in and said, "Sir, I know that you are hard to work for. You harvest what you don't plant and gather crops where you haven't scattered seed. **25** I was frightened and went out and hid your money in the ground. Here is every single coin!"

26 The master of the servant told him, "You are lazy and good-for-nothing! You know I harvest what I don't plant and gather crops where I haven't scattered seed. **27** You could have at least put my money in the bank, so I could have earned interest on it."

28 Then the master said, "Now your money will be taken away and given to the servant with 10,000 coins! **29** Everyone who has something will be given more, and they will have more than enough. But everything will be taken from those who don't have anything. **30** You are a worthless servant, and you will be thrown out into the dark

25.27 *bank:* Bankers in Jesus' day changed foreign money for the local money. They also helped businesses by investing money and giving out loans. Most people, however, did not give their money to bankers. They often buried or hid it. As a result, they didn't earn any profit or interest.

26.2 *Passover:* Passover celebrates how God helped the people of Israel escape from slavery in Egypt (Exod 12.1-27). It was to be celebrated on the fourteenth day of the first month starting at twilight. The Festival of Thin Bread began the next day and lasted for seven days (Lev 23.4-8; Num 28.16-25).

Passover and the Festival of Thin Bread

26.3 *chief priests and the nation's leaders . . . at the home of Caiaphas the high priest:* The Romans appointed Caiaphas to be the high priest in Jerusalem, and he served from A.D. 18 to 26. The high priest also was in charge of a powerful council made up of priests and other Jewish leaders. The Romans allowed this council to make most decisions about local matters. **(See the article People of the Law: The Religion of Israel on pg 1794.)**

26.5 *must not do it during Passover:* Many people would have been in the city to celebrate Passover. The leaders didn't want so many people to see Jesus arrested. They were afraid that the followers of Jesus might riot against them.

where people will cry and grit their teeth in pain."

The Final Judgment

³¹When the Son of Man comes in his glory with all his angels, he will sit on his royal throne. ³²The people of all nations will be brought before him, and he will separate them, as shepherds separate their sheep from their goats. ³³He will place the sheep on his right and the goats on his left. ³⁴Then the king will say to those on his right, "My father has blessed you! Come and receive the kingdom that was prepared for you before the world was created. ³⁵When I was hungry, you gave me something to eat, and when I was thirsty, you gave me something to drink. When I was a stranger, you welcomed me, ³⁶and when I was naked, you gave me clothes to wear. When I was sick, you took care of me, and when I was in jail, you visited me."

³⁷Then the ones who pleased the Lord will ask, "When did we give you something to eat or drink? ³⁸When did we welcome you as a stranger or give you clothes to wear ³⁹or visit you while you were sick or in jail?"

⁴⁰The king will answer, "Whenever you did it for any of my people, no matter how unimportant they seemed, you did it for me."

⁴¹Then the king will say to those on his left, "Get away from me! You are under God's curse. Go into the everlasting fire prepared for the devil and his angels! ⁴²I was hungry, but you did not give me anything to eat, and I was thirsty, but you did not give me anything to drink. ⁴³I was a stranger, but

ʸ**26.6** *leprosy:* See the note at 8.2.

you did not welcome me, and I was naked, but you did not give me any clothes to wear. I was sick and in jail, but you did not take care of me."

⁴⁴Then the people will ask, "Lord, when did we fail to help you when you were hungry or thirsty or a stranger or naked or sick or in jail?"

⁴⁵The king will say to them, "Whenever you failed to help any of my people, no matter how unimportant they seemed, you failed to do it for me."

⁴⁶Then Jesus said, "Those people will be punished forever. But the ones who pleased God will have eternal life."

The Plot To Kill Jesus
(Mark 14.1,2; Luke 22.1,2; John 11.45-53)

26 When Jesus had finished teaching, he told his disciples, ²"You know two days from now will be Passover. This is when the Son of Man will be handed over to his enemies and nailed to a cross."

³At that time the chief priests and the nation's leaders were meeting at the home of Caiaphas the high priest. ⁴They planned how they could sneak around and have Jesus arrested and put to death. ⁵But they said, "We must not do it during Passover, because the people will riot."

At Bethany
(Mark 14.3-9; John 12.1-8)

⁶Jesus was in the town of Bethany, eating at the home of Simon, who had leprosy.ʸ ⁷A woman came in with a bottle of expensive perfume and poured it on Jesus' head. ⁸But when his disciples saw this, they became angry and complained, "Why such a waste? ⁹We could have sold this perfume for a lot of money and given it to the poor."

"Whenever you did it for any of my people, no matter how unimportant they seemed, you did it for me." Matt 25.40

[10]Jesus knew what they were thinking, and he said:

Why are you bothering this woman? She has done a beautiful thing for me. [11]You will always have the poor with you, but you won't always have me. [12]She has poured perfume on my body to prepare it for burial.[z] [13]You may be sure that wherever the good news is told all over the world, people will remember what she has done. And they will tell others.

Judas and the Chief Priests
(Mark 14.10,11; Luke 22.3-6)

[14]Judas Iscariot[a] was one of the twelve disciples. He went to the chief priests [15]and asked, "How much will you give me if I help you arrest Jesus?" They paid Judas 30 silver coins, [16]and from then on he started looking for a good chance to betray Jesus.

Jesus Eats the Passover Meal with His Disciples
(Mark 14.12-21; Luke 22.7-13; John 13.21-30)

[17]On the first day of the Festival of Thin Bread, Jesus' disciples came to him and asked, "Where do you want us to prepare the Passover meal?"

[18]Jesus told them to go to a certain man in the city and tell him, "Our teacher says, 'My time has come! I want to eat the Passover meal with my disciples in your home.'" [19]They did as Jesus told them and prepared the meal.

[20-21]When Jesus was eating with his twelve disciples that evening, he said, "One of you will surely hand me over to my enemies."

[22]The disciples were very sad, and each one said to Jesus, "Lord, you can't mean me!"

[23]He answered, "One of you men who has eaten with me from this dish will betray me. [24]The Son of Man will die, as the Scriptures say. But it's going to be terrible for the one who betrays me! That man would be better off if he had never been born."

[25]Judas said, "Teacher, you surely don't mean me!"

"That's what you say!" Jesus replied. But later, Judas did betray him.

The Lord's Supper
(Mark 14.22-26; Luke 22.14-23; 1 Corinthians 11.23-25)

[26]During the meal Jesus took some bread in his hands. He blessed the bread and broke it. Then he gave it to his disciples and said, "Take this and eat it. This is my body."

[27]Jesus picked up a cup of wine and gave thanks to God. He then gave it to his disciples and said, "Take this and drink it. [28]This is my blood, and with it God makes his agreement with you. It will be poured out, so that many people will have their sins forgiven. [29]From now on I am not going to drink any wine, until I drink new wine with you in my Father's kingdom." [30]Then they sang a hymn and went out to the Mount of Olives.

Peter's Promise
(Mark 14.27-31; Luke 22.31-34; John 13.36-38)

[31]Jesus said to his disciples, "During this very night, all of you will reject me, as the Scriptures say,

'I will strike down
    the shepherd,

● 26.12 *poured perfume . . . to prepare it for burial:* Giving someone a proper burial was very important. Sometimes people anointed the dead with oil and put spices on the body to help preserve it. Jesus said the woman was preparing his body for burial, but what she did is also a reminder that Jesus is God's anointed one.

● 26.26-28 *This is my body . . . This is my blood:* A young lamb was always sacrificed and eaten as part of the Passover celebration. Jesus used the bread and wine to show how his life would be sacrificed to forgive sins. This sacrifice was the basis for the new agreement (covenant) between God and God's new people. Christians celebrate this event in a ceremony that is called the Lord's Supper, Holy Communion, or Eucharist.

---

[z]**26.12** *poured perfume on my body to prepare it for burial:* The Jewish people taught that giving someone a proper burial was even more important than helping the poor.   [a]**26.14** *Iscariot:* See the note at 10.4.

26.36 *Gethsemane*: Gethsemane was probably on the east side of the Kidron Valley in the area near the Mount of Olives. (See Map 13 on pg 1891.)

and the sheep
    will be scattered.'
32But after I am raised to life, I will go ahead of you to Galilee."

33Peter spoke up, "Even if all the others reject you, I never will!"

34Jesus replied, "I promise you before a rooster crows tonight, you will say three times that you don't know me." **35**But Peter said, "Even if I have to die with you, I will never say I don't know you."

All the others said the same thing.

Jesus Prays
(Mark 14.32-42; Luke 22.39-46)

36Jesus went with his disciples to a place called Gethsemane. When they got there, he told them, "Sit here while I go over there and pray."

37Jesus took along Peter and the two brothers, James and John.[b] He was very sad and troubled, **38**and he said to them, "I am so sad that I feel as if I am dying. Stay here and keep awake with me."

39Jesus walked on a little way. Then he knelt with his face to the ground and prayed, "My Father, if it is possible, don't make me suffer by drinking from this cup.[c] But do what you want, and not what I want."

40He came back and found his disciples sleeping. So he said to Peter, "Can't any of you stay awake with me for just one hour? **41**Stay awake and pray that you won't be tested. You want to do what is right, but you are weak."

42Again Jesus went to pray and said, "My Father, if there is no other way, and I must suffer, I will still do what you want."

43Jesus came back and found them sleeping again. They simply could not keep their eyes open. **44**He left them and prayed the same prayer once more.

45Finally, Jesus returned to his disciples and said, "Are you still sleeping and resting?[d] The time has come for the Son of Man to be handed over to sinners. **46**Get up! Let's go. The one who will betray me is already here."

Jesus Is Arrested
(Mark 14.43-50; Luke 22.47-53; John 18.3-12)

47Jesus was still speaking, when Judas the betrayer came up. He was one of the twelve disciples, and a large mob armed with swords and clubs was with him. They had been sent by the chief priests and the nation's leaders. **48**Judas had told them ahead of time, "Arrest the man I greet with a kiss."[e]

49Judas walked right up to Jesus and said, "Hello, teacher." Then Judas kissed him.

50Jesus replied, "My friend, do what you came for."[f]

The men grabbed Jesus and arrested him. **51**One of Jesus' followers pulled out a sword. He struck the servant of the high priest and cut off his ear.

52But Jesus told him, "Put your sword away. Anyone who lives by fighting will die by fighting. **53**Don't you know that I could ask my Father, and he would at once send me more than twelve armies of angels? **54**But then, how could the words of the Scriptures come true, which say this must happen?"

55Jesus said to the mob, "Why do you come with swords and clubs to arrest me

[b]**26.37** *the two brothers, James and John*: The Greek text has "the two sons of Zebedee" (see 27.56). [c]**26.39** *by drinking from this cup*: In the Scriptures "to drink from a cup" sometimes means to suffer (see the note at 20.22). [d]**26.45** *Are you still sleeping and resting*: Or "You may as well keep on sleeping and resting." [e]**26.48** *the man I greet with a kiss*: It was the custom for people to greet each other with a kiss on the cheek. [f]**26.50** *do what you came for*: Or "why are you here?"

Jesus told him, "Put your sword away. Anyone who lives by fighting will die by fighting." MATT 26.52

like a criminal? Day after day I sat and taught in the temple, and you didn't arrest me. [56]But all this happened, so that what the prophets wrote would come true."

All Jesus' disciples left him and ran away.

Jesus Is Questioned by the Council

(Mark 14.53-65; Luke 22.54,55,63-71; John 18.13,14,19-24)

[57]After Jesus had been arrested, he was led off to the house of Caiaphas the high priest. The nation's leaders and the teachers of the Law of Moses were meeting there. [58]But Peter followed along at a distance and came to the courtyard of the high priest's palace. He went in and sat down with the guards to see what was going to happen.

[59]The chief priests and the whole council wanted to put Jesus to death. So they tried to find some people who would tell lies about him in court.[g] [60]But they could not find any, even though many did come and tell lies. At last, two men came forward [61]and said, "This man claimed he could tear down God's temple and build it again in three days."

[62]The high priest stood up and asked Jesus, "Why don't you say something in your own defense? Don't you hear the charges they are making against you?" [63]But Jesus did not answer. So the high priest said, "With the living God looking on, you must tell the truth. Are you the Messiah, the Son of God?"[h]

[64]"That is what you say!" Jesus answered. "But I tell all of you,

'Soon you will see
    the Son of Man

sitting at the right side[i]
    of God All-Powerful
and coming on the clouds
    of heaven.'"

[65]The high priest then tore his robe and said, "This man claims to be God! We don't need any more witnesses! You have heard what he said. [66]What do you think?"

They answered, "He is guilty and deserves to die!" [67]Then they spit in his face and hit him with their fists. Others slapped him [68]and said, "You think you are the Messiah! So tell us who hit you!"

Peter Says He Doesn't Know Jesus

(Mark 14.66-72; Luke 22.56-62; John 18.15-18,25-27)

[69]While Peter was sitting out in the courtyard, a servant girl came up to him and said, "You were with Jesus from Galilee."

[70]But in front of everyone Peter said, "That isn't so! I don't know what you are talking about!"

[71]When Peter had gone out to the gate, another servant girl saw him and said to some people there, "This man was with Jesus from Nazareth."

[72]Again Peter denied it, and this time he swore, "I don't even know that man!"

[73]A little while later some people standing there walked over to Peter and said, "We know you are one of them. We can tell it because you talk like someone from Galilee."

[74]Peter began to curse and swear, "I don't know that man!"

Right then a rooster crowed, [75]and Peter remembered that Jesus had said, "Before a rooster crows, you will say three times you

26.57,58 *house of Caiaphas . . . high priest's palace:* The word translated as "palace" can also refer to the courtyard of the high priest's house. So the action in these verses is taking place at the same location, not two different ones.

26.59,60 *whole council . . . two men came forward:* In addition to the chief priests, this council was made up of local government and Jewish religious leaders. They had the authority to decide cases of local matters and to see that people obeyed laws. The Law of Moses taught that two witnesses were needed before a person could be put to death (see Num 35.30).

26.63 *Messiah, the Son of God:* "Son of God" was one of the titles used for the kings of Israel (Ps 2.7).

26.66 *deserves to die:* The high priest and the council thought Jesus was claiming to be God, which the Law said was a very terrible sin. A person who claimed to be God was guilty of shaming God's name (blasphemy) and could be sentenced to death.

---

[g]26.59 *some people who would tell lies about him in court:* The Law of Moses taught that two witnesses were necessary before a person could be put to death (see verse 60).   [h]26.63 *Son of God:* One of the titles used for the kings of Israel.   [i]26.64 *right side:* See the note at 22.44.

don't know me." Then Peter went out and cried bitterly.

Jesus Is Taken to Pilate
(Mark 15.1; Luke 23.1,2; John 18.28-32)

27 Early the next morning all the chief priests and the nation's leaders met and decided that Jesus should be put to death. **2**They tied him up and led him away to Pilate the governor.

The Death of Judas
(Acts 1.18,19)

3Judas had betrayed Jesus, but when he learned that Jesus had been sentenced to death, he was sorry for what he had done. He returned the 30 silver coins to the chief priests and leaders **4**and said, "I have sinned by betraying a man who has never done anything wrong."

"So what? That's your problem," they replied. **5**Judas threw the money into the temple and then went out and hanged himself.

6The chief priests picked up the money and said, "This money was paid to have a man killed. We can't put it in the temple treasury." **7**Then they had a meeting and decided to buy a field that belonged to someone who made clay pots. They wanted to use it as a graveyard for foreigners. **8**This is why people still call that place "Field of Blood." **9**So the words of the prophet Jeremiah came true,

"They took
the thirty silver coins,
the price of a person
among the people of Israel.
10They paid it
for a potter's field,j

as the Lord
had commanded me."

Pilate Questions Jesus
(Mark 15.2-5; Luke 23.3-5; John 18.33-38)

11Jesus was brought before Pilate the governor, who asked him, "Are you the king of the Jews?"

"Those are your words!" Jesus answered. **12**And when the chief priests and leaders brought their charges against him, he did not say a thing.

13Pilate asked him, "Don't you hear what crimes they say you have done?" **14**But Jesus did not say anything, and the governor was greatly amazed.

The Death Sentence
(Mark 15.6-15; Luke 23.13-26; John 18.39—19.16)

15During Passover the governor always freed a prisoner chosen by the people. **16**At that time a well-known terrorist named Jesus Barabbask was in jail. **17**So when the crowd came together, Pilate asked them, "Which prisoner do you want me to set free? Do you want Jesus Barabbas or Jesus who is called the Messiah?" **18**Pilate knew the leaders had brought Jesus to him because they were jealous.

19While Pilate was judging the case, his wife sent him a message. It said, "Don't have anything to do with that innocent man. I have had nightmares because of him."

20But the chief priests and the leaders convinced the crowds to ask for Barabbas to be set free and for Jesus to be killed. **21**Pilate asked the crowd again, "Which of these two men do you want me to set free?"

"Barabbas!" they shouted.

22Pilate asked them, "What am I to do with Jesus, who is called the Messiah?"

j**27.10** *a potter's field*: Perhaps a field owned by someone who made clay pots. But it may have been a field where potters came to get clay or to make pots or to throw away their broken pieces of pottery.   k**27.16** *Jesus Barabbas*: Here and in verse 17 many manuscripts have "Barabbas."

They all yelled, "Nail him to a cross!"
²³Pilate answered, "But what crime has he done?"

"Nail him to a cross!" they yelled even louder.

²⁴Pilate saw that there was nothing he could do and that the people were starting to riot. So he took some water and washed his hands^l in front of them and said, "I won't have anything to do with killing this man. You are the ones doing it!"

²⁵Everyone answered, "We and our own families will take the blame for his death!"

²⁶Pilate set Barabbas free. Then he ordered his soldiers to beat Jesus with a whip and nail him to a cross.

Soldiers Make Fun of Jesus
(Mark 15.16-21; John 19.2,3)

²⁷The governor's soldiers led Jesus into the fortress^m and brought together the rest of the troops. ²⁸They stripped off Jesus' clothes and put a scarlet robeⁿ on him. ²⁹They made a crown out of thorn branches and placed it on his head, and they put a stick in his right hand. The soldiers knelt down and pretended to worship him. They made fun of him and shouted, "Hey, you king of the Jews!" ³⁰Then they spit on him. They took the stick from him and beat him on the head with it.

Jesus Is Nailed to a Cross
(Mark 15.22-32; Luke 23.27-43; John 19.17-27)

³¹When the soldiers had finished making fun of Jesus, they took off the robe. They put his own clothes back on him and led him off to be nailed to a cross. ³²On the way they met a man named Simon who was from Cyrene, and they forced him to carry Jesus' cross.

³³They came to a place named Golgotha, which means "Place of a Skull."^o ³⁴There they gave Jesus some wine mixed with a drug to ease the pain. But when Jesus tasted what it was, he refused to drink it.

³⁵The soldiers nailed Jesus to a cross and gambled to see who would get his clothes. ³⁶Then they sat down to guard him. ³⁷Above his head they put a sign that told why he was nailed there. It read, "This is Jesus, the King of the Jews." ³⁸The soldiers also nailed two criminals on crosses, one to the right of Jesus and the other to his left.

³⁹People who passed by said terrible things about Jesus. They shook their heads and ⁴⁰shouted, "So you're the one who claimed you could tear down the temple and build it again in three days! If you are God's Son, save yourself and come down from the cross!"

⁴¹The chief priests, the leaders, and the teachers of the Law of Moses also made fun of Jesus. They said, ⁴²"He saved others, but he can't save himself. If he is the king of Israel, he should come down from the cross! Then we will believe him. ⁴³He trusted God, so let God save him, if he wants to. He even said he was God's Son." ⁴⁴The two criminals also said cruel things to Jesus.

The Death of Jesus
(Mark 15.33-41; Luke 23.44-49; John 19.28-30)

⁴⁵At noon the sky turned dark and stayed that way until three o'clock. ⁴⁶Then about that time Jesus shouted, "Eli, Eli,

---

^l27.24 *washed his hands*: To show that he was innocent.   ^m27.27 *fortress*: The place where the Roman governor stayed. It was probably at Herod's palace west of Jerusalem, though it may have been Fortress Antonia north of the temple, where the Roman troops were stationed.   ⁿ27.28 *scarlet robe*: This was probably a Roman soldier's robe.   ^o27.33 *Place of a Skull*: The place was probably given this name because it was near a large rock in the shape of a human skull.

● 27.24 *Pilate . . . washed his hands*: Pilate did this to show that it was the leaders' decision to put Jesus to death on a cross, not his; although an execution would not have happened without his final approval.

● 27.32 *a man named Simon . . . from Cyrene*: Cyrene was a city in North Africa. Simon was probably a Jew who came to Jerusalem to celebrate Passover and the Festival of Thin Bread.

● 27.33 *Golgotha . . . "Place of a Skull"*: The Latin translation of Golgotha is *calvaria*, which entered the English language as Calvary. This place of execution was on a hill outside the walls of Jerusalem, and was probably intended to intimidate people entering the city. **(See Map 13 on pg 1891.)**

⊂⋈   Crucifixion

● 27.34 *wine mixed with a drug to ease the pain*: The drug was probably a juice made from the bitter and poisonous herb called gall. This juice could have made Jesus unconscious or even made him die faster.

● 27.46 *Eli . . . sabachthani*: This statement comes from the Hebrew Psalm 22.1, but is quoted here in Aramaic, the language spoken by Jews in Palestine at this time.

27.47-49 *Elijah . . . Elijah will come:* The name "Elijah" sounds like "Eli," which means "my god." The Jewish people expected the prophet Elijah to come and prepare the way for the Messiah (see Mal 4.5,6) and so many thought Jesus was calling for Elijah.

27.56 *Mary Magdalene:* Her name probably means that she was from Magdala, a town on the western edge of Lake Galilee. Other Gospels tell how Jesus healed her (see Mark 16.9; Luke 8.2,3). As a follower of Jesus, she may have traveled with a group of Jesus' closest friends.

27.57 *Joseph from the town of Arimathea:* Arimathea was a small village in the hilly area called Ephraim, which was about 20 miles northwest of Jerusalem. Because Joseph was rich, he probably had money to pay Pilate and the guards, so he could take the body.

28.1 *Sabbath was over:* The Jewish Sabbath lasted from sundown on Friday until sundown on Saturday. When the daylight came on the next morning, which was Sunday, the women could walk to the tomb and put spices on Jesus' body.

lema sabachthani?"P which means, "My God, my God, why have you deserted me?"

⁴⁷Some of the people standing there heard Jesus and said, "He's calling for Elijah."q ⁴⁸One of them at once ran and grabbed a sponge. He soaked it in wine, then put it on a stick and held it up to Jesus.

⁴⁹Others said, "Wait! Let's see if Elijah will comer and save him." ⁵⁰Once again Jesus shouted, and then he died.

⁵¹At once the curtain in the temples was torn in two from top to bottom. The earth shook, and rocks split apart. ⁵²Graves opened, and many of God's people were raised to life. ⁵³They left their graves, and after Jesus had risen to life, they went into the holy city, where they were seen by many people.

⁵⁴The officer and the soldiers guarding Jesus felt the earthquake and saw everything else that happened. They were frightened and said, "This man really was God's Son!"

⁵⁵Many women had come with Jesus from Galilee to be of help to him, and they were there, looking on at a distance. ⁵⁶Mary Magdalene, Mary the mother of James and Joseph, and the mother of James and Johnt were some of these women.

Jesus Is Buried
(Mark 15.42-47; Luke 23.50-56; John 19.38-42)

⁵⁷That evening a rich disciple named Joseph from the town of Arimathea ⁵⁸went and asked for Jesus' body. Pilate gave orders for it to be given to Joseph, ⁵⁹who took the body and wrapped it in a clean linen cloth. ⁶⁰Then Joseph put the body in his own tomb that had been cut into solid rocku and had never been used. He rolled a big stone against the entrance to the tomb and went away.

⁶¹All this time Mary Magdalene and the other Mary were sitting across from the tomb.

⁶²On the next day, which was a Sabbath, the chief priests and the Pharisees went together to Pilate. ⁶³They said, "Sir, we remember what this liar said while he was still alive. He claimed in three days he would come back from death. ⁶⁴So please order the tomb to be carefully guarded for three days. If you don't, his disciples may come and steal his body. They will tell the people he has been raised to life, and this last lie will be worse than the first one."v

⁶⁵Pilate said to them, "All right, take some of your soldiers and guard the tomb as well as you know how." ⁶⁶So they sealed it tight and placed soldiers there to guard it.

Jesus Is Alive
(Mark 16.1-8; Luke 24.1-12; John 20.1-10)

28 The Sabbath was over, and it was almost daybreak on Sunday when Mary Magdalene and the other Mary went to see the tomb. ²Suddenly a strong earthquake struck, and the Lord's angel came down from heaven. He rolled away the stone and sat on it. ³The angel looked as bright as lightning, and his clothes were

P**27.46** *Eli . . . sabachthani:* These words are in Hebrew.   q**27.47** *Elijah:* In Aramaic the name "Elijah" sounds like "Eli," which means "my God."   r**27.49** *Elijah will come:* See the note at 16.14.
s**27.51** *curtain in the temple:* There were two curtains in the temple. One was at the entrance, and the other separated the holy place from the most holy place that the Jewish people thought of as God's home on earth. The second curtain is probably the one that is meant.   t**27.56** *of James and John:* The Greek text has "of Zebedee's sons" (see 26.37).   u**27.60** *tomb . . . solid rock:* Some of the Jewish people buried their dead in rooms carved into solid rock. A heavy stone was rolled against the entrance.
v**27.64** *the first one:* Probably the belief that Jesus is the Messiah.

white as snow. **4**The guards shook from fear and fell down, as though they were dead.

5The angel said to the women, "Don't be afraid! I know you are looking for Jesus, who was nailed to a cross. **6**He isn't here! God has raised him to life, just as Jesus said he would. Come, see the place where his body was lying. **7**Now hurry! Tell his disciples he has been raised to life and is on his way to Galilee. Go there, and you will see him. This is what I came to tell you."

8The women were frightened and yet very happy, as they hurried from the tomb and ran to tell his disciples. **9**Suddenly Jesus met them and greeted them. They went near him, held on to his feet, and worshiped him. **10**Then Jesus said, "Don't be afraid! Tell my followers to go to Galilee. They will see me there."

Report of the Guard

11While the women were on their way, some soldiers who had been guarding the tomb went into the city. They told the chief priests everything that had happened. **12**So the chief priests met with the leaders and decided to bribe the soldiers with a lot of money. **13**They said to the soldiers, "Tell everyone that Jesus' disciples came during the night and stole his body while you were asleep. **14**If the governor[w] hears about this, we will talk to him. You won't have anything to worry about." **15**The soldiers took the money and did what they were told. The people of Judea still tell each other this story.

What Jesus' Followers Must Do
(Mark 16.14-18; Luke 24.36-49; John 20.19-23; Acts 1.6-8)

16Jesus' eleven disciples went to a mountain in Galilee, where Jesus had told them to meet him. **17**They saw him and worshiped him, but some of them doubted. **18**Jesus came to them and said:

I have been given all authority in heaven and on earth! **19**Go to the people of all nations and make them my disciples. Baptize them in the name of the Father, the Son, and the Holy Spirit, **20**and teach them to do everything I have told you. I will be with you always, even until the end of the world.

28.7 *Galilee:* This is the home area of Jesus in northern Palestine. **(See Map 12 on pg 1890.)**

28.19 *Baptize:* People who were baptized were usually dunked in a pool or stream of water. Jesus says that this was to be done in the name of God— the Father, Son, and Holy Spirit. Baptism was done to show that a person was now part of God's new people. Other New Testament writers describe baptism as dying to the old self and being born to a new life in Christ (see Rom 6.3,4).

Baptism

---

[w]**28.14** *governor:* Pontius Pilate.

Jesus said, "Go to the people of all nations and make them my disciples." MATT 28.19

Reflection Questions About Matthew 1.1—28.20

1. After John baptized Jesus, the Holy Spirit led Jesus into the desert (4.1-11). What happened there? How did Jesus respond to the things the devil suggested?

2. Who did Jesus choose to be his first followers (4.18-22)? What do you think Jesus meant when he told them that they would "bring in people instead of fish"? How can Jesus' followers today "bring in people"?

3. In the section known as the Sermon on the Mount (5.1—7.27), Jesus taught many things. Choose five of Jesus' teachings that you find most challenging. How can applying these lessons improve your life and strengthen your faith?

4. What is the purpose of prayer (6.5-15)? What sorts of things does Jesus want his followers to pray for? What is the relationship of prayer and forgiveness?

5. Jesus chose Matthew, a tax collector, to be one of his disciples (9.9-13). Why was this consid-ered unusual? What did Jesus say to the Phar-isees who criticized him for this? How do you treat people that society calls "sinners"?

6. What is the good news that Jesus talks about (11.4-6)? Who are messengers of the good news today? What message do they tell, and why is it good news?

7. Jesus uses a number of images and parables to describe the kingdom of heaven (13.1-52). Choose one of these and explain what you think it means.

8. Read what Jesus had to say about the Law of Moses (22.36-40). Explain what you think Jesus means in 22.40.

9. Jesus told his disciples, "Always be ready!" (25.13) How does one "get ready" for Jesus?

10. After God raised Jesus to life, what did Jesus tell his followers to do (28.19,20)? What does this message mean for Jesus' followers today?

mark

Sometimes good news needs to be kept secret until the time is right. The big secret in MARK is the answer to the question, "Who is Jesus?"

WHAT MAKES MARK SPECIAL?

The first verse announces that MARK is the "good news about Jesus Christ, the Son of God." The rest of the book describes how Jesus showed that he truly is the Son of God. MARK is the shortest and probably the oldest of the four Gospels included in the New Testament. It tells about many of Jesus' miracles and healings. But according to MARK, the most powerful miracle of Jesus is his suffering and death. The first person in the Gospel who appears to understand this miracle is a Roman officer who sees Jesus die on the cross and says, "This man really was the Son of God!" (15.39).

MARK provides answers to some important questions like:
• How does Jesus fulfill prophecies made in the Old Testament?
• How is Jesus the Son of God and how will Jesus be seen in the future as the Son of Man?
• How and why did Jesus die, and how will he return?
• How should the new people of God live?

Reading MARK is a little like reading a mystery. The author gives clues to help people discover Jesus' true identity. Throughout the book, Jesus reminds people, and even the demons, not to tell anyone who he really is or what he has done. Just before the end of the book, a Roman army officer identifies Jesus as the Son of God, which is how he is described at the beginning.

WHAT'S THE STORY BEHIND THE SCENE?

MATTHEW and LUKE include most of what is written in MARK, but they arrange the material differently and add to it. Because the book explains Aramaic words and Jewish customs to readers, scholars think that Mark wrote the Gospel so that Gentiles or non-Jewish Christians could understand it. The apostle Peter is especially important in this Gospel, and since Mark is connected with Peter in 1 Peter 5.13, it was believed by the second century A.D. that it was Mark who wrote the Gospel.

HOW IS MARK CONSTRUCTED?

MARK can be outlined in the following way:

Jesus prepares for his work (1.1-20)
Jesus does the work of God's kingdom in Galilee (1.21—9.50)
    Healings, miracles, and stories (1.21—8.26)
    Jesus is the Messiah (8.27—9.13)
    More work in Galilee (9.14-50)
Jesus teaches and works miracles in Judea (10.1-52)
Jesus in Jerusalem (11.1—15.47)
    Teachings in the temple (11.1—12.44)
    God's coming kingdom (13.1-37)
    Jesus prepares for his death (14.1-42)
    The final hours (14.43—15.47)
Jesus lives (16.1-20)

Mark is the earliest Gospel and most likely was written for a community of Gentiles in Rome around A.D. 70. It encourages readers to understand that suffering was a necessary part of Jesus' identity, and invites them to realize, as does the Roman army officer at the foot of the cross, that Jesus "really was the Son of God." Mark was written in a popular dramatic style. Though the author immediately lets the reader know who Jesus is, the story is told so that the reader can share the discovery with Jesus' disciples that Jesus is the Son of God. Mark often shows Jesus through the eyes of the disciple Peter. This Gospel does not have many long speeches, but instead tries to touch the hearts of those who hear it or read it with lively, simple, and direct writing.

Outline

The Preaching of John the Baptist

(Matthew 3.1-12; Luke 3.1-18; John 1.19-28)

1 This is the good news about Jesus Christ, the Son of God.[a] [2]It began just as God had said in the book written by Isaiah the prophet,

"I am sending my messenger
to get the way ready
    for you.
[3]In the desert
    someone is shouting,
'Get the road ready
    for the Lord!
Make a straight path
    for him.'"

[4]So John the Baptist showed up in the desert and told everyone, "Turn back to God and be baptized! Then your sins will be forgiven."

[5]From all Judea and Jerusalem crowds of people went to John. They told how sorry they were for their sins, and he baptized them in the Jordan River.

[6]John wore clothes made of camel's hair. He had a leather strap around his waist and ate grasshoppers and wild honey.

[7]John also told the people, "Someone more powerful is going to come. And I am not good enough even to stoop down and untie his sandals.[b] [8]I baptize you with water, but he will baptize you with the Holy Spirit!"

The Baptism of Jesus

(Matthew 3.13-17; Luke 3.21,22)

[9]About that time Jesus came from Nazareth in Galilee, and John baptized him in the Jordan River. [10]As soon as Jesus came out of the water, he saw the sky open and the Holy Spirit coming down to him like a dove. [11]A voice from heaven said, "You are my own dear Son, and I am pleased with you."

[a]1.1 the Son of God: These words are not in some manuscripts.   [b]1.7 untie his sandals: This was the duty of a slave.

1.2 *Isaiah the prophet:* A prophet in Judah from about 740 to 701 B.C.

1.4 *John the Baptist:* John was a prophet who preached in the desert. He baptized people with water, symbolizing the old way of life being washed away. John encouraged people to turn back to God and to be forgiven for their sins.

John the Baptist

1.4 *your sins will be forgiven:* People "sin" when they turn away from God and disobey God's commands. Forgiveness is God's way of pardoning those who are sorry for their sins.

1.5 *Judea and Jerusalem . . . Jordan River:* Judea was in the southern part of Palestine. Jerusalem was the most important center of worship in Jesus' day, because the temple was located there. The Jordan River, the longest river in Palestine, flows from the slopes of Mount Hermon to the Dead Sea. **(See Map 3 on pg 1881.)**

1.8 *baptize you with the Holy Spirit:* Baptism in the name of Jesus would make people completely new by giving them the gift of the Holy Spirit. The Holy Spirit is God's power at work in the world.

Holy Spirit

Baptism

This is the good news about Jesus Christ, the Son of God. MARK 1.1

1.13 *Satan . . . angels:* The word *Satan* means "adversary." Satan was also known as the devil ("accuser") or Beelzebul, the ruler of the demons. The word "angel" in English is based on the Greek word *angelos,* which means "messenger." Angels act both as messengers and servants of God.

Angels

1.15 *God's kingdom:* God's kingdom refers to the eternal rule of God, and this rule includes instructions on how people are to live in obedience to God.

1.16 *Lake Galilee:* Lake Galilee is located in the northern part of the Jordan River Valley. It is also known as the Sea of Galilee or Lake Gennesaret (Luke 5.1), and the Romans called it the Sea of Tiberias (John 6.1; 21.1).

Fish and Fishing

1.21 *Sabbath:* Sabbath was the seventh day of the week, the day that God rested after the work of creation (Gen 2.2,3). Sabbath means "rest," and it was a rule for all Jewish people to stop working on the Sabbath (Exod 20.8-11; Deut 5.12-15).

1.24 *God's Holy One:* The evil spirit knows who Jesus really is and calls him a name that probably refers to Jesus as being God's chosen Messiah.

Jesus and Satan
(Matthew 4.1-11; Luke 4.1-13)

[12]At once God's Spirit made Jesus go into the desert. [13]He stayed there for 40 days while Satan tested him. Jesus was with the wild animals, but angels took care of him.

Jesus Begins His Work
(Matthew 4.12-17; Luke 4.14,15)

[14]After John was arrested, Jesus went to Galilee and told the good news that comes from God.[c] [15]He said, "The time has come! God's kingdom will soon be here.[d] Turn back to God and believe the good news!"

Jesus Chooses Four Fishermen
(Matthew 4.18-22; Luke 5.1-11)

[16]As Jesus was walking along the shore of Lake Galilee, he saw Simon and his brother Andrew. They were fishermen and were casting their nets into the lake. [17]Jesus said to them, "Follow me! I will teach you how to bring in people instead of fish." [18]Right then the two brothers dropped their nets and went with him. [19]Jesus walked on and soon saw James and John, the sons of Zebedee. They were in a boat, mending their nets. [20]At once Jesus asked them to come with him. They left their father in the boat with the hired workers and went with him.

A Man with an Evil Spirit
(Luke 4.31-37)

[21]Jesus and his disciples went to the town of Capernaum. Then on the next Sabbath he went into the synagogue and started teaching. [22]Everyone was amazed at his teaching. He taught with authority, and not like the teachers of the Law of Moses. [23]Suddenly a man with an evil spirit[e] in him entered the synagogue and yelled, [24]"Jesus from Nazareth, what do you want with us? Have you come to destroy us? I know who you are! You are God's Holy One."

[25]Jesus told the evil spirit, "Be quiet and come out of the man!" [26]The spirit shook him. Then it gave a loud shout and left.

[27]Everyone was completely surprised and kept saying to each other, "What is this? It must be some new kind of powerful teaching! Even the evil spirits obey him." [28]News about Jesus quickly spread all over Galilee.

Jesus Heals Many People
(Matthew 8.14-17; Luke 4.38-41)

[29]As soon as Jesus left the synagogue with James and John, they went home with Simon and Andrew. [30]When they got there, Jesus was told that Simon's mother-in-law was sick in bed with fever. [31]Jesus went to her. He took hold of her hand and helped her up. The fever left her, and she served them a meal.

[32]That evening after sunset,[f] all who were sick or had demons in them were brought to Jesus. [33]In fact, the whole town gathered around the door of the house. [34]Jesus healed all kinds of terrible diseases and forced out a lot of demons. But the demons knew who he was, and he did not let them speak.

[35]Very early the next morning before

---

[c]**1.14** *that comes from God:* Or "that is about God."   [d]**1.15** *will soon be here:* Or "is already here."
[e]**1.23** *evil spirit:* A Jewish person who had an evil spirit was considered "unclean" and was not allowed to eat or worship with other Jewish people.   [f]**1.32** *after sunset:* The Sabbath was over, and a new day began at sunset.

daylight, Jesus got up and went to a place where he could be alone and pray. [36]Simon and the others started looking for him. [37]And when they found him, they said, "Everyone is looking for you!"

[38]Jesus replied, "We must go to the nearby towns, so that I can tell the good news to those people. This is why I have come." [39]Then Jesus went to their synagogues everywhere in Galilee, where he preached and forced out demons.

Jesus Heals a Man
(Matthew 8.1-4; Luke 5.12-16)

[40]A man with leprosy[g] came to Jesus and knelt down.[h] He begged, "You have the power to make me well, if only you wanted to."

[41]Jesus felt sorry for[i] the man. So he put his hand on him and said, "I want to! Now you are well." [42]At once the man's leprosy disappeared, and he was well.

[43]After Jesus strictly warned the man, he sent him on his way. [44]He said, "Don't tell anyone about this. Just go and show the priest that you are well. Then take a gift to the temple as Moses commanded, and everyone will know that you have been healed."[j]

[45]The man talked about it so much and told so many people, that Jesus could no longer go openly into a town. He had to stay away from the towns, but people still came to him from everywhere.

Jesus Heals a Man Who Could Not Walk
(Matthew 9.1-8; Luke 5.17-26)

[2]Jesus went back to Capernaum, and a few days later people heard that he was at home.[k] [2]Then so many of them came to the house that there wasn't even standing room left in front of the door.

Jesus was still teaching [3]when four people came up, carrying a man on a mat because he could not walk. [4]But because of the crowd, they could not get him to Jesus. So they made a hole in the roof[l] above him and let the man down in front of everyone.

[5]When Jesus saw how much faith they had, he said to the man, "My friend, your sins are forgiven."

[6]Some of the teachers of the Law of Moses were sitting there. They started wondering, [7]"Why would he say such a thing? He must think he is God! Only God can forgive sins."

[8]At once, Jesus knew what they were thinking, and he said, "Why are you thinking such things? [9]Is it easier for me to tell this man his sins are forgiven or to tell him to get up and pick up his mat and go on home? [10]I will show you that the Son of Man has the right to forgive sins here on earth." So Jesus said to the man, [11]"Get up! Pick up your mat and go on home."

[12]The man got right up. He picked up his mat and went out while everyone watched in amazement. They praised God and said, "We have never seen anything like this!"

[g]1.40 leprosy: In biblical times the word "leprosy" was used for many different kinds of skin diseases. [h]1.40 and knelt down: These words are not in some manuscripts. [i]1.41 felt sorry for: Some manuscripts have "was angry with." [j]1.44 everyone will know that you have been healed: People with leprosy had to be examined by a priest and told that they were well (that is, "clean") before they could once again live a normal life in the Jewish community. The gift that Moses commanded was the sacrifice of some lambs together with flour mixed with olive oil. [k]2.1 at home: Or "in the house" (perhaps Simon Peter's home). [l]2.4 roof: In Palestine the houses usually had a flat roof. Stairs on the outside led up to the roof that was made of beams and boards covered with packed earth.

2.1 Capernaum: This city was an important fishing town on the northern shore of Lake Galilee. It was located on the "high road," the major trade route between Egypt to the southwest and Syria to the northeast. In Jesus' day, Capernaum was a base for Roman soldiers who enforced the collection of taxes. (See Map 12 on pg 1890.)

2.10 Son of Man: The Bible often uses "Son of Man" simply to mean a human being, but the name was given a special meaning in DANIEL, where it refers to a savior—the person God will chose to rule over the world and its people. In the Gospels, Jesus uses the term in both ways to refer to himself.

Son of Man

2.16 *Pharisees:* The name *Pharisee* comes from Hebrew words that may mean "separate ones" or "pure ones." They believed in following God's law as closely as possible.

2.28 *Son of Man is Lord over the Sabbath:* What Jesus, the Son of Man, teaches and does has even more authority than the Law of Moses, which includes laws about the Sabbath.

Jesus Chooses Levi
(Matthew 9.9-13; Luke 5.27-32)

[13]Once again, Jesus went to the shore of Lake Galilee. A large crowd gathered around him, and he taught them. [14]As he walked along, he saw Levi, the son of Alphaeus. Levi was sitting at the place for paying taxes, and Jesus said to him, "Follow me!" So he got up and went with Jesus.

[15]Later, Jesus and his disciples were having dinner at Levi's house.[m] Many tax collectors[n] and other sinners had become followers of Jesus, and they were also guests at the dinner.

[16]Some of the teachers of the Law of Moses were Pharisees, and they saw Jesus eating with sinners and tax collectors. So they asked his disciples, "Why does he eat with tax collectors and sinners?"

[17]Jesus heard them and answered, "Healthy people don't need a doctor, but sick people do. I didn't come to invite good people to be my followers. I came to invite sinners."

People Ask about Going without Eating
(Matthew 9.14-17; Luke 5.33-39)

[18]The followers of John the Baptist and the Pharisees often went without eating.[o] Some people came and asked Jesus, "Why do the followers of John and those of the Pharisees often go without eating, while your disciples never do?"

[19]Jesus answered:

The friends of a bridegroom don't go without eating while he is still with them. [20]But the time will come when he will be taken from them. Then they will go without eating.

[21]No one patches old clothes by sewing on a piece of new cloth. The new piece would shrink and tear a bigger hole.

[22]No one pours new wine into old wineskins. The wine would swell and burst the old skins.[p] Then the wine would be lost, and the skins would be ruined. New wine must be put into new wineskins.

A Question about the Sabbath
(Matthew 12.1-8; Luke 6.1-5)

[23]One Sabbath Jesus and his disciples were walking through some wheat fields. His disciples were picking grains of wheat as they went along.[q] [24]Some Pharisees asked Jesus, "Why are your disciples picking grain on the Sabbath? They are not supposed to do that!"

[25]Jesus answered, "Haven't you read what David did when he and his followers were hungry and in need? [26]It was during the time of Abiathar the high priest. David went into the house of God and ate the sacred loaves of bread that only priests are allowed to eat. He also gave some to his followers."

[27]Jesus finished by saying, "People were not made for the good of the Sabbath. The Sabbath was made for the good of people. [28]So the Son of Man is Lord over the Sabbath."

[m]2.15 *Levi's house:* Or "Jesus' house." [n]2.15 *tax collectors:* These were usually Jewish people who paid the Romans for the right to collect taxes. They were hated by other Jews who thought of them as traitors to their country and to their religion. [o]2.18 *without eating:* The Jewish people sometimes went without eating (also called "fasting") to show their love for God or to show sorrow for their sins. [p]2.22 *swell and burst the old skins:* While the juice from grapes was becoming wine, it would swell and stretch the skins in which it had been stored. If the skins were old and stiff, they would burst. [q]2.23 *went along:* It was the custom to let hungry travelers pick grains of wheat.

A Man with a Paralyzed Hand

(Matthew 12.9-14; Luke 6.6-11)

3 The next time Jesus went into the synagogue, a man with a paralyzed hand was there. **2**The Pharisees[r] wanted to accuse Jesus of doing something wrong, and they kept watching to see if Jesus would heal him on the Sabbath.

3Jesus told the man to stand up where everyone could see him. **4**Then he asked, "On the Sabbath should we do good deeds or evil deeds? Should we save someone's life or destroy it?" But no one said a word.

5Jesus was angry as he looked around at the people. Yet he felt sorry for them because they were so stubborn. Then he told the man, "Stretch out your hand." He did, and his bad hand was healed.

6The Pharisees left. And at once they started making plans with Herod's followers[s] to kill Jesus.

Large Crowds Come to Jesus

7Jesus led his disciples down to the shore of the lake. Large crowds followed him from Galilee, Judea, **8**and Jerusalem. People came from Idumea, as well as other places east of the Jordan River. They also came from the region around the towns of Tyre and Sidon. All of these crowds came because they had heard what Jesus was doing. **9**He even had to tell his disciples to get a boat ready to keep him from being crushed by the crowds. **10**After Jesus had healed many people, the other sick people begged him to let them touch him. **11**And whenever any evil spirits saw Jesus, they would fall to the ground and shout, "You are the Son of God!" **12**But Jesus warned the spirits not to tell who he was.

Jesus Chooses His Twelve Apostles

(Matthew 10.1-4; Luke 6.12-16)

13Jesus decided to ask some of his disciples to go up on a mountain with him, and they went. **14**Then he chose twelve of them to be his apostles,[t] so they could be with him. He also wanted to send them out to preach **15**and to force out demons. **16**Simon was one of the twelve, and Jesus named him Peter. **17**There were also James and John, the two sons of Zebedee. Jesus called them Boanerges, which means "Thunderbolts." **18**Andrew, Philip, Bartholomew, Matthew, Thomas, James son of Alphaeus, and Thaddaeus were also apostles. The others were Simon, known as the Eager One,[u] **19**and Judas Iscariot,[v] who later betrayed Jesus.

Jesus and the Ruler of Demons

(Matthew 12.22-32; Luke 11.14-23; 12.10)

20Jesus went back home,[w] and once again such a large crowd gathered that there was no chance even to eat. **21**When Jesus' family heard what he was doing, they thought he was crazy and went to get him under control.

3.6 *Herod's followers:* Political followers of Herod Antipas, the son of Herod the Great. Herod Antipas ruled over Galilee and Perea from 4 B.C. to A.D. 39. The formal name for his title was tetrarch, but the people sometimes also called him a king (Matt 14.9).

3.8 *Idumea . . . Tyre and Sidon:* Idumea was the hill country south of the Dead Sea, which in the Old Testament is called Seir or Edom (Gen 32.3; Num 20.14-21). Tyre and Sidon were important non-Jewish port cities on the Mediterranean Sea in northern Palestine in what is now Lebanon. (See Map 12 on pg 1890.)

3.16-19 *the twelve . . . apostles:* A *disciple* means a follower who learns from a master teacher. The term *apostle* refers to a person chosen and sent by a leader to do a special job. Jesus gave these disciples the power to preach and force out evil spirits.

3.30 *evil spirit:* Evil spirits were understood to work for Satan. In Jesus' day, evil spirits or demons were believed to be the cause of many kinds of sickness and mental illness. A Jewish person who had an evil spirit was considered "unclean" and was not allowed to eat or worship with other Jews. People were afraid that the illness caused by the evil spirit would "rub off" on them, so unclean people were isolated from the group.

3.31 *Jesus' mother and brothers:* Jesus' mother is Mary (Luke 1.26—2.52). Jesus' family came to try to get him under control because they thought he was crazy. Mark 6.3 mentions the names of four brothers and says that he also had sisters.

4.2 *used stories to teach:* "Stories" is a translation of a Greek word that is often translated as "parables," and which means "to put things together in order to compare them." Usually parables are short stories told to teach a lesson.

Stories (Parables)

4.3 *farmer went out to scatter seed in a field:* Before planting seeds, a farmer usually prepared an area of ground by breaking it up and clearing it. Then he would plant or sow the seeds by scattering them a handful at a time. After that he would plow the seeds into the ground. **(See the article How People Made a Living in the Time of Jesus on pg 1813.)**

²²Some teachers of the Law of Moses came from Jerusalem and said, "This man is under the power of Beelzebul, the ruler of demons! He is even forcing out demons with the help of Beelzebul."

²³Jesus told the people to gather around him. Then he spoke to them in riddles and said:

How can Satan force himself out? ²⁴A nation whose people fight each other won't last very long. ²⁵And a family that fights won't last long either. ²⁶So if Satan fights against himself, that will be the end of him.

²⁷How can anyone break into the house of a strong man and steal his things, unless he first ties up the strong man? Then he can take everything.

²⁸I promise you that any of the sinful things you say or do can be forgiven, no matter how terrible those things are. ²⁹But if you speak against the Holy Spirit, you can never be forgiven. That sin will be held against you forever.

³⁰Jesus said this because the people were saying that he had an evil spirit in him.

Jesus' Mother and Brothers

(Matthew 12.46-50; Luke 8.19-21)

³¹Jesus' mother and brothers came and stood outside. Then they sent someone with a message for him to come out to them. ³²The crowd sitting around Jesus told him, "Your mother and your brothers and sisters^x are outside and want to see you."

³³Jesus asked, "Who is my mother and who are my brothers?" ³⁴Then he looked at the people sitting around him and said, "Here are my mother and my brothers. ³⁵Anyone who obeys God is my brother or sister or mother."

^x**3.32** *and sisters:* These words are not in some manuscripts.

A Story about a Farmer

(Matthew 13.1-9; Luke 8.4-8)

4 The next time Jesus taught beside Lake Galilee, a big crowd gathered. It was so large that he had to sit in a boat out on the lake, while the people stood on the shore. ²He used stories to teach them many things, and this is part of what he taught:

³Now listen! A farmer went out to scatter seed in a field. ⁴While the farmer was scattering the seed, some of it fell along the road and was eaten by birds. ⁵Other seeds fell on thin, rocky ground and quickly started growing because the soil wasn't very deep. ⁶But when the sun came up, the plants were scorched and dried up, because they did not have deep roots. ⁷Some other seeds fell where thornbushes grew up and choked out the plants. So they did not produce any grain. ⁸But a few seeds did fall on good ground where the plants grew and produced 30 or 60 or even 100 times as much as was scattered.

⁹Then Jesus said, "If you have ears, pay attention."

Why Jesus Used Stories

(Matthew 13.10-17; Luke 8.9,10)

¹⁰When Jesus was alone with the twelve apostles and some others, they asked him about these stories. ¹¹He answered:

I have explained the secret about God's kingdom to you, but for others I can use only stories. ¹²The reason is,

"These people will look
   and look, but never see.
They will listen and listen,
   but never understand.
If they did,

they would turn to God
and be forgiven."

Jesus Explains the Story about the Farmer
(Matthew 13.18-23; Luke 8.11-15)

¹³Jesus then told them:

If you don't understand this story, you won't understand any others. ¹⁴What the farmer is spreading is really the message about the kingdom. ¹⁵The seeds that fell along the road are the people who hear the message. But Satan soon comes and snatches it away from them. ¹⁶The seeds that fell on rocky ground are the people who gladly hear the message and accept it at once. ¹⁷But they don't have roots, and they don't last very long. As soon as life gets hard or the message gets them in trouble, they give up.

¹⁸The seeds that fell among the thornbushes are also people who hear the message. ¹⁹But they start worrying about the needs of this life. They are fooled by the desire to get rich and to have all kinds of other things. So the message gets choked out, and they never produce anything. ²⁰The seeds that fell on good ground are the people who hear and welcome the message. They produce 30 or 60 or even 100 times as much as was planted.

Light
(Luke 8.16-18)

²¹Jesus also said:

You don't light a lamp and put it under a clay pot or under a bed. Don't you put a lamp on a lampstand? ²²There is nothing hidden that will not be made public. There is no secret that will not be well known. ²³If you have ears, pay attention!

²⁴Listen carefully to what you hear! The way you treat others will be the way you will be treated—and even worse. ²⁵Everyone who has something will be given more. But people who don't have anything will lose what little they have.

Another Story about Seeds

²⁶Again Jesus said:

God's kingdom is like what happens when a farmer scatters seed in a field. ²⁷The farmer sleeps at night and is up and around during the day. Yet the seeds keep sprouting and growing, and he doesn't understand how. ²⁸It is the ground that makes the seeds sprout and grow into plants that produce grain. ²⁹Then when harvest season comes and the grain is ripe, the farmer cuts it with a sickle.ʸ

A Mustard Seed
(Matthew 13.31,32; Luke 13.18,19)

³⁰Finally, Jesus said:

What is God's kingdom like? What story can I use to explain it? ³¹It is like what happens when a mustard seed is planted in the ground. It is the smallest seed in all the world. ³²But once it is planted, it grows larger than any garden plant. It even puts out branches that are big enough for birds to nest in its shade.

ʸ**4.29** *sickle*: A knife with a long curved blade, used to cut grain and other crops.

4.21 *lamp . . . clay pot:* In Jesus' day, people used small clay lamps that burned olive oil. Putting a clay pot over the lamp would put the lamp out or keep its light from being seen. In the Bible, God's Word is compared to a "lamp that gives light wherever I walk" (Ps 119.105).

4.31 *mustard seed:* In Jesus' day, the smallest quantity of something was compared with the tiny black "mustard seed." This seeds was used to flavor food and to keep it fresh. It also contained oil and was used as a medicine. The mustard plant does not usually grow as tall as most trees, but a mustard plant can grow taller than an average adult. The stem can be as thick as an adult's arm, so Jesus is not exaggerating when he says that the mustard seed grew into a tree.

5.7 *Son of God in heaven*: The demons know who Jesus is. Often heaven is described as a place "up there," but in the Bible it simply refers to the place where God rules. Jesus often talks about how God's rule will be total some time in the future, and that living under God's rule will be the reward for those who are faithful.

5.9 *My name is Lots*: The term translated here as "Lots" can also be translated as "Legion." A Roman army legion was made up of 6,000 men.

5.11 *large herd of pigs*: Jewish people considered pigs to be an unclean animal, and they would never have raised pigs. The fact that a large herd of pigs was near Gerasa shows that this was likely a Gentile area where few Jews lived.

Purity (Clean and Unclean)

The Reason for Teaching with Stories
(Matthew 13.34,35)

³³Jesus used many other stories when he spoke to the people, and he taught them as much as they could understand. ³⁴He did not tell them anything without using stories. But when he was alone with his disciples, he explained everything to them.

A Storm
(Matthew 8.23-27; Luke 8.22-25)

³⁵That evening, Jesus said to his disciples, "Let's cross to the east side." ³⁶So they left the crowd, and his disciples started across the lake with him in the boat. Some other boats followed along. ³⁷Suddenly a storm struck the lake. Waves started splashing into the boat, and it was about to sink. ³⁸Jesus was in the back of the boat with his head on a pillow, and he was asleep. His disciples woke him and said, "Teacher, don't you care that we're about to drown?" ³⁹Jesus got up and ordered the wind and the waves to be quiet. The wind stopped, and everything was calm. ⁴⁰Jesus asked his disciples, "Why were you afraid? Don't you have any faith?" ⁴¹Now they were more afraid than ever and said to each other, "Who is this? Even the wind and the waves obey him!"

A Man with Evil Spirits
(Matthew 8.28-34; Luke 8.26-39)

5 Jesus and his disciples crossed Lake Galilee and came to shore near the town of Gerasa.ᶻ ²When he was getting out of the boat, a man with an evil spirit quickly ran to him ³from the graveyardᵃ where he had been living. No one was able to tie the man up anymore, not even with a chain. ⁴He had often been put in chains and leg irons, but he broke the chains and smashed the leg irons. No one could control him. ⁵Night and day he was in the graveyard or on the hills, yelling and cutting himself with stones.

⁶When the man saw Jesus in the distance, he ran up to him and knelt down. ⁷He shouted, "Jesus, Son of God in heaven, what do you want with me? Promise me in God's name that you won't torture me!" ⁸The man said this because Jesus had already told the evil spirit to come out of him.

⁹Jesus asked, "What is your name?"

The man answered, "My name is Lots, because I have 'lots' of evil spirits." ¹⁰He then begged Jesus not to send them away.

¹¹Over on the hillside a large herd of pigs was feeding. ¹²So the evil spirits begged Jesus, "Send us into those pigs! Let us go into them." ¹³Jesus let them go, and they went out of the man and into the pigs. The whole herd of about 2,000 pigs rushed down the steep bank into the lake and drowned.

¹⁴The men taking care of the pigs ran to the town and the farms to spread the news. Then the people came out to see what had happened. ¹⁵When they came to Jesus, they saw the man who had once been full of demons. He was sitting there with his clothes on and in his right mind, and they were terrified.

¹⁶Everyone who had seen what had happened told about the man and the pigs. ¹⁷Then the people started begging Jesus to leave their part of the country.

¹⁸When Jesus was getting into the boat, the man begged to go with him. ¹⁹But

---

ᶻ5.1 *Gerasa*: Some manuscripts have "Gadara," and others have "Gergesa." ᵃ5.3 *graveyard*: It was thought that demons and evil spirits lived in graveyards.

The disciples said to each other, "*Who is this? Even the wind and the waves obey him!*" MARK 4.41

Jesus would not let him. Instead, he said, "Go home to your family and tell them how much the Lord has done for you and how good he has been to you."

²⁰The man went away into the region near the ten cities known as Decapolis[b] and began telling everyone how much Jesus had done for him. Everyone who heard what had happened was amazed.

A Dying Girl and a Sick Woman
(Matthew 9.18-26; Luke 8.40-56)

²¹Once again Jesus got into the boat and crossed Lake Galilee.[c] Then as he stood on the shore, a large crowd gathered around him. ²²The person in charge of the synagogue was also there. His name was Jairus, and when he saw Jesus, he went over to him. He knelt at Jesus' feet ²³and started begging him for help. He said, "My little daughter is about to die! Please come and touch her, so she will get well and live." ²⁴Jesus went with Jairus. Many people followed along and kept crowding around.

²⁵In the crowd was a woman who had been bleeding for twelve years. ²⁶She had gone to many doctors, and they had not done anything except cause her a lot of pain. She had paid them all the money she had. But instead of getting better, she only got worse.

²⁷The woman had heard about Jesus, so she came up behind him in the crowd and barely touched his clothes. ²⁸She had said to herself, "If I can just touch his clothes, I will be healed." ²⁹As soon as she touched them, her bleeding stopped, and she knew she was healed.

³⁰At that moment Jesus felt power go out from him. He turned to the crowd and asked, "Who touched my clothes?"

³¹His disciples said to him, "Look at all these people crowding around you! How can you ask who touched you?" ³²But Jesus turned to see who had touched him.

³³The woman knew what had happened to her. So she came trembling with fear and knelt down in front of Jesus. Then she told him the whole story.

³⁴Jesus said to the woman, "You are now well because of your faith. May God give you peace! You are healed, and you will no longer be in pain."

³⁵While Jesus was still speaking, some people came from Jairus' home and said, "Your daughter has died! Why bother the teacher anymore?"

³⁶Jesus heard[d] what they said, and he said to Jairus, "Don't worry. Just have faith!"

³⁷Jesus did not let anyone go with him except Peter and the two brothers, James and John. ³⁸They went home with Jairus and saw the people crying and making a lot of noise.[e] ³⁹Then Jesus went inside and said to them, "Why are you crying and carrying on like this? The child isn't dead. She is just asleep." ⁴⁰But the people laughed at him.

After Jesus had sent them all out of the house, he took the girl's father and mother and his three disciples and went to where she was. ⁴¹⁻⁴²He took the twelve-year-old girl by the hand and said, "Talitha, koum!"[f] which means, "Little girl, get up!" The girl got right up and started walking around.

Everyone was greatly surprised. ⁴³But Jesus ordered them not to tell anyone what had happened. Then he said, "Give her something to eat."

5.19 *the Lord:* The Greek word for "Lord" is *kyrios,* which may mean master or may be used to address someone as "sir." When it is used for Jesus, it emphasizes his authority and power.

Lord (Title for Jesus)

5.22 *synagogue:* The Greek word for *synagogue* means "gathering." In the Bible, a synagogue was any group of people who met together to worship and to study the Scriptures.

Synagogues

Faith

5.26 *doctors:* In New Testament times, there were doctors who helped people when they were sick or injured. Though they had many skills, their knowledge of what actually caused diseases was limited. **(See the article Miracles, Magic, and Medicine on pg 1820.)**

---

[b]**5.20** *the ten cities known as Decapolis:* A group of ten cities east of Samaria and Galilee, where the people followed the Greek way of life. [c]**5.21** *crossed Lake Galilee:* To the west side. [d]**5.36** *heard:* Or "ignored." [e]**5.38** *crying and making a lot of noise:* The Jewish people often hired mourners for funerals. [f]**5.41,42** *Talitha, koum:* These words are in Aramaic, a language spoken in Palestine during the time of Jesus.

● 6.3 *James, Joseph, Judas, and Si-mon his brothers:* Little is known about Jesus' brothers and sisters, except for James, who became an important leader in the church. James saw Jesus raised from death (1 Cor 15.7) and was head of the Jewish-Christian church in Jerusalem (Acts 15.13; 21.18; Gal 1.19). Church tradition says that James was put to death some time before A.D. 70.

● 6.15 *Elijah:* Elijah was a prophet in Israel over 800 years before Jesus was born. Later prophets expected God to send Elijah back to earth to warn people of God's judgment (Mal 3.1-4; 4.5,6) and prepare the way for the Messiah.

CR   Elijah

The People of Nazareth Turn against Jesus
(Matthew 13.53-58; Luke 4.16-30)

6 Jesus left and returned to his home-town[g] with his disciples. [2]The next Sabbath he taught in the synagogue. Many of the people who heard him were amazed and asked, "How can he do all this? Where did he get such wisdom and the power to work these miracles? [3]Isn't he the carpen-ter,[h] the son of Mary? Aren't James, Joseph, Judas, and Simon his brothers? Don't his sisters still live here in our town?" The peo-ple were upset because of what he was doing.

[4]But Jesus said, "Prophets are honored by everyone, except the people of their home-town and their relatives and their own family." [5]Jesus could not work any mira-cles there, except to heal a few sick people by placing his hands on them. [6]He was sur-prised that the people did not have any faith.

Instructions for the Twelve Apostles
(Matthew 10.5-15; Luke 9.1-6)

Jesus taught in all the neighboring vil-lages. [7]Then he called together his twelve apostles and sent them out two by two with power over evil spirits. [8]He told them, "You may take along a walking stick. But don't carry food or a traveling bag or any money. [9]It's all right to wear sandals, but don't take along a change of clothes. [10]When you are welcomed into a home,

stay there until you leave that town. [11]If any place won't welcome you or listen to your message, leave and shake the dust from your feet[i] as a warning to them."

[12]The apostles left and started telling everyone to turn to God. [13]They forced out many demons and healed a lot of sick people by putting olive oil[j] on them.

The Death of John the Baptist
(Matthew 14.1-12; Luke 9.7-9)

[14]Jesus became so well-known that Herod the ruler[k] heard about him. Some people thought he was John the Baptist, who had come back to life with the power to work miracles. [15]Others thought he was Elijah[l] or some other prophet who had lived long ago. [16]But when Herod heard about Jesus, he said, "This must be John! I had his head cut off, and now he has come back to life."

[17-18]Herod had earlier married Herodias, the wife of his brother Philip. But John had told him, "It isn't right for you to take your brother's wife!" So, in order to please Hero-dias, Herod arrested John and put him in prison.

[19]Herodias had a grudge against John and wanted to kill him. But she could not do it [20]because Herod was afraid of John and protected him. He knew that John was a good and holy man. Even though Herod was confused by what John said,[m] he was glad to listen to him. And he often did.

[21]Finally, Herodias got her chance when Herod gave a great birthday celebration for himself and invited his officials, his army officers, and the leaders of Galilee. [22]The

---

[g]6.1 *hometown:* Nazareth.   [h]6.3 *carpenter:* The Greek word may also mean someone who builds or works with stone or brick.   [i]6.11 *shake the dust from your feet:* This was a way of showing rejection.   [j]6.13 *olive oil:* The Jewish people used olive oil as a way of healing people. Sometimes olive oil is a symbol for healing by means of a miracle (see James 5.14).   [k]6.14 *Herod the ruler:* Herod Antipas, the son of Herod the Great.   [l]6.15 *Elijah:* Many of the Jewish people expected the prophet Elijah to come and prepare the way for the Messiah.   [m]6.20 *was confused by what John said:* Some manuscripts have "did many things because of what John said."

daughter of Herodias[n] came in and danced for Herod and his guests. She pleased them so much that Herod said, "Ask for anything, and it's yours! [23]I swear that I will give you as much as half of my kingdom, if you want it."

[24]The girl left and asked her mother, "What do you think I should ask for?"

Her mother answered, "The head of John the Baptist!"

[25]The girl hurried back and told Herod, "Here and now on a serving plate I want the head of John the Baptist!"

[26]Herod was very sorry for what he had said. But he did not want to break the promise he had made in front of his guests. [27]At once he ordered a guard to cut off John's head there in prison. [28]The guard put the head on a serving plate and took it to the girl. Then she gave it to her mother.

[29]When John's followers learned that he had been killed, they took his body and put it in a tomb.

Jesus Feeds Five Thousand
(Matthew 14.13-21; Luke 9.10-17; John 6.1-14)

[30]After the apostles returned to Jesus,[o] they told him everything they had done and taught. [31]But so many people were coming and going that Jesus and the apostles did not even have a chance to eat. Then Jesus said, "Let's go to a place[p] where we can be alone and get some rest." [32]They left in a boat for a place where they could be alone. [33]But many people saw them leave and figured out where they were going. So people from every town ran on ahead and got there first.

[34]When Jesus got out of the boat, he saw the large crowd that was like sheep without a shepherd. He felt sorry for the people and started teaching them many things.

[35]That evening the disciples came to Jesus and said, "This place is like a desert, and it's already late. [36]Let the crowds leave, so they can go to the farms and villages near here and buy something to eat."

[37]Jesus replied, "You give them something to eat."

But they asked him, "Don't you know it would take almost a year's wages[q] to buy all of these people something to eat?"

[38]Then Jesus said, "How much bread do you have? Go and see!"

They found out and answered, "We have five small loaves of bread[r] and two fish." [39]Jesus told his disciples to tell the people to sit down on the green grass. [40]They sat down in groups of 100 and groups of 50. [41]Jesus took the five loaves and the two fish. He looked up toward heaven and blessed the food. Then he broke the bread and handed it to his disciples to give to the people. He also divided the two fish, so everyone could have some.

[42]After everyone had eaten all they wanted, [43]Jesus' disciples picked up twelve large baskets of leftover bread and fish. [44]There were 5,000 men who ate the food.

Jesus Walks on the Water
(Matthew 14.22-33; John 6.15-21)

[45]At once, Jesus made his disciples get into the boat and start back across to Bethsaida. But he stayed until he had sent the

6.26 *did not want to break the promise that he had made:* Rulers were expected to do what they said they would do. So when Herod made his promise to the daughter of his wife in the presence of important guests, he could not take it back.

6.29 *tomb:* Tombs were usually carved out of the soft limestone hillsides in Palestine. Many times a large circular stone was used to seal the entrance to the tomb.

6.41 *blessed the food . . . broke the bread:* This same language is used when Jesus later shares a final meal with his disciples (14.22-26).

6.43 *twelve large baskets:* Twelve is an important number in Jewish culture and religion. (See the chart Numbers in the Bible on pg 1844.)

6.45 *Bethsaida:* A Jewish town just east of where the Jordan River empties into the northern end of Lake Galilee.

6.52 *true meaning of the loaves of bread*: Even though they witnessed Jesus' miracles, they did not yet understand who Jesus really was.

6.53 *town of Gennesaret*: This town was located on the northwestern side of Lake Galilee, south of Capernaum, where Jesus lived. It was probably located on a narrow plain that was also known as Gennesaret. (See Map 12 on pg 1890.)

6.56 *marketplace*: In Jesus' day, every village in Palestine had a market, usually located on a street or in an open area.

At the Market

7.1 *Pharisees and several teachers of the Law of Moses from Jerusalem*: Jesus' teachings and miracle-working were attracting attention among the Jewish leaders in Jerusalem, who were willing to travel many miles to the north to hear what Jesus had to say.

7.2 *without first washing their hands*: According to the Law of Moses, if people touched something impure before they ate, any food they touched would also be ritually impure. So the Law required them to wash their hands before eating.

crowds away. [46]Then he told them goodbye and went up on the side of a mountain to pray. [47]Later in the evening he was still there by himself, and the boat was somewhere in the middle of the lake. [48]He could see that the disciples were struggling hard, because they were rowing against the wind. Not long before morning, Jesus came toward them. He was walking on the water and was about to pass the boat.

[49]When the disciples saw Jesus walking on the water, they thought he was a ghost, and they started screaming. [50]All of them saw him and were terrified. But at this same time he said, "Don't worry! I am Jesus. Don't be afraid." [51]He then got into the boat with them, and the wind died down. The disciples were completely confused. [52]Their minds were closed, and they could not understand the true meaning of the loaves of bread.

Jesus Heals Sick People in Gennesaret
(Matthew 14.34-36)

[53]Jesus and his disciples crossed the lake and brought the boat to shore near the town of Gennesaret. [54]As soon as they got out of the boat, the people recognized Jesus. [55]So they ran all over that part of the country to bring their sick people to him on mats. They brought them each time they heard where he was. [56]In every village or farm or marketplace where Jesus went, the people brought their sick to him. They begged him to let them just touch his clothes, and everyone who did was healed.

The Teaching of the Ancestors
(Matthew 15.1-9)

7 Some Pharisees and several teachers of the Law of Moses from Jerusalem came and gathered around Jesus. [2]They noticed that some of his disciples ate without first washing their hands.[s]

[3]The Pharisees and many others obey the teachings of their ancestors. They always wash their hands in the proper way[t] before eating. [4]None of them will eat anything they buy in the market until it is washed. They also follow a lot of other teachings, such as washing cups, pitchers, and bowls.[u]

[5]The Pharisees and teachers asked Jesus, "Why don't your disciples obey what our ancestors taught us to do? Why do they eat without washing their hands?"

[6]Jesus replied:

You are nothing but show-offs! The prophet Isaiah was right when he wrote that God had said,
"All of you praise me
  with your words,
but you never really
  think about me.
[7]It is useless for you
  to worship me,
when you teach rules
  made up by humans."

[8]You disobey God's commands in order to obey what humans have taught. [9]You are good at rejecting God's commands so that you can follow your own teachings! [10]Didn't Moses command you to respect your father and mother? Didn't he tell you to put to death all who curse their par-

[s]7.2 *without first washing their hands*: The Jewish people had strict laws about washing their hands before eating, especially if they had been out in public. [t]7.3 *in the proper way*: The Greek text has "with the fist," but the exact meaning is not clear. It could mean "to the wrist" or "to the elbow." [u]7.4 *bowls*: Some manuscripts add "and sleeping mats."

ents? [11]But you let people get by without helping their parents when they should. You let them say that what they own has been offered to God.[v] [12]You won't let those people help their parents. [13]And you ignore God's commands in order to follow your own teaching. You do a lot of other things just as bad.

What Really Makes People Unclean
(Matthew 15.10-20)

[14]Jesus called the crowd together again and said, "Pay attention and try to understand what I mean. [15-16]The food that you put into your mouth doesn't make you unclean and unfit to worship God. The bad words that come out of your mouth are what make you unclean."[w]

[17]After Jesus and his disciples had left the crowd and gone into the house, they asked him what these sayings meant. [18]He answered, "Don't you know what I am talking about by now? You surely know that the food you put into your mouth cannot make you unclean. [19]It doesn't go into your heart, but into your stomach, and then out of your body." By saying this, Jesus meant that all foods were fit to eat. [20]Then Jesus said:

What comes from your heart is what makes you unclean. [21]Out of your heart come evil thoughts, vulgar deeds, stealing, murder, [22]unfaithfulness in marriage, greed, meanness, deceit, indecency, envy, insults, pride, and foolishness. [23]All of these come from your heart, and they are what make you unfit to worship God.

A Woman's Faith
(Matthew 15.21-28)

[24]Jesus left and went to the region near the town of Tyre, where he stayed in someone's home. He did not want people to know he was there, but they found out anyway. [25]A woman whose daughter had an evil spirit in her heard where Jesus was. And at once she came and knelt down at his feet. [26]The woman was Greek and had been born in the part of Syria known as Phoenicia. She begged Jesus to force the demon out of her daughter. [27]But Jesus said, "The children must first be fed! It isn't right to take away their food and feed it to dogs."[x]

[28]The woman replied, "Lord, even puppies eat the crumbs that children drop from the table."

[29]Jesus answered, "That's true! You may go now. The demon has left your daughter." [30]When the woman got back home, she found her child lying on the bed. The demon had gone.

Jesus Heals a Man Who Was Deaf and Could Hardly Talk

[31]Jesus left the region around Tyre and went by way of Sidon toward Lake Galilee. He went through the land near the ten cities known as Decapolis.[y] [32]Some people brought to him a man who was deaf and could hardly talk. They begged Jesus just to touch him.

[7.11 has been offered to God: According to Jewish custom, when people said something was offered to God, it belonged to God and could not then be given to anyone else. The teachers of the Law said that everything they owned had been given to God. That's why they wouldn't use what they had given to God, not even to help their parents.

7.15-16 unclean and unfit: The Law of Moses taught that what people ate and touched could make them unfit to worship God. But Jesus said that what people eat doesn't make them unclean. Rather, it's what they say, because their words reflect what they believe.

Purity (Clean and Unclean)]

[v]7.11 has been offered to God: According to Jewish custom, when anything was offered to God, it could not be used for anyone else, not even for a person's parents. [w]7.15,16 unclean: Some manuscripts add, "If you have ears, pay attention." [x]7.27 feed it to dogs: Some Jewish people referred to Gentiles as dogs. [y]7.31 the ten cities known as Decapolis: See the note at 5.20.

8.4 *like a desert:* Jesus' feeding of the 5,000 people in the desert would have reminded his listeners of how God fed the Israelite people as they wandered in the desert many centuries earlier, after leaving Egypt (Exod 16; Num 11).

8.8-9 *seven large baskets:* Seven was a sacred number in the ancient Near East. It symbolized completeness or perfection. **(See the chart Numbers in the Bible on pg 1844.)**

8.15 *the yeast of the Pharisees and of Herod:* Jesus was saying that the teaching of the Pharisees (2.16) and the actions of Herod Antipas (3.6) affect the whole people of God just as a little yeast affects a whole batch of dough. See also Luke 12.1.

[33]After Jesus had taken him aside from the crowd, he stuck his fingers in the man's ears. Then he spit and put it on the man's tongue. [34]Jesus looked up toward heaven, and with a groan he said, "Effatha!"[z] which means "Open up!" [35]At once the man could hear, and he had no more trouble talking clearly.

[36]Jesus told the people not to say anything about what he had done. But the more he told them, the more they talked about it. [37]They were completely amazed and said, "Everything he does is good! He even heals people who cannot hear or talk."

Jesus Feeds Four Thousand
(Matthew 15.32-39)

8 One day another large crowd gathered around Jesus. They had not brought along anything to eat. So Jesus called his disciples together and said, [2]"I feel sorry for these people. They have been with me for three days, and they don't have anything to eat. [3]Some of them live a long way from here. If I send them away hungry, they might faint on their way home."

[4]The disciples said, "This place is like a desert. Where can we find enough food to feed such a crowd?"

[5]Jesus asked them how much food they had. They replied, "Seven small loaves of bread."[a]

[6]After Jesus told the crowd to sit down, he took the seven loaves and gave thanks. He then broke the loaves and handed them to his disciples, who passed them out to the crowd. [7]They also had a few little fish, and after Jesus had blessed these, he told the disciples to pass them around.

[8-9]The crowd of about 4,000 people ate all they wanted, and the leftovers filled seven large baskets.

As soon as Jesus had sent the people away, [10]he got into the boat with the disciples and crossed to the territory near Dalmanutha.[b]

A Sign from Heaven
(Matthew 16.1-4)

[11]The Pharisees came out and started an argument with Jesus. They wanted to test him by asking for a sign from heaven. [12]Jesus groaned and said, "Why are you always looking for a sign? I can promise you that you will not be given one!" [13]Then he left them. He again got into a boat and crossed over to the other side of the lake.

The Yeast of the Pharisees and of Herod
(Matthew 16.5-12)

[14]The disciples had forgotten to bring any bread, and they had only one loaf with them in the boat. [15]Jesus warned them, "Watch out! Guard against the yeast of the Pharisees and of Herod."[c]

[16]The disciples talked this over and said to each other, "He must be saying this because we don't have any bread."

[17]Jesus knew what they were thinking and asked, "Why are you talking about not having any bread? Don't you understand? Are your minds still closed? [18]Are your eyes blind and your ears deaf? Don't you remember [19]how many baskets of leftovers you picked up when I fed those 5,000 people with only five small loaves of bread?"

"Yes," the disciples answered. "There were twelve baskets."

[z]**7.34** *Effatha:* This word is in Aramaic, a language spoken in Palestine during the time of Jesus. [a]**8.5** *small loaves of bread:* See the note at 6.38. [b]**8.10** *Dalmanutha:* The place is unknown. [c]**8.15** *Herod:* Herod Antipas, the son of Herod the Great.

²⁰Jesus then asked, "And how many baskets of leftovers did you pick up when I broke seven small loaves of bread for those 4,000 people?"

"Seven," they answered.

²¹"Don't you know what I am talking about by now?" Jesus asked.

Jesus Heals a Blind Man at Bethsaida

²²As Jesus and his disciples were going into Bethsaida, some people brought a blind man to him and begged him to touch the man. ²³Jesus took him by the hand and led him out of the village, where he spit into the man's eyes. He placed his hands on the blind man and asked him if he could see anything. ²⁴The man looked up and said, "I see people, but they look like trees walking around."

²⁵Once again Jesus placed his hands on the man's eyes, and this time the man stared. His eyes were healed, and he saw everything clearly. ²⁶Jesus said to him, "You may return home now, but don't go into the village."

Who Is Jesus?

(Matthew 16.13-20; Luke 9.18-21)

²⁷Jesus and his disciples went to the villages near the town of Caesarea Philippi. As they were walking along, he asked them, "What do people say about me?"

²⁸The disciples answered, "Some say you are John the Baptist or maybe Elijah.^d Others say you are one of the prophets."

²⁹Then Jesus asked, "But who do you say I am?"

"You are the Messiah!" Peter replied.

³⁰Jesus warned the disciples not to tell anyone about him.

Jesus Speaks about His Suffering and Death

(Matthew 16.21-28; Luke 9.22-27)

³¹Jesus began telling his disciples what would happen to him. He said, "The nation's leaders, the chief priests, and the teachers of the Law of Moses will make the Son of Man suffer terribly. He will be rejected and killed, but three days later he will rise to life." ³²Then Jesus explained clearly what he meant.

Peter took Jesus aside and told him to stop talking like that. ³³But when Jesus turned and saw the disciples, he corrected Peter. He said to him, "Satan, get away from me! You are thinking like everyone else and not like God."

³⁴Jesus then told the crowd and the disciples to come closer, and he said:

If any of you want to be my followers, you must forget about yourself. You must take up your cross and follow me. ³⁵If you want to save your life,^e you will destroy it. But if you give up your life for me and for the good news, you will save it. ³⁶What will you gain, if you own the whole world but destroy yourself? ³⁷What could you give to get back your soul?

³⁸Don't be ashamed of me and my message among these unfaithful and sinful people! If you are, the Son of Man will be ashamed of you when he comes in the glory of his Father with the holy angels.

9 I can assure you that some of the people standing here will not die be-

---

^d8.28 *Elijah:* See the note at 6.15.   ^e8.35 *life:* In verses 35-37 the same Greek word is translated "life," "yourself," and "soul."

8.29 *Messiah: Messiah* comes from the Hebrew word that means "the chosen one." When Peter calls Jesus the Messiah, this means that Jesus was God's chosen one. In Greek the word for "anointed one" is *christos* (Christ).

Messiah (Chosen One)

8.31 *nation's leaders, the chief priests, and the teachers of the Law of Moses:* The Romans allowed the chief priests and other leaders, like the Pharisees and Sadducees, to form a council that made decisions about local matters.

8.31 *Son of Man . . . will be rejected and killed:* Jesus was talking about his trial, his death on a cross, and the fact that God would bring him back to life.

9.2 *Peter, James, and John:* These three disciples are often with Jesus at important times.

9.4 *Elijah and Moses:* God chose Moses to lead the Hebrew people out of slavery in Egypt (Exod 3–14) and to receive the Ten Commandments. Elijah was a prophet who encouraged the people of Israel to worship God. Moses and Elijah were chosen to tell God's people to live a new way of life, just as Jesus was telling his disciples.

Elijah

Moses

9.9 *the Son of Man had been raised from death:* Jesus knew that most people were looking for a political leader who could rule the country like a king, or who would be a miracle-worker. But Jesus' true mission would only be completed when he died to defeat sin and overcame death by being raised to life.

9.11 *Elijah must come before the Messiah:* Since the prophet Elijah was expected to return before God's Messiah appeared, many may have wondered: If Jesus is the Messiah, why haven't we seen Elijah?

9.12,13 *Elijah . . . has already come:* When Jesus says that Elijah has already come and been mistreated (9.13), he may be talking about John the Baptist.

fore they see God's kingdom come with power.

The True Glory of Jesus

(Matthew 17.1-13; Luke 9.28-36)

2Six days later Jesus took Peter, James, and John with him. They went up on a high mountain, where they could be alone. There in front of the disciples, Jesus was completely changed. **3**And his clothes became much whiter than any bleach on earth could make them. **4**Then Elijah and Moses appeared and were talking with Jesus.

5Peter said to Jesus, "Teacher, it is good for us to be here! Let us make three shelters, one for you, one for Moses, and one for Elijah." **6**But Peter and the others were terribly frightened, and he did not know what he was talking about.

7The shadow of a cloud passed over and covered them. From the cloud a voice said, "This is my Son, and I love him. Listen to what he says!" **8**At once the disciples looked around, but they saw only Jesus.

9As Jesus and his disciples were coming down the mountain, he told them not to say a word about what they had seen, until the Son of Man had been raised from death. **10**So they kept it to themselves. But they wondered what he meant by the words "raised from death."

11The disciples asked Jesus, "Don't the teachers of the Law of Moses say that Elijah must come before the Messiah does?"

12Jesus answered:

Elijah certainly will come^f to get everything ready. But don't the Scriptures also say that the Son of Man must suffer terribly and be rejected? **13**I can assure you that Elijah has already come. And people treated him just as

^f**9.12** *Elijah certainly will come:* See the note at 6.15.

they wanted to, as the Scriptures say they would.

Jesus Heals a Boy

(Matthew 17.14-20; Luke 9.37-43a)

14When Jesus and his three disciples came back down, they saw a large crowd around the other disciples. The teachers of the Law of Moses were arguing with them. **15**The crowd was really surprised to see Jesus, and everyone hurried over to greet him.

16Jesus asked, "What are you arguing about?"

17Someone from the crowd answered, "Teacher, I brought my son to you. A demon keeps him from talking. **18**Whenever the demon attacks my son, it throws him to the ground and makes him foam at the mouth and grit his teeth in pain. Then he becomes stiff. I asked your disciples to force out the demon, but they couldn't do it."

19Jesus said, "You people don't have any faith! How much longer must I be with you? Why do I have to put up with you? Bring the boy to me."

20They brought the boy, and as soon as the demon saw Jesus, it made the boy shake all over. He fell down and began rolling on the ground and foaming at the mouth.

21Jesus asked the boy's father, "How long has he been like this?"

The man answered, "Ever since he was a child. **22**The demon has often tried to kill him by throwing him into a fire or into water. Please have pity and help us if you can!"

23Jesus replied, "Why do you say 'if you can'? Anything is possible for someone who has faith!"

24At once the boy's father shouted, "I do

From the cloud a voice said, "This is my Son, and I love him. Listen to what he says!" MARK 9.7

have faith! Please help me to have even more."

25When Jesus saw that a crowd was gathering fast, he spoke sternly to the evil spirit that had kept the boy from speaking or hearing. He said, "I order you to come out of the boy! Don't ever bother him again."

26The spirit screamed and made the boy shake all over. Then it went out of him. The boy looked dead, and almost everyone said he was. 27But Jesus took hold of his hand and helped him stand up.

28After Jesus and the disciples had gone back home and were alone, they asked him, "Why couldn't we force out that demon?"

29Jesus answered, "Only prayer can force out this kind of demon."

Jesus Again Speaks about His Death
(Matthew 17.22,23; Luke 9.43b-45)

30Jesus left with his disciples and started through Galilee. He did not want anyone to know about it, 31because he was teaching the disciples that the Son of Man would be handed over to people who would kill him. But three days later he would rise to life. 32The disciples did not understand what Jesus meant, and they were afraid to ask.

Who Is the Greatest?
(Matthew 18.1-5; Luke 9.46-48)

33Jesus and his disciples went to his home in Capernaum. After they were inside the house, Jesus asked them, "What were you arguing about along the way?" 34They had been arguing about which one of them was the greatest, and so they did not answer.

35After Jesus sat down and told the twelve disciples to gather around him, he said, "If you want the place of honor, you must become a slave and serve others!"

36Then Jesus asked a child to stand near him. He put his arm around the child and said, 37"When you welcome even a child because of me, you welcome me. And when you welcome me, you welcome the one who sent me."

For or against Jesus
(Luke 9.49,50)

38John said, "Teacher, we saw a man using your name to force demons out of people. But he wasn't one of us, and we told him to stop."

39Jesus said to his disciples:

Don't stop him! No one who works miracles in my name will soon turn and say something bad about me. 40Anyone who isn't against us is for us. 41And anyone who gives you a cup of water in my name, just because you belong to me, will surely be rewarded.

Temptations To Sin
(Matthew 18.6-9; Luke 17.1,2)

42It will be terrible for people who cause even one of my little followers to sin. Those people would be better off thrown into the ocean with a heavy stone tied around their necks. 43-44So if your hand causes you to sin, cut it off! You would be better off to go into life paralyzed than to have two hands and be thrown into the fires of hell that never go out.g 45-46If your foot causes you to sin, chop it off. You

g9.43,44 *never go out*: Some manuscripts add, "The worms there never die, and the fire never stops burning."

9.30 *Galilee:* Galilee was the northern part of Palistine west of the Jordan River and the Sea of Galilee. The area was part of the northern kingdom of Israel that the Assyrians conquered in 722 B.C. Later, it was ruled by the Babylonians, Persians, Greeks, and Syrians. In 63 B.C., the Romans made it part of their empire and ruled it during the time Jesus lived. Jesus grew up in Nazareth (Matt 2.19-23), a small town that is never mentioned in the Jewish Scriptures (Old Testament). **(See Map 11 on pg 1889.)**

9.43-44 *fires of hell:* In the New Testament, the place of judgment for evildoers is often pictured as a place of fiery torture (Matt 5.22; Luke 16.23,24 and Rev 20.14).

CR   Fire

CR   Hell

10.3 *Law of Moses:* Refers to the first five books of the Old Testament— GENESIS, EXODUS, LEVITICUS, NUMBERS, DEUTERONOMY. These books include a number of laws that explain how people were to live and worship.

10.13 *children:* Jesus used children as an example because they were not considered powerful or wise like adults. Jesus wanted to show that being wise or powerful is not the way to get into the kingdom of God. Being humble and faithful is.

10.17 *eternal life:* By the time of Jesus, many Jewish people had come to believe in and hope for life after death. But some, like the Sadducees, did not accept the concept of eternal life, because it was not specifically mentioned in the Law of Moses.

 formation   Eternal Life

would be better off to go into life lame than to have two feet and be thrown into hell.[h] [47]If your eye causes you to sin, get rid of it. You would be better off to go into God's kingdom with only one eye than to have two eyes and be thrown into hell. [48]The worms there never die, and the fire never stops burning.

[49]Everyone must be salted with fire.[i]

[50]Salt is good. But if it no longer tastes like salt, how can it be made salty again? Have salt among you and live at peace with each other.[j]

Teaching about Divorce
(Matthew 19.1-12; Luke 16.18)

10 After Jesus left, he went to Judea and then on to the other side of the Jordan River. Once again large crowds came to him, and as usual, he taught them.

[2]Some Pharisees wanted to test Jesus. So they came up to him and asked if it was right for a man to divorce his wife. [3]Jesus asked them, "What does the Law of Moses say about this?"

[4]They answered, "Moses allows a man to write out divorce papers and send his wife away."

[5]Jesus replied, "Moses gave you this law because you are so heartless. [6]But in the beginning God made a man and a woman. [7]That's why a man leaves his father and mother and gets married. [8]He becomes like one person with his wife. Then they are no longer two people, but one. [9]And no

one should separate a couple that God has joined together."

[10]When Jesus and his disciples were back in the house, they asked him about what he had said. [11]He told them, "A man who divorces his wife and marries someone else is unfaithful to his wife. [12]A woman who divorces her husband[k] and marries again is also unfaithful."

Jesus Blesses Little Children
(Matthew 19.13-15; Luke 18.15-17)

[13]Some people brought their children to Jesus so he could bless them by placing his hands on them. But his disciples told the people to stop bothering him.

[14]When Jesus saw this, he became angry and said, "Let the children come to me! Don't try to stop them. People who are like these little children belong to the kingdom of God.[l] [15]I promise you that you cannot get into God's kingdom, unless you accept it the way a child does." [16]Then Jesus took the children in his arms and blessed them by placing his hands on them.

A Rich Man
(Matthew 19.16-30; Luke 18.18-30)

[17]As Jesus was walking down a road, a man ran up to him. He knelt down, and asked, "Good teacher, what can I do to have eternal life?"

[18]Jesus replied, "Why do you call me good? Only God is good. [19]You know the commandments. 'Do not murder. Be faith-

[h]9.45,46 *thrown into hell:* Some manuscripts add, "The worms there never die, and the fire never stops burning."   [i]9.49 *salted with fire:* Some manuscripts add "and every sacrifice will be seasoned with salt." The verse may mean that Christ's followers must suffer because of their faith.
[j]9.50 *Have salt among you and live at peace with each other:* This may mean that when Christ's followers have to suffer because of their faith, they must still try to live at peace with each other.   [k]10.12 *A woman who divorces her husband:* Roman law let a woman divorce her husband, but Jewish law did not let a woman do this.   [l]10.14 *People who are like these little children belong to the kingdom of God:* Or "The kingdom of God belongs to people who are like these little children."

ful in marriage. Do not steal. Do not tell lies about others. Do not cheat. Respect your father and mother.'"

20The man answered, "Teacher, I have obeyed all these commandments since I was a young man."

21Jesus looked closely at the man. He liked him and said, "There's one thing you still need to do. Go sell everything you own. Give the money to the poor, and you will have riches in heaven. Then come with me."

22When the man heard Jesus say this, he went away gloomy and sad because he was very rich.

23Jesus looked around and said to his disciples, "It's hard for rich people to get into God's kingdom!" **24**The disciples were shocked to hear this. So Jesus told them again, "It's terribly hard[m] to get into God's kingdom! **25**In fact, it's easier for a camel to go through the eye of a needle than for a rich person to get into God's kingdom."

26Jesus' disciples were even more amazed. They asked each other, "How can anyone ever be saved?"

27Jesus looked at them and said, "There are some things that people cannot do, but God can do anything."

28Peter replied, "Remember, we left everything to be your followers!"

29Jesus told him:

You can be sure that anyone who gives up home or brothers or sisters or mother or father or children or land for me and for the good news **30**will be rewarded. In this world they will be given 100 times as many houses and brothers and sisters and mothers and children and pieces of land, though

they will also be mistreated. And in the world to come, they will have eternal life. **31**But many who are now first will be last, and many who are now last will be first.

Jesus Again Tells about His Death

(Matthew 20.17-19; Luke 18.31-34)

32The disciples were confused as Jesus led them toward Jerusalem, and his other followers were afraid. Once again, Jesus took the twelve disciples aside and told them what was going to happen to him. He said:

33We are now on our way to Jerusalem where the Son of Man will be handed over to the chief priests and the teachers of the Law of Moses. They will sentence him to death and hand him over to foreigners,[n] **34**who will make fun of him and spit on him. They will beat him and kill him. But three days later he will rise to life.

The Request of James and John

(Matthew 20.20-28)

35James and John, the sons of Zebedee, came up to Jesus and asked, "Teacher, will you do us a favor?"

36Jesus asked them what they wanted, **37**and they answered, "When you come into your glory, please let one of us sit at your right side and the other at your left."[o]

38Jesus told them, "You don't really know what you're asking! Are you able to drink from the cup[p] that I must soon drink from or be baptized as I must be baptized?"[q]

---

[m]**10.24** *hard:* Some manuscripts add "for people who trust in their wealth." Others add "for the rich."   [n]**10.33** *foreigners:* The Romans who ruled Judea at this time.   [o]**10.37** *right side . . . left:* The most powerful people in a kingdom sat at the right and left side of the king.   [p]**10.38** *drink from the cup:* In the Scriptures a "cup" is sometimes used as a symbol of suffering. To "drink from the cup" would be to suffer.   [q]**10.38** *as I must be baptized:* Baptism is used with the same meaning that "cup" has in this verse.

● **10.23** *It's hard for rich people to get into God's kingdom:* The wealthy were considered to be blessed by God, especially if they had lived according to the Law of Moses. But Jesus warns that having wealth can actually make it harder for people to get into God's kingdom, especially for those who trust their wealth instead of God.

● **10.25** *a camel to go through the eye of a needle:* Camels are large animals. Jesus' outlandish statement emphasized the point he was making.

■ **10.29,30** *good news . . . eternal life:* The "world to come" in MARK may be heaven, or it may be a future time when the Son of Man (Jesus) returns to gather his chosen ones from all over the earth.

11.1 *Bethphage and Bethany near the Mount of Olives:* Bethphage was a little village on the road from Jericho approaching Jerusalem. Bethany, a small village about two miles east of Jerusalem, is on the slopes of the Mount of Olives.

The Mount of Olives is a ridge about two and a half miles long. Its name comes from the olive trees that grew on its slopes. It is located about half a mile east of the temple area in Jerusalem. Because it was about 300 to 500 feet higher than the temple area, it was a perfect place for Jesus to show his disciples the temple area while he taught them what was going to happen to the temple. **(See Maps 12 and 13 on pgs 1890 and 1891.)**

⊂R   Slaves and Servants in the Time of Jesus

[39]"Yes, we are!" James and John answered.

Then Jesus replied, "You certainly will drink from the cup from which I must drink. And you will be baptized just as I must! [40]But it isn't for me to say who will sit at my right side and at my left. This is for God to decide."

[41]When the ten other disciples heard this, they were angry with James and John. [42]But Jesus called the disciples together and said:

You know that those foreigners who call themselves kings like to order their people around. And their great leaders have full power over the people they rule. [43]But don't act like them. If you want to be great, you must be the servant of all the others. [44]And if you want to be first, you must be everyone's slave. [45]The Son of Man did not come to be a slave master, but a slave who will give his life to rescue[r] many people.

Jesus Heals Blind Bartimaeus
(Matthew 20.29-34; Luke 18.35-43)

[46]Jesus and his disciples went to Jericho. And as they were leaving, they were followed by a large crowd. A blind beggar by the name of Bartimaeus son of Timaeus was sitting beside the road. [47]When he heard that it was Jesus from Nazareth, he shouted, "Jesus, Son of David,[s] have pity on me!" [48]Many people told the man to stop, but he shouted even louder, "Son of David, have pity on me!"

[49]Jesus stopped and said, "Call him over!"

They called out to the blind man and said, "Don't be afraid! Come on! He is calling for you." [50]The man threw off his coat as he jumped up and ran to Jesus.

[51]Jesus asked, "What do you want me to do for you?"

The blind man answered, "Master,[t] I want to see!"

[52]Jesus told him, "You may go. Your eyes are healed because of your faith."

At once the man could see, and he went down the road with Jesus.

Jesus Enters Jerusalem
(Matthew 21.1-11; Luke 19.28-40; John 12.12-19)

11 Jesus and his disciples reached Bethphage and Bethany near the Mount of Olives. When they were getting close to Jerusalem, Jesus sent two of them on ahead. [2]He told them, "Go into the next village. As soon as you enter it, you will find a young donkey that has never been ridden. Untie the donkey and bring it here. [3]If anyone asks why you are doing this, say, 'The Lord[u] needs it and will soon bring it back.'"

[4]The disciples left and found the donkey tied near a door that faced the street. While they were untying it, [5]some of the people standing there asked, "Why are you untying the donkey?" [6]They told them what Jesus had said, and the people let them take it.

[7]The disciples led the donkey to Jesus. They put some of their clothes on its back, and Jesus got on. [8]Many people spread clothes on the road, while others spread branches they had cut from the fields.[v]

[9]In front of Jesus and behind him, people went along shouting,

[r]**10.45** *rescue:* The Greek word often, though not always, means the payment of a price to free a slave or a prisoner. [s]**10.47** *Son of David:* The Jewish people expected the Messiah to be from the family of King David, and for this reason the Messiah was often called the "Son of David." [t]**10.51** *Master:* A Hebrew word that may also mean "Teacher." [u]**11.3** *The Lord:* Or "The master of the donkey." [v]**11.8** *spread . . . branches from the fields:* This was one way that the Jewish people welcomed a famous person.

Jesus said, *"If you want to be great, you must be the servant of all the others."* MARK 10.43

"Hooray!^w
God bless the one who comes
　　in the name of the Lord!
[10]God bless the coming kingdom
　　of our ancestor David.
Hooray for God
　　in heaven above!"

[11]After Jesus had gone to Jerusalem, he went into the temple and looked around at everything. But since it was already late in the day, he went back to Bethany with the twelve disciples.

Jesus Puts a Curse on a Fig Tree
(Matthew 21.18,19)

[12]When Jesus and his disciples left Bethany the next morning, he was hungry. [13]From a distance Jesus saw a fig tree covered with leaves, and he went to see if there were any figs on the tree. But there were none, because it wasn't the season for figs. [14]So Jesus said to the tree, "Never again will anyone eat fruit from this tree!" The disciples heard him say this.

Jesus in the Temple
(Matthew 21.12-17; Luke 19.45-48; John 2.13-22)

[15]After Jesus and his disciples reached Jerusalem, he went into the temple and began chasing out everyone who was selling and buying. He turned over the tables of the moneychangers and the benches of those who were selling doves. [16]Jesus would not let anyone carry things through the temple. [17]Then he taught the people and said, "The Scriptures say, 'My house should be called a place of worship for all nations.' But you have made it a place where robbers hide!"

[18]The chief priests and the teachers of the Law of Moses heard what Jesus said, and they started looking for a way to kill him. They were afraid of him, because the crowds were completely amazed at his teaching. [19]That evening, Jesus and the disciples went outside the city.

A Lesson from the Fig Tree
(Matthew 21.20-22)

[20]As the disciples walked past the fig tree the next morning, they noticed that it was completely dried up, roots and all. [21]Peter remembered what Jesus had said to the tree. Then Peter said, "Teacher, look! The tree you put a curse on has dried up."

[22]Jesus told his disciples:

Have faith in God! [23]If you have faith in God and don't doubt, you can tell this mountain to get up and jump into the sea, and it will. [24]Everything you ask for in prayer will be yours, if you only have faith.

[25-26]Whenever you stand up to pray, you must forgive what others have done to you. Then your Father in heaven will forgive your sins.^x

A Question about Jesus' Authority
(Matthew 21.23-27; Luke 20.1-8)

[27]Jesus and his disciples returned to Jerusalem. And as he was walking through the temple, the chief priests, the nation's leaders, and the teachers of the Law of Moses came over to him. [28]They asked, "What right do you have to do these things? Who gave you this authority?"

---

^w[11.9] *Hooray:* This translates a word that can mean "please save us." But it is most often used as a shout of praise to God.　^x[11.25,26] *your sins:* Some manuscripts add, "But if you do not forgive others, God will not forgive you."

● 11.15 *selling and buying . . . moneychangers:* Jewish people came to the temple to buy animals to make a sacrifice to God. Many sellers set up animal pens and cages in the outer court of the temple and moneychangers set up tables for those who needed to change their money. Sometimes the people selling animals and the moneychangers cheated their customers.

◌ Money Changing in the Temple

● 11.25-26 *stand up to pray:* People in Jesus' day usually prayed in public at the temple or in their meeting places (synagogues). It was traditional to stand with arms raised when praying to God. Jesus emphasized the importance of praying for forgiveness.

◌ Prayer

In front of Jesus and behind him, people went along shouting, "Hooray! God bless the one who comes in the name of the Lord!" MARK 11.9

12.1 *vineyard:* The vineyard is a place where grapes are grown. Grapevines need lots of special care. Branches that aren't producing need to be cut off, and the soil around the vines needs to be loosened and weeded. Many workers were required to care for and protect the grapevines. Vineyards were usually located on stony hillsides and enclosed by walls for protection. Many were bordered by a high tower where someone could watch over the valuable fruit. Vineyards also had a pit (wine press) where the grapes were crushed into juice.

12.14 *pay taxes to the Emperor:* Jews in Palestine had to pay taxes to the Romans, who controlled their land. The emperor was the highest Roman leader. If Jesus answered "No," the leaders could accuse him of rebelling against the Romans.

[29]Jesus answered, "I have just one question to ask you. If you answer it, I will tell you where I got the right to do these things. [30]Who gave John the right to baptize? Was it God in heaven or merely some human being?"

[31]They thought it over and said to each other, "We can't say that God gave John this right. Jesus will ask us why we didn't believe John. [32]On the other hand, these people think that John was a prophet. So we can't say it was merely some human who gave John the right to baptize."

They were afraid of the crowd [33]and told Jesus, "We don't know."

Jesus replied, "Then I won't tell you who gave me the right to do what I do."

Renters of a Vineyard
(Matthew 21.33-46; Luke 20.9-19)

12 Jesus then told them this story:
A farmer once planted a vineyard. He built a wall around it and dug a pit to crush the grapes in. He also built a lookout tower. Then he rented out his vineyard and left the country.

[2]When it was harvest time, he sent a servant to get his share of the grapes. [3]The renters grabbed the servant, beat him up, and sent him away without a thing.

[4]The owner sent another servant, but the renters beat him on the head and insulted him terribly. [5]Then the man sent another servant, and they killed him. He kept sending servant after servant. They beat some of them and killed some.

[6]The owner had a son he loved very much. Finally, he sent his son to the renters because he thought they would respect him. [7]But they said to themselves, "Someday he will own this vineyard. Let's kill him! That way we can have it all for ourselves." [8]So they grabbed the owner's son, killed him, and threw his body out of the vineyard.

[9]Jesus asked, "What do you think the owner of the vineyard will do? He will come and kill those renters and let someone else have his vineyard. [10]You surely know that the Scriptures say,

'The stone the builders
    tossed aside
is now the most important
    stone of all.
[11]This is something
    the Lord has done,
        and it is amazing to us.'"

[12]The leaders knew that Jesus was really talking about them, and they wanted to arrest him. But because they were afraid of the crowd, they let him alone and left.

Paying Taxes
(Matthew 22.15-22; Luke 20.20-26)

[13]The Pharisees got together with Herod's followers.[y] Then they sent some men to trick Jesus into saying something wrong. [14]They went to him and said, "Teacher, we know that you are honest. You treat everyone with the same respect, no matter who they are. And you teach the truth about what God wants people to do. Tell us, should we pay taxes to the Emperor or not?"

[15]Jesus knew what they were up to, and he said, "Why are you trying to test me? Show me a coin!"

[y]**12.13** *Herod's followers:* People who were political followers of the family of Herod the Great and his son Herod Antipas.

¹⁶They brought him a silver coin, and he asked, "Whose picture and name are on it?"

"The Emperor's," they answered.

¹⁷Then Jesus told them, "Give the Emperor what belongs to him and give God what belongs to God." The men were amazed at Jesus.

Life in the Future World
(Matthew 22.23-33; Luke 20.27-40)

¹⁸The Sadducees did not believe that people would rise to life after death. So some of them came to Jesus and said:

¹⁹Teacher, Moses wrote that if a married man dies and has no children, his brother should marry the widow. Their first son would then be thought of as the son of the dead brother. ²⁰There were once seven brothers. The first one married, but died without having any children. ²¹The second brother married his brother's widow, and he also died without having children. The same thing happened to the third brother, ²²and finally to all seven brothers. At last the woman died. ²³When God raises people from death, whose wife will this woman be? After all, she had been married to all seven brothers.

²⁴Jesus answered:

You are completely wrong! You don't know what the Scriptures teach. And you don't know anything about the power of God. ²⁵When God raises people to life, they won't marry. They will be like the angels in heaven. ²⁶You surely know about people being raised to life. You know that in the story about Moses and the burning bush,

God said, "I am the God worshiped by Abraham, Isaac, and Jacob."^z ²⁷He isn't the God of the dead, but of the living. You Sadducees are all wrong.

The Most Important Commandment
(Matthew 22.34-40; Luke 10.25-28)

²⁸One of the teachers of the Law of Moses came up while Jesus and the Sadducees were arguing. When he heard Jesus give a good answer, he asked him, "What is the most important commandment?"

²⁹Jesus answered, "The most important one says: 'People of Israel, you have only one Lord and God. ³⁰You must love him with all your heart, soul, mind, and strength.' ³¹The second most important commandment says: 'Love others as much as you love yourself.' No other commandment is more important than these."

³²The man replied, "Teacher, you are certainly right to say there is only one God. ³³It is also true that we must love God with all our heart, mind, and strength, and that we must love others as much as we love ourselves. These commandments are more important than all the sacrifices and offerings that we could possibly make."

³⁴When Jesus saw that the man had given a sensible answer, he told him, "You are not far from God's kingdom." After this, no one dared ask Jesus any more questions.

About David's Son
(Matthew 22.41-46; Luke 20.41-44)

³⁵As Jesus was teaching in the temple, he said, "How can the teachers of the Law of

12.16 *silver coin:* This coin was probably a denarius. In the time of Jesus, a denarius had a picture of the Emperor Tiberius on one side. On the other side were the words: "Tiberius Caesar Augustus, son of the divine Augustus." The coin was used to pay taxes to Caesar.

12.18 *Sadducees:* The Sadducees were a wealthy group of Jews who worked closely with the priests. Their name probably comes from "Zadok," the name of a major priestly family (2 Sam 20.25; 1 Kgs 1.39-45). They taught that the most important act was to go to the temple and offer sacrifices there. The Pharisees believed in the possibility of life after death, but the Sadducees did not (Acts 23.8), since this was not specifically mentioned in the Law of Moses.

12.33 *sacrifices and offerings:* Before the destruction of Jerusalem by the Romans in A.D. 70, faithful Jews were to bring offerings and make sacrifices at the temple there. But several of Israel's prophets also spoke of the importance of helping others (Isa 1.10-17, Hos 6.6, Amos 5.21-24). **(See the chart Sacrifices and Offerings on pg 1828.)**

^z**12.26** *I am the God worshiped by Abraham, Isaac, and Jacob:* Jesus argues that if God is worshiped by these three, they must still be alive, because he is the God of the living.

12.38-40 *the teachers of the Law of Moses . . . long robes . . . pray long prayers:* These teachers were Jewish scholars who studied the Law of Moses and tried to teach others how to live by what that Law taught. Jesus lists a number of things that showed how teachers of the Law of Moses liked to be noticed for what they were doing. The long robes were meant to be worn at prayer, but it sounds like the teachers were making sure people recognized them by wearing them in public. Also, taking the best seats at a banquet or praying long prayers gave the impression that they were more important than others in God's eyes. Some teachers even accepted large sums of money from widows for giving advice or for praying for them. Sometimes the widows even gave over their houses in payment.

13.1 *temple:* The temple mentioned here was built in Jerusalem under the leadership of Herod the Great. Work began in 20 B.C., and construction continued in Jesus' day (John 2.20). The temple sat on a huge stone platform that was nearly a mile around at the base. It was built above the bedrock where King Solomon had built the first temple over 900 years earlier. Jesus' prophecy (13.2) came true when the Romans captured Jerusalem from Jewish rebels and destroyed the temple in A.D. 70. **(See the article People of the Law: The Religion of Israel on pg 1794.)**

Moses say the Messiah will come from the family of King David? [36]The Holy Spirit led David to say,

'The Lord said to my Lord:
Sit at my right side[a]
until I make your enemies
into a footstool for you.'

[37]If David called the Messiah his Lord, how can the Messiah be his son?"[b]

The large crowd enjoyed listening to Jesus teach.

Jesus Condemns the Pharisees and the Teachers of the Law of Moses

(Matthew 23.1-36; Luke 20.45-47)

[38]As Jesus was teaching, he said:

Guard against the teachers of the Law of Moses! They love to walk around in long robes and be greeted in the market. [39]They like the front seats in the synagogues and the best seats at banquets. [40]But they cheat widows out of their homes and pray long prayers just to show off. They will be punished most of all.

A Widow's Offering

(Luke 21.1-4)

[41]Jesus was sitting in the temple near the offering box and watching people put in their gifts. He noticed that many rich people were giving a lot of money. [42]Finally, a poor widow came up and put in two coins worth only a few pennies. [43]Jesus told his disciples to gather around him. Then he said:

I tell you that this poor widow has put in more than all the others. [44]Everyone else gave what they didn't need. But she is very poor and gave

everything she had. Now she doesn't have a cent to live on.

The Temple Will Be Destroyed

(Matthew 24.1,2; Luke 21.5,6)

13 As Jesus was leaving the temple, one of his disciples said to him, "Teacher, look at these beautiful stones and wonderful buildings!"

[2]Jesus replied, "Do you see these huge buildings? They will certainly be torn down! Not one stone will be left in place."

Warning about Trouble

(Matthew 24.3-14; Luke 21.7-19)

[3]Later, as Jesus was sitting on the Mount of Olives across from the temple, Peter, James, John, and Andrew came to him in private. [4]They asked, "When will these things happen? What will be the sign that they are about to take place?"

[5]Jesus answered:

Watch out and don't let anyone fool you! [6]Many will come and claim to be me. They will use my name and fool many people.

[7]When you hear about wars and threats of wars, don't be afraid. These things will have to happen first, but that isn't the end. [8]Nations and kingdoms will go to war against each other. There will be earthquakes in many places, and people will starve to death. But this is just the beginning of troubles.

[9]Be on your guard! You will be taken to courts and beaten with whips in their synagogues. And because of me, you will have to stand before rulers and kings to tell about your faith. [10]But before the end comes, the good news must be preached to all nations.

[a]**12.36** *right side:* The place of power and honor.   [b]**12.37** *David . . . his son:* See the note at 10.47.

[11]When you are arrested, don't worry about what you will say. You will be given the right words when the time comes. But you will not really be the ones speaking. Your words will come from the Holy Spirit.

[12]Brothers and sisters will betray each other and have each other put to death. Parents will betray their own children, and children will turn against their parents and have them killed. [13]Everyone will hate you because of me. But if you keep on being faithful right to the end, you will be saved.

The Horrible Thing

(Matthew 24.15-21; Luke 21.20-24)

[14]Someday you will see that "Horrible Thing" where it should not be.[c] Everyone who reads this must try to understand! If you are living in Judea at that time, run to the mountains. [15]If you are on the roof[d] of your house, don't go inside to get anything. [16]If you are out in the field, don't go back for your coat. [17]It will be an awful time for women who are expecting babies or nursing young children. [18]Pray that it won't happen in winter.[e] [19]This will be the worst time of suffering since God created the world, and nothing this terrible will ever happen again. [20]If the Lord doesn't make the time shorter, no one will be left alive. But because of his chosen and special ones, he will make the time shorter. [21]If someone should say, "Here is the Messiah!" or "There he is!" don't believe it. [22]False messiahs and false prophets will come and work miracles and signs. They will even try to fool God's chosen ones. [23]But be on your guard! That's why I am telling you these things now.

When the Son of Man Appears

(Matthew 24.29-31; Luke 21.25-28)

[24]In those days, right after this time of suffering,

"The sun will become dark,
   and the moon
      will no longer shine.
[25]The stars will fall,
   and the powers in the sky[f]
      will be shaken."

[26]Then the Son of Man will be seen coming in the clouds with great power and glory. [27]He will send his angels to gather his chosen ones from all over the earth.

A Lesson from a Fig Tree

(Matthew 24.32-35; Luke 21.29-33)

[28]Learn a lesson from a fig tree. When its branches sprout and start putting out leaves, you know summer is near. [29]So when you see all these things happening, you will know that the time has almost come.[g] [30]You can be sure that some of the people of this generation will still be alive when all this happens. [31]The sky and the earth will not last forever, but my words will.

13.14 "Horrible Thing" where it should not be: Jesus was probably referring to the prophecy that someone would set up an idol in the holy place in the temple and make people worship it instead of God (Dan 9.27; 11.31; and 12.11). In 168 B.C., the Syrian ruler Antiochus IV Epiphanes had done just that. Jesus is saying that a similar horrible thing is going to occur again, probably in the temple.

13.28 fig tree: In Jesus' day the fruit (figs) that grew on this tree was an important source of food. The first fig crop ripens in June and is eaten fresh. The second crop is harvested about two months later and is usually dried in the sun and eaten during the winter months.

[c]13.14 where it should not be: Probably the holy place in the temple.   [d]13.15 roof: See the note at 2.4.
[e]13.18 in winter: In Palestine the winters are cold and rainy and make travel difficult.   [f]13.25 the powers in the sky: In ancient times people thought that the stars were spiritual powers.   [g]13.29 the time has almost come: Or "he (that is, the Son of Man) will soon be here."

Jesus said, "The sky and the earth will not last forever, but my words will." MARK 13.31

14.1 *Passover and the Festival of Thin Bread:* An important pilgrimage festival when Jewish men were expected to go to the temple in Jerusalem and to make sacrifices and celebrate. On the fifteenth of the Jewish month called Nisan, all yeast was to be removed from homes (Exod 12.15-20), and the Passover lambs were to be killed. The Passover meal took place after sunset and included the offering and eating of the sacrificial lamb, thin bread, and other special foods, and drinking wine. **(See the chart Pilgrimage Festivals on pg 1799.)**

Passover and the Festival of Thin Bread

14.13 *a man carrying a jar of water:* Usually this kind of work was done by a woman, so a man carrying water would have been easy to spot.

No One Knows the Day or Time
(Matthew 24.36-44)

32No one knows the day or the time. The angels in heaven don't know, and the Son himself doesn't know. Only the Father knows. **33**So watch out and be ready! You don't know when the time will come. **34**It is like what happens when a man goes away for a while and places his servants in charge of everything. He tells each of them what to do, and he orders the guard to keep alert. **35**So be alert! You don't know when the master of the house will come back. It could be in the evening or at midnight or before dawn or in the morning. **36**But if he comes suddenly, don't let him find you asleep. **37**I tell everyone just what I have told you. Be alert!

A Plot To Kill Jesus
(Matthew 26.1-5; Luke 22.1,2; John 11.45-53)

14 It was now two days before Passover and the Festival of Thin Bread. The chief priests and the teachers of the Law of Moses were planning how they could sneak around and have Jesus arrested and put to death. **2**They were saying, "We must not do it during the festival, because the people will riot."

At Bethany
(Matthew 26.6-13; John 12.1-8)

3Jesus was eating in Bethany at the home of Simon, who once had leprosy,[h] when a woman came in with a very expensive bottle of sweet-smelling perfume.[i] After breaking it open, she poured the perfume on Jesus' head. **4**This made some of the guests angry, and they complained, "Why such a waste? **5**We could have sold this perfume for more than 300 silver coins and given the money to the poor!" So they started saying cruel things to the woman. **6**But Jesus said:

Leave her alone! Why are you bothering her? She has done a beautiful thing for me. **7**You will always have the poor with you. And whenever you want to, you can give to them. But you won't always have me here with you. **8**She has done all she could by pouring perfume on my body to prepare it for burial. **9**You may be sure that wherever the good news is told all over the world, people will remember what she has done. And they will tell others.

Judas and the Chief Priests
(Matthew 26.14-16; Luke 22.3-6)

10Judas Iscariot[j] was one of the twelve disciples. He went to the chief priests and offered to help them arrest Jesus. **11**They were glad to hear this, and they promised to pay him. So Judas started looking for a good chance to betray Jesus.

Jesus Eats with His Disciples
(Matthew 26.17-25; Luke 22.7-14,21-23; John 13.21-30)

12It was the first day of the Festival of Thin Bread, and the Passover lambs were being killed. Jesus' disciples asked him, "Where do you want us to prepare the Passover meal?"

13Jesus said to two of the disciples, "Go into the city, where you will meet a man

[h]**14.3** *leprosy:* In biblical times the word "leprosy" was used for many different skin diseases. [i]**14.3** *sweet-smelling perfume:* The Greek text has "perfume made of pure spikenard," a plant used to make perfume. [j]**14.10** *Iscariot:* See the note at 3.19.

carrying a jar of water.^k Follow him, ¹⁴and when he goes into a house, say to the owner, 'Our teacher wants to know if you have a room where he can eat the Passover meal with his disciples.' ¹⁵The owner will take you upstairs and show you a large room furnished and ready for you to use. Prepare the meal there."

¹⁶The two disciples went into the city and found everything just as Jesus had told them. So they prepared the Passover meal.

¹⁷⁻¹⁸While Jesus and the twelve disciples were eating together that evening, he said, "The one who will betray me is now eating with me."

¹⁹This made the disciples sad, and one after another they said to Jesus, "You surely don't mean me!"

²⁰He answered, "It is one of you twelve men who is eating from this dish with me. ²¹The Son of Man will die, just as the Scriptures say. But it is going to be terrible for the one who betrays me. That man would be better off if he had never been born."

The Lord's Supper
(Matthew 26.26-30; Luke 22.14-23; 1 Corinthians 11.23-25)

²²During the meal Jesus took some bread in his hands. He blessed the bread and broke it. Then he gave it to his disciples and said, "Take this. It is my body."

²³Jesus picked up a cup of wine and gave thanks to God. He gave it to his disciples, and they all drank some. ²⁴Then he said, "This is my blood, which is poured out for many people, and with it God makes his agreement. ²⁵From now on I will not drink any wine, until I drink new wine in God's kingdom." ²⁶Then they sang a hymn and went out to the Mount of Olives.

Peter's Promise
(Matthew 26.31-35; Luke 22.31-34; John 13.36-38)

²⁷Jesus said to his disciples, "All of you will reject me, as the Scriptures say,

'I will strike down
   the shepherd,
and the sheep
   will be scattered.'

²⁸But after I am raised to life, I will go ahead of you to Galilee."

²⁹Peter spoke up, "Even if all the others reject you, I never will!"

³⁰Jesus replied, "This very night before a rooster crows twice, you will say three times that you don't know me."

³¹But Peter was so sure of himself that he said, "Even if I have to die with you, I will never say I don't know you!"

All the others said the same thing.

Jesus Prays
(Matthew 26.36-46; Luke 22.39-46)

³²Jesus went with his disciples to a place called Gethsemane, and he told them, "Sit here while I pray."

³³Jesus took along Peter, James, and John. He was sad and troubled and ³⁴told them, "I am so sad that I feel as if I am dying. Stay here and keep awake with me."

³⁵⁻³⁶Jesus walked on a little way. Then he knelt down on the ground and prayed, "Father,^l if it is possible, don't let this happen to me! Father, you can do anything. Don't make me suffer by drinking from this cup.^m But do what you want, and not what I want."

³⁷When Jesus came back and found the disciples sleeping, he said to Simon Peter, "Are you asleep? Can't you stay awake for just one hour? ³⁸Stay awake and pray that

^k14.13 *a man carrying a jar of water*: A male slave carrying water could mean that the family was rich.
^l14.35,36 *Father*: The Greek text has "Abba," which is an Aramaic word meaning "father."
^m14.35,36 *by drinking from this cup*: See the note at 10.38.

14.22-24 *my body . . . my blood . . . and with it God makes his agreement*: Jesus used the bread and wine to show how his body would be killed and his blood poured out as a sacrifice to forgive sins. Jesus' death would be the basis for a new agreement (covenant) between God and God's new people.

14.32 *Gethsemane*: The exact location is not known, but it was probably on the east side of the Kidron Valley in an area near the Mount of Olives. (See Map 13 on pg 1891.)

14.41 *Son of Man . . . sinners:* Here Jesus is talking about how he will be handed over to Jewish and Roman authorities.

14.53 *high priest:* Caiaphas was the high priest in Jerusalem from A.D. 18 to 26.

14.55 *find someone to accuse Jesus of a crime:* The Law of Moses stated that two witnesses were needed before a person could be put to death (Num 35.30).

14.61 *Son of the glorious God:* "Son of God" was one of the titles used for kings. If the high priest could get Jesus to claim that he was the Son of God, he could tell the Romans that Jesus was claiming to be king, which would have been treason under Roman law.

you won't be tested. You want to do what is right, but you are weak."

[39]Jesus went back and prayed the same prayer. [40]But when he returned to the disciples, he found them sleeping again. They simply could not keep their eyes open, and they did not know what to say.

[41]When Jesus returned to the disciples the third time, he said, "Are you still sleeping and resting?[n] Enough of this! The time has come for the Son of Man to be handed over to sinners. [42]Get up! Let's go. The one who will betray me is already here."

Jesus Is Arrested
(Matthew 26.47-56; Luke 22.47-53; John 18.3-12)

[43]Jesus was still speaking, when Judas the betrayer came up. He was one of the twelve disciples, and a mob of men armed with swords and clubs were with him. They had been sent by the chief priests, the nation's leaders, and the teachers of the Law of Moses. [44]Judas had told them ahead of time, "Arrest the man I greet with a kiss.[o] Tie him up tight and lead him away."

[45]Judas walked right up to Jesus and said, "Teacher!" Then Judas kissed him, [46]and the men grabbed Jesus and arrested him.

[47]Someone standing there pulled out a sword. He struck the servant of the high priest and cut off his ear.

[48]Jesus said to the mob, "Why do you come with swords and clubs to arrest me like a criminal? [49]Day after day I was with you and taught in the temple, and you didn't arrest me. But what the Scriptures say must come true."

[50]All of Jesus' disciples ran off and left him. [51]One of them was a young man who was wearing only a linen cloth. And when the men grabbed him, [52]he left the cloth behind and ran away naked.

Jesus Is Questioned by the Council
(Matthew 26.57-68; Luke 22.54,55,63-71; John 18.13,14,19-24)

[53]Jesus was led off to the high priest. Then the chief priests, the nation's leaders, and the teachers of the Law of Moses all met together. [54]Peter had followed at a distance, and when he reached the courtyard of the high priest's house, he sat down with the guards to warm himself beside a fire.

[55]The chief priests and the whole council tried to find someone to accuse Jesus of a crime, so they could put him to death. But they could not find anyone to accuse him. [56]Many people did tell lies against Jesus, but they did not agree on what they said. [57]Finally, some men stood up and lied about him. They said, [58]"We heard him say he would tear down this temple that we built. He also claimed that in three days he would build another one without any help." [59]But even then they did not agree on what they said.

[60]The high priest stood up in the council and asked Jesus, "Why don't you say something in your own defense? Don't you hear the charges they are making against you?" [61]But Jesus kept quiet and did not say a word. The high priest asked him another question, "Are you the Messiah, the Son of the glorious God?"[P]

[62]"Yes, I am!" Jesus answered.

"Soon you will see
     the Son of Man

[n]**14.41** *Are you still sleeping and resting:* Or "You may as well keep on sleeping and resting."
[o]**14.44** *greet with a kiss:* It was the custom for people to greet each other with a kiss on the cheek.
[P]**14.61** *Son of the glorious God:* "Son of God" was one of the titles used for the kings of Israel.

sitting at the right side^q
of God All-Powerful,
and coming with the clouds
of heaven."

⁶³At once the high priest ripped his robe apart and shouted, "Why do we need more witnesses? ⁶⁴You heard him claim to be God! What is your decision?" They all agreed he should be put to death.

⁶⁵Some of the people started spitting on Jesus. They blindfolded him, hit him with their fists, and said, "Tell us who hit you!" Then the guards took charge of Jesus and beat him.

Peter Says
He Doesn't Know Jesus
(Matthew 26.69-75; Luke 22.56-62; John 18.15-18,25-27)

⁶⁶While Peter was still in the courtyard, a servant girl of the high priest came up ⁶⁷and saw Peter warming himself by the fire. She stared at him and said, "You were with Jesus from Nazareth!"

⁶⁸Peter replied, "That isn't true! I don't know what you're talking about. I don't have any idea what you mean." He went out to the gate, and a rooster crowed.^r

⁶⁹The servant girl saw Peter again and said to the people standing there, "This man is one of them!"

⁷⁰"No, I'm not!" Peter replied.

A little while later some of the people said to Peter, "You certainly are one of them. You're a Galilean!"

⁷¹This time Peter began to curse and swear, "I don't even know the man you're talking about!"

⁷²At once the rooster crowed a second time. Then Peter remembered that Jesus had told him, "Before a rooster crows twice, you will say three times that you don't know me." So Peter started crying.

Pilate Questions Jesus
(Matthew 27.1,2,11-14; Luke 23.1-5; John 18.28-38)

15 Early the next morning the chief priests, the nation's leaders, and the teachers of the Law of Moses met together with the whole Jewish council. They tied up Jesus and led him off to Pilate. ²He asked Jesus, "Are you the king of the Jews?"

"Those are your words," Jesus answered. ³The chief priests brought many charges against Jesus. ⁴Then Pilate questioned him again, "Don't you have anything to say? Don't you hear what crimes they say you have done?" ⁵But Jesus did not answer, and Pilate was amazed.

The Death Sentence
(Matthew 27.15-26; Luke 23.13-25; John 18.39—19.16)

⁶During Passover, Pilate always freed one prisoner chosen by the people. ⁷And at that time there was a prisoner named Barabbas. He and some others had been arrested for murder during a riot. ⁸The crowd now came and asked Pilate to set a prisoner free, just as he usually did.

⁹Pilate asked them, "Do you want me to free the king of the Jews?" ¹⁰Pilate knew that the chief priests had brought Jesus to him because they were jealous. ¹¹But the chief priests told the crowd to ask Pilate to free Barabbas.

¹²Then Pilate asked the crowd, "What do you want me to do with this man you say is^s the king of the Jews?"

^q**14.62** *right side*: See the note at 12.36.   ^r**14.68** *a rooster crowed*: These words are not in some manuscripts.   ^s**15.12** *this man you say is*: These words are not in some manuscripts.

15.13 *Nail him to a cross*: This was the most common way the Romans used to put criminals and other troublemakers to death. Dying on a cross was a very slow and painful death.

Crucifixion

15.21 *Simon from Cyrene . . . father of Alexander and Rufus*: Cyrene was a city in North Africa. Simon was probably a Jew who was in Jerusalem to celebrate Passover. Alexander and Rufus may have been known by the first readers of Mark, but nothing else is said about them in the Bible, unless Rufus is the one Paul greets in Rom 16.13.

15.22 *Golgotha, which means "Place of a Skull"*: The place was probably near a large rock in the shape of a skull. **(See Map 13 on pg 1891.)**

15.32 *Messiah, the king of Israel*: The people expected the Messiah to have great power from God. Because Jesus did not save himself, many didn't believe he could be the Messiah.

¹³They yelled, "Nail him to a cross!"

¹⁴Pilate asked, "But what crime has he done?"

"Nail him to a cross!" they yelled even louder.

¹⁵Pilate wanted to please the crowd, so he set Barabbas free. Then he ordered his soldiers to beat Jesus with a whip and nail him to a cross.

Soldiers Make Fun of Jesus

(Matthew 27.27-30; John 19.2,3)

¹⁶The soldiers led Jesus inside the courtyard of the fortress[t] and called together the rest of the troops. ¹⁷They put a purple robe[u] on him, and on his head they placed a crown they had made out of thorn branches. ¹⁸They made fun of Jesus and shouted, "Hey, you king of the Jews!" ¹⁹Then they beat him on the head with a stick. They spit on him and knelt down and pretended to worship him.

²⁰When the soldiers had finished making fun of Jesus, they took off the purple robe. They put his own clothes back on him and led him off to be nailed to a cross. ²¹Simon from Cyrene happened to be coming in from a farm, and they forced him to carry Jesus' cross. Simon was the father of Alexander and Rufus.

Jesus Is Nailed to a Cross

(Matthew 27.31-44; Luke 23.27-43; John 19.17-27)

²²The soldiers took Jesus to Golgotha, which means "Place of a Skull."[v] ²³There

they gave him some wine mixed with a drug to ease the pain, but he refused to drink it.

²⁴They nailed Jesus to a cross and gambled to see who would get his clothes. ²⁵It was about nine o'clock in the morning when they nailed him to the cross. ²⁶On it was a sign that told why he was nailed there. It read, "This is the King of the Jews." ²⁷⁻²⁸The soldiers also nailed two criminals on crosses, one to the right of Jesus and the other to his left.[w]

²⁹People who passed by said terrible things about Jesus. They shook their heads and shouted, "Ha! So you're the one who claimed you could tear down the temple and build it again in three days. ³⁰Save yourself and come down from the cross!"

³¹The chief priests and the teachers of the Law of Moses also made fun of Jesus. They said to each other, "He saved others, but he can't save himself. ³²If he is the Messiah, the king of Israel, let him come down from the cross! Then we will see and believe." The two criminals also said cruel things to Jesus.

The Death of Jesus

(Matthew 27.45-56; Luke 23.44-49; John 19.28-30)

³³About noon the sky turned dark and stayed that way until around three o'clock. ³⁴Then about that time Jesus shouted, "Eloi, Eloi, lema sabachthani?"[x] which means, "My God, my God, why have you deserted me?"

³⁵Some of the people standing there

[t]**15.16** *fortress*: The place where the Roman governor stayed. It was probably at Herod's palace west of Jerusalem, though it may have been Fortress Antonia, north of the temple, where the Roman troops were stationed.   [u]**15.17** *purple robe*: This was probably a Roman soldier's robe.   [v]**15.22** *Place of a Skull*: The place was probably given this name because it was near a large rock in the shape of a human skull.   [w]**15.27-28** *left*: Some manuscripts add, "So the Scriptures came true which say, 'He was accused of being a criminal.'"   [x]**15.34** *Eloi . . . sabachthani*: These words are in Aramaic, a language spoken in Palestine during the time of Jesus.

heard Jesus and said, "He is calling for Elijah."[y] [36]One of them ran and grabbed a sponge. After he had soaked it in wine, he put it on a stick and held it up to Jesus. He said, "Let's wait and see if Elijah will come[z] and take him down!" [37]Jesus shouted and then died.

[38]At once the curtain in the temple[a] tore in two from top to bottom.

[39]A Roman army officer was standing in front of Jesus. When the officer saw how Jesus died, he said, "This man really was the Son of God!"

[40-41]Some women were looking on from a distance. They and many others had come with Jesus to Jerusalem. But even before this they had been his followers and had helped him while he was in Galilee. Mary Magdalene and Mary the mother of the younger James and of Joseph were two of these women. Salome was also one of them.

Jesus Is Buried

(Matthew 27.57-61; Luke 23.50-56; John 19.38-42)

[42]It was now the evening before the Sabbath, and the Jewish people were getting ready for that sacred day. [43]A man named Joseph from Arimathea was brave enough to ask Pilate for the body of Jesus. Joseph was a highly respected member of the Jewish council, and he was also waiting for God's kingdom to come. [44]Pilate was surprised to hear that Jesus was already dead, and he called in the army officer to find out if Jesus had been dead very long. [45]After the officer told him, Pilate let Joseph have Jesus' body.

[46]Joseph bought a linen cloth and took the body down from the cross. He had it wrapped in the cloth, and he put it in a tomb that had been cut into solid rock. Then he rolled a big stone against the entrance to the tomb.

[47]Mary Magdalene and Mary the mother of Joseph were watching and saw where the body was placed.

Jesus Is Alive

(Matthew 28.1-8; Luke 24.1-12; John 20.1-10)

16 After the Sabbath, Mary Magdalene, Salome, and Mary the mother of James bought some spices to put on Jesus' body. [2]Very early on Sunday morning, just as the sun was coming up, they went to the tomb. [3]On their way, they were asking one another, "Who will roll the stone away from the entrance for us?" [4]But when they looked, they saw that the stone had already been rolled away. And it was a huge stone!

[5]The women went into the tomb, and on the right side they saw a young man in a white robe sitting there. They were alarmed.

[6]The man said, "Don't be alarmed! You are looking for Jesus from Nazareth, who was nailed to a cross. God has raised him to life, and he isn't here. You can see the place where they put his body. [7]Now go and tell his disciples, and especially Peter, that he will go ahead of you to Galilee. You will see him there, just as he told you."

[8]When the women ran from the tomb, they were confused and shaking all over. They were too afraid to tell anyone what had happened.

---

[y]**15.35** *Elijah*: The name "Elijah" sounds something like "Eloi," which means "my God." [z]**15.36** *see if Elijah will come*: See the note at 6.15. [a]**15.38** *curtain in the temple*: There were two curtains in the temple. One was at the entrance, and the other separated the holy place from the most holy place that the Jewish people thought of as God's home on earth. The second curtain is probably the one which is meant.

15.38,39 *curtain in the temple . . . Roman army officer . . . Son of God*: For the author of MARK, the fact that this curtain was torn at the death of Jesus meant that Jesus' death was the sacrifice that made it possible for all people, including Gentiles (non-Jews) to enter into God's presence.

This officer in the Roman army would have been a Gentile. For the author, it was significant that a Gentile was the first person after Jesus' death to recognize Jesus as the "Son of God." This shows that the good news that Jesus died as a sacrifice for the sins of human beings is for all people, Jews and Gentiles alike.

15.43 *Joseph from Arimathea*: Arimathea was a small village in the hilly area called Ephraim, which was about 20 miles northwest of Jerusalem. Joseph was a respected member of the Jewish council, so he risked his reputation by helping to give Jesus a good burial.

Burial

16.1 *spices*: These were probably myrrh and aloes. **(See the chart Spices and Perfumes on pg 1835.)**

16.6 *God has raised him to life*: God brought Jesus back to life from death. This act is also called the resurrection.

Resurrection

16.9 *One Old Ending:* When you read chapter 16 you will notice that MARK has three different endings. This is because the Greek manuscripts of MARK differ from one another. Many of the oldest and most important manuscripts stop at verse 8; others include verses 9-20; and still others have only a shortened ending.

16.9 *Mary Magdalene:* Mary Magdalene's name probably means that she was from Magdala, a town on the western edge of Lake Galilee. Luke 8.2 tells how Jesus healed her. As a follower of Jesus, she may have traveled with a group of Jesus' closest friends.

The author of MARK states that Mary Magdalene was one of several women who had witnessed Jesus' death on the cross. With her were Mary the mother of James and Joseph, and Salome. The other Mary and her sons are hard to identify, though they were probably known to many of MARK's earliest readers. James may be the James who is mentioned as the son of Alphaeus (Mark 3.18; Acts 1.13), but this is not certain. Salome may have been the wife of one of Jesus' disciples.

16.14 *eleven disciples:* Judas Iscariot was no longer part of the group at this time. Other New Testament books report that Judas committed suicide after Jesus was arrested (Matt 27.3-10; Acts 1.16-20).

ONE OLD ENDING TO MARK'S GOSPEL[b]

Jesus Appears to Mary Magdalene

(Matthew 28.9,10; John 20.11-18)

[9]Very early on the first day of the week, after Jesus had risen to life, he appeared to Mary Magdalene. Earlier he had forced seven demons out of her. [10]She left and told his friends, who were crying and mourning. [11]Even though they heard that Jesus was alive and that Mary had seen him, they still would not believe it.

Jesus Appears to Two Disciples

(Luke 24.13-35)

[12]Later, Jesus appeared in another form to two disciples, as they were on their way out of the city. [13]But when these disciples told what had happened, the others would not believe either.

What Jesus' Followers Must Do

(Matthew 28.16-20; Luke 24.36-49; John 20.19-23; Acts 1.6-8)

[14]Afterwards, Jesus appeared to his eleven disciples as they were eating. He scolded them because they were too stubborn to believe the ones who had seen him after he had been raised to life. [15]Then he told them:

Go and preach the good news to everyone in the world. [16]Anyone who believes me and is baptized will be saved. But anyone who refuses to believe me will be condemned. [17]Everyone who believes me will be able to do wonderful things. By using my name they will force out demons, and they will speak new languages. [18]They will handle snakes and will drink poison and not be hurt. They will also heal sick people by placing their hands on them.

Jesus Returns to Heaven

(Luke 24.50-53; Acts 1.9-11)

[19]After the Lord Jesus had said these things to the disciples, he was taken back up to heaven where he sat down at the right side[c] of God. [20]Then the disciples left and preached everywhere. The Lord was with them, and the miracles they worked proved that their message was true.

ANOTHER OLD ENDING TO MARK'S GOSPEL[d]

[9-10]The women quickly told Peter and his friends what had happened. Later, Jesus sent the disciples to the east and to the west with his sacred and everlasting message of how people can be saved forever.

---

[b]16.9 *One Old Ending to Mark's Gospel:* Verses 9-20 are not in some manuscripts.   [c]16.19 *right side:* See the note at 12.36.   [d]16.9,10 *Another Old Ending to Mark's Gospel:* Some manuscripts and early translations have both this shorter ending and the longer one (verses 9-20).

"Go and preach the good news to everyone in the world. Anyone who believes me and is baptized will be saved."
MARK 16.15,16

Reflection Questions About Mark 1.1—16.10

1. MARK begins with the words, "This is the good news about Jesus Christ." What is this "good news"? Give two or three examples from the first nine chapters to support your definition.

2. Read 3.1-6. What did Jesus do that made the Pharisees angry? What is the answer to Jesus' question in 3.4? Why?

3. Jesus used parables (stories) to teach the good news. Chapter 4 has three stories about seeds and planting. How is the message similar in each story? What is the key message?

4. Read 9.33-35. How does Jesus' teaching go against what our modern world often teaches? Is Jesus' teaching easy or difficult to follow? Why?

5. Describe the meeting between Jesus and the rich young man (10.17-22). What happened at the end of their meeting? Why?

6. What did Jesus say are the two most important commandments (12.28-33)?

7. Summarize Jesus' teachings about the future (13.1-37). Are his words comforting or frightening, or both? Why?

8. What promise did Peter make to Jesus (14.27-31)? Was he able to keep it? Why or why not? What does it mean to deny Jesus? How does this denial take place in today's world?

9. What did the Roman army officer guarding Jesus' cross realize (15.39)? What makes this important in MARK?

10. Why was Joseph of Arimathea's burial of Jesus an act of courage? What is the most courageous thing you have ever done? Why did you do it? Does it take courage to be a follower of God? Explain.

luke

"Timing is everything," as the saying goes. Read LUKE
*to learn how God chose Jesus, and sent him to earth
when the time was right.*

WHAT MAKES LUKE SPECIAL?

LUKE is the first part of a two-volume work that includes ACTS. This is clear from the introductions to
both books (see Luke 1.1-4 and Acts 1.1-5). These
books, considered together, give readers a panoramic
view of the foundation of Christianity.

WHAT'S THE STORY BEHIND THE SCENE?

LUKE was probably created after A.D. 70 from at least
three different sources: the book of MARK, a collection of Jesus' sayings that the writer of MATTHEW
also used, and a collection of stories not included in
any other Gospel. Some familiar stories told by Jesus
are found only in LUKE: "The Good Samaritan"
(10.25-37), "One Sheep" (15.1-7), and "Two Sons"
(15.11-32). LUKE is the only Gospel that tells how Jesus visited the home of the hated tax collector
named Zacchaeus (19.1-10) and promised life in paradise to a dying criminal (23.39-43).

LUKE, like the book of ACTS, often mentions God's
Holy Spirit. LUKE also shows how important prayer
was to Jesus (3.21; 6.12; 9.18; and 23.34,46). From
LUKE we learn of three stories that Jesus used in
teaching about prayer (11.5-9; 18.1-8, also 9-14). Another key theme is that God sent Jesus to be the Savior of all people, not only Jews but also Gentiles.

Jesus' concern for the poor is an important
theme in LUKE. The good news is preached to them
(4.18; 7.22); they receive God's blessings (6.20); and
they are invited to a great banquet (14.13,21). A poor
beggar named Lazarus is taken to heaven by angels
(16.20,22). Jesus also commands his disciples to
sell what they have and give the money to the poor
(12.33).

HOW IS LUKE CONSTRUCTED?

In the following outline, LUKE is organized around
important events in Jesus' life and the places where
these events happen.

Preparing the way for Jesus (1.1—4.13)
    Why Luke wrote this book (1.1-4)
    Two miraculous births (1.5—2.21)
    Jesus as a child (2.22-52)
    Jesus is God's own Son (3.1—4.13)
Jesus Preaches and Heals in Galilee (4.14—9.50)
    Mixed reactions toward Jesus (4.14-37)
    Jesus heals many people and chooses his disci-
    ples (4.38—5.32)
    Jesus continues his work in Galilee (5.33—9.17)
    Who Jesus is and what he must do (9.18-50)
Jesus goes to Jerusalem (9.51—19.27)
    Followers and unbelievers (9.51—10.42)
    Jesus teaches many things (11.1—12.59)
    Teachings about the Kingdom of God
    (13.1—14.35)
    The lost are found (15.1-32)
    Faithful servants (16.1—19.27)
Jesus' final week in Jerusalem (19.28—23.56)
    Jesus teaches in Jerusalem (19.28—21.38)
    The last days of Jesus: his trial and death
    (22.1—23.56)
Jesus rises from death and appears to the disciples
    (24.1-53)

Luke and Acts were composed as one history. Luke—the story of Jesus' life, ministry, death, and resurrection—is completed by Acts, which shows how Jesus' disciples spread the good news of Jesus Christ throughout the Roman Empire in the first century. Written in the eloquent and compelling literary style popular among history writers at that time, this Gospel shows Jesus' ministry as the fulfillment of God's promise and saving love to his people. The book is rich in historical details. It also contains a number of stories about Jesus as well as parables (stories) Jesus taught that are not contained in the other Gospels. Scholars have pointed out that Luke "takes the long view," demonstrating how the events and timing of Jesus' ministry fit perfectly into God's plan for his creation.

Outline

1

Many people have tried to tell the story of what God has done among us. ²They wrote what we had been told by the ones who were there in the beginning and saw what happened. ³So I made a careful study[a] of everything and then decided to write and tell you exactly what took place. Honorable Theophilus, ⁴I have done this to let you know the truth about what you have heard.

An Angel Tells about the Birth of John

⁵When Herod was king of Judea, there was a priest by the name of Zechariah from the priestly group of Abijah. His wife Elizabeth was from the family of Aaron.[b] ⁶Both of them were good people and pleased the Lord God by obeying all that he had commanded. ⁷But they did not have children. Elizabeth could not have any, and both Zechariah and Elizabeth were already old.

⁸One day Zechariah's group of priests were on duty, and he was serving God as a priest. ⁹According to the custom of the priests, he had been chosen to go into the Lord's temple that day and to burn incense,[c] ¹⁰while the people stood outside praying.

¹¹All at once an angel from the Lord appeared to Zechariah at the right side of the altar. ¹²Zechariah was confused and afraid when he saw the angel. ¹³But the angel told him:

Don't be afraid, Zechariah! God has heard your prayers. Your wife Elizabeth will have a son, and you must name him John. ¹⁴His birth will make you very happy, and many people will be glad. ¹⁵Your son will be a great servant of the Lord. He must never drink wine or beer, and the power of the Holy Spirit will be with him from the time he is born.

¹⁶John will lead many people in

ᵃ**1.3** *a careful study:* Or "a study from the beginning."   ᵇ**1.5** *Aaron:* The brother of Moses and the first priest.   ᶜ**1.9** *burn incense:* This was done twice a day, once in the morning and again in the late afternoon.

1.17 *Elijah:* The prophet Elijah lived in Israel more than 800 years before Jesus was born. Later prophets expected God to send Elijah back to earth to warn people of God's judgment (Mal 3.1-4; 4.5,6). Some people thought John the Baptist was Elijah come back again (see Mark 6.14,15).

Elijah

1.19 *Gabriel:* This angel first appears in DANIEL as a messenger who brings Daniel the wisdom to understand a vision (Dan 8.16; 9.21).

1.31 *Jesus:* In Hebrew Jesus means "the Lord saves."

1.32 *God Most High:* This name for God goes back to the time of Abraham (Gen 14.17-22).

Names of God

1.35 *Holy Spirit:* The Holy Spirit—God's power at work in the world—is very important in LUKE. The Holy Spirit does miraculous things like causing the virgin Mary to become pregnant.

Holy Spirit

Son of God

Israel to turn back to the Lord their God. **17**He will go ahead of the Lord with the same power and spirit that Elijah[d] had. And because of John, parents will be more thoughtful of their children. And people who now disobey God will begin to think as they ought to. This is how John will get people ready for the Lord.

18Zechariah said to the angel, "How will I know this is going to happen? My wife and I are both very old."

19The angel answered, "I am Gabriel, God's servant, and I was sent to tell you this good news. **20**You have not believed what I have said. So you will not be able to say a thing until all this happens. But everything will take place when it is supposed to."

21The crowd was waiting for Zechariah and kept wondering why he was staying in the temple so long. **22**When he did come out, he could not speak, and they knew he had seen a vision. He motioned to them with his hands, but did not say a thing.

23When Zechariah's time of service in the temple was over, he went home. **24**Soon after this, his wife was expecting a baby, and for five months she did not leave the house. She said to herself, **25**"What the Lord has done for me will keep people from looking down on me."[e]

An Angel Tells about the Birth of Jesus

26One month later God sent the angel Gabriel to the town of Nazareth in Galilee **27**with a message for a virgin named Mary. She was engaged to Joseph from the family

of King David. **28**The angel greeted Mary and said, "You are truly blessed! The Lord is with you."

29Mary was confused by the angel's words and wondered what they meant. **30**Then the angel told Mary, "Don't be afraid! God is pleased with you, **31**and you will have a son. His name will be Jesus. **32**He will be great and will be called the Son of God Most High. The Lord God will make him king, as his ancestor David was. **33**He will rule the people of Israel forever, and his kingdom will never end."

34Mary asked the angel, "How can this happen? I am not even married!"

35The angel answered, "The Holy Spirit will come down to you, and God's power will come over you. So your child will be called the holy Son of God. **36**Your relative Elizabeth is also going to have a son, even though she is old. No one thought she could ever have a baby, but in three months she will have a son. **37**Nothing is impossible for God!"

38Mary said, "I am the Lord's servant! Let it happen as you have said." And the angel left her.

Mary Visits Elizabeth

39A short time later Mary hurried to a town in the hill country of Judea. **40**She went into Zechariah's home, where she greeted Elizabeth. **41**When Elizabeth heard Mary's greeting, her baby moved within her.

The Holy Spirit came upon Elizabeth. **42**Then in a loud voice she said to Mary:

God has blessed you more than any other woman! He has also blessed the

[d]**1.17** *Elijah:* The prophet Elijah was known for his power to work miracles.   [e]**1.25** *keep people from looking down on me:* When a married woman could not have children, it was thought that the Lord was punishing her.

child you will have. **43**Why should the mother of my Lord come to me? **44**As soon as I heard your greeting, my baby became happy and moved within me. **45**The Lord has blessed you because you believed that he will keep his promise.

Mary's Song of Praise

46Mary said:
  With all my heart
    I praise the Lord,
47and I am glad
    because of God my Savior.
48God cares for me,
    his humble servant.
  From now on,
    all people will say
    God has blessed me.
49God All-Powerful has done
  great things for me,
    and his name is holy.
50He always shows mercy
  to everyone
    who worships him.
51The Lord has used
  his powerful arm
    to scatter those
    who are proud.
52 God drags strong rulers
    from their thrones
  and puts humble people
    in places of power.
53God gives the hungry
    good things to eat,
  and sends the rich away
    with nothing.
54God helps his servant Israel
  and is always merciful
    to his people.
55The Lord made this promise

to our ancestors,
  to Abraham and his family
    forever!

56Mary stayed with Elizabeth about three months. Then she went back home.

The Birth of John the Baptist

57When Elizabeth's son was born, **58**her neighbors and relatives heard how kind the Lord had been to her, and they too were glad. **59**Eight days later they did for the child what the Law of Moses commands.**f** They were going to name him Zechariah, after his father. **60**But Elizabeth said, "No! His name is John."

61The people argued, "No one in your family has ever been named John." **62**So they motioned to Zechariah to find out what he wanted to name his son. **63**Zechariah asked for a writing tablet. Then he wrote, "His name is John." Everyone was amazed. **64**At once, Zechariah started speaking and praising God.

65All the neighbors were frightened because of what had happened, and everywhere in the hill country people kept talking about these things. **66**Everyone who heard about this wondered what this child would grow up to be. They knew the Lord was with him.

Zechariah Praises the Lord

67The Holy Spirit came upon Zechariah, and he began to speak:

68Praise the Lord,
    the God of Israel!
  He has come

---

f1.59 *what the Law of Moses commands:* This refers to circumcision. It is the cutting off of skin from the private part of Jewish boys eight days after birth to show that they belong to the Lord.

1.46-55 *With all my heart . . . and his family forever:* Mary's song is a prayer that praises God and is like the song that Hannah sang when God gave her a son (1 Sam 2.1-10). Mary's song is also known by some Christians as the *Magnificat*, which in Latin means "magnify." This song introduces an important theme in Luke: God is a friend of poor people.

1.55 *our ancestors, to Abraham:* This refers to the people of Israel, all of whom can trace their families back to Abraham and Sarah. God made an agreement (covenant) with Abraham many centuries before Jesus was born (Gen 12.1-3; 17.4-8). Abraham agreed to follow God, and God promised Abraham that he and Sarah would be the parents of a great nation (Gen 15.1-6).

CR   Abraham

CR   Israel

CR   Circumcision

1.68-79 *Praise the Lord . . . into a life of peace:* Zechariah praised God and offered a prophecy or vision of what his son, John, would do. Zechariah's song is in the form of a blessing much like those found in Psalms. See Ps 41.13; 106.48.

1.69 *David his servant:* This refers to Israel's King David.

David

1.70 *holy prophets:* The prophets of Israel were special messengers who spoke for God. They told about God's promise to send a Messiah who would save the people (see Isa 7.14; 9.6,7; Mic 5.2). (See the article Prophets and Prophecy on pg 1791.)

1.80 *desert until the time he was sent:* The time between John's birth and his preaching in the desert was about 30 years. John probably lived in the desert of Judea, which is between Jerusalem and the Dead Sea. (See Map 12 on pg 1890.)

2.1 *Emperor Augustus:* The Roman emperor at the time Jesus was born. Emperor Augustus greatly improved the organization of the whole Roman Empire, and led the empire to control almost all the land surrounding the Mediterranean Sea. The stability and peace enforced by the Roman Empire, called the *Pax Romana* in Latin, allowed Christianity to spread rapidly throughout the ancient world. (See the article The World of Jesus: Peoples, Powers, and Politics on pg 1801.)

2.1 *names . . . listed in record books:* This was done so that everyone living in Roman-held territories could be made to pay taxes to the Roman emperor. All the people were supposed to register in their hometowns (2.3).

to save his people.
⁶⁹Our God has given us
  a mighty Savior^g
from the family
  of David his servant.
⁷⁰Long ago the Lord promised
  by the words
  of his holy prophets
⁷¹to save us from our enemies
  and from everyone
  who hates us.
⁷²God said he would be kind
  to our people and keep
  his sacred promise.
⁷³He told our ancestor Abraham
⁷⁴that he would rescue us
  from our enemies.
  Then we could serve him
  without fear,
⁷⁵by being holy and good
  as long as we live.

⁷⁶You, my son, will be called
  the prophet of God Most High.
  You will go ahead of the Lord
  to get everything ready
  for him.
⁷⁷You will tell his people
  that they can be saved
  when their sins
  are forgiven.
⁷⁸God's love and kindness
  will shine upon us
  like the sun that rises
  in the sky.^h
⁷⁹On us who live

in the dark shadow
  of death
this light will shine
  to guide us
  into a life of peace.

⁸⁰As John grew up, God's Spirit gave him great power. John lived in the desert until the time he was sent to the people of Israel.

The Birth of Jesus
(Matthew 1.18-25)

2 About that time Emperor Augustus gave orders for the names of all the people to be listed in record books.^i ²These first records were made when Quirinius was governor of Syria.^j

³Everyone had to go to their own hometown to be listed. ⁴So Joseph had to leave Nazareth in Galilee and go to Bethlehem in Judea. Long ago Bethlehem had been King David's hometown, and Joseph went there because he was from David's family.

⁵Mary was engaged to Joseph and traveled with him to Bethlehem. She was soon going to have a baby, ⁶and while they were there, ⁷she gave birth to her first-born^k son. She dressed him in baby clothes^l and laid him on a bed of hay, because there was no room for them in the inn.

The Shepherds

⁸That night in the fields near Bethlehem some shepherds were guarding their sheep. ⁹All at once an angel came down to them

^g1.69 *a mighty Savior:* The Greek text has "a horn of salvation." In the Scriptures animal horns are often a symbol of great strength.   ^h1.78 *like the sun that rises in the sky:* Or "like the Messiah coming from heaven."   ^i2.1 *names . . . listed in record books:* This was done so that everyone could be made to pay taxes to the Emperor.   ^j2.2 *Quirinius was governor of Syria:* It is known that Quirinius made a record of the people in A.D. 6 or 7. But the exact date of the record taking that Luke mentions is not known.   ^k2.7 *first-born:* The Jewish people said that the first-born son in each of their families belonged to the Lord.   ^l2.7 *dressed him in baby clothes:* The Greek text has "wrapped him in wide strips of cloth," which was how young babies were dressed.

from the Lord, and the brightness of the Lord's glory flashed around them. The shepherds were frightened. [10]But the angel said, "Don't be afraid! I have good news for you, which will make everyone happy. [11]This very day in King David's hometown a Savior was born for you. He is Christ the Lord. [12]You will know who he is, because you will find him dressed in baby clothes and lying on a bed of hay."

[13]Suddenly many other angels came down from heaven and joined in praising God. They said:

[14]"Praise God in heaven!
　Peace on earth to everyone
　　who pleases God."

[15]After the angels had left and gone back to heaven, the shepherds said to each other, "Let's go to Bethlehem and see what the Lord has told us about." [16]They hurried off and found Mary and Joseph, and they saw the baby lying on a bed of hay.

[17]When the shepherds saw Jesus, they told his parents what the angel had said about him. [18]Everyone listened and was surprised. [19]But Mary kept thinking about all this and wondering what it meant.

[20]As the shepherds returned to their sheep, they were praising God and saying wonderful things about him. Everything they had seen and heard was just as the angel had said.

[21]Eight days later Jesus' parents did for him what the Law of Moses commands.[m] And they named him Jesus, just as the angel had told Mary when he promised she would have a baby.

Simeon Praises the Lord

[22]The time came for Mary and Joseph to do what the Law of Moses says a mother is supposed to do after her baby is born.[n]

They took Jesus to the temple in Jerusalem and presented him to the Lord, [23]just as the Law of the Lord says, "Each first-born[o] baby boy belongs to the Lord." [24]The Law of the Lord also says parents have to offer a sacrifice, giving at least a pair of doves or two young pigeons. So that is what Mary and Joseph did.

[25]At this time a man named Simeon was living in Jerusalem. Simeon was a good man. He loved God and was waiting for him to save the people of Israel. God's Spirit came to him [26]and told him that he would not die until he had seen Christ the Lord.

[27]When Mary and Joseph brought Jesus to the temple to do what the Law of Moses says should be done for a new baby, the Spirit told Simeon to go into the temple. [28]Simeon took the baby Jesus in his arms and praised God,

[29]"Lord, I am your servant,
　and now I can die in peace,
　because you have kept
　　your promise to me.
[30]With my own eyes I have seen
　what you have done
　　to save your people,
[31]and foreign nations
　will also see this.
[32]Your mighty power is a light
　for all nations,
　and it will bring honor
　　to your people Israel."

● 2.11 *King David's hometown:* Bethlehem.

■ 2.11 *Savior . . . Christ:* A savior is one who rescues or sets people free. See Isa 43.11; Matt 1.21. "Christ" is from the Greek word, *Christos*, which means Messiah or "chosen one."

⊗ Messiah (Chosen One)

■ 2.13 *angels:* The word "angel" means "messenger." In the Bible, angels act both as messengers and as servants of God.

⊗ Angels

⊗ Law

● 2.28-32 *Simeon . . . praised God:* Simeon's song is also known to some Christians as the "Nunc Dimittis," which in Latin means, "Now you let [me] leave."

■ 2.32 *a light for all nations:* Simeon was referring to Isaiah 42.6; 49.6; 52.10. See also Acts 13.46,47, where Paul and Barnabas say that they have been chosen to carry on the work of Jesus by taking his message to the Gentiles (all nations).

[m]2.21 *what the Law of Moses commands:* See the note at 1.59.   [n]2.22 *after her baby is born:* After a Jewish mother gave birth to a son, she was considered "unclean" and had to stay home until he was circumcised (see the note at 1.59). Then she had to stay home for another 33 days, before offering a sacrifice to the Lord.   [o]2.23 *first-born:* See the note at 2.7.

2.36 *prophet Anna . . . from the tribe of Asher:* Little is known about the prophet Anna or her father Phanuel. Though most prophets were male, LUKE has a number of examples of women who, like Anna, spoke God's messages or participated as Jesus' followers. One of the twelve tribes of Israel was named for Asher, one of Jacob's twelve sons (Gen 30.9-12).

2.41 *Passover:* Passover was celebrated as a remembrance of how God helped the people of Israel escape from slavery in Egypt (Exod 12.1-27; Deut 16.1-8).

Passover and the Festival of Thin Bread

2.42 *twelve years old:* At twelve years old, Jewish boys prepared to take their full place in the religious community when they turned thirteen.

2.46 *teachers:* Probably refers to men who taught the Law of Moses and the Jewish Scriptures.

33 Jesus' parents were surprised at what Simeon had said. 34 Then he blessed them and told Mary, "This child of yours will cause many people in Israel to fall and others to stand. The child will be like a warning sign. Many people will reject him, 35 and you, Mary, will suffer as though you had been stabbed by a dagger. But all this will show what people are really thinking."

Anna Speaks about the Child Jesus

36 The prophet Anna was also there in the temple. She was the daughter of Phanuel from the tribe of Asher, and she was very old. In her youth she had been married for seven years, but her husband died. 37 And now she was 84 years old.[p] Night and day she served God in the temple by praying and often going without eating.[q]

38 At this time Anna came in and praised God. She spoke about the child Jesus to everyone who hoped for Jerusalem to be set free.

The Return to Nazareth

39 After Joseph and Mary had done everything that the Law of the Lord commands, they returned home to Nazareth in Galilee. 40 The child Jesus grew. He became strong and wise, and God blessed him.

The Boy Jesus in the Temple

41 Every year Jesus' parents went to Jerusalem for Passover. 42 And when Jesus was twelve years old, they all went there as usual for the celebration. 43 After Passover his parents left, but they did not know that Jesus had stayed on in the city. 44 They thought he was traveling with some other people, and they went a whole day before they started looking for him. 45 When they could not find him with their relatives and friends, they went back to Jerusalem and started looking for him there.

46 Three days later they found Jesus sitting in the temple, listening to the teachers and asking them questions. 47 Everyone who heard him was surprised at how much he knew and at the answers he gave.

48 When his parents found him, they were amazed. His mother said, "Son, why have you done this to us? Your father and I have been very worried, and we have been searching for you!"

49 Jesus answered, "Why did you have to look for me? Didn't you know that I would be in my Father's house?"[r] 50 But they did not understand what he meant.

51 Jesus went back to Nazareth with his parents and obeyed them. His mother kept on thinking about all that had happened.

52 Jesus became wise, and he grew strong. God was pleased with him and so were the people.

The Preaching of John the Baptist

(Matthew 3.1-12; Mark 1.1-8; John 1.19-28)

3 For 15 years[s] Emperor Tiberius had ruled that part of the world. Pontius Pilate was governor of Judea, and Herod[t] was the ruler of Galilee. Herod's brother, Philip, was the ruler in the countries of Iturea and Trachonitis, and Lysanias was

[p] **2.37** *And now she was 84 years old:* Or "And now she had been a widow for 84 years." [q] **2.37** *without eating:* The Jewish people sometimes went without eating (also called "fasting") to show their love for God or to show sorrow for their sins. [r] **2.49** *in my Father's house:* Or "doing my Father's work." [s] **3.1** *For 15 years:* This was either A.D. 28 or 29, and Jesus was about 30 years old (see 3.23). [t] **3.1** *Herod:* Herod Antipas, the son of Herod the Great.

the ruler of Abilene. **2**Annas and Caiaphas were the Jewish high priests.**u**

At that time God spoke to Zechariah's son John, who was living in the desert. **3**So John went along the Jordan Valley, telling the people, "Turn back to God and be baptized! Then your sins will be forgiven." **4**Isaiah the prophet wrote about John when he said,

"In the desert
    someone is shouting,
'Get the road ready
    for the Lord!
Make a straight path
    for him.
5Fill up every valley
and level every mountain
    and hill.
Straighten the crooked paths
and smooth out
    the rough roads.
6Then everyone will see
    the saving power of God.'"

7Crowds of people came out to be baptized, but John said to them, "You bunch of snakes! Who warned you to run from the coming judgment? **8**Do something to show that you really have given up your sins. Don't start saying you belong to Abraham's family. God can turn these stones into children for Abraham.**v** **9**An ax is ready to cut the trees down at their roots. Any tree that doesn't produce good fruit will be cut down and thrown into a fire."

10The crowds asked John, "What should we do?"

11John told them, "If you have two coats, give one to someone who doesn't have any. If you have food, share it with someone else."

12When tax collectors**w** came to be baptized, they asked John, "Teacher, what should we do?"

13John told them, "Don't make people pay more than they owe."

14Some soldiers asked him, "And what about us? What do we have to do?"

John told them, "Don't force people to pay money to make you leave them alone. Be satisfied with your pay."

15Everyone became excited and wondered, "Could John be the Messiah?"

16John said, "I am just baptizing with water. But someone more powerful is going to come, and I am not good enough even to untie his sandals.**x** He will baptize you with the Holy Spirit and with fire. **17**His threshing fork**y** is in his hand, and he is ready to separate the wheat from the husks. He will store the wheat in his barn and burn the husks with a fire that never goes out."

18In many different ways John preached the good news to the people. **19**But to Herod the ruler, he said, "It was wrong for you to take Herodias, your brother's wife." John also said Herod had done many other bad things. **20**Finally, Herod put John in jail, and this was the worst thing he had done.

3.8 *children for Abraham:* John warned the Jewish people not to think that they could live any way they wanted, just because they were descendants of Abraham and Sarah. See also John 8.33.

Sin

3.12 *tax collectors:* The Romans issued contracts for the right to collect taxes. These contracts were usually given to wealthy foreigners, who hired local people to collect taxes. Tax collectors usually took from people more than was actually demanded by Rome. Most Jews in Jesus' day hated tax collectors, considered them ritually unclean, and treated them as traitors.

3.16 *baptizing . . . Holy Spirit and with fire:* Baptizing people with water symbolized the old way of life being washed away. Fire may be connected with God's judgment or with the Holy Spirit (Acts 2.3).

Baptism

The Holy Spirit

Fire

---

u3.2 *Annas and Caiaphas . . . high priests:* Annas was high priest from A.D. 6 until 15. His son-in-law Caiaphas was high priest from A.D. 18 until 37.   **v3.8** *children for Abraham:* The Jewish people thought they were God's chosen people because of God's promises to their ancestor Abraham.   **w3.12** *tax collectors:* These were usually Jewish people who paid the Romans for the right to collect taxes. They were hated by other Jews who thought of them as traitors to their country and to their religion.   **x3.16** *untie his sandals:* This was the duty of a slave.   **y3.17** *threshing fork:* After Jewish farmers had trampled out the grain, they used a large fork to pitch the grain and the husks into the air. Wind would blow away the light husks, and the grain would fall back to the ground, where it could be gathered up.

3.23-38 *son of Joseph . . . God:* Family roots were very important to the Jewish people. They believed that the Messiah would come from the family of David (Isa 11.1-11). LUKE traces Jesus' personal history all the way back to Adam and to God. Compare this list of ancestors (called a genealogy) with the one MATTHEW provides at Matthew 1.1-17.

4.1 *Jordan River . . . desert:* The desert of Judea stretched about 20 miles eastward from the highlands around Jerusalem down to the Jordan River and the Dead Sea. **(See Map 12 on pg 1890.)**

Baptism

4.2 *40 days:* The 40 days and nights Jesus spent in the desert are the same number of days that Moses (Exod 24.18; 34.28) and Elijah (1 Kgs 19.8) spent preparing for the important work they had to do among God's people. **(See the chart Numbers in the Bible on pg 1844.)**

4.3 *devil:* By the time of Jesus, the devil (Satan), was identified as the leader of the forces that are against God and God's people.

Satan

4.14 *Galilee:* Jesus' home region.

4.14 *power of the Spirit:* LUKE often notes that God's Spirit is at work directing Jesus and others.

The Baptism of Jesus
(Matthew 3.13-17; Mark 1.9-11)

²¹While everyone else was being baptized, Jesus himself was baptized. Then as he prayed, the sky opened up, ²²and the Holy Spirit came down upon him in the form of a dove. A voice from heaven said, "You are my own dear Son, and I am pleased with you."

The Ancestors of Jesus
(Matthew 1.1-17)

²³When Jesus began to preach, he was about 30 years old. Everyone thought he was the son of Joseph. But his family went back through Heli, ²⁴Matthat, Levi, Melchi, Jannai, Joseph, ²⁵Mattathias, Amos, Nahum, Esli, Naggai, ²⁶Maath, Mattathias, Semein, Josech, Joda;

²⁷Joanan, Rhesa, Zerubbabel, Shealtiel, Neri, ²⁸Melchi, Addi, Cosam, Elmadam, Er, ²⁹Joshua, Eliezer, Jorim, Matthat, Levi;

³⁰Simeon, Judah, Joseph, Jonam, Eliakim, ³¹Melea, Menna, Mattatha, Nathan, David, ³²Jesse, Obed, Boaz, Salmon, Nahshon;

³³Amminadab, Admin, Arni, Hezron, Perez, Judah, ³⁴Jacob, Isaac, Abraham, Terah, Nahor, ³⁵Serug, Reu, Peleg, Eber, Shelah;

³⁶Cainan, Arphaxad, Shem, Noah, Lamech, ³⁷Methuselah, Enoch, Jared, Mahalaleel, Kenan, ³⁸Enosh, and Seth. The family of Jesus went all the way back to Adam and then to God.

Jesus and the Devil
(Matthew 4.1-11; Mark 1.12,13)

4 When Jesus returned from the Jordan River, the power of the Holy Spirit

ᶻ**4.2** *went without eating:* See the note at 2.37.

was with him, and the Spirit led him into the desert. ²For 40 days Jesus was tested by the devil, and during that time he went without eating.ᶻ When it was all over, he was hungry.

³The devil said to Jesus, "If you are God's Son, tell this stone to turn into bread."

⁴Jesus answered, "The Scriptures say, 'No one can live only on food.' "

⁵Then the devil led Jesus up to a high place and quickly showed him all the nations on earth. ⁶The devil said, "I will give all this power and glory to you. It has been given to me, and I can give it to anyone I want to. ⁷Just worship me, and you can have it all."

⁸Jesus answered, "The Scriptures say:
'Worship the Lord your God
    and serve only him!' "

⁹Finally, the devil took Jesus to Jerusalem and had him stand on top of the temple. The devil said, "If you are God's Son, jump off. ¹⁰⁻¹¹The Scriptures say:
'God will tell his angels
    to take care of you.
They will catch you
    in their arms,
and you will not even hurt
    your feet on the stones.' "

¹²Jesus answered, "The Scriptures also say, 'Don't try to test the Lord your God!' "

¹³After the devil had finished testing Jesus in every way possible, he left him for a while.

Jesus Begins His Work
(Matthew 4.12-17; Mark 1.14,15)

¹⁴Jesus returned to Galilee with the power of the Spirit. News about him spread everywhere. ¹⁵He taught in the Jewish synagogues, and everyone praised him.

A voice from heaven said, "You are my own dear Son, and I am pleased with you." LUKE 3.22

The People of Nazareth Turn against Jesus

(Matthew 13.53-58; Mark 6.1-6)

[16]Jesus went back to Nazareth, where he had been brought up, and as usual he went to the synagogue on the Sabbath. When he stood up to read from the Scriptures, [17]he was given the book of Isaiah the prophet. He opened it and read,

[18]"The Lord's Spirit
    has come to me,
  because he has chosen me
    to tell the good news
      to the poor.
  The Lord has sent me
    to announce freedom
      for prisoners,
    to give sight to the blind,
    to free everyone
      who suffers,
[19]and to say, 'This is the year
    the Lord has chosen.'"

[20]Jesus closed the book, then handed it back to the man in charge and sat down. Everyone in the synagogue looked straight at Jesus. [21]Then Jesus said to them, "What you have just heard me read has come true today."

[22]All the people started talking about Jesus and were amazed at the wonderful things he said. They kept on asking, "Isn't he Joseph's son?"

[23]Jesus answered:

You will certainly want to tell me this saying, "Doctor, first make yourself well." You will tell me to do the same things here in my own hometown that you heard I did in Capernaum. [24]But you can be sure that no prophets are liked by the people of their own hometown.

[25]Once during the time of Elijah there was no rain for three and a half years, and people everywhere were starving. There were many widows in Israel, [26]but Elijah was sent only to a widow in the town of Zarephath near the city of Sidon. [27]During the time of the prophet Elisha, many men in Israel had leprosy.[a] But no one was healed, except Naaman who lived in Syria.

[28]When the people in the synagogue heard Jesus say this, they became so angry [29]that they got up and threw him out of town. They dragged him to the edge of the cliff on which the town was built, because they wanted to throw him down from there. [30]But Jesus slipped through the crowd and got away.

A Man with an Evil Spirit

(Mark 1.21-28)

[31]Jesus went to the town of Capernaum in Galilee and taught the people on the Sabbath. [32]His teaching amazed them because he spoke with power. [33]There in the synagogue was a man with an evil spirit. He yelled out, [34]"Hey, Jesus of Nazareth, what do you want with us? Are you here to get rid of us? I know who you are! You are God's Holy One."

[35]Jesus ordered the evil spirit to be quiet and come out. The demon threw the man to the ground in front of everyone and left without harming him.

[36]They all were amazed and kept saying to each other, "What kind of teaching is this? He has power to order evil spirits out of people!" [37]News about Jesus spread all over that part of the country.

[a]4.27 *leprosy*: In biblical times the word "leprosy" was used for many different kinds of skin diseases.

4.16 *Sabbath*: The Jewish day of rest. The Sabbath was the seventh day of the week, the day that God rested after creating the world (Gen 2.2,3). **(See the chart Pilgrimage Festivals on pg 1799.)**

4.16 *Scriptures*: These are the Jewish Scriptures, which Christians call the Old Testament.

4.17 *Isaiah the prophet*: Isaiah was a prophet in Judah from about 740 to 701 B.C.

4.20 *book*: The books of the Jewish Scriptures were written on long parchment or leather scrolls.

Scrolls

4.25-27 *many widows . . . Naaman*: See 1 Kgs 17.1-15 and 2 Kgs 5.1-14. Both the widow of Zarephath and Naaman of Syria were Gentiles. Jesus told these stories to show how God cares about all people.

4.33-35 *evil spirit . . . demon*: Demons are evil spirits that work for the devil. In Jesus' day, demons were believed be the cause of many kinds of sickness and mental illness. This demon recognized who Jesus was and called him "God's Holy One." (See the article Miracles, Magic, and Medicine on pg 1820.)

4.38 *Simon's home:* Simon, also known as Peter, was one of the first of the Jesus' disciples.

4.43 *good news about God's kingdom:* Jesus first told why he was sent in 4.18,19. This is the "good news." God's kingdom is anywhere God's people do what God wants them to do, like serving others and telling the good news.

4.44 *Judea:* This is the Greek name for the territory of Palestine that had once been known as Judah. The capital and religious center for the Jewish people was Jerusalem, in Judea. **(See Map 12 on pg 1890.)**

5.8 *I am a sinner:* Peter recognized God's glory in Jesus. This made Peter realize that he himself was sinful.

Sin

5.10 *James and John, the sons of Zebedee:* James and John became disciples of Jesus (5.11; 6.14). He nicknamed them "Boanerges," which means "Thunderbolts" (Mark 3.17).

5.14 *Don't tell anyone about this:* Jesus often told people he helped not to tell what he had done for them (Mark 3.10-12; 7.34-36). He may have wanted the miracle to speak for itself. On the other hand, he may have wanted to avoid drawing crowds of people who were more interested in miracles than in hearing about God's new kingdom.

Jesus Heals Many People

(Matthew 8.14-17; Mark 1.29-34)

[38]Jesus left the synagogue and went to Simon's home. When Jesus got there, he was told that Simon's mother-in-law was sick with a high fever. [39]So Jesus went over to her and ordered the fever to go away. Right then she was able to get up and serve them a meal.

[40]After the sun had set, people with all kinds of diseases were brought to Jesus. He put his hands on each one of them and healed them. [41]Demons went out of many people and shouted, "You are the Son of God!" But Jesus ordered the demons not to speak because they knew he was the Messiah.

[42]The next morning Jesus went out to a place where he could be alone, and crowds came looking for him. When they found him, they tried to stop him from leaving. [43]But Jesus said, "People in other towns must hear the good news about God's kingdom. This is why I was sent." [44]So he kept on preaching in the synagogues in Judea.[b]

Jesus Chooses His First Disciples

(Matthew 4.18-22; Mark 1.16-20)

5 Jesus was standing on the shore of Lake Gennesaret,[c] teaching the people as they crowded around him to hear God's message. [2]Near the shore he saw two boats left there by some fishermen who had gone to wash their nets. [3]Jesus got into the boat that belonged to Simon and asked him to row it out a little way from the shore. Then Jesus sat down[d] in the boat to teach the crowd.

[4]When Jesus had finished speaking, he told Simon, "Row the boat out into the deep water and let your nets down to catch some fish."

[5]"Master," Simon answered, "we have worked hard all night long and have not caught a thing. But if you tell me to, I will let the nets down." [6]They did this and caught so many fish that their nets began ripping apart. [7]Then they signaled for their partners in the other boat to come and help them. The men came, and together they filled the two boats so full that they both began to sink.

[8]When Simon Peter saw this happen, he knelt down in front of Jesus and said, "Lord, don't come near me! I am a sinner." [9]Peter and everyone with him were completely surprised at all the fish they had caught. [10]His partners James and John, the sons of Zebedee, were surprised too.

Jesus told Simon, "Don't be afraid! From now on you will bring in people instead of fish." [11]The men pulled their boats up on the shore. Then they left everything and went with Jesus.

Jesus Heals a Man

(Matthew 8.1-4; Mark 1.40-45)

[12]Jesus came to a town where there was a man who had leprosy.[e] When the man saw Jesus, he knelt down to the ground in front of Jesus and begged, "Lord, you have the power to make me well, if only you wanted to."

[13]Jesus put his hand on him and said, "I want to! Now you are well." At once the man's leprosy disappeared. [14]Jesus told him, "Don't tell anyone about this, but go and show yourself to the priest. Offer a gift

[b]4.44 *Judea:* Some manuscripts have "Galilee."   [c]5.1 *Lake Gennesaret:* Another name for Lake Galilee.   [d]5.3 *sat down:* Teachers in the ancient world, including Jewish teachers, usually sat down when they taught.   [e]5.12 *leprosy:* See the note at 4.27.

to the priest, just as Moses commanded, and everyone will know that you have been healed."f

15News about Jesus kept spreading. Large crowds came to listen to him teach and to be healed of their diseases. 16But Jesus would often go to some place where he could be alone and pray.

Jesus Heals a Man Who Could Not Walk
(Matthew 9.1-8; Mark 2.1-12)

17One day some Pharisees and experts in the Law of Moses sat listening to Jesus teach. They had come from every village in Galilee and Judea and from Jerusalem.

God had given Jesus the power to heal the sick, 18and some people came carrying a man on a mat because he could not walk. They tried to take him inside the house and put him in front of Jesus. 19But because of the crowd, they could not get him to Jesus. So they went up on the roof,g where they removed some tiles and let the mat down in the middle of the room.

20When Jesus saw how much faith they had, he said to the man, "My friend, your sins are forgiven."

21The Pharisees and the experts began arguing, "Jesus must think he is God! Only God can forgive sins."

22Jesus knew what they were thinking, and he said, "Why are you thinking this? 23Is it easier for me to tell this man that his sins are forgiven or to tell him to get up and walk? 24But now you will see that the Son of Man has the right to forgive sins

here on earth." Jesus then said to the man, "Get up! Pick up your mat and walk home."

25At once the man stood up in front of everyone. He picked up his mat and went home, giving thanks to God. 26Everyone was amazed and praised God. What they saw surprised them, and they said, "We have seen a great miracle today!"

Jesus Chooses Levi
(Matthew 9.9-13; Mark 2.13-17)

27Later, Jesus went out and saw a tax collectorh named Levi sitting at the place for paying taxes. Jesus said to him, "Follow me." 28Levi left everything and went with Jesus.

29In his home Levi gave a big dinner for Jesus. Many tax collectors and other guests were also there.

30The Pharisees and some of their teachers of the Law of Moses grumbled to Jesus' disciples, "Why do you eat and drink with these tax collectors and other sinners?"

31Jesus answered, "Healthy people don't need a doctor, but sick people do. 32I didn't come to invite good people to turn to God. I came to invite sinners."

People Ask about Going without Eating
(Matthew 9.14-17; Mark 2.18-22)

33Some people said to Jesus, "John's followers often pray and go without eating,i and so do the followers of the Pharisees. But your disciples never go without eating or drinking."

5.17 *Pharisees and experts in the Law of Moses:* The Pharisees met in homes to pray and to study the Jewish Scriptures. The experts in the Law of Moses were teachers who studied the first five books of the Jewish Scriptures. Like the Pharisees, they believed that only God could forgive sins. **(See the article The World of Jesus: Peoples, Powers, and Politics on pg 1801.)**

Son of Man

5.27 *tax collector named Levi:* Levi is also called Matthew (Matt 9.9-13). He was probably collecting taxes from people and merchants as they traveled past him on a major highway.

5.33 *John's followers:* This refers to followers of John the Baptist.

---

f5.14 *everyone will know that you have been healed:* People with leprosy had to be examined by a priest and told they were well (that is, "clean") before they could once again live a normal life in the Jewish community. The gift that Moses commanded was the sacrifice of some lambs together with flour mixed with olive oil.   g5.19 *roof:* In Palestine the houses usually had a flat roof. Stairs on the outside led up to the roof, which was made of beams and boards covered with packed earth. Luke says that the roof was made of (clay) tiles, which were also used for making roofs in New Testament times.   h5.27 *tax collector:* See the note at 3.12.   i5.33 *without eating:* See the note at 2.37.

Jesus answered, "Healthy people don't need a doctor, but sick people do." LUKE 5.31

5.34 *bridegroom:* Jesus was referring to himself.

6.2 *picking grain on the Sabbath:* The Pharisees believed that all Jews should be strict about following the Laws of Moses. One important law said that it was wrong to do any work on the Sabbath (see Exod 20.10; Deut 5.14). The Pharisees said that picking grain on the Sabbath broke this law.

6.5 *Son of Man:* What Jesus teaches and does has more authority than the Law of Moses, which includes the laws about the Sabbath. See also Heb 2.1—3.6.

6.9 *On the Sabbath . . . good deeds:* Jesus showed by his actions that doing good on the Sabbath is not against God's Law.

6.12 *mountain:* Jesus went to a mountain to pray before selecting his apostles. In LUKE , mountains are often associated with important moments in Jesus' ministry.

6.13 *disciples . . . twelve . . . apostles:* A disciple is a follower who learns from a master teacher, and an apostle is someone who is sent to others to carry the teacher's actions and message. The number of disciples (twelve) is the same number as the tribes of Israel. These twelve were later called apostles, as were a few others such as Paul (1 Cor 9.1). **(See the chart Jesus' Twelve Disciples on pg 1837.)**

---

[34]Jesus told them, "The friends of a bridegroom don't go without eating while he is still with them. [35]But the time will come when he will be taken from them. Then they will go without eating."

[36]Jesus then told them these sayings:

No one uses a new piece of cloth to patch old clothes. The patch would shrink and make the hole even bigger.

[37]No one pours new wine into old wineskins. The new wine would swell and burst the old skins.[j] Then the wine would be lost, and the skins would be ruined. [38]New wine must be put only into new wineskins.

[39]No one wants new wine after drinking old wine. They say, "The old wine is better."

A Question about the Sabbath

(Matthew 12.1-8; Mark 2.23-28)

6 One Sabbath when Jesus and his disciples were walking through some wheat fields,[k] the disciples picked some wheat. They rubbed the husks off with their hands and started eating the grain.

[2]Some Pharisees said, "Why are you picking grain on the Sabbath? You're not supposed to do that!"

[3]Jesus answered, "You surely have read what David did when he and his followers were hungry. [4]He went into the house of God and took the sacred loaves of bread that only priests were supposed to eat. He not only ate some himself, but even gave some to his followers."

[5]Jesus finished by saying, "The Son of Man is Lord over the Sabbath."

A Man with a Paralyzed Hand

(Matthew 12.9-14; Mark 3.1-6)

[6]On another Sabbath[l] Jesus was teaching in a synagogue, and a man with a paralyzed right hand was there. [7]Some Pharisees and teachers of the Law of Moses kept watching Jesus to see if he would heal the man. They did this because they wanted to accuse Jesus of doing something wrong.

[8]Jesus knew what they were thinking, so he told the man to stand up where everyone could see him. And the man stood up. [9]Then Jesus asked, "On the Sabbath should we do good deeds or evil deeds? Should we save someone's life or destroy it?"

[10]After he had looked around at everyone, he told the man, "Stretch out your hand." He did, and his bad hand became completely well.

[11]The teachers and the Pharisees were furious and started saying to one another, "What can we do about Jesus?"

Jesus Chooses His Twelve Apostles

(Matthew 10.1-4; Mark 3.13-19)

[12]About that time Jesus went off to a mountain to pray, and he spent the whole night there. [13]The next morning he called his disciples together and chose twelve of them to be his apostles. [14]One was Simon, and Jesus named him Peter. Another was Andrew, Peter's brother. There were also James, John, Philip, Bartholomew, [15]Matthew, Thomas, and James the son of Alphaeus. The rest of the apostles were Simon, known as the Eager

---

[j]**5.37** *swell and burst the old skins:* While the juice from grapes was becoming wine, it would swell and stretch the skins in which it had been stored. If the skins were old and stiff, they would burst.
[k]**6.1** *walking through some wheat fields:* It was the custom to let hungry travelers pick grains of wheat.
[l]**6.6** *On another Sabbath:* Some manuscripts have a reading which may mean "the Sabbath after the next."

One,[m] [16]Jude, who was the son of James, and Judas Iscariot,[n] who later betrayed Jesus.

Jesus Teaches, Preaches, and Heals
(Matthew 4.23-25)

[17]Jesus and his apostles went down from the mountain and came to some flat, level ground. Many other disciples were there to meet him. Large crowds of people from all over Judea, Jerusalem, and the coastal towns of Tyre and Sidon were there too. [18]These people had come to listen to Jesus and to be healed of their diseases. All who were troubled by evil spirits were also healed. [19]Everyone was trying to touch Jesus, because power was going out from him and healing them all.

Blessings and Troubles
(Matthew 5.1-12)

[20]Jesus looked at his disciples and said:
God will bless you people
who are poor.
His kingdom belongs to you!
[21]God will bless
you hungry people.
You will have plenty
to eat!
God will bless you people
who are now crying.
You will laugh!

[22]God will bless you when others hate you and won't have anything to do with you. God will bless you when people insult you and say cruel things about you, all because you are a follower of the Son of Man. [23]Long ago your own people did these same things to the prophets. So when this happens to you, be happy and jump for joy! You will have a great reward in heaven.

[24]But you rich people
are in for trouble.
You have already had
an easy life!
[25]You well-fed people
are in for trouble.
You will go hungry!
You people
who are laughing now
are in for trouble.
You are going to cry
and weep!

[26]You are in for trouble when everyone says good things about you. That is what your own people said about those prophets who told lies.

Love for Enemies
(Matthew 5.38-48; 7.12a)

[27]This is what I say to all who will listen to me:
Love your enemies, and be good to everyone who hates you. [28]Ask God to bless anyone who curses you, and pray for everyone who is cruel to you. [29]If someone slaps you on one cheek, don't stop that person from slapping you on the other cheek. If someone wants to take your coat, don't try to

6.17 *down from the mountain . . . to some flat, level ground:* It is not clear exactly where this was. What Jesus teaches in 6.20-49 is sometimes called the "Sermon on the Plain." Notice that many of the things that Jesus says here are similar to what he says while teaching from the mountainside in Matthew 5.1—7.29.

6.23 *heaven:* Living under God's rule in heaven will be the reward for those who are faithful.

Heaven

6.29 *someone slaps you on one cheek:* A slap on the cheek was a very bad insult.

[m]6.15 *known as the Eager One:* The word "eager" translates the Greek word "zealot," which was a name later given to the members of a Jewish group that resisted and fought against the Romans. [n]6.16 *Iscariot:* This may mean "a man from Kerioth" (a place in Judea). But more probably it means "a man who was a liar" or "a man who was a betrayer."

Jesus said, "*Love your enemies, and be good to everyone who hates you.*" LUKE 6.27

keep back your shirt. ³⁰Give to everyone who asks and don't ask people to return what they have taken from you. ³¹Treat others just as you want to be treated.

³²If you love only someone who loves you, will God praise you for that? Even sinners love people who love them. ³³If you are kind only to someone who is kind to you, will God be pleased with you for that? Even sinners are kind to people who are kind to them. ³⁴If you lend money only to someone you think will pay you back, will God be pleased with you for that? Even sinners lend to sinners because they think they will get it all back.

³⁵But love your enemies and be good to them. Lend without expecting to be paid back.° Then you will get a great reward, and you will be the true children of God in heaven. He is good even to people who are unthankful and cruel. ³⁶Have pity on others, just as your Father has pity on you.

Judging Others
(Matthew 7.1-5)

³⁷Jesus said:

Don't judge others, and God won't judge you. Don't be hard on others, and God won't be hard on you. Forgive others, and God will forgive you. ³⁸If you give to others, you will be given a full amount in return. It will be packed down, shaken together, and spilling over into your lap. The way you treat others is the way you will be treated.

³⁹Jesus also used some sayings as he spoke to the people. He said:

Can one blind person lead another

blind person? Won't they both fall into a ditch? ⁴⁰Are students better than their teacher? But when they are fully trained, they will be like their teacher.

⁴¹You can see the speck in your friend's eye, but you don't notice the log in your own eye. ⁴²How can you say, "My friend, let me take the speck out of your eye," when you don't see the log in your own eye? You show-offs! First, get the log out of your own eye; then you can see how to take the speck out of your friend's eye.

A Tree and Its Fruit
(Matthew 7.17-20; 12.34b,35)

⁴³A good tree cannot produce bad fruit, and a bad tree cannot produce good fruit. ⁴⁴You can tell what a tree is like by the fruit it produces. You cannot pick figs or grapes from thornbushes. ⁴⁵Good people do good things because of the good in their hearts, but bad people do bad things because of the evil in their hearts. Your words show what is in your heart.

Two Builders
(Matthew 7.24-27)

⁴⁶Why do you keep on saying that I am your Lord, when you refuse to do what I say? ⁴⁷Anyone who comes and listens to me and obeys me ⁴⁸is like someone who dug down deep and built a house on solid rock. When a flood came and the river rushed against the house, it was built so well that it didn't even shake. ⁴⁹But anyone who hears what I say and doesn't obey me is like someone whose house wasn't built on solid rock. As soon as the

°6.35 *without expecting to be paid back:* Some manuscripts have "without giving up on anyone."

river rushed against that house, it was smashed to pieces!

Jesus Heals an Army Officer's Servant
(Matthew 8.5-13; John 4.43-54)

7 After Jesus had finished teaching the people, he went to Capernaum. **2**In this town an army officer's servant was sick and about to die. The officer liked his servant very much. **3**And when he heard about Jesus, he sent some Jewish leaders to ask him to come and heal the servant.

4The leaders went to Jesus and begged him to do something. They said, "This man deserves your help! **5**He loves our nation and even built us a synagogue." **6**So Jesus went with them.

When Jesus wasn't far from the house, the officer sent some friends to tell him, "Lord, don't go to any trouble for me! I am not good enough for you to come into my house. **7**And I am certainly not worthy to come to you. Just say the word, and my servant will get well. **8**I have officers who give orders to me, and I have soldiers who take orders from me. I can say to one of them, 'Go!' and he goes. I can say to another, 'Come!' and he comes. I can say to my servant, 'Do this!' and he will do it."

9When Jesus heard this, he was so surprised that he turned and said to the crowd following him, "In all of Israel I've never found anyone with this much faith!" **10**The officer's friends returned and found the servant well.

A Widow's Son

11Soon Jesus and his disciples were on their way to the town of Nain, and a big crowd was going along with them. **12**As they came near the gate of the town, they saw people carrying out the body of a widow's only son. Many people from the town were walking along with her.

13When the Lord saw the woman, he felt sorry for her and said, "Don't cry!" **14**Jesus went over and touched the stretcher on which the people were carrying the dead boy. They stopped, and Jesus said, "Young man, get up!" **15**The boy sat up and began to speak. Jesus then gave him back to his mother.

16Everyone was frightened and praised God. They said, "A great prophet is here with us! God has come to his people."

17News about Jesus spread all over Judea and everywhere else in that part of the country.

John the Baptist
(Matthew 11.1-19)

18-19 John's followers told John everything that was being said about Jesus. So he sent two of them to ask the Lord, "Are you the one we should be looking for? Or must we wait for someone else?"

20When these messengers came to Jesus, they said, "John the Baptist sent us to ask, 'Are you the one we should be looking for? Or are we supposed to wait for someone else?' "

21At that time Jesus was healing many people who were sick or in pain or were troubled by evil spirits, and he was giving sight to a lot of blind people. **22**Jesus said to the messengers sent by John, "Go and tell John what you have seen and heard. Blind people are now able to see, and the lame can walk. People who have leprosyP are being healed, and the deaf can now hear. The dead are raised to life, and the poor are hearing the good news. **23**God will bless

P7.22 *leprosy*: See the note at 4.27.

7.2 *army officer:* The Greek text says that this officer was a centurion, a leader of 100 men. A centurion commanded and trained his men to fight and die at his command. Since this is Galilee, it is possible that the centurion served in the army of Herod Antipas.

7.3 *Jewish leaders:* These were probably respected local leaders who worked with the government authorities in Capernaum.

7.11 *Nain:* This small town was in southern Galilee. **(See Map 12 on pg 1890.)**

7.12 *people carrying out the body:* The Jewish people usually took the dead body to a tomb on the same day the person died. The family of a dead person often hired professional mourners for funerals. The family and other mourners would wail (cry out loud) and beat on their chests or tear their clothes to show their sadness (see Gen 37.34; Deut 34.8; 1 Sam 31.13).

7.14,15 *Jesus . . . touched the stretcher . . . back to his mother:* Jewish people in the crowd would have been reminded of the prophet Elijah who used God's power to raise a widow's dead son (1 Kgs 17.8-24). The Gospels tell of two other times Jesus raised people from the dead: the daughter of Jairus (Luke 8.40-56) and Lazarus (John 11.38-44).

7.27 *God calls John his messenger:* Jesus says that John is a messenger sent from God (Exod 23.20; Mal 3.1) to prepare the way for Jesus.

7.32-34 *children sitting in the market:* Jesus said that some of the Jewish people and their religious leaders were like quarreling children. Some children wanted to play a joyful game, but others wanted to play a sad game. Jesus is saying that some leaders didn't agree with John's ways, because they were so strict. And they didn't like Jesus' ways, because they weren't strict enough.

7.35 *Wisdom:* Wise people were honored in Jewish society. True wisdom was said to come from God's Law (Ps 19.7). Here Jesus is saying that Wisdom is made visible by the good we do for others.

Wisdom

7.39 *what kind of woman is touching him:* It is not clear what the woman's sin was. According to Jewish law, someone who touched a sinner would become unclean and would have to live apart from the Jewish community. Simon was a Pharisee who always tried to avoid contact with anyone who could make him unclean. That is why he was surprised that Jesus let the woman touch him.

everyone who doesn't reject me because of what I do."

²⁴After John's messengers had gone, Jesus began speaking to the crowds about John:

What kind of person did you go out to the desert to see? Was he like tall grass blown about by the wind? ²⁵What kind of man did you really go out to see? Was he someone dressed in fine clothes? People who wear expensive clothes and live in luxury are in the king's palace. ²⁶What then did you go out to see? Was he a prophet? He certainly was! I tell you that he was more than a prophet. ²⁷In the Scriptures, God calls John his messenger and says, "I am sending my messenger ahead of you to get things ready for you." ²⁸No one ever born on this earth is greater than John. But whoever is least important in God's kingdom is greater than John.

²⁹Everyone had been listening to John. Even the tax collectors⁹ had obeyed God and had done what was right by letting John baptize them. ³⁰But the Pharisees and the experts in the Law of Moses refused to obey God and be baptized by John.

³¹Jesus went on to say:

What are you people like? What kind of people are you? ³²You are like children sitting in the market and shouting to each other,

"We played the flute,
    but you would not dance!
We sang a funeral song,
    but you would not cry!"

³³John the Baptist did not go around eating and drinking, and you said, "John has a demon in him!" ³⁴But be-

cause the Son of Man goes around eating and drinking, you say, "Jesus eats and drinks too much! He is even a friend of tax collectors and sinners." ³⁵Yet Wisdom is shown to be right by what its followers do.

Simon the Pharisee

³⁶A Pharisee invited Jesus to have dinner with him. So Jesus went to the Pharisee's home and got ready to eat.ʳ

³⁷When a sinful woman in that town found out that Jesus was there, she bought an expensive bottle of perfume. ³⁸Then she came and stood behind Jesus. She cried and started washing his feet with her tears and drying them with her hair. The woman kissed his feet and poured the perfume on them.

³⁹The Pharisee who had invited Jesus saw this and said to himself, "If this man really were a prophet, he would know what kind of woman is touching him! He would know that she is a sinner."

⁴⁰Jesus said to the Pharisee, "Simon, I have something to say to you."

"Teacher, what is it?" Simon replied.

⁴¹Jesus told him, "Two people were in debt to a moneylender. One of them owed him 500 silver coins, and the other owed him 50. ⁴²Since neither of them could pay him back, the moneylender said that they didn't have to pay him anything. Which one of them will like him more?"

⁴³Simon answered, "I suppose it would be the one who had owed more and didn't have to pay it back."

"You are right," Jesus said.

[44]He turned toward the woman and said to Simon, "Have you noticed this woman? When I came into your home, you didn't give me any water so I could wash my feet. But she has washed my feet with her tears and dried them with her hair. [45]You didn't greet me with a kiss, but from the time I came in, she has not stopped kissing my feet. [46]You didn't even pour olive oil on my head,[s] but she has poured expensive perfume on my feet. [47]So I tell you that all her sins are forgiven, and that is why she has shown great love. But anyone who has been forgiven for only a little will show only a little love."

[48]Then Jesus said to the woman, "Your sins are forgiven."

[49]Some other guests started saying to one another, "Who is this who dares to forgive sins?"

[50]But Jesus told the woman, "Because of your faith, you are now saved.[t] May God give you peace!"

Women Who Helped Jesus

8 Soon after this, Jesus was going through towns and villages, telling the good news about God's kingdom. His twelve apostles were with him, [2]and so were some women who had been healed of evil spirits and all sorts of diseases. One of the women was Mary Magdalene,[u] who once had seven demons in her. [3]Joanna, Susanna, and many others had also used what they owned to help Jesus[v] and his disciples. Joanna's husband Chuza was one of Herod's officials.[w]

A Story about a Farmer
(Matthew 13.1-9; Mark 4.1-9)

[4]When a large crowd from several towns had gathered around Jesus, he told them this story:

[5]A farmer went out to scatter seed in a field. While the farmer was doing this, some of the seeds fell along the road and were stepped on or eaten by birds. [6]Other seeds fell on rocky ground and started growing. But the plants did not have enough water and soon dried up. [7]Some other seeds fell where thornbushes grew up and choked the plants. [8]The rest of the seeds fell on good ground where they grew and produced a hundred times as many seeds.

When Jesus had finished speaking, he said, "If you have ears, pay attention!"

Why Jesus Used Stories
(Matthew 13.10-17; Mark 4.10-12)

[9]Jesus' disciples asked him what the story meant. [10]So he answered:

I have explained the secrets about God's kingdom to you. But for others I use stories, so they will look, but not see, and they will hear, but not understand.

8.2 *Mary Magdalene:* Her name means that she was from Magdala, a small town on the shore of Lake Galilee. Some say that she was the sinful woman in 7.36-50, but the Bible gives no hint that this is true. She was present when Jesus was crucified (Luke 23.49; Mark 15.40,41), and saw where he was buried (Luke 23.55; Mark 15.47). She brought spices to the tomb to prepare Jesus' body for burial (Luke 24.1; Mark 16.1) and so became the first person to see Jesus after he was raised from death (Luke 24.9,10; Mark 16.9).

8.3 *Joanna, Susanna and . . . Joanna's husband Chuza:* Joanna and Susanna probably traveled with Jesus (Luke 23.49) and helped in his ministry. This is the only place in the Bible where Susanna is mentioned. Joanna is mentioned again in 24.10. Chuza was a manager who worked for Herod Antipas.

8.5 *A farmer went out to scatter seed in a field:* Before planting seeds, farmers prepared the ground by using a metal-tipped, wood-frame plow pulled by animals, or, depending on the size or slope of the land, by using a hand tool such as a hoe or digging stick. After breaking up the ground, farmers scattered seeds on the ground a handful at a time. After scattering seeds, the farmer would plow the seed into the ground. **(See the article How People Made a Living in the Time of Jesus on pg 1813.)**

---

[s]**7.44-46** *washed my feet . . . greet me with a kiss . . . pour olive oil on my head:* Guests in a home were usually offered water so they could wash their feet, because most people either went barefoot or wore sandals and would come in the house with very dusty feet. Guests were also greeted with a kiss on the cheek, and special ones often had sweet-smelling olive oil poured on their head. [t]**7.50** *saved:* Or "healed." The Greek word may have either meaning. [u]**8.2** *Magdalene:* Meaning "from Magdala," a small town on the western shore of Lake Galilee. There is no hint that she is the sinful woman in 7.36-50. [v]**8.3** *used what they owned to help Jesus:* Women often helped Jewish teachers by giving them money. [w]**8.3** *Herod's officials:* Herod Antipas, the son of Herod the Great.

8.16 *lamp:* In Jesus' day, people used clay lamps that burned olive oil, and were small enough to hold in one's hand. Alhough this lamp parable uses the sense of sight, and the previous parable uses the sense of hearing, Jesus is making the same point: "Pay attention to how you listen!" (8.18). See also Matt 5.15; Luke 11.33.

8.19 *Jesus' mother and brothers:* Mark 6.3 gives the names of four brothers and says that Jesus also had sisters.

8.26 *town of Gerasa:* Gerasa was probably located about 20 miles east of the Jordan River. It was one of the ten cities that formed what was known as the Decapolis, or "ten towns." Its population, architecture, and style of life were mostly Greek.

Jesus Explains the Story about a Farmer
(Matthew 13.18-23; Mark 4.13-20)

11This is what the story means: The seed is God's message, **12**and the seeds that fell along the road are the people who hear the message. But the devil comes and snatches the message out of their hearts, so they will not believe and be saved. **13**The seeds that fell on rocky ground are the people who gladly hear the message and accept it. But they don't have deep roots, and they believe only for a little while. As soon as life gets hard, they give up. **14**The seeds that fell among the thornbushes are also people who hear the message. But they are so eager for riches and pleasures that they never produce anything. **15**Those seeds that fell on good ground are the people who listen to the message and keep it in good and honest hearts. They last and produce a harvest.

Light
(Mark 4.21-25)

16No one lights a lamp and puts it under a bowl or under a bed. A lamp is always put on a lampstand, so people who come into a house will see the light. **17**There is nothing hidden that will not be found. There is no secret that will not be well known. **18**Pay attention to how you listen! Everyone who has something will be given more, but people who have nothing will lose what little they think they have.

Jesus' Mother and Brothers
(Matthew 12.46-50; Mark 3.31-35)

19Jesus' mother and brothers went to see him, but because of the crowd they could not get near him. **20**Someone told Jesus, "Your mother and brothers are standing outside and want to see you." **21**Jesus answered, "My mother and my brothers are those people who hear and obey God's message."

A Storm
(Matthew 8.23-27; Mark 4.35-41)

22One day, Jesus and his disciples got into a boat, and he said, "Let's cross the lake."ˣ They started out, **23**and while they were sailing across, he went to sleep.

Suddenly a storm struck the lake, and the boat started sinking. They were in danger. **24**So they went to Jesus and woke him up, "Master, Master! We are about to drown!"

Jesus got up and ordered the wind and waves to stop. They obeyed, and everything was calm. **25**Then Jesus asked the disciples, "Don't you have any faith?"

But they were frightened and amazed. They said to each other, "Who is this? He can give orders to the wind and the waves, and they obey him!"

A Man with Demons in Him
(Matthew 8.28-34; Mark 5.1-20)

26Jesus and his disciples sailed across Lake Galilee and came to shore near the town of Gerasa.ʸ **27**As Jesus was getting out of the boat, he was met by a man from this town. The man had demons in him. He had gone

ˣ**8.22** *cross the lake:* To the eastern shore of Lake Galilee, where most of the people were not Jewish.
ʸ**8.26** *Gerasa:* Some manuscripts have "Gergesa."

naked for a long time and no longer lived in a house, but in the graveyard.[z]

²⁸The man saw Jesus and screamed. He knelt down in front of him and shouted, "Jesus, Son of God Most High, what do you want with me? I beg you not to torture me!" ²⁹He said this because Jesus had already told the evil spirit to go out of him.

The man had often been attacked by the demon. And even though he had been bound with chains and leg irons and kept under guard, he smashed whatever bound him. Then the demon would force him out into lonely places.

³⁰Jesus asked the man, "What is your name?"

He answered, "My name is Lots." He said this because there were "lots" of demons in him. ³¹They begged Jesus not to send them to the deep pit,[a] where they would be punished.

³²A large herd of pigs was feeding there on the hillside. So the demons begged Jesus to let them go into the pigs, and Jesus let them go. ³³Then the demons left the man and went into the pigs. The whole herd rushed down the steep bank into the lake and drowned.

³⁴When the men taking care of the pigs saw this, they ran to spread the news in the town and on the farms. ³⁵The people went out to see what had happened, and when they came to Jesus, they also found the man. The demons had gone out of him, and he was sitting there at the feet of Jesus. He had clothes on and was in his right mind. But the people were terrified.

³⁶Then all who had seen the man healed told about it. ³⁷Everyone from around Gerasa[b] begged Jesus to leave, because they were so frightened.

When Jesus got into the boat to start back, ³⁸the man who had been healed begged to go with him. But Jesus sent him off and said, ³⁹"Go back home and tell everyone how much God has done for you." The man then went all over town, telling everything that Jesus had done for him.

A Dying Girl and a Sick Woman
(Matthew 9.18-26; Mark 5.21-43)

⁴⁰Everyone had been waiting for Jesus, and when he came back, a crowd was there to welcome him. ⁴¹Just then the man in charge of the synagogue came and knelt down in front of Jesus. His name was Jairus, and he begged Jesus to come to his home ⁴²because his twelve-year-old child was dying. She was his only daughter.

While Jesus was on his way, people were crowding all around him. ⁴³In the crowd was a woman who had been bleeding for twelve years. She had spent everything she had on doctors,[c] but none of them could make her well.

⁴⁴As soon as she came up behind Jesus and barely touched his clothes, her bleeding stopped.

⁴⁵"Who touched me?" Jesus asked.

While everyone was denying it, Peter said, "Master, people are crowding all around and pushing you from every side."[d]

⁴⁶But Jesus answered, "Someone touched me, because I felt power going out from me." ⁴⁷The woman knew that she could not hide, so she came trembling and knelt down in front of Jesus. She told everyone why she had touched him and that she had been healed at once.

⁴⁸Jesus said to the woman, "You are now

8.28 *Son of God:* The demons knew that Jesus was God's Son, even if people did not fully believe or understand who Jesus was. Compare this verse to 4.35.

8.31 *deep pit:* The place where evil spirits were kept and punished. This pit may be the place later described as "hell."

8.32 *herd of pigs:* Jewish people did not have pigs, since the Law of Moses said they could not eat pork. This shows that the area was Gentile, not Jewish.

8.43 *doctors:* In New Testament times, physicians helped people when they were sick or injured. Though physicians of the time had many skills—Greek science had already began to study anatomy, physiology, and surgery—the physicians' knowledge of what caused diseases was limited. **(See the article Miracles, Magic, and Medicine on pg 1820.)**

---

[z]**8.27** *graveyard:* It was thought that demons and evil spirits lived in graveyards. [a]**8.31** *deep pit:* The place where evil spirits are kept and punished. [b]**8.37** *Gerasa:* See the note at 8.26. [c]**8.43** *She had spent everything she had on doctors:* Some manuscripts do not have these words. [d]**8.45** *from every side:* Some manuscripts add "and you ask, 'Who touched me?'"

8.51 *Peter, John, James:* Three of the twelve apostles (disciples). All three of them were fishermen when Jesus called them to follow him. James and John were brothers (Luke 5.1-10). All three would see Jesus' true glory (transfiguration) on a mountaintop (Luke 9.28-36), and all of them were with Jesus when he prayed in Gethsemane before his arrest (Mark 14.33).

8.55 *give her something to eat:* Eating was a sign that the girl was alive and not just a spirit. Compare this with Luke 24.30-43. After God raised Jesus from the dead, he met two of his disciples on the road to Emmaus. They recognized him when he shared a meal with them. Later, when he appeared to his disciples, he also ate with them.

9.7 *Herod the ruler:* This is Herod Antipas, one of the sons of Herod the Great. The formal name for Herod's title was "tetrarch," which meant someone who ruled a fourth of a province. Jesus called Herod a fox (13.32), because he thought Herod was clever and dangerous.

9.10 *Bethsaida:* Bethsaida was a Jewish town just east of where the Jordan River empties into Lake Galilee. **(See Map 12 on pg 1890.)**

well because of your faith. May God give you peace!"

⁴⁹While Jesus was speaking, someone came from Jairus' home and said, "Your daughter has died! Why bother the teacher anymore?"

⁵⁰When Jesus heard this, he told Jairus, "Don't worry! Have faith, and your daughter will get well."

⁵¹Jesus went into the house, but he did not let anyone else go with him, except Peter, John, James, and the girl's father and mother. ⁵²Everyone was crying and weeping for the girl. But Jesus said, "The child isn't dead. She is just asleep." ⁵³The people laughed at him because they knew she was dead.

⁵⁴Jesus took hold of the girl's hand and said, "Child, get up!" ⁵⁵She came back to life and got right up. Jesus told them to give her something to eat. ⁵⁶Her parents were surprised, but Jesus ordered them not to tell anyone what had happened.

Instructions for the Twelve Apostles
(Matthew 10.5-15; Mark 6.7-13)

9 Jesus called together his twelve apostles and gave them complete power over all demons and diseases. ²Then he sent them to tell about God's kingdom and to heal the sick. ³He told them, "Don't take anything with you! Don't take a walking stick or a traveling bag or food or money or even a change of clothes. ⁴When you are welcomed into a home, stay there until you leave that town. ⁵If people won't welcome you, leave the town and shake the dust from your feet[e] as a warning to them."

⁶The apostles left and went from village to village, telling the good news and healing people everywhere.

Herod Is Worried
(Matthew 14.1-12; Mark 6.14-29)

⁷Herod[f] the ruler heard about all that was happening, and he was worried. Some people were saying John the Baptist had come back to life. ⁸Others were saying Elijah had come[g] or one of the prophets from long ago had come back to life. ⁹But Herod said, "I had John's head cut off! Who is this I hear so much about?" Herod was eager to meet Jesus.

Jesus Feeds Five Thousand
(Matthew 14.13-21; Mark 6.30-44; John 6.1-14)

¹⁰The apostles came back and told Jesus everything they had done. He then took them with him to the village of Bethsaida, where they could be alone. ¹¹But a lot of people found out about this and followed him. Jesus welcomed them. He spoke about God's kingdom and healed everyone who was sick.

¹²Late in the afternoon the twelve apostles came to Jesus and said, "Send the crowd to the villages and farms around here. They need to find a place to stay and something to eat. There is nothing in this place. It's like a desert!"

¹³Jesus answered, "You give them something to eat."

But they replied, "We have only five small loaves of bread[h] and two fish. If we are going to feed all these people, we will have to go and buy food." ¹⁴There were about 5,000 men in the crowd.

Jesus said to his disciples, "Tell the people

[e]9.5 *shake the dust from your feet:* This was a way of showing rejection. [f]9.7 *Herod:* Herod Antipas, the son of Herod the Great. [g]9.8 *Elijah had come:* Many of the Jewish people expected the prophet Elijah to come and prepare the way for the Messiah. [h]9.13 *small loaves of bread:* These would have been flat and round or in the shape of a bun.

to sit in groups of 50." [15]They did this, and all the people sat down. [16]Jesus took the five loaves and the two fish. He looked up toward heaven and blessed the food. Then he broke the bread and fish and handed them to his disciples to give to the people.

[17]Everyone ate all they wanted. What was left over filled twelve baskets.

Who Is Jesus?

(Matthew 16.13-19; Mark 8.27-29)

[18]When Jesus was alone praying, his disciples came to him, and he asked them, "What do people say about me?"

[19]They answered, "Some say you are John the Baptist or Elijah[i] or a prophet from long ago who has come back to life."

[20]Jesus then asked, "But who do you say I am?"

Peter answered, "You are the Messiah sent from God."

[21]Jesus strictly warned his disciples not to tell anyone about this.

Jesus Speaks about His Suffering and Death

(Matthew 16.20-28; Mark 8.30—9.1)

[22]Jesus told his disciples, "The nation's leaders, the chief priests, and the teachers of the Law of Moses will make the Son of Man suffer terribly. They will reject him and kill him, but three days later he will rise to life."

[23]Then Jesus said to all the people:

If any of you want to be my followers, you must forget about yourself. You must take up your cross every day and follow me. [24]If you want to save your life,[j] you will destroy it. But if you

give up your life for me, you will save it. [25]What will you gain, if you own the whole world but destroy yourself or waste your life? [26]If you are ashamed of me and my message, the Son of Man will be ashamed of you when he comes in his glory and in the glory of his Father and the holy angels. [27]You can be sure some of the people standing here will not die before they see God's kingdom.

The True Glory of Jesus

(Matthew 17.1-8; Mark 9.2-8)

[28]About eight days later Jesus took Peter, John, and James with him and went up on a mountain to pray. [29]While he was praying, his face changed, and his clothes became shining white. [30]Suddenly Moses and Elijah were there speaking with him. [31]They appeared in heavenly glory and talked about all that Jesus' death[k] in Jerusalem would mean.

[32]Peter and the other two disciples had been sound asleep. All at once they woke up and saw how glorious Jesus was. They also saw the two men who were with him.

[33]Moses and Elijah were about to leave, when Peter said to Jesus, "Master, it is good for us to be here! Let us make three shelters, one for you, one for Moses, and one for Elijah." But Peter did not know what he was talking about.

[34]While Peter was still speaking, a shadow from a cloud passed over, and they were frightened as the cloud covered them. [35]From the cloud a voice spoke, "This is my chosen Son. Listen to what he says!"

[36]After the voice had spoken, Peter, John, and James saw only Jesus. For some

9.17 *twelve baskets:* The Jewish people believed that twelve was an especially sacred number. **(See the chart Numbers in the Bible on pg 1844.)**

9.22 *nation's leaders, the chief priests, and the teachers of the Law of Moses:* The nation's leaders were wealthy older men who had ties to the chief priests. Together, they formed a group that was given some authority by the Romans to make decisions about the local affairs of the Jewish people.

9.26 *Father and the holy angels:* Jesus often referred to God as "Father" (see John 15–17).

9.28 *Peter, John, and James:* These disciples were the same ones who went with Jesus into the home of Jairus (8.51).

9.28 *mountain:* The exact location of this mountain is not clear.

9.30 *Moses and Elijah:* Moses was very important in the history of Israel. God revealed his name, "I Am," to Moses and chose him to lead the people out of slavery in Egypt. Moses' face glowed with light when he met God on Mount Sinai (Exod 34.29,30). Both Moses and Elijah were chosen to call God's people to live a new way of life, just as Jesus was.

Moses

Elijah

[i]9.19 *Elijah:* See the note at 9.8. [j]9.24 *life:* In verses 24,25 a Greek word which often means "soul" is translated "life" and "yourself." [k]9.31 *Jesus' death:* In Greek this is "his departure," which probably includes his rising to life and his return to heaven.

9.51 *Jerusalem:* Jerusalem was the religious center for the Jewish people. Although the Romans controlled Jerusalem in Jesus' day, the Jewish people were still allowed to worship at the temple. Jesus went to the temple to face the Jewish religious leaders, who were against him, and to preach his message to the Jewish people who worshiped there. **(See the article People of the Law: The Religion of Israel on pg 1794.)**

Jerusalem

9.52 *Samaritan village:* The exact location of this village is not known. Samaria was a region north of Jerusalem. In Jesus' day, the Jews and the Samaritans distrusted one another. The Samaritans had their own temple (on Mt. Gerizim) and their own priests. In addition, they followed their own version of the Law of Moses.

time they kept quiet and did not say anything about what they had seen.

Jesus Heals a Boy
(Matthew 17.14-18; Mark 9.14-27)

37The next day Jesus and his three disciples came down from the mountain and were met by a large crowd. **38**Just then someone in the crowd shouted, "Teacher, please do something for my son! He is my only child! **39**A demon often attacks him and makes him scream. It shakes him until he foams at the mouth, and it won't leave him until it has completely worn the boy out. **40**I begged your disciples to force out the demon, but they couldn't do it."

41Jesus said to them, "You people are stubborn and don't have any faith! How much longer must I be with you? Why do I have to put up with you?"

Then Jesus said to the man, "Bring your son to me." **42**While the boy was being brought, the demon attacked him and made him shake all over. Jesus ordered the demon to stop. Then he healed the boy and gave him back to his father. **43**Everyone was amazed at God's great power.

Jesus Again Speaks about His Death
(Matthew 17.22,23; Mark 9.30-32)

While everyone was still amazed at what Jesus was doing, he said to his disciples, **44**"Pay close attention to what I am telling you! The Son of Man will be handed over to his enemies." **45**But the disciples did not know what he meant. The meaning was hidden from them. They could not understand it, and they were afraid to ask.

Who Is the Greatest?
(Matthew 18.1-5; Mark 9.33-37)

46Jesus' disciples were arguing about which one of them was the greatest. **47**Jesus knew what they were thinking, and he had a child stand there beside him. **48**Then he said to his disciples, "When you welcome even a child because of me, you welcome me. And when you welcome me, you welcome the one who sent me. Whichever one of you is the most humble is the greatest."

For or against Jesus
(Mark 9.38-40)

49John said, "Master, we saw a man using your name to force demons out of people. But we told him to stop, because he isn't one of us."

50"Don't stop him!" Jesus said. "Anyone who isn't against you is for you."

A Samaritan Village Refuses To Receive Jesus

51Not long before it was time for Jesus to be taken up to heaven, he made up his mind to go to Jerusalem. **52**He sent some messengers on ahead to a Samaritan village to get things ready for him. **53**But he was on his way to Jerusalem, so the people there refused to welcome him. **54**When the disciples James and John saw what was happening, they asked, "Lord, do you want us to call down fire from heaven to destroy these people?"^l

55But Jesus turned and corrected them for what they had said.^m **56**Then they all went on to another village.

^l**9.54** *to destroy these people:* Some manuscripts add "as Elijah did." ^m**9.55** *what they had said:* Some manuscripts add, "and said, 'Don't you know what spirit you belong to? The Son of Man did not come to destroy people's lives, but to save them.' "

Jesus said to his disciples, "*Whichever one of you is the most humble is the greatest.*" LUKE 9.48

Three People Who Wanted To Be Followers

(Matthew 8.19-22)

[57] Along the way someone said to Jesus, "I'll follow you anywhere!"

[58] Jesus said, "Foxes have dens, and birds have nests, but the Son of Man doesn't have a place to call his own."

[59] Jesus told someone else to come with him. But the man said, "Lord, let me wait until I bury my father."[n]

[60] Jesus answered, "Let the dead take care of the dead, while you go and tell about God's kingdom."

[61] Then someone said to Jesus, "I want to follow you, Lord, but first let me go back and take care of things at home."

[62] Jesus answered, "Anyone who starts plowing and keeps looking back isn't worth a thing to God's kingdom!"

The Work of the Seventy-Two Followers

10 Later the Lord chose 72 [o] other followers and sent them out two by two to every town and village where he was about to go. [2] He said to them:

A large crop is in the fields, but there are only a few workers. Ask the Lord in charge of the harvest to send out workers to bring it in. [3] Now go, but remember, I am sending you like lambs into a pack of wolves. [4] Don't take along a moneybag or a traveling bag or sandals. And don't waste time greeting people on the road.[P] [5] As soon as you enter a home, say, "God bless this home with peace." [6] If the people living there are peace-loving, your prayer for peace will bless them. But if they are not peace-loving, your prayer will return to you. [7] Stay with the same family, eating and drinking whatever they give you, because workers are worth what they earn. Don't move around from house to house.

[8] If the people of a town welcome you, eat whatever they offer. [9] Heal their sick and say, "God's kingdom will soon be here!"[q]

[10] But if the people of a town refuse to welcome you, go out into the street and say, [11] "We are shaking the dust from our feet[r] as a warning to you. And you can be sure that God's kingdom will soon be here!"[s] [12] I tell you that on the day of judgment the people of Sodom will get off easier than the people of that town!

The Unbelieving Towns

(Matthew 11.20-24)

[13] You people of Chorazin are in for trouble! You people of Bethsaida are also in for trouble! If the miracles that took place in your towns had happened in Tyre and Sidon, the people there would have turned to God long ago. They would have dressed in sackcloth and put ashes on their heads.[t] [14] On the day of judgment the people

[n]9.59 *bury my father*: The Jewish people taught that giving someone a proper burial was even more important than helping the poor. [o]10.1 *72*: Some manuscripts have "70." According to Jewish tradition, there were 70 nations on earth. But the ancient Greek translation of the Old Testament has "72" in place of "70." Jesus probably chose this number of followers to show that his message was for everyone in the world. [P]10.4 *waste time greeting people on the road*: In those days a polite greeting could take a long time. [q]10.9 *will soon be here*: Or "is already here." [r]10.11 *shaking the dust from our feet*: This was a way of showing rejection. [s]10.11 *will soon be here*: Or "is already here." [t]10.13 *dressed in sackcloth . . . ashes on their heads*: This was one way that people showed how sorry they were for their sins.

10.1 *72*: According to Genesis 10, where the descendants of Noah are listed, there were 70 nations on earth.

10.13 *Chorazin . . . Bethsaida . . . Tyre and Sidon*: Chorazin, Bethsaida, and Capernaum were Jewish towns on the northern end of Lake Galilee. Tyre and Sidon were important non-Jewish port cities on the Mediterranean Sea coast. While the people in these Jewish towns did not respond to Jesus' message and miracles, Jesus says that the people in cities like Tyre and Sidon would be more willing to turn to God. **(See Map 12 on pg 1890.)**

10.13 *sackcloth and . . . ashes*: Sackcloth is dark cloth (see Rev 6.12) made of camel's hair or goat's hair. The Greek word for "ashes" in this verse refers to a kind of smoky soot. People wore sackcloth or put ashes on their head in times of deep sadness or when they wanted to show that they were sorry for their sins (see Esth 4.1,3; Job 2.8).

10.14 *day of judgment*: Referring to a time when God would judge the people of the world. Those who put their trust in Christ would be saved, but those who did not would experience God's anger and punishment (see Matt 13.47-50; 25.31-46; John 12.44-50).

Day of the LORD

10.16 *the one who sent me:* Jesus is referring to God. See also Matt 10.40; Mark 9.37; Luke 9.48; John 13.20.

10.20 *names are written in heaven:* Living under God's rule will be the reward for those who are faithful. Hebrews 12.23 also says that the names of the faithful will be written down in heaven. References to a "book" of life can be found in Ps 69.28; Dan 12.1; Phil 4.3; Rev 3.5.

10.25 *eternal life:* By the time of Jesus, many Jewish people had come to believe in and hope for life after death. However, some, like the Sadducees, did not accept the concept of eternal life, because it was not specifically mentioned in the Law of Moses. Jesus says that all who have faith in him will have eternal life. **(See the article The World of Jesus: Peoples, Powers, and Politics on pg 1801.)**

Eternal Life

10.31 *priest:* Jewish priests were descendants of Moses' brother Aaron (see Num 18.20-32). A priest knew that touching a dead body or the blood of an injured man would make him unclean according to the Law of Moses. If he became unclean, he would have to go through a cleansing ceremony before he could serve in the temple again.

Israel's Priests

of Tyre and Sidon will get off easier than you will. [15] People of Capernaum, do you think you will be honored in heaven? Well, you will go down to hell!

[16] My followers, whoever listens to you is listening to me. Anyone who says "No" to you is saying "No" to me. And anyone who says "No" to me is really saying "No" to the one who sent me.

The Return of the Seventy-Two

[17] When the 72[u] followers returned, they were excited and said, "Lord, even the demons obeyed when we spoke in your name!"

[18] Jesus told them:

I saw Satan fall from heaven like a flash of lightning. [19] I have given you the power to trample on snakes and scorpions and to defeat the power of your enemy Satan. Nothing can harm you. [20] But don't be happy because evil spirits obey you. Be happy that your names are written in heaven!

Jesus Thanks His Father
(Matthew 11.25-27; 13,16,17)

[21] At that same time, Jesus felt the joy that comes from the Holy Spirit,[v] and he said:

My Father, Lord of heaven and earth, I am grateful that you hid all this from wise and educated people and showed it to ordinary people. Yes, Father, this is what pleased you.

[22] My Father has given me everything, and he is the only one who knows the Son. The only one who really knows the Father is the Son. But

the Son wants to tell others about the Father, so they can know him too.

[23] Jesus then turned to his disciples and said to them in private, "You are really blessed to see what you see! [24] Many prophets and kings were eager to see what you see and to hear what you hear. But I tell you they did not see or hear."

The Good Samaritan

[25] An expert in the Law of Moses stood up and asked Jesus a question to see what he would say. "Teacher," he asked, "what must I do to have eternal life?"

[26] Jesus answered, "What is written in the Scriptures? How do you understand them?"

[27] The man replied, "The Scriptures say, 'Love the Lord your God with all your heart, soul, strength, and mind.' They also say, 'Love your neighbors as much as you love yourself.' "

[28] Jesus said, "You have given the right answer. If you do this, you will have eternal life."

[29] But the man wanted to show that he knew what he was talking about. So he asked Jesus, "Who are my neighbors?"

[30] Jesus replied:

As a man was going down from Jerusalem to Jericho, robbers attacked him and grabbed everything he had. They beat him up and ran off, leaving him half dead.

[31] A priest happened to be going down the same road. But when he saw the man, he walked by on the other side. [32] Later a temple helper[w] came to the same place. But when he saw the man who had been beaten up, he also went by on the other side.

[u]**10.17** *72:* See the note at 10.1. [v]**10.21** *the Holy Spirit:* Some manuscripts have "his spirit."
[w]**10.32** *temple helper:* A man from the tribe of Levi, whose job it was to work around the temple.

33A man from Samaria then came traveling along that road. When he saw the man, he felt sorry for him **34**and went over to him. He treated his wounds with olive oil and wine[x] and bandaged them. Then he put him on his own donkey and took him to an inn, where he took care of him. **35**The next morning he gave the innkeeper two silver coins and said, "Please take care of the man. If you spend more than this on him, I will pay you when I return."

36Then Jesus asked, "Which one of these three people was a real neighbor to the man who was beaten up by robbers?"

37The expert in the Law of Moses answered, "The one who showed pity."

Jesus said, "Go and do the same!"

Martha and Mary

38The Lord and his disciples were traveling along and came to a village. When they got there, a woman named Martha welcomed him into her home. **39**She had a sister named Mary, who sat down in front of the Lord and was listening to what he said. **40**Martha was worried about all that had to be done. Finally, she went to Jesus and said, "Lord, doesn't it bother you that my sister has left me to do all the work by myself? Tell her to come and help me!"

41The Lord answered, "Martha, Martha! You are worried and upset about so many things, **42**but only one thing is necessary. Mary has chosen what is best, and it will not be taken away from her."

Prayer

(Matthew 6.9-13; 7.7-11)

11 When Jesus had finished praying, one of his disciples said to him, "Lord, teach us to pray, just as John taught his followers to pray."

2So Jesus told them, "Pray in this way:
'Father, help us
    to honor your name.
Come and set up
    your kingdom.
3Give us each day
    the food we need.[y]
4Forgive our sins,
  as we forgive everyone
    who has done wrong to us.
And keep us
    from being tempted.'"

5Then Jesus went on to say:

Suppose one of you goes to a friend in the middle of the night and says, "Let me borrow three loaves of bread. **6**A friend of mine has dropped in, and I don't have a thing for him to eat." **7**And suppose your friend answers, "Don't bother me! The door is bolted, and my children and I are in bed. I cannot get up to give you something." **8**He may not get up and give you the bread, just because you are his friend. But he will get up and give you as much as you need, simply because you are not ashamed to keep on asking.

9So I tell you to ask and you will receive, search and you will find, knock and the door will be opened for you. **10**Everyone who asks will receive, everyone who searches will find, and the door will be opened for everyone

10.38 *village:* This is Bethany, where Mary and Martha lived with their brother Lazarus (John 11.1). Bethany was about two miles east of Jerusalem.

10.38-40 *Martha . . . sister named Mary:* Martha was concerned with practical matters like preparing food and offering hospitality to a traveler (the Greek word is also used to refer to the "service" of a disciple). Mary was more interested in listening to Jesus teach. In JOHN, Martha did not understand what Jesus said about rising from the dead (John 11.17-27).

Sin

[x]**10.34** *olive oil and wine:* In New Testament times these were used as medicine. Sometimes olive oil is a symbol for healing by means of a miracle (see James 5.14). [y]**11.3** *the food we need:* Or "food for today" or "food for the coming day."

11.15 *Beelzebul, the ruler of the demons:* The name Beelzebul comes from a title of the Canaanite god Baal meaning "prince Baal" or "lord of power." The Hebrew people changed the name slightly to Beelzebub (Matt 12.24), meaning "lord of the flies." See also Matt 9.34.

11.23 *gather in the crop:* Jesus is referring to the harvest of believers. Those who do not join with Jesus in this task are against him and his message. See also Mark 9.40.

11.29,30 *what happened to Jonah . . . a sign to the people of Nineveh:* The prophet Jonah refused God's command to bring a message to the Assyrians, and tried to hide from God by taking a ship heading in the opposite direction from Nineveh. God sent a powerful storm and Jonah was thrown from the ship. God sent a big fish that swallowed Jonah. Jonah remained inside the fish for three days before being spit out (Jonah 3.4). Jesus is comparing the time he would spend in the grave with the time Jonah spent inside the big fish (see also Matt 16.4; Mark 8.12).

who knocks. **11**Which one of you fathers would give your hungry child a snake if the child asked for a fish? **12**Which one of you would give your child a scorpion if the child asked for an egg? **13**As bad as you are, you still know how to give good gifts to your children. But your heavenly Father is even more ready to give the Holy Spirit to anyone who asks.

Jesus and the Ruler of Demons
(Matthew 12.22-30; Mark 3.20-27)

14Jesus forced a demon out of a man who could not talk. And after the demon had gone out, the man started speaking, and the crowds were amazed. **15**But some people said, "He forces out demons by the power of Beelzebul, the ruler of the demons!"

16Others wanted to put Jesus to the test. So they asked him to show them a sign from God. **17**Jesus knew what they were thinking, and he said:

A kingdom where people fight each other will end up in ruin. And a family that fights will break up. **18**If Satan fights against himself, how can his kingdom last? Yet you say that I force out demons by the power of Beelzebul. **19**If I use his power to force out demons, whose power do your own followers use to force them out? They are the ones who will judge you. **20**But if I use God's power to force out demons, it proves that God's kingdom has already come to you.

21When a strong man arms himself and guards his home, everything he owns is safe. **22**But if a stronger man comes and defeats him, he will carry

off the weapons in which the strong man trusted. Then he will divide with others what he has taken. **23**If you are not on my side, you are against me. If you don't gather in the crop with me, you scatter it.

Return of an Evil Spirit
(Matthew 12.43-45)

24When an evil spirit leaves a person, it travels through the desert, looking for a place to rest. But when it doesn't find a place, it says, "I will go back to the home I left." **25**When it gets there and finds the place clean and fixed up, **26**it goes off and finds seven other evil spirits even worse than itself. They all come and make their home there, and that person ends up in worse shape than before.

Being Really Blessed

27While Jesus was still talking, a woman in the crowd spoke up, "The woman who gave birth to you and nursed you is blessed!"

28Jesus replied, "That's true, but the people who are really blessed are the ones who hear and obey God's message!"ᶻ

A Sign from God
(Matthew 12.38-42; Mark 8.12)

29As crowds were gathering around Jesus, he said:

You people of today are evil! You keep looking for a sign from God. But what happened to Jonahᵃ is the only sign you will be given. **30**Just as Jonah

ᶻ**11.28** *That's true, but the people who are really blessed . . . message:* Or "That's not true, the people who are blessed . . . message." ᵃ**11.29** *what happened to Jonah:* Jonah was in the stomach of a big fish for three days and nights (see Matthew 12.40).

Jesus said, "The people who are really blessed are the ones who hear and obey God's message!" LUKE 11.28

was a sign to the people of Nineveh, the Son of Man will be a sign to the people of today. **31**When the judgment comes, the Queen of the South[b] will stand there with you and condemn you. She traveled a long way to hear Solomon's wisdom, and yet here is something far greater than Solomon. **32**The people of Nineveh will also stand there with you and condemn you. They turned to God when Jonah preached, and yet here is something far greater than Jonah.

Light
(Matthew 5.15; 6.22,23)

33No one lights a lamp and then hides it or puts it under a clay pot. A lamp is put on a lampstand, so everyone who comes into the house can see the light. **34**Your eyes are the lamp for your body. When your eyes are good, you have all the light you need. But when your eyes are bad, everything is dark. **35**So be sure your light isn't darkness. **36**If you have light, and nothing is dark, then light will be everywhere, as when a lamp shines brightly on you.

Jesus Condemns the Pharisees and Teachers of the Law of Moses
(Matthew 23.1-36; Mark 12.38-40; Luke 20.45-47)

37When Jesus finished speaking, a Pharisee invited him home for a meal. Jesus went and sat down to eat.[c] **38**The Pharisee was surprised that he did not wash his hands[d] before eating. **39**So the Lord said to him:

You Pharisees clean the outside of cups and dishes, but on the inside you are greedy and evil. **40**You fools! Didn't God make both the outside and the inside?[e] **41**If you would only give what you have to the poor, everything you do would please God.

42You Pharisees are in for trouble! You give God a tenth of the spices from your gardens, such as mint and rue. But you cheat people, and you don't love God. You should be fair and kind to others and still give a tenth to God.

43You Pharisees are in for trouble! You love the front seats in the synagogues, and you like to be greeted with honor in the market. **44**But you are in for trouble! You are like unmarked graves[f] that people walk on without even knowing it.

45A teacher of the Law of Moses spoke up, "Teacher, you said cruel things about us." **46**Jesus replied:

You teachers are also in for trouble! You load people down with heavy burdens, but you won't lift a finger to help them carry the loads. **47**Yes, you are really in for trouble. You build monuments to honor the prophets your own people murdered long ago. **48**You must think that was the right thing for your people to do, or else you would not have built monuments for the prophets they murdered.

49Because of your evil deeds, the

[b]**11.31** *South*: Sheba, probably a country in southern Arabia. [c]**11.37** *sat down to eat*: See the note at 7.36. [d]**11.38** *did not wash his hands*: The Jewish people had strict laws about washing their hands before eating, especially if they had been out in public. [e]**11.40** *Didn't God make both the outside and the inside*: Or "Doesn't the person who washes the outside always wash the inside too?" [f]**11.44** *unmarked graves*: Tombs were whitewashed to keep anyone from accidentally touching them. A person who touched a dead body or a tomb was considered unclean and could not worship with other Jewish people.

11.31,32 *the Queen of the South*: This refers to the Queen of Sheba. Jesus is saying that if Gentiles like the people of Nineveh (Jonah 3.5) or the Queen of Sheba (1 Kgs 10.1-10; 2 Chr 9.1-12) could learn from Jewish prophets and kings, why can't the leaders of Judah recognize God's message from one of their own people, namely Jesus?

11.38,39 *did not wash his hands*: The Jewish Law taught that what people ate and touched could make them unfit to worship God. This is why they washed their hands and cleansed their dishes before eating. However, Jesus was saying that what a person was like inside is more important than following laws that only make a person clean on the outside.

   Purity (Clean and Unclean)

11.42 *give God a tenth*: The Pharisees followed the law about giving one-tenth of everything back to the Lord (see Deut 14.22 and Lev 27.30), even one-tenth of the spices in their gardens. Jesus told them that helping others was just as important.

11.46 *heavy burdens*: Refers to the laws taught by the Pharisees and teachers of the Law of Moses. Jesus suggests that these teachers liked to lay down rules, but were not willing to help those who struggled to keep them. (See the article People of the Law: The Religion of Israel on pg 1794.)

11.49 *Wisdom of God:* Jesus is quoting from an unknown source. God sent messengers before Jesus, but the Jewish people turned their backs on them or even killed them. They failed to listen to what God was saying to them.

12.5 *hell:* In Greek the word for hell is *gehenna,* which is a form of the Hebrew words that mean "Valley of Hinnom." Even before Jesus was born, some Jewish teachers said that the place where wicked people go when they die is like the burning Valley of Hinnom.

Hell

12.6 *Five sparrows . . . few cents:* The Roman coin referred to here is an assarius, which equals only about one-sixteenth of what a common laborer earned for one day's work. The Law of Moses did not forbid the eating of sparrows. They were cheap, and an average person could afford them.

Wisdom of God said, "I will send prophets and apostles to you. But you will murder some and mistreat others." [50] You people living today will be punished for all the prophets who have been murdered since the beginning of the world. [51] This includes every prophet from the time of Abel to the time of Zechariah,[g] who was murdered between the altar and the temple. You people will certainly be punished for all of this.

[52] You teachers of the Law of Moses are really in for trouble! You carry the keys to the door of knowledge about God. But you never go in, and you keep others from going in.

[53] Jesus was about to leave, but the teachers and the Pharisees wanted to get even with him. They tried to make him say what he thought about other things, [54] so they could catch him saying something wrong.

Warnings

12 As thousands of people crowded around Jesus and were stepping on each other, he told his disciples:

Be sure to guard against the dishonest teaching[h] of the Pharisees! It is their way of fooling people. [2] Everything that is hidden will be found out, and every secret will be known. [3] Whatever you say in the dark will be heard when it is day. Whatever you whisper in a closed room will be shouted from the housetops.

The One To Fear
(Matthew 10.28-31)

[4] My friends, don't be afraid of people. They can kill you, but after that, there is nothing else they can do. [5] God is the one you must fear. Not only can he take your life, but he can throw you into hell. God is certainly the one you should fear!

[6] Five sparrows are sold for only a few cents, but God doesn't forget a single one of them. [7] Even the hairs on your head are counted. So don't be afraid! You are worth much more than many sparrows.

Telling Others about Christ
(Matthew 10.32,33; 12.32; 10.19,20)

[8] If you tell others that you belong to me, the Son of Man will tell God's angels that you are my followers. [9] But if you reject me, you will be rejected in front of them. [10] If you speak against the Son of Man, you can be forgiven, but if you speak against the Holy Spirit, you cannot be forgiven.

[11] When you are brought to trial in the synagogues or before rulers or officials, don't worry about how you will defend yourselves or what you will say. [12] At that time the Holy Spirit will tell you what to say.

A Rich Fool

[13] A man in a crowd said to Jesus, "Teacher, tell my brother to give me my

[g]**11.51** *from the time of Abel . . . Zechariah:* Genesis is the first book in the Jewish Scriptures, and it tells that Abel was the first person to be murdered. Second Chronicles is the last book in the Jewish Scriptures, and the last murder that it tells about is that of Zechariah. [h]**12.1** *dishonest teaching:* The Greek text has "yeast," which is used here of a teaching that is not true (see Matthew 16.6,12).

share of what our father left us when he died."

[14]Jesus answered, "Who gave me the right to settle arguments between you and your brother?"

[15]Then he said to the crowd, "Don't be greedy! Owning a lot of things won't make your life safe."

[16]So Jesus told them this story:

A rich man's farm produced a big crop, [17]and he said to himself, "What can I do? I don't have a place large enough to store everything."

[18]Later, he said, "Now I know what I'll do. I'll tear down my barns and build bigger ones, where I can store all my grain and other goods. [19]Then I'll say to myself, 'You have stored up enough good things to last for years to come. Live it up! Eat, drink, and enjoy yourself.' "

[20]But God said to him, "You fool! Tonight you will die. Then who will get what you have stored up?"

[21]"This is what happens to people who store up everything for themselves, but are poor in the sight of God."

Worry

(Matthew 6.25-34)

[22]Jesus said to his disciples:

I tell you not to worry about your life! Don't worry about having something to eat or wear. [23]Life is more than food or clothing. [24]Look at the crows! They don't plant or harvest, and they don't have storehouses or barns. But God takes care of them. You are much more important than any birds. [25]Can worry make you live longer?[i] [26]If you don't have power over small things, why worry about everything else?

[27]Look how the wild flowers grow! They don't work hard to make their clothes. But I tell you Solomon with all his wealth[j] wasn't as well clothed as one of these flowers. [28]God gives such beauty to everything that grows in the fields, even though it is here today and thrown into a fire tomorrow. Won't he do even more for you? You have such little faith!

[29]Don't keep worrying about having something to eat or drink. [30]Only people who don't know God are always worrying about such things. Your Father knows what you need. [31]But put God's work first, and these things will be yours as well.

Treasures in Heaven

(Matthew 6.19-21)

[32]My little group of disciples, don't be afraid! Your Father wants to give you the kingdom. [33]Sell what you have and give the money to the poor. Make yourselves moneybags that never wear out. Make sure your treasure is safe in heaven, where thieves cannot steal it and moths cannot destroy it. [34]Your heart will always be where your treasure is.

Faithful and Unfaithful Servants

(Matthew 24.45-51)

[35]Be ready and keep your lamps burning [36]just like those servants who wait up for their master to return

12.27 *Solomon with all his wealth:* The Jewish people thought that King Solomon was the richest person who had ever lived. See also 1 Kgs 10.4-7; 2 Chr 9.3-6.

Solomon

12.30 *Your Father:* Jesus is referring to God.

Slaves and Servants in the Time of Jesus

[i]**12.25** *live longer:* Or "grow taller." [j]**12.27** *Solomon with all his wealth:* The Jewish people thought that Solomon was the richest person who had ever lived.

Jesus said, "Don't be greedy! Owning a lot of things won't make your life safe." LUKE 12.15

12.54 *cloud coming up in the west:* Weather systems usually travel from west to east. This is true in Palestine, where there are occasional heavy rainstorms in the winter.

from a wedding feast. As soon as he comes and knocks, they open the door for him. [37]Servants are fortunate if their master finds them awake and ready when he comes! I promise you he will get ready and let his servants sit down so he can serve them. [38]Those servants are really fortunate if their master finds them ready, even though he comes late at night or early in the morning. [39]You would surely not let a thief break into your home, if you knew when the thief was coming. [40]So always be ready! You don't know when the Son of Man will come.

[41]Peter asked Jesus, "Did you say this just for us or for everyone?"

[42]The Lord answered:

Who are faithful and wise servants? Who are the ones the master will put in charge of giving the other servants their food supplies at the proper time? [43]Servants are fortunate if their master comes and finds them doing their job. [44]A servant who is always faithful will surely be put in charge of everything the master owns.

[45]But suppose one of the servants thinks that the master won't return until late. Suppose that servant starts beating all the other servants and eats and drinks and gets drunk. [46]If that happens, the master will come on a day and at a time when the servant least expects him. That servant will then be punished and thrown out with the servants who cannot be trusted.

[47]If servants are not ready or willing to do what their master wants them to do, they will be beaten hard. [48]But servants who don't know what their master wants them to do will not be beaten so hard for doing wrong. If God has been generous with you, he will expect you to serve him well. But if he has been more than generous, he will expect you to serve him even better.

Not Peace, but Trouble
(Matthew 10.34-36)

[49]I came to set fire to the earth, and I wish it were already on fire! [50]I am going to be put to a hard test. And I will have to suffer a lot of pain until it is over. [51]Do you think that I came to bring peace to earth? No indeed! I came to make people choose sides. [52]A family of five will be divided, with two of them against the other three. [53]Fathers and sons will turn against one another, and mothers and daughters will do the same. Mothers-in-law and daughters-in-law will also turn against each other.

Knowing What To Do
(Matthew 16.2,3; 5.25,26)

[54]Jesus said to all the people:

As soon as you see a cloud coming up in the west, you say, "It's going to rain," and it does. [55]When the south wind blows, you say, "It's going to get hot," and it does. [56]Are you trying to fool someone? You can predict the weather by looking at the earth and sky, but you don't really know what's going on right now. [57]Why don't you understand the right thing to do? [58]When someone accuses you of something, try to settle things before you are taken to court. If you don't, you will be dragged before the judge. Then the judge will hand you over to the jailer, and you will be locked up. [59]You won't get out until you have paid the last cent you owe.

Turn Back to God

13 About this same time Jesus was told that Pilate had given orders for some people from Galilee to be killed while they were offering sacrifices. ²Jesus replied:

Do you think that these people were worse sinners than everyone else in Galilee just because of what happened to them? ³Not at all! But you can be sure that if you don't turn back to God, every one of you will also be killed. ⁴What about those 18 people who died when the tower in Siloam fell on them? Do you think they were worse than everyone else in Jerusalem? ⁵Not at all! But you can be sure that if you don't turn back to God, every one of you will also die.

A Story about a Fig Tree

⁶Jesus then told them this story:

A man had a fig tree growing in his vineyard. One day he went out to pick some figs, but he didn't find any. ⁷So he said to the gardener, "For three years I have come looking for figs on this tree, and I haven't found any yet. Chop it down! Why should it take up space?"

⁸The gardener answered, "Master, leave it for another year. I'll dig around it and put some manure on it to make it grow. ⁹Maybe it will have figs on it next year. If it doesn't, you can have it cut down."

Healing a Woman on the Sabbath

¹⁰One Sabbath, Jesus was teaching in a synagogue, ¹¹and a woman was there who had been crippled by an evil spirit for 18 years. She was completely bent over and could not straighten up. ¹²When Jesus saw the woman, he called her over and said,

"You are now well." ¹³He placed his hands on her, and at once she stood up straight and praised God.

¹⁴The man in charge of the synagogue was angry because Jesus had healed someone on the Sabbath. So he said to the people, "Each week has six days when we can work. Come and be healed on one of those days, but not on the Sabbath."

¹⁵The Lord replied, "Are you trying to fool someone? Won't any one of you untie your ox or donkey and lead it out to drink on a Sabbath? ¹⁶This woman belongs to the family of Abraham, but Satan has kept her bound for 18 years. Isn't it right to set her free on the Sabbath?" ¹⁷Jesus' words made his enemies ashamed. But everyone else in the crowd was happy about the wonderful things he was doing.

A Mustard Seed and Yeast

(Matthew 13.31-33; Mark 4.30-32)

¹⁸Jesus said, "What is God's kingdom like? What can I compare it with? ¹⁹It is like what happens when someone plants a mustard seed in a garden. The seed grows as big as a tree, and birds nest in its branches."

²⁰Then Jesus said, "What can I compare God's kingdom with? ²¹It is like what happens when a woman mixes yeast into three batches of flour. Finally, all the dough rises."

The Narrow Door

(Matthew 7.13,14,21-23)

²²As Jesus was on his way to Jerusalem, he taught the people in the towns and villages. ²³Someone asked him, "Lord, are only a few people going to be saved?"

Jesus answered:

²⁴Do all you can to go in by the narrow door! A lot of people will try to get in, but will not be able to. ²⁵Once the owner of the house gets up and

13.1 *Pilate:* The Roman governor in charge of Judea from A.D. 26 to 36. Several first-century Jewish historians reported that Pilate was a cruel leader who was disrespectful of the Jewish temple and religious customs. Normally, however, Roman leaders did not interfere with the everyday work and worship at the temple.

Pontius Pilate

13.2 *sinners:* Those who rebel against God and disobey God's Law. People in Jesus' day generally believed that bad things happened to someone who was sinful. Jesus is saying that all people are sinful and need to turn to God.

13.14 *healed . . . on the Sabbath:* Doing any kind of work on the Sabbath, including healing someone, was against the Jewish Law.

13.16 *Satan:* In Jesus' day, Satan and demons were often thought to be responsible for sickness and other physical and mental problems. (See the article Miracles, Magic, and Medicine on pg 1820.)

13.21 *yeast:* Yeast is mixed with water and flour to cause the dough to rise, so the bread will not be flat when baked. Bread that has no yeast is flat and is called "thin bread" (unleavened bread). Thin bread was served at special times, such as Passover.

13.28 *Abraham, Isaac:* The Jewish people Jesus was talking to would have known that God made an agreement with Abraham, the ancestor of all Jewish people (Gen 12.1-3; 17.1-9). See also Matt 22.13; 25.30.

Abraham

13.29 *feast in God's kingdom:* This feast refers to a future time when God will bring together faithful people not only from the people of Israel but also from every nation. Jesus compares this time to a feast because a feast was a time of celebration. See also Matt 8.11,12.

13.31 *Pharisees:* The Pharisees may have been trying to scare Jesus into leaving for Judea.

13.33 *Jerusalem:* A number of the prophets had also been killed when they brought unpopular messages to Jerusalem.

13.35 *temple:* This is the temple that Herod the Great built in Jerusalem. Work began in 20 B.C. and continued into Jesus' day (see John 2.20). **(See the article People of the Law: The Religion of Israel on pg 1794.)**

locks the door, you will be left standing outside. You will knock on the door and say, "Sir, open the door for us!"

But the owner will answer, "I don't know a thing about you! "

²⁶Then you will start saying, "We dined with you, and you taught in our streets."

²⁷But he will say, "I really don't know who you are! Get away from me, you evil people!"

²⁸Then when you have been thrown outside, you will weep and grit your teeth because you will see Abraham, Isaac, Jacob, and all the prophets in God's kingdom. ²⁹People will come from all directions and sit down to feast in God's kingdom. ³⁰There the ones who are now least important will be the most important, and those who are now most important will be least important.

Jesus and Herod

³¹At that time some Pharisees came to Jesus and said, "You had better get away from here, because Herodᵏ wants to kill you!"

³²Jesus said to them:

Go tell that fox, "I am going to force out demons and heal people today and tomorrow, and three days later I'll be through." ³³But I am going on my way today and tomorrow and the next day. After all, Jerusalem is the place where prophets are killed.

Jesus Loves Jerusalem
(Matthew 23.37-39)

³⁴Jerusalem, Jerusalem! Your people have killed the prophets and have

stoned the messengers who were sent to you. I have often wanted to gather your people, as a hen gathers her chicks under her wings. But you wouldn't let me. ³⁵Now your temple will be deserted. You won't see me again until the time when you say,

"Blessed is the one who comes
in the name of the Lord."

Jesus Heals a Sick Man

14 One Sabbath, Jesus was having dinner in the home of an important Pharisee, and everyone was carefully watching Jesus. ²All of a sudden a man with swollen legs stood up in front of him. ³Jesus turned and asked the Pharisees and the teachers of the Law of Moses, "Is it right to heal on the Sabbath?" ⁴But they did not say a word.

Jesus took hold of the man. Then he healed him and sent him away. ⁵Afterwards, Jesus asked the people, "If your son or ox falls into a well, wouldn't you pull him out at once, even on the Sabbath?" ⁶There was nothing they could say.

How To Be a Guest

⁷Jesus saw how the guests had tried to take the best seats. So he told them:

⁸When you are invited to a wedding feast, don't sit in the best place. Someone more important may have been invited. ⁹Then the one who invited you will come and say, "Give your place to this other guest!" You will be embarrassed and will have to sit in the worst place.

¹⁰When you are invited to be a guest, go and sit in the worst place. Then the

ᵏ**13.31** *Herod:* Herod Antipas, the son of Herod the Great.

one who invited you may come and say, "My friend, take a better seat!" You will then be honored in front of all the other guests. [11]If you put yourself above others, you will be put down. But if you humble yourself, you will be honored.

[12]Then Jesus said to the man who had invited him:

When you give a dinner or a banquet, don't invite your friends and family and relatives and rich neighbors. If you do, they will invite you in return, and you will be paid back. [13]When you give a feast, invite the poor, the paralyzed, the lame, and the blind. [14]They cannot pay you back. But God will bless you and reward you when his people rise from death.

The Great Banquet
(Matthew 22.1-10)

[15]After Jesus had finished speaking, one of the guests said, "The greatest blessing of all is to be at the banquet in God's kingdom!"

[16]Jesus told him:

A man once gave a great banquet and invited a lot of guests. [17]When the banquet was ready, he sent a servant to tell the guests, "Everything is ready! Please come."

[18]One guest after another started making excuses. The first one said, "I bought some land, and I've got to look it over. Please excuse me."

[19]Another guest said, "I bought five teams of oxen, and I need to try them out. Please excuse me."

[20]Still another guest said, "I've just now married, and I can't be there."

[21]The servant told his master what happened, and the master became so angry he said, "Go as fast as you can to every street and alley in town! Bring in everyone who is poor or paralyzed or blind or lame."

[22]When the servant returned, he said, "Master, I've done what you told me, and there is still plenty of room for more people."

[23]His master then told him, "Go out along the back roads and make people come in, so my house will be full. [24]Not one of the guests I first invited will get even a bite of my food!"

Being a Disciple
(Matthew 10.37,38)

[25]Large crowds were walking along with Jesus, when he turned and said:

[26]You cannot be my disciple, unless you love me more than you love your father and mother, your wife and children, and your brothers and sisters. You cannot follow me unless you love me more than you love your own life.

[27]You cannot be my disciple unless you carry your own cross and follow me.

[28]Suppose one of you wants to build a tower. What is the first thing you will do? Won't you sit down and figure out how much it will cost and if you have enough money to pay for it? [29]Otherwise, you will start building the tower, but not be able to finish. Then everyone who sees what is happening will laugh at you. [30]They will say, "You started building, but could not finish the job."

[31]What will a king do if he has only 10,000 soldiers to defend himself against a king who is about to attack him with 20,000 soldiers? Before he goes out to battle, won't he first sit down and decide if he can win? [32]If he thinks he won't be able to defend himself, he will

14.14 *when his people rise from death*: Jesus is talking about the future time when God will bring his faithful followers back from death to live under God's everlasting rule (Dan 12.2; John 5.28,29; 1 Thes 4.16; Rev 20.11-15).

Resurrection

14.19 *teams of oxen*: A team of oxen could be as few as two oxen tied or yoked together.

14.27 *cross*: The cross was a symbol for suffering, since the Romans used it as a way to put criminals or rebels to death. Death on a cross was usually slow and painful, and was most often the result of suffocation. See also Matt 10.38; 16.24; Mark 8.34; Luke 9.23.

Crucifixion

A man said to Jesus, *"The greatest blessing of all is to be at the banquet in God's kingdom!"* LUKE 14.15

14.34 *salt*: Salt was used to flavor food. It was also used to preserve food, especially meat and fish. Salt that has lost its taste was no longer useful.

15.1 *sinners*: "Sinners" was the name given to people who are unclean or disobedient according to the Law of Moses. Jesus wanted to show how much God cared for sinners and wanted to welcome them into the community of God's people.

15.4 *go look for the lost sheep*: A good shepherd in Jesus' time would not have been likely to leave his whole herd unattended in order to go search for one lost sheep.

15.8 *ten silver coins*: The coins mentioned here are Greek drachmas. One drachma was worth the price of one sheep, and it would take five drachmas to buy an ox.

15.12 *my share of the property*: In a Jewish family, the sons inherited the family's goods and property from their father. Usually the older son received a greater share, often twice as much as his younger brothers.

Purity (Clean and Unclean)

send messengers and ask for peace while the other king is still a long way off. [33] So then, you cannot be my disciple unless you give away everything you own.

Salt and Light
(Matthew 5.13; Mark 9.50)

[34] Salt is good, but if it no longer tastes like salt, how can it be made to taste salty again? [35] It is no longer good for the soil or even for the manure pile. People simply throw it out. If you have ears, pay attention!

One Sheep
(Matthew 18.12-14)

15 Tax collectors[l] and sinners were all crowding around to listen to Jesus. [2] So the Pharisees and the teachers of the Law of Moses started grumbling, "This man is friendly with sinners. He even eats with them."

[3] Then Jesus told them this story:

[4] If any of you has 100 sheep, and one of them gets lost, what will you do? Won't you leave the 99 in the field and go look for the lost sheep until you find it? [5] And when you find it, you will be so glad that you will put it on your shoulder [6] and carry it home. Then you will call in your friends and neighbors and say, "Let's celebrate! I've found my lost sheep."

[7] Jesus said, "In the same way there is more happiness in heaven because of one sinner who turns to God than over 99 good people who don't need to."

One Coin

[8] Jesus told the people another story:

What will a woman do if she has ten silver coins and loses one of them? Won't she light a lamp, sweep the floor, and look carefully until she finds it? [9] Then she will call in her friends and neighbors and say, "Let's celebrate! I've found the coin I lost."

[10] Jesus said, "In the same way God's angels are happy when even one person turns to him."

Two Sons

[11] Jesus told them yet another story:

Once a man had two sons. [12] The younger son said to his father, "Give me my share of the property." So the father divided his property between his two sons.

[13] Not long after that, the younger son packed up everything he owned and left for a foreign country, where he wasted all his money in wild living. [14] He had spent everything, when a bad famine spread through that whole land. Soon he had nothing to eat.

[15] He went to work for a man in that country, and the man sent him out to take care of his pigs.[m] [16] He would have been glad to eat what the pigs were eating,[n] but no one gave him a thing.

[17] Finally, he came to his senses and said, "My father's workers have plenty to eat, and here I am, starving to death! [18] I will go to my father and say to him, 'Father, I have sinned against

[l]**15.1** *Tax collectors*: See the note at 3.12. [m]**15.15** *pigs*: The Jewish religion taught that pigs were not fit to eat or even to touch. A Jewish man would have felt terribly insulted if he had to feed pigs, much less eat with them. [n]**15.16** *what the pigs were eating*: The Greek text has "(bean) pods," which came from a tree in Palestine. These were used to feed animals. Poor people sometimes ate them too.

God in heaven and against you. **19**I am no longer good enough to be called your son. Treat me like one of your workers.'"

20The younger son got up and started back to his father. But when he was still a long way off, his father saw him and felt sorry for him. He ran to his son and hugged and kissed him.

21The son said, "Father, I have sinned against God in heaven and against you. I am no longer good enough to be called your son."

22But his father said to the servants, "Hurry and bring the best clothes and put them on him. Give him a ring for his finger and sandals° for his feet. **23**Get the best calf and prepare it, so we can eat and celebrate. **24**This son of mine was dead, but has now come back to life. He was lost and has now been found." And they began to celebrate.

25The older son had been out in the field. But when he came near the house, he heard the music and dancing. **26**So he called one of the servants over and asked, "What's going on here?"

27The servant answered, "Your brother has come home safe and sound, and your father ordered us to kill the best calf." **28**The older brother got so angry that he would not even go into the house.

His father came out and begged him to go in. **29**But he said to his father, "For years I have worked for you like a slave and have always obeyed you. But you have never even given me a little goat, so that I could give a dinner for my friends. **30**This other son of yours

wasted your money on prostitutes. And now that he has come home, you ordered the best calf to be killed for a feast."

31His father replied, "My son, you are always with me, and everything I have is yours. **32**But we should be glad and celebrate! Your brother was dead, but he is now alive. He was lost and has now been found."

A Dishonest Manager

16 Jesus said to his disciples:
A rich man once had a manager to take care of his business. But he was told that his manager was wasting money. **2**So the rich man called him in and said, "What is this I hear about you? Tell me what you have done! You are no longer going to work for me."

3The manager said to himself, "What shall I do now that my master is going to fire me? I can't dig ditches, and I'm ashamed to beg. **4**I know what I'll do, so that people will welcome me into their homes after I've lost my job."

5Then one by one he called in the people who were in debt to his master. He asked the first one, "How much do you owe my master?"

6"A hundred barrels of olive oil," the man answered.

So the manager said, "Take your bill and sit down and quickly write '50.'"

7The manager asked someone else who was in debt to his master, "How much do you owe?"

"A thousand sacks^P of wheat," the man replied.

°**15.22** *ring . . . sandals*: These show that the young man's father fully accepted him as his son. A ring was a sign of high position in the family. Sandals showed that he was a son instead of a slave, since slaves did not usually wear sandals.   ^P**16.7** *A thousand sacks*: The Greek text has "100 measures," and each measure is about 10 or 12 sacks.

● 16.6 *hundred barrels of olive oil:* One of these barrels was called a *batos* in Greek (from the Hebrew word *bath*). Each batos held about eight or nine gallons.

The father said . . . "This son of mine was dead, but has now come back to life. He was lost and has now been found."
LUKE 15.23,24

16.8 *people of this world . . . people who belong to the light:* The "people of this world" do not follow God or are opposed to God's purposes. In some parts of the New Testament, the "world" is often pictured as evil and as God's enemy (Rom 12.2; Gal 4.3; Jas 1.27). In the Bible, light is used to describe those people or things that reveal God's truth (see Isa 49.6; John 1.3,4). The followers of Jesus are also called "people of the light" (Eph 5.8).

16.9 *wicked wealth:* Jesus is not saying that money is evil, but that people sometimes get money by cheating others. Money and possessions can also be used to make friends and to serve others. Money can run out, but God offers something more valuable: an eternal home (living with God forever).

16.16 *the Law of Moses and the Books of the Prophets:* The Law of Moses refers to the first five books of the Bible. The Law gives the early history of God's people and lists the rules that God gave the people through Moses about how to live right. The Books of the Prophets include those books written by God's special messengers. **(See the articles Prophets and Prophecy on pg 1791 and What Books Belong in the Bible? on pg 1764.)**

Law

The manager said, "Take your bill
and write '800.' "
8The master praised his dishonest
manager for looking out for himself so
well. That's how it is! The people of
this world look out for themselves better than the people who belong to the
light.
9My disciples, I tell you to use wicked
wealth to make friends for yourselves.
Then when it is gone, you will be welcomed into an eternal home. 10Any-
one who can be trusted in little matters
can also be trusted in important matters. But anyone who is dishonest in
little matters will be dishonest in important matters. 11If you cannot be
trusted with this wicked wealth, who
will trust you with true wealth? 12And
if you cannot be trusted with what belongs to someone else, who will give
you something that will be your own?
13You cannot be the slave of two masters. You will like one more than the
other or be more loyal to one than to
the other. You cannot serve God and
money.

Some Sayings of Jesus

(Matthew 11.12,13; 5.31,32; Mark 10.11,12)

14The Pharisees really loved money. So
when they heard what Jesus said, they
made fun of him. 15But Jesus told them:
You are always making yourselves
look good, but God sees what is in
your heart. The things that most people think are important are worthless
as far as God is concerned.
16Until the time of John the Baptist, people had to obey the Law of
Moses and the Books of the Prophets.[q]
But since God's kingdom has been
preached, everyone is trying hard to
get in. 17Heaven and earth will disappear before the smallest letter of the
Law does.
18It is a terrible sin[r] for a man to divorce his wife and marry another
woman. It is also a terrible sin for a
man to marry a divorced woman.

Lazarus and the Rich Man

19There was once a rich man who
wore expensive clothes and every day
ate the best food. 20But a poor beggar
named Lazarus was brought to the
gate of the rich man's house. 21He was
happy just to eat the scraps that fell
from the rich man's table. His body
was covered with sores, and dogs kept
coming up to lick them. 22The poor
man died, and angels took him to the
place of honor next to Abraham.[s]
The rich man also died and was
buried. 23He went to hell[t] and was suffering terribly. When he looked up and
saw Abraham far off and Lazarus at his
side, 24he said to Abraham, "Have pity
on me! Send Lazarus to dip his finger
in water and touch my tongue. I'm
suffering terribly in this fire."
25Abraham answered, "My friend,
remember that while you lived, you
had everything good, and Lazarus had
everything bad. Now he is happy, and
you are in pain. 26And besides, there is

[q] **16.16** *the Law of Moses and the Books of the Prophets*: The Jewish Scriptures, that is, the Old Testament. [r] **16.18** *a terrible sin*: The Greek text uses a word that means the sin of being unfaithful in marriage. [s] **16.22** *the place of honor next to Abraham*: The Jewish people thought that heaven would be a banquet that God would give for them. Abraham would be the most important person there, and the guest of honor would sit next to him. [t] **16.23** *hell*: The Greek text has "hades," which the Jewish people often thought of as the place where the dead wait for the final judgment.

a deep ditch between us, and no one from either side can cross over."

27But the rich man said, "Abraham, then please send Lazarus to my father's home. **28**Let him warn my five brothers, so they won't come to this horrible place."

29Abraham answered, "Your brothers can read what Moses and the prophets[u] wrote. They should pay attention to that."

30Then the rich man said, "No, that's not enough! If only someone from the dead would go to them, they would listen and turn to God."

31So Abraham said, "If they won't pay attention to Moses and the prophets, they won't listen even to someone who comes back from the dead."

Faith and Service
(Matthew 18.6,7,21,22; Mark 9.42)

17 Jesus said to his disciples:
There will always be something that causes people to sin. But anyone who causes them to sin is in for trouble. A person who causes even one of my little followers to sin **2**would be better off thrown into the ocean with a heavy stone tied around their neck. **3**So be careful what you do.

Correct any followers[v] of mine who sin, and forgive the ones who say they are sorry. **4**Even if one of them mistreats you seven times in one day and says, "I am sorry," you should still forgive that person.

5The apostles said to the Lord, "Make our faith stronger!"

6Jesus replied:

If you had faith no bigger than a tiny mustard seed, you could tell this mulberry tree to pull itself up, roots and all, and to plant itself in the ocean. And it would!

7If your servant comes in from plowing or from taking care of the sheep, would you say, "Welcome! Come on in and have something to eat"? **8**No, you wouldn't say that. You would say, "Prepare me something to eat. Get ready to serve me, so I can have my meal. Then later on you can eat and drink." **9**Servants don't deserve special thanks for doing what they are supposed to do. **10**And that's how it should be with you. When you've done all you should, then say, "We are merely servants, and we have simply done our duty."

Ten Men with Leprosy

11On his way to Jerusalem, Jesus went along the border between Samaria and Galilee. **12**As he was going into a village, ten men with leprosy[w] came toward him. They stood at a distance **13**and shouted, "Jesus, Master, have pity on us!"

14Jesus looked at them and said, "Go show yourselves to the priests."[x]

On their way they were healed. **15**When one of them discovered that he was healed, he came back, shouting praises to God. **16**He bowed down at the feet of Jesus and thanked him. The man was from the country of Samaria.

17Jesus asked, "Weren't ten men healed? Where are the other nine? **18**Why was this foreigner the only one who came back to thank God?" **19**Then Jesus told the man,

● **16.31** *they won't listen:* Jesus is saying that some people, including many of the Pharisees he is talking to, will not be convinced by his message even after he is raised from death.

● **17.6** *mulberry tree:* The mulberry tree was first grown in Persia. It can grow to a height of about 20 feet and is usually very wide at the top. Its berries turn black when ripe and contain a sweet red juice.

● **17.16** *man was from the country of Samaria:* Those who heard this story may have been surprised that it was the Samaritan who thanked Jesus. But like other non-Jews ("foreigners") in LUKE, he is healed because of his faith (see also 7.1-17).

---

[u]**16.29** *Moses and the prophets:* The Jewish Scriptures, that is, the Old Testament.   [v]**17.3** *followers:* The Greek text has "brothers," which is often used in the New Testament for followers of Jesus. [w]**17.12** *leprosy:* See the note at 4.27.   [x]**17.14** *show yourselves to the priests:* See the note at 5.14.

"If you had faith no bigger than a tiny mustard seed, you could tell this mulberry tree to pull itself up, roots and all, and to plant itself in the ocean. And it would!" LUKE 17.6

17.26,27 *Noah:* God chose the good and faithful Noah to build a big boat (ark) that would save his family and other living things from the flood (see Gen 6–9).

17.28,29 *Lot . . . Sodom:* Lot, the nephew of Abraham, ran into trouble in Sodom, which was a very evil city (see Gen 18.16—19.29). God destroyed the evil people who lived there, but rescued Lot and his family. The location of Sodom is not known, but it may have been near the south end of the Dead Sea.

17.32 *what happened to Lot's wife:* She turned into a block of salt when she disobeyed God by turning around to look at the destruction of Sodom (see Gen 19.26).

17.35-36 *grinding wheat:* Usually women sifted the harvested wheat grains and crushed (ground) them in a mill to make flour. A simple mill would have had a flat rock surface where grain could be pounded or rolled with a rock or wooden tool.

18.3 *widow . . . fair treatment in court:* In Jewish culture, a woman who had lost her husband sometimes had no one else to stand up for her or to take care of her.

"You may get up and go. Your faith has made you well."

God's Kingdom

(Matthew 24.23-28,37-41)

²⁰Some Pharisees asked Jesus when God's kingdom would come. He answered, "God's kingdom isn't something you can see. ²¹There is no use saying, 'Look! Here it is' or 'Look! There it is.' God's kingdom is here with you."^y

²²Jesus said to his disciples:

The time will come when you will long to see one of the days of the Son of Man, but you will not. ²³When people say to you, "Look there," or "Look here," don't go looking for him. ²⁴The day of the Son of Man will be like lightning flashing across the sky. ²⁵But first he must suffer terribly and be rejected by the people of today. ²⁶When the Son of Man comes, things will be just as they were when Noah lived. ²⁷People were eating, drinking, and getting married right up to the day when Noah went into the big boat. Then the flood came and drowned everyone on earth.

²⁸When Lot^z lived, people were also eating and drinking. They were buying, selling, planting, and building. ²⁹But on the very day Lot left Sodom, fiery flames poured down from the sky and killed everyone. ³⁰The same will

happen on the day when the Son of Man appears.

³¹At that time no one on a rooftop^a should go down into the house to get anything. No one in a field should go back to the house for anything. ³²Remember what happened to Lot's wife.^b

³³People who try to save their lives will lose them, and those who lose their lives will save them. ³⁴On that night two people will be sleeping in the same bed, but only one will be taken. The other will be left. ³⁵⁻³⁶Two women will be together grinding wheat, but only one will be taken. The other will be left.^c

³⁷Then Jesus' disciples spoke up, "But where will this happen, Lord?"

Jesus said, "Where there is a corpse, there will always be vultures."^d

A Widow and a Judge

18 Jesus told his disciples a story about how they should keep on praying and never give up:

²In a town there was once a judge who didn't fear God or care about people. ³In that same town there was a widow who kept going to the judge and saying, "Make sure that I get fair treatment in court."

⁴For a while the judge refused to do anything. Finally, he said to himself, "Even though I don't fear God or care

^y**17.21** *here with you:* Or "in your hearts."   ^z**17.27,28** *Noah . . . Lot:* When God destroyed the earth by a flood, he saved Noah and his family. And when God destroyed the cities of Sodom and Gomorrah and the evil people who lived there, he rescued Lot and his family (see Genesis 19.1-29). ^a**17.31** *rooftop:* See the note at 5.19.   ^b**17.32** *what happened to Lot's wife:* She turned into a block of salt when she disobeyed God (see Genesis 19.26).   ^c**17.35,36** *will be left:* Some manuscripts add, "Two men will be in the same field, but only one will be taken. The other will be left."   ^d**17.37** *Where there is a corpse, there will always be vultures:* This saying may mean that when anything important happens, people soon know about it. Or the saying may mean that whenever something bad happens, curious people gather around and stare. But the word translated "vulture" also means "eagle" and may refer to the Roman army, which had an eagle as its symbol.

about people, [5]I will help this widow because she keeps on bothering me. If I don't help her, she will wear me out." [6]The Lord said:

Think about what that crooked judge said. [7]Won't God protect his chosen ones who pray to him day and night? Won't he be concerned for them? [8]He will surely hurry and help them. But when the Son of Man comes, will he find on this earth anyone with faith?

A Pharisee and a Tax Collector

[9]Jesus told a story to some people who thought they were better than others and who looked down on everyone else:

[10]Two men went into the temple to pray.[e] One was a Pharisee and the other a tax collector.[f] [11]The Pharisee stood over by himself and prayed,[g] "God, I thank you that I am not greedy, dishonest, and unfaithful in marriage like other people. And I am really glad that I am not like that tax collector over there. [12]I go without eating[h] for two days a week, and I give you one tenth of all I earn."

[13]The tax collector stood off at a distance and did not think he was good enough even to look up toward heaven. He was so sorry for what he had done that he pounded his chest and prayed, "God, have pity on me! I am such a sinner."

[14]Then Jesus said, "When the two men went home, it was the tax collector and not the Pharisee who was pleasing to God. If you put yourself above others, you will be put down. But if you humble yourself, you will be honored."

Jesus Blesses Little Children
(Matthew 19.13-15; Mark 10.13-16)

[15]Some people brought their little children for Jesus to bless. But when his disciples saw them doing this, they told the people to stop bothering him. [16]So Jesus called the children over to him and said, "Let the children come to me! Don't try to stop them. People who are like these children belong to God's kingdom.[i] [17]You will never get into God's kingdom unless you enter it like a child!"

A Rich and Important Man
(Matthew 19.16-30; Mark 10.17-31)

[18]An important man asked Jesus, "Good Teacher, what must I do to have eternal life?"

[19]Jesus said, "Why do you call me good? Only God is good. [20]You know the commandments: 'Be faithful in marriage. Do not murder. Do not steal. Do not tell lies about others. Respect your father and mother.'"

[21]He told Jesus, "I have obeyed all these commandments since I was a young man."

[22]When Jesus heard this, he said, "There is one thing you still need to do. Go and sell everything you own! Give the money to the poor, and you will have riches in heaven. Then come and be my follower." [23]When the man heard this, he was sad, because he was very rich.

[24]Jesus saw how sad the man was. So he said, "It's terribly hard for rich people to

18.12 go without eating . . . give you one tenth of all I earn: To go without eating is also called "fasting." Giving a tenth of everything you earn is called "tithing."

18.19,20 the commandments: The five commandments Jesus recites here are part of the Ten Commandments that God gave to Moses on Mount Sinai. See Exod 20.1-17 and Deut 5.1-21.

---

[e]18.10 into the temple to pray: Jewish people usually prayed there early in the morning and late in the afternoon.   [f]18.10 tax collector: See the note at 3.12.   [g]18.11 stood over by himself and prayed: Some manuscripts have "stood up and prayed to himself."   [h]18.12 without eating: See the note at 2.37.
[i]18.16 People who are like these children belong to God's kingdom: Or "God's kingdom belongs to people who are like these children."

18.25 *camel:* Camels are large animals that can be very nasty and stubborn. Jesus used such a bold statement to emphasize the truth of what he was saying.

18.35 *Jericho:* Joshua 5.13—6.26 describes how the people of Israel destroyed Jericho after crossing the Jordan River into the land of Canaan.

18.35 *blind man:* He is called Bartimaeus in Mark 10.46.

18.37 *Jesus from Nazareth:* Because Jesus was a common male name at this time, Jesus was often identified by adding his hometown to his name.

19.2 *Zacchaeus:* This is the only mention of Zacchaeus in the New Testament.

19.3-4 *sycamore tree:* The sycamore tree mentioned here is not the same as the North American species. This sycamore tree belongs to the same family as the mulberry and fig trees. It is a broad tree with strong branches. Its fruit doesn't taste very good but it was eaten by some poor people.

get into God's kingdom! [25]In fact, it's easier for a camel to go through the eye of a needle than for a rich person to get into God's kingdom."

[26]When the crowd heard this, they asked, "How can anyone ever be saved?"

[27]Jesus replied, "There are some things that people cannot do, but God can do anything."

[28]Peter said, "Remember, we left everything to be your followers!"

[29]Jesus answered, "You can be sure that anyone who gives up home or wife or brothers or family or children because of God's kingdom [30]will be given much more in this life. And in the future world they will have eternal life."

Jesus Again Tells about His Death
(Matthew 20.17-19; Mark 10.32-34)

[31]Jesus took the twelve apostles aside and said:

We are now on our way to Jerusalem. Everything that the prophets wrote about the Son of Man will happen there. [32]He will be handed over to foreigners,[j] who will make fun of him, mistreat him, and spit on him. [33]They will beat him and kill him, but three days later he will rise to life.

[34]The apostles did not understand what Jesus was talking about. They could not understand, because the meaning of what he said was hidden from them.

Jesus Heals a Blind Beggar
(Matthew 20.29-34; Mark 10.46-52)

[35]When Jesus was coming close to Jericho, a blind man sat begging beside the

road. [36]The man heard the crowd walking by and asked what was happening. [37]Some people told him that Jesus from Nazareth was passing by. [38]So the blind man shouted, "Jesus, Son of David,[k] have pity on me!" [39]The people who were going along with Jesus told the man to be quiet. But he shouted even louder, "Son of David, have pity on me!"

[40]Jesus stopped and told some people to bring the blind man over to him. When the blind man was getting near, Jesus asked, [41]"What do you want me to do for you?"

"Lord, I want to see!" he answered.

[42]Jesus replied, "Look and you will see! Your eyes are healed because of your faith." [43]At once the man could see, and he went with Jesus and started thanking God. When the crowds saw what happened, they praised God.

Zacchaeus

19 Jesus was going through Jericho, [2]where a man named Zacchaeus lived. He was in charge of collecting taxes[l] and was very rich. [3-4]Jesus was heading his way, and Zacchaeus wanted to see what he was like. But Zacchaeus was a short man and could not see over the crowd. So he ran ahead and climbed up into a sycamore tree.

[5]When Jesus got there, he looked up and said, "Zacchaeus, hurry down! I want to stay with you today." [6]Zacchaeus hurried down and gladly welcomed Jesus.

[7]Everyone who saw this started grumbling, "This man Zacchaeus is a sinner! And Jesus is going home to eat with him."

[8]Later that day Zacchaeus stood up and said to the Lord, "I will give half of my property to the poor. And I will now pay

[j]18.32 *foreigners:* The Romans, who ruled Judea at this time.   [k]18.38 *Son of David:* The Jewish people expected the Messiah to be from the family of King David, and for this reason the Messiah was often called the "Son of David."   [l]19.2 *in charge of collecting taxes:* See the note at 3.12.

back four times as much[m] to everyone I have ever cheated."

[9]Jesus said to Zacchaeus, "Today you and your family have been saved,[n] because you are a true son of Abraham.[o] [10]The Son of Man came to look for and to save people who are lost."

A Story about Ten Servants
(Matthew 25.14-30)

[11]The crowd was still listening to Jesus as he was getting close to Jerusalem. Many of them thought that God's kingdom would soon appear, [12]and Jesus told them this story:

A prince once went to a foreign country to be crowned king and then to return. [13]But before leaving, he called in ten servants and gave each of them some money. He told them, "Use this to earn more money until I get back."

[14]But the people of his country hated him, and they sent messengers to the foreign country to say, "We don't want this man to be our king."

[15]After the prince had been made king, he returned and called in his servants. He asked them how much they had earned with the money they had been given.

[16]The first servant came and said, "Sir, with the money you gave me I have earned ten times as much."

[17]"That's fine, my good servant!" the king said. "Since you have shown that you can be trusted with a small amount, you will be given ten cities to rule."

[18]The second one came and said, "Sir, with the money you gave me, I have earned five times as much."

[19]The king said, "You will be given five cities."

[20]Another servant came and said, "Sir, here is your money. I kept it safe in a handkerchief. [21]You are a hard man, and I was afraid of you. You take what isn't yours, and you harvest crops you didn't plant."

[22]"You worthless servant!" the king told him. "You have condemned yourself by what you have just said. You knew I am a hard man, taking what isn't mine and harvesting what I've not planted. [23]Why didn't you put my money in the bank? On my return, I could have had the money together with interest."

[24]Then he said to some other servants standing there, "Take the money away from him and give it to the servant who earned ten times as much."

[25]But they said, "Sir, he already has ten times as much!"

[26]The king replied, "Those who have something will be given more. But everything will be taken away from those who don't have anything. [27]Now bring me the enemies who didn't want me to be their king. Kill them while I watch!"

Jesus Enters Jerusalem
(Matthew 21.1-11; Mark 11.1-11; John 12.12-19)

[28]When Jesus had finished saying all this, he went on toward Jerusalem. [29]As he was getting near Bethphage and Bethany on

19.9 *saved:* After admitting his sin, he is rescued and placed under God's care.

God's Saving Love (Salvation)

19.9 *true son of Abraham:* The Jewish people were also called the sons and daughters of Abraham. Here, Jesus says Zacchaeus is truly one of God's special people.

19.11 *God's kingdom:* Some thought a great earthly ruler, like King David, would defeat the Romans and win back Israel's land and freedom. Others thought the whole world would be changed when God's kingdom came.

19.23 *interest:* Bankers used the money given to them to make more money by buying and selling. Some of the bankers' profits were returned as interest to the people who gave the banker money to invest.

19.29 *Bethphage and Bethany on the Mount of Olives:* Bethphage, which means "house of figs," was a little village on the road between Jericho and Jerusalem. Bethany is on the slopes of the Mount of Olives. Luke 24.50 suggests that Bethany was where Jesus went up to heaven. The Mount of Olives is a ridge about two and a half miles long to the east of the Kidron Valley and Jerusalem. It rises about 300 to 500 feet above the temple area in Jerusalem. (See Map 13 on pg 1891.)

Jerusalem

[m]**19.8** *pay back four times as much:* Both Jewish and Roman law said that a person must pay back four times the amount that was taken.   [n]**19.9** *saved:* Zacchaeus was Jewish, but it is only now that he is rescued from sin and placed under God's care.   [o]**19.9** *son of Abraham:* As used in this verse, the words mean that Zacchaeus is truly one of God's special people.

The king said, "Since you have shown that you can be trusted with a small amount, you will be given ten cities to rule." LUKE 19.17

19.37 *starting down the Mount of Olives:* If Jesus entered the city by way of the temple gate , crowds could have been lined up for over a mile. People in the temple area could have watched Jesus ride down from the Mount of Olives, across the Kidron Valley, and back up the road that led to the temple gate. **(See Map 13 on pg 1891.)**

19.43 *Jerusalem, the time will come:* Jesus' predictions did come true. In A.D. 66, the Jews rebelled and forced the Romans out of Jerusalem. As recorded by the Jewish historian Josephus, a large Roman army used siege warfare (surrounded) Jerusalem, and in A.D. 70, the city's defenses collapsed. The Romans destroyed many of the city walls and burned the temple.

God's Saving Love (Salvation)

19.47 *chief priests, the teachers . . . and some other important people:* These groups had the most to lose if the people accepted Jesus and his teachings. Jesus challenged their authority and power, which made them mad enough to want to kill Jesus. **(See the articles People of the Law: The Religion of Israel on pg 1794 and The World of Jesus: Peoples, Powers, and Politics on pg 1801.)**

the Mount of Olives, he sent two of his disciples on ahead. [30]He told them, "Go into the next village, where you will find a young donkey that has never been ridden. Untie the donkey and bring it here. [31]If anyone asks why you are doing this, just say, 'The LordP needs it.'"

[32]They went off and found everything just as Jesus had said. [33]While they were untying the donkey, its owners asked, "Why are you doing that?"

[34]They answered, "The LordP needs it."

[35]Then they led the donkey to Jesus. They put some of their clothes on its back and helped Jesus get on. [36]And as he rode along, the people spread clothes on the roadq in front of him. [37]When Jesus started down the Mount of Olives, his large crowd of disciples were happy and praised God because of all the miracles they had seen. [38]They shouted,

"Blessed is the king who comes
   in the name of the Lord!
Peace in heaven
   and glory to God."

[39]Some Pharisees in the crowd said to Jesus, "Teacher, make your disciples stop shouting!"

[40]But Jesus answered, "If they keep quiet, these stones will start shouting."

[41]When Jesus came closer and could see Jerusalem, he cried [42]and said:

It is too bad that today your people don't know what will bring them peace! Now it is hidden from them. [43]Jerusalem, the time will come when your enemies will build walls around you to attack you. Armies will surround you and close in on you from

every side. [44]They will level you to the ground and kill your people. Not one stone in your buildings will be left on top of another. This will happen because you did not see that God had come to save you.r

Jesus in the Temple
(Matthew 21.12-17; Mark 11.15-19; John 2.13-22)

[45]When Jesus entered the temple, he started chasing out the people who were selling things. [46]He told them, "The Scriptures say, 'My house should be a place of worship.' But you have made it a place where robbers hide!"

[47]Each day, Jesus kept on teaching in the temple. So the chief priests, the teachers of the Law of Moses, and some other important people tried to have him killed. [48]But they could not find a way to do it, because everyone else was eager to listen to him.

A Question about Jesus' Authority
(Matthew 21.23-27; Mark 11.27-33)

20 One day, Jesus was teaching in the temple and telling the good news. So the chief priests, the teachers, and the nation's leaders [2]asked him, "What right do you have to do these things? Who gave you this authority?"

[3]Jesus replied, "I want to ask you a question. [4]Who gave John the right to baptize? Was it God in heaven or merely some human being?"

[5]They talked this over and said to each other, "We can't say God gave John this right. Jesus will ask us why we didn't believe John. [6]And we can't say it was merely

P19.31,34 *The Lord:* Or "The master of the donkey."   q19.36 *spread clothes on the road:* This was one way that the Jewish people welcomed a famous person.   r19.44 *that God had come to save you:* The Jewish people looked for the time when God would come and rescue them from their enemies. But when Jesus came, many of them refused to obey him.

some human who gave John the right to baptize. The crowd will stone us to death, because they think John was a prophet."

⁷So they told Jesus, "We don't know who gave John the right to baptize."

⁸Jesus replied, "Then I won't tell you who gave me the right to do what I do."

Renters of a Vineyard
(Matthew 21.33-46; Mark 12.1-12)

⁹Jesus told the people this story:

A man once planted a vineyard and rented it out. Then he left the country for a long time. ¹⁰When it was time to harvest the crop, he sent a servant to ask the renters for his share of the grapes. But they beat up the servant and sent him away without anything. ¹¹So the owner sent another servant. The renters also beat him up. They insulted him terribly and sent him away without a thing. ¹²The owner sent a third servant. He was also beaten terribly and thrown out of the vineyard.

¹³The owner then said to himself, "What am I going to do? I know what. I'll send my son, the one I love so much. They will surely respect him!"

¹⁴When the renters saw the owner's son, they said to one another, "Someday he will own the vineyard. Let's kill him! Then we can have it all for ourselves." ¹⁵So they threw him out of the vineyard and killed him.

Jesus asked, "What do you think the owner of the vineyard will do? ¹⁶I'll tell you what. He will come and kill those renters and let someone else have his vineyard."

When the people heard this, they said, "This must never happen!"

¹⁷But Jesus looked straight at them and said, "Then what do the Scriptures mean when they say, 'The stone the builders tossed aside is now the most important stone of all'? ¹⁸Anyone who stumbles over this stone will get hurt, and anyone it falls on will be smashed to pieces."

¹⁹The chief priests and the teachers of the Law of Moses knew that Jesus was talking about them when he was telling this story. They wanted to arrest him right then, but they were afraid of the people.

Paying Taxes
(Matthew 22.15-22; Mark 12.13-17)

²⁰Jesus' enemies kept watching him closely, because they wanted to hand him over to the Roman governor. So they sent some men who pretended to be good. But they were really spies trying to catch Jesus saying something wrong. ²¹The spies said to him, "Teacher, we know you teach the truth about what God wants people to do. And you treat everyone with the same respect, no matter who they are. ²²Tell us, should we pay taxes to the Emperor or not?"

²³Jesus knew they were trying to trick him. So he told them, ²⁴"Show me a coin." Then he asked, "Whose picture and name are on it?"

"The Emperor's," they answered.

²⁵Then he told them, "Give the Emperor what belongs to him and give God what belongs to God." ²⁶Jesus' enemies could not catch him saying anything wrong there in front of the people. They were amazed at his answer and kept quiet.

Life in the Future World
(Matthew 22.23-33; Mark 12.18-27)

²⁷The Sadducees did not believe that people would rise to life after death. So some of them came to Jesus ²⁸and said:

Teacher, Moses wrote that if a married man dies and has no children, his brother should marry the widow. Their

20.9 *vineyard:* A vineyard was a very valuable possession. Many vineyards had walls around them and a watchtower where someone could keep an eye out for robbers or stray animals that might eat or damage the vines.

20.18 *this stone:* Jesus was describing himself as this important stone.

20.22 *pay taxes to the Emperor:* In Jesus' time, Judea was part of the Roman Empire, so the people in Judea had to pay taxes to the Roman government. The highest Roman leader was called the Emperor, who ruled the empire from Rome.

20.24 *coin:* This coin was probably a denarius, which was roughly the amount paid to a laborer for a day's work. In the time of Jesus, a denarius had a picture of Emperor Tiberius on one side. On the other side were the words: "Tiberius Caesar Augustus, son of the divine Augustus."

20.27 *Sadducees:* The Sadducees were a wealthy group of Jews who worked closely with the priests in the temple. They taught that the most important thing in life was going to the temple and offering sacrifices there. The Sadducees did not believe that God brought people back to life from death, because it was not directly taught in the Law of Moses. **(See the article The World of Jesus: Peoples, Powers, and Politics on pg 1801.)**

"Give the Emperor what belongs to him and give God what belongs to God." Luke 20.25

■ **20.36** *will be like the angels and . . . God's children:* Jesus taught that people will be raised to life and will live forever as angels do. Those who are worthy to be God's children won't have to worry about something like who they are married to.

● **21.1** *offering box:* These funnel-shaped boxes were located in the court of women in the temple area.

● **21.2** *few cents:* The Greek has *lepton,* which was the smallest Greek coin. It was worth only half of the smallest Roman coin.

first son would then be thought of as the son of the dead brother.

²⁹There were once seven brothers. The first one married, but died without having any children. ³⁰The second one married his brother's widow, and he also died without having any children. ³¹The same thing happened to the third one. Finally, all seven brothers married this woman and died without having any children. ³²At last the woman died. ³³When God raises people from death, whose wife will this woman be? All seven brothers had married her.

³⁴Jesus answered:

The people in this world get married. ³⁵But in the future world no one who is worthy to rise from death will either marry ³⁶or die. They will be like the angels and will be God's children, because they have been raised to life.

³⁷In the story about the burning bush, Moses clearly shows that people will live again. He said, "The Lord is the God worshiped by Abraham, Isaac, and Jacob."ˢ ³⁸So the Lord isn't the God of the dead, but of the living. This means that everyone is alive as far as God is concerned.

³⁹Some of the teachers of the Law of Moses said, "Teacher, you have given a good answer!" ⁴⁰From then on, no one dared to ask Jesus any questions.

About David's Son

(Matthew 22.41-46; Mark 12.35-37)

⁴¹Jesus asked, "Why do people say that the Messiah will be the son of King David?ᵗ ⁴²In the book of Psalms, David himself says,

'The Lord said to my Lord,
    Sit at my right sideᵘ
⁴³until I make your enemies
    into a footstool for you.'
⁴⁴David spoke of the Messiah as his Lord, so how can the Messiah be his son?"

Jesus and the Teachers of the Law of Moses

(Matthew 23.1-36; Mark 12.38-40; Luke 11.37-54)

⁴⁵While everyone was listening to Jesus, he said to his disciples:

⁴⁶Guard against the teachers of the Law of Moses! They love to walk around in long robes, and they like to be greeted in the market. They want the front seats in the synagogues and the best seats at banquets. ⁴⁷But they cheat widows out of their homes and then pray long prayers just to show off. These teachers will be punished most of all.

A Widow's Offering

(Mark 12.41-44)

21 Jesus looked up and saw some rich people tossing their gifts into the offering box. ²He also saw a poor widow putting in a few cents. ³And he said, "I tell you that this poor woman has put in more than all the others. ⁴Everyone else gave what they didn't need. But she is very poor and gave everything she had."

The Temple Will Be Destroyed

(Matthew 24.1,2; Mark 13.1,2)

⁵Some people were talking about the beautiful stones used to build the temple

ˢ**20.37** *The Lord is the God worshiped by Abraham, Isaac, and Jacob:* Jesus argues that if God is worshiped by these three, they must be alive, because he is the God of the living.   ᵗ**20.41** *the son of King David:* See the note at 18.38.   ᵘ**20.42** *right side:* The place of power and honor.

and about the gifts that had been placed in it. Jesus said, 6"Do you see these stones? The time is coming when not one of them will be left in place. They will all be knocked down."

Warning about Trouble
(Matthew 24.3-14; Mark 13.3-13)

7Some people asked, "Teacher, when will all this happen? How can we know when these things are about to take place?" 8Jesus replied:

Don't be fooled by those who will come and claim to be me. They will say, "I am Christ!" and "Now is the time!" But don't follow them. 9When you hear about wars and riots, don't be afraid. These things will have to happen first, but this isn't the end.

10Nations will go to war against one another, and kingdoms will attack each other. 11There will be great earthquakes, and in many places people will starve to death and suffer terrible diseases. All sorts of frightening things will be seen in the sky.

12Before all this happens, you will be arrested and punished. You will be tried in your synagogues and put in jail. Because of me you will be placed on trial before kings and governors. 13But this will be your chance to tell about your faith. 14Don't worry about what you will say to defend yourselves. 15I will give you the wisdom to know what to say. None of your enemies will be able to oppose you or to say that you are wrong. 16You will be betrayed by your own parents, brothers, family, and friends. Some of you will even be killed. 17Because of me, you will be hated by everyone. 18But don't worry!V 19You will be saved by being faithful to me.

Jerusalem Will Be Destroyed
(Matthew 24.15-21; Mark 13.14-19)

20When you see Jerusalem surrounded by soldiers, you will know that it will soon be destroyed. 21If you are living in Judea at this time, run to the mountains. If you are in the city, leave it. And if you are out in the country, don't go back into the city. 22This time of punishment is what is written about in the Scriptures. 23It will be an awful time for women who are expecting babies or nursing young children! Everywhere in the land people will suffer horribly and be punished. 24Some of them will be killed by swords. Others will be carried off to foreign countries. Jerusalem will be overrun by foreign nations until their time comes to an end.

When the Son of Man Appears
(Matthew 24.29-31; Mark 13.24-27)

25Strange things will happen to the sun, moon, and stars. The nations on earth will be afraid of the roaring sea and tides, and they won't know what to do. 26People will be so frightened that they will faint because of what is happening to the world. Every power in the sky will be shaken.W 27Then the Son of Man will be seen, coming in a cloud with power and great glory.

■ 21.8 *Christ:* This comes from the Greek word *christos*, which means "anointed one."

● 21.12 *your synagogues:* What Jesus said later came true. Acts tells how some of Jesus' disciples were put on trial in the Jewish synagogues and at the temple (see Acts 4.1-22; 5.17-42; 6.8—8.2; 17.1-9; 21.27—26.32).

⌗ Temple Offerings

● 21.26 *Every power in the sky will be shaken:* In ancient times, some thought that the stars were spiritual powers. Others compared the stars to nations on earth. So this verse may mean that God would shake earthly powers (nations) or the spiritual powers that opposed God.

V21.18 *But don't worry:* The Greek text has "Not a hair of your head will be lost," which means, "There's no need to worry." W21.26 *Every power in the sky will be shaken:* In ancient times people thought that the stars were spiritual powers.

[28]When all of this starts happening, stand up straight and be brave. You will soon be set free.

A Lesson from a Fig Tree
(Matthew 24.32-35; Mark 13.28-31)

[29]Then Jesus told them a story:

When you see a fig tree or any other tree [30]putting out leaves, you know that summer will soon come. [31]So, when you see these things happening, you know that God's kingdom will soon be here. [32]You can be sure that some of the people of this generation will still be alive when all of this takes place. [33]The sky and the earth won't last forever, but my words will.

A Warning

[34]Don't spend all of your time thinking about eating or drinking or worrying about life. If you do, the final day will suddenly catch you [35]like a trap. This day will surprise everyone on earth. [36]Watch out and keep praying that you can escape all that is going to happen and that the Son of Man will be pleased with you.

[37]Jesus taught in the temple each day, and he spent each night on the Mount of Olives. [38]Everyone got up early and came to the temple to hear him teach.

A Plot To Kill Jesus
(Matthew 26.1-5,14,16; Mark 14.1,2,10,11; John 11.45-53)

22 The Festival of Thin Bread, also called Passover, was near. [2]The chief priests and the teachers of the Law of Moses were looking for a way to get rid of Jesus, because they were afraid of what the people might do. [3]Then Satan entered the heart of Judas Iscariot,[x] who was one of the twelve apostles.

[4]Judas went to talk with the chief priests and the officers of the temple police about how he could help them arrest Jesus. [5]They were very pleased and offered to pay Judas some money. [6]He agreed and started looking for a good chance to betray Jesus when the crowds were not around.

Jesus Eats with His Disciples
(Matthew 26.17-25; Mark 14.12-21; John 13.21-30)

[7]The day had come for the Festival of Thin Bread, and it was time to kill the Passover lambs. [8]So Jesus said to Peter and John, "Go and prepare the Passover meal for us to eat."

[9]But they asked, "Where do you want us to prepare it?"

[10]Jesus told them, "As you go into the city, you will meet a man carrying a jar of water.[y] Follow him into the house [11]and say to the owner, 'Our teacher wants to know where he can eat the Passover meal with his disciples.' [12]The owner will take you upstairs and show you a large room ready for you to use. Prepare the meal there."

[13]Peter and John left. They found everything just as Jesus had told them, and they prepared the Passover meal.

The Lord's Supper
(Matthew 26.26-30; Mark 14.22-26; 1 Corinthians 11.23-25)

[14]When the time came for Jesus and the apostles to eat, [15]he said to them, "I have very much wanted to eat this Passover

meal with you before I suffer. [16]I tell you I will not eat another Passover meal until it is finally eaten in God's kingdom."

[17]Jesus took a cup of wine in his hands and gave thanks to God. Then he told the apostles, "Take this wine and share it with each other. [18]I tell you that I will not drink any more wine until God's kingdom comes."

[19]Jesus took some bread in his hands and gave thanks for it. He broke the bread and handed it to his apostles. Then he said, "This is my body, which is given for you. Eat this as a way of remembering me!"

[20]After the meal he took another cup of wine in his hands. Then he said, "This is my blood. It is poured out for you, and with it God makes his new agreement. [21]The one who will betray me is here at the table with me! [22]The Son of Man will die in the way that has been decided for him, but it will be terrible for the one who betrays him!"

[23]Then the apostles started arguing about who would ever do such a thing.

An Argument about Greatness

[24]The apostles got into an argument about which one of them was the greatest. [25]So Jesus told them:

Foreign kings order their people around, and powerful rulers call themselves everyone's friends.[z] [26]But don't be like them. The most important one of you should be like the least important, and your leader should be like a servant. [27]Who do people think is the greatest, a person who is served or one who serves? Isn't it the one who is served? But I have been with you as a servant.

[28]You have stayed with me in all my troubles. [29]So I will give you the right to rule as kings, just as my Father has given me the right to rule as a king. [30]You will eat and drink with me in my kingdom, and you will each sit on a throne to judge the twelve tribes of Israel.

Jesus' Disciples Will Be Tested
(Matthew 26.31-35; Mark 14.27-31; John 13.36-38)

[31]Jesus said, "Simon, listen to me! Satan has demanded the right to test each one of you, as a farmer does when he separates wheat from the husks.[a] [32]But Simon, I have prayed that your faith will be strong. And when you have come back to me, help the others."

[33]Peter said, "Lord, I am ready to go with you to jail and even to die with you."

[34]Jesus replied, "Peter, I tell you that before a rooster crows tomorrow morning, you will say three times that you don't know me."

Moneybags, Traveling Bags, and Swords

[35]Jesus asked his disciples, "When I sent you out without a moneybag or a traveling bag or sandals, did you need anything?"

"No!" they answered.

[36]Jesus told them, "But now, if you have a moneybag, take it with you. Also take a traveling bag, and if you don't have a sword,[b] sell some of your clothes and buy one. [37]Do this because the Scriptures say, 'He was considered a criminal.' This was written about me, and it will soon come true."

[z]22.25 everyone's friends: This translates a Greek word that rulers sometimes used as a title for themselves or for special friends. [a]22.31 separates wheat from the husks: See the note at 3.17.
[b]22.36 moneybag . . . traveling bag . . . sword: These were things that someone would take on a dangerous journey. Jesus was telling his disciples to be ready for anything that might happen. They seem to have understood what he meant (see 22.49-51).

22.19 *bread:* This probably would have been the thin bread that was made for the Passover meal and the Festival of Thin Bread.

22.20 *God makes his new agreement:* God made an agreement with Moses when God gave Moses the Law for the Israelites. Jesus is announcing that God is about to create a new agreement that will apply to all people.

God's Saving Love (Salvation)

Agreements (Covenants)

22.30 *twelve tribes of Israel:* Originally the twelve tribes of Israel referred to the Hebrew descendants of Jacob's twelve sons (see Gen 32.20-32; 35.23-26). Because the priestly line of Levi did not hold land (Num 1.47-53), it was no longer considered one of the twelve tribes. Joseph's descendants formed two separate tribes (Ephraim and Manasseh). **(See the article From Joshua to the Exile: The People of Israel in the Promised Land on pg 1783.)**

22.42 *drinking from this cup*: Here to "drink from this cup" means to suffer. Jesus knew that God had planned that he would have to suffer and die to fulfill God's purposes (see 9.22; 18.31-33; 22.20-22).

22.54 *house of the high priest*: The council of Jewish leaders who questioned Jesus may have met at the house of Caiaphas. **(See the article People of the Law: The Religion of Israel on pg 1794.)**

22.59 *Galilee*: Peter came from Galilee and spoke with an accent that was different from the accent of people in Jerusalem. That is how these people could tell Peter was from Galilee.

38The disciples said, "Lord, here are two swords!"

"Enough of that!" Jesus replied.

Jesus Prays

(Matthew 26.36-46; Mark 14.32-42)

39Jesus went out to the Mount of Olives, as he often did, and his disciples went with him. **40**When they got there, he told them, "Pray that you won't be tested."

41Jesus walked on a little way before he knelt down and prayed, **42**"Father, if you will, please don't make me suffer by drinking from this cup.[c] But do what you want, and not what I want."

43Then an angel from heaven came to help him. **44**Jesus was in great pain and prayed so sincerely that his sweat fell to the ground like drops of blood.[d]

45Jesus got up from praying and went over to his disciples. They were asleep and worn out from being so sad. **46**He said to them, "Why are you asleep? Wake up and pray that you won't be tested."

Jesus Is Arrested

(Matthew 26.47-56; Mark 14.43-50; John 18.3-11)

47While Jesus was still speaking, a crowd came up. It was led by Judas, one of the twelve apostles. He went over to Jesus and greeted him with a kiss.[e]

48Jesus asked Judas, "Are you betraying the Son of Man with a kiss?"

49When Jesus' disciples saw what was about to happen, they asked, "Lord, should we attack them with a sword?" **50**One of the disciples even struck at the high priest's servant with his sword and cut off the servant's right ear.

51"Enough of that!" Jesus said. Then he touched the servant's ear and healed it.

52Jesus spoke to the chief priests, the temple police, and the leaders who had come to arrest him. He said, "Why do you come out with swords and clubs and treat me like a criminal? **53**I was with you every day in the temple, and you didn't arrest me. But this is your time, and darkness[f] is in control."

Peter Says
He Doesn't Know Jesus

(Matthew 26.57,58,67-75; Mark 14.53,54,66-72;
John 18.12-18, 25-27)

54Jesus was arrested and led away to the house of the high priest, while Peter followed at a distance. **55**Some people built a fire in the middle of the courtyard and were sitting around it. Peter sat there with them, **56**and a servant girl saw him. Then after she had looked at him carefully, she said, "This man was with Jesus!"

57Peter said, "Woman, I don't even know that man!"

58A little later someone else saw Peter and said, "You are one of them!"

"No, I'm not!" Peter replied.

59About an hour later another man insisted, "This man must have been with Jesus. They both come from Galilee."

60Peter replied, "I don't know what you are talking about!" Right then, while Peter was still speaking, a rooster crowed.

61The Lord turned and looked at Peter. And Peter remembered that the Lord had said, "Before a rooster crows tomorrow morning, you will say three times that you don't know me." **62**Then Peter went out and cried bitterly.

[c]**22.42** *drinking from this cup*: In the Scriptures "to drink from a cup" sometimes means to suffer.
[d]**22.43,44** *Then an angel . . . like drops of blood*: Verses 43,44 are not in some manuscripts.
[e]**22.47** *greeted him with a kiss*: It was the custom for people to greet each other with a kiss on the cheek.   [f]**22.53** *darkness*: Darkness stands for the power of the devil.

63The men who were guarding Jesus made fun of him and beat him. **64**They put a blindfold on him and said, "Tell us who struck you!" **65**They kept on insulting Jesus in many other ways.

Jesus Is Questioned by the Council
(Matthew 26.59-66; Mark 14.55-64; John 18.19-24)

66At daybreak the nation's leaders, the chief priests, and the teachers of the Law of Moses got together and brought Jesus before their council. **67**They said, "Tell us! Are you the Messiah?"

Jesus replied, "If I said so, you wouldn't believe me. **68**And if I asked you a question, you wouldn't answer. **69**But from now on, the Son of Man will be seated at the right side of God All-Powerful."

70Then they asked, "Are you the Son of God?"**g**

Jesus answered, "You say I am!"**h**

71They replied, "Why do we need more witnesses? He said it himself!"

Pilate Questions Jesus
(Matthew 27.1,2,11-14; Mark 15.1-5; John 18.28-38)

23 Everyone in the council got up and led Jesus off to Pilate. **2**They started accusing him and said, "We caught this man trying to get our people to riot and to stop paying taxes to the Emperor. He also claims that he is the Messiah, our king."

3Pilate asked Jesus, "Are you the king of the Jews?"

"Those are your words," Jesus answered.

4Pilate told the chief priests and the crowd, "I don't find him guilty of anything."

5But they all kept on saying, "He has been teaching and causing trouble all over Judea. He started in Galilee and has now come all the way here."

Jesus Is Brought before Herod

6When Pilate heard this, he asked, "Is this man from Galilee?" **7**After Pilate learned that Jesus came from the region ruled by Herod,**i** he sent him to Herod, who was in Jerusalem at that time.

8For a long time Herod had wanted to see Jesus and was very happy because he finally had this chance. He had heard many things about Jesus and hoped to see him work a miracle.

9Herod asked him a lot of questions, but Jesus did not answer. **10**Then the chief priests and the teachers of the Law of Moses stood up and accused him of all kinds of bad things.

11Herod and his soldiers made fun of Jesus and insulted him. They put a fine robe on him and sent him back to Pilate. **12**That same day Herod and Pilate became friends, even though they had been enemies before this.

The Death Sentence
(Matthew 27.15-26; Mark 15.6-15; John 18.39—19.16)

13Pilate called together the chief priests, the leaders, and the people. **14**He told them, "You brought Jesus to me and said he was a troublemaker. But I have questioned him here in front of you, and I have not found him guilty of anything that you say he has done. **15**Herod didn't find him guilty either and sent him back. This man doesn't deserve to be put to death! **16-17**I will just have him beaten with a whip and set free."**j**

---

g22.70 *Son of God:* This was one of the titles used for the kings of Israel.   **h22.70** *You say I am:* Or "That's what you say."   **i23.7** *Herod:* Herod Antipas, the son of Herod the Great.   **j23.16,17** *set free:* Some manuscripts add, "Pilate said this, because at every Passover he was supposed to set one prisoner free for the Jewish people."

23.18 *Barabbas:* His name means "son of Abba." He was a violent criminal who apparently caused riots and murdered people (see Matt 27.15-20; Mark 15.6-11).

23.20 *Nail him to a cross:* The people wanted Jesus to die by means of the Roman method of execution called crucifixion. Jesus was put to death for political reasons, not because he had broken the Law of Moses.

⚫ Crucifixion

23.26 *a man named Simon from Cyrene:* Cyrene was a city in North Africa. Simon was probably in Jerusalem to celebrate the Passover and Festival of Thin Bread.

23.33 *"The Skull":* This place was Golgotha, which may have gotten its name because it was near a large rock shaped like a human skull or from the fact that the Romans performed executions there. **(See Map 13 on pg 1891.)**

23.36 *wine:* This may have been wine mixed with a bitter and poisonous herb called gall (Matt 27.34), or with bile. Such a mixture could have made Jesus die faster and possibly with less pain.

23.38 *Above him was a sign:* Usually Roman soldiers would put a sign above the head of the person to tell what the person was accused of doing. Since Jesus was not really found guilty of any crime, they put up the words, "This is the King of the Jews."

[18]But the whole crowd shouted, "Kill Jesus! Give us Barabbas!" [19]Now Barabbas was in jail because he had started a riot in the city and had murdered someone.

[20]Pilate wanted to set Jesus free, so he spoke again to the crowds. [21]But they kept shouting, "Nail him to a cross! Nail him to a cross!"

[22]Pilate spoke to them a third time, "But what crime has he done? I have not found him guilty of anything for which he should be put to death. I will have him beaten with a whip and set free."

[23]The people kept on shouting as loud as they could for Jesus to be put to death. [24]Finally, Pilate gave in. [25]He freed the man who was in jail for rioting and murder, because he was the one the crowd wanted to be set free. Then Pilate handed Jesus over for them to do what they wanted with him.

Jesus Is Nailed to a Cross
(Matthew 27.31-44; Mark 15.21-32; John 19.17-27)

[26]As Jesus was being led away, some soldiers grabbed hold of a man named Simon who was from Cyrene. He was coming in from the fields, but they put the cross on him and made him carry it behind Jesus.

[27]A large crowd was following Jesus, and in the crowd a lot of women were crying and weeping for him. [28]Jesus turned to the women and said:

Women of Jerusalem, don't cry for me! Cry for yourselves and for your children. [29]Someday people will say, "Women who never had children are really fortunate!" [30]At that time everyone will say to the mountains, "Fall on us!" They will say to the hills, "Hide us!" [31]If this can happen when the wood is green, what do you think will happen when it is dry?[k]

[32]Two criminals were led out to be put to death with Jesus. [33]When the soldiers came to the place called "The Skull,"[l] they nailed Jesus to a cross. They also nailed the two criminals to crosses, one on each side of Jesus.

[34-35]Jesus said, "Father, forgive these people! They don't know what they're doing."[m]

While the crowd stood there watching Jesus, the soldiers gambled for his clothes. The leaders insulted him by saying, "He saved others. Now he should save himself, if he really is God's chosen Messiah!"

[36]The soldiers made fun of Jesus and brought him some wine. [37]They said, "If you are the king of the Jews, save yourself!"

[38]Above him was a sign that said, "This is the King of the Jews."

[39]One of the criminals hanging there also insulted Jesus by saying, "Aren't you the Messiah? Save yourself and save us!"

[40]But the other criminal told the first one off, "Don't you fear God? Aren't you getting the same punishment as this man? [41]We got what was coming to us, but he didn't do anything wrong." [42]Then he said to Jesus, "Remember me when you come into power!"

[43]Jesus replied, "I promise that today you will be with me in paradise."[n]

[k]*23.31 If this can happen when the wood is green, what do you think will happen when it is dry:* This saying probably means, "If this can happen to an innocent person, what do you think will happen to one who is guilty?" [l]*23.33 "The Skull":* The place was probably given this name because it was near a large rock in the shape of a human skull. [m]*23.34,35 Jesus said, "Father, forgive these people! They don't know what they're doing":* These words are not in some manuscripts. [n]*23.43 paradise:* In the Greek translation of the Old Testament, this word is used for the Garden of Eden. In New Testament times it was sometimes used for the place where God's people are happy and at rest, as they wait for the final judgment.

The Death of Jesus

(Matthew 27.45-56; Mark 15.33-41; John 19.28-30)

44Around noon the sky turned dark and stayed that way until the middle of the afternoon. **45**The sun stopped shining, and the curtain in the temple[o] split down the middle. **46**Jesus shouted, "Father, I put myself in your hands!" Then he died.

47When the Roman officer saw what had happened, he praised God and said, "Jesus must really have been a good man!"

48A crowd had gathered to see the terrible sight. Then after they had seen it, they felt brokenhearted and went home. **49**All of Jesus' close friends and the women who had come with him from Galilee stood at a distance and watched.

Jesus Is Buried

(Matthew 27.57-61; Mark 15.42-47; John 19.38-42)

50-51 There was a man named Joseph, who was from Arimathea in Judea. Joseph was a good and honest man, and he was eager for God's kingdom to come. He was also a member of the council, but he did not agree with what they had decided. **52**Joseph went to Pilate and asked for Jesus' body. **53**He took the body down from the cross and wrapped it in fine cloth. Then he put it in a tomb that had been cut out of solid rock and had never been used. **54**It was Friday, and the Sabbath was about to begin.[p] **55**The women who had come with Jesus from Galilee followed Joseph and watched how Jesus' body was placed in the tomb. **56**Then they went to prepare some sweet-smelling spices for his burial. But on the Sabbath they rested, as the Law of Moses commands.

Jesus Is Alive

(Matthew 28.1-10; Mark 16.1-8; John 20.1-10)

24 Very early on Sunday morning the women went to the tomb, carrying the spices they had prepared. **2**When they found the stone rolled away from the entrance, **3**they went in. But they did not find the body of the Lord[q] Jesus, **4**and they did not know what to think.

Suddenly two men in shining white clothes stood beside them. **5**The women were afraid and bowed to the ground. But the men said, "Why are you looking in the place of the dead for someone who is alive? **6**Jesus isn't here! He has been raised from death. Remember that while he was still in Galilee, he told you, **7**'The Son of Man will be handed over to sinners who will nail him to a cross. But three days later he will rise to life.' " **8**Then they remembered what Jesus had said.

9-10 Mary Magdalene, Joanna, Mary the mother of James, and some other women were the ones who had gone to the tomb. When they returned, they told the eleven apostles and the others what had happened. **11**The apostles thought it was all nonsense, and they would not believe.

12But Peter ran to the tomb. And when he stooped down and looked in, he saw only the burial clothes. Then he returned, wondering what had happened.[r]

● **23.53** *put it in a tomb:* Some of the Jewish people buried their dead in rooms carved into soft limestone rock.

▣ Burial

● **23.56** *sweet-smelling spices:* These were probably spices called myrrh and aloes (see John 19.39). Many cultures in the Middle East used aloe for medicine and for embalming the dead.

● **23.56** *on the Sabbath they rested:* After preparing the spices, the women could not actually walk to the tomb and prepare the body because the Law of Moses would not allow them to do this kind of work on the Sabbath (see Exod 20.10; Deut 5.14). They waited until the next morning, which was Sunday.

● **24.9-10** *Mary the mother of James:* Mary the mother of James is also mentioned in Mark 16.1. Who she was, or which James was her son, is not clear. She may have been the mother of one of the two disciples named James.

● **24.9-10** *eleven apostles:* These are Jesus' handpicked followers (see 6.12-16). There are only eleven because Judas, who betrayed Jesus, is no longer with them. Matthew 27.3-5 reports that Judas committed suicide.

---

[o]**23.45** *curtain in the temple:* There were two curtains in the temple. One was at the entrance, and the other separated the holy place from the most holy place that the Jewish people thought of as God's home on earth. The second curtain is probably the one which is meant.   [p]**23.54** *the Sabbath was about to begin:* The Sabbath begins at sunset on Friday.   [q]**24.3** *the Lord:* These words are not in some manuscripts.   [r]**24.12** *what had happened:* Verse 12 is not in some manuscripts.

24.13 *two of Jesus' disciples:* These were followers of Jesus but not two of Jesus' twelve closest apostles.

24.13 *Emmaus:* Emmaus was a small village in Judea. Its exact location is not certain. Archaeologists think that Emmaus could be one of three different places. One of the most likely is Amwas, which is about 20 miles from Jerusalem.

24.18 *Cleopas:* He was a follower of Jesus mentioned only here in LUKE, and nothing else is known about him.

24.32 *Scriptures:* These are the Jewish Scriptures, which Christians call the Old Testament.

24.39 *my hands and my feet:* Sometimes large nails were driven through the wrists and feet of a person who was being put to death on a cross. Jesus wanted them to see his wounds so that they would realize who he was.

Jesus Appears to Two Disciples
(Mark 16.12,13)

[13] That same day two of Jesus' disciples were going to the village of Emmaus, which was about seven miles from Jerusalem. [14] As they were talking and thinking about what had happened, [15] Jesus came near and started walking along beside them. [16] But they did not know who he was.

[17] Jesus asked them, "What were you talking about as you walked along?"

The two of them stood there looking sad and gloomy. [18] Then the one named Cleopas asked Jesus, "Are you the only person from Jerusalem who didn't know what was happening there these last few days?"

[19] "What do you mean?" Jesus asked.

They answered:

Those things that happened to Jesus from Nazareth. By what he did and said he showed that he was a powerful prophet, who pleased God and all the people. [20] Then the chief priests and our leaders had him arrested and sentenced to die on a cross. [21] We had hoped that he would be the one to set Israel free! But it has already been three days since all this happened. [22] Some women in our group surprised us. They had gone to the tomb early in the morning, [23] but did not find the body of Jesus. They came back, saying they had seen a vision of angels who told them that he is alive. [24] Some men from our group went to the tomb and found it just as the women had said. But they didn't see Jesus either.

[25] Then Jesus asked the two disciples, "Why can't you understand? How can you be so slow to believe all that the prophets said? [26] Didn't you know that the Messiah would have to suffer before he was given his glory?" [27] Jesus then explained everything written about himself in the Scriptures, beginning with the Law of Moses and the Books of the Prophets.[s]

[28] When the two of them came near the village where they were going, Jesus seemed to be going farther. [29] They begged him, "Stay with us! It's already late, and the sun is going down." So Jesus went into the house to stay with them.

[30] After Jesus sat down to eat, he took some bread. He blessed it and broke it. Then he gave it to them. [31] At once they knew who he was, but he disappeared. [32] They said to each other, "When he talked with us along the road and explained the Scriptures to us, didn't it warm our hearts?" [33] So they got up and returned to Jerusalem.

The two disciples found the eleven apostles and the others gathered together. [34] And they learned from the group that the Lord was really alive and had appeared to Peter. [35] Then the disciples from Emmaus told what happened on the road and how they knew he was the Lord when he broke the bread.

What Jesus' Followers Must Do
(Matthew 28.16-20; Mark 16.14-18; John 20.19-23; Acts 1.6-8)

[36] While Jesus' disciples were talking about what had happened, Jesus appeared and greeted them. [37] They were frightened and terrified because they thought they were seeing a ghost.

[38] But Jesus said, "Why are you so frightened? Why do you doubt? [39] Look at my hands and my feet and see who I am! Touch me and find out for yourselves. Ghosts don't have flesh and bones as you see I have."

[s]24.27 *the Law of Moses and the Books of the Prophets:* See the note at 16.16.

Jesus said to his disciples, "*Look at my hands and my feet and see who I am!*" LUKE 24.39

40After Jesus said this, he showed them his hands and his feet. 41The disciples were so glad and amazed that they could not believe it. Jesus then asked them, "Do you have something to eat?" 42They gave him a piece of broiled fish. 43He took it and ate it as they watched.

44Jesus said to them, "While I was still with you, I told you that everything written about me in the Law of Moses, the Books of the Prophets, and in the Psalms[t] had to happen."

45Then he helped them understand the Scriptures. 46He told them:

The Scriptures say that the Messiah must suffer, then three days later he will rise from death. 47They also say that all people of every nation must be told in my name to turn to God, in order to be forgiven. So beginning in Jerusalem, 48you must tell everything that has happened. 49I will send you the one my Father has promised,[u] but you must stay in the city until you are given power from heaven.

Jesus Returns to Heaven
(Mark 16.19,20; Acts 1.9-11)

50Jesus led his disciples out to Bethany, where he raised his hands and blessed them. 51As he was doing this, he left and was taken up to heaven.[v] 52After his disciples had worshiped him,[w] they returned to Jerusalem and were very happy. 53They spent their time in the temple, praising God.

24.43 *ate it as they watched*: This was another way Jesus showed that he was not a ghost.

24.44 *Law of Moses . . . Psalms*: The Jewish Scriptures are made up of three parts: 1) the Law of Moses, 2) the Books of the Prophets, 3) and the Writings, which includes Psalms. (See the article Different Kinds of Literature in the Bible on pg 1770.)

24.49 *the one my Father has promised*: Jesus is talking about the Holy Spirit. Acts 2 tells how this promise came true on the day of Pentecost.

24.53 *temple*: The temple in Jerusalem.

[t]24.44 *Psalms*: The Jewish Scriptures were made up of three parts: (1) the Law of Moses, (2) the Books of the Prophets, (3) and the Writings, which included the Psalms. Sometimes the Scriptures were just called the Law or the Law (of Moses) and the Books of the Prophets. [u]24.49 *the one my Father has promised*: Jesus means the Holy Spirit. [v]24.51 *and was taken up to heaven*: These words are not in some manuscripts. [w]24.52 *After his disciples had worshiped him*: These words are not in some manuscripts.

Reflection Questions About Luke 1.1—24.53

1. Describe how each of the following reacted to the birth of Jesus: (a) the shepherds, (b) Simeon, (c) Anna (2.1-38). What is the promise that Simeon sings about? What would you say is special about Jesus' birth?

2. In what ways does the devil test Jesus (4.1-13)? How does Jesus challenge this testing? Has anyone ever tried to persuade you to do something that you knew was wrong? How did you handle it? Where do you turn for help in facing temptations or times of testing?

3. What can we learn from Jesus' teachings about loving our enemies and about judging others (6.27-36; 6.37-42)? When are these teachings hard to follow?

4. How is love expressed in the story about the good Samaritan (10.25-37)? How do you respond to Jesus' question, "Who is my neighbor?"

5. Describe what Jesus says about being his disciple (14.25-31). What do you think this means for the way you live your life?

6. Compare the story of the rich and important man (18.18-30) with the story of Zacchaeus (19.1-10). What strikes you about each man and his meeting with Jesus?

7. Why did Jesus cry when he approached Jerusalem (19.41-44)? Compare this passage with 21.1-4,20-24. What does Jesus say is going to happen?

8. How did Jesus settle the argument among the disciples who were discussing which one of them was the greatest (22.24-30)? Think of situations today where people want to be "Number 1." What can be learned from Jesus' teachings about power and service (see also 9.46-48)?

9. How did the disciples react to what they were told by the women who had gone to the tomb (24.1-12)? Why do you think they acted that way? Do you find the women's story hard to believe or not?

10. Why didn't the two disciples who met Jesus on the road to Emmaus recognize him right away? At what point do they recognize him? Why (24.13-35)? What does Jesus tell his followers to do? What does he promise will happen (24.45-48)?

john

Signs point us in the right direction. As you read John, *watch for the signs (miracles) that point out how Jesus is God's powerful Son.*

WHAT MAKES JOHN SPECIAL?

John tells about the life and words of Jesus in a way that is different from the other Gospels. The key events in Jesus' life are mentioned, but John pays a lot of attention to three questions:

Who is Jesus? In John, Jesus is described in many different ways. For example, the author calls Jesus the "Word," which was present with God when God created and gave life to everything. John the Baptist calls Jesus the "Lamb of God who takes away the sin of the world" (1.29). Jesus describes himself as: the Messiah (4.25,26); the bread that gives life (6.35); and the good shepherd (10.14), among others.

What did Jesus do that proves that he is God's Son? John describes many miracles that point to the deeper meaning of Jesus' actions and words. When Jesus changes water into wine, calms the storm on the lake, feeds the hungry crowd, heals the sick, and brings the dead to life, he shows that he is God's Son and that he is doing what God sent him to do: bring new life to all people.

What was the relationship between the followers of Jesus and those who were against him? This Gospel helps us better understand the struggle between those who followed Jesus' new teachings and those who felt they could not do that and still remain loyal to the teachings of the Law of Moses.

WHAT'S THE STORY BEHIND THE SCENE?

The Gospel seems to have been written down a number of years after Jesus died and was raised from death, probably after the Romans destroyed the temple and ended a Jewish uprising in A.D. 70. After this time, Jewish people who accepted the teachings of Jesus began to be banned from the Jewish synagogues to keep them from spreading the message about Jesus there.

HOW IS JOHN CONSTRUCTED?

The basic outline of John can be described in the following way:

Who Jesus is (1.1-51)
Jesus' seven miracles (2.1—11.44)
    Miracle one—Jesus at a wedding in Cana (2.1-12)
    Jesus in Judea and Samaria (2.13—4.42)
    Miracle two—Jesus heals an official's son (4.43-54)
    Miracle three—Jesus heals a sick man (5.1-47)
    Miracle four—Jesus feeds 5,000 (6.1-15)
    Miracle five—Jesus walks on the water (6.16-21)
    Jesus teaches in Galilee and Judea (6.22—8.59)
    Miracle six—Jesus heals a man born blind (9.1-41)
    The good shepherd and the true flock (10.1-42)
    Miracle seven—Jesus brings Lazarus to life (11.1-44)
Jesus' final days (11.45—19.42)
    Preparations for Jesus' death (11.45—12.50)
    Jesus prepares his followers (13.1—17.26)
    Jesus' arrest, trial, and death on a cross (18.1—19.42)
Jesus appears to his followers (20.1—21.25)

ohn, the fourth Gospel, focuses on Jesus' role as the Messiah and as the eternal Word of God who was present with God at the beginning of creation. This makes John quite different from the previous three Gospels—Matthew, Mark, and Luke—which focus on providing historical accounts to show that Jesus was the fulfillment of God's promise to Israel. For this reason, many scholars believe John was written to answer those who doubted Jesus was the Messiah. John describes seven miracles ("signs") of Jesus and uses these miracles to show the profound teachings of Jesus and to point to him as the Son of God. By using metaphors to describe Jesus—such as water, light, a gate, and bread—John tries to lead readers into the kingdom of God that Jesus has prepared for them.

Outline

The Word of Life

1 In the beginning was the one
who is called the Word.
The Word was with God
and was truly God.
2From the very beginning
the Word was with God.

3And with this Word,
God created all things.
Nothing was made
without the Word.
Everything that was created
4 received its life from him,
and his life gave light
to everyone.
5The light keeps shining
in the dark,
and darkness has never
put it out.ª
6God sent a man named John,
7who came to tell

about the light
and to lead all people
to have faith.
8John wasn't this light.
He came only to tell
about the light.

9The true light that shines
on everyone
was coming into the world.
10The Word was in the world,
but no one knew him,
though God had made the world
with his Word.
11He came into his own world,
but his own nation
did not welcome him.
12Yet some people accepted him
and put their faith in him.
So he gave them the right
to be the children of God.
13They were not God's children
by nature or because

ª**1.5** *put it out:* Or "understood it."

■ 1.1-3 *In the beginning . . . the Word:* This same phrase is used at the very beginning of Genesis 1, which describes how God created all things. The Greek word translated here as "Word" also means "reason" or "purpose." In the Jewish Scriptures (Old Testament), God used Wisdom to create the world (Prov 8.22,23). The Word also shows God's power, a power that was able to create simply by speaking (see "God said" in Gen 1). In John 1.1-3, "the Word" refers to Jesus Christ, who brings God's message to all people and reveals God's power and purpose. These verses show that even though Jesus is God's Son born as a human being, he is also truly God, because he has existed with God from the beginning of time.

■ 1.4,5 *light . . . darkness:* Light and darkness are important images in JOHN. John uses the opposites "light" and "darkness" to refer to the struggle between those who accept Jesus and those who refuse to believe.

ରୀ John the Baptist

● 1.11 *his own nation:* Jesus was Jewish. He came to his own people as God's chosen one (Messiah), but many people from his own country did not believe in him or accept his message.

■ 1.12 *children of God:* This phrase is used to describe those who trust Jesus as God's true light.

*In the beginning was the one who is called the Word.
The Word was with God and was truly God.* JOHN 1.1

1.14 *The Word became a human being:* Jesus lived as a human being in order to show God's glory. Sometimes this is referred to as the "incarnation."

1.17 *The Law was given by Moses:* Jesus did not intend to throw out the Law of Moses but he wanted to show how people could fill their lives with "kindness and truth."

Law

Israel's Priests

Messiah (Chosen One)

Elijah

1.24 *Pharisees:* These religious Jews believed in following God's law as closely as possible. **(See the article The World of Jesus: Peoples, Powers, and Politics on pg 1801.)**

1.33 *baptize with the Holy Spirit:* Just as God poured the Spirit on Jesus (1.32), Jesus will pour out the Spirit on those who follow him.

Baptism

Holy Spirit

1.34 *Son of God:* John is claiming that Jesus is the one God has chosen to rule over Israel.

Son of God

of any human desires.
God himself was the one
    who made them his children.

¹⁴The Word became
    a human being
    and lived here with us.
We saw his true glory,
    the glory of the only Son
    of the Father.
From him the complete gifts
    of undeserved grace and truth
    have come down to us.

¹⁵John spoke about him and shouted, "This is the one I told you would come! He is greater than I am, because he was alive before I was born."

¹⁶Because of all that the Son is, we have been given one blessing after another.[b] ¹⁷The Law was given by Moses, but Jesus Christ brought us undeserved kindness and truth. ¹⁸No one has ever seen God. The only Son, who is truly God and is closest to the Father, has shown us what God is like.

John the Baptist Tells about Jesus

(Matthew 3.1-12; Mark 1.1-8; Luke 3.15-17)

¹⁹⁻²⁰The religious authorities in Jerusalem sent priests and temple helpers to ask John who he was. He told them plainly, "I am not the Messiah." ²¹Then when they asked him if he were Elijah, he said, "No, I am not!" And when they asked if he were the Prophet,[c] he also said "No!"

²²Finally, they said, "Who are you then? We have to give an answer to the ones who sent us. Tell us who you are!"

²³John answered in the words of the prophet Isaiah, "I am only someone shouting in the desert, 'Get the road ready for the Lord!'"

²⁴Some Pharisees had also been sent to John. ²⁵They asked him, "Why are you baptizing people, if you are not the Messiah or Elijah or the Prophet?"

²⁶John told them, "I use water to baptize people. But here with you is someone you don't know. ²⁷Even though I came first, I am not good enough to untie his sandals." ²⁸John said this as he was baptizing east of the Jordan River in Bethany.[d]

The Lamb of God

²⁹The next day, John saw Jesus coming toward him and said:

Here is the Lamb of God who takes away the sin of the world! ³⁰He is the one I told you about when I said, "Someone else will come, who is greater than I am, because he was alive before I was born." ³¹I didn't know who he was. But I came to baptize you with water, so that everyone in Israel would see him.

³²I was there and saw the Spirit come down on him like a dove from heaven. And the Spirit stayed on him. ³³Before this I didn't know who he was. But the one who sent me to baptize with water had told me, "You will see the Spirit come down and stay on someone. Then you will know that he is the one who will baptize with the Holy Spirit." ³⁴I saw this happen, and I tell you that he is the Son of God.

[b]**1.16** *one blessing after another:* Or "one blessing in place of another." [c]**1.21** *the Prophet:* Many of the Jewish people expected God to send them a prophet who would be like Moses, but with even greater power (see Deuteronomy 18.15,18). [d]**1.28** *Bethany:* An unknown village east of the Jordan with the same name as the village near Jerusalem.

The First Disciples of Jesus

35The next day, John was there again, and two of his followers were with him. **36**When he saw Jesus walking by, he said, "Here is the Lamb of God!" **37**John's two followers heard him, and they went with Jesus.

38When Jesus turned and saw them, he asked, "What do you want?"

They answered, "Rabbi, where do you live?" The Hebrew word "Rabbi" means "Teacher."

39Jesus replied, "Come and see!" It was already about four o'clock in the afternoon when they went with him and saw where he lived. So they stayed on for the rest of the day.

40One of the two men who had heard John and had gone with Jesus was Andrew, the brother of Simon Peter. **41**The first thing Andrew did was to find his brother and tell him, "We have found the Messiah!" The Hebrew word "Messiah" means the same as the Greek word "Christ."

42Andrew brought his brother to Jesus. And when Jesus saw him, he said, "Simon son of John, you will be called Cephas." This name can be translated as "Peter."**e**

Jesus Chooses Philip and Nathanael

43-44 The next day Jesus decided to go to Galilee. There he met Philip, who was from Bethsaida, the hometown of Andrew and Peter. Jesus said to Philip, "Follow me."

45Philip then found Nathanael and said,

"We have found the one that Moses and the Prophets**f** wrote about. He is Jesus, the son of Joseph from Nazareth."

46Nathanael asked, "Can anything good come from Nazareth?"

Philip answered, "Come and see."

47When Jesus saw Nathanael coming toward him, he said, "Here is a true descendant of our ancestor Israel. And he isn't deceitful."**g**

48"How do you know me?" Nathanael asked.

Jesus answered, "Before Philip called you, I saw you under the fig tree."

49Nathanael said, "Rabbi, you are the Son of God and the King of Israel!"

50Jesus answered, "Did you believe me just because I said that I saw you under the fig tree? You will see something even greater. **51**I tell you for certain you will see heaven open and God's angels going up and coming down on the Son of Man."**h**

Jesus at a Wedding in Cana

2 Three days later Mary, the mother of Jesus, was at a wedding feast in the village of Cana in Galilee. **2**Jesus and his disciples had also been invited and were there.

3When the wine was all gone, Mary said to Jesus, "They don't have any more wine."

4Jesus replied, "Mother, my time hasn't yet come!**i** You must not tell me what to do."

5Mary then said to the servants, "Do whatever Jesus tells you to do."

6At the feast there were six stone water

---

e1.42 *Peter:* The Aramaic name "Cephas" and the Greek name "Peter" each mean "rock." **f**1.45 *Moses and the Prophets:* The Jewish Scriptures, that is, the Old Testament. **g**1.47 *Israel . . . isn't deceitful:* Israel (meaning "a man who wrestled with God" or "a prince of God") was the name that the Lord gave to Jacob (meaning "cheater" or "deceiver"), the famous ancestor of the Jewish people. **h**1.51 *going up and coming down on the Son of Man:* When Jacob (see the note at verse 47) was running from his brother Esau, he had a dream in which he saw angels going up and down on a ladder from earth to heaven (see Genesis 28.10-22). **i**2.4 *my time hasn't yet come:* The time when the true glory of Jesus would be seen, and he would be recognized as God's Son (see 12.23).

1.36 *Lamb of God:* John the Baptist said that Jesus was like the lamb that would be silently led to be slaughtered (1.29; see also Isa 1.29; 53.4-12) in order to restore God's people. "The Lamb" also refers to the lamb that was killed by the priests at the Passover Feast (Exod 12), which was celebrated each year to remind the people how God had set Israel free from slavery in Egypt.

1.40 *Andrew:* Andrew was a fisherman who came from Bethsaida, but he lived in Capernaum (Mark 1.29) with his brother Simon Peter.

1.41 *Messiah . . . Christ:* Both *Messiah* (Hebrew) and *Christos* (Greek) mean "anointed one," or one chosen by God to lead God's people.

1.43-44 *Galilee . . . Bethsaida:* Galilee was the area west of the upper Jordan River and the Sea of Galilee. Bethsaida was a fishing village on the northeast shore of Lake Galilee. **(See Map 12 on pg 1890.)**

Israel

Son of Man

2.1 *Mary, the mother of Jesus:* Mary lived in Nazareth, which was about ten miles south of Cana in Galilee.

2.6 *jars...for washing themselves:* According to the Law of Moses, if people touched something unclean before they ate, any food they touched would also be made unclean.

Purity (Clean and Unclean)

2.12 *Capernaum:* See Map 12 on pg 1890.

2.14 *people selling...moneychangers:* In the Court of the Gentiles at the temple, priests made lots of money buying and selling animals for the sacrifices that were required by the Law of Moses.

Money Changing in the Temple

2.19 *in three days I will build it again:* Jesus was claiming that his body—not the actual temple—would be destroyed and that God would raise him from death in three days (2.21).

2.22 *Scriptures:* The Jewish Scriptures, which Christians call the Old Testament.

2.23 *Jerusalem:* The capital city of Judea in southern Palestine.

Jerusalem

3.3 *God's kingdom:* God's kingdom is not simply a place. It is what happens when God rules and God's people do what God wants them to do, like serving others and telling the good news about Jesus.

jars that were used by the people for washing themselves in the way that their religion said they must. Each jar held about 20 or 30 gallons. [7]Jesus told the servants to fill them to the top with water. Then after the jars had been filled, [8]he said, "Now take some water and give it to the man in charge of the feast."

The servants did as Jesus told them, [9]and the man in charge drank some of the water that had now turned into wine. He did not know where the wine had come from, but the servants did. He called the bridegroom over [10]and said, "The best wine is always served first. Then after the guests have had plenty, the other wine is served. But you have kept the best until last!"

[11]This was Jesus' first miracle,[j] and he did it in the village of Cana in Galilee. There Jesus showed his glory, and his disciples put their faith in him. [12]After this, he went with his mother, his brothers, and his disciples to the town of Capernaum, where they stayed for a few days.

Jesus in the Temple

(Matthew 21.12,13; Mark 11.15-17; Luke 19.45,46)

[13]Not long before the Jewish festival of Passover, Jesus went to Jerusalem. [14]There he found people selling cattle, sheep, and doves in the temple. He also saw moneychangers sitting at their tables. [15]So he took some rope and made a whip. Then he chased everyone out of the temple, together with their sheep and cattle. He turned over the tables of the moneychangers and scattered their coins.

[16]Jesus said to the people who had been selling doves, "Get those doves out of here! Don't make my Father's house a marketplace."

[17]The disciples then remembered that the Scriptures say, "My love for your house burns in me like a fire."

[18]The Jewish leaders asked Jesus, "What miracle[j] will you work to show us why you have done this?"

[19]"Destroy this temple," Jesus answered, "and in three days I will build it again!"

[20]The leaders replied, "It took 46 years to build this temple. What makes you think you can rebuild it in three days?"

[21]But Jesus was talking about his body as a temple. [22]And when he was raised from death, his disciples remembered what he had told them. Then they believed the Scriptures and the words of Jesus.

Jesus Knows What People Are Like

[23]In Jerusalem during Passover many people put their faith in Jesus, because they saw him work miracles.[j] [24]But Jesus knew what was in their hearts, and he would not let them have power over him. [25]No one had to tell him what people were like. He already knew.

Jesus and Nicodemus

3 There was a man named Nicodemus who was a Pharisee and a Jewish leader. [2]One night he went to Jesus and said, "Rabbi, we know that God has sent you to teach us. You could not work these miracles, unless God were with you."

[3]Jesus replied, "I tell you for certain that you must be born from above[k] before you can see God's kingdom!"

[4]Nicodemus asked, "How can a grown man ever be born a second time?"

[5]Jesus answered:

[j]2.11,18,23 *miracle:* The Greek text has "sign." In the Gospel of John the word "sign" is used for the miracle itself and as a way of pointing to Jesus as the Son of God.   [k]3.3 *from above:* Or "in a new way." The same Greek word is used in verses 7,31.

I tell you for certain that before you can get into God's kingdom, you must be born not only by water, but by the Spirit. [6]Humans give life to their children. Yet only God's Spirit can change you into a child of God. [7]Don't be surprised when I say that you must be born from above. [8]Only God's Spirit gives new life. The Spirit is like the wind that blows wherever it wants to. You can hear the wind, but you don't know where it comes from or where it is going.

[9]"How can this be?" Nicodemus asked.

[10]Jesus replied:

How can you be a teacher of Israel and not know these things? [11]I tell you for certain we know what we are talking about because we have seen it ourselves. But none of you will accept what we say. [12]If you don't believe when I talk to you about things on earth, how can you possibly believe if I talk to you about things in heaven? [13]No one has gone up to heaven except the Son of Man, who came down from there. [14]And the Son of Man must be lifted up, just as the metal snake was lifted up by Moses in the desert.[l] [15]Then everyone who has faith in the Son of Man will have eternal life.

[16]God loved the people of this world so much that he gave his only Son, so that everyone who has faith in him will have eternal life and never really die. [17]God did not send his Son into the world to condemn its people. He sent him to save them! [18]No one who has faith in God's Son will be condemned. But everyone who doesn't have faith in him has already been condemned for not having faith in God's only Son.

[19]The light has come into the world, and people who do evil things are judged guilty because they love the dark more than the light. [20]People who do evil hate the light and won't come to the light, because it clearly shows what they have done. [21]But everyone who lives by the truth will come to the light, because they want others to know that God is really the one doing what they do.

Jesus and John the Baptist

[22]Later, Jesus and his disciples went to Judea, where he stayed with them for a while and was baptizing people.

[23-24]John had not yet been put in jail. He was at Aenon near Salim, where there was a lot of water, and people were coming there for John to baptize them.

[25]John's followers got into an argument with a Jewish man[m] about a ceremony of washing.[n] [26]They went to John and said, "Rabbi, you spoke about a man when you were with him east of the Jordan. He is now baptizing people, and everyone is going to him."

[27]John replied:

No one can do anything unless God in heaven allows it. [28]You surely remember how I told you that I am not the Messiah. I am only the one sent ahead of him.

3.6 *child of God:* The Jewish people believed that they were God's children because they were descendants of Abraham. Jesus is saying that being a child of God no longer has to do simply with being born into a Jewish family or following the Law of Moses. See also Gal 3.1-5,26-29.

3.10 *a teacher of Israel:* As a Pharisee, Nicodemus was also a teacher of the Jewish Scriptures.

3.14 *metal snake was lifted up by Moses in the desert:* Jesus is saying that he would be lifted up like the snake Moses lifted up to cure the people of snake bites in the desert (Num 21.4-9). Jesus would be nailed to a cross, and whoever believed in him would be saved from death.

Eternal Life

Heaven

3.22 *Judea:* "Judea" is the Latin name that was used for the territory that once had been called "Judah." In the time of Jesus, Judea was under Roman rule. **(See Map 12 on pg 1890.)**

3.23-24 *Aenon near Salim:* The exact location of this place is not known.

Purity (Clean and Unclean)

---

[l]**3.14** *just as the metal snake was lifted up by Moses in the desert:* When the Lord punished the people of Israel by sending snakes to bite them, he told Moses to hold a metal snake up on a pole. Everyone who looked at the snake bites was cured of the snake bites (see Numbers 21.4-9). [m]**3.25** *a Jewish man:* Some manuscripts have "some Jewish men." [n]**3.25** *about a ceremony of washing:* The Jewish people had many rules about washing themselves and their dishes, in order to make themselves fit to worship God.

Jesus said, "God loved the people of this world so much that he gave his only Son, so that everyone who has faith in him will have eternal life." JOHN 3.16

4.4 *Samaria:* Samaria was an area in central Palestine between Judea and Galilee. The Jews living in Judea in Jesus' day did not like Samaritans, because they thought the Samaritans were not faithful to the God of Israel. (See Map 12 on pg 1890.)

4.6-8 *A Samaritan woman came to draw water:* The woman mentioned here went to the well during the hottest part of the day when few other people would do so.

4.9 *Jews and Samaritans:* Jewish people who were strict about following certain purity laws were not supposed to drink from a Samaritan's cup or bucket.

4.12 *Our ancestor Jacob:* Like the Jews living in Judea, the Samaritans were descendants of the earliest ancestors of Israel.

4.15 *give me . . . that water:* The woman thinks Jesus is going to give her a private supply of water that will never run out. Then she wouldn't have to go to the well each day in the hot sun.

4.16 *bring your husband:* Jesus knew that the woman had lived with many men and that she had no husband (either because she was divorced or her last husband had died).

---

[29] At a wedding the groom is the one who gets married. The best man is glad just to be there and to hear the groom's voice. That's why I am so glad. [30] Jesus must become more important, while I become less important.

The One Who Comes from Heaven

[31] God's Son comes from heaven and is above all others. Everyone who comes from the earth belongs to the earth and speaks about earthly things. The one who comes from heaven is above all others. [32] He speaks about what he has seen and heard, and yet no one believes him. [33] But everyone who does believe him has shown that God is truthful. [34] The Son was sent to speak God's message, and he has been given the full power of God's Spirit. [35] The Father loves the Son and has given him everything. [36] Everyone who has faith in the Son has eternal life. But no one who rejects him will ever share in that life, and God will be angry with them forever.

4 Jesus knew that the Pharisees had heard that he was winning and baptizing more followers than John was. [2] But Jesus' disciples were really the ones doing the baptizing, and not Jesus himself.

Jesus and the Samaritan Woman

[3] Jesus left Judea and started for Galilee again. [4] This time he had to go through Samaria, [5] and on his way he came to the town of Sychar. It was near the field that

---

Jacob had long ago given to his son Joseph. [6-8] The well that Jacob had dug was still there, and Jesus sat down beside it because he was tired from traveling. It was noon, and after Jesus' disciples had gone into town to buy some food, a Samaritan woman came to draw water from the well. Jesus asked her, "Would you please give me a drink of water?"

[9] "You are a Jew," she replied, "and I am a Samaritan woman. How can you ask me for a drink of water when Jews and Samaritans won't have anything to do with each other?"[o]

[10] Jesus answered, "You don't know what God wants to give you, and you don't know who is asking you for a drink. If you did, you would ask me for the water that gives life."

[11] "Sir," the woman said, "you don't even have a bucket, and the well is deep. Where are you going to get this life-giving water? [12] Our ancestor Jacob dug this well for us, and his family and animals got water from it. Are you greater than Jacob?"

[13] Jesus answered, "Everyone who drinks this water will get thirsty again. [14] But no one who drinks the water I give will ever be thirsty again. The water I give will become in that person a flowing fountain that gives eternal life."

[15] The woman replied, "Sir, please give me a drink of that water! Then I won't get thirsty and have to come to this well again."

[16] Jesus told her, "Go and bring your husband."

[17-18] The woman answered, "I don't have a husband."

"That's right," Jesus replied, "you're tell-

---

[o]4.9 *won't have anything to do with each other*: Or "won't use the same cups." The Samaritans lived in the land between Judea and Galilee. They worshiped God differently from the Jews and did not get along with them.

ing the truth. You don't have a husband. You have already been married five times, and the man you are now living with isn't your husband."

¹⁹The woman said, "Sir, I can see that you are a prophet. ²⁰My ancestors worshiped on this mountain,P but you Jews say Jerusalem is the only place to worship."

²¹Jesus said to her:

Believe me, the time is coming when you won't worship the Father either on this mountain or in Jerusalem. ²²You Samaritans don't really know the one you worship. But we Jews do know the God we worship, and by using us, God will save the world. ²³But a time is coming, and it is already here! Even now the true worshipers are being led by the Spirit to worship the Father according to the truth. These are the ones the Father is seeking to worship him. ²⁴God is Spirit, and those who worship God must be led by the Spirit to worship him according to the truth.

²⁵The woman said, "I know that the Messiah will come. He is the one we call Christ. When he comes, he will explain everything to us."

²⁶"I am that one," Jesus told her, "and I am speaking to you now."

²⁷The disciples returned about this time and were surprised to find Jesus talking with a woman. But none of them asked him what he wanted or why he was talking with her.

²⁸The woman left her water jar and ran back into town, where she said to the people, ²⁹"Come and see a man who told me everything I have ever done! Could he be the Messiah?" ³⁰Everyone in town went out to see Jesus.

³¹While this was happening, Jesus' disciples were saying to him, "Teacher, please eat something."

³²But Jesus told them, "I have food you don't know anything about."

³³His disciples started asking each other, "Has someone brought him something to eat?"

³⁴Jesus said:

My food is to do what God wants! He is the one who sent me, and I must finish the work that he gave me to do. ³⁵You may say there are still four months until harvest time. But I tell you to look, and you will see that the fields are ripe and ready to harvest.

³⁶Even now the harvest workers are receiving their reward by gathering a harvest that brings eternal life. Then everyone who planted the seed and everyone who harvests the crop will celebrate together. ³⁷So the saying proves true, "Some plant the seed, and others harvest the crop." ³⁸I am sending you to harvest crops in fields where others have done all the hard work.

³⁹A lot of Samaritans in that town put their faith in Jesus because the woman had said, "This man told me everything I have ever done." ⁴⁰They came and asked him to stay in their town, and he stayed on for two days.

⁴¹Many more Samaritans put their faith in Jesus because of what they heard him say. ⁴²They told the woman, "We no longer have faith in Jesus just because of what you told us. We have heard him ourselves, and we are certain that he is the Savior of the world!"

P4.20 this mountain: Mount Gerizim, near the city of Shechem.

● 4.19 a prophet: Prophets sometimes had visions about things that would happen in the future. More often prophets were faithful people who observed what was happening around them and brought a message from God that fit the situation. (See the article Prophets and Prophecy on pg 1791.)

■ 4.23 true worshipers are being led by the Spirit: Jesus is saying that true worship does not depend on being at a certain place. Rather, true worship happens when people are led by God's Spirit.

■ 4.34 My food is to do what God wants: In JOHN, Jesus often talks about doing the work that God sent him to do. Here he calls this work his "food." See also 3.16,17,34; 5.26; 6.27,33-35; 17.1,2. Later, Jesus describes doing what God wants him to do as drinking from the cup (18.11), an image that is often used in the Bible as a symbol of suffering (Isa 51.17,22; Jer 25.15,17).

■ 4.35 four months until harvest . . . fields are ripe and ready to harvest: The grain harvest for the area was still months away, but Jesus is saying that the harvest (gathering) of many new followers is ready right away.

■ 4.37 Some plant the seed, and others harvest the crop: Those who plant the seed are those who tell God's message to others; those who harvest are those who help others trust in Jesus.

4.43-44 *Prophets:* Many Samaritans in the area around Sychar believed Jesus was God's chosen Messiah, but Jesus knew that many people in his own home area of Nazareth in Galilee would not accept him as the Messiah.

4.46 *official in Capernaum:* The Greek word describing this "official" suggests that he was a royal officer who served the king (Herod Antipas). Because Jesus healed the boy at the very moment he said he would, the official and his whole family put their faith in Jesus (4.53).

5.7 *when the water is stirred up:* The water may have been stirred occasionally by a spring. Some believed an angel of God stirred the waters.

5.9 *Sabbath:* This Jewish day of rest begins at sunset on Friday. It ends with a blessing at sunset on Saturday. The Sabbath is the seventh day of the week, the day that God rested after the work of creation (Gen 2.2,3). Jewish law forbade Jews and their servants from working on the Sabbath (Exod 20.8-11; Deut 5.12-15). Carrying bedding was considered work, so it was not allowed.

5.14 *don't sin anymore:* People sin when they turn away from God and disobey God's Law. Jesus' warning to the man he healed does not mean that the man's illness was caused by sin. **(See the article Miracles, Magic, and Medicine on pg 1820.)**

Jesus Heals an Official's Son

(Matthew 8.5-13; Luke 7.1-10)

43-44 Jesus had said, "Prophets are honored everywhere, except in their own country." Then two days later he left **45** and went to Galilee. The people there welcomed him, because they had gone to the festival in Jerusalem and had seen everything he had done.

46 While Jesus was in Galilee, he returned to the village of Cana, where he had turned the water into wine. There was an official in Capernaum whose son was sick. **47** And when the man heard that Jesus had come from Judea, he went and begged him to keep his son from dying.

48 Jesus told the official, "You won't have faith unless you see miracles and wonders!"

49 The man replied, "Lord, please come before my son dies!"

50 Jesus then said, "Your son will live. Go on home to him." The man believed Jesus and started back home.

51 Some of the official's servants met him along the road and told him, "Your son is better!" **52** He asked them when the boy got better, and they answered, "The fever left him yesterday at one o'clock."

53 The boy's father realized that at one o'clock the day before, Jesus had told him, "Your son will live!" So the man and everyone in his family put their faith in Jesus.

54 This was the second miracle[q] that Jesus worked after he left Judea and went to Galilee.

Jesus Heals a Sick Man

5 Later, Jesus went to Jerusalem for another Jewish festival.[r] **2** In the city near the sheep gate was a pool with five porches, and its name in Hebrew was Bethzatha.[s]

3-4 Many sick, blind, lame, and paralyzed people were lying close to the pool.[t]

5 Beside the pool was a man who had been sick for 38 years. **6** When Jesus saw the man and realized that he had been crippled for a long time, he asked him, "Do you want to be healed?"

7 The man answered, "Sir, I don't have anyone to put me in the pool when the water is stirred up. I try to get in, but someone else always gets there first."

8 Jesus told him, "Pick up your mat and walk!" **9** Right then the man was healed. He picked up his mat and started walking around. The day on which this happened was a Sabbath.

10 When the Jewish leaders saw the man carrying his mat, they said to him, "This is the Sabbath! No one is allowed to carry a mat on the Sabbath."

11 But he replied, "The man who healed me told me to pick up my mat and walk."

12 They asked him, "Who is this man that told you to pick up your mat and walk?" **13** But he did not know who Jesus was, and Jesus had left because of the crowd.

14 Later, Jesus met the man in the temple and told him, "You are now well. But don't sin anymore or something worse might happen to you." **15** The man left and told the leaders that Jesus was the one who had healed him. **16** They started making a lot of

[q] **4.54** *miracle*: See the note at 2.11. [r] **5.1** *another Jewish festival*: Either the Festival of Shelters or Passover. [s] **5.2** *Bethzatha*: Some manuscripts have "Bethesda" and others have "Bethsaida." [t] **5.3,4** *pool*: Some manuscripts add, "They were waiting for the water to be stirred, because an angel from the Lord would sometimes come down and stir it. The first person to get into the pool after that would be healed."

trouble for Jesus because he did things like this on the Sabbath.

¹⁷But Jesus said, "My Father has never stopped working, and this is why I keep on working." ¹⁸Now the leaders wanted to kill Jesus for two reasons. First, he had broken the law of the Sabbath. But even worse, he had said God was his Father, which made him equal with God.

The Son's Authority

¹⁹Jesus told the people:

I tell you for certain the Son cannot do anything on his own. He can do only what he sees the Father doing, and he does exactly what he sees the Father do. ²⁰The Father loves the Son and has shown him everything he does. The Father will show him even greater things, and you will be amazed. ²¹Just as the Father raises the dead and gives life, so the Son gives life to anyone he wants to.

²²The Father doesn't judge anyone, but he has made his Son the judge of everyone. ²³The Father wants all people to honor the Son as much as they honor him. When anyone refuses to honor the Son, this is the same as refusing to honor the Father who sent him. ²⁴I tell you for certain that everyone who hears my message and has faith in the one who sent me has eternal life and will never be condemned. They have already gone from death to life.

²⁵I tell you for certain the time will come, and it is already here, when all of the dead will hear the voice of the Son of God. And those who listen to it will live! ²⁶The Father has the power to give life, and he has given that same power to the Son. ²⁷And he has given

his Son the right to judge everyone, because he is the Son of Man.

²⁸Don't be surprised! The time will come when all of the dead will hear the voice of the Son of Man, ²⁹and they will come out of their graves. Everyone who has done good things will rise to life, but everyone who has done evil things will rise and be condemned.

³⁰I cannot do anything on my own. The Father sent me, and he is the one who told me how to judge. I judge with fairness, because I obey him, and I don't just try to please myself.

Witnesses to Jesus

³¹If I speak for myself, there is no way to prove I am telling the truth. ³²But there is someone else who speaks for me, and I know what he says is true. ³³You sent messengers to John, and he told them the truth. ³⁴I don't depend on what people say about me, but I tell you these things so that you may be saved. ³⁵John was a lamp that gave a lot of light, and you were glad to enjoy his light for a while.

³⁶But something more important than John speaks for me. I mean the things that the Father has given me to do! All of these speak for me and prove that the Father sent me. ³⁷The Father who sent me also speaks for me, but you have never heard his voice or seen him face to face. ³⁸You have not believed his message, because you refused to have faith in the one he sent.

³⁹You search the Scriptures, because you think you will find eternal life in them. The Scriptures tell about me, ⁴⁰but you refuse to come to me for eternal life.

● 5.16 *did things like this on the Sabbath:* Doing any kind of work on the Sabbath was a serious offense according to the law of Moses (Exod 31.14,15; 35.2). However during Jesus' day when the Roman Empire controlled Judea, Jewish leaders did not actually have the authority to execute people for this crime. It is not clear exactly how the Jewish leaders "started making trouble" for Jesus.

■ 5.17 *My Father:* In this Gospel, Jesus often refers to God as his Father (3.35; 5.20-30; 15.1,16; 17). For Jesus to call God his Father was to claim a special relationship with God and authority in relation to God's people (Ps 2.6,7). Since the Jewish leaders believed no human being could be equal with God, they thought Jesus was dishonoring the Law of Moses by saying God was his Father (5.18).

■ 5.25 *time will come, and it is already here:* Jesus is saying that those who hear his message of forgiveness and new life have life that will never end. This includes those who have already died as faithful people.

● 5.39,40 *You search the Scriptures . . . for eternal life:* The "Scriptures" are the Jewish Scriptures, which Christians call the Old Testament. The teachers followed the teachings of Scripture as a guide to living as God expected. Jesus is saying that those same Scriptures point to him as the way to eternal life.

5.45-47 *You have put your hope in Moses:* Jesus was referring to the Law of Moses, which was an important part of the Jewish Scriptures. When Jesus says "Moses wrote about me," he is referring to the overall message of the first five books of the Jewish Scriptures, traditionally called the Books of Moses.

6.11 *Jesus took the bread:* Over a thousand years earlier, God miraculously fed the Israelite people in the desert wilderness of Sinai with bread (manna) that came down from heaven (Exod 16.1-35; Num 11.7-9). Those who saw Jesus' miracle of feeding 5,000 may have been reminded of God's earlier miracle.

6.13 *twelve large baskets:* Twelve is a very significant number to the Jewish people because Israel was made up of twelve tribes. (See the chart Numbers in the Bible on pg 1844.)

6.16 *lake:* Meaning Lake Galilee.

6.19 *Jesus walking on the water:* Jesus' miracle of walking on the water may have reminded the disciples of two miracles God had done earlier: controlling the waters of creation (Gen 1.1-13) and saving the Israelite people when Moses parted the waters of the Red Sea (Exod 14.21-31).

I Am

Names of God

⁴¹I don't care about human praise, ⁴²but I do know that none of you love God. ⁴³I have come with my Father's authority, and you have not welcomed me. But you will welcome people who come on their own. ⁴⁴How could you possibly believe? You like to have your friends praise you, and you don't care about praise that the only God can give!

⁴⁵Don't think that I will be the one to accuse you to the Father. You have put your hope in Moses, yet he is the very one who will accuse you. ⁴⁶Moses wrote about me, and if you had believed Moses, you would have believed me. ⁴⁷But if you don't believe what Moses wrote, how can you believe what I say?

Feeding Five Thousand
(Matthew 14.13-21; Mark 6.30-44; Luke 9.10-17)

6 Jesus crossed Lake Galilee, which was also known as Lake Tiberias. ²A large crowd had seen him work miracles to heal the sick, and those people went with him. ³⁻⁴It was almost time for the Jewish festival of Passover, and Jesus went up on a mountain with his disciples and sat down.ᵘ

⁵When Jesus saw the large crowd coming toward him, he asked Philip, "Where will we get enough food to feed all these people?" ⁶He said this to test Philip, since he already knew what he was going to do.

⁷Philip answered, "Don't you know that it would take almost a year's wagesᵛ just to buy only a little bread for each of these people?"

⁸Andrew, the brother of Simon Peter,

was one of the disciples. He spoke up and said, ⁹"There is a boy here who has five small loavesʷ of barley bread and two fish. But what good is that with all these people?"

¹⁰The ground was covered with grass, and Jesus told his disciples to tell everyone to sit down. About 5,000 men were in the crowd. ¹¹Jesus took the bread in his hands and gave thanks to God. Then he passed the bread to the people, and he did the same with the fish, until everyone had plenty to eat.

¹²The people ate all they wanted, and Jesus told his disciples to gather up the leftovers, so that nothing would be wasted. ¹³The disciples gathered them up and filled twelve large baskets with what was left over from the five barley loaves.

¹⁴After the people had seen Jesus work this miracle,ˣ they began saying, "This must be the Prophetʸ who is to come into the world!" ¹⁵Jesus realized that they would try to force him to be their king. So he went up on a mountain, where he could be alone.

Jesus Walks on the Water
(Matthew 14.22-27; Mark 6.45-52)

¹⁶That evening, Jesus' disciples went down to the lake. ¹⁷They got into a boat and started across for Capernaum. Later that evening Jesus had still not come to them, ¹⁸and a strong wind was making the water rough.

¹⁹When the disciples had rowed for three or four miles, they saw Jesus walking on the water. He kept coming closer to the boat, and they were terrified. ²⁰But he said, "I am Jesus!ᶻ Don't be afraid!" ²¹The disci-

ᵘ**6.3,4** *sat down:* Possibly to teach. Teachers in the ancient world, including Jewish teachers, usually sat down to teach. ᵛ**6.7** *almost a year's wages:* The Greek text has "200 silver coins." Each coin was worth the average day's wages for a worker. ʷ**6.9** *small loaves:* These would have been flat and round or in the shape of a bun. ˣ**6.14** *miracle:* See the note at 2.11. ʸ**6.14** *the Prophet:* See the note at 1.21. ᶻ**6.20** *I am Jesus:* The Greek text has "I am" (see the note at 8.24).

ples wanted to take him into the boat, but suddenly the boat reached the shore where they were headed.

The Bread That Gives Life

²²The people who had stayed on the east side of the lake knew that only one boat had been there. They also knew that Jesus had not left in it with his disciples. But the next day ²³some boats from Tiberias sailed near the place where the crowd had eaten the bread for which the Lord had given thanks. ²⁴They saw that Jesus and his disciples had left. Then they got into the boats and went to Capernaum to look for Jesus. ²⁵They found him on the west side of the lake and asked, "Rabbi, when did you get here?"

²⁶Jesus answered, "I tell you for certain that you are not looking for me because you saw the miracles,[a] but because you ate all the food you wanted. ²⁷Don't work for food that spoils. Work for food that gives eternal life. The Son of Man will give you this food, because God the Father has given him the right to do so."

²⁸"What exactly does God want us to do?" the people asked.

²⁹Jesus answered, "God wants you to have faith in the one he sent."

³⁰They replied, "What miracle will you work, so that we can have faith in you? What will you do? ³¹For example, when our ancestors were in the desert, they were given manna[b] to eat. It happened just as the Scriptures say, 'God gave them bread from heaven to eat.' "

³²Jesus then told them, "I tell you for certain that Moses wasn't the one who gave you bread from heaven. My Father is the one who gives you the true bread from heaven. ³³And the bread that God gives is the one who came down from heaven to give life to the world."

³⁴The people said, "Sir, give us this bread and don't ever stop!"

³⁵Jesus replied:

I am the bread that gives life! No one who comes to me will ever be hungry. No one who has faith in me will ever be thirsty. ³⁶I have told you already that you have seen me and still do not have faith in me. ³⁷Everything and everyone that the Father has given me will come to me, and I won't turn any of them away.

³⁸I didn't come from heaven to do what I want! I came to do what the Father wants me to do. He sent me, ³⁹and he wants to make certain that none of the ones he has given me will be lost. Instead, he wants me to raise them to life on the last day.[c] ⁴⁰My Father wants everyone who sees the Son to have faith in him and to have eternal life. Then I will raise them to life on the last day.

⁴¹The people started grumbling because Jesus had said he was the bread that had come down from heaven. ⁴²They were asking each other, "Isn't he Jesus, the son of Joseph? Don't we know his father and mother? How can he say that he has come down from heaven?"

⁴³Jesus told them:

Stop grumbling! ⁴⁴No one can come to me, unless the Father who sent me makes them want to come. But if they do come, I will raise them to life on the

---

[a]6.26 *miracles:* The Greek text has "signs" here and "sign" in verse 30 (see the note at 2.11).
[b]6.31 *manna:* When the people of Israel were wandering through the desert, the Lord gave them a special kind of food to eat. It tasted like a wafer and was called "manna," which in Hebrew means, "What is this?"   [c]6.39 *the last day:* When God will judge all people.

6.23,24 *Tiberias . . . Capernaum:* Tiberias was a city on the west coast of Lake Galilee, built around A.D. 25 by Herod Antipas to honor the emperor, Tiberius Caesar. When the people didn't find Jesus on the east side of the lake, they sailed back to Capernaum. **(See Map 12 on pg 1890.)**

6.35 *I am the bread that gives life:* Jesus compares himself to the miraculous gift of manna that God sent from heaven. Just as God sent the manna, God sends Jesus to bring life.

Bread

6.39 *the last day:* Jesus is referring to the time when God will judge all people. Those who have faith in Jesus, the Son, will be raised up to life (6.40), that is, have eternal life.

Eternal Life

Day of the LORD

Jesus replied: "I am the bread that gives life!" JOHN 6.35

■ **6.53 eat . . . drink . . . Son of Man:** This is probably a reference to the Lord's Supper, which Jesus' followers share in response to his command (Matt 26.26-30; Mark 14.22-26; Luke 22.14-23; 1 Cor 11.23-29).

⊂⧽ Son of Man

● **6.59 synagogue in Capernaum:** The Greek word that is translated here as "synagogue" means "gathering." A Roman army officer built a place of worship for the Jewish people in Capernaum (Luke 7.5).

⊂⧽ Synagogues

● **6.67 twelve disciples:** These are the ones whom Jesus called to be his special apostles (Matt 10.1-4).

● **6.70,71 a demon . . . Judas . . . Iscariot:** Demons were understood to be the helpers of Satan and God's enemies. Jesus is saying that Judas, one of Jesus' twelve special disciples, would betray him. "Iscariot" may mean "a man from Kerioth" (a place in Judea). Or, "a man who was a liar" or "a man who was a betrayer" (Matt 10.4).

● **7.1 Judea . . . Galilee:** In chapter 6, Jesus is reported as being in Capernaum, which is in Galilee. JOHN does not explain when Jesus returned to Judea.

last day. **45**One of the prophets wrote, "God will teach all of them." And so everyone who listens to the Father and learns from him will come to me. **46**The only one who has seen the Father is the one who has come from him. No one else has ever seen the Father. **47**I tell you for certain that everyone who has faith in me has eternal life.

48I am the bread that gives life! **49**Your ancestors ate manna[d] in the desert, and later they died. **50**But the bread from heaven has come down, so that no one who eats it will ever die. **51**I am that bread from heaven! Everyone who eats it will live forever. My flesh is the life-giving bread I give to the people of this world.

52They started arguing with each other and asked, "How can he give us his flesh to eat?"

53Jesus answered:

I tell you for certain that you won't live unless you eat the flesh and drink the blood of the Son of Man. **54**But if you do eat my flesh and drink my blood, you will have eternal life, and I will raise you to life on the last day. **55**My flesh is the true food, and my blood is the true drink. **56**If you eat my flesh and drink my blood, you are one with me, and I am one with you. **57**The living Father sent me, and I have life because of him. Now everyone who eats my flesh will live because of me. **58**The bread that comes down from heaven isn't like what your ancestors ate. They died, but whoever eats this bread will live forever. **59**Jesus was teaching in a synagogue in Capernaum when he said these things.

The Words of Eternal Life

60Many of Jesus' disciples heard him and said, "This is too hard for anyone to understand."

61Jesus knew that his disciples were grumbling. So he asked, "Does this bother you? **62**What if you should see the Son of Man go up to heaven where he came from? **63**The Spirit is the one who gives life! Human strength can do nothing. The words that I have spoken to you are from that life-giving Spirit. **64**But some of you refuse to have faith in me." Jesus said this, because from the beginning he knew who would have faith in him. He also knew which one would betray him.

65Then Jesus said, "You cannot come to me, unless the Father makes you want to come. That is why I have told these things to all of you."

66Because of what Jesus said, many of his disciples turned their backs on him and stopped following him. **67**Jesus then asked his twelve disciples if they also were going to leave him. **68**Simon Peter answered, "Lord, there is no one else that we can go to! Your words give eternal life. **69**We have faith in you, and we are sure that you are God's Holy One."

70Jesus told his disciples, "I chose all twelve of you, but one of you is a demon!" **71**Jesus was talking about Judas, the son of Simon Iscariot.[e] He would later betray Jesus, even though he was one of the twelve disciples.

Jesus' Brothers Don't Have Faith in Him

7 Jesus decided to leave Judea and to start going through Galilee because

[d]**6.49** *manna:* See the note at 6.31.   [e]**6.71** *Iscariot:* This may mean "a man from Kerioth" (a place in Judea). But more probably it means "a man who was a liar" or "a man who was a betrayer."

the leaders of the people wanted to kill him. [2] It was almost time for the Festival of Shelters, [3]and Jesus' brothers said to him, "Why don't you go to Judea? Then your disciples can see what you are doing. [4]No one does anything in secret, if they want others to know about them. So let the world know what you are doing!" [5]Even Jesus' own brothers had not yet become his followers.

[6]Jesus answered, "My time hasn't yet come,[f] but your time is always here. [7]The people of this world cannot hate you. They hate me, because I tell them that they do evil things. [8]Go on to the festival. My time hasn't yet come, and I am not going." [9]Jesus said this and stayed on in Galilee.

Jesus at the Festival of Shelters

[10]After Jesus' brothers had gone to the festival, he went secretly, without telling anyone.

[11]During the festival the leaders of the people looked for Jesus and asked, "Where is he?" [12]The crowds even got into an argument about him. Some were saying, "Jesus is a good man," while others were saying, "He is lying to everyone." [13]But the people were afraid of their leaders, and none of them talked in public about him.

[14]When the festival was about half over, Jesus went into the temple and started teaching. [15]The leaders were surprised and said, "How does this man know so much? He has never been taught!"

[16]Jesus replied:

I am not teaching something I thought up. What I teach comes from the one who sent me. [17]If you really want to obey God, you will know if what I teach comes from God or from

me. [18]If I wanted to bring honor to myself, I would speak for myself. But I want to honor the one who sent me. This is why I tell the truth and not a lie. [19]Didn't Moses give you the Law? Yet none of you obey it! So why do you want to kill me?

[20]The crowd replied, "You're crazy! What makes you think someone wants to kill you?"

[21]Jesus answered:

I worked one miracle,[g] and it amazed you. [22]Moses commanded you to circumcise your sons. But it wasn't really Moses who gave you this command. It was your ancestors, and even on the Sabbath you circumcise your sons [23]in order to obey the Law of Moses. Why are you angry with me for making someone completely well on the Sabbath? [24]Don't judge by appearances. Judge by what is right.

[25]Some of the people from Jerusalem were saying, "Isn't this the man they want to kill? [26]Yet here he is, speaking for everyone to hear. And no one is arguing with him. Do you suppose the authorities know he is the Messiah? [27]But how could that be? No one knows where the Messiah will come from, but we know where this man comes from."

[28]As Jesus was teaching in the temple, he shouted, "Do you really think you know me and where I came from? I didn't come on my own! The one who sent me is truthful, and you don't know him. [29]But I know the one who sent me, because I came from him."

[30]Some of the people wanted to arrest Jesus right then. But no one even laid a hand on him, because his time had not yet come.[h] [31]A lot of people in the crowd put

---

[f]7.6 My time hasn't yet come: See the note at 2.4. [g]7.21 one miracle: The healing of the sick man (5.1-18; see also the note at 2.11). [h]7.30 his time had not yet come: See the note at 2.4.

● 7.3 Jesus' brothers: These may be Jesus' actual brothers, or they may be cousins and half-brothers.

■ 7.10 he went secretly: Jesus goes in secret rather than attracting attention to himself. He knows that there is danger in having people believe in him just because of his miracles.

● 7.14 temple: The center of Jewish worship in Jerusalem. Herod greatly expanded this important building as a way of trying to win the favor of the Jewish people. During the time of the festivals, many visitors came to Jerusalem to offer sacrifices at the temple and Jesus would have been able to speak to large crowds of people. (See the article People of the Law: The Religion of Israel on pg 1794.)

■ 7.16 the one who sent me: Jesus was referring to God, the Father.

● 7.19 Didn't Moses give you the Law?: Jesus tells his listeners that they have not really understood what God was saying in the Law.

● 7.21 I worked one miracle: Jesus is talking about his healing of the man who was crippled (5.1-18).

● 7.22 Moses commanded you to circumcise your sons: Jesus teaches that if it is acceptable to circumcise on the Sabbath, then it should be acceptable to treat the whole body, as he did when he healed the man who was crippled.

⊗   Circumcision

7.32 *Pharisees . . . chief priests . . . temple police:* Chief priests were members of a group in charge of the temple in Jerusalem. The temple police guarded the temple area and helped the council of Jewish leaders in Jerusalem keep order among the Jewish people.

7.50 *Nicodemus . . . the council:* The Jewish council was made up of religious and civic leaders, including the chief priests, Pharisees, and Sadducees. The Romans, who ruled Palestine, allowed the local leaders in each part of their empire to decide cases against those who broke religious laws and to make people obey local laws.

7.51 *Our Law:* The Law of Moses taught that two witnesses were needed before a person could be convicted of a crime (Deut 17.4-7; 19.15) and put to death (Num 35.30).

7.52 *no prophet is to come from Galilee:* Since Jesus is from Nazareth in Galilee, they don't believe he could be the Messiah. What the leaders didn't realize was that Jesus was born in Bethlehem in Judea, the hometown of King David, and that he was a descendant of David. It was from the family of King David that a Messiah was to come (2 Sam 7.16,17; Isa 11.1).

8.1 *Mount of Olives:* The Mount of Olives got its name because of all the olive trees that grew on its slopes. **(See Map 13 on pg 1891.)**

their faith in him and said, "When the Messiah comes, he surely won't perform more miracles[i] than this man has done!"

Officers Sent To Arrest Jesus

[32]When the Pharisees heard the crowd arguing about Jesus, they got together with the chief priests and sent some temple police to arrest him. [33]But Jesus told them, "I will be with you a little while longer, and then I will return to the one who sent me. [34]You will look for me, but you won't find me. You cannot go where I am going."

[35]The people asked each other, "Where can he go to keep us from finding him? Is he going to some foreign country where our people live? Is he going there to teach the Greeks?[j] [36]What did he mean by saying that we will look for him, but won't find him? Why can't we go where he is going?"

Streams of Life-Giving Water

[37]On the last and most important day of the festival, Jesus stood up and shouted, "If you are thirsty, come to me and drink! [38]Have faith in me, and you will have life-giving water flowing from deep inside you, just as the Scriptures say." [39]Jesus was talking about the Holy Spirit, who would be given to everyone that had faith in him. The Spirit had not yet been given to anyone, since Jesus had not yet been given his full glory.[k]

The People Take Sides

[40]When the crowd heard Jesus say this, some of them said, "He must be the

Prophet!"[l] [41]Others said, "He is the Messiah!" Others even said, "Can the Messiah come from Galilee? [42]The Scriptures say that the Messiah will come from the family of King David. Doesn't this mean that he will be born in David's hometown of Bethlehem?" [43]The people started taking sides against each other because of Jesus. [44]Some of them wanted to arrest him, but no one laid a hand on him.

The Leaders Refuse To Have Faith in Jesus

[45]When the temple police returned to the chief priests and Pharisees, they were asked, "Why didn't you bring Jesus here?"

[46]They answered, "No one has ever spoken like this man!"

[47]The Pharisees said to them, "Have you also been fooled? [48]Not one of the chief priests or the Pharisees has faith in him. [49]And these people who don't know the Law are under God's curse anyway."

[50]Nicodemus was there at the time. He was a member of the council, and was the same one who had earlier come to see Jesus.[m] He said, [51]"Our Law doesn't let us condemn people before we hear what they have to say. We cannot judge them before we know what they have done."

[52]Then they said, "Nicodemus, you must be from Galilee! Read the Scriptures, and you will find that no prophet is to come from Galilee."

A Woman Caught in Sin

8 [53]Everyone else went home, [1]but Jesus walked out to the Mount of Olives.

[i]**7.31** *miracles:* See the note at 2.11. [j]**7.35** *Greeks:* Perhaps Gentiles or Jews who followed Greek customs. [k]**7.39** *had not yet been given his full glory:* In the Gospel of John, Jesus is given his full glory both when he is nailed to the cross and when he is raised from death to sit beside his Father in heaven. [l]**7.40** *the Prophet:* See the note at 1.21. [m]**7.50** *who had earlier come to see Jesus:* See 3.1-21.

[2]Then early the next morning he went to the temple. The people came to him, and he sat down[n] and started teaching them.

[3]The Pharisees and the teachers of the Law of Moses brought in a woman who had been caught in bed with a man who wasn't her husband. They made her stand in the middle of the crowd. [4]Then they said, "Teacher, this woman was caught sleeping with a man who isn't her husband. [5]The Law of Moses teaches that a woman like this should be stoned to death! What do you say?"

[6]They asked Jesus this question, because they wanted to test him and bring some charge against him. But Jesus simply bent over and started writing on the ground with his finger.

[7]They kept on asking Jesus about the woman. Finally, he stood up and said, "If any of you have never sinned, then go ahead and throw the first stone at her!" [8]Once again he bent over and began writing on the ground. [9]The people left one by one, beginning with the oldest. Finally, Jesus and the woman were there alone.

[10]Jesus stood up and asked her, "Where is everyone? Isn't there anyone left to accuse you?"

[11]"No sir," the woman answered.

Then Jesus told her, "I am not going to accuse you either. You may go now, but don't sin anymore."[o]

Jesus Is the Light for the World

[12]Once again Jesus spoke to the people. This time he said, "I am the light for the world! Follow me, and you won't be walking in the dark. You will have the light that gives life."

[13]The Pharisees objected, "You are the only one speaking for yourself, and what you say isn't true!"

[14]Jesus replied:

Even if I do speak for myself, what I say is true! I know where I came from and where I am going. But you don't know where I am from or where I am going. [15]You judge in the same way that everyone else does, but I don't judge anyone. [16]If I did judge, I would judge fairly, because I would not be doing it alone. The Father who sent me is here with me. [17]Your Law requires two witnesses to prove that something is true. [18]I am one of my witnesses, and the Father who sent me is the other one.

[19]"Where is your Father?" they asked.

"You don't know me or my Father!" Jesus answered. "If you knew me, you would know my Father."

[20]Jesus said this while he was still teaching in the place where the temple treasures were stored. But no one arrested him, because his time had not yet come.[p]

You Cannot Go Where I Am Going

[21]Jesus also told them, "I am going away, and you will look for me. But you cannot go where I am going, and you will die with your sins unforgiven."

[22]The people asked, "Does he intend to kill himself? Is that what he means by saying we cannot go where he is going?"

[23]Jesus answered, "You are from below, but I am from above. You belong to this world, but I don't. [24]This is why I said you will die with your sins unforgiven. If you

8.5 *The Law . . . stoned to death:* According to the Law of Moses, a woman caught sleeping with a man who is not her husband, and the man she slept with, are both to be killed by stoning (Lev 20.10,22; Deut 22.22-24). The witnesses are supposed to be the first ones to throw the stones. Only the woman is mentioned in this passage.

8.12 *I am the light for the world:* Jesus is defending his message as true. He has come into the world to help people see who God really is and to show them that God wants to give new life to all people.

8.20 *the place where the temple treasures were stored:* It is not likely that Jesus spoke with the Pharisees inside the temple storage rooms, since only the priests were allowed to go into them. This verse could refer to the part of the temple known as "the court of the women," where offering boxes for the temple treasury were located (Luke 21.1).

Temple Offerings

8.23 *You are from below, but I am from above:* Jesus is referring to the fact that he was sent from God in heaven (above). When he uses the word "below," he is referring to "the world," which is often described in the Scriptures as being opposed to God (15.18-19; Gal 6.14).

---

[n]**8.2** *sat down:* See the note at 6.3,4.   [o]**8.11** *don't sin anymore:* Verses 1-11 are not in some manuscripts. In other manuscripts these verses are placed after 7.36 or after 21.25 or after Luke 21.38, with some differences in the text.   [p]**8.20** *his time had not yet come:* See the note at 2.4.

don't have faith in me for who I am,[q] you will die, and your sins will not be forgiven."

[25]"Who are you?" they asked Jesus.

Jesus answered, "I am exactly who I told you at the beginning. [26]There is a lot more I could say to condemn you. But the one who sent me is truthful, and I tell the people of this world only what I have heard from him."

[27]No one understood that Jesus was talking to them about the Father.

[28]Jesus went on to say, "When you have lifted up the Son of Man,[r] you will know who I am. You will also know that I don't do anything on my own. I say only what my Father taught me. [29]The one who sent me is with me. I always do what pleases him, and he will never leave me."

[30]After Jesus said this, many of the people put their faith in him.

The Truth Will Set You Free

[31]Jesus told the people who had faith in him, "If you keep on obeying what I have said, you truly are my disciples. [32]You will know the truth, and the truth will set you free."

[33]They answered, "We are Abraham's children! We have never been anyone's slaves. How can you say we will be set free?"

[34]Jesus replied:

I tell you for certain that anyone who sins is a slave of sin! [35]And slaves don't stay in the family forever, though the Son will always remain in the family. [36]If the Son gives you freedom, you are free! [37]I know that you are from Abraham's family. Yet you want to kill me, because my message isn't really in your hearts. [38]I am telling you what my Father has shown me, just as you are doing what your father has taught you.

Your Father Is the Devil

[39]The people said to Jesus, "Abraham is our father!"

Jesus replied, "If you were Abraham's children, you would do what Abraham did. [40]Instead, you want to kill me for telling you the truth that God gave me. Abraham never did anything like that. [41]But you are doing exactly what your father does."

"Don't accuse us of having someone else as our father!" they said. "We just have one father, and he is God."

[42]Jesus answered:

If God were your Father, you would love me, because I came from God and now I am here. He sent me. I did not come on my own. [43]Why can't you understand what I am talking about? Can't you stand to hear what I am saying? [44]Your father is the devil, and you do exactly what he wants. He has always been a murderer and a liar. There is nothing truthful about him. He speaks on his own, and everything he says is a lie. Not only is he a liar himself, but he is also the father of all lies. [45]Everything I have told you is true, and you still refuse to have faith in me. [46]Can any of you accuse me of sin? If you cannot, why won't you have faith in me? After all, I am telling you the truth. [47]Anyone who belongs to God will listen to his message. But you refuse to listen, because you don't belong to God.

[q]8.24 *I am:* For the Jewish people the most holy name of God is "Yahweh," which may be translated "I am." In the Gospel of John "I am" is sometimes used by Jesus to show that he is that one. [r]8.28 *lifted up the Son of Man:* See the note at 7.39.

Jesus and Abraham

48The people told Jesus, "We were right to say that you are a Samaritan[s] and that you have a demon in you!"

49Jesus answered, "I don't have a demon in me. I honor my Father, and you refuse to honor me. **50**I don't want honor for myself. But there is one who wants me to be honored, and he is also the one who judges. **51**I tell you for certain that if you obey my words, you will never die."

52Then the people said, "Now we are sure that you have a demon. Abraham is dead, and so are the prophets. How can you say that no one who obeys your words will ever die? **53**Are you greater than our father Abraham? He died, and so did the prophets. Who do you think you are?"

54Jesus replied, "If I honored myself, it would mean nothing. My Father is the one who honors me. You claim that he is your God, **55**even though you don't really know him. If I said I didn't know him, I would be a liar, just like all of you. But I know him, and I do what he says. **56**Your father Abraham was really glad to see me."

57"You are not even 50 years old!" they said. "How could you have seen Abraham?"

58Jesus answered, "I tell you for certain that even before Abraham was, I was, and I am."[t] **59**The people picked up stones to kill Jesus, but he hid and left the temple.

Jesus Heals a Man Born Blind

9 As Jesus walked along, he saw a man who had been blind since birth. **2**Jesus' disciples asked, "Teacher, why was this man born blind? Was it because he or his parents sinned?"

3"No, it wasn't!" Jesus answered. "But because of his blindness, you will see God work a miracle for him. **4**As long as it is day, we must do what the one who sent me wants me to do. When night comes, no one can work. **5**While I am in the world, I am the light for the world."

6After Jesus said this, he spit on the ground. He made some mud and smeared it on the man's eyes. **7**Then he said, "Go wash off the mud in Siloam Pool." The man went and washed in Siloam, which means "One Who Is Sent." When he had washed off the mud, he could see.

8The man's neighbors and the people who had seen him begging wondered if he really could be the same man. **9**Some of them said he was the same beggar, while others said he only looked like him. But he told them, "I am that man."

10"Then how can you see?" they asked.

11He answered, "Someone named Jesus made some mud and smeared it on my eyes. He told me to go and wash it off in Siloam Pool. When I did, I could see."

12"Where is he now?" they asked.

"I don't know," he answered.

The Pharisees Try To Find Out What Happened

13-14 The day when Jesus made the mud and healed the man was a Sabbath. So the people took the man to the Pharisees. **15**They asked him how he was able to see, and he answered, "Jesus made some mud and smeared it on my eyes. Then after I washed it off, I could see."

16Some of the Pharisees said, "This man Jesus doesn't come from God. If he did, he would not break the law of the Sabbath."

Others asked, "How could someone who is a sinner work such a miracle?"[u]

---

[s]8.48 *Samaritan:* See 4.9 and the note there. [t]8.58 *I am:* See the note at 8.24. [u]9.16 *miracle:* See the note at 2.11.

8.52 *Abraham is dead, and so are the prophets:* The people do not understand what Jesus means when he tells them that they will never die if they obey him (7.51). At this time, there were differing opinions about eternal life.

8.56 *Abraham was really glad to see me:* Jesus is saying that Abraham was able to see how the promises God made to Abraham would be fulfilled.

9.2 *because he or his parents sinned:* At the time of Jesus, some believed that a person who was blind was being punished by God for sinning, or for the sin of his or her parents (Exod 20.5).

9.4 *When night comes:* Night is a place of darkness, which often symbolizes a lack of understanding. Jesus may also be referring to a time of judgment.

9.7 *Siloam Pool:* This pool is actually a reservoir that was constructed inside the walls of Jerusalem at the time of King Hezekiah (715–687 B.C.). It was located in the valley below and south of the Jerusalem temple. Those who knew the Jewish Scriptures would have been reminded of the time when the prophet Elisha told Naaman, the man with leprosy, to go wash in the Jordan River (2 Kgs 5.1-14). Like the man born blind, Naaman was healed. **(See Map 13 on pg 1891.)**

9.13-14 *Sabbath:* When Jesus healed the blind man, he was accused of violating the Sabbath law (9.16).

9.22-23 *no one was to have any-thing to do with:* The Jewish leaders were going to reject (9.34) anyone who became a follower of Jesus.

Messiah (Chosen One)

9.24 *Jesus is a sinner:* The leaders thought Jesus was a sinner because he did not follow the Law of Moses.

9.41 *If you were blind:* Jesus is saying that those who are blind spiritually but open to the truth are not guilty. But those who claim they understand the truth (based on the Law of Moses) but will not trust Jesus continue to be guilty.

10.2-3 *gatekeeper . . . gate:* The gatekeeper decided who or what got into the sheep pen. Often the gate-keeper was the shepherd himself, who counted the sheep as they entered the pen for the night. The gate was the only way to go into or out of the pen.

10.2-3 *sheep . . . shepherd's voice:* In the Scriptures, sheep and flocks of sheep are symbols for God's people. A "Good Shepherd" was an early Christian symbol for Christ, and these symbols have been discovered in stone carvings dating back to the third century A.D.

Shepherds

Since the Pharisees could not agree among themselves, ¹⁷they asked the man, "What do you say about this one who healed your eyes?"

"He is a prophet!" the man told them. ¹⁸But the Jewish leaders would not believe that the man had once been blind. They sent for his parents ¹⁹and asked them, "Is this the son that you said was born blind? How can he now see?"

²⁰The man's parents answered, "We are certain that he is our son, and we know that he was born blind. ²¹But we don't know how he got his sight or who gave it to him. Ask him! He is old enough to speak for himself."

²²⁻²³The man's parents said this because they were afraid of their leaders. The leaders had already agreed that no one was to have anything to do with anyone who said Jesus was the Messiah.

²⁴The leaders called the man back and said, "Swear by God to tell the truth! We know that Jesus is a sinner."

²⁵The man replied, "I don't know if he is a sinner or not. All I know is that I used to be blind, but now I can see!"

²⁶"What did he do to you?" they asked. "How did he heal your eyes?"

²⁷The man answered, "I have already told you once, and you refused to listen. Why do you want me to tell you again? Do you also want to become his disciples?"

²⁸The leaders insulted the man and said, "You are his follower! We are followers of Moses. ²⁹We are sure God spoke to Moses, but we don't even know where Jesus comes from."

³⁰"How strange!" the man replied. "He healed my eyes, and yet you don't know where he comes from. ³¹We know that God listens only to people who love and obey him. God doesn't listen to sinners. ³²And this is the first time in history anyone has ever given sight to someone born blind. ³³Jesus could not do anything unless he came from God."

³⁴The leaders told the man, "You have been a sinner since the day you were born! Do you think you can teach us anything?" Then they said, "You can never come back into any of our synagogues!"

³⁵When Jesus heard what had happened, he went and found the man. Then Jesus asked, "Do you have faith in the Son of Man?"

³⁶He replied, "Sir, if you will tell me who he is, I will put my faith in him."

³⁷"You have already seen him," Jesus answered, "and right now he is talking with you."

³⁸The man said, "Lord, I put my faith in you!" Then he worshiped Jesus.

³⁹Jesus told him, "I came to judge the people of this world. I am here to give sight to the blind and to make blind everyone who can see."

⁴⁰When the Pharisees heard Jesus say this, they asked, "Are we blind?"

⁴¹Jesus answered, "If you were blind, you would not be guilty. But now that you claim to see, you will keep on being guilty."

A Story about Sheep

10 Jesus said:
I tell you for certain only thieves and robbers climb over the fence instead of going in through the gate to the sheep pen. ²⁻³But the gatekeeper opens the gate for the shepherd, and he goes in through it. The sheep know their shepherd's voice. He calls each of them by name and leads them out.

⁴When he has led out all of his sheep, he walks in front of them, and they follow, because they know his voice. ⁵The sheep will not follow strangers. They don't recognize a stranger's voice, and they run away.

[6]Jesus told the people this story. But they did not understand what he was talking about.

Jesus Is the Good Shepherd

[7]Jesus said:

I tell you for certain that I am the gate for the sheep. [8]Everyone who came before me was a thief or a robber, and the sheep did not listen to any of them. [9]I am the gate. All who come in through me will be saved. Through me they will come and go and find pasture. [10]A thief comes only to rob, kill, and destroy. I came so everyone would have life, and have it fully. [11]I am the good shepherd, and the good shepherd gives up his life for his sheep. [12]Hired workers are not like the shepherd. They don't own the sheep, and when they see a wolf coming, they run off and leave the sheep. Then the wolf attacks and scatters the flock. [13]Hired workers run away because they don't care about the sheep.

[14]I am the good shepherd. I know my sheep, and they know me. [15]Just as the Father knows me, I know the Father, and I give up my life for my sheep. [16]I have other sheep that are not in this sheep pen. I must also bring them together, when they hear my voice. Then there will be one flock of sheep and one shepherd.

[17]The Father loves me, because I give up my life, so I may receive it back again. [18]No one takes my life from me. I give it up willingly! I have the power to give it up and the power to receive it back again, just as my Father commanded me to do.

[19]The people took sides because of what Jesus had told them. [20]Many of them said, "He has a demon in him! He is crazy! Why listen to him?"

[21]But others said, "How could anyone with a demon in him say these things? No one like this could give sight to a blind person!"

Jesus Is Rejected

[22]That winter, Jesus was in Jerusalem for the Temple Festival. [23]One day he was walking in the part of the temple known as Solomon's Porch,[v] [24]and the people gathered all around him. They said, "How long are you going to keep us guessing? If you are the Messiah, tell us plainly!"

[25]Jesus answered:

I have told you, and you refused to believe me. The things I do by my Father's authority show who I am. [26]But since you are not my sheep, you don't believe me. [27]My sheep know my voice, and I know them. They follow me, [28]and I give them eternal life, so that they will never be lost. No one can snatch them out of my hand. [29]My Father gave them to me, and he is greater than all others.[w] No one can snatch them from his hands, [30]and I am one with the Father.

[31]Once again the people picked up stones in order to kill Jesus. [32]But he said, "I have shown you many good things my Father sent me to do. Which one are you going to stone me for?"

[33]They answered, "We are not stoning you because of any good thing you did. We are stoning you because you did a terrible thing. You are just a man, and here you are claiming to be God!"

[v]10.23 *Solomon's Porch*: A public place with tall columns along the east side of the temple.
[w]10.29 *he is greater than all others*: Some manuscripts have "they are greater than all others."

10.7 *I am the gate for the sheep*: As the gate for the sheep (his followers), Jesus stands guard and protects them. He also determines who will go through the gate.

10.8 *a thief or a robber*: Jesus is talking about those who have been teaching the people (God's sheep or flock) the Law of Moses in a way that led them away from the truth about what God wants.

10.16 *one flock . . . and one shepherd*: Jesus will help his followers become "one" in spite of their differences (see also Gal 3.26-29).

10.22 *Temple Festival*: This festival is also known as Hanukkah.

10.31 *the people picked up stones*: Anyone who disobeyed the Law of Moses in a way that threatened the purity of the community was to be killed by the joint action of the group (Lev 24.15,16; Deut 21.18-21; 22.20-22). The group would throw big stones to crush and bury the one who was accused of being a threat to all of God's people.

10.33 *you are claiming to be God*: The Jewish leaders accused Jesus of claiming he was God. Since they believed he was only a man, and not God, they said that Jesus was guilty of one of the most horrible offenses against God (blasphemy), which was punishable by death.

11.1-2 *Lazarus . . . had two sisters, Mary and Martha:* The name Lazarus in Hebrew means "God helps." Martha and Mary are mentioned in Luke 10.38-42. Mary is also the one who pours perfume on Jesus' feet in 12.3.

11.1-2 *Bethany:* A small village about two miles east of Jerusalem. **(See Map 12 on pg 1890.)**

11.11 *Lazarus is asleep:* Jesus meant that Lazarus was dead (11.13). Jesus would "wake him up" by bringing him back to life from the dead.

11.16 *Thomas:* Thomas was one of Jesus' twelve close apostles (disciples). His Aramaic name means "Twin." Thomas is sometimes known as "doubting Thomas," because he refused at first to believe that Jesus had been raised from death.

11.17 *tomb:* Tombs were usually carved out of the soft limestone hillsides in Palestine. Most tombs had more than one room and burial chamber. Each chamber held one body. A large circular stone was sometimes used to seal the entrance to the tomb.

11.24 *raised to life on the last day:* Martha apparently believed in the hope of life after death.

Eternal Life

[34]Jesus replied:

In your Scriptures doesn't God say, "You are gods"? [35]You can't argue with the Scriptures, and God spoke to those people and called them gods. [36]So why do you accuse me of a terrible sin for saying that I am the Son of God? After all, it is the Father who prepared me for this work. He is also the one who sent me into the world. [37]If I don't do as my Father does, you should not believe me. [38]But if I do what my Father does, you should believe because of that, even if you don't have faith in me. Then you will know for certain that the Father is one with me, and I am one with the Father.

[39]Again they wanted to arrest Jesus. But he escaped [40]and crossed the Jordan to the place where John had earlier been baptizing. While Jesus was there, [41]many people came to him. They were saying, "John didn't work any miracles, but everything he said about Jesus is true." [42]A lot of those people also put their faith in Jesus.

The Death of Lazarus

11 [1-2]A man by the name of Lazarus was sick in the village of Bethany. He had two sisters, Mary and Martha. This was the same Mary who later poured perfume on the Lord's head and wiped his feet with her hair. [3]The sisters sent a message to the Lord and told him that his good friend Lazarus was sick.

[4]When Jesus heard this, he said, "His sickness won't end in death. It will bring glory to God and his Son."

[5]Jesus loved Martha and her sister and brother. [6]But he stayed where he was for two more days. [7]Then he said to his disciples, "Now we will go back to Judea."

[x]11.24 *the last day:* When God will judge all people.

[8]"Teacher," they said, "the people there want to stone you to death! Why do you want to go back?"

[9]Jesus answered, "Aren't there twelve hours in each day? If you walk during the day, you will have light from the sun, and you won't stumble. [10]But if you walk during the night, you will stumble, because you don't have any light." [11]Then he told them, "Our friend Lazarus is asleep, and I am going there to wake him up."

[12]They replied, "Lord, if he is asleep, he will get better." [13]Jesus really meant that Lazarus was dead, but they thought he was talking only about sleep.

[14]Then Jesus told them plainly, "Lazarus is dead! [15]I am glad I wasn't there, because now you will have a chance to put your faith in me. Let's go to him."

[16]Thomas, whose nickname was "Twin," said to the other disciples, "Come on. Let's go, so we can die with him."

Jesus Brings Lazarus to Life

[17]When Jesus got to Bethany, he found that Lazarus had already been in the tomb four days. [18]Bethany was only about two miles from Jerusalem, [19]and many people had come from the city to comfort Martha and Mary because their brother had died.

[20]When Martha heard that Jesus had arrived, she went out to meet him, but Mary stayed in the house. [21]Martha said to Jesus, "Lord, if you had been here, my brother would not have died. [22]Yet even now I know that God will do anything you ask."

[23]Jesus told her, "Your brother will live again!"

[24]Martha answered, "I know he will be raised to life on the last day,[x] when all the dead are raised."

[25]Jesus then said, "I am the one who

Jesus said, *"I am the one who raises the dead to life!"*
JOHN 11.25

raises the dead to life! Everyone who has faith in me will live, even if they die. **26**And everyone who lives because of faith in me will never really die. Do you believe this?"

27"Yes, Lord!" she replied. "I believe you are the Christ, the Son of God. You are the one we hoped would come into the world."

28After Martha said this, she went and privately said to her sister Mary, "The Teacher is here, and he wants to see you." **29**As soon as Mary heard this, she got up and went out to Jesus. **30**He was still outside the village where Martha had gone to meet him. **31**Many people had come to comfort Mary, and when they saw her quickly leave the house, they thought she was going out to the tomb to cry. So they followed her.

32Mary went to where Jesus was. Then as soon as she saw him, she knelt at his feet and said, "Lord, if you had been here, my brother would not have died."

33When Jesus saw that Mary and the people with her were crying, he was terribly upset **34**and asked, "Where have you put his body?"

They replied, "Lord, come and you will see."

35Jesus started crying, **36**and the people said, "See how much he loved Lazarus."

37Some of them said, "He gives sight to the blind. Why couldn't he have kept Lazarus from dying?"

38Jesus was still terribly upset. So he went to the tomb, which was a cave with a stone rolled against the entrance. **39**Then he told the people to roll the stone away. But Martha said, "Lord, you know that Lazarus has been dead four days, and there will be a bad smell."

40Jesus replied, "Didn't I tell you that if you had faith, you would see the glory of God?"

41After the stone had been rolled aside, Jesus looked up toward heaven and prayed, "Father, I thank you for answering my prayer. **42**I know that you always answer my prayers. But I said this, so the people here would believe you sent me."

43When Jesus had finished praying, he shouted, "Lazarus, come out!" **44**The man who had been dead came out. His hands and feet were wrapped with strips of burial cloth, and a cloth covered his face.

Jesus then told the people, "Untie him and let him go."

The Plot To Kill Jesus

(Matthew 26.1-5; Mark 14.1,2; Luke 22.1,2)

45Many of the people who had come to visit Mary saw the things Jesus did, and they put their faith in him. **46**Others went to the Pharisees and told what Jesus had done. **47**Then the chief priests and the Pharisees called the council together and said, "What should we do? This man is working a lot of miracles.*y* **48**If we don't stop him now, everyone will put their faith in him. Then the Romans will come and destroy our temple and our nation."*z*

49One of the council members was Caiaphas, who was also high priest that year. He spoke up and said, "You people don't have any sense at all! **50**Don't you know it is better for one person to die for the people than for the whole nation to be destroyed?" **51**Caiaphas did not say this on his own. As high priest that year, he was prophesying that Jesus would die for the nation. **52**Yet Jesus would not die just for

CR　Son of God

● **11.39** *a bad smell:* A body that had been dead for four days would have begun to decay, causing a bad odor to come from the tomb. Martha was concerned with the practical fact that the body would smell when Jesus goes in to look at it.

● **11.44** *strips of burial cloth:* In Jesus' day, dead bodies were usually wrapped in strips of linen cloth. Sometimes sweet-smelling spices and ointments were also put on the body. A single piece of cloth was used to cover the face of the person who had died.

CR　Burial

● **11.48** *destroy our temple and our nation:* The Jewish leaders were afraid that Jesus would lead his followers to rebel against Rome and that the Roman army would then destroy their nation and the temple. They were also afraid that if many people started to follow Jesus and his teachings, their own power would be lessened.

● **11.49** *Caiaphas:* Caiaphas was the high priest in Jerusalem from A.D. 18 to 37. As head of the priests in the temple, Caiaphas had great power among the religious and political leaders of Israel.

11.52 *bring together all of God's scattered people:* Though God had chosen Israel (the Jewish nation), people of all nations are invited to be part of God's new family.

11.53 *council:* They probably hoped to arrest and kill Jesus during the time of the upcoming Passover Festival.

11.54 *Ephraim:* This village was probably north of Jerusalem on the border of the Judean desert toward the Jordan River.

12.4 *Judas Iscariot:* Judas was the disciple in charge of the moneybag that was used to support Jesus and the disciples and to give to the poor.

12.5 *300 silver coins:* One silver coin was equal to one day's pay for a worker. The ointment was worth nearly a year's wages.

12.7 *for the day of my burial:* Without knowing, Mary was preparing Jesus ahead of time for his burial.

≪ Burial

12.10 *chief priests made plans to kill Lazarus:* They wanted to kill Lazarus because he was living proof of Jesus' power (12.11).

12.15 *donkey:* See Zechariah 9.9, which predicts the coming of Israel's king on a donkey. Roman leaders, on the other hand, usually rode large horses when they entered a city in a parade.

the Jewish nation. He would die to bring together all of God's scattered people. ⁵³From that day on, the council started making plans to put Jesus to death.

⁵⁴Because of this plot against him, Jesus stopped going around in public. He went to the town of Ephraim, which was near the desert, and he stayed there with his disciples.

⁵⁵It was almost time for Passover. Many of the Jewish people who lived out in the country had come to Jerusalem to get themselves ready[a] for the festival. ⁵⁶They looked around for Jesus. Then when they were in the temple, they asked each other, "You don't think he will come here for Passover, do you?"

⁵⁷The chief priests and the Pharisees told the people to let them know if any of them saw Jesus. This is how they hoped to arrest him.

At Bethany
(Matthew 26.6-13; Mark 14.3-9)

12 Six days before Passover Jesus went back to Bethany, where he had raised Lazarus from death. ²A meal had been prepared for Jesus. Martha was doing the serving, and Lazarus himself was there. ³Mary took a very expensive bottle of perfume[b] and poured it on Jesus' feet. She wiped them with her hair, and the sweet smell of the perfume filled the house. ⁴A disciple named Judas Iscariot[c] was there. He was the one who was going to betray Jesus, and he asked, ⁵"Why wasn't this perfume sold for 300 silver coins and the money given to the poor?" ⁶Judas did not

really care about the poor. He asked this because he carried the moneybag and sometimes would steal from it.

⁷Jesus replied, "Leave her alone! She has kept this perfume for the day of my burial. ⁸You will always have the poor with you, but you won't always have me."

A Plot To Kill Lazarus

⁹A lot of people came when they heard that Jesus was there. They also wanted to see Lazarus, because Jesus had raised him from death. ¹⁰So the chief priests made plans to kill Lazarus. ¹¹He was the reason that many of the people were turning from them and putting their faith in Jesus.

Jesus Enters Jerusalem
(Matthew 21.1-11; Mark 11.1-11; Luke 19.28-40)

¹²The next day a large crowd was in Jerusalem for Passover. When they heard that Jesus was coming for the festival, ¹³they took palm branches and went out to greet him.[d] They shouted,

"Hooray![e]
God bless the one who comes
in the name of the Lord!
God bless the King
of Israel!"

¹⁴Jesus found a donkey and rode on it, just as the Scriptures say,

¹⁵"People of Jerusalem,
don't be afraid!
Your King is now coming,
and he is riding
on a donkey."

[a]11.55 *get themselves ready:* The Jewish people had to do certain things to prepare themselves to worship God.   [b]12.3 *very expensive bottle of perfume:* The Greek text has "expensive perfume made of pure spikenard," a plant used to make perfume.   [c]12.4 *Iscariot:* See the note at 6.71.   [d]12.13 *took palm branches and went out to greet him:* This was one way the people welcomed a famous person.   [e]12.13 *Hooray:* This translates a word that can mean "please save us." But it is most often used as a shout of praise to God.

[16]At first, Jesus' disciples did not understand. But after he had been given his glory,[f] they remembered all this. Everything had happened exactly as the Scriptures said it would.

[17-18]A crowd had come to meet Jesus because they had seen him call Lazarus out of the tomb. They kept talking about him and this miracle.[g] [19]But the Pharisees said to each other, "There is nothing we can do! Everyone in the world is following Jesus."

Some Greeks Want To Meet Jesus

[20]Some Greeks[h] had gone to Jerusalem to worship during Passover. [21]Philip from Bethsaida in Galilee was there too. So they went to him and said, "Sir, we would like to meet Jesus." [22]Philip told Andrew. Then the two of them went to Jesus and told him.

The Son of Man Must Be Lifted Up

[23]Jesus said:

The time has come for the Son of Man to be given his glory.[i] [24]I tell you for certain that a grain of wheat that falls on the ground will never be more than one grain unless it dies. But if it dies, it will produce lots of wheat. [25]If you love your life, you will lose it. If you give it up in this world, you will be given eternal life. [26]If you serve me, you must go with me. My servants will be with me wherever I am. If you serve me, my Father will honor you.

[27]Now I am deeply troubled, and I don't know what to say. But I must not ask my Father to keep me from this time of suffering. In fact, I came into the world to suffer. [28]So Father, bring glory to yourself.

A voice from heaven then said, "I have already brought glory to myself, and I will do it again!" [29]When the crowd heard the voice, some of them thought it was thunder. Others thought an angel had spoken to Jesus.

[30]Then Jesus told the crowd, "That voice spoke to help you, not me. [31]This world's people are now being judged, and the ruler of this world[j] is already being thrown out! [32]If I am lifted up above the earth, I will make everyone want to come to me." [33]Jesus was talking about the way he would be put to death.

[34]The crowd said to Jesus, "The Scriptures teach that the Messiah will live forever. How can you say that the Son of Man must be lifted up? Who is this Son of Man?"

[35]Jesus answered, "The light will be with you for only a little longer. Walk in the light while you can. Then you won't be caught walking blindly in the dark. [36]Have faith in the light while it is with you, and you will be children of the light."

The People Refuse To Have Faith in Jesus

After Jesus had said these things, he left and went into hiding. [37]He had worked a lot of miracles[k] among the people, but they were still not willing to have faith in him. [38]This happened so that what the prophet Isaiah had said would come true,

"Lord, who has believed
our message?
And who has seen
your mighty strength?"

[f]**12.16** *had been given his glory*: See the note at 7.39.   [g]**12.17,18** *miracle*: See the note at 2.11.
[h]**12.20** *Greeks*: Perhaps Gentiles who worshiped with the Jews. See the note at 7.35.   [i]**12.23** *be given his glory*: See the note at 7.39.   [j]**12.31** *world*: In the Gospel of John "world" sometimes refers to the people who live in this world and to the evil forces that control their lives.   [k]**12.37** *miracles*: See the note at 2.11.

12.27 *I came into the world to suffer*: Jesus knows that he will fulfill God's purposes by suffering death on a cross. His death would also bring glory to God the Father (7.39 and 2.4).

12.28,29 *voice from heaven ... thunder*: The voice is from God, but some think the voice is thunder and others think it is an angel. Thunder is linked with God's voice in the Bible (Exod 19.6; Ps 29; 1 Sam 7.9,10; Rev 14.2).

12.31 *ruler of this world*: This is one of John's names for the devil, sometimes called Satan, who is the leader of the forces in the world that are against God and God's people (8.44; 14.30; and 16.11).

12.32 *lifted up above the earth*: Jesus used these words to refer both to the time when he will be nailed to a cross (12.33) and when he will be raised from death to live with God in heaven.

12.34 *Messiah will live forever*: No specific passage in the Jewish Scriptures says this, but the people may be referring to the promise that the family of King David would rule forever (2 Sam 5; Ps 89.36; Isa 9.7). The people didn't understand why—if Jesus was the Messiah—he would have to be "lifted up," which here means put to death on a cross.

12.42 *Pharisees . . . given orders:* The Pharisees were in charge of many of the Jewish synagogues. Some Jewish leaders had secretly put their faith in Jesus, but they were afraid to be open about this, for fear that they would be thrown out of the Jewish synagogues by the Pharisees.

12.44 *Everyone who has faith in me:* Jesus is saying that when people put their trust in him it is the same as putting their trust in God.

Faith

13.1 *before Passover:* In JOHN, it is not clear just how long before the Passover this meal takes place. In the other Gospels, Jesus' last supper with the disciples is the Passover meal (see Mark 14.12, for example).

Satan

13.5 *began washing his disciples' feet:* In ancient Jewish society, it was the duty of the servant to wash his or her master's feet. Jesus takes the job of a servant and washes his disciples' feet. The foot washing is a symbol of his great servant act to come, dying on the cross for the sins of the world.

13.6 *Simon Peter:* Peter's questions and argument are understandable, since Jesus was the master.

13.11 *except for one of you:* Jesus was talking about Judas (13.2).

39The people could not have faith in Jesus, because Isaiah had also said,

40"The Lord has blinded
  the eyes of the people,
and he has made
  the people stubborn.
He did this so that they
  could not see
  or understand,
and so that they
  would not turn to the Lord
  and be healed."

41Isaiah said this, because he saw the glory of Jesus and spoke about him.[l] 42Even then, many of the leaders put their faith in Jesus, but they did not tell anyone about it. The Pharisees had already given orders for the people not to have anything to do with anyone who had faith in Jesus. 43And besides, the leaders liked praise from others more than they liked praise from God.

Jesus Came To Save the World

44In a loud voice Jesus said:

Everyone who has faith in me also has faith in the one who sent me. 45And everyone who has seen me has seen the one who sent me. 46I am the light that has come into the world. No one who has faith in me will stay in the dark.

47I am not the one who will judge those who refuse to obey my teachings. I came to save the people of this world, not to be their judge. 48But everyone who rejects me and my teachings will be judged on the last day[m] by what I have said. 49I don't speak on my own. I say only what the Father who sent me has told me to say. 50I know that his commands will bring

eternal life. This is why I tell you exactly what the Father has told me.

Jesus Washes the Feet of His Disciples

13 It was before Passover, and Jesus knew that the time had come for him to leave this world and to return to the Father. He had always loved his followers in this world, and he loved them to the very end.

2Even before the evening meal started, the devil had made Judas, the son of Simon Iscariot,[n] decide to betray Jesus. 3Jesus knew he had come from God and would go back to God. He also knew that the Father had given him complete power. 4So during the meal Jesus got up, removed his outer garment, and wrapped a towel around his waist. 5He put some water into a large bowl. Then he began washing his disciples' feet and drying them with the towel he was wearing.

6But when he came to Simon Peter, this disciple asked, "Lord, are you going to wash my feet?"

7Jesus answered, "You don't really know what I am doing, but later you will understand."

8"You will never wash my feet!" Peter replied.

"If I don't wash you," Jesus told him, "you don't really belong to me."

9Peter said, "Lord, don't wash just my feet. Wash my hands and my head."

10Jesus answered, "People who have bathed and are clean all over need to wash just their feet. And you, my disciples, are clean, except for one of you." 11Jesus knew who would betray him. That is why he said, "except for one of you."

---

[l]**12.41** *he saw the glory of Jesus and spoke about him:* Or "he saw the glory of God and spoke about Jesus." [m]**12.48** *the last day:* See the note at 6.39. [n]**13.2** *Iscariot:* See the note at 6.71.

12After Jesus had washed his disciples' feet and had put his outer garment back on, he sat down again.**o** Then he said:

Do you understand what I have done? **13**You call me your teacher and Lord, and you should, because that is who I am. **14**And if your Lord and teacher has washed your feet, you should do the same for each other. **15**I have set the example, and you should do for each other exactly what I have done for you. **16**I tell you for certain that servants are not greater than their master, and messengers are not greater than the one who sent them. **17**You know these things, and God will bless you, if you do them.

18I am not talking about all of you. I know the ones I have chosen. But what the Scriptures say must come true. And they say, "The man who ate with me has turned against me!" **19**I am telling you this before it all happens. Then when it does happen, you will believe who I am.**p** **20**I tell you for certain that anyone who welcomes my messengers also welcomes me, and anyone who welcomes me welcomes the one who sent me.

Jesus Tells What Will Happen to Him
(Matthew 26.20-25; Mark 14.17-21; Luke 22.21-23)

21After Jesus had said these things, he was deeply troubled and told his disciples, "I tell you for certain that one of you will betray me." **22**They were confused about what he meant. And they just stared at each other.

23Jesus' favorite disciple was sitting next to him at the meal, **24**and Simon motioned for this disciple to find out which one Jesus meant. **25**So the disciple leaned toward Jesus and asked, "Lord, which one of us are you talking about?"

26Jesus answered, "I will dip this piece of bread in the sauce and give it to the one I was talking about."

Then Jesus dipped the bread and gave it to Judas, the son of Simon Iscariot.**q** **27**Right then Satan took control of Judas.

Jesus said, "Judas, go quickly and do what you have to do." **28**No one at the meal understood what Jesus meant. **29**But because Judas was in charge of the money, some of them thought that Jesus had told him to buy something they needed for the festival. Others thought that Jesus had told him to give some money to the poor. **30**Judas took the piece of bread and went out.

It was already night.

The New Command

31After Judas had gone, Jesus said:

Now the Son of Man will be given glory, and he will bring glory to God. **32**Then, after God is given glory because of him, God will bring glory to him, and God will do it very soon. **33**My children, I will be with you for only a little while longer. Then you will look for me, but you won't find me. I tell you just as I told the people, "You cannot go where I am going." **34**But I am giving you a new command. You must love each other, just as I have loved you. **35**If you love each other, everyone will know that you are my disciples.

o13.12 *sat down again:* On special occasions the Jewish people followed the Greek and Roman custom of lying down on their left side and leaning on their left elbow, while eating with their right hand. **p13.19** *I am:* See the note at 8.24. **q13.26** *Iscariot:* See the note at 6.71.

13.12 *sat down:* This means that Jesus returned to his place at the meal.

13.13 *Lord:* The Greek word for "Lord" is *Kyrios,* which may mean "master" or may be used to address someone as "Sir." When applied to Jesus, the word emphasizes his authority and power.

Lord (Title for Jesus)

I am

13.23 *Jesus' favorite disciple:* In JOHN, one disciple is singled out as being Jesus' favorite (19.26 and 20.2). It is not clear exactly which disciple this may be.

13.24 *Simon:* This is Simon Peter.

Son of Man

13.34 *new command . . . love each other:* Jesus' love for his followers is to be the standard for how they will love one another (John 15.12,17; 1 John 3.23; 2 John 5).

Jesus said to his disciples; "I am giving you a new command. You must love each other, just as I have loved you." JOHN 13.34

13.38 *before a rooster crows:* Since roosters crowed at dawn, Jesus is saying that Peter will deny that he knows Jesus three times before the next sunrise.

14.2 *many rooms in my Father's house:* Jesus is talking about heaven.

Heaven

14.6 *Without me, no one can go to the Father:* Jesus here claims that he is the "way" people can learn the "truth" about God and find "life" with God.

I Am

14.9 *Father:* Jesus is saying that Philip and the other disciples will be able to do what Jesus has been doing— preaching the good news and working miracles (14.12). They will be able to do this because of the gift of the Holy Spirit.

Holy Spirit

14.22 *The other Judas, not Judas Iscariot:* This Judas may be Judas, the son of James mentioned in Luke 6.16 and Acts 1.13.

Peter's Promise

(Matthew 26.31-35; Mark 14.27-31; Luke 22.31-34)

36Simon Peter asked, "Lord, where are you going?"

Jesus answered, "You can't go with me now, but later on you will."

37Peter asked, "Lord, why can't I go with you now? I would die for you!"

38"Would you really die for me?" Jesus asked. "I tell you for certain before a rooster crows, you will say three times that you don't even know me."

Jesus Is the Way to the Father

14 Jesus said to his disciples, "Don't be worried! Have faith in God and have faith in me.[r] **2**There are many rooms in my Father's house. I wouldn't tell you this, unless it was true. I am going there to prepare a place for each of you. **3**After I have done this, I will come back and take you with me. Then we will be together. **4**You know the way to where I am going."

5Thomas said, "Lord, we don't even know where you are going! How can we know the way?"

6"I am the way, the truth, and the life!" Jesus answered. "Without me, no one can go to the Father. **7**If you had really known me, you would have known the Father. But from now on, you do know him, and you have seen him."

8Philip said, "Lord, show us the Father. That is all we need."

9Jesus replied:

Philip, I have been with you for a long time. Don't you know who I am? If you have seen me, you have seen the Father. How can you ask me to show you the Father? **10**Don't you believe that I am one with the Father and that the Father is one with me? What I say isn't said on my own. The Father who lives in me does these things.

11Have faith in me when I say that the Father is one with me and that I am one with the Father. Or else have faith in me simply because of the things I do. **12**I tell you for certain that if you have faith in me, you will do the same things I am doing. You will do even greater things, now that I am going back to the Father. **13**Ask me, and I will do whatever you ask. This way the Son will bring honor to the Father. **14**I will do whatever you ask me to do.

The Holy Spirit Is Promised

15Jesus said to his disciples:

If you love me, you will do as I command. **16**Then I will ask the Father to send you the Holy Spirit who will help[s] you and always be with you. **17**The Spirit will show you what is true. The people of this world cannot accept the Spirit, because they don't see or know him. But you know the Spirit, who is with you and will keep on living in you.

18I won't leave you like orphans. I will come back to you. **19**In a little while the people of this world won't be able to see me, but you will see me. And because I live, you will live. **20**Then you will know I am one with the Father. You will know you are one with me, and I am one with you. **21**If you love me, you will do what I have said, and my Father will love you. I will also love you and show you what I am like. **22**The other Judas, not Judas Iscariot,[t]

[r]**14.1** *Have faith in God and have faith in me:* Or "You have faith in God, so have faith in me."   [s]**14.16** *help:* The Greek word may mean "comfort," "encourage," or "defend."   [t]**14.22** *Iscariot:* See the note at 6.71.

Jesus said, *"I am the way, the truth, and the life!"*
JOHN 14.6

then spoke up and asked, "Lord, what do you mean by saying that you will show us what you are like, but you will not show the people of this world?"

²³Jesus replied:

If anyone loves me, they will obey me. Then my Father will love them, and we will come to them and live in them. ²⁴But anyone who doesn't love me, won't obey me. What they have heard me say doesn't really come from me, but from the Father who sent me.

²⁵I have told you these things while I am still with you. ²⁶But the Holy Spirit will come and help[u] you, because the Father will send the Spirit to take my place. The Spirit will teach you everything and will remind you of what I said while I was with you.

²⁷I give you peace, the kind of peace only I can give. It isn't like the peace this world can give. So don't be worried or afraid.

²⁸You have already heard me say I am going and I will also come back to you. If you really love me, you should be glad I am going back to the Father, because he is greater than I am.

²⁹I am telling you this before I leave, so when it does happen, you will have faith in me. ³⁰I cannot speak with you much longer, because the ruler of this world is coming. But he has no power over me. ³¹I obey my Father, so everyone in the world might know that I love him.

It is time for us to go now.

Jesus Is the True Vine

15 Jesus said to his disciples:

I am the true vine, and my Father is the gardener. ²He cuts away every branch of mine that doesn't produce fruit. But he trims clean every branch that does produce fruit, so that it will produce even more fruit. ³You are already clean because of what I have said to you.

⁴Stay joined to me, and I will stay joined to you. Just as a branch cannot produce fruit unless it stays joined to the vine, you cannot produce fruit unless you stay joined to me. ⁵I am the vine, and you are the branches. If you stay joined to me, and I stay joined to you, then you will produce lots of fruit. But you cannot do anything without me. ⁶If you don't stay joined to me, you will be thrown away. You will be like dry branches that are gathered up and burned in a fire.

⁷Stay joined to me and let my teachings become part of you. Then you can pray for whatever you want, and your prayer will be answered. ⁸When you become fruitful disciples of mine, my Father will be honored. ⁹I have loved you, just as my Father has loved me. So remain faithful to my love for you. ¹⁰If you obey me, I will keep loving you, just as my Father keeps loving me, because I have obeyed him.

¹¹I have told you this to make you as completely happy as I am. ¹²Now I tell you to love each other, as I have loved you. ¹³The greatest way to show love for friends is to die for them. ¹⁴And you are my friends, if you obey me. ¹⁵Servants don't know what their master is doing, and so I don't speak to you as my servants. I speak to you as my friends, and I have told you everything my Father has told me.

¹⁶You did not choose me. I chose you and sent you out to produce fruit,

[u]**14.26** *help:* See the note at 14.16.

14.27 *peace:* The peace that Jesus gives here is more than simple contentment or the absence of conflict. It is complete well-being and wholeness of mind, body, and spirit.

14.28 *going back to the Father:* Jesus is talking about going back to heaven to rule beside God the Father (Luke 24.50,51).

15.1,2 *true vine . . . more fruit:* Jesus says that he is the main vine of the plant, which produces many smaller branches. A farmer who takes care of fruit-bearing vines needs to trim away (prune) old branches that are not giving fruit. Only those branches that stay connected to the vine (Jesus) can produce fruit (15.5). The kind of "fruit" Jesus wants his followers to produce is based on loving God and other people. God's people, Israel, are sometimes pictured in the Jewish Scriptures as a vineyard that did not produce the kind of grapes the owner expected (Isa 5.1-7).

15.15 *Servants:* The word in the New Testament usually translated as "servant" actually means a slave, not a servant hired to do a certain job. Slaves or servants were not considered to be equal to their masters, and masters would not have talked with them as equals, the way two friends would talk together.

Slaves and Servants in the Time of Jesus

15.21 *will do to you exactly what they did to me:* Jesus is saying that some people of the "world" who are not followers of Jesus will treat Jesus' followers badly. Some of Jesus' followers will be put to death, just as Jesus was.

15.22 *sin:* Jesus came to offer all people a chance to turn to God and believe the truth. Many chose not to believe in Jesus' new message.

16.7 *Holy Spirit . . . help you:* The Spirit will show how wrong the world is about sin and reveal the right way to live. The Spirit teaches the truth about God and God's purposes.

Holy Spirit

16.8 *truth . . . God's justice:* Many believed that the laws and rules based on the Law of Moses were the whole truth about what God expected of God's people. Jesus made it clear that some had missed the true message of the Law and misunderstood what God expected. God's justice was meant for all people, not a select group from Israel. Those who did not believe Jesus would have to face God's judgment.

the kind of fruit that will last. Then my Father will give you whatever you ask for in my name.[v] [17]So I command you to love each other.

The World's Hatred

[18]If the people of this world[w] hate you, just remember that they hated me first. [19]If you belonged to the world, its people would love you. But you don't belong to the world. I have chosen you to leave the world behind, and this is why its people hate you. [20]Remember how I told you that servants are not greater than their master. So if people mistreat me, they will mistreat you. If they do what I say, they will do what you say.

[21]People will do to you exactly what they did to me. They will do it because you belong to me, and they don't know the one who sent me. [22]If I had not come and spoken to them, they would not be guilty of sin. But now they have no excuse for their sin.

[23]Everyone who hates me also hates my Father. [24]I have done things no one else has ever done. If they had not seen me do these things, they would not be guilty. But they did see me do these things, and they still hate me and my Father too. [25]This is why the Scriptures are true when they say, "People hated me for no reason."

[26]I will send you the Spirit who comes from the Father and shows what is true. The Spirit will help[x] you and will tell you about me. [27]Then you will also tell others about me, because you have been with me from the beginning.

[16] I am telling you these things, so that you will not turn away. [2]You will be chased out of the synagogues. And the time will come when people will kill you and think they are doing God a favor. [3]They will do these things because they don't know either the Father or me. [4]I am saying this to you now, so that when the time comes, you will remember what I have said.

The Work of the Holy Spirit

I was with you at the first, and so I didn't tell you these things. [5]But now I am going back to the Father who sent me, and none of you asks me where I am going. [6]You are very sad from hearing all of this. [7]But I tell you I am going to do what is best for you. This is why I am going away. The Holy Spirit cannot come to help[x] you until I leave. But after I am gone, I will send the Spirit to you.

[8]The Spirit will come and show the people of this world the truth about sin and God's justice and the judgment. [9]The Spirit will show them that they are wrong about sin, because they didn't have faith in me. [10]They are wrong about God's justice, because I am going to the Father, and you won't see me again. [11]And they are wrong about the judgment, because God has already judged the ruler of this world.

[12]I have much more to say to you, but right now it would be more than you could understand. [13]The Spirit shows what is true and will come and guide you into the full truth. The Spirit doesn't speak on his own. He will tell you only what he has heard

[v]**15.16** *in my name:* Or "because you are my followers." [w]**15.18** *world:* See the note at 12.31.
[x]**15.26; 16.7** *help:* See the note at 14.16.

from me, and he will let you know what is going to happen. **14**The Spirit will bring glory to me by taking my message and telling it to you. **15**Everything the Father has is mine. This is why I have said that the Spirit takes my message and tells it to you.

Sorrow Will Turn into Joy

16Jesus told his disciples, "For a little while you won't see me, but after a while you will see me."

17They said to each other, "What does Jesus mean by saying that for a little while we won't see him, but after a while we will see him? What does he mean by saying he is going to the Father? **18**What is this 'little while' that he is talking about? We don't know what he means."

19Jesus knew they had some questions, so he said:

You are wondering what I meant when I said that for a little while you won't see me, but after a while you will see me. **20**I tell you for certain that you will cry and be sad, but the world will be happy. You will be sad, but later you will be happy.

21When a woman is about to give birth, she is in great pain. But after it is all over, she forgets the pain and is happy, because she has brought a child into the world. **22**You are now very sad. But later I will see you, and you will be so happy that no one will be able to change the way you feel. **23**When that time comes, you won't have to ask me about anything. I tell you for certain the Father will give you whatever you ask for in my name. **24**You have not asked for anything in

this way before, but now you must ask in my name.ʸ Then it will be given to you, so you will be completely happy.

25I have used examples to explain to you what I have been talking about. But the time will come when I will speak to you plainly about the Father and will no longer use examples like these. **26**You will ask the Father in my name,ᶻ and I won't have to ask him for you. **27**God the Father loves you because you love me, and you believe I have come from him. **28**I came from the Father into the world, but I am leaving the world and returning to the Father.

29The disciples said, "Now you are speaking plainly to us! You are not using examples. **30**At last we know that you understand everything, and we don't have any more questions. Now we believe you truly have come from God."

31Jesus replied:

Do you really believe me? **32**The time will come and is already here when all of you will be scattered. Each of you will go back home and leave me by myself. But the Father will be with me, and I won't be alone. **33**I have told you this, so that you might have peace in your hearts because of me. While you are in the world, you will have to suffer. But cheer up! I have defeated the world.ᵃ

Jesus Prays

17 After Jesus had finished speaking to his disciples, he looked up toward heaven and prayed:

Father, the time has come for you to bring glory to your Son, in order that

16.20 *you will cry . . . but the world will be happy:* Jesus was talking about the sadness and fear his followers would feel when he was put to death on a cross (19.17-30). This sadness would be severe, like the pain a woman feels before she gives birth to a baby. However, those who do not have faith in Jesus ("the world"), will be happy to get rid of him.

16.32 *you will be scattered . . . leave me by myself:* Even though the disciples said they knew who Jesus really was, his trial and death would test their courage and faith. Jesus tells them that they will not, at first, stand by him in his suffering (18.15-18,25-27; Mark 14.50,51).

ʸ**16.23,24** *in my name . . . in my name:* Or "as my disciples . . . as my disciples." ᶻ**16.26** *in my name:* Or "because you are my followers." ᵃ**16.33** *world:* See the note at 12.31.

Jesus said to his disciples, "God the Father loves you because you love me, and you believe that I have come from him." JOHN 16.27

Eternal Life

17.12 *the one who had to be lost:* Jesus was talking about Judas Iscariot.

Satan

Truth

17.23 *Then this world's people will know:* Jesus prays that his followers will be one with God and one with each other. The "unity" that Jesus' followers show will help convince the world (unbelievers) that Jesus really did come from God.

he may bring glory to you. **2**And you gave him power over all people, so he would give eternal life to everyone you give him. **3**Eternal life is to know you, the only true God, and to know Jesus Christ, the one you sent. **4**I have brought glory to you here on earth by doing everything you gave me to do. **5**Now, Father, give me back the glory I had with you before the world was created.

6You have given me some followers from this world, and I have shown them what you are like. They were yours, but you gave them to me, and they have obeyed you. **7**They know that you gave me everything I have. **8**I told my followers what you told me, and they accepted it. They know I came from you, and they believe you are the one who sent me. **9**I am praying for them, but not for those who belong to this world.[b] My followers belong to you, and I am praying for them. **10**All I have is yours, and all you have is mine, and they will bring glory to me.

11Holy Father, I am no longer in the world. I am coming to you, but my followers are still in the world. So keep them safe by the power of the name you have given me. Then they will be one with each other, just as you and I are one. **12**While I was with them, I kept them safe by the power you have given me. I guarded them, and not one of them was lost, except the one who had to be lost. This happened so that what the Scriptures say would come true.

13I am on my way to you. But I say these things while I am still in the world, so my followers will have the same complete joy that I do. **14**I have

told them your message. But the people of this world hate them, because they don't belong to this world, just as I don't.

15Father, I don't ask you to take my followers out of the world, but keep them safe from the evil one. **16**They don't belong to this world, and neither do I. **17**Your word is the truth. So let this truth make them completely yours. **18**I am sending them into the world, just as you sent me. **19**I have given myself completely for their sake, so they may belong completely to the truth.

20I am not praying just for these followers. I am also praying for everyone else who will have faith because of what my followers will say about me. **21**I want all of them to be one with each other, just as I am one with you and you are one with me. I also want them to be one with us. Then the people of this world will believe that you sent me.

22I have honored my followers in the same way you honored me, in order that they may be one with each other, just as we are one. **23**I am one with them, and you are one with me, so they may become completely one. Then this world's people will know that you sent me. They will know that you love my followers as much as you love me.

24Father, I want everyone you have given me to be with me, wherever I am. Then they will see the glory you have given me, because you loved me before the world was created. **25**Good Father, the people of this world don't know you. But I know you, and my followers know that you sent me. **26**I

[b]**17.9** *world:* See the note at 12.31.

told them what you are like, and I will tell them even more. Then the love you have for me will become part of them, and I will be one with them.

Jesus Is Betrayed and Arrested
(Matthew 26.47-56; Mark 14.43-50; Luke 22.47-53)

18 When Jesus had finished praying, he and his disciples crossed the Kidron Valley and went into a garden.[c] [2]Jesus had often met there with his disciples, and Judas knew where the place was.

[3-5]Judas had promised to betray Jesus. So he went to the garden with some Roman soldiers and temple police, who had been sent by the chief priests and the Pharisees. They carried torches, lanterns, and weapons. Jesus already knew everything that was going to happen, but he asked, "Who are you looking for?"

They answered, "We are looking for Jesus from Nazareth!"

Jesus told them, "I am Jesus!"[d] [6]At once they all backed away and fell to the ground.

[7]Jesus again asked, "Who are you looking for?"

"We are looking for Jesus from Nazareth," they answered.

[8]This time Jesus replied, "I have already told you that I am Jesus. If I am the one you are looking for, let these others go. [9]Then everything will happen, just as I said, 'I did not lose anyone you gave me.' "

[10]Simon Peter had brought along a sword. He pulled it out and struck at Malchus, the servant of the high priest, cutting off his right ear. [11]Jesus told Peter, "Put your sword away. I must drink from the cup[e] that the Father has given me."

Jesus Is Brought to Annas
(Matthew 26.57,58; Mark 14.53,54; Luke 22.54)

[12]The Roman officer and his men, together with the temple police, arrested Jesus and tied him up. [13]They took him first to Annas, who was the father-in-law of Caiaphas, the high priest that year. [14]This was the same Caiaphas who had told the Jewish leaders, "It is better if one person dies for the people."

Peter Says He Doesn't Know Jesus
(Matthew 26.69,70; Mark 14.66-68; Luke 22.55-57)

[15]Simon Peter and another disciple followed Jesus. That disciple knew the high priest, and he followed Jesus into the courtyard of the high priest's house. [16]Peter stayed outside near the gate. But the other disciple came back out and spoke to the girl at the gate. She let Peter go in, [17]but asked him, "Aren't you one of that man's followers?"

"No, I am not!" Peter answered.

[18]It was cold, and the servants and temple police had made a charcoal fire. They were warming themselves around it, when Peter went over and stood near the fire to warm himself.

Jesus Is Questioned by the High Priest
(Matthew 26.59-66; Mark 14.55-64; Luke 22.66-71)

[19]The high priest questioned Jesus about his followers and his teaching. [20]But Jesus told him, "I have spoken freely in front of everyone. And I have always taught in our

18.1 *Kidron Valley:* This valley runs just east of the temple mount in Jerusalem. Across the Kidron Valley to the east is a high hill known as the Mount of Olives. Near the bottom of that slope was a grove of olive trees, which other Gospels call Gethsemane (Mark 14.32; Matt 26.36). The hill is where the prophet Zechariah (14.1-4) said God would appear and defeat his enemies. It is in this place that Jesus' enemies arrest him. **(See Map 13 on pg 1891.)**

18.3-5 *Roman soldiers...Jesus from Nazareth:* The chief priests and Pharisees may have persuaded the Roman soldiers to make the arrest by saying that Jesus was a dangerous rebel. Jesus was often identified by adding his hometown (Nazareth) to his name, since there were probably many Jewish men named Jesus at the time he lived.

I Am

18.15 *another disciple:* The other disciple who risks his life to go with Jesus before the high priest is probably the same as Jesus' "favorite disciple," who stood at the foot of the cross, and who went with Peter to the tomb.

18.19 *high priest:* In the other Gospels, Jesus goes on trial in front of the high priest and a whole council of Jewish leaders (see Matt 26.57-68; Luke 22.66-71; Mark 14.55-65.)

[c]18.1 *garden:* The Greek word is usually translated "garden," but probably referred to an olive orchard. [d]18.3-5 *I am Jesus:* The Greek text has "I am" (see the note at 8.24). [e]18.11 *drink from the cup:* In the Scriptures a cup is sometimes used as a symbol of suffering. To "drink from the cup" is to suffer.

Synagogues

18.24 *Annas sent him to Caiaphas the high priest:* This verse makes it sound as if Annas was the one questioning Jesus in 18.19, though he was not really the high priest.

18.27 *Once more Peter denied it:* This is the third time Peter denies knowing Jesus.

18.28 *the building where the Roman governor stayed:* Pilate's official residence was in Caesarea, the provincial capital city on the Mediterranean coast. When he was in Jerusalem, Pilate lived at the Antonia Fortress, which overlooked the temple area from the northwest. **(See Map 13 on pg 1891.)**

Pontius Pilate

18.31 *we are not allowed to put anyone to death:* It is most likely that the Roman authorities did not allow Jewish officials to put anyone to death without a clear case of guilt.

18.33 *king of the Jews:* If Jesus admitted to being a real king, he could be put on trial as a political rebel. This crime against Roman authority was punishable by death on a cross.

synagogues and in the temple, where all of our people come together. I have not said anything in secret. ²¹Why are you questioning me? Why don't you ask the people who heard me? They know what I have said."

²²As soon as Jesus said this, one of the temple police hit him and said, "That's no way to talk to the high priest!"

²³Jesus answered, "If I have done something wrong, say so. But if not, why did you hit me?" ²⁴Jesus was still tied up, and Annas sent him to Caiaphas the high priest.

Peter Again Denies that He Knows Jesus

(Matthew 26.71-75; Mark 14.69-72; Luke 22.58-62)

²⁵While Simon Peter was standing there warming himself, someone asked him, "Aren't you one of Jesus' followers?"

Again Peter denied it and said, "No, I am not!"

²⁶One of the high priest's servants was there. He was a relative of the servant whose ear Peter had cut off, and he asked, "Didn't I see you in the garden with that man?"

²⁷Once more Peter denied it, and right then a rooster crowed.

Jesus Is Tried by Pilate

(Matthew 27.1,2,11-14; Mark 15.1-5; Luke 23.1-5)

²⁸It was early in the morning when Jesus was taken from Caiaphas to the building where the Roman governor stayed. But the crowd waited outside. Any of them who had gone inside would have become

unclean and would not be allowed to eat the Passover meal.^f

²⁹Pilate came out and asked, "What charges are you bringing against this man?"

³⁰They answered, "He is a criminal! That's why we brought him to you."

³¹Pilate told them, "Take him and judge him by your own laws."

The crowd replied, "We are not allowed to put anyone to death." ³²And so what Jesus said about his death^g would soon come true.

³³Pilate then went back inside. He called Jesus over and asked, "Are you the king of the Jews?"

³⁴Jesus answered, "Are you asking this on your own or did someone tell you about me?"

³⁵"You know I'm not a Jew!" Pilate said. "Your own people and the chief priests brought him to you. What have you done?"

³⁶Jesus answered, "My kingdom doesn't belong to this world. If it did, my followers would have fought to keep me from being handed over to our leaders. No, my kingdom doesn't belong to this world."

³⁷"So you are a king," Pilate replied.

"You are saying that I am a king," Jesus told him. "I was born into this world to tell about the truth. And everyone who belongs to the truth knows my voice."

³⁸Pilate asked Jesus, "What is truth?"

Jesus Is Sentenced to Death

(Matthew 27.15-31; Mark 15.6-20; Luke 23.13-25)

Pilate went back out and said, "I don't find this man guilty of anything! ³⁹And since I usually set a prisoner free for you at

^f**18.28** *would have become unclean and would not be allowed to eat the Passover meal:* Jewish people who came in close contact with foreigners right before Passover were not allowed to eat the Passover meal. ^g**18.32** *about his death:* Jesus had said that he would die by being "lifted up," which meant that he would die on a cross. The Romans killed criminals by nailing them on a cross, but they did not let the Jews kill anyone in this way.

Passover, would you like for me to set free the king of the Jews?"

40They shouted, "No, not him! We want Barabbas." Now Barabbas was a terrorist.**h**

19 Pilate gave orders for Jesus to be beaten with a whip. **2**The soldiers made a crown out of thorn branches and put it on Jesus. Then they put a purple robe on him. **3**They came up to him and said, "Hey, you king of the Jews!" They also hit him with their fists.

4Once again Pilate went out. This time he said, "I will have Jesus brought out to you again. Then you can see for yourselves that I have not found him guilty."

5Jesus came out, wearing the crown of thorns and the purple robe. Pilate said, "Here is the man!"**i**

6When the chief priests and the temple police saw him, they yelled, "Nail him to a cross! Nail him to a cross!"

Pilate told them, "You take him and nail him to a cross! I don't find him guilty of anything."

7The crowd replied, "He claimed to be the Son of God! Our law says that he must be put to death."

8When Pilate heard this, he was terrified. **9**He went back inside and asked Jesus, "Where are you from?" But Jesus did not answer.

10"Why won't you answer my question?" Pilate asked. "Don't you know I have the power to let you go free or to nail you to a cross?"

11Jesus replied, "If God had not given you the power, you couldn't do anything at all to me. But the one who handed me over to you did something even worse."

12Then Pilate wanted to set Jesus free. But the crowd again yelled, "If you set this man free, you are no friend of the Emperor! Anyone who claims to be a king is an enemy of the Emperor."

13When Pilate heard this, he brought Jesus out. Then he sat down on the judge's bench at the place known as "The Stone Pavement." In Aramaic this pavement is called "Gabbatha." **14**It was about noon on the day before Passover, and Pilate said to the crowd, "Look at your king!"

15"Kill him! Kill him!" they yelled. "Nail him to a cross!"

"So you want me to nail your king to a cross?" Pilate asked.

The chief priests replied, "The Emperor is our king!" **16**Then Pilate handed Jesus over to be nailed to a cross.

Jesus Is Nailed to a Cross
(Matthew 27.32-44; Mark 15.21-32; Luke 23.26-43)

Jesus was taken away, **17**and he carried his cross to a place known as "The Skull."**j** In Aramaic this place is called "Golgotha." **18**There Jesus was nailed to the cross, and on each side of him a man was also nailed to a cross.

19Pilate ordered the charge against Jesus to be written on a board and put above the cross. It read, "Jesus of Nazareth, King of the Jews." **20**The words were written in Hebrew, Latin, and Greek.

The place where Jesus was taken wasn't far from the city, and many of the people read the charge against him. **21**So the chief priests went to Pilate and said, "Why did you write that he is King of the Jews? You should have written, 'He claimed to be King of the Jews.'"

h18.40 *terrorist*: Someone who stirred up trouble against the Romans in the hope of gaining freedom for the Jewish people. **i19.5** *"Here is the man!"*: Or "Look at the man!" **j19.17** *The Skull*: The place was probably given this name because it was near a large rock in the shape of a human skull.

19.1,2 *beaten . . . crown out of thorn branches*: In the Roman Empire, often before a condemned person was nailed to a cross (crucified) he would be mocked and beaten. The "crown" that the soldiers placed on Jesus' head may have been made from the branches of the spiny burnet plant that grows in Palestine.

19.4 *I have not found him guilty*: See also Matt 27.24, which reports that Pilate washed his hands in front of the crowd as a sign that he was not responsible for Jesus' death.

Crucifixion

19.11 *the one who handed me over to you*: The "one" mentioned here might be Judas, Caiaphas, or even Satan.

19.12 *Emperor*: At this time the Roman Emperor was Tiberius Caesar, who ruled the Roman Empire from A.D. 14 to 37.

19.14 *noon on the day before Passover*: At the time Jesus was being put on trial and sentenced to die on the cross, the Passover lambs were being slaughtered and prepared for the next day's Passover meal.

19.15 *"The Emperor is our king"*: Though the chief priests are supposed to serve God, they showed their loyalty to the Roman emperor in order to get Pilate to sentence Jesus to death.

19.29 *jar of cheap wine:* Sometimes inexpensive wine or vinegar was mixed with a drug called gall (Matt 27.34). This mixture reduced some of the pain that the person on the cross was feeling.

19.30 *Everything is done:* Jesus' words show not only that his earthly life was done, but also that the work God had sent him to do, to sacrifice himself for the sins of the world (1.29), had been completed.

19.31 *a special day for the Jewish people:* Since the Passover was set by the phase of the moon, it could be on any day of the week. In Israel, a day began at sundown. Here, the next day was also the Sabbath, so it was important that the dead body of Jesus not be left to decay on that doubly holy day. And anyone who touched a dead body would have to go through purification rites before being able to celebrate the Passover.

Crucifixion

19.38 *Joseph from Arimathea:* Joseph was from Arimathea, a small village 20 miles northwest of Jerusalem. Because Joseph was rich (Matt 27.57), he had money enough to prepare Jesus' body for a proper burial.

²²But Pilate told them, "What is written will not be changed!"

²³After the soldiers had nailed Jesus to the cross, they divided up his clothes into four parts, one for each of them. But his outer garment was made from a single piece of cloth, and it did not have any seams. ²⁴The soldiers said to each other, "Let's not rip it apart. We will gamble to see who gets it." This happened so the Scriptures would come true, which say,

"They divided up my clothes
and gambled
for my garments."

The soldiers then did what they had decided.

²⁵Jesus' mother stood beside his cross with her sister and Mary the wife of Clopas. Mary Magdalene was standing there too.ᵏ ²⁶When Jesus saw his mother and his favorite disciple with her, he said to his mother, "This man is now your son." ²⁷Then he said to the disciple, "She is now your mother." From then on, that disciple took her into his own home.

The Death of Jesus

(Matthew 27.45-56; Mark 15.33-41; Luke 23.44-49)

²⁸Jesus knew that he had now finished his work. And in order to make the Scriptures come true, he said, "I am thirsty!" ²⁹A jar of cheap wine was there. Someone then soaked a sponge with the wine and held it up to Jesus' mouth on the stem of a hyssop plant. ³⁰After Jesus drank the wine,

he said, "Everything is done!" He bowed his head and died.

A Spear Is Stuck in Jesus' Side

³¹The next day would be both a Sabbath and the Passover. It was a special day for the Jewish people,ˡ and they did not want the bodies to stay on the crosses during this day. So they asked Pilate to break the men's legsᵐ and take their bodies down. ³²The soldiers first broke the legs of the other two men who were nailed there. ³³But when they came to Jesus, they saw he was already dead, and they did not break his legs.

³⁴One of the soldiers stuck his spear into Jesus' side, and blood and water came out. ³⁵We know this is true, because it was told by someone who saw it happen. Now you can have faith too. ³⁶All this happened so that the Scriptures would come true, which say, "No bone of his body will be broken" ³⁷and "They will see the one in whose side they stuck a spear."

Jesus Is Buried

(Matthew 27.57-61; Mark 15.42-47; Luke 23.50-56)

³⁸Joseph from Arimathea was one of Jesus' disciples. He had kept it secret though, because he was afraid of the Jewish leaders. But now he asked Pilate to let him have Jesus' body. Pilate gave him permission, and Joseph took it down from the cross.

³⁹Nicodemus also came with about 75 pounds of spices made from myrrh and

ᵏ**19.25** *Jesus' mother stood beside his cross with her sister and Mary the wife of Clopas. Mary Magdalene was standing there too:* The Greek text may also be understood to include only three women ("Jesus' mother stood beside the cross with her sister, Mary the mother of Clopas. Mary Magdalene was standing there too.") or merely two women ("Jesus' mother was standing there with her sister Mary of Clopas, that is, Mary Magdalene."). "Of Clopas" may mean "daughter of" or "mother of."
ˡ**19.31** *a special day for the Jewish people:* Passover could be any day of the week. But according to the Gospel of John, Passover was on a Sabbath in the year that Jesus was nailed to a cross.   ᵐ**19.31** *break the men's legs:* This was the way that the Romans sometimes speeded up the death of a person who had been nailed to a cross.

aloes. This was the same Nicodemus who had visited Jesus one night.[n] 40The two men wrapped the body in a linen cloth, together with the spices, which was how the Jewish people buried their dead. 41In the place where Jesus had been nailed to a cross, there was a garden with a tomb that had never been used. 42The tomb was nearby, and since it was the time to prepare for the Sabbath, they were in a hurry to put Jesus' body there.

Jesus Is Alive

(Matthew 28.1-10; Mark 16.1-8; Luke 24.1-12)

20 On Sunday morning while it was still dark, Mary Magdalene went to the tomb and saw that the stone had been rolled away from the entrance. 2She ran to Simon Peter and to Jesus' favorite disciple and said, "They have taken the Lord from the tomb! We don't know where they have put him."

3Peter and the other disciple started for the tomb. 4They ran side by side, until the other disciple ran faster than Peter and got there first. 5He bent over and saw the strips of linen cloth lying inside the tomb, but he did not go in.

6When Simon Peter got there, he went into the tomb and saw the strips of cloth. 7He also saw the piece of cloth that had been used to cover Jesus' face. It was rolled up and in a place by itself. 8The disciple who got there first then went into the tomb, and when he saw it, he believed. 9At that time Peter and the other disciple did not know that the Scriptures said Jesus would rise to life. 10So the two of them went back to the other disciples.

Jesus Appears to Mary Magdalene

(Mark 16.9-11)

11Mary Magdalene stood crying outside the tomb. She was still weeping, when she stooped down 12and saw two angels inside. They were dressed in white and were sitting where Jesus' body had been. One was at the head and the other was at the foot. 13The angels asked Mary, "Why are you crying?"

She answered, "They have taken away my Lord's body! I don't know where they have put him."

14As soon as Mary said this, she turned around and saw Jesus standing there. But she did not know who he was. 15Jesus asked her, "Why are you crying? Who are you looking for?"

She thought he was the gardener and said, "Sir, if you have taken his body away, please tell me, so I can go and get him."

16Then Jesus said to her, "Mary!"

She turned and said to him, "Rabboni." The Aramaic word "Rabboni" means "Teacher."

17Jesus told her, "Don't hold on to me! I have not yet gone to the Father. But tell my disciples I am going to the one who is my Father and my God, as well as your Father and your God." 18Mary Magdalene then went and told the disciples she had seen the Lord. She also told them what he had said to her.

Jesus Appears to His Disciples

(Matthew 28.16-20; Mark 16.14-18; Luke 24.36-49)

19The disciples were afraid of the Jewish leaders, and on the evening of that same Sunday they locked themselves in a room. Suddenly, Jesus appeared in the middle of

---

[n]19.39 *Nicodemus who had visited Jesus one night:* See 3.1-21.

19.41 *garden with a tomb:* The tomb and garden must have been near Golgotha. This would have made it easier to finish the task of preparing and burying the body before the Sabbath.

20.1 *Sunday morning:* Early on the morning after the Sabbath ended.

20.1 *Mary Magdalene:* Her name probably means that she was from Magdala, a town on the western edge of Lake Galilee. Other Gospels tell how Jesus healed her (Mark 16.9; Luke 8.2). See also 19.25.

Angels

20.19 *disciples were afraid of the Jewish leaders:* Jesus' followers were afraid that they would be identified and harassed for their beliefs, so they hid out in a locked room.

20.20 *showed them his hands and his side:* Jesus had nails driven through his hands (or possibly wrists) when he was put to death. A soldier later pierced his side with a spear.

Crucifixion

20.22 *Receive the Holy Spirit:* Jesus gave the Holy Spirit to the disciples as he had earlier promised.

20.23 *forgive anyone's sins:* In giving the Holy Spirit, Jesus gave the disciples the power and the right to forgive sins. It had been believed that only God could forgive sins (see Mark 2.7), but here Jesus says that his followers will now share that task. The Christian church's power to forgive sins is also based on being "sent" by Jesus (20.21).

20.28 *my ... God:* Thomas is convinced that Jesus has been raised from the dead, because he can see the wounds Jesus received when he was put to death on the cross.

20.31 *these are written:* Verses 30,31 have often been called the "theme verses" of JOHN. John tells about Jesus' miracles (signs), so that people who were not able to see and hear Jesus in person would have faith in Jesus.

the group. He greeted them [20] and showed them his hands and his side. When the disciples saw the Lord, they became very happy.

[21] After Jesus had greeted them again, he said, "I am sending you, just as the Father has sent me." [22] Then he breathed on them and said, "Receive the Holy Spirit. [23] If you forgive anyone's sins, they will be forgiven. But if you don't forgive their sins, they will not be forgiven."

Jesus and Thomas

[24] Although Thomas the Twin was one of the twelve disciples, he wasn't with the others when Jesus appeared to them. [25] So they told him, "We have seen the Lord!"

But Thomas said, "First, I must see the nail scars in his hands and touch them with my finger. I must put my hand where the spear went into his side. I won't believe unless I do this!"

[26] A week later the disciples were together again. This time, Thomas was with them. Jesus came in while the doors were still locked and stood in the middle of the group. He greeted his disciples [27] and said to Thomas, "Put your finger here and look at my hands! Put your hand into my side. Stop doubting and have faith!"

[28] Thomas replied, "You are my Lord and my God!"

[29] Jesus said, "Thomas, do you have faith because you have seen me? The people who have faith in me without seeing me are the ones who are really blessed!"

Why John Wrote His Book

[30] Jesus worked many other miracles[o] for his disciples, and not all of them are written in this book. [31] But these are written so that you will put your faith in Jesus as the Messiah and the Son of God. If you have faith in[P] him, you will have true life.

Jesus Appears to Seven Disciples

21 Jesus later appeared to his disciples along the shore of Lake Tiberias. [2] Simon Peter, Thomas the Twin, Nathanael from Cana in Galilee, and the brothers James and John,[q] were there, together with two other disciples. [3] Simon Peter said, "I'm going fishing!"

The others said, "We will go with you." They went out in their boat. But they didn't catch a thing that night.

[4] Early the next morning Jesus stood on the shore, but the disciples did not realize who he was. [5] Jesus shouted, "Friends, have you caught anything?"

"No!" they answered.

[6] So he told them, "Let your net down on the right side of your boat, and you will catch some fish."

They did, and the net was so full of fish that they could not drag it up into the boat. [7] Jesus' favorite disciple told Peter, "It's the Lord!" When Simon heard it was the Lord, he put on the clothes he had taken off while he was working. Then he jumped into the water. [8] The boat was only about 100 yards from shore. So the other disciples stayed in the boat and dragged in the net full of fish.

[9] When the disciples got out of the boat,

[o]20.30 *miracles:* See the note at 2.11. [P]20.31 *put your faith in . . . have faith in:* Some manuscripts have "keep on having faith in . . . keep on having faith in." [q]21.2 *the brothers James and John:* Greek "the two sons of Zebedee."

These are written so that you will put your faith in Jesus as the Messiah and the Son of God. If you have faith in him, you will have true life. JOHN 20.31

they saw some bread and a charcoal fire with fish on it. ¹⁰Jesus told his disciples, "Bring some of the fish you just caught." ¹¹Simon Peter got back into the boat and dragged the net to shore. In it were 153 large fish, but still the net did not rip.

¹²Jesus said, "Come and eat!" But none of the disciples dared ask who he was. They knew he was the Lord. ¹³Jesus took the bread in his hands and gave some of it to his disciples. He did the same with the fish. ¹⁴This was the third time Jesus appeared to his disciples after he was raised from death.

Jesus and Peter

¹⁵When Jesus and his disciples had finished eating, he asked, "Simon son of John, do you love me more than the others do?"ʳ

Simon Peter answered, "Yes, Lord, you know I do!"

"Then feed my lambs," Jesus said. ¹⁶Jesus asked a second time, "Simon son of John, do you love me?"

Peter answered, "Yes, Lord, you know I love you!"

"Then take care of my sheep," Jesus told him. ¹⁷Jesus asked a third time, "Simon son of John, do you love me?"

Peter was hurt because Jesus had asked him three times if he loved him. So he told Jesus, "Lord, you know everything. You know I love you."

Jesus replied, "Feed my sheep. ¹⁸I tell you for certain that when you were a young man, you dressed yourself and went wherever you wanted to go. But when you are old, you will hold out your hands. Then others will wrap your belt around you and lead you where you don't want to go."

¹⁹Jesus said this to tell how Peter would die and bring honor to God. Then he said to Peter, "Follow me!"

Jesus and His Favorite Disciple

²⁰Peter turned and saw Jesus' favorite disciple following them. He was the same one who had sat next to Jesus at the meal and had asked, "Lord, who is going to betray you?" ²¹When Peter saw this disciple, he asked Jesus, "Lord, what about him?"

²²Jesus answered, "What is it to you, if I want him to live until I return? You must follow me." ²³So the rumor spread among the other disciples that this disciple would not die. But Jesus did not say he would not die. He simply said, "What is it to you, if I want him to live until I return?"

²⁴This disciple is the one who told all of this. He wrote it, and we know he is telling the truth.

²⁵Jesus did many other things. If they were all written in books, I don't suppose there would be room enough in the whole world for all the books.

● 21.9 *bread and . . . fish:* In John these are not simply food. The bread represents the bread of the Lord's Supper and is a reminder that Jesus is the bread that gives life (6.34). In the early church a favorite symbol for Jesus was the fish.

● 21.15 *Simon son of John:* Simon Peter.

■ 21.15,16 *feed my lambs . . . my sheep:* Jesus called himself the good shepherd (10.14). His followers are his flock of lambs (sheep). Jesus tells Peter to take care of his sheep ("followers") by feeding them the message of Jesus, which includes offering forgiveness (20.23).

■ 21.18,19 *you will hold out your hands . . . bring honor to God:* The phrase "hold out your hands" probably means that Peter would die on a cross just as Jesus had. Peter's freedom would be taken away and he would be led where he does not want to go. Even so, his death would bring honor to God, just as Jesus' death glorified God.

● 21.24 *This disciple is the one who told all of this:* According to this verse, "Jesus' favorite disciple" (see 21.20) is the one who wrote this true account of Jesus' words and works, though he had to choose them from the many stories and memories of what Jesus said and did (21.25).

ʳ21.15 *more than the others do?:* Or "more than you love these things?"

Reflection Questions About John 1.1—21.25

1. Who is the "Word" of God, and what did this Word do? What other titles for Jesus are suggested in John 1? What makes each of these titles important?

2. What do the many miracles in chapters 2—11 say about Jesus? What effect did Jesus' miracles have on people?

3. What did Jesus mean when he described himself as "the bread that gives life" (6.35)? As the source of "life-giving water" (7.38,39)? As "the light for the world" (8.12)? As "the good shepherd" (10.14)?

4. What did Jesus do that made the leaders angry enough to kill him (5.17,18)? Why did they want to get rid of Jesus?

5. When Jesus says he has come to give sight to the blind and make blind everyone who can see, what does he mean (9.39)? In your life, what would you like to "see" more clearly?

6. What is the "new command" Jesus gave his followers (13.34,35)? How can this command be followed?

7. How did Jesus promise to help his followers after he left to be with the Father (16.5-15)?

8. How did Jesus reply to Pilate's question (18.33-37)? What is Jesus' kingdom?

9. What task did Jesus give to his disciples when he met them after he was raised from death (20.21-23)? What does this mean for the church today?

10. What command did Jesus give to Peter (21.15-19)? What did that mean for Peter? What does it mean for Jesus' followers (the church) today?

acts

What's the first thing you do when you hear good news? How do you share that news with others? Read ACTS to discover how the good news about Jesus spread everywhere!

WHAT MAKES ACTS SPECIAL?

ACTS is the second volume of a two-part work written by the same person who wrote LUKE. As ACTS begins, Jesus is about to go up to heaven, but before he does, he tells his disciples to "tell everyone about me in Jerusalem, in all Judea, in Samaria, and everywhere in the world." Then he promises to send the Holy Spirit who will give power to all his followers (1.8). The writer of ACTS wanted to show that nothing could stop the good news about Jesus from spreading everywhere.

ACTS also tells how the earliest followers struggled to decide who could belong to God's people. Since Jesus' first followers were Jews, many thought Jesus' message was only for Jews. Yet the Holy Spirit showed that Jesus welcomes people from every nation and race to be part of God's people.

WHAT'S THE STORY BEHIND THE SCENE?

The writer of LUKE and ACTS tells about the people and places the apostles visited and about how those who spread the good news did miracles in Jesus' name. ACTS also tells about Saul of Tarsus (Paul), a loyal Jew who was dedicated to ending the Jesus movement (Acts 8.1-3; 9.1-2). While he was on a trip to arrest some of Jesus' followers, Saul saw Jesus in a vision. That vision changed his life. He became a follower of Jesus and one of the greatest preachers of the good news. Much of the second half of ACTS tells about Paul's preaching, journeys, and experiences. He took the message about Jesus as far as Rome, the world's most important city at that time (28.16-31).

HOW IS ACTS CONSTRUCTED?

ACTS can be divided in the following way:

The Spirit gives power to Jesus' followers (1.1—2.47)
    The apostles prepare to receive God's power (1.1-26)
    God sends the Holy Spirit (2.1-47)
The church in Jerusalem (3.1—8.3)
    Peter and John (3.1—4.22)
    Life among the early followers in Jerusalem (4.23—5.42)
    Leaders for the new church (6.1—8.3)
The good news preached in Judea and Samaria (8.4—9.31)
    Philip, Peter, and John in Samaria (8.4-40)
    God chooses Saul (9.1-31)
The good news goes out to the Gentile world (9.32—15.35)
    Peter preaches and lives the good news (9.32—11.18)
    The growing church faces trouble (11.19—12.25)
    Saul and Barnabas journey to tell the good news (13.1—14.28)
    An important meeting in Jerusalem (15.1-35)
The good news reaches Asia Minor, Greece, and Rome (15.36—28.31)
    Paul's second journey (15.36—18.23)
    Paul's third journey (18.24—21.16)
    Paul in Jerusalem (21.17—23.22)
    Paul in Caesarea (23.23—26.32)
    Paul brings the good news to Rome (27.1—28.31)

A cts continues the story its author began in Luke, and like the Gospel it emphasizes the fulfillment of Scripture, the importance of the Holy Spirit and prayer, and the Christian duty to care for the poor. Acts tells the story of the early church—the coming of the Holy Spirit and the ministries and missionary journeys of the apostles Peter, John, James, and Paul, and of other important early church leaders, like Stephen, Barnabas, Priscilla and Aquila, and Lydia. The author sets the tone early in the book by telling how Jesus sent the Holy Spirit to give Jesus' followers the power to tell everyone everywhere the good news about Jesus. By the end of Acts, Paul has brought the good news to Rome, the capital of the Roman Empire. This story of what God's Holy Spirit and the faithful followers of Jesus can do is intended to inspire others who face difficult times because of their faith.

Outline

Theophilus, I first wrote to you[a] about all that Jesus did and taught from the very first [2]until he was taken up to heaven. But before he was taken up, he gave orders to the apostles he had chosen with the help of the Holy Spirit.

[3]For 40 days after Jesus had suffered and died, he proved in many ways that he had been raised from death. He appeared to his apostles and spoke to them about God's kingdom. [4]While he was still with them, he said:

Don't leave Jerusalem yet. Wait here for the Father to give you the Holy Spirit, just as I told you he has promised to do. [5]John baptized with water, but in a few days you will be baptized with the Holy Spirit.

Jesus Is Taken to Heaven

[6]While the apostles were still with Jesus, they asked him, "Lord, are you now going to give Israel its own king again?"[b]

[7]Jesus said to them, "You don't need to know the time of those events that only the Father controls. [8]But the Holy Spirit will come upon you and give you power. Then you will tell everyone about me in Jerusalem, in all Judea, in Samaria, and everywhere in the world." [9]After Jesus had said this and while they were watching, he was taken up into a cloud. They could not see him, [10]but as he went up, they kept looking up into the sky.

Suddenly two men dressed in white clothes were standing there beside them. [11]They said, "Why are you men from Galilee standing here and looking up into the sky? Jesus has been taken to heaven.

[a]**1.1** *I first wrote to you*: The Gospel of Luke. [b]**1.6** *are you now going to give Israel its own king again*: Or "Are you now going to rule Israel as its king?"

But he will come back in the same way you have seen him go."

Someone To Take the Place of Judas

12-13 The Mount of Olives was about half a mile from Jerusalem. The apostles who had gone there were Peter, John, James, Andrew, Philip, Thomas, Bartholomew, Matthew, James the son of Alphaeus, Simon, known as the Eager One,[c] and Judas the son of James.

After the apostles returned to the city, they went upstairs to the room where they had been staying. **14**The apostles often met together and prayed with a single purpose in mind.[d] The women and Mary the mother of Jesus would meet with them, and so would his brothers. **15**One day there were about 120 of the Lord's followers meeting together, and Peter stood up to speak to them. **16-17**He said:

My friends, long ago by the power of the Holy Spirit, David said something about Judas, and what he said has now happened. Judas was one of us and had worked with us, but he brought the mob to arrest Jesus. **18**Then Judas bought some land with the money he was given for doing that evil thing. He fell headfirst into the field. His body burst open, and all his insides came out. **19**When the people of Jerusalem found out about this, they called the place Akeldama, which in the local language means "Field of Blood."

20In the book of Psalms it says,

"Leave his house empty,

and don't let anyone
   live there."
It also says,
   "Let someone else
      have his job."

21-22 So we need someone else to help us tell others that Jesus has been raised from death. He must also be one of the men who was with us from the very beginning. He must have been with us from the time the Lord Jesus was baptized by John until the day he was taken to heaven. **23**Two men were suggested: One of them was Joseph Barsabbas, known as Justus, and the other was Matthias. **24**Then they all prayed, "Lord, you know what everyone is like! Show us the one you have chosen **25**to be an apostle and to serve in place of Judas, who got what he deserved." **26**They drew names, and Matthias was chosen to join the group of the eleven apostles.

The Coming of the Holy Spirit

2 On the day of Pentecost[e] all the Lord's followers were together in one place. **2**Suddenly there was a noise from heaven like the sound of a mighty wind! It filled the house where they were meeting. **3**Then they saw what looked like fiery tongues moving in all directions, and a tongue came and settled on each person there. **4**The Holy Spirit took control of everyone, and they began speaking whatever languages the Spirit let them speak. **5**Many religious Jews from every country in the world were living in Jerusalem.

Suddenly there was a noise from heaven like the sound of a mighty wind! ACTS 2.2

⁶And when they heard this noise, a crowd gathered. But they were surprised, because they were hearing everything in their own languages. ⁷They were excited and amazed, and said:

Don't all these who are speaking come from Galilee? ⁸Then why do we hear them speaking our very own languages? ⁹Some of us are from Parthia, Media, and Elam. Others are from Mesopotamia, Judea, Cappadocia, Pontus, Asia, ¹⁰Phrygia, Pamphylia, Egypt, parts of Libya near Cyrene, Rome, ¹¹Crete, and Arabia. Some of us were born Jews, and others of us have chosen to be Jews. Yet we all hear them using our own languages to tell the wonderful things God has done. ¹²Everyone was excited and confused. Some of them even kept asking each other, "What does all this mean?" ¹³Others made fun of the Lord's followers and said, "They are drunk."

Peter Speaks to the Crowd

¹⁴Peter stood with the eleven apostles and spoke in a loud and clear voice to the crowd:

Friends and everyone else living in Jerusalem, listen carefully to what I have to say! ¹⁵You are wrong to think that these people are drunk. After all, it is only nine o'clock in the morning. ¹⁶But this is what God told the prophet Joel to say,

¹⁷"When the last days come,
  I will give my Spirit
    to everyone.
  Your sons and daughters
    will prophesy.
  Your young men
    will see visions,
  and your old men
    will have dreams.

¹⁸In those days I will give
  my Spirit to my servants,
  both men and women,
    and they will prophesy.

¹⁹I will work miracles
  in the sky above
and wonders
  on the earth below.
There will be blood and fire
  and clouds of smoke.
²⁰The sun will turn dark,
  and the moon
    will be as red as blood
before the great
  and wonderful day
    of the Lord appears.
²¹Then the Lord
  will save everyone
    who asks for his help."

²²Now, listen to what I have to say about Jesus from Nazareth. God proved he sent Jesus to you by having him work miracles, wonders, and signs. All of you know this. ²³God had already planned and decided that Jesus would be handed over to you. So you took him and had evil men put him to death on a cross. ²⁴But God set him free from death and raised him to life. Death could not hold him in its power. ²⁵What David said are really the words of Jesus,

"I always see the Lord
  near me,
and I will not be afraid
  with him at my right side.
²⁶Because of this,
  my heart will be glad,
  my words will be joyful,
  and I will live in hope.
²⁷The Lord won't leave me
  in the grave.
I am his holy one,

2.29-31 *our ancestor David . . . knew this would happen:* When Peter says David was a prophet, he means that David spoke God's message in Psalms, and that Jesus' being raised to life fulfills what David had spoken about centuries earlier.

◌ David

2.36 *Lord and Christ:* Christ comes from the Greek word, *Christos,* which means "chosen one" and means the same thing as the Hebrew title, Messiah.

◌ Lord (Title for Jesus)

◌ Messiah (Chosen One)

2.38 *forgiveness of your sins:* People sin when they turn away from God and disobey God's Law. Being baptized in Jesus' name brings the promise of God's forgiveness.

◌ Sin

2.42 *broke bread . . . together:* Jesus used the bread and wine to show how his life would be sacrificed to forgive sins, which was the basis for a new agreement (covenant) between God and God's new people. Christians celebrate this event in the meal that is called the Lord's Supper, Holy Communion, or the Eucharist.

2.47 *being saved:* This is another way to describe being baptized in Jesus' name and having sins forgiven.

◌ God's Saving Love (Salvation)

and he won't let
my body decay.
²⁸He has shown me
the path to life,
and he makes me glad
by being near me."

²⁹My friends, it is right for me to speak to you about our ancestor David. He died and was buried, and his tomb is still here. ³⁰But David was a prophet, and he knew that God had made a promise he would not break. He had told David someone from his own family would someday be king. ³¹David knew this would happen, and so he told us Christ would be raised to life. He said God would not leave him in the grave or let his body decay. ³²All of us can tell you that God has raised Jesus to life!

³³Jesus was taken up to sit at the right side[f] of God, and he was given the Holy Spirit, just as the Father had promised. Jesus is also the one who has given the Spirit to us, and this is what you are now seeing and hearing. ³⁴David didn't go up to heaven. So he wasn't talking about himself when he said, "The Lord told my Lord to sit at his right side, ³⁵until he made my Lord's enemies into a footstool for him." ³⁶Everyone in Israel should then know for certain that God has made Jesus both Lord and Christ, even though you put him to death on a cross.

³⁷When the people heard this, they were very upset. They asked Peter and the other apostles, "Friends, what should we do?"

³⁸Peter said to them, "Turn to God and be baptized, every one of you, in the name of Jesus Christ for the forgiveness of your sins, and you will receive the gift of the Holy Spirit. ³⁹This promise is for you and your children. It is for everyone our Lord God will choose, no matter where they live."

⁴⁰Peter told them many other things as well. Then he said, "I beg you to save yourselves from what will happen to all these evil people." ⁴¹On that day about 3,000 believed his message and were baptized. ⁴²They spent their time learning from the apostles, and they were like family to each other. They also broke bread[g] and prayed together.

Life among the Lord's Followers

⁴³Everyone was amazed by the many miracles and wonders that the apostles worked. ⁴⁴All the Lord's followers often met together, and they shared everything they had. ⁴⁵They would sell their property and possessions and give the money to whoever was in need. ⁴⁶Day after day they met together in the temple. They broke bread[h] together in different homes and shared their food happily and freely, ⁴⁷while praising God. Everyone liked them, and each day the Lord added to their group others who were being saved.

Peter and John Heal a Lame Man

3 The time of prayer[i] was about three o'clock in the afternoon, and Peter and John were going into the temple. ²A man who had been born lame was being

[f]**2.33** *right side:* The place of honor and power.   [g]**2.42** *broke bread:* They ate together and celebrated the Lord's Supper.   [h]**2.46** *broke bread:* See the note at 2.42.   [i]**3.1** *The time of prayer:* Many of the Jewish people prayed in their homes at regular times each day (see Daniel 6.11), and on special occasions they prayed in the temple.

carried to the temple door. Each day he was placed beside this door, known as the Beautiful Gate. He sat there and begged from the people who were going in.

³The man saw Peter and John entering the temple, and he asked them for money. ⁴But they looked straight at him and said, "Look up at us!"

⁵The man stared at them and thought he was going to get something. ⁶But Peter said, "I don't have any silver or gold! But I will give you what I do have. In the name of Jesus Christ from Nazareth, get up and start walking." ⁷Peter then took him by the right hand and helped him up.

At once the man's feet and ankles became strong, ⁸and he jumped up and started walking. He went with Peter and John into the temple, walking and jumping and praising God. ⁹Everyone saw him walking around and praising God. ¹⁰They knew he was the beggar who had been lying beside the Beautiful Gate, and they were completely surprised. They could not imagine what had happened to the man.

Peter Speaks in the Temple

¹¹While the man kept holding on to Peter and John, the whole crowd ran to them in amazement at the place known as Solomon's Porch.ʲ ¹²Peter saw that a crowd had gathered, and he said:

Friends, why are you surprised at what has happened? Why are you staring at us? Do you think we have some power of our own? Do you think we were able to make this man walk because we are so religious? ¹³The God that Abraham, Isaac, Jacob, and our other ancestors worshiped has brought honor to his Servantᵏ Jesus. He is the one you betrayed. You turned against him when he was being tried by Pilate, even though Pilate wanted to set him free.

¹⁴You rejected Jesus, who was holy and good. You asked for a murderer to be set free, ¹⁵and you killed the one who leads people to life. But God raised him from death, and all of us can tell you what he has done. ¹⁶You see this man, and you know him. He put his faith in the name of Jesus and was made strong. Faith in Jesus made this man completely well while everyone was watching.

¹⁷My friends, I am sure you and your leaders didn't know what you were doing. ¹⁸But God had his prophets tell that his Messiah would suffer, and now he has kept this promise. ¹⁹So turn to God! Give up your sins, and you will be forgiven. ²⁰Then the time will come when the Lord will give you fresh strength. He will send you Jesus, his chosen Messiah. ²¹But Jesus must stay in heaven until God makes all things new, just as his holy prophets promised long ago.

²²Moses said, "The Lord your God will choose one of your own people to be a prophet, just as he chose me. Listen to everything he tells you. ²³No one who disobeys this prophet will be one of God's people any longer."

²⁴Samuel and all the other prophets who came later also spoke about what is now happening. ²⁵You are really the ones God told his prophets to speak to. And you were given the promise God made to your ancestors. He said to Abraham, "All nations on earth will be blessed because of someone from your

3.2 *Beautiful Gate:* Perhaps the Nicanor Gate. People with physical problems, who were considered ritually unclean, were not allowed into the temple. Nevertheless, they could sit by its gates and beg for money.

3.11 *Solomon's Porch:* A public place with tall columns along the east side of the temple, it was named for King Solomon, who built the first Jewish temple in Jerusalem.

Lᴏʀᴅ (YHWH)

Pontius Pilate

3.14 *a murderer:* Peter is talking about Barabbas. See Matt 27.15-26; Mark 15.6-15; Luke 23.13-23.

3.24 *Samuel and all the other prophets:* Samuel was mainly known as a judge (leader), though Peter calls him a prophet. Samuel anointed the first two kings of Israel, Saul and David.

ʲ**3.11** *Solomon's Porch*: A public place with tall columns along the east side of the temple.
ᵏ**3.13** *Servant*: Or "Son."

4.1 *temple guard . . . Sadducees:* The Jewish leaders assigned a group of men to serve as the temple guard. Guards kept order in the busy temple area and made sure that no one broke the laws of the temple. The captain of the temple guard came from a priestly family and was close in rank to the high priest.

The Sadducees were a wealthy group of Jews who worked closely with the priests. They taught that the most important thing in life was going to the temple and offering sacrifices there. This sometimes caused the Sadducees to oppose the Pharisees, a group who thought that obeying the Law in a personal way was more important than following all the rules about temple worship and sacrifice. The Pharisees believed in life after death, but the Sadducees did not.

Israel's Priests

4.5 *leaders, the elders, and the teachers of the Law:* The leaders were probably a group of wealthy men who were connected to the priests and the temple. The elders may have been a highly respected group of teachers who were very familiar with the Law of Moses. The teachers of the Law of Moses carefully studied the first five books of the Jewish Scriptures, called the Torah.

family." [26]God sent his chosen Son[1] to you first, because God wanted to bless you and make each one of you turn away from your sins.

Peter and John Are Brought in Front of the Council

4 The apostles were still talking to the people, when some priests, the captain of the temple guard, and some Sadducees arrived. [2]These men were angry because the apostles were teaching the people that the dead would be raised from death, just as Jesus had been raised from death. [3]It was already late in the afternoon, and they arrested Peter and John and put them in jail for the night. [4]But a lot of people who had heard the message believed it. So by now there were about 5,000 followers of the Lord.

[5]The next morning the leaders, the elders, and the teachers of the Law of Moses met in Jerusalem. [6]The high priest Annas was there, as well as Caiaphas, John, Alexander, and other members of the high priest's family. [7]They brought in Peter and John and made them stand in the middle while they questioned them. They asked, "By what power and in whose name have you done this?"

[8]Peter was filled with the Holy Spirit and told the nation's leaders and the elders:

[9]You are questioning us today about a kind deed in which a man who could not walk was healed. [10]But there is something we must tell you and everyone else in Israel. This man is standing here completely well because of the power of Jesus Christ from Nazareth. You put Jesus to death on a cross, but God raised him to life. [11]He is the stone you builders thought was worthless,

[3.26] Son: Or "Servant."

and now he is the most important stone of all. [12]Only Jesus has the power to save! His name is the only one in all the world that can save anyone.

[13]The officials were amazed to see how brave Peter and John were, and they knew that these two apostles were only ordinary men and not well educated. The officials were certain these men had been with Jesus. [14]But they could not deny what had happened. The man who had been healed was standing there with the apostles.

[15]The officials commanded them to leave the council room. Then the officials said to each other, [16]"What can we do with these men? Everyone in Jerusalem knows about this miracle, and we cannot say it didn't happen. [17]But to keep this thing from spreading, we will warn them never again to speak to anyone about the name of Jesus." [18]So they called the two apostles back in and told them they must never, for any reason, teach anything about the name of Jesus.

[19]Peter and John answered, "Do you think God wants us to obey you or to obey him? [20]We cannot keep quiet about what we have seen and heard."

[21-22]The officials could not find any reason to punish Peter and John. So they threatened them and let them go. The man who was healed by this miracle was more than 40 years old, and everyone was praising God for what had happened.

Peter and Others Pray for Courage

[23]As soon as Peter and John had been set free, they went back and told the others everything the chief priests and the leaders had said to them. [24]When the rest of the Lord's followers heard this, they prayed together and said:

Master, you created heaven and earth, the sea, and everything in them. 25And by the Holy Spirit you spoke to our ancestor David. He was your servant, and you told him to say:

"Why are all the Gentiles
so furious?
Why do people
make foolish plans?
26The kings of earth
prepare for war,
and the rulers
join together
against the Lord
and his Messiah."

27Here in Jerusalem, Herod[m] and Pontius Pilate got together with the Gentiles and the people of Israel. Then they turned against your holy Servant[n] Jesus, your chosen Messiah. 28They did what you in your power and wisdom had already decided would happen.

29Lord, listen to their threats! We are your servants. So make us brave enough to speak your message. 30Show your mighty power, as we heal people and work miracles and wonders in the name of your holy Servant[o] Jesus. 31After they had prayed, the meeting place shook. They were all filled with the Holy Spirit and bravely spoke God's message.

Sharing Possessions

32The group of followers all felt the same way about everything. None of them claimed that their possessions were their own, and they shared everything they had with each other. 33In a powerful way the apostles told everyone that the Lord Jesus was now alive. God greatly blessed his followers,[p] 34and no one went in need of anything. Everyone who owned land or houses would sell them and bring the money 35to the apostles. Then they would give the money to anyone in need.

36-37Joseph was one of the followers who had sold a piece of property and brought the money to the apostles. He was a Levite from Cyprus, and the apostles called him Barnabas, which means "one who encourages others."

Peter Condemns Ananias and Sapphira

5 Ananias and his wife Sapphira also sold a piece of property. 2But they agreed to cheat and keep some of the money for themselves.

So when Ananias took the rest of the money to the apostles, 3Peter said, "Why has Satan made you keep back some of the money from the sale of the property? Why have you lied to the Holy Spirit? 4The property was yours before you sold it, and even after you sold it, the money was still yours. What made you do such a thing? You didn't lie to people. You lied to God!"

5As soon as Ananias heard this, he dropped dead, and everyone who heard about it was frightened. 6Some young men came in and wrapped up his body. Then they took it out and buried it.

7Three hours later Sapphira came in, but she did not know what had happened to her husband. 8Peter asked her, "Tell me, did you sell the property for this amount?"

"Yes," she answered, "that's the amount."

9Then Peter said, "Why did the two of

4.27 *Herod and Pontius Pilate:* This is Herod Antipas, the son of Herod the Great. He was the governor of Galilee from 4 B.C. to A.D. 39. Even though his home was in Caesarea, he was in Jerusalem when Jesus was arrested (Luke 23.7).

4.36-37 *Joseph . . . called him Barnabas:* Joseph was from the Levite tribe, which meant that the men in his family worked in the temple. The Levites did not actually own inherited land in Palestine, but since this man lived on the island of Cyprus he probably was allowed to purchase land there. Barnabas became an important leader in the early church. He went with Paul on one of his missionary trips. (See Map 15 on pg 1893.)

5.1 *Ananias and his wife Sapphira:* All we know about this couple is what we read in Acts. They are shown as a bad example of sharing. Their actions would likely have reminded the Jewish followers of the sin of Achan, who stole things that had been set aside for the Lord (Josh 7).

Satan

---

[m]4.27 *Herod:* Herod Antipas, the son of Herod the Great. [n]4.27 *Servant:* See the note at 3.13. [o]4.30 *Servant:* See the note at 3.13. [p]4.33 *God greatly blessed his followers:* Or "Everyone highly respected his followers."

5.9 *test the Lord's Spirit:* Another way of saying "lying to God's Spirit." It was important that the believers could trust each other. Keeping the money was not a sin, since it was rightfully their money. Pretending to be generous was the sin.

5.11 *The church:* The Greek word for "church" is *ekklesia*, which means "assembly" and can refer to any kind of gathering of people.

Church

5.16 *troubled by evil spirits:* Evil spirits, or demons, work for the devil. In Peter's day, demons were thought to be the primary cause of many kinds of sickness and mental illness.

5.17 *high priest:* At this time Caiaphas would have been the high priest.

Israel's Priests

5.19 *angel from the Lord:* The word "angel" in English is based on the Greek word *angelos,* which means "messenger." In the Bible, angels frequently play an important part in seeing that God's will is carried out.

Angels

5.21 *council:* The high priest, the chief priests, and other prominent Jewish citizens formed a council of Jewish leaders. The Roman rulers gave this council the right to make decisions about some local matters that affected the Jewish people.

you agree to test the Lord's Spirit? The men who buried Ananias are by the door, and they will carry you out!" [10]At once she fell at Peter's feet and died.

When the young men came back in, they found Sapphira lying there dead. So they carried her out and buried her beside her husband. [11]The church members were afraid, and so was everyone else who heard what had happened.

Peter's Unusual Power

[12]The apostles worked many miracles and wonders among the people. All of the Lord's followers often met in the part of the temple known as Solomon's Porch.[q] [13]No one outside their group dared join them, even though everyone liked them very much.

[14]Many men and women started having faith in the Lord. [15]Then sick people were brought out to the road and placed on mats. It was hoped that Peter would walk by, and his shadow would fall on them and heal them. [16]A lot of people living in the towns near Jerusalem brought those who were sick or troubled by evil spirits, and they were all healed.

Trouble for the Apostles

[17]The high priest and all the other Sadducees who were with him became jealous. [18]They arrested the apostles and put them in the city jail. [19]But that night an angel from the Lord opened the doors of the jail and led the apostles out. The angel said, [20]"Go to the temple and tell the people everything about this new life." [21]So they went into the temple before sunrise and started teaching.

The high priest and his men called together their council, which included all of Israel's leaders. Then they ordered the apostles to be brought to them from the jail. [22]The temple police who were sent to the jail did not find the apostles. They returned and said, [23]"We found the jail locked tight and the guards standing at the doors. But when we opened the doors and went in, we didn't find anyone there." [24]The captain of the temple police and the chief priests listened to their report, but they did not know what to think about it.

[25]Just then someone came in and said, "Now those men you put in jail are in the temple, teaching the people!" [26]The captain went with some of the temple police and brought the apostles back. But they did not use force. They were afraid that the people might start throwing stones at them.

[27]When the apostles were brought before the council, the high priest said to them, [28]"We told you plainly not to teach in the name of Jesus. But look what you have done! You have been teaching all over Jerusalem, and you are trying to blame us for his death."

[29]Peter and the apostles replied:

We don't obey people. We obey God. [30]You killed Jesus by nailing him to a cross. But the God our ancestors worshiped raised him to life [31]and made him our Leader and Savior. Then God gave him a place at his right side,[r] so that the people of Israel would turn back to him and be forgiven. [32]We are here to tell you about all this, and so is the Holy Spirit, who is God's gift to everyone who obeys God.

[33]When the council members heard this, they became so angry they wanted to kill the apostles. [34]But one of the members was the Pharisee Gamaliel, a highly respected

[q]5.12 *Solomon's Porch:* See the note at 3.11.   [r]5.31 *right side:* See the note at 2.33.

teacher. He ordered the apostles to be taken out of the room for a little while. [35]Then he said to the council:

Men of Israel, be careful what you do with these men. [36]Not long ago Theudas claimed to be someone important, and about 400 men joined him. But he was killed, and all his followers were scattered. That was the end of that.

[37]Later, when the people of our nation were being counted, Judas from Galilee showed up. A lot of people followed him, but he was killed, and all his followers were scattered.

[38]So I advise you to stay away from these men. Leave them alone. If what they are planning is something of their own doing, it will fail. [39]But if God is behind it, you cannot stop it anyway, unless you want to fight against God.

The council members agreed with what he said, [40]and they called the apostles back in. They had them beaten with a whip and warned them not to speak in the name of Jesus. Then they let them go.

[41]The apostles left the council and were happy, because God had considered them worthy to suffer for the sake of Jesus. [42]Every day they spent time in the temple and in one home after another. They never stopped teaching and telling the good news that Jesus is the Messiah.

Seven Leaders for the Church

6 A lot of people were now becoming followers of the Lord. But some of the ones who spoke Greek started complaining about the ones who spoke Aramaic. They complained that the Greek-speaking widows were not given their share when the food supplies were handed out each day.

[2]The twelve apostles called the whole group of followers together and said, "We should not give up preaching God's message in order to serve at tables.[s] [3]My friends, choose seven men who are respected and wise and filled with God's Spirit. We will put them in charge of these things. [4]We can spend our time praying and serving God by preaching."

[5]This suggestion pleased everyone, and they began by choosing Stephen. He had great faith and was filled with the Holy Spirit. Then they chose Philip, Prochorus, Nicanor, Timon, Parmenas, and also Nicolaus, who worshiped with the Jewish people[t] in Antioch. [6]These men were brought to the apostles. Then the apostles prayed and placed their hands on the men to show they had been chosen to do this work. [7]God's message spread, and many more people in Jerusalem became followers. Even a large number of priests put their faith in the Lord.

Stephen Is Arrested

[8]God gave Stephen the power to work great miracles and wonders among the people. [9]But some men from Cyrene and Alexandria were members of a group who called themselves "Free Men."[u] They started arguing with Stephen. Some others from Cilicia and Asia also argued with him. [10]But they were no match for Stephen, who spoke with the great wisdom that the

[s]6.2 *to serve at tables*: This may mean either that they were in charge of handing out food to the widows or that they were in charge of the money, since the Greek word "table" may also mean "bank."   [t]6.5 *worshiped with the Jewish people*: This translates the Greek word "proselyte" that means a Gentile who had accepted the Jewish religion.   [u]6.9 *Free Men*: A group of Jewish men who had once been slaves, but had been freed.

● 5.36,37 *Theudas . . . Judas*: Theudas probably led some kind of revolt against the Roman rulers occupying Palestine. Judas from Galilee, possibly the founder of the group known as the Zealots, led a rebellion against Rome in A.D. 6. (See the article The World of Jesus: Peoples, Powers, and Politics on pg 1801.)

■ 5.42 *good news*: The good news is the message Jesus brought about God's kingdom and the message Jesus' followers brought about what Jesus did.

● 6.1 *ones who spoke Greek . . . ones who spoke Aramaic*: After Alexander the Great (356–323 B.C.) conquered the Near East, Greek language and culture dominated the ancient world. Greek was a kind of universal language. Educated people spoke and understood Greek as well as their native languages. Aramaic, the native language of much of Palestine and Syria, was a language close to Hebrew and was used by most Jews in everyday activities.

● 6.5 *Antioch*: This Greek city in Syria became an important center for the early Christian outreach to the Gentiles. (See Map 14 on pg 1892.)

● 6.7 *priests*: This statement is noteworthy because these leaders generally opposed the new followers of Jesus.

7.9 *Joseph*: Joseph was Jacob's first son by his favorite wife, Rachel, and a grandson of Abraham.

7.9 *Egypt*: At this time Egypt was a powerful country to the southwest of Canaan. **(See Map 2 on pg 1880.)**

7.16 *Shechem*: A town in central Canaan where Jacob's body was taken to be buried along with the bodies of other Israelites who had died in Egypt (see Gen 46.1-7; 49.33). Abraham bought land at Hebron (Gen 23.3-18) where he (Gen 25.9-11), Isaac (Gen 35.28-29), and Jacob (Gen 50.7-13) were buried. Jacob bought land at Shechem and built an altar to the Lord there (Gen 33.19). His son Joseph was later buried there (Josh 24.32). Stephen actually has summarized all this history by making the point that the earliest ancestors were buried in Canaan, not in Egypt.

Spirit gave him. [11]So they talked some men into saying, "We heard Stephen say terrible things against Moses and God!"

[12]They turned the people and their leaders and the teachers of the Law of Moses against Stephen. Then they all grabbed him and dragged him in front of the council.

[13]Some men agreed to tell lies about Stephen, and they said, "This man keeps on saying terrible things about this holy temple and the Law of Moses. [14]We have heard him claim that Jesus from Nazareth will destroy this place and change the customs Moses gave us." [15]Then all the council members stared at Stephen. They saw that his face looked like the face of an angel.

Stephen's Speech

7 The high priest asked Stephen, "Are they telling the truth about you?" [2]Stephen answered:

Friends, listen to me. Our glorious God appeared to our ancestor Abraham while he was still in Mesopotamia, before he had moved to Haran. [3]God told him, "Leave your country and your relatives and go to a land that I will show you." [4]Then Abraham left the land of the Chaldeans and settled in Haran.

After his father died, Abraham came and settled in this land where you now live. [5]God didn't give him any part of it, not even a square foot. But God did promise to give it to him and his family forever, even though Abraham didn't have any children. [6]God said Abraham's descendants would live for a while in a foreign land. There they would be slaves and would be mistreated 400 years. [7]But he also said, "I will punish the nation that makes them slaves. Then later they will come and worship me in this place."

[8]God said to Abraham, "Every son in each family must be circumcised to show you have kept your agreement with me." So when Isaac was eight days old, Abraham circumcised him. Later, Isaac circumcised his son Jacob, and Jacob circumcised his twelve sons. [9]These men were our ancestors.

Joseph was also one of our famous ancestors. His brothers were jealous of him and sold him as a slave to be taken to Egypt. But God was with him [10]and rescued him from all his troubles. God made him so wise that the Egyptian king Pharaoh thought highly of him. The king even made Joseph governor over Egypt and put him in charge of everything he owned.

[11]Everywhere in Egypt and Canaan the grain crops failed. There was terrible suffering, and our ancestors could not find enough to eat. [12]But when Jacob heard there was grain in Egypt, he sent our ancestors there for the first time. [13]It was on their second trip that Joseph told his brothers who he was, and the king learned about Joseph's family.

[14]Joseph sent for his father and his relatives. In all, there were 75 of them. [15]His father went to Egypt and died there, just as our ancestors did. [16]Later their bodies were taken back to Shechem and placed in the tomb that Abraham had bought from the sons of Hamor.

[17]Finally, the time came for God to do what he had promised Abraham. By then the number of our people in Egypt had greatly increased. [18]Another king was ruling Egypt, and he didn't know anything about Joseph. [19]He tricked our ancestors and was cruel to them. He even made them leave their babies outside, so they would die.

20During this time Moses was born. He was a very beautiful child, and for three months his parents took care of him in their home. 21Then when they were forced to leave him outside, the king's daughter found him and raised him as her own son. 22Moses was given the best education in Egypt. He was a strong man and a powerful speaker.

23When Moses was 40 years old, he wanted to help the Israelites because they were his own people. 24One day he saw an Egyptian mistreating one of them. So he rescued the man and killed the Egyptian. 25Moses thought the rest of his people would realize God was going to use him to set them free. But they didn't understand.

26The next day Moses saw two of his own people fighting, and he tried to make them stop. He said, "Men, you are both Israelites. Why are you so cruel to each other?"

27But the man who had started the fight pushed Moses aside and asked, "Who made you our ruler and judge? 28Are you going to kill me, just as you killed that Egyptian yesterday?" 29When Moses heard this, he ran away to live in the country of Midian. His two sons were born there.

30Forty years later, an angel appeared to Moses from a burning bush in the desert near Mount Sinai. 31Moses was surprised by what he saw. He went closer to get a better look, and the Lord said, 32"I am the God who was worshiped by your ancestors, Abraham, Isaac, and Jacob." Moses started shaking all over and didn't dare to look at the bush.

33The Lord said to him, "Take off your sandals, because the place where you are standing is holy. 34With my own eyes I have seen the suffering of my people in Egypt. I have heard their groans and have come down to rescue them. Now I am sending you back to Egypt."

35This was the same Moses that the people rejected by saying, "Who made you our leader and judge?" God's angel had spoken to Moses from the bush. And God had even sent the angel to help Moses rescue the people and be their leader.

36In Egypt and at the Red Sea^v and in the desert, Moses rescued the people by working miracles and wonders for 40 years. 37Moses is the one who told the people of Israel, "God will choose one of your people to be a prophet, just as he chose me." 38Moses brought our people together in the desert, and the angel spoke to him on Mount Sinai. There he was given these life-giving words to pass on to us. 39But our ancestors refused to obey Moses. They rejected him and wanted to go back to Egypt.

40The people said to Aaron, "Make some gods to lead us! Moses led us out of Egypt, but we don't know what's happened to him now." 41Then they made an idol in the shape of a calf. They offered sacrifices to the idol and were pleased with what they had done.

42God turned his back on his people and left them. Then they worshiped the stars in the sky, just as it says in the Book of the Prophets, "People of Israel, you didn't offer sacrifices and offerings

---

^v7.36 Red Sea: This name comes from the Bible of the early Christians, a translation made into Greek about 200 B.C. It refers to the body of water that the Israelites crossed and was one of the marshes or fresh water lakes near the eastern part of the Nile Delta, where they lived and where the towns of Exodus 13.17—14.9 were located.

7.20 Moses: For many Jews, Moses was the most important person in their history. He led the Hebrew people out of slavery in Egypt, and God chose to give him the Law that the Israelite people were to live by. The story of Moses that Stephen tells in 7.20-44 is given in the books of Exodus, Leviticus, Numbers, and Deuteronomy.

Moses

7.29 country of Midian: Midian was the land east of the Gulf of Aqabah. (See Map 3 on pg 1881.)

7.29 His two sons: Moses' sons were Gershom and Eliezer.

7.33 sandals: Removing sandals was considered an act of respect for God and God's holy place. See also Josh 5.15.

7.42,43 God turned his back … carried off beyond Babylonia: The prophets often told the people of Israel how they had turned their back on God. Stephen's quotes from Amos 5.25-27 (Septuagint) recalled that the people had worshiped the god Molech and kept the star of the god Rephan.

When people of the northern kingdom (Israel) turned their backs on God and were defeated by the Assyrians in 721 B.C. many of them were carried off to Damascus and other parts of Assyria. About 130 years later, the southern kingdom (Judah) was defeated by the Babylonians who took many of its people into exile in Babylon.

Exile

The Sacred Tent

7.47 *King Solomon who built a house:* Solomon, David's son, was a wise and wealthy king who built the first temple.

7.48 *Most High God:* This name for God was very old. In Israel's history, it dates to the time of Abraham. Abraham met Melchizedek, the King of Salem, who was called "a priest of God Most High" (Gen 14.17-22).

Names of God

7.56 *Son of Man:* Jesus called himself the Son of Man as a way of drawing attention to the fact that he is a human being who represents God's faithful people.

Son of Man

to me during those 40 years in the desert. [43]Instead, you carried the tent where the god Molech is worshiped, and you took along the star of your god Rephan. You made those idols and worshiped them. So now I will have you carried off beyond Babylonia."

[44]The tent where our ancestors worshiped God was with them in the desert. This was the same tent that God had commanded Moses to make. And it was made like the model that Moses had seen. [45]Later it was given to our ancestors, and they took it with them when they went with Joshua. They carried the tent along as they took over the land from those people that God had chased out for them. Our ancestors used this tent until the time of King David. [46]He pleased God and asked him if he could build a house of worship for the people[w] of Israel. [47]And it was finally King Solomon who built a house for God.[x]

[48]But the Most High God doesn't live in houses made by humans. It is just as the prophet said, when he spoke for the Lord,

[49]"Heaven is my throne,
 and the earth
  is my footstool.
 What kind of house
  will you build for me?
 In what place will I rest?
[50]I have made everything."

[51]You stubborn and hardheaded people! You are always fighting against the Holy Spirit, just as your ancestors did. [52]Is there one prophet that your ancestors didn't mistreat? They killed the prophets who told about the coming of the One Who Obeys God.[y] And now you have turned against him and killed him. [53]Angels gave you God's Law, but you still don't obey it.

Stephen Is Stoned to Death

[54]When the council members heard Stephen's speech, they were angry and furious. [55]But Stephen was filled with the Holy Spirit. He looked toward heaven, where he saw our glorious God and Jesus standing at his right side.[z] [56]Then Stephen said, "I see heaven open and the Son of Man standing at the right side of God!"

[57]The council members shouted and covered their ears. At once they all attacked Stephen [58]and dragged him out of the city. Then they started throwing stones at him. The men who had brought charges against him put their coats at the feet of a young man named Saul.[a]

[59]As Stephen was being stoned to death, he called out, "Lord Jesus, please welcome me!" [60]He knelt down and shouted, "Lord, don't blame them for what they have done." Then he died.

8 [1-2]Saul approved the stoning of Stephen. Some faithful followers of the Lord buried Stephen and mourned very much for him.

Saul Makes Trouble for the Church

At that time the church in Jerusalem suffered terribly. All of the Lord's followers, except the apostles, were scattered

---

[w]**7.46** *people:* Some manuscripts have "God." [x]**7.47** *God:* Or "the people." [y]**7.52** *One Who Obeys God:* That is, Jesus. [z]**7.55** *standing at his right side:* The "right side" is the place of honor and power. "Standing" may mean that Jesus is welcoming Stephen (see verse 59). [a]**7.58** *Saul:* Better known as Paul, who became a famous follower of Jesus.

Stephen said, "I see heaven open and the Son of Man standing at the right side of God!" ACTS 7.56

everywhere in Judea and Samaria. ³Saul started making a lot of trouble for the church. He went from house to house, arresting men and women and putting them in jail.

The Good News Is Preached in Samaria

⁴The Lord's followers who had been scattered went from place to place, telling the good news. ⁵Philip went to the city of Samaria and told the people about Christ. ⁶They crowded around Philip because they were eager to hear what he was saying and to see him work miracles. ⁷Many people with evil spirits were healed, and the spirits went out of them with a shout. A lot of paralyzed and lame people were also healed. ⁸Everyone in that city was very glad because of what was happening.

⁹For some time a man named Simon had lived there and had amazed the people of Samaria. He practiced witchcraft and claimed to be somebody great. ¹⁰Everyone, rich and poor, crowded around him. They said, "This man is the power of God called 'The Great Power.' "

¹¹For a long time, Simon had used witchcraft to amaze the people, and they kept crowding around him. ¹²But when they believed what Philip was saying about God's kingdom and about the name of Jesus Christ, they were all baptized. ¹³Even Simon believed and was baptized. He stayed close to Philip, because he marveled at all the miracles and wonders.

¹⁴The apostles in Jerusalem heard that some people in Samaria had accepted God's message, and they sent Peter and John. ¹⁵When the two apostles arrived, they prayed that these people would be given the Holy Spirit. ¹⁶Before this, the Holy Spirit had not been given to any of them, though some of them had been baptized in the name of the Lord Jesus. ¹⁷Peter and John then placed their hands on everyone who had faith in the Lord, and they were given the Holy Spirit.

¹⁸Simon noticed that the Spirit was given only when the apostles placed their hands on the people. So he brought money ¹⁹and said to Peter and John, "Let me have this power too! Then anyone I place my hands on will also be given the Holy Spirit."

²⁰Peter said to him, "You and your money will both end up in hell if you think you can buy God's gift! ²¹You don't have any part in this, and God sees that your heart isn't right. ²²Get rid of these evil thoughts and ask God to forgive you. ²³I can see that you are jealous and bound by your evil ways."

²⁴Simon said, "Please pray to the Lord, so that what you said won't happen to me."

²⁵After Peter and John had preached about the Lord, they returned to Jerusalem. On their way they told the good news in many villages of Samaria.

Philip and an Ethiopian Official

²⁶The Lord's angel said to Philip, "Go south[b] along the desert road that leads from Jerusalem to Gaza."[c] ²⁷So Philip left.

An important Ethiopian official happened to be going along that road in his chariot. He was the chief treasurer for Candace, the Queen of Ethiopia. The official had gone to Jerusalem to worship ²⁸and was now on his way home. He was sitting in his chariot, reading the book of the prophet Isaiah.

---

b8.26 Go south: Or "About noon go."   **c**8.26 the desert road that leads from Jerusalem to Gaza: Or "the road that leads from Jerusalem to Gaza in the desert."

● 8.3 Saul: This man later became an important leader (apostle) in the early church. After becoming a follower of Jesus, he began to use his Greek name, Paul. His letters to churches and individuals in the Mediterranean world would become an important part of the New Testament.

∝ Paul (Saul) of Tarsus

● 8.5 Philip: Philip was one of the seven men chosen to be a leader in the new church (6.5).

● 8.9 Simon . . . practiced witchcraft: Also known as Simon the magician, his witchcraft was to call up the spirits of the dead or to tell fortunes. **(See the article Miracles, Magic, and Medicine on pg 1820.)**

■ 8.20 hell: The Greek word for hell in this verse is apoleia, which means a place of complete destruction.

∝ Hell

■ 8.21 heart isn't right: The heart was thought to be the place where a person's true inner self, thoughts, and intentions came from.

● 8.28 book of . . . Isaiah: The scroll called ISAIAH that is found in the Jewish Scriptures (Old Testament).

∝ Scrolls

8.40 Azotus ... all the way to Caesarea: Caesarea was about 40 miles north of Azotus on the Mediterranean coast. Herod named this city in honor of Emperor Caesar Augustus, who had made Herod "king" of Judea. Herod, who was famous for his building projects, built an aqueduct and a fortress in Caesarea, and turned the harbor into a major seaport. **(See Map 12 on pg 1890.)**

9.2 Damascus: One of the oldest, continuously inhabited cities in the Near East. Under the Romans it became one of the major cities in the Greek-style confederacy called the Decapolis. Damascus was a major center for trade between Palestine and the Mediterranean world. Saul knew that if he did not stop the Christian message in Damascus, the message could spread everywhere.

9.2 the Lord's Way: In ACTS, "Lord's Way," "God's Way," or simply the "The Way" refer to the group of people who had become followers of Jesus Christ.

9.11 city of Tarsus: Saul grew up in Tarsus, which was located in Cilicia, a Roman province of Asia Minor. Its location on a trade route through the Tarsus Mountains allowed for a mix of cultures and ideas. Tarsus was famous as a center of learning—on the level of Athens in Greece and Alexandria in Egypt. **(See Map 14 on pg 1892.)**

29The Spirit told Philip to catch up with the chariot. 30Philip ran up close and heard the man reading aloud from the book of Isaiah. Philip asked him, "Do you understand what you are reading?"

31The official answered, "How can I understand unless someone helps me?" He then invited Philip to come up and sit beside him.

32The man was reading the passage that said,

"He was led like a sheep
 on its way to be killed.
He was silent as a lamb
whose wool
 is being cut off,
and he did not say
 a word.
   33He was treated like a nobody
 and did not receive
 a fair trial.
How can he have children,
if his life
 is snatched away?"

34The official said to Philip, "Tell me, was the prophet talking about himself or about someone else?" 35So Philip began at this place in the Scriptures and explained the good news about Jesus.

36-37As they were going along the road, they came to a place where there was some water. The official said, "Look! Here is some water. Why can't I be baptized?"d 38He ordered the chariot to stop. Then they both went down into the water, and Philip baptized him.

39After they had come out of the water, the Lord's Spirit took Philip away. The official never saw him again, but he was very happy as he went on his way.

40Philip later appeared in Azotus. He went from town to town, all the way to Caesarea, telling people about Jesus.

Saul Becomes a Follower of the Lord
(Acts 22.6-16; 26.12-18)

9 Saul kept on threatening to kill the Lord's followers. He even went to the high priest 2and asked for letters to the leaders of the synagogues in Damascus. He did this because he wanted to arrest and take to Jerusalem any man or woman who had accepted the Lord's Way.e 3When Saul had almost reached Damascus, a bright light from heaven suddenly flashed around him. 4He fell to the ground and heard a voice saying, "Saul! Saul! Why are you so cruel to me?"

5"Who are you?" Saul asked.

"I am Jesus," the Lord answered. "I am the one you are so cruel to. 6Now get up and go into the city, where you will be told what to do."

7The men with Saul stood there speechless. They had heard the voice, but they had not seen anyone. 8Saul got up from the ground, and when he opened his eyes, he could not see a thing. Someone then led him by the hand to Damascus, 9and for three days he was blind and did not eat or drink.

10A follower named Ananias lived in Damascus, and the Lord spoke to him in a vision. Ananias answered, "Lord, here I am."

11The Lord said to him, "Get up and go to the house of Judas on Straight Street. When you get there, you will find a man named Saul from the city of Tarsus. Saul is praying, 12and he has seen a vision. He saw

d8.36,37 Why can't I be baptized: Some manuscripts add, "Philip replied, 'You can, if you believe with all your heart.' The official answered, 'I believe that Jesus Christ is the Son of God.' " e9.2 accepted the Lord's Way: In the book of Acts, this means to become a follower of the Lord Jesus.

a man named Ananias coming to him and putting his hands on him, so he could see again."

¹³Ananias replied, "Lord, a lot of people have told me about the terrible things this man has done to your followers in Jerusalem. ¹⁴Now the chief priests have given him the power to come here and arrest anyone who worships in your name."

¹⁵The Lord said to Ananias, "Go! I have chosen him to tell foreigners, kings, and the people of Israel about me. ¹⁶I will show him how much he must suffer for worshiping in my name."

¹⁷Ananias left and went into the house where Saul was staying. Ananias placed his hands on him and said, "Saul, the Lord Jesus has sent me. He is the same one who appeared to you along the road. He wants you to be able to see and to be filled with the Holy Spirit."

¹⁸Suddenly something like fish scales fell from Saul's eyes, and he could see. He got up and was baptized. ¹⁹Then he ate and felt much better.

Saul Preaches in Damascus

For several days Saul stayed with the Lord's followers in Damascus. ²⁰Soon he went to the synagogues and started telling people that Jesus is the Son of God. ²¹Everyone who heard Saul was amazed and said, "Isn't this the man who caused so much trouble for those people in Jerusalem who worship in the name of Jesus? Didn't he come here to arrest them and take them to the chief priests?"

²²Saul preached with such power that he completely confused the Jewish people in Damascus, as he tried to show them that Jesus is the Messiah.

²³Later some of them made plans to kill Saul, ²⁴but he found out about it. He learned that they were guarding the gates of the city day and night in order to kill him. ²⁵Then one night his followers let him down over the city wall in a large basket.

Saul in Jerusalem

²⁶When Saul arrived in Jerusalem, he tried to join the followers. But they were all afraid of him, because they did not believe he was a true follower. ²⁷Then Barnabas helped him by taking him to the apostles. He explained how Saul had seen the Lord and how the Lord had spoken to him. Barnabas also said when Saul was in Damascus, he had spoken bravely in the name of Jesus.

²⁸Saul moved about freely with the followers in Jerusalem and told everyone about the Lord. ²⁹He was always arguing with the Jews who spoke Greek, and so they tried to kill him. ³⁰But the followers found out about this and took Saul to Caesarea. From there they sent him to the city of Tarsus.

³¹The church in Judea, Galilee, and Samaria now had a time of peace and kept on worshiping the Lord. The church became stronger, as the Holy Spirit encouraged it and helped it grow.

Peter Heals Aeneas

³²While Peter was traveling from place to place, he visited the Lord's followers who lived in the town of Lydda. ³³There he met a man named Aeneas, who for eight years had been sick in bed and could not move. ³⁴Peter said to Aeneas, "Jesus Christ has healed you! Get up and make up your bed."ᶠ At once he stood up.

ᶠ9.34 and make up your bed: Or "and fix something to eat."

9.15 *foreigners:* "Foreigners" here means Gentiles (non-Jews).

Gentiles

9.20 *synagogues:* "Synagogue" comes from a Greek word that means "gathering." In the Bible, a synagogue was any group of people who met together to worship the Lord and study the Scriptures.

Synagogues

9.26 *Jerusalem:* Most of the apostles and many other followers of Jesus were still in Jerusalem, the center of the Jewish religion.

9.31 *Judea, Galilee, and Samaria:* Judea, Galilee, and Samaria were regions of Palestine. The first part of Jesus' promise to the apostles was coming to pass (see 1.8). (See Map 1 on pg 1879.)

9.31 *church:* The church here refers not to a single congregation but to all the followers of Jesus wherever they lived.

9.32 *town of Lydda:* Lydda was about 35 miles northwest of Jerusalem and 11 miles southeast of Joppa. Since around 145 B.C. it had been a Jewish town. The fact that there were followers of the Lord here shows that the church was spreading west of Jerusalem as well as the northeast.

9.35 *Sharon:* Sharon was a fertile strip of land that stretched 50 miles along the Mediterranean Sea coast between Mount Carmel in the north and Joppa in the south.

9.36 *Joppa:* When Peter arrived in the port city of Joppa, there was already a Christian community living there. Joppa dates back to the eighteenth century B.C. It was controlled by the Egyptians from around 1500 to 1225 B.C. Later, it became a Phoenician city. Today, this city is called Jaffa and is a suburb of Tel Aviv, Israel.

9.43 *who made leather:* Leather making, also called tanning, is an ancient craft that involves processing animal skins for use as clothing, tents, and household items. Because leather makers soaked animal skins in foul-smelling solutions, their work areas were unpleasant. Leather workers usually lived outside of town.

10.1 *Cornelius ... The Italian Unit:* Cornelius was a Roman centurion. A Roman army legion was divided into ten units (regiments), and each unit had a special name. The group Cornelius commanded was part of the unit called the "Italian." A centurion was in charge of about one-sixth of a regiment, or about 100 men.

10.3 *vision:* In the Bible, God's Spirit, or a messenger of God such as an angel, speaks to the deepest thoughts of a person, providing a clear picture of something they are to do or to say. This is called a "vision."

35Many people in the towns of Lydda and Sharon saw Aeneas and became followers of the Lord.

Peter Brings Dorcas Back to Life

36In Joppa there was a follower named Tabitha. Her Greek name was Dorcas, which means "deer." She was always doing good things for people and had given much to the poor. **37**But she got sick and died, and her body was washed and placed in an upstairs room. **38**Joppa wasn't far from Lydda, and the followers heard that Peter was there. They sent two men to say to him, "Please come with us as quickly as you can!" **39**At once, Peter went with them.

The men took Peter upstairs into the room. Many widows were there crying. They showed him the coats and clothes that Dorcas had made while she was still alive.

40After Peter had sent everyone out of the room, he knelt down and prayed. Then he turned to the body of Dorcas and said, "Tabitha, get up!" The woman opened her eyes, and when she saw Peter, she sat up. **41**He took her by the hand and helped her to her feet.

Peter called in the widows and the other followers and showed them that Dorcas had been raised from death. **42**Everyone in Joppa heard what had happened, and many of them put their faith in the Lord. **43**Peter stayed on for a while in Joppa in the house of a man named Simon, who made leather.

Peter and Cornelius

10 In Caesarea there was a man named Cornelius, who was the captain of a group of soldiers called "The Italian Unit." **2**Cornelius was a very religious man. He worshiped God, and so did everyone else who lived in his house. He had given a lot of money to the poor and was always praying to God.

3One afternoon at about three o'clock,[g] Cornelius had a vision. He saw an angel from God coming to him and calling him by name. **4**Cornelius was surprised and stared at the angel. Then he asked, "What is this all about?"

The angel answered, "God has heard your prayers and knows about your gifts to the poor. **5**Now send some men to Joppa for a man named Simon Peter. **6**He is staying with Simon the leather maker, who lives in a house near the sea." **7**After saying this, the angel left.

Cornelius called in two of his servants and one of his soldiers who worshiped God. **8**He explained everything to them and sent them off to Joppa.

9The next day about noon these men were coming near Joppa. Peter went up on the roof[h] of the house to pray **10**and became very hungry. While the food was being prepared, he fell sound asleep and had a vision. **11**He saw heaven open, and something came down like a huge sheet held up by its four corners. **12**In it were all kinds of animals, reptiles, and birds. **13**A voice said to him, "Peter, get up! Kill these and eat them." **14**But Peter said, "Lord, I can't do that! I've never eaten anything that is unclean and not fit to eat."[i]

[g]**10.3** *at about three o'clock:* Probably while he was praying (see 3.1 and the note there). [h]**10.9** *roof:* In Palestine the houses usually had a flat roof. Stairs on the outside led up to the roof, which was made of beams and boards covered with packed earth. [i]**10.14** *unclean and not fit to eat:* The Law of Moses taught that some foods were not fit to eat.

15The voice spoke to him again, "When God says that something can be used for food, don't say it isn't fit to eat."

16This happened three times before the sheet was suddenly taken back to heaven.

17Peter was still wondering what all this meant, when the men sent by Cornelius came and stood at the gate. They had found their way to Simon's house 18and were asking if Simon Peter was staying there.

19While Peter was still thinking about the vision, the Holy Spirit said to him, "Threej men are here looking for you. 20Hurry down and go with them. Don't worry, I sent them."

21Peter went down and said to the men, "I am the one you are looking for. Why have you come?"

22They answered, "Captain Cornelius sent us. He is a good man who worships God and is liked by the Jewish people. One of God's holy angels told Cornelius to send for you, so he could hear what you have to say." 23Peter invited them to spend the night.

The next morning, Peter and some of the Lord's followers in Joppa left with the men who had come from Cornelius. 24The next day they arrived in Caesarea where Cornelius was waiting for them. He had also invited his relatives and close friends.

25When Peter arrived, Cornelius greeted him. Then he knelt at Peter's feet and started worshiping him. 26But Peter took hold of him and said, "Stand up! I am nothing more than a human."

27As Peter entered the house, he was still talking with Cornelius. Many people were there, 28and Peter said to them, "You know that we Jews are not allowed to have anything to do with other people. But God has shown me that he doesn't think anyone is unclean or unfit. 29I agreed to come here, but I want to know why you sent for me."

30Cornelius answered:

Four days ago at about three o'clock in the afternoon I was praying at home. Suddenly a man in bright clothes stood in front of me. 31He said, "Cornelius, God has heard your prayers, and he knows about your gifts to the poor. 32Now send to Joppa for Simon Peter. He is visiting in the home of Simon the leather maker, who lives near the sea."

33I sent for you at once, and you have been good enough to come. All of us are here in the presence of the Lord God, so that we can hear what he has to say.

34Peter then said:

Now I am certain that God treats all people alike. 35God is pleased with everyone who worships him and does right, no matter what nation they come from. 36This is the same message that God gave to the people of Israel, when he sent Jesus Christ, the Lord of all, to offer peace to them.

37You surely know what happenedk everywhere in Judea. It all began in Galilee after John had told everyone to be baptized. 38God gave the Holy Spirit and power to Jesus from Nazareth. He was with Jesus, as he went around doing good and healing everyone who was under the power of the devil. 39We all saw what Jesus did both in Israel and in the city of Jerusalem.

Jesus was put to death on a cross. 40But three days later, God raised him to life and let him be seen. 41Not everyone saw him. He was seen only by

10.30 a man in bright clothes: This is how Cornelius described the angel.

10.37 John: This is John the Baptist.

10.43 *Every one of the prophets:* Israel's prophets lived between 200 and 800 years before Jesus. None of them mentioned Jesus by name, but many talked about how God would restore the Israelite people or make a new start with them. Others talked about one who would be a Messiah (Chosen Leader) for the people.

10.45 *Jewish followers of the Lord:* Most of the very earliest followers of Jesus were Jewish, as were Jesus and his first disciples.

Gentiles

11.1 *apostles and followers in Judea:* These are the rest of the twelve apostles and others who lived in and around Jerusalem. At this time, Jerusalem was still the center for the followers of Jesus.

11.3 *stayed in the homes of Gentiles . . . ate with them:* The Law of Moses said Jewish people were not to spend time with Gentiles (non-Jews) or eat food Gentiles had touched. They were shocked that Peter had done this and thought this had made Peter unclean.

Gentiles

Purity (Clean and Unclean)

11.12,13 *a man who told us:* Peter is referring to Captain Cornelius.

us, who ate and drank with him after he was raised from death. We were the ones God chose to tell others about him.

⁴²God told us to announce clearly to the people that Jesus is the one he has chosen to judge the living and the dead. ⁴³Every one of the prophets has said that all who have faith in Jesus will have their sins forgiven in his name.

⁴⁴While Peter was still speaking, the Holy Spirit took control of everyone who was listening. ⁴⁵Some Jewish followers of the Lord had come with Peter, and they were surprised that the Holy Spirit had been given to Gentiles. ⁴⁶Now they were hearing Gentiles speaking unknown languages and praising God.

Peter said, ⁴⁷"These Gentiles have been given the Holy Spirit, just as we have! I am certain that no one would dare stop us from baptizing them." ⁴⁸Peter ordered them to be baptized in the name of Jesus Christ, and they asked him to stay on for a few days.

Peter Reports to the Church in Jerusalem

11 The apostles and the followers in Judea heard that Gentiles had accepted God's message. ²So when Peter came to Jerusalem, some of the Jewish followers started arguing with him. They wanted Gentile followers to be circumcised, and ³they said, "You stayed in the homes of Gentiles, and you even ate with them!"

⁴Then Peter told them exactly what had happened:

⁵I was in the town of Joppa and was praying when I fell sound asleep and had a vision. I saw heaven open, and

¹11.8 *unclean and not fit to eat:* See the note at 10.14.

something like a huge sheet held by its four corners came down to me. ⁶When I looked in it, I saw animals, wild beasts, reptiles, and birds. ⁷I heard a voice saying to me, "Peter, get up! Kill these and eat them."

⁸But I said, "Lord, I can't do that! I've never taken a bite of anything that is unclean and not fit to eat."¹

⁹The voice from heaven spoke to me again, "When God says that something can be used for food, don't say it isn't fit to eat." ¹⁰This happened three times before it was all taken back into heaven.

¹¹Suddenly three men from Caesarea stood in front of the house where I was staying. ¹²The Holy Spirit told me to go with them and not to worry. Then six of the Lord's followers went with me to the home of a man ¹³who told us that an angel had appeared to him. The angel had ordered him to send to Joppa for someone named Simon Peter. ¹⁴Then Peter would tell him how he and everyone in his house could be saved.

¹⁵After I started speaking, the Holy Spirit was given to them, just as the Spirit had been given to us at the beginning. ¹⁶I remembered that the Lord had said, "John baptized with water, but you will be baptized with the Holy Spirit." ¹⁷God gave those Gentiles the same gift that he gave us when we put our faith in the Lord Jesus Christ. So how could I have gone against God?

¹⁸When they heard Peter say this, they stopped arguing and started praising God. They said, "God has now let Gentiles turn to him, and he has given life to them!"

The Church in Antioch

[19]Some of the Lord's followers had been scattered because of the terrible trouble that started when Stephen was killed. They went as far as Phoenicia, Cyprus, and Antioch, but they told the message only to the Jews.

[20]Some of the followers from Cyprus and Cyrene went to Antioch and started telling Gentiles[m] the good news about the Lord Jesus. [21]The Lord's power was with them, and many people turned to the Lord and put their faith in him. [22]News of what was happening reached the church in Jerusalem. Then they sent Barnabas to Antioch.

[23]When Barnabas got there and saw how God had blessed them with undeserved grace, he was very glad. So he begged them to remain faithful to the Lord with all their hearts. [24]Barnabas was a good man of great faith, and he was filled with the Holy Spirit. Many more people turned to the Lord.

[25]Barnabas went to Tarsus to look for Saul. [26]He found Saul and brought him to Antioch, where they met with the church for a whole year and taught many of its people. There in Antioch the Lord's followers were first called Christians.

[27]During this time some prophets from Jerusalem came to Antioch. [28]One of them was Agabus. Then with the help of the Spirit, he told that there would be a terrible famine everywhere in the world. And it happened when Claudius was Emperor.[n] [29]The followers in Antioch decided to send whatever help they could to the followers in Judea. [30]So they appointed Barnabas and Saul to take their gifts to the church leaders in Jerusalem.

Herod Causes Trouble for the Church

12 At that time King Herod[o] caused terrible suffering for some members of the church. [2]He ordered soldiers to cut off the head of James, the brother of John. [3]When Herod saw that this pleased the Jewish people, he had Peter arrested during the Festival of Thin Bread. [4]He put Peter in jail and ordered four squads of soldiers to guard him. Herod planned to put him on trial in public after the festival.

[5]While Peter was being kept in jail, the church never stopped praying to God for him.

Peter Is Rescued

[6]The night before Peter was to be put on trial, he was asleep and bound by two chains. A soldier was guarding him on each side, and two other soldiers were guarding the entrance to the jail. [7]Suddenly an angel from the Lord appeared, and light flashed around in the cell. The angel poked Peter in the side and woke him up. Then he said, "Quick! Get up!"

The chains fell off his hands, [8]and the angel said, "Get dressed and put on your sandals." Peter did what he was told. Then the angel said, "Now put on your coat and follow me." [9]Peter left with the angel, but he thought everything was only a dream. [10]They went past the two groups of soldiers, and when they came to the iron gate to the city, it opened by itself. They went out and were going along the street, when all at once the angel disappeared.

[11]Peter now realized what had happened,

11.19 *the terrible trouble . . . when Stephen was killed:* The execution of Stephen created fear among the early Christians. Christians began to move out of Jerusalem and Judea to places where they could gather and worship in peace.

11.19,20 *Phoenicia, Cyprus, and Antioch:* The region of Phoenicia stretched about 120 miles along the northeastern Mediterranean Sea coast. Its most important cities were Tyre and Sidon. Cyprus, at this time part of the Roman Empire, is an island in the northeastern Mediterranean Sea, about 100 miles west of the coast of Syria. Antioch was a Greek city in Syria that became an important center for the early Christian outreach to the Gentiles.

11.28 *Agabus:* He is a follower of Jesus who had received the gift of prophecy from the Holy Spirit (1 Cor 12.7-11).

12.2 *James, the brother of John:* James and John were two of the apostles, the sons of Zebedee (see Matt 4.21). Jesus had predicted that the brothers would drink from the cup that he must soon drink from (Matt 20.22, 23), which meant they would also suffer and die at the hands of enemies.

---

[m]**11.20** *Gentiles:* This translates a Greek word that may mean "people who speak Greek" or "people who live as Greeks do." Here the word seems to mean "people who are not Jews." Some manuscripts have "Greeks," which also seems to mean "people who are not Jews." [n]**11.28** *when Claudius was Emperor:* A.D. 41–54. [o]**12.1** *Herod:* Herod Agrippa I, the grandson of Herod the Great.

12.12 *Mary the mother of John . . . Mark:* Mary may have been the aunt of Barnabas (Col 4.10). Her home was probably a meeting place for followers of Jesus. John Mark is mentioned again in 12.25. He had been a co-worker of Paul.

12.17 *James:* The brother of Jesus (Matt 13.55; Mark 6.3). Later, James became the head of the Jewish-Christian church in Jerusalem (Acts 15.13; 21.18; Gal 1.19), where he helped resolve differences between the Jewish and Gentile followers of Jesus (15.22-29; see also Gal 2.9).

13.1 *Simeon . . . Lucius . . . Manaen:* Simeon is a Jewish name, but Niger is Latin meaning "black." This may mean that he had dark skin. Lucius came from Cyrene to preach in Antioch. Manaen had lived in the court of Herod Antipas, who had ruled Galilee at the time of Jesus.

13.4 *Seleucia:* Seleucia was a free Roman city in Syria not far from Antioch. (See Map 15 on pg 1893.)

and he said, "I am certain that the Lord sent his angel to rescue me from Herod and from everything the Jewish leaders planned to do to me." ¹²Then Peter went to the house of Mary the mother of John whose other name was Mark. Many of the Lord's followers had come together there and were praying.

¹³Peter knocked on the gate, and a servant named Rhoda came to answer. ¹⁴When she heard Peter's voice, she was too excited to open the gate. She ran back into the house and said Peter was standing there.

¹⁵"You are crazy!" everyone told her. But she kept saying it was Peter. Then they said, "It must be his angel."ᴾ ¹⁶But Peter kept on knocking, until finally they opened the gate. They saw him and were completely amazed.

¹⁷Peter motioned for them to keep quiet. Then he told how the Lord had led him out of jail. He also said, "Tell Jamesᑫ and the others what has happened." After that, he left and went somewhere else.

¹⁸The next morning the soldiers who had been on guard were terribly worried and wondered what had happened to Peter. ¹⁹Herod ordered his own soldiers to search for him, but they could not find him. Then he questioned the guards and had them put to death. After this, Herod left Judea to stay in Caesarea for a while.

Herod Dies

²⁰Herod and the people of Tyre and Sidon were very angry with each other. But their country got its food supply from the region that he ruled. So a group of them went to see Blastus, who was one of Herod's high officials. They convinced Blastus that they wanted to make peace between their cities and Herod, ²¹and a day was set for them to meet with him.

Herod came dressed in his royal robes. He sat down on his throne and made a speech. ²²The people shouted, "You speak more like a god than a man!" ²³At once an angel from the Lord struck him down because he took the honor that belonged to God. Later, Herod was eaten by worms and died.

²⁴God's message kept spreading. ²⁵And after Barnabas and Saul had done the work they were sent to do, they went back to Jerusalemʳ with John, whose other name was Mark.

Barnabas and Saul Are Chosen and Sent

13 The church at Antioch had several prophets and teachers. They were Barnabas, Simeon, also called Niger, Lucius from Cyrene, Manaen, who was Herod'sˢ close friend, and Saul. ²While they were worshiping the Lord and going without eating,ᵗ the Holy Spirit told them, "Appoint Barnabas and Saul to do the work for which I have chosen them." ³Everyone prayed and went without eating for a while longer. Next, they placed their hands on Barnabas and Saul to show that they had been appointed to do this work. Then everyone sent them on their way.

Barnabas and Saul in Cyprus

⁴After Barnabas and Saul had been sent by the Holy Spirit, they went to Seleucia.

P12.15 *his angel:* Probably meaning "his guardian angel." ᑫ12.17 *James:* The brother of the Lord. ʳ12.25 *went back to Jerusalem:* Some manuscripts have "left Jerusalem," and others have "went to Antioch." ˢ13.1 *Herod's:* Herod Antipas, the son of Herod the Great. ᵗ13.2 *going without eating:* The Jews often went without eating as a way of showing how much they loved God. This is also called "fasting."

From there they sailed to the island of Cyprus. [5]They arrived at Salamis and began to preach God's message in the synagogues. They also had John[u] as a helper.

[6]Barnabas and Saul went all the way to the city of Paphos on the other end of the island, where they met a Jewish man named Bar-Jesus. He practiced witchcraft and was a false prophet. [7]He also worked for Sergius Paulus, who was very smart and was the governor of the island. Sergius Paulus wanted to hear God's message, and he sent for Barnabas and Saul. [8]But Bar-Jesus, whose other name was Elymas, was against them. He even tried to keep the governor from having faith in the Lord.

[9]Then Saul, better known as Paul, was filled with the Holy Spirit. He looked straight at Elymas [10]and said, "You son of the devil! You are a liar, a crook, and an enemy of everything that is right. When will you stop speaking against the true ways of the Lord? [11]The Lord is going to punish you by making you completely blind for a while."

Suddenly the man's eyes were covered by a dark mist, and he went around trying to get someone to lead him by the hand. [12]When the governor saw what had happened, he was amazed at this teaching about the Lord. So he put his faith in the Lord.

Paul and Barnabas in Antioch of Pisidia

[13]Paul and the others left Paphos and sailed to Perga in Pamphylia. But John[v] left them and went back to Jerusalem. [14]The rest of them went on from Perga to Antioch in Pisidia. Then on the Sabbath they went to the synagogue and sat down.

[15]After the reading of the Law and the Prophets,[w] the leaders sent someone over to tell Paul and Barnabas, "Friends, if you have anything to say that will help the people, please say it."

[16]Paul got up. He motioned with his hand and said:

People of Israel, and everyone else who worships God, listen! [17]The God of Israel chose our ancestors, and he let our people prosper while they were living in Egypt. Then with his mighty power he led them out, [18]and for about 40 years he took care of[x] them in the desert. [19]He destroyed seven nations in the land of Canaan and gave their land to our people. [20]All this happened in about 450 years.

Then God gave our people judges until the time of the prophet Samuel, [21]but the people demanded a king. So for 40 years God gave them King Saul, the son of Kish from the tribe of Benjamin. [22]Later, God removed Saul and let David rule in his place. God said about him, "David the son of Jesse is the kind of person who pleases me most! He does everything I want him to do."

[23]God promised that someone from David's family would come to save the people of Israel, and this one is Jesus. [24]But before Jesus came, John was telling everyone in Israel to turn back to God and be baptized. [25]Then, when John's work was almost done, he said, "Who do you people think I am? Do you think I am the Promised One? He will come later, and I am not good enough to untie his sandals."

[26]Now listen, you descendants of Abraham! Pay attention, all of you

---

[u]**13.5** *John:* Whose other name was Mark (see 12.12,25). [v]**13.13** *John:* See the note at 13.5.
[w]**13.15** *the Law and the Prophets:* The Jewish Scriptures, that is, the Old Testament.   [x]**13.18** *took care of:* Some manuscripts have "put up with."

● **13.6** *Paphos:* Paphos became the capital of the Roman province of Cyprus in 22 B.C. Paul and Barnabas visited the city around A.D. 46. **(See Map 15 on pg 1893.)**

● **13.6** *Bar-Jesus . . . false prophet:* "Bar" is Aramaic for "son of." So, this man was named "son of Jesus." Many Jewish men were named Jesus, the Greek form of the Hebrew name Joshua. The witchcraft Bar-Jesus practiced probably included casting spells, telling fortunes, and doing magic.

● **13.7** *Sergius Paulus:* He was the Roman governor of Cyprus.

● **13.9** *Saul, better known as Paul:* Saul was his Jewish name. Paul was his Greek name. In Greek-speaking areas, he would have been more widely known by using his Greek name.

■ **13.10** *son of the devil:* This was Paul's way of saying that Elymas's deceitful ways made him closely related to the devil.

Satan

● **13.14** *Sabbath:* This Jewish day of rest (Sabbath) began at sunset on Friday and ended with a blessing at sunset on Saturday. The Sabbath was also a day when people gathered to read and discuss the Scriptures.

● **13.24** *John:* This is John the Baptist.

13.45 *Jewish people:* This does not mean all the Jewish people, since some Jewish people had invited Paul and Barnabas back to the next Sabbath meeting. It refers to Jewish people who did not believe what Paul was saying about Jesus. They thought Paul was trying to destroy the Law of Moses and the Jewish beliefs.

Eternal Life

Gentiles who are here to worship God! Listen to this message about how to be saved, because it is for everyone. **27**The people of Jerusalem and their leaders didn't realize who Jesus was. And they didn't understand the words of the prophets they read each Sabbath. So they condemned Jesus just as the prophets had said.

28-29 They did exactly what the Scriptures said they would. Even though they couldn't find any reason to put Jesus to death, they still asked Pilate to have him killed.

After Jesus had been put to death, he was taken down from the cross*y* and placed in a tomb. **30**But God raised him from death! **31**Then for many days Jesus appeared to his followers who had gone with him from Galilee to Jerusalem. Now they are telling our people about him.

32God made a promise to our ancestors. And we are here to tell you the good news **33**that he has kept this promise to us. It is just as the second Psalm says about Jesus,

"You are my son because today
I have become your Father."

34God raised Jesus from death and will never let his body decay. It is just as God said,

"I will make to you
the same holy promises
that I made to David."

35And in another psalm it says, "God will never let the body of his Holy One decay."

36When David was alive, he obeyed God. Then after he died, he was buried in the family grave, and his body de-cayed. **37**But God raised Jesus from death, and his body did not decay.

38My friends, the message is that Jesus can forgive your sins! The Law of Moses could not set you free from all your sins. **39**But everyone who has faith in Jesus is set free. **40**Make sure what the prophets have said doesn't happen to you. They said,

41"Look, you people
who make fun of God!
Be amazed
and disappear.
I will do something today
that you won't believe,
even if someone
tells you about it!"

42As Paul and Barnabas were leaving the synagogue, the people begged them to say more about these same things on the next Sabbath. **43**After the service, many Jews and a lot of Gentiles who worshiped God went with them. Paul and Barnabas begged them all to remain faithful to God, who had treated them with undeserved grace.

44The next Sabbath almost everyone in town came to hear the message about the Lord.*z* **45**When the Jewish people saw the crowds, they were very jealous. They insulted Paul and spoke against everything he said.

46But Paul and Barnabas bravely said:

We had to tell God's message to you before we told it to anyone else. But you rejected the message! This proves that you don't deserve eternal life. Now we are going to the Gentiles. **47**The Lord has given us this command,

"I have placed you here
as a light
for the Gentiles.

*y***13.28,29** *cross:* This translates a Greek word that means "wood," "pole," or "tree." *z***13.44** *the Lord:* Some manuscripts have "God."

You are to take
the saving power of God
to people everywhere on earth."

[48]This message made the Gentiles glad, and they praised what they had heard about the Lord.[a] Everyone who had been chosen for eternal life then put their faith in the Lord.

[49]The message about the Lord spread all over this region. [50]But the Jewish leaders went to some of the important men in the town and to some respected women who were religious. They turned them against Paul and Barnabas and started making trouble for them. They even chased them out of this part of the country.

[51]Paul and Barnabas shook the dust from that place off their feet[b] and went on to the city of Iconium.

[52]But the Lord's followers in Antioch were very happy and were filled with the Holy Spirit.

Paul and Barnabas in Iconium

14 Paul and Barnabas spoke in the synagogue in Iconium, just as they had done at Antioch, and many Jews and Gentiles[c] put their faith in the Lord. [2]But the Jews who did not have faith in him made the other Gentiles angry and turned them against the Lord's followers.

[3]Paul and Barnabas stayed there for a while, having faith in the Lord and bravely speaking his message. The Lord gave them the power to work miracles and wonders, and he showed that their message his gift of undeserved grace was true.

[4]The people of Iconium did not know what to think. Some of them believed the Jewish group, and others believed the apostles. [5]Finally, some Gentiles and Jews, together with their leaders, decided to make trouble for Paul and Barnabas and to stone them to death.

[6-7]But when the two apostles found out what was happening, they escaped to the region of Lycaonia. They preached the good news there in the towns of Lystra and Derbe and in the nearby countryside.

Paul and Barnabas in Lystra

[8]In Lystra there was a man who had been born with paralyzed feet and had never been able to walk. [9]The man was listening to Paul speak, when Paul saw that he had faith in Jesus and could be healed. So he looked straight at the man [10]and shouted, "Stand up!" The man jumped up and started walking around.

[11]When the crowd saw what Paul had done, they yelled out in the language of Lycaonia, "The gods have turned into humans and have come down to us!" [12]The people then gave Barnabas the name Zeus, and they gave Paul the name Hermes,[d] because he did the talking.

[13]The temple of Zeus was near the entrance to the city. Its priest and the crowds wanted to offer a sacrifice to Barnabas and Paul. So the priest brought some bulls and flowers to the city gates. [14]When the two apostles found out about this, they tore their clothes in horror and ran to the crowd, shouting:

[15]Why are you doing this? We are humans just like you. Please give up all this foolishness. Turn to the living

---

14.1 *Iconium:* Iconium was an important commercial city in the province of Galatia in Asia Minor. It was about 100 miles east of Antioch in Pisidia. Highways from Syria to Ephesus and Rome went through Iconium. **(See Map 15 on pg 1893.)**

14.6-7 *Lycaonia . . . Lystra and Derbe:* Lycaonia was a district in the region of Galatia. It was east of the province of Pisidia and north of the Taurus Mountains. Lystra was about 20 miles southwest of Iconium. Derbe was about 60 miles southeast of Lystra. **(See Map 15 on pg 1893.)**

14.12 *Hermes:* Hermes, similar to the Roman god Mercury, was considered the messenger of the other gods. Since Paul talked the most, the people called him "Hermes." **(See the chart Greek and Roman Gods and Goddesses on pgs 1838–39.)**

Religion in the Roman World

14.15 *the living God:* Paul was talking about Israel's God. He was comparing the living God to gods like Zeus, which were imaginary or simply made of stone.

---

[a]**13.48** *the Lord:* See the note at 13.44. [b]**13.51** *shook the dust from that place off their feet:* This was a way of showing rejection. [c]**14.1** *Gentiles:* The Greek text has "Greeks," which probably means people who were not Jews. But it may mean Gentiles who worshiped with the Jews. [d]**14.12** *Hermes:* The Greeks thought of Hermes as the messenger of the other gods, especially of Zeus, their chief god.

14.21 *Derbe . . . Lystra, Iconium, and Antioch in Pisidia:* Paul and Barnabas had the courage to return to cities where the leaders had made trouble for them, so they could encourage the new followers of Jesus.

14.24 *Pisidia to Pamphylia:* Pisidia was a district in the province of Galatia. Antioch was in this district. Pamphylia was a smaller district located southeast of Pisidia. (See Map 15 on pg 1893.)

14.25 *Attalia:* Attalia was a seaport on the coast of Pamphylia.

15.1 *Judea:* Judea was the area around Jerusalem. Many of the apostles and church leaders still lived there.

15.1 *could not be saved, unless they were circumcised:* Paul and Barnabas argued that this outward sign was not necessary for anyone to be part of God's new people.

Circumcision

15.5 *Gentiles . . . must be circumcised:* This is an argument that Paul faced many times (see Gal 2.3,11-21; 5.1-18).

God, who made the sky, the earth, the sea, and everything in them. ¹⁶In times past, God let each nation go its own way. ¹⁷But he showed he was there by the good things he did. God sends rain from heaven and makes your crops grow. He gives food to you and makes your hearts glad. ¹⁸Even after Paul and Barnabas had said all this, they could hardly keep the people from offering a sacrifice to them.

¹⁹Some Jewish leaders from Antioch and Iconium came and turned the crowds against Paul. They hit him with stones and dragged him out of the city, thinking he was dead. ²⁰But when the Lord's followers gathered around Paul, he stood up and went back into the city. The next day he and Barnabas went to Derbe.

Paul and Barnabas Return to Antioch in Syria

²¹Paul and Barnabas preached the good news in Derbe and won some people to the Lord. Then they went back to Lystra, Iconium, and Antioch in Pisidia. ²²They encouraged the followers and begged them to remain faithful. They told them, "We have to suffer a lot before we can get into God's kingdom." ²³Paul and Barnabas chose some leaders for each of the churches. Then they went without eating^e and prayed that the Lord would take good care of these leaders who had trusted in the Lord.

²⁴Paul and Barnabas went on through Pisidia to Pamphylia, ²⁵where they preached in the town of Perga. Then they went down to Attalia ²⁶and sailed to Antioch in Syria. It was there that they had been placed in God's care for the work they had now completed.^f

²⁷After arriving in Antioch, they called the church together. They told the people what God had helped them do and how he had made it possible for the Gentiles to believe. ²⁸Then they stayed there with the followers for a long time.

15 Some people came from Judea and started teaching the Lord's followers that they could not be saved, unless they were circumcised as Moses had taught. ²This caused trouble, and Paul and Barnabas argued with them about this teaching. So it was decided to send Paul and Barnabas and a few others to Jerusalem to discuss this problem with the apostles and the church leaders.

The Church Leaders Meet in Jerusalem

³The men who were sent by the church went through Phoenicia and Samaria, telling how the Gentiles had turned to God. This news made the Lord's followers very happy. ⁴When the men arrived in Jerusalem, they were welcomed by the church, including the apostles and the leaders. They told them everything God had helped them do. ⁵But some Pharisees had become followers of the Lord. They stood up and said, "Gentiles who have faith in the Lord must be circumcised and told to obey the Law of Moses."

⁶The apostles and church leaders met to discuss this problem about Gentiles. ⁷They had talked it over for a long time, when Peter got up and said:

My friends, you know that God decided long ago to let me be the one from your group to preach the good news to the Gentiles. God did this so they would hear and obey him. ⁸He knows what is in everyone's heart.

^e**14.23** *went without eating:* See the note at 13.2.   ^f**14.26** *the work they had now completed:* See 13.1-3.

And he showed he had chosen the Gentiles, when he gave them the Holy Spirit, just as he had given his Spirit to us. ⁹God treated them in the same way that he treated us. They put their faith in him, and he made their hearts pure.

¹⁰Now why are you trying to make God angry by placing a heavy burden on these followers? This burden was too heavy for us or our ancestors. ¹¹But we believe that we will be saved by the gift of undeserved grace from our Lord Jesus Christ, just as the Gentiles are.

¹²Everyone kept quiet and listened as Barnabas and Paul told how God had given them the power to work a lot of miracles and wonders for the Gentiles.

¹³After they had finished speaking, James^g said:

My friends, listen to me! ¹⁴Simon Peter^h has told how God first came to the Gentiles and made some of them his own people. ¹⁵This agrees with what the prophets wrote,

¹⁶"I, the Lord, will return
    and rebuild
        David's fallen house.
    I will build it from its ruins
        and set it up again.
¹⁷Then other nations
    will turn to me
        and be my chosen ones.
    I, the Lord, say this.
¹⁸I promised it long ago."

¹⁹And so, my friends, I don't think we should place burdens on the Gentiles who are turning to God. ²⁰We should simply write and tell them not to eat anything that has been offered to idols. They should be told not to eat the meat of any animal that has been strangled or that still has blood in it. They must also not commit any terrible sexual sins.^i

²¹We must remember that the Law of Moses has been preached in city after city for many years, and every Sabbath it is read in our synagogues.

A Letter to Gentiles Who Had Faith in the Lord

²²The apostles, the leaders, and all the church members decided to send some men to Antioch along with Paul and Barnabas. They chose Silas and Judas Barsabbas,^j who were two leaders of the Lord's followers. ²³They wrote a letter that said:

We apostles and leaders send friendly greetings to all of you Gentiles who are followers of the Lord in Antioch, Syria, and Cilicia.

²⁴We have heard that some people from here have terribly upset you by what they said. But we did not send them! ²⁵So we met together and decided to choose some men and to send them to you along with our good friends Barnabas and Paul. ²⁶These men have risked their lives for our Lord Jesus Christ. ²⁷We are also sending Judas and Silas, who will tell you in person the same things that we are writing.

²⁸The Holy Spirit has shown us that we should not place any extra burden on you. ²⁹But you should not eat anything offered to idols. You should not

■ 15.11 *saved by the gift of undeserved grace:* Paul makes the argument here and in many of his letters that all people—Jews and Gentiles alike—are saved by God's grace, not by following certain laws or rituals.

● 15.13 *James:* Jesus' brother was one of the leaders of the church in Jerusalem.

● 15.22 *Silas and Judas Barsabbas:* Silas received the gift of being a prophet. Like Paul, he was a Roman citizen, and is probably the person Paul mentioned in 2 Cor 1.19; 1 Thes 1.1. Judas Barsabbas may have been the brother of Joseph Barsabbas, who was mentioned in 1.23.

^g15.13 *James:* The Lord's brother.   ^h15.14 *Simon Peter:* The Greek text has "Simeon," which is another form of the name "Simon." The apostle Peter is meant.   ^i15.20 *not commit any terrible sexual sins:* This probably refers to the laws about the wrong kind of marriages that are forbidden in Leviticus 18.6-18 or to some serious sexual sin.   ^j15.22 *Judas Barsabbas:* He may have been a brother of Joseph Barsabbas (see 1.23), but the name "Barsabbas" was often used by the Jewish people.

15.36 *cities:* Paul was talking about the cities mentioned in Acts 13.1—14.28. (See Map 15 on pg 1893.)

15.41 *Syria:* Syria was a Roman province north of Palestine in the northeastern corner of the Mediterranean Sea. Antioch and Damascus were its most important cities. (See Map 14 on pg 1892.)

16.1 *Timothy:* An important coworker of Paul who is mentioned frequently in Paul's letters.

16.6 *Phrygia and Galatia . . . Asia:* Phrygia was a region in Asia Minor that included parts of the Roman provinces of Asia and Galatia. The province of Galatia extended from the eastern part of Phrygia north to the central part of Asia Minor. Paul's letter to the churches in Galatia, included in the New Testament, is called GALATIANS. Asia was a Roman province west of Phrygia that bordered on the Aegean Sea. Pergamum and Ephesus were two of its most important cities. (See Map 15 on pg 1893.)

16.10 *we began looking:* This is the first time the author of ACTS uses the word "we." This may suggest that the information he begins to relate here is from personal experience. Alternatively, it may suggest that the author is working from another person's firsthand account of Paul's travels.

eat any meat that still has the blood in it or any meat of any animal that has been strangled. You must also not commit any terrible sexual sins. If you follow these instructions, you will do well.

We send our best wishes.

[30]The four men left Jerusalem and went to Antioch. Then they called the church members together and gave them the letter. [31]When the letter was read, everyone was pleased and greatly encouraged. [32]Judas and Silas were prophets, and they spoke a long time, encouraging and helping the Lord's followers.

[33]The men from Jerusalem stayed on in Antioch for a while. And when they left to return to the ones who had sent them, the followers wished them well. [34-35]But Paul and Barnabas stayed on in Antioch, where they and many others taught and preached about the Lord.[k]

Paul and Barnabas Go Their Separate Ways

[36]Sometime later Paul said to Barnabas, "Let's go back and visit the Lord's followers in the cities where we preached his message. Then we will know how they are doing." [37]Barnabas wanted to take along John, whose other name was Mark. [38]But Paul did not want to, because Mark had left them in Pamphylia and had stopped working with them.

[39]Paul and Barnabas argued, then each of them went his own way. Barnabas took Mark and sailed to Cyprus, [40]but Paul took Silas and left after the followers had placed them in God's care. [41]They traveled through Syria and Cilicia, encouraging the churches.

Timothy Works with Paul and Silas

16 Paul and Silas went back to Derbe and Lystra, where there was a follower named Timothy. His mother was also a follower. She was Jewish, and his father was Greek. [2]The Lord's followers in Lystra and Iconium said good things about Timothy, [3]and Paul wanted him to go with them. But Paul first had him circumcised, because all the Jewish people around there knew that Timothy's father was Greek.[l]

[4]As Paul and the others went from city to city, they told the followers what the apostles and leaders in Jerusalem had decided, and they urged them to follow these instructions. [5]The churches became stronger in their faith, and each day more people put their faith in the Lord.

Paul's Vision in Troas

[6]Paul and his friends went through Phrygia and Galatia, but the Holy Spirit would not let them preach in Asia. [7]After they arrived in Mysia, they tried to go into Bithynia, but the Spirit of Jesus would not let them. [8]So they went on through[m] Mysia until they came to Troas.

[9]During the night, Paul had a vision of someone from Macedonia who was standing there and begging him, "Come over to Macedonia and help us!" [10]After Paul had seen the vision, we began looking for a way to go to Macedonia. We were sure that God had called us to preach the good news there.

[k]15.34,35 Verse 34, which says that Silas decided to stay on in Antioch, is not in some manuscripts. [l]16.3 *had him circumcised . . . Timothy's father was Greek:* Timothy would not have been acceptable to the Jews unless he had been circumcised, and Greeks did not circumcise their sons. [m]16.8 *went on through:* Or "passed by."

Lydia Becomes a Follower of the Lord

[11]We sailed straight from Troas to Samothrace, and the next day we arrived in Neapolis. [12]From there we went to Philippi, which is a Roman colony in the first district of Macedonia.[n]

We spent several days in Philippi. [13]Then on the Sabbath we went outside the city gate to a place by the river, where we thought there would be a Jewish meeting place for prayer. We sat down and talked with the women who came. [14]One of them was Lydia, who was from the city of Thyatira and sold expensive purple cloth. She was a worshiper of the Lord God, and he made her willing to accept what Paul was saying. [15]Then after she and her family were baptized, she kept on begging us, "If you think I really do have faith in the Lord, come stay in my home." Finally, we accepted her invitation.

Paul and Silas Are Put in Jail

[16]One day on our way to the place of prayer, we were met by a slave girl. She had a spirit in her that gave her the power to tell the future. By doing this she made a lot of money for her owners. [17]The girl followed Paul and the rest of us, and she kept yelling, "These men are servants of the Most High God! They are telling you how to be saved."

[18]This went on for several days. Finally, Paul got so upset that he turned and said to the spirit, "In the name of Jesus Christ, I order you to leave this girl alone!" At once the evil spirit left her.

[19]When the girl's owners realized they had lost all chances for making more money, they grabbed Paul and Silas and dragged them into court. [20]They told the officials, "These Jews are upsetting our city! [21]They are telling us to do things we Romans are not allowed to do."

[22]The crowd joined in the attack on Paul and Silas. Then the officials tore the clothes off the two men and ordered them to be beaten with a whip. [23]After they had been badly beaten, they were put in jail, and the jailer was told to guard them carefully. [24]The jailer did as he was told. He put them deep inside the jail and chained their feet to heavy blocks of wood.

[25]About midnight Paul and Silas were praying and singing praises to God, while the other prisoners listened. [26]Suddenly a strong earthquake shook the jail to its foundations. The doors opened, and the chains fell from all the prisoners.

[27]When the jailer woke up and saw that the doors were open, he thought that the prisoners had escaped. He pulled out his sword and was about to kill himself. [28]But Paul shouted, "Don't harm yourself! No one has escaped."

[29]The jailer asked for a torch and went into the jail. He was shaking all over as he knelt down in front of Paul and Silas. [30]After he had led them out of the jail, he asked, "What must I do to be saved?"

[31]They replied, "Have faith in the Lord Jesus and you will be saved! This is also true for everyone who lives in your home."

[32]Then Paul and Silas told him and everyone else in his house about the Lord. [33]While it was still night, the jailer took them to a place where he could wash their cuts and bruises. Then he and everyone in his home were baptized. [34]They were very glad they had put their faith in God. After this, the jailer took Paul and Silas to his home and gave them something to eat.

[35]The next morning the officials sent

16.12 *Philippi*: Philippi was named after Philip II, the father of Alexander the Great. In the fourth century B.C., Philip made the city into a fortress and the capital of his growing kingdom. At the time of Paul, Philippi was a Roman colony and many Roman soldiers lived there after they retired. (See Map 16 on pg 1894.)

16.14 *Lydia . . . Thyatira*: Lydia was a businesswoman who came from Thyatira, which was in the Roman province of Asia.

16.16 *slave girl . . . had a spirit*: The Greek words translated here are "pythonic spirit." A mythical serpent (Python) guarded the oracle (prophet) at Delphi in Greece. The term "pythonic" was used to describe persons who spoke by the power of this type of spirit.

16.21 *things we Romans are not allowed to do*: The officials were probably charging Paul and Silas with "proselytizing," which meant trying to encourage people to practice a new religion.

16.27 *pulled out his sword . . . to kill himself*: If a guard allowed a prisoner to escape, he was expected to give up his life (12.19).

God's Saving Love (Salvation)

[n]16.12 *in the first district of Macedonia*: Some manuscripts have "and the leading city of Macedonia."

16.37 *Roman citizens:* Only a small number of people living in the Roman Empire were citizens, and they had special rights and privileges. (See the article The World of Jesus: Peoples, Powers, and Politics on pg 1801.)

17.7 *break the laws of the Roman Emperor:* Anyone who claimed to be a king or said that anyone besides the Roman Emperor was king was breaking Roman law.

17.10 *Berea . . . synagogue:* Berea was about 50 miles southwest of Thessalonica in a different district of Macedonia. A Jewish group met regularly in Berea for study and worship.

17.14 *down to the coast:* This is the northwest coast of the Aegean Sea. Paul could have sailed to Athens, or he could have walked on a road that followed the coast of Macedonia south of Berea and into Achaia, the southern province of Greece. (See Map 15 on pg 1893.)

17.15 *Athens:* People settled in Athens as early as 3000 B.C. By about 440 B.C. it was the main center of Greece and the greatest cultural city in the Mediterranean world. Athenian culture was one of the main sources of the Greek science, reason, philosophy, mathematics, and medicine that spread through the ancient Near East.

some police with orders for the jailer to let Paul and Silas go. ³⁶The jailer told Paul, "The officials have ordered me to set you free. Now you can leave in peace."

³⁷But Paul told the police, "We are Roman citizens,º and the Roman officials had us beaten in public without giving us a trial. They threw us into jail. Now do they think they can secretly send us away? No, they cannot! They will have to come here themselves and let us out."

³⁸When the police told the officials that Paul and Silas were Roman citizens, the officials were afraid. ³⁹So they came and apologized. They led them out of the jail and asked them to please leave town. ⁴⁰But Paul and Silas went straight to the home of Lydia, where they saw the Lord's followers and encouraged them. Then they left.

Trouble in Thessalonica

17 After Paul and his friends had traveled through Amphipolis and Apollonia, they went on to Thessalonica. A synagogue was in that city. ²So as usual, Paul went there to worship, and on three Sabbaths he spoke to the people. He used the Scriptures ³to show them that the Messiah had to suffer, but that he would rise from death. Paul also told them that Jesus is the Messiah he was preaching about. ⁴Some of them believed what Paul had said, and they became followers with Paul and Silas. Some Gentilesᴾ and many important women also believed the message.

⁵The Jewish leaders were jealous and got some troublemakers who hung around the marketplace to start a riot in the city. They wanted to drag Paul and Silas out to the mob, and so they went straight to Jason's home. ⁶But when they did not find them there, they dragged out Jason and some of the Lord's followers. They took them to the city authorities and shouted, "Paul and Silas have been upsetting things everywhere. Now they have come here, ⁷and Jason has welcomed them into his home. All of them break the laws of the Roman Emperor by claiming that someone named Jesus is king."

⁸The officials and the people were upset when they heard this. ⁹So they made Jason and the other followers pay bail before letting them go.

People in Berea Welcome the Message

¹⁰That same night the Lord's followers sent Paul and Silas on to Berea, and after they arrived, they went to the synagogue. ¹¹The people in Berea were much nicer than those in Thessalonica, and they gladly accepted the message. Day after day they studied the Scriptures to see if these things were true. ¹²Many of them put their faith in the Lord, including some important Greek women and several men.

¹³When the Jewish leaders in Thessalonica heard that Paul had been preaching God's message in Berea, they went there and caused trouble by turning the crowds against Paul.

¹⁴At once the followers sent Paul down to the coast, but Silas and Timothy stayed in Berea. ¹⁵Some men went with Paul as far as Athens, and then returned with instructions for Silas and Timothy to join him as soon as possible.

º16.37 *Roman citizens:* Only a small number of the people living in the Roman Empire were citizens, and they had special rights and privileges. ᴾ17.4 *Gentiles:* See the note at 14.1.

Paul in Athens

[16]While Paul was waiting in Athens, he was upset to see all the idols in the city. [17]He went to the synagogue to speak to the Jews and to anyone who worshiped with them. Day after day he also spoke to everyone he met in the market. [18]Some of them were Epicureans[q] and some were Stoics,[r] and they started arguing with him.

People were asking, "What is this know-it-all trying to say?"

Some even said, "Paul must be preaching about foreign gods! That's what he means when he talks about Jesus and about people rising from death."[s]

[19]They brought Paul before a council called the Areopagus, and said, "Tell us what your new teaching is all about. [20]We have heard you say some strange things, and we want to know what you mean."

[21]More than anything else the people of Athens and the foreigners living there loved to hear and to talk about anything new. [22]So Paul stood up in front of the council and said:

People of Athens, I see that you are very religious. [23]As I was going through your city and looking at the things you worship, I found an altar with the words, "To an Unknown God." You worship this God, but you don't really know him. So I want to tell you about him. [24]This God made the world and everything in it. He is Lord of heaven and earth, and he doesn't live in temples built by human hands. [25]He doesn't need help from anyone. He gives life, breath, and everything else to all people. [26]From

one person God made all nations who live on earth, and he decided when and where every nation would be. [27]God has done all this, so that we will look for him and reach out and find him. He isn't far from any of us, [28]and he gives us the power to live, to move, and to be who we are. "We are his children," just as some of your poets have said. [29]Since we are God's children, we must not think that he is like an idol made out of gold or silver or stone. He isn't like anything that humans have thought up and made. [30]In the past, God forgave all this because people did not know what they were doing. But now he says that everyone everywhere must turn to him. [31]He has set a day when he will judge the world's people with fairness. And he has chosen the man Jesus to do the judging for him. God has given proof of this to all of us by raising Jesus from death.

[32]As soon as the people heard Paul say a man had been raised from death, some of them started laughing. Others said, "We will hear you talk about this some other time." [33]When Paul left the council meeting, [34]some of the men put their faith in the Lord and went with Paul. One of them was a council member named Dionysius. A woman named Damaris and several others also put their faith in the Lord.

Paul in Corinth

18 Paul left Athens and went to Corinth, [2]where he met Aquila, a Jewish man from Pontus. Not long before

---

[q]17.18 *Epicureans:* People who followed the teaching of a man named Epicurus, who taught that happiness should be the main goal in life. [r]17.18 *Stoics:* Followers of a man named Zeno, who taught that people should learn self-control and be guided by their consciences. [s]17.18 *people rising from death:* Or "a goddess named 'Rising from Death.'"

18.3 *tent makers*: Tents in Paul's day were often made from leather. Paul often talks in his letters about working with his hands (1 Cor 4.12; 1 Thes 2.9; 2 Thes 3.8).

18.12 *Gallio was governor of Achaia*: Gallio was the brother of the famous Roman philosopher Seneca. An ancient inscription found at Delphi shows that Gallio was the ruler (proconsul) of Achaia in A.D. 51–52.

18.13 *worship God . . . against our Law*: The Jewish leaders accused Paul of breaking the Roman rule against proselytizing. Paul did not get to defend himself, but later he argued that the good news about Christ was clearly based on the faith of his Jewish ancestors. Therefore, his preaching was not a new religion, but a new message based on Jewish Scriptures and its teachings.

18.17 *Sosthenes*: It is not clear whether Sosthenes was beaten by Greeks in the crowd or by his own Jewish people.

18.19 *Ephesus*: Ephesus was the capital of the Roman province of Asia and a very important center for trading.

18.24 *Apollos*: Apollos grew up in Alexandria, a city in Egypt with a large Jewish population. It is not surprising that Apollos knew the Jewish Scriptures well. See also 1 Cor 1.12; 3.4-6.

this, Aquila had come from Italy with his wife Priscilla, because Emperor Claudius had ordered the Jewish people to leave Rome.[t] Paul went to see Aquila and Priscilla ³and found out they were tent makers. Paul was also a tent maker, so he stayed with them, and they worked together.

⁴Every Sabbath, Paul went to the synagogue. He spoke to Jews and Gentiles[u] and tried to win them over. ⁵But after Silas and Timothy came from Macedonia, he spent all his time preaching to the Jews about Jesus the Messiah. ⁶Finally, they turned against him and insulted him. So he shook the dust from his clothes[v] and told them, "Whatever happens to you will be your own fault! I am not to blame. From now on I am going to preach to the Gentiles."

⁷Paul then moved into the house of a man named Titius Justus, who worshiped God and lived next door to the synagogue. ⁸Crispus was the leader of the synagogue. He and everyone in his family put their faith in the Lord. Many others in Corinth also heard the message, and all the people who had faith in the Lord were baptized.

⁹One night, Paul had a vision, and in it the Lord said, "Don't be afraid to keep on preaching. Don't stop! ¹⁰I am with you, and you won't be harmed. Many people in this city belong to me." ¹¹Paul stayed on in Corinth for a year and a half, teaching God's message to the people.

¹²While Gallio was governor of Achaia, some of the Jewish leaders got together and grabbed Paul. They brought him into court ¹³and said, "This man is trying to make our people worship God in a way that is against our Law!"

¹⁴Even before Paul could speak, Gallio said, "If you were charging this man with a crime or some other wrong, I would have to listen to you. ¹⁵But since this concerns only words, names, and your own law, you will have to take care of it yourselves. I refuse to judge such matters." ¹⁶Then he sent them out of the court. ¹⁷The crowd grabbed Sosthenes, the Jewish leader, and beat him up in front of the court. But none of this mattered to Gallio.

Paul Returns to Antioch in Syria

¹⁸After Paul had stayed for a while with the Lord's followers in Corinth, he told them goodbye and sailed on to Syria with Aquila and Priscilla. But before he left, he had his head shaved[w] at Cenchreae because he had made a promise to God.

¹⁹The three of them arrived in Ephesus, where Paul left Priscilla and Aquila. He then went into the synagogue to talk with the people there. ²⁰They asked him to stay longer, but he refused. ²¹He told them goodbye and said, "If God lets me, I will come back."

²²Paul sailed to Caesarea, where he greeted the church. Then he went on to Antioch. ²³After staying there for a while, he left and visited several places in Galatia and Phrygia. He helped the followers there to become stronger in their faith.

Apollos in Ephesus

²⁴A Jewish man named Apollos came to Ephesus. Apollos had been born in the city of Alexandria. He was a very good speaker

[t]18.2 *Emperor Claudius had ordered the Jewish people to leave Rome*: Probably A.D. 49, though it may have been A.D. 41.   [u]18.4 *Gentiles*: Here the word is "Greeks." But see the note at 14.1.   [v]18.6 *shook the dust from his clothes*: This means the same as shaking dust from the feet (see the note at 13.51). [w]18.18 *he had his head shaved*: Paul had promised to be a "Nazirite" for a while. This meant that for the time of the promise, he could not cut his hair or drink wine. When the time was over, he would have to cut his hair and offer a sacrifice to God.

and knew a lot about the Scriptures. ²⁵He also knew much about the Lord's Way,^x and he spoke about it with great excitement. What he taught about Jesus was right, but all he knew was John's message about baptism.

²⁶Apollos started speaking bravely in the synagogue. But when Priscilla and Aquila heard him, they took him to their home and helped him understand God's Way even better.

²⁷Apollos decided to travel through Achaia. So the Lord's followers wrote letters, encouraging the followers there to welcome him. After Apollos arrived in Achaia, he was a great help to everyone who had put their faith in the Lord Jesus because of God's gift of undeserved grace. ²⁸He got into fierce arguments with the Jewish people, and in public he used the Scriptures to prove that Jesus is the Messiah.

Paul in Ephesus

19 While Apollos was in Corinth, Paul traveled across the hill country to Ephesus, where he met some of the Lord's followers. ²He asked them, "When you put your faith in Jesus, were you given the Holy Spirit?"

"No!" they answered. "We have never even heard of the Holy Spirit."

³"Then why were you baptized?" Paul asked.

They answered, "Because of what John taught."^y

⁴Paul replied, "John baptized people so they would turn to God. But he also told them someone else was coming, and they should put their faith in him. Jesus is the one

that John was talking about." ⁵After the people heard Paul say this, they were baptized in the name of the Lord Jesus. ⁶Then Paul placed his hands on them. The Holy Spirit was given to them, and they spoke unknown languages and prophesied. ⁷There were about twelve men in this group.

⁸For three months Paul went to the synagogue and talked bravely with the people about God's kingdom. He tried to win them over, ⁹but some of them were stubborn and refused to believe. In front of everyone they said terrible things about God's Way. Paul left and took the followers with him to the lecture hall of Tyrannus. He spoke there every day ¹⁰for two years, until every Jew and Gentile^z in Asia had heard the Lord's message.

The Sons of Sceva

¹¹God gave Paul the power to work great miracles. ¹²People even took handkerchiefs and aprons that had touched Paul's body, and they carried them to everyone who was sick. All of the sick people were healed, and the evil spirits went out.

¹³Some Jewish men started going around trying to force out evil spirits by using the name of the Lord Jesus. They said to the spirits, "Come out in the name of that same Jesus that Paul preaches about!"

¹⁴Seven sons of a high priest named Sceva were doing this, ¹⁵when an evil spirit said to them, "I know Jesus! And I have heard about Paul. But who are you?" ¹⁶Then the man with the evil spirit jumped on them and beat them up. They ran out of the house, naked and bruised.

¹⁷When the Jews and Gentiles^a in

19.6 *Holy Spirit was given to them:* After being baptized in Jesus' name, and through the laying on of hands, the Holy Spirit came to these new believers. Two gifts of the Spirit, prophecy and speaking in unknown languages (tongues), are mentioned here. See also Acts 2.4,11; 10.44-46.

19.9 *lecture hall of Tyrannus:* Tyrannus was a philosopher who probably lectured in this hall, which may have been a kind of school.

19.14 *sons of . . . Sceva:* Sceva and his sons may have been related to the high priestly family in Jerusalem, but he was not the official high priest.

^x**18.25** *the Lord's Way:* See the note at 9.2.   ^y**19.3** *Then why were you baptized? . . . Because of what John taught:* Or "In whose name were you baptized? . . . We were baptized in John's name."   ^z**19.10** *Gentile:* The text has "Greek" (see the note at 14.1).   ^a**19.17** *Gentiles:* The text has "Greeks" (see the note at 14.1).

Ephesus heard about this, they were so frightened that they praised the name of the Lord Jesus. [18]Many who were followers now started telling everyone about the evil things they had been doing. [19]Some who had been practicing witchcraft even brought their books and burned them in public. These books were worth about 50,000 silver coins. [20]So the Lord's message spread and became even more powerful.

The Riot in Ephesus

[21]After all this had happened, Paul decided[b] to visit Macedonia and Achaia on his way to Jerusalem. Paul had said, "From there I will go on to Rome." [22]So he sent his two helpers, Timothy and Erastus, to Macedonia. But he stayed on in Asia for a while.

[23]At that time there was serious trouble because of the Lord's Way.[c] [24]A silversmith named Demetrius had a business that made silver models of the temple of the goddess Artemis. Those who worked for him earned a lot of money. [25]Demetrius brought together everyone who was in the same business and said:

Friends, you know we make a good living at this. [26]But you have surely seen and heard how this man Paul is upsetting a lot of people, not only in Ephesus, but almost everywhere in Asia. He claims that the gods we humans make are not really gods at all. [27]Everyone will start saying terrible things about our business. They will stop respecting the temple of the goddess Artemis, who is worshiped in Asia and all over the world. Our great goddess will be forgotten!

[28]When the workers heard this, they got angry and started shouting, "Great is Artemis, the goddess of the Ephesians!" [29]Soon the whole city was in a riot, and some men grabbed Gaius and Aristarchus, who had come from Macedonia with Paul. Then everyone in the crowd rushed to the place where the town meetings were held.

[30]Paul wanted to go out and speak to the people, but the Lord's followers would not let him. [31]A few of the local officials were friendly to Paul, and they sent someone to warn him not to go.

[32]Some of the people in the meeting were shouting one thing, and others were shouting something else. Everyone was completely confused, and most of them did not even know why they were there.

[33]Several of the Jewish leaders pushed a man named Alexander to the front of the crowd and started telling him what to say. He motioned with his hand and tried to explain what was going on. [34]But when the crowd saw that he was Jewish, they all shouted for two hours, "Great is Artemis, the goddess of the Ephesians!"

[35]Finally, a town official made the crowd be quiet. Then he said:

People of Ephesus, who in the world doesn't know that our city is the center for worshiping the great goddess Artemis? Who doesn't know that her image which fell from heaven is right here? [36]No one can deny this, and so you should calm down and not do anything foolish. [37]You have brought men in here who have not robbed temples or spoken against our goddess.

[38]If Demetrius and his workers have a case against these men, we have courts and judges. Let them take their complaints there. [39]But if you want to do more than that, the matter will have to be brought before the city

[b]19.21 *Paul decided*: Or "Paul was led by the Holy Spirit." [c]19.23 *the Lord's Way*: See the note at 9.2.

council. **40**We could easily be accused of starting a riot today. There is no excuse for it! We cannot even give a reason for this uproar. **41**After saying this, he told the people to leave.

Paul Goes through Macedonia and Greece

20 When the riot was over, Paul sent for the followers and encouraged them. He then told them goodbye and left for Macedonia. **2**As he traveled from place to place, he encouraged the followers with many messages. Finally, he went to Greece*d* **3**and stayed there for three months.

Paul was about to sail to Syria. But some of the Jewish leaders plotted against him, so he decided to return by way of Macedonia. **4**With him were Sopater, son of Pyrrhus from Berea, and Aristarchus and Secundus from Thessalonica. Gaius from Derbe was also with him, and so were Timothy and the two Asians, Tychicus and Trophimus. **5**They went on ahead to Troas and waited for us there. **6**After the Festival of Thin Bread, we sailed from Philippi. Five days later we met them in Troas and stayed there for a week.

Paul's Last Visit to Troas

7On the first day of the week*e* we met to break bread together.*f* Paul spoke to the people until midnight because he was leaving the next morning. **8**In the upstairs room where we were meeting, there were a lot of lamps. **9**A young man by the name of Eutychus was sitting on a window sill.

While Paul was speaking, the young man got very sleepy. Finally, he went to sleep and fell three floors all the way down to the ground. When they picked him up, he was dead. **10**Paul went down and bent over Eutychus. He took him in his arms and said, "Don't worry! He's alive." **11**After Paul had gone back upstairs, he broke bread, and ate with us. He then spoke until dawn and left. **12**Then the followers took the young man home alive and were very happy.

The Voyage from Troas to Miletus

13Paul decided to travel by land to Assos. The rest of us went on ahead by ship, and we were to take him aboard there. **14**When he met us in Assos, he came aboard, and we sailed on to Mitylene. **15**The next day we came to a place near Chios, and the following day we reached Samos. The day after that we sailed to Miletus. **16**Paul had decided to sail on past Ephesus, because he did not want to spend too much time in Asia. He was in a hurry and wanted to be in Jerusalem in time for Pentecost.*g*

Paul Says Goodbye to the Church Leaders of Ephesus

17From Miletus, Paul sent a message for the church leaders at Ephesus to come and meet with him. **18**When they got there, he said:

You know everything I did during the time I was with you when I first came to Asia. **19**Some of the Jews plotted against me and caused me a lot of sorrow and trouble. But I served

*d***20.2** *Greece:* Probably Corinth. *e***20.7** *On the first day of the week:* Since the Jewish day began at sunset, the meeting would have begun in the evening. *f***20.7** *break bread together:* See the note at 2.46. *g***20.16** *in time for Pentecost:* The Jewish people liked to be in Jerusalem for this festival (see the note at 2.1).

19.40 *accused of starting a riot:* Since Ephesus was part of the Roman Empire, it had to follow Roman laws. The Romans had strict rules against starting riots. So the city official tells the crowd that they might all get in trouble with the Roman authorities if they kept shouting and complaining.

20.13 *Assos:* Since the others had to sail the 40 miles around the peninsula, they may have arrived in Assos at about the same time as Paul. (See Map 16 on pg 1894.)

20.14,15 *Mitylene . . . Miletus:* Mitylene was a harbor on the southeast shore of the island of Lesbos. Chios was a large island off the coast of Asia. Paul decided not to go in to dock at Ephesus, because he would have lost time, so he headed directly for Samos and then Miletus. (See Map 16 on pg 1894.)

20.16 *Pentecost:* Paul spent Passover in Macedonia, probably at Philippi. That meant he had fewer than 50 days to travel from Macedonia to Jerusalem for the Pentecost celebration.

20.17 *Ephesus:* Ephesus was a day's journey north of Miletus. Even though Paul wanted to get to Jerusalem for Pentecost, he took time to talk with the church leaders from Ephesus.

20.22 *Jerusalem . . . I must obey God's Spirit:* Paul knew that Jewish leaders and leaders of the followers of Jesus were probably still arguing with each other. He realized that going there might not be safe, but he was driven by the Spirit to go.

⟨R   Jerusalem

21.7,8   *Ptolemais . . . Caesarea:* Originally Ptolemais was known as Acco. When the Greeks ruled the area, the city was named after the ruling family, the Ptolemies. Ptolemais came under Roman rule in 65 B.C.

the Lord and was humble. [20]When I preached in public or taught in your homes, I didn't hold back from telling anything that would help you. [21]I told Jews and Gentiles to turn to God and have faith in our Lord Jesus.

[22]I don't know what will happen to me in Jerusalem, but I must obey God's Spirit and go there. [23]In every city I visit, I am told by the Holy Spirit that I will be put in jail and will be in trouble in Jerusalem. [24]But I don't care what happens to me, as long as I finish the work the Lord Jesus gave me to do. And this work is to tell the good news about God's gift of undeserved grace.

[25]I have gone from place to place, preaching to you about God's kingdom, but now I know that none of you will ever see me again. [26]I tell you today I am no longer responsible for any of you! [27]I have told you everything God wants you to know. [28]Look after yourselves and everyone the Holy Spirit has placed in your care. Be like shepherds to God's church. It is the flock he bought with the blood of his own Son.[h]

[29]I know that after I am gone, others will come like fierce wolves to attack you. [30]Some of your own people will tell lies to win over the Lord's followers. [31]Be on your guard! Remember how day and night for three years I kept warning you with tears in my eyes.

[32]I now place you in God's care. Remember the message about his gift of undeserved grace! This message can help you and give you what belongs to you as God's people. [33]I have never wanted anyone's money or clothes.

[34]You know how I have worked with my own hands to make a living for myself and my friends. [35]By everything I did, I showed how you should work to help everyone who is weak. Remember that our Lord Jesus said, "More blessings come from giving than from receiving."

[36]After Paul had finished speaking, he knelt down with all of them and prayed. [37]Everyone cried and hugged and kissed him. [38]They were especially sad because Paul had told them, "You will never see me again."

Then they went with him to the ship.

Paul Goes to Jerusalem

21 After saying goodbye, we sailed straight to Cos. The next day we reached Rhodes and from there sailed on to Patara. [2]We found a ship going to Phoenicia, so we got on board and sailed off.

[3]We came within sight of Cyprus and then sailed south of it on to the port of Tyre in Syria, where the ship was going to unload its cargo. [4]We found the Lord's followers and stayed with them for a week. The Holy Spirit had told them to warn Paul not to go on to Jerusalem. [5]But when the week was over, we started on our way again. All the men, together with their wives and children, walked with us from the town to the seashore. We knelt on the beach and prayed. [6]Then after saying goodbye to each other, we got into the ship, and they went back home.

[7]We sailed from Tyre to Ptolemais, where we greeted the followers and stayed with them for a day. [8]The next day we went to Caesarea and stayed with Philip, the preacher. He was one of the seven men

[h]**20.28** *the blood of his own Son:* Or "his own blood."

who helped the apostles, ⁹and he had four unmarriedⁱ daughters who prophesied.

¹⁰We had been in Caesarea for several days, when the prophet Agabus came to us from Judea. ¹¹He took Paul's belt, and with it he tied up his own hands and feet. Then he told us, "The Holy Spirit says that some of the Jewish leaders in Jerusalem will tie up the man who owns this belt. They will also hand him over to the Gentiles." ¹²After Agabus said this, we and the followers living there begged Paul not to go to Jerusalem.

¹³But Paul answered, "Why are you crying and breaking my heart? I am not only willing to be put in jail for the Lord Jesus, but I am even willing to die for him in Jerusalem!"

¹⁴Since we could not get Paul to change his mind, we gave up and prayed, "Lord, please make us willing to do what you want."

¹⁵Then we got ready to go to Jerusalem. ¹⁶Some of the followers from Caesarea went with us and took us to stay in the home of Mnason. He was from Cyprus and had been a follower from the beginning.

Paul Visits James

¹⁷When we arrived in Jerusalem, the Lord's followers gladly welcomed us. ¹⁸Paul went with us to see James^j the next day, and all the church leaders were present. ¹⁹Paul greeted them and told how God had used him to help the Gentiles. ²⁰Everyone who heard this praised God and said to Paul:

My friend, you can see how many tens of thousands of our people have become followers! And all of them are eager to obey the Law of Moses. ²¹But

they have been told that you are teaching those who live among the Gentiles to disobey this Law. They claim that you are telling them not to circumcise their sons or to follow our customs.

²²What should we do now that our people have heard you are here? ²³Please do what we ask, because four of our men have made special promises to God. ²⁴Join with them and prepare yourself for the ceremony that goes with the promises. Pay the cost for their heads to be shaved. Then everyone will learn that the reports about you are not true. They will know you do obey the Law of Moses.

²⁵Some while ago we told the Gentile followers what we think they should do. We instructed them not to eat anything offered to idols. They were told not to eat any meat with blood still in it or the meat of an animal that has been strangled. They were also told not to commit any terrible sexual sins.^k

²⁶The next day Paul took the four men with him and got himself ready at the same time they did. Then he went into the temple and told when the final ceremony would take place and when an offering would be made for each of them.

Paul Is Arrested

²⁷When the period of seven days for the ceremony was almost over, some of the Jewish people from Asia saw Paul in the temple. They got a large crowd together and started attacking him. ²⁸They were shouting, "Friends, help us! This man goes around everywhere, saying bad things

ⁱ21.9 *unmarried:* Or "virgin." ^j21.18 *James:* The Lord's brother. ^k21.25 *not to commit any terrible sexual sins:* See the note at 15.20.

● 21.11 *Gentiles:* Here Agabus means the non-Jewish authorities.

● 21.16 *Mnason:* Nothing else is known of Mnason, but he must have had a house large enough to hold a number of guests.

● 21.23 *four of our men have made special promises to God:* They were talking about the Nazirite vows (Num 6.5, 13-21; 8.5).

● 21.27 *Jewish people from Asia:* They were probably in Jerusalem for the Pentecost Festival.

21.28 *bringing in Gentiles:* Jewish laws said that non-Jews (Gentiles) were not allowed within the temple, except in a special area called the Court of the Gentiles.

21.29 *Trophimus from Ephesus:* Trophimus was a Gentile. Paul probably did not bring him into the forbidden area of the temple, because this would have put Trophimus' life in danger.

21.31 *commander:* The Greek word here is *chiliarch*, one who commanded one thousand soldiers (a regiment). Perhaps this is Claudius Lysias, the commander who is named in 23.26.

21.34 *fortress:* This is Antonia Fortress, which overlooked the temple area from the northwest. It was connected to the temple area by steps. Roman soldiers lived in the fortress in special barracks. (See Map 12 on pg 1890.)

21.38 *that Egyptian who started a riot:* The Jewish historian Josephus wrote about an Egyptian who had led a group of terrorists out to the Mount of Olives. The Romans soldiers killed hundreds of the terrorists, but their leader escaped.

about our nation and about the Law of Moses and about this temple. He has even brought shame to this holy temple by bringing in Gentiles." ²⁹Some of them thought that Paul had brought Trophimus from Ephesus into the temple, because they had seen them together in the city.

³⁰The whole city was in an uproar, and the people turned into a mob. They grabbed Paul and dragged him out of the temple. Then suddenly the doors were shut. ³¹The people were about to kill Paul when the Roman army commander heard that all Jerusalem was starting to riot. ³²So he quickly took some soldiers and officers and ran to where the crowd had gathered.

As soon as the mob saw the commander and soldiers, they stopped beating Paul. ³³The army commander went over and arrested him and had him bound with two chains. Then he tried to find out who Paul was and what he had done. ³⁴Part of the crowd shouted one thing, and part of them shouted something else. But they were making so much noise that the commander could not find out a thing. Then he ordered Paul to be taken into the fortress. ³⁵As they reached the steps, the crowd became so wild that the soldiers had to lift Paul up and carry him. ³⁶The crowd followed and kept shouting, "Kill him! Kill him!"

Paul Speaks to the Crowd

³⁷When Paul was about to be taken into the fortress, he asked the commander, "Can I say something to you?"

"How do you know Greek?" the commander asked. ³⁸"Aren't you that Egyptian who started a riot not long ago and led 4,000 terrorists into the desert?"

³⁹"No!" Paul replied. "I am a Jew from Tarsus, an important city in Cilicia. Please let me speak to the crowd."

⁴⁰The commander told him he could speak, so Paul stood on the steps and motioned to the people. When they were quiet, he spoke to them in Aramaic:[l]

22 "My friends and leaders of our nation, listen as I explain what happened!" ²When the crowd heard Paul speak to them in Aramaic, they became even quieter. Then Paul said:

³I am a Jew, born in the city of Tarsus in Cilicia. But I grew up here in Jerusalem where I was a student of Gamaliel and was taught to follow every single law of our ancestors. In fact, I was just as eager to obey God as any of you are today.

⁴I made trouble for everyone who followed the Lord's Way,[m] and I even had some of them killed. I had others arrested and put in jail. I didn't care if they were men or women. ⁵The high priest and all the council members can tell you this is true. They even gave me letters to the Jewish leaders in Damascus, so that I could arrest people there and bring them to Jerusalem to be punished.

⁶One day about noon I was getting close to Damascus, when a bright light from heaven suddenly flashed around me. ⁷I fell to the ground and heard a voice asking, "Saul, Saul, why are you so cruel to me?"

⁸"Who are you?" I answered.

The Lord replied, "I am Jesus from Nazareth! I am the one you are so cruel to." ⁹Those who were traveling with me saw the light, but did not hear the voice.

[l]21.40 *Aramaic:* Or "Hebrew." Aramaic is a Semitic language closely related to Hebrew.
[m]22.4 *followed the Lord's Way:* See the note at 9.2.

¹⁰I asked, "Lord, what do you want me to do?"

Then he told me, "Get up and go to Damascus. When you get there, you will be told what to do." ¹¹The light had been so bright that I couldn't see. And the others had to lead me by the hand to Damascus.

¹²In that city there was a man named Ananias, who faithfully obeyed the Law of Moses and was well liked by all the Jewish people living there. ¹³He came to me and said, "Saul, my friend, you can now see again!"

At once I could see. ¹⁴Then Ananias told me, "The God that our ancestors worshiped has chosen you to know what he wants done. He has chosen you to see the One Who Obeys Godⁿ and to hear his voice. ¹⁵You must tell everyone what you have seen and heard. ¹⁶What are you waiting for? Get up! Be baptized, and wash away your sins by praying to the Lord."

¹⁷After this I returned to Jerusalem and went to the temple to pray. There I had a vision ¹⁸of the Lord who said to me, "Hurry and leave Jerusalem! The people won't listen to what you say about me."

¹⁹I replied, "Lord, they know that in many of our synagogues I arrested and beat people who had faith in you. ²⁰Stephen was killed because he spoke for you, and I stood there and cheered them on. I even guarded the clothes of the men who murdered him."

²¹But the Lord told me to go, and he promised to send me far away to the Gentiles.

²²The crowd listened until Paul said this. Then they started shouting, "Get rid of this man! He doesn't deserve to live." ²³They kept shouting. They waved their clothes around and threw dust into the air.

Paul and the Roman Army Commander

²⁴The Roman commander ordered Paul to be taken into the fortress and beaten with a whip. He did this to find out why the people were screaming at Paul. ²⁵While the soldiers were tying Paul up to be beaten, he asked the officer standing there, "Is it legal to beat a Roman citizen before he has been tried in court?"

²⁶When the officer heard this, he went to the commander and said, "What are you doing? This man is a Roman citizen!"

²⁷The commander went to Paul and asked, "Tell me, are you a Roman citizen?"

"Yes," Paul answered.

²⁸The commander then said, "I paid a lot of money to become a Roman citizen."^o

But Paul replied, "I was born a Roman citizen."

²⁹The men who were about to beat and question Paul quickly backed off. And the commander himself was frightened when he realized that he had put a Roman citizen in chains.

Paul Is Tried by the Council

³⁰The next day the commander wanted to know the real reason why the Jewish leaders had brought charges against Paul. So he had Paul's chains removed, and he ordered the chief priests and the whole council to meet. Then he had Paul led in and made him stand in front of them.

23 Paul looked straight at the council members and said, "My friends, to this day I have served God with a clear conscience!"

ⁿ**22.14** *One Who Obeys God:* See the note at 7.52.　^o**22.28** *Roman citizen:* See the note at 16.37.

22.25 *Roman citizen:* As a Roman citizen Paul had certain rights, including the chance to argue his case directly to the Roman emperor. Only a small number of people in the Roman Empire had the rights of a citizen, which included the privileges of voting, holding office, entering into a legal marriage, and holding property. Along with these privileges came the duties to pay taxes and serve in the army, if called to do so.

22.30 *the whole council:* This council had the right to decide if someone had broken a Jewish law and to determine the punishment.

23.2 *Ananias the high priest:* Ananias, the son of Nedebeus, served as high priest from A.D. 48 to 58. He had a reputation for cruelty and for siding with the Roman authorities. He was killed by Jewish rebels at the beginning of the Jewish War of A.D. 66–70.

23.5 *Scriptures:* The law Paul is referring to is described in Exodus 22.28.

23.6 *Sadducees . . . Pharisees:* Paul knew his comment about the dead being raised to life would start an argument between these two groups.

23.16 *Paul's nephew:* He was the son of Paul's sister, whose name is not known.

²Then Ananias the high priest ordered the men standing beside Paul to hit him on the mouth. ³Paul turned to the high priest and said, "You whitewashed wall!P God will hit you. You sit there to judge me by the Law of Moses. But at the same time you order men to break the Law by hitting me."

⁴The men standing beside Paul asked, "Don't you know you are insulting God's high priest?"

⁵Paul replied, "Oh! I didn't know he was the high priest. The Scriptures do tell us not to speak evil about a leader of our people."

⁶When Paul saw that some of the council members were Sadducees and others were Pharisees, he shouted, "My friends, I am a Pharisee and the son of a Pharisee. I am on trial simply because I believe that the dead will be raised to life."

⁷As soon as Paul said this, the Pharisees and the Sadducees got into a big argument, and the council members started taking sides. ⁸The Sadducees do not believe in angels or spirits or that the dead will rise to life. But the Pharisees believe in all of these, ⁹and so there was a lot of shouting. Some of the teachers of the Law of Moses were Pharisees. Finally, they became angry and said, "We don't find anything wrong with this man. Maybe a spirit or an angel really did speak to him."

¹⁰The argument became fierce, and the commander was afraid that Paul would be pulled apart. So he ordered the soldiers to go in and rescue Paul. Then they took him back into the fortress.

¹¹That night the Lord stood beside Paul and said, "Don't worry! Just as you have told others about me in Jerusalem, you must also tell about me in Rome."

A Plot To Kill Paul

¹²⁻¹³The next morning more than 40 Jewish men got together and vowed that they would not eat or drink anything until they had killed Paul. ¹⁴Then some of them went to the chief priests and the nation's leaders and said, "We have promised God that we would not eat a thing until we have killed Paul. ¹⁵You and everyone in the council must go to the commander and pretend that you want to find out more about the charges against Paul. Ask for him to be brought before your court. Meanwhile, we will be waiting to kill him before he gets there."

¹⁶When Paul's nephew heard about the plot, he went to the fortress and told Paul about it. ¹⁷So Paul said to one of the army officers, "Take this young man to the commander. He has something to tell him."

¹⁸The officer took him to the commander and said, "The prisoner named Paul asked me to bring this young man to you, because he has something to tell you."

¹⁹The commander took the young man aside and asked him in private, "What do you want to tell me?"

²⁰He answered, "Some men are planning to ask you to bring Paul down to the Jewish council tomorrow. They will claim they want to find out more about him. ²¹But please don't do what they say. More than 40 men are going to attack Paul. They have made a vow not to eat or drink anything until they have killed him. Even now they are waiting to hear what you decide."

²²The commander sent the young man away after saying to him, "Don't let anyone know you told me this."

P23.3 *whitewashed wall:* Someone who pretends to be good, but really isn't.

Paul Is Sent to Felix the Governor

23The commander called in two of his officers and told them, "By nine o'clock tonight have 200 soldiers ready to go to Caesarea. Take along 70 men on horseback and 200 foot soldiers with spears. **24**Get a horse ready for Paul and make sure he gets safely through to Felix the governor." **25**The commander wrote a letter that said:

26Greetings from Claudius Lysias to the Honorable Governor Felix:

27Some Jews grabbed this man and were about to kill him. But when I found out that he was a Roman citizen, I took some soldiers and rescued him. **28**I wanted to find out what they had against him. So I brought him before their council **29**and learned that the charges concern only their religious laws. This man isn't guilty of anything for which he should die or even be put in jail.

30As soon as I learned that there was a plot against him, I sent him to you and told their leaders to bring charges against him in your court.

31The soldiers obeyed the commander's orders, and that same night they took Paul to the city of Antipatris. **32**The next day the foot soldiers returned to the fortress and let the soldiers on horseback take him the rest of the way. **33**When they came to Caesarea, they gave the letter to the governor and handed Paul over to him.

34The governor read the letter. Then he asked Paul and found out that he was from Cilicia. **35**The governor said, "I will listen to your case as soon as the people come to bring their charges against you." After saying this, he gave orders for Paul to be kept as a prisoner in Herod's palace.⁹

Paul Is Accused in the Court of Felix

24 Five days later Ananias the high priest, together with some of their leaders and a lawyer named Tertullus, went to the governor to present their case against Paul. **2**So Paul was called in, and Tertullus stated the case against him:ʳ

Honorable Felix, you have brought our people a long period of peace, and because of your concern our nation is much better off. **3**All of us are always grateful for what you have done. **4**I don't want to bother you, but please be patient with us and listen to me for just a few minutes.

5This man has been found to be a real pest and troublemaker for our people all over the world. He is also a leader of a group called Nazarenes. **6-8**When he tried to disgrace the temple, we arrested him.ˢ If you question him, you will find out for yourself that our charges are true.

9The Jewish crowd spoke up and agreed with what Tertullus had said.

Paul Defends Himself

10The governor motioned for Paul to speak, and he began:

I know that you have judged the people of our nation for many years, and I am glad to defend myself in your court.

⁹**23.35** *Herod's palace:* The palace built by Herod the Great and used by the Roman governors of Palestine. ʳ**24.2** *Paul was called in, and Tertullus stated the case against him:* Or "Tertullus was called in and stated the case against Paul." ˢ**24.6-8** *we arrested him:* Some manuscripts add, "We wanted to judge him by our own laws. But Lysias the commander took him away from us by force. Then Lysias ordered us to bring our charges against this man in your court."

23.23 *Caesarea:* The Roman governor of the region lived in Caesarea.

23.24 *Felix the governor:* In A.D. 52, the Emperor Claudius appointed Antonius Felix as military governor (procurator) of Judea. He ruled for about eight years. Felix could not stop the terrorists called the *Sicarii,* who killed people they suspected were friendly to the Romans. Felix knew something about Christianity and liked talking to Paul, but he kept him in prison anyway.

23.29 *charges concern only their religious laws:* The Romans allowed the Jewish people to decide cases that involved Jewish laws or customs, as long as they did not break any Roman law or cause a riot. Paul was a Roman citizen, so the commander saw it as his duty to protect Paul's rights.

24.1 *a lawyer named Tertullus:* Here " lawyer" means someone who was familiar with both Roman and Jewish law. Tertullus was probably a Jew who may have grown up outside of Palestine and who had been trained in Roman law.

24.5 *Nazarenes:* Probably a term used to describe the followers of Jesus who came from Nazareth. On the other hand, Tertullus could be saying that Paul was part of the Nazirite group who separated themselves and made special vows.

Making Promises (Vows)

24.24 *Drusilla:* She was Felix's third wife and the daughter of Herod Agrippa I. She had married Azizus, the king of Emesa, when she was 15, but left him to marry Felix.

24.27 *Porcius Festus became governor:* Although exact dates are uncertain, Porcius Festus was governor (procurator) in Judea from A.D. 60 to 62.

[11]It was no more than twelve days ago that I went to worship in Jerusalem. You can find this out easily enough. [12]Never once did the Jews find me arguing with anyone in the temple. I didn't cause trouble in the synagogues or in the city itself. [13]There is no way that they can prove these charges they are now bringing against me.

[14]I admit that their leaders think the Lord's Way[t] which I follow is based on wrong beliefs. But I still worship the same God that my ancestors worshiped. And I believe everything written in the Law of Moses and in the Prophets.[u] [15]I am just as sure as these people are that God will raise from death everyone, good or evil. [16]And because I am sure, I try my best to have a clear conscience in whatever I do for God or for people.

[17]After being away for several years, I returned here to bring gifts for the poor people of my nation and to offer sacrifices. [18]This is what I was doing when I was found going through a ceremony in the temple. I wasn't with a crowd, and there was no uproar. [19]Some Jews from Asia were there at that time, and if they have anything to say against me, they should be here now. [20]Or ask the ones who are here. They can tell you that they didn't find me guilty of anything when I was tried by their own council. [21]The only charge they can bring against me is what I shouted out in court, when I said, "I am on trial today because I believe that the dead will be raised to life!"

[22]Felix knew a lot about the Lord's Way.[v] But he brought the trial to an end and said, "I will make my decision after Lysias the commander arrives." [23]He then ordered the army officer to keep Paul under guard, but not to lock him up or to stop his friends from helping him.

Paul Is Kept under Guard

[24]Several days later Felix and his wife Drusilla, who was Jewish, went to the place where Paul was kept under guard. They sent for Paul and listened while he spoke to them about having faith in Christ Jesus. [25]But Felix was frightened when Paul started talking to them about doing right, about self-control, and about the coming judgment. So he said to Paul, "That's enough for now. You may go. But when I have time I will send for you." [26]After this, Felix often sent for Paul and talked with him, because he hoped that Paul would offer him a bribe.

[27]Two years later Porcius Festus became governor in place of Felix. But since Felix wanted to do the Jewish leaders a favor, he kept Paul in jail.

Paul Asks To Be Tried by the Roman Emperor

25 Three days after Festus had become governor, he went from Caesarea to Jerusalem. [2]There the chief priests and some Jewish leaders told him about their charges against Paul. They also asked Festus [3]if he would be willing to bring Paul to Jerusalem. They begged him to do this because they were planning to attack and kill Paul on the way. [4]But Festus told them, "Paul will be kept in Caesarea, and I am soon going there myself. [5]If he has done anything wrong, let your leaders go with me and bring charges against him there."

[t]*24.14 the Lord's Way:* See the note at 9.2. [u]*24.14 Law of Moses . . . the Prophets:* The Jewish Scriptures, that is, the Old Testament. [v]*24.22 the Lord's Way:* See the note at 9.2.

⁶Festus stayed in Jerusalem for eight or ten more days before going to Caesarea. Then the next day he took his place as judge and had Paul brought into court. ⁷As soon as Paul came in, the leaders from Jerusalem crowded around him and said he was guilty of many serious crimes. But they could not prove anything. ⁸Then Paul spoke in his own defense, "I have not broken the Law of my people. And I have not done anything against either the temple or the Emperor."

⁹Festus wanted to please the leaders. So he asked Paul, "Are you willing to go to Jerusalem and be tried by me on these charges?"

¹⁰Paul replied, "I am on trial in the Emperor's court, and that's where I should be tried. You know very well I have not done anything to harm the Jewish nation. ¹¹If I had done something deserving death, I would not ask to escape the death penalty. But I am not guilty of any of these crimes, and no one has the right to hand me over to these people. I now ask to be tried by the Emperor himself."

¹²After Festus had talked this over with members of his council, he told Paul, "You have asked to be tried by the Emperor, and to the Emperor you will go!"

Paul Speaks to Agrippa and Bernice

¹³A few days later King Agrippa and Bernice came to Caesarea to visit Festus. ¹⁴They had been there for several days, when Festus told the king about the charges against Paul. He said:

Felix left a man here in jail, ¹⁵and when I went to Jerusalem, the chief priests and the Jewish leaders came and asked me to find him guilty. ¹⁶I told them it isn't the Roman custom to hand a man over to people who are

bringing charges against him. He must first have the chance to meet them face to face and to defend himself against their charges.

¹⁷So when they came here with me, I wasted no time. On the very next day I took my place on the judge's bench and ordered him to be brought in. ¹⁸But when the men stood up to make their charges against him, they did not accuse him of any of the crimes that I thought they would. ¹⁹Instead, they argued with him about some of their beliefs and about a dead man named Jesus, who Paul said was alive.

²⁰Since I did not know how to find out the truth about all this, I asked Paul if he would be willing to go to Jerusalem and be put on trial there. ²¹But Paul asked to be kept in jail until the Emperor could decide his case. So I ordered him to be kept here until I could send him to the Emperor.

²²Then Agrippa said to Festus, "I would also like to hear what this man has to say." Festus answered, "You can hear him tomorrow."

²³The next day Agrippa and Bernice made a big show as they came into the meeting room. High ranking army officers and leading citizens of the town were also there. Festus then ordered Paul to be brought in ²⁴and said:

King Agrippa and other guests, look at this man! Every Jew from Jerusalem and Caesarea has come to me, demanding for him to be put to death. ²⁵I have not found him guilty of any crime deserving death. But because he has asked to be judged by the Emperor, I have decided to send him to Rome. ²⁶I have to write some facts about this man to the Emperor. So I have brought him before all of you, but

25.11 *I now ask to be tried by the Emperor:* Nero was the Roman emperor at this time. As a Roman citizen, Paul had the right to have his case heard by the emperor or the emperor's representative in Rome. It was the highest court that could hear a case.

25.13 *King Agrippa and Bernice:* This was Herod Agrippa II. The Emperor Claudius allowed him to rule over areas north and east of Lake Galilee and parts of Perea. When the Jews revolted against the Romans in A.D. 66, Agrippa II was on the side of the Romans. Bernice was the sister of Agrippa II. She married her uncle Herod of Chalcis when she was only 13. After he died, she went to live with her brother. Even after she married Polomon of Cilicia she continued her incestuous relationship with Agrippa II.

25.23 *High ranking army officers and leading citizens:* A number of Roman units called regiments were stationed in Caesarea. All of their commanders were at the meeting. The leading citizens included both influential local Jews and Roman authorities.

26.18 *from darkness to light:* In the Bible, darkness refers to places of pain and suffering (Ps 107.10) or confusion (Eccl 2.14). God's opponents are called the rulers of darkness (Eph 6.12), who will be "thrown outside into the dark" (Matt 22.13). Light is used in the Bible to describe God or God's word (1 John 1.5; Ps 119.105) and those people or things that reveal God's truth (Isa 49.6).

especially before you, King Agrippa. After we have talked about his case, I will then have something to write. [27]It makes no sense to send a prisoner to the Emperor without stating the charges against him.

Paul's Defense before Agrippa

26 Agrippa told Paul, "You may now speak for yourself."

Paul stretched out his hand and said:

[2]King Agrippa, I am glad for this chance to defend myself before you today on all these charges my own people have brought against me. [3]You know a lot about our religious customs and the beliefs that divide us. So I ask you to listen patiently to me.

[4-5]All the Jews have known me since I was a child. They know what kind of life I have lived in my own country and in Jerusalem. And if they were willing, they could tell you I was a Pharisee, a member of a group that is stricter than any other. [6]Now I am on trial because I believe the promise God made to our people long ago.

[7]Day and night our twelve tribes have earnestly served God, waiting for his promised blessings. King Agrippa, because of this hope, some of our leaders have brought charges against me. [8]Why should any of you doubt that God raises the dead to life?

[9]I once thought that I should do everything I could to oppose Jesus from Nazareth. [10]I did this first in Jerusalem, and with the authority of the chief priests I put many of God's people in jail. I even voted for them to be killed. [11]I often had them punished in our synagogues, and I tried to make

them give up their faith. In fact, I was so angry with them, that I went looking for them in foreign cities.

[12]King Agrippa, one day I was on my way to Damascus with the authority and permission of the chief priests. [13]About noon I saw a light brighter than the sun. It flashed from heaven on me and on everyone traveling with me. [14]We all fell to the ground. Then I heard a voice say to me in Aramaic,[w] "Saul, Saul, why are you so cruel to me? It's foolish to fight against me!"

[15]"Who are you?" I asked.

Then the Lord answered, "I am Jesus! I am the one you are so cruel to. [16]Now stand up. I have appeared to you, because I have chosen you to be my servant. You are to tell others what you have learned about me and what I will show you later."

[17]The Lord also said, "I will protect you from the Jews and from the Gentiles that I am sending you to. [18]I want you to open their eyes, so they will turn from darkness to light and from the power of Satan to God. Then their sins will be forgiven, and by faith in me they will become part of God's holy people."

[19]King Agrippa, I obeyed this vision from heaven. [20]First I preached to the people in Damascus, and then I went to Jerusalem and all over Judea. Finally, I went to the Gentiles and said, "Stop sinning and turn to God! Then prove what you have done by the way you live."

[21]That is why some men grabbed me in the temple and tried to kill me. [22]But all this time God has helped me, and I have preached both to the rich and to the poor. I have told them only

[w]26.14 *Aramaic:* Or "Hebrew." Aramaic is a Semitic language closely related to Hebrew.

what the prophets and Moses said would happen. [23]I told them how the Messiah would suffer and be the first to be raised from death, so he could bring light to his own people and to the Gentiles.

[24]Before Paul finished defending himself, Festus shouted, "Paul, you're crazy! Too much learning has driven you out of your mind."

[25]But Paul replied, "Honorable Festus, I am not crazy. What I am saying is true, and it makes sense. [26]None of these things happened off in a corner somewhere. I am sure that King Agrippa knows what I am talking about. That's why I can speak so plainly to him."

[27]Then Paul said to Agrippa, "Do you believe what the prophets said? I know you do."

[28]Agrippa asked Paul, "In such a short time do you think you can talk me into being a Christian?"

[29]Paul answered, "Whether it takes a short time or a long time, I wish you and everyone else who hears me today would become just like me! Except, of course, for these chains."

[30]Then King Agrippa, Governor Festus, Bernice, and everyone who was with them got up. [31]But before they left, they said, "This man isn't guilty of anything. He doesn't deserve to die or to be put in jail."

[32]Agrippa told Festus, "Paul could have been set free, if he had not asked to be tried by the Roman Emperor."

Paul Is Taken to Rome

27 When it was time for us to sail to Rome, Captain Julius from the Emperor's special troops was put in charge of Paul and the other prisoners. [2]We went aboard a ship from Adramyttium that was about to sail to some ports along the coast of Asia. Aristarchus from Thessalonica in Macedonia sailed on the ship with us.

[3]The next day we came to shore at Sidon. Captain Julius was very kind to Paul. He even let him visit his friends, so they could give him whatever he needed. [4]When we left Sidon, the winds were blowing against us, and we sailed close to the island of Cyprus to be safe from the wind. [5]Then we sailed south of Cilicia and Pamphylia until we came to the port of Myra in Lycia. [6]There the army captain found a ship from Alexandria that was going to Italy. So he ordered us to board that ship.

[7]We sailed along slowly for several days and had a hard time reaching Cnidus. The wind would not let us go any farther in that direction, so we sailed past Cape Salmone, where the island of Crete would protect us from the wind. [8]We went slowly along the coast and finally reached a place called Fair Havens, not far from the town of Lasea.

[9]By now we had already lost a lot of time, and sailing was no longer safe. In fact, even the Great Day of Forgiveness[x] was past. [10]Then Paul spoke to the crew of the ship, "Men, listen to me! If we sail now, our ship and its cargo will be badly damaged, and many lives will be lost." [11]But Julius listened to the captain of the ship and its owner, rather than to Paul.

[12]The harbor at Fair Havens wasn't a good place to spend the winter. Because of this, almost everyone agreed that we should at least try to sail along the coast of Crete as far as Phoenix. It had a harbor that

[x]**27.9** *Great Day of Forgiveness*: This Jewish festival took place near the end of September. The sailing season was dangerous after the middle of September, and it was stopped completely between the middle of November and the middle of March.

26.27 *what the prophets said*: Paul was asking if Agrippa believed the writings of the prophets found in the Jewish Scriptures. **(See the article What Books Belong in the Bible? on pg 1764.)**

26.32 *Paul could have been set free*: Since Paul asked to have his case heard in front of the Roman emperor, he could not be set free.

27.1 *Captain Julius*: Julius is not mentioned anywhere else except in this chapter of Acts.

27.3,4 *Sidon . . . Cyprus*: Sidon was a port on the coast of Phoenicia about 70 miles north of Caesarea. The winds must have been from a westerly direction for Cyprus to give them protection. **(See Map 16 on pg 1894.)**

27.6 *Alexandria . . . Italy*: Alexandria was a great city on the northern coast of Egypt near the mouth of the Nile River. Rome was in Italy, their final destination. **(See Map 16 on pg 1894.)**

27.12 *Phoenix*: Phoenix, on the southern coast of Crete, was about 80 miles west of Fair Havens. Phoenix had a better harbor that gave more protection from winter storms. **(See Map 16 on pg 1894.)**

27.14 *"The Northeaster"*: This was a hurricane-like wind called the Euraquillo that came from the northeast and blew the ship away from the coast.

27.17 *sandbanks in the gulf of Syrtis:* This gulf was south of Italy and west of the province of Cyrenaica in Africa. The sandbanks were most likely quicksand, which would swallow up a ship that was blown into it. **(See Map 16 on pg 1894.)**

27.24 *Emperor:* The Emperor at this time was Nero, who ruled from A.D. 54 to 68. He was the son of Claudius' fourth wife, Agrippina. Though his rule began with acts of generosity and public assistance, Nero became more and more brutal and irresponsible, even having his mother and wife killed. He also became increasingly unpopular with Roman citizens. When a terrible fire destroyed much of Rome in A.D. 64, Nero put the blame on Christians. The apostles Peter and Paul are believed to have been executed in the persecution that followed.

27.27 *Mediterranean Sea:* The Roman Empire controlled all the lands surrounding the sea. **(See Map 10 on pg 1888.)**

27.28 *measured:* The sailors dropped a weighted rope overboard in order to measure how deep the water was.

opened toward the southwest and northwest,[y] and we could spend the winter there.

The Storm at Sea

[13]When a gentle wind from the south started blowing, the men thought it was a good time to do what they had planned. So they pulled up the anchor, and we sailed along the coast of Crete. [14]But soon a strong wind called "The Northeaster" blew against us from the island. [15]The wind struck the ship, and we could not sail against it. So we let the wind carry the ship.

[16]We went along the island of Cauda on the side that was protected from the wind. We had a hard time holding the lifeboat in place, [17]but finally we got it where it belonged. Then the sailors wrapped ropes around the ship to hold it together. They lowered the sail and let the ship drift along, because they were afraid it might hit the sandbanks in the gulf of Syrtis.

[18]The storm was so fierce that the next day they threw some of the ship's cargo overboard. [19]Then on the third day, with their bare hands they threw overboard some of the ship's gear. [20]For several days we could not see either the sun or the stars. A strong wind kept blowing, and we finally gave up all hope of being saved.

[21]Since none of us had eaten anything for a long time, Paul stood up and told the men:

You should have listened to me! If you had stayed on in Crete, you would not have had this damage and loss. [22]But now I beg you to cheer up, because you will be safe. Only the ship will be lost.

[23]I belong to God, and I worship him. Last night he sent an angel [24]to tell me, "Paul, don't be afraid! You will stand trial before the Emperor. And because of you, God will save the lives of everyone on the ship." [25]Cheer up! I am sure that God will do exactly what he promised. [26]But we will first be shipwrecked on some island.

[27]For 14 days and nights we had been blown around over the Mediterranean Sea. But about midnight the sailors realized we were getting near land. [28]They measured and found that the water was about 120 feet deep. A little later they measured again and found it was only about 90 feet. [29]The sailors were afraid that we might hit some rocks, and they let down four anchors from the back of the ship. Then they prayed for daylight.

[30]The sailors wanted to escape from the ship. So they lowered the lifeboat into the water, pretending that they were letting down some anchors from the front of the ship. [31]But Paul said to Captain Julius and the soldiers, "If the sailors don't stay on the ship, you won't have any chance to save your lives." [32]The soldiers then cut the ropes that held the lifeboat and let it fall into the sea.

[33]Just before daylight Paul begged the people to eat something. He told them, "For 14 days you have been so worried that you haven't eaten a thing. [34]I beg you to eat something. Your lives depend on it. Do this and not one of you will be hurt."

[35]After Paul had said this, he took a piece of bread and gave thanks to God. Then in front of everyone, he broke the bread and ate some. [36]They all felt encouraged, and each of them ate something. [37]There were 276 people on the ship, [38]and after everyone had eaten, they threw the cargo of wheat into the sea to make the ship lighter.

[y]**27.12** *southwest and northwest:* Or "northeast and southeast."

The Shipwreck

39Morning came, and the ship's crew saw a coast they did not recognize. But they did see a cove with a beach. So they decided to try to run the ship aground on the beach. **40**They cut the anchors loose and let them sink into the sea. At the same time they untied the ropes that were holding the rudders. Next, they raised the sail at the front of the ship and let the wind carry the ship toward the beach. **41**But it ran aground on a sandbank. The front of the ship stuck firmly in the sand, and the rear was being smashed by the force of the waves.

42The soldiers decided to kill the prisoners to keep them from swimming away and escaping. **43**But Captain Julius wanted to save Paul's life, and he did not let the soldiers do what they had planned. Instead, he ordered everyone who could swim to jump into the water and head for shore. **44**Then he told the others to hold on to planks of wood or parts of the ship. At last, everyone safely reached shore.

On the Island of Malta

28 When we came ashore, we learned that the island was called Malta. **2**The local people were very friendly, and they welcomed us by building a fire, because it was rainy and cold.

3After Paul had gathered some wood and had put it on the fire, the heat caused a snake to crawl out, and it bit him on the hand. **4**When the local people saw the snake hanging from Paul's hand, they said to each other, "This man must be a murderer! He didn't drown in the sea, but the goddess of justice will kill him anyway."

5Paul shook the snake off into the fire and wasn't harmed. **6**The people kept thinking that Paul would either swell up or suddenly drop dead. They watched him for a long time, and when nothing happened to him, they changed their minds and said, "This man is a god."

7The governor of the island was named Publius, and he owned some of the land around there. Publius was very friendly and welcomed us into his home for three days. **8**His father was in bed, sick with fever and stomach trouble, and Paul went to visit him. Paul healed the man by praying and placing his hands on him.

9After this happened, everyone on the island brought their sick people to Paul, and they were all healed. **10**The people were very respectful to us, and when we sailed, they gave us everything we needed.

From Malta to Rome

11Three months later we sailed in a ship that had been docked at Malta for the winter. The ship was from Alexandria in Egypt and was known as "The Twin Gods."ᶻ **12**We arrived in Syracuse and stayed for three days. **13**From there we sailed to Rhegium. The next day a south wind began to blow, and two days later we arrived in Puteoli. **14**There we found some of the Lord's followers, who begged us to stay with them. A week later we left for the city of Rome.

15Some of the followers in Rome heard about us and came to meet us at the Market of Appius and at the Three Inns. When Paul saw them, he thanked God and was encouraged.

28.1 *Malta:* The ship had sailed or drifted nearly 600 miles since it left Phoenix on Crete.

28.4 *the goddess of justice:* Possibly the Greek goddess Dike, the daughter of Zeus and Themis.

28.7 *Publius:* The Greek term translated as governor means "chief," or "number one" leader.

28.13 *Rhegium . . . Puteoli:* Rhegium was located at the southern tip of Italy. Puteoli was located on the bay of Naples about 75 miles south of Rome, and was the main seaport for Rome.

28.14 *Rome:* Rome, the capital of the Roman Empire, was built on a group of hills along the Tiber River. In Paul's day, Rome had at least 13 synagogues and many shrines for various Roman gods. Although it isn't known who first brought the good news about Jesus to Rome, there were probably Christians meeting there by the mid-40s. (See Map 10 on pg 1888.)

ᶻ**28.11** *known as "The Twin Gods":* Or "carried on its bow a wooden carving of the Twin Gods." These gods were Castor and Pollux, two of the favorite gods among sailors.

28.21 *Judea:* The area where Jerusalem, the center of the Jewish religion, was located. By Paul's day the extensive network of Roman roads and improved sea travel significantly aided communication from one part of the Roman Empire to the other.

28.22 *this new group:* Meaning the followers of Jesus of Nazareth.

Paul in Rome

[16]We arrived in Rome, and Paul was allowed to live in a house by himself with a soldier to guard him.

[17]Three days after we got there, Paul called together some of the Jewish leaders and said:

My friends, I have never done anything to hurt our people, and I have never gone against the customs of our ancestors. But in Jerusalem I was handed over as a prisoner to the Romans. [18]They looked into the charges against me and wanted to release me. They found that I had not done anything deserving death. [19]The Jewish leaders disagreed, so I asked to be tried by the Emperor.

But I don't have anything to say against my own nation. [20]I am bound by these chains because of what we people of Israel hope for. This is why I have called you here to talk about this hope of ours.

[21]The leaders replied, "No one from Judea has written us a letter about you. And not one of them has come here to report on you or to say anything against you. [22]But we would like to hear what you have to say. We understand that people everywhere are against this new group."

[23]They agreed on a time to meet with Paul, and many of them came to his house. From early morning until late in the afternoon, Paul talked to them about God's kingdom. He used the Law of Moses and the Books of the Prophets[a] to try to win them over to Jesus.

[24]Some of the leaders agreed with what Paul said, but others did not. [25]Since they could not agree among themselves, they started leaving. But Paul said, "The Holy Spirit said the right thing when he sent Isaiah the prophet [26]to tell our ancestors,

'Go to these people
    and tell them:
You will listen and listen,
    but never understand.
You will look and look,
    but never see.
[27]All of you
    have stubborn hearts.
Your ears are stopped up,
    and your eyes are covered.
You cannot see or hear
    or understand.
If you could,
you would turn to me,
    and I would heal you.'"

[28-29]Paul said, "You may be sure that God wants to save the Gentiles! And they will listen."[b]

[30]For two years Paul stayed in a rented house and welcomed everyone who came to see him. [31]He bravely preached about God's kingdom and taught about the Lord Jesus Christ, and no one tried to stop him.

---

[a]28.23 *Law of Moses and the Books of the Prophets:* The Jewish Bible, that is, the Old Testament.
[b]28.28,29 *And they will listen:* Some manuscripts add, "After Paul said this, the people left, but they got into a fierce argument among themselves."

Reflection Questions About Acts 1.1—28.30

1. What instructions did Jesus give the apostles before he went up to heaven (1.3-9)? How can followers of Jesus today carry out these instructions?

2. Describe the coming of the Holy Spirit (2.1-13). What happened as a result? How is the Holy Spirit at work in the world today?

3. Describe life among the Lord's followers as described in 2.43-47. Is this a good model for the church today?

4. What is the special problem described in 6.1-7 that the early church faced? How did the apostles deal with it? How does your church handle conflicts and differences of opinion?

5. Why was Saul going to Damascus? What happened to change his plans (9.1-19)? What did God tell Saul to do (9.19-31)? What caused the change in Saul's attitude? How does God "change" lives today?

6. What was important about Peter's vision and his meeting with Cornelius (chapter 10)? Peter says that he is certain that "God treats all people alike" (10.34). What did that mean for the early church? What might it mean for Christ's followers today? Are all people treated the same in your community?

7. What major problem was discussed in Jerusalem (15.1-21)? What decision was made about the problem (15.22-35)? What effect did their decision have on the early church?

8. What was Paul's message to the people of Athens (17.16-34)? How did Paul get the people to listen to what he had to say? What were some of the different ways people responded to what Paul said? Have you shared your faith with others? If so, how did they respond?

9. What happened to Paul when he returned to Jerusalem (21.17-26)? Who was trying to kill him, and why? Who helped him?

10. Choose one scene from Paul's difficult trip to Rome, and describe what happened (27.1—28.15). How did Paul and the others respond to the situation?

romans

*How do people become acceptable to God? Read what
Paul said to the Jewish and Gentile Christians about
God's powerful way of saving people from their sin and
accepting them as people of God.*

WHAT MAKES ROMANS SPECIAL?

In this letter, Paul supplies his most detailed summary of the good news about Jesus Christ. ROMANS is more than a letter. It is a well-organized essay that has profoundly influenced Christian doctrine and faith. Jewish and Gentile Christians in the early church often disagreed about what made a person acceptable to God, and how followers of Christ should live. In ROMANS, Paul announces that the good news is "God's powerful way of saving all people who have faith, whether they are Jews or Gentiles" (1.16).

Paul wrote this letter late in his life, sometime around A.D. 56, probably from Corinth, to introduce himself to the followers of Christ in Rome. The followers in Rome probably included Gentile Christians as well as Jewish Christians who had returned after being thrown out years earlier (see Acts 18.1-4) for rioting. Jewish Christians living in Rome continued to follow the Law of Moses, but Gentile Christians did not. Who was right? What place did the Law of Moses have for Gentile Christians?

In ROMANS, Paul teaches that the good news is based on God's promise to Israel's ancestor Abraham, whose faith made him acceptable to God. The Law, given to Moses and the people of Israel, reveals how God's people should live. God sent Jesus Christ to forgive sins and make people acceptable because of their faith, something that the Law on its own cannot do. Paul says that only people who have faith in Jesus Christ can become fully acceptable to God.

WHAT'S THE STORY BEHIND THE SCENE?

Long before Paul planned his trip to Rome, a group of believers in Jesus Christ lived in the city. Paul hoped to visit them on his way to Spain (15.28). Paul's immediate plan was to travel to the church in Jerusalem, bringing money collected in Macedonia and Achaia (15.26-29). ACTS reports that Paul was taken to Rome as a prisoner of the Roman emperor (Acts 27,28). The Bible does not say if he ever preached the good news in Spain.

HOW IS ROMANS CONSTRUCTED?

ROMANS is written in the Greek letter-writing style of the first century A.D. Writers identified themselves (1.1-6), named persons they were addressing (1.8), and offered a greeting. As with most of Paul's letters, a prayer follows his greeting (1.8-15), and the letter closes with a greeting and blessing (16.1-27). It can be outlined as follows:

Paul introduces himself and the good news (1.1-17)
Everyone is guilty before God (1.18—3.20)
How God accepts people (3.21—4.25)
Living the new life of faith (5.1—8.39)
God reaches out to the people of Israel (9.1—11.36)
Life in the body of Christ (12.1—15.13)
Paul's plans and personal greetings (15.14—16.27)

Romans is a long letter written by the apostle Paul to the church in Rome, a community of both Gentile and Jewish Christians. At the time of writing the letter, Paul was planning to visit Rome. Paul's purpose in writing seems to have been to introduce himself and his teachings about the good news of Jesus Christ to the Roman church and to seek their support for his planned missionary work in Spain. In writing to a people he has not yet met, Paul provides the most complete account of his teachings about Christ, salvation, faith, relations between Jews and Gentiles, relations between Christians and secular authorities, and living a new life grounded in Christian love.

Outline

1

From Paul, a servant of Christ Jesus. God chose me to be an apostle, and he appointed me to preach the good news [2]that he promised long ago by what his prophets said in the holy Scriptures. [3-4]This good news is about his Son, our Lord Jesus Christ! As a human, he was from the family of David. But the Holy Spirit[a] proved that Jesus is the powerful Son of God,[b] because he was raised from death.

[5]Jesus was kind to me and chose me to be an apostle,[c] so that people of all nations would obey and have faith. [6]You are some of those people chosen by Jesus Christ.

[7]This letter is to all of you in Rome. God loves you and has chosen you to be his very own people.

I pray that God our Father and our Lord Jesus Christ will be kind to you and will bless you with peace!

A Prayer of Thanks

[8]First, I thank God in the name of Jesus Christ for all of you. I do this because people everywhere in the world are talking about your faith. [9]God has seen how I never stop praying for you, while I serve him with all my heart and tell the good news about his Son.

[10]In all my prayers, I ask God to make it possible for me to visit you. [11]I want to see you and share with you the same blessings that God's Spirit has given me. Then you will grow stronger in your faith. [12]What I am saying is that we can encourage each other by the faith that is ours.

[13]My friends, I want you to know that I have often planned to come for a visit. But something has always kept me from doing it. I want to win followers to Christ in Rome, as I have done in many other places. [14-15]It doesn't matter if people are civilized

---

[a]1.4 *the Holy Spirit:* Or "his own spirit of holiness." [b]1.4 *proved that Jesus is the powerful Son of God:* Or "proved in a powerful way that Jesus is the Son of God." [c]1.5 *Jesus was kind to me and chose me to be an apostle:* Or "Jesus was kind to us and chose us to be his apostles."

● 1.1 *Paul, a servant of Christ:* Paul was also known by his Jewish name, Saul. Paul often described himself as a servant, which literally means "slave" of Christ.

◌ Paul (Saul) of Tarsus

● 1.1 *apostle . . . to preach the good news:* Here, apostle means someone chosen by God to spread the message about Jesus, which is also called the "good news," or "gospel."

● 1.2 *prophets:* The prophets of Israel were special messengers who spoke for God. Paul quoted from many prophets to show that God's earlier plans were being fulfilled in Jesus Christ. **(See the article Prophets and Prophecy on pg 1791.)**

● 1.2 *holy Scriptures:* The holy Scriptures here refers to the Jewish Scriptures, which Christians often refer to as the Old Testament.

■ 1.3-4 *his Son, our Lord Jesus Christ:* Paul proclaimed that Jesus was God's Son, which is what Jesus is often called in the Gospels (John 1.49; Mark 15.39). The Greek word for "Lord" is *Kyrios*, which emphasizes authority and power. "Christ" comes from the Greek word *Christos*, which means the same thing as the Hebrew title, "Messiah."

◌ Son of God

◌ Messiah (Chosen)

◌ Lord (Title for Jesus)

1.16 *saving all people who have faith:* This is a very important theme in all of Paul's letters, but especially in RO-MANS. Here "saving" means that God freed humans from sin and the powers of evil. Salvation comes to those who have faith in Jesus as God's Son and as the Savior of the world.

God's Saving Love (Salvation)

Eternal Life

Faith

Gentiles

1.18 *heaven:* People often think of heaven as a place "up there," but it is most often described in the Bible simply as the place where God rules.

Heaven

1.19,20 *God has shown . . . from the beginning of creation:* Paul argues that everyone should be able to understand how God wants people to live by seeing how God has created the world.

1.21 *minds are in the dark:* Since Jesus called himself "the light for the world," the "dark" is a place for people who decide not to follow Jesus (John 8.12).

and educated, or if they are uncivilized and uneducated. I must tell the good news to everyone. That's why I am eager to visit all of you in Rome.

The Power of the Good News

[16]I am proud of the good news! It is God's powerful way of saving all people who have faith, whether they are Jews or Gentiles. [17]The good news tells how God accepts everyone who has faith, but only those who have faith.[d] It is just as the Scriptures say, "The people God accepts because of their faith will live."[e]

Everyone Is Guilty

[18]From heaven God shows how angry he is with all the wicked and evil things that sinful people do to crush the truth. [19]They know everything that can be known about God, because God has shown it all to them. [20]God's eternal power and character cannot be seen. But from the beginning of creation, God has shown what these are like by all he has made. That's why those people don't have any excuse. [21]They know about God, but they don't honor him or even thank him. Their thoughts are useless, and their stupid minds are in the dark. [22]They claim to be wise, but they are fools. [23]They don't worship the glorious and eternal God. Instead, they worship idols that are made to look like humans who cannot live forever, and like birds, animals, and reptiles. [24]So God let these people go their own way. They did what they wanted to do, and their filthy thoughts made them do shameful things with their bodies. [25]They gave up the truth about God for a lie, and they

worshiped God's creation instead of God, who will be praised forever. Amen.

[26]God let them follow their own evil desires. Women no longer wanted to have sex in a natural way, and they did things with each other that were not natural. [27]Men behaved in the same way. They stopped wanting to have sex with women and had strong desires for sex with other men. They did shameful things with each other, and what has happened to them is punishment for their foolish deeds.

[28]Since these people refused even to think about God, he let their useless minds rule over them. That's why they do all sorts of indecent things. [29]They are evil, wicked, and greedy, as well as mean in every possible way. They want what others have, and they murder, argue, cheat, and are hard to get along with. They gossip, [30]say cruel things about others, and hate God. They are proud, conceited, and boastful, always thinking up new ways to do evil.

These people don't respect their parents. [31]They are stupid, unreliable, and don't have any love or pity for others. [32]They know God has said that anyone who acts this way deserves to die. But they keep on doing evil things, and they even encourage others to do them.

God's Judgment Is Fair

2 Some of you accuse others of doing wrong. But there is no excuse for what you do. When you judge others, you condemn yourselves, because you are guilty of doing the very same things. [2]We know that God is right to judge everyone who behaves in this way. [3]Do you really think God won't punish you, when you behave ex-

[d]**1.17** *but only those who have faith:* Or "and faith is all that matters."   [e]**1.17** *The people God accepts because of their faith will live:* Or "The people God accepts will live because of their faith."

I am proud of the good news! It is God's powerful way of saving all people who have faith, whether they are Jews or Gentiles. ROM 1.16

actly like the people you accuse? **4**You surely don't think much of God's wonderful goodness or of his patience and willingness to put up with you. Don't you know that the reason God is good to you is because he wants you to turn to him?

5But you are stubborn and refuse to turn to God. So you are making things even worse for yourselves on that day when he will show how angry he is and will judge the world with fairness. **6**God will reward each of us for what we have done. **7**He will give eternal life to everyone who has patiently done what is good in the hope of receiving glory, honor, and life that lasts forever. **8**But he will show how angry and furious he can be with every selfish person who rejects the truth and wants to do evil. **9**All who are wicked will be punished with trouble and suffering. It doesn't matter if they are Jews or Gentiles. **10**But all who do right will be rewarded with glory, honor, and peace, whether they are Jews or Gentiles. **11**God doesn't have any favorites!

12Those people who don't know about God's Law will still be punished for what they do wrong. And the Law will be used to judge everyone who knows what it says. **13**God accepts those who obey his Law, but not those who simply hear it.

14Some people naturally obey the Law's commands, even though they don't have the Law. **15**This proves that the conscience is like a law written in the human heart. And it will show whether we are forgiven or condemned, **16**when God appoints Jesus Christ to judge everyone's secret thoughts, just as my message says.

The Jews and the Law

17Some of you call yourselves Jews. You trust in the Law and take pride in God. **18**By reading the Scriptures you learn how God wants you to behave, and you discover what is right. **19**You are sure that you are a guide for the blind and a light for all who are in the dark. **20**And since there is knowledge and truth in God's Law, you think you can instruct fools and teach young people.

21But how can you teach others when you refuse to learn? You preach it is wrong to steal. But do you steal? **22**You say people should be faithful in marriage. But are you faithful? You hate idols, yet you rob their temples. **23**You take pride in the Law, but you disobey the Law and bring shame to God. **24**It is just as the Scriptures tell us, "You have made foreigners say insulting things about God."

25Being circumcised is worthwhile, if you obey the Law. But if you don't obey the Law, you are no better off than people who are not circumcised. **26**In fact, if they obey the Law, they are as good as anyone who is circumcised. **27**So everyone who obeys the Law, but has never been circumcised, will condemn you. Even though you are circumcised and have the Law, you still don't obey its teachings.

28Just because you live like a Jew and are circumcised doesn't make you a real Jew. **29**To be a real Jew you must obey the Law. True circumcision is something that happens deep in your heart, not something done to your body. And besides, you should want praise from God and not from humans.

3 What good is it to be a Jew? What good is it to be circumcised? **2**It is good in a lot of ways! First of all, God's messages were spoken to the Jews. **3**It is true that some of them did not believe the message. But does this mean that God cannot be trusted, just because they did not have faith? **4**No, indeed! God tells the truth, even if everyone else is a liar. The Scriptures say about God,

2.7 *eternal life:* By the time of Jesus, many Jewish people had come to believe in life after death. Some thought that life after death would be similar to life on earth. Paul talks of eternal life as being raised to new life with Christ (6.4-8).

Eternal Life

2.12 *God's Law:* Paul is referring to the Law of Moses. According to Paul, people who believe that God will accept them because they follow the Law, will also be judged according to the Law. **(See the article People of the Law: The Religion of Israel on pg 1794.)**

Law

2.15 *forgiven or condemned:* Sin occurs whenever people rebel against God and disobey God's Word. Forgiveness removes sin. Paul says that forgiveness comes from Jesus, who died to take away sins (3.25,26). Those who do not trust in God will be condemned, punished, and may not be able to share the promise of eternal life.

2.25 *Being circumcised:* Paul is saying that being circumcised is an important part of the Law of Moses. If someone chooses not to obey the Law, however, circumcision cannot make that person "a real Jew" (2.28).

Circumcision

3.8 *Some people even claim that we are saying this:* Some of Paul's opponents claimed that Paul was asking people to disobey the Law of Moses, just so that God could show his love by forgiving them. Paul's opponents thought that all followers of Jesus should also obey the laws and traditions that were part of the Law of Moses.

3.22 *God . . . accepts people:* One of the major themes in Paul's writings. This is the way to be in a "right" relationship with God. See also Gal 3.26-29.

3.23 *sinned and fallen short of God's glory:* "Falling short of God's glory" means that people cannot perfectly follow God's Law or live according to all God's purposes.

Sin

3.25-26 *God sent Christ to be our sacrifice:* Since Christ has been sacrificed for our sins, God can show mercy on sinners.

The Sacred Chest

3.28 *acceptable to God:* The Greek word translated here as "acceptable to God" is often translated as "justified." People are acceptable to God because they have faith (put their trust) in Christ Jesus.

"Your words
will be proven true,
and in court
you will win your case."

⁵If our evil deeds show how right God is, then what can we say? Is it wrong for God to become angry and punish us? What a foolish thing to ask. ⁶But the answer is, "No." Otherwise, how could God judge the world? ⁷Since your lies bring great honor to God by showing how truthful he is, you may ask why God still says you are a sinner. ⁸You might as well say, "Let's do something evil, so that something good will come of it!" Some people even claim that we are saying this. But God is fair and will judge them as well.

No One Is Good

⁹What does all this mean? Does it mean that we Jews are better off[f] than the Gentiles? No, it doesn't! Jews, as well as Gentiles, are ruled by sin, just as I have said. ¹⁰The Scriptures tell us,
"No one is acceptable to God!
¹¹Not one of them understands
or even searches for God.
¹²They have all turned away
and are worthless.
There isn't one person
who does right.
¹³ Their words are like
an open pit,
and their tongues are good
only for telling lies.
Each word is as deadly
as the fangs of a snake,
¹⁴and they say nothing
but bitter curses.
¹⁵These people quickly
become violent.
¹⁶Wherever they go,
they leave ruin
and destruction.
¹⁷They don't know how
to live in peace.
¹⁸ They don't even fear God."

¹⁹We know that everything in the Law was written for those who are under its power. The Law says these things to stop anyone from making excuses and to let God show that the whole world is guilty. ²⁰God doesn't accept people simply because they obey the Law. No, indeed! All the Law does is to point out our sin.

God's Way of Accepting People

²¹Now we see how God does make us acceptable to him. The Law and the Prophets[g] tell how we become acceptable, and it isn't by obeying the Law of Moses. ²²God treats everyone alike. He accepts people only because they have faith in Jesus Christ. ²³All of us have sinned and fallen short of God's glory. ²⁴But God treats us much better than we deserve, and because of Christ Jesus, he freely accepts us and sets us free from our sins. ²⁵⁻²⁶God sent Christ to be our sacrifice. Christ offered his life's blood, so by faith in him we could come to God. And God did this to show that in the past he was right to be patient and forgive sinners. This also shows that God is right when he accepts people who have faith in Jesus.

²⁷What is left for us to brag about? Not a thing! Is it because we obeyed some law? No! It is because of faith. ²⁸We see that people are acceptable to God because they have faith, and not because they obey the

[f]**3.9** *better off:* Or "worse off."   [g]**3.21** *The Law and the Prophets:* The Jewish Scriptures, that is, the Old Testament.

Law. ²⁹Does God belong only to the Jews? Isn't he also the God of the Gentiles? Yes, he is! ³⁰There is only one God, and he accepts Gentiles as well as Jews, simply because of their faith. ³¹Do we destroy the Law by our faith? Not at all! We make it even more powerful.

The Example of Abraham

4 Well then, what can we say about our ancestor Abraham? ²If he became acceptable to God because of what he did, then he would have something to brag about. But he would never be able to brag about it to God. ³The Scriptures say, "God accepted Abraham because Abraham had faith in him."

⁴Money paid to workers isn't a gift. It is something they earn by working. ⁵But you cannot make God accept you because of something you do. God accepts sinners only because they have faith in him. ⁶In the Scriptures David talks about the blessings that come to people who are acceptable to God, even though they don't do anything to deserve these blessings. David says,

⁷⁻⁸"What a blessing
  when God forgives our sins
    and our evil deeds.
  What a blessing
  when the Lord erases our sins
    from his book."

⁹Are these blessings meant for circumcised people or for those who are not circumcised? Well, the Scriptures say that God accepted Abraham because Abraham had faith in him. ¹⁰But when did this happen? Was it before or after Abraham was circumcised? Of course, it was before. ¹¹Abraham let himself be circumcised to show he had been accepted because of his faith even before he was circumcised. This makes Abraham the father of all who are acceptable to God because of their faith, even though they are not circumcised. ¹²This also makes Abraham the father of everyone who is circumcised and has faith in God, as Abraham did before he was circumcised.

The Promise Is for All Who Have Faith

¹³God promised Abraham and his descendants that he would give them the world. This promise wasn't made because Abraham had obeyed a law, but because his faith in God made him acceptable. ¹⁴If Abraham and his descendants were given this promise because they had obeyed a law, then faith would mean nothing, and the promise would be worthless.

¹⁵God becomes angry when his Law is broken. But where there isn't a law, it cannot be broken. ¹⁶Everything depends on having faith in God, so that God's promise is assured by his gift of undeserved grace. This promise isn't only for Abraham's descendants who have the Law. It is for all who are Abraham's descendants because they have faith, just as he did. Abraham is the ancestor of us all. ¹⁷The Scriptures say that Abraham would become the ancestor of many nations. This promise was made to Abraham because he had faith in God, who raises the dead to life and creates new things.

¹⁸God promised Abraham a lot of descendants. And when it all seemed hopeless, Abraham still had faith in God and became the ancestor of many nations. ¹⁹Abraham's faith never became weak, not even when he was nearly 100 years old. He knew he was almost dead and that his wife Sarah could not have children. ²⁰But Abraham never doubted or questioned God's promise. His faith made him strong, and he gave all the credit to God.

3.31 *Do we destroy the Law:* Paul does not want to destroy the Law, since it shows what God expects. The problem comes when people make following the Law more important than faith in God.

Abraham

4.6 *Scriptures David:* King David ruled Israel from around 1010 to 970 B.C., and was understood to be the author of Psalms.

David

4.7,8 *What a blessing . . . from his book:* Paul is quoting Psalm 32.1,2, a psalm that is traditionally credited to King David.

4.9 *circumcised:* Paul points out that Abraham was circumcised after God had accepted him because of his faith. That makes Abraham the father of those who are circumcised and those who are not.

4.16 *Abraham's descendants . . . Abraham is the ancestor of us all:* Paul argues that a person's nationality does not matter. Anyone can be a descendant of Abraham because of his or her faith in God.

4.24 God . . . raised our Lord Jesus to life: Paul is referring to how Jesus rose to life three days after dying on a cross (Matt 28.1-10; Acts 2.22-24). This "rising" is sometimes called the "resurrection."

⃝ℜ Resurrection

5.2 God's gift of undeserved grace: This phrase translates the Greek word *charis*, which Paul often uses in place of the Hebrew *hesed* (meaning "mercy"). Early Christian believers used *charis*—a word that could also mean "graciousness," "kindness," "favor," or "gift"—to express God's loving kindness and the unearned mercy God extends to humanity because of the sacrifice Jesus made on their behalf.

5.9 sacrificed his life's blood: Paul argues that God's sacrifice of Jesus was an act of God's undeserved kindness (grace) that freed us from God's anger.

5.12 Adam sinned, and that sin brought death: Adam, the first human created by God, sinned by disobeying God in the Garden of Eden (Gen 2.15-17; 3.1-24). Human beings had been created to live with God forever, but Adam's sin made all people sin and die.

5.15 the gift: The gift is the new life that God gives to those who trust in Jesus Christ, the one who brought forgiveness and made people acceptable to God.

²¹Abraham was certain that God could do what he had promised. ²²So God accepted him, ²³just as we read in the Scriptures. But these words were not written only for Abraham. ²⁴They were written for us, since we will also be accepted because of our faith in God, who raised our Lord Jesus to life. ²⁵God gave Jesus to die for our sins, and he raised him to life, so that we would be made acceptable to God.

What It Means To Be Acceptable to God

5 By faith we have been made acceptable to God. And now, thanks to our Lord Jesus Christ, we have peace[h] with God. ²Christ has also introduced us[i] to God's gift of undeserved grace on which we now take our stand. So we are happy, as we look forward to sharing in the glory of God. ³But that's not all! We gladly suffer,[j] because we know that suffering helps us to endure. ⁴And endurance builds character, which gives us a hope ⁵that will never disappoint us. All of this happens because God has given us the Holy Spirit, who fills our hearts with his love.

⁶Christ died for us at a time when we were helpless and sinful. ⁷No one is really willing to die for an honest person, though someone might be willing to die for a truly good person. ⁸But God showed how much he loved us by having Christ die for us, even though we were sinful.

⁹But there is more! Now that God has accepted us because Christ sacrificed his life's blood, we will also be kept safe from God's anger. ¹⁰Even when we were God's enemies, he made peace with us, because his Son died for us. Yet something even

greater than friendship is ours. Now that we are at peace with God, we will be saved by the life of his Son. ¹¹And in addition to everything else, we are happy because God sent our Lord Jesus Christ to make peace with us.

Adam and Christ

¹²Adam sinned, and that sin brought death into the world. Now everyone has sinned, and so everyone must die. ¹³Sin was in the world before the Law came. But no record of sin was kept, because there was no Law. ¹⁴Yet death still had power over all who lived from the time of Adam to the time of Moses. This happened, though not everyone disobeyed a direct command from God, as Adam did.

In some ways Adam is like Christ who came later. ¹⁵But the gift of God's undeserved grace was very different from Adam's sin. That one sin brought death to many others. Yet in an even greater way, Jesus Christ alone brought God's gift of undeserved grace to many people.

¹⁶There is a lot of difference between Adam's sin and God's gift. That one sin led to punishment. But God's gift made it possible for us to be acceptable to him, even though we have sinned many times. ¹⁷Death ruled like a king because Adam had sinned. But that cannot compare with what Jesus Christ has done. God has treated us with undeserved grace, and he has accepted us because of Jesus. And so we will live and rule like kings.

¹⁸Everyone was going to be punished because Adam sinned. But because of the good thing that Christ has done, God accepts us and gives us the gift of life. ¹⁹Adam

[h]**5.1** *we have peace:* Some manuscripts have "let us have peace." [i]**5.2** *introduced us:* Some manuscripts add "by faith." [j]**5.3** *We gladly suffer:* Or "Let us gladly suffer."

By faith we have been made acceptable to God.
ROM 5.1

disobeyed God and caused many others to be sinners. But Jesus obeyed him and will make many others acceptable to God.

20The Law came, so that the full power of sin could be seen. Yet where sin was powerful, God's gift of undeserved grace was even more powerful. 21Sin ruled by means of death. But God's gift of grace now rules, and God has accepted us because of Jesus Christ our Lord. This means that we will have eternal life.

Dead to Sin but Alive because of Christ

6 What should we say? Should we keep on sinning, so that God's gift of undeserved grace will show up even better? 2No, we should not! If we are dead to sin, how can we go on sinning? 3Don't you know that all who share in Christ Jesus by being baptized also share in his death? 4When we were baptized, we died and were buried with Christ. We were baptized, so we would live a new life, as Christ was raised to life by the glory of God the Father.

5If we shared in Jesus' death by being baptized, we will be raised to life with him. 6We know that the persons we used to be were nailed to the cross with Jesus. This was done, so our sinful bodies would no longer be the slaves of sin. 7We know sin doesn't have power over dead people.

8As surely as we died with Christ, we believe we will also live with him. 9We know that death no longer has any power over Christ. He died and was raised to life, never again to die. 10When Christ died, he died for sin once and for all. But now he is alive, and he lives only for God. 11In the same way, you must think of yourselves as dead to the power of sin. But Christ Jesus has given life to you, and you live for God.

12Don't let sin rule your body. After all, your body is bound to die, so don't obey its desires 13or let any part of it become a slave of evil. Give yourselves to God, as people who have been raised from death to life. Make every part of your body a slave that pleases God. 14Don't let sin keep ruling your lives. You are ruled by God's undeserved grace and not by the Law.

Slaves Who Do What Pleases God

15What does all this mean? Does it mean we are free to sin, because we are ruled by God's gift of undeserved grace and not by the Law? Certainly not! 16Don't you know that you are slaves of anyone you obey? You can be slaves of sin and die, or you can be obedient slaves of God and be acceptable to him. 17You used to be slaves of sin. But I thank God that with all your heart you followed the example set forth in the teaching you received.18Now you are set free from sin and are slaves who please God.

19I am using these everyday examples, because in some ways you are still weak. You used to let the different parts of your body be slaves of your evil thoughts. But now you must make every part of your body serve God, so that you will belong completely to him.

20When you were slaves of sin, you didn't have to please God. 21But what good did you receive from the things you did? All you have to show for them is your shame, and they lead to death. 22Now you have been set free from sin, and you are God's slaves. This will make you holy and will lead you to eternal life. 23Sin pays off with death. But God's gift is eternal life given by Jesus Christ our Lord.

7.2 *the Law says:* Paul is likely teaching the traditional understanding of faithfulness in marriage, rather than a specific part of the Law of Moses.

7.4 *part of the body of Christ:* Now that Christ has come, people can join themselves to him just as a husband and wife join in marriage. They are free to do this because the power of the Law, which they had been "married to," is dead in their lives.

7.6 *obeying his Spirit:* Paul says that the new life God offers is life that is led by the Holy Spirit.

7.7 *Does this mean that the Law is sinful:* Some of Paul's opponents were saying that he was making the Law into an evil or sinful thing. Paul wants to make it clear that this is not at all what he teaches. He goes on to explain that the function of God's Law was to show what sin was really like.

7.8 *without the Law, sin is dead:* Without God's Law, no one would know what sin is. Hearing the Law makes a person aware of sin, but that doesn't mean that the Law causes sin. Because the Law and its commands are holy and good, the Law exposes the evil of sin.

7.14 *the Law is spiritual. But I am merely a human:* For Paul, the Law was an expression of God's perfect will, but Paul was human and therefore a slave to sin.

An Example from Marriage

7 My friends, you surely understand enough about law to know that laws only have power over people who are alive. ²For example, the Law says that a man's wife must remain his wife as long as he lives. But once her husband is dead, she is free ³to marry someone else. However, if she goes off with another man while her husband is still alive, she is said to be unfaithful.

⁴That is how it is with you, my friends. You are now part of the body of Christ and are dead to the power of the Law. You are free to belong to Christ, who was raised to life so we could serve God. ⁵When we thought only of ourselves, the Law made us have sinful desires. It made every part of our bodies into slaves who are doomed to die. ⁶But the Law no longer rules over us. We are like dead people, and it cannot have any power over us. Now we can serve God in a new way by obeying his Spirit, and not in the old way by obeying the written Law.

The Battle with Sin

⁷Does this mean that the Law is sinful? Certainly not! But if it had not been for the Law, I would not have known what sin is really like. For example, I would not have known what it means to want something that belongs to someone else, unless the Law had told me not to do this. ⁸It was sin that used this command as a way of making me have all kinds of desires. But without the Law, sin is dead.

⁹Before I knew about the Law, I was alive. But as soon as I heard that command, sin came to life, ¹⁰and I died. The very command that was supposed to bring life to me, instead brought death. ¹¹Sin used this command to trick me, and because of it I

died. ¹²Still, the Law and its commands are holy and correct and good.

¹³Am I saying something good caused my death? Certainly not! It was sin that killed me by using something good. Now we can see how terrible and evil sin really is. ¹⁴We know that the Law is spiritual. But I am merely a human, and I have been sold as a slave to sin. ¹⁵In fact, I don't understand why I act the way I do. I don't do what I know is right. I do the things I hate. ¹⁶Although I don't do what I know is right, I agree that the Law is good. ¹⁷So I am not the one doing these evil things. The sin that lives in me is what does them.

¹⁸I know that my selfish desires won't let me do anything that is good. Even when I want to do right, I cannot. ¹⁹Instead of doing what I know is right, I do wrong. ²⁰And so, if I don't do what I know is right, I am no longer the one doing these evil things. The sin that lives in me is what does them.

²¹The Law has shown me that something in me keeps me from doing what I know is right. ²²With my whole heart I agree with the Law of God. ²³But in every part of me I discover something fighting against my mind, and it makes me a prisoner of sin that controls everything I do. ²⁴What a miserable person I am. Who will rescue me from this body that is doomed to die? ²⁵Thank God! Jesus Christ will rescue me.

So with my mind I serve the Law of God, although my selfish desires make me serve the law of sin.

Living by the Power of God's Spirit

8 If you belong to Christ Jesus, you won't be punished. ²The Holy Spirit will give you life that comes from Christ Jesus and will set you[k] free from sin and death. ³The

[k]**8.2** *you:* Some manuscripts have "me."

Law of Moses cannot do this, because our selfish desires make the Law weak. But God set you free when he sent his own Son to be like us sinners and to be a sacrifice for our sin. God used Christ's body to condemn sin. [4]He did this, so that we would do what the Law commands by obeying the Spirit instead of our own desires.

[5]People who are ruled by their desires think only of themselves. Everyone who is ruled by the Holy Spirit thinks about spiritual things. [6]If our minds are ruled by our desires, we will die. But if our minds are ruled by the Spirit, we will have life and peace. [7]Our desires fight against God, because they do not and cannot obey God's laws. [8]If we follow our desires, we cannot please God.

[9]You are no longer ruled by your desires, but by God's Spirit, who lives in you. People who don't have the Spirit of Christ in them don't belong to him. [10]But Christ lives in you. So you are alive because God has accepted you, even though your bodies must die because of your sins. [11]Yet God raised Jesus to life! God's Spirit now lives in you, and he will raise you to life by his Spirit.

[12]My dear friends, we must not live to satisfy our desires. [13]If you do, you will die. But you will live, if by the help of God's Spirit you say "No" to your desires. [14]Only those people who are led by God's Spirit are his children. [15]God's Spirit doesn't make us slaves who are afraid of him. Instead, we become his children and call him our Father.[l] [16]God's Spirit makes us sure that we are his children. [17]His Spirit lets us know that together with Christ we will be given

what God has promised. We will also share in the glory of Christ, because we have suffered with him.

A Wonderful Future for God's People

[18]I am sure what we are suffering now cannot compare with the glory that will be shown to us. [19]In fact, all creation is eagerly waiting for God to show who his children are. [20]Meanwhile, creation is confused, but not because it wants to be confused. God made it this way in the hope [21]that creation would be set free from decay and would share in the glorious freedom of his children. [22]We know that all creation is still groaning and is in pain, like a woman about to give birth.

[23]The Spirit makes us sure about what we will be in the future. But now we groan silently, while we wait for God to show that we are his children.[m] This means that our bodies will also be set free. [24]And this hope is what saves us. But if we already have what we hope for, there is no need to keep on hoping. [25]However, we hope for something we have not yet seen, and we patiently wait for it.

[26]In certain ways we are weak, but the Spirit is here to help us. For example, when we don't know what to pray for, the Spirit prays for us in ways that cannot be put into words. [27]All of our thoughts are known to God. He can understand what is in the mind of the Spirit, as the Spirit prays for God's people. [28]We know that God is always at work for the good of everyone who loves him.[n] They are the ones God has

---

[l]**8.15** *our Father*: The Greek text uses the Aramaic word "Abba" (meaning "father"), which shows the close relation between the children and their father.   [m]**8.23** *to show that we are his children*: These words are not in some manuscripts. The translation of the remainder of the verse would then read, "while we wait for God to set our bodies free."   [n]**8.28** *God is always at work for the good of everyone who loves him*: Or "All things work for the good of everyone who loves God" or "God's Spirit always works for the good of everyone who loves God."

■ **8.5** *spiritual things:* By spiritual things, Paul means the things that are from God and that are pleasing to God.

■ **8.9** *Spirit of Christ:* The Holy Spirit is present in everyone who trusts in Jesus Christ.

■ **8.14** *those . . . led by God's Spirit are his children:* This statement was directed to everyone, but especially to those who believed that a person could be a child of God simply by following the Law of Moses, or by being born into a family that was descended from Abraham and Sarah.

■ **8.18** *suffering now . . . compare with the glory that will be shown to us:* All who trust in Jesus can look toward a future free of pain—the promise of eternal life. Paul offered hope of a future day when all God's children would live under God's care and love forever.

■ **8.23** *The Spirit makes us sure about what we will be in the future:* God's people can endure suffering and difficulties because they know that God's Spirit is within them and continues to support and encourage them. This is how they can be sure they will be saved and why they wait patiently for it.

■ **8.26** *the Spirit prays for us:* Paul says that the Spirit's work includes praying for those who cannot find words to pray for themselves.

9.1 *the Holy Spirit is a witness to my conscience:* Paul has described the "conscience" as a law written on the human heart. Here, Paul says that the Holy Spirit acts as his teacher, speaking to his conscience and shaping his innermost thoughts and desires.

9.7-9 *when God made the promise to Abraham . . . you will already have a son:* See Gen 16; 21.8-20. God's promises were made to the descendants of Abraham and Sarah's son Isaac. Abraham did have other children, like Ishmael, his son with Sarah's slave Hagar.

chosen for his purpose, [29] and he has always known who his chosen ones would be. He had decided to let them become like his own Son, so his Son would be the first of many children. [30] God then accepted the people he had already decided to choose, and he has shared his glory with them.

God's Love

[31] What can we say about all this? If God is on our side, can anyone be against us? [32] God did not keep back his own Son, but he gave him for us. If God did this, won't he freely give us everything else? [33] If God says his chosen ones are acceptable to him, can anyone bring charges against them? [34] Or can anyone condemn them? No indeed! Christ died and was raised to life, and now he is at God's right side,[o] speaking to him for us. [35] Can anything separate us from the love of Christ? Can trouble, suffering, and hard times, or hunger and nakedness, or danger and death? [36] It is exactly as the Scriptures say,

"For you we face death
　all day long.
We are like sheep
　on their way
　　to be butchered."

[37] In everything we have won more than a victory because of Christ who loves us. [38] I am sure that nothing can separate us from God's love—not life or death, not angels or spirits, not the present or the future, [39] and not powers above or powers below. Nothing in all creation can separate us from God's love for us in Christ Jesus our Lord!

God's Choice of Israel

9 I am a follower of Christ, and the Holy Spirit is a witness to my conscience. So I tell the truth and I am not lying when I say [2] my heart is broken and I am in great sorrow. [3] I would gladly be placed under God's curse and be separated from Christ for the good of my own people. [4] They are the descendants of Israel, and they are also God's chosen people. God showed them his glory. He made agreements with them and gave them his Law. The temple is theirs and so are the promises that God made to them. [5] They have those famous ancestors, who were also the ancestors of the Christ.[P] I pray that God, who rules over all, will be praised forever![q] Amen.

[6] It cannot be said that God broke his promise. After all, not all of the people of Israel are the true people of God. [7-8] In fact, when God made the promise to Abraham, he meant only Abraham's descendants by his son Isaac. God was talking only about Isaac when he promised [9] Sarah, "At this time next year I will return, and you will already have a son."

[10] Don't forget what happened to the twin sons of Isaac and Rebekah. [11-12] Even before they were born or had done anything good or bad, the Lord told Rebekah that her older son would serve the younger one. The Lord said this to show he makes his own choices and it wasn't because of anything either of them had done. [13] That's why the Scriptures say that the Lord liked Jacob more than Esau.

[14] Are we saying God is unfair? Certainly not! [15] The Lord told Moses that he has pity and mercy on anyone he wants to. [16] Every-

[o]8.34 *right side:* The place of power and honor.　[P]9.5 *Christ:* Or "Messiah."　[q]9.5 *Christ. I pray that God, who rules over all, will be praised forever:* Or "Christ, who rules over all. I pray that God will be praised forever" or "Christ. And I pray that Christ, who is God and rules over all, will be praised forever."

Nothing in all creation can separate us from God's love for us in Christ Jesus our Lord! ROM 8.39

thing then depends on God's mercy and not on what people want or do. [17]In the Scriptures the Lord says to the king of Egypt, "I let you become king, so that I could show you my power and be praised by all people on earth." [18]Everything depends on what God decides to do, and he can either have pity on people or make them stubborn.

God's Anger and Mercy

[19]Someone may ask, "How can God blame us, if he makes us behave in the way he wants us to?" [20]But, my friend, I ask, "Who do you think you are to question God? Does the clay have the right to ask the potter why he shaped it the way he did? [21]Doesn't a potter have the right to make a fancy bowl and a plain bowl out of the same lump of clay?"

[22] God wanted to show his anger and reveal his power against everyone who deserved to be destroyed. But instead, he patiently put up with them. [23]He did this by showing how glorious he is when he has pity on the people he has chosen to share in his glory. [24]Whether Jews or Gentiles, we are these chosen ones, [25]just as the Lord says in the book of Hosea,

"Although they are not
my people,
  I will make them my people.
I will treat with love
those nations
  that have never been loved.

[26]"Once they were told,
  'You are not my people.'
But in that very place
they will be called
  children of the living God."

[27]And this is what the prophet Isaiah said about the people of Israel,
"The people of Israel
  are as many
as the grains of sand
  along the beach.
But only a few who are left
  will be saved.
[28]The Lord will be quick
  and sure to do on earth
what he has warned
  he will do."

[29]Isaiah also said,
"If the Lord All-Powerful
had not spared some
  of our descendants,
we would have been destroyed
like the cities of Sodom
  and Gomorrah."[r]

Israel and the Good News

[30]What does all of this mean? It means that the Gentiles were not trying to be acceptable to God, but they found that he would accept them if they had faith. [31-32]It also means that the people of Israel were not acceptable to God. And why not? It was because they were trying[s] to be acceptable by obeying the Law instead of by having faith in God. The people of Israel fell over the stone that makes people stumble, [33]just as God says in the Scriptures,
"Look! I am placing in Zion
a stone to make people
  stumble and fall.
But those who have faith
in that one will never
  be disappointed."

[r]9.29 *Sodom and Gomorrah*: During the time of Abraham the Lord destroyed these two cities because their people were so sinful.   [s]9.31,32 *because they were trying*: Or "while they were trying" or "even though they were trying."

9.18 *Everything depends on what God decides*: Paul emphasizes that God is the one who is in control of giving mercy or making people stubborn.

9.25 *Hosea*: Hosea was a prophet in Israel during the time Uzziah was king of Judah (783–746 B.C.) and Jeroboam II was king of Israel (786–746 B.C.). An important theme in HOSEA concerns Hosea's wife Gomer who left him for another man. She is compared to the people of Israel, who left God to follow idols and foreign gods.

9.25 *Although they are not my people*: Paul is quoting from both Hosea 2.23 and 1.10. These prophecies deal with how God will invite people from all nations to be God's children.

9.27 *Isaiah*: Isaiah was a prophet in Judah from about 740 to 701 B.C.

9.31-32 *the stone that makes people stumble*: Paul is referring to Jesus.

9.33 *Zion*: Zion was the name of a hilltop fortress captured by King David, which later became his royal city, Jerusalem. Because the temple was built there, Zion also was considered the place where God lived among his people.

Zion

Israel

10.6 *people whose faith makes them acceptable:* Paul means that those who have faith in Christ realize that being made acceptable to God is something God gives to people, not something people can achieve on their own.

10.19 *Moses:* God gave the Law to Moses who passed it on to the people of Israel.

Moses

10 Dear friends, my greatest wish and my prayer to God is for the people of Israel to be saved. [2] I know they love God, but they don't understand [3] what makes people acceptable to him. So they refuse to trust God, and they try to be acceptable by obeying the Law. [4] But Christ makes the Law no longer necessary[t] for those who become acceptable to God by faith.

Anyone Can Be Saved

[5] Moses said a person could become acceptable to God by obeying the Law. He did this when he wrote, "If you want to live, you must do all the Law commands."

[6] But people whose faith makes them acceptable to God will never ask, "Who will go up to heaven to bring Christ down?" [7] Neither will they ask, "Who will go down into the world of the dead to raise him to life?"

[8] All who are acceptable because of their faith simply say, "The message is as near as your mouth or your heart." And this is the same message we preach about faith. [9] So you will be saved, if you honestly say, "Jesus is Lord," and if you believe with all your heart that God raised him from death. [10] God will accept you and save you, if you truly believe this and tell it to others.

[11] The Scriptures say no one who has faith will be disappointed, [12] no matter if that person is a Jew or a Gentile. There is only one Lord, and he is generous to everyone who asks for his help. [13] All who call out to the Lord will be saved.

[14] How can people have faith in the Lord and ask him to save them, if they have never heard about him? And how can they hear, unless someone tells them? [15] And how can anyone tell them without being sent by the Lord? The Scriptures say it is a beautiful sight to see even the feet of someone coming to preach the good news. [16] Yet not everyone has believed the message. For example, the prophet Isaiah asked, "Lord, has anyone believed what we said?"

[17] No one can have faith without hearing the message about Christ. [18] But am I saying that the people of Israel did not hear? No, I am not! The Scriptures say,

"The message was told
   everywhere on earth.
It was announced
   all over the world."

[19] Did the people of Israel understand or not? Moses answered this question when he told that the Lord had said,

"I will make Israel jealous
   of people
who are a nation
   of nobodies.
I will make them angry
   with people
who don't understand
   a thing."

[20] Isaiah was fearless enough to tell that the Lord had said,

"I was found by people
   who were not looking
   for me.
I appeared to the ones
   who were not asking
   about me."

[21] And Isaiah said about the people of Israel,

"All day long the Lord
   has reached out
to people who are stubborn
   and refuse to obey."

God Has Not Rejected His People

11 Am I saying that God has turned his back on his people? Certainly not! I am one of the people of Israel, and I

---

[t] *10.4 But Christ makes the Law no longer necessary:* Or "But Christ gives the full meaning to the Law."

myself am a descendant of Abraham from the tribe of Benjamin. **2**God did not turn his back on his chosen people. Don't you remember reading in the Scriptures how Elijah complained to God about the people of Israel? **3**He said, "Lord, they killed your prophets and destroyed your altars. I am the only one left, and now they want to kill me."

4But the Lord told Elijah, "I still have 7,000 followers who have not worshiped Baal." **5**It is the same way now. God treated the people of Israel with undeserved grace, and so a few of them are still his followers. **6**This happened because of God's undeserved kindness and not because of anything they have done. It could not have happened except for God's gift of undeserved grace.

7This means that only a chosen few of the people of Israel found what all of them were searching for. And the rest of them were stubborn, **8**just as the Scriptures say,

"God made them so stupid
    that their eyes are blind,
and their ears
    are still deaf."

9Then David said,
"Turn their meals
    into bait for a trap,
so that they will stumble
and be given
    what they deserve.
10Blindfold their eyes!
    Don't let them see.
Bend their backs
beneath a burden
    that will never be lifted."

Gentiles Will Be Saved

11Do I mean that the people of Israel fell, never to get up again? Certainly not! Their failure made it possible for the Gentiles to be saved, and this will make the people of Israel jealous. **12**But if the rest of the world's people were helped so much by their sin and loss, they will be helped even more by their full return.

13I am now speaking to you Gentiles, and as long as I am an apostle to you, I will take pride in my work. **14**I hope in this way to make some of my own people jealous enough to be saved. **15**When Israel rejected God,**u** the rest of the people in the world were able to turn to him. So when God makes friends with Israel, it will be like bringing the dead back to life. **16**If part of a batch of dough is made holy by being offered to God, then all of the dough is holy. If the roots of a tree are holy, the rest of the tree is holy too.

17You Gentiles are like branches of a wild olive tree made to be part of a cultivated olive tree. You have taken the place of some branches that were cut away from it. And because of this, you enjoy the blessings that come from being part of that cultivated tree. **18**But don't think you are better than the branches that were cut away. Just remember you are not supporting the roots of this tree. Its roots are supporting you.

19Maybe you think those branches were cut away, so you could be put in their place. **20**That's true enough. But they were cut away because they did not have faith, and you are where you are because you do have faith. So don't be proud, but be afraid. **21**If God cut away those natural branches, couldn't he do the same to you?

22Now you see both how kind and how hard God can be. He was hard on those who fell, but he was kind to you. And he will keep on being kind to you, if you keep on trusting in his kindness. Otherwise, you will be cut away too.

u11.15 *When Israel rejected God:* Or "When Israel was rejected."

11.1 I *from the tribe of Benjamin:* The tribe took its name from the youngest son of Jacob (Israel).

11.2 *Elijah:* Over 800 years before Jesus was born, the prophet Elijah preached against worshiping other gods, especially the Canaanite god Baal.

Elijah

11.12 *their sin and loss:* Referring to Israel's rejection of Jesus, God's Messiah.

11.16 *batch of dough . . . roots of a tree:* Paul uses two images to show that the holiness of a part of a group can lead to the holiness of an entire group. The first followers of Jesus among the people of Israel (the part) make the Gentiles holy and acceptable to God.

11.17 *like branches of a wild olive tree:* Inserting the branches or leaves of one plant into the stalks or branches of another is called "grafting." Since ancient times, farmers have used grafting to improve the flavor and quality of fruit. Paul argues that the Gentiles are like branches cut from a wild tree and grafted into a cultivated tree. "Gentile" branches have been grafted into the tree, which stands for the whole people of God.

11.36 *Amen:* In biblical Hebrew, this word means "truthful, reliable." It is also used as a way of saying, "Yes, it is so!" That is why it is often spoken at the end of a prayer.

12.1 *offer your bodies . . . as a living sacrifice:* Offering sacrifices was an important part of the Jewish religion as well as other religions of Paul's day. However, Paul says that God's new followers don't need to offer dead animals or to make other sacrifices to please God. Rather, they are to offer their whole selves in living service to God.

CR Temple Offerings

12.2 *world:* For Paul, the "world" stands for the present age, in which most of the things people put their trust in are against God.

12.5 *body of Christ:* This is another way Paul describes the whole group of Jesus' followers, the Christian church.

12.6 *different gifts:* God's Spirit gives different gifts to the followers of Jesus to be used in God's service. To receive the gift of prophecy is to receive a special ability to hear God's message and tell it to others. Paul mentions other gifts such as serving others, teaching, giving money in a generous way, and leadership. See also 1 Cor 12.4-11.

²³If those other branches will start having faith, they will be made a part of that tree again. God has the power to put them back. ²⁴After all, it wasn't natural for branches to be cut from a wild olive tree and to be made part of a cultivated olive tree. So it is much more likely that God will join the natural branches back to the cultivated olive tree.

The People of Israel Will Be Brought Back

²⁵My friends, I don't want you Gentiles to be too proud of yourselves. So I will explain the mystery of what has happened to the people of Israel. Some of them have become stubborn, and they will stay like that until the complete number of you Gentiles has come in. ²⁶In this way all of Israel will be saved, as the Scriptures say,

"From Zion someone will come
    to rescue us.
Then Jacob's descendants
    will stop being evil.
²⁷This is what the Lord
    has promised to do
when he forgives their sins."

²⁸The people of Israel are treated as God's enemies, so the good news can come to you Gentiles. But they are still the chosen ones, and God loves them because of their famous ancestors. ²⁹God doesn't take back the gifts he has given or disown the people he has chosen.

³⁰At one time you Gentiles rejected God. But now Israel has rejected God, and you have been shown mercy. ³¹And because of the mercy shown to you, they will also be shown mercy. ³²All people have disobeyed God, and that's why he treats them as prisoners. But he does this, so that he can have mercy on all of them.

³³Who can measure the wealth and wisdom and knowledge of God? Who can understand his decisions or explain what he does?

³⁴"Has anyone known
    the thoughts of the Lord
    or given him advice?
³⁵Has anyone loaned
    something to the Lord
    that must be repaid?"

³⁶Everything comes from the Lord. All things were made because of him and will return to him. Praise the Lord forever! Amen.

Christ Brings New Life

12 Dear friends, God is good. So I beg you to offer your bodies to him as a living sacrifice, pure and pleasing. That's the most sensible way to serve God. ²Don't be like the people of this world, but let God change the way you think. Then you will know how to do everything that is good and pleasing to him.

³I realize God has treated me with undeserved grace, and so I tell each of you not to think you are better than you really are. Use good sense and measure yourself by the amount of faith that God has given you. ⁴A body is made up of many parts, and each of them has its own use. ⁵That's how it is with us. There are many of us, but we each are part of the body of Christ, as well as part of one another.

⁶God has also given each of us different gifts to use. If we can prophesy, we should do it according to the amount of faith we have. ⁷If we can serve others, we should serve. If we can teach, we should teach. ⁸If we can encourage others, we should encourage them. If we can give, we should be generous. If we are leaders, we should do our best. If we are good to others, we should do it cheerfully.

Dear friends, God is good. I beg you to offer your bodies to him as a living sacrifice, pure and pleasing. That's the most sensible way to serve God. ROM 12.1

Rules for Christian Living

⁹Be sincere in your love for others. Hate everything that is evil and hold tight to everything that is good. ¹⁰Love each other as brothers and sisters and honor others more than you do yourself. ¹¹Never give up. Eagerly follow the Holy Spirit and serve the Lord. ¹²Let your hope make you glad. Be patient in time of trouble and never stop praying. ¹³Take care of God's needy people and welcome strangers into your home.

¹⁴Ask God to bless everyone who mistreats you. Ask him to bless them and not to curse them. ¹⁵When others are happy, be happy with them, and when they are sad, be sad. ¹⁶Be friendly with everyone. Don't be proud and feel that you know more than others. Make friends with ordinary people.ᵛ ¹⁷Don't mistreat someone who has mistreated you. But try to earn the respect of others, ¹⁸and do your best to live at peace with everyone.

¹⁹Dear friends, don't try to get even. Let God take revenge. In the Scriptures the Lord says,

> "I am the one to take revenge
> and pay them back."

²⁰The Scriptures also say,

> "If your enemies are hungry,
> give them something to eat.
> And if they are thirsty,
> give them something
> to drink.
> This will be the same
> as piling burning coals
> on their heads."

²¹Don't let evil defeat you, but defeat evil with good.

Obey Rulers

13 Obey the rulers who have authority over you. Only God can give authority to anyone, and he puts these rulers in their places of power. ²People who oppose the authorities are opposing what God has done, and they will be punished. ³Rulers are a threat to evil people, not to good people. There is no need to be afraid of the authorities. Just do right, and they will praise you for it. ⁴After all, they are God's servants, and it is their duty to help you.

If you do something wrong, you ought to be afraid, because these rulers have the right to punish you. They are God's servants who punish criminals to show how angry God is. ⁵But you should obey the rulers because you know it is the right thing to do, and not just because of God's anger.

⁶You must also pay your taxes. The authorities are God's servants, and it is their duty to take care of these matters. ⁷Pay all that you owe, whether it is taxes and fees or respect and honor.

Love

⁸Let love be your only debt! If you love others, you have done all that the Law demands. ⁹In the Law there are many commands, such as, "Be faithful in marriage. Do not murder. Do not steal. Do not want what belongs to others." But all of these are summed up in the command that says, "Love others as much as you love yourself." ¹⁰No one who loves others will harm them. So love is all that the Law demands.

12.13 *Take care of God's needy people and welcome strangers:* Paul and other apostles in the early church were concerned about receiving offerings to give to the poor, and wanted to continue the Jewish custom of welcoming strangers into one's home for food or rest.

13.1 *Only God can give authority to anyone:* Paul believed that God was in control of putting people in places of power. Those who opposed earthly rulers were opposing God.

13.3,4 *Rulers . . . are God's servants:* Paul argues that the followers of Jesus should obey authorities because they are God's servants. Obeying the authorities meant paying taxes to support the government and the Roman military. This was difficult for the followers of Jesus who knew that their taxes went to support Roman emperors, who did not believe in God or even declared that they were gods. However, if a small group of Jesus' followers caused trouble for the government, the government could stop the good news from spreading throughout the Roman Empire.

ᵛ**12.16** *Make friends with ordinary people:* Or "Do ordinary jobs."

If you love others, you have done all that the Law demands. ROM 13.8

The Day When Christ Returns

¹¹You know what sort of times we live in, and so you should live properly. It is time to wake up. You know that the day when we will be saved is nearer now than when we first put our faith in the Lord. ¹²Night is almost over, and day will soon appear. We must stop behaving as people do in the dark and be ready to live in the light. ¹³So behave properly, as people do in the day. Don't go to wild parties or get drunk or be vulgar or indecent. Don't quarrel or be jealous. ¹⁴Let the Lord Jesus Christ be as near to you as the clothes you wear. Then you won't try to satisfy your selfish desires.

Don't Criticize Others

14 Welcome all the Lord's followers, even those whose faith is weak. Don't criticize them for having beliefs that are different from yours. ²Some think it is all right to eat anything, while those whose faith is weak will eat only vegetables. ³But you should not criticize others for eating or for not eating. After all, God welcomes everyone. ⁴What right do you have to criticize someone else's servants? Only their Lord can decide if they are doing right, and the Lord will make sure that they do right.

⁵Some of the Lord's followers think one day is more important than another. Others think all days are the same. But each of you should make up your own mind. ⁶Any followers who count one day more important than another day do it to honor their Lord. And any followers who eat meat give thanks to God, just like the ones who don't eat meat.

⁷Whether we live or die, it must be for God, rather than for ourselves. ⁸Whether we live or die, it must be for the Lord. Alive or dead, we still belong to the Lord. ⁹This is because Christ died and rose to life, so that he would be the Lord of the dead and of the living. ¹⁰Why do you criticize other followers of the Lord? Why do you look down on them? The day is coming when God will judge all of us. ¹¹In the Scriptures God says,

"I swear by my very life
that everyone will kneel down
and praise my name!"

¹²And so, each of us must give an account to God for what we do.

Don't Cause Problems for Others

¹³We must stop judging others. We must also make up our minds not to upset anyone's faith. ¹⁴The Lord Jesus has made it clear to me that God considers all foods fit to eat. But if you think some foods are unfit to eat, then for you they are not fit.

¹⁵If you are hurting others by the foods you eat, you are not guided by love. Don't let your appetite destroy someone Christ died for. ¹⁶Don't let your right to eat bring shame to Christ. ¹⁷God's kingdom isn't about eating and drinking. It is about pleasing God, about living in peace, and about true happiness. All this comes from the Holy Spirit. ¹⁸If you serve Christ in this way, you will please God and be respected by people. ¹⁹We should try^w to live at peace and help each other have a strong faith.

²⁰Don't let your appetite destroy what God has done. All foods are fit to eat, but it is wrong to cause problems for others by what you eat. ²¹It is best not to eat meat or drink wine or do anything else that causes problems for other followers of the Lord. ²²What you believe about these things should be kept between you and God. You

^w14.19 *We should try:* Some manuscripts have "We try."

are fortunate, if your actions don't make you have doubts. **23**But if you do have doubts about what you eat, you are going against your beliefs. And you know that is wrong, because anything you do against your beliefs is sin.

Please Others and Not Yourself

15 If our faith is strong, we should be patient with the Lord's followers whose faith is weak. We should try to please them instead of ourselves. **2**We should think of their good and try to help them by doing what pleases them. **3**Even Christ did not try to please himself. But as the Scriptures say, "The people who insulted you also insulted me." **4**And the Scriptures were written to teach and encourage us by giving us hope. **5**God is the one who makes us patient and cheerful. I pray that he will help you live at peace with each other, as you follow Christ. **6**Then all of you together will praise God, the Father of our Lord Jesus Christ.

The Good News Is for Jews and Gentiles

7Honor God by accepting each other, as Christ has accepted you. **8**I tell you that Christ came as a servant of the Jews to show that God has kept the promises he made to their famous ancestors. Christ also came, **9**so that the Gentiles would praise God for being kind to them. It is just as the Scriptures say,

"I will tell the nations
     about you,
   and I will sing praises
     to your name."

10The Scriptures also say to the Gentiles, "Come and celebrate with God's people." **11**Again the Scriptures say,

"Praise the Lord,
   all you Gentiles.
All you nations, come
   and worship him."

12Isaiah says,
"Someone from David's family
   will come to power.
He will rule the nations,
   and they will put their hope
     in him."

13I pray that God, who gives hope, will bless you with complete happiness and peace because of your faith. And may the power of the Holy Spirit fill you with hope.

Paul's Work as a Missionary

14My friends, I am sure that you are very good and that you have all the knowledge you need to teach each other. **15**But I have spoken to you plainly and have tried to remind you of some things. God treated me with undeserved grace! **16**He chose me to be a servant of Christ Jesus for the Gentiles and to do the work of a priest in the service of his good news. God did this so that the Holy Spirit could make the Gentiles into a holy offering, pleasing to him. **17**Because of Christ Jesus, I can take pride in my service for God. **18**In fact, all I will talk about is how Christ let me speak and work, so that the Gentiles would obey him. **19**Indeed, I will tell how Christ worked miracles and wonders by the power of the Holy Spirit. I have preached the good news about him all the way from Jerusalem to Illyricum. **20**But I have always tried to preach where people have never heard about Christ. I am like a builder who doesn't build on someone else's foundation. **21**It is just as the Scriptures say,

"All who haven't been told
   about him

● 15.8 *Christ came as a servant of the Jews:* Paul repeats his belief that Jesus came to fulfill God's promise to send a chosen Messiah to the Jewish people.

● 15.9 *I will tell the nations:* "Nations" refers to all the Gentile nations.

● 15.10 *Come and celebrate with God's people:* Paul stresses that all the nations would be invited to worship God and to be part of God's new people.

■ 15.16 *priest in the service of his good news:* Jewish priests served God by making sure the rituals described in the Law of Moses were obeyed and by preparing special offerings and sacrifices. Paul says that he serves God by preaching the good news to the Gentiles.

● 15.19 *Jerusalem to Illyricum:* Jerusalem was the capital of Judea and the center for Israel's worship and government. Illyricum was a Roman province on the eastern coast of the Adriatic Sea. The Bible does not say that Paul went to Illyricum, but he may have preached to some Illyrians while in Macedonia, who then took his message home with them. Paul suggests that the good news about Jesus has spread in a huge territorial circle throughout the Roman Empire. **(See Map 13 on pg 1891.)**

15.24 *stop off on my way to Spain:* The Bible does not say if Paul ever went to Spain. Some think that he may have gone to Spain after being released from house arrest in Rome (Acts 28; Phil 1.13). Others think Paul was put to death in Rome. (See Map 10 on pg 1888.)

16.1 *Phoebe . . . a leader in the church at Cenchreae:* Phoebe is only mentioned here in the New Testament. This is evidence that some women held leadership positions in the early church. Cenchreae was a seaport located seven miles southeast of the city of Corinth. (See the chart Leaders of House Churches in the New Testament on pg 1840 and Map 15 on pg 1893.)

16.3 *Priscilla and Aquila:* This couple had lived in Rome, but were driven out along with other members of the Jewish community in about A.D. 49. They later worked as tent makers with Paul. See also Acts 18.18-26; 1 Cor 16.19; and 2 Tim 4.19.

16.5,6 *Epaenetus . . . Mary:* The New Testament does not mention Epaenetus anywhere else, and it is not clear who Mary is.

16.8-15 *Ampliatus . . . Olympas:* None of the many names in these verses is mentioned anywhere else in the New Testament. Tryphaena, Tryphosa, Persis, Julia, and Olympas are women's names, giving more evidence of the leadership roles women held in the early church.

will see him,
and those who haven't heard about him
will understand."

Paul's Plan To Visit Rome

[22] My work has always kept me from coming to see you. [23] Now there is nothing left for me to do in this part of the world, and for years I have wanted to visit you. [24] So I plan to stop off on my way to Spain. Then after a short, but refreshing, visit with you, I hope you will quickly send me on.

[25-26] I am now on my way to Jerusalem to deliver the money that the Lord's followers in Macedonia and Achaia collected for God's needy people. [27] This is something they really wanted to do. But sharing their money with the Jews was also like paying back a debt, because the Jews had already shared their spiritual blessings with the Gentiles. [28] After I have safely delivered this money, I will visit you and then go on to Spain. [29] And when I do arrive in Rome, I know it will be with the full blessings of Christ.

[30] My friends, by the power of the Lord Jesus Christ and by the love that comes from the Holy Spirit, I beg you to pray sincerely with me and for me. [31] Pray that God will protect me from the unbelievers in Judea, and that his people in Jerusalem will be pleased with what I am doing. [32] Ask God to let me come to you and have a pleasant and refreshing visit. [33] I pray that God, who gives peace, will be with all of you. Amen.

Personal Greetings

16 I have good things to say about Phoebe, who is a leader in the church at Cenchreae. [2] Welcome her in a way that is proper for someone who has faith in the Lord and is one of God's own people. Help her in any way you can. After all, she has proved to be a respected leader for many others, including me.

[3] Give my greetings to Priscilla and Aquila. They have not only served Christ Jesus together with me, [4] but they have even risked their lives for me. I am grateful for them and so are all the Gentile churches. [5] Greet the church that meets in their home.

Greet my dear friend Epaenetus, who was the first person in Asia to have faith in Christ.

[6] Greet Mary, who has worked so hard for you.

[7] Greet my relatives[x] Andronicus and Junia, who were in jail with me. They are highly respected by the apostles and were followers of Christ before I was.

[8] Greet Ampliatus, my dear friend whose faith is in the Lord.

[9] Greet Urbanus, who serves Christ along with us.

Greet my dear friend Stachys.

[10] Greet Apelles, a faithful servant of Christ.

Greet Aristobulus and his family.

[11] Greet Herodion, who is a relative[y] of mine.

Greet Narcissus and the others in his family, who have faith in the Lord.

[12] Greet Tryphaena and Tryphosa, who work hard for the Lord.

Greet my dear friend Persis. She also works hard for the Lord.

[13] Greet Rufus, that special servant of the Lord, and greet his mother, who has been like a mother to me.

[14] Greet Asyncritus, Phlegon, Hermes, Patrobas, and Hermas, as well as our friends who are with them.

[x]**16.7** *relatives:* Or "Jewish friends." [y]**16.11** *relative:* Or "Jewish friend."

¹⁵Greet Philologus, Julia, Nereus and his sister, and Olympas, and all of God's people who are with them.

¹⁶Be sure to give each other a warm greeting.

All of Christ's churches greet you.

¹⁷My friends, I beg you to watch out for anyone who causes trouble and divides the church by refusing to do what all of you were taught. Stay away from them! ¹⁸They want to serve themselves and not Christ the Lord. Their flattery and fancy talk fool people who don't know any better. ¹⁹I am glad that everyone knows how well you obey the Lord. But still, I want you to understand what is good and not have anything to do with evil. ²⁰Then God, who gives peace, will soon crush Satan under your feet. I pray that our Lord Jesus will be kind to you.

²¹Timothy, who works with me, sends his greetings, and so do my relatives,ᶻ Lucius, Jason, and Sosipater.

²²I, Tertius, also send my greetings. I am a follower of the Lord, and I wrote this letter.ᵃ

²³⁻²⁴Gaius welcomes me and the whole church into his home, and he sends his greetings.

Erastus, the city treasurer, and our dear friend Quartus send their greetings too.ᵇ

Paul's Closing Prayer

²⁵Praise God! He can make you strong by means of my good news, which is the message aboutᶜ Jesus Christ. For ages and ages this message was kept secret, ²⁶but now at last it has been told. The eternal God commanded his prophets to write about the good news, so that all nations would obey and have faith. ²⁷And now, because of Jesus Christ, we can praise the only wise God forever! Amen.ᵈ

16.20 *Satan*: Satan means "adversary."

Satan

16.21 *Timothy*: Timothy, the son of a Jewish Christian mother and a Gentile father became a member of God's people because of Paul (Acts 16.1-3).

16.21 *Lucius, Jason, and Sosipater*: A Lucius is mentioned in Acts 13.1, and the name Jason is mentioned in Acts 17.5-9, but it is not clear if these are the same persons Paul names. Sosipater may be a variation of the name Sopater, who is mentioned in Acts 20.4.

16.22 *Tertius*: The person who wrote down the words Paul dictated. A physical problem apparently made it impossible for Paul to write down these words himself. See also 2 Cor 10.10; 12.7; Gal 4.13-16; 6.11.

16.23-24 *Gaius . . . Erastus . . . Quartus*: The name "Gaius" also occurs in Acts 19.29; 20.4; 1 Cor 1.14; and 3 John 1, but it is not the same person in each case. Erastus and Quartus are not mentioned anywhere else in the New Testament. The fact that Erastus was a city treasurer shows that the good news of Jesus had reached not only the poor, but wealthy people as well.

ᶻ**16.21** *relatives*: See the note at verse 7.   ᵃ**16.22** *I wrote this letter*: Paul probably dictated this letter to Tertius.   ᵇ**16.23,24** *send their greetings too*: Some manuscripts add, "I pray that our Lord Jesus Christ will always bless you with undeserved grace. Amen."   ᶜ**16.25** *about*: Or "from."   ᵈ**16.27** *Amen*: Some manuscripts have verses 25-27 after 14.23. Others have the verses here and after 14.23, and one manuscript has them after 15.33.

Reflection Questions About Romans 1.1—16.27

1. How does Paul describe the "good news" (1.16,17)?

2. How do people "crush the truth" (1.18—2.16)? How does Paul describe God's judgment (2.2-11)? What does Paul say about the human conscience?

3. What is the real purpose of the Law (3.19,20)? If following the Law is not the way to be saved or accepted by God, what is (3.21-30)? Does this mean that the Law is useless or should be thrown out (3.31)?

4. According to Paul, what is the relationship between suffering and having hope (5.3-5)? How do God's people have hope?

5. How did God show how much he loved us (5.6-11)?

6. What does it mean to be a slave to sin? What does it mean to be a slave to God (6.15-23)?

7. How do people come to have faith in the Lord (10.14-17)? What does this mean for modern Christians?

8. What does it mean to offer your body as a living sacrifice (12.1)? Paul compares the followers of Christ to one body. Each part of the body has special gifts. What are some of those gifts (12.6-8)? Which of these gifts do you have? What other gifts do you have that can be used to serve God?

9. Why did Paul encourage the followers of Christ in his day to obey their earthly rulers? What about rulers who are opposed to God and God's people? Should they be obeyed and followed? Why or why not?

10. What request does Paul make of the followers in Rome (15.30-32)?

1 corinthians

Faith in Jesus Christ makes us friends with God and all of God's followers. Learn how Paul planted seeds of faith among the people at Corinth, and how his "faith-planting" also made his friendship with them grow and blossom.

WHAT MAKES 1 CORINTHIANS SPECIAL?

FIRST CORINTHIANS provides a clear idea of the kind of questions faced by one early group of Jesus' followers. It also shows Paul's teaching on a number of issues. This letter is well-known for its chapters on the gifts of the Holy Spirit, and for Paul's teaching that love is the best gift of all (12–14). Chapter 15 includes Paul's statement that God has defeated death and promises new life and a "spiritual" body to everyone faithful to Jesus.

Paul visited Corinth and taught the good news about Jesus Christ (see Acts 18.1-17). During this time, he became close to the followers of Christ who lived in Corinth. He wrote to them because they were his friends and because he had heard about certain arguments and disputes among them. He was especially concerned about the way the Corinthian Christians were dividing themselves into different groups (1.10—4.21) and about the way they were treating one another (5.1—6.20). He also wrote to answer their questions about marriage (7.1-40) and about eating food offered to idols (8.1-13). They had earlier sent these questions to Paul in a letter (7.1). Finally, Paul wanted to let the Corinthian Christians know that he intended to return to Corinth and stay with them for a while (16.5).

WHAT'S THE STORY BEHIND THE SCENE?

Although this letter is called 1 CORINTHIANS, it is not the first one Paul wrote to this church. In this letter, he mentions that he had written an earlier one (5.9).

The city of Corinth was located on a narrow strip of land that had a seaport to both the east and west. It was a very worldly city, influenced by people of many cultures. People who lived in Corinth had a long tradition of devotion to the love goddess, Aphrodite. Paul's letter addresses some of the struggles the Corinthian Christians continued to face because of the many influences present in the city.

HOW IS 1 CORINTHIANS CONSTRUCTED?

FIRST CORINTHIANS is probably a single letter, though it may include other letters Paul wrote to the followers at Corinth. It can be outlined as follows:

Greetings and a prayer of thanks (1.1-9)
Be united by the cross of Christ (1.10—2.16)
Trust the teaching of God's apostles (3.1—4.21)
Advice about problems in relationships (5.1—7.40)
Honor God and not idols (8.1—11.1)
Guidance for worship and the use of spiritual gifts (11.2—14.40)
The meaning of Christ's victory over death (15.1-58)
Future plans and final greetings (16.1-24)

orinth was an important port city in ancient Greece. During the first century A.D., Corinth was part of the Roman Empire and home to a large Jewish community. Paul preached the good news to the Jewish and Gentile Corinthians and helped to found the Christian church there. Later, when he was in Ephesus, Paul learned that the Christians in Corinth were divided into factions and arguing among themselves. He had written to them once to give them advice on godly living and received at least one letter from them seeking his advice on specific matters. The letter known as 1 Corinthians contains Paul's answers to the community's questions and includes teachings on marriage, rules for worship, how to celebrate the Lord's Supper, the importance of spiritual gifts, and the meaning of Jesus' being raised from death. In this letter, Paul not only gives later generations important historical information about the early church, but he also produces profound and beautifully expressed teachings that have guided Christians throughout the ages.

Outline

1 From Paul, chosen by God to be an apostle of Christ Jesus, and from Sosthenes, who is also a follower.

2To God's church in Corinth. Christ Jesus chose you to be his very own people, and you worship in his name, as we and all others do who call him Lord.

3My prayer is that God our Father and the Lord Jesus Christ will be kind to you and will bless you with peace!

4I never stop thanking my God for treating you with undeserved grace by giving you Christ Jesus, **5**who helps you speak and understand so well. **6**Now you are certain that everything we told you about our Lord Christ Jesus is true. **7**You are not missing out on any blessings, as you wait for him to return. **8**And until the day Christ does return, he will keep you completely innocent. **9**God can be trusted, and he chose you to be partners with his Son, our Lord Jesus Christ.

Taking Sides

10My dear friends, as a follower of our Lord Jesus Christ, I beg you to get along with each other. Don't take sides. Always try to agree in what you think. **11**Several people from Chloe's family[a] have already reported to me that you keep arguing with each other. **12**They have said that some of you claim to follow me, while others claim to follow Apollos or Peter[b] or Christ.

13Has Christ been divided up? Was I nailed to a cross for you? Were you baptized in my name? **14**I thank God[c] that I didn't baptize any of you except Crispus and Gaius. **15**Not one of you can say that you were baptized in my name. **16**I did baptize the family[d] of

---

[a]**1.11** *family*: Family members and possibly slaves and others who may have lived in the house.
[b]**1.12** *Peter*: The Greek text has "Cephas," which is an Aramaic name meaning "rock." Peter is the Greek name with the same meaning.   [c]**1.14** *I thank God*: Some manuscripts have "I thank my God."   [d]**1.16** *family*: See the note at 1.11.

1.17,18 *good news ... message about the cross:* This message is the good news that Jesus died on a cross to defeat death and sin, and then was raised from death. "Lost people" do not have faith in Jesus, but rely on human wisdom. To them the message about the cross is foolish.

1.20-27 *wisdom of this world ... foolish things:* For Paul, the "world" stands for things that are against God (Rom 12.2; Gal 4.3; 6.14). God chose something that seemed to be a defeat— the cross of Christ—to be the instrument that brings new life to human beings. This seemed foolish to those who expected God to act in a more forceful way.

2.1 *mystery:* Paul says the good news is God's own plan, which human beings cannot understand on their own. The main part of this mystery is that God provided the perfect sacrifice for human sins when Jesus died on the cross (see Rom 3.25-26).

2.7 *God's hidden and mysterious wisdom:* According to Paul, this wisdom was a part of God's plan from the very beginning (see also Rom 16.25).

Wisdom

Stephanas, but I don't remember if I baptized anyone else. [17]Christ did not send me to baptize. He sent me to tell the good news without using words that sound wise and would make the cross of Christ lose its power.

Christ Is God's Power and Wisdom

[18]The message about the cross doesn't make any sense to lost people. But for those of us who are being saved, it is God's power at work. [19]As God says in the Scriptures,

"I will destroy the wisdom
    of all who claim
        to be wise.
I will confuse those
    who think they know
        so much."

[20]What happened to those wise people? What happened to those experts in the Scriptures? What happened to the ones who think they have all the answers? Didn't God show that the wisdom of this world is foolish? [21]God was wise and decided not to let the people of this world use their wisdom to learn about him.

Instead, God chose to save only those who believe the foolish message we preach. [22]Jews ask for miracles, and Greeks want something that sounds wise. [23]But we preach that Christ was nailed to a cross. Most Jews have problems with this, and most Gentiles think it is foolish. [24]Our message is God's power and wisdom for the Jews and the Greeks that he has chosen. [25]Even when God is foolish, he is wiser than everyone else, and even when God is weak, he is stronger than everyone else.

[26]My dear friends, remember what you were when God chose you. The people of this world didn't think that many of you were wise. Only a few of you were in places of power, and not many of you came from important families. [27]But God chose the foolish things of this world to put the wise to shame. He chose the weak things of this world to put the powerful to shame. [28]What the world thinks is worthless, useless, and nothing at all is what God has used to destroy what the world considers important. [29]God did all this to keep anyone from bragging to him. [30]You are God's children. He sent Christ Jesus to save us and to make us wise, acceptable, and holy. [31]So if you want to brag, do what the Scriptures say and brag about the Lord.

Telling about Christ and the Cross

2 Friends, when I came and told you the mystery[e] that God had shared with us, I didn't use big words or try to sound wise. [2]In fact, while I was with you, I made up my mind to speak only about Jesus Christ, who had been nailed to a cross.

[3]At first, I was weak and trembling with fear. [4]When I talked with you or preached, I didn't try to prove anything by sounding wise. I simply let God's Spirit show his power. [5]That way you would have faith because of God's power and not because of human wisdom.

[6]We do use wisdom when speaking to people who are mature in their faith. But it isn't the wisdom of this world or of its rulers, who will soon disappear. [7]We speak of God's hidden and mysterious wisdom that God decided to use for our glory long before the world began. [8]The rulers of this world didn't know anything about this wisdom. If they had known about it, they

[e]2.1 *mystery:* Some manuscripts have "testimony."

would not have nailed the glorious Lord to a cross. **9**But it is just as the Scriptures say,

"What God has planned
for people who love him
is more than eyes have seen
or ears have heard.
It has never even
entered our minds!"

10God's Spirit has shown you everything. His Spirit finds out everything, even what is deep in the mind of God. **11**You are the only one who knows what is in your own mind, and God's Spirit is the only one who knows what is in God's mind. **12**But God has given us his Spirit. This is why we don't think the same way that the people of this world think. This is also why we can recognize the blessings God has given us.

13Every word we speak was taught to us by God's Spirit, not by human wisdom. And this same Spirit helps us teach spiritual things to spiritual people.**f** **14**This is why only someone who has God's Spirit can understand spiritual blessings. Anyone who doesn't have God's Spirit thinks these blessings are foolish. **15**People who are guided by the Spirit can make all kinds of judgments, but they cannot be judged by others. **16**The Scriptures ask,

"Has anyone ever known
the thoughts of the Lord
or given him advice?"
But we understand what Christ is thinking.**g**

Working Together for God

3 My friends, you are acting like the people of this world. That's why I could not speak to you as spiritual people. You are like babies as far as your faith in Christ is concerned. **2**So I had to treat you like babies and feed you milk. You could not take solid food, and you still cannot, **3**because you are not yet spiritual. You are jealous and argue with each other. This proves you are not spiritual and you are acting like the people of this world.

4Some of you say you follow me, and others claim to follow Apollos. Isn't this how ordinary people behave? **5**Apollos and I are merely servants who helped you to have faith. It was the Lord who made it all happen. **6**I planted the seeds, Apollos watered them, but God made them sprout and grow. **7**What matters isn't those who planted or watered, but God who made the plants grow. **8**The one who plants is just as important as the one who waters. And each one will be paid for what they do. **9**Apollos and I work together for God, and you are God's garden and God's building.

Only One Foundation

10God treated me with undeserved grace and let me become an expert builder. I laid a foundation on which others have built. But we must each be careful how we build, **11**because Christ is the only foundation. **12-13**Whatever we build on this foundation will be tested by fire on the day of judgment. Then everyone will find out if we have used gold, silver, and precious stones, or wood, hay, and straw. **14**We will be rewarded if our building is left standing. **15**But if it is destroyed by the fire, we will lose everything. Yet we ourselves will be saved, like someone escaping from flames.

16All of you surely know you are God's temple and his Spirit lives in you. **17**Together you are God's holy temple, and God will destroy anyone who destroys his temple.

f2.13 *teach spiritual things to spiritual people*: Or "compare spiritual things with spiritual things."
g2.16 *we understand what Christ is thinking*: Or "we think as Christ does."

2.12 *God has given us his Spirit*: God's Spirit reveals the truth, which is not a truth the people of the world would otherwise understand or believe. See John 14.15-17; Acts 2.1-12; and Gal 5.22-25.

3.3 *you are not yet spiritual*: Paul was concerned that the Corinthians were not living like people led by God's Spirit. Though they had become followers of Christ, they continued to argue with each other. Many returned to their "worldly" lives, ignoring Paul's message (5.1—6.20).

3.6-10 *I planted the seeds, Apollos watered them . . . I laid a foundation*: Paul and Apollos had different jobs to do. Paul started the church in Corinth, and Apollos helped it grow. However, the real foundation of this new "building" is Christ.

3.12-13 *tested by fire on the day of judgment*: This refers to a time when God will examine how people have lived and whether they have been faithful. In the New Testament, the place of judgment for evildoers is often pictured as a place of fiery torture (Luke 16.23; Rev 20.14). Paul pictures the kind of fire used to melt valuable metal. Wood, hay, or straw would burn. Gold and silver would melt. Precious stones would not be burned at all. Paul states that his teaching will be tested by God's fire of judgment. If it has been a good teaching, it will survive the fire just like a precious stone.

Fire

All of you surely know you are God's temple and his Spirit lives in you. Together you are God's holy temple.
1 Cor 3.16,17

4.5 *until the Lord returns. He will show what is hidden:* When Jesus comes back, Paul says that he will reveal all of God's mysterious plans, which human minds have a hard time understanding.

4.9 *God has put us apostles in the worst possible place:* Paul and other apostles had faced hunger, thirst, ridicule, punishment, and jail.

4.17 *Timothy:* Paul sent Timothy to carry on the teaching Paul had begun. Timothy was the son of a Jewish Christian mother and a Gentile father from Lystra. See also 2 Cor 1.1; 1 Thes 1.1; Phlm 1.

4.19 *the ones . . . bragging:* This probably refers to those who are identified as the "super apostles" in 2 Cor 12.11. These super apostles claimed to have special wisdom that made them superior to Paul and the other apostles.

4.20 *God's kingdom:* God's kingdom is God's rule over people, both in this world and the next. This kingdom is made visible in the actions of Christ and of God's faithful people.

[18]Don't fool yourselves! If any of you think you are wise in the things of this world, you will have to become foolish before you can be truly wise. [19]This is because God considers the wisdom of this world to be foolish. It is just as the Scriptures say, "God catches the wise when they try to outsmart him." [20]The Scriptures also say, "The Lord knows that the plans made by wise people are useless." [21-22]So stop bragging about what anyone has done. Paul and Apollos and Peter[h] all belong to you. In fact, everything is yours, including the world, life, death, the present, and the future. Everything belongs to you, [23]and you belong to Christ, and Christ belongs to God.

The Work of the Apostles

4 Think of us as servants of Christ who have been given the work of explaining God's mysterious ways. [2]And since our first duty is to be faithful to the one we work for, [3]it doesn't matter to me if I am judged by you or even by a court of law. In fact, I don't judge myself. [4]I don't know of anything against me, but this doesn't prove I am right. The Lord is my judge. [5]So don't judge anyone until the Lord returns. He will show what is hidden in the dark and what is in everyone's heart. Then God will be the one who praises each of us.

[6]Friends, I have used Apollos and myself as examples to teach you the meaning of the saying, "Follow the rules." I want you to stop saying one of us is better than the other. [7]What is so special about you? What do you have that you were not given? And if it was given to you, how can you brag? [8]Are you already satisfied? Are you now rich? Have you become kings while we are

still nobodies? I wish you were kings. Then we could have a share in your kingdom.

[9]It seems to me that God has put us apostles in the worst possible place. We are like prisoners on their way to death. Angels and the people of this world just laugh at us. [10]Because of Christ we are thought of as fools, but Christ has made you wise. We are weak and hated, but you are powerful and respected. [11]Even today we go hungry and thirsty and don't have anything to wear except rags. We are mistreated and don't have a place to live. [12]We work hard with our own hands, and when people abuse us, we wish them well. When we suffer, we are patient. [13]When someone curses us, we answer with kind words. Until now we are thought of as nothing more than the trash and garbage of this world.

[14]I am not writing to embarrass you. I want to help you, just as parents help their own dear children. [15]Ten thousand people may teach you about Christ, but I am your only father. You became my children when I told you about Christ Jesus, [16]and I want you to be like me. [17]This is why I sent Timothy to you. I love him like a son, and he is a faithful servant of the Lord. Timothy will tell you what I do to follow Christ and how it agrees with what I always teach about Christ in every church.

[18]Some of you think I am not coming for a visit, and so you are bragging. [19]But if the Lord lets me come, I will soon be there. Then I will find out if the ones who are doing all this bragging really have any power. [20]God's kingdom isn't just a lot of words. It is power. [21]What do you want me to do when I arrive? Do you want me to be hard on you or to be kind and gentle?

[h]3.21,22 *Peter:* See the note at 1.12.

Immoral Followers

5 I have heard terrible things about some of you. In fact, you are behaving worse than Gentiles. A man is even sleeping with his own stepmother.[i] ²You are proud, when you ought to feel bad enough to chase away anyone who acts like this.

³⁻⁴I am with you only in my thoughts. But in the name of our Lord Jesus I have already judged this man, as though I were with you in person. So when you meet together and the power of the Lord Jesus is with you, I will be there too. ⁵You must then hand that man over to Satan. His body will be destroyed, but his spirit will be saved when the Lord Jesus returns.

⁶Stop being proud! Don't you know how a little yeast can spread through the whole batch of dough? ⁷Get rid of the old yeast! Then you will be like fresh bread made without yeast, and this is what you are. Our Passover lamb is Christ, who has already been sacrificed. ⁸So don't celebrate the festival by being evil and sinful, which is like serving bread made with yeast. Be pure and truthful and celebrate by using bread made without yeast.

⁹In my other letter[j] I told you not to have anything to do with immoral people. ¹⁰But I wasn't talking about the people of this world. You would have to leave this world to get away from everyone who is immoral or greedy or who cheats or worships idols. ¹¹I was talking about your own people who are immoral or greedy or worship idols or curse others or get drunk or cheat. Don't even eat with them! ¹²Why should I judge outsiders? Aren't we supposed to judge only church members? ¹³God judges everyone else. The Scriptures say, "Chase away any of your own people who are evil."

Taking Each Other to Court

6 When one of you has a complaint against another, do you take your complaint to a court of sinners? Or do you take it to God's people? ²Don't you know that God's people will judge the world? And if you are going to judge the world, can't you settle small problems? ³Don't you know we will judge angels? And if this is so, we can surely judge everyday matters. ⁴Why do you take everyday complaints to judges who are not respected by the church? ⁵I say this to your shame. Aren't any of you wise enough to act as a judge between one follower and another? ⁶Why should one of you take another to be tried by unbelievers?

⁷When one of you takes another to court, all of you lose. It would be better to let yourselves be cheated and robbed. ⁸But instead, you cheat and rob other followers.

⁹Don't you know that evil people won't have a share in the blessings of God's kingdom? Don't fool yourselves! No one who is immoral or worships idols or is unfaithful in marriage or is a pervert or behaves like a homosexual ¹⁰will share in God's kingdom. Neither will any thief or greedy person or drunkard or anyone who curses and cheats others. ¹¹Some of you used to be like that. But now the name of our Lord Jesus Christ and the power of God's Spirit have washed you and made you holy and acceptable to God.

---

[i]**5.1** *is even sleeping with his own stepmother*: Or "has even married his own stepmother."   [j]**5.9** *other letter*: An unknown letter that Paul wrote to the Christians at Corinth before he wrote this one.

● **5.1,2** *Gentiles . . . You are proud*: Most Gentiles (non-Jews) would have been unfamiliar with the Law of Moses. Some of the Corinthian Christians took Paul's message to mean that they didn't have to obey God's Law, and began doing immoral things.

● **5.6,7** *a little yeast . . . old yeast*: Paul argues that a few bad examples can influence all the people in the Corinthian church to do evil things. Getting rid of old yeast refers to the Jewish practice of throwing out all dough containing yeast just before Passover each year (Exod 13.3-10).

■ **5.7** *Our Passover lamb is Christ*: Paul compares Jesus' death with the sacrifice of the Passover lamb. Just as the blood of the lamb was used to save the Israelites from the angel of death, Jesus' death was a sacrifice that saved people from sin and death (Rom 3.25-26).

Ⓡ   Passover and the Festival of Thin Bread

● **6.1** *court of sinners . . . God's people*: "Sinners" here refers to worldly people who are judges for the state or government. "God's people" means the followers of Christ in Corinth.

■ **6.11** *Lord Jesus Christ . . . God's Spirit*: This verse may refer to baptism, in which the followers of Christ are "washed," made holy, and become acceptable to God.

Ⓡ   Baptism

6.12 *We can do anything we want to:* Even though obeying the Law of Moses cannot "save" a person, it still shows people how to live in a way that honors God and respects the best interests of others.

○‍R   Eternal Life

○‍R   Resurrection

6.15 *your bodies are part of the body of Christ:* God's Spirit lives in Christ's true followers and makes them God's temple, so they are united with Jesus' own body.

6.20 *God paid a great price for you:* God provided the perfect sacrifice for human sins when Jesus died on the cross (Rom 3.25-26).

7.1 *your letter:* The Corinthians had sent a letter to Paul asking him a number of questions. The question in 7.1 has to do with sexual relations. Some thought it was acceptable to have sexual relations outside of marriage, but Paul defended the Law of Moses, which called for married couples to be faithful to each other. Others believed that avoiding sex made them more spiritual. Paul says that this is also untrue, and gives his own advice in 7.2-40. He makes clear that some of this advice was his "opinion."

○‍R   Satan

Honor God with Your Body

¹²Some of you say, "We can do anything we want to." But I tell you not everything is good for us. So I refuse to let anything have power over me. ¹³You also say, "Food is meant for our bodies, and our bodies are meant for food." But I tell you that God will destroy them both. We are not supposed to do indecent things with our bodies. We are to use them for the Lord who is in charge of our bodies. ¹⁴God will raise us from death by the same power he used when he raised our Lord to life.

¹⁵Don't you know that your bodies are part of the body of Christ? Is it right for me to join part of the body of Christ to a prostitute? No, it isn't! ¹⁶Don't you know that a man who does that becomes part of her body? The Scriptures say, "The two of them will be like one person." ¹⁷But anyone who is joined to the Lord is one in spirit with him.

¹⁸Don't be immoral in matters of sex. That is a sin against your own body in a way no other sin is. ¹⁹You surely know that your body is a temple where the Holy Spirit lives. The Spirit is in you and is a gift from God. You are no longer your own. ²⁰God paid a great price for you. So use your body to honor God.

Questions about Marriage

7 Now I will answer the questions you asked in your letter. You asked, "Is it best for people not to marry?"ᵏ ²Well, having your own husband or wife should keep you from doing something immoral. ³Husbands and wives should be fair with each other about having sex. ⁴A wife belongs to her husband instead of to herself,

and a husband belongs to his wife instead of to himself. ⁵So don't refuse sex to each other, unless you agree not to have sex for a little while, in order to spend time in prayer. Then Satan won't be able to tempt you because of your lack of self-control. ⁶In my opinion that is what should be done, though I don't know of anything the Lord said about this matter. ⁷I wish all of you were like me, but God has given different gifts to each of us.

⁸My advice for the unmarried and for widows is that it is acceptable for them to remain single, just as I am. ⁹But if you don't have enough self-control, then go ahead and get married. After all, it is better to marry than to burn with desire.ˡ

¹⁰I instruct married couples to stay together, and this is exactly what the Lord himself taught. A wife who leaves her husband ¹¹should either stay single or go back to her husband. And a husband should not leave his wife.

¹²I don't know of anything else the Lord said about marriage. All I can do is to give you my own advice. If your wife isn't a follower of the Lord, but is willing to stay with you, don't divorce her. ¹³If your husband isn't a follower, but is willing to stay with you, don't divorce him. ¹⁴Your husband or wife who isn't a follower is made holy by having you as a partner. This also makes your children holy and keeps them from being unclean in God's sight.

¹⁵If your husband or wife isn't a follower of the Lord and decides to divorce you, then you should agree to it. You are no longer bound to that person. After all, God chose you and wants you to live at peace. ¹⁶And besides, how do you know if you will be able to save your husband or wife who isn't a follower?

Obeying the Lord at All Times

[17]In every church I tell the people to stay as they were when the Lord Jesus chose them and God called them to be his own. Now I say the same thing to you. [18]If you are already circumcised, don't try to change it. If you are not circumcised, don't get circumcised. [19]Being circumcised or uncircumcised isn't really what matters. The important thing is to obey God's commands. [20]So don't try to change what you were when God chose you. [21]Are you a slave? Don't let that bother you. But if you can win your freedom, you should. [22]When the Lord chooses slaves, they become his free people. And when he chooses free people, they become slaves of Christ. [23]God paid a great price for you. So don't become slaves of anyone else. [24]Stay what you were when God chose you.

Unmarried People

[25]I don't know of anything the Lord said about people who have never been married.[m] But I will tell you what I think. And you can trust me, because the Lord has treated me with kindness. [26]We are now going through hard times, and I think it is best for you to stay as you are. [27]If you are married, stay married. If you are not married, don't try to get married. [28]It isn't wrong to marry, even if you have never been married before. But those who marry will have a lot of trouble, and I want to protect you from this.

[29]My friends, what I mean is that the Lord will soon come,[n] and it won't matter if you are married or not. [30]It will be all the same if you are crying or laughing, or if you are buying or are completely broke. [31]It won't make any difference how much good you are getting from this world or how much you like it. This world as we know it is now passing away.

[32]I want all of you to be free from worry. An unmarried man worries about how to please the Lord. [33]But a married man has more worries. He must worry about the things of this world, because he wants to please his wife. [34]So he is pulled in two directions. Unmarried women and women who have never been married[o] worry only about pleasing the Lord, and they keep their bodies and minds pure. But a married woman worries about the things of this world, because she wants to please her husband. [35]What I am saying is for your own good—it isn't to limit your freedom. I want to help you to live right and to love the Lord above all else.

[36]But suppose you are engaged to someone old enough to be married, and you want her so much that all you can think about is getting married. Then go ahead and marry.[p] There is nothing wrong with that. [37]But it is better to have self-control and to make up your mind not to marry. [38]It is perfectly all right to marry, but it is better not to get married at all.

[39]A wife should stay married to her husband until he dies. Then she is free to marry again, but only to a man who is a

---

[m]7.25 *people who have never been married:* Or "virgins." [n]7.29 *the Lord will soon come:* Or "there's not much time left" or "the time for decision comes quickly." [o]7.34 *women who have never been married:* Or "virgins." [p]7.36 *But suppose you are engaged … go ahead and marry:* Verses 36-38 may also be translated: [36]"If you feel that you are not treating your grown daughter right by keeping her from getting married, then let her marry. You won't be doing anything wrong. [37]But it is better to have self-control and make up your mind not to let your daughter get married. [38]It is all right for you to let her marry. But it is better if you don't let her marry at all."

● 7.17 *church:* The Greek word for "church" is *ekklesia*, a term that referred to any gathering of people. In the New Testament "church" often refers to all the followers of Christ, but it can also refer to individual congregations, as it does in this verse.

❧ Church

● 7.18,19 *circumcised:* Some early Christians insisted that all males be circumcised. Paul teaches here, as in his other letters, that circumcision is not necessary to join God's people.

❧ Circumcision

■ 7.22 *slaves of Christ:* Paul thought of himself and other followers of Christ as Christ's slaves or servants (Rom 1.1; Phil 1.1). All believers belong to the Lord because of the "great price" that was paid for them. Among God's new people, all are equal, whether they are "free" or "slaves" in the Roman system of government (Gal 3.26-29).

8.6 *Jesus Christ is . . . Lord. Everything was made by him:* Christians said that Jesus was God's Son, but he was also present with God when God created the world (John 1.2, 3).

8.10 *eat in the temple of an idol:* Some Corinthian Christians may have been invited to feasts in the local temples, where food offered to idols was served. Paul reminded the followers that eating this food is not bad. Eating the food does not mean they believe in the idol. However, if others see the follower eating the food and eat it too, it may cause them to feel terribly guilty. Followers of Christ need to be careful not to cause misunderstandings for others.

9.2 *Others may think that I am not an apostle:* Because Paul had not been a follower of Jesus from the very beginning, some thought he was not really an apostle. They questioned his authority and teaching.

9.4-6 *Barnabas and I . . . support ourselves:* Barnabas went with Paul on one of his missionary trips (Acts 13.1—15.2). Paul argues that he and Barnabas (see Gal 2) have the right to be given food and drink and even to make a living by being preachers of the good news, the way the other apostles do. Paul felt it would be right for the Corinthians and others to support him, just as other workers earned pay for what they did.

follower of the Lord. **40**However, I think I am obeying God's Spirit when I say she would be happier to stay single.

Food Offered to Idols

8 In your letter you asked me about food offered to idols. All of us know something about this subject. But knowledge makes us proud of ourselves, while love makes us helpful to others. **2**In fact, people who think they know so much don't know anything at all. **3**But God has no doubts about who loves him.

4Even though food is offered to idols, we know that none of the idols in this world are alive. After all, there is only one God. **5**Many things in heaven and on earth are called gods and lords, but none of them really are gods or lords. **6**We have only one God, and he is the Father. He created everything, and we live for him. Jesus Christ is our only Lord. Everything was made by him, and by him life was given to us.

7Not everyone knows these things. In fact, many people have grown up with the belief that idols have life in them. So when they eat meat offered to idols, they are bothered by a weak conscience. **8**But food doesn't bring us any closer to God. We are no worse off if we don't eat, and we are no better off if we do.

9Don't cause problems for someone with a weak conscience, just because you have the right to eat anything. **10**You know all this, and so it doesn't bother you to eat in the temple of an idol. But suppose a person with a weak conscience sees you and decides to eat food that has been offered to idols. **11**Then what you know has destroyed someone Christ died for. **12**When you sin by hurting a follower with a weak conscience, you sin against Christ. **13**So if I

hurt one of the Lord's followers by what I eat, I will never eat meat as long as I live.

The Rights of an Apostle

9 I am free. I am an apostle. I have seen the Lord Jesus and have led you to have faith in him. **2**Others may think that I am not an apostle, but you are proof that I am an apostle to you.

3When people question me, I tell them **4**that Barnabas and I have the right to our food and drink. **5**We each have the right to marry one of the Lord's followers and to take her along with us, just as the other apostles and the Lord's brothers and Peter⁹ do. **6**Are we the only ones who have to support ourselves by working at another job? **7**Do soldiers pay their own salaries? Don't people who raise grapes eat some of what they grow? Don't shepherds get milk from their own goats?

8-9I am not saying this on my own authority. The Law of Moses tells us not to muzzle an ox when it is grinding grain. But was God concerned only about an ox? **10**No, he wasn't! He was talking about us. This was written in the Scriptures so that all who plow and all who grind the grain will look forward to sharing in the harvest.

11When we told the message to you, it was like planting spiritual seed. So we have the right to accept material things as our harvest from you. **12**If others have the right to do this, we have an even greater right. But we haven't used this right of ours. We are willing to put up with anything to keep from causing trouble for the message about Christ.

13Don't you know that people who work in the temple make their living from what is brought to the temple? Don't you know that a person who serves at the altar is

9.5 *Peter:* See the note at 1.12.

We have only one God, and he is the Father. He created everything, and we live for him. 1 Cor 8.6

given part of what is offered? ¹⁴In the same way, the Lord wants everyone who preaches the good news to make a living from preaching this message.

¹⁵But I have never used these privileges of mine, and I am not writing this because I want to start now. I would rather die than have someone rob me of the right to take pride in this. ¹⁶I don't have any reason to brag about preaching the good news. Preaching is something God told me to do, and if I don't do it, I am doomed. ¹⁷If I preach because I want to, I will be paid. But even if I don't want to, it is still something God has sent me to do. ¹⁸What pay am I given? It is the chance to preach the good news free of charge and not to use the privileges that are mine because I am a preacher.

¹⁹I am not anyone's slave. But I have become a slave to everyone, so I can win as many people as possible. ²⁰When I am with the Jews, I live like a Jew to win Jews. They are ruled by the Law of Moses, and I am not. But I live by the Law to win them. ²¹And when I am with people who are not ruled by the Law, I forget about the Law to win them. Of course, I never really forget about the law of God. In fact, I am ruled by the law of Christ. ²²When I am with people whose faith is weak, I live as they do to win them. I do everything I can to win everyone I possibly can. ²³I do all this for the good news, because I want to share in its blessings.

A Race and a Fight

²⁴You know that many runners enter a race, and only one of them wins the prize. So run to win! ²⁵Athletes work hard to win a crown that cannot last, but we do it for a crown that will last forever. ²⁶I don't run

^r**10.9** *Christ:* Some manuscripts have "the Lord."

without a goal. And I don't box by beating my fists in the air. ²⁷I keep my body under control and make it my slave, so I won't lose out after telling the good news to others.

Don't Worship Idols

10 Friends, I want to remind you that all our ancestors walked under the cloud and went through the sea. ²This was like being baptized and becoming followers of Moses. ³All of them also ate the same spiritual food ⁴and drank the same spiritual drink, which flowed from the spiritual rock that followed them. That rock was Christ. ⁵But most of them did not please God. So they died, and their bodies were scattered all over the desert.

⁶What happened to them is a warning to keep us from wanting to do the same evil things. ⁷They worshiped idols, just as the Scriptures say, "The people sat down to eat and drink. Then they got up to dance around." So don't worship idols. ⁸Some of those people did shameful things, and in a single day about 23,000 died. Don't do shameful things as they did. ⁹And don't try to test Christ,^r as some of them did and were later bitten by poisonous snakes. ¹⁰Don't even grumble, as some of them did and were killed by the destroying angel. ¹¹These things happened to them as a warning to us. All this was written in the Scriptures to teach us who live in these last days.

¹²Even if you think you can stand up to temptation, be careful not to fall. ¹³You are tempted in the same way that everyone else is tempted. But God can be trusted not to let you be tempted too much, and he will show you how to escape from your temptations.

9.16 *preaching:* Paul told about how Jesus chose him to preach the good news to both Jews and Gentiles (see Gal 1.16; 2.6-8; see also Acts 9.1-15; 13.44-49).

Law

9.25 *a crown:* Winners of athletic contests in ancient Corinth were awarded a crown made of fresh leaves. This crown is temporary, but the crown that lasts forever is the reward the followers of Jesus will receive for being faithful.

10.1 *our ancestors walked . . . went through the sea:* Paul's ancestors were the people of Israel who had escaped from slavery in Egypt. God saved the people by opening a path through the sea (Exod 14.21-29).

Moses

10.16,17 *drink from the cup . . . eat the bread:* At the Last Supper, Jesus used bread and wine to show how his body would be broken and his blood poured out as a sacrifice to forgive sins.

10.26 *The earth and everything in it:* Paul is quoting Psalm 24.1 to say that all food comes from God and is all right to eat. See also Mark 7.15,16; Acts 10.1—11.18.

10.33—11.1 *I always try to please others . . . the example of Christ:* Paul believed that at times it was necessary to avoid doing things that might offend new followers of Christ. Jesus taught that his followers must be willing to be like servants to others (Mark 10.23-25).

11.3 *the head:* Paul later describes the followers of Jesus as the "body of Christ" (12.12). Jesus is the head of this body. Although Paul says in Galatians 3.28 that men and women are one in Christ, he also taught the Corinthian Christians what the Jewish Scriptures say about the first woman being formed from a man (Gen 1.26,27; 2.18-25).

11.6 *wear something on her head:* Paul argues that whenever women pray or prophesy in public, they should either keep their hair tied up on their head or cover it in some way, since unkempt hair was equated with adultery and prostitution in ancient Jewish culture.

[14]My friends, you must keep away from idols. [15]I am speaking to you as people who have enough sense to know what I am talking about. [16]When we drink from the cup we ask God to bless, isn't that sharing in the blood of Christ? When we eat the bread we break, isn't that sharing in the body of Christ? [17]By sharing in the same loaf of bread, we become one body, even though there are many of us.

[18]Aren't the people of Israel sharing in the worship when they gather around the altar and eat the sacrifices offered there? [19]Am I saying that either the idols or the food sacrificed to them is anything at all? [20]No, I am not! This food is really sacrificed to demons and not to God. I don't want you to have anything to do with demons. [21]You cannot drink from the cup of demons and still drink from the Lord's cup. You cannot eat at the table of demons and still eat at the Lord's table. [22]We would make the Lord jealous if we did this. And we are not stronger than the Lord.

Always Honor God

[23]Some of you say, "We can do whatever we want to!" But I tell you not everything may be good or helpful. [24]We should think about others and not about ourselves. [25]However, when you buy meat in the market, go ahead and eat it. Keep your conscience clear by not asking where the meat came from. [26]The Scriptures say, "The earth and everything in it belong to the Lord."

[27]If an unbeliever invites you to dinner, and you want to go, then go. Eat whatever you are served. Don't cause a problem for someone's conscience by asking where the food came from. [28-29]But if you are told it has been sacrificed to idols, don't cause a problem by eating it. I don't mean a problem for yourself, but for the one who told you. Why should my freedom be limited by someone else's conscience? [30]If I give thanks for what I eat, why should anyone accuse me of doing wrong?

[31]When you eat or drink or do anything else, always do it to honor God. [32]Don't cause problems for Jews or Greeks or anyone else who belongs to God's church. [33]I always try to please others instead of myself, in the hope that many of them will

11 be saved. [1]You must follow my example, as I follow the example of Christ.

Rules for Worship

[2]I am proud of you, because you always remember me and obey the teachings I gave you. [3]Now I want you to know that Christ is the head of all men, and a man is the head of a woman. But God is the head of Christ. [4]This means that any man who prays or prophesies with something on his head brings shame to his head.

[5]But any woman who prays or prophesies without something on her head brings shame to her head. In fact, she may as well shave her head.[s] [6]A woman should wear something on her head. It is a disgrace for a woman to shave her head or cut her hair. But if she refuses to wear something on her head, let her cut off her hair.

[7]Men were created to be like God and to bring honor to God. This means a man should not wear anything on his head. Women were created to bring honor to men. [8]It was the woman who was made

[s]11.5 *she may as well shave her head:* A woman's hair was a mark of beauty, and it was shameful for a woman to cut her hair short or to shave her head, so that she looked like a man.

from a man, and not the man who was made from a woman. **9**He wasn't created for her. She was created for him. **10**And so, because of this, and also because of the angels, a woman ought to wear something on her head, as a sign of her authority.**t**

11As far as the Lord is concerned, men and women need each other. **12**It is true that the first woman came from a man, but all other men have been given birth by women. Yet God is the one who created everything. **13**Ask yourselves if it is proper for a woman to pray without something on her head. **14**Isn't it unnatural and disgraceful for men to have long hair? **15**But long hair is a beautiful way for a woman to cover her head. **16**This is how things are done in all of God's churches,**u** and this is why none of you should argue about what I have said.

Rules for the Lord's Supper

17Your worship services do you more harm than good. I am certainly not going to praise you for this. **18**I am told you can't get along with each other when you worship, and I am sure that some of what I have heard is true. **19**You are bound to argue with each other, but it is easy to see which of you have God's approval.

20When you meet together, you don't really celebrate the Lord's Supper. **21**You even start eating before everyone gets to the meeting, and some of you go hungry, while others get drunk. **22**Don't you have homes where you can eat and drink? Do you hate God's church? Do you want to embarrass people who don't have anything? What can I say to you? I certainly cannot praise you.

The Lord's Supper
(Matthew 26.26-29; Mark 14.22-25; Luke 22.14-20)

23I have already told you what the Lord Jesus did on the night he was betrayed. And it came from the Lord himself.

He took some bread in his hands. **24**Then after he had given thanks, he broke it and said, "This is my body, which is given for you. Eat this and remember me."

25After the meal, Jesus took a cup of wine in his hands and said, "This is my blood, and with it God makes his new agreement with you. Drink this and remember me."

26The Lord meant that when you eat this bread and drink from this cup, you tell about his death until he comes.

27But if you eat the bread and drink the wine in a way that isn't worthy of the Lord, you sin against his body and blood. **28**This is why you must examine the way you eat and drink. **29**If you fail to understand that you are the body of the Lord, you will condemn yourselves by the way you eat and drink. **30**This is why many of you are sick and weak and why a lot of others have died. **31**If we carefully judge ourselves, we won't be punished. **32**But when the Lord judges and punishes us, he does it to keep us from being condemned with the rest of the world.

33My dear friends, you should wait until everyone gets there before you start eating. **34**If you really are hungry, you can eat at home. Then you won't condemn yourselves when you meet together.

After I arrive, I will instruct you about the other matters.

---

t11.10 *as a sign of her authority:* Or "as a sign that she is under someone's authority."   **u11.16** *This is how things are done in all of God's churches:* Or "There is no set rule for this in any of God's churches."

● **11.17** *Your worship services:* The problems that were dividing the Corinthians when they came together for worship included a misunderstanding of the Lord's Supper (11.20-34) and a disorderly use of spiritual gifts, which upset the worship gathering (12.1—14.40).

● **11.20-22** *you don't really celebrate the Lord's Supper:* The Corinthian Christians quarreled even when they gathered to share the bread and wine of the Lord's Supper. Some ate and drank all the bread and wine without waiting for the others, and some drank until they were drunk. This showed that they misunderstood the significance of the Lord's Supper.

● **11.23** *what the Lord Jesus did on the night he was betrayed:* By sharing in the Lord's Supper, the followers of Jesus remembered that they were united by his death until he returns.

● **11.29** *you will condemn yourselves:* Paul told the Corinthians to examine how they were celebrating the Lord's Supper. This examination should encourage them to see that they are the body of the Lord, and that they should not live or act in a way that dishonors the Lord.

● **11.34** *After I arrive:* Paul intended to return to visit the Corinthian Christians.

Spiritual Gifts

12.3 God's Spirit: This is the Holy Spirit, which carries out God's purposes in the world. The Spirit teaches and guides the people of God so that they can bear witness to the good news and become the kind of people God wants them to be. Here, Paul also describes how the Spirit gives God's people special gifts.

Holy Spirit

12.10 speak different kinds of languages . . . tell what these languages mean: Those who had these special gifts could speak or interpret languages they had never learned. This is also known as "speaking in tongues."

12.12 body of Christ: Christ is the head of the body, which is made up of followers who are one because they share in the one loaf and the one cup of the Lord's Supper (10.16,17).

12.13 God's Spirit baptized each of us: The gift of the Holy Spirit was connected to baptism in Jesus' name. After being baptized in Jesus' name, and through the laying on of hands, the Holy Spirit came to new believers (Acts 4.8; 13.3,9,52; 19.5,6). This is what Paul meant when he says "we drink from that same Spirit."

13.1 angels: The word "angel" in English is based on the Greek word *angelos,* which means "messenger." In the Bible, angels are God's messengers.

Spiritual Gifts

12 My friends, you asked me about spiritual gifts. [2]I want you to remember that before you became followers of the Lord, you were led in all the wrong ways by idols that cannot even talk. [3]Now I want you to know that if you are led by God's Spirit, you will say that Jesus is Lord, and you will never curse Jesus.

[4]There are different kinds of spiritual gifts, but they all come from the same Spirit. [5]There are different ways to serve the same Lord, [6]and we can each do different things. Yet the same God works in all of us and helps us in everything we do.

[7]The Spirit has given each of us a special way of serving others. [8]Some of us can speak with wisdom, while others can speak with knowledge, but these gifts come from the same Spirit. [9]To others the Spirit has given great faith or the power to heal the sick [10]or the power to work mighty miracles. Some of us are prophets, and some of us recognize when God's Spirit is present.[v] Others can speak different kinds of languages, and still others can tell what these languages mean. [11]But it is the Spirit who does all this and decides which gifts to give to each of us.

One Body with Many Parts

[12] The body of Christ has many different parts, just as any other body does. [13]Some of us are Jews, and others are Gentiles. Some of us are slaves, and others are free. But God's Spirit baptized each of us and made us part of the body of Christ. Now we each drink from that same Spirit.[w]

[14]Our bodies don't have just one part. They have many parts. [15]Suppose a foot says, "I'm not a hand, and so I'm not part of the body." Wouldn't the foot still belong to the body? [16]Or suppose an ear says, "I'm not an eye, and so I'm not part of the body." Wouldn't the ear still belong to the body? [17]If our bodies were only an eye, we couldn't hear a thing. And if they were only an ear, we couldn't smell a thing. [18]But God has put all parts of our body together in the way that he decided is best.

[19]A body isn't really a body, unless there is more than one part. [20]It takes many parts to make a single body. [21]That's why the eyes cannot say they don't need the hands. That's also why the head cannot say it doesn't need the feet. [22]In fact, we cannot get along without the parts of the body that seem to be the weakest. [23]We take special care to dress up some parts of our bodies. We are modest about our personal parts, [24]but we don't have to be modest about other parts.

God put our bodies together in such a way that even the parts that seem the least important are valuable. [25]He did this to make all parts of the body work together smoothly, with each part caring about the others. [26]If one part of our body hurts, we hurt all over. If one part of our body is honored, the whole body will be happy.

[27]Together you are the body of Christ. Each one of you is part of his body. [28]First, God chose some people to be apostles and prophets and teachers for the church. But he also chose some to work miracles or heal the sick or help others or be leaders or speak different kinds of languages. [29]Not everyone is an apostle. Not everyone is a

[v]**12.10** *and some of us . . . present:* Or "and some of us recognize the difference between God's Spirit and other spirits." [w]**12.13** *Some of us are Jews . . . that same Spirit:* Verse 13 may also be translated, "God's Spirit is inside each of us, and all around us as well. So it doesn't matter that some of us are Jews and others are Gentiles and that some are slaves and others are free. Together we are one body."

prophet. Not everyone is a teacher. Not everyone can work miracles. **30**Not everyone can heal the sick. Not everyone can speak different kinds of languages. Not everyone can tell what these languages mean. **31**I want you to desire the best gifts.**x** So I will show you a much better way.

Love

13 What if I could speak all languages of humans and even of angels? If I did not love others, I would be nothing more than a noisy gong or a clanging cymbal. **2**What if I could prophesy and understand all mysteries and all knowledge? And what if I had faith that moved mountains? I would be nothing, unless I loved others. **3**What if I gave away all that I owned and let myself be burned alive?**y** I would gain nothing, unless I loved others. **4**Love is patient and kind, never jealous, boastful, proud, or **5**rude. Love isn't selfish or quick tempered. It doesn't keep a record of wrongs that others do. **6**Love rejoices in the truth, but not in evil. **7**Love is always supportive, loyal, hopeful,

and trusting.
8Love never fails!

Everyone who prophesies
will stop,
and unknown languages
will no longer
be spoken.
All that we know
will be forgotten.
9We don't know everything,
and our prophecies
are not complete.
10But what is perfect
will someday appear,
and what isn't perfect
will then disappear.

11When we were children,
we thought and reasoned
as children do.
But when we grew up,
we quit our childish ways.
12Now all we can see of God
is like a cloudy picture
in a mirror.
Later we will see him
face to face.
We don't know everything,
but then we will,
just as God completely
understands us.
13For now there are faith,
hope, and love.
But of these three,
the greatest is love.

Speaking Unknown Languages and Prophesying

14 Love should be your guide. Be eager to have the gifts that come from

---

x12.31 *I want you to desire the best gifts:* Or "You desire the best gifts."   **y13.3** *and let myself be burned alive:* Some manuscripts have "so that I could brag."

Angels

■ **13.2** *prophesy:* The act of telling God's truth about the present and future is to "prophesy." Prophecy is the message that is told.

■ **13.4-13** *Love:* Of the several Greek words for "love," *storge* (love among family members) and *eros* (sexual love) do not occur in the New Testament, though *philia*, which means "friendly" does occur. The special word for love used in these verses is the Greek word *agape*, which refers to God's love (John 3.16; Rom 5.5-8) and describes the kind of self-giving love God's followers are to show toward others (Mark 12.31; Rom 13.9; Lev 19.18).

Love

■ **13.10-12** *what is perfect will someday appear . . . then we will:* These phrases probably are a reference to that future day when Jesus will return.

● **13.12** *cloudy picture in a mirror:* The bronze mirrors used in the ancient world would not have given clear reflections. Mirrors using glass and metal were not widely produced until late in the 12th century A.D.

Love is patient and kind, never jealous, boastful, proud, or rude. 1 Cor 13.4,5

14.2-4 *speak languages that others don't know:* This gift of the Spirit helped the person who received it to praise God. People who came into Christian gathering might have been amazed at the unusual ability, but they received no benefit from a message they could not understand.

14.5 *I prefer that you would prophesy:* Paul regarded prophecy as a gift that helped the whole body of Christ more than the gift of speaking in unknown languages.

14.8 *bugle call:* Besides being used in battle, horns were used at the temple in Jerusalem to call people to worship.

14.15 *pray with my spirit, and . . . pray with my mind:* Praying with the spirit refers to praying in different languages that had not been learned. Praying with the mind refers to all sorts of ways people pray when they are aware of what they are saying.

14.24,25 *realize that they are sinners . . . what is hidden in their hearts:* Sin is turning away from God and failing to live as God intended. Prophecy that reveals God's true word can also make people realize that they have sinned. It encourages them to tell, or confess, what is hidden in their hearts.

Sin

the Holy Spirit, especially the gift of prophecy. ²If you speak languages that others don't know, God will understand what you are saying, though no one else will know what you mean. You will be talking about mysteries that only the Spirit understands. ³But when you prophesy, you will be understood, and others will be helped. They will be encouraged and made to feel better.

⁴By speaking languages that others don't know, you help only yourself. But by prophesying you help everyone in the church. ⁵I am glad for you to speak unknown languages, although I prefer that you would prophesy. In fact, prophesying does much more good than speaking unknown languages, unless someone can help the church by explaining what you mean.

⁶My friends, what good would it do, if I came and spoke unknown languages to you and didn't explain what I meant? How would I help you, unless I told you what God had shown me or gave you some knowledge or prophecy or teaching? ⁷If all musical instruments sounded alike, how would you know the difference between a flute and a harp? ⁸If a bugle call isn't clear, how would you know to get ready for battle?

⁹This is how it is when you speak unknown languages. If no one can understand what you are talking about, you will only be talking to the wind. ¹⁰There are many different languages in this world, and all of them make sense. ¹¹But if I don't understand the language that someone is using, we will be like foreigners to each other. ¹²If you really want spiritual gifts, choose the ones that will be most helpful to the church.

¹³When we speak languages that others don't know, we should pray for the power to explain what we mean. ¹⁴For example, if I use an unknown language in my prayers, my spirit prays but my mind is useless. ¹⁵Then what should I do? There are times when I should pray with my spirit, and times when I should pray with my mind. Sometimes I should sing with my spirit, and at other times I should sing with my mind.

¹⁶Suppose some strangers are in your worship service, when you are praising God with your spirit. If they don't understand you, how will they know to say, "Amen"? ¹⁷You may be worshiping God in a wonderful way, but no one else will be helped. ¹⁸I thank God that I speak unknown languages more than any of you. ¹⁹But words that make sense can help the church. This is why in church I had rather speak five words that make sense than to speak 10,000 words in a language that others don't know.

²⁰My friends, stop thinking like children. Think like mature people and be as innocent as tiny babies. ²¹In the Scriptures the Lord says,

"I will use strangers
   who speak unknown languages
      to talk to my people.
They will speak to them
   in foreign languages,
but still my people
   won't listen to me."

²²Languages others don't know may mean something to unbelievers, but not to the Lord's followers. Prophecy, on the other hand, is for followers, not for unbelievers. ²³Suppose everyone in your worship service started speaking unknown languages, and some outsiders or some unbelievers come in. Won't they think you are crazy? ²⁴But suppose all of you are prophesying when those unbelievers and outsiders come in. They will realize that they are sinners, and they will want to

change their ways because of what you are saying. **25**They will tell what is hidden in their hearts. Then they will kneel down and say to God, "We are certain that you are with these people."

Worship Must Be Orderly

26My friends, when you meet to worship, you must do everything for the good of everyone there. That's how it should be when someone sings or teaches or tells what God has said or speaks an unknown language or explains what the language means. **27**No more than two or three of you should speak unknown languages during the meeting. You must take turns, and someone should always be there to explain what you mean. **28**If no one can explain, you must keep silent in church and speak only to yourself and to God.

29Two or three persons may prophesy, and everyone else must listen carefully. **30**If someone sitting there receives a message from God, the speaker must stop and let the other person speak. **31**Let only one person speak at a time, then all of you will learn something and be encouraged. **32**A prophet should be willing to stop and let someone else speak. **33**God wants everything to be done peacefully and in order.

When God's people meet in church, **34**the women must not be allowed to speak. They must keep quiet and listen, as the Law of Moses teaches. **35**If there is something they want to know, they can ask their husbands when they get home. It is disgraceful for women to speak in church.

36God's message did not start with you people, and you are not the only ones it has reached.

37If you think of yourself as a prophet or a spiritual person, you will know I am writing only what the Lord has commanded. **38**So don't pay attention to anyone who ignores what I am writing. **39**My friends, be eager to prophesy and don't stop anyone from speaking languages that others don't know. **40**But do everything properly and in order.

Christ Was Raised to Life

15 My friends, I want you to remember the message I preached and that you believed and trusted. **2**You will be saved by this message, if you hold firmly to it. But if you don't, your faith was all for nothing.

3I told you the most important part of the message exactly as it was told to me. This part is:

Christ died for our sins,
     as the Scriptures say.
4He was buried,
     and three days later
   he was raised to life,
     as the Scriptures say.
5Christ appeared to Peter,[z]
     then to the twelve.
6After this, he appeared
   to more than five hundred
     other followers.
   Most of them are still alive,
     but some have died.
7He also appeared to James,
     then to all of the apostles.

8Finally, he appeared to me, even though I am like someone who was born at the wrong time.[a]

9I am the least important of all the apostles. In fact, I caused so much trouble for

---

z15.5 *Peter:* See the note at 1.12.   **a**15.8 *who was born at the wrong time:* The meaning of these words in Greek is not clear.

14.30 *If someone . . . receives a message from God:* In the Corinthian church, it apparently was common for different people to speak a message from God. The people had to respect each other and allow someone who had a prophecy to speak when the message came from the Spirit. Without this, many people might start speaking at the same time, which would cause confusion.

14.34 *women must not be allowed to speak:* Paul was not talking about a specific rule in the Law of Moses but about a "law" as commonly interpreted by tradition. See verse 11.5, which seems to assume that women do speak and pray during worship.

14.37 *a spiritual person:* A "spiritual person" is someone who is led by God's Spirit or has been given some spiritual gift.

    Spiritual Gifts

    God's Saving Love (Salvation)

15.5,6 *the twelve . . . five hundred other followers:* "The twelve" refers to the close group of Christ's followers, also known as the disciples (Matt 10.2-4). It is not clear who the "five hundred followers" are, since they are not mentioned anywhere else in the New Testament.

15.7 *James . . . the apostles:* The James mentioned here is Jesus' brother (Mark 6.3; Gal 1.19; Acts 12.17; 15.13).

When you meet to worship, you must do everything for the good of everyone there. 1 COR 14.26

15.12 *some of you say the dead will not be raised to life:* Apparently, some of the followers of Christ in Corinth did not believe that dead people could be raised from death to eternal life. Some may have believed that the body of a dead person stays in the ground while the soul comes back to life apart from the body. This is called the "immortality of the soul." Paul's teachings about life after death are different from this view.

Resurrection

15.17 *Unless Christ was raised to life . . . you are still living in your sins:* Paul said that God's mysterious wisdom sent Jesus to die on a cross to forgive sins (1 Cor 2.1,4). If God did not raise Jesus from death, Paul says, God's promise of forgiveness of sins could not be true.

15.21 *we will die because of Adam:* Adam and Eve disobeyed God by eating fruit from the tree that gave the power to know the difference between right from wrong (Gen 3.20). This sin caused death to come into the world, but the forgiveness Jesus brings will overcome sin and death.

15.29 *Why are they being baptized for those dead people:* Some people were being baptized on behalf of friends or relatives who had died before being baptized into the Christian faith. Paul says that such baptizing is not necessary.

God's church that I don't even deserve to be called an apostle. [10]But God treated me with undeserved grace! He made me what I am, and his grace wasn't wasted. I worked much harder than any of the other apostles, although it was really God's grace at work and not me. [11]But it doesn't matter if I preached or if they preached. All of you believed the message just the same.

God's People Will Be Raised to Life

[12]If we preach that Christ was raised from death, how can some of you say the dead will not be raised to life? [13]If they won't be raised to life, Christ himself wasn't raised to life. [14]And if Christ wasn't raised to life, our message is worthless, and so is your faith. [15]If the dead won't be raised to life, we have told lies about God by saying he raised Christ to life, when he really did not.

[16]So if the dead won't be raised to life, Christ wasn't raised to life. [17]Unless Christ was raised to life, your faith is useless, and you are still living in your sins. [18]And those people who died after putting their faith in him are completely lost. [19]If our hope in Christ is good only for this life, we are worse off than anyone else.

[20]But Christ has been raised to life! And he makes us certain that others will also be raised to life. [21]Just as we will die because of Adam, we will be raised to life because of Christ. [22]Adam brought death to all of us, and Christ will bring life to all of us. [23]But we must each wait our turn. Christ was the first to be raised to life, and his people will be raised to life when he returns. [24]Then after Christ has destroyed all powers and forces, the end will come, and he will give the kingdom to God the Father. [25]Christ will rule until he puts all his enemies under his power, [26]and the last

enemy he destroys will be death. [27]When the Scriptures say he will put everything under his power, they don't include God. It was God who put everything under the power of Christ. [28]After everything is under the power of God's Son, he will put himself under the power of God, who put everything under his Son's power. Then God will mean everything to everyone.

[29]If the dead are not going to be raised to life, what will people do who are being baptized for them? Why are they being baptized for those dead people? [30]And why do we always risk our lives [31]and face death every day? The pride that I have in you because of Christ Jesus our Lord is what makes me say this. [32]What do you think I gained by fighting wild animals in Ephesus? If the dead are not raised to life,

"Let's eat and drink.
    Tomorrow we die."

[33]Don't fool yourselves. Bad friends will destroy you. [34]Be sensible and stop sinning. You should be embarrassed that some people still don't know about God.

What Our Bodies Will Be Like

[35]Some of you have asked, "How will the dead be raised to life? What kind of bodies will they have?" [36]Don't be foolish. A seed must die before it can sprout from the ground. [37]Wheat seeds and all other seeds look different from the sprouts that come up. [38]This is because God gives everything the kind of body he wants it to have. [39]People, animals, birds, and fish are each made of flesh, but none of them are alike. [40]Everything in the heavens has a body, and so does everything on earth. But each one is very different from all the others. [41]The sun isn't like the moon, the moon isn't like the stars, and each star is different.

[42]That's how it will be when our bodies are raised to life. These bodies will die, but

the bodies that are raised will live forever. 43These ugly and weak bodies will become beautiful and strong. 44As surely as there are physical bodies, there are spiritual bodies. And our physical bodies will be changed into spiritual bodies.

45The first man was named Adam, and the Scriptures tell us that he was a living person. But Jesus, who may be called the last Adam, is a life-giving spirit. 46We see that the one with a spiritual body did not come first. He came after the one who had a physical body. 47The first man was made from the dust of the earth, but the second man came from heaven. 48Everyone on earth has a body like the body of the one who was made from the dust of the earth. And everyone in heaven has a body like the body of the one who came from heaven. 49Just as we are like the one who was made out of earth, we will be like the one who came from heaven.

50My friends, I want you to know that our bodies of flesh and blood will decay. This means they cannot share in God's kingdom, which lasts forever. 51I will explain a mystery to you. Not every one of us will die, but we will all be changed. 52It will happen suddenly, quicker than the blink of an eye. At the sound of the last trumpet the dead will be raised. We will all be changed, so we will never die again. 53Our dead and decaying bodies will be changed into bodies that won't die or decay. 54The bodies we now have are weak and can die. But they will be changed into bodies that are eternal. Then the Scriptures will come true,

> "Death has lost the battle!
> 55Where is its victory?
> Where is its sting?"

56Sin is what gives death its sting, and the Law is the power behind sin. 57But thank God for letting our Lord Jesus Christ give us the victory!

58My dear friends, stand firm and don't be shaken. Always keep busy working for the Lord. You know that everything you do for him is worthwhile.

A Collection for God's People

16 When you collect money for God's people, I want you to do exactly what I told the churches in Galatia to do. 2That is, each Sunday each of you must put aside part of what you have earned. If you do this, you won't have to take up a collection when I come. 3Choose some followers to take the money to Jerusalem. I will send them on with the money and with letters which show that you approve of them. 4If you think I should go along, they can go with me.

Paul's Travel Plans

5After I have gone through Macedonia, I hope to see you 6and visit with you for a while. I may even stay all winter, so that you can help me on my way to wherever I will be going next. 7If the Lord lets me, I would rather come later for a longer visit than to stop off now for only a short visit. 8I will stay in Ephesus until Pentecost, 9because there is a wonderful opportunity for me to do some work here. But there are also many people who are against me.

10When Timothy arrives, give him a friendly welcome. He is doing the Lord's work, just as I am. 11Don't let anyone mistreat him. I am looking for him to return to me together with the other followers. So when he leaves, send him off with your blessings.

12I have tried hard to get our friend Apollos to visit you with the other followers. He doesn't want to come just now, but he will come when he can.

15.44 *spiritual bodies:* Paul teaches that those who are raised to life from death will have a completely new body. The popular belief in Paul's day was that death would release the soul from the body, which rotted away, while the soul lived forever.

15.45-49 *Adam . . . Jesus:* Paul calls Jesus the "last Adam," because he was the human who ended the curse of death brought on by the first Adam's sin. Those who have faith in Jesus now have human bodies that are like the first Adam, but they will have spiritual bodies like Jesus after they are raised from death.

15.51 *Not every one of us will die, but we will all be changed:* Paul taught that when Jesus comes back, some people will be transformed into heavenly, or spiritual, bodies (1 Thes 4.15-17).

15.52 *At the sound of the last trumpet the dead will be raised:* See Matt 24.31; John 5.25; 1 Thes 4.16; and Rev 8.2—11.19.

Second Coming

Eternal Life

Resurrection

15.56 *the Law is the power behind sin:* Paul does not mean that the Law of Moses causes people to sin, but that because the Law tells people what they shouldn't do, it actually makes people want to sin.

The bodies we now have are weak and can die. But they will be changed into bodies that are eternal. 1 Cor 15.54

16.19 *the churches in Asia:* Asia was an important Roman province in the western part of Asia Minor. **(See Map 16 on pg 1894.)**

16.19 *Aquila and Priscilla:* This couple was driven out of Rome along with the rest of the Jewish community around A.D. 49 by the Emperor Claudius. They moved to Corinth (Acts 18.1-4) and later to Ephesus (Acts 18.18-26) where they worked as tent makers with Paul. See also Rom 16.3; 2 Tim 4.19.

16.21 *I am signing this letter myself:* Paul probably dictated the letter to someone who wrote it down for him.

Personal Concerns and Greetings

[13]Keep alert. Be firm in your faith. Stay brave and strong. [14]Show love in everything you do.

[15]You know that Stephanas and his family were the first in Achaia to have faith in the Lord. They have done all they can for God's people. My friends, I ask you [16]to obey leaders like them and to do the same for all others who work hard with you.

[17]I was glad to see Stephanas and Fortunatus and Achaicus. Having them here was like having you. [18]They made me feel much better, just as they made you feel better. You should appreciate people like them.

[19]Greetings from the churches in Asia. Aquila and Priscilla, together with the church that meets in their house, send greetings in the name of the Lord.

[20]All the Lord's followers send their greetings.

Give each other a warm greeting.

[21]I am signing this letter myself: PAUL.

[22]I pray that God will put a curse on everyone who doesn't love the Lord. And may the Lord come soon.

[23]I pray the Lord Jesus will be kind to you.

[24]I love everyone who belongs to Christ Jesus.

Reflection Questions About 1 Corinthians 1.1—16.24

1. What controversy or argument is taking place among the Christians at Corinth (1.10-12; 3.1-6)? What does Paul say about this (1.13-17; 3.6-23)?

2. Why does the message about Christ dying on a cross seem like foolishness to some people (1.18-25)? Why did God choose this "foolish" way to save people and make them wise, acceptable, and holy (1.26-31)?

3. Who were "the ones doing all this bragging" (4.18-21)? What were they bragging about? Why did this cause problems for the rest of the church at Corinth?

4. Why did Paul suggest that the Corinthian Christians settle disputes among themselves rather than suing each other in court (6.1-8)? Should modern Christians consider following this advice? Why?

5. Summarize Paul's key teachings about marriage (7.1-40).

6. Why does Paul talk to the Corinthian Christians about worshiping idols (10.1-22)? What idols exist in modern society?

7. List the spiritual gifts described in chapter 12. What is the purpose of these gifts?

8. Why does Paul say that "love" is the greatest gift of the Spirit (13.1-13)?

9. What is the message that Paul says has the power to "save" (15.1-7)? What would make this message "worthless" (15.12-15)? Is the modern world skeptical about Jesus' rising from death? Why or why not? How can the church deal with this kind of skepticism?

10. How does Paul answer the Corinthians' questions in 15.35? What is your picture of life in God's perfect kingdom (heaven)?

2 corinthians

What Paul wrote to the Corinthian Christians was true and meant to be helpful, but some took his words the wrong way. Read 2 CORINTHIANS to discover how Paul pleads with them to "make room in their hearts for him" once again.

WHAT MAKES 2 CORINTHIANS SPECIAL?

This letter gives insights into Paul's personal relationship with the Corinthian Christians, especially how he answers the attacks made against him. While he has many supporters, some challenge his authority as an apostle. Others criticize him for the way he speaks and writes, while others think he is unfriendly and too harsh in his comments.

Paul lived and worked among Christ's followers in Corinth. Later in his travels, he wrote to encourage them and to answer their questions. He also promised to visit them (1 Cor 16.5,6). At the beginning of 2 CORINTHIANS, Paul explains why he changed his mind. Paul also defends himself as a true apostle of Christ and encourages the Corinthians to give money to help Christians in other parts of the Roman world.

As Paul defends himself as an apostle of Christ, he shares a number of important teachings:
- Forgive others (2.5-17)
- God's new agreement comes from the Holy Spirit, not the Law (3.1-18)
- Anyone who belongs to Christ is a new person (5.17-21)
- Give generously to help God's people in Jerusalem (8.1-15; 9.1-15)
- Paul's account of how God changed his life (12.1-9).

WHAT'S THE STORY BEHIND THE SCENE?

Paul wrote a series of letters to the church in Corinth. These include an earlier letter mentioned in 1 Corinthians 5.9 and the letter we know as 1 CORINTHIANS. He also mentions a letter he wrote when he was sad (2 Cor 2.3,4). SECOND CORINTHIANS may be two letters written by Paul that circulated together and were eventually combined. The first one is made up of chapters 1–9, and the second, chapters 10–13. It is possible that 6.14—7.1 is a fragment of yet another letter, since it breaks the flow of thought from 6.11-13 to 7.2. Paul probably stayed in Corinth first in about A.D. 50–51 and wrote 1 CORINTHIANS around A.D. 53–54, after he had gone back to Jerusalem (Acts 18). The two letters that form 2 CORINTHIANS were written some time after that.

HOW IS 2 CORINTHIANS CONSTRUCTED?

Although 2 CORINTHIANS is probably not one single letter, its beginning and ending are typical of the greetings that people in Paul's day would use to open and close letters. The letter can be outlined in this way:

Greetings and prayers of thanks (1.1-11)
Paul wants to make peace with his opponents
  (1.12—6.13; 7.2-16)
A possible fragment from another letter
  (6.14—7.16)
Paul encourages the Corinthians to be generous
  givers (8.1—9.15)
Paul defends himself as a true apostle of Christ
  (10.1—12.21)
Final warnings and greetings (13.1-13)

Second Corinthians is one of Paul's most emotionally volatile and personal letters. Like 1 Corinthians, it was addressed to the Christian church in the Greek port city of Corinth. It is not clear whether Paul wrote this letter on a single occasion or whether some parts of 2 Corinthians were written at different times but brought together by those who first collected and preserved all the writings they understood to be from Paul. This may explain why the tone and themes of the letter sometimes change abruptly. Even though the historical context of parts of 2 Corinthians may be difficult to place, it seems clear that much of the letter was written after 1 Corinthians. By this time, Paul's relationship with the Corinthian church had worsened because certain "false apostles" were questioning his right to be called an apostle. In spite of this conflict, 2 Corinthians includes some of Paul's most profound teaching—on forgiveness, finding strength in weakness, the importance of giving generously, and the new life that is available to everyone because of what Christ has done.

Outline

1 From Paul, chosen by God to be an apostle of Jesus Christ, and from Timothy, who is also a follower.

To God's church in Corinth and to all of God's people in Achaia.

²I pray that God our Father and the Lord Jesus Christ will be kind to you and will bless you with peace!

Paul Gives Thanks

³Praise God, the Father of our Lord Jesus Christ! The Father is a merciful God, who always gives us comfort. ⁴He comforts us when we are in trouble, so that we can share this same comfort with others in trouble. ⁵We share in the terrible sufferings of Christ, but also in the wonderful comfort he gives. ⁶We suffer in the hope that you will be comforted and saved. And because we are comforted, you will also be comforted, as you patiently endure suffering like ours. ⁷You never disappoint us. You suffered as much as we did, and we know that you will be comforted as we were.

⁸My friends, I want you to know what a hard time we had in Asia. Our sufferings were so horrible and so unbearable that death seemed certain. ⁹In fact, we felt sure we were going to die. But this made us stop trusting in ourselves and start trusting God, who raises the dead to life. ¹⁰God saved us from the threat of death,ᵃ and we are sure that he will do it again and again. ¹¹Please help us by praying for us. Then many people will give thanks for the blessings we receive in answer to all these prayers.

Paul's Change of Plans

¹²We can be proud of our clear conscience. We have always lived honestly and sincerely, especially when we were with you. And we were guided by God's gift of undeserved grace instead of by the wisdom

---

ᵃ**1.10** *the threat of death*: Some manuscripts have "many threats of death."

1.1 *Timothy:* Paul sent Timothy to the Corinthians to carry on the teaching Paul had begun (1 Cor 4.17; 16.10).

1.3 *comfort:* The "comfort" that God gave to Paul and to the Corinthians is the strength and hope that helped them face suffering, threats, and even death.

1.6 *saved:* Here the word "saved" points to what God has done and is still doing to free humans from sin and the powers of evil. "Being saved" also can refer to receiving "eternal life."

God's Saving Love (Salvation)

Eternal Life

1.8 *what a hard time we had in Asia:* At the time of Paul, Asia was the name of a Roman province in the southwest part of what is now Turkey. Paul does not explain what kind of suffering he had experienced in Ephesus, but it probably included torture and the threat of death. **(See Map 15 on pg 1893.)**

1.12 *wisdom of this world:* Paul is referring to human wisdom that ignores God's wisdom or God's purposes. Paul's conscience and actions were not guided by popular human wisdom. Rather he was guided by God's kindness. For Paul, the "world" stood for all things that are against God.

Wisdom

1.19 Son of God: The title "son of God" was given to the king God chose to rule over the people of Israel (Ps 2.6-8). By calling Jesus the Son of God, Paul is claiming that Jesus is the one God has chosen to rule over the new Israel.

Son of God

1.19 Silas: This probably refers to the Silas who was said in Acts 15.32 to have the gift of being a prophet. Like Paul, Silas was a Roman citizen. He accompanied Paul on his later journeys.

1.22 put his Spirit in our hearts: Paul is referring to the Holy Spirit. In 1 Corinthians 12–14, Paul describes how the Holy Spirit gives special gifts to individual followers in order to strengthen the whole body of Christ, the church.

Holy Spirit

Faith

2.3,4 I wrote as I did . . . I was suffering terribly: Paul did not want to visit the Corinthians when he was angry with them, and they were upset by his remarks. The way the Corinthians had been acting must have been very painful for Paul.

2.6 the wrong that person did: Apparently one particular person had been attacking Paul's teachings. Paul encourages the Corinthians to forgive this person.

of this world. [13]I am not writing anything you cannot read and understand. I hope you will understand it completely, [14]just as you already partly understand us. Then when our Lord Jesus returns, you can be as proud of us as we are of you.

[15]I was so sure of your pride in us that I had planned to visit you first of all. In this way you would have the blessing of two visits from me—[16]once on my way to Macedonia and again on my return from there. Then you could send me on to Judea. [17]Do you think I couldn't make up my mind about what to do? Or do I seem like someone who says "Yes" or "No" simply to please others? [18]God can be trusted, and so can I, when I say our answer to you has always been "Yes" and never "No." [19]This is because Jesus Christ the Son of God is always "Yes" and never "No." And he is the one Silas,[b] Timothy, and I told you about.

[20]Christ says "Yes" to all God's promises. This is why we have Christ to say "Amen"[c] for us to the glory of God. [21]And so God makes it possible for you and us to stand firmly together with Christ. God is also the one who chose us [22]and put his Spirit in our hearts to show that we belong only to him.

[23]God is my witness that I stayed away from Corinth, just to keep from being hard on you. [24]We are not bosses who tell you what to believe. We are working with you to make you glad, because your faith is strong.

2 I have decided not to make my next visit with you so painful. [2]If I make you feel bad, who would be left to cheer me up, except the people I had made to feel bad? [3]The reason I want to be happy is to make you happy. I wrote as I did because I didn't want to visit you and be made to feel

bad, when you should make me feel happy. [4]At the time I wrote, I was suffering terribly. My eyes were full of tears, and my heart was broken. But I didn't want to make you feel bad. I only wanted to let you know how much I cared for you.

Forgiveness

[5]I don't want to be hard on you. But if one of you has made someone feel bad, I am not really the one who has been made to feel bad. Some of you are the ones. [6]Most of you have already pointed out the wrong that person did, and this is punishment enough for what was done.

[7]When people sin, you should forgive and comfort them, so they won't give up in despair. [8]You should make them sure of your love for them.

[9]I also wrote because I wanted to test you and find out if you would follow my instructions. [10]I will forgive anyone you forgive. Yes, for your sake and with Christ as my witness, I have forgiven whatever needed to be forgiven. [11]I have done this to keep Satan from getting the better of us. We all know what goes on in his mind.

[12]When I went to Troas to preach the good news about Christ, I found that the Lord had already prepared the way. [13]But I was worried when I didn't find my friend Titus there. So I left the other followers and went on to Macedonia.

[14]I am grateful that God always makes it possible for Christ to lead us to victory. God also helps us spread the knowledge about Christ everywhere, and this knowledge is like the smell of perfume. [15-16]In fact, God thinks of us as a perfume that brings Christ to everyone. For people who are being saved, this perfume has a sweet

[b]**1.19 Silas:** The Greek text has "Silvanus," which is another form of the name Silas.   [c]**1.20 Amen:** The word "amen" is used here with the meaning of "yes."

smell and leads them to a better life. But for people who are lost, it has a bad smell and leads them to a horrible death.

No one really has what it takes to do this work. [17]A lot of people try to get rich from preaching God's message. But we are God's sincere messengers, and by the power of Christ we speak our message with God as our witness.

God's New Agreement

3 Are we once again bragging about ourselves? Do we need letters to you or from you to tell others about us? Some people do need letters telling about them. [2]But you are our letter, and you are in our[d] hearts for everyone to read and understand. [3]You are like a letter written by Christ and delivered by us. But you are not written with pen and ink or on tablets made of stone. You are written in our hearts by the Spirit of the living God.

[4]We are sure about all this. Christ makes us sure in the very presence of God. [5]We don't have the right to claim that we have done anything on our own. God gives us what it takes to do all we do. [6]He makes us worthy to be the servants of his new agreement that comes from the Holy Spirit and not from a written Law. After all, the Law brings death, but the Spirit brings life.

[7]The Law of Moses brought only the promise of death, even though it was carved on stones and given in a wonderful way. Still the Law made Moses' face shine so brightly the people of Israel could not look at it, even though it was a fading glory. [8]So won't the agreement the Spirit brings to us be even more wonderful? [9]If something that brings the death sentence is glorious, won't something that makes us acceptable to God be even more glorious?

[10]In fact, the new agreement is so wonderful that the Law is no longer glorious at all. [11]The Law was given with a glory that faded away. But the glory of the new agreement is much greater, because it will never fade away.

[12]This wonderful hope makes us feel like speaking freely. [13]We are not like Moses. His face was shining, but he covered it to keep the people of Israel from seeing the brightness fade away. [14]The people were stubborn, and something still keeps them from seeing the truth when the Law is read. Only Christ can take away the covering that keeps them from seeing.

[15]When the Law of Moses is read, they have their minds covered over [16]with a covering that is removed only for those who turn to the Lord. [17]The Lord and the Spirit are one and the same, and the Lord's Spirit sets us free. [18]So our faces are not covered. They show the bright glory of the Lord, as the Lord's Spirit makes us more and more like our glorious Lord.

Treasure in Clay Jars

4 God has been kind enough to trust us with this work. This is why we never give up. [2]We don't do shameful things that must be kept secret. And we don't try to fool anyone or twist God's message around. God is our witness that we speak only the truth, so others will be sure we can be trusted. [3]If there is anything hidden about our message, it is hidden only to someone who is lost.

[4]The god who rules this world has blinded the minds of unbelievers. They cannot see the light, which is the good news about our glorious Christ, who shows what God is like. [5]We are not preaching about ourselves. Our message is

[d]**3.2** *our:* Some manuscripts have "your."

2.17 *people try to get rich . . . sincere messengers:* It was considered acceptable for those who preached the good news to expect to be supported by the churches who received them. "Sincere" messengers—people called by the Spirit to preach the good news—would not try to get rich from their ministry.

3.6 *new agreement:* God's new agreement with his people was announced by the prophet Jeremiah (31.31-33). The new agreement is one given by God to bring the forgiveness of sins. According to Paul, the Law brought death (Rom 3.20; 7.8-11).

3.7 *The Law of Moses:* When Moses came down from Mount Sinai with the Ten Commandments, his face was shining with God's glory (Exod 34.29-35).

Law

Moses

3.15,16 *minds covered over with a covering:* Paul means that the people of Israel did not understand the true purpose of the Law of Moses. Paul says, this covering can only be removed when people interpret the Law by faith in Jesus as the Christ.

4.3 *someone who is lost:* The "lost" are those who do not have faith in Jesus. To them the message about Jesus and his death on the cross is foolish (1 Cor 1.18).

4.13,14 *faith . . . God raised the Lord Jesus to life:* God raised Jesus to life three days after he died on a cross (Matt 28.1-10; Acts 2.22-24).

Faith

Resurrection

4.17 *eternal glory:* Paul mentions a future time when Jesus will give all who follow him new life and new spiritual bodies (1 Cor 15.45-57; Rom 8.18).

Eternal Life

5.1 *Our bodies are like tents:* Paul compares life to a journey. The bodies that human beings "travel in" through life are not permanent. God will provide a permanent new spiritual body after death (1 Cor 15).

5.14 *if one person died:* Jesus died for everyone. Those who follow Jesus have died to sin, and have been given new life.

5.16 *we once judged Christ in this way:* Paul may be referring to the fact that, earlier in his life, he joined others who made trouble for the followers of Jesus. See Phil 3.6; Acts 8.1-3 and 9.1,2.

that Jesus Christ is Lord. He also sent us to be your servants. **6**The Scriptures say, "God commanded light to shine in the dark." Now God is shining in our hearts to let you know that his glory is seen in Jesus Christ.

7We are like clay jars in which this treasure is stored. The real power comes from God and not from us. **8**We often suffer, but we are never crushed. Even when we don't know what to do, we never give up. **9**In times of trouble, God is with us, and when we are knocked down, we get up again. **10-11**We face death every day because of Jesus. Our bodies show what his death was like, so his life can also be seen in us. **12**This means that death is working in us, but life is working in you.

13In the Scriptures it says, "I spoke because I had faith." We have this same kind of faith. So we speak **14**because we know that God raised the Lord Jesus to life. And just as God raised Jesus, he will also raise us to life. Then he will bring us into his presence together with you. **15**All of this has been done for you, so more and more people will know how kind God is and will praise and honor him.

Faith in the Lord

16We never give up. Our bodies are gradually dying, but we ourselves are being made stronger each day. **17**These little troubles are getting us ready for an eternal glory that will make all our troubles seem like nothing. **18**Things that are seen don't last forever, but things that are not seen are eternal. This is why we keep our minds on the things that cannot be seen.

5 Our bodies are like tents that we live in here on earth. But when these tents are destroyed, we know that God will give each of us a place to live. These homes will not be buildings someone has made, but they are in heaven and will last forever.

2While we are here on earth, we sigh because we want to live in that heavenly home. **3**We want to put it on like clothes and not be naked.

4These tents we now live in are like a heavy burden, and we groan. But we don't do this just because we want to leave these bodies that will die. It is because we want to change them for bodies that will never die. **5**God is the one who makes all this possible. He has given us his Spirit to make us certain he will do it. **6**So always be cheerful!

As long as we are in these bodies, we are away from the Lord. **7**But we live by faith, not by what we see. **8**We should be cheerful, because we would rather leave these bodies and be at home with the Lord. **9**But whether we are at home with the Lord or away from him, we still try our best to please him. **10**After all, Christ will judge each of us for the good or the bad that we do while living in these bodies.

Bringing People to God

11We know what it means to respect the Lord, and we encourage everyone to turn to him. God himself knows what we are like, and I hope you also know what kind of people we are. **12**We are not trying once more to brag about ourselves. But we want you to be proud of us, when you are with those who are not sincere and brag about what others think of them.

13If we seem out of our minds, it is between God and us. But if we are in our right minds, it is for your good. **14**We are ruled by Christ's love for us. We are certain that if one person died for everyone else, then all of us have died. **15**And Christ did die for all of us. He died so we would no longer live for ourselves, but for the one who died and was raised to life for us.

16We are careful not to judge people by what they seem to be, though we once judged Christ in this way. ¹⁷Anyone who belongs to Christ is a new person. The past is forgotten, and everything is new. ¹⁸God has done it all! He sent Christ to make peace between himself and us, and he has given us the work of making peace between himself and others.

¹⁹What we mean is that God was in Christ, offering peace and forgiveness to the people of this world. And he has given us the work of sharing his message about peace. ²⁰We were sent to speak for Christ, and God is begging you to listen to our message. We speak for Christ and sincerely ask you to make peace with God. ²¹Christ never sinned! But God treated him as a sinner, so Christ could make us acceptable to God.

6 We work together with God, and we beg you to make good use of God's gift of undeserved grace. ²In the Scriptures God says,

"When the time came,
  I listened to you,
and when you needed help,
  I came to save you."

That time has come. This is the day for you to be saved.

³We don't want anyone to find fault with our work, and so we try hard not to cause problems. ⁴But in everything and in every way we show we truly are God's servants. We have always been patient, though we have had a lot of trouble, suffering, and hard times. ⁵We have been beaten, put in jail, and hurt in riots. We have worked hard and have gone without sleep or food. ⁶But we have kept ourselves pure and have been understanding, patient, and kind. The Holy Spirit has been with us, and our love has been real. ⁷We have spoken the truth, and God's power has worked in us. In all our struggles we have said and done only what is right.

⁸Whether we were honored or dishonored or praised or cursed, we always told the truth about ourselves. But some people said we did not. ⁹We are unknown to others, but well known to you. We seem to be dying, and yet we are still alive. We have been punished, but never killed, ¹⁰and we are always happy, even in times of suffering. Although we are poor, we have made many people rich. And though we own nothing, everything is ours.

¹¹Friends in Corinth, we are telling the truth when we say there is room in our hearts for you. ¹²We are not holding back on our love for you, but you are holding back on your love for us. ¹³I speak to you as I would speak to my own children. Please make room in your hearts for us.

The Temple of the Living God

¹⁴Stay away from people who are not followers of the Lord! Can someone who is good get along with someone who is evil? Are light and darkness the same? ¹⁵Is Christ a friend of Satan?^e Can people who follow the Lord have anything in common with those who don't? ¹⁶Do idols belong in the temple of God? We are the temple of the living God, as God himself says,

"I will live with these people
  and walk among them.
I will be their God,
and they will be
  my people."

¹⁷The Lord also says,
"Leave them and stay away!
Don't touch anything
  that isn't clean.

^e**6.15** *Satan:* The Greek text has "Beliar," which is another form of the Hebrew word "Belial," meaning "wicked" or "useless." The Jewish people sometimes used this as a name for Satan.

5.18 *God . . . sent Christ to make peace:* Christ's death took away sin and made it possible for God and people to be at peace once again. Sometimes this word for peace is translated as "reconciliation."

6.10 *made many people rich . . . everything is ours:* Paul is referring to the riches of the good news about Jesus, not to money or belongings. Those who trust in Jesus have more than the world could ever offer.

Satan

6.16 *idols . . . We are the temple of the living God:* Those who worship idols are in darkness and are friends of Satan. Some Corinthian Christians were probably invited to celebrations in local temples built to honor idols. At the feasts, they may have been served food and drink that had been offered to gods. By eating and drinking, they gave the appearance of worshiping the idols in the temple.

Paul said that God's Spirit was present in every follower of Jesus, so each Christian's body is like the temple (1 Cor 3.16). Christ's followers should try to stay away from things like worshiping idols, which can make their lives unclean.

7.2 *Make a place for us:* The possible fragment from another letter ends at 7.1. Verse 2 continues the thought that begins in 6.13.

7.5 *Macedonia . . . .We were faced with all kinds of problems:* When Paul visited Philippi in Macedonia, he ran into opposition and was thrown in jail (Acts 16.16-40). He also faced trouble in Thessalonica, the capital of Macedonia (Acts 17.1-8).

7.8 *my letter:* There is no copy of this letter, which apparently criticized some of the Corinthian Christians. Some of the issues that Paul mentioned are probably similar to things he mentioned in the letters that make up 1 CORINTHIANS.

8.1 *Macedonia:* Macedonia was the northern part of what is now Greece and became part of the Roman Empire in 168 B.C. Paul visited and wrote letters to the cities of Thessalonica and Philippi, located in Macedonia. In 1 Corinthians 1.15,16, Paul may have been talking about his return to Ephesus, or possibly his return to Jerusalem (see also Acts 21.1-17).

8.2 *going through hard times:* The churches in Macedonia faced some kind of suffering and difficulty which Paul never completely describes, although Paul mentions this in other letters (Phil 1.29,30; 1 Thes 1.6; 2.14; 3.3,4).

Then I will welcome you
18 and be your Father.
You will be my sons
and my daughters,
as surely as I am God,
the All-Powerful."

7 My friends, God has made us these promises. So we should stay away from everything that keeps our bodies and spirits from being clean. We should honor God and try to be completely like him.

The Church Makes Paul Happy

2Make a place for us in your hearts! We haven't mistreated or hurt anyone. We haven't cheated anyone. 3I am not saying this to be hard on you. But, as I have said before, you will always be in our thoughts, whether we live or die. 4I trust you completely.[f] I am always proud of you, and I am greatly encouraged. In all my trouble I am still very happy.

5After we came to Macedonia, we didn't have any chance to rest. We were faced with all kinds of problems. We were troubled by enemies and troubled by fears. 6But God cheers up people in need, and this is what he did when he sent Titus to us. 7Of course, we were glad to see Titus, but what really made us glad is the way you cheered him up. He told how sorry you were and how concerned you were about me. And this made me even happier.

8I don't feel bad anymore, even though my letter[g] hurt your feelings. I did feel bad at first, but I don't now. I know that the letter hurt you for a while. 9Now I am happy, but not because I hurt your feelings. It is because God used your hurt feelings to make you turn back to him, and none of you were harmed by us. 10When God makes you feel sorry enough to turn to him and be saved, you don't have anything to feel bad about. But when this world makes you feel sorry, it can cause your death.

11Just look what God has done by making you feel sorry! You sincerely want to prove you are innocent. You are angry. You are shocked. You are eager to see that justice is done. You have proved that you were completely right in this matter. 12When I wrote you, it wasn't to accuse the one who was wrong or to take up for the one who was hurt. I wrote, so God would show you how much you do care for us. 13And we were greatly encouraged.

Although we were encouraged, we felt even better when we saw how happy Titus was, because you had shown he had nothing to worry about. 14We had told him how much we thought of you, and you did not disappoint us. Just as we have always told you the truth, so everything we told him about you has also proved to be true. 15Titus loves all of you very much, especially when he remembers how you obeyed him and how you trembled with fear when you welcomed him. 16It makes me really glad to know I can depend on you.

Generous Giving

8 My friends, we want you to know that the churches in Macedonia[h] have shown others God's gift of undeserved grace. 2Although they were going through

[f]7.4 *I trust you completely:* Or "I have always spoken the truth to you" or "I can speak freely to you."
[g]7.8 *my letter:* There is no copy of this letter that Paul wrote to the church at Corinth.   [h]8.1 *churches in Macedonia:* The churches that Paul had started in Philippi and Thessalonica. The church in Berea is probably also meant.

hard times and were very poor, they were glad to give generously. ³They gave as much as they could afford and even more, simply because they wanted to. ⁴They even asked and begged us to let them have the joy of giving their money for God's people. ⁵And they did more than we had hoped. They gave themselves first to the Lord and then to us, just as God wanted them to do.

⁶Titus was the one who got you started doing this good thing, so we begged him to help you finish what you had begun. ⁷You do everything better than anyone else. You have stronger faith. You speak better and know more. You are eager to give, and you love us better.ⁱ Now you must give more generously than anyone else.

⁸I am not ordering you to do this. I am simply testing how real your love is by comparing it with the concern that others have shown. ⁹You know our Lord Jesus Christ treated us with undeserved grace by giving up all his riches, so you could become rich.

¹⁰A year ago you were the first ones to give, and you gave because you wanted to. So listen to my advice. ¹¹I think you should finish what you started. If you give according to what you have, you will prove you are as eager to give as you were to think about giving. ¹²It doesn't matter how much you have. What matters is how much you are willing to give from what you have.

¹³I am not trying to make life easier for others by making life harder for you. But it is only fair ¹⁴for you to share with them when you have so much, and they have so little. Later, when they have more than enough, and you are in need, they can share with you. Then everyone will have a fair share, ¹⁵just as the Scriptures say,

"Those who gathered
too much

had nothing left.
Those who gathered
only a little
had all they needed."

Titus and His Friends

¹⁶I am grateful that God made Titus care as much about you as we do. ¹⁷When we begged Titus to visit you, he said he would. He wanted to because he cared so much for you. ¹⁸With Titus we are also sending one of the Lord's followers who is well known in every church for spreading the good news. ¹⁹The churches chose this follower to travel with us while we carry this gift that will bring praise to the Lord and show how much we hope to help. ²⁰We don't want anyone to find fault with the way we handle your generous gift. ²¹But we want to do what pleases the Lord and what people think is right.

²²We are also sending someone else with Titus and the other follower. We approve of this man. In fact, he has already shown us many times that he wants to help. And now he wants to help even more than ever, because he trusts you so much. ²³Titus is my partner, who works with me to serve you. The other two followers are sent by the churches, and they bring honor to Christ. ²⁴Treat them in such a way that the churches will see your love and will know why we bragged about you.

The Money for God's People

9 I don't need to write you about the money you plan to give for God's people. ²I know how eager you are to give. And I have proudly told the Lord's followers in Macedonia that you people in Achaia have been ready for a whole year. Now your

ⁱ8.7 *you love us better*: Some manuscripts have "we love you better."

8.4 *money for God's people*: Another way of translating the phrase that means "ministry to the saints," which refers to the original group of Jesus' followers in Jerusalem. These "saints" had little money to continue their work in Jerusalem, so Christians in other cities and lands were asked to support them. This special offering is mentioned elsewhere (1 Cor 16.1-3,15; Rom 15.25,26,31; 2 Cor 9).

8.6 *Titus*: Titus was a Gentile Christian who worked closely with Paul and who had accompanied Paul on a trip to Jerusalem (Gal 2.1-3).

8.14 *you have so much*: The followers of Christ in Corinth were richer than some of the other churches, so Paul encouraged them to give more money, or their "fair share."

8.15 *Those who gathered too much*: Paul is quoting Exodus 16.17,18, which describes how the Israelite people gathered God's gift of manna in the wilderness.

8.18 *one of the Lord's followers*: This unnamed person was well-known and respected for spreading the good news about Jesus, and had a reputation for encouraging churches to give generously to the fund that Titus was collecting.

It doesn't matter how much you have. What matters is how much you are willing to give from what you have. 2 COR 8.12

9.12 *What you are doing*: Refers to the money offering that the Corinthians were collecting. Paul wanted to bring money to the followers of Jesus in Jerusalem because many of them were poor, and because the Jerusalem church was the center of the early Christian church. (See Map 15 on pg 1893.)

ᴄᴿ   Paul (Saul) of Tarsus

10.2 *act like the people of this world*: Some people claimed that Paul was nice when he was with them but nasty when he was away. Others claimed that Paul and his co-workers acted like the people of this world. For Paul, the "world" stood for the people and things that were opposed to God.

10.4 *God's power*: Paul is talking about the power of the Holy Spirit, which helps him and other apostles say and do things that convince people that the good news about Jesus is true.

10.10 *Paul's letters are harsh*: At least one letter Paul wrote to the Corinthians had some harsh words that offended some of the followers. This may be the letter mentioned in 1 Corinthians 5.9 or the letter mentioned in 2 Corinthians 2.1-4. Some claimed that Paul was not a powerful speaker. In 1 Corinthians 2.3, Paul admits that when he first came to the Corinthians, he was weak and trembling with fear.

desire to give has made them want to give. ³This is why I am sending Titus and the two others to you. I want you to be ready, just as I promised. This will prove we were not wrong to brag about you.

⁴Some followers from Macedonia may come with me, and I want them to find that you have the money ready. If you don't, I would be embarrassed for trusting you to do this. But you would be embarrassed even more. ⁵So I have decided to ask Titus and the others to spend some time with you before I arrive. This way they can arrange to collect the money you have promised. Then you will have the chance to give because you want to, and not because you feel forced to.

⁶Remember this saying,
"A few seeds make
    a small harvest,
but a lot of seeds make
    a big harvest."

⁷Each of you must make up your own mind about how much to give. But don't feel sorry that you must give and don't feel you are forced to give. God loves people who love to give. ⁸God can bless you with everything you need, and you will always have more than enough to do all kinds of good things for others. ⁹The Scriptures say,
"God freely gives his gifts
    to the poor,
    and always does right."
¹⁰God gives seed to farmers and provides everyone with food. He will increase what you have, so you can give even more to those in need. ¹¹You will be blessed in every way, and you will be able to keep on being generous. Then many people will thank God when we deliver your gift.

¹²What you are doing is much more than a service that supplies God's people

with what they need. It is something that will make many others thank God. ¹³The way in which you have proved yourselves by this service will bring honor and praise to God. You believed the message about Christ, and you obeyed it by sharing generously with God's people and with everyone else. ¹⁴Now they are praying for you and want to see you, because God used you to bless them so very much. ¹⁵Thank God for his gift that is too wonderful for words!

Paul Defends His Work for Christ

10 Do you think I am a coward when I am with you and brave when I am far away? Well, I ask you to listen, because Christ himself was humble and gentle. ²Some people have said we act like the people of this world. So when I arrive, I expect I will have to be firm and forceful in what I say to them. Please don't make me treat you that way. ³We live in this world, but we don't act like its people ⁴or fight our battles with the weapons of this world. Instead, we use God's power that can destroy fortresses. We destroy arguments ⁵and every bit of pride that keeps anyone from knowing God. We capture people's thoughts and make them obey Christ. ⁶And when you completely obey him, we will punish anyone who refuses to obey.

⁷You judge by appearances.ʲ If any of you think you are the only ones who belong to Christ, then think again. We belong to Christ as much as you do. ⁸Maybe I brag a little too much about the authority that the Lord gave me to help you and not to hurt you. Yet I am not embarrassed to brag. ⁹And I am not trying to scare you with my letters. ¹⁰Some of you are saying, "Paul's letters are harsh and powerful. But in per-

ʲ10.7 *You judge by appearances*: Or "Take a close look at yourselves."

God loves people who love to give.   2 Cᴏʀ 9.7

son, he is a weakling and has nothing worth saying." [11]Those people had better understand that when I am with you, I will do exactly what I say in my letters.

[12]We won't dare compare ourselves with those who think so much of themselves. But they are foolish to compare themselves with themselves. [13]We won't brag about something we don't have a right to brag about. We will only brag about the work God has sent us to do, and you are part of that work. [14]We are not bragging more than we should. After all, we did bring the message about Christ to you.

[15]We don't brag about what others have done, as if we had done those things ourselves. But I hope as you become stronger in your faith, we will be able to reach many more of the people around you.[k] That has always been our goal. [16]Then we will be able to preach the good news in other lands where we cannot take credit for work someone else has already done. [17]The Scriptures say, "If you want to brag, then brag about the Lord." [18]You may brag about yourself, but the only approval that counts is the Lord's approval.

Paul and the False Apostles

11 Please put up with a little of my foolishness. [2]I am as concerned about you as God is. You were like a virgin bride I had chosen only for Christ. [3]But now I fear that you will be tricked, just as Eve was tricked by that lying snake. I am afraid that you might stop thinking about Christ in an honest and sincere way. [4]We told you about Jesus, and you received the Holy Spirit and accepted our message. But you let some people tell you about another Jesus. Now you are ready to receive an-

other spirit and accept a different message. [5]I think I am as good as any of those super apostles. [6]I may not speak as well as they do, but I know as much. And this has already been made perfectly clear to you.

[7]Was it wrong for me to lower myself and honor you by preaching God's message free of charge? [8]I robbed other churches by taking money from them to serve you. [9]Even when I was in need, I still didn't bother you. In fact, some of the Lord's followers from Macedonia brought me what I needed. I have not been a burden to you in the past, and I will never be a burden. [10]As surely as I speak the truth about Christ, no one in Achaia can stop me from bragging about this. [11]And it isn't because I don't love you. God himself knows how much I do love you.

[12]I plan to go on doing just what I have always done. Then those people won't be able to brag about doing the same things we are doing. [13]Anyway, they are no more than false apostles and dishonest workers. They only pretend to be apostles of Christ. [14]And it is no wonder. Even Satan tries to make himself look like an angel of light. [15]So why does it seem strange for Satan's servants to pretend to do what is right? Someday they will get exactly what they deserve.

Paul's Sufferings for Christ

[16]I don't want any of you to think I am a fool. But if you do, then let me be a fool and brag a little. [17]When I do all this bragging, I do it as a fool and not for the Lord. [18]Yet if others want to brag about what they have done, so will I. [19]And since you are so smart, you will gladly put up with a fool. [20]In fact, you let people make slaves

[k]**10.15** *we will be able to reach many more of the people around you*: Or "you will praise us even more because of our work among you."

● **10.15** *We don't brag:* Some of Paul's critics were also acting as if their message were their own, rather than giving credit to Paul, or to the Spirit of God.

● **11.2** *You were like a virgin bride:* In the Jewish and Greek cultures of Paul's day, a woman who had not had sexual intercourse (a virgin) was highly valued as a bride. Paul may be suggesting that he is like a father who wants to protect his virgin daughter (the Corinthian Christians) until the time of her marriage to the most suitable husband (Christ).

● **11.5** *super apostles:* Apparently, the super apostles were charming and persuasive public speakers, and seem to have been asking for money to support their preaching and teaching. They may also be the ones that Paul lists as "braggers" in 1 Corinthians 4.19. The super apostles claimed to have special wisdom that was beyond Paul and the other apostles.

● **11.7** *preaching God's message free of charge:* Paul did not ask to be paid while he was teaching and preaching among them (1 Cor 9.1-23). This meant that he had to rely on money gifts from other churches while he was in Corinth (11.8,9).

● **11.15** *Satan's servants:* The false apostles mentioned in 11.13.

The Scriptures say, "If you want to brag, then brag about the Lord." 2 COR 10.17

11.22 *Hebrews . . . from the family of Abraham:* Like Paul, the false apostles were Jewish. Paul is sure that descendants of the people of Israel will be part of the new people of God. In Paul's day, many different groups tried to define who God's people were, but Paul is convinced that those who follow Jesus Christ are the real people of God.

12.2-4 *the third heaven . . . paradise:* Paul begins to describe his vision as if it had happened to someone else, but he is really talking about himself. In Paul's day, people argued about just how many levels heaven had. The third was said to be where God dwells.

Heaven

Paradise

12.8 *suffering:* It is not clear exactly what kind of suffering this was. It may have been some kind of ongoing physical problem or sickness (Gal 4.13, 14), mental anxiety, sadness (2 Cor 11.28), or the persecution he faced (Gal 5.11; 2 Cor 11.24-29). Paul asked God to take this suffering away, but God allowed these difficulties to happen so that Paul would continue to rely on the strength that God provides rather than relying on his own strength. Paul realized that God's kindness and power was all he needed. That is why he was able to say, "when I am weak, I am strong" (12.10).

of you and cheat you and steal from you. Why, you even let them strut around and slap you in the face. ²¹I am ashamed to say we are too weak to behave in such a way.

If they can brag, so can I, but it is a foolish thing to do. ²²Are they Hebrews? So am I. Are they Jews? So am I. Are they from the family of Abraham? Well, so am I. ²³Are they servants of Christ? I am a fool to talk this way, but I serve him better than they do. I have worked harder and have been put in jail more times. I have been beaten with whips more and have been in danger of death more often.

²⁴Five times my own people gave me 39 lashes with a whip. ²⁵Three times the Romans beat me with a big stick, and once my enemies stoned me. I have been shipwrecked three times, and I even had to spend a night and a day in the sea. ²⁶During my many travels, I have been in danger from rivers, robbers, my own people, and foreigners. My life has been in danger in cities, in deserts, at sea, and with people who only pretended to be the Lord's followers.

²⁷I have worked and struggled and spent many sleepless nights. I have gone hungry and thirsty and often had nothing to eat. I have been cold from not having enough clothes to keep me warm. ²⁸Besides everything else, each day I am burdened down, worrying about all the churches. ²⁹When others are weak, I am weak too. When others are tricked into sin, I get angry.[l]

³⁰If I have to brag, I will brag about how weak I am. ³¹God, the Father of our Lord Jesus, knows I am not lying. And God is to

be praised forever! ³²The governor of Damascus at the time of King Aretas had the city gates guarded, so he could capture me. ³³But I escaped by being let down in a basket through a window in the city wall.

Visions from the Lord

12 I have to brag. There is nothing to be gained by it, but I must brag about the visions and other things that the Lord has shown me. ²I know about one of Christ's followers who was taken up into the third heaven 14 years ago. I don't know if the man was still in his body when it happened, but God certainly knows.

³As I said, only God really knows if this man was in his body at the time. ⁴But he was taken up into paradise,[m] where he heard things too wonderful to tell. ⁵I will brag about that man, but not about myself, except to say how weak I am.

⁶Yet even if I did brag, I would not be foolish. I would simply be speaking the truth. But I will try not to say too much. That way, none of you will think more highly of me than you should because of what you have seen me do and say. ⁷Of course, I am now referring to the wonderful things I saw. One of Satan's angels was sent to make me suffer terribly, so that I would not feel too proud.[n]

⁸Three times I begged the Lord to make this suffering go away. ⁹But he replied, "My gift of undeserved grace is all you need. My power is strongest when you are weak." So if Christ keeps giving me his power, I will gladly brag about how weak I

[l]11.29 *When others are tricked into sin, I get angry:* Or "When others stumble into sin, I hurt for them."
[m]12.4 *paradise:* In the Greek translation of the Old Testament, this word is used for the Garden of Eden. In New Testament times it was sometimes used for the place where God's people are happy and at rest, as they wait for the final judgment.   [n]12.7 *Of course . . . too proud:* Or "Because of the wonderful things I saw, one of Satan's angels was sent to make me suffer terribly, so I would not feel too proud."

So if Christ keeps giving me his power, I will gladly brag about how weak I am.   2 COR 12.9

am. [10]Yes, I am glad to be weak or insulted or mistreated or to have troubles and sufferings, if it is for Christ. Because when I am weak, I am strong.

Paul's Concern
for the Lord's Followers at Corinth

[11]I have been making a fool of myself. But you forced me to do it, when you should have been speaking up for me. I may be nothing at all, but I am as good as those super apostles. [12]When I was with you, I was patient and worked all the powerful miracles and signs and wonders of a true apostle. [13]You missed out on only one blessing the other churches received. That is, you didn't have to support me. Forgive me for doing you wrong.

[14]I am planning to visit you for the third time. But I still won't make a burden of myself. What I really want is you, and not what you have. Children are not supposed to save up for their parents, but parents are supposed to take care of their children. [15]So I will gladly give all I have and all I am. Will you love me less for loving you too much? [16]You agree that I wasn't a burden to you. Maybe that's because I was trying to catch you off guard and trick you. [17]Were you cheated by any of those I sent to you? [18]I urged Titus to visit you, and I sent another follower with him. But Titus didn't cheat you, and we felt and behaved the same way he did.

[19]Have you been thinking all along that we have been defending ourselves to you? Actually, we have been speaking to God as followers of Christ. But, my friends, we did it all for your good.

[20]I am afraid when I come, we won't be pleased with each other. I fear that some of you may be arguing or jealous or angry or selfish or gossiping or insulting each other.

I even fear that you may be proud and acting like a mob. [21]I am afraid God will make me ashamed when I visit you again. I will feel like crying because many of you have never given up your old sins. You are still doing things that are immoral, indecent, and shameful.

Final Warnings and Greetings

13 I am on my way to visit you for the third time. And as the Scriptures say, "Any charges must be proved true by at least two or three witnesses." [2]During my second visit I warned you that I would punish you and anyone else who doesn't stop sinning. I am far away from you now, but I give you the same warning. [3]This should prove to you that I am speaking for Christ. When he corrects you, he won't be weak. He will be powerful! [4]Although he was weak when he was nailed to the cross, he now lives by the power of God. We are weak, just as Christ was. But you will see that we will live by the power of God, just as Christ does.

[5]Test yourselves and find out if you really are true to your faith. If you pass the test, you will discover that Christ is living in you. But if Christ isn't living in you, you have failed. [6]I hope you will discover we have not failed. [7]We pray you will stop doing evil things. We don't pray like this to make ourselves look good, but to get you to do right, even if we are failures.

[8]All we can do is to follow the truth and not fight against it. [9]Even though we are weak, we are glad that you are strong, and we pray you will do even better. [10]I am writing these things to you before I arrive. This way I won't have to be hard on you when I use the authority the Lord has given me. I was given this authority, so I could help you and not destroy you.

12.12 *miracles and signs and wonders of a true apostle:* When Jesus chose his twelve apostles, he gave them the power to force out evil spirits, to heal diseases, and even to raise the dead to life (Matt 10.1,8). Paul also identifies the ability to work miracles and the power to heal the sick as two special gifts the Holy Spirit gives to some of God's people (1 Cor 12.28,29). Though he was not one of the original twelve apostles, Paul had the same powers they did (Acts 13.9-12; 19.11,12; 28.3-6).

12.13 *you didn't have to support me:* Paul reminded the Corinthians once again that, unlike the super apostles, he didn't ask them to support him with money (1 Cor 9.1; 2 Cor 11.7-10).

12.14 *visit you for a third time:* Paul first visited the Corinthians when he founded the church there (Acts 18.1-17). His second visit was the painful visit described in 2 Corinthians 2.1.

12.18 *Titus:* Paul reminded the Corinthians that Titus did not ask for money either.

13.2 *stop sinning:* The sins mentioned here probably refer to sexual immorality (1 Cor 5), worshiping idols (1 Cor 8; 2 Cor 6.14—7.1), and the offensive behavior of some who took part in the Lord's Supper (1 Cor 11.17-34).

Test yourselves and find out if you really are true to your faith. If you pass the test, you will discover that Christ is living in you. 2 COR 13.5

13.12 *warm greeting:* This phrase translates Greek words that mean "holy kiss."

13.12 *All God's people:* Paul brought greetings from all the followers of Christ, or from all the followers in the place where he was writing this letter.

[11]Goodbye, my friends. Do better and pay attention to what I have said. Try to get along and live peacefully with each other. Now I pray that God, who gives love and peace, will be with you. [12]Give each other a warm greeting. All God's people send their greetings.

[13]I pray that the Lord Jesus Christ will bless you and be kind to you! May God bless you with his love, and may the Holy Spirit join all your hearts together.

Reflection Questions About 2 Corinthians 1.1—13.13

1. What does Paul mean when he says that "Christ says 'Yes' to all God's promises" (1.20)?

2. What does Paul mean when he says "the Law brings death, but the Spirit brings life" (3.5-17)? What does this have to do with the "new agreement" Paul mentions?

3. Paul describes his suffering in 6.9,10. How does Paul's view of life differ from many modern views about happiness and wealth?

4. Read what Paul has to say about being hurt and made to feel sorry (7.8-10). What is the difference between the hurt that God "causes" and the hurt caused by the world (7.10)?

5. In chapters 8 and 9, Paul encourages the Corinthians to be generous givers. What does the saying about seeds in 9.6 have to do with giving, or with serving God in other ways?

6. What is the purpose of giving, whether it is money, time, or special abilities?

7. In chapter 10, Paul discusses bragging. Who seems to be doing this bragging, and what do they seem to be bragging about? Is it ever right to brag (10.17)?

8. Who were the "super apostles," and how were they affecting the church at Corinth (11.1-21)?

9. What has Paul's life been like as an apostle (11.21-33)? Why can he brag about how weak he is (11.30—12.10)? How can weaknesses be turned into strengths or into something positive?

10. Think about your own church. In your opinion, what are its strengths and weaknesses? What can you do to communicate your concerns, encouragement, or thanks to those who are in charge?

galatians

What someone believes says a lot about them. Find out why the apostle Paul had to defend himself and his message about Christ.

WHAT MAKES GALATIANS SPECIAL?

GALATIANS is a very personal letter that provides help in understanding Paul's character and his strong beliefs. The letter also gives some details about Paul's early life. Most of all, GALATIANS provides an inside view of a major controversy in the early Christian church. This controversy and Paul's response to it had a great effect on the way God's message about Jesus Christ was preached. Paul taught that people become God's children by faith in Jesus Christ (3.26), not by following the Law of Moses. Further, Christ sets God's children free from the Law (5.1), and the Holy Spirit guides them (5.16) to be loving, kind, and good (5.22,23).

Paul wrote to persuade the Galatians that he was a true apostle of Jesus Christ, and that his message about Jesus was the only true one (1.6-9). On an earlier visit, Paul had brought the good news about Christ to the Galatians (1.7,8). Paul later learned that false teachers were telling the Galatians that they must obey the Law of Moses in order to be God's children. These false teachers claimed that they were following the rules kept by the leaders of the Christian church in Jerusalem, including Jesus' own brother, James (1.19). Paul tells the Galatians that the Jerusalem apostles accept him as an apostle, and that they agree with him that Gentiles (non-Jews) can be part of the new people of God without following the Law of Moses or Jewish traditions.

WHAT'S THE STORY BEHIND THE SCENE?

Galatia was an area in northern central Asia Minor (modern-day Turkey). Many of the people who lived there were descended from a group of people called "Celts" who settled in the region well before 200 B.C. In the time of Paul, the Romans ruled this region, which the Roman emperor Augustus named Galatia in 25 B.C. It is not clear exactly where or when Paul wrote GALATIANS.

HOW IS GALATIANS CONSTRUCTED?

GALATIANS is a letter, or "epistle," that begins with a brief greeting (1.1-4) and ends with a short blessing (6.18). Paul uses the letter to present his case against the false teachers that are causing trouble for the Galatian believers and to defend himself and his message about Christ. Notice these things in the following outline:

Paul defends his apostleship and his message
　(1.1—2.21)
Faith in Christ is the way to become God's children
　(3.1—4.31)
Christ gives freedom, and the Spirit guides
　(5.1—6.10)
Final warnings (6.11-18)

Galatians is Paul's letter to the churches in Galatia, an area in northern or central Asia Minor ruled by the Romans. Paul and Barnabas most likely had visited many of these churches when they traveled through this region. Even though Paul isn't addressing one specific church, the churches in Galatia seem to share a common problem which Paul wants to correct. Apparently some false teachers, most likely from Jerusalem, visited these churches after Paul had been there and were teaching that Christians needed to be circumcised and obey all the Laws of Moses in order to share in the blessings that come from following Israel's Messiah (Christ). Paul answers them by asserting that faith in Jesus, not mere obedience to the Law of Moses, is the key to being put right with God. Paul also defends his authority as an apostle, and states that all who accept Christ are guided by the Holy Spirit and are part of God's people.

Outline

1

¹⁻²From the apostle Paul and from all the Lord's followers with me.

I was chosen to be an apostle by Jesus Christ and by God the Father, who raised him from death. No mere human chose or appointed me to this work.

To the churches in Galatia:

³I pray that God the Father and our Lord Jesus Christ will be kind to you and will bless you with peace! ⁴Christ obeyed God our Father and gave himself as a sacrifice for our sins to rescue us from this evil world. ⁵God will be given glory forever and ever. Amen.

The Only True Message

⁶I am shocked that you have so quickly turned from God, who chose you with his gift of undeserved grace.ᵃ You have believed another message, ⁷when there is really only one true message. But some people are causing you trouble and want to make you turn away from the good news about Christ. ⁸I pray that God will punish anyone who preaches anything different from our message to you! It doesn't matter if that person is one of us or an angel from heaven. ⁹I have said it before, and I will say it again. I hope God will punish anyone who preaches anything different from what you have already believed.

¹⁰I am not trying to please people. I want to please God. Do you think I am trying to please people? If I were doing that, I would not be a servant of Christ.

How Paul Became an Apostle

¹¹My friends, I want you to know that no one made up the message I preach. ¹²It wasn't given or taught to me by some mere human. My message came directly from Jesus Christ when he appeared to me.

¹³You know how I used to live as a Jew. I was cruel to God's church and even tried to destroy it. ¹⁴I was a much better Jew than anyone else my own age, and I obeyed

---

ᵃ**1.6** *his gift of undeserved grace:* Some manuscripts have "the gift of Christ's undeserved grace."

1.1-2 *apostle Paul:* In GALATIANS, apostle means someone chosen by God to spread the message about Jesus Christ. Paul claims that God, and not any human being, chose him to be an apostle.

Paul (Saul) of Tarsus

1.1-2 *Galatia:* Galatia is a province located in central Asia Minor which Paul is known to have visited on his missionary journeys (see Acts 13—14.23; 16.6; 18.23). The name of the province is a form of the word "Gauls," the name of a Celtic tribe who controlled much of this region from the third to the second century B.C. Galatia was made into a Roman province in 25 B.C.

1.7 *some people are causing you trouble:* The troublemakers insisted that Gentile (non-Jewish) believers like the Galatians must follow certain Jewish rites, including circumcision. They also claimed that—because Paul said Gentiles didn't have to follow the Law of Moses or take part in Jewish ceremonies—he was not a true apostle.

1.10 *I am not trying to please people:* Paul was probably being accused of being a "people-pleaser" because he did not insist that Gentile males be circumcised as a symbol of God's agreement with Abraham.

Circumcision

1.12 *My message came directly from Jesus:* How Paul became a follower of Jesus is described in Acts 9.1-18.

1.18 *Peter:* An apostle of Jesus and important leader in the early church (see Matt 16.13-20).

1.21 *regions of Syria and Cilicia:* Paul was born in Tarsus in Cilicia (Acts 9.11; 22.3), a center of Greek culture. **(See Map 14 on pg 1892.)**

1.22 *Judea:* The earliest churches began in Jerusalem, in Judea. **(See Map 12 on pg 1890.)**

2.1 *Barnabas . . . Titus:* Barnabas was from Cyprus and was a member of the Jewish tribe of Levi. See also Acts 9.27 and Acts 13.1—14.28. Titus was a Gentile Christian who worked with Paul in Corinth (2 Cor 8.3-6) and in Ephesus (Acts 19.1—20.1).

2.9 *James . . . John:* James was Jesus' brother (1.19). John is probably the apostle John (Matt 4.21).

2.11 *Antioch:* Antioch in Syria was the third largest city in the Roman Empire.

2.12 *Peter . . . stopped eating with Gentiles:* The Law of Moses said it was wrong to eat certain foods and to share meals with Gentiles or with Jews who did not keep the purity laws. Peter had earlier agreed that these rules were not required of Gentile followers of Jesus (Acts 11.1-18), but appears to have changed his position due to pressure from followers of James.

every law our ancestors had given us. [15]But even before I was born, God had chosen me by his gift of undeserved grace and had decided [16]to show me his Son, so I would announce his message to the Gentiles. I didn't talk this over with anyone. [17]I didn't say a word, not even to the men in Jerusalem who were apostles before I was. Instead, I went at once to Arabia, and afterwards I returned to Damascus.

[18]Three years later I went to visit Peter[b] in Jerusalem and stayed with him for 15 days. [19]The only other apostle I saw was James, the Lord's brother. [20]And in the presence of God I swear I am telling the truth.

[21]Later, I went to the regions of Syria and Cilicia. [22]But no one who belonged to Christ's churches in Judea had ever seen me in person. [23]They had only heard that the one who had been cruel to them was now preaching the message that he had once tried to destroy. [24]And because of me, they praised God.

2 Fourteen years later I went to Jerusalem with Barnabas. I also took along Titus. [2]But I went there because God had told me to go, and I explained the good news I had been preaching to the Gentiles. Then I met privately with the ones who seemed to be the most important leaders. I wanted to make sure my work in the past and my future work would not be for nothing.

[3]Titus went to Jerusalem with me. He was a Greek, but still he wasn't forced to be circumcised. [4]We went there because of those who pretended to be followers and had sneaked in among us as spies. They had come to take away the freedom Christ Jesus had given us, and they were trying to make us their slaves. [5]But we wanted you to have the true message. This is why we didn't give in to them, not even for a second.

[6]Some of them were supposed to be important leaders, but I didn't care who they were. God doesn't have any favorites! None of these so-called special leaders added anything to my message. [7]They realized God had sent me with the good news for Gentiles, and he had sent Peter with the same message for Jews. [8]God, who had sent Peter on a mission to the Jews, was now using me to preach to the Gentiles.

[9]James, Peter,[b] and John realized that God had given me the message about his gift of undeserved grace. And these men are supposed to be the backbone of the church. They even gave Barnabas and me a friendly handshake. This was to show that we would work with Gentiles and that they would work with Jews. [10]They only asked us to remember the poor, and this was something I had always been eager to do.

Paul Corrects Peter at Antioch

[11]When Peter came to Antioch, I told him face to face that he was wrong. [12]He used to eat with Gentile followers of the Lord, until James sent some Jewish followers. Peter was afraid of the Jews and soon stopped eating with Gentiles. [13]He and the others hid their true feelings so well that even Barnabas was fooled. [14]But when I saw they were not really obeying the truth that is in the good news, I corrected Peter in front of everyone and said:

Peter, you are a Jew, but you live like a Gentile. So how can you force Gentiles to live like Jews?

[15]We are Jews by birth and are not sinners like Gentiles. [16]But we know

[b]1.18; 2.9 *Peter:* The Greek text has "Cephas," which is an Aramaic name meaning "rock." Peter is the Greek name with the same meaning.

that God accepts only those who have faith in Jesus Christ. No one can please God by simply obeying the Law. So we put our faith in Christ Jesus, and God accepted us because of our faith.

[17]When we Jews started looking for a way to please God, we discovered that we are sinners too. Does this mean that Christ is the one who makes us sinners? No, it doesn't! [18]But if I tear down something and then build it again, I prove that I was wrong at first. [19]It was the Law itself that killed me and freed me from its power, so I could live for God.

I have been nailed to the cross with Christ. [20]I have died, but Christ lives in me. And I now live by faith in the Son of God, who loved me and gave his life for me. [21]I don't turn my back on God's gift of undeserved grace. If we can be acceptable to God by obeying the Law, it was useless for Christ to die.

Faith Is the Only Way

3 You stupid Galatians! I told you exactly how Jesus Christ was nailed to a cross. Has someone now put an evil spell on you? [2]I want to know only one thing. How were you given God's Spirit? Was it by obeying the Law of Moses or by hearing about Christ and having faith in him? [3]How can you be so stupid? Do you think that by yourself you can complete what God's Spirit started in you? [4]Have you gone through all of this for nothing? Is it all really for nothing? [5]God gives you his Spirit and works miracles in you. But does he do this because you obey the Law of

Moses or because you have heard about Christ and have faith in him?

[6]The Scriptures say that God accepted Abraham because Abraham had faith. [7]And so, you should understand that everyone who has faith is a child of Abraham.[c] [8]Long ago the Scriptures said God would accept the Gentiles because of their faith. This is why God told Abraham the good news that all nations would be blessed because of him. [9]This means everyone who has faith will share in the blessings given to Abraham because of his faith.

[10]Anyone who tries to please God by obeying the Law is under a curse. The Scriptures say, "Everyone who doesn't obey everything in the Law is under a curse." [11]No one can please God by obeying the Law. The Scriptures also say, "The people God accepts because of their faith will live."[d]

[12]The Law isn't based on faith. It promises life only to people who obey its commands. [13]But Christ rescued us from the Law's curse, when he became a curse in our place. This is because the Scriptures say that anyone who is nailed to a tree is under a curse. [14]And because of what Jesus Christ has done, the blessing promised to Abraham was taken to the Gentiles. This happened so that by faith we would be given the promised Holy Spirit.

The Law and the Promise

[15]My friends, I will use an everyday example to explain what I mean. Once someone agrees to something, no one else can change or cancel the agreement.[e] [16]That is how it is with the promises God made to

---

2.16 *No one can please God by simply obeying the Law:* This statement was at the heart of Paul's message, the good news about Christ. The Law here refers to the Law of Moses.

ᗑ Law

2.19 *the Law . . . killed me:* Paul means that the Law of Moses shows people that they are sinners and cannot please God (2.17; see also Rom 3.20). When people discover this, they are then free to put their faith in Jesus. Faith in Jesus Christ gives new life, which is something the Law cannot give (Phil 3.8,9).

2.19,20 *I have been nailed to the cross . . . I have died:* Though the cross was a symbol of death to the world, it meant new life to Paul. Christ's death frees people from the "Law's curse" (3.13). Paul does not mean that he was literally nailed to a cross, but that his old life under the Law became a new life based on faith in Christ.

ᗑ Holy Spirit

ᗑ Abraham

3.13 *Law's curse:* Paul argues that God's Law is a curse because no one can follow it perfectly. Jesus took the place of all people and died under a curse, so that all who trust in him will be freed from the curse of the Law.

---

[c]**3.7** *a child of Abraham:* God chose Abraham, and so it was believed that anyone who was a child of Abraham was also a child of God (see the note at 3.29).   [d]**3.11** *The people God accepts because of their faith will live:* Or "The people God accepts will live because of their faith."   [e]**3.15** *Once someone . . . cancel the agreement:* Or "Once a person makes out a will, no one can change or cancel it."

3.16 *Abraham and his descendant:* The Greek word for "descendant" can mean one or many descendants. In this verse, Paul uses it to mean "Christ."

3.17 *430 years before the Law was given:* God gave the Law to Moses and the Israelite people centuries after giving his promises to Abraham.

3.19 *angels gave the Law to Moses:* No Scripture passage says this directly, but it was believed according to Jewish tradition that angels played a role in giving the Law at Sinai (Deut 33.2).

3.27 *baptized:* Water is used in baptism to show how a person is made new and becomes part of God's family. In ROMANS, Paul says that baptism is like dying and being buried with Christ (Rom 6.3-5). The old life of slavery to sin dies, and a new person is born.

Baptism

4.4 *God sent his Son:* Jesus was the son of a Jewish woman named Mary (Matt 1.18-25; Luke 1.26-56; 2.1-20), and as a Jew he obeyed the Law of Moses.

4.6 *God has sent the Spirit . . . into our hearts:* In Bible times, people believed the human will was located in the heart. If Christ's Spirit is present in someone's heart, that person will have the power to live according to God's will.

Abraham and his descendant.f The promises were not made to many descendants, but only to one, and that one is Christ. 17What I am saying is that the Law cannot change or cancel God's promise made 430 years before the Law was given. 18If we have to obey the Law in order to receive God's blessings, those blessings don't really come to us because of God's promise. But God was kind to Abraham and made him a promise.

19What is the use of the Law? It was given later to show that we sin. But it was only supposed to last until the coming of that descendantg who was given the promise. In fact, angels gave the Law to Moses, and he gave it to the people. 20There is only one God, and the Law did not come directly from him.

Slaves and Children

21Does the Law disagree with God's promises? No, it doesn't! If any law could give life to us, we could become acceptable to God by obeying that law. 22But the Scriptures say that sin controls everyone, so that God's promises will be for anyone who has faith in Jesus Christ.

23The Law controlled us and kept us under its power until the time came when we would have faith. 24In fact, the Law was to be our teacher until Christ came. Then we could have faith and be acceptable to God. 25But once a person has learned to have faith, there is no more need to have the Law as a teacher.

26All of you are God's children because of your faith in Christ Jesus. 27And when you were baptized, it was as though you had put on Christ in the same way you put on new clothes. 28Faith in Christ Jesus is what makes each of you equal with each other, whether you are a Jew or a Greek, a slave or a free person, a man or a woman. 29So if you belong to Christ, you are now part of Abraham's family,h and you will be given what God has promised. 1Children who are under age are no better off than slaves, even though everything their parents own will someday be theirs. 2This is because children are placed in the care of guardians and teachers until the time their parents have set. 3This is how it was with us. We were like children ruled by the powers of this world.

4But when the time was right, God sent his Son, and a woman gave birth to him. His Son obeyed the Law, 5 so he could set us free from the Law, and we could become God's children. 6Now that we are his children, God has sent the Spirit of his Son into our hearts. And his Spirit tells us that God is our Father. 7You are no longer slaves. You are God's children, and you will be given what he has promised.

Paul's Concern for the Galatians

8Before you knew God, you were slaves of gods that are not real. 9But now you know God, or better still, God knows you. How can you turn back and become the slaves of those weak and pitiful powers?i 10You even celebrate certain days, months, seasons, and years. 11I am afraid I have wasted my time working with you.

12My friends, I beg you to be like me, just as I once tried to be like you. Did you mistreat me 13when I first preached to you? No you didn't, even though you knew I had come there because I was sick. [14]My illness must have caused you some trouble, but you didn't hate me or turn me away because of it. You welcomed me as though I were one of God's angels or even Christ Jesus himself. [15]Where is that good feeling now? I am sure if it had been possible, you would have taken out your own eyes and given them to me. [16]Am I now your enemy, just because I told you the truth?

[17]Those people may be paying you a lot of attention, but it isn't for your good. They only want to keep you away from me, so you will pay them a lot of attention. [18]It is always good to give your attention to something worthwhile, even when I am not with you. [19]My children, I am in terrible pain until Christ may be seen living in you. [20]I wish I were with you now. Then I would not have to talk this way. You really have me puzzled.

Hagar and Sarah

[21]Some of you would like to be under the rule of the Law of Moses. But do you know what the Law says? [22]In the Scriptures we learn that Abraham had two sons. The mother of one of them was a slave, while the mother of the other one had always been free. [23]The son of the slave woman was born in the usual way. But the son of the free woman was born because of God's promise.

[24]All of this has another meaning as well. Each of the two women stands for one of the agreements God made with his people. Hagar, the slave woman, stands for the agreement that was made at Mount Sinai. Everyone born into her family is a slave. [25]Hagar also stands for Mount Sinai in Arabia[j] and for the present city of Jerusalem. She[k] and her children are slaves.

[26]But our mother is the city of Jerusalem in heaven above, and she isn't a slave. [27]The Scriptures say about her,

"You have never had children,
    but now you can be glad.
You have never given birth,
    but now you can shout.
Once you had no children,
    but now you will have
more children than a woman
    who has been married
    for a long time."

[28]My friends, you were born because of this promise, just as Isaac was. [29]But the child who was born in the natural way made trouble for the child who was born because of the Spirit. The same thing is happening today. [30]The Scriptures say, "Get rid of the slave woman and her son! He won't be given anything. The son of the free woman will receive everything." [31]My friends, we are children of the free woman and not of the slave.

Christ Gives Freedom

5 Christ has set us free! This means we are really free. Now hold on to your freedom and don't ever become slaves of the Law again.

[2]I, Paul, promise you that Christ won't do you any good if you get circumcised. [3]If you do, you must obey the whole Law. [4]And if you try to please God by obeying the Law, you have cut yourself off from Christ and his gift of undeserved grace.

4.14,15 *My illness . . . your own eyes:* Paul was sick when he first came to Galatia, which here sounds like it may have been some kind of eye disease.

4.22 *Abraham had two sons:* Because he didn't believe God's promise to give him a son by his wife Sarah, Abraham had a son by Hagar, Sarah's slave. Hagar's son was named Ishmael (Gen 16.1-16). Later, Sarah and Abraham had a child named Isaac. Isaac was the child God had promised, and his descendants became the people of Israel. Anyone who follows the Law is a slave like Hagar and her son. But those who have faith in Christ are like the descendants of Sarah, because she was the mother of the child born according to God's promise.

4.29 *child who was born in the natural way:* Paul is speaking of Ishmael (Gen 21.9,10).

---

[j]**4.25** *Hagar also stands for Mount Sinai in Arabia:* Some manuscripts have "Sinai is a mountain in Arabia." This sentence would then be translated: "Sinai is a mountain in Arabia, and Hagar stands for the present city of Jerusalem."   [k]**4.25** *She:* "Hagar" or "Jerusalem."

5.11 *preach that people need to be circumcised:* Apparently, the trouble-makers were claiming that Paul approved of circumcision, but he denies it.

Circumcision

5.18 *Law of Moses:* Paul means that evil, selfish desires lead to death. Those who think they can save themselves from death by following the Law of Moses are also wrong.

5.21 *God's kingdom:* God's rule over people, both in this life and in the next.

6.1 *trapped in sin:* People sin when they turn their backs on God and disobey God's Law.

Sin

6.2 *the law of Christ:* The law of Christ is to love one another as Christ has loved human beings (John 13.34; 1 Cor 9.21; 1 John 2.7-11; 4.10-12). Followers of Christ love one another because they have been accepted by God and have received God's Spirit, not because they want to win God's approval.

Eternal Life

Heaven

Hell

⁵But the Spirit makes us sure God will accept us because of our faith in Christ. ⁶If you are a follower of Christ Jesus, it makes no difference whether you are circumcised or not. All that matters is your faith that makes you love others.

⁷You were doing so well until someone made you turn from the truth. ⁸And that person was certainly not sent by the one who chose you. ⁹A little yeast can change a whole batch of dough, ¹⁰but you belong to the Lord. This makes me certain you will do what I say, instead of what someone else tells you to do. Whoever is causing trouble for you will be punished.

¹¹My friends, if I still preach that people need to be circumcised, why am I in so much trouble? The message about the cross would no longer be a problem, if I told people to be circumcised. ¹²I wish everyone who is upsetting you would not only get circumcised, but would cut off much more!

¹³My friends, you were chosen to be free. So don't use your freedom as an excuse to do anything you want. Use it as an opportunity to serve each other with love. ¹⁴All the Law says can be summed up in the command to love others as much as you love yourself. ¹⁵But if you keep attacking each other like wild animals, you had better watch out or you will destroy yourselves.

God's Spirit and Our Own Desires

¹⁶If you are guided by the Spirit, you won't obey your selfish desires. ¹⁷The Spirit and your desires are enemies of each other. They are always fighting each other and keeping you from doing what you feel you should. ¹⁸But if you obey the Spirit, the Law of Moses has no control over you.

¹⁹People's desires make them give in to immoral ways, filthy thoughts, and shameful deeds. ²⁰They worship idols, practice witchcraft, hate others, and are hard to get along with. People become jealous, angry, and selfish. They not only argue and cause trouble, but they are ²¹envious. They get drunk, carry on at wild parties, and do other evil things as well. I told you before, and I am telling you again: No one who does these things will share in the blessings of God's kingdom.

²²God's Spirit makes us loving, happy, peaceful, patient, kind, good, faithful, ²³gentle, and self-controlled. There is no law against behaving in any of these ways. ²⁴And because we belong to Christ Jesus, we have killed our selfish feelings and desires. ²⁵God's Spirit has given us life, and so we should follow the Spirit. ²⁶But don't be conceited or make others jealous by claiming to be better than they are.

Help Each Other

6 My friends, you are spiritual. So if someone is trapped in sin, you should gently lead that person back to the right path. But watch out, and don't be tempted yourself. ²You obey the law of Christ when you offer each other a helping hand.

³If you think you are better than others, when you really aren't, you are wrong. ⁴Do your own work well, and then you will have something to be proud of. But don't compare yourself with others. ⁵We each must carry our own load.

⁶Share every good thing you have with anyone who teaches you what God has said.

⁷You cannot fool God, so don't make a fool of yourself! You will harvest what you plant. ⁸If you follow your selfish desires, you will harvest destruction, but if you follow the Spirit, you will harvest eternal life. ⁹Don't get tired of helping others. You will

God's Spirit makes us loving, happy, peaceful, patient, kind, good, faithful, gentle, and self-controlled. GAL 5.22,23

be rewarded when the time is right, if you don't give up. [10]We should help people whenever we can, especially if they are followers of the Lord.

Final Warnings

[11]You can see what big letters I make when I write with my own hand.

[12]Those people who are telling you to get circumcised are only trying to show how important they are. And they don't want to get into trouble for preaching about the cross of Christ. [13]They are circumcised, but they don't obey the Law of Moses. All they want is to brag about having you circumcised. [14]But I will never brag about anything except the cross of our Lord Jesus Christ. Because of his cross, the world is dead as far as I am concerned, and I am dead as far as the world is concerned.

[15]It doesn't matter if you are circumcised or not. All that matters is that you are a new person.

[16]If you follow this rule, you will belong to God's true people. God will treat you with undeserved kindness and will bless you with peace.

[17]On my own body are scars that prove I belong to Christ Jesus. So I don't want anyone to bother me anymore.

[18]My friends, I pray that the Lord Jesus Christ will be kind to you! Amen.

6.14 *the world is dead:* For Paul, the "world" stands for those people and things that are opposed to God and God's purposes.

6.17 *scars:* In Greek, this word also means the scars made to mark a slave or an animal, which are also called "brands." Paul says he is physically branded by scars that he received from those who persecuted him because of his belief in Jesus Christ. In 2 Corinthians 11.23-26 Paul describes how he had been beaten many times in the past.

Reflection Questions About Galatians 1.1—6.18

1. How were certain people trying to make the Galatians turn away from the good news about Christ (1.7; 3.1-14; 5.1-15; 6.12-15)? Why was this a problem?

2. Both Peter and Paul were respected leaders in the early church. Describe in your own words the conflict between Paul and Peter (2.11-21). What did Peter do that upset Paul? What did Paul say to "correct" Peter? How do leaders in churches today handle conflicts and differences of opinion?

3. Paul says that "Christ has set us free!" (5.1). In what ways are Christians free? What does this kind of freedom include? What, if anything, are its limits?

4. Compare the list in 5.19-21 with the list in 5.22,23. Where do the items in each list come from? What does Paul mean when he says that "God's Spirit has given us life" (5.25)?

5. What does Paul mean when he says, "you will harvest what you plant" (6.7)? Think about your life a year from now . . . five years from now. How do the decisions you make today affect your future?

ephesians

Why is being part of a team, a group, or a family so important? Read this letter to the Ephesians to find out how everyone who has faith in Christ Jesus is part of the "same body" and belongs to God's family.

WHAT MAKES EPHESIANS SPECIAL?

EPHESIANS summarizes many of Paul's important teachings. It begins by describing how God raised Christ, who rules beside God in heaven. The letter explains how Christ has brought both Gentiles and Jews together by "breaking down the wall of hatred" that separated them (2.14). Those who have faith in Jesus have been chosen by God's Spirit to be part of one body, which is the church. This body has "one Lord, one faith, and one baptism" (4.5). Christ has chosen some people in the church to have gifts as apostles, prophets, missionaries, pastors, and teachers (4.11). The final chapters of the letter offer practical instructions for living as God's people—including a description of the spiritual "armor" that God gives to his people, so they can withstand the devil and the rulers of darkness (6.10-17).

Many of Paul's letters give clues about why Paul wrote them. EPHESIANS, however, does not mention any particular issues or questions in the Ephesian church. Acts 19,20 may offer a clue. Those chapters describe how Paul told people in Ephesus about Jesus Christ. Later, he argued with those who worshiped Artemis, the favorite goddess in Ephesus. The local leader refused to punish Paul when a riot almost broke out, but Paul left the city. Paul later met the leaders of the Ephesian church and gave them courage to face their problems. The difficulty among the Ephesian followers was that some members, in spite of Paul's teachings, were trying to divide followers into groups. So EPHESIANS addresses the problem of unity within the church.

WHAT'S THE STORY BEHIND THE SCENE?

Many ancient manuscripts say that this letter was addressed to "the saints who are in Ephesus." Yet, some biblical manuscripts—including the oldest—do not name the Ephesians as recipients of the letter. The Greek writing style and vocabulary used in EPHESIANS differs somewhat from Paul's other letters. In addition, Paul spent about three years in Ephesus starting a congregation (Acts 18.19-21; 19.1-20; 20.17-38); however, the author and readers of this letter don't seem to have met (1.15). All the same, because of its similarities to Paul's writings, especially his letter to the COLOSSIANS, EPHESIANS has been linked with the apostle.

HOW IS EPHESIANS CONSTRUCTED?

The letter can be outlined as follows:

Greetings, blessings, and prayers (1.1-23)
Christ brings unity and peace to the people of God (2.1—3.21)
Living as the body of Christ, the people of light (4.1—6.24)

Ephesians is a letter addressed to the Christians of Ephesus, an important port city in Asia Minor. Although it is not easy to identify the historical context of the church at Ephesus, Ephesians repeats a number of important teachings of Paul. The letter puts a strong emphasis on the importance of the unity of the church that results from what Christ had done for humankind. Whether followers are Jewish or Gentile, they are one in Christ Jesus. The letter also explains the difference between the old life of sin, and the new life the Holy Spirit will create for those who are faithful to Jesus. The letter gives lists of rules for Christian behavior and tells how Christians are to use the strength of the Lord to become strong in the fight against evil.

Outline

1

From Paul, chosen by God to be an apostle of Christ Jesus.

To God's people who live in Ephesus and[a] are faithful followers of Christ Jesus.

[2]I pray that God our Father and our Lord Jesus Christ will be kind to you and will bless you with peace!

Christ Brings Spiritual Blessings

[3]Praise the God and Father of our Lord Jesus Christ for the spiritual blessings that Christ has brought us from heaven! [4]Before the world was created, God had Christ choose us to live with him and to be his holy and innocent and loving people. [5]God was kind[b] and decided that Christ would choose us to be God's own adopted children. [6]God treated us with undeserved grace because of the Son he dearly loves, and so we should praise God.

[7-8]Christ sacrificed his life's blood to set us free, which means our sins are now for-given. Christ did this because of God's gift of undeserved grace to us. God has great wisdom and understanding, [9]and by what Christ has done, God has shown us his own mysterious ways. [10]Then when the time is right, God will do all he has planned, and Christ will bring together everything in heaven and on earth.

[11]God always does what he plans, and this is why he appointed Christ to choose us. [12]He did this so we Jews would bring honor to him and be the first ones to have hope because of him. [13]Christ also brought you the truth, which is the good news about how you can be saved. You put your faith in Christ and were given the prom-ised Holy Spirit to show you belong to God. [14]The Spirit also makes us sure we will be given what God has stored up for his people. Then we will be set free, and God will be honored and praised.

[a]1.1 *live in Ephesus and*: Some manuscripts do not have these words. [b]1.4,5 *holy and innocent and loving people.* [5]*God was kind*: Or "holy and innocent people. God was loving [5]and kind."

● 1.1 *Paul...an apostle of Christ Jesus*: In EPHESIANS, "apostle" means someone chosen by God to spread the message about Jesus Christ. "Christ" is from the Greek word *Christos*, which means "Messiah" or "chosen one."

◌ Paul (Saul of Tarsus)

◌ Messiah (Chosen One)

■ 1.3 *spiritual blessings...heaven*: The spiritual blessings include forgive-ness (1.7,8), wisdom and understand-ing (1.17), faith (2.8), and special gifts to serve God and the church. When the writer of EPHESIANS says that Christ is in heaven he is making it clear that Christ rules and is present in all things.

◌ Heaven

■ 1.4 *Before the world...had Christ choose us*: Christ is the Word that was with God in the beginning of time, who helped God create all things (John 1.1-3). This means that when Christ chose people to be part of God's family, it was part of God's plan from the beginning.

■ 1.7-8 *Christ sacrificed...sins are now forgiven*: The Greek word trans-lated as "sacrificed" has the meaning of paying a debt. Jesus bought forgiveness for all people, and paid for it with his blood. (See also Rom 3.24-26; 1 Cor 1.30; and Heb 9.15.) Forgiveness removes sin, and allows people to turn back to God and become acceptable to God once again.

◌ God's Saving Love (Salvation)

1.18 *light will flood your hearts:* In the Bible, light is used to describe God or God's word (Ps 119.105; John 1.3,4; 1 John 1.5). The followers of Jesus are also called "people of the light" (Eph 5.8).

1.22,23 *church . . . the body of Christ:* Since Christ is the "head of everything," he is also the head of the church, which is called the body of Christ (Rom 12.5; 1 Cor 12.27; Col 1.17,18).

Church

2.2 *ways of this world . . . devil:* Here, the "world" stands for all the forces that are against God. The devil, sometimes called Satan, is the leader of these forces.

Satan

2.6 *raised us from death . . . given us a place beside Christ:* Often Paul talks of being raised to new life as something that happens in the future (Rom 6.5-8; 8.18-25; 1 Cor 15; Phil 3.11). Here Paul may be talking about the new life that comes from being baptized (Rom 6.3,4; Col 2.12).

2.15 *the Law of Moses:* Though the author of EPHESIANS says that Jesus came to "destroy the Law of Moses," other New Testament letters say that faith in Jesus does not destroy the Law, but shows how people can become truly obedient (Rom 3.31; Col 2.14). Even though God's Law was holy and good, it could not save anyone. The Law could only point out how people sin (Rom 3.20; 7.7-12; Gal 3.12-14; 2.15,16).

Paul's Prayer

¹⁵I have heard about your faith in the Lord Jesus and your love for all God's people. ¹⁶So I never stop being grateful for you, as I mention you in my prayers. ¹⁷I ask the glorious Father and God of our Lord Jesus Christ to give you his Spirit. The Spirit will make you wise and let you understand what it means to know God. ¹⁸My prayer is that light will flood your hearts and you will understand the hope given to you when God chose you. Then you will discover the glorious blessings that will be yours together with all God's people.

¹⁹I want you to know about the great and mighty power that God has for us followers. It is the same wonderful power he used ²⁰when he raised Christ from death and let him sit at his right side[c] in heaven. ²¹There Christ rules over all forces, authorities, powers, and rulers. He rules over all beings in this world and will rule in the future world as well. ²²God has put all things under the power of Christ, and for the good of the church he has made him the head of everything. ²³The church is the body of Christ and is filled with Christ who completely fills everything.[d]

From Death to Life

2 In the past you were dead because you sinned and fought against God. ²You followed the ways of this world and obeyed the devil. He rules the world, and his spirit has power over everyone who doesn't obey God. ³Once we were also ruled by the selfish desires of our bodies and minds. We had made God angry, and we were going to be punished like everyone else.

⁴⁻⁵But God was merciful! We were dead because of our sins, but God loved us so much he made us alive with Christ, and God's gift of undeserved grace is what saves you. ⁶God raised us from death to life with Christ Jesus, and he has given us a place beside Christ in heaven. ⁷God did this so in the future world he could show how truly good and kind he is to us because of what Christ Jesus has done. ⁸You were saved by faith in God, who treats us much better than we deserve.[e] This is God's gift to you, and not anything you have done on your own. ⁹It isn't something you have earned, so there is nothing you can brag about. ¹⁰God planned for us to do good things and to live as he has always wanted us to live. This is why he sent Christ to make us what we are.

United by Christ

¹¹Don't forget that you are Gentiles. In fact, you used to be called "uncircumcised" by those who take pride in being circumcised. ¹²At that time you did not know about Christ. You were foreigners to the people of Israel, and you had no part in the promises God had made to them. You were living in this world without hope and without God, ¹³and you were far from God. But Christ offered his life's blood as a sacrifice and brought you near God.

¹⁴Christ has made peace between Jews and Gentiles, and he has united us by breaking down the wall of hatred that separated us. Christ gave his own body ¹⁵to destroy the Law of Moses with all its rules and commands. He even brought Jews and Gentiles together as though we were only one person, when he united us in peace. ¹⁶On

[c]**1.20** *right side:* The place of power and honor.   [d]**1.23** *and is filled with Christ who completely fills everything:* Or "which completely fills Christ and fully completes his work."   [e]**2.8** *treats us much better than we deserve:* The Greek word *charis,* traditionally rendered "grace," is translated here and other places in the CEV to express the overwhelming kindness of God.

the cross Christ did away with our hatred for each other. He also made peace[f] between us and God by uniting Jews and Gentiles in one body. [17]Christ came and preached peace to you Gentiles, who were far from God, and peace to us Jews, who were near God. [18]And because of Christ, all of us can come to the Father by the same Spirit.

[19]You Gentiles are no longer strangers and foreigners. You are citizens with everyone else who belongs to the family of God. [20]You are like a building with the apostles and prophets as the foundation and with Christ as the most important stone. [21]Christ is the one who holds the building together and makes it grow into a holy temple for the Lord. [22]And you are part of that building Christ has built as a place for God's own Spirit to live.

Paul's Mission to the Gentiles

3 Christ Jesus made me his prisoner, so I could help you Gentiles. [2]You have surely heard about God's gift of undeserved grace in choosing me to help you. [3]In fact, this letter tells you a little about how God has shown me his mysterious ways. [4]As you read the letter, you will also find out how well I really do understand the mystery about Christ. [5]No one knew about this mystery until God's Spirit told it to his holy apostles and prophets. [6]And the mystery is this: Because of Christ Jesus, the good news has given the Gentiles a share in the promises God gave to the Jews. God has also let the Gentiles be part of the same body.

[7]God treated me with kindness. His power worked in me, and it became my job to spread the good news. [8]I am the least important of all God's people. But God was kind and chose me to tell the Gentiles that because of Christ there are blessings that cannot be measured. [9]God, who created everything, wanted me to help everyone understand the mysterious plan that had always been hidden in his mind. [10]Then God would use the church to show the powers and authorities in the spiritual world that he has many different kinds of wisdom.

[11]God did this according to his eternal plan. And he was able to do what he had planned because of all Christ Jesus our Lord had done. [12]Christ now gives us courage and confidence, so we can come to God by faith. [13]This is why you should not be discouraged when I suffer for you. After all, it will bring honor to you.

Christ's Love for Us

[14]I kneel in prayer to the Father. [15]All beings in heaven and on earth receive their life from him.[g] [16]God is wonderful and glorious. I pray that his Spirit will make you become strong followers [17]and that Christ will live in your hearts because of your faith. Stand firm and be deeply rooted in his love. [18]I pray that you and all God's people will understand what is called wide or long or high or deep.[h] [19]I want you to know all about Christ's love, although it is too wonderful to be measured. Then your lives will be filled with all that God is.

[20-21]I pray that Christ Jesus and the church will forever bring praise to God. His power at work in us can do far more than we dare ask or imagine. Amen.

20.20-21 *building . . . a holy temple:* The temple was the central place where God's presence was experienced among the people of Israel (2 Chr 5.11—6.2; Hab 2.20). Paul says that those who have been given the Holy Spirit now form God's holy temple (1 Cor 3.16,17). They are made holy because of God's presence.

2.20 *apostle and prophets:* The apostles were special messengers chosen to bring the good news to all people. The "prophets" may refer either to the prophets of Israel (800 to 400 B.C.) or to prophets of the early Christian church who had received the Holy Spirit's gift of prophecy.

3.1 *prisoner:* This may refer to Paul's own imprisonment by Roman authorities. It may also refer to how Christ has captured Paul's mind and heart so he could preach to the Gentiles (Acts 9.15,16).

[f]2.16 *He also made peace:* Or "The cross also made peace." [g]3.15 *receive their life from him:* Or "know who they really are because of him." [h]3.18 *what is called wide or long or high or deep:* This may refer to the heavenly Jerusalem or to God's love or wisdom or to the meaning of the cross.

4.4-6 *the same body . . . Father of all people:* EPHESIANS gives seven different examples of how the followers of Christ are unified. Verse 4.4 says they are part of one body, follow one Spirit (2.18), and share one hope (1.18). Verse 4.5 says that they claim one Lord (1.3), one faith (1.13), and one baptism. Ultimately, the followers of Christ are unified by worship of one God (4.6).

Baptism

4.9,10 *"he went up," . . . went deep into the earth:* Jesus was taken up to heaven 40 days after God had raised him from death (Luke 24.50,51; Acts 1.3,6-11; 2.33). The writer of 1 PETER says that when Jesus was put to death, he preached to the spirits being kept in prison (1 Pet 3.19), which may refer to the spirits of the dead who were imprisoned in Sheol, the place of the dead.

4.11 *apostles, prophets:* Here, Christ chooses some people for special tasks. The New Testament often identifies the Holy Spirit as the one who gives out such gifts and abilities (1 Cor 12–14). In ROMANS, Paul says that God gives such gifts (Rom 12.4-8).

4.18 *dark:* In the Bible, "the dark" refers to places of pain (Ps 107.10) or confusion (Eccl 2.14). God's opponents are called "rulers of darkness" (Eph 6.12). Those who oppose God may "be thrown outside into the dark" (Matt 22.13).

Unity with Christ

4 As a prisoner of the Lord, I beg you to live in a way that is worthy of the people God has chosen to be his own. [2]Always be humble and gentle. Patiently put up with each other and love each other. [3]Try your best to let God's Spirit keep your hearts united. Do this by living at peace. [4]All of you are part of the same body. There is only one Spirit of God, just as you were given one hope when you were chosen to be God's people. [5]We have only one Lord, one faith, and one baptism. [6]There is one God who is the Father of all people. Not only is God above all others, but he works by using all of us, and he lives in all of us.

[7]Christ has generously divided out his gifts to us. [8]As the Scriptures say,

"When he went up
    to the highest place,
he led away many prisoners
    and gave gifts to people."

[9]When it says, "he went up," it means that Christ had been deep in the earth. [10]This also means that the one who went deep into the earth is the same one who went into the highest heaven, so he would fill the whole universe. [11]Christ chose some of us to be apostles, prophets, missionaries, pastors, and teachers, [12]so his people would learn to serve and his body would grow strong. [13]This will continue until we are united by our faith and by our understanding of the Son of God. Then we will be mature, just as Christ is, and we will be completely like him.[i] [14]We must stop acting like children. We must not let deceitful people trick us by their false teachings, which are like winds that toss us around from place to place. [15]Love should always make us tell the truth. Then we will grow in every way and be more like Christ, the head [16]of the body. Christ holds it together and makes all of its parts work perfectly, as it grows and becomes strong because of love.

The Old Life and the New Life

[17]As a follower of the Lord, I order you to stop living like stupid, godless people. [18]Their minds are in the dark, and they are stubborn and ignorant and have missed out on the life that comes from God. They no longer have any feelings about what is right, [19]and they are so greedy they do all kinds of indecent things.

[20-21]But this isn't what you were taught about Jesus Christ. He is the truth, and you heard about him and learned about him. [22]You were told that your foolish desires will destroy you and that you must give up your old way of life with all its bad habits. [23]Let the Spirit change your way of thinking [24]and make you into a new person. You were created to be like God, and so you must please him and be truly holy.

Rules for the New Life

[25]We are part of the same body. Stop lying and start telling each other the truth. [26]Don't get so angry that you sin. Don't go to bed angry [27]and don't give the devil a chance. [28]If you are a thief, quit stealing. Be honest and work hard, so you will have something to give to people in need. [29]Stop all your dirty talk. Say the right thing at the right time and help others by what you say.

[i]*4.13 and we will be completely like him:* Or "and he is completely perfect."

30Don't make God's Spirit sad. The Spirit makes you sure that someday you will be free from your sins.

31Stop being bitter and angry and mad at others. Don't yell at one another or curse each other or ever be rude. 32Instead, be kind and merciful, and forgive others, just as God forgave you because of Christ.

5 Do as God does. After all, you are his dear children. 2Let love be your guide. Christ loved usj and offered his life for us as a sacrifice that pleases God.

3You are God's people, so don't let it be said that any of you are immoral or indecent or greedy. 4Don't use dirty or foolish or filthy words. Instead, say how thankful you are. 5Being greedy, indecent, or immoral is just another way of worshiping idols. You can be sure people who behave in this way will never be part of the kingdom that belongs to Christ and to God.

Living as People of Light

6Don't let anyone trick you with foolish talk. God punishes everyone who disobeys him and saysk foolish things. 7So don't have anything to do with anyone like that.

8You used to be like people living in the dark, but now you are people of the light because you belong to the Lord. So act like people of the light 9and make your light shine. Be good and honest and truthful, 10as you try to please the Lord. 11Don't take part in doing those worthless things that are done in the dark. Instead, show how wrong they are. 12It is disgusting even to talk about what is done in the dark. 13But the light will show what these things are really like. 14Light shows up everything,l just as the Scriptures say,

"Wake up from your sleep
and rise from death.
Then Christ will shine on you."

15Act like people with good sense and not like fools. 16These are evil times, so make every minute count. 17Don't be stupid. Instead, find out what the Lord wants you to do. 18Don't destroy yourself by getting drunk, but let the Spirit fill your life. 19When you meet together, sing psalms, hymns, and spiritual songs, as you praise the Lord with all your heart. 20Always use the name of our Lord Jesus Christ to thank God the Father for everything.

Wives and Husbands

21Honor Christ and put others first. 22A wife should put her husband first, as she does the Lord. 23A husband is the head of his wife, as Christ is the head and the Savior of the church, which is his own body. 24Wives should always put their husbands first, as the church puts Christ first.

25A husband should love his wife as much as Christ loved the church and gave his life for it. 26He made the church holy by the power of his word, and he made it pure by washing it with water. 27Christ did this, so he would have a glorious and holy church, without faults or spots or wrinkles or any other flaws.

28In the same way, a husband should love his wife as much as he loves himself. A husband who loves his wife shows he loves himself. 29None of us hate our own bodies. We provide for them and take good care of them, just as Christ does for the church, 30because we are each part of his body. 31As the Scriptures say, "A man leaves his father

j5.2 us: Some manuscripts have "you." k5.6 says: Or "does." l5.14 Light shows up everything: Or "Everything that is seen in the light becomes light itself."

■ 5.5 the kingdom that belongs to Christ and to God: This is the only place in the New Testament using the phrase, "kingdom that belongs to Christ." Like the similar terms "kingdom of God" (Mark 1.15; Luke 4.43) and "kingdom of heaven" (Matt 3.2), it means God's rule over people, both in this life and in the life to come. See also 1 Cor 15.24,25.

■ 5.14 Wake up . . . . Christ will shine on you: This phrase resembles Isaiah 26.19 and 60.1. Some form of this quotation may have been used as an early Christian hymn or baptism ceremony.

■ 5.18 let the Spirit fill your life: God's people are to avoid anger (4.26), dirty talk (4.29; 5.4), cursing others (4.31), greed or immorality (5.3), and intoxication (5.18).

● 5.21-25 Honor Christ and put others first: In Paul's day, people accepted certain levels of authority in households. The writer of EPHESIANS seems to be adding to this the idea of equality by telling Jesus' followers to "put others first."

■ 5.28 love: The kind of self-giving love mentioned in this verse is commanded in Leviticus 19.8, repeated by Jesus (Matt 19.19; 22.39), and taught by Paul (Rom 13.9).

You used to be like people living in the dark, but now you are people of the light because you belong to the Lord. EPH 5:8

6.1-4 *Children . . . Parents:* Because children "belong to the Lord," parents should respect them and teach them about the Lord. The writer repeats one of the Ten Commandments (Exod 20.12; Deut 5.16) to remind Christians that the obedience of children is a path to one of God's promises.

6.5-9 *Slaves . . . Slave owners:* To show ownership, masters forced their slaves to wear collars. A slave wearing a collar would not be able to find work as a free person.

Slaves and Servants in the Time of Jesus

Satan

6.13 *that evil day:* Refers to a time of testing. This may be in the present (5.16) or some time in the future (1 Cor 3.10-15; Rev 2.10).

6.14-1 *belt . . . shield:* The belt referred to here was a soldier's belt—a broad belt usually made of leather that provided support for a soldier as well as a place to attach other equipment. This broad belt circled a soldier just as God's truth surrounds the believer. A soldier's shield was often a large rectangle of wood covered with canvas and animal hide. Just before battle, soldiers dipped their shields in water so that when flaming arrows hit the shield, they would fizzle out. In the same way, faith is able to put out the flaming arrows of the evil one.

and mother to get married, and he becomes like one person with his wife." [32]This is a great mystery, but I understand it to mean Christ and his church. [33]So each husband should love his wife as much as he loves himself, and each wife should respect her husband.

Children and Parents

6 Children, you belong to the Lord, and you do the right thing when you obey your parents. The first commandment with a promise says, [2]"Obey your father and your mother, [3]and you will have a long and happy life."

[4]Parents, don't be hard on your children. Raise them properly. Teach them and instruct them about the Lord.

Slaves and Masters

[5]Slaves, you must obey your earthly masters. Show them great respect and be as loyal to them as you are to Christ. [6]Try to please them at all times, and not just when you think they are watching. You are slaves of Christ, so with your whole heart you must do what God wants you to do. [7]Gladly serve your masters, as though they were the Lord himself, and not simply people. [8]You know that you will be rewarded for any good things you do, whether you are slaves or free.

[9]Slave owners, you must treat your slaves with this same respect. Don't threaten them. They have the same Master in heaven that you do, and he doesn't have favorites.

The Fight against Evil

[10]Finally, let the mighty strength of the Lord make you strong. [11]Put on all the armor that God gives, so you can defend yourself against the devil's tricks. [12]We are not fighting against humans. We are fighting against forces and authorities and against rulers of darkness and powers in the spiritual world. [13]So put on all the armor that God gives. Then when that evil day[m] comes, you will be able to defend yourself. And when the battle is over, you will still be standing firm.

[14]Be ready! Let the truth be like a belt around your waist, and let God's justice protect you like armor. [15]Your desire to tell the good news about peace should be like shoes on your feet. [16]Let your faith be like a shield, and you will be able to stop all the flaming arrows of the evil one. [17]Let God's saving power be like a helmet, and for a sword use God's message that comes from the Spirit.

[18]Never stop praying, especially for others. Always pray by the power of the Spirit. Stay alert and keep praying for God's people. [19]Pray that I will be given the message to speak and that I may fearlessly explain the mystery about the good news. [20]I was sent to do this work, and this is the reason I am in jail. So pray that I will be brave and will speak as I should.

Final Greetings

[21-22]I want you to know how I am getting along and what I am doing. This is why I am sending Tychicus to you. He is a dear friend, as well as a faithful servant of the Lord. He will tell you how I am doing, and he will cheer you up.

[23]I pray that God the Father and the Lord Jesus Christ will give peace, love, and faith to every follower! [24]May God be kind to everyone who keeps on loving our Lord Jesus Christ.

[m]6.13 *that evil day:* Either the present (see 5.16) or "the day of death" or "the day of judgment."

Reflection Questions About Ephesians 1.1—6.24

1. What is the "truth" that Christ brought (1.13)? How does this truth differ from other kinds of truth?

2. Who belongs to God's family (2.14-19)? How does someone become part of God's family?

3. What seven things do the people of God share (4.4-6)? Choose one of these things and describe in your own words what it means.

4. List the things that are part of a Christian's "old life," and list the "rules" for the "new life" (4.17—5.5).

5. Take time to re-read the description of "the armor that God gives" (6.10-17). Which pieces of *your* spiritual armor need shining, reinforcing, or sharpening?

philippians

God's messengers may be imprisoned, but the truth about Christ cannot be locked up. Read PHILIPPIANS *to find out how the apostle Paul found courage in times of trouble.*

WHAT MAKES PHILIPPIANS SPECIAL?

The apostle Paul wrote this letter to the Lord's followers at Philippi while he was in jail in a city he does not name. Even though he faced difficult times, Paul wanted to remind the Philippians to remain faithful to the good news about Christ that Paul had first preached to them (Acts 16.12-40; Phil 4.15-17). Paul reminds the Philippians that they may have to face suffering, just as he has suffered (1.30; 2.17,18), but they should not be afraid of such suffering, since "Christ gives . . . the strength to face anything" (4.13). Paul's strong words of faith in this short letter have given encouragement to Christians ever since it was first written.

Paul wanted to thank the Philippians for helping him with their gifts and prayers (1.5; 4.10-19) and to tell them what had been happening to him since he was arrested by the Romans. Paul was also aware of problems among the followers in the church he had organized at Philippi some time earlier. The Christians there were arguing about whether or not the new followers of Jesus needed to obey the Law of Moses (3.2-11).

WHAT'S THE STORY BEHIND THE SCENE?

The author of ACTS reports that Philippi was the very first city Paul visited after he crossed over to southeastern Europe from Asia Minor (Acts 16.11,12). Philippi was an important city of Macedonia, located on the eastern end of the major highway called the Egnatian Way, which merchants and the Roman army used to carry goods and supplies between the eastern part of the empire and Rome in the west. Philippi was named after Philip II, the father of Alexander the Great. Philip made the city into a fortress and the capital of his growing kingdom in the fourth century B.C.

PHILIPPIANS is considered one of Paul's Prison Letters (along with EPHESIANS, COLOSSIANS, and PHILEMON) because Paul most likely wrote it from jail. It is not known exactly how many times Paul was in jail or in how many different places. ACTS, however, says that Paul was imprisoned in Ephesus (Acts 19.1-21) and Caesarea (Acts 24.24—26.32), and was under house arrest in Rome (Acts 28.11-30). Paul may have written PHILIPPIANS from one of these cities or from some other city in the eastern Mediterranean, where Roman guards were stationed (1.13).

HOW IS PHILIPPIANS CONSTRUCTED?

Paul begins his letter with a Christian form of the words of greeting traditionally used in formal Greek letter writing, and he ends with a final greeting (4.21-23). As in many of Paul's letters, the introduction is followed by prayers of thanksgiving for the people he addresses. In the rest of the letter, Paul gives news about his present situation, offers advice and encouragement to the Philippian Christians, and expresses his thanks for the help they had given him in the past.

PHILIPPIANS can be outlined in the following way:

Paul greets and gives thanks for the Philippians (1.1-11)
Living for Christ, God's humble servant (1.12—2.18)
Encouragement and advice (2.19—4.9)
Final words of thanks and greeting (4.10-23)

Philippi was an important city in ancient Greece located midway on a key travel route between western Asia Minor and Rome. Paul had helped establish the church here and the letter has many of the hallmarks of a friendship letter, indicating that Paul had great affection for this community of believers. Most likely the letter was written from prison in Rome, Caesarea, or Ephesus. Paul thanks the Philippians for their prayers and gifts, uses a beautiful hymn to teach them about true humility, warns them against false teaching, encourages them in their faith in Jesus, and explains how God has strengthened him since he was arrested by the Romans.

Outline

1

From Paul and Timothy, servants of Christ Jesus.

To all God's people who belong to Christ Jesus at Philippi and to all your bishops and deacons.

²I pray that God our Father and the Lord Jesus Christ will be kind to you and will bless you with peace!

Paul's Prayer for the Church in Philippi

³Every time I think of you, I thank my God. ⁴And whenever I mention you in my prayers, it makes me happy. ⁵This is because you have taken part with me in spreading the good news from the first day you heard about it. ⁶God is the one who began this good work in you, and I am certain that he won't stop before it is complete on the day that Christ Jesus returns.

⁷You have a special place in my heart. So it is only natural for me to feel the way I do. All of you have helped in the work God has given me, as I defend the good news and tell about it here in jail. ⁸God himself knows how much I want to see you. He knows I care for you in the same way Christ Jesus does.

⁹I pray that your love will keep on growing and you will fully know and understand ¹⁰how to make the right choices. Then you will still be pure and innocent when Christ returns. And until that day, ¹¹Jesus Christ will keep you busy doing good deeds that bring glory and praise to God.

What Life Means to Paul

¹²My dear friends, I want you to know that what has happened to me has helped to spread the good news. ¹³The Roman guards and all the others know I am here in jail because I serve Christ. ¹⁴Now most of the Lord's followers have become brave and are fearlessly telling the message.[a]

¹⁵Some are preaching about Christ

---

[a]**1.14** *the message:* Some manuscripts have "the Lord's message," and others have "God's message."

1.1 *Paul and Timothy:* As a Pharisee, Paul had been a strict follower of the Law of Moses. Now he identifies himself as a servant of Christ Jesus. Timothy was the son of a Jewish Christian mother and a Gentile father from Lystra. He is named as Paul's coworker in many of Paul's letters (1 Cor 4.17; 2 Cor 1.1; 1 Thes 1.1; Phlm 1).

Paul (Saul) of Tarsus

1.1 *bishops and deacons:* Bishops were the top leaders of each group of Jesus' followers in Philippi. Deacons helped meet the direct needs of the people in the churches by handling the distribution of food and money.

1.2 *God our Father . . . Lord:* Paul uses the term "Father" in many of his letters to describe God (Gal 1.2,3; 1 Cor 1.3; Rom 1.7). When it is used for Jesus, "Lord" emphasizes his authority and power.

Lord (Title for Jesus)

1.5 *spreading the good news:* The good news (or "gospel") is both the message about Jesus and the message Jesus brings about God's kingdom.

Second Coming

1.7 *here in jail:* Paul may have been writing from some city in the eastern Mediterranean where Roman guards were stationed (1.13), or from Rome itself, where he was put under house arrest (Acts 28.16,30,31).

1.19 the Spirit of Christ Jesus: Paul mentions the Holy Spirit a number of times in this letter. The Spirit acts as a helper to keep Paul safe (1.19), as one who brings unity to the followers of Jesus (2.1), and as the One who leads the Lord's followers in true worship (3.3).

Holy Spirit

1.23 die and be with Christ: Paul believes that those who are faithful followers of Christ will be with Christ after they die.

Eternal Life

1.28 enemies: Paul may be talking about the people he later describes as "dogs" (3.2) who were trying to turn the people away from the good news, or he may be referring to any group who made trouble for Christ's followers at Philippi.

1.30 You saw me suffer . . . Now you must suffer: Paul was badly beaten and put in prison the first time he was in Philippi (Acts 16.16-40). Now he is in prison again. Regardless of the circumstances, Paul sees his suffering as an opportunity to serve Christ.

2.6 Christ was truly God: This same idea is expressed in John 1.1-18 and Colossians 1.15-20. The authors of the New Testament and the teachings of the early church leaders agreed that Jesus was truly God, but also truly human (2.7). Verses 6 to 11 are probably an early Christian hymn that the Philippians might have known.

because they are jealous and envious of us. Others are preaching because they want to help. [16]They love Christ and know I am here to defend the good news about him. [17]But the ones who are jealous of us are not sincere. They just want to cause trouble for me while I am in jail. [18]But that doesn't matter. All that matters is that people are telling about Christ, whether they are sincere or not. This is what makes me glad.

I will keep on being glad, [19]because I know that your prayers and the help that comes from the Spirit of Christ Jesus will keep me safe. [20]I honestly expect and hope I will never do anything to be ashamed of. Whether I live or die, I always want to be as brave as I am now and bring honor to Christ.

[21]If I live, it will be for Christ, and if I die, I will gain even more. [22]I don't know what to choose. I could keep on living and doing something useful. [23]It is a hard choice to make. I want to die and be with Christ, because this would be much better. [24-25]But I know that all of you still need me. This is why I am sure I will stay on to help you grow and be happy in your faith. [26]Then, when I visit you again, you will have good reason to take great pride in Christ Jesus because of me.[b]

[27]Above all else, you must live in a way that brings honor to the good news about Christ. Then, whether I visit you or not, I will hear that all of you think alike. I will know that you are working together and are struggling side by side to get others to believe the good news.

[28]Be brave when you face your enemies. Your courage will show them that they are going to be destroyed, and it will show you

that you will be saved. God will make all of this happen, [29]and he has blessed you. Not only do you have faith in Christ, but you suffer for him. [30]You saw me suffer, and you still hear about my troubles. Now you must suffer in the same way.

True Humility

2 Christ encourages you, and his love comforts you. God's Spirit unites you, and you are concerned for others. [2]Now make me completely happy! Live in harmony by showing love for each other. Be united in what you think, as if you were only one person. [3]Don't be jealous or proud, but be humble and consider others more important than yourselves. [4]Care about them as much as you care about yourselves [5]and think the same way that Christ Jesus thought:[c]

> [6]Christ was truly God.
> But he did not try to remain[d]
> equal with God.
> [7]Instead he gave up everything[e]
> and became a slave,
> when he became
> like one of us.
>
> [8]Christ was humble.
> He obeyed God and even died
> on a cross.
> [9]Then God gave Christ
> the highest place
> and honored his name
> above all others.
>
> [10]So at the name of Jesus
> everyone will bow down,
> those in heaven, on earth,

[b]**1.26** *take great pride in Christ Jesus because of me:* Or "take great pride in me because of Christ Jesus." [c]**2.5** *think the same way that Christ Jesus thought:* Or "think the way you should because you belong to Christ Jesus." [d]**2.6** *remain:* Or "become." [e]**2.7** *he gave up everything:* Greek, "he emptied himself."

and under the earth.
¹¹And to the glory
of God the Father
everyone will openly agree,
"Jesus Christ is Lord!"

Lights in the World

¹²My dear friends, you always obeyed when I was with you. Now that I am away, you should obey even more. So work with fear and trembling to discover what it really means to be saved. ¹³God is working in you to make you willing and able to obey him.

¹⁴Do everything without grumbling or arguing. ¹⁵Then you will be the pure and innocent children of God. You live among people who are crooked and evil, but you must not do anything they can say is wrong. Try to shine as lights among the people of this world, ¹⁶as you hold firmly to^f the message that gives life. Then on the day when Christ returns, I can take pride in you. I can also know that my work and efforts were not useless.

¹⁷Your faith in the Lord and your service are like a sacrifice offered to him. And my own blood may have to be poured out with the sacrifice.^g If this happens, I will be glad and rejoice with you. ¹⁸In the same way, you should be glad and rejoice with me.

Timothy and Epaphroditus

¹⁹I want to be encouraged by news about you. So I hope the Lord Jesus will soon let me send Timothy to you. ²⁰I don't have anyone else who cares about you as much as he does. ²¹The others think only about what interests them and not about what

concerns Christ Jesus. ²²But you know what kind of person Timothy is. He has worked with me like a son in spreading the good news. ²³I hope to send him to you, as soon as I find out what is going to happen to me. ²⁴And I feel sure the Lord will also let me come soon.

²⁵I think I ought to send my dear friend Epaphroditus back to you. He is a follower and a worker and a soldier of the Lord, just as I am. You sent him to look after me, ²⁶but now he is eager to see you. He is worried, because you heard he was sick. ²⁷In fact, he was very sick and almost died. But God was kind to him, and also to me, and he kept me from being burdened down with sorrow.

²⁸Now I am more eager than ever to send Epaphroditus back again. You will be glad to see him, and I won't have to worry any longer. ²⁹Be sure to give him a cheerful welcome, just as people who serve the Lord deserve. ³⁰He almost died working for Christ, and he risked his own life to do for me what you could not.

Being Acceptable to God

3 Finally, my dear friends, be glad that you belong to the Lord. It doesn't bother me to write the same things to you that I have written before. In fact, it is for your own good.

²Watch out for those people who behave like dogs! They are evil and want to do more than just circumcise you. ³But we are the ones who are truly circumcised, because we worship by the power of God's Spirit^h and take pride in Christ Jesus. We don't brag about what we have done, ⁴although I could. Others may brag about

---

2.11 *Jesus Christ is Lord:* When people said in public, "Jesus is Lord," it showed that they believed that Jesus was truly God and that he was the master of their lives.

2.12 *to be saved:* Different words in the Bible are translated as "salvation," "save," and "savior." All of them point to what God does to free humans from sin and the powers of evil.

God's Saving Love (Salvation)

Eternal Life

2.15 *shine as lights:* Many biblical writers use "light" to describe God or God's word (Ps 119.105; 1 John 1.5), and those people or things that reveal God's truth (Isa 49.6). The followers of Jesus are sometimes called "children of light" (John 12.36; Eph 5.8) and "light for the whole world" (Matt 5.14-16).

2.17 *my own blood . . . the sacrifice:* The Law of Moses required that the Jewish people offer sacrifices to God. Here Paul says that faith in the Lord and lives of service are the sacrifices that God expects (2.17). Paul believes his own blood may be poured out or sacrificed by people who want to make trouble for followers of Christ. If this should happen, Paul says, he would be glad to be able to serve God in this way.

---

^f**2.16** *hold firmly to:* Or "offer them." ^g**2.17** *my own blood may have to be poured out with the sacrifice:* Offerings of water or wine were sometimes poured out when animals were sacrificed on the altar. ^h**3.3** *by the power of God's Spirit:* Some manuscripts have "sincerely."

3.5 the tribe of Benjamin . . . a true Hebrew: Paul reminded the Philippian Christians that he was from a Jewish family (the people of Israel). Israel had twelve tribes named for the sons of Jacob (Gen 49.1-28). Paul belonged to the tribe named for Jacob's youngest son, Benjamin (Rom 11.1).

Israel

3.5 *Pharisee . . . Law of Moses:* The name "Pharisee" may come from a word meaning "pure ones." They were especially strict about obeying the Law of Moses and opposed those who taught anything different. The Law of Moses refers to the first five books of the Jewish Scriptures—Genesis, Exodus, Leviticus, Numbers, and Deuteronomy.

Law

3.9 *faith in Christ:* As a follower of Christ, Paul now believed that God accepted those who had faith in Christ rather than those who tried to gain God's favor by obeying the Law of Moses.

3.11 *I also may be raised to life:* Paul is talking about being raised to life from death.

Resurrection

Eternal Life

Second Coming

themselves, but I have more reason to brag than anyone else. [5]I was circumcised when I was eight days old,[i] and I am from the nation of Israel and the tribe of Benjamin. I am a true Hebrew. As a Pharisee, I strictly obeyed the Law of Moses. [6]And I was so eager I even made trouble for the church. I did everything the Law demands in order to please God.

[7]But Christ has shown me that what I once thought was valuable is worthless. [8]Nothing is as wonderful as knowing Christ Jesus my Lord. I have given up everything else and count it all as garbage. All I want is Christ [9]and to know that I belong to him. I could not make myself acceptable to God by obeying the Law of Moses. God accepted me simply because of my faith in Christ. [10]All I want is to know Christ and the power that raised him to life. I want to suffer and die as he did, [11]so that somehow I also may be raised to life.

Running toward the Goal

[12]I have not yet reached my goal, and I am not perfect. But Christ has taken hold of me. So I keep on running and struggling to take hold of the prize. [13]My friends, I don't feel I have already arrived. But I forget what is behind, and I struggle for what is ahead. [14]I run toward the goal, so I can win the prize of being called to heaven. This is the prize God offers because of what Christ Jesus has done. [15]All of us who are mature should think in this same way. And if any of you think differently, God will make it clear to you. [16]But we must keep going in the direction that we are now headed.

[17]My friends, I want you to follow my example and learn from others who closely follow the example we set for you. [18]I often warned you that many people are living as enemies of the cross of Christ. And now with tears in my eyes, I warn you again [19]that they are headed for hell! They worship their stomachs and brag about the disgusting things they do. All they can think about are the things of this world.

[20]But we are citizens of heaven and are eagerly waiting for our Savior to come from there. Our Lord Jesus Christ [21]has power over everything, and he will make these poor bodies of ours like his own glorious body.

4 Dear friends, I love you and long to see you. Please keep on being faithful to the Lord. You are my pride and joy.

Paul Encourages the Lord's Followers

[2]Euodia and Syntyche, you belong to the Lord, so I beg you to stop arguing with each other. [3]And, my true partner,[j] I ask you to help them. These women have worked together with me and with Clement and with the others in spreading the good news. Their names are now written in the book of life.[k]

[4]Always be glad because of the Lord! I will say it again: Be glad. [5]Always be gentle with others. The Lord will soon be here. [6]Don't worry about anything, but pray about everything. With thankful hearts offer up your prayers and requests to God. [7]Then, because you belong to Christ Jesus, God will bless you with peace that no one can completely understand. And this peace will control the way you think and feel.

[8]Finally, my friends, keep your minds on

[i]**3.5** *when I was eight days old:* Jewish boys are circumcised eight days after birth.   [j]**4.3** *partner:* Or "Syzygus," a person's name.   [k]**4.3** *the book of life:* A book in which the names of God's people are written.

Don't worry about anything, but pray about everything. With thankful hearts offer up your prayers and requests to God. Phil 4.6

whatever is true, pure, right, holy, friendly, and proper. Don't ever stop thinking about what is truly worthwhile and worthy of praise. [9]You know the teachings I gave you, and you know what you heard me say and saw me do. So follow my example. And God, who gives peace, will be with you.

Paul Gives Thanks for the Gifts He Was Given

[10]The Lord has made me very grateful that at last you have thought about me once again. Actually, you were thinking about me all along, but you didn't have any chance to show it. [11]I am not complaining about having too little. I have learned to be satisfied with[l] whatever I have. [12]I know what it is to be poor or to have plenty, and I have lived under all kinds of conditions. I know what it means to be full or to be hungry, to have too much or too little. [13]Christ gives me the strength to face anything.

[14]It was good of you to help me when I was having such a hard time. [15]My friends at Philippi, you remember what it was like when I started preaching the good news in Macedonia.[m] After I left there, you were the only church that became my partner by giving blessings and by receiving them in return. [16]Even when I was in Thessalonica, you helped me more than once. [17]I am not trying to get something from you, but I want you to receive the blessings that come from giving.

[18]I have been paid back everything, and with interest. I am completely satisfied with the gifts you sent with Epaphroditus. They are like a sweet-smelling offering or like the right kind of sacrifice that pleases God. [19]I pray that God will take care of all your needs with the wonderful blessings that come from Christ Jesus! [20]May God our Father be praised forever and ever. Amen.

Final Greetings

[21]Give my greetings to all who are God's people because of Christ Jesus.

The Lord's followers here with me send you their greetings.

[22]All of God's people send their greetings, especially those in the service of the Emperor.

[23]I pray that our Lord Jesus Christ will be kind to you and will bless your life!

4.15 *Macedonia:* A region in the northern part of Greece. Paul is talking about his first visit to Philippi (Acts 16.12-40).

4.16 *Thessalonica:* The capital of Macedonia. The Egnatian Way enters Thessalonica from the east, and passes under the Arch of Galerius, which commemorates the Roman victory over the Persians in A.D. 298.

4.22 *in the service of the Emperor:* May refer to some of the Roman soldiers who guarded Paul (1.13).

[l]**4.11** *be satisfied with:* Or "get by on."   [m]**4.15** *when I started preaching the good news in Macedonia:* Paul is talking about his first visit to Philippi (see Acts 16.12-40).

Reflection Questions About Philippians 1.1—4.23

1. What difference does it make knowing that Paul wrote his letter to the Philippians while he was a prisoner?

2. Paul describes choosing between living and dying as a difficult choice to make (1.21-26). Why is this so? What do you live for? What would you be willing to die for?

3. What does Paul mean when he says, "faith in the Lord and . . . service are like a sacrifice offered to him" (2.17)? What does it mean to be a servant of God?

4. Re-read Paul's advice in 4.4-6. Of all the things he commands, which would be the easiest for you to do? Which would be the hardest? Why?

5. Paul says "I have learned to be satisfied with whatever I have" (4.11). Have there been times in your life when you had very little? When you've had a lot? What do you need to be equally satisfied in either circumstance?

colossians

People are often searching for what is "real" in life.
Read COLOSSIANS *to find out about the real life that*
Christ brings.

WHAT MAKES COLOSSIANS SPECIAL?

The apostle Paul writes in his letters about the great change that is soon to come when Christ returns to conquer the powers of evil and to rule over the entire world. However, COLOSSIANS describes what Jesus Christ has already done. When Christ died on the cross, all the forces opposed to God were already defeated (2.15,20). This letter also includes a beautiful hymn that explains who Christ is (1.15-20). He is God's Son (1.15) and the head of "his body, which is the church" (1.18). The author goes on to say he is the key to God's mystery (2.2).

The author of COLOSSIANS wanted to encourage the Christians in Colossae to keep following Christ Jesus (2.6) and not to be fooled by false teachings or tricked into following any of the many religious ideas and practices that were being taught in Asia Minor at that time (2.8,16-23). The author also wanted to convince the Colossians to "live a life that honors the Lord" (1.10). This meant that they were to leave behind the bad things that were part of their old life (3.1-9) and live as God's special people who are kind, humble, meek, patient, forgiving, and loving (3.12-14). The author's advice also included some rules about how family members were to treat each other.

WHAT'S THE STORY BEHIND THE SCENE?

Colossae was a small inland city in Asia Minor, east of the major port city of Ephesus and close to the cities of Laodicea and Hierapolis. All four cities are mentioned in this letter. The writer of COLOSSIANS had never actually been to Colossae, but he was pleased to learn that the Christians there were strong in their faith (1.3-7; 2.6,7). Instead, the Colossians had heard the good news about Jesus from Epaphras, one of Paul's co-workers, who had once lived in Colossae (1.7; 4.12,13).

Some scholars believe this letter may have been written by one of Paul's followers in the decades after Paul's death in A.D. 64 or 65, rather than by Paul himself. It was not unusual in the ancient world for a follower to honor his or her teacher by writing something in the teacher's name.

HOW IS COLOSSIANS CONSTRUCTED?

COLOSSIANS is a letter that includes opening and concluding greetings that are similar to the ones found in several of Paul's letters. The opening greeting (1.1,2) is nearly identical to the opening of EPHESIANS (Eph 1.1,2). The letter can be outlined in this way:

Greetings, prayers, and a hymn to Christ (1.1-23)
Paul teaches the truth about Christ (1.24—2.19)
Living the new life in Christ (2.20—4.6)
Final greetings and advice (4.7-18)

This letter was written to the Christian community in Colossae, a small city in Asia Minor that would later be destroyed by an earthquake. The church in Colossae was established not by Paul, but by Epaphras, a Christian leader who is mentioned several times in the letter and who was in prison with Paul at the time the letter was written. The letter warns the Colossian Christians against false teachings that value special or mystical knowledge over faith. It also warns against religious practices that include the worship of angels and extreme self-denial. Reminding his readers that Christ is the key to God's mystery, the author explains what it means to be raised to life with Christ. The letter urges the Colossians to let this message about Jesus fill their lives, and it lists rules for Christian living.

Outline

1

¹From Paul, chosen by God to be an apostle of Christ Jesus, and from Timothy, who is also a follower.

²To God's people who live in Colossae and are faithful followers of Christ.

I pray that God our Father will be kind to you and will bless you with peace!

A Prayer of Thanks

³Each time we pray for you, we thank God, the Father of our Lord Jesus Christ. ⁴We have heard of your faith in Christ and of your love for all God's people, ⁵because what you hope for is kept safe for you in heaven. You first heard about this hope when you believed the true message, which is the good news.

⁶The good news is spreading all over the world with great success. It has spread in this same way among you, ever since the first day you learned the truth about God's wonderful kindness ⁷from our good friend Epaphras. He works together with us for Christ and is a faithful worker for you.[a] ⁸He is also the one who told us about the love that God's Spirit has given you.

The Person and Work of Christ

⁹We have not stopped praying for you since the first day we heard about you. In fact, we always pray that God will show you everything he wants you to do and that you may have all the wisdom and understanding his Spirit gives. ¹⁰Then you will live a life that honors the Lord, and you will always please him by doing good deeds. You will come to know God even better. ¹¹His glorious power will make you patient and strong enough to endure anything, and you will be truly happy.

¹²I pray that you will be grateful to God for letting you[a] have part in what he has promised his people in the kingdom of light. ¹³God rescued us from the dark

---

a 1.7,12 *you:* Some manuscripts have "us."

1.14 *forgives our sins:* Sin is rebellion against God and disobedience to God's Law. Forgiveness removes sin as a barrier between the sinner and God. According to the Jewish Scriptures (Old Testament), sinners could be forgiven by turning back to God and by making a sacrifice commanded by the Law of Moses. Jesus died to take away sins (Rom 3.25,26; Eph 1.7,8).

◌ Sin

1.18 *head of his body . . . the church:* Christ is the head of the whole church, which Paul frequently called "the body of Christ" (Rom 12.5; 1 Cor 12.27; Eph 1.22,23).

◌ Church

1.18 *first to be raised from death:* After Jesus was put to death on a cross, God raised him from death (Matt 27.31—28.7; Acts 2.22-24,32).

◌ Resurrection

1.26,27 *secret . . . mystery:* The secret is the good news that Jesus Christ has saved people from sin and death (Rom 16.25,26). The author of EPHESIANS describes this mystery as God accepting Gentiles and giving them a share of the same promises he gave to the Jews (Eph 3.3-6).

1.27 *Gentiles:* Most of the people in Colossae were not Jewish.

◌ Gentiles

power of Satan and brought us into the kingdom of his dear Son, **14**who forgives our sins and sets us free.

15Christ is exactly like God,
  who cannot be seen.
He is the first-born Son,
  superior to all creation.
16Everything was created by him,
  everything in heaven
    and on earth,
  everything seen and unseen,
including all forces
    and powers,
and all rulers
    and authorities.
All things were created
    by God's Son,
and everything was made
    for him.

17God's Son was before all else,
  and by him everything
    is held together.
18He is the head of his body,
  which is the church.
He is the very beginning,
  the first to be raised
    from death,
so that he would be
  above all others.

19God himself was pleased
  to live fully in his Son.
20And God was pleased
  for him to make peace
by sacrificing his blood
  on the cross,
so that all beings in heaven
  and on earth
would be brought back to God.

b1.24 *continue:* Or "complete."

21You used to be far from God. Your thoughts made you his enemies, and you did evil things. **22**But his Son became a human and died. So God made peace with you, and now he lets you stand in his presence as people who are holy and faultless and innocent. **23**But you must stay deeply rooted and firm in your faith. You must not give up the hope you received when you heard the good news. It was preached to everyone on earth, and I myself have become a servant of this message.

Paul's Service to the Church

24I am glad I can suffer for you. I am pleased also that in my own body I can continue**b** the suffering of Christ for his body, the church. **25**God's plan was to make me a servant of his church and to send me to preach his complete message to you. **26**For ages and ages this message was kept secret from everyone, but now it has been explained to God's people. **27**God did this because he wanted you Gentiles to understand his wonderful and glorious mystery. And the mystery is that Christ lives in you, and he is your hope of sharing in God's glory.

28We announce the message about Christ, and we use all our wisdom to warn and teach everyone, so all of Christ's followers will grow and become mature. **29**This is why I work so hard and use the mighty power he gives me.

2 I want you to know what a struggle I am going through for you, for God's people at Laodicea, and for all of those followers who have never met me. **2**I do it to encourage them. Then as their hearts are joined together in love, they will be wonderfully blessed with complete understanding. And they will truly know Christ. Not only is he the key to God's mystery, [3]but all wisdom and knowledge are hidden away in him. [4]I tell you these things to keep you from being fooled by fancy talk. [5]Even though I am not with you, I keep thinking about you. I am glad to know that you are living as you should and your faith in Christ is strong.

Christ Brings Real Life

[6]You have accepted Christ Jesus as your Lord. Now keep on following him. [7]Plant your roots in Christ and let him be the foundation for your life. Be strong in your faith, just as you were taught. And be grateful. [8]Don't let anyone fool you by using senseless arguments. These arguments may sound wise, but they are only human teachings. They come from the powers of this world[c] and not from Christ. [9]God lives fully in Christ. [10]And you are fully grown because you belong to Christ, who is over every power and authority. [11]Christ has also taken away your selfish desires, just as circumcision removes flesh from the body. [12]And when you were baptized, it was the same as being buried with Christ. Then you were raised to life because you had faith in the power of God, who raised Christ from death. [13]You were dead, because you were sinful and were not God's people. But God let Christ make you[d] alive, when he forgave all our sins. [14]God wiped out the charges that were against us for disobeying the Law of Moses. He took them away and nailed them to the cross. [15]There Christ defeated all powers and forces. He let the whole world see them being led away as prisoners when he celebrated his victory.

[16]Don't let anyone tell you what you must eat or drink. Don't let them say you must celebrate the New Moon festival, the Sabbath, or any other festival. [17]These things are only a shadow of what was to come. But Christ is real! [18]Don't be cheated by people who make a show of acting humble and who worship angels.[e] They brag about seeing visions. But it is all nonsense, because their minds are filled with selfish desires. [19]They are no longer part of Christ, who is the head of the whole body. Christ gives the body its strength, and he uses its joints and muscles to hold it together, as it grows by the power of God.

Christ Brings New Life

[20]You died with Christ. Now the forces of the universe[f] don't have any power over you. Why do you live as if you had to obey such rules as, [21]"Don't handle this. Don't taste that. Don't touch this."? [22]After these things are used, they are no longer good for anything. So why be bothered with the rules that humans have made up? [23]Obeying these rules may seem to be the smart thing to do. They appear to make you love God more and to be very humble and to have control over your body. But they don't really have any power over our desires.

3 You have been raised to life with Christ. Now set your heart on what is in heaven, where Christ rules at God's

[c]**2.8** *powers of this world:* Spirits and unseen forces were thought to control human lives and were believed to be connected with the movements of the stars.   [d]**2.13** *you:* See the note at 1.7.   [e]**2.18** *worship angels:* Or "worship with angels (in visions of heaven)."   [f]**2.20** *forces of the universe:* See the note at 2.8.

Wisdom

2.12 *baptized . . . buried with Christ:* Being baptized is like dying to sin and being raised to life, just as Jesus died and then was raised to life by God (Rom 6.3-6).

Baptism

2.13 *You were dead . . . Christ . . . forgave all our sins:* The writer means that sin leads to separation from God, which is worse than death. Jesus defeated evil and death when he died on the cross and was raised to life by God. He also promised forgiveness to those who had faith in him.

Eternal Life

2.14 *Law of Moses . . . cross:* The Law of Moses refers to the set of instructions that God gave to Moses and the people of Israel at Mount Sinai. When Jesus died on the cross, he removed the guilt (the "charges") that came from disobeying the Law of Moses.

2.18 *acting humble . . . worship angels:* Those who made a show of being humble may have been the pious people mentioned in 2.16. The worship of angels may refer to some kind of mystery cult in which the participants worshiped certain heavenly beings or had visions of angels.

3.4 *when he appears:* Paul often wrote in his letters about a day when Jesus would come back (1 Cor 1.8,9; 15.20-28; 1 Thes 4.13-18; Phil 1.6; 3.20,21).

Second Coming

3.5 *wrong kind of sex . . . worshiping idols:* Those who have a new life in Christ are to avoid having sexual relations forbidden by the Law of Moses and impure sexual thoughts and desires (Matt 5.27,28, 31,32; Rom 1.24-27; 1 Cor 5.1-5; Gal 5.19; Eph 5.3). The Bible says greed is as bad as worshiping idols (Matt 6.24; Eph 5.5).

3.9 *your old way of life:* The Colossians had been doing things that were opposed to the will of God and the new life that comes from Jesus. What they were doing may have been like what Paul criticized the Corinthians for doing (1 Cor 5,6; 10,11).

Slaves and Servants in the Time of Jesus

3.18,19 *wife . . . husband:* Just as wives are to honor their husbands and put them first, husbands are to love their wives as much as Christ loved the church. See also 1 Pet 3.7; Gal 3.28,29; Eph 5.22-25.

3.22—4.1 *Slaves . . . Slave owners:* The writer argues that when slaves serve their masters they are really serving Christ, who will punish evil people, including evil slave owners.

right side.[g] [2] Think about what is up there, not about what is here on earth. [3] You died, which means that your life is hidden with Christ, who sits beside God. [4] Christ gives meaning to your[h] life, and when he appears, you will also appear with him in glory.

[5] Don't be controlled by your body. Kill every desire for the wrong kind of sex. Don't be immoral or indecent or have evil thoughts. Don't be greedy, which is the same as worshiping idols. [6] God is angry with people who disobey him by doing[i] these things. [7] And this is exactly what you did, when you lived among people who behaved in this way. [8] But now you must stop doing such things. You must quit being angry, hateful, and evil. You must no longer say insulting or cruel things about others. [9] And stop lying to each other. You have given up your old way of life with its habits. [10] Each of you is now a new person. You are becoming more and more like your Creator, and you will understand him better. [11] It doesn't matter if you are a Greek or a Jew, or if you are circumcised or not. You may even be a barbarian or a Scythian,[j] and you may be a slave or a free person. Yet Christ is all that matters, and he lives in all of us.

[12] God loves you and has chosen you as his own special people. So be gentle, kind, humble, meek, and patient. [13] Put up with each other, and forgive anyone who does you wrong, just as Christ has forgiven you. [14] Love is more important than anything else. It is what ties everything completely together.

[15] Each one of you is part of the body of Christ, and you were chosen to live together in peace. So let the peace that comes from Christ control your thoughts. And be grateful. [16] Let the message about Christ completely fill your lives, while you use all your wisdom to teach and instruct each other. With thankful hearts, sing psalms, hymns, and spiritual songs to God. [17] Whatever you say or do should be done in the name of the Lord Jesus, as you give thanks to God the Father because of him.

Some Rules for Christian Living

[18] A wife must put her husband first. This is her duty as a follower of the Lord.

[19] A husband must love his wife and not abuse her.

[20] Children must always obey their parents. This pleases the Lord.

[21] Parents, don't be hard on your children. If you are, they might give up.

[22] Slaves, you must always obey your earthly masters. Try to please them at all times, and not just when you think they are watching. Honor the Lord and serve your masters with your whole heart. [23] Do your work willingly, as though you were serving the Lord himself, and not just your earthly master. [24] In fact, the Lord Christ is the one you are really serving, and you know he will reward you. [25] But Christ has no favorites! He will punish evil people, just as they deserve.

4 Slave owners, be fair and honest with your slaves. Don't forget that you have a Master in heaven.

[2] Never give up praying. And when you pray, keep alert and be thankful. [3] Be sure to pray that God will make a way for us to spread his message and explain the mystery about Christ, even though I am in jail

[g]3.1 *right side:* The place of power and honor.   [h]3.4 *your:* Some manuscripts have "our."   [i]3.6 *people who disobey him by doing:* Some manuscripts do not have these words.   [j]3.11 *a barbarian or a Scythian:* Barbarians were people who could not speak Greek and would be in the lower class of society. Scythians were people who were known for their cruelty.

Let the message about Christ completely fill your lives, while you use all your wisdom to teach and instruct each other.
COL 3.16

for doing this. [4]Please pray that I will make the message as clear as possible.

[5]When you are with unbelievers, always make good use of the time. [6]Be pleasant and hold their interest when you speak the message. Choose your words carefully and be ready to give answers to anyone who asks questions.

Final Greetings

[7]Tychicus is the dear friend, who faithfully works and serves the Lord with us, and he will give you the news about me. [8]I am sending him to cheer you up by telling you how we are getting along. [9]Onesimus, the dear and faithful follower from your own group, is coming with him. The two of them will tell you everything that has happened here.

[10]Aristarchus is in jail with me. He sends greetings to you, and so does Mark, the cousin of Barnabas. You have already been told to welcome Mark, if he visits you. [11]Jesus, who is known as Justus, sends his greetings. These three men are the only Jewish followers who have worked with me for the kingdom of God. They have given me much comfort.

[12]Your own Epaphras, who serves Christ Jesus, sends his greetings. He always prays hard that you may fully know what the Lord wants you to do and that you may do it completely. [13]I have seen how much trouble he has gone through for you and for the followers in Laodicea and Hierapolis.

[14]Our dear doctor Luke sends you his greetings, and so does Demas.

[15]Give my greetings to the followers at Laodicea, especially to Nympha and the church that meets in her home.

[16]After this letter has been read to your people, be sure to have it read in the church at Laodicea. And you should read the letter that I have sent to them.[k]

[17]Remind Archippus to do the work that the Lord has given him to do.

[18]I am signing this letter myself: PAUL. Don't forget that I am in jail.
I pray that God will be kind to you.

4.7 *Tychicus:* Tychicus, whose name means "lucky," was from Asia Minor. He traveled with Paul (Acts 20.4,5) and delivered messages for him (Eph 6.21,22; 2 Tim 4.12; Titus 3.12).

4.9 *Onesimus:* Onesimus, whose name means "useful," had been a slave of Philemon (see the book of PHILEMON).

4.10-17 *Aristarchus . . . Archippus:* Most of the people mentioned in these verses are mentioned elsewhere in the New Testament:
Aristarchus (Acts 19.29; 20.4,5; 27.2, Phlm 24)
Mark (Acts 11.27-30; 12.12,24,25; 13.13; 15.36-39; 2 Tim 4.11)
Epaphras (Col 1.7; Phlm 23)
Luke (Phlm 24; 2 Tim 4.11)
Demas (Phlm 24; 2 Tim 4.10)
Archippus (Phlm 2)
Jesus (Justus) and Nympha are mentioned only here in COLOSSIANS.

4.13 *Laodicea and Hierapolis:* Laodicea was located about twelve miles west of Colossae. Hierapolis was a city famous for its dye and textile industry. It was located six miles away from Laodicea in the Upper Lycus Valley.

4.18 *I am signing this letter myself:* This seems to indicate that the letter was dictated to a secretary of some sort.

---

[k]**4.16** *the letter that I have sent to them:* This is the only mention of the letter to the church at Laodicea.

Reflection Questions About Colossians 1.1—4.18

1. What does Paul pray for concerning the Colossians (1.9-12)? What does it mean to "live a life that honors the Lord"?

2. What is the message that Paul says had been kept secret for ages and ages, and why is it important to the Colossians (1.24-28)?

3. How is Paul's message different from the message that others are trying to teach the Colossians (2.8-23)? What messages in the world today pull people away from the new life that God offers in Christ Jesus?

4. Paul says those who trust in Christ are "new persons" (3.10) and God's "own special people" (3.12). What are some of the things God's people should not do (3.5-9)? What are the qualities God's people should begin to practice (3.12-17)?

5. Take the time to re-read what Paul had to say about spreading the message and explaining the mystery about Christ (4.2-6). What advice does he give about how to treat unbelievers? Which of Paul's points will help you most the next time you try to share your faith with someone?

1 thessalonians

What happens when we die? Find out what Paul says about this when he writes to his good friends in Thessalonica.

WHAT MAKES 1 THESSALONIANS SPECIAL?

This letter may have been written as early as A.D. 43 and is most likely the oldest of Paul's letters. First Thessalonians may even be the earliest of all New Testament writings. This short letter gives us a look at the relationship Paul had with the Thessalonian church. Over half the letter is devoted to his prayers and thanksgiving for their faith. Paul is like a pastor who is concerned for his congregation and thankful for the time he has spent with them. Repeatedly, Paul uses phrases like "You know" and "You remember," and reminds the Thessalonians what they have learned from him. It is clear that he is writing to people who already follow Jesus Christ.

Paul wanted to greet the Thessalonians and thank them for their faithfulness. He also wanted them to know that he intended to visit them again (3.11). Apparently, some of the Thessalonian followers had questions about what would happen to followers who had died before Christ returned, so Paul included an answer to this question (4.13-18). He followed up this advice by reminding them to be on the lookout for Christ's return at all times (5.1-11). As in most of his letters, Paul offers advice about how to live in a way that pleases God (4.1-12).

WHAT'S THE STORY BEHIND THE SCENE?

Cassander, a general of Alexander the Great, founded Thessalonica in 316 B.C. and named it after Alexander's stepsister. Built in foothills and along slopes, Thessalonica rises above its harbor to the Aegean Sea. The Romans conquered the area in 168 B.C. and made Thessalonica capital of the Roman province of Macedonia. The city was located on a major east-west highway, and served the Romans as a military and commercial base. Many of its people had worshiped idols before becoming Christians (1.9). They were now faithful to the Lord, and because of them the Lord's message had spread everywhere in the region (1.7,8).

The author of Acts describes Paul's ministry among the Thessalonians (Acts 17.1-10). It's not certain how long Paul stayed in Thessalonica. In this letter, Paul says that he worked long and hard to support himself (2.9) while starting the church in Thessalonica. This suggests that he stayed for at least several months.

HOW IS 1 THESSALONIANS CONSTRUCTED?

The letter can be outlined in the following way:

The Thessalonians' faith and Paul's work
  (1.1—3.13)
Christian living and Christ's return (4.1—5.22)
Final greetings (5.23-28)

First Thessalonians was most likely the first of the New Testament books to be written. While many of Paul's letters were written to help Christians who were challenged by false teachings, 1 Thessalonians was written to thank the Christians in Thessalonica for remaining faithful to Jesus, and Paul's affection for this community in northern Greece is evident throughout the letter. He reminds them of the hard work involved in spreading Christ's message and lets them know he would like to visit them again. Paul devotes the rest of this short letter to teachings about how to live in a way that pleases God. He also describes what will happen when Christ returns and urges the followers to remain watchful.

Outline

1

From Paul, Silas,[a] and Timothy.

To the church in Thessalonica, the people of God the Father and of the Lord Jesus Christ.

I pray that God will be kind to you and will bless you with peace!

²We thank God for you and always mention you in our prayers. Each time we pray, ³we tell God our Father about your faith and loving work and about your firm hope in our Lord Jesus Christ.

The Thessalonians' Faith and Example

⁴My dear friends, God loves you, and we know he has chosen you to be his people. ⁵When we told you the good news, it was with the power and assurance that come from the Holy Spirit, and not simply with words. You knew what kind of people we were and how we helped you. ⁶So, when you accepted the message, you followed our example and the example of the Lord.

You suffered, but the Holy Spirit made you glad.

⁷You became an example for all the Lord's followers in Macedonia and Achaia. ⁸And because of you, the Lord's message has spread everywhere in those regions. Now the news of your faith in God is known all over the world, and we don't have to say a thing about it. ⁹Everyone is talking about how you welcomed us and how you turned away from idols to serve the true and living God. ¹⁰They also tell how you are waiting for his Son Jesus to come from heaven. God raised him from death, and on the day of judgment Jesus will save us from God's anger.

Paul's Work in Thessalonica

2

My friends, you know our time with you wasn't wasted. ²As you remember, we had been mistreated and insulted at Philippi. But God gave us the courage to tell you the good news about him, even

[a]**1.1** *Silas:* The Greek text has "Silvanus," another form of the name Silas.

1.1 *Paul, Silas and Timothy:* Timothy is named as Paul's co-worker in many of Paul's letters (1 Cor 16.10; 2 Cor 1.1; Phlm 1). Paul sent Timothy to help the Thessalonians settle some disputes (3.2-6). The apostles and church leaders in Jerusalem sent Silas along with Paul to start new churches among the Gentiles (Acts 15.22). They were put in prison in Philippi (Acts 16.16-40) and later were attacked by a mob at Thessalonica (Acts 17.1-9).

Paul (Saul) of Tarsus

Church

Faith

1.5 *good news . . . Holy Spirit:* The good news is both the message about Jesus and the message Jesus brings about God's kingdom. Those who believe the good news will become part of God's new family of followers.

1.10 *waiting for his Son . . . heaven . . . day of judgment Jesus will save us:* Paul often wrote about a day when Jesus would come back (see 1 Cor 15.20-28; Phil 1.10). Those who have faith in Christ will be saved (John 12.44-50), but those who reject God will experience God's punishment (1 Thes 5.1-11).

Son of God

Heaven

God's Saving Love (Salvation)

Second Coming

2.3 *we didn't try to fool or trick anyone:* Paul claimed that his message came straight from God, and that his actions were honest and pure (2.9,10). Others may have tried to teach another message in order to make money (2.5) or to get a reputation (2.6), but Paul did not.

2.14 *like God's churches in Judea:* The Christian church began in Jerusalem in Judea (Acts 1,2). The earliest followers were Jewish, like Jesus and his twelve apostles. Many of these followers were treated badly (Acts 3–7). When the Thessalonians listened to Paul's teachings and began to follow Jesus Christ, their own Gentile neighbors made trouble for them (see Acts 17.5).

Church

2.15 *Those evil people:* Paul is referring specifically to those Jewish leaders who rejected Jesus and his claim to be God's Son. They cooperated with the Roman authorities in seeing that he was executed. Each of the Gospels reports the arrest, trial, and death of Jesus. It is not clear which prophets the author has in mind. See Acts 7.52; Jer 26.20-24.

2.16 *Gentiles:* Gentiles refers to those people who are not Jewish. Paul was chosen by God to bring the good news to all people, but his special mission was to the Gentiles (Acts 9.15; 15.12; Gal 2.1-9).

Gentiles

though many people caused us trouble. [3]We didn't have any hidden motives when we won you over, and we didn't try to fool or trick anyone. [4]God was pleased to trust us with his message. We didn't speak to please people, but to please God who knows our motives.

[5]You also know we didn't try to flatter anyone. God himself knows what we did wasn't a cover-up for greed. [6]We were not trying to get you or anyone else to praise us. [7]But as apostles, we could have demanded help from you. After all, Christ is the one who sent us. We chose to be like children or like a mother[b] nursing her baby. [8]We cared so much for you, and you became so dear to us, that we were willing to give our lives for you when we gave you God's message.

[9]My dear friends, you surely haven't forgotten our hard work and hardships. You remember how night and day we struggled to make a living, so we could tell you God's message without being a burden to anyone. [10]Both you and God are witnesses that we were pure and honest and innocent in our dealings with you followers of the Lord. [11]You also know we did everything for you that parents would do for their own children. [12]We begged, encouraged, and urged each of you to live in a way that would honor God. He is the one who chose you to share in his own kingdom and glory.

[13]We always thank God that you believed the message we preached. It came from him, and it isn't something made up by humans. You accepted it as God's message, and now he is working in you. [14]My friends, you did just like God's churches in Judea and like the other followers of Christ Jesus there. And so, you were mistreated by your own people, in the same way they were mistreated by their people.

[15]Those evil people killed the Lord Jesus and the prophets, and they even chased us away. God doesn't like what they do and neither does anyone else. [16]They keep us from speaking his message to the Gentiles and from leading them to be saved. They have always gone too far with their sins. Now God has finally become angry and will punish them.

Paul Wants To Visit the Church Again

[17]My friends, we were kept from coming to you for a while, but we never stopped thinking about you. We were eager to see you and tried our best to visit you in person. [18]We really wanted to come. I myself tried several times, but Satan always stopped us. [19]After all, when the Lord Jesus appears, who else but you will give us hope and joy and be like a glorious crown for us? [20]You alone are our glory and joy!

3 Finally, we couldn't stand it any longer. We decided to stay in Athens by ourselves [2]and send our friend Timothy to you. He works with us as God's servant and preaches the good news about Christ. We wanted him to make you strong in your faith and to encourage you. [3]We didn't want any of you to be discouraged by all these troubles. You knew we would have to suffer, [4]because when we were with you, we told you this would happen. And we did suffer, as you well know. [5]At last, when I could not wait any longer, I sent Timothy to find out about your faith. I hoped Satan had not tempted you and made all our work useless.

[6]Timothy has now come back from his visit with you and has told us about your faith and love. He also said that you always have happy memories of us and that you

[b]2.7 *like children or like a mother:* Some manuscripts have "as gentle as a mother."

want to see us as much as we want to see you.

[7] My friends, even though we have a lot of trouble and suffering, your faith makes us feel better about you. [8] Your strong faith in the Lord is like a breath of new life. [9] How can we possibly thank God enough for all the happiness you have brought us? [10] Day and night we sincerely pray that we will see you again and help you to have an even stronger faith.

[11] We pray that God our Father and our Lord Jesus will let us visit you. [12] May the Lord make your love for each other and for everyone else grow by leaps and bounds. This is how our love for you has grown. [13] And when our Lord comes with all his people, I pray he will make your hearts pure and innocent in the sight of God the Father.

A Life That Pleases God

4 Finally, my dear friends, since you belong to the Lord Jesus, we beg and urge you to live as we taught you. Then you will please God. You are already living that way, but try even harder. [2] Remember the instructions we gave you as followers of the Lord Jesus. [3] God wants you to be holy, so don't be immoral in matters of sex. [4] Respect and honor your wife.[c] [5] Don't be a slave of your desires or live like people who don't know God. [6] You must not cheat any of the Lord's followers in matters of sex.[d] Remember, we warned you that he punishes everyone who does such things. [7] God didn't choose you to be filthy, but to be pure. [8] So if you don't obey these rules, you are not really disobeying us. Instead, you are disobeying God, who gives you his Holy Spirit.

[9] We don't have to write you about the need to love each other. God has taught you to do this, [10] and you already have shown your love for all his people in Macedonia. But, my dear friends, we ask you to do even more. [11] Try your best to live quietly, to mind your own business, and to work hard, just as we taught you to do. [12] Then you will be respected by people who are not followers of the Lord, and you won't have to depend on anyone.

The Lord's Coming

[13] My friends, we want you to understand how it will be for those followers who have already died. Then you won't grieve over them and be like people who don't have any hope. [14] We believe Jesus died and was raised to life. We also believe that when God brings Jesus back again, he will bring with him all who had faith in Jesus before they died. [15] Our Lord Jesus told us that when he comes, we won't go up to meet him ahead of his followers who have already died.

[16] With a loud command and with the shout of the chief angel and a blast of God's trumpet, the Lord will return from heaven. Then those who had faith in Christ before they died will be raised to life. [17] Next, all of us who are still alive will be taken up into the clouds together with them to meet the Lord in the sky. From that time on we will all be with the Lord forever. [18] Encourage each other with these words.

5 I don't need to write you about the time or date when all this will happen. [2] You surely know that the Lord's return[e] will be as a thief coming at night. [3] People will think they are safe and secure. But destruction will suddenly strike them like

4.3 be holy, so don't be immoral: The Greek word translated here as "be holy" means to be set apart or chosen to do what God wants. Holy living includes avoiding immoral sexual behavior (Acts 15.20,29; 21.25; 1 Cor 5.1; Gal 5.19). In Thessalonica, sexual intercourse was sometimes practiced as part of certain pagan ceremonies.

4.8 if you don't obey these rules: The Thessalonian followers did not become God's children by keeping the rules set out in the Law of Moses; instead, the way they lived showed that they were part of God's people.

4.8 Holy Spirit: The Holy Spirit is the unseen power of God carrying out God's purposes in the world. For Paul, the Holy Spirit is present in the lives of Christ's followers to help them live in a way that pleases God.

Holy Spirit

4.16 raised to life: Those who have died but had faith in Jesus will be given a new life with a new spiritual body (1 Cor 15.35-44,51,52).

Resurrection

End Times

4.17 taken up into the clouds: Christ's followers who are still alive when Christ returns will be taken up to heaven in the same way that God took Jesus up to heaven.

Heaven

[c]**4.4** *your wife:* Or "your body."   [d]**4.6** *in matters of sex:* Or "in business."   [e]**5.2** *the Lord's return:* The Greek text has "the day of the Lord."

Try your best to live quietly, to mind your own business, and to work hard, just as we taught you to do. 1 Thes 4.11

5.5 *light . . . day . . . night . . . dark:* In the Bible, light is used to describe God or God's word (Ps 119.105; John 1.3, 4; 1 John 1.5), and people or things that reveal God's truth (Isa 49.6). The followers of Jesus are sometimes called "children of light" (Rom 12.36; Eph 5.8). God's opponents are called the rulers of darkness (Eph 6.12), and those who do not do what God expects risk being "thrown outside into the dark" (Matt 22.13).

5.19,20 *Don't turn away God's Spirit or ignore prophecies:* Paul described the first of the Holy Spirit in 1 Corinthians 12–14. **(See the article Prophets and Prophecy on pg 1791.)**

Spiritual Gifts

5.21 *Put everything to the test:* Paul knew that Christians were not the only ones who claimed to have visions or special messages from God. It was important for Christians to test everything they heard to make sure it agreed with what Paul taught.

5.23 *peace . . . spirit, soul, and body:* The kind of peace Paul talks about here includes more than just peace of mind or freedom from conflict. It includes a sense of well-being and the setting right of any disagreements among the members of God's people.

5.26 *warm greeting:* This can also be translated as "holy kiss."

the pains of a woman about to give birth. And they won't escape.

⁴My dear friends, you don't live in darkness, and so that day won't surprise you like a thief. ⁵You belong to the light and live in the day. We don't live in the night or belong to the dark. ⁶Others may sleep, but we should stay awake and be alert. ⁷People sleep during the night, and some even get drunk. ⁸But we belong to the day. So we must stay sober and let our faith and love be like a suit of armor. Our firm hope that we will be saved is our helmet.

⁹God doesn't intend to punish us, but wants us to be saved by our Lord Jesus Christ. ¹⁰Christ died for us, so we could live with him, whether we are alive or dead when he comes. ¹¹This is why you must encourage and help each other, just as you are already doing.

Final Instructions and Greetings

¹²My friends, we ask you to be thoughtful of your leaders who work hard and tell you how to live for the Lord. ¹³Show them great respect and love because of their work. Try to get along with each other.

¹⁴My friends, we beg you to warn anyone who isn't living right. Encourage anyone who feels left out, help all who are weak, and be patient with everyone. ¹⁵Don't be hateful to people, just because they are hateful to you. Rather, be good to each other and to everyone else.

¹⁶Always be joyful ¹⁷and never stop praying. ¹⁸Whatever happens, keep thanking God because of Jesus Christ. This is what God wants you to do.

¹⁹Don't turn away God's Spirit ²⁰or ignore prophecies. ²¹Put everything to the test. Accept what is good ²²and don't have anything to do with evil.

²³I pray that God, who gives peace, will make you completely holy. And may your spirit, soul, and body be kept healthy and faultless until our Lord Jesus Christ returns. ²⁴The one who chose you can be trusted, and he will do this.

²⁵Friends, please pray for us.

²⁶Give the Lord's followers a warm greeting.

²⁷In the name of the Lord I beg you to read this letter to all his followers.

²⁸I pray that our Lord Jesus Christ will be kind to you!

Reflection Questions About 1 Thessalonians 1.1—5.28

1. How had the Thessalonians been an example for other Christians in the area around them (1.7-9)?

2. In 2.1-12, Paul describes his work in Thessalonica. What does he say was his motivation for preaching? What does he imply would be wrong motives for preaching the good news?

3. Paul sent his friend Timothy to remind the Thessalonians of what Paul had first taught them (3.1-6). Why is it important for Christians to be reminded often about the message about Christ?

4. What was a special concern for some of the Thessalonians (4.13-15)? What did Paul say to calm their fears?

5. Some people consider 1 THESSALONIANS the "warmest" or "most affectionate" letter Paul wrote to a group of followers. Which of Paul's statements do you find the most encouraging?

2 thessalonians

Sometimes hearing or seeing something more than once can help us understand it better. Many of Paul's teachings from 1 THESSALONIANS are repeated and reinforced in this short letter.

WHAT MAKES 2 THESSALONIANS SPECIAL?

As in 1 THESSALONIANS, the author thanks God that the Thessalonian Christians continue to grow in faith and love, in spite of the difficulties and suffering they are going through. The author tells them that they are a good example for other churches. The letter also gives further insight into the apostle's beliefs about the return of Christ and his teachings about how to prepare for this event.

Some members of the Thessalonian church were upset because people were saying that Christ had already come back again, and that they had missed this event. But Paul tells them what will happen when Christ does return: the "wicked one" and unbelievers will be punished (2.12), and those who are faithful to Christ will be saved (2.13). The Thessalonians are told to pray for the spread of the good news (3.1-5), and warned to listen to Paul's teachings and avoid being lazy (3.6-13).

WHAT'S THE STORY BEHIND THE SCENE?

This letter was probably written shortly after 1 THESSALONIANS. Even though the members of the Thessalonian church were good examples of faith and love, some of them were listening to false teachings about Christ's return (2.1-5). The author explains more about the Lord's return and the Lord's victory over the "evil one." The author concludes by reminding them that the belief that Christ would return soon is no excuse to quit working.

Scholars believe this letter may have been written by one of Paul's followers after Paul died. It was not unusual in the ancient world for a follower to honor his or her teacher by writing something in the teacher's name.

HOW IS 2 THESSALONIANS CONSTRUCTED?

The letter can be outlined as follows:

The truth about Christ's return (1.1—2.17)
Prayers and warnings (3.1-18)

Second Thessalonians was written some time after 1 Thessalonians and echoes the format and themes of the earlier letter. The author thanks God for the Thessalonians' steady faith in God, which has remained strong in spite of the troubles and sufferings they are experiencing. Perhaps because they were being persecuted, some in the Thessalonian church were listening to false teachings, claiming that Jesus had already returned. The Christians there are told not to be fooled by such false claims. The letter repeats what Paul had previously taught them about Christ's return—that unbelievers will be punished and the faithful saved—and it concludes with a warning against laziness, followed by encouragement to never tire of doing what is right.

Outline

1

From Paul, Silas,[a] and Timothy.

To the church in Thessalonica, the people of God our Father and of the Lord Jesus Christ.

[2]I pray that God our Father and the Lord Jesus Christ will be kind to you and will bless you with peace!

When Christ Returns

[3]My dear friends, we always have good reason to thank God for you, because your faith in God and your love for each other keep growing all the time. [4]This is why we brag about you to all of God's churches. We tell them how patient you are and how you keep on having faith, even though you are going through a lot of trouble and suffering.

[5]All this shows that God judges fairly and is making you fit to share in his kingdom for which you are suffering. [6]It is only right for God to punish everyone who is causing you trouble, [7]but he will give you relief from your troubles. God will do the same for us, when the Lord Jesus comes from heaven with his powerful angels [8]and with a flaming fire.

Our Lord Jesus will punish anyone who doesn't know God and won't obey his message. [9]Their punishment will be eternal destruction, and they will be kept far from the presence of our Lord and his glorious strength. [10]This will happen on the day when the Lord returns to be praised and honored by all who have faith in him and belong to him. This includes you, because you believed what we said.

[11]God chose you, and we keep praying that God will make you worthy of being his people. We pray for God's power to help you do all the good things you hope to do and your faith makes you want to do. [12]Then, because of the undeserved grace of God and our Lord Jesus Christ, you will bring honor to the name of our Lord Jesus, and he will bring honor to you.

---

[a]1.1 *Silas:* The Greek text has "Silvanus," which is another form of the name Silas.

■ 1.1 *God our Father . . . Lord Jesus Christ:* Jesus often referred to God as "Father" (see John 14, for example). Paul uses this same term in many of his letters to describe God (Rom 1.7; 1 Cor 1.3; Gal 1.2,3). The Greek word for "Lord" is *Kyrios,* which may mean "Master" or "Sir." When used for Jesus, it emphasizes his authority and power. The word "Christ" is from the Greek word, *Christos,* a title that means "Messiah" or "chosen one."

Lord (Title for Jesus)

Messiah (Chosen One)

● 1.4 *we brag about you to all of God's churches:* Probably refers to the churches in Achaia and Macedonia (1 Thes 1.7,8). The Thessalonians have been patient and faithful in spite of the trouble and suffering they have experienced.

■ 1.5 *share in his kingdom:* Paul is not saying that Christians must suffer to be part of this kingdom, but that those who follow Christ are likely to face suffering and opposition.

● 1.6 *punish everyone who is causing you trouble:* Apparently, the Thessalonians' own Gentile neighbors made trouble for them when they listened to Paul's teachings and began to follow Jesus.

2.1 *we will be gathered:* Paul describes how the followers of Jesus who have died and those still living will be taken up to be with Christ (1Thes 4.13-17).

2.2 *people who claim the Lord has already come:* Because of confusion caused by false teachers, some Thessalonians were uncertain about the meaning of Christ's return to earth.

2.3 *wicked one:* This person would be against God's Law and would even claim to be God (2.4). Satan may use this wicked person to work miracles that will fool people into thinking he is truly God (2.9). See also Dan 11.29-39; 1 John 2.18.

2.7 *someone is holding him back:* It is not clear who this "someone" is. Some scholars think it may have been the Roman government, which kept order in the empire so that no group could try to destroy Christ's followers. Others think that this "someone" may refer to the Holy Spirit, or to an angel like Michael (1 Thes 4.16), or the angel of the pit (Rev 20.1-3).

2.10 *Lost people:* The word "lost" points to those people who will die because they refuse to have faith in Jesus Christ.

2.10 *could be saved:* "Being saved" can also refer to receiving "eternal life."

God's Saving Love (Salvation)

The Lord's Return

2 When our Lord Jesus returns, we will be gathered up to meet him. So I ask you, my friends, [2]not to be easily upset or disturbed by people who claim the Lord[b] has already come. They may say they heard this directly from the Holy Spirit, or from someone else, or even that they read it in one of our letters. [3]But don't be fooled! People will rebel against God. Then before the Lord returns, the wicked[c] one who is doomed to be destroyed will appear. [4]He will brag and oppose everything holy or sacred. He will even sit in God's temple and claim to be God. [5]Don't you remember I told you this while I was still with you?

[6]You already know what is holding this wicked one back until it is time for him to come. [7]His mysterious power is already at work, but someone is holding him back. And the wicked one won't appear until this someone is out of the way. [8]Then he will appear, but the Lord Jesus will kill him simply by breathing on him. He will be completely destroyed by the Lord's glorious return.

[9]When the wicked one appears, Satan will pretend to work all kinds of miracles, wonders, and signs. [10]Lost people will be fooled by his evil deeds. They could be saved, but they will refuse to love the truth and accept it. [11]So God will make sure they are fooled into believing a lie. [12]All of them will be punished, because they would rather do evil than believe the truth.

Be Faithful

[13]My friends, the Lord loves you, and it is only natural for us to thank God for you.

God chose you to be the first ones to be saved.[d] His Spirit made you holy, and you put your faith in the truth. [14]God used our preaching as his way of inviting you to share in the glory of our Lord Jesus Christ. [15]My friends, this is why you must remain faithful and follow closely what we taught you in person and by our letters.

[16]God our Father loves us. He treats us with undeserved grace and has given us eternal comfort and a wonderful hope. We pray that our Lord Jesus Christ and God our Father [17]will encourage you and help you always to do and say the right thing.

Pray for Us

3 Finally, our friends, please pray for us. This will help the message about the Lord to spread quickly, and others will respect it, just as you do. [2]Pray that we may be kept safe from worthless and evil people. After all, not everyone has faith. [3]But the Lord can be trusted to make you strong and protect you from harm. [4]He has made us sure that you are obeying what we taught you and that you will keep on obeying. [5]I pray that the Lord will guide you to be as loving as God and as patient as Christ.

Warnings against Laziness

[6]My dear friends, in the name of[e] the Lord Jesus, I beg you not to have anything to do with any of your people who loaf around and refuse to obey the instructions we gave you. [7]You surely know that you should follow our example. We didn't waste our time loafing, [8]and we didn't accept food from anyone without paying for it. We didn't want to be a burden to any of

[b]**2.2** *Lord:* The Greek text has "day of the Lord."   [c]**2.3** *wicked:* Some manuscripts have "sinful."
[d]**2.13** *God chose you to be the first ones to be saved:* Some manuscripts have "From the beginning God chose you to be saved."   [e]**3.6** *in the name of:* Or "as a follower of."

you, so night and day we worked as hard as we could.

⁹We had the right not to work, but we wanted to set an example for you. ¹⁰We also gave you this rule: If you don't work, you don't eat. ¹¹Now we learn that some of you just loaf around and won't do any work, except the work of a busybody. ¹²So, for the sake of our Lord Jesus Christ, we ask and beg these people to settle down and start working for a living. ¹³Dear friends, you must never become tired of doing right.

¹⁴Be on your guard against any followers who refuse to obey what we have written in this letter. Put them to shame by not having anything to do with them. ¹⁵Don't consider them your enemies. Instead, speak kindly to them as you would to any other follower.

Final Prayer

¹⁶I pray that the Lord, who gives peace, will always bless you with peace. May the Lord be with all of you.

¹⁷I always sign my letters as I am now doing: PAUL.

¹⁸I pray that our Lord Jesus Christ will be kind to all of you.

3.11 *some of you just loaf around:* Some church members probably took advantage of the kindness of others. It is also possible that some of them argued that they did not have to work, since Jesus was coming back soon anyway.

3.17 *sign my letters:* This seems to indicate that the letter was dictated to a secretary of some sort.

I pray that the Lord, who gives peace, will always bless you with peace. 2 THES 3.16

Reflection Questions About 2 Thessalonians 1.1—3.18

1. Why does the author of 2 THESSALONIANS so often mention that he has been praying for the Thessalonians (1.2; 2.17; 3.16-18)? What is the value of prayer?

2. What does the author mean by his statement that the "Lord Jesus will punish anyone who doesn't know God and won't obey his message" (1.8)? What does it mean to know God? What does it mean to obey God's message?

3. What false teaching was spread in the Thessalonian church (2.1,2)? Why is this teaching dangerous or harmful?

4. Re-read 2.13-17. What does this passage teach about God's love, faithfulness, hope, and the importance of doing and saying the right thing? When in your life have you experienced God's kindness (2.16)? How did this change the way you thought or acted toward others?

5. What advice does the author have for the Thessalonian Christians as they wait for Christ's return (3.6-13)? What are some of the hazards of laziness? What can you do to avoid becoming "tired of doing right"?

1 timothy

Who gives you advice when you need it? Read this letter to find out what kind of advice Timothy received about being a leader in the church.

WHAT MAKES 1 TIMOTHY SPECIAL?

FIRST and SECOND TIMOTHY and TITUS are often called the "Pastoral Letters," since they deal with the responsibilities of those who were in charge of some of the first Christian churches. FIRST TIMOTHY provided many helpful standards and guidelines for organizing the new Christian faith communities. Although personally addressed to Timothy, it served as a leadership manual for the early churches.

FIRST TIMOTHY was written to warn about false teaching and to offer advice for all God's people. The letter also tells the church how its leaders are to be chosen, what titles are to be given to them, and what responsibilities they are to take on.

WHAT'S THE STORY BEHIND THE SCENE?

Timothy, the son of a Jewish Christian mother and a Gentile father from Lystra (Acts 16.1), was guided in his faith by Paul (1 Cor 4.17). He is named as Paul's co-worker in many of Paul's letters (2 Cor 1.1; 1 Thes 1.1; Phlm 1). Paul had great confidence in Timothy (1 Cor 16.10; 2 Cor 1.19), who served as his messenger and is often mentioned as a co-sender of many of Paul's letters (2 CORINTHIANS, 1,2 THESSALONIANS, PHILIPPIANS, PHILEMON). Timothy traveled and worked with Paul (Rom 16.21; Phil 2.19; Acts 16.1-3). Because of their shared faith, Timothy was like a son to Paul (1.2).

This letter may have been written toward the end of Paul's life, or, as some scholars believe, it may have been written in Paul's name by one of his followers after Paul's death. The structure of the church and certain teachings that appear in this letter indicate that the letter may have been written as much as a generation or two after Paul died. It was not unusual in the ancient world for followers to honor their teacher by writing something in the teacher's name.

HOW IS 1 TIMOTHY CONSTRUCTED?

The letter can be outlined in the following way:

Instructions for church life (1.1—3.13)
True faith and warnings about false teachings (3.14—4.5)
Advice to Timothy and other church leaders (4.6—6.21)

First and Second Timothy and the book of Titus are often called the "Pastoral Letters," because they address issues facing many of the first Christian churches. Because 1 Timothy provides guidelines for choosing church leaders and for organizing new faith communities, it served as a leadership manual in the early Christian church. The letter is addressed to Timothy, who traveled with Paul and assisted him in his ministry. The key concern of the letter is to spread the good news about Jesus, and the author seeks to do this in two different ways. First, he warns against false teachings that would cause arguments and divisions among Christians. Second, he gives instructions for building a solid and stable faith community by providing rules for worship, dress, Christian behavior, social responsibility within the Christian community, and the selection of worthy church leaders.

Outline

1

From Paul.

God our Savior and Christ Jesus commanded me to be an apostle of Christ Jesus, who gives us hope.

[2] Timothy, because of our faith, you are like a son to me. I pray that God our Father and our Lord Jesus Christ will be kind and merciful to you. May they bless you with peace!

Warning against False Teaching

[3] When I was leaving for Macedonia, I asked you to stay on in Ephesus and warn certain people there to stop spreading their false teachings. [4] You needed to warn them to stop wasting their time on senseless stories and endless lists of ancestors. Such things only cause arguments. They don't help anyone to do God's work that can only be done by faith.

[5] You must teach people to have genuine love, as well as a good conscience and true faith. [6] There are some who have given up these for nothing but empty talk. [7] They want to be teachers of the Law of Moses. But they don't know what they are talking about, even though they think they do.

[8] We know the Law is good, if it is used in the right way. [9] We also understand it wasn't given to control people who please God, but to control lawbreakers, criminals, godless people, and sinners. It is for wicked and evil people, and for murderers, who would even kill their own parents. [10] The Law was written for people who are sexual perverts or who live as homosexuals or are kidnappers or liars or won't tell the truth in court. It is for anything else that opposes the correct teaching [11] of the good news the glorious and wonderful God has given me.

Being Thankful for God's Kindness

[12] I thank Christ Jesus our Lord, who has given me the strength for my work because he knew he could trust me. [13] I used to say terrible and insulting things about

him, and I was cruel. But Christ had mercy on me because I didn't know what I was doing, and I had not yet put my faith in him. [14]Christ Jesus our Lord treated me with undeserved grace and has greatly blessed my life with faith and love just like his own.

[15]"Christ Jesus came into the world to save sinners." This saying is true, and it can be trusted. I was the worst sinner of all! [16]But since I was worse than anyone else, God had mercy on me and let me be an example of the endless patience of Christ Jesus. He did this so that others would put their faith in Christ and have eternal life. [17]I pray that honor and glory will always be given to the only God, who lives forever and is the invisible and eternal King! Amen.

[18]Timothy, my son, the instructions I am giving you are based on what some prophets[a] once said about you. If you follow these instructions, you will fight like a good soldier. [19]You will be faithful and have a clear conscience. Some people have made a mess of their faith because they didn't listen to their consciences. [20]Two of them are Hymenaeus and Alexander. I have given these men over to the power of Satan, so they will learn not to oppose God.

How To Pray

2 First of all, I ask you to pray for everyone. Ask God to help and bless them all, and tell God how thankful you are for each of them. [2]Pray for kings and others in power, so we may live quiet and peaceful lives as we worship and honor God. [3]This kind of prayer is good, and it pleases God our Savior. [4]God wants everyone to be saved and to know the whole truth, which is,

[5]There is only one God,
and Christ Jesus
is the only one
who can bring us
to God.
Jesus was truly human,
and he gave himself
to rescue all of us.
[6]God showed us this
at the right time.

[7]This is why God chose me to be a preacher and an apostle of the good news. I am telling the truth. I am not lying. God sent me to teach the Gentiles about faith and truth.

[8]I want everyone everywhere to lift innocent hands toward heaven and pray, without being angry or arguing with each other.

[9]I would like for women to wear modest and sensible clothes. They should not have fancy hairdos, or wear expensive clothes, or put on jewelry made of gold or pearls. [10]Women who claim to love God should do helpful things for others, [11]and they should learn by being quiet and paying attention. [12]They should be silent and not be allowed to teach or to tell men what to do. [13]After all, Adam was created before Eve, [14]and the man Adam wasn't the one who was fooled. It was the woman Eve who was completely fooled and sinned. [15]But women will be saved by having children,[b] if they stay faithful, loving, holy, and modest.

1.16 eternal life: Paul talks of eternal life as being raised to new life with Christ (Rom 6.4-8; 1 Cor 15.20-55).

Eternal Life

1.20 Hymenaeus and Alexander: Hymenaeus is mentioned in 2 Timothy 2.17 as someone who claimed that Jesus had already returned. Alexander is mentioned in 2 Timothy 4.14. What he did to hurt Paul is not clear.

Satan

2.2 Pray for kings and others in power: It was important for Christians to show respect to authorities so that they could avoid trouble. In this way, they could hope to gain respect for their beliefs, gain new members, and lessen the risk of being persecuted.

2.7 faith: Paul often describes faith as trusting in Christ (Rom 3.27-31; Gal 2.16; Phil 3.9), but here "faith" is used more in the sense of a set of beliefs about right living.

2.9 women . . . gold or pearls: This suggests that there were people in Timothy's congregation who loved money and liked to show off their wealth (6.5-10,17).

Church Officials

3 It is true that[c] anyone who desires to be a church official[d] wants to be something worthwhile. [2]That's why officials must have a good reputation and be faithful in marriage.[e] They must be self-controlled, sensible, well-behaved, friendly to strangers, and able to teach. [3]They must not be heavy drinkers or troublemakers. Instead, they must be kind and gentle and not love money.

[4]Church officials must be in control of their own families, and they must see that their children are obedient and always respectful. [5]If they don't know how to control their own families, how can they look after God's people?

[6]They must not be new followers of the Lord. If they are, they might become proud and be doomed along with the devil. [7]Finally, they must be well-respected by people who are not followers. Then they won't be trapped and disgraced by the devil.

Church Officers

[8]Church officers[f] should be serious. They must not be liars, heavy drinkers, or greedy for money. [9]And they must have a clear conscience and hold firmly to what God has shown us about our faith. [10]They must first prove themselves. Then if no one has anything against them, they can serve as officers.

[11]Women[g] must also be serious. They must not gossip or be heavy drinkers, and they must be faithful in everything they do.

[12]Church officers must be faithful in marriage.[h] They must be in full control of their children and everyone else in their home. [13]Those who serve well as officers will earn a good reputation and will be highly respected for their faith in Christ Jesus.

The Mystery of Our Religion

[14]I hope to visit you soon. But I am writing these instructions, [15]so if I am delayed, you will know how everyone who belongs to God's family ought to behave. After all, the church of the living God is the strong foundation of truth.

[16]Here is the great mystery of our religion:

Christ[i] came as a human.
The Spirit proved
    that he pleased God,
and he was seen by angels.

Christ was preached
    to the nations.
People in this world
    put their faith in him,
and he was taken up to glory.

People Will Turn from Their Faith

4 God's Spirit clearly says that in the last days many people will turn from their faith. They will be fooled by evil spirits and by teachings that come from demons. [2]They will also be fooled by the false claims of liars whose consciences have lost all feeling. These liars [3]will forbid people to marry

3.15 *church of the living God:* Here "church" refers to all the people who had become followers of Jesus Christ, rather than to any single local congregation.

Church

3.16 *Spirit . . . angels:* The Holy Spirit teaches and guides the people of God so that they can become the kind of people God wants them to be.

Holy Spirit

Angels

4.1 *in the last days . . . evil spirits . . . demons:* The "last days" refers to a time just before the end of the world, or to the time when God will judge the world. A number of New Testament passages say that false teachings will be spread during this time (2 Thes 2.1-12; 2 Tim 3.1-9; 2 Pet 3.3). Evil spirits and demons are connected to the power of the devil, or Satan.

End Times

4.2,3 *liars will forbid people to marry or to eat certain foods:* Certain groups taught a very strict way of life called "asceticism." Ascetics abstained from sexual relations and limited their diet to certain foods or fasted (went without eating) in order to prove how devoted they were to God.

[c]3.1 *It is true that:* These words may be taken with 2.15. If so, that verse would be translated: "It is true that women will be saved . . . holy, and modest." And 3.1 would be translated, "Anyone who desires . . . something worthwhile." [d]3.1 *church official:* Or "bishop." [e]3.2 *be faithful in marriage:* Or "be the husband of only one wife." [f]3.8 *Church officers:* Or "Deacons." [g]3.11 *Women:* Either church officers or the wives of church officers. [h]3.12 *be faithful in marriage:* See the note at 3.2. [i]3.16 *Christ:* The Greek text has "he," probably meaning "Christ." Some manuscripts have "God."

4.8-9 *Exercise is good*: The source of this saying is not known. However, it seems to be related to the saying in 1 Timothy 6.6.

4.13 *Scriptures*: This most likely refers to the Jewish Scriptures (Old Testament). Though the writings included in the New Testament circulated among the churches, they were not yet considered part of "the Scriptures."

4.14 *gift you were given*: "The gift" probably refers to Timothy's ability to teach and preach the good news. This special gift was given to Timothy by the Holy Spirit.

Spiritual Gifts

4.14 *blessed you*: The "blessing" of a new leader was done when other church leaders laid their hands on the chosen person's head. This practice is also described in the Jewish Scriptures (Old Testament). In the New Testament, this way of touching someone's head was used in healing (Mark 1.41), giving a blessing (Mark 10.16), choosing someone for a special task (Acts 6.6; 1 Tim 5.22), or passing on the gifts of the Holy Spirit (Acts 8.17; 19.6). In modern times, choosing someone for a special task in the church is often called "ordaining" or "commissioning."

5.1 *older man*: Refers to older men who were experienced church leaders.

or to eat certain foods. But God created these foods to be eaten with thankful hearts by his followers who know the truth. [4]Everything God created is good. And if you give thanks, you may eat anything. [5]What God has said and your prayer will make it fit to eat.

Paul's Advice to Timothy

[6]If you teach these things to other followers, you will be a good servant of Christ Jesus. You will show you have grown up on the teachings about our faith and on the good instructions you have obeyed. [7]Don't have anything to do with worthless, senseless stories. Work hard to be truly religious. [8-9]As the saying goes,

"Exercise is good
    for your body,
but religion helps you
    in every way.
It promises life
    now and forever."

These words are worthwhile and should not be forgotten. [10]We have put our hope in the living God, who is the Savior of everyone, but especially of those who have faith. This is why we work and struggle so hard.[j]

[11]Teach these things and tell everyone to do what you say. [12]Don't let anyone make fun of you, just because you are young. Set an example for other followers by what you say and do, as well as by your love, faith, and purity.

[13]Until I arrive, be sure to keep on reading the Scriptures in worship, and don't stop preaching and teaching. [14]Use the gift you were given when the prophets spoke and the group of church leaders[k] blessed

you by placing their hands on you. [15]Remember these things and think about them, so everyone can see how well you are doing. [16]Be careful about the way you live and about what you teach. Keep on doing this, and you will save not only yourself, but the people who hear you.

How To Act toward Others

5 Don't correct an older man. Encourage him, as you would your own father. Treat younger men as you would your own brother, [2]and treat older women as you would your own mother. Show the same respect to younger women that you would to your sister.

[3]Take care of any widow who is really in need. [4]But if a widow has children or grandchildren, they should learn to serve God by taking care of her, as she once took care of them. This is what God wants them to do. [5]A widow who is really in need is one who doesn't have any relatives. She has faith in God, and she keeps praying to him night and day, asking for his help.

[6]A widow who thinks only about having a good time is already dead, even though she is still alive.

[7]Tell all this to everyone, so they will do the right thing. [8]People who don't take care of their relatives, and especially their own families, have given up their faith. They are worse than someone who doesn't have faith in the Lord.

[9]For a widow to be put on the list of widows, she must be at least 60 years old, and she must have been faithful in marriage.[l] [10]She must also be well-known for doing all sorts of good things, such as raising children, giving food to strangers, welcoming

[j]4.10 *struggle so hard*: Some manuscripts have "are treated so badly." [k]4.14 *group of church leaders*: Or "group of elders" or "group of presbyters." This translates one Greek word, and it is related to the one used in 5.17,19. [l]5.9 *been faithful in marriage*: Or "been the wife of only one husband."

God's people into her home,[m] helping people in need, and always making herself useful.

[11]Don't put young widows on the list. They may later have a strong desire to get married. Then they will turn away from Christ [12]and become guilty of breaking their promise to him. [13]Besides, they will become lazy and get into the habit of going from house to house. Next, they will start gossiping and become busybodies, talking about things that are none of their business.

[14]I would prefer that young widows get married, have children, and look after their families. Then the enemy won't have any reason to say insulting things about us. [15]Look what's already happened to some of the young widows! They have turned away to follow Satan.

[16]If a woman who is a follower has any widows in her family, she[n] should help them. This will keep the church from having that burden, and then the church can help widows who are really in need.

Church Leaders

[17]Church leaders[o] who do their job well deserve to be paid[p] twice as much, especially if they work hard at preaching and teaching. [18]It is just as the Scriptures say, "Don't muzzle an ox when you are using it to grind grain." You also know the saying, "Workers are worth their pay."

[19]Don't listen to any charge against a church leader, unless at least two or three people bring the same charges. [20]But if any of the leaders should keep on sinning, they must be corrected in front of the whole group, as a warning to everyone else.

[21]In the presence of God and Christ Jesus and their chosen angels, I order you to follow my instructions! Be fair with everyone, and don't have any favorites.

[22]Don't be too quick to accept people into the service of the Lord[q] by placing your hands on them.

Don't sin because others do, but stay close to God.

[23]Stop drinking only water. Take a little wine to help your stomach trouble and the other illnesses you often have.

[24]Some people get caught in their sins almost at once, even before the time of judgment. But other people's sins don't show up until later. [25]It is the same with good deeds. Some are easily seen, but none of them can be hidden.

6 If you are a slave, you should respect and honor your owner. This will keep people from saying bad things about God and about our teaching. [2]If any of you slaves have owners who are followers, you should show them respect. After all, they are also followers of Christ, and he loves them. So you should serve and help them the best you can.

False Teaching and True Wealth

These are the things you must teach and tell the people to do. [3]Anyone who teaches something different disagrees with the correct and godly teaching of our Lord Jesus Christ. [4]Those people who disagree are proud of themselves, but they don't really know a thing. Their minds are sick, and they like to argue over words. They cause jealousy, disagreements, unkind words, evil suspicions, [5]and nasty quarrels. They

---

5.16 *widows in her family:* Christian family members were to take care of their relatives, including widows. The church was to help only those widows who didn't have family members to take care of their needs.

5.17 *Church leaders:* This Greek word, *presbyteroi*, can be translated "elders," "presbyters," or "priests." This probably refers to all those who held a special office in the church, including church officials (bishops).

5.20 *sinning . . . corrected in front of the whole group:* This teaching about how to correct those who have sinned is very similar to what Jesus taught his disciples (Matt 18.15-17). Since the leader's actions affected the whole group of followers, the leader's hearing and punishment should be public, in front of all the followers.

6.1 *slave:* In some New Testament letters, slaves are encouraged to be loyal to their masters (Eph 6.5-8; Col 3.22-24), but see Gal 3.26-29.

Slaves and Servants in the Time of Jesus

6.5 *These people:* Some false teachers wanted to make lots of money by teaching religion. But being part of the church does not include gaining wealth, and people who love money cause trouble.

---

[m]**5.10** *welcoming God's people into her home:* The Greek text has "washing the feet of God's people." In New Testament times most people either went barefoot or wore sandals, and a host would often wash the feet of special guests.   [n]**5.16** *woman . . . she:* Some manuscripts have "man or woman . . . that person."   [o]**5.17** *church leaders:* Or "elders" or "presbyters."   [p]**5.17** *paid:* Or "honored" or "respected."   [q]**5.22** *to accept people into the service of the Lord:* Or "to forgive people."

6.13 *Pontius Pilate:* Pontius Pilate was the Roman governor in charge of Judea from A.D. 26 to 36. Pilate said that Jesus was not guilty of anything, but the leaders of the Jewish people in Jerusalem insisted that Pilate have Jesus put to death (Luke 23.1-5; John 18.33-37).

6.14 *until our Lord . . . returns:* Paul believed that Jesus was going to return to earth very soon, perhaps during his own lifetime (Phil 3.20; 4.5; 1 Thes 5.1-11).

Second Coming

6.16 *God lives . . . in light:* In the Bible, light is used to describe God or God's word (Ps 119.105; John 1.3,4; 1 John 1.5), and those people or things that reveal God's truth (Isa 49.6). The followers of Jesus are also called "children of light" (John 12.36,46; Eph 5.8). In the Jewish Scriptures (Old Testament), God brings light (Gen 1.3) and often is described as appearing in some kind of light (Exod 3.2,3; 13.20-22).

have wicked minds and have missed out on the truth.

These people think religion is supposed to make you rich. ⁶And religion does make your life rich, by making you content with what you have. ⁷We didn't bring anything into this world, and we won'tʳ take anything with us when we leave. ⁸So we should be satisfied just to have food and clothes. ⁹People who want to be rich fall into all sorts of temptations and traps. They are caught by foolish and harmful desires that drag them down and destroy them. ¹⁰The love of money causes all kinds of trouble. Some people want money so much they have given up their faith and caused themselves a lot of pain.

Fighting a Good Fight for the Faith

¹¹Timothy, you belong to God, so keep away from all these evil things. Try your best to please God and to be like him. Be faithful, loving, dependable, and gentle. ¹²Fight a good fight for the faith and claim eternal life. God offered it to you when you clearly told about your faith, while so many people listened. ¹³Now I ask you to make a promise. Make it in the presence of God, who gives life to all, and in the presence of Christ Jesus, who openly told Pontius Pilate about his faith. ¹⁴Promise to obey completely and fully all that you have been told until our Lord Jesus Christ returns.

¹⁵The glorious God
is the only Ruler,
the King of kings
and Lord of lords.
At the time that God
has already decided,
he will send Jesus Christ
back again.

¹⁶Only God lives forever!
And he lives in light
that no one can come near.
No human has ever seen God
or ever can see him.
God will be honored,
and his power
will last forever. Amen.

¹⁷Warn the rich people of this world not to be proud or to trust in wealth that is easily lost. Tell them to have faith in God, who is rich and blesses us with everything we need to enjoy life. ¹⁸Instruct them to do as many good deeds as they can and to help everyone. Remind the rich to be generous and share what they have. ¹⁹This will lay a solid foundation for the future, so they will know what true life is like.

²⁰Timothy, guard what God has placed in your care! Don't pay any attention to godless and stupid talk that sounds smart but really isn't. ²¹Some people have even lost their faith by believing this talk.

I pray that the Lord will be kind to all of you!

ʳ6.7 *we won't:* Some manuscripts have "we surely won't."

Fight a good fight for the faith and claim eternal life.
1 Tim 6.12

Reflection Questions About 1 Timothy 1.1—6.21

1. This letter refers several times to the close relationship between the apostle Paul and his "son" Timothy (1.2,18; 3.14; 4.11; and 6.11-14,20). How do you think sharing a common faith in God can strengthen a relationship? How can Christians help one another strengthen their individual relationships with God?

2. The author of this letter gives Timothy much advice about how to deal with false teachers who are having a bad influence on the people of Timothy's church. What are some of these "false teachings" based on (1.4; 4.6; 6.20; also 4.1-5)? What, according to the author, is "the whole truth" (2.4-6; 4.16)? What are some of the things he suggests followers of Christ do (and not do) in order to "be faithful and have a clear conscience" (2.1; 4.7; 4.16; 5.1-3; 6.11)?

3. FIRST TIMOTHY is a kind of "Manual for Church Leaders." What does the author say church leaders should be like, and what kind of behavior is expected of them (3.1-13)? Why do you think the standards are so high (3.15; 4.16; 6.19)? In your opinion, what are the five most important traits of a church leader, pastor, or priest?

4. Timothy seems to have been "young" for a church leader at this time. What special advice did the letter writer give Timothy about being a respected and effective leader (4.12; 5.1,2)? How much does your own church encourage young people to be involved, to lead worship, and to serve?

5. What special warnings did the letter writer have for people who thought religion was supposed to make them rich (6.3-10)? How can religion make a person's life "rich"? Are you "content with what you have"?

2 timothy

Soldiers are taught to be disciplined and to be prepared for almost anything, including suffering or death. Read this letter to find out why Timothy is told to be a good soldier of Christ Jesus.

WHAT MAKES 2 TIMOTHY SPECIAL?

This second letter to Timothy is more personal than the first one. Timothy is like a "dear child" to Paul, who always remembers Timothy in his prayers (1.2,3). Timothy's mother and grandmother are mentioned by name in this letter, and Timothy is reminded how Paul placed his hands on him as a special sign that the Spirit was guiding Timothy's work.

The situation of the early Christian church changed throughout the first century A.D. Eventually, the leaders of the church were in danger of being put in jail or punished by the Roman authorities. And within the church, people were coming up with new ideas that did not fit with the original message of the good news about Jesus' death on the cross and his being raised from death. The writer tells Timothy to be a "good soldier" of Christ Jesus and to learn to endure suffering (2.1,3). Some who claim to be followers of the Lord are already trapped by the devil, so the writer warns Timothy to run from those temptations that often catch young people (2.20-26; 3.1-9). He tells Timothy to keep preaching God's message, even if it is not the popular thing to do (4.2), and to be patient with the people in his care (4.3-5).

WHAT'S THE STORY BEHIND THE SCENE?

In this letter, Paul is pictured as being in jail as he writes to Timothy (1.8,16,17), and as someone who expects to be put to death soon (4.6). Timothy was like a son to Paul (1 Tim 1.2), because they had traveled and worked closely together (Rom 16.21; 1 Cor 16.10; Phil 2.19; Acts 16.1-3).

Like 1 TIMOTHY, this letter may have been written toward the end of Paul's life, or it may have been written in his name by one of his followers perhaps as much as a generation or two after Paul's death. Writing in another person's name was not considered dishonest or unusual in the first century. Instead, it was considered a way of honoring that person and his work.

HOW IS 2 TIMOTHY CONSTRUCTED?

The letter can be outlined in the following way:

Encouragement and warnings for Timothy
   (1.1—2.26)
Courage and faithfulness to the end (3.1—4.8)
Final instructions and greetings (4.9-22)

Second Timothy, like 1 Timothy and Titus, is often called a "Pastoral Letter." Pastoral letters address various issues facing many of the first Christian churches. Like 1 Timothy, 2 Timothy is addressed to Paul's co-worker Timothy, who traveled and ministered with the apostle. The letter depicts Paul as being in jail and close to death. In this personal letter, Timothy is addressed as "a dear child" who has been trusted with the treasure of the good news about Jesus, and who should guard it carefully with the help of the Holy Spirit. The writer tells Timothy to be a "good soldier" of Christ Jesus, to endure suffering, to keep his mind on Jesus, and to run from temptations. Even though God has laid a solid foundation in the church, the last days will bring hard times for all who belong to Christ. Timothy is advised to remain faithful, and no matter how unpopular or difficult the situation, to work hard to spread the good news about Jesus.

Outline

1

From Paul, an apostle of Christ Jesus. God himself chose me to be an apostle, and he gave me the promised life that Jesus Christ makes possible.

²Timothy, you are like a dear child to me. I pray that God our Father and our Lord Christ Jesus will be kind and merciful to you and will bless you with peace!

Do Not Be Ashamed of the Lord

³Night and day I mention you in my prayers. I am always grateful for you, as I pray to the God my ancestors and I have served with a clear conscience. ⁴I remember how you cried, and I want to see you, because this would make me truly happy. ⁵I also remember the genuine faith of your mother Eunice. Your grandmother Lois had the same sort of faith, and I am sure you have it as well. ⁶So I ask you to make full use of the gift God gave you when I placed my hands on you.ᵃ Use it well.

⁷God's Spiritᵇ doesn't make cowards out of us. The Spirit gives us power, love, and self-control.

⁸Don't be ashamed to speak for our Lord. And don't be ashamed of me, just because I am in jail for serving him. Use the power that comes from God and join with me in suffering for telling the good news.

⁹God saved us and chose us
    to be his holy people.
We did nothing
    to deserve this,
but God planned it
    because he is so kind.
Even before time began
God planned for Christ Jesus
    to show kindness to us.

¹⁰Now Christ Jesus has come
    to offer us God's gift
    of undeserved grace.
Christ our Savior defeated death

ᵃ**1.6** *when I placed my hands on you:* Church leaders placed their hands on people who were being appointed to preach or teach (see 1 Timothy 4.14).   ᵇ**1.7** *God's Spirit:* Or "God."

1.10 *shines like a light:* In the Bible, light is often used to describe God or God's word (Ps 119.105; John 1.3,4; 1 John 1.5), and those people or things that reveal God's truth (Isa 49.6). Here "light" refers to the "good news."

1.14 *treasure . . . Holy Spirit:* The treasure is the true message about Christ that Timothy has received from Paul. The Holy Spirit teaches and guides the people of God so that they can become the kind of people God wants them to be.

Holy Spirit

1.15 *everyone in Asia has turned against me:* At the time of Paul, "Asia" referred to a province in the western section of what is now Turkey. Paul mentions the suffering he experienced in Ephesus (2 Cor 1.8), which probably included torture and the threat of death. See also Acts 20.17-19. (See Map 16 on pg 1894.)

1.15 *Phygelus and Hermogenes:* This is the only time these names are mentioned in the New Testament, so it is not clear just how they opposed Paul.

2.8 *family of David:* A number of New Testament passages refer to the fact that Jesus was a descendant of David, Israel's greatest king (Matt 1.1-17; Luke 2.1-4; Rom 1.1-4).

David

and brought us
  the good news.
It shines like a light
and offers life
  that never ends.

[11]My work is to be a preacher, an apostle, and a teacher.[c] [12]This is why I am suffering now. But I am not ashamed! I know the one I have faith in, and I am sure he can guard until the last day what he has trusted me with.[d] [13]Now follow the example of the correct teaching I gave you, and let the faith and love of Christ Jesus be your model. [14]You have been trusted with a wonderful treasure. Guard it with the help of the Holy Spirit, who lives within us.

[15]You know that everyone in Asia has turned against me, especially Phygelus and Hermogenes. [16]I pray that the Lord will be kind to the family of Onesiphorus. He often cheered me up and wasn't ashamed of me when I was put in jail. [17]Then after he arrived in Rome, he searched everywhere until he found me. [18]I pray that the Lord Jesus will ask God to show mercy to Onesiphorus on the day of judgment. You know how much he helped me in Ephesus.

A Good Soldier of Christ Jesus

2 Timothy, my child, you must let Christ Jesus make you strong by his gift of undeserved grace. [2]You have often heard me teach. Now I want you to tell these same things to followers who can be trusted to tell others.

[3]As a good soldier of Christ Jesus you must endure your share of suffering. [4]Soldiers on duty don't work at outside jobs. They try only to please their commanding officer. [5]No one wins an athletic contest without obeying the rules. [6]And farmers who work hard are the first to eat what grows in their field. [7]If you keep in mind what I have told you, the Lord will help you understand completely.

[8]Keep your mind on Jesus Christ! He was from the family of David and was raised from death, just as my good news says. [9]And because of this message, I am locked up in jail and treated like a criminal. But God's good news isn't locked in jail, [10]and so I am willing to put up with anything. Then God's special people will be saved and given eternal glory because they belong to Christ Jesus. [11]Here is a true message:
  "If we died with Christ,
    we will live with him.
[12]If we don't give up,
    we will rule with him.
If we deny
    that we know him,
he will deny
    that he knows us.
[13]If we are not faithful,
    he will still be faithful.
Christ cannot deny
    who he is."

An Approved Worker

[14]Don't let anyone forget these things. And with God[e] as your witness, you must warn them not to argue about words. These arguments don't help anyone. In fact, they ruin everyone who listens to them. [15]Do your best to win God's approval as a worker who doesn't need to be ashamed and who teaches only the true message.

[16]Keep away from worthless and useless talk. It only leads people farther away from God. [17]That sort of talk is like a sore that

[c]**1.11** *teacher:* Some manuscripts add "of the Gentiles." [d]**1.12** *what he has trusted me with:* Or "what I have trusted him with." [e]**2.14** *God:* Some manuscripts have "the Lord," and others have "Christ."

As a good soldier of Christ Jesus you must endure your share of suffering. 2 TIM 2.3

won't heal. And Hymenaeus and Philetus have been talking this way [18]by teaching that the dead have already been raised to life. This is far from the truth, and it is destroying the faith of some people.

[19]But the foundation God has laid is solid. On it is written, "The Lord knows who his people are. So everyone who worships the Lord must turn away from evil."

[20]In a large house some dishes are made of gold or silver, while others are made of wood or clay. Some of these are special, and others are not. [21]This is also how it is with people. The ones who stop doing evil and make themselves pure will become special. Their lives will be holy and pleasing to their Master, and they will be able to do all kinds of good deeds.

[22]Run from temptations that capture young people. Always do the right thing. Be faithful, loving, and easy to get along with. Worship with people whose hearts are pure. [23]Stay away from stupid and senseless arguments. These only lead to trouble, [24]and God's servants must not be troublemakers. They must be kind to everyone, and they must be good teachers and very patient.

[25]Be humble when you correct people who oppose you. Maybe God will lead them to turn to him and learn the truth. [26]They have been trapped by the devil, and he makes them obey him, but God may help them escape.

What People Will Be Like in the Last Days

3 You can be certain that in the last days there will be some very hard times. [2]People will love only themselves and money. They will be proud, stuck-up,

rude, and disobedient to their parents. They will also be ungrateful, godless, [3]heartless, and hateful. Their words will be cruel, and they will have no self-control or pity. These people will hate everything good. [4]They will be sneaky, reckless, and puffed up with pride. Instead of loving God, they will love pleasure. [5]Even though they will make a show of being religious, their religion won't be real. Don't have anything to do with such people.

[6]Some men fool whole families, just to get power over those women who are slaves of sin and are controlled by all sorts of desires. [7]These women always want to learn something new, but they never can discover the truth. [8]Just as Jannes and Jambres[f] opposed Moses, these people are enemies of the truth. Their minds are sick, and their faith isn't real. [9]But they won't get very far with their foolishness. Soon everyone will know the truth about them, just as Jannes and Jambres were found out.

Paul's Last Instructions to Timothy

[10]Timothy, you know what I teach and how I live. You know what I want to do and what I believe. You have seen how patient and loving I am, and how in the past I put up with [11]trouble and suffering in the cities of Antioch, Iconium, and Lystra. Yet the Lord rescued me from all those terrible troubles. [12]In fact, anyone who belongs to Christ Jesus and wants to live right will have trouble from others. [13]But evil people who pretend to be what they are not will become worse than ever, as they fool others and are fooled themselves.

[14]Keep on being faithful to what you were taught and to what you believed.

[f]**3.8** *Jannes and Jambres:* These names are not found in the Old Testament. But many believe these were the names of the two Egyptian magicians who opposed Moses when he wanted to lead the people of Israel out of Egypt (see Exodus 7.11,22).

2.22 *temptations that capture young people:* This could refer to a number of things such as false teachings (4.3), lack of self control (3.3), and loving pleasure rather than loving God (3.4).

Satan

3.1 *last days:* Refers to a time just before the end of the present age, or the time when God will judge the world. A number of New Testament passages say that false teachings would be common during this time.

End Times

3.6 *men fool whole families . . . women who are slaves of sin:* One strategy the false teachers used was to influence certain women in order to gain control of their families.

3.8 *Jannes and Jambres:* These names are not found in the Old Testament. But according to Jewish tradition these were the names of the two Egyptian magicians who opposed Moses. See Exod 7.11,22.

3.11 *trouble and suffering in . . . Antioch:* This refers to the city of Antioch in Pisidia (Acts 13.14-52), where Paul and Barnabas preached the good news with success.

3.15,16 *Holy Scriptures . . . God's Word:* This refers to the Jewish Scriptures (Old Testament). The writings included in the New Testament were not yet collected as Scripture and would not have been widely available for study.

⊂ℜ   Second Coming

4.6 *drink offering:* The water or wine offered by Jewish priests in the temple. See Num 28.7; Phil 2.17.

4.7,8 *finished the race . . . a crown:* Winners of athletic contests were often awarded with a "crown" made of fresh leaves. The leaves of this crown eventually died, but a crown that lasts forever will be the reward of Jesus' faithful followers.

4.10 *Dalmatia:* Dalmatia was a remote coastal region on the Adriatic Sea in what is modern-day Croatia. Though partially brought under Roman control in 228 B.C., the people of Dalmatia often revolted against Roman rule.

⊂ℜ   Scrolls

4.17 *hungry lions:* It is not clear here whether the author is talking about actual animals or about Paul's human opponents. See also 1 Cor 15.32.

After all, you know who taught you these things. ¹⁵Since childhood, you have known the Holy Scriptures that are able to make you wise enough to have faith in Christ Jesus and be saved. ¹⁶Everything in the Scriptures is God's Word. All of it is useful for teaching and helping people and for correcting them and showing them how to live. ¹⁷The Scriptures train God's servants to do all kinds of good deeds.

4 When Christ Jesus comes as king, he will be the judge of everyone, whether they are living or dead. So with God and Christ as witnesses, I command you ²to preach God's message. Do it willingly, even if it isn't the popular thing to do. You must correct people and point out their sins. But also cheer them up, and when you instruct them, always be patient. ³The time is coming when people won't listen to good teaching. Instead, they will look for teachers who will please them by telling them only what they are itching to hear. ⁴They will turn from the truth and eagerly listen to senseless stories. ⁵But you must stay calm and be willing to suffer. You must work hard, telling the good news and to do your job well.

⁶Now the time has come for me to die. My life is like a drink offering[g] being poured out on the altar. ⁷I have fought well. I have finished the race, and I have been faithful. ⁸So a crown will be given to me for pleasing the Lord. He judges fairly, and on the day of judgment he will give a crown to me and to everyone else who wants him to appear with power.

Personal Instructions

⁹Come to see me as soon as you can. ¹⁰Demas loves the things of this world so much that he left me and went to Thessalonica. Crescens has gone to Galatia, and Titus has gone to Dalmatia. ¹¹Only Luke has stayed with me.

Mark can be very helpful to me, so please find him and bring him with you. ¹²I sent Tychicus to Ephesus.

¹³When you come, bring the coat I left at Troas with Carpus. Don't forget to bring the scrolls, especially the ones made of leather.[h]

¹⁴Alexander, the metalworker, has hurt me in many ways. But the Lord will pay him back for what he has done. ¹⁵Alexander opposes what we preach, so you had better watch out for him.

¹⁶When I was first put on trial, no one helped me. In fact, everyone deserted me. I hope it won't be held against them. ¹⁷But the Lord stood beside me. He gave me the strength to tell his full message, so that all Gentiles would hear it. And I was kept safe from hungry lions. ¹⁸The Lord will always keep me from being harmed by evil, and he will bring me safely into his heavenly kingdom. Praise him forever and ever! Amen.

Final Greetings

¹⁹Give my greetings to Priscilla and Aquila and to the family of Onesiphorus.

²⁰Erastus stayed at Corinth.

Trophimus was sick when I left him at Miletus.

²¹Do your best to come before winter.

Eubulus, Pudens, Linus, and Claudia send you their greetings, and so do the rest of the Lord's followers.

²²I pray that the Lord will bless your life and will be kind to you.

[g]**4.6** *drink offering:* Water or wine was sometimes poured out as an offering when an animal sacrifice was made.   [h]**4.13** *the ones made of leather:* A scroll was a kind of rolled up book, and it could be made out of paper (called "papyrus") or leather (that is, animal skin) or even copper.

Reflection Questions About 2 Timothy 1.1—4.22

1. What three qualities does God's Spirit give (1.7)? Why would these things be important to a young leader of the church like Timothy? How are they important for Christians living today?

2. In 2.3-7, three types of people are described as hard workers. What qualities did these different workers have that the author wants Timothy to imitate? Which type of worker do you think best depicts the life of a Christian? Why?

3. Read the advice given to Timothy in 2.22-26. Why is this advice important to a leader in the church? In your opinion, what difficult temptations do Christians face today? Where do you find strength to face temptations?

4. In 3.1-5, the author gives Timothy a brief description of how difficult the "last days" will be. What does the author say people will be like at that time?

5. What is the difference between those who "listen to good teaching" and those who only listen to "what they are itching to hear" (4.3)? Do you see this difference in people today?

titus

In a world full of different ideas and lifestyles, how do people discover the truth about God and being part of God's people? Read TITUS and find out.

WHAT MAKES TITUS SPECIAL?

Titus was a close friend of Paul who worked with him in Asia Minor and Greece and who was connected with the church in Corinth (see 2 Cor 2.13; 7.5-7,13-15; 8.6,16-24; 12.14-18; Gal 2.1-3). Titus apparently received this letter while he was still on the island of Crete, where Paul had left Titus to develop leaders for the churches in each town (Titus 1.5; Acts 27.7-13).

This letter was written to encourage Titus to continue teaching the truth about the faith and to instruct people how to live their lives as God wants. Apparently, some people in the churches on Crete were trying to fool some of the followers by teaching false things (1.10-14; 3.9,10). The letter also provides instructions for church leaders and all the people of God.

WHAT'S THE STORY BEHIND THE SCENE?

TITUS focuses on instructions to church leaders about following correct beliefs and living in a proper way. This concern for how authority should be maintained within the churches may indicate that TITUS is one of Paul's later letters, or even that the letter was written in Paul's name a number of years after he died. Writing a letter in a person's name was considered a way of honoring that person's life and teachings and was a common practice in that age.

HOW IS TITUS CONSTRUCTED?

The letter may be outlined in the following way:

Church leaders and false teachers (1.1-16)
What to believe and how to live as God's people
(2.1—3.15)

Titus was a co-worker of Paul's who had traveled with the apostle during his ministry in Asia Minor and Greece. He had been especially helpful to Paul in his dealings with the much troubled church at Corinth. During their travels, Paul and Titus had visited the large Greek island of Crete. Paul had asked Titus to remain in Crete and appoint church leaders for the Christian churches in each of its towns. Like 1 and 2 Timothy, this letter is considered a "Pastoral Letter" because it addresses key issues faced by many of the first Christian churches. Here, the author describes the kind of people who should be selected as church leaders. The letter lists the kind of virtues Titus should encourage in the congregations he oversees, and reminds Titus to set a good example for others. The author also tells Titus not to encourage troublemakers or people who would spread false teachings about Jesus. Instead of engaging in useless arguments, Christians should devote their energies to living their faith.

Outline

1 From Paul, a servant of God and an apostle of Jesus Christ.

I encourage God's own people to have more faith and to understand the truth about religion. [2]Then they will have the hope of eternal life God promised long ago. And God never tells a lie! [3]So, at the proper time, God our Savior gave this message and told me to announce what he had said.

[4]Titus, because of our faith, you are like a son to me. I pray that God our Father and Christ Jesus our Savior will be kind to you and will bless you with peace!

What Titus Was To Do in Crete

[5]I left you in Crete to do what had been left undone and to appoint leaders[a] for the churches in each town. As I told you, [6]they must have a good reputation and be faithful in marriage.[b] Their children must be followers of the Lord and not have a reputation for being wild and disobedient.

[7]Church officials[c] are in charge of God's work, and so they must also have a good reputation. They must not be bossy, quick-tempered, heavy drinkers, bullies, or dishonest in business. [8]Instead, they must be friendly to strangers and enjoy doing good things. They must also be sensible, fair, pure, and self-controlled. [9]They must stick to the true message they were taught, so their good teaching can help others and correct everyone who opposes it.

[10]There are many who don't respect authority, and they fool others by talking nonsense. This is especially true of some Jewish followers. [11]But you must make them be quiet. They are after money, and they upset whole families by teaching what they should not. [12]It is like one of their own prophets once said,

"The people of Crete
    always tell lies.
They are greedy and lazy
    like wild animals."

---

[a]**1.5** *leaders*: Or "elders" or "presbyters" or "priests." [b]**1.6** *be faithful in marriage*: Or "be the husband of only one wife." [c]**1.7** *Church officials*: Or "Bishops."

■ 1.1 *faith and . . . the truth about religion*: In Paul's letters, the word "faith" usually refers to trust in Jesus Christ. Here faith seems to refer to "correct beliefs," a later Christian understanding of this word. The word translated as "religion" means "proper way of life." This term does not appear in any of Paul's earlier letters.

✆ Eternal Life

● 1.5 *Crete*: Crete is a large island in the Mediterranean Sea southeast of Greece. Crete was the home of the Minoan culture that thrived between 2000 and 1100 B.C. **(See Map 16 on pg 1894.)**

● 1.10,11 *don't respect authority . . . fool others*: The "nonsense" described here may refer to Jewish members of the churches of Crete insisting that all the male followers of Jesus be circumcised. Paul and Titus had already settled this issue earlier, when they met with other church leaders in Jerusalem (see Gal 2.1-10). Other followers apparently tried to get money for themselves from other members by claiming that they had the real truth (see also 1 Tim 6.5). Some false teachers tried to influence the women in order to control their whole families.

● 1.12 *The people . . . animals*: This quote is from the Greek philosopher named Epimenides, who is believed to have lived on Crete around 600 B.C.

1.14 *senseless Jewish stories and human commands:* Exaggerated stories about people mentioned in the genealogies in GENESIS were taught in various Jewish writings of the time, and in the writing of religious groups known as Gnostics (see also 1 Tim 1.3,4; 4.7; 2 Tim 4.4). **(See the article Religions and Philosophies in Bible Times on pg 1816.)**

2.4,5 *younger women . . . puts her own husband first:* In Paul's day wives were to serve their husbands. Christian women who served their husbands and took care of their children were also serving Christ (Eph 5.21-25).

2.9 *slaves . . . owners:* The author reminds Titus that slaves should respect their masters, and masters should take care of their slaves and treat them well (Eph 6.5-9).

Slaves and Servants in the Time of Jesus

2.11 *save all people:* Here the word "save" points to what God does to free humans from sin and the powers of evil.

God's Saving Love (Salvation)

2.13 *glorious return of . . . Savior Jesus Christ:* Paul often talked in his letters about a day when Jesus would come back (1 Cor 15.20-28; Phil 1.10; 2.16; 3.20,21).

Second Coming

[13]This surely is a true saying. And you should be hard on such people, so you can help them grow stronger in their faith. [14]Don't pay any attention to any of those senseless Jewish stories and human commands. These are made up by people who won't obey the truth.

[15]Everything is pure for someone whose heart is pure. But nothing is pure for an unbeliever with a dirty mind. That person's mind and conscience are destroyed. [16]Such people claim to know God, but their actions prove they really don't. They are disgusting. They won't obey God, and they are too worthless to do anything good.

Instructions for Different Groups of People

2 Titus, you must teach only what is correct. [2]Tell the older men to have self-control and to be serious and sensible. Their faith, love, and patience must never fail.

[3]Tell the older women to behave as those who love the Lord should. They must not gossip about others or be slaves of wine. They must teach what is proper, [4]so the younger women will be loving wives and mothers. [5]Each of the younger women must be sensible and kind, as well as a good homemaker, who puts her own husband first. Then no one can say insulting things about God's message.

[6]Tell the young men to have self-control in everything.

[7]Always set a good example for others. Be sincere and serious when you teach. [8]Use clean language that no one can criticize. Do this, and your enemies will be too ashamed to say anything against you.

[9]Tell slaves always to please their owners by obeying them in everything. Slaves must not talk back to their owners [10]or steal from them. They must be completely honest and trustworthy. Then everyone will show great respect for what is taught about God our Savior.

God's Kindness and the New Life

[11]God has shown us undeserved grace by coming to save all people. [12]He taught us to give up our wicked ways and our worldly desires and to live decent and honest lives in this world. [13]We are filled with hope, as we wait for the glorious return of our great God and Savior Jesus Christ.[d] [14]He gave himself to rescue us from everything evil and to make our hearts pure. He wanted us to be his own people and to be eager to do right.

[15]Teach these things, as you use your full authority to encourage and correct people. Make sure you earn everyone's respect.

Doing Helpful Things

3 Remind your people to obey the rulers and authorities and not to be rebellious. They must always be ready to do something helpful [2]and not say cruel things or argue. They should be gentle and kind to everyone. [3]We used to be stupid, disobedient, and foolish, as well as slaves of all sorts of desires and pleasures. We were evil and jealous. Everyone hated us, and we hated everyone.

[4]God our Savior showed us
how good and kind he is.
[5]He saved us because

[d]**2.13** *the glorious return of our great God and Savior Jesus Christ:* Or "the glorious return of our great God and our Savior Jesus Christ" or "the return of Jesus Christ, who is the glory of our great God and Savior."

Always set a good example for others. TITUS 2.7

of his mercy,
and not because
of any good things
we have done.

God washed us by the power
of the Holy Spirit.
He gave us new birth
and a fresh beginning.
⁶God sent Jesus Christ
our Savior
to give us his Spirit.

⁷Jesus treated us much better
than we deserve.
He made us acceptable to God
and gave us the hope
of eternal life.

⁸This message is certainly true.

These teachings are useful and helpful for everyone. I want you to insist that the people follow them, so that all who have faith in God will be sure to do good deeds. ⁹But don't have anything to do with stupid arguments about ancestors. And stay away from disagreements and quarrels about the Law of Moses. Such arguments are useless and senseless.

¹⁰Warn troublemakers once or twice. Then don't have anything else to do with them. ¹¹You know their minds are twisted, and their own sins show how guilty they are.

Personal Instructions and Greetings

¹²I plan to send Artemas or Tychicus to you. After he arrives, please try your best to meet me at Nicopolis. I have decided to spend the winter there.

¹³When Zenas the lawyer and Apollos get ready to leave, help them as much as you can, so they won't have need of anything.

¹⁴Our people should learn to spend their time doing something useful and worthwhile.

¹⁵Greetings to you from everyone here. Greet all of our friends who share in our faith.

I pray that the Lord will be kind to all of you!

■ **3.5** *washed us by the power of the Holy Spirit:* This probably refers to baptism. Paul taught that in baptism the followers of Christ are raised to new life (see Rom 6.3-5). This is the "new birth" mentioned in 3.5.

◌੪ Baptism

◌੪ Holy Spirit

◌੪ Roman Empire

◌੪ Sin

● **3.12** *Artemas or Tychicus:* This is the only time Artemas is mentioned in the Bible. Tychicus was one of Paul's co-workers. Paul trusted Tychicus to deliver messages and get information for him (Acts 20.4; Eph 6.21,22; Col 4.7,8; and 2 Tim 4.12).

● **3.12** *Nicopolis:* A port city on the western coast of Achaia. Travel by boat on the Mediterranean Sea was very dangerous during the winter months. This may be why the writer decided to stay in Nicopolis during the winter.

● **3.13** *Zenas . . . Apollos:* This is the only time Zenas is mentioned in the Bible. Apollos may be the same person mentioned in 1 Corinthians 3.1-9; 16.12, and in Acts 18.24.

◌੪ Lord (Title for Jesus)

Reflection Questions About Titus 1.1—3.15

1. According to the author of TITUS, how are appointed church leaders and officials to live (1.5-9)? Do you think church leaders, pastors, and priests are expected to live according to a higher set of standards than anyone else? Why or why not?

2. The author of TITUS says, "Everything is pure for someone whose heart is pure" (Titus 1.15). What does this mean?

3. According to TITUS, how did God show his kindness (2.11-14; 3.4-7)?

4. Why was Titus instructed to remind the people in his care to obey the government rulers and authorities (3.1)? What might have been the consequences if they were rebellious? What do you think of this advice? Compare Titus 3.1 to Acts 5.27-29. What do you make of the difference between these passages?

5. What was the most important thing you learned from reading TITUS?

philemon

Every society has laws and standards that it expects its people to live by. Read this short letter to find out what Paul had to say about God's love—how it can help the Lord's followers to do even more than what society expects of them.

WHAT MAKES PHILEMON SPECIAL?

This letter is typical of the kinds of letters people wrote in the Roman world. It is the shortest and most personal of Paul's letters. The way it is written suggests that Paul and Philemon were close friends. Most of the people mentioned in this letter, including Philemon's slave Onesimus, are also mentioned in COLOSSIANS (Col 4.7-9).

Philemon was a wealthy man who probably lived in Colossae. Like many wealthy people in the Roman world, he owned slaves. But he was also a Christian who used his large house for church meetings (Phlm 2). Paul is writing on behalf of Onesimus who had escaped from Philemon's household. Onesimus had become a follower of the Lord and a valuable friend to Paul. Paul is writing to say that he is sending Onesimus back to Philemon and to encourage Philemon to accept Onesimus as a friend and as a follower of the Lord.

WHAT'S THE STORY BEHIND THE SCENE?

Paul may have written this letter while he was in prison in Ephesus, or he may have written it from Rome where he was forced to live in a house guarded by a soldier who made sure Paul did not go out and who could keep an eye on the kind of visitors he received (Acts 28.16-21).

Paul's concern is that Philemon treats his returning slave with kindness and love. He knew that Roman law allowed slave-owners to punish escaped slaves harshly, and he does not question Philemon's right to own slaves. In fact, Paul seems to accept slavery as part of society in his day (1 Cor 7.20-22). In his letters he urged slaves to obey their masters. But more importantly, he urged masters to be kind to their slaves (Col 3.22,23—4.1). In GALATIANS, Paul says that slaves and free persons who have faith in Christ are equal with each other in God's family (Gal 3.26-28).

HOW IS PHILEMON CONSTRUCTED?

The letter may be outlined in the following way:

Greetings and a prayer for Philemon (1-3)
Message to Philemon about his slave, Onesimus (4-22)
Final greetings and a prayer (23-25)

This short letter was written by the apostle Paul while he was in prison at an undisclosed location. It is addressed to three people who are leaders of a church that meets in the home of one or more of them, but Philemon is clearly the principal addressee. The letter is highly personal and a masterpiece of persuasive rhetoric. In it Paul asks Philemon to be reconciled to a man named Onesimus, a fellow Christian, and to receive him as he would receive Paul himself. It is not clear how Onesimus has wronged Philemon, but Paul is willing to compensate Philemon for any loss his friend may have suffered because of Onesimus. Although Paul can use his authority as an apostle to make Philemon do as he asks, he prefers to appeal to him as a fellow Christian and asks Philemon to act out of sincere love.

Outline

[1]From Paul, who is in jail for serving Christ Jesus, and from Timothy, who is like a brother because of our faith.

Philemon, you work with us and are very dear to us. This letter is to you [2]and to the church that meets in your home. It is also to our dear friend Apphia and to Archippus, who serves the Lord as we do.

[3]I pray that God our Father and our Lord Jesus Christ will be kind to you and will bless you with peace!

Philemon's Love and Faith

[4]Philemon, each time I mention you in my prayers, I thank God. [5]I hear about your faith in our Lord Jesus and about your love for all God's people. [6]As you share your faith with others, I pray they may come to know all the blessings Christ has given us. [7]My friend, your love has made me happy and has greatly encouraged me. It has also cheered the hearts of God's people.

Paul Speaks to Philemon about Onesimus

[8]Christ gives me the courage to tell you what to do. [9]But I would rather ask you to do it simply because of love. Yes, as someone[a] in jail for Christ, [10]I beg you to help Onesimus![b] He is like a son to me because I led him to Christ here in jail. [11]Before this, he was useless to you, but now he is useful both to you and to me.

[12]Sending Onesimus back to you makes me very sad. [13]I would like to keep him here with me, where he could take your place in helping me while I am here in prison for preaching the good news. [14]But I won't do anything unless you agree to it first. I want your act of kindness to come from your heart, and not be something you feel forced to do.

[15]Perhaps Onesimus was taken from you for a little while so you could have him back for good, [16]but not as a slave. Onesimus is

[a]9 *someone*: Greek "a messenger" or "an old man."
[b]10 *Onesimus*: In Greek this name means "useful."

☙   Paul, (Saul) of Tarsus

●   1 *Paul . . . Philemon:* Paul was also known by his Jewish name, Saul (see Acts 7.57—8.3; 9.1-30). Paul had been a strict follower of the Law of Moses and tried to make trouble for the early followers of Jesus (Gal 1.13; Phil 3.5,6), but Jesus chose him to be his apostle and to preach the good news (Acts 9.1-19).

●   2 *the church that meets in your home:* The Greek word translated as "church" is *ekklesia*, and it originally referred to any gathering of people. In Paul's day Christians met in homes that were large enough for these kinds of gatherings. Here they came together for preaching, teaching, worship, sharing the Lord's Supper (Eucharist), and for social events. (See the chart Leaders of House Churches in the New Testament on pg 1840.)

☙   Church

●   10 *Onesimus:* In Greek, the name Onesimus means "useful." Onesimus was a slave who may have run away from his master Philemon. Onesimus eventually reached the city where Paul was in jail or under house arrest. Verse 18 implies that Onesimus may have taken money or property from Philemon. Paul got to know Onesimus while he was in jail, although it is not clear whether Onesimus was also a prisoner. Paul feels especially fond of Onesimus because he had led Onesimus to Christ.

As you share your faith with others, I pray they may come to know all the blessings Christ has given us. PHLM 6

19 *you owe me your life:* This probably means that Paul first told Philemon about the good news of God's love. When Philemon accepted this message by faith, he received new life in Christ.

22 *get a room ready for me:* Paul intended to visit Philemon. This may indicate that Paul was not imprisoned far away in Rome, but may have been in Ephesus or some other city nearer to where Philemon lived.

23 *Epaphras:* He is also mentioned as a worker with Paul in Colossians 1.7; 4.12.

24 *Mark, Aristarchus, Demas, and Luke:* These followers are all mentioned in Colossians 4.10-14. Mark worked with Paul and Barnabas, and is mentioned several times in ACTS (Acts 12.12, 25; 13.13; 15.36-39). Aristarchus was from Thessalonica in Greece, but traveled with Paul (Acts 19.29; 20.4,5), including his final journey to Rome (Acts 27.2). Demas is mentioned in 2 Timothy 4.10, where his actions are criticized. Luke is mentioned in Colossians 4.14, where he is called a doctor. Although it is not certain who wrote LUKE or ACTS, they have been traditionally considered his works.

much more than a slave. To me he is a dear friend, but to you he is even more, both as a person and as a follower of the Lord.

¹⁷If you consider me a friend because of Christ, then welcome Onesimus as you would welcome me. ¹⁸If he has cheated you or owes you anything, charge it to my account. ¹⁹With my own hand I write: I, PAUL, WILL PAY YOU BACK. But don't forget you owe me your life. ²⁰My dear friend and follower of Christ our Lord, please cheer me up by doing this for me.

²¹I am sure you will do all I have asked, and even more. ²²Please get a room ready for me. I hope your prayers will be answered, and I can visit you.

²³Epaphras is also here in jail for being a follower of Christ Jesus. He sends his greetings, ²⁴and so do Mark, Aristarchus, Demas, and Luke, who work together with me.

²⁵I pray that the Lord Jesus Christ will be kind to you!

Reflection Questions About Philemon 1-25

1. Paul tells Philemon that he is in jail "for serving Christ Jesus" (1). What do you think this means? Can you think of other people who have been imprisoned because of their faith? How can Christians help people in this situation?

2. Everything we know about the wealthy Christian Philemon and his slave Onesimus is contained in this letter. What significant change has Onesimus experienced since leaving his master's house (10)?

3. Why does Paul think Onesimus is now useful both to Philemon and himself (11)?

4. If Onesimus had intentionally run away from his master, Roman law would have allowed Philemon to punish him severely, perhaps even putting him to death. What does Paul encourage Philemon to do instead (12-20)?

5. What does PHILEMON have to say about how Christians should treat one another? What can be learned from Paul's example and the actions he took on behalf of his friend Onesimus?

hebrews

The Jewish people had a high priest who offered sacrifices in the temple so that the people would be forgiven. Yet how could the new Christians be forgiven? Read Hebrews to find out.

WHAT MAKES HEBREWS SPECIAL?

Although HEBREWS is often referred to as a "letter," it is really a carefully organized speech or a sermon that makes its main points very clearly. HEBREWS uses both the Jewish Scriptures and ideas from Greek culture and philosophy to explain the new Christian faith. It answers very basic questions about the Christian faith and explains how important Jesus really is.

Many religious people in the first century, both Jews and Gentiles, had questions about the religion of the early Christians. HEBREWS states that Christianity, though based in the Jewish religion, is quite different in important ways. The main difference is Christ Jesus, who is the perfect high priest and who offered his own life as a perfect sacrifice for sin once for all time (9.23—10.18). By dying and returning from death he has opened the way for all people to come to God (4.14—5.10; 7.1—8.13). The forgiveness and new life that Jesus offers comes only by faith. Christians are to keep their eyes and minds focused on Jesus, who leads them in this race and makes their faith complete (12.2,3).

WHAT'S THE STORY BEHIND THE SCENE?

It is not clear who wrote HEBREWS, or when it was written. The letter was likely written after A.D. 60 and before A.D. 95, when parts of HEBREWS appear in a letter written by Clement of Rome.

The identity of the letter's audience is also unclear. Some members of the audience have gone through hard times, being mistreated in public and having their belongings taken away (10.32-34). Some followers have quit meeting for worship, perhaps because Christ has not returned as soon as they expected (10.25). This suggests that the audience was a second generation of Christians.

HOW IS HEBREWS CONSTRUCTED?

The argument of the book is developed in five major themes. Each main theme is followed by sections that teach how God's people should live.

God chose Jesus to purify and renew the world (1.1-14)
"Listen to the message that saves" (2.1-4)
Jesus' way of saving God's people is greater than Moses' way (2.5—3.6)
"Hold on to faith and enter the place of rest" (3.7—4.13)
Jesus is the great high priest (4.14—5.10)
"Turn away from deeds that bring death" (5.11—6.12)
Jesus' sacrifice makes a new agreement (6.13—10.18)
"Prepare for the day of the Lord's coming" (10.19-39)
Faith has always been the way to belong to God (11.1-40)
"Run the race of faith" (12.1—13.25)

Although the letter to the Hebrews contains many of the features common to first century letters in the Greco-Roman world, it does not begin with the standard introduction and greeting. Perhaps, therefore, it is best to think of Hebrews less as a personal letter addressed to a single congregation than as a long and powerful sermon that was intended to be circulated among a number of churches. Its main purpose is to tell people how important Jesus really is. Using references to the Jewish Scriptures (Old Testament), the author shows how Jesus Christ's ministry, death, and being raised to life fulfilled ancient prophecies. The author then shows how Christ's sacrificial death offers a new way of asking God to forgive sins. In this way, Christ created a new agreement between God and God's people. Not only does Jesus prepare the way for the future, he helps the faithful understand past events. With the new understanding Jesus reveals come new responsibilities for the faithful. Each step in the author's presentation of this new agreement is balanced with a list of responsibilities that Christians are to embrace. As Jesus' followers, they have been given a kingdom that cannot be shaken.

Outline

1 Long ago in many ways and at many
times God's prophets spoke his message to our ancestors. ²But now at last, God
sent his Son to bring his message to us. God
created the universe by his Son, and everything will someday belong to the Son.
³God's Son has all the brightness of God's
own glory and is like him in every way. By
his own mighty word, he holds the universe together.

After the Son had washed away our sins,
he sat down at the right side[a] of the glorious God in heaven. ⁴He had become much
greater than the angels, and the name he
was given is far greater than any of theirs.

God's Son Is Greater than Angels

⁵God has never said
   to any of the angels,
"You are my Son, because today
   I have become your Father!"

Neither has God said
   to any of them,
"I will be his Father,
   and he will be my Son!"

⁶When God brings his first-born Son[b]
into the world, he commands all of his angels to worship him.
⁷And when God speaks about the angels,
he says,
"I change my angels into wind
   and my servants
      into flaming fire."

⁸But God says about his Son,
"You are God,
   and you will rule
      as King forever!
Your[c] royal power
   brings about justice.
⁹You loved justice
   and hated evil,

---

[a]**1.3** *right side*: The place of honor and power.   [b]**1.6** *first-born Son*: The first son born into a family had
certain privileges that the other children did not have. In 12.23 (see note) "first-born" refers to
God's special people.   [c]**1.8** *Your*: Some manuscripts have "His."

1.1 *God's prophets spoke his message to our ancestors*: This refers to the
ancient Jewish prophets whose words
are recorded in the Jewish Scriptures,
which Christians call the Old Testament. In HEBREWS, God's message often refers to the promises God made to
Abraham and to the Law God gave
Moses and the people. **(See the article
Prophets and Prophecy on pg 1791.)**

◈ Abraham

1.3 *his own mighty word*: The
"mighty word" that Christ uses to hold
creation together is as powerful as the
words God used to create the universe
(Gen 1).

1.3 *washed away our sins*: The Law
of Moses stated that people who had
sinned had become ritually unclean.
People who were ritually unclean were
required to go through a washing ceremony so they could once again take
their place among God's people. But
now, the writer says, Jesus forgives sins
by washing them away.

◈ Sin

1.4 *angels*: In the Bible, angels are
beings in a special relationship with
God, who carry out God's will. The author of HEBREWS states that God's Son
(Christ) was also a messenger, but that
because of his special relationship to
God, he is greater than any angel, and
all angels worship him.

◈ Angels

---

*God created the universe by his Son, and everything
will someday belong to the Son.* HEB 1.2

2.2 *message spoken by angels*: Acts 7.53 mentions that God's Law was given by the angels.

2.4 *miracles and wonders*: The writer is referring to wonders like God's helping the people of Israel pass through the Red Sea in order to escape from slavery in Egypt (Exod 14) and providing them with food called manna while they wandered in the desert (Num 11.4-9).

2.4 *Holy Spirit*: The Holy Spirit is the power of God carrying out God's purposes in the world. The Spirit teaches and guides people so they can become the kind of people God wants them to be.

Holy Spirit

2.9 *lower than the angels*: The writer means that when Jesus was fully human, he was temporarily lower than the angels.

2.9 *Jesus died for everyone*: Jesus died in order to defeat death and overcome sin and evil. God raised Jesus from death and gave him a place of honor in heaven, where he rules with God (see Eph 1.19-22).

2.11 *holy...family*: The word "holy" here means "chosen" or "set apart" for God. The "family" here is God's family, which is made up of those who have faith in Christ.

and so I, your God,
have chosen you.
I appointed you
and made you happier
than any of your friends."

[10]The Scriptures also say,
"In the beginning, Lord,
you were the one
who laid the foundation
of the earth
and created the heavens.
[11]They will all disappear
and wear out like clothes,
but you will last forever.
[12]You will roll them up
like a robe
and change them
like a garment.
But you are always the same,
and you will live forever."

[13]God never said to any
of the angels,
"Sit at my right side
until I make your enemies
into a footstool for you!"

[14]Angels are merely spirits sent to serve people who are going to be saved.

This Great Way of Being Saved

2 We must give our full attention to what we were told, so we won't drift away. [2]The message spoken by angels proved to be true, and all who disobeyed or rejected it were punished as they deserved. [3]So if we refuse this great way of being saved, how can we hope to escape? The Lord himself was the first to tell about it, and people who heard the message proved to us that it was true. [4]God himself showed that his message was true by working all kinds of powerful miracles and wonders. He also gave his Holy Spirit to anyone he chose to.

The One Who Leads Us To Be Saved

[5]We know that God did not put the future world under the power of angels. [6]Somewhere in the Scriptures someone says to God,
"What makes you care
about us humans?
Why are you concerned
for weaklings such as we?
[7]You made us lower
than the angels
for a while.
Yet you have crowned us
with glory and honor.[d]
[8]And you have put everything
under our power!"

God has put everything under our power and has not left anything out of our power. But we still don't see it all under our control. [9]What we do see is Jesus, who for a little while was made lower than the angels. Because of God's gift of undeserved grace, Jesus died for everyone. And now that Jesus has suffered and died, he is crowned with glory and honor! [10]Everything belongs to God, and all things were created by his power. So God did the right thing when he made Jesus perfect by suffering, as Jesus led many of God's children to be saved and to share in his glory. [11]Jesus and the people he makes holy all belong to the same family. This is why he isn't ashamed to call them his brothers and sisters. [12]He even said to God,

[d]2.7 *and honor*: Some manuscripts add "and you have placed us in charge of all you created."

"I will tell them your name
and sing your praises
when they come together
to worship."

[13]He also said,
"I will trust God."

Then he said,
"Here I am with the children
God has given me."

[14]We are people of flesh and blood. This is why Jesus became one of us. He died to destroy the devil, who had power over death. [15]But he also died to rescue all of us who live each day in fear of dying. [16]Jesus clearly did not come to help angels, but he did come to help Abraham's descendants. [17]He had to be one of us, so he could serve God as our merciful and faithful high priest and sacrifice himself for the forgiveness of our sins. [18]And now that Jesus has suffered and was tempted, he can help anyone else who is tempted.

Jesus Is Greater than Moses

3 My friends, God has chosen you to be his holy people. So think about Jesus, the one we call our apostle and high priest! [2]Jesus was faithful to God, who appointed him, just as Moses was faithful in serving all[e] God's people. [3]But Jesus deserves more honor than Moses, just as the builder of a house deserves more honor than the house. [4]Of course, every house is built by someone, and God is really the one who built everything. [5]Moses was a faithful servant and told God's people what would be said in the future. [6]But Christ is the Son in charge of God's people. And we are those people, if we keep on being brave and don't lose hope.

A Rest for God's People

[7]It is just as the Holy Spirit says,

"If you hear God's voice today,
[8] don't be stubborn!
Don't rebel like those people
who were tested
in the desert.
*[9f]For forty years your ancestors
tested God and saw
the things he did.

[10]"Then God got tired of them
and said,
'You people never
show good sense,
and you don't understand
what I want you to do.'
[11]God became angry
and told the people,
'You will never enter
my place of rest!' "

[12]My friends, watch out! Don't let evil thoughts or doubts make any of you turn from the living God. [13]You must encourage one another each day. And you must keep on while there is still a time that can be called "today." If you don't, then sin may fool some of you and make you stubborn. [14]We were sure about Christ when we first became his people. So let's hold tightly to our faith until the end. [15]The Scriptures say,
"If you hear his voice today,
don't be stubborn
like those who rebelled."

[e]**3.2** *all:* Some manuscripts do not have "all."   [f]**3.9** When an asterisk (*) occurs before a verse number, it indicates that this verse and the following have been combined.

● **2.17** *high priest and sacrifice:* On the Great Day of Forgiveness (Lev 16.1-34; Exod 28.1-39), the high priest of Israel entered the most holy place in the temple to offer sacrifices, asking God to take away the sins of the people. Like the high priest, Jesus offered a sacrifice for all people's sins. The sacrifice he brought was himself (see Rom 3.25,26).

● **3.5** *Moses:* **See the chart Key Events in Moses' Life on pg 1841.**

⊙ Moses

■ **3.6** *Christ:* "Christ" is from the Greek word *Christos,* and has the same meaning as the Hebrew word Messiah, or "chosen one." God chose Jesus to lead God's people.

● **3.8,9** *tested in the desert . . . your ancestors tested God:* After escaping from Egypt, the people of Israel wandered for many years in the desert. By complaining and disobeying God's commands (Exod 15.23; 17.7; Deut 6.16; Num 14.21-23), they tested God.

We were sure about Christ when we first became his people.

So let's hold tightly to our faith until the end. HEB 3.14

4.1 *the place of rest:* The Israelite people who left Egypt were headed for Canaan, where they hoped to make their home in a land of plenty and peace. The generation of Israelites that disobeyed God in the desert was not allowed to enter this place of rest. However, God has provided a place of rest in heaven for those who have faith in Christ. In this place of rest, they will live with God forever.

Eternal Life

4.7 *David:* King David lived about 1,000 years before Jesus was born, and was considered by many to be Israel's greatest ruler.

David

4.8 *Joshua:* Before Moses died, Joshua was chosen to lead the people into Canaan (Deut 31.1-8). The Israelite people conquered much of the land and did experience some periods of peace (Josh 21.44), but nothing like the "place of rest" still to come.

4.9,10 *Sabbath:* The writer compares the new day of rest to the Jewish Sabbath. Sabbath means "rest" or to "stop working" and was a rule for all Jewish people (Exod 20.8-11; Deut 5.12-15).

5.4 *Aaron:* God chose Aaron, Moses' brother, to be the first high priest (Exod 28.1—29.35).

Israel's Priests

[16]Who were those people that heard God's voice and rebelled? Weren't they the same ones that came out of Egypt with Moses? [17]Who were the people that made God angry for 40 years? Weren't they the ones that sinned and died in the desert? [18]And who did God say would never enter his place of rest? Weren't they the ones that disobeyed him? [19]We see that those people did not enter the place of rest because they did not have faith.

4 The promise to enter the place of rest is still good, and we must take care that none of you miss out. [2]We have heard the message, just as they did. But they failed to believe what they heard, and the message did not do them any good. [3]Only people who have faith will enter the place of rest. It is just as the Scriptures say,

"God became angry
    and told the people,
'You will never enter
    my place of rest!'"

God said this, even though everything has been ready from the time of creation. [4]In fact, somewhere the Scriptures say that by the seventh day, God had finished his work, and so he rested. [5]We also read that he later said, "You people will never enter my place of rest!" [6]This means that the promise to enter is still good, because those who first heard about it disobeyed and did not enter. [7]Much later God told David to make the promise again, just as I have already said,

"If you hear his voice today,
    don't be stubborn!"

[8]If Joshua had really given the people rest, there would not be any need for God to talk about another day of rest. [9]But God has promised us a Sabbath when we will rest, even though it has not yet come. [10]On that day God's people will rest from their work, just as God rested from his work.

[11]We should do our best to enter the place of rest, so none of us will disobey and miss going there, as they did. [12]God's word is alive and powerful! It is sharper than any double-edged sword. His word can cut through our spirits and souls and through our joints and marrow, until it discovers the desires and thoughts of our hearts. [13]Nothing is hidden from God! He sees through everything, and we will have to tell him the truth.

Jesus Is the Great High Priest

[14]We have a great high priest, who has gone into heaven, and he is Jesus the Son of God. This is why we must hold on to what we have said about him. [15]Jesus understands every weakness of ours, because he was tempted in every way that we are. But he did not sin! [16]So whenever we are in need, we should come bravely before the throne of our merciful God. There we will be treated with undeserved grace, and we will find help.

5 Every high priest is appointed to help others by offering gifts and sacrifices to God because of their sins. [2]A high priest has weaknesses of his own, and he feels sorry for foolish and sinful people. [3]This is why he must offer sacrifices for his own sins and for the sins of others. [4]But no one can have the honor of being a high priest simply by wanting to be one. Only God can choose a priest, and God is the one who chose Aaron.

[5]This is how it was with Christ. He became a high priest, but not just because he wanted the honor of being one. It was God who told him,

"You are my Son, because today
    I have become your Father!"

[6]In another place, God says,

"You are a priest forever
just like Melchizedek."[g]

[7]God had the power to save Jesus from death. And while Jesus was on earth, he begged God with loud crying and tears to save him. He truly worshiped God, and God listened to his prayers. [8]Jesus is God's own Son, but still he had to suffer before he could learn what it really means to obey God. [9]Suffering made Jesus perfect, and now he can save forever all who obey him. [10]This is because God chose him to be a high priest like Melchizedek.

Warning against Turning Away

[11]Much more could be said about this subject. But it is hard to explain, and all of you are slow to understand. [12]By now you should have been teachers, but once again you need to be taught the simplest things about what God has said. You need milk instead of solid food. [13]People who live on milk are like babies who don't really know what is right. [14]Solid food is for mature people who have been trained to know right from wrong.

6 We must try to become mature and start thinking about more than just the basic things we were taught about Christ. We shouldn't need to keep talking about why we ought to turn from deeds that bring death and why we ought to have faith in God. [2]And we shouldn't need to keep teaching about baptisms[h] or about the laying on of hands[i] or about people being raised from death and the future judgment. [3]Let's grow up, if God is willing.

[4-6]But what about people who turn away after they have already seen the light and have received the gift from heaven and have shared in the Holy Spirit? What about those who turn away after they have received the good message of God and the powers of the future world? There is no way to bring them back. What they are doing is the same as nailing the Son of God to a cross and insulting him in public!

[7]A field is useful to farmers, if there is enough rain to make good crops grow. In fact, God will bless such a field. [8]But land that produces only thornbushes is worthless. It is likely to fall under God's curse, and in the end it will be set on fire.

[9]My friends, we are talking this way. But we are sure that you are doing those really good things people do when they are being saved. [10]God is always fair. He will remember how you helped his people in the past and how you are still helping them. You belong to God, and he won't forget the love you have shown his people. [11]We wish each of you would always be eager to show how strong and lasting your hope really is. [12]Then you would never be lazy. You would be following the example of those who had faith and were patient until God kept his promise to them.

God's Promise Is Sure

[13]No one is greater than God. So he made a promise in his own name when he said to Abraham, [14]"I, the Lord, will bless you with many descendants!" [15]Then after Abraham had been very patient, he was given what God had promised. [16]When anyone wants to settle an argument, they make a vow by using the name of someone

[g]5.6 Melchizedek: When Melchizedek is mentioned in the Old Testament, he is described as a priest who lived before Aaron. Nothing is said about his ancestors or his death (see 7.3 and Genesis 14.17-20). [h]6.2 baptisms: Or "ceremonies of washing." [i]6.2 laying on of hands: This was a ceremony in which church leaders and others put their hands on people to show that those people were chosen to do some special kind of work.

6.17 *vow:* According to the Law of Moses, someone who made a vow in God's name was responsible to carry out that vow (Exod 22.11). The vow could not be taken back. In the same way God could not take back the promises made to Abraham (Gen 12.1-3).

Making Promises (Vows)

6.19 *hope reaches behind the curtain:* The "hope that reaches beyond the curtain" is the hope that Christians have because Jesus became the high priest, sacrificed himself for their sins, and entered heaven.

7.5 *give a tenth . . . descendants of Levi:* According to the Law of Moses, the people of Israel were to give one-tenth of what they possessed to God. These gifts were given to the priests, who were descendants of Levi, one of the sons of Jacob (Gen 35.23-26; Num 18.20-32).

7.13-15 *our Lord . . . Judah . . . who is like Melchizedek:* Jesus' earthly father, Joseph, came from the royal tribe of Judah (Gen 49.8-10; see also Matt 1.1-17). Melchizedek was not part of the priestly tribe of Levi either. The writer of HEBREWS says that Melchizedek and Jesus did not become high priests because of the Law of Moses. They became high priests because their lives can never end (7.16), unlike the priests from the tribe of Levi, who eventually die (7.8).

or something greater than themselves. [17]So when God wanted to prove for certain his promise to his people could not be broken, he made a vow. [18]God cannot tell lies! And so his promises and vows are two things that can never be changed.

We have run to God for safety. Now his promises should greatly encourage us to take hold of the hope that is right in front of us. [19]This hope is like a firm and steady anchor for our souls. In fact, hope reaches behind the curtain[j] and into the most holy place. [20]Jesus has gone there ahead of us, and he is our high priest forever, just like Melchizedek.[k]

The Priestly Family of Melchizedek

7 Melchizedek was both king of Salem and priest of God Most High. He was the one who went out and gave Abraham his blessing, when Abraham returned from killing the kings. [2]Then Abraham gave him a tenth of everything he had.

The meaning of the name Melchizedek is "King of Justice." But since Salem means "peace," he is also "King of Peace." [3]We are not told he had a father or mother or ancestors or beginning or end. He is like the Son of God and will be a priest forever.[l]

[4]Notice how great Melchizedek was! Our famous ancestor Abraham gave him a tenth of what he had taken from his enemies. [5]The Law teaches that even Abraham's descendants must give a tenth of what they possess. And they are to give this to their own relatives, who are the descendants of Levi and are priests. [6]Although

Melchizedek wasn't a descendant of Levi, Abraham gave him a tenth of what he had. Then Melchizedek blessed Abraham, who had been given God's promise. [7]Everyone agrees a person who gives a blessing is greater than the one who receives the blessing.

[8]Priests are given a tenth of what people earn. But all priests die, except Melchizedek, and the Scriptures teach that he is alive. [9]Levi's descendants are now the ones who receive a tenth from people. We could even say that when Abraham gave Melchizedek a tenth, Levi also gave him a tenth. [10]This is because Levi was born later into the family of Abraham, who gave a tenth to Melchizedek.

[11]Even though the Law of Moses says the priests must be descendants of Levi, those priests cannot make anyone perfect. So there needs to be a priest like Melchizedek, rather than one from the priestly family of Aaron.[m] [12]And when the rules for selecting a priest are changed, the Law must also be changed.

[13]The person we are talking about is our Lord, who came from a tribe that had never had anyone to serve as a priest at the altar. [14]Everyone knows he came from the tribe of Judah, and Moses never said priests would come from that tribe.

[15]All of this becomes clearer, when someone who is like Melchizedek is appointed to be a priest. [16]That person wasn't appointed because of his ancestors, but because his life can never end. [17]The Scriptures say about him,

"You are a priest forever, just like Melchizedek."

[j]6.19 *behind the curtain:* In the tent that was used for worship, a curtain separated the "holy place" from the "most holy place," which only the high priest could enter. [k]6.20 *Melchizedek:* See the note at 5.6. [l]7.3 *will be a priest forever:* See the note at 5.6. [m]7.11 *descendants of Levi . . . from the priestly family of Aaron:* Levi was the ancestor of the tribe from which priests and their helpers (called "Levites") were chosen. Aaron was the first high priest.

[18]In this way a weak and useless command was put aside, [19]because the Law cannot make anything perfect. At the same time, we are given a much better hope, and it can bring us close to God.

[20-21]God himself made a promise when this priest was appointed. But he did not make a promise like this when the other priests were appointed. The promise he made is,

"I, the Lord, promise that you
      will be a priest forever!
And I will never
      change my mind!"

[22]This means that Jesus guarantees us a better agreement with God. [23]There have been a lot of other priests, and all of them have died. [24]But Jesus will never die, and so he will be a priest forever! [25]He is forever able to save[n] the people he leads to God, because he always lives to speak to God for them.

[26]Jesus is the high priest we need. He is holy and innocent and faultless, and not at all like us sinners. Jesus is honored above all beings in heaven, [27]and he is better than any other high priest. Jesus doesn't need to offer sacrifices each day for his own sins and then for the sins of the people. He offered a sacrifice once for all, when he gave himself. [28]The Law appoints priests who have weaknesses. But God's promise, which came later than the Law, appoints his Son. And he is the perfect high priest forever.

A Better Promise

8 What I mean is we have a high priest who sits at the right side[o] of God's great throne in heaven. [2]He also serves as the priest in the most holy place[p] inside the real tent there in heaven. This tent of worship was set up by the Lord, not by humans.

[3]Since all priests must offer gifts and sacrifices, Christ also needed to have something to offer. [4]If he were here on earth, he would not be a priest at all, because here the Law appoints other priests to offer sacrifices. [5]But the tent where they serve is just a copy and a shadow of the real one in heaven. Before Moses made the tent, he was told, "Be sure to make it exactly like the pattern you were shown on the mountain!" [6]Now Christ has been appointed to serve as a priest in a much better way, and he has given us much assurance of a better agreement.

[7]If the first agreement with God had been all right, there would not have been any need for another one. [8]But the Lord found fault with it and said,

"I tell you the time will come,
   when I will make
      a new agreement
   with the people of Israel
      and the people of Judah.
[9]It won't be like the agreement
   that I made
      with their ancestors,
   when I took them by the hand
      and led them out of Egypt.
They broke their agreement
   with me,
   and I stopped caring
      about them!

[10]"But now I tell the people
of Israel
      this is my new agreement:
'The time will come

7.22 *Jesus guarantees us a better agreement:* God's new agreement is based on Jesus, who was sacrificed to forgive sins. This does not mean that the old agreement based on the Law of Moses is worthless (Matt 5.17; Rom 3.31). It means that trusting Jesus, the perfect high priest, is the way to be saved (Gal 3.1-14).

Agreements (Covenants)

8.2 *most holy place inside the real tent:* Though the most holy place was in the sacred tent (and later in the temple) the writer says that the most holy place is now in the real tent (heaven).

8.6 *agreement:* In the "first agreement," God promised to protect and bless the people of Israel and to give them a land to call their own. In return, the people were commanded to follow the Law, which included rules concerning correct worship and instructions about how to live together in peace and justice. Above all, the people were to remain faithful to God alone. The people were unable to live up to the first agreement, so God made a new agreement that was not written on stone tablets but directly on their hearts and minds (Jer 31.31-34).

● 9.2-4 *the tent . . . sacred chest:* For a detailed description of the sacred tent and the holy objects in it, see Exodus 25–27 and 36.8—38.31.

The Sacred Tent

● 9.10 *rules about physical things:* These rules refer to the rules in the Law of Moses that apply to proper eating and drinking, and to special cleansing ceremonies required to restore a person to ritual purity (Lev 11.1—15.32).

● 9.13 *people who become unclean:* According to the Law of Moses, a number of things could make a person unclean (Lev 11–15; 16.15,16; 17.10–18.30).

Purity (Clean and Unclean)

when I, the Lord,
will write my laws
    on their minds and hearts.
I will be their God,
    and they will be
    my people.
[11] Not one of them
will have to teach another
    to know me, their Lord.'

"All of them will know me,
    no matter who they are.
[12] I will treat them with kindness,
even though they are wicked.
    I will forget their sins."

[13] When the Lord talks about a new agreement, he means that the first one is out of date. And anything that is old and useless will soon disappear.

The Tent in Heaven

9 The first promise included rules for worship and a tent for worship here on earth. [2] The first part of the tent was called the holy place, and a lampstand, a table, and the sacred loaves of bread were kept there. [3] Behind the curtain was the most holy place. [4] The gold altar for burning incense was in this holy place. The gold-covered sacred chest was also there, and inside it were three things. First, there was a gold jar filled with manna.[q] Then there was Aaron's walking stick that sprouted.[r] Finally, there were the flat stones with the Ten Com-

mandments written on them. [5] On top of the chest were the glorious creatures with wings[s] opened out above the place of mercy.[t]

Now isn't the time to go into detail about these things. [6] But this is how everything was when the priests went each day into the first part of the tent to do their duties. [7] However, only the high priest could go into the second part of the tent, and he went in only once a year. Each time he carried blood to offer for his sins and for any sins that the people had committed without meaning to.

[8] All of this is the Holy Spirit's way of saying no one could enter the most holy place while the tent was still the place of worship. [9] This also has a meaning for today. It shows we cannot make our consciences clear by offering gifts and sacrifices. [10] These rules are merely about such things as eating and drinking and ceremonies for washing ourselves. And rules about physical things will last only until the time comes to change them for something better.

[11] Christ came as the high priest of the good things that are now here.[u] He also went into a much better tent that wasn't made by humans and that doesn't belong to this world. [12] Then Christ went once for all into the most holy place and freed us from sin forever. He did this by offering his own blood instead of the blood of goats and bulls.

[13] According to the Law of Moses, those people who become unclean are not fit to worship God. Yet they will be considered

q9.4 *manna:* When the people of Israel were wandering through the desert, the Lord provided them with food that could be made into thin wafers. This food was called manna, which in Hebrew means "What is it?"   r9.4 *Aaron's walking stick that sprouted:* According to Numbers 17.1-11, Aaron's walking stick sprouted and produced almonds to show that the Lord was pleased with him and Moses.   s9.5 *glorious creatures with wings:* Two of these creatures (called "cherubim" in Hebrew and Greek) with outspread wings were on top of the sacred chest and were symbols of God's throne.   t9.5 *place of mercy:* The lid of the sacred chest, which was thought to be God's throne on earth.   u9.11 *that are now here:* Some manuscripts have "that were coming."

Christ went once for all into the most holy place and freed us from sin forever. He did this by offering his own blood.
HEB 9.12

clean, if they are sprinkled with the blood of goats and bulls and with the ashes of a sacrificed calf. [14]But Christ was sinless, and he offered himself as an eternal and spiritual sacrifice to God. This is why his blood is much more powerful and makes our[v] consciences clear. Now we can serve the living God and no longer do things that lead to death.

[15]Christ died to rescue those who had sinned and broken the old agreement. Now he brings his chosen ones a new agreement with its guarantee of God's eternal blessings! [16]In fact, making an agreement of this kind is like writing a will. This is because the one who makes the will must die before it is of any use. [17]In other words, a will doesn't go into effect as long as the one who made it is still alive.

[18]Blood was also used[w] to put the first agreement into effect. [19]Moses told the people all the Law said they must do. Then he used red wool and a hyssop plant to sprinkle the people and the book of the Law with the blood of bulls and goats[x] and with water. [20]He told the people, "With this blood God makes his agreement with you." [21]Moses also sprinkled blood on the tent and on everything else used in worship. [22]The Law says that almost everything must be sprinkled with blood, and no sins can be forgiven unless blood is offered.

Christ's Great Sacrifice

[23]These things are only copies of what is in heaven, and so they had to be made holy by these ceremonies. But the real things in heaven must be made holy by something better. [24]This is why Christ did not go into a tent made by humans and was only a copy of the real one. Instead, he went into heaven and is now there with God to help us.

[25]Christ did not have to offer himself many times. He wasn't like a high priest who goes into the most holy place each year to offer the blood of an animal. [26]If he had offered himself every year, he would have suffered many times since the creation of the world. But instead, near the end of time he offered himself once and for all, so he could be a sacrifice that does away with sin.

[27]We die only once, and then we are judged. [28]So Christ died only once to take away the sins of many people. But when he comes again, it will not be to take away sin. He will come to save everyone who is waiting for him.

10 The Law of Moses is like a shadow of the good things to come. This shadow isn't the good things themselves, because it cannot free people from sin by the sacrifices offered year after year. [2]If there were worshipers who already have their sins washed away and their consciences made clear, there would not be any need to go on offering sacrifices. [3-4]But the blood of bulls and goats cannot take away sins. It only reminds people of their sins from one year to the next.

[5]When Christ came into the world, he said to God,

"Sacrifices and offerings
    are not what you want,
but you have given me
    my body.
[6]No, you are not pleased
with animal sacrifices
    and offerings for sin."

[7]Then Christ said,
    "And so, my God,

9.14 *eternal and spiritual sacrifice:* Jesus went directly into the presence of God to make the perfect sacrifice for the sins of humanity. His "spiritual sacrifice" changes people and lasts forever, while sacrifices made by the priests were outward acts that had only a temporary effect.

9.23,24 *copies of what is in heaven:* The blood offerings described in 9.18-22 were physical acts that reminded the people of their relationship with God, but these acts were replaced by the offering Christ made to God.

9.25 *Christ . . . high priest:* Because Christ's sacrifice was the perfect sacrifice, it only had to be done once for all time.

Day of the LORD

9.28 *when he comes again:* The New Testament says Jesus will return to earth (Phil 1.10; 2.16; 3.20,21; 1 Thes 4.13-18). Those who follow Christ are to look forward to this day with hope, because Jesus will save them (1 Thes 5.1-11).

Second Coming

10.3-4 *It only reminds people of their sins:* The Law of Moses cannot actually wash away sins or save; it can only remind people that they have sinned (see also Rom 3.20).

---

[v]9.14 *our:* Some manuscripts have "your," and others have "their."   [w]9.18 *Blood was also used:* Or "There also had to be a death."   [x]9.19 *blood of bulls and goats:* Some manuscripts do not have "and goats."

10.27 *terrible judgment and a furious fire:* God's enemies sin by rejecting the good news about Jesus even after they have heard it. They face God's terrible judgment, which includes a fiery punishment. In the New Testament, the place of judgment for evildoers is often pictured as a place of fiery torture (see Matt 5.22; Luke 16.23,24; Rev 20.14).

Fire

Hell

10.32 *the light:* In the Bible, light is used to describe God or God's word (Ps 119.105; 1 John 1.5), and those people or things that reveal God's truth (Isa 49.6). The followers of Jesus are also called "children of light" (John 12.36; Eph 5.8).

10.33,34 *you were abused . . . your possessions be taken:* At the time HEBREWS was written, some Christians were being viewed with suspicion. For example, some Christians did not take part in business groups that had secret vows and ceremonies that went against the Christian faith. Because of this, they were sometimes singled out for various kinds of abuse and mistreatment. Some even had their possessions taken from them. Other Christians faced persecution from the Roman government when they refused to worship the emperor as if he were a god. After the Roman emperor Nero blamed the great fire in Rome (A.D. 64) on the Christians—probably to avoid being blamed himself—Roman persecution of Christians increased.

I have come to do
what you want,
as the Scriptures say."

⁸The Law teaches that offerings and sacrifices must be made because of sin. But why did Christ mention these things and say that God did not want them? ⁹Well, it was to do away with offerings and sacrifices and to replace them. This is what he meant by saying to God, "I have come to do what you want." ¹⁰So we are made holy because Christ obeyed God and offered himself once for all.

¹¹The priests do their work each day, and they keep on offering sacrifices that can never take away sins. ¹²But Christ offered himself as a sacrifice that is good forever. Now he is sitting at God's right side,ʸ ¹³and he will stay there until his enemies are put under his power. ¹⁴By his one sacrifice he has forever set free from sin the people he brings to God.

¹⁵The Holy Spirit also speaks of this by telling us that the Lord said,

¹⁶"When the time comes,
I will make an agreement
with them.
I will write my laws
on their minds and hearts.
¹⁷Then I will forget
about their sins
and no longer remember
their evil deeds."

¹⁸When sins are forgiven, there is no more need to offer sacrifices.

Encouragement and Warning

¹⁹My friends, the blood of Jesus gives us courage to enter the most holy place ²⁰by a new way that leads to life! And this way

ʸ10.12 *right side:* See the note at 1.3.

takes us through the curtain that is Christ himself.

²¹We have a great high priest who is in charge of God's house. ²²So let's come near God with pure hearts and a confidence that comes from having faith. Let's keep our hearts pure, our consciences free from evil, and our bodies washed with clean water. ²³We must hold tightly to the hope we say is ours. After all, we can trust the one who made the agreement with us. ²⁴We should keep on encouraging each other to be thoughtful and to do helpful things. ²⁵Some people have given up the habit of meeting for worship, but we must not do that. We should keep on encouraging each other, especially since you know that the day of the Lord's coming is getting closer.

²⁶No sacrifices can be made for people who decide to sin after they find out about the truth. ²⁷They are God's enemies, and all they can look forward to is a terrible judgment and a furious fire. ²⁸If two or more witnesses accused someone of breaking the Law of Moses, that person could be put to death. ²⁹But it is much worse to dishonor God's Son and to disgrace the blood of the promise that made us holy. And it is just as bad to insult the Holy Spirit, who shows us mercy. ³⁰We know that God has said he will punish and take revenge. We also know that the Scriptures say the Lord will judge his people. ³¹It is a terrible thing to fall into the hands of the living God!

³²Don't forget all the hard times you went through when you first received the light. ³³Sometimes you were abused and mistreated in public, and at other times you shared in the sufferings of others. ³⁴You were kind to people in jail. And you gladly let your possessions be taken away, because you knew you had something better, something that would last forever.

We have a great high priest who is in charge of God's house. So let's come near God with pure hearts and a confidence that comes from having faith. HEB 10.21,22

[35]Keep on being brave! It will bring you great rewards. [36]Learn to be patient, so you will please God and be given what he has promised. [37]As the Scriptures say,

"God is coming soon!
    It won't be very long.
[38]The people God accepts
    will live because
        of their faith.[z]
    But he isn't pleased
        with anyone
            who turns back."

[39]We are not like those people who turn back and get destroyed. We will keep on having faith until we are saved.

The Great Faith of God's People

11 Faith makes us sure of what we hope for and gives us proof of what we cannot see. [2]It was their faith that made our ancestors pleasing to God.

[3]Because of our faith, we know that the world was made at God's command. We also know that what can be seen was made out of what cannot be seen.

[4]Because Abel had faith, he offered God a better sacrifice than Cain did. God was pleased with him and his gift, and even though Abel is now dead, his faith still speaks for him.

[5]Enoch had faith and did not die. He pleased God, and God took him up to heaven. This is why his body was never found. [6]But without faith no one can please God. We must believe that God is real and rewards everyone who searches for him.

[7]Because Noah had faith, he was warned about something that had not yet hap-

pened. He obeyed and built a boat that saved him and his family. In this way the people of the world were judged, and Noah was given the blessings that come to everyone who pleases God.

[8]Abraham had faith and obeyed God. He was told to go to the land that God had said would be his, and he left for a country he had never seen. [9]Because Abraham had faith, he lived as a stranger in the promised land. He lived there in a tent, and so did Isaac and Jacob, who were later given the same promise. [10]Abraham did this, because he was waiting for the eternal city God had planned and built.

[11]Even when Sarah was too old to have children, she had faith that God would do what he had promised, and she had a son. [12]Her husband Abraham was almost dead, but he became the ancestor of many people. In fact, there are as many of them as there are stars in the sky or grains of sand along the seashore.

[13]Every one of those people died. But they still had faith, even though they had not received what they had been promised. They were glad just to see these things from far away, and they agreed that they were only strangers and foreigners on this earth. [14]When people talk this way, it is clear they are looking for a place to call their own. [15]If they had been talking about the land where they had once lived, they could have gone back at any time. [16]But they were looking forward to a better home in heaven. This is why God wasn't ashamed for them to call him their God. He even built a city for them.

[17-18]Abraham had been promised that Isaac, his only son,[a] would continue his family. But when Abraham was tested, he

---

11.1 *Faith:* Here, faith means trusting in God rather than observing certain rituals or following a particular set of teachings.

Faith

11.2 *our ancestors:* In chapter 11, the writer says that some of the first people mentioned in GENESIS pleased God because of their faith, and are forever part of God's people. Most of these people lived before the Law was given to Moses. **(See the chart People of Faith Mentioned in Hebrews 11 on pgs 1842–43.)**

11.10 *eternal city:* This is the place of rest (4.1) and the heavenly tent (9.11) where Christ went to be with God. It is the heavenly place where those who are faithful to God will be with God forever. See also Rev 21.3; 21.10—22.5.

11.17-18 *Isaac, his only son:* God promised Abraham a son who would be the father of a great nation (Gen 15.4,5). Although Abraham had a son by a slave woman named Hagar, Abraham's son Isaac was considered his "only son," because he was born as the result of God's promise to Abraham. According to the writer of HEBREWS, Abraham was willing to sacrifice his only son (Gen 22.1-19), because he was sure God could raise people back to life.

---

[z]10.38 *The people God accepts will live because of their faith:* Or "The people God accepts because of their faith will live." [a]11.17,18 *his only son:* Although Abraham had a son by a slave woman, his son Isaac was considered his only son, because he was born as a result of God's promise to Abraham.

Faith makes us sure of what we hope for and gives us proof of what we cannot see. HEB 11.1

11.23 *the king's orders:* The king of Egypt ordered all Israelite baby boys to be killed (Exod 1.22) in order to reduce the growing Israelite population in Egypt (Exod 1.12—2.10).

11.27 *Moses had seen the invisible God:* God appeared to Moses in a burning bush (Exod 3.1-6). However, the God of Israel was not to be pictured or represented by any kind of a statue (Exod 20.2-6; Isa 45.20—46.7).

11.30 *Jericho:* Jericho was a key Canaanite city that guarded the Jordan River Valley. Joshua 5.13—6.26 describes how the Israelites conquered this ancient city.

11.35 *the dead are raised to life:* This refers to the promise that those who were faithful to God would be raised to new life, just as God raised Jesus from death.

Resurrection

had faith and was willing to sacrifice Isaac, [19]because he was sure that God could raise people to life. This was just like getting Isaac back from death.

[20]Isaac had faith, and he promised blessings to Jacob and Esau. [21]Later, when Jacob was about to die, he leaned on his walking stick and worshiped. Then because of his faith he blessed each of Joseph's sons. [22]And right before Joseph died, he had faith that God would lead the people of Israel out of Egypt. So he told them to take his bones with them.

[23]Because Moses' parents had faith, they kept him hidden until he was three months old. They saw that he was a beautiful child, and they were not afraid to disobey the king's orders.[b] [24]Then after Moses grew up, his faith made him refuse to be called the king's grandson. [25]He chose to be mistreated with God's people instead of having the good time that sin could bring for a little while. [26]Moses knew that the treasures of Egypt were not as wonderful as what he would receive from suffering for the Messiah,[c] and he looked forward to his reward.

[27]Because of his faith, Moses left Egypt. Moses had seen the invisible God and wasn't afraid of the king's anger. [28]His faith also made him celebrate Passover. He sprinkled the blood of animals on the doorposts, so that the first-born sons of the people of Israel would not be killed by the destroying angel.

[29]Because of their faith, the people walked through the Red Sea[d] on dry land. But when the Egyptians tried to do it, they were drowned.

[30]God's people had faith, and when they had walked around the city of Jericho for seven days, its walls fell down.

[31]Rahab had been a prostitute, but she had faith and welcomed the spies. So she wasn't killed with the people who disobeyed.

[32]What else can I say? There isn't enough time to tell about Gideon, Barak, Samson, Jephthah, David, Samuel, and the prophets. [33]Their faith helped them conquer kingdoms, and because they did right, God made promises to them. They closed the jaws of lions [34]and put out raging fires and escaped from the swords of their enemies. Although they were weak, they were given the strength and power to chase foreign armies away.

[35]Some women received their loved ones back from death. Many of these people were tortured, but they refused to be released. They were sure they would get a better reward when the dead are raised to life. [36]Others were made fun of and beaten with whips, and some were chained in jail. [37]Still others were stoned to death or sawed in two[e] or killed with swords. Some had nothing but sheep skins or goat skins to wear. They were poor, mistreated, and tortured. [38]The world did not deserve these good people, who had to wander in deserts and on mountains and had to live in caves and holes in the ground.

[39]All of them pleased God because of their faith! But still they died without being given what had been promised. [40]This was because God had something better in store for us. And he did not want them to reach the goal of their faith without us.

[b]11.23 *the king's orders:* The king of Egypt ordered all Israelite baby boys to be left outside of their homes, so they would die or be killed. [c]11.26 *the Messiah:* Or "Christ." [d]11.29 *Red Sea:* This name comes from the Bible of the early Christians, a translation made into Greek about 200 B.C. It refers to the body of water that the Israelites crossed and was one of the marshes or fresh water lakes near the eastern part of the Nile Delta, where they lived and where the towns of Exodus 13.17—14.9 were located. [e]11.37 *sawed in two:* Some manuscripts have "tested" or "tempted."

A Large Crowd of Witnesses

12 Such a large crowd of witnesses is all around us! So we must get rid of everything that slows us down, especially the sin that just won't let go. And we must be determined to run the race that is ahead of us. [2]We must keep our eyes on Jesus, who leads us and makes our faith complete. He endured the shame of being nailed to a cross, because he knew later on he would be glad he did. Now he is seated at the right side[f] of God's throne! [3]So keep your mind on Jesus, who put up with many insults from sinners. Then you won't get discouraged and give up.

[4]None of you have yet been hurt[g] in your battle against sin. [5]But you have forgotten that the Scriptures say to God's children,

"When the Lord punishes you,
    don't make light of it,
and when he corrects you,
    don't be discouraged.
[6]The Lord corrects the people
    he loves
and disciplines those
    he calls his own."

[7]Be patient when you are being corrected! This is how God treats his children. Don't all parents correct their children? [8]God corrects all his children, and if he doesn't correct you, then you don't really belong to him. [9]Our earthly fathers correct us, and we still respect them. Isn't it even better to be given true life by letting our spiritual Father correct us?

[10]Our human fathers correct us for a short time, and they do it as they think best. But God corrects us for our own good, because he wants us to be holy, as he is. [11]It is never fun to be corrected. In fact, at the time it is always painful. But if we learn to obey by being corrected, we will do right and live at peace.

[12]Now stand up straight! Stop your knees from shaking [13]and walk a straight path. Then lame people will be healed, instead of getting worse.

Warning against Turning from God

[14]Try to live at peace with everyone! Live a clean life. If you don't, you will never see the Lord. [15]Make sure no one misses out on God's wonderful kindness. Don't let anyone become bitter and cause trouble for the rest of you. [16]Watch out for immoral and ungodly people like Esau, who sold his future blessing[h] for only one meal. [17]You know how he later wanted it back. But there was nothing he could do to change things, even though he begged his father and cried.

[18]You have not come to a place like Mount Sinai[i] that can be seen and touched. There is no flaming fire or dark cloud or storm [19]or trumpet sound. The people of Israel heard a voice speak. But they begged it to stop, [20]because they could not obey its commands. They were even told to kill any animal that touched the mountain. [21]The sight was so frightening that Moses said he shook with fear.

[22]You have now come to Mount Zion and to the heavenly Jerusalem. This is the city of the living God, where thousands and thousands of angels have come to celebrate.

[f]**12.2** *right side:* See the note at 1.3. [g]**12.4** *hurt:* Or "killed." [h]**12.16** *sold his future blessing:* As the first-born son, Esau had certain privileges that were known as a "birthright." [i]**12.18** *a place like Mount Sinai:* The Greek text has "a place," but the writer is referring to the time that the Lord spoke to the people of Israel from Mount Sinai (see Exodus 19.16-25).

12.1 *large crowd of witnesses:* Those who have been faithful to God since the beginning of time, including those mentioned in Hebrews 11. This crowd was like the kind of crowd that filled the seats of an arena or amphitheater to watch an athletic contest.

12.1 *sin...run the race:* The apostle Paul also compares the life of faith to running a race. He said the goal of the race is being invited to live with God in heaven (Phil 3.12-16). To reach this goal, Christians need to "keep their eyes on Jesus," their leader, who has already run this race and reached the goal.

12.9 *our spiritual Father:* This means "God."

12.10 *to be holy:* "Holy" can mean "set apart" (or "chosen") by God in order to serve God.

Holiness

12.16 *Esau...sold his...blessing:* As Isaac's first-born son, Esau had certain privileges that were known as a "birthright." He sold this birthright to his younger brother Jacob for some stew (Gen 25.27-34). The writer says that those who do not live godly lives are throwing away their rights as God's children, just as Esau threw away his birthright.

We must keep our eyes on Jesus, who leads us and makes our faith complete. Heb 12.2

12.25 people did not escape: The people of God often disobeyed the Law that God had given them at Mount Sinai (Exod 20.22). Even God's chosen people did not escape punishment when they disobeyed.

12.28 kingdom that cannot be shaken: This kingdom is God's heavenly kingdom, which cannot be destroyed because it is perfect and will last forever (Heb 7.22—8.13; 9.15).

13.9 certain foods: The Law of Moses had rules about what could be eaten. The writer states that following food rules is not as important as relying on God's kindness.

13.12 Jesus himself suffered outside the city gate: Jesus was put to death on a cross at a place called "the Skull," which was outside Jerusalem's city walls (Luke 23.26-49). **(See Map 13 on pg 1891.)**

²³Here you will find all of God's dearest children,^j whose names are written in heaven. And you will find God himself, who judges everyone. Here also are the spirits of those good people who have been made perfect. ²⁴And Jesus is here! He is the one who makes God's new agreement with us, and his sprinkled blood says much better things than the blood of Abel.^k

²⁵Make sure you obey the one who speaks to you. The people did not escape, when they refused to obey the one who spoke to them at Mount Sinai. Do you think you can possibly escape, if you refuse to obey the one who speaks to you from heaven? ²⁶When God spoke the first time, his voice shook only the earth. This time he has promised to shake the earth once again, and heaven too.

²⁷The words "once again" mean that these created things will someday be shaken and removed. Then what cannot be shaken will last. ²⁸We should be grateful we were given a kingdom that cannot be shaken. And in this kingdom we please God by worshiping him and by showing him great honor and respect. ²⁹Our God is like a destructive fire!

Service That Pleases God

13 Keep being concerned about each other as the Lord's followers should. ²Be sure to welcome strangers into your home. By doing this, some people have welcomed angels as guests, without even knowing it.

³Remember the Lord's people who are in jail and be concerned for them. Don't forget those who are suffering, but imagine you are there with them.

⁴Have respect for marriage. Always be faithful to your partner, because God will punish anyone who is immoral or unfaithful in marriage.

⁵Don't fall in love with money. Be satisfied with what you have. The Lord has promised that he will not leave us or desert us. ⁶This should make you feel like saying,

"The Lord helps me!
Why should I be afraid
    of what people
    can do to me?"

⁷Don't forget about your leaders who taught you God's message. Remember what kind of lives they lived and try to have faith like theirs.

⁸Jesus Christ never changes! He is the same yesterday, today, and forever. ⁹Don't be fooled by any kind of strange teachings. It is better to receive strength from God's gift of undeserved grace than to depend on certain foods. After all, these foods don't really help the people who eat them. ¹⁰But we have an altar where even the priests who serve in the place of worship have no right to eat.

¹¹After the high priest offers the blood of animals as a sin offering, the bodies of those animals are burned outside the camp. ¹²Jesus himself suffered outside the city gate, so his blood would make people holy. ¹³This is why we should go outside the camp to Jesus and share in his disgrace. ¹⁴On this earth we don't have a city that lasts forever, but we are waiting for such a city.

¹⁵Our sacrifice is to keep offering praise to God in the name of Jesus. ¹⁶But don't forget to help others and to share your possessions with them. This too is like offering a sacrifice that pleases God.

^j12.23 *all of God's dearest children:* The Greek text has "the gathering of the first-born children" (see the note at 1.6).   ^k**12.24** *blood of Abel:* Cain and Abel were the two sons of Adam and Eve. Cain murdered Abel (see Genesis 4.1-16).

Jesus Christ never changes! He is the same yesterday, today, and forever. HEB 13.8

[17]Obey your leaders and do what they say. They are watching over you, and they must answer to God. So don't make them sad as they do their work. Make them happy. Otherwise, they won't be able to help you at all. [18]Pray for us. Our consciences are clear, and we always try to live right. [19]I especially want you to pray that I can visit you again soon.

Final Prayers and Greetings

[20]God gives peace, and he raised our Lord Jesus Christ from death. Now Jesus is like a Great Shepherd whose blood was used to make God's eternal agreement with his flock.[l] [21]I pray God will make you ready to obey him and that you will always be eager to do right. May Jesus help you do what pleases God. To Jesus Christ be glory forever and ever! Amen.

[22]My friends, I have written only a short letter to encourage you, and I beg you to pay close attention to what I have said.

[23]By now you surely must know that our friend Timothy is out of jail. If he gets here in time, I will bring him with me when I come to visit you.

[24]Please give my greetings to your leaders and to the rest of the Lord's people.

His followers from Italy send you their greetings.

[25]I pray that God will be kind to all of you![m]

13.18 *Pray for us:* The unknown writer of HEBREWS may have been writing from prison.

13.20 *our Lord Jesus Christ … Great Shepherd:* The Greek word for "Lord" is *Kyrios*. When used for Jesus, it emphasizes his authority and power. The word "Christ" is from the Greek word *Christos*, which means "Messiah" or "anointed one." Jesus called himself the Good Shepherd (John 10.10-16).

Messiah (Chosen One)

Lord (Title for Jesus)

13.23 *Timothy:* This may be the same person who was Paul's helper (Acts 16.1-3) and the church leader whose name appears on two New Testament letters, 1 and 2 TIMOTHY.

13.24 *Italy:* The writer of HEBREWS may have been in Rome, the capital of the Roman Empire, which was located in Italy. **(See Map 14 on pg 1892.)**

---

[l]**13.20** *whose blood was used to make God's eternal agreement with his flock:* See 9.18-22. [m]**13.25** *to all of you:* Some manuscripts add "Amen."

Reflection Questions About Hebrews 1.1—13.25

1. How does the first chapter of HEBREWS picture Jesus? List a number of things that describe who he is and what he does.

2. Why does the writer say that "the Law of Moses is like a shadow of the good things to come" (10.1-18)?

3. How did the ancestors of Israel please God (11.1,2)? What word would you use to describe your own faith in God? Why?

4. In 12.1-3 the writer compares the Christian life with a race that is being run in front of a large crowd of witnesses. How are these witnesses like the home team's crowd at a game? How is the Christian life like a race? Where do Christians get help to run this race?

5. What kinds of service are pleasing to God (13.1-7)? In what particular way(s) can God's followers serve God and others?

james

How can faith be "dead"? The writer of JAMES gives advice about how Christians can keep their faith alive.

WHAT MAKES JAMES SPECIAL?

JAMES begins like a letter that is written to Christians scattered throughout the Roman Empire (1.1), but it really is more like a short book of instructions on how God's people should live and treat others. The advice in the book is clear and to the point: If you are poor, don't despair! Don't give up when your faith is being tested. Don't get angry quickly. Don't favor the rich over the poor. Help others, and control your tongue and your desires. Rely on God's wisdom. Resist the devil. Don't brag about what you are going to do. If you are rich, use your money to help the poor. Be patient and kind, and pray for those who need God's help.

For the writer of JAMES, faith means action! This letter says that the faith of a person who does not do kind deeds is as good as dead. The writer challenges God's people to obey "the most important law in the Scriptures"—to love others as much they love themselves (2.8).

WHAT'S THE STORY BEHIND THE SCENE?

This letter is written to "the twelve tribes scattered all over the world" (1.1). This does not refer to the people of Israel but to Christians, who viewed themselves as heirs of the Jewish tradition. The author of the book calls himself James, which in Greek is *Iakobos,* a form of the Hebrew name "Jacob."

Church tradition has said that the book was written by James, the brother of Jesus. It is filled with teachings that are similar to the teachings of Jesus in the Gospels. However, the general language and style of the letter suggest that the writer was also familiar with the terms used by the broader Greek culture of the first century. This means that the writer probably lived many years after James the brother of Jesus (Mark 6.3) or James the disciple (Matt 4.21).

HOW IS JAMES CONSTRUCTED?

After a brief greeting, the letter offers advice about living as God's people. The letter can be outlined in the following way:

Ask for God's wisdom and patience (1.1-18)
Show that your faith is alive (1.19—2.26)
Watch what you say, and be wise (3.1—5.6)
Be patient, kind, and prayerful (5.7-20)

James addressed this letter to all of the Lord's followers scattered throughout the Roman Empire and intended it as a guide for how Christians should live in their communities. Readers are encouraged to seek God's wisdom and remain faithful, even when facing times of testing and temptation. A key theme is that true faith is shown in acts of love. Faith that doesn't lead people to do good deeds, James argues, is dead. Christians are urged to listen to God's message and obey it. James advises his readers to be patient—despite persecution and hardship—and to constantly renew their faith through prayer.

Outline

1 From James, a servant of God and of our Lord Jesus Christ.

Greetings to the twelve tribes scattered all over the world.[a]

Faith and Wisdom

[2]My friends, be glad, even if you have a lot of trouble. [3]You know you learn to endure by having your faith tested. [4]But you must learn to endure everything, so you will be completely mature and not lacking in anything.

[5]If any of you need wisdom, you should ask God, and it will be given to you. God is generous and won't correct you for asking. [6]But when you ask for something, you must have faith and not doubt. Anyone who doubts is like an ocean wave tossed around in a storm. [7-8]If you are that kind of person, you can't make up your mind, and you surely can't be trusted. So don't expect the Lord to give you anything at all.

Poor People and Rich People

[9]Any of God's people who are poor should be glad he thinks so highly of them. [10]But any who are rich should be glad when God makes them humble. Rich people will disappear like wild flowers [11]scorched by the burning heat of the sun. The flowers lose their blossoms, and their beauty is destroyed. This is how the rich will disappear, as they go about their business.

Trials and Temptations

[12]God will bless you, if you don't give up when your faith is being tested. He will reward you with a glorious life,[b] just as he rewards everyone who loves him.

---

[a]**1.1** *twelve tribes scattered all over the world*: James is saying that the Lord's followers are like the tribes of Israel that were scattered everywhere by their enemies. [b]**1.12** *a glorious life*: The Greek text has "the crown of life." In ancient times an athlete who had won a contest was rewarded with a crown of flowers as a sign of victory.

■ 1.1 *Lord Jesus Christ:* The Greek word for "Lord" is *Kyrios*, which can mean master or can be used to address someone as "Sir." "Christ" is a title that comes from the Greek word *Christos*, meaning "Messiah" or "chosen one."

◌ Lord (Title for Jesus)

◌ Messiah (Chosen One)

■ 1.3 *faith:* In the Gospels and in Paul's letters, faith usually means trust in God. This is the meaning of faith in 1.3 and 1.6, and in 2.1. In other parts of JAMES, faith seems to refer to correct beliefs and actions (2.17,18,22,26).

■ 1.5 *wisdom:* JAMES offers wisdom and practical advice about how people with faith are to live. In the Jewish community, wisdom was highly valued, and parents understood that they were to teach their children wisdom based on God's Law (Deut 6.1-9).

◌ Wisdom

● 1.10 *Rich people:* Rich people may be tempted to ignore God and rely on their possessions and power. The writer is saying that poor Christians are actually better off than rich ones, because those without money and power need to depend on God.

1.15 Our desires make us sin: Selfish desires make people serve the law of sin (Rom 7.25), and sin "pays off with death" (Rom 6.23).

Sin

God's Saving Love (Salvation)

1.25 perfect law that sets you free: This may refer to the commandment to "love others as much as we love ourselves" (2.8). Or it may refer to the will of God as revealed in the Jewish Scriptures (Old Testament) and in the life and teachings of Jesus Christ.

2.3 give the best seat: Some early followers of Jesus may have been tempted to give special treatment to rich or powerful people, because these people could finance or protect their local churches. The writer warns Christians not to favor rich people while ignoring the poor. See also Luke 14.7-14.

The Poor

2.8 most important law . . . love others: This law, found in Leviticus 19.18, was emphasized by Jesus as well (Mark 12.28-31).

2.11 God's Law: This refers to the Law of Moses, which described how God expected the people to live, worship, and treat each other.

Law

¹³Don't blame God when you are tempted! God cannot be tempted by evil, and he doesn't use evil to tempt others. ¹⁴We are tempted by our own desires that drag us off and trap us. ¹⁵Our desires make us sin, and when sin is finished with us, it leaves us dead. ¹⁶Don't be fooled, my dear friends. ¹⁷Every good and perfect gift comes down from the Father who created all the lights in the heavens. He is always the same and never makes dark shadows by changing. ¹⁸He wanted us to be his own special people,[c] and so he sent the true message to give us new birth.

Hearing and Obeying

¹⁹My dear friends, you should be quick to listen and slow to speak or to get angry. ²⁰If you are angry, you cannot do any of the good things God wants done. ²¹You must stop doing anything immoral or evil. Instead be humble and accept the message planted in you to save you.

²²Obey God's message! Don't fool yourselves by just listening to it. ²³If you hear the message and don't obey it, you are like people who stare at themselves in a mirror ²⁴and forget what they look like as soon as they leave. ²⁵But you must never stop looking at the perfect law that sets you free. God will bless you in everything you do, if you listen and obey, and don't just hear and forget.

²⁶If you think you are being religious, but can't control your tongue, you are fooling yourself, and your religion is useless. ²⁷Religion that pleases God the Father must be pure and spotless. You must help needy orphans and widows and not let this world make you evil.

Warning against Having Favorites

2 My friends, if you have faith in our glorious Lord Jesus Christ, you won't treat some people better than others. ²Suppose a rich person wearing fancy clothes and a gold ring comes to one of your meetings. And suppose a poor person dressed in worn-out clothes also comes. ³You must not give the best seat to the one in fancy clothes and tell the one who is poor to stand at the side or sit on the floor. ⁴This is the same as saying that some people are better than others, and you would be acting like a crooked judge.

⁵My dear friends, pay attention. God has given a lot of faith to the poor people in this world. God has also promised them a share in his kingdom that he will give to everyone who loves him. ⁶You mistreat the poor. But isn't it the rich who boss you around and drag you off to court? ⁷Aren't they the ones who make fun of your Lord?

⁸You will do all right, if you obey the most important law[d] in the Scriptures. It is the law that commands us to love others as much as we love ourselves. ⁹But if you treat some people better than others, you have done wrong, and the Scriptures teach that you have sinned.

¹⁰If you obey every law except one, you are still guilty of breaking them all. ¹¹The same God who told us to be faithful in marriage also told us not to murder. So even if you are faithful in marriage, but murder someone, you still have broken God's Law.

[c]*1.18 his own special people:* The Greek text has "the first of his creatures." The Law of Moses taught that the first-born of all animals and the first part of the harvest were special and belonged to the Lord.   [d]*2.8 most important law:* The Greek text has "royal law," meaning the one given by the king (that is, God).

¹²Speak and act like people who will be judged by the law that sets us free. ¹³Do this, because on the day of judgment there will be no pity for those who have not had pity on others. But even in judgment, God is merciful!ᵉ

Faith and Works

¹⁴My friends, what good is it to say you have faith, when you don't do anything to show you really do have faith? Can this kind of faith save you? ¹⁵If you know someone who doesn't have any clothes or food, ¹⁶you shouldn't just say, "I hope all goes well for you. I hope you will be warm and have plenty to eat." What good is it to say this, unless you do something to help? ¹⁷Faith that doesn't lead us to do good deeds is all alone and dead!

¹⁸Suppose someone disagrees and says, "It is possible to have faith without doing kind deeds."

I would answer, "Prove that you have faith without doing kind deeds, and I will prove that I have faith by doing them." ¹⁹You surely believe there is only one God. That's fine. Even demons believe this, and it makes them shake with fear.

²⁰Does some stupid person want proof that faith without deeds is useless? ²¹Well, our ancestor Abraham pleased God by putting his son Isaac on the altar to sacrifice him. ²²Now you see how Abraham's faith and deeds worked together. He proved his faith was real by what he did. ²³This is what the Scriptures mean by saying, "Abraham had faith in God, and God accepted him." That's how Abraham became God's friend.

²⁴You can now see that we please God by what we do and not only by what we believe. ²⁵For example, Rahab had been a prostitute. But she pleased God when she welcomed the spies and sent them home by another way.

²⁶Anyone who doesn't breathe is dead, and faith that doesn't do anything is just as dead!

The Tongue

3 My friends, we should not all try to become teachers. In fact, teachers will be judged more strictly than others. ²All of us do many wrong things. But if you can control your tongue, you are mature and able to control your whole body.

³By putting a bit into the mouth of a horse, we can turn the horse in different directions. ⁴It takes strong winds to move a large sailing ship, but the captain uses only a small rudder to make it go in any direction. ⁵Our tongues are small too, and yet they brag about big things.

It takes only a spark to start a forest fire! ⁶The tongue is like a spark. It is an evil power that dirties the rest of the body and sets a person's entire life on fire with flames that come from hell itself. ⁷All kinds of animals, birds, reptiles, and sea creatures can be tamed and have been tamed. ⁸But our tongues get out of control. They are restless and evil, and always spreading deadly poison.

⁹⁻¹⁰My dear friends, with our tongues we speak both praises and curses. We praise our Lord and Father, and we curse people who were created to be like God, and this isn't right. ¹¹Can clean water and dirty water both flow from the same spring? ¹²Can a fig tree produce olives or a grapevine produce figs? Does fresh water come from a well full of salt water?

ᵉ2.13 *But even in judgment, God is merciful:* Or "So be merciful, and you will be shown mercy on the day of judgment."

2.13 *day of judgment:* The New Testament letters mention a day when Jesus will return (1 Cor 15.20-28; 1 Thes 4.13-18; Phil 1.10; 2.16; 3.20,21). On this day, God would judge the people of the world (Matt 13.47-50; 25.31-46; John 12.44-50).

☞ Second Coming

☞ Day of the LORD (Judgment Day)

2.18 *faith without doing kind deeds:* Some Christian teachers may have claimed that good deeds were not necessary if a person had faith in God's promises. JAMES contrasts two kinds of faith: genuine faith which can be seen in good works and kind deeds, and "imitation faith" that never expresses itself in good works and so cannot be considered real faith at all.

2.21 *Abraham . . . Isaac:* Abraham was considered the father of all the Israelite people. God promised that Abraham would have many descendants who would become a great nation (Gen 15.4,5; 17.1-5). To make this promise come true, God gave Abraham and his wife Sarah a son named Isaac in their old age. God later commanded Abraham to offer his son Isaac as a sacrifice (Gen 22.1-18). Abraham showed his faith by preparing to do what God asked. At the last moment, God stopped Abraham from killing his son, provided a ram as an acceptable sacrifice, and praised Abraham for his faith.

☞ Abraham

You can see now that we please God by what we do and not only by what we believe. JAS 2.24

3.15 *wisdom . . . devil:* Wisdom that doesn't come from above (that is, from God) is here called "earthly wisdom." Earthly wisdom that produces evil is said to come from the devil, also known as Satan, the leader of the evil forces that are against God and God's people. In Greek, the word for devil means "the accuser."

☞ Satan

4.2 *You should pray for it:* Prayer is the act of communicating with God. When people pray, they may be thanking or praising God, asking God for forgiveness, or asking God for help or wisdom. Here the writer of JAMES is telling Christians to pray in order to receive God's forgiveness and help.

☞ Prayer

4.4 *love the world:* Here, the "world" refers to the evil people and forces that oppose God. By "love the world," the writer may be referring to selfish living, or to believing in wealth and power as a measure of success. The New Testament does not condemn pleasure, except when that pleasure becomes a false idol that turns people away from God.

Wisdom from Above

[13]Are any of you wise or sensible? Then show it by living right and by being humble and wise in everything you do. [14]But if your heart is full of bitter jealousy and selfishness, don't brag or lie to cover up the truth. [15]This kind of wisdom doesn't come from above. It is earthly and selfish and comes from the devil himself. [16]Whenever people are jealous or selfish, they cause trouble and do all sorts of cruel things. [17]But the wisdom that comes from above leads us to be pure, friendly, gentle, sensible, kind, helpful, genuine, and sincere. [18]When peacemakers plant seeds of peace, they will harvest justice.

Friendship with the World

4 Why do you fight and argue with each other? Isn't it because you are full of selfish desires that fight to control your body? [2]You want something you don't have, and you will do anything to get it. You will even kill! But you still cannot get what you want, and you won't get it by fighting and arguing. You should pray for it. [3]Yet even when you do pray, your prayers are not answered, because you pray just for selfish reasons.

[4]You people aren't faithful to God! Don't you know if you love the world, you are God's enemies? And if you decide to be a friend of the world, you make yourself an enemy of God. [5]Do you doubt the Scriptures that say, "God truly cares about the Spirit he has put in us"?[f] [6]In fact, God treats us with even greater kindness, just as the Scriptures say,

"God opposes everyone
    who is proud,

but he blesses all who are humble
    with undeserved grace."

[7]Surrender to God! Resist the devil, and he will run from you. [8]Come near to God, and he will come near to you. Clean up your lives, you sinners. Purify your hearts, you people who can't make up your mind. [9]Be sad and sorry and weep. Stop laughing and start crying. Be gloomy instead of glad. [10]Be humble in the Lord's presence, and he will honor you.

Saying Cruel Things about Others

[11]My friends, don't say cruel things about others! If you do, or if you condemn others, you are condemning God's Law. And if you condemn the Law, you put yourself above the Law and refuse to obey either it [12]or God who gave it. God is our judge, and he can save or destroy us. What right do you have to condemn anyone?

Warning against Bragging

[13]You should know better than to say, "Today or tomorrow we will go to the city. We will do business there for a year and make a lot of money!" [14]What do you know about tomorrow? How can you be so sure about your life? It is nothing more than mist that appears for only a little while before it disappears. [15]You should say, "If the Lord lets us live, we will do these things." [16]Yet you are stupid enough to brag, and it is wrong to be so proud. [17]If you don't do what you know is right, you have sinned.

[f]**4.5** *God truly cares about the Spirit he has put in us:* One possible meaning for the difficult Greek text; other translations are possible, such as, "the Spirit that God put in us truly cares."

The wisdom that comes from above leads us to be pure, friendly, gentle, sensible, kind, helpful, genuine, and sincere.
JAS 3.17

Warning to the Rich

5 You rich people should cry and weep! Terrible things are going to happen to you. **2**Your treasures have already rotted, and moths have eaten your clothes. **3**Your money has rusted, and the rust will be evidence against you, as it burns your body like fire. Yet you keep on storing up wealth in these last days. **4**You refused to pay the people who worked in your fields, and now their unpaid wages are shouting out against you. The Lord All-Powerful has surely heard the cries of the workers who harvested your crops.

5While here on earth, you have thought only of filling your own stomachs and having a good time. But now you are like fat cattle on their way to be butchered. **6**You have condemned and murdered innocent people, who couldn't even fight back.

Be Patient and Kind

7My friends, be patient until the Lord returns. Think of farmers who wait patiently for the autumn and spring rains to make their valuable crops grow. **8**Be patient like those farmers and don't give up. The Lord will soon be here! **9**Don't grumble about each other or you will be judged, and the judge is right outside the door.

10My friends, follow the example of the prophets who spoke for the Lord. They were patient, even when they had to suffer.

11In fact, we praise the ones who endured the most. You remember how patient Job was and how the Lord finally helped him. The Lord did this because he is so merciful and kind.

12My friends, above all else, don't take an oath. You must not swear by heaven or by earth or by anything else. "Yes" or "No" is all you need to say. If you say anything more, you will be condemned.

13If you are having trouble, you should pray. And if you are feeling good, you should sing praises. **14**If you are sick, ask the church leaders[g] to come and pray for you. Ask them to put olive oil[h] on you in the name of the Lord. **15**If you have faith when you pray for sick people, they will get well. The Lord will heal them, and if they have sinned, he will forgive them.

16If you have sinned, you should tell each other what you have done. Then you can pray for one another and be healed. The prayer of an innocent person is powerful, and it can help a lot. **17**Elijah was just as human as we are, and for three and a half years his prayers kept the rain from falling. **18**But when he did pray for rain, it fell from the skies and made the crops grow.

19My friends, if any followers have wandered away from the truth, you should try to lead them back. **20**If you turn sinners from the wrong way, you will save them from death, and many of their sins will be forgiven.

---

g5.14 *church leaders*: Or "elders" or "presbyters."   **h5.14** *olive oil*: The Jewish people used olive oil for healing.

5.1 *rich people*: The writer is not warning against riches, since money can be used to serve others. Instead, the warning is directed to people who love money so much that they turn away from God. It is the "love" of money that causes all kinds of trouble (1 Tim 6.10).

5.11 *Job*: The book of JOB in the Old Testament tells the story of Job, a faithful man who lost his family, his possessions, and his health (Job 1.1—2.10). Though Job questioned why he was suffering, he continued to trust in God (Job 19.23-27; 42.1-6), and God helped him (Job 42.7-17).

5.15 *sinned, he will forgive*: The Law of Moses taught that sins could be taken away by sacrificing a young goat on the Great Day of Forgiveness (Lev 16.1-22). The prophets said that God was willing to forgive those who turned away from sin and turned back to God (Isa 1.18; Jer 35.3). Christians believe that God sent Jesus Christ to free people from sin by dying on a cross (Rom 3.21-26).

5.17 *Elijah*: The prophet Elijah lived over 800 years before Jesus was born. His name means, "My god is Yahweh," the Hebrew name for Israel's God.

Elijah

5.19 *truth*: This refers to the truth about God and the good news about Jesus Christ, especially as the writer of JAMES proclaims it.

Truth

Reflection Questions About James 1.1—5.20

1. Apparently, JAMES was written to people who were having their faith tested (1.3). Name some ways the faith of the early Christians was tested. Does this kind of testing still occur today in the world?

2. What does the writer of JAMES say about hearing and obeying (1.19-27)? Which piece of advice do you find most challenging?

3. The writer of JAMES was aware that the church included both rich and poor people (1.9-11; 2.1-9; 5.1-6). What does he say about how Christians are to treat rich people and poor people? What warnings does he give to rich people?

4. The writer of JAMES has much to say about how Christians are to speak to others (1.19; 3.1-12; 4.11-17). What are the dangers of speaking rashly or in anger? Of bragging? What are some positive ways in which Christians can speak out?

5. Take the time to re-read 2.14-26. Do you agree or disagree with the following statements?
   a. It is possible to have faith without doing kind deeds.
   b. Faith that doesn't lead us to do good deeds is dead.
   c. Faith is trust in God, and doesn't need to be proved by good deeds.

1 peter

The writer of 1 PETER declares, "Once you were nobody. Now you are God's people" (2.10). Read this letter to discover the challenges and joys that are in store for people who follow Jesus.

WHAT MAKES 1 PETER SPECIAL?

FIRST PETER is written in the form of an ancient Greek letter. The letter's main message (1.3—5.11) makes use of themes and styles that are found in many New Testament writings. Like the Gospels, it tells of the importance of Jesus' death and God's raising him back to life. It also repeats Jesus' teachings concerning trust in God, the importance of being humble and joyful even in times of suffering. Like ACTS, it mentions the work of Peter, Silvanus (Silas), and Mark. It provides a picture of the early church, which met in private homes. FIRST PETER also appears to include parts of creeds or hymns that were used in Christian worship of the time (1.20; 2.21-25; 3.18-22).

FIRST PETER encourages Christians to follow Christ's example, to live good lives, and tells Christians to expect suffering—themes that are also found in the letters of Paul. The letter uses Christian family images like the ones found in 1 JOHN. Like HEBREWS, it describes how people who hate or fear the followers of Jesus may make trouble for them and exclude them from society.

The letter was written to Christians scattered over northern Asia Minor. The writer wants those who read the letter to realize that they may have to face suffering because of their faith. Suffering, however, cannot defeat them, because Jesus suffered and died to forgive their sins, and God raised Jesus from death.

Many other important themes are presented in 1 PETER. It teaches that God is at work in Jesus Christ to create a new people, and that God's new people (the church) are chosen to live a holy life and be a holy nation. The letter urges God's new people to respect the Roman emperor and Roman law, but to honor Christ and obey God above everything else, even if it means suffering or losing friends.

WHAT'S THE STORY BEHIND THE SCENE?

The letter has traditionally been connected to Jesus' disciple Peter, and includes greetings from Silvanus and Mark, who worked closely with the apostle Paul. However, many who have studied the sophisticated language and the style of writing in this letter believe it is unlikely that Peter, a Galilean fisherman (Mark 1.16,17; 3.16) with little education (Acts 4.13), could be the letter's author. Instead, they believe, it was most likely written in Peter's name, a common way to honor someone at the time.

This letter may have been written during the reign of the emperor Domitian (A.D. 81–96), when the Jewish and Christian movements clearly separated, and the Roman authorities actively began to persecute Christians. Previously, Christians were considered a sect of the Jewish religion and were protected by the Roman government. (One exception to this was the emperor Nero's persecution of Christians in Rome around A.D. 64.)

HOW IS 1 PETER CONSTRUCTED?

This important letter can be outlined as follows:

Chosen, protected, and saved (1.1-12)
Living as God's holy people (1.13—3.22)
Serving and suffering to the end (4.1—5.14)

This letter was written to Christians in the remote Roman territories of northern Asia Minor. Living with limited rights as resident aliens, the groups addressed in 1 Peter were also suffering from discrimination, prejudice, and abuse because they were Christians. Aware of their suffering, the author offers his readers words of encouragement and tells them how kind God really is and why it is important that they continue to place their faith in God. Using great literary skill, the author shows his readers that they are God's chosen and special people who have been rescued by Christ and who together make up a holy nation. Christians are encouraged to live as Christ's servants, even if it means suffering, because suffering for Christ is a sign that God's glorious Spirit is with them.

Outline

1

From Peter, an apostle of Jesus Christ,
To God's people who are scattered like foreigners in Pontus, Galatia, Cappadocia, Asia, and Bithynia.

²God the Father decided to choose you as his people, and his Spirit has made you holy. You have obeyed Jesus Christ and are sprinkled with his blood.[a]

I pray that God will be kind to you and will keep on giving you peace!

A Real Reason for Hope

³Praise God, the Father of our Lord Jesus Christ. God is so good, and by raising Jesus from death, he has given us new life and a hope that lives on. ⁴God has something stored up for you in heaven, where it will never decay or be ruined or disappear.

⁵You have faith in God, whose power will protect you until the last day.[b] Then he will save you, just as he has always planned to do. ⁶On that day you will be glad, even if you have to go through many hard trials for a while. ⁷Your faith will be like gold that has been tested in a fire. And these trials will prove that your faith is worth much more than gold that can be destroyed. They will show that you will be given praise and honor and glory when Jesus Christ returns.

⁸You have never seen Jesus, and you don't see him now. But still you love him and have faith in him, and no words can tell how glad and happy ⁹you are to be saved. This is why you have faith.

¹⁰Some prophets told how God would treat you with undeserved grace, and they searched hard to find out more about the way you would be saved. ¹¹The Spirit of Christ was in them and was telling them how Christ would suffer and would then

---

[a]**1.2** *sprinkled with his blood*: According to Exodus 24.3-8 the people of Israel were sprinkled with the blood of cows to show they would keep their agreement with God. Peter says that it is the blood of Jesus that seals the agreement between God and his people (see Hebrews 9.18-21).   [b]**1.5** *the last day*: When God will judge all people.

1.18 rescued from the useless way of life: The Greek word translated here as "rescued," often, though not always, means paying a price to free a slave or prisoner. Their "useless way of life" describes how they had lived before they became God's obedient children (see 1.14; 4.1-4).

1.19 rescued by the precious blood of Christ . . . lamb: The New Testament refers to Christ's death on the cross as a sacrifice to forgive sins (Rom 3.25,26). He is also compared to the spotless lamb, whose blood has power to bring forgiveness (see Heb 9.23-28; 1 John 1.7).

Blood

2.4,5 the living stone . . . living stones: The prophet Isaiah compared the chosen one (Messiah) to a cornerstone (Isa 28.16). Cornerstones were usually large stones placed in the corner of a building's foundation. Later, Jesus compared himself to such a stone (Mark 12.1-12). See also Acts 4.8-12; Rom 9.30-33.

Those who trust in Jesus as the cornerstone, the author says, will become living stones themselves. They will be built into a spiritual house. Other New Testament writers also use images of God's people as a temple (see 1 Cor 3.16,17; Eph 2.19-22; Rev 3.12).

be given great honor. So they searched to find out exactly who Christ would be and when this would happen. [12]But they were told that they were serving you and not themselves. They preached to you by the power of the Holy Spirit, who was sent from heaven. And their message was only for you, even though angels would like to know more about it.

Chosen To Live a Holy Life

[13]Be alert and think straight. Put all your hope in how God will treat you with undeserved grace when Jesus Christ appears. [14]Behave like obedient children. Don't let your lives be controlled by your desires, as they used to be. [15]Always live as God's holy people should, because God is the one who chose you, and he is holy. [16]That's why the Scriptures say, "I am the holy God, and you must be holy too."

[17]You say that God is your Father, but God doesn't have favorites! He judges all people by what they do. So you must honor God while you live as strangers here on earth. [18]You were rescued[c] from the useless way of life you learned from your ancestors. But you know you were not rescued by such things as silver or gold that don't last forever. [19]You were rescued by the precious blood of Christ, that spotless and innocent lamb. [20]Christ was chosen even before the world was created, but because of you, he did not come until these last days. [21]And when he did come, it was to lead you to have faith in God, who raised him from death and honored him in a glorious way. This is why you have put your faith and hope in God.

[22]You obeyed the truth,[d] and your souls were made pure. Now you sincerely love each other. But you must keep on loving with all your heart. [23]Do this because God has given you new birth by his message that lives on forever. [24]The Scriptures say,

"Humans wither like grass,
    and their glory fades
        like wild flowers.
Grass dries up,
    and flowers fall
        to the ground.
[25]But what the Lord has said
    will stand forever."

Our good news to you is what the Lord has said.

A Living Stone and a Holy Nation

2 Stop being hateful! Quit trying to fool people, and start being sincere. Don't be jealous or say cruel things about others. [2]Be like newborn babies who are thirsty for the pure spiritual milk that will help you grow and be saved. [3]You have already found out how good the Lord really is.

[4]Come to Jesus Christ. He is the living stone people have rejected, but which God has chosen and highly honored. [5]And now you are living stones being used to build a spiritual house. You are also a group of holy priests, and with the help of Jesus Christ you will offer sacrifices that please God. [6]It is just as God says in the Scriptures,

"Look! I am placing in Zion
    a choice and precious
        cornerstone.
No one who has faith
    in this one
        will be disappointed."

[7]You are followers of the Lord, and this stone is precious to you. But it isn't pre-

[c]**1.18 rescued:** The Greek word often, though not always, means payment of a price to free a slave or prisoner.   [d]**1.22 You obeyed the truth:** Some manuscripts add "by the power of the Spirit."

You obeyed the truth, and your souls were made pure.
Now you sincerely love each other.   1 PET 1.22

cious to those who refuse to follow him. They are the builders who tossed aside the stone that turned out to be the most important one of all. **8**They disobeyed the message and stumbled and fell over this stone, because they were doomed.

9But you are God's chosen and special people. You are a group of royal priests and a holy nation. God has brought you out of darkness into his marvelous light. Now you must tell all the wonderful things he has done. The Scriptures say,

10"Once you were nobody.
    Now you are God's people.
At one time no one
    had mercy on you.
Now God has treated you
    with kindness."

Live as God's Servants Should

11Dear friends, you are foreigners and strangers on this earth. So I beg you not to surrender to those desires that fight against you. **12**Always let others see you behaving properly, even though they may still accuse you of doing wrong. Then on the day of judgment, they will honor God by telling the good things they saw you do.

13The Lord wants you to obey all human authorities, especially the Emperor, who rules over everyone. **14**You must also obey governors, because they are sent by the Emperor to punish criminals and to praise good citizens. **15**God wants you to silence stupid and ignorant people by doing right. **16**You are free, but still you are God's servants, and you must not use your freedom as an excuse for doing wrong. **17**Respect everyone and show special love for God's people. Honor God and respect the Emperor.

The Example of Christ's Suffering

18Servants, you must obey your masters and always show respect to them. Do this, not only to those who are kind and thoughtful, but also to those who are cruel. **19**God will bless you, even if others treat you unfairly for being loyal to him. **20**You don't gain anything by being punished for some wrong you have done. But God will bless you, if you have to suffer for doing something good. **21**After all, God chose you to suffer as you follow in the footsteps of Christ, who set an example by suffering for you.

22Christ did not sin
    or ever tell a lie.
23Although he was abused,
    he never tried to get even.
And when he suffered,
    he made no threats.
Instead, he had faith in God,
    who judges fairly.
24Christ carried the burden
    of our sins.
He was nailed to the cross,
so we would stop sinning
    and start living right.
By his cuts and bruises
    you are healed.
25You had wandered away
    like sheep.
Now you have returned
    to the one
who is your shepherd
    and protector.

Wives and Husbands

3 If you are a wife, you must put your husband first. Even if he opposes our message, you will win him over by what you do. No one else will have to say anything to him, **2**because he will see how you

■ **2.9** *royal priests and a holy nation:* In Exodus, God tells Moses to tell the people of Israel that they will be God's "holy nation" and serve him "as priests" (Exod 19.6). Though God chose the Israelites to be his special people in the past, God's new people is made up of all who have faith (Rom 11.1-29; Gal 3.22-29).

● **2.13-17** *human authorities . . . Emperor:* The Roman emperor and his government protected the lives and property of law-abiding people and punished criminals. Christians could turn suspicion and fear concerning their worship practices into respect if they obeyed the local laws and were good neighbors. Nero was the Roman emperor from A.D. 54 to 68, and would have been the emperor in power at the time of Peter's death.

● **2.18** *Servants . . . obey your masters:* Slavery was common in the Roman world. The early church included both slaves and slaveholders. The way slaves and masters behaved toward each other could affect how others viewed God.

◯ Slaves and Servants in the Time of Jesus

■ **2.21** *the footsteps of Christ:* Christians will suffer and be mistreated, but they are not to fight those who mistreat them, just as Jesus did not fight those who had put him to death.

3.1-5 *fancy hairdos:* It is easier for a woman who honors God to convince her husband to believe in God than it is for a woman who is overly concerned with wearing fancy hairdos or expensive clothes.

3.6 *Sarah:* Sarah faithfully followed Abraham when God called them to leave their homeland to go to Canaan (Gen 12—23).

Abraham

3.18 *Christ died . . . his spirit was made alive:* This verse is probably a very early Christian hymn that celebrates how Christ died to forgive sins, and God raised him to life.

3.19 *the spirits . . . being kept in prison:* Here, "the spirits" seem to be those who disobeyed God in the time of Noah and so were destroyed by God in the great flood (3.20). Christ's preaching to them proved his power even over the disobedient.

3.20,21 *Noah . . . flood waters were like baptism:* Noah was faithful to God when others were not (Gen 6.1—7.24). God saved Noah and his family from the great flood. Now God's new people, the followers of Jesus, are saved by baptism, whose waters are a reminder of God's saving acts. In 1 Corinthians 10.1,2, God's saving of the Israelites at the Red Sea is also compared to baptism.

honor God and live a pure life. **3**Don't depend on things like fancy hairdos or gold jewelry or expensive clothes to make you look beautiful. **4**Be beautiful in your heart by being gentle and quiet. This kind of beauty will last, and God considers it very special.

5Long ago those women who worshiped God and put their hope in him made themselves beautiful by putting their husbands first. **6**For example, Sarah obeyed Abraham and called him her master. You are her true children, if you do right and don't let anything frighten you.

7If you are a husband, you should be thoughtful of your wife. Treat her with honor, because she isn't as strong as you are, and she shares with you in the gift of life. Then nothing will stand in the way of your prayers.

Suffering for Doing Right

8Finally, all of you should agree and have concern and love for each other. You should also be kind and humble. **9**Don't be hateful and insult people just because they are hateful and insult you. Instead, treat everyone with kindness. You are God's chosen ones, and he will bless you. The Scriptures say,

10"Do you really love life?
  Do you want to be happy?
Then stop saying cruel things
  and quit telling lies.
11Give up your evil ways
  and do right,
as you find and follow
  the road to peace.
12The Lord watches over
  everyone who obeys him,
and he listens
  to their prayers.

e3.22 right side: The place of honor and power.

But he opposes everyone
  who does evil."

13Can anyone really harm you for being eager to do good deeds? **14**Even if you have to suffer for doing good things, God will bless you. So stop being afraid and don't worry about what people might do. **15**Honor Christ and let him be the Lord of your life.

Always be ready to give an answer when someone asks you about your hope. **16**Give a kind and respectful answer and keep your conscience clear. This way you will make people ashamed for saying bad things about your good conduct as a follower of Christ. **17**You are better off to obey God and suffer for doing right than to suffer for doing wrong.

18Christ died once for our sins.
  An innocent person died
    for those who are guilty.
  Christ did this
    to bring you to God,
  when his body
    was put to death
  and his spirit
    was made alive.

19Christ then preached to the spirits that were being kept in prison. **20**They had disobeyed God while Noah was building the boat, but God had been patient with them. Eight people went into that boat and were brought safely through the flood.

21Those flood waters were like baptism that now saves you. But baptism is more than just washing your body. It means turning to God with a clear conscience, because Jesus Christ was raised from death. **22**Christ is now in heaven, where he sits at the right side[e] of God. All angels, authorities, and powers are under his control.

Being Faithful to God

4 Christ suffered here on earth. Now you must be ready to suffer as he did, because suffering shows that you have stopped sinning. [2]It means you have turned from your own desires and want to obey God for the rest of your life. [3]You have already lived long enough like people who don't know God. You were immoral and followed your evil desires. You went around drinking and partying and carrying on. In fact, you even worshiped disgusting idols. [4]Now your former friends wonder why you have stopped running around with them, and they curse you for it. [5]But they will have to answer to God, who judges the living and the dead. [6]The good news has even been preached to the dead,[f] so that after they have been judged for what they have done in this life, their spirits will live with God.

[7]Everything will soon come to an end. So be serious and be sensible enough to pray.

[8]Most important of all, you must sincerely love each other, because love wipes away many sins.

[9]Welcome people into your home and don't grumble about it.

[10]Each of you has been blessed with one of God's many wonderful gifts to be used in the service of others. So use your gift well. [11]If you have the gift of speaking, preach God's message. If you have the gift of helping others, do it with the strength that God supplies. Everything should be done in a way that will bring honor to God because of Jesus Christ, who is glorious and powerful forever. Amen.

Suffering for Being a Christian

[12]Dear friends, don't be surprised or shocked that you are going through testing that is like walking through fire. [13]Be glad for the chance to suffer as Christ suffered. It will prepare you for even greater happiness when he makes his glorious return.

[14]Count it a blessing when you suffer for being a Christian. This shows that God's glorious Spirit is with you. [15]But you deserve to suffer if you are a murderer, a thief, a crook, or a busybody. [16]Don't be ashamed to suffer for being a Christian. Praise God that you belong to him. [17]God has already begun judging his own people. And if his judgment begins with us, imagine how terrible it will be for those who refuse to obey his message. The Scriptures say,

[18]"If good people barely escape,
    what will happen to sinners
    and to others
        who don't respect God?"

[19]If you suffer for obeying God, you must have complete faith in your faithful Creator and keep on doing right.

Helping Christian Leaders

5 Church leaders, I am writing to encourage you. I too am a leader, as well as a witness to Christ's suffering, and I will share in his glory when it is shown to us.

[2]Just as shepherds watch over their sheep, you must watch over everyone God has placed in your care. Do it willingly in order to please God, and not simply because you think you must. Let it be something you want to do, instead of something

---

4.1,2 stopped sinning: Christians should show faith in God by refusing to do the evil things their neighbors do, even if it means being persecuted (1 Pet 1.14; 2.11,12; 3.8,9; 4.14-19).

Sin

4.3 were immoral . . . followed your evil desires: The partying and drunkenness mentioned here is probably a reference to the kind of wild banquets held by many trade groups and social clubs in Asia Minor. Some Christians may have been members of these groups or clubs, because they were considered a good place to make business contacts and friends. The idols mentioned here might have been statues representing Artemis, the goddess who was known as the goddess of fertility (see Acts 19.23-29).

4.7 Everything will soon come to an end: The writer believed that Christ would come back very soon and change the world.

4.10,11 God's many wonderful gifts: In other New Testament writings, these gifts are said to come from the Holy Spirit (Rom 12.3-8; 1 Cor 12.4-31).

5.1 witness to Christ's suffering: Peter, one of Jesus' apostles, was present when Jesus suffered on the cross.

---

[f]*4.6 the dead:* Either people who died after becoming followers of Christ or the people of Noah's day (see 3.19).

5.4 *Chief Shepherd . . . crown that will never lose its glory:* See also John 10.10-18; Heb 13.20, which describe Jesus as the Good Shepherd. In ancient times an athlete who had won a contest was rewarded with a crown of flowers as a sign of victory.

Shepherd

Satan

Eternal Life

5.12 *Silvanus:* Silvanus was a Christian prophet, who was probably also known as Silas (Acts 15.22-41; 16.9—17.15; 2 Cor 1.19; 1 Thes 1.1; 2 Thes 1.1).

5.13 *Babylon:* This may be a secret name for the city of Rome (see also Rev 18.1-24). In the first century A.D. Babylon was no longer a dominant world power, but Rome was.

Babylon

5.13 *Mark:* Mark went with Paul and Barnabas from the Syrian city of Antioch to Jerusalem in order to deliver money needed by the church there (Acts 11.27-30; 12.12,25; 13.13). Later, Mark (John Mark) left Paul and worked with Barnabas (Acts 15.36-39). See also Col 4.10-14; Phlm 24.

5.14 *warm greeting:* This phrase translates a Greek word that means "holy kiss."

you do merely to make money. **3**Don't be bossy to those people who are in your care, but set an example for them. **4**Then when Christ the Chief Shepherd returns, you will be given a crown that will never lose its glory.

5All of you young people should obey your elders. In fact, everyone should be humble toward everyone else. The Scriptures say,

"God opposes proud people,
but he helps everyone
who is humble."

6Be humble in the presence of God's mighty power, and he will honor you when the time comes. **7**God cares for you, so turn all your worries over to him.

8Be on your guard and stay awake. Your enemy, the devil, is like a roaring lion, sneaking around to find someone to attack. **9**But you must resist the devil and stay strong in your faith. You know that all over the world the Lord's followers are suffering just as you are. **10**But God shows undeserved kindness to everyone. That's why he appointed Christ Jesus to choose you to share in his eternal glory. You will suffer for a while, but God will make you complete, steady, strong, and firm. **11**God will be in control forever! Amen.

Final Greetings

12Silvanus helped me write this short letter, and I consider him a faithful follower of the Lord. I wanted to encourage you and tell you how kind God really is, so you will keep on having faith in him.

13Greetings from the Lord's followers in Babylon.g They are God's chosen ones.

Mark, who is like a son to me, sends his greetings too.

14Give each other a warm greeting. I pray that God will give peace to everyone who belongs to Christ.h

---

g5.13 *Babylon:* This may be a secret name for the city of Rome. h5.14 *Christ:* Some manuscripts add "Amen."

Reflection Questions About 1 Peter 1.1—5.14

1. What does the writer mean when he says that God has given God's people "new life and a hope that lives on" (1.3)? How will this hope be tested (1.6,7; 2.18-21; 4.1,12-19)? Why are the Lord's followers to be glad for the chance to suffer (4.13,14)?

2. How have God's people been rescued from the useless way of life they learned from their ancestors (1.18; 4.3,4)? How are they to live instead?

3. Chapter 2.1-12 uses a number of images to describe God's chosen people: living stones, holy (or royal) priests, a holy nation, foreigners, and strangers. What does each image tell you about what it means to be one of Christ's followers?

4. What advice does the writer give to servants (2.18-21), wives (3.1-6), and husbands (3.7)? What important advice is given to all of God's people, no matter who they are (3.8-15; 4.8-10)?

5. A number of times the writer mentions the importance of being obedient and humble (1.14-16; 3.8-12; 4.8-11; 5.5-7). What does being humble have to do with being one of God's people? Do you think that humble people can be successful in the modern world?

2 peter

Christ Jesus came into the world to be its Savior and to choose a people to call his own. One day he will return to welcome his people into a glorious kingdom that will last forever. Read 2 PETER to see how Christians are to live in the meantime.

WHAT MAKES 2 PETER SPECIAL?

SECOND PETER is written in the form of an ancient Greek letter, but it is actually intended to be the farewell message, or last testament, of the apostle Peter. The writer warns Christians about false teachers who are trying to lead the Lord's followers away from the truth. When false teachers are at work, he says, Christians must stick to their faith and show others how to live right by living right themselves. Christians must never forget that the Lord's return is certain, even though it has not happened as quickly as some expected. In the meantime, they are to wait patiently and obey God by living pure and spotless lives.

WHAT'S THE STORY BEHIND THE SCENE?

This letter claims the apostle Peter as its author. Most scholars believe a follower of Peter wrote this letter after Peter had died—as a way of honoring Peter and as a way of defending the teachings of the early apostles against new opponents. Consider the following clues:

1. The style of the book more closely reflects the Greek culture of the second century A.D. than any other New Testament book. The apostle Peter was an uneducated Galilean fisherman, who probably died around A.D. 65 in Rome.

2. The writer mentions Paul's letters as if they are being considered as Scripture for the Christian church (3.15,16). Paul probably died about the same time as Peter, and it seems unlikely that Paul's letters would have been regarded as Christian Scripture until a few years after Paul's death.

3. Many New Testament letters expressed hope that Christ would soon return (Phil 1.20; 2.16; 3.20,21; 1 Thes 4.13-18). Yet in 2 PETER, false teachers are making fun of the Christians who hope for the Lord's return, saying the church's first leaders "have already died, and the world hasn't changed a bit" (3.4). Peter was part of the first generation of church leaders. The writer emphasizes being patient about the Lord's return and not losing hope, since God isn't being slow about keeping his promises (3.9). This would not have been an important concern during Peter's lifetime.

HOW IS 2 PETER CONSTRUCTED?

The letter can be outlined as follows:

Please God and hold firmly to the truth (1.1-21)
Watch out for false prophets and false teachers (2.1-22)
Be ready, because the Lord will return (3.1-18)

Second Peter addresses unnamed Christian congregations that have been misled by false prophets—church members posing as teachers who deny or contradict the beliefs and values handed down by the first apostles. These false teachers apparently had caused some Christians to wonder why the Lord had not yet returned. The author directs Christians to live in a way that pleases God. Rather than listen to clever speculation, Christians should pay close attention to the message of Jesus and allow their hearts to be guided by the Holy Spirit. The letter concludes by explaining that the Lord is not slow to return, but is patiently allowing everyone to turn away from sin.

Outline

1

From Simon Peter, a servant and an apostle of Jesus Christ.

To everyone who shares with us in the privilege of believing that our God and Savior Jesus Christ will do what is just and fair.[a]

²I pray that God will be kind to you and will let you live in perfect peace! May you keep learning more and more about God and our Lord Jesus.

Living as the Lord's Followers

³We have everything we need to live a life that pleases God. It was all given to us by God's own power, when we learned he had invited us to share in his wonderful goodness. ⁴God made great and marvelous promises, so his nature would become part of us. Then we could escape our evil desires and the corrupt influences of this world.

⁵Do your best to improve your faith by adding goodness, understanding, ⁶self-control, patience, devotion to God, ⁷con-cern for others, and love. ⁸If you keep growing in this way, it will show that what you know about our Lord Jesus Christ has made your lives useful and meaningful. ⁹But if you don't grow, you are like someone who is nearsighted or blind, and you have forgotten that your past sins are forgiven.

¹⁰My friends, you must do all you can to show God has really chosen and selected you. If you keep on doing this, you won't stumble and fall. ¹¹Then our Lord and Savior Jesus Christ will give you a glorious welcome into his kingdom that will last forever.

¹²You are holding firmly to the truth you were given. But I am still going to remind you of these things. ¹³In fact, I think I should keep on reminding you until I leave this body. ¹⁴And our Lord Jesus Christ has already told me that I will soon leave it behind. ¹⁵This is why I am doing my best to make sure that each of you remembers all of this after I am gone.

[a]**1.1** *To everyone who . . . just and fair:* Or "To everyone whose faith in the justice and fairness of our God and Savior Jesus Christ is as precious as our own faith."

● 1.1 *everyone:* This letter may have been intended for followers of Christ in Asia Minor.

■ 1.1 *God and Savior Jesus Christ:* Savior means "one who delivers." As Savior, Jesus Christ has the power to deliver all people from sin and death. The word "Christ" is from the Greek word *Christos,* which means "Messiah" or "chosen one," so it can be placed before or after Jesus' name.

CR   Messiah (Chosen One)

■ 1.5-7 *improve your faith . . . love:* In most New Testament writings, faith means trust in Christ, but here it means doing things that show that Jesus' followers are really one with God. This would set the followers apart from false teachers and reckless, proud, and senseless people who will be destroyed by their own corrupt deeds (2.10-13).

SECOND PETER was written at a time when Christianity was competing with other popular religions and philosophies in the Roman world. Readers would have been familiar with the list of things mentioned in verses 5-7, because they were found in popular philosophies. But Christian "growth" was to be based on faith in Christ and would result in love.

■ 1.11 *a glorious welcome into his kingdom:* Christ will welcome those who are faithful to him into his heavenly kingdom (1 Cor 15.12-57; 1 Thes 4.13-18; 1 Pet 5.10,11).

CR   Heaven

We have everything we need to live a life that pleases God. 2 PET 1.3

1.19-21 *prophets . . . guided by the Spirit of God:* Just as the Jewish prophets of the Old Testament spoke by the Spirit of God, only followers who are led by God's Spirit can truly understand what the Scriptures mean.

1.19 *until daylight comes:* The coming of daylight, or dawn, refers to the new day that Christ will bring when he returns.

2.1 *false prophets spoke to . . . Israel:* The Jewish Scriptures (Old Testament) often mention false prophets, who encouraged the people of Israel to disobey God's commands (see 1 Kgs 18.1-39; Jer 14.13-16).

2.1 *Master:* This refers to Jesus Christ, who died as a sacrifice to forgive the sins of all people (Rom 3.25-26; Heb 2.14-18).

2.4 *angels that sinned . . . thrown into . . . hell:* This may refer to the angels who liked the human women on earth so much that they came down and had sex with them (Gen 6.1,2; Jude 6).

Hell

2.7-8 *Lot:* Lot went to live in the valley near Sodom after separating from his uncle Abraham (Gen 13.1-13; 19.1-16).

The Message about the Glory of Christ

[16]When we told you about the power and the return of our Lord Jesus Christ, we were not telling clever stories someone had made up. But with our own eyes we saw his true greatness. [17]God, our great and wonderful Father, truly honored him by saying, "This is my own dear Son, and I am pleased with him." [18]We were there with Jesus on the holy mountain and heard this voice speak from heaven.

[19]All of this makes us even more certain that what the prophets said is true. So you should pay close attention to their message, as you would to a lamp shining in some dark place. You must keep on paying attention until daylight comes and the morning star rises in your hearts. [20]But you need to realize that no one alone can understand any of the prophecies in the Scriptures. [21]The prophets did not think these things up on their own, but they were guided by the Spirit of God.

False Prophets and Teachers

2 Sometimes false prophets spoke to the people of Israel. False teachers will also sneak in and speak harmful lies to you. But these teachers don't really belong to the Master who paid a great price for them, and they will quickly destroy themselves. [2]Many people will follow their evil ways and cause others to tell lies about the true way. [3]They will be greedy and cheat you with smooth talk. But long ago God decided to punish them, and God doesn't sleep.

[4]God did not have pity on the angels that sinned. He had them tied up and thrown into the dark pits of hell until the time of judgment. [5]And during Noah's time, God did not have pity on the ungodly people of the world. He destroyed them with a flood, though he did save eight people, including Noah, who preached the truth.

[6]God punished the cities of Sodom and Gomorrah[b] by burning them to ashes, and this is a warning to anyone else who wants to sin.

[7-8]Lot lived right and was greatly troubled by the terrible way those wicked people were living. He was a good man, and day after day he suffered because of the evil things he saw and heard. So the Lord rescued him. [9]This shows that the Lord knows how to rescue godly people from their sufferings and to punish evil people while they wait for the day of judgment.

[10]The Lord is especially hard on people who disobey him and don't think of anything except their own filthy desires. They are reckless and proud and are not afraid of cursing the glorious beings in heaven. [11]Although angels are more powerful than these evil beings,[c] even the angels don't dare to accuse them to the Lord.

[12]These people are no better than senseless animals that live by their feelings and are born to be caught and killed. They speak evil of things they don't know anything about. But their own corrupt deeds will destroy them. [13]They have done evil, and they will be rewarded with evil.

They think it is fun to have wild parties during the day. They are immoral, and the meals they eat with you are spoiled by the shameful and selfish way they carry on.[d]

[b]**2.6** *Sodom and Gomorrah:* During the time of Abraham the Lord destroyed these cities because the people there were so evil (see Genesis 19.24).   [c]**2.11** *evil beings:* Or "evil teachers."   [d]**2.13** *and the meals they eat with you are spoiled by the shameful and selfish way they carry on:* Some manuscripts have "and the meals they eat with you are spoiled by the shameful way they carry on during your feasts of Christian love."

[14]All they think about is having sex with someone else's husband or wife. There is no end to their wicked deeds. They trick people who are easily fooled, and their minds are filled with greedy thoughts. But they are headed for trouble!

[15]They have left the true road and have gone down the wrong path by following the example of the prophet Balaam. He was the son of Beor and loved what he got from being a crook. [16]But a donkey corrected him for this evil deed. It spoke to him with a human voice and made him stop his foolishness.

[17]These people are like dried up water holes and clouds blown by a windstorm. The darkest part of hell is waiting for them. [18]They brag out loud about their stupid nonsense. And by being vulgar and crude, they trap people who have barely escaped from living the wrong kind of life. [19]They promise freedom to everyone. But they are merely slaves of filthy living, because people are slaves of whatever controls them.

[20]When they learned about our Lord and Savior Jesus Christ, they escaped from the filthy things of this world. But they are again caught up and controlled by these filthy things, and now they are in worse shape than they were at first. [21]They would have been better off if they had never known about the right way. Even after they knew what was right, they turned their backs on the holy commandments they were given. [22]What happened to them is just like the true saying,

> "A dog will come back
>   to lick up its own vomit.
> A pig that has been washed
>   will roll in the mud."

The Lord Will Return

3 My dear friends, this is the second letter I have written to encourage you to do some honest thinking. I don't want you to forget [2]what God's prophets said would happen. You must never forget what the holy prophets taught in the past. And you must remember what the apostles told you our Lord and Savior has commanded us to do.

[3]But first you must realize that in the last days some people won't think about anything except their own selfish desires. They will make fun of you [4]and say, "Didn't your Lord promise to come back? Yet the first leaders have already died, and the world hasn't changed a bit."

[5]They will say this because they want to forget that long ago the heavens and the earth were made at God's command. The earth came out of water and was made from water. [6]Later it was destroyed by the waters of a mighty flood. [7]But God has commanded the present heavens and earth to remain until the day of judgment. Then they will be set on fire, and ungodly people will be destroyed.

[8]Dear friends, don't forget that for the Lord one day is the same as 1,000 years, and 1,000 years is the same as one day. [9]The Lord isn't slow about keeping his promises, as some people think he is. In fact, God is patient, because he wants everyone to turn from sin and no one to be lost.

[10]The day of the Lord's return will surprise us like a thief. The heavens will disappear with a loud noise, and the heat will melt the whole universe.[e] Then the earth and everything on it will be seen for what they are.[f]

2.15,16 *Balaam . . . a donkey:* King Balak of Moab hired Balaam to curse the people of Israel (Num 22.4-35).

2.19 *They promise freedom to everyone:* Some false teachers may have been twisting the truth about Christian freedom (3.16). The apostle Paul taught that Christians are free because of Christ, but this did not mean that they could use this freedom to do anything they felt like doing (see Gal 5.13). See also John 8.31-36; Rom 6.16.

2.21 *holy commandments:* This may refer to the commandment to love God and love one's neighbor (Mark 12.28-31) or to the Ten Commandments (Exod 20.1-17; Deut 5.1-21).

3.1 *the second letter:* The letter known as 1 PETER had already been passed around the churches.

3.2 *apostles:* "Apostles" refers to the earliest followers of Jesus who were chosen to spread the message about Jesus. What "our Lord and Savior has commanded us to do" probably refers back to 2.21.

3.4 *the first leaders have already died:* This may refer to the apostles who were the very first generation of leaders in the church.

---

[e]3.10 *the whole universe:* Probably the sun, moon, and stars, or the elements that everything in the universe is made of.   [f]3.10 *will be seen for what they are:* Some manuscripts have "will go up in flames."

Fire

3.13 *new heaven and a new earth:* This idea can also be found in Isaiah 65.17; 66.22; and Revelation 21.1.

3.16 *Paul . . . in all his letters . . . Scriptures:* The writer considered Paul's letters to be Scripture for the Christian church. This is evidence that this letter was written quite late in the first century A.D., because it took that long for Paul's letters to be circulated among the churches and to gain authority as Scripture.

Those who were "twisting" what Paul taught may have used his teaching on freedom from the Law (Rom 3.27-31; Gal 5.1) as an excuse to do anything they wanted. Or they may have argued that Paul was wrong in teaching that the Lord would soon come back (Rom 13.11,12; Phil 4.5; 1 Thes 4.15).

[11]Everything will be destroyed. So you should serve and honor God by the way you live. [12]You should look forward to the day when God judges everyone, and you should try to make it come soon.[g] On that day the heavens will be destroyed by fire, and everything else will melt in the heat. [13]But God has promised us a new heaven and a new earth, where justice will rule. We are really looking forward to this!

[14]My friends, while you are waiting, you should make certain the Lord finds you pure, spotless, and living at peace. [15]Don't forget that the Lord is patient because he wants people to be saved. This is also what our dear friend Paul said when he wrote you with the wisdom God had given him. [16]Paul talks about these same things in all his letters, but part of what he says is hard to understand. Some ignorant and unsteady people even destroy themselves by twisting what he said. They do the same thing with other Scriptures too.

[17]My dear friends, you have been warned ahead of time! So don't let the errors of evil people lead you down the wrong path and make you lose your balance. [18]Let the gift of undeserved grace and the understanding that come from our Lord and Savior Jesus Christ help you keep on growing. Praise Jesus now and forever! Amen.[h]

[g]3.12 *and you should try to make it come soon:* Or "and you should eagerly desire for that day to come."
[h]3.18 *Amen:* Some manuscripts do not have "Amen."

Let the gift of undeserved grace and the understanding that come from our Lord and Savior Jesus Christ help you keep on growing. 2 PET 3.18

Reflection Questions About 2 Peter 1.1—3.18

1. How were the readers of 2 PETER encouraged to "keep growing" (1.5-8)? What is the purpose for growing in faith (1.10,11)?

2. What false teachings and immoral things did the followers of Christ face (2.1-3,10-22)? Do these sorts of things go on where you live? If so, how are people (and churches in particular) dealing with them?

3. Why did some people make fun of their Christian neighbors who expected Jesus to return during their lifetime (3.3,4)? According to the writer of 2 PETER, why has God been patient about bringing the day of judgment (3.8,9)?

4. According to the writer, what will the day of the Lord's return be like (3.10-13)? Do you look forward to the day of the Lord's return?

5. How are Christ's followers to act as they wait for his return (3.14-18)?

1 john

Who are the children of light and the children of darkness? Read 1 John and find out.

WHAT MAKES 1 JOHN SPECIAL?

Though 1 John is called a letter, it does not have many of the features of a typical ancient Greek letter. For example, it does not have a formal greeting. Because it calls Jesus the "Word of God" and emphasizes that Christians should love one another, 1 John has always been linked with the Gospel of John. The book also provides a look at how the early church settled disagreements between true followers of Jesus and those who had false ideas.

First John and the other letters of John seem to have been written to encourage the followers of Christ to remain faithful to the truth: Jesus, God's Son, was truly human, and really shed his blood to take away sins (1.7). Some followers were falsely claiming that Jesus was a purely spiritual being, not a human. These teachers also believed that spiritual life was greater than moral life and spiritual knowledge was more important than moral rules. They taught that moral rules were only for people who couldn't see beyond the physical level of life. For example, they believed that their spiritual rebirth made it impossible for them to sin, so they had no sins to confess (1.9,10).

Besides believing that Jesus "had a truly human body" (4.2) and is truly God's Son (2.22; 3.23), God's true children ("the children of light") are those who also obey God and love one another (3.11-24). Only those who believe that Jesus Christ was truly human and who love one another really have eternal life.

WHAT'S THE STORY BEHIND THE SCENE?

This book was probably written late in the first century or very early in the second century. At that time, the early church was trying to determine what made someone a true child of God. It was a time of many new and competing religions. One trend among these new religions was toward Gnosticism, a movement that described the physical world as purely evil and the spiritual world as the only good. Gnostics believed that the goal of humans was to get special knowledge that would free them from the real world. They claimed that this superior knowledge separated them from this corrupt world. However, the writer of 1 John shows that God made the world and sent Jesus to free the world from evil and to unite the physical world with God.

HOW IS 1 JOHN CONSTRUCTED?

The book does not have a formal opening greeting or final greeting, though it was likely intended to be a letter (1.4). The book may be outlined in the following way:

Living in the light (1.1—2.17)
The devil's children and God's children
    (2.18—3.10)
Love that comes from God (3.11—4.21)
Faith that brings victory over the world (5.1-21)

First John is written as a sermon and lacks the opening greeting, thanksgiving, and closing greeting that mark most New Testament letters. The author's key purpose is to defend Christian communities against false prophets and to remind them that as children of God they are to live in the light and love one another. The "enemies of Christ" that he warns against have apparently left the church, and have persuaded many members to join them. In order to warn Christians against the teachings of these false prophets, the author of 1 John explains what it means to be a child of God. True Christians live in the truth of God's light, have faith in God's son Jesus Christ, believe that Jesus had a human body, obey God, and love others with the kind of love that comes from God.

Outline

1

The Word that gives life
 was from the beginning,
and this is the one
 our message is about.

Our ears have heard,
 our eyes have seen,
and our hands have touched
 this Word.

[2]The one who gives life appeared! We saw it happen, and we are witnesses to what we have seen. Now we are telling you about this eternal life that was with the Father and appeared to us. [3]We are telling you what we have seen and heard, so you may share in this life with us. And we share in it with the Father and with his Son Jesus Christ. [4]We are writing to tell you these things, because this makes us[a] truly happy.

God Is Light

[5]Jesus told us God is light and doesn't have any darkness in him. Now we are telling you. [6]If we say we share in life with God and keep on living in the dark, we are lying and are not living by the truth. [7]But if we live in the light, as God does, we share in life with each other. And the blood of his Son Jesus washes all our sins away. [8]If we say we have not sinned, we are fooling ourselves, and the truth isn't in our hearts. [9]But if we confess our sins to God, he can always be trusted to forgive us and take our sins away.

[10]If we say we have not sinned, we make God a liar, and his message isn't in our hearts.[b]

---

[a]**1.4** *us:* Some manuscripts have "you." [b]**1.10** *and his message isn't in our hearts:* Or "because we have not accepted his message."

■ 1.1 *The Word that gives life:* The Greek word *Logos*, translated here as "Word," also means "reason" or "purpose." Here the "Word" refers to Jesus Christ, who brings life. Jesus was truly God because he was present with God at the time of creation (John 1.2), but he also came as a human being who could be seen and touched and heard.

■ 1.1 *from the beginning:* See also Gen 1.1—2.4, which describes how God created all things at the beginning.

■ 1.2 *eternal life:* "Eternal life" here refers to Christ Jesus himself, and to God's promise that those who have faith in Jesus will live forever with God.

◯ Eternal Life

■ 1.6 *truth:* Though Jesus died and was raised from death in order to defeat sin and death, his followers need to continue to confess their sins. This true teaching about Jesus is in contrast to the false teaching that Jesus was not really human and that his followers were free to live however they wished.

◯ Truth

■ 1.7 *blood of his Son Jesus washes . . . sins away:* The New Testament teaches that God gave his Son as a sacrifice for sins (see Acts 2.23; Rom 3.25,26; Heb 2.16,17; 9.25,26). Those who "sin" reject the truth about God and God's promises.

◯ Sin

Notes (left column)

2.1 *My children:* The writer uses the term "children" for all the true followers of Jesus, no matter what age they might be.

2.2 *Christ is the sacrifice:* Jesus' death was a sacrifice that removes sins as a barrier between God and those who trust in Jesus.

2.7 *new commandment:* This is the command that Jesus gave his disciples in John 13.34,35. It builds on the old commandment from the Law of Moses: "I command you to love others as much as you love yourself" (Lev 19.18).

2.13 *one who was there from the beginning:* The Word, Jesus.

2.18 *the last hour . . . the enemy of Christ:* The "last hour" probably refers to a time just before the end of the world, or the time when God will judge the world. False teachings will be widespread during this time (see also 2 Pet 3.3; 2 Thes 2.1-12; 2 Tim 3.1-9; 4.3,4). The Greek word translated here as "enemy of Christ" is *antichristos* (antichrist). This person's teachings are compared to the teachings of Christ's enemies who have already appeared. Only 1, 2, and 3 JOHN use this term (1 John 2.18,22; 4.3; 2 John 7), but see also 2 Thes 2.1-12 and Rev 12–14.

Christ Helps Us

2 My children, I am writing this so you won't sin. But if you do sin, Jesus Christ always does the right thing, and he will speak to the Father for us. [2]Christ is the sacrifice that takes away our sins and the sins of all the world's people.

[3]When we obey God, we are sure we know him. [4]But if we claim to know him and don't obey him, we are lying and the truth isn't in our hearts. [5]We truly love God only when we obey him as we should, and then we know we belong to him. [6]If we say we are his, we must follow the example of Christ.

The New Commandment

[7]My dear friends, I am not writing to give you a new commandment. It is the same one you were first given, and it is the message you heard. [8]But it really is a new commandment, and you know its true meaning, just as Christ does. You can see the darkness fading away and the true light already shining.

[9]If we claim to be in the light and hate someone, we are still in the dark. [10]But if we love others, we are in the light, and we don't cause problems for them.[c] [11]If we hate others, we are living and walking in the dark. We don't know where we are going, because we can't see in the dark.

[12]Children, I am writing you,
because your sins
have been forgiven
in the name of Christ.
[13]Parents, I am writing you,
because you have known
the one who was there
from the beginning.
Young people, I am writing you,
because you have defeated
the evil one.
[14]Children, I am writing you,
because you have known
the Father.
Parents, I am writing you,
because you have known
the one who was there
from the beginning.
Young people, I am writing you,
because you are strong.
God's message is firm
in your hearts,
and you have defeated
the evil one.

[15]Don't love the world or anything that belongs to the world. If you love the world, you cannot love the Father. [16]Our foolish pride comes from this world, and so do our selfish desires and our desire to have everything we see. None of this comes from the Father. [17]The world and the desires it causes are disappearing. But if we obey God, we will live forever.

The Enemy of Christ

[18]Children, this is the last hour. You heard that the enemy of Christ would appear at this time, and many of Christ's enemies have already appeared. So we know the last hour is here. [19]These people came from our own group, yet they were not really part of us. If they had been part of us, they would have stayed with us. But they left, which proves they did not belong to our group.

[c]2.10 *and we don't cause problems for them:* Or "and we can see anything that might make us fall."

20Christ, the Holy One,d has blessede you, and now all of you understand.f 21I did not need to write you about the truth, since you already know it. You also know that liars do not belong to the truth. 22And a liar is anyone who says Jesus isn't truly Christ. Anyone who says this is an enemy of Christ and rejects both the Father and the Son. 23If we reject the Son, we reject the Father. But if we say we accept the Son, we have the Father. 24Keep thinking about the message you first heard, and you will always be one in your heart with the Son and with the Father. 25The Song has promised ush eternal life.

26I am writing to warn you about those people who are misleading you. 27But Christ has blessed you with the Holy Spirit.i Now the Spirit stays in you, and you don't need any teachers. The Spirit is truthful and teaches you everything. So stay one in your heart with Christ, just as the Spirit has taught you to do.

Children of God

28Children, stay one in your hearts with Christ. Then when he returns, we will have confidence and won't have to hide in shame. 29You know Christ always does right and everyone who does right is a child of God.

3 Think how much the Father loves us. He loves us so much that he lets us be called his children, as we truly are. But since the people of this world did not know who Christj is, they don't know who we are. 2My dear friends, we are already God's children, though what we will be hasn't yet been seen. But we do know when Christ returns, we will be like him, because we will see him as he truly is. 3This hope makes us keep ourselves holy, just as Christk is holy.

4Everyone who sins breaks God's law, because sin is the same as breaking God's law. 5You know Christ came to take away our sins. He isn't sinful, 6and people who stay one in their hearts with him won't keep on sinning. If they do keep on sinning, they don't know Christ, and they have never seen him.

7Children, don't be fooled. Anyone who does right is good, just like Christ himself. 8Anyone who keeps on sinning belongs to the devil. He has sinned from the beginning, but the Son of God came to destroy all that he has done. 9God's children cannot keep on being sinful. His life-giving powerl lives in them and makes them his children, so they cannot keep on sinning. 10You can tell God's children from the devil's children, because those who belong to the devil refuse to do right or to love each other.

2.24 *heart*: To be one with the Son and Father in "your heart" means that true followers let God's message (truth) fill their thoughts and affect their actions. They also openly say that Jesus is the Son of God (4.15)

Holy Spirit

Second Coming

3.4 *breaks God's law*: To break God's law here may refer to breaking the Law of Moses, or it may refer to the lawless behavior the apostle Paul describes in Romans 1.18-32.

3.9 *life-giving power*: This may refer to the Holy Spirit that is given to all who are God's children (2.27-29).

d2.20 *Christ, the Holy One*: The Greek text has "the Holy One" which may refer either to Christ or to God the Father.   e2.20 *blessed*: This translates a word which means "to pour olive oil on (someone's head)." In Old Testament times it was the custom to pour olive oil on a person's head when that person was chosen to be a priest or a king. Here the meaning is not clear. It may refer to the ceremony of pouring olive oil on the followers of the Lord right before they were baptized or it may refer to the gift of the Holy Spirit which they were given at baptism (see verse 27).   f2.20 *now all of you understand*: Some manuscripts have "you understand all things."   g2.25 *The Son*: The Greek text has "he" and may refer to God the Father.   h2.25 *us*: Some manuscripts have "you."   i2.27 *Christ has blessed you with the Holy Spirit*: The Greek text has "You received a pouring on of olive oil from him" (see verse 20). The "pouring on of olive oil" is here taken to refer to the gift of the Holy Spirit, and "he" may refer either to Christ or to the Father.   j3.1 *Christ*: The Greek text has "he" and may refer to God.   k3.3 *Christ*: The Greek text has "that one" and may refer to God.   l3.9 *His life-giving power*: The Greek text has "his seed."

Think how much the Father loves us. He loves us so much that he lets us be called his children, as we truly are.

1 JOHN 3.1

3.12 *Cain . . . murdered his own brother:* See Gen 4.1-16.

3.23 *faith . . . love:* Faith is trust in Jesus Christ as God's Son and as the Savior of the world. The importance of love can also be seen in JOHN (John 13.34,35; 15.12-17) where Jesus tells his followers to love one another with the kind of love he has shown for them.

Faith

4.1,2 *false prophets . . . Christ had a truly human body:* This likely refers to the false teachers who were denying that Jesus was truly a human being. Even though they claimed to have the Spirit of God, they really were one with the spirit of the enemy of Christ.

Love Each Other

[11]From the beginning you were told we must love each other. [12]Don't be like Cain, who belonged to the devil and murdered his own brother. Why did he murder him? He did it because his brother was good, and he was evil. [13]My friends, don't be surprised if the people of this world hate you. [14]Our love for each other proves we have gone from death to life. But if you don't love each other, you are still under the power of death.

[15]If you hate each other, you are murderers, and we know murderers do not have eternal life. [16]We know what love is because Jesus gave his life for us. This is why we must give our lives for each other. [17]If we have all we need and see one of our own people in need, we must have pity on that person, or else we cannot say we love God. [18]Children, you show love for others by truly helping them, and not merely by talking about it.

[19]When we love others, we know we belong to the truth, and we feel at ease in the presence of God. [20]But even if we don't feel at ease, God is greater than our feelings, and he knows everything. [21]Dear friends, if we feel at ease in the presence of God, we will have the courage to come near him. [22]He will give us whatever we ask, because we obey him and do what pleases him. [23]God wants us to have faith in his Son Jesus Christ and to love each other. This is also what Jesus taught us to do. [24]If we obey God's commandments, we will stay one in our hearts with him, and he will stay one with us. The Spirit he has given us is proof that we are one with him.

God Is Love

4 Dear friends, don't believe everyone who claims to have the Spirit of God. Test them all to find out if they really do come from God. Many false prophets have already gone out into the world, [2]and you can know which ones come from God. His Spirit says that Jesus Christ had a truly human body. [3]But when someone doesn't say this about Jesus, you know this person has a spirit that doesn't come from God and is the enemy of Christ. You knew this enemy was coming into the world and now is already here.

[4]Children, you belong to God, and you have defeated these enemies. God's Spirit[m] is in you and is more powerful than the one who is in the world. [5]These enemies belong to this world, and the world listens to them, because they speak its language. [6]We belong to God, and everyone who knows God will listen to us. But the people who don't know God won't listen to us. This is how we can tell the Spirit that speaks the truth from the one that tells lies.

[7]My dear friends, we must love each other. Love comes from God, and when we love each other, it show we have been given new life. We are now God's children, and we know him. [8]God is love, and anyone who doesn't love others has never known him. [9]God showed his love for us when he sent his only Son into the world to give us life. [10]Real love isn't our love for God, but his love for us. God sent his Son to be the sacrifice by which our sins are forgiven. [11]Dear friends, since God loved us this much, we must love each other.

[12]No one has ever seen God. But if we love each other, God lives in us, and his love is truly in our hearts.

[m]4.4 *God's Spirit:* The Greek text has "he" and may refer to the Spirit or to God or to Jesus.

13God has given us his Spirit. This is how we know we are one with him, just as he is one with us. **14**God sent his Son to be the Savior of the world. We saw his Son and are now telling others about him. **15**God stays one with everyone who openly says Jesus is the Son of God. This is how we stay one with God **16**and are sure God loves us.

God is love. If we keep on loving others, we will stay one in our hearts with God, and he will stay one with us. **17**If we truly love others and live as Christ did in this world, we won't be worried about the day of judgment. **18**A real love for others will chase those worries away. The thought of being punished is what makes us afraid. It shows we have not really learned to love.

19We love because God loved us first. **20**But if we say we love God and don't love each other, we are liars. We cannot see God. So how can we love God, if we don't love the people we can see? **21**The commandment that God has given us is: "Love God and love each other!"

Victory over the World

5 If we believe Jesus is truly Christ, we are God's children. Everyone who loves the Father will also love his children. **2**If we love and obey God, we know we will love his children. **3**We show our love for God by obeying his commandments, and they are not hard to follow.

4Every child of God can defeat the world, and our faith is what gives us this victory. **5**No one can defeat the world without having faith in Jesus as the Son of God.

Who Jesus Is

6Water and blood came out from the side of Jesus Christ. It wasn't just water, but water and blood.**n** The Spirit tells about this, because the Spirit is truthful. **7**In fact, there are three who tell about it. **8**They are the Spirit, the water, and the blood, and they all agree.

9We believe what people tell us. But we can trust what God says even more, and God is the one who has spoken about his Son. **10**If we have faith in God's Son, we have believed what God has said. But if we don't believe what God has said about his Son, it is the same as calling God a liar. **11**God has also said he gave us eternal life and this life comes to us from his Son. **12**And so, if we have God's Son, we have this life. But if we don't have the Son, we don't have this life.

Knowing about Eternal Life

13All of you have faith in the Son of God, and I have written to let you know you have eternal life. **14**We are certain God will hear our prayers when we ask for what pleases him. **15**And if we know God listens when we pray, we are sure our prayers have already been answered.

16Suppose you see one of our people commit a sin that isn't a deadly sin. You can pray, and this person will be given eternal life. But the sin must not be one that is deadly. **17**Everything that is wrong is sin, but not all sins are deadly.

18We are sure God's children do not keep on sinning. God's own Son protects them, and the devil cannot harm them.

n5.6 *Water and blood came out from the side of Jesus Christ. It wasn't just water, but water and blood:* See John 19.34. It is also possible to translate, "Jesus Christ came by the water of baptism and by the blood of his death! He was not only baptized, but he bled and died." The purpose of the verse is to tell that Jesus was truly human and that he really died.

4.16 *God is love:* See John 3.16.

4.21 *Love God and love each other:* See Deut 6.4 and Lev 19.18. These commandments from the Law of Moses are the basis for Jesus' new commandment to love (Matt 22.34-40).

Love

5.1 *Jesus is truly Christ, we are God's children:* Just as God has chosen Jesus, so Jesus has chosen his followers to be God's children.

5.7,8 *three . . . the Spirit, the water, and the blood:* Three things tell God's people that they really belong to God: The Spirit is God's power and the helper, which Jesus said he would send to his followers after he was taken from them (John 16.5-15). Water is connected with baptism, which Jesus experienced when he was baptized by John the Baptist (Matt 3.13-17). Baptism also shows that God's new people have washed away the sins of the old way of life and have new life in Christ (Rom 6.3-5). Blood recalls the death of Jesus on the cross (John 19.34,35), as well as the Last Supper. Jesus said that the cup of wine he shared with his disciples was his blood, which God uses to make his agreement to forgive sins (Matt 26.27,28).

5.16 *sin must not be one that is deadly:* A deadly sin was one that was beyond forgiveness (see also Heb 6.4-6).

Every child of God can defeat the world, and our faith is what gives us this victory. 1 JOHN 5.4

5.21 *idols:* The author of 1 JOHN knew that there were many religions that did not follow the teachings of Christ. Many followers of these religions worshiped false gods, such as the gods and goddesses worshiped by the Greeks and Romans. Often statues (idols) intended to depict these gods were placed in temples where they could be worshiped and where offerings could be made in their honor. **(See the chart Greek and Roman Gods and Goddesses on pgs 1838–39.)**

[19] We are certain we come from God and the rest of the world is under the power of the devil.

[20] We know that Jesus Christ the Son of God has come and has shown us the true God. And because of Jesus, we now belong to the true God who gives eternal life.

[21] Children, you must stay away from idols.

Reflection Questions About 1 John 1.1—5.21

1. According to 1 JOHN, what does it mean to "live in the light" and to live "in the dark" (1.5-10; 2.9-11)?

2. FIRST JOHN reveals a number of conflicts that were happening in the early church. What seems to have caused some of these conflicts (1.8-10; 2.18-26; 4.1-3)? What conflicts do you see happening in the church today? How can these conflicts be resolved?

3. Why is it important for Christians to show love for one another (3.7-18; 4.7-18)?

4. Who are God's children (5.1)?

5. Who has eternal life (5.11,12)?

2 john

*How should God's children respond to those who attack
the truth about Jesus Christ? Read 2 JOHN and find out.*

WHAT MAKES 2 JOHN SPECIAL?

SECOND JOHN reads like a letter with standard greetings and conclusions. It encourages Christ's followers to love each other and to obey the truth. The
"special woman" (2 John 1) and the "special sister"
(2 John 13) probably refer to two different groups of
the Lord's followers rather than to two individuals.

WHAT'S THE STORY BEHIND THE SCENE?

Besides encouraging the Lord's followers, the letter
warns them about the liars and enemies of Christ
who were claiming that Jesus Christ was not truly
a human being. The writer says that the Lord's followers should not welcome these liars into their
homes.

HOW IS 2 JOHN CONSTRUCTED?

This short book in the style of a letter may be outlined in the following way:

Greetings (1-3)
Obeying the truth and living in love (4-13)

This letter, from a church leader to a Christian worship group, is the shortest book of the Bible. It takes up many of the concerns of 1 John and urges the recipients to love Jesus, love each other, and remain steady in their faith. It warns them against false teachers, and tells the Christians not to welcome these "liars" into their homes or even to greet them.

Outline

¹From the church leader.ᵃ

To a very special woman and her children.ᵇ I truly love all of you, and so does everyone else who knows the truth. ²We love you because the truth is now in our hearts, and it will be there forever.

³I pray that God the Father and Jesus Christ his Son will be kind and merciful to us! May they give us peace and truth and love.

Truth and Love

⁴I was very glad to learn that some of your children are obeying the truth, as the Father told us to do. ⁵Dear friend, I am not writing to tell you and your children to do something you have not done before. I am writing to tell you to love each other, which is the first thing you were told to do.

⁶Love means that we do what God tells us. And from the beginning, he told you to love him.

⁷Many liars have gone out into the world. These deceitful liars are saying that Jesus Christ did not have a truly human body. But they are liars and the enemies of Christ. ⁸So be sure not to lose what weᶜ have worked for. If you do, you won't be given your full reward. ⁹Don't keep changing what you were taught about Christ, or else God will no longer be with you. But if you hold firmly to what you were taught, both the Father and the Son will be with you. ¹⁰If people won't agree to this teaching, don't welcome them into your home or even greet them. ¹¹Greeting them is the same as taking part in their evil deeds.

ᵃ1 *church leader*: Or "elder" or "presbyter."   ᵇ1 *very special woman and her children*: A group of the Lord's followers who met together for worship. "The children of your . . . sister" (see verse 13) is another group of followers. "Very special" (here and verse 13) probably means "chosen (by the Lord)."   ᶜ8 *we*: Some manuscripts have "you."

1 *A very special woman and her children*: Most likely, this letter was not written to a specific woman. The "special woman and her children" (verse 1) and "the children of your very special sister" (verse 13) are probably poetic ways of referring to churches in two different cities. The writer of 2 JOHN may have used this expression to protect the churches mentioned in case the letter was intercepted by someone who didn't like Christians and might have made trouble for the sender or recipient. Some early churches, however, did meet in the homes of wealthy women who had become followers of Christ (Acts 16.14,15; Rom 16.1,2; 1 Cor 16.19; Col 4.15).

2 *the truth is now in our hearts*: Here "truth" probably refers to the truth about God's love revealed in Jesus, God's Son, whose blood washes away sins (1 John 1.7). This true teaching about Jesus is in contrast to the false teaching that Jesus did not really have a human body (verse 7). In this passage the words translated "in our hearts" actually means "within us."

Truth

8 *your full reward*: This refers to eternal life, which is promised to those who have faith in Jesus Christ and who obey God. See John 3.16; 1 John 2.24,25; 3.15; 4.17; 5.10-12.

Love means that we do what God tells us. 2 JOHN 6

13 *the children of your very special sister*: This probably means the followers of Christ who are part of a church, which the writer here calls "very special sister."

Final Greetings

¹²I have much more to tell you, but I don't want to write it with pen and ink. I want to come and talk to you in person, because that will make us[d] really happy.

¹³Greetings from the children of your very special sister.[e]

[d]12 *us*: Some manuscripts have "you."   [e]13 *sister*: See the note at verse 1.

Reflection Questions About 2 John 1-12

1. What does 2 JOHN say about love?

2. What does 2 JOHN say about truth?

3. What particular lie was being passed among the Christian churches?

4. How were God's people supposed to act toward those who were spreading this lie (7-10)?

5. How do Christians today show love for God and for others?

3 john

How should Christians support those who travel around telling the good news? Read 3 JOHN and find out.

WHAT MAKES 3 JOHN SPECIAL?

Like 2 JOHN, this short book is in the style of a letter and has a standard greeting and conclusion. However, it is written to a specific person named Gaius.

The writer offers prayers and thanks for his friend Gaius, who has been welcoming the followers of the Lord who traveled to Gaius' area with the message about Jesus.

WHAT'S THE STORY BEHIND THE SCENE?

A leader of Gaius' church group named Diotrephes was refusing to welcome any of the Lord's followers and was urging others not to welcome them either. So, Gaius is encouraged to keep welcoming the Lord's followers even if Diotrephes does not.

HOW IS 3 JOHN CONSTRUCTED?

THIRD JOHN may be outlined in the following way:

Greetings (1-4)
Helping the Lord's followers (5-15)

This letter is a personal plea from a church leader to Gaius, a friend and fellow church leader. The writer praises Gaius for his strong faith and for his hospitality to a group of Christians who are traveling and sharing the good news with others. The writer also warns him about Diotrephes, a self-appointed church leader who has been gossiping, acting inhospitably toward others, and causing division in the church. Gaius is encouraged to do kind deeds and to regard a man named Demetrius as one who teaches what is true.

Outline

¹From the church leader.ᵃ

To my dear friend Gaius.

I love you because we follow the truth, ²dear friend, and I pray all goes well for you. I hope you are as strong in body, as I know you are in spirit. ³It makes me very happy when the Lord's followers come by and speak openly of how you obey the truth. ⁴Nothing brings me greater happiness than to hear that my childrenᵇ are obeying the truth.

Working Together

⁵Dear friend, you have always been faithful in helping other followers of the Lord, even the ones you didn't know before. ⁶They have told the church about your love. They say you were good enough to welcome them and to send them on their mission in a way God's servants deserve. ⁷When they left to tell others about the Lord, they decided not to accept help from anyone who wasn't a follower. ⁸We must support people like them, so we can take part in what they are doing to spread the truth.

⁹I wrote to the church. But Diotrephes likes to be the number-one leader, and he won't pay any attention to us. ¹⁰So if I come, I will remind him of how he has been attacking us with gossip. Not only has he been doing this, but he refuses to welcome any of the Lord's followers who come by. And when other church members want to welcome them, he puts them out of the church.

¹¹Dear friend, don't imitate the evil deeds of others, but follow the example of people who do kind deeds. They are God's children, but those who are always doing evil have never seen God.

¹²Everyone speaks well of Demetrius, and so does the true message that he teaches. I also speak well of him, and you know what I say is true.

---

1 *Gaius:* A follower of the Lord with a reputation for obeying the truth about Jesus Christ. The writer ("church leader") may have been the one who brought Gaius to trust in Christ. The writer praises Gaius because he has encouraged his church community to welcome traveling preachers and teachers who have come to his town.

3 *obey the truth:* Gaius obeyed the truth about Jesus by trusting that Jesus was God's Son, the -Messiah "chosen one." This true teaching about Jesus is in contrast to the false teaching that Jesus did not have a truly human body and was not God's Son (see 1 John 2.18-23; 4.1-3; 2 John 7).

Truth

6 *their mission:* Probably to tell the good news about Jesus (8).

9 *Diotrephes:* Diotrephes is not mentioned anywhere else in the Bible. He apparently was one of the leaders in the same church that Gaius belonged to. Diotrephes had attacked the person who sent this letter by telling lies and spreading gossip about him, and he refused to welcome anyone who was associated with the leader.

12 *Demetrius:* The leader praises Demetrius for his truthful teaching about Christ. It is possible that Demetrius had delivered this letter to the church in advance of the church leader's visit and had been rejected by Diotrephes.

Follow the example of people who do kind deeds. They are God's children. 3 JOHN 11

Final Greetings

13I have much more to say to you, but I don't want to write it with pen and ink. **14**I hope to see you soon, and then we can talk in person.

15I pray that God will bless you with peace!

Your friends send their greetings. Please give a personal greeting to each of our friends.

Reflection Questions About 3 John 1-15

1. What seems to be the "truth" mentioned by the author of this letter (1-8,12)?

2. Who is attacking the truth in Gaius' church?

3. Based on this brief letter, how would you describe Gaius' church (congregation)?

4. What kinds of problems was Diotrephes causing in Gaius' church (9,10)? What problems have you observed happening when someone wants to be considered "the number one leader" in a church group?

5. Why is it important to encourage and welcome those who follow the Lord, especially those who teach and preach the truth?

jude

How should God's chosen people stand up for what they believe? Read JUDE and find out.

WHAT MAKES JUDE SPECIAL?

This letter gives a strong warning to Christians about false teachers and prophets who are trying to lead the Lord's followers away from the truth. The author uses a number of examples from the Jewish Scriptures (Old Testament) and even refers to two documents from Jewish literature not included in the Bible: *The Assumption of Moses* and *1 Enoch*. You may notice also that many verses of this letter are used in 2 PETER (compare 2 Pet 2.1-8 with Jude 4-16).

The writer of JUDE was worried about "godless" people who had sneaked into and claimed to be part of Christ's followers. These godless ones argued that they could live in an immoral way, because God was so kind and would always forgive them. They even denied that Jesus Christ was their only Lord (Jude 4). Readers of Jude were encouraged to defend the faith against the teachings of godless people. And Christians themselves are to be faithful to Christ by living moral lives that are "in step with God's love" (Jude 21). This means avoiding sinful behavior, helping those who have doubts, and rescuing those who need to be saved.

WHAT'S THE STORY BEHIND THE SCENE?

The writer of this short book is identified as Jude, the traditional English form of the Greek name Ju-das and the Hebrew name Judah. "Judah" was the name of one of the sons of Jacob (Gen 29.35) and both King David and Jesus were members of the Israelite tribe that was named after him (Luke 3.33).

James and Jude (Judas) are named as Jesus' brothers in the Gospels (Matt 13.55; Mark 6.3). James was a leader of the early church in Jerusalem (see Acts 15.13; Gal 1.19). It is possible that Jude was also a leader in the early Jewish Christian church in Palestine. It's not clear who the original readers of the letter were (Jude 1,2). They may have been early Jewish Christians who were familiar with the Jewish Scriptures, or, as some scholars have suggested, the letter may have been written after Jesus' brothers, James and Judas, had died. These scholars propose that the style of the letter, and the situation it describes, seem to come from a time later than the first generation of Jesus' followers. For the most part, the kinds of false teachings the author is addressing in this letter were not big problems for the earlier followers of Jesus.

HOW IS JUDE CONSTRUCTED?

This letter may be outlined in the following way:

Greetings and a prayer (1,2)
Defending the faith against false teachers (3-25)

Jude is a very short letter written to warn early Christians against false teachers and prophets and to urge them to defend the faith that God has given them. According to Jude, many godless people had joined Christian communities. These godless teachers and prophets claimed it was acceptable to live immoral lives because God would forgive them. Jude tries to encourage Christians to unite against such false teachings. Using examples from the Old Testament and from Jewish literature, he argues that it is important to keep in step with God's love while waiting for the Lord Jesus Christ to give them eternal life. The letter closes with a beautiful prayer which identifies Jesus as the true Lord and only source of salvation.

Outline

¹From Jude, a servant of Jesus Christ and the brother of James.

To all who are chosen and loved by God the Father and are kept safe by Jesus Christ.

²I pray that God will greatly bless you with mercy, peace, and love!

False Teachers

³My dear friends, I really wanted to write you about God's saving power at work in our lives. But instead, I must write and ask you to defend the faith that God has once for all given to his people. ⁴Some godless people have sneaked in among us and are saying, "God treats us much better than we deserve, and so it is all right to be immoral." They even deny we must obey Jesus Christ as our only Master and Lord. But long ago the Scriptures warned that these godless people were doomed.

⁵Don't forget what happened to those people the Lord rescued from Egypt. Some of them did not have faith, and he later destroyed them. ⁶You also know about the angelsª who didn't do their work and left their proper places. God chained them with everlasting chains and is now keeping them in dark pits until the great day of judgment. ⁷We should also be warned by what happened to the cities of Sodom and Gomorrahᵇ and the nearby towns. Their people became immoral and committed all sorts of sexual sins. Then God made an example of them and punished them with eternal fire.

⁸The people I am talking about are behaving just like those dreamers who destroyed their own bodies. They reject all authority and insult angels. ⁹Even Michael, the chief angel, didn't dare to insult the devil, when the two of them were arguing

---

ª6 *angels*: This may refer to the angels who liked the women on earth so much that they came down and married them (see Genesis 6.2). ᵇ7 *Sodom and Gomorrah*: During the time of Abraham the Lord destroyed these cities because the people there were so evil. ᶜ9 *Michael . . . the body of Moses*: This refers to what was said in an ancient Jewish book about Moses.

■ 3 *God's saving power . . . defend the faith*: Here the word "saving" points to what God does in order to free humans from sin and the powers of evil. The Holy Spirit who helps Jesus' followers "keep in step with God's love" (20, 21) gives this saving power.

◎ God's Saving Love (Salvation)

● 4 *godless people . . . sneaked in*: The godless people who sneaked in among the Christians were teaching false things about God's overwhelming love, also referred to as "God's grace." The godless people described here apparently twisted this message and used it as an excuse to live as they wanted (see also Rom 6.1,15; 2 Pet 2.19; 3.16).

● 4 *Scriptures warned . . . godless people were doomed*: A number of Bible passages warn that God will judge and destroy evil people (see, for example, Jer 14.13-16; Ps 94). See also verses 14-18.

● 5 *what happened to those people*: God rescued the Hebrew people from slavery in Egypt. However, because of their complaining and lack of faith, God did not allow them to enter the promised land of Canaan (Exod 12.51; Num 14.26-30).

11 *Cain's example . . . Balaam:* In GENESIS, Cain is named as the first person to commit murder (Gen 4.1-16). Balaam was an ancient prophet from Mesopotamia.

12 *they spoil the meals you eat together:* Early Christians shared meals called "love feasts" as well as celebrating the Lord's Supper (also known as Communion or Eucharist). See also 1 Cor 11.17-32.

14 *Enoch . . . Adam:* See Gen 5.18, 21-24. Enoch truly loved God. In the centuries around the time of Christ, a number of prophetic writings written in Enoch's name were widely read in the Near East. The quotation in these verses is from a book known as *1 Enoch* (1.9).

17 *warning . . . given by the apostles:* Here "apostles" means those chosen by God to spread the message about Jesus Christ. The message about godless people doing evil things near the end of time can also be found in 1 Timothy 4.1; 2 Timothy 3.1-9; 2 Peter 2.1; 3.3,4.

Holy Spirit

Eternal Life

about the body of Moses.[c] All Michael said was, "The Lord will punish you!"

[10]But these people insult powers they don't know anything about. They are like senseless animals that end up getting destroyed, because they live only by their feelings. [11]Now they are in for real trouble. They have followed Cain's example[d] and have made the same mistake that Balaam[e] did by caring only for money. They have also rebelled against God, just as Korah did.[f] Because of all this, they will be destroyed.

[12]These people are filthy minded, and by their shameful and selfish actions they spoil the meals you eat together. They are like clouds blown along by the wind, but never bringing any rain. They are like leafless trees, uprooted and dead, and unable to produce fruit. [13]Their shameful deeds show up like foam on wild ocean waves. They are like wandering stars forever doomed to the darkest pits of hell.

[14]Enoch was the seventh person after Adam, and he was talking about these people when he said:

Look! The Lord is coming with thousands and thousands of holy angels [15]to judge everyone. He will punish all those ungodly people for all the evil things they have done. The Lord will surely punish those ungodly sinners for every evil thing they have ever said about him.

[16]These people grumble and complain and live by their own selfish desires. They brag about themselves and flatter others to get what they want.

More Warnings

[17]My dear friends, remember the warning you were given by the apostles of our Lord Jesus Christ. [18]They told you that near the end of time, selfish and godless people would start making fun of God. [19]And now these people are already making you turn against each other. They think only about this life, and they don't have God's Spirit.

[20]Dear friends, keep building on the foundation of your most holy faith, as the Holy Spirit helps you to pray. [21]And keep in step with God's love, as you wait for our Lord Jesus Christ to show how kind he is by giving you eternal life. [22]Be helpful to[g] all who may have doubts. [23]Rescue any who need to be saved, as you would rescue someone from a fire. Then with fear in your own hearts, have mercy on everyone who needs it. But hate even the clothes of those who have been made dirty by their filthy deeds.

Final Prayer

[24-25]Offer praise to God our Savior because of our Lord Jesus Christ! Only God can keep you from falling and make you pure and joyful in his glorious presence. Before time began and now and forever, God is worthy of glory, honor, power, and authority. Amen.

[d]11 *Cain's example:* Cain murdered his brother Abel.   [e]11 *Balaam:* According to the biblical account, Balaam refused to curse the people of Israel for profit (see Numbers 22.18; 24.13), though he led them to be unfaithful to the Lord (see Numbers 25.1-3; 31.16). But by New Testament times, some Jewish teachers taught that Balaam was greedy and did accept money to curse them.   [f]11 *just as Korah did:* Together with Dathan and Abiram, Korah led a rebellion against Moses and Aaron (see Numbers 16.1-35; 26.9,10).   [g]22 *Be helpful to:* Some manuscripts have "Correct."

Keep in step with God's love, as you wait for our Lord Jesus Christ to show how kind he is by giving you eternal life. JUDE 21

Reflection Questions About Jude 1-25

1. How were the "godless people" described in this letter twisting the truth about God (4)?

2. The godless people were willing to take advantage of God's kindness, and they used it as an excuse for immoral behavior. How would a "godly person" complete the following sentence? "God treats us much better than we deserve, and so . . ."

3. What selfish and shameful actions spoiled the Christians' love feasts and celebrations of the Lord's Supper (12)?

4. According to the writer, what will happen to those who do such shameful deeds (13)?

5. How can the Christians "keep in step with God's love" (21-23)?

revelation

War! Disasters! Famine! Armagedon! Revelation, the final book of the Bible, shows how God ends evil and prepares a new city of peace for his chosen people.

WHAT MAKES REVELATION SPECIAL?

The word translated as "revelation" (1.1) comes from the Greek word *apokalypsis,* meaning a revealing or an unveiling. Revelation belongs to a kind of writing called apocalyptic literature. Apocalyptic writings try to reveal the secrets of heaven to human beings, and often describe visions of how human history will end. Apocalyptic passages can be found in other books of the Bible such as Daniel 7–12 and Mark 13, but Revelation is the only book of the Bible made up entirely of apocalyptic writing.

Revelation excites the imagination. This complicated book features brilliant visions of a coming Day of the Lord. These visions are expressed through many symbols, including people shaped like animals or beasts, predictions about when God will bring the world to an end, and colors and numbers that have secret meanings. **(See the chart Numbers in the Bible on pg 1844.)** Over half the verses in Revelation are directly or indirectly based on Old Testament passages. This is important for understanding the meaning of the book.

The writer of Revelation received a special message from God and shared it with seven churches in Asia, but the message is really for all Christians. The book shows the struggle of the church against the enemies of God. That struggle begins in the story of seven earthly churches and ends with a vision of God's victory, and the new heaven and earth that God will create. This was a powerful message of hope for early Christians who had to suffer or die for their faith. They learned that, in spite of the cruel power of the Roman Empire, Jesus (the Lamb of God) would win the final victory.

WHAT'S THE STORY BEHIND THE SCENE?

The identity of John is still debated today. John was a common name among Jews and Christians, and he never claims to be one of the twelve disciples. The date of the book's composition is also in question. Domitian (ruled A.D. 81–91) was the first Roman emperor who tried to force Christians to worship the emperor as a god. The emperor Trajan (ruled A.D. 98–117) commanded that everyone worship the Roman emperors who had died. Since Revelation seems to address Christians who were persecuted for not worshiping the emperor, many scholars think it was likely written late in Domitian's reign or even later, when Trajan ruled. Other scholars, however, believe the book was written earlier, just before the destruction of Jerusalem in A.D. 70.

HOW IS REVELATION CONSTRUCTED?

Revelation can be outlined in the following way:

John's prophecy and prayer (1.1-8)
Vision for the seven churches (1.9—3.22)
Vision of God and the Lamb (4.1—5.14)
Opening the seven seals (6.1—8.5)
The seven trumpets (8.6—11.19)
The opponents of God (12.1—13.18)
Visions of God's judgment and protection
   (14.1—16.21)
Victory over the enemies of God (17.1—20.15)
God makes all things new (21.1—22.5)
Final promises, blessings, and warnings (22.6-21)

Revelation is an example of apocalyptic writing, which is a type of Jewish literature containing symbolism, visions, and predictions of future events. It most likely was written to provide encouragement and hope to believers in the early Christian churches who were suffering from persecution by the Roman emperors Vespasian and Domitian. The author, who identifies himself simply as "John, a follower together with all of you," was probably using the conventions of apocalyptic writing as a way to hide his message from the enemies of the early Christians. Revelation suggests that the troubles and evil of the world would increase before a new age of the world would begin, when Jesus and the church would rule with justice and love. The book begins with John describing a vision from God sent by Jesus through an angel. John is then instructed to write letters to seven churches in Asia, giving them both words of encouragement and warnings. The rest of the Revelation is a vision of a long battle between God's forces and the forces of evil, concluding with the defeat of Satan, and the creation of a new heaven and earth illuminated by the glory of God.

Outline

1

This is what God showed to Jesus Christ, so that he could tell his servants what must happen soon. Christ then sent his angel with the message to his servant John. ²And John told everything he had seen about God's message and about what Jesus Christ had said and done.

³God will bless everyone who reads this prophecy to others,ᵃ and he will bless everyone who hears and obeys it. The time is almost here.

⁴From John to the seven churches in Asia.ᵇ

> I pray that you
>   will be blessed
> with kindness and peace
> from God, who is and was
>   and is coming.
> May you receive
>   kindness and peace
> from the seven spirits
> before the throne of God.
> ⁵May kindness and peace
>   be yours
> from Jesus Christ,
>   the faithful witness.
>
> Jesus was the first
>   to conquer death,
> and he is the ruler
>   of all earthly kings.
> Christ loves us,
>   and by his blood
> he set us free
>   from our sins.
> ⁶He lets us rule as kings
> and serve God his Father
>   as priests.
> To him be glory and power
>   forever and ever! Amen.
> ⁷Look! He is coming
>   with the clouds.
> Everyone will see him,

ᵃ**1.3** *who reads this prophecy to others*: A public reading, in a worship service. ᵇ**1.4** *Asia*: The section 1.4—3.22 is in the form of a letter. Asia was in the eastern part of the Roman Empire and is present day Turkey.

■ 1.1 *what God showed to Jesus Christ ... his angel*: "Christ" is the Greek translation of the Hebrew word "Messiah." It is a title that means, "chosen one." The word "angel" (Greek, *angelos*) means "messenger."

◌ Messiah (Chosen One)

◌ Angels

● 1.3 *God will bless everyone who reads this prophecy to others*: This is the first of seven different blessings in this book (see also Rev 14.13; 16.15; 19.9; 20.6; 22.7; 22.14). "Prophecy" here refers to the contents of John's visions and the message he received from Jesus.

■ 1.5 *set us free from our sins*: Jesus came to save people from sin, which leads to death (see Rom 3.24).

◌ Sin

■ 1.6 *serve God his Father as priests*: In JOHN, Jesus often calls God his Father (3.35; 5.17-30; 15.1,16; 17). For Jesus to call God his Father was to claim a special relationship with God and the authority to rule over God's people (see Ps 2.6-8). The writer of 1 PETER refers to God's new people as "holy" or "royal" priests (1 Pet 2.5, 9), who will offer sacrifices of holy living.

◌ Israel's Priests

1.8 *Alpha and Omega:* The first and last letters of the Greek alphabet—α and Ω—(like "A" and "Z" in English) were sometimes used to mean "first" and "last" in any list of things. John uses this expression twice in REVELATION: in the beginning of the book (1.8,17) and toward the end of the book (21.6). The prophet Isaiah uses a similar expression to describe the completeness and totality of God (Isa 44.6; 48.12).

1.10 *the Lord's day:* Sunday, the day when Jesus was raised from death, and when many Christians worship.

1.10 *the Spirit:* The Holy Spirit took control of John, which probably means the things God wanted John to see were revealed in a kind of trance or dream.

Holy Spirit

1.12 *seven gold lampstands:* A golden lampstand with seven lamps, called a *menorah* in Hebrew, was kept in the sacred tent of Israel (see Exod 25.31-39; Zech 4.1-6). In this passage, the seven lampstands are the seven churches (1.20). In the Bible, the number seven often stands for completeness. As used here, it may mean that John's book was to be read to all churches. **(See the chart Numbers in the Bible on pg 1844.)**

1.16 *seven stars:* The seven stars are the angels of the seven churches. See also Matt 17.1,2.

even the ones who stuck
a sword through him.
All people on earth
will weep because of him.
Yes, it will happen! Amen.

[8]The Lord God says, "I am Alpha and Omega,[c] the one who is and was and is coming. I am God All-Powerful!"

A Vision of the Risen Lord

[9]I am John, a follower together with all of you. We suffer because Jesus is our king, but he gives us the strength to endure. I was sent to Patmos Island,[d] because I had preached God's message and had told about Jesus. [10]On the Lord's day the Spirit took control of me, and behind me I heard a loud voice that sounded like a trumpet. [11]The voice said, "Write in a book what you see. Then send it to the seven churches in Ephesus, Smyrna, Pergamum, Thyatira, Sardis, Philadelphia, and Laodicea."[e]

[12]When I turned to see who was speaking to me, I saw seven gold lampstands. [13]There with the lampstands was someone who seemed to be the Son of Man.[f] He was wearing a robe that reached down to his feet, and a gold cloth was wrapped around his chest. [14]His head and his hair were white as wool or snow, and his eyes looked like flames of fire. [15]His feet were glowing like bronze being heated in a furnace, and his voice sounded like the roar of a waterfall. [16]He held seven stars in his right hand, and a sharp double-edged sword was coming from his mouth. His face was shining as bright as the sun at noon.

[17]When I saw him, I fell at his feet like a dead person. But he put his right hand on me and said:

Don't be afraid! I am the first, the last, [18]and the living one. I died, but now I am alive forever, and I have the keys to death and the world of the dead.[g] [19]Write what you have seen and what is and what will happen after these things. [20]I will explain the mystery of the seven stars you saw at my right side and the seven gold lampstands. The seven stars are the angels[h] of the seven churches, and the lampstands are the seven churches.

The Letter to Ephesus

2 This is what you must write to the angel of the church in Ephesus:
I am the one who holds the seven stars in my right hand, and I walk among the seven gold lampstands. Listen to what I say.

[2]I know everything you have done, including your hard work and how you have endured. I know you won't put up with anyone who is evil. When some people pretended to be apostles, you tested them and found out they were liars. [3]You have endured and gone through hard times because of me, yet you have not given up.

[4]But I do have something against you! And it is this: You don't have as much love as you used to. [5]Think about where you have fallen from, and then turn back and do as you did at

[c]**1.8** *Alpha and Omega:* The first and last letters of the Greek alphabet, which sometimes mean "first" and "last." [d]**1.9** *Patmos Island:* A small island where prisoners were sometimes kept by the Romans. [e]**1.11** *Ephesus . . . Laodicea:* Ephesus was in the center with the six other cities forming a half-circle around it. [f]**1.13** *Son of Man:* That is, Jesus. [g]**1.18** *keys to death and the world of the dead:* That is, power over death and the world of the dead. [h]**1.20** *angels:* Perhaps guardian angels that represent the churches, or they may be church leaders or messengers sent to the churches.

first. If you don't turn back, I will come and take away your lampstand. [6]But there is one thing you are doing right. You hate what the Nicolaitans[i] are doing, and so do I.

[7]If you have ears, listen to what the Spirit says to the churches. I will let everyone who wins the victory eat from the life-giving tree in God's wonderful garden.

The Letter to Smyrna

[8]This is what you must write to the angel of the church in Smyrna:

I am the first and the last. I died, but now I am alive! Listen to what I say.

[9]I know how much you suffer and how poor you are, but you are rich. I also know the cruel things being said about you by people who claim to be God's people. But they are not really God's people. They are a group that belongs to Satan.

[10]Don't worry about what you will suffer. The devil will throw some of you into jail, and you will be tested and made to suffer for ten days. But if you are faithful until you die, I will reward you with a glorious life.[j]

[11]If you have ears, listen to what the Spirit says to the churches. Whoever wins the victory will not be hurt by the second death.[k]

The Letter to Pergamum

[12]This is what you must write to the angel of the church in Pergamum:

I am the one who has the sharp double-edged sword! Listen to what I say.

[13]I know you live where Satan has his throne.[l] But you have kept true to my name. Right there where Satan lives, my faithful witness Antipas[m] was taken from you and put to death. Even then you did not give up your faith in me.

[14]I do have a few things against you. Some of you are following the teaching of Balaam.[n] Long ago he told Balak to teach the people of Israel to eat food that had been offered to idols and to be immoral. [15]Now some of you are following the teaching of the Nicolaitans.[o] [16]Turn back! If you don't, I will come quickly and fight against these people. And my words will cut like a sword.

[17]If you have ears, listen to what the Spirit says to the churches. To everyone who wins the victory, I will give some of the hidden food.[p] I will also

---

[i]**2.6** *Nicolaitans:* Nothing else is known about these people, though it is possible that they claimed to be followers of Nicolaus from Antioch (see Acts 6.5).   [j]**2.10** *a glorious life:* The Greek text has "a crown of life." In ancient times an athlete who had won a contest was rewarded with a crown of flowers as a sign of victory.   [k]**2.11** *second death:* The first death is physical death, and the "second death" is eternal death.   [l]**2.13** *where Satan has his throne:* The meaning is uncertain, but it may refer to the city as a center of pagan worship or of Emperor worship.   [m]**2.13** *Antipas:* Nothing else is known about this man, who is mentioned only here in the New Testament.   [n]**2.14** *Balaam:* According to Numbers 22–24, Balaam refused to disobey the Lord. But in other books of the Old Testament, he is spoken of as evil (see Deuteronomy 23.4,5; Joshua 13,22; 24.9,10; Nehemiah 13.2).   [o]**2.15** *Nicolaitans:* See the note at 2.6.   [p]**2.17** *hidden food:* When the people of Israel were going through the desert, the Lord provided a special food for them. Some of this was placed in a jar and stored in the sacred chest (see Exodus 16). According to later Jewish teaching, the prophet Jeremiah rescued the sacred chest when the temple was destroyed by the Babylonians. He hid the chest in a cave, where it would stay until God came to save his people.

2.8 *Smyrna:* About 70 years before REVELATION was written, a temple in honor of the Roman emperor Tiberius was built and dedicated at this port city. See also Isa 44.6; 48.12.

2.9 *how poor you are:* Some Christians at Smyrna were most likely poor immigrants from Galilee and Judea who had fled Palestine during the Jewish War of A.D. 66–74.

2.9 *claim to be God's people:* This may have been a group of local Jewish leaders who accused the Christians of causing trouble or of being disloyal to the Roman authorities.

2.10 *devil:* Here "the devil" may refer to those who did the devil's work.

Satan

2.12 *Pergamum:* A city in Asia Minor famous for its large library and its many temples honoring various gods. On a hill overlooking the city stood a huge altar built to the god Zeus. Pergamum was also the center for the worship of Asclepios, the god of healing. Under Roman rule, the city may have been home to as many as 200,000 people.

2.13 *Antipas:* Antipas probably refused to take part in worshiping the emperor. His death was likely meant to scare Christians into leaving their faith behind.

2.18 *Thyatira:* This city was well known for making and trading cloth, dye, brass, leather, and pottery. It was located along a Roman road that connected Pergamum to Laodicea See also Acts 16.14,15.

2.20 *do immoral things . . . idols:* Business groups sometimes held banquets in temples to honor various gods. If Christians did not participate in these feasts, they might be rejected by the business community. Yet if they did join in the activities, they would be unfaithful to Christ.

2.27-28 *morning star:* This usually refers to the planet Venus. Here it is used as a name for Christ (see 22.16). See also Num 24.17; 2 Pet 1.19.

3.1 *Sardis:* In Roman times, this ancient city was the capital of the Roman province of Lydia, and a center for emperor worship. Sardis was destroyed by a great earthquake in A.D.17 and was completely rebuilt.

3.3 *turn from your sins . . . wake up:* John compares followers in Sardis to their ancient ancestors who had been surprised by sneak attacks. See also Matt 24.43,44; Luke 12.39,40.

3.4 *white clothes:* A traditional symbol of inner purity. See also Dan 7.9.

give each one a white stone[q] with a new name[r] written on it. No one will know that name except the one who is given the stone.

The Letter to Thyatira

[18]This is what you must write to the angel of the church in Thyatira:

I am the Son of God! My eyes are like flames of fire, and my feet are like bronze. Listen to what I say.

[19]I know everything about you, including your love, your faith, your service, and how you have endured. I know you are doing more now than you have ever done before. [20]But I still have something against you because of that woman Jezebel.[s] She calls herself a prophet, and you let her teach and mislead my servants to do immoral things and to eat food offered to idols. [21]I gave her a chance to turn from her sins, but she did not want to stop doing these immoral things.

[22]I am going to strike down Jezebel. Everyone who does these immoral things with her will also be punished, if they don't stop. [23]I will even kill her followers.[t] Then all the churches will see that I know everyone's thoughts and feelings. I will treat each of you as you deserve.

[24]Some of you in Thyatira don't follow Jezebel's teaching. You don't know anything about what her followers call the "deep secrets of Satan." So I won't

burden you down with any other commands. [25]But until I come, you must hold firmly to the teaching you have.

[26]I will give power over the nations to everyone who wins the victory and keeps on obeying me until the end. [27-28]I will give each of them the same power my Father has given me. They will rule the nations with an iron rod and smash those nations to pieces like clay pots. I will also give them the morning star.[u]

[29]If you have ears, listen to what the Spirit says to the churches.

The Letter to Sardis

3 This is what you must write to the angel of the church in Sardis:

I have the seven spirits of God and the seven stars. Listen to what I say.

I know what you are doing. Everyone may think you are alive, but you are dead. [2]Wake up! You have only a little strength left, and it is almost gone. So try to become stronger. I have found that you are not completely obeying God. [3]Remember the teaching you were given and heard. Hold firmly to it and turn from your sins. If you don't wake up, I will come when you least expect it, just as a thief does.

[4]A few of you in Sardis have not dirtied your clothes with sin. You will walk with me in white clothes, because you are worthy. [5]Everyone who wins the victory will wear white clothes. Their

[q]2.17 *white stone:* The meaning of this is uncertain, though it may be the same as a ticket that lets a person into God's banquet where the "hidden food" is eaten. Or it may be a symbol of victory. [r]2.17 *a new name:* Either the name of Christ or God or the name of the follower who is given the stone. [s]2.20 *Jezebel:* Nothing else is known about her. This may have been her real name or a name that was given to her because she was like Queen Jezebel, who opposed the Lord (see 1 Kings 19.1,2; 21.1-26). [t]2.23 *her followers:* Or "her children." [u]2.27, 28 *the morning star:* Probably thought of as the star that signals the end of night and the beginning of day. In 22.16 Christ is called the "morning star."

names will not be erased from the book of life,[v] and I will tell my Father and his angels that they are my followers.

[6]If you have ears, listen to what the Spirit says to the churches.

The Letter to Philadelphia

[7]This is what you must write to the angel of the church in Philadelphia:

I am the one who is holy and true, and I have the keys that belonged to David.[w] When I open a door, no one can close it. And when I close a door, no one can open it. Listen to what I say.

[8]I know everything you have done. And I have placed before you an open door no one can close. You were not very strong, but you obeyed my message and did not deny you are my followers.[x] [9]Now you will see what I will do with those people who belong to Satan's group. They claim to be God's people, but they are liars. I will make them come and kneel down at your feet. Then they will know that I love you.

[10]You obeyed my message and endured. So I will protect you from the time of testing everyone in all the world must go through. [11]I am coming soon. So hold firmly to what you have, and no one will take away the crown you will be given as your reward.

[12]Everyone who wins the victory will be made into a pillar in the temple of my God, and they will stay there forever. I will write on each of them the name of my God and the name of his city. It is the new Jerusalem my God will send down from heaven. I will also write on them my own new name.

[13]If you have ears, listen to what the Spirit says to the churches.

The Letter to Laodicea

[14]This is what you must write to the angel of the church in Laodicea:

I am the one called Amen![y] I am the faithful and true witness and the source[z] of God's creation. Listen to what I say.

[15]I know everything you have done, and you are not cold or hot. I wish you were either one or the other. [16]But since you are lukewarm and neither cold nor hot, I will spit you out of my mouth. [17]You claim to be rich and successful and to have everything you need. But you don't know how bad off you really are. You are pitiful, poor, blind, and naked.

[18]Buy your gold from me. It has been refined in a fire, and it will make you rich. Buy white clothes from me. Wear them and you can cover up your shameful nakedness. Buy medicine for your eyes, so you will be able to see.

[19]I correct and punish everyone I love. So make up your minds to turn away from your sins. [20]Listen! I am standing and knocking at your door. If you hear my voice and open the door, I will come in and we will eat together. [21]Everyone who wins the victory will sit with me on my throne, just as I won the victory and sat with my Father on his throne.

3.7 *keys that belonged to David:* God promised David that one of his descendants would rule a kingdom that would last forever (2 Sam 7.11-16; Isa 9.6,7). Jesus, a descendant of David, is the chosen king who fulfills these ancient prophecies.

David

Messiah (Chosen One)

3.10 *time of testing:* This refers to a time before Jesus will return to judge the world (2 Pet 3.10-13; Rev 6.10; 16.14,15). Many Bible passages say that before Christ returned, there would be a time of trouble and testing for the followers of Christ (1 John 2.18; 2 Pet 3.3,4; 2 Tim 3.1-9).

End Times

3.12 *a pillar in the temple:* The Christians of Philadelphia had seen solidly-built temples collapse under the force of earthquakes. When they heard that God's people would be pillars that stood forever, they knew that they would be like the living stones (1 Pet 2.5).

3.18 *Buy your gold . . . white clothes . . . medicine:* John tells rich people of Laodicea to trade their gold jewelry for the gold "refined in a fire," which may refer to the blood of Christ who gave his life to forgive them (see 1 Pet 1.18,19), or to the rich spiritual life that comes by suffering for Christ. Just as salve helped heal eye diseases, so the truth about Jesus would open the Laodiceans' eyes to spiritual life.

---

[v]**3.5** *book of life:* The book in which the names of God's people are written.   [w]**3.7** *the keys that belonged to David:* The keys stand for authority over David's kingdom.   [x]**3.8** *did not deny you are my followers:* Or "did not say evil things about me."   [y]**3.14** *Amen:* Meaning "Trustworthy."   [z]**3.14** *source:* Or "beginning."

4.4-10 *Twenty-four other thrones:* The number of elders given here most likely represents the sum of the twelve patriarchs of GENESIS (therefore, all the tribes of Israel) and the twelve apostles of Jesus. Together these symbolize all of God's chosen people.

4.6 *glass sea:* The clear, glass sea may be a symbol for purity.

4.6-9 *four living creatures:* These living creatures represent the people of God, just as the four creatures in DANIEL represent the evil empires that try to rule the world (Dan 7). The many eyes likely symbolize that they can see everything in every direction. The lion, bull, human, and eagle faces probably represent authority, strength, wisdom, and swiftness, all valued things in creation. These living creatures never stop praising God, echoing the words of the six-winged creatures in the prophet Isaiah's vision of the Lord (Isa 6.2,3).

5.2 *a mighty angel ask . . . "Who is worthy":* The scroll represents God's plan for the future. To break the seals is to cause these events to happen. No human being is worthy to understand and carry out that plan, except Jesus the Lamb.

5.6 *Lamb:* Though John may have expected to see a lion, he saw a lamb that showed signs of once being slaughtered. Christ is pictured as the Lamb of God, as in John 1.29.

[22]If you have ears, listen to what the Spirit says to the churches.

Worship in Heaven

4 After this, I looked and saw a door that opened into heaven. Then the voice that had spoken to me at first and that sounded like a trumpet said, "Come up here! I will show you what must happen next." [2]Right then the Spirit took control of me, and there in heaven I saw a throne and someone sitting on it. [3]The one who was sitting there sparkled like precious stones of jasper[a] and carnelian.[b] A rainbow that looked like an emerald[c] surrounded the throne.

[4]Twenty-four other thrones were in a circle around that throne. And on each of these thrones there was an elder dressed in white clothes and wearing a gold crown. [5]Flashes of lightning and roars of thunder came out from the throne in the center of the circle. Seven torches, which are the seven spirits of God, were burning in front of the throne. [6]Also in front of the throne was something that looked like a glass sea, clear as crystal.

Around the throne in the center were four living creatures covered front and back with eyes. [7]The first creature was like a lion, the second one was like a bull, the third one had the face of a human, and the fourth was like a flying eagle. [8]Each of the four living creatures had six wings, and their bodies were covered with eyes. Day and night they never stopped singing,

"Holy, holy, holy is the Lord,
　　the all-powerful God,

who was and is
　　and is coming!"

[9]The living creatures kept praising, honoring, and thanking the one who sits on the throne and who lives forever and ever. [10]At the same time the 24 elders knelt down before the one sitting on the throne. And as they worshiped the one who lives forever, they placed their crowns in front of the throne and said,

[11]"Our Lord and God,
　　you are worthy
　　to receive glory,
　　　honor, and power.
　　You created all things,
　　and by your decision they are
　　　and were created."

The Scroll and the Lamb

5 In the right hand of the one sitting on the throne I saw a scroll[d] that had writing on the inside and on the outside. And it was sealed in seven places. [2]I saw a mighty angel ask with a loud voice, "Who is worthy to open the scroll and break its seals?" [3]No one in heaven or on earth or under the earth was able to open the scroll or look inside it.

[4]I cried hard because no one was found worthy to open the scroll or look inside it. [5]Then one of the elders said to me, "Stop crying and look! The one who is called both the 'Lion from the Tribe of Judah'[e] and 'King David's Great Descendant'[f] has won the victory. He will open the scroll and its seven seals."

[6]Then I looked and saw a Lamb standing

[a]4.3 *jasper:* Usually green or clear.　[b]4.3 *carnelian:* Usually deep-red or reddish-white.　[c]4.3 *emerald:* A precious stone, usually green.　[d]5.1 *scroll:* A roll of paper or special leather used for writing on. Sometimes a scroll would be sealed on the outside with one or more pieces of wax.　[e]5.5 *'Lion from the Tribe of Judah':* In Genesis 49.9 the tribe of Judah is called a young lion, and King David was from Judah.　[f]5.5 *'King David's Great Descendant':* The Greek text has "the root of David" which is a title for the Messiah based on Isaiah 11.1,10.

Day and night they never stopped singing, "Holy, holy, holy is the Lord, the all-powerful God, who was and is and is coming!" REV 4.8

in the center of the throne surrounded by the four living creatures and the elders. The Lamb looked as if it had once been killed. It had seven horns and seven eyes, which are the seven spirits[g] of God, sent out to all the earth.

⁷The Lamb went over and took the scroll from the right hand of the one who sat on the throne. ⁸After he had taken it, the four living creatures and the 24 elders knelt down before him. Each of them had a harp and a gold bowl full of incense,[h] which are the prayers of God's people. ⁹Then they sang a new song,

"You are worthy
  to receive the scroll
and open its seals,
  because you were killed.
And with your own blood
  you bought for God
people from every tribe,
  language, nation, and race.
¹⁰You let them become kings
  and serve God as priests,
and they will rule on earth."

¹¹As I looked, I heard the voices of a large number of angels around the throne and the voices of the living creatures and of the elders. There were millions and millions of them, ¹²and they were saying in a loud voice,

"The Lamb who was killed
  is worthy to receive power,
riches, wisdom, strength,
  honor, glory, and praise."

¹³Then I heard all beings in heaven and on the earth and under the earth and in the sea offer praise. Together, all of them were saying,

"Praise, honor, glory,
  and strength
    forever and ever
to the one who sits
  on the throne
    and to the Lamb!"

¹⁴The four living creatures said "Amen," while the elders knelt down and worshiped.

Opening the Seven Seals

6 At the same time I saw the Lamb open the first of the seven seals, I heard one of the four living creatures shout with a voice like thunder. It said, "Come out!" ²Then I saw a white horse. Its rider carried a bow and was given a crown. He had already won some victories, and he went out to win more.

³When the Lamb opened the second seal, I heard the second living creature say, "Come out!" ⁴Then another horse came out. It was fiery red. And its rider was given the power to take away all peace from the earth, so people would slaughter one another. He was also given a big sword.

⁵When the Lamb opened the third seal, I heard the third living creature say, "Come out!" Then I saw a black horse, and its rider had a balance scale in one hand. ⁶I heard what sounded like a voice from somewhere among the four living creatures. It said, "A quart of wheat will cost you a whole day's wages! Three quarts of barley will cost you a day's wages too. But don't ruin the olive oil or the wine."

⁷When the Lamb opened the fourth seal, I heard the voice of the fourth living creature say, "Come out!" ⁸Then I saw a pale

[g]5.6 *the seven spirits:* Some manuscripts have "the spirits."   [h]5.8 *incense:* A material that produces a sweet smell when burned. Sometimes it is a symbol for the prayers of God's people.

■ 5.9,10 *you bought . . . rule on earth:* Unlike the ancient people of God who had to obey kings and priests, the new people will have power ("become kings") and be able to come to God on their own ("serve God as priests"). See Exod 19.6; Rev 1.6. The new people of God include not only the people of Israel but followers of Christ from every nation on earth.

● 6.2 *white horse:* This horse and the rider carrying a bow together symbolize military victory. The Parthians, who lived on the eastern borders of the Roman Empire, used a bow and arrow as their main weapon. This verse could be suggesting that Parthians might successfully invade the Roman Empire. The crown is a symbol of victory and authority.

● 6.4 *horse . . . was fiery red:* This horse symbolizes fierce and bloody war, including revolution.

● 6.5 *black horse, and its rider had a balance scale:* The black horse probably is meant to symbolize famine, death caused by a shortage of food. Black was associated with death because the world of the dead (Hades) was thought to be a land of darkness.

■ 6.8 *pale green horse . . . Death's Kingdom:* Green is the color of rotting flesh. This verse gives a picture of dead bodies scattered about as the result of the war, famine, and disease that would follow. Wild animals are eating the decaying bodies. "Death's Kingdom" refers to Hades.

The angels *were saying in a loud voice,* "The Lamb who was killed is worthy to receive power, riches, wisdom, strength, honor, glory, and praise." Rev 5.12

6.9,10 *souls . . . punish the people:* These martyrs are asking God when he will judge and punish the people who killed them. Christians living at the time of John's vision would have had Christian friends or neighbors who were put in prison, tortured, or killed because they refused to worship the emperor.

6.16 *one who sits on the throne and from the anger of the Lamb:* Meaning God and Christ.

6.17 *That terrible day:* The day when God will judge the world.

7.1-2 *four angels:* These angels have the power to damage the earth. They will also protect God's people so they can survive and be part of God's new creation.

7.4 *144,000:* This is a symbolic number for the 12 tribes of Israel multiplied by 12 and then by 1,000. Among other things, the number 12 was considered a symbol of completeness. So this group represents the complete people of God. **(See the chart Numbers in the Bible on pg 1844.)**

7.5-8 *Judah . . . Benjamin:* These verses list the names of the tribes of Israel.

Israel

green horse. Its rider was named Death, and Death's Kingdom followed close behind. They were given power over one fourth of the earth, and they could kill its people with swords, famines, diseases, and wild animals.

⁹When the Lamb opened the fifth seal, I saw under the altar the souls of everyone who had been killed for speaking God's message and telling about their faith. ¹⁰They shouted, "Master, you are holy and faithful! How long will it be before you judge and punish the people of this earth who killed us?"

¹¹Then each of those who had been killed was given a white robe and told to rest for a little while. They had to wait until the complete number of the Lord's other servants and followers would be killed.

¹²When I saw the Lamb open the sixth seal, I looked and saw a great earthquake. The sun turned as dark as sackcloth,ⁱ and the moon became red as blood. ¹³The stars in the sky fell to earth, just like figs shaken loose by a windstorm. ¹⁴Then the sky was rolled up like a scroll,ʲ and all mountains and islands were moved from their places.

¹⁵The kings of the earth, its famous people, and its military leaders hid in caves or behind rocks on the mountains. They hid there together with the rich and the powerful and with all the slaves and free people. ¹⁶Then they shouted to the mountains and the rocks, "Fall on us! Hide us from the one who sits on the throne and from the anger of the Lamb. ¹⁷That terrible day has come! God and the Lamb will show their anger, and who can face it?"

The 144,000 Are Marked for God

7 ¹⁻²After this I saw four angels. Each one was standing on one of the earth's four corners. The angels held back the four winds, so that no wind would blow on the earth or on the sea or on any tree. These angels had also been given the power to harm the earth and the sea. Then I saw another angel come up from where the sun rises in the east, and he was ready to put the mark of the living God on people. He shouted to the four angels, ³"Don't harm the earth or the sea or any tree! Wait until I have marked the foreheads of the servants of our God."

⁴Then I heard how many people had been marked on the forehead. There were 144,000, and they came from every tribe of Israel:

⁵12,000 from Judah,
12,000 from Reuben,
12,000 from Gad,
⁶12,000 from Asher,
12,000 from Naphtali,
12,000 from Manasseh,
⁷12,000 from Simeon,
12,000 from Levi,
12,000 from Issachar,
⁸12,000 from Zebulun,
12,000 from Joseph, and
12,000 from Benjamin.

People from Every Nation

⁹After this, I saw a large crowd with more people than could be counted. They were from every race, tribe, nation, and language, and they stood before the throne and before the Lamb. They wore white robes and held palm branches in their hands, ¹⁰as they shouted,
"Our God, who sits
upon the throne,
has the power
to save his people,
and so does the Lamb."

ⁱ6.12 *sackcloth:* A rough, dark-colored cloth made from goat or camel hair and used to make grain sacks. It was worn in times of trouble or sorrow.   ʲ6.14 *scroll:* See the note at 5.1.

[11]The angels who stood around the throne knelt in front of it with their faces to the ground. The elders and the four living creatures knelt there with them. Then they all worshiped God [12]and said,

> "Amen! Praise, glory, wisdom,
> thanks, honor, power,
> and strength belong to our God
> forever and ever! Amen!"

[13]One of the elders asked me, "Do you know who these people are that are dressed in white robes? Do you know where they come from?"

[14]"Sir," I answered, "you must know." Then he told me:

> "These are the ones
> who have gone through
> the great suffering.
> They have washed their robes
> in the blood of the Lamb
> and have made them white.
> [15]And so they stand
> before the throne of God
> and worship him in his temple
> day and night.
> The one who sits on the throne
> will spread his tent
> over them.
> [16]They will never hunger
> or thirst again,
> and they won't be troubled
> by the sun
> or any scorching heat.

> [17]The Lamb in the center
> of the throne
> will be their shepherd.
> He will lead them to streams
> of life-giving water,
> and God will wipe all tears
> from their eyes."

k8.3 *incense:* See the note at 5.8.

The Seventh Seal Is Opened

8 When the Lamb opened the seventh seal, there was silence in heaven for about half an hour. [2]I noticed that the seven angels who stood before God were each given a trumpet.

[3]Another angel, who had a gold container for incense,[k] came and stood at the altar. This one was given a lot of incense to offer with the prayers of God's people on the gold altar in front of the throne. [4]Then the smoke of the incense, together with the prayers of God's people, went up to God from the hand of the angel.

[5]After this, the angel filled the incense container with fire from the altar and threw it on the earth. Thunder roared, lightning flashed, and the earth shook.

The Trumpets

[6]The seven angels now got ready to blow their trumpets.

[7]When the first angel blew his trumpet, hail and fire mixed with blood were thrown down on the earth. A third of the earth, a third of the trees, and a third of all green plants were burned.

[8]When the second angel blew his trumpet, something like a great fiery mountain was thrown into the sea. A third of the sea turned to blood, [9]a third of the living creatures in the sea died, and a third of the ships were destroyed.

[10]When the third angel blew his trumpet, a great star fell from heaven. It was burning like a torch, and it fell on a third of the rivers and on a third of the springs of water. [11]The name of the star was Bitter, and a third of the water turned bitter. Many people died because the water was so bitter.

■ 7.14 *washed their robes in the blood of the Lamb:* Meaning that Christ has forgiven them. The white clothes show that their lives have been made pure.

■ 7.17 *shepherd:* In the Bible, God and Jesus are pictured as shepherds (see Ps 23.1; Ezek 34.11-30; John 10.7-16).

■ 8.2 *trumpet:* The trumpets given to the seven angels represent a series of judgments against those who had disobeyed God.

■ 8.6 *seven angels:* This probably refers to a specific group of angels who were above the others, according to some Jewish traditions.

■ 8.8 *great fiery mountain . . . thrown into the sea:* In the ancient world, volcanoes, like earthquakes, were often seen as punishment from the gods. REVELATION was likely written after the eruption of Mount Vesuvius in A.D. 79. That erupting volcano buried the city of Pompeii and destroyed many ships in its harbor.

■ 8.10,11 *a great star fell . . . Bitter:* The word translated as "Bitter" sounds like the name of a tree (wormwood) that grew in Palestine. Its leaves were used to make medicine, and its roots contained a bitter juice. At Marah, Moses made bitter water fit to drink when he threw a piece of wood into it (Exod 15.22-25). Here the reverse is happening. See also Jer 9.15.

8.12 *no light:* This punishment sounds like an eclipse of the sun or moon. Here it means that the light of God is being taken from many on earth.

9.1 *star fall . . . deep pit:* The fifth angel symbolizes plagues that spread over the peoples of the earth. The deep pit here refers to the underworld, a watery cave where the evil and the disobedient spirits waited to be judged.

Hell

9.3-10 *Locusts . . . like a scorpion's tail:* In the Bible locusts are frequently used as a symbol of God's anger and the punishment in store for God's enemies. These locusts have stinging tails like scorpions, and injure those who do not have God's mark on their foreheads.

Locusts

9.14 *Euphrates River:* This river marked the eastern boundary of the land God promised to give Abraham (see Gen 15.18; Deut 11.24; Josh 1.4). At the time of John's vision, the Euphrates River was the eastern boundary of the Roman Empire. Across the river lived the Parthians, who were fierce warriors. **(See Map 10 on pg 1888.)**

9.21 *practicing witchcraft:* Witchcraft, forbidden by the Law of Moses (Lev 19.26), was practiced by some people living in the Roman Empire. Practicing witchcraft most likely meant calling the spirits of the dead to do unusual things (see Acts 8.9-11).

[12]When the fourth angel blew his trumpet, a third of the sun, a third of the moon, and a third of the stars were struck. They each lost a third of their light. So during a third of the day there was no light, and a third of the night was also without light.

[13]Then I looked and saw a lone eagle flying across the sky. It was shouting, "Trouble, trouble, trouble to everyone who lives on earth! The other three angels are now going to blow their trumpets."

9 When the fifth angel blew his trumpet, I saw a star[l] fall from the sky to earth. It was given the key to the tunnel that leads down to the deep pit. [2]As it opened the tunnel, smoke poured out like the smoke of a great furnace. The sun and the air turned dark because of the smoke. [3]Locusts[m] came out of the smoke and covered the earth. They were given the same power that scorpions have.

[4]The locusts were told not to harm the grass on the earth or any plant or any tree. They were to punish only those people who did not have God's mark on their foreheads. [5]The locusts were allowed to make them suffer for five months, but not to kill them. The suffering they caused was like the sting of a scorpion. [6]In those days people will want to die, but they will not be able to. They will hope for death, but it will escape from them.

[7]These locusts looked like horses ready for battle. On their heads they wore something like gold crowns, and they had human faces. [8]Their hair was like a woman's long hair, and their teeth were like those of a lion. [9]On their chests they wore armor made of iron. Their wings roared like an army of horse-drawn chariots rushing into battle. [10]Their tails were like a scorpion's tail with a stinger that had the power to hurt someone for five months. [11]Their king was the angel in charge of the deep pit. In Hebrew his name was Abaddon, and in Greek it was Apollyon.[n]

[12]The first horrible thing has now happened! But wait. Two more horrible things will happen soon.

[13]Then the sixth angel blew his trumpet. I heard a voice speak from the four corners of the gold altar that stands in the presence of God. [14]The voice spoke to this angel and said, "Release the four angels who are tied up beside the great Euphrates River." [15]The four angels had been prepared for this very hour and day and month and year. Now they were set free to kill a third of all people.

[16]By listening, I could tell there were more than 200,000,000 war horses. [17]In my vision their riders wore fiery-red, dark-blue, and yellow armor on their chests. The heads of the horses looked like lions, with fire and smoke and sulfur coming out of their mouths. [18]One third of all people were killed by the three terrible troubles caused by the fire, the smoke, and the sulfur. [19]The horses had powerful mouths, and their tails were like poisonous snakes that bite and hurt.

[20]The people who lived through these terrible troubles did not turn away from the idols they had made, and they did not stop worshiping demons. They kept on worshiping idols that were made of gold, silver, bronze, stone, and wood. Not one of these idols could see, hear, or walk. [21]No one stopped murdering or practicing witchcraft or being immoral or stealing.

[l]**9.1** *star:* In the ancient world, stars were often thought of as living beings, such as angels.
[m]**9.3** *Locusts:* A type of grasshopper that comes in swarms and causes great damage to crops.
[n]**9.11** *Abaddon . . . Apollyon:* The Hebrew word "Abaddon" and the Greek word "Apollyon" each mean "destruction."

The Angel and the Little Scroll

10 I saw another powerful angel come down from heaven. This one was covered with a cloud, and a rainbow was over his head. His face was like the sun, his legs were like columns of fire, [2]and with his hand he held a little scroll[o] that had been unrolled. He stood there with his right foot on the sea and his left foot on the land. [3]Then he shouted with a voice that sounded like a growling lion. Thunder roared seven times.

[4]After the thunder stopped, I was about to write what it had said. But a voice from heaven shouted, "Keep it secret! Don't write these things."

[5]The angel I had seen standing on the sea and the land then held his right hand up toward heaven. [6]He made a promise in the name of God who lives forever and who created heaven, earth, the sea, and every living creature. The angel said, "You won't have to wait any longer. [7]God told his secret plans to his servants the prophets, and it will all happen by the time the seventh angel sounds his trumpet."

[8]Once again the voice from heaven spoke to me. It said, "Go and take the open scroll from the hand of the angel standing on the sea and the land."

[9]When I went over to ask the angel for the little scroll, the angel said, "Take the scroll and eat it! Your stomach will turn sour, but the taste in your mouth will be sweet as honey." [10]I took the little scroll from the hand of the angel and ate it. The taste was sweet as honey, but my stomach turned sour.

[11]Then some voices said, "Keep on telling what will happen to the people of many nations, races, and languages, and also to kings."

The Two Witnesses

11 An angel gave me a measuring stick and said:

Measure around God's temple. Be sure to include the altar and everyone worshiping there. [2]But don't measure the courtyard outside the temple building. Leave it out. It has been given to those people who don't know God, and they will trample all over the holy city for 42 months. [3]My two witnesses will wear sackcloth,[P] while I let them preach for 1,260 days.

[4]These two witnesses are the two olive trees and the two lampstands that stand in the presence of the Lord who rules the earth. [5]Any enemy who tries to harm them will be destroyed by the fire that comes out of their mouths. [6]They have the power to lock up the sky and to keep rain from falling while they are prophesying. And whenever they want to, they can turn water to blood and cause all kinds of terrible troubles on earth.

[7]After the two witnesses have finished preaching God's message, the beast that lives in the deep pit will come up and fight against them. It will win the battle and kill them. [8]Their bodies will be left lying in the streets of the same great city where their Lord was nailed to a cross. And this city is spiritually like the city of Sodom or the country of Egypt.

[9]For three and a half days the people of every nation, tribe, language, and race will stare at the bodies of these two witnesses and refuse to let them be buried. [10]Everyone on earth will celebrate and be happy. They will give gifts to each other, because of what happened to the two prophets who caused them so much trouble. [11]But three and a half days later, God will breathe

[o]**10.2** *scroll*: See the note at 5.1.   [P]**11.3** *sackcloth*: See the note at 6.12.

10.1 *powerful angel*: Before the seventh trumpet sounds, two visions show how God continues to speak to his people.

10.7 *secret plans . . . the prophets*: This refers to the prophets of ancient Israel who spoke God's messages of hope and judgment. The secret plan probably refers to what God promised to do by raising Christ from death.

11.1 *Measure around God's temple*: The temple here may refer to all of God's true followers, who, like the courtyard, will be trampled by people who don't know God. John is to measure the people of God to see if they are being faithful.

11.2 *42 months*: In 167 B.C., Antiochus IV Epiphanes, a Syrian king, set up pagan images in the temple and commanded the Jewish people to worship them. The images remained in the temple for three and a half years, until the Jewish people, led by the Maccabees, defeated the forces of Antiochus and reclaimed and purified the temple. See also Dan 12.7.

11.3 *two witnesses*: The identity of these two is not clear.

11.8 *great city . . . Sodom . . . Egypt*: The "great city" is Jerusalem, where God had once been present in the temple. Now, in John's vision, it has become a symbol of evil and opposition to God—just like the immoral city Sodom (see Gen 18.16—19.29) and Israel's ancient oppressor Egypt (see Exod 1).

11.14 *The second horrible thing:* The first horrible thing was the destruction that occurred after the fifth angel blew his trumpet. The beast killing the Lord's two witnesses is the second horrible thing.

11.15 *Chosen One:* This phrase translates the Greek word *Christos,* meaning Messiah.

Messiah (Chosen One)

The Sacred Chest

12.1-6 *a woman . . . a place that God had prepared for her:* The woman in these verses is probably a symbol for Israel or for the whole people of God.

12.3,4 *dragon with seven heads and ten horns . . . wanted to eat her child:* The dragon is identified in 12.9 as the devil, God's chief opponent. The seven heads and ten horns may refer to the men who struggled to gain control of the Roman Empire, or to Rome itself, which was built on seven hills. The stars being pulled down from the sky may symbolize the Roman emperors' claims to be gods. The newborn child that the dragon wanted to eat is Jesus.

12.6 *1,260 days:* This equals three and a half years, or the 42 months mentioned in 11.2.

life into their bodies. They will stand up, and everyone who sees them will be terrified.

¹²The witnesses then heard a loud voice from heaven, saying, "Come up here." And while their enemies were watching, they were taken up to heaven in a cloud. ¹³At that same moment there was a terrible earthquake that destroyed a tenth of the city. Seven thousand people were killed, and the rest were frightened and praised the God who rules in heaven.

¹⁴The second horrible thing has now happened! And the third one will be here soon.

The Seventh Trumpet

¹⁵At the sound of the seventh trumpet, loud voices were heard in heaven. They said,

"Now the kingdom
    of this world
belongs to our Lord
    and to his Chosen One!
And he will rule
    forever and ever!"

¹⁶Then the 24 elders, who were seated on thrones in God's presence, knelt down and worshiped him. ¹⁷They said,

"Lord God All-Powerful,
    you are and you were,
    and we thank you.
You used your great power
    and started ruling.
¹⁸When the nations got angry,
    you became angry too!
Now the time has come
    for the dead
    to be judged.
It is time for you to reward

your servants the prophets
    and all your people
who honor your name,
    no matter who they are.
It is time to destroy everyone
    who has destroyed
    the earth."

¹⁹The door to God's temple in heaven was then opened, and the sacred chest⁹ could be seen inside the temple. I saw lightning and heard roars of thunder. The earth trembled and huge hailstones fell to the ground.

The Woman and the Dragon

12 Something important appeared in the sky. It was a woman whose clothes were the sun. The moon was under her feet, and a crown made of twelve stars was on her head. ²She was about to give birth, and she was crying because of the great pain.

³Something else appeared in the sky. It was a huge red dragon with seven heads and ten horns, and a crown on each of its seven heads. ⁴With its tail, it dragged a third of the stars from the sky and threw them down to the earth. Then the dragon turned toward the woman, because it wanted to eat her child as soon as it was born.

⁵The woman gave birth to a son, who would rule all nations with an iron rod. The boy was snatched away. He was taken to God and placed on his throne. ⁶The woman ran into the desert to a place that God had prepared for her. There she would be taken care of for 1,260 days.

---

⁹**11.19** *sacred chest:* In Old Testament times the sacred chest was kept in the tent used for worship. It was the symbol of God's presence with his people and also of his agreement with them.

Michael Fights the Dragon

[7]A war broke out in heaven. Michael and his angels were fighting against the dragon and its angels. [8]But the dragon lost the battle. It and its angels were forced out of their places in heaven [9]and were thrown down to the earth. Yes, that old snake and his angels were thrown out of heaven! That snake, who fools everyone on earth, is known as the devil and Satan. [10]Then I heard a voice from heaven shout,

"Our God has shown
his saving power,
   and his kingdom has come!
God's own Chosen One
   has shown his authority.
Satan accused our people
in the presence of God
   day and night.
Now he has been thrown out!

[11]"Our people defeated Satan
   because of the blood[r]
of the Lamb
   and the message of God.
They were willing
   to give up their lives.

[12]"The heavens should rejoice,
   together with everyone
   who lives there.
But pity the earth
   and the sea,
because the devil
was thrown down
   to the earth.
He knows his time is short,
   and he is very angry."

[13]When the dragon realized it had been thrown down to the earth, it tried to make trouble for the woman who had given birth to a son. [14]But the woman was given two wings like those of a huge eagle, so she could fly into the desert. There she would escape from the snake and be taken care of for a time, two times, and half a time.

[15]The snake then spewed out water like a river to sweep the woman away. [16]But the earth helped her and swallowed the water that had come from the dragon's mouth. [17]This made the dragon terribly angry with the woman. So it started a war against the rest of her children. They are the people who obey God and are faithful to what Jesus did and taught. [18]The dragon[s] stood on the beach beside the sea.

The Two Beasts

13 I looked and saw a beast coming up from the sea. This one had ten horns and seven heads, and a crown was on each of its ten horns. On each of its heads were names that were an insult to God. [2]The beast I saw had the body of a leopard, the feet of a bear, and the mouth of a lion. The dragon handed over its own power and throne and great authority to this beast. [3]One of its heads seemed to have been fatally wounded, but now it was well. Everyone on earth marveled at this beast, [4]and they worshiped the dragon who had given its authority to the beast. They also worshiped the beast and said, "No one is like this beast! No one can fight against it."

[5]The beast was allowed to brag and claim to be God, and for 42 months it was allowed to rule. [6]The beast cursed God, and it cursed the name of God. It even cursed the place where God lives, as well as everyone who lives in heaven with God. [7]It was allowed to fight against God's people and defeat them. It was also given authority over the people of every tribe, nation,

[r]**12.11** *blood:* Or "death."   [s]**12.18** *The dragon:* The text has "he," and some manuscripts have "I."

12.7 *Michael and his angels:* Michael was considered a chief angel who was the special protector of Israel and who would save the people of Israel from destruction in the last days (Dan 12.1). Michael will protect God's new people, the church. (See also Dan 10.13,21; Jude 9).

Angels

12.11 *the Lamb:* Christ's death and resurrection defeated Satan.

12.14 *a time, two times, and half a time:* Meaning one year, two years, and a half year, which totals three and a half years.

12.15 *snake then spewed out water:* The flood of water symbolizes the troubles that the forces of evil would pour out upon people.

13.1 *beast coming up from the sea:* This may symbolize the Roman Empire, whose armies came across the sea to attack parts of Asia Minor. The heads, horns, and crowns likely refer to the series of Roman emperors, whose names became an insult to God because they insisted on being worshiped as if they were gods and punished or imprisoned Christians who refused. The beast (Rome and its emperors) received power from the dragon (Satan).

13.3 *One of its heads:* May refer to how the Roman emperors struggled to gain and keep power and how they fought many battles to keep control.

John heard a voice from heaven shout, "Our God has shown his saving power, and his kingdom has come! God's Chosen One has shown his authority." REV 12.10

13.11 *another beast . . . two horns like a lamb:* This probably refers to a particular governor in the eastern part of the Roman Empire who was assigned the job of forcing people, especially Christians, to take part in ceremonies honoring the Roman emperor as a god.

13.13-15 *second beast fooled people . . . wounded:* These miracles probably refer to magic tricks and rehearsed events meant to impress people. It may even have included some kind of ventriloquism that made the idols appear to speak. Those who did not worship the idol of the beast were punished or put to death.

13.16,17 *a mark . . . stood for the name of the beast:* This may refer to some sort of mark that showed a person took part in ceremonies worshiping the emperor. It may also refer to the Roman coins that had the image of the emperor on them.

13.18 *the number of the beast . . . 666:* In both Greek and Hebrew, letters of the alphabet were used as numbers. The number of the beast symbolizes incompleteness and imperfection, since six is the sacred number seven minus one. Repeating it three times (666) emphasizes just how imperfect the number is. Many scholars believe this number stood for the Roman emperor Nero.

14.1 *Mount Zion:* Where the temple in Jerusalem had been.

language, and race. ⁸The beast was worshiped by everyone whose name wasn't written before the time of creation in the book of the Lamb who was killed.ᵗ

⁹If you have ears,
  then listen!
¹⁰If you are doomed
  to be captured,
    you will be captured.
If you are doomed
  to be killed by a sword,
    you will be killed
      by a sword.

This means God's people must learn to endure and be faithful!

¹¹I now saw another beast. This one came out of the ground. It had two horns like a lamb, but spoke like a dragon. ¹²It worked for the beast whose fatal wound had been healed. And it used all its authority to force the earth and its people to worship that beast. ¹³It worked mighty miracles, and while people watched, it even made fire come down from the sky.

¹⁴This second beast fooled people on earth by working miracles for the first one. Then it talked them into making an idol in the form of the beast that did not die after being wounded by a sword. ¹⁵It was allowed to put breath into the idol, so it could speak. Everyone who refused to worship the idol of the beast was put to death. ¹⁶All people were forced to put a mark on their right hand or forehead. Whether they were powerful or weak, rich or poor, free people or slaves, ¹⁷they all had to have this mark, or else they could not buy or sell anything. This mark stood for the

name of the beast and for the number of its name.

¹⁸You need wisdom to understand the number of the beast! But if you are smart enough, you can figure this out. Its number is 666, and it stands for a person.

The Lamb and His 144,000 Followers

14 I looked and saw the Lamb standing on Mount Zion!ᵘ With him were 144,000, who had his name and his Father's name written on their foreheads. ²Then I heard a sound from heaven that was like a roaring flood or loud thunder or even like the music of harps. ³And a new song was being sung in front of God's throne and in front of the four living creatures and the elders. No one could learn that song, except the 144,000 who had been rescued from the earth. ⁴All of these are pure virgins, and they follow the Lamb wherever he leads. They have been rescued to be presented to God and the Lamb as the most precious peopleᵛ on earth. ⁵They never tell lies, and they are innocent.

The Messages of the Three Angels

⁶I saw another angel. This one was flying across the sky and had the eternal good news to announce to the people of every race, tribe, language, and nation on earth. ⁷The angel shouted, "Worship and honor God! The time has come for him to judge everyone. Kneel down before the one who created heaven and earth, the oceans, and every stream."

⁸A second angel followed and said, "The

ᵗ**13.8** *wasn't written . . . was killed:* Or "not written in the book of the Lamb who was killed before the time of creation." ᵘ**14.1** *Mount Zion:* Another name for Jerusalem. ᵛ**14.4** *the most precious people:* The Greek text has "the first people." The Law of Moses taught that the first-born of all animals and the first part of the harvest were special and belonged to the Lord.

great city of Babylon has fallen! This is the city that made all nations drunk and immoral. Now God is angry, and Babylon has fallen."

[9]Finally, a third angel came and shouted:

Here is what will happen if you worship the beast and the idol and have the mark of the beast on your hand or forehead. [10]You will have to drink the wine that God gives to everyone who makes him angry. You will feel his mighty anger, and you will be tortured with fire and burning sulfur, while the holy angels and the Lamb look on.

[11]If you worship the beast and the idol and accept the mark of its name, you will be tortured day and night. The smoke from your torture will go up forever and ever, and you will never be able to rest.

[12]God's people must learn to endure. They must also obey his commands and have faith in Jesus.

[13]Then I heard a voice from heaven say, "Put this in writing. From now on, the Lord will bless everyone who has faith in him when they die."

The Spirit answered, "Yes, they will rest from their hard work, and they will be rewarded for what they have done."

The Earth Is Harvested

[14]I looked and saw a bright cloud, and someone who seemed to be the Son of Man[w] was sitting on the cloud. He wore a gold crown on his head and held a sharp sickle[x] in his hand. [15]An angel came out of the temple and shouted, "Start cutting with your sickle! Harvest season is here,

and all crops on earth are ripe." [16]The one on the cloud swung his sickle and harvested the crops.

[17]Another angel with a sharp sickle then came out of the temple in heaven. [18]After this, an angel with power over fire came from the altar and shouted to the angel who had the sickle. He said, "All grapes on earth are ripe! Harvest them with your sharp sickle." [19]The angel swung his sickle on earth and cut off its grapes. He threw them into a pit[y] where they were trampled on as a sign of God's anger. [20]The pit was outside the city, and when the grapes were mashed, blood flowed out. The blood turned into a river that was about 200 miles long and almost deep enough to cover a horse.

The Last of the Terrible Troubles

15 After this, I looked at the sky and saw something else that was strange and important. Seven angels were bringing the seven last terrible troubles. When these are ended, God will no longer be angry.

[2]Then I saw something that looked like a glass sea mixed with fire, and people were standing on it. They were the ones who had defeated the beast and the idol and the number that tells the name of the beast. God had given them harps, [3]and they were singing the song his servant Moses and the Lamb had sung. They were singing,

"Lord God All-Powerful,
    you have done great
        and marvelous things.
You are the ruler
    of all nations,
and you do what is
    right and fair.

---

[w]14.14 *Son of Man*: See the note at 1.13.   [x]14.14 *sickle*: A knife with a long curved blade, used to cut grain and other crops.   [y]14.19 *pit*: It was the custom to put grapes in a pit (called a wine press) and stomp on them to make juice that would later turn to wine.

● 14.8 *The great city of Babylon*: Here "Babylon" stands for Rome. Because Rome has been evil and caused other nations to be immoral, the second angel announces that it will fall.

⊙ Babylon

■ 14.10 *wine . . . fire and burning sulfur*: To drink the wine of God's anger means to receive God's punishment. Fire and burning are often connected with God's judgment of those who reject him.

■ 14.18,19 *grapes*: The prophets of Israel spoke of God's people as a vineyard where grapes are grown (Isa 5). They also compare God's judgment on the people for their disobedience to the harvesting of grapes (Joel 3.13). Similar images are used here to describe what will happen to people who reject God.

⊙ Wine

■ 15.2 *a glass sea mixed with fire*: Like the Red Sea in Exodus, the glass sea symbolizes the boundary set by God to protect God's people from their enemies (Exod 14).

● 15.2 *harps*: A small five- or six-stringed instrument also known as a lyre.

● 15.3 *Moses*: Moses helped save the people of Israel. Jesus Christ, the Lamb, is the Savior of all people.

⊙ Moses

God's people must learn to endure. They must also obey his commands and have faith in Jesus. Rev 14.12

15.5 *sacred tent:* The ancient people of Israel were commanded to create a tent that would be the place where God would live among them. They carried this tent with them as they wandered in the desert after leaving Egypt (Num 17.7; 18.4). The real tent of God's presence (temple) is here seen in heaven (see also Heb 8.1-5).

16.13 *evil spirit . . . false prophet:* Three evil spirits appear. One that looks like a frog comes from the dragon (Satan). Frogs were thought to represent the ability to trick people by lying. A second evil spirit came out of the mouth of the beast (the Roman Empire). A third came out of the mouth of the false prophet.

⁴Lord, who doesn't honor
 and praise your name?
You alone are holy,
 and all nations will come
  and worship you,
because you have shown
 that you judge
  with fairness."

⁵After this, I noticed something else in heaven. The sacred tent used for a temple was open. ⁶And the seven angels who were bringing the terrible troubles were coming out of it. They were dressed in robes of pure white linen and wore belts made of pure gold. ⁷One of the four living creatures gave each of the seven angels a bowl made of gold. These bowls were filled with the anger of God who lives forever and ever. ⁸The temple quickly filled with smoke from the glory and power of God. No one could enter it until the seven angels had finished pouring out the seven last troubles.

The Bowls of God's Anger

16 From the temple I heard a voice shout to the seven angels, "Go and empty the seven bowls of God's anger on the earth."

²The first angel emptied his bowl on the earth. At once ugly and painful sores broke out on everyone who had the mark of the beast and worshiped the idol.

³The second angel emptied his bowl on the sea. At once the sea turned into blood like that of a dead person, and every living thing in the sea died.

⁴The third angel emptied his bowl into the rivers and streams. At once they turned to blood. ⁵Then I heard the angel, who has power over water, say,

"You have always been,
 and you always will be
  the holy God.
You had the right
 to judge in this way.
⁶They poured out the blood^z
 of your people
  and your prophets.
So you gave them blood
 to drink as they deserve!"
⁷After this, I heard
 the altar shout,
"Yes, Lord God All-Powerful,
 your judgments are honest
  and fair."

⁸The fourth angel emptied his bowl on the sun, and it began to scorch people like fire. ⁹Everyone was scorched by its great heat, and all of them cursed the name of God who had power over these terrible troubles. But no one turned to God and praised him.

¹⁰The fifth angel emptied his bowl on the throne of the beast. At once darkness covered its kingdom, and its people began biting their tongues in pain. ¹¹And because of their painful sores, they cursed the God who rules in heaven. But still they did not stop doing evil things.

¹²The sixth angel emptied his bowl on the great Euphrates River, and it completely dried up to make a road for the kings from the east. ¹³An evil spirit that looked like a frog came out of the mouth of the dragon. One also came out of the mouth of the beast, and another out of the mouth of the false prophet. ¹⁴These evil spirits had the power to work miracles. They went to every king on earth, to bring them together for a war against God All-Powerful. But that will be the day of God's great victory.

^z**16.6** *They poured out the blood:* A way of saying, "They murdered."

[15]Remember Christ says, "When I come, it will surprise you like a thief! But God will bless you, if you are awake and ready. Then you won't have to walk around naked and be ashamed."

[16]Those armies came together in a place that in Hebrew is called Armagedon.[a]

[17]As soon as the seventh angel emptied his bowl in the air, a loud voice from the throne in the temple shouted, "It's done!" [18]There were flashes of lightning, roars of thunder, and the worst earthquake in all history. [19]The great city of Babylon split into three parts, and the cities of other nations fell. So God made Babylon drink from the wine cup filled with his anger. [20]Every island ran away, and the mountains disappeared. [21]Hailstones, weighing about 100 pounds each, fell from the sky on people. Finally, the people cursed God, because the hail was so terrible.

The Prostitute and the Beast

17 One of the seven angels who had emptied the bowls came over and said to me, "Come on! I will show you how God will punish that shameless prostitute who sits on many oceans. [2]Every king on earth has slept with her, and her shameless ways are like wine that has made everyone on earth drunk."

[3]With the help of the Spirit, the angel took me into a desert, where I saw a woman sitting on a red beast. The beast was covered with names that were an insult to God, and it had seven heads and ten horns. [4]The woman was dressed in purple and scarlet robes, and she wore jewelry made of gold, precious stones, and pearls. In her hand she held a gold cup filled with the filthy and nasty things she had done. [5]On her forehead a mysterious name was written:

I AM THE GREAT CITY OF BABYLON,
THE MOTHER OF EVERY IMMORAL
AND FILTHY THING ON EARTH.

[6]I could tell that the woman was drunk on the blood of God's people who had given their lives for Jesus. This surprising sight amazed me, [7]and the angel said:

Why are you so amazed? I will explain the mystery about this woman and about the beast she is sitting on, with its seven heads and ten horns. [8]The beast you saw is one that used to be and no longer is. It will come back from the deep pit, but only to be destroyed. Everyone on earth whose names were not written in the book of life[b] before the time of creation will be amazed. They will see this beast that used to be and no longer is, but will be once more.

[9]Anyone with wisdom can figure this out. The seven heads that the woman is sitting on stand for seven hills. These heads are also seven kings. [10]Five of the kings are dead. One is ruling now, and the other one has not yet come. But when he does, he will rule for only a little while.

[11]You also saw a beast that used to be and no longer is. That beast is one of the seven kings who will return as the eighth king, but only to be destroyed.

[12]The ten horns you saw are ten more kings, who have not yet come into power, and they will rule with the beast for only a short time. [13]They all think alike and will give their power and authority to the beast. [14]These kings will go to war against the Lamb.

[a]**16.16** *Armagedon:* The Hebrew form of the name would be "Har Megiddo," meaning "Hill of Megiddo," where many battles were fought in ancient times (see Judges 5.19; 2 Kings 23.29,30).
[b]**17.8** *book of life:* See the note at 3.5.

■ **17.1** *shameless prostitute:* Refers to Rome, the empire's capital city, with its evil way of life and its shameless pride. The other nations and rulers that Rome has conquered are like those who have slept with the prostitute (17.2).

■ **17.3** *woman sitting on a red beast:* The woman is likely meant to be a symbol for Rome, the same immoral woman as in 17.1.

● **17.4** *purple and scarlet robes:* The color purple symbolized royalty (see Judg 8.26; Dan 5.7). Scarlet may be connected with the blood of God's people.

● **17.6** *drunk on the blood of God's people:* Certain Roman leaders were responsible for putting many Christians to death.

■ **17.9-11** *seven heads...seven kings:* Ancient Rome was built on seven hills. The "seven heads" stand for the emperors (here called "kings") of Rome. Which seven emperors John means is not clear.

■ **17.12,13** *ten horns...are ten more kings:* This may refer to ten more Roman emperors who give power to the beast (Satan), or to ten world rulers who give power to the Roman Empire.

■ **17.14** *Lamb:* The worldly kings (17.12,13) will fight against the Lamb, meaning that they will persecute Jesus' followers and the church (see 19.11-21).

17.16 *start hating the shameless woman:* The nations that support Rome will eventually turn against it and defeat it.

18.2 *demons:* Evil spirits that serve Satan.

18.3 *evil and immoral wine:* Wine here is used to symbolize how Rome's authority and attitudes attracted people, and how Rome used this attraction to control the world. Just as someone can become intoxicated and lose good judgment from drinking too much wine, so people could be fooled by Rome's military power and wealth.

But he will defeat them, because he is Lord over all lords and King over all kings. His followers are chosen and special and faithful.

[15]The oceans you saw the prostitute sitting on are crowds of people from all races and languages. [16]The ten horns and the beast will start hating the shameless woman. They will strip off her clothes and leave her naked. Then they will eat her flesh and throw the rest of her body into a fire. [17]God is the one who made these kings all think alike and decide to give their power to the beast. And they will do this until what God has said comes true.

[18]The woman you saw is the great city that rules over all kings on earth.

The Fall of Babylon

18 I saw another angel come from heaven. This one had great power, and the earth was bright because of his glory. [2]The angel shouted,

> "Fallen! Powerful Babylon
>   has fallen
> and is now the home
>   of demons.
> It is the den
>   of every filthy spirit
> and of all unclean birds,
> and every dirty
>   and hated animal.
> [3]Babylon's evil and immoral wine
>   has made all nations drunk.
> Every king on earth
>   has slept with her,
> and every merchant on earth
> is rich because of
>   her evil desires."

[4]Then I heard another voice
  from heaven shout,

> "My people, you must escape
>   from Babylon.
> Don't take part in her sins
>   and share her punishment.
> [5]Her sins are piled
>   as high as heaven.
> God has remembered the evil
>   she has done.
> [6]Treat her as she
>   has treated others.
> Make her pay double
>   for what she has done.
> Make her drink twice as much
> of what she mixed
>   for others.
> [7]That woman honored herself
>   with a life of luxury.
> Reward her now
>   with suffering and pain.

> "Deep in her heart
> Babylon said,
>   'I am the queen!
> Never will I be a widow
> or know what it means
>   to be sad.'
> [8]And so, in a single day
> she will suffer the pain
>   of sorrow, hunger, and death.
> Fire will destroy
>   her dead body,
> because her judge
>   is the powerful Lord God."

[9]Every king on earth who slept with her and shared in her luxury will mourn. They will weep, when they see the smoke from that fire. [10]Her sufferings will frighten them, and they will stand at a distance and say,

> "Pity that great
>   and powerful city!
> Pity Babylon!
> In a single hour
>   her judgment has come."

11Every merchant on earth will mourn, because there is no one to buy their goods. **12**There won't be anyone to buy their gold, silver, jewels, pearls, fine linen, purple cloth, silk, scarlet cloth, sweet-smelling wood, fancy carvings of ivory and wood, as well as things made of bronze, iron, or marble. **13**No one will buy their cinnamon, spices, incense, myrrh, frankincense,*c* wine, olive oil, fine flour, wheat, cattle, sheep, horses, chariots, slaves, and other humans.

14Babylon, the things
your heart desired
have all escaped
from you.
Every luxury
and all your glory
will be lost forever.
You will never
get them back.

15The merchants had become rich because of her. But when they saw her sufferings, they were terrified. They stood at a distance, crying and mourning. **16**Then they shouted,

"Pity the great city
of Babylon!
She dressed in fine linen
and wore purple
and scarlet cloth.
She had jewelry
made of gold
and precious stones
and pearls.
17Yet in a single hour
her riches disappeared."

Every ship captain and passenger and sailor stood at a distance, together with everyone who does business by traveling on the sea. **18**When they saw the smoke from her fire, they shouted, "This was the greatest city ever!"

19They cried loudly, and in their sorrow they threw dust on their heads, as they said,

"Pity the great city
of Babylon!
Everyone who sailed the seas
became rich
from her treasures.
But in a single hour
the city was destroyed.
20The heavens should be happy
with God's people
and apostles and prophets.
God has punished her
for them."

21A powerful angel then picked up a huge stone and threw it into the sea. The angel said,

"This is how the great city
of Babylon
will be thrown down,
never to rise again.
22The music of harps and singers
and of flutes and trumpets
will no longer be heard.
No workers will ever
set up shop in that city,
and the sound
of grinding grain
will be silenced forever.
23Lamps will no longer shine
anywhere in Babylon,
and couples will never again
say wedding vows there.
Her merchants ruled
the earth,
and by her witchcraft
she fooled all nations.
24On the streets of Babylon

*c***18.13** *myrrh, frankincense:* Myrrh was a valuable sweet-smelling powder often used in perfume. Frankincense was a valuable powder that was burned to make a sweet smell.

18.11 *Every merchant on earth will mourn:* The Roman Empire controlled the seaports and highways throughout the Mediterranean world. The merchants had to follow Roman laws and pay taxes to Rome. In return, the Empire protected them and provided a huge market for buying and selling their goods.

18.13 *slaves, and other humans:* The Romans took people from the many lands they had captured and made them slaves, bringing many of them to Rome to serve in the homes of wealthy Roman leaders and in the court of the emperor. In the late first century, slaves made up nearly half the population of Rome. "Other humans" here may refer to people who were made to fight and die in arenas to entertain the Roman leaders and crowds.

Slaves and Servants in the Time of Jesus

18.20 *apostles and prophets:* Here "apostles" means those chosen by God to spread the message about Jesus Christ. The apostles included the twelve closest followers of Jesus named in the Gospels and other important teachers, such as Paul.

18.21 *huge stone:* Refers to a millstone, which was used to crush grain into flour. Just as a large stone would quickly sink if thrown into the sea, so Rome's end would be violent and sudden.

19.1 *power to save*: Here the word "saved" points to what God has done and is still doing to free humans from sin and the powers of evil. "Being saved" can also refer to receiving "eternal life."

God's Saving Love (Salvation)

Eternal Life

19.7 *wedding day of the Lamb . . . his bride*: This is a day of celebration when Christ (the Lamb) and his people (the bride) will be united. It also signals that God is about to defeat Satan for all time. Israel's prophets used the idea of marriage as a way to describe the relationship between God and the people of Israel (see Isa 54.1-8; Ezek 16.7,8; Hos 2.19,20). In the New Testament, the church is pictured as the wife of Christ (Eph 5.23-32).

19.11 *rider was called Faithful and True*: The rider is Christ, who appears as a military leader going to war. The many crowns he wears symbolize his authority. In John's day, kings often wore several crowns, one for each country they ruled.

19.13 *robe that was covered with blood . . . "Word of God"*: The blood is Christ's who won a victory over sin and death by shedding his blood on the cross (see Rom 3.24,25; Rev 5.6,9; 7.14; 12.11). Jesus is the "Word of God" (see John 1.1-3, 14; Heb 4.12).

is found the blood
of God's people
and of his prophets,
and everyone else."

19 After this, I heard what sounded like a lot of voices in heaven, and they were shouting,
"Praise the Lord!
To our God belongs
the glorious power to save,
²because his judgments
are honest and fair.
That filthy prostitute
ruined the earth
with shameful deeds,
But God has judged her
and made her pay
the price for murdering
his servants."

³Then the crowd shouted,
"Praise the Lord!
Smoke will never stop rising
from her burning body."

⁴After this, the 24 elders and the four living creatures all knelt before the throne of God and worshiped him. They said, "Amen! Praise the Lord!"

The Marriage Supper of the Lamb

⁵From the throne a voice said,
"If you worship
and fear our God,
give praise to him,
no matter who you are."

⁶Then I heard what seemed to be a large crowd that sounded like a roaring flood and loud thunder all mixed together. They were saying,
"Praise the Lord!
Our Lord God All-Powerful
now rules as king.
⁷So we will be glad and happy
and give him praise.
The wedding day of the Lamb
is here,
and his bride is ready.
⁸She will be given
a wedding dress
made of pure
and shining linen.
This linen stands for
the good things
God's people have done."

⁹Then the angel told me, "Put this in writing. God will bless everyone who is invited to the wedding feast of the Lamb." The angel also said, "These things God has said are true."

¹⁰I knelt at the feet of the angel and began to worship him. But the angel said, "Don't do that! I am a servant, just like you and everyone else who tells about Jesus. Don't worship anyone but God. Everyone who tells about Jesus does it by the power of the Spirit."

The Rider on the White Horse

¹¹I looked and saw heaven was open, and a white horse was there. Its rider was called Faithful and True, and he is always fair when he judges or goes to war. ¹²He had eyes like flames of fire, and he was wearing a lot of crowns. His name was written on him, but he was the only one who knew what the name meant. ¹³The rider wore a robe that was covered with[d] blood, and he was known as "The

[d]19.13 *covered with*: Some manuscripts have "sprinkled with."

Word of God." **14**He was followed by armies from heaven that rode on white horses and were dressed in pure white linen. **15**From his mouth a sharp sword went out to attack the nations. He will rule them with an iron rod and will show the fierce anger of God All-Powerful by trampling the grapes in the pit where wine is made. **16**On the part of the robe that covered his thigh was written, "KING OF KINGS AND LORD OF LORDS."

17I then saw an angel standing on the sun, and he shouted to all the birds flying in the sky, "Come and join in God's great feast! **18**You can eat the flesh of kings, rulers, leaders, horses, riders, free people, slaves, important people, and everyone else."

19I also saw the beast and all kings of the earth come together. They fought against the rider on the white horse and against his army. **20**But the beast was captured and so was the false prophet. This is the same prophet who had worked miracles for the beast, so he could fool everyone who had the mark of the beast and worshiped the idol. The beast and the false prophet were thrown alive into a lake of burning sulfur. **21**But the rest of their army was killed by the sword that came from the mouth of the rider on the horse. Then birds stuffed themselves on the dead bodies.

The Thousand Years

20 I saw an angel come down from heaven, carrying the key to the deep pit and a big chain. **2**He chained the dragon for 1,000 years. It is that old snake, who is also known as the devil and Satan. **3**Then the angel threw the dragon into the pit. He locked and sealed it, so 1,000 years would go by before the dragon could fool

the nations again. But after that, it would have to be set free for a little while.

4I saw thrones, and sitting on those thrones were the ones who had been given the right to judge. I also saw the souls of the people who had their heads cut off because they had told about Jesus and preached God's message. They were the same ones who had not worshiped the beast or the idol, and they had refused to let its mark be put on their foreheads or hands. They will come to life and rule with Christ for 1,000 years.

5-6 These people are the first to be raised to life, and they are especially blessed and holy. The second death**e** has no power over them. They will be priests for God and Christ and will rule with them for 1,000 years.

No other dead people were raised to life until 1,000 years later.

Satan Is Defeated

7At the end of the 1,000 years, Satan will be set free. **8**He will fool the countries of Gog and Magog, which are at the far ends of the earth, and their people will follow him into battle. They will have as many followers as there are grains of sand along the beach, **9**and they will march all the way across the earth. They will surround the camp of God's people and the city God loves. But fire will come down from heaven and destroy the whole army. **10**Then the devil who fooled them will be thrown into the lake of fire and burning sulfur. He will be there with the beast and the false prophet, and they will be in pain day and night forever and ever.

e20.5, 6 *second death:* See the note at 2.11.

20.2 *1,000 years . . . Satan:* The 1,000 years of peace or calm begin when Satan is imprisoned in the pit. This number likely is meant to symbolize the fact that the final victory over Satan and death will not come immediately, or even during the lifetime of John's readers. The 1,000 years are measured in God's time, not human time (see Ps 90.4; 2 Pet 3.8).

20.4 *souls of the people who had their heads cut off:* Christians who were put to death because they preached about Jesus and refused to take part in emperor worship are known as martyrs. These martyrs will be raised to life and rule with God.

20.8 *Gog and Magog:* The prophet Ezekiel tells of a wicked ruler named Gog from the land of Magog who was supposed to attack the people of Israel from the north (Ezek 38.2-16). However, in this verse Gog and Magog are both countries that represent all the worldly powers that are against God and God's people.

20.10 *lake of fire and burning sulfur:* This is the second and final time that the devil and those who followed him are thrown into the pit and lake of burning sulfur.

20.12 *book of life was opened . . . dead were judged:* Other New Testament passages talk about how God will judge the world and its people at the end of time (see Matt 7.22; 13.49,50; 25.31-46).

21.1 *new heaven and a new earth:* In this vision, the first earth, which had become filled with evil, war, sickness, and pollution, is gone. In its place will be a new earth.

21.2 *New Jerusalem . . . like a bride:* Jerusalem was the center of the religious life of the people of Israel and the place where they had built the Lord's temple. That it was "holy" meant that it was set apart for God's use in the world. John sees the New Jerusalem as "coming down" from God, which shows how God comes down to live among his chosen people. The city is also described as a bride who is ready to meet her husband (God). Note that 21.3,4 mention no temple. The New Jerusalem has no temple because in the new heaven and earth, God will live openly among the people (21.3,22).

Jerusalem

21.12, 14 *twelve tribes of Israel . . . twelve apostles:* The holy city brings together the people of Israel and the Christian church—all who put their trust in God.

The Judgment
at the Great White Throne

11I saw a great white throne with someone sitting on it. Earth and heaven tried to run away, but there was no place for them to go. **12**I also saw all the dead people standing in front of that throne. Every one of them was there, no matter who they had once been. Several books were opened, and then the book of life[f] was opened. The dead were judged by what those books said they had done.

13The sea gave up the dead people who were in it, and death and its kingdom also gave up their dead. Then everyone was judged by what they had done. **14**Afterwards, death and its kingdom were thrown into the lake of fire. This is the second death.[g] **15**Anyone whose name wasn't written in the book of life was thrown into the lake of fire.

The New Heaven
and the New Earth

21 I saw a new heaven and a new earth. The first heaven and the first earth had disappeared, and so had the sea. **2**Then I saw New Jerusalem, the holy city, coming down from God in heaven. It was like a bride dressed in her wedding gown and ready to meet her husband.

3I heard a loud voice shout from the throne:

God's home is now with his people. He will live with them, and they will be his own. Yes, God will make his home among his people. **4**He will wipe all tears from their eyes, and there will be no more death, suffering, crying, or

pain. These things of the past are gone forever.

5Then the one sitting on the throne said:

I am making everything new. Write down what I have said. My words are true and can be trusted. **6**Everything is finished! I am Alpha and Omega,[h] the beginning and the end. I will freely give water from the life-giving fountain to everyone who is thirsty. **7**All who win the victory will be given these blessings. I will be their God, and they will be my people.

8But I will tell you what will happen to cowards and to everyone who is unfaithful or dirty-minded or who murders or is sexually immoral or uses witchcraft or worships idols or tells lies. They will be thrown into that lake of fire and burning sulfur. This is the second death.[i]

The New Jerusalem

9I saw one of the seven angels who had the bowls filled with the seven last terrible troubles. The angel came to me and said, "Come on! I will show you the one who will be the bride and wife of the Lamb." **10**Then with the help of the Spirit, he took me to the top of a very high mountain. There he showed me the holy city of Jerusalem coming down from God in heaven.

11The glory of God made the city bright. It was dazzling and crystal clear like a precious jasper stone. **12**The city had a high and thick wall with twelve gates, and each one of them was guarded by an angel. On each of the gates was written the name of one of the twelve tribes of Israel. **13**Three of

[f]**20.12** *book of life:* See the note at 3.5.   [g]**20.14** *second death:* See the note at 2.11.   [h]**21.6** *Alpha and Omega:* See the note at 1.8.   [i]**21.8** *second death:* See the note at 2.11.

these gates were on the east, three were on the north, three more were on the south, and the other three were on the west. [14]The city was built on twelve foundation stones. On each of the stones was written the name of one of the Lamb's twelve apostles.

[15]The angel who spoke to me had a gold measuring stick to measure the city and its gates and its walls. [16]The city was shaped like a cube, because it was just as high as it was wide. When the angel measured the city, it was about 1,500 miles high and 1,500 miles wide. [17]Then the angel measured the wall, and by our measurements it was about 216 feet high.

[18]The wall was built of jasper, and the city was made of pure gold, clear as crystal. [19]Each of the twelve foundations was a precious stone. The first was jasper,[j] the second was sapphire, the third was agate, the fourth was emerald, [20]the fifth was onyx, the sixth was carnelian, the seventh was chrysolite, the eighth was beryl, the ninth was topaz, the tenth was chrysoprase, the eleventh was jacinth, and the twelfth was amethyst. [21]Each of the twelve gates was a solid pearl. The streets of the city were made of pure gold, clear as crystal.

[22]I did not see a temple there. The Lord God All-Powerful and the Lamb were its temple. [23]And the city did not need the sun or the moon. The glory of God was shining on it, and the Lamb was its light. [24]Nations will walk by the light of that city, and kings will bring their riches there. [25]Its gates are always open during the day, and night never comes. [26]The glorious treasures of nations will be brought into the city. [27]But nothing unworthy will be allowed to enter. No one who is dirty-minded or who tells lies will be there. Only those whose names are written in the Lamb's book of life[k] will be in the city.

22 The angel showed me a river that was crystal clear, and its waters gave life. The river came from the throne where God and the Lamb were seated. [2]Then it flowed down the middle of the city's main street. On each side of the river are trees[l] that grow a different kind of fruit each month of the year. The fruit gives life, and the leaves are used as medicine to heal the nations.

[3]God's curse will no longer be on the people of that city. He and the Lamb will be seated there on their thrones, and its people will worship God [4]and will see him face to face. God's name will be written on the foreheads of the people. [5]Never again will night appear, and no one who lives there will ever need a lamp or the sun. The Lord God will be their light, and they will rule forever.

The Coming of Christ

[6]Then I was told:

These words are true and can be trusted. The Lord God controls the spirits of his prophets, and he is the one who sent his angel to show his servants what must happen very soon. [7]Remember, I am coming soon! God

21.16 *city was shaped like a cube:* In ancient symbolism, the cube was considered the perfect shape.

21.25 *its gates are always open . . . night never comes:* This symbolizes how God welcomes all whose names are in the book of life. The gates are open because no evil thing or person can enter (21.27). The never-ending light shows that the powers of darkness (evil) have been defeated forever.

22.1 *river:* The river in New Jerusalem is like the life-giving rivers God created to flow in the Garden of Eden (Gen 2.10-14). See also Ezek 47.1-12; Zech 14.8.

22.3 *God's curse:* When Adam and Eve ate from the tree that gave power to know right and wrong (Gen 2.17; 3.6), God cursed them and sent them out of the Garden so they could never eat fruit from the other tree, the one that would let them live forever (Gen 3.22). In the New Jerusalem, God's people are able to eat fruit from the tree that gives life, because the curse of sin has been removed forever.

22.7 *I am coming soon:* This phrase is repeated three times in the final verses. It is both a promise and a warning. The message is that followers of Christ always need to be ready for Christ's return.

⊕ End Times

⊕ Second Coming

[j]**21.19** *jasper:* The precious and semi-precious stones mentioned in verses 19, 20 are of different colors. Jasper is usually green or clear; sapphire is blue; agate has circles of brown and white; emerald is green; onyx has different bands of color; carnelian is deep-red or reddish-white; chrysolite is olive-green; beryl is green or bluish-green; topaz is yellow; chrysoprase is apple-green; jacinth is reddish-orange; and amethyst is deep purple. [k]**21.27** *book of life:* See the note at 3.5. [l]**22.2** *trees:* The Greek has "tree," which is used in a collective sense of trees on both sides of the heavenly river.

22.17 *the bride:* "The bride" here refers to the New Jerusalem (the new people of God). See also Matt 22.1-10; Eph 5.22-32.

22.17 *everyone who hears this:* REVELATION was intended to be read in services of worship.

will bless everyone who pays attention to the message of this book.

⁸My name is John, and I am the one who heard and saw these things. Then after I had heard and seen all this, I knelt down and began to worship at the feet of the angel who had shown it to me.

⁹But the angel said,

Don't do that! I am a servant, just like you. I am the same as a follower or a prophet or anyone else who obeys what is written in this book. God is the one you should worship.

¹⁰Don't keep the prophecies in this book a secret. These things will happen soon.

¹¹Evil people will keep on being evil, and everyone who is dirty-minded will still be dirty-minded. But good people will keep on doing right, and God's people will always be holy.

¹²Then I was told:

I am coming soon! And when I come, I will reward everyone for what they have done. ¹³I am Alpha and Omega,ᵐ the first and the last, the beginning and the end.

¹⁴God will bless all who have washed their robes. They will each have the right to eat fruit from the tree that gives life, and they can enter the gates of the city. ¹⁵But outside the city will be dogs, witches, immoral people, murderers, idol worshipers, and everyone who loves to tell lies and do wrong.

¹⁶I am Jesus! And I am the one who sent my angel to tell all of you these things for the churches. I am David's Great Descendant,ⁿ and I am also the bright morning star.ᵒ

¹⁷The Spirit and the bride say, "Come!" Everyone who hears thisᵖ should say, "Come!"

If you are thirsty, come! If you want life-giving water, come and take it. It's free!

¹⁸Here is my warning for everyone who hears the prophecies in this book:

If you add anything to them, God will make you suffer all the terrible troubles written in this book. ¹⁹If you take anything away from these prophecies, God will not let you have part in the life-giving tree and in the holy city described in this book.

²⁰The one who has spoken these things says, "I am coming soon!"

So, Lord Jesus, please come soon!

²¹I pray that the Lord Jesus will be kind to all of you.

ᵐ**22.13** *Alpha and Omega:* See the note at 1.8.   ⁿ**22.16** *David's Great Descendant:* See the note at 5.5. ᵒ**22.16** *the bright morning star:* Probably thought of as the brightest star (see 2.27, 28).   ᵖ**22.17** *who hears this:* The reading of the book of Revelation in a service of worship.

Reflection Questions About Revelation 1.1—22.21

1. Who was John, and why was he on Patmos Island (1.4,9)? What happened to him while was there (1.9-11)?

2. In John's vision, what was happening at the "throne" (chapters 4,5)? Who are the 24 elders (4.4,10)?

3. Who is the Lamb (5.6-13)? What is the scroll (book) with the seven seals (5.1-5; 6.1—8.1)? What animals are connected with the opening of the first four seals? What does each represent?

4. What happens when each of the first six angels blows their trumpets (8.2—9.21)? What is revealed when the seventh and last trumpet is sounded (10.1-19)?

5. What happens when the seventh trumpet is sounded (11.15-19)? Who are the woman and the dragon (12.1-6)? After fighting in heaven with the angel Michael, who does the dragon make trouble for (12.13-18)? What do you think this battle represents?

6. Who is the beast that comes up from the sea (13.1-4)? From where did it get its power? How long was the beast allowed to rule (13.5)? What is significant about this amount of time? What was the second beast able to do (13.11-18)?

7. What messages were given by the three angels (14.6-12)? What effect might these messages have had on early Christians living in a society that was often hostile to the Christian faith? What was in the seven bowls of anger (16.1-21)?

8. Who or what is the "prostitute"? What is the prostitute's connection to the beast (17.1-18)?

9. What does Babylon stand for (18.1-24)? Why do kings and merchants mourn when Babylon falls (18.9-18)? What happens to the beast and the dragon (19.19—20.3,7-15)?

10. Describe the new heaven and new earth (21.1-8). What is the New Jerusalem (21.9—22.5)? How is the New Jerusalem like the Garden of Eden (Gen 1,2)?

how the bible came to us

The Bible is like a small library that contains many books written by many authors. The word "Bible" comes from the Greek word *biblia,* meaning "books." It took well over one thousand years for all of these books to be written down, and it was many more years before the list of books now known as the Bible came together in one large book.

PASSING STORIES ALONG

Before anything in the Bible was written down, people told stories about God and God's relationship with the people we now read about in the Bible. This stage of relating stories by word of mouth lasted for many years as families passed along the stories of their ancestors to each new generation. In the case of the Jewish Scriptures (Old Testament), some stories were told for centuries before they were written down in a final form.

WRITING DOWN THE BIBLE STORIES

Eventually, as human societies in the Near East began to develop forms of writing that were easy to learn and use (around 1800 B.C.), people began to write down the stories, songs (psalms), and prophecies that would one day become a part of the Bible. These were written on papyrus, a paper-like material made from reeds, or on vellum, which was made from dried animal skins. The books found in the Old Testament were not written down at one time. This process took centuries. While some books were being written and collected, others were still being passed on in storytelling fashion.

The very first manuscripts of the books that make up the Old and New Testaments have never been found, and most likely wore out from continued use, or were destroyed centuries ago. However, copies of these manuscripts were made by hand and became valued possessions of synagogues, churches, and monasteries. Before these copies wore out, new copies were made, and then eventually copies were made from these copies—and so on, from one generation to the next. Some very old copies of both the Old and New Testament writings have been preserved, and they are now stored in museums and libraries around the world.

COLLECTING THE JEWISH SCRIPTURES

It is not possible to know exactly when all the books of the Jewish Scriptures were finally collected. Some of the writings in the Jewish Scriptures may go back as far as 1300 B.C., but the process of bringing the books together may not have begun until around 400 B.C. This collecting of books continued while new books were being written as late as the second century B.C. The process of deciding which books would be part of the official Jewish Scriptures went on until almost A.D. 100. This work was often done by Jewish rabbis (teachers).

PREPARING THE BIBLE FOR A CHANGING WORLD

During this time, the Jewish Scriptures were translated into Greek. This translation is called the Septuagint, which means "seventy," and is often identified by the Roman numeral for seventy (LXX). The legend of how the Septuagint came to be, and how it got its name is told in a document called the *Letter of Aristeas*. The legend says that seventy-two scholars began translating the Jewish Scriptures from Hebrew, all at the same time. The *Letter* goes on to say that they all finished at the same time, in seventy-two days, and that all seventy-two scholars discovered that their translations were exactly the same! The translation was named for all the "seventy" numbers in that story. This Greek version of the Bible was used by Jewish people scattered throughout the Roman world, because most of them spoke Greek instead of Hebrew. The oldest copies of the Septuagint date from the second century B.C., more than one hundred years before Jesus was born. The Septuagint was also the main version of the Jewish Scriptures used by early Christians.

It is not exactly clear how it was decided which books should be considered holy enough to be included in the Jewish Scriptures. We do know that around A.D. 100, a group of Jewish scholars met at Jamnia, a center of Jewish learning west of Jerusalem. At Jamnia, the scholars debated which books should be in the Jewish Scriptures. Probably these scholars' discussions were a large part of the Jewish community's decision that thirty-nine books should be on the holy list (canon). Seven books, sometimes called the Deuterocanonical books (meaning "second list"), were not included on the list. Today, most Protestant churches follow the original list of thirty-nine books and call it the Old Testament. The Roman Catholic, Anglican (Episcopal), and Eastern Orthodox churches include the Deuterocanonical books in their Old Testament.

THE STORIES OF CHRIST AND HIS FIRST FOLLOWERS

Jesus and most of his followers were Jewish, and so they used and quoted the Jewish Scriptures. After Jesus died and was raised to life around A.D. 30, the stories about Jesus, as well as his sayings, were passed on by word of mouth. It wasn't until about A.D. 65

that these stories and sayings began to be gathered and written down in books known as the Gospels, which make up about half of what Christians call the New Testament. The earliest writings of the New Testament, however, are probably some of the letters that the apostle Paul wrote to groups of Jesus' followers who were scattered throughout the Roman Empire. The first of these letters, probably 1 THESSALONIANS, may have been written as early as A.D. 50. Other New Testament writings were written in the late first century or early second century A.D.

The New Testament books were written in Greek, an international language during this period of the Roman Empire. They were often passed on and read as single books or letters. For nearly three hundred years (A.D. 100–400), the early church leaders and councils argued about which New Testament writings should be considered holy and treated with the same respect given to the Jewish Scriptures. In A.D. 367, Athanasius, the bishop of Alexandria, wrote a letter that listed the twenty-seven books he said Christians should consider authoritative. His list included the books already in widest use in the Christian churches, and the writings he named are the same twenty-seven books that today we call the New Testament.

TRANSLATING THE BIBLE

When the New Testament books were written, the Greek language was understood all over the Mediterranean world. But by the late second century A.D., local languages were becoming popular again, especially in local churches. Translations of the Bible were then made into Latin, the language of Rome; Coptic, a language of Egypt; and Syriac, a language of Syria. In A.D. 383, Pope Damasus I assigned a scholar priest named Jerome to create an official translation of the Bible into Latin. It took Jerome about twenty-seven years to translate the whole Bible. His translation came to be known as the Vulgate and served as the standard version of the Bible in Western Europe for the next thousand years.

By the Middle Ages, only scholars could read and

understand Latin. But by the time Johannes Gutten-berg invented the modern printing press (around 1456), the use of national languages was becoming acceptable and widespread in official, educational, and religious settings. As more people began to learn to read, there was a new demand for the Bible in national languages. Translators like Martin Luther, William Tyndale, Cassiodoro de Reina, and Giovanni Diodati began to translate the Bible into the languages that people spoke in their everyday lives.

The process of Bible translating continues today, and it has been helped by some recent discoveries.

Many ancient Greek manuscripts of the New Testa-ment have been found in the last 150 years. In 1947, some very old manuscripts of the Jewish Scriptures were found in caves at Qumran, Murabba'at, and other locations just west of the Dead Sea in Israel, and have become known as the Dead Sea Scrolls. These manuscripts, which date from between the third century B.C. and the first century A.D., have helped modern scholars better understand the wording of texts and to make decisions about how to best translate specific verses or words.

what books belong in the bible?

The Bible as Christians know it today did not begin as one large volume—with Old and New Testaments. It came into being as part of a selection process called "canonization." The Greek word for "canon" can mean many things, such as "measuring rod" or "ruler." At first, the early church leaders used "canon" to mean a "standard," and later a "list" or "catalog" of authoritative writings. There were many books circulating among the churches throughout the Roman world that were read and studied by the early church. It was important for the church leaders at that time to go through a process of deciding which books were holy and had authority for God's people. This process did not happen overnight. In some cases, it took hundreds of years from the time they were written to decide which of the many writings that were being read should be part of Holy Scripture, that is, the Bible.

THE HEBREW SCRIPTURES AND THE OLD TESTAMENT

The books in the Old Testament section of this edition are translations of the Hebrew Scriptures still used by the Jewish people in their worship services today. These books were written by many different authors over a period of hundreds of years. The introductions to the individual books of the Old Testament offer some suggestions about where and when these books may have been written, so this article will not try to deal with this issue.

The Old Testament developed in stages and its books were collected in groups. Before the process of collecting books and putting them in some kind of order took place, individual manuscripts were hand-copied and passed among groups. The earliest literature of the Jewish people may date as far back as the time of Moses or earlier (about 1300 B.C.). Other literature found in the Old Testament (for instance DANIEL) may have been written as late as the second century B.C. That would mean that the literature collected into the Old Testament was written over a period of 1000 years or more!

While the writing of Hebrew manuscripts was taking place, the process of collecting and editing was also going on. One important collection of books was called "The Law," which included the first five books of the Bible. "The Law" is also called by its Hebrew name, *Torah*, and by the name *Pentateuch*, which is the Greek term for a five-volume book. Another collection was called "The Prophets." In the Jewish Bible, this collection includes certain books that Christians would call "history books." The last major group of books to be collected was simply called "The Writings." They contain books of poetry and wise sayings, and books that Christians would consider prophetic or historical in nature. Because different religious traditions arrange these books differently, a chart has been provided on pgs 1768–69 for easy reference.

It is not known exactly how or when the books of the Old Testament were selected and approved for inclusion in the Hebrew Scriptures, but it is certain that the books of the *Torah* were accepted as authoritative almost from the time they were written. There is also some evidence that the list of authoritative books was not finalized until after A.D. 100. Only the books on this final list were considered to be Scripture by the Jewish people.

The chart called **Books of the Hebrew Scriptures, or "Tanak,"** shows the three main sections of the Hebrew Scriptures: The Law, The Prophets, and The Writings. If you compare this list to the chart called **The Old Testament in Christian Bibles** on pgs 1768–69, you'll notice that all of these books are included in the Old Testaments of Christian Bibles, though they are grouped differently and placed in a slightly different order. The Hebrew word for Bible is *Tanak* (sometimes spelled *Tanakh*). This is an acronym, or a word made from the first letters of the Hebrew words for each of the three main sections: *Torah, Nevi'im,* and *Kethuvim.*

If you further examine **The Old Testament in Christian Bibles** chart, you'll notice that some Christian traditions include other books in their Old Testaments as well. These additional writings are known as "Apocryphal" or "Deuterocanonical" books. The term "apocrypha" comes from a Greek word meaning "hidden," and today suggests books that have been "set aside" or given secondary status. The term "deuterocanonical," a word that Catholics prefer to use when referring to many of these same books, means books that came into the canon at a later (secondary) date, in order to distinguish them from the Hebrew Scriptures discussed above. In the 1600s, some Protestant Christians began to use only the Jewish list of Old Testament books, while the Roman Catholic and Eastern Orthodox Christians continued to use some or all of the Apocryphal/Deuterocanonical books as well. Some of these books are discussed in the following section on Greek versions of the Jewish Scriptures.

BOOKS OF THE HEBREW SCRIPTURES, OR "TANAK"

TORAH (The Law)	NEVI'IM (The Prophets)	KETHUVIM (The Writings)
GENESIS	JOSHUA	PSALMS
EXODUS	JUDGES	JOB
LEVITICUS	SAMUEL (1 & 2 SAM)	PROVERBS
NUMBERS	KINGS (1 & 2 KGS)	RUTH
DEUTERONOMY	ISAIAH	SONG OF SONGS
	JEREMIAH	ECCLESIASTES
	EZEKIEL	LAMENTATIONS
	BOOK OF THE TWELVE	ESTHER
	Hosea	DANIEL
	Joel	EZRA-NEHEMIAH
	Amos	CHRONICLES (1 & 2 CHR)
	Obadiah	
	Jonah	
	Micah	
	Nahum	
	Habakkuk	
	Zephaniah	
	Haggai	
	Zechariah	
	Malachi	

GREEK VERSIONS OF THE JEWISH SCRIPTURES

In the third century B.C., Jewish scholars in Alexandria, Egypt, translated the Hebrew Scriptures into Greek, since many Jewish people lived in Greek-speaking areas of the Mediterranean world, and spoke Greek on an everyday basis. This Greek version of the Jewish Scriptures is known as the Septuagint (commonly abbreviated LXX).

Some of the Jewish scholars in Egypt did not agree about what books should be included in the official list of Scriptures, even though a canon was being agreed upon by another group of Jewish scholars in Palestine. For example, some of the Egyptian scholars would allow only documents written in Hebrew or Aramaic (a Semitic language similar to Hebrew). Other Greek-speaking Jews included documents originally written in Greek (some of them from as late as the first century A.D.). These Greek writings included:

Historical writings: *1 Esdras* (a Greek version of ESDRA in the Hebrew Bible, with some additions); *Judith; Tobit; 1–4 Maccabees;* and

Poetic and prophetic writings, wisdom, and tales: *Sirach* (sometimes called *Ecclesiasticus*); *Wisdom of Solomon; Baruch; Letter of Jeremiah; Susanna; Prayer of Azariah and the Song of the Three Young Men;* and *Bel and the Dragon.*

Though most of these titles may not sound familiar to many Christians today, many of the early Christians seem to have accepted them as part of their Scriptures. Aside from these documents, there were also additions to the Greek translation of the Hebrew book of ESTHER that was made in the second and first centuries B.C. And some of the tales listed above were added to the Greek translation of DANIEL.

The Roman Catholic Bible still includes many of these books, along with the fuller versions of the books of ESTHER and DANIEL. The Greek Orthodox Bible includes many of these books, plus a few others, such as the *Prayer of Manasseh* and an extra psalm (151). Many Protestant Bibles now follow the list called "Hebrew Scriptures" shown in the chart on pg 1765, and exclude the "extra" books. Some editions do include them, but place them between the Old and New Testaments or at the end of the Bible.

THE NEW TESTAMENT

Jesus and his disciples spoke Aramaic and used the Hebrew version of the Jewish Scriptures, but the apostle Paul and many other early Christians spoke Greek and used the Greek version of the Jewish Scriptures (Septuagint). Of the many Old Testament passages quoted or referred to in the New Testament, most are taken from the Septuagint. Though a small number of Christians, by the third and fourth centuries, thought that the Jewish Scriptures should not be part of the Christian Bible, most believed, as did the writers of the New Testament, that the Jewish Scriptures were the Word of God. They considered these writings to be holy and authoritative, and to be suitable for instructing Christians about God and faith (see Mark 7.13; Rom 3.2; 2 Tim 3.16; Heb 1.1). After all, they would have argued, Jesus said that he did not come to do away with the Law and the Prophets, but to give them their full meaning (Matt 5.17-19).

The twenty-seven books that are included in the present New Testament were written by a number of different authors, the earliest ones being written as early as A.D. 50 and none being written any later than the early part of the second century. The letters of Paul are probably the oldest writings included in the New Testament. MATTHEW, MARK, LUKE, and JOHN (the Gospels) were probably written between A.D. 60, ten years before the temple was destroyed in Jerusalem, and A.D. 100. Most scholars agree that MARK was probably the first Gospel written, since MATTHEW and LUKE seem to take many of their details and the order of events directly from MARK. Some of the other letters and REVELATION were probably some of the last books to be written, since they seem to give a picture of the situations Christians faced at the end of the first century and in the early part of the second century A.D.

The books included in the present New Testament were not the only letters or Gospels written by Christians during the first and second centuries. It took many years of debate between church leaders and scholars to settle on an accepted list (canon) of New Testament books. Various church leaders proposed different lists in the three hundred years that followed the writing of the New Testament books, but the list proposed in A.D. 367 by Athanasius, a bishop of Alexandria, is the accepted list that nearly all Christian traditions accept today.

How did the church leaders decide which books should become part of the accepted list? There were probably three "tests" they used to make their decision. First, a book had to have some connection with one of the early apostles. This meant that either the apostle was judged to be the writer of the book, or the material was thought to capture the key teachings of that apostle. Second, the book or letter had to be in agreement with the Jewish Scriptures and other accepted New Testament writings. The third test had to do with usage. Was the book or letter accepted and being used by a majority of Christians? If so, the case for including it as part of the New Testament was stronger.

The Protestant, Roman Catholic, and Eastern Orthodox churches all generally consider the twenty-seven books of the New Testament to be "canonical" and usually list them in the same order in their Bibles.

THE OLD TESTAMENT IN CHRISTIAN BIBLES

The Old Testament in Christian Bibles contains all of the books included in the Jewish Scriptures. Some Christian traditions, however, also include books that are not part of the Hebrew Bible. Most of these books were included in the Septuagint, a Greek translation of the Hebrew Bible that was used by the apostles and the early Christians.

The Protestant Old Testament contains only the books found in the Hebrew Bible, but arranges them in a different order. The Catholic Old Testament contains all of these books plus the other books that were part of the Septuagint. The Orthodox Old Testament includes all of these books, plus *3 & 4 Maccabees, Prayer of Manasseh, and Psalm 151* which are included in the Orthodox Bible because they appear in some versions of the Septuagint. The list below shows the order in which these books usually appear in Bibles printed for each of these Christian traditions.

PROTESTANT	CATHOLIC	ORTHODOX
GENESIS	GENESIS	GENESIS
EXODUS	EXODUS	EXODUS
LEVITICUS	LEVITICUS	LEVITICUS
NUMBERS	NUMBERS	NUMBERS
DEUTERONOMY	DEUTERONOMY	DEUTERONOMY
JOSHUA	JOSHUA	JOSHUA
JUDGES	JUDGES	JUDGES
RUTH	RUTH	RUTH
1 SAMUEL	1 SAMUEL	1 KINGDOMS (1 SAM)
2 SAMUEL	2 SAMUEL	2 KINGDOMS (2 SAM)
1 KINGS	1 KINGS	3 KINGDOMS (1 KGS)
2 KINGS	2 KINGS	4 KINGDOMS (2 KGS)
1 CHRONICLES	1 CHRONICLES	1 CHRONICLES
2 CHRONICLES	2 CHRONICLES	2 CHRONICLES
EZRA	EZRA	[1 ESDRAS]
NEHEMIAH	NEHEMIAH	[2 ESDRAS (EZRA + NEH)]
ESTHER	*TOBIT*	*ESTHER (with additions)*[1]
JOB	*JUDITH*	*JUDITH*
PSALMS	*ESTHER (with additions)*[1]	*TOBIT*
PROVERBS	*1 MACCABEES*	*1 MACCABEES*
ECCLESIASTES	*2 MACCABEES*	*2 MACCABEES*
SONG OF SONGS	JOB	*[3 MACCABEES]*
ISAIAH	PSALMS	PSALMS (+ *PS 151*)
JEREMIAH	PROVERBS	*PRAYER OF MANASSEH*
LAMENTATIONS	ECCLESIASTES	JOB
EZEKIEL	SONG OF SONGS	PROVERBS

PROTESTANT	CATHOLIC	ORTHODOX
DANIEL	*WISDOM OF SOLOMON*	ECCLESIASTES
HOSEA	*SIRACH*[2]	SONG OF SONGS
JOEL	ISAIAH	*WISDOM OF SOLOMON*
AMOS	JEREMIAH	*SIRACH*[2]
OBADIAH	LAMENTATIONS	HOSEA
JONAH	*BARUCH*	AMOS
MICAH	*(with Letter of Jeremiah)*	MICAH
NAHUM	EZEKIEL	JOEL
HABAKKUK	*DANIEL (with additions)*[3]	OBADIAH
ZEPHANIAH	HOSEA	JONAH
HAGGAI	JOEL	NAHUM
ZECHARIAH	AMOS	HABAKKUK
MALACHI	OBADIAH	ZEPHANIAH
	JONAH	HAGGAI
	MICAH	ZECHARIAH
	NAHUM	MALACHI
	HABAKKUK	ISAIAH
	ZEPHANIAH	JEREMIAH
	HAGGAI	*BARUCH*
	ZECHARIAH	LAMENTATIONS
	MALACHI	*LETTER OF JEREMIAH*
		EZEKIEL
		DANIEL (with additions)[3]
		[4 MACCABEES
		(in Appendix)]

Books listed in the Catholic and Orthodox columns that are printed in *italic* are part of the tradtional Protestant Apocrypha. Books that are in brackets are traditionally included only in Orthodox Bibles.

[1]ESTHER in Catholic and Orthodox Bibles includes six additional passages that are found in the Greek translation of the Hebrew Book of ESTHER.

[2]SIRACH is also known as *Ecclesiasticus.*

[3]DANIEL in Catholic and Orthodox Bibles includes additional sections sometimes printed with the titles: "Prayer of Azariah and the Song of the Three Young Men," "Susanna," and "Bel and the Dragon."

different kinds of literature in the bible

Most books fall into one particular category of literature or another. An instruction booklet for building something uses technical language; a novel uses some kind of narrative structure; a book of poetry may use rhymed or non-rhymed verse; and a book of history uses factual prose writing. The type of book usually determines the literary form used. The Bible is bound as one large book, but it is really made up of many different books using many different kinds of literature. This makes the Bible both challenging and exciting to read.

When studying the books of the Bible, it is important to look not only at the information a book contains but also at the literary form that the author has used. The kind of literature used can give clues about what the author was trying to say. For example, look at 1 Samuel 1.1-28 and compare it to 1 Samuel 2.1-10. These passages from the same book use two different kinds of writing. The first section is more like prose, or story, while the second section is a prayer or song in poetic form.

Noticing the change from prose to poetry can give a reader more to think about regarding the text. A brief example from the New Testament is the story of Jesus' birth. Luke 2.1-21 tells of the events of Jesus' birth and gives many details regarding the birth itself. In contrast, JOHN does not use a story to tell about Jesus' birth. Instead, it begins with a poem (1.1-14), which refers to Jesus as "the Word" and "the true light" that became "a human being." How do these different kinds of literature influence the way we think about who Jesus is? Why has the writer of each of these Gospels emphasized different aspects of Jesus' birth and identity? Looking at how a writer chooses to share information can open the way for new ways of understanding what the Bible has to say.

The Bible includes a great number of types of literature. Some forms of literature describe an entire book. In the Bible the most important of these forms are laws and rules, history, poetry and songs, wisdom sayings and proverbs, Gospels, letters, and apocalyptic writings. Other forms of literature describe sections within a book. The most important of these forms are prose narrative, prayers, parables, prophecies (oracles), and long family lists (genealogies).

LITERARY FORMS FOR WHOLE BOOKS

Laws and rules. Many ancient Near Eastern cultures developed law codes. One of the most famous was the Code developed by the Babylonian leader named Hammurabi (ruled from about 1792 to 1750 B.C.). The first five books of the Jewish Scriptures (Old Testament) make up the section known as the Law, or Torah. Not all of the literature in these five books includes laws, but much does. These laws include both laws that forbid things ("Do not . . . ") and laws that encourage things ("Do . . . "), and were given to the people of Israel in order to help them worship correctly and treat one another with respect and care. The most well-known law literature in the Bible is the Ten Commandments (Exod 20.1-17; Deut 5.6-21. Other examples are found in Exodus 21.1—23.19; Leviticus 1.1—7.36; Numbers 6.1-21; 35.16-34; Deuteronomy 14.3—17.7; James 4.11,12.

History. In the Old Testament, history writings tell the story of Israel's history from the settlement of Canaan in 1250 B.C. to the fall of Jerusalem in 587 B.C. These books describe the activities of such important figures as the prophets Elijah and Elisha, and the kings of Israel and Judah, including King David and King Solomon. These books also include information about the events of the two Israelite kingdoms after the split in 931 B.C. Examples of history books in the Old Testament are JOSHUA and 1 and 2 KINGS. In the New Testament, ACTS tells the history of the early church.

Poetry and songs. This is a large category that includes different forms. Poetry is used especially in PSALMS, JOB, and the SONG OF SONGS. But poetry can be found in many books of the Bible. Some poems in the Bible are examples of old hymns or songs. Many of the psalms were meant for use in worship and prayer. The speeches of the prophets include poetic forms of language. Translating Hebrew poetry into English is not simple, and sometimes special techniques that are effective in the original language cannot be meaningfully carried over into English. One important feature of Hebrew poetry is the repeating of a single idea in two similar but different ways. This is called "parallelism" and an example is Psalm 22.9,10. Other examples of poetry in the Old Testament include: Exodus 15.1-18; Job 22.21-30; Psalm 23; Isaiah 5.1-7; and Jonah 2.2-9. Poetry is also used in the New Testament. Some examples are Luke 1.46-55; Philippians 2.6-11; and Revelation 15.3,4.

Wisdom sayings and proverbs. The large division of the Old Testament called "Wisdom and Worship" literature includes poetry, psalms, stories, and more. Here, wisdom sayings and proverbs have a unique style which makes them read like common sense reflections about the world, God, and the place of human beings. Wisdom sayings fill a book like PROVERBS, but they can also be found in other books. Books like ECCLESIASTES and JOB offer wisdom along with the kinds of philosophic reflections listed above. Wisdom writings usually do not give much direct information about Israel's history. Instead, they raise questions about moral issues, and ask hard questions about life. Some of these Wisdom writings are attributed to Solomon because he was known as Israel's wisest king, but were probably written after his time and credited to him as a way of honoring him. In addition to the books already mentioned, Psalm 1 and Psalm 37 are good examples of wisdom literature. Wisdom sayings are also an important part of the New Testament. Examples can be found in Jesus' "Sermon on the Mount" (Matt 5–7) and in James 3.2-8; and 4.13-17.

Gospels. MATTHEW, MARK, LUKE, and JOHN are the four books of the New Testament which tell about the life and teachings of Jesus. These books are called "Gospels." The word "gospel" comes from the Old English word *godspel,* which is a strict translation of the Greek word *euangelion,* meaning "good news."

Letters. A number of books in the New Testament are letters written by the apostle Paul or others. These letters are written in the formal Greek letter-writing style of the first century A.D. The person writing a letter is identified first (Rom 1.1-6). This is followed by the name of the persons being written to, and a greeting (Rom 1.7). The largest section of a letter is the "body" (Rom 1.16—15.35). In most of Paul's letters, a prayer of thanksgiving follows the greeting (Rom 1.8-15), and a final greeting and blessing closes the letter (Rom 16.1-27). Within each letter a number of different kinds of literature can be found, including prayers, instructions, teaching, wisdom, warnings, hymns or songs, and personal news.

Some writings in the New Testament that have also been called "letters" deal with more general questions that would be of concern to Christian communities almost anywhere. HEBREWS is an example of this type. Brief letters to the Seven Churches of Asia Minor appear in Revelation 2,3. The Bible books that are letters or written in the style of letters can be found after ACTS and before REVELATION.

Apocalyptic writings. "Apocalyptic" comes from the Greek word *apokalypsis,* meaning "a revealing or an unveiling." This type of literature is sometimes called prophecy. Like prophecy, apocalyptic writings deal with future events, but apocalyptic writings have certain other features that make them unique. For instance, apocalyptic literature contains visions from God, people appearing in the shape of animals or beasts, colors and numbers that have secret meanings, and predictions about a coming Day of the LORD. They were usually written during times of trouble and speak of a time when God will bring in a new creation, and everyone who has been faithful will live with God forever. DANIEL and REVELATION are two books most commonly identified as apocalyptic literature.

LITERARY FORMS FOR SECTIONS IN BOOKS

Prose narrative. Prose is a term that describes many forms of narrative and descriptive literature. Prose is often used when telling stories about people and historical events. It can include dialogue. Most of the Bible is written in prose. A very common form of prose in the Bible is the story. Some stories are short and are told in a few chapters within a book like the stories of Noah (Gen 6–10) and Joseph (Gen 37.1—47.26). Other stories take up a whole book, like RUTH, or ESTHER. As described earlier, the Gospels tell the story of Jesus' life, death, and resurrection. But the Gospels contain other stories as well, such as the story of John the Baptist (Matt 3.1-17; 11.1-19; 14.1-12). ACTS tells many stories about Peter, Paul, and other followers of Jesus who preached the good news about Jesus Christ.

Prayers. Prayers appear in the Bible in both prose and poetry. What makes "prayer" a unique category of literature is that it expresses direct communication between people and their God. PSALMS contains many prayers that are written in poetic form. Some psalm prayers were written for group worship when all the people came together to ask for God's help (Ps 79; 80), to give thanks to God at the time of har-

vest (Ps 126), or to celebrate the crowning of a new king (Ps 21). Other psalm prayers are more personal. They were used as individual prayers expressing sadness, asking for help, giving thanks, or asking for forgiveness (see Ps 12; 51; 120; 138). Prayers can be found throughout the Bible. (Some examples are Gen 18.27,28; Exod 17.4; Judg 5.2-31; 1 Sam 2.1-10; 1 Kgs 3.6-9; Jon 2.2-9; Luke 11.2-4; 22.42; John 17.1-26; Rom 16.25-27; and Heb 13.21.) Perhaps the most famous prayer in the Bible is the one Jesus taught his disciples (Matt 6.9-13).

Prophecies. Prophecies, or prophetic speeches, make up a large portion of the Old Testament. Many prophetic speeches (also called oracles) begin with the phrase "The LORD has said" or "The LORD God says." This phrase makes it clear that the message given by the prophets is not their own, but comes from God. Prophetic speeches often look like Hebrew poetry and even use some of the features of poetry, such as parallelism. The books of prophecy in the Old Testament often combine a story giving information about the prophet and his work along with his prophetic messages from God. Vivid examples of prophecies in the Old Testament include Isa 1.2-31; 10.24-27; Jer 2; Ezek 36.22-32; Amos 5.4-27; and Zech 9.1-17. The New Testament includes examples of prophetic speeches as well, especially when telling the stories of John the Baptist and Jesus (Matt 3.1-12; 24.1-31).

Parables. Parables are stories about familiar, everyday things that were told in order to teach an important truth about God and life in God's kingdom. The Gospels show that Jesus used parables frequently when talking to his disciples and to the crowd who came to hear him speak. Parables can be very short (Matt 13.44-48 is made up of three very short parables); or they can be somewhat longer, involving several characters or images (Luke 10.30-37; 15.11-32).

Long family lists (genealogies). A number of long family lists appear in the Bible. They trace the family background of important figures in Israel's history and show how people are related to one another. One particularly important list found at the beginning of MATTHEW traces Jesus' family line back to King David (Matt 1.1-17). The author of MATTHEW included this genealogy in his Gospel to show that Jesus was descended from King David and that he was the Messiah that the prophets said would come to save the people. Although it is not always clear why a list of a person's ancestors is given in the Bible, it is clear that for the people of Israel, and other people in the ancient Near East, family connections were important. Some other genealogies and lists of names are found in Genesis 5.1-32; 1 Chronicles 1–8; Ezra 8.2-14.

translating
the bible

Translation is the process of communicating a message into a language that is different from the one in which the message was originally written. The message may be in a song, a poem, a story, a telephone message, or a sermon. But if a person cannot understand that message because it is written or told in an unfamiliar language, the message must be translated. Without translation, that message will never be communicated to a new audience. This is especially important when the Bible is the message to be communicated.

The Bible is made up of many individual books that were written and told long ago in various languages quite unfamiliar to us today. These books came together over a period of more than a thousand years to form what we know as the Bible. These books were originally written in ancient Hebrew and Aramaic (for the Hebrew Scriptures/Old Testament) and in Greek (for the New Testament). Without Bible translation, people today would have to learn these three languages in order to read and understand the words of the Bible.

THE BEGINNINGS OF BIBLE TRANSLATION

The work of translating the Bible began around 250 B.C. when a group of Jewish scholars translated the Hebrew Scriptures into Greek because many Jewish people were living in places where Greek was the everyday language. This translation is known as the Septuagint. The purpose of the Septuagint was clear: to communicate the Hebrew Scriptures in the language familiar to most of the Jewish people in these particular places.

Since that first Bible translation, the words of both the Hebrew Scriptures and the New Testament have been translated into hundreds of languages. These languages include ancient languages (like Coptic, Arabic, Latin, and Syriac), as well as more recent, modern languages (like Portuguese, Russian, Navajo, Danish, Spanish, and English). The purpose behind all these Bible translations is the same as that behind the Septuagint: to put the words of the Bible into a language that people will understand.

TRANSLATING THE BIBLE INTO ENGLISH

The story of the translation of the Bible into English is long and complex. The chart called **The Bible in English,** shown on pg 1776, helps to sort through many of the difficulties in understanding this history. It is important to remember, though, that each of these English Bible translations set out to make versions of the Bible that were reliable and understandable to their audiences.

One of the most important Bible translators was William Tyndale (1484–1536), often called "The Father of the English Bible." Tyndale wanted to make the Scriptures understandable to all people. But due to the political and religious tensions that existed throughout Europe at the time, he was unable to do his translation in England. So he went to Germany, where he published his New Testament in February,

1526. Though he experienced a great deal of opposition, he continued his work of translating the Old Testament from Hebrew, and he published the Pentateuch (GENESIS through DEUTERONOMY) in 1530. In 1536, Tyndale was found guilty of heresy, and in October of that same year, he was executed.

Tyndale's influence can still be seen in what is surely the most significant English Bible translation ever done, the King James Version of the Bible, published in 1611. The King James Version (also called the Authorized Version) was prepared at the request of King James I of England at a time when several versions of the English Bible were in use (most notably the Geneva Bible, favored by Puritans, and the Bishops' and Great Bibles used by the official Church of England). Although there was resistance to the King James Version at first, it eventually won wide acceptance and became the standard English version of the Bible in the English-speaking world for three centuries. The style of the King James Version is at times unfamiliar to us today because of its very literal dependence on Hebrew and Greek sources. Still, it remains one of the most widely used English translations of the Bible today.

WHY SO MANY ENGLISH BIBLE TRANSLATIONS?

Since the publication of the King James Version, there have been dozens of English Bible translations. With so many different English Bible translations done over the past several hundred years, the Bible reader today must wonder why there are so many of them.

First, languages constantly change. New words are always being added and others take on different or added meanings. For example, only recently have we begun using the word "internet" as part of everyday speech. And when we hear the word "cool" in a conversation today, it is not always referring to the weather! These two words are examples of how the English language has recently changed.

Second, Bible scholars are always learning new things. New knowledge about ancient Israel and the Near East helps scholars better understand the historical and cultural context from which the Bible emerged. For example, we understand much more clearly today the way the various social classes interacted in the ancient world, as well as the more intimate workings of families, clans, and tribes in ancient Israel. Such discoveries sometimes affect how we understand the words and stories of the Bible.

Third, archaeologists continue to discover new documents and libraries. Discoveries often help translators better understand the ancient Hebrew and Greek languages, and that helps them translate the Bible more accurately. For example, the King James Version translates 1 Samuel 17.22 like this: "And David left his carriage in the hand of the keeper of the carriage, and ran into the army." The translators had difficulty with one of the Hebrew words in the manuscripts they used, and translated "his carriage" and "keeper of the carriage" based on the context of the narrative. When translators learned more about the Hebrew language and its vocabulary, they understood that the verse did not talk about David's "carriage," but about the "carried things" or "baggage" that he had with him for the soldiers in the army. And so, the translators of the Revised Standard Version (published in 1952) were able to translate the same verse more accurately: "And David left the things in charge of the keeper of the baggage, and ran to the ranks."

With so many translations of the Bible available today in English and other languages, it is important to remember that no matter who does a Bible translation or which basic approach is used, the purpose is to make the Bible reliable and understandable to those who want to read and hear its message of justice, hope, and love. Without the skill, sacrifice, and efforts of Bible translators, the message of the Bible might have been lost to us forever.

THE BIBLE IN ENGLISH

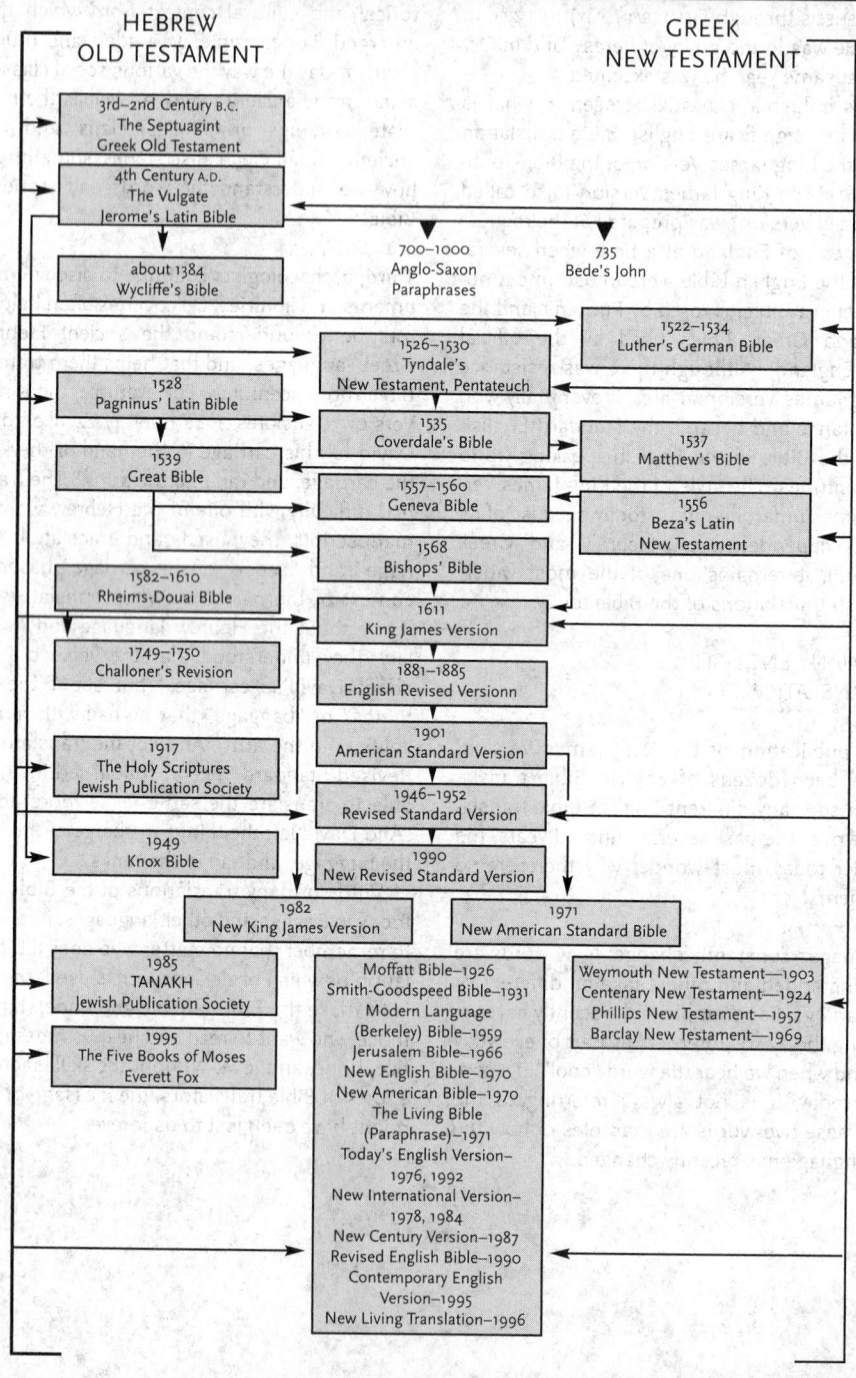

HEBREW
OLD TESTAMENT

GREEK
NEW TESTAMENT

3rd–2nd Century B.C.
The Septuagint
Greek Old Testament

4th Century A.D.
The Vulgate
Jerome's Latin Bible

about 1384
Wycliffe's Bible

700–1000
Anglo-Saxon
Paraphrases

735
Bede's John

1522–1534
Luther's German Bible

1526–1530
Tyndale's
New Testament, Pentateuch

1528
Pagninus' Latin Bible

1535
Coverdale's Bible

1537
Matthew's Bible

1539
Great Bible

1557–1560
Geneva Bible

1556
Beza's Latin
New Testament

1582–1610
Rheims-Douai Bible

1568
Bishops' Bible

1611
King James Version

1749–1750
Challoner's Revision

1881–1885
English Revised Versionn

1901
American Standard Version

1917
The Holy Scriptures
Jewish Publication Society

1946–1952
Revised Standard Version

1949
Knox Bible

1990
New Revised Standard Version

1982
New King James Version

1971
New American Standard Bible

1985
TANAKH
Jewish Publication Society

1995
The Five Books of Moses
Everett Fox

Moffatt Bible–1926
Smith-Goodspeed Bible–1931
Modern Language
(Berkeley) Bible–1959
Jerusalem Bible–1966
New English Bible–1970
New American Bible–1970
The Living Bible
(Paraphrase)–1971
Today's English Version–
1976, 1992
New International Version–
1978, 1984
New Century Version–1987
Revised English Bible–1990
Contemporary English
Version–1995
New Living Translation–1996

Weymouth New Testament—1903
Centenary New Testament—1924
Phillips New Testament—1957
Barclay New Testament—1969

archaeology and the bible

Archaeology studies past human cultures by examining the physical objects they have left behind. It includes excavating (digging) to recover objects that have been buried for long periods of time. To help gather the most information possible, many other specialists work on digs with archaeologists. These include architects, geologists, soil specialists, photographers, language and script specialists, bone and animal specialists, pottery restorers, and aerial photographers, as well as many students and volunteers.

HOW HAS ARCHAEOLOGY AFFECTED THE STUDY OF THE BIBLE?

The recovery of physical objects—especially written documents—has greatly improved biblical understanding. Archaeology has provided much information about the history and culture of ancient Israel and its surrounding neighbors. Archaeology has also helped us to understand the history, culture, and religion of the people who lived in Bible lands long before the Israelites settled there. It would be difficult to understand the Bible without some knowledge of the history and culture of the ancient Near East.

WHAT ANCIENT WRITINGS REVEAL

Bible translators sometimes have difficulty rendering accurate translations of certain Hebrew words until these words (or words similar to them) are discovered in other ancient writings. When ancient writings are compared with biblical words, the meaning of the Hebrew becomes clearer.

One important document discovered by archaeologists is the Cyrus Cylinder, a 10-inch long clay barrel. This was written in the Akkadian language in the 500's B.C. The inscription tells how King Cyrus of Persia defeated the kingdom of Babylonia. It also tells that Cyrus was generous toward his new subjects and allowed them to practice their own religions. Similarly, EZRA tells that Cyrus allowed the people of Judah to return to their homeland with what remained of the treasures that the Babylonians had taken from the temple in Jerusalem (Ezra 1.1-11). Other ancient documents, which describe events reported in EZRA and NEHEMIAH, have also been discovered through archaeology.

One of the most exciting archaeological finds ever occurred in 1947 when a shepherd boy wandered into a cave searching for a lost sheep. He found many ancient clay jars containing scrolls. The cave was located just west of the Dead Sea, so these important documents have come to be known as the "Dead Sea Scrolls." These scrolls include a variety of writings about the Essene community that lived in the wilderness area near these caves from around 250 B.C. to A.D. 68. The Essenes were a group of very religious people who left Jerusalem for religious and political reasons, and settled in the secluded location around Qumran. Perhaps the most interesting documents discovered there were the scrolls of Old Testament books, the oldest copies of Hebrew Scriptures currently in existence. Of these, the most precious find is the "Isaiah Scroll." It contains a complete copy of ISAIAH, which was copied around 150–50 B.C.

ANCIENT TEXTS RELATED TO THE OLD TESTAMENT

ANCIENT DOCUMENT AND DATE	LANGUAGE	DESCRIPTION
Gilgamesh Epic (around 1700 B.C.; some sources circulated as early as 2100 B.C.)	Akkadian	Gilgamesh, the ruler of Uruk, has many adventures and meets Utnapishtim, the only survivor of a great flood.
Enuma Elish (around 1200 B.C.)	Akkadian	A story written on seven stone tablets which tells of the Babylonian god Marduk and how the world was created.
Code of Hammurabi (around 1750 B.C.)	Akkadian	A listing of laws for the people of the kingdom of Babylonia. It has many laws similar to the Law of Moses in the Bible. Moses lived about 400 years after Hammurabi.
Ras-Shamra Tablets (around 1450 B.C.)	Ugaritic	Tells of the adventures of Canaanite gods and rulers which helps us better understand Canaanite religion and Old Testament poetry.
Amarna Letters (around 1350 B.C.)	Canaanite Akkadian	Hundreds of letters written by Canaanite scribes give information about political, social, and religious relationships between Canaan and Egypt during the rule of Egyptian Pharaohs, Amenhotep III and Akhenaten.
Merneptah Stele (around 1210 B.C.)	Egyptian	Also known as the "Israel Stele," it describes the victory of Egyptian king Merneptah over peoples from the west, including "Israel." Shows that by this time a people known as "Israel" existed in Canaan.
Gezer Calendar (around 925 B.C.)	Hebrew	A student from Israel (northern kingdom) describes the seasons, the crops, and the yearly farm work done in Israel.
Moabite Stone (around 850 B.C.)	Moabite	Describes how Mesha, king of Moab, rebelled against one of the kings of Israel who followed King Omri (see 2 Kgs 3.4).
Clay Prism of Sennacherib (around 690 B.C.)	Akkadian	The Annals Of Sennacherib describe how Sennacherib of Assyria surrounded Jerusalem and made King Hezekiah of Judah a prisoner in his own city.
Lachish Letters (around 590 B.C.)	Hebrew	Writings on pottery fragments tell about the difficult days in Jerusalem before the Babylonians surrounded the city.
Cyrus Cylinder (around 539 B.C.)	Akkadian	Describes how King Cyrus of Persia defeated the Babylonians and tells of his policies toward the peoples he ruled over and describes their gods.
Dead Sea Scrolls (some as early as 250 B.C., others as late as A.D. 70)	Hebrew Aramaic Greek	Hundreds of scrolls and scroll fragments, including the oldest existing copies of Old Testament books and passages. Some documents describe the religious community, believed to be Essenes, who wrote and collected these documents.

UNEARTHING THE PAST

Archaeology has helped to confirm some of the events reported in the Bible. Although it cannot "prove" every detail found in the Bible (since the Bible was written thousands of years ago), many archaeological excavations have provided useful evidence that in some cases supports what the Bible says. For example, archaeological evidence shows that there were many Philistines in Palestine around 1000 B.C., and that they were most likely a threat to the Israelites. This may be one reason why the people of Israel felt the need for a strong ruler (king) so that they could better defend themselves (1 Sam 8).

Also, archaeological studies of village sites in Judea dating from the sixth century B.C. show that many of them had been abandoned for a number of years before being used again. This supports the Bible's extensive description of how the Babylonians took many of the people away from Judah and into exile in Babylon from 586 B.C. to about 538 B.C.

Other important archaeological finds are those uncovered at:

Jericho, where many layers of civilizations have been unearthed, the oldest dating from before 5000 B.C., several thousand years before the Israelites conquered it (Josh 5.13—6.27). Archaeologists also uncovered the ruins of a building near Jericho from a later period. It has been identified as the winter palace of Herod the Great.

Shechem, Mount Gerizim, and Samaria, all sites in central Palestine, which are important because they were centers of royal power and worship for the northern tribes of Israel.

Megiddo, where the famous "Stables of Solomon" were found (1 Kgs 9.19). The site at Megiddo is about 70 feet deep, so several strata (layers) of material have been uncovered.

Jerusalem, where a tunnel known as "Hezekiah's Tunnel" was found. This tunnel was used to bring water into the city during the Assyrian siege in 701 B.C. (2 Kgs 20.20).

Capernaum, where an early synagogue (Jewish meeting place) was found that may relate to Mark 1.21. A fisherman's house that dates from the first century A.D. was also found nearby.

Ephesus, where the temple of Artemis was unearthed along with writings that mention the silver statues of this temple, possibly similar to those mentioned in Acts 19.24.

LEARNING ABOUT HOW PEOPLE LIVED

Some archaeological finds provide us with information on what life was like in biblical times. We have glimpses of how the royal and military rulers governed their countries; how people earned a living, produced food and goods; how buildings were built; how people worshiped, what they believed about how the world came into existence, and what they believed the future held for them.

Archaeological discoveries of ivory carvings, religious figurines, pottery, jewelry, and even animal and human bones have provided additional clues about the culture of biblical times. Skeletons found from the time of Jesus show that the average height of people was just over five feet. They also confirm that people were indeed nailed to crosses (crucified) as a form of capital punishment as described in the Gospels. Other archaeological discoveries reveal much about the types of architecture and building projects undertaken by the Romans who ruled over Palestine during the time of Jesus. All of these discoveries are useful to people who want to understand the biblical world.

the ancient world:
peoples, powers,
and politics

Hundreds of years before the people of Israel took over the land known as Canaan, their ancestors came from Mesopotamia, a land between the Tigris and Euphrates rivers far to the east. In fact, the word Mesopotamia means, "land between two rivers." Israelites trace their history back to Abraham, whose father Terah came from Ur (Gen 11.26-28). With Terah, Abraham and his wife Sarah traveled north along the Euphrates River Valley to a place called Haran, which was located in the far northwestern part of Mesopotamia. Terah wanted to settle in the land of Canaan, to the southwest and near the Mediterranean Sea, but he died in Haran (Gen 11.31,32). At Haran, God spoke to Abraham and told him to go to Canaan, the land promised to Abraham's descendants. Abraham followed God's commands and went to Canaan around 1900 B.C.

How did God's people become the nation of Israel? When did they live in the land God promised to give them? To understand these key events of the Bible, it will be helpful to look back to the centuries before Abraham was born.

A TIME BEFORE ABRAHAM AND SARAH

The most important civilizations of the ancient Near East developed in great river valleys. In the east was Mesopotamia, located in the river valleys and plains between the Tigris and Euphrates rivers. In the west was Egypt, which grew to be a strong nation beside the Nile River, the longest river in the world. In between lay the land of Canaan, west of the Jordan River. The Jordan River, fed by mountain streams, flowed past fertile land that could be used for growing crops. Perhaps even more important, Canaan was a land bridge that connected Egypt and other peoples of the Mediterranean kingdoms to the people of Mesopotamia, Babylonia, and Assyria.

Discoveries at Jericho show that people lived in villages in Canaan, Egypt, and Mesopotamia even before 5000 B.C. However, the first true civilization arose around 4000 B.C. in southern Mesopotamia near the Persian Gulf. At that time, the Sumerian people moved into the area, possibly from south central Asia. The Sumerians built cities, made canals to bring water to their fields, and created hand-painted pottery. Around 3500 B.C., they invented a system of writing called cuneiform. From 2860 to 2360 B.C., the Sumerian culture was made up of a number of powerful city-states. Each city-state had its own ruler and another leader who was in charge of the city's temple, which was built to honor the god of that city.

The Akkadian people also lived in Mesopotamia, just north of the Sumerians. Around 2360 B.C., the Akkadian rulers gained power and created a true empire in Mesopotamia. They built palaces, which replaced the temples as the centers of power. Gradually, their language began to replace the Sumerian language.

While cultures were developing in Mesopotamia, Egyptian culture was developing in Africa. Before 3000 B.C., Egypt was divided into two main kingdoms, one in Upper Egypt (south of Cairo), and the other in Lower Egypt. Around 2900 B.C., Egypt began to unite into one kingdom. This period (2675–2180 B.C.) is known as the Old Kingdom.

During this period, many cities sprang up in Canaan as well, but no single city-state dominated the others. The language of the Canaanites was likely the ancestor of the Hebrew language, the language spoken by the Israelite people.

Two centuries or so before the time of Abraham, the great kingdoms in both Mesopotamia and Egypt suffered chaotic and difficult times. The Guti and other peoples from the north invaded Mesopotamia and defeated the Akkadians. Eventually, in Egypt, rival pharaohs each claimed to be the true leader of Egypt. Without one leader, local towns formed their own governments. Then, nomadic peoples (wandering herders) entered Egypt, causing more confusion. Irrigation of fields was not kept up, which led to food shortages and starvation. In Canaan, nomadic peoples invaded and destroyed many cities. The area became dotted with small, poorly constructed villages.

In the century before Abraham, the Sumerian people, led by the kings of Ur, defeated the Guti people, and once again ruled Mesopotamia. But soon after, the Sumerian language began to disappear as the Sumerian and Akkadian peoples became more mixed. The Akkadian language became an important international language used throughout much of the ancient Near East. In Egypt, a powerful family in the city of Thebes (Upper Nile) was able to reunite the land and finally put an end to confusion. Egypt then entered a stable and prosperous period known as the Middle Kingdom.

FROM ABRAHAM TO THE TIME OF MOSES

During the nearly six hundred years between the time of Abraham and the time of Moses, Amorite people, who were centered in Babylon, ruled the land of Mesopotamia. Later, the Assyrians from the north took over the area. Cities such as Mari and Babylon became powerful and had many beautiful temples and palaces. When Hittite invaders from the north defeated the Babylonians and ended their rule, much of the Near East entered another period of disorder and turmoil.

Also around this time, Egypt had moved into a period known as the Middle Kingdom (around 2181 B.C.). The Middle Kingdom lasted until the Hyksos people invaded around 1800 B.C. The Hyksos were probably from northwest of Mesopotamia, north of the Mediterranean Sea, and they may have worshiped the gods of the Canaanites. The Hyksos ruled in Egypt for nearly two hundred years, until Egyptian rulers, who created what is known as the New Kingdom around 1600 B.C., drove the Hyksos out of Egypt.

Some time around the beginning of the New Kingdom, the descendants of Jacob (Israel) traveled to Egypt seeking food, because of a famine in Canaan. Chapters 12–50 of GENESIS tell about Abraham and Sarah's journeys and how their children and grandchildren lived as wandering herders. One of Abraham's grandsons, Jacob, was also known by the name Israel, which means "one who wrestles with God." Jacob had twelve sons, including Joseph, who became an important leader in Egypt (Gen 41.37-57). At the end of GENESIS, Jacob and his family, who were the ancestors of the people of Israel, travel to Egypt.

They apparently stayed on in Egypt for many generations. Eventually, these descendants of Abraham, who were known as Hebrews, became slaves in Egypt (Exod 1.8-14). A child called Moses was born to Hebrew parents in Egypt at a time when the pharaoh of Egypt was trying to reduce the Hebrew population by killing Hebrew male babies (Exod 1.1-22). Moses' mother and sister were able to save Moses from this fate and eventually he was adopted by pharaoh's daughter and raised in the royal household (Exod 2.1-10). When he was a young man, Moses killed an Egyptian guard and had to escape from Egypt (Exod 2.11-15). He later returned

(Exod 4.18-20), probably during the reign of the Egyptian pharaoh Rameses II (1279–1212 B.C.). Finally, with God's help, Moses led the Hebrew people out of Egypt and toward the land God had promised to give Abraham and his descendants—Canaan.

ONE GOD, ONE PEOPLE

The people who left Egypt with Moses were not yet known as the people of Israel. They did not yet really know the God who had chosen Abraham and who called Moses to return to Egypt to free his people. This God was known by the name "I Am," or Yahweh in Hebrew (Exod 3.13-15). Yahweh later gave the Law to Moses as the people wandered in the Sinai desert. The very first commandment in the Law said that the people were not to worship any other gods except Yahweh (Exod 20.1-3). While the peoples of the ancient Near East worshiped many gods, the people who eventually entered Canaan and became known as the people of Israel were to worship and follow only one God.

The people of Israel lived in a world that had seen many conflicts and wars. Control of Egypt, Mesopotamia, and Canaan had changed many times. Wars would be part of Israel's history as well. But the Israelite people also lived in a world that had already made great progress in terms of building, writing, and art. Just as God had acted in history to open the way for them, they now were about to take their place in world history and make contributions that continue to affect us today.

from joshua to the exile: the people of israel in the promised land

Moses led the people of Israel in the desert for forty years after they escaped from slavery in Egypt. When the people were camped in the lowlands of Moab on the east side of the Jordan River, Moses died, and Joshua became their new leader. The promise God made more than five hundred years earlier to Abraham (Gen 12.1,2; 15.7-21) and repeated to Joshua (Josh 1.1-8) was about to be fulfilled. Abraham's descendants, the people of Israel, were ready to take over the land of Canaan.

THE PEOPLE OF ISRAEL ENTER THE PROMISED LAND

The story of how the people of Israel conquered the people of Canaan is told in JOSHUA. Like the biblical books that tell how Moses led the people (Exod, Num, Deut), JOSHUA is full of miracles. Before the people of Israel could enter Canaan, they had to cross the Jordan River. Once again, God was with them and helped them in a miraculous way. Just as God had helped Moses by opening up the waters of the Red Sea (Exod 14), so God made the Jordan River stop flowing when the priests of Israel stepped into the river (Josh 3.15-17).

After they crossed the river and came to Gilgal, the people made a monument using twelve rocks, one rock for each tribe of Israel. They set up camp, and prepared to capture Jericho, a walled city located along an important east-west trade route in the fertile Jordan River valley. The conquest of Jericho is another miraculous story. After the Israelite priests and army marched around the city for seven days as the LORD had instructed, the priests blew their trumpets and the people shouted. The walls of the city fell flat and the Israelites captured the city (Josh 6). From Jericho, the people moved into other parts of Canaan, capturing cities in battle, and making agreements with people already living in the land.

THE TRIBES OF ISRAEL AND THEIR LANDS

Eventually Joshua gave different parts of the land of Canaan to each of Israel's twelve tribes (Josh 13–21). These tribes were like big extended families, with the oldest male (father) serving as the center of authority. As the tribes took ownership of their land, they built towns, grew crops, and raised herds of sheep and goats. The land these tribes owned was believed to have been assigned by God, and could not be sold or given to anyone else. If that did happen, the land was eventually to be returned to the tribe that first owned it. This would happen during the Year of the Celebration which was celebrated approximately every fifty years (Lev 25.8-17, 23-28).

The tribe of Levi did not get their own land, because they were given a special task and would not be farmers or herders. The Law of Moses said they would be in charge of offering sacrifices to God (Deut 18.1). Other tribes were to provide these sacrifices, and the Levites were allowed to keep some of the food sacrifices for themselves. Thus, the Levites (priests from the tribe of Levi) had an important place as the religious leaders of the other tribes: they would be the priests for all Israel.

JUDGES ARE CHOSEN TO RULE THE PEOPLE OF ISRAEL

After Joshua died, the tribes of Israel continued to fight the Canaanites (Judg 1), but they did not drive out all the people who had lived in the land. In addition, the tribes of Israel were surrounded by other peoples who were not friendly.

At this time, the Israelites began to forget the promises they had made to the LORD while Joshua was still alive. Some of them worshiped the Canaanite gods, Baal and Astarte, as well as idols of other gods from nearby lands. The LORD was so angry that he let the surrounding nations raid Israel's lands and steal their crops and possessions (Judg 2.6-15). When the people cried out for help, God felt sorry for them. Help came from special leaders known as judges. The "judges" sometimes settled legal cases (see Judg 4.4,5), but most were better known as military leaders chosen by God to lead the Israelites in battle against their enemies. The lives of these judges are described in JUDGES, chapters 3–16.

SAMUEL: PROPHET, PRIEST, AND LEADER

Near the end of the period of the judges, a boy named Samuel was born to Hannah and Elkanah (1 Sam 1). They took him to Shiloh, where he was dedicated to the LORD by the priest Eli. Samuel stayed with Eli in Shiloh and helped Eli serve the LORD. While Samuel was still very young (1 Sam 3), the LORD chose him to be his special servant and he grew up to be the LORD's prophet (1 Sam 3.19—4.1; 7.3-5). Samuel also served as a priest (1 Sam 7.9-10), as a leader (1 Sam 7.15), and is sometimes called the last of Israel's judges.

KINGS AND KINGDOMS

When Samuel was old, the leaders of Israel's tribes asked him to choose a king to rule over them, because all the lands around them were ruled by kings. Samuel believed that a king would not treat the people well (1 Sam 8.9-18), and he thought that the people's request for a king showed their lack of trust in the LORD (1 Sam 10.17-19). However, when Samuel prayed about the situation, the LORD told him to give the people a king (1 Sam 8.1-22). This was a milestone in the history of the Israelite people. Earlier, they had been a loosely connected group of tribes with one God but separate leaders. Now, they were about to become a single nation made up of tribes united not only by one God, but also by a king.

From the time of Saul (about 1030 to 1010 B.C.) and David (1010 to 970 B.C.) to the reign of Zedekiah (597 to 587 B.C.), the people of ancient Israel were ruled by kings. Some kings were strong rulers who remained faithful to God, but other kings led their people away from worshiping God, made bad agreements with Israel's enemies, and treated the people cruelly and unfairly. The history of the kings is told in 1 and 2 SAMUEL, 1 and 2 KINGS, and is retold in 1 and 2 CHRONICLES.

THE JUDGES OF ISRAEL

JUDGE	YEARS OF SERVICE	CHIEF ENEMY	ACCOMPLISHMENTS	SCRIPTURE PASSAGE
Othniel	40	Northern Syria	Helped Israel defeat King Cushan Rishathaim of Northern Syria and brought Israel forty years of peace.	Judg 3.7-11
Ehud	80	Moabites and Amalekites	Killed King Eglon of Moab and defeated the Moabites, who had joined with the Amalekites to attack Israel.	Judg 3.12-30
Shamgar	10	Philistines	Rescued Israel by killing 600 Philistines.	Judg 3.31
Deborah and Barak	40	Canaanites	Defeated the army of Canaanite King Jabin of Hazor and his commander Sisera.	Judg 4.1–5.31
Gideon	40	Midianites and Amalekites	Built an altar for worshiping the LORD and pulled down the altar where his father had worshiped the Canaanite god Baal. Defeated the Midianites who had joined with the Amalekites to steal Israel's livestock and crops. Honored the LORD by refusing to be made king.	Judg 6.1–8.35
Tola	23	Not stated in the Bible	The Bibles says he rescued Israel but gives very little information about this judge.	Judg 10.1,2
Jair	22	Not stated in the Bible	The Bible says little about this judge's accomplishments, but it does say he had thirty sons, each one in charge of a town in Gilead.	Judg 10.3-5
Jephthah	6	Ammonites and Ephraimites	Defeated the Ammonites who had invaded Gilead. Battled the army of the Israelite tribe of Ephraim.	Judg 11.1–12.7
Ibzan	7	Not stated in the Bible	The Bible says little about this judge's accomplishments, but it does say he had thirty daughters and thirty sons.	Judg 12.8-10
Elon	10	Not stated in the Bible	The Bible gives no specific information about this judge's accomplishments.	Judg 12.11,12
Abdon	8	Not stated in the Bible	The Bible says little about this judge's accomplishments, but it does say he had forty sons. and thirty grandsons.	Judg 12.13-15
Samson	20	Philistines	Took revenge on the Philistine leaders and people who burned his wife and family.	Judg 13.1—16.31

SAUL: ISRAEL'S FIRST KING

The period of the kings is divided into two main parts. The first part is the time of the United Israelite Kingdom, when there was just one king for all of the Israelite people and tribes. Samuel chose Saul to be the first king of Israel (1 Sam 9,10) and he was accepted by tribal leaders because of his courage and military abilities (1 Sam 11). He ruled for about twenty years and helped bring the tribes together and to defeat some of Israel's enemies. Yet Saul was also a troubled man who was unfaithful to God at times (1 Sam 13;15).

DAVID BECOMES ISRAEL'S KING

While Saul was still king the LORD told Samuel to go to Bethlehem to find the next king. This turned out to be David, the youngest son of Jesse (1 Sam 16.1-13). David soon entered Saul's court as a special servant who played the harp to console the troubled king (1 Sam 16.14-23). Another account of David's life shows him to be a brave soldier who trusted in the LORD. David killed the giant Philistine Goliath (1 Sam 17.1-54) and impressed the king so much that Saul made him a high officer in the army (1 Sam 18.5). Eventually, Saul became suspicious of David and jealous of his military successes. Saul tried several times to have David killed, but was never successful. Eventually, Saul committed suicide after being injured in battle against the Philistines (1 Sam 31.1-13).

After Saul's death, the people of Israel were briefly divided between loyalty to Saul's only living son, Ishbosheth, and to David, the powerful military leader. David became king of the people of Judah at Hebron (2 Sam 2.4), and then king of all of Israel after the murder of Saul's son (2 Sam 5.1-3). He then conquered the Jebusite city Jerusalem and made it the capital of the United Israelite Kingdom (2 Sam 5.6-12). He put the sacred chest on the hilltop where the temple would later be built (2 Sam 6.1-19). The prophet Nathan told David that God would dwell in the great temple in Jerusalem some day. But he said that David's son would build it, not David (2 Sam 7.1-17).

David defeated the Philistines in battle and took control of all the land east of the Jordan River and north of Damascus in Syria as far as the Euphrates River (2 Sam 8). PSALMS and books of the prophets portray David as a model king who had a close relationship with God. In many ways, he became a symbol of new life for God's people and of God's rule in the world (2 Sam 23.5; Ps 89.3,4; Isa 9.1-7; Jer 33.14-26; Mic 5.2-5). However, David was not always perfect (2 Sam 11;12).

SOLOMON: ISRAEL'S WISEST KING

David's son, Solomon, became king after David died and ruled from about 970 to 931 B.C. Solomon was known as a wise man (1 Kgs 2.9; 3.12,28; 4.29-34), and he was in charge of building Israel's first temple in Jerusalem (1 Kgs 5–8). He expanded David's kingdom, built an enormous palace (1 Kgs 7.1-12) and many fortresses, established store cities, and made Israel a very rich country (1 Kgs 4.20-28). In doing this, Solomon married foreign wives and let them to set up shrines and monuments to other gods (1 Kgs 11.1-13), things which were certainly not pleasing to the LORD.

THE KINGDOM IS DIVIDED

When Solomon died around 922 B.C., his son Rehoboam became king. Shortly after that, the ten northern tribes rebelled against the king and formed their own kingdom. This period of Israel's history became known as the Divided Kingdom.

The tribes of Judah and Benjamin in the south became known as the kingdom of Judah (or the southern kingdom). The other tribes to the north formed the kingdom of Israel (or the northern kingdom). Each kingdom had its own king. In Judah, the kings continued to be descendants of King David, but in Israel the tribal and military leaders fought to become king. Jerusalem remained the capital of Judah, and the people of Judah still worshiped the LORD in its temple. But in Israel, King Jeroboam I made a shrine in Bethel so that people could offer sacrifices there instead of going to the temple in Jerusalem (1 Kgs 12.25-33). Later, Samaria became the capital city of Israel (1 Kgs 16.24-29).

ISRAEL: THE NORTHERN KINGDOM

In the northern kingdom of Israel, some rulers allowed people to worship idols such as the Canaanite god Baal. This practice was condemned by a number of prophets who preached in Israel during this time. For example, the prophet Elijah spoke out against King Ahab and his wife Queen Jezebel, who encouraged the worship of Baal and supported Baal's prophets (see 1 Kings 18.1—19.18).

The practice of allowing the worship other gods led to Israel's downfall. They fought civil wars with Judah and battled with neighbors like Syria and Moab. Eventually, the Assyrians invaded Israel and attacked the capital city of Samaria. In 722 B.C., the city was conquered. Many of the Israelites were captured and taken away to Assyria as prisoners. Israelites who remained often married people the Assyrians had brought in to settle the land. The northern kingdom of Israel never regained its power as a nation.

JUDAH: THE SOUTHERN KINGDOM

Meanwhile, Judah in the south had its own problems. Though many of its kings, such as Hezekiah and especially Josiah, were faithful to God and followed the teachings of the Law of Moses (2 Kgs 18.1-8; 2 Kgs 22.1—23.25), other kings, like Manasseh, did things to make the LORD angry (2 Kgs 21.1-18). Eventually Judah could no longer hold out against the attacks of its powerful neighbors. The kingdom of Babylon finally invaded and destroyed Jerusalem and its temple in 587 B.C. Many of the people of Judah were taken to Babylon as prisoners. During the next fifty years, this group of Israelites remained in Babylon and could not return to their own land. This period is known as "the exile."

THE KINGS OF ISRAEL

This chart lists all of the kings of Israel starting with the three who ruled the United Israelite Kingdom. After Solomon's death, the northern tribes broke away from the southern tribes and continued to call themselves Israel. The southern tribes came to be known as Judah. The prophets, shown in *italics*, sometimes spoke to the people of the northern or southern kingdoms, and sometimes to both.

DATE	THE UNITED ISRAELITE KINGDOM		
1050 B.C.		Saul (1030–1010)	*Eli*
1000 B.C.	*Nathan*	David (1010–970)	*Samuel*
950 B.C.		Solomon (970–931)	

DATE	Judah (Southern Kingdom)	The Kingdom Divides *Prophets*	Israel (Northern Kingdom)
950 B.C.	Rehoboam (931–913) Abijah (913–911) Asa (911–870)		Jeroboam (931–910) Nadab (910–909) Baasha (909–886)
900 B.C.	Jehoshaphat (870–848)	*Elijah*	Elah (886–885) Zimri (7 days in 885) Omri (885–874) Ahab (874–853) Ahaziah (853–852)
850 B.C.	Jehoram (848–841) Ahaziah (of Judah, 841) Queen Athaliah (841–835) Joash (835–796)	*Elisha*	Joram (852–841) Jehu (841–814)
800 B.C.	Amaziah (796–781) Uzziah (781–740)	*Jonah*	Jehoahaz (814–798) Jehoash (798–783) Jeroboam II (783–743)
750 B.C.	Jotham (740–736) Ahaz (736–716) Hezekiah (716–687)	*Amos* *Isaiah* *Micah*	*Hosea* Zechariah (6 mos. in 743) Shallum (1 mo. in 743) Menahem (743–738) Pekah (737–732) Hoshea (732–723)
700 B.C.	Manasseh (687–642)		Assyrians defeat Israel and capture its capital, Samaria, 722. Kingdom of Israel ends.
650 B.C.	Amon (642–640) Josiah (640–609) Joahaz (3 mos. in 609) Jehoiakim (609–598) Jehoiachin (3 mos. in 598) Zedekiah (598–587)	*Zephaniah (640–609)* *Nahum (663–612)* *Jeremiah* *Habakkuk (620–597)* *Ezekiel*	
600 B.C.	Babylonians defeat Judah and destroy Jerusalem, 587 or 586. The exile in Babylon, 586–538.		

All dates are approximate.

after the exile: god's people return to judea

IN BABYLON

The Bible provides little information about the years in the sixth century B.C. when many of the Israelite people lived in exile in Babylon. Though the people could no longer worship God in the temple in Jerusalem, the Babylonians allowed them to gather and practice their religion. The Israelites told the stories of their ancestors, heard the words of prophets, and studied the Law of Moses. Some believe that it was during the time of the exile that some of Israel's priests added to the old Scriptures and wrote new ones, so the people would not forget who they were and where they came from.

BACK HOME IN JUDEA

Between the years 597 to 582 B.C., many of the Jewish people had been sent into exile. In 539 B.C., Cyrus of Persia conquered Babylonia. About one year later, he gave the Jewish people permission to return to their homeland of Judea. The books of EZRA and NEHEMIAH in the Old Testament tell about the hundred-year period that followed the time of the exile. The books of the prophets Haggai and Zechariah also come from this time. Sometime between 500 and 425 B.C., the priest named Ezra encouraged the people to take back their Jewish traditions and to obey the Law of Moses. He went so far as to force Jewish men to give up their foreign wives (Ezra 9,10).

Two religious issues were most important to the people who had returned from exile: (1) worship of the God of Israel in the rebuilt temple in Jerusalem, and (2) study of the Law of Moses to see how God's people were to live in the present situation. Also in this period, Nehemiah served for a time as governor of Judea and helped supervise the rebuilding of Jerusalem's walls. Though the people had the freedom to worship as they wished, their land was still under control of the Persians.

OUTSIDE OF JUDEA

While some of the Jewish people were settling back in Jerusalem, others stayed in the lands ruled by Persia or moved on to other major cities in the eastern Mediterranean world. Some of these groups developed their own collections of the Jewish Scriptures and their own methods of interpreting them. Jewish groups also appeared in Syria and Asia Minor, in North Africa, and on islands in the Mediterranean. Many Jewish writings of the period after the exile come from Alexandria in Egypt, where Jewish teachers read their Scriptures along with Greek philosophy. These teachers believed that this approach would help people to understand the basic truths of the Bible.

THE INFLUENCE OF ALEXANDER THE GREAT

Between 336 B.C. and 323 B.C., Alexander the Great conquered much of the eastern Mediterranean world, including Egypt, Palestine (where Jerusalem was located), and much of Persia. After Alexander died, these lands were ruled for over a century by his generals or those who followed them. The most important of these rulers were the Seleucids, who controlled Syria, and the Ptolemies, who controlled Egypt. One or the other of these royal families ruled Palestine, the land of the Jewish people, for much of this time. However, in 168 B.C. the Seleucid king, Antiochus IV, began to try to stop people from practicing the Jewish religion. He declared that it was forbidden to study the Law of Moses, observe the Sabbath, or practice circumcision. Antiochus IV also set up a statue of the Greek god Zeus in the Jewish temple. His actions deeply offended the Jewish people.

Greek, Roman, and Persian philosophies and ideas influenced Jewish writings of the time. This influence is apparent in many of the books that are included in some editions of the Bible and known as "deuterocanonical" or "apocryphal."

The religion of the Jewish people after the exile in Babylon did not move toward one single pattern or style. People were practicing Judaism and living as Jews in a variety of ways. This was the situation when Jesus came to teach the people many new things about God and God's kingdom.

THE JEWISH PEOPLE RECLAIM THEIR LAND

The Jewish people revolted against the Seleucid king, Antiochus IV. The rebellion broke out suddenly. Soon the rebellion had a leader named Judas Maccabeus. (One of the possible meanings for his last name is "the hammer.") Led by Judas Maccabeus, the small bands of Jewish fighters defeated the mighty army of Antiochus. This revolt is described in 1 and 2 *MACCABEES*.) Eventually the rebels purified the temple, an event still remembered by Jews today in the celebration of Hanukkah.

Finally, the Maccabees set up their own government. Those Maccabean rulers who came after Judas called themselves by the title of king, even though they were not descendants of King David or from the tribe of Judah. This upset many Jews, who did not like the Maccabeans' cruel style of control and the agreements they made with Rome in order to remain in power. The rule of the Maccabees lasted until the Roman general Pompey invaded Jerusalem and brought all the land under direct Roman control in 63 B.C.

Because they were bitterly disappointed over the Maccabean political rule, some of the Jewish people turned to other kinds of religions or philosophies. For example, one group of Jews became very disappointed with the temple priests in Jerusalem who seemed to love the wealth and power connected with running the temple. This group withdrew from Jewish society and lived as a separate community in a barren area near the Dead Sea. They remained there, living in complete obedience to God's Law as they understood it. They believed that God would help them drive out the present priests and rebuild the city of Jerusalem and the temple. In the middle of the twentieth century, many books and writings of this group were discovered in a place called Qumran near the Dead Sea. These writings are known as the Dead Sea Scrolls. Included in these scrolls is the oldest surviving copy of ISAIAH, as well as the rule books for this community.

prophets and prophecy

A prophet is someone who speaks God's message. The message the prophet speaks is called a "prophecy." In general culture, prophets are sometimes compared with fortunetellers or those who predict future events. The prophets of the Old Testament, however, were somewhat different. Their task was to observe what was happening around them and then to deliver God's message for that situation. Their messages were given both to God's people and to those who did not trust in Israel's God. Sometimes the message was a warning to the people or their leaders that they were not obeying God, and that they should change their ways. Sometimes the prophets brought words of hope in tough times, or said that even though things were bad in the present, God would make things better in the future.

PROPHETS IN THE OLD TESTAMENT

The Old Testament includes fifteen books written by or called by the names of different prophets, but these are not the only prophets who had an impact on the people of Israel. Some prophets were connected with other temples or kings, and some acted on their own. Using the very broad definition of prophet as one who speaks God's message, people from Israel's earliest history were called prophets: Abraham (Gen 20.7), Aaron (Exod 7.1), Miriam (Exod 15.20), Moses (Deut 18.18; 34.10), and Deborah (Judg 4.4). Moses certainly passed God's message to the people of Israel, but he also spoke to God for them. This was also the task of prophets.

Samuel, the last of Israel's judges, was known as a prophet (1 Sam 3.20).

Some prophets described in the Old Testament went into a kind of trance when they prophesied. They lost control of their speech and actions and were not aware of what was happening around them. Some of these prophets were defeated in a contest with Israel's prophet, Elijah (875–845 B.C.), to try to prove who was stronger, Israel's God *Yahweh*, or the Canaanite god, Baal. The prophets of Baal acted as if they were caught up in a trance and began to dance. They even used their swords to cut themselves until blood poured out (1 Kgs 18.24-29).

Other Old Testament prophets include Balaam of Pethor near the Euphrates River, who was hired by the king of Moab to put a curse on Israel (Num 22.2—24.25). The prophet Nathan gave King David the good news that his descendants would always rule the people of Israel (2 Sam 7.11-16), but Nathan also delivered God's angry message after David had arranged the death of a man named Uriah so that he could have Uriah's wife Bathsheba. Because of this evil action, Nathan told David that David and Bathsheba's son would die (2 Sam 12.1-14). Another prophet named Micaiah warned King Ahab that he would die in battle against the Syrian army (1 Kgs 22.5-38). Elisha became Elijah's assistant and eventually took his place (1 Kgs 19.19-21; 2 Kgs 2.1-18). He was the prophet who healed Naaman (2 Kgs 5.1-14). Another prophet, Huldah, gave advice to King Josiah (640–609 B.C.) when Josiah asked what he should do with *The Book of God's Law* that had been found in the temple (2 Kgs 22.14-20).

THE WRITINGS OF THE PROPHETS

After the death of King Solomon, the kingdom of Israel split into two sections (northern and southern) around 931 B.C. Each kingdom had its own temple and king, and prophets in both kingdoms of Israel gave warnings and encouragement to the rulers and the people. The first books of the prophets probably date back to just after 800 B.C. The prophecies of Amos and Hosea were written for the rulers and the people of the northern kingdom (Israel). They warned the leaders and the rich people to care for the poor and stop worshiping idols.

About the same time, the prophets Micah and Isaiah delivered their prophecies in the southern kingdom (Judah). Isaiah warned that a king would come from the east to take over the land and force the people to leave. He called the people to obey God in order to avoid the punishment that he predicted, but he also gave them the promise that God would help them triumph in the end.

Jeremiah, Zephaniah, Nahum, and Habakkuk were prophets in Judah before Babylon defeated it in 586 B.C. and took many of its people taken captive. About the time Jeremiah was finishing his work as a prophet, Ezekiel began to bring God's message to the people. His prophecies were given to the people of Judah before they were taken away from their homes and forced to live in exile, and continued into the period of the exile in Babylon, where Ezekiel was also taken as captive. The last part of his prophecy includes a great vision of the future when God would rebuild the temple in Jerusalem and bring a new day for God's people (Ezek 40–46).

After the people of Judah were allowed to leave Babylon and return home, the prophets Haggai and Zechariah delivered God's message. Speaking around 520 B.C., Haggai told the people that God wanted them to rebuild the temple. About the same time, Zechariah told the people the LORD's chosen king would again rule in Jerusalem and that all people on earth would someday worship Israel's God. Still later came the prophecies of Malachi, who told the priests to be faithful to the agreement the LORD had made with Israel. The prophet Obadiah probably wrote some time after 587 B.C. when the country of Edom helped Babylon defeat Judah. And the prophet Joel delivered his message of judgment and hope after the people returned from captivity in Babylon.

Unlike other prophetic books, JONAH gives only one sentence of what Jonah preached (3.4). The rest of the book tells about how Jonah tried to run away when God told him to preach to the people of Nineveh, the capital of Assyria, who were enemies of Israel. The first half of DANIEL tells about Daniel and what happened to him in Babylon. The second half of DANIEL tells of Daniel's vision of the future when God would help bring victory to his people. Daniel's vision belongs to a kind of writing known as "apocalyptic."

PROPHECY AND THE NEW TESTAMENT

The New Testament focuses on the life and work of Jesus Christ. The New Testament writers used the Jewish Scriptures, especially the writings of the prophets, to show that Jesus was God's promised Messiah. For example, MATTHEW often uses the phrase, "just as the prophet had said" which is followed by a quote from one of the Old Testament prophets (Matt 1.22; 2.5-6,17-18; 4.14-16). Each quote is meant to show that Jesus' life fulfills what one of the prophets said hundreds of years earlier. In his letters, the apostle Paul quoted the Old Testament prophets to show that Jesus was God's chosen one who had come to save all people, Jews and Gentiles alike (Rom 9.25,26,33; 15.11,12).

The New Testament writers also used the words of the prophet Isaiah to show that John the Baptist was the one who had been sent to prepare the way for Jesus (Matt 3.1-3; Luke 3.3-6). And John preached like a prophet, telling the people to turn to God and get ready for the one (Jesus) who would baptize them with the Holy Spirit (Mark 1.7,8; Luke 3.15-17).

Jesus quoted the Old Testament prophets to show that he was the Son of Man who would come from heaven with power and great glory (Matt

24.29,30 quotes Joel 2.10; Matt 26.64 quotes Dan 7.13,14). Jesus also said that he was the shepherd who would be rejected and struck down (Matt 26.31 quotes Zech 13.7). He applied the writing of the prophet Isaiah to himself, explaining why he had come to earth (Luke 4.16-21 quotes Isa 61.1). Paul said it was because God's purpose for people and all creation was fulfilled in Jesus (1 Cor 15.20-28), who overcame the powers of evil.

PROPHECY AND THE CHURCH

Some of the followers of Jesus received the special gift of prophecy from God's Spirit (Rom 12.6; 1 Cor 12.27-31). These New Testament prophets were to use this gift to speak God's messages of truth (1 Cor 14.29-32). God's followers are also warned to watch out for false prophets who would try to lead them away from the truth about God (1 Tim 6.2-10; 2 Pet 2.1-3). REVELATION warns of a false prophet who would perform fake miracles and make false predictions in an effort to trick God's people (Rev 13.11-15), and the faithful are told to listen only to the message of God's true prophets (Rev 22.18,19).

people of the law: the religion of israel

The faith of Israel, now more commonly known as the Jewish faith, did not begin as a set of religious practices or system of beliefs. Rather, it began when God commanded Abraham to leave his home and take his wife Sarah and family to a new land called Canaan. Along with this command, God promised Abraham three things: (1) Abraham would have many descendants who would become a great nation; (2) his descendants would be famous and have a land they could call their own; and (3) God would bless Abraham's descendants, and everyone on earth would be blessed because of them (Gen 12.1-3; 15.1-6; 17.1-8).

In return for these promises, Abraham and his descendants were to trust in God alone and obey what God told them to do. A special agreement (also known as a "covenant") had been formed. Abraham confirmed this agreement with God by having his son and all his male descendants circumcised (Gen 17.9-27). Having male children circumcised became an important sign of belonging to God's special people.

The faith of Israel was unique among the religions of the ancient world because they believed that God (*Yahweh*) had selected them to be his special (chosen) people. They believed God acted in history and was involved in the life of the whole community. God's relationship was with all the people, not just with a few individuals or the community's leaders. They believed only in *Yahweh* and did not worship any other gods.

THE LORD GIVES HIS CHOSEN PEOPLE THE LAW

The Bible describes how God was at work in the history of the Hebrew people (later called Israelites). When they went to Egypt to escape a famine (Gen 42), God took care of them. Later, God helped them escape from slavery in Egypt (Exod 12–14). The festival called Passover commemorates this important event, and is observed by Jewish people today.

God made an important agreement with the Israelite people at Mount Sinai, a place in the desert where Moses and the Israelites arrived after escaping from Egypt (Exod 19.1-2). At Sinai, God gave the Law to Moses and the people. This Law includes the Ten Commandments (Exod 20.2-17; Deut 5.6-21) and other instructions about how the Israelite people should live together and worship God. Other sections of this Law of Moses are given in Exodus 19–34, LEVITICUS, and DEUTERONOMY. The Law includes rules about making sacrifices to God, about how to treat others, and about who would be in charge of Israel's worship. It also included instructions about observing special festivals and holy days and explained what should happen if someone broke a law. At this point in their history, the people of Israel did not need a system of government or a constitution because they were supposed to live according to the Law of Moses. God promised that if the people followed the Law they would be rewarded. But if they were unfaithful to God and did not live according to the Law, they could expect to be punished (Exod 20.5,6; Lev 25.14-46).

THE PEOPLE ENTER THE LAND
GOD PROMISED THEM

In addition to the Law, God also gave Moses instructions for making a sacred tent (also known as the Tabernacle). The people would gather to worship God and offer sacrifices (Exod 25–30). This tent had three sections:

The outer area. This is where animals were sacrificed and burned on an altar. There was also a bronze bowl in this area for the priests to wash their hands (Exod 27.1-19; 30.17-21).

A holy place. This area had a table, a golden candlestick, and an altar where incense was burned. The altar and table were made of acacia wood and covered with gold. A special kind of bread called Sacred Bread, or the Bread of the Presence was kept on the table. Twelve loaves of bread, one for each of Israel's tribes, were to be set out on the table every Sabbath (the day of rest), and only the priests were permitted to eat it (Lev 24.5-9). The lampstand was made of gold and had seven branches that curved upward. An oil-burning lamp was placed on each of the seven branches (Exod 25.31-40). The lampstand had seven branches probably because seven was a holy number that symbolized the Sabbath, the seventh day of the week (the day God rested after creating the world; see Gen 2.1,2).

The most holy place (holy of holies). This is where God was said to be present and where the sacred chest (or ark) containing the stone tablets of the Law was kept. The sacred chest was covered with gold and measured about four feet long and was just over two feet wide and high. Gold rings were put on each side, so the people could carry the chest with them when they moved from place to place (Exod 25.10-22). The lid of the box (traditionally called the mercy seat), was where God "sat" (was present) to be among the people, to receive their sacrifices, and to meet a representative of the people (Exod 26.34). Only Moses, and later the high priest, were allowed to enter the most holy place. It was separated from the rest of the tent by a curtain (Exod 27.21) and inside was a lamp that was to be kept burning (Exod 27.20).

Each of the areas of the sacred tent was separated from the others by curtains. A frame made of 48 acacia wood planks supported the whole tent, and it measured about 150 feet by 75 feet. The people carried the sacred tent and sacred chest with them as they journeyed. When they finally entered Canaan, they divided it among Israel's twelve tribes. At this point, there was no single leader and no government in charge of the people. What the people shared in common was their faith in *Yahweh*, which their tribal leaders renewed at the central place of worship at Shechem (Josh 24.1-28).

The agreement God had made with Abraham and Sarah was beginning to take shape. *Yahweh* had led the people of Israel out of slavery in Egypt and had helped them get their own land. With each new generation, the people of Israel grew in number and began to enjoy the blessings of living in the promised land. But the people had a difficult time being completely loyal to God, so problems arose.

JUDGES describes how God raised up special leaders, called judges, to help the people in times of crisis. Israelites lived in this way for many years, until the people begged the judge and prophet named Samuel to give them a king like the ones who ruled neighboring countries. God eventually told Samuel to choose Saul as Israel's first king (1 Sam 8–10). Later, David was made king (1 Sam 16). David captured Jerusalem and made it the capital of Israel and the single place of worship for all the tribes (2 Sam 5,6). He even set up the sacred tent in Jerusalem on a hill that was known as Zion.

David's son Solomon built the first temple to take the place of the sacred tent. The temple was built using cedar, olive wood, and brick, with beautiful decorations made of gold and ivory. Like the sacred tent, the temple had three areas, but in the temple a large olive wood door, instead of a curtain, separated the holy place from the most holy place

(1 Kgs 6.1-38; 7.13—8.13). It took seven years to build Solomon's temple, which was dedicated sometime between 960 and 950 B.C. during the Festival of Shelters (1 Kgs 8.62-65).

After King Solomon died, the ten northern tribes of Israel broke away and made Shechem and then Tirzah their capital. They created several places of worship (1 Kgs 12.25-33), and some of the northern leaders, such as Ahab and Jezebel, encouraged the people to worship the Canaanite god Baal (1 Kgs 18). They also built idols to worship the local gods (1 Kgs 14.15). This was one of the things God and God's prophets had warned the people not to do. Because the people did not remain loyal to *Yahweh* alone, they were punished. In 722 B.C. the Assyrians invaded (Israel) the northern kingdom and took most of the people from their homeland to live in Assyria (2 Kgs 17). The people of the southern kingdom (Judah) saw this as God's punishment for the northern tribes' disobedience to God.

Later the people of Judah also disobeyed God and were invaded by the Babylonians, who destroyed Jerusalem and the temple in 586 B.C. Solomon's temple had stood for nearly four hundred years, but the Babylonian invasion put a temporary end to worship at the temple. Israel's priests and prophets were forced to discover how Israel's faith could survive in exile, far away from Jerusalem in captivity in Babylon.

ISRAEL RETURNS AND REBUILDS THE TEMPLE

The people of Israel lived in exile in Babylon for about fifty years, but the priests and teachers of Israel did not let their faith die. Although the temple was destroyed, and they were far from home, they still had God's Word in the Scriptures and in their hearts. Some scholars believe that the time of exile marked a renewed commitment to God and to studying Scripture. The Jewish people probably continued to meet for worship, but they had to do so in private homes.

In 540 B.C. the Persians defeated the Babylonians. The Persian ruler, Cyrus, followed the Persian cus-

tom of allowing captured people to return to their homelands and to worship freely, as long as they promised not to start a revolt against the Persians. Many, but not all Israelites, did return to Judah beginning in 539 B.C. They completed work on a new, smaller temple ("the second temple") in 515 B.C. (Ezra 3–6). The prophet Haggai said it could not compare with Solomon's temple (Hag 2.3), but it was used for more than four hundred years, somewhat longer than Solomon's temple was used.

Two men, Ezra and Nehemiah, were especially important leaders during the first hundred years after the people returned to Judah from exile. Ezra, a Jewish priest and scribe, studied the Law of Moses and taught it to the people (Neh 8). Copies of the Law of Moses and the historical records were recovered, edited, and again became the basic guidelines for the relationship between the God and the people of Israel. Nehemiah, who was appointed by the Persian king to be governor of Judah, supervised the reconstruction of the walls of Jerusalem (Neh 2–6).

During the centuries after the second temple was built and before Jesus was born, the people of Israel were often under the rule of foreign powers. This caused them to start thinking of themselves more as a religious group than as a nation with physical boundaries and a political leadership of its own. At this time, the most important feature of Israel's religion, which had come to be known as Judaism, was its stress on keeping the Law of Moses. To be a Jew meant following the Law of Moses. This included observing all the religious festivals as well as the special rules for priests and worship in the temple.

HEROD REBUILDS AND ENLARGES THE TEMPLE

In 37 B.C., the Romans named a local leader ruler of Judah. In 20 B.C., Herod received permission to rebuild and expand the temple. Most of the building was completed in a year and a half, but work continued on the temple for another forty to fifty years, into the time when Jesus began his teaching (John 2.20). This expanded second temple, sometimes called "Herod's temple," was built on a huge four-sided platform that was almost a mile around its base. Some of its stones are still in place today on the temple site in Jerusalem. What is left of this "temple mount" can be seen clearly at the site called the "Western Wall" (or "Wailing Wall"), where many Jews still go to pray. The temple itself was surrounded by a large wall that had many different entrances. In addition to the traditional sections discussed earlier—an altar area where burnt offerings were sacrificed by the priests, a holy area, where only priests were allowed, and the most holy place (or holy of holies), where only the high priest was allowed to go—the second temple also included a women's court.

The religious life of the temple went on in clear view of the Romans, who occupied the Antonia Fortress built right outside the northwest corner of the wall surrounding the temple area. This fortress was the living quarters for a large number of Roman soldiers, whose job was to keep peace in Jerusalem (Acts 21.34-37). The Roman governor's official residence was in Caesarea, but he usually stayed at this fortress while in Jerusalem.

During the time of Herod's temple, the Romans were in charge of Jerusalem and Judea. They did, however, allow a council of local Jewish leaders, including the high priest and other important religious and business leaders, to have some control over settling local matters, especially those having to do with the temple and religious issues. For example, no Gentile (non-Jew) was allowed in the inner parts of the temple. If someone broke this law, the Jewish leaders could call upon the Roman authorities to put the offender to death.

Jesus' prediction that the temple would be destroyed (Mark 13.1,2) came to pass when the Romans destroyed Herod's temple while putting down a Jewish revolt that lasted between A.D. 64 and 70. The Roman emperor Hadrian (A.D. 117–138) crushed a second Jewish revolt about A.D. 131. In 132, Hadrian built a temple to honor the Roman god Jupiter on the same site, and in the seventh century A.D., Muslims built a mosque called the Dome of the Rock on the temple site. The shrine and mosque are still standing today, as are a few parts of Herod's original temple area.

THE ROLE OF ISRAEL'S PRIESTS

According to the agreement God made with Moses, all the people of Israel were to serve God as priests (Exod 19.5,6). They would be God's holy nation among all the other nations. The Law of Moses also set aside special priests to represent the whole people in their relationship with God. The priests of Israel were to be from the tribe of Levi. Those who were not born into this tribe could not serve as priests.

The priesthood of Israel appears to fall into three levels. In the lowest level were those Levites who were not direct descendants of Moses' brother Aaron (see Num 3.5-13). They were to help the priests and take care of the furnishings in the sacred tent (and later, in the temple). At the next level were the priests who were responsible for offering sacrifices and leading the worship. These priests were also from the Levite tribe, but had to be direct descendants of Aaron. The Levites and the priests were divided into twenty-four groups or shifts. Each group served in the temple for one week on a rotating basis. With twenty-four groups, a particular priest might serve for a total of two or, very occasionally, three weeks each year. At the head of the priesthood was the high priest. He was in charge of the other priests, and was the only priest who could enter the most holy place to offer sacrifices on the Great Day of Forgiveness (Lev 16.1-25).

When the Jewish people returned to Jerusalem after exile in Babylon, the Persian king would not allow them to have their own king. Because they could not have a king, the high priest became an even more significant person in the life of the people. In the centuries before Jesus and during Jesus' lifetime, the high priest was the head of the temple and of the Jewish people.

WORSHIP AND FESTIVALS

The worship practices of Israel included the offering of prayers, and Scripture reading. Selected texts were read for certain occasions, and sometimes songs were sung. PSALMS includes prayers and songs that were sung or said in worship by the whole people or used by individuals in private prayer. The text of Deuteronomy 6.4 ("Hear, O Israel," called the *Shema*) was to be said in prayer every morning and evening.

One of the most important aspects of the religious life of the Jewish people, both before and after the exile, was the keeping of the Sabbath (Exod 20.8-11; 31.12-17). On the Sabbath, the seventh day of the week, Jews are commanded not to do any work and to rest, just as God rested after creating the world in six days (Gen 1.1—2.4). The Sabbath is also devoted to prayer and to remembering how God brought the Israelite people out of slavery in Egypt. On this day, they and their children, their servants, their visitors, and even their livestock should rest and not work (Deut 5.12-15).

The festival celebrations that were commanded in the Law of Moses and established by Jewish tradition greatly influenced Israel's life of faith. These celebrations can be grouped according to the time they were to take place as well as by purpose.

THE CALENDAR IN THE ANCIENT WORLD

As in other parts of the ancient Near East, the people of Israel developed a calendar that was based on the yearly movement of the sun and on the phases of the moon. The year was divided into twelve months, based on the observation that the moon's phases changed about twelve times in the period of days that made up a year. The number of days in the lunar (moon-based) year was about eleven days shorter than the solar (sun-based) year, so the Israelites periodically added an extra month to the calendar to make sure that the festivals they celebrated would continue to fall at their expected times in relation to the weather patterns (seasons) and agricultural cycles (planting and harvesting).

Early in Israelite history the year was considered to begin in the beginning of the seventh month (around the fall fruit harvest). Later, it was considered to begin in the spring on the first new moon after the vernal equinox (one of two times in the year when day and night are equal in length).

Time was measured, however, more often by seasons than by names of months. The year was divided into the dry season (April to September) and the rainy season (October to March). These, in turn, were divided into times for planting grain (November to December) and harvesting (April to June). Further, specific agricultural activities were undertaken in specific months. For example, wheat was harvested in March and April, grapes matured in June and July, and summer fruit was picked in August and September.

The months themselves had religious significance for the people of Israel. The beginning of each month (when the moon is "new") was considered a holy time and New Moon Festivals were celebrated (Num 28.11-15). Most of the yearly religious festivals had traditional associations with agricultural events as well as to the events in Jewish history they commemorated.

SABBATH: A WEEKLY FESTIVAL

The word Sabbath is from the Hebrew verb *shabbat*, "to stop" or "to rest," and refers to the seventh day of the week, from sunset on Friday to sunset on Saturday. The ancient Israelites, like modern Jews, worship on the Sabbath and rest from their work.

The Bible's description of the Sabbath's origin is found in Genesis 2.1-3. These verses come at the end of the creation story and tell how God rested from the work of creation on the seventh day and made it a special, holy day. In EXODUS, a connection is made between God's resting from creation and Israel's command to rest from work on the Sabbath and to worship the LORD (Exod 20.8-11; 31.17). This resting from work was not for the Israelites alone, but for their animals and servants (including

PILGRIMAGE FESTIVALS

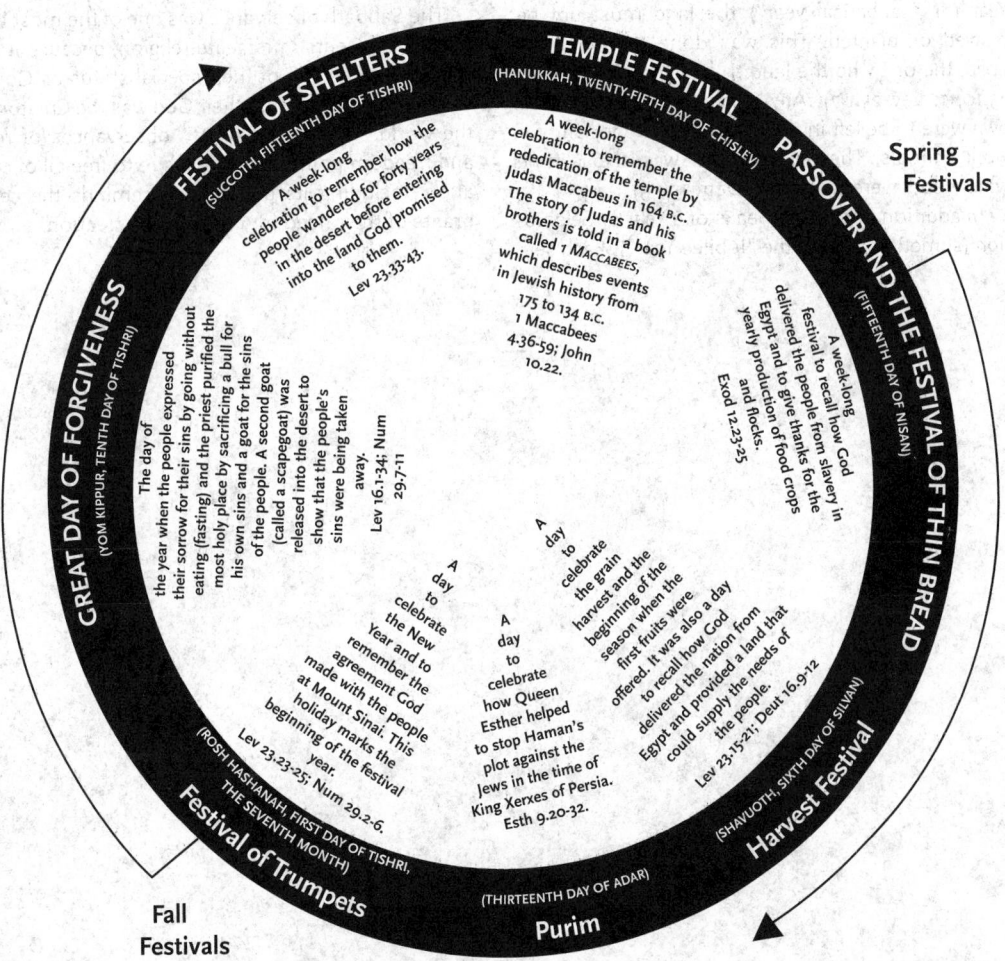

FESTIVAL OF SHELTERS
(SUCCOTH, FIFTEENTH DAY OF TISHRI)

A week-long celebration to remember how the people wandered for forty years in the desert before entering into the land God promised to them. Lev 23.33-43.

TEMPLE FESTIVAL
(HANUKKAH, TWENTY-FIFTH DAY OF CHISLEV)

A week-long celebration to remember the rededication of the temple by Judas Maccabeus in 164 B.C. The story of Judas and his brothers is told in a book called 1 MACCABEES, which describes events in Jewish history from 175 to 134 B.C. 1 Maccabees 4.36-59; John 10.22.

PASSOVER AND THE FESTIVAL OF THIN BREAD
(FIFTEENTH DAY OF NISAN)

A week-long festival to recall how God delivered the people from slavery in Egypt and to give thanks for the yearly production of food crops and flocks. Exod 12.23-25.

Spring Festivals

GREAT DAY OF FORGIVENESS
(YOM KIPPUR, TENTH DAY OF TISHRI)

The day of the year when the people expressed their sorrow for their sins by going without eating (fasting) and the priest purified the most holy place by sacrificing a bull for his own sins and a goat for the sins of the people. A second goat (called a scapegoat) was released into the desert to show that the people's sins were being taken away. Lev 16.1-34; Num 29.7-11

A day to celebrate the New Year and to remember the agreement God made with the people at Mount Sinai. This holiday marks the beginning of the festival year. Lev 23.23-25; Num 29.2-6.

Festival of Trumpets
(ROSH HASHANAH, FIRST DAY OF TISHRI, THE SEVENTH MONTH)

A day to celebrate how Queen Esther helped to stop Haman's plot against the Jews in the time of King Xerxes of Persia. Esth 9.20-32.

(THIRTEENTH DAY OF ADAR)

Purim

A day to celebrate the grain harvest and the beginning of the season when the first fruits were offered. It was also a day to recall how God delivered the nation from Egypt and provided a land that could supply the needs of the people. Lev 23.15-21; Deut 16.9-12

Harvest Festival
(SHAVUOTH, SIXTH DAY OF SILVAN)

Fall Festivals

Three times a year, Jewish men were required to go to Jerusalem to celebrate these special festivals:

Festival of Shelters
Passover and the Festival of Thin Bread
Harvest Festival

slaves), as well; and for any foreigners who lived in Israel (Exod 23.12; Deut 5.14-15).

Related to the weekly Sabbath observance is the biblical command that every seven years land must be allowed to rest for a full year. During this Seventh Year (or "sabbatical year") the land must not be plowed or planted. This was done to honor the LORD, the one who the land truly belonged to (Exod 23.10,11; Lev 25.1-7). Any crops that grew on their own were to be left in the fields for the poor and for work animals. The Seventh Year was also a time when debts were cancelled (Deut 15.1-3).

In addition, the Bible speaks of a Year of Celebration (sometimes called the "Jubilee Year"). Each seventh Sabbatical Year (that is, every forty-nine years), land that had been sold was to be returned to its original owner, and all slaves were to freed to their families (Lev 25.8-34). This year began on the "Great Day of Forgiveness" with the blowing of the ram's horn.

The Sabbath observance was one of the most important elements in Israelite religion, because it reminded the people of their special status as God's chosen people and that their God was the Creator of the world. The three Sabbath observances of rest and freedom point to God's desire to free all of creation, including its people, and reminds the celebrants of their need for continual re-creation.

the world of jesus: peoples, powers, and politics

Jesus was born in the town of Bethlehem in the province of Judea during the reign of Augustus Caesar, the first Roman ruler called emperor. About sixty years earlier, the Romans had invaded Palestine as they continued expanding their great empire throughout the lands surrounding the Mediterranean Sea and beyond. At the time of Augustus, the Roman Empire ruled over fifty million people from many different nationalities—from Palestine and Syria in the east to Spain in the west, including most of northern Africa and much of Europe. Because the Romans were well organized and had a strong army, their empire was actually very stable. Travel and trade between areas was easier than it had ever been.

PALESTINE BEFORE ROMAN RULE

In Palestine, the centuries leading up to Jesus' birth were not politically stable. The Jewish people who returned to Judah from exile in Babylon were allowed to rebuild their cities and the temple in Jerusalem, but they were still ruled by the Persians. Then the Greeks, led by Alexander the Great, defeated the Persians, and drove them out of Palestine. Alexander's generals and their descendants ruled the land for many years, bringing with them Greek (Hellenistic) culture. One Greek ruler from the Seleucid family (Antiochus IV Epiphanes) tried to force the Hellenistic way of life on the Jewish people in Palestine. When he put up a statue of a pagan god in the holy Jewish temple in 168 B.C., Jewish people were enraged and rebelled. Led by Judas Maccabeus, the people defeated the Seleucids, reclaimed the temple, and created their own government.

For nearly one hundred years the Jewish people were again in charge of the land, led by members of Judas Maccabeus' family (the Hasmoneans), who took over as kings and priests of Israel. Yet many thought that the Hasmonean rulers were just as selfish and cruel as the foreign kings who had ruled before them, so Jews did not fight back when the Romans invaded the country in 63 B.C.

ROMAN RULE IN PALESTINE

Though many peoples and cultures contributed to the cultural life in Palestine in Jesus' day, the Romans were by far the most powerful. They controlled the land with strong, well-trained armies. The Roman emperor appointed a governor (procurator) who was in charge of collecting taxes and preventing the people from rebelling against Rome. The Romans placed heavy taxes on land, on goods and food that were bought and sold, and on inheritances. They also charged tolls for people traveling through the areas they controlled. The taxes went to support the Roman army and to maintain control of

Palestine. Farmers and the poor suffered most under this system of taxes.

The Romans made contracts with local people to collect taxes. These local tax collectors (publicans) would often collect much more than the amount they were supposed to turn over to the Romans. They kept the rest. Tax collectors were often seen as traitors by the Jewish religious leaders. Some called them sinners, and said they were not welcome to be part of the Jewish people or to worship with them. When Jesus ate with tax collectors and welcomed them (Luke 5.27-32; 19.1-10), he offended those who wanted to keep the tax collectors apart from Jewish social life.

Roman policy was to respect local customs and the laws of the peoples they ruled. They let local people form councils to control local affairs. In Judea, the local ruling council (Sanhedrin) consisted of the high priest, the chief priests, and wealthy supporters of the Roman government. Their participation in the work of the council made them become even wealthier. The Romans also set up rulers in the areas that were under their control. These local kings and governors reported to the Roman senate or to the emperor's representatives.

In 37 B.C., the Romans appointed Herod the Great as king of Palestine, partly because Herod's father had helped the Romans take control of the region. Herod ruled until 4 B.C. and was responsible for rebuilding the temple in Jerusalem, which attracted many worshipers and visitors from all over the Roman Empire. The high priest, who was in charge of the temple, held his position because of support of the Roman authorities.

When Herod died, his three sons were appointed by the Romans to rule Galilee and Perea, the land east of the Jordan River. Under the Herods, priests and their supporters on the council gained greater power and wealth. Although John the Baptist and Jesus were born during the time of Herod the Great, it was Herod's son, Herod Antipas, who was in power when they came to trial. Herod Antipas ordered the death of John the Baptist (Matt 14.1-12). During Jesus' trial, the Roman governor, Pontius Pilate, sent Jesus to see Herod Antipas because Jesus was from Galilee, the area under this Herod's rule. Usually, the Roman governors did not want to be mixed up in local problems and arguments. It was only after the leaders of the people almost started a riot and argued that Jesus claimed to be a king of the Jews, that Pilate sentenced Jesus to death. Their claim meant Jesus was considered guilty of rebellion against Rome and could be put to death according to Roman law.

CLASS AND RANK IN THE ROMAN EMPIRE

The Roman Empire had a class structure based on wealth, birth, and citizenship. At the very top of Roman society was the emperor, who was the empire's "first citizen." Some emperors even declared themselves equal with the gods. Below the emperor were six hundred senators, who were the empire's wealthiest citizens. Next came a group known as "knights," who had reached a certain level of wealth. They were well educated and often served in the government of the empire. Beneath them were wealthy local citizens, known as "honorable men," who formed city councils.

Below these top groups was the large group of ordinary working people. They were divided into levels. First came those who were not wealthy but still had the privileges of Roman citizenship. Rome recognized only a small group of its subjects as full citizens. Citizens had the freedom and protection of their personal rights. For example, the apostle Paul was able to have his trial in Rome because he was a Roman citizen (Acts 16.37; 22.27). Jesus was not a Roman citizen, so he could be condemned to death without a formal trial by the personal decision of the Roman governor, Pontius Pilate.

Lower than citizens in the class structure were a large group of non-citizens who were free but did not have the special privileges allowed to Roman citizens. And beneath these non-citizens, at the very bottom of the class structure, were slaves, who could legally be bought or sold, beaten or tortured, as their owners saw fit. Slaves worked mostly as

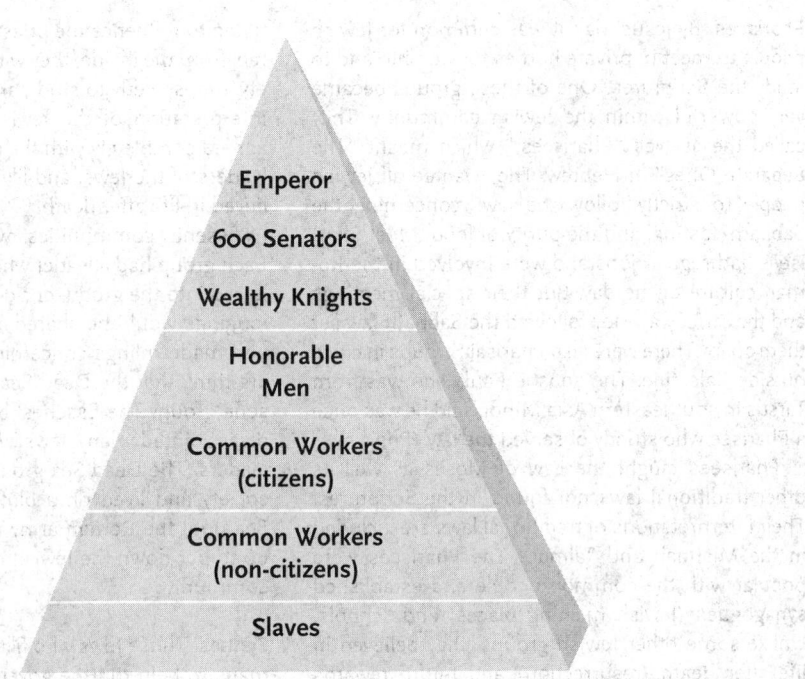

Emperor

600 Senators

Wealthy Knights

Honorable
Men

Common Workers
(citizens)

Common Workers
(non-citizens)

Slaves

household servants for the rich. At the time of Jesus, almost one-third of the population of Italy were slaves. Slavery was very common and accepted throughout the Roman Empire in Jesus' day.

JEWISH GROUPS IN PALESTINE

The local councils allowed by the Romans usually included the wealthy and powerful people in a region. These councils were free to make laws and to force people in that region to obey them. The chief priests and the rich people who worked with the Roman authorities formed the Jewish council based in Jerusalem. The Greek word for this council was the *synedrion*. After the Romans destroyed the temple in A.D. 70, the Jews began to use this name spelled in Hebrew (*Sanhedrin*) for the group that replaced the priests as the organizers and lawmakers of the Jewish people in Jerusalem. This group began to write

down formulas for applying the Law of Moses. These interpretations developed into what today are known as the "Mishnah" and "Talmud."

Jews in the time of Jesus had different opinions about what it meant to be the people of God. Here is a summary of some of the key groups that formed and how each one interpreted the Law of Moses:

Zealots. Zealots were Jewish nationalists who tried to organize revolts against the Romans. Attempts to win freedom and create an independent Jewish state failed in A.D. 70 and again in A.D. 135. Scholars disagree about whether this term applies to a single, well-organized group or to any number of groups of dissatisfied Jews who wanted to be rid of their Roman rulers. The *CEV* translates zealot as "Eager One." In the New Testament, the term is even applied to one of the followers of Jesus (Luke 6.15; Acts 1.13).

Pharisees. By Jesus' day, it was common for Jewish people to meet in private homes for worship and to study the Scriptures. One of these groups became very powerful within the Jewish community. They called themselves "Pharisees," which meant "The Separate Ones" in Hebrew. They wanted all Jewish people to strictly follow the laws concerning the Sabbath, fasting, and the purity of food. Most Pharisees had regular jobs and were involved in the Roman culture of the day. But their special meetings and the strict way they followed the Sabbath law set them apart. There were also Pharisaic groups in cities outside Palestine. The apostle Paul, who was from Tarsus in southeastern Asia Minor, said he was once a Pharisee who strictly observed the law (Phil 3.5).

Pharisees taught the Law of Moses as well as other traditional laws not found in the Scriptures. Their interpretations of traditional laws are included in the Mishnah and Talmud. The Pharisees were popular with the common people and established synagogues (Jewish meeting places) and schools. Unlike some other Jewish groups, they believed in life after death (resurrection) and future rewards and punishments (see Acts 23.6).

Sadducees. This group's name may come from Zadok, the high priest of Israel at the time of King David. The Sadducees stayed close to the priestly families and tried to influence the business of the temple. They were willing to work with the Romans when they came to rule Palestine. Unlike the Pharisees, the Sadducees did not accept interpretations of the Law, but believed in following only the Law of Moses. They also did not believe that the dead were raised to life (Mark 12.18; Acts 23.8). As long as the Sadducees followed the main teachings of the Law and stayed friendly with the Romans, they expected to continue in positions of power and wealth among their people. After the Jewish revolt led to the destruction of the temple in A.D. 70, the Sadducees no longer existed as a group.

Essenes. The Essenes may have been formed at about the same time as the Sadducees. Instead of trying to influence the priesthood and religion of Israel from the inside, they withdrew from Jewish society, met secretly to study, and had their own special interpretation of the Jewish Scriptures. They disagreed completely with the priests and other official leaders of the Jews, and like the Pharisees, they believed in life after death.

Essene communities were highly structured. Each group had a leader who controlled who was allowed into the group, decided how property and belongings would be shared among group members, and made rulings concerning the law. Some scholars think that the Dead Sea community was an Essene group. The Essenes' beliefs show how deeply disappointed many Jews were with their religious leaders. The Dead Sea group withdrew from Jewish society and lived on a bluff overlooking the Dead Sea until the Roman army invaded the land in A.D. 66 to put down the Jewish revolt and destroyed the community.

Scribes. Those Jews who filled jobs set up by the Romans to help run the government in the land were called "scribes." Because they could read and write in a time when many people could not, they were very valuable to kings and governments. In the Jewish Scriptures (Old Testament), they are shown as having the authority to write legal papers. Scribes are identified as keepers of government records (2 Kgs 18.18). Like Jeremiah's scribe Baruch, they took dictation and then read it aloud for people to hear (Jer 36.4-18). Scribes also worked as secretaries of state and treasurers.

In the New Testament, scribes are described as working as lawyers (Luke 5.17) and judges (Matt 23.2). Because of their extensive learning, they knew about interpreting the law, and sometimes argued with Jesus about the meaning of traditional Jewish laws (Matt 9.3; 15.1; Mark 2.16; 7.1-2; Luke 5.30; 6.7). The scribes were not the same as the Pharisees, but Pharisees and chief priests paid the scribes for legal advice. The scribes saw Jesus as a threat to law and order as set up by the Romans.

Samaritans. Another group mentioned a few times in the New Testament are the Samaritans. The ancestors of the Samaritans came from the ten Israelite tribes that rebelled against King Solomon's son Rehoboam and formed a separate kingdom known as Israel, or the northern kingdom. They had their own temple on Mount Gerizim near Shechem, and their own priests. They followed the laws about the Sabbath in a very strict way, and they said that their holy Mount Gerizim was more important than Mount Zion, where the temple in Jerusalem was located. The Jewish people did not like the Samaritans and believed they were not really part of God's chosen people. The writers of the Gospels, however, record that Jesus reached out to them (Luke 17.11-19; John 4.3-9), and used one as a positive example when explaining to an expert in the Law of Moses what it means to have compassion and be a neighbor (Luke 10.25-37).

Jesus faced this complicated situation as he tried to preach his message of good news. When he defended the poor and reached out to accept people such as tax collectors, Samaritans, and prostitutes, he offended local religious leaders.

trade and travel

The story of trade and travel in the ancient Near East tells how those civilizations developed. The Bible, other documents of the times, and archaeological discoveries give a general picture of how ancient peoples traded with one another, where the most important trade centers were, and how they traveled and transported their goods to these marketplaces.

EARLY ISRAELITES

The Bible tells us how Abraham moved with Sarah and their family from Ur in Chaldea (at the head of the Persian Gulf) to Canaan in Palestine (Gen 11.26—12.9). Like other nomadic peoples, Abraham and his descendants lived in tents, temporary dwellings that were easy to set up and take down. Abraham's grandson Jacob moved his whole family to Egypt because there was a famine in Canaan where they lived (Gen 46.5-28). His sons and their families remained in Egypt for many years until Moses led them out of Egypt. They lived there in tents for forty years as they made their way back to the land of Canaan. Besides the sheep and oxen they took with them, they may have had donkeys and camels to carry them and their belongings (Gen 12.16; 22.3; 24.10; 42.26).

The earliest Israelites traded in animals, milk, cheese, and wool. Even after they settled in Canaan, the Israelites were farmers and herders, but few were professional merchants. However, the geography of the ancient Near East encouraged rapid change. Canaan (later known as Palestine), was a land bridge that connected northern Africa and Asia Minor with the rest of the Near East. Wandering peoples, merchants, skilled workers, and armies used this land bridge to pass from one part of the ancient world to another. They brought special skills, ideas, and products over this land bridge. Egyptians, Babylonians, Assyrians, Hittites, Greeks, Persians, and desert nomads influenced the Israelites. From about 1000 B.C. on, the Israelites became increasingly involved in trading beyond their local marketplaces.

In early Bible times, trade between countries was limited to diplomatic exchanges between kings and had little impact on the economic life of ordinary people. Most peoples created enough goods and services in their local economies to satisfy their daily needs. However, in later times, trade would increase as transportation improved, making possible the spread of ideas, culture, and material wealth. Unfortunately, this would also give rise to wars and the struggles to maintain empires.

LOCAL TRADING AND LOCAL ECONOMIES

Ancient Palestine was an agricultural society. People traded farm products and animals from their flocks in the marketplaces. Farmers brought wheat and barley, grapes and wine, olives and olive oil, figs, dates, and nuts to markets in nearby towns and cities. Herders brought milk, cheese, and butter to city markets all year round. The busiest time of the year for trading was in the late spring when herders also brought young lambs and goats to market.

In ancient Palestine, items changed hands by a kind of trading called bartering since gold and silver were not plentiful enough to be used to buy things.

The use of money in the form of minted coins was not used in Palestine until after the exile (beginning around 538 B.C.). The Persians who controlled Palestine during this time introduced the use of coins in buying and selling.

TRADING WITH THE OUTSIDE WORLD

After the tribes of Israel were united under King David (around 1000 B.C.), international trade began to increase. Israelite rulers built storage cellars and warehouses to store wine, grain, and olive oil taken from local farmers as a form of taxation. The kings used these items in their courts or traded them with neighboring countries. This practice created the need for professional traders (merchants) who specialized in the business of buying and selling.

The Bible reports that trade with other nations increased during King Solomon's reign (961–922 B.C.). Solomon needed wood, gold, and precious stones to build and furnish his palace and the temple he built for the LORD in Jerusalem. He traded with King Hiram of Tyre and a trade agreement between them gave Hiram the right to use Israel's port at Ezion-Geber on the Red Sea. In return, Hiram sent Solomon experienced sailors to help the Israelites' journey to Ophir (believed to be in either India or Africa) to obtain gold (1 Kgs 9.26-28). Solomon also traded with the Queen of Sheba (1 Kgs 10.1-10). He bought horses from Musri (Egypt) and Kue (in today's southeast Turkey) for his many chariots (1 Kgs 10.28, 29). In addition, Solomon probably charged foreign traders tolls or taxes to pass through Israel's territory.

TRADE IN OLD TESTAMENT TIMES

International trade increased during the reign of Solomon. First Kings 5–10 and Ezekiel 27 list many of the products traded in ancient times and identify which countries were involved in the international trading of these goods.

COUNTRY OR REGION	PRODUCT
Spain	Silver, iron, tin, lead
Greece, Tubal (Asia Minor), Meshech	Slaves, bronze
Beth-Togarmah (Armenia)	Various breeds of horses, mules
Edom	Purple cloth, linen, embroidery; emeralds, rubies, coral
Judah, Israel	High-quality wheat, figs, olives and olive oil, honey, spices
Damascus	Wine, wool
Vedan and Javan (Mesopotamia)	Iron, spices
Dedan	Saddle blankets
Arabia	Lambs, sheep, goats, gold
Kedar	Lambs, sheep, goats
Sheba, Raamah	Gems, gold, rare spices
Haran, Canneh, Eden, Sheba, Asshur, Chilmad (Mesopotamia and Assyria)	Expensive clothing, purple and embroidered cloth, colored rugs, rope
Ophir (location uncertain)	Gems, gold, juniper wood
Musri (Egypt), Kue (Turkey)	Horses, chariots

ISRAEL'S IMPORTS AND EXPORTS

Israel's main exports continued to be farm products, such as olive oil, wine, and grains (1 Kgs 5.11; Ezek 27.17). They also produced and exported dried nuts (such as pistachios and almonds), perfume, and spices (Gen 43.11). Other important products were dates, figs, wool, and clothing made from wool.

Israel imported raw materials such as tin, lead, silver, copper, iron, gold (1 Kgs 10.10-12), and timber (1 Kgs 5.6-9). White linen cloth probably came regularly from Egypt and Syria, while purple-dyed wool and cloth came from Phoenicia. Though Israelites made pottery, they imported special pottery from the island of Cyprus and from Greece. Gems, ivory, spices, and other things came to Israel by camel caravans across the desert and by sea from southern Arabia, Ethiopia, and India (1 Kgs 10.2,10,22).

PAYING FOR MERCHANDISE

As trade increased in Israel during the time of Solomon, so did the use of gold and silver to pay for goods. Around this time, merchants and a special group of moneychangers began to weigh and test gold and silver pieces to judge their value and purity. Even so, exchanging one kind of merchandise for another continued to be the main way of doing business.

In Jesus' day, Roman coins were the only form of money that could be used to pay taxes to the Roman government (see Luke 20.20-26), though coins of other countries were used in buying and selling. The Bible mentions workers being paid for a day's wage (Matt 20.1,2), and describes the requirement to pay annual temple taxes (Matt 17.24-27). Each of these passages probably refers to a denarius, a coin from Cappadocia. This was also probably the coin Jesus mentioned in Matt 22.19. The thirty silver coins that Judas was paid to help the authorities arrest Jesus (Matt 26.15) probably amounted to the wage of a typical laborer for approximately four months of work.

TRAVEL

Travel in biblical times, besides being difficult and slow, could also be very dangerous. Robbers were a hazard to travelers and merchants as they walked along foot paths. The story of the Good Samaritan (Luke 10.25-27) is an example of the constant danger. Travelers sometimes faced unfriendly or even hostile people in certain areas or towns. Wild animals, such as lions and bears, could also be a serious threat for travelers (Judg 14.5,6; 1 Sam 17.34-36; 2 Kgs 2.23-25).

Sea travel was also dangerous (2 Cor 11.25,26). Wind and waves could easily sink a small boat or push it off course. Weather around the Mediterranean Sea was even more stormy in winter, so very few ships tried to sail during winter (Acts 27.27; 28.11). Pirates sometimes raided merchant ships as they moved their cargo on the open sea.

TRAVEL OVER LAND

Most travel in Bible times was done on foot. People walked along paths or roads known as "ways." Many places in the Bible describe individuals or groups of people traveling by foot. Depending on the condition of the road, people could walk up to twenty miles in a day. If the road was not good shape, or if people were loaded down with goods and supplies, the distance they could cover in a day would be much less.

Roads. Ancient roads were well-worn paths for travel and carrying goods from place to place. As wheeled transportation became more common, roads were widened and elevated so they didn't flood over as much, and were sometimes paved. Roads led through major religious centers, such as Jerusalem, Samaria, and Damascus in the Near East; Ephesus in Asia Minor; and Athens on the Greek peninsula. Merchants often set up markets in these places. Some sold religious objects or gifts for presenting

BANKING AND MONEY IN THE ANCIENT WORLD

Ancient economies developed from a barter system, in which one kind of merchandise is exchanged for another. International trade at first involved only exchanges between rulers and did not affect the lives of ordinary people. Silver, gold, and precious stones were used as money. Refining techniques increased the purity of precious metals and made accurate coinages possible. Yet even as the economy in cities became ever more sophisticated and complex, many rural areas continued to function in a barter system.

DATE	HISTORICAL EVENT	BANKING MILESTONE
10,000–6000 B.C.	Ancient people develop agriculture and tend livestock.	Barter system: cattle and grain are used as money.
3000–2000 B.C.	Banking begins in Mesopotamia.	Writing is used to keep trade accounts.
2250–2150 B.C.	Rulers of Cappodocia (Turkey) guarantee quality of silver ingots.	The official guarantee of the purity and weight of the silver increases their acceptance as money.
about 1750 B.C.	The Code of Hammurabi is written.	It includes laws governing banking operations.
about 640 B.C.	The first true coins are minted in Lydia (Asia Minor).	The coins are minted of "electrum," a natural mixture of gold and silver.
about 600 B.C.	The first surviving record of a merchant banker (Pythius) in the ancient world is written.	Pythius trades throughout Asia Minor.
after 538 B.C.	Minted coins begin to be used in Palestine.	The Persians introduce coinage to Palestine after the Israelite people return from exile.
336–323 B.C.	Alexander the Great helps pay his troops with captured Persian gold.	Trade is stimulated throughout the ancient world.
323–30 B.C.	Ptolemy Dynasty in Egypt creates first unified banking system.	A central bank is created in Alexandria.

to the various gods. In Jerusalem, pilgrims could buy small animals and grains from merchants to make sacrificial offerings at the temple during special festivals.

The Persians began to build major highways throughout the Near East around 600 B.C. Greek rulers who succeeded Alexander the Great extended and improved roads in Egypt and Syria. But the Romans built the best highways of ancient times. Roman roads were built to make it easier for the Roman army to move freely through the territories it conquered. As the Roman Empire grew, roads were built from the southern Jordan Valley across Asia Minor, throughout Europe, and even in remote places like northern Britain. Roman roads were wide enough for chariots and wagons going in different directions to pass each other. Some of these roads, which date from before the time of Jesus, can still be seen today.

Main travel routes. The most important road that passed through ancient Israel was the Great Coastal Highway, or the Way of the Sea. This road connected Egypt in the south with Mesopotamia, Syria, Phoenicia, and the Land of the Hittites in the north. The King's Highway was another very important road. It went from Egypt to Israel across the southern desert, and then turned north along the eastern side of the Great Rift Valley (the long, north-south valley that contains the Dead Sea, Jordan River, and Lake Galilee), and on to Damascus.

By the time the apostle Paul and other early Christians began to take the good news about Jesus Christ to the far corners of the Roman Empire, the value of the Roman road system was clear. Paul traveled on the Egnatian Way through Macedonia. On his final journey to Rome he traveled from Puteoli, a major port for the nearby cities of Napoli and Pompeii, to the capital city on one of the most famous highways in Italy, the Appian Way. The highways developed by the Romans made it easier for Christian preachers to spread the good news about Jesus, and for groups of Christians to keep in touch with and support one another.

Caravans. Groups of merchants, pilgrims, or travelers joined together for protection as they traveled with their pack animals (either donkeys or camels, depending on the terrain). Trade and travel by caravans go back as far as recorded history (see, for example, Gen 37.25).

As civilizations developed, caravans became very important to the economies of cities and empires. Cities could rise or fall depending on their closeness to important caravan routes; and empires had important interests in protecting trade routes. (See Judges 5.6,7.) Caravans were usually large and their valuable cargo required the protection of soldiers or armed guards. Wealthy travelers, like Abraham, bought slaves to use as armed guards (see Gen 14.14).

Land caravans contributed to trade in Palestine as they moved from Asia Minor following the western edge of the Syrian Desert. They supplied the markets of Aleppo, Hamath, and Damascus before heading south into Palestine. From there, they would travel to Egypt or to places near the Red Sea.

In the deserts of the ancient Near East, Egypt and northern Africa, camels were the animal most often used in caravans. Some nomads who invaded the Israelite people rode on camels (Judg 6.3-5; 7.12; 1 Sam 30.17). Camels are the best pack animals for desert travel because they are strong, have natural protection from the environment, and can travel long distances without needing to stop for water.

Vehicles. Archaeologists guess that the invention of the wheel occurred sometime between 10,000 and 8000 B.C. From existing evidence, it appears that wheels were attached to carts no later than 4000 B.C. when the inhabitants of the ancient Mesopotamian city of Sumer placed sledges on wheels to transport goods. At first, wheels were solid disks of wood. Wheels with spokes were first introduced around 2700 B.C.

In ancient times, two-wheeled carts and four-wheeled wagons were used to transport people and goods. Wheeled vehicles were efficient on good roads and on the level plains of Palestine. They were not as reliable on rocky and dangerous mountain roads and so were not initially used for long-distance travel. Later, Roman engineers introduced wagons with undercarriages and a pivoting front axle for easier maneuvering.

Many ancient peoples used chariots as early as 3000 B.C. Chariots were two-wheeled vehicles that one or more horses pulled. Chariots were used for hunting by kings and in warfare. The speed and mobility of chariots made a decisive factor in military campaigns. The dominance of the Egyptians, Assyrians, and Babylonians at different periods in Bible times is partly due to their use of chariots in battle. During the time of Solomon and the divided kingdom, Israel also made extensive use of chariots (1 Kgs 4.26; 2 Chr 1.14; 9.25). A horse and chariot could easily travel thirty miles in a day, and up to forty-five miles a day when necessary.

WATER TRAVEL

Ships. Israel's King Solomon built a fleet of ships at Ezion-Geber (1 Kgs 9.26-28; 2 Chr 8.17,18). These ships were used to carry goods back and forth to Ophir. But since Israel did not have ports on the Mediterranean Sea, Israelites never built a strong navy and had to rely on merchants from other countries for trading and sea travel. Little mention is made of sea-going ships in the New Testament, except those that the apostle Paul sailed on during his trip to Rome (Acts 20.38; 21.6; 27.2; 28.11). At this time, passengers like Paul had to travel on merchant ships that carried grain or other cargo (Acts 21.1-3; 27.10). The Romans had a very active "grain fleet," which brought grain from Egypt to Rome. When space allowed, these cargo ships also took passengers.

Small boats and fishing craft. Within Israel, however, smaller boats were important to the economy of the area around Lake Galilee, especially during the Roman period. Archaeologists have discovered the remains of a small boat in this freshwater lake that dates from the time of Jesus. Such small boats were used for both fishing and transportation. They are often mentioned in the Gospels (Matt 14.22; Mark 1.19; Luke 5.2; John 6.19).

SPECIAL REASONS FOR TRAVEL

Holy travel. The people of Israel traveled to special holy places such as Shiloh, Dan, Bethel, and Jerusalem to worship and celebrate religious festivals (1 Sam 1; 1 Kgs 12.26-33; 2 Kgs 10.18-24; Amos 5.4,5). Joshua called the people of Israel together at Shechem (Josh 24). And King Solomon gathered the people in Jerusalem to celebrate the Festival of Shelters and to dedicate the temple they had built for the LORD there (1 Kgs 8.1-13, 62-65).

At the time of Jesus, it was the custom for the people of Israel to travel to Jerusalem three times each year to celebrate the major pilgrimage festivals—Passover, the Harvest Festival (Pentecost), and the Festival of Shelters. In ACTS, Luke describes how the early apostles of Jesus traveled around preaching and teaching the good news. More than half of the book tells about Paul's many travels by land and sea.

Wars. A major reason for travel concerned the movement of military forces. Israel's armies often traveled outside their boundaries to battle with unfriendly neighbors (see 2 Sam 8.1-12). Israel itself was attacked by invaders from other lands including Egypt, Assyria, and Babylonia. In 331 B.C. Alexander the Great passed through Palestine on his way to invade Egypt. His army was said to have traveled as far as forty-five miles in one day. Later, when the Roman army became the most powerful army in the world, they could conquer large areas partly because they built good roads that made it possible for their troops and supplies to move quickly and easily.

Communication. Land or sea travel was the means of sending messages to different places. The Old Testament mentions messengers who carried news, orders, and other messages from the king to his own military commanders or to rulers in neighboring countries (2 Sam 2.5; 3.14; 11.19).

COMMON FORMS OF TRANSPORTATION IN THE ANCIENT WORLD

MEANS OF TRANSPORTATION	DISTANCES	EXAMPLES
Walking	About 20 miles per day	Peter walks 40 miles from Joppa to Caesarea in two days (Acts 10.23-25).
Camels	As a pack animal, a camel can carry as much as 1,000 lbs. and travel almost 30 miles per day. As a saddle animal, a camel can take its rider as far as 100 miles a day.	An Ishmaelite camel caravan takes spices from Gilead to Egypt (Gen 37.25). Rebekah and her traveling companions get on camels and leave with Abraham's servant (Gen 24.61).
Donkeys	About 20 miles per day. Donkeys were used for transporting goods, and were not used for riding except by women, children, or those too weak to walk.	The "Good Samaritan" uses his donkey to transport the man wounded by thieves (Luke 10.34).
Horses	From 25 to 35 miles per day. If people changed horses throughout the day, they could travel greater distances.	With a change of horses at Antipatris, Paul is taken by military escort from Jerusalem to Caesarea, approx. 60 miles, in two days (Acts 23.23-31).
Chariots	Horse-drawn chariots covered distances similar to horses alone, and were used by royalty or wealthy people.	An important Ethiopian official rides from Jerusalem to Gaza (Acts 8.28).
Sailing boats	Seagoing boats were probably not built until around 3000 B.C. when the river peoples of Egypt and southern Iraq built reed boats. With the right conditions, sailing vessels could average from 5 to 6 knots (5 to 7 miles) per hour.	Jonah runs from the LORD by boarding a ship traveling to Spain (Jon 1.3).

The Roman imperial post carried messages important to the Roman Empire. A messenger would journey by carriage, changing horses at staging posts along the way. In the New Testament, Paul and other church leaders communicated with groups of Christians living in various parts of the Mediterranean world by sending letters that messengers delivered by hand. As civilization became more connected by trading, the Christian message of hope traveled throughout the ancient world.

how people made a living in the time of jesus

The Bible describes a wide range of cultures and lifestyles. The time from Abraham to the time of the early church spans a period of about two thousand years. Some peoples were "nomads," living in small groups, keeping flocks of sheep and goats, and traveling from place to place in order to feed and protect their animals. Others lived more settled lives, farming or working in towns and urban areas. Most of the "jobs" described in this article were still practiced by at least some part of the population of Palestine at the time of Jesus.

HERDING AND FARMING

Herding and farming are the two central ways of life mentioned in the Bible. GENESIS reports that one of Adam and Eve's sons herded sheep while the other farmed the land (Gen 4.2). The earliest ancestors of the people of Israel, including Abraham and Sarah, survived by keeping herds and flocks of animals (Gen 13.1-3). The importance of herding and farming in ancient Israelite society is shown by the Bible's special instructions about eating (Lev 11), sacrificing animals (Lev 1), and sacrificing grain (Lev 2).

Keeping herds of animals like sheep and goats was common among the many generations of the people of Israel. At first, these herders (shepherds) were wandering nomads who lived in tents and had very little personal property. Closer to the time of Je-

sus, when urban life was more developed, shepherds may also have lived in or near villages. They had the right to let their flocks feed in nearby pastures and would have been hired by landowners who needed help to harvest their fields. When food supplies got scarce near the villages, shepherds would move their herds to mountain pastures in the hot summer or to warmer valleys in the winter.

When the Israelites settled in Canaan, farming became a more important way of making a living for them. Grains, such as wheat and barley, were used for making bread, and were the most important crop. Unlike farmers in Egypt and Mesopotamia, Israelite farmers did not need to depend on irrigation for water. Even though the rainy season in Palestine was rather short and the soil was often rocky, the farmers' know-how in clearing and fertilizing the land usually produced fine crops. The Israelite farmers learned how to grow crops according to the yearly cycle of rainy and dry spells. They also learned to adjust the crops to what was best for the different kinds of land: fertile plains, rocky hills, and semi-barren areas.

Farming shaped the economic and social life of the people. For example, some of the major religious festivals in Israel—the Harvest Festival and the Festival of Shelters—were coordinated with the farming cycle. The Harvest Festival, also called the Festival of Weeks, celebrated the wheat harvest in the spring (Exod 23.16; 34.22; Lev 23.15-22; Num 28.26-31; Deut 16.9). The

Festival of Shelters (or Booths) is an autumn holiday for the occasion of the planting and gathering of crops, and the annual harvest (Exod 23.16; 34.22; Lev 23.33-43; Num 29.12-39; Deut 16.13-17; Ezek 45.25). Another feature of the life of Israel was the sabbatical year, the one year in every seven when farmers would let the land rest. This followed the pattern of working only six days out of each week according to God's command to rest on seventh day, called the Sabbath (Exod 23.10-12). This sabbatical rest for fields also had practical benefits, since it increased the long-term fertility of the land.

The people may also have practiced crop rotation, further improving the soil (Isa 28.23-29). The orderly way in which the farmers grew their crops was to match God's plan for the Israelite people and for the good of creation. From a religious perspective, however, DEUTERONOMY makes it clear that a large harvest also depended on how the people of Israel obeyed God's commandments (Deut 11.10-17).

FISHING

Fishing was a far less important source of food and income for the people of Israel, since the Philistines and others controlled the seacoast. What fish were available usually came from Lake Galilee and the Jordan River. Since fishing is mentioned so little in the Jewish Scriptures (Old Testament), some scholars think it was not important to the economy of Israel. It is possible that the fishing industry was more prosperous in the time of Jesus than it had been earlier, since when Jesus called James and John to be his disciples, they left the family fishing business to their father and the "hired workers" (Mark 1.19-20).

SPECIAL SKILLS AND CRAFTS

As the Israelites became more settled in and near cities, they became involved in many other types of work. Skilled workers were highly respected, since people needed their skills and products to live comfortably. Those who worked on special crafts were builders, stonemasons (stonecutters), carpenters, wood-carvers, boat-builders, and silversmiths, glass workers, potters, leather workers, weavers, and fullers, who worked with cleaning and texturing old and new cloth. The Bible tells us that Jesus grew up helping his father Joseph, who was a carpenter (Matt 13.55). And the apostle Paul apparently made a living at the craft of tentmaking (Acts 18.3).

SERVANTS AND SLAVES

Many people, free and slave, provided personal services as laborers. These servants included household servants, employed by wealthy people. Such servants might work as cooks, maids, groundskeepers, tutors, or in helping to care for children. Loyal household workers were highly valued. A royal servant called a cupbearer (Gen 40.11; Neh 1.11) brought food and drink to a ruler. Others served as midwives (Gen 35.16-18), doctors (2 Chr 16.12; Mark 5.25-26), nurses (usually a woman who fed another woman's baby), moneychangers (Matt 21.12), innkeepers (Luke 2.7; 10.35), and prostitutes (Gen 38.14-18; Josh 2.1).

Often the Bible is not clear when describing the work of servants, because the word "servant" may mean either a slave or a person hired to do some task. Slavery in many forms was common in Bible times. Some people sold themselves into slavery to pay back a debt, or because they were desperately poor and that was the only way they could get food and shelter. Many slaves in Bible times were prisoners of war. Most slaves performed household work rather than fieldwork or manual labor. There are some rules regarding slavery in the Bible, including ones that put a limit on the customs for slavery and recommended when a term of slavery should end (Exod 21.2-6; Lev 25.10,38-41). There was also some expectation that slaves would be treated fairly and without cruelty (Deut 23.15-16).

MILITARY AND GOVERNMENT WORK

A number of jobs were related to maintaining governments and kingdoms. At the top of the social structure were kings, queens and emperors, diplomats and ambassadors, senators and governors (Acts 13.7). Within the palace, there were deputies, counselors, interpreters (Gen 42.23), and messengers (Num 20.14; 1 Kgs 20.5; 2 Chr 32.31). The interests of the leaders and the nation were protected by armies which were made up of military officers (Matt 8.9; Acts 21.32), soldiers, and armor-bearers (Judg 9.54; 1Sam 14.6). To maintain the government, additional workers were needed, such as tax collectors (Luke 19.1-2), keepers of records and secretaries (2 Sam 8.16,17), and lawyers (Acts 24.1; Titus 3.13). Some rulers hired musicians (1 Sam 16.14-23) and others paid for advice from astrologers or fortunetellers (Isa 19.3).

SPECIAL SERVANTS OF GOD

For years, the temple in Jerusalem was the center of the religious life of the people of Israel. Work on the temple and other religious centers supported many artisans, such as architects, builders, goldsmiths, silversmiths, and sculptors, who used their skills to build and decorate temples and shrines (1 Kgs 5.13-18). According to the Law of Moses, the members of the tribe of Levi were to work as priests, serving all the people of God. Since the Levites were not given their own land, they were allowed to keep a portion of the sacrifices that the Israelite people offered to God (Josh 13.14). A high priest was in charge of the temple, and supported by chief priests, gatekeepers (1 Chr 9.17-32), temple workers (Ezra 2.43-54), and guards (1 Chr 9.17-32).

Many of the kings of Israel and Judah also employed prophets (1 Chr 21.9; 2 Chr 19.1-2) who helped them make decisions based on God's will, and who warned them of the consequences of their actions. Other prophets worked independently as preachers (1 Sam 9.6-21). By the time of Jesus, a growing number of teachers known as scribes and Pharisees earned money as teachers of the Law.

religions and philosophies in bible times

The faith of Israel and the faith of the early Christians developed in cultural contexts rich in other religious traditions. The people of Israel encountered religions with many similar beliefs and rituals in Palestine and Egypt. Christianity came into being as one among many religions and philosophies spread around the Mediterranean world by merchants and soldiers.

THE PEOPLE OF ISRAEL AND CANAANITE RELIGIONS

The people of Israel believed in one God. This belief is known as "monotheism." Many of the other religions in the ancient Mediterranean world recognized a number of different gods. When the Israelite people entered Canaan well over one thousand years before Jesus was born, they came into contact with the various gods of their neighbors. The Law of Moses commanded God's people to remain loyal to the one true God, *Yahweh*, who had led them out of slavery in Egypt and into the Promised Land of Canaan (Exod 20.1-5). Once they settled there, they were often tempted to follow the other gods, and often did.

The Gods of Israel's Neighbors. Among the Canaanites, one of the most common names for god was El. The Canaanites did not believe that El was the only god, but they did believe that El was the one who ruled over all the other gods. They believed El was the creator of the universe and the kind, compassionate father of the whole human race. El was worshiped in Palestine before the Israelites took over the land. In the Jewish Scriptures, "El" also frequently refers to the God of Israel. Some examples of the use of this name are found in the Old Testament.

Some of the enemies of El were known as Yamm (the sea), Mot (death) and Leviathan (the sea monster). See Psalm 104.26 and Isaiah 27.1.

Another name for a god in the ancient Near East was Baal, which means "master," "husband," and "lord." Baal was worshiped by the Canaanites as a god of fertility who ensured good and abundant crops. Baal was also connected to storms that came into Syria and Palestine from the sea in the winter and early spring. Since rain was essential for the growth of crops, people believed that the storms that came from the sea were powerful gods.

Some people in the ancient world believed goddesses provided fertility for crops and flocks and helped human beings to have children. The Canaanite goddess Asherah, who was also known as Astarte, was pictured as the mother of the gods. She was identified as the wife of El. The term "Asherah" was also used for sacred poles that were put up in hilltop shrines as symbols of fertility (1 Kgs 14.23; 16.33). The goddess Anat was also a fertility god-

NAMES OF GOD

NAME	PLACE USED	SCRIPTURE PASSAGE
El Elyon (God Most High)	Jerusalem	Gen 14.18-20
El Olam (God of Eternity)	Beersheba	Gen 21.33
El Berith (God of the Covenant)	Shechem	Judg 9.46
El Shaddai (God All-Powerful or God of the Mountains)	Bethel	Gen 17.1; 35.9-11; Exod 6.3

dess. She was famous for performing acts of violence against those who opposed her. An important city in Israel, Anathoth, was named for her (Josh 21.9-19; Jer 1.1; 11.21). This means that Anat was probably worshiped in this town at an earlier time. Even during the time when Nehemiah (about 445 B.C.) was helping restore Israel to the land and reminding the people to practice God's law after the exile in Babylon, the city's name remained Anathoth (Neh 7.26-38; 11.32).

The Philistine people who lived in the narrow strip of land between Judah and the Mediterranean Sea often battled with Israel. Their chief god was Dagon (1 Sam 5.1-5). The people of Moab, another of Israel's enemies when the Israelites were settling in Canaan, worshiped the god named Chemosh.

When the people of Israel worshiped other gods, God punished them. Ahab, the king of Israel, married Jezebel, the daughter of the king Ethbaal of Sidon. Part of Jezebel's name, Zebul, was a form of Baal's name. Ahab went against the Law of Moses when he built a temple with an altar to worship Baal in his capital city, Samaria (1 Kgs 16.31-32), and when he allowed Jezebel to encourage him to support hundreds of prophets of Asherah (1 Kgs 18.19). Many of the people of Israel were led to worship *Yahweh,* Israel's God, as well as Baal and Asherah. This worship broke the commandment God had given to Moses: "Do not worship any god except me." Because of their sins, God allowed Israel's neighbors to defeat them and carry many of the people into exile (2 Kgs 17).

Other Religions Outside of Palestine. In the ancient world, many cities or city-states had their own gods. Often people would build altars and places of worship (shrines) where they could bring sacrifices for their gods. These sacrifices were intended to please the gods in the hope that they would then protect the people of the city and give them good crops.

Astrology, the belief that the sun and the stars control human life, came out of Babylonia and had a great influence throughout the Greek and Roman empires. The people of Israel rejected this belief in the influence of the stars as contrary to monotheism. They believed that God created the sun, moon, and stars (Gen 1.14-19; Ps 8.3; 147.4). Since these heavenly bodies are created, they cannot be gods.

In Egypt the cults of Isis, Osiris, and Serapis were popular. In Syria, Israel's northern neighbor, people worshiped the great sky-god named Hadad, and helped spread the belief in astrology, common in Babylonia, to the Greeks. From Persia, a nation that conquered the Babylonians and ruled Palestine before the Greeks invaded the land, came the cult of Mazdaism. This was connected to the religion taught by Zoroaster, a teacher whose ideas would later influence Gnostic beliefs. The most important of the cults popular in Asia Minor was the cult of Cybele, also known as the Great Mother. The Greeks identified Cybele with Rhea, the mother of the Greek gods, and with Artemis, who is mentioned in the Bible as the goddess of the Ephesians (Acts 19.21-41).

THE CHRISTIAN CHURCH
IN THE GREEK WORLD

In the centuries before Jesus was born, the number of religions, cults, and forms of philosophy in the Mediterranean world had grown rapidly. The letters of the New Testament provide glimpses of how various religions, philosophies, and cult teachings opposed Christian followers. (For examples, see 1 Cor 8; 10; Gal 1.6-9; 1 John 2.26,27; Rev 2.2-6,14-16,20-25).

Greek Religions. The greatest religious influences and new philosophies came from the ancient Greeks. When Alexander the Great and his heirs took over Syria and Palestine after 330 B.C., they gave new names to the local gods and goddesses and introduced new deities.

Various "mystery cults" were popular throughout the Greek world as well. Mystery cults had secret beliefs, so becoming a member usually required going through initiation ceremonies or practicing specific kinds of rites or sacraments. To many people at this time, Christians also seemed to be a mystery cult, because when they celebrated the Lord's Supper, Christians ate the bread and drank the wine that Jesus described as his body and blood (Mark 14.22-24).

Other religions in the first century were based on fate, fortune, astrology, and magic. Some people believed that the supreme god was Tyche ("Fortune"), who ruled the lives of human beings. If someone became rich, it was because of Fortune; if that person suddenly lost his or her wealth, it was also because of Fortune. Similarly, some people believed in a ruler known as "Fate." Fate was thought to determine everything that would happen in the universe, including the actions of all people.

Greek Philosophies. In Greece during the third and fourth centuries before Christ, the Greek philosophers Socrates, Plato, and Aristotle were concerned with how people could live a virtuous life that was in harmony with their city, their culture, and the natural world. Disciples of these great teachers would later form schools of philosophy. By the time of the early Christian church, the teachings of these schools had spread throughout the Mediterranean world. Plato and Aristotle especially had a profound effect on later Christian writers and thinkers.

Gnostics is a term historians have given to a number of religious groups in the second and third centuries A.D. *Gnosis* is the Greek word for knowledge, and Gnostics believed they possessed a special or secret knowledge. Gnostics believed that Jesus was a godlike being (rather than a living person) who had been sent to restore people's knowledge of their origin in the true God. According to the Gnostics, Christians might achieve a lower form of salvation through their faith, but real salvation came through a superior knowledge *(gnosis)* of the life of the spirit and soul. In the early centuries after Christ, Gnosticism was a serious challenge to the early church, leading to the rise of elitist sects within Christianity.

Emperor Worship. The Jews and early Christians faced the problem of emperor worship in the centuries just before and after Jesus was born. Beginning in the fourth century B.C., Alexander the Great (356–323 B.C.), who conquered much of the Near East, claimed that he was divine. The Greek rulers who seized power after Alexander likewise demanded that their subjects honor them as gods. Roman emperors, whose armies conquered Palestine in 63 B.C., also claimed that they were gods. The Roman emperor Gaius Caligula (ruled A.D. 37–41) wanted to put up a statue of himself in the temple, but he died before he could make this happen. Around the end of the first century, the emperor Domitian ordered people to address him as "Lord and God." REVELATION pictures a prostitute and a horrible beast which likely symbolized the Roman

Empire's attempt to destroy God's people and their worship of "the Lamb" (Christ), and to force Christians to worship the emperor instead (Rev 17).

THE BIBLE AND THE BELIEFS
OF THE ANCIENT WORLD

As Jews and Christians moved away from Jerusalem after the destruction of the temple in A.D. 70 and settled in other parts of the Roman Empire, they encountered the various religions and philosophies described in this article, and many others as well.

Many of these systems of belief were not compatible with the monotheism of Judaism and Christianity. Sometimes, however, they adopted or adapted some of the teachings from these other systems of thought in response to the situations they faced. In light of these situations, both the Jewish Scriptures (Old Testament) and the New Testament contain direct and indirect references to these other forms of belief. It is, therefore, important to become aware of these other beliefs in order to understand the Bible more fully.

miracles, magic, and medicine

The Bible is a book of faith, telling the story of how God acted in history to protect and save humankind. Miracles are an important part of that story. God's actions in miracles on behalf of the faithful are contrasted with the situation of those who looked to other gods and relied on magic, reading the stars, or calling on the spirits of the dead. Throughout the Bible, the miracles of God are extraordinary acts. Many of these miracles can be described in the categories shown on the chart on pg 1821.

The people praised God for these miracles, including God's amazing actions in Israel's history (Deut 7.19; 11.1-4; 34.10-12). The writers of PSALMS and the later teachers of the Law of Moses saw God working in miracles to preserve and reward the Israelite people, and to keep them living in God's ways (Ps 105; 107; 136; see also Neh 9).

Throughout the Bible, miracles are presented as signs that point to a larger meaning. This is evident, for example, in the descriptions of the Israelites' experiences in the desert of Sinai, which show God's special purpose for the people. Not only do they survive their ordeal, but they are brought into the land God promised to them so that they can worship the LORD (Deut 4.23-34; 6.21-25; 26.5-11; Josh 24.17). Miracles also helped the Israelites believe God's promises because the Israelites could see them being fulfilled. Even a Babylonian king came to believe that Israel's God had miraculous power after he saw how God preserved the three faithful young Israelite men in the fiery furnace (Dan 3).

JESUS' MIRACLES SHOW GOD'S LOVE AND POWER

The New Testament reports Jesus' many miracles. Yet, when Jesus' opponents tried to test him by making him perform a miracle to prove that God was with him, Jesus refused (Matt 16.1-4; Mark 8.11,12; John 4.48; 6.26-34). Also, Jesus sometimes warned people not to tell anyone about his miracles (Mark 1.44; 5.43), possibly because non-believers would have thought Jesus was just a magician. Often, it seemed that Jesus' miracles only worked for people who believed (Mark 2.5-12; 5.34). His miracles were not for showing off. Instead, they demonstrated God's love for the people (Luke 4.18-21) and announced the presence of the Kingdom of God.

MIRACLES IN THE EARLY CHURCH

At the time of the early church, public miracles helped people recognize that God was at work (Acts 2.19-22, 43; 4.30; 5.12,13; 8.13). At the same time, some people wrongly thought that the ability to heal and do miracles was a result of magical powers. In Acts 8.9-24 a magician named Simon claimed to be converted to Christianity, but he still had to learn that God's power was a gift, and not some magic power that could be bought. The apostle Paul claimed that God helped him perform miracles to confirm the good news about Jesus and Paul's own role as an apostle (2 Cor 12.12). He also told of Jesus' miracles to help people believe (Rom 15.15-19).

HOW GOD USES MIRACLES

TYPE OF MIRACLE	SCRIPTURE PASSAGES
God's power revealed to the people	Gen 15.17; Exod 3.1-6; Josh 3.14-17; 1 Kgs 18.16-39; Luke 8.22-25; John 2.1-12; 6.16-21; Acts 2
God helps women unable to have children	Gen 17.1-21; Judg 13; 1 Sam 1; Luke 1.5-25
God's power used to judge evildoers and rebellious people	Gen 6–9; 19.23-29; Exod 7.14—12.30; 2 Sam 12.1-23; 1 Kgs 18.1-40; Jer 18; Acts 5.1-11
God helps Israel in battle	Josh 5.13—6.27; 10.1-15; Judg 6.33—8.3; 1 Sam 17.41-54
God saves or delivers people from trouble	Exod 14; Dan 3,6; Acts 12.6-12; 16.16-34
God provides food and other blessings	Exod 16.1—17.7; 2 Kgs 4.1-7; Luke 5.1-11; John 6.5-15; 21.1-14
God heals and restores health	Num 21. 4-9; 2 Kgs 5.1-19; Mark 5.21-43; Luke 18.35-43; Acts 3.1-10
God's purposes and glory revealed in a vision	Isa 6; Ezek 1; Zech 1.7—5.11; Acts 9.1-19; 10.1-48
God overcomes death	2 Kgs 4.18-37; Matt 28.1-7; Luke 7.11-17; John 11.1-44; Acts 9.36-43
God chooses servants and gives them special gifts	Gen 41; Exod 4.1-12; Judg 6.11-24; 1 Sam 3.1-18; Dan 2; Luke 1.26-38; Acts 2.1-13; 1 Cor 12.1-11

MAGIC, SORCERY, AND WITCHCRAFT

In the ancient world, the belief in magic, sorcery, and witchcraft were common. The people of Israel claimed that the miracles performed by their prophets and leaders were different from these things because they were based on God's power.

The writers of the Scriptures often contrasted these "true" miracles with unusual acts done by the prophets and priests of other peoples and religions. For example, Joseph used God's help to interpret the dreams of the king of Egypt after the king's own magicians and wise men could not (Gen 41.1-36).

Later, when the Egyptian king's magicians turned their walking sticks into snakes, Moses and his brother Aaron used God's power to do the same thing, and their snake ate the snakes created by the Egyptians (Exod 7.8-13). This showed the superiority of the God of Israel. In another case, Elijah showed that the power of Israel's God was greater than that of the god Baal when God helped Elijah win a contest against the prophets of Baal (1 Kgs 18.16-40).

Witchcraft was forbidden by the Law of Moses (Lev 19.26), because relying on spirits or powers other than God showed a lack of faith and trust in the one true God. Disobeying the command against

SOME WELL-KNOWN MIRACLES OF JESUS

MIRACLE	SCRIPTURE PASSAGES
Turns water into wine in Cana	John 2.1-11
Orders the wind and waves to be quiet	Mark 4.35-41
Walks on water on Lake Galilee	Matthew 14.22-33
With five loaves and two fishes, feeds a crowd of more than 5,000 people	Matthew 14.13-21
Raises his friend Lazarus to life	John 11.17-44
Raises a dead girl to life	Matthew 9.18-26
Gives sight to a man born blind	John 9.1-41
Cures the woman who had been bleeding for twelve years	Matthew 9.20-22
Cures a man of evil spirits and sends the spirits into a herd of pigs	Mark 5.1-20
Heals ten men with leprosy	Luke 17.11-19
Heals a crippled man in Capernaum	Mark 2.1-12
Heals a man who was deaf and could hardly talk	Mark 7.31-37
Heals the high priest's servant after the man's ear is cut off	Luke 22.49-52

witchcraft could lead to harsh punishment (Exod 22.18; Deut 18.10-13). When King Saul, Israel's first king, was afraid of the approaching Philistine army, he did not pray to God for help. Instead, he broke the law forbidding witchcraft and asked a woman from Endor who talked to spirits to call on Samuel, who died some time before (1 Sam 28.4-20). In another example, when the people of the northern kingdom (Israel) disobeyed God by worshiping the stars and using magic, or by worshiping idols like Asherah and Baal, God became so furious with them that he allowed them to be defeated by the Assyrians and carried away as prisoners (2 Kgs 17.16-18).

Parts of the New Testament make clear that sorcery and fortunetelling were caused by evil spirits. In one case, a slave girl lost her power to tell fortunes after Paul ordered an evil spirit to leave her. This angered her owners because she could no longer make money for them by telling fortunes (Acts 16.16-19). In GALATIANS, Paul includes witchcraft on the list of "shameful deeds" done by those who obey their own selfish desires instead of obeying God's Spirit (Gal 5.20). And in REVELATION, a beast fooled people by doing magical miracles, such as making an idol speak as if it were alive (Rev 13.11-15).

MEDICINE AND HEALING

What does the Bible reveal about healers in the ancient world? In one part of the Old Testament, it says that King Asa's death may have been from depending only on human healers, and not asking for God's help (2 Chr 16.12-13). Also, the prophet Jeremiah questions whether medicine or doctors can truly provide healing (Jer 8:22). After all, God is seen as the main healer in the Old Testament (Exod 15.26; Ps 41.1-4; Jer 17.14; Hos 6.1). In fact, often the priests were seen as healers on God's behalf (Lev 13.1-3; 14.1-32).

Some parts of the Bible reflect the belief that disease and sickness are caused by failing to live according to God's Law (Deut 28.21-23, 27-29, 34,35), while health and well-being were seen as the reward for trusting God (Exod 15.26; Deut 7.12-15;). Other parts of the Bible question this belief (Job 2; 42.7; Eccl 8.10-13, 9.2; John 9.1-7). People with certain diseases were set apart from the rest of God's people because they were considered unclean (Lev 13; Num 12.9-14). While this was done primarily for religious reasons, those who had these diseases were not allowed to worship or be among their friends and neighbors until they were cured and had gone through a ritual cleansing ceremony (Lev 14).

Jesus knew these laws about sickness and being cleansed, but he also showed himself to be a great healer. Many of Jesus' miracles included healing people considered unclean. He encouraged the ten men he healed of leprosy to show themselves to the priests, probably so they could go through the ritual cleansing and be welcomed back into the community of God's people (Luke 17.1-16). Another time, Jesus' power healed a woman who had spent all her money and had gone to many doctors without finding a cure (Mark 5.25-34). Jesus offered his healing also to those who were not part of the Jewish people (Luke 4.23-29), just as the prophets before him had done (1 Kgs 17.1-24; 2 Kgs 5.14). This was surely amazing to many people, and was a way of showing that God's love is for everyone.

The Bible tends to teach trust in God and prayer and fasting as the way to be healed from illness, rather than trusting in human doctors or healers. The Bible is not always against doctors and medicine though, and biblical authors were not aware of modern scientific techniques. After all, Luke, a companion of the apostle Paul, was said to be a physician (Col 4.14). Also, modern medicine can be seen in light of the biblical command to love one's neighbor (Lev 19.18; Luke 10.25-37). In fact, Jesus told his followers to go heal the sick (Luke 10.9). The Bible also stresses the value and dignity of human life, teaching that all human beings are created by God and in God's likeness (Gen 1.26-27). This belief has probably influenced the practice and ethics of modern medicine as well.

The Bible's accounts of miracles, magic, and medicine are all stories about God's power and love. They are not scientific explanations of supernatural events, but a faithful witness to the all-powerful nature of God, the Creator.

appendix

JACOB'S CHILDREN AND THEIR MOTHERS			
LEAH	**ZILPAH** (Leah's servant)	**BILHAH** (Rachel's servant)	**RACHEL**
Reuben (1)	Gad (7)	Dan (5)	Joseph (12)
Simeon (2)	Asher (8)	Naphtali (6)	Benjamin (13)
Levi (3)			
Judah (4)			
Issachar (9)			
Zebulun (10)			
Dinah (11)			

Note: The numbers after Jacob's children's names indicate their birth order as given in Genesis 29; 30; 35.16-26.

EGYPTIAN KINGS (PHARAOHS) IN THE BIBLE

KING	IDENTITY OR POSSIBLE IDENTITY	SCRIPTURE PASSAGES
Unnamed	Knew Abraham and Sarah	Gen 12.14-20
Unnamed	Put Joseph in charge of food supply in Egypt	Gen 41.37-57
Sety I (Sethos) (1291–127 B.C.)	Possibly the "new king" (Exod 1.8) who was pharaoh during the Hebrews' time of slavery in Egypt	Exod 1–14
Rameses II (1279–1212 B.C.)	Followed Sety I and may have been the pharaoh at the time of Hebrews' exodus from Egypt	Exod 1–14
Unnamed	Father of King Solomon's Egyptian wife	1 Kgs 3.1; 7.8
Shishak (c. 945–924 B.C.)	Raided the Jerusalem temple during the reign of Rehoboam of Judah (c. 922–915) but let King Jeroboam of Israel (c. 922–901) hide in his palace	1 Kgs 14.25,26; 2 Chr 12.2-9
So (727–720 B.C.)	This may have been Pharaoh Osorkon IV, who was sent a message by King Hoshea of Israel (732–724) just before the Israelites rebelled against the king of Assyria.	2 Kgs 17.1-4
Tirhakah (c. 690–664 B.C.)	Called "King of Ethiopia," who battled with Assyria during the reign of King Hezekiah of Judah	2 Kgs 19.9; Isa 37.9
Neco (610–595 B.C.)	Killed King Josiah of Judah (640–609) at Megiddo, replaced Jehoahaz with Jehoiakim as Judah's ruler, and was defeated by King Nebuchadnezzar of Babylon	2 Kgs 23.29-34; 2 Chr 35.20—36.4
Hophra (589–570 B.C.)	The prophet Jeremiah said Hophra would be captured by his enemy Nebuchadnezzar of Babylonia.	Jer 43.6-13; 44.30
Other unnamed pharaohs	Little is known about these.	1 Kgs 11.14-22; 2 Kgs 18.21; 1 Chr 4.17-18

EGYPTIAN DYNASTIES

DYNASTIES AND ACHIEVEMENTS	APPROX. DATES
Pre-dynastic and early dynastic periods Early Egyptian village groups began to band together.	3400–2950 B.C.
First and Second Dynasties The Nile River valley and delta were brought under one ruler.	2950–2675 B.C.
Old Kingdom—Third to Sixth Dynasties The great pyramids were built near Memphis.	2675–2180 B.C.
First Intermediate Period—Seventh to Tenth Dynasties Outsiders controlled the delta—Libyans from the west and Asians from the east.	2180–1970 B.C.
Middle Kingdom—Eleventh to Twelfth Dynasties Egypt was again unified with its capital at Thebes. This period was the high point of Egyptian art. Abraham was in Egypt during this period (Gen 12).	1970–1756 B.C.
Second Intermediate Period—Thirteenth to Seventeenth Dynasties Egypt was ruled by the Hyksos, Asian invaders who had high technical and military skills. They were based in the delta and had traded with Syria and Palestine. Possibly Joseph, and then Jacob and his sons were in Egypt during this time.	1756–1520 B.C.
New Kingdom—Eighteenth to Twentieth Dynasties Many famous Egyptian rulers lived in this period, including Amenhotep; Queen Hastshepsut; Amenhotep IV, also known as Akhenaton, who worshiped only Aton, god of the sun; Tutankhamen, also known as King Tut, who restored the worship of Amon, the chief traditional god of the Egyptians; Rameses II, who may have been the Egyptian king when the Hebrews were led out of Egypt by Moses in a great exodus.	1539–1075 B.C.
Third Intermediate Period—Twenty-first to Twenty-fifth Dynasties A pharaoh from one of these dynasties gave his daughter in marriage to Solomon (1 Kgs 9.16). The Egyptians could not prevent the Assyrians from invading Egypt.	1075–656 B.C.
Late Period—Twenty-sixth to Thirty-first Dynasties After struggles with the Assyrians and support by the Greeks, the Persians took over the Near East, including Egypt. Then Alexander the Great of Macedonia took over Egypt in 332 B.C. Alexander built a new capital city on the Mediterranean Sea coast at the very northern edge of the Nile River delta. This city was called Alexandria. For six hundred years it was one of the great centers of learning in the whole world.	664–343 B.C.
Ptolemaic Dynasty—Final Period When Alexander the Great died, one of his generals, Ptolemy Soter, seized control of Egypt and founded the Ptolemaic Dynasty. The Ptolemies fought with the Seleucid dynasty of northern Syria for control of Palestine. Egypt became more dependent on the Roman Empire. After the Ptolemaic queen Cleopatra fell from power in 30 B.C., Egypt was directly ruled by Rome.	332 B.C.–A.D. 324

DISASTERS (PLAGUES)

DISASTER	WHAT HAPPENED?	EXODUS PASSAGE
1	Nile River's water is turned into blood	7.14-24
2	Frogs swarm all over the land	8.1-15
3	Gnats cover all humans and animals	8.16-19
4	Flies swarm everywhere and fill the houses	8.20-24
5	Egyptian livestock killed by a disease	9.1-7
6	Humans and animals are covered with sores	9.8-12
7	Hail, thunder, and rain knock down the crops	9.13-35
8	Locusts eat up all the plants	10.1-20
9	Darkness covers the whole land	10.21-29
10	Death of all first-born Egyptian males and animals	12.29-30

SACRIFICES AND OFFERINGS

The practice of offering objects to the gods was common in the ancient world. Offerings were made to give thanks, to ask for something like plenty of rainfall or good crops, and to keep the gods from becoming angry or to make them happy. The laws God gave to Moses and the people called for a number of specific kinds of sacrifices or offerings. The objects offered for sacrifice were sometimes brought by the common people and their leaders, but only the priests could perform the sacrifices, which were to be offered to Israel's LORD (*Yahweh*), and to him alone.

The five basic kinds of sacrifices offered by Israel's priests are as follows:

TYPE OF SACRIFICE	OBJECT TO BE SACRIFICED	REASON FOR SACRIFICE	LEVITICUS PASSAGES
Sacrifices to please the LORD ("whole burnt offerings")	Bull, male sheep or goat without blemish, or a dove or pigeon for the poor	To worship God, show devotion to God, and to ask for God's forgiveness; the entire object is burned	1.1-17; 6.8-13; 8.18-21; 16.23,24
Sacrifices to give thanks to the LORD ("grain offerings")	A mixture of fine wheat flour, olive oil and incense; bread baked without yeast or honey in loaves or wafers or fried in flat wafers; salt added sometimes; sometimes used along with burnt offerings or peace offerings	To worship God by giving thanks; to recognize that God is the giver of blessings and provides good things	2.1-16; 6.14-23
Sacrifices to ask the LORD's blessing ("peace offerings" or "well-being offerings")	Fat and certain inner organs from a bull, cow, sheep, or goat that has nothing wrong with it; various kinds of bread made without yeast	To worship God and ask for God's blessing; some of the meat is kept and eaten (7.28-35)	3.1-17; 7.11-36
Sacrifices to ask forgiveness ("sin offerings")	• A young bull for the high priest and the whole nation • A male goat for a tribal leader • A female goat or lamb for ordinary people • Two doves or pigeons for the poor • Two pounds of fine flour for the very poor • Two goats and a ram on the Great Day of Forgiveness (one goat carries the sins of the whole nation into the wilderness)	To ask for God's forgiveness; to make amends for specific unintentional sins; to become clean after becoming ritually unclean	4.1–5.13; 6.24-30; 8.14-17; 16.3-22
Sacrifices to make things right ("guilt offerings")	A ram that has nothing wrong with it, or the price of the ram in addition to paying back what was stolen or destroyed plus twenty percent	To make up for cheating the LORD or unintentionally destroying something that belonged to the LORD; to make up for robbing or cheating another person	5.14—6.7; 7.1-6

ISRAEL COUNTED TWICE

NUMBERS describes two censuses organized by Moses. The LORD asked Moses to make a list of all the men twenty years or older who would be able to fight in battle. The first census took place at Sinai a year after the Israelites came out of Egypt. It counted the generation of Israelites the LORD would not allow to enter Canaan, because of their lack of trust in God (Num 14.21-35). The second census took place in the hills of Moab (Num 26) about thirty-eight years later. It counted the generation that would eventually enter Canaan. Between the censuses, some tribes lost many people as a punishment for disobeying God. The LORD also asked Moses to count all the men and boys in the Levi tribe who were at least one month old. The Levites would not own land because the LORD had assigned them the special task of caring for the sacred tent.

TRIBES ENTITLED TO LAND AND REQUIRED TO FIGHT IN BATTLE

Israel's tribes	Numbers 1.20-46	Numbers 26.1-65
Reuben	46,500	43,730
Simeon	59,300	22,200
Gad	45,650	40,500
Judah	74,600	76,500
Issachar	54,400	64,300
Zebulun	57,400	60,500
Ephraim	40,500	32,500
Manasseh	32,200	52,700
Benjamin	35,400	45,600
Dan	62,700	64,400
Asher	41,500	53,400
Naphtali	53,400	45,400
SUBTOTALS	**603, 550**	**601,730**

PRIESTLY TRIBES IN CHARGE OF THE SACRED TENT

Levites	22,000	23,000
TOTAL	**625,550**	**624,730**

ISRAEL ON THE MARCH

The LORD gave Moses instructions about how the Israelites were to arrange their camp during the time they wandered in the Sinai Desert (see Num 2.1–31). When the Israelites moved to the next place the LORD chose for them, they were to march in the formation shown here. Levites carrying the sacred chest would lead the way. Judah would lead the first row of warrior tribes, and Dan would lead the tribes responsible for protecting the Israelites from behind (see Num 10.11–28).

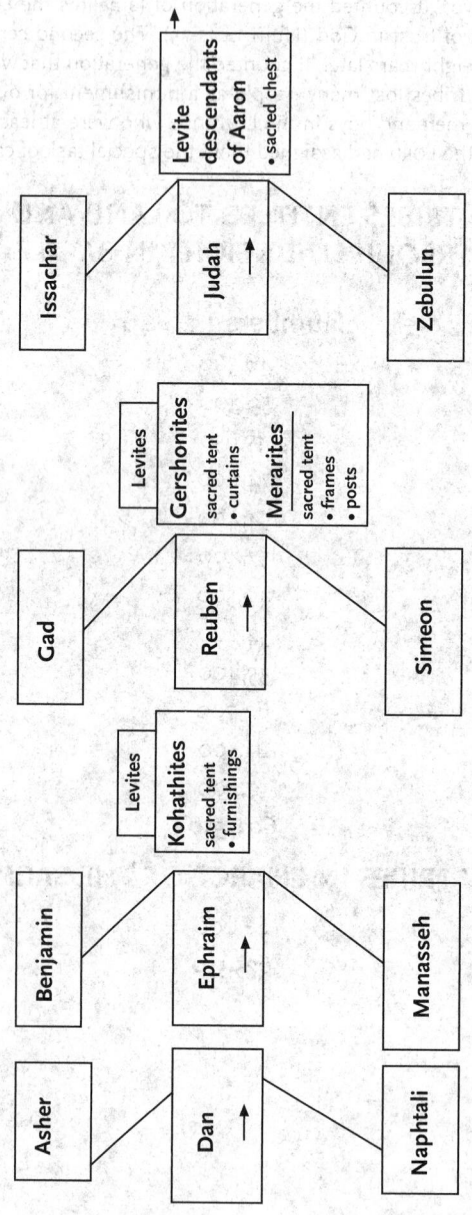

COURT RECORDS AND SOURCES FOR 1 AND 2 KINGS

The author of 1 and 2 Kings drew upon existing material to tell the stories of the kings of Israel and Judah. Some of the sources were probably court records kept by officials who served these kings. Today, the source documents no longer exist. Many people, however, find evidence of these texts in the Scripture passages listed below.

SOURCE DOCUMENTS	SCRIPTURE PASSAGES
A book about Solomon and his wisdom	1 Kings 11.41
The History of the Kings of Judah	1 Kings 14.29; 15.6-7, 23; 22.43-46; 2 Kings 8.23; 12.19; 14.18-20; 15.6, 36; 16.19; 20.20; 21.17, 24-26; 23.28; 24.5
The History of the Kings of Israel	1 Kings 14.19; 15.31; 16.5-7, 14, 20, 27; 22.39; 2 Kings 1.18; 10.34; 13.8, 12; 14.15, 28; 15.11-12, 14-16, 21, 26, 31
The Book of God's Law	2 Kings 22.8,11; 23.2,21

KEY EVENTS IN DAVID'S LIFE

EVENTS	SCRIPTURE PASSAGES	RELATED PSALMS
The LORD chooses David to be king	1 Sam 16.1-13	78
David plays the harp for king Saul	1 Sam 16.14-23	
David kills Goliath	1 Sam 17.1-54	
Saul becomes jealous of David	1 Sam 18.6-30	
David's marriage to Michal	1 Sam 18.20-28; 19.9-17; 2 Sam 6.20-23	59
David's friendship with Jonathan	1 Sam 18.1-4; 20.1-42; 23.14-18; 2 Sam 1.1-27	54, 63
David meets and marries Abigail	1 Sam 25.1-44	
David becomes king of Judah	2 Sam 2.1-7	
David becomes king of Israel	2 Sam 5.1-5; 1 Chr 11.1-3	
David captures Jerusalem	2 Sam 5.6-12; 1 Chr 11.4-9; 14.1-2	
David brings the sacred chest to Jerusalem	2 Sam 6.1-19; 1 Chr 13.1-14; 15.1—16.43	
David and Bathsheba	2 Sam 11.1—12.25	51
Solomon is born	2 Sam 12.24,25	
Absalom rebels against his father David	2 Sam 15.1-12	3
Absalom dies and David mourns	2 Sam 18.7—19.8	
David counts the people	2 Sam 24.1-25	
David gives instructions to his son Solomon	1 Kgs 2.1-9	
David dies	1 Kgs 2.10-12	

KINDS OF PSALMS

PSALMS is a collection of prayers and songs that were written to be used in private devotion, public worship, and for teaching. This chart identifies a variety of psalms according to some general categories and some specific topics they address. Many psalms can fit into more than one of these categories. The ones listed here are just a sampling of the riches to be found in PSALMS.

LAMENTS

Times of national crisis	44; 60; 74; 80; 83
Times of personal crisis or hardship	10; 22; 35; 42; 43; 102

PRAYERS AND PLEAS FOR HELP

Help in times of trouble	6; 23; 25; 41; 57; 91
Deliverance from enemies	35; 68; 129; 137
Forgiveness	32; 38; 39; 51; 130

THANKSGIVING

Deliverance	18; 70; 77; 98
Victory over enemies	21; 52; 124
God's care and healing	30; 108; 126; 127; 145

PRAISE

God's goodness	100; 103
God as creator	8; 104; 148
God as Ruler (King) of all	29; 46; 93; 96; 99
God acts in world events	78; 105; 106; 114
Wisdom and God's Law	1; 19; 37; 119

SONGS FOR WORSHIP

In the holy temple	84; 87; 122; 134
For leader and congregation	24; 136; 149; 150

KINDS OF PROVERBS

The wise sayings found in Proverbs can be grouped in a number of ways. At a very general level, the sayings can be described as statements of truth—"Kind words are like honey" (16.24); or as instructions—"Accept correction, and you will find life" (10.17). But the sayings can also be described by the form or pattern they take. One common pattern follows the form of Hebrew poetry known as "parallelism." In parallel statements, the second part either agrees with the first or provides its opposite. This chart gives some of the patterns or forms used in creating the proverbs.

FORM OR PATTERN OF PROVERB	EXAMPLES

1. Opposite parallel
The same statement or instruction is given twice, but in opposite ways.
	Hatred stirs up trouble;
	  love overlooks the wrongs that others do. (10.12)
	
	Always do the right thing, and you will live;
	  keep on doing wrong, and you will die. (11.19)

2. Similar parallel
The same statement or instruction is given twice in similar ways. The same idea is restated in different words. Sometimes, the second line makes the point more strongly than the first line did.
	God's people avoid evil ways,
	  and they protect themselves by watching where they go. (16.17)
	
	Use wisdom and understanding to establish your home;
	  let good sense fill the rooms with priceless treasures. (24.3,4)

3. Single statement Some proverbs are a single statement describing some truth. These are often short, bold statements or simple warnings.	Even fools seem smart when they are quiet. (17.28) You may think you are on the right road and still end up dead. (14.12)

4. Statement with an explanation
The first line is a concrete image which is then explained by the second line.
	Just as iron sharpens iron,
	  friends sharpen the minds of each other. (27.17)
	
	An angry ruler is like a roaring lion—
	  make either one angry, and you are dead. (20.2)

5. Comparison
Some proverbs use striking images that compare one thing or person to another. These are called "metaphors."
	A beautiful woman who acts foolishly
	  is like a gold ring on the snout of a pig. (11.22)
	
	Our inner thoughts are a lamp from the Lord. (20.27)
	
	A ruler who mistreats the poor is like a roaring lion
	  or a bear hunting for food. (28.15)

6. Descriptive list Usually three or four answers that follow a statement based on an unspoken question.	There are three or four things I cannot understand: How eagles fly so high or snakes crawl on rocks, how ships sail the ocean or people fall in love. (30.18,19)

7. "If-then" statement and "or-else" instruction
The second part explains the consequences of doing or not doing something. The "or-else" is usually implied but not stated.
	If you obey God,
	  you will have something to leave your grandchildren. (13.22)
	
	Make fun of wisdom, and you will never find it. (14.6)
	
	It's better to take hold of a mad dog by the ears
	  than to take part in someone else's argument. (26.17)

SPICES AND PERFUMES

In the ancient Near East, most spices were considered to be a valuable luxury (1 Kgs 10.10,25; Ezek 27.17-22), especially those that had to be imported by traders and merchants from lands far away. Spices were used for cooking, for making fragrant incense (Exod 30.34-38), and for making perfumes. Spices added fragrance to oils and ointments used for grooming and for those used in holy ceremonies (Exod 25.6; 30.23-25). The following chart provides a description of the spices mentioned in Song 4.13,14 and lists some other Bible texts where they are mentioned.

SPICE	DESCRIPTION AND USE	BIBLE PASSAGES
Henna	This small tree has light green spear-shaped leaves, thorny branches, and sweet-smelling flowers. It grows wild in warmer areas of Palestine, such as Jericho and the oasis of En-Gedi (Song 1.14). Its leaves are dried, crushed, and mixed with warm water to make a dye used for coloring fingernails and toenails. Some wealthy women wore little bags filled with fragrant henna flowers around their necks.	Song 4.13
Nard	Also known as spikenard, this plant grows in the Himalayan countries of Bhutan, Nepal, and Kashmir. The fragrant root and lower stems were dried and used in a perfumed ointment. Since perfume made from the nard plant had to be imported to the Near East from India, it was expensive.	Song 1.12; 4.13; probably also Mark 14.3; John 12.3
Saffron	This probably came from the blue-flowered saffron crocus, which may have grown in Palestine in ancient times. Part of the flower was dried and crushed to make a yellow dye used for coloring food, clothing, and walls. It was also mixed with oil and used as a cooking spice, as an ingredient for perfume, and to make medicine.	Song 4.14
Calamus	This probably refers to a fragrant long-stemmed reed or cane that was imported to Palestine. It was used in making the sweet smelling anointing oil (Exod 30.23, "cane") used by Israel's holy priests.	Song 4.14; Isa 43.24, "delicious spices"; Jer 6.20
Cinnamon	Cinnamon comes from an evergreen tree that did not grow in the Near East. Its brown inner bark was easily cut and peeled off. Cinnamon had to be imported to the Near East from countries as far away as Ceylon and Malaysia. It was used as a cooking spice, perfume fragrance, and as an ingredient in holy oil.	Exod 30.23; Prov 7.17; Song 4.14; Rev 18.13
Frankincense	This white gummy resin comes from the wood of Boswellia shrubs or trees that grow in India, Somalia, and Arabia. It is uncertain whether they grew in Palestine. Frankincense resin was pounded into a valuable powder that was burned to make a sweet smell. It was an ingredient in various ointments and in the holy incense burned by Israel's priests. It was also burned along with various sacrifices offered by the priests.	Exod 30.34-38; Song 4.14; Matt 2.11; Rev 18.13; probably also Lev 6.14,15
Myrrh	Myrrh comes from a bush or tree that grows in Arabia and on the coast of East Africa. Some myrrh trees may have grown in Palestine, but most myrrh was imported, making it an expensive luxury. A light-colored sticky substance, or resin, flows from the branches of the myrrh tree. After it is exposed to the air it hardens and turns brown. Myrrh resin was crushed and used in making expensive perfumes and ointments, including the holy oil for dedication and ordination (Exod 30.23-33). Myrrh was also used for embalming the dead (John 19.39).	Esth 2.12; Ps 45.8; Prov 7.7; Song 1.13; 3.6; 4.6,14; 5.1,5,13; Matt 2.11; probably also Mark 15.23
Aloes	Aloes may either refer to the fragrant resin from the tall eaglewood tree that grows in southeast Asia and northern India, or it may refer to the aloe plant, which has thick leaves that form a tight rose shape. Aloe resin has a pleasing smell but it tastes very bitter. Aloes had to be imported to the Near East and were expensive. They were used for making perfumes, medicines, and for embalming the dead.	Ps 45.8; Prov 7.17; Song 4.14; John 19.39

WEIGHTS AND MEASURES IN ANCIENT ISRAEL

KIND OF MEASURE	FRACTIONS	STANDARD	MULTIPLES
Dry (grain)		ephah (about 1/2 bushel)	homer = 10 ephahs (about 5 bushels)
Liquid (olive oil)		bath (about 5 1/2 gallons)	cor = 10 baths (about 55 gallons)
Weight	gerah = 1/20 shekel	shekel (about 2/5 ounce)	mina = 60 shekels (about 24 ounces)

APOCALYPTIC WRITINGS AND THE BIBLE

A brief list of some apocalyptic writings is given below. Apocalyptic writings appear not only in some of the books of the Bible, but also in other Near Eastern writings from the centuries just before and after the birth of Christ.

Jewish apocalypses not included in the Hebrew Bible	Old Testament books with apocalyptic elements	New Testament books with apocalyptic elements	Jewish or Christian apocalypses not included in the New Testament	Writings from other cultures with apocalyptic elements
1 Enoch	Daniel	Revelation	Apocalypse of Peter	Dynastic Prophecy; Uruk Prophecy (ancient Babylon)
4 Ezra; 2 and 3 Baruch	Ezekiel; Isaiah	Matthew (24–25); Mark (13)	Shepherd of Hermas	Vision of the Netherworld (ancient Assyrian)
Apocalypse of Abraham	Joel; Zechariah	Luke (21); 1 Thessalonians (4.13-18)	Ascension of Isaiah	Sibylline Oracles (originally ancient Greek)

JESUS' TWELVE DISCIPLES

The Gospels of Matthew, Mark, and Luke list the twelve disciples of Jesus. Notice how the disciples are listed differently in each Gospel. The reason for this difference is not clear.

MATTHEW 10.2-4	MARK 3.14-19	LUKE 6.13-16
Simon (Peter)	Simon (Peter)	Simon (Peter)
Andrew, Peter's brother	James and John, sons of Zebedee (Boanerges)	Andrew, Peter's brother
James and John, sons of Zebedee	Andrew	James
Philip	Philip	John
Bartholomew	Bartholomew	Philip
Thomas	Matthew	Bartholomew
Matthew the tax collector	Thomas	Matthew
James the son of Alphaeus	James son of Alphaeus	Thomas
Thaddaeus	Thaddaeus	James the son of Alphaeus
Simon, the Eager One	Simon, the Eager One	Simon, the Eager One
Judas Iscariot	Judas Iscariot	Jude
		Judas Iscariot

GREEK AND ROMAN GODS AND GODDESSES

The ancient Greeks had no word for "religion," but they worshiped many gods and goddesses, and believed they controlled much of life and the natural world. In Greek religion, the responsibility of the worshiper was to believe that the gods existed and to make ritual sacrifices to please them and gain their approval. The ancient Romans also worshiped many gods, some of them modeled after the Greek gods. The ancient Greeks pictured their gods with colorful personalities, but the Romans did not give their gods personalities until the Greeks began to influence them. The Romans believed that it did not matter what the worshipers thought of the gods as long as they performed the proper rituals.

God	Worshiped as	Relation to other gods	Beliefs about	Symbols	Center of Worship	Worshiped from
Zeus (also the Roman god Jupiter)	chief god	father of the gods	ruled clouds and rain, decided outcomes of battles, hurled thunderbolts, was celebrated in festival of Olympia (Olympic Games)	the eagle, the color white, the element tin	Olympia (Athens) and Capitoline Hill (Rome)	800 B.C.–A.D. 400
Apollo	god of music, archery, poetry, prophecy, and healing	son of Zeus, brother of Artemis, father of Asclepios	killed mythical monsters, leader of Muses (spirits of art), sometimes pictured as Helios, the sun god	The laurel, bow and arrow, lyre, lions	Delos, Delphi	1300 B.C.–A.D. 400
Artemis (also the Roman goddess Diana)	virgin goddess of animals and hunting	daughter of Zeus, sister of Apollo	presided over nature, helped Hera give birth to Apollo	bow and arrow, wild animals, the moon	Antioch, Delos, Ephesus	800 B.C.–A.D. 400
Asclepios (also the Roman god Aesculapius)	mortal man believed to have become the god of physicians and healing	son of Apollo and a mortal woman	lived as a mortal, killed by Zeus for bringing a human back to life	a rod with twin snakes coiled around it	Epidauros, Kos, Pergamum (Asia)	800 B.C.–A.D. 400
Athena (also the Roman goddess Minerva)	chief goddess, goddess of war	daughter of Zeus, born without a mother	symbol of discipline and self-control, helped legendary heroes in battle, brought the olive tree to mankind	the owl, the skin of a sacrificial goat	Athens, Sparta, and throughout Greece	800 B.C.–A.D. 400

GREEK AND ROMAN GODS AND GODDESSES

God	Worshiped as	Relation to other gods	Beliefs about	Symbols	Center of Worship	Worshiped from
Hera (also the Roman goddess Juno)	goddess of marriage and childbirth	wife of Zeus	takes revenge against others who loved Zeus, celebrated in the *Heraia* (New Year Festival), and Olympic Women's Games	the cow, the peacock, the cuckoo	Sparta, Plataea	800 B.C.– A.D. 400
Hermes (also the Roman god Mercury)	messenger of the gods, god of boundaries, shepherds, heralds (messengers), and thieves	son of Zeus, brother of Apollo	only god able to travel to the underworld (Hades) and back	winged sandals, magical herald's staff, the element Mercury	Arcadia, also posts with head of Mercury erected at crossroads	800 B.C.– A.D. 400
Hephaestus (also the Roman god Vulcan)	god of fire and blacksmiths	son of Zeus and Hera	only disabled (lame) god, made special shields and weapons for Greek gods and heroes	fire, volcanoes	Lemnos, Athens, Ephesus (Asia)	1500 B.C.– A.D. 400
Demeter (also the Roman god Ceres)	goddess of agriculture	sister of Zeus	searched for her daughter Persephone who had been kidnapped by Hades, god of the dead	pigs, a basket filled with flowers, fruit, and grain,	throughout Greece, and particularly at Eleusis	at least 800 B.C.–A.D. 400
Dionysus (also the Roman god Bacchus or Liber)	god, of fruitfulness, wine, and intoxication	son of Zeus	lavish drinking and sexual rites (Bacchanalia) held in his honor	the ivy wreath and the *kantharos* (large two-handled goblet)	Pylos, Keos, Phyrigia (Asia), and Lydia (Asia)	at least 1500 B.C.– A.D. 400
Hades (also the Roman god Pluto)	god of the dead and ruler of the underworld, which was also called "Hades"	brother of Zeus and Poseidon	supervised the trial and punishment of the wicked after death, never moved by prayer or sacrifice	a black chariot drawn by four black horses, a two-pronged harpoon, a key	only on Pylos	800 B.C.– A.D. 400
Poseidon (also the Roman god Neptune)	god of the sea and of water, also the god of earthquakes	brother of Zeus and Hades, father of the winged horse Pegasus	ruled the oceans from a palace made of coral and jewels on the bottom of the sea, drove a chariot pulled by horses	the trident, the dolphin, the tuna	Colonus, also Mt. Mykale (Turkey), and Berytus (Syria)	1600 B.C.– A.D. 400

LEADERS OF HOUSE CHURCHES
IN THE NEW TESTAMENT

The Greek word for "church" (*ekklesia*) means "assembly" or "gathering." The first churches met in homes of Christians to pray, sing hymns, read the Scriptures, and share "love meals" together. Although little is known about the individuals listed here, they are remembered as early followers of Christ who opened their homes for Christian fellowship or who led local groups of Christians.

LEADERS	CITY	SCRIPTURE PASSAGE
Phoebe	Cenchreae	Rom 16.1,2
Gaius	Corinth	Rom 16.23,24; 1 Cor 1.14
Priscilla and Aquila	Ephesus	Acts 18.1-26; Rom 16.3-5; 1 Cor 16.19
Philemon	Colossae	Phlm 2
Nympha	Laodicea	Col 4.15

KEY EVENTS IN MOSES' LIFE

EVENT	SCRIPTURE PASSAGE
The birth of Moses	Exod 2.1-10
Moses kills an Egyptian and escapes to the land of Midian	Exod 2.11-15
Moses marries Zipporah, a Midianite	Exod 2.21,22
God speaks to Moses from the burning bush	Exod 3.1—4.17
Moses and Aaron confront the king of Egypt and the LORD brings about the ten disasters (plagues)	Exod 5.1—12.30
Moses leads the people of Israel out of Egypt and across the Red Sea	Exod 12.31-42; 13.17—14.31
The LORD makes the bitter waters at Marah drinkable	Exod 15.22-25
The LORD sends bread (manna) from heaven	Exod 16.1-36; Num 11.4-9
The LORD gives water from a rock	Exod 17.1-7; Num 20.1-13
Moses receives the Ten Commandments at Mount Sinai	Exod 20.1-17; Deut 5.1-21
Moses receives laws concerning civil matters	Exod 21.1—23.9; Num 30.1-16; 35.9—36.13; Deut 15.1-18; 16.18-20; 17.8-20; 19.1—25.16
Moses receives instructions about the sacred tent and other religious matters	Exod 25.1—31.18; 35.1—40.38; Lev 1—27; Num 19.1-22; 28.1—29.40; Deut 12.1—14.29; 15.19—16.17
The people make an idol in the shape of a bull and Moses breaks the stones on which the LORD's commandments were written	Exod 32.1-35; Deut 9.6-29
The LORD gives a second set of commandments	Exod 34.1-9; Deut 10.1-5
Moses' face shines from being in the LORD's presence on Mount Sinai	Exod 34.29-35
The LORD gives Moses instructions about making the tribe of Levi into priests to serve in the sacred tent	Num 3.5-13; 8.5-26; 18.1-32; Deut 10.8,9
Korah, Dathan, and Abiram rebel against Moses' leadership	Num 16.1-40
Moses makes a bronze snake to heal the people bitten by poisonous snakes	Num 21.4-9
The LORD refuses to let Moses enter Canaan	Deut 3.23-29; 32.48-52
The LORD gives Moses the most important commandment	Deut 6.1-9
Moses blesses the tribes of Israel	Deut 33.1-29
The death of Moses	Deut 34.1-8

PEOPLE OF FAITH MENTIONED IN HEBREWS

PERSON	DESCRIPTION	ACT OF FAITH	KEY BIBLE PASSAGES
Abel	Adam and Eve's second son, younger brother of Cain. Cain killed Abel when Abel offered a better sacrifice to the LORD.	Offered the best parts of a lamb as a sacrifice to the LORD	Gen 4.1-16
Enoch	Little information is given about Enoch in the Bible. Instead of saying he died, the Bible says that God "took him away."	"truly loved God"	Gen 5.21-26
Noah	Son of Lamech and great-grandson of Enoch. His name sounds like the Hebrew word for "comfort."	Believed God's warning that God was going to destroy the evil people of the world in a flood. Built a large boat (ark) as God commanded to save his family and animals.	Gen 6.1—9.17
Abraham	A descendant of Noah's son Shem and the son of Terah. Husband of Sarah and father of Isaac. He was named Abram at birth, but God changed his name to Abraham which sounds like the Hebrew for "father of many nations" (Gen 17.4-5).	Left the security of his homeland, when God called him to go to a new land where God would give him many descendants	Gen 12.1-9; 17.1-8; see also Rom 4
Sarah	Wife of Abraham and mother of Isaac. She was originally named Sarai but God changed her name to Sarah (both names mean "princess" (Gen 17.15).	Was too old to have children, but she had faith that God would give her a child anyway	Gen 18.1-15; 21.1-8
Isaac	Abraham and Sarah's son. Although Abraham had a son by his wife's slave Hagar, Isaac is called Abraham's "only son" because he was born as the result of God's promise to Abraham.	Gave a blessing to his sons Jacob and Esau	Gen 27.1-40
Jacob	Son of Isaac and Rebekah, and twin brother of Esau. His name was changed to Israel (Gen 32.22-28) which means "a man who wrestles with God." The twelve tribes of Israel were named after his sons. God's promise to Abraham and Isaac was repeated to Jacob (Gen 28.13-15).	Blessed his grandsons Ephraim and Manasseh (Joseph's sons)	Gen 48.1-22

PEOPLE OF FAITH MENTIONED IN HEBREWS

PERSON	DESCRIPTION	ACT OF FAITH	KEY BIBLE PASSAGES
Joseph	Son of Jacob and Rachel. He was sold by his brothers to a passing caravan of traders and taken to Egypt where he became an important official in the kings court.	Used his position in the Egyptian government to save his family when they went to Egypt during a time of famine in Caanan. Also, trusted that God would lead the Hebrew people of Israel out of Egypt.	Gen 37–50; especially 50.22-25.
Moses	A Hebrew born in Egypt who was adopted into the royal household. The LORD appeared to him and commanded him to lead the Hebrew people out of slavery in Egypt; later the LORD gave him the Law on Mount Sinai.	Refused to be considered the king's grandson; led the Hebrew people out of Egypt; celebrated Passover	Exod 1–15; 19–34
Rahab	A Canaanite prostitute who lived in Jericho before the Israelites conquered the city	Helped two Israelite spies escape Jericho so they could make a report to their commanders	Josh 2.1,3; 6.21-25
Gideon, Barak, Samson, and Jephthah	Leaders (also called "judges") of the tribes of Israel before Israel had a king	Performed acts of heroism and helped the Israelites to gain control of the land (Canaan) promised to Abraham and his descendants	Judg 4–16
David	A great warrior and Israel's greatest king. He made Jerusalem the capital of Israel and had the sacred chest brought there. He was the father of Solomon, a wise king who built the first temple in Jerusalem.	Slew the giant Goliath and helped the Israelites to conquer Canaan	1 Sam 16.1—1 Kgs 2.11; especially, 1 Sam 17
Samuel	Samuel was a prophet and the last judge of Israel. He poured oil on the heads of Saul and David to show that God had chosen them to be kings of Israel.	Led the people of Israel as a judge and prophet	1 Sam 1.1—25.1

NUMBERS IN THE BIBLE

Certain numbers had special meanings in the ancient world and to the writers of the Bible. This chart gives some key examples. Keep in mind, however, that sometimes these numbers represent actual quantities and are not intended to be understood symbolically.

ONE

Monotheism, uniqueness, and unity.

"The LORD our God is the only true God!" *Deut 6.4*
"We have only one Lord, one faith, and one baptism." *Eph 4.5*

THREE

Completeness or totality. Many ancient religions considered three a divine number.

Three men visited Abraham at Mamre *Gen 18.1-15*
Three annual festivals (Thin Bread, Harvest, & Shelters) *Exod 23.14-19*
Number of days and nights Jonah was inside the big fish *Jonah 1.17*
Number of days between Jesus' death and resurrection *Mark 8.31; 1 Cor 15.4*

FOUR

Totality of the created world. Most cultures speak of four winds or directions, and divide the year into four seasons.

Number of rivers flowing out of the garden of Eden *Gen 2.10*
Four living creatures of Ezekiel's vision *Ezek 1.4-28* (see also *Rev 4.1-8*)
Four horses and riders of John's vision *Rev 6.1-8*

SEVEN

Completeness and perfection. Like three it was considered a sacred number to many cultures in the ancient world.

Number of days in the week based on Creation story *Gen 1.1—2.3*
The "seventh" day is a holy day of rest (Sabbath) *Exod 20.8-11*
The Israelites were to let the land rest every "seventh" year (sabbatical year) *Exod 23.10,11*
Every fiftieth year (7 x 7 + 1) the Israelites were to celebrate a Year of Celebration (Jubilee) to mark a time of freedom and forgiveness *Lev 25.8-55*
Temple furnishings and decorations were often done in seven parts *1 Kgs 7.17; Ezek 40.22, 26*
Number of times blood is to be sprinkled during sacrificial ceremonies *Lev 4.6, 17; 14.7; Num 19.4*
Number of several items mentioned in REVELATION (lampstands, stars, churches, seals, trumpets, bowls) *Rev 1; 6–11;15–16*
Number of times Jesus said to forgive (seven times seventy) *Matt 18.21,22*

TEN

Because ten is the sum of three and seven it sometimes represents complete perfection.

The number of times "God said" is repeated in the Hebrew text of the Creation story *Gen 1.1-31*
The Ten Commandments *Exod 20.1-17; Deut 5.1-22*

TWELVE

Also a number of completeness and perfection.

Number of Jacob's sons and the number of tribes of Israel *Gen 35.23-26;49.1-28*
Number of gates to Jerusalem in Ezekiel's vision *Ezek 48.30* (see also *Rev 21.11-21*)
Number of Jesus' apostles *Matt 10.1-4; Mark 3.13-19; Luke 6.12-16*

FORTY

A long, but limited period of time.

Number of days it rained during the great Flood *Gen 7.4, 17-18*
Number of days Moses stayed on Mount Sinai *Exod 24.17-18*
Number of years the Israelites wandered in the desert *Num 14.33,34; Deut 2.7; 29.4-6*
Number of days Jesus fasted in the desert *Matt 4.2; Mark 1.12,13; Luke 4.2*
Number of years a favored king is said to rule *2 Sam 5.4; 1 Kgs 11.41,42; 2 Chr 24.1*

a mini dictionary for the bible

Aaron The brother of Moses. Only he and his descendants were to serve as priests and offer sacrifices for the people of Israel (see Exodus 4.14-16; 28.1; Numbers 16.1—18.7).

Ab The fifth month in the Hebrew calendar; it falls around mid-July to mid-August.

Abel The second son of Adam and Eve and the younger brother of Cain. Abel was killed by Cain after God accepted Abel's offering and refused to accept Cain's (see Genesis 4.1-11).

Abib or Nisan The first month in the Hebrew calendar; it falls around mid-March to mid-April.

Abraham or Abram The first of the three great ancestors of the people of Israel. Abraham was the husband of Sarah and the father of Isaac. At first Abraham's name was Abram, meaning "Great Father." Then, when Abram was ninety-nine years old, God changed Abram's name to Abraham, which means "Father of Many People." Abraham trusted God, and so God promised that Abraham and his wife Sarah would have a son and more descendants than could be counted. God also promised that Abraham would be a blessing to everyone on earth (see Genesis 12.1-7; 17.1—18.15).

acacia A flowering tree that produces a hard, durable wood. The sacred chest, the altars, and certain other wooden objects in the sacred tent were made of acacia wood.

A.D. *Anno Domini.* Latin for "In the year of the Lord." Used to date events that happened after Christ's birth. "A.D." is often used before the number of the year. The numbering system now in use was developed about A.D. 525. The plan was that the year of Christ's birth would be A.D. 1, and then the years would be numbered before and after. But an error was made in assigning A.D. 1, and by the time the error was discovered, the numbering system could not be changed. And so, the correct year of Christ's birth according to the numbering system is probably 6 B.C. See also "B.C."

Adam The first man and the husband of Eve (see Genesis 1.26—3.21).

Adar The twelfth month in the Hebrew calendar; it falls around mid-February to mid-March.

Agrippa (1) Herod Agrippa I was king of Judea A.D. 41—44 and mistreated Christians (see Acts 12.1-5). (2) Agrippa II was the son of Herod Agrippa and ruled parts of Palestine from A.D. 53—93 or later. He and his sister Bernice listened to Paul defend himself (see Acts 25.13—26.32).

aloes A sweet-smelling spice that was mixed with myrrh and used as a perfume.

altar A raised structure where sacrifices and offerings were presented to God or to pagan gods. Altars could be made of rocks, packed earth, metal, or pottery. See Genesis 8.20; 13.18; 33.20.

Amalekites A nomadic nation living mostly in the area south and east of the Dead Sea. They were enemies of Israel.

Amen A Hebrew word used after a prayer or a blessing and meaning that what had been said was right and true.

Ammon A nation that lived east of Israel. According to Genesis 19.30-38, the people of Ammon descended from Lot, a nephew of Abraham.

Amorites Usually a name for all the non-Israelite nations who lived in Canaan, but in some passages it may refer to one nation scattered in several areas of Canaan.

Anakim Perhaps a group of very large people who lived in Palestine before the Israelites. See Numbers 13.33 and Deuteronomy 2.10,11,21.

Andrew One of Jesus' twelve closest disciples (called "apostles") and the brother of Simon Peter. See "apostle."

angel A supernatural being who tells God's messages to people or protects those who belong to God. See Genesis 16.7-12; Numbers 22.22-35; Luke 1.11-28.

Antipas (1) Herod Antipas, son of Herod the Great (see "Herod"). (2) An otherwise unknown Christian at Pergamum, who was killed because he was a follower of Christ (see Revelation 2.13).

apostle A person chosen and sent by Christ to take his message to others. Lists of the names of Christ's twelve apostles can be found in Matthew 10.2-4; Mark 3.16-19; Luke 6.14-16; Acts 1.12,13. Later, others such as Paul and James the brother of Jesus also became known as apostles.

Aramaic A language closely related to Hebrew. In New Testament times Aramaic was spoken by many Jews including Jesus. Parts of Ezra and Daniel were written in Aramaic (see Ezra 4.8—6.18; 7.12-26; Daniel 2.4b—7.28).

Asher (1) Jacob's eighth son, and his second by Leah's servant Zilpah. (2) One of the twelve tribes of Israel. When the Israelites left Egypt, the tribe of Asher occupied land along the Mediterranean coast from Mount Carmel to the border with the city of Tyre (see Joshua 19.24-31).

Asia A Roman province in what is today the nation of Turkey.

Assyria An empire of Old Testament times, whose capital city Nineveh was located in what is today northern Iraq. In 722 B.C. Assyria conquered the kingdom of Israel and took many Israelites as captives. The Assyrians then forced people from other parts of its empire to settle on Israel's land (see 2 Kings 18.9-12).

Astarte A Canaanite goddess. Those who worshiped her believed that she gave them fertile land and many children, and that she helped their animals give birth to lots of young.

Augustus A title meaning "honored," which was given to Octavian by the Romans when he began ruling the Roman world in 27 B.C. He was the Roman Emperor when Jesus was born (Luke 2.1).

Baal A term meaning "lord" that was originally used for each of the local gods of Canaan. Later it was applied only to the chief god of Canaan, who was believed to have power to bring about fertility in people, animals, and the earth.

Babylonia A large empire of Old Testament times, whose capital city Babylon was located in what is today Iraq. The Babylonians defeated the southern kingdom of Judah in 586 B.C. and forced many of its people to live in Babylonia (see 2 Kings 25.1-12).

Balaam A prophet from the town of Pethor (exact location unknown). Balaam was hired by the king of Moab to put a curse on Israel, but instead Balaam blessed Israel (see Numbers 22–24).

Bartholomew One of Jesus' twelve closest disciples (called "apostles"). He is mentioned in all New Testament lists of the apostles, but nowhere else. See "apostle."

Bashan The highlands and wooded hills of southern Syria. Bashan was just north of the region of Gilead and was known for its fat cattle and fine grain.

B.C. Before Christ. Used to date events that happened before Christ's birth. "B.C." is used after the number of the year. For more about dates, see "A.D."

Benjamin (1) Jacob's twelfth son, and his second by his wife Rachel. He was Joseph's younger brother. (2) One of the twelve tribes of Israel. When the Israelites left Egypt, the tribe of Benjamin occupied land between Bethel and Jerusalem (see Joshua 18.11-28). Israel's first king, Saul, was from this tribe (see 1 Samuel 9.21). When the northern tribes of Israel broke away following the death of Solomon, only the tribes of Benjamin and Judah were left to form the southern kingdom.

Bul or Marchesvan The eighth month in the Hebrew calendar; it falls around mid-October to mid-November.

Cain The first son of Adam and Eve; Cain killed his brother Abel after God accepted Abel's offering and refused to accept Cain's (see Genesis 4.1-17).

Canaan The area now covered by Israel plus Gaza, the West Bank of Jordan, Lebanon, and southern Syria (see Numbers 34.1-12). Many passages use the term to refer only to the area south of Lebanon.

Canaanites The nations who lived in Canaan before the Israelites. Many Canaanites continued to live there even after the Israelites occupied the land.

cedar A tall tree once common in the Lebanon mountains and used for many of the royal building projects in Jerusalem.

Cephas See "Peter."

chariot A two-wheeled cart that was open at the back and was pulled by horses. It was the ancient equivalent of an armored vehicle and was often the symbol of royalty or riches (see Exodus 14.7; 2 Kings 2.11).

Chislev The ninth month in the Hebrew calendar; it falls around mid-November to mid-December.

Christ (1) A Greek word meaning "the Chosen One" and used to translate the Hebrew word "Messiah," often referring to the one that many of the Jews believed God was going to send to rescue them from their enemies. (2) The term "Christ" is used in the New Testament both as a title and as a name for Jesus.

circumcise To cut off the foreskin of the male organ. This was done for Israelite boys eight days after they were born to show that they belonged to God's people (see Genesis 17.9-14).

cistern A hole or pit used for storing rainwater. Cisterns were sometimes dug in the ground and lined with stones and plaster, and at other times they were cut into the rock. The CEV sometimes translates "cistern" as "well."

clan A group of families who were related to each other and who often lived close to each other. A group of clans made up a tribe.

clean and unclean (1) In Old Testament times, a person who was acceptable to worship God was called "clean." A person who had certain kinds of diseases, who had touched a dead body, or who had broken certain laws became "unclean," and was unacceptable to worship God. If a person was unclean because of disease, the disease would have to be cured before the person could be clean again. And becoming clean involved performing certain ceremonies that sometimes included sacrifices. (2) Animals that were acceptable as food were called "clean." Those that were not acceptable were called "unclean" (see Leviticus 11.1-47; Deuteronomy 14.3-21). (3) Many things including tools, dishes, houses, and land could also become unclean and unusable, especially if they were touched by something unclean. Some unclean objects had to be destroyed, but others could be made clean by being washed or placed in a fire for a short time.

commandments God's rules for his people to live by. The most famous are the Ten Commandments (see Exodus 20.1-17; Deuteronomy 5.6-21).

council (1) A group of leaders who meet and make decisions for their people. (2) The Old Testament refers to God's council as a group of angels who meet and talk with God in heaven (see Job 15.8; Jeremiah 23.18-22).

cross A wooden structure to which Romans either nailed or tied condemned prisoners, who hung there until they died. It was made of two pieces of lumber crossed in a "**T**," "**t**," or "**X**" shape. Jesus was put to death on a cross (see Matthew 27.31-56).

Cush The Hebrew name for Ethiopia (see "Ethiopia").

Dagon The chief god of the Philistines (see Judges 16.23).

Dan (1) Jacob's fifth son, and his first by Rachel's servant Bilhah. (2) One of the twelve tribes of Israel. When the Israelites left Egypt, the tribe of Dan first occupied land west of Judah, Benjamin, and Ephraim (see Joshua 19.40-48). But after the Philistines took control of this area, part of the tribe then moved to the northernmost area of Israel.

David King of Israel from about 1010–970 B.C. David was the most famous king Israel ever had, and many of the people of Israel hoped that one of his descendants would always be their king (see 1 Samuel 16–30; 2 Samuel 1–24; 1 Kings 1–2).

Deborah A prophet and judge who helped lead Israel to defeat King Jabin of Hazor (see Judges 4–5).

demons and evil spirits Supernatural beings that do harmful things to people and sometimes cause them to do bad things. In the New Testament they are sometimes called "unclean spirits," because people under their power were thought to be unclean and unfit to worship God. See Mark 5.1-13; 7.24-30.

devil The chief of the demons and evil spirits, also known as "Satan." See Job 1.6—2.7; Matthew 4.1-11; Luke 4.1-13; John 8.44.

disciples Those who were followers of Jesus and learned from him. The term often refers to his twelve apostles. See "apostle."

Edomites A nation living in Edom or Seir, an area south and southeast of the Dead Sea. According to Genesis 36.1-43, the Edomites descended from Esau, Jacob's brother.

elder An older person of wisdom who had special influence and authority within a secular or religious community.

Elijah A prophet who spoke for God in the early ninth century B.C. and who opposed the evil King Ahab and Queen Jezebel of the northern kingdom. Many Jews in later centuries thought Elijah would return to get everything ready for the day of judgment or for the coming of the Messiah. See 1 Kings 17–21; 2 Kings 1–2; Malachi 4.1-6; Matthew 17.10,11; Mark 9.11,12.

Elisha A prophet who assisted Elijah and later took his place. Elisha spoke for God in the late ninth century B.C., and was the prophet who healed Naaman (see 1 Kings 19.19-21; 2 Kings 2–9; 13.14-21).

Elul The sixth month in the Hebrew calendar; it falls around mid-August to mid-September.

Ephraim (1) Joseph's son, the younger brother of Manasseh (see Genesis 48). (2) One of the largest tribes of Israel. Ephraim occupied the land north of Benjamin and south of West Manasseh (see Joshua 16.1-10; 17.14-18).

Epicureans People who followed the teachings of a man named Epicurus (died around 270 B.C.), who taught that happiness should be the main goal in life.

Esau The older son of Isaac and Rebekah, and the brother of Jacob. Esau was also known as Edom and as the ancestor of the Edomites. See Genesis 25.20-34; 26.34; 28.6-9; 32.1—33.16.

eternal life Life that is the gift of God and that never ends. See John 3.16; 10.27,28; 11.25,26.

Ethanim or Tishri The seventh month in the Hebrew calendar; it falls around mid-September to mid-October.

Ethiopia In the CEV, "Ethiopia" is often used to translate the Hebrew name "Cush," which was a region south of Egypt that included parts of the present countries of Ethiopia and Sudan. See Genesis 2.13; Isaiah 11.11; 18.1,2; 20.1-6.

Eve The first woman and the wife of Adam (see Genesis 1.26—3.21).

evil spirits See "demons."

exile The time in Israel's history (597–539 B.C.) when the Babylonians took away many of the people of Jerusalem and Judah as prisoners of war and made them live in Babylonia. The northern tribes had been taken away by Assyria in 722 B.C. See Jeremiah 52.1-30.

fasting See "going without eating."

Felix The Roman governor of Palestine A.D. 52–60, who listened to Paul speak and kept him in jail (see Acts 23.24—24.27).

Festival of Purim See "Purim."

Festival of Shelters A Jewish religious festival in the early fall celebrating the period of forty years when the people of Israel walked through the desert and lived in small shelters. This happy celebration began on the fifteenth day of Tishri, and for the next seven days, the people lived in small shelters made of tree branches. The name of this festival in Hebrew is "Sukkoth." See Leviticus 23.33-43; Nehemiah 8.13-18.

Festival of Thin Bread A seven-day Jewish festival right after Passover. During this festival the Israelites ate a thin, flat bread made without yeast to remind themselves how God freed the people of Israel from slavery in Egypt and made them into a nation. The name of this festival in Hebrew is "Mazzoth." See Exodus 12.17-20.

Festival of Trumpets or New Moon Festival A Jewish religious festival held on the day of the new moon, the day when only a thin edge of the moon can be seen. This day was always the first day of the month for the Hebrew calendar. The New Moon Festival was a time for rest from work, and a time for worship, sacrifices, celebration, and eating. See 1 Samuel 20.5,18,24. The New Moon Festival in the month of Tishri in the early fall was also called "the Festival of Trumpets," and it involved even more sacrifices. See Leviticus 23.23-25; Numbers 29.1-6.

Festus The Roman governor after Felix, who sent Paul to stand trial in Rome (see Acts 24.27—26.32).

flax The stalks of the flax plants were harvested, soaked in water, and dried. Then their fibers were separated and spun into thread, which was woven to make linen cloth that was used for many purposes, including special priestly garments.

fortuneteller A person who thought they could learn about the future and what God wanted people to do by watching birds in flight, looking at the livers of animals, and by rolling dice, all of which was forbidden in Israel. See 2 Kings 17.16-18; 21.4-7; Zechariah 10.2.

Gad (1) Jacob's seventh son, and his first by Leah's servant Zilpah. (2) One of the twelve tribes of Israel. When the Israelites left Egypt, the tribe of Gad occupied land east of the Jordan River from the northern end of the Dead Sea north to the Jabbok River (see Joshua 13.24-28).

generation One way of describing a group of people who live during the same period of time. In the Bible the time of one generation is often understood to be about forty years.

Gentiles A term used in the New Testament of non-Jewish people in contrast to the Jewish people.

Gethsemane A garden or olive orchard on the Mount of Olives (see Mark 14.32). See also "Mount of Olives."

Gilead A region east of the Jordan River. Moab lay to the south of Gilead, and Bashan was to the north.

Girgashites One of the nations that lived in Canaan before the Israelites.

glory Something seen, heard, or felt that shows a person or thing is important, wonderful, or powerful. When God appeared to people, his glory was often seen as a bright light or as fire and smoke. Jesus' glory was seen when he performed miracles, when he was lifted up on the cross, and when he was raised from death.

God's kingdom God's rule over people, both in this life and in the next.

God's tent See "sacred tent."

going without eating This was a way of showing sorrow, or of asking for God's help. It is also called "fasting."

Great Day of Forgiveness The tenth day of Tishri in the early fall. On this one day of the year, the high priest was allowed to go into the most holy part of the temple and sprinkle some of the blood of a sacrificed bull on the sacred chest. This was done so that the people's sins would be forgiven. In English this holy day has traditionally been called "the Day of Atonement," and its name in Hebrew is "Yom Kippur." See Leviticus 16.1-34; Numbers 29.7-11.

Greek The language used throughout the Mediterranean world in New Testament times, and the language in which the New Testament was written.

Hagar A slave of Sarah, the wife of Abraham. When Sarah could not have any children, she followed the ancient custom of letting her husband have a child by Hagar, her slave. The boy's name was Ishmael (see Genesis 16; 21.9-21).

Harvest Festival A Jewish festival held in mid-spring, fifty days after Passover. At this festival Israelites celebrated the wheat harvest. Also called "Pentecost," "the Feast of Weeks," or by its Hebrew name, "Shavuoth." See Leviticus 23.15-21; Deuteronomy 16.9-12; Acts 2.1.

Hebrew (1) An older term for "Israelite" or "Jewish." (2) The language used by most of the people of Israel until the Exile. But after the people returned, more and more people spoke Aramaic instead. Most of the Old Testament was written in Hebrew.

Hermes The Greek god of skillful speaking and the messenger of the other Greek gods (see Acts 14.12).

Herod (1) Herod the Great was the king of all Palestine from 37 to 4 B.C., and so he was king at the time Jesus was born. (2) Herod Antipas was the son of Herod the Great and was the ruler of Galilee 4 B.C.—A.D. 39. (3) Herod Agrippa I, the grandson of Herod the Great, ruled Palestine A.D. 41–44.

high priest See "priest."

Hinnom Valley A valley west and south of Jerusalem, where human sacrifice was sometimes made in Old Testament times (see "Molech").

Hittites A nation whose capital city was located in what is now Turkey. The Hittites had an empire that at times controlled some kingdoms in Canaan before 1200 B.C., and many Hittites remained in Canaan even after the Israelites came.

Hivites A nation that lived in Canaan before the Israelites, probably related to the Horites.

Holy One (1) A name for God used in the Old Testament (see Psalms 71.22; 89.18; Isaiah 43.3). (2) In the New Testament it is used of the promised Savior (see Mark 1.24; Luke 4.34; John 6.69; Acts 2.27; 13.35; 1 John 2.20). See also "Savior."

holy place The main room of the sacred tent and of the temple. This room contained the sacred bread, the golden incense altar, and the golden lamp stand. A curtain or wall separated the holy place from the most holy place. A priest would go into the holy place once each morning and evening to burn incense on the golden altar (see also "most holy place").

Horites A nation that lived in Canaan before the Israelites. The Horites were also known as "Hurrians."

hyssop A bush with clusters of small branches. In religious ceremonies, hyssop was sometimes dipped in a liquid and then used to sprinkle people or objects (see Exodus 12.22).

incense A material that makes a sweet smell when burned. It was used in the worship of God (see Exodus 30.34-38).

Isaac The second of the three great ancestors of the people of Israel. He was the son of Abraham and Sarah, and he was the father of Esau and Jacob. See Genesis 21.1-8; 22.1-19; 24.1—28.9.

Ishmael The son of Abraham and Hagar. See Genesis 16.1-16; 21.9-21.

Israel (1) Another name for Jacob (see Genesis 32.22-32). See also "Jacob." (2) The nation made up of the twelve tribes descended from Jacob (see "twelve tribes of Israel"). (3) The northern kingdom, after the northern tribes broke away following the death of Solomon (see 1 Kings 12.1-20).

Issachar (1) Jacob's ninth son, and his fifth by his wife Leah. (2) One of the twelve tribes of Israel. When the Israelites left Egypt, the tribe of Issachar occupied land southwest of Lake Galilee (see Joshua 19.17-23).

Iyyar or Ziv The second month in the Hebrew calendar; it falls around mid-April to mid-May.

Jacob The third great ancestor of the people of Israel. Jacob was the son of Isaac and Rebekah, and his name was changed to Israel when he struggled with God at Peniel near the Jabbok River (see Genesis 32.22-32).

James Two of Jesus' closest disciples (called "apostles") and one of his brothers were named James. One of the apostles was called James the son of Zebedee and is usually mentioned along with his brother John (Matthew 4.21,22; 17.1; 20.20-23). The other apostle was called James son of Alphaeus. See "apostle."

Jebusites A group of Canaanite people who lived at Jebus, also known as Jerusalem (see 2 Samuel 5.6-9).

Jew At first this was a geographical term, referring generally to those people who lived in the territory of Judah. Later it became a religious term, referring to anyone who accepted the Jewish religion. See also "Hebrew."

John Several people in the New Testament are called John. (1) John the Baptist, a prophet in Jesus' day who preached that people should turn away from their sins and announced the coming of God's Chosen One (Messiah). See Luke 1.5-25,57-80; 7.18-35; 9.7-9. (2) John the son of Zebedee, one of Jesus' twelve closest disciples (called "apostles") and brother of James. (3) John of Patmos, a leader in the early church and author of Revelation (see Revelation 1.1-11).

Joseph Jacob's eleventh son, and his first by his wife Rachel. Joseph was sold as a slave by his brothers, but later he became governor of Egypt. See Genesis 37.12-36; 41.1-57.

Judah (1) Jacob's fourth son by his wife Leah. (2) One of the twelve tribes of Israel. When the Israelites left Egypt, the tribe of Judah occupied the hill country west of the Dead Sea (see Joshua 15.1-12). When the ten northern tribes of Israel broke away following the death of Solomon, only the tribes of Judah and Benjamin were left to form the southern kingdom, and it was also called "Judah."

Judas A common Jewish name in Jesus' day. Two of Jesus' closest disciples (called "apostles") had this name: (1) Judas, also known as Jude or Thaddeus, the son of James; (2) Judas Iscariot, the disciple who betrayed Jesus (see John 12.4-6; 13.21-30; 18.1-5). See "apostle."

judges Leaders chosen by the Lord for the people of Israel after the time of Joshua and before Saul was made Israel's first king.

Kadesh A town in the desert of Paran southwest of the Dead Sea, near the southern border of Israel and the western border of Edom. Israel camped at Kadesh while the twelve tribal leaders explored Canaan (see Numbers 13–14).

kingdom of heaven See "God's kingdom."

Law and the Prophets A term used in New Testament times to refer to the sacred writings of the Jewish people. The Law and the Prophets were two of the three sections of the Old Testament, but the expression sometimes refers to the entire Old Testament.

Law of the Lord or Law of Moses Usually refers to the first five books of the Old Testament, but sometimes to the entire Old Testament.

Levi (1) Jacob's third son by his wife Leah. (2) One of the tribes of Israel. The men of this tribe were to be the special servants of the Lord at the sacred tent and later at the temple, and so the people of this tribe were not given tribal land. Instead, they were given towns scattered throughout the other twelve tribes (see also "Levites"). (3) One of Jesus' twelve closest disciples (called "apostles"). He is also known as Matthew. See "apostle."

Leviathan A legendary sea monster representing revolt and evil, also known from Canaanite writings. See Psalms 74.13,14; 104.26.

Levites Those Israelites who belonged to the tribe of Levi. God chose the men of one Levite family, the descendants of Aaron, to be Israel's priests. The other men from this tribe helped with the work in the sacred tent and later in the temple (see Numbers 3.5-10).

local shrine See "place of worship."

locust A type of grasshopper that comes in huge swarms and causes great damage to plant life. See Joel 1.2—2.11.

LORD In the Old Testament the word "LORD" in capital letters stands for the Hebrew consonants YHWH, the personal name of God. Ancient Hebrew did not have vowel letters, and so anyone reading Hebrew would have to know what vowels to put with the consonants. It is not known for certain what vowel sounds were originally used with the consonants YHWH. The word "Lord" represents the Hebrew term Adonai, the usual word for "lord." By late Old Testament times, Jews considered God's personal name too holy to be pronounced. So they said Adonai, "Lord," whenever they read YHWH. When the Jewish scribes first translated the Hebrew Scriptures into ancient Greek, they translated the personal name of God as Kurios, "Lord." Since that time, most translations, including the *Contemporary English Version*, have followed their example and have avoided using the personal name of God.

Lot A nephew of Abraham and the ancestor of the Moabites and Ammonites. See Genesis 11.26-28; 13.1-13; 14.8-16; 19.1-38.

Manasseh (1) Joseph's son, the older brother of Ephraim (see Genesis 48). (2) One of the twelve tribes of Israel. When the Israelites left Egypt, the tribe of Manasseh occupied two areas of land. East Manasseh occupied the land east of the Jordan River and north of the Jabbok River in the areas of Bashan and northern Gilead; West Manasseh occupied the land west of the Jordan River and to the north of Ephraim (see Joshua 17).

Marchesvan or Bul The eighth month in the Hebrew calendar; it falls around mid-October to mid-November.

Mary A common name for Jewish women in Jesus' day. Several key women in the New Testament are called Mary. (1) Mary, the wife of Joseph and mother of Jesus (see Matthew 1.18-25; Luke 1.26-56; 2.1-52; John 2.1-12). (2) Mary of Bethany, a friend of Jesus and the sister of Lazarus and Martha (see Luke 10.38-42; John 11.1-44). (3) Mary Magdalene, one of Jesus' female disciples (Luke 8.1,2; 24.9,10; John 20.11-18). According to Luke, Jesus cast seven demons out of Mary Magdalene.

Matthew One of Jesus' twelve closest disciples (called "apostles"). He is also known as Levi. See "apostle."

Medes A nation that lived in what is today northwest Iran. Their kingdom, called "Media," later became one of the most important provinces of the Persian Empire, and Persian laws were referred to as the laws of the Medes and Persians (see Esther 1.19; Daniel 6.8,12,15).

Messiah See "Christ."

Midianites A nomadic nation that lived mainly in the desert along the eastern shore of the Gulf of Aqaba.

Milcom The national god of the Ammonites. Some Israelites offered human sacrifices to Molech in Hinnom Valley near Jerusalem. Also called Molech.

Moab A nation that lived east of the Dead Sea. According to Genesis 19.30-38, the people of Moab descended from Lot, the nephew of Abraham. Moab is sometimes depicted in the Old Testament as one of Israel's enemies (see Isaiah 15—16; Jeremiah 48).

Molech See "Milcom."

Moses The prophet who led the people of Israel when God rescued them from slavery in Egypt. Moses also received laws from God and gave them to Israel. See Exodus 2–12; 19–24; Numbers 12.6-8.

most holy place The inner room of the sacred tent and of the temple. In the sacred tent this room contained only the sacred chest; in Solomon's temple, the most holy place also held statues of winged creatures. Only the high priest could enter the most holy place, and even he could enter it only once a year on the Great Day of Forgiveness. The most holy place has traditionally been called "the holy of holies."

Mount of Olives A mountain just east of Jerusalem, across Kidron Valley from the temple. Gethsemane, a place where Jesus and his disciples often went to pray, was on this mountain, and so were the villages of Bethany, Bethphage, and Bahurim (see Matthew 26.36; Mark 14.32; Luke 22.39; John 18.1,2).

myrrh A valuable sweet-smelling powder used in perfume.

Naphtali (1) Jacob's sixth son, and his second by Rachel's servant Bilhah. (2) One of the twelve tribes of Israel. When the Israelites left Egypt, the tribe of Naphtali occupied land north and west of Lake Galilee (see Joshua 19.32-39).

Nazarenes A name that was sometimes used for the followers of Jesus, who came from the small town of Nazareth (see Acts 24.5).

Nazirites A person who took a special vow of self-dedication. Such a person was not to drink beer or wine, cut his hair, or touch a dead body (see Numbers 6.1-21). The vow could be taken for a certain period of time, but some persons were dedicated to God as Nazirites from their birth.

New Moon Festival See "Festival of Trumpets."

Nisan or Abib The first month in the Hebrew calendar; it falls around mid-March to mid-April.

Noah When God destroyed the world by a flood, Noah and his family were kept safe in a big boat that God had told him to build. See Genesis 6–9.

offerings See "sacrifices."

Passover A Jewish festival held on the fourteenth day of Abib in the early spring. At Passover the Israelites celebrated the time God rescued them from slavery in Egypt. The name of this festival in Hebrew is "Pesach." See Exodus 12.1-27; Numbers 28.16-25.

Paul An important leader in the early church. Although he was not one of Jesus' twelve closest disciples, his claim to be an apostle was based on having received his message directly from Jesus Christ (see Galatians 1.11—2.21). He wrote many of the Letters in the New Testament; Romans is considered his masterpiece. He was also known by his Jewish name, Saul (see Acts 7.57—8.3; 9.1-30).

Peniel A place near the Jabbok River where Jacob wrestled with God. Then God changed Jacob's name to Israel (see Genesis 32.22-32).

Pentecost See "Harvest Festival."

Perizzites A nation that lived in the central hill country of Canaan, before the Israelites.

Persia A large empire of Old Testament times, whose capital was located in what is now southern Iran. It is sometimes called "the Medo-Persian Empire," because of the importance of the province of Media.

Peter One of Jesus' twelve closest disciples (called "apostles"). Jesus gave him the keys to the kingdom of heaven (see Matthew 16.13-20) and he became an important leader in the early church (see Acts 2—5; 9.32—12.19; 15.3-21). Peter was also known as Cephas or Simon. See "apostle."

Pharisees A group of Jews who thought they could best serve God by strictly obeying the laws of the Old Testament as well as their own rules, traditions, and teachings.

Philip One of Jesus' twelve closest disciples (called "apostles"). He was from Bethsaida, the hometown of apostles Simon and Andrew.

Philistines The land along the Mediterranean coast controlled by the Philistine people was called "Philistia." There were five main cities, each with its own ruler: Ashdod, Ashkelon, Ekron, Gath, and Gaza. The Philistines were often at war with Israel.

Phoenicia The territory along the Mediterranean Sea controlled by the cities of Tyre, Sidon, Arvad, and Byblos. The coast of modern Lebanon covers about the same area.

place of worship A place to worship God or pagan gods. These places were often on a hill outside of a town and have traditionally been called "high places." In the CEV they are sometimes called "local shrines."

priest A man who led the worship in the sacred tent or in the temple and who offered sacrifices. Some of the more important priests were called "chief priests," and the most important priest was called the "high priest."

prophet Someone who speaks God's message, which at times included telling what would happen in the future. Sometimes when the Spirit of God took control of prophets, they lost some or all control over their speech and actions or were not aware of what was happening around them.

proverb A wise saying that is short and easy to remember.

psalm A Hebrew poem. Psalms were often written in such a way that they could be prayed or sung by an individual or a group. Some of the psalms thank and praise God, while others ask God to take away sins, punish enemies, or give protection, comfort, or mercy.

Purim A Jewish festival on the fourteenth and fifteenth of Adar, near the end of winter, when the Jews celebrated how they were saved from Haman, the evil prime minister of Persia who wanted to have them killed (see Esther 9.20-32).

Rebekah The wife of Isaac, and the mother of Jacob and Esau (see Genesis 24.1-67; 25.19-28).

Red Sea Hebrew *yam suph,* "Sea of Reeds," one of the marshes or fresh water lakes, near the eastern part of the Nile Delta. This identification is based on Exodus 13.17—14.9, which lists the towns on the route of the Israelites before crossing the sea. In the Greek translation of the Scriptures made about 200 B.C., the "Sea of Reeds" was named "Red Sea." In some places in the Bible the name "Red Sea" may be used when only the part of the sea known as the Gulf of Suez is intended (as in Exodus 10.19), or when the Gulf of Aqaba is intended (Exodus 23.31).

reed Several kinds of tall plants related to the grass family can be called "reeds." Some varieties are hollow, and some grow in shallow water. The stems were strong and could be up to 18 feet long and 3 inches across at the base.

Rephaim Perhaps a group of very large people who lived in Palestine before the Israelites (see Deuteronomy 2.11,20).

Reuben (1) Jacob and Leah's first son. (2) One of the twelve tribes of Israel. When the Israelites left Egypt, the tribe of Reuben occupied land east of the Dead Sea, from the Arnon River in the south to the northern end of the Dead Sea (see Joshua 13.15-23).

Roman Empire The political and military power that controlled the area around the Mediterranean Sea and Western Europe in New Testament times and into the fifth century A.D. Its capital was Rome.

Sabbath The seventh day of the week, from sunset on Friday to sunset on Saturday. Israelites worshiped on the Sabbath and rested from their work. See Exodus 20.8-11; 23.10-12).

sackcloth A rough, dark-colored cloth made from goat or camel hair. Sackcloth was usually used to make grain sacks, but clothing made from it was worn in times of trouble or sorrow.

sacred chest The chest or box that contained the two flat stones with the Ten Commandments written on them. The chest was covered with gold, and two golden statues of winged creatures were on the lid of the chest. These winged creatures and the chest represented God's throne on earth. Two wooden poles, one on each side, were put through rings at the corners of the chest, so that the Levites could carry the chest without touching it. The chest was kept in the most holy place (see Exodus 25.10-22).

sacred pole A symbol of Asherah, a fertility goddess (see 2 Chronicles 14.3); it is sometimes referred to as a "a sacred tree."

sacred tent The tent where the people of Israel worshiped God before the temple was built. It has traditionally been called "the tabernacle" (see Exodus 26).

sacrifices These gifts to God included certain animals, grains, fruits, and sweet-smelling spices. Israelites offered sacrifices to give thanks to God, to ask for his forgiveness and his blessing, and to make a payment for a wrong. Some sacrifices were completely burned on the altar. In the case of other sacrifices, a portion was given to the Lord and burned on the altar, then the rest was eaten by the priests or the worshipers who had offered the sacrifice.

sacrifices to ask the Lord's blessing Traditionally called "peace offerings" or "offerings of well-being." A main purpose was to ask for the Lord's blessing, and so in the CEV they are sometimes called "sacrifices to ask the Lord's blessing" (see Leviticus 3).

sacrifices to give thanks to the Lord Traditionally called "grain offerings." A main purpose of such sacrifices was to thank the Lord with a gift of grain, and so in the CEV they are sometimes called "sacrifices to give thanks to the Lord" (see Leviticus 2).

sacrifices to make things right Traditionally called "guilt offerings." A main purpose was to make things right when a person had cheated someone or the Lord. These sacrifices were also made when a person had broken certain religious rules (see Leviticus 5.14—6.7).

sacrifices to please the Lord Traditionally called "whole burnt offerings" because the whole animal was burned on the altar. While these sacrifices did involve forgiveness for sin, a main purpose was to please the Lord with the smell of the smoke from the sacrifice, and so in the CEV they are often called "sacrifices to please the Lord" (see Leviticus 1).

Sadducees A small and powerful group of Jews in New Testament times. They were closely connected with the high priests and accepted only the first five books of the Old Testament as their Bible. They also did not believe in life after death.

Samaria (1) The capital city of the northern kingdom of Israel beginning with the rule of King Omri (ruled 885–874 B.C.). (2) In New Testament times, a district between Judea and Galilee, named for the city of Samaria. The people of this district, called "Samaritans," worshiped God differently from the Jews, and these two groups refused to have anything to do with one another.

Samuel A prophet and the last judge of Israel (see "judges"). When the people of Israel wanted to have a king to rule over them like the neighboring nations had, Samuel poured oil on the head of Saul to show that Saul was the one God chose to be king (see 1 Samuel 8–10).

Sarah The wife of Abraham and the mother of Isaac. At first her name was Sarai, but when she was old, God promised her that she would have a son, and he changed her name to Sarah. Both names mean "princess." See Genesis 11.29,30; 17.15-19; 18.9-15; 21.1-7.

Satan See "devil."

Saul (1) Israel's first king (see 1 Samuel 8–31). (2) Another name for the apostle Paul (see "Paul").

save In biblical terms, this refers to the act of God in rescuing people from sin and placing them under his care.

Savior In biblical terms, this may refer either to God himself, or to Jesus Christ, the one God sent to save people from sin.

scepter A decorated rod, often made of gold, that a king held in his hand as a symbol of royal power.

scribe An authority in the interpretation of the Jewish Scriptures.

Scriptures Although this term now refers to the whole Bible, in the New Testament it refers to the Old Testament (see 1 Timothy 4.13; 2 Timothy 3.15-17).

scroll A roll of paper or special thin leather used for writing on.

Shebat The eleventh month of the Hebrew calendar; it falls around mid-January to mid-February.

Sidon See "Phoenicia."

Simeon (1) Jacob and Leah's second son. (2) One of the twelve tribes of Israel. When the Israelites left Egypt, the tribe of Simeon occupied land southwest of Judah, and was later practically absorbed into Judah (see Joshua 19.1-9).

Simon A common man's name in Jesus' day. Two of Jesus' disciples were called Simon, (1) Simon Peter, also called Cephas (see "Peter"), and (2) Simon, "the Eager One." See "apostle."

sin Disobeying God by refusing to do what God demands.

Sivan The third month in the Hebrew calendar; it falls around mid-May to mid-June.

Solomon A son of King David and Bathsheba. After David's death, Solomon ruled Israel from about 970 to 931 B.C. Solomon built the temple in Jerusalem and was widely known for his wisdom. See 1 Kings 1–11. The Hebrew text indicates that he wrote many of the proverbs and two of the psalms.

Son of Man A title often used by Jesus to refer to himself (see Mark 8.31; 9.31; 10.45). This title is also found in the Hebrew text of Daniel 7.13. In Ezekiel the term is used numerous times to refer to Ezekiel.

Stoics Followers of a man named Zeno (died 262 B.C.), who taught that people should learn self-control and be guided by their consciences.

Synagogue A Greek word meaning "gathering." Synagogues were places where Jews met every Sabbath day for public worship and the reading of Scripture (see Luke 4.16-30). In Jesus' day, these meeting places mostly took place in people's homes where they served as centers for Jewish social life and as schools for Jewish children (see Acts 9.20; 13.5). When the Romans destroyed the Jerusalem temple in A.D. 70, synagogues became more important in the religious life of Jews. In the second and third centuries, as houses were remodeled to be better able to serve the many functions of these religious gatherings, the word "synagogue" began to be used for the buildings themselves.

Tammuz The fourth month in the Hebrew calendar; it falls around mid-June to mid-July.

taxes and tax collectors Taxes are special fees collected by rulers. Taxes are usually calculated as a percentage of the value of a person's crops, property, or income. Taxes were collected at markets, city gates, ports, and border crossings. In New Testament times, Jews were hired by the Roman government to collect taxes from other Jews, and these tax collectors were hated by their own people.

Tebeth The tenth month of the Hebrew calendar; it falls around mid-December to mid-January.

temple (1) A building used as a place of worship. (2) King Solomon built Israel's first temple for the worship of the Lord in Jerusalem. Another temple was begun on its ruins following the return from exile in Babylonia (538 B.C.). In 20 B.C., Herod the Great began a new temple on the same site, but it was not entirely finished before the destruction of Jerusalem by the Romans in A.D. 70.

Temple Festival In 165 B.C. the Jewish people recaptured the temple in Jerusalem from their enemies and made it fit for worship again. They celebrated this event each year by an eight-day festival that began on the twenty-fifth day of the month of Chislev in the late fall. This festival is traditionally called "the Festival of Dedication," or in Hebrew, "Hanukkah."

Thaddeus One of Jesus' twelve closest disciples (called "apostles"). He was also known as Judas or Jude the son of James. See "apostle."

Thomas One of Jesus' twelve closest disciples (called "apostles"). He was also known as "the Twin." See "apostle."

threshing The process of separating grain from its husks. Grain was spread out at a "threshing place," a flat area of stone or packed earth. People or animals walked on the grain or dragged heavy boards across it to remove the husks. Then the grain and husks were tossed into the air with a special shovel called a "threshing fork." The wind would blow the light husks away, but the heavy grain would fall back to the surface of the threshing place.

Tishri or Ethanim The seventh month of the Hebrew calendar; it falls around mid-September to mid-October.

tribe A large group of people descended from a common ancestor. See also "clan" and "twelve tribes of Israel."

twelve tribes of Israel The Bible speaks of all the people in a tribe as having descended from one of the twelve sons of Jacob. The tribes of Ephraim and Manasseh were a little different, because the people in those tribes descended from the two sons of Joseph, who was one of Jacob's sons. That would make a total of thirteen tribes, but the Bible always counts only twelve. In some passages Ephraim and Manasseh are counted as one tribe, and in other passages the Levi tribe is left out, probably because they were designated for priestly service to all the tribes, and as such, were scattered throughout the land belonging to the other tribes. People from other nations were sometimes allowed to become Israelites (see Exodus 12.38; Deuteronomy 23.7,8; Ruth 1–4), and these people would then belong to one of the tribes.

Tyre See "Phoenicia."

unclean See "clean and unclean."

Way In the book of Acts the Christian life is sometimes called "the Way" or "the Lord's Way" or "God's Way" (see Acts 9.2; 19.9,23; 24.22).

wine-pit A hollow place cut into the rock where the juice was squeezed from grapes to make wine.

winged creature These supernatural beings represented the presence of God and supported his throne in Ezekiel 1.4-25; 10.1-22. Statues of winged creatures were on top of the sacred chest, and larger ones were in the most holy place in the temple built by Solomon. Wood carvings of winged creatures decorated the inside walls and doors of the temple, and figures of winged creatures were woven into the curtain separating the holy place from the most holy place in the sacred tent. The traditional term for winged creature is "cherub" (or "cherubim" for more than one).

wisdom Often refers to the common sense and practical skill needed to solve everyday problems, but in some places in the Bible it also refers to the ability to find answers to the hard questions about the meaning of life. See 1 Kings 3.1-15; 10.1-10; Proverbs 3.13-18; 8.1-36; 1 Corinthians 1.18—2.16.

Year of Celebration According to the Law of Moses, land that had been sold was to be returned to its original owner and all slaves were to be freed and returned to their families during this special year celebrated once every fifty years. Also known as the Jubilee Year. See Leviticus 25.8-34.

yoke A strong, heavy, wooden collar that fit around the neck of an ox, so that the ox could pull a plow or a cart.

Zebulun (1) Jacob's tenth son, and the youngest of his wife Leah's six sons. (2) One of the twelve tribes of Israel. When the Israelites left Egypt, the tribe of Zebulun occupied land north of Manasseh from the eastern end of Mount Carmel to Mount Tabor (see Joshua 19.10-16).

Zeus The chief god of the Greeks (see Acts 14.12).

Zion Another name for Jerusalem. Zion sometimes refers specifically to the hill in Jerusalem where the temple was built (see 2 Samuel 5.6-10; Psalm 78.68,69).

Ziv or Iyyar The second month in the Hebrew calendar; it falls around mid-April to mid-May.

what's in the bible

The following are summary capsules for each book of the Bible. It will be obvious from how brief the descriptions are that they are not complete. They should, however, serve as a quick and handy guide to the content of the whole Bible.

Old Testament

GENESIS: In this book of beginnings the stories are about creation, early relationships between God and people, and God's promise to bless Abraham and his descendants.

EXODUS: The name Exodus means "departure" and this book tells about how God led the Israelites out of a life of hardship and slavery in Egypt. God made a covenant with them and gave them the Law to order their lives.

LEVITICUS: This book is named for the priestly tribe of Levi and is made up of laws concerning rituals and ceremonies.

NUMBERS: The Israelites wandered in the wilderness for 40 years before entering Canaan, the promised land. The name of the book comes from two censuses taken during the journey.

DEUTERONOMY: Moses gave three farewell speeches shortly before he died. In them he reviewed the laws of God for the Israelites. This book gets its name—"second law"—from this review.

JOSHUA: Joshua led the Israelite armies into victory over the Canaanites. The book ends with the division of the land among the tribes of Israel.

JUDGES: The Israelites often fell away from God and into the hands of oppressors. God sent "judges" to lead and deliver them.

RUTH: Love and dedication between Ruth and her mother-in-law, Naomi, are the focus of this story.

1 SAMUEL: Samuel was the leader of Israel between the time of Judges and the time of Saul, the first king of Israel. When Saul's leadership failed, David was anointed by Samuel to be king.

2 SAMUEL: Under David's rule, the new nation was strong and unified. But after David committed adultery and murder, his family and nation suffered.

1 KINGS: This book starts with stories about Solomon's reign over Israel. After the death of Solomon, the kingdom went to war with itself, north against south. The result was two nations, Israel in the north and Judah in the south.

2 KINGS: Israel was conquered by Assyria in 721 B.C. Judah was defeated by Babylon in 586 B.C. These events were seen as judgment upon the people because they did not follow the laws of God.

1 CHRONICLES: This book begins with genealogies from Adam to David and then recounts the incidents of David's reign.

2 CHRONICLES: This book covers the same period as 2 Kings but the emphasis is on Judah, the southern kingdom, and its rulers.

EZRA: God's people returned to Jerusalem after being held captive in Babylon for several decades. One of the leaders was Ezra. This book contains his charge to the people to be true to the law of God.

NEHEMIAH: After the Temple was rebuilt, the protective wall around Jerusalem was restored. Nehemiah brought this effort to completion. He also worked with Ezra to restore religious fervor among the people.

ESTHER: This book tells the story of the Jewish queen of Persia who exposed a plot to destroy her people and thus saved all the Jews in that country from destruction.

JOB: The question, "Why do innocent people suffer?" is address in the story of Job.

PSALMS: These 150 prayers and hymns were used by the Hebrew people to express their relationship with God. They cover the whole range of human emotions from joy to anger, from hope to despair.

PROVERBS: This is a book of wise sayings and ethical and common sense teachings on how to live a godly life.

ECCLESIASTES: In a quest for happiness and the meaning of life, this writer, known as "the Philosopher," asks many questions that are still raised in today's society.

SONG OF SONGS: This poem describes the joy and ecstasy of love. It has been understood both as a picture of God's love for Israel and of Christ's love for the Church.

ISAIAH: The prophet Isaiah brought the message of God's judgment on the nations, pointed to a future king like David, and promised a time of comfort and peace.

JEREMIAH: Before Babylon destroyed Judah, Jeremiah foretold God's judgment. While his message was largely of destruction, he also pointed toward a new covenant with God.

LAMENTATIONS: As Jeremiah had warned, Jerusalem fell to the Babylonians. This book records five "laments" for the fallen city.

EZEKIEL: Ezekiel's message was given to the Jews held captive in Babylon. He used stories and parables to speak about judgement, hope and restoration.

DANIEL: Daniel remained faithful to God while facing many pressures as a captive in Babylon. This book includes Daniel's prophetic visions.

HOSEA: Hosea used his commitment to his wife in the face of her unfaithfulness to illustrate the "adultery" Israel had committed against God, whose faithful love never ceased.

JOEL: After a locust plague in Judah, Joel urged the people to repent.

AMOS: During an era of prosperity, this Judean prophet preached judgment on the rich leaders of Israel. Amos urged them to consider the poor and oppressed rather than their own self-satisfaction.

OBADIAH: Obadiah prophesied judgment on Edom, a neighboring country.

JONAH: Jonah did not want to preach to the Ninevites, an enemy people. When he finally brought God's message to them, they repented.

MICAH: Micah's message to Judah was a prophecy of judgment as well as forgiveness and hope for restoration. Especially notable is his single verse summary of what God requires of us (6.8).

NAHUM: Nahum announced that God would destroy the people of Nineveh because of their cruelty in war.

HABAKKUK: Habakkuk's book features a dialogue between Habakkuk and God about suffering and justice.

ZEPHANIAH: Zephaniah announced the day of the Lord, which would bring judgment on Judah and other surrounding nations. This coming day would be one of doom for many, but a humble and faithful remnant will survive to bless the whole world.

HAGGAI: After the people returned from exile, Haggai reminded them to give God their highest priority and to rebuild the Temple before working on their own homes.

ZECHARIAH: Like Haggai, Zechariah urged the people to rebuild the Temple, assuring them of God's help and blessing. His visions point to a glorious future.

MALACHI: After the exiles returned, they became complacent about their religious life. Malachi tried to stir them up by preaching about the day of the Lord.

New Testament

MATTHEW: This Gospel includes many Old Testament quotations, thus appealing to a Jewish audience and presenting Jesus as the Messiah promised in the Hebrew Scriptures. Matthew told the story of Jesus from birth to resurrection and placed emphasis on his teaching.

MARK: Mark wrote a short, action-packed Gospel. He emphasized Jesus' miracles and his life of suffering. His aim was to deepen the faith and commitment of the believers in the community to which he wrote.

LUKE: In this Gospel, the availability of salvation for all people is emphasized. Luke proclaimed this message by showing Jesus' involvement with people who are poor, needy, and on the fringes of society.

JOHN: The Gospel of John stands apart from the others. John organized his message around seven signs that point to Jesus as the Son of God. His writing style is reflective and filled with striking images.

ACTS: When Jesus left his disciples, the Holy Spirit came to abide with them. Written by Luke as the sequel to his Gospel, Acts records key events in the history of the work of the early Christian Church to spread the Gospel throughout the Mediterranean world.

ROMANS: In this important letter, Paul wrote to the Romans about life in the Spirit, which is given to believers in Christ through faith. The apostle tells them about God's great kindness and declares that because of Jesus Christ, God accepts us and sets us free from our sins.

1 CORINTHIANS: This letter deals with the problems the church in Corinth was experiencing: dissension, immorality, public worship, and confusion about spiritual gifts.

2 CORINTHIANS: In this letter, Paul wrote about his relationship with the church of Corinth and the effects of certain false apostles on his ministry.

GALATIANS: This letter addresses freedom from the law through Christ. Paul declares that it is by faith that all who believe are put right with God.

EPHESIANS: A central theme to this letter is that God's eternal purpose is to bring together from many nations and peoples the universal Church of Jesus Christ.

PHILIPPIANS: This letter emphasizes the joy found in any situation when a person believes in Christ. Paul wrote it while in prison.

COLOSSIANS: In this letter Paul tells the people of Colossae to make Christ the center of their faith and to put aside their superstitions.

1 THESSALONIANS: In this letter Paul gives advice to the people of Thessalonica concerning Christ's return.

2 THESSALONIANS: This letter discusses the same topics as the first. Paul teaches the people a way to be ready for the Lord.

1 TIMOTHY: This letter served as a guide to Timothy, a young leader in the church. It contains advice about worship, ministry, and relationships within the church.

2 TIMOTHY: This is Paul's last letter. In it he offers a final challenge to his co-worker.

TITUS: Titus was ministering in Crete. In this letter, Paul gave him advice on how to help Christians follow Christ.

PHILEMON: In this letter, Philemon is urged to forgive his runaway slave, Onesimus, and accept him as a friend in Christ.

HEBREWS: The letter to the Hebrews challenges new Christians to move beyond their traditional rituals and ceremonies and believe that Christ has fulfilled them all.

JAMES: James advises putting beliefs into practice and offers practical ways for Christians to live out their faith.

1 PETER: This letter was written to comfort early Christians who were being persecuted for their faith.

2 PETER: In this letter Peter warns against false teachers and urges Christians to stay loyal to God.

1 JOHN: This letter explains basic truths about the Christian life, with emphasis on the command to love one another.

2 JOHN: This letter, addressed to "the dear Lady and to her children," warns against false teachers.

3 JOHN: In contrast to 2 John, this letter states the need to welcome people who preach Christ.

JUDE: Jude warns against the influence of evil ones outside the fellowship of believers.

REVELATION: This book was written to encourage persecuted believers and affirm their faith that God will care for them. Using visions and symbols, the writer illustrates the triumph of good over evil and the creation of a new heaven and new earth.

how to read the bible

Set aside time each day to read from your Bible. Try to make it the same time each day. Be realistic. Commit yourself only to as much time as you honestly feel that you can stick to on an ongoing basis. Before you begin reading ask for God's guidance and blessing. Some people have found that keeping a daily notebook is helpful. Use the following steps to get the most out of your daily Bible reading:

1. Select a passage (perhaps one from one of the lists that follow).

2. Examine its context:

   a. What kind of book is it drawn from? A biographical book such as one of the Gospel accounts of Jesus' life; a long historical book, such as *The Second Book of Samuel*, which tells of the reign of King David; a brief letter to a person *(The Letters of Paul to Timothy)* or to a specific church *(The Letters of Paul to the Corinthians)*?

   b. What is the overall purpose/intent of this book? (Do not do lengthy research, but feel free to read the opening and closing paragraphs as well as section headings and introductions if your Bible has them.)

   c. What occurs or is discussed in the passage immediately preceding and following the passage you chose?

3. Read the passage quickly for sense.

4. Identify key words or phrases. Are there words or thoughts that are repeated throughout the passage? Are any cause and effect relationships established? (These are often signaled by words like *if* and *then, therefore, because, since,* and *so.*) Are any comparisons made or similarities pointed out? Are any two people, things or concepts contrasted?

5. Read the passage again and ask yourself what the intent or purpose of the passage is. Try to find out what the author is saying. Be honest; don't just look for what you want to hear. The Bible has many strong messages that can change lives!

6. What do you learn about God from this passage? What do you learn about human nature? Ask yourself how this message applies to you. Is there anything you need to change in your life in order to be a more faithful child of God or more loving to your neighbor? Ask for God's help in making this change.

7. Re-read the passage one more time. Is there one verse you would like to commit to memory? Why not write it on an index card and carry it with you throughout the day as a study aid?

8. Thank God for what he has shown you, and ask for his help as you seek to apply this lesson in your life.

9. Share what you have learned with someone else.

famous passages of the bible

Stories from the Old Testament

Early Beginnings

Creation and Sin
Genesis 2.4—3.24

The First Murder
Genesis 4.1-15

Noah and the Flood
Genesis 6.1—9.17

The Tower of Babel (Babylon)
Genesis 11.1-9

The Call of Abraham
Genesis 12.1-9

The Destruction of Sodom and Gomorrah
Genesis 19.1-28

Hagar and Ishmael
Genesis 16.1-15; 21.9-21

The Birth of Isaac
Genesis 21.1-8

Abraham's Offering of Isaac
Genesis 22.1-19

The Story of Jacob
Genesis 25.19—35.29

The Story of Joseph
Genesis 37—50

Moses in Egypt
Exodus 1—14

Moses' Desert Wanderings
Exodus 15.22—20.26;
Exodus 31.18—34.35;
Numbers 20.1—21.25

The Ten Commandments
Exodus 20.1-17;
Deuteronomy 5.1-21

The King of Moab and Balaam
Numbers 22—24

People of Great Faith in the Old Testament

Rahab Helps the Israelite Spies
Joshua 2

Joshua, Military Strategist
Joshua 3; 6

Deborah, a Woman of Power and Judgment
Judges 4—5

Gideon, the Conqueror
Judges 6.11—8.32

Samson, a Man of Great Strength
Judges 13—16

Ruth, a Woman of Loyalty and Devotion
Ruth 1—4

Samuel, a Prophet Who Listened to God
1 Samuel 1—3; 7—10; 12; 15; 16

Saul, Israel's First King
1 Samuel 8—11; 13; 15; 28; 31

David, the Shepherd King
1 Samuel 16—27; 29.1—30.25;
2 Samuel 2; 11; 12; 15.1-8; 18;
1 Kings 1.1-31; 2.1-11

Solomon, the Wise King
1 Kings 2.12—11.43

Elijah, a Great Prophet
1 Kings 17—19; 21; 2 Kings 1

Elisha, His Successor
2 Kings 2; 4.1—7.2; 13.14-21

Nehemiah, a Heroic Builder
Nehemiah 1; 2; 4

Esther, a Brave Queen
Esther 1—10

Daniel, a Prophet of Courage
Daniel 1—6

Jonah, the Reluctant Missionary
Jonah 1—4

Stories from the New Testament

The Life of Jesus

The Birth of Jesus
Matthew 1.18—2.15; Luke 2.1-20

Jesus Is Named and Presented in the Temple
Luke 2.21-40

The Boy Jesus
Luke 2.41-52

The Baptism of Jesus
Matthew 3; Mark 1.1-11; Luke 3.21,22

The Temptation of Jesus
Matthew 4.1-11; Mark 1.12,13;
Luke 4.1-13

Jesus Calls His First Disciples
Matthew 4.18-22; Mark 1.16-20;
Luke 5.1-11

Jesus Chooses Twelve Apostles
Matthew 10.1-4; Mark 3.13-19;
Luke 6.12-16

The Transfiguration of Jesus
Matthew 17.1-13; Mark 9.2-13

Jesus' Death and Resurrection

Jesus' Entry into Jerusalem
Matthew 21.1-11; Mark 11.1-11;
Luke 19.29-44; John 12.12-19

The Last Supper of Jesus
Matthew 26.17-35; Mark 14.12-26;
Luke 22.1-38

Jesus Prays in Gethsemane
Matthew 26.36-46; Mark 14.32-42;
Luke 22.39-46

The Teachings and Parables of Jesus

What is a parable?

Parables are stories that use typical everyday situations in order to teach important truths. Jesus used many parables to teach his followers about the Kingdom of God.

Other New Testament Stories

The Birth of John the Baptist
Luke 1.57-66

John the Baptist Is Executed
Matthew 14.1-12; Mark 6.14-29

Peter Receives the Keys to the Kingdom of Heaven
Matthew 16.13-20

The Holy Spirit Comes on Pentecost
Acts 2

Stephen, the First Martyr
Acts 6.5-15; 7.54-60

Philip Baptizes the Ethiopian Official
Acts 8.26-39

The Conversion of Paul
Acts 9.1-31

Peter and Cornelius
Acts 10

Peter in Prison
Acts 12.1-19

The Baptism of Lydia
Acts 16.11-15

Paul in Prison
Acts 16.16-40

The Riot in Ephesus
Acts 19.23-41

Paul's Voyage to Rome
Acts 27; 28

Other Famous Passages

Songs of the Bible

Moses' Song of Deliverance
Exodus 15.1-18

Deborah and Barak's Song of Victory
Judges 5.1-31

Hannah's Song of Praise
1 Samuel 2.1-10

David's Song of Lament
2 Samuel 1.17-27

David's Song of Victory
2 Samuel 22; Psalm 18

Solomon's Love Song
Song of Songs 2.10-15

Mary's Song of Praise
Luke 1.46-55

A Hymn to Christ Jesus
Philippians 2.6-11

Prayers of the Bible

Solomon's Personal Prayer
1 Kings 3.5-10

Solomon's Public Prayer
1 Kings 8.22-61
2 Chronicles 6.12-42

Hezekiah's Temple Prayer
2 Kings 19.15-19; Isaiah 37.14-20

David's Prayer of Thanksgiving
2 Samuel 7.18-29; 1 Chronicles 17.16-27

Job's Prayer
Job 42.1-6

Jeremiah's Prayer
Jeremiah 32.16-25

Daniel's Prayer
Daniel 9.3-19

Jonah's Prayer
Jonah 2.1-9

The Lord's Prayer
Matthew 6.9-13

Jesus' Prayer in Gethsemane
Matthew 26.36-44

Jesus' Prayer for His Disciples
John 17

The Disciples' Prayer
Acts 4.24-31

Paul's Prayer for Believers
Ephesians 3.14-21

Special Blessings from the Bible

Invocations and Openings
Psalm 19.14; 1 Corinthians 1.3;
1 Timothy 1.2; 2 John 3;
Revelation 1.4-6

Dismissals and Closings
Numbers 6.24-26; 1 Kings 8.57,58;
Romans 15.5,6,13; Romans 16.25-27;
2 Corinthians 13.13; Ephesians 6.23,24;
Philippians 4.7; Hebrews 13.20,21;
Jude 24,25

finding help in the bible

Help in Special Circumstances

Being a friend
Proverbs 17.17; Luke 10.25-37;
John 15.11-17; Romans 16.1,2

Being a leader
Isaiah 11.1-9; Isaiah 32.1-8;
1 Timothy 3.1-7; 2 Timothy 2.14-26;
Titus 1.5-9

Caring for the aged and widowed
Genesis 47.1-12; Ruth 1; Proverbs 23.22;
1 Timothy 5.3-8

**Celebrating the birth/
adoption of a child**
Psalm 100; Proverbs 22.6;
Luke 18.15-17; John 16.16-22

Celebrating a graduation
Psalm 119.105,106; Proverbs 9.10-12;
Galatians 5.16-26; Philippians 4.4-9

Celebrating a marriage
Genesis 2.18-24; Song of Songs 8.6,7;
Ephesians 5.21-33; Colossians 2.6,7

Celebrating a wedding anniversary
Psalm 100; 1 Corinthians 13

Controlling your temper
Proverbs 14.17, 29; 15.18; 19.11; 29.22;
Ecclesiastes 7.9; Galatians 5.16-26

Controlling your tongue
Psalm 12; Psalm 19.14; Proverbs 11.13;
Proverbs 26.20; 2 Thessalonians 2.16,17;
James 3.1-12

Discovering God's will
Psalm 15; Micah 6.6-8; Matthew 5.14-16;
Luke 9.21-27; Romans 13.8-14;
2 Peter 1.3-9; 1 John 4.7-21

Encountering a cult
Matthew 7.15-20; 2 Peter 2;
1 John 4.1-6; Jude

Encountering peer pressure
Proverbs 1.7-19; Romans 12.1,2;
Galatians 6.1-5; Ephesians 5.1-20

Entering college
Proverbs, 2.1-8; Proverbs 3.1-18;
Proverbs 4.1-27; Proverbs 23.12;
Romans 8.1-17; 1 Corinthians 1.18-31

Entering military service
2 Samuel 22.2-51; Psalm 91;
Ephesians 6.10-20; 2 Timothy 2.1-13

Experiencing the death of a loved one
Job 19.25-27; John 11.25-27; John 14.1-7;
Romans 8.31-39; Romans 14.7-9;
1 Thessalonians 4.13-18

Experiencing illness
Psalm 23; Mark 1.29-34; Mark 6.53-56;
James 5.14-16

Experiencing suffering and persecution
Psalm 109; Psalm 119.153-160;
Matthew 5.3-12; John 15.18—16.4;
Romans 8.18-30; 2 Corinthians 4.1-15;
Hebrews 12.1-11; 1 Peter 4.12-19

Facing a difficult decision
1 Kings 3; Esther 4–7; Psalm 139;
Daniel 2.14-23; Colossians 3.12-17

Facing a divorce
Psalm 25; Matthew 19.1-9;
Philippians 3.1-11

Facing homelessness
Psalm 90.1,2; Isaiah 65.17-25
Lamentations 3.19-24; Luke 9.57-62;
Revelation 21.1-4

Facing imprisonment
Lamentations 3.34-36; Matthew 25.31-46;
Luke 4.16-21

Facing life alone
1 Corinthians 7.25-38;
1 Corinthians 12.1-31

Facing a natural disaster
Genesis 8.1—9.17; Job 36.22—37.13;
Psalms 29,124; Psalm 36.5-9;
Jeremiah 31.35-37; Romans 8.31-39;
1 Peter 1.3-12

Facing a trial or lawsuit
Psalm 26; Isaiah 50.4-11; Matthew 5.25, 26;
Luke 18.1-8

Losing your job
Jeremiah 29.10-14; Luke 16.1-13;
Philippians 4.10-13

Losing your property and possessions
Job 1.13-22; Job 42.7-17; Isaiah 30.19-26;
Isaiah 41.17-20; Romans 8.18-39

Managing your time
Proverbs 12.11; Proverbs 28.19;
Mark 13.32-37; Luke 21.34-36;
1 Timothy 4.11-16; Titus 3.8-14

Moving into a new home
Psalm 127.1,2; Proverbs 24.3,4; John 14.1-7;
Ephesians 3.14-21; Revelation 3.20,21

Overcoming addiction
Psalm 40.1-5,11-17; Psalm 116.1-7;
Proverbs 23.29-35; 2 Corinthians 5.16-21;
Ephesians 4.22-24

Overcoming a grudge
Leviticus 19.17,18; Matthew 5.23-26;
Luke 6.27-36; Ephesians 4.25-32

Overcoming prejudice
Matthew 7.1-5; Acts 10.34-36;
Galatians 3.26-29; Ephesians 2.11-22;
Colossians 3.5-11; James 2.1-13

Overcoming pride
Psalm 131; Mark 9.33-37; Luke 14.7-11;
Luke 18.9-14; Luke 22.24-27;
Romans 12.14-16; 1 Corinthians 1.18-41;
2 Corinthians 12.1-10

Overcoming procrastination
Matthew 22.1-14; Matthew 25.1-13;
2 Corinthians 6.1,2

Raising children
Proverbs 22.6; Ephesians 6.4; Colossians 3.21

Respecting civil authorities
Mark 12.13-17; Romans 13.1-7;
Titus 3.1,2; 1 Peter 2.13-17

Respecting parents
Exodus 20.12; Proverbs 23.22;
Ephesians 6.1-3; Colossians 3.20

Retiring from your job
Numbers 6.24-26; Psalm 145;
Matthew 25.31-46, Romans 12.1,2;
Philippians 3.12-21; 2 Peter 1.2

Seeking forgiveness
Psalm 32.1-5; Psalm 51; Proverbs 28.13;
Joel 2.12-17; Matthew 6.14-15; Luke 15;
Philemon; Hebrews 4.14-16; 1 John 1.5-10

Seeking God's help
Psalms 5, 57, 86, 121, 130;
Psalm 119.169-176; Matthew 7.7-12

Seeking justice
Psalms 10, 17, 75, 94; Isaiah 42.1-7;
Isaiah 61.1-9; Amos 5.21-24;
Habakkuk 1.1-2.4

Seeking salvation
John 3.1-21; Romans 1.16, 17;
Romans 3.21-31; Romans 5.1-11;
Romans 10.5-13; Ephesians 1.3-14;
Ephesians 2.1-10

Seeking strength
Psalms 46, 138; Isaiah 40.27-31;
Isaiah 51.12-16; Ephesians 6.10-20;
2 Thessalonians 2.16, 17

Seeking truth
Psalm 119.153-160; John 8.31-47;
John 14.6-14; John 16.4b-15;
1 Timothy 2.1-7

Sharing your gifts
Exodus 35.20-29; Malachi 3.6-12;
Luke 21.1-4; Acts 2.43-47;
Acts 4.32-37; Romans 12.9-13;
1 Corinthians 16.1-4; 2
Corinthians 8.1-15; 2 Corinthians 9.6-15

Starting a new job
Proverbs 11.3; Proverbs 22.29;
Romans 12.3-11; 1 Thessalonians 5.12-18;
2 Thessalonians 3.6-13; 1 Peter 4.7-11

Understanding your relationship with God
Deuteronomy 5.1-22; Psalm 139;
John 15.1-17; Romans 5.1-11;
Romans 8.1-17

Understanding your relationship with others
Deuteronomy 5.16-21; Proverbs 3.27-35;
Matthew 18.15-17; Matthew 18.21-35;
Romans 14.13-23; Romans 15.1-6;
Galatians 6.1-10; Colossians 3.12-17;
1 John 4.7-12

Worrying about the future
Isaiah 35; Isaiah 60; Jeremiah 29.10-14;
1 Peter 1.3-5; Revelation 21.1-8

Worrying about growing old
Psalm 37.23-29; Isaiah 46.3,4

Worrying about money
Proverbs 11.7; Ecclesiastes 5.10-20;
Matthew 6.24-34; Luke 12.13-21;
1 Timothy 6.6-10

Experiencing Troublesome Feelings

Afraid?
Psalms 27, 91; Isaiah 41.5-13; Mark 4.35-41;
Hebrews 13.5,6; 1 John 4.13-18

Afraid of death?
Psalm 23; Psalm 63.1-8; John 6.35-40;
Romans 8.18-39; 1 Corinthians 15.35-57;
1 Corinthians 5.1-10; 2 Timothy 1.8-10

Angry?
Proverbs 15.1; Matthew 5.21-24;
Romans 12.17-21; Ephesians 4.26-32,
James 1.19-21

Anxious? Worried?
Psalm 25; Matthew 6.24-34;
Matthew 10.26-31; 1 Peter 1.3-5; 1 Peter 5.7

Depressed?
Psalms 16, 43, 130; Isaiah 61.1-4;
Jeremiah 15.10-21; Lamentations 3.55-57;
John 3.14-17; Ephesians 3.14-21

Disappointed? Let down?
Psalm 55; Psalm 62.1-8; Jeremiah 20.7-18

Discouraged?
Psalm 34; Isaiah 12.1-6; Romans 15.13;
2 Corinthians 4.16-18; Philippians 4.10-13;
Colossians 1.9-14; Hebrews 6.9-12

Doubting your faith in God?
Psalms 8, 146; Proverbs 30.5;
Matthew 7.7-12; Luke 17.5,6;
John 20.24-31; Romans 4.13-25;
Hebrews 11; 1 John 5.13-15

Frustrated?
Job 21.1-16; Job 24.1-17; Job 36.1-26;
Matthew 7.13,14

Impatient?
Psalm 13; Psalm 37.1-7; Psalm 40.1-5;
Ecclesiastes 3.1-15; Lamentations 3.25-33;
Hebrews 6.13-20; James 5.7-11

Insecure? Lacking confidence?
Deuteronomy 31.1-8; Psalm 73.21-26;
Psalm 108; Philippians 4.10-20;
1 John 3.19-24

Jealous?
Psalm 49; Proverbs 23.17; James 3.13-18

Lonely?
Psalms 22, 42; John 14.15-31a

Overwhelmed? Experiencing stress?
Isaiah 55.1-9; Matthew 11.25-30;
John 4.1-30; 2 Corinthians 6.3-10;
Revelation 22.17

Rejected?
Psalm 38; Isaiah 52.13—53.12;

Matthew 9.9-13; Luke 4.16-30;
John 15.18—16.4; Ephesians 1.3-14;
1 Peter 2.1-10

Tempted?
Psalm 19.12-14; Psalm 141; Luke 4.1-13;
Hebrews 2.11-18; Hebrews 4.14-16;
James 1.12-18

Tempted by sex?
2 Samuel 11.1—12.25;
1 Corinthians 6.12-20;
Galatians 5.16-26

Tired? Weary?
Psalm 3.5,6; Psalm 4.4-8; Isaiah 35.1-10;
Matthew 11.25-30; 2 Thessalonians 3.16;
Hebrews 4.1-11

Feeling useless? Inferior?
Isaiah 6.1-8; Jeremiah 1.4-10;
Galatians 1.11-24; Ephesians 4.1-16;
1 Peter 2.4-10

Vengeful?
Matthew 5.38-42; Romans 12.17-2

how to use this book

THE BEGINNINGS: EVENTS IN PREHISTORY	THE ANCESTORS OF THE ISRAELITES 1900 TO 1700 B.C.	THE ISRAELITES IN EGYPT AND THE WILDERNESS 1700 TO 1250 B.C.
Creation.	Beginning around 1900 B.C. Abraham comes to Palestine.	1700–1290 B.C. The descendants of Jacob are enslaved in Egypt.
Adam and Eve in the Garden.	Isaac is born to Abraham.	1290 B.C. Moses leads the Israelites out of Egypt.
Cain and Abel.	Jacob is born to Isaac.	
Noah and the Flood.	Jacob has twelve sons, who become the ancestors of the twelve tribes of Israel. The most prominent of these sons is Joseph, who becomes advisor to the King of Egypt.	1290–1250 B.C. The Israelites wander in the wilderness. During this time Moses receives the Law on Mount Sinai.
The Tower of Babel.		

In the beginning God created the heavens and the earth.
(Gen 1.1)

The LORD said to Abraham, "Look at the sky and see if you can count the stars. That's how many descendants you will have."
(Gen 15.5)

Moses and Aaron went to the king of Egypt and told him, "The LORD God says, 'Let my people go into the desert, so they can honor me with a celebration there.'"
(Exod 5.1)

ARCHAEOLOGICAL AGES

Archaeologists classify ancient civilizations according to a series of technological "Ages." By naming an Age by the common technology and objects of an ancient civilization, archaeologists describe how advanced that civilization was.

AGE	TECHNOLOGY	APPROXIMATE TIME PERIOD
Stone Age	Making and using stone tools	2,000,000 to 6000 B.C.
Pottery Age (Late Stone Age)	Making and using clay pottery	6000 to 5000 B.C.
Copper Age	Making and using cast copper utensils	5000 to 3000 B.C.
Bronze Age	Making and using bronze (cast copper and tin) tools	3000 to 1200 B.C.
Iron Age	Making and using iron tools	1200 to 300 B.C.

THE CONQUEST AND SETTLEMENT OF CANAAN 1250 TO 1030 B.C.	THE UNITED ISRAELITE KINGDOM 1030 TO 931 B.C.	THE TWO ISRAELITE KINGDOMS 931 TO 687 B.C.		
	KINGS	*KINGS* JUDAH (SOUTHERN KINGDOM)	*PROPHETS*	*KINGS* ISRAEL (NORTHERN KINGDOM)
1250 B.C. Joshua leads the first stage of the invasion of Canaan.	**1030–1010 B.C.** Saul	**931–913 B.C. Rehoboam**		**931–910 B.C. Jeroboam**
	1010–970 B.C. David	**913–911 B.C. Abijah**		**910–909 B.C. Nadab**
Israel remains a loose confederation of tribes, and leadership is exercised by heroic figures known as the Judges.	**970–931 B.C.** Solomon	**911–870 B.C. Asa**		**909–886 B.C. Baasha**
				886–885 B.C. Elah
	David said, "A ruler who obeys God and does right is like the sunrise on a cloudless day." (2 Sam 23.3,4)			**7 days IN 885 B.C. Zimri**
				885–874 B.C. Omri
The LORD said to Joshua, *"Now you must lead Israel across the Jordan River into the land I'm giving to all of you. Wherever you go, I'll give you that land, as I promised Moses."* (Josh 1.2,3)		**870–848 B.C. Jehoshaphat**	Elijah	**874–853 B.C. Ahab**
				853–852 B.C. Ahaziah
				852–841 B.C. Joram
		848–841 B.C. Jehoram		**841–814 B.C. Jehu**
		841 B.C. Ahaziab	Elisha	
		841–835 B.C. Queen Athaliah		
		835–796 B.C. Joash		
				814–798 B.C. Jehoahaz
		796–781 B.C. Amaziah		**798–783 B.C. Jehoash**
		781–740 B.C. Uzziah	Jonah	**783–743 B.C. Jeroboam II**
			Amos	**6 mo. in 743 B.C. Zechariah**
				1 mo. in 743 B.C. Shallum
				743–738 B.C. Menahem
		740–736 B.C. Jotham	Hosea	**738–737 B.C. Pekahiah**
		736–716 B.C. Ahaz	Micah Isaiah	**737–732 B.C. Pekah**
				732–723 B.C. Hoshea
				722 B.C. *FALL OF SAMARIA*
		716–687 B.C. Hezekiah		

THE LAST YEARS OF THE KINGDOM OF JUDAH 687 TO 586 B.C.		THE EXILE AND THE RESTORATION 586 TO 443 B.C.

KINGS	PROPHETS	PROPHETS

687–642 B.C.
Manasseh

642–640 B.C.
Amon

640–609 B.C.
Josiah — Zephaniah

3 MO. IN 609 B.C.
Joahaz — Nahum

609–598 B.C.
Jehoiakim — Jeremiah

3 MO. IN 598 B.C.
Jehoiachin — Habakkuk?

598–587 B.C.
Zedekiah — Ezekiel

JULY 587 OR 586 B.C.
FALL OF JERUSALEM

586 B.C.
The Judeans taken into exile in Babylonia after the fall of Jerusalem.

539 B.C.
Persian rule begins.

538 B.C.
Edict of Cyprus allows Jews to return. — Haggai / Zechariah

520 B.C.
Foundations of new temple are laid. — Obadiah / Daniel

445–443 B.C.
The walls of Jerusalem are restored. — Malachi / Joel?

The Babylonian soldiers . . .
carried off the bronze things used
for worship at the temple . . .
The people of Judah had been carried away
as captives from their own country.
(2 Kgs 25.13,14,21)

Cyrus told the people of his kingdom,
"The LORD God will watch over and
encourage any of his people who want
to go back to Jerusalem and help
build the temple."
(Ezra 1.2–3)

A WORD ABOUT DATES

The initials B.C. have traditionally been an abbreviation for "Before Christ." Based on information presented in LUKE, then, Jesus was born at least four years before the years known as A.D. began. (A.D. stands for the Latin phrase "in the year of our Lord.") Christian dating was actually not introduced until A.D. 526 by a monk named Dionysius Exiguus. He was given the job of creating a calendar for the feasts of the church. He fixed the birth of Jesus in the Roman year 754, which was selected as the first year of the Christian era beginning on January 1. Dionysius apparently misjudged Herod's reign by about five years.

The initials B.C.E. (Before the Common Era) and C.E. (in the Common Era) are sometimes used in place of the traditional B.C. and A.D.

All dates in this timeline are approximate.

THE TIME BETWEEN THE TESTAMENTS 333 TO 4 B.C.	THE TIME OF THE NEW TESTAMENT 6 B.C. TO A.D. 70

333 B.C.
Alexander the Great establishes Greek rule in Palestine.

323–198 B.C.
The Ptolemies, descendants of one of Alexander's generals, who had been given the position of ruler over Egypt, rule Palestine.

198–166 B.C.
The Seleucids, descendants of one of Alexander's generals, who had acquired the rule of Syria, rule Palestine.

166–63 B.C.
Jewish revolt under Judas Maccabeus reestablishes Jewish independence. Judas' family and descendants, the Hasmoneans, rule Palestine.

63 B.C.
The Roman general Pompey takes Jerusalem.

37–4 B.C.
Puppet kings appointed by Rome rule Palestine. One of these is Herod the Great.

"Then the greatest kingdom of all will be given to the chosen ones of God Most High. His kingdom will be eternal, and all others will serve and obey him."
(Dan 7.27)

Birth of Jesus.

Ministry of John the Baptist; baptism of Jesus and beginning of his public ministry.

around A.D. 32
Death and resurrection of Jesus.

A.D. 37
Conversion of Paul (Saul of Tarsus).

A.D. 41–65
Ministry of Paul.

A.D. 65
Final imprisonment of Paul.

A.D. 70
Herod's temple destroyed.

Jesus said, "I am the light for the world! Follow me, and . . . you will have the light that gives life."
(John 8.12)

A MOMENT WITH SCRIPTURE

Many people have found that taking a moment each morning to read the Bible and pray is a wonderful way to prepare themselves for whatever the day has to offer. This daily Bible reading plan is designed to introduce you to many of the important stories and key themes that have made God's Word such a source of comfort and strength for people who turn to it regularly for guidance.

Most of the passages selected can be easily read in less than five minutes. Before reading the passage for the day, ask God to clear your mind and open your heart to receive God's Word. Some Bible readers have found it helpful to keep a journal of the insights they gain while reading the Scriptures. Many have found that taking time to thank God and to remember others in prayer further enriches their devotional experience.

JANUARY

1　A Story of Creation
　❏ Gen 1.1—2.4
2　The Preaching of John the Baptist
　❏ Mark 1.1-8
3　Jesus Is Baptized and Tested
　❏ Matt 3.13—4.11
4　The Garden of Eden
　❏ Gen 2.5-25
5　Jesus Begins His Work in Galilee
　❏ Luke 4.14-30
6　The Trouble with Sin
　❏ Gen 3.1-24
7　Warnings about False Prophets
　❏ Matt 7.15-23
8　A Man with Evil Spirits
　❏ Mark 1.21-28
9　The First Murder
　❏ Gen 4.1-16
10　Jesus Turns Water into Wine
　❏ John 2.1-12
11　God Warns Noah about a Coming Flood
　❏ Gen 6.1-22
12　The Flood Comes
　❏ Gen 7.1-24
13　Jesus and Nicodemus
　❏ John 3.1-21
14　The Floodwaters Dry Up
　❏ Gen 8.1-19
15　God's Promise to Noah
　❏ Gen 9.1-17
16　Jesus Heals a Crippled Man
　❏ Mark 2.1-12
17　Jesus Chooses Twelve To Be His Apostles
　❏ Matt 9.9-13; 10.1-4
18　A Promise to Abraham and Sarah
　❏ Gen 17.1-27
19　Jesus and the Ruler of Demons
　❏ Mark 3.20-30
20　The LORD Tests Abraham
　❏ Gen 22.1-19
21　Jesus and the Samaritan Woman
　❏ John 4.3-26
22　Jacob's Name Is Changed to Israel
　❏ Gen 32.22-32
23　Jesus Heals an Army Officer's Servant
　❏ Luke 7.1-10

24　Joseph and His Brothers
　❏ Gen 37.1-11
25　Jesus Raises a Widow's Son to Life
　❏ Luke 7.11-17
26　A Story about a Dishonest Manager
　❏ Luke 16.1-13
27　Jesus Heals a Sick Man
　❏ John 5.1-18
28　Joseph Is Taken to Egypt
　❏ Gen 37.12-36
29　A Storm on Lake Galilee
　❏ Mark 4.35-41
30　Joseph Interprets the King's Dreams
　❏ Gen 41.1-36
31　Another Man with Evil Spirits
　❏ Mark 5.1-20

FEBRUARY

1　Joseph Is Made Governor of Egypt
　❏ Gen 41.37-57
2　Jesus Heals a Dying Girl and a Sick Woman
　❏ Mark 5.21-43
3　Joseph's Brothers Go to Egypt
　❏ Gen 42.1-24
4　Wisdom and Foolishness
　❏ Prov 9.1-18
5　Joseph's Brothers Return to Egypt
　❏ Gen 43.1-34
6　The Death of John the Baptist
　❏ Mark 6.14-29
7　Joseph Sends for Jacob
　❏ Gen 45.1-28
8　Salt and Light
　❏ Matt 5.13-16
9　Jesus Feeds Five Thousand
　❏ John 6.1-15
10　Jacob and His Family Go to Egypt
　❏ Gen 46.1-7,28-34
11　The People of Israel Suffer in Egypt
　❏ Exod 1.1-22
12　Jesus Walks on Water
　❏ Matt 14.22-33
13　Moses Escapes from Egypt
　❏ Exod 2.1-25
14　Love Never Fails
　❏ 1 Cor 13.1-13

11 A Time of Suffering before the Son of Man
   Appears
    ❏ Matt 24.15-31
12 Choose Life
    ❏ Deut 30.1-20
13 No One Knows the Day or Time
    ❏ Matt 24.36-44
14 The Song of Moses
    ❏ Deut 32.1-43
15 Putting God First
    ❏ Matt 6.19-21,24-34
16 Jesus Is Honored and Betrayed
    ❏ Matt 26.1-16
17 Joshua Becomes Israel's Leader
    ❏ Josh 1.1-9
18 The Last Supper (part 1)
    ❏ Matt 26.17-25
19 The Last Supper (part 2)
    ❏ Matt 26.26-35
20 The Bread that Gives Life
    ❏ John 6.28-40
21 Jesus Washes the Feet of His Disciples
    ❏ John 13.1-20
22 Jesus Is the True Vine
    ❏ John 15.1-17
23 Jesus Prays in Gethsemane
    ❏ Matthew 26.36-46
24 The People of Israel Cross the Jordan River
    ❏ Josh 3.1-17
25 Jesus Prays for His Followers (part 1)
    ❏ John 17.1-19
26 Jesus Prays for His Followers (part 2)
    ❏ John 17.20-26
27 The Capture of Jericho
    ❏ Josh 5.13—6.20
28 We Will Worship and Obey the LORD
    ❏ Josh 24.1-28
29 Jesus Is Arrested
    ❏ Matt 26.47-56
30 Israel's Disobedience
    ❏ Judg 2.6-19

MAY

1 Jesus Is Questioned by the Council
    ❏ Matt 26.57-68
2 Deborah and Barak
    ❏ Judg 4.1-24
3 Peter Says He Doesn't Know Jesus
    ❏ Matt 26.69-75
4 Deborah's Song
    ❏ Judg 5.1-31
5 Jesus and Pontius Pilate
    ❏ Matt 27.1-14
6 Gideon Will Defeat the Midianites
    ❏ Judg 6.11-24
7 Jesus Is Sentenced To Die
    ❏ Matt 27.15-26
8 Gideon Needs Proof from the LORD
    ❏ Judg 6.33-40

9 Jesus Is Nailed to a Cross
    ❏ Matt 27.27-44
10 Delilah Tricks Samson
    ❏ Judg 16.1-20
11 The Death of Jesus
    ❏ Matt 27.45-56
12 Jesus Is the Great High Priest
    ❏ Heb 4.14—5.10
13 Jesus Is Buried
    ❏ Matt 27.57-66
14 Samson's Strength Returns
    ❏ Judg 16.21-31
15 Jesus Is Alive
    ❏ Matt 28.1-10
16 Christ Was Raised to Life
    ❏ 1 Cor 15.1-11
17 Jesus Appears to Two Disciples
    ❏ Luke 24.13-35
18 God's People Will Be Raised to Life
    ❏ 1 Cor 15.12-34
19 Jesus and Thomas
    ❏ John 20.24-29
20 What Our Bodies Will Be Like
    ❏ 1 Cor 15.35-58
21 Jesus Questions Peter
    ❏ John 21.15-19
22 Ruth and Naomi
    ❏ Ruth 1.1-22
23 Ruth Meets Boaz
    ❏ Ruth 2.1-23
24 Boaz Promises to Take Care of Ruth
    ❏ Ruth 3.1-18
25 Ruth and Boaz Are Married
    ❏ Ruth 4.12-22
26 What Jesus' Followers Must Do
    ❏ Matt 28.16-20
27 Jesus Is Taken to Heaven
    ❏ Acts 1.1-11
28 From Death to Life
    ❏ Eph 2.1-10
29 Someone To Take the Place of Judas
    ❏ Acts 1.12-26
30 The Prophet Samuel Is Born
    ❏ 1 Sam 1.1-20
31 The Holy Spirit Is Promised to Jesus' Disciples
    ❏ John 14.15-31

JUNE

1 A Story about a Farmer
    ❏ Luke 8.4-15
2 Hannah's Song
    ❏ 1 Sam 2.1-10
3 The Work of the Holy Spirit
    ❏ John 16.1-15
4 The LORD Speaks to Samuel
    ❏ 1 Sam 3.1-18
5 The Philistines Capture the Sacred Chest
    ❏ 1 Sam 4.1-11

SEPTEMBER

OCTOBER

1 Jerusalem Will Be at Peace
   ❑ Zech 8.1-17
2 What People Desire and What God's Spirit Offers
   ❑ Gal 5.16-26
3 The LORD Is a Strong Shield
   ❑ Ps 28.1-9
4 Help Each Other
   ❑ Gal 6.1-10
5 Judgment on Jerusalem and Judah
   ❑ Isa 3.1-15
6 Israel's Sin Is Like a Crack in a Wall
   ❑ Isa 30.8-17
7 The Old Life and the New Life
   ❑ Eph 4.17-24
8 Habakkuk Praises the LORD's Power
   ❑ Hab 3.1-15
9 Running toward the Goal
   ❑ Phil 3.12-21
10 Always Be Glad because of the Lord
   ❑ Phil 4.4-9
11 God Is a Mighty Fortress
   ❑ Ps 46.1-11
12 The Power of Prayer
   ❑ 1 Tim 2.1-8
13 The LORD Purifies and Calls the Prophet Isaiah
   ❑ Isa 6.1-13
14 False Teaching and True Wealth
   ❑ 1 Tim 6.3-10
15 Obey the LORD
   ❑ Ps 1.1-6
16 Love and Giving
   ❑ Matt 5.43—6.4
17 Fighting a Good Fight for the Faith
   ❑ 1 Tim 6.11-19
18 Daniel in a Pit of Lions
   ❑ Dan 6.1-24
19 A Good Soldier of Christ Jesus
   ❑ 2 Tim 2.1-13
20 God's Love for Israel
   ❑ Hos 11.1-11
21 How To Be an Approved Worker
   ❑ 2 Tim 2.14-26
22 The Fierce Anger of the LORD
   ❑ Nah 1.1-6
23 Warning against Having Favorites
   ❑ Jas 2.1-13
24 A Glorious New Temple
   ❑ Hag 2.1-9
25 Controlling the Tongue
   ❑ Jas 3.1-12
26 It's Wise To Be Honest
   ❑ Prov 11.1-11
27 Be Patient and Kind
   ❑ Jas 5.7-20
28 All Creation Praises the LORD
   ❑ Ps 148.1-14
29 The New Commandment
   ❑ 1 John 2.7-17
30 God Is Love
   ❑ 1 John 4.1-21
31 The Fight against Evil
   ❑ Eph 6.10-20

NOVEMBER

1 Powerful Leaders Are Condemned
   ❑ Mic 2.1-11
2 See that Justice Is Done
   ❑ Mic 6.6-8
3 A Reason for Hope
   ❑ 1 Pet 1.3-12
4 Ezekiel Condemns Jerusalem's Leaders
   ❑ Ezek 11.1-13
5 The LORD Is the Good Shepherd
   ❑ Ezek 34.1-16
6 A Living Stone and a Holy Nation
   ❑ 1 Pet 2.1-10
7 Dry Bones Live Again
   ❑ Ezek 37.1-14
8 The Stream Flowing from the New Temple
   ❑ Ezek 47.1-12
9 Suffering for Doing Right
   ❑ 1 Pet 3.8-22
10 God's Love Never Fails
   ❑ Ps 136.1-26
11 Helping Christian Leaders To Do Their Best
   ❑ 1 Pet 5.1-11
12 Wise Sayings about Foolishness
   ❑ Prov 18.1-19
13 Living As the Lord's Followers
   ❑ 2 Pet 1.3-15
14 Jeremiah's Letter to the Exiles in Babylonia
   ❑ Jer 29.1-14
15 A New Agreement with Israel and Judah
   ❑ Jer 31.31-37
16 A Large Crowd of Witnesses
   ❑ Heb 12.1-13
17 Trust the LORD
   ❑ Isa 40.21-31
18 Jerusalem's People Are Coming Home
   ❑ Isa 60.1-9
19 A New Day for Jerusalem
   ❑ Isa 65.17-25
20 God's Kindness and the New Life
   ❑ Titus 2.11-15
21 Everything Has Its Time
   ❑ Eccl 3.1-8
22 Being Kind and Doing Good
   ❑ Titus 3.1-11
23 Choose Good and Not Evil
   ❑ Amos 5.10-15
24 Visions of Coming Punishment
   ❑ Amos 7.1-9
25 The New Heaven and the New Earth
   ❑ Rev 21.1-8
26 The LORD Is Merciful
   ❑ Jer 3.12-20
27 The New Jerusalem (part 1)
   ❑ Rev 21.9-21
28 The New Jerusalem (part 2)
   ❑ Rev 21.22—22.5

READ THROUGH THE BIBLE IN A YEAR

Have you ever read the entire Bible all the way through? If you set aside just twenty or thirty minutes a day, you can do just that in one year. By following this reading plan you will read part of the Old and New Testaments each day. When the reading plan directs you to a new book of the Bible, be sure to read the Introduction to that book so that you will be alert to its key themes, characters, and passages. Begin today and discover the riches of God's Word!

JANUARY

1 ☐ Luke 5.27-39 ☐ Gen 1-2 ☐ Ps 1
2 ☐ Luke 6.1-26 ☐ Gen 3-5 ☐ Ps 2
3 ☐ Luke 6.27-49 ☐ Gen 6-7 ☐ Ps 3
4 ☐ Luke 1.1-17 ☐ Gen 8-10 ☐ Ps 4
5 ☐ Luke 7.18-50 ☐ Gen 11 ☐ Ps 5
6 ☐ Luke 8.1-25 ☐ Gen 12 ☐ Ps 6
7 ☐ Luke 8.26-56 ☐ Gen 13-14 ☐ Ps 7
8 ☐ Luke 9.1-27 ☐ Gen 15 ☐ Ps 8
9 ☐ Luke 9.28-62 ☐ Gen 16 ☐ Ps 9
10 ☐ Luke 10.1-20 ☐ Gen 17 ☐ Ps 10
11 ☐ Luke 10.21-42 ☐ Gen 18 ☐ Ps 11
12 ☐ Luke 11.1-28 ☐ Gen 19 ☐ Ps 12
13 ☐ Luke 11.29-54 ☐ Gen 20 ☐ Ps 13
14 ☐ Luke 12.1-31 ☐ Gen 21 ☐ Ps 14
15 ☐ Luke 12.32-59 ☐ Gen 22 ☐ Ps 15
16 ☐ Luke 13.1-17 ☐ Gen 23 ☐ Ps 16
17 ☐ Luke 13.18-35 ☐ Gen 24 ☐ Ps 17
18 ☐ Luke 14.1-24 ☐ Gen 25 ☐ Ps 18
19 ☐ Luke 14.25-35 ☐ Gen 26 ☐ Ps 19
20 ☐ Luke 15 ☐ Gen 27.1-45 ☐ Ps 20
21 ☐ Luke 16 ☐ Gen 27.46-28.22 ☐ Ps 21
22 ☐ Luke 17 ☐ Gen 29.1-30 ☐ Ps 22
23 ☐ Luke 18.1-17 ☐ Gen 29.31—30.43 ☐ Ps 23
24 ☐ Luke 18.18-43 ☐ Gen 31 ☐ Ps 24
25 ☐ Luke 19.1-27 ☐ Gen 32-33 ☐ Ps 25
26 ☐ Luke 19.28-48 ☐ Gen 34 ☐ Ps 26
27 ☐ Luke 20.1-26 ☐ Gen 35-36 ☐ Ps 27
28 ☐ Luke 20.27-47 ☐ Gen 37 ☐ Ps 28
29 ☐ Luke 21 ☐ Gen 38 ☐ Ps 29
30 ☐ Luke 22.1-38 ☐ Gen 39 ☐ Ps 30
31 ☐ Luke 22.39-71 ☐ Gen 40 ☐ Ps 31

FEBRUARY

1 ☐ Luke 23.1-25 ☐ Gen 41 ☐ Ps 32
2 ☐ Luke 23.26-56 ☐ Gen 42 ☐ Ps 33
3 ☐ Luke 24.1-12 ☐ Gen 43 ☐ Ps 34
4 ☐ Luke 24.13-53 ☐ Gen 44 ☐ Ps 35
5 ☐ Heb 1 ☐ Gen 45.1—46.27 ☐ Ps 36
6 ☐ Heb 2 ☐ Gen 46.28—47.31 ☐ Ps 37
7 ☐ Heb 3.1—4.13 ☐ Gen 48 ☐ Ps 38
8 ☐ Heb 4.14—6.12 ☐ Gen 49-50 ☐ Ps 39
9 ☐ Heb 6.13-20 ☐ Exod 1-2 ☐ Ps 40

10 ☐ Heb 7 ☐ Exod 3-4 ☐ Ps 41
11 ☐ Heb 8 ☐ Exod 5.1—6.27 ☐ Prov 1
12 ☐ Heb 9.1-22 ☐ Exod 6.28—8.32 ☐ Prov 2
13 ☐ Heb 9.23—10.18 ☐ Exod 9-10 ☐ Prov 3
14 ☐ Heb 10.19-39 ☐ Exod 11-12 ☐ Prov 4
15 ☐ Heb 11.1-22 ☐ Exod 13-14 ☐ Prov 5
16 ☐ Heb 11.23-40 ☐ Exod 15 ☐ Prov 6.1—7.5
17 ☐ Heb 12 ☐ Exod 16-17 ☐ Prov 7.6-27
18 ☐ Heb 13 ☐ Exod 18-19 ☐ Prov 8
19 ☐ Matt 1 ☐ Exod 20-21 ☐ Prov 9
20 ☐ Matt 2 ☐ Exod 22-23 ☐ Prov 10
21 ☐ Matt 3 ☐ Exod 24 ☐ Prov 11
22 ☐ Matt 4 ☐ Exod 25-27 ☐ Prov 12
23 ☐ Matt 5.1-20 ☐ Exod 28-29 ☐ Prov 13
24 ☐ Matt 5.21-48 ☐ Exod 30-32 ☐ Prov 14
25 ☐ Matt 6.1-18 ☐ Exod 33-34 ☐ Prov 15
26 ☐ Matt 6.19-34 ☐ Exod 35-36 ☐ Prov 16
27 ☐ Matt 7 ☐ Exod 37-38 ☐ Prov 17
28 ☐ Matt 8.1-13 ☐ Exod 39-40 ☐ Prov 18

MARCH

1 ☐ Matt 8.14-34 ☐ Lev 1-2 ☐ Prov 19
2 ☐ Matt 9.1-17 ☐ Lev 3-4 ☐ Prov 20
3 ☐ Matt 9.18-38 ☐ Lev 5-6 ☐ Prov 21
4 ☐ Matt 10.1-25 ☐ Lev 7-8 ☐ Prov 22
5 ☐ Matt 10.26-42 ☐ Lev 9-10 ☐ Prov 23
6 ☐ Matt 11.1-19 ☐ Lev 11-12 ☐ Prov 24
7 ☐ Matt 11.20-30 ☐ Lev 13 ☐ Prov 25
8 ☐ Matt 12.1-21 ☐ Lev 14 ☐ Prov 26
9 ☐ Matt 12.22-50 ☐ Lev 15-16 ☐ Prov 27
10 ☐ Matt 13.1-23 ☐ Lev 17-18 ☐ Prov 28
11 ☐ Matt 13.24-58 ☐ Lev 19 ☐ Prov 29
12 ☐ Matt 14.1-21 ☐ Lev 20-21 ☐ Prov 30
13 ☐ Matt 14.22-36 ☐ Lev 22-23 ☐ Prov 31
14 ☐ Matt 15.1-20 ☐ Lev 24-25 ☐ Eccl 1.1-11
15 ☐ Matt 15.21-39 ☐ Lev 26-27 ☐ Eccl 1.12—2.26
16 ☐ Matt 16 ☐ Num 1-2 ☐ Eccl 3.1-15
17 ☐ Matt 17 ☐ Num 3-4 ☐ Eccl 3.16—4.16
18 ☐ Matt 18.1-20 ☐ Num 5-6 ☐ Eccl 5
19 ☐ Matt 18.21-35 ☐ Num 7-8 ☐ Eccl 6
20 ☐ Matt 19.1-15 ☐ Num 9-10 ☐ Eccl 7
21 ☐ Matt 19.16-30 ☐ Num 11-12 ☐ Eccl 8
22 ☐ Matt 20.1-16 ☐ Num 13-14 ☐ Eccl 9.1-12
23 ☐ Matt 20.17-34 ☐ Num 15-16 ☐ Eccl 9.13—10.20

24 ❑ Matt 21.1-27 ❑ Num 17-18 ❑ Eccl 11.1-8
25 ❑ Matt 21.28-46 ❑ Num 19-20 ❑ Eccl 11.9—12.14
26 ❑ Matt 22.1-22 ❑ Num 21 ❑ Song 1.1—2.7
27 ❑ Matt 22.23-46 ❑ Num 22.1-40 ❑ Song 2.8—3.5
28 ❑ Matt 23.1-12 ❑ Num 22.41—23.26 ❑ Song 3.6—5.1
29 ❑ Matt 23.13-39 ❑ Num 23.27—24.25 ❑ Song 5.2—6.3
30 ❑ Matt 24.1-31 ❑ Num 25-27 ❑ Song 6.4-8.4
31 ❑ Matt 24.32-51 ❑ Num 28-29 ❑ Song 8.5-14

APRIL

1 ❑ Matt 25.1-30 ❑ Num 30-31 ❑ Job 1
2 ❑ Matt 25.31-46 ❑ Num 32-34 ❑ Job 2
3 ❑ Matt 26.1-25 ❑ Num 35-36 ❑ Job 3
4 ❑ Matt 26.26-46 ❑ Deut 1-2 ❑ Job 4
5 ❑ Matt 26.47-75 ❑ Deut 3-4 ❑ Job 5
6 ❑ Matt 27.1-31 ❑ Deut 5-6 ❑ Job 6
7 ❑ Matt 27.32-66 ❑ Deut 7-8 ❑ Job 7
8 ❑ Matt 28 ❑ Deut 9-10 ❑ Job 8
9 ❑ Acts 1 ❑ Deut 11-12 ❑ Job 9
10 ❑ Acts 2.1-13 ❑ Deut 13-14 ❑ Job 10
11 ❑ Acts 2.14-47 ❑ Deut 15-16 ❑ Job 11
12 ❑ Acts 3 ❑ Deut 17-18 ❑ Job 12
13 ❑ Acts 4.1-22 ❑ Deut 19-20 ❑ Job 13
14 ❑ Acts 4.23-37 ❑ Deut 21-22 ❑ Job 14
15 ❑ Acts 5.1-16 ❑ Deut 23-24 ❑ Job 15
16 ❑ Acts 5.17-42 ❑ Deut 25-27 ❑ Job 16
17 ❑ Acts 6 ❑ Deut 28 ❑ Job 17
18 ❑ Acts 7.1-22 ❑ Deut 29-30 ❑ Job 18
19 ❑ Acts 7.23—8.1a ❑ Deut 31-32 ❑ Job 19
20 ❑ Acts 8.1b-25 ❑ Deut 33-34 ❑ Job 20
21 ❑ Acts 8.26-40 ❑ Josh 1-2 ❑ Job 21
22 ❑ Acts 9.1-25 ❑ Josh 3.1—5.1 ❑ Job 22
23 ❑ Acts 9.26-43 ❑ Josh 5.2—6.27 ❑ Job 23
24 ❑ Acts 10.1-33 ❑ Josh 7-8 ❑ Job 24
25 ❑ Acts 10.34-48 ❑ Josh 9-10 ❑ Job 25
26 ❑ Acts 11.1-18 ❑ Josh 11-12 ❑ Job 26
27 ❑ Acts 11.19-30 ❑ Josh 13-14 ❑ Job 27
28 ❑ Acts 12 ❑ Josh 15-17 ❑ Job 28
29 ❑ Acts 13.1-25 ❑ Josh 18-19 ❑ Job 29
30 ❑ Acts 13.26-52 ❑ Josh 20-21 ❑ Job 30

MAY

1 ❑ Acts 14 ❑ Josh 22 ❑ Job 31
2 ❑ Acts 15.1-21 ❑ Josh 23-24 ❑ Job 32
3 ❑ Acts 15.22-41 ❑ Judg 1 ❑ Job 33
4 ❑ Acts 16.1-15 ❑ Judg 2-3 ❑ Job 34
5 ❑ Acts 16.16-40 ❑ Judg 4-5 ❑ Job 35
6 ❑ Acts 17.1-15 ❑ Judg 6 ❑ Job 36
7 ❑ Acts 17.16-34 ❑ Judg 7-8 ❑ Job 37

8 ❑ Acts 18 ❑ Judg 9 ❑ Job 38
9 ❑ Acts 19.1-20 ❑ Judg 10.1—11.33 ❑ Job 39
10 ❑ Acts 19.21-41 ❑ Judg 11.34—12.15 ❑ Job 40
11 ❑ Acts 20.1-16 ❑ Judg 13 ❑ Job 41
12 ❑ Acts 20.17-38 ❑ Judg 14-15 ❑ Job 42
13 ❑ Acts 21.1-36 ❑ Judg 16 ❑ Ps 42
14 ❑ Acts 21.37—22.29 ❑ Judg 17-18 ❑ Ps 43
15 ❑ Acts 22.30—23.22 ❑ Judg 19 ❑ Ps 44
16 ❑ Acts 23.23—24.9 ❑ Judg 20 ❑ Ps 45
17 ❑ Acts 24.10-27 ❑ Judg 21 ❑ Ps 46
18 ❑ Acts 25 ❑ Ruth 1-2 ❑ Ps 47
19 ❑ Acts 26.1-18 ❑ Ruth 3-4 ❑ Ps 48
20 ❑ Acts 26.19-32 ❑ 1 Sam 1.1—2.10 ❑ Ps 49
21 ❑ Acts 27.1-12 ❑ 1 Sam 2.11-36 ❑ Ps 50
22 ❑ Acts 27.13-44 ❑ 1 Sam 3 ❑ Ps 51
23 ❑ Acts 28.1-16 ❑ 1 Sam 4-5 ❑ Ps 52
24 ❑ Acts 28.17-31 ❑ 1 Sam 6-7 ❑ Ps 53
25 ❑ Rom 1.1-15 ❑ 1 Sam 8 ❑ Ps 54
26 ❑ Rom 1.16-32 ❑ 1 Sam 9.1—10.16 ❑ Ps 55
27 ❑ Rom 2.1-3.8 ❑ 1 Sam 10.17—11.15 ❑ Ps 56
28 ❑ Rom 3.9-31 ❑ 1 Sam 12 ❑ Ps 57
29 ❑ Rom 4 ❑ 1 Sam 13 ❑ Ps 58
30 ❑ Rom 5 ❑ 1 Sam 14 ❑ Ps 59
31 ❑ Rom 6 ❑ 1 Sam 15 ❑ Ps 60

JUNE

1 ❑ Rom 7 ❑ 1 Sam 16 ❑ Ps 61
2 ❑ Rom 8 ❑ 1 Sam 17.1-54 ❑ Ps 62
3 ❑ Rom 9.1-29 ❑ 1 Sam 17.55—18.30 ❑ Ps 63
4 ❑ Rom 9.30—10.21 ❑ 1 Sam 19 ❑ Ps 64
5 ❑ Rom 11.1-24 ❑ 1 Sam 20 ❑ Ps 65
6 ❑ Rom 11.25-36 ❑ 1 Sam 21-22 ❑ Ps 66
7 ❑ Rom 12 ❑ 1 Sam 23-24 ❑ Ps 67
8 ❑ Rom 13 ❑ 1 Sam 25 ❑ Ps 68
9 ❑ Rom 14 ❑ 1 Sam 26 ❑ Ps 69
10 ❑ Rom 15.1-13 ❑ 1 Sam 27-28 ❑ Ps 70
11 ❑ Rom 15.14-33 ❑ 1 Sam 29-31 ❑ Ps 71
12 ❑ Rom 16 ❑ 2 Sam 1 ❑ Ps 72
13 ❑ Mark 1.1-20 ❑ 2 Sam 2.1—3.1 ❑ Dan 1
14 ❑ Mark 1.21-45 ❑ 2 Sam 3.2-39 ❑ Dan 2.1-23
15 ❑ Mark 2 ❑ 2 Sam 4-5 ❑ Dan 2.24-49
16 ❑ Mark 3.1-19 ❑ 2 Sam 6 ❑ Dan 3
17 ❑ Mark 3.20-35 ❑ 2 Sam 7-8 ❑ Dan 4
18 ❑ Mark 4.1-20 ❑ 2 Sam 9-10 ❑ Dan 5
19 ❑ Mark 4.21-41 ❑ 2 Sam 11-12 ❑ Dan 6
20 ❑ Mark 5.1-20 ❑ 2 Sam 13 ❑ Dan 7
21 ❑ Mark 5.21-43 ❑ 2 Sam 14 ❑ Dan 8
22 ❑ Mark 6.1-29 ❑ 2 Sam 15 ❑ Dan 9
23 ❑ Mark 6.30-56 ❑ 2 Sam 16 ❑ Dan 10.1-21
24 ❑ Mark 7.1-13 ❑ 2 Sam 17 ❑ Dan 11.1-19
25 ❑ Mark 7.14-37 ❑ 2 Sam 18 ❑ Dan 11.20-45

26	❑ Mark 8.1-21	❑ 2 Sam 19	❑ Dan 12
27	❑ Mark 8.22—9.1	❑ 2 Sam 20-21	❑ Hos 1.1—2.1
28	❑ Mark 9.2-50	❑ 2 Sam 22	❑ Hos 2.2-23
29	❑ Mark 10.1-31	❑ 2 Sam 23	❑ Hos 3
30	❑ Mark 10.32-52	❑ 2 Sam 24	❑ Hos 4.1-11a

JULY

1	❑ Mark 11.1-14	❑ 1 Kgs 1	❑ Hos 4.11b—5.4
2	❑ Mark 11.15-33	❑ 1 Kgs 2	❑ Hos 5.5-15
3	❑ Mark 12.1-27	❑ 1 Kgs 3	❑ Hos 6.1—7.2
4	❑ Mark 12.28-44	❑ 1 Kgs 4-5	❑ Hos 7.3-16
5	❑ Mark 13.1-13	❑ 1 Kgs 6	❑ Hos 8
6	❑ Mark 13.14-37	❑ 1 Kgs 7	❑ Hos 9.1-16
7	❑ Mark 14.1-31	❑ 1 Kgs 8	❑ Hos 9.17—10.15
8	❑ Mark 14.32-72	❑ 1 Kgs 9	❑ Hos 11.1-11
9	❑ Mark 15.1-20	❑ 1 Kgs 10	❑ Hos 11.12—12.14
10	❑ Mark 15.21-47	❑ 1 Kgs 11	❑ Hos 13
11	❑ Mark 16	❑ 1 Kgs 12.1-31	❑ Hos 14
12	❑ 1 Cor 1.1-17	❑ 1 Kgs 12.32—13.34	❑ Joel 1
13	❑ 1 Cor 1.18-31	❑ 1 Kgs 14	❑ Joel 2.1-11
14	❑ 1 Cor 2	❑ 1 Kgs 15.1-32	❑ Joel 2.12-32
15	❑ 1 Cor 3	❑ 1 Kgs 15.33—16.34	❑ Joel 3
16	❑ 1 Cor 4	❑ 1 Kgs 17	❑ Amos 1
17	❑ 1 Cor 5	❑ 1 Kgs 18	❑ Amos 2.1—3.2
18	❑ 1 Cor 6	❑ 1 Kgs 19	❑ Amos 3.3—4.3
19	❑ 1 Cor 7.1-24	❑ 1 Kgs 20	❑ Amos 4.4-13
20	❑ 1 Cor 7.25-40	❑ 1 Kgs 21	❑ Amos 5
21	❑ 1 Cor 8	❑ 1 Kgs 22	❑ Amos 6
22	❑ 1 Cor 9	❑ 2 Kgs 1-2	❑ Amos 7
23	❑ 1 Cor 10	❑ 2 Kgs 3	❑ Amos 8
24	❑ 1 Cor 11.1-16	❑ 2 Kgs 4	❑ Amos 9
25	❑ 1 Cor 11.17-34	❑ 2 Kgs 5	❑ Obad
26	❑ 1 Cor 12	❑ 2 Kgs 6.1—7.2	❑ Jonah 1
27	❑ 1 Cor 13	❑ 2 Kgs 7.3-20	❑ Jonah 2
28	❑ 1 Cor 14.1-25	❑ 2 Kgs 8	❑ Jonah 3
29	❑ 1 Cor 14.26-40	❑ 2 Kgs 9	❑ Jonah 4
30	❑ 1 Cor 15.1-34	❑ 2 Kgs 10	❑ Mic 1
31	❑ 1 Cor 15.35-58	❑ 2 Kgs 11	❑ Mic 2

AUGUST

1	❑ 1 Cor 16	❑ 2 Kgs 12-13	❑ Mic 3
2	❑ 2 Cor 1.1—2.4	❑ 2 Kgs 14	❑ Mic 4.1—5.1
3	❑ 2 Cor 2.5—3.18	❑ 2 Kgs 15-16	❑ Mic 5.2-15
4	❑ 2 Cor 4.1-5.10	❑ 2 Kgs 17	❑ Mic 6
5	❑ Cor 5.11—6.13	❑ 2 Kgs 18	❑ Mic 7
6	❑ 2 Cor 6.14-7.16	❑ 2 Kgs 19	❑ Nah 1
7	❑ 2 Cor 8	❑ 2 Kgs 20-21	❑ Nah 2
8	❑ 2 Cor 9	❑ 2 Kgs 22.1—23.35	❑ Nah 3
9	❑ 2 Cor 10	❑ 2 Kgs 23.36—24.20	❑ Hab 1
10	❑ 2 Cor 11	❑ 2 Kgs 25	❑ Hab 2

11	❑ 2 Cor 12	❑ 1 Chr 1-2	❑ Hab 3
12	❑ 2 Cor 13	❑ 1 Chr 3-4	❑ Zeph 1
13	❑ John 1.1-18	❑ 1 Chr 5-6	❑ Zeph 2
14	❑ John 1.19-34	❑ 1 Chr 7-8	❑ Zeph 3
15	❑ John 1.35-51	❑ 1 Chr 9	❑ Hag 1-2
16	❑ John 2	❑ 1 Chr 10-11	❑ Zech 1
17	❑ John 3.1-21	❑ 1 Chr 12	❑ Zech 2
18	❑ John 3.22-36	❑ 1 Chr 13-14	❑ Zech 3
19	❑ John 4.1-26	❑ 1 Chr 15.1—16.6	❑ Zech 4
20	❑ John 4.27-42	❑ 1 Chr 16.7-43	❑ Zech 5
21	❑ John 4.43-54	❑ 1 Chr 17	❑ Zech 6
22	❑ John 5.1-18	❑ 1 Chr 18-19	❑ Zech 7
23	❑ John 5.19-47	❑ 1 Chr 20.1—22.1	❑ Zech 8
24	❑ John 6.1-21	❑ 1 Chr 22.2—23.32	❑ Zech 9
25	❑ John 6.22-59	❑ 1 Chr 24	❑ Zech 10
26	❑ John 6.60-71	❑ 1 Chr 25-26	❑ Zech 11
27	❑ John 7.1-24	❑ 1 Chr 27-28	❑ Zech 12
28	❑ John 7.25-52	❑ 1 Chr 29	❑ Zech 13
29	❑ John 8.1-20	❑ 2 Chr 1.1—2.16	❑ Zech 14
30	❑ John 8.21-47	❑ 2 Chr 2.17-5.1	❑ Mal 1.1—2.9
31	❑ John 8.48-59	❑ 2 Chr 5.2-14	❑ Mal 2.10-16

SEPTEMBER

1	❑ John 9.1-23	❑ 2 Chr 6	❑ Mal 2.17—3.18
2	❑ John 9.24-41	❑ 2 Chr 7	❑ Mal 4
3	❑ John 10.1-21	❑ 2 Chr 8	❑ Ps 73
4	❑ John 10.22-42	❑ 2 Chr 9	❑ Ps 74
5	❑ John 11.1-27	❑ 2 Chr 10-11	❑ Ps 75
6	❑ John 11.28-57	❑ 2 Chr 12-13	❑ Ps 76
7	❑ John 12.1-26	❑ 2 Chr 14-15	❑ Ps 77
8	❑ John 12.27-50	❑ 2 Chr 16-17	❑ Ps 78.1-20
9	❑ John 13.1-20	❑ 2 Chr 18	❑ Ps 78.21-37
10	❑ John 13.21-38	❑ 2 Chr 19	❑ Ps 78.38-55
11	❑ John 14.1-14	❑ 2 Chr 20.1—21.1	❑ Ps 78.56-72
12	❑ John 14.15-31	❑ 2 Chr 21.2—22.12	❑ Ps 79
13	❑ John 15.1—16.4a	❑ 2 Chr 23	❑ Ps 80
14	❑ John 16.4b-33	❑ 2 Chr 24	❑ Ps 81
15	❑ John 17	❑ 2 Chr 25	❑ Ps 82
16	❑ John 18.1-18	❑ 2 Chr 26	❑ Ps 83
17	❑ John 18.19-38a	❑ 2 Chr 27-28	❑ Ps 84
18	❑ John 18.38b—19.16a	❑ 2 Chr 29	❑ Ps 85
19	❑ John 19.16b-42	❑ 2 Chr 30	❑ Ps 86
20	❑ John 20.1-18	❑ 2 Chr 31	❑ Ps 87
21	❑ John 20.19-31	❑ 2 Chr 32	❑ Ps 88
22	❑ John 21	❑ 2 Chr 33	❑ Ps 89.1-18
23	❑ 1 John 1	❑ 2 Chr 34	❑ Ps 89.19-37
24	❑ 1 John 2	❑ 2 Chr 35	❑ Ps 89.38-52
25	❑ 1 John 3	❑ 2 Chr 36	❑ Ps 90
26	❑ 1 John 4	❑ Ezra 1-2	❑ Ps 91
27	❑ 1 John 5	❑ Ezra 3-4	❑ Ps 92
28	❑ 2 John	❑ Ezra 5-6	❑ Ps 93

29 ❏ 3 John ❏ Ezra 7-8 ❏ Ps 94
30 ❏ Jude ❏ Ezra 9-10 ❏ Ps 95

OCTOBER

1 ❏ Rev 1 ❏ Neh 1-2 ❏ Ps 96
2 ❏ Rev 2 ❏ Neh 3 ❏ Ps 97
3 ❏ Rev 3 ❏ Neh 4 ❏ Ps 98
4 ❏ Rev 4 ❏ Neh 5.1—7.4 ❏ Ps 99
5 ❏ Rev 5 ❏ Neh 7.5—8.12 ❏ Ps 100
6 ❏ Rev 6 ❏ Neh 8.13—9.37 ❏ Ps 101
7 ❏ Rev 7 ❏ Neh 9.38—10.39 ❏ Ps 102
8 ❏ Rev 8 ❏ Neh 11 ❏ Ps 103
9 ❏ Rev 9 ❏ Neh 12 ❏ Ps 104.1-23
10 ❏ Rev 10 ❏ Neh 13 ❏ Ps 104.24-35
11 ❏ Rev 11 ❏ Esth 1 ❏ Ps 105.1-25
12 ❏ Rev 12 ❏ Esth 2 ❏ Ps 105.26-45
13 ❏ Rev 13 ❏ Esth 3-4 ❏ Ps 106.1-23
14 ❏ Rev 14 ❏ Esth 5.1—6.13 ❏ Ps 106.24-48
15 ❏ Rev 15 ❏ Esth 6.14—8.17 ❏ Ps 107.1-22
16 ❏ Rev 16 ❏ Esth 9-10 ❏ Ps 107.23-43
17 ❏ Rev 17 ❏ Isa 1-2 ❏ Ps 108
18 ❏ Rev 18 ❏ Isa 3-4 ❏ Ps 109.1-19
19 ❏ Rev 19 ❏ Isa 5-6 ❏ Ps 109.20-31
20 ❏ Rev 20 ❏ Isa 7-8 ❏ Ps 110
21 ❏ Rev 21-22 ❏ Isa 9-10 ❏ Ps 111
22 ❏ 1 Thes 1 ❏ Isa 11-13 ❏ Ps 112
23 ❏ 1 Thes 2.1-16 ❏ Isa 14-16 ❏ Ps 113
24 ❏ 1 Thes 2.17—3.13 ❏ Isa 17-19 ❏ Ps 114
25 ❏ 1 Thes 4 ❏ Isa 20-22 ❏ Ps 115
26 ❏ 1 Thes 5 ❏ Isa 23-24 ❏ Ps 116
27 ❏ 2 Thes 1 ❏ Isa 25-26 ❏ Ps 117
28 ❏ 2 Thes 2 ❏ Isa 27-28 ❏ Ps 118
29 ❏ 2 Thes 3 ❏ Isa 29-30 ❏ Ps 119.1-32
30 ❏ 1 Tim 1 ❏ Isa 31-33 ❏ Ps 119.33-64
31 ❏ 1 Tim 2 ❏ Isa 34-35 ❏ Ps 119.65-96

NOVEMBER

1 ❏ 1 Tim 3 ❏ Isa 36-37 ❏ Ps 119.97-120
2 ❏ 1 Tim 4 ❏ Isa 38-39 ❏ Ps 119.121-144
3 ❏ 1 Tim 5.1-22 ❏ Jer 1-2 ❏ Ps 119.145-176
4 ❏ 1 Tim 5.23—6.21 ❏ Jer 3-4 ❏ Ps 120
5 ❏ 2 Tim 1 ❏ Jer 5-6 ❏ Ps 121
6 ❏ 2 Tim 2 ❏ Jer 7-8 ❏ Ps 122
7 ❏ 2 Tim 3 ❏ Jer 9-10 ❏ Ps 123
8 ❏ 2 Tim 4 ❏ Jer 11-12 ❏ Ps 124
9 ❏ Titus 1 ❏ Jer 13-14 ❏ Ps 125
10 ❏ Titus 2 ❏ Jer 15-16 ❏ Ps 126
11 ❏ Titus 3 ❏ Jer 17-18 ❏ Ps 127
12 ❏ Phlm ❏ Jer 19-20 ❏ Ps 128
13 ❏ Jas 1 ❏ Jer 21-22 ❏ Ps 129

14 ❏ Jas 2 ❏ Jer 23-24 ❏ Ps 130
15 ❏ Jas 3 ❏ Jer 25-26 ❏ Ps 131
16 ❏ Jas 4 ❏ Jer 27-28 ❏ Ps 132
17 ❏ Jas 5 ❏ Jer 29-30 ❏ Ps 133
18 ❏ 1 Pet 1 ❏ Jer 31-32 ❏ Ps 134
19 ❏ 1 Pet 2 ❏ Jer 33-34 ❏ Ps 135
20 ❏ 1 Pet 3 ❏ Jer 35-36 ❏ Ps 136
21 ❏ 1 Pet 4 ❏ Jer 37-38 ❏ Ps 137
22 ❏ 1 Pet 5 ❏ Jer 39-40 ❏ Ps 138
23 ❏ 2 Pet 1 ❏ Jer 41-42 ❏ Ps 139
24 ❏ 2 Pet 2 ❏ Jer 43-44 ❏ Ps 140
25 ❏ 2 Pet 3 ❏ Jer 45-46 ❏ Ps 141
26 ❏ Gal 1 ❏ Jer 47-48 ❏ Ps 142
27 ❏ Gal 2 ❏ Jer 49-50 ❏ Ps 143
28 ❏ Gal 3.1-18 ❏ Jer 51-52 ❏ Ps 144
29 ❏ Gal 3.19—4.20 ❏ Lam 1-2 ❏ Ps 145
30 ❏ Gal 4.21-31 ❏ Lam 3-4 ❏ Ps 146

DECEMBER

1 ❏ Gal 5.1-15 ❏ Lam 5 ❏ Ps 147
2 ❏ Gal 5.16-26 ❏ Ezek 1 ❏ Ps 148
3 ❏ Gal 6 ❏ Ezek 2-3 ❏ Ps 149
4 ❏ Eph 1 ❏ Ezek 4-5 ❏ Ps 150
5 ❏ Eph 2 ❏ Ezek 6-7 ❏ Isa 40
6 ❏ Eph 3 ❏ Ezek 8-9 ❏ Isa 41
7 ❏ Eph 4.1-16 ❏ Ezek 10-11 ❏ Isa 42
8 ❏ Eph 4.17-32 ❏ Ezek 12-13 ❏ Isa 43
9 ❏ Eph 5.1-20 ❏ Ezek 14-15 ❏ Isa 44
10 ❏ Eph 5.21-33 ❏ Ezek 16 ❏ Isa 45
11 ❏ Eph 6 ❏ Ezek 17 ❏ Isa 46
12 ❏ Phil 1.1-11 ❏ Ezek 18 ❏ Isa 47
13 ❏ Phil 1.12-30 ❏ Ezek 19 ❏ Isa 48
14 ❏ Phil 2.1-11 ❏ Ezek 20 ❏ Isa 49
15 ❏ Phil 2.12-30 ❏ Ezek 21-22 ❏ Isa 50
16 ❏ Phil 3 ❏ Ezek 23 ❏ Isa 51
17 ❏ Phil 4 ❏ Ezek 24 ❏ Isa 52
18 ❏ Col 1.1-23 ❏ Ezek 25-26 ❏ Isa 53
19 ❏ Col 1.24—2.19 ❏ Ezek 27-28 ❏ Isa 54
20 ❏ Col 2.20—3.17 ❏ Ezek 29-30 ❏ Isa 55
21 ❏ Col 3.18—4.18 ❏ Ezek 31-32 ❏ Isa 56
22 ❏ Luke 1.1-25 ❏ Ezek 33 ❏ Isa 57
23 ❏ Luke 1.26-56 ❏ Ezek 34 ❏ Isa 58
24 ❏ Luke 1.57-80 ❏ Ezek 35-36 ❏ Isa 59
25 ❏ Luke 2.1-20 ❏ Ezek 37 ❏ Isa 60
26 ❏ Luke 2.21-52 ❏ Ezek 38-39 ❏ Isa 61
27 ❏ Luke 3.1-20 ❏ Ezek 40-41 ❏ Isa 62
28 ❏ Luke 3.21-38 ❏ Ezek 42-43 ❏ Isa 63
29 ❏ Luke 4.1-30 ❏ Ezek 44-45 ❏ Isa 64
30 ❏ Luke 4.31-44 ❏ Ezek 46-47 ❏ Isa 65
31 ❏ Luke 5.1-26 ❏ Ezek 48 ❏ Isa 66

HOW TO LOOK UP A SCRIPTURE REFERENCE

Here's a helpful hint for those who are unfamiliar with looking up Bible passages. Like many books, the Bible is divided into units (here called "books" of the Bible); and each book is divided into chapters. However, unlike most books, chapters are divided into much smaller units called "verses" (usually consisting of a sentence or two). Both chapters and verses are numbered. This provides a very convenient and useful system for identifying specific verses in the Bible. References to Bible passages will be listed in the following way.

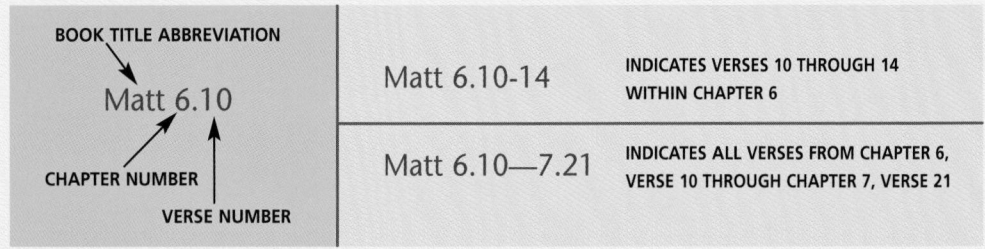

BOOK TITLE ABBREVIATION		
Matt 6.10	Matt 6.10-14	INDICATES VERSES 10 THROUGH 14 WITHIN CHAPTER 6
CHAPTER NUMBER VERSE NUMBER	Matt 6.10—7.21	INDICATES ALL VERSES FROM CHAPTER 6, VERSE 10 THROUGH CHAPTER 7, VERSE 21

The more you look up Scripture references, the sooner you will become familiar with the abbreviations used and this system of notation. In the meantime, the "Alphabetical Listing with Abbreviations" located immediately after the "Contents" page will help you become familiar with any abbreviations you don't recognize.

MAP 1

The Ancient Near East, 1800 to 1400 B.C.

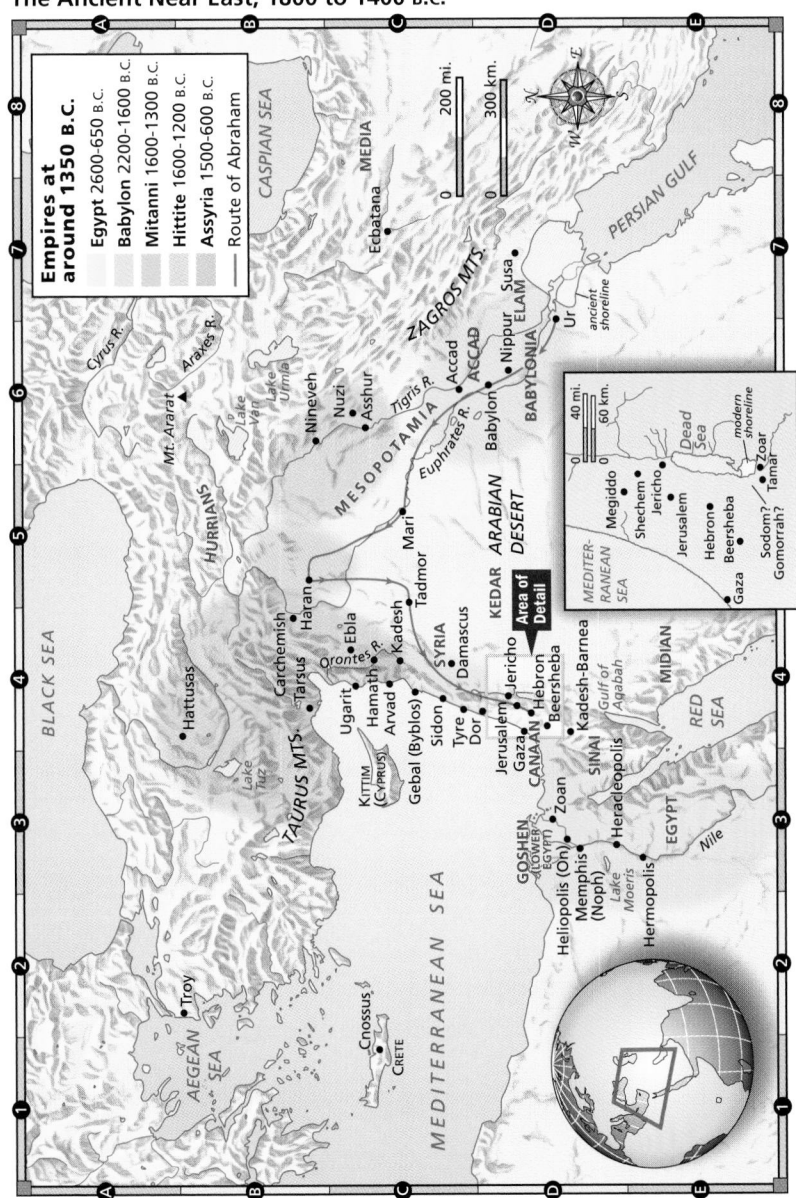

MAP 2
Egypt and Sinai, 1400 to 1200 B.C.

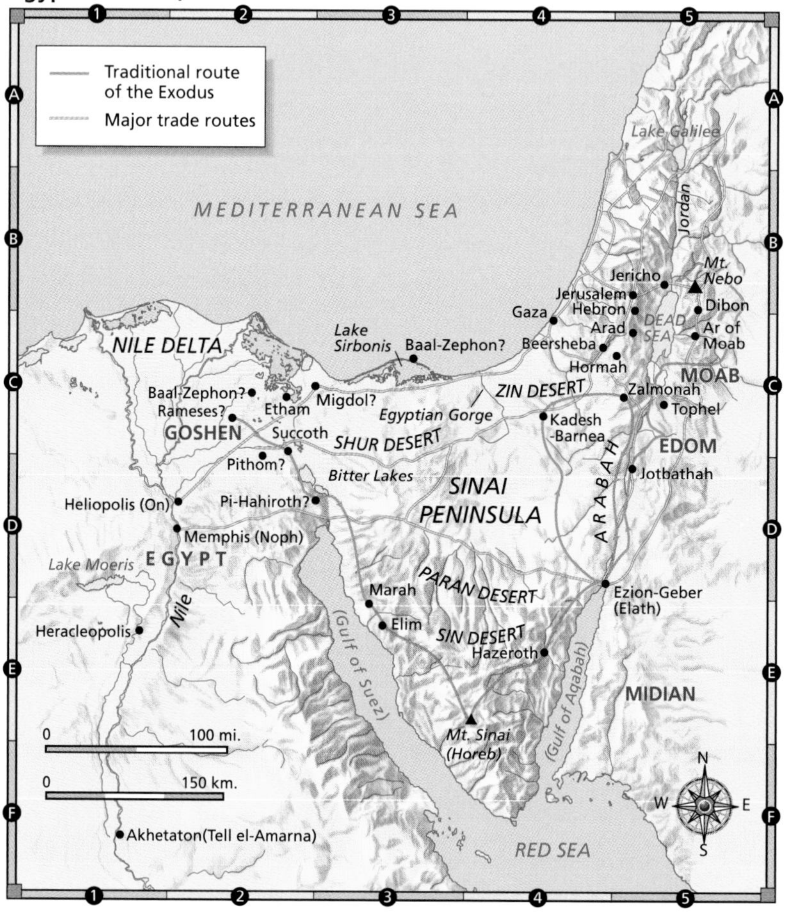

Traditional route
of the Exodus

Major trade routes

MEDITERRANEAN SEA

Lake Galilee

Jordan

Jericho
Jerusalem
Mt. Nebo
Gaza
Hebron
Dibon
Lake Sirbonis
Baal-Zephon?
Arad
DEAD SEA
Ar of Moab
Beersheba
ZIN DESERT
Hormah
MOAB
Baal-Zephon?
Zalmonah
Rameses?
Etham
Migdol?
Egyptian Gorge
Tophel
NILE DELTA
GOSHEN
Succoth
Kadesh -Barnea
SHUR DESERT
EDOM
Pithom?
Bitter Lakes
Jotbathah
Heliopolis (On)
Pi-Hahiroth?
SINAI PENINSULA
A R A B A H
Memphis (Noph)
Lake Moeris
E G Y P T
Marah
PARAN DESERT
Ezion-Geber (Elath)
Elim
SIN DESERT
Heracleopolis
Hazeroth
MIDIAN
Nile
(Gulf of Suez)
(Gulf of Aqabah)

0   100 mi.
0   150 km.

Mt. Sinai (Horeb)

N
W   E
S

Akhetaton(Tell el-Amarna)

RED SEA

MAP 3

Division of Canaan, 1200 to 1030 B.C.

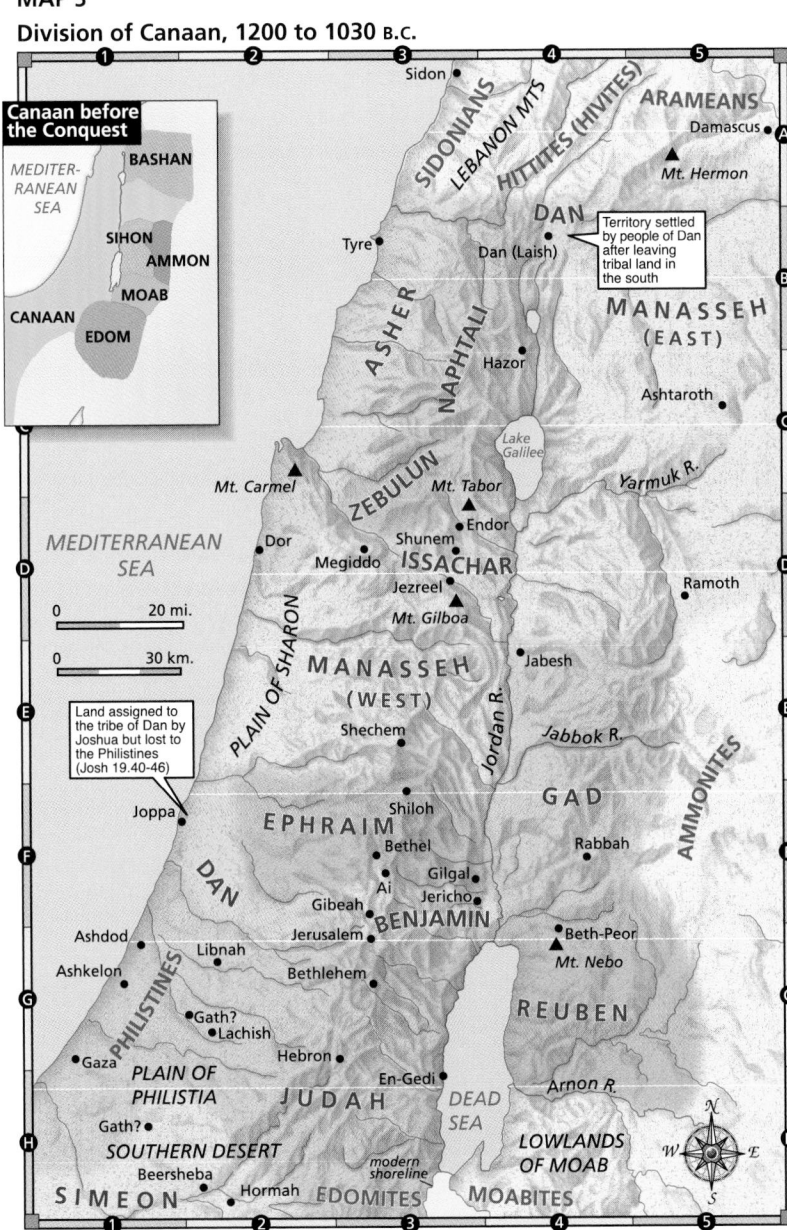

Canaan before the Conquest

MEDITERRANEAN SEA

BASHAN

SIHON

AMMON

MOAB

CANAAN

EDOM

Sidon

SIDONIANS

LEBANON MTS

HITTITES (HIVITES)

ARAMEANS

Damascus

Mt. Hermon

DAN

Territory settled by people of Dan after leaving tribal land in the south

Tyre

Dan (Laish)

ASHER

NAPHTALI

MANASSEH (EAST)

Hazor

Ashtaroth

Lake Galilee

Mt. Carmel

ZEBULUN

Mt. Tabor

Yarmuk R.

Endor

MEDITERRANEAN SEA

Dor

Shunem

ISSACHAR

Megiddo

Ramoth

Jezreel

0   20 mi.

Mt. Gilboa

0   30 km.

Jabesh

MANASSEH (WEST)

PLAIN OF SHARON

Jordan R.

Jabbok R.

Shechem

Land assigned to the tribe of Dan by Joshua but lost to the Philistines (Josh 19.40-46)

GAD

AMMONITES

Joppa

EPHRAIM

Shiloh

DAN

Bethel

Rabbah

Ai

Gilgal

Gibeah

Jericho

Ashdod

Jerusalem

BENJAMIN

Beth-Peor

Libnah

Mt. Nebo

Ashkelon

Bethlehem

PHILISTINES

Gath?

REUBEN

Lachish

Hebron

Gaza

En-Gedi

Arnon R.

PLAIN OF PHILISTIA

JUDAH

DEAD SEA

N

Gath?

LOWLANDS OF MOAB

W   E

SOUTHERN DESERT

S

Beersheba

modern shoreline

SIMEON

Hormah

EDOMITES

MOABITES

MAP 4

United Israelite Kingdom,
Israel in the Time of Kings Saul, David and Solomon, 1000 to 924 B.C.

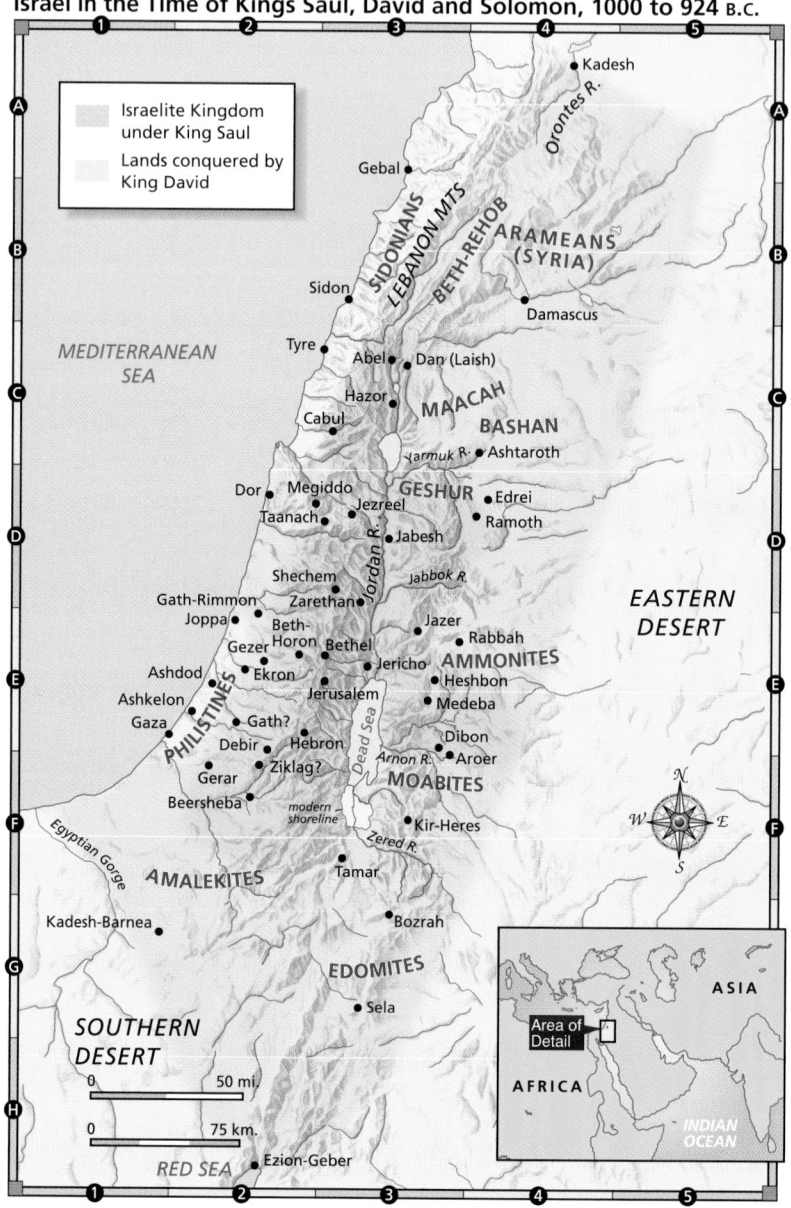

Israelite Kingdom under King Saul

Lands conquered by King David

MEDITERRANEAN SEA

Kadesh

Gebal

SIDONIANS

LEBANON MTS

Orontes R.

BETH-REHOB

ARAMEANS (SYRIA)

Sidon

Damascus

Tyre

Abel

Dan (Laish)

Hazor

Cabul

MAACAH

BASHAN

Yarmuk R.

Ashtaroth

Dor

Megiddo

Jezreel

GESHUR

Edrei

Taanach

Ramoth

Jordan R.

Jabesh

Shechem

Jabbok R.

Gath-Rimmon

Zarethan

EASTERN DESERT

Joppa

Beth-Horon

Bethel

Jazer

Gezer

Rabbah

Ashdod

Ekron

Jericho

AMMONITES

Ashkelon

Jerusalem

Heshbon

Gaza

PHILISTINES

Gath?

Medeba

Debir

Hebron

Dibon

Gerar

Ziklag?

Arnon R.

Aroer

Beersheba

MOABITES

modern shoreline

Dead Sea

Egyptian Gorge

Kir-Heres

Zered R.

AMALEKITES

Tamar

Kadesh-Barnea

Bozrah

EDOMITES

SOUTHERN DESERT

Sela

0   50 mi.

0   75 km.

RED SEA

Ezion-Geber

ASIA

Area of Detail

AFRICA

INDIAN OCEAN

MAP 5

Jerusalem in Old Testament Times,
The Growth of David's City, 960 to 44 B.C.

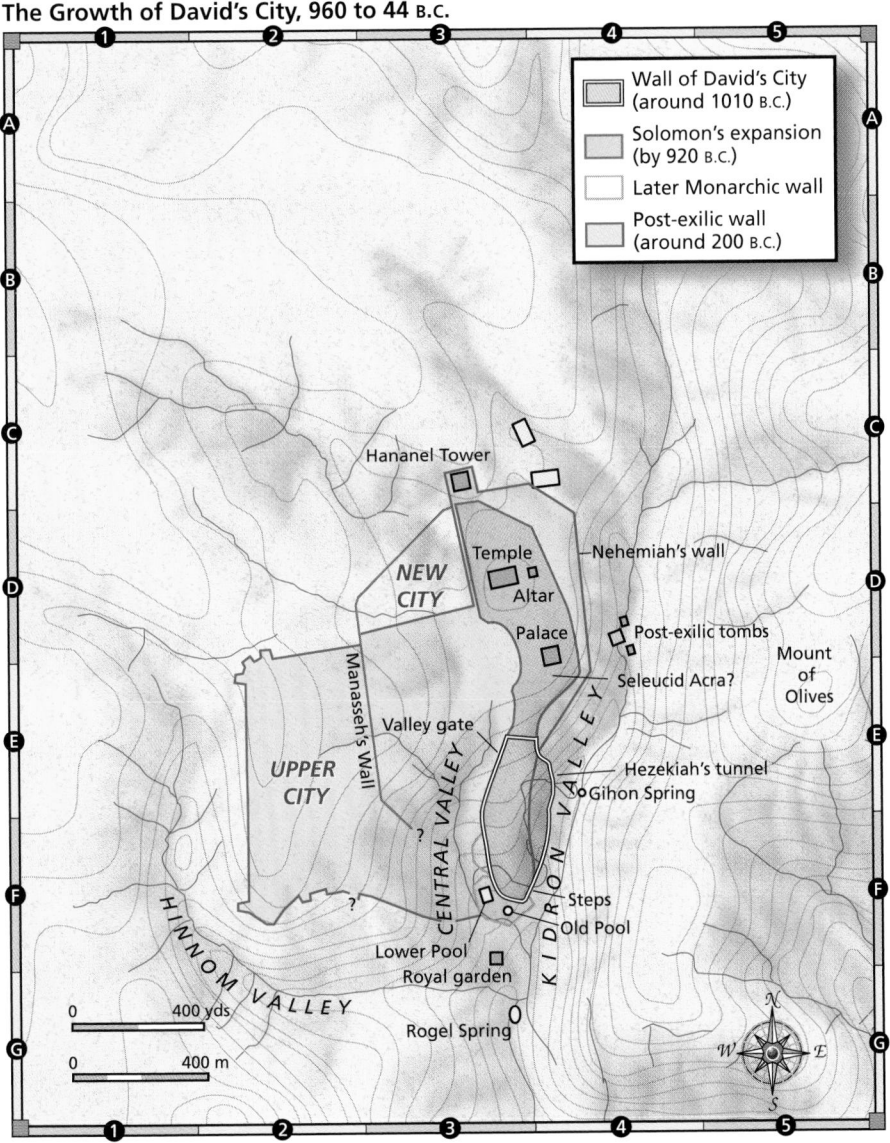

Wall of David's City
(around 1010 B.C.)

Solomon's expansion
(by 920 B.C.)

Later Monarchic wall

Post-exilic wall
(around 200 B.C.)

Hananel Tower

NEW
CITY

Temple
Altar

Nehemiah's wall

Palace

Post-exilic tombs

Mount
of
Olives

Seleucid Acra?

Manasseh's Wall

Valley gate

UPPER
CITY

CENTRAL VALLEY

Hezekiah's tunnel

Gihon Spring

KIDRON VALLEY

Steps

Old Pool

HINNOM VALLEY

Lower Pool

Royal garden

0   400 yds

0   400 m

Rogel Spring

N
W   E
S

MAP 6

The Kingdoms of Israel and Judah, 924 to 722 B.C.

maps

MAP 7

Assyrian and Babylonian Kingdoms, 9th to 6th Centuries B.C.

Assyrian Kingdom about 824 B.C.
Assyrian Kingdom about 640 B.C.
Babylonian Kingdom about 550 B.C.

CASPIAN SEA

BLACK SEA

Cyrus R.

URARTU

Araxes R.

Abydos
MESHECH
Gordion
TUBAL
ARMENIA
Sardis

PHRYGIA
KUE
Haran
Gozan
ASSYRIA
Miletus
Tarsus
Arpad
Carchemish
Nineveh
LYCIA
CILICIA
Aleppo
Tiphsah
Asshur
CRETE
RHODES
Tadmor
Euphrates R.
Tigris R.
ECBATANA
CYPRUS
Arvad
Ecbatana

MEDITERRANEAN SEA
Sidon
Damascus
MEDIA
Tyre
KEDAR
Hamath
Kedesh
Sippar
Samaria
AMMON
Babylon
BABYLONIA
Susa
Gaza
Jerusalem
Erech
ELAM
Tahpanhes
MOAB
Ur
Athribis
JUDAH
EDOM
ancient
Heliopolis
SINAI
Sela
shoreline
EGYPT
Memphis
Ezion-Geber
ARABIAN DESERT
PERSIAN GULF
Hermopolis
ARABIA
Siut
Nile
LIBYAN DESERT
Abydos
RED SEA
Thebez

Syene

Major Powers 670-550 B.C.

Kingdom
of Lydia
670-546 B.C.

Kingdom
of the Medes
612-550 B.C.

Babylonian
Kingdom
550 B.C.

MEDITERRANEAN
SEA

Kingdom
of Egypt
663-525 B.C.

N
W   E
S

0   400 mi.
0   600 km.

MAP 8

Persian Kingdom, 550 to 330 B.C.

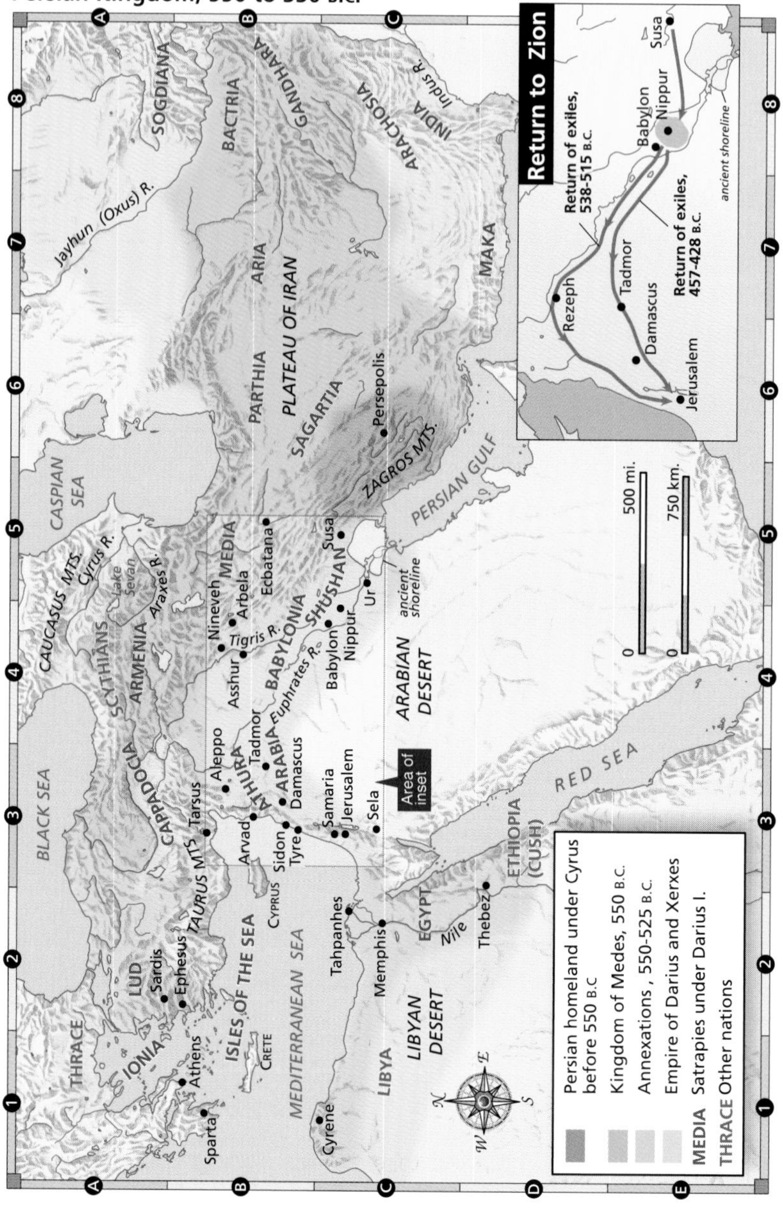

Return to Zion

Return of exiles, 538-515 B.C.

Return of exiles, 457-428 B.C.

Susa

Nippur

Babylon

Rezeph

Tadmor

Damascus

Jerusalem

ancient shoreline

SOGDIANA

BACTRIA

GANDHARA

ARACHOSIA

INDIA

Indus R.

MAKA

Jayhun (Oxus) R.

ARIA

PARTHIA

PLATEAU OF IRAN

SAGARTIA

Persepolis

ZAGROS MTS.

PERSIAN GULF

CASPIAN SEA

CAUCASUS MTS.

Cyrus R.

Lake Sevan

Araxes R.

ARMENIA

SCYTHIANS

MEDIA

Nineveh

Asshur

Arbela

Ecbatana

Tigris R.

BABYLONIA

SHUSHAN

Susa

ASSYRIA

Euphrates R.

Babylon

Nippur

Ur

ancient shoreline

ARABIAN DESERT

500 mi.

750 km.

BLACK SEA

CAPPADOCIA

TAURUS MTS.

Tarsus

Aleppo

Tadmor

ARABIA

Damascus

Arvad

Sidon

Tyre

CYPRUS

Samaria

Jerusalem

Sela

Area of inset

RED SEA

ETHIOPIA (CUSH)

THRACE

LUD

IONIA

Sardis

Ephesus

Athens

Sparta

ISLES OF THE SEA

Crete

MEDITERRANEAN SEA

Tahpanhes

Memphis

EGYPT

Nile

Thebez

LIBYA

LIBYAN DESERT

Cyrene

Persian homeland under Cyrus before 550 B.C.

Kingdom of Medes, 550 B.C.

Annexations, 550-525 B.C.

Empire of Darius and Xerxes

MEDIA Satrapies under Darius I.

THRACE Other nations

MAP 9

Palestine in the Time of the Maccabees, 175 to 63 B.C.

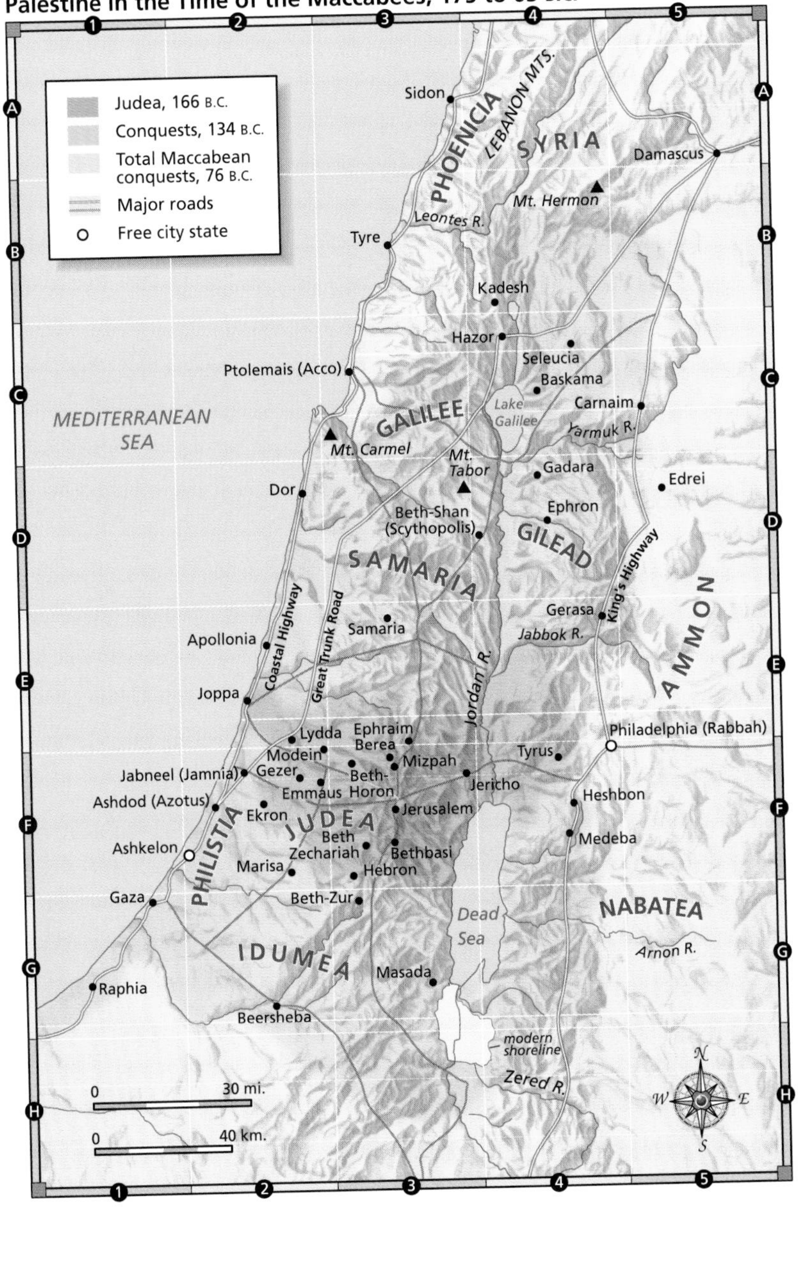

Legend:
- Judea, 166 B.C.
- Conquests, 134 B.C.
- Total Maccabean conquests, 76 B.C.
- Major roads
- ○ Free city state

MEDITERRANEAN SEA

PHOENICIA
LEBANON MTS.
SYRIA
GALILEE
SAMARIA
GILEAD
AMMON
JUDEA
PHILISTIA
IDUMEA
NABATEA

Sidon
Damascus
Mt. Hermon
Tyre
Leontes R.
Kadesh
Hazor
Seleucia
Baskama
Ptolemais (Acco)
Carnaim
Lake Galilee
Yarmuk R.
Mt. Carmel
Mt. Tabor
Gadara
Edrei
Dor
Ephron
Beth-Shan (Scythopolis)
Gerasa
Jabbok R.
Samaria
Apollonia
Coastal Highway
Great Trunk Road
King's Highway
Jordan R.
Joppa
Ephraim
Berea
Lydda
Modein
Gezer
Mizpah
Tyrus
Philadelphia (Rabbah)
Jabneel (Jamnia)
Beth-Horon
Emmaus
Jericho
Ashdod (Azotus)
Ekron
Jerusalem
Heshbon
Ashkelon
Beth Zechariah
Bethbasi
Medeba
Marisa
Hebron
Gaza
Beth-Zur
Dead Sea
Masada
Raphia
Beersheba
modern shoreline
Zered R.
Arnon R.

0   30 mi.
0   40 km.

N
W   E
S

MAP 10

Growth of the Roman Empire, 27 B.C. to A.D. 180

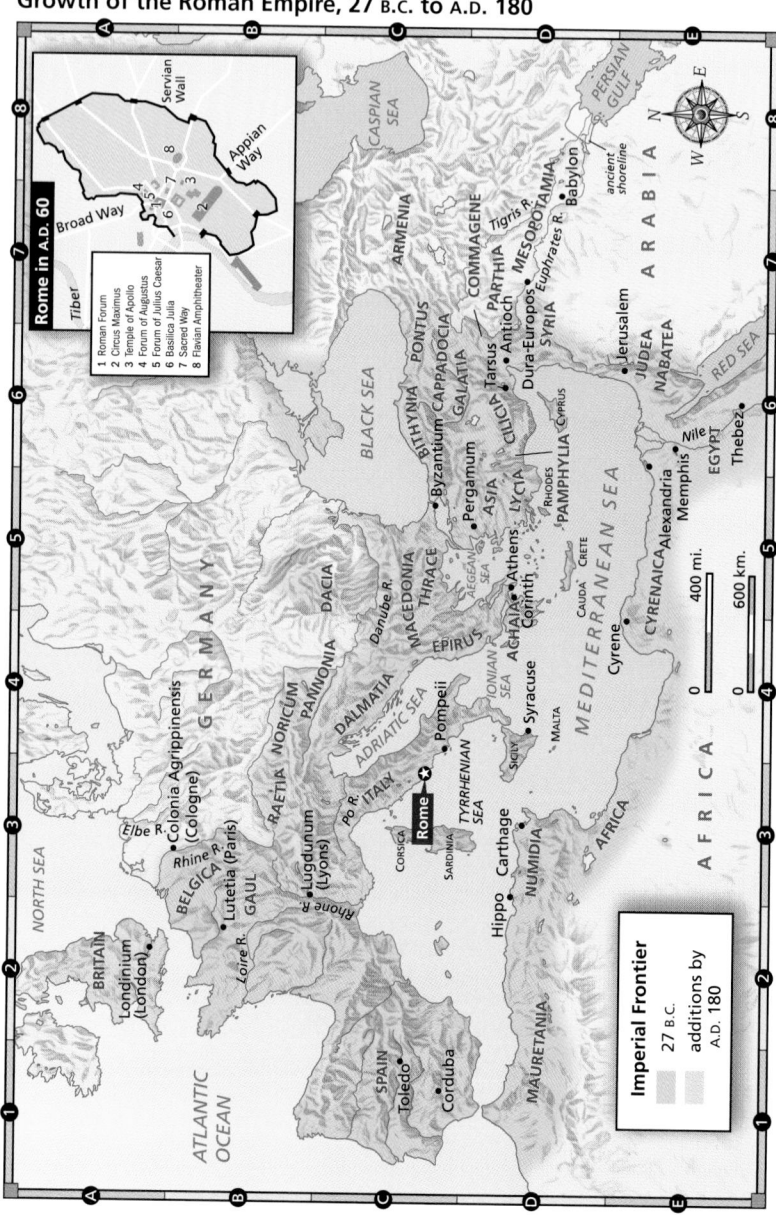

MAP 11

Palestine Under the Herods, 4 B.C. to A.D. 44

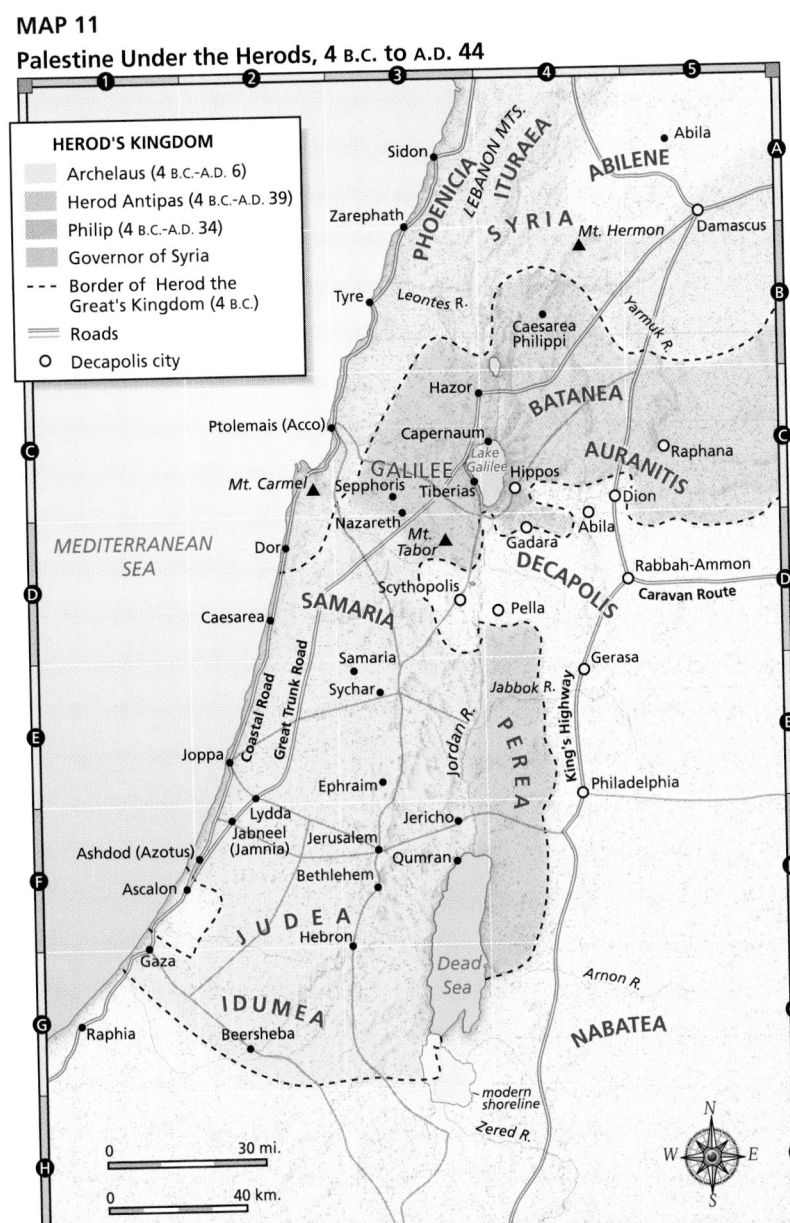

HEROD'S KINGDOM
- Archelaus (4 B.C.-A.D. 6)
- Herod Antipas (4 B.C.-A.D. 39)
- Philip (4 B.C.-A.D. 34)
- Governor of Syria
- - - - Border of Herod the Great's Kingdom (4 B.C.)
- Roads
- ○ Decapolis city

Abila

PHOENICIA
LEBANON MTS.
ITURAEA
ABILENE

Sidon

Zarephath

SYRIA

Mt. Hermon

Damascus

Tyre
Leontes R.

Caesarea Philippi

Yarmuk R.

Hazor
BATANEA

Ptolemais (Acco)

Capernaum

AURANITIS

Raphana

Mt. Carmel
GALILEE
Lake Galilee
Hippos

Sepphoris
Tiberias
Dion

Nazareth
Mt. Tabor
Abila

Gadara
DECAPOLIS

Dor
Rabbah-Ammon

MEDITERRANEAN SEA

Scythopolis
SAMARIA
Caravan Route

Caesarea
Pella

Samaria
Gerasa

Sychar
Jabbok R.

Joppa
Coastal Road
Great Trunk Road
Jordan R.
PEREA
King's Highway

Ephraim
Philadelphia

Lydda
Jabneel (Jamnia)
Jericho

Ashdod (Azotus)
Jerusalem
Qumran

Bethlehem

Ascalon
JUDEA
Hebron

Gaza
Dead Sea
Arnon R.

IDUMEA
NABATEA

Raphia
Beersheba

modern shoreline

Zered R.

0   30 mi.

0   40 km.

N
W   E
S

MAP 12

Palestine in the Time of Jesus, A.D. 6 to 30

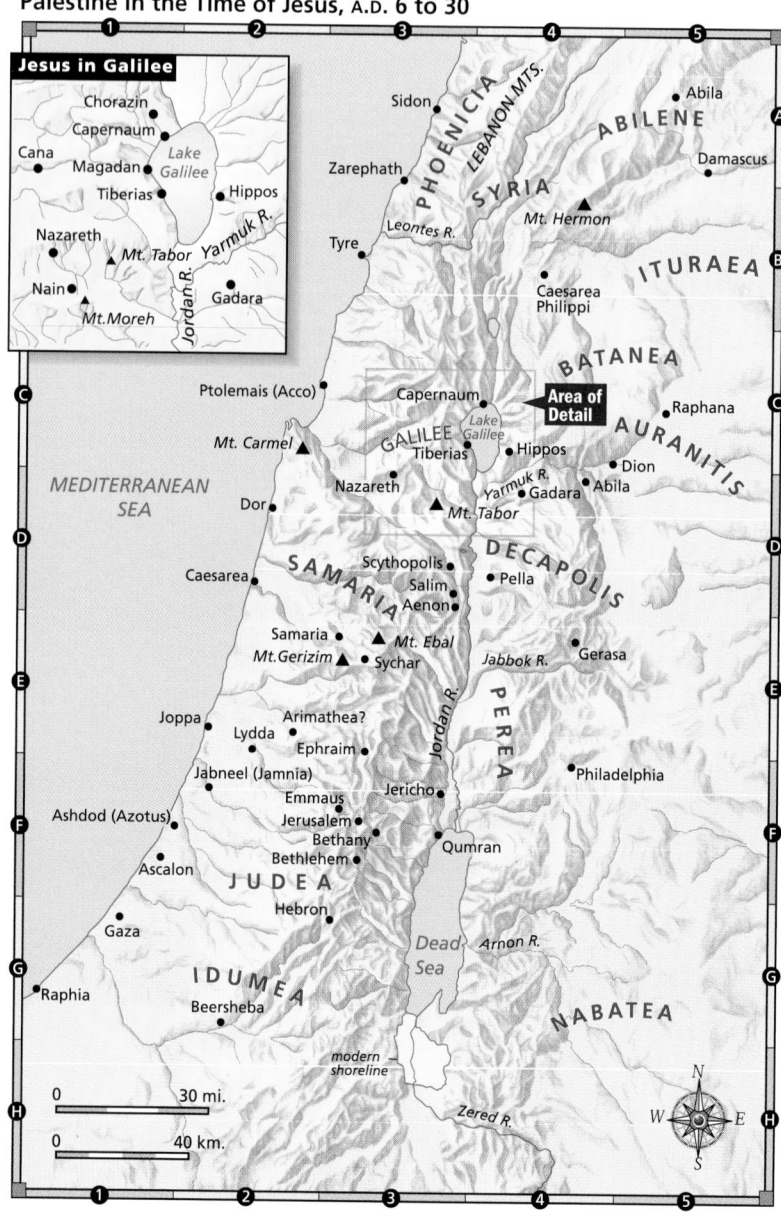

Jesus in Galilee

Chorazin
Capernaum
Cana
Magadan
Lake Galilee
Tiberias
Hippos
Nazareth
Mt. Tabor
Yarmuk R.
Jordan R.
Nain
Mt. Moreh
Gadara

Sidon
Abila
PHOENICIA
LEBANON MTS.
ABILENE
Zarephath
SYRIA
Damascus
Leontes R.
Mt. Hermon
Tyre
ITURAEA
Caesarea Philippi
BATANEA
Ptolemais (Acco)
Capernaum
Area of Detail
Raphana
Lake Galilee
AURANITIS
Mt. Carmel
GALILEE
Tiberias
Hippos
Dion
Nazareth
Yarmuk R.
Abila
MEDITERRANEAN SEA
Dor
Gadara
Mt. Tabor
Scythopolis
DECAPOLIS
Caesarea
SAMARIA
Salim
Pella
Aenon
Samaria
Mt. Ebal
Mt. Gerizim
Sychar
Jabbok R.
Gerasa
Joppa
Arimathea?
Lydda
Ephraim
PEREA
Jabneel (Jamnia)
Emmaus
Jericho
Philadelphia
Ashdod (Azotus)
Jerusalem
Bethany
Bethlehem
Qumran
Ascalon
JUDEA
Hebron
Gaza
Dead Sea
Arnon R.
IDUMEA
Raphia
Beersheba
NABATEA
modern shoreline
Zered R.

0   30 mi.
0   40 km.

MAP 13
Jerusalem in the Time of Jesus, Around A.D. 30

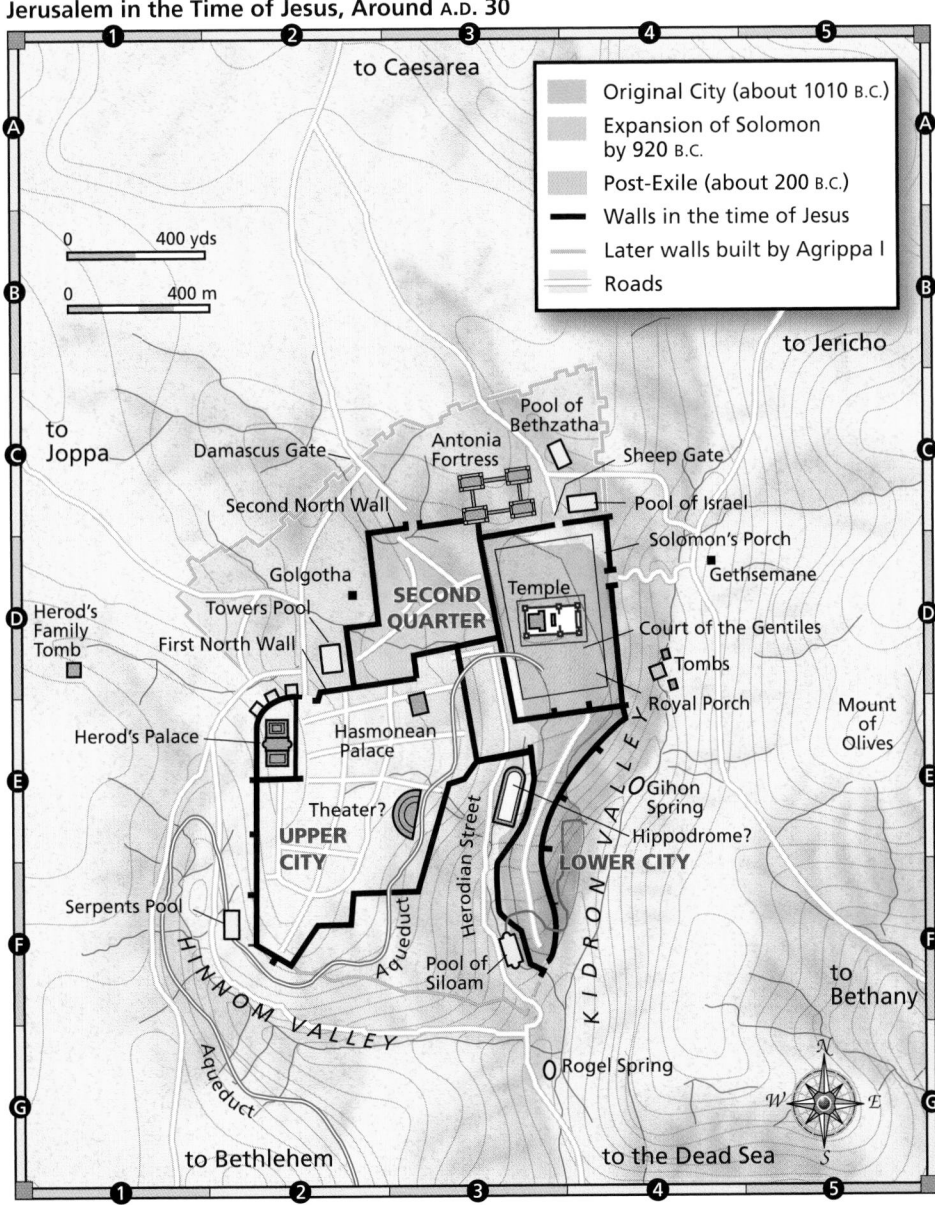

to Caesarea

Original City (about 1010 B.C.)

Expansion of Solomon
by 920 B.C.

Post-Exile (about 200 B.C.)

Walls in the time of Jesus

Later walls built by Agrippa I

Roads

to Jericho

to
Joppa

0   400 yds

0   400 m

Pool of
Bethzatha

Damascus Gate

Antonia
Fortress

Sheep Gate

Second North Wall

Pool of Israel

Solomon's Porch

Golgotha

Temple

Gethsemane

Towers Pool

SECOND
QUARTER

Herod's
Family
Tomb

First North Wall

Court of the Gentiles

Tombs

Royal Porch

Mount
of
Olives

Herod's Palace

Hasmonean
Palace

Theater?

Gihon
Spring

UPPER
CITY

Hippodrome?

LOWER CITY

Serpents Pool

Aqueduct

Herodian Street

KIDRON VALLEY

to
Bethany

Pool of
Siloam

HINNOM VALLEY

Aqueduct

Rogel Spring

N
W   E
S

to Bethlehem

to the Dead Sea

MAP 14

World of the New Testament, Around A.D. **50**

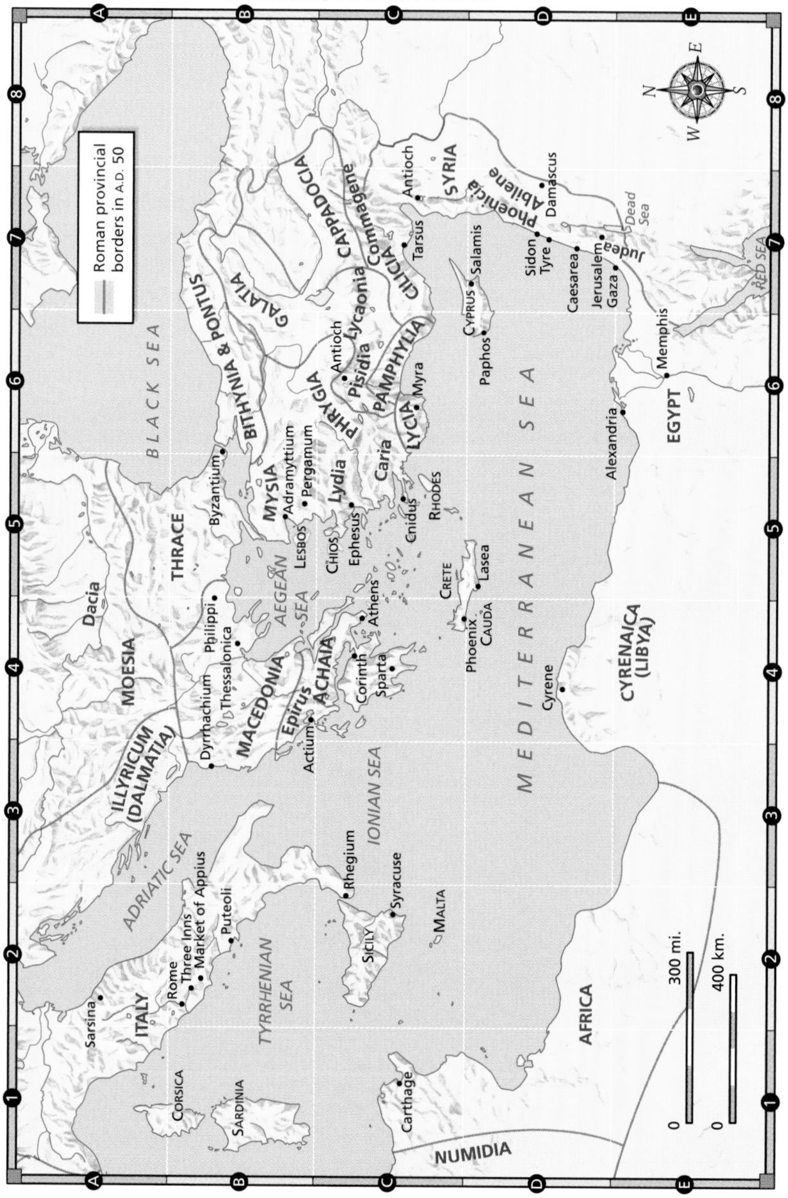

Roman provincial borders in A.D. 50

ITALY
Sarsina
Rome
Three Inns
Market of Appius
Puteoli
CORSICA
SARDINIA
TYRRHENIAN SEA
ADRIATIC SEA
ILLYRICUM (DALMATIA)
MOESIA
Dacia
THRACE
BLACK SEA
Dyrrhachium
Thessalonica
Philippi
MACEDONIA
Epirus
Actium
ACHAIA
Corinth
Sparta
Athens
AEGEAN SEA
IONIAN SEA
Rhegium
Syracuse
SICILY
MALTA
Carthage
NUMIDIA
AFRICA
MEDITERRANEAN SEA
CYRENAICA (LIBYA)
Cyrene
CRETE
CAUDA
Phoenix
Lasea
RHODES
Cnidus
Ephesus
Chios
LESBOS
Caria
Lydia
Pergamum
Adramyttium
MYSIA
BITHYNIA & PONTUS
GALATIA
PHRYGIA
Antioch
Pisidia
Lycaonia
PAMPHYLIA
LYCIA
Myra
CAPPADOCIA
Commagene
CILICIA
Tarsus
Antioch
SYRIA
Abilene
Damascus
Phoenicia
Sidon
Tyre
Caesarea
Judea
Jerusalem
Gaza
Dead Sea
RED SEA
CYPRUS
Salamis
Paphos
Memphis
Alexandria
EGYPT
Byzantium
300 mi.
400 km.
0

N
W E
S

MAP 15

Paul's First and Second Journeys

BLACK SEA

THRACE

MACEDONIA

Philippi

Apollonia · Neapolis

Thessalonica

Berea

SAMOTHRACE

BYZANTIUM

MYSIA

BITHYNIA

ASIA

GALATIA

Troas

AEGEAN SEA

Pergamum

Thyatira

Sardis

Smyrna

LYDIA

Ephesus

PHRYGIA

Antioch

Iconium

CAPPADOCIA

ACHAIA

Corinth

Cenchreae

Athens

Colossae

Lystra

Tarsus

Miletus

Perga

Derbe

CILICIA

Sparta

Attalia

PAMPHYLIA

Seleucia

Cnidus

LYCIA

Antioch

Rhodes

RHODES

Patara Myra

CRETE

Salamis

Phoenix

CAUDA

Lasea

CYPRUS

Fair Havens

Paphos

SYRIA

MEDITERRANEAN SEA

Sidon

PHOENICIA

ABILENE

Tyre

Caesarea

Jerusalem

CYRENAICA

Alexandria

JUDEA

EGYPT

Paul's first journey

Paul's second journey

Roman provincial boundaries

0   200 mi.

0   300 km.

N

W   E

S

RED SEA

MAP 16
Paul's Third Journey and His Journey to Rome

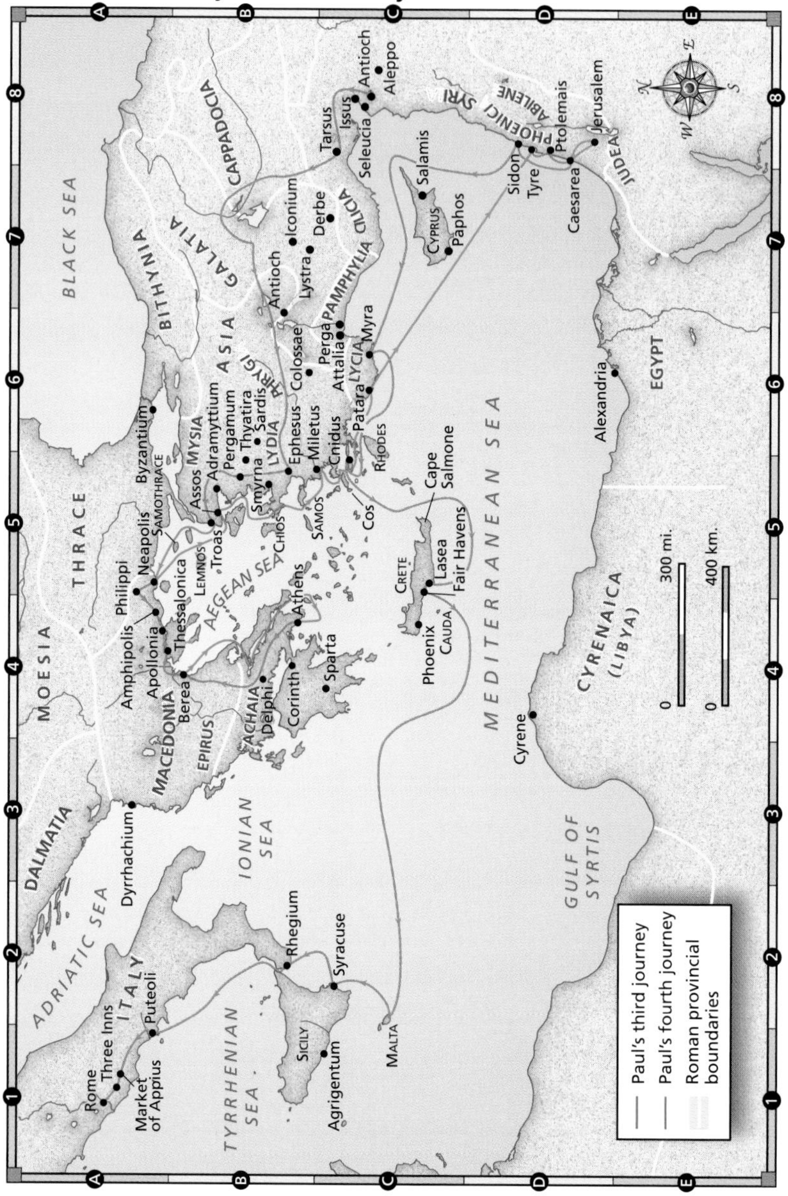

Paul's third journey
Paul's fourth journey
Roman provincial boundaries